2013
Writer's
MARKET
DELUXE EDITION

includes a 1-year online subscription to

Where & How to Sell What You Write

THE ULTIMATE MARKET RESEARCH TOOL FOR WRITERS

To register your *2013 Writer's Market Deluxe Edition* book and **start your 1-year online subscription**, scratch off the block below to reveal your activation code*, then go to www.WritersMarket.com. Find the box that says "Have an Activation Code?" then click on "Sign Up Now" and enter your contact information and activation code. It's that easy!

UPDATED MARKET LISTINGS FOR YOUR INTEREST AREA

EASY-TO-USE SEARCHABLE DATABASE • RECORD-KEEPING TOOLS

PROFESSIONAL TIPS & ADVICE • INDUSTRY NEWS

*valid through 12/31/13

WritersMarket.com

Where & How to Sell What You Write

Activate your WritersMarket.com subscription to get instant access to:

- **UPDATED LISTINGS IN YOUR WRITING GENRE:** Find additional listings that didn't make it into the book, updated contact information and more. WritersMarket.com provides the most comprehensive database of verified markets available anywhere.

- **EASY-TO-USE SEARCHABLE DATABASE:** Looking for a specific magazine or book publisher? Just type in its name. Or widen your prospects with the Advanced Search. You can also search for listings that have been recently updated!

- **PERSONALIZED TOOLS:** Store your best-bet markets, and use our popular recording-keeping tools to track your submissions. Plus, get new and updated market listings, query reminders, and more—every time you log in!

- **PROFESSIONAL TIPS & ADVICE:** From pay rate charts to sample query letters, and from how-to articles to Q&A's with literary agents, we have the resources freelance writers need.

YOU'LL GET ALL OF THIS WITH YOUR INCLUDED SUBSCRIPTION TO

WritersMarket.com

Where & How to Sell What You Write

13TH ANNUAL EDITION

2013

Writer's
MARKET
DELUXE EDITION

Robert Lee Brewer, Editor

WD

**WRITER'S DIGEST
BOOKS**

WritersDigest.com
Cincinnati, Ohio

2013 Writer's Market. Copyright © 2012 F + W Media, Inc. Published by Writer's Digest Books, an imprint of F+W Media, Inc., 10151 Carver Road, Suite 200, Blue Ash, Ohio 45242. Printed and bound in the United States of America. All rights reserved. No part of this book may be reproduced in any form or by any electronic or mechanical means including information storage and retrieval systems without permission in writing from the publisher, except by a reviewer, who may quote brief passages in a review.

Publisher: Phil Sexton

Writer's Market website: www.writersmarket.com
Writer's Digest website: www.writersdigest.com

Distributed in Canada by Fraser Direct
100 Armstrong Avenue
Georgetown, Ontario, Canada L7G 5S4
Tel: (905) 877-4411

Distributed in the U.K. and Europe by F&W Media International
Brunel House, Newton Abbot, Devon, TQ12 4PU, England
Tel: (+44) 1626-323200, Fax: (+44) 1626-323319
E-mail: postmaster@davidandcharles.co.uk

Distributed in Australia by Capricorn Link
P.O. Box 704, Windsor, NSW 2756 Australia
Tel: (02) 4577-3555

Library of Congress Catalog Number 31-20772
ISSN: 0084-2729
ISBN-13: 978-1-59963-593-4
ISBN-13: 978-1-59963-594-1 (*Writer's Market Deluxe Edition*)
ISBN-10: 1-59963-593-3
ISBN-10: 1-59963-594-1 (*Writer's Market Deluxe Edition*)

Attention Booksellers: This is an annual directory of F + W Media, Inc. Return deadline for this edition is December 31, 2013.

Edited by: Robert Lee Brewer
Cover designed by: Jessica Boonstra
Interior designed by: Claudean Wheeler
Production coordinated by: Greg Nock
Cover illustration by: Joshua Roflow

CONTENTS

FROM THE EDITOR..1

HOW TO USE *WRITER'S MARKET*...2

FINDING WORK

BEFORE YOUR FIRST SALE...7

QUERY LETTER CLINIC..16

PERFECT PITCH:
    by Marc Acito...27

FEATURE ARTICLE WRITING:
    by Chuck Sambuchino..34

WHEN WORKING FOR FREE PAYS:
    by Sue Bradford Edwards...43

SELF-PUBLISHING CHECKLIST...48

FINDING FREELANCE OPPORTUNITIES ONLINE:
    by Carol Tice...51

FUNDS FOR WRITERS 101:
    by C. Hope Clark..57

GHOSTWRITING 101:
    by Eva Shaw...63

PUBLISHERS & THEIR IMPRINTS...69

MANAGING WORK

THE WRITING ENTREPRENEUR
    by J.M. Lacey...75

CONTRACTS 101
    by Cindy Ferraino...81

MAKING THE MOST OF THE MONEY YOU EARN
    by Sage Cohen..88

REPURPOSING WRITING FOR PLATFORM AND PROFIT:
    by Sage Cohen..94

RECORD KEEPING AND PRICING
by Daniel Dern... 100

SUBMISSION TRACKER.. 110

DIVERSIFYING DURING TOUGH TIMES:
by Melissa Crytzer Fry 112

LAUNCHING YOUR FREELANCE BUSINESS
by I.J. Schecter 118

HOW MUCH SHOULD I CHARGE?
by Lynn Wasnak 126

PROMOTING WORK

BUILD A PLATFORM:
by Jeff Yeager... 144

HOW TO IMPROVE YOUR PRESENTATION SKILLS:
by Brenda Collins.. 153

THE ART OF PROMOTING:
by Kerrie Flanagan.. 158

BLOGGING BASICS:
by Robert Lee Brewer.. 161

TWITTER CHEAT SHEET FOR WRITERS
by Robert Lee Brewer.. 167

FACEBOOK VS.LINKEDIN:
by Robert Lee Brewer.. 170

AUTHOR PLATFORM 2.O:
by Jane Friedman.. 175

MARKETS

LITERARY AGENTS.. 182

BOOK PUBLISHERS... 221

CONSUMER MAGAZINES.. 468

Animal 470

Art and Architecture 476

Associations 479

Astrology, Metaphysical
and New Age 483

Automotive and Motorcycle 485

Aviation 487

Business and Finance 490

Career, College and Alumni 497

Child Care and Parental
    Guidance 499

Comic Books 508

Consumer Service and Business
    Opportunity 508

Contemporary Culture 508

Disabilities 513

Entertainment 516

Ethnic and Minority 519

Food and Drink 525

Games and Puzzles 527

Gay and Lesbian Interest 528

General Interest 531

Health and Fitness 537

History 541

Hobby and Craft 546

Home and Garden 558

Humor 565

Inflight 565

Juvenile 567

Literary and Little 575

Men's 612

Military 612

Music Consumer 614

Mystery 615

Nature, Conservation
    and Ecology 616

Personal Computers 621

Photography 621

Politics and World Affairs 621

Psychology and Self-Improvement 622

Regional 623

Religious 657

Retirement 674

Rural 675

Science 677

Science Fiction, Fantasy
    and Horror 681

Sex 684

Sports 685

Teen and Young Adult 717

Travel, Camping and Trailer 718

Women's 724

TRADE JOURNALS 732

Advertising, Marketing and PR 733

Art, Design and Collectibles 734

Auto and Truck 737

Aviation and Space 739

Beauty and Salon 740

Beverages and Bottling 743

Book and Bookstore 744

Brick, Glass and Ceramics 745

Building Interiors 746

Business Management 747

Church Administration
    and Ministry 750

Clothing 754

Construction and Contracting 754

Drugs, Health Care and
    Medical Products 757

Education and Counseling 757

Electronics and
    Communication 760

Energy and Utilities 761

Engineering and Technology 762

Entertainment and the Arts 764

Farm 766

Finance 771

Florist, Nurseries and
    Landscapers 772

Government and Public Service ...773
Groceries and Food Products 775
Home Furnishings and
    Household Goods 777
Hospitals, Nursing and
    Nursing Homes 777
Hotels, Motels, Clubs, Resorts
    and Restaurants 778
Industrial Operations 780
Information Systems 780
Insurance 781
Jewelry 782
Journalism and Writing 782
Law 787
Lumber 789
Machinery and Metal 790
Maintenance and Safety 792
Management and Supervision 792

Marine and Maritime Industries .793
Medical 793
Music Trade 797
Paper 799
Pets 799
Plumbing, Heating, Air Conditioning
    and Refrigeration 800
Printing 800
Professional Photography 801
Real Estate 801
Resources and Waste Reduction ...803
Selling and Merchandising 804
Sport Trade 807
Stone, Quarry and Mining 809
Toy, Novelty and Hobby 810
Transportation 810
Travel Trade 811
Veterinary 812

CONTESTS & AWARDS 813

Playwriting & Scriptwriting...........814
Arts Councils & Fellowships 818
Fiction...821
Nonfiction 830
Writing for Children &
    Young Adults 836

General 842
Journalism...843
Translation..844
Poetry..845
Multiple Writing Areas...................863

RESOURCES

PROFESSIONAL ORGANIZATIONS 872
GLOSSARY 877

INDEX

GENERAL INDEX..883

FROM THE EDITOR

Without going back through previous editions of *Writer's Market*, I can make a safe guess as to a recurring theme: the change constantly happening in the publishing and media industries. It's a popular topic, and the only constant in publishing and media is, yes, change.

Over the years, the more experienced writers have probably noticed the way the business has changed in small ways each year to add up to dramatic changes over time. For instance, postal submissions have been almost completely replaced by e-mail and online submission forms. Self-publishing, which was once frowned upon, is where some authors are now finding their greatest successes.

However, one thing has not changed: *Writer's Market* still strives to provide writers with the best information available to help them get their writing published and get paid for their writing. If anything, this reference has stepped up its game by sharing how writers can manage and promote their work effectively.

As always, this book is loaded with opportunities to get published and paid for your writing, whether you're searching for book publishers, magazines, contests, or literary agents. Some things just never change.

Until next we meet, keep writing and marketing what you write.

Robert Lee Brewer
Senior Content Editor
Writer's Market and WritersMarket.com
http://writersdigest.com/editor-blogs/poetic-asides
http://robertleebrewer.blogspot.com
http://twitter.com/robertleebrewer

PHOTO: Al Parrish

HOW TO USE
WRITER'S MARKET

Writer's Market is here to help you decide where and how to submit your writing to appropriate markets. Each listing contains information about the editorial focus of the market, how it prefers material to be submitted, payment information, and other helpful tips.

WHAT'S INSIDE?

Since 1921, *Writer's Market* has been giving you the information you need to knowledgeably approach a market. We've continued to develop improvements to help you access that information more efficiently.

NAVIGATIONAL TOOLS. We've designed the pages of *Writer's Market* with you, the writer, in mind. Within the pages you will find **readable market listings** and **accessible charts and graphs**. One such chart can be found in the ever-popular "How Much Should I Charge?" article.

Since 1921, *Writer's Market* has been giving you the information you need to knowledgeably approach a market. We've designed it with you, the writer, in mind.

We've taken all of the updated information in this feature and put it into an easy-to-read and navigate chart, making it convenient for you to find the rates that accompany the freelance jobs you're seeking.

ICONS. There are a variety of icons that appear before each listing. A complete Key to Icons & Abbreviations appears on the right. Icons let you know whether a listing is new to the book (⊕), a book publisher accepts only agented writers (Ⓐ), comparative pay rates for a magazine ($</span>-<span>$$$$), and more.

ACQUISITION NAMES, ROYALTY RATES AND ADVANCES. In the Book Publishers section, we identify acquisition editors with the boldface word **Contact** to help you get your manuscript to the right person. Royalty rates and advances are also highlighted in boldface, as is other important information on the percentage of first-time writers and unagented writers the company publishes, the number of books published, and the number of manuscripts received each year.

EDITORS, PAY RATES, AND PERCENTAGE OF MATERIAL WRITTEN BY FREELANCE WRITERS. In the Consumer Magazines and Trade Journals sections, we identify to whom you should send your query or article with the boldface word **Contact**. The amount (percentage) of material accepted from freelance writers, and the pay rates for features, columns and departments, and fillers are also highlighted in boldface to help you quickly identify the information you need to know when considering whether to submit your work.

QUERY FORMATS. We asked editors how they prefer to receive queries and have indicated in the listings whether they prefer them by mail, e-mail, fax or phone. Be sure to check an editor's individual preference before sending your query.

ARTICLES. Many of the articles are new to this edition. Writers who want to improve their submission techniques should read the articles in the **Finding Work** section. The **Managing Work** section is geared more toward post-acceptance topics, such as contract negotiation and organization. With self-promotion a

KEY TO ICONS & ABBREVIATIONS

⊕	market new to this edition
Ⓐ	market accepts agented submissions only
⦸	market does not accept unsolicited submissions
☺	award-winning market
○	Canadian market
●	market located outside of the U.S. and Canada
◐	online opportunity
$	market pays 0-9¢/word or $0-$150/article
$$	market pays 10-49¢/word or $151-$750/article
$$$	market pays 50-99¢/word or $751-$1,500/article
$$$$	market pays $1/word or over $1,500/article
○	comment from the editor of *Writer's Market*
⚷	tips to break into a specific market
ms, mss	manuscript(s)
b&w	black & white (photo)
SASE	self-addressed, stamped envelope
SAE	self-addressed envelope
IRC	International Reply Coupon, for use when mailing to countries other than your own

big key in freelance success, there is a section of articles dedicated to this topic too: **Promoting Work**.

IMPORTANT LISTING INFORMATION

1) Listings are based on editorial questionnaires and interviews. They are not advertisements; publishers do not pay for their listings. The markets are not endorsed by *Writer's Market* editors. F + W Media, Inc., Writer's Digest Books, and its employees go to great effort to ascertain the validity of information in this book. However, transactions between users of the information and individuals and/or companies are strictly between those parties.

2) All listings have been verified before publication of this book. If a listing has not changed from last year, then the editor said the market's needs have not changed and the previous listing continues to accurately reflect its policies.

3) *Writer's Market* reserves the right to exclude any listing.

4) When looking for a specific market, check the index. A market may not be listed for one of these reasons:
   - It doesn't solicit freelance material.
   - It doesn't pay for material.
   - It has gone out of business.
   - It has failed to verify or update its listing for this edition.
   - It hasn't answered *Writer's Market* inquiries satisfactorily. (To the best of our ability, and with our readers' help, we try to screen fradulent listings.)

IF WRITER'S MARKET IS NEW TO YOU . . .

A quick look at the **Contents** pages will familiarize you with the arrangement of *Writer's Market*. The three largest sections of the book are the market listings of Book Publishers; Consumer Magazines; and Trade Journals. You will also find other sections of market listings for Literary Agents; and Contests & Awards. More opportunities can be found on WritersMarket.com.

Narrowing your search

After you've identified the market categories that interest you, you can begin researching specific markets within each section.

Consumer Magazines and Trade Journals are categorized by subject within their respective sections to make it easier for you to identify markets for your work. If you want to publish an article dealing with parenting, you could look under the Child Care & Parental Guidance category of Consumer Magazines to find an appropriate market. You would want to keep in mind, however, that magazines in other categories might also be interested in your article. (For example, women's magazines publish such material.)

Contests & Awards are categorized by genre of writing. If you want to find journalism contests, you would search the Journalism category; if you have an unpublished novel, check the Fiction category.

Interpreting the markets

Once you've identified companies or publications that cover the subjects in which you're interested, you can begin evaluating specific listings to pinpoint the markets most receptive to your work and most beneficial to you.

In evaluating individual listings, check the location of the company, the types of material it is interested in seeing, submission requirements, and rights and payment policies. Depending on your personal concerns, any of these items could be a deciding factor as you determine which markets you plan to approach. Many listings also include a reporting time.

Check the Glossary for unfamiliar words. Specific symbols and abbreviations are explained in the Key to Icons & Abbreviations appearing on the back inside cover. The most important abbreviation is SASE—self-addressed, stamped envelope.

A careful reading of the listings will reveal that many editors are very specific about their needs. Your chances of success increase if you follow directions to the letter. Often companies do not accept unsolicited manuscripts and return them unread. If a company does not accept unsolicited manuscripts, it is indicated in the listing with a (⊘) icon. (Note: You may still be able to query a market that does not accept unsolicited manuscripts.)

Whenever possible, obtain submission guidelines before submitting material. You can usually obtain guidelines by sending a SASE to the address in the listing. Magazines often post their guidelines on their websites, and many book publishers do so as well. Most of the listings indicate how writer's guidelines are made available. You should also familiarize yourself with the company's publications. Many of the listings contain instructions on how to obtain sample copies, catalogs or market lists. The more research you do upfront, the better your chances of acceptance, publication and payment.

Guide to listing features

Following is an example of the market listings you'll find in each section of *Writer's Market*. Note the callouts that identify various format features of the listing.

EASY-TO-USE REFERENCE ICONS

DIRECT E-MAIL ADDRESSES

SPECIFIC CONTACT NAMES

DETAILED SUBMISSION GUIDELINES

SPECIFIC PAY RATES

$ THE GEORGIA REVIEW

The University of Georgia, Athens GA 30602-9009. (706)542-3481. Fax: (706)542-0047. E-mail: garev@uga.edu. Website: www.uga.edu/garev. **Contact:** Stephen Corey, editor. **99% freelance written**. Quarterly journal. Our readers are educated, inquisitive people who read a lot of work in the areas we feature, so they expect only the best in our pages. All work submitted should show evidence that the writer is at least as well-educated and well-read as our readers. Essays should be authoritative but accessible to a range of readers. Estab. 1947. Circ. 3,500. Byline given. Pays on publication. No kill fee. Publishes ms an average of 6 months after acceptance. Accepts queries by mail. Responds in 2 weeks to queries. Responds in 2-3 months to mss. Sample copy for $10. Guidelines available online.

- No simultaneous or electronic submissions.

NONFICTION Needs essays. For the most part we are not interested in scholarly articles that are narrow in focus and/or overly burdened with footnotes. The ideal essay for *The Georgia Review* is a provocative, thesis-oriented work that can engage both the intelligent general reader and the specialist. **Buys 12-20 mss/year.** Send complete ms. **Pays $40/published page.**

PHOTOS Send photos. Reviews 5x7 prints or larger. Offers no additional payment for photos accepted with ms.

FICTION "We seek original, excellent writing not bound by type. Ordinarily we do not publish novel excerpts or works translated into English, and we strongly discourage authors from submitting these." **Buys 12-20 mss/year.** Send complete ms. **Pays $40/published page.**

POETRY "We seek original, excellent poetry. We do not accept submissions via fax or e-mail. If a submission is known to be included in a book already accepted by a publisher, please notify us of this fact (and of the anticipated date of book publication) in a cover letter." Reads year-round, but submissions postmarked May 15-August 15 will be returned unread. Guidelines available for SASE or on website. Responds in 2-3 months. Always sends prepublication galleys. Acquires first North American serial rights. Reviews books of poetry. "Our poetry reviews range from 500-word 'Book Briefs' on single volumes to 5,000-word essay reviews on multiple volumes." Buys 60-75 poems/year. Submit maximum 5 poems. **Pays $3/line.**

TIPS "Unsolicited manuscripts will not be considered from May 15-August 15 (annually); all such submissions received during that period will be returned unread. Check website for submission guidelines."

BEFORE YOUR FIRST SALE

Everything in life has to start somewhere and that somewhere is always at the beginning. Stephen King, Stephenie Meyer, John Grisham, Nora Roberts—they all had to start at the beginning. It would be great to say becoming a writer is as easy as waving a magic wand over your manuscript and "Poof!" you're published, but that's not how it happens. While there's no one true "key" to becoming successful, a long, well-paid writing career *can* happen when you combine four elements:

- Good writing
- Knowledge of writing markets
- Professionalism
- Persistence

Good writing is useless if you don't know which markets will buy your work or how to pitch and sell your writing. If you aren't professional and persistent in your contact with editors, your writing is just that—your writing. But if you are a writer who embraces the above four elements, you have a good chance at becoming a paid, published writer who will reap the benefits of a long and successful career.

As you become more involved with writing, you may read articles or talk to editors and authors with conflicting opinions about the right way to submit your work. The truth is, there are many different routes a writer can follow to get published, but no matter which route you choose, the end is always the same—becoming a published writer.

The following information on submissions has worked for many writers, but it is by no means the be-all-end-all of proper submission guidelines. It's very easy to get wrapped up in the specifics of submitting (Should I put my last name on every page of my manuscript?) and ignore the more important issues (Will this idea on ice fishing in Alaska be appropriate for a regional magazine in Seattle?). Don't allow yourself to become so blinded by submission procedures that you forget common sense. If you use your common sense and develop professional, courteous relations with editors, you will eventually find your own submission style.

DEVELOP YOUR IDEAS, THEN TARGET THE MARKETS

Writers often think of an interesting story, complete the manuscript, and then begin the search for a suitable publisher or magazine. While this approach is common for fiction, poetry and screenwriting, it reduces your chances of success in many nonfiction writing areas. Instead, try choosing categories that interest you and study those sections in *Writer's Market*. Select several listings you consider good prospects for your type of writing. Sometimes the individual listings will even help you generate ideas.

Next, make a list of the potential markets for each idea. Make the initial contact with markets using the method stated in the market listings. If you exhaust your list of possibilities, don't give up. Instead, reevaluate the idea or try another angle. Continue developing ideas and approaching markets. Identify and rank potential markets for an idea and continue the process.

As you submit to the various publications listed in *Writer's Market*, it's important to remember that every magazine is published with a particular audience and slant in mind. Probably the number one complaint we receive from editors is the submissions they receive are completely wrong for their magazines or book line. The first mark of professionalism is to know your market well. Gaining that knowledge starts with *Writer's Market*, but you should also do your own detective work. Search out back issues of the magazines you wish to write for, pick up recent issues at your local newsstand, or visit magazines' websites—anything that will help you figure out what subjects specific magazines publish. This research is also helpful in learning what topics have been covered ad nauseum—the topics you should stay away from or approach in a fresh way. Magazines' websites are invaluable as most post the current issue of the magazine, as well as back issues, and most offer writer's guidelines.

The same advice is true for submitting to book publishers. Research publisher websites for their submission guidelines, recently published titles and their backlist. You can use this information to target your book proposal in a way that fits with a publisher's other titles while not directly competing for sales.

Prepare for rejection and the sometimes lengthy wait. When a submission is returned, check your file folder of potential markets for that idea. Cross off the market that rejected the idea. If the editor has given you suggestions or reasons why the manuscript was not accepted, you might want to incorporate these suggestions when revising your manuscript.

After revising your manuscript mail it to the next market on your list.

Take rejection with a grain of salt

Rejection is a way of life in the publishing world. It's inevitable in a business that deals with such an overwhelming number of applicants for such a limited number of positions. Anyone who has published has lived through many rejections, and writers with thin skin are at a distinct disadvantage. A rejection letter is not a personal attack. It simply indicates your submission is not appropriate for that market. Writers who let rejection dissuade them from pursuing their dream or who react to an editor's "No" with indignation or fury do themselves a disservice. Writers who let rejection stop them do not get published. Resign yourself to facing rejection now. You will live through it, and you'll eventually overcome it.

QUERY AND COVER LETTERS

A query letter is a brief, one-page letter used as a tool to hook an editor and get him interested in your idea. When you send a query letter to a magazine, you are trying to get an editor to buy your idea or article. When you query a book publisher, you are attempting to get an editor interested enough in your idea to request your book proposal or your entire manuscript. (Note: Some book editors prefer to receive book proposals on first contact. Check individual listings for which method editors prefer.)

Here are some basic guidelines to help you create a query that's polished and well-organized. For more tips see "Query Letter Clinic" article.

- **LIMIT IT TO ONE PAGE, SINGLE-SPACED**, and address the editor by name (Mr. or Ms. and the surname). *Note*: Do not assume that a person is a Mr. or Ms. unless it is obvious from the name listed. For example, if you are contacting a D.J. Smith, do not assume that D.J. should be preceded by Mr. or Ms. Instead, address the letter to D.J. Smith.

- **GRAB THE EDITOR'S ATTENTION WITH A STRONG OPENING.** Some magazine queries, for example, begin with a paragraph meant to approximate the lead of the intended article.

- **INDICATE HOW YOU INTEND TO DEVELOP THE ARTICLE OR BOOK.** Give the editor some idea of the work's structure and content.

- **LET THE EDITOR KNOW IF YOU HAVE PHOTOS** or illustrations available to accompany your magazine article.

- **MENTION ANY EXPERTISE OR TRAINING THAT QUALIFIES YOU** to write the article or book. If you've been published before, mention it; if not, don't.

- **END WITH A DIRECT REQUEST TO WRITE THE ARTICLE.** Or, if you're pitching a book, ask for the go-ahead to send in a full proposal or the entire manuscript. Give the editor an idea of the expected length and delivery date of your manuscript.

A common question that arises is: If I don't hear from an editor in the reported response time, how do I know when I can safely send the query to another market? Many writers find it helpful to indicate in their queries that if they don't receive a response from the editor (slightly after the listed reporting time), they will assume the editor is not interested. It's best to take this approach, particularly if your topic is timely.

A brief, single-spaced cover letter is helpful when sending a manuscript as it helps personalize the submission. However, if you have previously queried the editor, use the cover letter to politely and briefly remind the editor of that query—when it was sent, what it contained, etc. "Here is the piece on low-fat cooking that I queried you about on December 12. I look forward to hearing from you at your earliest convenience." Do not use the cover letter as a sales pitch.

If you are submitting to a market that accepts unsolicited manuscripts, a cover letter is useful because it personalizes your submission. You can, and should, include information about the manuscript, yourself, your publishing history, and your qualifications.

In addition to tips on writing queries, the "Query Letter Clinic" article offers eight example query letters, some that work and some that don't, as well as comments on why the letters were either successful or failed to garner an assignment or contract.

Querying for fiction

Fiction is sometimes queried, but more often editors prefer receiving material. Many fiction editors won't decide on a submission until they have seen the complete manuscript. When submitting a fiction book idea, most editors prefer to see at least a synopsis and sample chapters (usually the first three). For fiction published in magazines, most editors want to see the complete short story manuscript. If an editor does request a query for fiction, it should include a description of the main theme and story line, including the conflict and resolution. Take a look at individual listings to see what editors prefer to receive.

QUERY LETTER RESOURCES

The following list of books provide you with more detailed information on writing query letters, cover letters, and book proposals. All titles are published by Writer's Digest Books.

- *Formatting & Submitting Your Manuscript*, 3rd Edition, by Chuck Sambuchino
- *How to Write Attention-Grabbing Query & Cover Letters*, by John Wood
- *How to Write a Book Proposal*, 4th Edition, by Michael Larsen
- *Writer's Market Companion*, 2nd Edition, by Joe Feiertag and Mary Cupito

---

THE SYNOPSIS

Most fiction books are sold by a complete manuscript, but most editors and agents don't have the time to read a complete manuscript of every wannabe writer. As a result, publishing decision makers use the synopsis and sample chapters to help the screening process of fiction. The synopsis, on its most basic level, communicates what the book is about.

The length and depth of a synopsis can change from agent to agent or publisher to publisher. Some will want a synopsis that is 1-2 single-spaced pages; others will want a synopsis that can run up to 25 double-spaced pages. Checking your listings in *Writer's Market*, as well as double-checking with the listing's website, will help guide you in this respect.

The content should cover all the essential points of the novel from beginning to end and in the correct order. The essential points include main characters, main plot points, and, yes, the ending. Of course, your essential points will vary from the editor who wants a 1-page synopsis to the editor who wants a 25-page synopsis.

NONFICTION BOOK PROPOSALS

Most nonfiction books are sold by a book proposal—a package of materials that details what your book is about, who its intended audience is, and how you intend to write the book. It includes some combination of a cover or query letter, an overview, an outline, author's information sheet, and sample chapters. Editors also want to see information about the audience for your book and about titles that compete with your proposed book.

Submitting a nonfiction book proposal

A proposal package should include the following items:

- **A COVER OR QUERY LETTER.** This letter should be a short introduction to the material you include in the proposal.
- **AN OVERVIEW.** This is a brief summary of your book. It should detail your book's subject and give an idea of how that subject will be developed.
- **AN OUTLINE.** The outline covers your book chapter by chapter and should include all major points covered in each chapter. Some outlines are done in traditional outline form, but most are written in paragraph form.
- **AN AUTHOR'S INFORMATION SHEET.** This information should acquaint the editor with your writing background and convince him of your qualifications regarding the subject of your book.
- **SAMPLE CHAPTERS.** Many editors like to see sample chapters, especially for a first book. Sample chapters show the editor how you write and develop ideas from your outline.
- **MARKETING INFORMATION.** Facts about how and to whom your book can be successfully marketed are now expected to accompany every book proposal. If you can provide information about the audience for your book and suggest ways the book publisher can reach those people, you will increase your chances of acceptance.

- **COMPETITIVE TITLE ANALYSIS.** Check the *Subject Guide to Books in Print* for other titles on your topic. Write a one- or two-sentence synopsis of each. Point out how your book differs and improves upon existing topics.

For more information on nonfiction book proposals, read Michael Larsen's *How to Write a Book Proposal* (Writer's Digest Books).

A WORD ABOUT AGENTS

An agent represents a writer's work to publishers, negotiates contracts, follows up to see that contracts are fulfilled, and generally handles a writer's business affairs, leaving the writer free to write. Effective agents are valued for their contacts in the publishing industry, their knowledge about who to approach with certain ideas, their ability to guide an author's career, and their business sense.

While most book publishers listed in *Writer's Market* publish books by unagented writers, some of the larger houses are reluctant to consider submissions that have not reached them through a literary agent. Companies with such a policy are noted by an (**A**) icon at the beginning of the listing, as well as in the submission information within the listing.

Writer's Market includes a list of literary agents who are all members of the Association of Authors' Representatives and who are also actively seeking new and established writers.

MANUSCRIPT FORMAT

You can increase your chances of publication by following a few standard guidelines regarding the physical format of your manuscript. It should be your goal to make your manuscript readable. Follow these suggestions as you would any other suggestions: Use what works for you and discard what doesn't.

In general, when submitting a manuscript, you should use white, 8½×11, 20 lb. paper, and you should also choose a legible, professional looking font (i.e., Times New Roman)— no all-italic or artsy fonts. Your entire manuscript should be double-spaced with a 1½-inch margin on all sides of the page. Once you are ready to print your manuscript, you should print either on a laser printer or an ink-jet printer.

MANUSCRIPT FORMATTING SAMPLE

1 Your Name   50,000 Words **3**
Your Street Address
City State ZIP Code
Day and Evening Phone Numbers
E-mail Address

Website (if applicable)
2

TITLE

by

4 Your Name

5 You can increase your chances of publication by following a few standard guidelines regarding the physical format of your article or manuscript. It should be your goal to make your manuscript readable. Use these suggestions as you would any other suggestions: Use what works for you and discard what doesn't.

In general, when submitting a manuscript, you should use white, 8½×11, 20-lb. bond paper, and you should also choose a legible, professional-looking font (i.e., Times New Roman)—no all-italic or artsy fonts. Your entire manuscript should be double-spaced with a 1½-inch margin on all sides of the page. Once you are ready to print your article or manuscript, you should print either on a laser printer or an inkjet printer.

Remember, articles should be written after you send a one-page query letter to an editor, and the editor then asks you to write the article. If, however, you are sending an article "on spec" to an editor, you should send both a query letter and the complete article.

Fiction and poetry is a little different from nonfiction articles, in that it is rarely queried. More often than not, poetry and fiction editors want to review the complete manuscript before making a final decision.

1 Type your real name (even if you use a pseudonym) and contact information **2** Double-space twice **3** Estimated word count **4** Type your title in capital letters, double-space and type "by," double-space again, and type your name (or pseudonym if you're using one) **5** Double-space twice, then indent first paragraph and start text of your manuscript **6** On subsequent pages, type your name, a dash, and the page number in the upper left or right corner

ESTIMATING WORD COUNT

Many computers will provide you with a word count of your manuscript. Your editor will count again after editing the manuscript. Although your computer is counting characters, an editor or production editor is more concerned about the amount of space the text will occupy on a page. Several small headlines or subheads, for instance, will be counted the same by your computer as any other word of text. However, headlines and subheads usually employ a different font size than the body text, so an editor may count them differently to be sure enough space has been estimated for larger type.

For short manuscripts, it's often quickest to count each word on a representative page and multiply by the number of pages. You can get a very rough count by multiplying the number of pages in your manuscript by 250 (the average number of words on a double-spaced typewritten page).

PHOTOGRAPHS AND SLIDES

In some cases, the availability of photographs and slides can be the deciding factor as to whether an editor will accept your submission. This is especially true when querying a publication that relies heavily on photographs, illustrations or artwork to enhance the article (i.e., craft magazines, hobby magazines, etc.). In some instances, the publication may offer additional payment for photographs or illustrations.

Check the individual listings to find out which magazines review photographs and what their submission guidelines are. Most publications prefer you do not send photographs with your submission. However, if photographs or illustrations are available, you should indicate that in your query. As with manuscripts, never send the originals of your photographs or illustrations. Instead, send digital images, which is what most magazine and book publishers prefer to use.

SEND PHOTOCOPIES

If there is one hard-and-fast rule in publishing, it's this: *Never* send the original (or only) copy of your manuscript. Most editors cringe when they find out a writer has sent the only copy of their manuscript. You should always send copies of your manuscript.

Some writers choose to send a self-addressed, stamped postcard with a photocopied submission. In their cover letter they suggest if the editor is not interested in their manuscript, it may be tossed out and a reply sent on the postcard. This method is particularly helpful when sending your submissions to international markets.

MAILING SUBMISSIONS

No matter what size manuscript you're mailing, always include a self-addressed, stamped envelope (SASE) with sufficient return postage. The website for the U.S. Postal Service (www.

usps.com) and the website for the Canadian Post (www.canadapost.ca) both have postage calculators if you are unsure how much postage to affix.

A book manuscript should be mailed in a sturdy, well-wrapped box. Enclose a self-addressed mailing label and paper clip your return postage to the label. However, be aware that some book publishers do not return unsolicited manuscripts, so make sure you know the practice of the publisher before sending any unsolicited material.

Types of mail service

There are many different mailing service options available to you whether you are sending a query letter or a complete manuscript. You can work with the U.S. Postal Service, United Parcel Service, Federal Express, or any number of private mailing companies. The following are the five most common types of mailing services offered by the U.S. Postal Service.

- **FIRST CLASS** is a fairly expensive way to mail a manuscript, but many writers prefer it. First-Class mail generally receives better handling and is delivered more quickly than Standard mail.
- **PRIORITY MAIL** reaches its destination within two or three days.
- **STANDARD MAIL** rates are available for packages, but be sure to pack your materials carefully because they will be handled roughly. To make sure your package will be returned to you if it is undeliverable, print "Return Postage Guaranteed" under your address.
- **CERTIFIED MAIL** must be signed for when it reaches its destination.
- **REGISTERED MAIL** is a high-security method of mailing where the contents are insured. The package is signed in and out of every office it passes through, and a receipt is returned to the sender when the package reaches its destination.

MAILING MANUSCRIPTS

- Fold manuscripts under five pages into thirds, and send in a #10 SASE.
- Mail manuscripts five pages or more unfolded in a 9×12 or 10×13 SASE.
- For return envelope, fold the envelope in half, address it to yourself, and add a stamp, or, if going to Canada or another international destination, International Reply Coupons (available at most post office branches).
- Don't send by Certified Mail—this is a sign of an amateur.

QUERY LETTER CLINIC

Many great writers ask year after year, "Why is it so hard to get published?" In many cases, these writers have spent years—and possibly thousands of dollars on books and courses—developing their craft. They submit to the appropriate markets, yet rejection is always the end result. The culprit? A weak query letter.

The query letter is often the most important piece of the publishing puzzle. In many cases, it determines whether an editor or agent will even read your manuscript. A good query letter makes a good first impression; a bad query letter earns a swift rejection.

THE ELEMENTS OF A QUERY LETTER

A query letter should sell editors or agents on your idea or convince them to request your finished manuscript. The most effective query letters get into the specifics from the very first line. It's important to remember that the query is a call to action, not a listing of features and benefits.

In addition to selling your idea or manuscript, a query letter can include information on the availability of photographs or artwork. You can include a working title and projected word count. Depending on the piece, you might also mention whether a sidebar might be appropriate and the type of research you plan to conduct. If appropriate, include a tentative deadline and indicate whether the query is being simultaneously submitted.

Biographical information should be included as well, but don't overdo it unless your background actually helps sell the article or proves that you're the only person who could write your proposed piece.

THINGS TO AVOID IN A QUERY LETTER

The query letter is not a place to discuss pay rates. This step comes after an editor has agreed to take on your article or book. Besides making an unprofessional impression on an editor, it can also work to your disadvantage in negotiating your fee. If you ask for too much, an editor may not even contact you to see if a lower rate might work. If you ask for too little, you may start an editorial relationship where you are making far less than the normal rate.

You should also avoid rookie mistakes, such as mentioning that your work is copyrighted or including the copyright symbol on your work. While you want to make it clear that you've researched the market, avoid using flattery as a technique for selling your work. It often has the opposite effect of what you intend. In addition, don't hint that you can rewrite the piece, as this only leads the editor to think there will be a lot of work involved in shaping up your writing.

Also, never admit several other editors or agents have rejected the query. Always treat your new audience as if they are the first place on your list of submission possibilities.

HOW TO FORMAT YOUR QUERY LETTER

It's OK to break writing rules in a short story or article, but you should follow the rules when it comes to crafting an effective query. Here are guidelines for query writing.

- Use a normal font and typeface, such as Times New Roman and 10- or 12-point type.
- Include your name, address, phone number, e-mail address and website, if possible.
- Use a one-inch margin on paper queries.
- Address a specific editor or agent. (Note: The listings in *Writer's Market* provide a contact name for most submissions. It's wise to double-check contact names online or by calling.)
- Limit query letter to one single-spaced page.
- Include self-addressed, stamped envelope or postcard for response with post submissions. Use block paragraph format (no indentations). Thank the editor for considering your query.

WHEN AND HOW TO FOLLOW UP

Accidents do happen. Queries may not reach your intended reader. Staff changes or interoffice mail snafus may end up with your query letter thrown away. Or the editor may have set your query off to the side for further consideration and forgotten it. Whatever the case may be, there are some basic guidelines you should use for your follow-up communication.

Most importantly, wait until the reported response time, as indicated in *Writer's Market* or their submission guidelines, has elapsed before contacting an editor or agent. Then, you should send a short and polite e-mail describing the original query sent, the date it was sent, and asking if they received it or made a decision regarding its fate.

The importance of remaining polite and businesslike when following up cannot be stressed enough. Making a bad impression on an editor can often have a ripple effect—as that editor may share his or her bad experience with other editors at the magazine or publishing company. Also, don't call.

HOW THE CLINIC WORKS

As mentioned earlier, the query letter is the most important weapon for getting an assignment or a request for your full manuscript. Published writers know how to craft a well-written, hard-hitting query. What follows are eight queries: four are strong; four are not. Detailed comments show what worked and what did not. As you'll see, there is no cut-and-dried "good" query format; every strong query works on its own merit.

GOOD NONFICTION MAGAZINE QUERY

Jimmy Boaz, editor
American Organic Farmer's Digest
8336 Old Dirt Road
Macon GA 00000

Dear Mr. Boaz,

There are 87 varieties of organic crops grown in the United States, but there's only one farm producing 12 of these—Morganic Corporation.

Located in the heart of Arkansas, this company spent the past decade providing great organic crops at a competitive price helping them grow into the ninth leading organic farming operation in the country. Along the way, they developed the most unique organic offering in North America.

As a seasoned writer with access to Richard Banks, the founder and president of Morganic, I propose writing a profile piece on Banks for your Organic Shakers department. After years of reading this riveting column, I believe the time has come to cover Morganic's rise in the organic farming industry. ③

This piece would run in the normal 800-1,200 word range with photographs available of Banks and Morganic's operation.

I've been published in *Arkansas Farmer's Deluxe, Organic Farming Today* and in several newspapers. ④

Thank you for your consideration of this article. I hope to hear from you soon.

Sincerely,

Jackie Service
34 Good St.
Little Rock AR 00000
jackie.service9867@email.com

① My name is only available on our magazine's website and on the masthead. This writer has done her research. ② Here's a story that hasn't been pitched before. I didn't know Morganic was so unique in the market. I want to know more. ③ The writer has access to her interview subject, and she displays knowledge of the magazine by pointing out the correct section in which her piece would run. ④ While I probably would've assigned this article based off the idea alone, her past credits do help solidify my decision.

BAD NONFICTION MAGAZINE QUERY

Dear Gentlemen, **1**

I'd like to write the next great article you'll ever publish. My writing credits include amazing pieces I've done for local and community newspapers and for my college English classes. I've been writing for years and years. **2**

Your magazine may not be a big one like *Rolling Stone or Sports Illustrated,* but I'm willing to write an interview for you anyway. I know you need material, and I need money. (Don't worry. I won't charge you too much.) **3**

Just give me some people to interview, and I'll do the best job you've ever read. It will be amazing, and I can re-write the piece for you if you don't agree. I'm willing to re-write 20 times if needed. **4**

You better hurry up and assign me an article though, because I've sent out letters to lots of other magazines, and I'm sure to be filled up to capacity very soon. **5**

Later gents,

Carl Bighead
76 Bad Query Lane
Big City NY 00000

1 This is sexist, and it doesn't address any contact specifically. **2** An over-the-top claim by a writer who does not impress me with his publishing background. **3** Insults the magazine and then reassures me he won't charge too much? **4** While I do assign material from time to time, I prefer writers pitch me their own ideas after studying the magazine. **5** I'm sure people aren't going to be knocking down his door anytime soon.

GOOD FICTION MAGAZINE QUERY

Marcus West
88 Piano Drive
Lexington KY 00000

August 8, 2011 **1**

Jeanette Curic, editor
Wonder Stories
45 Noodle Street
Portland OR 00000

Dear Ms. Curic,

Please consider the following 1,200-word story, "Turning to the Mel-on," a quirky coming-of-age story with a little magical realism thrown in the mix. **2**

After reading *Wonder Stories* for years, I think I've finally written something that would fit with your audience. My previous short story credits include *Stunned Fiction Quarterly* and *Faulty Mindbomb.* **3**

Thank you in advance for considering "Turning to Melon."

Sincerely,

Marcus West
(123) 456-7890
marcusw87452@email.com

Encl: Manuscript and SASE **4**

1 Follows the format we established in our guidelines. Being able to follow directions is more important than many writers realize. **2** Story is in our word count, and the description sounds like the type of story we would consider publishing. **3** It's flattering to know he reads our magazine. While it won't guarantee publication, it does make me a little more hopeful that the story I'm reading will be a good fit. Also, good to know he's been published before. **4** I can figure it out, but it's nice to know what other materials were included in the envelope. This letter is not flashy, but it gives me the basics and puts me in the right frame of mind to read the actual story.

BAD FICTION MAGAZINE QUERY

To: curic@wonderstories808.com ❶
Subject: A Towering Epic Fantasy

Hello there. ❷

I've written a great fantasy epic novel short story of about 25,000 words that may be included in your magazine if you so desire. ❸

More than 20 years, I've spent chained to my desk in a basement writing out the greatest story of our modern time. And it can be yours if you so desire to have it. ❹

Just say the word, and I'll ship it over to you. We can talk money and movie rights after your acceptance. I have big plans for this story, and you can be part of that success. ❺

Yours forever (if you so desire), ❻

Harold
(or Harry for friends)

❶ We do not consider e-mail queries or submissions. ❷ This is a little too informal. ❸ First off, what did he write? An epic novel or short story? Second, 25,000 words is way over our 1,500-word max. ❹ I'm lost for words. ❺ Money and movie rights? We pay moderate rates and definitely don't get involved in movies. ❻ I'm sure the writer was just trying to be nice, but this is a little bizarre and kind of creepy. I do not so desire more contact with "Harry."

GOOD NONFICTION BOOK QUERY

To: corey@bigbookspublishing.com
Subject: Query: Become a Better Parent in 30 Days **1**

Dear Mr. Corey,

2 As a parent of six and a high school teacher for more than 20 years, I know first hand that being a parent is difficult work. Even harder is being a good parent. My proposed title **3** *Taking Care of Yourself and Your Kids: A 30-day Program to Become a Better Parent While Still Living Your Life* would show how to handle real-life situations and still be a good parent.

This book has been years in the making, as it follows the outline I've used successfully in my summer seminars I give on the topic to thousands of parents every year. It really works, because past participants contact me constantly to let me know what a difference my classes have made in their lives. **4**

In addition to marketing and selling *Taking Care of Yourself and Your Kids* at my summer seminars, I would also be able to sell it through my website and promote it through my weekly e-newsletter with over 25,000 subscribers. Of course, it would also make a very nice trade title that I think would sell well in bookstores and possibly retail outlets, such as Wal-Mart and Target. **5**

Please contact me for a copy of my full book proposal today. **6**

Thank you for your consideration.

Marilyn Parent
8647 Query St.
Norman OK 00000
mparent8647@email.com
www.marilynsbetterparents.com

1 Effective subject line. Lets me know exactly what to expect when I open the e-mail. **2** Good lead. Six kids and teaches high school. I already trust her as an expert. **3** Nice title that would fit well with others we currently offer. **4** Her platform as a speaker definitely gets my attention. **5** 25,000 e-mail subscribers? She must have a very good voice to gather that many readers. **6** I was interested after the first paragraph, but every paragraph after made it impossible to not request her proposal.

BAD NONFICTION BOOK QUERY

To: info@bigbookspublishing.com
Subject: a question for you **1**

I really liked this book by Mega Book Publishers called *Build Better Trains in Your Own Backyard.* It was a great book that covered all the basics of model train building. My father and I would read from it together and assemble all the pieces, and it was magical like Christmas all through the year. Why wouldn't you want to publish such a book? **2**

Well, here it is. I've already copyrighted the material for 2006 and can help you promote it if you want to send me on a worldwide book tour. As you can see from my attached digital photo, I'm not the prettiest person, but I am passionate. **3**

There are at least 1,000 model train builders in the United States alone, and there might be even more than that. I haven't done enough research yet, because I don't know if this is an idea that appeals to you. If you give me maybe $500, I could do that research in a day and get back to you on it. **4**

Anyway, this idea is a good one that brings back lots of memories for me.

Jacob **5**

1 The subject line is so vague I almost deleted this e-mail as spam without even opening it. **2** The reason we don't publish such a book is easy—we don't do hobby titles. **3** I'm not going to open an attachment from an unknown sender via e-mail. Also, copyrighting your work years before pitching is the sign of an amateur. **4** 1,000 possible buyers is a small market, and I'm not going to pay a writer to do research on a proposal. **5** Not even a last name? Or contact information? At least I won't feel guilty for not responding.

GOOD FICTION BOOK QUERY

Jeremy Mansfield, editor
Novels R Us Publishing
8787 Big Time Street
New York NY 00000

Dear Mr. Mansfield,

My 62,000-word novel, *The Cat Walk,* is a psychologically complex thriller in the same mold as James Patterson's Alex Cross novels, but with a touch of the supernatural a la Stephenie Meyer. **1**

Rebecca Frank is at the top of the modeling world, posing for magazines in exotic locales all over the world and living life to its fullest. Despite all her success, she feels something is missing in her life. Then she runs into Marcus Hunt, a wealthy bachelor with cold blue eyes and an ambiguous past.

Within 24 hours of meeting Marcus, Rebecca's understanding of the world turns upside down, and she finds herself fighting for her life and the love of a man who may not have the ability to return her the favor.

Filled with demons, serial killers, trolls, maniacal clowns and more, *The Cat Walk* follows Rebecca through a gauntlet of trouble and turmoil, leading up to a final climactic realization that may lead to her own unraveling. **2**

The Cat Walk should fit in well with your other titles, such as *Bone Dead* and *Carry Me Home*, though it is a unique story. Your website mentioned supernatural suspense as a current interest, so I hope this is a good match. **3**

My short fiction has appeared in many mystery magazines, including a prize-winning story in *The Mysterious Oregon Quarterly.* This novel is the first in a series that I'm working on (already half-way through the second). **4**

As stated in your guidelines, I've included the first 30 pages. Thank you for considering *The Cat Walk.*

Sincerely,

Merry Plentiful
54 Willow Road
East Lansing MI 00000
merry865423@email.com

---

1 Novel is correct length and has the suspense and supernatural elements we're seeking. **2** The quick summary sounds like something we would write on the back cover of our paperbacks. That's a good thing, because it identifies the triggers that draw a response out of our readers. **3** She mentions similar titles we've done and that she's done research on our website. She's not afraid to put in a little extra effort. **4** At the moment, I'm not terribly concerned that this book could become a series, but it is something good to file away in the back of my mind for future use.

BAD FICTION BOOK QUERY

Jeremy Mansfield
Novels R Us Publishing
8787 Big Time Street
New York NY 00000

Dear Editor,

My novel has an amazing twist ending that could make it a worldwide phenomenon overnight while you are sleeping. It has spectacular special effects that will probably lead to a multi-million dollar movie deal that will also spawn action figures, lunch boxes, and several other crazy subsidiary rights. I mean, we're talking big-time money here. **①**

I'm not going to share the twist until I have a signed contract that authorizes me to a big bank account, because I don't want to have my idea stolen and used to promote whatever new initiative "The Man" has in mind for media nowadays. Let it be known that you will be rewarded handsomely for taking a chance on me. **②**

Did you know that George Lucas once took a chance on an actor named Harrison Ford by casting him as Han Solo in Star Wars? Look at how that panned out. Ford went on to become a big actor in the Indiana Jones series, *The Fugitive, Blade Runner*, and more. It's obvious that you taking a risk on me could play out in the same dramatic way. **③**

I realize that you've got to make money, and guess what? I want to make money too. So we're on the same page, you and I. We both want to make money, and we'll stop at nothing to do so.

If you want me to start work on this amazing novel with an incredible twist ending, just send a one-page contract agreeing to pay me a lot of money if we hit it big. No other obligations will apply. If it's a bust, I won't sue you for millions. **④**

Sincerely,

Kenzel Pain
92 Bad Writer Road
Austin TX 00000

① While I love to hear enthusiasm from a writer about his or her work, this kind of unchecked excitement is worrisome for an editor. **②** I need to know the twist to make a decision on whether to accept the manuscript. Plus, I'm troubled by the paranoia and emphasis on making a lot of money. **③** I'm confused. Does he think he's Harrison Ford? **④** So that's the twist: He hasn't even written the novel yet. There's no way I'm going to offer a contract for a novel that hasn't been written by someone with no experience or idea of how the publishing industry works.

PERFECT PITCH:

Pitches That Never Fail

....

by Marc Acito

"*A first-time novelist sets the record at a writers conference for the most pitches, leading to a multiple-book deal, awards, translations, excellent reviews and a movie option. An inspiring true success story, a literary version of Seabiscuit, except the horse is a writer.*"

As pitches go, this one's devoid of conflict, but that's the point. This scenario actually happened to me. Hence my qualification for writing this article.

My writing students get nervous when I ask them to pitch their works-in-progress on the first day of class, particularly if they're just starting. "I wouldn't know how to describe it," they say. "I don't know what it's about."

....

A pitch is simply another story that you're telling. A very, very short one.

....

And therein lies the problem. To some degree, we can't know what our novel/memoir/screenplay/play/nonfiction book is entirely about until we've gotten it down. But I contend that thinking about the pitch ahead of time helps focus a writer's goals for a piece. It's not just a commercial concern, it's an artistic one.

Writers are storytellers and a pitch is simply another story that you're telling. A very, very short one. Rather than view pitching as if you were a salesman in a bad suit hawking used cars, imagine that you're a pitcher for the Yankees and that the agent or editor is the catcher: They're on your team, so they really want to catch the ball.

Or, put another way, you're a different kind of pitcher, this one full of cool, refreshing water that will fill their empty glass.

But first you've got to get their attention.

THE HOOK

"I need something to grab me right away that tells me exactly why I should want to read this submission (of all the submissions on my desk)," says Christina Pride, senior editor at Hyperion.

A hook is exactly what it sounds like—a way to grab a reader like a mackerel and reel them in. It's not a plot summary, but more like the ad campaign you'd see on a movie poster. Veteran Hollywood screenwriter Cynthia Whitcomb, who teaches the pitching workshop at the Willamette Writers Conference in Portland, Oregon, recommends that writers of all genres start with a hooky tagline like this one from *Raiders of the Lost Ark:*

> *"If adventure had a name, it'd be Indiana Jones."*

That's not just first-rate marketing, it's excellent storytelling.

Here are some of my other favorite taglines for movies based on books, so you can see how easily the concept works for novels:

- "Help is coming from above." (*Charlotte's Web*)
- "From the moment they met it was murder." (*Double Indemnity*)
- "The last man on earth is not alone." (*I am Legend*)
- "Love means never having to say you're sorry." (*Love Story*)

The last one actually isn't true; love means always saying you're sorry, even when you're not, but the thought is provocative and provocation is exactly what you want to do.

When I pitched my first novel, *How I Paid for College,* I always started the same way. First, I looked the catcher right in the eye (this is very important—how else are they going to catch the ball?). Then I said,

> *"Embezzlement. Blackmail. Fraud…High School."*

I began my query letters the same way.

"I always begin my proposals with a question," says Jennifer Basye Sander, co-author of *The Complete Idiots Guide to Getting Published.* "I want to get an editor nodding their head in agreement right away."

No, you're not asking something like, "Are you ready to rock 'n roll?" but instead an open-ended conversation starter like, "Can you be forgiven for sending an innocent man to jail?" (Ian McEwan's *Atonement*) or "What does it take to climb Mount Everest?" (Jon Krakauer's *Into Thin Air*). Particularly useful are "what if?" questions like "What if an amnesiac didn't know he was the world's most wanted assassin?" (Robert Ludlum's *The Bourne Identity*) or "What if Franklin Delano Roosevelt had been defeated by Charles Lindbergh in 1940?" (*The Plot Against America*, Philip Roth).

Acito employs humor in his novels, but there's nothing funny about the effectiveness of his pitches.

The same also holds true for nonfiction. If you sat down in front of an agent and asked, "What if you could trim your belly fat and use it to fuel your car?" trust me, they'd listen. Questions like that make the catcher want to know more. Which is exactly what you do by creating…

THE LOG LINE

No, it's not a country western dance done in a timber mill. And without realizing it, you're already a connoisseur of the genre, having read thousands of log lines in *TV Guide* or imdb. com or the *New York Times* Bestseller List. A log line is a one-sentence summary that states the central conflict of your story. For example:

> *"A teen runaway kills the first person she encounters, then is pursued by the dead woman's sister as she teams up with three strangers to kill again."*

Recognize it? That's *The Wizard of Oz.*
  Here's another:

> *"The son of a carpenter leaves on an adventure of self-discovery, rejects sin, dies and rises again transformed."*

Obviously, that's *Pinocchio.*
  Okay, seriously, here's the one I did for *How I Paid for College*:

> *"A talented but irresponsible teenager schemes to steal his college tuition money when his wealthy father refuses to pay for him to study acting at Juilliard."*

It's not genius, but it captured the story succinctly by identifying the protagonist, the antagonist, and the conflict between them. In other words, the essential element for any compelling story.

AND HERE'S THE PITCH...

Pitches are often referred to as "elevator pitches" because they should last the length of your average elevator ride—anywhere from 30 seconds to two minutes. Or, for a query letter, one page single-spaced. That's about 350 words, including "Dear Mr. William Morris" and "Your humble servant, Desperate Writer."

Essentially, the pitch is identical to a book jacket blurb: it elaborates on the set-up, offers a few further complications on the central conflict, then gives an indication of how it wraps up. When it comes to the ending, "don't be coy," says Erin Harris, a literary agent at the Irene Skolnick Agency in Manhattan. "Spoil the secrets, and let me know what really happens." Agents and editors want a clear idea of what kind of ride they're getting on before investing hours in your manuscript. Make it easy for them to do their jobs selling it.

> Agents and editors want a clear idea of what kind of ride they're getting on before investing hours in your manuscript.

Nowhere was this clearer to me than when I read the jacket copy of my first novel and saw that it was virtually identical to my query letter.

Indeed, your best practice for learning how to pitch is to read jacket descriptions (leaving out the part about the author being a "bold, original new voice"—that's for others to say).

Or think of it as a very short story, following the structure attributed to writer Alice Adams: Action, Backstory, Development, Climax, End.

It's as easy as ABDCE.

"The best queries convey the feeling that the author understands what the scope, structure, voice, and audience of the book really are," says Rakesh Satyal, senior editor at HarperCollins to authors such as Paul Coelho, Armistead Maupin and Clive Barker. "To misunderstand or miscommunicate any of these things can be truly detrimental."

That's the reason we often resort to the Hollywoody jargon of it's "This meets that," as in "It's *No Country for Old Men* meets *Little Women*." Or it's...

- ...*Die Hard* on a bus (*Speed*)
- ...*Die Hard* in a plane (*Con Air*)
- ...*Die Hard* in a phone booth (*Phone Booth*)
- ...*Die Hard* in a skyscraper (no, wait, that's *Die Hard*).

HOW I PAID FOR COLLEGE

A Tale of Sex, Theft, Friendship and Musical Theater

A novel by Marc Acito

Embezzlement…Blackmail…Fraud…High School.

How I Paid for College is a 97,000-word comic novel about a talented but irresponsible teenager who schemes to steal his college tuition money when his wealthy father refuses to pay for acting school. The story is just true enough to embarrass my family.

It's 1983 in Wallingford, New Jersey, a sleepy bedroom community outside of Manhattan. Seventeen-year-old Edward Zanni, a feckless Ferris Bueller type, is Peter Panning his way through a carefree summer of magic and mischief, sending underwear up flagpoles and re-arranging lawn animals in compromising positions. The fun comes to a screeching halt, however, when Edward's father remarries and refuses to pay for Edward to study acting at Juilliard.

In a word, Edward's screwed. He's ineligible for scholarships because his father earns too much. He's unable to contact his mother because she's off somewhere in Peru trying to commune with the Incan spirits. And, in a sure sign he's destined for a life in the arts, Edward's incapable of holding down a job. ("One little flesh wound is all it takes to get fired as a dog groomer, even if you artfully arrange its hair so the scar doesn't show.")

So Edward turns to his loyal (but immoral) misfit friends to help him steal the tuition money from his father. Disguising themselves as nuns and priests (because who's going to question the motives of a bunch of nuns and priests?) they merrily scheme their way through embezzlement, money laundering, identity theft, forgery and blackmail.

But along the way Edward also learns the value of friendship, hard work and how you're not really a man until you can beat up your father. (Metaphorically, that is.)

How I Paid for College is a farcical coming-of-age story that combines the first-person-smart-ass tone of David Sedaris with the byzantine plot twists of Armistead Maupin. I've written it with the HBO-watching, NPR-listening, Vanity Fair-reading audience in mind.

As a syndicated humor columnist, I'm familiar with this audience. For the past three years, my bi-weekly column, "The Gospel According to Marc," has appeared in 18 alternative newspapers in major markets, including Los Angeles, Chicago and Washington, DC. During that time I've amassed a personal mailing list of over 1,000 faithful readers.

How I Paid for College is a story for anyone who's ever had a dream…and a scheme.

www.MarcAcito.com

(503) 246-2208

Marc@MarcAcito.com

5423 SW Cameron Road, Portland, OR 97221

"I appreciate when agents and authors offer good comp titles," confirms Hyperion's Christina Pride. "It's good shorthand to help me begin to position the book in my mind right from the outset in terms of sensibility and potential audience."

Agent Erin Harris agrees. "For example," she says, "the premise of one book meets the milieu of another book." As in *Pride and Prejudice and Zombies*, an idea I will forever regret not thinking of myself.

When citing comp titles, be certain to invoke the most commercially successful and well-known works to which you can honestly liken yourself. No agent wants to earn 15 percent of *Obscure Literary Title* meets *Total Downer by Author Who Committed Suicide*.

So I steered clear of my lesser-known influences and focused on the big names, saying, "*How I Paid for College* is a farcical coming-of-age story that combines the first-person-smart-ass tone of David Sedaris with the byzantine plot twists of Armistead Maupin."

That line also made it onto the jacket copy.

My book hasn't changed, but I continue to update the pitch as I develop the movie. What started as "*Ferris Bueller* meets *High School Musical*," turned into "A mash-up of *Ocean's 11* and *Glee*." By the time the movie actually gets made it'll be "*iTunes Implant Musical Experience* meets *Scheming Sentient Robots*."

"A word of caution," Harris adds. "Please do not liken your protagonist to Holden Caulfield or your prose style to that of Proust. Truly, it's best to steer clear of the inimitable."

Speaking of the inimitable, while the titles of *Catcher in the Rye* and *Remembrance of Things Past* are poetically evocative, they wouldn't distinguish themselves from the pack in the Too-Much-Information Age. Nowadays, your project is competing for attention with a video of a toddler trapped behind a couch. (I'm serious, Google it, it's got all the makings of great drama: a sympathetic protagonist, conflict, complications, laughter, tears and an uplifting ending. All in two minutes and 27 seconds.)

So while it's not a dictum of the publishing industry (though, given the nosedive the industry has taken, what do *they* know?), I think 21st century writers would do well to title their works in ways that accommodate the searchable keyword culture of the Internet.

In other words, *To Kill a Mockingbird* was fine for 1960, but if you tried promoting it today, you'd end up at the PETA website.

Like the logline, the catchiest titles actually describe what the book is about. Consider:

- *Eat, Pray, Love*
- *Diary of a Wimpy Kid*
- *Sh*t My Dad Says*
- *A Portrait of the Artist as a Young Man*

In those cases, the title is the synopsis. Similarly, some titles, while less clear, include an inherent mystery or question:

- *Sophie's Choice*

- *The Hunger Games*
- *And Then There Were None*
- *The Hitchhiker's Guide to the Galaxy*

Lastly, even if the reader can't know automatically what the title means, it helps if it's simple and memorable, like:

- *Twilight*
- *Valley of the Dolls*
- *The Thorn Birds*
- *Captain Underpants*

One way to tell if you've got an effective title is to submit it to the "Have you read…?" test. If it feels natural coming at the end of that sentence, you're on the right track.

Granted, straightforward titles are easier if you're writing nonfiction like *Trim Your Belly Fat and Use it to Fuel Your Car*. As is the final part of the pitch.

BUILDING A PLATFORM

Along with branding, platform is one of the most overused buzz words of the last decade. "If you are writing nonfiction," Erin Harris says, "it's important to describe your platform and to be a qualified expert on the subject about which you're writing"

In other words, if you're going to write *Teach Your Cat to Tap Dance* you better deliver a tap-dancing cat, along with research about the market for such a book.

For first-time novelists this can prove challenging. But Harris says that every credit truly helps: "If you have pieces published in literary magazines, if you have won awards, or if you have an MFA, my interest is piqued."

That last advice should also pique the interest of every fledgling writer out there. In my case, what actually got me an agent wasn't just the pitch, it was the fact that I met best-selling novelist Chuck Palahniuk at a workshop and he'd read a column of mine in a small alternative newspaper. Ultimately, it's not about who you know, it's about who knows you. So publish wherever you can. You never know who's reading.

Write on.

MARC ACITO is the award-winning author of the comic novels *How I Paid for College* and *Attack of the Theater People*. *How I Paid for College* won the Ken Kesey Award for Fiction, was a Top Teen Pick by the American Library Association and is translated into five languages the author cannot read. A regular contributor to NPR's *All Things Considered*, he teaches story structure online and at NYU. www.MarcAcito.com

FEATURE ARTICLE WRITING:

The Query in 3 Parts

by Chuck Sambuchino

If you want to write freelance articles for editors, the query letter is your best and most effective tool. It's essentially a one-page business plan for your idea—explaining what the idea is, why it will be a good fit for their publication, and why you're a qualified writer for the assignment.

You see, editors for magazines, newspapers and websites have one thing in common: They're all incredibly busy. They have very little time for anything, so they need to consider article ideas quickly, and that's where your query comes in. It's your pitch, and you have one short page to get their attention and convince them to pay you money in exchange for an assignment. Although there is no "perfect" or "surefire" way to structure a query, I have adopted and slowly tried to refine a three-part approach that seems to work well. Read on, and dig deeper into what comprises a successful, eye-catching query letter.

THE FIRST SECTION: THE HOOK

Nothing works better in a query letter than hooking an editor right away with your idea. By the end of the first sentence, they should be intrigued and want to know more. The first paragraph is designed to pique interest and give them a taste of what your article will be about. It's also the best chance you have in a query to show the flavor of your writing—your voice, for lack of a better term. If the article is going to be light and funny, your intro should reflect that. If it's going to be heavy and serious, make sure your query is, too. Keep in mind that if you are contacting a person you know or through a referral, that is always a great way to start—explaining your connection.

If you don't have a connection or referral, here are a few ways to get an editor's attention immediately with your query:

Start with an eye-catching fact

> Alaska not only has the country's highest ratio of low birth weight babies, the percentage is actually going up yearly.

> Last year's dreaded recession brought countless white wedding plans to a screeching halt. According to David Bridal's recent national survey, 75% of American brides-to-be are searching high and low for a way to still have the wedding of their dreams—without spending a fortune.

With an approach like this, you're aiming to immediately tell the editor that what you have to say is news—and it's important.

Use an interesting tidbit

> There are 87 varieties of organic crops grown in the United States, but there's only one farm producing 12 of these—Morganic Corporation.

> If I asked you which sports hobby was the most popular for retirees in South Florida, you may say bowling or shuffleboard. Perhaps some would even throw out softball or darts—but all those guesses would be wrong. The truth is: The mini-golf movement has hit South Florida big time, and it's taking over everywhere.

When you have a story that isn't hard news (perhaps a feature or profile), an interesting fact works well. Think of it like this: You learned about something and were interested enough to research more and pitch an article. Try to get us interested in the subject just like you were.

Start in media res—in the middle of a story

> It was 2:14 a.m. when a drunk driver smashed into the bedroom of Mike Edson's condo and took the life of his wife.

> I'm right in the middle of my weeklong quest to find the best cheeseburger in DC when a monstrosity known only as "The Goliath" is dropped in front of me on a plate. It's less of a burger than it is a defining moment in your life. I notice my hands are shaking as I reach to pick it up—all three pounds of it.

When your piece focuses on a front-to-back narrative (that can involve you or others), you can always just show an interesting moment right in the middle. This gets us editors asking questions such as "How did he get to this moment?" "Does he finish the burger?" "What was his final decision as to the best burger in the city?" In other words, I want to know more.

THE SECOND SECTION: THE SPECS

If you've done your job, the editor is still reading your query. You've caught their attention with the first sentence then expounded on your idea by putting more meat on the bones. The second part of the query letter is where you take a step back and start to talk about the specs of the article itself. A safe way is to start this paragraph with "I propose an article on …"

With a paragraph or two, your goal is to explain more about the size and scope of the piece, what the article will look like on the page, and, finally, prove to the editor that you read their publication and are familiar with the type of content readers like to see.

Mind the Details

Here are things you want to address/include:

- Estimated length (word count).
- Targeted section of the magazine. Where will this article appear in the publication?
- What kind of story is it? Feature? Profile? Column?
- The slant, if it needs explaining. For example, let's say you hear about a local woman who's planting a rose in town for every soldier that dies fighting the war on terror. You could pitch an article about her to a gardening magazine, a military/patriotic magazine, and a local interest magazine. But each one will need a different focus— a different slant.
- Do you have access to people you will interview? If you are proposing to profile famous screenwriter Charlie Kaufman for *Creative Screenwriting*, you will need to say that you have access to him somehow. Do you want to sit down with Kevin Garnett? How can you secure an interview?
- Do you have access to images or will you provide art/pictures? If you're writing for *Popular Woodworking* or *Ohio Game and Fish*, will you be taking your own photos to provide with the piece? You increase your chances of success if you do so.
- Any sources lined up—or at least the names of whom you would interview. If you are writing a piece on low birth weight, to continue that example, you should quickly list the names of people you will consult and interview for the piece. With luck, you've already spoken with one and have a quote you can include in the query.

THE THIRD SECTION: THE BIO

If an editor is still reading your query by the end, she must love the idea and feel it has promise for their publication. What a writer must do now is convince her as to why they're the ideal person to compose this piece. In other words, she's looking for credentials—a bio.

Elements of a Bio

- Do you have any qualifications of relevance? For example, if you're writing for *Men's Fitness,* do you hold any degrees or certifications in the health field?
- Have you written about this subject before?
- What publications have you written for, if any?

If you have enclosed or attached clips (previously published samples of your writing), say so. You can attach PDF scans of a piece, or simply paste a link to an online article. Ideally, you want to show them clips that have some comparison to what you want to write about. For instance, if you want to do a profile of gymnast who is considered the most promising eight-year-old in the world in her field, then do you have any sample profiles for the editor to see? Mentioning that you write about cars for the local paper shows that you're a professional, but doesn't yet convince her that you can tackle a profile on an eight-year-old.

And if You Have No Credits?

Keep in mind that if you have no clips to include, don't embellish or exaggerate. Just skip the clips part. Thank the editor for considering the submission and wrap up with "Sincerely, (Name)."

The higher you aim for an assignment, the more editors will demand credentials and credits. If you query the local parenting magazine that's usually found for free in supermarkets, you don't need a slew of impressive articles in your pocket. You probably just need a good idea and professional-looking query. But if you want to write for a mid-size magazine like *The Pastel Journal* or *Girlfriends Magazine*, you will likely need some bylines to your name.

QUERY FAQ

Do queries have a specific font or format? Your best bet is to use a normal font and typeface, such as Times New Roman or Arial. Use 10- or 12-point font.

Should I discuss payment in a query? No. If you've done your research, you should have a general idea of what a magazine pays. The payment discussion will come up organically as the conversation goes along. Bringing up payment too quickly may show that you're hard to work with.

Who do I address the letter to? Every publication has a submissions editor—meaning, an individual who is in charge of reviewing queries and accepting good ideas. With a tiny website or magazine, there is likely a staff of one, and the top editor is reviewing everything. For larger publications, such as our magazines here at our publishing house—*Writer's Digest* or *Watercolor Artist*—the top editor is not the contact person for submissions. Seek out a copy of the publication's submission guidelines to get the name of the submissions editor. If in doubt, contact the publication by e-mail or phone and simply ask who to address the letter to and the best e-mail address to use.

Should I mention the work is copyrighted? No. The editors already know this, and mentioning what the editors already know comes off amateurish.

Do editors want to know if it's a simultaneous submission? You don't *have* to mention it, but yes, editors appreciate knowing.

What if the query has been rejected in the past? Don't mention it when contacting editors. Letting them know this just makes the idea sound worse. They get to thinking, "If four other people have rejected it, the idea must not be worth it…"

What if the material's been published before? Let editors know. If what you're pitching is a reprinted article or an excerpt from a book you wrote, that's A-OK—just let them know upfront.

Should writers submit via e-mail vs. snail mail? Once again, check the submission guidelines to see how publications like to get queries. Over the past decade, there has been a gradual yet large shift toward e-queries—and that's a good thing. E-mail queries are quicker and less expensive. If you have the option to submit either way, it makes no real difference.

Can I follow up if I don't hear back? Sure, but check guidelines first. If a magazine says they respond to ideas within six weeks, I'd wait eight before following up. In your follow-up, be polite and humble, simply mentioning that you had not heard back and are afraid the first e-mail got lost in cyberspace, which is why you're resubmitting the original query below (just cut and paste it again).

How do you end a query? A safe bet is always to thank the editor for their time and sign off. If you're querying an agent, ask if you can send some pages of your work (or the full proposal for nonfiction).

BOOK QUERIES

Book queries are slightly different than article queries whether you're submitting to a literary agent or directly to a publisher. Again, there is no surefire format, but they are still one page long and you can still employ a three-part structure—but the three parts will be:

PART 1: THE BASICS. Provide the title, word count and genre/category. Also, why are you contacting this agent/editor? Explain why you picked this agent/editor out of all your options. Explain why they're a great match for your book. Try to establish a connection. If you are contacting by referral, or because you met them at a writers' conference, say so upfront.

PART 2: THE PITCH. This is where you explain what your project is about in 3-10 sentences. If you're writing a novel or memoir, go to the nearest Barnes & Noble and start looking at the backs of DVD boxes and the inside covers of novels. This will get you in the mindset of writing a concise and compelling pitch paragraph. You will see how a pitch is composed and how they're designed to pique your interest but not reveal the ending.

PART 3: THE BIO. Again, list who you are and what credits you have. If you are writing nonfiction, this section—explaining your platform and marketing ability—will be the most important aspect of the letter.

GOOD ARTICLE QUERY

John Q. Writer **7**
123 Author Lane Writerville, USA
johnqwriter@email.com
(323) 555-0000

Jan. 30, 2009

Jane Smith, managing editor
New Mexico Magazine
4200 Magazine Blvd. Santa Fe, NM 87501

Ms. Smith: **1**

According to the Bible, it took two days for God to create all living creatures. **9** The way New Mexican Regina Gordon sees it, the 48-Hour Film Project involves the same amount of time—with only a slightly less complicated task.

1 Always address the correct editor **2** Estimated word count **3** Highlight qualifications quickly and effectively **4** Be polite **5** Signature. If you're mailing the letter, leave enough room here to sign your cursive signature. **6** Detail your enclosures **7** One of many letterhead styles you can use **8** Targeting a specific section of the magazine shows you're familiar with the publication **9** A lead designed to hook and pique interest

"Every second counts, when you have 48 hours to make a film." That's the motto of the 48-Hour Film Project (www.48hourfilm.com), a nationwide event that challenges local filmmakers to form teams and create four-minute movies—from script to set design to finished product—in 48 hours or less. Albuquerque is no stranger to the fray, and will again participate in the competition in 2009.

Also returning in 2009 is the city's area producer: Gordon. More than 20 area teams competed in 2008—with all of these guerilla filmmakers reporting to one woman—Gordon—who must substitute passion, adrenaline, and insane amounts of coffee for sleep she certainly won't get. So what drives her and other participants to exhaust themselves like they do? I propose an **2** 800-word short profile on Gordon and, with it, New Mexico's involvement in the project for *New Mexico Magazine*. (I've already touched based with Gordon.) I believe that a Gordon feature would be a great fit for the "Introducing" section **8** of your magazine. To give readers a feel for what a kinetic, exciting, shoot-from-the-hip experience this is, I would interview Langston to hear anecdotes from last year and discover what lies in store for this year—as a sense of community for the project continues to build in the area.

3 In 2003, I covered Philadelphia's involvement in the project for *Artspike* magazine. Thank you for considering this piece. My résumé and clips are enclosed.

4 Respectfully,
5

John Q. Writer

Encl.: Clips and résumé **6**

BAD ARTICLE QUERY

Richard D. Bonehead
123 Mistake Lane Rejectionville, USA

March 24, 2009

Editors
Atlanta Journal-Constitution
2

Dear Sir/Ma'am: **3**

I have an idea for a newspaper article. I have a feeling that it would be a controversial and explosive story that would sell a whole bunch of copies—its **4** that good. What I want to do is give you some of my early thoughts, and if you're interested, we can talk some specifics over the phone (though bear with me; my cell phone gets bad reception).

This is what I'm thinking. I write an article on how the social networking juggernaut MySpace **5** is affecting the dating scene in the ATL. Cool, huh? I know that I could have pitched this) to *Atlanta Magazine* or even *People*, but I figured I would give you a shot. For the article, I would need some ideas for sources, and probably some upfront money to buy a laptop. At this point, I'm thinking the article will run about 5,000 words. **6**

My writing influences are Stephen King, James Patterson and Joe Eszterhas. I've blogged on MySpace plenty of times before and I also regularly comment on website forums and message boards, so I think I have the necessary experience to tackle such an article. **7**

I'm offering a seven-day window on this query because I think that's fair. After all, this is a sizzling topic. Please get back to me right quick.

Peace,

Richard D. Bonehead

1 No e-mail or phone number included **2** Address is missing **3** Not targeting a specific editor shows lack of basic research **4** This simple grammatical error could have been caught with some proofreading **5** Idea is not fleshed out and no indication of how to hook readers **6** Proposed length is way too long for virtually any publication **7** While you want to list credentials, something worse would be to list meaningless accomplishments

GOOD QUERY TO AGENT

(2) Dorien Orion
123 Author Lane
Writerville, USA
(323) 555-0000
johnqwriter@email.com

Mollie Glick

Foundry Literary + Media
33 West 17th St. PH
New York, NY 10011

Dear Ms. Glick: (3)

I am a psychiatrist, published author, and expert for the national media seeking representation for my memoir (1) titled, *Queen of the Road: The True Tale of 47 States, 22,000 Miles, 200 Shoes, 2 Cats, 1 Poodle, a Husband, and a Bus with a Will of Its Own*. Because you are interested in unique voices, I thought we might be a good match.

When Tim first announced he wanted to "chuck it all" and travel around the country in a converted bus for a year, (4) I gave this profound and potentially life-altering notion all the thoughtful consideration it deserved. "Why can't you be like a normal husband with a midlife crisis and have an affair or buy a Corvette?" I asked, adding, "I will never, ever, EVER live on a bus."

What do you get when you cram married shrinks — one in a midlife crisis, the other his materialistic, wise-cracking wife — two cats who hate each other and a Standard Poodle who loves licking them all, into a bus for a year? *Queen of the Road* is a memoir of my dysfunctional, multi-species family's travels to and travails in the 49 continental states.

(5) As a psychiatrist, award-winning author (*I Know You Really Love Me*, Macmillan/Dell) and frequent media expert on psychiatric topics, (including "Larry King," "GMA," "48 Hours," *The New York Times* and *People Magazine*), my life has centered on introspection, analysis and storytelling. Yet, I count among my greatest accomplishments that last year, our bus was featured as the centerfold of *Bus Conversions Magazine*, thus fulfilling my life-long ambition of becoming a Miss September.

If you are interested in sample pages, I would be happy to send them to you via e-mail or snail mail.

Best wishes,

Doreen Orion

Note how this is a nonfiction book, but memoirs are treated as novels because they read like novels. *(Comments provided by Mollie Glick of Foundry Literary + Media.)*

> (1) Note how books are "titled," not "entitled." (2) Including full contact information (3) Always address your query to a specific agent. (4) It doesn't take long for Doreen to provide the hook, or "elevator pitch," and quickly explain what her memoir is about. (5) Lastly, Doreen sums up her platform nicely. Her writing credits are impressive, and she's obviously got the connections in place to spread the word about this book once it comes out.

BAD QUERY TO AGENT

Big Time Literary Agency
200 W. Broadway
New York, NY 10125

Dear Agent: **2**

I have just completed my first novel and would like to sell it to a publisher. I have never had a book published but I know this novel will be a bestseller. I'm looking for an agent to help me. I would really appreciate it if you could read over the enclosed chapters and give me some advice on whether you think this a good novel **6** and if it needs any extra work to make it a bestseller.

The Subject of Susan is about 60,000 words long and is geared toward an **4** adult audience. It is all about a headstrong woman named Susan and her trials and tribulations throughout the 1950s and beyond as she makes her way in the legal world after graduating from law school as the only woman in her graduating class. **1**

This is my first novel **3** and while I am not familiar with the legal world, since I'm not a lawyer, I find the subject fascinating and think readers will too. I've written a lot of short stories dealing with women's lives but they were much more romanticized than the story of Susan. Susan is someone you would know in real life. I have spent the last 20 years of my life raising my children **7** and think I have what it takes to become a successful writer.

I own the **5** copyright on this book and would like to discuss possible advances and royalties with you sometime soon.

Thank you very much,

John Q. Writer

1 There is nothing here to indicate how this book will distinguish itself from the thousands of other similar books that have been published. How will this book be different? **2** Always address your query to a specific agent. **3** Never mention that you're a first-time writer or that you have never been published—it singles you out as an amateur. **4** This is vague and tells the agent very little about the book. There is no "hook" to capture the agent's attention. **5** Don't mention copyright information or payment expectations. This is a query to assess an agent's interest in your novel. **6** Don't ask an agent for advice or criticism—that's not the agent's job nor the purpose of the query letter. **7** Don't draw attention to your lack of experience as a writer, and don't mention anything about yourself that is not pertinent to the novel. Keep all your information focused on the book itself.

CHUCK SAMBUCHINO is a freelancer as well as the editor of *Guide to Literary Agents* (www.guidetoliteraryagents.com/blog). He also helmed the third edition of *Formatting & Submitting Your Manuscript* (Writer's Digest Books) and is the author of *How to Survive a Garden Gnome Attack* (Ten Speed Press). More than 600 of his articles have appeared in print.

WHEN WORKING FOR FREE PAYS:

When It Makes Sense to Donate Your Writing Skills

by Sue Bradford Edwards

Like many writers I know, when I was a beginner, I sometimes wrote for free. It didn't bring the paycheck I so badly wanted, but I earned a byline which became a line in my resume. Soon I had the credits I needed to approach paying markets like the ones listed in *Writer's Market*.

Although I still occasionally write for free, it often brings criticism from my peers. "This is a business. You can't give anything away if you want to make a living."

Then I read Arthur Slade's blog posts about giving his e-book away. At a conference, Jody Feldman told me about her free Skype visits. At another event, Louise Jackson mentioned her free speaking engagements. Then an editor raved about an author who initially paid for her own promotional items, to be rewarded with bountiful support from the publicity department.

They do it, because even established writers are on the lookout for readers and book sales. One of the best ways to connect with the readers who will buy your work involves writing for free.

YOUR WRITTEN WORDS

Writing for free doesn't have to be as complex as writing a novel. In fact, it can be as easy as creating a 300-word blog entry. "Writing posts for your own blog and writing guest posts for other people's blogs that are read by your target readership are both excellent ways of writing for free in order to connect with people likely to be interested in your material," says author Phyllis Zimbler Miller.

If you don't have the time to maintain your own blog with several entries a week, then write for others. Approach authors whose blogs you like and offer to write a guest post. You can also find bloggers seeking writers through directories. "BloggerLinkUp.com is a free source of blog owners looking for guest posts," says Miller. Using BloggerLinkUp.com you can also list your availability to write on a particular topic.

"You can also write insightful comments on other people's blog posts or on relevant group discussions on LinkedIn, for example. These insightful comments can introduce your writing to your target readership," says Miller.

E-books can work in much the same way. For a limited time, Canadian young adult novelist Arthur Slade gave away an already published book in e-book format. The benefits? Additional reviews on Amazon, through which Slade made his book available, but also additional sales once the give-away ended. "When the books went from 'free' status to 'paid' status they suddenly jumped up the charts. This process really bumped up my sales," says Slade.

These kinds of freebies encourage readers to spread the word. Impressive posts can be Tweeted, forwarded and posted on Facebook walls. E-books are easy for readers to share, especially when they are free and all it takes is forwarding a link. Hook readers with these free reads and they will often pay to read even more of your work.

But your writing isn't the only way to connect with readers. You can also do it face-to-face.

FACE TIME

From writer's conferences to fan cons, adult readers pay to hear their favorite authors speak in person. Young readers may not be able to pay an entrance fee, but students read, and to encourage this schools bring in authors as speakers and some receive large honorariums.

Why then speak for free? "Once I show them what I can do, they will likely ask me to speak later for pay. I often mention this to them ahead of time," says middle grade novelist Louise Jackson. "There's no doubt that it has paid off for me. In effect, I am giving a free sample, the quality of which I am totally convinced. This is a time-honored method of getting business and I think it is sometimes a valid one. I spoke to a small librarian's group for free. When one of the librarians in that group later became an officer of a much larger professional group and she had control of some funds, she paid me to speak to their convention."

Not willing to pay travel expenses to speak for free? Don't overlook Skype, an online service that offers free video calling. "I give away free 15-minute Skype chats with schools who have studied my books," says Slade. "I do this because I see Skype as being a new way to communicate and by giving it away free I am able to educate the educators about its benefits. I did around 20 free ones before I was 'booked' for a paid one." Such payoffs seem slight until you realize how they add up. One of these Skype visits has turned into an annual paying event.

Middle grade novelist Jody Feldman, who lives in Missouri, picked up on Skype after receiving a teacher's request. "A teacher in Florida who led a book discussion group contacted me. 'We're about to start reading *The Gollywhopper Games*,' she said. 'Might you be able to meet with our group for 10-15 minutes when we discuss your book?'" reports Feldman. "Who was I to say no?"

But that's not the only way Feldman uses these free visits. "I've been asking the educators if they have an extra five minutes for our Skype so I can read the students a chapter of *The Seventh Level*. They usually contact me in conjunction with *The Gollywhopper Games* and the fact that it's been on numerous state lists. When I read the *Seventh Level* chapter, students rush the library to check out the book. So I warn the contacting teacher and they make sure their library has at least one copy," says Feldman.

Speaking for free may seem like a gamble, but the payoff can be big. As a professor, Jackson spoke for free in a school district that gave positions to her student teachers. It was a win-win situation for Jackson's students and the school district and later for Jackson as well. "When the district had some extra Title One money, maybe eight years after my previous work, they brought me in as a visiting author and bought 32 classroom sets of my newest novel. I had a great time speaking in four schools to all the 4th and 5th grades, each of which had read the book and done projects to share with me and their parents." Speaking for free led to a large block of sales Jackson hadn't anticipated.

In spite of the payoffs, there are things to consider when asked to speak for free, especially for a school visit. Schools are more vested if they pay a speaker than if they don't. Says Feldman, "If someone needs to cut a check of any size, there's more buy-in with the school, the educators and the students." Without monetary commitment, the school feels less compelled to commit to making the visit a success. Any venue who normally pays other speakers but brings you in for free may value your efforts less. When speaking for free, you also have to consider travel costs. If they are too high, consider Skype.

But Skype isn't the only way to avoid travel costs. You can also create videos or radio programming at no cost. "One such audio technique is creating a free online radio show on BlogTalkRadio.com, where anyone can have a targeted program," says Miller. "From November 2008 to November 2009 I was co-host with Nancy Brown of YourMilitary.com on a BlogTalkRadio show that featured information for military personnel, their families and veterans. I often blogged at www.mrslieutenant.blogspot.com about the people we interviewed, which helped get attention for my novel, *Mrs. Lieutenant*." Listeners can phone in questions or submit them through the site, both of which allow for greater interaction. The shows are also archived for easy access. All of this increases contact with your audience and draws in potential readers.

Another way to hook readers is to draw them into your story world. To do this, you need a different kind of freebie.

FREE LOOT

If you write for adults or teens, start with a top-notch site. Some authors, like librarian and young adult novelist Kelly Creagh, give their readers something more. "The web is the go-to place for teens when they want to find more information on anything," says Creagh. "I wanted to invest in something that would catch my readers' attention and also, since *Nevermore* is a series, give them a reason to return to the site."

Creagh gives them a complex site that pulls them in using things that appear in her story. "The song that is available on my website as a free download is one that makes an appearance in the novel. Though only a fragment of the song appears in *Nevermore*, I wrote the lyrics to the entire song so that music could be created to go with it. Having a freebee like this is fun for teens who, today, are carrying around their music on their ipods and phones. They can carry part of the story with them. It's another item they can share with their friends." This drive to share something incredible fuels word-of-mouth about your book.

Creagh's efforts, which included not only the site and song but also a temporary tattoo, purple pens, an Edgar Allan Poe action figure, and a Poe T-shirt, caught the attention and enthusiasm of her publisher and they've done more than send out review copies. "My publishers created a widget for Nevermore which I can display on my website. Nevermore was also featured on Simon and Schuster's teen community page PulseIT," says Creagh. "If you want to get your publishers on board with publicizing your book, do your best to meet them halfway. Be prepared to invest some of your advance into marketing materials. Think about your audience and the best ways to reach them. For teens, the Internet is an ideal place for marketing."

Creagh's must-have publicity item, even in this electronic age? The bookmark. "I share bookmarks with booksellers, librarians and teens. The bookmarks are great to have at signings because they add an extra freebie incentive to purchasing the novel, especially if you can sign them. Also, if you're at a signing and you have someone who might be interested in buying a copy but is uncertain, you can always send them home with a bookmark which should most certainly display your website address," says Creagh. "Sometimes I'll leave stacks of bookmarks in coffee shops or other places that have an area for business cards. The bookmark becomes your business card."

Freebies offer you a way to connect with potential readers. Adults read blogs. Teens and tweens flock to YouTube. Younger readers hurry home after school visits to tell Mom and Dad about the Author. Find something that readers can pass on to their friends and watch word of mouth at work, especially if it is something that could have come from your story world. The key is to look for what matches your comfort zone, resources and type of writing. What will it give your reader? What will it tell them about you? Be creative.

It should be do-able. You are, after all, a writer.

FOR A CAUSE

Sometimes the goal isn't an immediate payback or pulling in readers. Sometimes authors give their time and work away because they believe in a cause.

"I am committed to the goals of a group called the Rainbow Network that works with the rural poor in Nicaragua. The development officer is a good friend with whom I also attend church. He asked me to write a picture book about Rainbow's work," says Louise Jackson. "I paid for my own trip to Nicaragua and wrote 'H is for Hope.' I also gave them the copyright."

There hasn't been any monetary payback for this particular freebie but Jackson holds that the psychic paybacks have been more than worth the effort.

SUE BRADFORD EDWARDS works from her home in St. Louis, Missouri. Her how-tos for writers have appeared in Writer's Digest, the *Children's Writer's and Illustrator's Market*, *Children's Writer* newsletter, and the *Writer's Guide*. In addition, she writes fiction and nonfiction for children as well as devotional literature. Find out more about her and her work at One Writer's Journey (suebe.wordpress.com).

SELF-PUBLISHING CHECKLIST

Below is a checklist of essential hurdles to clear when self-publishing your book. This list makes the assumption that you've already completed and polished your manuscript. For more information on self-publishing, check out *The Complete Guide to Self-Publishing*, by Tom and Marilyn Ross (Writer's Digest).

☐ **CREATE PRODUCTION SCHEDULE.** Put a deadline for every step of the process of self-publishing your book. A good rule of thumb is to double your estimates on how long each step will take. It's better to have too much time and hit your dates than constantly have to extend deadlines.

☐ **FIND EDITOR.** Don't skimp on your project and do all the editing yourself. Even editors need editors. Try to find an editor you trust, whether through a recommendation or a search online. Ask for references if the editor is new to you.

☐ **FIND DESIGNER.** Same goes here. Find a good designer to at least handle the cover. If you can have a designer lay out the interior pages too, that's even better.

☐ **DEFINE THE TARGET AUDIENCE.** In nonfiction this is an important step, because knowing the needs of the audience can help with the editing process. Even if you're writing fiction or poetry, it's a good idea to figure out who your audience is, because this will help you with the next few steps.

☐ **FIGURE OUT A PRINT AND DISTRIBUTION PLAN.** This plan should first figure out what the end product will be: printed book, e-book, app, or a combination of options. Then, the plan will define how the products will be created and distributed to readers.

- [ ] **SET PUBLICATION DATE.** The publication date should be set on your production schedule above. Respect this deadline more than all the others, because the marketing and distribution plans will most likely hinge on this deadline being met.

- [ ] **PLOT OUT YOUR MARKETING PLAN.** The smartest plan is to have a soft launch date of a week or two (just in case). Then, hard launch into your marketing campaign, which could be as simple as a book release party and social networking mentions, or as involved as a guest blog tour and paid advertising. With self-publishing, it's usually more prudent to spend energy and ideas than money on marketing—at least in the beginning.

- [ ] **HAVE AN EXCELLENT TITLE.** For nonfiction, titles are easy. Describe what your book is covering in a way that is interesting to your target audience. For fiction and poetry, titles can be a little trickier, but attempt to make your title easy to remember and refer.

- [ ] **GET ENDORSEMENT.** Time for this should be factored into the production schedule. Contact some authors or experts in a field related to your title and send them a copy of your manuscript to review. Ask them to consider endorsing your book, and if they do, put that endorsement on the cover. Loop in your designer to make this look good.

- [ ] **REGISTER COPYRIGHT.** Protect your work. Go to http://copyright.gov for more information on how to register your book.

- [ ] **SECURE ISBN.** An ISBN code helps booksellers track and sell your book. To learn more about securing an ISBN, go to www.isbn.org.

- [ ] **CREATE TABLE OF CONTENTS AND INDEX (FOR NONFICTION).** The table of contents (TOC) helps organize a nonfiction title and give structure for both the author and the reader. An index serves a similar function for readers, making it easier for them to find the information they want to find. While an index is usually not necessary for fiction or poetry, most poetry collections do use a table of contents to make it easy to locate individual poems.

- [ ] **INCLUDE AUTHOR BIO.** Readers want to know about the authors of the books they read. Make this information easy to find in the back of the book.

- [ ] **INCLUDE CONTACT INFORMATION.** In the front of the book, preferably on the copyright and ISBN page, include all contact information, including mailing address and website. E-mail address is optional, but the more options you give the better chance you'll be contacted.

☐ **EXECUTE MARKETING PLAN.** Planning is important, but execution is critical to achieving success. If you're guest posting, finish posts on time and participate in comments section of your blog post. If you're making bookstore appearances, confirm dates and show up a little early—plus invite friends and family to attend.

☐ **KEEP DETAILED ACCOUNTING RECORDS.** For tax purposes, you'll need to keep records of how much money you invest in your project, as well as how much you receive back. Keep accurate and comprehensive records from day one, and you'll be a much happier self-published author.

FINDING FREELANCE OPPORTUNITIES ONLINE:

How to Start Making Money Online

by Carol Tice

Print markets have been hard-hit by the economic downturn, especially newspapers. But there's another part of the freelance-writing marketplace that's still growing—and it's as close as your computer.

Demand for writers is strong online, and expected to keep growing as readers increasingly consume news and read magazines via the Internet. To make their online product stand out, many print publications assign online-exclusive features. There are also a growing number of former print magazines that are now only published online, including *U.S. News & World Report*, *eWeek* and *PC Magazine*. Though the *Writers Market* only recently began tracking online publications, there are already over 100 online consumer and trade publication markets included in this guide.

Publications aren't the only digital writing opportunity, either. Increasingly, businesses use website content including blog posts as an affordable way to find new customers and keep existing customers loyal. Changes to how Google ranks websites have brought lower search rankings for sites using duplicate content—and that means more businesses need writers to create unique material for their site.

"Google's 2011 algorithm update has created an even stronger demand from clients for richer, original, and better-quality content," says Ed Gandia, co-author of *The Wealthy Freelancer.* "It's definitely good news."

AVOIDING SCAMS

Many writers have already discovered the dark underbelly of the online writing markets: writing "opportunities" at appallingly low rates—$10 per written piece or even less—and outright scams. Fly-by-night startups promise only exposure and a link to your website, or possibly a few pennies if readers click on your page's ads.

Some website editors may request several sample articles on a specific topic before deciding to make a hire. Often, the work is then simply published without payment or permission.

Avoid ripoffs with a few simple steps:

- **RESEARCH YOUR MARKET.** Remember that anyone can put up a website. Find the business name and then do Internet searches to see what's being said. The best on-line markets are usually long-established publications and businesses. Try to get a sense of the organization's size, too, as bigger markets often pay better. Don't take claims about "big traffic" on a site at face value, either—check web-traffic ranking sites such as Alexa (http://www.alexa.com/) to get a more reliable measure of a site's readership.

- **GET FULL CONTACT INFORMATION.** Would you write for a print magazine that provided no street address or phone number, where the editor didn't give you her last name? I hope not. Don't treat online markets any differently.

- **ASK AROUND.** Before you write for an online market, tap your writer networks to see if anyone has written for the site previously. Other writers may be able to give you a reality check on whether it's a legitimate market.

- **SIGN ON THE DOTTED LINE.** If a website wants you to start writing to meet a short deadline and says a contract will follow later, be wary. Get a contract that spells out payment, payment terms, deadlines, and ownership rights before you start work.

SPECIAL SKILLS FOR BLOGGERS

With some online markets, writing can be as simple as e-mailing your editor a Word document with your article. But writers with other skills—social-media savvy, experience using key words to get search rankings, and knowledge of blogging software such as WordPress—have a definite edge, especially in landing blogging assignments.

For instance, at AOL's community-news network Patch.com, editors favor writers who understand how to promote their pieces on Twitter and other social-media platforms, says editor-in-chief Brian Farnham.

"Social media is part of our DNA," says Farnham. "If you know how to do it, it doesn't just benefit us—it benefits your personal brand."

Writing a personal niche blog and promoting it in social media is a great way to gain experience and create a writing sample to show editors. Your blog can also be a showcase that demonstrates you understand online writing style.

Online readers tend to be skimmers and scanners, preferring articles with bulleted or numbered lists or bolded subheads, notes Christina Hoffmann, editor of the National Association of Realtors' HouseLogic (http://www.houselogic.com/) website for homeowners.

Launched in early 2010, the site aims to publish one new story each business day, assigns $1-a-word features, and also pays bloggers at competitive rates.

BREAK-IN OPPORTUNITY: ONLINE LOCAL NEWS

Community or "hyperlocal" sites offer decent pay to new writers with an interest in reporting on local events. These sites feature neighborhood news stories that are off the radar of big-city papers. The big gorilla of this niche is AOL's Patch.com (http://www.patch.com/), but your region may also have independent sites that do well and offer writer pay. One example is the popular West Seattle Blog, which gets more than 1 million monthly pageviews.

Launched in 2009, Patch has since grown to over 860 sites in communities across the U.S. Editor-in-chief Brian Farnham says Patch continues to expand where it sees a community need or a big news story. For instance, Patch added sites in New Hampshire, Iowa and South Carolina in late 2011 to get a ringside seat for presidential-primary coverage.

Most Patch sites have relationships with at least two regular freelance writers, says Farnham. Good story pitches have a new slant on a local issue, and writers should be ready to turn stories around quickly.

"We love people with a reporter's soul and the motivation to get out there," he says. "Not everyone wants to cover a city council meeting for three hours."

Rates vary, depending on length and whether fieldwork is required, but generally run $50-100 per story—similar to what you might get at a local alternative city paper. Editors are accessible, with email addresses listed at the top of their Patch's home page.

The best time to break in is when a new Patch starts up, Farnham says. As the sites mature, they have fewer paid assignments and rely more on feeds from unpaid community bloggers. On the plus side, if you get accepted to freelance at one local Patch, it's easy to pitch other area Patches for additional assignments.

Shorter sentences and shorter paragraphs are typical online compared with print markets, says Hoffmann. Additionally, online assignments often require writers to include links to relevant related materials and mentioned resources. "Internal" links that send readers back to older content on the same website are also important.

Pay tends to be lower for blogging work than for articles—$50 to $100 a post is considered a good blog-post rate. Major corporations and established media companies tend to be good payers, says longtime financial writer Lydia Dishman, who has blogged for websites owned by *Forbes* magazine, CBS, and American Express, among others. Dishman says her experience in social media definitely helped her land her blogging gigs. Writers with a journalism background such as Dishman are well-positioned for blogging, as many have deadline-writing experience and understand libel issues, which are a prime concern for website owners.

Paid blogging may call for posting as often as every business day, so you'll need to know how to scan relevant news sources online to develop a constant supply of story ideas on your topic. One quick method is to set up Google alerts (http://www.google.com/alerts) on key industry phrases.

"You need to be tapped into everywhere there might be news on your industry," she says.

FINDING YOUR FIRST ONLINE MARKETS

If you haven't written for online markets and are looking to break in, start with websites of local businesses you frequent, or an industry where you have experience. For instance, when copywriter Sean Platt broke into writing online, targeting local florists to write web copy made sense, as he'd previously owned a flower shop. He's since branched out to other industries, writing for companies in the legal, tax, and health insurance fields. One of his specialties is creating white papers for companies to use as free downloads to build customer interest.

"I wouldn't even leave your city," says Platt, who writes the GhostwriterDad blog. "Just look for the people who are making money online. Those are the people who can afford to pay you."

To discover good online markets, scan news sites for announcements about new websites or editor changes at online publications. For business clients, read the business pages of your local paper or press-release sites to find local companies that are promoting their success, says Platt. Then, study their website along with competitors' to spot missing elements you could pitch as a writing project. A blog that hasn't been updated in months is always a good entry point.

One challenge to cracking online markets is locating contact names. Where most print publications have a masthead page that lists editor contact information, finding out who to contact at an online magazine or information portal can take a bit more sleuthing.

If the "About" or "Contact" pages aren't helpful, try searching Google for "editor <publication name>." Alternatively, try searching for the company on LinkedIn to see if you can turn up editor names. Another social-media resource for finding editors is MuckRack (http://muckrack.com/), which tracks media players' activity on Twitter. If the site lists a phone number, simply call to ask who you could send a pitch. Most online markets prefer e-mail submissions.

ONLINE ARTICLE MARKETS

If you are currently writing for any print publications, begin your online-market search with a look at their website. Compare it with the magazine to see if they are creating unique content or "online exclusives." If so, try to learn their needs from your current editor or get an introduction to the online features editor. This is how I crossed over from writing for *Entrepreneur*'s print magazine to blogging for their website.

Online publications have a bad reputation for offering low pay compared with print. But ad dollars have gravitated away from print and to the Internet in the past few years—for instance, digital-ad revenue at *The Atlantic* topped print-ad revenue for the first time in fall 2011. That growing online revenue is helping to lift online writing rates.

Increasingly stiff competition for Internet readers in many topic niches is also inspiring rate hikes. For instance, after several years of commissioning only $100 short how-to business articles, in 2009 the portal Allbusiness.com (http://www.allbusiness.com/) looked to differentiate the site by assigning in-depth, reported features to experienced business writers at much higher rates, notes former senior editor David Hennessy. (The site ceased making assignments completely in early 2012 as owner Dun & Bradstreet contemplated its sale—an example of the rapid change that characterizes today's online media markets.)

Where most print publications have a masthead page that lists editor contact information, finding out who to contact at an online magazine or information portal can take a bit more sleuthing.

At base, querying online article markets is a similar process to querying in print. Study your target website carefully—"Follow the brand on Facebook and Twitter too," Hoffmann says—then, query editors with fresh ideas that haven't been covered on the site before. HouseLogic's Hoffmann likes to see "buzzy, engaging ideas."

Writers' most common mistake? "I don't get a sense the writer looked at our site to see if we already have content on that angle," she says.

As with most online sites, Hoffmann would like to see article pitches for HouseLogic that are both newsy and could use relevant industry key words and phrases that receive a high volume of online searches, says Hoffmann.

To prep an online query, you can discover popular search terms using Google's free Keyword Tool (https://adwords.google.com/select/KeywordToolExternal).

BUSINESS WEBSITES

To stay competitive, businesses are spending more to keep their websites fresh, says copywriter-author Ed Gandia. One of his favorite copywriting assignments is a "website refresh," where a medium-to-large business's website of 50 pages or more is revamped with fresh content. Gandia recommends targeting companies selling high-margin products such as software that are frequently updated. That creates a need for regular rewrites.

Writing web content can be a great initial project, as it allows you to learn a lot about a business, notes Gandia. You can then propose additional projects such as white papers, case studies, virtual brochures or updated brand messaging. Rates can range from $50 an hour and up to $200 an hour or more, as you acquire expertise in a company or industry.

Think you won't know what to write? Ask lots of questions of the business owner. Then study competitors' sites and ask the client which ones they think do the best job.

"Your swipe file," he says, "is right there online."

Carol Tice has more than a decade of freelance-writing experience, for publications including *Entrepreneur, Seattle Times, Seattle Magazine,* and *Alaska Airlines* magazine, and clients including Costco, American Express, and Dun & Bradstreet. She writes the Make a Living Writing blog (http://www.makealivingwriting.com) and serves as Den Mother of the writers' learning and support community, Freelance Writers Den (http://freelancewritersden.com).

FUNDS FOR WRITERS 101:

Find Money You Didn't Know Existed

....

by C. Hope Clark

When I completed writing my novel over a decade ago, I imagined the next step was simply to find a publisher and watch the book sell. Like most writers, my goal was to earn a living doing what I loved so I could walk away from the day job. No such luck. Between rejection and newfound knowledge that a novel can take years to sell enough for a single house payment, I opened my mind to other writing avenues. After researching in depth, I learned that there's no *one* way to find funds to support your writing; instead there are *many*. So many, in fact, that I felt the need to share the volume of knowledge I collected, and I called it FundsforWriters.com.

Funds are money. But obtaining those funds isn't necessarily a linear process, or a one-dimensional path. As a serious writer, you study all options at your fingertips, entertaining financial resources that initially don't make sense as well as the obvious. In the end, it's about publishing. In the interim, it's about identifying the fiscal resources to get you there.

GRANTS

Grants come from government agencies, nonprofits, businesses and even generous individuals. They do not have to be repaid, as long as you use the grant as intended. No two are alike. Therefore, you must do your homework to find the right match between your grant need and the grant provider's mission. Grantors like being successful at their mission just as you like excelling at yours. So they screen applicants, ensuring they fit the rules and show promise to follow through.

Don't fear grants. Sure, you're judged by a panel, and rejection is part of the game, but you already know that as a writer. Gigi Rosenberg, author of *The Artist's Guide to Grant Writing*, states, "If one funder doesn't want to invest in your project, find another who does.

And if nobody does, then begin it any way you can. Once you've started, that momentum will help your project find its audience and its financial support."

TYPES OF GRANTS

Grants can send you to retreats, handle emergencies, provide mentors, pay for conferences, or cover travel. They also can be called awards, fellowships, residencies, or scholarships. But like any aspect of your writing journey, define how any tool, even a grant, fits into your plans. Your mission must parallel a grantor's mission.

The cream-of-the-crop grants have no strings attached. Winning recipients are based upon portfolios and an application that defines a work-in-progress. You don't have to be a Pulitzer winner, but you must prove your establishment as a writer.

You find most of these opportunities in state arts commissions. Find them at www.nasaa-arts.org or as a partner listed at the National Endowment for the Arts website, www.nea.gov. Not only does your state's arts commission provide funding, but the players can direct you to other grant opportunities, as well as to artists who've gone before you. Speaking to grant winners gives you a wealth of information and a leg up in designing the best application.

Foundations and nonprofits fund the majority of grants. Most writers' organizations are nonprofits. Both the Mystery Writers of America (www.mysterywriters.org) and Society of Children's Book Writers and Illustrators (www.scbwi.org) offer scholarships and grants.

Many retreats are nonprofits. Journalist and freelancer Alexis Grant, (http://alexis-grant.com/) tries to attend a retreat a year. Some ask her to pay, usually on a sliding scale based upon income, and others provide scholarships. Each time, she applies with a clear definition of what she hopes to gain from the two to five-week trips. "It's a great way to get away from the noise of everyday responsibilities, focus on writing well and meet other people who prioritize writing. I always return home with a new perspective." A marvelous resource to find writing retreats is the Alliance of Artists Communities (http://www.artist-communities.org/).

Laura Lee Perkins won four Artist-in-Residence slots with the National Park Service (http://nps.gov). The federal agency has 43 locations throughout the United States where writers and artists live for two to four weeks. From Acadia National Park in Maine to Sleeping Bear Dunes National Lakeshore in Michigan, Laura spoke to tourists about her goals to write a book about Native American music. "Memories of the US National Parks' beauty and profound serenity will continue to enrich my work. Writers find unparalleled inspiration, quietude, housing, interesting staff, and a feeling of being in the root of your artistic desires."

Don't forget writers' conferences. While they may not advertise financial aid, many have funds available in times of need. Always ask as to the availability of a scholarship or work-share program that might enable your attendance.

Grants come in all sizes. FundsforWriters posts most emergency grants on its grants page (www.fundsforwriters.com/grants.htm) as well as periodic new grant opportunities such as the Sustainable Arts Foundation (www.sustainableartsfoundation.org) that offers grants twice a year to writers and artists with children under the age of 18, or the Awesome Foundation (www.awecomefoundation.org), which gives $1,000 grants to "awesome" creative projects.

Novelist Joan Dempsey won an Elizabeth George Foundation grant (http://www.elizabethgeorgeonline.com/foundation/index.htm) in early 2012. "I applied to the Foundation for a research grant that included three trips to places relevant to my novel-in-progress, trips I otherwise could not have afforded. Not only does the grant provide travel funds, but it also provides validation that I'm a serious writer worthy of investment, which is great for my psyche and my resume."

FISCAL SPONSORSHIP

Nonprofits have access to an incredibly large number of grants that individuals do not, and have the ability to offer their tax-exempt status to groups and individuals involved in activities related to their mission. By allowing a nonprofit to serve as your grant overseer, you may acquire funds for your project.

Deborah Marshall is President of the Missouri Writers Guild (www.missouriwritersguild.org) and founder of the Missouri Warrior Writers Project, with ample experience with grants in the arts. "Although grant dollars are available for individual writers, writing the grant proposal becomes difficult without significant publication credits. Partnering with a nonprofit organization, whether it is a writing group, service, community organization, or any 501(c)3, can fill in those gaps to make a grant application competitive. Partnering not only helps a writer's name become known, but it also assists in building that all-important platform."

Two excellent groups that offer fiscal sponsorship for writers are The Fractured Atlas (www.fracturedatlas.org) and Artspire (www.artspire.org) sponsored by the New York Foundation for the Arts and open to all US citizens. Visit The Foundation Center (www.foundationcenter.org) for an excellent tutorial guide to fiscal sponsorship.

CROWD SOURCING

Crowd sourcing is a co-op arrangement where people support artists directly, much like the agricultural co-op movement where individuals fund farming operations in exchange for fresh food. Kickstarter (www.kickstarter.com) has made huge strides in making this funding method successful in the arts.

Basically, the writer proposes his project, and for a financial endorsement as low as $1, donors receive some token in return, like an autographed book, artwork, or bookmark.

The higher the donation, the bigger the *wow* factor in the gift. Donors do not receive ownership in the project.

Meagan Adele Lopez (www.ladywholunches.net) presented her debut self-published book *Three Questions* to Kickstarter readers, requesting $4,400 to take her book on tour, create a book trailer, pre-order books, and redesign the cover. Eighty-eight backers pledged a total of $5,202. She was able to hire an editor and a company that designed film trailers. For every $750 she received over her plan, she added a new city to her book tour.

Other crowd sourcing companies are up and coming to include Culture 360 (www.culture360.org) that serves Asia and Europe, and Indie GoGo (www.indiegogo.com), as well as Rocket Hub (www.rockethub.com). And nothing stops you from simply asking those you know to support your project. The concept is elementary.

CONTESTS

Contests offer financial opportunity, too. Of course you must win, place or show, but many writers overlook the importance that contests have on a career. These days, contests not only open doors to publishing, name recognition, and money, but listing such achievements in a query letter might make an agent or publisher take a second glance. Noting your wins on a magazine pitch might land a feature assignment. Mentioning your accolades to potential clients could clinch a freelance deal.

I used contests as a barometer when fleshing out my first mystery novel, *A Lowcountry Bribe*, Bell Bridge Books. After I placed in several contests, earned a total of $750, and reached the semi-finals of the Amazon Breakthrough Novel Award (www.createspace.com/abna), my confidence grew strong enough to pitch agents. My current agent admits that the contest wins drew her in.

Contests can assist in sales of existing books, not only aiding sales but also enticing more deals for future books . . . or the rest of your writing profession.

Whether writing short stories, poetry, novels or nonfiction, contests abound. As with any call for submission, study the rules. Double checking with entities that screen, like FundsforWriters.com and WinningWriters.com, will help alleviate concerns when selecting where to enter.

FREELANCING

A thick collection of freelancing clips can make an editor sit up and take notice. You've been vetted and accepted by others in the business, and possibly established a following. The more well known the publications, the brighter your aura.

Sooner or later in your career, you'll write an article. In the beginning, articles are a great way to gain your footing. As your career develops, you become more of an expert, and are expected to enlighten and educate about your journey and the knowledge you've acquired. Articles are, unarguably, one of the best means to income and branding for writers.

Trade magazines, national periodicals, literary journals, newsletters, newspapers and blogs all offer you a chance to present yourself, earn money, and gain readers for a platform. Do not discount them as income earners.

Linda Formichelli, of Renegade Writer fame (www.therenegadewriter.com) leaped into freelance magazine writing because she simply loved to write, and that love turned her into an expert. "I never loved working to line someone else's pockets." A full-time freelancer since 1997, with credits like *Family Circle*, *Redbook*, and *Writer's Digest*, she also writes articles, books, e-courses, and e-books about her profession as a magazine writer.

JOBS

Part-time, full-time, temporary or permanent, writing jobs hone your skills, pad your resume, and present avenues to movers and shakers you wouldn't necessarily meet on your own. Government and corporate managers hire writers under all sorts of guises like Social Media Specialist and Communications Specialist, as well as the expected Reporter and Copywriter.

Alexis Grant considers her prior jobs as catapults. "Working at a newspaper (*Houston Chronicle*) and a news magazine (*US News & World Report*) for six years provided the foundation for what I'm doing now as a freelancer. Producing stories regularly on tight deadlines will always make you a better writer."

Joan Dempsey chose to return to full-time work and write her novel on the side, removing worries about her livelihood. "My creative writing was suffering trying to freelance. So, I have a day job that supports me now." She still maintains her Facebook presence to continue building her platform for her pending novel.

DIVERSIFICATION

Most importantly, however, is learning how to collect all your funding options and incorporate them into your plan. The successful writer doesn't perform in one arena. Instead, he thrives in more of a three-ring circus.

Grant states it well. "For a long while I thought of myself as only a journalist, but there are so many other ways to use my skills. Today my income comes from three streams: helping small companies with social media and blogging (the biggest source), writing and selling e-guides and courses (my favorite), and taking freelance writing or editing assignments."

Formichelli is proud of being flexible. "When I've had it with magazine writing, I put more energy into my e-courses, and vice versa. Heck, I'm even a certified personal trainer, so if I get really sick of writing I can work out. But a definite side benefit to diversifying is that I'm more protected from the feast-or-famine nature of writing."

Sometimes pursuing the more common sense or lucrative income opportunity can open doors for the dream. When my novel didn't sell, I began writing freelance articles. Then I established FundsforWriters, using all the grant, contest, publisher and market research I did for myself. A decade later, once the site thrived with over 45,000 readers, I used the very research I'd gleaned for my readers to find an agent and sign a publishing contract . . . for the original novel started so long ago.

You can fight to fund one project or study all resources and fund a career. Opportunity is there. Just don't get so wrapped up in one angle that you miss the chance to invest more fully in your future.

C. HOPE CLARK manages FundsforWriters.com, a site selected for *Writer's Digest's* 101 Best Websites for Writers for the past twelve years. She is also author of *A Lowcountry Bribe*, the first in The Palmetto State Mystery Series published by Bell Bridge Books . She lives on the banks of Lake Murray, South Carolina and presents to several writers conferences each year.

GHOSTWRITING 101

by Eva Shaw

What do *Jersey Shore*'s Snooki, B.B. King, Hillary Clinton, Richard Petty and Michelle Obama in common? They're friendly with ghosts. These people and countless others have hired ghostwriters to write for them.

Celebrities, entrepreneurs, academics, sports stars, business movers and shakers, media darlings, scientists, politicians, reality-wannabe flashes in the pan, even kids who have seen heaven, along with regular people who have a story to tell or information to share routinely engage ghostwriters to capture their words for print. It's estimated that 60 to perhaps 80 percent of published nonfiction books are ghosted. Among those in the know, it's said that some of the big names in fiction work with or have hired ghosts.

IT'S REWARDING

Curious how you can boost your writing career by ghostwriting? Let's walk through the process and then decide. Ghosts write a multitude of projects including novels, nonfiction books, essays, articles, blogs, reports, speeches and columns. To make it simple for your crash course in ghosting, let's refer to projects as "books."

Ghostwriting is rewarding on countless career levels but novices often have misconceptions about it. Once in a while I'll even meet a hopeful writer who sneers and says, "It's immoral to be a ghostwriter." Not so. Actually so way not so.

Sure it's not for every writer, but becoming a ghost can skyrocket a career regardless of the genre. Imagine collecting outstanding clips, have "your" work appear in a multitude of publications, able to give knock-out references, and build a rock-solid platform? Think about how having those perks would help when you're ready to sell that novel or submit a nonfiction book proposal. Exactly. You'd have credibility to spare and your own writing business.

In our service-oriented society, ghostwriting is a field with growth potential. When I began ghosting years back, ghosts were hush-hush. Today ghostwriters, sometimes called collaborators, editors or even "great helpers," are part of the publishing team that brings a multitude of projects to market.

> I make it clear to my clients that their agent, editor or publisher must be aware of our relationship.

Agents, editors and publishers appreciate working with a professional writer and there's no need for a ghost to stay in the closet. I make it clear to my clients that their agent, editor or publisher must be aware of our relationship.

Why do clients hire a ghost? The reasons include:

- The client may be an adequate writer, but doesn't want to write the book.
- The client realizes that good writing requires expertise; it's more efficient when performed by a professional.
- The client may not have the skills or talent to write.
- The client may not have the time to write.

Why don't more writers ghost? Perhaps it is the fear of the unknown or not being quite as sure of their craft as they would like others to believe. Ghostwriting requires you to be a better-than-average writer and have first-rate people skills.

THE GHOSTING PROCESS

The process for all ghosting is similar whether you're writing a book or an article although the steps might be in a different order.

- The client approaches you or you find the client.
- You send or provide samples of your writing and give references.
- You meet, review the project, and work out the project.
- You discuss all the financial details. (FYI: I talked with other ghosts and we have much in common when it comes to money. We usually split our fees into two to four parts, with half of the fee due on the contract's signing.)
- If needed, an attorney or agent might look over the contract to make sure it outlines exactly what your role will be.
- A timeline for completion of the project is developed and agreed upon.
- You write the book. You work on as many drafts as necessary until you're satisfied and know your client will be, too.
- You give the draft to the client. The client reviews it, makes changes or comments, and you go back to work.

- You rewrite the book and present the final draft.
- You're paid the final installment and the client says, "Good bye."

SIMPLE AS 1, 2, 3

Clients are everywhere. Really.

1. Tell everyone you know that you are a ghostwriter. Go ahead. Whether you live in a hamlet or a metropolis, there are people who need your writing services, but they won't know until you explain how and what you do. While plenty of ghosts advertise their services, that's expensive. Instead, I ask for referrals—that's been working extremely well for 20 years.
2. Pitch the publishing industry. Publishers (big and small), agents, editors and book packagers seek out ghostwriters. Why not write some sizzling queries and offer your services? Too few ghosts do this.
3. Keep your eyes out for clients. Did you just read an article or meet someone who has an amazing story or a fascinating career? You're looking at a potential ghosting client. Approach this person for an article interview, place the article, and then consider if she or he just might want to write a book (using you as a ghost).

THE UNVARNISHED TRUTH

When the project is completed, some clients will bid you farewell especially if you've been hired as a contractor. Most of mine stay with me for the long run. How so? I provide a service that's fast, on deadline, efficient and cost effective. I'm honorable, confidential, and competitive in pricing, provide references and always go the extra distance.

....

Ghosting isn't always rosy. Sometimes there's a bad match between the ghost and the client.

....

Why bother? Clients go out of their way to recommend me to others. I've written for doctors, lawyers, movie stars, high-profile CEOs, artists, entrepreneurs, fitness and health experts and others with stories to share. I call my clients the "authors" of the material and keep their names and our projects private unless the client permits me to share the info. I'm often privy to a lifestyle or opinions unknown to the public; my clients trust me with their work and lives.

Ghostwriting isn't always rosy. Sometimes there's a bad match between the ghost and client or the client decides to write the material themselves. With corporate clients, budgets are snatched away or the corporation goes in another direction. Once I was fired when

I confronted a client because she asked me to plagiarize, hotly claimed the writing as her own. It stings. If it does happen to you, dust off your britches and try again.

IT'S THE VOICE

There is an art to capturing your client and it starts with listening. You not only must know how to write, but be able to listen and then translate the voice of your client into words that reflect the flair, style, phrases, unusual slang, witticisms, and elements that make the client sound unique. Clients talk about soft markets, bottom lines, team play, cosmic consciousness, and billions of expressions. Some use elongated, complex sentences interspersed with statistics; others prefer short, snappy, slightly whimsical phrases. Duplicating word patterns is the essence of ghostwriting. Here's a secret: All ghostwriting clients want to have their written material sound intelligent and smooth, even if their speaking patterns and words are not.

....

There is an art to capturing clients and it starts with listening.

....

If you haven't done so already, start listening to how people speak. How do their speech patterns differ? Next time you're watching the evening news, why not practice "ghosting" with the anchors? In addition to words, watch how they use their hands, change their expressions, move their eyes, and even hesitate when thinking. This info conveys the distinct persona of clients.

INTERVIEWING CLIENTS

Yes, you should interview clients although you don't have to tell them you're doing so. At your first meeting, most clients want to know: Do you like the project's idea? What is your background? What's your experience? Are you available? What's this going to cost? Be ready with answers and you'll be considered a pro.

What should you look for in a client? That depends, however, at your meeting, if the client's comments or behavior checks any items below, proceed with eyes wide open.

- The client is late more than once for a meeting and without a reasonable excuse.
- The client is overbearing.
- The client doesn't let you ask questions.
- The client has trouble staying on the topic.
- The client forgets your name or that your time is valuable.
- The client insists you agree right then to write the book, without knowing all the details.
- The client balks or pales when you discuss money.
- The client wants you to write for free.

Before you decide to accept a ghosting gig, ponder the project and ask yourself some questions about this potential client and their book.

- Can the client afford my services?
- Will I be able to sleep if I disagree with the book's ideas or topics?
- What's my gut-level feeling about the client and the book?
- How committed is the client to the book?
- Can I be totally at ease with the client?
- Will the client allow me to be truthful?

Be sure to ask your potential clients questions. I do. The following questions give insight into a client's motivation and help me decide if a client is right. There are no wrong answers.

- Why are you hiring a ghost? Most will say they don't have the time or talent to write.
- What is your goal for the project? If money is the goal, that's okay.
- What working arrangement do you visualize with the ghost?
- Where are you in the writing process?
- Who else have you worked with? Ugly comments? Could be a red flag.
- Who will buy your book and why? You might have to educate a client on this because, as you know, there has to be a market for the book.
- What is the budget for a ghostwriter?
- What do you want from a ghost?

MONEY FOR WORDS

As a ghost, you'll set your own prices and determine your worth. There are no absolutes when it comes to the fees ghosts charge and the fees can fluctuate depending on your location, the client and your experience. If you already have an hourly fee for writing, then estimate how long this book (or whatever) project will take you to complete.

Most ghosts calculate how much to charge by the amount of work required and the time it will take to complete the work. If you're offered $5,000 to ghost a book that might sound great, but if it will take you a year with countless meetings and revisions, you might be working for less than minimum wage.

....

Most ghosts calculate how much to charge by the amount of work required and the time it will take to complete the work.

....

Since it will be up to you to decide on the fee, how is that approached? Here's what I say: "Dr. Jones, what is your budget for a ghostwriter?" By calling the fee "the budget" it eliminates personal involvement and returns it all to the business of writing.

What can you expect? It's been my experience that ghostwriting articles or columns, the fees are between $25 and $100/hour. Ghosting an article for a popular magazine, rates are $1/word or from $300-3,000 per project. If you're writing continuing columns for a local publication, the fees may be $50-300. When ghostwriting a book the rates range from $5,000 to many zeros over that.

ON YOUR MARK...

If you can put your ego aside and think of ghostwriting as a business, you will succeed. There are clients everywhere, from a local tax attorney who needs a workbook for her seminar to a neighbor who wants you to write a memoir just for her family. After scores of ghosting projects, my best advice is: Give it a try. Be friendly and sincere. Have a good contract. Have fun.

Ghosting isn't for every writer. That's good. It means there's more lucrative work for you and me.

Eva Shaw, Ph.D. (www.evashaw.com) is the ghostwriter/author of 70 books, many best sellers and award winners. Under her byline, they include: *Ghostwriting for Fun & Profit, Writeriffic 2: Creativity Training for Writers, Write Your Book in 20 Minutes, Shovel It: Nature's Health Plan, What to Do When a Loved One Dies, For the Love of Children, There's No Business Like Show Business, Insider's Guide to San Diego, The Sun Never Sets,* and more. Eva's work has been featured in publications such as *USA Today, Shape, Country Living, San Diego Union Tribune, Los Angeles Times, Costco Connection, Publisher's Weekly, Washington Post, the Wall Street Journal* plus she has ghosted more than 1000 columns, articles and short stories. She's a regular presenter at writing conferences and teaches six different online writing courses (with Education to Go, www.ed2go.com) that are available worldwide. She lives and writes in Carlsbad CA with husband Joseph and their rambunctious Welsh terrier, Miss Rosy Geranium.

PUBLISHERS & THEIR IMPRINTS

The publishing world is in constant transition. With all the buying, selling, reorganizing, consolidating, and dissolving, it's hard to keep publishers and their imprints straight. To help make sense of these changes, here's a breakdown of major publishers (and their divisions)—who owns whom and which imprints are under each company umbrella. Keep in mind that this information changes frequently. The website of each publisher is provided to help you keep an eye on this ever-evolving business.

HACHETTE BOOK GROUP USA

www.hachettebookgroup.com

CENTER STREET

FAITHWORDS

GRAND CENTRAL PUBLISHING
- Business Plus
- 5 Spot
- Forever
- Forever Yours
- GCP African American
- Grand Central Life & Style
- Twelve
- Vision

HACHETTE BOOK GROUP DIGITAL MEDIA
Hachette Audio

LITTLE, BROWN AND COMPANY
- Back Bay Books
- Bulfinch
- Mulholland Books
- Reagan Arthur Books

LITTLE, BROWN BOOKS FOR YOUNG READERS
- LB Kids
- Poppy

ORBIT

YEN PRESS

HARLEQUIN ENTERPRISES

www.harlequin.com

HARLEQUIN

Harlequin American Romance
Harlequin Bianca
Harlequin Blaze
Harlequin Deseo
Harlequin Historical
Harlequin Intrigue
Harlequin Tiffany
Harlequin Teen
Harlequin Medical Romance
Harlequin NASCAR
Harlequin Presents
Harlequin Romance
Harlequin Superromance
Harlequin eBooks
Harlequin Special Releases
Harlequin Nonfiction
Harlequin Historical Undone

HQN BOOKS

LUNA

MIRA

KIMANI PRESS

Kimani Press Arabesque
Kimani Press Kimani Romance
Kimani Press Kimani TRU
Kimani Press New Spirit
Kimani Press Sepia
Kimani Press Special Releases
Kimani Press eBooks

RED DRESS INK

SILHOUETTE

Silhouette Desire
Silhouette Nocturne
Silhouette Nocturne Bites
Silhouette Romantic Suspense
Silhouette Special Edition
Silhouette eBooks

SPICE

SPICE Books
SPICE Briefs

STEEPLE HILL

Steeple Hill Café©
Steeple Hill Love Inspired
Steeple Hill Love Inspired Historical
Steeple Hill Love Inspired Suspense
Steeple Hill Women's Fiction
Steeple Hill eBooks

WORLDWIDE LIBRARY

Rogue Angel
Worldwide Mystery
Worldwilde Library eBooks

HARLEQUIN CANADA

HARLEQUIN U.K.

Mills & Boon

HARPERCOLLINS

www.harpercollins.com

HARPERCOLLINS GENERAL BOOKS GROUP

Amistad
Avon
Avon Inspire
Avon Red
Broadside Books
Caedmon
Collins Design
Ecco
Harper
Harper Business
Harper Design

Harper Luxe

Harper paperbacks

Harper Perennial

Harper Perennial Modern Classics

Harper Voyager

HarperAudio

HarperBibles

HarperCollins e-Books

HarperOne

ItBooks

Rayo

William Morrow

HARPERCOLLINS CHILDREN'S BOOKS

Amistad

Balzer + Bray

Collins

Greenwillow Books

HarperCollins Children's Audio

HarperFestival

HarperTeen

Rayo

Katherine Tegen Books

Walden Pond Press

HARPERCOLLINS U.K.

Fourth Estate

HarperPress

HarperPerennial

The Friday Project

HarperThorsons/Element

HarperNonFiction

HarperTrue

HarperSport

HarperFiction

> Voyager
>
> Blue Door
>
> Angry Robot
>
> Avon U.K.

HarperCollins Childrens Books

Collins

> Collins Geo
>
> Collins Education
>
> Collins Language

HARPERCOLLINS CANADA

HarperCollinsPublishers

Collins Canada

HarperPerennial Canada

HarperTrophyCanada

Phyllis Bruce Books

HARPERCOLLINS AUSTRALIA

HarperCollins

Angus & Robertson

HarperSports

Fourth Estate

Harper Perennial

Collins

Voyager

HARPERCOLLINS INDIA

HARPERCOLLINS NEW ZEALAND

HarperCollins

HarperSports

Flamingo

Voyager

Perennial

ZONDERVAN

Zonderkids

Editorial Vida

Youth Specialties

MACMILLAN US (HOLTZBRINCK)

http://us.macmillan.com

MACMILLAN

Farrar, Straus & Giroux

Faber and Faber, Inc

Farrar, Straus

Hill & Wang

HENRY HOLT & CO.

Henry Holt Books for Young Readers

Holt Paperbacks

Metropolitan

Times

MACMILLAN CHILDREN'S

Feiwel & Friends

Farrar, Straus and Giroux Books
for Young Readers

Kingfisher

Holt Books for Young Readers

Priddy Books

Roaring Brook Press

First Second

Square Fish

PICADOR

PALGRAVE MACMILLAN

TOR/FORGE BOOKS

Tor

Forge

Orb

Tor/Seven Seas

ST. MARTIN'S PRESS

Minotaur Press

Thomas Dunne Books

BEDFORD, FREEMAN & WORTH
PUBLISHING GROUP

BEDFORD/ST. MARTIN'S

HAYDEN-MCNEIL

W.H. FREEMAN

WORTH PUBLISHERS

MACMILLAN KIDS

YOUNG LISTENERS

MACMILLAN AUDIO

PENGUIN GROUP (USA), INC.

www.penguingroup.com

PENGUIN ADULT DIVISION

Ace

Alpha

Amy Einhorn Books/Putnam

Avery

Berkley

Blue Rider Press

Current

Dutton

G.P. Putnam's Sons

Gotham

HP Books

Hudson Street Press

Jove

NAL

Pamela Dorman Books

Penguin

Penguin Press

Perigree

Plume

Portfolio

Prentice Hall Press

RIVERHEAD

Sentinel

Tarcher

Viking Press

Price Stern Sloan

YOUNG READERS DIVISION

Dial Books for Young Readers

Dutton Children's Books

Firebird

Frederick Warne

G.P. Putnam's Sons Books for Young Readers

Grosset & Dunlap

Philomel

PUFFIN BOOKS

Razorbill

Speak

Viking Books for Young Readers

RANDOM HOUSE, INC. (BERTELSMANN)

www.randomhouse.com

CROWN PUBLISHING GROUP

Amphoto Books

Backstage Books

Billboard Books

Broadway Business

Clarkson Potter

Crown

Crown Archetype

Crown Business

Crown Forum

Doubleday Religion

Harmony

Image Books

Potter Craft

Potter Style

Ten Speed Press

Three Rivers Press

Waterbrook Multnomah

Watson-Guptill

KNOPF DOUBLEDAY PUBLISHING GROUP

Alfred A. Knopf

Anchor Books

Doubleday

Everyman's Library

Nan A. Talese

Pantheon Books

Schocken Books

Vintage

RANDOM HOUSE PUBLISHING GROUP

Ballantine Books

Bantam

Del Rey

Del Rey/Lucas Books

Del Rey/Manga

Delacorte

Dell

The Dial Press

The Modern Library

One World

Presidio Press

Random House Trade Group

Random House Trade Paperbacks

Spectra

Spiegel and Grau

Triumph Books

Villard Books

RANDOM HOUSE AUDIO PUBLISHING GROUP

Listening Library

Random House Audio

RANDOM HOUSE CHILDREN'S BOOKS

Kids@Random

Golden Books

Princeton Review

Sylvan Learning

RANDOM HOUSE DIGITAL PUBLISHING GROUP

Books on Tape

Fodor's Travel

Living Language

Listening Library

Random House Audio

RH Large Print

RANDOM HOUSE INTERNATIONAL
RH Australia
RH of Canada Limited
RH India
RH Mondadori
RH New Zealand
RH South America
RH Group (UK)
Transworld Ireland
Verlagsgruppe RH

SIMON & SCHUSTER

www.simonandschuster.com

SIMON & SCHUSTER ADULT PUBLISHING
Atria Books/Beyond Words
Folger Shakespeare Library
Free Press
Gallery Books
Howard Books
Pocket Books

Scribner
Simon & Schuster
Threshold Editions
The Touchstone & Fireside Group
Pimsleur
Simon & Schuster Audioworks

SIMON & SCHUSTER CHILDREN'S PUBLISHING
Aladdin Paperbacks
Atheneum Books for Young Readers
Bench Lane Books
Little Simon®
Margaret K. McElderry Books
Paula Wiseman Books
Simon & Schuster Books for Young Readers
Simon Pulse
Simon Spotlight®

SIMON & SCHUSTER INTERNATIONAL
Simon & Schuster Australia
Simon & Schuster Canada
Simon & Schuster UK

THE WRITING ENTREPRENEUR

....

by J.M. Lacey

If you are writing full time, or even part time, and you claim the business on your taxes, you are an entrepreneur. Running a business comes with unique challenges and perks. If you are a sole proprietorship, or LLC, and you have no staff, you are marketing your own business, managing contracts and filing your own taxes. So how do you enjoy writing while simultaneously running a business? How can social networking ease your burden? Do your business cards scream amateur? How can you get a client to sign a contract—on your terms? And what really is considered tax deductible for a writer?

THE HAPPY WRITER

Before you even begin your writing business, there are some things to consider to help you build your career.

Kelly James-Enger, author of *Six Figure Freelancing–The Writer's Guide to Making More Money* and freelancer for the last 14 years, says that finding a niche, something you're good at, will help stem the tide of financial insecurity. "Specializing helps set you apart from everyone else and it's easier to get assignments."

To maintain a happy, balanced writing life, she also offers some tips for writers:

- **CHOOSE A MARKET YOU'D LIKE TO WRITE FOR MORE THAN ONCE,** then focus on building relationships.
- **HAVE A DAILY PRODUCTION GOAL,** such as how many queries you plan to send.
- **THINK LONG TERM.** Make sure what you do is leading you in the direction you want to reach.
- **CONSIDER WHAT THE MARKET WILL BEAR,** not just what you want to do. "Don't have all your money come from one source," she adds. "Diversify what you can do."

- **BE CAREFUL ABOUT WORKING NON-STOP.** Have a set time to turn off the e-mail and computer. Avoid working weekends and nights.

GETTING CLIENTS

Things that seem small to you—business cards, websites, stationery—can make a big impression. Prospects will never know how well you write if they can't get past a non-professional set-up.

Get simple, classy, clean and sophisticated cards professionally printed. Include your phone number, mailing, web and e-mail addresses, if you want paying clients to contact you. Your stationery should be the same.

Your website is going to be your most important marketing tool. Make sure your site is personalized, professional and provides the information your prospect will need, such as articles, client list, and portfolio.

....

Your website is going to be your most important marketing tool.

....

There are many books and articles that will tell you to save money and go ahead and design your own site. I disagree 100 percent. Unless you have had training in marketing, design, SEO and html construction, your site will look homemade. Plus, you are too intimate with your own business to have an objective outlook.

Websites aren't as expensive as they used to be, but you will have to dish out a few to several hundred dollars, depending on your needs. To run a business, you have to spend money, and if you pour your investment into anything, it should be your website. Write your own content and save money, but hand the rest over to the professionals. To keep more dollars in your wallet, offer to do a trade with your designer—materials for them and a website for you.

"But I'm a writer," you say, "what does design matter?" If your site looks thrown together, prospects will think your writing is treated the same. And frankly, if your site is difficult to navigate—too much scrolling, tiny fonts, unorganized, dark background—they'll give up looking. No one has that much time or patience.

You also need a professional e-mail address, so get rid of your Yahoo, Gmail and Hotmail, and use your real name. JMLacey@jmlacey.com sounds a lot better than trixie_partygirl@hotmail.com. Save that for your personal accounts.

Next, find work by writing letters, making cold calls, sending e-mails and getting out there. Target businesses (or magazines) for whom you'd like to write. My first major client came via a cold call to another prospect. After I met with the initial contact, she referred me to someone else. I contacted that business immediately, and within three days, I had snagged that client and am still with them over two years later working on multiple projects.

Can social networking help? Yes, if you use it wisely. Join groups like LinkedIn, Facebook and Twitter, but make sure anytime you type a comment or message, it's with the purpose of building your business. You can direct people to your site and blog, but don't ask for their business. Try to type messages and/or guide them to helpful articles and information. Remember the WIIFM—What's In It For Me? It's about *them,* not you. Eventually, your readers will gain confidence in your expert abilities. Be cautious that your networking habits do not become time suckers. Try to have a set time each day, and a set amount of time, to check in with all your networks and forums.

CONTRACTS

Once you have a client, how do you get paid on your terms?

As you establish your business and writing credentials, try to have a solid, though not inflexible idea, of how much you will be paid. Understand what to charge for your level of expertise and geographical area. Most clients, especially corporate clients, prefer project fees instead of hourly rates. So have a base in your head, if you can, of how long something will take you, and come up with a reasonable fee.

Figure out how much you're willing to go down if the client tries to negotiate. Be confident in your figure, but be agreeable with the client. Before I type the contract, I usually state the estimate then ask: "Will that work within your budget?" You want to avoid going too low just to get that project, but don't quote so high you quote yourself out of a job. It takes trial and error, but after a while, you'll learn and gain confidence.

Make sure your contract covers everything unexpected because once you quote a price you can't retract and ask for more. For example, my contracts outline the project and everything that goes with it—three edits, one additional meeting (even via phone), conception, content and design. If the project goes over what was agreed upon—additional edits, meetings, pages, etc.—I charge the additional fee stated in the contract. I also charge extra for commercial photos and anything that might crop up as I go along. But I have to have it covered or I lose money. And don't forget to include the deadline.

Most important, be certain the contract states what you will be paid and when. For my new clients, especially for large projects, I always ask for one-third to one-half down payment. If I'm hiring outside contractors, such as a web designer, I will ask for my contractor's fee in full, if I can, just in case the project flops. All my clients know they will receive an invoice when they've approved the final draft, and my invoice states "payment due upon receipt."

Some commercial clients have their own contracts written by lawyers who really should use writers. If you don't understand something, ask. Contracts are for negotiating. Include your requirements, like the additional charges for extra work. You want to be comfortable signing that contract.

Do not do the work or research until you have it in writing. People will try to get you to "look" at their stuff so you can get a handle on what they want. That's fine, but either wait until you have the contract, or tell them you charge for your research. The reason? You want people to respect you as a professional from the start. Otherwise, they will expect more for nothing.

Do not do the work or research until you have it in writing.

Target clients that will pay you what you are worth. Again, use your discretion, but be firm. If they start out by saying, "I don't have much money," run, because they don't and you have a business to operate. If they tell you, "We can market you," then unless they are a marketing agency, they can't do anything to help you that you can't do. To run your business effectively, establish yourself as a professional by not catering to the low-paying, time-sucking gigs that will get you nowhere except homeless.

TAX DEDUCTIONS

If you claim your writing on your taxes, then it isn't a hobby. This means that almost everything you do and buy for your business is tax deductible.

So what can you deduct? Pretty much anything office-related (computer, pens), books, magazine subscriptions and conferences are among your deductions. And anything you need that will help you in your research, such as travel expenses. In my case, CDs and concert tickets are included in my write-offs as a classical music writer.

Building your writing business takes time. It can take several months to a few years, but it will happen. The more effort you put into it, the sooner it will thrive. But above all, your professional habits will only increase your chances of being successful.

NEGOTIATING TIPS FOR WRITERS FROM AN EDITOR

While being an editor pays the bills around here, I always see a writer when I look in the mirror. And just to show you how much I care about my fellow writers, I'm going to make my life as an editor potentially more difficult by sharing my negotiating tips for writers.

Different editors surely approach negotiation in their own unique ways, but these are my tips for handling editors like myself.

- **ALWAYS TRY TO NEGOTIATE.** I loathe negotiating. Judging by the lack of negotiation from most of my freelancers, I've concluded that most of them loathe negotiating too. But I think it's important for writers to at least try to negotiate from the beginning, because I take those writers a little more seriously, especially if they...

- **DELIVER THE GOODS ON EACH ASSIGNMENT.** Write an amazing article with great sources and examples, and I'm more likely to offer you a better contract the next time around. If I don't, I may be trying to maintain the status quo, but you should try to nudge me again. And I emphasize nudging.

- **DON'T MAKE YOUR DEMANDS A "MY-WAY-OR-THE-HIGHWAY" SITUATION.** That is, don't make it that kind of situation unless you're willing to take the highway. There have been situations, especially when I'm working with a new freelancer, in which I'm not able or willing to go over my initial offer. There have been very good pitches that I let walk, because I couldn't (or wouldn't) go higher. Believe me, I always wish I could offer more, but I have to fill my pages with great content (not squander it all on a handful of articles). That said...

- **PITCH ME WITH AN IDEA THAT IS UNIQUE AND TRULY HELPFUL FOR MY AUDIENCE.** If you pitch me on an interview or list of query tips, I'm less likely to get excited than if you pitch me on an article that tells writers how to make a living off Twitter in 30 days (and actually have the track record to back up that claim). For instance, Lynn Wasnak, who puts together our "How Much Should I Charge?" piece, is far and away my top paid freelancer, because she has to survey professionals in several different fields of writing. It's a unique piece that is truly helpful for my audience. As such, she has greater negotiating power. Still...

- **CHOOSE YOUR BATTLES.** I advise negotiating each time you get a new assignment. Maybe I'll give a little, maybe I won't. But please pick your battles about what you want to negotiate. Don't fight over every single clause in your contract. That gets annoying on my end, and I'm just too busy to enjoy being annoyed. Related to that...

- **DON'T BE A PEST.** I'm more willing to negotiate with writers who complete their assignments on time and don't contact me every couple days with a revision of an already turned in piece or who try to re-negotiate the fee on an article after I've already assigned the piece. I like it when writers ask questions and want to make sure they understand an assignment, but I don't like to have to constantly haggle over things after we've come to an agreement. That's a good way to not receive any more assignments in the future.

- **THINK OF CREATIVE WAYS TO NEGOTIATE.** Offer to write a sidebar for an extra fee—or a series of blog posts. If the editor is unable to offer more money, ask for more complimentary copies. Or some other related comp that the editor may be able to send your way. Editors like to make writers happy (especially if they do a great job), so help them help you get more out of your relationship.

—ROBERT LEE BREWER

J.M. LACEY (http://jmlacey.com) is an independent writer, marketing and public relations professional. She has over 14 years worth of experience in journalism, marketing, public relations, and sales, working for both the corporate and nonprofit sectors. She maintains a classical music blog (http://seasonkt.com) and works with small to large businesses creating websites, advertisements, biographies and other marketing and publicity needs. She is also a public speaker and teaches workshops on writing for businesses and on marketing at writing and corporate conferences.

CONTRACTS 1 O 1

....

by Cindy Ferraino

After you do a victory dance about getting the book deal you always dreamed about or your article hitting the top of the content list of a popular magazine, the celebration quickly comes to a halt when you realize you are not at the finish line yet. Your heart begins to beat faster because you know the next possible hurdle is just around the corner—the contract. For many, the idea of reviewing a contract is like being back in first grade. You know you have to listen to the teacher when you could be playing outside. You know you have to read this contract but why because there are terms in there that look like an excerpt from a foreign language syllabus.

Before I changed my status to self-employed writer, I was working as a grants and contracts administrator at a large medical university in Philadelphia. I helped shepherd the MD and PhD researchers through the channels of grants and contracts administration. While the researchers provided the technical and scientific pieces that could potentially be the next cure for diabetes, heart disease or cancer, I was there to make sure they did their magic within the confines of a budget and imposed contractual regulations. The budget process was easy but when it came to contract regulations—oh well, that was a different story. I became familiar with the terms such as indemnifications, property and intellectual rights and conditions of payments. In addition to the budget process, I was an integral part of reviewing and negotiating a grant or contract that had the best interests for every party involved.

After my son was born, I left the university and my contracts background went on a brief hiatus. Once my son went off to school, I began freelance writing. After a few writing gigs sprinkled with a few too many rejection slips, I landed an assignment for *Dog Fancy* magazine. I was thrilled and eagerly anticipated the arrival of a contract in my inbox. As

PAYMENT TYPES

There are any number of different arrangements for publishers to pay writers. However, here are three of the most common and what they mean.

- Pays on acceptance. This means that a publisher pays (or cuts a check) for the writer upon acceptance of the manuscript. This is usually the best deal a writer can hope to receive.
- Pays on publication. In these cases, a publisher pays (or cuts a check) for the writer by the publication date of the manuscript. For magazines, this could mean several months after the manuscript was accepted and approved. For books, this could mean more than a year.
- Pays after publication. Sometimes contracts will specify exactly how long after publication. Be wary of contracts that leave it open-ended.

I opened the document, the hiatus had lifted. I read through the contract and was able to send it back within a few hours.

For many new freelancers or writers who have been around the block, contract administration is not something that they can list as a perk on their resume. Instead of searching through the Yellow Pages for a contract lawyer or trying to call in a special favor to a writer friend, there are some easy ways for a newbie writer or even a seasoned writer to review a contract before putting a smiley face next to the dotted line.

TAKE A DEEP BREATH, THEN READ ON

Remember breaking those seals on test booklets and the voice in the background telling you "Please read the directions slowly." As you tried to drown out the voice because your stomach was in knots, little did you know that those imparting words of wisdom would come in handy as you perspired profusely over the legal jargon that unfolded before your eyes. The same words go for contracts.

Many writers, including myself, are anxious to get an assignment under way but the contract carrot continues to loom over our creative minds. "I'm surprised by writers who just skim a contract and then sign it without understanding what it means, "says Kelly James-Enger. James-Enger is the author of books including *Six Figure Freelancing: The Writer's Guide to Making More* (Random House, 2005) and blog Dollarsanddeadlines. blogspot.com. "Most of the language in magazine contracts isn't that complicated, but it can be confusing when you're new to the business."

When I receive a contract from a new publisher or editor, I make a second copy. My children call it "my sloppy copy." I take out a highlighter and begin to mark up the key points of the contract: beginning and end date, conditions of payment, how my relationship is defined by the publisher and what the outline of the article should look like.

The beginning and end date of a contract is crucial. After I recently negotiated a contract, the editor changed the due date of the article in an e-mail. I made sure the contract was changed to reflect the new due date. The conditions of the payments are important because it will describe when the writer will be paid and by what method. Most publishers have turned to incremental payment schedules or payments to be made online like Pay-Pal. How the publisher considers your contractor status is important. If you're a freelance contract writer, the contract should reflect that as well as identify you as an independent contractor for IRS tax purposes. Finally, the contract will highlight an outline of what your article or proposal should look like.

After I recently negotiated a contract, the editor changed the due date of the article in an e-mail. I made sure the contract was changed to reflect the new due date.

As you slowly digest the terms you are about to agree to for your assignment or book project, you gain a better understanding of what an editor or publisher expects from you and when.

CUTTING TO THE LEGAL CHASE

Once you have had a chance to review a contract, you may be scratching your head and saying, "Okay, now what does this all mean to me as a writer?" James-Enger describes three key areas where writers should keep sharp on when it comes to contracts—Indemnification, Pay and Exclusivity provisions.

INDEMNIFICATION is a publisher's way of saying if something goes wrong, we are not responsible. If a claim is brought against another writer's work, a publisher does not want to be responsible for the legal aftermath but you could be the one receiving a notice in the mail. James-Enger warns writers to be on the lookout for indemnification clauses. "In the U.S., anyone can sue anyone over just about anything," she says. "I'm okay with agreeing to indemnification clauses that specify breaches of contract because I know I'm not going to plagiarize, libel or misquote anyone. But I can't promise that the publication will never be sued by anyone whether or not I actually breached the contract."

CONTRACT TIPS

Even seasoned freelancers can find themselves intimidated by contracts. Here are a few things to consider with your contract:

- **KEEP COPY ON RECORD.** If the contract is sent via e-mail, keep a digital copy, but also print up a hard copy and keep it in an easy-to-find file folder.

- **CHECK FOR RIGHTS.** It's almost never a good idea to sell all rights. But you should also pay attention to whether you're selling any subsidiary or reprint rights. The more rights you release the more payment you should expect (and demand).
- **WHEN PAYMENT.** Make sure you understand when you are to be paid and have it specified in your contract. You may think that payment will come when the article is accepted or published, but different publishers have different policies. Get it in writing.
- **HOW MUCH PAYMENT.** The contract should specify exactly how much you are going to be paid. If there is no payment listed on the contract, the publisher could use your work for free.
- **TURN IN CONTRACT BEFORE ASSIGNMENT.** Don't start working until the contract is signed, and everything is official. As a freelancer, time is as important as money. Don't waste any of your time and effort on any project that is not yet contracted.

PAY is where you want the publisher "to show you the money." Writers need to be aware of how publishers will discuss the terms of payment in the contract. James-Enger advises to have "payment on acceptance." This means you will be paid when the editor agrees to accept your manuscript or article. If there is "no payment on acceptance," some publishers will pay when the article is published. "Push for payment whenever you can," she says.

EXCLUSIVITY PROVISIONS are where a particular publisher will not allow the writer to publish an article or manuscript that is "about the same or similar subject" during the time the publisher runs the piece. Because of the nature of the writing business, James-Enger feels writers need to negotiate this part of the contract. "I specialize in health, fitness and nutrition, and I'm always writing about a similar subject," she says.

WHEN TO HEAD TO THE BARGAINING TABLE

Recently, I became an independent contractor for the American Composites Manufacturing Association (ACMA). When I reviewed the terms of the contract, I was concerned how my independent contractor status was identified. Although I am not an ACMA employee, I wanted to know if I could include my ACMA publications on my resume. Before I signed the contract, I questioned this issue with my editor. My editor told me I may use this opportunity to put on my resume. I signed the contract and finished my assignment.

Writers should be able to talk to an editor or a publisher if there is a question about a term or clause in a contract. "Don't be afraid to talk to the editor about the changes you'd like to make to a contract," James-Enger says. "You don't know what you'll get or if an editor is willing to negotiate it, until you ask."

When writers have to approach an editor for changes to a contract, James-Enger advises writers to act professionally when it comes to the negotiations. "I start out with saying—I am really excited to be working with you on this story and I appreciate the assignment, but I have a couple of issues with the contract that I'd like to talk to you about," she says. "Sure I want a better contract but I also want to maintain a good working relationship with my editor. A scorched-earth policy doesn't benefit any freelancer in the long run."

In today's economy, writers are a little more reluctant to ask for a higher rate for an article.

Negotiating payment terms is a tricky subject for some writers. Writers want to get the most bang for their buck but they don't want to lose a great writing assignment. Do your research first before you decide to ask an editor for more money to complete the assignment. Double check the publisher's website or look to see if the pay scale is equivalent to other publishers in the particular industry. Some publishers have a set publishing fee whereas others may have a little more wiggle room depending on the type of the assignment given. In today's economy, writers are a little more reluctant to ask for a higher rate for an article. If the publisher seems to be open to discussion about the pay scale, just make sure you approach the situation in a professional manner so as to not turn the publisher away from giving you another assignment.

WHO WILL OWN YOUR WRITING?

Besides payment terms, another area that writers may find themselves on the other end of the negotiation table is with ownership rights. We all want to take credit for the work that we have poured our heart and soul into. Unfortunately, the business of publishing has different ways of saying how a writer can classify their work. Ownership rights vary but the biggest one that writers have a hard time trying to build up a good case against is "all rights." "All rights" is exactly what it means: *hope you are not in love with what you have just written because you will not be able to use it again.*

RIGHTS AND WHAT THEY MEAN

A creative work can be used in many different ways. As the author of the work, you hold all rights to the work in question. When you agree to have your work published, you are granting a publisher the right to use your work in any number of ways. Whether that right is to publish the manuscript for the first time in a publication, or to publish it as many times and in as many ways as a publisher wishes, is up to you—it all depends on the agreed-upon terms. As a general rule, the more rights you license away, the less control you have over your work and the money you're paid. You should strive to keep as many rights to your work as you can.

Writers and editors sometimes define rights in a number of different ways. Below you will find a classification of terms as they relate to rights.

- **FIRST SERIAL RIGHTS.** Rights that the writer offers a newspaper or magazine to publish the manuscript for the first time in any periodical. All other rights remain with the writer. Sometimes the qualifier "North American" is added to these rights to specify a geographical limitation to the license. When content is excerpted from a book scheduled to be published, and it appears in a magazine or newspaper prior to book publication, this is also called first serial rights.
- **ONE-TIME RIGHTS.** Nonexclusive rights (rights that can be licensed to more than one market) purchased by a periodical to publish the work once (also known as simultaneous rights). That is, there is nothing to stop the author from selling the work to other publications at the same time.
- **SECOND SERIAL (REPRINT) RIGHTS.** Nonexclusive rights given to a newspaper or magazine to publish a manuscript after it has already appeared in another newspaper or magazine.
- **ALL RIGHTS.** This is exactly what it sounds like. "All rights" means an author is selling every right he has to a work. If you license all rights to your work, you forfeit the right to ever use the work again. If you think you may want to use the article again, you should avoid submitting to such markets or refuse payment and withdraw your material.
- **ELECTRONIC RIGHTS.** Rights that cover a broad range of electronic media, including websites, CD/DVDs, video games, smart phone apps, and more. The contract should specify if—and which—electronic rights are included. The presumption is unspecified rights remain with the writer.
- **SUBSIDIARY RIGHTS.** Rights, other than book publication rights, that should be covered in a book contract. These may include various serial rights; movie, TV, audio, and other electronic rights; translation rights, etc. The book contract should specify who controls the rights (author or publisher) and what percentage of sales from the licensing of these rights goes to the author.
- **DRAMATIC, TV, AND MOTION PICTURE RIGHTS.** Rights for use of material on the stage, on TV, or in the movies. Often a one-year option to buy such rights is offered (generally for 10 percent of the total price). The party interested in the rights then tries to sell the idea to other people—actors, directors, studios, or TV networks. Some properties are optioned numerous times, but most fail to become full productions. In those cases, the writer can sell the rights again and again.

Sometimes editors don't take the time to specify the rights they are buying. If you sense that an editor is interested in getting stories, but doesn't seem to know what his and the writer's responsibilities are, be wary. In such a case, you'll want to explain what rights you're offering (preferably one-time or first serial rights only) and that you expect additional payment for subsequent use of your work.

The Copyright Law that went into effect January 1, 1978, states writers are primarily selling one-time rights to their work unless they—and the publisher—agree otherwise in writing. Book rights are covered fully by contract between the writer and the book publisher.

In recent months, I have written for two publications that I had given "all rights" to the company. My rationale is that I knew I would never need to use those articles again but I did make sure I was able to include those articles for my byline to show that I have publishing experience.

If you feel that you want to reuse or recycle an article that you had written a few years ago, you might want to consider negotiating an "all rights" clause or maybe going to another publisher. "We don't take all rights so there is no reason for authors to request we change the rights clause," says Angela Hoy, author and owner of WritersWeekly.com and Booklocker.com. "Our contracts were rated 'Outstanding' by Mark Levine (author of *The Fine Print of Self-Publishing*) and has also been called the clearest and fairest in the industry."

James-Enger is also an advocate of negotiating contracts that include an "all rights" clause. "I hate 'all rights' contracts, and try to avoid signing them as they preclude me from ever reselling the piece as a reprint to other markets," she says. "I explain that to editors, and I have been able to get editors to agree to let me retain nonexclusive reprint rights even when they buy all rights—which still lets me market the piece as a reprint." James-Enger also advises that "if the publisher demands all rights, then negotiate if the payment is sub-standard."

So if you are just receiving a contract in the mail for the first time or you are working with a new publisher, you should not be afraid of the legal lingo that blankets the message "we want to work with you." Contracts are meant to protect both the interests of the publishers and writers. Publishers want the commitment from writers that he or she will provide their best work and writers want to be recognized for their best work. But between those contracts lines, the legal lingo can cause writers to feel they need a law degree to review the contract. No, just sit back and relax and enjoy the prose that will take your writing to the next level.

....

CINDY FERRAINO has been blessed with a variety of assignments, including newspaper articles, magazine articles, ghost-written articles, stories for books, and most recently authoring a book on accounting and bookkeeping terminology, *The Complete Dictionary of Accounting & Bookkeeping Terms Explained Simply* (Atlantic Publishing Group).

....

MAKING THE MOST OF THE MONEY YOU EARN

....

by Sage Cohen

Writers who manage money well can establish a prosperous writing life that meets their short-term needs and long-term goals. This article will introduce the key financial systems, strategies, attitudes and practices that will help you cultivate a writing life that makes the most of your resources and sustains you over time.

DIVIDING BUSINESS AND PERSONAL EXPENSES

If you are reporting your writing business to the IRS, it is important that you keep the money that flows from this source entirely separate from your personal finances. Here's what you'll need to accomplish this:

- **BUSINESS CHECKING ACCOUNT:** Only two types of money go into this account: money you have been paid for your writing and/or "capital investments" you make by depositing your own money to invest in the business. And only two types of payments are made from this account: business-related expenses (such as: subscriptions, marketing and advertisement, professional development, fax or phone service, postage, computer software and supplies), and "capital draws" which you make to pay yourself.

- **BUSINESS SAVINGS ACCOUNT OR MONEY MARKET ACCOUNT:** This account is the holding pen where your quarterly tax payments will accumulate and earn interest. Money put aside for your retirement account(s) can also be held here.

- **BUSINESS CREDIT CARD:** It's a good idea to have a credit card for your business as a means of emergency preparedness. Pay off the card responsibly every month and this will help you establish a good business credit record, which can be useful down the line should you need a loan for any reason.

When establishing your business banking and credit, shop around for the best deals, such as highest interest rates, lowest (or no) monthly service fees, and free checking. Mint.com is a good source for researching your options.

EXPENSE TRACKING AND RECONCILING

Once your bank accounts are set up, it's time to start tracking and categorizing what you earn and spend. This will ensure that you can accurately report your income and itemize your deductions when tax time rolls around every quarter. Whether you intend to prepare your taxes yourself or have an accountant help you, immaculate financial records will be the key to speed and success in filing your taxes.

For the most effective and consistent expense tracking, I highly recommend that you use a computer program such as QuickBooks. While it may seem simpler to do accounting by hand, I assure you that it isn't. Even a luddite such as I, who can't comprehend the most basic principles of accounting, can use QuickBooks with great aplomb to plug in the proper categories for income and expenses, easily reconcile bank statements, and with a few clicks prepare all of the requisite reports that make it easy to prepare taxes.

PAYING BILLS ONLINE

While it's certainly not imperative, you might want to check out your bank's online bill pay option if you're not using this already. Once you've set up the payee list, you can make payments in a few seconds every month or set up auto payments for expenses that are recurring. Having a digital history of bills paid can also come in handy with your accounting.

MANAGING TAXES

Self-employed people need to pay quarterly taxes. A quick, online search will reveal a variety of tax calculators and other online tools that can help you estimate what your payments should be. Programs such as TurboTax are popular and useful tools for automating and guiding you step-by-step through tax preparation. An accountant can also be helpful in understanding your unique tax picture, identifying and saving the right amount for taxes each quarter, and even determining SEP IRA contribution amounts (described later in this article). The more complex your finances (or antediluvian your accounting skills), the more likely that you'll benefit from this kind of personalized expertise.

Once you have forecasted your taxes either with the help of a specialized, tax-planning program or an accountant, you can establish a plan toward saving the right amount for quarterly payments. For example, once I figured out what my tax bracket was and the approximate percentage of income that needed to be set aside as taxes, I would immediately transfer a percentage of every deposit to my savings account, where it would sit and grow a little interest until quarterly tax time came around. When I could afford to do so, I would also set aside the appropriate percentage of SEP IRA contribution from each deposit so that I'd be ready at end-of-year to deposit as much as I possibly could for retirement.

THE PRINCIPLE TO COMMIT TO IS THIS: Get that tax-earmarked cash out of your hot little hands (i.e., checking account) as soon as you can, and create whatever deterrents you need to leave the money in savings so you'll have it when you need it.

INTELLIGENT INVESTING FOR YOUR CAREER

Your writing business will require not only the investment of your time but also the investment of money. When deciding what to spend and how, consider your values and your budget in these three, key areas:

EDUCATION	MARKETING AND PROMOTION	KEEPING THE WHEELS TURNING
Subscriptions to publications in your field	URL registration and hosting for blogs and websites	Technology and application purchase, servicing and back-up
Memberships to organizations in your field	Contact database subscription (such as Constant Contact) for communicating with your audiences	Office supplies and furniture
Books: on topics you want to learn, or in genres you are cultivating	Business cards and stationery	Insurances for you and/or your business
Conferences and seminars	Print promotions (such as direct mail), giveaways and schwag	Travel, gas, parking
Classes and workshops	Online or print ad placement costs	Phone, fax and e-mail

This is not an absolute formula for spending, by any means—just a snapshot of the types of expenses you may be considering and negotiating over time. My general rule would be: start small and modest with the one or two most urgent and/or inexpensive items in each list, and grow slowly over time as your income grows.

The good news is that these legitimate business expenses may all be deducted from your income—making your net income and tax burden less. Please keep in mind that the IRS allows losses as long as you make a profit for at least three of the first five years you are in business. Otherwise, the IRS will consider your writing a non-deductible hobby.

PREPARATION AND PROTECTION FOR THE FUTURE

As a self-employed writer, in many ways your future is in your hands. Following are some of the health and financial investments that I'd recommend you consider as you build and nurture The Enterprise of You. Please understand that these are a layperson's suggestions. I am by no means an accountant, tax advisor or financial planning guru. I am simply a person who has educated herself on these topics for the sake of her own writing business, made the choices I am recommending and benefited from them. I'd like you to benefit from them, too.

SEP IRAS

Individual Retirement Accounts (IRAs) are investment accounts designed to help individuals save for retirement. But I do recommend that you educate yourself about the Simplified Employee Pension Individual Retirement Account (SEP IRA) and consider opening one if you don't have one already.

A SEP IRA is a special type of IRA that is particularly beneficial to self-employed people. Whereas a Roth IRA has a contribution cap of $5,000 or $6,000, depending on your age, the contribution limit for self-employed people in 2011 is approximately 20% of adjusted earned income, with a maximum contribution of $49,000. Contributions for a SEP IRA are generally 100% tax deductible and investments grow tax deferred. Let's say your adjusted earned income this year is $50,000. This means you'd be able to contribute $10,000 to your retirement account. I encourage you to do some research online or ask your accountant if a SEP IRA makes sense for you.

CREATING A 9-MONTH SAVINGS BUFFER

When you're living month-to-month, you are extremely vulnerable to fluctuation in the economy, client budget changes, life emergencies and every other wrench that could turn a good working groove into a frightening financial rut. The best way to prepare for the unexpected is to start (or continue) developing a savings buffer. The experts these days are suggesting that we accumulate nine months of living expenses to help us navigate transition in a way that we feel empowered rather than scared and desperate to take the next thing that comes along.

....

When I paid off one of my credit cards in full, I added that monthly payment to the monthly savings transfer.

....

I started creating my savings buffer by opening the highest-interest money market account I could find and setting up a modest, monthly automatic transfer from my checking account. Then, when I paid off my car after five years of monthly payments, I added my car payment amount to the monthly transfer. (I'd been paying that amount for five years, so I was pretty sure I could continue to pay it to myself.) When I paid off one of my credit cards in full, I added that monthly payment to the monthly savings transfer. Within a year, I had a hefty sum going to savings every month before I had time to think about it, all based on expenses I was accustomed to paying, with money that had never been anticipated in the monthly cash flow.

What can you do today—and tomorrow—to put your money to work for your life, and start being as creative with your savings as you are with language?

DISABILITY INSURANCE

If writing is your livelihood, what happens if you become unable to write? I have writing friends who have become incapacitated and unable to work due to injuries to their brains, backs, hands and eyes. Disability insurance is one way to protect against such emergencies and ensure that you have an income in the unlikely event that you're not physically able to earn one yourself.

Depending on your health, age and budget, monthly disability insurance payments may or may not be within your means or priorities. But you won't know until you learn more about your coverage options. I encourage you to investigate this possibility with several highly rated insurance companies to get the lay of the land for your unique, personal profile and then make an informed decision.

HEALTH INSURANCE

Self-employed writers face tough decisions about health insurance. If you are lucky, there is someone in your family with great health coverage that is also available to you. Without the benefit of group health insurance, chances are that self-insuring costs are high and coverage is low. Just as in disability insurance, age and health status are significant variables in costs and availability of coverage. (Once again, I am no expert on this topic; only a novice who has had to figure things out for myself along the way, sharing the little I know with you.)

Ideally, of course, you'll have reasonably-priced health insurance that helps make preventive care and health maintenance more accessible and protects you in case of a major medical emergency. The following are a few possibilities to check out that could reduce costs and improve access to health coverage:

- Join a group that aggregates its members for group coverage, such as a Chamber of Commerce or AARP. Ask an insurance agent in your area if there are any other group coverage options available to you.

- Consider a high-deductible health plan paired with a Health Savings Account (HSA). Because the deductible is so high, these plans are generally thought to be most useful for a major medical emergency. But an HSA paired with such a plan allows you to put aside a chunk of pre-tax change every year that can be spent on medical expenses or remain in the account where it can be invested and grow. 2011 HSA investment limits, for example, are: $3,050 for individual coverage and $6,150 for family coverage.

Establishing effective financial systems for your writing business will take some time and energy at the front end. I suggest that you pace yourself by taking an achievable step or two each week until you have a baseline of financial management that works for you. Then, you can start moving toward some of your bigger, longer-term goals. Once it's established, your solid financial foundation will pay you in dividends of greater efficiency, insight and peace of mind for the rest of your writing career.

SAGE COHEN is the author of *The Productive Writer* and *Writing the Life Poetic,* both from Writer's Digest Books. She's been nominated for a Pushcart Prize, won first prize in the Ghost Road Press Poetry contest and published dozens of poems, essays and articles on the writing life. Sage holds an MFA in creative writing from New York University and a BA from Brown University. Since 1997, she has been a freelance writer serving clients including Intuit, Blue Shield, Adobe, and Kaiser Permanente..

PHOTO © Nyla Alisia

REPURPOSING WRITING FOR PLATFORM AND PROFIT

by Sage Cohen

Anything worth writing about is worth writing about repeatedly. The greater your command on a topic, the more leverage you have in the realm of publishing, income generation and platform building. Plus, when you consolidate knowledge by adapting writing in ways that improve your performance and results, you gain confidence in what you know and your ability to communicate it. Eventually, you may even come to consider yourself—and be considered by others—an expert in your chosen field. This article suggests strategies and systems that can help you maximize the value of your work by repurposing writing for fresh markets and media.

A STRATEGIC APPROACH TO CREATING CONTINUED VALUE FROM YOUR THINKING AND WRITING

Instead of starting from scratch each time you pitch an article, workshop, or class, I propose that you leverage the knowledge base you've already cultivated, while finding a new dimension to explore or a new audience to educate. I call this process repurposing.

Repurposing works best when you start cultivating a consciousness about what you're writing now, what you want to be writing more of over time, and charting out the path between the two. These simple steps can take you there.

Take stock of what you have already written.

Investigate your files, archives, clips, and notebooks to see what topics or themes are taking up the most real estate. Check out not only the themes you've been assigned by editors or clients, but also the writing you choose to do. Make a diagram or chart that helps you measure how much of each type of source information you already have on hand. Let's say you come up with this list of themes about which you could write and have written authoritatively: mortgage banking, health and wellness, positive discipline for preschoolers, and providing inspiration and instruction for writers.

Decide which theme(s) you'd enjoy exploring more deeply

I invite you to prioritize your list of themes in order of what you most want to pursue moving forward. Make sure you choose a topic that truly interests you, or else you're likely to limit your productivity through your own resistance.

Let's say you believe you should be writing about mortgage banking because that's been profitable for you, but what you really love writing about is skills and strategies for improving writing. I'd argue this: When you're writing about something that is of great interest to you, you'll have far more energy for exploring its nuances and finding surprising ways to publish and profit from it.

If you're just getting started, or you would like to start from scratch with a topic you've never covered before, no problem. Write that down at the top of your list. Everyone has to start repurposing somewhere.

Define the types of people you might want to reach.

Let's assume that your number one interest from the list you just made is "providing inspiration and instruction for writers." Now ask yourself what types of people would benefit from knowing about this? The obvious answer is, of course: Writers. But there could be dozens or even hundreds of sub-categories, and then sub-sub categories that could help you identify publications, speaking and teaching opportunities, and other media through which you might customize content that connects with each of these groups. Here's a sample brainstorm:

POETS	CREATIVE NONFICTION WRITERS	FICTION WRITERS	FREELANCE WRITERS (FOR MAGAZINES)	COPY WRITERS (FOR BUSINESS / MARKETING / ADVERTISING)
Members of writing organizations				
Blog readers / online media consumers				
Students: college / high school / elementary / adult education				
Magazine / literary publication subscribers				
Book club members				
Writing groups				
People who attend writing conferences				
Audiences at community literary events / lectures / readings				

Each of these groups could be broken down further into the following sub-categories:

- Writers wanting to publish / author
- Writers wanting to improve their craft
- Writers wanting to improve their process
- Writers with bad habits who want to learn better habits
- Writers wanting to make more money
- Writers wanting to know how to run their own writing business
- Writers wanting to understand and navigate brand or platform
- Writers wanting to get inspired
- Writers wanting to use social media more effectively

Spend some time getting as detailed as you can about the types of people who might be interested in your topic—including where they might go to learn about this topic, and the types of knowledge they might be seeking. (Don't worry yet about if you actually want to speak to all of these audiences. The point here is to dream big and capture a wide range of possibilities.)

Identify fresh ways to reach subsets of your identified audience

Staying with the "providing inspiration and instruction for writers" theme, let's say you just published an article about transforming fear into courage in a writing trade magazine. Now you want to find fresh ways to spin and sell this content. If you focused on the same general audience but targeted different sub-sets and/or media, you might consider the following:

- Present at writing conferences, high schools, or writing groups on this topic.
- Use the article's knowledge base as a jumping-off point for developing a 25-page e-book on the topic.
- Offer a tele-class (or a series of tele-classes) where you teach writers about how to get a handle on their relationship with fear.
- Condense or expand your 10 best tips on fear in the writing life and offer them as a series for targeted subscribers, such as rewarding subscribers to your blog or website with a 10-week, free e-mail series, or pitching this content to literary blogs or other organizations as content for their readers.
- Create and sell a daily e-mail series where you offer writers one bite-sized thought, quote or tip about fear for (you define the time range).

You see what I mean? You could keep going and going and going with new ways to explore and package and market your interest in writers' relationship with fear. I call this process of finding and using new formats, media or experiences through which you reach similar audiences *lateral* repurposing.

Tap unprecedented markets

Another approach to repurposing, which I call *vertical* repurposing, involves re-slanting content for completely new markets or audiences. Because fear is something that every human negotiates at one time or another, there are likely to be principles in our example piece that translate to people of every stripe.

First, I recommend naming for yourself the universal, translatable nugget of truth that you believe you are offering. In this case, let's say: *Behaviors and attitudes that help you work with your fear to eliminate procrastination and perfectionism.*

Then, have fun brainstorming the various audiences you might target and channels through which you might reach them. The sky is literally the limit. A few examples of the result of this work might be:

- Offer a workshop (and accompanying training materials) to corporate teams or departments who want employees to become more productive.
- Pitch a piece to a psychology trade magazine on how fear influences human development and performance —and what can be done about it.
- Pitch an article to a performance arts publication that addresses their unique creative concerns in the context of fear.
- Write an article in publications for educators teaching them how to identify and address the signs of fear in low-performing students.
- Train entrepreneurs in "feeling the fear and doing it anyway."

Make a game plan

You've done the important work of brainstorming possibilities. Now it's time to get as specific as possible about how you intend to proceed with repurposing. I'm a big fan of making extremely detailed work plans—because they help prove to me that what I want to do is actually within my reach. Even if I don't follow the plan at all, which often I don't, I move forward anchored in a sense of certainty that it's only a matter of time before I accomplish what I've set out to do.

- Choose a piece of writing from your preferred arsenal of work. Again, make sure the topic still holds some interest for you.
- Make yourself a blueprint of possibilities that identifies who you want to pitch or sell or present it to next, why it might matter to them, and the ways that you might reach this audience. For example, I have culled some of the possibilities suggested above:

Lateral Repurposing Possibilities for Fear Article

MARKET OR CHANNEL	AUDIENCE	WHY THIS IS RELEVANT TO THEM	PIECE/S TO PITCH OR SELL
[Name of] Writing Conference	Conference attendees	Website says 50% of attendees want to learn about writing process and productivity.	Workshop on fear in the writing life
My Blog about the Writing Life	My blog subscribers, Facebook friends, Twitter followers	They've subscribed to or visited my blog to get tips on writing more effectively.	25-page e-book and/or daily e-mail series focused on transforming your relationship with fear in 30 days
Tele-class through [Name of Writer who features guest writing teachers]	[Name of Writer's] audience, my blog subscribers, Facebook friends, Twitter followers	They signed up to learn about tackling fear in the writing life.	FREE: Present class material distilled from workshop above and/or OFFERS of a 25-page e-book and/or daily e-mail series focused on transforming your relationship with fear in 30 days

Vertical Repurposing Possibilities for Fear Article

MARKET OR CHANNEL	AUDIENCE	WHY THIS IS RELEVANT TO THEM	PIECE/S TO PITCH OR SELL
Corporations	Employee teams or departments	It can help teams collaborate more effectively and become more productive.	Workshop, educational collateral, and/or training materials
Psychology Trade Magazine	People interested in human psychology	Provide education about the impact of fear on human development.	Magazine article
Education Trade Magazine	Educators	Help them identify and address fear's role in low academic performance.	Magazine article

You can refer to these lists again and again —and add to them over time to track the evolution of your expertise for preferred audiences and markets.

Repurpose

With all of the strategic heavy lifting complete, you can now choose one of the possibilities you've articulated above and do whatever next step makes sense to take your work forward, such as: create the product to sell, write the query, submit a proposal to the conference, etc. I suggest the following guidelines to steer your thinking and writing:

- Read your original piece a few times, ideally out loud at least once. This helps you re-establish your connection with what you already know about this topic. Then put it out of sight.
- Start a working draft; at the top, write down everything you know you are striving to accomplish, such as: word count, market or channel / audience, target publication / media / delivery channel.
- Draft a detailed outline or do a 10-minute free write (whatever your style may be) to capture in writing the essence of what you want to accomplish with this piece.
- Research and write as you would any article or query or [whatever you have determined your deliverable to be].
- This piece should reflect the next step in your investigation of this topic. Compare it to the original to ensure there are no exact overlaps or repeats of language. This new piece should read in some way fresh and new and authentically distinguished from all of your other writing about [fear in the writing life]. (Echoing similar strategies or tips is not necessarily a problem, as long as the audience and/or market are significantly different from those of the original.)
- If you are sending this out for publication, briefly explain in your query of the success you've already had on this topic (what you've published, where you've presented) and how it's relevant to the current application that you are proposing. The delicate dance here is demonstrating that you have established expertise, while also making it clear that you have something fresh and engaging to say to this publication's readers. (The same principle is true if you are marketing a writing product yourself.)

REPEAT AND PROSPER!

You can stay engaged in repurposing consciousness by asking yourself one simple question every time you write something: "Who else could benefit from knowing about this?" (Simply apply this process to flesh out the answer to that question.) Once you've repurposed a piece of writing a few times, you'll get a feel for how vast the opportunities might be for everything you write. And you'll be on your way to establishing a practice that can boost your confidence and expertise while fortifying your platform and your profits.

RECORD KEEPING AND PRICING

....

by Daniel Dern

Being a writer includes many tasks besides the actual act of writing. There's research, marketing, computer maintenance, and, unless you are doing writing strictly as a hobby, financial recordkeeping—keeping track of the money you spend and receive related to your writing activities.

For example, I've been doing freelance writing since 1973, ranging from part-time to full-time... and, along with the writing, research, marketing and sales, et cetera, done my own recordkeeping.

This recordkeeping doesn't have to be complicated or expensive. It's gotten simple bordering on automatic, depending on how you do it.

You'll need to spend a few hours learning what to do and why, and setting up to do it. Jeff Hecht, a full-time science and technology writer who has also sold some science fiction, points out, "You need to understand something about accounting and taxes, even if you use an accountant, because you have to know what's deductible and what isn't, what records to keep, and what information you will have to provide."

After that, it's a few minutes every day or so.

Here's some of my current thoughts and advice on recordkeeping.

[**NOTE:** From a tax perspective, this article assumes you are a) a U.S. taxpayer, and b) doing your business activities as an unincorporated individual, which means you file your business income/expense tax information using a Form 1040 Schedule C. If you're already incorporated, or not a U.S. taxpayer, you should know what's in this article already, and some things won't apply to you... but keep reading, you may still learn something useful.)

WHY KEEP FINANCIAL RECORDS OF YOUR BUSINESS

There are several important reasons to keep financial records.

One, so you know how much money you have to pay taxes on (which in turn impacts Reason Number Two).

For example, if you have $65,439 of business income for a calendar year, and $16,222 in business-related expenses, then you have taxable business income of $65,439 - $16,222 = $49,217... the amount you have to report on your Form 1040 under BUSINESS INCOME OR LOSS (which currently is Form 1040 Line 12).

Another way to look at this is: If you don't keep good records of your expenses (which are harder than logging your revenues, as a rule), you'll pay more taxes than you have to, since those business expenses are reducing your total income, which is what you're paying taxes on. Your business expenses become pre-tax rather than post-tax spending... and between Federal income tax, the roughly 16 percent SE (Social Security and Medicare) tax, and any state or city income taxes, that can be between 20 and 50 percent, so good recordkeeping can legitimately lower your tax obligation by as much as several thousand dollars a year in taxes. (Depending, of course, on how much you earned, and what your business expenses were—which only good recordkeeping will tell you.)

Convinced yet?

Two, recordkeeping lets you know how well/poorly you're doing in terms of writing as a business activity, income and expensewise. Are you earning less or more than you are spending? Are you earning more—after expenses—than you would working at some other job?

Three, recordkeeping may help you analyze your writing from a business perspective and see what, if anything, might merit being changed. For example, are there seasonal peaks or slumps in work loads? Do some clients (customers) take too long to pay? Are some clients not paying? Do your phone bills seem too high? Can you get some of your supplies at better prices, by changing how you order or switching suppliers? Are you spending more on some events or activities than the resulting business justifies? Accurate records tell you what your gut may only suspect (or might not even suspect).

Rick Telberg, president and chief executive of Bay Street Group, which provides custom research, marketing, strategic consulting, and other services to the professional tax, accounting, and finance sector, stresses the importance of good, organized record-keeping. "Just because you're a writer doesn't mean you are not in business."

WHAT ARE FINANCIAL RECORDS?

Briefly, my definition: "records," a.k.a. "books" or "bookkeeping," means the list of business-related income and business-related expenses.

A BRIEF RECOMMENDATION FOR INVOICE IDS

Include the year, an absolute tracking number, the client ID, and per-client tracking number—and have this data be part of the file name! So, for example, I have invoice "numbers" like:

Dern-2011-035/SmartBear-01

which would be in a file named:

Dern-2011-SmartBear-01-TestingMobileDevices

Business-related INCOME—in accountant-speak, "Accounts Receivable"—as a writer includes money you earn selling articles, stories, books, podcasts—and possibly from writing services, like copyediting, proposal writing, rewriting—and from writing-related activities, e.g., speaking, doing readings, and teaching.

Business-related EXPENDITURES—"Accounts Payable"—refers to money spent to enable you to write. For example, a computer and printer, monthly broadband Internet service, an annual subscription to *Writer's Digest*, professional memberships like SCBWI, office supplies, and professional activities. (More on this below.)

Broadly, "business records" means a list of your relevant monetary transactions. Each item includes the date (month, day, year) and amount.

Income records also include:

- Source—the name of who paid you, e.g., JOE'S FISH MARKET, Susanna Creamcheese, Nicholas' Pizza, Corner Computing.
- Nature of work, e.g. "Royalties, Jan-Mar 2012, Ice Fishing On Mars," "Article, 100 Uses For Old Socks," "Fiction, "Refunds For That Bridge In Brooklyn."

And, if you have invoices (not everyone will), the invoice ID.

FIGURE 1 shows examples of business income records.

FIGURE 1: SAMPLE RECORDS OF BUSINESS INCOME

DATE	INVOICE#	CLIENT#	CLIENT	AMOUNT	PROJECT
Jan 04, 2011	2010-047	NSD-03	NSDuckToll mag	$350.00	Article, "Think Fast! Videoing Your Toller," 800 words
Jan 05, 2011	2010-050	SmartBear-03	SmartBear	$575.00	Article, "Testing Mobile Devices," 2,300 words
Jan 17, 2011	2011-002	CGL-01	Cambridge Globe	$75.00	Article, "Tollers Tolling In The Snow," 400 words
Jan 23, 2011	n/a		DogHouse Press	$382.50	Royalties, 2010 Q2, "Toller Tales: The Restless Urge To Fetch (3rd ed)
Feb 27, 2011	2011-004	FruitBat-01	FruitBatCo	$1,200.00	Case history, "Tablet computers Save $ For Fruit Bat Owners"

Business expense records include, in addition to the date and amount:

- Company, organization, etc. for vendor, supplier, store, etc., their name, e.g., Staples, U.S. Post Office, Fedex, Kinko's, Amazon, AT&T Wireless, Verizon, SouthWest Air, Holiday Inn. For smaller transactions, possibly a general description, like "local newsstand," "yard sale," "airport food," "books from Ernest."
- Nature of item. E.g., broadband, cell phone service, toner for laser printer, stamps, *Maximum PC* magazine (2-year renewal), library fines, batteries, iTunes card, plane fare to SCBWI Winter Conference, etc.

and, depending on how you make payments and how you keep your records:

- Transaction Info, e.g. check #, credit card name, "cash," PayPal
- Notes—details or other miscellaneous information, e.g. "Meet with editor to discuss schedule," "research on hummingbirds, for story," etc.

FIGURE 2 shows examples of business expense records.

FIGURE 2: SAMPLE RECORDS OF BUSINESS EXPENSES

DATE	CATEGORY	WHO	AMOUNT	METHOD	WHAT/NOTES
Jan 12, 2011	DUES&SUBS	Writers Digest	$19.96	Check 437	Renewal, 1 year (8 issues)
Jan 15, 2011	UTILITIES	KiboComm	$89.37	Check 442	Broadband & office tel.
Jan 16, 2011	DUES&SUBS	NSDuckTollClub	$25.00	Check 445	Dues, 1 year
Jan 18, 2011	OFF SUPL	Staples	$23.42	Amex	Paper, binders, misc

It's important—arguably essential—to keep records in a way that lets you find and check specific items, and also lets you get categorized totals. The first reason is to let you check and verify items; the second reason is for having properly sorted totals in preparation for doing your taxes.

"Good recordkeeping means that when it's time to do your taxes, you've got everything in the right place, and, ideally, already sorted and totaled."

"Good recordkeeping means that when it's time to do your taxes, you've got everything in the right place, and, ideally, already sorted and totaled," says Rick Telberg—versus, say, having thrown everything into the proverbial shoebox throughout the year. "It's amazing what 15 minutes a week will yield you in reduced time and aggravation at tax time. Even if you use an accountant to do your taxes, you'll save money by needing less of their time."

WHAT QUALIFIES AS A BUSINESS EXPENSE?

What's a business expense? Your opinion may vary from that of your peers, customers, or friends—for example, you might think that an $800 Barca-Lounger chair for your living room, or a $600 treadmill for your basement, contribute to your "business thinking time" and therefore qualify as business expenses. However, your opinion isn't what matters.

For purposes of doing your taxes, the U.S. Internal Revenue Service (IRS) determines and defines very clearly what constitutes a qualifying expense, and, in some cases, what percentage of a given expense you can claim.

For the official answers, see Instructions for Schedule C: Profit or Loss From A Business.

I also strongly recommend the IRS' Publication 334, Tax Guide for Small Business (For Individuals Who Use Schedule C or C-EZ). Pub 334 tells you exactly what the government wants to know, and what its rules are. Both are available free, as a download, or in hardcopy on request from the IRS, and your local library probably has a copy.

HOW TO CHARGE: SIZE OR TIME

Many writing projects are priced roughly based on word count, but have a fixed price. For example, a 1,500-word article on "Testing Mobile Devices" for one client might be $500, while an 1,800-word one on "Comparing Drupal to Joomla," for a different client, $1,200.

Other projects, like working on a brochure, or doing research, might be a hourly rate, against "Not to Exceed" amounts.

It's essential to establish bounds and limits on project pricing and effort. Your client wants to have a clear cap on the price. You need to have a clear cap on effort for that price, e.g., "Additional drafts, $75/hour," or "If you want an additional 350-word sidebar, that's another $250."

The IRS also has a publication specifically about recordkeeping: Publication 552 (01/2011), Recordkeeping for Individuals.

I urge you to get a copy of each, and read it, slowly and carefully, two or three times. You don't have to do this every year, but it's definitely worth doing at least once. After that, you can just read the "What's New" section.

You may also want to buy or borrow a book or two that explains these. But the IRS is, by definition, the official source regarding what they want. Other books are bound to be correct, and may be clearer, or provide more examples, but the IRS instructions and Publication 334 are your primary sources.

I also suggest you cultivate a business relationship with an accountant or two. Even if you end up doing all your own recordkeeping, bookkeeping and tax prep, it's helpful to have a knowledgeable industry expert on tap for the occasional question or advice. (Be prepared to pay for their time, of course!)

So, what qualifies? Professional memberships and publications are legitimate business expenses, for example. For writers, subscriptions to daily newspapers, e.g., the *New York Times, Washington Post*, and *Boston Globe* are. Ditto a desk, and a chair—even a good ergonomic Herman-Miller Aeron chair (which I haven't yet sprung for) qualifies. Some things may fall into gray areas. Again, read the instructions in the IRS instructions! And feel free to ask fellow writers...but don't accept their opinions blindly.

HOW MUCH TO CHARGE: SETTING (OR AGREEING ON) PRICES

Here's some quick guidelines to setting prices—taken largely from my article "How to Set Prices for Your Services: A Step-by-Step Guide to Calculating What You Must—or CAN—Charge" (http://www.dern.com/hw2price.shtml).

The advice here assumes you are writing for a living. Even if you aren't, it's still worth thinking through your prices—and you shouldn't be undercutting prices of people who are doing this for a living.

First, you need to know how much you would have to charge, to make a living—earn your target salary. This information is the basis for actually setting or agreeing on prices. (Or for deciding you need to look for a new occupation.)

The short answer here (see my "How to set price" article for the long answer) is: Double your current (or target) annual salary, and multiply by between 1.5 and 2, to determine how much you need to earn to replace your salary and benefits, and cover business expenses. Then divide by 1,400—the number of billable/salable hours you have in a year—to get your target hourly rate.

For example: If you were earning $50,000/year, 50,000 times 2 divided by 1,400 equals around $70/hour. If times 1.5, around $55/hour.

Once you know what you have to charge, you can also consider other strategies to base your prices on, which take into account factors like circumstance, bargaining strength, etc.:

- Going Rates. What do your fellow professionals charge; what are prospects paying?
- Paying for Priority. If someone needs immediate, drop-everything service, that often is worth 25-50% more. (Don't be greedy, though.)

Remember that it's legitimate to have sets of prices, such as for large corporations versus start-ups and small businesses; discounts for companies referring or sub-contracting to you; and fixed prices for standard types of projects.

> And note: Companies that work regularly with writers (like magazines, and PR agencies) should have set rates and simply tell you what they pay. (But feel free to try and negotiate.)

To help keep track of business expenses (which makes it easier to do the recordkeeping):

- When you buy things, where possible, do business transactions separate from non-business ones. E.g., if you're buying business supplies and school supplies at Staples, CostCo, or wherever, separate the piles, and get them rung up separately.
- Consider a separate checking account and a separate credit card for your business, versus the ones you use for personal expenses. (The separate credit card is particularly good, as interest you pay here is a business expense.)

CATEGORIZING EXPENSES—WHAT INFORMATION DOES THE GOVERNMENT WANT FROM YOU?

Since records for your tax forms are a major goal of business recordkeeping, it makes sense to do your recordkeeping in a way that matches what the government wants.

That means tagging or otherwise categorizing items using the list in Schedule C Part II: EXPENSES, which currently includes (i.e., this is a partial list):

- Advertising
- Car and truck expenses—parking, tolls, and per-mile
- Depreciation and section 179 expense deductions
- Insurance (other than health)—e.g., Business Owner's Policy
- Interest: (Mortgage, other)
- Legal and professional services—accountant, etc.
- Office expense—paper, toner, USB sticks, etc.
- Supplies (not included in Part III)
- Utilities—business phone line, broadband Internet
- Other Expenses—stuff that doesn't readily fall into the other categories

Some of these categories are specific, some are broad. There is no specific category, for example, for "computers"—and it's not necessarily clear where "Web domain registration fees" would go. However, since all numbers end up going into one total—and you're entering totals, not each line item—there's room for judgement calls, or putting those categories into "Other Expenses."

In my recordkeeping, I've typically had more categories than Schedule C has—although over the years, I've combined and simplified some categories—and then combined category totals as needed in my year-end process. For example, my categories include "BOOKS,

MAGAZINES AND MULTIMEDIA" and "DUES AND SUBSCRIPTIONS," both of which get put on my Schedule C under "Other Expenses."

HOW DO YOU KEEP RECORDS?

You need to keep records in a way that's consistent, and clear—and easy for you to do. IRS Publication 552 (01/2011), Recordkeeping for Individuals can help you with this.

These records should be "journaled," that is, written, or entered into a computer file, in a day-by-date order. You might not enter items right when they happen, but it's a bad idea to get more than a few days behind.

Ideally, do this in a way that makes totaling them up easy—like having separate columns for each of the categories that your tax forms want, per above.

You don't need a computer or special software to do this.

You can do this with pen and paper (which I did, for years). For example, with a notebook using accounting paper—or plain old paper. This may be easier if you have a separate column or page for each category.

I began using pen/pencil, accounting paper (a mix of two, three, four and five-column) in a three-ring binder, along with a simple calculator and several folders for filing receipts for the year.

....
There's nothing fancy sophisticated about my spreadsheet. It's just a bunch of columns.
....

A computer will help, though, if used properly.

For example, in the past few years, I've (finally!) started using a spreadsheet, done with Microsoft Excel, and five or 10 three-tab manilla folders for filing receipts.

There's nothing fancy sophisticated about my spreadsheet. It's just a bunch of columns— DATE, VENDOR/SUPPLIER, ITEM(S), CHECK#/ETC, NOTES, and a column for each category, e.g., BOOKS, DUES & SUBSCRIPTIONS, INSURANCE, OFFICE EXPENSES, etc. I have a summing (add items up) row, at the top, for each column; each time I enter a new item, the TOTAL cell automatically updates itself.

(I'll post a generic copy of the spreadsheet to my dern.com website—look for "STUFF I SAID I'D POST"—which you're welcome to use.)

Total cost—less than buying that accounting paper and another three-ring binder, since I already have the computer and a copy of Microsoft Office. Plus the dozen-ish manilla file folders.

You don't have to use a spreadsheet. (I'm doing single-entry bookkeeping, and brief forays into other software were more frustrating than helpful...but I am looking into some new ones that handle expense entry.)

Telberg states, "There's no shortage of software you can run on your computer, or Internet-based services you can use via your Web browser, to keep your records, such as QuickBooks, Quicken Home & Business, FreshBooks, ShowBox, Outright, and Wave Accounting." Some of these, Telberg notes, are just doing bookkeeping, some also offer business tasks like invoicing and analysis.

....

What's important is that you use the tools, enter items on a regular basis, and make sure you're got a regular backup of your data!

....

There are a growing number of mobile phone apps, such as ProOnGo Expense (which I haven't tried yet) that can help you record transactions when you are away from your office, by taking pictures of expense receipts and doing a lot of the data entry for you.

What's important is that you use the tools, enter items on a regular basis, and make sure you've got a regular backup of your data! If the file is on your computer, make sure you've got an online backup; if the file is online, make sure you've got a backup locally, or elsewhere online.

SAVING AND FILING RECEIPTS AND RELATED PAPERWORK

For petty expenses, say, under $25, the IRS (and whatever other organizations you might have to show your records to) will take your word for it. In general, get a receipt—and save and file it—whenever possible.

I file and save my receipts—including revenue receipts—using three-tab manilla folders that correspond to my expense categories, one set of folders per year. Like my recordkeeping categories, I've reduced the number of file folder categories over the years. (I don't, for no particular reason, simply have a folder for each recordkeeping category. Go figure.)

To make it easy to find a receipt after I've filed it, when I've entered an item into my business records, I circle and check off the amount on the receipt, and, if it isn't already clear, what the actual item is. If it's a bill that I've paid, I include the date paid and check number, to make it easier to verify without having to dig through my checkbook. Then I file it, trying to put the newest one in the front of the folder.

If you've done a good job of entering this information into your records, you'll almost never actually look at these receipts again. But when you do need to find one, you'll be grateful you're organized.

In terms of keeping receipts, consider getting a scanner—digital copies are now acceptable. (Again, make sure you've got backups!) See IRS Publication 552 for more details about paper versus digital receipts.

And enter the amounts and file the receipts when you get home. Don't wait until the end of the month—or year—to sort, file and enter!

Again, the key is to get, save, enter and file receipts regularly.

SUMMARY: KEEPING PROPER RECORDS REGULARLY IS EASIER AND BETTER THAN NOT

Like I said above, the most important use for this information is to provide the numbers you need for tax purposes, namely, filling out U.S. Form 1040 Schedule C. If you've done your recordkeeping right, you've got all your information in and up-to-date, and the totals are there. If, like me, you've got a few more categories than the Schedule C uses, you'll spend a few minutes adding those totals up.

Otherwise, you're in for days of avoidable stress come April.

And you'll be able to see how well (or poorly) you've done, in terms of writing as a business, and have the information to help decide how you can do better, what expenses to try and cut, or where to spend more.

All for a pad of paper, or little to no additional software, and a few minutes a day.

DANIEL P. DERN has been a freelance writer since 1973 and is based in Newton Center, MA, whose written everything from technology and business journalism and PR, to science fiction, and his Dern Grim Bedtime Tales. His website is www.dern.com, and his blogs include Trying Technology (http://www.TryingTechnology.com) and Dern's PR Tips (http://www.DernsPRTips. com). Contact Daniel at dern@pair.com.

SUBMISSION TRACKER

Recordkeeping is an important tool for the successful freelance writer. It's important to keep accurate records for tax season, but it's equally important to keep accurate submission records. Failure to do so could lead to some embarrassing double submissions or result in missed opportunities to follow up. Plus, an organized writer always impresses editors and agents.

On the next page is a sample submission tracker spreadsheet. You can make copies of the one in this book to help you keep records, or you can create a similar spreadsheet on your computer using a spreadsheet program. WritersMarket.com also provides submission tracking tools as part of the My Markets feature of the site.

This submission tracker has nine columns:

- **MANUSCRIPT TITLE.** This is the title of your manuscript.
- **MARKET.** This is the name of the magazine, book publisher, contest, or other entity to which you've submitted your manuscript.
- **CONTACT NAME.** This is the name of the editor, agent, or other contact who's received your work.
- **DATE SENT.** The date you submitted your manuscript.
- **DATE RETURNED.** The date your manuscript was rejected.
- **DATE ACCEPTED.** The date your manuscript was accepted.
- **DATE PUBLISHED.** The date your manuscript was published.
- **PAYMENT RECEIVED.** Detail any payment received.
- **COMMENTS.** This column is for any other notes about your experience with the market.

SUBMISSION TRACKER

MANUSCRIPT TITLE	MARKET	CONTACT NAME	DATE SENT	DATE RETURNED	DATE ACCEPTED	DATE PUBLISHED	PAYMENT RECEIVED	COMMENTS

DIVERSIFYING DURING TOUGH TIMES

by Melissa Crytzer Fry

Are you one of the thousands of writers affected by the economic slump, scraping for clients and competing in the ever-more-crowded freelance workspace? Or maybe you're just getting started and are finding it isn't as easy as you'd hoped.

I can relate. The perfect storm of my career began brewing in 2009 when my three largest clients announced some big changes: *We're hiring in house. Our freelance budget was eliminated. We're asking freelancers to become part-time employees (and we're cutting your pay by more than half.)*

I had to scramble. I had to think. What can I do now? What industries *are* successful in the recession? How can I sell myself to those markets?

Fortunately, I had already begun to branch out beyond my safety net of higher education and corporate copywriting. I started writing for a local university's research magazine. Soon the 'safe' liberal arts research stories I'd written led to biological sciences stories, and then alternative energy and solar articles, and then engineering writing assignments.

Bingo. I would market myself as a science writer—something I had *never* envisioned in my writing career, but something I realized I *could* do, I *was* doing. And so can you. Worried that science isn't your thing? It doesn't have to be. You might be surprised at what *is* your thing if you look beyond what you *think* you can do to what you *can* do.

KEYS TO SURVIVAL: FLEXIBILITY & ADAPTABILITY

Learning and writing about the sciences taught me two biological survival techniques that apply in many other scenarios, including freelance writing: *flexibility* and *adaptation.*

Like the intelligent and elastic octopus, you must stretch yourself and become flexible in the types of industries and media for which you write. Like the adaptive coyote that now calls the southwest, midwest *and* southeast its home, you must expand your territory. You must embrace projects that are outside your experience and initial comfort level. You must diversify.

"Sure, the economy is lousy, but there are still plenty of businesses that are cranking right along—you may just need to look a little harder," says Jake Poinier, an Ariz.-based freelance writer, "and become more of an omnivore."

Poinier targets multiple businesses, industries, topics, media types and even company sizes. He writes articles for magazines and newspapers, ghostwrites and offers corporate copywriting and editorial services.

When he lost two five-figure clients during the past three years—one to bankruptcy, one who hired in-house—diversification helped keep his business stable. "If a single organization ever became 25 percent or more of my income, I'd be nervous," he says.

And while diversification is important, Mass.-based freelancer Susan Johnston cautions writers not to overdo it. "Over-diversification can lead to burnout and sloppy work. If you try to edit textbooks, write blog posts, teach a class, finish your novel and manage Twitter accounts for clients all at once, you may wind up doing none of those things well. Finding that balance where you have a variety of projects but you're not overextended is key."

Johnston has struck the balance writing website articles about small business and personal finance topics, as well as copywriting for nonprofits and retail companies. She also teaches freelancing at her local adult education center and has published two e-books on related topics: *LinkedIn and Lovin' It* and *The Urban Muse: Guide to Online Writing Markets*.

THREE ESSENTIAL SKILLS TO BRANCH OUT IN YOUR BUSINESS

If you are shaking your head and saying, "I'm just not that prolific in my writing. I'm a niche writer," then take a deep breath. You really only need three key skills to expand your writing projects:

- Inquisitiveness
- Solid interviewing skills
- Research and preparation skills

The most important requirement is interest. Are you genuinely curious about the industries and projects you're seeking?

Let's face it, people who are excited about a topic ask lots of questions. Just think back to the guided tours you've experienced and the overzealous question-asker in the group. Be *that* guy, while using your professional interviewing skills. You don't need to have a background in silicon solar cell manufacturing to write about alternative energy or be a cardiologist to write about heart health. You simply need to be inquisitive and interested.

My fascination with science—plus strong research, preparation and interview skills—led to a successful shift in my writing career. Prior to a project meeting or interview, I always contact the client or interviewee, requesting recommended reading materials that will help me prepare. I do my own research as well. When I'm writing a topic new to me, I never allow myself to enter a meeting or interview unprepared.

Johnston doesn't let lack of familiarity affect her target markets, either. "I did not formally study business or finance in college, but I've always been interested in these topics, so I read widely, listen to podcasts, and talk to as many experts as I can, asking lots of questions," she explains. "I also started writing softer personal finance topics at first, such as online shopping or saving money at the grocery store, rather than complex topics like retirement plans or mortgages. I cover those now, but I do a lot of research to get up to speed."

DETERMINING NEW MARKETS: QUESTIONS TO ASK YOURSELF

Ensuring a good project fit or organizational camaraderie is simply good business (and makes your writing experience more enjoyable).

John Soares, a Calif.-based freelance writer working for higher education textbook companies, stresses the importance of self-analysis. "Freelancers must make a list of all their potential specialties," he says. "What jobs have you had in what industries? What was your major in college? What are your hobbies?"

Soares credits his success during two economic slumps (present and early 2000s) with analysis that ultimately led to the expansion of his business. He branched out by writing an e-book, *Writing College Textbook Supplements: The Definitive Guide to Winning High-Paying Assignments in the College Textbook Publishing Market,* as well as a companion blog for freelancers.

No matter your industry or experience, ask yourself these key questions before targeting new clients:

- What kind of writing do I want to do?
- Do my interests and life experiences complement certain industries or companies?
- Is there freelance demand in those markets?
- Is this a company or publication I want to write for regularly?
- Does the work offer a good balance in terms of pay, portfolio value and promise of long-term income?
- How will I differentiate myself from other freelancers?
- Do I have more than one idea to pitch?

HOW TO "BREAK IN" TO NEW MARKETS

Writers who succeed in today's sluggish market are often those with a certain level of business sophistication. Employing a combination of both "soft" and "hard" business skills can prepare you for greater success:

Take chances.

Consider going after business that represents more of a personal interest than a professional one. "I recently sold my first piece to a sailing magazine," says Poinier. "Honestly, I was a bit nervous about getting a rejection. But when the editor sent me back a note that she loved it, it was the first magazine assignment in ages that excited me on any kind of emotional level."

Consider creative business alternatives.

Have you ever considered publishing an e-book, writing book jacket copy, editing fiction? Would you enjoy teaching at your community college or sharing professional insight at the local business development center?

Creative projects add vigor to your routine and often provide residual benefits. Johnston's teaching position with adult learners represents only a small portion of her income, but the benefits include free education courses *and* a new repertoire of writing topics. "I've learned about floral design, cupcake baking, buying a condo, fashion writing. Many of my students have really great ideas that help me get fired up about my own writing."

Network the old fashioned way.

Make it a priority to keep in touch with key non-current client contacts, colleagues from past jobs, editors and friends. Schedule time each week for coffee or lunch with at least one contact, or send an e-mail or handwritten note to an out-of-state colleague. But more than that, embrace your role as a support person and friend.

"One of the toughest challenges is when an editor or client leaves her position," explains Poinier. "All of a sudden, my existing relationship with the publisher or business is in possible jeopardy, through no fault of mine. My immediate thought is: can I help her with a resume or networking connection? I need to trust that the solid, long-term ties to that person will result in work once she lands elsewhere."

Target the right companies.

How do you know which companies to target? The safest option is to stick with mid-size and larger businesses, when possible. "They have the most money to pay freelancers," Soares says. And they are often more financially stable.

Online entities that sell a product or service rather than content only also tend to be safer choices. "The health of those markets isn't reliant on advertising dollars or affiliate income," explains Johnston. Those product and service companies that have a robust online presence and hire freelance journalists to write for their blog or website, she says, also often have an ongoing need for content *and* pay well.

Hone your sales, marketing and relationship skills.

Today's successful writers understand that the health of their business relies on two factors: retaining existing clients and acquiring new ones. While you can gain sales and marketing knowledge from classes, books and blogs, Poinier suggests a more personal approach: contact the best salesperson you know. "Buy him lunch or dinner in exchange for a brain-picking session."

Texas-based freelancer Natalia Sylvester, a creative writing graduate, is largely self-taught in marketing. At the early stages of her career, she registered for mediabistro's Freelance Marketplace, poring over the site's marketing and copywriting articles. "There is so much information readily available online today that there is almost no excuse not to learn a new topic," she explains. "Writers should never think, 'I don't have enough experience with that.'"

Embrace new technology, new knowledge.

Don't be afraid to learn. If you're not willing to embrace new technology, you could be forfeiting your next assignment. Website content management systems (CMS) like WordPress, social media programs such as Twitter, HootSuite and Facebook, project management software like Basecamp, and blog publishing systems such as Movable Type are all programs that can be learned. "Many work similarly or are intuitive," says Johnston. "Don't be afraid of jumping in and learning those tools."

Use social media to your advantage.

Social media relationships, like real-life relationships, involve work—often over a significant length of time. Sylvester will tell you that genuine social media connections are vitally important to survival during economic downturns. She's currently working on a monthly contract basis with a Twitter contact. "When he needed a writer, he thought of me," she says. "Ideally that's how you want it to work. You have a conversation for a year. You build a relationship."

Soares has also found social media success. "It's important to have a complete profile on LinkedIn and to make a lot of quality connections to people in your industry. Editors and business owners *do* look for freelance writers on LinkedIn, and you want to show up in the search results."

EXERCISE PATIENCE

Keep in mind the results of your diversification efforts *may* take time.

My solar-energy client emerged after sending a query and sample packet two years earlier (fortunately, my samples were shuffled from employee to employee until they were ready to call). Johnston broke into a major women's magazine after 10 rejections from the same editor. Other freelancers have reported project query-to-assignment lag times of up to five years.

That's why it's so important to continue getting your name out there. As Poinier warns, "No matter how great a writer you are, the odds are that no one is going to discover you by accident. It takes a concerted strategic effort to put yourself out there, and in a down market, you will likely hear 'no' more often. Whether it's cold calls, queries or letters of introduction, you can't take it personally."

You keep trying, keep adapting, until you get the call.

MELISSA CRYTZER FRY continues to adapt and diversify, adding fiction to her skill set. Her novel-in-progress earned a semifinalist nod in the 2011 William Faulkner-William Wisdom Writing Competition. At her ranch in southern Arizona with her husband (amid javelin, coyotes and rattlesnakes), she blogs and continues to work with clients in the solar and signage industries, institutions of higher education and nonprofits. http://melissacrytzerfry.com

LAUNCHING YOUR FREELANCE BUSINESS

....

by I.J. Schecter

Starting something from scratch takes guts, faith and a healthy dose of stubborn optimism. Some would argue that deciding to launch a freelance writing practice requires a touch of masochism, too. But let's look at this rationally. First, you aren't starting from scratch; you're starting with talent, knowledge, skill, connections, and, probably, the moral support of a good number of people. Second, starting a writing business is no more or less difficult than starting any other type of business, whether a bakery, real estate brokerage or piano-tuning service. Third, you're peddling an extremely valuable product. Most businesses figure out pretty fast that if they don't know how to communicate, they're going to have a hard time winning customers. And in today's world of short attention spans and stimulus overload, the ability to communicate succinctly and powerfully is more valuable than ever.

PRE-WORK

Before putting your name out there, there are a few things you need to take care of. At the top of the list is getting business cards and letterhead printed. When you do start to tell people about your practice, the last thing you want is to be stuck without a card to hand over. And after you do offer it, hopefully prompting a discussion about your potential client's needs, you'll want to send a follow-up letter immediately—but on your own stationery, not some generic one. From the moment you decide to freelance professionally, you must think of yourself as a brand. Most writers feel hesitant about marketing themselves in any specific way because they don't want to cut off other opportunities. But when you're starting out, establishing a firm brand perception—that is, a clear statement about what you do and why it's valuable—is more important than appearing able do it all. Demonstrate expertise in a few specific areas, and others will inevitably find their way into your lap.

SELLING YOURSELF

Almost all writers share an aversion to self-selling—but it's mostly a function of unfair conditioning. That is, they assume they hate marketing themselves before they even try because other writers have convinced them one can't be a good writer and a good salesman at the same time.

The truth is plenty of good writers are natural salesmen, too, but they feel the superficial selling part undermines the authentic writing part. Take a moment to think about it and you'll realize all business-people have to market themselves just like writers do. A restaurateur needs to do more than just open his doors to generate traffic. An investment broker must go beyond merely getting a license if he hopes to suc-

> **TAX TIP**
>
> Sure, self-employment doesn't come with medical and dental, but it does offer plenty of opportunities for tax write-offs. Among the expenses you can potentially deduct are car, phone, restaurant meals, postage, magazine purchases, and, if you work from home, a portion of your monthly mortgage (or rent) and utilities. Have a chat with your accountant about this and hold onto your receipts so calculations are easy come tax season. You'll be glad you did.

ceed. A psychologist wanting to build a practice ought to take a few steps in addition to simply hanging a shingle. And a writer needs to do more than just write. "This job is about sales as much as it is about writing," says Toronto-based freelancer Ian Harvey. "One of the simple rules guiding my practice is this: Hustle, hustle, hustle."

So how does a writer generate buzz? There are several ways: letters, flyers, brochures, newsletters, blogs, samples, cold calls, and so on. When I launched my practice, the first thing I did (after getting business cards and letterhead printed, of course) was to send out hundreds of introductory letters—to those I knew, to those I didn't know, to people, to businesses . . . to just about everyone whose address I could get. I discriminated little in this initial blitz, though naturally with each letter I dropped into the mailbox I became even more nervous that all the money, time and effort I was expending might lead nowhere.

Then I received a phone call. One of my letters had gone to a high school acquaintance working at a company that manufactured and distributed musical compilations on CD. She had received my letter just as her boss was looking for a writer to help write snappy liner notes. Years later, this company remains one of my biggest corporate clients.

Another of my letters went to an old colleague. He had become the head of an executive degree program at a local university and was preparing to design the program brochure, for which a writer was sorely needed. I won the assignment, which led to another three.

The lesson? You truly never know where work is going to come from. More important, you can't count on finding yourself in the right place at the right time; you have to create the possibility of being there.

GROWING PAINS

There are two parts to selling yourself. First is developing the nerve to do it. Second is developing the right type of skin: rhino. "Rejections are part of the game," says Harvey, "but this is the only game in which rejection doesn't mean no. It means not now, or not for me, or not for me right now. It doesn't mean no forever." While it's fair to spend a little time—very little—getting annoyed or frustrated at rejection, it's best to take that annoyed or frustrated energy and pour it into something productive. Few businesses explode overnight; the ones that end up successful demand lots of grunt work up front, reach a minimum threshold after a few years, and then begin to grow in earnest.

WHERE IS YOUR STAPLER?

Many writers and other artists claim that their extreme lack of organization is simply an occupational hazard. Others practically boast about it, claiming it as a distinct imprint of creativity. Whether or not creative types are naturally disinclined toward self-organization, the sooner you decide to get organized and stay organized, the more successful you and your practice will become. Why? Two reasons, one physical, the other mental.

Physically speaking, when your work environment is organized, you spend more time writing and less time trying to locate the calculator or paper clips or this file or that folder. Simple odds dictate that using your time more productively will lead to more work.

The mental aspect is just as important. We all know how aggravating it is having to scramble to find that copy of the current contract for that magazine when we've forgotten what the word count was, or trying desperately to remember where we put the CD with the backup copy of that article after the electrical storm has wiped out our operating system with the deadline looming.

It stands to reason that the less energy you need to put into non-writing activities, the more energy you can direct toward your actual work, improving its overall quality and thereby making you a more desirable commodity. Sure, a little anxiety can be healthy for writing, but it should be anxiety borne of the drive to produce stellar work, not anxiety based on wondering where the stamps got to for the umpteenth time.

Organizing yourself is probably a lot easier than you imagine, and you might even be surprised at how good a little structure makes you feel.

Start small: Buy a box of multicolored file folders, some labels, some CDs or a memory stick, and several upright magazine files. Label one of the magazine files **Contracts**, then place in it different file folders labeled with the subject area for a given contract. For me, these folders include, among others, Bridal, Fitness, Golf, Men's, Gardening, and, of course, Writing and Publishing.

Label another of the magazine files **Current Assignments** and a third **Story Ideas**, and populate them as you did the first. Use consistent colors for specific topics—in other words, gardening always gets a yellow file folder whether it's in the **Story Ideas** or the **Contracts** file. This will make for easy cross-referencing.

And that's just a start. Odds are this small bit of organization will spur you, and soon you'll be creating files for every aspect of your work—character sketches, source notes, dialogue snippets, conferences and retreats, news items.

"Organization is everything," says freelancer Heather Cook, author of *Rookie Reiner: Surviving and Thriving in the Show Pen* (Trafalgar Square Books). "From maintaining accurate records for tax purposes to structuring a weekly plan to include marketing and administrative tasks, it allows me to stay focused and efficient—and that makes my overall work better."

It's imperative you commit to the up-front part. "Most businesses fail because the proprietors underestimate the amount of work required to get the business off the ground and overestimate the revenue in the first year or two," says Paul Lima, a professional writer for over 25 years and author of *The Six-Figure Freelancer*. Adds Vancouver-based freelancer Teresa Murphy, author of more than 1,000 magazine articles, "You need the ability to work 15 hours a day and love it, day in and day out. That means holidays, summer weekends and all-nighters when clients have rush projects. I've worked Boxing Day, New Year's Eve, Easter Sunday until midnight."

Of course, if you've decided to take the plunge in the first place, no doubt you've got this much passion and then some, because, like these professionals, you've realized that, despite the challenges of the writing life, nothing in the world makes you feel happier or more fulfilled.

GAINING, AND SUSTAINING, MOMENTUM

Investing the time and energy at the outset will lead to a point of critical mass—that first small group of people interested in your work, the first pebble in your pond. This could include a magazine editor, the president of a company or a friend needing some editing help. To help that first small ripple expand outward, you need to embed two vital behavioral principles.

1. OVERDELIVERY. Whether you're writing an article for your local newspaper, a marketing brochure for a multinational conglomerate or an essay for your best friend's medical school application, do the very best job you can. Your writing is judged every time you put pen to paper or fingers to keys. Force yourself to knock the ball out of the park at every opportunity and you'll develop the kind of reputation that leads to positive word of mouth, constant repeat business and sparkling testimonials.

2. PROFESSIONALISM. From editors to executives, just about everyone is stretched thin these days—and that's why being known as someone easy to work with can distinguish you from other writers who also deliver solid work. Acting like a professional means a number of things. Dressing a certain way. Acting a certain way. Hitting deadlines. Returning calls and e-mails promptly.

> In this business just like any other, people, and circumstances, will irk you—but in almost every case it behooves you to take the high road.

It also means not ever being petty, spiteful or antagonistic. Following the publication of my first short story collection, I lucked into a chance to set up a small table at a prominent outdoor literary festival. Beside me was the editor of an esteemed literary journal—along with her large dog, in a cage a few feet behind us. The dog began barking his head off just as people starting checking out the book tables, and he didn't stop for an hour, scaring off just about anyone who wandered anywhere near me and my book. The woman did nothing. I didn't just want to offer her a few choice words; I wanted to write her a scathing letter several pages long. Friends and family urged me to resist, and, though it was hard, I did. A few years later, when I sent this editor a story for consideration in her journal, she accepted it (though she had no recollection of me from the festival), creating a writing credit that remains one of my most important. The moral? In this business just like any other, people, and circumstances, will irk you—but in almost every case it behooves you to take the high road. Reacting emotionally can only harm you; staying cool can only benefit you.

THE NUMBERS GAME

Writing is dynamic and fluid; it can be endlessly revised, massaged, tweaked, twisted and reversed back over itself. For this reason, it's essential that you get every one of your assignments in writing (no pun intended; OK, slightly intended). Commercial assignments will usually come with a contract; corporate assignments almost never will. To address this, prepare two versions of your own standard agreement. For commercial gigs, this document should include a brief description of the assignment, word count, pay rate, and deadline, along with all the other legal bits you can find by looking up any typical freelance contract. For corporate assignments, it should include a more detailed description of the project (including each piece of work if there are multiple parts), the agreed timeline, the fee (either an overall flat rate or an hourly rate), and, crucially, a definition of completion. For example, in my standard corporate agreement, I have a clause indicating that, for the agreed-upon fee, I will deliver the described work by the noted deadline and then allow two rounds of requested revisions or suggestions from the client, after which I will start charging extra. This creates clear mutual expectations between the client and me and helps avoid awkward conversations toward the end of the project when the senior partner tries to add an arbitrary comma for the third time.

For corporate work, you'll also have to develop the skill of estimating. It's one thing to name an hourly rate when a potential client first asks; it's another to try to come up with a total number of hours based on his incredibly vague description of the assignment. But come up with one you must—only to be met with, in some cases, a response gently questioning why the work ought to take so long. Here we have a quandary: By and large, people vastly underestimate how long good writing actually takes. I've found the best way to deal with this is to be truthful. I tell my clients up front that writing and communications work tends to take quite a bit longer than non-writers imagine, and that, in fact, most projects end up taking 20 percent more hours than I initially estimate because the client themselves didn't realize going in how much would be involved. As long as I deliver good work, this ceases to be an issue.

> It's one thing to name an hourly rate when a potential client first asks; it's another to try to come up with a total number of hours based on his incredibly vague description of the assignment.

How much or how little should you charge for your work? It depends—based on your experience, where you live, and a host of other factors. Make sure, before you enter any negotiation, that you've decided upon the lowest figure you're willing to accept. Or, as freelancer Colette van Haaren puts it, "You need three things in this business: a good nose to sniff out stories, a thick skin for when rejection hits, and a backbone for when you have to negotiate."

SURE I'M WORKING HARD. IN MY HEAD

Only about half my time is spent actually working on assignments. The other half is spent crafting queries, doing research, maintaining correspondence, or, to be honest, just brainstorming. My favorite part of being a writer is that I can work anywhere, since so much of the work is done between my ears. Often someone will ask me a question, and, when I don't answer, my wife will murmur to him or her, "Oh, he's just working." And she's right.

I also believe, however, that the luxury of being able to do mental work represents an important responsibility. During spells when my plate isn't full with deadlines, I don't rest on my laurels. Instead, I record ideas, I query like crazy, I read other writers, I think about new marketing angles. In short, given the nature of my profession, I have no excuse for down time. "If you don't care about your business, no one else will," says freelancer Sharon Aschaiek. "Use slow times to indirectly generate more work—develop new pitches, follow up with previous editors and clients, explore new marketing avenues. Even use the time to take care of accounting and administrative issues. Just don't let yourself get complacent."

ANSWERING THE QUESTION

Friends familiar with your long-time desire to write may good-naturedly tease you about the risk of giving up your thankless but stable 9-to-5 grind to tackle something so daunting. Former colleagues may wonder aloud about your decision. Busybody aunts will gossip about how no one makes money writing and what a nice doctor or lawyer you would have made.

Change their perception by embracing and celebrating your decision rather than timidly defending it. When people ask, "So what are you doing now?" answer with pride and conviction. Don't say, "I thought I'd give freelancing a go and see how it works out," or "I'm going to try being a freelance writer, though I'm not really sure what that means."

Have your "elevator speech"—a business term for the 30-second spiel that describes what you do—always at the ready. When people ask me what I do, I respond, "I'm a freelance writer and communications consultant." If they want to know more, I tell them my practice is divided evenly between commercial writing, like magazine features, and corporate writing, which entails everything from marketing brochures to ghostwriting business books. Suddenly they're intrigued. They see writing as a real, viable, honest-to-goodness business—not because I've dropped figures but because I've spoken about it in a clear, confident manner.

Let's stop apologizing for being writers. I love being one, and I bet you do, too. Tell anyone who asks.

THE BOTTOM LINE

Is freelancing hard work? Sure—damned hard. But it's no harder than any other profession. Like every job, it requires a combination of skill, thoroughness and dependability. The difference is you don't have anyone defining the parameters of the job for you or providing incentives to succeed. The discipline and drive have to come solely from you. Or, in the words of full-time freelancer and book author Lisa Bendall, "All the talent in the world won't help if you aren't willing to put in the time at your desk and actually work. You've got to crack your own whip."

Now get cracking!

I.J. SCHECTER (www.ijschecter.com) is an award-winning writer, interviewer and essayist based in Toronto. His bestselling collection, *Slices: Observations from the Wrong Side of the Fairway* (John Wiley & Sons), is available in bookstores and online. Schecter is also the author of *102 Ways to Earn Money Writing 1,500 Words or Less* (Writer's Digest Books). Schecter provides corporate, creative and technical writing services to a diverse range of clients spanning the globe.

HOW MUCH SHOULD I CHARGE?

....

by Lynn Wasnak

If you're a beginning freelance writer, or don't know many other freelancers, you may wonder how anyone manages to earn enough to eat and pay the rent by writing or performing a mix of writing-related tasks. Yet, smart full-time freelance writers and editors annually gross $35,000 and up—sometimes into the $150,000-200,000 range. These top-earning freelancers rarely have names known to the general public. (Celebrity writers earn fees far beyond the rates cited in this survey.) But, year after year, they sustain themselves and their families on a freelance income, while maintaining control of their hours and their lives.

Such freelancers take writing and editing seriously—it's their business.

Periodically, they sit down and think about the earning potential of their work, and how they can make freelancing more profitable and fun. They know their numbers: what it costs to run their business; what hourly rate they require; how long a job will take. Unless there's a real bonus (a special clip, or a chance to try something new) these writers turn down work that doesn't meet the mark and replace it with a better-paying project.

If you don't know your numbers, take a few minutes to figure them out. Begin by choosing your target annual income—whether it's $25,000 or $100,000. Add in fixed expenses: social security, taxes, and office supplies. Don't forget health insurance and something for your retirement. Once you've determined your annual gross target, divide it by 1,000 billable hours—about 21 hours per week—to determine your target hourly rate.

Remember—this rate is flexible. You can continue doing low-paying work you love as long as you make up for the loss with more lucrative jobs. But you must monitor your rate of earning if you want to reach your goal. If you slip, remind yourself you're in charge. As a freelancer, you can raise prices, chase better-paying jobs, work extra hours, or adjust your spending."

"Sounds great," you may say. "But how do I come up with 1,000 billable hours each year? I'm lucky to find a writing-related job every month or two, and these pay a pittance."

That's where business attitude comes in: network, track your time, join professional organizations, and study the markets. Learn how to query, then query like mad. Take chances by reaching for the next level. Learn to negotiate for a fee you can live on—your plumber does! Then get it in writing.

You'll be surprised how far you can go, and how much you can earn, if you believe in your skills and act on your belief. The rates that follow are a guide to steer you in the right direction.

This report is based on input from sales finalized in 2009 and 2010 only. The data is generated from voluntary surveys completed by members of numerous professional writers' and editors' organizations and specialty groups. We thank these responding groups, listed below, and their members for generously sharing information. If you would like to contribute your input, e-mail lwasnak@fuse.net for a survey.

PARTICIPATING ORGANIZATIONS

Here are the organizations surveyed to compile the "How Much Should I Charge?" pay rate chart. You can also find Professional Organizations in the Resources.

- American Independent Writers (AIW), (202)775-5150. Website: www.amerindy writers.org.
- American Literary Translators Association (ALTA), (972)883-2093. Website: www. utdallas.edu/alta/.
- American Medical Writers Association (AMWA), (301)294-5303. Website: www. amwa.org.
- American Society of Journalists & Authors (ASJA), (212)997-0947. Website: www. asja.org.
- American Society of Media Photographers (ASMP), (215)451-2767. Website: www. asmp.org.
- American Society of Picture Professionals (ASPP), (703)299-0219. Website: www. aspp.com.
- American Translators Association (ATA), (703)683-6100. Website: www.atanet.org.
- Angela Hoy's Writers Weekly. Website: www.writersweekly.com.
- Association of Independents in Radio (AIR), (617)825-4400. Website: www.air media.org.
- Association of Personal Historians (APH). Website: www.personalhistorians.org.
- Educational Freelancers Association (EFA), (212)929-5400. Website: www.the-efa.org.

- Freelance Success (FLX), (877) 731-5411. Website: www.freelancesucess.com.
- International Association of Business Communicators (IABC), (415)544-4700. Website: www.iabc.com.
- Investigative Reporters & Editors (IRE), (573)882-2042. Website: www.ire.org.
- Media Communicators Association International (MCA-I), (888)899-6224. Website: www.mca-i.org.
- National Cartoonists Society (NCS), (407)647-8839. Website: www.reuben.org/main.asp.
- National Writers Union (NWU), (212)254-0279. Website: www.nwu.org.
- National Association of Science Writers (NASW), (510)647-9500. Website: www.nasw.org.
- Society of Professional Journalists (SPJ), (317)927-8000. Website: www.spj.org.
- Society for Technical Communication (STC), (703)522-4114. Website: www.stc.org.
- Women in Film (WIF). Website: www.wif.org.
- Writer's Guild of America East (WGAE), (212)767-7800. Website: www.wgaeast.org.
- Writer's Guild of America West (WGA), (323)951-4000. Website: www.wga.org.

LYNN WASNAK (www.lynnwasnak.com) was directed to the market for her first paid piece of deathless prose ("Fossils in Your Driveway" published by *Journeys* in 1968 for $4) by *Writer's Market*. In the 40 years since, she's made her living as a freelancer and has never looked back.

ADVERTISING & PUBLIC RELATIONS

	PER HOUR			PER PROJECT			OTHER		
	HIGH	LOW	AVG	HIGH	LOW	AVG	HIGH	LOW	AVG
Advertising copywriting	$150	$35	$83	$9,000	$150	$2752	$3/word	25¢/word	$1.56/word
Advertising editing	$125	$20	$64	n/a	n/a	n/a	$1/word	25¢/word	65¢/word
Advertorials	$180	$50	$92	$1,875	$200	$479	$3/word	75¢/word	$1.57/word
Business public relations	$180	$30	$84	n/a	n/a	n/a	$500/day	$200/day	$356/day
Campaign development or product launch	$150	$35	$95	$8,750	$1,500	$4,540	n/a	n/a	n/a
Catalog copywriting	$150	$25	$71	n/a	n/a	n/a	$350/item	$25/item	$116/item
Corporate spokesperson role	$180	$70	$107	n/a	n/a	n/a	$1,200/day	$500/day	$740/day
Direct-mail copywriting	$150	$35	$84	$8,248	$500	$2,839	$4/word $400/page	$1/word $200/page	$2.17/word $314/page
Event promotions/publicity	$125	$30	$75	n/a	n/a	n/a	n/a	n/a	$500/day
Press kits	$180	$30	$82	n/a	n/a	n/a	$850/60sec	$120/60sec	$456/60sec
Press/news release	$180	$30	$78	$1,500	$125	$700	$2/word $750/page	40¢/word $150/page	$1.17/word $348/page
Radio commercials	$99	$30	$72	n/a	n/a	n/a	$850/60sec	$120/60sec	$456/60sec

	PER HOUR			PER PROJECT			OTHER		
	HIGH	LOW	AVG	HIGH	LOW	AVG	HIGH	LOW	AVG
Speech writing/editing for individuals or corporations	$167	$35	$90	$10,000	$2,700	$5,036	$350/minute	$100/minute	$204/minute
BOOK PUBLISHING									
Abstracting and abridging	$125	$30	$74	n/a	n/a	n/a	$2/word	$1/word	$1.48/word
Anthology editing	$80	$23	$51	$7,900	$1,200	$4,588	n/a	n/a	n/a
Book chapter	$100	$35	$60	$2,500	$1,200	$1,758	20¢/word	8¢/word	14¢/word
Book production for clients	$100	$40	$67	n/a	n/a	n/a	$17.50/page	$5/page	$10/page
Book proposal consultation	$125	$25	$66	$1,500	$250	$788	n/a	n/a	n/a
Book publicity for clients	n/a	n/a	n/a	$10,000	$500	$2,000		n/a	n/a
Book query critique	$100	$50	$72	$500	$75	$202	n/a	n/a	n/a
Children's book writing	$75	$35	$50	n/a	n/a	n/a	$5/word $5,000/adv	$1/word $450/adv	$2.75/word $2,286/adv
Content editing (scholarly/textbook)	$125	$20	$51	$15,000	$500	$4,477	$20/page	$3/page	$6.89/page
Content editing (trade)	$125	$19	$54	$20,000	$1,000	$6,538	$20/page	$3.75/page	$8/page
Copyediting (trade)	$100	$16	$46	$5,500	$2,000	$3,667	$6/page	$1/page	$4.22/page

	PER HOUR			PER PROJECT			OTHER		
	HIGH	LOW	AVG	HIGH	LOW	AVG	HIGH	LOW	AVG
Encyclopedia articles	n/a	n/a	n/a	n/a	n/a	n/a	50¢/word $3,000/item	15¢/word $50/item	35¢/word $933/item
Fiction book writing (own)	n/a	n/a	n/a	n/a	n/a	n/a	$40,000/adv	$525/adv	$14,193/adv
Ghostwriting, as told to	$125	$35	$67	$47,000	$5,500	$22,892	$100/page	$50/page	$87/page
Ghostwriting, no credit	$125	$30	$73	n/a	n/a	n/a	$3/word $500/page	50¢/word $50/page	$1.79/word $206/page
Guidebook writing/editing	n/a	n/a	n/a	n/a	n/a	n/a	$14,000/adv	$10,000/adv	$12,000/adv
Indexing	$60	$22	$35	n/a	n/a	n/a	$12/page	$2/page	$4.72/page
Manuscript evaluation and critique	$100	$23	$66	$2,000	$150	$663	n/a	n/a	n/a
Manuscript typing	n/a	n/a	$20	n/a	n/a	n/a	$3/page	95¢/page	$1.67/page
Movie novelizations	n/a	n/a	n/a	$15,000	$5,000	$9,159	n/a	n/a	n/a
Nonfiction book writing (collaborative)	$125	$40	$80	n/a	n/a	n/a	$110/page $75,000/adv	$50/page $1,300/adv	$80/page $22,684/adv
Nonfiction book writing (own)	$125	$40	$72	n/a	n/a	n/a	$110/page $50,000/adv	$50/page $1,300/adv	$80/page $14,057/adv
Novel synopsis (general)	$60	$30	$45	$450	$150	$292	$100/page	$10/page	$37/page

	PER HOUR			PER PROJECT			OTHER		
	HIGH	LOW	AVG	HIGH	LOW	AVG	HIGH	LOW	AVG
Personal history writing/editing (for clients)	$125	$30	$60	$40,000	$750	$15,038	n/a	n/a	n/a
Proofreading	$75	$15	$31	n/a	n/a	n/a	$5/page	$2/page	$3.26/page
Research for writers or book publishers	$150	$15	$52	n/a	n/a	n/a	$600/day	$450/day	$525/day
Rewriting/structural editing	$120	$25	$67	$50,000	$2,500	$13,929	15¢/word	6¢/word	11¢/word
Translation—literary	n/a	n/a	n/a	$10,000	$7,000	$8,500	20¢/target word	6¢/target word	11¢/target word
Translation—nonfiction/technical	n/a	n/a	n/a	n/a	n/a	n/a	35¢/target word	8¢/target word	16¢/target word
BUSINESS									
Annual reports	$180	$45	$92	$15,000	$500	$5,708	$600	$100	$349
Brochures, booklets, flyers	$150	$30	$81	$15,000	$300	$4,215	$2.50/word $800/page	35¢/word $50/page	$1.21/word $341/page
Business editing (general)	$150	$25	$70	n/a	n/a	n/a	n/a	n/a	n/a
Business letters	$150	$30	$74	n/a	n/a	n/a	$2/word	$1/word	$1.47/word
Business plan	$150	$30	$82	$15,000	$200	$4,100	n/a	n/a	n/a

	PER HOUR			PER PROJECT			OTHER		
	HIGH	LOW	AVG	HIGH	LOW	AVG	HIGH	LOW	AVG
Business writing seminars	$200	$60	$107	$8,600	$550	$2,919	n/a	n/a	n/a
Consultation on communications	$180	$40	$95	n/a	n/a	n/a	$1,200/day	$500/day	$823/day
Copyediting for business	$125	$25	$60	n/a	n/a	n/a	$4/page	$2/page	$3/page
Corporate histories	$180	$35	$86	160,000	$5,000	$54,500	$2/word	$1/word	$1.50/word
Corporate periodicals, editing	$125	$35	$69	n/a	n/a	n/a	$2.50/word	75¢/word	$1.42/word
Corporate periodicals, writing	$135	$35	$78	n/a	n/a	$1,875	$3/word	$1/word	$1.71/word
Corporate profiles	$180	$35	$88	n/a	n/a	$3,000	$2/word	$1/word	$1.50/word
Ghostwriting for business execs	$150	$25	$84	$3,000	$500	$1,393	$2.50/word	50¢/word	$2/word
Ghostwriting for businesses	$250	$35	$109	$3,000	$500	$1,756	n/a	n/a	n/a
Newsletters, desktop publishing/production	$135	$35	$71	$6,600	$1,000	$3,480	$750/page	$150/page	$429/page
Newsletters, editing	$125	$25	$67	n/a	n/a	$3,600	$230/page	$150/page	$185/page
Newsletters, writing	$125	$25	$77	$6,600	$800	$3,567	$5/word $1,250/page	$1/word $150/page	$2.30/word $514/page

	PER HOUR			PER PROJECT			OTHER		
	HIGH	LOW	AVG	HIGH	LOW	AVG	HIGH	LOW	AVG
Translation services for business use	$75	$35	$52	n/a	n/a	n/a	$35/ target word $1.40/ target line	6¢/ target word $1/ target line	$2.30/ target word $1.20/ target line
Resume writing	$100	$60	$72	$500	$150	$287	n/a	n/a	n/a
COMPUTER, INTERNET & TECHNICAL									
Blogging—paid	n/a	n/a	$100	$2,000	$500	$1,240	$500/post	$6/post	$49/post
E-mail copywriting	$125	$35	$85	n/a	n/a	$300	$2/word	30¢/word	91¢/word
Educational webinars	$500	$0	$195	n/a	n/a	n/a	n/a	n/a	n/a
Hardware/Software help screen writing	$95	$60	$81	$6,000	$1,000	$4,000	n/a	n/a	n/a
Hardware/Software manual writing	$165	$30	$80	$23,500	$5,000	$11,500	n/a	n/a	n/a
Internet research	$95	$25	$55	n/a	n/a	n/a	n/a	n/a	n/a
Keyword descriptions	n/a	n/a	n/a	n/a	n/a	n/a	$200/page	$135/page	$165/page
Online videos for clients	$95	$60	$76	n/a	n/a	n/a	n/a	n/a	n/a

	PER HOUR			PER PROJECT			OTHER		
	HIGH	LOW	AVG	HIGH	LOW	AVG	HIGH	LOW	AVG
Social media postings for clients	$95	$30	$62	n/a	n/a	$500	n/a	n/a	$10/word
Technical editing	$150	$25	$65	n/a	n/a	n/a	n/a	n/a	n/a
Technical writing	$160	$30	$80	n/a	n/a	n/a	n/a	n/a	n/a
Web editing	$100	$25	$57	n/a	n/a	n/a	$10/page	$3/page	$5.67/page
Webpage design	$150	$35	$80	$4,000	$200	$1,278	n/a	n/a	n/a
Website or blog promotion	n/a	n/a	n/a	$650	$195	$335	n/a	n/a	n/a
Website reviews	n/a	n/a	n/a	$900	$50	$300	n/a	n/a	n/a
Website search engine optimization	$89	$60	$76	$50,000	$8,000	$12,000	n/a	n/a	n/a
White papers	$135	$25	$82	$10,000	$2,500	$4,927	n/a	n/a	n/a
EDITORIAL/DESIGN PACKAGES									
Desktop publishing	$150	$25	$67	n/a	n/a	n/a	$750/page	$30/page	$202/page
Photo brochures	$125	$65	$87	$15,000	$400	$3,869	$65/picture	$35/picture	$48/picture
Photography	$100	$50	$71	$10,500	$50	$2,100	$2,500/day	$500/day	$1,340/day

	PER HOUR			PER PROJECT			OTHER		
	HIGH	LOW	AVG	HIGH	LOW	AVG	HIGH	LOW	AVG
Photo research	$75	$25	$49	n/a	n/a	n/a	n/a	n/a	n/a
Picture editing	$100	$40	$64	n/a	n/a	n/a	$65/picture	$35/picture	$53/picture
EDUCATIONAL & LITERARY SERVICES									
Author appearances at national events	n/a	n/a	n/a	n/a	n/a	n/a	$500/hour $30,000/event	$100/hour $500/event	$285/hour $5,000/event
Author appearances at regional events	n/a	n/a	n/a	n/a	n/a	n/a	$1,500/event	$50/event	$615/event
Author appearances at local groups	$63	$40	$47	n/a	n/a	n/a	$400/event	$75/event	$219/event
Authors presenting in schools	$125	$25	$78	n/a	n/a	n/a	$350/class	$50/class	$183/class
Educational grant and proposal writing	$100	$35	$67	n/a	n/a	n/a	n/a	n/a	n/a
Manuscript evaluation for theses/dissertations	$100	$15	$53	$1,550	$200	$783	n/a	n/a	n/a
Poetry manuscript critique	$100	$25	$62	n/a	n/a	n/a	n/a	n/a	n/a
Private writing instruction	$60	$50	$57	n/a	n/a	n/a	n/a	n/a	n/a

	PER HOUR			PER PROJECT			OTHER		
	HIGH	LOW	AVG	HIGH	LOW	AVG	HIGH	LOW	AVG
Readings by poets, fiction writers	n/a	n/a	n/a	n/a	n/a	n/a	$3,000/event	$50/event	$225/event
Short story manuscript critique	$150	$30	$75	$175	$50	$112	n/a	n/a	n/a
Teaching adult writing classes	$125	$35	$82	n/a	n/a	n/a	$800/class $5,000/course	$150/class $500/course	$450/class $2,667/course
Writer's workshop panel or class	$220	$30	$92	n/a	n/a	n/a	$5,000/day	$60/day	$1,186/day
Writing for scholarly journals	$100	$40	$63	$450	$100	$285	n/a	n/a	n/a
FILM, VIDEO, TV, RADIO, STAGE									
Book/novel summaries for film producers	n/a	n/a	n/a	n/a	n/a	n/a	$34/page	$15/page	$23/page $120/book
Business film/video scriptwriting	$150	$50	$97	n/a	n/a	$600	$1,000/run min	$50/run min	$334/run min $500/day
Comedy writing for entertainers	n/a	n/a	n/a	n/a	n/a	n/a	$150/joke $500/group	$5/joke $100/group	$50/joke $283/group
Copyediting audiovisuals	$90	$22	$53	n/a	n/a	n/a	n/a	n/a	n/a
Educational or training film/video scriptwriting	$125	$35	$81	n/a	n/a	n/a	$500/run min	$100/run min	$245/run min

	PER HOUR			PER PROJECT			OTHER		
	HIGH	LOW	AVG	HIGH	LOW	AVG	HIGH	LOW	AVG
Feature film options	First 18 months, 10% WGA minimum; 10% minimum each 18-month period thereafter.								
TV options	First 180 days, 5% WGA minimum; 10% minimum each 180-day period thereafter.								
Industrial product film/video scriptwriting	$150	$30	$99	n/a	n/a	n/a	$500/run min	$100/run min	$300/run min
Playwriting for the stage	5-10% box office/Broadway, 6-7% box office/off-Broadway, 10% box office/regional theatre.								
Radio editorials	$70	$50	$60	n/a	n/a	n/a	$200/run min $400/day	$45/run min $250/day	$124/run min $325/day
Radio interviews	n/a	n/a	n/a	$1,500	$150	$683	n/a	n/a	n/a
Screenwriting (original screenplay-including treatment)	n/a	n/a	n/a	n/a	n/a	n/a	$117,602	$62,642	$90,122
Script synopsis for agent or film	$2,344/30 min, $4,441/60 min, $6,564/90 min								
Script synopsis for business	$75	$45	$62	n/a	n/a	n/a	n/a	n/a	n/a
TV commercials	$99	$60	$81	n/a	n/a	n/a	$2,500/30 sec	$150/30 sec	$1,204/30 sec
TV news story/feature	$1,455/5 min, $2,903/10 min, $4,105/15 min								
TV scripts (non-theatrical)	Prime Time: $33,681/60 min, $47,388/90 min / Not Prime Time: $12,857/30 min, $23,370/60 min, $35,122/90 min								

	PER HOUR			PER PROJECT			OTHER		
	HIGH	LOW	AVG	HIGH	LOW	AVG	HIGH	LOW	AVG
TV scripts (teleplay/MOW)	$68,150/120 min								
MAGAZINES & TRADE JOURNALS									
Article manuscript critique	$125	$25	$64	n/a	n/a	n/a	n/a	n/a	n/a
Arts query critique	$100	$50	$75	n/a	n/a	n/a	n/a	n/a	n/a
Arts reviewing	$95	$60	$79	$325	$100	$194	$1.20/word	8¢/word	58¢/word
Book reviews	n/a	n/a	n/a	$900	$25	$338	$1.50/word	15¢/word	68¢/word
City magazine calendar	n/a	n/a	n/a	$250	$50	$140	$1/word	30¢/word	70¢/word
Comic book/strip writing	$200 original story, $500 existing story, $35 short script.								
Consultation on magazine editorial	$150	$30	$81	n/a	n/a	n/a	n/a	n/a	$100/page
Consumer magazine column	n/a	n/a	n/a	$2,500	$75	$898	$2.50/word	37¢/word	$1.13/word
Consumer front-of-book	n/a	n/a	n/a	$850	$350	$600	n/a	n/a	n/a
Content editing	$125	$25	$57	$6,500	$2,000	$3,819	15¢/word	6¢/word	11¢/word
Contributing editor	n/a	n/a	n/a	n/a	n/a	n/a	$156,000/ contract	$20,000/ contract	$51,000/ contract

	PER HOUR			PER PROJECT			OTHER		
	HIGH	LOW	AVG	HIGH	LOW	AVG	HIGH	LOW	AVG
Copyediting magazines	$100	$18	$50	n/a	n/a	n/a	$10/page	$2.90/page	$5.68/page
Fact checking	$125	$15	$46	n/a	n/a	n/a	n/a	n/a	n/a
Gag writing for cartoonists	$35/gag; 25% sale on spec.								
Ghostwriting articles (general)	$200	$30	$102	$3,500	$1,100	$2,229	$10/word	60¢/word	$2.25/word
Magazine research	$100	$15	$47	n/a	n/a	n/a	$500/item	$100/item	$200/item
Proofreading	$75	$15	$35	n/a	n/a	n/a	n/a	n/a	n/a
Reprint fees	n/a	n/a	n/a	$1,500	$20	$461	$1.50/word	10¢/word	73¢/word
Rewriting	$125	$20	$68	n/a	n/a	n/a	n/a	n/a	$50/page
Trade journal feature article	$122	$40	$80	$4,950	$150	$1,412	$3/word	20¢/word	$1.16/word
Transcribing interviews	$180	$90	$50	n/a	n/a	n/a	$3/min	$1/min	$2/min
MEDICAL/SCIENCE									
Medical/scientific conference coverage	$125	$50	$85	n/a	n/a	n/a	$800/day	$300/day	$600/day
Medical/scientific editing	$125	$21	$73	n/a	n/a	n/a	$12.50/page $600/day	$3/page $500/day	$4.40/page $550/day

	PER HOUR			PER PROJECT			OTHER		
	HIGH	LOW	AVG	HIGH	LOW	AVG	HIGH	LOW	AVG
Medical/scientific writing	$250	$30	$95	$5,000	$1,000	$3,354	$2/word	25¢/word	$1.12/word
Medical/scientific multimedia presentations	$100	$50	$75	n/a	n/a	n/a	$100/slide	$50/slide	$77/slide
Medical/scientific proofreading	$125	$18	$64	n/a	n/a	$500	$3/page	$2.50/page	$2.75/page
Pharmaceutical writing	$125	$90	$105	n/a	n/a	n/a	n/a	n/a	n/a
NEWSPAPERS									
Arts reviewing	$69	$30	$53	$200	$15	$101	60¢/word	6¢/word	36¢/word
Book reviews	$69	$45	$58	$350	$15	$140	60¢/word	25¢/word	44¢/word
Column, local	n/a	n/a	n/a	$600	$25	$206	$1/word	38¢/word	65¢/word
Column, self-syndicated	n/a	n/a	n/a	n/a	n/a	n/a	$35/insertion	$4/insertion	$16/insertion
Copyediting	$35	$15	$27	n/a	n/a	n/a	n/a	n/a	n/a
Editing/manuscript evaluation	$75	$25	$35	n/a	n/a	n/a	n/a	n/a	n/a
Feature writing	$79	$40	$63	$1,040	$85	$478	$1.60/word	10¢/word	59¢/word
Investigative reporting	n/a	n/a	n/a	n/a	n/a	n/a	$10,000/grant	$250/grant	$2,250/grant

	PER HOUR			PER PROJECT			OTHER		
	HIGH	LOW	AVG	HIGH	LOW	AVG	HIGH	LOW	AVG
Obituary copy	n/a	n/a	n/a	$225	$35	$124	n/a	n/a	n/a
Proofreading	$45	$15	$23	n/a	n/a	n/a	n/a	n/a	n/a
Stringing	n/a	n/a	n/a	$2,400	$40	$525	n/a	n/a	n/a
NONPROFIT									
Grant writing for nonprofits	$150	$19	$70	$3,000	$500	$1,852	n/a	n/a	n/a
Nonprofit annual reports	$100	$30	$64	n/a	n/a	n/a	n/a	n/a	n/a
Nonprofit writing	$150	$20	$77	$17,600	$200	$4,706	n/a	n/a	n/a
Nonprofit editing	$125	$25	$54	n/a	n/a	n/a	n/a	n/a	n/a
Nonprofit fundraising literature	$110	$35	$74	$3,500	$300	$1,597	$1,000/day	$500/day	$767/day
Nonprofit presentations	$100	$50	$73	n/a	n/a	n/a	n/a	n/a	n/a
Nonprofit public relations	$100	$20	$60	n/a	n/a	n/a	n/a	n/a	n/a
POLITICS/GOVERNMENT									
Government agency writing/editing	$100	$20	$57	n/a	n/a	n/a	$1.25/word	25¢/word	75¢/word

	PER HOUR			PER PROJECT			OTHER		
	HIGH	LOW	AVG	HIGH	LOW	AVG	HIGH	LOW	AVG
Government grant writing/editing	$150	$19	$68	n/a	n/a	n/a	n/a	n/a	n/a
Government-sponsored research	$100	$35	$66	n/a	n/a	n/a	n/a	n/a	$600/day
Public relations for political campaigns	$150	$40	$86	n/a	n/a	n/a	n/a	n/a	n/a
Speechwriting for government officials	$200	$30	$96	$4,500	$1,000	$2,750	$200/run min	$110/run min	$155/run min
Speechwriting for political campaigns	$150	$60	$101	n/a	n/a	n/a	$200/run min	$100/run min	$162/run min

BUILD A PLATFORM:

Or You'll Miss the Train

....

by Jeff Yeager

"Jeff, you're a wonderful writer!"

Coming from the seasoned New York literary agent, I just wanted those words to hang there, in suspended celebration, while we enjoyed a leisurely lunch at the trendy Manhattan eatery she'd chosen for our meeting. Even though I'm not a dessert fan, I started thinking that maybe I'd stick around after all for some crème brûlée and an espresso or two.

"But the fact is," she continued, "there are lots of wonderful writers—and even lots of truly great writers—who never get a book published." Darn it, so much for basking in the moment. I hadn't even started my salad. Check please!

"The thing that interests me about you, and frankly the reason I agreed to meet with you today, is your platform. I know you're just starting out, but I think publishers will be impressed with the exposure you're already getting and what that means for your platform going forward." I thoughtfully crunched on a crouton from my salad, hoping to suggest that I was contemplating the wisdom of the agent's words. But I'm too honest to be a good bluffer.

"That's fantastic!" I said, enthusiastically spraying the woman I hoped would be my future agent in a shower of soggy crouton crumbs.

"Look," I continued, trying to divert my gaze from what appeared to be an entire crushed baguette clinging to the front of the poor agent's Ann Taylor dress suit. "I really hope you'll agree to represent me, and I want you to know that I always believe in being honest. So I have to confess: I have absolutely no idea what a *platform* is … although I'm delighted that you think I have such a good one."

WHAT THE HECK IS A PLATFORM?

With that awkward self-confessional a few short years ago, I began my journey—and more importantly my education—into the über competitive, promotion-driven world of book publishing.

Simply put, a platform is a writer's capacity to help promote and market his own work to potential readers. It's a writer's ability to attract a fan base of his own, outside of the promotional efforts of his publisher. It's a writer's ability to get his message out to the world.

Ideally, a platform has more than just one plank. For example, it's more than just a strong website or a weekly column in your local newspaper, although either of those planks would be a terrific start. It's a combination of assets, skills, expertise, activities, and professional connections that both strengthen each other and enhance the writer's chances for commercial success.

....

Ideally, a platform has more than just one plank.

....

In my case I was lucky enough to inadvertently receive some national television exposure early in my writing career (see 2008 *Writer's Market* Freelance Success Stories), which I then opportunistically parlayed into more press exposure and a growing network of media contacts. By the time I went looking for a literary agent to represent me in a book deal, I'd only had a few articles published and most of those were online. And while the media visibility I'd received prior to that point was not inconsequential, it wasn't nearly enough to carry a book.

But it was a start, and it proved to an agent—and then to a publisher—that I had the wherewithal to build a viable platform; that I was a horse worth betting on. That was two book deals ago, and my platform has since grown to include professional speaking and television reporting gigs, as well as blogging on a number of high traffic websites and authoring articles for a range of national publications.

At first blush my story might seem plucky to the point of being irrelevant to the careers of most writers. After all, how many newbie writers make their media debut on NBC's *Today* show, as I did? But what I've come to appreciate about platform building is this: Even with luck, you need persistence and promotional savvy, and—even without luck—persistence and promotional savvy is probably all you need.

It's also true what they say about making your own luck. Or, as quote-meister H. Jackson Brown, Jr. puts it, "Opportunity dances with those already on the dance floor." The key to building a successful promotional platform is to make sure you're always out there on the dance floor, shakin' what you got.

PRIORITIES AND GETTING STARTED

Given the laundry list of possible tactics for developing a platform (see sidebar), you need to set priorities in order to use your time and resources effectively, while at the same time remaining flexible enough to quickly act on unanticipated opportunities as they come your way. After all, you never know who's going to ask you to dance once you're out there on the floor.

Logically, the first step is to identify the target audience(s) for your writing. The more focused you can be in defining your audience, the more effective you'll be in reaching out to them. For example, if you're writing a book about dieting, you're obviously looking to reach people who would like to lose weight. But can you be even more specific? Maybe your niche is really middle-aged women hoping to lose weight, or parents who want to help their kids lose weight. Or say you write young adult fiction. Does it appeal more to boys or girls, teens or preteens, urban kids or rural kids, or particular YA book discussion groups, etc.?

Now that you know who your audience is, you need to figure out where and how you can best reach them. This is when the brainstorming really starts. What websites or online discussion boards do they frequent? What magazines and other print publications do they read? Are there certain TV or radio shows that appeal to them? Are there any special events they attend, or clubs or associations they join? In short, what are their favorite dance floors?

Identifying publications, media, and other forums through which you can reach your target audience is a never ending process, because they're constantly changing and you're always looking to expand your platform. When you've tapped into one forum, for example a website that caters to middle-aged women hoping to lose weight, always ask the people you meet there what other websites they visit, magazines they read, books they've enjoyed, and so on. I call this a *progressive focus group*, relying on everyone I meet in my target audience to educate me further about themselves and where I can find more folks just like them.

10 WAYS TO BUILD YOUR PLATFORM

1. Create your own website, keep it current with a blog and other updated content, and make it interactive with forums, contests, surveys, newsletters, a guestbook, etc.

2. Write articles, stories, op-eds, and even letters to the editor for magazines, newsletters, and other print publications read by your target audience.

3. Contact other high-traffic websites frequented by your target audience, offer to guest blog or contribute content to them (even for free), link your site to theirs, and participate in their networking forums.

4. Position yourself as *the* go-to source for information regarding your area of expertise by joining related professional organizations, earning certifications, and registering

with online and print directories like LinkedIn.com and *Poets & Writers*, as well as social networking sites like Facebook and Twitter.

5. Send periodic press releases about yourself, your activities, or some timely aspect of your work/field to targeted print and broadcast media, and offer to sit for an interview—you might be surprised by the response.

6. Hold a publicity event—or dare I say a publicity stunt or gimmick? Challenge your church group to see how much weight they can lose by following the instructions in the diet book you're writing, or hype the mystery novel you're writing by hiding clues around town to the location of the buried treasure—the real treasure might be the media exposure you generate.

7. Give talks, teach classes, offer workshops about your specialty at libraries, schools, churches, and online—but make sure the press knows all about it.

8. Get involved as a volunteer or board member with nonprofit organizations related to your field of interest/expertise; it looks good on your resume and they can be valuable marketing partners for your work.

9. Partner with or co-author a book with a well established, widely recognized expert or celebrity, or try publishing your book through an established franchise like the *Dummies* or *Chicken Soup* serials, where your personal platform is less of a factor.

10. Post your own book trailers and other video content on YouTube, create your own podcasts, or publish your own e-zine—even amateurish efforts can catch fire.

IT'S ALL ABOUT CONTENT

Once you've identified your target audience and started building a list of dance floors where they hang out, it's time to introduce yourself, to get to know them, and to make sure they get to know *you*. For most writers, this means providing content; content that helps to establish your reputation, builds name recognition (AKA "brand recognition"), and ideally creates for you a positive notoriety or even celebrity status among members of your target audience.

If you're a nonfiction writer, you typically provide content from the perspective of being an expert in the field (again, a weight loss expert, for example). If you write fiction, the content you provide is hopefully deemed desirable because of your creative and literary prowess. Who wouldn't want to read the words posted on some obscure website by a future J.K. Rowling?

Content, of course, can take many different forms. It's an article or story you get paid handsomely to write for a national magazine, as well as something you write without compensation for an association newsletter read by your target audience. It's the content of your own website and the guest blogs you write for another high-traffic website frequented by your target audience, and it's also every word you type in a chat room where your audience hangs out, even if it's just passing the time of day. It's the talk you give at the local library about what you do for a living. It's the interview you give on radio or national TV.

> Remember, the most valuable words many authors have ever written are the words they most wish they could take back.

The content you provide is the basic building block of your platform, so make sure you have plenty of it and that it reflects the quality and style you want to be associated with. Remember, the most valuable words many authors have ever written are the words they most wish they could take back.

A VIRTUAL PLATFORM?

There's no denying that the Internet has had a profound impact on the enterprises of writing and publishing, and also on the ability of an author to develop a platform. Pre-Internet, writers had to rely on traditional print and broadcast media, as well as public appearances and other in-person networking, to gain visibility and establish credibility.

But is it possible to build a promotional platform entirely through online activities—a *virtual platform*, if you will? If you have your own winning website, soft-market yourself through online chat rooms, maybe blog or contribute content to other sites, will that do the trick?

Timothy Ferriss, author of the bestselling book *The 4 Hour Workweek*, attributes much of his success to viral marketing, particularly his efforts to befriend fellow bloggers who then hyped his book. But viral or old school, it all comes back to content. Ferriss said in an interview with Leo Babauta on writetodone.com, "Marketing can get you an initial wave of customers, but you need a good product to go viral … Focus on making yourself a credible expert vs. pushing a book."

Clearly a strong presence on the Internet can not only be a major plank in an author's platform, but it's also a logical place for many writers to begin building their platforms.

"The barriers (e.g. cost, skill, etc.) for gaining exposure through the Internet are very low," says Kristine Puopolo, Senior Editor with Doubleday Broadway Publishing. "The good news is that almost anyone can publish a blog or create his own website. The bad news is that almost *everyone does* publish a blog and create his own website," she says. Getting noticed on the information superhighway has become increasingly difficult as traffic congestion has increased. "The Internet is a terrific place to create buzz about a book or an author," Puopolo says. "But success is getting that buzz picked up by other media, like TV and print."

So if you were hoping to build your platform solely by sitting at a computer keyboard, Google "try again." Even Ferriss says that his relationships with fellow bloggers were not forged so much over the Internet or even by phone, but by speaking at events they attended and—talk about old school—joining them for some beers afterwards.

5 TOP-O-MIND TIPS

Keep these things in mind as you build your platform, or you'll kick yourself later:

BUILD RELATIONSHIPS, NOT JUST A ROLADEX FILE. Do you still see yourself in the writing business five years from now? Nurture the relationships you develop with press contacts, readers, and the other folks you encounter in the publishing industry, rather than just milking them for a one-off interview, etc. Keep in touch, do them favors, and treat them as friends so that they'll be glad to help you out again in the future.

NO PUBLICITY IS BAD PUBLICITY... or at least that's the way the saying goes. And it's true in a great many cases, particularly when you're just starting out and you're relatively unknown. But also remember that it can be hard to shake an unfavorable reputation once the publicity Gods have saddled you with one, so think twice before jumping at publicity for publicity's sake.

MAILING LISTS ARE GOLDEN. Capturing the names and contact information for everyone you meet—from readers and potential readers to press contacts and booksellers—is key to building your platform. Distribute sign-up lists at your events, collect business cards religiously, and start building a computerized database of your contacts from day one.

REMEMBER THE "SOFT" IN "SOFT-MARKETING." Particularly when it comes to promoting yourself online, in social networking forums, chat rooms, etc., tread lightly. First get to know the community and contribute content that's not self-promotional before you ever start talking about yourself and your writing. I've never encountered an online forum that doesn't have an eager Spam Master (or ten) to bounce you out if you come on too strong with self-promotion.

RECOGNIZE YOUR STRENGTHS AND WEAKNESSES. It's a truly rare and talented writer who has the skills, resources, and time to develop a robust platform without outside help. Consider hiring a publicist, getting professional "media training," taking a public speaking class, or securing other professional assistance to compliment your strengths and weaknesses.

COMMON MYTHS ABOUT PLATFORMS

THAT'S NOT MY JOB, MAN. Talk to anyone in the publishing business, and the answer is always the same: Gone are the days when authors were just expected to write books and publishers were expected to market them, if those golden days ever existed in the first place. Luke Dempsey knows how it works from both sides of the desk. He's the editor-in-chief of Hudson Street Press, a division of Penguin USA, and he's also author of *A Supremely Bad Idea*, published by Bloomsbury in 2008. "These days book promotion is, at best, a partnership between an author and a publisher. If an author has a strong platform, it's also more likely that the publisher will get excited about the project and put their backs into it as well."

ONLY NONFICTION AUTHORS NEED A PLATFORM. It's true that the publishing industry has historically expected most nonfiction authors to have a strong promotional platform of their own. After all, nonfiction writers are usually considered experts regarding their subject matter, and their expertise should be both in demand and validated by appearing in the media, serving as a source, and writing articles and other content related to their field. But as the book industry has become more competitive, fiction writers are now commonly expected to come to the table with a promotional platform as well.

"It used to be that fiction sold pretty much just as a result of good reviews," Puopolo says. "But with so many books on the market today and the increased competition for media attention, a fiction author with a compelling personal story, winning personality, or a degree of celebrity definitely has a leg up." Puopolo says that fiction writers can develop their platforms using some of the same techniques as nonfiction writers (e.g. blogs, personal appearances, etc.), and also with things like "virtually hosting" book discussion groups online or by phone, joining local and national literary organizations, and participating in other genre specific forums. Fiction or nonfiction, Puopolo says effective platforms grow out of the "authenticity" of the author. "Follow who and what you are. Don't try to be something that you aren't."

OKAY, I'VE BUILT MY PLATFORM. NOW I CAN GET BACK TO WRITING. As you probably appreciate by now, your platform is not a static set of achievements, but an evolving portfolio of capacities which will hopefully grow and expand along with your writing career. Everything you write, every media appearance you make, every book talk you give, opens a new avenue for extending and strengthening your platform. You need to start building your platform as soon as you start writing—not when you go shopping for a book deal—and the process continues as long as you continue writing. When it comes to your platform as a writer, it's true what they say: "If you're not growing, you're dying."

CREATING EFFECTIVE PRESS RELEASES

by Lisa Abeyta

I often hear from other writers who take one of my workshops or online classes that they do not know how to market their own work. Writing the entire novel was an easier task than approaching stores, newspapers, or online venues about carrying their book. But whether a writer landed a coveted spot with a major publisher, chose to go with a small local press or ventured into the world of print on demand and vanity presses, it often falls on the shoulders of the author to market their own book. A few fortunate authors will gain access to a publicist through their publisher, but many will be completely on their own.

Writing a press release does not have to be a daunting task. In fact, for anyone who has already written a query letter, you are well on your way to mastering a press release. The goal is the same: catch the reader's attention right away, build interest in your project, and motivate the reader to act on your request.

BASIC PRESS RELEASE FORMAT

Beyond the basics of not using all caps (nobody wants to be shouted at, even if you're excited) and checking your grammar, start your press release with the following headline: For Immediate Release. The next line should be in bold and should contain the headline of your press release. Follow this with a very brief paragraph summarizing the content below and then with the body of the press release. Finish with a short About the Author paragraph and end with your contact information, including your address, phone number, email and website.

QUALITY CONTENT IS A MUST

One of the best ways to get your press release past the intern who screens the incessant influx of information is to write your release as a completed article. If your text is compelling, interesting, and complete, you have a much better shot of finding that same text in the Sunday Arts section of the paper. Editors are busy people, and the gift of print-ready text is hard to pass up.

Years ago, when I was working as an artist's representative, I sent press packages to media outlets ahead of each performance in a new city. Editors would often print the press release verbatim, although some would call the artist and conduct an interview. But the press release did its job either way by gaining invaluable publicity before a performance.

Study articles about authors and books. Learn the voice and tone of those articles. Mimic it in your own writing, and you'll be far more likely to generate interest in your project.

WHERE TO SEND YOUR RELEASE

A press release can be a stand alone product or as part of a press package. A package should contain a headshot of yourself and art from your book, both printed and on cd in low and high resolution where possible. The more options you provide, the more likely art will accompany any story published from your press release. It should also include a press copy of the book when possible. You can also attach a sheet with upcoming appearances, other titles, and any other pertinent information.

Press releases can be e-mailed directly to the appropriate editors or reviewers or uploaded to a variety of online PR distribution sites. And while these sites are great for getting the word out on the web, it is still recommended that you take the time to directly contact the editors who will possibly run your story in print or online. And remember to follow up your press releases with a personal phone call. Nothing will set you apart from the pile of press releases like a friendly follow-up call.

There has been a proliferation of online distribution sites focusing on public relations. Someof these include www/PRWeb.com, www.PRLeap.com, and www.24-7pressrelease.com, and www.epressreleases.com. While many of these sites offer free basic online distribution, there are additional fee-based products for you to consider.

MORE THAN A MEANS TO AN END

Another common misconception, particularly among new authors, is that platform building is simply a step—perhaps even a necessary evil—in getting your book published.

But here's a bright point to end on: From a business perspective, a robust platform *is* an author's business. In manufacturing terms, it's the sum total of *product lines* that a writer has with which to earn a living. And the payout is that in many cases the non-writing product lines that make up an author's platform may grow to be even more lucrative than writing.

Stacey Glick, a literary agent with the prestigious firm Dystel and Goderich in New York, says it best. "The thing you need to understand is that most authors can no longer afford to be one dimensional; that is, just authors," she told me. "An author's appeal to a publisher is largely his platform, and his platform in turn benefits from the books he writes. Round and round you go."

And I always value Glick's advice. After all, she's not only my agent, but she didn't even send me the dry cleaning bill for her Ann Taylor dress suit.

....

JEFF YEAGER is the author of *The Ultimate Cheapskate's Road Map to True Riches: A Practical (and Fun) Guide to Enjoying Life More by Spending Less* and *The Cheapskate Next Door: The Surprising Secrets of Americans Living Happily Below Their Means* (both by Broadway). Yeager has appeared as a guest on CNN, ABC News, CNBC, FOX News, PBS, and dozens of local TV stations around the country. www.ultimatecheapskate.com

....

HOW TO IMPROVE YOUR PRESENTATION SKILLS

by Brenda Collins

Given the emerging power and popularity of social media, do you still need to put your physical face on your author brand? Do you have to give presentations or workshops? According to many successful editors, agents and writers, the answer is "yes". In this competitive publishing environment, authors have to be skilled marketers. The experts report that live events can be very beneficial to an author's career. The good news is you can learn how to present effectively even if the thought scares you now.

"For certain audiences," notes Holly Root, of the Waxman Literary Agency, "it's absolutely expected that an author would be willing to appear—for instance, a very newsy nonfiction title, or a book with a huge publicity push, or a novel for kids, where school visits would be key. For the majority of novelists, it is optional, the kind of thing that if done well can be a terrific boost. The more people who know about you, the better your chances some of them will be your kind of readers." Root believes that appearances by one of her authors, Lisa Patton, absolutely contributed to her books becoming bestsellers.

If the thought of speaking in front of a crowd makes your stomach churn, you are not alone. Several studies have shown that public speaking is the number one fear for most people, followed by fear of death.

In my experience, though, even an introvert can become a great public speaker. When I was 10 years old, I stood in front of my Grade 5 class to give my first speech—and burst into tears. With practice, and maturity, I now deliver talks to audiences of all sizes. You just need the right skills, techniques and experience.

PREPARATION

Preparation is the secret to successful presentations. Preparation will ease the jitters when first you look out at your audience. Preparation will help you hide the fact you've lost your place in your notes. Preparation will ensure your presentation doesn't run too long or too short. And, more than anything else, preparation will make sure you say something that is worth the time your audience spends listening to you.

DEFINE OBJECTIVE

Jot down, in plain language, one sentence stating what you want to achieve through the presentation. That is not the same as what you want to say. Ask yourself why you are giving this particular presentation to this particular audience. What should they take away from it? This becomes your *key message*, which will shape the rest of your presentation. For example, "My presentation objective is to give writers the tools they need to deliver effective presentations with confidence."

REFINE CONTENT & STRUCTURE

List the important points you want to make in the presentation. For some this may be a neat list of bullet points, but for less linear thinkers, also known as *pantsers*, it could be a mind map, bubble drawing, or just scribbles all over a page.

Guided by your key message, arrange your notes so that each point flows naturally into the next, like a story plot. Think—beginning, middle, and end. This is your opportunity to make sure your message is clear.

Presentation structure is quite standardized. Your opening is like a novel or magazine article. You need to hook your audience right from the beginning with a relevant quotation, personal anecdote, a rhetorical question or other device.

There's a saying, "Tell them what you're going to say—, tell them—, then tell them what you told them!" That forms the body of your presentation: your objective, main points and summary.

Finally, you wrap up your presentation by linking back to your opening. Think of your opening and closing as the bookends of your presentation holding it all together for your audience.

EDIT

Eliminate unnecessary information and conflicting messages. Presentations are rarely too short; often they are too long. As operatic soprano and self-help guru Dorothy Sarnoff once noted, "Make sure you have finished speaking before your audience has finished listening."

Some of your revisions can help you prepare for audience questions. Don't worry about anticipating all possible questions. If you do not have the answer, either throw the question out to the audience to generate discussion or ask for the questioner's card so you can get back with an answer later.

AVOID DEATH BY POWERPOINT

Decide if and where you are going to use slides, handouts or other aids. Slides are *not* mandatory. In fact, they can be a distraction, and there's always a risk that the technology won't work on the big day.

Only use a slide or handout if it illustrates something that is otherwise hard to visualize or if it will support audience participation.

If you do want to use slides, there are a few rules.

- Assume two minutes talk time per slide to calculate how many you should have. Remember to number them.
- A picture or graph is worth a thousand words. Use them where possible.
- No more than three or four short bullets per slide. Overwhelming detail or animation is confusing.
- Use a clear (sans serif), large (minimum 24 point) font size.
- Use a consistent color scheme, of three or four high contrast colors at most. Remember some people have difficulty distinguishing between certain color combinations e.g. red-green, blue-yellow.

If you will be using slides, tell the organizers beforehand to ensure you'll have the equipment you need and that technical help will be available.

With or without technology, always have a contingency plan. Overhead lamps burn out. The projector provided might not work with your laptop, the thumb drive you had your presentation on could get lost. Bring a hard copy of your slides and notes so you can go ahead without a computer if need be.

The organizer may determine when handouts are distributed but, if you have a choice, consider these options.

BEFORE: Makes it easy for your audience to follow along with you and take notes. However, they also may be reading instead of listening to you and the paper rattling can be distracting.

DURING: This is my least favorite. It is difficult to distribute the handout quickly enough to be relevant to the point you're making without breaking the flow of your presentation.

AFTER: My preference is to let the audience know they will receive the slides at the end of the presentation so they can focus on what I'm saying but avoid taking unnecessary notes.

REHEARSE, REHEARSE, AND REHEARSE SOME MORE

One of the ways I learned to overcome the mind-numbing fear was to practice the presentation until I could give it in my sleep.

For notes, only write down key words, in large print so they are easy to read. Use these sparingly as memory joggers, not as a script. The fastest way to bore an audience is to read your presentation word for word.

Practice where you will pause throughout your presentation. You need time to take a breath and your audience needs time to digest your point before you move onto the next one.

Rehearse not only what you're going to say, but how. Use your voice and body language to make it interesting. Bob Mayer, best-selling author of over 40 books, publisher, and skilled professional speaker, notes, "as much as it is presenting information, it is also a form of entertainment. While content is important, presenting in an energetic and exciting manner is also important."

A run-through in front of the mirror is good. Even better is a trusted friend who will tell you if you unconsciously use any "ah, um, you know, like" empty fillers.

No friends available? Try recording your practice run, on video if possible. Early in my career, I was taped as part of a media training course. Watching that video was a shocker. As I spoke, my hands were flailing around as if I was swatting at wasps. You don't have to tie your hands behind your back but make sure you don't hold a pointer, pen or any other object you might play with if you're nervous. If you like putting your hands in your pockets, make sure there are no coins in there. You want your entire posture to project confidence and calm.

Your dress rehearsal should include the outfit you plan to wear for the presentation. What you wear should be appropriate and comfortable. You also want to be sure your shoes won't squeak and your jewelry won't rattle as you move.

THE BIG DAY

You are ready. Standing at the side of the stage, you hear your name called. Wait! If you want to deliver your presentation with energy and composure—I'm remembering my embarrassing episode of stage fright in Grade 5—the delivery of your presentation starts at least an hour before you get to the podium. You arrive before anyone else so that you can scope out the room in advance, place some water within easy reach, make sure your notes are in order, set up and test out any equipment you've requested.

With your environment arranged, you focus on making sure you are ready. My eldest brother had a long and successful career as an on-air morning show host on national public radio. He had to wake up his mouth and voice before flipping on the microphone. He might tighten and stretch his face muscles, rotate his lower jaw to loosen the jaw muscles, and recite a tongue twister, like "Rita wrote a ridiculous rhythm about racoons" or other sound combinations. Try it and your opening will slide out more smoothly.

Right before you begin is also the time to release any pent-up tension from your body by rolling your shoulders, stretching your neck, pulling your arms over your head and behind your back to open up your chest. Then take three deep abdominal breaths, straighten your shoulders and walk out to the podium with confidence.

While presenting, stay aware of your audience. If they are yawning or drooping, do not take it personally, especially if it's after lunch. Have you slipped into a monotone, or started reading your slides? Add an anecdote or stretch break to wake them up.

Presentations are both an art and a science. Consult your library or bookstore to learn more about giving presentations. I can add a few final lessons that the books often miss, and that I learned the hard way:

- Keep a bottle of water at hand for when your tongue threatens to stick to the roof of your mouth.
- Never drink coffee before you give a talk. Let's just say it makes men perspire and ladies glisten.
- When it comes to mistakes of any kind, laugh and the audience with laugh with you.
- If your talk is after lunch when everyone feels sluggish, turn down the thermostat a degree or two. You don't want to see their breath, but just enough to keep the audience feeling refreshed.
- Memorize your first three slides. I find that if nerves hit when I first look out at the audience, I can rely on rote to get started and usually by the fourth slide I've found my groove.

Writers are skilled wordsmiths. Presentations are one more way we can use our talent in crafting, polishing and delivering words to an audience. Any writer can learn to give presentations but Alicia Rasley, an award-winning author and nationally known teacher of writing workshops, advises, "Give presentations because it excites you, because it's fun, because you get to meet new people and see new places."

As Emily Ohanjanians, Associate Editor, HQN Books (Harlequin) says, "It is certainly not easy for everyone, but just be confident in who you are and what you have to say. After all, if people read your writing, you must have something good to say!"

....

BRENDA COLLINS has long believed that, for writers to succeed, writing talent must be supplemented with strong business skills. To support that view, she has published articles and delivered workshops to hundreds of writers on career planning, professional networking and presentation skills. Collins also serves annually as a judge for an international mystery / suspense fiction-writing contest. Her paranormal novella, *Witch in the Wind*, is available on Amazon. Prior to becoming a freelance writer, Collins spent 25 years in the corporate world where her work included award winning technical and corporate writing.

....

THE ART OF PROMOTING:

Advice From the Trenches

....

by Kerrie Flanagan

Author book promotion is not what it used to be. Both traditional and newer online strategies are needed to create an effective marketing plan because publishers now expect authors to carry the majority of the PR responsibilities. Marketing can feel overwhelming for an author but the good news is there are those who have found success in navigating this vast territory.

PLAN AN EVENT

To ensure a good turnout at a book signing or book launch, put in a little extra time to make it an event people will remember. Acclaimed YA author Laura Resau has perfected this idea over the years with the release of each of her books.

"Be creative and think outside the box," says Resau. "Include all ages if possible. Create a fun, lively, warm atmosphere. Make it a party that YOU would attend."

For the launch party of her fourth book, *The Indigo Notebook*, set in Ecuador, her Ecuadorian friend danced and explained the folklore behind the dance. With her latest book, *The Ruby Notebook*, set in France, she hired an accordionist who played while the young kids danced and the crowd enjoyed French pastries. She sets aside time to read excerpts and autograph books.

To promote the event, she uses listservs, her blog, Facebook, an e-newsletter, plus she enlists the help of her friends and writing group members to spread the word. She also sends postcard invitations with the book cover image on front.

"I think people are more likely to come to the release if they have the postcard hanging on their fridge staring at them every day for weeks before the event," she says.

An event can also happen online. For three years in a row, Christina Katz, author of *Get Known Before the Book Deal* and *Writer Mama*, hosted The Writer Mama Back-to-School Giveaway where she gave away a book on her blog every day for 30 days.

"I connected fellow authors with readers and in the process got to know my readers a lot better," said Katz. "One thing authors need to understand about marketing books today is that if you are not having an ongoing conversation with your fans, you are really missing out on the wealth of opportunities."

SPEAK UP

LeAnn Thieman, co-author of 11 Chicken Soup for the Soul books including the *New York Times* best-seller, *Chicken Soup for the Nurses Soul*, finds radio is an effective promotional outlet.

"There are over 10,000 radio stations in the United States, many with hosts looking for people to interview every day," said Thieman. "When I am going to be in an area for a speaking event or even just visiting, I call the local stations to see if they are interested in interviewing me on my topic, one I creatively relate to what's happening in the world today."

She advises authors to send a copy of their book and a synopsis to the station before the interview. Provide them with questions they can ask and have three to four talking points of your own ready. Weave your own sound bites and messages into the interview, but never overtly promote your book.

Greg Campbell, the best-selling nonfiction author of *Blood Diamonds: Tracing The Deadly Path Of The World's Most Precious Stones*, found promoting himself as an expert speaker to universities, nonprofits and trade shows to be an effective way to promote his books.

"When Scott Selby and I published *Flawless: Inside the Largest Diamond Heist in History*," Campbell said, "we searched for major trade shows on security and offered to speak to attendees about the real-life security failures described in the book. We ended up as keynote speakers at the International Security Conference in Las Vegas, with about 500 people in the audience."

With the help of their publisher, Selby and Campbell arranged to have the local Barnes & Noble set up a table to sell books at the event.

GET SOCIAL

Most authors would agree that staying connected with readers via social media is crucial in any successful publicity plan.

Campbell recently had social media thrust upon him by a pair of fans disappointed in his anemic online presence. They set up a Facebook author fan page as well as an author page on Goodreads.com for him. It pushed him to embrace social media.

"The fact that it took my readers to force me into this realm proved that there were readers out there hungry for information and new content," he said. "Even if it's just 140-character tweets. My education into this realm is continuing, but I plan to begin tweeting and blogging about the content of my newest book several months before it hits the shelves. In this way, I hope to have primed the pump and created online buzz for it long before it's available."

Jane Porter, author of six novels, including her latest, *She's Gone Country*, makes a point to stay connected with her readers.

"Sites like Facebook and Twitter have proved invaluable in providing a different platform to meet with my readers and spread the word," said Porter. "The more accessible you are the more readers get a chance to listen to what you have to share."

Romance author Ashley March finds blog tours highly successful. "I researched blogs and online romance community sites which had good followings and scheduled around 20 days where I visited each website with either an interview or guest blog. I always included a giveaway as a way to create more enthusiasm."

She attributes the buzz and success of her debut novel, *Seducing the Duchess*, with this blog tour.

PARTNER WITH YOUR PUBLISHER

Although publishers do expect authors to take on the role of publicist, it doesn't mean they are not willing to help at all. With her debut novel March took the lead and found her publisher eager to support her efforts.

They sent her book to every major romance reviewer online, provided her with her books to use as giveaways and when she couldn't reach someone at a blog she really wanted to visit, the publisher coordinated that specific blog visit for her. Because of the publisher's support, her March Madness blog party was a success.

"Throughout my debut experience," says March, "I truly felt like we were partners, and that's a great feeling to have."

Katz sums it up best. "Consistent and constant self-promotion are key to publishing success, regardless of whether you self-publish or traditionally publish...It's not any one self-promotion technique an author uses, it's using all of them."

KERRIE FLANAGAN is a freelance writer and the director of Northern Colorado Writers, an organization that supports and encourages writers of all levels and genres. Over the past decade she has published more than 125 articles in national and regional publications, enjoyed two years as contributing editor for Journey magazine, worked in PR for the Fort Collins CVB and for various authors and started The Writing Bug blog. www.KerrieFlanagan.com

PHOTO: Desiree Suchy

BLOGGING BASICS:

Get the Most Out of Your Blog

....

by Robert Lee Brewer

In these days of publishing and media change, writers have to build platforms and learn how to connect to audiences if they want to improve their chances of publication and overall success. There are many methods of audience connection available to writers, but one of the most important is through blogging.

Since I've spent several years successfully blogging—both personally and professionally—I figure I've got a few nuggets of wisdom to pass on to writers who are curious about blogging or who already are.

Here's my quick list of tips:

1. **START BLOGGING TODAY.** If you don't have a blog, use Blogger, WordPress, or some other blogging software to start your blog today. It's free, and you can start off with your very personal "Here I am, world" post.

2. **START SMALL.** Blogs are essentially very simple, but they can get very complicated (for people who like complications). However, I advise bloggers start small and evolve over time.

3. **USE YOUR NAME IN YOUR URL.** This will make it easier for search engines to find you when your audience eventually starts seeking you out by name. For instance, my url is http://robertleebrewer.blogspot.com. If you try Googling "Robert Lee Brewer," you'll notice that My Name Is Not Bob is one of the top 5 search results (behind my other blog: Poetic Asides).

4. **UNLESS YOU HAVE A REASON, USE YOUR NAME AS THE TITLE OF YOUR BLOG.** Again, this helps with search engine results. My Poetic Asides blog includes my name in the title, and it ranks higher than My Name Is Not Bob. However, I felt the play on my name was worth the trade off.

5. **FIGURE OUT YOUR BLOGGING GOALS.** You should return to this step every couple months, because it's natural for your blogging goals to evolve over time. Initially, your blogging goals may be to make a post a week about what you have written, submitted, etc. Over time, you may incorporate guests posts, contests, tips, etc.

6. **BE YOURSELF.** I'm a big supporter of the idea that your image should match your identity. It gets too confusing trying to maintain a million personas. Know who you are and be that on your blog, whether that means you're sincere, funny, sarcastic, etc.

7. **POST AT LEAST ONCE A WEEK.** This is for starters. Eventually, you may find it better to post once a day or multiple times per day. But remember: Start small and evolve over time.

8. **POST RELEVANT CONTENT.** This means that you post things that your readers might actually care to know.

9. **USEFUL AND HELPFUL POSTS WILL ATTRACT MORE VISITORS.** Talking about yourself is all fine and great. I do it myself. But if you share truly helpful advice, your readers will share it with others, and visitors will find you on search engines.

10. **TITLE YOUR POSTS IN A WAY THAT GETS YOU FOUND IN SEARCH ENGINES.** The more specific you can get the better. For instance, the title "Blogging Tips" will most likely get lost in search results. However, the title "Blogging Tips for Writers" specifies which audience I'm targeting and increases the chances of being found on the first page of search results.

11. **LINK TO POSTS IN OTHER MEDIA.** If you have an e-mail newsletter, link to your blog posts in your newsletter. If you have social media accounts, link to your blog posts there. If you have a helpful post, link to it in relevant forums and on message boards.

12. **WRITE WELL, BUT BE CONCISE.** At the end of the day, you're writing blog posts, not literary manifestos. Don't spend a week writing each post. Try to keep it to an hour or two tops and then post. Make sure your spelling and grammar are good, but don't stress yourself out too much.

13. **FIND LIKE-MINDED BLOGGERS.** Comment on their blogs regularly and link to them from yours. Eventually, they may do the same. Keep in mind that blogging is a form of social media, so the more you communicate with your peers the more you'll get out of the process.

14. **RESPOND TO COMMENTS ON YOUR BLOG.** Even if it's just a simple "Thanks," respond to your readers if they comment on your blog. After all, you want your readers to be engaged with your blog, and you want them to know that you care they took time to comment.

15. **EXPERIMENT.** Start small, but don't get complacent. Every so often, try something new. For instance, the biggest draw to my Poetic Asides blog are the poetry prompts

and challenges I issue to poets. Initially, that was an experiment—one that worked very well. I've tried other experiments that haven't panned out, and that's fine. It's all part of a process.

SEO TIPS FOR WRITERS

Most writers may already know what SEO is. If not, SEO stands for *search engine optimization*. Basically, a site or blog that practices good SEO habits should improve its rankings in search engines, such as Google and Bing. Most huge corporations have realized the importance of SEO and spend enormous sums of time, energy and money on perfecting their SEO practices. However, writers can improve their SEO without going to those same extremes.

In this section, I will use the terms of *site pages* and *blog posts* interchangeably. In both cases, you should be practicing the same SEO strategies (when it makes sense).

Here are my top tips on ways to improve your SEO starting today:

1. **USE APPROPRIATE KEYWORDS.** Make sure that your page displays your main keyword(s) in the page title, content, URL, title tags, page header, image names and tags (if you're including images). All of this is easy to do, but if you feel overwhelmed, just remember to use your keyword(s) in your page title and content (especially in the first and last 50 words of your page).

2. **USE KEYWORDS NATURALLY.** Don't kill your content and make yourself look like a spammer to search engines by overloading your page with your keyword(s). You don't get SEO points for quantity but for quality. Plus, one of the main ways to improve your page rankings is when you...

3. **DELIVER QUALITY CONTENT.** The best way to improve your SEO is by providing content that readers want to share with others by linking to your pages. Some of the top results in search engines can be years old, because the content is so good that people keep coming back. So, incorporate your keywords in a smart way, but make sure it works organically with your content.

4. **UPDATE CONTENT REGULARLY.** If your site looks dead to visitors, then it'll appear that way to search engines too. So update your content regularly. This should be very easy for writers who have blogs. For writers who have sites, incorporate your blog into your site. This will make it easier for visitors to your blog to discover more about you on your site (through your site navigation tools).

5. **LINK BACK TO YOUR OWN CONTENT.** If I have a post on Blogging Tips for Writers, for instance, I'll link back to it if I have a Platform Building post, because the two complement each other. This also helps clicks on my blog, which helps SEO. The one caveat is that you don't go crazy with your linking and that you make sure your links are relevant. Otherwise, you'll kill your traffic, which is not good for your page rankings.

6. **LINK TO OTHERS YOU CONSIDER HELPFUL.** Back in 2000, I remember being ordered by my boss at the time (who didn't last too much longer afterward) to ignore any competitive or complementary websites—no matter how helpful their content—because they were our competitors. You can try basing your online strategy on these principles, but I'm nearly 100 percent confident you'll fail. It's helpful for other sites and your own to link to other great resources. I shine a light on others to help them out (if I find their content truly helpful) in the hopes that they'll do the same if ever they find my content truly helpful for their audience.

7. **GET SPECIFIC WITH YOUR HEADLINES.** If you interview someone on your blog, don't title your post with an interesting quotation. While that strategy may help get readers in the print world, it doesn't help with SEO at all. Instead, title your post as "Interview With (insert name here)." If you have a way to identify the person further, include that in the title too. For instance, when I interview poets on my Poetic Asides blog, I'll title those posts like this: Interview With Poet Erika Meitner. Erika's name is a keyword, but so are the terms *poet* and *interview*.

8. **USE IMAGES.** Many expert sources state that the use of images can improve SEO, because it shows search engines that the person creating the page is spending a little extra time and effort on the page than a common spammer. However, I'd caution anyone using images to make sure those images are somehow complementary to the content. Don't just throw up a lot of images that have no relevance to anything. At the same time...

9. **OPTIMIZE IMAGES THROUGH STRATEGIC LABELING.** Writers can do this by making sure the image file is labeled using your keyword(s) for the post. Using the Erika Meitner example above (which does include images), I would label the file "Erika Meitner headshot.jpg"—or whatever the image file type happens to be. Writers can also improve image SEO through the use of captions and ALT tagging. Of course, at the same time, writers should always ask themselves if it's worth going through all that trouble for each image or not. Each writer has to answer that question for him (or her) self.

10. **USE YOUR SOCIAL MEDIA PLATFORM TO SPREAD THE WORD.** Whenever you do something new on your site or blog, you should share that information on your other social media sites, such as Twitter, Facebook, LinkedIn, online forums, etc. This lets your social media connections know that something new is on your site/blog. If it's relevant and/or valuable, they'll let others know. And that's a great way to build your SEO.

Programmers and marketers could get even more involved in the dynamics of SEO optimization, but I think these tips will help most writers out immediately and effectively while still allowing plenty of time and energy for the actual work of writing.

BLOG DESIGN TIPS FOR WRITERS

Design is an important element to any blog's success. But how can you improve your blog's design if you're not a designer? I'm just an editor with an English Lit degree and no formal training in design. However, I've worked in media for more than a decade now and can share some very fundamental and easy tricks to improve the design of your blog.

Here are my seven blog design tips for writers:

1. **USE LISTS.** Whether they're numbered or bullet points, use lists when possible. Lists break up the text and make it easy for readers to follow what you're blogging.

2. **BOLD MAIN POINTS IN LISTS.** Again, this helps break up the text while also highlighting the important points of your post.

3. **USE HEADINGS.** If your posts are longer than 300 words and you don't use lists, then please break up the text by using basic headings.

4. **USE A READABLE FONT.** Avoid using fonts that are too large or too small. Avoid using cursive or weird fonts. Times New Roman or Arial works, but if you want to get "creative," use something similar to those.

5. **LEFT ALIGN.** English-speaking readers are trained to read left to right. If you want to make your blog easier to read, avoid centering or right aligning your text (unless you're purposefully calling out the text).

6. **USE SMALL PARAGRAPHS.** A good rule of thumb is to try and avoid paragraphs that drone on longer than five sentences. I usually try to keep paragraphs to around three sentences myself.

7. **ADD RELEVANT IMAGES.** Personally, I shy away from using too many images. My reason is that I only like to use them if they're relevant. However, images are very powerful on blogs, so please use them—just make sure they're relevant to your blog post.

If you're already doing everything on my list, keep it up! If you're not, then you might want to re-think your design strategy on your blog. Simply adding a header here and a list there can easily improve the design of a blog post.

GUEST POSTING TIPS FOR WRITERS

Recently, I've broken into guest posting as both a guest poster and as a host of guest posts (over at my Poetic Asides blog). So far, I'm pretty pleased with both sides of the guest posting process. As a writer, it gives me access to an engaged audience I may not usually reach. As a blogger, it provides me with fresh and valuable content I don't have to create. Guest blogging is a rare win-win scenario.

That said, writers could benefit from a few tips on the process of guest posting:

1. **PITCH GUEST POSTS LIKE ONE WOULD PITCH ARTICLES TO A MAGAZINE.** Include what your hook is for the post, what you plan to cover, and a little about who you are.

Remember: Your post should somehow benefit the audience of the blog you'd like to guest post.

2. **OFFER PROMOTIONAL COPY OF BOOK (OR OTHER GIVEAWAYS) AS PART OF YOUR GUEST POST.** Having a random giveaway for people who comment on a blog post can help spur conversation and interest in your guest post, which is a great way to get the most mileage out of your guest appearance.

3. **CATER POSTS TO AUDIENCE.** As the editor of *Writer's Market* and *Poet's Market*, I have great range in the topics I can cover. However, if I'm writing a guest post for a fiction blog, I'll write about things of interest to a novelist—not a poet.

4. **MAKE PERSONAL, BUT PROVIDE NUGGET.** Guest posts are a great opportunity for you to really show your stuff to a new audience. You could write a very helpful and impersonal post, but that won't connect with readers the same way as if you write a very helpful and personal post that makes them want to learn more about you (and your blog, your book, your Twitter account, etc.). Speaking of which...

5. **SHARE LINKS TO YOUR WEBSITE, BLOG, SOCIAL NETWORKS, ETC.** After all, you need to make it easy for readers who enjoyed your guest post to learn more about you and your projects. Start the conversation in your guest post and keep it going on your own sites, profiles, etc. And related to that...

6. **PROMOTE YOUR GUEST POST THROUGH YOUR NORMAL CHANNELS ONCE THE POST GOES LIVE.** Your normal audience will want to know where you've been and what you've been doing. Plus, guest posts lend a little extra "street cred" to your projects. But don't stop there...

7. **CHECK FOR COMMENTS ON YOUR GUEST POST AND RESPOND IN A TIMELY MANNER.** Sometimes the comments are the most interesting part of a guest post (no offense). This is where readers can ask more in-depth or related questions, and it's also where you can show your expertise on the subject by being as helpful as possible. And guiding all seven of these tips is this one:

8. **PUT SOME EFFORT INTO YOUR GUEST POST.** Part of the benefit to guest posting is the opportunity to connect with a new audience. Make sure you bring your A-game, because you need to make a good impression if you want this exposure to actually help grow your audience. Don't stress yourself out, but put a little thought into what you submit.

ONE ADDITIONAL TIP: Have fun with it. Passion is what really drives the popularity of blogs. Share your passion and enthusiasm, and readers are sure to be impressed.

TWITTER CHEAT SHEET FOR WRITERS

by Robert Lee Brewer

With the publishing (and/or media) industry changing at the speed of light, so are the roles of writers (or content providers), editors (or content managers), agents (or content strategists), etc. One big change for writers (even in fiction, poetry, and other fields) is that they are expected to take an active role in building their own platforms via online and real world networking and exposure. One great tool for this online is Twitter.

It's easy (and free) enough to create a Twitter account, but how can writers take advantage of this social networking tool? What can they logically expect to gain from using it? What is a hashtag anyway? Well, hopefully, this cheat sheet will help.

First, let's look at some basic terminology:

- **TWEET** = Any message sent out to everyone on Twitter. Unless you direct message (DM) someone, everything on Twitter is a Tweet and viewable by anyone.
- **RT** = Retweet. Twitter created a RT-ing tool that makes for easy retweets, but the standard convention is to put an RT and cite the source before reposting something funny or useful that someone else has shared. For example, if I tweeted "Nouns are verbs waiting to happen," you could RT me this way: RT @robertleebrewer Nouns are verbs waiting to happen.
- **DM** = Direct message. These are private and only between people who DM each other.
- **# = HASHTAG.** These are used in front a word (or set of letters) to allow people to easily communicate on a specific topic. For instance, I tweet poetry with other poets on Twitter by using the hashtag #poettalk. Poets can click on the "poettalk" after the hashtag (no space) or they can search on the term "poettalk" in Twitter (right-hand toolbar).

- **#FF** = Follow Friday. This is a nice way to show support for other tweeters on Twitter. On Friday.

Second, here are 10 things you can do to optimize your use of Twitter:

1. **USE YOUR REAL NAME IF POSSIBLE.** Make it easy for people you know or meet to find you on Twitter.

2. **ADD A PROFILE PICTURE.** Preferably this will be a picture of you. People connect better with other people, not cartoons, book covers, logos, etc.

3. **LINK TO A WEBSITE.** Hopefully, you have a blog or website you can link to in your profile. If you don't have a website or blog, make one. Now. And then, link to it from your Twitter profile.

4. **WRITE YOUR BIO.** Make this memorable in some way. You don't have to be funny or cute, but more power to you if you can do this and still make it relevant to who you are.

5. **TWEET REGULARLY.** It doesn't matter if you have only 2 followers (and one is your mom); you still need to tweet daily (or nearly daily) for Twitter to be effective. And remember: If you don't have anything original to add, you can always RT something funny or useful from someone else.

6. **TWEET RELEVANT INFORMATION.** Don't be the person who tweets like this: "I am making a salad;" "I am eating a salad;" "That salad was good;" "I wonder what I'm going to eat next;" etc. These tweets are not interesting or relevant. However, if your salad eating experience rocked your world in a unique way, feel free to share: "Just ate the best salad ever. Now, I'm ready to write a novel."

7. **LINK AND DON'T LINK.** It's good to link to other places and share things you're doing or that you've found elsewhere. At the same time, if all you do is link, people may think you're just trying to sell them stuff all the time.

8. **HAVE A PERSONALITY.** Be yourself. You don't have to be overly cute, funny, smart, etc. Just be yourself and remember that Twitter is all about connecting people. So be a person.

9. **FOLLOW THOSE WORTH FOLLOWING.** Just because you're being followed you don't have to return the follow. For instance, if some local restaurant starts following me, I'm not going to follow them back, because they aren't relevant to me or to my audience.

10. **COMMUNICATE WITH OTHERS.** I once heard someone refer to Twitter as one big cocktail party, and it's true. Twitter is all about communication. If people talk to you or RT you, make sure you talk back and/or thank them. (*Here's a secret: People like to feel involved and acknowledged. I like it; you like it; and so does everyone else.*)

And, of course, if you're not already, please follow me on Twitter @robetleebrewer (http://twitter.com/robertleebrewer)

HERE ARE SOME EXTRA RESOURCES:

- **TwitterGrader.com** (http://twittergrader.com) This site allows you to enter your profile at any given time and find out how you're doing (according to them) in using Twitter effectively. Of course, the grade you receive is bound to not be perfect, but it is a good measuring stick.
- **What the Hashtag?** (http://wthashtag.com) This site allows you to search for hashtags, run reports on them, get transcripts between specific time periods, and more.
- **Hootsuite** (http://hootsuite.com) This is one of many tools that give the ability to Tweet and track your account without even going to Twitter. Many (maybe even most) people use these. There are others, such as TweetDeck, Seesmic, etc. Find one that you like and let it make your social networking life easier to manage.
- **bit.ly** (http://bit.ly) This is one of many URL shortening services out there, which is very helpful when tweeting URL links, since they can easily eat into your 140-character limit on Twitter. This particular one makes it easy for you to track clicks, though I'm sure that's fairly standard.

FACEBOOK VS. LINKEDIN:

Tips for Using Two Social Networking Sites

by Robert Lee Brewer

Many writers ask why start a LinkedIn account if they already have a Facebook, or conversely, why start a Facebook if they already have a LinkedIn? That's a fair question, but the answer is simple: Both these sites cater to different audiences, and both of these audiences are important to writers.

LinkedIn is the more professional site of the two. Many professionals use it to make meaningful connections with other like-minded professionals. HR departments use the site to find potential job candidates, and potential job candidates use their LinkedIn profiles as their resumes.

Facebook is a lot less professional, but smart writers treat this site as an important piece to their marketing puzzle. In fact, it's natural for writers to have more fun with their Facebook profiles, but they should still remember that editors, agents, writers, and other professionals may be interested in linking up on Facebook.

FACEBOOK TIPS FOR WRITERS

As of the writing of this article, Facebook is the most popular social networking website on the Internet. Chances are good that you already have a profile on this site and have already collected several friends, both those you know in real life and those you've only met through using other social networking sites. (If you don't have a Facebook profile, then you should create one now, since they're free.) However, you may or may not be optimizing your Facebook use.

Here are some tips for writers who are either new to Facebook or who aren't sure if they're using it the correct way:

1. **COMPLETE YOUR PROFILE.** You don't have to include EVERYTHING, but I'd suggest at least covering these bases: Current City, Birthday (you don't have to include the year), Bio, Education and Work, Contact Information.

2. **MAKE EVERYTHING PUBLIC.** As a writer, you should be using sites like Facebook and Twitter to connect with other writers, editors, agents, and your audience. So make it easy for them to find you and learn more about you by making everything available to the public. That said...

3. **THINK ABOUT YOUR AUDIENCE, FRIENDS, FAMILY, BOSS, FORMER TEACHERS, ETC., IN EVERYTHING YOU DO ON FACEBOOK.** Like it or not, you have to understand that if you are completely public on Facebook (and you should be if you want to connect with your audience) that you need to think about what you do on Facebook before you do it. Because Facebook isn't like Vegas: What happens on Facebook could easily go viral. But don't get paranoid; just use common sense.

....

Even though it's virtual, you want your profile to be as human as possible so that you can connect with others.

....

4. **INCLUDE A PROFILE PICTURE OF YOURSELF.** Don't use a picture of a cute animal, house pet, your children, an animated character, a famous celebrity, a model, etc. Just a nice pic of yourself. Even though it's virtual, you want your profile to be as human as possible so that you can connect with others.

5. **UPDATE YOUR STATUS REGULARLY.** You shouldn't update your status every hour, but once a day is a good pace. This just lets others on Facebook know that you are actively using the site.

6. **COMMUNICATE WITH FRIENDS ON FACEBOOK.** Don't stalk your friends; communicate with them. If you like a friend's status update, comment on it—or at the very least, click the Like button (to acknowledge that you liked their update). Speaking of friends...

7. **BE SELECTIVE ABOUT FRIENDS YOU ADD.** Don't blindly accept every friend request, because some may be bogus, and others may be from serial frienders (people who are trying to hit their friend limits). You want quality friends who share your interests or who you know from the "real world."

8. **BE SELECTIVE ABOUT ADDING APPS.** I'm not a huge fan of apps, because they are a distraction and time killer on Facebook. But there are some that could be useful.

However, don't waste a month of your life playing Farmville or Mafia Wars; you'd be better off completing a crossword or sudoku puzzle.

9. **JOIN RELEVANT GROUPS.** For writers, there are an abundance of groups you could join, from professional organizations to those based around magazines, publishers and literary events. These are great places to connect with other writers. On that same note...

10. **FOLLOW RELEVANT FAN PAGES.** There are many who once had groups that migrated over to using fan pages, so there are fan pages for writing organizations, magazines, publishers, literary events, and more. (I even have a fan page on Facebook; just search for Robert Lee Brewer.)

BONUS TIP: If you have a blog, you can feed your Facebook profile automatically by using the Notes function. All you have to do is go to Notes, click the "Edit import settings" link, and enter your blog url in the correct field. (Note: I had to enter my full url, including the forward slash at the end, before the Notes function accepted my url.)

OTHER SOCIAL NETWORKING SITES

This book contains articles on Twitter, Facebook, and LinkedIn, but there are many other powerful social networking sites on the Internet. Here's a list of some of them:

- **Bebo** (http://bebo.com)
- **Classmates** (http://classmates.com)
- **Digg** (http://digg.com)
- **Flickr** (http://flickr.com)
- **Google+** (http://plus.google.com)
- **Habbo** (http://habbo.com)
- **Hi5** (http://hi5.com)
- **MeetUp** (http://meetup.com)
- **Ning** (http://ning.com)
- **Orkut** (http://orkut.com)
- **Pinterest** (http://pinterest.com)
- **Reddit** (http://reddit.com)
- **StumbleUpon** (http://stumbleupon.com)
- **Yelp** (http://yelp.com)
- **YouTube** (http://youtube.com)
- **Zorpia** (http://zorpia.com)

LINKEDIN TIPS FOR WRITERS

If Twitter and Facebook are the social networks where writers can just "hang out," then LinkedIn is the one where writers can "network" and make meaningful connections. Some writers may even be able to make connections with editors (like myself) and agents.

Many writers may not use LinkedIn anywhere near as much as they use Facebook or Twitter, but I believe in making yourself easy to find. Having a completed and optimized LinkedIn profile could lead to connections with editors, event coordinators, and other writers.

Here are a few tips I've picked up over time on how to use LinkedIn:

1. **USE YOUR OWN HEAD SHOT FOR YOUR AVATAR. I** recommend this on all social networks, because people want to make "real" connections on these sites. It's hard to take a picture of a family pet or cartoon character seriously.

2. **COMPLETE YOUR PROFILE.** There are many steps to completing your profile, including completing your resume and getting a few recommendations from connections, which leads to the next tip...

3. **GIVE THOUGHTFUL RECOMMENDATIONS TO RECEIVE THEM.** Give if you wish to receive. The recommendations you write will make you feel and look better, but the recommendations you receive in return will truly rock your solar system. Of course, to make and receive recommendations, you'll need to...

4. **SEARCH FOR CONNECTIONS YOU ALREADY HAVE.** These could be "real world" connections and/or connections from other social networks. The ones who are (or have been) most valuable to you are the best to make at first. Then...

5. **MAKE MEANINGFUL CONNECTIONS WITH OTHERS.** Search for other writers, editors, agents, or whoever you think might benefit your writing career. But don't ever spam. Look for meaningful connections and include a note about why you're contacting them through LinkedIn. Remember: Social networking is about *who* you know, not *how many*.

6. **ACCEPT INVITATIONS.** While I think it's a good rule of thumb to be selective about who you invite to connect with you, I also don't see any harm in accepting invitations with abandon—unless they are obviously not a good fit. My reasoning here is that you never know why someone is contacting you. Of course, you can always kill the connection later if it's not working.

7. **MAKE YOUR PROFILE EASY TO FIND.** If possible, work your name into your LinkedIn url. For instance, you can view my LinkedIn profile at http://www.linkedin.

com/in/robertleebrewer. Also, connect to your profile in blog posts and on other social networks.

8. **TAILOR YOUR PROFILE TO THE VISITOR.** It's easy to make me-centric profiles on social networks, because they're asking questions about you. However, remember that these descriptions are more beneficial to you if you're filling them out for the prospective connections you can make on social networking sites. Make it easy for them to figure out who you are, what you do, and how you might improve their lives. As such...

9. **UPDATE YOUR PROFILE REGULARLY WITH USEFUL CONTENT.** You can feed blog posts into your profile easily, and that will keep your profile active. You can also update your status by feeding in tweets or Facebook updates, but I refrain from doing that myself. My reasoning is that my updates are slightly different for each place. However, I can make meaningful tweets and LinkedIn status updates simultaneously by simply adding an #in hashtag to the tweet in question.

10. **JOIN (AND PARTICIPATE) IN GROUPS.** Heck, start your own group if you feel so inclined. Of course, participating in groups will require an extra level of engagement with the site, so this last tip is more an extra credit assignment for those who want to unlock the full potential of LinkedIn.

AUTHOR PLATFORM 2.0

by Jane Friedman

You've been through the drill already. You know about establishing your own website, being active on social media, plus networking up and down the food chain. You've heard all the advice about building your online and offline presence—and perhaps you've landed a book deal because of your strong platform.

But platform building is a career-long activity. It doesn't stop once your website goes live, or after you land a book deal. In fact, your continued career growth depends on extending your reach and uncovering new opportunities. So what's next?

I'll break it down into three categories:

- Optimize your online presence.
- Make your relationships matter.
- Diversify your content.

OPTIMIZE YOUR ONLINE PRESENCE

First things first. You need your own domain (e.g., JaneFriedman.com is the domain I own), and you should be self-hosted. If you're still working off Blogger or Wordpress.com, then you won't be able to implement all of my advice due to the limitations of having your site owned or hosted by someone else.

Once you truly own your site, hire a professional website designer to customize the look and feel to best convey your personality or brand. If you don't yet have a grasp on what your "personality" is, then hold off on a site revamp until you do. Or you might start simple, by getting a professionally designed header that's unique to your site.

Website and blog must-haves

Here's a checklist of things you should implement aside from a customized design.

- Readers should be able to subscribe to your blog posts via e-mail or RSS. You should be able to track the number of people who are signing up, and see when they are signing up.
- Customize the e-mails sent to anyone who subscribes to your blog posts. This can be done if you use Feedburner (free service) or MailChimp (free up to 2,000 names). Each e-mail that your readers receive should have the same look and feel as your website or whatever branding you typically use. You should also be able to see how many people open these e-mails and what they click on.
- If you do not actively blog, start an e-mail newsletter and post the sign-up form on your site. This way you can stay in touch with people who express interest in your news and updates. Again, MailChimp is a free e-mail newsletter delivery service for up to 2,000 names. You should also have e-newsletter sign-up forms with you at speaking engagements.
- Install Google Analytics, which offers valuable data on who visits your site, when they visit, what content they look at, how long they stay, etc.
- Add social sharing buttons to your site and each post, so people can easily share your content on Facebook, Google, etc. This functionality might have to be manually added if you have a self-hosted site.

Review your metrics

As I hope you noticed, many of the above items relate to metrics and measurement. Advance platform building requires that you study your numbers. Especially think about the following:

- How do people find your site? For example, if you're dumping a lot of energy into Twitter to drive traffic to your blog posts, but very few people visit your site from Twitter, that means your strategy is not working, and you might need to course correct.
- What content is the most popular on your site? This is like a neon sign, telling you what your readers want. Whatever it is, consider how you can build on it, repurpose it, or expand it.
- What causes a spike in traffic, followers, or subscribers? When you achieve spikes, you've done something right. How can you repeat the success?
- What's extending your reach? Most days, you're probably talking to the same crowd you were yesterday. But every so often, you'll be opened up to a new audience—and from that you can find new and loyal readers. Identify activities that have a broad ripple effect, and make you heard beyond your existing circles. (In Google Analytics, this would mean tracking how new visitors find you.)

Advanced social media monitoring and involvement

Just about everyone by now has a Facebook profile or page, a LinkedIn profile, a Twitter account, etc. But static profiles can only do so much for you. Social media becomes more valuable when you decide how to interact and how to facilitate valuable discussion among your followers. Here are a few areas to consider.

- Implement an advanced commenting system. Sometimes the most valuable part of a blog is having a comments section where people can contribute and interact with each other. But this usually means actively filtering the good comments from the bad. Using a robust system like Disqus or Livefyre (and paying for access to their filtering tools) can help you develop a quality discussion area that rewards the most thoughtful contributors.

- Add a forum or discussion board. Very popular bloggers, who may have hundreds of comments on a post, will often add a forum or discussion board so their community can interact in an extended way. If your site is Wordpress-based, plug-ins can help you add a forum to your site in one step. Or you can consider using a private Facebook group or Ning (ning.com) as the base for your community.

- Use HootSuite to be strategic with your social media updates. HootSuite is a free, Web-based software that helps you schedule updates primarily for Twitter, but also for other sites. It also helps you analyze the effectiveness of your tweets (e.g, how many people clicked on a link you tweeted?).

- Use Paper.li (free service) to automatically curate the best daily tweets, updates, and posts on whatever subject you're an expert on—based on the people or organizations you follow and trust. Sometimes curating is one of the best services you can provide for your community—not only do you provide valuable content, you help people understand *who else* provides valuable content!

A final word about social media: Everyone knows about the usual suspects (Facebook, Twitter, Google Plus). Make sure you're not missing a more niche, devoted community on your topic. For example, All About Romance (www.likesbooks.com) is a very popular site for readers and authors of romance.

MAKE YOUR RELATIONSHIPS MATTER

A key component to platform is the relationships you have and grow. Often when you see a successful author, it's only the *visible* aspects of their online presence or content that are apparent. What you can't see is all of the relationship-building and behind-the-scenes conversations that contribute to a more impactful and amplified reach.

Am I saying you have to know big-name people to have a successful platform? No! Do you need to build relationships with successful or authoritative people (or organizations/businesses) in your community? Yes. Here's how to amplify your efforts.

Make a list of who's interacting with you the most

Regardless of where it's happening (on your site or on social media), take note of who is reading, commenting on, or sharing your content. These are people who are already paying attention, like what you're doing, and are receptive to further interaction.

If you're ignoring these people, then you're missing an opportunity to develop a more valuable relationship (which will likely lead to new ones), as well as reward and empower those you're already engaged with.

What does "rewarding" and "empowering" look like? You might drop a personal note, offer an e-book or product for free, or involve them somehow in your online content. You might have a special newsletter for them. Do what makes sense—there are many ways to employ this principle. Christina Katz, who teaches classes to writers, creates "Dream Teams" of writers who are selected from previous students. It's a great idea that rewards both Christina and the students she coaches.

Make a list of your mentors and how you can help them

You should have a list (or wish list!) of mentors. If not, develop one. We all have people who are doing something we dream of, or operate a few steps beyond where we're currently at.

....

Do not approach this as something you're going to "get something" out of, or it will backfire.

....

If you're not already closely following your mentors on their most active channels of communication (blog, Twitter, Facebook, etc), then start. Begin commenting, sharing, and being a visible fan of what they do. Consider other ways you can develop the relationship, e.g., interview them on your blog or review their book. But most of all, brainstorm how you can serve them.

If you engage mentors in an intelligent way (not in a needy "look at me" sort of way), then you may develop a more meaningful relationship when they reach out to acknowledge your efforts. But be careful: Do not approach this as something you're going to "get something" out of, or it will backfire.

Do watch for opportunities that mentors will inevitably offer (e.g., "I'm looking for someone to help moderate my community. Who wants to help?") I once helped an author arrange a book event when he stopped in Cincinnati, and that helped solidify a relationship that had only been virtual up until that point.

Finally, don't forget a time-honored way to cozy up to mentors: offer a guest post for their blog. Just make sure that what you contribute is of the highest quality possible—more high quality than what you'd demand for your own site. If you bring a mentor considerable traffic, you'll earn their attention and esteem.

Look for partnerships with peers

Who is attempting to reach the same audience as you? Don't see them as competitors. Instead, align with them to do bigger and better things. You can see examples of partnership everywhere in the writing community, such as:

- Writer Unboxed website (where I participate)
- Jungle Red Writers blog
- The Kill Zone blog

We all have different strengths. Banding together is an excellent way to extend your platform in ways you can't manage on your own. When presented with opportunities to collaborate, say yes whenever you'll be exposed to a new audience or diversify your online presence.

Stay alert to your influencers and who you influence

There are many ways to identify important people in your community, but if you're not sure where to start, try the following.

- Blog rolls. Find just one blog that you know is influential. See who they're linking to and recommending. Identify sites that seem to be on everyone's "best of" list—or try searching for "best blogs" + your niche.
- Klout. This social media tool attempts to measure people's authority online by assigning a score. It will summarize who you influence, and who you are influenced by.
- If you use the Disqus commenting system, it will identify the most active commenters on your site.

DIVERSIFY YOUR CONTENT

Writers can easily fall into the trap of thinking only about new *written* content. It's a shame, because by repurposing existing content into new mediums, you can open yourself up to entirely new audiences.

For example, I have a friend who has a long solo commute by car, plus he walks his dogs while listening to his iPod. Nearly all of his media consumption is podcast driven. He rarely reads because his lifestyle doesn't support it. That means that if he can't get his content in audio form, he won't buy it.

Envision a day in the life of your readers. Are they likely to be using mobile devices? Tablets? (Guess what: Google Analytics tells you the percentage of mobile and tablet visits to your site!) Do your readers like to watch videos on YouTube? Do they buy e-books? Are they on Twitter?

If you adapt your content to different mediums, you will uncover a new audience who didn't know you existed. While not all content is fit for adaptation, brainstorm a list of all the content you currently own rights to, and think of ways it could be repurposed or redistributed.

....

If you adapt your content to different mediums, you will uncover a new audience who didn't know you existed.

....

A popular repurposing project for longtime bloggers is to compile and edit a compilation of best blog posts, and make it available as an e-book (free or paid). Some bloggers will even do that with a handful of blog posts that can serve as a beginner or introductory guide to a specific topic. Fiction writers: How about a sampler of your work in e-book or PDF form? Poets: How about a podcast of you reading some of your favorite poems?

Some forms or mediums you might want to explore:

- Creating podcasts and distributing through your own site (or via iTunes)
- Creating videocasts and distributing through YouTube or Vimeo (did you know that YouTube is now the No. 2 search engine?)
- Creating tips or lessons in e-mail newsletter form
- Creating PDFs (free or paid), and using Scribd to help distribute
- Creating online tutorials or offering critiques through tools such as Google Hangouts, Google Docs, and/or Screencast.com
- Creating slide presentations and distributing through SlideShare

The only limit is your imagination!

HOUSEKEEPING

On a final note, I'd like to share a few housekeeping tips that can help boost your image and authority online. While they may seem trivial, they go a long way in making a good impression and spreading the word about what you do.

- Get professional headshots that accurately convey your brand or personality—what people know you and love you for.
- For your social media profiles, completely fill out *all* fields and maximize the functionality. This is important for search and discoverability. For instance, on LinkedIn, add keywords that cover all of your skill sets, pipe in your Twitter account and blog posts, and give complete descriptions of all positions you've held. On Google Plus, list all the sites that you're a contributor for. On Facebook, allow people to subscribe to your public updates even if they aren't your friends.

- Gather updated testimonials and blurbs, and use them on your site and/or your social media profiles if appropriate.

However you decide to tackle the next stage of your platform development, ensure consistency. Whether it's your website, e-newsletter, Facebook profile, business cards, or letterhead, be consistent in the look and feel of your materials and in the message you send. Unless you are appealing to different audiences with different needs, broadcast a unified message no matter where and how people find you. Believe me—it doesn't get boring. Instead, it helps people remember who you are and what you stand for.

JANE FRIEDMAN is a former publishing and media exec who now teaches full-time at the University of Cincinnati. She has spoken on writing, publishing, and the future of media at more than 200 events since 2001, including South by Southwest, BookExpo America, and the Association of Writers and Writing Programs. Find out more at http://janefriedman.com.

LITERARY AGENTS

//

The literary agencies listed in this section are open to new clients and are members of the Association of Authors' Representatives (AAR), which means they do not charge for reading, critiquing, or editing. Some agents in this section may charge clients for office expenses such as photocopying, foreign postage, long-distance phone calls, or express mail services. Make sure you have a clear understanding of what these expenses are before signing any agency agreement.

FOR MORE...

The *2013 Guide to Literary Agents* (Writer's Digest Books) offers more than 800 literary agents, as well as information on writers' conferences. It also offers a wealth of information on the author/agent relationship and other related topics.

SUBHEADS

Each listing is broken down into subheads to make locating specific information easier. In the first section, you'll find contact information for each agency. Further information is provided which indicates an agency's size, its willingness to work with a new or previously unpublished writer, and its general areas of interest.

MEMBER AGENTS Agencies comprised of more than one agent list member agents and their individual specialties to help you determine the most appropriate person for your query letter.

REPRESENTS Here agencies specify what nonfiction and fiction subjects they consider.

8→ Look for the key icon to quickly learn an agent's areas of specialization or specific strengths.

HOW TO CONTACT In this section agents specify the type of material they want to receive, how they want to receive it, and how long you should wait for their response.

TERMS Provided here are details of an agent's commission, whether a contract is offered, and what additional office expenses you might have to pay if the agent agrees to represent you. Standard commissions range from 10-15 percent for domestic sales, and 15-20 percent for foreign or dramatic sales.

TIPS Agents offer advice and additional instructions for writers looking for representation.

2M COMMUNICATIONS, LTD.

33 W. 17 St., PH, New York NY 10011. (212)741-1509. **Fax:** (212)691-4460. **E-mail:** morel@2mcommunications. com. **Website:** www.2mcommunications.com. **Contact:** Madeleine Morel. Member of AAR. Represents 100 clients. 20% of clients are new/unpublished writers. Currently handles: nonfiction books 100%.

REPRESENTS Nonfiction books. **Considers these nonfiction areas:** autobiography, biography, child guidance, cooking, cultural interests, diet/nutrition, ethnic, foods, health, history, medicine, music, parenting, self-help, women's issues, women's studies, cookbooks.

⚭ Only represents ghostwriters and works with major literary agents and publishing houses whose "platformed" authors require help.

HOW TO CONTACT Query with SASE. Submit outline, 3 sample chapters. Accepts simultaneous submissions. Responds in 1 week to queries. Responds in 1 month to mss. Obtains most new clients through recommendations from others, solicitations.

TERMS Agent receives 15% commission on domestic sales. Agent receives 20% commission on foreign sales. Offers written contract, binding for 2 years. Charges clients for postage, photocopying, long-distance calls, faxes.

DOMINICK ABEL LITERARY AGENCY, INC.

146 W. 82nd St., #1A, New York NY 10024. (212)877-0710. **Fax:** (212)595-3133. **E-mail:** dominick@dalainc. com. Member AAR. Represents 100 clients. Currently handles: adult fiction and nonfiction.

HOW TO CONTACT Query via e-mail.

TERMS Agent receives 15% commission on domestic sales. Agent receives 20% commission on foreign sales.

ADAMS LITERARY

7845 Colony Rd., C4 #215, Charlotte NC 28226. (704)542-1440. **Fax:** (704)542-1450. **E-mail:** info@adamsliterary.com; submissions@adamsliterary.com. **Website:** www.adamsliterary.com. **Contact:** Tracey Adams, Josh Adams, Quinlan Lee. Member of AAR. Other memberships include SCBWI and WNBA. Currently handles: juvenile books.

⚭ Represents "The finest children's book authors and artists."

HOW TO CONTACT Contact through online form on website only. Send e-mail if that is not operating correctly. "All submissions and queries must be made through the online form on our website. We will not

review—and will promptly recycle—any unsolicited submissions or queries we receive by post. Before submitting your work for consideration, please carefully review our complete guidelines." Responds in 6 weeks. "While we have an established client list, we do seek new talent—and we accept submissions from both published and aspiring authors and artists."

TERMS Agent receives 15% commission on domestic sales; 20% on foreign sales. Offers written contract.

TIPS "Guidelines are posted (and frequently updated) on our website."

ALIVE COMMUNICATIONS, INC.

7680 Goddard St., Suite 200, Colorado Springs CO 80920. (719)260-7080. **Fax:** (719)260-8223. **E-mail:** submissions@alivecom.com. **Website:** www.alivecom.com. **Contact:** Rick Christian. Member of AAR. Other memberships include Authors Guild. Represents 100+ clients. 5% of clients are new/unpublished writers. Currently handles: nonfiction books 50%, novels 40%, juvenile books 10%.

MEMBER AGENTS Rick Christian, president (blockbusters, bestsellers); Lee Hough (popular/commercial nonfiction and fiction, thoughtful spirituality, children's); Andrea Heinecke (thoughtful/inspirational nonfiction, women's fiction/nonfiction, popular/commercial nonfiction & fiction); Joel Kneedler popular/commercial nonfiction and fiction, thoughtful spirituality, children's).

REPRESENTS Nonfiction books, novels, short story collections, novellas. **Considers these nonfiction areas:** autobiography, biography, business, child guidance, economics, how-to, inspirational, parenting, personal improvement, religious, self-help, women's issues, women's studies. **Considers these fiction areas:** adventure, contemporary issues, crime, family saga, historical, humor, inspirational, literary, mainstream, mystery, police, religious, satire, suspense, thriller.

⚭ This agency specializes in fiction, Christian living, how-to and commercial nonfiction. Actively seeking inspirational, literary and mainstream fiction, and work from authors with established track records and platforms. Does not want to receive poetry, scripts or dark themes.

HOW TO CONTACT Query via e-mail. "Be advised that this agency works primarily with well-established, best-selling, and career authors. Always looking for a breakout, blockbuster author with genuine talent." New clients come through recommendations from others.

TERMS Agent receives 15% commission on domestic sales. Offers written contract; 2-month notice must be given to terminate contract.

TIPS Rewrite and polish until the words on the page shine. Endorsements and great connections may help, provided you can write with power and passion. Network with publishing professionals by making contacts, joining critique groups, and attending writers' conferences in order to make personal connections and to get feedback. Alive Communications, Inc., has established itself as a premiere literary agency. We serve an elite group of authors who are critically acclaimed and commercially successful in both Christian and general markets.

BETSY AMSTER LITERARY ENTERPRISES

6312 SW Capitol Hwy #503, Portland OR 97239. **Website:** www.amsterlit.com. **Contact:** Betsy Amster. Estab. 1992. Member of AAR. Represents more than 65 clients. 35% of clients are new/unpublished writers. Currently handles: nonfiction books 65%, novels 35%.

REPRESENTS Nonfiction books, novels. **Considers these nonfiction areas:** art & design, biography, business, child guidance, cooking/nutrition, current affairs, ethnic, gardening, health/medicine, history, memoirs, money, parenting, popular culture, psychology, science/technology, self-help, sociology, travelogues, social issues, women's issues. **Considers these fiction areas:** ethnic, literary, women's, high quality. ✂⊶ "Actively seeking strong narrative nonfiction, particularly by journalists; outstanding literary fiction (the next Richard Ford or Jhumpa Lahiri); witty, intelligent commerical women's fiction (the next Elinor Lipman or Jennifer Weiner); mysteries that open new worlds to us; and high-profile self-help and psychology, preferably research based." Does not want to receive poetry, children's books, romances, western, science fiction, action/adventure, screenplays, fantasy, techno-thrillers, spy capers, apocalyptic scenarios, or political or religious arguments.

HOW TO CONTACT For adult titles: b.amster.assistant@gmail.com. See submission requirements online at website. The requirements have changed and only e-mail submissions are accepted. Accepts simultaneous submissions. Responds in 1 month to queries. Responds in 2 months to mss. Obtains most new clients through recommendations from others, solicitations, conferences.

TERMS Agent receives 15% commission on domestic sales. Agent receives 20% commission on foreign sales. Offers written contract, binding for 1 year; 3-month notice must be given to terminate contract. Charges for photocopying, postage, long distance phone calls, messengers, galleys/books used in submissions to foreign and film agents and to magazines for first serial rights.

ARCADIA

31 Lake Place N., Danbury CT 06810. **E-mail:** arcadialit@sbcglobal.net. **Contact:** Victoria Gould Pryor. Member of AAR.

REPRESENTS nonfiction books, literary and commercial fiction. **Considers these nonfiction areas:** biography, business, current affairs, health, history, psychology, science, true crime, women's, investigative journalism; culture; classical music; life transforming self-help. ✂⊶ "I'm a very hands-on agent, which is necessary in this competitive marketplace. I work with authors on revisions until whatever we present to publishers is as strong as possible. Arcadia represents talented, dedicated, intelligent and ambitious writers who are looking for a long-term relationship based on professional success and mutual respect." Does not want to receive science fiction/fantasy, horror, humor or children's/YA. "We are only able to read fiction submissions from previously published authors."

HOW TO CONTACT No unsolicited submissions. Query with SASE. This agency accepts e-queries (no attachments).

THE BALKIN AGENCY, INC.

P.O. Box 222, Amherst MA 01004. (413)322-8697; (978)656-8389. **Fax:** (413)322-8697. **E-mail:** rick62838@crocker.com; christinawardlit@mac.com. **Website:** http://wardbalkin.com. **Contact:** Rick Balkin, president. Christina Ward: P.O. Box 7144, Lowell, MA 01852. Member of AAR. Represents 50 clients. 10% of clients are new/unpublished writers. Currently handles: nonfiction books 85%, 5% reference books .

REPRESENTS Nonfiction books. **Considers these nonfiction areas:** animals, anthropology, current affairs, health, history, how to, nature, popular culture, science, sociology, translation, biography, et al.

☛ This agency specializes in adult nonfiction. Does not want to receive fiction, poetry, screenplays, children's books or computer books.

HOW TO CONTACT Query with SASE. Submit proposal package, outline. Responds in 1 week to queries. Responds in 2 weeks to mss. Obtains most new clients through recommendations from others.

TERMS Agent receives 15% commission on domestic sales. Agent receives 20% commission on foreign sales. Offers written contract, binding for 1 year. This agency charges clients for photocopying and express or foreign mail.

TIPS "I do not take on books described as bestsellers or potential bestsellers. Any nonfiction work that is either unique, paradigmatic, a contribution, truly witty, or a labor of love is grist for my mill."

LORETTA BARRETT BOOKS, INC.

220 E. 23rd St., 11th Floor, New York NY 10010. (212)242-3420. **E-mail:** query@lorettabarrettbooks.com. **Website:** www.lorettabarrettbooks.com. **Contact:** Loretta A. Barrett, Nick Mullendore, Gabriel Davis. Estab. 1990. Member of AAR. Currently handles: nonfiction books 50%, novels 50%.

REPRESENTS Nonfiction books, novels. **Considers these nonfiction areas:** biography, child guidance, current affairs, ethnic, government, health/nutrition, history, memoirs, money, multicultural, nature, popular culture, psychology, religion, science, self help, sociology, spirituality, sports, women's, young adult, creative nonfiction. **Considers these fiction areas:** contemporary, psychic, adventure, detective, ethnic, family, historical, literary, mainstream, mystery, thriller, young adult.

☛ "The clients we represent include both fiction and nonfiction authors for the general adult trade market. The works they produce encompass a wide range of contemporary topics and themes including commercial thrillers, mysteries, romantic suspense, popular science, memoirs, narrative fiction and current affairs." No children's, juvenile, cookbooks, gardening, science fiction, fantasy novels, historical romance.

HOW TO CONTACT See guidelines online. Use e-mail (no attachments) or if by post, query with SASE. For hardcopy queries, please send a 1-2 page query letter and a synopsis or chapter outline for your project. In your letter, please include your contact information, any relevant background information on yourself or your project, and a paragraph of description of your project. If you are submitting electronically, then all of this material may be included in the body of your e-mail. Accepts simultaneous submissions. Responds in 3-6 weeks to queries.

TERMS Agent receives 15% commission on domestic sales. Agent receives 20% commission on foreign sales. Offers written contract. Charges clients for shipping and photocopying.

FAYE BENDER LITERARY AGENCY

19 Cheever Place, Brooklyn NY 11231. **E-mail:** info@fbliterary.com. **Website:** www.fbliterary.com. **Contact:** Faye Bender. Estab. 2004. Member of AAR.

REPRESENTS Nonfiction books, novels, juvenile. **Considers these nonfiction areas:** biography, memoirs, popular culture, women's issues, women's studies, young adult, narrative; health; popular science. **Considers these fiction areas:** commercial, literary, women's, young adult (middle-grade).

☛ "I choose books based on the narrative voice and strength of writing. I work with previously published and first-time authors." Faye does not represent picture books, genre fiction for adults (western, romance, horror, science fiction, fantasy), business books, spirituality, or screenplays.

HOW TO CONTACT Query with SASE and 10 sample pages via mail or e-mail (no attachments). Guidelines online. "Please do not send queries or submissions via registered or certified mail, or by FedEx or UPS requiring signature. We will not return unsolicited submissions weighing more than 16 ounces, even if an SASE is attached. We do not respond to queries via phone or fax."

TIPS "Please keep your letters to the point, include all relevant information, and have a bit of patience."

VICKY BIJUR LITERARY AGENCY

333 West End Ave., Apt. 5B, New York NY 10023. **E-mail:** assistant@vickybijuragency.com. Estab. 1988. Member of AAR.

REPRESENTS Nonfiction books, novels. **Considers these nonfiction areas:** cooking, government, health, history, psychology, psychiatry, science, self help, sociology, biography; child care/development; environmental studies; journalism; social sciences.

☛ Does not want science fiction, fantasy, horror, romance, poetry, children's.

HOW TO CONTACT Accepts e-mail queries. Fiction: query and first chapter (if e-mailed, please paste chapter into body of e-mail as I don't open attachments from unfamiliar senders). Nonfiction: query and proposal. No phone or fax queries.

DAVID BLACK LITERARY AGENCY

335 Adams St., #2710, Brooklyn NY 11201-3724. (718)852-5500. **Contact:** David Black, owner. Member of AAR. Represents 150 clients. Currently handles: nonfiction books 90%, novels 10%.

MEMBER AGENTS David Black; Susan Raihofer (general nonfiction, literary fiction); Gary Morris (commercial fiction, psychology); Joy E. Tutela (general nonfiction, literary fiction); Leigh Ann Eliseo; Linda Loewenthal (general nonfiction, health, science, psychology, narrative).

REPRESENTS Nonfiction books, novels. **Considers these nonfiction areas:** autobiography, biography, business, economics, finance, government, health, history, inspirational, law, medicine, military, money, multicultural, psychology, religious, sports, war, women's issues, women's studies. **Considers these fiction areas:** literary, mainstream, commercial.

8—☛ This agency specializes in business, sports, politics, and novels.

HOW TO CONTACT Query with SASE. For nonfiction works, send a formal proposal that includes an overview, author bio, chapter outline, a marketing/publicity section, a competition section, and at least one sample chapter. Please also include writing samples, such as newspaper or magazine clips if relevant. (See questions in Guidelines online.) When submitting fiction, please include a synopsis, author bio, and the first 3 chapters of the book (25-50 pages). Accepts simultaneous submissions. Responds in 2 months to queries.

TERMS Agent receives 15% commission on domestic sales. Charges clients for photocopying and books purchased for sale of foreign rights.

BOOKENDS, LLC

136 Long Hill Rd., Gillette NJ 07933. **Website:** www.bookends-inc.com; bookendslitagency.blogspot.com. **Contact:** Kim Lionetti, Jessica Alvarez, Lauren Ruth. Member of AAR. RWA, MWA Represents 50+ clients. 10% of clients are new/unpublished writers. Currently handles: nonfiction books 50%, novels 50%.

MEMBER AGENTS Jessica Faust (**no long accepting unsolicited material**) (fiction: romance, erotica, women's fiction, mysteries and suspense; nonfiction: business, finance, career, parenting, psychology, women's issues, self-help, health, sex); Kim Lionetti (Kim is only currently considering romance, women's fiction, and young adult queries. If your book is in any of these 3 categories, please be sure to specify "Romance," "Women's Fiction," or "Young Adult" in your e-mail subject line. Any queries that do not follow these guidelines will not be considered); Jessica Alvarez (romance, women's fiction, erotica, romantic suspense); Lauren Ruth.

REPRESENTS Nonfiction books, novels. **Considers these nonfiction areas:** business, child, ethnic, gay, health, how-to, money, psychology, religion, self-help, sex, true crime, women's. **Considers these fiction areas:** detective, cozies, mainstream, mystery, romance, thrillers, women's.

8—☛ "BookEnds is currently accepting queries from published and unpublished writers in the areas of romance (and all its sub-genres), erotica, mystery, suspense, women's fiction, and literary fiction. We also do a great deal of nonfiction in the areas of self-help, business, finance, health, pop science, psychology, relationships, parenting, pop culture, true crime, and general nonfiction." BookEnds does not want to receive children's books, screenplays, science fiction, poetry, or technical/military thrillers.

HOW TO CONTACT Review website for guidelines, as they change. BookEnds is no longer accepting unsolicited proposal packages or snail mail queries. Send query in the body of e-mail to only one agent.

BOOKS & SUCH LITERARY AGENCY

52 Mission Circle, Suite 122, PMB 170, Santa Rosa CA 95409. **E-mail:** representation@booksandsuch.biz. **Website:** www.booksandsuch.biz. **Contact:** Janet Kobobel Grant, Etta Wilson, Rachel Kent, Mary Keeley. Member of AAR. Member of CBA (associate), American Christian Fiction Writers. Represents 150 clients. 5% of clients are new/unpublished writers. Currently handles: nonfiction books 50%, novels 50%.

REPRESENTS Nonfiction books, novels. **Considers these nonfiction areas:** humor, religion, self help, women's. **Considers these fiction areas:** contemporary, family, historical, mainstream, religious, romance.

8—☛ This agency specializes in general and inspirational fiction, romance, and in the Christian booksellers market. Actively seeking well-crafted material that presents Judeo-Christian values, if only subtly.

HOW TO CONTACT Query via e-mail only, no attachments. Accepts simultaneous submissions. Responds in 1 month to queries. "If you don't hear from us asking to see more of your writing within 30 days after you have sent your e-mail, please know that we have read and considered your submission but determined that it would not be a good fit for us." Obtains most new clients through recommendations from others, conferences.

TERMS Agent receives 15% commission on domestic sales. Agent receives 20% commission on foreign sales. Offers written contract; 2-month notice must be given to terminate contract. No additional charges.

TIPS "The heart of our agency's motivation is to develop relationships with the authors we serve, to do what we can to shine the light of success on them, and to help be a caretaker of their gifts and time."

BARBARA BRAUN ASSOCIATES, INC.

7 E. 14th St., Suite 19F, New York NY 10003. **Fax:** (212)604-9023. **E-mail:** bbasubmissions@gmail.com. **Website:** www.barbarabraunagency.com. **Contact:** Barbara Braun. Member of AAR.

MEMBER AGENTS Barbara Braun; John F. Baker.

REPRESENTS Nonfiction books, novels. **Considers these nonfiction areas:** "We represent both literary and commercial and serious nonfiction, including psychology, biography, history, women's issues, social and political issues, cultural criticism, as well as art, architecture, film, photography, fashion and design." **Considers these fiction areas:** literary and commercial.

⌗—⚲ "Our fiction is strong on women's stories, historical and multicultural stories, as well as mysteries and thrillers. We're interested in narrative nonfiction and books by journalists. We do not represent poetry, science fiction, fantasy, horror, or screenplays. Look online for more details."

HOW TO CONTACT "E-mail submissions only, marked 'query' in subject line. We no longer accept submissions by regular mail. Your query should include: a brief summary of your book, word count, genre, any relevant publishing experience, and the first 5 pages of your ms pasted into the body of the e-mail. (No attachments—we will not open these.)"

TERMS Agent receives 15% commission on domestic sales. Agent receives 20% commission on foreign sales.

TIPS "Our clients' books are represented throughout Europe, Asia, and Latin America by various sub-agents. We are also active in selling motion picture rights to the books we represent, and work with various Hollywood agencies."

BRICK HOUSE LITERARY AGENTS

80 Fifth Ave., Suite 1101, New York NY 10011. **Website:** www.brickhouselit.com. **Contact:** Sally Wofford-Girand. Member of AAR.

MEMBER AGENTS Sally Wofford-Girand; Jenni Ferrari-Adler; Kezia Toth, assistant.

REPRESENTS nonfiction books, narrative nonfiction. **Considers these nonfiction areas:** cultural interests, ethnic, history, memoirs, nature, science, women's issues, women's studies, biography; food writing; lifestyle; science; natural history. **Considers these fiction areas:** literary, general & juvenile fiction.

⌗—⚲ Sally's particular areas of interest are: history, memoir, women's issues, cultural studies, and fiction that is both literary and hard to put down (novels like *The Road* or *Blindness).* Jenni Ferrari-Adler specializes in representing novels, food narrative and cookbooks, and narrative nonfiction. Actively seeking history, memoir, women's issues, cultural studies, literary fiction, and quality commerical fiction.

HOW TO CONTACT "E-m ail query letter (in body of e-mail—not as attachment) and first page to either Sally or Jenni. We will ask to see more if interested and are sorry that we cannot respond to all queries."

CURTIS BROWN, LTD.

10 Astor Place, New York NY 10003-6935. (212)473-5400. **E-mail:** gknowlton@cbltd.com. **Website:** www.curtisbrown.com. **Contact:** Ginger Knowlton. Alternate address: Peter Ginsberg, president at CBSF, 1750 Montgomery St., San Francisco CA 94111. (415)954-8566. Member of AAR. Signatory of WGA.

MEMBER AGENTS Ginger Clark; Katherine Fausset; Holly Frederick, VP; Emilie Jacobson; Elizabeth Hardin; Ginger Knowlton, executive vice president; Timothy Knowlton, CEO; Laura Blake Peterson; Mitchell Waters. San Francisco Office: Peter Ginsberg (president).

REPRESENTS Nonfiction books, novels, short story collections, juvenile. **Considers these nonfiction areas:** agriculture horticulture, americana, crafts, interior, juvenile, New Age, young, animals, anthropology, art, biography, business, child, computers, cooking, current affairs, education, ethnic, gardening, gay, government, health, history, how-to, humor, language, memoirs, military, money, multicultural, music, nature, philosophy, photography, popular culture, psychology, recreation, regional, religion, science, self-help, sex, sociology, software, spirituality, sports, film, translation, travel, true crime, women's, creative nonfiction. **Considers these fiction areas:** contemporary, glitz, New Age, psychic, adventure, comic, confession, detective, erotica, ethnic, experimental, family, fantasy, feminist, gay, gothic, hi lo, historical, horror, humor, juvenile, literary, mainstream, military, multicultural, multimedia, mystery, occult, picture books, plays, poetry, regional, religious, romance, science, short, spiritual, sports, thriller, translation, western, youn, women's.

HOW TO CONTACT Prefers to read materials exclusively. *No unsolicited mss.* Query with SASE. If a picture book, send only one picture book ms. Considers simultaneous queries, "but please tell us." Returns material only with SASE. Responds in 3 weeks to queries; 5 weeks to mss. Obtains most new clients through recommendations from others, solicitations, conferences.

TERMS Agent receives 15% commission on domestic sales; 20% on foreign sales. Offers written contract. 75 days notice must be given to terminate contract. Offers written contract. Charges for some postage (overseas, etc.).

BROWNE & MILLER LITERARY ASSOCIATES

410 S. Michigan Ave., Suite 460, Chicago IL 60605-1465. (312)922-3063. **E-mail:** mail@browneandmiller. com. **Website:** www.browneandmiller.com. **Contact:** Danielle Egan-Miller. Estab. 1971. Member of AAR. Other memberships include RWA, MWA, Author's Guild. Represents 150 clients. 2% of clients are new/unpublished writers. Currently handles: nonfiction books 25%, novels 75%.

REPRESENTS Nonfiction books, most genres of commercial adult fiction and nonfiction, as well as select young adult projects. **Considers these nonfiction areas:** agriculture, animals, anthropology, archeology, autobiography, biography, business, child guidance, cooking, crafts, cultural interests, current affairs, economics, environment, ethnic, finance, foods, health, hobbies, horticulture, how-to, humor, inspirational, investigative, medicine, memoirs, money, nature, nutrition, parenting, personal improvement, popular culture, psychology, religious, satire, science, self-help, sociology, sports, technology, true crime, women's issues, women's studies. **Considers these fiction areas:** contemporary issues, crime, detective, erotica, ethnic, family saga, glitz, historical, inspirational, literary, mainstream, mystery, police, religious, romance, sports, suspense, thriller, paranormal.

☛ "We are partial to talented newcomers and experienced authors who are seeking hands-on career management, highly personal representation, and who are interested in being full partners in their books' successes. We are editorially focused and work closely with our authors through the whole publishing process, from proposal to after publication. We are most interested in commercial women's fiction, especially elegantly crafted, sweeping historicals; edgy, fresh teen/chick/mom/lady lit; and CBA women's fiction by established authors. We are also very keen on literary historical mysteries and literary YA novels. Topical, timely nonfiction projects in a variety of subject areas are also of interest, especially prescriptive how-to, self-help, sports, humor, and pop culture." Does not represent poetry, short stories, plays, original screenplays, articles, children's picture books, software, horror, or sci-fi novels.

HOW TO CONTACT Only accepts e-mail queries. Inquiring authors may initially submit one chapter and a synopsis. *No unsolicited mss.* Prefers to read material exclusively. Put submission in the subject line. Send no attachments. Also has online submission form. Responds in 2-4 months to queries. Obtains most new clients through referrals, queries by professional/marketable authors.

TERMS Agent receives 15% commission on domestic sales. Agent receives 20% commission on foreign sales. Offers written contract, binding for 2 years. Charges clients for photocopying, overseas postage.

TIPS "If interested in agency representation, be well informed."

SHEREE BYKOFSKY ASSOCIATES, INC.

P.O. Box 706, Brigantine NJ 08203. **E-mail:** shereebee@aol.com. **E-mail:** submitbee@aol.com. **Website:** www.shereebee.com. **Contact:** Sheree Bykofsky. Member of AAR. Other memberships include ASJA,

WNBA. Currently handles: nonfiction books 80%, novels 20%.

MEMBER AGENTS Janet Rosen, associate.

REPRESENTS Nonfiction books, novels. **Considers these nonfiction areas:** Americana, animals, architecture, art, autobiography, biography, business, child guidance, cooking, crafts, creative nonfiction, cultural interests, current affairs, dance, design, economics, education, environment, ethnic, film, finance, foods, gardening, gay, government, health, history, hobbies, humor, language, law, lesbian, memoirs, metaphysics, military, money, multicultural, music, nature, New Age, nutrition, parenting, philosophy, photography, popular culture, politics, psychology, recreation, regional, religious, science, sex, sociology, spirituality, sports, translation, travel, true crime, war, anthropology, creative nonfiction. **Considers these fiction areas:** contemporary issues, literary, mainstream, mystery, suspense.

> ☛ This agency specializes in popular reference nonfiction, commercial fiction with a literary quality, and mysteries. "I have wide-ranging interests, but it really depends on quality of writing, originality, and how a particular project appeals to me (or not). I take on fiction when I completely love it—it doesn't matter what area or genre." Does not want to receive poetry, material for children, screenplays, Westerns, horror, science fiction, or fantasy.

HOW TO CONTACT We only accept e-queries now and will only respond to those in which we are interested. E-mail short queries to submitbee@aol.com. Please, no attachments, snail mail, or phone calls. One-page query, one-page synopsis, and first page of manuscript in the body of the e-mail. Non-fiction: One-page query in the body of the e-mail. We cannot open attached Word files or any other types of attached files. These will be deleted. Accepts simultaneous submissions. Responds in 1 month to requested mss. Obtains most new clients through recommendations from others.

TERMS Agent receives 15% commission on domestic sales. Agent receives 20% commission on foreign sales. Offers written contract, binding for 1 year. Charges for postage, photocopying, fax.

TIPS "Read the agent listing carefully and comply with guidelines."

MARIA CARVAINIS AGENCY, INC.

1270 Avenue of the Americas, Suite 2320, New York NY 10019. (212)245-6365. **Fax:** (212)245-7196. **E-mail:** mca@mariacarvainisagency.com. **Contact:** Maria Carvainis, Chelsea Gilmore. Member of AAR. Signatory of WGA. Other memberships include Authors Guild, Women's Media Group, ABA, MWA, RWA. Represents 75 clients. 10% of clients are new/unpublished writers. Currently handles: nonfiction books 35%, novels 65%.

REPRESENTS Nonfiction books, novels. **Considers these nonfiction areas:** autobiography, biography, business, economics, history, memoirs, science, technology, women's issues, women's studies. **Considers these fiction areas:** contemporary issues, historical, literary, mainstream, mystery, suspense, thriller, women's, young adult, middle grade.

> ☛ Does not want to receive science fiction or children's picture books.

HOW TO CONTACT Query with SASE. No e-mail accepted. Responds in up to 3 months to mss and to queries 1 month. Obtains most new clients through recommendations from others, conferences, query letters.

TERMS Agent receives 15% commission on domestic sales. Agent receives 20% commission on foreign sales. Offers written contract. Charges clients for foreign postage and bulk copying.

CASTIGLIA LITERARY AGENCY

1155 Camino Del Mar, Suite 510, Del Mar CA 92014. (858)755-8761. **Fax:** (858)755-7063. **E-mail:** deborah@castigliaagency.com; win@castiglioagency.com. **Website:** home.earthlink.net/~mwgconference/id22.html. Member of AAR. Other memberships include PEN. Represents 65 clients. Currently handles: nonfiction books 55%, novels 45%.

MEMBER AGENTS Julie Castiglia; Winifred Golden (science fiction, ethnic, commercial and thriller novels, plus narrative nonfiction and some health books—prefers referrals); Sally Van Haitsma (actively looking for good proposals by way of query letters, and her wish list covers literary and women's fiction, current affairs, architecture, pop culture, and science fiction); Deborah Ritchken (narrative nonfiction, food/cookbooks, design, France, literary fiction, no genre fiction).

REPRESENTS Nonfiction books, novels. **Considers these nonfiction areas:** animals, anthropology, archeology, autobiography, biography, business, child guidance, cooking, cultural interests, current affairs, economics, environment, ethnic, finance, foods, health, history, inspirational, language, literature, medicine, money, nature, nutrition, psychology, religious, science, technology, women's issues, women's studies. **Considers these fiction areas:** contemporary issues, ethnic, literary, mainstream, mystery, suspense, women's.

✂ Does not want to receive horror, screenplays, poetry or academic nonfiction.

HOW TO CONTACT No unsolicited submissions. Query with SASE. No e-mail submissions accepted. Obtains most new clients through recommendations from others, solicitations, conferences.

TERMS Agent receives 15% commission on domestic sales. Agent receives 25% commission on foreign sales. Offers written contract; 6-week notice must be given to terminate contract.

TIPS "Be professional with submissions. Attend workshops and conferences before you approach an agent."

THE CHOATE AGENCY, LLC

1320 Bolton Rd., Pelham NY 10803. **E-mail:** mickey@thechoateagency.com. **Website:** www.thechoateagency.com. **Contact:** Mickey Choate. Estab. 2004. Member of AAR.

REPRESENTS Nonfiction books, novels. **Considers these nonfiction areas:** history; memoirs by journalists, military or political figures, biography; cookery/food; journalism; military science; narrative; politics; general science; natural science, wine/spirits. **Considers these fiction areas:** historical, mystery, thriller, select literary fiction, strong commercial fiction.

✂ The agency does not handle genre fiction, chic-lit, cozies, romance, self-help, confessional memoirs, spirituality, pop psychology, religion, how-to, New Age titles, children's books, poetry, self-published works, or screenplays.

HOW TO CONTACT Query with brief synopsis and bio. This agency prefers e-queries, but accepts snail mail queries with SASE.

FRANCES COLLIN, LITERARY AGENT

P.O. Box 33, Wayne PA 19087-0033. **E-mail:** queries@francescollin.com. **Website:** www.francescollin.com. **Contact:** Sarah Yake, associate agent. Member of AAR. Represents 90 clients. 1% of clients are new/unpublished writers. Currently handles: nonfiction books 50%, fiction 50%.

REPRESENTS Nonfiction books, fiction, young adult.

✂ Does not want to receive cookbooks, craft books, poetry, screenplays, or books for young children.

HOW TO CONTACT Query via e-mail describing project (text in the body of the e-mail only, no attachments) to queries@francescollin.com. "Please note that all queries are reviewed by both agents." No phone or fax queries. Accepts simultaneous submissions.

TERMS Agent receives 15% commission on domestic sales. Agent receives 20% commission on foreign sales. Offers written contract.

THE CREATIVE CULTURE, INC.

47 E. 19th St., Third Floor, New York NY 10003. (212)680-3510. **Fax:** (212)680-3509. **Website:** www.thecreativeculture.com/about. **Contact:** Debra Goldstein. Estab. 1998. Member of AAR.

MEMBER AGENTS Debra Goldstein (self-help, creativity, fitness, inspiration, lifestyle); Mary Ann Naples (health/nutrition, lifestyle, narrative nonfiction, practical nonfiction, literary fiction, animals/vegetarianism); Laura Nolan (literary fiction, parenting, self-help, psychology, women's studies, current affairs, science); Karen Gerwin (pop culture, lifestyle, parenting, humor, memoir/narrative nonfiction, women's interests, and a very limited selection of fiction [no genre categories, i.e. thrillers, romance, sci-fi/fantasy, etc.]); Matthew Elblonk (literary fiction, humor, pop culture, music and young adult. Interests also include commercial fiction, narrative non-fiction, science, and he is always on the lookout for something slightly quirky or absurd).

REPRESENTS Nonfiction books, novels.

✂ We are known for our emphasis on lifestyle books that enhance readers' overall well-being, be it through health, inspiration, entertainment, thought-provoking ideas, life management skills, beauty and fashion, or food. Does not want to receive children's books, poetry, screenplays or science fiction.

HOW TO CONTACT Query with bio, book description, 4-7 sample pages (fiction only), SASE. We only reply if interested. Please see the titles page to get a sense of the books we represent. Responds in 2 months to queries.

DARHANSOFF & VERRILL LITERARY AGENTS

236 W. 26th St., Suite 802, New York NY 10001. (917)305-1300. **Fax:** (917)305-1400. **E-mail:** chuck@

dvagency.com. **Website:** www.dvagency.com. Member of AAR. Represents 120 clients. 10% of clients are new/unpublished writers. Currently handles: nonfiction books 25%, novels 60%, story collections 15%.
MEMBER AGENTS Liz Darhansoff; Chuck Verrill; Michele Mortimer.
REPRESENTS Novels, juvenile books, narrative nonfiction, literary fiction, mystery & suspense, young adult.
HOW TO CONTACT Queries welcome via website or with SASE. Obtains most new clients through recommendations from others.

LIZA DAWSON ASSOCIATES

350 Seventh Ave., Suite 2003, New York NY 10001. (212)465-9071. **Fax:** (212)947-0460. **E-mail:** queryliza@lizadawsonassociates.com. **Website:** www.lizadawsonassociates.com. **Contact:** Anna Olswanger. Member of AAR. Other memberships include MWA, Women's Media Group. Represents 50+ clients. 30% of clients are new/unpublished writers. Currently handles: nonfiction books 60%, novels 40%.
MEMBER AGENTS Liza Dawson (plot-driven literary fiction, historicals, thrillers, suspense, parenting books, history, psychology [both popular and clinical], politics, narrative nonfiction and memoirs); Caitlin Blasdell (science fiction, fantasy (both adult and young adult), parenting, business, thrillers and women's fiction); Anna Olswanger (gift books for adults, young adult fiction and nonfiction, children's illustrated books, and Judaica); Havis Dawson (business books, how-to and practical books, spirituality, fantasy, Southern-culture fiction and military memoirs); David Austern (fiction and nonfiction, with an interest in young adult, pop culture, sports, and male-interest works).
REPRESENTS Nonfiction books, novels and gift books (Olswanger only). **Considers these nonfiction areas:** autobiography, biography, business, health, history, medicine, memoirs, parenting, politics, psychology, sociology, women's issues, women's studies. **Considers these fiction areas:** literary, mystery, regional, suspense, thriller, African-American (Miller only), fantasy and science fiction (Blasdell only).
8—⚊ "This agency specializes in readable literary fiction, thrillers, mainstream historicals, women's fiction, academics, historians, business, journalists and psychology."
HOW TO CONTACT Query with first 5 pages. Query by e-mail only. No phone calls. Responds in 4 weeks

to queries; 8 weeks to mss. Obtains most new clients through recommendations from others, conferences.
TERMS Agent receives 15% commission on domestic sales. Agent receives 20% commission on foreign sales. Offers written contract. Charges clients for photocopying and overseas postage.

DEFIORE & CO.

47 E. 19th St., 3rd Floor, New York NY 10003. (212)925-7744. **Fax:** (212)925-9803. **E-mail:** info@defioreandco.com; submissions@defioreandco.com. **Website:** www.defioreandco.com. **Contact:** Lauren Gilchrist. Member of AAR. Represents 75 clients. 50% of clients are new/unpublished writers. Currently handles: nonfiction books 70%, novels 30%.
MEMBER AGENTS Brian DeFiore (popular nonfiction, business, pop culture, parenting, commercial fiction); Laurie Abkemeier (memoir, parenting, business, how-to/self-help, popular science); Kate Garrick (literary fiction, memoir, popular non-fiction); Debra Goldstein (health and diet, wellness); Laura Nolan (cookbooks, memoir, non-fiction); Matthew Elblonk (young adult, popular culture, narrative non-fiction); Karen Gerwin (popular culture, memoir); Caryn Karmatz-Rudy (popular fiction, self-help, narrative non-fiction).
REPRESENTS Nonfiction books, novels. **Considers these nonfiction areas:** autobiography, biography, business, child guidance, cooking, economics, foods, how-to, inspirational, money, multicultural, parenting, popular culture, psychology, religious, self-help, sports, young adult, middle grade. **Considers these fiction areas:** ethnic, literary, mainstream, mystery, suspense, thriller.
8—⚊ "Please be advised that we are not considering children's picture books, poetry, adult science fiction and fantasy, romance, or dramatic projects at this time."
HOW TO CONTACT Query with SASE or e-mail to submissions@defioreandco.com. Please include the word "Query" in the subject line. All attachments will be deleted; please insert all text in the body of the e-mail. For more information about our agents, their individual interests, and their query guidelines, please visit our "About Us" page. Accepts simultaneous submissions. Responds in 3 weeks to queries. Responds in 2 months to mss. Obtains most new clients through recommendations from others.
TERMS Agent receives 15% commission on domestic sales. Agent receives 20% commission on foreign

sales. Offers written contract; 10-day notice must be given to terminate contract. Charges clients for photocopying and overnight delivery (deducted only after a sale is made).

SANDRA DIJKSTRA LITERARY AGENCY

1155 Camino del Mar, PMB 515, Del Mar CA 92014. (858)755-3115. **Fax:** (858)794-2822. **E-mail:** elise@dijkstraagency.com. **Website:** www.dijkstraagency.com. Member of AAR. Other memberships include Authors Guild, PEN West, Poets and Editors, MWA. Represents 100+ clients. 30% of clients are new/unpublished writers. Currently handles: nonfiction books 50%, novels 45%, juvenile books 5%.

MEMBER AGENTS Sandra Dijkstra; Elise Capron; Jill Marr; Taylor Martindale.

REPRESENTS Nonfiction books, novels. **Considers these nonfiction areas:** Americana, animals, anthropology, archeology, art, business, child guidance, cooking, cultural interests, diet/nutrition, economics, environment, ethnic, foods, gay/lesbian, government, health, history, inspirational, language, law, literature, medicine, memoirs, military, money, parenting, politics, psychology, regional, science, self-help, sociology, technology, travel, war, women's issues, women's studies, Asian studies, juvenile nonfiction, accounting, transportation. **Considers these fiction areas:** erotica, ethnic, fantasy, juvenile, literary, mainstream, mystery, picture books, science fiction, suspense, thriller, graphic novels.

⚲➝ Does not want to receive Westerns, screenplays, short story collections or poetry.

HOW TO CONTACT "Please see guidelines on our website and please note that we now only accept e-mail submissions. Due to the large number of unsolicited submissions we receive, we are now *only* able to respond those submissions in which we are interested. Unsolicited submissions in which we are not interested will receive no response." Accepts simultaneous submissions. Responds in about 6 weeks to queries. Obtains most new clients through recommendations from others, solicitations, conferences.

TERMS Agent receives 15% commission on domestic sales. Agent receives 20% commission on foreign sales. Offers written contract. Charges clients for expenses for foreign postage and copying costs if a client requests a hard copy submission to publishers.

TIPS "Be professional and learn the standard procedures for submitting your work. Be a regular patron of bookstores, and study what kind of books are being published and will appear on the shelves next to yours. Read! Check out your local library and bookstores—you'll find lots of books on writing and the publishing industry that will help you. At conferences, ask published writers about their agents. Don't believe the myth that an agent has to be in New York to be successful. We've already disproved it!"

DREISBACH LITERARY MANAGEMENT

P.O. Box 5379, El Dorado Hills CA 95762. (916)804-0833. **E-mail:** verna@dreisbachliterary.com. **Website:** www.dreisbachliterary.com. **Contact:** Verna Dreisbach. Estab. 2007.

REPRESENTS Considers these nonfiction areas: animals, biography, business, health, multicultural, parenting, travel, true crime, women's issues. **Considers these fiction areas:** commercial, literary, mystery, thriller, young adult.

⚲➝ "The agency has a particular interest in books with a political, economic, or social context. Open to most types of nonfiction. Fiction interests include literary, commercial, and YA. Verna's first career as a law enforcement officer gives her a genuine interest and expertise in the genres of mystery, thriller, and true crime." Does not want to receive sci-fi, fantasy, horror, poetry, screenplay, Christian, or children's books

HOW TO CONTACT E-mail queries only please. No attachments in the query; they will not be opened. No unsolicited mss.

DUNHAM LITERARY, INC.

156 Fifth Ave., Suite 625, New York NY 10010-7002. (212)929-0994. **E-mail:** query@dunhamlit.com. **Website:** www.dunhamlit.com. **Contact:** Jennie Dunham. Member of AAR. SCBWI Represents 50 clients. 15% of clients are new/unpublished writers. Currently handles: nonfiction books 25%, novels 25%, juvenile books 50%.

MEMBER AGENTS Blair Hewes. Represents authors of literary and commercial fiction, narrative non fiction, and books for children of all ages. She is interested in representing authors of nonfiction books in the categories of pop culture, historical biography, lifestyle, and women's issues. She is not interested in westerns, hard-boiled crime fiction, or political or medical thrillers.

REPRESENTS Nonfiction books, novels, short story collections, juvenile. **Considers these nonfiction ar-**

eas: anthropology, archeology, autobiography, biography, cultural interests, environment, ethnic, government, health, history, language, law, literature, medicine, popular culture, politics, psychology, science, technology, women's issues, women's studies. **Considers these fiction areas:** ethnic, juvenile, literary, mainstream, picture books, young adult.

HOW TO CONTACT Query with SASE. Responds in 1 week to queries; 2 months to mss. Obtains most new clients through recommendations from others, solicitations.

TERMS Agent receives 15% commission on domestic sales. Agent receives 20% commission on foreign sales.

DYSTEL & GODERICH LITERARY MANAGEMENT

1 Union Square W., Suite 904, New York NY 10003. (212)627-9100. **Fax:** (212)627-9313. **E-mail:** mbourret@dystel.com. **Website:** www.dystel.com. **Contact:** Michael Bourret; Jim McCarthy. Member of AAR. SCBWI. Represents 617 clients. 50% of clients are new/unpublished writers. Currently handles: nonfiction books 65%, novels 35%.

MEMBER AGENTS Jane Dystel; Stacey Glick; Michael Bourret; Jim McCarthy; Jessica Papin; Lauren Abramo; Chasya Milgrom; Rachel Oakley.

REPRESENTS Nonfiction books, novels, cookbooks. **Considers these nonfiction areas:** animals, anthropology, archeology, autobiography, biography, business, child guidance, cultural interests, current affairs, economics, ethnic, gay/lesbian, health, history, humor, inspirational, investigative, medicine, metaphysics, military, New Age, parenting, popular culture, psychology, religious, science, technology, true crime, women's issues, women's studies. **Considers these fiction areas:** action, adventure, crime, detective, ethnic, family saga, gay, lesbian, literary, mainstream, mystery, police, suspense, thriller.

➤ ⚑ "This agency specializes in cookbooks and commercial and literary fiction and nonfiction. We are actively seeking fiction for all ages, in all genres. We're especially interested in quality young adult fiction, from realistic to paranormal, and all kinds of middle grade, from funny boy books to more sentimental fare. Though we are open to author/illustrators, we are not looking for picture book manuscripts. And, while we would like to see more YA memoir, nonfiction is not something we usually handle." No plays, screenplays, or poetry.

HOW TO CONTACT Query with SASE. Please include the first 3 chapters in the body of the email. Email queries preferred (Michael Bourret only accepts email queries); will accept mail. See website for full guidelines. Accepts simultaneous submissions. Responds in 6 to 8 weeks to queries; within 8 weeks to mss. Obtains most new clients through recommendations from others, solicitations, conferences.

TERMS Agent receives 15% commission on domestic sales. Agent receives 19% commission on foreign sales. Offers written contract.

TIPS "DGLM prides itself on being a full-service agency. We're involved in every stage of the publishing process, from offering substantial editing on mss and proposals, to coming up with book ideas for authors looking for their next project, negotiating contracts and collecting monies for our clients. We follow a book from its inception through its sale to a publisher, its publication, and beyond. Our commitment to our writers does not, by any means, end when we have collected our commission. This is one of the many things that makes us unique in a very competitive business."

THE ELAINE P. ENGLISH LITERARY AGENCY

4710 41st St. NW, Suite D, Washington DC 20016. (202)362-5190. **Fax:** (202)362-5192. **E-mail:** queries@elaineenglish.com. **E-mail:** elaine@elaineenglish.com. **Website:** www.elaineenglish.com/literary.php. **Contact:** Elaine English, Lindsey Skouras. Member of AAR. Represents 20 clients. 25% of clients are new/unpublished writers. Currently handles: novels 100%.

REPRESENTS Novels. **Considers these fiction areas:** historical, multicultural, mystery, suspense, thriller, women's, romance (single title, historical, contemporary, romantic, suspense, chick lit, erotic), general women's fiction. The agency is slowly but steadily acquiring in all mentioned areas.

➤ ⚑ Actively seeking women's fiction, including single-title romances, and young adult fiction. Does not want to receive any science fiction, time travel, or picture books.

HOW TO CONTACT Generally prefers e-queries sent to queries@elaineenglish.com. If requested, submit synopsis, first 3 chapters, SASE. Please check website for further details. Responds in 4-8 weeks to queries; 3 months to requested submissions. Obtains most new clients through recommendations from others, conferences, submissions.

TERMS Agent receives 15% commission on domestic sales. Agent receives 20% commission on foreign sales. Offers written contract; 30-day notice must be given to terminate contract. Charges only for shipping expenses; generally taken from proceeds.

FELICIA ETH LITERARY REPRESENTATION

555 Bryant St., Suite 350, Palo Alto CA 94301-1700. (650)375-1276. **Fax:** (650)401-8892. **E-mail:** felicia-eth@aol.com. **Contact:** Felicia Eth. Member of AAR. Represents 25-35 clients. Currently handles: nonfiction books 75%, novels 25% adult.

REPRESENTS nonfiction books, novels. **Considers these nonfiction areas:** animals, anthropology, autobiography, biography, business, child guidance, cultural interests, current affairs, economics, ethnic, gay/lesbian, government, health, history, investigative, law, medicine, parenting, popular culture, politics, psychology, science, sociology, technology, true crime, women's issues, women's studies. **Considers these fiction areas:** literary, mainstream.

→ This agency specializes in high-quality fiction (preferably mainstream/contemporary) and provocative, intelligent, and thoughtful nonfiction on a wide array of commercial subjects.

HOW TO CONTACT Query with SASE. Accepts simultaneous submissions. Responds in 3 weeks to queries. Responds in 4-6 weeks to mss.

TERMS Agent receives 15% commission on domestic sales. Agent receives 20% commission on foreign sales. Agent receives 20% commission on film sales. Charges clients for photocopying and express mail service.

TIPS "For nonfiction, established expertise is certainly a plus—as is magazine publication—though not a prerequisite. I am highly dedicated to those projects I represent, but highly selective in what I choose."

DIANA FINCH LITERARY AGENCY

116 W. 23rd St., Suite 500, New York NY 10011. E-mail: diana.finch@verizon.net. **Website:** dianafinchliteraryagency.blogspot.com/. **Contact:** Diana Finch. Member of AAR. Represents 40 clients. 20% of clients are new/unpublished writers. Currently handles: nonfiction books 85%, novels 15%, juvenile books 5%, multimedia 5%.

REPRESENTS Nonfiction books, novels, scholarly. **Considers these nonfiction areas:** autobiography, biography, business, child guidance, computers, cultural interests, current affairs, dance, economics, environment, ethnic, film, government, health, histo-

ry, how-to, humor, investigative, juvenile nonfiction, law, medicine, memoirs, military, money, music, parenting, photography, popular culture, politics, psychology, satire, science, self-help, sports, technology, theater, translation, true crime, war, women's issues, women's studies, computers, electronic. **Considers these fiction areas:** action, adventure, crime, detective, ethnic, historical, literary, mainstream, police, thriller, young adult.

→ Actively seeking narrative nonfiction, popular science, memoir and health topics. "Does not want romance, mysteries, or children's picture books."

HOW TO CONTACT Query with SASE or via e-mail (no attachments). Accepts simultaneous submissions. Obtains most new clients through recommendations from others.

TERMS Agent receives 15% commission on domestic sales. Agent receives 20% commission on foreign sales. Offers written contract. "I charge for photocopying, overseas postage, galleys, and books purchased, and try to recoup these costs from earnings received for a client, rather than charging outright."

TIPS "Do as much research as you can on agents before you query. Have someone critique your query letter before you send it. It should be only 1 page and describe your book clearly—and why you are writing it—but also demonstrate creativity and a sense of your writing style."

FINEPRINT LITERARY MANAGEMENT

240 West 35th St., Suite 500, New York NY 10001. (212)279-1282. **E-mail:** stephany@fineprintlit.com. **Website:** www.fineprintlit.com. Member of AAR.

MEMBER AGENTS Peter Rubie, CEO (nonfiction interests include narrative nonfiction, popular science, spirituality, history, biography, pop culture, business, technology, parenting, health, self help, music, and food; fiction interests include literate thrillers, crime fiction, science fiction and fantasy, military fiction and literary fiction); Stephany Evans, president (nonfiction interests include health and wellness—especially women's health, spirituality, lifestyle, home renovating/decorating, entertaining, food and wine, popular reference, and narrative nonfiction; fiction interests include stories with a strong and interesting female protagonist, both literary and upmarket commercial—including chick lit, romance, mystery, and light suspense); June Clark (nonfiction: entertainment, self-help, parenting, reference/how-to books, teen books, food and wine, style/beauty, and prescriptive business titles); Diane Freed (nonfiction: health/fitness, women's issues, memoir, baby boomer trends, parenting, popular culture, self-help, humor, young adult, and topics of New England regional interest); Meredith Hays (both fiction and nonfiction: commercial and literary; she is interested in sophisticated women's fiction such as urban chick lit, pop culture, lifestyle, animals, and absorbing nonfiction accounts); Janet Reid (mysteries and offbeat literary fiction); Colleen Lindsay; Marissa Walsh; Ward Calhoun; Laura Wood.

REPRESENTS Nonfiction books, novels. **Considers these nonfiction areas:** business, child guidance, cooking, dance, diet/nutrition, economics, foods, government, health, history, humor, law, medicine, memoirs, music, parenting, politics, psychology, science, spirituality, true crime, women's issues, women's studies, narrative nonfiction, young adult, popular science. **Considers these fiction areas:** crime, detective, fantasy, literary, military, mystery, police, romance, science fiction, suspense, war, women's, young adult.

HOW TO CONTACT Query with SASE. Submit synopsis and first two chapters for fiction; proposal for nonfiction. Do not send attachments or manuscripts without a request. See contact page onilne at website for e-mails. Obtains most new clients through recommendations from others, solicitations.

TERMS Agent receives 15% commission on domestic sales. Agent receives 20% commission on foreign sales.

JEANNE FREDERICKS LITERARY AGENCY, INC.

221 Benedict Hill Rd., New Canaan CT 06840. (203)972-3011. **Fax:** (203)972-3011. **E-mail:** jeanne. fredericks@gmail.com. **Website:** www.jeannefredericks.com. **Contact:** Jeanne Fredericks. Member of AAR. Other memberships include Authors Guild. Represents 90 clients. 10% of clients are new/unpublished writers. Currently handles: nonfiction books 100%.

REPRESENTS Nonfiction books. **Considers these nonfiction areas:** animals, autobiography, biography, child guidance, cooking, decorating, foods, gardening, health, history, how-to, interior design, medicine, parenting, photography, psychology, self-help, women's issues.

8→ This agency specializes in quality adult nonfiction by authorities in their fields. Does not want to receive children's books or fiction.

HOW TO CONTACT Query first with SASE, then send outline/proposal, 1-2 sample chapters, SASE, or by e-mail, if requested. See submission guidelines online first. Accepts simultaneous submissions. Responds in 3-5 weeks to queries. Responds in 2-4 months to mss. Obtains most new clients through recommendations from others, solicitations, conferences.

TERMS Agent receives 15% commission on domestic sales. Agent receives 25% commission on foreign sales with co-agent. Offers written contract, binding for 9 months; 2-month notice must be given to terminate contract. Charges client for photocopying of whole proposals and mss, overseas postage, priority mail, express mail services.

TIPS "Be sure to research competition for your work and be able to justify why there's a need for your book. I enjoy building an author's career, particularly if he/she is professional, hardworking, and courteous. Aside from 20 years of agenting experience, I've had 10 years of editorial experience in adult trade book publishing that enables me to help an author polish a proposal so that it's more appealing to prospective editors. My MBA in marketing also distinguishes me from other agents."

THE FRIEDRICH AGENCY

19 West 21st St, Suite 201, New York NY 10010. **E-mail:** mfriedrich@friedrichagency.com; pcirone@ friedrichagency.com; lcarson@friedrichagency.com. **Website:** www.friedrichagency.com. **Contact:** Molly Friedrich. Member of AAR. Represents 50+ clients.

MEMBER AGENTS Molly Friedrich, Founder and Agent (open to queries); Paul Cirone, Foreign Rights Director and Agent (open to queries); Lucy Carson, assistant.

REPRESENTS Full-length fiction and nonfiction.

HOW TO CONTACT Query with SASE by mail, or e-mail. See guidelines on website.

GELFMAN SCHNEIDER LITERARY AGENTS, INC.

250 W. 57th St., Suite 2122, New York NY 10107. (212)245-1993. **Fax:** (212)245-8678. **E-mail:** mail@gelfmanschneider.com. **Website:** www.gelfmanschneider.com. **Contact:** Jane Gelfman, Deborah Schneider. Member of AAR. Represents 300+ clients. 10% of clients are new/unpublished writers.

REPRESENTS Fiction and nonfiction books. **Considers these fiction areas:** literary, mainstream, mystery, women's.

⚋➤ Does not want to receive romance, science fiction, westerns, or children's books.

HOW TO CONTACT Query with SASE. Send queries via snail mail only. No unsolicited mss. Please send a query letter, a synopsis, and a sample chapter only. Responds in 1 month to queries; 2 months to mss.

TERMS Agent receives 15% commission on domestic sales. Agent receives 20% commission on foreign sales. Agent receives 15% commission on film sales. Offers written contract. Charges clients for photocopying and messengers/couriers.

BARRY GOLDBLATT LITERARY, LLC

320 Seventh Ave., #266, Brooklyn NY 11215. **Fax:** (718)360-5453. **Website:** www.bgliterary.com. **Contact:** Barry Goldblatt. Member of AAR. SCBWI

MEMBER AGENTS Barry Goldblatt, Joe Monti, Beth Fleisher (kids work and graphic novels; she is particularly interested in finding new voices in middle grade and young adult fantasy, science fiction, mystery, historicals and action adventure).

REPRESENTS Juvenile books. **Considers these fiction areas:** picture books, young adult, middle grade, all genres.

⚋➤ This agency specializes in children's books of all kinds from picture books to young adult novels, across all over genres.

HOW TO CONTACT E-mail queries query@bgliterary.com, and include the first 5 pages and a synopsis of the novel pasted into the text of the e-mail. No attachments or links.

ASHLEY GRAYSON LITERARY AGENCY

1342 W. 18th St., San Pedro CA 90732. **Fax:** (310)514-1148. **E-mail:** graysonagent@earthlink.net. **Website:** www.graysonagency.com/blog. Estab. 1976. Member of AAR. Represents 100 clients. 5% of clients are new/unpublished writers. Currently handles: nonfiction books 20%, novels 50%, juvenile books 30%.

MEMBER AGENTS Ashley Grayson (fantasy, mystery, thrillers, young adult); Carolyn Grayson (chick lit, mystery, children's, nonfiction, women's fiction, romance, thrillers); Denise Dumars (mind/body/spirit, women's fiction, dark fantasy/horror); Lois Winston (women's fiction, chick lit, mystery).

REPRESENTS Nonfiction books, novels. **Considers these nonfiction areas:** business, computers, economics, history, investigative, popular culture, science, self-help, sports, technology, true crime, mind/body/spirit, lifestyle. **Considers these fiction areas:** fantasy, juvenile, multicultural, mystery, romance, science fiction, suspense, women's, young adult, chick lit.

⚋➤ "We prefer to work with published (traditional print), established authors. We will give first consideration to authors who come recommended to us by our clients or other publishing professionals. We accept a very small number of new, previously unpublished authors. The agency is temporarily closed to queries from writers who are not published at book length (self published or print-on-demand do not count). There are only three exceptions to this policy: (1) Unpublished authors who have received an offer from a reputable publisher, who need an agent before beginning contract negotiations; (2) Authors who are recommended by a published author, editor or agent who has read the work in question; (3) Authors whom we have met at conferences and from whom we have requested submissions. Authors who are recognized within their field or area may still query with proposals. We are seeking more mysteries and thrillers."

HOW TO CONTACT Agency open to fiction authors with publishing credits (no self-published). For nonfiction, only writers with platforms will be considered. Responds to queries in 1 month; mss in 2-3 months.

TERMS Agent receives 15% commission on domestic sales. Agent receives 20% commission on foreign sales.

TIPS "We do request revisions as they are required. We are long-time agents, professional and known in the business. We perform professionally for our clients and we ask the same of them."

SANFORD J. GREENBURGER ASSOCIATES, INC.

55 Fifth Ave., New York NY 10003. (212)206-5600. **Fax:** (212)463-8718. **E-mail:** queryHL@sjga.com. **Website:** www.greenburger.com. Member of AAR. Represents 500 clients.

MEMBER AGENTS Heide Lange; Faith Hamlin; Dan Mandel; Matthew Bialer; Courtney Miller-Callihan, Michael Harriot, Brenda Bowen (authors and illustrators of children's books for all ages as well as graphic novelists); Lisa Gallagher.

REPRESENTS Nonfiction books and novels. **Considers these nonfiction areas:** Americana, animals, anthropology, archeology, architecture, art, biography, business, computers, cooking, crafts, current affairs, decorating, diet/nutrition, design, education, environment, ethnic, film, foods, gardening, gay/lesbian, government, health, history, horticulture, how-to, humor, interior design, investigative, juvenile nonfiction, language, law, literature, medicine, memoirs, metaphysics, military, money, multicultural, music, New Age, philosophy, photography, popular culture, psychology, recreation, regional, romance, science, sex, sociology, software, sports, theater, translation, travel, true crime, women's issues, women's studies, young adult, software. **Considers these fiction areas:** action, adventure, crime, detective, ethnic, family saga, feminist, gay, glitz, historical, humor, lesbian, literary, mainstream, mystery, police, psychic, regional, satire, sports, supernatural, suspense, thriller.

HOW TO CONTACT Submit query, first 3 chapters, synopsis, brief bio, SASE. Accepts simultaneous submissions. Responds in 2 months to queries and mss. Responds to mss. Obtains most new clients through recommendations from others.

TERMS Agent receives 15% commission on domestic sales. Agent receives 20% commission on foreign sales. Charges for photocopying and books for foreign and subsidiary rights submissions.

GREYHAUS LITERARY

3021 20th St., PL SW, Puyallup WA 98373. **E-mail:** scott@greyhausagency.com. **Website:** www.greyhausagency.com. **Contact:** Scott Eagan, member RWA. Estab. 2003.

REPRESENTS Novels. **Considers these fiction areas:** romance, women's.

⚷━ "We specialize in romance, women's fiction and YA romance." Actively seeking contemporary romance, and stories that are 75,000-100,000 words in length. Does not want sci-fi, fantasy, inspirational, literary, futuristic, erotica, writers targeting e-pubs, young adult.

HOW TO CONTACT Send a query, the first 3 pages and a synopsis of no more than 3 pages. There is also a submission form on this agency's website.

THE JOY HARRIS LITERARY AGENCY, INC.

381 Park Avenue S, Suite 428, New York NY 10016. (212)924-6269. **Fax:** (212)725-5275. **E-mail:** submissions@jhlitagent.com; contact@jhlitagent.com.

Website: joyharrisliterary.com. **Contact:** Joy Harris. Member of AAR. Represents more than 100 clients. Currently handles: nonfiction books 50%, novels 50%.

REPRESENTS Nonfiction books, novels, and young adult. **Considers these fiction areas:** ethnic, experimental, family saga, feminist, gay, glitz, hi-lo, historical, humor, lesbian, literary, mainstream, multicultural, multimedia, mystery, regional, satire, short story collections, spiritual, suspense, translation, women's, young adult.

⚷━ We do not accept unsolicited manuscripts, and are not accepting poetry, screenplays, or self-help submissions at this time.

HOW TO CONTACT Visit our website for guidelines. Query with sample chapter, outline/proposal, SASE. Accepts simultaneous submissions. Responds in 2 months to queries. Obtains most new clients through recommendations from clients and editors.

TERMS Agent receives 15% commission on domestic sales. Agent receives 20% commission on foreign sales. Charges clients for some office expenses.

RICHARD HENSHAW GROUP

22 West 23rd Street, 5th Floor, New York NY 10010. **E-mail:** submissions@henshaw.com. **Website:** http://www.richh.addr.com. **Contact:** Rich Henshaw. Member of AAR. Other memberships include SinC, MWA, HWA, SFWA, RWA. 20% of clients are new/unpublished writers. Currently handles: nonfiction books 35%, novels 65%.

REPRESENTS Nonfiction books, novels. **Considers these nonfiction areas:** animals, autobiography, biography, business, child guidance, cooking, current affairs, dance, economics, environment, foods, gay/lesbian, health, humor, investigative, money, music, New Age, parenting, popular culture, politics, psychology, science, self-help, sociology, sports, technology, true crime, women's issues, women's studies, electronic. **Considers these fiction areas:** action, adventure, crime, detective, ethnic, family saga, historical, humor, literary, mainstream, mystery, police, psychic, romance, satire, science fiction, sports, supernatural, suspense, thriller.

⚷━ This agency specializes in thrillers, mysteries, science fiction, fantasy and horror.

HOW TO CONTACT Query with SASE. Accepts multiple submissions. Responds in 3 weeks to queries. Responds in 6 weeks to mss. Obtains most new clients through recommendations from others, solicitations, conferences.

TERMS Agent receives 15% commission on domestic sales. Agent receives 20% commission on foreign sales. No written contract. Charges clients for photocopying and book orders.

TIPS "While we do not have any reason to believe that our submission guidelines will change in the near future, writers can find up-to-date submission policy information on our website. Always include a SASE with correct return postage."

KIRCHOFF/WOHLBERG, INC.

897 Boston Post Rd., Madison CT 06443. (203)245-7308. **Fax:** (203)245-3218. **E-mail:** rzollshan@kirchoffwohlberg.com. **Website:** www.kirchoffwohlberg.com. **Contact:** Ronald Zollshan. Memberships include SCBWI, Society of Illustrators, SPAR, Bookbuilders of Boston, New York Bookbinders' Guild, AIGA.

☛ This agency specializes in juvenile fiction and nonfiction through young adult.

HOW TO CONTACT "Submit by mail to address above. We welcome the submission of mss from first-time or established children's book authors. Please enclose an SASE, but note that while we endeavor to read all submissions, we cannot guarantee a reply or their return." Accepts simultaneous submissions.

TERMS Offers written contract, binding for at least 1 year. Agent receives standard commission, depending upon whether it is an author only, illustrator only, or an author/illustrator.

HARVEY KLINGER, INC.

300 W. 55th St., Suite 11V, New York NY 10019. (212)581-7068. **E-mail:** queries@harveyklinger.com. **Website:** www.harveyklinger.com. **Contact:** Harvey Klinger. Member of AAR. Represents 100 clients. 25% of clients are new/unpublished writers. Currently handles: nonfiction books 50%, novels 50%.

MEMBER AGENTS David Dunton (popular culture, music-related books, literary fiction, young adult, fiction, and memoirs); Sara Crowe (children's and young adult authors, adult fiction and nonfiction, foreign rights sales); Andrea Somberg (literary fiction, commercial fiction, romance, sci-fi/fantasy, mysteries/thrillers, young adult, middle grade, quality narrative nonfiction, popular culture, how-to, self-help, humor, interior design, cookbooks, health/fitness).

REPRESENTS Nonfiction books, novels. **Considers these nonfiction areas:** autobiography, biography, cooking, diet/nutrition, foods, health, investigative, medicine, psychology, science, self-help, spirituality, sports, technology, true crime, women's issues, women's studies. **Considers these fiction areas:** action, adventure, crime, detective, family saga, glitz, literary, mainstream, mystery, police, suspense, thriller.

☛ This agency specializes in big, mainstream, contemporary fiction and nonfiction.

HOW TO CONTACT Use online e-mail submission form, or query with SASE. No phone or fax queries. Don't send unsolicited manuscripts or e-mail attachments. Responds in 2 months to queries and mss. Obtains most new clients through recommendations from others.

TERMS Agent receives 15% commission on domestic sales. Agent receives 25% commission on foreign sales. Offers written contract. Charges for photocopying mss and overseas postage for mss.

LINDA KONNER LITERARY AGENCY

10 W. 15th St., Suite 1918, New York NY 10011-6829. (212)691-3419. **E-mail:** ldkonner@cs.com. **Website:** www.lindakonnerliteraryagency.com. **Contact:** Linda Konner. Member of AAR. Signatory of WGA. Other memberships include ASJA. Represents 85 clients. 30-35% of clients are new/unpublished writers. Currently handles: nonfiction books 100%.

REPRESENTS Nonfiction books. **Considers these nonfiction areas:** diet/nutrition, gay/lesbian, health, medicine, money, parenting, popular culture, psychology, self-help, women's issues, biography (celebrity), African American and Latino issues, relationships.

☛ This agency specializes in health, self-help, and how-to books. Authors/co-authors must be top experts in their field with a substantial media platform.

HOW TO CONTACT Query by e-mail or by mail with SASE, synopsis, author bio, sufficient return postage. Prefers to read materials exclusively for 2 weeks. Accepts simultaneous submissions. Obtains most new clients through recommendations from others, occasional solicitation among established authors/journalists.

TERMS Agent receives 15% commission on domestic sales. Agent receives 25% commission on foreign sales. Offers written contract. Charges one-time fee for domestic expenses; additional expenses may be incurred for foreign sales.

BARBARA S. KOUTS, LITERARY AGENT

P.O. Box 560, Bellport NY 11713. (631)286-1278. **Fax:** (631) 286-1538. **Contact:** Barbara S. Kouts. Member of AAR. Represents 50 clients. 10% of clients are new/unpublished writers.

REPRESENTS Juvenile.

8—ᴦ This agency specializes in children's books.

HOW TO CONTACT Query with SASE. Accepts queries by mail only. Accepts simultaneous submissions. Responds in 1 week to queries; 2 months to mss. Obtains most new clients through recommendations from others, solicitations, conferences.

TERMS Agent receives 10% commission on domestic sales. Agent receives 20% commission on foreign sales. This agency charges clients for photocopying.

TIPS "Write, do not call. Be professional in your writing."

STUART KRICHEVSKY LITERARY AGENCY, INC.

381 Park Ave. S., Suite 428, New York NY 10016. (212)725-5288. **Fax:** (212)725-5275. **E-mail:** query@skagency.com. **Website:** www.skagency.com. Member of AAR.

MEMBER AGENTS Stuart Krichevsky; Shana Cohen (science fiction, fantasy); Jennifer Puglisi (assistant).

REPRESENTS Nonfiction books, novels.

HOW TO CONTACT Submit query, synopsis, 1 sample page via e-mail (no attachments). Snail mail queries also acceptable. Obtains most new clients through recommendations from others, solicitations.

MICHAEL LARSEN/ELIZABETH POMADA, LITERARY AGENTS

1029 Jones St., San Francisco CA 94109-5023. (415)673-0939. **E-mail:** larsenpoma@aol.com. **Website:** www.larsen-pomada.com. **Contact:** Mike Larsen, Elizabeth Pomada. Member of AAR. Other memberships include Authors Guild, ASJA, PEN, WNBA, California Writers Club, National Speakers Association. Represents 100 clients. 40-45% of clients are new/unpublished writers. Currently handles: nonfiction books 70%, novels 30%.

MEMBER AGENTS Michael Larsen (nonfiction); Elizabeth Pomada (fiction & narrative nonfiction).

REPRESENTS **Considers these nonfiction areas:** anthropology, archeology, architecture, art, autobiography, biography, business, current affairs, diet/nutrition, design, economics, environment, ethnic, film, foods, gay/lesbian, health, history, how-to, humor, inspirational, investigative, law, medicine, memoirs, metaphysics, money, music, New Age, popular culture, politics, psychology, religious, satire, science, self-help, sociology, sports, travel, women's issues, women's studies, futurism. **Considers these fiction areas:** action, adventure, contemporary issues, crime, detective, ethnic, experimental, family saga, feminist, gay, glitz, historical, humor, inspirational, lesbian, literary, mainstream, mystery, police, religious, romance, satire, suspense, chick lit.

8—ᴦ We have diverse tastes. We look for fresh voices and new ideas. We handle literary, commercial and genre fiction, and the full range of nonfiction books. Actively seeking commercial, genre, and literary fiction. Does not want to receive children's books, plays, short stories, screenplays, pornography, poetry or stories of abuse.

HOW TO CONTACT Query with SASE. **Elizabeth Pomada** handles literary and commercial fiction, romance, thrillers, mysteries, narrative non-fiction and mainstream women's fiction. If you have completed a novel, **please e-mail the first 10 pages and 2-page synopsis to larsenpoma@aol.com**. Use 14-point typeface, double-spaced, as an e-mail letter with no attachments. For nonfiction, please read Michael's *How to Write a Book Proposal* book—available through your library or bookstore, and through our website—so you will know exactly what editors need. Then, before you start writing, send him the title, subtitle, and your promotion plan via conventional mail (with SASE) or e-mail. If sent as e-mail, please include the information in the body of your e-mail with NO attachments. Please allow up to 2 weeks for a response. Responds in 8 weeks to pages or submissions.

TERMS Agent receives 15% commission on domestic sales. Agent receives 20% (30% for Asia) commission on foreign sales. May charge for printing, postage for multiple submissions, foreign mail, foreign phone calls, galleys, books, legal fees.

TIPS "We love helping writers get the rewards and recognition they deserve. If you can write books that meet the needs of the marketplace and you can promote your books, now is the best time ever to be a writer. We must find new writers to make a living, so we are very eager to hear from new writers whose work will interest large houses, and non-fiction writers who can promote their books. For a list of recent sales, helpful info, and three ways to make yourself irresistible to any publisher, please visit our website."

SARAH LAZIN BOOKS

126 Fifth Ave., Suite 300, New York NY 10011. (212)989-5757. **Fax:** (212)989-1393. **E-mail:** manuela@lazinbooks.com; slazin@lazinbooks.com. **Contact:** Sarah Lazin. Member of AAR. Represents 75+ clients. Currently handles: nonfiction books 80%, novels 20%. **MEMBER AGENTS** Sarah Lazin; Manuela Jessel. **REPRESENTS** Nonfiction books, novels. **Considers these nonfiction areas:** narrative nonfiction, history, politics, contemporary affairs, popular culture, music, biography and memoir.

8—π Works with companies who package their books; handles some photography.

HOW TO CONTACT Query with SASE. No e-mail queries. Only accepts queries on referral.

TERMS Agent receives 15% commission on domestic sales. Agent receives 20% commission on foreign sales.

LESCHER & LESCHER, LTD.

346 E. 84th St., New York NY 10028. (212)396-1999. **Fax:** (212)396-1991. **E-mail:** cl@lescherltd.com. **Contact:** Carolyn Larson, agent. Member of AAR. Represents 150 clients. Currently handles: nonfiction books 80%, novels 20%. **REPRESENTS** Nonfiction books, novels. **Considers these nonfiction areas:** biography, cooking, current affairs, history, law, memoirs, popular culture, cookbooks/wines, narrative nonfiction. **Considers these fiction areas:** commercial, literary, mystery, suspense.

8—π Does not want to receive screenplays, science fiction, or romance.

HOW TO CONTACT Query with SASE. Obtains most new clients through recommendations from others.

TERMS Agent receives 15% commission on domestic sales. Agent receives 10% commission on foreign sales.

LEVINE GREENBERG LITERARY AGENCY, INC.

307 Seventh Ave., Suite 2407, New York NY 10001. (212)337-0934. **Fax:** (212)337-0948. **E-mail:** submit@levinegreenberg.com. **Website:** www.levinegreenberg.com. Member of AAR. Represents 250 clients. 33% of clients are new/unpublished writers. Currently handles: nonfiction books 70%, novels 30%.

MEMBER AGENTS James Levine, Daniel Greenberg, Stephanie Kip Rostan, Lindsay Edgecombe, Danielle Svetcov, Elizabeth Fisher, Victoria Skurnick. **REPRESENTS** Nonfiction books, novels. **Considers these nonfiction areas:** New Age, animals, art, biography, business, child, computers, cooking, gardening, gay, health, money, nature, religion, science, self help, sociology, spirituality, sports, women's. **Considers these fiction areas:** literary, mainstream, mystery, thriller, psychological, women's.

8—π This agency specializes in business, psychology, parenting, health/medicine, narrative nonfiction, spirituality, religion, women's issues, and commercial fiction.

HOW TO CONTACT See website for full submission procedure at "How to Submit." Or use our e-mail address if you prefer, or online submission form. Do not submit directly to agents. Prefers electronic submissions. Cannot respond to submissions by mail. Obtains most new clients through recommendations from others.

TERMS Agent receives 15% commission on domestic sales. Agent receives 20% commission on foreign sales. Offers written contract. Charges clients for out-of-pocket expenses—telephone, fax, postage, photocopying—directly connected to the project.

TIPS "We focus on editorial development, business representation, and publicity and marketing strategy."

LIVING WORD LITERARY AGENCY

P.O. Box 40974, Eugene OR 97414. **E-mail:** livingwordliterary@gmail.com. **Website:** livingwordliterary.wordpress.com. **Contact:** Kimberly Shumate/Agent. Estab. 2008. Member Evangelical Christian Publishers Association

REPRESENTS Considers nonfiction areas: health, parenting, self-help, relationships. **Considers fiction areas:** inspirational, adult fiction, Christian living.

8—π Does not want to receive cookbooks, children's books, science fiction or fantasy, memoirs, screenplays or poetry.

HOW TO CONTACT Submit a query with short synopsis and first chapter via Word document. Agency only responds if interested.

LOWENSTEIN ASSOCIATES INC.

121 W. 27th St., Suite 601, New York NY 10001. (212)206-1630. **Fax:** (212)727-0280. **E-mail:** assistant@bookhaven.com. **Website:** www.lowensteinassociates.com. **Contact:** Barbara Lowenstein. Mem-

ber of AAR. Represents 150 clients. 20% of clients are new/unpublished writers. Currently handles: nonfiction books 60%, novels 40%.

MEMBER AGENTS Barbara Lowenstein, president (nonfiction interests include narrative nonfiction, health, money, finance, travel, multicultural, popular culture, and memoir; fiction interests include literary fiction and women's fiction); Kathleen Ortiz, associate agent and foreign rights manager at Lowenstein Associates. She is seeking children's books (chapter, middle grade, and young adult) and young adult nonfiction.

REPRESENTS Nonfiction books, novels. **Considers these nonfiction areas:** animals, anthropology, archeology, autobiography, biography, business, child guidance, current affairs, education, ethnic, film, government, health, history, how-to, language, literature, medicine, memoirs, money, multicultural, parenting, popular culture, psychology, science, sociology, travel, music; narrative nonfiction; science; film. **Considers fiction areas:** crime, detective, erotica, ethnic, fantasy, feminist, historical, literary, mainstream, mystery, police, romance, suspense, thriller, young adult.

8—π"This agency specializes in health, business, creative nonfiction, literary fiction and commercial fiction—especially suspense, crime and women's issues. We are a full-service agency, handling domestic and foreign rights, film rights and audio rights to all of our books." Lowenstein is currently looking for writers who have a platform and are leading experts in their field, including business, women's issues, psychology, health, science and social issues, and is particularly interested in strong new voices in fiction and narrative nonfiction.

HOW TO CONTACT Please send us a one-page query letter, along with the first 10 pages pasted in the body of the message (if fiction; for nonfiction, please send only a query letter), by e-mail. Please put the word QUERY and the title of your project in the subject field of your e-mail and address it to the agent of your choice. Please do not send an attachment. We reply to all queries and generally send a response within 2-4 weeks. By mail: For Fiction: Mail a query letter, short synopsis, first chapter and a SASE For Nonfiction: Mail a query letter, proposal, if available, or else a project overview and a SASE. Responds in 4 weeks to queries. Obtains most new clients through recommendations from others, solicitations, conferences.

TERMS Agent receives 15% commission on domestic sales. Agent receives 20% commission on foreign sales. Offers written contract. Charges for large photocopy batches, messenger service, international postage.

TIPS "Know the genre you are working in and read! Also, please see our website for details on which agent to query for your project."

LYONS LITERARY, LLC

27 West 20th St., Suite 10003, New York NY 10011. (212)255-5472. **Fax:** (212)851-8405. **E-mail:** info@lyonsliterary.com. **Website:** www.lyonsliterary.com. **Contact:** Jonathan Lyons. Member of AAR. Other memberships include Author's Guild, American Bar Association, NY State Bar Associaton, New York State Intellectual Property Law Section. Represents 37 clients. 15% of clients are new/unpublished writers. Currently handles: nonfiction books 60%, novels 40%.

REPRESENTS Nonfiction books, novels. **Considers these nonfiction areas:** animals, autobiography, biography, cooking, crafts, cultural interests, current affairs, diet/nutrition, ethnic, foods, gay/lesbian, government, health, history, hobbies, how-to, humor, law, medicine, memoirs, military, money, multicultural, popular culture, politics, psychology, science, sociology, sports, technology, translation, travel, true crime, women's issues, women's studies. **Considers these fiction areas:** contemporary issues, crime, detective, fantasy, feminist, gay, historical, humor, lesbian, literary, mainstream, mystery, police, psychic, regional, satire, science fiction, sports, supernatural, suspense, thriller, women's, chick lit.

8—π"With my legal expertise and experience selling domestic and foreign language book rights, paperback reprint rights, audio rights, film/TV rights and permissions, I am able to provide substantive and personal guidance to my clients in all areas relating to their projects. In addition, with the advent of new publishing technology, Lyons Literary, LLC is situated to address the changing nature of the industry while concurrently handling authors' more traditional needs."

HOW TO CONTACT Only accepts queries through online submission form. Accepts simultaneous submissions. Responds in 8 weeks to queries. Responds in 12 weeks to mss. Obtains most new clients through recommendations from others.

TERMS Agent receives 15% commission on domestic sales. Agent receives 20% commission on foreign sales. Offers written contract.

TIPS "Please submit electronic queries through our website submission form."

DONALD MAASS LITERARY AGENCY

121 W. 27th St., Suite 801, New York NY 10001. (212)727-8383. **E-mail:** info@maassagency.com. **Website:** www.maassagency.com. Member of AAR. Other memberships include SFWA, MWA, RWA. Represents more than 100 clients. 5% of clients are new/unpublished writers. Currently handles: novels 100%.

MEMBER AGENTS Donald Maass (mainstream, literary, mystery/suspense, science fiction, romance); Jennifer Jackson (commercial fiction, romance, science fiction, fantasy, mystery/suspense); Cameron McClure (literary, mystery/suspense, urban, fantasy, narrative nonfiction and projects with multicultural, international, and environmental themes, gay/lesbian); Stacia Decker (fiction, memoir, narrative nonfiction, pop-culture [cooking, fashion, style, music, art], smart humor, upscale erotica/erotic memoir and multicultural fiction/nonfiction); Amy Boggs (fantasy/science fiction, especially urban fantasy, paranormal romance, steampunk, YA/children's, and alternate history. historical fiction, multicultural fiction, westerns).

REPRESENTS Considers these nonfiction areas: , narrative nonfiction (and see J.L's bio for subject interest). **Considers these fiction areas:** crime, detective, fantasy, historical, horror, literary, mainstream, mystery, police, psychic, science fiction, supernatural, suspense, thriller, women's, romance (historical, paranormal, and time travel).

⚷ This agency specializes in commercial fiction, especially science fiction, fantasy, mystery and suspense. Actively seeking to expand in literary fiction and women's fiction. We are fiction specialists. All genres are welcome. Does not want to receive nonfiction, picture books, prescriptive nonfiction, or poetry.

HOW TO CONTACT Query with SASE. Returns material only with SASE. Accepts simultaneous submissions. Responds in 2 weeks to queries. Responds in 3 months to mss.

TERMS Agent receives 15% commission on domestic sales. Agent receives 20% commission on foreign sales.

TIPS We are fiction specialists, also noted for our innovative approach to career planning. Few new clients are accepted, but interested authors should query with a SASE. Works with subagents in all principle foreign countries and Hollywood. No prescriptive nonfiction, picture books, or poetry will be considered.

CAROL MANN AGENCY

55 Fifth Ave., New York NY 10003. (212)206-5635. **Fax:** (212)675-4809. **Website:** www.carolmannagency.com/. **Contact:** Eliza Dreier. Member of AAR. Represents roughly 200 clients. 15% of clients are new/unpublished writers. Currently handles: nonfiction books 90%, novels 10%.

MEMBER AGENTS Carol Mann (health/medical, religion, spirituality, self-help, parenting, narrative nonfiction, current affairs); Laura Yorke; Gareth Esersky; Myrsini Stephanides (nonfiction areas of interest: pop culture and music, humor, narrative nonfiction and memoir, cookbooks; fiction areas of interest: offbeat literary fiction, graphic works, and edgy YA fiction). Joanne Wyckoff (nonfiction areas of interest: memoir, narrative nonfiction, personal narrative, psychology, women's issues, education, health and wellness, parenting, serious self-help, natural history); fiction.

REPRESENTS Nonfiction books, novels. **Considers these nonfiction areas:** anthropology, archeology, architecture, art, autobiography, biography, business, child guidance, cultural interests, current affairs, design, ethnic, government, health, history, law, medicine, money, music, parenting, popular culture, politics, psychology, self-help, sociology, sports, women's issues, women's studies. **Considers these fiction areas:** commercial, literary.

⚷ This agency specializes in current affairs, self-help, popular culture, psychology, parenting, and history. Does not want to receive genre fiction (romance, mystery, etc.).

HOW TO CONTACT Please see website for submission guidelines. Responds in 4 weeks to queries.

TERMS Agent receives 15% commission on domestic sales. Agent receives 20% commission on foreign sales. Offers written contract.

MANUS & ASSOCIATES LITERARY AGENCY, INC.

425 Sherman Ave., Suite 200, Palo Alto CA 94306. (650)470-5151. **Fax:** (650)470-5159. **E-mail:** manuslit@manuslit.com. **Website:** www.manuslit.

com. **Contact:** Jillian Manus, Jandy Nelson, Penny Nelson. Member of AAR. Represents 75 clients. 30% of clients are new/unpublished writers. Currently handles: nonfiction books 70%, novels 30%.

MEMBER AGENTS Jandy Nelson, jandy@manuslit.com (self-help, health, memoirs, narrative nonfiction, women's fiction, literary fiction, multicultural fiction, thrillers). Nelson is currently on sabbatical and not taking on new clients. Jillian Manus, jillian@manuslit.com (political, memoirs, self-help, history, sports, women's issues, Latin fiction and nonfiction, thrillers); Penny Nelson, penny@manuslit.com (memoirs, self-help, sports, nonfiction); Dena Fischer (literary fiction, mainstream/commercial fiction, chick lit, women's fiction, historical fiction, ethnic/cultural fiction, narrative nonfiction, parenting, relationships, pop culture, health, sociology, psychology); Janet Wilkens Manus (narrative fact-based crime books, religion, pop psychology, inspiration, memoirs, cookbooks); Stephanie Lee (not currently taking on new clients).

REPRESENTS Nonfiction books, novels. **Considers these nonfiction areas:** autobiography, biography, business, child guidance, cultural interests, current affairs, economics, environment, ethnic, health, how-to, medicine, memoirs, money, parenting, popular culture, psychology, science, self-help, technology, women's issues, women's studies, Gen X and Gen Y issues; creative nonfiction. **Considers these fiction areas:** literary, mainstream, multicultural, mystery, suspense, thriller, women's, quirky/edgy fiction.

8—m "Our agency is unique in the way that we not only sell the material, but we edit, develop concepts, and participate in the marketing effort. We specialize in large, conceptual fiction and nonfiction, and always value a project that can be sold in the TV/feature film market." Actively seeking high-concept thrillers, commercial literary fiction, women's fiction, celebrity biographies, memoirs, multicultural fiction, popular health, women's empowerment and mysteries. No horror, romance, science fiction, fantasy, western, young adult, children's, poetry, cookbooks, or magazine articles.

HOW TO CONTACT Query with SASE. If requested, submit outline, 2-3 sample chapters. All queries should be sent to the California office. Accepts simultaneous submissions. Responds in 3 months to queries. Responds in 3 months to mss. Obtains most new

clients through recommendations from others, solicitations, conferences.

TERMS Agent receives 15% commission on domestic sales. Agent receives 20-25% commission on foreign sales. Offers written contract, binding for 2 years; 60-day notice must be given to terminate contract. Charges for photocopying and postage/UPS.

TIPS "Research agents using a variety of sources."

THE EVAN MARSHALL AGENCY

6 Tristam Place, Pine Brook NJ 07058-9445. (973)882-1122. **Fax:** (973)882-3099. **E-mail:** evanmarshall@optonline.net. **Contact:** Evan Marshall. Member of AAR. Other memberships include MWA, Sisters in Crime. Currently handles: novels 100%.

REPRESENTS **Considers these fiction areas:** action, adventure, erotica, ethnic, frontier, historical, horror, humor, inspirational, literary, mainstream, mystery, religious, satire, science fiction, suspense, western, romance (contemporary, gothic, historical, regency).

HOW TO CONTACT Do not query. Currently accepting clients only by referal from editors and our own clients. Responds in 1 week to queries. Responds in 3 months to mss. Obtains most new clients through recommendations from others.

TERMS Agent receives 15% commission on domestic sales. Agent receives 20% commission on foreign sales. Offers written contract.

MARTIN LITERARY MANAGEMENT

7683 SE 27th St., #307, Mercer Island WA 98040. (206)486-1773. **Fax:** (206)466-1774. **E-mail:** sharlene@martinliterarymanagement.com; andrew@martinliterarymanagement.com. **Website:** www.MartinLiteraryManagement.com. **Contact:** Sharlene Martin. 75% of clients are new/unpublished writers.

MEMBER AGENTS Sharlene Martin (nonfiction). Andrew Wetzel, associate agent (fiction).

REPRESENTS **Considers these nonfiction areas:** autobiography, biography, business, child guidance, current affairs, economics, health, history, how-to, humor, inspirational, investigative, medicine, memoirs, parenting, popular culture, psychology, satire, self-help, true crime, women's issues, women's studies.

8—m This agency has strong ties to film/TV. Actively seeking nonfiction that is highly commercial and that can be adapted to film. "We are being inundated with queries and submissions that are wrongfully being submitted to us, which only results in more frustration for the writers."

HOW TO CONTACT Query via e-mail with MS Word only. No attachments on queries; place letter in body of e-mail. Accepts simultaneous submissions. Responds in 2 weeks to queries. Responds in 3-4 weeks to mss. Obtains most new clients through recommendations from others.

TERMS Agent receives 15% commission on domestic sales; 25% commission on foreign sales. Offers written contract, binding for 1 year; 1-month notice must be given to terminate contract. Charges author for postage and copying if material is not sent electronically. 99% of materials are sent electronically to minimize charges to author for postage and copying.

TIPS "Have a strong platform for nonfiction. Please don't call. I welcome e-mail. I'm very responsive when I'm interested in a query and work hard to get my clients' materials in the best possible shape before submissions. Do your homework prior to submission and only submit your best efforts. Please review our website carefully to make sure we're a good match for your work. If you read my book, *Publish Your Nonfiction Book: Strategies For Learning the Industry, Selling Your Book and Building a Successful Career* (Writer's Digest Books) you'll know exactly how to charm me."

MARGRET MCBRIDE LITERARY AGENCY

P.O. Box 9128, La Jolla CA 92038. (858)454-1550. **Fax:** (858)454-2156. **E-mail:** staff@mcbridelit.com. **Website:** www.mcbrideliterary.com. **Contact:** Michael Daley, submissions manager. Member of AAR. Other memberships include Authors Guild.

REPRESENTS Nonfiction, novels. **Considers nonfiction areas:** autobiography, biography, business, cooking, cultural interests, current affairs, economics, ethnic, foods, government, health, history, how-to, law, medicine, money, popular culture, politics, psychology, science, self-help, sociology, technology, women's issues, style. **Considers fiction areas:** action, adventure, crime, detective, historical, humor, literary, mainstream, mystery, police, satire, suspense, thriller.

8—➤ This agency specializes in mainstream fiction and nonfiction. Please do not send: screenplays, romance, poetry, or children's.

HOW TO CONTACT The agency is only accepting new clients by referral at this time. Query with synopsis, bio, SASE. Do not fax queries. Accepts simultaneous submissions. Responds in 4-6 weeks to queries. Responds in 6-8 weeks to mss.

TERMS Agent receives 15% commission on domestic sales. Agent receives 25% commission on foreign sales. Charges for overnight delivery and photocopying.

MENDEL MEDIA GROUP, LLC

115 W. 30th St., Suite 800, New York NY 10001. (646)239-9896. **Fax:** (212)685-4717. **E-mail:** scott@mendelmedia.com. **Website:** www.mendelmedia.com. Member of AAR. Represents 40-60 clients.

REPRESENTS Nonfiction books, novels, scholarly, with potential for broad/popular appeal. **Considers these nonfiction areas:** Americana, animals, anthropology, architecture, art, biography, business, child guidance, cooking, current affairs, dance, diet/nutrition, education, environment, ethnic, foods, gardening, gay/lesbian, government, health, history, how-to, humor, investigative, language, medicine, memoirs, military, money, multicultural, music, parenting, philosophy, popular culture, psychology, recreation, regional, religious, science, self-help, sex, sociology, software, spirituality, sports, true crime, war, women's issues, women's studies, Jewish topics, creative nonfiction. **Considers these fiction areas:** action, adventure, contemporary issues, crime, detective, erotica, ethnic, feminist, gay, glitz, historical, humor, inspirational, juvenile, lesbian, literary, mainstream, mystery, picture books, police, religious, romance, satire, sports, thriller, young adult, Jewish fiction.

8—➤ "I am interested in major works of history, current affairs, biography, business, politics, economics, science, major memoirs, narrative nonfiction, and other sorts of general nonfiction. Actively seeking new, major or definitive work on a subject of broad interest, or a controversial, but authoritative, new book on a subject that affects many people's lives. I also represent more light-hearted nonfiction projects, such as gift or novelty books, when they suit the market particularly well. Does not want queries about projects written years ago that were unsuccessfully shopped to a long list of trade publishers by either the author or another agent. I am specifically not interested in reading short, category romances (regency, time travel, paranormal, etc.), horror novels, supernatural stories, poetry, original plays, or film scripts."

HOW TO CONTACT Query with SASE. Do not e-mail or fax queries. For nonfiction, include a complete, fully edited book proposal with sample chapters. For fiction, include a complete synopsis and no more than 20 pages of sample text. Responds in 2 weeks to queries. Responds in 4-6 weeks to mss. Obtains most new clients through recommendations from others.

TERMS Agent receives 15% commission on domestic sales. Agent receives 20% commission on foreign sales.

TIPS "While I am not interested in being flattered by a prospective client, it does matter to me that she knows why she is writing to me in the first place. Is one of my clients a colleague of hers? Has she read a book by one of my clients that led her to believe I might be interested in her work? Authors of descriptive nonfiction should have real credentials and expertise in their subject areas, either as academics, journalists, or policy experts, and authors of prescriptive nonfiction should have legitimate expertise and considerable experience communicating their ideas in seminars and workshops, in a successful business, through the media, etc."

HOWARD MORHAIM LITERARY AGENCY

30 Pierrepont St., Brooklyn NY 11201. (718)222-8400. **Fax:** (718)222-5056. **Website:** www.morhaimliterary.com. Member of AAR.

MEMBER AGENTS Howard Morhaim, Kate McKean, Katie Menick.

⊶ Actively seeking fiction, nonfiction, and young adult novels.

HOW TO CONTACT Query via e-mail with cover letter and three sample chapters. See each agent's listing for specifics.

WILLIAM MORRIS AGENCY, INC.

1325 Avenue of the Americas, New York NY 10019. (212)586-5100. **Fax:** (212)246-3583. **Website:** www.wma.com. **Contact:** Literary Department Coordinator. Alternate address: One William Morris Place, Beverly Hills CA 90212. (310)285-9000. **Fax:** (310)859-4462. Member of AAR.

MEMBER AGENTS Owen Laster; Jennifer Rudolph Walsh; Suzanne Gluck; Joni Evans; Tracy Fisher; Mel Berger; Jay Mandel; Peter Franklin; Lisa Grubka; Jonathan Pecursky.

REPRESENTS Nonfiction books, novels, TV, movie scripts, feature film.

⊶ Does not want to receive screenplays.

HOW TO CONTACT Query with synopsis, publication history, SASE. Send book queries to the NYC address. Accepts simultaneous submissions.

TERMS Agent receives 15% commission on domestic sales. Agent receives 20% commission on foreign sales.

TIPS "If you are a prospective writer interested in submitting to the William Morris Agency in **London**, please follow these guidelines: For all queries, please send a cover letter, synopsis, and the first three chapters (up to 50 pages) by e-mail only to: dkar@wmeentertainment.com."

JEAN V. NAGGAR LITERARY AGENCY, INC.

216 E. 75th St., Suite 1E, New York NY 10021. (212)794-1082. **E-mail:** jweltz@jvnla.com; jvnla@jvnla.com; jregel@jvnla.com; atasman@jvnla.com; atasman@jvnla.com. **Website:** www.jvnla.com. **Contact:** Jean Naggar. Member of AAR. Other memberships include PEN, Women's Media Group, Women's Forum, SCBWI. Represents 450 clients. 20% of clients are new/unpublished writers. Currently handles: nonfiction 35%, novels 45%, juvenile 15%, scholarly 5%.

MEMBER AGENTS Jennifer Weltz (subrights, children's, adults); Jessica Regel (young adult, adult, subrights); Jean Naggar (taking no new clients); Alice Tasman (adult, children's); Elizabeth Evans (adult nonfiction, some fiction and YA).

REPRESENTS Nonfiction books, novels. **Considers these nonfiction areas:** biography, child guidance, current affairs, government, health, history, juvenile nonfiction, law, medicine, memoirs, New Age, parenting, politics, psychology, self-help, sociology, travel, women's issues, women's studies. **Considers these fiction areas:** action, adventure, crime, detective, ethnic, family saga, feminist, historical, literary, mainstream, mystery, police, psychic, supernatural, suspense, thriller.

⊶ This agency specializes in mainstream fiction and nonfiction and literary fiction with commercial potential.

HOW TO CONTACT Query via e-mail. Prefers to read materials exclusively. No fax queries. Responds in 1 day to queries. Responds in 2 months to mss. Obtains most new clients through recommendations from others.

TERMS Agent receives 15% commission on domestic sales. Agent receives 20% commission on foreign sales. Offers written contract. Charges for overseas mailing, messenger services, book purchases, long-distance telephone, photocopying—all deductible from royalties received.

TIPS "Use a professional presentation. Because of the avalanche of unsolicited queries that flood the agency every week, we have had to modify our policy. We will now only guarantee to read and respond to queries from writers who come recommended by someone we know. Our areas are general fiction and nonfiction—no children's books by unpublished writers, no multimedia, no screenplays, no formula fiction, and no mysteries by unpublished writers. We recommend patience and fortitude: the courage to be true to your own vision, the fortitude to finish a novel and polish it again and again before sending it out, and the patience to accept rejection gracefully and wait for the stars to align themselves appropriately for success."

NELSON LITERARY AGENCY

1732 Wazee St., Suite 207, Denver CO 80202. (303)292-2805. **E-mail:** query@nelsonagency.com. **Website:** www.nelsonagency.com. **Contact:** Kristin Nelson, president and senior literary agent; Sara Megibow, associate literary agent. Member of AAR. RWA, SCBWI, SFWA.

REPRESENTS Novels, select nonfiction. **Considers these nonfiction areas:** memoirs. **Considers these fiction areas:** commercial, literary, mainstream, women's, chick lit (includes mysteries), romance (includes fantasy with romantic elements, science fiction, fantasy, young adult).

☞ NLA specializes in representing commercial fiction and high-caliber literary fiction. Actively seeking Latina writers who tackle contemporary issues in a modern voice (think *Dirty Girls Social Club*). Does not want short story collections, mysteries (except chick lit), thrillers, Christian, horror, or children's picture books.

HOW TO CONTACT Query by e-mail only.

HAROLD OBER ASSOCIATES

425 Madison Ave., New York NY 10017. (212)759-8600. **Fax:** (212)759-9428. **Website:** www.haroldober.com. **Contact:** Appropriate agent. Member of AAR. Represents 250 clients. 10% of clients are new/unpublished writers. Currently handles: nonfiction books 35%, novels 50%, juvenile books 15%.

MEMBER AGENTS Phyllis Westberg; Pamela Malpas; Craig Tenney (few new clients, mostly Ober backlist); Jake Elwell (previously with Elwell & Weiser).

HOW TO CONTACT Submit concise query letter addressed to a specific agent with the first 5 pages of the ms or proposal and SASE. No fax or e-mail. Does not handle filmscripts or plays. Responds as promptly as possible. Obtains most new clients through recommendations from others.

TERMS Agent receives 15% commission on domestic sales. Agent receives 20% commission on foreign sales. Charges clients for express mail/package services.

HELEN F. PRATT INC.

1165 Fifth Ave., New York NY 10029. (212)722-5081. **Fax:** (212)722-8569. **E-mail:** hfpratt@verizon.net. **Contact:** Helen F. Pratt. Member of AAR. Currently handles: other 100% illustrated books and nonfiction.

MEMBER AGENTS Helen Pratt (illustrated books, fashion/decorative design nonfiction); Seamus Mullarky (does not accept unsolicited queries).

REPRESENTS nonfiction books, illustrated books. **Considers these nonfiction areas:** , biography, cookbooks, gardening, memoirs, psychology, and especially gardening. **Considers these fiction areas:** children's and young adult.

HOW TO CONTACT Query with SASE. Include illustrations if possible.

AARON M. PRIEST LITERARY AGENCY

708 3rd Ave., 23rd Floor, New York NY 10017-4201. (212)818-0344. **Fax:** (212)573-9417. **Website:** www.aaronpriest.com. Estab. 1974. Member of AAR. Currently handles: nonfiction books 25%, novels 75%.

MEMBER AGENTS Aaron Priest, querypriest@aaronpriest.com (thrillers, commercial fiction, biographies); Lisa Erbach Vance, queryvance@aaronpriest.com (general fiction, international fiction, thrillers, upmarket women's fiction, historical fiction, narrative nonfiction, memoir); Lucy Childs Baker, querychilds@aaronpriest.com (literary and commercial fiction, memoir, edgy women's fiction); Nicole Kenealy, querykenealy@aaronpriest.com (young adult fiction, narrative nonfiction, how-to, political, and pop-culture, literary and commercial fiction, specifically dealing with social and cultural issues).

☞ Does not want poetry, screenplays or sci-fi.

HOW TO CONTACT Query using appropriate e-mail listed online. "Please do not submit to more than 1 agent. We urge you to check our website and consider each agent's emphasis before submitting. Your query letter should be about one page long and describe your work as well as your background. You may also paste the first chapter of your work in the body of the e-mail. Do not send attachments." Accepts simultaneous submissions. Responds in 3 weeks, only if interested.

TERMS Agent receives 15% commission on domestic sales. This agency charges for photocopying and postage expenses.

HELEN REES LITERARY AGENCY

14 Beacon St., Suite 710, Boston MA 02108. (617)227-9014. **Fax:** (617)227-8762. **E-mail:** reesagency@reesagency.com. **Website:** http://reesagency.com. **Contact:** Joan Mazmanian, Ann Collette, Helen Rees, Lorin Rees. Estab. 1983. Member of AAR. Other memberships include PEN. Represents more than 100 clients. 50% of clients are new/unpublished writers. Currently handles: nonfiction books 60%, novels 40%.

MEMBER AGENTS Ann Collette (literary, mystery, thrillers, suspense, vampire, and women's fiction; in nonfiction, she prefers true crime, narrative nonfiction, military and war, work to do with race and class, and work set in or about Southeast Asia. Ann can be reached at: Agent10702@aol.com). Lorin Rees (literary fiction, memoirs, business books, self-help, science, history, psychology, and narrative nonfiction. lorin@reesagency.com).

REPRESENTS Nonfiction books, novels. **Considers these nonfiction areas:** autobiography, biography, business, current affairs, economics, government, health, history, law, medicine, money, politics, women's issues, women's studies. **Considers these fiction areas:** historical, literary, mainstream, mystery, suspense, thriller.

HOW TO CONTACT Query with SASE, outline, 2 sample chapters. No unsolicited e-mail submissions. No multiple submissions. Responds in 3-4 weeks to queries. Obtains most new clients through recommendations from others, conferences, submissions.

TERMS Agent receives 15% commission on domestic sales. Agent receives 20% commission on foreign sales.

REGAL LITERARY AGENCY

236 W. 26th St., #801, New York NY 10001. (212)684-7900. **Fax:** (212)684-7906. **E-mail:** info@regal-literary.com. **Website:** www.regal-literary.com. **Contact:** Barbara Marshall. London Office: 36 Gloucester Ave., Primrose Hill, London NW1 7BB, United Kingdom, uk@regal-literary.com Estab. 2002. Member of AAR. Represents 70 clients. 20% of clients are new/unpublished writers.

⚓ Actively seeking literary fiction and narrative nonfiction. Does not want romance, science fiction, horror, screenplays.

HOW TO CONTACT "Query with SASE. No phone calls or e-mail queries. Submissions should consist of a 1-page query letter detailing the book in question, as well as the qualifications of the author. For fiction, submissions may also include the first 10 pages of the novel or one short story from a collection. We do not consider romance, science fiction, poetry, or screenplays." Accepts simultaneous submissions. Responds in 2-3 weeks to queries. Responds in 4-12 weeks to mss.

TERMS Agent receives 15% commission on domestic sales. Agent receives 20% commission on foreign sales. "We charge no reading fees."

TIPS "We are deeply committed to every aspect of our clients' careers, and are engaged in everything from the editorial work of developing a great book proposal or line editing a fiction manuscript to negotiating state-of-the-art book deals and working to promote and publicize the book when it's published. We are at the forefront of the effort to increase authors' rights in publishing contracts in a rapidly changing commercial environment. We deal directly with co-agents and publishers in every foreign territory and also work directly and with co-agents for feature film and television rights, with extraordinary success in both arenas. Many of our clients' works have sold in dozens of translation markets, and a high proportion of our books have been sold in Hollywood. We have strong relationships with speaking agents, who can assist in arranging author tours and other corporate and college speaking opportunities when appropriate. We also have a staff publicist and marketer to help promote our clients and their work."

JODIE RHODES LITERARY AGENCY

8840 Villa La Jolla Dr., Suite 315, La Jolla CA 92037-1957. **Website:** jodierhodesliterary.com. **Contact:** Jodie Rhodes, president. Member of AAR. Represents 74 clients. 60% of clients are new/unpublished writers. Currently handles: nonfiction books 45%, novels 35%, juvenile books 20%.

MEMBER AGENTS Jodie Rhodes; Clark McCutcheon (fiction); Bob McCarter (nonfiction).

REPRESENTS Nonfiction books, novels. **Considers these nonfiction areas:** autobiography, biography, child guidance, cultural interests, ethnic, government, health, history, law, medicine, memoirs, military, parenting, politics, science, technology, war, women's issues, women's studies. **Considers these fiction areas:** ethnic, family saga, historical, literary, mainstream, mystery, suspense, thriller, women's, young adult.

⚓ "Actively seeking witty, sophisticated women's books about career ambitions and relationships; edgy/trendy young adult and teen books; narrative nonfiction on groundbreaking scientific discoveries, politics, economics, military; and important current affairs by prominent scientists and academic professors." Does not want to receive erotica, horror, fantasy, romance, science fiction, religious/inspirational, or children's books (does accept YA/teen).

HOW TO CONTACT Query with brief synopsis, first 30-50 pages, SASE. Do not call. Do not send complete ms unless requested. This agency does not return unrequested material weighing a pound or more that requires special postage. Include e-mail address with query. Accepts simultaneous submissions. Responds in 3 weeks to queries. Obtains most new clients through recommendations from others, agent sourcebooks.

TERMS Agent receives 15% commission on domestic sales. Agent receives 20% commission on foreign sales. Offers written contract; 1-month notice must be given to terminate contract. Charges clients for fax, photocopying, phone calls, postage. Charges are itemized and approved by writers upfront.

TIPS "Think your book out before you write it. Do your research, know your subject matter intimately, and write vivid specifics, not bland generalities. Care deeply about your book. Don't imitate other writers. Find your own voice. We never take on a book we don't believe in, and we go the extra mile for our writers. We welcome talented, new writers."

☺ THE RIGHTS FACTORY

P.O. Box 499, Station C, Toronto ON M6J 3P6 Canada. (416)966-5367. **Website:** www.therightsfactory.com. **MEMBER AGENTS** Sam Hiyate, Alisha Sevigny, Ali McDonald.

☛ "The Rights Factory is an agency that deals in intellectual property rights to entertainment products, including books, comics and graphic novels, film, television, and video games. We license rights in every territory by representing three types of clients."

HOW TO CONTACT There is a submission form on this agency's website.

ANGELA RINALDI LITERARY AGENCY

P.O. Box 7877, Beverly Hills CA 90212-7877. (310)842-7665. **Fax:** (310)837-8143. **E-mail:** amr@rinaldiliterary.com. **Website:** www.rinaldiliterary.com. **Contact:** Angela Rinaldi. Member of AAR. Represents 50 clients. Currently handles: nonfiction books 50%, novels 50%.

REPRESENTS Nonfiction books, novels, TV and motion picture rights (for clients only). **Considers these nonfiction areas:** biography, business, health books that address specific issues, career, personal finance, self help, true crime, women's issues/studies, current issues, psychology, popular reference, prescriptive and proactive self help, books by journalists, academics, doctors and therapists, based on their research, motivational. **Considers these fiction areas:** commercial/literary fiction, upmarket contemporary women's fiction, suspense, literary historical thrillers like Elizabeth Kostova's *The Historian*, gothic suspense like Diane Setterfield's *The Thirteenth Tale* and Matthew Pearl's *The Dante Club*, women's book club fiction—novels where the story lends itself to discussion like Kim Edwards' *The Memory Keeper's Daughter*.

☛ Actively seeking commercial and literary fiction. Does not want to receive humor, techno thrillers, KGB/CIA espionage, drug thrillers, Da Vinci-code thrillers, category romances, science fiction, fantasy, horror, westerns, film scripts, poetry, category romances, magazine articles, religion, occult, supernatural.

HOW TO CONTACT For fiction send first 3 chapters, brief synopsis, SASE or brief e-mail inquiry with the first 10 pages pasted into the e-mail—no attachments unless asked for. For nonfiction, query with detailed letter or outline/proposal, SASE or e-mail—no attachments unless asked for. Do not send certified or metered mail. Responds in 6 weeks to queries that are posted; e-mail queries 2-3 weeks.

TERMS Agent receives 15% commission on domestic sales. Agent receives 25% commission on foreign sales. Offers written contract.

ANN RITTENBERG LITERARY AGENCY, INC.

15 Maiden Lane, Suite 206, New York NY 10038. **Website:** www.rittlit.com. **Contact:** Ann Rittenberg, president; Penn Whaling, associate. Member of AAR. Currently handles: fiction 75%, nonfiction 25%.

REPRESENTS Considers these nonfiction areas: memoirs, women's issues, women's studies. **Considers these fiction areas:** literary, thriller, upmarket fiction.

☞ This agent specializes in literary fiction and literary nonfiction. Does not want to receive screenplays, straight genre fiction, poetry, self-help.

HOW TO CONTACT Query with SASE. Submit outline, 3 sample chapters, SASE. Query via postal mail *only*. Accepts simultaneous submissions. Responds in 6 weeks to queries. Responds in 2 months to mss. Obtains most new clients through referrals from established writers and editors.

TERMS Agent receives 15% commission on domestic sales. Agent receives 20% commission on foreign sales. Offers written contract. This agency charges clients for photocopying only.

RLR ASSOCIATES, LTD.

Literary Department, 7 W. 51st St., New York NY 10019. (212)541-8641. **Fax:** (212)262-7084. **E-mail:** sgould@rlrassociates.net. **Website:** www.rlrassociates.net. **Contact:** Scott Gould. Member of AAR. Represents 50 clients. 25% of clients are new/unpublished writers. Currently handles: nonfiction books 70%, novels 25%, story collections 5%.

REPRESENTS Nonfiction books, novels, short-story collections, scholarly. **Considers these nonfiction areas:** animals, anthropology, archeology, art, autobiography, biography, business, child guidance, cooking, cultural interests, current affairs, decorating, diet/nutrition, economics, education, environment, ethnic, foods, gay/lesbian, government, health, history, humor, inspirational, interior design, language, law, memoirs, money, multicultural, music, parenting, photography, popular culture, politics, psychology, religious, science, self-help, sociology, sports, technology, translation, travel, true crime, women's issues, women's studies. **Considers these fiction areas:** action, adventure, cartoon, comic books, crime, detective, ethnic, experimental, family saga, feminist, gay, historical, horror, humor, lesbian, literary, mainstream, multicultural, mystery, police, satire, sports, suspense.

☞ "We provide a lot of editorial assistance to our clients and have connections." Actively seeking fiction, current affairs, history, art, popular culture, health and business. Does not want to receive screenplays.

HOW TO CONTACT Query by either e-mail or mail. Accepts simultaneous submissions. Responds in 4-8 weeks to queries. Obtains most new clients through recommendations from others.

TERMS Agent receives 15% commission on domestic sales. Agent receives 20% commission on foreign sales. Offers written contract.

TIPS "PLEASE check out our website for more details on our agency."

B.J. ROBBINS LITERARY AGENCY

5130 Bellaire Ave., North Hollywood CA 91607-2908. **E-mail:** Robbinsliterary@gmail.com. **E-mail:** amy.bjrobbinsliterary@gmail.com. **Contact:** (Ms.) B.J. Robbins, or Amy Maldonado. Member of AAR. Represents 40 clients. 50% of clients are new/unpublished writers. Currently handles: nonfiction books 50%, novels 50%.

REPRESENTS Nonfiction books, novels. **Considers these nonfiction areas:** autobiography, biography, cultural interests, current affairs, dance, ethnic, film, health, humor, investigative, medicine, memoirs, music, popular culture, psychology, self-help, sociology, sports, theater, travel, true crime, women's issues, women's studies. **Considers these fiction areas:** crime, detective, ethnic, literary, mainstream, mystery, police, sports, suspense, thriller.

HOW TO CONTACT Query with SASE. Submit outline/proposal, 3 sample chapters, SASE. Accepts e-mail queries (no attachments). Accepts simultaneous submissions. Responds in 2-6 weeks to queries. Responds in 6-8 weeks to mss. Obtains most new clients through conferences, referrals.

TERMS Agent receives 15% commission on domestic sales. Agent receives 20% commission on foreign sales. Offers written contract; 3-month notice must be given to terminate contract. This agency charges clients for postage and photocopying (only after sale of ms).

THE ROSENBERG GROUP

23 Lincoln Ave., Marblehead MA 01945. (781)990-1341. **Fax:** (781)990-1344. **Website:** www.rosenberggroup.com. **Contact:** Barbara Collins Rosenberg. Estab. 1998. Member of AAR. Recognized agent of the RWA. Represents 25 clients. 15% of clients are new/unpublished writers. Currently handles: nonfiction books 30%, novels 30%, scholarly books 10%, 30% college textbooks.

REPRESENTS Nonfiction books, novels, textbooks, college textbooks only. **Considers these nonfiction areas:** current affairs, foods, popular culture, psychology, sports, women's issues, women's studies, women's health, wine/beverages. **Considers these fiction areas:** romance, women's.

☞ Ms. Rosenberg is well-versed in the romance market (both category and single title). She is a frequent speaker at romance conferences. Actively seeking romance category or single title in contemporary romantic suspense, and the historical subgenres. Does not want to receive inspirational, time travel, futuristic or paranormal.

HOW TO CONTACT Query with SASE. No e-mail or fax queries; will not respond. See guidelines on website. Responds in 2 weeks to queries. Responds in 4-6 weeks to mss. Obtains most new clients through recommendations from others, solicitations, conferences.

TERMS Agent receives 15% commission on domestic sales. Agent receives 15% commission on foreign sales. Offers written contract; 1-month notice must be given to terminate contract. Charges maximum of $350/year for postage and photocopying.

RITA ROSENKRANZ LITERARY AGENCY

440 West End Ave., #15D, New York NY 10024-5358. (212)873-6333. **Website:** www.ritarosenkranzliterary-agency.com. **Contact:** Rita Rosenkranz. Member of AAR. Represents 35 clients. 30% of clients are new/unpublished writers. Currently handles: nonfiction books 99%, novels 1%.

REPRESENTS Considers nonfiction areas: animals, anthropology, art, autobiography, biography, business, child guidance, computers, cooking, crafts, cultural interests, current affairs, dance, decorating, economics, ethnic, film, gay, government, health, history, hobbies, how-to, humor, inspirational, interior design, language, law, lesbian, literature, medicine, military, money, music, nature, parenting, personal improvement, photography, popular culture, politics, psychology, religious, satire, science, self-help, sports, technology, theater, war, women's issues, women's studies.

☞ "This agency focuses on adult nonfiction, stresses strong editorial development and refinement before submitting to publishers, and brainstorms ideas with authors." Actively seeks authors who are well paired with their subject, either for professional or personal reasons.

HOW TO CONTACT Send query letter only (no proposal) via regular mail or e-mail. Submit proposal package with SASE only on request. No fax queries. Accepts simultaneous submissions. Responds in 2 weeks to queries. Obtains most new clients through directory listings, solicitations, conferences, word of mouth.

TERMS Agent receives 15% commission on domestic sales; 20% commission on foreign sales. Offers written contract, binding for 3 years; 3-month written notice must be given to terminate contract. Charges clients for photocopying. Makes referrals to editing services.

TIPS "Identify the current competition for your project to make sure the project is valid. A strong cover letter is very important."

ROSS YOON AGENCY

1666 Connecticut Ave. NW, Suite 500, Washington DC 20009. (202)328-3282. **Fax:** (202)328-9162. **E-mail:** submissions@rossyoon.com. **Website:** http://rossyoon.com. **Contact:** Jennifer Manguera. Member of AAR. Represents 200 clients. 75% of clients are new/unpublished writers. Currently handles: nonfiction books 95%.

MEMBER AGENTS Gail Ross (represents important commercial nonfiction in a variety of areas and counts top doctors, CEO's, prize-winning journalists, and historians among her clients. She and her team work closely with first-time authors; gail@rossyoon.com), Howard Yoon (nonfiction topics ranging from current events and politics to culture to religion and history, to smart business; he is also looking for commercial fiction by published authors; howard@rossyoon.com).

REPRESENTS Nonfiction books. **Considers these nonfiction areas:** anthropology, archeology, autobiography, biography, business, cultural interests, economics, education, environment, ethnic, gay/lesbian, government, health, inspirational, investigative, law, medicine, money, politics, psychology, religious, science, self-help, sociology, sports, technology, true crime. **Considers these fiction areas:** , occasional commercial fiction.

☞ "This agency specializes in adult trade nonfiction."

HOW TO CONTACT "Send proposals by e-mail with a cover letter, résumé, brief synopsis of your work, and several sample chapters. We also accept query letters. No longer accepting submissions by mail." Accepts simultaneous submissions. Responds in 4-6 weeks to queries. Obtains most new clients through recommendations from others.

TERMS Agent receives 15% commission on domestic sales. Agent receives 25% commission on foreign sales. Charges for office expenses.

JANE ROTROSEN AGENCY LLC

318 E. 51st St., New York NY 10022. (212)593-4330. **Fax:** (212)935-6985. **Website:** www.janerotrosen.com.

Estab. 1974. Member of AAR. Other memberships include Authors Guild. Represents more than 100 clients. Currently handles: nonfiction books 30%, novels 70%.
MEMBER AGENTS Jane R. Berkey; Andrea Cirillo; Annelise Robey; Meg Ruley; Christina Hogrebe; Peggy Gordijn, director of rights.
REPRESENTS Nonfiction books, novels. **Considers these nonfiction areas:** autobiography, biography, business, child guidance, cooking, current affairs, diet/nutrition, economics, environment, foods, health, how-to, humor, investigative, medicine, money, parenting, popular culture, psychology, satire, self-help, sports, true crime, women's issues, women's studies. **Considers these fiction areas:** crime, family saga, historical, mystery, police, romance, suspense, thriller, women's.
HOW TO CONTACT Query with SASE to the attention of "Submissions." Find appropriate agent contact/e-mail on website. Responds in 2 weeks to writers who have been referred by a client or colleague. Responds in 2 months to mss. Obtains most new clients through recommendations from others.
TERMS Agent receives 15% commission on domestic sales. Agent receives 20% commission on foreign sales. Offers written contract, binding for 3 years; 2-month notice must be given to terminate contract. Charges clients for photocopying, express mail, overseas postage, book purchase.

THE DAMARIS ROWLAND AGENCY

420 E 23rd St., Suite 6F, New York NY 10010-5040. **Contact:** Damaris Rowland. Member of AAR.
REPRESENTS Nonfiction books, novels.
✂━ This agency specializes in women's fiction, literary fiction and nonfiction, and pop fiction.
HOW TO CONTACT Query with synopsis, SASE. Obtains most new clients through recommendations from others, solicitations, conferences.
TERMS Agent receives 15% commission on domestic sales. Agent receives 20% commission on foreign sales. Offers written contract.

RUSSELL & VOLKENING

50 W. 29th St., Suite 7E, New York NY 10001. (212)684-6050. **Fax:** (212)889-3026. **Website:** www.randvinc.com. **Contact:** Jesseca Salky (adult, general fiction and nonfiction, memoirs: jesseca@randvinc.com); Carrie Hannigan (children's and young adult), Josh Getzler (mysteries, thrillers, literary and commercial fiction, young adult and middle grade, particularly adventures and mysteries for boys; e-mail queries only with cover letter and first 5 pages: josh@randvinc.com); Joy Azmitia (chick-lit, multicultural fiction, romance, humor, and nonfiction in the areas of travel, pop culture, and philosophy: joy@randvinc.com). Member of AAR. Represents 140 clients. 20% of clients are new/unpublished writers. Currently handles: nonfiction books 45%, novels 50%, story collections 3%, novella 2%.
REPRESENTS Nonfiction books, novels. **Considers these nonfiction areas:** anthropology, architecture, art, autobiography, biography, business, cooking, cultural interests, current affairs, design, education, environment, ethnic, film, gay/lesbian, government, health, history, language, law, military, money, music, photography, popular culture, politics, psychology, science, sociology, sports, technology, true crime, war, women's issues, women's studies, creative nonfiction. **Considers these fiction areas:** action, adventure, crime, detective, ethnic, literary, mainstream, mystery, picture books, police, sports, suspense, thriller.
✂━ This agency specializes in literary fiction and narrative nonfiction. Actively seeking novels.
HOW TO CONTACT Query only with SASE to appropriate person. Responds in 4 weeks to queries.
TERMS Agent receives 15% commission on domestic sales. Agent receives 20% commission on foreign sales. Charges clients for standard office expenses relating to the submission of materials.
TIPS "If the query is cogent, well written, well presented, and is the type of book we'd represent, we'll ask to see the manuscript. From there, it depends purely on the quality of the work."

THE SAGALYN AGENCY

4922 Fairmont Ave., Suite 200, Bethesda MD 20814. (301)718-6440. **Fax:** (301)718-6444. **E-mail:** query@sagalyn.com. **Website:** www.sagalyn.com. Estab. 1980. Member of AAR. Currently handles: nonfiction books 85%, novels 5%, scholarly books 10%.
MEMBER AGENTS Raphael Sagalyn; Bridget Wagner, Shannon O'Neill.
REPRESENTS Nonfiction books. **Considers these nonfiction areas:** autobiography, biography, business, economics, history, inspirational, memoirs, popular culture, science, technology, journalism.
✂━ Does not want to receive stage plays, screenplays, poetry, science fiction, fantasy, romance, children's books or young adult books.

HOW TO CONTACT Please send e-mail queries only (no attachments). Include 1 of these words in the subject line: query, submission, inquiry.

TIPS "We receive 1,000-1,200 queries a year, which in turn lead to 2 or 3 new clients. Query via e-mail only. See our website for sales information and recent projects."

VICTORIA SANDERS & ASSOCIATES

241 Avenue of the Americas, Suite 11 H, New York NY 10014. (212)633-8811. **Fax:** (212)633-0525. **E-mail:** queriesvsa@gmail.com. **Website:** www.victoriasanders.com. **Contact:** Victoria Sanders, Diane Dickensheid. Estab. 1992. Member of AAR. Signatory of WGA. Represents 135 clients. 25% of clients are new/unpublished writers. Currently handles: nonfiction books 30%, novels 70%.

MEMBER AGENTS Tanya McKinnon, Victoria Sanders, Chris Kepner (open to all types of books as long as the writing is exceptional. Include the first three chapters in the body of the e-mail. At the moment, he is especially on the lookout for quality nonfiction).

REPRESENTS Nonfiction books, novels. **Considers these nonfiction areas:** autobiography, biography, cultural interests, current affairs, dance, ethnic, film, gay/lesbian, government, history, humor, language, law, literature, music, popular culture, politics, psychology, satire, theater, translation, women's issues, women's studies. **Considers these fiction areas:** action, adventure, contemporary issues, ethnic, family saga, feminist, gay, lesbian, literary, thriller.

HOW TO CONTACT Query by e-mail only.

TERMS Agent receives 15% commission on domestic sales. Agent receives 20% commission on foreign sales. Offers written contract. Charges for photocopying, messenger, express mail. If in excess of $100, client approval is required.

TIPS "Limit query to letter (no calls) and give it your best shot. A good query is going to get a good response."

HAROLD SCHMIDT LITERARY AGENCY

415 W. 23rd St., #6F, New York NY 10011. **Contact:** Harold Schmidt, Acquisitions. Estab. 1984. Member of AAR. Represents 3 clients.

REPRESENTS Considers these fiction areas: contemporary issues, gay, literary, original quality fiction with unique narrative voices, high quality psychological suspense and thrillers, likes offbeat/quirky.

8—📌 Actively seeking novels.

HOW TO CONTACT Query with by mail with SASE or e-mail; do not send material without being asked. No telephone or e-mail queries. We will respond if interested. Do not send material unless asked as it cannot be read or returned.

SUSAN SCHULMAN LITERARY AGENCY

454 W. 44th St., New York NY 10036. (212)713-1633. **Fax:** (212)581-8830. **E-mail:** schulmanqueries@yahoo.com. **Contact:** Susan Schulman. Estab. 1980. Member of AAR. Signatory of WGA. Other memberships include Dramatists Guild. 10% of clients are new/unpublished writers. Currently handles: nonfiction books 50%, novels 25%, juvenile books 15%, stage plays 10%.

MEMBER AGENTS Linda Kiss, director of foreign rights; Katherine Stones, theater; Emily Uhry, submissions editor.

REPRESENTS Considers these nonfiction areas: anthropology, archeology, autobiography, biography, business, child guidance, cooking, cultural interests, current affairs, dance, diet/nutrition, economics, education, environment, ethnic, foods, gay/lesbian, government, health, history, how-to, inspirational, investigative, language, law, literature, medicine, memoirs, money, music, parenting, popular culture, politics, psychology, religious, self-help, sociology, sports, true crime, women's issues, women's studies. **Considers these fiction areas:** action, adventure, crime, detective, feminist, historical, humor, inspirational, juvenile, literary, mainstream, mystery, picture books, police, religious, suspense, women's, young adult.

8—📌 "We specialize in books for, by and about women and women's issues including self-help books, fiction and theater projects. We also handle film, television and allied rights for several agencies as well as foreign rights for several publishing houses." Actively seeking nonfiction. Considers plays. Does not want to receive poetry, TV scripts or concepts for television.

HOW TO CONTACT Query with SASE. Submit outline, synopsis, author bio, 3 sample chapters. Accepts simultaneous submissions. Responds in 6 weeks to queries/mss. Obtains most new clients through recommendations from others, solicitations, conferences.

TERMS Agent receives 15% commission on domestic sales. Agent receives 20% commission on foreign sales. Offers written contract; 30-day notice must be given to terminate contract.

TIPS "Keep writing!" Schulman describes her agency as "professional boutique, long-standing, eclectic."

SCOVIL GALEN GHOSH LITERARY AGENCY, INC.

276 Fifth Ave., Suite 708, New York NY 10001. (212)679-8686. **Fax:** (212)679-6710. **E-mail:** info@sgglit.com. **Website:** www.sgglit.com. **Contact:** Russell Galen. Estab. 1992. Member of AAR. Represents 300 clients. Currently handles: nonfiction books 60%, novels 40%.

MEMBER AGENTS Jack Scovil, jackscovil@sgglit.com; Russell Galen, russellgalen@sgglit.com (novels that stretch the bounds of reality; strong, serious nonfiction books on almost any subject that teach something new; no books that are merely entertaining, such as diet or pop psych books; serious interests include science, history, journalism, biography, business, memoir, nature, politics, sports, contemporary culture, literary nonfiction, etc.); Anna Ghosh, annaghosh@sgglit.com (strong nonfiction proposals on all subjects, as well as adult commercial and literary fiction by both unpublished and published authors; serious interests include investigative journalism, literary nonfiction, history, biography, memoir, popular culture, science, adventure, art, food, religion, psychology, alternative health, social issues, women's fiction, historical novels and literary fiction); Ann Behar, annbehar@sgglit.com (juvenile books for all ages).

REPRESENTS Nonfiction books, novels.

HOW TO CONTACT E-mail queries strongly preferred. Accepts simultaneous submissions.

THE SEYMOUR AGENCY

475 Miner St., Canton NY 13617. (315)386-1831. **E-mail:** marysue@twcny.rr.com; nicole@theseymouragency.com. **Website:** www.theseymouragency.com. **Contact:** Mary Sue Seymour, Nicole Resciniti. Member of AAR. Signatory of WGA. Other memberships include RWA, Authors Guild. Represents 50 clients. 5% of clients are new/unpublished writers. Currently handles: nonfiction books 50%, other 50% fiction.

MEMBER AGENTS Mary Sue Seymour (accepts queries in Christian, inspirational, romance, and nonfiction; Nicole Resciniti (accepts queries in same categories as Ms. Seymour in addition to action/suspense/thriller, mystery, sci-fi, fantasy, and YA/children's).

REPRESENTS nonfiction books, novels. **Considers these nonfiction areas:** business, health, how-to, self help, Christian books; cookbooks; any well-written

nonfiction that includes a proposal in standard format and 1 sample chapter. **Considers these fiction areas:** action, fantasy, mystery, religious, romance, science fiction, suspense, thriller, young adult.

HOW TO CONTACT Query with SASE, synopsis, first 50 pages for romance. Accepts e-mail queries. Accepts simultaneous submissions. Responds in 1 month to queries. Responds in 3 months to mss.

TERMS Agent receives 12-15% commission on domestic sales.

DENISE SHANNON LITERARY AGENCY, INC.

20 W. 22nd St., Suite 1603, New York NY 10010. (212)414-2911. **Fax:** (212)414-2930. **E-mail:** info@deniseshannonagency.com. **E-mail:** submissions@deniseshannonagency.com. **Website:** www.deniseshannonagency.com. **Contact:** Denise Shannon. Estab. 2002. Member of AAR.

REPRESENTS Nonfiction books, novels. **Considers these nonfiction areas:** biography, business, health, narrative nonfiction; politics; journalism; memoir; social history. **Considers these fiction areas:** literary.

☛ "We are a boutique agency with a distinguished list of fiction and nonfiction authors."

HOW TO CONTACT Query by e-mail to: submissions@deniseshannonagency.com, or mail with SASE. Submit query with description of project, bio, SASE. See guidelines online.

TIPS "Please do not send queries regarding fiction projects until a complete manuscript is available for review. We request that you inform us if you are submitting material simultaneously to other agencies."

WENDY SHERMAN ASSOCIATES, INC.

27 W. 24th St., New York NY 10010. (212)279-9027. **E-mail:** wendy@wsherman.com; submissions@wsherman.com. **Website:** www.wsherman.com. **Contact:** Wendy Sherman. Member of AAR. Represents 50 clients. 30% of clients are new/unpublished writers.

MEMBER AGENTS Wendy Sherman, Kim Perel.

REPRESENTS **Considers these nonfiction areas:** memoirs, psychology, narrative; practical. **Considers these fiction areas:** mainstream, Mainstream fiction that hits the sweet spot between literary and commercial.

☛ "We specialize in developing new writers, as well as working with more established writers. My experience as a publisher has proven to be a great asset to my clients."

HOW TO CONTACT Query via e-mail Accepts simultaneous submissions. Responds in 1 month to queries. Obtains most new clients through recommendations from others.

TERMS Agent receives 15% commission on domestic sales; 20% commission on foreign and film sales. Offers written contract.

TIPS "The bottom line is: Do your homework. Be as well prepared as possible. Read the books that will help you present yourself and your work with polish. You want your submission to stand out."

ROSALIE SIEGEL, INTERNATIONAL LITERARY AGENCY, INC.

1 Abey Dr., Pennington NJ 08534. (609)737-1007. **Fax:** (609)737-3708. **Website:** http://rosaliesiegel.com. **Contact:** Rosalie Siegel. Member of AAR. Represents 35 clients. 10% of clients are new/unpublished writers. Currently handles: nonfiction books 45%, novels 45%, 10% YA and short story collections for current clients.

HOW TO CONTACT Obtains most new clients through referrals from writers and friends.

TERMS Agent receives 15% commission on domestic sales; 20% commission on foreign sales. Offers written contract; 2-month notice must be given to terminate contract. Charges clients for photocopying.

SPENCERHILL ASSOCIATES

P.O. Box 374, Chatham NY 12037. (518)392-9293. **Fax:** (518)392-9554. **E-mail:** submissions@spencerhillassociates.com. **Website:** www.spencerhillassociates.com. **Contact:** Karen Solem or Jennifer Schober (please refer to their website for the latest information). Member of AAR. Represents 96 clients. 10% of clients are new/unpublished writers.

MEMBER AGENTS Karen Solem; Jennifer Schober.

REPRESENTS Considers these fiction areas: crime, detective, historical, inspirational, literary, mainstream, police, religious, romance, thriller, young adult.

8—⚮ "We handle mostly commercial women's fiction, historical novels, romance (historical, contemporary, paranormal, urban fantasy), thrillers, and mysteries. We also represent Christian fiction only—no nonfiction." No nonfiction, poetry, science fiction, picture books, or scripts.

HOW TO CONTACT Query submissions@spencerhillassociates.com with synopsis and first three chapters attached as a .doc or .rtf file. "Please note: We no longer accept queries via the mail." Responds in 6-8 weeks to queries "if we are interested in pursuing."

TERMS Agent receives 15% commission on domestic sales. Agent receives 20% commission on foreign sales. Offers written contract; 3-month notice must be given to terminate contract.

PHILIP G. SPITZER LITERARY AGENCY, INC

50 Talmage Farm Lane, East Hampton NY 11937. (631)329-3650. **Fax:** (631)329-3651. **E-mail:** Luc. Hunt@spitzeragency.com. **Website:** www.spitzeragency.com. **Contact:** Luc Hunt. Member of AAR. Represents 60 clients. 10% of clients are new/unpublished writers. Currently handles: nonfiction books 35%, novels 65%.

REPRESENTS Nonfiction books, novels. **Considers these nonfiction areas:** biography, history, investigative, sports, travel, true crime. **Considers these fiction areas:** crime, detective, literary, mainstream, mystery, police, sports, suspense, thriller.

8—⚮ This agency specializes in mystery/suspense, literary fiction, sports and general nonfiction (no how-to).

HOW TO CONTACT Query with SASE. Responds in 2 weeks to queries. Responds in 6 weeks to mss. Obtains most new clients through recommendations from others.

TERMS Agent receives 15% commission on domestic sales. Agent receives 20% commission on foreign sales. Charges clients for photocopying.

STEELE-PERKINS LITERARY AGENCY

26 Island Ln., Canandaigua NY 14424. (585)396-9290. **Fax:** (585)396-3579. **E-mail:** pattiesp@aol.com. **Contact:** Pattie Steele-Perkins. Member of AAR. Other memberships include RWA. Currently handles: novels 100%.

REPRESENTS Considers fiction areas: romance, women's, category romance, romantic suspense, historical, contemporary, multi-cultural, and inspirational.

HOW TO CONTACT Submit synopsis and one chapter via e-mail (no attachments) or snail mail. Snail mail submissions require SASE. Accepts simultaneous submissions. Responds in 6 weeks to queries. Obtains most new clients through recommendations from others, queries/solicitations.

TERMS Agent receives 15% commission on domestic sales. Offers written contract, binding for 1 year; 1-month notice must be given to terminate contract.

TIPS "Be patient. E-mail rather than call. Make sure what you are sending is the best it can be."

STERLING LORD LITERISTIC, INC.

65 Bleecker St., 12th Floor, New York NY 10012. (212)780-6050. **Fax:** (212)780-6095. **E-mail:** info@sll.com. **Website:** www.sll.com. Member of AAR. Signatory of WGA. Represents 600 clients. Currently handles: nonfiction books 50%, novels 50%.

MEMBER AGENTS Sterling Lord; Peter Matson; Philippa Brophy (represents journalists, nonfiction writers and novelists, and is most interested in current events, memoir, science, politics, biography, and women's issues); Chris Calhoun; Claudia Cross (a broad range of fiction and nonfiction, from literary fiction to commercial women's fiction and romance novels, to cookbooks, lifestyle titles, memoirs, serious nonfiction on religious and spiritual topics, and books for the CBA marketplace); Robert Guinsler (literary and commercial fiction, journalism, narrative nonfiction with an emphasis on pop culture, science and current events, memoirs and biographies); Laurie Liss (commercial and literary fiction and nonfiction whose perspectives are well developed and unique); Judy Heiblum (fiction and nonfiction writers, looking for distinctive voices that challenge the reader, emotionally or intellectually. She works with journalists, academics, memoirists, and essayists, and is particularly interested in books that explore the intersections of science, culture, history and philosophy. In addition, she is always looking for writers of literary fiction with fresh, uncompromising voices); Neeti Madan (memoir, journalism, history, pop culture, health, lifestyle, women's issues, multicultural books and virtually any intelligent writing on intriguing topics. Neeti is looking for smart, well-written commercial novels, as well as compelling and provocative literary works); George Nicholson (writers and illustrators for children); Jim Rutman; Ira Silverberg; Douglas Stewart (literary fiction, narrative nonfiction, and young adult fiction).

HOW TO CONTACT Query with SASE by snail mail. Include synopsis of the work, a brief proposal or the first three chapters of the manuscript, and brief bio or resume. Does not respond to unsolicited e-mail queries. Responds in 1 month to mss.

TERMS Agent receives 15% commission on domestic sales. Agent receives 20% commission on foreign sales. Offers written contract. Charges clients for photocopying.

ROBIN STRAUS AGENCY, INC.

229 E. 79th St., Suite 5A, New York NY 10075. (212)472-3282. **Fax:** (212)472-3833. **E-mail:** info@robinstrausagency.com. **Website:** www.robinstrausagency.com/. **Contact:** Ms. Robin Straus. Estab. 1983. Member of AAR.

REPRESENTS Represents high quality adult fiction and nonfiction including literary and commercial fiction, narrative nonfiction, women's fiction, memoirs, history, biographies, books on psychology, popular culture and current affairs, science, parenting, and cookbooks.

➤ Does *not* represent juvenile, young adult, science fiction/fantasy, horror, romance, Westerns, poetry or screenplays.

HOW TO CONTACT If you prefer to submit your queries electronically, please note that we do not download manuscripts. All materials must be included in the body of the e-mail. We do not respond to any submissions that do not include a SASE. No metered postage.

TERMS Agent receives 15% commission on domestic sales. Agent receives 20% commission on foreign sales. Offers written contract. Charges for photocopying, express mail services, messenger and foreign postage, galleys and books for submissions, etc. as incurred.

PAM STRICKLER AUTHOR MANAGEMENT

134 Main St., New Paltz NY 12561. (845)255-0061. **E-mail:** pamstrickleragency@gmail.com. **Website:** www.pamstrickler.com. **Contact:** Pamela Dean Strickler. Member of AAR. Also an associate member of the Historical Novel Society and member of RWA.

REPRESENTS Considers these fiction areas: historical, romance, women's.

➤ Does not want nonfiction or children's books.

HOW TO CONTACT Please, no unsolicited manuscripts. Prefer e-mail queries, including a one-page letter with a brief description of your plot, plus the first 10 pages of your novel all pasted into the body of the e-mail. Unknown attachments will not be opened.

THE STRINGER LITERARY AGENCY, LLC

E-mail: stringerlit@comcast.net. **Website:** www.stringerlit.com. **Contact:** Marlene Stringer.

REPRESENTS Considers these nonfiction areas: history, military, music, parenting, science, sports, middle grade. **Considers these fiction areas:** fantasy, historical, mystery, romance, science fiction, thriller, women's, young adult.

⚲— This agency specializes in fiction. Does not want picture books, plays, short stories or poetry.

HOW TO CONTACT Electronic submissions only. Accepts simultaneous submissions.

TIPS "If your manuscript falls between categories, or you are not sure of the category, query and we'll let you know if we'd like to take a look. We strive to respond as quickly as possible. If you have not received a response in the time period indicated, please re-query."

THE STROTHMAN AGENCY, LLC

197 Eighth St., Flagship Wharf - 611, Charlestown MA 02129. (617)742-2011. **Fax:** (617)742-2014. **E-mail:** strothmanagency@gmail.com. **Website:** www.strothmanagency.com. **Contact:** Wendy Strothman, Lauren MacLeod. Member of AAR. Other memberships include Authors' Guild. Represents 50 clients. Currently handles: nonfiction books 70%, novels 10%, scholarly books 20%.

REPRESENTS Nonfiction books, novels, scholarly, young adult and middle grade. **Considers these nonfiction areas:** business, current affairs, environment, government, history, language, law, literature, politics, travel. **Considers these fiction areas:** literary, young adult, middle grade.

⚲— "Because we are highly selective in the clients we represent, we increase the value publishers place on our properties. We specialize in narrative nonfiction, memoir, history, science and nature, arts and culture, literary travel, current affairs, and some business. We have a highly selective practice in literary fiction, young adult and middle grade fiction, and nonfiction. We are now opening our doors to more commercial fiction but from authors who have a platform. If you have a platform, please mention it in your query letter. The Strothman Agency seeks out scholars, journalists, and other acknowledged and emerging experts in their fields. We are now actively looking for authors of well-written young-adult fiction and nonfiction. Browse the Latest News to get an idea of the types of books that we represent. For more about what we're looking for, read Pitching an Agent: The Strothman Agency on the publishing website www.strothmanagency.com." Does not want to receive commercial fiction, romance, science fiction or self-help.

HOW TO CONTACT Accepts queries only via e-mail at strothmanagency@gmail.com. See submission guidelines online. Accepts simultaneous submissions. Responds in 4 weeks to queries. Responds in 6 weeks to mss. Obtains most new clients through recommendations from others.

TERMS Agent receives 15% commission on domestic sales. Agent receives 20% commission on foreign sales. Offers written contract; 30-day notice must be given to terminate contract.

EMMA SWEENEY AGENCY, LLC

245 E 80th St., Suite 7E, New York NY 10075. **E-mail:** queries@emmasweeneyagency.com. **Website:** www.emmasweeneyagency.com. Member of AAR. Represents 80 clients. 5% of clients new/unpublished writers. Currently handles: nonfiction books 50%, novels 50%.

MEMBER AGENTS Emma Sweeney, president; Eva Talmadge, rights manager and agent (represents literary fiction, young adult novel, and narrative nonfiction. Considers these nonfiction areas: popular science, pop culture and music history, biography, memoirs, cooking, and anything relating to animals. Considers these fiction areas: literary [of the highest writing quality possible], young adult; eva@emmasweeneyagency.com); Justine Wenger, junior agent/assistant (justine@emmasweeneyagency.com).

⚲— "We specialize in quality fiction and nonfiction. Our primary areas of interest include literary and women's fiction, mysteries and thrillers, science, history, biography, memoir, religious studies and the natural sciences." Does not want romance, Westerns or screenplays.

HOW TO CONTACT Send query letter and first 10 pages in body of e-mail (no attachments) to queries@emmasweeneyagency.com. No snail mail queries.

TERMS Agent receives 15% commission on domestic sales. Agent receives 10% commission on foreign sales.

PATRICIA TEAL LITERARY AGENCY

2036 Vista Del Rosa, Fullerton CA 92831-1336. Phone/**Fax:** (714)738-8333. **Contact:** Patricia Teal. Member of AAR. Other memberships include RWA, Authors Guild. Represents 20 clients.

REPRESENTS Nonfiction books, novels. **Considers nonfiction areas:** animals, autobiography, biography, child guidance, health, how-to, investigative, medicine, parenting, psychology, self-help, true crime, women's issues, women's studies. **Considers fiction areas:** glitz, mainstream, mystery, romance, suspense.

☞ This agency specializes in women's fiction, commercial how-to, and self-help nonfiction. Does not want to receive poetry, short stories, articles, science fiction, fantasy, or regency romance.

HOW TO CONTACT Published authors only may query with SASE. Accepts simultaneous submissions. Responds in 10 days to queries. Responds in 6 weeks to mss. Obtains most new clients through conferences, recommendations from authors and editors.

TERMS Agent receives 10-15% commission on domestic sales. Agent receives 20% commission on foreign sales. Offers written contract, binding for 1 year. Charges clients for ms copies.

TIPS "Include SASE with all correspondence. I am taking on published authors only."

TESSLER LITERARY AGENCY, LLC

27 W. 20th St., Suite 1003, New York NY 10011. (212)242-0466. **Fax:** (212)242-2366. **E-mail:** michelle@tessleragency.com. **Website:** www.tessleragency.com. **Contact:** Michelle Tessler. AAR member.
REPRESENTS Nonfiction books, novels.
☞ "The Tessler Agency is a full-service boutique agency that represents writers of literary fiction and high-quality nonfiction in the following categories: popular science, reportage, memoir, history, biography, psychology, business and travel."

HOW TO CONTACT Submit query through website only.

S©OTT TREIMEL NY

434 Lafayette St., New York NY 10003. (212)505-8353. **E-mail:** general@scotttreimelny.com. **Website:** ScottTreimelNY.blogspot.com; www.ScottTreimelNY.com. **Contact:** John M. Cusick. Member of AAR. Other memberships include Authors Guild, SCBWI. 10% of clients are new/unpublished writers. Currently handles: other 100% junvenile/teen books.
REPRESENTS Nonfiction books, novels, juvenile, children's, picture books, young adult.
☞ This agency specializes in tightly focused segments of the trade and institutional markets. Career clients.

HOW TO CONTACT Submissions accepted only via website.

TERMS Agent receives 15% commission on domestic sales. Agent receives 20% commission on foreign sales. Offers verbal or written contract. Charges clients for photocopying, express postage, messengers, and books needed to sell foreign, film and other rights.

TIPS "We look for dedicated authors and illustrators able to sustain longtime careers in our increasingly competitive field. I want fresh, not derivative story concepts with overly familiar characters. We look for gripping stories, characters, pacing, and themes. We remain mindful of an authentic (to the age) point-of-view, and look for original voices. We spend significant time hunting for the best new work, and do launch debut talent each year. It is best *not* to send manuscripts with lengthy submission histories already."

TRIDENT MEDIA GROUP

41 Madison Ave., 36th Floor, New York NY 10010. (212)262-4810. **E-mail:** ellen.assistant@tridentmedia-group.com. **Website:** www.tridentmediagroup.com. **Contact:** Ellen Levine. Member of AAR.
MEMBER AGENTS Kimberly Whalen, whalen.assistant@tridentmediagroup (commercial fiction and nonfiction, women's fiction, suspense, paranormal, and pop culture); Eileen Cope, ecope@tridentmedia-group.com (narrative nonfiction, history, biography, pop culture, health, literary fiction and short story collections); Scott Miller, smiller@tridentmediagroup.com (thrillers, crime, mystery, young adult, children's, narrative nonfiction, current events, military, memoir, literary fiction, graphic novels, pop culture); Alex Glass aglass@tridentmediagroup (thrillers, literary fiction, crime, middle grade, pop culture, young adult, humor and narrative nonfiction); Melissa Flashman, mflashman@tridentmediagroup.com (narrative nonfiction, serious nonfiction, pop culture, lifstyle); Alyssa Henkin, ahenkin@tridentmediagroup.com (juvenile, children's, young adult); Stephanie Maclean (romance, women's fiction and young adult); Don Fehr (literary and commercial novelists, narrative nonfiction, memoirs, biography, travel, science/medical/health related titles); Alanna Ramirez (literary fiction, narrative nonfiction, memoir, pop culture, food and wine, and lifestyle books); John Silbersack (commercial and literary fiction, science fiction and fantasy, narrative nonfiction, young adult, thrillers).
REPRESENTS Nonfiction books, novels, short story collections, juvenile. **Considers these nonfiction areas:** autobiography, biography, current affairs, government, humor, law, memoirs, military, multicultural, popular culture, politics, true crime, war, women's issues, women's studies, young adult. **Considers these**

fiction areas: crime, detective, humor, juvenile, literary, military, multicultural, mystery, police, short story collections, suspense, thriller, women's, young adult.

8—➤ Actively seeking new or established authors in a variety of fiction and nonfiction genres.

HOW TO CONTACT Query with SASE or via e-mail. Check website for more details.

TIPS "If you have any questions, please check FAQ page before e-mailing us."

VERITAS LITERARY AGENCY

601 Van Ness Ave., Opera Plaza, Suite E, San Francisco CA 94102. (415)647-6964. **Fax:** (415)647-6965. **E-mail:** submissions@veritasliterary.com. **Website:** www.veritasliterary.com. **Contact:** Katherine Boyle. Member of AAR. Other memberships include Author's Guild.

REPRESENTS Nonfiction books, novels. **Considers these nonfiction areas:** current affairs, memoirs, popular culture, politics, true crime, women's issues, young adult, narrative nonfiction, art and music biography, natural history, health and wellness, psychology, serious religion (no New Age) and popular science. **Considers these fiction areas:** commercial, fantasy, literary, mystery, science fiction, young adult.

8—➤ Does not want romance, poetry or children's books.

HOW TO CONTACT This agency accepts short queries or proposals via e-mail only. "If you are sending a proposal or a manuscript after a positive response to a query, please write 'requested material' on the subject line and include the initial query letter."

WALES LITERARY AGENCY, INC.

P.O. Box 9426, Seattle WA 98109-0426. (206)284-7114. **E-mail:** waleslit@waleslit.com. **Website:** www.waleslit.com. **Contact:** Elizabeth Wales, Neal Swain. Member of AAR. Other memberships include Book Publishers' Northwest, Pacific Northwest Booksellers Association, PEN. Represents 60 clients. 10% of clients are new/unpublished writers. Currently handles: nonfiction books 60%, novels 40%.

8—➤ This agency specializes in quality fiction and nonfiction. Does not handle screenplays, children's literature, genre fiction or category nonfiction.

HOW TO CONTACT Accepts queries sent with cover letter and SASE, and e-mail queries with no attachments. No phone or fax queries. Accepts simultaneous submissions. Responds in 2 weeks to queries, 2 months to mss.

TERMS Agent receives 15% commission on domestic sales. Agent receives 20% commission on foreign sales.

TIPS "We are especially interested in work that espouses a progressive cultural or political view, projects a new voice, or simply shares an important, compelling story. We also encourage writers living in the Pacific Northwest, West Coast, Alaska, and Pacific Rim countries, and writers from historically underrepresented groups, such as gay and lesbian writers and writers of color, to submit work (but does not discourage writers outside these areas). Most importantly, whether in fiction or nonfiction, the agency is looking for talented storytellers."

WEED LITERARY

27 West 20th St., New York NY 10011. **E-mail:** info@weedliterary.com. **Website:** www.weedliterary.com. **Contact:** Elisabeth Weed. Estab. 2007.

REPRESENTS Nonfiction, fiction, novels. **Considers these fiction areas:** literary, women's.

8—➤ This agency specializes in upmarket women's fiction. Does not want to receive picture books, mysteries, thrillers, romance or military.

HOW TO CONTACT Send a query letter.

THE WENDY WEIL AGENCY, INC.

232 Madison Ave., Suite 1300, New York NY 10016. (212)685-0030. **Fax:** (212)685-0765. **E-mail:** wweil@wendyweil.com. **Website:** www.wendyweil.com. Estab. 1987. Member of AAR. Currently handles: nonfiction books 20%, novels 80%.

MEMBER AGENTS Wendy Weil (commercial fiction, women's fiction, family saga, historical fiction, short stories); Emily Forland; Emma Patterson.

8—➤ "The Wendy Weil Agency, Inc. represents fiction and nonfiction for the trade market. We work with literary and commercial fiction, mystery/thriller, memoir, narrative nonfiction, journalism, history, current affairs, books on health, science, popular culture, lifestyle, social activism, and art history. It is a full-service literary agency that handles around 100 authors, among them Pulitzer Prize winners, National Book Award winners, *New York Times* bestsellers." Does not want screenplays or textbooks.

HOW TO CONTACT "Accepts queries by regular mail and e-mail; however, we cannot guarantee a response to electronic queries. Query letters should be no more than 2 pages, which should include a bit about yourself and an overview of your project. If you'd like, you're welcome to include a separate synopsis along with your query. For queries via regular mail, please be sure to include a SASE for our reply. Snail mail queries are preferred." Responds in 4-6 weeks. Obtains most new clients through recommendations from others, solicitations.

WM CLARK ASSOCIATES

186 Fifth Ave., Second Floor, New York NY 10010. (212)675-2784. **Fax:** (347)-649-9262. **E-mail:** general@wmclark.com. **Website:** www.wmclark.com. Estab. 1997. Member of AAR. 50% of clients are new/unpublished writers. Currently handles: nonfiction books 50%, novels 50%.

REPRESENTS Considers nonfiction areas: architecture, art, autobiography, biography, cultural interests, current affairs, dance, design, ethnic, film, history, inspirational, memoirs, music, politics, popular culture, religious, science, sociology, technology, theater, translation, travel memoir, Eastern philosophy. **Considers fiction areas:** contemporary issues, ethnic, historical, literary, mainstream, Southern fiction.

8—⚼William Clark represents a wide range of titles across all formats to the publishing, motion picture, television, and new media fields on behalf of authors of first fiction and award-winning, best-selling narrative nonfiction, international authors in translation, chefs, musicians, and artists. Offering individual focus and a global presence, the agency undertakes to discover, develop, and market today's most interesting content and the talent that create it, and forge sophisticated and innovative plans for self-promotion, reliable revenue streams, and an enduring creative career. Referral partners are available to provide services including editorial consultation, media training, lecture booking, marketing support, and public relations. Agency does not respond to screenplays or screenplay pitches. It is advised that before querying you browse our Book List, which is available on our website.

HOW TO CONTACT Accepts queries via online form only at www.wmclark.com/queryguidelines.html. We respond to all queries submitted via this form. Responds in 1-2 months to queries.

TERMS Agent receives 15% commission on domestic sales. Agent receives 20% commission on foreign sales. Offers written contract.

WRITERS HOUSE

21 W. 26th St., New York NY 10010. (212)685-2400. **Fax:** (212)685-1781. **E-mail:** mmejias@writershouse.com; smalk@writershouse.com. **Website:** www.writershouse.com. **Contact:** Michael Mejias. Estab. 1973. Member of AAR. Represents 440 clients. 50% of clients are new/unpublished writers. Currently handles: nonfiction books 25%, novels 40%, juvenile books 35%.

MEMBER AGENTS Albert Zuckerman (major novels, thrillers, women's fiction, important nonfiction).

REPRESENTS nonfiction books, novels, juvenile. **Considers these nonfiction areas:** animals, art, autobiography, biography, business, child guidance, cooking, decorating, diet/nutrition, economics, film, foods, health, history, humor, interior design, juvenile nonfiction, medicine, military, money, music, parenting, psychology, satire, science, self-help, technology, theater, true crime, women's issues, women's studies. **Considers these fiction areas:** adventure, cartoon, contemporary issues, crime, detective, erotica, ethnic, family saga, fantasy, feminist, frontier, gay, hi-lo, historical, horror, humor, juvenile, literary, mainstream, military, multicultural, mystery, New Age, occult, picture books, police, psychic, regional, romance, spiritual, sports, thriller, translation, war, Westerns, women's, young adult, cartoon.

8—⚼This agency specializes in all types of popular fiction and nonfiction. Does not want scholarly, professional, poetry, plays, or screenplays.

HOW TO CONTACT Query with SASE. Please send us a query letter of no more than 2 pages, which includes your credentials, an explanation of what makes your book unique and special, and a synopsis. (If submitting to Steven Malk: Writers House, 7660 Fay Ave., #338H, La Jolla, CA 92037) Responds in 6-8 weeks to queries. Obtains most new clients through recommendations from authors and editors.

TERMS Agent receives 15% commission on domestic sales. Agent receives 20% commission on foreign sales. Offers written contract, binding for 1 year. Agency charges fees for copying mss/proposals and overseas airmail of books.

TIPS "Do not send manuscripts. Write a compelling letter. If you do, we'll ask to see your work. Follow submission guidelines and please do not simultaneously submit your work to more than one Writers House agent."

BOOK PUBLISHERS

The markets in this year's Book Publishers section offer opportunities in nearly every area of publishing. Large, commercial houses are here as are their smaller counterparts.

When you have compiled a list of publishers interested in books in your subject area, read the detailed listings. Pare down your list by cross-referencing two or three subject areas and eliminating the listings only marginally suited to your book. When you have a good list, send for those publishers' catalogs and manuscript guidelines, or check publishers' websites, which often contain catalog listings, manuscript preparation guidelines, current contact names, and other information helpful to prospective authors. You want to use this information to make sure your book idea is in line with a publisher's list but is not a duplicate of something already published.

You should also visit bookstores and libraries to see if the publisher's books are well represented. When you find a couple of books the house has published that are similar to yours, write or call the company to find out who edited those books. This extra bit of research could be the key to getting your proposal to precisely the right editor.

Publishers prefer different methods of submission on first contact. Most like to see a one-page query with SASE, especially for nonfiction. Others will accept a brief proposal package that might include an outline and/or a sample chapter. Some publishers will accept submissions from agents only. Each listing in the Book Publishers section includes specific submission methods, if provided by the publisher. Make sure you read each listing carefully to find out exactly what the publisher wants to receive.

When you write your one-page query, give an overview of your book, mention the intended audience, the competition for your book (check local bookstore shelves), and what sets your book apart from the competition. You should also include any previous publishing experience or special training relevant to the subject of your book. For more on queries, read "Query Letter Clinic."

Personalize your query by addressing the editor individually and mentioning what you know about the company from its catalog or books. Never send a form letter as a query. Envelopes addressed to "Editor" or "Editorial Department" end up in the dreaded slush pile. Try your best to send your query to the appropriate editor. Editors move around all the time, so it's in your best interest to look online or call the publishing house to make sure the editor you are addressing your query to is still employed by that publisher.

AUTHOR-SUBSIDY PUBLISHERS' NOT INCLUDED

Writer's Market is a reference tool to help you sell your writing, and we encourage you to work with publishers that pay a royalty. Subsidy publishing involves paying money to a publishing house to publish a book. The source of the money could be a government, foundation or university grant, or it could be the author of the book. If one of the publishers listed in this book offers you an author-subsidy arrangement (sometimes called "cooperative publishing," "co-publishing," or "joint venture"); or asks you to pay for part or all of the cost of any aspect of publishing (editing services, manuscript critiques, printing, advertising, etc.); or asks you to guarantee the purchase of any number of the books yourself, we would like you to inform us of that company's practices immediately.

PUBLISHERS, THEIR IMPRINTS, AND HOW THEY ARE RELATED

In this era of big publishing—and big mergers—the world of publishing has grown even more intertwined. In "Publishers & Their Imprints" we list the imprints and divisions of the largest conglomerate publishers.

Keep in mind that most of the major publishers listed in this family tree do not accept unagented submissions or unsolicited manuscripts. You will find many of these publishers and their imprints listed within the Book Publishers section, and many contain only basic contact information. If you are interested in pursuing any of these publishers, we advise you to see each publisher's website for more information.

23 HOUSE PUBLISHING

405 Moseley St., Jefferson TX 75657. **Fax:** (214)367-4343. **E-mail:** editor@23house.com. **Website:** www.23house.com. Estab. 1998. Publishes trade paperback originals and electronic book format. Accepts simultaneous submissions. Catalog and guidelines online.

○ "We are looking for regional titles around the U.S., specifically in the folklore and supernatural genre. An idea of the market for the book should be included as part of the proposal.""

NONFICTION Haunted locations, interesting history, etc. "We are looking for regional nonfiction titles that can build an audience in specific locations in the U.S. Submit proposal via e-mail, and we'll go from there."

TIPS "Please check our current needs on the guidelines section of our website. If you're pitching a book to us, we're as interested in the market for it as we are the work itself."

ABBEVILLE FAMILY

Abbeville Press, 137 Varick St., New York NY 10013. (212)366-5585. **Fax:** (212)366-6966. **E-mail:** cvance@abbeville.com. **Website:** www.abbeville.com. **Contact:** Cynthia Vance, ms/art acquisitions/director. Estab. 1977. **Publishes 8 titles/year. 10% of books from first-time authors.**

○ Not accepting unsolicited mss.

FICTION Picture books: animal, anthology, concept, contemporary, fantasy, folktales, health, hi-lo, history, humor, multicultural, nature/environment, poetry, science fiction, special needs, sports, suspense. Average word length 300-1,000 words. Please refer to website for submission policy. Not accepting unsolicited mss. If you wish to have your ms or materials returned, SASE with proper postage must be included.

ABC-CLIO

Acquisitions Department, P.O. Box 1911, Santa Barbara CA 93116. (805)968-1911. **E-mail:** ccasey@abc-clio.com. **Website:** www.abc-clio.com; www.greenwood.com. **Contact:** Cathleen Casey. Estab. 1955. **Publishes 600 titles/year. 20% of books from first-time authors. 90% from unagented writers. Pays variable royalty on net price.** Accepts simultaneous submissions. Catalog and guidelines online.

⚸ ABC-CLIO is an award-winning publisher of reference titles, academic and general interest books, electronic resources, and books for librarians and other professionals. Today, ABC-CLIO publishes under 5 well-respected imprints.

NONFICTION Subjects include business, child guidance, education, government, history, humanities, language, music, psychology, religion, social sciences, sociology, sports, women's issues. No memoirs, drama. Query with proposal package, including scope, organization, length of project, whether a complete ms is available or when it will be, CV or résumé and SASE.

TIPS "Looking for reference materials and materials for educated general readers. Many of our authors are college professors who have distinguished credentials and who have published research widely in their fields."

ABRAMS BOOKS FOR YOUNG READERS

115 W. 18th St., New York NY 10011. **Website:** www.abramsyoungreaders.com.

○ Abrams no longer accepts unsolicited manuscripts or queries.

HARRY N. ABRAMS INC.

Subsidiary of La Martiniere Group, 115 West 18th St., 6th Floor, New York NY 10011. (212)206-7715. **Fax:** (212)519-1210. **E-mail:** abrams@abramsbooks.com. **Website:** www.abramsbooks.com. **Contact:** Managing editor. Estab. 1951. Publishes hardcover and a few paperback originals. **Publishes 250 titles/year.** Responds in 6 months (if interested) to queries.

○ Does not accept unsolicited materials.

NONFICTION Subjects include art, architecture, nature, environment, recreation, outdoor. Requires illustrated material for art and art history, museums. Submit queries, proposals, and mss via mail with SASE. No e-mail submissions. Reviews artwork/photos.

TIPS "We are one of the few publishers who publish almost exclusively illustrated books. We consider ourselves the leading publishers of art books and high-quality artwork in the U.S. Once the author has signed a contract to write a book for our firm the author must finish the manuscript to agreed-upon high standards within the schedule agreed upon in the contract."

ABSEY & CO.

23011 Northcrest Dr., Spring TX 77389. (281)257-2340. **E-mail:** abseyandco@aol.com; info@absey.biz. **Website:** www.absey.biz. **Contact:** Edward Wilson, editor-in-chief. Responds to mss in 6-9 months.

⚸ "We accept mainstream fiction and nonfiction, poetry, educational books, especially those dealing in language arts. We do not accept e-mail submissions of manuscripts. Submit: A brief cover letter; a chapter by chapter outline; an author's information sheet (please focus on relevantqualifications and previous publishing experience); two or three sample chapters; SASE."

TIPS Absey publishes a few titles every year. We like the author and the illustrator working together to create something magical. Authors and illustrators have input into every phase of production."

ⒶACE SCIENCE FICTION AND FANTASY

Imprint of the Berkley Publishing Group, Penguin Group (USA), Inc., 375 Hudson St., New York NY 10014. (212)366-2000. **Website:** www.penguin.com. **Contact:** Anne Sowards, editor; Jessica Webb, editorial assistant. Estab. 1953. Publishes hardcover, paperback, and trade paperback originals and reprints. **Publishes 75 titles/year. Pays royalty. Pays advance.** Publishes book 1-2 years after acceptance of ms. Responds in 2 months to queries. Responds in 6 months to mss. Guidelines for #10 SASE.

⌐Ace publishes science fiction and fantasy exclusively.

FICTION Subjects include fantasy, science fiction. No other genre accepted. No short stories. Due to the high volume of manuscripts received, most Penguin Group (USA) Inc. imprints do not normally accept unsolicited manuscripts. Query first with SASE.

ACME PRESS

P.O. Box 1702, Westminster MD 21158-1702. (410)848-7577. **Contact:** (Ms.) E.G. Johnston, man. ed. Estab. 1991. Publishes hardcover and trade paperback originals. **Publishes 1-2 titles/year. Pays 25 author's copies and 50% of profits. Pays small advance.** Publishes book 1 year after acceptance of ms. Accepts simultaneous submissions. Responds in 2 weeks to queries; 2 months to mss. Catalog and guidelines for #10 SASE. Does not accept electronic submissions.

NONFICTION Please include the following contact information in your cover letter and on your manuscript: Byline (name as you want it to appear if published), mailing address, phone number, and e-mail. Include a self-addressed stamped envelope (SASE). If a SASE is not enclosed, you will only hear from us if we are interested in your work. Include the genre (e.g., fiction, et al) of your work in the address.

FICTION Subjects include humor. "We accept submissions on any subject if the material is humorous;

prefer full-length novels. No cartoons or art (text only). No pornography, poetry, short stories, or children's material." Submit first 3-5 chapters, synopsis.

TIPS "We are always looking for the great comic novel."

ACROPOLIS BOOKS INC.

DeVorss and Company, 533 Constitution Ave., Camarillo CA 93012. (805)322-9010 or (800)843-5743. **Fax:** (800)843-6960. **E-mail:** service@devross.com; contact@acropolisbooks.com. **Website:** www.acropolisbooks.com.

⌐"Acropolis Books is dedicated to the publication and preservation of the works of Joel S. Goldsmith, an international teacher of practical mysticism who devoted his life to the discovery and teaching of spiritual principles which he called the Infinite Way."

ⒶACTION PUBLISHING

P.O. Box 391, Glendale CA 91209. (323)478-1667. **Fax:** (323)478-1767. **Website:** www.actionpublishing.com. Estab. 1996. **Pays authors royalty based on wholesale price. Offers advances against royalties.**

◯ *Only interested in agented material.*

FICTION Picture book: fantasy. Middle readers: adventure.

TIPS "We use a small number of photos. Promo is kept on file for reference if potential interest. If you are sending a book proposal, send query letter first with web link to sample photos if available."

ADAMS-BLAKE PUBLISHING

8041 Sierra St., Fair Oaks CA 95628. (916)962-9296. **Website:** www.adams-blake.com. **Contact:** Monica Blane, acquisitions editor. Estab. 1992. Publishes only e-books. **Publishes 5 titles/year. 50 queries received/year. 15 mss received/year. 80% of books from first-time authors. 99% from unagented writers. Pays 10% royalty on wholesale price.** Publishes book 2 months after acceptance. Accepts simultaneous submissions. Responds in 2 month on queries, proposals and mss.

NONFICTION Subjects include business, economics, computers, electronics, counseling, career guidance, labor, money, finance. "We like titles in sales and marketing, but which are targeted to a specific industry. We don't look for retail trade titles but more to special markets where we sell 10,000 copies to a company to give to their employees." Query with SASE. Submit proposal package, including outline, 1 sample chapter and marketing information—Demographics of readership, pricing, etc.

TIPS "If you have a book that a large company might buy and give away at sales meetings, send us a query. We like books on sales, especially in specific industries—Like 'How to Sell Annuities' or 'How to Sell High-Tech.' We look for the title that a company will buy several thousand copies of at a time. We often 'personalize' for the company. We especially like short books, 50,000 words (more or less)."

ADAMS-HALL PUBLISHING

P.O. Box 491002, Los Angeles CA 90049. (800)888-4452. **E-mail:** adamshallpublish@aol.com. **Website:** www.adams-hall.com. **Contact:** Sue Ann Bacon, editorial director. Publishes hardcover and trade paperback originals and reprints. **Publishes 3-4 titles/year. Pays negotiable advance.** Responds in 1 month.

NONFICTION Subjects include money, finance, business. Small successful house that aggressively promotes select titles. Only interested in business or personal finance titles with broad appeal. Submit query, title, synopsis, your qualifications, a list of three competitive books and how it's widely different from other books. Do not send ms or sample chapters.

ADAMS MEDIA

Division of F+W Media, Inc., 57 Littlefield St., Avon MA 02322. (508)427-7100. **Fax:** (800)872-5628. **E-mail:** paula.munier@fwmedia.com. **E-mail:** submissions@adamsmedia.com. **Website:** www.adamsmedia.com. **Contact:** Paula Munier. Estab. 1980. Publishes hardcover originals, trade paperback originals and reprints. **Publishes more than 250 titles/year. 5,000 queries received/year. 1,500 mss received/year. 40% of books from first-time authors. 40% from unagented writers. Pays standard royalty or makes outright purchase. Pays variable advance.** Publishes book 12-18 months after acceptance. Accepts simultaneous submissions. Responds in 3 months to queries. Guidelines online.

⚲ Adams Media publishes commercial nonfiction, including self-help, inspiration, women's issues, pop psychology, relationships, business, careers, pets, parenting, New Age, gift books, cookbooks, how-to, reference, and humor. Does not return unsolicited materials. Does not accept electronic submissions.

ADDICUS BOOKS, INC.

P.O. Box 45327, Omaha NE 68145. (402)330-7493. **Fax:** (402)330-1707. **E-mail:** info@addicusbooks.com. **Web-**site: www.addicusbooks.com. Estab. 1994. **Publishes 10 titles/year. 90% of books from first-time authors. 95% from unagented writers.** Publishes book 9 months after acceptance. Responds in 1 month to proposals. Catalog and guidelines available on website.

⚲ Addicus Books, Inc. seeks mss with strong national or regional appeal. "We are dedicated to producing high-quality nonfiction books. Our focus is on consumer health titles, and we continue to develop our growing line of books. Our authors, many of whom are physicians, are experts in their fields. Our editors, who are among the best, work diligently to make sure the text in every single book is clear and concise, while our graphics specialists strive to produce attractive books inside and out. In addition to working with a master book distributor, IPG Books of Chicago, which delivers books to stores and libraries, we continually seek special sales channels, outside traditional bookstores."

NONFICTION Subjects include business, economics, health, psychology, regional, consumer health, investing, self-help. "We are expanding our line of consumer health titles. Query with a brief e-mail. Tell us what your book is about, who the audience is, and how that audience would be reached. If we are interested, we may ask for a proposal, outlining the nature of your work. See proposal guidelines on our website. Do not send entire ms unless requested. When querying electronically, send only 1-page e-mail, giving an overview of your book and its market Please do not send hard copies by certified mail or return receipt requested. Additional submission guidelines online."

TIPS "We are looking for compact, concise books on consumer health topics."

AERONAUTICAL PUBLISHERS

1 Oakglade Circle, Hummelstown PA 17036-9525. (717)566-0468. **Fax:** (717)566-6423. **E-mail:** info@possibilitypress.com. **Website:** www.aeronautical-publishers.com. **Contact:** Mike Markowski, publisher. Estab. 1981. Publishes trade paperback originals. **Pays variable royalty.** Responds in 2 months to queries. Guidelines online.

⚲ "Our mission is to help people learn more about aviation and model aviation through the written word."

NONFICTION Subjects include history, aviation, hobbies, recreation., radio control, free flight, indoor models, micro radio control, home-built aircraft, ul-tralights, and hang gliders. Prefers submission by mail. Include SASE. See guidelines online. Reviews artwork/photos. Do not send originals.

TIPS "Our focus is on books of short to medium length that will serve the emerging needs of the hobby. We also want to help youth get started, while enhancing everyone's enjoyment of the hobby. We are looking for authors who are passionate about the hobby, and will champion their book and the messages of their books, supported by efforts at promoting and selling their books."

AFFLUENT PUBLISHING CORPORATION

Affluent Publishing, 1040 Avenues of the Americas, 24th Floor, New York NY 10018. **Website:** www.affluent-publishing.com. **Contact:** JB Hamilton, editor (mainstream/contemporary). I. Smushkin, editor (suspense, mystery). Estab. 2008. **Publishes 3 titles/year. 50% of books from first-time authors. 50% from unagented writers. Pays 10-15% royalty on retail price.** Publishes book 24 months after acceptance of ms. Accepts simultaneous submissions. Responds in 2-4 months on queries. Guidelines online.

Ｏ Does not accept e-mail submissions.

FICTION Subjects include adventure, ethnic, literary, mainstream, mystery, romance, suspense, young adult. Query with SASE.

TIPS "Please follow the submission guidelines posted on our website."

AHSAHTA PRESS

MFA Program in Creative Writing, Boise State University, 1910 University Dr., MS 1525, Boise ID 83725. (208)426-4210. **E-mail:** ahsahta@boisestate.edu. **E-mail:** jholmes@boisestate.edu. **Website:** ahsahtapress.boisestate.edu. **Contact:** Janet Holmes, director. Estab. 1974. Publishes trade paperback originals. **Publishes 7 titles/year. 800 mss received/year. 15% of books from first-time authors. 100% from unagented writers. Pays 8% royalty on retail price.** Publishes book 2 years after acceptance. Accepts simultaneous submissions. Responds in 3 months to mss. Catalog online.

POETRY "We are booked years in advance and are not currently reading manuscripts, with the exception of the Sawtooth Poetry Prize competition, from which we publish 2-3 mss per year." Submit complete ms. Considers multiple and simultaneous submissions. Reading period is temporarily suspended due to backlog, but the press publishes runners-up as well

as winners of the Sawtooth Poetry Prize. Forthcoming, new, and backlist titles available on website. Most backlist titles: $9.95; most current titles: $17.50.

TIPS "Ahsahta's motto is that poetry is art, so our readers tend to come to us for the unexpected—poetry that makes them think, reflect, and even do something they haven't done before."

ALADDIN/PULSE

1230 Avenue of the Americas, 4th Floor, New York NY 10020. (212)698-2707. **Fax:** (212)698-7337. **Website:** www.simonsays.com. **Contact:** Bethany Buck, vice president/publisher (Aladdin/Pulse); Ellen Krieger, vice president/associate publisher (Aladdin); Liesa Abrams, executive editor (Aladdin); Emily Lawrence, associate editor (Aladdin); Kate Angelella, assistant editor (Aladdin); Jennifer Klonsky, editorial director (Pulse); Anica Rissi, editor (Pulse); Michael del Rosario, associate editor (Pulse); Karin Paprocki, art acquisitions (Aladdin); Russell Gordon, art acquisitions (Simon Pulse). Publishes hardcover/paperback imprints of Simon & Schuster Children's Publishing Children's Division.

Aladdin publishes picture books, beginning readers, chapter books, middle grade and tween fiction and nonfiction, and graphic novels and nonfiction in hardcover and paperback, with an emphasis on commercial, kid-friendly titles. Simon Pulse publishes original teen series, single-title fiction, and select nonfiction, in hardcover and paperback.

FICTION Accepts query letters with proposals (Aladdin); accepts query letters (Simon Pulse).

ALDINE TRANSACTION

Imprint of Transaction Publishers, Rutgers—The State University of New Jersey, 35 Berrue Circle, Piscataway NJ 08854. **E-mail:** trans@transactionpub.com. **Contact:** Irving Louis Horowitz, editorial director. Publishes hardcover and academic paperback originals. Accepts simultaneous submissions. Catalog available free.

NONFICTION Subjects include anthropology, archeology, humanities, psychology, evolutionary, sociology, criminology, social psychology (not clinical). Aldine's authors are academics with PhDs and strong publication records. No poetry or fiction. "Send an inquiry to our general trans@transactionpub.com mailbox marked 'Manuscript Inquiry.' Please do not send your manuscript or sample chapters via e-mail;

electronic files submitted as attachments on speculation are not opened. You may send a hard copy of your complete ms to the attention of our Editorial Director at the address above. Include biographical information and information about your previously published work, and a cover letter with your full contact information."

TIPS Audience is professors and upper level and graduate students. Never send unsolicited mss; always query before sending anything.

ALLWORTH PRESS

An imprint of Skyhorse Publishing, 307 West 36th St., 11th Floor, New York NY 10010. (212)777-8395. **Fax:** (212)777-8261. **E-mail:** pub@allworth.com. **E-mail:** bporter@allworth.com. **Website:** www.allworth.com. **Contact:** Bob Porter, associate publisher. Tad Crawford, publisher. Estab. 1989. Publishes hardcover and trade paperback originals. **Publishes 12-18 titles/year. Pays advance.** Responds in 1 month to queries. Responds in 2 months to proposals. Catalog and guidelines free.

8—☞ "Allworth Press publishes business and self-help information for artists, designers, photographers, authors and film and performing artists, as well as books about business, money and the law for the general public. The press also publishes the best of classic and contemporary writing in art and graphic design. Currently emphasizing photography, graphic & industrial design, performing arts, fine arts and crafts, et al."

NONFICTION Subjects include art, architecture, business, economics, film, cinema, stage, music, dance, photography, film, television, graphic design, performing arts, writing, as well as business and legal guides for the public. "We are currently accepting query letters for practical, legal, and technique books targeted to professionals in the arts, including designers, graphic and fine artists, craftspeople, photographers, and those involved in film and the performing arts." Query.

TIPS "We are helping creative people in the arts by giving them practical advice about business and success."

ALONDRA PRESS, LLC

4119 Wildacres Dr., Houston TX 77072. **E-mail:** lark@alondrapress.com. **Website:** www.alondrapress.com. **Contact:** Pennelope Leight, fiction editor; Solomon Tager, nonfiction editor. Estab. 2007. Publishes trade paperback originals and reprints. **Publishes 4 titles/year. 75% of books from first-time authors. 75% from unagented writers.** Publishes book 8 months after acceptance. Accepts simultaneous submissions. Responds in 1 month to queries/proposals; 3 months to mss. Guidelines online.

NONFICTION Subjects include anthropology, archaeology, history, philosophy, psychology, translation. Submit complete ms.

FICTION Subjects include literary, all fiction genres. "Just send us a few pages in an e-mail attachment, or the entire manuscript. We will look at it quickly and tell you if it interests us."

TIPS "Be sure to read our guidelines before sending a submission. We will not respond to authors who do not observe our simple guidelines. Send your submissions in an e-mail attachment only."

ALPINE PUBLICATIONS

38262 Linman Road, Crawford CO 81415. (970)921-5005. **Fax:** (970)921-5081. **E-mail:** alpinepubl@aol.com. **Website:** alpinepub.com. **Contact:** Ms. B.J. McKinney, publisher. Estab. 1975. Publishes hardcover and trade paperback originals and reprints. **Publishes 6-10 titles/year. 40% of books from first-time authors. 95% from unagented writers. Pays 8-15% royalty on wholesale price. Pays advance.** Publishes book 18 months after acceptance. Accepts simultaneous submissions. Responds in 1-3 weeks to queries; 1 month to proposals and mss. Catalog available free. Guidelines online.

NONFICTION Subjects include animals. Alpine specializes in books that promote the enjoyment of and responsibility for companion animals with emphasis on dogs and horses. No biographies. Reviews artwork/photos. Send photocopies.

TIPS "Our audience is pet owners, breeders, exhibitors, veterinarians, animal trainers, animal care specialists, and judges. Our books are in-depth and most are heavily illustrated. Look up some of our titles before you submit. See what is unique about our books. Write your proposal to suit our guidelines."

☼ THE ALTHOUSE PRESS

University of Western Ontario, Faculty of Education, 1137 Western Rd., London ON N6G 1G7, Canada. (519)661-2096. **Fax:** (519)661-3714. **E-mail:** press@uwo.ca. **Website:** www.edu.uwo.ca/althousepress. **Contact:** Katherine Butson, editorial assistant. Publishes trade paperback originals and reprints. **Pub-**

lishes 1-5 titles/year. **50-100 queries received/year. 14 mss received/year. 50% of books from first-time authors. 100% from unagented writers. Pays $300 advance.** Publishes book 18 months after acceptance. Accepts simultaneous submissions. Responds in 1-2 months to queries; 4 months to mss. Catalog available free. Guidelines online.

❧ "The Althouse Press publishes both scholarly research monographs in education and professional books and materials for educators in elementary schools, secondary schools, and faculties of education. De-emphasizing curricular or instructional materials intended for use by elementary or secondary school students."

NONFICTION Subjects include education, scholarly. "Do not send incomplete mss that are only marginally appropriate to our market and limited mandate." Reviews artwork/photos. Send photocopies.

TIPS "Audience is practicing teachers and graduate education students."

AMACOM BOOKS

American Management Association, 1601 Broadway, New York NY 10019-7406. (212)586-8100. **Fax:** (212)903-8168. **E-mail:** cparisi@amanet.org; ekadin@amanet.org; rnirkind@amanet.org. **Website:** www.amacombooks.org; www.amanet.org. **Contact:** Ellen Kadin, executive editor (marketing, career, personal development); Robert Nirkind, senior editor (sales, customer service, project management, finance); Christina Parisi, executive editor (human resources, leadership, training, management). Estab. 1923. Publishes hardcover and trade paperback originals, professional books.

❧ AMACOM is the publishing arm of the American Management Association, the world's largest training organization for managers and their organizations—advancing the skills of individuals to drive business success. AMACOM's books are intended to enhance readers' personal and professional growth, and to help readers meet the challenges of the future by conveying emerging trends and cutting-edge thinking.

NONFICTION Subjects include all business topics. Publishes books for consumer and professional markets, including general business, management, strategic planning, human resources, manufacturing, project management, training, finance, sales, marketing, customer service, career, technology applications, history, real estate, parenting, communications and biography. Submit proposals including brief book description and rationale, TOC, author bio and platform, intended audience, competing books and sample chapters. Proposals returned with SASE only.

AMADEUS PRESS

Hal Leonard Publishing Group, Hal Leonard Corp., 33 Plymouth St., Suite 302, Montclair NJ 07402. (973)337-5034. **Fax:** (973)337-5227. **Website:** www.amadeuspress.com. **Contact:** John Cerullo, publisher.

❧ "Amadeus Press welcomes submissions pertaining to classical and traditional music and opera. Send proposal including: a letter describing the purpose and audience for your book, along with your background and qualifications; please indicate which word-processing software you use as we ask that final ms be submitted on disk; an outline or table of contents and an estimate of the length of the completed ms in numbers of words or double-spaced pages; a sample chapter or two, printed out (no electronic file transfers, please); sample illustrations as well as an estimate of the total numbers and types (for example, pen-and-ink artwork for line drawings, black-and-white glossy photographic prints, camera-ready music examples) of illustrations planned for your book; your schedule to complete the book. Generally, we ask authors to submit book proposals early in the writing process as this allows us to give editorial advice during the development phase and cuts down the amount of revisions needed later. Due to the large volume of submissions, you may not receive a response from us. If you wish to have the materials you submit returned to you, please so indicate and include return postage."

AMBASSADOR BOOKS, INC.

Paulist Press, 997 MacArthur Blvd., Mahwah NJ 07430. (201)825-7300; (800)218-1903. **Fax:** (800)836-3161. **E-mail:** info@paulistpress.com; ggoggins@paulistpress.com; jconlan@paulistpress.com. **Website:** www.ambassadorbooks.com. Publishes hardcover and trade paperback originals. **Publishes 12 titles/year. 500 queries received/year. 100 mss received/year. 50% of books from first-time authors. 90% from unagented writers. Pays 8-10% royalty on net sales.** Publishes book 1 year after acceptance. Responds in up to 4 months to queries. Catalog online for download, or write for paper catalog.

8—☛ "We are a Christian publishing company seeking spirituality-focused books for children and adults."

NONFICTION Subjects include creative nonfiction, regional, religion, spirituality, sports., spiritual seeking, spirituality of sports, Catholic themes, intellectual exploration of religious topics, spiritual self-help. Adult books must have spiritual theme. Children's books published as Ambassador Children's Books, and must have spiritual or self-help topic and 32-page format for ages 3-7, and under 100 pages for juvenile biography and religious topics for ages 8-13. Books with a spiritual theme. Query with proposal and SASE or submit complete ms. Reviews artwork/photos. Send photocopies.

FICTION Not accepted except in adult or juvenile fables. Query with SASE or submit complete ms.

AMBER COMMUNICATIONS GROUP, INC.

1334 E. Chandler Blvd., Suite 5-D67, Phoenix AZ 85048. **Website:** www.amberbooks.com. **Contact:** Tony Rose, publisher. Estab. 1998. Publishes trade paperback and mass market paperback originals. Catalog free or online.

8—☛ Amber Communications Group, Inc. is the nation's largest African-American publisher of self-help books and music biographies.

NONFICTION Subjects include beauty, fashion, history, celebrity memoirs, biographies, multicultural., personal finance, relationship advice. Submit proposal or outline with author biography. Please do not e-mail or mail mss unless requested by publisher. Reviews artwork/photos. Send photocopies, not originals.

FICTION Wants African-American topics and interest. Submit proposal or outline.

TIPS "The goal of Amber Communications Group is to expand our catalog comprised of self-help books, and celebrity bio books; and expand our fiction department in print and on software, which pertain to, about, and are for the African-American population."

AMERICAN BAR ASSOCIATION PUBLISHING

321 N. Clark St., Chicago IL 60654. (312)988-5000. **Fax:** (312)988-6030. **Website:** www.ababooks.org. **Contact:** Kathleen A. Welton, director of book publishing. Estab. 1878. Publishes hardcover and trade paperback originals. **Publishes 100 titles/year. 50 queries received/**

year. **20% of books from first-time authors. 95% from unagented writers.** Publishes book 6 months after acceptance. Accepts simultaneous submissions. Responds in 1 month to queries and proposals; 3 months to mss. Catalog and guidelines online.

8—☛ "We are interested in books that help lawyers practice law more effectively, whether it's how to handle clients, structure a real estate deal, or take an antitrust case to court."

NONFICTION Subjects include business, economics, computers, electronics, money, finance, software., legal practice. "Our market is not, generally, the public. Books need to be targeted to lawyers who are seeking solutions to their practice problems. We rarely publish scholarly treatises." All areas of legal practice. Query with SASE.

TIPS "ABA books are written for busy, practicing lawyers. The most successful books have a practical, reader-friendly voice. If you can build in features like checklists, exhibits, sample contracts, flow charts, and tables of cases, please do so. The Association also publishes over 60 major national periodicals in a variety of legal areas. Contact Tim Brandhorst, Deputy Director of book publishing, at the above address for guidelines."

AMERICAN CARRIAGE HOUSE PUBLISHING

P.O. Box 1330, Nevada City CA 95959. (530)432-8860. **Fax:** (530)432-7379. **E-mail:** editor@americancarriagehousepublishing.com. **Website:** www.americancarriagehousepublishing.com. **Contact:** Lynn Taylor, editor (parenting, reference, child, women). Estab. 2004. Publishes trade paperback and electronic originals. **Publishes 10 titles/year. 10% of books from first-time authors. 100% from unagented writers. Pays outright purchase of $300-3,000.** Publishes book 1 year after acceptance. Accepts simultaneous submissions. Responds in 6 months to queries, proposals, and mss. Catalog free on request.

NONFICTION Subjects include child guidance, education, parenting, womens issues, womens studies, young adult. Query with SASE. Reviews artwork/photos. Send photocopies.

FICTION Subjects include religious, spiritual, young adult. Query with SASE.

AMERICAN CATHOLIC PRESS

16565 S. State St., South Holland IL 60473. (312)331-5845. **Fax:** (708)331-5484. **E-mail:** acp@acpress.org.

Website: www.acpress.org. **Contact:** Rev. Michael Gilligan, PhD, editorial director. Estab. 1967. Publishes hardcover originals and hardcover and paperback reprints. **Publishes 4 titles/year. Makes outright purchase of $25-100.** Guidelines online.

NONFICTION Subjects include education, music, dance, religion, spirituality. "We publish books on the Roman Catholic liturgy—for the most part, books on religious music and educational books and pamphlets. We also publish religious songs for church use, including Psalms, as well as choral and instrumental arrangements. We are interested in new music, meant for use in church services. Books, or even pamphlets, on the Roman Catholic Mass are especially welcome. We have no interest in secular topics and are not interested in religious poetry of any kind."

TIPS "Most of our sales are by direct mail, although we do work through retail outlets."

AMERICAN CHEMICAL SOCIETY

Publications/Books Division, 1155 16th St. NW, Washington DC 20036. (202)452-2120. **Fax:** (202)452-8913. **E-mail:** b_hauserman@acs.org. **Website:** pubs.acs.org/books/. **Contact:** Bob Hauserman, acquisitions editor. Estab. 1876. Publishes hardcover originals. **Publishes 35 titles/year. Pays royalty.** Accepts simultaneous submissions. Responds in 2 months to proposals. Catalog available free. Guidelines online.

✂━ American Chemical Society publishes symposium-based books for chemistry.

NONFICTION Subjects include science. Emphasis is on meeting-based books. Log in to submission site.

AMERICAN CORRECTIONAL ASSOCIATION

206 N. Washington St., Suite 200, Alexandria VA 22314. (703)224-0194. **Fax:** (703)224-0179. **E-mail:** aliceh@aca.org; susanc@aca.org; rgibson@aca.org. **Website:** www.aca.org. **Contact:** Alice Heiserman, manager of publications and research. Estab. 1870. Publishes trade paperback originals. **Publishes 18 titles/year. 90% of books from first-time authors. 100% from unagented writers.** Publishes book 1 year after acceptance. Responds in 4 months to queries. Catalog available free. Guidelines online.

✂━ "American Correctional Association provides practical information on jails, prisons, boot camps, probation, parole, community corrections, juvenile facilities and rehabilitation programs, substance abuse programs, and other areas of corrections."

NONFICTION "We are looking for practical, how-to texts or training materials written for the corrections profession. We are especially interested in books on management, development of first-line supervisors, and security-threat group/management in prisons." No autobiographies or true-life accounts by current or former inmates or correctional officers, theses, or dissertations. No fiction or poetry. Query with SASE. Reviews artwork/photos.

TIPS "Authors are professionals in the field of corrections. Our audience is made up of corrections professionals and criminal justice students. No books by inmates or former inmates. This publisher advises out-of-town freelance editors, indexers, and proofreaders to refrain from requesting work from them."

AMERICAN COUNSELING ASSOCIATION

5999 Stevenson Ave., Alexandria VA 22304. (703)823-9800. **Fax:** (703)823-4786. **E-mail:** cbaker@counseling.org. **Website:** www.counseling.org. **Contact:** Carolyn C. Baker, director of publications. Estab. 1952. Publishes paperback originals. **Publishes 10-12 titles/year. 1% of books from first-time authors. 90% from unagented writers.** Accepts simultaneous submissions. Responds in 1 month to queries. Guidelines available free.

✂━ "The American Counseling Association is dedicated to promoting public confidence and trust in the counseling profession. We publish scholarly texts for graduate level students and mental health professionals. We do not publish books for the general public."

NONFICTION Subjects include education, gay, lesbian, health, multicultural, psychology, religion, sociology, spirituality, women's issues. ACA does not publish self-help books or autobiographies. Query with SASE. Submit proposal package, outline, 2 sample chapters, vitae.

TIPS "Target your market. Your books will not be appropriate for everyone across all disciplines."

AMERICAN FEDERATION OF ASTROLOGERS

6535 S. Rural Rd., Tempe AZ 85283. (480)838-1751. **Fax:** (480)838-8293. **E-mail:** info@astrologers.com. **Website:** www.astrologers.com. Estab. 1938. Publishes trade paperback originals and reprints. **Publishes 10-15 titles/year. 10 queries received/year. 20** mss received/year. **50% of books from first-time authors. 100% from unagented writers. Pays 10% royalty.** Publishes book 10 months after acceptance of ms. Accepts simultaneous submissions. Responds in 6 months to mss. Catalog available free. Guidelines available on website.

⌘ American Federation of Astrologers publishes astrology books, calendars, charts, and related aids.

NONFICTION "Our market for beginner books, Sun-sign guides, and similar material is limited and we thus publish very few of these. The ideal word count for a book-length manuscript published by AFA is about 40,000 words, although we will consider manuscripts from 20,000 to 60,000 words." Submit complete ms.

TIPS "AFA welcomes articles for *Today's Astrologer*, our monthly journal for members, on any astrological subject. Most articles are 1,500-3,000 words, but we do accept shorter and longer articles. Follow the guidelines online for book manuscripts. You also can e-mail your article to info@astrologers.com, but any charts or illustrations must be submitted as attachments and not embedded in the body of the e-mail or in an attached document."

⊘ AMERICAN PRESS

60 State St., Suite 700, Boston MA 02109. (617)247-0022. **E-mail:** americanpress@flash.net. **Website:** www.americanpresspublishers.com. **Contact:** Jana Kirk, editor. Estab. 1911. Publishes college textbooks. **Publishes 25 titles/year. 350 queries received/year. 100 mss received/year. 50% of books from first-time authors. 90% from unagented writers. Pays 5-15% royalty on wholesale price.** Publishes book 9 months after acceotance. after acceptance of ms. Responds in 3 months to queries.

NONFICTION Subjects include agriculture, anthropology, archeology, art, architecture, business, economics, education, government, politics, health, medicine, history, horticulture, music, dance, psychology, science, sociology, sports. "We prefer that our authors actually teach courses for which the manuscripts are designed." Query, or submit outline with tentative TOC. *No complete mss.*

AMERICAN QUILTER'S SOCIETY

Schroeder Publishing, P.O. Box 3290, Paducah KY 42002. (270)898-7903. **Fax:** (270)898-1173. **E-mail:** editor@aqsquilt.com. **Website:** www.americanquil-

ter.com. **Contact:** Andi Reynolds, executive book editor (primarily how-to and patterns, but other quilting books sometimes published, including quilt-related fiction). Estab. 1984. Publishes trade paperbacks. **Publishes 20-24 titles/year. 100 queries received/year. Multiple submissions okay. 60% of books from first-time authors. Pays 5% royalty on retail price.** Publishes book 18 months after acceptance. Accepts simultaneous submissions. Responds in 2 months to proposals. Proposal guidelines online.

⌘ "American Quilter's Society publishes how-to and pattern books for quilters (beginners through intermediate skill level). We are not the publisher for non-quilters writing about quilts."

NONFICTION No queries; proposals only. Note: 1 or 2 completed quilt projects must accompany proposal.

AMERICAN WATER WORKS ASSOCIATION

6666 W. Quincy Ave., Denver CO 80235. (303)347-6278. **Fax:** (303)794-7310. **E-mail:** mkozyra@awwa.org. **Website:** www.awwa.org/communications/books. **Contact:** Scott Millard, manager, business and product development. Estab. 1881. Publishes hardcover and trade paperback originals. Responds in 4 months to queries. Catalog and guidelines free.

⌘ "AWWA strives to advance and promote the safety and knowledge of drinking water and related issues to all audiences—from kindergarten through post-doctorate."

NONFICTION Subjects include nature, environment, science, software, drinking water- and wastewater-related topics, operations, treatment, sustainability. Query with SASE. Submit outline, bio, 3 sample chapters. Reviews artwork/photos. Send photocopies.

TIPS "See website to download submission instructions."

AMERICA WEST PUBLISHERS

P.O. Box 2208, Carson City NV 89702. (775)885-0700. **Fax:** (877)726-2632. **E-mail:** global@nohoax.com. **Website:** www.nohoax.com. **Contact:** George Green, president. Estab. 1985. Publishes hardcover and trade paperback originals and reprints. **Publishes 20 titles/year. 90% of books from first-time authors. 90% from unagented writers. Pays 10% royalty on wholesale price. Pays $300 average advance.** Publishes book 6 months after acceptance. Accepts simultaneous submissions. Responds in 1 month to queries. Catalog and guidelines free.

8—π "America West seeks the other side of the picture, political cover-ups, and new health alternatives."

NONFICTION Subjects include business, economics, government, politics, including cover-up, health, medicine, holistic self-help, New Age., UFO-metaphysical. Submit outline, sample chapters. Reviews artwork/photos.

TIPS "We currently have materials in all bookstores that have areas of UFOs; also political and economic nonfiction."

AMHERST MEDIA INC.

175 Rano St., Suite 200, Buffalo NY 14207. (716)874-4450. **Fax:** (716)874-4508. **E-mail:** submissions@amherstmedia.com. **Website:** www.amherstmedia.com. **Contact:** Craig Alesse, publisher. Estab. 1974. Publishes trade paperback originals and reprints. **Publishes 30 titles/year. 60% of books from first-time authors. 90% from unagented writers. Pays 6-8% royalty. Pays advance.** Publishes book 1 year after acceptance. Accepts simultaneous submissions. Responds in 2 months to queries. Catalog free and online (catalog@amherstmedia.com). Guidelines free and available online.

8—π Publishes how-to photography books.

NONFICTION Subjects include photography. Looking for well-written and illustrated photo books. Query with outline, 2 sample chapters, and SASE. Reviews artwork/photos.

TIPS "Our audience is made up of beginning to advanced photographers. If I were a writer trying to market a book today, I would fill the need of a specific audience and self-edit in a tight manner."

⊘ AMIGADGET PUBLISHING CO.

P.O. Box 1696, Lexington SC 29071. **E-mail:** amigadget@fotoartista.com. **Website:** www.fotoartista.com/amigadget. **Contact:** Jay Gross, editor-in-chief. Publishes trade paperbacks. **Publishes 1 title/year.**

NONFICTION Query via e-mail only. *All unsolicited mss returned unopened.*

TIPS "We are not currently seeking new paper publishing projects, and and we do not publish fiction."

AMSTERDAM PRESS

6199 State Hwy 43, Amsterdam OH 43903. (740)543-4333. **E-mail:** editor@amsterdampress.net. **Website:** www.amsterdampress.net. **Contact:** Cindy Kelly, editor. Estab. 2007. Responds in 1-3 months.

8—π Amsterdam Press publishes chapbooks and broadsides, wants "poetry of place, poetry grounded in sense images, poetry that leaps, and has a clear voice." Does not want "esoteric poetry that focuses on the universal." Mss are selected through open submission. Chapbooks are 36 pgs, laser-printed, saddle-stitched, with card cover and black and white art/graphics.

POETRY Query first, with a few sample poems and a cover letter with brief bio and publication credits. Chapbook mss may include previously published poems. "Previously published poetry must be recognized on a separate page of mss."

AMULET BOOKS

Abrams Books for Young Readers, 115 W. 18th St., New York NY 10001. **Website:** www.amuletbooks.com. **Contact:** Susan Van Metre, vice president/publisher; Tamar Brazis, editorial director; Cecily Kaiser, publishing director. Estab. 2004. **10% of books from first-time authors.**

○ *Does not accept unsolicited mss or queries.*

ANACUS PRESS AND ECOPRESS

Imprint of Finney Co., 8075 215th St. W, Lakeville MN 55044. (952)469-6699. **Fax:** (952)469-1968. **E-mail:** feedback@finneyco.com. **Website:** www.ecopress.com. **Contact:** Alan Krysan, president. Publishes trade paperbacks. **Publishes variable number of titles/year. Pays 10% royalty on wholesale price.** Responds in 10-12 weeks to queries. Catalog online.

NONFICTION Subjects include recreation, regional, travel, travel guides, travelogue. environmental, eco-friendly. Query with SASE.

TIPS "Audience is cyclists and armchair adventurers."

⊕ ANAPHORA LITERARY PRESS

104 Banff Dr., Apt. 101, Edinboro PA 16412. (814)273-0004. **E-mail:** pennsylvaniajournal@gmail.com. **Website:** www.anaphoraliterary.wordpress.com. **Contact:** Anna Faktorovich, editor-in-chief (general interest). Estab. 2007. Format publishes in trade paperback originals and reprints; mass market paperback originals and reprints. **Publishes 3 titles/year. 200 queries/year; 100 mss/year 50% of books from first-time authors. 100% from unagented writers. Pays 10-30% royalty on retail price.** "We currently publish journals, which are authored by several people. If we publish a novel or a critical book by a single author, we will share our profits with the

author." Publishes book 2 months after acceptance of ms. Accepts simultaneous submissions. Responds in 1 month on queries, proposals, and mss. Catalog and guidelines online.

NONFICTION Subjects include communications, contemporary culture, creative nonfiction, education, entertainment, games, government, hobbies, humanities, language, literary criticism, literature, memoirs, multicultural, New Age, philosophy, politics, recreation, regional, travel, women's issues, academic, legal, business, journals, edited and un-edited dissertations. "We are actively seeking quality writing that is original, innovative, enlightening, intellectual and otherwise a pleasure to read. Our primary focus in nonfiction is literary criticism; but, there are many other areas of interest. Send a query letter if you are considering submitting anything in the other fields listed above." Query with SASE. Submit proposal package, including: outline, 1 sample chapter. Submit completed ms.

FICTION Subjects include adventure, comic books, confession, contemporary, experimental, fantasy, feminist, gothic, historical, humor, literary, mainstream, military, mystery, occult, picture books, plays, poetry, poetry in translation, regional, short story collections, suspense, war. "We are actively seeking submissions at this time. The genre is not as important as the quality of work. You should have a completed full-length ms ready to be e-mailed or mailed upon request." Looking for single and multiple-author books in fiction (poetry, novels, and short story collections). Query with SASE. Submit proposal package, including synopsis, 1 sample chapter, and completed ms.

POETRY Looking for single and multiple-author books in poetry. Query. Submit 10 sample poems. Submit complete ms.

TIPS "Our audience is academics, college students and graduates, as well as anybody who loves literature. Regardless of profits, we love publishing great books and we enjoy reading submissions. So, if you are reading this book because you love writing and hope to publish as soon as possible, send a query letter or a submission to us. But, remember—proofread your work (most of our editors are English instructors)."

Ⓐ ANDREWS MCMEEL UNIVERSAL

1130 Walnut St., Kansas City MO 64106-2109. (816)932-6700. **Website:** www.amuniversal.com. **Contact:** Christine Schillig, vice president/editorial director. Estab. 1973. Publishes hardcover and paperback originals. **Publishes 200 titles/year. Pays royalty on retail price or net receipts. Pays advance.**

⚷━➤ Andrews McMeel publishes general trade books, humor books, miniature gift books, calendars, and stationery products.

NONFICTION Subjects include contemporary culture, general trade, relationships. Also produces gift books. Agented submissions only.

ANGOOR PRESS LLC

2734 Bruchez Pkwy., Unit 103, Denver CO 80234. E-mail: submissions@angoorpress.com. **Website:** www.angoorpress.com. **Contact:** Carolina Maine, Founder, Editor. Estab. 2010. **Publishes 10 titles/year. 50-100% of books from first-time authors. 100% from unagented writers. Pays 5%-20% on wholesale price in royalties.** Publishes book 6-12 months after acceptance of ms. Responds 3 months to proposals and manuscripts. No catalog available. Manuscript guidelines are free by request.

NONFICTION Subjects include contemporary culture, religion. "Essays submitted must be in line with Catholic teaching. Must include author bio." Submit proposal package, and essays in via PDF e-mail attachment.

FICTION Subjects include adventure, confession, contemporary, ethnic, literary, mainstream, poetry, religious, spiritual. Submit proposal package, including market search, author bio and book marketing plan.

POETRY Submit 2-5 number of sample poems and complete ms.

ANHINGA PRESS

P.O. Box 3665, Tallahassee FL 32315. (850)422-1408. **Fax:** (850)442-6323. **E-mail:** info@anhinga.org. **Website:** www.anhinga.org. **Contact:** Rick Campbell, editor. Publishes hardcover and trade paperback originals. **Publishes 5 titles/year. Pays 10% royalty on retail price. Offers Anhinga Prize of $2,000.** Accepts simultaneous submissions. Responds in 3 months to queries, proposals, and mss. Catalog and contest for #10 SASE or online. Guidelines online.

⚷━➤ Publishes only full-length collections of poetry (60-80 pages). No individual poems or chapbooks.

POETRY Query with SASE and 10-page sample (not full ms) by mail. No e-mail queries.

⃠ⓒ ANNICK PRESS, LTD.

15 Patricia Ave., Toronto ON M2M 1H9, Canada. (416)221-4802. **Fax:** (416)221-8400. **E-mail:** annick-

press@annickpress.com. **Website:** www.annick-press.com. **Contact:** Rick Wilks, director; Colleen MacMillan, associate publisher; Sheryl Shapiro, creative director. Publishes picture books, juvenile and YA fiction and nonfiction; specializes in trade books. **Publishes 25 titles/year. 5,000 queries received/year. 3,000 mss received/year. 20% of books from first-time authors. 80-85% from unagented writers. Pays authors royalty of 5-12% based on retail price. Offers advances (average amount: $3,000). Pays illustrators royalty of 5% minimum.** Publishes book Publishes a book 2 years after acceptance. Catalog and guidelines online.

Does not accept unsolicited mss.

ANVIL PRESS

P.O. Box 3008 MPO, Vancouver BC V6B 3X5, Canada. (604)876-8710. **Fax:** (604)879-2667. **E-mail:** info@anvilpress.com. **E-mail:** christine@anvilpress.com. **Website:** www.anvilpress.com. **Contact:** Brian Kaufman. Estab. 1988. Publishes trade paperback originals. **Publishes 8-10 titles/year. 300 queries received/year. 80% of books from first-time authors. 70% from unagented writers. Pays advance.** Publishes book 8 months after acceptance of ms. Accepts simultaneous submissions. Responds in 2 months to queries. Responds in 6 months to mss. Catalog for 9×12 SAE with 2 first-class stamps. Guidelines online. "Anvil Press publishes contemporary adult fiction, poetry, and drama, giving voice to up-and-coming Canadian writers, exploring all literary genres, discovering, nurturing, and promoting new Canadian literary talent. Currently emphasizing urban/suburban themed fiction and poetry; de-emphasizing historical novels."

FICTION Subjects include experimental, literary, short story collections. Contemporary, modern literature; no formulaic or genre. Query with SASE.

POETRY "Get our catalog, look at our poetry. We do very little poetry, maybe 1-2 titles per year."

TIPS "Audience is young, informed, educated, aware, with an opinion, culturally active (films, books, the performing arts). No U.S. authors. Research the appropriate publisher for your work."

APA BOOKS

American Psychological Association, 750 First St., NE, Washington DC 20002. (800)374-2721 or (202)336-5500. **Website:** www.apa.org/books. Publishes hard-cover and trade paperback originals. Catalog and guidelines online.

NONFICTION Subjects include education, gay, lesbian, multicultural, psychology, science, social sciences, sociology, women's issues/studies. Submit cv and prospectus with TOC, intended audience, selling points, and outside competition.

TIPS "Our press features scholarly books on empirically supported topics for professionals and students in all areas of psychology."

APPALACHIAN MOUNTAIN CLUB BOOKS

5 Joy St., Boston MA 02108. (617)523-0636. **Fax:** (617)523-0722. **E-mail:** amcpublications@outdoors.org. **Website:** www.outdoors.org. Estab. 1876. Publishes hardcover and trade paperback originals. Accepts simultaneous submissions. Guidelines online.

"AMC Books are written and published by the experts in the Northeast outdoors. Our mission is to publish authoritative, accurate, and easy-to-use books and maps based on AMC's expertise in outdoor recreation, education, and conservation. We are committed to producing books and maps that appeal to novices and day visitors as well as outdoor enthusiasts in our core activity areas of hiking and paddling. By advancing the interest of the public in outdoor recreation and helping our readers to access backcountry trails and waterways, and by using our books to educate the public about safety, conservation, and stewardship, we support AMC's mission of promoting the protection, enjoyment, and wise use of the Northeast outdoors. We work with the best professional writers possible and draw upon the experience of our programs staff and chapter leaders from Maine to Washington, D.C."

NONFICTION Subjects include nature, environment, recreation, regional, Northeast outdoor recreation, literary nonfiction, guidebooks. Maps that are based on our direct work with land managers and our on-the-ground collection of data on trails, natural features, and points of interest. AMC Books also publishes narrative titles related to outdoor recreation, mountaineering, and adventure, often with a historical perspective. "Appalachian Mountain Club publishes hiking guides, paddling guides, nature, conservation, and mountain-subject guides for America's Northeast. We connect recreation to conservation and education." Query with proposal and the first 3 chapters of your ms to the publications department at AMCpublications@outdoors.org. You can also send them via US Postal Service to AMC Books Editor, Appalachian Mountain Club, 5 Joy Street, Boston, MA 02108 with SASE. Reviews artwork/photos. Send on a disk or via weblink.

TIPS "Our audience is outdoor recreationists, conservation-minded hikers and canoeists, family outdoor lovers, armchair enthusiasts. Visit our website for proposal submission guidelines and more information."

Ⓐ ARCADE PUBLISHING

307 W. 57th St., 11th Floor, New York NY 10018. (212)643-6816. **Fax:** (212)643-6819. **Website:** www.arcadepub.com. **Contact:** Jeannette Seaver, publisher/executive editor; Cal Barksdale, executive editor; Casey Ebro, editor; Tessa Aye, assistant editor. Estab. 1988. Publishes hardcover originals, trade paperback reprints. **Publishes 35 titles/year. 5% of books from first-time authors. Pays royalty on retail price and 10 author's copies. Pays advance.** Publishes book 18 months after acceptance. Responds in 2 months to queries. Catalog and guidelines for #10 SASE.

☞ "Arcade prides itself on publishing top-notch literary nonfiction and fiction, with a significant proportion of foreign writers."

NONFICTION Subjects include history, memoirs, nature, environment, travel, popular science, current events. Agented submissions only. Reviews artwork/photos. Send photocopies.

FICTION Subjects include literary, mainstream, contemporary, short story collections, translation. No romance, historical, science fiction. Agented submissions only.

ARCADIA PUBLISHING

420 Wando Park Blvd., Mt. Pleasant SC 29464. (843)853-2070. **Fax:** (843)853-0044. **E-mail:** publishingnortheast@arcadiapublishing.com; publishingsouth@arcadiapublishing.com; publishingwest@arcadiapublishing.com; publishingmidwest@arcadiapublishing.com. **Website:** www.arcadiapublishing.com. Estab. 1993. Publishes trade paperback originals. **Publishes 600 titles/year. Pays 8% royalty on retail price.** Publishes book 9 months after acceptance. Accepts simultaneous submissions. Catalog online. Guidelines available free.

☞ "Arcadia publishes photographic vintage regional histories. We have more than 3,000 Im-

ages of America series in print. We have expanded our California program."

NONFICTION Subjects include history, local, regional. "Arcadia accepts submissions year-round. Our editors seek proposals on local history topics and are able to provide authors with detailed information about our publishing program as well as book proposal submission guidelines. Due to the great demand for titles on local and regional history, we are currently searching for authors to work with us on new photographic history projects. Please contact one of our regional publishing teams if you are interested in submitting a proposal." Specific proposal form to be completed.

TIPS "Writers should know that we only publish history titles. The majority of our books are on a city or region, and contain vintage images with limited text."

⊕ ARCHAIA

1680 Vine St., Suite 912, Los Angeles CA 90028. **E-mail:** editorial@archaia.com, submissions@archaia.com. **Website:** www.archaia.com. **Contact:** Submissions Editor.

⊘ ARC PUBLICATIONS

Nanholme Mill, Shaw Wood Rd., Todmorden, Lancashire OL14 6DA, England. **E-mail:** info@arcpublications.co.uk. **Website:** www.arcpublications.co.uk. **Contact:** Tony Ward, managing editor. Angele Jarman, director of development. Estab. 1969.

POETRY Publishes "contemporary poetry from new and established writers from the UK and abroad, specializing in the work of world poets writing in English, and the work of overseas poets in translation. *At present we are not accepting submissions but keep updated by visiting the website.*"

ARCTOS PRESS

P.O. Box 401, Sausalito CA 94966. (415)331-2503. **E-mail:** runes@aol.com. **Website:** www.arctospress.com. **Contact:** CB Follett, editor. Estab. 1997.

POETRY "We publish quality, perfect-bound books and anthologies of poetry, usually theme-oriented, in runs of 1,500. as well as individual poetry collections such as *Prism*, poems by David St. John; *Fire Is Favorable to the Dreamer*, poems by Susan Terris; J.D. Whitney, Lowell Jaeger, and others. *We do not accept unsolicited manuscripts.*"

A-R EDITIONS, INC.

8551 Research Way, Suite 180, Middleton WI 53562. (608)203-2565. **Fax:** (608)831-8200. **E-mail:** pamela.

whitcomb@areditions.com; james.zychowicz@aredi-tions.com. **Website:** www.areditions.com. **Contact:** Pamela Whitcomb, managing editor (Recent Researches Series); James L. Zychowicz, managing editor (Computer Music and Digital Audio Series, and MLA's Index and Bibliography, Technical Reports, and Basic Manual Series). Estab. 1962. **Publishes 30 titles/year. 40 queries received/year. 30 mss received/year. 75% of books from first-time authors. 100% from unagented writers. Pays royalty or honoraria.** Responds in 1 month to queries; 3 months to proposals; 6 months to mss. Catalog and guidelines online.

NONFICTION Subjects include computers, electronics, music, dance, software, historical music editions. Computer Music and Digital Audio Series titles deal with issues tied to digital and electronic media, and include both textbooks and handbooks in this area. Query with SASE. Submit outline. "All material submitted in support of a proposal becomes the property of A-R Editions. Please send photocopies of all important documents (retain your originals). We suggest that you send your proposal either with delivery confirmation or by a service that offers package tracking to avoid misdirected packages."

⊕ ARKHAM BRIDGE PUBLISHING

P.O. Box 2346, Everett WA 98213. **E-mail:** arkhambridgepublishing@arkhambridgepublishing.com; submissions@arkhambridgepublishing.com. **Website:** www.arkhambridgepublishing.com. **Contact:** James Davis, senior editor. Estab. 2009. **Publishes 1-3 titles/year. 100% of books from first-time authors. 100% from unagented writers.** Accepts simultaneous submissions. Responds in 1 month. Catalog and guidelines free on request with SAE or online.

&—⚓ "Arkham Bridge Publishing is a book and periodical publisher based in Washington State, aiming to bring works by new authors to the national market. We publish many genres, but especially aim to publish science-fiction, fantasy, and alternate history works."

NONFICTION Subjects include agriculture, alternative lifestyles, Americana, animals, anthropology, archeology, architecture, art, astrology, automotive, business, child guidance, communications, community, computers, contemporary culture, cooking, counseling, crafts, creative nonfiction, education, entertainment, environment, ethnic, gardening, gay, government, health, history, hobbies, horticulture,

house and home, humanities, labor, language, law, lesbian, literary criticism, literature, marine subjects, medicine, memoirs, military, money, multicultural, music, nature, New Age, nutrition, parenting. Submit completed ms. Reviews artwork.

FICTION Subjects include adventure, comic books, confession, contemporary, erotica, ethnic, experimental, fantasy, feminist, gay, gothic, hi-lo, historical, horror, humor, juvenile, lesbian, literary, mainstream, military, multicultural, multimedia, mystery, occult, poetry, regional, religious, romance, science fiction, short story collections, spiritual, sports, suspense, translation, western. "Arkham Bridge is looking to expand into more fiction markets with more titles, and will accept and review all fiction submissions." Submit completed ms.

TIPS "Arkham Bridge Publishing is looking to expand and grow, having only one book title and two magazine titles at this time. We see no problem with receiving and reviewing a greater quantity of queries and manuscripts, and we intend to begin publishing between one and three titles each year."

◌ ARSENAL PULP PRESS

#101-211 East Georgia St., Vancouver BC V6A 1Z6, Canada. (604)687-4233. **Fax:** (604)687-4283. **E-mail:** info@arsenalpulp.com. **Website:** www.arsenalpulp.com. **Contact:** Editorial Board. Estab. 1980. Publishes trade paperback originals, and trade paperback reprints. **Publishes 14-20 titles/year. 500 queries received/year. 300 mss received/year. 30% of books from first-time authors. 100% from unagented writers.** Publishes book 1 year after acceptance of ms. Accepts simultaneous submissions. Responds in 2 months to queries. Responds in 4 months to proposals and manuscripts. Catalog for 9×12 SAE with IRCs or online. Guidelines online.

NONFICTION Subjects include art, architecture, cooking, foods, nutrition, creative nonfiction, ethnic, Canadian, cultural studies, aboriginal issues, gay, health, lesbian, history, cultural, language, literature, multicultural, political/sociological studies, regional studies and guides, in particular for British Columbia, sex, sociology, travel, women's issues/studies, youth culture., film, visual art. Rarely publishes non-Canadian authors. No poetry at this time. We do not publish children's books. Each submission must include: a synopsis of the work, a chapter by chapter outline for non-fiction, writing credentials, a 50-page excerpt from the manuscript (*do not send more, it will be a waste of postage; if we like what we see, we'll ask for the rest of the manuscript*), and a marketing analysis. If our editorial board is interested, you will be asked to send the entire manuscript. We do not accept discs or submissions by fax or e-mail, and we do not discuss concepts over the phone. Send submissions to: Editorial Board Reviews artwork/photos.

FICTION Subjects include ethnic, general, feminist, gay, lesbian, literary, multicultural, short story collections. No children's books or genre fiction, i.e., westerns, romance, horror, mystery, etc. Submit proposal package, outline, clips, 2-3 sample chapters.

ARTE PUBLICO PRESS

University of Houston, 452 Cullen Performance Hall, Houston TX 77204-2004. **Fax:** (713)743-3080. **E-mail:** submapp@mail.uh.edu. **Website:** www.artepublicopress.com. **Contact:** Nicolas Kanellos, editor. Estab. 1979. Publishes hardcover originals, trade paperback originals and reprints. **Publishes 25-30 titles/year. 1,000 queries received/yeare. 2,000 mss received/year. 50% of books from first-time authors. 80% from unagented writers. Pays 10% royalty on wholesale price. Provides 20 author's copies; 40% discount on subsequent copies. Pays $1,000-3,000 advance.** Publishes book 2 years after acceptance. Accepts simultaneous submissions. Responds in 1 month to queries & to proposals. Responds in 4 months to mss. Catalog available free. Guidelines online.

Arte Publico Press is the oldest and largest publisher of Hispanic literature for children and adults in the United States. "We are a showcase for **Hispanic** literary creativity, arts and culture. Our endeavor is to provide a national forum for U.S.-Hispanic literature."

NONFICTION Subjects include ethnic, language, literature, regional, translation, women's issues/studies. Hispanic civil rights issues for new series: The Hispanic Civil Rights Series. Query with SASE. Submit outline, 2 sample chapters.

FICTION Subjects include contemporary, ethnic, literary, mainstream. "Written by U.S.-Hispanics." Query with SASE. Submit outline/proposal, clips, 2 sample chapters. Submit complete ms.

POETRY Submit 10 sample poems.

TIPS "Include cover letter in which you 'sell' your book—why should we publish the book, who will

want to read it, why does it matter, etc. Use our ms submission online form. Format files accepted are: Word, plain/text, rich/text files. Other formats will not be accepted. Manuscript files cannot be larger than 5MB. Once editors review your ms, you will receive an e-mail with the decision. Revision process could take up to four (4) months."

ASA, AVIATION SUPPLIES & ACADEMICS

7005 132 Place SE, Newcastle WA 98059. (425)235-1500. **E-mail:** feedback@asa2fly.com. **Website:** www. asa2fly.com. Catalog available free.

"ASA is an industry leader in the development and sales of aviation supplies, publications, and software for pilots, flight instructors, flight engineers and aviation technicians. All ASA products are developed by a team of researchers, authors and editors."

NONFICTION "We are primarily an aviation publisher. Educational books in this area are our specialty; other aviation books will be considered." All subjects must be related to aviation education and training. Query with outline. Send photocopies.

TIPS "Two of our specialty series include ASA's *Focus Series*, and ASA *Aviator's Library*. Books in our *Focus Series* concentrate on single-subject areas of aviation knowledge, curriculum and practice. The *Aviator's Library* is comprised of titles of known and/or classic aviation authors or established instructor/authors in the industry, and other aviation specialty titles."

ASABI PUBLISHING

Three West Enterprises, (813)579-3506. **E-mail:** submissions@asabipublishing.com. **E-mail:** submissions@asabipublishing.com. **Website:** www.asabipublishing.com. **Contact:** Tressa Sanders, publisher. Estab. 2004. Publishes hardcover, mass market and trade paperback originals. **Publishes 24 titles/year. Accepts submissions electronically only. 90% of books from first-time authors. 90% from unagented writers. Pays 10% royalty on wholesale or list price. Pays up to $500 advance.** Publishes book 6 months after acceptance. Accepts simultaneous submissions. Responds in 1 month to queries and proposals, 2-6 months to mss. Catalog online. Guidelines available online and by e-mail.

FICTION Subjects include adventure, confession, erotica, ethnic, experimental, fantasy, gay, horror, juvenile, lesbian, mystery, romance, science fiction, short story collections, suspense, young adult. Submit 4 sample chapters or completed ms.

ASCE PRESS

American Society of Civil Engineers, 1801 Alexander Bell Dr., Reston VA 20191. (703)295-6275. **Fax:** (703)295-6278. **E-mail:** bkulamer@asce.org. **Website:** www.asce.org/pubs. Estab. 1989. **Publishes 10-15 titles/year. 20% of books from first-time authors. 100% from unagented writers.** Guidelines online.

8—🠶 "ASCE Press publishes technical volumes that are useful to practicing civil engineers and civil engineering students, as well as allied professionals. We publish books by individual authors and editors to advance the civil engineering profession. Currently emphasizing geotechnical, structural engineering, sustainable engineering and engineering history. De-emphasizing highly specialized areas with narrow scope."

NONFICTION "We are looking for topics that are useful and instructive to the engineering practitioner." Query with proposal, sample chapters, CV, TOC, and target audience.

TIPS "As a traditional publisher of scientific and technical materials, ASCE Press applies rigorous standards to the expertise, scholarship, readability and attractiveness of its books."

ASHLAND POETRY PRESS

401 College Avenue, Ashland OH 44805. (419)289-5957. **Fax:** (419)289-5255. **E-mail:** app@ashland.edu. **Website:** www.ashland.edu/aupoetry. **Contact:** Sarah M. Wells, managing editor. Estab. 1969. Publishes trade paperback originals. **Publishes 2-3 titles/year. 360 mss received/year. 50% of books from first-time authors. 100% from unagented writers. Makes outright purchase of $500-1,000.** Publishes book 10 months after acceptance. Accepts simultaneous submissions. Responds in 1 month to queries; 6 months to mss. Catalog and guidelines online.

POETRY "We accept unsolicited manuscripts through the Snyder Prize competition each spring-the deadline is April 30. Judges are mindful of dedication to craftsmanship and thematic integrity."

TIPS "We rarely publish a title submitted off the transom outside of our Snyder Prize competition."

ASM PRESS

Book division for the American Society for Microbiology, 1752 N. St., NW, Washington DC 20036. (202)737-3600. **Fax:** (202)942-9342. **E-mail:** lwilliams@asmusa.org. **Website:** www.asmpress.org. **Contact:** Lindsay Williams (proposal submissions-books); Gregory Payne, senior editor (all microbiology and related sciences); Eleanor Riemer, consulting editor (food microbiology). Estab. 1899. Publishes hardcover, trade paperback and electronic originals. **Publishes 30 titles/year. 40% of books from first-time authors. 95% from unagented writers. Pays 5-15% royalty on wholesale price. Pays $1,000-10,000 advance.** Publishes book 6-9 months after acceptance. Accepts simultaneous submissions. Responds in 1 month to queries; 2 months to proposals; 4 months to mss. Catalog and guidelines online.

NONFICTION Subjects include agriculture, animals, education, health, medicine, history, horticulture, nature, environment, science., microbiology and related sciences. "Must have bona fide academic credentials in which they are writing." Query with SASE or by e-mail. Submit proposal package, outline, prospectus. Proposals for journal articles must be submitted to the journals department at: journals@asmusa.com. Reviews artwork/photos. Send photocopies.

TIPS "Credentials are most important."

ASTRAGAL PRESS

Finney Company, 8075 215th St. West, Lakeville MN 55044. (866)543-3045. **Fax:** (952)669-1968. **E-mail:** feedback@finneyco.com. **Website:** www.astragalpress.com. Estab. 1983. Publishes trade paperback originals and reprints. Accepts simultaneous submissions. Catalog and guidelines free.

8—🠶 "Our primary audience includes those interested in antique tool collecting, metalworking, carriage building, early sciences and early trades, and railroading."

NONFICTION Wants books on early tools, trades & technology, and railroads. Query with SASE. Submit sample chapters, TOC, book overview, illustration descriptions. Submit complete ms.

TIPS "We sell to niche markets. We are happy to work with knowledgeable amateur authors in developing titles."

Ⓐ⊘ ATHENEUM BOOKS FOR YOUNG READERS

Simon & Schuster, 1230 Avenue of the Americas, New York NY 10020. **Website:** http://imprints.simonandschuster.biz/atheneum; www.simonsayskids.com. **Contact:** Caitlyn Dlouhy, editorial director; Justin

Chanda, VP/publisher; Namrata Tripathi, executive editor; Emma Dryden, vice president. Estab. 1960. Publishes hardcover originals. Accepts simultaneous submissions. Guidelines for #10 SASE.

🔑➤ "Atheneum Books for Young Readers publishes books aimed at children, pre-school through high school." Publishes hardcover originals, picture books for young kids, nonfiction for ages 8-12 and novels for middle-grade and young adults. Types of books include biography, historical fiction, history, nonfiction. Publishes 60 titles/year. 100% require freelance illustration. Catalog free by request. Approached by hundreds of freelance artists/year.

NONFICTION Subjects include Americana, animals, art, architecture, business, economics, government, politics, health, medicine, history, music, dance, nature, environment, photography, psychology, recreation, religion, science, sociology, sports, travel. Publishes hardcover originals, picture books for young kids, nonfiction for ages 8-12 and novels for middle-grade and young adults. Types of books include biography, historical fiction, history, nonfiction. Publishes 60 titles/year. 100% require freelance illustration. Catalog free by request. *Query only for all submissions.*

FICTION Subjects include adventure, ethnic, experimental, fantasy, gothic, historical, horror, humor, mainstream, contemporary, mystery, science fiction, sports, suspense, western, animal. All in juvenile versions. "We have few specific needs except for books that are fresh, interesting and well written. Fad topics are dangerous, as are works you haven't polished to the best of your ability. We also don't need safety pamphlets, ABC books, coloring books and board books. In writing picture book texts, avoid the coy and `cutesy,' such as stories about characters with alliterative names. *Query only. No unsolicited mss.*" No paperback romance-type fiction.

TIPS "Study our titles."

A.T. PUBLISHING

23 Lily Lake Rd., Highland NY 12528. (845)691-2021. **E-mail:** tjp2@optonline.net. **Contact:** Anthony Prizzia, publisher (education); John Prizzia, publisher. Estab. 2001. Publishes trade paperback originals. **Publishes 1-3 titles/year. 5-10 queries received/year; 5-10 100% of books from first-time authors. 100% from unagented writers. Pays 15-25% royalty on retail price. Makes outright purchase of $500-2,500.**

Pays $500-1,000 advance. Accepts simultaneous submissions. Responds in 1 month to queries; 2 months to proposals; 4 months to mss.

NONFICTION Subjects include cooking, foods, nutrition, education, recreation, science, sports. Query with SASE. Submit complete ms. Reviews artwork/photos. Send photocopies.

TIPS "Audience is people interested in a variety of topics, general. Submit typed manuscript for consideration, including a SASE for return of ms."

ATRIAD PRESS, LLC

13820 Methuen Green, Dallas TX 75240. (972)671-0002. **Fax:** (214)367-4343. **E-mail:** ginnie@atriadpress.com. **E-mail:** editor@atriadpress.com. **Website:** www.atriadpress.com; www.hauntedencounters.com. **Contact:** Mitchel Whitington, senior editor. Estab. 2002. Publishes trade paperback originals. **Writers selected for this collection of personal ghost tales will receive a copy of the book in which their story appears. Authors can purchase additional copies of the books at discounted prices, and re-sell them at book signings, speaking engagements, etc. for additional revenue. A photo and brief bio of the author will be included at the end of the story.** Accepts simultaneous submissions. Catalog and guidelines online.

🔑➤ "We are seeking books on supernatural happenings focused on the State of Texas. The first two titles in this series are: *True Tales of Texas Ghosts: Living in a Haunted House* and *True Tales of Texas Ghosts: Spirits in the Workplace.* A submission should be based on a true, supernatural encounter that you have personally experienced in the State of Texas. Length requirements are somewhat flexible, but stories should be 1,000-2,000 words. Longer stories will be considered."

NONFICTION "Atriad Press publishes nonfiction Texas genre books only." No poetry, children's books or fiction, please. No family memoirs, either, unless your family was famous, or better yet, infamous. No extreme violence, explicit sexual content, strong language, or any other elements that makes them inappropriate for a teenaged audience. Does not want UFO or angels. Query first. "We prefer e-mail rather than postal mail."

TIPS "Manuscripts should be written on an adult level, but please keep in mind that we market to school libraries. Approximate length should be 65,000 words. The market for ghost stories ranges from young to old. Please check your manuscript carefully for errors in spelling and structure."

AUTUMN HOUSE PRESS

87½ Westwood St., Pittsburgh PA 15211. (412)381-261. **E-mail:** info@autumnhouse.org. **Website:** www.autumnhouse.org. **Contact:** Michael Simms, editor-in-chief (fiction). Sharon Dilworth, fiction editor Estab. 1998. Hardcover, trade paperback, and electronic originals. Format: acid-free paper; offset printing; perfect and casebound (cloth) bound; sometimes contains illustrations. Average print order: 1,500. Debut novel print order: 1,500. **Publishes 8 titles/year. 1,000 mss/year 10% of books from first-time authors. 100% from unagented writers. Pays 7% royalty on wholesale price Pays $0-2,500 advance.** Publishes book 9 months from acceptance to publication after acceptance of ms. Accepts simultaneous submissions. Responds in 1-3 days on queries and proposals; 3 months on mss. Catalog free on request. Guidelines online; free on request; or for #10 SASE.

FICTION Subjects include literary. "We are pleased to announce the fourth annual Autumn House Fiction Contest. For the 2011 contest, the preliminary judge is John Fried, and the final judge is Stewart O'Nan; the winner will be awarded publication of a full-length manuscript and $2,500. The postmark deadline for entries is June 30, 2011. For further questions, feel free to e-mail us, message us on Twitter, or ask us through our Facebook Fan Page. The winners will receive book publication, $1,000 advance against royalties, and a $1,500 travel grant to participate in the 2012 Autumn House Master Authors Series in Pittsburgh. The deadline is June 30, 2011. *We ask that all submissions from authors new to Autumn House come through one of our annual contests.* All finalists will be considered for publication. The final judge for the Fiction Prize is Stewart O'Nan. Fiction submissions should be approximately 200-300 pages. All fiction sub-genres (short stories, short-shorts, novellas, or novels) or any combination of sub-genres are eligible. Submit only through our annual contest. See guidelines online. Submit completed ms."

POETRY Since 2003, the annual Autumn House Poetry Contest has awarded publication of a full-length manuscript and $2,500 to the winner. For the 2011 contest, the preliminary judge is Thom Ward, and the final judge is Denise Duhamel. The postmark deadline for entries is June 30, 2011. For further questions, feel free to e-mail us, message us on Twitter, or ask us through our Facebook Fan Page. The deadline is June 30, 2011. *We ask that all submissions from authors new to Autumn House come through one of our annual contests.* All finalists will be considered for publication. The final judge for the Poetry Prize is Denise Duhamel. Submit only through our annual contest.

TIPS "The competition to publish with Autumn House is very tough. Submit only your best work."

Ⓐ AVALON BOOKS

Thomas Bouregy & Sons, Inc., 160 Madison Ave., 5th Floor, New York NY 10016. (212)598-0222. **Fax:** (212)979-1862. **E-mail:** editorial@avalonbooks.com; avalon@avalonbooks.com; lbrown@avalonbooks.com. **Website:** www.avalonbooks.com. **Contact:** Lia Brown, editor. Estab. 1950. Publishes hardcover originals. **Publishes 60 titles/year. Pays 10% royalty. Pays $1,000 advance.** Publishes book Publishes a book 12-18 months after acceptance. Responds in 2-3 months to queries. Guidelines online.

FICTION "We publish contemporary romances, historical romances, mysteries and westerns. Time period and setting are the author's preference. The historical romances will maintain the high level of reading expected by our readers. The books shall be wholesome fiction, without graphic sex, violence or strong language. We do accept unagented material. We no longer accept e-mail queries. When submitting, include a query letter, a 2-3 page (and no longer) synopsis of the entire ms, and the first three chapters. All submissions must be typed and double spaced. If we think that your novel might be suitable for our list, we will contact you and request that you submit the entire manuscript. **Please note that any unsolicited full manuscripts will not be returned.** There is no need to send your partial to any specific editor at Avalon. The editors read all the genres that are listed above. Address your letter to: **The Editors**."

TIPS "Avalon Books are geared and marketed for librarians to purchase and distribute."

AVON BOOKS

Harper Collins Publishers, 10 E. 53 Street, New York NY 10022. **Website:** www.harpercollins.com. **Contact:** Michael Morrison, publisher. Estab. 1941. Publishes hardcover and paperback originals and reprints. **Publishes 400 titles/year.**

○ *Does not accept unsolicited mss.*

☞ "Avon has been publishing award-winning books since 1941. It is recognized for having pioneered the historical romance category and continues to bring the best of commercial literature to the broadest possible audience."

FICTION Subjects include historical, literary, mystery, romance, science fiction, young adult. Query with SASE. Send SASE or IRC.

⊕ AZRO PRESS

PMB 342, 1704 Llano St. B, Santa Fe NM 87505. (505)989-3272. **Fax:** (505)989-3832. **E-mail:** books@azropress.com; book@cybermesa.com. **Website:** www.azropress.com. **Contact:** Gae Eisenhardt. Estab. 1997. **Pays authors royalty of 5-10% based on wholesale price. Pays illustrators by the project ($2,000) or royalty of 5%.** Publishes book 1-2 years after acceptance. Accepts simultaneous submissions. Responds to queries/mss in 3-4 months. Catalog available for #10 SASE and 3 first-class stamps or online.

○ "We like to publish illustrated children's books by Southwestern authors and illustrators. We are always looking for books with a Southwestern look or theme."

NONFICTION Picture books: animal, geography, history. Young readers: geography, history. Query or submit complete ms.

FICTION Picture books: animal, history, humor, nature/environment. Young readers: adventure, animal, hi-lo, history, humor. Average word length: picture books—1,200; young readers—2,000-2,500. Query or submit complete ms.

TIPS "We are not currently accepting new manuscripts. Please see our website for acceptance date."

BACKBEAT BOOKS

Hal Leonard Publishing Group, 33 Plymouth St., Suite 302, Montclair NJ 07042. (800)637-2852. **E-mail:** medison@halleonard.com. **Website:** www.backbeatbooks.com. **Contact:** Mike Edison, senior editor (rock, jazz, pop culture). Kristina Radke, publicity Publishes hardcover and trade paperback originals; trade paperback reprints. **Publishes 24 titles/year.**

NONFICTION Subjects include music (rock & roll)., pop culture. Query by e-mail.

BAEN BOOKS

P.O. Box 1188, Wake Forest NC 27588. (919)570-1640. **E-mail:** artdirector@baen.com. **Website:** www.baen.

com. Estab. 1983. Responds to mss within 12-18 months.

☞ "We publish only science fiction and fantasy. Writers familiar with what we have published in the past will know what sort of material we are most likely to publish in the future: powerful plots with solid scientific and philosophical underpinnings are the sine qua non for consideration for science fiction submissions. As for fantasy, any magical system must be both rigorously coherent and integral to the plot, and overall the work must at least strive for originality."

FICTION "Style: Simple is generally better; in our opinion good style, like good breeding, never calls attention to itself. Length: 100,000-130,000 words Generally we are uncomfortable with manuscripts under 100,000 words, but if your novel is really wonderful send it along regardless of length. Query letters are not necessary. We prefer to see complete mss accompanied by a synopsis. We prefer not to see simultaneous submissions. Electronic submissions are strongly preferred. *We no longer accept submissions by e-mail.* Send ms by using the submission form."

⊕ BAILIWICK PRESS

309 East Mulberry St., Fort Collins CO 80524. (970) 672-4878. **Fax:** (970) 672-4731. **E-mail:** info@bailiwickpress.com. **Website:** www.bailiwickpress.com.

☞ "We're a micro-press that produces books and other products that inspire and tell great stories. Our motto is 'books with something to say.' We are now considering submissions, agented and unagented, for children's and young adult fiction. We're looking for smart, funny, and layered writing that kids will clamor for. Illustrated fiction is desired but not required. (Illustrators are also invited to send samples.) Make us laugh out loud, ooh and aah, and cry, 'Eureka!' Please read the Aldo Zelnick series to determine if we might be on the same page, then fill out our submission form. Please do not send submissions via snail mail. You must complete the online submission form to be considered. If, after completing and submitting the form, you also need to send us an e-mail attachment (such as sample illustrations or excerpts of graphics), you may e-mail them to info@bailiwickpress.com."

⊘ BAKER ACADEMIC

Division of Baker Publishing Group, 6030 E. Fulton Rd., Ada MI 49301. (616)676-9185. **Fax:** (616)676-2315. **Website:** www.bakeracademic.com. Estab. 1939. Publishes hardcover and trade paperback originals. **Publishes 50 titles/year. 10% of books from first-time authors. 85% from unagented writers. Pays advance.** Publishes book 1 year after acceptance. Catalog for 9½×12½ SAE with 3 first-class stamps. Guidelines for #10 SASE.

○ "Baker Academic publishes religious academic and professional books for students and church leaders. Does not accept unsolicited queries. We will consider unsolicited work only through one of the following avenues. Materials sent to our editorial staff through a professional literary agent will be considered. In addition, our staff attends various writers' conferences at which prospective authors can develop relationships with those in the publishing industry. You may also submit your work to the following ms submission service, which serve sas a liaison between publishers and prospective authors: Christian Manuscript Submissions, an online service of the Evangelical Christian Publishers' Association: Website: www.christianmanuscriptsubmissions.com; E-mail: info@christianmanuscriptsubmissions.com."

NONFICTION Subjects include anthropology, archeology, education, psychology, religion, women's issues/studies., Biblical studies, Christian doctrine, books for pastors and church leaders, contemporary issues.

Ⓐ⊘ BAKER BOOKS

6030 East Fulton Rd., Ada MI 49301. **Website:** www.bakerbooks.com. Estab. 1939. Publishes in hardcover and trade paperback originals, and trade paperback reprints. Catalog for 9½×12½ envelope and 3 first-class stamps. Guidelines for #10 SASE and online.

NONFICTION Subjects include childe guidance, psychology, religion, women's issues/studies, Christian doctrines. "We will consider unsolicited work only through one of the following avenues. Materials sent through a literary agent will be considered; various writers' conferences; also to one or more of the following manuscript submission services, which serve as a liaison between publishers and prospective authors:

Authonomy.com, The Writer's Edge, and Christian Manuscript Submissions, an online service of the Evangelical Christian Publishers' Association. You may contact these organizations at these addresses: Authonomy.com, www.authonomy.com/christian. The Writer's Edge, P.O. Box 1266, Wheaton, IL 60189, writersedgeservice.com, info@writersedgeservice.com. Christian Manuscript Submissions, www.christianmanuscriptsubmissions.com, and info@christianmanuscriptsubmissions.com. Baker Academic welcomes book proposals from prospective authors holding relevant academic credentials (which usually means a Ph.D. or similar degree in the field of the proposed book and a teaching position at a recognized institution of higher learning). If you have been in previous conversation with a Baker Academic editor, you may send your proposal to that editor. Otherwise, your proposal may be sent by post or e-mail to: Submissions, Baker Academic, PO Box 6287, Grand Rapids, MI 49516-6287 or submissions@bakeracademic.com."

TIPS "We are not interested in historical fiction, romances, science fiction, biblical narratives or spiritual warfare novels. Do not call to 'pass by' your idea."

BALZER & BRAY

HarperCollins Children's Books, 10 E. 53rd St., New York NY 10022. **Website:** www.harpercollinschildrens.com. Estab. 2008. **Publishes 10 titles/year. Offers advances. Pays illustrators by the project.** Publishes book 18 months after acceptance.

NONFICTION All levels: animal, biography, concept, cooking, history, multicultural, music/dance, nature/environment, science, self-help, social issues, special needs, sports. "We will publish very few non-fiction titles, maybe 1-2 per year."

FICTION Picture Books, Young Readers: adventure, animal, anthology, concept, contemporary, fantasy, history, humor, multicultural, nature/environment, poetry, science fiction, special needs, sports, suspense. Middle Readers, Young Adults/Teens: adventure, animal, anthology, contemporary, fantasy, history, humor, multicultural, nature/environment, poetry, science fiction, special needs, sports, suspense.

Ⓐ BANCROFT PRESS

P.O. Box 65360, Baltimore MD 21209-9945. (410)358-0658. **Fax:** (410)764-1967. **E-mail:** bruceb@bancroftpress.com; HDemchick@bancroftpress.com (if bancrof account is down). **Website:** www.bancroftpress.com. **Contact:** Bruce Bortz, editor/publisher (health, investments, politics, history, humor, literary novels, mystery/thrillers, chick lit, young adult). Publishes hardcover and trade paperback originals. **Publishes 4-6 titles/year. Pays 6-8% royalty. Pays various royalties on retail price. Pays $750 advance.** Publishes book up to 3 years after acceptance of ms. Accepts simultaneous submissions. Responds in 6-12 months to queries, proposals and manuscripts. Guidelines online.

⚷ "Bancroft Press is a general trade publisher. We publish young adult fiction and adult fiction, as well as occasional nonfiction. Our only mandate is 'books that enlighten.'"

NONFICTION Subjects include business, economics, government, politics, health, medicine, money, finance, regional, sports, women's issues/studies., popular culture. "We advise writers to visit the website." All quality books on any subject of interest to the publisher. Submit proposal package, outline, 2 sample chapters, competition/market survey.

FICTION Subjects include ethnic, general, feminist, gay, lesbian, historical, humor, literary, mainstream, contemporary, military, war, mystery, amateur sleuth, cozy, police procedural, private eye/hardboiled, regional, science fiction, hard science fiction/technological, soft/sociological, translation, frontier sage, traditional, young adult, historical, problem novels, series, thrillers.

TIPS "We advise writers to visit our website and to be familiar with our previous work. Patience is the number one attribute contributors must have. It takes us a very long time to get through submitted material, because we are such a small company. Also, we only publish 4-6 books per year, so it may take a long time for your optioned book to be published. We like to be able to market our books to be used in schools and in libraries. We prefer fiction that bucks trends and moves in a new direction. We are especially interested in mysteries and humor (especially humorous mysteries)."

ⒶⓄ BANTAM BOOKS

Imprint of Random House Children's Books/Random House, Inc., 1745 Broadway, New York NY 10019. (212)782-9000. **Website:** www.randomhouse.com/kids; www.randomhouse.com/teens.

○ *Not seeking mss at this time.*

BARRICADE BOOKS, INC.

185 Bridge Plaza N., Suite 309, Fort Lee NJ 07024. (201)944-7600. **Fax:** (201)917-4951. **Website:** www.barricadebooks.com. **Contact:** Carole Stuart, publisher. Estab. 1991. Publishes hardcover and trade paperback originals, trade paperback reprints. **Publishes 12 titles/year. 200 queries received/year. 100 mss received/year. 80% of books from first-time authors. 50% from unagented writers. Pays 10-12% royalty on retail price for hardcover. Pays advance.** Publishes book 18 months after acceptance. Responds in 1 month to queries.

⚷ "Barricade Books publishes nonfiction, mostly of the controversial type, and books we can promote with authors who can talk about their topics on radio and television and to the press."

NONFICTION Subjects include business, economics, ethnic, gay, lesbian, government, politics, health, medicine, history, nature, environment, psychology, sociology, true crime. We look for quality non-fiction manuscripts—preferably with a controversial lean. Query with SASE. Submit outline, 1-2 sample chapters. Material will not be returned or responded to without SASE. We do not accept proposals on disk or via e-mail. Reviews artwork/photos.

TIPS "Do your homework. Visit bookshops to find publishers who are doing the kinds of books you want to write. Always submit to a person—not just `Editor.'"

BASIC HEALTH PUBLICATIONS, INC.

28812 Top of the World Dr., Laguna Beach CA 92651. (949)715-7327. **Fax:** (949)715-7328. **Website:** www.basichealthpub.com. **Contact:** Norman Goldfind, publisher. Estab. 2001. Publishes hardcover trade paperback and mass market paperback originals and reprints. Accepts simultaneous submissions. Catalog online. Guidelines for #10 SASE.

NONFICTION Subjects include health, medicine. "We are very highly focused on health, alternative medicine, nutrition, and fitness. Must be well researched and documented with appropriate references. Writing should be aimed at lay audience but also be able to cross over to professional market." Submit proposal package, outline, 2-3 sample chapters, introduction.

TIPS "Our audience is over 30, well educated, middle to upper income. We prefer writers with professional credentials (M.D.s, PhD.s, N.D.s, etc.), or writers with backgrounds in health and medicine."

BAYLOR UNIVERSITY PRESS

One Bear Place 97363, Waco TX 76798. (254)710-3164; 3522. **Fax:** (254)710-3440. **E-mail:** carey_newman@baylor.edu. **Website:** www.baylorpress.com. **Contact:** Dr. Carey C. Newman, director. Publishes hardcover and trade paperback originals. **Publishes 30 titles/year. Pays 10% royalty on wholesale price.** Publishes book 1 year after acceptance. Accepts simultaneous submissions. Responds in 2 months to proposals. Guidelines online.

8—π "We publish contemporary and historical scholarly works about culture, religion, politics, science, and the arts."

NONFICTION Submit outline, 1-3 sample chapters.

BEARMANOR MEDIA

P.O. Box 1129, Duncan OK 73534. (580)252-3547. **Fax:** (814)690-1559. **E-mail:** books@benohmart.com. **Website:** www.bearmanormedia.com. **Contact:** Ben Ohmart, publisher. Estab. 2000. Publishes trade paperback originals and reprints. **Publishes 70 titles/year. 90% of books from first-time authors. 90% from unagented writers. Negotiable per project. Pays upon acceptance.** Accepts simultaneous submissions. Responds only if interested. Catalog vailable online, or free with a 9×12 SASE submission.

NONFICTION Subjects include old-time radio, voice actors, old movies, classic television. Query with SASE. E-mail queries preferred. Submit proposal package, outline, list of credits on the subject.

TIPS "My readers love the past. Radio, old movies, old television. My own tastes include voice actors and scripts, especially of radio and television no longer available. I prefer books on subjects that haven't previously been covered as full books. It doesn't matter to me if you're a first-time author or have a track record. Just know your subject!"

BEDFORD/ST. MARTIN'S

Division of Macmillan Publishers, Boston Office, 75 Arlington St., Boston MA 02116. (617)399-4000. **E-mail:** contactus@bedfordstmartins.com; ddennison@bedfordstmartins.com. **Website:** www.bedfordstmartins.com. **Contact:** Donna Lee Dennison, senior art director. Estab. 1981. **Publishes 200 titles/year.** Catalog online.

8—π Publishes college textbooks. Subjects include English composition, literature, history, communications, philosophy, music. Photos used for text illustrations, promotional materials, book covers.

BEHRMAN HOUSE INC.

11 Edison Place, Springfield NJ 07081. (973)379-7200. **Fax:** (973)379-7280. Estab. 1921. **12% of books from first-time authors. Pays authors royalty of 3-10% based on retail price or buys ms outright for $1,000-5,000. Offers advance. Pays illustrators by the project (range: $500-5,000).** Publishes book 18 months after acceptance. Accepts simultaneous submissions. Responds in 1 month to queries; 2 months to mss. Catalog free on request.

8—π Publishes books on all aspects of Judaism: history, cultural, textbooks, holidays. "Behrman House publishes quality books of Jewish content—history, Bible, philosophy, holidays, ethics—for children and adults."

NONFICTION All levels: Judaism, Jewish educational textbooks. Average word length: young reader—1,200; middle reader—2,000; young adult—4,000. Submit outline/synopsis and sample chapters.

FICTION Submit outline/synopsis, sample chapters.

TIPS Looking for "religious school texts" with Judaic themes or general trade Judaica.

FREDERIC C. BEIL, PUBLISHER, INC.

609 Whitaker St., Savannah GA 31401. (912)233-2446. **Fax:** (912)233-6456. **E-mail:** books@beil.com. **Website:** www.beil.com. **Contact:** Mary Ann Bowman, editor. Estab. 1982. Publishes hardcover originals and reprints. **Publishes 13 titles/year. 3,500 queries received/year. 13 mss received/year. 80% of books from first-time authors. 100% from unagented writers. Pays 7 ½% royalty on retail price.** Publishes book 20 months after acceptance of ms. Accepts simultaneous submissions. Responds in 1 week to queries. Catalog available free.

NONFICTION Subjects include art, architecture, history, language, literature., book arts. Query with SASE. Reviews artwork/photos. Send photocopies.

FICTION Subjects include historical, literary, regional, short story collections, translation., biography. Query with SASE.

TIPS "Our objectives are (1) to offer to the reading public carefully selected texts of lasting value; (2) to adhere to high standards in the choice of materials and in bookmaking craftsmanship; (3) to produce books that exemplify good taste in format and design; and (4) to maintain the lowest cost consistent with quality."

BELLEVUE LITERARY PRESS

New York University School of Medicine, Dept. of Medicine, NYU School of Medicine, 550 First Avenue, OBV 612, New York NY 10016. (212) 263-7802. **E-mail:** BLPsubmissions@gmail.com. **Website:** http://blpress.org. Estab. 2005.

➤ "Publishes literary and authoritative fiction and nonfiction at the nexus of the arts and the sciences, with a special focus on medicine. As our authors explore cultural and historical representations of the human body, illness, and health, they address the impact of scientific and medical practice on the individual and society."

NONFICTION "If you have a completed manuscript, a sample of a manuscript or a proposal that fits our mission as a press feel free to submit it to us by postal mail. Please keep in mind that at this time we are unable to return manuscripts. We will also accept short proposals by e-mail. You may submit them to either Erika Goldman or her assistant Leslie Hodgkins at: leslie.hodgkins@med.nyu.edu."

TIPS "We are a project of New York University's School of Medicine and while our standards reflect NYU's excellence in scholarship, humanistic medicine, and science, our authors need not be affiliated with NYU. We are not a university press and do not receive any funding from NYU. Our publishing operations are financed exclusively by foundation grants, private donors, and book sales revenue."

BENBELLA BOOKS

10300 N. Central Expy., Suite 400, Dallas TX 75231, United States. **Website:** www.benbellabooks.com. **Contact:** Glenn Yeffeth, publisher. Estab. 2001. Publishes hardcover and trade paperback originals. **Publishes 20-25 titles/year. Pays 6-15% royalty on retail price.** Publishes book 10 months after acceptance. Accepts simultaneous submissions. Guidelines online.

NONFICTION Subjects include pop contemporary culture, cooking, foods, nutrition, health, medicine, literary criticism, money, finance, science. Submit proposal package, including: outline, 2 sample chapters (via e-mail).

☺ BENDALL BOOKS

P.O. BOX 115, Mill Bay BC V0R2P0, CA. (250)743-2946. **Fax:** (250)743-2910. **E-mail:** admin@bendall-

books.com. **Website:** www.bendallbooks.com. **Contact:** Mary Moore, publisher. Publishes trade paperback originals. **Publishes 1 title/year. 30 queries received/year. 5 mss received/year. 50% of books from first-time authors. 100% from unagented writers. Pays 5-15% royalty on wholesale price.** Publishes book 1 year after acceptance. Catalog available free. Guidelines online.

NONFICTION Subjects include education.

BENTLEY PUBLISHERS

1734 Massachusetts Ave., Cambridge MA 02138. (617)547-4170. **Fax:** (617)876-9235. **E-mail:** michael.bentley@bentleypublishers.com. **Website:** www.bentleypublishers.com. **Contact:** Michael Bentley, president. Estab. 1950. Publishes hardcover and trade paperback originals and reprints. Catalog and guidelines online and with 9x12 SASE with 4 first-class stamps.

➤ "Bentley Publishers publishes books for automotive enthusiasts. We are interested in books that showcase good research, strong illustrations, and valuable technical information." Automotive subjects only. Query with SASE. Submit sample chapters, bio, synopsis, target market. Reviews artwork/photos.

NONFICTION Subjects include Automotive subjects only. Query with SASE. Submit sample chapters, bio, synopsis, target market. Rreviews artwork/photos.

TIPS "Our audience is composed of serious, intelligent automobile, sports car, and racing enthusiasts, automotive technicians and high-performance tuners."

❷⊘ THE BERKLEY PUBLISHING GROUP

Penguin Group (USA) Inc., 375 Hudson St., New York NY 10014. **Website:** http://us.penguingroup.com/. **Contact:** Leslie Gelbman, president and publisher. Estab. 1955. Publishes paperback and mass market originals and reprints. **Publishes 500 titles/year.**

➤ "Due to the high volume of manuscripts received, most Penguin Group (USA) Inc. imprints do not normally accept unsolicited manuscripts. The preferred and standard method for having manuscripts considered for publication by a major publisher is to submit them through an established literary agent."

NONFICTION Subjects include business, economics, child guidance, creative nonfiction, gay, lesbian, health, medicine, history, New Age, psychology, true crime, job-seeking communication. No memoirs or personal stories. *Prefers agented submissions.*

FICTION Subjects include adventure, historical, literary, mystery, romance, spiritual, suspense, western, young adult. No occult fiction. *Prefers agented submissions.*

BERRETT-KOEHLER PUBLISHERS, INC.

235 Montgomery St., Suite 650, San Francisco CA 94104. (415)288-0260. **Fax:** (415)362-2512. **E-mail:** bkpub@bkpub.com. **Website:** www.bkconnection.com. **Contact:** Jeevan Sivasubramaniam, senior managing editor. Publishes hardcover & trade paperback originals, mass market paperback originals, hardcover & trade paperback reprints. **Publishes 40 titles/year. 1,300 queries received/year. 800 mss received/year. 20-30% of books from first-time authors. 70% from unagented writers. Pays 10-20% royalty.** Publishes book 10 months after acceptance. Accepts simultaneous submissions. Responds in 1 month to queries, proposals and mss. Catalog and guidelines online.

⊶ "Berrett-Koehler Publishers' mission is to publish books that support the movement toward a world that works for all. Our titles promote positive change at personal, organizational and societal levels." Please see proposal guidelines online.

NONFICTION Subjects include business, economics, community, government, politics, New Age, spirituality. Submit proposal package, outline, bio, 1-2 sample chapters. Hard-copy proposals only. Do not e-mail, fax, or phone please. Reviews artwork/photos. Send photocopies or originals with SASE.

TIPS "Our audience is business leaders. Use common sense, do your research."

⊘ BETHANY HOUSE PUBLISHERS

Baker Publishing Group, 6030 E. Fulton Rd., Ada MI 49301. (616)676-9185. **Fax:** (616)676-9573. **Website:** www.bethanyhouse.com. Estab. 1956. Publishes hardcover and trade paperback originals, mass market paperback reprints. **Publishes 90-100 titles/year. 2% of books from first-time authors. 50% from unagented writers. Pays royalty on net price. Pays advance.** Publishes book Publishes a book 1 year after acceptance. Accepts simultaneous submissions. Responds in 3 months to queries. Catalog for 9×12 envelope and 5 first-class stamps. Guidelines online.

◗ *All unsolicited mss returned unopened.*

NONFICTION Subjects include child guidance., Biblical disciplines, personal and corporate renewal, emerging generations, devotional, marriage and family, applied theology, inspirational.

FICTION Subjects include historical, young adult., contemporary.

TIPS Bethany House Publishers' publishing program relates Biblical truth to all areas of life—whether in the framework of a well-told story, of a challenging book for spiritual growth, or of a Bible reference work. We are seeking high-quality fiction and nonfiction that will inspire and challenge our audience.

BETTERWAY HOME BOOKS

Imprint of F+W Media, Inc., 10151 Carver Rd., Suite 200, Cincinnati OH 45242. (513)531-2690, ext. 11467. **E-mail:** jacqueline.musser@fwmedia.com. **Website:** www.betterwaybooks.com. **Contact:** Jacqueline Musser, acquisitions editor. Publishes trade paperback and hardcover originals. **Publishes 6-8 titles/year. 6 queries received/year. 60% of books from first-time authors. 95% from unagented writers. Pays 8-10% royalty on wholesale price. Pays $2,500-3,000 advance.** Publishes book 18 months after acceptance. Accepts simultaneous submissions. Responds in 3 month to queries and proposals.

NONFICTION Subjects include gardening, house and home., home organization, homemaking, simple living, homesteading skills, personal finance. Query with SASE. Submit proposal package, outline, 1 sample chapter. Reviews artwork/photos. Send photocopies and PDFs (if submitting electronically).

TIPS "Looking for authors with a strong web following in their book topic."

BICK PUBLISHING HOUSE

307 Neck Rd., Madison CT 06443. (203)245-0073. **Fax:** (203)245-5990. **E-mail:** bickpubhse@aol.com. **Website:** www.bickpubhouse.com. **Contact:** Dale Carlson, president. Estab. 1994. Publishes trade paperback originals. **Publishes 4 titles/year. 100 queries received/year; 100 mss received/year. 55% of books from first-time authors. 55% from unagented writers. Pays $500-1,000 advance.** Publishes book 1 year after acceptance. Responds in 1 month to queries; 2 months to proposals; 3 months to mss. Catalog available free. Guidelines for #10 SASE.

NONFICTION Subjects include health, medicine, disability/special needs, psychology., young adult or teen science, psychology, wildlife rehabilitation. Query with SASE. Submit proposal package, outline, résumé, 3 sample chapters.

TIPS "Read our books!"

BIRDSONG BOOKS

1322 Bayview Rd., Middletown DE 19709. (302)378-7274. **E-mail:** birdsong@birdsongbooks.com. **Website:** www.BirdsongBooks.com. **Contact:** Nancy Carol Willis, president. Estab. 1998. Publishes book 2-3 years after acceptance. Accepts simultaneous submissions. Responds to mss in 3 months.

✎ "Birdsong Books seeks to spark the delight of discovering our wild neighbors and natural habitats. We believe knowledge and understanding of nature fosters caring and a desire to protect the Earth and all living things. Our emphasis is on North American animals and habitats, rather than people."

NONFICTION Picture books, young readers: activity books, animal, nature/environment. Average word length: picture books—800-1,000 plus content for 2-4 pages of back matter. Submit complete ms package with SASE.

TIPS "We are a small independent press actively seeking manuscripts that fit our narrowly defined niche. We are only interested in nonfiction, natural science picture books or educational activity books about North American animals and habitats. We are not interested in fiction stories based on actual events. Our books include several pages of back matter suitable for early elementary classrooms. Mailed submissions with SASE only. No e-mail submissions or phone calls, please. Cover letters should sell author/illustrator and book idea."

BKMK PRESS

University of Missouri - Kansas City, 5101 Rockhill Rd., Kansas City MO 64110-2499. (816)235-2558. **Fax:** (816)235-2611. **E-mail:** bkmk@umkc.edu. **Website:** www.umkc.edu/bkmk. **Contact:** Ben Furnish, managing editor. Estab. 1971. Publishes trade paperback originals. **Publishes 4/year titles/year.** Accepts simultaneous submissions. Responds in 4-6 months to queries. Guidelines online.

✎ "BkMk Press publishes fine literature. Reading period January-June."

NONFICTION Creative nonfiction essays. Submit 25-50 pp. sample and SASE.

FICTION Subjects include literary, short story collections. Query with SASE.

POETRY Submit 10 sample poems and SASE.

TIPS "We skew toward readers of literature, particularly contemporary writing. Because of our limited number of titles published per year, we discourage apprentice writers or `scattershot' submissions."

BLACK DOME PRESS CORP.

1011 Route 296, Hensonville NY 12439. (518)734-6357. **Fax:** (518)734-5802. **E-mail:** blackdomep@aol.com. **Website:** www.blackdomepress.com. Estab. 1990. Publishes cloth and trade paperback originals and reprints. Accepts simultaneous submissions. Catalog and guidelines online.

○ Do not send the entire work. Mail a cover letter, table of contents, introduction, sample chapter (or two), and your CV or brief biography to the Editor. Please do not send computer disks or submit your proposal via e-mail. If your book will include illustrations, please send us copies of sample illustrations. Do not send originals.

NONFICTION Subjects include history, nature, environment, photography, regional, New York state., Native Americans, grand hotels, genealogy, colonial life, French & Indian War (NYS), American Revolution (NYS), quilting, architecture, railroads, hiking and kayaking guidebooks. New York state regional material only. Submit proposal package, outline, bio.

TIPS "Our audience is comprised of New York state residents, tourists, and visitors."

BLACK HERON PRESS

P.O. Box 13396, Mill Creek WA 98082. **Website:** www.blackheronpress.com. **Contact:** Jerry Gold, publisher. Estab. 1984. Publishes hardcover and trade paperback originals, trade paperback reprints. **Publishes 4 titles/year. 1,500 queries received/year. 50% of books from first-time authors. 90% from unagented writers. Pays 8% royalty on retail price.** Publishes book 2 years after acceptance. Accepts simultaneous submissions. Responds in 6 months to queries and mss. Catalog available online and for 6" x 9" SAE with 3 first-class stamps. Guidelines available for #10 SASE.

✎ "Black Heron Press publishes primarily literary fiction."

NONFICTION Subjects include military, war. Submit proposal package, include cover letter & first 30-50 pages of your completed novel. "We do not review artwork."

FICTION Subjects include confession, erotica, literary (regardless of genre), military, war, sci-fi, young adult., Some science fiction—not fantasy, not Dungeons & Dragons—that makes or implies a social statement. "All of our fiction is character driven. We don't want to see fiction written for the mass market. If it sells to the mass market, fine, but we don't see ourselves as a commercial press." Submit proposal package, including cover letter & first 40-50 pages pages of your completed novel.

TIPS "Our Readers love good fiction—they are scattered among all social classes, ethnic groups, and zip code areas. If you can't read our books, at least check out our titles on our website."

BLACK LAWRENCE PRESS

115 Center Ave., Aspinwall PA 15215. **E-mail:** editors@blacklawrencepress.com. **E-mail:** submissions@blacklawrencepress.com. **Website:** www.blacklawrencepress.com. **Contact:** Diane Goettel, executive editor. Estab. 2003.

Black Lawrence Press seeks "to publish intriguing books of literature: novels, short story collections, poetry. Will also publish the occasional translation (from the German and French)." Has published poetry by D.C. Berry, James Reidel, and Stefi Weisburd. Publishes 10-12 books/year, mostly poetry and fiction. Manuscripts are selected through open submission and competition (see below). Books are 48-400 pages, offset-printed or high-quality POD, perfect-bound, with matte 4-color cover.

POETRY "Regular submissions are considered on a year-round basis. Please check the general submissions page on our website for the most up-to-date guidelines information before submitting." Responds in up to 4 months for mss, "sometimes longer depending on backlog." Pays royalties. Sample books available through website.

⊕ BLACK MOUNTAIN PRESS

109 Roberts, Asheville NC 28801. (828)273-3332. **E-mail:** jackmoe@theBlackMountainPress.com. **Website:** www.theBlackMountainPress.com. **Contact:** Jack Moe, editor (how-to, poetry); James Robiningski (short story collections, novels). Estab. 1994. Publishes hardcover, trade paperback, and electronic originals. **Publishes 4 titles/year. 150 mss received/year. 90% of books from first-time authors. 100% from unagented writers. Pays 5-10% royalty on retail price. Pays $100-500 advance.** Publishes book 5 months after acceptance. Accepts simultaneous submissions. Responds in 4-6 months to mss. Catalog and guidelines online.

NONFICTION Subjects include architecture, art, language, literature, sports. "We are concentrating more on literary projects for the next 2 years." Submit complete ms. Reviews artwork. Send digital photos only on CD or DVD.

FICTION Subjects include comic books, experimental, literary, poetry, poetry in translation, short story collections., graphic novels. "Creative literary fiction and poetry or collection of short stories are wanted for the next few years." Submit complete ms.

POETRY Submit complete ms.

TIPS "Don't be afraid of sending your anti-government, anti-religion, anti-art, anti-literature, experimental, avant-garde efforts here. But don't send your work before it's fully cooked, we do, however, enjoy fresh, natural, and sometimes even raw material, just don't send in anything that is "glowing" unless it was savaged from a FoxNews book-burning event."

⊕ BLACK OCEAN

P.O. Box 52030, Boston MA 02205. **Fax:** (617)849-5678. **E-mail:** carrie@blackocean.org. **Website:** www.blackocean.org. **Contact:** Carrie Olivia Adams, poetry editor. Estab. 2006. **Publishes 3 titles/year.** Responds in 6 months to mss.

POETRY Wants poetry that is well-considered, risks itself, and by its beauty and/or bravery disturbs a tiny corner of the universe. Manuscripts are selected through open submission. Books are 60+ pages. Book/chapbook mss may include previously published poems. We have an open submission period in May of each year; specific guidelines are updated and posted on our website in the months preceding.

BLACK ROSE WRITING

P.O. Box 1540, Castroville TX 78009. **E-mail:** creator@blackrosewriting.com. **Website:** www.blackrosewriting.com. **Contact:** Reagan Rothe. Estab. 2006. Publishes majority trade paperback, occasional hard cover or children's book. **Publishes 75+ titles/year.** Accepts simultaneous submissions. Responds in 1-2 months to mss. Please check submission guidelines before contacting by e-mail.

NONFICTION Subjects include science, sports, young adult, general. Query via e-mail. Submit synopsis and author bio. Please allow 3-4 weeks for response.

FICTION Subjects include adventure, fantasy, historical, horror, humor, juvenile, mainstream, mystery, picture books, plays, romance, short story collections, sports, western, young adult., detective. Query via e-mail. Submit synopsis and author bio. Please allow 3-4 weeks for response.

TIPS "Please query via e-mail first with synopsis and author information. Allow 3-4 weeks for response. Always spell-check and try and sent an edited manuscript. Do not forward your initial contact e-mails."

BLACK VELVET SEDUCTIONS PUBLISHING

1350-C W. Southport, Box 249, Indianapolis IN 46217. (888)556-2750. **E-mail:** lauriesanders@blackvelvetseductions.com. **Website:** www.blackvelvetseductions.com. **Contact:** Laurie Sanders, acquisitions editor. Estab. 2005. Publishes trade paperback and electronic originals and reprints. **Publishes about 20 titles/year. 500 queries received/year. 1,000 mss received/year. 90% of books from first-time authors. 100% from unagented writers. Pays 10% royalty for paperbacks; 50% royalty for electronic books.** Publishes book 6-12 months after acceptance of ms. Accepts simultaneous submissions. Responds in 6 months to queries. Responds in 8 months to proposals. Responds in 8-12 months to mss. Catalog free or online. Guidelines online (guidelines@blackvelvetseductions.com).

➤ "We publish two types of material: 1) romance novels and short stories and 2) romantic stories involving spanking between consenting adults. We look for well-crafted stories with a high degree of emotional impact. No first person point of view. All material must be in third person point of view." Publishes trade paperback and electronic originals. "We have a high interest in republishing backlist titles in electronic and trade paperback formats once rights have reverted to the author." Accepts only complete mss. Query with SASE. Submit complete ms.

FICTION Subjects include erotic romance, historical romance, multicultural romance, romance, short story collections romantic stories, romantic suspense, western romance. All stories must have a strong romance element. "There are very few sexual taboos in our erotic line. We tend to give our authors the widest latitude. If it is safe, sane, and consensual we will allow our authors latitude to show us the eroticism. However, we will not consider manuscripts with any of the following: bestiality (sex with animals), necrophilia (sex with dead people), pedophillia (sex with children)." Only accepts electronic submissions.

TIPS "We publish romance and erotic romance. We look for books written in very deep point of view."

JOHN F. BLAIR, PUBLISHER

1406 Plaza Dr., Winston-Salem NC 27103. (336)768-1374. **Fax:** (336)768-9194. **Website:** www.blairpub.com. **Contact:** Carolyn Sakowski, president. Estab. 1954. **Pays royalties. Pays negotiable advance.** Publishes book 18 months after acceptance. Responds in 3-6 months.

FICTION "We specialize in regional books, with an emphasis on nonfiction categories such as history, travel, folklore, and biography. We publish only one or two works of fiction each year. Fiction submitted to us should have some connection with the Southeast. We do not publish children's books, poetry, or category fiction such as romances, science fiction, or spy thrillers. We do not publish collections of short stories, essays, or newspaper columns. Any fiction submitted should have some connection with the Southeast, either through setting or author's background. Send a cover letter, giving a synopsis of the book. Include the first two chapters (at least 50 pages) of the manuscript. You may send the entire manuscript if you wish. If you choose to send only samples, please include the projected word length of your book and estimated completion date in your cover letter. Send a biography of the author, including publishing credits and credentials."

TIPS "We are primarily interested in nonfiction titles. Most of our titles have a tie-in with North Carolina or the southeastern United States, we do not accept short-story collections. Please enclose a cover letter and outline with the manuscript. We prefer to review queries before we are sent complete mss. Queries should include an approximate word count."

BLOOMBERG PRESS

Imprint of Bloomberg L.P., 731 Lexington Ave., New York NY 10022. **Website:** www.bloomberg.com/books. Estab. 1995. Publishes hardcover and trade paperback originals. **Publishes 18-22 titles/year. 200 queries received/year. 20 mss received/year. 45% from unagented writers. Pays negotiable, competitive royalty. Pays negotiable advance for trade books.** Publishes book 9 months after acceptance. Accepts simultaneous submissions. With SASE, responds in 1 month to queries. Catalog for 10×13 envelope and 5 First-Class stamps.

➤ Bloomberg Press publishes professional books for practitioners in the financial markets. We publish commercially successful, very high-quality books that stand out clearly from the competition by their brevity, ease of use, sophistication, and abundance of practical tips and strategies; books readers need, will use, and appreciate.

NONFICTION Subjects include business, economics, money, finance, professional books on finance, investment and financial services, and books for financial advisors. We are looking for authorities and for experienced service journalists. Do not send us unfocused books containing general information already covered by books in the marketplace. We do not publish business, management, leadership, or career books. Submit outline, sample chapters, SAE with sufficient postage. Submit complete ms.

TIPS *Bloomberg Professional Library*: Audience is upscale, financial professionals—traders, dealers, brokers, planners and advisors, financial managers, money managers, company executives, sophisticated investors. Authors are experienced financial journalists and/or financial professionals nationally prominent in their specialty for some time who have proven an ability to write a successful book. Research Bloomberg and look at our books in a library or bookstore, and peruse our website.

BLOOMING TREE PRESS

P.O. Box 140934, Austin TX 78714. (512)921-8846. **Fax:** (512)873-7710. **E-mail:** e-mail@bloomingtreepress.com. **Website:** www.bloomingtreepress.com. **Contact:** Miriam Hees, publisher; Madeline Smoot, publisher (CBAY Books); Anna Herrington, editorial director (Blooming Tree Children's and Tire Swing Books); Bradford Hees, publisher (Ready Blade graphic novels/comics); Theresa Tabi, art director. Estab. 2000. Publishes hardcover, trade paperback, and mass market paperback originals. **Publishes 8-15 titles/year. 10,000 queries received/year. 1,200 mss received/year. 80% of books from first-time authors. 90% from unagented writers. Pays 8-12% royalty on wholesale price.** Publishes book 2 years after acceptance. Accepts simultaneous submissions. Responds in 3 months to queries; 6 months to proposals and mss. Catalog and guidelines online.

"Blooming Tree Press is dedicated to producing high quality book for the young and the young at heart. It is our hope that you will find your dreams between the pages of our books."

FICTION Subjects include adventure, comic books, fantasy, historical, humor, juvenile, literary, mystery, picture books, romance, science fiction, short story collections, spiritual, young adult. *Agented submissions only.* Unsolicited mss returned unopened.

TIPS "During submission times follow the guidelineslisted on our Website. Send a crisp and clean one-page query letter statingyour project, why it is right for the market, and a little about yourself. Write what you know, not what's 'in.' Remember, every great writer/illustratorstarted somewhere. Keep submitting; don't ever give up."

BLOOMSBURY CHILDREN'S BOOKS

Imprint of Bloomsbury USA, 175 Fifth Ave., New York NY 10010. **E-mail:** bloomsbury.kids@bloomsburyusa.com. **Website:** www.bloomsburykids.com. **Publishes 60 titles/year. 25% of books from first-time authors. Pays royalty. Pays advance.** Accepts simultaneous submissions. Responds in 6 months to queries; 6 months to ms. *Agented submissions only.* Guidelines online.

FICTION Subjects include adventure, fantasy, historical, humor, juvenile, multicultural, mystery, picture books, poetry, science fiction, sports, suspense, young adult, animal, anthology, concept, contemporary, folktales, problem novels. Query with SASE. Submit clips, first 3 chapters with SASE.

BLUEBRIDGE

Imprint of United Tribes Media, Inc., P.O. Box 601, New York NY 10536. (914)301-5901. **E-mail:** janguerth@bluebridgebooks.com. **Website:** www.bluebridgebooks.com. **Contact:** Jan-Erik Guerth, publisher (general nonfiction). Estab. 2004. Publishes hardcover and trade paperback originals. **Publishes 6-8 titles/year. 1,000 queries received/year. Pays variable advance.** Accepts simultaneous submissions. Responds in 1 month to queries and proposals.

BlueBridge is an independent publisher of international nonfiction based near New York City. The BlueBridge mission: Thoughtful Books for Mind and Spirit.

NONFICTION Subjects include Americana, anthropology, archaeology, art, architecture, business, economics, child guidance, contemporary culture, creative nonfiction, ethnic, gardening, gay, lesbian, government, politics, health, medicine, history, humanities, language, literature, literary criticism, multicultural, music, dance, nature, environment, philosophy, psychology, religion, science, social sciences, sociology, spirituality, travel, women's issues, world affairs. Query with SASE or preferably by e-mail.

TIPS "We target a broad general nonfiction audience."

BLUE LIGHT PRESS

1563 45th Ave., San Francisco CA 94122. **E-mail:** bluelightpress@aol.com. **Website:** www.bluelightpress.com. **Contact:** Diane Frank, chief editor. Estab. 1988.

⚷ "We like poems that are imagistic, emotionally honest, and push the edge—where the writer pushes through the imagery to a deeper level of insight and understanding. No rhymed poetry. Books are elegantly designed and artistic." Chapbooks are 30 pages, digest-sized, professionally printed, with original cover art.

POETRY "We have an online poetry workshop with a wonderful group of American and international poets—open to new members 3 times per year. Send an e-mail for info. We work in person with local poets, and will edit/critique poems by mail; $40 for four poems." Does not accept e-mail submissions. **Deadlines:** January 30 full-sized ms. and June 15 for chapbooks. "Read our guidelines before sending your ms."

BLUE MOON BOOKS, INC.

327 Elk Ave., PO Box 908, Crested Butte CO 81224. (970)349-0504. **E-mail:** bluemoonbookscb@yahoo.com. **Website:** http://bluemoonbookscb.com. Estab. 1987. Publishes trade paperback and mass market paperback originals. Catalog available free.

⚷ Blue Moon Books is strictly an erotic press; largely fetish-oriented material, B&D, S&M, etc.

FICTION Subjects include erotica. *No unsolicited mss.*

⊕ BLUE MOUNTAIN PRESS

Blue Mountain Arts, Inc., P.O. Box 4219, Boulder CO 80306. (800)525-0642. **E-mail:** BMPbooks@sps.com. **Website:** www.sps.com. **Contact:** Patti Wayant, editorial director. Estab. 1971. Publishes hardcover originals, trade paperback originals, electronic originals. **Pays royalty on wholesale price.** Publishes book 6-8 months after acceptance. Accepts simultaneous submissions. Responds in 2-4 months to queries, mss, and proposals. Guidelines available by e-mail.

NONFICTION Subjects include spirituality, womens issues, young adult., family, love, inspirational. Query with SASE. Submit proposal package including outline and 3-5 sample chapters.

POETRY "We publish poetry appropriate for gift books, self-help books, and personal growth books.

We do not publish chapbooks or literary poetry." Query. Submit 10+ sample poems.

BLUE POPPY PRESS

Imprint of Blue Poppy Enterprises, Inc., 1990 57th Court Unit A, Boulder CO 80301. (303)447-8372. **Fax:** (303)245-8362. **E-mail:** info@bluepoppy.com. **Website:** www.bluepoppy.com. **Contact:** Bob Flaws, editor-in-chief. Estab. 1981. Publishes hardcover and trade paperback originals. **Publishes 3-4 titles/year. 50 queries received/year. 5-10 mss received/year. 30-40% of books from first-time authors. 100% from unagented writers. Pays 8-12% royalty.** Publishes book 1 year after acceptance. Responds in 1 month to queries. Catalog available free. Guidelines online.

○ "Blue Poppy Press is dedicated to expanding and improving the English language literature on acupuncture and Asian medicine for both professional practitioners and lay readers."

NONFICTION Subjects include ethnic, health, medicine. We only publish books on acupuncture and Oriental medicine by authors who can read Chinese and have a minimum of 5 years clinical experience. We also require all our authors to use Wiseman's *Glossary of Chinese Medical Terminology* as their standard for technical terms. Query with SASE. Submit outline, 1 sample chapter.

TIPS "Audience is practicing acupuncturists interested in alternatives in healthcare, preventive medicine, Chinese philosophy, and medicine."

⊕ BLUE RIVER PRESS

Cardinal Publishers Group, 2402 N. Shadeland Ave., Suite A, Indianapolis IN 46219. (317)352-8200. **Fax:** (317)352-8202. **E-mail:** tdoherty@cardinalpub.com; editorial@cardinalpub.com. **Website:** www.cardinalpub.com. **Contact:** Tom Doherty, president (adult nonfiction). Estab. 2000. Publishes hardcover, trade paperback and electronic originals and reprints. **Publishes 8-12 titles/year. 60 queries received/year. 25% of books from first-time authors. 80% from unagented writers. Pays 10-15% on wholesale price. Outright purchase of $500-5,000. Offers advance up to $5,000.** Publishes book 6 months after acceptance. Accepts simultaneous submissions. Responds to queries in 2 months. Catalog for #10 SASE or online. Guidelines available by e-mail at info@cardinalpub.com.

NONFICTION "Most non-religious adult nonfiction subjects are of interest. We like concepts that can develop into series products. Most of our books are paperback or hardcover in the categories of sport, business, health, fitness, lifestyle, yoga, and educational books for teachers and students."

BNA BOOKS

Imprint of The Bureau of National Affairs, Inc., 1801 S. Bell St., Arlington VA 22202. (703)341-5777. **Fax:** (703)341-1610. **E-mail:** books@bna.com. **Website:** www.bnabooks.com. **Contact:** Jim Fattibene, acquisitions manager. Estab. 1929. Publishes hardcover and softcover originals. Accepts simultaneous submissions. Catalog and guidelines online.

○ BNA Books publishes professional reference books written by lawyers, for lawyers.

NONFICTION No fiction, biographies, bibliographies, cookbooks, religion books, humor, or trade books. Submit detailed TOC or outline, CV, intended market, estimated word length.

TIPS "Our audience is made up of practicing lawyers and law librarians. We look for authoritative and comprehensive treatises that can be supplemented or revised every year or 2 on legal subjects of interest to those audiences."

BOA EDITIONS, LTD.

250 N. Goodman St., Suite 306, Rochester NY 14607. (585)546-3410. **Fax:** (585)546-3913. **E-mail:** conners@boaeditions.org; hall@boaeditions.org. **Website:** www.boaeditions.org. **Contact:** Peter Conners, editor. Melissa Hall, Development Director/Office Manager Estab. 1976. Publishes hardcover and trade paperback originals. **Publishes 11-13 titles/year. 1,000 queries received/year. 700 mss received/year. 15% of books from first-time authors. 90% from unagented writers. Negotiates royalties. Pays variable advance.** Publishes book 18 months after acceptance. Accepts simultaneous submissions. Responds in 1 week to queries; 5 months to mss. Catalog and guidelines online.

⚏ "BOA Editions publishes distinguished collections of poetry, fiction and poetry in translation. Our goal is to publish the finest American contemporary poetry, fiction and poetry in translation."

FICTION Subjects include literary, poetry, poetry in translation, short story collections. "We now publish literary fiction through our American Reader Series. While aesthetic quality is subjective, our fiction will be by authors more concerned with the artfulness of their writing than the twists and turns of plot. Our strongest current interest is in short story collections (and short-short story collections), although we will consider novels. We strongly advise you to read our first published fiction collections. *We are temporarily closed to novel/collection submissions.*"

POETRY "Readers who, like Whitman, expect of the poet to 'indicate more than the beauty and dignity which always attach to dumb real objects. They expect him to indicate the path between reality and their souls,' are the audience of BOA's books." BOA Editions, a Pulitzer Prize-winning, not-for-profit publishing house acclaimed for its work, reads poetry mss for the American Poets Continuum Series (new poetry by distinguished poets in mid- and late career), the Lannan Translations Selection Series (publication of 2 new collections of contemporary international poetry annually, supported by The Lannan Foundation of Santa Fe, NM), The A. Poulin, Jr. Poetry Prize (to honor a poet's first book; mss considered through competition), and The America Reader Series (short fiction and prose on poetics). "Please adhere to the general submission guidelines for each series." Check website for reading periods for the American Poets Continuum Series and The Lannan Translation Selection Series. "Please adhere to the general submission guidelines for each series."

⊕ BOBO STRATEGY

2506 N. Clark, #301, Chicago IL 60614. **E-mail:** info@bobostrategy.com. **E-mail:** submissions@bobostrategy.com. **Website:** www.bobostrategy.com. **Contact:** Chris Cunliffe, editor-in-chief. Estab. 2008. Trade paperback originals. **Publishes 1-5 titles/year. Pays 0-10% royalty on retail price; outright purchase up to $2,500.** Publishes book Acceptance to publication time is 6 months. after acceptance of ms. Accepts simultaneous submissions. Responds in 1 month on queries and proposals; responds in 2 months on mss. Catalog online. Guidelines available by e-mail.

⚏ "We seek writing that brings clarity and simplicity to the complex. If your idea is good, we may be willing to take a chance on you."

NONFICTION Subjects include architecture, art, chess, creative nonfiction, government, humanities, memoirs, politics, regional, travel, world affairs. Query with SASE; submit proposal package, including: outline, 1 sample chapter. E-mail preferred. Reviews artwork; send photocopies. E-mail preferred.

FICTION Subjects include poetry, regional, short story collections. True Query; submit proposal package, including: synopsis, 1 sample chapter. E-mail preferred.

BOLD STROKES BOOKS, INC.

P.O. Box 249, Valley Falls NY 12185. (518)753-6642. **Fax:** (518)753-6648. **E-mail:** publisher@boldstrokes-books.com. **E-mail:** submissions@boldstrokesbooks.com. **Website:** www.boldstrokesbooks.com. **Contact:** Len Barot, president; Lee Ligon, operations manager; Cindy Cresap, senior consulting editor and production manager. Publishes trade paperback originals and reprints; electronic originals and reprints. **Publishes 60+ titles/year. 300 queries/year; 300 mss/year. 10-20% of books from first-time authors. 95% from unagented writers. Pays 7-10% royalty on retail price.** Publishes book 16 months after acceptance. Responds in 1 month to queries; 2 months to proposals; 4 months to mss. Catalog free. Guidelines online.

NONFICTION Subjects include gay, lesbian, memoirs, young adult. Submit completed ms with bio, cover letter, and synopsis electronically only.

FICTION Subjects include adventure, erotica, fantasy, gay, gothic, historical, horror, lesbian, literary, mainstream, mystery, romance, science fiction, suspense, western, young adult. "Submissions should have a gay, lesbian, transgendered, or bisexual focus and should be positive and life-affirming." Submit completed ms with bio, cover letter, and synopsis—electronically only.

TIPS "We are particularly interested in authors who are interested in craft enhancement, technical development, and exploring and expanding traditional genre definitions and boundaries and are looking for a long-term publishing relationship ."

THE BOLD STRUMMER, LTD.

P.O. Box 2037, Westport CT 06880-2037. (203)227-8588. **Fax:** (203)227-8775. **E-mail:** theboldstrummer@msn.com. **Website:** www.boldstrummerltd.com. **Contact:** Nicholas Clarke. Estab. 1973. Publishes hardcover and trade paperback originals and reprints. Niche publisher now concentrates solely on books about the guitar, including books about flamenco and all its aspects. **Publishes 3 titles/year.**

Guitar related reading and instruction books.

NONFICTION Contact through online form.

BOREALIS PRESS, LTD.

8 Mohawk Crescent, Napean ON K2H 7G6, Canada. (613)829-0150. **Fax:** (613)829-7783. **E-mail:** drt@bore-alispress.com. **Website:** www.borealispress.com. Estab. 1972. Publishes hardcover and paperback originals and reprints. **Publishes 20 titles/year. 80% of books from first-time authors. 95% from unagented writers. Pays 10% royalty on net receipts; plus 3 free author's copies.** Publishes book 18 months after acceptance. Responds in 2 months to queries; 4 months to mss. Catalog and guidelines online.

NONFICTION Subjects include government, politics, history, language, literature, regional. Only material Canadian in content. Looks for style in tone and language, reader interest, and maturity of outlook. Query with SASE. Submit outline, 2 sample chapters. *No unsolicited mss.* Reviews artwork/photos.

FICTION Subjects include adventure, ethnic, historical, juvenile, literary, mainstream, contemporary, romance, short story collections, young adult. Only material Canadian in content and dealing with significant aspects of the human situation. Query with SASE. Submit clips, 1-2 sample chapters. *No unsolicited mss.*

BOTTOM DOG PRESS, INC.

P.O. Box 425, Huron OH 44839. **E-mail:** LsmithDog@smithdocs.net. **Website:** http://smithdocs.net. **Contact:** Larry Smith, director. Allen Frost and Laura Smith, associate editors

Bottom Dog Press, Inc., "is a nonprofit literary and educational organization dedicated to publishing the best writing and art from the Midwest." Has published poetry by Jeff Gundy, Jim Daniels, Maj Ragain, Diane di Prima, and Sue Doro. Publishes the Midwest Series, Working Lives Series, and Harmony Series (105 books to date).

BRANDEN PUBLISHING CO., INC.

P.O. Box 812094, Wellesley MA 02482. (781)235-3634. **Fax:** (781)235-3634. **E-mail:** branden@brandenbooks.com. **Website:** www.brandenbooks.com. **Contact:** Adolph Caso, editor. Estab. 1909. Publishes hardcover and trade paperback originals, reprints, and software. **Publishes 15 titles/year. 80% of books from first-time authors. 90% from unagented writers.** Publishes book 10 months after acceptance. Responds in 1 month to queries.

"Branden publishes books by or about women, children, military, Italian-American, or African-American themes."

NONFICTION Subjects include Americana, art, architecture, computers, electronics, contemporary culture, education, ethnic, government, politics, health, medicine, history, military, war, music, dance, photography, sociology, software., classics. "Especially looking for about 10 manuscripts on national and international subjects, including biographies of well-known individuals. Currently specializing in Americana, Italian-American, African-American." No religion or philosophy. *No unsolicited mss.* Paragraph query only with SASE. No telephone, e-mail, or fax inquiries. Reviews artwork/photos.

FICTION Subjects include ethnic, histories, integration, historical, literary, military, war, religious, historical-reconstructive, short story collections, translation. Looking for contemporary, fast pace, modern society. No science, mystery, experimental, horror, or pornography. *No unsolicited mss.* Query with SASE. Paragraph query only with author bio.

NICHOLAS BREALEY PUBLISHING

20 Park Plaza, Suite 1115A, Boston MA 02116. (617)523-3801. **Fax:** (617)523-3708. **E-mail:** info@nicholasbrealey.com; submissions@nicholasbrealey.com. **Website:** www.nicholasbrealey.com. **Contact:** Vanessa Descalzi, assistant editor and digital director. Estab. 1992.

8—ᴨ "Nicholas Brealey Publishing has a reputation for publishing high-quality and thought-provoking business books with international appeal. Over time our list has grown to focus also on adjacent fields like careers, professional and personal development and crossing cultures—and we are now expanding further into narrative non-fiction, notably adventure and travel writing. We welcome fresh ideas and new insights in all of these subject areas." Submit via e-mail and follow the guidelines on the website.

BRENNER INFORMATION GROUP

Imprint of Brenner Microcomputing, Inc., P.O. Box 721000, San Diego CA 92172. (858)538-0093. **E-mail:** brenner@brennerbooks.com. **Website:** www.brennerbooks.com. **Contact:** Deedee Ade, acquisitions manager (pricing & ranges). Estab. 1982. Publishes trade paperback and electronic originals specializing in pricing and performance time standards. **Publishes 4 titles/year. 4 ms and 6 queries received/year. 1% of books from first-time authors. 1% from unagented writers. Pays 5-15% royalty on wholesale price. Pays $0-1,000 advance.** Publishes book 1 year after accep-

tance. Accepts simultaneous submissions. Responds in 1 month to queries, proposals, and mss.

BREWERS PUBLICATIONS

Imprint of Brewers Association, 736 Pearl St., Boulder CO 80302. (303)447-0816. **Fax:** (303)447-2825. **E-mail:** kristi@brewersassociation.org; webmaster@brewersassociation.org. **Website:** beertown.org. **Contact:** Kristi Switzer, publisher. Estab. 1986. Publishes hardcover and trade paperback originals. **Publishes 2 titles/year. 50% of books from first-time authors. 100% from unagented writers. Pays small advance.** Publishes book 9 months after acceptance. Accepts simultaneous submissions. Responds in 3 months to relevant queries. "Only those submissions relevant to our needs will receive a response to queries.". Guidelines online.

8—ᴨ "Brewers Publications is the largest publisher of books on beer-related subjects."

NONFICTION "We only publish nonfiction books of interest to amateur and professional brewers. Our authors have many years of brewing experience and in-depth practical knowledge of their subject. We are not interested in fiction, drinking games or beer/bar reviews. If your book is not about how to make beer, then do not waste your time or ours by sending it. Those determined to fit our needs will subscribe to and read *Zymurgy* and *The New Brewer*." Query first with proposal and sample chapter.

☉ BRICK BOOKS

Box 20081, 431 Boler Rd., London ON N6K 4G6, Canada. (519)657-8579. **E-mail:** brick.books@sympatico.ca. **Website:** www.brickbooks.ca. **Contact:** Don McKay, Stan Dragland, Barry Dempster, editors. Estab. 1975. Publishes trade paperback originals. **Publishes 7 titles/year. 30 queries received/year. 100 mss received/year 30% of books from first-time authors. 100% from unagented writers.** Publishes book 2 years after acceptance. Responds in 3-4 months to queries. Catalog free or online. Guidelines online.

8—ᴨ Brick Books has a reading period of January 1-April 30. Mss received outside that period will be returned. No multiple submissions. Pays 10% royalty in book copies only.

POETRY Submit only poetry.

TIPS "Writers without previous publications in literary journals or magazines are rarely considered by Brick Books for publication."

⊕ BRICK ROAD POETRY PRESS, INC.

P.O. Box 751, Columbus GA 31902. (706)649-3080. **Fax:** (706)649-3094. **E-mail:** editor@brickroadpoetrypress.com. **Website:** www.brickroadpoetrypress.com. **Contact:** Ron Self and Keith Badkowski, co-editors/founders. Estab. 2009.

POETRY Publishes poetry only: books (single author collections), e-zine, and annual anthology. "We prefer poetry that offers a coherent human voice, a sense of humor, attentiveness to words and language, narratives with surprise twists, persona poems, and/or philosophical or spiritual themes explored through the concrete scenes and images." Does not want overemphasis on rhyme, intentional obscurity or riddling, highfalutin vocabulary, greeting card verse, overt religious statements of faith and/or praise, and/or abstractions. Publishes 10-12 poetry books/year and 1 anthology/year. Accepted poems meeting our theme requirements are published on our website. Mss accepted through open submission and competition. Books are 110 pages, print-on-demand, perfect-bound, paperback with full color art or photograph covers. "We accept .doc, .rtf, or .pdf file formats. We prefer electronic submissions but will reluctantly consider hard copy submissions by mail if USPS Flat Rate Mailing Envelope is used and with the stipulation that, should the author's work be chosen for publication, an electronic version (.doc or .rtf) must be prepared in a timely manner and at the poet's expense." Please include cover letter with poetry publication/recognition highlights and something intriguing about your life story or ongoing pursuits. "We would like to develop a connection with the poet as well as the poetry." Please include the collection title in the cover letter. "We want to publish poets who are engaged in the literary community, including regular submission of work to various publications and participation in poetry readings, workshops, and writers' groups. That said, we would never rule out an emerging poet who demonstrates ability and motivation to move in that direction." Pays royalties and 15 author copies. Initial print run of 150, print-on-demand thereafter. "Submit up to 5 poems per submission via our online submission manager. Poems accepted will be published on our website. Inclusion in a print anthology will be considered as well."

TIPS "The best way to discover all that poetry can be and to expand the limits of your own poetry is to read expansively. We recommend the following poets: Kim Addonizio, Ken Babstock, Coleman Barks, Billy Collins, Morri Creech, Alice Friman, Beth A. Gylys, Jane Hirshfield, Jane Kenyon, Ted Kooser, Stanley Kunitz, Thomas Lux, Barry Marks, Michael Meyerhofer, Linda Pastan, Mark Strand, and Natasha D. Trethewey."

◐ BRIGHTER BOOKS PUBLISHING HOUSE

Brighter Brains, Inc., 4825 Fairbrook Crescent, Nanaimo B.C. V9T 6M6, Canada. (250)585-7372. **E-mail:** info@brighterbooks.com; submissions@brighterbooks.com. **Website:** www.brighterbooks.com. **Contact:** Angela Souza, senior/chief editor. Dean Jurgensen, senior editor (sciences, technology, information). Estab. 2009. Publishes hardcover and electronic originals; hardcover and trade paperback reprints; trade paperback originals and reprints. **Publishes 10-15 titles/year. 50% of books from first-time authors. 50% from unagented writers. Pays royalty on wholesale price. Advances are negotiable.** Publishes book 1 year after acceptance. Accepts simultaneous submissions. Responds in 2 months to queries and proposals; 3-4 months to mss. Catalog available online. Guidelines online and by e-mail at info@brighterbooks.com.

NONFICTION Subjects include animals, art/architecture, child guidance/parenting, computers/electronics, crafts, education, entertainment/games, hobbies, money/finance for kids, nature/environment, science. "We focus on high-quality reading for children and also unique methods of teaching things to both adults and children." Query with SASE. Submit proposal package, including: outline, 3 sample chapters, and introduction. Submit completed ms for picture books and younger readers. Reviews artwork/photos. "We prefer digital samples, but photocopies are fine as well."

FICTION Subjects include adventure, fantasy, humor, juvenile, multicultural, multimedia, mystery, picture books, science fiction, young adult. "We are looking for a return to the quality of writing found in classical works of literature. We want to publish truly great fiction, no matter the target audience or age level. We believe that by exposing children and young adults to excellent literature on a day-to-day basis, we can change their lives, making them better thinkers, more creative and well-adjusted. Books change people, and we want to do our part to make it a positive change." Query with SASE. Submit proposal package, including synopsis, 3 sampe chapters. Submit completed ms for picture books and young readers.

TIPS "Our fiction readers are smart boys and girls of all ages who are looking for characters they can relate to, and love to read. Our El-Hi readers are looking for a different way of learning school subjects. They may have learning difficulties with traditional methods. Our adult readers are well educated, and looking for well-written books about their subject of interest. 55% of work must be Canadian or Resident. However, we are still looking for talent worldwide."

BRIGHT MOUNTAIN BOOKS, INC.

206 Riva Ridge Dr., Fairview NC 28730. (828)628-1768. **Fax:** (828)628-1755. **E-mail:** booksbmb@charter. net. **Website:** www.brightmountainbooks.com. **Contact:** Cynthia F. Bright, senior editor. Martha Fullington, editor Estab. 1983. Publishes trade paperback originals and reprints. **Publishes 3 titles/year. 50% of books from first-time authors. 100% from unagented writers. Pays royalty.** Responds in 1 month to queries; 5 months to mss.

NONFICTION Subjects include history, regional. "Our current emphasis is on regional titles set in the Southern Appalachians and Carolinas, which can include nonfiction by local writers." Query with SASE.

BRIGHT RING PUBLISHING, INC.

P.O. Box 31338, Bellingham WA 98228. (360)592-9201. **Fax:** (360)592-4503. **E-mail:** maryann@brightring. com. **Website:** www.brightring.com. **Contact:** Mary-Ann Kohl, editor. Estab. 1985.

○ *Bright Ring is no longer accepting manuscript submissions.*

BROADWAY BOOKS

The Crown Publishing Group/Random House, 1745 Broadway, New York NY 10019. (212)782-9000. **Fax:** (212)782-9411. **Website:** www.broadwaybooks.com. **Contact:** William Thomas, editor-in-chief. Estab. 1995. Publishes hardcover and trade paperback books. **Receives thousands of mss/year. Pays royalty on retail price. Pays advance.**

○ "Broadway publishes high quality general interest nonfiction and fiction for adults."

NONFICTION Subjects include business, economics, child guidance, contemporary culture, cooking, foods, nutrition, gay, lesbian, government, politics, health, medicine, history, memoirs, money, finance, multicultural, New Age, psychology, sex, spirituality, sports, travel, narrative, womens' issues, women's

studies., current affairs, motivational/inspirational, popular culture, consumer reference. *Agented submissions only.*

BROKEN JAW PRESS

Box 596, STN A, Fredericton NB E3B 5A6, Canada. (506)454-5127. **E-mail:** editors@brokenjaw.com. **Website:** www.brokenjaw.com. "Publishes almost exclusively Canadian-authored literary trade paperback originals and reprints." **Publishes 3-6 titles/year. 20% of books from first-time authors. 100% from unagented writers. Pays 10% royalty on retail price. Pays $0-500 advance.** Publishes book 18 months after acceptance. Responds in 1 year to mss. Catalog for 6×9 SAE with 2 first-class Canadian stamps in Canada or download PDF from website. Guidelines online.

○ *Currently not accepting unsolicited mss and queries.*

NONFICTION Subjects include history, literature, literary criticism, regional, women's issues/studies., contemporary culture.

FICTION Subjects include Literary novel and short story collections, poetry.

TIPS "Unsolicited queries and manuscripts are not welcome at this time."

BROOKS BOOKS

3720 N. Woodridge Dr., Decatur IL 62526. **E-mail:** brooksbooks@sbcglobal.net. **Website:** www.brooksbookshaiku.com. **Contact:** Randy Brooks, editor (haiku poetry, tanka poetry). Publishes hardcover, trade paperback, and electronic originals. **Publishes 2-3 titles/year. 100 queries received/year. 25 mss received/year. 10% of books from first-time authors. 100% from unagented writers. Outright purchase based on wholesale value of 10% of a press run.** Publishes book 1 year after acceptance. Responds in 2 months to queries; 3 months to proposals and mss. Catalog free on request or online. Guidelines free on request, for #10 SASE.

POETRY "We celebrate English language haiku by promoting & publishing in a variety of media. Our goal is to share our joy of the art of reading & writing haiku through our little chapbook-size magazine, *Mayfly*. Also, we celebrate the art of haiga, lifetime contributions of haiku writers, the integration of visual arts (photography or painting) and contemporary English language haiku by leading poets. Query.

TIPS "The best haiku capture human perception—moments of being alive conveyed through sensory images. They do not explain nor describe nor provide philosophical or political commentary. Haiku are gifts of the here and now, deliberately incomplete so that the reader can enter into the haiku moment to open the gift and experience the feelings and insights of that moment for his or her self. Our readership includes the haiku community, readers of contemporary poetry, teachers and students of Japanese literature and contemporary Japanese poetics."

BRONZE MAN BOOKS

Bronze Man Books, Millikin University, 1184 W. Main, Decatur IL 62522. (217)424-6264. **Website:** www.bronzemanbooks.com. **Contact:** Dr. Randy Brooks, editorial board (Area of interest: children's books, fiction, poetry, nonfiction); Edwin Walker, editorial board (art, exhibits, graphic design). Estab. 2006. Publishes hardcover, trade paperback, & mass market paperback originals. **Publishes 3-4 titles/year. Receives 45 queries/year; 25 mss/year. 80% of books from first-time authors. 100% from unagented writers. Outright purchase based on wholesale value of 10% of a press run.** Publishes book 6 months after acceptance. Responds in 1 month to queries, 2 months to proposals, 3 months to mss. Catalog free on request.

NONFICTION Subjects include art, architecture, children's, graphic design, exhibits. "We do not publish author subsidy books." Query with SASE; submit proposal package, including outline and 3 sample chapters. Reviews artwork/photos. Send photocopies.

FICTION Subjects include art, exhibits, graphic design, general. Submit completed ms.

POETRY Submit completed ms.

TIPS "The art books are intended for serious collectors and scholars of contemporary art, especially of artists from the Midwestern U.S. These books are published in conjunction with art exhibitions at Millikin University or the Decatur Area Arts Council. The children's books have our broadest audience, and the literary chapbooks are intended for readers of contemporary fiction, drama, and poetry."

THE BRUCEDALE PRESS

P.O. Box 2259, Port Elgin ON N0H 2C0, Canada. (519)832-6025. **E-mail:** brucedale@bmts.com. **Website:** www.bmts.com/~brucedale. Publishes hardcover and trade paperback originals. **Publishes 3 titles/year. 50 queries received/year. 30 mss received/year. 75% of books from first-time authors. 100% from un-**agented writers. Pays royalty.** Publishes book 1 year after acceptance. Accepts simultaneous submissions. Catalog for #10 SASE (Canadian postage or IRC) or online. Guidelines online.

○ *Accepts works by Canadian authors only. Submissions accepted in September and March only.*

NONFICTION Subjects include history, language, literature, memoirs, military, war, nature, environment, photography. Reviews artwork/photos.

FICTION Subjects include fantasy, feminist, historical, humor, juvenile, literary, mainstream, contemporary, mystery, plays, poetry, romance, short story collections, young adult.

TIPS Our focus is very regional. In reading submissions, I look for quality writing with a strong connection to the Queen's Bush area of Ontario. All authors should visit our website, get a catalog, and read our books before submitting.

BUSTER BOOKS

16 Lion Yard, Tremadoc Rd., London WA SW4 7NQ, United Kingdom. 020 7720 8643. **Fax:** 022 7720 8953. **E-mail:** enquiries@michaelomarabooks.com. **Website:** www.mombooks.com.

○— "We are dedicated to providing irresistible and fun books for children of all ages. We typically publish black-and-white nonfiction for children aged 8-12 novelty titles-including doodle books."

NONFICTION Prefers synopsis and sample text over complete ms.

TIPS "We do not accept fiction submissions. Please do not send original artwork as we cannot guarantee its safety." Visit website before submitting.

BY LIGHT UNSEEN MEDIA

P.O. Box 1233, Pepperell MA 01463. (978) 433-8866. **Fax:** (978) 433-8866. **E-mail:** vyrdolak@bylightunseenmedia.com. **Website:** www.bylightunseenmedia.com. **Contact:** Inanna Arthen, owner/editor-in-chief. Estab. 2006. Publishes hardcover, paperback and electronic originals; trade paperback reprints. **Publishes 5 titles/year. 20 mss received/year; 5 queries received/year. 80% of books from first-time authors. 100% from unagented writers. Pays royalty of 20-50% on net as explicitly defined in contract. Payment quarterly. Pays $200 advance.** Publishes book 4 months after acceptance. Accepts simultaneous submissions. Responds in 3 months to queries/proposals/mss. Catalog available online. Guidelines online.

NONFICTION Subjects include alternative lifestyles, contemporary culture, creative nonfiction, history, language, literary criticism, literature, New Age, science, social sciences., folklore, popular media. "We are a niche small press that will *only* consider nonfiction on the theme of vampires (vampire folklore, movies, television, literature, vampires in culture, etc.). We're especially interested in academic or other well-researched material, but will consider self-help/New Age types of books (e.g. the kind of material published by Llewellyn). We use digital printing so all interiors would need to be black and white, including illustrations." Submit proposal package including outline, 3 sample chapters, brief author bio. *All unsolicited mss will be returned unopened.* Reviews artwork. Send photocopies/scanned PDF/jpeg.

FICTION Subjects include fantasy, gay, gothic, horror, lesbian, mystery, occult, science fiction, short story collections, suspense, western, young adult., magical realism, thriller. "We are a niche small press that *only* publishes fiction relating in some way to vampires. Within that guideline, we're interested in almost any genre that includes a vampire trope, the more creative and innovative, the better. We do not publish anthologies." Submit proposal package including synopsis, 3 sample chapters, brief author bio. *We encourage electronic submissions. All unsolicited mss will be returned unopened.*

TIPS "We strongly urge authors to familiarize themselves with the vampire genre and not imagine that they're doing something new and amazingly different just because they're not imitating the current fad. Our submission guidelines list two online articles we recommend prospective authors read: "7 Wrong Things You Should Know About Vampire Folklore," and "Think Outside the Coffin: Writing the Vampire Novel." We're looking for strong characters and good story-telling, not gimmicks. Our most successful promotional tag line is "vampire stories for grown-ups." That gives a good idea of what we're selling (and buying from authors)."

⊕ C&R PRESS

812 Westwood Ave., Chattanooga TN 37405. (423)645-5375. **Website:** www.crpress.org. **Contact:** Chad Prevost, editorial director and publisher; Ryan G. Van Cleave, executive director and publisher. Estab. 2006. Publishes hardcover, trade paperback, mass market paperback, and electronic originals. **Publish-**es 8 titles/year. 20% of books from first-time authors. 75% from unagented writers.** Publishes book 1 year after acceptance. Accepts simultaneous submissions. Responds in up to 1 month on queries and proposals, 1-2 months on mss. Catalog and guidelines online.

NONFICTION Subjects include contemporary culture, creative nonfiction, memoirs. Submit complete ms and query via e-mail. "C&R is a green company and we prefer all submissions to be done electronically."

FICTION Subjects include experimental, literary, poetry, regional. "We want dynamic, exciting literary fiction and we want to work with authors (not merely books) who are engaged socially and driven to promote their work because of their belief in the product, and because it's energizing and exciting to do so and a vital part of the process." Submit complete ms via e-mail.

POETRY "We remain committed to our annual first book of poetry contest, the De Novo Award. However, we also feature 1-2 monthly paid reading periods when we consider any and all poetry projects. Please check the website for updated guidelines." Submit complete ms.

⊘ CALAMARI PRESS

Via Titta Scarpetta #28, Rome 00153, Italy. **E-mail:** derek@calamaripress.net. **Website:** www.calamaripress.com. Publishes paperback originals. **Publishes 1-2/year titles/year. Pays in author's copies.** Publishes book Manuscript published 2-6 months after acceptance. Responds to mss in 2 weeks. Writer's guidelines on website.

&⊶ Calamari Press publishes books of literary text and art. Publishes 1-2 books/year. Manuscripts are selected by invitation. Occasionally has open submission period— check website. Helps to be published in *SleepingFish* first." See separate listing in magazines/journals. Order books through the website, Powell's, or SPD.

FICTION Query with outline/synopsis and 3 sample chapters. Accepts queries by e-mail only. Include brief bio. Send SASE or IRC for return of ms.

CALKINS CREEK

Boyds Mills Press, 815 Church St., Honesdale PA 18431. **Website:** www.calkinscreekbooks.com. Estab. 2004. **Pays authors royalty or work purchased outright.** Guidelines available on website.

&⊶ We aim to publish books that are a well-written blend of creative writing and extensive research, which emphasize important events, people, and places in U.S. history."

NONFICTION All levels: history. Submit outline/synopsis and 3 sample chapters.

FICTION All levels: history. Submit outline/synopsis and 3 sample chapters.

TIPS "Read through our recently published titles and review our catalog. When selecting titles to publish, our emphasis will be on important events, people, and places in U.S. history. Writers are encouraged to submit a detailed bibliography, including secondary and primary sources, and expert reviews with their submissions."

CAMINO BOOKS, INC.

P.O. Box 59026, Philadelphia PA 19102. (215)413-1917. **Fax:** (215)413-3255. **Website:** www.caminobooks. com. **Contact:** E. Jutkowitz, publisher. Estab. 1987. Publishes hardcover and trade paperback originals. **Publishes 6-10 titles/year. 20% of books from first-time authors. Pays $2,000 average advance.** Publishes book 1 year after acceptance. Responds in 2 weeks to queries. Guidelines online.

→ "Camino Books was founded in 1987 for the purpose of publishing quality nonfiction books of regional interest to people in the Middle Atlantic states. Our list is especially strong in titles about cooking, travel, gardening, and history, but we also publish biographies, local reference books, and books concerning parenting and important health issues. We occasionally publish books of national interest as well. We currently publish about 6 to 10 books per year, and we are always looking for new material and projects."

NONFICTION Subjects include agriculture, Americana, art, architecture, child guidance, cooking, foods, nutrition, ethnic, gardening, government, politics, history, regional, travel. Query with SASE. Submit outline, sample chapters.

TIPS "The books must be of interest to readers in the Middle Atlantic states, or they should have a clearly defined niche, such as cookbooks."

⊘ CANDLEWICK PRESS

99 Dover St., Somerville MA 02144. (617)661-3330. **Fax:** (617)661-0565. **E-mail:** bigbear@candlewick. com. **Website:** www.candlewick.com. **Contact:** Deb Wayshak, executive editor (fiction); Joan Powers, editor-at-large (picture books); Liz Bicknell, editorial director/associate publisher (poetry, picture books, fiction); Mary Lee Donovan, executive editor (picture books, nonfiction/fiction); Hilary Van Dusen, senior editor (nonfiction/fiction); Sarah Ketchersid, senior editor (board, toddler); Joan Powers, editor-at-large. Estab. 1991. Publishes hardcover and trade paperback originals, and reprints. **Publishes 200 titles/year. 5% of books from first-time authors. Pays authors royalty of 2½-10% based on retail price. Offers advance.**

🔑 *Candlewick Press is not accepting queries or unsolicited mss at this time.*

NONFICTION Picture books: concept, biography, geography, nature/environment. Young readers: biography, geography, nature/environment.

FICTION Subjects include juvenile, picture books, young adult. Picture books: animal, concept, contemporary, fantasy, history, humor, multicultural, nature/environment, poetry. Middle readers, young adults: contemporary, fantasy, history, humor, multicultural, poetry, science fiction, sports, suspense/mystery. "We do not accept editorial queries or submissions online. If you are an author or illustrator and would like us to consider your work, please read our submissions policy (online) to learn more."

TIPS *"We no longer accept unsolicited mss.* See our website for further information about us."

CAROLRHODA BOOKS, INC.

1251 Washington Ave. N., Minneapolis MN 55401. **Website:** www.lernerbooks.com. Estab. 1959.

→ "We will continue to seek targeted solicitations at specific reading levels and in specific subject areas. The company will list these targeted solicitations on our website and in national newsletters, such as the SCBWI Bulletin."

CARSTENS PUBLICATIONS, INC.

Hobby Book Division, 108 Phil Hardin Rd., Newton NJ 07860. (973)383-3355. **Fax:** (973)383-4064. **E-mail:** carstens@carstens-publications.com. **Website:** www.carstens-publications.com. **Contact:** Henry R. Carstens, publisher. Estab. 1933. Publishes paperback originals. **Publishes 8 titles/year. 100% from unagented writers. Pays 10% royalty on retail price. Pays advance.** Publishes book 1 year after acceptance. Responds in 2 months to queries. Catalog for #10 SASE.

→ Carstens specializes in books about railroads, model railroads, and airplanes for hobbyists.

NONFICTION Authors must know their field intimately because our readers are active modelers. Writers cannot write about somebody else's hobby with authority. If they do, we can't use them. Our railroad books presently are primarily photographic essays on specific railroads. Query with SASE. Reviews artwork/photos.

TIPS We need lots of good photos. Material must be in model, hobby, railroad, and transportation field only.

CARTWHEEL BOOKS

557 Broadway, New York NY 10012. **Website:** www. scholastic.com. **Contact:** Rotem Moscovich, editor; Jeffrey Salane, editor; Daniel Moreton, executive art director. Estab. 1991. **Publishes 100 titles/year. Pays advance against royalty or flat fee.** Publishes book Publishes a book 2 years after acceptance. Responds in 6 months to mss.

> *Cartwheel Books is no longer accepting unsolicited mss. All unsolicited materials will be returned unread.*

NONFICTION Picture books, young readers: seasonal/curricular topics involving animals (polar animals, ocean animals, hibernation), nature (fall leaves, life cycles, weather, solar system), history (first Thanksgiving, MLK Jr., George Washington, Columbus). "Most of our nonfiction is either written on assignment or is within a series. We do not want to see any arts/crafts or cooking." Average word length: picture books—100-1,500; young readers—100-2,000. For previously published or agented authors, submit complete ms. SASE required with all submissions.

FICTION Picture books, young readers: seasonal/holiday, humor, family/love. Average word length: picture books—100-500; easy readers—100-1,500. For previously published or agented authors, submit complete ms. SASE required with all submissions.

TIPS "With each Cartwheel list, we seek a pleasing balance of board books and novelty books, hardcover picture books and gift books, nonfiction, paperback storybooks and easy readers. Cartwheel seeks to acquire projects that speak to young children and their world: new and exciting novelty formats, fresh seasonal and holiday stories, curriculum/concept-based titles, and books for beginning readers. Our books are inviting and appealing, clearly marketable, and have inherent educational and social value. We strive to provide the earliest readers with relevant and exciting books that will ultimately lead to a lifetime of reading, learning, and wondering. Know what types of books

we do. Check out bookstores or catalogs first to see where your work would fit best, and why."

CATHOLIC UNIVERSITY OF AMERICA PRESS

620 Michigan Ave. NE, 240 Leahy Hall, Washington DC 20064. (202)319-5052. **Fax:** (202)319-4985. **E-mail:** cua-press@cua.edu. **Website:** cuapress.cua. edu. **Contact:** James C. Kruggel, acquisitions editor (philosophy, theology); Dr. David J. McGonagle, director (all other fields). Estab. 1939. **Publishes 30-35 titles/year. 50% of books from first-time authors. 100% from unagented writers. Pays variable royalty on net receipts.** Publishes book 18 months after acceptance. Responds in 5 days to queries. Catalog on request. Guidelines online.

The Catholic University of America Press publishes in the fields of history (ecclesiastical and secular), literature and languages, philosophy, political theory, social studies, and theology. "We have interdisciplinary emphasis on patristics, and medieval studies. We publish works of original scholarship intended for academic libraries, scholars and other professionals and works that offer a synthesis of knowledge of the subject of interest to a general audience or suitable for use in college and university classrooms."

NONFICTION Subjects include government, politics, history, language, literature, philosophy, religion., Church-state relations. No unrevised doctoral dissertations. Length: 40,000-120,000 words. Query with outline, sample chapter, CV, and list of previous publications.

TIPS Scholarly monographs and works suitable for adoption as supplementary reading material in courses have the best chance.

CAVE HOLLOW PRESS

P.O. Drawer J, Warrensburg MO 64093. **E-mail:** gbcrump@cavehollowpress.com. **Website:** www.cavehollowpress.com. **Contact:** G.B. Crump, editor. Estab. 2001. Publishes trade paperback originals. **Publishes 1 title/year. 70 queries received/year. 6 mss received/year. 80% of books from first-time authors. 100% from unagented writers. Pays 7-12% royalty on wholesale price. Pays negotiable amount in advance.** Publishes book 1 year after acceptance of ms. Accepts simultaneous submissions. Responds in 1-2 months to queries and proposals. Responds in 3-6 months to mss. Catalog for #10 SASE. Guidelines available free.

FICTION Subjects include : mainstream, contemporary. "Our website is updated frequently to reflect the current type of fiction Cave Hollow Press is seeking." Query with SASE.

TIPS "Our audience varies based on the type of book we are publishing. We specialize in Missouri and Midwest regional fiction. We are interested in talented writers from Missouri and the surrounding Midwest. Check our submission guidelines on the website for what type of fiction we are interested in currently."

MARSHALL CAVENDISH CHILDREN'S BOOKS

99 White Plains Rd., Tarrytown NY 10591. (914)332-8888. **Fax:** (914)332-1082. **E-mail:** mcc@marshall-cavendish.com. **Website:** www.marshallcavendish.us. **Contact:** Margery Cuyler, publisher. **Publishes 60-70 titles/year. Pays authors/illustrators advance and royalties.**

○ *Marshall Cavendish is no longer accepting unsolicited mss. However, the company will continue to consider agented mss.*

CAXTON PRESS

312 Main St., Caldwell ID 83605. (208)459-7421. **Fax:** (208)459-7450. **E-mail:** sgipson@caxtonpress.com. **Website:** caxtonpress.com. **Contact:** Wayne Cornell, editor (Western Americana, regional nonfiction). Estab. 1907. Publishes hardcover and trade paperback originals. **Publishes 6-10 titles/year. 50% of books from first-time authors. 60% from unagented writers. Pays royalty. Pays advance.** Publishes book 18 months after acceptance. Accepts simultaneous submissions. Responds in 3 months to queries. Catalog for 9×12 envelope and first-class stamps. Guidelines online.

8—¶ "Western Americana nonfiction remains our focus. We define Western Americana as almost any topic that deals with the people or culture of the west, past and present. Currently emphasizing regional issues—primarily Pacific Northwest. De-emphasizing coffee table or photograph-intensive books."

NONFICTION Subjects include Americana, history, regional. "We need good Western Americana, especially the Northwest, emphasis on serious, narrative nonfiction." Query. Reviews artwork/photos.

TIPS "Books to us never can or will be primarily articles of merchandise to be produced as cheaply as possible and to be sold like slabs of bacon or packages of cereal over the counter. If there is anything that is really worthwhile in this mad jumble we call the 21st century, it should be books."

CEDAR FORT, INC.

2373 W. 700 S, Springville UT 84663. (801)489-4084. **Fax:** (801)489-1097. **Website:** www.cedarfort.com. **Contact:** Shersta Gatica, acquisitions editor. Estab. 1986. Publishes hardcover, trade paperback originals and reprints, mass market paperback and electronic reprints. **Publishes 120 titles/year. Receives 200 queries/year; 600 mss/year. 60% of books from first-time authors. 95% from unagented writers. Pays 10-12% royalty on wholesale price. Pays $2,000-50,000 advance.** Publishes book 10-14 months after acceptance. Responds in 1 month on queries; 2 months on proposals; 4 months on mss. Catalog and guidelines online.

8—¶ "Each year we publish well over 100 books, and many of those are by first-time authors. At the same time, we love to see books from establishedauthors. As one of the largest book publishers in Utah, we have the capability and enthusiasm to make your book a success, whether you are a newauthor or a returning one. We want to publish uplifting and edifying books that help people think about what is important in life, books people enjoyreading to relax and feel better about themselves, and books to help improve lives. We like to publish a wide variety of books. We are always on thelookout for new and exciting material that will capture the public's interest. However, there are a few genres with which we are very selective. Werarely take biographies, autobiographies, or memoirs unless they have a very strong selling point (such as Mafia to Mormon). We do not publishpoetry. Although we do put out several children's books each year, we are extremely selective. Our children's books must have strong religious ormoral values, and must contain outstanding writing and an excellent storyline."

NONFICTION Subjects include agriculture, Americana, animals, anthropology, archeology, business, child guidance, communications, cooking, crafts, creative nonfiction, economics, education, foods, gardening, health, history, hobbies, horticulture, house and home, military, nature, recreation, regional, religion, social sciences, spirituality, war, womens issues, young adult. Query with SASE; submit proposal package, including outline, 2 sample chapters; or submit completed ms. Reviews artwork as part of the ms package. Send photocopies.

FICTION Subjects include adventure, contemporary, fantasy, historical, humor, juvenile, literary, mainstream, military, multicultural, mystery, regional, religious, romance, science fiction, spiritual, sports, suspense, war, western, young adult. Submit completed ms.

TIPS "Our audience is rural, conservative, mainstream. The first page of your ms is very important because we start reading every submission, but good writing and plot keep us reading."

⊕ CELLAR DOOR PUBLISHING, LLC

3439 NE Sandy Blvd., Suite 309, Portland OR 97232-1959. **Website:** www.cellardoorpublishing.com. Estab. 2004. Publishes hardcover originals, trade paperback originals and electronic originals. **Publishes 3-4 titles/year. Pays a percentage of sales on royalty.** Accepts simultaneous submissions. Guidelines available via e-mail.

⚬—ᴛ "Cellar Door Publishing specializes in the publication of high-quality illustrated literature and graphic novels. We are looking for all genres and age groups. We encourage creators to experiment with format and content, though it is not required. We do accept a limited number of submissions for books without illustrations. This is generally reserved for books that are either unique in content or controversial in nature, or literary projects that can be released in a serialized format."

NONFICTION Nonfiction submissions will also be considered if they fall into one of our categories. Submit online. Reviews artwork/photos. Send photocopies.

FICTION Subjects include adventure, comic books, erotica, experimental, fantasy, gothic, historical, horror, humor, juvenile, literary, mainstream, contemporary, multimedia, mystery, occult, picture books, romance, science fiction, suspense, western, young adult., translation. "We currently accept unsolicited submissions via online submission form and comic book conventions only. We no longer accept unsolicited submissions through traditional mail. To submit book proposals for consideration, please use the online submission form."

⊕ CENTER FOR THANATOLOGY RESEARCH & EDUCATION, INC.

391 Atlantic Ave., Brooklyn NY 11217. (718)858-3026. **E-mail:** thanatology@pipeline.com. **Website:** www.thanatology.org. Estab. 1980. **Publishes 7 titles/year. 10 queries received/year. 3 mss received/year. 15% of books from first-time authors. 100% from unagented writers. Pays 10% royalty on wholesale price.** Publishes book 9 months after acceptance. Responds in 1 month to queries and proposals. Catalog and guidelines free.

NONFICTION Subjects include education, health, medicine, humanities, psychology, religion, social sciences, sociology, women's issues/studies, anthropology. All proposals we feel are applicable are sent to a board of professional readers for comment. Query. Reviews artwork/photos. Send photocopies.

POETRY We are open to appropriate submissions. Query.

TIPS "We serve 2 different audiences: One is physicians/social workers/nurses dealing with dying patients and bereaved families. The second relates to all aspects of cemetery lore: recording, preservation, description, art of."

⊕ CENTER ONE PUBLISHING

P.O. Box 651, Kingsley MI 49649. (708)441-4297. **E-mail:** contactus@centeronepublishing.com. **Website:** www.centeronepublishing.com. **Contact:** Ann Dine, acquisitions editor; Justin Dine, publisher. Estab. 2010. Publishes trade paperback originals, trade paperback reprints, electronic originals, electronic reprints. **Publishes 8-16 titles/year. 100% of books from first-time authors. 100% from unagented writers. Pays royalty of 6-12% on retail price.** Publishes book 1 year after acceptance. Accepts simultaneous submissions. Responds to queries in 3-6 months. Catalogue available online. Guidelines online.

FICTION Subjects include adventure, fantasy, humor, mystery, romance, science fiction, short story collections. Submit proposal package electronically. Include synopsis, 3 sample chapters, and a brief explanation about writing goals.

TIPS "Queries need to be submitted electronically in legible format. All information requested by form must be provided. Only information requestion by form should be provided. Please read all submissions guidelines on website."

CENTERSTREAM PUBLISHING

P.O. Box 17878, Anaheim Hills CA 92817. (714)779-9390. **Fax:** (714)779-9390. **E-mail:** Centerstrm@aol.com. **Website:** www.centerstream-usa.com. **Contact:** Ron Middlebrook, Cindy Middlebrook, owners. Estab. 1980. Publishes music hardcover and mass market paperback originals, trade paperback and mass market paperback reprints. **Publishes 12 titles/year. 15 queries received/year. 15 mss received/year. 80% of books from first-time authors. 100% from unagented writers. Pays 10-15% royalty on wholesale price. Pays $300-3,000 advance.** Publishes book 8 months after acceptance. Accepts simultaneous submissions. Responds in 3 months to queries. Catalog and guidelines for #10 SASE.

⚷ Centerstream publishes music history and instructional books, all instruments plus DVDs.

NONFICTION Query with SASE.

CHALICE PRESS

1221 Locust St., Suite 670, St. Louis MO 63103. (314)231-8500. **Fax:** (314)231-8524. **E-mail:** submissions@chalicepress.com. **Website:** www.chalicepress.com. **Contact:** Cyrus N. White, president and publisher. Publishes hardcover and trade paperback originals. **Publishes 35 titles/year. 300 queries received/year. 250 mss received/year. 10% of books from first-time authors. 100% from unagented writers.** Publishes book 1 year after acceptance. Accepts simultaneous submissions. Responds in 1 month to queries; 2 months to proposals; 3 months to mss. Catalog and guidelines online.

NONFICTION Subjects include religion., Christian spirituality. Submit proposal package, outline, 1-2 sample chapters.

TIPS "We publish for professors, church ministers, and lay Christian readers."

⊕ CHANNEL LAKE, INC.

P.O. Box 1771, New York NY 10156-1771. (800)592-1566. **Fax:** (866)794-5507. **E-mail:** info@channellake.com; submissions@channellake.com. **Website:** www.touristtown.com; www.channellake.com. **Contact:** Dirk Vanderwilt, publisher (travel guide books). Estab. 2005. Trade paperback originals. **Publishes 8-10 titles/year. 75% of books from first-time authors. 75% from unagented writers. Pays 6-10% royal on retail price.** Publishes book 3 months after acceptance of ms. Accepts simultaneous submissions. Responds in 1 month on queries, proposals, and manu-

scripts. Catalog available online at www.touristtown.com. Guidelines free on request.

NONFICTION Subjects include travel guide books. "We strongly suggest that you query us before sending a completed manuscript. Our editorial team has very strict content and formatting requirements. Contact us for details." Query.

TIPS "Our books are 'local interest' and 'travel books' that are marketed and sold near or in the destination city. Our audience is primarily tourists and vacationers to the destination city. Query first for ms guidelines. The query should include the destination city (U.S. only) that you are interested in writing about."

CHARLESBRIDGE PUBLISHING

85 Main St., Watertown MA 02472. (617)926-0329. **Fax:** (617)926-5720. **E-mail:** tradeart@charlesbridge.com. **Website:** www.charlesbridge.com. Estab. 1980. Publishes hardcover and trade paperback nonfiction and fiction, children's books for the trade and library markets. **Publishes 30 titles/year. 10-20% of books from first-time authors. 80% from unagented writers. Pays royalty. Pays advance.** Publishes book 2-4 years after acceptance. Responds in 3 months. If you have not heard back from us after 3 months, you may assume we do not have a place for your project and submit it elsewhere. Guidelines online.

⚷ "Charlesbridge publishes high-quality books for children, with a goal of creating lifelong readers and lifelong learners. Our books encourage reading and discovery in the classroom, library, and home. We believe that books for children should offer accurate information, promote a positive worldview, and embrace a child's innate sense of wonder and fun. To this end, we continually strive to seek new voices, new visions, and new directions in children's literature."

NONFICTION Subjects include animals, creative nonfiction, history, multicultural, nature, environment, science, social science. Strong interest in nature, environment, social studies, and other topics for trade and library markets. *Exclusive submissions only.* "Charlesbridge accepts unsolicited manuscripts submitted exclusively to us for a period of three months. 'Exclusive Submission' should be written on all envelopes and cover letters." Please submit only one or two chapters at a time. For nonfiction books longer than 30 manuscript pages, send a detailed proposal, a chapter outline, and one to three chapters of text. Manuscripts should be typed and double-spaced. Please do not submit material by e-mail, by fax, or on a computer disk. Illustrations are not necessary. Please make a copy of your manuscript, as we cannot be responsible for submissions lost in the mail. Include your name and address on the first page of your manuscript and in your cover letter. Be sure to list any previously published work or relevant writing experience.

FICTION Strong stories with enduring themes. Charlesbridge publishes both picture books and transitional bridge books (books ranging from early readers to middle-grade chapter books). Our fiction titles include lively, plot-driven stories with strong, engaging characters. No alphabet books, board books, coloring books, activity books, or books with audiotapes or CD-ROMs. *Exclusive submissions only.* "Charlesbridge accepts unsolicited manuscripts submitted exclusively to us for a period of three months. 'Exclusive Submission' should be written on all envelopes and cover letters. Please submit only one or two manuscript(s) at a time. For picture books and shorter bridge books, please send a complete ms. For fiction books longer than 30 manuscript pages, please send a detailed plot synopsis, a chapter outline, and three chapters of text. Manuscripts should be typed and double-spaced. Please do not submit material by e-mail, by fax, or on a computer disk. Illustrations are not necessary. Please make a copy of your manuscript, as we cannot be responsible for submissions lost in the mail. Include your name and address on the first page of your manuscript and in your cover letter. Be sure to list any previously published work or relevant writing experience."

TIPS "To become acquainted with our publishing program, we encourage you to review our books and visit our website (www.charlesbridge.com), where you will find our catalog. To request a printed catalog, please send a 9×12 SASE with $2.50 in postage."

CHARLES RIVER MEDIA

Course Technology PTR, Cengage Learning, Inc., 20 Channel Center St., Boston MA 02210. **E-mail:** info@gameprogramminggems.com. **E-mail:** emi.smith@cengage.com. **Website:** www.gameprogramminggems.com. **Contact:** Emi Smith, senior acquisitions editor. **Publishes 60 titles/year. 1,000 queries received/year. 250 mss received/year. 20% of books from first-time authors. 90% from unagented writ-**

ers. **Pays 5-20% royalty on wholesale price. Pays $3,000-20,000 advance.** Publishes book 4 months after acceptance. Accepts simultaneous submissions. Responds in 2 weeks to queries. Catalog for #10 SASE. Guidelines online.

- "Now an imprint of Course Technology PTR. Our publishing program concentrates on 6 major areas: Internet, networking, game development, programming, engineering, and graphics. The majority of our titles are considered intermediate, not high-level research monographs, and not for lowest-level general users."

NONFICTION Subjects include computers, electronics. Query with SASE. Submit proposal package, outline, résumé, 2 sample chapters. Reviews artwork/photos. Send photocopies and GIF, TIFF, or PDF files.

TIPS "We are very receptive to detailed proposals by first-time or nonagented authors. Consult our website for proposal outlines. Manuscripts must be completed within 6 months of contract signing."

CHELSEA GREEN PUBLISHING CO.

P.O. Box 428, White River Junction VT 05001. (802)295-6300. **Fax:** (802)295-6444. **E-mail:** submissions@chelseagreen.com; jpraded@chelseagreen.com. **Website:** www.chelseagreen.com. **Contact:** Joni Praded, editorial director. Estab. 1984. Publishes hardcover and trade paperback originals and reprints. **Publishes 18-25 titles/year. 600-800 queries received/year. 200-300 mss received/year. 30% of books from first-time authors. 80% from unagented writers. Pays royalty on publisher's net. Pays $2,500-10,000 advance.** Publishes book 18 months after aceeptance. after acceptance of ms. Responds in 2 weeks to queries; 1 month to proposals/mss. Catalog free or online. Guidelines online.

- "Chelsea Green's Science writers series publishes books on cutting-edge topics that advance science and the role it can play in preserving or creating sustainable civilizations and ecosystems."

NONFICTION Subjects include agriculture, alternative lifestyles, ethical & sustainable business, environment, foods, organic gardening, health, green building, progressive politics, science, social justice, simple living, renewable energy; and other sustainability topics. We only rarely publish cookbooks. We prefer electronic queries and proposals via e-mail (as a single attachment). If sending via snail mail, submissions will only be returned with SASE. Please review our guidelines carefully before submitting. Reviews artwork/photos.

FICTION We do not publish fiction or children's books.

TIPS "Our readers and our authors are passionate about finding sustainable and viable solutions to contemporary challenges in the fields of energy, food production, economics, and building. It would be helpful for prospective authors to have a look at several of our current books, as well as our website."

CHEMICAL PUBLISHING CO., INC.

P.O. Box 676, Revere MA 02151. (888)439-3976. **Fax:** (888)439-3976. **E-mail:** info@chemical-publishing. com. **Website:** www.chemical-publishing.com. **Contact:** B. Carr, publisher. Estab. 1934. Publishes hardcover originals. **Publishes 10-15 titles/year. 20 queries received/year. 50% of books from first-time authors. 100% from unagented writers. Pays 10% royalty on retail price or makes negotiable outright purchase. Pays negotiable advance.** Publishes book 8 months after acceptance. Responds in 3 weeks to queries; 5 weeks to proposals; 1 months to mss.

○ "We invite the submission of manuscripts whether they are technical, scientific or serious popular expositions. All submitted manuscripts and planned works will receive prompt attention. The staff will consider finished and proposed manuscripts by authors whose works have not been previously published as sympathetically as those by experienced authors. Please do not hesitate to consult us about such mss or about your ideas for writing them."

NONFICTION Subjects include agriculture, cooking, foods, nutrition, health, medicine, nature, environment, science., analytical methods, chemical technology, cosmetics, dictionaries, engineering, environmental science, food technology, formularies, industrial technology, medical, metallurgy, textiles. Submit outline, a few pages of 3 sample chapters, SASE. Download CPC submission form online and include with submission. Reviews, artwork and photos should also be part of the manuscript package.

TIPS Audience is professionals in various fields of chemistry, corporate and public libraries, college libraries. We request a fax letter with an introduction of

the author and the kind of book written. Afterwards, we will reply. If the title is of interest, then we will request samples of the manuscript.

CHICAGO REVIEW PRESS

814 N. Franklin St., Chicago IL 60610. (312)337-0747. **Fax:** (312)337-5110. **E-mail:** frontdesk@chicagoreviewpress.com. **Website:** www.chicagoreviewpress. com. **Contact:** Cynthia Sherry, publisher; Allison Felus, managing editor. Estab. 1973. **Pays authors royalty of 7-12% based on retail price. Offers advances of $3,000-6,000. Pays illustrators by the project (range varies considerably). Pays photographers by the project (range varies considerably).** Publishes book Publishes a book 1-2 years after acceptance. Accepts simultaneous submissions. Responds to queries/mss in 2 months. Catalog available for $3. Ms guidelines available for $3.

⊶ "Chicago Review Press publishes high-quality, nonfiction, educational activity books that extend the learning process through hands-on projects and accurate and interesting text. We look for activity books that are as much fun as they are constructive and informative."

NONFICTION Young readers, middle readers and young adults: activity books, arts/crafts, multicultural, history, nature/environment, science. "We're interested in hands-on, educational books; anything else probably will be rejected." Average length: young readers and young adults—144-160 pages. Enclose cover letter and no more than a table of contents and 1-2 sample chapters; prefers not to receive e-mail queries.

TIPS "We're looking for original activity books for small children and the adults caring for them—new themes and enticing projects to occupy kids' imaginations and promote their sense of personal creativity. We like activity books that are as much fun as they are constructive. Please write for guidelines so you'll know what we're looking for."

CHILDREN'S BRAINS ARE YUMMY (CBAY) BOOKS

P.O. Box 92411, Austin TX 78709. (512)789-1004. **Fax:** (512)473-7710. **E-mail:** submissions@cbaybooks.com. **Website:** www.cbaybooks.com. **Contact:** Madeline Smoot, publisher. Estab. 2008. **Publishes 8 titles/year. 30% of books from first-time authors. 0% from unagented writers. Pays authors royalty 10%-15% based on wholesale price. Offers**

advances against royalties. Average amount $500. Responds in 3 months to mss. Brochure and Guidelines online.

�—➔ "CBAY Books currently focuses on quality fantasy and science fiction books for the middle grade and teen markets. Although we are exploring the possibility of publishing fantasy and science fiction books in the future, we are not seeking submissions for them at this time. We do welcome books that mix genres—a fantasy mystery for example—but since our press currently has a narrow focus, all submissions need to have fantasy or science fiction elements to fit in with our list."

FICTION Subjects include adventure, mystery, science fiction, suspense., folktales. Accepts international material. Submit outline/synopsis and 3 sample chapters.

TIPS "CBAY Books only accepts unsolicited submissions from authors at specific times for specific genres. Please check the website to see if we are accepting books at this time. Manuscripts received when submissions are closed are not read."

CHILDREN'S PRESS/FRANKLIN WATTS

Imprint of Scholastic, Inc., 90 Old Sherman Turnpike, Danbury CT 06816. **Website:** scholastic.com/library-publishing; http://www.scholastic.com/internationalschools/childrenspress.htm. Estab. 1946. Publishes nonfiction hardcover originals. Catalog for #10 SASE.

◖ "Children's Press publishes 90% nonfiction for the school and library market, and 10% early reader fiction and nonfiction. Our books support textbooks and closely relate to the elementary and middle-school curriculum. Franklin Watts publishes nonfiction for middle and high school curriculum."

NONFICTION Subjects include animals, anthropology, archeology, art, architecture, ethnic, health, medicine, history, hobbies, multicultural, music, dance, nature, environment, science, sports., general children's nonfiction. We publish nonfiction books that supplement the school curriculum. No fiction, poetry, folktales, cookbooks or novelty books. Query with SASE.

TIPS Most of this publisher's books are developed in-house; less than 5% come from unsolicited submissions. However, they publish several series for which they always need new books. Study catalogs to discover possible needs.

◕ CHILD'S PLAY (INTERNATIONAL) LTD.

Children's Play International, Ashworth Rd. Bridgemead, Swindon, Wiltshire SN5 7YD, United Kingdom. **E-mail:** allday@childs-play.com; neil@childs-play.com; office@childs-play.com. **Website:** www.childs-play.com. **Contact:** Sue Baker, Neil Burden, manuscript acquisitions. Annie Kubler, art director Estab. 1972. **Publishes 45 titles/year. 20% of books from first-time authors.** Publishes book 2 years after acceptance. Accepts simultaneous submissions. Responds to queries in 10 weeks; mss in 15 weeks.

�—➔ Specializes in nonfiction, fiction, educational material, multicultural material. Produces 30 picture books/year; 10 young readers/year; 2 middle readers/year. "A child's early years are more important than any other. This is when children learn most about the world around them and the language they need to survive and grow. Child's Play aims to create exactly the right material for this all-important time."

NONFICTION Picture books: activity books, animal, concept, multicultural, music/dance, nature/environment, science. Young readers: activity books, animal, concept, multicultural, music/dance, nature/environment, science. Average word length: picture books—2,000; young readers—3,000. Recently published *Roly Poly Discovery,* by Kees Moerbeek (ages 3+ years, novelty).

FICTION Picture books: adventure, animal, concept, contemporary, folktales, multicultural, nature/environment. Young readers: adventure, animal, anthology, concept, contemporary, folktales, humor, multicultural, nature/environment, poetry. Average word length: picture books—1,500; young readers—2,000. Recently published *Snug,* by Carol Thompson (ages 0-2, picture book); *The Lost Stars,* by Hannah Cumming (ages 4-8 yrs, picture book); *Uuggh!,* by Claudia Boldt (ages 4-8 yrs, picture book); *First Time Doctor/Dentist/Hospital/Vet,* by Jess Stockham (ages 2-5 yrs, picture book); New Baby Series, by Rachel Fuller (ages 1-3, board book).

TIPS "Look at our website to see the kind of work we do before sending. Do not send cartoons. We do not publish novels. We do publish lots of books with pictures of babies/toddlers."

CHILD WELFARE LEAGUE OF AMERICA

E-mail: books@cwla.org. **Website:** www.cwla.org/pubs. Publishes hardcover and trade paperback originals. Accepts simultaneous submissions. Catalog and guidelines online.

NONFICTION Subjects include child guidance, sociology. Submit complete ms and proposal with outline, TOC, sample chapter, intended audience, and SASE.

TIPS We are looking for positive, kid-friendly books for ages 3-9. We are looking for books that have a positive message—a feel-good book.

CHIVALRY BOOKSHELF

3305 Mayfair Ln., Highland Village TX 75077. (978)418-4774. **Fax:** (978)418-4774. **E-mail:** brian@chivalrybookshelf.com; csr@chivalrybookshelf.com. **Website:** www.chivalrybookshelf.com. **Contact:** Brian R. Price, publisher (history, art, philosophy, political science, military, martial arts, fencing). Estab. 1996. Publishes hardcover and trade paperback originals and reprints. **Publishes 12 titles/year. 75 queries received/year. 25 mss received/year. 50% of books from first-time authors. 90% from unagented writers. Pays 5-12% royalty.** Publishes book 6 months after acceptance. Responds in 1 month to queries/proposals; 2 months to mss. Catalog available free. Guidelines online.

NONFICTION Subjects include art, architecture, creative nonfiction, education, government, politics, history, military, war, recreation, sports, martial arts/fencing especially, translation. "Chivalry Bookshelf began focusing on new works and important reprints relating to arms and armour, medieval knighthood, and related topics. Since then, we have become the largest publisher of books relating to 'Western' or 'historical' martial arts, including translations, interpretations, and fascimile reproductions done in partnership with major museums such as the J. Paul Getty Museum and the British Royal Armouries." Query with SASE if mailing, e-mail or fax. Submit proposal package, outline, 1 sample chapter, sample illustrations. Submit complete ms. Reviews artwork/photos.

TIPS "The bulk of our books are intended for serious amateur scholars and students of history and martial arts. The authors we select tend to have a strong voice, are well read in their chosen field, and submit relatively clean manuscripts."

CHOSEN BOOKS

A division of Baker Publishing Group, 3985 Bradwater St., Fairfax VA 22031. (703)764-8250. **Fax:** (703)764-3995. **E-mail:** jcampbell@chosenbooks.com. **Website:** www.chosenbooks.com. **Contact:** Jane Campbell, editorial director. Estab. 1971. Publishes hardcover and trade paperback originals. **Publishes 20 titles/year. 10% of books from first-time authors. 99% from unagented writers. Pays small advance.** Publishes book 18 months after acceptance. Accepts simultaneous submissions. Responds in 3 months to queries. Guidelines sent electronically on request.

🔑 "We publish well-crafted books that recognize the gifts and ministry of the Holy Spirit, and help the reader live a more empowered and effective life for Jesus Christ."

NONFICTION "We publish books reflecting the current acts of the Holy Spirit in the world, books with a charismatic Christian orientation, or thematic first-person narrative. Query briefly by e-mail first." No New Age, poetry, fiction, autobiographies, biographies, compilations, Bible studies, booklets, academic, or children's books. Submit synopsis, chapter outline, 2 chapters, résumé and SASE or e-mail address. No computer disks. E-mail attachments OK.

TIPS "We look for solid, practical advice for the growing and maturing Christian from authors with professional or personal experience platforms. No chronicling of life events, please. Narratives have to be theme-driven. State the topic or theme of your book clearly in your query."

● CHRISTIAN BOOKS TODAY LTD

136 Main St., Buckshaw Village Chorley, Lancashire PR7 7BZ, United Kingdom. **E-mail:** md@christianbookstoday.com; submissions@christianbookstoday.com. **Website:** www.christianbookstoday.com. **Contact:** Jason Richardson, MD (nonfiction); Lynda McIntosh, editor (fiction). Estab. 2009. Publishes trade paperback originals/reprints and electronic originals/reprints. **Publishes 39 titles/year. 75% of books from first-time authors. 100% from unagented writers. Pays 10% royalty on retail price or 50% of title profit.** Publishes book 6 months after acceptance. Accepts simultaneous submissions. Responds in 1 month to queries; 2 months to proposals and mss. Catalog and guidelines available online.

NONFICTION Subjects include spirituality., Christian/Catholic. "We are not looking for nonfiction at this time. Please send us your fiction."

FICTION Subjects include adventure, mainstream, poetry, religious, spiritual, Catholic/Christian.

"We're looking for writers who write about life, failures and all! Tackle the big issues but in a tasteful way. Deal with divorce, blended families, ecumenism, atheists, creationism, crazy preachers, celebrity culture, sexuality. Life doesn't conform to expectations – neither did Christ. Tackle the difficult and brutal. How do we as Christians deal with the messiness? Moralizing doesn't appeal to a broader audience. In your cover letter tell us how you intend to market the book, what sets it apart. No fantasy or sci-fi please." Submit "cover letter, chapter by chapter outline, first 3 chapters & SASE. Or via the member section of our website."

TIPS "We appeal to a general Christian readership. We are not interested in Hallmark stories, nor fantasy, or mysticism. We want work by Christians rather than Christian writing. If you want to take a risk in subject, you are particularly encouraged to submit. We actively seek out writers who want to build a career with us and who understand we do what we do because we love it."

CHRISTIAN ED. PUBLISHERS

P.O. Box 26639, San Diego CA 92196. (858)578-4700. **E-mail:** crogers@cehouse.com. **Website:** www.christianedwarehouse.com. **Contact:** Janet Ackelson, assistant editor. Acquisitions: Janet Ackelson, assistant editor; Carol Rogers, managing editor; Nicole Tom, production coordinator. **Work purchased outright from authors for 3¢/word. Pays illustrators $18-20/page.** Publishes book Publishes assignments 1 year after acceptance. Responds in 1 month. Catalog available for 9×12 SAE and 4 first-class stamps. Ms and art guidelines available for SASE or via e-mail.

NONFICTION Publishes Bible curriculum and take-home papers for all ages.

FICTION Young readers: contemporary. Middle readers: adventure, contemporary, suspense/mystery. "All fiction is on assignment only."

TIPS "Read our guidelines carefully before submitting. Do not send unsolicited manuscripts. All writing and illustrating is done on assignment only and must be age-appropriate (preschool-6th grade). Ask for a writer's application"

CHRISTIAN FOCUS PUBLICATIONS

Geanies House, Tain Ross-shire IV20 1TW, United Kingdom. 44 (0) 1862 871 011. **Fax:** 44 (0) 1862 871 699. **E-mail:** info@christianfocus.com. **Website:** www.christianfocus.com. **Contact:** Catherine Mackenzie, publisher. Estab. 1975. **Publishes 22-32 titles/year. 2% of books from first-time authors.** Publishes book 1 year after acceptance. Responds to queries in 2 weeks; mss in 3 months.

⟿ Specializes in Christian material, nonfiction, fiction, educational material.

NONFICTION All levels: activity books, biography, history, religion, science. Average word length: picture books—5,000; young readers—5,000; middle readers—5,000-10,000; young adult/teens—10,000-20,000. Query or submit outline/synopsis and 3 sample chapters. Will consider electronic submissions and previously published work.

FICTION Picture books, young readers, adventure, history, religion. Middle readers: adventure, problem novels, religion. Young adult/teens: adventure, history, problem novels, religion. Average word length: young readers—5,000; middle readers—max 10,000; young adult/teen—max 20,000. Query or submit outline/synopsis and 3 sample chapters. Will consider electronic submissions and previously published work.

TIPS "Be aware of the international market as regards writing style/topics as well as illustration styles. Our company sells rights to European as well as Asian countries. Fiction sales are not as good as they were. Christian fiction for youngsters is not a product that is performing well in comparison to nonfiction such as Christian biography/Bible stories/church history, etc."

CHRONICLE BOOKS

680 Second St., San Francisco CA 94107. **Website:** www.chroniclekids.com. **Contact:** Acquisitions: Victoria Rock, founding publisher and editor-at-large; Andrea Menotti, senior editor; Julie Romeis, editor; Melissa Manlove, editor; Naomi Kirsten, assistant editor; Mary Colgan, assistant editor. **Publishes 90 titles/year. Generally pays authors in royalties based on retail price, "though we do occasionally work on a flat fee basis." Advance varies. Illustrators paid royalty based on retail price or flat fee.** Publishes book Publishes a book 1-3 years after acceptance. Responds to queries in 1 month. Catalog for 9x12 SAE and 8 first-class stamps. Ms guidelines for #10 SASE.

NONFICTION Picture books, young readers, middle readers, young adults: "We are open to a very wide range of topics." Submit complete ms (picture books); submit outline/synopsis and 3 sample chapters (for older readers). Will not respond to submissions unless interested. Will not consider submissions by fax, e-mail or disk. Do not include SASE; do not send original materials. No submissions will be returned; to confirm receipt, include a SASP.

FICTION Picture books, young readers, middle readers, young adults: "We are open to a very wide range of topics." Submit complete ms (picture books); submit outline/synopsis and 3 sample chapters (for older readers). Will not respond to submissions unless interested. Will not consider submissions by fax, e-mail or disk. Do not include SASE; do not send original materials. No submissions will be returned; to confirm receipt, include a SASP.

TIPS "Chronicle Books publishes an eclectic mixture of traditional and innovative children's books. We are interested in taking on projects that have a unique bent to them—be it subject matter, writing style, or illustrative technique. As a small list, we are looking for books that will lend us a distinctive flavor. We are also interested in growing our fiction program for older readers, including chapter books, middle grade, and young adult projects."

CHRONICLE BOOKS FOR CHILDREN

680 Second St., San Francisco CA 94107. (415)537-4200. **Fax:** (415)537-4460. **E-mail:** frontdesk@chroniclebooks.com. **Website:** www.chroniclekids.com. Publishes hardcover and trade paperback originals. **Publishes 50-60 titles/year. 30,000 queries received/year. 6% of books from first-time authors. 25% from unagented writers. Pays 8% royalty. Pays variable advance.** Publishes book Publishes a book 18-24 months after acceptance. Accepts simultaneous submissions. Responds in 2-4 weeks to queries; 6 months to mss. Catalog for 9x12 envelope and 3 first-class stamps. Guidelines online.

- "Chronicle Books for Children publishes an eclectic mixture of traditional and innovative children's books. Our aim is to publish books that inspire young readers to learn and grow creatively while helping them discover the joy of reading. We're looking for quirky, bold artwork and subject matter. Currently emphasizing picture books. De-emphasizing young adult."

NONFICTION Subjects include animals, art, architecture, multicultural, nature, environment, science. Query with synopsis. Reviews artwork/photos.

FICTION Subjects include mainstream, contemporary, multicultural, young adult., picture books. We do not accept proposals by fax, via e-mail, or on disk.

When submitting artwork, either as a part of a project or as samples for review, do not send original art.

TIPS "We are interested in projects that have a unique bent to them—be it in subject matter, writing style, or illustrative technique. As a small list, we are looking for books that will lend our list a distinctive flavor. Primarily we are interested in fiction and nonfiction picture books for children ages up to eight years, and nonfiction books for children ages up to twelve years. We publish board, pop-up, and other novelty formats as well as picture books. We are also interested in early chapter books, middle grade fiction, and young adult projects."

CHURCH GROWTH INSTITUTE

P.O. Box 7, Elkton MD 21922. (434)525-0022. **Fax:** (434)525-0608. **E-mail:** cgimail@churchgrowth.org. **Website:** www.churchgrowth.org. **Contact:** Cindy Spear, administrator/resource development director. Estab. 1978. Publishes electronic books (pdf), 3-ring-bound manuals, mixed media resource packets. **Publishes 3 titles/year. Pays 6% royalty on retail price.** Publishes book 1 year after acceptance. Accepts simultaneous submissions. Responds in 3 months to queries. Catalog for 9×12 envelope and 4 first-class stamps.

- "Our mission is to provide practical resources to help pastors, churches, and individuals reach their potential for Christ; to promote spiritual and numerical growth in churches, thereby leading Christians to maturity and lost people to Christ; and to equip pastors so they can equip their church members to do the work of the ministry."

NONFICTION Subjects include education, religion, church-growth related., ministry, how-to manuals, spiritual growth, relationship-building, evangelism. "Accepted manuscripts will be adapted to our resource packet, manual, or inventory format. All material must be practical and easy for the average Christian to understand. Material should originate from a conservative Christian view and cover topics that will help churches grow, through leadership training, self-evaluation, and new or unique ministries, or enhancing existing ministries. Self-discovery inventories regarding spiritual growth, relationship improvement, etc. are hot items." Query, or submit outline and brief explanation of what the packet will accomplish in the local church and whether it is leadership or lay oriented. Queries accepted by mail or e-mail. No phone queries. Reviews artwork/photos. Send photos or images on CD (in TIFF, EPS, or PDF format).

RECENT TITLE(S) *Fruits of the Spirit Assessment*; *Serving God Where You Fit Best*; *How to Develop and Use the Gift of Exhortation*.

TIPS "We are not accepting textbooks, and are publishing few new printed materials this year-most are online or downloads. Concentrate on how-to manuals and ministry evaluation and diagnostic tools and spiritual or relationship-oriented 'inventories' for individual Christians."

CHURCH PUBLISHING INC.

4775 Linglestown Rd., Harrisburg PA 17112. 800-223-6602. **Fax:** (212) 779-3392. **E-mail:** nabryan@cpg.org. **Website:** www.churchpublishing.org. **Contact:** Nancy Bryan, editorial director. Estab. 1884.

"With a religious publishing heritage dating back to 1918 and headquartered today in New York City, CPI is an official publisher of worship materials and resources for The Episcopal Church, plus a multi-faceted publisher and supplier to the broader ecumenical marketplace. In the nearly 100 years since its first publication, Church Publishing has emerged as a principal provider of liturgical and musical resources for The Episcopal Church, along with works on church leadership, pastoral care and Christian formation. With its growing portfolio of professional books and resources, Church Publishing was recognized in 1997 as the official publisher for the General Convention of the Episcopal Church in the United States. Simultaneously through the years, Church Publishing has consciously broadened its program, reach, and service to the church by publishing books for and about the worldwide Anglican Communion."

TIPS "Prefer using freelancers who are located in central Pennsylvania and are available for meetings when necessary."

CLARION BOOKS

Houghton Mifflin Co., 215 Park Ave. S., New York NY 10003. **Website:** www.houghtonmifflinbooks.com; www.hmco.com. **Contact:** Dinah Stevenson, vice president and publisher; Jennifer B. Greene, senior editor (contemporary fiction, picture books for all ages, nonfiction); Jennifer Wingertzahn, editor (fiction, picture books); Lynne Polvino, editor (fiction, nonfiction, pic-

ture books); Christine Kettner, art director. Estab. 1965. Publishes hardcover originals for children. **Publishes 50 titles/year. Pays 5-10% royalty on retail price. Pays minimum of $4,000 advance.** Publishes book Publishes a book 2 years after acceptance. Responds in 2 months to queries. Guidelines for #10 SASE or online.

"We are no longer responding to your unsolicited submission unless we are interested in publishing it. Please do not include a SASE. Submissions will be recycled, and you will not hear from us regarding the status of your submission unless we are interested. We regret that we cannot respond personally to each submission, but we do consider each and every submission we receive."

NONFICTION Subjects include Americana, history, language, literature, nature, environment, photography, holiday. No unsolicited mss. Query with SASE. Submit proposal package, sample chapters, SASE. Reviews artwork/photos. Send photocopies.

FICTION Subjects include adventure, historical, humor, suspense, strong character studies, contemporary. "Clarion is highly selective in the areas of historical fiction, fantasy, and science fiction. A novel must be superlatively written in order to find a place on the list. Mss that arrive without an SASE of adequate size will *not* be responded to or returned. Accepts fiction translations." Submit complete ms. No queries, please. Send to only *one* Clarion editor.

TIPS "Looks for freshness, enthusiasm—in short, life."

CLARITY PRESS, INC.

3277 Roswell Rd. NE, Suite 469, Atlanta GA 30305. (877)613-1495. **Fax:** (877)613-7868. **E-mail:** claritypress@usa.net. **Website:** www.claritypress.com. **Contact:** Diana G. Collier, editorial director (contemporary social justice issues). Estab. 1984. Publishes hardcover and trade paperback originals. **Publishes 4 titles/year.** Accepts simultaneous submissions. Responds to queries if interested.

NONFICTION Subjects include ethnic, world affairs., human rights/socioeconomic and minority issues. Publishes books on contemporary global issues in U.S., Middle East and Africa. No fiction. Query by e-mail only with synopsis, TOC, résumé, publishing history.

TIPS "Check our titles on the website."

CLEAR LIGHT PUBLISHERS

823 Don Diego, Santa Fe NM 87505. (505)989-9590. **Fax:** (505)989-9519. **E-mail:** market@clearlightbooks.

com. **Website:** http://clearlightbooks.com/. **Contact:** Harmon Houghton, publisher. Estab. 1981. Publishes hardcover and trade paperback originals. **Publishes 20-24 titles/year. 100 queries received/year. 10% of books from first-time authors. 50% from unagented writers. Pays 10% royalty on wholesale price. Offers advance, a percent of gross potential.** Publishes book Publishes a book 1 year after acceptance. Accepts simultaneous submissions. Responds in 3 months to queries. Catalog free. Guidelines online.

8—¬ "Clear Light publishes books that accurately depict the positive side of human experience and inspire the spirit."

NONFICTION Subjects include Americana, anthropology, archeology, art, architecture, cooking, foods, nutrition, ethnic, history, nature, environment, philosophy, photography, regional, Southwest. Middle readers and young adults: multicultural, American Indian and Hispanic only. Submit complete ms with SASE. "No e-mail submissions. Authors supply art. Manuscripts not considered without art or artist's renderings." Reviews artwork/photos. Send photocopies.

CLEIS PRESS

Cleis Press & Viva Editions, 2246 Sixth St., Berkeley CA 94710. (510)845-8000 or (800)780-2279. **Fax:** (510)845-8001. **E-mail:** cleis@cleispress.com. **E-mail:** bknight@cleispress.com. **Website:** www.cleispress.com and www.vivaeditions.com. **Contact:** Brenda Knight, associate publisher. Kara Wuest, publishing coordinator; Frédérique Delacoste, art director Estab. 1980. Publishes books that inform, enlighten, and entertain. Areas of interest include gift, inspiration, health, family and childcare, self-help, women's issues, reference, cooking. "We do our best to bring readers quality books that celebrate life, inspire the mind, revive the spirit, and enhance lives all around. Our authors are practical visionaries; people who offer deep wisdom in a hopeful and helpful manner." **Publishes 45 titles/year. 2,000 10% of books from first-time authors. 90% from unagented writers. Pays royalty on retail price.** Publishes book 2 years after acceptance of ms. Responds in 1 month to queries.

8—¬ Cleis Press publishes provocative, intelligent books in the areas of sexuality, gay and lesbian studies, erotica, fiction, gender studies, and human rights.

NONFICTION Subjects include gay, lesbian, women's issues/studies, sexual politics. "Cleis Press is in-

terested in books on topics of sexuality, human rights and women's and gay and lesbian literature." Query or submit outline and sample chapters

FICTION Subjects include feminist, gay, lesbian, literary. "We are looking for high quality fiction and nonfiction. Submit complete ms."

TIPS "Be familiar with publishers' catalogs; be absolutely aware of your audience; research potential markets; present fresh new ways of looking at your topic; avoid `PR' language and include publishing history in query letter."

CLEVELAND STATE UNIVERSITY POETRY CENTER

2121 Euclid Ave., RT 1841, Cleveland OH 44115. (216)687-3986. **Fax:** (216)687-6943. **E-mail:** poetry-center@csuohio.edu. **Website:** www.csuohio.edu/poetrycenter. **Contact:** Michael Dumanis or Rita Grabowski, managers. Estab. 1962.

POETRY The Cleveland State University Poetry Center publishes "full-length collections by established and emerging poets, through competition and solicitation, as well as occasional poetry anthologies, texts on poetics, and novellas. Eclectic in its taste and inclusive in its aesthetic, with particular interest in lyric poetry and innovative approaches to craft. Not interested in light verse, devotional verse, doggerel, or poems by poets who have not read much contemporary poetry." "Most manuscripts we publish are accepted through the competitions. All manuscripts sent for competitions are considered for publication. Outside of competitions, manuscripts are accepted by solicitation only."

CLOVER PARK PRESS

P.O. Box 5067-WS, Santa Monica CA 90409. **E-mail:** submissions@cloverparkpress.com. **Website:** www.cloverparkpress.com. **Contact:** Martha Grant, acquisitions editor. Estab. 1991. Publishes hardcover and trade paperback originals. **Publishes 1-3 titles/year. 800 queries received/year. 500 mss received/year. 90% of books from first-time authors. 80% from unagented writers. Pays royalty. Makes outright purchase. Pays modest advance.** Publishes book less than 1 year after acceptance. Accepts simultaneous submissions. Responds in 1-4 months to queries, proposals, and to mss. Catalog online. Guidelines for #10 SASE. Current list and guidelines available on website.

NONFICTION Subjects include California (history, natural history, travel, culture or the arts), creative nonfiction, multicultural, nature, environment, regional, science, travel, women's issues/studies, world affairs. No fiction, poetry, children's, photography, true crime, diaries, journals, memoirs, new age, or books about abuse, alcoholism or addiction. Query with SASE. Proposal package should contain outline, bio, 30-50 pages (including the first chapter), SASE. Begin your query by e-mail with WS-Query. E-mail queries preferred. Do not telephone.

TIPS "Our audience is primarily women, high school, and college students, readers with curiosity about the world. Initial contact by e-mail or query letter. We welcome good writing. Have patience, we will respond."

COACH HOUSE BOOKS

401 Huron St. on bpNichol Lane, 80 bpNichol Lane, Toronto ON M5S 3J4, Canada. (416)979-2217. **Fax:** (416)977-1158. **E-mail:** editor@chbooks.com. **Website:** www.chbooks.com. **Contact:** Alana Wilcox, editor. Publishes trade paperback originals by Canadian authors. **Publishes 16 titles/year. 80% of books from first-time authors. 100% from unagented writers. Pays 10% royalty on retail price.** Publishes book 1 year after acceptance of ms. Responds in 6 months to queries. Guidelines online.

NONFICTION Query with SASE.

FICTION Subjects include experimental, literary, plays. "Electronic submissions of fiction and drama are welcome. (The spacing often gets garbled in poetry, so we prefer hard copies of poetry submissions.) If submitting electronically, please e-mail a Word file – no PDFs please – to editor@chbooks.com. You can include the cover letter and CV as a separate file or as a part of the MS. Be patient. We try to respond promptly, but we do receive hundreds of submissions, so it may take us months to get back to you." Consult website for submissions policy.

POETRY Consult website for guidelines. Query.

TIPS "We are not a general publisher, and publish only Canadian poetry, fiction, artist books and drama. We are interested primarily in innovative or experimental writing."

COFFEE HOUSE PRESS

79 13th NE, Suite 110, Minneapolis MN 55413. (612)338-0125. **Fax:** (612)338-4004. **E-mail:** info@coffeehousepress.org. **Website:** www.coffeehousepress.org. **Contact:** Chris Fischbach, associate publisher. Estab. 1984. Publishes hardcover and trade paperback originals. **Publishes 16-18 titles/year.** Responds in 4-6 weeks to queries; up to 6 months to mss. Catalog and guidelines online.

This successful nonprofit small press has received numerous grants from various organizations including the NEA, the McKnight Foundation and Target. Books published by Coffee House Press have won numerous honors and awards. Example: The Book of Medicines by Linda Hogan won the Colorado Book Award for Poetry and the Lannan Foundation Literary Fellowship.

FICTION Fiction Seeks literary novels, short story collections and poetry. Query first with outline and samples (20-30 pages).

POETRY As of September 1, 2010, Coffee House Press will only accept submissions during two annual reading periods: September 1-October 31 and March 1-April 30. Submissions postmarked outside of these two reading periods will not be considered or returned. In addition, until further notice, Coffee House Press will not accept unsolicited poetry submissions. Please check our web page periodically for future updates to this policy.

TIPS Look for our books at stores and libraries to get a feel for what we like to publish. No phone calls, e-mails, or faxes."

COLLEGE PRESS PUBLISHING CO.

P.O.Box 1132, 2111 N. Main Street, Suite C, Joplin MO 64801. (800)289-3300. **Fax:** (417)623-1929. **Website:** www.collegepress.com. Estab. 1959. Publishes hardcover and trade paperback originals and reprints. Accepts simultaneous submissions. Responds in 3 months to proposals; 2 months to mss. Catalog for 9×12 envelope and 5 first-class stamps. Guidelines online.

College Press is a traditional Christian publishing house. Seeks proposals for Bible studies, topical studies (biblically based), apologetic studies, historical biographies of Christians, Sunday/Bible School curriculum (adult electives).

NONFICTION Seeks Bible studies, topical studies, apologetic studies, historical biographies of Christians, and Sunday/Bible school curriculum. No poetry, games/puzzles, books on prophecy from a premillennial or dispensational viewpoint, or any book without a Christian message. Query with SASE. Always send a proposal or query letter first and requested mss to: Acquisitions Editor.

TIPS "Our core market is Christian Churches/ Churches of Christ and conservative evangelical

Christians. Have your material critically reviewed prior to sending it. Make sure that it is non-Calvinistic and that it leans more amillennial (if it is apocalyptic writing)."

⊘ COMMON COURAGE PRESS

One Red Barn Rd., Box 702, Monroe ME 04951. (207)525-0900. **Fax:** (207)525-3068. **Website:** www.commoncouragepress.com. Estab. 1991. Publishes hardcover and trade paperback originals and trade paperback reprints. Catalog and guidelines online.

○ *"We are not accepting unsolicited submissions at this time.* Nonfiction leftist, activist, political, history, feminist, media issues are our niche."

NONFICTION Subjects include anthropology, archeology, creative nonfiction, ethnic, gay, lesbian, government, politics, health, medicine, history, military, war, multicultural, nature, environment, science. Unsolicited mss returned unopened. Reviews artwork/photos.

TIPS Audience consists of left-wing activists, college audiences.

CONARI PRESS

Red Wheel/Weiser, LLC., 665 Third St., Suite 400, San Francisco CA 94107. **E-mail:** info@redwheelweiser.com; submissions@rwwbooks.com. **Website:** www.redwheelweiser.com. **Contact:** Pat Bryce, acquisitions editor. Estab. 1987.

8→ "Conari Press, an imprint of Red Wheel/Weiser, publishes books on topics ranging from spirituality, personal growth, and relationships to women's issues, parenting, and social issues. Our mission is to publish quality books that will make a difference in people's lives—how we feel about ourselves and how we relate to one another. We value integrity, compassion, and receptivity, both in the books we publish and in the way we do business."

NONFICTION Inspire, literally to breathe life into. That's what Conari Press books aim to do — inspire all walks of life, mind, body, and spirit; inspire creativity, laughter, gratitude, good food, good health, and all good things in life. We publish wellness and recovery books, particularly 12-step books, books on health and eating, books especially for women, and books on spirituality, personal growth, parenting, and social issues. Submit proposal, including: an overview of the book; a complete table of contents; a market/audience analysis, including similar titles; an up-to-date listing of your own marketing and publicity experience and/or plans; your vita and/or qualifications to write the book; and two or three sample chapters. Send cover letter including author information and brief description of proposed work.

TIPS "Review our website to make sure your work is appropriate."

CONCORDIA PUBLISHING HOUSE

3558 S. Jefferson Ave., St. Louis MO 63118. (314)268-1187. **Fax:** (314)268-1329. **E-mail:** publicity@cph.org; rosemary.parkinson@cph.org. **Website:** www.cph.org. **Contact:** Peggy Kuethe, senior editor (children's product, adult devotional, women's resources); Dawn Weinstock, managing production editor (adult nonfiction on Christian spirituality and culture, academic works of interest in Lutheran markets). Estab. 1869. Publishes hardcover and trade paperback originals. **Pays authors royalties based on retail price or work purchased outright ($750-2,000).** Responds in 1 month to queries; 3 months to mss. Ms guidelines for 1 first-class stamp and a #10 envelope.

NONFICTION Subjects include child guidance, religion, science., child guidance in Christian context, inspirational. Picture books, young readers, young adults: Bible stories, activity books, arts/crafts, concept, contemporary, religion. "All books must contain explicit Christian content." Submit complete ms (picture books); submit outline/synopsis and samples for longer mss. May also query.

TIPS "Do not send finished artwork with the manuscript. If sketches will help in the presentation of the manuscript, they may be sent. If stories are taken from the Bible, they should follow the Biblical account closely. Liberties should not be taken in fantasizing Biblical stories."

CONSORTIUM PUBLISHING

640 Weaver Hill Rd., West Greenwich RI 02817. (401)397-9838. **Fax:** (401)392-1926. **E-mail:** ConsortiumPub@msn.com. **Website:** consortiumpublishing.tripod.com/consortiumpub/index.html. **Contact:** John M. Carlevale, chief of publications. Estab. 1990. Publishes trade paperback originals and reprints. **Publishes 12 titles/year. 150 queries received/year. 50 mss received/year. 50% of books from first-time authors. 95% from unagented writers. Pays 10-15% royalty.** Publishes book 3 months after acceptance.

Responds in 2 months to queries. Catalog online and ms guidelines for #10 SASE.

8—ᴥ "Consortium publishes books for all levels of the education market."

NONFICTION Subjects include business, economics, child guidance, education, government, politics, health, medicine, history, music, dance, nature, environment, psychology, science, sociology, women's issues/studies. Query, or submit proposal package, including TOC, outline, 1 sample chapter, and SASE. Reviews artwork/photos. Send photocopies.

TIPS "Audience is college and high school students and instructors, elementary school teachers and other trainers."

Ⓐ ⦿ CONSTABLE & ROBINSON, LTD.

3 The Lanchesters, 162 Fulham Palace Rd., London En WG 9ER, United Kingdom. 0208-741-3663. **Fax:** 0208-748-7562. **E-mail:** enquiries@constablerobinson.com. **Website:** http://constablerobinson.co.uk/. **Contact:** Krystyna Green, editorial director (crime fiction). lpoliticsautobiographyQuery with SASE. Submit synopsis, SAE.Reviews artwork/photos. Send photocopies. Publishes hardcover and trade paperback originals. **Publishes 60 titles/year. 3,000 queries/year; 1,000 mss/year. Pays royalty. Pays advance.** Publishes book 1 year after acceptance of ms. Accepts simultaneous submissions. Responds in 1 month to queries and proposals; 3 months to mss. Catalog available free.

NONFICTION Subjects include health, history, medicine, military, photography, politics, psychology, science, travel, war. Query with SASE. Submit synopsis. Reviews artwork/photos. Send photocopies.

TIPS Constable & Robinson Ltd. is looking for "crime novels with good, strong identities. Think about what it is that makes your book(s) stand out from the others. We do not publish thrillers."

CONSUMER PRESS

13326 SW 28 St., Suite 102, Ft. Lauderdale FL 33330. (954)370-9153. **E-mail:** info@consumerpress.com. **Contact:** Joseph Pappas, editorial director. Estab. 1989. Publishes trade paperback originals. **Publishes 2-5 titles/year. Pays royalty on wholesale price or on retail price, as per agreement.** Catalog available free.

Ⓞ "Consumer Press is a full-spectrum publishing company specializing in literary works by noted personalities. Known for innovation and excellence in copy development, book de-

sign, publicity, and distribution, we provide an array of related services for the seasoned or first-time author. Our staff collaborates closely with clients from planning to promotion, with a focus on perennial exposure and global recognition of each title."

NONFICTION Subjects include child guidance, health, medicine, money, finance, women's issues/studies., homeowner guides, building/remodeling, food/nutrition. Query with SASE, call, e-mail, or use online submission form.

⦸ COPPER CANYON PRESS

P.O. Box 271, Bldg. 313, Port Townsend WA 98368. (360)385-4925. **Fax:** (360)385-4985. **E-mail:** poetry@coppercanyonpress.org. **Website:** www.coppercanyonpress.org. Estab. 1972. Publishes trade paperback originals and occasional cloth-bound editions. **Publishes 18 titles/year. 2,000 queries received/year. 1,500 mss received/year. 0% of books from first-time authors. 95% from unagented writers. Pays royalty.** Publishes book 2 years after acceptance. Responds in 4 months to queries. Catalog & Guidelines online.

8—ᴥ "Copper Canyon Press is dedicated to publishing poetry in a wide range of styles and from a full range of the world's cultures."

POETRY *No unsolicited mss.*

TIPS "CCP publishes poetry exclusively and is the largest poetry publisher in the U.S. We will not review queries if guidelines are not followed. We will read queries from poets who have published a book. Please read our query guidelines."

CORWIN PRESS, INC.

2455 Teller Rd., Thousand Oaks CA 91320. (800)818-7243. **Fax:** (805)499-2692. **E-mail:** cathy.hernandez@corwinpress.com. **Website:** www.corwinpress.com. **Contact:** Cathy Hernandez, acquisitions editor (content, curriculum). Hudson Perigo, executive editor (classroom management, new teacher induction, general teaching methods); Jessica Allan, senior acquisitions editor (science, special education, gifted education, early childhood education, and counseling). Estab. 1990. Publishes hardcover and paperback originals. **Publishes 240 titles/year.** Publishes book 7 months after acceptance. Responds in 1-2 months to queries. Guidelines online.

NONFICTION Subjects include education. Seeking fresh insights, conclusions, and recommendations for action. Prefers theory or research-based books that provide real-world examples and practical, hands-on strategies to help busy educators be successful. Professional-level publications for administrators, teachers, school specialists, policymakers, researchers and others involved with Pre K-12 education. No textbooks that simply summarize existing knowledge or mass-market books. Query with SASE.

COTEAU BOOKS

Thunder Creek Publishing Co-operative Ltd., 2517 Victoria Ave., Regina SK S4P 0T2, Canada. (306)777-0170. **Fax:** (306)522-5152. **E-mail:** coteau@coteaubooks.com. **Website:** www.coteaubooks.com. **Contact:** Geoffrey Ursell, publisher. Estab. 1975. Publishes trade paperback originals and reprints. **Publishes 16 titles/year. 200 queries received/year. 200 mss received/year. 25% of books from first-time authors. 90% from unagented writers. Pays 10% royalty on retail price.** Responds in 3 months to queries and mss. Catalog available free. Guidelines online.

⚡ "Our mission is to publish the finest in Canadian fiction, nonfiction, poetry, drama, and children's literature, with an emphasis on Saskatchewan and prairie writers. De-emphasizing science fiction, picture books."

NONFICTION Subjects include creative nonfiction, ethnic, history, language, literature, memoirs, regional, sports, travel. *Canadian authors only.* Submit bio, 3-4 sample chapters, SASE.

FICTION Subjects include ethnic, fantasy, feminist, gay, lesbian, historical, humor, juvenile, literary, mainstream, contemporary, multicultural, multimedia, mystery, plays, poetry, regional, short story collections, spiritual, sports, teen/young adult., novels/short fiction, adult/middle years. *Canadian authors only.* No science fiction. No children's picture books. Submit bio, complete ms, SASE.

POETRY Submit 20-25 sample poems and complete ms.

TIPS "Look at past publications to get an idea of our editorial program. We do not publish romance, horror, or picture books but are interested in juvenile and teen fiction from Canadian authors. Submissions, even queries, must be made in hard copy only. We do not accept simultaneous/multiple submissions. Check our website for new submission timing guidelines."

COUNCIL ON SOCIAL WORK EDUCATION

1701 Duke St., Suite 200, Alexandria VA 22314. (703)683-8080. **Fax:** (703)683-8099. **E-mail:** info@ cswe.org. **Website:** www.cswe.org. **Contact:** Elizabeth Simon, publications manager. Estab. 1952. Publishes trade paperback originals. **Publishes 4 titles/year. 12 queries received/year. 8 mss received/year. 25% of books from first-time authors. 100% from unagented writers. Pays sliding royalty scale, starting at 10%.** Publishes book 1 year after acceptance. Responds in 2 months to queries; 3 months to proposals and mss. Catalog and guidelines free via website or with SASE.

⚡ "Council on Social Work Education produces books and resources for social work educators, students and practitioners."

NONFICTION Subjects include education, sociology. social work. Books for social work and other educators. Query via e-mail only with proposal package, including CV, outline, expected audience, and 2 sample chapters.

TIPS "Audience is Social work educators and students and others in the helping professions. Check areas of publication interest on website."

THE COUNTRYMAN PRESS

P.O. Box 748, Woodstock VT 05091. (802)457-4826. **Fax:** (802)457-1678. **E-mail:** countrymanpress@ wwnorton.com; khummel@wwnorton.com. **Website:** www.countrymanpress.com. Estab. 1973. Publishes hardcover originals, trade paperback originals and reprints. **Publishes 60 titles/year. 1,000 queries received/year. 30% of books from first-time authors. 70% from unagented writers. Pays 5-15% royalty on retail price. Pays $1,000-5,000 advance.** Publishes book 18 months after acceptance. Accepts simultaneous submissions. Responds in 2 months to proposals. Catalog available free. Guidelines online.

⚡ "Countryman Press publishes books that encourage physical fitness and appreciation for and understanding of the natural world, self-sufficiency, and adventure."

NONFICTION Subjects include cooking, foods, nutrition, gardening, history, nature, environment, recreation, regional, travel., country living. "We publish several series of regional recreation guidebooks—hiking, bicycling, walking, fly-fishing, canoeing, kayaking—and are looking to expand them. We're also looking for books of national interest on travel, gardening, rural living, nature, and fly-fishing." Submit proposal package, outline, bio, 3 sample chapters, market information, SASE. Reviews artwork/photos. Send photocopies.

COVENANT COMMUNICATIONS, INC.

920 E. State Rd., American Fork UT 84003. (801)756-9966. **Fax:** (801)756-1049. **E-mail:** info@covenant-lds; submissions@covenant-lds.com. **Website:** www.covenant-lds.com. **Contact:** Kathryn Jenkins, managing editor. Estab. 1958. **Publishes 80-100 titles/year. 350 queries, 1,200 mss 60% of books from first-time authors. 99% from unagented writers. Pays 6 ½-15% royalty on retail price.** Publishes book 6 months to a year after acceptance of ms. Accepts simultaneous submissions. Responds in 1 month on queries & proposals; 4 months on manuscripts. Guidelines online.

8——➤ "Currently emphasizing inspirational, doctrinal, historical, biography. Our fiction is also expanding, and we are looking for new approaches to LDS literature and storytelling."

NONFICTION Subjects include history, religion, spirituality. "We target an exclusive audience of members of The Church of Jesus Christ of Latter-day Saints. All mss must be written for that audience." Submit complete ms. Reviews artwork. Send photocopies.

FICTION Subjects include adventure, historical, mystery, regional, religious, romance, spiritual, suspense. "We publish exclusively to the 'Mormon' (The Church of Jesus Christ of Latter-Day Saints) market. Fiction must feature characters who are members of that church, grappling with issues relevant to that religion." Submit complete ms.

TIPS "Our audience is exclusively LDS (Latter-Day Saints, 'Mormon')." We do not accept manuscripts that do not have a strong LDS theme or feature strong LDS characters.

COWLEY PUBLICATIONS

Rowman & Littlefield, 4501 Forbes Blvd., Suite 200, Lanham MD 20706. **Website:** www.rowmanlittlefield.com/imprints/cowley.shtml. **Contact:** Sarah Stanton, acquisitions editor. Estab. 1979. Publishes cloth and paperback originals. **Publishes 5-10 titles/year. 500 queries received/year. 300 mss received/year. 50% of books from first-time authors. 90% from unagented writers. Pays 8-15% royalty on net. Pays $0-3,000 advance.** Publishes book 18 months after acceptance. Accepts simultaneous submissions. Responds in 3 months to queries and proposals. Catalog and guidelines online.

NONFICTION Subjects include religion, spirituality,. "We publish books and resources for those seeking spiritual and theological formation. We are com-

mitted to developing a new generation of writers and teachers who will encourage people to think and pray in new ways about spirituality, reconciliation, and the future. We are interested in the many ways that faith and spirituality intersect with the world, in arts, social concerns, ethics, and so on." Query with SASE. Submit proposal package, outline, 1 sample chapter, other materials as specified online.

CQ PRESS

2300 N Street, NW, Suite 800, Washington DC 20037. (202)729-1800. **E-mail:** ckiino@cqpress.com; sstesney@cqpress.com; dghart@cqpress.com; mburt@cqpress.com. **Website:** www.cqpress.com. Estab. 1945. Publishes hardcover and online paperback titles. Accepts simultaneous submissions. Catalog available free.

NONFICTION Subjects include government, politics, history. "We are interested in American government, public administration, comparative government, and international relations." Submit proposal package, outline, bio.

TIPS Our books present important information on American government and politics, and related issues, with careful attention to accuracy, thoroughness, and readability.

CRABTREE PUBLISHING COMPANY

PMB 59051, 350 Fifth Ave., 59th Floor, New York NY 10118. (212)496-5040; (800)387-7650. **Fax:** (800)355-7166. **Website:** www.crabtreebooks.com. Estab. 1978.

8——➤ Crabtree Publishing Company is dedicated to producing high-quality books and educational products for K-8+. Each resource blends accuracy, immediacy, and eye-catching illustration with the goal of inspiring nothing less than a life-long interest in reading and learning in children. The company began building its reputation in 1978 as a quality children's non-fiction book publisher with acclaimed author Bobbie Kalman's first series about the early pioneers. The Early Settler Life Series became a mainstay in schools as well as historic sites and museums across North America.

TIPS "Since our books are for younger readers, lively photos of children and animals are always excellent." Portfolio should be diverse and encompass several subjects rather than just 1 or 2; depth of coverage of subject should be intense so that any publishing company could, conceivably, use all or many of a photographer's photos in a book on a particular subject."

CRAFTSMAN BOOK CO.

6058 Corte Del Cedro, Carlsbad CA 92011. (760)438-7828 or (800)829-8123. **Fax:** (760)438-0398. **Website:** www.craftsman-book.com. **Contact:** Laurence D. Jacobs, editorial manager. Estab. 1957. Publishes paperback originals. **Publishes 12 titles/year. 85% of books from first-time authors. 98% from unagented writers. Pays 7 ½-12 ½% royalty on wholesale price or retail price.** Publishes book 2 years after acceptance. Accepts simultaneous submissions. Responds in 2 months to queries. Catalog and guidelines free.

☛ Publishes how-to manuals for professional builders. Currently emphasizing construction software.

NONFICTION All titles are related to construction for professional builders. Query with SASE. Reviews artwork/photos.

TIPS "The book submission should be loaded with step-by-step instructions, illustrations, charts, reference data, forms, samples, cost estimates, rules of thumb, and examples that solve actual problems in the builder's office and in the field. It must cover the subject completely, become the owner's primary reference on the subject, have a high utility-to-cost ratio, and help the owner make a better living in his chosen field."

CREATIVE COMPANY

P.O. Box 227, Mankato MN 56002. (800)445-6209. **Fax:** (507)388-2746. **E-mail:** info@thecreativecompany.us. **Website:** www.thecreativecompany.us. **Contact:** Aaron Frisch. Estab. 1932. **Publishes 140 titles/year.** Publishes book Publishes a book 2 years after acceptance. Responds in 3 months to queries/mss. Guidelines available for SAE.

☛ The Creative Company has two imprints: Creative Editions (picture books), and Creative Education (nonfiction series).

NONFICTION Picture books, young readers, young adults: animal, arts/crafts, biography, careers, geography, health, history, hobbies, multicultural, music/dance, nature/environment, religion, science, social issues, special needs, sports. Average word length: young readers—500; young adults—6,000. Recently published *Empire State Building*, by Kate Riggs (age 7, young reader); *The Assassination of Archduke Ferdinand*, by Valerie Bodden (age 14, young adult/teen).

Submit outline/synopsis and 2 sample chapters, along with division of titles within the series.

TIPS "We are accepting nonfiction, series submissions only. Fiction submissions will not be reviewed or returned. Nonfiction submissions should be presented in series (4, 6, or 8) rather than single."

CREATIVE EDITIONS

The Creative Company, P.O. Box 227, Mankato MN 56002. (800)445-6209. **E-mail:** info@thecreativecompany.us; artdirector@thecreativecompany.us. **Website:** www.thecreativecompany.us. Estab. 1989. Catalog availble online.

☛ All Creative Editions and Creative Paperbacks titles are distributedto the retail and library wholesale markets by Chronicle Books

TIPS "Creative Editions publishes unique books for the book-lover. Emphasis is on aesthetics and quality. Completed manuscripts are more likely to be accepted than preliminary proposals. Please do not send slides or other valuable materials."

CREATIVE HOMEOWNER

24 Park Way, Upper Saddle River NJ 07458. (201)934-7100, ext. 375. **Fax:** (201)934-8971 or (201)934-7541. **E-mail:** info@creativehomeowner.com; rweisman@creativehomeowner.com; mdolan@creativehomeowner.com. **Website:** www.creativehomeowner.com. **Contact:** Rich Weisman, president; Mary Dolan, photo researcher. Estab. 1978. Publishes trade paperback originals. Catalog available free.

☛ Creative Homeowner is a leading and trusted source for the best information, inspiration, and instruction related to the house and home. Over the past 25 years, Creative Homeowner has grown significantly to include titles covering all aspects of decorating and design; home repair and improvement; house plans; and gardening and landscaping. Creative Homeowner's books and online information are known by consumers for their complete and easy-to-follow instructions, up-to-date information, and extensive use of color photography. Among its best-selling titles are *Decorating with Architectural Trimwork, Wiring, and Landscaping with Stone.*

NONFICTION Subjects include gardening, home remodeling/building. Query, or submit proposal package, including competitive books (short analysis), outline, and SASE. Reviews artwork/photos.

● CRESCENT MOON PUBLISHING

P.O. Box 393, Maidstone Kent ME14 5XU, UK. (44) (162)272-9593. **E-mail:** cresmopub@yahoo.co.uk. **Website:** www.crescentmoon.org.uk. **Contact:** Jeremy Robinson, director (arts, media, cinema, literature); Cassidy Hushes (visual arts). Estab. 1988. Publishes hardcover and trade paperback originals. **Publishes 25 titles/year. 300 queries received/year. 400 mss received/year. 1% of books from first-time authors. 1% from unagented writers. Pays royalty. Pays negotiable advance.** Publishes book 18 months after acceptance of ms. Accepts simultaneous submissions. Responds in 2 months to queries; 4 months to proposals and mss. Catalog and guidelines free.

8—⚷ "Our mission is to publish the best in contemporary work, in poetry, fiction, and critical studies, and selections from the great writers. Currently emphasizing nonfiction (media, film, music, painting). De-emphasizing children's books."

NONFICTION Subjects include Americana, art, architecture, gardening, government, politics, language, literature, music, dance, philosophy, religion, travel, women's issues/studies, cinema, the media, cultural studies. Query with SASE. Submit outline, 2 sample chapters, bio. Reviews artwork/photos. Send photocopies.

FICTION Subjects include erotica, experimental, feminist, gay, lesbian, literary, short story collections, translation. "We do not publish much fiction at present but will consider high quality new work." Query with SASE. Submit outline, clips, 2 sample chapters, bio.

POETRY "We prefer a small selection of the poet's very best work at first. We prefer free verse or non-rhyming poetry. Do not send too much material." Query and submit 6 sample poems.

TIPS "Our audience is interested in new contemporary writing."

⊘ CRICKET BOOKS

Imprint of Carus Publishing, 70 E. Lake St., Suite 300, Chicago IL 60601. (603)924-7209. **Fax:** (603)924-7380. **Website:** www.cricketmag.com. **Contact:** Submissions Editor. Estab. 1999. Publishes hardcover originals. **Publishes 5 titles/year. Pays up to 10% royalty on retail price. Average advance: $1,500 and up.** Publishes book 18 months after acceptance.

○ *Currently not accepting queries or mss. Check website for submissions details and updates.*

FICTION Subjects include juvenile, adventure, easy-to-read, fantasy/science fiction, historical, horror, mystery/suspense, problem novels, sports, westerns.

TIPS "Take a look at the recent titles to see what sort of materials we're interested in, especially for nonfiction. Please note that we aren't doing the sort of strictly educational nonfiction that other publishers specialize in."

⊕ CRIMSON ROMANCE

Adams Media, a division of F+W Media, Inc., 57 Littlefield St., Avon MA 02322. (508)427-7100. **E-mail:** editorcrimson@gmail.com. **Contact:** Jennifer Lawler, editor. Publishes electronic originals.

8—⚷ "Direct to e-book imprint of Adams Media."

FICTION "We're open to romance submissions in five popular subgenres: romantic suspense, contemporary, paranormal, historical, and erotic romance. Within those subgenres, we are flexible about what happens. It's romance, so there must be a happily-ever-after, but we're open to how your characters get there. You won't come up against preconceived ideas about what can or can't happen in romance or what kind of characters you can or can't have. Our only rule is everyone has to be a consenting adult. Other than that, we're looking for smart, savvy heroines, fresh voices, and new takes on old favorite themes. We're looking for full-length novels, and while we prefer to work on the shorter end of the spectrum (50,000 words, give or take), we're not going to rule you out because you go shorter or longer. If you have a finished novel you'd like for us to consider, please just drop editor Jennifer Lawler a line at editorcrimson@gmail.com with a brief description of your work–please, no attachments until I know you're not a spambot. That's it! I'll get back to you as quickly as I can–within a few days for queries and within a few weeks if I request a full."

CROSS-CULTURAL COMMUNICATIONS

239 Wynsum Ave., Merrick NY 11566. (516)869-5635. **Fax:** (516)379-1901. **E-mail:** cccpoetry@aol.com. **Website:** www.cross-culturalcommunications.com. **Contact:** Stanley H. Barkan, publisher/editor-in-chief (bilingual poetry); Bebe Barkan, Mia Barkan Clarke, art editors (complementary art to poetry editions). Estab. 1971. Publishes hardcover and trade paperback originals. **Publishes 10 titles/year. 200 queries received/year. 50 mss received/year. 25% of books from first-time authors. 100% from unagented writers.** Publishes book 1 year after acceptance. Responds

in 1 month to proposals; 2 months to mss. Catalog (sample flyers) for #10 SASE.

NONFICTION Subjects include language, literature, memoirs, multicultural. "Query first; we basically do not want the focus on nonfiction." Query with SASE. Reviews artwork/photos. Send photocopies.

FICTION Subjects include historical, multicultural, poetry, poetry in translation, translation., Bilingual poetry. Query with SASE.

POETRY For bilingual poetry submit 3-6 short poems in original language with English translation, a brief (3-5 lines) bio of the author and translator(s).

⊘ CROSSQUARTER PUBLISHING GROUP

P.O. Box 23749, Santa Fe NM 87502. **E-mail:** info@crossquarter.com. **Website:** www.crossquarter.com. **Contact:** Anthony Ravenscroft, acquisitions. Publishes trade paperback originals and reprints. **Publishes 5-10 titles/year. 1,200 queries received/year. 90% of books from first-time authors. Pays 8-10% royalty on wholesale or retail price.** Publishes book 1-2 years after acceptance. Accepts simultaneous submissions. Responds in 3 months to queries. Catalog for $1.75. Guidelines online.

> "We emphasize personal sovereignty, self responsibility and growth with pagan or pagan-friendly emphasis for young adults and adults."

NONFICTION Subjects include health, medicine, nature, environment, New Age, philosophy, psychology, religion, pagan only, spirituality., autobiography. Query with SASE. Reviews artwork/photos. Send photocopies.

FICTION Subjects include science fiction., visionary fiction. Query with SASE.

RECENT TITLE(S) *Parasitic People and Other Daily Hazards*, by Norm Dubeski; *The Mirrors of Castaway Time*, by Douglas Arvidson; *Polyamory*, by Anthony Ravenscroft; *Extinction*, by John Lee Schneider.

TIPS "Our audience is earth-conscious people looking to grow into balance of body, mind, heart and spirit."

CROWN BOOKS FOR YOUNG READERS

1540 Broadway, New York NY 10171. (212)572-2600 or (800)200-3552. **Website:** www.randomhouse.com/kids.

> Random House Children's Publishing only accepts submissions through agents.

Ⓐ CROWN BUSINESS

Random House, Inc., 1745 Broadway, New York NY 10019. (212)572-2275. **Fax:** (212)572-6192. **E-mail:** crownbiz@randomhouse.com. **Website:** crownpub-

lishing.com. Estab. 1995. Publishes hardcover and trade paperback originals. Accepts simultaneous submissions. Catalog online.

> *Agented submissions only.*

NONFICTION Subjects include business, economics, money, finance, management. Query with proposal package including outline, 1-2 sample chapters, market analysis and information on author platform.

Ⓐ⊘ CROWN PUBLISHING GROUP

Imprint of Random House, Inc., 1745 Broadway, New York NY 10019. (212)782-9000. **E-mail:** CrownBiz@randomhouse.com. **Website:** www.randomhouse.com/crown. Estab. 1933. Publishes popular fiction and nonfiction hardcover originals.

> *Agented submissions only.* See website for more details.

CYCLE PUBLICATIONS INC.

Van der Plas Publications, 1282 Seventh Ave., San Francisco CA 94112. (415)665-8214. **Fax:** (415)753-8572. **E-mail:** rvdp@cyclepublishing.com. **Website:** www.cyclepublishing.com. Estab. 1985.

> "Van der Plas Publications / Cycle Publishing was started in 1997 with four books. Since then, we have introduced about 4 new books each year, and in addition to our "mainstay" of cycling books, we now also have books on manufactured housing, golf, baseball, and strength training. Our offices are located in San Francisco, where we do editorial work, as well as administration, publicity, and design. Our books are warehoused in Kimball, Michigan, which is close to the companies that print most of our books and is conveniently located to supply our book trade distributors and the major book wholesalers."

CYCLOTOUR GUIDE BOOKS

P.O. Box 10585, Rochester NY 10585. (585)244-6157. **Fax:** (585)244-6157. **E-mail:** cyclotour@cyclotour.com. **Website:** www.cyclotour.com. Estab. 1994. Publishes trade paperback originals. **Publishes 2 titles/year. Receives 25 queries/year and 2 mss/year. 50% of books from first-time authors. 100% from unagented writers.** Publishes book 2 years after acceptance. Accepts simultaneous submissions. Responds in 1 month to queries, proposals, and mss. Catalog and guidelines online.

NONFICTION Subjects include sports (bicycle only), travel (bicycle tourism). No narrative accounts of their bicycle tour without distance indicators. Query with SASE. Reviews artwork/photos as part of ms package. Send photocopies.

TIPS "Check your grammar and spelling. Write logically."

⊘ DA CAPO PRESS

Perseus Books Group, 11 Cambridge Center, Cambridge MA 02142. (617)252-5200. **Website:** www.dacapopress.com. Estab. 1975. Publishes hardcover originals and trade paperback originals and reprints. **Publishes 115 titles/year. 500 queries received/year. 300 mss received/year. 25% of books from first-time authors. 1% from unagented writers. Pays 7-15% royalty. Pays $1,000-225,000 advance.** Publishes book 1 year after acceptance. Catalog and guidelines online.

NONFICTION Subjects include art, architecture, contemporary culture, creative nonfiction, government, politics, history, language, literature, memoirs, military, war, social sciences, sports, translation, travel, world affairs.

DANIEL & DANIEL PUBLISHERS, INC.

P.O. Box 2790, McKinleyville CA 95519. (707)839-3495. **Fax:** (707)839-3242. **E-mail:** dandd@danielpublishing.com. **Website:** www.danielpublishing.com. **Contact:** John Daniel, publisher. Estab. 1980. Publishes hardcover originals and trade paperback originals. **Publishes 12 titles/year. 50% of books from first-time authors. 90% from unagented writers. Pays 10%-60% royalty on wholesale price. Pays $0-500 advance for John Daniel & Co. Pays $1,000 advance for Perseverance Press. No advance for Fithian Press.** Publishes book 1 year after acceptance. Accepts simultaneous submissions. Responds in 1 month to queries and proposals; 2 months to mss. Catalog and guidelines online.

○ Accepts simultaneous submissions for John Daniel & Co. and Fithian Press; but acquisitions for Perseverance Press are by invitation only.

NONFICTION Subjects include : creative nonfiction, memoirs. "We seldom publish books over 70,000 words. Other than that, we're looking for books that are important and well-written." Query with SASE. Submit proposal package, outline, 5 pages.

FICTION Subjects include : literary, short story collections. Query with SASE. Submit proposal package, clips, 5 pages.

POETRY "We publish very little poetry, I'm sorry to say." Query and submit complete ms.

TIPS "Audience includes literate, intelligent general readers. We are very small and very cautious, and we publish fewer books each year, so any submission to us is a long shot. But we welcome your submissions, by mail or e-mail only, please. We don't want submissions by phone, fax or disk."

DANTE UNIVERSITY OF AMERICA PRESS, INC.

P.O. Box 812158, Wellesley MA 02482. **Fax:** (781)790-1056. **E-mail:** danteu@danteuniversity.org. **Website:** www.danteuniversity.org/dpress.html. **Contact:** Josephine Tanner, president. Estab. 1975. Publishes hardcover and trade paperback originals and reprints plus Kindle and Nook editions. **Publishes 5 titles/year. 50% of books from first-time authors. 50% from unagented writers. Pays royalty. Pays negotiable advance.** Publishes book 10 months after acceptance. Responds in 2 months to queries.

✂━ "The Dante University Press exists to bring quality, educational books pertaining to our Italian heritage as well as the historical and political studies of America. Profits from the sale of these publications benefit the Foundation, bringing Dante University closer to a reality."

NONFICTION Subjects include history, Italian-American, humanities, translation, from Italian and Latin., general scholarly nonfiction, Renaissance thought and letter, Italian language and linguistics, Italian-American culture, bilingual education. Query with SASE. Reviews artwork/photos.

FICTION Translations from Italian and Latin. Query with SASE.

POETRY There is a chance that we would use Renaissance poetry translations.

MAY DAVENPORT, PUBLISHERS

26313 Purissima Rd., Los Altos Hills CA 94022. (650)947-1275. **Fax:** (650)947-1373. **E-mail:** mdbooks@earthlink.net. **Website:** www.maydavenportpublishers.com. **Contact:** May Davenport, editor/publisher. Estab. 1976. Publishes hardcover and paperback originals. **Publishes 4 titles/year. 95% of books from first-time authors. 100% from unagented writers. Pays 15% royalty on retail price (if book sells). Pays no advance.** Publishes book 12 months after acceptance of ms. Responds in 1 month to queries. Catalog and guidelines for #10 SASE.

✂━ "May Davenport publishes literature for teenagers (before they graduate from high school) as supplementary literary material in English courses nationwide. Looking particularly for authors able to write for the teen Internet generation who don't like to read in-depth. Currently emphasizing more upper-level subjects for teens."

NONFICTION Subjects include Americana, language, literature., humorous memoirs for children/young adults. "For children ages 6-8: stories to read with pictures to color in 500 words. For preteens and young adults: Exhibit your writing skills and entertain them with your literary tools." Query with SASE.

FICTION Subjects include humor, literary. "We want to focus on novels junior and senior high school teachers can read aloud, share with their reluctant readers in their classrooms." Query with SASE.

TIPS "Just write your fictional novel humorously. If you can't write that way, create youthful characters so teachers, as well as 15-18-year-old high school readers, will laugh at your descriptive passages and contemporary dialogue. Avoid 1-sentence paragraphs. The audience we want to reach is today's high-tech teens who are talented with digital cameras hooked up to computers. Show them what you can do 'in print' for them and their equipment."

JONATHAN DAVID PUBLISHERS INC.

68-22 Eliot Ave., Middle Village NY 11379. (718)456-8611. **Fax:** (718)894-2818. **E-mail:** submission@jdbooks.com. **Website:** www.jdbooks.com. **Contact:** David Kolatch, editorial director. Estab. 1948. Publishes hardcover and trade paperback originals and reprints. **Publishes 20-25 titles/year. 50% of books from first-time authors. 90% from unagented writers. Pays royalty, or makes outright purchase.** Publishes book 18 months after acceptance. Responds in 1 month to queries and proposals; 2 months to mss. Catalog and guidelines online.

Jonathan David publishes popular Judaica.

NONFICTION Subjects include cooking, foods, nutrition, creative nonfiction, ethnic, multicultural, religion, sports. Query with SASE. Submit proposal package, outline, résumé, 3 sample chapters. Reviews artwork/photos. Send photocopies.

DAW BOOKS, INC.

Penguin Group (USA), 375 Hudson St., New York NY 10014-3658. (212)366-2096. **Fax:** (212)366-2090. **Website:** www.dawbooks.com. **Contact:** Peter Stampfel, submissions editor. Estab. 1971. Publishes hardcover and paperback originals and reprints. **Publishes**

50-60 titles/year. Pays in royalties with an advance negotiable on a book-by-book basis. Responds in 3 months to mss. Guidelines online.

Simultaneous submissions not accepted, unless prior arrangements are made by agent.

FICTION "Currently seeking modern urban fantasy and paranormals. We like character-driven books with appealing protagonists, engaging plots, and well-constructed worlds. We accept both agented and unagented manuscripts.". Submit entire ms, cover letter, SASE.

DAWBERT PRESS, INC.

Submissions Department, P.O. Box 67, Duxbury MA 02331. (781)934-7202. **E-mail:** editor@dawbert.com. **Website:** www.dawbert.com. **Contact:** Allison Elliott, editor. Publishes mass market paperbacks. **Publishes 3 titles/year. Pays 5-10% royalty on retail price.** Accepts simultaneous submissions. Guidelines online.

NONFICTION Subjects include travel., recreation. We publish only travel and recreation books. Submit outline. Reviews artwork/photos. Send photocopies.

DAWN PUBLICATIONS

12402 Bitney Springs Rd., Nevada City CA 95959. (530)274-7775. **Fax:** (530)274-7778. **Website:** www.dawnpub.com. **Contact:** Glenn Hovemann, editor. Estab. 1979. Publishes hardcover and trade paperback originals. **Publishes 6 titles/year. 2,500 queries or mss received/year. 15% of books from first-time authors. 90% from unagented writers. Pays advance.** Publishes book 1-2 years after acceptance. Accepts simultaneous submissions. Responds in 2 months to queries. Catalog and guidelines online.

"Dawn Publications is dedicated to inspiring in children a sense of appreciation for all life on earth. Dawn looks for nature awareness and appreciation titles that promote a relationship with the natural world and specific habitats, usually through inspiring treatment and nonfiction."

NONFICTION Subjects include animals, nature, environment.

TIPS "Publishes mostly creative nonfiction with lightness and inspiration." Looking for "picture books expressing nature awareness with inspirational quality leading to enhanced self-awareness." Does not publish anthropomorphic works; no animal dialogue.

DBS PRODUCTIONS

P.O. Box 1894, Charlottesville VA 22903. (800)745-1581. **Fax:** (434)293-5502. **E-mail:** info@dbs-sar.com. **Website:** www.dbs-sar.com. **Contact:** Bob Adams, publisher. Estab. 1989. Publishes hardcover and trade paperback originals. **Publishes 4 titles/year. 10 queries received/year. 10% of books from first-time authors. 100% from unagented writers. Pays 5-20% royalty on retail price.** Publishes book 1 year after acceptance. Responds in 2 weeks to queries. Catalog available on request or on website. Guidelines for #10 SASE.

NONFICTION Subjects include health, medicine. Submit proposal package, outline, 2 sample chapters. Reviews artwork/photos. Send photocopies.

DELACORTE PRESS BOOKS FOR YOUNG READERS

Imprint of Random House Children's Books/Random House, Inc., 1745 Broadway, New York NY 10019. (212)782-9000. **Website:** www.randomhouse.com/kids; www.randomhouse.com/teens.

Although not currently accepting unsolicited mss, mss are being sought for 2 contests: Delacorte Dell Yearling Contest for a First Middle-Grade Novel and Delacorte Press Contest for a First Young Adult Novel. Submission guidelines can be found online at www.randomhouse.com/kids/writingcontests.

DEL REY BOOKS

Imprint of Random House Publishing Group, 1745 Broadway, 18th Floor, New York NY 10019. (212)782-9000. **E-mail:** delrey@randomhouse.com. **Website:** www.randomhouse.com. Estab. 1977. Publishes hardcover, trade paperback, and mass market originals and mass market paperback reprints. **Pays royalty on retail price. Pays competitive advance.**

Del Rey publishes top level fantasy, alternate history, and science fiction.

FICTION Subjects include fantasy, should have the practice of magic as an essential element of the plot, science fiction, well-plotted novels with good characterizations, exotic locales and detailed alien creatures., alternate history. Agented submissions only.

TIPS "Del Rey is a reader's house. Pay particular attention to plotting, strong characters, and dramatic, satisfactory conclusions. It must be/feel believable. That's what the readers like. In terms of mass market, we basically created the field of fantasy bestsellers. Not that it didn't exist before, but we put the mass into mass market."

DEMONTREVILLE PRESS, INC.

P.O. Box 835, Lake Elmo MN 55042. **E-mail:** publisher@demontrevillepress.com. **Website:** www.demont-

revillepress.com. **Contact:** Kevin Clemens, publisher (automotive fiction and nonfiction). Estab. 2006. Publishes trade paperback originals and reprints. **Publishes 4 titles/year. 150 queries received/year. 100 mss received/year. 90% of books from first-time authors. 90% from unagented writers. Pays 20% royalty on sale price.** Publishes book 18 months after acceptance. Accepts simultaneous submissions. Responds in 3 months to queries; 4 months to proposals; 6 months to mss. Catalog and guidelines online.

NONFICTION Subjects include current events, automotive, environment, motorcycle. "We want novel length automotive or motorcycle historicals and/or adventures. Environmental energy and infrastructure books wanted." Submit proposal package online, outline, 3 sample chapters, bio. Reviews artwork/photos. Do not send photos until requested.

FICTION Subjects include current events, environment, adventure, mystery, sports, young adult, automotive, motorcycle. "We want novel length automotive or motorcycle historicals and/or adventures." Submit proposal package, 3 sample chapters, clips, bio.

TIPS "Environmental, energy and transportation nonfiction works are now being accepted. Automotive and motorcycle enthusiasts, adventurers, environmentalists and history buffs make up our audience."

THE DENALI PRESS

P.O. Box 021535, Juneau AK 99802. (907)586-6014. **Fax:** (907)463-6780. **E-mail:** denalipress@alaska.com. **Website:** www.denalipress.com. **Contact:** Alan Schorr, editorial director; Sally Silvas-Ottumwa, editorial associate. Estab. 1986. Publishes trade paperback originals. **Publishes 5 titles/year. 50% of books from first-time authors. 80% from unagented writers. Pays 10% royalty on wholesale price. Makes outright purchase. Pays advance.** Publishes book 1 year after acceptance. Accepts simultaneous submissions. Responds in 1 month to queries.

The Denali Press looks for reference works suitable for the educational, professional, and library market. Though we publish books on a variety of topics, our focus is most broadly centered on multiculturalism, public policy, Alaskana, and general reference works.

NONFICTION Subjects include Americana, anthropology, archeology, ethnic, government, politics, history, multicultural, recreation, regional. We need reference books—ethnic, refugee, and minority concerns. Query with SASE. Submit outline, sample chapters. *All unsolicited mss returned unopened.*

☼⊘ DESCRIBE ADONIS PRESS

297 Blake Blvd. #4, Ottawa ON K1L 6L6, Canada. **Website:** http://vallance22.hpage.com. Estab. 2002.
POETRY Describe Adonis Press publishes Japanese form poetry only, "especially haiku, but also senryu, renga, tanka, etc." Does not want any other form or genre of poetry. Publishes one poetry book/year, 5 chapbooks/year on average. Contact with up to 12 haikus via e-mail attachment in rtf form only. E-mail is through website form at http://vallance22.hpage.com. Format should be single-spaced with three blank lines between each haiku; subject line should read: "Submission of hiaku (or haikus) by [your name]." Must use Georgia Font 11 points, or, if absolutely unable to use that, in Times New Roman 11 point font. See website for complete guidelines and contact.

ⒶDIAL BOOKS FOR YOUNG READERS

Imprint of Penguin Group USA, 345 Hudson St., New York NY 10014. (212)366-2000. **Website:** www.penguin.com/youngreaders. **Contact:** Lauri Hornik, president/publisher; Kathy Dawson, associate publisher; Kate Harrison, senior editor; Liz Waniewski, editor; Alisha Niehaus, editor; Jessica Garrison, editor; Lily Malcom, art director. Estab. 1961. Publishes hardcover originals. **Publishes 50 titles/year. 5,000 queries received/year. 20% of books from first-time authors. Pays royalty. Pays varies advance.** Responds in 4-6 months to queries. Catalog for 9 X12 envelope and 4 first-class stamps.

&⊶ "Dial Books for Young Readers publishes quality picture books for ages 18 months-6 years; lively, believable novels for middle readers and young adults; and occasional nonfiction for middle readers and young adults."

NONFICTION "Due to the overwhelming number of unsolicited manuscripts we receive, Dial will no longer respond to your unsolicited submission unless interested in publishing it. Please do not include SASE with your submission. You will not hear from Dial regarding the status of your submission unless we are interested, in which case you can expect a reply from us within four months. We accept entire picture book manuscripts and a maximum of 10 pages for longer works (novels, easy-to-reads). When submitting a portion of a longer work, please provide an accompanying cover letter that briefly describes your manuscript's plot, genre (i.e., easy-to-read, middle grade or YA novel), the intended age group, and your publishing credits, if any."

FICTION Subjects include adventure, fantasy, juvenile, picture books, young adult. Especially looking for lively and well-written novels for middle grade and young adult children involving a convincing plot and believable characters. The subject matter or theme should not already be overworked in previously published books. The approach must not be demeaning to any minority group, nor should the roles of female characters (or others) be stereotyped, though we don't think books should be didactic, or in any way message-y. No topics inappropriate for the juvenile, young adult, and middle grade audiences. No plays. Accepts unsolicited queries and up to 10 pages for longer works and unsolicited mss for picture books.

TIPS "Our readers are anywhere from preschool age to teenage. Picture books must have strong plots, lots of action, unusual premises, or universal themes treated with freshness and originality. Humor works well in these books. A very well-thought-out and intelligently presented book has the best chance of being taken on. Genre isn't as much of a factor as presentation."

⊘ DISKUS PUBLISHING

P.O. Box 43, Albany IN 47320. **E-mail:** editor@diskuspublishing.com. **Website:** www.diskuspublishing.com. **Contact:** Joyce McLaughlin, inspirational and children's editor; Holly Janey, submissions editor. Estab. 1996. Publishes e-books. **Publishes 50 titles/year. Pays 40% royalty.** Publishes book 6-8 months after accetance. after acceptance of ms. Accepts simultaneous submissions. Catalog for #10 SASE. Guidelines for #10 SASE or online.

⬗ *At this time DiskUs Publishing is closed for submissions. We will reopen for submissions in the near future. We get thousands of submissions each month and our editors need time to get through the current ones. Keep checking our website for updates on the status of our submissions reopen date.*

FICTION Subjects include adventure, ethnic, general, fantasy, space fantasy, historical, horror, humor, juvenile, literary, mainstream, contemporary, military, war, multicultural, general, mystery, religious, romance, science fiction, short story collections, suspense, western, young adult. "We are actively seeking confessions for our Diskus Confessions line. As well as short stories for our Quick Pick line. We only accept e-mailed submissions for these lines." Submit publishing history, bio, estimated word count and genre. Submit complete ms.

ⓐ DISNEY HYPERION BOOKS FOR CHILDREN

114 Fifth Ave., New York NY 10011-5690. **Website:** www.hyperionbooksforchildren.com.

NONFICTION Narrative nonfiction for elementary schoolers.

FICTION Picture books, early readers, middle readers, young adults: adventure, animal, anthology (short stories), contemporary, fantasy, history, humor, multicultural, poetry, science fiction, sports, suspense/mystery. Middle readers, young adults: commercial fiction. *All submissions must come via an agent.*

DIVERSION PRESS

P.O. Box 3930, Clarksville TN 37043. **E-mail:** diversionpress@yahoo.com. **Website:** www.diversionpress. com. Estab. 2008. Publishes hardcover, trade and mass market paperback originals. **Publishes 5-10 titles/year. 75% of books from first-time authors. 100% from unagented writers. Pays 10% royalty on wholesale price.** Publishes book 1-2 years after acceptance. Responds in 2 weeks to queries. Responds in 1 month to proposals. Guidelines online.

○ Prefers submissions via e-mail. Does not accept unsolicited mss.

NONFICTION Subjects include Americana, animals, community, contemporary culture, education, ethnic, government, politics, health, medicine, history, hobbies, humanities, language, literature, literary criticism, memoirs, military, war, multicultural, philosophy, psychology, recreation, regional, science, social sciences, sociology, travel, women's issues/studies, world affairs. "The editors have doctoral degrees and are interested in a broad range of academic works. We are also interested in how-to, slice of life, and other nonfiction areas." Does not review works that are sexually explicit, religious, or put children in a bad light. Send query/proposal first. Mss accepted by request only. Reviews artwork/photos. Send photocopies.

FICTION Subjects include adventure, fantasy, gothic, historical, horror, humor, literary, mainstream, contemporary, mystery, poetry, science fiction, short story collections, suspense, young adult. "We will happily consider any children's or young adult books if they are illustrated. If your story has potential to become a series, please address that in your proposal. Fiction short stories and poetry will be considered for our anthology series. See website for details on how to submit your ms."

POETRY "Poetry will be considered for anthology series and our poetry award." Submit 5 sample poems.

TIPS "Read our website and blog prior to submitting. We like short, concise queries. Tell us why your book is different, not like other books. Give us a realistic idea of what you will do to market your book—that you will actually do. We will ask for more information if we are interested."

⊕ DIVERTIR

P.O. Box 232, North Salem NH 03073. **E-mail:** info@ divertirpublishing.com; query@divertirpublishing. com. **Website:** http://divertirpublishing.com/. **Contact:** Dr. Kenneth Tupper, Publisher (nonfiction);. Estab. 2009. Format publishes in trade paperback and electronic originals. **Publishes 6-12 titles/year. 100% of books from first-time authors. 100% from unagented writers. Pays 10-15% royalty on wholesale price (for novels and nonfiction); outright purchase: $10-50 (for short stories) with additional bonus payments to authors when certain sales milestones are met.** Publishes book 6-9 months after acceptance of ms. Responds in 1-2 months on queries; 3-4 months on proposals and mss. Catalog and guidelines online.

NONFICTION Subjects include astrology, community, contemporary culture, cooking, crafts, creative nonfiction, government, history, hobbies, New Age, photography, politics, psychic, psychology, religion, spirituality, world affairs. "We are particularly interested in the following: political/social commentary, current events, history, humor and satire, crafts and hobbies, inspirational, self-help, religious and spiritual, and metaphysics." Reviews artwork/photos as part of the ms package. Submit electronically.

FICTION Subjects include adventure, contemporary, fantasy, gothic, historical, horror, humor, literary, mainstream, mystery, occult, poetry, religious, romance, science fiction, short story collections, spiritual, translation, young adult. "We are particularly interested in the following: science fiction, fantasy, historical, alternate history, contemporary mythology, mystery and suspense, paranormal, and urban fantasy. Electronically submit proposal package, including synopsis and query letter with author's bio.

POETRY Query.

TIPS "We are currently accepting submissions in the following areas: Fictional Satire (submissions deadline 3/15), Noir (submissions deadline 5/15), Poetry (submissions deadline 3/15). Please see our Author Info page (online) for more information."

DK PUBLISHING

375 Hudson St., New York NY 10014. **Website:** www. dk.com.

> DK Publishing does not accept unagented mss or proposals.

DNA PRESS & NARTEA PUBLISHING

DNA Press, P.O. Box 9311, Glendale CA 91226. **E-mail:** editors@dnapress.com. **Website:** www.dna-press.com. Estab. 1998. Publishes hardcover and trade paperback originals. **Publishes 10 titles/year. 500 queries received/year. 400 mss received/year. 90% of books from first-time authors. 100% from unagented writers. Pays 10-15% royalty.** Publishes book 8 months after acceptance. Accepts simultaneous submissions. Responds in 6 weeks to mss. Catalog and guidelines free.

> Book publisher for young adults, children, and adults.

NONFICTION "We publish business, real estate and investment books." Reviews artwork/photos.

FICTION Subjects include juvenile, science fiction, young adult. All books should be oriented to explaining science even if they do not fall 100% under the category of science fiction. Submit complete ms.

TIPS Quick response, great relationships, high commission/royalty.

DOG-EARED PUBLICATIONS

P.O. Box 620863, Middletown WI 53562. (608)831-1410. **Fax:** (608)831-1410. **E-mail:** field@dog-eared.com. **Website:** www.dog-eared.com. **Contact:** Nancy Field, publisher. Estab. 1977. **Pays author royalty based on wholesale price. Offers advance.** Brochure available for SASE and 1 first-class stamp or on website.

> The home of Dog-eared Publications is a perfect place to create children's nature books! Perched on a hilltop in Middleton, Wisconsin, we are surrounded by wild meadows and oak

forests where deer, wild turkeys, and even bobcats leave their marks.

NONFICTION Middle readers: activity books, animal, nature/environment, science. Average word length: varies. *Currently not accepting unsolicited mss.*

DORAL PUBLISHING, INC.

3 Burroughs, Irvine CA 92618. (800)633-5385. **E-mail:** doralpub@mindspring.com. **Website:** www. doralpub.com. **Contact:** Alvin Grossman, publisher; Joe Liddy, marketing manager (purebred dogs). Estab. 1986. Publishes hardcover and trade paperback originals. **Publishes 10 titles/year. 30 queries received/year. 15 mss received/year. 85% from unagented writers. Pays 10% royalty on wholesale price.** Publishes book 6 months after acceptance. Responds in 2 months to queries. Catalog available free. Guidelines for #10 SASE.

> "Doral Publishing publishes only books about dogs and dog-related topics, mostly geared for pure-bred dog owners and showing. Currently emphasizing breed books."

NONFICTION Subjects include animals, health, medicine. "We are looking for new ideas. No flowery prose. Manuscripts should be literate, intelligent, but easy to read. Subjects must be dog-related." Query with SASE. Submit outline, 2 sample chapters. Reviews artwork/photos. Send photocopies.

FICTION Subjects include juvenile. Subjects must center around dogs. Either the main character should be a dog or a dog should play an integral role. Query.

TIPS "We are currently expanding and are looking for new topics and fresh ideas while staying true to our niche. While we will steadfastly maintain that market—we are always looking for excellent breed books—we also want to explore more 'mainstream' topics."

DORCHESTER PUBLISHING CO., INC.

200 Madison Ave., Suite 2000, New York NY 10016. (212)725-8811. **Fax:** (212)532-1054. **E-mail:** submissions@dorchesterpub.com. **Website:** www.dorchesterpub.com. **Pays advance.** Guidelines online.

> Dorchester Publishing is not currently accepting unsolicited mss.

FICTION E-mail a 3-7 page synopsis and the complete ms as Word or .rtf attachments to submissions@dorchesterpub.com. Or if you prefer mail. please query or submit synopsis and first three chapters only—**no complete mss unless specifically requested.** Include a sase for your response.

DOUBLEDAY BOOKS FOR YOUNG READERS

1540 Broadway, New York NY 10036. (212)782-9000. **Website:** www.randomhouse.com/kids.

○ Only accepts mss submitted by an agent. Trade picture book list, from preschool to age 8.

Ⓐ DOUBLEDAY RELIGIOUS PUBLISHING

The Crown Publishing Group, a Division of Random House, Inc., 1745 Broadway, New York NY 10019. (212)782-9000. **Website:** www.randomhouse.com; http://crownpublishing.com. Estab. 1897. Publishes hardcover and trade paperback originals and reprints. Accepts simultaneous submissions.

○ "Random House, Inc. does not accept unsolicited submissions, proposals, manuscripts, or submission queries via e-mail at this time. If you would like to have your work or manuscript considered for publication by a major book publisher, we recommend that you work with an established literary agent. Each agency has manuscript submission guidelines."

NONFICTION Agented submissions only.

DOVER PUBLICATIONS, INC.

31 E. Second St., Mineola NY 11501. (516)294-7000. **Fax:** (516)873-1401. **E-mail:** hr@doverpublications. com. **Website:** www.doverpublications.com. **Contact:** John Grafton (math/science reprints). Estab. 1941. Publishes trade paperback originals and reprints. **Publishes 660 titles/year. Makes outright purchase.** Accepts simultaneous submissions. Catalog online.

NONFICTION Subjects include agriculture, Americana, animals, anthropology, archeology, art, architecture, cooking, foods, nutrition, health, medicine, history, hobbies, language, literature, music, dance, nature, environment, philosophy, photography, religion, science, sports, translation, travel. Publishes mostly reprints. Accepts original paper doll collections, game books, coloring books (juvenile). Query with SASE. Reviews artwork/photos.

DOWN EAST BOOKS

Imprint of Down East Enterprise, Inc., P.O. Box 679, Camden ME 04843. (207)594-9544, 800-766-1670. **Fax:** (207)594-7215. **E-mail:** jviehman@downeast. com; editorial@downeast.com. **E-mail:** submissions@downeast.com. **Website:** www.downeast.com. **Contact:** Paul Doiron, editor-in-chief. John Viehman, publisher Estab. 1967. Publishes hardcover and trade paperback originals, trade paperback reprints.

Publishes 24-30 titles/year. 50% of books from first-time authors. 90% from unagented writers. Pays $500 average advance. Publishes book 1 year after acceptance. Accepts simultaneous submissions. Responds in 3 months to queries. Send SASE for ms guidelines. Send 9×12 SASE for guidelines, plus recent catalog.

⌿ Down East Books publishes books that capture and illuminate the unique beauty and character of New England's history, culture, and wild places.

NONFICTION Subjects include Americana, history, nature, environment, recreation, regional, sports. Books about the New England region, Maine in particular. All of our regional books must have a Maine or New England emphasis. Query with SASE. Do not send CD, DVD, or disk. Reviews artwork/photos.

FICTION Subjects include juvenile, mainstream, contemporary, regional. We publish 2-4 juvenile titles/year (fiction and nonfiction), and 0-1 adult fiction titles/year. Query with SASE.

DOWN THE SHORE PUBLISHING

Box 100, West Creek NJ 08092. **Fax:** (609)597-0422. **E-mail:** dtsbooks@comcast.net. **Website:** www.down-the-shore.com. Publishes hardcover and trade paperback originals and reprints. **Publishes 4-10 titles/year. Pays royalty on wholesale or retail price, or makes outright purchase.** Accepts simultaneous submissions. Responds in 3 months to queries. Catalog for 8×10 SAE with 2 first-class stamps or on website. Guidelines online.

⌿ "Bear in mind that our market is regional-New Jersey, the Jersey Shore, the mid-Atlantic, and seashore and coastal subjects."

NONFICTION Subjects include Americana, art, architecture, history, nature, environment, regional. Query with SASE. Submit proposal package, 1-2 sample chapters, synopsis. Reviews artwork/photos. Send photocopies.

FICTION Subjects include regional. Query with SASE. Submit proposal package, clips, 1-2 sample chapters.

POETRY "We do not publish poetry, unless it is to be included as part of an anthology."

TIPS "Carefully consider whether your proposal is a good fit for our established market."

Ⓐ⊘ DRAGONFLY

Imprint of Random House Children's Books/Random House, Inc., 1745 Broadway, New York NY 10019. (212)782-9000. **Website:** www.randomhouse.com.

Quality reprint paperback imprint for paperback books. *Does not accept mss.*

DREAMLAND BOOKS INC.

P.O. Box 1714, Minnetonka MN 55345. (612)281-4704. **E-mail:** dreamlandbooks@inbox.com. **Website:** www.dreamlandbooks.inc.com. Estab. 2008.

FICTION "We are not accepting children's story submissions at this time. However, if you have a master or doctoral degree in creative writing, literature, or like field and already have at least one non-vanity book published, we welcome query letters."

POETRY "We are accpeting poetry and flash story submissions for our poetry journal Cellar Door Poetry. We accept all forms of poetry, but will not publish any work that promotes violence or pornography."

DUFOUR EDITIONS

P.O. Box 7, 124 Byers Road, Chester Springs PA 19425. (610)458-5005 or (800)869-5677. **Fax:** (610)458-7103. **E-mail:** orders@dufoureditions.com. **Website:** www.dufoureditions.com. Estab. 1948. Publishes hardcover originals, trade paperback originals and reprints. **Publishes 3-4 titles/year. 200 queries received/year. 15 mss received/year. 20-30% of books from first-time authors. 80% from unagented writers. Pays $100-500 advance.** Publishes book 18 months after acceptance of ms. Accepts simultaneous submissions. Responds in 3 months to queries. Responds in 3 months to proposals. Responds in 6 months to mss. Catalog available free.

↳ We publish literary fiction by good writers which is well received and achieves modest sales. De-emphsazing poetry and nonfiction.

NONFICTION Subjects include history, translation. Query with SASE. Reviews artwork/photos. Send photocopies.

FICTION Subjects include literary, short story collections, translation. We like books that are slightly off-beat, different and well-written. Query with SASE.

POETRY Query.

TIPS Audience is sophisticated, literate readers especially interested in foreign literature and translations, and a strong Irish-Celtic focus, as well as work from U.S. writers. Check to see if the publisher is really a good match for your subject matter.

DUNDURN PRESS, LTD.

3 Church St., Suite 500, Toronto ON M5E 1M2, Canada. (416)214-5544. **E-mail:** info@dundurn.com. **E-mail:** submissions@dundurn.com. **Website:** www.dundurn.com. **Contact:** Kirk Howard, president and publisher. Estab. 1972. **600 queries received/year. 25% of books from first-time authors. 50% from unagented writers.** Publishes book 1 year after acceptance. Accepts simultaneous submissions. Responds in 3 months to queries. Guidelines online.

NONFICTION Subjects include art, architecture, history, Canadian and military, war, music, dance, drama, regional., art history, theater, serious and popular nonfiction. Submit cover letter, synopsis, CV, sample chapters, SASE/IRC, or submit complete ms. Accepts submissions via postal mail only.

FICTION Subjects include literary, mystery, young adult. No romance, science fiction, or experimental. Submit sample chapters, synopsis, author fee, SASE/IRCs, or submit complete ms. Accepts submissions via postal mail only.

DUNEDIN ACADEMIC PRESS LTD

Hudson House, 8 Albany St., Edinburgh EH1 3QB, United Kingdom. (44)(131)473-2397. **E-mail:** mail@dunedinacademicpress.co.uk. **Website:** www.dunedinacademicpress.co.uk. **Contact:** Anthony Kinahan, director. Estab. 2001. **Publishes 15-20 titles/year. 10% of books from first-time authors. 90% from unagented writers. Pays royalty.** Catalog and proposal Guidelines online.

↳ "Ask for and look over our author proposal guidelines before submitting. Synopses and ideas welcome. Approach first by e-mail, outlining proposal and identifying the market."

NONFICTION, vocal music, earth science. Reviews artwork/photos.

TIPS "Although located in Scotland, Dunedin's list contains authors and subjects from the wider academic world and DAP's horizons are far broader than our immediate Scottish environment. One of the strengths of Dunedin is that we are able to offer our authors that individual support that comes from dealing with a small independent publisher committed to growth through careful treatment of its authors."

THOMAS DUNNE BOOKS

Imprint of St. Martin's Press, 175 Fifth Ave., New York NY 10010. (212)674-5151. **Website:** www.thomasdunnebooks.com. Estab. 1986. Publishes hardcover and trade paperback originals, and reprints. Accepts simultaneous submissions. Catalog and guidelines free.

Accepts agented submissions only.

NONFICTION Subjects include government, politics, history, sports., political commentary. Author's attention to detail is important. We get a lot of manuscripts that are poorly proofread and just can't be considered. Agents submit query, or an outline and 1 sample pages. Reviews artwork/photos. Send photocopies.

FICTION Subjects include mainstream, contemporary, mystery, suspense., thrillers, women's. Agents submit query.

DUQUESNE UNIVERSITY PRESS

600 Forbes Ave., Pittsburgh PA 15282. (412)396-6610. **Fax:** (412)396-5984. **E-mail:** wadsworth@duc.edu. **Website:** www.dupress.duq.edu. **Contact:** Susan Wadsworth-Booth, director. Estab. 1927. Publishes hardcover and trade paperback originals. **Publishes 8-12 titles/year. 400 queries received/year. 65 mss received/year. 30% of books from first-time authors. 95% from unagented writers. Pays royalty on net price. Pays (some) advance.** Publishes book 1 year after acceptance. Responds in 1 month to proposals; 3 months to mss. Catalog and guidelines for #10 SASE. Guidelines online.

⌐⟶ "Duquesne publishes scholarly monographs in the fields of literary studies (medieval & Renaissance), continental philosophy, ethics, religious studies and existential psychology. Interdisciplinary works are also of interest. Duquesne University Press does NOT publish fiction, poetry, children's books, technical or "hard" science works, or unrevised theses or dissertations."

NONFICTION Subjects include language, literature, philosophy, continental, psychology, existential, religion. "We look for quality of scholarship." For scholarly books, query or submit outline, 1 sample chapter, and SASE.

Ⓐ DUTTON (ADULT TRADE)

Penguin Group, Inc., 375 Hudson St., New York NY 10014. (212)366-2000. **Website:** us.penguingroup.com. **Contact:** Brian Tart, publisher; Erika Imranyi, Editor. Estab. 1852. **Pays royalty.** Publishes book 18 months after acceptance.

◯ "Query letters *only* (must include SASE). A query letter should be typed and, ideally, fit on one page. Please include a brief synopsis of your manuscript and your publishing credits, if any."

FICTION Subjects include adventure, mainstream.

TIPS "Write the complete ms and submit it to an agent or agents. They will know exactly which editor will be interested in a project."

DUTTON CHILDREN'S BOOKS

Penguin Group (USA), Inc., 375 Hudson St., New York NY 10014. **E-mail:** duttonpublicity@us.penguingroup.com. **Website:** www.penguin.com. **Contact:** Sara Reynolds, art director. Estab. 1852. Publishes hardcover originals as well as novelty formats. **Publishes 100 titles/year. 15% of books from first-time authors. Pays royalty on retail price. Pays advance.**

⌐⟶ Dutton Children's Books publishes high-quality fiction and nonfiction for readers ranging from preschoolers to young adults on a variety of subjects. Currently emphasizing middlegrade and young adult novels that offer a fresh perspective. De-emphasizing photographic nonfiction and picture books that teach a lesson. Approximately 80 new hardcover titles are published every year, fiction and nonfiction for babies through young adults.

NONFICTION Subjects include animals, history, US, nature, environment, science. Query with SASE.

FICTION Dutton Children's Books has a diverse, general interest list that includes picture books; easy-to-read books; and fiction for all ages, from first chapter books to young adult readers. Query with SASE.

EAGLE'S VIEW PUBLISHING

168 W. 12th St., Ogden UT 84310. (801)393-3991. **Fax:** (801)393-4647. **E-mail:** sales@eaglefeathertrading.com. **Website:** www.eaglesviewpub.com. **Contact:** Denise Knight, editor-in-chief. Estab. 1982. Publishes trade paperback originals. **Publishes 2-4 titles/year. 40 queries received/year. 20 mss received/year. 90% of books from first-time authors. 100% from unagented writers. Pays 8-10% royalty on net selling price.** Publishes book 1 year after acceptance. Accepts simultaneous submissions. Responds in 1 year to proposals. Catalog and guidelines for $4.00.

⌐⟶ "Eagle's View primarily publishes how-to craft books with a subject related to historical or contemporary Native American/Mountain Man/frontier crafts/bead crafts. Currently emphasizing bead-related craft books. De-emphasizing history except for historical Indian crafts."

NONFICTION Subjects include anthropology, archaeology, Native American crafts, ethnic, Native American, history, American frontier historical patterns and books, hobbies, crafts, especially beadwork. Submit outline, 1-2 sample chapters. Reviews artwork/photos. Send photocopies and sample illustrations.

TIPS "We will not be publishing any new beaded earrings books for the foreseeable future. We are interested in other craft projects using seed beads, especially books that feature a variety of items, not just different designs for 1 item."

EAKIN PRESS

P.O. Box 21235, Waco TX 76702. (254)235-6161. **Fax:** (254)235-6230. **Website:** www.eakinpress.com. **Contact:** Kris Gholson, associate publisher. Estab. 1978. Publishes hardcover and paperback originals and reprints. Accepts simultaneous submissions. Responds in up to 1 year to queries. Guidelines online.

- "Our top priority is to cover the history and culture of the Southwest, especially Texas and Oklahoma. We also have successfully published titles related to ethnic studies. We publish very little fiction, other than for children."

NONFICTION Subjects include Americana, Western, business, economics, cooking, foods, nutrition, ethnic, history, military, war, regional, sports., African American studies. Juvenile nonfiction: includes biographies of historic personalities, prefer with Texas or regional interest, or nature studies; and easy-read illustrated books for grades 1-3. Submit sample chapters, bio, synopsis, publishing credits, SASE.

FICTION Subjects include historical, juvenile. Juvenile fiction for grades K-12, preferably relating to Texas and the Southwest or contemporary. No adult fiction. Query or submit outline/synopsis

EASTLAND PRESS

P.O. Box 99749, Seattle WA 98139. (206)217-0204. **Fax:** (206)217-0205. **E-mail:** info@eastlandpress.com. **Website:** www.eastlandpress.com. **Contact:** John O'Connor, Managing Editor. Estab. 1981. Publishes hardcover and trade paperback originals. **Publishes 4-6 titles/year. 25 queries received/year. 30% of books from first-time authors. 90% from unagented writers. Pays 12-15% royalty on receipts.** Publishes book 1-2 years after acceptance of ms. Accepts simultaneous submissions. Responds in 1 month.

- "Eastland Press is interested in textbooks for practitioners of alternative medical therapies, primarily Chinese and physical therapies, and related bodywork."

NONFICTION Subjects include health, medicine. "We prefer that a manuscript be completed or close to completion before we will consider publication. Proposals are rarely considered, unless submitted by a published author or teaching institution." Submit outline and 2-3 sample chapters. Reviews artwork/photos. Send photocopies.

ⓐ ⊘ THE ECCO PRESS

10 E. 53rd St., New York NY 10022. (212)207-7000. **Fax:** (212)702-2460. **Website:** www.harpercollins.com. **Contact:** Daniel Halpern, editor-in-chief. Estab. 1970. **Publishes 60 titles/year. Pays royalty. Pays negotiable advance.** Publishes book 1 year after acceptance.

FICTION Literary, short story collections. "We can publish possibly one or two original novels a year." Query with SASE.

TIPS "We are always interested in first novels and feel it's important that they be brought to the attention of the reading public."

☺ ÉCRITS DES FORGES

992-A, rue Royale, Trois-Riviéres QC G9A 4H9, Canada. (819)840-8492. **Website:** www.ecritsdesforges. com. **Contact:** Stéphane Despatie, director. Estab. 1971. **Pays royalties of 10-20%.** Responds to queries in 6 months.

POETRY Écrits des Forges publishes poetry only that is "authentic and original as a signature. We have published poetry from more than 1,000 poets coming from most of the francophone countries: Andreé Romus (Belgium), Amadou Lamine Sall (Sénégal), Nicole Brossard, Claude Beausoleil, Jean-Marc Desgent, and Jean-Paul Daoust (Québec)." Publishes 45-50 paperback books of poetry/year. Books are usually 80-88 pages, digest-sized, perfect-bound, with 2-color covers with art. Query first with a few sample poems and a cover letter with brief bio and publication credits. Order sample books by writing or faxing.

EDCON PUBLISHING GROUP

30 Montauk Blvd., Oakdale NY 11769. (631)567-7227. **Fax:** (631)567-8745. **E-mail:** dale@edconpublishing. com. **Website:** www.edconpublishing.com. **Work purchased outright from authors for up to $1,000.** Publishes book 6 months after acceptance. Accepts simultaneous submissions. Catalog available online.

- Looking for educational games and nonfiction work in the areas of math, science, reading and social studies.

NONFICTION Grades 1-12, though primarily 6-12 remedial.

FICTION Submit outline/synopsis and 1 sample chapter. Submission kept on file unless return is requested. Include SASE for return.

◎ EDGE SCIENCE FICTION AND FANTASY PUBLISHING/TESSERACT BOOKS

Hades Publications, Box 1714, Calgary AB T2P 2L7, Canada. (403)254-0160. **Fax:** (403)254-0456. **E-mail:** publisher@hadespublications.com. **Website:** www.edgewebsite.com. **Contact:** Editorial Manager. Estab. 1996.

TIPS "Send us your best, polished, completed manuscript. Use proper manuscript format. Take the time before you submit to get a critique from people who can offer you useful advice. When in doubt, visit our website for helpful resources, FAQs and other tips."

EDUCATOR'S INTERNATIONAL PRESS, INC.

18 Colleen Rd., Troy NY 12180. (518)271-9886. **Fax:** (518)266-9422. **E-mail:** bill@edint.com. **Website:** www.edint.com. **Contact:** William Clockel, publisher. Estab. 1996. Publishes hardcover and trade paperback originals and reprints. Accepts simultaneous submissions. Catalog and guidelines free.

⚷━► "Educator's International publishes books in all aspects of education, broadly conceived, from pre-kindergarten to postgraduate. We specialize in texts, professional books, videos and other materials for students, faculty, practitioners and researchers. We also publish a full list of books in the areas of women's studies, and social and behavioral sciences."

NONFICTION Subjects include education, language, literature, philosophy, psychology, software, women's studies. Submit TOC, outline, 2-3 chapters, résumé with SASE. Reviews artwork/photos.

TIPS Audience is professors, students, researchers, individuals, libraries.

EDUPRESS, INC.

P.O. Box 8610, Madison WI 53708. (920)563-9571 ext. 332. **Fax:** (920)563-7395. **E-mail:** edupress@highsmith.com; LBowie@highsmith.com. **Website:** www.edupressinc.com. **Contact:** Liz Bowie. Estab. 1979. **Work purchased outright from authors.** Publishes book 1-2 years after acceptance. Responds in 2-4 months to queries and mss. Catalog available on website.

⚷━► Edupress, Inc., publishes supplemental curriculum resources for PK-6th grade. Currently emphasizing reading and math materials, as well as science and social studies.

NONFICTION Submit complete ms via mail or e-mail with "Manuscript Submission" as the subject line.

TIPS "We are looking for unique, research-based, quality supplemental materials for Pre-K through eighth grade. We publish all subject areas in many different formats, including games. Our materials are intended for classroom and home schooling use."

EERDMANS BOOKS FOR YOUNG READERS

2140 Oak Industrial Dr. NE, Grand Rapids MI 49505. **E-mail:** youngreaders@eerdmans.com; gbrown@eerdmans.com. **Website:** www.eerdmans.com/youngreaders. **Contact:** Shannon White, acquisitions editor. **6,000 mss received/year. Pays 5-7% royalty on retail.** Publishes book Publishes middle reader and YA books 1 year after acceptance; publishes picture books in 2-3 years. after acceptance of ms. Responds to mss in 3-4 months.

⚷━► "We are seeking books that encourage independent thinking, problem-solving, creativity, acceptance, kindness. Books that encourage moral values without being didactic or preachy. "Board books, picture books, middle reader fiction, young adult fiction, nonfiction, illustrated storybooks. A submission stands out when it's obvious that someone put time into it—the publisher's name and address are spelled correctly, the package is neat, and all of our submission requirements have been followed precisely. We look for short, concise cover letters that explain why the ms fits with our list, and/or how the ms fills an important need in the world of children's literature. Send exclusive ms submissions to acquisitions editor. We regret that due to the volume of material we receive, we cannot comment on ms we are unable to accept."

NONFICTION Middle readers: biography, history, multicultural, nature/environment, religion, social issues. Young adults/teens: biography, history, multicultural, nature/environment, religion, social issues. Average word length: middle readers—35,000; young adult books—35,000. Reviews artwork/photos. Send color photocopies rather than original art.

FICTION Picture books: animal, contemporary, folktales, history, humor, multicultural, nature/environment, poetry, religion, special needs, social issues, sports, suspense. Young readers: animal, contemporary, fantasy, folktales, history, humor, multicultural, poetry, religion, special needs, social issues, sports, suspense. Middle readers: adventure, contemporary, fantasy, history, humor, multicultural, nature/

environment, problem novels, religion, social issues, sports, suspense. Young adults/teens: adventure, contemporary, fantasy, folktales, history, humor, multicultural, nature/environment, problem novels, religion, sports, suspense. Average word length: picture books—1,000; middle readers—15,000; young adult—45,000. "Right now we are not acquiring books that revolve around a holiday. (No Christmas, Thanksgiving, Easter, Halloween, Fourth of July, Hanukkah books.) We do not publish retold or original fairy tales, nor do we publish books about witches or ghosts or vampires." Send exclusive ms submissions (marked so on outside of envelope) to acquisitions editor.

TIPS "Find out who Eerdmans is before submitting a manuscript. Look at our website, request a catalog, and check out our books."

WILLIAM B. EERDMANS PUBLISHING CO.

2140 Oak Industrial Dr. NE, Grand Rapids MI 49505. (616)459-4591. **Fax:** (616)459-6540. **E-mail:** info@eerdmans.com. **Website:** www.eerdmans.com. **Contact:** Jon Pott, editor-in-chief. Estab. 1911. Publishes hardcover and paperback originals and reprints. Accepts simultaneous submissions. Responds in 4 weeks to queries, possibly longer for mss. Please include e-mail and/or SASE. Catalog and guidelines free.

◯ Will not respond to or accept mss, proposals, or queries sent by e-mail or fax.

NONFICTION Subjects include history, religious, language, literature, philosophy, of religion, psychology, regional, history, religion, sociology, translation., Biblical studies. "We prefer that writers take the time to notice if we have published anything at all in the same category as their manuscript before sending it to us." Query with TOC, 2-3 sample chapters, and SASE for return of ms. Reviews artwork/photos.

FICTION Subjects include religious, children's, general, fantasy. Query with SASE.

EGMONT USA

443 Park Ave. S, New York NY 10016. (212)685-0102. **E-mail:** Suite 806. **Website:** www.egmontusa.com. **Contact:** Elizabeth Law, vice president/publisher; Regina Griffin, executive editor. Estab. 2008. **25% of books from first-time authors. Pays authors royalties based on retail price.** Publishes book 18 months after acceptance. Accepts simultaneous submissions. Responds to queries in 4 weeks; mss in 6 weeks.

◯ "Unfortunately, Egmont USA is not currently able to accept unsolicited submissions; we only accept submissions from literary agents."

FICTION Picture books: animal, concept, contemporary, humor, multicultural. Young readers: adventure, animal, contemporary, humor, multicultural. Middle readers: adventure, animal, contemporary, fantasy, humor, multicultural, problem novels, science fiction, special needs. Young adults/teens: adventure, animal, contemporary, humor, multicultural, problem novels, science fiction, special needs. Query or submit completed ms.

EDWARD ELGAR PUBLISHING INC.

Edward Elgar Publishing Inc., The William Pratt House, 9 Dewey Court, Northampton MA 01060. (413)584-5551. **Fax:** (413)584-9933. **E-mail:** elgarsubmissions@e-elgar.com; submissions@e-elgar.co.uk. **Website:** www.e-elgar.com. **Contact:** Alan Sturmer; Tara Gorvine. Estab. 1986.

◯ "We are actively commissioning new titles and are happy to consider and advise on ideas for monograph books, textbooks, professional law books and academic journals at any stage. Please complete a proposal form in as much detail as possible. We review all prososals with our academic advisors."

⊕ ELIXIRIST

P.O. Box 17132, Sugar Land TX 77496. **E-mail:** support@elixirist.com; submissions@elixirist.com. **Website:** www.elixirist.com. **Contact:** Juanita Samborski, Acquisitions Editor (romance, comedy, chicklit, urban fantasy); Sean Samborski, Publisher (speculative, comedy, horror, literary). Estab. 2010. Format publishes in trade paperback, mass market paperback, and electronic originals. **Publishes 12/year titles/year. 50% of books from first-time authors. 100% from unagented writers. Pays 6-12% royalty on retail price.** Publishes book 6-12 months after acceptance of ms. Accepts simultaneous submissions. Responds in 12 months on queries, proposals, and mss. Catalog and guidelines available for SASE.

⚷ A small, commercial publisher dealing primarily in the print market in multiple genre formats.

NONFICTION Subjects include Americana, community, creative nonfiction, dance, hobbies, humanities, literary criticism, memoirs, music, philosophy, public affairs, sex, social sciences, sociology, sports, travel, womens issues, womens studies, world affairs, young adult. Query with SASE; submit proposal package, including outline and 3 sample chapters. Reviews artwork/photos as part of the ms package.

FICTION Subjects include adventure, comic books, contemporary, experimental, fantasy, gothic, historical, horror, humor, juvenile, literary, mainstream, mystery, occult, religious, romance, science fiction, sports, suspense, western, young adult, speculative subgenres. Query with SASE; submit synopsis and 3 sample chapters.

TIPS "We publish novels in genres ranging from young adult to literary, multi-genres appealing to both male and female readers."

ELLORA'S CAVE PUBLISHING, INC.

1056 Home Ave., Akron OH 44310. **E-mail:** service@ellorascave.com; submissions@ellorascave.com. **Website:** www.ellorascave.com. **Contact:** Raelene Gorlinsky, managing editor; Kelli collins, editor-in-chief. Estab. 2000. Publishes electronic originals and reprints; print books. **Pays 37.5% royalty on gross (cover price).** Accepts simultaneous submissions. Responds in 2 months to queries and proposals; 2-6 months to mss. Guidelines online.

FICTION Erotic romance of every subgenre, including gay/lesbian, menage and more, and BDSM. All must be under genre romance. All must have erotic content or author must be willing to add sex during editing. Submit query letter, full synopsis, first three chapters, and last chapter.

TIPS "Our audience is romance readers who want explicit sexual detail. They come to us because we offer not erotica, but Romantica™—sex with romance, plot, emotion. In addition to erotic romance with happy-ever-after endings, we also publish pure erotica, detailing sexual adventure, experimentation, and coming of age."

✪ ELOHI GADUGI / THE HABIT OF RAINY NIGHTS PRESS

900 NE 81st Ave., #209, Portland OR 97213. **E-mail:** editors@elohigadugi.org. **Website:** http://rainynightspress.org. **Contact:** Patricia McLean, nonfiction editor (narrative nonfiction); Duane Poncy, fiction editor (general fiction, native American); Ger Killeen, poetry editor. Estab. 2003. Format publishes in electronic originals. **Publishes 2-3 projected print titles/year, 5-6 projected ebook titles/year/ titles/year. Receives 60-100 queries/year. 90% of books from first-time authors. 100%**

from unagented writers. **Pays 20-25% royalty on retail price (60-70% of wholesale for e-books).** Publishes book 9-12 months after acceptance. Accepts simultaneous submissions. Responds in 1-2 months on queries; 2-3 months on mss. Catalog and guidelines online.

NONFICTION Subjects include creative nonfiction, environment, ethnic, memoirs, multicultural, nature. "At this time we are only interested in Native American culture and narrative nonfiction which addresses contemporary environmental, social, political, or indigenous issues from a progressive viewpoint." Submit completed ms using submission manager on website. Reviews artwork/photos; writers should send jpeg digital images.

FICTION Subjects include contemporary, ethnic, fantasy, historical, literary, mainstream, multicultural, mystery, science fiction, suspense, translation, young adult. "We publish emerging writers whose fiction explores the important concerns of the contemporary world with depth and compassion. Have a strong narrative voice and character-driven story. We don't particularly care for the current trend of books about 'me.' We are not adverse to magical realism, poetic language, and books that take a chance." romance, Christian, new age, vampires, zombies, superheros Submit using submission manager on website.

POETRY "All poetry should have a strong narrative quality. Have something to say!" No academic or experimental poetry. Submit 5-6 sample poems; submit complete ms.

TIPS "Respect your work. Make sure it is ready for publication. Polish, polish, polish. We cannot consider books that need a lot of basic cleaning up. Have something to say—we are not interested in using up vital resources to publish fluff."

EMIS, INC.

P.O. Box 270666, Fort Collins CO 80527. (214)349-0077; (800)225-0694. **Fax:** (970)672-8606. **Website:** www.emispub.com. **Contact:** Lynda Blake, president. Publishes trade paperback originals. **Publishes 2 titles/year. Pays 12% royalty on retail price.** Responds in 3 months to queries. Catalog available free. Guidelines available free.

NONFICTION Subjects include health, medicine, psychology. women's health/medicine. Submit 3 sample chapters with SASE.

TIPS Audience is medical professionals and medical product manufacturers and distributors.

ⓐⓞ ENCOUNTER BOOKS

900 Broadway, Suite 601, New York NY 10003. (212)871-6310. **Fax:** (212)871-6311. **E-mail:** read@encounterbooks.com. **Website:** www.encounterbooks.com. **Contact:** Roger Kimball, editor and president. Hardcover originals and trade paperback reprints. Accepts simultaneous submissions. Catalog free or online. Guidelines online.

�'➤ Encounter Books publishes serious nonfiction—books that can alter our society, challenge our morality, stimulate our imaginations—in the areas of history, politics, religion, biography, education, public policy, current affairs, and social sciences. Encounter Books is an activity of Encounter for Culture and Education, a tax-exempt, non profit corporation dedicated to strengthening the marketplace of ideas and engaging in educational activities to help preserve democratic culture.

NONFICTION Subjects include child guidance, education, ethnic, government, politics, health, medicine, history, language, literature, memoirs, military, war, multicultural, philosophy, psychology, religion, science, sociology, women's issues/studies., gender studies. Submit proposal package, including outline and 1 sample chapter, SASE. Do not send via e-mail.

⊕ ENETE ENTERPRISES

3600 Mission #10, San Diego CA 92109. **E-mail:** EneteEnterprises@gmail.com. **Website:** www.EneteEnterprises.com. **Contact:** Shannon Enete, editor. Estab. 2011. Publishes hardcover originals, trade paperback originals, mass market paperback originals, electronic originals. **Publishes 6 titles/year. Receives 55 queries/year; 20 ms/year. 95% of books from first-time authors. 100% from unagented writers. Pays royalties of 1-15%.** Publishes book 3-6 months after acceptance. Accepts simultaneous submissions. Responds to queries/proposals in 1 month; mss in 1-3 months. Guidelines available on website.

NONFICTION Subjects include cooking, creative nonfiction, education, foods, gay, government, health, lesbian, medicine, memoirs, multicultural, nutrition, photography, politics, science, spirituality, travel, world affairs. "Actively seeking books about healthcare / medicine. More specifically: back care, emergency medicine, international medicine, healthcare, insurance, EMT or Paramedic, or alternative medi-

cine." Submit query, proposal, or ms by e-mail. Reviews artwork.

FICTION Subjects include adventure, gay, lesbian, romance, science fiction. "We are looking for new fiction that could grow into a series of books." Submit query, proposal, or ms by e-mail.

TIPS "Send me your best work. Do not rush a draft."

ENGLISH TEA ROSE PRESS

The Wild Rose Press, P.O. Box 708, Adams Basin NY 14410-0708. (585)752-8770. **E-mail:** queryus@thewildrosepress.com. **Website:** www.thewildrosepress.com. **Contact:** Nicole D'Arienzo, editor. Estab. 2006. Format publishes in paperback originals, reprints, and e-books in a POD format. *Does not accept unsolicited mss.* **Pays royalty of 7% minimum; 35% maximum.** Publishes book 1 year after acceptance of ms. Responds to queries in 4 weeks; to mss in 12 weeks. Writer's guidelines available on website.

○ *Does not accept unsolicited mss.* Agented fiction less than 1%. Always comments on rejected mss. Sends prepublication galleys to author.

FICTION Wants contemporary, futuristic/time travel, gothic, historical, regency, romantic suspense, erotic, and paranormal romances. Plans several anthologies "in several lines of the company in the next year, including Cactus Rose, Yellow Rose, American Rose, Black Rose, and Scarlet Rose.". Send query letter with outline and a list of publishing credits. Include estimated word count, brief bio, and list of publishing credits.

TIPS "Polish your manuscript, make it as error free as possible, and follow our submission guidelines."

ENSLOW PUBLISHERS INC.

Box 398, 40 Industrial Rd., Berkeley Heights NJ 07922. (908)771-0925. **Fax:** (908)771-0925. **E-mail:** info@enslow.com. **Website:** www.enslow.com. **Contact:** Brian D. Enslow, vice president. Estab. 1978. **Publishes 200 titles/year. 30% of books from first-time authors. Pays authors royalties or work purchased outright.** Publishes book 18 months after acceptance. Responds to queries and mss in 2 weeks. Catalog/ms guidelines available for $3, along with an 8½×11 SASE and $2 postage.

○ Enslow Imprint MyReportLinks.com Books produces books on animals, states, presidents, continents, countries, and a variety of other topics for middle readers and young adults, and offers links to online sources of information on topics covered in books.

NONFICTION Young readers, middle readers, young adults: animal, arts/crafts, biography, careers, geography, health, history, multicultural, nature/environment, science, social issues, sports. Middle readers, young adults: hi-lo. "Enslow is moving into the elementary (grades 3-4) level and is looking for authors who can write biography and suggest other nonfiction themes at this level." Average word length: young readers—2,000; middle readers—5,000; young adult—18,000. Query.

Ⓐ⊘ EOS

Imprint of HarperCollins General Books Group, 10 E. 53rd St., New York NY 10022. (212)207-7000. **Website:** www.eosbooks.com. Estab. 1998. Publishes hardcover originals, trade and mass market paperback originals, and reprints. **Pays royalty on retail price. Pays variable advance.** Guidelines for #10 SASE.

Eos publishes quality science fiction/fantasy with broad appeal.

FICTION Subjects include fantasy, science fiction. No horror or juvenile. Agented submissions only. *All unsolicited mss returned.*

TIPS "Query via e-mail. Your query should be brief—no more than a 2-page description of your book. Do not send chapters or full synopsis at this time. You will receive a response—either a decline or a request for more material—in approximately 1-2 months."

EPICENTER PRESS, INC.

P.O. Box 82368, Kenmore WA 98028. **Fax:** (425)481-8253. **E-mail:** info@epicenterpress.com; laelmorgan@cs.com. **Website:** www.epicenterpress.com. **Contact:** Lael Morgan, acquisitions editor. Estab. 1987. Publishes hardcover and trade paperback originals. **Publishes 4-8 titles/year. 200 queries received/year. 100 mss received/year. 75% of books from first-time authors. 90% from unagented writers.** Publishes book 1-2 years after acceptance. Responds in 3 months to queries. Catalog and guidelines on website.

"We are a regional press founded in Alaska whose interests include but are not limited to the arts, history, environment, and diverse cultures and lifestyles of the North Pacific and high latitudes."

NONFICTION Subjects include animals, ethnic, history, nature, environment, recreation, regional, women's issues. "Our focus is Alaska and the Pacific Northwest. We do not encourage nonfiction titles from outside this region." Submit outline and 3 sample chapters. Reviews artwork/photos. Send photocopies.

⊘ ERIE CANAL PRODUCTIONS

4 Farmdale St., Clinton NY 13323. **E-mail:** eriecanal@juno.com. **Website:** www.eriecanalproductions.com. **Contact:** Scott Fiesthumel, president. Estab. 2001. Publishes trade paperback originals. **Publishes 1-2 titles/year. 50% of books from first-time authors. 100% from unagented writers. Pays negotiable royalty on net profits.** Responds in 1 month to queries. Catalog available free.

NONFICTION Subjects include Americana, history, sports. Query with SASE. *All unsolicited mss returned unopened.*

TIPS "We publish nonfiction books that look at historical places, events, and people along the traditional route of the Erie Canal through New York State."

ESCAPE COLLECTIVE PUBLISHING

P.O. Box 8821, Olympia WA 98509. **E-mail:** admin@escapecollective.com. **E-mail:** longfic@escapecollective.com; anthology@escapecollective.com. **Website:** www.escapecollective.com. **Contact:** Alexandra J. Ash, editor; Patrick Jennings-Mapp, editor. Estab. 2010. Publishes electronic originals. **Publishes 4 titles/year. 90% of books from first-time authors. 100% from unagented writers.** Publishes book 3 months after acceptance. Accepts simultaneous submissions. Responds in 1 month to queries; 3 months to mss. Catalog available online. Guidelines online.

FICTION Subjects include adventure, experimental, fantasy, gothic, horror, mystery, occult, romance, science fiction, suspense, young adult. No fan fiction, realist (mainstream/literary) fiction, nonfiction, erotica, Christian/religious themes, poetry, children's stories, art, graphic novels, previously published work, unedited mss. Submit proposal package, including 2-5 page synopsis and 1 sample chapter. "In the e-mail subject line, put Submission: The Title-Your Last Name-The Genre-Length."

TIPS "Be professional and courteous and we will return the favor! Read our submission guidelines and blog and review our published works for an idea of what we like."

ETC PUBLICATIONS

1456 Rodeo Rd., Palm Springs CA 92262. (760)316-9695; (866)514-9969. **Fax:** (760)316-9681. **Website:** www.etcpublications.com. **Contact:** Dr. Richard W.

Hostrop, publisher (education and social sciences); Lee Ona S. Hostrop, editorial director (history and works suitable below the college level). Estab. 1972. **Publishes 6-12 titles/year. 75% of books from first-time authors. 90% from unagented writers. Offers 5-15% royalty, based on wholesale and retail price.** Publishes book 9 months after acceptance.

☛ ETC publishes works that further learning as opposed to entertainment.

NONFICTION Subjects include education, translation, in above areas. Submit complete ms with SASE. Reviews artwork/photos.

TIPS Special consideration is given to those authors who are capable and willing to submit their completed work in camera-ready, typeset form. We are particularly interested in works suitable for both the Christian school market and homeschoolers; e.g., state history texts below the high school level with a Christian-oriented slant.

F+W CRIME

10151 Carver Road, Suite 200, Blue Ash OH 45242. (513)531-2690. **Website:** fwmedia.com. **Contact:** Benjamin LeRoy, publisher and community leader.

◯ With acquisition of Tyrus Books, F+W Media, Inc., will enter the fiction marketplace with Benjamin LeRoy.

FICTION F+W Crime will release as many as 200 e-book only titles. Currently not open to submissions.

F+W MEDIA, INC. (BOOK DIVISION)

1213 Sherman Ave. #306, Madison WI 53704. **E-mail:** info@tyrusbooks.com. **Website:** tyrusbooks.com. **Contact:** Sara Domville, President; David Blansfield, President.

◯ F+W Media, Inc., is composed of several enthusiast communities, including fine art, horticulture, writing, woodworking, graphic design, collectibles, outdoors, and more. Please see individual listings for specific submission information about the company's imprints.

FABER & FABER INC.

Farrar, Straus & Giroux, 18 W. 18th St., New York NY 10011. (212)741-6900. **Website:** us.macmillan.com/faberandfaber.aspx. Estab. 1976. Responds in 6-8 weeks.

NONFICTION "All submissions must be submitted through the mail—we do not accept electronic submissions, or submissions delivered in person. Please include a cover letter describing your submission, along with the first 50 pages of the manuscript."

POETRY "All submissions must be submitted through the mail—we do not accept electronic submissions, or submissions delivered in person. Please include a cover letter describing your submission, along with the first 50 pages of the manuscript. If you are submitting poems, please include 3-4 poems."

FABER & FABER LTD

3 Queen Square, London WC1N 3AU United Kingdom. 020 7465 0045. **Fax:** 020 7465 0034. **Website:** www.faber.co.uk. **Contact:** Lee Brackstone, Hannah Griffiths, Angus Cargill, (fiction); Walter Donohue, (film); Dinah Wood, (plays); Julian Loose, Neil Belton, (nonfiction); Paul Keegan, (poetry); Belinda Matthews, (music); Suzy Jenvy, Julia Wells, (children's). Estab. 1925. Publishes hardcover and paperback originals and reprints. **Publishes 200 titles/year. Pays royalty. Pays varying advances with each project.** Accepts simultaneous submissions. Responds in 3 months to mss. Catalog online.

☛ Faber & Faber have rejuvenated their nonfiction, music and children's titles in recent years and the film and drama lists remain market leaders.

NONFICTION Subjects include art, architecture, contemporary culture, cooking, foods, nutrition, creative nonfiction, government, politics, history, humanities, literary criticism, memoirs, military, war, multicultural, music, dance, psychology, recreation, science, sports, travel, world affairs., Children's. *No unsolicited nonfiction submissions.*

FICTION Subjects include adventure, ethnic, experimental, fantasy, historical, humor, literary, mystery, plays, poetry, short story collections, spiritual, sports, suspense, young adult. *No unsolicited fiction submissions.*

POETRY Address poetry to 'Poetry Submissions Department' and include an SAE for return. For more information, ring 020 7465 0045. Submit 6 sample poems.

TIPS Explore the website and downloadable Catalogues thoroughly to get a feel for the lists in all categories and genres.

FACTS ON FILE, INC.

Infobase Publishing, 132 W. 31st St., 17th Floor, New York NY 10001. (800)322-8755. **Fax:** (800)678-3633. **E-mail:** llikoff@factsonfile.com; custserv@factsonfile.com. **Website:** www.factsonfile.com. **Contact:** Laurie Likoff, editorial director (science, fashion, natural history); Frank Darmstadt (science & technology, nature, reference); Owen Lancer, senior editor (American history, women's studies); James Chambers, trade editor (health, pop culture, true crime, sports); Jeff Soloway, acquisitions editor (language/literature). Estab. 1941. Publishes hardcover originals and reprints. **Publishes 135-150 titles/year. 25% from unagented writers. Pays 10% royalty on retail price. Pays $5,000-10,000 advance.** Accepts simultaneous submissions. Responds in 2 months to queries. Catalog available free. Guidelines online.

8— Facts on File produces high-quality reference materials on a broad range of subjects for the school library market and the general nonfiction trade.

NONFICTION Subjects include contemporary culture, education, health, medicine, history, language, literature, multicultural, recreation, religion, sports., careers, entertainment, natural history, popular culture. "We publish serious, informational books for a targeted audience. All our books must have strong library interest, but we also distribute books effectively to the trade. Our library books fit the junior and senior high school curriculum." No computer books, technical books, cookbooks, biographies (except YA), pop psychology, humor, fiction or poetry. Query or submit outline and sample chapter with SASE. No submissions returned without SASE.

TIPS "Our audience is school and public libraries for our more reference-oriented books and libraries, schools and bookstores for our less reference-oriented informational titles."

FAIRLEIGH DICKINSON UNIVERSITY PRESS

285 Madison Ave., M-GH2-01, Madison NJ 07940. (973)443-8564. **Fax:** (973)443-8364. **E-mail:** fdupress@fdu.edu. **Website:** www.fdupress.org. **Contact:** Harry Keyishian, director. Estab. 1967. Publishes hardcover originals and occasional paperbacks. **Publishes 30-40 titles/year. 33% of books from first-time authors. 95% from unagented writers.** Publishes book 1 year after acceptance. Responds in 2 weeks to queries.

8— Fairleigh Dickinson publishes scholarly books for the academic market, in the humanities and social sciences.

NONFICTION Subjects include agriculture, art, architecture, business, economics, contemporary culture, ethnic, film, cinema, stage, gay, lesbian, government, politics, history, local, literary criticism, multicultural, music, dance, philosophy, psychology, regional, religion, sociology, translation, women's issues/studies, world affairs., Civil War, film, Jewish studies, scholarly editions. "The Press discourages submissions of unrevised dissertations. We do look for scholarly editions of literary works in all fields, in English, or translation. We welcome inquiries about essay collections if the majority of the material is previously unpublished; that the essays have a unifying and consistent theme, and that the editors provide a substantial scholarly introduction." No nonscholarly books. We do not publish textbooks, or original fiction, poetry or plays. Query with outline, detailed abstract, and sample chapters (if possible). Reviews artwork/photos. Send only copies of illustrations during the evaluation process.

TIPS "Press books are reviewed regularly in leading academic circles. Each year between 150,000-200,000 brochures are mailed to announce new works. Research must be up-to-date. Poor reviews result when bibliographies and notes don't reflect current research. We follow Chicago Manual of Style (15th edition) in scholarly citation. We welcome proposals for essay collections, including unpublished conference papers if they relate to a strong central theme and have scholarly merit. For further details, consult our online catalog."

FARCOUNTRY PRESS

P.O. Box 5630, Helena MT 59604. (800)821-3874. **Fax:** (406)443-5480. **E-mail:** shirley.machonis@farcountrypress.com. **Website:** www.farcountrypress.com. **Contact:** Shirley Machonis.

8— The award-winning publisher specializes in softcover and hardcover photography books showcasing the nation's cities, states, national parks, and wildlife. *Farcountry* also publishes several children's series (science/nature, history), as well as guidebooks, cookbooks, and regional history titles nationwide.

FARRAR, STRAUS & GIROUX

175 Fifth Ave., New York NY 10010. (212)741-6900. **Fax:** (212)633-2427. **E-mail:** childrens.editorial@fsgbooks.com. **Website:** www.fsgkidsbooks.com. **Contact:** Margaret Ferguson, editorial director; Wesley Adams, executive editor; Janine O'Malley, senior editor; Frances Foster, Frances Foster Books; Robbin Gourley, art director. Estab. 1946. Catalog available for 9×12 SASE with $1.95 postage. Ms guidelines for

SASE, with 1 first-class stamp, or can be viewed at www.fsgkidsbooks.com.

○ *As of January 2010, Farrar Straus & Giroux does not accept unsolicited manuscripts.* "We recommend finding a literary agent to represent you and your work."

NONFICTION All levels: all categories. "We publish only literary nonfiction."

FICTION All levels: all categories. "Original and well-written material for all ages."

TIPS "Study our catalog before submitting. We will see illustrators' portfolios by appointment. Don't ask for criticism and/or advice—due to the volume of submissions we receive, it's just not possible. Never send originals. Always enclose SASE."

ⓐⓄ FARRAR, STRAUS & GIROUX/ BOOKS FOR YOUNG READERS

Books for Young Readers, 175 Fifth Ave., New York NY 10010. (646)307-5151. **Website:** www.fsgkidsbooks.com. **Contact:** Children's Editorial Department. Estab. 1946. Publishes hardcover originals and trade paperback reprints. **Publishes 75 titles/year. 6,000 queries and mss received/year. 5% of books from first-time authors. 50% from unagented writers. Pays 2-6% royalty on retail price for paperbacks, 3-10% for hardcovers. Pays $3,000-25,000 advance.** Publishes book 18 months after acceptance of ms. Accepts simultaneous submissions. Responds in 2 months to queries. Responds in 3 months to mss. For catalog fax request or e-mail to: childrens.publicity@fsgbooks.com. Guidelines online.

⌐ "We publish original and well-written material for all ages."

FICTION Subjects include juvenile, picture books, young adult., nonfiction. True Do not query picture books; just send manuscript. Do not fax or e-mail queries or manuscripts. Query with SASE. Hard copy submissions only.

TIPS Audience is full age range, preschool to young adult. Specializes in literary fiction.

FATHER'S PRESS

2424 SE 6th St., Lee's Summit MO 64063. (816)600-6288. **E-mail:** mike@fatherspress.com. **Website:** www.fatherspress.com. **Contact:** Mike Smitley, owner (fiction, nonfiction). Estab. 2006. Publishes hardcover, trade paperback, and mass market paperback originals and reprints. **Publishes 6-10 titles/year. Pays 10-15% royalty on wholesale price.** Publishes book 6

months after acceptance of ms. Responds in 1 month to queries and proposals. Responds in 3 months to mss. Guidelines online.

NONFICTION Subjects include animals, cooking, foods, nutrition, creative nonfiction, history, military, war, nature, regional, religion, travel, women's issues, world affairs. Query with SASE. Unsolicited mss returned unopened. Call or e-mail first. Reviews artwork/photos. Send photocopies.

FICTION Subjects include adventure, historical, juvenile, literary, mainstream, contemporary, military, war, mystery, regional, religious, suspense, western, young adult. Query with SASE. Unsolicited mss returned unopened. Call or e-mail first.

FC2

Center for Publications, School of Arts and Sciences-UHV, 3007 N. Ben Wilson, Victoria TX 77901. **E-mail:** fc2.cmu@gmail.com. **Website:** http://fc2.org. **Contact:** Carmen Edington, managing editor. Estab. 1974. Publishes hardcover and paperback originals. **Pays 10% royalty.** Publishes book 1-3 years after acceptance. Accepts simultaneous submissions. Responds in 3 weeks to queries; 9-6 months to mss. Ms guidelines online.

⌐ Publisher of innovative fiction. Books: perfect/Smyth binding; illustrations. Average print order: 2,200. **Published some debut authors within the last year.** Plans 2 first novels this year. Averages 6 total titles, 6 fiction titles/year. Titles distributed through University of Alabama Press. No open submissions except through Ronald Sukenick Innovative Fiction Prize. Does not accept unsolicited mss. See website for contest info. Agented fiction 5%.

FICTION Subjects include experimental, feminist, gay, lesbian., innovative; modernist/postmodern; avant-garde; anarchist; minority; cyberpunk.

TIPS "Be familiar with our list."

FREDERICK FELL PUBLISHERS, INC.

2131 Hollywood Blvd., Suite 305, Hollywood FL 33020. (954)925-5242. **Fax:** (954)455-4243. **E-mail:** fellpub@aol.com. **Website:** www.fellpub.com. **Contact:** Barbara Newman, senior editor. Publishes hardcover and trade paperback originals. **Publishes 25 titles/year. 4,000 queries received/year. 1,000 mss received/year. 95% of books from first-time authors. 95% from unagented writers. Pays negotiable royalty on retail price. Pays up to $10,000 advance.** Publishes book

1 year after acceptance of ms. Accepts simultaneous submissions. Responds in 1 month to queries. Responds in 3 months to proposals. Guidelines online.

○ "Fell is now publishing 50 e-books per year."

NONFICTION Subjects include business, economics, child guidance, education, ethnic, film, cinema, stage, health, medicine, hobbies, money, finance, spirituality. "We are reviewing in all categories. Advise us of the top 3 competitive titles for your work and the reasons why the public would benefit by having your book published." Submit proposal package, including outline, 3 sample chapters, author bio, publicity ideas, market analysis. Reviews artwork/photos. Send photocopies.

TIPS "We are most interested in well-written, timely nonfiction with strong sales potential. We will not consider topics that appeal to a small, select audience. Learn markets and be prepared to help with sales and promotion. Show us how your book is unique or better than the competition."

FENCE BOOKS

Science Library 320, Univ. of Albany, 1400 Washington Ave., Albany NY 12222. (518)591-8162. **E-mail:** fence.fencebooks@gmail.com; robfence@gmail.com. **Website:** www.fenceportal.org. **Contact:** Rob Arnold, Submissions Manager. Hardcover originals. Guidelines online.

&— *"Fence is closed to submissions right now.* We'll have another reading period in the Spring. Fence Books offers 2 book contests (in addition to the National Poetry Series) with 2 sets of guidelines and entry forms on our website."

POETRY Enter National Poetry Series Contest. See Open Competition Guidelines online. Also the annual Fence Books Motherwell Prize 2011 ($5,000) for a first or second book of poetry by a woman. Submit 48-60 pages during the month of November; and Fence Modern Poets Series 2011, for a poet writing in English at any stage in his or her career. $25 entry fee. Submissions may be sent through regular USPS mail, UPS, Fedex-type couriers, or certified mail.

TIPS "At present Fence Books is a self-selecting publisher; mss come to our attention through our contests and through editors' investigations. We hope to become open to submissions of poetry and fiction mss in the near future."

FERGUSON PUBLISHING CO.

Infobase Publishing, 132 W. 31st St., 17th Floor, New York NY 10001. (800)322-8755. **E-mail:** editorial@ factsonfile.com. **Website:** www.infobasepublishing. com. Estab. 1940. Publishes hardcover and trade paperback originals. **Publishes 50 titles/year. Pays by project.** Responds in 6 months to queries. Guidelines online.

&— "We are primarily a career education publisher that publishes for schools and libraries. We need writers who have expertise in a particular career or career field (for possible full-length books on a specific career or field)."

NONFICTION "We publish work specifically for the elementary/junior high/high school/college library reference market. Works are generally encyclopedic in nature. Our current focus is career encyclopedias and young adult career sets and series. We consider manuscripts that cross over into the trade market." No mass market, poetry, scholarly, or juvenile books, please. Query or submit an outline and 1 sample chapter.

TIPS "We like writers who know the market—former or current librarians or teachers or guidance counselors."

DAVID FICKLING BOOKS

31 Beamont St., Oxford En OX1 2NP, United Kingdom. (018)65-339000. **Fax:** (018)65-339009. **E-mail:** DFickling@randomhouse.co.uk; tburgess@randomhouse.co.uk. **Website:** www.avidficklingbooks. co.uk. **Publishes 12 titles/year.** Responds to mss in 3 months.

FICTION Considers all categories. Recently published *Once Upon a Time in the North*, by Phillip Pullman; *The Curious Incident of the Dog in the Night-time*, by Mark Haddon; *The Boy in the Striped Pyjamas*, by John Boyne. Submit 3 sample chapters.

FIFTH HOUSE PUBLISHERS

Fitzhenry & Whiteside, 195 Allstate Parkway, Markham ON L3R 4&8, Canada. (403)571-5230; (800)387-9776. **E-mail:** stewart@fifthhousepublishers. ca. **Website:** www.fifthhousepublishers.ca. **Contact:** Stephanie Stewart, publisher. Estab. 1982.

&— "Fifth House Publishers, a Fitzhenry & Whiteside company, is committed to "bringing the West to the rest" by publishing approximately fifteen books a year about the land and people who make this region unique. We publish the acclaimed Going Wild series, Pierre Berton's History for Young Canadians, Keepers of Life, the Western Canadian Classics series, the Prairie Gardening series, and more. Our books are selected for their quality and contribution to the understanding of western-Canadian (and Canadian) history, culture, and environment."

FILTER PRESS, LLC

P.O. Box 95, Palmer Lake CO 80133. (719)481-2420; (888)570-2663. **Fax:** (719)481-2420. **E-mail:** info@filterpressbooks.com. **Website:** www.filterpressbooks.com. **Contact:** Doris Baker, president. Estab. 1957. Publishes trade paperback originals and reprints. **Publishes 4-6 titles/year. Pays 10-12% royalty on wholesale price.** Publishes book 18 months after acceptance.

NONFICTION Subjects include Americana, anthropology, archeology, ethnic, history, regional., crafts and crafts people of the Southwest. Query with outline and SASE. Reviews artwork/photos.

⟲ FINDHORN PRESS

Delft Cottage, Dyke, Forres Scotland IV36 2TF, United Kingdom. (44)(1309) 690-582. **Fax:** (44)(131) 777-2711. **E-mail:** submissions@findhornpress.com. **Website:** www.findhornpress.com. **Contact:** Thierry Bogliolo, publisher. Estab. 1971. Publishes trade paperback originals. **Publishes 20 titles/year. 1,000 queries received/year. 50% of books from first-time authors. 80% from unagented writers. Pays 10-15% royalty on wholesale price.** Publishes book 1 year after acceptance. Responds in 2-3 months to proposals. Catalog and guidelines online.

NONFICTION Subjects include health, nature, spirituality. No autobiographies.

FINNEY COMPANY, INC.

8075 215th St. W., Lakeville MN 55044. (952)469-6699. **Fax:** (952)469-1968. **E-mail:** feedback@finneyco.com. **Website:** www.finneyco.com. **Contact:** Alan E. Krysan, president. Publishes trade paperback originals. **Publishes 2 titles/year. Pays 10% royalty on wholesale price. Pays advance.** Publishes book 1 year after acceptance. Responds in 2-3 months to queries.

NONFICTION Subjects include business, economics, education., career exploration/development. Finney publishes career development educational materials. Query with SASE. Reviews artwork/photos.

⊕ FIRST EDITION DESIGN PUBLISHING

5202 Old Ashwood Dr., Sarasota FL 34233. (941)921-2607. **Fax:** (617)249-1694. **E-mail:** support@firsteditiondesign.com; submission@firsteditiondesign.com. **Website:** www.firsteditiondesignpublishing.

com. **Contact:** Deborah E. Gordon, executive editor; Tom Gahan, marketing director. Estab. 1985. **Publishes 750+ titles/year. 45% of books from first-time authors. 95% from unagented writers. Pays royalty 30-70% on retail price.** Publishes book Accept to publish time is one week to two months. after acceptance of ms. Accepts simultaneous submissions. Send SAE for catalog. Guidelines available free on request or online.

NONFICTION Subjects include agriculture, alternative lifestyles, Americana, animals, architecture, art, business, career guidance, contemporary culture, counseling, creative nonfiction, education, ethnic, gay, government, health, history, humanities, language, law, memoirs, military, money, multicultural, nature, New Age, philosophy, psychology, recreation, regional, religion, science, sex, social sciences, sociology, spirituality, womens issues, womens studies, world affairs, young adult. Send complete ms electronically.

FICTION Subjects include adventure, confession, ethnic, experimental, fantasy, feminist, gay, gothic, historical, horror, humor, literary, mainstream, multicultural, mystery, occult, poetry, regional, religious, romance, science fiction, short story collections, spiritual, suspense, western, young adult. Submit complete ms electronically.

POETRY Submit complete ms electronically.

TIPS "Follow our FAQs listed on our website."

◑ FITZHENRY & WHITESIDE LTD.

195 Allstate Pkwy., Markham ON L3R 4T8, Canada. (905)477-9700. **Fax:** (905)477-9179. **E-mail:** fitzkids@fitzhenry.ca; godwit@fitzhenry.ca; charkin@fitzhenry.ca. **Website:** www.fitzhenry.ca/. **Contact:** Sharon Fitzhenry, president; Cathy Sandusky, children's publisher; Christie Harkin, submissions editor. **Publishes 15 titles/year. 10% of books from first-time authors. Pays authors 8-10% royalty with escalations. Offers "respectable" advances for picture books, split 50/50 between author and illustrator. Pays illustrators by project and royalty. Pays photographers per photo.** Publishes book 1-2 years after acceptance.

✎ Emphasis on Canadian authors and illustrators, subject or perspective.

TIPS "We respond to quality."

FIVE STAR PUBLICATIONS, INC.

P.O. Box 6698, Chandler AZ 85246. (480)940-8182. **Fax:** (480)940-8787. **E-mail:** info@fivestarpublications.com. **Website:** www.fivestarpublications.com. **Contact:** Linda Radke, president. Estab. 1985.

☛ "Helps produce and market award-winning books."

TIPS Features the Purple Dragonfly Book Awards and Royal Dragonfly Book Awards, which were conceived and designed with children in mind. "Not only do we want to recognize and honor accomplished authors in the field of children's literature, but we also want to highlight and reward up-and-coming newly published authors, as well as younger published writers. In our efforts to include everyone, the awards are divided into distinct subject categories, ranging from books on the environment and cooking to books on sports and family issues. (Please see the complete categories list on the entry form on our website.)

🌑 FLARESTACK POETS

P.O. Box 14779, Birmingham, West Midlands B13 3GU, United Kingdom. **E-mail:** meria@btinternet.com; jacquierowe@hotmail.co.uk. **Website:** www.flarestackpoets.co.uk. **Contact:** Meredith Andrea and Jacqui Rowe. Estab. 2008. **Pays 25% royalty and 6 contributor's copies.** Responds in 6 weeks.

◒ *Currently not accepting submissions.*

POETRY Flarestack Poets wants "poems that dare outside current trends, even against the grain." Does not want "poems that fail to engage with either language or feeling." Publishes 8 chapbooks/year and 1 anthology. Manuscripts are selected through open submission and competition. "Our first chapbooks are winners of the 2009 Flarestack Poets Pamphlet competition. Thereafter we will consider open submissions." Chapbooks are 20-30 pages, professional photocopy, saddle-stitched, card cover. Query first with a few sample poems and a cover letter with brief bio and publication credits. Ms may include previously published poems.

FLASHLIGHT PRESS

527 Empire Blvd., Brooklyn NY 11225. (718)288-8300. **Fax:** (718)972-6307. **E-mail:** editor@flashlightpress.com. **Website:** www.flashlightpress.com. **Contact:** Shari Dash Greenspan, editor. Estab. 2004. Publishes hardcover and trade paperback originals. **1,200 queries received/year. 120 mss received/year. Pays 8-10% royalty on wholesale price.** Publishes book 36 months after acceptance of ms. Accepts simultaneous submissions. "Due to the large number of queries we receive, we are no longer able to send individual replies for queries we do not wish to pursue. You will receive an automated reply that we received your query." Responds in 3 months to mss. Catalog and guidelines online.

FICTION "Only publishes fiction (2 picture books/year), so we're extremely selective. Looking for gems."

TIPS "Our audience is 4-8 years old. Follow our online submissions guide."

FLOATING BRIDGE PRESS

PO Box 18814, Seattle WA 98118. **E-mail:** floatingbridgepress@yahoo.com. **Website:** www.floatingbridgepress.org. Estab. 1994.

POETRY Floating Bridge Press publishes chapbooks and anthologies by Washington State poets, selected through an annual competition (see below). For a sample chapbook or anthology, send $13 postpaid.

FLORICANTO PRESS

Inter American Development, 650 Castro St., Suite 120-331, Mountain View CA 94041-2055. (415)552-1879. **Fax:** (702)995-1410. **E-mail:** info@floricantopress.com. **Website:** www.floricantopress.com. **Contact:** Roberto Cabello-Argandona. Estab. 1982. Publishes hardcover and trade paperback originals and reprints. Catalog for #10 SASE. Guidelines online.

☛ "Floricanto Press is dedicated to promoting Latino thought and culture."

NONFICTION Subjects include anthropology, archeology, cooking, foods, nutrition, ethnic, Hispanic, health, medicine, history, language, literature, psychology, women's issues/studies. "We are looking primarily for nonfiction popular (but serious) titles that appeal to the general public on Hispanic subjects." Submit ms with word count, author bio, SASE.

TIPS "Audience is general public interested in Hispanic culture. We need authors that are willing to promote their work heavily."

FLORIDA ACADEMIC PRESS

P.O. Box 540, Gainesville FL 32602. (352)332-5104. **Fax:** (352)331-6003. **E-mail:** fapress@gmail.com. **Website:** www.floridaacademicpress.com. Max Vargas, CEO (fiction/nonfiction/scholarly) Estab. 1997. Hardcover and trade paperback originals. **Publishes 4-8 titles/year. 2,000 queries received/year. 1,200 mss received/year. 90% of books from first-time authors. 100% from unagented writers. 5-8% royalty on retail price and higher on sales of 2,500+ copies a year.** Publishes book 3 months after acceptance of ms.

Responds in 2 months on mss if rejected; 3-4 months if sent for external review. Catalog available online.

NONFICTION Subjects include government/politics, philosophy, psychology, social sciences, world affairs. We only assess complete mss that do not require extensive copy-editing. SASE returns. Submit completed ms only and CV. Query letters or works in progress of little interest—submit only final ms. Reviews artwork/photos. Send photocopies.

FICTION Subjects include historical, literary. No poetry, poetry in translation, religious or short story collections. Submit completed ms by hard copy only.

TIPS Considers complete mss only. "Manuscripts we decide to publish must be re-submitted by the author in ready-to-print PDF files. Match our needs—do not send blindly. Books we accept for publication must be submitted in camera-ready format. The Press covers all publication/promotional expenditures."

FLUX

Llewellyn Worldwide, Ltd., Llewellyn Worldwide, Ltd., 2143 Wooddale Dr., Woodbury MN 55125. (651)312-8613. **Fax:** (651)291-1908. **Website:** www.fluxnow.com; fluxnow.blogspot.com. **Contact:** Brian Farrey, acquisitions editor. Estab. 2005. **Publishes 21 titles/year. 50% of books from first-time authors. Pays royalties of 10-15% based on wholesale price.** Catalog and guidelines available on website.

◯ *Does not accept unsolicited mss.*

FICTION Young Adults: adventure, contemporary, fantasy, history, humor, problem novels, religion, science fiction, sports, suspense. Average word length: 50,000.

TIPS "Read contemporary teen books. Be aware of what else is out there. If you don't read teen books, you probably shouldn't write them. Know your audience. Write incredibly well. Do not condescend."

FLYING PEN PRESS LLC

1660 Niagara St., Denver CO 80228. (303)375-0499. **Fax:** (303)375-0499. **E-mail:** GeneralInquiries@FlyingPenPress.com; Publisher@FlyingPenPress.com. **E-mail:** Submissions@FlyingPenPress.com. **Website:** www.flyingpenpress.com. **Contact:** David A. Rozansky, publisher. Estab. 2007. Publishes trade paperback and electronic originals. **Publishes 5/2010 titles/year. Recevies 120 queries/year; 360 mss/year. 55% of books from first-time authors. 88% from unagented writers. Pays 35-46% royalty; share of gross profits (net receipts less printing costs). No**

advances. Publishes book 6 months after acceptance. Accepts simultaneous submissions. Responds in less than 1 month to queries/proposals; 6 months to mss. Catalog free on request; available online. Guidelines free on request and available online.

◯ *No unsolicited mss.*

NONFICTION Subjects include alternative lifestyles, Americana, animals, anthropology, archaeology, business, career guidance, child guidance, communications, community, computers, contemporary culture, counseling, creative nonfiction, economics, electronics, entertainment, environment, ethnic, finance, games, government, health, history, hobbies, humanities, labor, language, literature, medicine, memoirs, military, money, muticultural, nature, parenting, philosophy, politics, public affairs, recreation, regional (CO, S.W. U.S., Nat'l Parks, Rocky Mountains), science, social sciences, sociology, software, translation, transportation, travel, war, world affairs., aviation, aerospace, game books, travel guides, puzzle books. Submit book proposals and completed ms by e-mail only. Reviews artwork/photos. Send JPG, TIF, or PDF files.

FICTION Subjects include adventure, comic books, contemporary, ethnic, experimental, fantasy, gothic, historical, horror, humor, literary, mainstream, military, multicultural, mystery, regional, romance, science fiction, short story collections, sports, suspense, translation, western. "We have changed our focus to be platform centric. We seek ideas for series, and we invite trademark holders and blogging personalities to submit ideas for a line of books." Submit completed ms by e-mail only.

TIPS "Create a series concept that will attract readers, which we can then assign to writers for several books in the line. Trademarked characters, movie and TV tie-ins, and popular blogs are suitable platforms."

FOCAL PRESS

Imprint of Elsevier (USA), Inc., 30 Corporate Dr., Suite 400, Burlington MA 01803. **Fax:** (781)221-1615. **Website:** www.focalpress.com. **Contact:** Amorette Petersen, publishing director; for further editorial contacts, visit the contacts page on the company's Website. Estab. US, 1981; UK, 1938. Publishes hardcover and paperback originals and reprints. **Publishes 80-120 UK-US titles/year; entire firm publishes over 1,000 titles/year. 25% of books from first-time authors. 90% from unagented writers.** Publishes book

6 months after acceptance. Accepts simultaneous submissions. Responds in 2 months to queries. Catalog for #10 SASE. Guidelines online.

8—¬ "Focal Press provides excellent books for students, advanced amateurs, and working professionals involved in all areas of media technology. Topics of interest include photography (digital and traditional techniques), film/video, audio, broadcasting, and cinematography, through to journalism, radio, television, video, and writing. Currently emphasizing graphics, gaming, animation, and multimedia."

NONFICTION Subjects include film, cinema, stage, photography, film, cinematography, broadcasting, theater and performing arts, audio, sound and media technology. We do not publish collections of photographs or books composed primarily of photographs. To submit a proposal for consideration by Elsevier, please fill in the **proposal form** online. Once we have had a chance to review your proposal in line with our publishing plan and budget, we will contact you to discuss the next steps. Reviews artwork/photos.

Ⓐ FODOR'S TRAVEL PUBLICATIONS, INC.

Imprint of Random House, Inc., 1745 Broadway, New York NY 10019. **E-mail:** editors@fodors.com. **Website:** www.fodors.com. Estab. 1936. Publishes trade paperback originals. **Most titles are collective works, with contributions as works for hire. Most contributions are updates of previously published volumes.** Accepts simultaneous submissions. Responds in 2 months to queries. Catalog available free.

◯ "If you're interested in working for Fodor's as a travel writer, send your résumé and writing clips, together with a cover letter explaining your qualifications and areas of expertise, to editors@fodors.com. You may also mail materials to: Fodor's Travel Publications, Researcher Writer Positions, 1745 Broadway, 15th floor, New York, NY 10019. Remember that most Fodor's writers live in the areas they cover. Note that we do not accept unsolicited manuscripts."

8—¬ Fodor's publishes travel books on many regions and countries.

NONFICTION Subjects include travel. We are interested in unique approaches to favorite destinations. Writers seldom review our catalog or our list and often query about books on topics that we're already covering. Beyond that, it's important to review competition and to say what the proposed book will add. Do not send originals without first querying as to our interest in the project. We're not interested in travel literature or in proposals for general travel guidebooks. Agented submissions only. Submit proposal and résumé via mail.

TIPS In preparing your query or proposal, remember that it's the only argument Fodor's will hear about why your book will be a good one, and why you think it will sell; and it's also best evidence of your ability to create the book you propose. Craft your proposal well and carefully so that it puts your best foot forward.

FOREIGN POLICY ASSOCIATION

470 Park Ave. S., New York NY 10016. (212)481-8100. **Fax:** (212)481-9275. **E-mail:** info@fpa.org; rnolan@fpa.org. **Website:** www.fpa.org. Publishes 2 periodicals, an annual eight episode PBS Television series with DVD and an occasional hardcover and trade paperback original. Accepts simultaneous submissions. Catalog available free.

8—¬ The Foreign Policy Association, a nonpartisan, not-for-profit educational organization founded in 1918, is a catalyst for developing awareness, understanding of and informed opinion on US foreign policy and global issues. Through its balanced, nonpartisan publications, FPA seeks to encourage individuals in schools, communities and the workplace to participate in the foreign policy process.

NONFICTION Subjects include government, politics, history, foreign policy.

TIPS "Audience is students and people with an interest, but not necessarily any expertise, in foreign policy and international relations."

FORTRESS PRESS

P.O. Box 1209, Minneapolis MN 55440. (612)330-3300. **Website:** www.fortresspress.com. Publishes hardcover and trade paperback originals. **Pays royalty on retail price.** Accepts simultaneous submissions. Catalog free. Guidelines online.

8—¬ "Fortress Press publishes academic books in Biblical studies, theology, Christian ethics, church history, and professional books in pastoral care and counseling."

NONFICTION Subjects include religion, women's issues/studies., church history, African-American studies. Query with annotated TOC, brief CV, sample pages, SASE. Please study guidelines before submitting.

FORT ROSS INC.– INTERNATIONAL RIGHTS

26 Arthur Pl, Yonkers NY 10701. (914)375-6448. E-mail: fortross@optonline.net. **Website:** www.fortrossinc.com. **Contact:** Dr. Kartsev, executive director. Estab. 1992. Publishes in hardcover and paperback originals. Publishes book 12 months after acceptance of ms. Accepts simultaneous submissions. Responds in 1 month to queries and proposals; 3 months to mss.

⌐ "Generally, we publish Russia-related books in English or Russian. Sometimes we publish various fiction and nonfiction books in collaboration with the east European publishers in translation. We are looking mainly for well-established authors." Publishes paperback originals. 100 queries received/year; 100 mss received/year. Pays 6-8% royalty on wholesale price or makes outright purchase of $500-1,500; negotiable advance.

FORWARD MOVEMENT

412 Sycamore St., Cincinnati OH 45202. (513)721-6659; (800)543-1813. **Fax:** (513)721-0729. **E-mail:** rschmidt@forwarddaybyday.com. **Website:** www.forwardmovement.org. **Contact:** Rev. Dr. Richard H. Schmidt, editor and director. Estab. 1934. **Publishes 30 titles/year.** Responds in 1 month. Catalog and guidelines free. Guidelines online.

⌐ "Forward Movement was established to help reinvigorate the life of the church. Many titles focus on the life of prayer, where our relationship with God is centered, death, marriage, baptism, recovery, joy, the Episcopal Church and more. Currently emphasizing prayer/spirituality."

NONFICTION Subjects include religion. "We are an agency of the Episcopal Church.", "There is a special need for tracts of under 8 pages. (A page usually runs about 200 words.) On rare occasions, we publish a full-length book." Query with SASE or by e-mail with complete ms attached.

FICTION Subjects include juvenile.

TIPS "Audience is primarily Episcopalians and other Christians."

WALTER FOSTER PUBLISHING, INC.

3 Wrigley, Suite A, Irvine CA 92618. (800)426-0099. **Fax:** (949)380-7575. **E-mail:** info@walterfoster.com. **Website:** www.walterfoster.com. Estab. 1922. Publishes trade paperback originals.

⌐ "Walter Foster publishes instructional how-to/craft instruction as well as licensed products."

FOX CHAPEL PUBLISHING

1970 Broad St., East Petersburg PA 17520. (800)457-9112. **Fax:** (717)560-4702. **E-mail:** CustomerService@FoxChapelPublishing.com. **Website:** www.foxchapelpublishing.com. **Contact:** Peg Couch, acquisitions editor. Publishes hardcover and trade paperback originals and trade paperback reprints. **Publishes 25-40 titles/year. 50% of books from first-time authors. 100% from unagented writers. Pays royalty or makes outright purchase. Pays variable advance.** Publishes book 18 months after acceptance. Accepts simultaneous submissions. Responds in 2 months to queries.

⌐ Fox Chapel publishes woodworking, woodcarving, and design titles for professionals and hobbyists.

NONFICTION Submission guidelines on website. Reviews artwork/photos. Send photocopies.

TIPS "We're looking for knowledgeable artists, craftspeople and woodworkers, all experts in their fields, to write books of lasting value."

● FRANCES LINCOLN CHILDREN'S BOOKS

Frances Lincoln, 4 Torriano Mew, Torriano Ave., London NW5 2RZ, Wales. 00442072844009. **E-mail:** flcb@franceslincoln.com. **Website:** www.franceslincoln.com. Estab. 1977. **Publishes 100 titles/year. 6% of books from first-time authors.** Publishes book 18 months after acceptance. Accepts simultaneous submissions. Responds to mss in minimum of 6 weeks.

⌐ "Our company was founded by Frances Lincoln in 1977. We published our first books two years later, and we have been creating illustrated books of the highest quality ever since, with special emphasis on gardening, walking and the outdoors, art, architecture, design and landscape. In 1983, we started to publish illustrated books for children. Since then we have won many awards and prizes with both fiction and nonfiction children's books."

NONFICTION Picture books, young readers, middle readers, young adult: activity books, animal, biography, careers, cooking, graphic novels, history, multicultural, nature/environment, religion, social issues, special needs. Query by e-mail.

FICTION Picture books, young readers, middle readers, young adults: adventure, animal, anthology, fantasy, folktales, health, history, humor, multicultural, nature/environment, special needs, sports. Query by e-mail.

FREE SPIRIT PUBLISHING, INC.

217 Fifth Ave. N., Suite 200, Minneapolis MN 55401-1299. (612)338-2068. **Fax:** (612)337-5050. **E-mail:** acquisitions@freespirit.com. **Website:** www.freespirit.com. Estab. 1983. Publishes trade paperback originals and reprints. **Publishes 12-18 titles/year. 5% of books from first-time authors. 75% from unagented writers. Pays advance.** Catalog and guidelines online.

8—∗ "We believe passionately in empowering kids to learn to think for themselves and make their own good choices."

NONFICTION Subjects include child guidance, education, pre-K-12, study and social sciences skills, special needs, differentiation but not textbooks or basic skills books like reading, counting, etc., health, medicine, mental/emotional health for/about children, psychology for/about children, sociology for/about children. "Many of our authors are educators, mental health professionals, and youth workers involved in helping kids and teens." No fiction or picture storybooks, poetry, single biographies or autobiographies, books with mythical or animal characters, or books with religious or New Age content. "We are not looking for academic or religious materials, or books that analyze problems with the nation's school systems." Query with cover letter stating qualifications, intent, and intended audience and market analysis (how your book stands out from the field), along with outline, 2 sample chapters, résumé, SASE. Do not send original copies of work.

FICTION "Please review catalog and author guidelines (both available online) before submitting proposal." Responds to queries in 4-6 months. "If you'd like material returned, enclose a SASE with sufficient postage." Accepts queries only—not submissions—by e-mail.

TIPS "Our books are issue-oriented, jargon-free, and solution-focused. Our audience is children, teens, teachers, parents and youth counselors. We are especially concerned with kids' social and emotional well-being and look for books with ready-to-use strategies for coping with today's issues at home or in school—written in everyday language. We are not looking for

academic or religious materials, or books that analyze problems with the nation's school systems. Instead, we want books that offer practical, positive advice so kids can help themselves, and parents and teachers can help kids succeed."

FREESTONE/PEACHTREE, JR.

1700 Chattahoochee Ave., Atlanta GA 30318. (404)876-8761. **Fax:** (404)875-2578. **E-mail:** hello@peachtree-online.com. **Website:** www.peachtree-online.com. **Contact:** Helen Harriss, acquisitions; Loraine Joyner, art director; Melanie McMahon Ives, production manager. Estab. 1977. **Publishes 4-8 titles/year.** Publishes book 1-2 years after acceptance. Accepts simultaneous submissions. Responds in 6 months-1 year.

◑ Freestone and Peachtree, Jr. are imprints of Peachtree Publishers. See the listing for Peachtree for submission information. No e-mail or fax queries or submissions, please.

NONFICTION Picture books, young readers, middle readers, young adults: history, sports. Picture books: animal, health, multicultural, nature/environment, science, social issues, special needs.

FICTION Middle Readers: adventure, animal, history, nature/environment, sports. Young Adults: fiction, history, biography, mystery, adventure. Does not want to see science fiction, religion, or romance. Submit 3 sample chapters by postal mail only. No query necessary.

FRONT STREET

Boyds Mills Press, 815 Church St., Honesdale PA 18431. **Website:** www.frontstreetbooks.com. **Contact:** Acquisitions Editor. Estab. 1994. Publishes hardcover originals and trade paperback reprints. **Publishes 10-15 titles/year. 2,000 queries received/year. 5,000 mss received/year. 30% of books from first-time authors. 60% from unagented writers. Pays royalty on retail price. Pays advance.** Publishes book 1 year after acceptance of ms. Accepts simultaneous submissions. Responds in 3 months. Catalog and guidelines online.

8—∗ "We are an independent publisher of books for children and young adults."

FICTION Subjects include adventure, historical, humor, juvenile, literary, picture books, young adult, adventure, fantasy/science fiction fiction, historical, mystery/suspense, problem novels, sports. Query with SASE. Submit complete ms, if under 100 pages, with SASE. Keeps illustration samples on file. Reviews artwork/photos w/ms. Send photocopies. "High-quality fiction for children and young adults." Publishes hardcover originals and trade paperback reprints. Books: coated paper; offset printing; case binding; 4-color illustrations. Averages 15 fiction titles/year. Distributes titles through independent sales reps, wholesalers, and via order line directly from Front Street. Promotes titles through sales and professional conferences, sales reps, reviews, catalogs, website, and direct marketing.

POETRY Submit 25 sample poems.

TIPS "Read through our recently published titles and review our website. Check to see what's on the market and in our catalog before submitting your story. Feel free to query us if you're not sure."

FULCRUM PUBLISHING

4690 Table Mountain Dr., Suite 100, Golden CO 80403. **E-mail:** info@fulcrum-books.com. **Website:** www.fulcrum-books.com. **Contact:** T. Baker, acquisitions editor. Estab. 1984. **Pays authors royalty based on wholesale price. Offers advances.** Catalog available for SASE. Ms Guidelines online.

NONFICTION Middle and early readers: Western history, nature/ environment, Native American. Submit complete ms or submit outline/synopsis and 2 sample chapters. "Publisher does not send response letters unless we are interested in publishing."

TIPS "Research our line first. We look for books that appeal to the school market and trade. "

⊕ FUNNELBRAIN LLC

28310 Roadside Dr., Suite 229, Agoura Hills CA 91301. **E-mail:** writers@funnelbrain.com. **Website:** www.funnelbrain.com. **Contact:** Jack Dennison, executive chairman. Joe DeTuno, CEO Estab. 2008. Publishes electronic originals and reprints. **Publishes 100-1,000 titles/year. Pays 50% royalty on retail price.** Accepts simultaneous submissions. Responds in 1 month on queries, proposals, and mss. We typically respond within 5 business days. Catalog available online. Guidelines available online and by e-mail.

NONFICTION "We are looking for writers with expertise and enthusiasm in all academic subject areas, as well as non-academic subjects. We target an audience of middle school, high school, and college students, as well as lifelong learners. Writers will do well to focus on a particular niche where the writer has expertise. All queries should be via e-mail."

FICTION Fiction categories and requirements are the same as for nonfiction.

POETRY "We have no plans to publish poetry, but flashcards and quizzes about poetry are welcome."

TIPS "Writers submitting queries or proposals should describe their areas of expertise or interest and qualifications. If possible, writers should identify the particular niche audience they expect their flashcards to serve. While broad topics are welcome, more specific and narrowly focused topics will tend to perform better and face less competition."

FUTURECYCLE PRESS

313 Pan Will Rd., Mineral Bluff GA 30559. (706)622-4454. **E-mail:** submissions@futurecycle.org. **Website:** www.futurecycle.org. **Contact:** Robert S. King, director/editor-in-chief. Estab. 2007. **Pays 10% royalty and 25 author's copies.** Responds to mss in 3 months. Guidelines online.

POETRY Wants "poetry from highly skilled poets, whether well known or emerging. With a few exceptions, we are eclectic in our editorial tastes." Does not want concrete or visual poetry. Publishes 4 poetry books/year and 2 chapbooks/year. Ms. selected through open submission and competition. "We read unsolicited mss. but also conduct a yearly poetry book competition." Books are 60-90 pages; offset print, perfect-bound, with glossy, full color cover stock, b&w inside. Chapbooks are 20-40 pages, offset print, saddle-stitched. Submit complete ms, no need to query.

GAMBIT PUBLISHING

1725 W. Glenlake Ave., #1W, Chicago IL 60660. **E-mail:** gailglaser@gambitpublishingonline.com; editor@gambitpublishingonline.com. **Website:** www.gambitpublishingonline.com. **Contact:** Gail Glaser, editor (film, biography, popular culture). Publishes hardcover originals and reprints; trade paperback originals and reprints; mass market paperback originals and reprints; electronic originals and reprints. **Publishes 4 titles/year. 75% of books from first-time authors. 100% from unagented writers. Pays 10-60% royalty on retail price. No advance.** Publishes book 3 months after acceptance. Accepts simultaneous submissions. Responds in 1 month on queries, proposals, and mss. Catalog available online and for #10 SASE. Guidelines free by e-mail at website.

NONFICTION Subjects include architecture, art, contemporary culture, cooking, creative nonfiction, dance, entertainment, environment, games, history, hobbies, house and home, humanities, language, literary criticism, marine subjects, memoirs, military, money, multicultural, music, nature, photography, recreation, regional, sex, social sciences, travel, women's issues/studies, film, criticism. Reviews artwork only if necessary to the book. Send photocopies.

FICTION Subjects include adventure, comic books, contemporary, feminist, historical, humor, juvenile, literary, mainstream, military, multicultural, mystery, picture books, plays, poetry, regional, short story collections, suspense, war, western. "We're primarily interestsed in movies, tv, pop culture, but will look over many other subjects." Query with SASE. Submit proposal package, including synopsis, 2 sample chapters. Submit complete ms.

POETRY "We are open to most poetry." Query. Submit 3 sample poems. Submit complete ms.

GASLIGHT PUBLICATIONS

P.O. Box 1344, Studio City CA 91614. **Website:** http://playerspress.home.att.net/gaslight_catalogue.htm. **Contact:** Simon Waters, fiction editor (Sherlock Holmes only). Estab. 1960.

TIPS "Please send only Sherlock Holmes material. Other stuff just wastes time and money."

GAUTHIER PUBLICATIONS, INC.

Frog Legs Ink, P.O. Box 806241, Saint Clair Shores MI 48080. **Fax:** (586)279-1515. **E-mail:** info@gauthierpublications.com; submissions@gauthierpublications.com. **Website:** www.eatabook.com. **Contact:** Elizabeth Gauthier, creative director (children's/fiction). Hardcover originals and trade paperback originals. **Publishes 10 titles/year. 50% of books from first-time authors. 50% from unagented writers. Pays 5-10% royalty on retail price.** Guidelines available for #10 SASE, or online http://gauthierpublications.com, or by e-mail at: submissions@gauthierpublications.com.

Frog Legs Ink (imprint) is always looking for new writers and illustrators. We are currently looking for horror/thriller short stories for an upcoming collection.

NONFICTION Subjects include creative nonfiction, photography, self help. Query with SASE.

FICTION Subjects include adventure, confession, ethnic, experimental, fantasy, feminist, gothic, historical, horror, humor, juvenile, literary, mainstream, contemporary, military, war, multicultural, multimedia, mystery, plays, poetry, poetry in translation, regional, religious, romance. "We are particularly interested in mystery, thriller, graphic novels, horror and Young Adult areas for the upcoming year. We do, however, consider most subjects if they are intriguing and well written." Query with SASE. "Please do not send full ms unless we ask for it If we are interested we will request a few sample chapters and outline. Since we do take the time to read and consider each piece, response can take up to 8 weeks. Mailed submissions without SASE included are destroyed if we are not interested."

POETRY "We are particularly interested in mystery, thriller, graphic novels, horror and Young Adult areas for the upcoming year. We do, however, consider most subjects if they are intriguing and well written."Query with SASE.

GAY SUNSHINE PRESS AND LEYLAND PUBLICATIONS

P.O. Box 410690, San Francisco CA 94141-0690. **Website:** www.leylandpublications.com. **Contact:** Winston Leyland, editor. Estab. 1975. Publishes hardcover originals, trade paperback originals and reprints. **Publishes 2-3 titles/year. Pays royalty, or makes outright purchase.** Responds in 6 weeks to queries; 2 months to mss. Catalog for $1.

"Gay history, sex, politics, and culture are the focus of the quality books published by Gay Sunshine Press. Leyland Publications publishes books on popular aspects of gay sexuality and culture."

NONFICTION "We're interested in innovative literary nonfiction which deals with gay lifestyles." No long personal accounts, academic or overly formal titles. Query with SASE. *All unsolicited mss returned unopened.*

FICTION Subjects include erotica, experimental, historical, literary, mystery, science fiction, translation., All gay male material only. Interested in innovative well-written novels on gay themes; also short story collections. "We have a high literary standard for fiction. We desire fiction on gay themes of high literary quality and prefer writers who have already had work published in books or literary magazines. We also publish erotica—short stories and novels." Query with SASE. *All unsolicited mss returned.*

GEM GUIDES BOOK CO.

1275 W. Ninth St., Upland CA 91786. (626)855-1611. **Fax:** (626)855-1610. **E-mail:** gembooks@aol.com. **Website:** www.gemguidesbooks.com. **Contact:** Greg

Warner, editor. Estab. 1965. **Publishes 6-8 titles/year. 60% of books from first-time authors. 100% from unagented writers. Pays 6-10% royalty on retail price.** Publishes book 1 year after acceptance. Accepts simultaneous submissions. Responds in 5 months to queries.

➤ "Gem Guides prefers nonfiction books for the hobbyist in rocks and minerals; lapidary and jewelry-making; crystals and crystal healing; travel and recreation guide books for the West and Southwest; and other regional local interest. Currently emphasizing how-to, field guides, West/Southwest regional interest. De-emphasizing stories, history, poetry."

NONFICTION Subjects include history, Western, hobbies, rockhounding, prospecting, lapidary, jewelry craft, nature, recreation, regional, Western US, science, earth, travel. Query with outline/synopsis and sample chapters with SASE. Reviews artwork/photos.

TIPS "We have a general audience of people interested in recreational activities. Publishers plan and have specific book lines in which they specialize. Learn about the publisher and submit materials compatible with that publisher's product line."

GENESIS PRESS, INC.

P.O. Box 101, Columbus MS 39701. (888)463-4461. **Fax:** (662)329-9399. **E-mail:** customerservice@genesis-press.com. **Website:** www.genesis-press.com. Estab. 1993. Publishes hardcover and trade paperback originals and reprints. Responds in 2 months to queries. Responds in 4 months to mss. Guidelines online.

➤ Genesis Press is the largest privately owned African-American book publisher in the country. Genesis has steadily increased its reach, and now brings its readers everything from suspense and science fiction to Christian-oriented romance and non-fiction.

NONFICTION Submit outline, 3 sample chapters, SASE. If you would like your ms returned, you must follow all the rules on our website. Please use Priority or First Class mail-no Media Mail, Fed Ex, and no metered mail. We cannot return partials or manuscripts outside the US. No International Reply Coupons, please.

FICTION Subjects include adventure, erotica, ethnic, multicultural, mystery, romance, science fiction., women's. Submit clips, 3 sample chapters, SASE.

TIPS Be professional. Always include a cover letter and SASE. Follow the submission guidelines posted on our website or send SASE for a copy.

⊘ GHOST PONY PRESS

P.O. Box 260113, Madison WI 53726. **E-mail:** ghostponypress@hotmail.com. **Contact:** Ingrid Swanberg, editor/publisher. Estab. 1980.

POETRY Query first, with a few sample poems (5-10) and cover letter with brief bio and publication credits. Include SASE. Considers previously published material for book publication. Accepts submissions by postal mail only; no e-mail submissions. Editor sometimes comments briefly on rejected poems. No promised response time. "We currently have a considerable backlog."

GIBBS SMITH

P.O. Box 667, Layton UT 84041. (801)544-9800. **Fax:** (801)544-8853. **E-mail:** info@gibbs-smith.com. **Website:** www.gibbs-smith.com. **Contact:** Suzanne Taylor, associate publisher and creative director (children's activity books); Jennifer Grillone, art acquisitions. Estab. 1969. **Publishes 3 titles/year. 50% of books from first-time authors. 50% from unagented writers. Pays authors royalty of 2% based on retail price or work purchased outright ($500 minimum). Offers advances (average amount: $2,000).** Publishes book 1-2 years after acceptance. Accepts simultaneous submissions. Responds to queries and mss in 2 months. Catalog available for 9×12 SAE and $2.30 postage. Ms guidelines available by e-mail.

NONFICTION Middle readers: activity, arts/crafts, cooking, how-to, nature/environment, science. Average word length: picture books—under 1,000 words; activity books—under 15,000 words. Nonfiction: Submit an outline and writing samples for activity books; query for other types of books.

TIPS "We target ages 5-11. We do not publish young adult novels or chapter books."

⊘ GIFTED EDUCATION PRESS

10201 Yuma Ct., Manassas VA 20109. (703)369-5017. **E-mail:** mfisher345@comcast.net. **Website:** www. giftedpress.com. **Contact:** Maurice Fisher, publisher. Estab. 1981. Publishes trade paperback originals. **Publishes 5 titles/year. 20 queries received/year. 10 mss received/year. 90% of books from first-time authors. 100% from unagented writers. Pays 10% royalty on retail price.** Publishes book 4 months after acceptance. Accepts simultaneous submissions. Responds in 1 month to queries, proposals and mss. Catalog and guidelines online.

➤ "Searching for rigorous texts on teaching science, math and humanities to gifted students."

NONFICTION Subjects include child guidance, computers, electronics, education, history, humanities, philosophy, science, teaching, math, biology, Shakespeare, chemistry, physics, creativity. Query with SASE. *All unsolicited mss returned unopened.* Reviews artwork/photos.

TIPS "Audience includes teachers, parents, gift program supervisors, professors. "Be knowledgeable about your subject. Write clearly and don't use educational jargon."

GIVAL PRESS

Gival Press, LLC, P.O. Box 3812, Arlington VA 22203. (703)351-0079. **E-mail:** givalpress@yahoo.com. **Website:** www.givalpress.com. **Contact:** Robert L. Giron, editor-in-chief (area of interest: literary). Estab. 1998. Publishes trade paperback, electronic originals, and reprints. **Publishes 5-6 titles/year. over 200 queries received/year. 60 mss received/year. 50% of books from first-time authors. 70% from unagented writers. Royalties (% varies).** Publishes book 12 months after acceptance of ms. Accepts simultaneous submissions. Responds in 1 month to queries, 3 months to proposals & mss. Catalog available online, free on request/for #10 SASE. Guidelines available online, by e-mail, free on request/for #10 SASE.

NONFICTION Subjects include gay, lesbian, memoirs, multicultural, translation, womens issues, womens studies., scholarly. Submit between October-December only. Always query first via e-mail; provide plan/ms content, bio, and supportive material. Reviews artwork/photos; query first.

FICTION Subjects include gay, lesbian, literary, multicultural, poetry, translation. Always query first via e-mail; provide description, author's bio, and supportive material.

POETRY Query via e-mail; provide description, bio, etc.; submit 5-6 sample poems via e-mail.

TIPS "Our audience is those who read literary works with depth to the work. Visit our website—there is much to be read/learned from the numerous pages."

✚ GLASS PAGE BOOKS

P.O. Box 333, Signal Mountain TN 37377. **E-mail:** glasspage@comcast.net. **Website:** www.glasspagebooks.com. **Contact:** Pamela Alexander, owner/publisher. Estab. 2011. Publishes hardcover originals, trade paperback originals, mass market paperback originals, electronic originals. **Publishes 3-5 titles/year. 80% of books from first-time authors. 100%**

from unagented writers. **Pays 15-20% royalty on wholesale price.** Publishes book 10 months after acceptance. Accepts simultaneous submissions. Responds in 1 month to proposals; 2 months to mss. Catalogue available online. Ms Guidelines online.

NONFICTION Subjects include government, history, politics, social sciences, spirituality. Query with SASE.

FICTION Subjects include adventure, contemporary, fantasy, juvenile, literary, mainstream, romance, science fiction, suspense, young adult. Query with SASE.

TIPS "Our audience consists of lovers of adventure and fantasy sagas."

GLB PUBLISHERS

1028 Howard St., #503, San Francisco CA 94103. (415)621-8307. **E-mail:** glbpubs@glbpubs.com. **Website:** www.glbpubs.com. Estab. 1990. Hardcover, trade paperback, and electronic originals; trade paperback and electronic reprints. **Publishes 4-5 titles/year. Receives 50 queries/year; 40 mss/year. 20% of books from first-time authors. 90% from unagented writers. Pays 10-25% royalty on retail price.** Publishes book 2-3 months after acceptance. Responds in 2 weeks on queries and proposals; 1 month on mss. Catalog and guidelines free on request and online.

NONFICTION Subjects include alternative lifestyles, child guidance, contemporary culture, creative nonfiction, entertainment, ethnic, gay, government, health, history, humanities, lesbian, medicine, memoirs, multicultural, New Age, photography, politics, social sciences, travel, women's issues. Must apply to and be appropriate for gays, lesbians, bisexuals, transgenders. Submit completed ms. Reviews artwork/photos. Send originals or scanned files.

FICTION Subjects include adventure, erotica, fantasy, feminist, gay, gothic, historical, humor, literary, multicultural, mystery, plays, poetry, romance, science fiction, short story collections, suspense, western, young adult. "Must be gay, lesbian, bisexual, or transgender subjects." Submit completed ms.

POETRY Submit completed ms.

TIPS "Our audience consists of 'adults of all ages.'"

GLENBRIDGE PUBLISHING, LTD.

19923 E. Long Ave., Centennial CO 80016. (800)986-4135; (720)870-8381. **Fax:** (720)230-1209. **Website:** www.glenbridgepublishing.com. Estab. 1986. Publishes hardcover originals and reprints, trade paperback originals. **Publishes 6-8 titles/year. Pays 10% royalty.** Publishes book 1 year after acceptance.

Accepts simultaneous submissions. Responds in 2 months to queries. Catalog online. Guidelines for #10 SASE.

🔑 "Glenbridge has an eclectic approach to publishing. We look for titles that have long-term capabilities."

NONFICTION Subjects include Americana, animals, business, economics, education, environment, family, finance, parenting, writing, film, theatre, communication, cooking, foods, nutrition, health, medicine, history, philosophy, politics & government, psychology, sociology. Publishers for over 23 years, offering books from every genre, with the aim of uplifting, educating, and entertaining. Send e-mail on website. Query with outline/synopsis, sample chapters.

THE GLENCANNON PRESS

P.O. Box 1428, El Cerrito CA 94530. (510)528-4216. **Fax:** (510)528-3194. **E-mail:** merships@yahoo.com. **Website:** www.glencannon.com. **Contact:** Bill Harris (maritime, maritime children's). Estab. 1993. Publishes hardcover and paperback originals and hardcover reprints. **Publishes 4-5/year, 1 fiction title/year. Pays 10-20% royalty.** Publishes book 6-24 months after acceptance. Accepts simultaneous submissions. Responds in 1 month to queries; 2 months to mss.

🔑 "We publish quality books about ships and the sea." Average print order: 1,000. First novel print order: 750. Member PMA, BAIPA. Distributes titles through Baker & Taylor. Promotes titles through direct mail, magazine advertising and word of mouth. Accepts unsolicited mss. Often comments on rejected mss.

FICTION Subjects include adventure, contemporary, ethnic, humor, juvenile, mainstream, military, mystery, war, young adult. "We publish quality books about ships and the sea." Publishes hardcover and paperback originals and hardcover reprints. Books: Smyth: perfect binding; illustrations. Average print order: 1,000. First novel print order: 750. Averages 4-5 total titles, 1 fiction titles/year. Member PMA, BAIPA. Distributes titles through Baker & Taylor. Promotes titles through direct mail, magazine advertising and word of mouth. Submit complete ms. Include brief bio, list of publishing credits. Send SASE for return of ms or send a disposable ms and SASE for reply only.

TIPS "Write a good story in a compelling style."

🅐 DAVID R. GODINE, PUBLISHER

9 Hamilton Place, Boston MA 02108. (617)451-9600. **Fax:** (617)350-0250. **E-mail:** info@godine.com. **Website:** www.godine.com. Estab. 1970.

⭕ This publisher is no longer considering unsolicited manuscripts of any type.

NONFICTION Picture books: alphabet, animal, nature/environment. Young readers: activity books, animal, history, music/dance, nature/environment. Middle readers: activity books, animal, biography, history, music/dance, nature/environment. Young adults: biography, history, music/dance, nature/environment. Only interested in agented material. Query. Include SASE for return of material.

FICTION Picture books: adventure, animal, contemporary, folktales, nature/environment. Young readers: adventure, animal, contemporary, folk or fairy tales, history, nature/environment, poetry. Middle readers: adventure, animal, contemporary, folk or fairy tales, history, mystery, nature/environment, poetry. Young adults/teens: adventure, animal, contemporary, history, mystery, nature/environment, poetry. Only interested in agented material. Query. Include SASE for return of material.

TIPS "E-mail submissions are not accepted. Always enclose a SASE. Keep in mind that we do not accept unsolicited manuscripts and that we rarely use freelance illustrators."

GOLDEN WEST BOOKS

P.O. Box 80250, San Marino CA 91118. (626)458-8148. **Fax:** (626)458-8148. **E-mail:** trainbook@earthlink.net. **Website:** www.goldenwestbooks.com. **Contact:** Donald Duke, publisher. Publishes hardcover originals. **Publishes 3-4 titles/year. 8-10 queries received/year. 5 mss received/year. 75% of books from first-time authors. 100% from unagented writers. Pays 8-10% royalty on wholesale price.** Publishes book 3 months after acceptance. Responds in 3 months to queries. Catalog and guidelines free.

🔑 "Golden West Books specializes in railroad history."

NONFICTION Subjects include Americana, history. Query with SASE. Reviews artwork/photos.

GOLLEHON PRESS, INC.

6157 28th St. SE, Grand Rapids MI 49546. (616)949-3515. **Fax:** (616)949-8674. **E-mail:** editorial@gollehonbooks.com. **Website:** www.gollehonbooks.com. **Contact:** Lori Adams, editor. Publishes hardcover, trade paperback, and mass market paperback originals. **Publishes 6-8 titles/year. 100 queries received/year. 30 mss received/year. 85% of books from first-time authors. 90% from unagented writers. Pays 7% royalty on retail price. Pays $500-1,000 advance.** Publishes book 6 months after acceptance. Accepts simultaneous submissions. Responds in 1 month (if interested) to proposals; 2 months to mss. Catalog and guidelines online.

🔑 "Currently emphasizing theology (life of Christ), political, current events, pets (dogs only, rescue/heroic), self-help, and gardening. *No unsolicited mss*; brief proposals only with first 5 pages of Chapter 1. Writer must have strong credentials to author work."

NONFICTION Submit brief proposal package only with bio and first 5 pages of Chapter 1. "We do not return materials unless we specifically request the full manuscript." Reviews artwork/photos. Send Writer must be sure he/she owns all rights to photos, artwork, illustrations, etc., submitted for consideration (all submissions must be free of any third-party claims). Never send original photos or art.

TIPS "Mail brief book proposal, bio, and a few sample pages only. We will request a full manuscript if interested. We cannot respond to all queries. Full manuscript will be returned if we requested it, and if writer provides SASE. We do not return proposals. Simultaneous submissions are encouraged."

⊕ GOODMAN BECK PUBLISHING

P.O. Box 253, Attn: Senior Editor, Norwood NJ 07648-2428. (201)403-3097. **E-mail:** info@goodmanbeck.com. **Website:** www.goodmanbeck.com. Estab. 2007. Publishes trade paperback originals and reprints; mass market paperback originals and reprints. **Publishes 5-6 titles/year. 65% of books from first-time authors. 90% from unagented writers. Pays 10% royalty on retail price.** Publishes book 6-9 months after acceptance. Accepts simultaneous submissions. Responds in 1 month on queries/proposals; 2 months on mss.

🔑 "Our primary interest at this time is mental health, personal growth, aging well, positive psychology, accessible spirituality, and self-help."

NONFICTION Subjects include creative nonfiction, health, medicine, philosophy, psychology, spirituality. No religious or political works, textbooks, or how-to books at this time. Query with SASE. Reviews artwork/photos. Send photocopies.

FICTION Subjects include contemporary, mainstream, mystery, poetry, short story collections, suspense. "Fiction books should be able to generate a passionate response from our adult readers." No science fiction, romance novels. Query with SASE.

POETRY "We are interested in zen-inspired haiku and non-embellished, non-rhyming, egoless poems. Read Mary Oliver." Query, submit 3 sample poems.

TIPS "Your book should be enlightening and marketable. Be prepared to have a comprehensive marketing plan. You will be very involved."

☺ GOOSE LANE EDITIONS

500 Beaverbrook Ct., Suite 330, Fredericton, New Brunswick E3B 5X4, Canada. (506)450-4251. **Fax:** (506)459-4991. **Website:** www.gooselane.com/submissions.php. **Contact:** Angela Williams, publishing assistant. Estab. 1954. Publishes hardcover and paperback originals and occasional reprints. **Publishes 16-20 titles/year. 20% of books from first-time authors. 60% from unagented writers. Pays 8-10% royalty on retail price. Pays $500-3,000, negotiable advance.** Responds in 6 months to queries.

🔑 "Goose Lane publishes literary fiction and nonfiction from well-read and highly skilled Canadian authors."

NONFICTION Subjects include art, architecture, history, language, literature, nature, environment, regional, women's issues/studies. Query with SASE.

FICTION Subjects include literary, novels, short story collections, contemporary. Our needs in fiction never change: Substantial, character-centered literary fiction. No children's, YA, mainstream, mass market, genre, mystery, thriller, confessional or science fiction. Query with SAE with Canadian stamps or IRCs. No U.S. stamps.

TIPS "Writers should send us outlines and samples of books that show a very well-read author with highly developed literary skills. Our books are almost all by Canadians living in Canada; we seldom consider submissions from outside Canada. If I were a writer trying to market a book today, I would contact the targeted publisher with a query letter and synopsis, and request manuscript guidelines. Purchase a recent book from the publisher in a relevant area, if possible. Always send an SASE with IRCs or suffient return postage in Canadian stamps for reply to your query and for any material you'd like returned should it not suit our needs. Specializes in high quality Canadian literary fiction, poetry, and nonfiction. We consider submissions from outside Canada only when the author is Canadian and the book is of extraordinary interest to Canadian readers. We do not publish books for children or for the young adult market."

GRAND CANYON ASSOCIATION

1824 S. Thompson St., Suite 205, Flagstaff AZ 86001. (928)863-3878. **Fax:** (928)779-7279. **E-mail:** tberger@grandcanyon.org. **Website:** www.grandcanyon.org. **Contact:** Todd R. Berger, director of publishing. (Grand Canyon-related geology, natural history, outdoor activities, human history, photography, ecology, etc., posters, postcards and other non-book products). Estab. 1932. Publishes hardcover originals and reprints, and trade paperback originals and reprints. **200 queries received/year. Pays royalty on wholesale price. Makes outright purchase.** Accepts simultaneous submissions. Responds in 2 months to queries, proposals and mss. Catalog online. Ms guidelines available by e-mail.

NONFICTION Subjects include Grand Canyon-related animals; anthropology; archaeology; architecture; children's books (fiction & nonfiction); general nonfiction; history; nature; environment; photography; recreation; regional; science; sports; travel; geology. The mission of the Grand Canyon Association (GCA) is to help preserve and protect Grand Canyon National Park by cultivating support through education and understanding of the park. Grand Canyon Association (GCA) is a non-profit organization established to support education, research, and other programs for the benefit of Grand Canyon National Park and its visitors. GCA operates bookstores throughout the park, publishes books and other materials related to the Grand Canyon region, supports wildlife surveys and other research, funds acquisitions for the park's research library, and produces a wide variety of free publications and exhibits for park visitors. Query with SASE. Submit proposal package, outline, 3-4 sample chapters, list of publication credits, and samples of previous work. Submit complete ms. Reviews artwork/photos. Send transparencies, color or b&w prints, or digital samples of images.

TIPS "Do not send any proposals that are not directly related to the Grand Canyon or do not have educational value about the Grand Canyon."

GRANITE PUBLISHING, LLC

P.O. Box 1429, Columbus NC 28722. (828)894-8444. **Fax:** (828)894-8454. **E-mail:** brian@granitepublishing.us; eileen@souledout.org. **Website:** www.granitepublishing.us/index.html. **Contact:** Brian Crissey. Publishes trade paperback originals and reprints. **Publishes 4 titles/year. 50 queries received/year. 150 mss received/year. 70% of books from first-time authors. 90% from unagented writers. Pays 7 ½-10% royalty.** Publishes book 16 months after acceptance. Accepts simultaneous submissions. Responds in 6 months to mss.

➤ "Granite Publishing strives to preserve the Earth by publishing books that develop new wisdom about our emerging planetary citizenship, bringing information from the outerworlds to our world. Currently emphasizing indigenous ideas, planetary healing."

NONFICTION Subjects include New Age., planetary paradigm shift. Submit proposal. Reviews artwork/photos. Send photocopies.

GRAPHIA

222 Berkeley St., Boston MA 02116. (617)351-5000. **E-mail:** eden_edwards@hmco.com; erica_zappy@hmco.com. **Website:** www.graphiabooks.com. **Contact:** Julia Richardson, acquisitions. Accepts simultaneous submissions. Responds to queries in 3 months.

➤ "Graphia publishes quality paperbacks for today's teen readers, ages 14 and up. From fiction to nonfiction, poetry to graphic novels, Graphia runs the gamut, all unified by the quality of writing that is the hallmark of this imprint."

NONFICTION Young adults: biography, history, multicultural, nature/environment, science, social issues. Query.

FICTION Young adults: adventure, contemporary, fantasy, history, humor, multicultural, poetry. Query.

GRAYWOLF PRESS

250 Third Ave. N., Suite 600, Minneapolis MN 55401. **E-mail:** wolves@graywolfpress.org. **Website:** www.graywolfpress.org. **Contact:** Katie Dublinski, editorial manager (nonfiction, fiction). Estab. 1974. Publishes trade cloth and paperback originals. **Publishes 23 titles/year. 3,000 queries received/year. 20% of books from first-time authors. 50% from unagented writers. Pays royalty on retail price. Pays $1,000-25,000 advance.** Publishes book 18 months after ac-

ceptance of ms. Responds in 3 months to queries. Catalog available free. Guidelines online.

8—🖝 "Graywolf Press is an independent, nonprofit publisher dedicated to the creation and promotion of thoughtful and imaginative contemporary literature essential to a vital and diverse culture."

NONFICTION Subjects include contemporary culture, language, literature, culture. Query with SASE.

FICTION Subjects include short story collections., literary novels. "Familiarize yourself with our list first." No genre books (romance, western, science fiction, suspense) Query with SASE. Please do not fax or e-mail.

POETRY "We are interested in linguistically challenging work." Query with SASE.

GREAT NORTHWEST PUBLISHING & DIST. CO., INC.

P.O. Box 212383, Anchorage AK 99521. (907)373-0122. **Fax:** (907)376-0122. **E-mail:** aob-billing@alaskaoutdoorbooks.com. **Website:** www.alaskaoutdoorbooks.com. **Contact:** Marvin Clark. Estab. 1979. Publishes hardcover originals, trade paperback originals, hardcover reprints and trade paperback reprints. **Publishes 2 titles/year. 75 queries received/year. 20 mss received/year. 80% of books from first-time authors. 100% from unagented writers. Pays 10% royalty on wholesale price.** Publishes book 18 months after acceptance. Accepts simultaneous submissions. Responds in 2 weeks to queries. Catalog online. Guidelines available free.

8—🖝 "Great Northwest Publishing now is able to offer hunters and outdoorsmen its 'Alaska Outdoor Books' library. Each volume is a carefully selected work, written by an authentic Alaska Big game hunting and outdoor authority."

NONFICTION Hunting and Alaska. "We are interested only in works from authors with personal knowledge or experience in the matters written about." Query with SASE. Submit complete ms. Reviews artwork/photos. Send photocopies.

TIPS Audience includes upscale outdoorsmen and others interested in the Alaska outdoors.

GREAT POTENTIAL PRESS

7025 E. 1st Ave. Suite 5, Scottsdale AZ 85251. (602)954-4200. **Fax:** (602)954-0185. **E-mail:** info@ giftedbooks.com. **Website:** www.giftedbooks.com. **Contact:** Janet Gore, editor; James T. Webb, Ph.D.,

president. Estab. 1986. Publishes trade paperback originals. **Publishes 6-10 titles/year. 75 queries received/year. 20-30 mss received/year. 50% of books from first-time authors. 100% from unagented writers. Pays 10% royalty on retail price.** Publishes book 1 year after acceptance. Accepts simultaneous submissions. Responds in 2 months to queries; 3 months to proposals; 4 months to mss. Catalog free or on website. Guidelines online.

8—🖝 Specializes in nonfiction books that address academic, social and emotional issues of gifted and talented children and adults.

NONFICTION Subjects include child guidance, education, multicultural, psychology, translation, travel, women's issues, gifted/talented children and adults, misdiagnosis of gifted, parenting gifted, teaching gifted, meeting the social and emotional needs of gifted and talented, and strategies for working with gifted children and adults. Submit proposal package, including preface or introduction, TOC, chapter outline, 2-3 sample chapters and an explanation of how work differs from similar published books.

TIPS "Mss should be clear, cogent, and well-written and should pertain to gifted, talented, and creative persons and/or issues."

GREAT QUOTATIONS PUBLISHING

8102 Lemont Rd., #300, Woodridge IL 60517. (630)390-3580. **Contact:** Ringo Suek, acquisitions editor (humor, relationships, Christian); Jan Stob, acquisitions editor (children's). Estab. 1991. **Publishes 30 titles/year. 1,500 queries received/year. 1,200 mss received/year. 50% of books from first-time authors. 80% from unagented writers.** Publishes book 6 months after acceptance. Accepts simultaneous submissions. Responds in 6 months with SASE to queries. Call them if no response. Catalog for $2. Guidelines for #10 SASE.

8—🖝 "Great Quotations seeks original material for the following general categories: humor, inspiration, motivation, success, romance, tributes to mom/dad/grandma/grandpa, etc. Currently emphasizing humor, relationships. De-emphasizing poetry, self-help. We publish new books twice a year, in July and in January."

NONFICTION Subjects include business, economics, child guidance, nature, environment, religion, sports, women's issues/studies. "We look for subjects with identifiable markets, appealing to the general public. We publish humorous books or others requiring multicolor illustration on the inside. We don't publish highly controversial subject matter." Submit outline, 2 sample chapters. Reviews artwork/photos. Send photocopies and transparencies.

TIPS "Our books are physically small and generally a very quick read with short sentences. They are available at gift shops and book shops throughout the country. We are aware that most of our books are bought on impulse and given as gifts. We need strong, clever, descriptive titles; beautiful cover art; and brief, positive, upbeat text. Be prepared to submit final ms on computer disk, according to our specifications. (It is not necessary to try to format the typesetting of your ms to look like a finished book.)"

GREAT SOURCE EDUCATION GROUP

Houghton Mifflin Harcourt, Editorial Department, 181 Ballardvale St., Wilmington MA 01887. **Website:** www.greatsource.com. Guidelines online.

- Great Source's main publishing efforts are instructional and focus on the school market. For all materials, the reading level must be appropriate to the skill level of the students and the nature of the materials.

NONFICTION Reading, writing, language arts, math, and science. Material must be appealing to students, proven classroom effective, be consistent with current research.

GREENE BARK PRESS

P.O. Box 1108, Bridgeport CT 06601. (610)434-2802. **Fax:** (610)434-2803. **E-mail:** service@greenebarkpress.com. **Website:** www.greenebarkpress.com. **Contact:** Thomas J. Greene, publisher; Tara Maroney, associate publisher. Estab. 1991. Publishes hardcover originals. **Publishes 1-5 titles/year. 100 queries received/year. 6,000 mss received/year. 60% of books from first-time authors. 100% from unagented writers. Pays 10-15% royalty on wholesale price.** Publishes book 1 year after acceptance of ms. Accepts simultaneous submissions. Responds in 2 months to queries; 6 months to mss. Guidelines for SASE.

- "We only publish children's fiction-all subjects-but in reading picture book format appealing to ages 3-9 or all ages."

FICTION Subjects include juvenile. Submit complete ms. No queries or ms by e-mail.

TIPS "Audience is children who read to themselves and others. Mothers, fathers, grandparents, godparents who read to their respective children, grandchildren. Include SASE, be prepared to wait, do not inquire by telephone."

GREENHAVEN PRESS

27500 Drake Rd., Farmington Hills MI 48331. **E-mail:** kristine.burns@cengage.com. **Website:** www.gale.com/greenhaven. **Contact:** Kristine Burns. Estab. 1970.

- Publishes 220 young adult academic reference titles/year. 50% of books by first-time authors. Greenhaven continues to print quality nonfiction anthologies for libraries and classrooms. Our well known Opposing Viewpoints series is highly respected by students and librarians in need of material on controversial social issues. Greenhaven accepts no unsolicited manuscripts. Send query, résumé, and list of published works by e-mail. Work purchased outright from authors; write-for-hire, flat fee.

NONFICTION Young adults (high school): controversial issues, social issues, history, literature, science, environment, health.

⊘ GREENWILLOW BOOKS

HarperCollins Publishers, 1350 Avenue of the Americas, New York NY 10019. (212)207-7000. **Website:** www.harperchildrens.com. **Contact:** Virginia Duncan, vice president/publisher; Paul Zakris, art director. Estab. 1974. Publishes hardcover originals and reprints. **Pays authors royalty. Offers advances. Pays illustrators royalty or by the project. Sends galleys to authors.**

- *Currently not accepting unsolicited mail, mss or queries.*

FICTION Subjects include fantasy, humor, literary, mystery, picture books, juvenile.

⊘ GREENWOOD PRESS

ABC-CLIO, 130 Cremona Dr., Santa Barbara CA 93117. (805)968-1911. **E-mail:** CustomerService@abc-clio.com. **Website:** www.abc-clio.com. **Contact:** Vince Burns, vice president of editorial. Publishes hardcover originals. **Publishes 200 titles/year. 1,000 queries received/year. 25% of books from first-time authors. Pays variable royalty on net price. Pays rare advance.** Publishes book 1 year after acceptance. Accepts simultaneous submissions. Responds in 6 months to queries. Catalog and guidelines online.

- Greenwood Press publishes reference materials for high school, public and academic libraries in the humanities and the social and hard sciences.

NONFICTION Subjects include humanities, literary criticism, social sciences., humanities and the social and hard sciences. Query with proposal package, including scope, organization, length of project, whether complete ms is available or when it will be, cv or résumé and SASE. *No unsolicited mss.*

GREENWOOD PUBLISHING GROUP

ABC-CLIO, 88 Post Rd. W, Box 5007, Westport CT 06881. (203)226-3571. **Fax:** (203)222-6009; 203-222-1502. **E-mail:** achiffolo@abc-clio.com. **Website:** www.greenwood.com. **Pays variable royalty on net price.** Accepts simultaneous submissions. Catalog and guidelines online.

NONFICTION Subjects include business, economics, child guidance, education, government, politics, history, humanities, language, literature, music, dance, psychology, religion, social sciences, sociology, sports, women's issues/studies. Query with proposal package, including scope, organization, length of project, whether a complete ms is available or when it will be, CV or résumé and SASE.

TIPS "No interest in fiction, drama, poetry—looking for reference materials and materials for educated general readers. Many of our authors are college professors who have distinguished credential and who have published research widely in their fields. Greenwood Publishing maintains an excellent website, providing complete catalog, ms guidelines and editorial contacts."

⊕ GREY GECKO PRESS

565 S. Mason Rd., Suite 154, Katy TX 77450. **E-mail:** info@greygeckopress.com; submissions@greygeckopress.com. **Website:** www.greygeckopress.com. **Contact:** Hilary Comfort, editor-in-chief; Jason Aydelotte, executive director. Estab. 2011. Publishes hardcover, trade paperback, and electronic originals. **Publishes 5-7 titles/year. 25 queries received/year; 15 mss received/year. 100% of books from first-time authors. 100% from unagented writers. Pays 50-85% royalties on wholesale price.** Publishes book 1-2 months after acceptance. Accepts simultaneous submissions. Responds in 2 weeks to queries and proposals; 1 months to mss. Catalog and guidelines for #10 SASE, by e-mail or online.

NONFICTION Subjects include architecture, art, contemporary culture, cooking, creative nonfiction, environment, foods, history, marine subjects, military, nature, photography, travel, war. "All nonfiction submissions are evaluated on a case by case basis. We focus mainly on fiction, but we'll take a look at nonfiction works. We prefer electronic submissions." Query with SASE. Submit proposal package including outline and 3 sample chapters. Reviews artwork. Send photocopies or link to photo website.

FICTION Subjects include adventure, contemporary, ethnic, fantasy, feminist, gay, historical, horror, humor, juvenile, lesbian, literary, mainstream, military, multicultural, mystery, occult, regional, romance, science fiction, short story collections, sports, suspense, war, western, young adult. "We do not publish extreme horror (e.g., "Hostel", "Saw", etc.). New and interesting stories by unpublished authors will always get our attention. Innovation is a core value of our company. We prefer electronic submissions but will accept: Query with SASE. Submit proposal package including synopsis and 3 sample chapters."

TIPS "Be willing to be a part of the Grey Gecko Family. Publishing with us is a partnership, not indentured servitude."

⊕ GRIT CITY PUBLICATIONS

309 Hill St., Pittsburgh PA 15140. (412)607-4592. **E-mail:** GritCityPublications@gmail.com. **Website:** www.GritCityPublications.com. **Contact:** Ron Gavalik, publisher. Estab. 2011. Publishes electronic originals. **90% of books from first-time authors. 100% from unagented writers. Pays 11.7-18.4% royalty on retail price. Does not offer advance.** Publishes book 3-6 months after acceptance. Responds to queries in 1 month; mss in 3. Catalog and guidelines online.

FICTION Subjects include adventure, confession, erotica, fantasy, gothic, historical, horror, military, mystery, occult, romance, science fiction, short story collections, suspense, war, western, young adult., humor (dark only). "Please keep in mind we seek genre fiction for transformation into our unique fiction medium that's not published anywhere else. That's what makes EmotoBooks a hit with our fans. GCP publishes EmotoBooks. We seek shorter works of 6,000-10,000 words for EmotoSingles. We also seek works over 15,000 words for EmotoSerials. EmotoSerials are either short-term (novella length) or long-term (novel length). Writers are also required to read our "How To Create EmotoBooks handbook." This is a free download from the Write Emotobooks page on the website. "Query EmotoSerials through e-mail; submit completed EmotoSingles only by e-mail.

TIPS "We ask writers to experience already published EmotoBooks to discover the new medium and learn our style."

✪⊘ GROSSET & DUNLAP PUBLISHERS

Penguin Putnam Inc., 345 Hudson St., New York NY 10014. **Website:** www.penguingroup.com. **Contact:** Francesco Sedita, vice president/publisher. Estab. 1898. Publishes hardcover (few) and mass market paperback originals. **Publishes 140 titles/year. Pays royalty. Pays advance.**

○ *Not currently accepting submissions.*

NONFICTION Subjects include nature, environment, science. "We do not accept e-mail submissions. Unsolicited manuscripts usually receive a response in 6-8 weeks."

FICTION Subjects include juvenile. All book formats except for picture books. Submit a summary and the first chapter or two for longer works. Agented submissions only.

TIPS Nonfiction that is particularly topical or of wide interest in the mass market; new concepts for novelty format for preschoolers; and very well-written easy readers on topics that appeal to primary graders have the best chance of selling to our firm.

◎ GROUNDWOOD BOOKS

110 Spadina Ave. Suite 801, Toronto ON M5V 2K4, Canada. (416)363-4343. **Fax:** (416)363-1071. **E-mail:** nfroman@groundwoodbooks.com. **Website:** www. groundwoodbooks.com. **10% of books from first-time authors. Offers advances.** Accepts simultaneous submissions. Responds to mss in 6-8 months.

⚷ Groundwood Books. Publishes 10 picture books/year; 3 young readers/year; 5 middle readers/year; 5 young adult titles/year, approximately 2 nonfiction titles/year.

FICTION Submit synopsis and sample chapters.

TIPS "Try to familiarize yourself with our list before submitting to judge whether or not your work is appropriate for Groundwood. Visit our website for guidelines (http://www.groundwoodbooks.com/gw_guidelines.cgm)."

GROUP PUBLISHING, INC.

1515 Cascade Ave., Loveland CO 80539. **Website:** www.group.com. **Contact:** Kerri Loesche, contract and copyright administrator. Estab. 1974. Publishes trade paperback originals. **Publishes 65 titles/year.**

500 queries received/year. 500 mss received/year. 40% of books from first-time authors. 95% from unagented writers. Pays up to 10% royalty on wholesale price or makes outright purchase or work for hire. Pays up to $1,000 advance. Publishes book 18 months after acceptance. Accepts simultaneous submissions. Responds in 1 month to queries; 6 months to proposals and mss. Catalog for 9x12 envelope and 2 first-class stamps. Guidelines available online at www.grouppublishing.com/submissions.asp.

⚷ "Our mission is to equip churches to help children, youth, and adults grow in their relationship with Jesus."

NONFICTION Subjects include education, religion. "We're an interdenominational publisher of resource materials for people who work with adults, youth or children in a Christian church setting. We also publish materials for use directly by youth or children (such as devotional books, workbooks or Bibles stories). Everything we do is based on concepts of active and interactive learning as described in *Why Nobody Learns Much of Anything at Church: And How to Fix It*, by Thom and Joani Schultz. We need new, practical, hands-on, innovative, out-of-the-box ideas—things that no one's doing... yet." Query with SASE. Submit proposal package, outline, 3 sample chapters, cover letter, introduction to book, and sample activities if appropriate.

TIPS "Our audience consists of pastors, Christian education directors, youth leaders, and Sunday school teachers."

➕ Ⓐ GROVE/ATLANTIC, INC.

841 Broadway, 4th Floor, New York NY 10003. (212)614-7850. **Fax:** (212)614-7886. **E-mail:** info@groveatlantic.com. **Website:** www.groveatlantic.com. **Contact:** Morgan Entrekin, publisher (fiction, history, spsports, current affairs); Elisabeth Schmitz, exec. editor (literary fiction, memoirs). Publishes hardcover and trade paperback originals, and reprints. **Publishes 100 titles/year. 1,000+ queries received/year. 1,000+ mss received/year. 10% of books from first-time authors. 0% from unagented writers. Pays 7 ½-12 ½% royalty. Makes outright purchase of $5-500,000.** Publishes book 9 months after acceptance of ms. Accepts simultaneous submissions. Responds in 1 month to queries. Responds in 2 months to proposals. Responds in 4 months to mss. Catalog online.

NONFICTION Subjects include art, architecture, business, economics, creative nonfiction, education, government, politics, language, literature, memoirs, military, war, philosophy, psychology, science, social sciences, sports, translation. Agented submissions only.

FICTION Subjects include erotica, horror, literary, science fiction, short story collections, suspense, western. Agented submissions only.

GRYPHON HOUSE, INC.

10770 Columbia Pike, Suite 201, Silver Spring MD 20901. (800)638-0928. **Fax:** (301)595-0051. **E-mail:** kathy@ghbooks.com. **Website:** www.gryphonhouse. com. **Contact:** Kathy Charner, editor-in-chief. Estab. 1981. Publishes trade paperback originals. **Publishes 12-15 titles/year. Pays royalty on wholesale price.** Responds in 3-6 months to queries. Guidelines online.

NONFICTION Subjects include child guidance, education, early childhood. Currently emphasizing social-emotional intelligence and classroom management; de-emphasizing literacy after-school activities. "We prefer to receive a letter of inquiry and/or a proposal, rather than the entire manuscript. Please include: the proposed title, the purpose of the book, table of contents, introductory material, 20-40 sample pages of the actual book. In addition, please describe the book, including the intended audience, why teachers will want to buy it, how it is different from other similar books already published, and what qualifications you possess that make you the appropriate person to write the book. If you have a writing sample that demonstrates that you write clear, compelling prose, please include it with your letter."

GRYPHON PUBLICATIONS

P.O. Box 209, Brooklyn NY 11228. **Website:** www. gryphonbooks.com. **Contact:** Gary Lovisi, owner/publisher. Publishes trade paperback originals and reprints. **Publishes 10 titles/year. 500 queries received/year. 1,000 mss received/year. 20% of books from first-time authors. 90% from unagented writers. Makes outright purchase by contract, price varies. Pays no advance.** Publishes book 1-2 years after acceptance. Responds in 1 month to queries. Catalog and guidelines for #10 SASE.

- ☞ "I publish very genre-oriented work (science fiction, crime, pulps) and nonfiction on these topics, authors and artists. It's best to query with an idea first."

NONFICTION Subjects include hobbies, language, literature, book collecting. "We need well-written,

well-researched articles, but query first on topic and length. Writers should not submit material that is not fully developed/researched." Query with SASE. Reviews artwork/photos. Send photocopies; slides, transparencies may be necessary later.

FICTION "We want cutting-edge fiction, under 3,000 words with impact."

TIPS "We are very particular about novels and book-length work. A first-timer has a better chance with a short story or article. On anything over 4,000 words do not send manuscript, send only query letter with SASE. Always query first with an SASE."

⊘☺ GUERNICA EDITIONS

Box 117, Station P, Toronto ON M5S 2S6, Canada. (416)658-9888. **Fax:** (416)657-8885. **E-mail:** antoniodalfonso@sympatico.ca. **Website:** www.guernicaeditions.com. **Contact:** Antonio D'Alfonso, editor/publisher (poetry, nonfiction, novels). Estab. 1978. Publishes trade paperback originals, reprints, and software. **Publishes 15 titles/year. 750 mss received/year. 20% of books from first-time authors. 99% from unagented writers. Pays 8-10% royalty on retail price, or makes outright purchase of $200-5,000. Pays $200-2,000 advance.** Publishes book 15 months after acceptance of ms. Responds in 1 month to queries. Responds in 6 months to proposals. Responds in 1 year to mss. Catalog online.

- ☞ "Guernica Editions is an independent press dedicated to the bridging of cultures. We do original and translations of fine works. We are seeking essays on authors and translations with less emphasis on poetry."

NONFICTION Subjects include art, architecture, creative nonfiction, ethnic, film, cinema, stage, gay, lesbian, government, politics, history, language, literature, lit-crit, memoirs, multicultural, music, dance, philosophy, psychology, regional, religion, sex, translation, women's issues. Query with SASE. *All unsolicited mss returned unopened.* Reviews artwork/photos. Send photocopies.

FICTION Subjects include erotica, feminist, gay, lesbian, literary, multicultural, plays, poetry, poetry in translation, translation. "We wish to open up into the fiction world and focus less on poetry. We specialize in European, especially Italian, translations." Query with SASE. *All unsolicited mss returned unopened.*

POETRY Feminist, gay/lesbian, literary, multicultural, poetry in translation. We wish to have writers in translation. Any writer who has translated Italian poetry is welcomed. Full books only. No single poems by different authors, unless modern, and used as an anthology. First books will have no place in the next couple of years. Query.

GULF PUBLISHING COMPANY

2 Greenway Plaza, Suite 1020, Houston TX 77046. (713)529-4301. **Fax:** (713)520-4433. **E-mail:** svb@gulfpub.com. **Website:** www.gulfpub.com. **Contact:** Katie Hammon. Estab. 1916. Publishes hardcover originals and reprints; electronic originals and reprints. **Publishes 12-15 titles/year. 3-5 queries and mss received in a year. 30% of books from first-time authors. 80% from unagented writers. Royalties on retail price. Pays $1,000-$1,500 advance.** Publishes book 8-9 months after acceptance. Accepts simultaneous submissions. Responds in 2 months to queries; 1 month to proposals and mss. Catalog free on request. Guidelines available by e-mail.

8—¬ "Gulf Publishing Company is the leading publisher to the oil and gas industry. Our specialized publications reach over 100,000 people involved in energy industries worldwide. Our magazines and catalogs help readers keep current with information important to their field and allow advertisers to reach their customers in all segments of petroleum operations. More than half of Gulf Publishing Company's editorial staff have engineering degrees. The others are thoroughly trained and experienced business journalists and editors."

NONFICTION Engineering. "We don't publish a lot in the year, therefore we are able to focus more on marketing and sales—we are hoping to grow in the future." Submit outline, 1-2 sample chapters, completed ms. Reviews artwork. Send high res. file formats with high dpi in b&w.

TIPS "Our audience would be engineers, engineering students, academia, professors, well managers, construction engineers. We recommend getting contributors to help with the writing process—this provides a more comprehensive overview for technical and scientific books. Work harder on artwork. It's expensive and time-consuming for a publisher to redraw a lot of the figures."

Ⓐ GUN DIGEST BOOKS

F+W Media, 700 E. State St., Iola WI 54990. (888)457-2873. **E-mail:** kevin.michalowski@fwmedia.com.

Website: www.gundigest.com; www.krause.com. **Contact:** Kevin Michalowski, senior editor (all aspects of firearms history, scholarship, nonpolitical literature). Estab. 1944. Hardcover, trade paperback, mass market paperback, and electronic originals (all). **Publishes 25 titles/year. 75 submissions received/year. 30% of books from first-time authors. 80% from unagented writers. 10 min. to 20% max. (rare) royalty on wholesale price. Pays advance between $2,800 and $5,000.** Publishes book 7 months after acceptance. Accepts simultaneous submissions. Responds immediately to queries; 2 months to proposals/ms. Catalog online at www.krause.com. Guidelines available by e-mail at corrina.peterson@fwmedia.com.

NONFICTION Firearms, hunting-related titles only. "Must have mainstream appeal and not be too narrowly focused." Submit proposal package, including outline, 2 sample chapters, and author bio; submit completed ms. Review artwork/photos (required); high-res digital only (.jpg, .tif).

TIPS "Our audience is shooters, collectors, hunters, outdoors enthusiasts. We prefer not to work through agents."

H&S PUBLISHING, LLC

Best Places On Earth, 4330 Kauai Beach Dr., Suite G21, Lihue HI 96766. (808)822-7449. **Fax:** (808)822-2312. **E-mail:** sales@hshawaii.com. **Website:** www.bestplaceshawaii.com. **Contact:** Rob Sanford, editor. Estab. 1985. Publishes hardcover and paperback orginals and reprints. Books: recycled paper; digital printing; perfect binding; illustrations. **Pays 15-35% royalty.** Accepts simultaneous submissions. Responds in 1 month to queries; 3 months to mss. Sometimes comments on rejected mss.

8—¬ "Small independent publishing house founded and run by published authors."

FICTION Subjects include adventure, contemporary, humor, literary, mainstream, mystery, regional, religious, suspense., new age/mystic, inspirational, religious thriller. Send 1st chapter and synopsis. Include estimated word count, why author wrote book, and marketing plan. Send SASE for return of ms or send a disposable ms and SASE for reply only.

TIPS "Do what you do best and enjoy most. Your writing is an outcome of the above."

H & W PUBLISHING INC

P.O. Box 53515, Cincinnati OH 45253. **Website:** www.handwpublishing.com. Estab. 2007. **Publishes**

2 titles/year. 90% of books from first-time authors. Pays authors royalty 5% and work purchased outright for $2,500-4,000. Pays illustrators by the project (range $1,800-3,500) and royalty of 3-5% based on retail price. Originals returned to artist at job's completion. Writers and artists guidelines available at www.handwpublishing.com. Publishes book 18 months after acceptance. Responds in 1 month to queries; 2 months to mss.

☛ Specializes in African American children's literature. "Our company empowers, inspires, and uplifts."

NONFICTION Young Readers: biography, social issues. Average word length: picture books—700; young readers—1,200. Submit complete ms or submit outline/synopsis.

FICTION Picture Books: concept, contemporary, humor, poetry, religion. Young Readers: adventure, contemporary, nature/environment, poetry. Middle Readers: contemporary, problem novels. Average word length: picture books—1,200; young readers—850; middle readers—2,500. Submit complete ms or submit outline/synopsis.

TIPS "We specialize in literature for African American children. Illustrations should be detailed and reflect positive images. Story lines should either be humorist, contemporary, or teach without being preachy. No books on slavery, please."

HACHAI PUBLISHING

527 Empire Blvd., Brooklyn NY 11225. (718)633-0100. **Fax:** (718)633-0103. **Website:** www.hachai.com. **Contact:** Devorah Leah Rosenfeld, editor. Estab. 1988. Publishes hardcover originals. **Publishes 4 titles/year. 75% of books from first-time authors. Work purchased outright from authors for $800-1,000.** Accepts simultaneous submissions. Responds in 2 months to mss. Catalog available free. Guidelines online.

☛ Hachai is dedicated to producing high quality Jewish children's literature, ages 2-10. Story should promote universal values such as sharing, kindness, etc.

NONFICTION Subjects include ethnic, religion. Submit complete ms. Reviews artwork/photos. Send photocopies.

FICTION Picture books and young readers: contemporary, historical fiction, religion. Middle readers: adventure, contemporary, problem novels, religion. Does not want to see fantasy, animal stories, romance,

problem novels depicting drug use or violence. Submit complete ms.

TIPS "We are looking for books that convey the traditional Jewish experience in modern times or long ago; traditional Jewish observance such as Sabbath and holidays and mitzvos such as mezuzah, blessings etc.; positive character traits (middos) such as honesty, charity, respect, sharing, etc. We are also interested in historical fiction for young readers (7-10) written with a traditional Jewish perspective and highlighting the relevance of Torah in making important choices. Please, no animal stories, romance, violence, preachy sermonizing. Write a story that incorporates a moral, not a preachy morality tale. Originality is the key. We feel Hachai publications will appeal to a wider readership as parents become more interested in positive values for their children."

⊕ HADLEY RILLE BOOKS

PO Box 25466, Overland Park KS 66225. **E-mail:** subs@hadleyrillebooks.com. **Website:** www.hadleyrillebooks.com. **Contact:** Eric T. Reynolds, editor/publisher.

FICTION We currently don't have any anthologies open for submissions, but we will in the future. Please check back periodically. We only accept e-mail queries and submissions.

TIPS "We aim to produce books that are aligned with current interest in the genres. Anthology markets are somewhat rare in SF these days, we feel there aren't enough good anthologies being published each year and part of our goal is to present the best that we can. We like stories that fit well within the guidelines of the particular anthology for which we are soliciting manuscripts. Aside from that, we want stories with strong characters (not necessarily characters with strong personalities, flawed characters are welcome). We want a sense of wonder and awe. We want to feel the world around the character and so scene description is important (however, this doesn't always require a lot of text, just set the scene well so we don't wonder where the character is). We strongly recommend workshopping the story or having it critiqued in some way by readers familiar with the genre. We prefer clichés be kept to a bare minimum in the prose and avoid re-working old story lines."

HALF HALT PRESS, INC.

P.O. Box 67, Boonsboro MD 21713. (301)733-7119. **Fax:** (301)733-7408. **E-mail:** mail@halfhaltpress.com.

Website: www.halfhaltpress.com. **Contact:** Elizabeth Rowland, publisher. Estab. 1986. Publishes 90% hardcover and trade paperback originals and 10% reprints. **Publishes 10 titles/year. 25% of books from first-time authors. 50% from unagented writers. Pays 10-12 ½% royalty on retail price.** Publishes book 1 year after acceptance.

⚬—⚯ "We publish high-quality nonfiction on equestrian topics—books that help riders and trainers do something better."

NONFICTION Subjects include animals, horses, sports. "We need serious instructional works by authorities in the field on horse-related topics, broadly defined." Query with SASE. Reviews artwork/photos.

TIPS "Writers have the best chance selling us well-written, unique works that teach serious horse people how to do something better. Offer a straightforward presentation, letting the work speak for itself, without hype or hard sell. Allow the publisher to contact the writer, without frequent calling to check status. As the publisher/author relationship becomes close and is based on working well together, early impressions may be important, even to the point of being a consideration in acceptance for publication."

ALEXANDER HAMILTON INSTITUTE

70 Hilltop Rd., Ramsey NJ 07446. (201)825-3377; (800) 879-2441. **Fax:** (201)825-8696. **E-mail:** editorial@legalworkplace.com. **Website:** www.legalworkplace.com. **Contact:** Brian L.P. Zevnik, editor-in-chief; Gloria Ju, editor. Estab. 1909. Publishes 3-ring binder and paperback originals. **Publishes 5-10 titles/year. 50 queries received/year. 10 mss received/year. 25% of books from first-time authors. 95% from unagented writers. Pays 5-8% royalty on retail price. Makes outright purchase of $3,500-7,000. Pays $3,500-7,000 advance.** Publishes book 10 months after acceptance. Accepts simultaneous submissions. Responds in 1 month to queries; 2 months to mss.

⚬—⚯ "Alexander Hamilton Institute publishes management books for upper-level managers and executives. Currently emphasizing legal issues for HR/personnel."

NONFICTION These books combine court case research and practical application of defensible programs. The main audience is US personnel executives and high-level management.

TIPS "We sell exclusively by direct mail or through electronic means to managers and executives. A writer must know his/her field and be able to communicate legal and practical systems and programs."

HAMPTON ROADS PUBLISHING CO., INC.

665 Third Street, Suite 400, San Francisco CA 94107. **E-mail:** submissions@hrpub.com; submissions@redwheelweiser.com. **Website:** www.hrpub.com. **Contact:** Ms. Pat Bryce, Acquisitions Editor. Estab. 1989. Publishes and distributes hardcover and trade paperback originals on subjects including metaphysics, health, complementary medicine, visionary fiction, and other related topics. **Publishes 35-40 titles/year. 1,000 queries received/year. 1,500 mss received/year. 50% of books from first-time authors. 70% from unagented writers. Pays royalty. Pays $1,000-50,000 advance.** Publishes book 1 year after acceptance of ms. Accepts simultaneous submissions. Responds in 2-4 months to queries. Responds in 1 month to proposals. Responds in 6-12 months to mss. Guidelines online.

⚬—⚯ "Our reason for being is to impact, uplift, and contribute to positive change in the world. We publish books that will enrich and empower the evolving consciousness of mankind. Though we are not necessarily limited in scope, we are most interested in manuscripts on the following subjects: Body/Mind/Spirit, Health and Healing, Self-Help. Please be advised that at the moment we are not accepting: Fiction or novelized material that does not pertain to body/mind/spirit, channeled writing."

NONFICTION Subjects include New Age, spirituality. Query with SASE. Submit synopsis, SASE. No longer accepting electronic submissions. Reviews artwork/photos. Send photocopies.

FICTION Subjects include literary, spiritual., Visionary fiction, past-life fiction based on actual memories. Fiction should have 1 or more of the following themes: spiritual, inspirational, metaphysical, i.e., past-life recall, out-of-body experiences, near-death experience, paranormal. Query with SASE. Submit outline, 2 sample chapters, clips. Submit complete ms.

HANCOCK HOUSE PUBLISHERS

Hancock Wildlife Foundation, 1431 Harrison Ave., Blaine WA 98230. (604)538-1114. **Fax:** (604)538-2262. **E-mail:** karen@hancockwildlife.org. **Website:** www.hancockwildlife.org. **Contact:** David Hancock. Estab. 1971. Publishes hardcover and trade paperback originals and reprints. **Publishes 12-20 titles/year. 50% of** books from first-time authors. **90% from unagented writers. Pays 10% royalty.** Publishes book 1 year after acceptance. Accepts simultaneous submissions. Catalog available free. Guidelines online.

- ✎ "Hancock House Publishers is the largest North American publisher of wildlife and Native Indian titles. We also cover Pacific Northwest, fishing, history, Canadiana, biographies. We are seeking agriculture, natural history, animal husbandry, conservation, and popular science titles with a regional (Pacific Northwest), national, or international focus. Currently emphasizing nonfiction wildlife, cryptozoology, guide books, native history, biography, fishing."

NONFICTION Subjects include agriculture, animals, ethnic, history, horticulture, nature, environment, regional. Centered around Pacific Northwest, local history, nature guide books, international ornithology, and Native Americans. Submit proposal package, outline, 3 sample chapters, selling points, SASE. Reviews artwork/photos. Send photocopies.

HANSER PUBLICATIONS

6915 Valley Ave., Cincinnati OH 45244. (513)527-8800; (800)950-8977. **Fax:** (513)527-8801. **E-mail:** info@hanserpublications.com. **Website:** www.hanserpublications.com. Estab. 1993. Publishes hardcover and paperback originals, and digital educational and training programs. **Publishes 10-15 titles/year. 100 queries received/year. 10-20 mss received/year. 50% of books from first-time authors. 100% from unagented writers.** Publishes book 10 months after acceptance. Accepts simultaneous submissions. Responds in 2 weeks to queries; 1 month to proposals/mss. Catalog available free. Guidelines online.

- ✎ "Hanser Publications publishes books and electronic media for the manufacturing (both metalworking and plastics) industries. Publications range from basic training materials to advanced reference books."

NONFICTION "We publish how-to texts, references, technical books, and computer-based learning materials for the manufacturing industries. Titles include award-winning management books, encyclopedic references, and leading references." Submit outline, sample chapters, résumé, preface, and comparison to competing or similar titles.

TIPS "E-mail submissions speed up response time."

HARLAN DAVIDSON INC.

aka Forum Press Inc., 773 Glenn Ave., Wheeling IL 60090. (847)541-9720. **Fax:** (847)541-9830. **E-mail:** harlandavidson@harlandavidson.com. **Website:** www.harlandavidson.com.

- ✎ "Serving the needs of instructors and students of history in colleges, universities, and high schools throughout North America, Harlan Davidson, Inc., remains an independent publisher of textbooks and supplements. We invite you to browse our site. All of our publications are available for purchase or as complimentary examination copies to qualified instructors."

Ⓐ HARPERBUSINESS

Imprint of HarperCollins General Books Group, 10 E. 53rd St., New York NY 10022. (212)207-7000. **Website:** www.harpercollins.com. Estab. 1991. Publishes hardcover, trade paperback originals and reprints. **Pays royalty on retail price. Pays advance.** Accepts simultaneous submissions.

- ✎ HarperBusiness publishes the inside story on ideas that will shape business practices with cutting-edge information and visionary concepts.

NONFICTION Subjects include business, economics., Marketing subjects. We don't publish how-to, textbooks or things for academic market; no reference (tax or mortgage guides), our reference department does that. Proposals need to be top notch. We tend not to publish people who have no business standing. Must have business credentials. Agented submissions only.

HARPERCOLLINS CHILDREN'S BOOKS/ HARPERCOLLINS PUBLISHERS

10 East 53rd, New York NY 10022. (212)207-6901. **E-mail:** Dana.fritts@Harpercollins.com; Mischa.Rosenberg@Harpercollins.com. **Website:** www.harpercollins.com. **Contact:** Mischa Rosenberg, assistant designer; Dana Fritts, designer. Publishes hardcover and paperback originals and paperback reprints. **Publishes 500 titles/year. Negotiate a flat fee upon acceptance.** Accepts simultaneous submissions. 1 month, will contact if interested. Available online.

NONFICTION *No unsolicited mss or queries.* Agented submissions only. Unsolicited mss returned unopened.

FICTION Subjects include picture books, young adult, chapter books, middle grade, early readers. "We look for a strong story line and exceptional literary talent." Agented submissions only. *All unsolicited mss returned.*

TIPS "We do not accept any unsolicited material."

HARVARD BUSINESS REVIEW PRESS

Imprint of Harvard Business School Publishing Corp., 60 Harvard Way, Boston MA 02163. (617)783-7400. **Fax:** (617)783-7489. **E-mail:** cschinke@harvardbusiness.org. **Website:** www.hbr.org. **Contact:** Courtney Schinke, editorial coordinator. Estab. 1984. Publishes hardcover originals and several paperback series. **Publishes 40-50 titles/year. Pays escalating royalty on retail price. Advances vary depending on author and market for the book.** Accepts simultaneous submissions. Responds in 1 month to proposals and mss. Catalog and guidelines online.

⚭ The Harvard Business Review Press publishes books for senior and general managers and business scholars. Harvard Business Review Press is the source of the most influential ideas and conversations that shape business worldwide.

NONFICTION Submit proposal package, outline, sample chapters.

TIPS "We do not publish books on real estate, personal finance or business parables."

THE HARVARD COMMON PRESS

535 Albany St., 5th Floor, Boston MA 02118. (617)423-5803. **Fax:** (617)695-9794. **E-mail:** info@harvardpress.com; editorial@harvardcommonpress.com. **Website:** www.harvardcommonpress.com. **Contact:** Valerie Cimino, executive editor. Estab. 1976. Publishes hardcover and trade paperback originals and reprints. **Publishes 16 titles/year. 20% of books from first-time authors. 40% from unagented writers. Pays royalty. Pays average $2,500-10,000 advance.** Publishes book 1 year after acceptance. Accepts simultaneous submissions. Responds in 2 months to queries. Catalog for 9x12 envelope and 3 first-class stamps. Guidelines for #10 SASE or online.

⚭ "We want strong, practical books that help people gain control over a particular area of their lives. Currently emphasizing cooking, child care/parenting, health. De-emphasizing general instructional books, travel."

NONFICTION Subjects include child guidance, cooking, foods, nutrition, health, medicine. A large percentage of our list is made up of books about cooking, child care, and parenting; in these areas we are looking for authors who are knowledgeable, if not experts, and who can offer a different approach to the subject. We are open to good nonfiction proposals that show evidence of strong organization and writing, and clearly demonstrate a need in the marketplace. First-time authors are welcome. Submit outline. Potential authors may also submit a query letter or e-mail of no more than 300 words, rather than a full proposal; if interested, we will ask to see a proposal. Queries and questions may be sent via e-mail. We will not consider e-mail attachments containing proposals. No phone calls, please.

TIPS "We are demanding about the quality of proposals; in addition to strong writing skills and thorough knowledge of the subject matter, we require a detailed analysis of the competition."

⚠⊘ HARVEST HOUSE PUBLISHERS

990 Owen Loop N, Eugene OR 97402. (541)343-0123. **Fax:** (541)302-0731. **Website:** www.harvesthousepublishers.com. Estab. 1974. Publishes hardcover, trade paperback, and mass market paperback originals and reprints. **Publishes 160 titles/year. 1,500 queries received/year. 1,000 mss received/year. 1% of books from first-time authors. Pays royalty.**

NONFICTION Subjects include anthropology, archeology, business, economics, child guidance, health, medicine, money, finance, religion, women's issues/studies., Bible studies. *No unsolicited mss.*

FICTION *No unsolicited mss, proposals, or artwork.* Agented submissions only.

TIPS "For first time/nonpublished authors we suggest building their literary résumé by submitting to magazines, or perhaps accruing book contributions."

HASTINGS HOUSE/DAYTRIPS PUBLISHERS

LINI LLC, P.O. Box 908, Winter Park FL 32790. (407)339-3600; (800)206-7822. **Fax:** (407)339-5900. **E-mail:** hastingshousebooks.com. **Website:** www.hastingshousebooks.com. **Contact:** Earl Steinbicker, senior travel editor (edits Daytrips Series). Publishes trade paperback originals and reprints. **Publishes 20 titles/year. 600 queries received/year. 900 mss received/year. 10% of books from first-time authors. 40% from unagented writers.** Publishes book 10 months after acceptance. Responds in 2 months to queries.

NONFICTION Subjects include travel. Submit outline. Query.

HATALA GEROPRODUCTS

P.O. Box 42, Greentop MO 63546. **E-mail:** editor@geroproducts.com. **Website:** www.geroproducts.com. **Contact:** Mark Hatala, Ph.D., president (psychology, travel, relationships). Estab. 2002. Publishes hardcover and trade paperback originals. **Publishes 3-4 titles/year. 120 queries received/year. 50 mss received/year. 30% of books from first-time authors. 80% from unagented writers. Pays 5-7½% royalty on retail price. Pays $250-500 advance.** Publishes book 18 months after acceptance. Accepts simultaneous submissions. Responds in 1 month to queries; 2 months to proposals and mss. Guidelines online.

NONFICTION Subjects include health, medicine, psychology, sex, travel, seniors, advice. Books should be of interest to older (60+) adults. Romance, relationships, advice, travel, how-to books are most appropriate. All books are larger print; so manuscripts should be around 50,000 words. Query with SASE. Submit proposal package, outline, 3 sample chapters, SASE.

TIPS "Audience is men and women (but particularly women) over age 60. Books need to be pertinent to the lives of older Americans. No memoirs or poetry."

HAWK PUBLISHING GROUP

7107 S. Yale Ave., #345, Tulsa OK 74136. (918)492-3677. **Fax:** (918)492-2120. **Website:** www.hawkpublishing.com. Estab. 1999. Publishes hardcover and trade paperback originals. **Publishes 6-8 titles/year. 25% of books from first-time authors. 50% from unagented writers. Pays royalty.** Publishes book 1-2 years after acceptance of ms. Accepts simultaneous submissions. Guidelines online.

⇨ "Please visit our website and read the submission guidelines before sending anything to us. The best way to learn what might interest us is to visit the website, read the information there, look at the books, and perhaps even read a few of them."

NONFICTION "Looking for subjects of broad appeal and interest."

FICTION Looking for good books of all kinds. Not interested in juvenile, poetry, or short story collections. Does not want childrens or young adult books. "Submissions will not be returned, so send only copies. No SASE. No submissions by e-mail or by 'cerified mail' or any other service that requires a signature." Replies only if interested. If you have not heard from us within 3 months after the receipt of your submission, you may safely assume that we were not able to find a place for it in our list."

TIPS "Prepare a professional submission and follow the guidelines. The simple things really do count; use 12 pt. pitch with 1-inch margins and only send what is requested."

HAYES SCHOOL PUBLISHING CO. INC.

321 Pennwood Ave., Wilkinsburg PA 15221. (412)371-2373. **Fax:** (800)543-8771. **E-mail:** chayes@hayespub.com. **Website:** www.hayespub.com. **Contact:** Clair N. Hayes. Estab. 1940. **Work purchased outright. Purchases all rights.**

⇨ Produces folders, workbooks, stickers, certificates. Wants to see supplementary teaching aids for grades K-12. Interested in all subject areas. Will consider simultaneous and electronic submissions. Query with description or complete ms. Responds in 6 weeks. SASE for return of submissions.

Ⓐ HAY HOUSE INC.

P.O. Box 5100, Carlsbad CA 92018. (760)431-7695. **Fax:** (760)431-6948. **E-mail:** editorial@hayhouse.com. **Website:** www.hayhouse.com. **Contact:** Patty Gift, East Coast acquisitions (pgift@hayhouse.com); Alex Freemon, West Coast acquisitions (afreemon@hayhouse.com). Estab. 1985. Publishes hardcover and trade paperback originals. **Publishes 50 titles/year. Pays standard royalty.** Accepts simultaneous submissions. Guidelines online.

⇨ "We publish books, audios, and videos that help heal the planet."

NONFICTION Subjects include cooking, foods, nutrition, education, health, medicine, money, finance, nature, environment, New Age, philosophy, psychology, sociology, women's issues/studies., mind/body/spirit. "Hay House is interested in a variety of subjects as long as they have a positive self-help slant to them. No poetry, children's books, or negative concepts that are not conducive to helping/healing ourselves or our planet." Accepts e-mail submissions from agents.

TIPS "Our audience is concerned with our planet, the healing properties of love, and general self-help principles. If I were a writer trying to market a book today, I would research the market thoroughly to make sure there weren't already too many books on the subject I was interested in writing about. Then I would make sure I had a unique slant on my idea. Simultaneous submissions from agents must include SASE's."

HEALTH COMMUNICATIONS, INC.

3201 SW 15th St., Deerfield Beach FL 33442. (954)360-0909, ext. 232. **Fax:** (954)360-0034. **E-mail:** Editorial@hcibooks.com. **Website:** www.hcibooks.com. Estab. 1976. Publishes hardcover and trade paperback nonfiction only. **Publishes 60 titles/year.** Responds in 3-6 months to queries and proposals. See submission guidelines online.

⚲ "While HCI is a best known for recovery publishing, today recovery is only one part of a publishing program that includes titles in self-help and psychology, health and wellness, spirituality, inspiration, women's and men's issues, relationships, family, teens and children, memoirs, mind/body/spirit integration, and gift books."

NONFICTION Subjects include child guidance, health, parenting, psychology, women's issues/studies, young adult, self-help.

WILLIAM S. HEIN & CO., INC.

1285 Main St., Buffalo NY 14209. (716)882-2600. **Fax:** (716)883-8100. **E-mail:** mail@wshein.com. **Website:** www.wshein.com. **Contact:** Sheila Jarrett, publications manager. Estab. 1961. **Publishes 30 titles/year. 80 queries received/year. 40 mss received/year. 30% of books from first-time authors. 100% from unagented writers. Pays 10-20% royalty on net price.** Publishes book 9 months after acceptance. Accepts simultaneous submissions. Responds in 3 months to queries. Catalog online. Guidelines: send e-mail for info and mss proposal form.

⚲ "William S. Hein & Co. publishes reference books for law librarians, legal researchers, and those interested in legal writing. Currently emphasizing legal research, legal writing, and legal education."

NONFICTION Subjects include education, government, politics, women's issues., world affairs, legislative histories.

◗ HEINEMANN EDUCATIONAL PUBLISHERS

P.O. Box 781940, Sandton 2146, South Africa. (27)(11)322-8600. **Fax:** 086 687 7822. **E-mail:** customerliaison@heinemann.co.za. **Website:** www.heinemann.co.za.

⚲ Interested in textbooks for primary schools, literature and textbooks for secondary schools, and technical publishing for colleges/universities.

NONFICTION Subjects include animals, art, architecture, business, economics, education, ethnic, health, medicine, history, humanities, language, literature, music, dance, psychology, regional, religion, science, social sciences, sports., math, engineering, management, nursing, marketing.

HELLGATE PRESS

P.O. Box 3531, Ashland OR 97520. (541)973-5154. **E-mail:** harley@hellgatepress.com. **Website:** www.hellgatepress.com. **Contact:** Harley B. Patrick, editor. Estab. 1996. **Publishes 15-20 titles/year. 85% of books from first-time authors. 95% from unagented writers. Pays royalty.** Publishes book 6-9 months after acceptance. Responds in 2 months to queries.

⚲ "Hellgate Press specializes in military history, other military topics, travel adventure, and historical/adventure fiction."

NONFICTION Subjects include history, memoirs, military, war, travel adventure. Query/proposal only with SASE or by e-mail. *Do not send mss.* Reviews artwork/photos. Send photocopies.

⊕ HELLICIOUS HORRORS EPUBLISHING

1863 E. 73rd St., Cleveland OH 44103. **E-mail:** nhobson@hellicioushorrors.com. **Website:** www.hellicioushorrors.com. **Contact:** Nina Hobson, editor; Anthony Graysen, managing editor. Estab. 2011. Responds in 1-3 weeks on queries. Submit by e-mail as a Word document only.

⚲ Hellicious Horrors Epublishing is devoted solely to horror e-books starring straight, bi, gay, lesbian, and transgender preteens through young adults.

NONFICTION Does not accept nonfiction.

HENDRICK-LONG PUBLISHING CO., INC.

10635 Tower Oaks, Suite D, Houston TX 77070. 832-912-READ. **Fax:** (832)912-7353. **E-mail:** hendricklong@att.net. **Website:** hendricklongpublishing.com. **Contact:** Vilma Long. Estab. 1969. Publishes hardcover and trade paperback originals and hardcover reprints. **Publishes 4 titles/year. 90% from unagented writers. Pays royalty on selling price. Pays advance.** Publishes book 18 months after acceptance of ms. Responds in 3 months to queries. Catalog for 8½×11 or 9×12 SASE with 4 first-class stamps. Guidelines online.

⚲ "Hendrick-Long publishes historical fiction and nonfiction about Texas and the Southwest for children and young adults."

NONFICTION Subjects include history, regional. Subject must be Texas related; other subjects cannot be considered. We are particularly interested in material from educators that can be used in the classroom as workbooks, math, science, history with a Texas theme or twist. Query, or submit outline and 2 sample chapters. Reviews artwork/photos. Send photocopies.

FICTION Subjects include juvenile, young adult. Query with SASE. Submit outline, clips, 2 sample chapters.

HENDRICKSON PUBLISHERS, INC.

140 Summit St., P.O. Box 3473, Peabody MA 01961. **Fax:** (978)573-8276. **E-mail:** editorial@hendrickson. com; orders@hendrickson.com. **Website:** www.hendrickson.com. **Contact:** Shirley Decker-Lucke, editorial director. Estab. 1983. Publishes trade reprints, bibles, and scholarly material in the areas of New Testament; Hebrew Bible; religion and culture; patristics; Judaism; and practical, historical, and Biblical theology. **Publishes 35 titles/year. 800 queries received/year. 10% of books from first-time authors. 90% from unagented writers.** Publishes book 1 year after acceptance. Responds in 3-4 months to queries. Catalog and guidelines for #10 SASE.

8—⚡ "Hendrickson is an academic publisher of books that give insight into Bible understanding (academically) and encourage spiritual growth (popular trade). Currently emphasizing Biblical helps and reference, ministerial helps, and Biblical studies."

NONFICTION Subjects include religion. "No longer accepting unsolicited manuscripts or book proposals. Cannot return material sent or respond to all queries." Submit outline, sample chapters, and CV.

HERITAGE BOOKS, INC.

100 Railroad Ave., #104, Westminster MD 21157. (866)282-2689. **E-mail:** Info@HeritageBooks.com. **E-mail:** Submissions@HeritageBooks.com. **Website:** www.heritagebooks.com. Estab. 1978. Publishes hardcover and paperback originals and reprints. **Publishes 200 titles/year. 25% of books from first-time authors. 100% from unagented writers. Pays 10% royalty on list price.** Accepts simultaneous submissions. Responds in 3 months to queries. Catalog and guidelines free.

8—⚡ "Our goal is to celebrate life by exploring all aspects of American life: settlement, development, wars, and other significant events, in-

cluding family histories, memoirs, etc. Currently emphasizing early American life, early wars and conflicts, ethnic studies."

NONFICTION Subjects include Americana, ethnic, origins and research guides, history, memoirs, military, war, regional, history. Query with SASE. Submit outline via e-mail. Reviews artwork/photos.

TIPS "The quality of the book is of prime importance; next is its relevance to our fields of interest."

✪ HERITAGE HOUSE PUBLISHING CO., LTD.

#340-1105 Pandora Ave., Victoria BC V8V 3P9, Canada. 250-360-0829. **E-mail:** editorial@heritagehouse. ca. **Website:** www.heritagehouse.ca. **Contact:** Vivian Sinclair, Managing Editor. Publishes mostly trade paperback and some hardcovers. **Publishes 25-30 titles/year. 200 queries received/year. 100 mss received/year. 50% of books from first-time authors. 90% from unagented writers. Pays 12-15% royalty on net proceeds. Advances are rarely paid.** Publishes book within 1-2 years of acceptance. after acceptance of ms. Accepts simultaneous submissions. Responds in 6 months to queries. Catalogue and Guidelines online.

8—⚡ "Heritage House publishes books that celebrate the historical and cultural heritage of Canada, particularly Western Canada and, to an extent, the Pacific Northwest. We also publish some titles of national interest and a series of books aimed at young and casual readers, called *Amazing Stories*. We accept simultaneous submissions, but indicate on your query that it is a simultaneous submission."

NONFICTION Subjects include history, regional, adventure, contemporary Canadian culture. Query with SASE. Include synopsis, outline, 2-3 sample chapters with indication of illustrative material available, and marketing strategy.

TIPS "Our books appeal to residents of and visitors to the northwest quadrant of the continent. We're looking for good stories and good storytellers. We focus on work by Canadian authors."

HEYDAY BOOKS

c/o Acquisitions Editor, Box 9145, Berkeley CA 94709-9145. **Fax:** (510)549-1889. **E-mail:** heyday@heydaybooks.com. **Website:** www.heydaybooks.com. **Contact:** Gayle Wattawa, acquisitions editor. Estab. 1974. Publishes hardcover originals, trade paperback originals and reprints. **Publishes 12-15 titles/year. 50% of books** from first-time authors. **90% from unagented writers. Pays 8% royalty on net price.** Publishes book 10 months after acceptance. Responds in 2 months to queries/mss. Catalog for 7×9 SAE with 3 first-class stamps.

↪ "Heyday Books publishes nonfiction books and literary anthologies with a strong California focus. We publish books about Native Americans, natural history, history, literature, and recreation, with a strong California focus."

NONFICTION Subjects include Americana, ethnic, history, nature, environment, recreation, regional, travel. Books about California only. Query with outline and synopsis. "Query or proposal by traditional post. Include a cover letter introducing yourself and your qualifications, a brief description of your project, a table of contents and list of illustrations, notes on the market you are trying to reach and why your book will appeal to them, a sample chapter, and a SASE if you would like us to return these materials to you." Reviews artwork/photos.

◉ HIBBARD PUBLISHERS

P.O. Box 73182, Lynnwood Ridge 0040, South Africa. (27)(12)804-3990. **Fax:** (27)(12)804-1240. **E-mail:** publisher@hibbard.co.za;tersia@hibbard.co.za. **Website:** www.hibbard.co.za.

↪ "Our mission is to take the products of our authors' dreams and efforts, and to transform and shape these into the best possible product for end users, i.e. readers, teachers, learners and their parents."

TIPS "When the pressure is on, we make use of the services of some of the best free-lancers in various fields."

⊘ HIDDENSPRING

997 Macarthur Blvd., Mahwah NJ 07430. (201)825-7300. **Fax:** (201)825-8345. **Website:** www.hiddenspringbooks.com. **Contact:** Paul McMahon, managing editor (nonfiction/spirituality). Publishes hardcover and trade paperback originals and reprints. **Publishes 10-12 titles/year. 5% of books from first-time authors. 10% from unagented writers. Royalty varies. Pays variable advance.**

◯ *Currently not accepting unsolicited submissions.*

NONFICTION Subjects include Americana, art, architecture, creative nonfiction, ethnic, history, multicultural, psychology, religion.

HIGHLAND PRESS PUBLISHING

P.O. Box 2292, High Springs FL 32655. (386) 454-3927. **Fax:** (386) 454-3927. **E-mail:** The.Highland. Press@gmail.com; Submissions.hp@gmail.com. **Website:** www.highlandpress.org. **Contact:** Leanne Burroughs, CEO (fiction); she will forward all mss to appropriate editor. Estab. 2005. Paperback originals. **Publishes 30/year titles/year. 90% from unagented writers. Pays royalties 7.5-8%** Publishes book within 18 months after acceptance of ms. Accepts simultaneous submissions. Responds in 8 weeks to queries; responds in 3-12 months to mss. Catalog and guidelines online.

↪ "With our focus on historical romances, Highland Press Publishing is known as your 'Passport to Romance.' We focus on historical romances and our award-winning anthologies. Our short stories/novellas are heart warming. As for our historicals, we publish historical novels like many of us grew up with and loved. History is a big part of the story and is tactfully woven throughout the romance." We have recently opened our submissions up to all genres, with the exception of erotica. Our newest lines are inspirational, regency, and young adult.

FICTION Send query letter. Query with outline/synopsis and sample chapters. Accepts queries by snail mail, e-mail. Include estimated word count, target market.

TIPS Special interests: Children's ms must come with illustrator. "We will always be looking for good historical manuscripts. In addition, we are actively seeking inspirational romances and Regency period romances." Numerous romance anthologies are planned. Topics and word count are posted on the Website. Writers should query with their proposal. After the submission deadline has passed, editors select the stories. "I don't publish based on industry trends. We buy what we like and what we believe readers are looking for. However, often this proves to be the genres and time-periods larger publishers are not currently interested in. Be professional at all times. Present your manuscript in the best possible light. Be sure you have run spell check and that the manuscript has been vetted by at least one critique partner, preferably more. Many times we receive manuscripts that have wonderful stories involved, but would take far too much time to edit to make it marketable."

HIGH TIDE PRESS

2081 Calistoga Dr., Suite 2N, New Lenox IL 60451. (815)717-3780. **Website:** www.hightidepress.com.

Contact: Monica Regan, senior editor. Estab. 1995. Publishes hardcover and trade paperback originals. **Publishes 2-3 titles/year. 20 queries received/year. 3 mss received/year. 50% of books from first-time authors. 100% from unagented writers. Pays royalty. Percentages vary.** Publishes book up to 1 year after acceptance. Accepts simultaneous submissions. Responds in 6 months to queries and proposals. Catalog and guidelines online.

8— "High Tide Press is a leading provider of resources for disability and nonprofit professionals - publications and training materials on intellectual/developmental disabilities, behavioral health, and nonprofit management."

NONFICTION Subjects include business, economics, education, health, medicine, how-to, human services, nonprofit management, psychology, reference., All of these topics as they relate to developmental, learning and intellectual disabilities, behavioral health, and human services management. "We do not publish personal stories. We produce materials for direct support staff, managers and professionals in the fields of disabilities and human services, as well as educators." Query via e-mail.

TIPS "Our readers are leaders and managers, mostly in the field of human services, and especially those who serve persons with intellectual disabilities or behavioral health needs."

HINKLER

45-55 Fairchild St., Heatherton VI 3202, Australia. (61)(3)9552-1333. **Fax:** (61)(3)9558-2566. **E-mail:** enquiries@hinkler.com.au; Stevie.Brockley@hinkler.com.au. **Website:** www.hinklerbooks.com. **Contact:** Stephen Ungar, CEO/publisher. Estab. 1993.

8— "Packaged entertainment affordable to every family."

HIPPOCRENE BOOKS INC.

171 Madison Ave., New York NY 10016. (718)454-2366. **E-mail:** info@hippocrenebooks.com. **Website:** www.hippocrenebooks.com. Estab. 1971.

8— "Over the last forty years, Hippocrene Books has become one of America's foremost publishers of foreign language reference books and ethnic cookbooks. As a small publishing house in a marketplace dominated by conglomerates, Hippocrene has succeeded by continually reinventing its list while maintaining a strong international and ethnic orientation."

HIPPOPOTAMUS PRESS

22 Whitewell Rd., Frome Somerset BA11 4EL, UK. (44)(173)466-6653. **E-mail:** rjhippopress@aol.com. **Contact:** R. John, editor; M. Pargitter (poetry); Anna Martin (translation). Estab. 1974. Publishes hardcover and trade paperback originals. **Publishes 6-12 titles/year. 90% of books from first-time authors. 90% from unagented writers. Pays 7 ½-10% royalty on retail price. Pays advance.** Publishes book 10 months after acceptance. Accepts simultaneous submissions. Responds in 1 month to queries. Catalog available free.

8— "Hippopotamus Press publishes first, full collections of verse by those well represented in the mainstream poetry magazines of the English-speaking world."

NONFICTION Subjects include language, literature, translation. Query with SASE. Submit complete ms.

POETRY "Read one of our authors—Poets often make the mistake of submitting poetry without knowing the type of verse we publish." Query and submit complete ms.

TIPS "We publish books for a literate audience. We have a strong link to the Modernist tradition. Read what we publish."

HISTORY PUBLISHING COMPANY, INC.

P.O. Box 700, Palisades NY 10964. **Fax:** (845)231-6167. **E-mail:** djb@historypublishingco.com. **Website:** www.historypublishingco.com. **Contact:** Don Bracken, editorial director. Estab. 2001. Publishes hardcover and trade paperback originals and electronic books. **Publishes 20 titles/year. 50% of books from first-time authors. 75% from unagented writers. Pays 7-10% royalty on wholesale list price. Does not pay advances to unpublished authors.** Publishes book 1 year after acceptance. Responds in 2 months to full mss. Guidelines on website.

NONFICTION Subjects include Nonfiction: Americana, business, economics, contemporary culture, creative nonfiction, government, politics, history, military, war, social sciences, sociology, world affairs. Query with SASE. Submit proposal package, outline, 3 sample chapters. Submit complete ms. Reviews artwork/photos. Send photocopies.

TIPS "We focus on an audience interested in the events that shaped the world we live in and the events of today that continue to shape that world. Focus on interesting and serious events that will appeal to the contemporary reader who likes easy-to-read history that flows from one page to the next."

HIS WORK CHRISTIAN PUBLISHING

P.O. Box 563, Ward Cove AK 99928. (206)274-8474. **Fax:** (614)388-0664. **E-mail:** hiswork@hisworkpub.com. **Website:** www.hisworkpub.com. **Contact:** Angela J. Perez, acquisitions editor. Estab. 2005. Publishes trade paperback and electronic originals and reprints; also, hardcover originals. **Publishes 3-5 titles/year. 100% from unagented writers. Pays 10-20% royalty on wholesale price.** Publishes book 1-2 years after acceptance. Accepts simultaneous submissions. Responds in 1-3 months to queries; 1-2 months to *requested* manuscripts. Catalog online. "Guidelines available online and updated regularly. Please check these before submitting to see what we are looking for."

NONFICTION Subjects include child guidance, cooking, foods, nutrition, creative nonfiction, gardening, health, medicine, history, hobbies, language, literature, memoirs, money, finance, music, dance, photography, recreation, religion, sports. "We only accept Christian material or material that does not go against Christian standards. This is a very strict policy that we enforce. Please keep this in mind before deciding to submit your work to us." Submit query/proposal package, 3 sample chapters, clips. Reviews artwork/photos. Send photocopies.

FICTION Subjects include humor, juvenile, mystery, picture books, poetry, religious, short story collections, sports, suspense, young adult. Submit query/proposal package, 3 sample chapters, clips.

POETRY "We only plan to publish 1-2 titles per year in poetry. Send us only your best work." Submit 15 sample poems.

TIPS "Audience is children and adults who are looking for the entertainment and relaxation you can only get from jumping into a good book. Submit only your best work to us. Submit only in the genres we are interested in publishing. Do not submit work that is not suitable for a Christian audience."

HOLIDAY HOUSE, INC.

425 Madison Ave., New York NY 10017. (212)688-0085. **Fax:** (212)421-6134. **E-mail:** info@holidayhouse.com. **Website:** holidayhouse.com. **Contact:** Mary Cash, editor-in-chief. Estab. 1935. Publishes hardcover originals and paperback reprints. **Publishes 50 titles/year. 5% of books from first-time**

authors. 50% from unagented writers. Pays royalty on list price, range varies. Agent's royalty. Publishes book 1-2 years after acceptance of ms. Responds in 4 months. Guidelines for #10 SASE.

⚷ "Holiday House publishes children's and young adult books for the school and library markets. We have a commitment to publishing first-time authors and illustrators. We specialize in quality hardcovers from picture books to young adult, both fiction and nonfiction, primarily for the school and library market."

NONFICTION Subjects include Americana, history, science, Judaica. Please send the entire manuscript, whether submitting a picture book or novel. All submissions should be directed to the Editorial Department, Holiday House, 425 Madison Ave., New York, NY 10017. Send your manuscript via U.S. Mail. We do not accept certified or registered mail. There is no need to include a SASE. We do not consider submissions by e-mail or fax. Please note that you do not have to supply illustrations. However, if you have illustrations you would like to include with your submission, you may send detailed sketches or photocopies of the original art. Do not send original art. Reviews artwork/photos. Send photocopies-no originals.

FICTION Subjects include adventure, historical, humor, literary, mainstream, contemporary., Judaica and holiday, animal stories for young readers. Children's books only. Query with SASE. No phone calls, please.

TIPS "We need manuscripts with strong stories and writing."

HOMA & SEKEY BOOKS

P.O. Box 103, Dumont NJ 07628. (201)384-6692. **Fax:** (201)384-6055. **E-mail:** info@homabooks.com. **E-mail:** submission@homabooks.com. **Website:** www.homabooks.com. **Contact:** Shawn Ye, editor (fiction and nonfiction). Estab. 1997. Publishes hardcover originals and trade paperback originals and reprints. **Publishes 10 titles/year. 300-500 queries received/year. 100-200 mss received/year. 50% of books from first-time authors. 90% from unagented writers. Pays 5-10% royalty on retail price.** Publishes book 1 year after acceptance of ms. Accepts simultaneous submissions. Responds in 2 months to queries. Responds in 3 months to proposals. Responds in 4 months to mss. Catalog and guidelines online.

NONFICTION Subjects include alternative, art, architecture, business, economics, contemporary culture, creative nonfiction, ethnic, health, medicine, history, language, literature, literary criticism, memoirs, multicultural, New Age, photography, social sciences, translation, travel, world affairs. We publish books on Asian topics. Books should have something to do with Asia. Submit proposal package, outline, 2 sample chapters. Submit complete ms. Reviews artwork/photos. Send photocopies.

FICTION Subjects include adventure, ethnic, feminist, historical, literary, multicultural, mystery, plays, poetry, poetry in translation, romance, short story collections, translation. We publish books on Asian topics. Books should be Asia-related. Submit proposal package, clips, 2 sample chapters. Submit complete ms.

POETRY We publish books on Asian topics. Poetry should have things to do with Asia. Submit complete ms.

✚Ⓐ HOPEWELL PUBLICATIONS

P.O. Box 11, Titusville NJ 08560. **Website:** www.hopepubs.com. **Contact:** E. Martin, publisher. Estab. 2002. Format publishes in hardcover, trade paperback, and electronic originals; trade paperback and electronic reprints. **Publishes 20-30 titles/year. Receives 2,000 queries/year; 500 mss/year. 25% of books from first-time authors. 75% from unagented writers. Pays royalty on retail price.** Publishes book 6-12 months after acceptance of ms. Accepts simultaneous submissions. Responds in 3 months on queries; 6 months on proposals; 9 months on mss. Catalog online. Guidelines online (e-mail query guidelines).

NONFICTION All nonfiction subjects acceptable. Query online using our online guidelines.

FICTION Subjects include adventure, contemporary, experimental, fantasy, gay, historical, humor, juvenile, literary, mainstream, mystery, plays, short story collections, spiritual, suspense, young adult. All fiction subjects acceptable. Query online using our online guidelines.

HOUGHTON MIFFLIN HARCOURT BOOKS FOR CHILDREN

Imprint of Houghton Mifflin Trade & Reference Division, 222 Berkeley St., Boston MA 02116. (617)351-5000. **Fax:** (617)351-1111. **E-mail:** children's_books@hmco.com. **Website:** www.houghtonmifflinbooks.com. **Contact:** Erica Zappy, associate editor; Kate O'Sullivan, senior editor; Anne Rider, executive editor; Margaret Raymo, editorial director. Publishes hardcover originals and trade paperback originals and reprints. **Publishes 100 titles/year. 5,000 que-**

ries received/year. **14,000 mss received/year. 10% of books from first-time authors. 60% from unagented writers. Pays 5-10% royalty on retail price. Pays variable advance.** Publishes book 2 years after acceptance. Accepts simultaneous submissions. Responds in 4-6 months to queries. Guidelines online.

○ Does not respond to or return mss unless interested.

NONFICTION Subjects include animals, anthropology, archeology, art, architecture, ethnic, history, language, literature, music, dance, nature, environment, science, sports. Interested in innovative books and subjects about which the author is passionate. Query with SASE. Submit sample chapters, synopsis. Reviews artwork/photos. Send photocopies.

FICTION Subjects include adventure, ethnic, historical, humor, juvenile, early readers, literary, mystery, picture books, suspense, young adult, board books. Submit complete ms.

TIPS Faxed or e-mailed manuscripts and proposals are not considered. Complete submission guidelines available on website.

Ⓐ HOUGHTON MIFFLIN HARCOURT CO.

222 Berkeley St., Boston MA 02116. (617)351-5000. **Website:** www.hmhco.com; www.hmhbooks.com. Estab. 1832. Publishes hardcover originals and trade paperback originals and reprints.

NONFICTION We are not a mass market publisher. Our main focus is serious nonfiction. We do practical self-help but not pop psychology self-help. Agented submissions only. Unsolicited mss returned unopened.

♻Ⓢ HOUSE OF ANANSI PRESS

110 Spadina Ave., Suite 801, Toronto ON M5V 2K4, Canada. (416)363-4343. **Fax:** (416)363-1017. **Website:** www.anansi.ca. Estab. 1967. **Pays 8-10% royalties. Pays $750 advance and 10 author's copies.** Publishes book Responds to queries within 1 year, to mss (if invited) within 4 months after acceptance of ms.

POETRY House of Anansi publishes literary fiction and poetry by Canadian and international writers. "We seek to balance the list between well-known and emerging writers, with an interest in writing by Canadians of all backgrounds. We publish Canadian poetry only, and poets must have a substantial publication record—if not in books, then definitely in journals and magazines of repute." Does not want "children's poetry or poetry by previously unpublished poets."

Canadian poets should query first with 10 sample poems (typed double-spaced) and a cover letter with brief bio and publication credits. Considers simultaneous submissions. Poems are circulated to an editorial board. Often comments on rejected poems.

HOW BOOKS

F+W Media, Inc., 10151 Carver Rd., Suite 200, Blue Ash OH 45242. (513)531-2690. **E-mail:** megan.patrick@fwmedia.com. **Website:** www.howdesign.com. **Contact:** Megan Patrick, content director. Estab. 1985. Publishes hardcover and trade paperback originals. **Publishes 15 titles/year. 50 queries received/year. 5 mss received/year. 50% of books from first-time authors. 50% from unagented writers. Pays 10% royalty on wholesale price. Pays $2,000-6,000 advance.** Publishes book 18-24 months. after acceptance of ms. Accepts simultaneous submissions. Responds in 1 month to queries and proposals. Responds in 3 months to mss. Catalog and guidelines online.

NONFICTION Graphic design, creativity, pop culture. "We look for material that reflects the cutting edge of trends, graphic design, and culture. Nearly all HOW Books are intensely visual, and authors must be able to create or supply art/illustration for their books." Query with SASE. Submit proposal package, outline, 1 sample chapter, sample art or sample design. Reviews artwork/photos. Send photocopies and PDF's (if submitting electronically).

TIPS "Audience comprised of graphic designers. Your art, design, or concept."

HQN BOOKS

Imprint of Harlequin, 233 Broadway, Suite 1001, New York NY 10279. **Website:** e.harlequin.com; www.hqn.com. **Contact:** Tracy Farrell, executive editor. Publishes hardcover, trade paperback, and mass market paperback originals. **Pays royalty. Pays advance.**

FICTION Subjects include romance, contemporary and historical. Accepts unagented material. Length: 90,000 words.

HUDSON HILLS PRESS, INC.

3556 Main St., Box 205, Manchester VT 05254. (802)362-6450. **Fax:** (802)362-6459. **E-mail:** editorial@hudsonhills.com. **Website:** www.hudsonhills.com. Estab. 1978. Publishes hardcover and paperback originals. **Publishes 15+ titles/year. 15% of books from first-time authors. 90% from unagented writers. Pays 4-6% royalty on retail price. Pays $3,500 average advance.** Publishes book 1 year after accep-

tance. Accepts simultaneous submissions. Responds in 2 months to queries. Catalog for 6×9 SAE with 2 first-class stamps.

☞ Hudson Hills Press publishes books about art and photography, including monographs.

NONFICTION Subjects include art, architecture, photography. Query first, then submit outline and sample chapters. Reviews artwork/photos.

HUNTER HOUSE PUBLISHERS

P.O. Box 2914, 1515 ½ Park Street, Alameda CA 94501. (510)865-5282. **E-mail:** ordering@hunterhouse.com; acquisitions@hunterhouse.com. **Website:** www.hunterhouse.com. **Contact:** Jeanne Brondino, acquisitions editor; Kiran S. Rana, publisher. Estab. 1978. Publishes trade paperback originals and reprints. **Publishes 10-12 titles/year. 300 queries received/year. 100 mss received/year. 50% of books from first-time authors. 90% from unagented writers. Pays 10-20% royalty on net receipts. Pays $500-3,000 advance.** Publishes book 18 months after acceptance. Accepts simultaneous submissions. Responds in 2 months to queries; 3 months to proposals. Catalog available online. Guidelines available online and by e-mail request.

☞ Hunter House publishes health books (especially women's health), self-help health, sexuality and couple relationships, violence prevention and intervention. De-emphasizing reference, self-help psychology.

NONFICTION Subjects include child guidance, community, health, medicine, nutrition, parenting, psychology, sex, women's issues., self-help, women's health, fitness, relationships, sexuality, personal growth, and violence prevention. Health books (especially women's health) should focus on self-help, health. Family books: Our current focus is sexuality and couple relationships, and alternative lifestyles to high stress. Community topics include violence prevention/violence intervention. We also publish specialized curriculam for counselors and educators in the areas of violence prevention and trauma in children. Query with proposal package, including synopsis, TOC, and chapter outline, two sample chapters, target audience information, competition, and what distinguishes the book. We look for computer printouts of good quality or e-mail. Please inform us if a ms is available on computer disk (IBM format is preferable). Reviews artwork/photos. Send photocopies. Proposals generally not returned, requested mss returned with SASE. Reviews artwork/photos as part of ms package.

FICTION We do not publish fiction, autobiography, or general children's books, so those types of works get returned right away.

TIPS "Audience is concerned people who are looking to educate themselves and their community about real-life issues that affect them. Please send as much information as possible about who your audience is, how your book addresses their needs, and how you reach that audience in your ongoing work. Include a marketing plan. Explain how you will help us market your book. Have a Facebook account, Twitter, or a blog. List any professional organization of which you are a member."

IBEX PUBLISHERS

P.O. Box 30087, Bethesda MD 20824. (301)718-8188. **Fax:** (301)907-8707. **E-mail:** info@ibexpub.com. **Website:** www.ibexpublishers.com. Estab. 1979. Publishes hardcover and trade paperback originals and reprints. **Publishes 10-12 titles/year. Payment varies.** Accepts simultaneous submissions. Catalog available free.

⌘ "IBEX publishes books about Iran and the Middle East and about Persian culture and literature."

NONFICTION Subjects include cooking, foods, nutrition, language, literature. Query with SASE, or submit proposal package, including outline and 2 sample chapters.

POETRY "Translations of Persian poets will be considered."

IBIS EDITIONS

P.O. Box 8074, German Colony Jerusalem 91080, Israel. **E-mail:** iibis@netvision.net.il. **Website:** www.ibiseditions.com. **Contact:** Peter Cole, editor (poetry). Adina Hoffman, editor (essays and criticism). Estab. 1998.

⌘ "Publishes Levant-related books of poetry and belletristic prose. The press publishes translations from Hebrew, Arabic, Greek, French, and the other languages of the region. New writing is published, though special attention is paid to overlooked works from the recent and distant past. Ibis aims to make a modest contribution to the literature of this part of the world by drawing together a group of writers and translators whom both politics and market-forces would otherwise keep far apart, or out of print altogether. Ibis is motivated by the belief that literary work, especially when translated into a common language, can serve as an important vehicle for the promotion of understanding between individuals and peoples, and for the discovery of common ground."

ICONOGRAFIX, INC.

1830A Hanley Rd., P.O. Box 446, Hudson WI 54016. (715)381-9755. **Fax:** (715)381-9756. **E-mail:** dcfrautschi@iconografixinc.com. **Website:** www.enthusiastbooks.com. **Contact:** Dylan Frautschi, editorial director. Estab. 1992. Publishes trade paperback originals. **Publishes 24 titles/year. 100 queries received/year. 20 mss received/year. 50% of books from first-time authors. 100% from unagented writers. Pays 8-12% royalty on wholesale price. Pays $1,000-3,000 advance.** Publishes book 1 year after acceptance. Accepts simultaneous submissions. Responds in 1 month to queries; 3 months to proposals and mss. Catalog and guidelines free.

⌘ "Iconografix publishes special, historical-interest photographic books for transportation equipment enthusiasts. Currently emphasizing emergency vehicles, buses, trucks, railroads, automobiles, auto racing, construction equipment, snowmobiles."

NONFICTION Subjects include Americana, photos from archives of historic places, objects, people, history, hobbies, military, war., transportation (older photos of specific vehicles). Interested in photo archives. Query with SASE, or submit proposal package, including outline. Reviews artwork/photos. Send photocopies.

IDEALS PUBLICATIONS INC.

2630 Elm Hill Pike, Suite 100, Nashville TN 37214. (615)781-1451. **E-mail:** kwest@guideposts.org. **Website:** www.idealsbooks.com. Estab. 1944.

⌘ "Ideals Publications publishes 20 to 25 new children's titles a year, primarily for two- to eight-year-olds. Our backlist includes more than 400 titles, and we publish picture books, activity books, board books, and novelty and sound books covering a wide array of topics, such as Bible stories, holidays, early learning, history, family relationships, and values. Our bestselling titles include *The Story of Christmas, The Story of Easter, Seaman's Journal, How Do I Love You ?, My Daddy and I*, and *The Story of Jesus.* Through our dedication to publishing high-quality and engaging books, we never forget our obligation to our littlest readers to help create those special moments with books."

FICTION Ideals Children's Books publishes fiction and nonfiction picture books for children ages 4 to 8. Subjects include holiday, inspirational, and patriotic themes; relationships and values; and general fiction. Mss should be no longer than 800 words. CandyCane Press publishes board books and novelty books for children ages 2 to 5. Subject matter is similar to Ideals Children's Books, with a focus on younger children. Mss should be no longer than 250 words.

IDW PUBLISHING

5080 Santa Fe, San Diego CA 92109. **E-mail:** letters@ idwpublishing.com. **Website:** www.idwpublishing. com. Estab. 1999. Publishes hardcover, mass market and trade paperback originals.

🔑 IDW Publishing currently publishes a wide range of comic books and graphic novels including titles based on Angel, Doctor Who, GI Joe, Star Trek, Terminator: Salvation, and Transformers. Creator-driven titles include Fallen Angel by Peter David and JK Woodward, Locke & Key by Joe Hill and Gabriel Rodriguez, and a variety of titles by writer Steve Niles including Wake the Dead, Epilogue, and Dead, She Said.

IDYLL ARBOR, INC.

39129 264th Ave. SE, Enumclaw WA 98022. (360)825-7797. **Fax:** (360)825-5670. **E-mail:** editors@idyllarbor. com. **Website:** www.idyllarbor.com. **Contact:** Tom Blaschko. Estab. 1984. Publishes hardcover and trade paperback originals, and trade paperback reprints. **Publishes 6 titles/year. 50% of books from first-time authors. 100% from unagented writers. Pays 8-15% royalty on wholesale price or retail price.** Publishes book 1 year after acceptance. Accepts simultaneous submissions. Responds in 1 month; 2 months to proposals; 6 months to mss. Catalog and guidelines free.

🔑 "Idyll Arbor publishes practical information on the current state and art of healthcare practice. Currently emphasizing therapies (recreational, aquatic, occupational, music, horticultural), and activity directors in long-term care facilities. Issues Press looks at problems in society from video games to returning veterans and their problems reintegrating into the civil-

ian world. Pine Winds Press publishes books about strange phenomena such as Bigfoot."

NONFICTION Subjects include health, medicine, for therapists, activity directors, psychology, recreational therapy., horticulture (used in long-term care activities or health care therapy). "Idyll Arbor is currently developing a line of books under the imprint Issues Press, which treats emotional issues in a clear-headed manner. The latest books are *Barrier-Free Theatre, Diet Myths BUSTED, and Visits from the Forest People.* Another series of *Personal Health* books explains a condition or a closely related set of medical or psychological conditions. The target audience is the person or the family of the person with the condition. We want to publish a book that explains a condition at the level of detail expected of the average primary care physician so that our readers can address the situation intelligently with specialists. We look for manuscripts from authors with recent clinical experience. Good grounding in theory is required, but practical experience is more important." Query preferred with outline and 1 sample chapter. Reviews artwork/photos. Send photocopies.

TIPS "The books must be useful for the health practitioner who meets face to face with patients or the books must be useful for teaching undergraduate and graduate level classes. We are especially looking for therapists with a solid clinical background to write on their area of expertise."

ILIUM PRESS

2407 S. Sonora Dr., Spokane WA 99037-9011. (509)928-7950. **E-mail:** contact@iliumpress.com; submissions@iliumpress.com. **Website:** www.iliumpress. com. **Contact:** John Lemon, Owner/editor (literature, epic poetry, how-to). Estab. 2010. Format publishes in trade paperback originals and reprints, electronic originals and reprints. **Publishes 5-10 titles/year. Pays 20%-50% royalties on wholesale price.** Publishes book 6 months after acceptance of ms. Responds in 1 month on queries/proposals and 3 months on manuscripts. Guidelines available on website www. iliumpress.com.

NONFICTION Subjects include contemporary culture, memoirs, music. "Mostly interested in alternative music bio and small business how-to that appeals to urban hipster crowd-DIY music, art, creative work and its promotion." Query with SASE (preferred). Submit proposal package, including outline, 3 sample chapters and SASE.

FICTION Subjects include adventure, erotica, literary, mystery, poetry, poetry in translation, science fiction., noir, gritty mystery; focus on epic narrative poetry; dystopiad sci-fi. "See website for guidelines and preferred styles." Query with SASE. Submit proposal package, including synopsis, 3 sample chapters and SASE.

POETRY "I am primarily interested in epic, narrative book-length poems. See website for details." Query. Submit 3 sample chapters.

TIPS "Read submission guidelines on my website."

ILLUMINATION ARTS

P.O. Box 1865, Bellevue WA 98009. **Website:** www.illumin.com. **Contact:** Ruth Thompson, editorial director. Estab. 1987. **Pays authors and illustrators royalty based on wholesale price. Book fliers available for SASE.**

NONFICTION Uses color artwork only. Reviews both ms submissions from authors and illustration packages from artists. Artists may query with color samples, résumé and promotional material to be kept on file or returned with SASE only. Responds within 3 months with SASE only. Samples returned with SASE or filed.

FICTION Word length: Prefers under 1,000, but will consider up to 1,500 words. Recently published *God's Promise*, by Maureen Moss, illustrated by Gerald Purnell; *Roonie B. Moonie: Lost and Alone*, by Janan Cain.

TIPS "Read our books or visit website to see what our books are like. Follow submission guidelines found on website. Be patient. We are unable to track unsolicited submissions."

IMAGE COMICS

Submissions, 2134 Allston Way, 2nd Floor, Berkeley CA 94704. **E-mail:** submissions@imagecomics.com. **Website:** www.imagecomics.com. **Contact:** Eric Stephenson, publisher. Estab. 1992.

Publishes comic books, graphic novels. See this company's website for detailed guidelines.

IMMEDIUM

P.O. Box 31846, San Francisco CA 94131. (415)452-8546. **Fax:** (360)937-6272. **E-mail:** submissions@immedium.com. **Website:** www.immedium.com. **Contact:** Amy Ma, acquisitions editor. Estab. 2005. Publishes hardcover and trade paperback originals. **Publishes 4 titles/year. 50 queries received/year. 25 mss received/year. 50% of books from first-time authors. 90% from unagented writers. Pays 5% royalty on**

wholesale price. **Pays on publication.** Publishes book 2 years after acceptance. Accepts simultaneous submissions. Responds in 1 month to queries; 2 months to proposals; 3 months to mss. Catalog available online. Guidelines online.

"*Immedium* focuses on publishing eye-catching children's picture books, Asian American topics, and contemporary arts, popular culture, and multicultural issues."

NONFICTION Subjects include art, architecture, multicultural. Query with SASE. Submit proposal package, outline, 2 sample chapters. Submit complete ms. Reviews artwork/photos. Send photocopies.

FICTION Subjects include comic books, picture books. Submit complete ms.

TIPS "Our audience is children and parents. Please visit our site."

IMPACT BOOKS

F+W Media, Inc., 10151 Carver Road, Suite 200, Blue Ash OH 45242. (513)531-2690. **Fax:** (513)531-2686. **E-mail:** pam.wissman@fwmedia.com. **Website:** www.northlightshop.com; www.impact-books.com. **Contact:** Pamela Wissman, editorial director (art instruction for fantasy, comics, manga, anime, popular culture, graffiti, science fiction, cartooning, body art). Estab. 2004. Publishes trade paperback originals and reprints. **Publishes 8-9 titles/year. 50 queries received/year. 10-12 mss received/year. 80% of books from first-time authors. 100% from unagented writers.** Publishes book 11 months after acceptance of ms. Accepts simultaneous submissions. Responds in 4 months to queries. Responds in 4 months to proposals. Responds in 2 months to mss. Catalog available free. Guidelines online.

IMPACT Books publishes titles that emphasize illustrated how-to-draw-manga, graffiti, fantasy and comics art instruction. Currently emphasizing fantasy art, traditional American comics styles, including humor; and Japanese-style (manga and anime) and graffiti. This market is for experienced artists who are willing to work with an IMPACT editor to produce a step-by-step how-to book about the artist's creative process. See also separate listing for F+W Media in this section.

NONFICTION Subjects include art, art instruction, contemporary culture, creative nonfiction, hobbies. Submit proposal package, outline, 1 sample chapter, at least 1 example of sample art. Reviews artwork/photos. Send digital art, hard copies, or anything that represents the art well, preferably in the form the author plans to submit art if contracted.

TIPS "Audience comprised primarily of 12- to 18-year-old beginners along the lines of comic buyers, in general—mostly teenagers—but also appealing to a broader audience of young adults 19-30 who need basic techniques. Art must appeal to teenagers and be submitted in a form that will reproduce well. Authors need to know how to teach beginners step-by-step. A sample step-by-step demonstration is important."

IMPACT PUBLISHERS, INC.

P.O. Box 6016, Atascadero CA 93423. **E-mail:** submissions@impactpublishers.com; publisher@impactpublishers.com. **Website:** www.impactpublishers.com. **Contact:** Freeman Porter, submissions editor; Jean Trumbull, production manager. Estab. 1970. **Publishes 3-5 titles/year. 20% of books from first-time authors. Pays authors royalty of 10-12%. Offers advances. Pays illustrators by the project. Catalog available for #10 SAE with 2 first-class stamps; ms guidelines available for SASE. All imprints included in a single catalog.** Accepts simultaneous submissions. Responds to queries/mss in 3 months.

NONFICTION Young readers, middle readers, young adults: self-help. Query or submit complete ms, cover letter, résumé.

TIPS "Please do not submit fiction, poetry or narratives."

INFORMATION TODAY, INC.

143 Old Marlton Pike, Medford NJ 08055. (609)654-6266. **Fax:** (609)654-4309. **E-mail:** jbryans@infotoday.com. **Website:** www.infotoday.com. **Contact:** John B. Bryans, editor-in-chief/publisher. Publishes hardcover and trade paperback originals. **Publishes 15-20 titles/year. 200 queries received/year. 30 mss received/year. 30% of books from first-time authors. 90% from unagented writers. Pays 10-15% royalty on wholesale price. Pays $500-2,500 advance.** Publishes book 9 months after acceptance. Accepts simultaneous submissions. Responds in 1 month to queries; 2 months to proposals; 3 months to mss. Catalog free or on website. Proposal guidelines free or via e-mail as attachment.

⚷→ "We look for highly-focused coverage of cutting-edge technology topics. Written by established experts and targeted to a tech-savvy readership. Virtually all our titles focus on how information is accessed, used, shared, and transformed into knowledge that can benefit people, business, and society. Currently emphasizing Internet/online technologies, including their social significance: biography, how-to, technical, reference, scholarly. De-emphasizing fiction."

NONFICTION Subjects include business, economics, computers, electronics, education, science., Internet and cyberculture. Query with SASE. Reviews artwork/photos. Send photocopies.

TIPS "Our readers include scholars, academics, indexers, librarians, information professionals (ITI imprint), as well as high-end consumer and business users of Internet/WWW/online technologies, and people interested in the marriage of technology with issues of social significance (i.e., cyberculture)."

INGALLS PUBLISHING GROUP, INC

P.O. Box 2500, Banner Elk NC 28604. (828)297-6884. **Fax:** (828)297-6880. **E-mail:** editor@ingallspublishinggroup.com; sales@ingallspublishinggroup.com. **Website:** www.ingallspublishinggroup.com. **Contact:** Rebecca Owen. Estab. 2001. Publishes hardcover originals, paperback originals and paperback reprints. **Pays 10% royalty.** Publishes book 6 months-2 years after acceptance. Accepts simultaneous submissions. Responds in 6 weeks to queries or mss. Guidelines online.

⚷→ "We are a small regional house focusing on popular fiction and memoir. At present, we are most interested in regional fiction, historical fiction and mystery fiction." Exploring digital technologies for printing and e-books. Member IBPA, MWA, SIBA. Accepts unsolicited mss. Query first. Will specifically request if interested in reading synopsis and 3 sample chapters. Accepts queries by e-mail. Include estimated word count, brief bio, list of publishing credits. Agented fiction 10%. Accepts electronic submissions. No submissions on disk. Often comments on rejected mss.

FICTION Subjects include historical, mystery, regional. Query first. Will specifically request if interested in reading synopsis and 3 sample chapters. Accepts queries by e-mail. Include estimated word count, brief bio, list of publishing credits. No submissions on disk.

☯ INSOMNIAC PRESS

520 Princess Ave., London ON N6B 2B8, Canada. (416)504-6270. **E-mail:** mike@insomniacpress.com.

Website: www.insomniacpress.com. **Contact:** Mike O'Connor, publisher. Gillian Urbankiewicz, assistant ed. Estab. 1992. Publishes trade paperback originals and reprints, mass market paperback originals, and electronic originals and reprints. **Publishes 20 titles/year. 250 queries received/year. 1,000 mss received/year. 50% of books from first-time authors. 80% from unagented writers. Pays 10-15% royalty on retail price. Pays $500-1,000 advance.** Publishes book 6 months after acceptance of ms. Accepts simultaneous submissions. Guidelines online.

NONFICTION Subjects include business, creative nonfiction, gay, lesbian, government, politics, health, medicine, language, literature, money, finance, multicultural, religion., true crime. Very interested in areas such as true crime and well-written and well-researched nonfiction on topics of wide interest. Query via e-mail, submit proposal package including outline, 2 sample chapters, or submit complete ms. Reviews artwork/photos. Send photocopies.

FICTION Subjects include comic books, ethnic, experimental, gay, lesbian, humor, literary, mainstream, multicultural, mystery, poetry, suspense. "We publish a mix of commercial (mysteries) and literary fiction." Query via e-mail, submit proposal.

POETRY "Our poetry publishing is limited to 2-4 books per year and we are often booked up a year or two in advance." Submit complete ms.

TIPS "We envision a mixed readership that appreciates up-and-coming literary fiction and poetry as well as solidly researched and provocative nonfiction. Peruse our website and familiarize yourself with what we've published in the past."

INTERLINK PUBLISHING GROUP, INC.

46 Crosby St., Northampton MA 01060. (413)582-7054. **Fax:** (413)582-7057. **E-mail:** info@interlinkbooks.com; editor@interlinkbooks.com. **Website:** www.interlinkbooks.com. **Contact:** Michel Moushabeck, publisher; Pam Thompson, editor. Estab. 1987. Publishes hardcover and trade paperback originals. **Publishes 90 titles/year. 30% of books from first-time authors. 50% from unagented writers. Pays 6-8% royalty on retail price. Pays small advance.** Publishes book 18 months after acceptance of ms. Accepts simultaneous submissions. Responds in 3-6 months to queries. Catalog and guidelines available free online.

Interlink is a independent publisher of a general trade list of adult fiction and nonfiction with an emphasis on books that have a wide appeal while also meeting high intellectual and literary standards.

NONFICTION Subjects include world travel, world literature, world history and politics, art, world music & dance, international cooking, children's books from around the world. Submit outline and sample chapters.

FICTION Subjects include ethnic., international adult. "We are looking for translated works relating to the Middle East, Africa or Latin America." No science fiction, romance, plays, erotica, fantasy, horror. Query with SASE. Submit outline, sample chapters.

TIPS "Any submissions that fit well in our publishing program will receive careful attention. A visit to our website, your local bookstore, or library to look at some of our books before you send in your submission is recommended."

INTERNATIONAL PRESS

P.O. Box 43502, Somerville MA 02143. (617)623-3855. **Fax:** (617)623-3101. **E-mail:** ipb-mgmt@intlpress.com. **Website:** www.intlpress.com. **Contact:** Brian Bianchini, general manager (research math and physics). Estab. 1992. Publishes hardcover originals and reprints. **Publishes 12 titles/year. 200 queries received/year. 500 mss received/year. 10% of books from first-time authors. 100% from unagented writers. Pays 3-10% royalty.** Publishes book 6 months after acceptance. Responds in 5 months to queries and proposals; 1 year to mss. Guidelines online.

International Press of Boston, Inc. is an academic publishing company that welcomes book publication inquiries from prospective authors on all topics in Mathematics and Physics. International Press also publishes high-level mathematics and mathematical physics book titles and textbooks.

NONFICTION Subjects include science. All our books will be in research mathematics. Authors need to provide ready to print latex files. Submit complete ms. Reviews artwork/photos. Send EPS files.

TIPS "Audience is PhD mathematicians, researchers and students."

INTERNATIONAL PUBLISHERS CO., INC.

235 W. 23 St., Floor 8, New York NY 10011. (212)366-9816. **Fax:** (212)366-9820. **E-mail:** service@intpubnyc.com. **Website:** www.intpubnyc.com. **Contact:** Betty Smith, president. Estab. 1924. Publishes hardcover

originals, trade paperback originals and reprints. **Publishes 5-6 titles/year. 50-100 mss received/year. 10% of books from first-time authors. Pays 5-7½% royalty on paperbacks; 10% royalty on cloth.** Publishes book 6 months after acceptance of ms. Accepts simultaneous submissions. Responds in 1 month to queries; 6 months to mss. Catalog online. Guidelines online.

8—☛ "International Publishers Co., Inc. emphasizes books based on Marxist science."

NONFICTION Subjects include art, architecture, economics, government, politics, history, philosophy. Books on labor, black studies, and women's studies based on Marxist science have high priority. Query, or submit outline, sample chapters, and SASE. Reviews artwork/photos.

INTERNATIONAL WEALTH SUCCESS

P.O. Box 186, Merrick NY 11570. (516)766-5850. **Fax:** (516)766-5919. **Website:** www.iwsmoney.com. **Contact:** Tyler G. Hicks, editor. Estab. 1967. **Publishes 10 titles/year. 100% of books from first-time authors. 100% from unagented writers. Pays 10% royalty on wholesale or retail price. Offers usual advance of $1,000, but this varies depending on author's reputation and nature of book. Buys all rights.** Publishes book 4 months after acceptance. Responds in 1 month to queries. Catalog and guidelines for 9x12 SAE with 3 first-class stamps.

NONFICTION Subjects include business, economics., financing, business success, venture capital, etc. Techniques, methods, sources for building wealth. Highly personal, how-to-do-it with plenty of case histories. Books are aimed at wealth builders and are highly sympathetic to their problems. These publications present a wide range of business opportunities while providing practical, hands-on, step-by-step instructions aimed at helping readers achieve their personal goals in as short a time as possible while adhering to ethical and professional business standards. Length: 60,000-70,000 words. Query.

TIPS "With the mass layoffs in large and medium-size companies there is an increasing interest in owning your own business. So we focus on more how-to, hands-on material on owning—and becoming successful in—one's own business of any kind. Our market is the BWB—Beginning Wealth Builder. This person has so little money that financial planning is something they never think of. Instead, they want to know what kind of a business they can get into to make some money without a large investment. Write for this market and you have millions of potential readers. Remember—there are a lot more people without money than with money."

⊘ INTERVARSITY PRESS

P.O. Box 1400, Downers Grove IL 60515-1426. **E-mail:** e-mail@ivpress.com. **Website:** www.ivpress.com/submissions. **Contact:** David Zimmerman, associate editor (Likewise); Cindy Bunch, Sr. editor (IVP Connect, Formatio); Mike Gibson, associate editor (academic, reference); Gary Deddo, sr. ed. (IVP Academic) or Dan Reid, sr. ed. (reference, academic); Al Hsu, assoc. ed. (IVP Books). Estab. 1947. Publishes hardcover originals, trade paperback and mass market paperback originals. **Publishes 110-130 titles/year. 450 queries received/year. 900 mss received/year. 13% of books from first-time authors. 86% from unagented writers. Pays 14-16% royalty on retail price. Outright purchase is $75-1,500. Pays negotiable advance.** Publishes book 18 months after acceptance. Accepts simultaneous submissions. Responds in 3 months to proposals "from pastors, professors, or previously published authors. We are unable to respond to other proposals or queries.". Catalog for 9×12 SAE and 5 first-class stamps, or online. Guidelines online.

8—☛ "InterVarsity Press publishes a full line of books from an evangelical Christian perspective targeted to an open-minded audience. We serve those in the university, the church, and the world, by publishing books from an evangelical Christian perspective."

NONFICTION Subjects include business, child guidance, contemporary culture, economics, ethinic, government, history, memoirs, multicultural, philosophy, psychology, religion, science, social sciences, sociology, spirituality, women's issues/studies. "InterVarsity Press publishes a full line of books from an evangelical Christian perspective targeted to an open-minded audience. We serve those in the university, the church, and the world, by publishing books from an evangelical Christian perspective." Very few business/economics, child guidance/parenting, memoirs. Query with SASE.

TIPS "The best way to submit to us is to go to a conference where one of our editors are. Networking is key. We're seeking writers who have good ideas and a presence/platform where they've been testing their ideas out (a church, university, on a prominent blog). We need authors who will bring resources to the table for helping to publicize and sell their books (speaking at seminars and conferences, writing for national magazines or newspapers, etc.)."

IRISH ACADEMIC PRESS

2 Brookside, Dundrum Road, Dundrum Dublin 14, Ireland. (353)(1)2989937. **Fax:** (353)(1)2982783. **E-mail:** info@iap.ie; lisa.hyde@iap.ie. **Website:** www.iap.ie. **Contact:** Lisa Hyde, editor. Estab. 1974. **Publishes 15 titles/year. Pays royalty.** Accepts simultaneous submissions. Guidelines available free.

○ Request submission guidelines before submitting.

NONFICTION Subjects include art, architecture, government, politics, history, literary criticism, military, war, womens issues, womens studies., genealogy, Irish history. Does not want fiction or poetry. Query with SASE. Submit proposal package, outline, résumé, publishing history, bio, target audience, competing books, SASE.

IRON GATE PUBLISHING

P.O. Box 999, Niwot CO 80544. (303)530-2551. **Fax:** (303)530-5273. **E-mail:** editor@irongate.com. **Website:** www.irongate.com. **Contact:** Dina C. Carson, publisher (how-to, genealogy, local history). Publishes hardcover and trade paperback originals. **Publishes 6-10 titles/year. 100 queries received/year. 20 mss received/year. 30% of books from first-time authors. 10% from unagented writers. Pays royalty on a case-by-case basis.** Publishes book 1 year after acceptance. Accepts simultaneous submissions. Responds in 2 months to proposals. Catalog and writer's guidelines free or online.

☞ "Our readers are people who are looking for solid, how-to advice on planning reunions or self-publishing a genealogy."

NONFICTION Hobbies, genealogy, local history, reunions, party planning. Query with SASE, or submit proposal package, including outline, 2 sample chapters, and marketing summary. Reviews artwork/photos. Send photocopies.

TIPS "Please look at the other books we publish and tell us in your query letter why your book would fit into our line of books."

ITALICA PRESS

595 Main St., Suite 605, New York NY 10044-0047. (212)935-4230. **Fax:** (212)838-7812. **E-mail:** inqui-ries@italicapress.com. **Website:** www.italicapress.com. **Contact:** Ronald G. Musto and Eileen Gardiner, publishers. Estab. 1985. Publishes trade paperback originals. **Publishes 6 titles/year. 600 queries received/year. 60 mss received/year. 5% of books from first-time authors. 100% from unagented writers. Pays 7-15% royalty on wholesale price; author's copies.** Publishes book 1 year after acceptance of ms. Accepts simultaneous submissions. Responds in 1 month to queries. Responds in 4 months to mss. Catalog and guidelines online.

☞ "Italica Press publishes English translations of modern Italian fiction and medieval and Renaissance nonfiction."

NONFICTION Subjects include translation. "We publish English translations of medieval and Renaissance source materials and English translations of modern Italian fiction." Query with SASE. Reviews artwork/photos. Send photocopies.

FICTION Query with SASE.

POETRY Poetry titles are always translations and generally dual language.

TIPS "We are interested in considering a wide variety of medieval and Renaissance topics (not historical fiction), and for modern works we are only interested in translations from Italian fiction by well-known Italian authors." *Only* fiction that has been previously published in Italian. 90% of proposals we receive are completely off base—but we are very interested in things that are right on target. Please send return postage if you want your *only* fiction that has been previously published in Italian. A *brief* call saves a lot of postage.

JAIN PUBLISHING CO.

P.O. Box 3523, Fremont CA 94539. (510)659-8272. **Fax:** (510)659-0501. **E-mail:** mail@jainpub.com. **Website:** www.jainpub.com. **Contact:** M. Jain, editor-in-chief. Estab. 1989. Publishes hardcover and paperback originals and reprints. **Publishes 12-15 titles/year. 300 queries received/year. 100% from unagented writers. Pays 5-15% royalty on net sales.** Publishes book 2 years after acceptance. Responds in 3 months to mss. Catalog and guidelines online.

☞ Jain Publishing Co. publishes college textbooks and supplements, as well as professional and scholarly references, e-books and e-courses. It also publishes in the areas of humanities and societies pertaining specifically to ask, commonly categorized as "Asian Studies".

NONFICTION Subjects include humanities, social sciences., Asian studies, medical, business, scientific/technical. Submit proposal package, publishing history. Reviews artwork/photos. Send photocopies.

ALICE JAMES BOOKS

238 Main St., Farmington ME 04938. (207)778-7071. **Fax:** (207)778-7766. **E-mail:** interns@alicejamesbooks.org; Frank@alicejamesbooks.org. **Website:** www.alicejamesbooks.org. **Contact:** Frank Giampietro, managing editor; Carey Salerno, executive director; Meg Willing, editorial assistant. Estab. 1973. Publishes trade paperback originals. **Publishes 6 titles/year. 1,000 mss received/year. 50% of books from first-time authors. 100% from unagented writers. Pays through competition awards.** Publishes book 1 year after acceptance. Accepts simultaneous submissions. Responds promptly to queries; 4 months to mss. Catalog for free or on website. Guidelines for #10 SASE or on website.

➥ "Alice James Books is a nonprofit cooperative poetry press. The founders' objectives were to give women access to publishing and to involve authors in the publishing process. The cooperative selects mss for publication through both regional and national competitions."

POETRY "Alice James Books is a nonprofit cooperative poetry press. The founders' objectives were to give women access to publishing and to involve authors in the publishing process. The cooperative selects mss for publication through both regional and national competitions." Seeks to publish the best contemporary poetry by both established and beginning poets, with particular emphasis on involving poets in the publishing process. Publishes flat-spined paperbacks of high quality, both in production and contents. Does not want children's poetry or light verse. Publishes 6 paperback books/year, 80 pages each, in editions of 1,500. Query.

TIPS "Send SASE for contest guidelines or check website. Do not send work without consulting current guidelines."

JEWISH LIGHTS PUBLISHING

LongHill Partners, Inc., Sunset Farm Offices, Rt. 4, P.O. Box 237, Woodstock VT 05091. (802)457-4000. **Fax:** (802)457-4004. **E-mail:** editorial@jewishlights.com; sales@jewishlights.com. **Website:** www.jewishlights.com. **Contact:** Tim Holtz, art acquisitions. Estab. 1990. Publishes hardcover and trade paperback originals, trade paperback reprints. **Publishes 30 titles/year. 50% of books from first-time authors. 75% from unagented writers. Pays authors royalty of 10% of revenue received; 15% royalty for subsequent printings.** Publishes book 1 year after acceptance. Accepts simultaneous submissions. Responds in 3 months to queries. Catalog and guidelines online.

➥ "Jewish Lights publishes books for people of all faiths and all backgrounds who yearn for books that attract, engage, educate and spiritually inspire. Our authors are at the forefront of spiritual thought and deal with the quest for the self and for meaning in life by drawing on the Jewish wisdom tradition. Our books cover topics including history, spirituality, life cycle, children, self-help, recovery, theology and philosophy. We do not publish autobiography, biography, fiction, haggadot, poetry or cookbooks. At this point we plan to do only two books for children annually, and one will be for younger children (ages 4-10)." Fiction/nonfiction: Query with outline/synopsis and 2 sample chapters; submit complete ms for picture books. Include SASE. Responds to queries/mss in 4 months.

NONFICTION Subjects include business, economics, with spiritual slant, finding spiritual meaning in one's work, health, medicine, healing/recovery, wellness, aging, life cycle, history, nature, environment, philosophy, religion, theology, spirituality, and inspiration, women's issues/studies. Picture book, young readers, middle readers: activity books, spirituality. "We do *not* publish haggadot, biography, poetry, or cookbooks." Reviews artwork/photos. Send photocopies. Works with 2 illustrators/year. Reviews ms/illustration packages from artists. Query. Illustrations only: Query with samples; provide résumé. Samples returned with SASE; samples filed.

FICTION Picture books, young readers, middle readers: spirituality. "We are not interested in anything other than spirituality."

TIPS "We publish books for all faiths and backgrounds that also reflect the Jewish wisdom tradition. Explain in your cover letter why you're submitting your project to us in particular. Make sure you know what we publish."

JIST PUBLISHING

7321 Shadeland Station, Suite 200, Indianapolis IN 46256. (317)613-4200. **Fax:** (317)845-1052. **E-mail:**

spines@jist.com. **Website:** www.jist.com. **Contact:** Susan Pines, associate publisher (career and education reference and library titles, assessments, videos, e-products); Lori Cates Hand, product line manager, trade and workbooks (career, job search, and education trade and workbook titles). Estab. 1981. Publishes hardcover and trade paperback originals. **Publishes 60 titles/year. Receives 40 submissions/year. 25% of books from first-time authors. 75% from unagented writers. Pays 8-10% royalty on net receipts. Pays advance: 12 months.** Accepts simultaneous submissions. Responds in 6 months to queries, proposals, and mss. Catalog and guidelines online.

⚷ "Our purpose is to provide quality job search, career development, occupational, and life skills information, products, and services that help people manage and improve their lives and careers-and the lives of others. Publishes practical, self-directed tools and training materials that are used in employment and training, education, and business settings. Whether reference books, trade books, assessment tools, workbooks, or videos, JIST products foster self-directed job-search attitudes and behaviors."

NONFICTION Subjects include : business, economics, education. Specializes in job search, career development, occupational information, character education, and domestic abuse topics. "We want text/workbook formats that would be useful in a school or other institutional setting. We also publish trade titles for all reading levels. Will consider books for professional staff and educators, appropriate software and videos." Submit proposal package, including outline, 1 sample chapter, and author résumé, competitive analysis, marketing ideas.

TIPS "Our audiences are students, job seekers, and career changers of all ages and occupations who want to find good jobs quickly and improve their futures. We sell materials through the trade as well as to institutional markets like schools, colleges, and one-stop career centers."

THE JOHNS HOPKINS UNIVERSITY PRESS

2715 N. Charles St., Baltimore MD 21218. (410)516-6900. **Fax:** (410)516-6968. **E-mail:** jmm@press.jhu.edu. **Website:** www.press.jhu.edu. **Contact:** Jacqueline C. Wehmueller, executive editor (consumer health, psychology and psychiatry, and history of medicine; jcw@press.jhu.edu); Matthew McAdam, editor (mxm@jhu@press.edu); Robert J. Brugger, senior acquisitions editor (American history; rjb@press.jhu.edu); Vincent J. Burke, exec. editor (biology; vjb@press.jhu.edu); Juliana McCarthy, acquisitions editor (humanities, classics, and ancient studies; jmm@press.jhu.edu); Ashleigh McKown, assistant editor (higher education, history of technology, history of science; aem@press.jhu.edu); Suzanne Flinchbaugh, Associate Editor (Political Science, Health Policy, and Co-Publishing Liaison; skf@press.jhu.edu; Greg Nicholl, Assistant Editor (Regional Books, Poetry and Fiction, and Anabaptist and Pietist Studies; gan@press.jhu.edu). Estab. 1878. Publishes hardcover originals and reprints, and trade paperback reprints. **Publishes 140 titles/year. Pays royalty.** Publishes book 1 year after acceptance.

NONFICTION Subjects include government, politics, health, medicine, history, humanities, literary criticism, regional, religion, science. Submit proposal package, outline, 1 sample chapter, curriculum vita. Reviews artwork/photos. Send photocopies.

POETRY "One of the largest American university presses, Johns Hopkins publishes primarily scholarly books and journals. We do, however, publish short fiction and poetry in the series Johns Hopkins: Poetry and Fiction, edited by John Irwin."

JOURNEYFORTH

Imprint of BJU Press, 1700 Wade Hampton Blvd., Greenville SC 29614. (864)242-5100, ext. 4350. **Fax:** (864)298-0268. **E-mail:** jb@bju.edu. **Website:** www.journeyforth.com. **Contact:** Nancy Lohr. Estab. 1974. Publishes paperback originals. **Publishes 25 titles/year. 10% of books from first-time authors. 8% from unagented writers. Pays royalty.** Publishes book 12-18 months after acceptance of ms. Does accept simultaneous submissions. Responds in 1 month to queries. Responds in 3 months to mss. Catalog available free. Guidelines available online at www.bjupress.com/books/freelance.php.

⚷ "Small independent publisher of trustworthy novels and biographies for readers pre-school through high school from a conservative Christian perspective, Christian living books, and Bible studies for adults."

NONFICTION Subjects include animals, contemporary culture, creative nonfiction, environment, history, music, nature, religion, spirituality, sports, young adult. Nonfiction Christian living, Bible studies, church and ministry, church history. We produce books for the adult Christian market that are from a conservative Christian worldview.

FICTION Subjects include adventure, historical, animal, easy-to-read, series, mystery, sports, children's/juvenile, suspense, young adult, western. Our fiction is all based on a moral and Christian worldview. Does not want short stories. Submit 5 sample chapters, synopsis, SASE.

TIPS "Study the publisher's guidelines. No picture books and no submissions by e-mail."

⊕ JUPITER GARDENS PRESS

Jupiter Gardens, LLC, PO Box 191, Grimes IA 50111-0191. **E-mail:** submissions@jupitergardens.com. **Website:** www.jupitergardens.com. **Contact:** Mary Wilson, publisher (romance, sf/f, new age). Estab. 2007. Format publishes in trade paperback originals and reprints; electronic originals and reprints. **Publishes 30+ titles/year. 40% royalty on retail price.** Publishes book 4 months after acceptance of ms. Accepts simultaneous submissions. Responds in 1 months on proposals, 2 months on mss. Catalog available online. Guidelines online.

NONFICTION Subjects include alternative lifestyles, animals, astrology, environment, gay, health, lesbian, medicine, nature, psychic, religion, sex, spirituality, womens issues, world affairs, young adult., romance, science fiction, fantasy, and metaphysical fiction & nonfiction. "We only publish metaphysical/New Age nonfiction, or nonfiction related to science fiction & fantasy." Submit proposal package, including: outline, 3 sample chapters, and promotional plan/market analysis.

FICTION Subjects include fantasy, gay, lesbian, occult, religious, romance, science fiction, spiritual, young adult, New Age/metaphysical. "We only publish romance (all sub-genres), science fiction & fantasy & metaphysical fiction. Our science fiction and fantasy covers a wide variety of topics, such as feminist fantasy, or more hard science fiction and fantasy which looks at the human condition. Our young adult imprint, Jupiter Storm, with thought provoking reads that explore the full range of speculative fiction, includes science fiction or fantasy and metaphysical fiction. These readers would enjoy edgy contemporary works. Our romance readers love seeing a couple, no matter the gender, overcome obstacles and grow in order to find true love. Like our readers, we believe that love can come in many forms." Submit proposal package, including synopsis, 3 sample chapters, and promotional plan/market analysis .

TIPS "No matter which line you're submitting to, know your genre and your readership. We publish a diverse catalog, and we're passionate about our main focus. We want romance that takes your breath away and leaves you with that warm feeling that love does conquer all. Our science fiction takes place in wild and alien worlds, and our fantasy transports readers to mythical realms and finds strange worlds within our own. And our metaphysical non-fiction will help readers gain new skills and awareness for the coming age. We want authors who engage with their readers and who aren't afraid to use social media to connect. Read and follow our submission guidelines."

KAEDEN BOOKS

P.O. Box 16190, Rocky River OH 44116. **E-mail:** lstenger@kaeden.com. **Website:** www.kaeden.com. **Contact:** Lisa Stenger, editor. Estab. 1986. Publishes paperback originals. **Publishes 12-20 titles/year. 1,000 mss received/year. 30% of books from first-time authors. 95% from unagented writers. Pays royalty. Makes outright purchase. Pays flat fee or royalty by individual arrangement with author depending on book.** Publishes book 6-9 months after acceptance of ms. Accepts simultaneous submissions. Responds in 12 months to mss. Catalog and guidelines online.

☞ "Children's book publisher for education K-2 market: reading stories, fiction/nonfiction, chapter books, science, and social studies materials."

NONFICTION Subjects include animals, creative nonfiction, science, social sciences. Submit complete ms. Reviews artwork/photos. Send photocopies.

FICTION Subjects include adventure, fantasy, historical, humor, mystery, short story collections, sports, suspense. Grades K-3 only. Send a disposable copy of ms and SASE.

TIPS "Our audience ranges from Kindergarten-2nd grade school children. We are an educational publisher. We are particularly interested in humorous stories with surprise endings and beginning chapter books."

KALMBACH PUBLISHING CO.

21027 Crossroads Circle, P.O. Box 1612, Waukesha WI 53187. (262)796-8776. **Fax:** (262)798-6468. **E-mail:** books@kalmbach.com. **Website:** www.corporate. kalmbach.com. **Contact:** Ronald Kovach, senior editor. Estab. 1934. Publishes paperback originals and reprints. **Publishes 40-50 titles/year. 50% of books from first-time authors. 99% from unagented writers. Pays 7% royalty on net receipts. Pays $1,500 advance.** Publishes book 18 months after acceptance. Responds in 2 months to queries.

NONFICTION "Focus on beading, wirework, and one-of-a-kind artisan creations for jewelry-making and crafts and in the railfan, model railroading, plastic modeling and toy train collecting/operating hobbies. Kalmbach publishes reference materials and how-to publications for hobbyists, jewelry-makers, and crafters." Query with 2-3 page detailed outline, sample chapter with photos, drawings, and how-to text. Reviews artwork/photos.

TIPS "Our how-to books are highly visual in their presentation. Any author who wants to publish with us must be able to furnish good photographs and rough drawings before we'll consider his or her book."

KAMEHAMEHA PUBLISHING

567 S. King St., Honolulu HI 96813. **Website:** www.KamehamehaPublishing.org. Estab. 1933. **Work purchased outright from authors or by royalty agreement.** Publishes book 2 years after acceptance. Responds in 3 months to queries and mss. Call or write for Catalog.

8—π "Kamehameha Schools Press publishes in the areas of Hawaiian history, Hawaiian culture, Hawaiian language and Hawaiian studies."

NONFICTION Young reader, middle readers, young adults: biography, history, multicultural, Hawaiian folklore.

FICTION Young reader, middle readers, young adults: biography, history, multicultural, Hawaiian folklore.

TIPS "Writers and illustrators must be knowledgeable in Hawaiian history/culture and be able to show credentials to validate their proficiency. Greatly prefer to work with writers/illustrators available in the Honolulu area."

Ⓐ KANE/MILLER BOOK PUBLISHERS

Kane/Miller: A Division of EDC Publishing, 4901 Morena Blvd., Suite 213, San Diego CA 92117. (858)456-0540. **Fax:** (858)456-9641. **E-mail:** info@kanemiller.com; submissions@kanemiller.com. **Website:** www.kanemiller.com. **Contact:** Kira Lynn, editorial department. Estab. 1985. Responds in 90 days.

8—π "Kane/Miller Book Publishers is a division of EDC Publishing, specializing in award-winning children's books from around the world. Our books bring the children of the world closer to each other, sharing stories and ideas, while exploring cultural differences and similarities. Although we continue to look for books from other countries, we are now actively seeking works that convey cultures and communities within the US. We are looking for picture book fiction and nonfiction on those subjects that may be defined as particularly American: sports such as baseball, historical events, American biographies, American folk tales, etc. We are committed to expanding our early and middlegrade fiction list. We're interested in great stories with engaging characters in all genres (mystery, fantasy, adventure, historical, etc.) and, as with picture books, especially those with particularly American subjects. All submissions sent via USPS should be sent to: Editorial Department. Please do not send anything requiring a signature. Work submitted for consideration may also be sent via e-mail. Please send either the complete picture book ms, the published book (with a summary and outline in English, if that is not the language of origin) or a synopsis of the work and two sample chapters. Do not send originals. Illustrators may send color copies, tear sheets, or other non-returnable illustration samples. If you have a website with additional samples of your work, please include the web address. Please do not send original artwork, or samples on CD. A SASE must be included if you send your submission via USPS; otherwise you will not receive a reply. If we wish to follow up, we will notify you."

NONFICTION Subjects include Americana, history, sports, young adult.

FICTION Subjects include adventure, fantasy, historical, juvenile, mystery, picture books. Picture Books: concept, contemporary, health, humor, multicultural. Young Readers: contemporary, multicultural, suspense. Middle Readers: contemporary, humor, multicultural, suspense.

KAR-BEN PUBLISHING

Lerner Publishing Group, 241 First Ave. N, Minneapolis MN 55401. (612)332-3344, ext. 229. **Fax:** 612-332-7615. **E-mail:** Editorial@Karben.com. **Website:**

www.karben.com. Estab. 1974. Publishes hardcover, trade paperback and electronic originals. **Publishes 10-15 titles/year. 800 mss received/year. 20% of books from first-time authors. 70% from unagented writers. Pays 3-5% royalty on NET price. Pays $500-2,500 advance.** Publishes book Most manuscripts published within 2 years. after acceptance of ms. Accepts simultaneous submissions. Responds in 6 weeks. Catalog available online; free upon request. Guidelines online.

NONFICTION Subjects include Jewish content children's books only. "In addition to traditional Jewish-themed stories about Jewish holidays, history, folktales and other subjects, we especially seek stories that reflect the rich diversity of the contemporary Jewish community." Picture books, young readers: activity books, arts/crafts, biography, careers, concept, cooking, history, how-to, multicultural, religion, social issues, special needs; must be of Jewish interest. No textbooks, games, or educational materials. Submit completed ms. Reviews artwork separately.

FICTION Subjects include juvenile; Jewish content only. "We seek picture book mss of about 1,000 words on Jewish-themed topics for children." Picture books: Adventure, concept, folktales, history, humor, multicultural, religion, special needs; must be on a Jewish theme. Average word length: picture books—1,000. Submit full ms. Picture books only.

TIPS "Authors: Do a literature search to make sure similar title doesn't already exist. Illustrators: Look at our online catalog for a sense of what we like—bright colors and lively composition."

KEY CURRICULUM PRESS

1150 65th St., Emeryville CA 94608. (800)995-6284. **Fax:** (800)541-2442. **Website:** www.keypress.com. Estab. 1971.

8—▪ "It's our mission to: Engage students with effective, relevant, high-quality mathematics and science instructional materials and software that open their eyes to math and science in the world around them, develop both conceptual understanding and skills, and ignite their interest in learning. Support mathematics and science educators by partnering with them to promote an inclusive and compelling learning environment that facilitates their success in meeting the educational needs of all students. Advocate for research, ideas, strategies, and policies that lead to excellence and equity in education, as well as a better educational experience for all students. Provide a respectful, collaborative, and forward-thinking workplace that promotes open communication, values people, nurtures their ideas, and helps Key Curriculum Press achieve sustainable growth."

TIPS "Provide website gallery. Call prior to dropping off portfolio."

☺ KIDS CAN PRESS

25 Dockside Dr., Toronto ON M5A 0B5, Canada. (416)479-7000. **Fax:** (416)960-5437. **E-mail:** info@kidscan.com; kkalmar@kidscan.com. **Website:** www.kidscanpress.com. Estab. 1973. Publishes book 18-24 months after acceptance. Responds in 6 months only if interesed.

○ *Kids Can Press is currently accepting unsolicited mss from Canadian adult authors only.*

NONFICTION Picture books: activity books, animal, arts/crafts, biography, careers, concept, health, history, hobbies, how-to, multicultural, nature/environment, science, social issues, special needs, sports. Young readers: activity books, animal, arts/crafts, biography, careers, concept, history, hobbies, how-to, multicultural. Middle readers: cooking, music/dance. Average word length: picture books 500-1,250; young readers 750-2,000; middle readers 5,000-15,000. Submit outline/synopsis and 2-3 sample chapters. For picture books submit complete ms.

FICTION Picture books, young readers: concepts. We do not accept young adult fiction or fantasy novels for any age. Adventure, animal, contemporary, folktales, history, humor, multicultural, nature/environment, special needs, sports, suspense/mystery. Average word length: picture books 1,000-2,000; young readers 750-1,500; middle readers 10,000-15,000; young adults over 15,000. Submit outline/synopsis and 2-3 sample chapters. For picture books submit complete ms.

☺ KINDRED PRODUCTIONS

1310 Taylor Ave., Winnipeg MB R3M 3Z6, Canada. (204)669-6575. **Fax:** (204)654-1865. **E-mail:** kindred@mbconf.ca. **Website:** www.kindredproductions.com. **Contact:** Renita Kornelsen, acquisitions. Publishes trade paperback originals and reprints. **Publishes 3 titles/year. 1% of books from first-time authors. 100% from unagented writers.** Publishes book 18 months after acceptance. Accepts simultaneous submissions. Responds in 3 months to queries; 5 months to mss. Guidelines available by e-mail request.

8— "Kindred Productions publishes, promotes, and markets print and nonprint resources that will shape our Christian faith and discipleship from a Mennonite Brethren perspective. Currently emphasizing Mennonite Brethren Resources. De-emphasizing personal experience, biographical. No children's books or fiction."

NONFICTION Subjects include religion, historical., i. "Our books cater primarily to our Mennonite Brethren denomination readers." Query with SASE. Submit outline, 2-3 sample chapters.

TIPS "Most of our books are sold to churches, religious bookstores, and schools. We are concentrating on books with a Mennonite Brethren perspective. We do not accept children's manuscripts."

KITSUNE BOOKS

P.O. Box 1154, Crawfordville FL 32326. **E-mail:** anne@kitsunebooks.com, lynn@kitsunebooks.com. **Website:** www.kitsunebooks.com. **Contact:** Anne Petty, editor; Lynn Holschuh, assistant editor. Estab. 2006. Publishes trade paperback originals and reprints. **Publishes 5-6 titles/year. 600+ queries received/year. 70 mss received/year. 20% of books from first-time authors. 50% from unagented writers. Pays 10% royalty on retail price. Pays $300-600 advance.** Publishes book 18 months after acceptance. Accepts simultaneous submissions. Responds in 2-4 weeks to queries; 1-3 months to proposals; 6-9 months to mss. Catalog and guidelines online.

NONFICTION Subjects include New Age, spirituality, literary memoirs, literary commentary, yoga/fitness. Write for the general reader, but demonstrate a thorough, authoritative knowledge of your subject. No cookbooks, how-to, specific religion books. Query via e-mail only. If you insist on sending a postal letter, you must include SASE. No hardcopy submissions unless requested. Reviews artwork/photos.

FICTION Subjects include literary, mainstream, contemporary, dark fantasy, short story collections, poetry, speculative, noir, magical realism. "We are looking for carefully written fiction that's slightly off the beaten path-interesting novels that don't fit easily into any one category. Graceful command of the language is a plus; technical command of grammar/language mechanics a must. Our latest short story collection is in the Raymond Carver tradition. Looking for au-

thors with a unique voice and style." No children's picture books, crime thrillers, mystery, romance, war, westerns, juvenile fiction. No chapbooks. Query via e-mail. No hardcopy submissions, no previously published material.

POETRY "You must be able to submit a complete collection, not just a random sampling of unrelated poems. The collection should have a clear theme or structure." Query and submit 3 sample poems.

TIPS "Our readership is eclectic, with a taste for the unusual, the artistic and the unexpected. Kitsune Books caters to lovers of literature and language, poetry, and well-designed and researched nonfiction. We prefer to deal with mss electronically rather than receiving printouts (saves trees). Please read our category guidelines carefully. We no longer accept genre fiction. Interesting fiction that doesn't fit easily into any one category will be considered. NO self-published material."

ALLEN A. KNOLL, PUBLISHERS

200 W. Victoria Street, Santa Barbara CA 93101. (805)564-3377. **E-mail:** bookinfo@knollpublishers. com. **Website:** www.knollpublishers.com. **Contact:** Submissions. Estab. 1990. Format publishes in hardcover originals.

Ⓐ ALFRED A. KNOPF

1745 Broadway, 21st Floor, New York NY 10019. **Website:** knopf.knopfdoubleday.com. Estab. 1915. Publishes hardcover and paperback originals. **Publishes 200 titles/year. Royalties vary. Offers advance.** Publishes book 1 year after acceptance. Responds in 2-6 months to queries.

FICTION Publishes book-length fiction of literary merit by known or unknown writers. Length: 40,000-150,000 words. *Agented submissions only.* Query with SASE or submit sample chapter(s).

KNOX ROBINSON PUBLISHING

244 Fifth Ave., Suite 1861, New York NY 10001. **E-mail:** info@knoxrobinsonpublishing.com. **Website:** www.knoxrobinsonpublishing.com. **Contact:** Dana Celeste Robinson, managing director (historical fiction, historical romance, fantasy). Estab. 2010. **Publishes 5 titles/year. Pays royalty.** Accepts simultaneous submissions. Responds in 1 month to queries and proposals; 3 monts to mss.

8— Knox Robinson Publishing is an independent, specialist publishing house committed to the production of fresh new historical fiction, historical romance and fantasy

FICTION Fiction subjects include historical fiction, historical romance and fantasy. "We are seeking historical fiction, historical romance and fantasy featuring new and innovative subjects and plots." Submit proposal package, including synopsis and first three chapters.

🌑 KOALA BOOKS

P.O. Box 626, Mascot NS 1460, Australia. (61)(02)9667-2997. **Fax:** (61)(02)9667-2881. **Website:** www.koalabooks.com.au. **Pays authors royalty of 10% based on retail price or work purchased outright occasionally.** Responds to mss in 3 months.

8—➤ "Koala Books is an independent wholly Australian-owned children's book publishing house. Our strength is providing quality books for children at competitive prices."

NONFICTION Submit complete ms, blurb, brief author bio, list of published works, SASE.

FICTION Submit complete ms, blurb, brief author bio, list of published works, SASE.

TIPS "Take a look at our website to get an idea of the kinds of books we publish. A few hours research in a quality children's bookshop would be helpful when choosing a publisher."

KOENISHA PUBLICATIONS

3196 53rd St., Hamilton MI 49419. (269)751-4100. **E-mail:** koenisha@macatawa.org. **Website:** www.koenisha.com. **Contact:** Sharolett Koenig, publisher; Earl Leon, acquisition editor. Publishes trade paperback originals. **Publishes 10-12 titles/year. 500 queries received/year. 500 mss received/year. 95% of books from first-time authors. 100% from unagented writers.** Publishes book 1 year after acceptance. Guidelines online.

NONFICTION *Not accepting submissions from new authors at this time.*

FICTION Subjects include humor, mainstream, contemporary, mystery, romance, suspense, young adult. "We do not accept manuscripts that contain unnecessary foul language, explicit sex or gratuitous violence." Query with SASE. Submit proposal package, clips, 3 sample chapters.

POETRY Submit 3 sample poems.

TIPS "We're not interested in books written to suit a particular line or house or because it's trendy. Instead write a book from your heart—the inspiration or idea that kept you going through the writing process."

KRAUSE PUBLICATIONS

A Division of F+W Media, Inc., 700 E. State St., Iola WI 54990. (715)445-2214. **Fax:** (715)445-4087. **Website:** www.krausebooks.com. **Contact:** Paul Kennedy (antiques and collectibles, music, sports, militaria, humor, numismatics); Corrina Peterson (firearms); Brian Lovett (outdoors); Brian Earnest (automotive). Publishes hardcover and trade paperback originals. **Publishes 80 titles/year. 200 queries received/year. 40 mss received/year. 50% of books from first-time authors. 95% from unagented writers. Pays advance. Photo budget.** Publishes book 18 months after acceptance. Responds in 3 months to proposals. Responds in 2 months to mss. Catalog for free or on website. Guidelines available free upon request.

8—➤ "We are the world's largest hobby and collectibles publisher."

NONFICTION Submit proposal package, including outline, table of contents, a sample chapter, and letter explaining your project's unique contributions. Reviews artwork/photos. Accepts only digital photography. Send sample photos.

TIPS Audience consists of serious hobbyists. "Your work should provide a unique contribution to the special interest."

KRBY CREATIONS, LLC

P.O. Box 327, Bay Head NJ 08742. **Fax:** (815)846-0636. **E-mail:** info@KRBYCreations.com; KRBYEnterprises@comcast.net. **Website:** www.KRBYCreations.com. Estab. 2003. **Pays authors royalty of 6-15% based on wholesale price. Catalog on website. Offers writer's guidelines by e-mail.** Publishes book 1 year after acceptance. Accepts simultaneous submissions. Responds to queries in 1 week; mss in 3 months.

NONFICTION Writers *must* request guidelines by e-mail prior to submitting mss. See website. Submissions without annotation found in guidelines will not be considered. Detailed contact guidelines available on website. Illustrator terms negotiable. Pays advance plus royalties for experienced Illustrators. Avoids work-for-hire contracts. 40-60% of illustrators are first-time children's picture book published.

FICTION Writers *must* request guidelines by e-mail prior to submitting mss. See website. Submissions without annotation found in guidelines will not be considered.

TIPS "Submit as professionally as possible; make your vision clear to us about what you are trying to capture.

Know your market/audience and identify it in your proposal. Tell us what is new/unique with your idea."

KREGEL PUBLICATIONS

Kregel, Inc., P.O. Box 2607, Grand Rapids MI 49501. (616)451-4775. **Fax:** (616)451-9330. **E-mail:** kregel-books@kregel.com. **Website:** www.kregelpublications.com. **Contact:** Dennis R. Hillman, publisher. Estab. 1949. Publishes hardcover and trade paperback originals and reprints. **Publishes 90 titles/year. 20% of books from first-time authors. 35% from unagented writers. Pays royalty on wholesale price. Pays negotiable advance.** Guidelines online.

- ✎ "Our mission as an evangelical Christian publisher is to provide—with integrity and excellence—trusted, Biblically based resources that challenge and encourage individuals in their Christian lives. Works in theology and Biblical studies should reflect the historic, orthodox Protestant tradition."

NONFICTION "We serve evangelical Christian readers and those in career Christian service."

FICTION Subjects include religious, children's, general, inspirational, mystery/suspense, relationships, young adult. Fiction should be geared toward the evangelical Christian market. Wants books with fast-paced, contemporary storylines presenting a strong Christian message in an engaging, entertaining style.

TIPS "Our audience consists of conservative, evangelical Christians, including pastors and ministry students."

LADYBUGPRESS

New Voices / LadybugPress, 16964 Columbia River Dr., Sonora CA 95370. (209)694-8340. **E-mail:** georgia@ladybugbooks.com. **Website:** www.ladybugbooks.com. **Contact:** Georgia Jones, editor-in-chief (new authors). Irma Hudson, editor (nonfiction). Estab. 1996. Publishes trade paperback and electronic originals. **Publishes 4-6 titles/year. 50 queries/year; 30 mss/year. 90% of books from first-time authors. 100% from unagented writers. Pays 40-45% royalty on wholesale price.** Publishes book 2 months after acceptance of ms. Accepts simultaneous submissions. Responds in 1 month on queries/proposals, 2 months/mss. Catalog and guidelines available online or by CD.

- ◯ Recently won a national book award for audio book and would love to see more high quality audio proposals. Owns print facility and likes seeing creative and color print proposals.

NONFICTION Subjects include alternative lifestyles, contemporary culture, creative nonfiction, dance, music, social sciences, women's issues, world affairs. Our primary interest is in women's issues and peace. Query with SASE; We prefer e-mail submissions. Reviews artwork/photos; send electronic files.

FICTION Subjects include contemporary, feminist, historical, literary, mainstream, poetry. "Our tastes are eclectic." Submit proposal package, including synopsis; prefers electronic submissions, georgia@ladybugbooks.com.

POETRY "We like new poets but can only do poetry in our subsidized program, Partners in Publishing." Query.

TIPS "We have a lot of information on our website, and have several related sites that give an overview of who we are and what we like to see. Take advantage of this and it will help you make good decisions about submissions."

LAKE CLAREMONT PRESS

P.O. Box 711, Chicago IL 60690. (312)226-8400. **Fax:** (312)226-8420. **E-mail:** sharon@lakeclaremont.com. **Website:** www.lakeclaremont.com. **Contact:** Sharon Woodhouse, publisher. Estab. 1994. Publishes trade paperback originals. **Publishes 2-3 titles/year. 250 queries received/year. 100 mss received/year. 50% of books from first-time authors. 100% from unagented writers. Pays 10-15% royalty on net sales. Pays $500-1,000 advance.** Publishes book 12-18 months after acceptance of ms. Accepts simultaneous submissions. Responds in 1 month to queries. Responds in 2 months to proposals. Responds in 2-6 months to mss. Catalog online.

- ✎ "We specialize in nonfiction books on the Chicago area and its history, particularly by authors with a passion or organizations with a mission."

NONFICTION Subjects include Americana, ethnic, history, nature, environment, regional, travel, women's issues, film/cinema/stage (regional)—as long as it is primarily a Chicago book. Query with SASE, or submit proposal package, including outline and 2 sample chapters, or submit complete ms (e-mail queries and proposals preferred).

TIPS "Please include a market analysis in proposals (who would buy this book and where) and an analysis of similar books available for different regions. Please know what else is out there."

WENDY LAMB BOOKS

Imprint of Random House Children's Books/Random House, Inc., 1745 Broadway, New York NY 10019. (212)782-9000. **Fax:** (212)782-9452. **E-mail:** wlamb@randomhouse.com; cmeckler@randomhouse.com. **Website:** www.randomhouse.com. Estab. 2001. Publishes hardcover originals. **Pays royalty.** Accepts simultaneous submissions. Guidelines for #10 SASE.

○ Literary fiction and nonfiction for readers 8-15.

FICTION Subjects include middle grade and young adult.

POETRY Submit 4 sample poems.

TIPS "Please note that we do not publish picture books. Please send the first 10 pages of your ms (or until the end of the first chapter) along with a cover letter, synopsis, and SASE. Before you submit, please take a look at some of our recent titles to get an idea of what we publish."

LAPWING PUBLICATIONS

1 Ballysillan Dr., Belfast BT14 8HQ, Northern Ireland. +44 2890 500 796. **Fax:** +44 2890 295 800. **E-mail:** lapwing.poetry@ntlworld.com. **Website:** www.lapwingpoetry.com. **Contact:** Dennis Greig, editor. Estab. 1989. **Pays 20 author's copies, no royalties.** Responds to queries in 1 month; mss in 2 months.

○ Lapwing will produce work only if and when resources to do so are available.

POETRY Lapwing publishes "emerging Irish poets and poets domiciled in Ireland, plus the new work of a suitable size by established Irish writers. Non-Irish poets are also published. Poets based in continental Europe have become a major feature. Emphasis on first collections preferably not larger than 80 pages. Logistically, publishing beyond the British Isles is always difficult for 'hard copy' editions. PDF copies via e-mail are £3 or 3€ per copy. No fixed upperl limit to number of titles per year. Hard copy prices are £8 to £10 per copy. No e-reader required." Wants poetry of all kinds, but, "no crass political, racist, sexist propaganda, even of a positive or 'pc' tenor." Has published Alastair Thomson, Clifford Ireson, Colette Wittorski, Gilberte de Leger, Aubrey Malone, and Jane Shaw Holiday. Pamphlets up to 32 pages, chapbooks up to 44 pages, books 48-112 pages; New Belfast binding, simulated perfect binding for books, otherwise saddle stitching. "Submit 6 poems in the first instance; depending on these, an invitation to submit more may follow." Considers simultaneous submissions.

Accepts e-mail submissions in body of message or in DOC format. Cover letter is required. "All submissions receive a first reading. If these poems have minor errors or faults, the writer is advised. If poor quality, the poems are returned. Those 'passing' first reading are retained, and a letter of conditional offer is sent." Often comments on rejected poems. "After initial publication, irrespective of the quantity, the work will be permanently available using 'print-on-demand' production; such publications will not always be printed exactly as the original, although the content will remain the same."

LAUREL-LEAF

Imprint of Random House Children's Books/Random House, Inc., 1745 Broadway, New York NY 10019. (212)782-9000. **Website:** www.randomhouse.com/teens.

○ Quality reprint paperback imprint for young adult paperback books. *Does not accept unsolicited mss.*

LAWYERS & JUDGES PUBLISHING CO.

P.O. Box 30040, Tucson AZ 85751. (520)323-1500. **Fax:** (520)323-0055. **E-mail:** sales@lawyersandjudges.com. **Website:** www.lawyersandjudges.com. **Contact:** Steve Weintraub, president. Estab. 1963. Publishes professional hardcover and trade paperback originals. **Publishes 20 titles/year. 200 queries received/year. 60 mss received/year. 15% of books from first-time authors. 100% from unagented writers.** Publishes book 5 months after acceptance. Accepts simultaneous submissions. Responds in 1 month to queries. Catalog available free. Guidelines available free.

⚷ "Lawyers & Judges is a highly specific publishing company, reaching the legal, accident reconstruction, insurance, and medical fields."

NONFICTION Submit proposal package, outline, sample chapters.

LECTIO PUBLISHERS

P.O. Box 11435, Randhart 1457, South Africa. Phone/**Fax:** (27)(11)907-3053. **E-mail:** lectio@iafrica.com. **Website:** www.lectio.co.za.

⚷ Publishes educational and health materials (comics, books, wall charts, teaching aids) used by government departments.

NONFICTION Subjects include health, medicine, science, social sciences, math, life skills, sexuality, arts/culture, technology.

LEE & LOW BOOKS

95 Madison Ave., #1205, New York NY 10016. (212)779-4400. **E-mail:** general@leeandlow.com. **Website:** www.leeandlow.com. **Contact:** Louise May, editor-in-chief (multicultural children's fiction/nonfiction). Jennifer Fox, senior editor; Emily Hazel, assistant editor Estab. 1991. Publishes hardcover originals and trade paperback reprints. **Publishes 12-14 titles/year. Receives 100 queries/year; 1,200 mss/ year. 20% of books from first-time authors. 50% from unagented writers. Pays net royalty. Pays authors advances against royalty. Pays illustrators advance against royalty. Photographers paid advance against royalty.** Publishes book 2 years after acceptance. Responds in 6 months to mss if interested. Catalog online. Guidelines available online or by written request with SASE.

⌘ "Our goals are to meet a growing need for books that address children of color, and to present literature that all children can identify with. We only consider multicultural children's books. Currently emphasizing material for 5-12 year olds. Sponsors a yearly New Voices Award for first-time picture book authors of color. Contest rules online or for SASE."

NONFICTION Picture books: concept. Picture books, middle readers: biography, history, multicultural, science and sports. Average word length: picture books-1,500-3,000. Submit complete ms. Reviews artwork/photos only if writer is also a professional illustrator or photographer. Send photocopies and nonreturnable art samples only.

FICTION Subjects include contemporary and historical fiction featuring people of color. Also accepts thematic or narrative poetry collections with a multicultural focus. Picture books, young readers: anthology, contemporary, history, multicultural, poetry. Picture book, middle reader: contemporary, history, multicultural, nature/environment, poetry, sports. Average word length: picture books—1,000-1,500 words. "We do not publish folklore or animal stories." Submit complete ms.

POETRY Submit complete ms.

TIPS "Check our website to see the kinds of books we publish. Do not send mss that don't fit our mission."

LEGACY PRESS

P.O. Box 261129, San Diego CA 92196. (858)277-1167. **E-mail:** editor@rainbowpublishers.com. **Website:** www.rainbowpublishers.com; www.legacypresskids. com. Estab. 1979. **For authors work purchased outright (range: $500 and up). Pays illustrators by the project (range: $300 and up). Sends galleys to authors.** Accepts simultaneous submissions. Responds to queries in 6 weeks, mss in 3 months.

⌘ Publishes 4 young readers/year; 4 middle readers/year; 4 young adult titles/year. 50% of books by first-time authors. "Our mission is to publish Bible-based, teacher resource materials that contribute to and inspire spiritual growth and development in kids ages 2-12."

NONFICTION Young readers, middle readers, young adult/teens: activity books, arts/crafts, how-to, reference, religion. Works with 25 illustrators/year. Reviews ms/illustration packages from artists. Submit ms with 2-5 pieces of final art. Illustrations only: Query with samples. Responds in 6 weeks. Samples returned with SASE; samples filed.

TIPS "Our Rainbow imprint publishes reproducible books for teachers of children in Christian ministries, including crafts, activities, games and puzzles. Our Legacy imprint publishes titles for children such as devotionals, fiction and Christian living. Please write for guidelines and study the market before submitting material."

✚ HAL LEONARD BOOKS

Hal Leonard Publishing Group, 33 Plymouth St., Suite 302, Montclair NJ 07042. (973)337-5034. **Fax:** (973)337-5227. **Contact:** John Cerullo, publisher. Kristina Radka **Publishes 30 titles/year.**

NONFICTION Subjects include music. Query with SASE.

⊘ LETHE PRESS

118 Heritage Ave., Maple Shade NJ 08052. (609)410-7391. **E-mail:** editor@lethepressbooks.com. **Website:** www.lethepressbooks.com. **Contact:** Steve Berman, publisher. Estab. 2001.

ARTHUR A. LEVINE BOOKS

Scholastic, Inc., 557 Broadway, New York NY 10012. (212)343-4436. **Fax:** (212)343-4890. **E-mail:** alevine@ scholastic.com; eclement@scholastic.com. **Website:** www.arthuralevinebooks.com. **Contact:** Arthur A. Levine, editorial director; Cheryl Klein, senior editor. Estab. 1996. Publishes hardback and soft cover prints and reprints. Publishes book Publishes a book 18 months after acceptance. Responds in 1 month to queries; 5 months to mss.

NONFICTION Works with 8 illustrators/year. Will review ms/illustration packages from artists. Query first. Illustrations only: Send postcard sample with tearsheets. Samples not returned.

FICTION Subjects include juvenile, picture books, young adult. "Arthur A. Levine is looking for distinctive literature, for children and young adults, for whatever's extraordinary." Averages 18-20 total titles/year.

LIFE CYCLE BOOKS

P.O. Box 1008, Niagara Falls NY 14304. (416)690-5860. **Fax:** (416)690-8532. **Website:** www.lifecyclebooks. com. **Contact:** Paul Broughton, general manager. Estab. 1973. Publishes trade paperback originals and reprints, and mass market reprints. **Publishes 6 titles/ year. 100+ queries received/year. 50% of books from first-time authors. 100% from unagented writers. Pays 8-10% royalty on wholesale price. Pays $250-1,000 advance.** Publishes book 1 year after acceptance. Responds in 1 month to queries, proposals, and mss. Catalog online.

NONFICTION Subjects include health, medicine, religion, social sciences, womens issues, womens studies. We specialize in human life issues. Query with SASE. Submit complete ms. Reviews artwork/photos.

LIGHTHOUSE POINT PRESS

100 First Ave., Suite 525, Pittsburgh PA 15222-1517. (412)323-9320. **Fax:** (412)323-9334. **E-mail:** ryearick@yearick-millea.com. **Contact:** Ralph W. Yearick, publisher (business/career/general nonfiction). Estab. 1993. Publishes hardcover and trade paperback originals. **Pays 5-10% royalty on retail price.** Responds in 6 months to queries.

☞ "Lighthouse Point Press specializes in business/career nonfiction titles, and books that help readers improve their quality of life. We do not re-publish self-published books."

NONFICTION Subjects include business, economics. "We are open to all types of submissions related to general nonfiction, but most interested in business/career manuscripts." Submit proposal package, outline, 1-2 sample chapters and bio. Complete ms preferred.

TIPS "When submitting a manuscript or proposal, please tell us what you see as the target market/audience for the book. Also, be very specific about what you are willing to do to promote the book."

LILLENAS PUBLISHING CO.

Imprint of Lillenas Drama Resources, P.O. Box 419527, Kansas City MO 64109. (816)931-1900. **Fax:** (816)412-8390. **E-mail:** drama@lillenas.com. **Website:** www. lillenasdrama.com. Publishes mass market paperback and electronic originals. **Publishes 50+ titles/year. Pays royalty on net price. Makes outright purchase.** Responds in 4-6 months to material. See guidelines online.

☞ "We purchase only original, previously unpublished materials. Also, we require that all scripts be performed at least once before it is submitted for consideration. We do not accept scripts that are sent via fax or e-mail. Direct all manuscripts to the Drama Resources Editor."

NONFICTION Subjects include religion, life issues. No musicals. Query with SASE. Submit complete ms.

FICTION "Looking for sketch and monologue collections for all ages – adults, children and youth. For these collections, we request 12 - 15 scripts to be submitted at one time. Unique treatments of spiritual themes, relevant issues and biblical messages are of interest. Contemporary full-length and one-act plays that have conflict, characterization, and a spiritual context that is neither a sermon nor an apologetic for youth and adults. We also need wholesome so-called secular full-length scripts for dinner theatres and schools." No musicals.

LINDEN PUBLISHING, INC.

2006 S. Mary, Fresno CA 93721. (559)233-6633. **Fax:** (559)233-6933. **E-mail:** richard@lindenpub.com. **Website:** www.lindenpub.com. **Contact:** Richard Sorsky, president; Kent Sorsky, vice president. Estab. 1976. Publishes trade paperback originals; hardcover and trade paperback reprints. **Publishes 10-12 titles/year. 30+ queries received/year. 5-15 mss received/year. 40% of books from first-time authors. 50% from unagented writers. Pays 7½ -12% royalty on wholesale price. Pays $500-6,000 advance.** Publishes book 18 months after acceptance. Responds in 1 month to queries and proposals. Catalog online. Guidelines available via e-mail.

NONFICTION Subjects include history, regional, hobbies, woodworking., Regional California history. Submit proposal package, outline, 3 sample chapters, bio. Reviews artwork/photos. Send electronic files, if available.

LIQUID SILVER BOOKS

E-mail: tracey@liquidsilverbooks.com. **Website:** www.liquidsilverbooks.com. **Contact:** Tracey West, acquisitions editor; Terri Schaefer, editorial director.

Estab. 1999. Publishes book 4-5 months after acceptance. Accepts simultaneous submissions. Responds to mss in 4-6 weeks.

FICTION Needs contemporary, gay and lesbian, paranormal, supernatural, sci-fi, fantasy, historical, suspense, and western romances. We do not accept literary Erotica submissions. E-mail entire ms as an attachment in .RTF format in Arial 12pt. "Include in the body of the e-mail: author bio, your thoughts on ePublishing, a blurb of your book, including title and series title if applicable. Ms must include Pen name, real name, snail mail and e-mail contact information on the first page, top left corner." More writer's Guidelines online.

LISTEN & LIVE AUDIO

P.O. Box 817, Roseland NJ 07068. **E-mail:** alisa@listenandlive.com. **Website:** www.listenandlive.com. **Contact:** Alisa Weberman, publisher. **Publishes 30+ titles/year.** Catalog available online.

⌛ Independent audiobook publisher. "We also license audiobooks for the download market. We specialize in the following genres: fiction, mystery, nonfiction, self-help, business, children's, and teen."

Ⓐ ⊘ LITTLE, BROWN AND CO.

Hachette Book Group USA, 237 Park Ave., New York NY 10017. (212)364-1100. **Website:** www.hachettebookgroup.com. Estab. 1837. Publishes hardcover originals and paperback originals and reprints.

○ "Unsolicited manuscripts, submissions, and queries will not be answered. If you are interested in having a manuscript considered for publication, we recommend that you first enlist the services of an established literary agent."

Ⓐ LITTLE, BROWN AND CO. ADULT TRADE BOOKS

237 Park Ave., New York NY 10017. **E-mail:** publicity@littlebrown.com. **Website:** www.hachettebookgroup.com. **Contact:** Michael Pietsch, publisher. Estab. 1837. Publishes hardcover originals and paperback originals and reprints. **Publishes 100 titles/year. Pays royalty. Offer advance.** Guidelines online.

⌛ "The general editorial philosophy for all divisions continues to be broad and flexible, with high quality and the promise of commercial success as always the first considerations."

FICTION Literary, mainstream/contemporary. *Agented submissions only.*

Ⓐ LITTLE, BROWN AND CO. BOOKS FOR YOUNG READERS

Hachette Book Group USA, 237 Park Ave., New York NY 10017. (212)364-1100. **Fax:** (212)364-0925. **E-mail:** pamela.gruber@hbgusa.com. **Website:** www.lb-kids.com; www.lb-teens.com. Estab. 1837. **Publishes 100-150 titles/year. Pays authors royalties based on retail price. Pays illustrators and photographers by the project or royalty based on retail price. Sends galleys to authors; dummies to illustrators. Pays negotiable advance.** Publishes book 2 years after acceptance. Accepts simultaneous submissions. Responds in 1 month to queries; 2 months to proposals and mss.

⌛ "Little, Brown and Co. Children's Publishing publishes all formats including board books, picture books, middle grade fiction, and nonfiction YA titles. We are looking for strong writing and presentation, but no predetermined topics." *Only interested in solicited agented material.* Fiction: Submit complete ms. Nonfiction: Submit cover letter, previous publications, a proposal, outline and 3 sample chapters. Do not send originals.

NONFICTION Subjects include animals, art, architecture, ethnic, gay, lesbian, history, hobbies, nature, environment, recreation, science, sports. Writers should avoid looking for the 'issue' they think publishers want to see, choosing instead topics they know best and are most enthusiastic about/inspired by. Middle readers, young adults: arts/crafts, history, multicultural, nature, self help, social issues, sports, science. Average word length: middle readers—15,000-25,000; young adults—20,000-40,000. *Agented submissions only.*

FICTION Subjects include adventure, fantasy, feminist, gay, lesbian, historical, humor, mystery, science fiction, suspense., chick lit, multicultural. Picture books: humor, adventure, animal, contemporary, history, multicultural, folktales. Young adults: contemporary, humor, multicultural, suspense/mystery, chick lit. Multicultural needs include "any material by, for and about minorities." Average word length: picture books—1,000; young readers—6,000; middle readers—15,000- 50,000; young adults—50,000 and up. *Agented submissions only.*

TIPS "In order to break into the field, authors and illustrators should research their competition and try to come up with something outstandingly different."

LITTLE TIGER PRESS

1 The Coda Centre, 189 Munster Rd., London En SW6 6AW, United Kingdom. 44)20-7385 6333. **E-mail:** info@littletiger.co.uk; jcollins@littletiger.co.uk. **Website:** www.littletigerpress.com.

FICTION Picture books: animal, concept, contemporary, humor. Average word length: picture books—750 words or less. Recently published *Gruff the Grump*, by Steve Smallman and Cee Biscoe (ages 3-7, picture book); *One Special Day*, by M. Christina Butler and Tina Macnaughton (ages 3-7, touch-and-feel, picture book).

TIPS "Every reasonable care is taken of the manuscripts and samples we receive, but we cannot accept responsibility for any loss or damage. Try to read or look at as many books on the Little Tiger Press list before sending in your material. Refer to our website www.littletigerpress.com for further details."

LIVINGSTON PRESS

University of West Alabama, Station 22, Livingston AL 35470. **E-mail:** jwt@uwa.edu. **Website:** www.livingstonpress.uwa.edu. **Contact:** Joe Taylor, director. Estab. 1974. Publishes hardcover and trade paperback originals. **Publishes 10-12 titles/year. 50% of books from first-time authors. 100% from unagented writers. Pays 150 contributor's copies, after sales of 1,500, standard royalty.** Publishes book 18 months after acceptance of ms. Accepts simultaneous submissions. Responds in 1 month to queries. Responds in 6 months-1 year to mss. Guidelines online.

Reads mss in March only.

FICTION Subjects include experimental, literary, short story collections., off-beat or Southern. "We are interested in form and, of course, style." Query with SASE.

TIPS "Our readers are interested in literature, often quirky literature that emphasizes form and style. Please visit our website for current needs."

LLEWELLYN PUBLICATIONS

Imprint of Llewellyn Worldwide, Ltd., 2143 Wooddale Dr., Woodbury MN 55125. (651)291-1970. **Fax:** (651)291-1908. **E-mail:** Publicity@llewellyn.com. **Website:** www.llewellyn.com. Estab. 1901. Publishes trade and mass market paperback originals. **Publishes 100+ titles/year. 30% of books from first-time authors. 50% from unagented writers. Pays 10% royalty on wholesale or retail price.** Accepts simultaneous submissions. Responds in 3 months

to queries. Catalog for 9×12 SAE with 4 first-class stamps.

"Llewellyn publishes New Age fiction and nonfiction exploring new worlds of mind and spirit. Currently emphasizing astrology, alternative health and healing, tarot. De-emphasizing fiction, channeling."

NONFICTION Subjects include cooking, foods, nutrition, health, medicine, nature, environment, New Age, psychology, women's issues/studies. Submit outline, sample chapters. Reviews artwork/photos.

LOFT PRESS, INC.

9293 Fort Valley Rd., Fort Valley VA 22652. (540)933-6210. **Website:** www.loftpress.com. **Contact:** Ann A. Hunter, editor-in-chief. **Publishes 8-16 titles/year. 850 queries received/year. 300 mss received/year. 75% of books from first-time authors. 100% from unagented writers.** Publishes book 6 months after acceptance of ms. Guidelines online.

NONFICTION Subjects include Americana, art, architecture, business, economics, computers, electronics, government, politics, history, language, literature, memoirs, philosophy, regional, religion, science. Submit proposal package, outline, 1 sample chapter. Reviews artwork/photos. Send photocopies.

FICTION Subjects include literary, poetry, regional, short story collections. Submit proposal package, 1 sample chapter, clips.

POETRY Submit 5 sample poems.

LOLLIPOP POWER BOOKS

120 Morris Street, Durham NC 27701. (919)560-2738. **Fax:** (919)560-2759. **E-mail:** carolinawrenpress@earthling.net; andreaselch@earthlink.net. **Website:** www.carolinawrenpress.org. Estab. 1976. **Pays authors royalty of 10% minimum based on retail price or work purchased outright from authors (range: $500-$2,000). Pays illustrators by the project (range: $500-$2,000).** Catalog available on website.

No open submissions at this time. "Please check our website to see if we have re-opened submissions."

NONFICTION "Send one example and link to website with further examples. We will respond only if interested. Samples not returned."

LOST HORSE PRESS

105 Lost Horse Lane, Sandpoint ID 83864. (208)255-4410. **Fax:** (208)255-1560. **E-mail:** losthorsepress@mindspring.com. **Website:** www.losthorsepress.org.

Contact: Christine Holbert, editor. Estab. 1998. Publishes hardcover and paperback originals. **Publishes 4 titles/year.** Publishes book 1-2 years after acceptance of ms.

FICTION Subjects include literary, poetry, regional, Pacific Northwest, short story collections.

LOUISIANA STATE UNIVERSITY PRESS
3990 W. Lakeshore Dr., Baton Rouge LA 70808. (225)578-6294. **Fax:** (225)578-6461. **E-mail:** mkc@lsu.edu. **Website:** www.lsu.edu/lsupress. **Contact:** MK Callaway, director. John Easterly, excecutive editor (poetry, fiction, literary studies); Rand Dotson, senior editor (U.S. History & Southern Studies). Estab. 1935. Publishes hardcover and paperback originals, and reprints. Publishes 8 poetry titles per year and 2 works of original fiction as part of the Yellow Shoe Fiction series. **Publishes 80-90 titles/year. 33% of books from first-time authors. 95% from unagented writers. Pays royalty.** Publishes book 1 year after acceptance. Responds in 1 month to queries. Catalog and guidelines free and online.

Publishes in the fall and spring.

NONFICTION Subjects include Americana, animals, anthropology, archeology, art, architecture, ethnic, government, politics, history, language, literature, literary criticism, memoirs, military, war, Civil & WWII, music, dance, Southern, jazz, nature, environment, philosophy, political, photography, regional, sociology, women's issues/studies, world affairs, geography and environmental studies. "We publish general interest books about Louisiana and the South, Atlantic and European and World History. Prizes are regularly awarded to LSU Press authors for the excellence of their general body of work. All books must undergo a rigorous approval process." Query with SASE. Submit proposal package, outline, sample chapters, cover letter, résumé. *No unsolicited submissions by e-mail attachment.*

FICTION Query with SASE. Submit proposal package, sample chapters, résumé, clips, and cover letter.

POETRY No unsolicited poetry mss. for the foreseeable future. "We have filled our slots until 2014."

LOVE SPELL
Dorchester Publishing, 200 Madison Ave., Suite 2000, New York NY 10016. (212)725-8811. **Fax:** (212)532-1054. **E-mail:** adavis@dorchesterpub.com; submissions@dorchesterpub.com. **Website:** www.dorchesterpub.com. **Contact:** Alissa Davis, editorial assistant.

Leah Hultenschmidt, Christopher Keeslar, senior editor; Alicia Condon, editorial director. Publishes mass market paperback originals. **Publishes 48 titles/year. 1,500-2,000 queries/year; 150-500 mss/year. 25-30% of books from first-time authors. Pays royalty on retail price. Pays variable advance.** Publishes book 1 year after acceptance. Responds in 6-8 months to mss. Catalog for free online or by calling (800)481-9191. Guidelines online.

FICTION Whimsical contemporaries. "Books industry-wide are getting shorter; we're interested in 70,000 - 90,000 words. **We are currently acquiring only the following: romance, horror, Westerns, and thrillers.** Authors should attach their full ms in a Word or .rtf document, along with a 3- to 7-page synopsis. The body of the e-mail should contain the material of a normal cover letter: contact information, including physical address and phone number; word count (70,000-90,000 words); the genre of the novel; and a brief, tantalizing description of the plot. If by mail: Query with SASE. Submit clips. No material will be returned without SASE."

TIPS "The best way to learn to write a Love Spell Romance is by reading several of our recent releases. The best-written stories are usually ones writers feel passionate about—so write from your heart! Also, the market is very tight these days so more than ever we are looking for refreshing, standout original fiction."

LOVING HEALING PRESS INC.
5145 Pontiac Trail, Ann Arbor MI 48105. (888)761-6268. **Fax:** (734)663-6861. **E-mail:** info@lovinghealing.com. **Website:** www.lovinghealing.com. **Contact:** Victor R. Volkman, senior editor (psychology, self-help, personal growth, trauma recovery). Estab. 2003. Publishes hardcover and trade paperback originals and reprints. **Publishes 20 titles/year. Receives 200 queries/year; 100 mss/year. 50% of books from first-time authors. 80% from unagented writers. Pays 6-12% royalty on retail price.** Publishes book 10 months after acceptance. Accepts simultaneous submissions. Responds in 1 month on queries and proposals, 2 months on mss. Catalog available online. Guidelines online.

NONFICTION Subjects include child guidance, health, memoirs, psychology., social work. We are primarily interested in self-help books which are person-centered and non-judgmental. Submit proposal package, including: outline, 3 sample chapters;

submit complete ms. Reviews artwork/photos as part of the ms package; send JPEG files.

FICTION Subjects include multicultural., social change. Submit complete ms.

LRP PUBLICATIONS, INC.

P.O. Box 980, Horsham PA 19044. (215)784-0860. **Fax:** (215)784-9639. **E-mail:** dshadovitz@lrp.com. **Website:** www.lrp.com. Estab. 1977. Publishes hardcover and trade paperback originals. **Pays royalty.** Catalog available free. Guidelines available free.

NONFICTION Subjects include business, economics, education. Submit proposal package, outline.

⊘ LUCENT BOOKS

Attn: Publisher - Lucent Books, 27500 Drake Rd., Farmington Hills MI 48331. **E-mail:** kristine.burns@cengage.com. **Website:** www.gale.com/lucent. **Contact:** Kristine Burns. Estab. 1988.

☞ Lucent Books is a nontrade publisher of nonfiction for the middle school audience providing students with resource material for academic studies and for independent learning.

NONFICTION Potential writers should familiarize themselves with the material. All are works for hire, by assignment only. *No unsolicited mss.* E-mail query with cover letter, résumé and list of publications to kristine.burns@cengage.com.

⊘ LUNA BISONTE PRODS

137 Leland Ave., Columbus OH 43214-7505. **E-mail:** bennett.23@osu.edu. **Website:** www.johnmbennett. net. **Contact:** John M. Bennett, editor/publisher. Estab. 1967.

POETRY "Interested in avant-garde and highly experimental work only." Query first, with a few sample poems and cover letter with brief bio and publication credits. "Keep it brief. Chapbook publishing usually depends on grants or other subsidies, and is usually by solicitation. **Will also consider subsidy arrangements on negotiable terms.**" A sampling of various Luna Bisonte Prods products is available for $20.

THE LYONS PRESS

The Globe Pequot Press, Inc., Box 480, 246 Goose Ln., Guilford CT 06437. (203)458-4500. **Fax:** (203)458-4668. **E-mail:** info@globepequot.com. **Website:** www. lyonspress.com. Estab. 1984 (Lyons & Burford), 1997 (The Lyons Press). Publishes hardcover and trade paperback originals and reprints. **Pays $3,000-25,000 advance.** Accepts simultaneous submissions. Responds in 4 months to queries, proposals and tmss. Catalog and guidelines online.

☞ The Lyons Press publishes practical and literary books, chiefly centered on outdoor subjects—natural history, all sports, gardening, horses, fishing, hunting, survival, self-reliant living, plus cooking, memoir, bio, non-fiction.

NONFICTION Subjects include agriculture, Americana, animals, art & reference, cooking, foods & wine, nutrition, history, military, war, nature, environment, recreation, sports., adventure, fitness, the sea, woodworking. Visit our website and note the featured categories. Query with SASE. Submit proposal package, outline, 3 sample chapters. marketing description. Reviews artwork/photos. Send photocopies and non-original prints.

◐ MAGENTA PUBLISHING FOR THE ARTS

151 Winchester St., Toronto ON M4X 1B5, Canada. **E-mail:** info@magentafoundation.org. **Website:** www. magentafoundation.org. **Contact:** Submissions. Estab. 2004.

◯ See website for open submissions and sign up for e-newsletter for alerts. "We are looking for complete bodies of work *only* (80% finished). Please do not send works in progress. We are looking for work in all related arenas of photography."

TIPS "Please do not contact the office to inquire about the state of your proposal."

MAGICAL CHILD

Shades of White, 301 Tenth Ave., Crystal City MO 63019. **E-mail:** acquisitions@magicalchildbooks.com. **Website:** www.magicalchildbooks.com. Estab. 2007. **Pays authors royalty based on retail price. Offers advances. Pays illustrators royalty based on wholesale price.** Accepts simultaneous submissions. Responds in 3 weeks to queries; 3-6 months to mss.

☞ "The Neo-Pagan Earth Religions Community is the fastest growing demographic in the spiritual landscape, and Pagan parents are crying out for books appropriate for the Pagan kids. It is our plan to fill this small, but growing need." Query or submit outline/synopsis for picture books only or submit outline/synopsis and 3 sample chapters.

NONFICTION Middle Readers: biography, history (Earth religions only for both). Average word length: middle readers—11,200-28,000.

FICTION Picture Books: adventure, contemporary, nature/environment, submit only stories appropriate for Earth Religions *not* Native American. Young Readers: adventure, contemporary, nature/environment. Middle Readers: adventure, contemporary, nature/environment, submit only stories appropriate for Earth Religions *not* Native American. Average word length: picture books—500-800; young readers—500-4,500; middle readers—11,200-28,000.

TIPS "Visit our submissions guidelines on the website. Follow the information provided there. We expect our authors to take an active role in promoting their books. If you can't do that, please don't submit your manuscript. *No calls, please.* Our list is *very* specific. Please do not send us manuscripts outside of our requested needs."

MAGINATION PRESS

750 First Street, NE, Washington DC 20002. (202)336-5618. **Fax:** (202)336-5624. **E-mail:** rteeter@apa.org. **Website:** www.apa.org/pubs/imagination/index.aspx. **Contact:** Kristine Enderle, managing editor. Estab. 1988. **Publishes 12 titles/year. 75% of books from first-time authors.** Publishes book Publishes a book 18-24 months after acceptance. Accepts simultaneous submissions. Responds to queries in 1-2 months; mss in 2-6 months.

8→ Magination Press is an imprint of the American Psychological Association. "We publish books dealing with the psycho/therapeutic resolution of children's problems and psychological issues with a strong self-help component." Submit complete ms. Materials returned only with SASE.

NONFICTION All levels: psychological and social issues, self-help, health, multicultural, special needs.

FICTION All levels: psychological and social issues, self-help, health, parenting concerns and, special needs. Picture books, middle school readers.

MAGNUS PRESS

P.O. Box 2666, Carlsbad CA 92018. (760)806-3743. **Fax:** (760)806-3689. **E-mail:** magnuspres@aol.com. **Website:** www.magnuspress.com. **Contact:** Warren Angel, editorial director. Estab. 1997. Publishes trade paperback originals and reprints. **Publishes 1-3 titles/year. 120 queries received/year. 75 mss received/year. 44% of books from first-time authors. 89% from unagented writers. Pays 6-15% royalty on retail price.** Publishes book 1 year after acceptance.

Accepts simultaneous submissions. Responds in 1 month to queries, proposals and mss. Catalog and guidelines for #10 SASE.

NONFICTION Subjects include religion, from a Christian perspective. "Writers must be well-grounded in Biblical knowledge and must be able to communicate effectively with the lay person." Submit proposal package, outline, sample chapters, bio.

TIPS "Magnus Press's audience is mainly Christian lay persons, but also includes anyone interested in spirituality and/or Biblical studies and the church. Study our listings and catalog; learn to write effectively for an average reader; read any one of our published books."

MANAGEMENT ADVISORY PUBLICATIONS

P.O. Box 81151, Wellesley Hills MA 02481. (781)235-2895. **Fax:** (781)235-5446. **E-mail:** info@masp.com. **Website:** www.masp.com. **Contact:** Jay Kuong, editor (corporate governance, compliance, security, audit, IT, business continuity). Estab. 1972. Publishes mass market paperback originals. **Publishes 2-10 titles/year. Receives 25 queries/year; 10 mss/year. 5% of books from first-time authors. Pays 5-10% royalty on wholesale price.** Publishes book 6 months after acceptance. Responds in 4 months on queries.

NONFICTION Subjects include business, computers, economics, electronics. Submit proposal package.

TIPS "Our audience is primarily business and IT professionals and University and Company libraries."

MANDALA PUBLISHING

Mandala Publishing and Earth Aware Editions, 10 Paul Dr., San Rafael CA 94903. **E-mail:** info@mandalapublishing.com. **Website:** www.mandalapublishing.com. Estab. 1989. Publishes hardcover, trade paperback, and electronic originals. **Publishes 12 titles/year. 200 queries received/year. 100 mss received/year. 40% of books from first-time authors. 100% from unagented writers. Pays 3-15% royalty on retail price.** Publishes book 8 months after acceptance. Accepts simultaneous submissions. Responds in 6 months to queries, proposals, and mss. Catalog online.

8→ "In the traditions of the East, wisdom, truth, and beauty go hand in- hand. This is reflected in the great arts, music, yoga, and philosophy of India. Mandala Publishing strives to bring to its readers authentic and accessible renderings of thousands of years of wisdom and philosophy from this unique culture-timeless treasures that are our inspirations and guides. At Mandala, we believe that the arts, health, ecology, and spirituality of the great Vedic traditions are as relevant today as they were in sacred India thousands of years ago. As a distinguished publisher in the world of Vedic literature, lifestyle, and interests today, Mandala strives to provide accessible and meaningful works for the modern reader."

NONFICTION Subjects include alternative, cooking, foods, nutrition, education, health, medicine, philosophy, photography, religion, spirituality. Query with SASE. Reviews artwork/photos. Send photocopies and thumbnails.

FICTION Subjects include juvenile, religious, spiritual. Query with SASE.

MANOR HOUSE PUBLISHING, INC.

452 Cottingham Crescent, Ancaster ON L9G 3V6, Canada. **E-mail:** mbdavie@manor-house.biz. **Website:** www.manor-house.biz. **Contact:** Mike Davie, president (novels, poetry, and nonfiction). Estab. 1998. Publishes hardcover, trade paperback, and mass market paperback originals reprints. **Publishes 5-6 titles/year. 30 queries received/year; 20 mss received/year. 90% of books from first-time authors. 90% from unagented writers. Pays 10% royalty on retail price.** Publishes book 1 year after acceptance. Accepts simultaneous submissions. Queries and mss to be sent by e-mail only. "We will respond in 30 days if interested-if not, there is no response. Do not follow up unless asked to do so.". Catalog online. Guidelines available via e-mail.

NONFICTION Subjects include alternative, anthropology, business, community, history, sex, social sciences, sociology, spirituality. "We are a Canadian publisher, so mss should be Canadian in content and aimed as much as possible at a wide, general audience. At this point in time, we are only publishing books by Canadian citizens residing in Canada." Query via e-mail. Submit proposal package, outline, bio, 3 sample chapters. Submit complete ms. Reviews artwork/photos. Send photocopies.

FICTION Subjects include adventure, experimental, gothic, historical, horror, humor, juvenile, literary, mystery, occult, poetry, regional, romance, short story collections, young adult. Stories should have

Canadian settings and characters should be Canadian, but content should have universal appeal to wide audience. Query via e-mail. Submit proposal package, clips, bio, 3 sample chapters. Submit complete ms.

POETRY Poetry should engage, provoke, involve the reader.

TIPS "Our audience includes everyone-the general public/mass audience. Self-edit your work first, make sure it is well written with strong Canadian content."

MANTRA LINGUA

Global House, 303 Ballards Ln., London N12 8NP, United Kingdom. (44)(208)445-5123. **E-mail:** jean@mantralingua.com. **Website:** www.mantralingua.com.

Mantra Lingua publishes dual-language books in English and more that 42 languages. They also publish talking books and resources with their Talking Pen technology, which brings sound and interactivity to their products. They will consider good contemporary stories, myths and folklore for picture books only.

FICTION Picture books, young readers, middle readers: folktales, multicultural stories, myths. Average word length: picture books—1,000-1,500; young readers—1,000-1,500. Submit outline/synopsis (250 words) via postal mail. Incluse SASE for returns.

MARINE TECHNIQUES PUBLISHING

126 Western Ave., Suite 266, Augusta ME 04330. (207)622-7984. **Fax:** (207)621-0821. **E-mail:** info@marinetechpublishing.com. **Website:** www.marine-techpublishing.com. **Contact:** James L. Pelletier, president/owner(commercial maritime); Maritime Associates Globally (commercial maritime). Estab. 1983. Trade paperback originals and reprints. **Publishes 2-5 titles/year. 100+ queries received/year. 40+ mss received/year. 50% of books from first-time authors. 75% from unagented writers. Pays 25-55% royalty on wholesale or retail price. Makes outright purchase.** Publishes book 1 year after acceptance. Accepts simultaneous submissions. Responds in 2 months to queries, proposals, and mss. Catalog and guidelines available online, by e-mail, and for #10 SASE for $5.

"Publishes only books related to the commercial marine/maritime industry."

NONFICTION Subjects include maritime education, marine subjects, counseling, career guidance, maritime labor, marine engineering, global water transportation, marine subjects, water transportation. "We are concerned with 'maritime related works' and not recreational boating, but rather commercial maritime industries, such as deep-sea water transportation, offshore oil & gas, inland towing, coastal tug boat, 'water transportation industries.'" Submit proposal package, including all sample chapters; submit completed ms. Reviews artwork/photos as part of the ms package; send photocopies.

FICTION Subjects include adventure, military, war, maritime. Must be commercial maritime/marine related. Submit proposal package, including all sample chapters. Submit complete ms.

TIPS "Audience consists of commercial marine/maritime firms, persons employed in all aspects of the marine/maritime commercial water-transportation-related industries and recreational fresh and salt water fields, persons interested in seeking employment in the commercial marine industry; firms seeking to sell their products and services to vessel owners, operators, and managers; shipyards, vessel repair yards, recreational and yacht boat building and national and international ports and terminals involved with the commercial marine industry globally worldwide, etc."

⊘ MARLOR PRESS, INC.

4304 Brigadoon Dr., St. Paul MN 55126. (651)484-4600. **E-mail:** marlin.marlor@minn.net. **Contact:** Marlin Bree, publisher. Estab. 1981. Publishes trade paperback originals. **Publishes 2 titles/year. 100 queries received/year. 25 mss received/year. 100% of books from first-time authors. Pays 8-10% royalty on wholesale price.** Publishes book 1 year after acceptance. Responds in 3-6 weeks to queries.

> ✂ "Currently emphasizing general interest nonfiction children's books and nonfiction boating books."

NONFICTION Subjects include travel, boating. Primarily how-to stuff. *No unsolicited mss.* No anecdotal reminiscences or biographical materials. No fiction or poetry. Query first; submit outline with sample chapters only when requested. Do not send full ms. Reviews artwork/photos.

MARTIN SISTERS PUBLISHING, LLC

P.O. Box 1749, Barbourville KY 40906-1499. **E-mail:** publisher@martinsisterspublishing.com. **Website:** www.martinsisterspublishing.com. **Contact:** Denise Melton, Publisher/Editor (Fiction/non-Fiction); Melissa Newman, Publisher/Editor (Fiction/non-Fiction). Estab. 2011. Firm/imprint publishes trade and mass market paperback originals; electronic originals. **Publishes 12 titles/year. 75% of books from first-time authors. 100% from unagented writers. Pays 7.5% royalty/max on retail price. No advance offered.** Publishes book Time between acceptance of ms and publication is 6 months. after acceptance of ms. Accepts simultaneous submissions. Responds in 1 month on queries, 2 months on proposals, 3-6 months on mss. Catalog and guidelines online.

NONFICTION Subjects include Americana, child guidance, contemporary culture, cooking, creative nonfiction, education, gardening, history, house and home, humanities, labor, language, law, literature, memoirs, money, nutrition, parenting, psychology, regional, sociology, spirituality, womens issues, womens studies, western. Send query letter only to submissions@martinsisterspublishing.com

FICTION Subjects include adventure, confession, fantasy, historical, humor, juvenile, literary, mainstream, military, mystery, poetry in translation, regional, religious, romance, science fiction, short story collections, spiritual, sports, suspense, war, western, young adult.

⟲ MASKEW MILLER LONGMAN

Subsidiary of Pearson Education and Caxton Publishers, P.O. Box 396, Cape Town 8000, South Africa. (27)(21)531-8103. **E-mail:** mmlwCape@mml.co.za. **Website:** www.mml.co.za.

> ✂ "The Maskew Miller Longman Group has over 100 years of publishing experience in southern Africa, with staff and offices in countries throughout southern, central and east Africa. As partners to government in the educational arena, we develop local materials for local needs. We are one of the leading educational publishers in Africa. We tap into global expertise: whether it be in education, technology or customer services, we benefit from being part of Pearson Education, which is the largest educational publisher in the world and which produces the best and most up-to-date learning material available. We publish in more than 50 languages, including all of South Africa's official languages as well as French, Portuguese, and numerous African languages in each of the countries in which we operate. Publishes teacher references and dictionaries for educational markets. Interested in all genres (poetry/novels/short stories/plays) of African language literature, as

well as material for the Young Africa and They Fought for Freedom series in English."

NONFICTION Subjects include education, literature, young adult.

MASTER BOOKS

P.O. Box 726, Green Forest AR 72638. (870)438-5288. **Fax:** (870)438-5120. **E-mail:** nlp@newleafpress.net; amanda@newleafpress.net. **Website:** www.masterbooks.net. **Contact:** Craig Forman, acquisitions editor. Estab. 1975. **10% of books from first-time authors. Pays authors royalty of 3-15% based on wholesale price.** Publishes book 1 year after acceptance. Responds to queries and mss in 4 months. Catalog available upon request. Guidelines available on website.

Publishes 3 middle readers/year; 2 young adult nonfiction titles/year; 15 adult trade books/year.

NONFICTION Picture books: activity books, animal, nature/environment, creation. Young readers, middle readers, young adults: activity books, animal, biography Christian, nature/environment, science, creation. Recently published *Passport to the World* (middle readers); *The Earth* (science book); *Demolishing Supposed Bible Contradictions*, compiled by Ken Ham (adult series). Submission guidelines on website.

TIPS "All of our children's books are creation-based, including topics from the Book of Genesis. We look also for home school educational material that would be supplementary to a home school curriculum."

MAUPIN HOUSE PUBLISHING, INC.

2416 NW 71st Place, Gainesville FL 32653. (800)524-0634. **Fax:** (352)373-5546. **E-mail:** info@maupinhouse.com. **Website:** www.maupinhouse.com. **Contact:** Julie Graddy, publisher (areas of interest: education, professional development). Publishes trade paperback originals and reprints. **Publishes 6-8 titles/year. 60% of books from first-time authors. 100% from unagented writers. Pays 10% royalty on retail price.** Publishes book 18 months after acceptance. Accepts simultaneous submissions. Responds in less than 1 month to queries, proposals, and mss. Catalog and guidelines free on request and available online and by e-mail at: publisher@maupinhouse.com.

"Maupin House publishes professional resource books for language arts teachers K-12."

NONFICTION Subjects include education, language arts, literacy and the arts, reading comprehension, writing workshop. "Study the website to understand our publishing preferences. Successful authors are all teachers or former teachers." Query with SASE or via e-mail. Submit proposal package, including outline, 1-2 sample chapters, and TOC/marketing ideas. Reviews artwork/photos as part of the mss package. Writers should send photocopies, digital.

TIPS "Our audience is K-12 educators, teachers. Be familiar with our publishing areas and tell us why your book idea is better/different than what is out there. How do you plan to promote it? Successful authors help promote books via speaking engagements, conferences, etc."

⊘ MAVERICK DUCK PRESS

E-mail: maverickduckpress@yahoo.com. **Website:** www.maverickduckpress.com. **Contact:** Kendall A. Bell, editor. Estab. 2005. **Pays 20 author's copies (out of a press run of 50).**

Maverick Duck Press is a "publisher of chapbooks from undiscovered talent. We are looking for fresh and powerful work that shows a sense of innovation or a new take on passion or emotion. Previous publication in print or online journals will increase your chances of us accepting your manuscript." Does not want "unedited work."

POETRY Send ms in Microsoft Word format with a cover letter with brief bio and publication credits. Chapbook mss may include previously published poems. "Previous publication is always a plus, as we may be more familiar with your work. Chapbook mss should have at least 20 poems."

🦆 MAVERICK MUSICALS AND PLAYS

89 Bergann Rd., Maleny QLD 4552, Australia. **Phone/Fax:** (61)(7)5494-4007. **E-mail:** helen@mavmuse.com. **Website:** www.mavmuse.com. Estab. 1978. Guidelines online.

FICTION Subjects include plays and musicals. "Looking for two-act musicals and one- and two-act plays. See website for more details."

⊘ MCBOOKS PRESS

ID Booth Building, 520 N. Meadow St., Ithaca NY 14850. (607)272-2114. **Fax:** (607)273-6068. **E-mail:** jackie@mcbooks.com. **Website:** www.mcbooks.com. **Contact:** Jackie Swift, editorial director. Estab. 1979. Publishes trade paperback and hardcover originals and reprints. **Publishes 6 titles/year. Pays 5-10% royalty on retail price. Pays $1,000-5,000 advance.** Accepts simultaneous submissions. Responds in 3 months to queries and proposals. Guidelines online.

NONFICTION *No unsolicited mss.* Query with SASE. "Give us a general outline of your book. Let us know how your book differs from what is currently on the market and what your qualifications are for writing it. Give us an idea how you would go about promoting/marketing your book."

FICTION Subjects include historical., nautical, naval and military historical, action/adventure historical. "We will consider any type of fiction except sci-fi, fantasy, religious, and children's." E-mail queries preferred. If querying by mail, include SASE. Send excerpt as RTF file attachment.

TIPS "In the current tough book market, the author's ability to use the internet for self promotion is almost as important as his/her ability to tell a great story really well. Unfortunately, writing ability alone is not enough. Show that you're savvy with personal web sites, blogs, and social networking."

THE MCDONALD & WOODWARD PUBLISHING CO.

431-B E. College St., Granville OH 43023. (740)321-1140. **Fax:** (740)321-1141. **E-mail:** mwpubco@mwpubco.com. **Website:** www.mwpubco.com. **Contact:** Jerry N. McDonald, publisher. Estab. 1986. Publishes hardcover and trade paperback originals. **Publishes 5 titles/year. 25 queries received/year. 20 mss received/year. Pays 10% royalty.** Accepts simultaneous submissions. Responds in less than 1 month to queries, proposals & mss. Catalog online. Guidelines free on request; by e-mail.

⌛ McDonald & Woodward publishes books in natural history, cultural history, and natural resources. Currently emphasizing travel, natural and cultural history, and natural resource conservation.

NONFICTION Subjects include animals, architecture, environment, history, nature, science, travel., natural history. Query with SASE. Reviews artwork/photos. Photos are not required.

FICTION Subjects include historical. Query with SASE.

TIPS Our books are meant for the curious and educated elements of the general population.

⊘ MARGARET K. McELDERRY BOOKS

Imprint of Simon & Schuster Children's Publishing Division, Simon & Schuster, 1230 Sixth Ave., New York NY 10020. (212)698-7200. **Website:** www.simonsayskids.com. **Contact:** Justin Chanda, vice president; Karen Wojtyla, editorial director; Gretchen Hirsch, associate editor; Emily Fabre, assistant editor. Ann Bobco, executive art director. Estab. 1971. **Publishes 30 titles/year. 15% of books from first-time authors. 50% from unagented writers. Pays authors royalty based on retail price. Pays illustrator royalty of by the project. Pays photographers by the project. Original artwork returned at job's completion. Offers $5,000-8,000 advance for new authors.** Guidelines for #10 SASE.

⌛ "Margaret K. McElderry Books publishes hardcover and paperback trade books for children from pre-school age through young adult. This list includes picture books, middle grade and teen fiction, poetry, and fantasy. The style and subject matter of the books we publish is almost unlimited. We do not publish textbooks, coloring and activity books, greeting cards, magazines, pamphlets, or religious publications."

NONFICTION Subjects include history., adventure. Looks for originality of ideas, clarity and felicity of expression, well-organized plot and strong characterization (fiction) or clear exposition (nonfiction); quality. Accept query letters with SASE only for picture books; query letter with first 3 chapters, SASE for middle grades and young adult novels. *No unsolicited mss.*

FICTION Subjects include adventure, fantasy, historical, mainstream, contemporary, mystery, picture books, young adult, or middle grade., All categories (fiction and nonfiction) for juvenile and young adult. We will consider any category. Results depend on the quality of the imagination, the artwork, and the writing. Average word length: picture books—500; young readers—2,000; middle readers—10,000-20,000; young adults—45,000-50,000. *No unsolicited mss.* Send query letter with SASE.

POETRY *No unsolicited mss.* Query and submit 3 sample poems.

TIPS "Read! The children's book field is competitive. See what's been done and what's out there before submitting. We look for high quality: an originality of ideas, clarity and felicity of expression, a well organized plot, and strong character-driven stories. We're looking for strong, original fiction, especially mysteries and middle grade humor. We are always interested in picture books for the youngest age reader. Study our titles."

MCFARLAND & CO., INC., PUBLISHERS

Box 611, Jefferson NC 28640. (336)246-4460. **Fax:** (336)246-5018. **E-mail:** info@mcfarlandpub.com. **Website:** www.mcfarlandpub.com. **Contact:** Steve Wilson, editorial director (automotive, general); David Alff, editor (general); Gary Mitchem, acquisitions editor (general, baseball). Estab. 1979. Publishes hardcover and quality paperback originals; a nontrade publisher. **Publishes 350 titles/year. 50% of books from first-time authors. 95% from unagented writers.** Publishes book 10 months after acceptance. Responds in 1 month to queries. Guidelines online.

☞ "McFarland publishes serious nonfiction in a variety of fields, including general reference, performing arts, popular culture, sports (particularly baseball); women's studies, librarianship, literature, Civil War, history and international studies. Currently emphasizing medieval history, automotive history. De-emphasizing memoirs."

NONFICTION Subjects include art, architecture, automotive, health, medicine, history, military, war/war, popular contemporary culture, music, dance, recreation, sociology, world affairs, sports (very strong)., African-American studies (very strong). Reference books are particularly wanted—fresh material (i.e., not in head-to-head competition with an established title). We prefer manuscripts of 250 or more double-spaced pages or at least 75,000 words. No fiction, New Age, exposes, poetry, children's books, devotional/inspirational works, Bible studies, or personal essays. Query with SASE. Submit outline, sample chapters. Reviews artwork/photos.

TIPS "We want well-organized knowledge of an area in which there is not information coverage at present, plus reliability so we don't feel we have to check absolutely everything. Our market is worldwide and libraries are an important part. McFarland also publishes six journals: the *Journal of Information Ethics, North Korean Review, Base Ball: A Journal of the Early Game-Black Ball: A Negro Leagues Journal, Clues: A Journal of Detection*, and *Minerva Journal of Women and War*."

⊕ MC PRESS

PO Box 4886, Ketchum ID 83340. **Fax:** (208)639-1231. **E-mail:** duptmor@mcpressonline.com. **Website:** www.mcpressonline.com. **Contact:** David Uptmor,

publisher. Estab. 2001. Publishes trade paperback originals. **Publishes 40 titles/year. 100 queries received/year. 50 mss received/year. 5% of books from first-time authors. 5% from unagented writers. Pays 10-16% royalty on wholesale price.** Publishes book 5 months after acceptance. Accepts simultaneous submissions. Responds in 1 month to queries/proposals/mss. Catalog and guidelines free.

NONFICTION Subjects include computers, electronics. "We specialize in computer titles targeted at IBM technologies." Submit proposal package, outline, 2 sample chapters, abstract. Reviews artwork/photos. Send photocopies.

ME & MI PUBLISHING

English-Spanish Foundation, 400 South Knoll, Suite B, Wheaton IL 60187. **Fax:** (630)588-9804. **Website:** www.memima.com. **Contact:** Mark Wesley, acquisition editor (pre-K-1). Estab. 2001. Publishes hardcover originals. **Publishes 10 titles/year. 30 queries received/year. 30 mss received/year. 30% of books from first-time authors. 70% from unagented writers. Pays 5% royalty on wholesale price. Makes outright purchase of $1,000-3,000.** Publishes book 1 year after acceptance. Accepts simultaneous submissions. Responds in 1 month to queries; 3 months to proposals; 4 months to mss. Catalog online. Guidelines available via e-mail.

NONFICTION Subjects include ethnic, language, literature, multicultural. Submit complete ms. Reviews artwork/photos. Send photocopies.

TIPS "Our audience is pre-K to 2nd grade. Our books are bilingual (Spanish and English)."

MEADOWBROOK PRESS

5451 Smetana Dr., Minnetonka MN 55343. **Fax:** (952)930-1940. **E-mail:** info@meadowbrookpress.com. **Website:** www.meadowbrookpress.com. Estab. 1974. Publishes trade paperback originals and reprints. **1,500 queries received/year. 20% of books from first-time authors. Pays 7 ½% royalty. Pays $50-100/poem plus 1 contributor's copy. Pays small advance.** Publishes book 2 years after acceptance. Accepts simultaneous submissions. Responds only if interested to queries. Catalog for #10 SASE. Guidelines online.

NONFICTION Subjects include child guidance, cooking, foods, nutrition, pregnancy. Publishes activity books, arts/crafts, how-to, poetry. Average word length: varies. Recently published *The Siblings' Busy Book* by Heather Kempskie & Lisa Hanson (activity book); *I Hope I Don't Strike Out*, by Bruce Lansky (poetry). No children's fiction, academic, or biography. Query or submit outline with sample chapters.

POETRY Meadowbrook Press is "currently seeking poems to be considered for future funny poetry book anthologies for children." Wants humorous poems aimed at children ages 6-12. "Poems should be fun, punchy, and refreshing. We're looking for new, hilarious, contemporary voices in children's poetry that kids can relate to." Has published poetry by Shel Silverstein, Jack Prelutsky, Jeff Moss, Kenn Nesbitt, and Bruce Lansky. Published anthologies include *Kids Pick the Funniest Poems*, *A Bad Case of the Giggles*, and *Miles of Smiles*. "Please take time to read our guidelines, and send your best work." Submit up to 10 poems at a time; 1 poem to a page with name and address on each; include SASE. Lines/poem: 25 maximum. Considers simultaneous submissions.

TIPS "Always send for guidelines before submitting material. Always submit nonreturnable copies; we do not respond to queries or submissions unless interested."

MEDICAL GROUP MANAGEMENT ASSOCIATION

104 Inverness Terrace E., Englewood CO 80112. (303)799-1111. **E-mail:** support@mgma.com; connexion@mgma.com. **Website:** www.mgma.com. Estab. 1926. Publishes professional and scholarly hardcover, paperback, and electronic originals, and trade paperback reprints. **Publishes 6 titles/year. 18 queries received/year. 6 mss received/year. 30% of books from first-time authors. 100% from unagented writers. Pays 8-17% royalty on net sales (twice a year). Pays $2,000-5,000 advance.** Publishes book 6 months after acceptance. Accepts simultaneous submissions. Responds in less than 3 weeks to queries; months to proposals and mss. Catalog online. Writer's guidelines online or via e-mail.

NONFICTION Subjects include audio, business, economics, education, health. Submit proposal package, outline, 3 sample chapters. Submit complete ms. Reviews artwork/photos. Send photocopies.

TIPS Audience includes medical practice managers and executives. Our books are geared at the business side of medicine.

MELLEN POETRY PRESS

P.O. Box 450, Lewiston NY 14092. (716)754-2266. **Fax:** (716)754-4056. **E-mail:** jrupnow@mellenpress.

com. **Website:** www.mellenpress.com. **Contact:** Dr. John Rupnow, acquisitions. Estab. 1973.

✂ "We are a non-subsidy academic publisher of books in the humanities and social sciences. Our sole criterion for publication is that a manuscript makes a contribution to scholarship. We publish monographs, critical editions, collections, translations, revisionist studies, constructive essays, bibliographies, dictionaries, grammars and dissertations. We publish in English, French, German, Spanish, Italian, Portuguese, Welsh and Russian. Our books are well reviewed and acquired by research libraries worldwide. The *Press* also publishes over 100 continuing series, several academic journals, and the research generated by several scholarly institutes."

MERIWETHER PUBLISHING LTD.

885 Elkton Dr., Colorado Springs CO 80907. (719)594-9916. **Fax:** (719)594-9916. **E-mail:** editor@meriwether.com. **Website:** www.meriwetherpublishing.com. **Contact:** Ted Zapel; Rhonda Wray. Estab. 1969. **75% of books from first-time authors. Pays authors royalty of 10% based on retail or wholesale price.** Publishes book 6-12 months after acceptance. Accepts simultaneous submissions. Responds to queries in 3 weeks, mss in 2 months or less.

✂ "Our niche is drama. Our books cover a wide variety of theatre subjects from play anthologies to theatrecraft. We publish books of monologs, duologs, short one-act plays, scenes for students, acting textbooks, how-to speech and theatre textbooks, improvisation and theatre games. Our Christian books cover worship on such topics as clown ministry, storytelling, banner-making, drama ministry, children's worship and more. We also publish anthologies of Christian sketches. We do not publish works of fiction or devotionals."

NONFICTION Middle readers: activity books, how-to, religion, textbooks. Young adults: activity books, drama/theater arts, how-to church activities, religion. Average length: 250 pages.

FICTION Middle readers, young adults: anthology, contemporary, humor, religion. "We publish plays, not prose-fiction. Our emphasis is comedy plays instead of educational themes."

TIPS "We are currently interested in finding unique treatments for theater arts subjects: scene books, how-to books, musical comedy scripts, monologs and short comedy plays for teens."

MERRIAM PRESS

133 Elm St., Suite 3R, Bennington VT 05201. (802)447-0313. **E-mail:** ray@merriam-press.com. **Website:** www.merriam-press.com. Estab. 1988. Publishes hardcover and softcover trade paperback originals and reprints. **Publishes 12+ titles/year. 70-90% of books from first-time authors. 100% from unagented writers. Pays 10% royalty on actual selling price.** Publishes book 6 months or less after acceptance. Responds quickly (e-mail preferred) to queries. Catalog available for $5 or visit website to view all available titles and access writer's guidelines and info.

NONFICTION Subjects include military, war, World War II. Query with SASE or by e-mail first. Reviews artwork/photos. Send photocopies on disk/flash drive/e-mail attachment.

TIPS "Our military history books are geared for military historians, collectors, model kit builders, wargamers, veterans, general enthusiasts. We now publish some fiction and poetry and will consider well-written books on a variety of historical topics."

MESSIANIC JEWISH PUBLISHERS

6120 Day Long Lane, Clarksville MD 21029. (410)531-6644. **E-mail:** website@messianicjewish.net. **Website:** www.messianicjewish.net. **Contact:** Janet Chaier, managing editor. Publishes hardcover and trade paperback originals and reprints. **Publishes 6-12 titles/year. Pays 7-15% royalty on wholesale price.** Guidelines available via e-mail.

NONFICTION Subjects include religion, Messianic Judaism, Jewish roots of the Christian faith. Text must demonstrate keen awareness of Jewish culture and thought, and Biblical literacy. Jewish themes only. Query with SASE. Unsolicited mss are not returned.

FICTION Subjects include religious. "We publish very little fiction. Jewish or Biblical themes are a must. Text must demonstrate keen awareness of Jewish culture and thought." Query with SASE. Unsolicited mss are not return

⊘ MIAMI UNIVERSITY PRESS

356 Bachelor Hall, Miami University, Oxford OH 45056. **E-mail:** tumakw@muohio.edu. **Website:** www.muohio.edu/mupress. **Contact:** Keith Tuma, editor; Dana Leonard, managing editor. Estab. 1992.

○ *Currently closed to unsolicited mss, except for submissions to novella contest; see website for information on the contest.*

MICHIGAN STATE UNIVERSITY PRESS

1405 S. Harrison Rd., Suite 25, East Lansing MI 48823-5202. (517)355-9543. **Fax:** (517)432-2611. **E-mail:** msupress@msu.edu. **Website:** http://msupress.msu.edu/. **Contact:** Martha Bates and Julie Loehr, acquisitions. Estab. 1947. Publishes hardcover and softcover originals. **Pays variable royalty.** Catalog and guidelines for 9×12 SASE or online.

○ Michigan State University Press has notably represented both scholarly publishing and the mission of Michigan State University with the publication of numerous award-winning books and scholarly journals. In addition, they publish nonfiction that addresses, in a more contemporary way, social concerns, such as diversity and civil rights. They also publish literary fiction and poetry.

NONFICTION Subjects include Nonfiction Americana, American Studies, business, economics, creative nonfiction, ethnic, Afro-American studies, government, politics, history, contemporary civil rights, language, literature, literary criticism, regional, Great Lakes regional, Canadian studies, women's studies, environmental studies, and American Indian Studies. Distributes books for: University of Calgary Press, University of Alberta Press, and University of Manitoba Press. Submit proposal/outline and sample chapter. Hard copy is preferred but e-mail proposals are also accepted. Initial submissions to MSU Press should be in the form of a short letter of inquiry and a sample chapter(s), as well as our preliminary Marketing Questionnaire, which can be downloaded from their website. We do not accept: Festschrifts, conference papers, or unrevised dissertations. (Festschrift: A complimentary or memorial publication usually in the form of a collection of essays, addresses, or biographical, bibliographic, scientific, of other contributions). Reviews artwork/photos.

MICROSOFT PRESS

E-mail: 4bkideas@microsoft.com. **Website:** www.microsoft.com/learning/books. **Publishes 80 titles/year. 25% of books from first-time authors. 90% from unagented writers.** Book proposal Guidelines online.

NONFICTION Subjects include software. A book proposal should consist of the following information:

a table of contents, a résumé with author biography, a writing sample, and a questionnaire. "We place a great deal of emphasis on your proposal. A proposal provides us with a basis for evaluating the idea of the book and how fully your book fulfills its purpose."

MID-LIST PRESS

4324 12th Ave S., Minneapolis MN 55407. (612)822-3733. **Fax:** (612)823-8387. **E-mail:** guide@midlist.org. **Website:** www.midlist.org. Estab. 1989. Publishes hardcover and trade paperback originals. **Publishes 3 titles/year.** Publishes book Publishes titles 18 months after acceptance. Accepts simultaneous submissions. Guidelines online.

8—➤ "Mid-List Press publishes books of high literary merit and fresh artistic vision by new and emerging writers."

FICTION No children's, juvenile, romance, young adult. See guidelines.

TIPS "Mid-List Press is an independent press. Mid-List Press."

⊘ MIDMARCH ARTS PRESS

300 Riverside Dr., New York NY 10025. (212)666-6990. **Fax:** (212)865-5509. **E-mail:** info@mid-marchartspress.org. **Website:** www.mid-marchartspress.org. **Publishes 4 titles/year.**

POETRY Query by letter or e-mail prior to submitting anything.

MILKWEED EDITIONS

1011 Washington Ave. S., Suite 300, Minneapolis MN 55415. (612)332-3192. **Fax:** (612)215-2550. **E-mail:** submissions@milkweed.org. **Website:** www.milkweed.org. Estab. 1979. Publishes hardcover, trade paperback, and electronic originals; trade paperback and electronic reprints. **Publishes 15-20 titles/year. 25% of books from first-time authors. 75% from unagented writers. Pays authors variable royalty based on retail price. Offers advance against royalties. Pays varied advance from $500-10,000.** Publishes book in 18 months. after acceptance of ms. Accepts simultaneous submissions. Responds in 6 months to queries, proposals, and mss. Catalog available online. Guidelines available online http://www.milkweed.org/content/blogcategory/.

8—➤ "Milkweed Editions publishes with the intention of making a humane impact on society, in the belief that literature is a transformative art uniquely able to convey the essential experiences of the human heart and spirit. To that end, Milkweed Editions publishes distinctive voices of literary merit in handsomely designed, visually dynamic books, exploring the ethical, cultural, and esthetic issues that free societies need continually to address."

NONFICTION Subjects include agriculture, animals, archaeology, art, contemporary culture, creative nonfiction, environment, gardening, gay, government, history, humanities, language, literature, multicultural, nature, politics, literary, regional, translation, women's issues, world affairs.

FICTION Subjects include experimental, short story collections, translation, young adult. Novels for adults and for readers 8-13. High literary quality. For adult readers: literary fiction, nonfiction, poetry, essays. Middle readers: adventure, contemporary, fantasy, multicultural, nature/environment, suspense/mystery. Does not want to see folktales, health, hi-lo, picture books, poetry, religion, romance, sports. Average length: middle readers—90-200 pages. No romance, mysteries, science fiction. Query with SASE, submit completed ms.

POETRY Query with SASE; submit completed ms

TIPS "We are looking for excellent writing with the intent of making a humane impact on society. Please read submission guidelines before submitting and acquaint yourself with our books in terms of style and quality before submitting. Many factors influence our selection process, so don't get discouraged. Nonfiction is focused on literary writing about the natural world, including living well in urban environments."

MILKWEEDS FOR YOUNG READERS

Milkweed Editions, Open Book Building, 1011 Washington Ave. S., Suite 300, Minneapolis MN 55415. (612)332-3192. **Fax:** (612)215-2550. **E-mail:** submissions@milkweed.org. **Website:** www.milkweed.org. **Contact:** The editors. Estab. 1984. Publishes hardcover and trade paperback originals. **Publishes 3-4 titles/year. 25% of books from first-time authors. 50% from unagented writers. Pays 7% royalty on retail price. Pays variable advance.** Publishes book 1 year after acceptance of ms. Accepts simultaneous submissions. Responds in 6 months to queries. Catalog for $1.50. Guidelines for #10 SASE or on the website.

8—➤ "We are looking first of all for high quality literary writing. We publish books with the intention of making a humane impact on society."

FICTION Subjects include adventure, fantasy, historical, humor, mainstream, contemporary., animal, environmental. Query with SASE. "Milkweed Editions now accepts manuscripts online through ou rSubmission Manager. If you're a first-time submitter, you'll need to fill in a simple form and then follow the instructions for selecting and uploading your manuscript. Please make sure that your manuscript follows the submission guidelines."

THE MILLBROOK PRESS

Lerner Publishing Group, 1251 Washington Ave N, Minneapolis MN 55401. **Website:** www.lernerbooks.com. **Contact:** Carol Hinz, editorial director.

○ "We do not accept unsolicited manuscripts from authors. Occasionally, we may put out a call for submissions, which will be announced on our website."

MODERN PUBLISHING

155 E. 55th St., New York NY 10022. (212)826-0850. **Fax:** (212)759-9069. **Website:** www.modernpublishing.com.

○ "Modern Publishing is currently focusing on licensed properties and coloring and activity books. We are no longer considering submissions that don't fall within those categories."

MOMENTUM BOOKS, LLC

117 W. Third St., Royal Oak MI 48067. (248)691-1800. **Fax:** (248)691-4531. **E-mail:** info@momentumbooks.com. **Website:** www.momentumbooks.com. **Contact:** Franklin Foxx, editor. Estab. 1987. **Publishes 6 titles/year. 100 queries received/year; 30 mss received/year. 95% of books from first-time authors. 100% from unagented writers. Pays 10-15% royalty.** Guidelines online.

⚷ Momentum Books publishes Midwest regional nonfiction.

NONFICTION History, sports, travel, automotive, current events, biography, entertainment. Submit proposal package, outline, 3 sample chapters, marketing outline.

TIPS Also, custom publishing services are available for authors who are considering self-publishing.

MONDIAL

203 W. 107th St., Suite 6C, New York NY 10025. (212)851-3252. **Fax:** (208)361-2863. **E-mail:** contact@mondialbooks.com. **Website:** www.mondialbooks.com; www.librejo.com. **Contact:** Andrew Moore, editor. Estab. 1996. Publishes trade paperback originals and reprints. **Publishes 20 titles/year. 2,000 queries received/year. 500 mss received/year. 20% of books from first-time authors. Pays 10% royalty on wholesale price.** Publishes book 4 months after acceptance of ms. Accepts simultaneous submissions. Guidelines online.

NONFICTION Subjects include alternative, ethnic, gay, lesbian, history, language, literature, literary criticism, memoirs, multicultural, philosophy, psychology, sex, sociology, translation. Submit proposal package, outline, 1 sample chapters. Send only electronically by e-mail.

FICTION Subjects include adventure, erotica, ethnic, gay, lesbian, historical, literary, mainstream, contemporary, multicultural, mystery, poetry, romance, short story collections, translation.

Ⓐ ⊘ MOODY PUBLISHERS

Moody Bible Institute, 820 N. LaSalle Blvd., Chicago IL 60610. (800)678-8812. **Fax:** (312)329-4157. **E-mail:** authors@moody.edu. **Website:** www.moodypublishers.org. Estab. 1894. Publishes hardcover, trade, and mass market paperback originals. **Publishes 60 titles/year. 1,500 queries received/year. 2,000 mss received/year. 1% of books from first-time authors. 80% from unagented writers. Royalty varies.** Publishes book 1 year after acceptance. Responds in 2-3 months to queries. Catalog for 9×12 envelope and 4 first-class stamps. Guidelines for SASE and on website.

⚷ "The mission of Moody Publishers is to educate and edify the Christian and to evangelize the non-Christian by ethically publishing conservative, evangelical Christian literature and other media for all ages around the world, and to help provide resources for Moody Bible Institute in its training of future Christian leaders."

NONFICTION Subjects include child guidance, money, finance, religion, spirituality, women's issues/studies. We are no longer reviewing queries or unsolicited manuscripts unless they come to us through an agent. Unsolicited proposals will be returned only if proper postage is included. We are not able to acknowledge the receipt of your unsolicited proposal. Does not accept unsolicited nonfiction submissions.

FICTION Subjects include fantasy, historical, mystery, religious, children's religious, inspirational, religious mystery/suspense, science fiction, young adult, adventure, fantasy/science fiction, historical, mystery/ suspense, series. Submit query letter, bio, one-page description of book, word count, table of contents, two chapters fully written, marketing information and SASE. "Mss should be neatly typed, double-spaced, on white letter-size typing paper. Grammar, style and punctuation should follow normal English usage. We use The Chicago Manual of Style (University of Chicago Press) for fine points."

TIPS "In our fiction list, we're looking for Christian storytellers rather than teachers trying to present a message. Your motivation should be to delight the reader. Using your skills to create beautiful works is glorifying to God."

✪ MOON SHADOW PRESS

Wakestone Press, 200 Brook Hollow Rd., Nashville TN 37205. (615)739-6428. **Website:** http://www.wakestonepress.com. **Contact:** Frank Daniels III, editor (youth fiction). Estab. 2010. Format publishes in hardcover and paperback originals; e-books. **Publishes 6-8 titles/year. 3% of books from first-time authors. 100% from unagented writers. Pays 7.5-15% royalty. Pays $2,000 advance (negotiable)** Publishes book 2 years after acceptance. Accepts simultaneous submissions. Responds to queries in 4 weeks; mss in 2 months. Catalogs available online. Send SASE for writer's guidelines.

✆— "Moon Shadow Press, an imprint of Wakestone Press, was founded on the belief that neither authors nor stories get proper attention. Wakestone looks for authors who, with the right team and support, can break out of the crowded, chaotic catalog of books to get their stories widely read. We love the current confusing pace of the publishing business with its challenges in distirbution, technology, marketing and consumption. We think that these market challenges are an exciting time to bring both new and old stories to readers in a way of forms and formats. Our experience in a wide range of publishing ventures has led us to understand that the media world is an either/and world, where readers want to have both short- and long-form stories, in print and digital formats, in multimedia and one-dimensional media. Our goal is to enable authors to tell and sell their stories and make them a part of our culture.

Currently Moon Shadow Press is working on publishing youth titles.

FICTION Subjects include adventure, fantasy, horror, juvenile. Needs work for the series *Galadria: Peter Huddleson and the Rites of Passage*, Miguel Lopez DeLeon.

TIPS "Be honest, be creative, be interesting."

MOON TIDE PRESS

P.O. Box 50184, Irvine CA 92619. **E-mail:** publisher@ moontidepress.com. **Website:** www.moontidepress. com. **Contact:** Michael Miller, publisher. Estab. 2006. **POETRY** Query first.

TIPS "Keep in mind that when we open and read your ms, it will probably be in the middle of a large stack of other submissions, and many of those will be well-meaning but undistinguished collections about the same few themes. So don't be afraid to take risks. Surprise and entertain us. Give us something that the next ten poets in the stack won't."

☯ MOOSE ENTERPRISE BOOK & THEATRE PLAY PUBLISHING

684 Walls Rd., Sault Ste. Marie ON P6A 5K6, Canada. (705) 779-3331. **Fax:** (705) 779-3331. **E-mail:** mooseenterprises@on.aibn.com. **Website:** www.moosehidebooks.com. **Contact:** Edmond Alcid. Estab. 1996. **Pays royalties.** Publishes book 1 year after acceptance. Responds to queries in 1 month; mss in 3 months. Ms guidelines available for SASE.

○ This publisher does not offer payment for stories published in its anthologies and/or book collections. Be sure to send a SASE for guidelines.

NONFICTION Middle readers, young adults: biography, history, multicultural. Query.

FICTION Middle readers, young adults: adventure, fantasy, humor, suspense/mystery, story poetry. Query.

TIPS "Do not copy trends; be yourself—give me something new, something different."

MOREHOUSE PUBLISHING CO.

Church Publishing Incorporated, 4475 Linglestown Rd., Harrisburg PA 17112. **Fax:** (717)541-8136. **E-mail:** dperkins@cpg.org. **Website:** www.morehouse-publishing.org. **Contact:** Davis Perkins. Frank Tedeschi Estab. 1884. Publishes hardcover and paperback originals. **Publishes 35 titles/year. 50% of books from first-time authors. Pays small advance.** Publishes book 18 months after acceptance. Accepts simultaneous submissions. Responds in 2-3 months to queries. Guidelines online.

8—π Morehouse Publishing publishes mainline Christian books, primarily Episcopal/Anglican works. Currently emphasizing Christian spiritual direction.

NONFICTION Subjects include religion, Christian, women's issues/studies., Christian spirituality, liturgies, congregational resources, issues around Christian life. Submit outline, résumé, 1-2 sample chapters, market analysis.

⊕ MORGAN JAMES PUBLISHING

Morgan James LLC, 5 Penn Plaza, 23rd Floor, New York NY 10001. (212)655-5470. **Fax:** (516)908-4496. **E-mail:** csauer@morganjamespublishing.com. **Website:** www.morganjamespublishing.com. **Contact:** Rick Frishman, publisher (general nonfiction, business); David Hancock, founder (entrepreneurial business). Estab. 2003. Publishes hardcover, trade paperback, and electronic originals. **Publishes 163 titles/year. 4,500 queries/year; 3,700 mss/year. 60% of books from first-time authors. 80% from unagented writers. Pays 20-30% royalty on wholesale price.** Publishes book 6 months after acceptance. Accepts simultaneous submissions. Responds in 1 month on queries, proposals and mss. Catalog and guidelines free on request.

NONFICTION Subjects include business, career guidance, child guidance, communications, computers, counseling, economics, education, electronics, finance, government, health, history, law, medicine, money, real estate, religion. "Best if book supports existing platform or business." Submit proposal package, including outline, 3 sample chapters; submit completed ms.

TIPS "Study www.morganjamespublishing.com."

MOTORBOOKS

Quayside Publishing Group, Motorbooks, MBI Publishing Company, 400 First Avenue North, Suite 300, Minneapolis MN 55401. (612)344-8100. **Fax:** (612)344-8691. **E-mail:** customerservice@quaysidepub.com. **Website:** www.motorbooks.com; http://www.qbookshop.com/motorbooks.com/. **Contact:** Lee Klancher, senior editor; Darwin Holmstrom (motorcycles); Peter Bodensteiner (racing, how-to); Dennis Pernu (Americana, trains & boats); Steve Gansen (military, aviation, tractors). Estab. 1973. Publishes hardcover and paperback originals. **Publishes 200 titles/year. 300 queries received/year. 50 mss received/year. 95% from unagented writers. Pays $5,000 average advance.** Publishes book 1 year after acceptance. Accepts simultaneous submissions. Responds in 6-8 months to proposals. Catalog available free. Guidelines for #10 SASE or online.

8—π "Motorbooks is one of the world's leading transportation publishers, covering subjects from classic motorcycles to heavy equipment to today's latest automotive technology. We satisfy our customers' high expectations by hiring top writers and photographers and presenting their work in handsomely designed books that work hard in the shop and look good on the coffee table."

NONFICTION Subjects include Americana, history, hobbies, military, war, photography, translation, nonfiction. State qualifications for doing book. Transportation-related subjects. Query with SASE. Reviews artwork/photos. Send photocopies.

MOTORCYCLING

Imprint of Far Horizons Media Company, P.O. Box 560989, Rockledge FL 32956. (321)690-2224. **Fax:** (321)690-0853. **E-mail:** postmaster@farhorizonsmedia.com. **Website:** www.farhorizonsmedia.com. Publishes trade paperback originals and limited hardback. **Publishes 15-25 titles/year. 100 queries received/year. 50 mss received/year. 50% of books from first-time authors. 99% from unagented writers.** Publishes book 3 months after acceptance. Responds in 1 month to queries. Guidelines available by e-mail.

○ Motorcycling publishes books on motorcycling and motorcycling history.

NONFICTION "General interest relating to touring, guide books, how-to subjects, and motorcycling history. We are interested in any title related to these fields. Query with a list of ideas. Include phone number. Our title plans rarely extend past 6 months, although we know the type and quantity of books we will publish over the next 2 years. We prefer good knowledge with simple-to-understand writing style containing a well-rounded vocabulary." Query with SASE. Reviews artwork/photos. Send photocopies and JPEG files on CD.

TIPS "All of our staff and editors are riders. As such, we publish what we would want to read relating to the subject. Our audience in general are active riders at the beginner and intermediate level of repair knowledge and riding skills, and history buffs wanting to learn more about the history of motorcycles in this country. Many are people new to motorcycles, attempting to learn all they can before starting out on that first long ride or even buying their first bike. Keep it easy and simple to follow. Use motorcycle jargon sparingly. Do not use complicated technical jargon, terms, or formulas without a detailed explanation of the same. Use experienced riders and mechanics as a resource for knowledge."

MOUNTAIN PRESS PUBLISHING CO.

P.O. Box 2399, Missoula MT 59806. (406)728-1900 or (800)234-5308. **Fax:** (406)728-1635. **E-mail:** info@mtnpress.com. **Website:** www.mountain-press.com. **Contact:** Jennifer Carey, editor. Estab. 1948. Publishes hardcover and trade paperback originals. **Publishes 15 titles/year. 50% of books from first-time authors. 90% from unagented writers. Pays 7-12% royalty on wholesale price.** Publishes book 2 years after acceptance. Responds in 3 months to queries. Catalog online.

⚬—ℼ "We are expanding our Roadside Geology, Geology Underfoot, and Roadside History series (done on a state-by-state basis). We are interested in well-written regional field guides—plants and flowers—and readable history and natural history."

NONFICTION Subjects include animals, history, Western, nature, environment, regional, science, Earth science. No personal histories or journals, poetry or fiction. Query with SASE. Submit outline, sample chapters. Reviews artwork/photos.

TIPS "Find out what kind of books a publisher is interested in and tailor your writing to them; research markets and target your audience. Research other books on the same subjects. Make yours different. Don't present your manuscript to a publisher—sell it. Give the information needed to make a decision on a title. Please learn what we publish before sending your proposal. We are a 'niche' publisher."

⊘ MOVING PARTS PRESS

10699 Empire Grade, Santa Cruz CA 95060. (831)427-2271. **E-mail:** frice@movingpartspress.com. **Website:** www.movingpartspress.com. **Contact:** Felicia Rice, poetry editor. Estab. 1977.

⚬—ℼ Moving Part Press publishes handsome, innovative books, broadsides, and prints that "explore the relationship of word and image, typography and the visual arts, the fine arts and popular culture." Published *Codex Espangliensis: from Columbus to the Border Patrol* (1998) with performance texts by Guillermo Goómez-Peñña and collage imagery by Enrique Chagoya; *Cosmogonie Intime/An Intimate Cosmogony* (2005), a limited edition artists' book with poems by Yves Peyreé, translated by Elizabeth R. Jackson, and drawings by Ray Rice.

POETRY *Does not accept unsolicited mss.*

MSI PRESS

38 Monterey St., San Juan Bautista CA 95045. **E-mail:** editor@msipress.com. **Website:** www.msipress.com. **Contact:** Betty Leaver, managing editor (foreign language, humanities, humor, spirituality). Estab. 2003. Publishes trade paperback originals. **Publishes 8-12 titles/year. 10% of books from first-time authors. 100% from unagented writers. 10% royalty on wholesale price.** Publishes book 6 months after acceptance. Accepts simultaneous submissions. 1 month to queries and proposals; 2 months to mss. Catalog available online. Guidelines available at e-mail address: info@msipress.com.

NONFICTION Subjects include education, health, medicine, humanities, language, literature, medicine, psychology, spirituality. "We are hoping to expand our spirituality, psychology, and self-help line." Submit proposal package, including: outline, 1 sample chapter, and professional résumé. Prefers electronic submissions. Reviews artwork/photos; send computer disk.

FICTION "We have no current plans to publish any more fiction."

TIPS "We are interested in helping to develop new writers who have good literacy skills but have limited or no publishing experience. We also have the capacity to work with authors with limited English skills whose first language is Arabic, Russian, Spanish, French, German, or Czech."

◑⊘ MULTICULTURAL BOOKS

307 Birchwood Ct., 6311 Gilbert Rd., Richmond BC V7C 3V7, Canada. (60447-0979. **E-mail:** jrmbooks@hotmail.com. **Website:** www.mbooksofbc.com; www.thehypertexts.com. **Contact:** Joe M. Ruggier, publisher. Estab. 1985. Responds to queries and mss 2 months.

⚬—ℼ "MBooks of BC is a small press. We publish poetry, prose and poetry leaflets, prose, translations, children's writing, sound recordings, fiction, and literary non-fiction. We also have a publishing services division. We belong to an international circle of poets and editors committed to reforming the prevailing order by bringing about a traditionalist revival in writing."

FICTION Authors who feel their work may be up to standard are welcome to query us with a sample or else submit an entire manuscript. All interested parties may consult our guidelines as well as our sample publication contract on website."

POETRY Query first, with a few sample poems and a cover letter with brief bio and publication credits. Book mss may include previously published poems. "The only criteria is quality of work and excellence."

Ⓐ MVP BOOKS

MBI Publishing and Quayside Publishing Group, 400 First Ave. N, Suite 300, Minneapolis MN 55401. (612)344-8160. **E-mail:** jleventhal@mbipublishing. com. **Website:** www.mvpbooks.com. **Contact:** Josh Leventhal, publisher. Estab. 2009. Publishes hardcover and trade paperback originals. **Publishes 15-20 titles/year. Pays royalty or fees. Pays advance.** Publishes book 1 year after acceptance. Responds in 3 months to queries.

✎ "We publish books for enthusiasts in a wide variety of sports, recreation, and fitness subjects, including heavily illustrated celebrations, narrative works, and how-to instructional guides."

NONFICTION Subjects include sports (baseball, football, basketball, hockey, surfing, golf, bicycling, martial arts, etc.); outdoor activities (hunting and fishing); health and fitness. No children's books. Query with SASE. "We consider queries from both first-time and experienced authors as well as agented or unagented projects. Submit outline." Reviews artwork/photos. Send sample digital images or transparencies (duplicates and tearsheets only).

MYSTIC RIDGE BOOKS

Subsidiary of Mystic Ridge Productions, Inc., 222 Main St., Suite 142, Farmington CT 06032. **Website:** www.mysticridgebooks.com. Estab. "Mystic Ridge Books (and its new children's line, MRB Kidz) is a rapidly growing publishing company—nationally known and respected—whose books are sold at fine booksellers. Our aim is to publish 'can't-put-me-down' books on a variety of interests for adults & children. For adults, we're offering books on personal betterment

and happiness, including but not limited to books on: relationships, intimacy, love, and a range of human interests. Look for self-help books, too, in the future. For children, MRB Kidz offers books that delight, entertain, educate, inspire and instill positive values. This line, though new, has drawn rave reviews from the press, teachers, librarians, parents and kids. Its authors have appeared on TV shows throughout the nation.". Publishes hardcover, trade paperback, & mass market paperback originals; trade paperback & mass market paperback reprints. **Publishes 6+ titles/year. 500+ queries received/year. 200+ mss received/year. 50% of books from first-time authors. 90% from unagented writers. Pays 10% royalty on wholesale price.** Publishes book 9 months after acceptance. Accepts simultaneous submissions. Responds in 3 months to queries, proposals, and mss. Catalog and guidelines online.

NONFICTION Subjects include audio, Americana, animals, anthropology, archeology, business, economics, child guidance, contemporary culture, cooking, foods, nutrition, creative nonfiction, government, politics, health, medicine, history, hobbies, language, literature, memoirs, money, finance, philosophy, psychology, recreation, science, sex, social sciences, spirituality, translation, womens issues, womens studies. "The writer should have a unique angle on a subject (it would be a plus if they are an expert in their field). The target readership should be fairly large. The writer must also be a good self-promoter, willing to be proactive in getting publicity." Query with SASE. Reviews artwork/photos. Send photocopies.

FICTION Subjects include young adult. "We are only looking for juvenile fiction at this time." Query with SASE.

TIPS "An agent is not necessary. Quality is key. It is helpful if the author has a dynamic, charismatic personality, who is intent on developing a high, public profile. No inquiries by phone, and no queries by certified mail or e-mail."

☺ NAPOLEON & COMPANY

235-1173 Dundas St. E, Toronto ON M4M 3P1, Canada. (416)465-9961. **Fax:** (416)465-3241. **E-mail:** napoleon@napoleonandcompany.com. **Website:** www. napoleonandcompany.com. **Contact:** A. Thompson, editor. Estab. 1990. Publishes hardcover and trade paperback originals and reprints. **Publishes 15 titles/ year. 200 queries received/year. 100 mss received/**

year. 50% of books from first-time authors. 75% from unagented writers. Publishes book 18 months after acceptance. Accepts simultaneous submissions. Responds in 1 month to queries; 3 months to proposals; 6 months to mss. Catalog and guidelines online.

○ "Napoleon is not accepting children's picture books at this time. Rendezvous Crime is not accepting mysteries. Check website for updates. We are accepting general adult fiction only for RendezVous Press and Darkstar Fiction."

NONFICTION Query with SASE. Submit outline, 1 sample chapter.

TIPS Canadian resident authors only.

NAR ASSOCIATES

P.O. Box 233, Barryville NY 12719. (845)557-8713. **Website:** www.aodceus.com. **Contact:** Nick Roes, acquisitions editor. Estab. 1977. Publishes trade paperback originals. **Publishes 6 titles/year. 10 queries received/year. 10 mss received/year. 80% of books from first-time authors. 100% from unagented writers. Makes outright purchase of $500.** Publishes book 1 month after acceptance. Accepts simultaneous submissions. Responds in 1 month to queries, proposals and mss. Catalog online. Guidelines available via e-mail.

NONFICTION Subjects include education, psychology., counseling techniques, professional ethics. "We publish home study courses for addiction and social work professionals." Query with SASE. Reviews artwork/photos. Send photocopies.

TIPS "Our audience consists of addiction counselors, social workers, and other counseling professionals. Use same format as existing coursework currently in publication."

NATIONAL ASSOCIATION FOR MUSIC EDUCATION

1806 Robert Fulton Dr., Reston VA 20191-4348. **Fax:** (703)860-1531. **E-mail:** ellaw@menc.org. **Website:** www.menc.org. **Contact:** Ella Wilcox, editor; Linda Brown, editor. Sue Rarus, Dir. of Informaton Resources and Publications Estab. 1907. **Pays royalty on retail price.**

NONFICTION Subjects include child guidance, education, multicultural, music, dance, music education. Mss evaluated by professional music educators. Submit proposal package, outline, 1-3 sample chapters, bio, CV, marketing strategy. For journal articles, submit electronically to http://mc.manuscriptcentral.com/mej. Authors will be required to set up an on-

line account on the SAGETRACK system powered by ScholarOne (this can take about 30 minutes). From their account, a new submission can be initiated.

TIPS "Look online for book proposal guidelines. No telephone calls. We are committed to music education books that will serve as the very best resources for music educators, students and their parents."

NATUREGRAPH PUBLISHERS, INC.

P.O. Box 1047, Happy Camp CA 96039. **Fax:** (530)493-5240. **E-mail:** nature@sisqtel.net. **Website:** www.naturegraph.com. **Contact:** Barbara Brown, owner. Estab. 1946. Publishes trade paperback originals. **Publishes 2 titles/year. 300 queries received/year. 12 mss received/year. 80% of books from first-time authors. 0% from unagented writers.** Publishes book 2 years after acceptance. Accepts simultaneous submissions. Responds in 1 month to queries; 2 months to mss. Catalog for #10 SASE.

NONFICTION Subjects include anthropology, archaeology, multicultural, nature, environment, science, natural history: biology, geology, ecology, astronomy., crafts.

TIPS "Please-always send a stamped reply envelope. Publishers get hundreds of manuscripts yearly."

THE NAUTICAL & AVIATION PUBLISHING COMPANY OF AMERICA

2055 Middleburg Ln., Mt. Pleasant SC 29464, United States. (843)856-0561. **Fax:** (843)856-3164. **E-mail:** nauticalaviationpublishing@comcast.net. **Website:** www.nauticalaviation.bizland.com. **Contact:** Denise K. James. Estab. 1979. Publishes hardcover and trade paperback originals and reprints. **Publishes 6 titles/year. Pays royalties.** Accepts simultaneous submissions. Catalog free on request. Guidelines free on request.

✂ Publishes military history and fiction.

NONFICTION Subjects include military, war, war history. Query with SASE; submit proposal package, outline.

FICTION Subjects include military, war fiction.

NAVAL INSTITUTE PRESS

US Naval Institute, 291 Wood Rd., Annapolis MD 21402. (410)268-6110. **Fax:** (410)295-1084. **E-mail:** cparkinson@usni.org; books@usni.org. **Website:** www.usni.org; www.nip.org. Estab. 1873. **Publishes 80-90 titles/year. 50% of books from first-time authors. 90% from unagented writers.** Guidelines online.

✂ "The Naval Institute Press publishes trade and scholarly nonfiction. We are interested in national and international security, naval, military, military jointness, intelligence, and special warfare, both current and historical."

NONFICTION Submit proposal package with outline, author bio, TOC, description/synopsis, sample chapter(s), page/word count, number of illustrations, ms completion date, intended market; or submit complete ms. Send SASE with sufficient postage for return of ms. Send by postal mail only. No e-mail submissions, please.

⊘ NAVPRESS, (THE PUBLISHING MINISTRY OF THE NAVIGATORS)

P.O. Box 35001, Colorado Springs CO 80935. **Fax:** (719)260-7223. **E-mail:** customerservice@navpress. com. **Website:** www.navpress.com. Estab. 1975. Publishes hardcover, trade paperback, direct and mass market paperback originals and reprints; electronic books and Bible studies. **Pays royalty. Pays low or no advances.** Catalog available free.

NONFICTION Subjects include child guidance, parenting, sociology, spirituality and contemporary culture, Christian living, marriage.

NBM PUBLISHING

40 Exchange Pl., Suite 1308, New York NY 10005. **E-mail:** nbmgn@nbmpub.com. **Website:** nbmpub.com. **Contact:** Terry Nantier, editor/art director. Estab. 1976.

➤ Publishes graphic novels for an audience of 18-34 year olds. Types of books include fiction, fantasy, mystery, science fiction, horror and social parodies. Circ. 5,000-10,000.

NEAL-SCHUMAN PUBLISHERS, INC.

100 William St., Suite 2004, New York NY 10038. (212)925-8650. **Fax:** (212)219-8916. **E-mail:** charles@ neal-schuman.com.; info@neal-schuman.com. **Website:** www.neal-schuman.com. **Contact:** Charles Harman, vice president/ director of publishing. Estab. 1976. Publishes trade paperback originals. **Publishes 36 titles/year. 150 queries received/year. 80% of books from first-time authors. 100% from unagented writers. Pays 10-15% royalty on wholesale price. Pays infrequent advance.** Publishes book 5 months after acceptance. Accepts simultaneous submissions. Responds in 1 month to queries, proposals, and mss. Catalog free. Mss

➤ "Neal-Schuman publishes books about library management, archival science, records management, digital curation, information literary,

the Internet and information technology. Especially submitting proposals for undergraduate information studies, archival science, records management, and knowledge management textbooks."

NONFICTION Subjects include computers, electronics, education, software., Internet guides, library and information science, archival studies, records management. Submit proposal package, outline, 1 sample chapter. Reviews artwork. Send photocopies.

TIPS "Our audience are professional librarians, archivists, and records managers."

NEW CANAAN PUBLISHING COMPANY LLC.

2384 N. Hwy 341, Rossville GA 30741. 423)285-8672. **Fax:** (678)306-1471. **E-mail:** info@newcanaanpublishing.com. **Website:** www.newcanaanpublishing. com. **50% of books from first-time authors. Pays authors royalty of 7-12% based on wholesale price. Royalty may be shared with illustrator where relevant. Pays illustrators royalty of 4-6% as share of total royalties.** Guidelines available on website.

💬 *New Canaan no longer reviews unsolicited mss.*

➤ "We seek books with strong educational or traditional moral content and books with Christian themes." Publishes 1 picture book/year; 1 young reader/year; 1 middle reader/year; 1 young adult title/year.

NONFICTION All levels: religion (Christian only), textbooks. Average word length: picture books—1,000-3,000; young readers—8,000-30,000; middle readers—8,000-40,000; young adults—15,000-50,000.

FICTION All levels: adventure, history, religion (Christianity), suspense/mystery. Picture books: Christian themes. Average word length: picture books—1,000-3,000; young readers—8,000-30,000; middle readers—8,000-40,000; young adults—15,000-50,000.

TIPS "We are small, so please be patient."

NEW FORUMS PRESS

New Forums, 1018 S. Lewis St., Stillwater OK 74074. (405)372-6158. **Fax:** (405)377-2237. **E-mail:** contact@ newforums.com; submissions@newforums.com. **Website:** www.newforums.com. **Contact:** Doug Dollar, president (interests: higher education, Oklahoma-Regional). Estab. 1981. Hardcover and trade paperback originals. **60% of books from first-time authors.**

100% from unagented writers. Use Author Guidelines online or call (800)606-3766 with any questions.

☛ "New Forums Press is an independent publisher offering works devoted to various aspects of professional development in higher education, home and office aides, and various titles of a regional interest. We welcome suggestions for thematic series of books and thematic issues of our academic journals—addressing a single issue, problem, or theory."

NONFICTION Subjects include business, finance, history, literature, money, music, politics, regional, sociology, young adult. "We are actively seeking new authors—send for review copies and author guidelines, and visit our website." Mss should be submitted as a Microsoft Word document, or a similar standard word processor document (saved in RTF rich text), as an attachment to an e-mail sent to submissions@newforums.com. Otherwise, submit your manuscript on 8 ½ x 11 inch white bond paper (one original). The name and complete address, telephone, fax number, and e-mail address of each author should appear on a separate cover page, so it can be removed for the blind review process.

⊕ NEW ISSUES POETRY & PROSE

Western Michigan University, 1903 W. Michigan Ave., Kalamazoo MI 49008-5463. (269)387-8185. **Fax:** (269)387-2562. **E-mail:** new-issues@wmich. edu. **Website:** wmich.edu/newissues. **Contact:** Managing Editor. Estab. 1996. **50% first time authors% of books from first-time authors. 95% unagented writers% from unagented writers.** Publishes book 18 months after acceptance of ms. Accepts simultaneous submissions. Guidelines available online, by e-mail, or by SASE.

FICTION Subjects include literary, poetry.

POETRY New Issues Poetry & Prose offers two contests annually. The Green Rose Prize is awarded to an author who has previously published at least one full-length book of poems. The New Issues Poetry Prize, an award for a first book of poems, is chosen by a guest judge. Past judges have included Philip Levine, C.K. Williams, C.D. Wright, and Campbell McGrath. New Issues does not read manuscripts outside our contests. Graduate students in the Ph.D. and M.F.A. programs of Western Michigan Univ. often volunteer their time reading manuscripts. Finalists are chosen by the editors. New Issues often publishes up to two additional manuscripts selected from the finalists.

⊕ ⤴ NEW LIBRI PRESS

4230 95th Ave. SE, Mercer Island WA 98040. **E-mail:** stasa@newlibri.com. **E-mail:** query@newlibri.com. **Website:** http://www.newlibri.com. **Contact:** Michael Muller, editor (nonfiction and foreign writers); Stanislav Fritz (literary). Estab. 2011. Publishes hardcover, trade paperback, mass market paperback, electronic original, electronic reprints. **Publishes 10 titles/year. 80% of books from first-time authors. 90% from unagented writers. Pays 20-35% royalty on wholesale price. No advance.** Publishes book 6-9 months after acceptance. Responds in 1 month on queries and mss; 2 months on proposals. Catalog not available yet.

NONFICTION Subjects include agriculture, automotive, business, child guidance, computers, cooking, creative nonfiction, economics, electronics, environment, gardening, hobbies, house and home, nature, parenting, recreation, science, sex, software, translation, travel. "Writers should know we embrace ebooks. This means that some formats and types of books work well and others don't." Prefers e-mail. Submit proposal package, including outline, 2 sample chapters, and summary of market from author's perspective; submit completed ms.

FICTION Subjects include adventure, experimental, fantasy, historical, horror, literary, mainstream, military, mystery, science fiction, translation, war, western, young adult. "Open to most ideas right now; this will change as we mature as a press." As a new press, we are more open than most and time will probably shape the direction. That said, trite as it is, we want good writing that is fun to read. While we currently are not looking for some sub-genres, if it is well written and a bit off the beaten path, submit to us. We are ebook friendly, which means some fiction may be less likely to currently sell(e.g. picture books would work only on an iPad or Color Nook as of this writing)." Submit proposal package, including snyopsis, 5 sample chapters; submit completed ms.

POETRY "Poetry is not our focus. We will probably only examine poetry in the author-subsidized model."

TIPS "Our audience is someone who is comfortable reading an ebook,or someone who is tired of the recycled authors of mainstream publishing, but still wants a good, relatively fast, reading experience. The industry is changing, while we accept for the traditional model, we are searching for writings who are interested in sharing the risk and controlling their own destiny. We embrace writers with no agent."

⊘ NEW NATIVE PRESS

P.O. Box 661, Cullowhee NC 28723. (828)293-9237. **E-mail:** newnativepress@hotmail.com. **Website:** www.newnativepress.com. **Contact:** Thomas Rain Crowe, publisher. Estab. 1979. **Publishes 2 titles/year.** Publishes book 1 year after acceptance. Responds to queries in 2 weeks.

POETRY Always comments on rejected poems. Query first, with 10 sample poems and cover letter with brief bio and publication credits.

NEW RIVERS PRESS

MSU Moorhead, 1104 Seventh Ave. S., Moorhead MN 56563. **E-mail:** kelleysu@mnstate.edu. **Website:** www.newriverspress.com. **Contact:** Suzanne Kelley, managing editor. Estab. 1968.

⚷ New Rivers Press publishes collections of poetry, novels or novellas, translations of contemporary literature, and collections of short fiction and nonfiction. "We continue to publish books regularly by new and emerging writers, but we also welcome the opportunity to read work of every character and to publish the best literature available nationwide. Each fall through the MVP competition, we choose 2 books, 1 of them Poetry and 1 of them Prose."

POETRY The Many Voices Prize (MVP) awards $1,000, a standard book contract, and publication of a book-length ms by New Rivers Press. All previously published poems must be acknowledged. Considers simultaneous submissions "if noted as such. If your manuscript is accepted elsewhere during the judging, you must notify New Rivers Press immediately. If you do not give such notification and your manuscript is selected, your signature on the entry form gives New Rivers Press permission to go ahead with publication." Submit 50-80 pages of poetry. Entry form (required) and guidelines available on website. **Entry fee:** $20. **Deadline:** submit September 15-November 1 (postmark). Book-length mss of poetry, short fiction, novellas, or creative nonfiction are all considered. No fax or e-mail submissions. Guidelines available on website.

NEWSAGE PRESS

P.O. Box 607, Troutdale OR 97060-0607. (503)695-2211. **E-mail:** info@newsagepress.com. **Website:** www.newsagepress.com. **Contact:** Maureen R. Michelson, publisher; Sherry Wachter, design. Estab. 1985. Publishes trade paperback originals. Guidelines online.

⚷ "We focus on nonfiction books. No `how to' books or cynical, despairing books. Photo-essay books in large format are no longer published by Newsage Press. No novels or other forms of fiction."

NONFICTION Subjects include animals, multicultural, nature, environment, womens issues, womens studies., death/dying. Submit 2 sample chapters, proposal (no more than 1 page), SASE.

NEW VICTORIA PUBLISHERS

P.O. Box 13173, Chicago IL 60613. (773)793-2244. **E-mail:** newvictoriapub@att.net; queries@newvictoria.com. **Website:** www.newvictoria.com. **Contact:** Patricia Feuerhaken, president. Estab. 1976. Publishes trade paperback originals. **Publishes 3 titles/year. Pays 10% royalty.** Publishes book 1 year after acceptance. Accepts simultaneous submissions. Catalog free on request; for #10 SASE; or online. Guidelines free on request; for #10 SASE; or online.

⚷ "Publishes mostly lesbian fiction—strong female protagonists. Most well known for Stoner McTavish mystery series." Distributes titles through Amazon Books, Bella books, Bulldog Books (Sydney, Australia), and Women and Children First Books (Chicago). Promotes titles "mostly through lesbian feminist media."

NONFICTION Subjects include alternative, biography, lesbian, history, language, poetry, fiction, literature, memoirs, multicultural, music/dance, mystery, nature, environment, New Age, erotica, translation, women's issues/studies, world affairs, contemporary culture, autobiography, biography, general nonfiction, humor, reference, science fiction. "We will consider well-researched nonfiction of interest to women, as well as lesbian feminist herstory, or biography of interest to a general as well as academic audience." Query with SASE. Reviews artwork/photos; send photocopies.

FICTION Lesbian, feminist fiction including adventure, erotica, fantasy, historical, humor, mystery (amateur sleuth), or science fiction. "Looking for strong feminist, well drawn characters, with a strong plot and action. We will consider any original, well written piece that appeals to the lesbian/feminist audience." Publishes anthologies or special editions. We advise you to look through our catalog or visit our website to see our past editorial decisions as well as what we are currently marketing. Our books average 80-100,000 words, or 200-220 single-spaced pages. Accepts unsolicited mss, but prefers query first. Submit outline, synopsis, and sample chapters (50 pages). No queries by e-mail or fax; please send SASE or IRC. No simultaneous submissions.

TIPS "We are especially interested in lesbian or feminist novels, ideally with a character or characters who can evolve through a series of books. Stories should involve a complex plot, accurate details, and protagonists with full emotional lives. Pay attention to plot and character development. Read guidelines carefully. Our books average 80-100,000 words, or 200-220 single-spaced pages."

NEXT DECADE, INC.

39 Old Farmstead Rd., Chester NJ 07930. (908)879-6625. **Fax:** (908)879-2920. **E-mail:** barbara@nextdecade.com. **Website:** www.nextdecade.com. **Contact:** Barbara Kimmel, president (reference); Carol Rose, editor. Publishes trade paperback originals. **Publishes 2-4 titles/year. Pays 8-15% royalty on wholesale price.** Responds in 1 month to queries. Catalog and guidelines online.

NONFICTION Subjects include health, medicine, women's, money, finance, multicultural., senior/retirement issues, real estate.

TIPS "We publish books that simplify complex subjects. We are a small, award-winning press that successfully publishes a handful of books each year."

⊘ NINETY-SIX PRESS

Furman University, 3300 Poinsett Hwy., Greenville SC 29613. (864)294-3152. **Fax:** (864)294-2224. **E-mail:** gil.allen@furman.edu. **Contact:** Gilbert Allen, editor. Estab. 1991.

POETRY "**We currently accept submissions by invitation only.**" For a sample, send $10.

NOMAD PRESS

2456 Christain St., White River Junction NJ 05001. (802)649-1995. **Fax:** (802)649-2667. **E-mail:** rachel@nomadpress.net; info@nomadpress.net. **Website:** www.nomadpress.net. **Contact:** Alex Kahan, publisher. Estab. 2001. **Pays authors royalty based on retail price or work purchased outright. Offers advance against royalties.** Publishes book 1 year after acceptance. Responds to queries in 3-4 weeks. Catalog available on website.

⚮ "We produce nonfiction children's activity books that bring a particular science or cul-

tural topic into sharp focus. Nomad Press does not accept unsolicited manuscripts. If authors are interested in contributing to our children's series, please send a writing résumé that includes relevant experience/expertise and publishing credits."

NONFICTION Middle readers: activity books, history, science. Average word length: middle readers—30,000.

TIPS "We publish a very specific kind of nonfiction children's activity book. Please keep this in mind when querying or submitting."

NORTH CAROLINA OFFICE OF ARCHIVES AND HISTORY

Historical Publications Section, 4622 Mail Service Center, Raleigh NC 27699. (919)733-7442. **Fax:** (919)733-1439. **E-mail:** historical.publications@ncdcr.gov. **Website:** www.ncpublications.com. **Contact:** Donna E. Kelly, administrator (North Carolina and southern history). Publishes hardcover and trade paperback originals. **Publishes 4 titles/year. 20 queries received/year. 25 mss received/year. 5% of books from first-time authors. 100% from unagented writers. Makes one-time payment upon delivery of completed ms.** Publishes book 2 years after acceptance. Accepts simultaneous submissions. Responds in 1 week to queries and to proposals; 2 months to mss. Guidelines for $3.

⚮ "We publish *only* titles that relate to North Carolina. The North Carolina Office of Archives and History also publishes the *North Carolina Historical Review*, a quarterly scholarly journal of history."

NONFICTION Subjects include history, related to North Carolina, military, war, related to North Carolina, regional, North Carolina and Southern history. Query with SASE. Reviews artwork/photos. Send photocopies.

NORTH LIGHT BOOKS

F+W Media, Inc., 10151 Carver Rd., Suite 200, Cincinnati OH 45242. **Fax:** (513)891-7153. **E-mail:** jamie.markle@fwmedia.com; pam.wissman@fwmedia.com; vanessa.lyman@fwmedia.com; ali.meyer@fwmedia.com. **Website:** www.fwmedia.com. **Contact:** Jamie Markle, fine art publisher; Ali Meyer, craft publisher; Pam Wissman, senior content director fine arts; Vanessa Lyman, editorial director craft. Publishes hardcover and trade paperback how-to books.

Publishes 70-75 titles/year. Pays 8% royalty on net receipts and $4,000 advance. Accepts simultaneous submissions. Responds in 2 months to queries. Catalog for 9×12 envelope and 6 first-class stamps.

⊶ "North Light Books publishes art and craft books, including watercolor, drawing, mixed media, acrylic, knitting, jewelry making, sewing, and needle arts that emphasize illustrated how-to art instruction. Currently emphasizing drawing including traditional, fantasy art, and Japanese-style comics as well as creativity and inspiration."

NONFICTION Subjects include hobbies, watercolor, realistic drawing, creativity, decorative painting, comics drawing, paper arts, knitting, collage and other craft instruction books. Interested in books on acrylic painting, basic drawing and sketching, journaling, pen and ink, colored pencil, decorative painting, and beading, art, how-to. Do not submit coffeetable art books without how-to art instruction. Query with SASE. Submit outline.

NORTIA PRESS

27525 Puerta Real, Ste. 100-467, Mission Viejo CA 92701. **E-mail:** acquisitions@nortiapress.com. **Website:** www.NortiaPress.com. Estab. 2009. Publishes trade paperback and electronic originals. **Publishes 6 titles/year. 0% of books from first-time authors. 80% from unagented writers. Pays negotiable royalties on wholesale price.** Publishes book 7 months after acceptance. Accepts simultaneous submissions. Responds in 1 month to queries; months to proposals.. Catalog and guidelines available for SASE with first-class stamps.

NONFICTION Subjects include business, community, economics, ethnic, government, health, humanities, medicine, memoirs, military, psychology, public affairs, religion, science, sex, social sciences, sociology, war, women's issues/studies.

FICTION Subjects include comic books, ethnic, feminist, historical, humor, literary, military, multicultural, regional, sports, war. "We focus mainly on literary and historical fiction, but are open to other genres. No vampire stories, science fiction, or erotica, please. Submit a brief e-mail query. Please include a short bio, approximate word count of book, and expected date of completion (fiction titles should be completed before sending a query). All unsolicited snail mail will be discarded without review."

TIPS "We specialize in working with experienced authors who seek a more collaborative and fulfilling relationship with their publisher. As such, we are less likely to accept pitches from first-time authors, no matter how good the idea. As with any pitch, please make your e-mail very brief and to the point, so the reader is not forced to skim it. Always include some biographic information. Your life is interesting."

ⓐ W.W. NORTON CO., INC.

500 Fifth Ave., New York NY 10110. **Fax:** (212)869-0856. **E-mail:** manuscripts@wwnorton.com. **Website:** www.wwnorton.com. Estab. 1923. **Publishes 300 titles/year. Pays royalty. Pays advance.** Accepts simultaneous submissions. Responds to queries in 2 months. Ms guidelines online.

FICTION Literary, poetry, poetry in translation, religious. High-qulity literary fiction. *Does not accept unagented submissions or unsolicited mss.* If you would like to submit your proposal (6 pages or less) by e-mail, paste the text of your query letter and/or sample chapter into the body of the e-mail message. Do not send attachments.

NOVA PRESS

11659 Mayfield Ave., Suite 1, Los Angeles CA 90049. (310)207-4078. **Fax:** (310)571-0908. **E-mail:** novapress@aol.com. **Website:** www.novapress.net. **Contact:** Jeff Kolby, president. Estab. 1993. Publishes trade paperback originals. **Publishes 4 titles/year.** Publishes book 6 months after acceptance. Catalog available free.

⊶ "Nova Press publishes only test prep books for college entrance exams (SAT, GRE, GMAT, LSAT, etc.), and closely related reference books, such as college guides and vocabulary books."

NONFICTION Subjects include education, software.

NURSESBOOKS.ORG

American Nurses Association, 8515 Georgia Ave., Suite 400, Silver Spring MD 20901. 1-800-274-4ANA. **Fax:** (301)628-5003. **E-mail:** anp@ana.org. **Website:** www.nursesbooks.org. **Contact:** Rosanne Roe, publisher; Eric Wurzbacher, editor/project manager; Camille Walker, business operations coordinator/project manager. Publishes professional paperback originals and reprints. **Publishes 10 titles/year. 50 queries received/year. 8-10 mss received/year. 75% of books from first-time authors. 100% from unagented writers.** Publishes book 4 months after acceptance. Responds in 3 months to proposals and mss. Catalog online. Guidelines available free.

8—⚲ "Nursebooks.org publishes books designed to help professional nurses in their work and careers. Through the publishing program, Nursebooks.org provides nurses in all practice settings with publications that address cutting edge issues and form a basis for debate and exploration of this century's most critical health care trends."

NONFICTION Subjects include advanced practice, computers, continuing education, ethics, health care policy, nursing administration, psychiatric and mental health, quality, nursing history, workplace issues, key clinical topics, such as geriatrics, pain management, public health, spirituality and home health. Submit outline, 1 sample chapter, CV, list of 3 reviewers and paragraph on audience and how to reach them. Reviews artwork/photos. Send photocopies.

OAK KNOLL PRESS

310 Delaware St., New Castle DE 19720. (302)328-7232. **Fax:** (302)328-7274. **E-mail:** Laura@oakknoll.com. **Website:** www.oakknoll.com. **Contact:** Laura R. Williams, publishing director. Estab. 1976. Publishes hardcover and trade paperback originals and reprints. **Publishes 40 titles/year. 250 queries received/year. 100 mss received/year. 50% of books from first-time authors. 100% from unagented writers.** Publishes book 1 year after acceptance. Accepts simultaneous submissions. Guidelines online.

8—⚲ "Oak Knoll specializes in books about books and manuals on the book arts: preserving the art and lore of the printed word."

NONFICTION Reviews artwork/photos. Send photocopies.

OAK TREE PRESS

140 E. Palmer, Taylorville IL 62568. (217)824-6500. **E-mail:** oaktreepub@aol.com. **E-mail:** queryotp@aol.com. **Website:** www.oaktreebooks.com. **Contact:** Billie Johnson, publisher (mysteries, romance, nonfiction); Sarah Wasson, acquisitions editor (all); Barbara Hoffman, senior editor (children's, young adult, educational). Estab. 1998. Publishes trade paperback and hardcover books. **Royalties based on sales. No advance.** Publishes book 9-18 months after acceptance. Responds in 4-6 weeks. Catalog and guidelines online.

8—⚲ "Oak Tree Press is an independent publisher that celebrates writers, and is dedicated to the

many great unknowns who are just waiting for the opportunity to break into print. We're looking for mainstream, genre fiction, narrative nonfiction, how-to. Sponsors 3 contests annually: Dark Oak Mystery, Timeless Love Romance and CopTales for true crime and other stories of law enforcement professionals."

FICTION Adventure, confession, ethnic, fantasy (romance), feminist, humor, mainstream/contemporary, mystery (amateur sleuth, cozy, police procedural, private eye/hard-boiled), new age/mystic, picture books, romance (contemporary, futuristic/time travel, romantic suspense), suspense, thriller/espionage, young adult (adventure, mystery/suspense, romance). Emphasis on mystery and romance novels. "No science fiction or fantasy novels, or stories set far into the future. Next, novels substantially longer than our stated word count are not considered, regardless of genre. We look for manuscripts of 70-90,000 words. If the story really charms us, we will bend some on either end of the range. No right-wing political or racist agenda, gratuitous sex or violence, especially against women, or depict harm of animals." Does not accept or return unsolicited mss. Query with SASE. Accepts queries by e-mail. Include estimated word count, brief bio, list of publishing credits, brief description of ms. Send SASE for return of ms or send a disposable ms and SASE for reply only.

TIPS "Perhaps my most extreme pet peeve is receiving queries on projects which we've clearly advertised we don't want: science fiction, fantasy, epic tomes, bigoted diatribes and so on. Second to that is a practice I call 'over-taping,' or the use of yards and yards of tape, or worse yet, the filament tape so that it takes forever to open the package. Finding story pitches on my voice mail is also annoying."

OBERLIN COLLEGE PRESS

50 N. Professor St., Oberlin College, Oberlin OH 44074. (440)775-8408. **Fax:** (440)775-8124. **E-mail:** oc.press@oberlin.edu. **Website:** www.oberlin.edu/ocpress. **Contact:** Linda Slocum, managing editor. Estab. 1969. Publishes hardcover and trade paperback originals. **Publishes 2-3 titles/year. Pays 7½-10% royalty.** Accepts simultaneous submissions. Responds promptly to queries; 2 months to mss.

POETRY *"FIELD Magazine*—submit 2-6 poems through website "submissions" tab; FIELD Translation Series—query with SASE and sample poems;

FIELD Poetry Series—*no unsolicited mss.* Enter mss in FIELD Poetry Prize ($1,000 and a standard royalty contract) held annually in May. Submit electronically through field poetry prize link on website at www. oberlin.edu/ocpress." Submit 2-6 sample poems.

TIPS "Queries for the FIELD Translation Series: send sample poems and letter describing project. Winner of the annual FIELD poetry prize determines publication. Do not send unsolicited manuscripts."

☯ OBRAKE BOOKS

Obrake Canada, Inc., 3401 Dufferin Street, P.O. Box 27538, Toronto, ON M6A3B8, Canada. **E-mail:** editors@obrake.com. **Website:** www.obrake.com. **Contact:** Echez Godoy, acquisitions editor (fiction-suspense, thriller, multicultural, science fiction, literary, romance, short story collection, mystery, ethnic, African based novels, African American characters and interest). Estab. 2006. Publishes hardcover and paperback originals, paperback reprints. **Publishes 10 titles/year.**

⚿ "We're a small independent publisher. We publish mainly thriller, suspense, romance, mystery, multicutural, and ethnic novels and short story collections." Average print order: 1,500. Debut novel print order: 1,500. **Published 1 new writer(s) last year.** Plans 3 debut novels this year. Averages 10 total titles/year; 7 fiction titles/year. Member Independent Publishers Association PMA (USA), Canadian Booksellers Association (CBA), Book Promoters Association of Canada (BPAC).

FICTION Looking for adventure, children's/juvenile (adventure, fantasy, historical, mystery), comics/graphic novels, erotica, ethnic/multicultural, feminist, gay, historical (general), horror (psychological, supernatural), lesbian, literary, mainstream, mystery/suspense, psychic/supernatural, regional, religious (mystery/suspense, thriller, romance), romance (contemporary, historical, romantic suspense), short story collections, thriller/espionage, young adult/teen (adventure, fantasy/science fiction, historical, horror, romance). Send query letter. Query with outline/synopsis and 3 sample chapters, 50 pages max. Accepts queries by snail mail, e-mail. Include estimated word count, brief bio. Send SASE or IRC for return of ms or disposable copy of ms and SASE/IRC for reply only. Agented fiction: 5%. Responds to queries in 3-6 weeks. Accepts unsolicited mss. Considers simultaneous submissions, submissions on CD or disk. Rarely critiques/comments on rejected mss. Responds to mss in 3-6 months.

TIPS "Visit our website and follow our submission guidelines."

OCEANVIEW PUBLISHING

595 Bay Isles Rd., Suite 120-G, Longboat Key FL 34228. **E-mail:** submissions@oceanviewpub.com. **Website:** www.oceanviewpub.com. **Contact:** Robert Gussin, CEO. Estab. 2006. Publishes hardcover and electronic originals. Responds in 3 months.

⚿ "Independent publisher of nonfiction and fiction, with primary interest in original mystery, thriller and suspense titles. Accepts new and established writers."

NONFICTION Accepts nonfiction but specializes in original mystery, thriller and suspense titles. Query first.

FICTION Subjects include mystery, suspense, thriller. Accepting adult mss with a primary interest in the mystery, thriller and suspense genres—from new & established writers. No children's or YA literature, poetry, cookbooks, technical manuals or short stories. Within body of e-mail only, include author's name and brief bio (Indicate if this is an agent submission), ms title and word count, author's mailing address, phone number and e-mail address. Attached to the e-mail should be the following: A synopsis of 750 words or fewer. The first 30 pages of the ms. Please note that we accept only Word documents as attachments to the submission e-mail. Do not send query letters or proposals.

OCTAMERON PRESS

1900 Mount Vernon Ave., Alexandria VA 22301. (703)836-5480. **Fax:** (703)836-5650. **E-mail:** octameron@aol.com. **Website:** www.octameron.com. **Contact:** Anna J. Leider, publisher. Estab. 1976.

◑ ONEWORLD PUBLICATIONS

10 Fitzroy Square, London W1T 5HP, United Kingdom. (44)(1865)310597. **Fax:** (44)(1865)310598. **E-mail:** submissions@oneworld-publications.com. **Website:** www.oneworld-publications.com. Estab. 1986. Publishes hardcover and trade paperback originals and trade paperback reprints. **Publishes 50 titles/year. 200 queries received/year; 50 mss received/year. 20% of books from first-time authors. 50% from unagented writers. Pays 10% royalty on wholesale price. For academic books; varies for**

trade titles. Pays $1,000-20,000 advance. Publishes book 15 months after acceptance. Catalog and guidelines online.

- ☛ "We publish accessible but authoritative books, mainly by academics or experts for a general readership and cross-over student market. Authors must be well qualified. Currently emphasizing current affairs, popular science, history, and psychology; de-emphasizing self-help."

NONFICTION Submit through online proposal form.

FICTION Subjects include politics, history, multicultural, philosophy, psychology, religion, science, sociology, women's issues/studies. Focusing on well-written literary and commercial fiction from a variety of cultures and periods, many exploring interesting issues and global problems.

TIPS "We don't require agents—just good proposals with enough hard information."

ONSTAGE PUBLISHING

190 Lime Quarry Rd., Suite 106-J, Madison AL 35758-8962. (256)461-0661. **E-mail:** onstage123@ knology.net. **Website:** www.onstagepublishing.com. **Contact:** Dianne Hamilton, senior editor. Estab. 1999. **80% of books from first-time authors. Pays authors/illustrators/photographers advance plus royalties.**

- ☛ At this time, we only produce fiction books for ages 8-18. We will not do anthologies of any kind. Query first for nonfiction projects as nonfiction projects must spark our interest. Now accepting e-mail queries and submissions. For submissions: Put the first 3 chapters in the body of the e-mail. Do not use attachments! We will no longer return any mss. Only an SASE envelope is needed. Send complete ms if under 20,000 words, otherwise send synopsis and first 3 chapters.

FICTION Middle readers: adventure, contemporary, fantasy, history, nature/environment, science fiction, suspense/mystery. Young adults: adventure, contemporary, fantasy, history, humor, science fiction, suspense/mystery. Average word length: chapter books—4,000-6,000 words; middle readers—5,000 words and up; young adults—25,000 and up. "We do not produce picture books."

TIPS "Study our titles and get a sense of the kind of books we publish, so that you know whether your project is likely to be right for us."

OOLIGAN PRESS

P.O. Box 751, Portland OR 97207. (503)725-9410. **E-mail:** ooligan@ooliganpress.pdx.edu. **Website:** www. ooliganpress.pdx.edu. Estab. 2001. Publishes trade paperback, and electronic originals and reprints. **Publishes 4-6 titles/year. 250-500 queries received/year. 100 mss received/year. 90% of books from first-time authors. 90% from unagented writers. Pays negotiable royalty on retail price.** Catalog and guidelines online.

NONFICTION Subjects include agriculture, alternative, anthropology, archeology, art, architecture, community, contemporary culture, cooking, foods, nutrition, creative nonfiction, education, ethnic, film, cinema, stage, gay, lesbian, government, politics, history, humanities, language, literature, literary criticism, memoirs, multicultural, music, dance, nature, environment, philosophy, regional, religion, social sciences, sociology, spirituality, translation, travel, women's issues/studies, world affairs, young adult. Young adult: open to all categories. Query with SASE. Submit proposal package, outline, 4 sample chapters, projected page count, audience, marketing ideas and a list of similar titles. Reviews artwork/photos.

FICTION Subjects include adventure, ethnic, experimental, fantasy, feminist, gay, lesbian, historical, horror, humor, literary, mainstream, contemporary, multicultural, mystery, plays, poetry, poetry in translation, regional, science fiction, short story collections, spiritual, suspense, translation, young adult., and middle grade. "Ooligan Press is a general trade press at Portland State University. As a teaching press, Ooligan makes as little distinction as possible between the press and the classroom. Under the direction of professional faculty and staff, the work of the press is done by students enrolled in the Book Publishing graduate program at PSU. We are especially interested in works with social, literary, or educational value. Though we place special value on local authors, we are open to all submissions, including translated works and writings by children and young adults. We do not currently publish picture books, board books, easy readers, or pop-up books or middle grade readers." Query with SASE. *"At this time we cannot accept science fiction or fantasy submissions."*

POETRY Ooligan is a general trade press that "specializes in publishing authors from the Pacific Northwest and/or works that have specific value to that community. We are limited in the number of poetry titles that we publish as poetry represents only a small percentage of our overall acquisitions. We are open to all forms of style and verse; however, we give special preference to translated poetry, prose poetry, and traditional verse. Although spoken word, slam, and rap poetry are of interest to the press, we will not consider such work if it does not translate well to the written page. Ooligan does not publish chapbooks." Query, submit 20 sample poems, submit complete ms.

TIPS "For children's books, our audience will be middle grades and young adult, with marketing to general trade, libraries, and schools. Good marketing ideas increase the chances of a manuscript succeeding."

OPEN COURT PUBLISHING CO.

70 E. Lake St., Suite 300, Chicago IL 60601. **Website:** www.opencourtbooks.com. Estab. 1887. Publishes hardcover and trade paperback originals. **Publishes 20 titles/year. Pays 5-15% royalty on wholesale price.** Publishes book 2 years after acceptance. Catalog and guidelines online.

NONFICTION Subjects include philosophy, Asian thought, religious studies and popular culture. Query with SASE. Submit proposal package, outline, 1 sample chapter, TOC, author's cover letter, intended audience.

TIPS "Audience consists of philosophers and intelligent general readers."

OPEN ROAD TRAVEL GUIDES

P.O. Box 284, Cold Spring Harbor NY 11724. (631)692-7172. **E-mail:** jopenroad@aol.com. **Website:** www.openroadguides.com. Estab. 1993. Publishes trade paperback originals. **Publishes 20-22 titles/year. 200 queries received/year. 75 mss received/year. 30% of books from first-time authors. 98% from unagented writers. Pays 5-6% royalty on retail price. Pays $1,000-3,500 advance.** Publishes book 3 months after acceptance of ms. Accepts simultaneous submissions. Responds in 1 month to queries. Responds in 2 months to proposals. Catalog online. Ms guidelines sent if proposal is accepted.

⛏ "Open Road publishes travel guides and has expanded into other areas with its new imprint, Cold Spring Press, particularly sports/fitness, topical, biographies, history, and fantasy."

NONFICTION Subjects include travel guides and travelogues. Query with SASE.

ORANGE FRAZER PRESS, INC.

P.O. Box 214, 37½ W. Main St., Wilmington OH 45177. (937)382-3196. **Fax:** (937)383-3159. **E-mail:** publisher@orangefrazer.com. **Website:** www.orangefrazer.com; www.orangefrazercustombooks.com. **Contact:** Marcy Hawley (custom book publishing); John Baskin (trade publishing). Publishes hardcover and trade paperback originals. **Publishes 25 titles/year. 50 queries received/year. 35 mss received/year. 80% of books from first-time authors. 100% from unagented writers. Pays 10% royalty on wholesale price. "50% of our books are author-subsidy published/year if the author can afford it." Pays advance.** Publishes book 10 months after acceptance of ms. Accepts simultaneous submissions. Responds in 6 months to proposals. Catalog and guidelines available free.

⛏ "Orange Frazer Press accepts nonfiction only: corporate histories, town celebrations, and anniversary books. We now focus mostly on custom books/self-publishing, but do still take on some trade books."

NONFICTION Subjects include audio, anthropology, archaeology, art, architecture, business, economics, cooking, foods, nutrition, education, history, nature, environment, photography, regional, sports, travel. "Sports and personalities are our main focus. Accepts Ohio nonfiction only." Submit proposal package, outline, 3 sample chapters, and marketing plan. Reviews artwork/photos. Send photocopies.

TIPS "For our commercial titles, we focus mainly on sports and biographies. Our readers are interested in sports or curious about famous persons/personalities. Also, we mainly publish custom books now—90% custom titles, 10% trade titles."

☺ ORCA BOOK PUBLISHERS

P.O. Box 5626, Stn. B, Victoria BC V8R 6S4, Canada. **Fax:** (877)408-1551. **E-mail:** orca@orcabook.com. **Website:** www.orcabook.com. **Contact:** Christi Howes, editor (picture books); Sarah Harvey, editor (young readers); Andrew Wooldridge, editor (juvenile and teen fiction); Bob Tyrrell, publisher (YA, teen). Estab. 1984. Publishes hardcover and trade paperback originals, and mass market paperback originals and reprints. **Publishes 30 titles/year. 2,500 queries received/year. 1,000 mss received/year. 20% of books from first-time authors. 75% from unagented writers. Pays 10% royalty.** Publishes book 12-18 months after acceptance. Responds in 1 month to queries; 2 months to proposals and mss. Catalog for 8½x11 SASE. Guidelines online.

🔾 Only publishes Canadian authors.

NONFICTION Subjects include multicultural, picture books. Only publishes Canadian authors. Query with SASE.

FICTION Subjects include hi-lo, juvenile (5-9), literary, mainstream, contemporary, young adult (10-18). Picture books: animals, contemporary, history, nature/environment. Middle readers: contemporary, history, fantasy, nature/environment, problem novels, graphic novels. Young adults: adventure, contemporary, hi-lo (Orca Soundings), history, multicultural, nature/environment, problem novels, suspense/mystery, graphic novels. Query with SASE. Submit proposal package, outline, clips, 2-5 sample chapters, SASE.

TIPS "Our audience is students in grades K-12. Know our books, and know the market."

ORCHARD BOOKS

557 Broadway, New York NY 10012. **E-mail:** mcroland@scholastic.com. **Website:** www.scholastic.com. **Contact:** Ken Geist, vice president/editorial director; David Saylor, vice president/creative director. **Publishes 20 titles/year. 10% of books from first-time authors. Most commonly offers an advance against list royalties.**

🔾 *Orchard is not accepting unsolicited manuscripts.*

FICTION All levels: animal, contemporary, history, humor, multicultural, poetry.

TIPS "Read some of our books to determine first whether your manuscript is suited to our list."

⊘ ORCHISES PRESS

P.O. Box 320533, Alexandria VA 22320. (703)683-1243. **E-mail:** lathbury@gmu.edu. **Website:** mason.gmu.edu/~lathbury. **Contact:** Roger Lathbury, editor-in-chief. Estab. 1983. Publishes hardcover and trade paperback originals and reprints. **Publishes 2-3 titles/year. 1% of books from first-time authors. 95% from unagented writers. Pays 36% of receipts after Orchises has recouped its costs.** Publishes book 1 year after acceptance. Accepts simultaneous submissions. Responds in 3 months to queries. Guidelines online.

🔾 *Orchises Press no longer reads unsolicited mss.*

NONFICTION No real restrictions on subject matter. Query with SASE. Reviews artwork/photos. Send photocopies.

POETRY Poetry must have been published in respected literary journals. Orchises Press is a general literary publisher specializing in poetry with selected reprints and textbooks. *Orchises Press no longer reads unsolicited mss.* Poetry must have been published in respected literary journals. Publishes free verse, but has strong formalist preferences. Query and submit 5 sample poems.

OTTN PUBLISHING

16 Risler St., Stockton NJ 08559. (609)397-4005. **Fax:** (609)397-4007. **E-mail:** inquiries@ottnpublishing.com. **Website:** www.ottnpublishing.com. Estab. 1998. Publishes hardcover and trade paperback originals. **Publishes 5-10 titles/year. Receives 50 queriesyear. 50% of books from first-time authors. 100% from unagented writers. Pays outright purchase of $1,200 to $5,000.** Publishes book 9 months after acceptance. Accepts simultaneous submissions. Responds in 6 months to queries. Catalog available online. Guidelines online.

NONFICTION Subjects include government, history, military, politics, war. Query with SASE.

TIPS Most of our books are published for the school library market, although we do publish some books for an adult audience.

OUR CHILD PRESS

P.O. Box 4379, Philadelphia PA 19118. Phone/fax: (610)308-8088. **E-mail:** info@ourchildpress.com. **Website:** www.ourchildpress.com. **Contact:** Carol Perrott, president. **90% of books from first-time authors. Pays authors royalty of 5-10% based on wholesale price. Pays illustrators royalty of 5-10% based on wholesale price.** Publishes book Publishes a book 6-12 months after acceptance. Responds to queries/mss in 6 months. Catalog for business-size SAE and 67 cents.

FICTION All levels: adoption, multicultural, special needs.

OUR SUNDAY VISITOR, INC.

200 Noll Plaza, Huntington IN 46750. **E-mail:** jlindsey@osv.com. **Website:** www.osv.com. **Contact:** Jacquelyn Lindsey; David Dziena; Bert Ghezzi; Cindy Cavnar; Tyler Ottinger, art director. Publishes paperback and hardbound originals. **Publishes 40-50 titles/year. Pays authors royalty of 10-12% net. Pays illustrators by the project (range: $25-1,500).** Publishes book 1-2 years after acceptance. Accepts simultaneous submissions. Responds in 2 months to

queries/mss. Catalog for 9×12 envelope and first-class stamps; ms Guidelines online.

☞ "We are a Catholic publishing company seeking to educate and deepen our readers in their faith. Currently emphasizing devotional, inspirational, Catholic identity, apologetics, and catechetics."

NONFICTION Prefers to see well-developed proposals as first submission with annotated outline and definition of intended market; Catholic viewpoints on family, prayer, and devotional books, and Catholic heritage books. Picture books, middle readers, young readers, young adults. Recently published *Little Acts of Grace*, by Rosemarie Gortler and Donna Piscitelli, illustrated by Mimi Sternhagen. Query, submit complete ms, or submit outline/synopsis and 2-3 sample chapters. Reviews artwork/photos.

TIPS "Stay in accordance with our guidelines."

OUTRIDER PRESS, INC.

2036 North Winds Dr., Dyer IN 46311. (219)322-7270. **Fax:** (219)322-7085. **E-mail:** outriderpress@sbcglobal.net. **Website:** www.outriderpress.com. **Contact:** Whitney Scott, editor. Estab. 1988. Publishes trade paperback originals. **Receives 2,400 queries/year; 200 mss/year. 90% from unagented writers. Pays honorarium.** Publishes book 6 months after acceptance. Responds in 6 weeks to queries; 4 months to proposals and mss. Guidelines online.

○ Accepts unsolicited mss. Query with SASE. Accepts queries by mail. Include estimated word count, brief bio, list of publishing credits. Accepts simultaneous submissions, electronic submissions, submissions on disk. Sometimes comments on rejected mss. In affiliation with Tallgrass Writers Guild, publishes an annual anthology with cash prizes. Anthology theme for 2012 is: "'Deep waters: rivers, lakes and seas.' As always, broadly interpreted with a variety of historic/geographic/psychological settings welcomed." Pays honorarium. Ms guidelines for SASE. Was a *Small Press Review* "Pick" for 2000. Sponsors an anthology competition for short stories, poetry, and creative nonfiction.

NONFICTION Subjects include creative nonfiction, language, literature, general nonfiction.

FICTION Subjects include contemporary, ethnic, experimental, feminist, gay, historical, humor, lesbian, literary, mainstream, short story collections., fantasy (space fantasy, sword and sorcery), family saga, horror (psychological/supernatural), mystery (amateur sleuth, cozy, police procedural, private eye/hardboiled), psychic/supernatural, romance (contemporary, futuristic/time travel), western (frontier saga, traditional). Ethnic, experimental, family saga, fantasy (space fantasy, sword and sorcery), feminist, gay/lesbian, historical, horror (psychological, supernatural), humor, lesbian, literary, mainstream/contemporary, mystery (amateur sleuth, cozy, police procedural, private eye/hard-boiled), new age/mystic, psychic/supernatural, romance (contemporary, futuristic/time travel, gothic, historical, regency period, romantic suspense), science fiction (soft/sociological), short story collections, thriller/espionage, western (frontier saga, traditional). Query with SASE.

TIPS "It's always best to familiarize yourself with our publications. We're especially fond of humor/irony."

ⒶTHE OVERLOOK PRESS

141 Wooster St., New York NY 10012. (212)673-2210. **Fax:** (212)673-2296. **E-mail:** sales@overlookny.com. **Website:** www.overlookpress.com. Estab. 1971. Publishes hardcover and trade paperback originals and hardcover reprints. **Publishes 100 titles/year.** Catalog available free.

☞ "Overlook Press publishes fiction, children's books, and nonfiction."

NONFICTION Subjects include art, architecture, film, cinema, stage, history, regional, New York State, current events, design, health/fitness, how-to, lifestyle, martial arts. The Overlook Press is an independent general-interest publisher. The publishing program consists of nearly 100 new books per year, evenly divided between hardcovers and trade paperbacks. The list is eclectic, but areas of strength include interesting fiction, history, biography, drama, and design. No pornography. Agented submissions only.

FICTION Subjects include literary, some commercial, foreign literature in translation. Agented submissions only.

RICHARD C. OWEN PUBLISHERS, INC.

P.O. Box 585, Katonah NY 10536. (914)232-3903; (800)262-0787. **E-mail:** richardowen@rcowen.com. **Website:** www.rcowen.com. **Contact:** Richard Owen, publisher. Estab. 1982. **Pays authors royalty of 5% based on net price or outright purchase (range: $25-500). Offers no advances. Pays illustrators by the**

project (range: $100-2,000) or per photo (range: $100-150). Publishes book Publishes a book 2-3 years after acceptance. Accepts simultaneous submissions. Responds to mss in 1 year. Catalog available with SASE. Ms guidelines with SASE or online.

8— "We publish child-focused books, with inherent instructional value, about characters and situations with which five-, six-, and seven-year-old children can identify—books that can be read for meaning, entertainment, enjoyment and information. We include multicultural stories that present minorities in a positive and natural way. Our stories show the diversity in America." Not interested in lesson plans, or books of activities for literature studies or other content areas. Submit complete ms and cover letter.

NONFICTION Subjects include art, architecture, history, nature, environment, recreation, science, sports, women's issues/studies, music, diverse culture, nature. Our books are for kindergarten, first- and second-grade children to read on their own. The stories are very brief—under 1,000 words—yet well structured and crafted with memorable characters, language, and plots. Picture books, young readers: animals, careers, history, how-to, music/dance, geography, multicultural, nature/environment, science, sports. Multicultural needs include: "Good stories respectful of all heritages, races, cultural—African-American, Hispanic, American Indian." Wants lively stories. No "encyclopedic" type of information stories. Average word length: under 500 words. Recently published *The Coral Reef.*

TIPS "We don't respond to queries or e-mails. Please do not fax or e-mail us. Because our books are so brief, it is better to send an entire manuscript. We publish story books with inherent educational value for young readers—books they can read with enjoyment and success. We believe students become enthusiastic, independent, life-long learners when supported and guided by skillful teachers using good books. The professional development work we do and the books we publish support these beliefs."

OXFORD UNIVERSITY PRESS

198 Madison Ave., New York NY 10016. (212)726-6000. **E-mail:** custserv.us@oup.com. **Website:** www.oup.com/us.

OZARK MOUNTAIN PUBLISHING, INC.

P.O. Box 754, Huntsville AR 72740, U.S. (479)738-2348. **Fax:** (479)738-2448. **E-mail:** info@ozarkmt.

com. **Website:** www.ozarkmt.com. **Contact:** Julie Degan, office manager (New Age/metaphysics/spiritual). Estab. 1991. Publishes trade paperback originals. **Publishes 8-10 titles/year. 50-75 queries; 150-200 mss. 50% of books from first-time authors. 95% from unagented writers. Pays 10-15% royalty on retail or wholesale price. Pays $250-500 advance.** Publishes book 6-9 months after acceptance. Accepts simultaneous submissions. Responds in 6 months to queries, 7 months on mss. Guidelines online.

NONFICTION Subjects include new age/metaphysical/body-mind-spirit, philosophy, spirituality. No phone calls please. Query with SASE. Submit 4-5 sample chapters.

TIPS "We envision our audience to be open minded, spiritually expanding. Please do not call to check on submissions. Do not submit electronically. Send hard copy only."

P & R PUBLISHING CO.

P.O. Box 817, Phillipsburg NJ 08865. **Fax:** (908)859-2390. **E-mail:** editorial@prpbooks.com. **Website:** www.prpbooks.com. Estab. 1930. Publishes hardcover originals and trade paperback originals and reprints. **Publishes 40 titles/year. 300 queries received/year. 100 mss received/year. 5% of books from first-time authors. 95% from unagented writers. Pays 10-14% royalty on wholesale price.** Accepts simultaneous submissions. Responds in 3 months to proposals. Guidelines online.

NONFICTION Subjects include history, religion, spirituality, translation. Only accepts electronic submission with completion of online Author Guidelines. Hard copy mss will not be returned.

TIPS "Our audience is evangelical Christians and seekers. All of our publications are consistent with Biblical teaching, as summarized in the Westminster Standards."

PACIFIC PRESS

P.O. Box 5353, Nampa ID 83653. (208)465-2500. **Fax:** (208)465-2531. **E-mail:** scocad@pacificpress.com. **E-mail:** booksubmissions@pacificpress.com;. **Website:** www.pacificpress.com/writers/books.htm. **Contact:** Scott Cady, acquisitions; Gerald Monks, creative director. Estab. 1874. **Publishes 5 titles/year. 5% of books from first-time authors. Pays author royalty of 6-15% based on wholesale price. Offers advances (average amount: $1,500). Pays illustrators royalty of 6-15% based on wholesale price. Pays photogra-**

phers 6-15% based on wholesale price. Publishes book Publishes a book in 6-12 months after acceptance. Responds to queries in 3 months; mss in 1 year. Catalog available on website. Ms guidelines for SASE.

8—π Pacific Press brings the Bible and Christian lifestyle to children. Publishes 1 picture book/year; 2 young readers/year; 2 middle readers/year.

NONFICTION Picture books, young readers, middle readers, young adults: religion. Average word length: picture books—100; young readers—1,000; middle readers—15,000; young adults—40,000. Query or submit outline/synopsis and 3 sample chapters.

FICTION Picture books, young readers, middle readers, young adults: religious subjects only. No fantasy. Average word length: picture books—100; young readers—1,000; middle readers—15,000; young adults—40,000. Recently published *A Child's Steps to Jesus* (3 vols), by Linda Carlyle; *Octopus Encounter*, by Sally Streib; *Sheperd Warrior*, by Bradley Booth. Query or submit outline/synopsis and 3 sample chapters.

TIPS Pacific Press is owned by the Seventh-day Adventist Church. The Press rejects all material that is not Bible-based.

PACIFIC VIEW PRESS

P.O. Box 2897, Berkeley CA 94702. (415)285-8538. **Fax:** (510)843-5835. **E-mail:** Nancy@pacificviewpress.com. **Website:** www.pacificviewpress.com. **Publishes 1-2 titles/year. 50% of books from first-time authors. Pays authors royalty of 8-12% based on wholesale price. Pays illustrators by project (range: $2,000-5,000).** Responds to queries in 3 months.

8—π "We publish unique, high-quality introductions to Asian cultures and history for children 8-12, for schools, libraries, and families. Our children's books focus on hardcover illustrated nonfiction. We look for titles on aspects of the history and culture of the countries and peoples of the Pacific Rim, especially China, presented in an engaging, informative and respectful manner. We are interested in books that all children will enjoy reading and using, and that parents and teachers will want to buy."

NONFICTION Young readers, middle readers: Asia-related multicultural only. Recently published *Cloud Weavers: Ancient Chinese Legends*, by Rena Krasno and Yeng-Fong Chiang (all ages); *Exploring Chinatown: A Children's Guide to Chinese Culture*, by Carol Stepanchuk (ages 8-12). Query with outline and sample chapter.

TIPS "We welcome proposals from persons with expertise, either academic or personal, in their area of interest. While we do accept proposals from previously unpublished authors, we would expect submitters to have considerable experience presenting their interests to children in classroom or other public settings and to have skill in writing for children."

PALARI PUBLISHING

P.O. Box 9288, Richmond VA 23227. (866)570-6724. **Fax:** (866)570-6724. **E-mail:** dave@palaribooks.com. **Website:** www.palaribooks.com. **Contact:** David Smitherman, publisher/editor. Estab. 1998. Publishes hardcover and trade paperback originals. **Pays royalty.** Publishes book 1 year after acceptance. Responds in 1 month to queries; 2-3 months to mss. Guidelines online.

8—π "Palari provides authoritative, well-written nonfiction that addresses topical consumer needs and fiction with an emphasis on intelligence and quality. We accept solicited and unsolicited manuscripts, however we prefer a query letter and SASE, describing the project briefly and concisely. This letter should include a complete address and telephone number. Palari Publishing accepts queries or any other submissions by e-mail, but prefers queries submitted by US mail. All queries must be submitted by mail according to our guidelines. Promotes titles through book signings, direct mail and the Internet."

NONFICTION Subjects include business, economics, memoirs.

FICTION Subjects include adventure, ethnic, gay, lesbian, historical, literary, mainstream, contemporary, multicultural. Tell why your idea is unique or interesting. Make sure we are interested in your genre before submitting. Query with SASE. Submit bio, estimated word count, list of publishing credits. Accepts queries via e-mail (prefer US Mail), fax.

TIPS "Send a good bio. I'm interested in a writer's experience and unique outlook on life."

PALETTES & QUILLS

330 Knickerbocker Ave., Rochester NY 14615. (585)456-0217. **E-mail:** palettesnquills@gmail.com. **Website:** www.palettesnquills.com. **Contact:** Donna M. Marbach, publisher/owner. Estab. 2002.

NONFICTION Does not want political and religious diatribes.

POETRY Palettes & Quills "is at this point, a poetry press only, and produces only a handful of publications each year, specializing in anthologies, individual chapbooks, and broadsides." Wants "work that should appeal to a wide audience." Does not want "poems that are sold blocks of text, long-lined and without stanza breaks. Wildly elaborate free-verse would be difficult and in all likelihood fight with art background, amateurish rhyming poem, overly sentimental poems, poems that use excessive profanity, or which denigrate other people, or political and religious diatribes." Query first with 3-5 poems and a cover letter with brief bio and publication credits for individual unsolicited chapbooks. May include previously published poems. Chapbook poets would get 20 copies of a run; broadside poets and artists get 5-10 copies and occasionally paid $10 for reproduction rights. Anthology poets get 1 copy of the anthology. All poets and artists get a discount on purchases that include their work.

PANTHEON BOOKS

Random House, Inc., 1745 Broadway, 3rd Floor, New York NY 10019. **E-mail:** pantheonpublicity@randomhouse.com. **Website:** www.pantheonbooks.com. Estab. 1942. Publishes hardcover and trade paperback originals and trade paperback reprints.

○ Pantheon Books publishes both Western and non-Western authors of literary fiction and important nonfiction. "We only accept mss submitted by an agent. You may still send a 20-50 page sample and a SASE to our slushpile. Allow 2-6 months for a response."

FICTION *Does not accept unsolicited mss.* Send SASE or IRC. No simultaneous submissions.

PARADISE CAY PUBLICATIONS

P.O. Box 29, Arcata CA 95518-0029. (800)736-4509. **Fax:** (707)822-9163. **E-mail:** info@paracay.com; jim@paracay.com. **Website:** www.paracay.com. **Contact:** Matt Morehouse, publisher. Publishes hardcover and trade paperback originals and reprints. **Publishes 5 titles/year. 360-480 queries received/year. 240-360 mss received/year. 10% of books from first-time authors. 100% from unagented writers. Pays 10-15% royalty on wholesale price. Makes outright purchase of $1,000-10,000. Does not normally pay advances to first-time or little-known authors.** Pub-

lishes book 4 months after acceptance. Responds in 1 month to queries/proposals; 2 months to mss. Catalog and guidelines free on request or online.

⌘ "Paradise Cay Publications, Inc. is a small independent publisher specializing in nautical books, videos, and art prints. Our primary interest is in manuscripts that deal with the instructional and technical aspects of ocean sailing. We also publish and will consider fiction if it has a strong nautical theme."

NONFICTION Subjects include cooking, foods, nutrition, recreation, sports, travel. Must have strong nautical theme. Include a cover letter containing a story synopsis and a short bio, including any plans to promote their work. The cover letter should describe the book's subject matter, approach, distinguishing characteristics, intended audience, author's qualifications, and why the author thinks this book is appropriate for Paradise Cay. Call first. Reviews artwork/photos. Send photocopies.

FICTION Subjects include adventure, nautical, sailing. All fiction must have a nautical theme. Query with SASE. Submit proposal package, clips, 2-3 sample chapters.

TIPS Audience is recreational sailors. Call Matt Morehouse (publisher).

PARADISE RESEARCH PUBLICATIONS, INC.

P.O. Box 837, Kihei HI 96753. (808)874-4876. **Fax:** (808)874-4876. **E-mail:** dickb@dickb.com. **Website:** www.dickb.com/index.shtml. Publishes trade paperback originals. **Publishes 3 titles/year. 5 queries received/year. 1 mss received/year. 20% of books from first-time authors. 100% from unagented writers. Pays 10% royalty.** Publishes book 3 months after acceptance. Accepts simultaneous submissions. Responds in 1 month to queries. Catalog online.

⌘ Paradise Research Publications wants only books on Alcoholics Anonymous and its spiritual roots.

NONFICTION Subjects include health, medicine, psychology, religion, spirituality, recovery, alcoholism, addictions, Christian recovery, history of Alcoholics Annonymous. Query with SASE.

PARAGON HOUSE PUBLISHERS

1925 Oakcrest Ave., Suite 7, St. Paul MN 55113. (651)644-3087. **Fax:** (651)644-0997. **E-mail:** paragon@paragonhouse.com. **Website:** www.paragonhouse.

com. **Contact:** Gordon Anderson, acquisitions editor. Estab. 1962. Publishes hardcover and trade paperback originals and trade paperback reprints. **Publishes 12-15 titles/year. 1,500 queries received/year. 150 mss received/year. 7% of books from first-time authors. 90% from unagented writers. Pays $500-1,000 advance.** Publishes book 1 year after acceptance. Accepts simultaneous submissions. Guidelines online.

> ⚷ "We publish general-interest titles and textbooks that provide the readers greater understanding of society and the world. Currently emphasizing religion, philosophy, economics, and society."

NONFICTION Subjects include government, politics, multicultural, nature, environment, philosophy, psychology, religion, sociology, women's issues, world affairs. Submit proposal package, outline, 2 sample chapters, market breakdown, SASE.

PARKWAY PUBLISHERS, INC.

421 Fairfield Lane, Blowing Rock NC 28605. (828)295-9829. **Fax:** (828)295-9829. **E-mail:** editor@parkway-publishers.com. **Website:** www.parkwaypublishers.com. **Contact:** Rao Aluri, president. Publishes hardcover and trade paperback originals. **Publishes 5-6 titles/year. 15-20 queries received/year. 20 mss received/year. 75% of books from first-time authors. 100% from unagented writers.** Publishes book 8 months after acceptance.

> ⚷ "Parkway Publishers, Inc. is primarily interested in non-fiction manuscripts about western North Carolina in particular and North Carolina and Appalachia in general. We prefer manuscripts of 150 to 250 pages long - double-spaced, 8.5" ×11" pages. We would like to receive a hardcopy rather than an e-mail submission. We are interested in books about the history of region, biographies, and tourist-oriented books. Will consider fiction if it highlights the region."

NONFICTION Subjects include history, biography, tourism, and natural history. Query with SASE. Submit complete ms.

PASSKEY PUBLICATIONS

P.O. Box 580465, Elk Grove CA 95758. (916)712-7446. **E-mail:** pineappleguides@yahoo.com. **Website:** www.passkeypublications.com. **Contact:** Christine P. Silva, president. Estab. 2007. Publishes trade paperback originals. **Publishes 15 titles/year. 375 queries/year;**

120 mss/year. 15% of books from first-time authors. 90% from unagented writers. Pay varies on retail price. Publishes book 1 year after acceptance. Accepts simultaneous submissions. Responds in 1 month on queries, proposals, and mss (for tax & accounting only). All others 1-3 months. Catalog and guidelines online www.passkeypublications.com.

NONFICTION Subjects include business, economics, finance, money, real estate., accounting, taxation, study guides for professional examinations. "Books on taxation and accounting are generally updated every year to reflect tax law changes, and the turnaround on a ms must be less than 3 months for accounting and tax subject matter. Books generally remain in publication only 11 months and are generally published every year for updates." Submit complete ms. Nonfiction mss only. Reviews artwork/photos as part of ms package. Send electronic files on disk, via e-mail, or jump drive.

TIPS "Accepting business, accounting, tax, finance and other related subjects only."

⊘ PATH PRESS, INC.

1229 Emerson St., Evanston IL 60201. (847)492-0177. **Fax:** (773)651-0210. **E-mail:** pathpressinc@aol.com. **Contact:** Bennett J. Johnson, president. Estab. 1969.

> ⚷ Path Press is a small publisher of books and poetry primarily "by, for, and about African American and Third World people." Open to all types of poetic forms; emphasis is on high quality. Books are "hardback and quality paperbacks."

POETRY Query first, with a few sample poems and cover letter with brief bio and publication credits. Submissions should be typewritten in ms format. Accepts submissions by e-mail (as attachment).

PAUL DRY BOOKS

1616 Walnut St., Suite 808, Philadelphia PA 19103. (215)231-9939. **Fax:** (215)231-9942. **E-mail:** pdry@pauldrybooks.com; editor@pauldrybooks.com. **Website:** http://pauldrybooks.com. Hardcover and trade paperback originals, trade paperback reprints. Catalog and guidelines online.

NONFICTION Subjects include agriculture, contemporary culture, history, literary criticism, memoirs, multicultural, philosophy, religion, translation, popular mathematics. Submit proposal package.

FICTION Subjects include literary, short story collections, translation, young adult, novels. Submit sample chapters, clips, bio.

TIPS "Our aim is to publish lively books 'to awaken, delight, & educate'—to spark conversation. We publish fiction and nonfiction, and essays covering subjects from Homer to Chekhov, bird watching to jazz music, New York City to shogunate Japan."

PAULINE BOOKS & MEDIA

50 St. Paula's Ave., Boston MA 02130. (617)522-8911. **Fax:** (617)541-9805. **E-mail:** design@paulinemedia. com; editorial@paulinemedia.com. **Website:** www. pauline.org. Estab. 1932. Publishes trade paperback originals and reprints. **Publishes 40 titles/year. 15% of books from first-time authors. 5% from unagented writers. Varies by project, but generally are royalties with advance. Flat fees sometimes considered for smaller works.** Publishes book Publishes a book 11 months after acceptance. Accepts simultaneous submissions. Responds in 2 months to queries, proposals, & mss. Catalog online. Guidelines available online & by e-mail.

- "Submissions are evaluated on adherence to Gospel values, harmony with the Catholic tradition, relevance of topic, and quality of writing." For board books and picture books, the entire manuscript should be submitted. For easy-to-read, young readers, and middle reader books, please send a cover letter accompanied by a synopsis and two sample chapters. "Electronic submissions are encouraged. We make every effort to respond to unsolicited submissions within 2 months."

NONFICTION Subjects include child guidance, religion, spirituality. Picture books, young readers, middle readers: religion. Average word length: picture books—500-1,000; young readers—8,000-10,000; middle readers—15,000-25,000. Recently published *God Made Wonderful Me!*, by Genny Monchamp; *O Holy Night*, by Maite Roche; *Starring Francie O'Lear*, by Maryann; *Adventures of Saint Paul*, by Oldrich Selucky; *Anna Mei, Cartoon Girl*, by Carol A. Grund; *Goodness Graces! Ten Short Stories about the Sacraments*, by Diana R. Jenkins. No biography/autobiography, poetry, or strictly nonreligious works considered. Submit proposal package, including outline, 1-2 sample chapters, cover letter, synopsis, intended audience and proposed length. Reviews artwork; send photocopies.

FICTION Subjects include juvenile. Children's fiction only. We are now accepting submissions for easy-to-read and middle reader chapter fiction. Please see our Writer's Guidelines. "Submit proposal package, including synopsis, 2 sample chapters, and cover letter; complete ms."

TIPS "Manuscripts may or may not be explicitly catechetical, but we seek those that reflect a positive worldview, good moral values, awareness and appreciation of diversity, and respect for all people. All material must be relevant to the lives of young readers and must conform to Catholic teaching and practice."

PAULIST PRESS

997 MacArthur Blvd., Mahwah NJ 07430. (201)825-7300. **Fax:** (201)825-8345. **E-mail:** info@paulistpress. com; dcrilly@paulistpress.com. **Website:** www.paulistpress.com. **Contact:** Donna Crilly, editorial. Estab. 1865. Publishes hardcover and electronic originals and electronic reprints. **Publishes 85 titles/year. Receives 250 submissions/year. 50% of books from first-time authors. 95% from unagented writers. Advance payment is $500, payable on publication. Illustrators sometimes receive a flat fee when all we need are spot illustrations. Pays advance.** Publishes book Publishes a book 12-18 months after acceptance. Accepts simultaneous submissions. Responds in 2 months to queries and proposals; 2-3 months on mss. Catalog online. Guidelines available online and by e-mail.

- "Paulist Press publishes ecumenical theology, Roman Catholic studies, and books on scripture, liturgy, spirituality, church history, and philosophy, as well as works on faith and culture. Our publishing is oriented toward adult-level nonfiction. We do not publish poetry."

FICTION Christian and Catholic themes. Submit résumé, ms, SASE. Accepts unsolicited mss, but most of our titles have been commissioned.

TIPS "Our typical reader is probably Roman Catholic and wants the content to be educational about Catholic thought and practice, or else the reader is a spiritual seeker who looks for discovery of God and the spiritual values that churches offer but without the church connection."

PAYCOCK PRESS

3819 N. 13th St., Arlington VA 22201. (703)525-9296. **E-mail:** hedgehog2@erols.com. **Website:** www.gargoylemagazine.com. **Contact:** Lucinda Ebersole and Richard Peabody. Estab. 1976. Publishes book 1 year after acceptance. Accepts simultaneous submissions. Responds to queries in 1 month; mss in 4 months.

⚷ "Too academic for underground, too outlaw for the academic world. We tend to be edgy and look for ultra-literary work." Publishes paperback originals. Books: POD printing. Average print order: 500. Averages 1 total title/year. Member CLMP. Distributes through Amazon and website.

FICTION Wants: experimental, literary, short story collections. Accepts unsolicited mss. Accepts queries by e-mail. Include brief bio. Send SASE for return of ms or send a disposable ms and SASE for reply only.

TIPS "Check out our website. Two of our favorite writers are Paul Bowles and Jeanette Winterson."

PEACE HILL PRESS

Affiliate of W.W. Norton, 18021 The Glebe Ln., Charles City VA 23030. (804)829-5043. **Fax:** (804)829-5704. **E-mail:** info@peacehillpress.com. **Website:** www.peacehillpress.com. **Contact:** Peter Buffington, acquisitions editor. Estab. 2001. Publishes hardcover and trade paperback originals. **Publishes 4-8 titles/year. Pays 6-10% royalty on retail price. Pays $500-1,000 advance.** Publishes book Publishes a book 18 months after acceptance. Accepts simultaneous submissions.

NONFICTION Subjects include education, history, language, literature. Submit proposal package, outline, 1 sample chapter. Reviews artwork/photos. Send photocopies.

FICTION Subjects include historical, juvenile, picture books, young adult. Submit proposal package, outline, 1 sample chapter.

PEACHTREE CHILDREN'S BOOKS

Peachtree Publishers, Ltd., 1700 Chattahoochee Ave., Atlanta GA 30318-2112. (404)876-8761. **Fax:** (404)875-2578. **E-mail:** hello@peachtree-online.com. **Website:** www.peachtree-online.com. **Contact:** Helen Harriss, submissions editor. Publishes hardcover and trade paperback originals. **Publishes 30 titles/year. 25% of books from first-time authors. 25% from unagented writers. Pays royalty on retail price.** Publishes book 1 year after acceptance. Accepts simultaneous submissions. Responds in 6 months and mss. Catalog for 6 first-class stamps. Guidelines online.

⚷ "We publish a broad range of subjects and perspectives, with emphasis on innovative plots and strong writing."

NONFICTION Subjects include animals, child guidance, creative nonfiction, education, ethnic, gardening, health, medicine, history, language, literature, literary criticism, multicultural, music, dance, nature, environment, recreation, regional, science, social sciences, sports, travel. No e-mail or fax queries of mss. Submit complete ms with SASE, or summary and 3 sample chapters with SASE.

FICTION Subjects include juvenile, picture books, young adult. Looking for very well-written middle grade and young adult novels. Juvenile, picture books, young adult. Looking for very well written middle grade and young adult novels. No adult fiction. No short stories. No collections of poetry or short stories; no romance or science fiction. Submit complete ms with SASE.

PECAN GROVE PRESS

Box AL, 1 Camino Santa Maria, San Antonio TX 78228. (210)436-3442. **Fax:** (210)436-3782. **E-mail:** phall@stmarytx.edu. **Website:** http://library.stmarytx.edu/pgpress. **Contact:** H. Palmer Hall, editor/director. Estab. 1988. **Pays poet 50% of proceeds after printing/binding costs are covered.**

⚷ Member, CLMP. Pecan Grove Press is a poetry-only press and conducts one national chapbook competition each year. Aside from that, the press publishes approximately 7-8 books and chapbooks each year outside of the competition. Manuscripts are selected through open submission. Books are 52-100 pages, off-set or laser print, perfect-bound with color index stock cover and full color art. Chapbooks are 32-45 pages, laser printed, perfect-bound, index stock cover with color in-house graphics.

POETRY Submit complete ms via submission manager on website only.

☺⊘ PEDLAR PRESS

P.O. Box 26, Station P, Toronto ON M5S 2S6, Canada. (416)534-2011. **E-mail:** feralgrl@interlog.com. **Website:** www.pedlarpress.com. **Contact:** Beth Follett, owner/editor. **Publishes 7 titles/year. Pays 10% royalty on retail price. Average advance: $200-400.** Publishes book 1 year after acceptance.

⚷ Distributes in Canada through LitDistCo.; in the US distributes directly through publisher.

FICTION Experimental, feminist, gay/lesbian, literary, picture books, short story collections. Canadian writers only. Query with SASE, sample chapter(s), synopsis.

TIPS "I select manuscripts according to my taste, which fluctuates. Be familiar with some if not most of Pedlar's recent titles."

PELICAN PUBLISHING COMPANY

1000 Burmaster St., Gretna LA 70053. (504)368-1175. **Fax:** (504)368-1195. **E-mail:** editorial@pelicanpub. com. **Website:** www.pelicanpub.com. **Contact:** Nina Kooij, editor-in-chief. Estab. 1926. Publishes hardcover, trade paperback and mass market paperback originals and reprints. **Publishes 70 titles/year. 15% of books from first-time authors. 95% from unagented writers. Pays authors in royalties; buys ms outright "rarely." Illustrators paid by "various arrangements." Advance considered.** Publishes book Publishes a book 9-18 months after acceptance. Responds in 1 month to queries; 3 months to mss. Catalog and guidelines online.

⌐☛🖎 "We believe ideas have consequences. One of the consequences is that they lead to a best-selling book. We publish books to improve and uplift the reader. Currently emphasizing business and history titles." Publishes 20 young readers/year; 3 middle readers/year. "Our children's books (illustrated and otherwise) include history, biography, holiday, and regional. Pelican's mission is to publish books of quality and permanence that enrich the lives of those who read them."

NONFICTION Subjects include Americana, especially Southern regional, Ozarks, Texas, Florida, and Southwest, art, architecture, ethnic, government, politics, special interest in conservative viewpoint, history, popular, multicultural, American artforms, but will consider others: jazz, blues, Cajun, R&B, regional, religion, for popular audience mostly, but will consider others, sports, motivational (with business slant). "We look for authors who can promote successfully. We require that a query be made first. This greatly expedites the review process and can save the writer additional postage expenses." Young readers: biography, history, holiday, multicultural. Middle readers: Louisiana history, holiday, regional. Query with SASE. Reviews artwork/photos.

FICTION Subjects include historical, juvenile, regional or historical focus. We publish maybe 1 novel a year, usually by an author we already have. Almost all pro-

posals are returned. Young readers: history, holiday, science, multicultural and regional. Middle readers: Louisiana History. Multicultural needs include stories about African-Americans, Irish-Americans, Jews, Asian-Americans, and Hispanics. Does not want animal stories, general Christmas stories, "day at school" or "accept yourself" stories. Maximum word length: young readers—1,100; middle readers—40,000. No young adult, romance, science fiction, fantasy, gothic, mystery, erotica, confession, horror, sex, or violence. Also no psychological novels. Query with SASE. Submit outline, clips, 2 sample chapters, SASE.

POETRY Pelican Publishing Company is a medium-sized publisher of popular histories, cookbooks, regional books, children's books, and inspirational/motivational books. Considers poetry for "hardcover children's books only (1,100 words maximum), preferably with a regional focus. However, our needs for this are very limited; we publish 20 juvenile titles per year, and most of these are prose, not poetry." Books are 32 pages, magazine-sized, include illustrations.

TIPS "We do extremely well with cookbooks, popular histories, and business. We will continue to build in these areas. The writer must have a clear sense of the market and knowledge of the competition. A query letter should describe the project briefly, give the author's writing and professional credentials, and promotional ideas."

☁ PEMMICAN PUBLICATIONS

150 Henry Ave., Main Floor RM 12, Winnipeg MB R3B 0J7, Canada. (204)589-6346. **Fax:** (204)589-2063. **E-mail:** mcilroy@pemmican.mb.ca. **Website:** www. pemmican.mb.ca. **Contact:** Randal McIlroy, managing editor. Estab. 1980. **Pays 10% royalty. Provides 10 author's copies. Average advance: $350.**

⌐☛🖎 Metis adult and children's books. Publishes paperback originals. Books: stapled-bound smaller books and perfect-bound larger ones; 4-color illustrations, where applicable. Average print order: 1,500. First novel print order: 1,000. **Published some debut authors within the last year.** Averages 6 total titles/year. Distributes titles through press releases, website, fax, catalogues, and book displays.

FICTION Needs stories by and about the Canadian Metis experience, especially from a modern adult or young-adult perspective. Recently published *Flight of the Wild Geese* (YA fiction), by T.D. Thompson; *Riv-*

er of Tears (adult fiction), by Linda Ducharme; and *Kawlija's Blueberry Promise* (children's fiction), by Audrey Guiboche. Accepts unsolicited mss by conventional mail only. Submit samples and synopsis. Send SASE for return of ms or send a disposable ms and SASE for reply only. Return postage for outside of Canada must be provided in IRC's. Accepts simultaneous submissions.

☼ PEMMICAN PUBLICATIONS, INC.

150 Henry Ave., Winnipeg MB R3B 0J7, Canada. (204)589-6346. **Fax:** (204)589-2063. **E-mail:** pemmican@pemmican.mb.ca. **Website:** www.pemmican.mb.ca. **Contact:** Randal McILroy, managing editor (Metis culture & heritage). Estab. 1980. Publishes trade paperback originals and reprints. **Publishes 5-6 titles/year. 120 queries received/year. 120 mss received/year. 50% of books from first-time authors. 100% from unagented writers. Pays 10% royalty on retail price.** Publishes book 1-2 years after acceptance. Accepts simultaneous submissions. Responds to queries, proposals, and mss in 3 months. Catalog available free with SASE. Guidelines online.

⚷➤ "Pemmican Publications is a Metis publishing house, with a mandate to publish books by Metis authors and illustrators and with an emphasis on culturally relevant stories. We encourage writers to learn a little about Pemmican before sending samples. Pemmican publishes titles in the following genres: Adult Fiction, which includes novels, story collections and anthologies; Non-Fiction, with an emphasis on social history and biography reflecting Metis experience; Children's and Young Adult titles; Aboriginal languages, including Michif and Cree."

NONFICTION Subjects include alternative, creative nonfiction, education, ethnic, history, language, literature, military, war, nature, environment. All mss must be Metis culture and heritage related. Submit proposal package including outline and 3 sample chapters. Reviews artwork/photos. Send photocopies.
FICTION Subjects include adventure, ethnic, historical, juvenile, literary, mystery, picture books, short story collections, sports, suspense, young adult. All manuscripts must be Metis culture and heritage related. Submit proposal package including outline and 3 sample chapters.
POETRY Submit 10 sample poems and complete ms.

TIPS "Our mandate is to promote Metis authors, illustrators and stories. No agent is necessary."

⚠⊘ PENGUIN GROUP USA

375 Hudson St., New York NY 10014. (212)366-2000. **Website:** www.penguin.com. **Contact:** Peter Stampfel, submission editor (DAW Books). Responds in 3 months generally. Guidelines online.

🔾 *No unsolicited mss.* Submit work through a literary agent.

FICTION "We publish first novels if they are of professional quality. A literary agent is not required for submission. We will not consider mss that are currently on submission to another publisher unless prior arrangements have been made with a literary agent. Please enclose a SASE with your submission for our correspondence. We ask that you only send us disposable copies of your ms, which will be recycled in the event they are not found suitable for publication. We regret that we are no longer able to return submitted ms copies, as the process resulted in too many difficulties with the postal service and unnecessary expense for the prospective authors. It may require up to three months or more for our editors to review a submission and come to a decision. If you want to be sure we have received your manuscript, please enclose a stamped, self-addressed postcard that we will return when your ms. It is not necessary for you to register or copyright your work before publication—it is protected by law as long as it has not been published. When published, we will copyright the book in the author's name and register that copyright with the Library of Congress. DAW Books is currently accepting manuscripts in the science fiction/fantasy genre. We publish science fiction and fantasy novels. The average length of the novels we publish varies but is almost never less than 80,000 words. Do not submit handwritten material." We do not want short stories, short story collections, novellas, or poetry. "Due to the high volume of mss we receive, Penguin Group (USA) Inc. imprints do not normally accept unsolicited mss. On rare occasion, however, a particular imprint may be open to reading such. The Penguin Group (USA) web site features a listing of which imprints (if any) are currently accepting unsolicited manuscripts." Continue to check website for updates to the list.

PENNY-FARTHING PRESS INC.

2000 W. Sam Houston Pkwy. S, Houston TX 77042. (713)780-0300 or (800)926-2669. **Fax:** (713)780-

4004. **E-mail:** submissions@pfpress.com; corp@pfpress.com. **Website:** www.pfpress.com. **Contact:** Ken White, publisher; Marlaine Maddox, editor-in-chief. Estab. 1998. Guidelines online.

8—☛ "Penny-Farthing Press officially opened its doors in 1998 with a small staff and a plan to create comic books and children's books that exemplified quality storytelling, artwork, and printing.Starting with only one book, The Victorian, Penny-Farthing Press has expanded its line to six titles, but keeps its yearly output small enough to maintain the highest quality. This "boutique approach" to publishing has won the recognition of the comics and fine arts industries, and PFP has won numerous awards including the Gutenberg D'Argent Medal and several Spectrum Awards."

FICTION "Please make sure all submissions include a synopsis that is brief and to the point. Remember, the synopsis is the "first impression" of your submission and you know what they say about first impressions. If you are submitting just one single-issue story (standard 32 pp.), you may send the full script with your submission. If you are submitting a story for any kind of series or graphic novel, please send only the first chapter of the series. If we like what we see, we will contact you to see more. If you are submitting a completed work (script, art work and lettering) copies of this may be sent instead."

ⓐ⊘ PERENNIAL

HarperCollins Publishers, 10 E. 53rd St., New York NY 10022. (212)207-7000. **Website:** www.harpercollins.com. **Contact:** Acquisitions Editor. Estab. 1963. Publishes trade paperback originals and reprints. Catalog available free.

8—☛ Perennial publishes a broad range of adult literary fiction and nonfiction paperbacks that create a record of our culture.

NONFICTION Subjects include Americana, animals, business, economics, child guidance, cooking, foods, nutrition, education, ethnic, gay, lesbian, history, language, literature, military, war, money, finance, music, dance, nature, environment, and environment, philosophy, psychology, self-help psychotherapy, recreation, regional, religion, spirituality, science, sociology, sports, translation, travel, womens issues, womens studies., mental health, health, classic literature. Our focus is ever-changing, adjusting to the market-

place. Mistakes writers often make are not giving their background and credentials-why they are qualified to write the book. A proposal should explain why the author wants to write this book; why it will sell; and why it is better or different from others of its kind. Agented submissions only.

FICTION Subjects include ethnic, feminist, literary. Agented submissions only.

POETRY Don't send poetry unless you have been published in several established literary magazines already. *Agented submissions only.*

TIPS See our website for a list of titles or write to us for a free catalog.

THE PERMANENT PRESS

Attn: Judith Shepard, 4170 Noyac Rd., Sag Harbor NY 11963. (631)725-1101. **Fax:** (631)725-8215. **E-mail:** judith@thepermanentpress.com; shepard@thepermanentpress.com. **Website:** www.thepermanentpress.com. **Contact:** Judith and Martin Shepard, acquisitions/co-publishers. Blog: www.thecockeyedpessimist.com Estab. 1978. Publishes in hardcover originals. Publishes book within 18 months after acceptance. Responds in weeks or months to queries and submissions.

8—☛ Mid-size, independent publisher of literary fiction. "We keep titles in print and are active in selling subsidiary rights." Average print order: 1,500. Averages 14 total titles. Accepts unsolicited mss. Pays 10-15% royalty on wholesale price. Offers $1,000 advance.

FICTION Promotes titles through reviews. Literary, mainstream/contemporary, mystery. Especially looking for high-line literary fiction, "artful, original and arresting." Accepts any fiction category as long as it is a "well-written, original full-length novel."

TIPS "We are looking for good books—be they 10th novels or first ones, it makes little difference. The fiction is more important than the track record. Send us the first 25 pages; it's impossible to judge something that begins on page 302. Also, no outlines—let the writing present itself."

⊘ PERUGIA PRESS

P.O. Box 60364, Florence MA 01062. **E-mail:** info@perugiapress.com. **Website:** www.perugiapress.com. **Contact:** Susan Kan, director. Estab. 1997.

PETER PAUPER PRESS, INC.

202 Mamaroneck Ave., White Plains NY 10601. **E-mail:** customerservice@peterpauper.com. **Website:**

www.peterpauper.com. **Contact:** Barbara Paulding, editorial director. Estab. 1928. Publishes hardcover originals. **Publishes 40-50 titles/year. 100 queries received/year. 150 mss received/year. 5% from unagented writers. Makes outright purchase only. Pays advance.** Publishes book 1 year after acceptance. Responds in 2 months to queries. Ms guidelines for #10 SASE or may request via e-mail.

➤ "PPP publishes small and medium format, illustrated gift books for occasions and in celebration of specific relationships such as mom, sister, friend, teacher, grandmother, granddaughter. PPP has expanded into the following areas: books for teens and tweens, activity books for children, organizers, books on popular topics of nonfiction for adults and licensed books by best-selling authors."

NONFICTION "We do not publish fiction or poetry. We publish brief, original quotes, aphorisms, and wise sayings. Please do not send us other people's quotes." Query with SASE.

TIPS "Our readers are primarily female, age 10 and over, who are likely to buy a 'gift' book or gift book set in a stationery, gift, book, or boutique store or national book chain. Writers should become familiar with our previously published work. We publish only small- and medium-format, illustrated, hardcover gift books and sets of between 1,000-4,000 words. We have much less interest in work aimed at men."

PFLAUM PUBLISHING GROUP

6162 N. 114th, Milwaukee WI 53225. (414)353-5528. **Fax:** (414)353-5529. **E-mail:** kcannizzo@pflaum.com. **Contact:** Karen A. Cannizzo, editorial director. **Publishes 20 titles/year. Payment may be outright purchase, royalty, or down payment plus royalty.** Catalog and guidelines free.

➤ "Pflaum Publishing Group, a division of Peter Li, Inc., serves the specialized market of religious education, primarily Roman Catholic. We provide high quality, theologically sound, practical, and affordable resources that assist religious educators of and ministers to children from preschool through senior high school."

NONFICTION Query with SASE.

⊘ PHILOMEL BOOKS

Imprint of Penguin Group (USA), Inc., 375 Hudson St., New York NY 10014. (212)414-3610. **Website:** www.

us.penguingroup.com. **Contact:** Michael Green, president/publisher; Annie Ericsson, junior designer. Estab. 1980. Publishes hardcover originals. **Publishes 8-10 titles/year. 5% of books from first-time authors. 20% from unagented writers. Pays authors in royalties. Average advance payment "varies." Illustrators paid by advance and in royalties. Pays negotiable advance.** Accepts simultaneous submissions. Catalog for 9×12 envelope and 4 first-class stamps. Guidelines for #10 SASE.

➤ "We look for beautifully written, engaging manuscripts for children and young adults."

NONFICTION Picture books.

FICTION Subjects include adventure, ethnic, fantasy, historical, juvenile, literary, picture books, regional, short story collections, translation, western, young adult. All levels: adventure, animal, boys, contemporary, fantasy, folktales, historical fiction, humor, sports, multicultural. Middle readers, young adults: problem novels, science fiction, suspense/mystery. No concept picture books, mass-market "character" books, or series. Average word length: picture books—1,000; young readers—1,500; middle readers—14,000; young adult—20,000. No series or activity books. No generic, mass-market oriented fiction. *No unsolicited mss.*

TIPS Wants "unique fiction or nonfiction with a strong voice and lasting quality. Discover your own voice and own story and persevere." Looks for "something unusual, original, well written. Fine art or illustrative art that feels unique. The genre (fantasy, contemporary, or historical fiction) is not so important as the story itself and the spirited life the story allows its main character."

PIANO PRESS

P.O. Box 85, Del Mar CA 92014. (619)884-1401. **Fax:** (858)755-1104. **E-mail:** pianopress@pianopress.com. **Website:** www.pianopress.com. **Contact:** Elizabeth C. Axford, editor. Estab. 1998. **Pays authors, illustrators, and photographers royalty of 5-10% based on retail price.** Publishes book 1 year after acceptance. Accepts simultaneous submissions. Responds to queries in 3 months; mss in 6 months. Catalog available for #10 SASE and 2 first-class stamps.

➤ "We publish music-related books, either fiction or nonfiction, coloring books, songbooks, and poetry."

NONFICTION Picture books, young readers, middle readers, young adults: multicultural, music/dance. Average word length: picture books—1,500-2,000.

FICTION Picture books, young readers, middle readers, young adults: folktales, multicultural, poetry, music. Average word length: picture books—1,500-2,000.

TIPS "We are looking for music-related material only for any juvenile market. Please do not send non-music-related materials. Query first before submitting anything."

PIATKUS BOOKS

Little, Brown Book Group, 100 Victoria Embankment, London WA EC4Y 0DY, United Kingdom. 0207 911 8000. **Fax:** 0207 911 8100. **E-mail:** info@littlebrown.co.uk. **Website:** piatkus.co.uk. **Contact:** Emma Beswetherick, senior editor. Donna Condon, editor; Kim Mackay, editorial assistant Estab. 1979. Publishes hardcover originals, paperback originals, and paperback reprints. **10% from unagented writers.** Publishes book 1 year after acceptance. Responds in 3 months to mss. Guidelines online.

Piatkus no longer accepts fiction proposals.

NONFICTION To submit a nonfiction proposal to Piatkus, please send a letter of enquiry outlining the work and 3 sample chapters. We do not accept e-mailed book proposals. Accepts unsolicited mss. Query with SASE or submit first 3 sample chapter(s), synopsis. Accepts queries by mail. Include estimated word count, brief bio, list of publishing credits. Send SASE for return of ms or send a disposable ms and SASE for reply only. Accepts simultaneous submissions. No submissions on disk or via e-mail. Rarely comments on rejected mss.

FICTION Quality family saga, historical, literary.

TIPS "Study our list before submitting your work."

PICADOR USA

Subsidiary of Holtzbrinck Publishers Holdings LLC, 175 Fifth Ave., New York NY 10010. (212)674-5151. **Fax:** (212)253-9627. **E-mail:** james.meader@picadorusa.com. **Website:** www.picadorusa.com. Estab. 1994. Publishes hardcover and trade paperback originals and reprints.

No unsolicited mss or queries. Agented submissions only.

PICCADILLY BOOKS, LTD.

P.O. Box 25203, Colorado Springs CO 80936. (719)550-9887. **Fax:** (719) 550-8810. **Website:** www.piccadillybooks.com. Estab. 1985. Publishes hardcover originals and trade paperback originals and reprints. **Publishes 5-8 titles/year. 70% of books from first-time authors. 95% from unagented writers.**

Pays 6-10% royalty on retail price. Publishes book 1 year after acceptance. Accepts simultaneous submissions. Responds only if interested, unless accompanied by a SASE to queries.

NONFICTION Subjects include cooking, foods, nutrition, health, medicine, performing arts. "Do your research. Let us know why there is a need for your book, how it differs from other books on the market, and how you will promote the book. No phone calls. We prefer to see the entire ms, but will accept a minimum of 3 sample chapters on your first inquiry. A cover letter is also required; please provide a brief overview of the book, information about similar books already in print and explain why yours is different or better. Tell us the prime market for your book and what you can do to help market it. Also, provide us with background information on yourself and explain what qualifies you to write this book."

TIPS "We publish nonfiction, general interest, self-help books currently emphasizing alternative health."

PICCADILLY PRESS

5 Castle Rd., London En NW1 8PR, United Kingdom. (44)(207)267-4492. **Fax:** (44)(207)267-4493. **E-mail:** books@piccadillypress.co.uk. **Website:** www.piccadillypress.co.uk. Responds to mss in 6 weeks.

NONFICTION Young adults: self help (humorous). Average word length: young adults—25,000-35,000. Submit outline/synopsis and 2 sample chapters.

FICTION Picture books: animal, contemporary, fantasy, nature/environment. Young adults: contemporary, humor, problem novels. Average word length: picture books—500-1,000; young adults—25,000-35,000. Submit complete ms for picture books or submit outline/synopsis and 2 sample chapters for YA. Enclose a brief cover letter and SASE for reply.

TIPS "Take a look in bookshops to see if there are many other books of a similar nature to yours—this is what your book will be competing against, so make sure there is something truly unique about your story. Looking at what else is available will give you ideas as to what topics are popular, but reading a little of them will also give you a sense of the right styles, language and length appropriate for the age-group."

PINEAPPLE PRESS, INC.

P.O. Box 3889, Sarasota FL 34230. (941)739-2219. **Fax:** (941)739-2296. **E-mail:** info@pineapplepress.com. **Website:** www.pineapplepress.com. **Contact:**

June Cussen, executive editor. Estab. 1982. Publishes hardcover and trade paperback originals. **Publishes 25 titles/year. 1,000 queries received/year. 500 mss received/year. 50% of books from first-time authors. 95% from unagented writers. Pays authors royalty of 10-15%.** Publishes book Publishes a book 1 year after acceptance. Accepts simultaneous submissions. Responds to queries/samples/mss in 2 months. Catalog for 9×12 SAE with $1.25 postage. Guidelines online.

⌐⊶ "We are seeking quality nonfiction on diverse topics for the library and book trade markets. Our mission is to publish good books about Florida."

NONFICTION Subjects include regional, Florida. Picture books: animal, history, nature/environmental, science. Young readers, middle readers, young adults: animal, biography, geography, history, nature/environment, science. We will consider most nonfiction topics when related to Florida. Query or submit outline/synopsis and intro and 3 sample chapters. Reviews artwork/photos. Send photocopies.

FICTION Subjects include regional, Florida. Picture books, young readers, middle readers, young adults: animal, folktales, history, nature/environment. Query or submit outline/synopsis and 3 sample chapters.

TIPS "Quality first novels will be published, though we usually only do one or two novels per year and they must be set in Florida. We regard the author/editor relationship as a trusting relationship with communication open both ways. Learn all you can about the publishing process and about how to promote your book once it is published. A query on a novel without a brief sample seems useless."

PIÑATA BOOKS

Imprint of Arte Publico Press, University of Houston, 452 Cullen Performance Hall, Houston TX 77204-2004. (713)743-2845. **Fax:** (713)743-3080. **E-mail:** submapp@mail.uh.edu. **Website:** www.artepublicopress.com. **Contact:** Nicolas Kanellos, director. Estab. 1994. Publishes hardcover and trade paperback originals. **Publishes 10-15 titles/year. 80% of books from first-time authors. Pays 10% royalty on wholesale price. Pays $1,000-3,000 advance.** Publishes book 2 years after acceptance. Accepts simultaneous submissions. Responds in 2-3 month to queries; 4-6 months to mss. Catalog and guidelines available via website or with #10 SASE.

NONFICTION Subjects include ethnic. Piñata Books specializes in publication of children's and young adult literature that authentically portrays themes, characters and customs unique to U.S. Hispanic culture. Query with SASE.

FICTION Subjects include adventure, juvenile, picture books, young adult. Send complete ms.

POETRY Appropriate to Hispanic theme. Submit 10 sample poems.

TIPS "Include cover letter with submission explaining why your manuscript is unique and important, why we should publish it, who will buy it, etc."

PITSPOPANY PRESS

Simcha Media, P.O. Box 5329, Englewood NJ 07631. (212)444-1657. **Fax:** (866)205-3966. **E-mail:** pitspop@netvision.net.il; stu@stuartschnee.com. **Website:** www.pitspopany.com. Estab. 1992. **Pays authors royalty or work purchased outright.** Publishes book 9 months after acceptance. Accepts simultaneous submissions. Responds to queries/mss in 6 weeks. Catalog on website. Writer's guidelines available for SASE.

⌐⊶ "Pitspopany Press is dedicated to bringing quality children's books of Jewish interest into the marketplace. Our goal is to create titles that will appeal to the esthetic senses of our readers and, at the same time, offer quality Jewish content to the discerning parent, teacher, and librarian. While the people working for Pitspopany Press embody a wide spectrum of Jewish belief and opinion, we insist that our titles be respectful of the mainstream Jewish viewpoints and beliefs. We are especially interested in chapter books for kids. Most of all, we are committed to creating books that all Jewish children can read, learn from, and enjoy."

NONFICTION All levels: activity books, animal, arts/crafts, biography, careers, concept, cooking, geography, health, history, hobbies, how-to, multicultural, music/dance, nature/environment, reference, religion, science, self help, social issues, special needs, sports. Submit outline/synopsis.

FICTION Picture books: animal, anthology, fantasy, folktales, history, humor, multicultural, nature/environment, poetry. Young readers: adventure, animal, anthology, concept, contemporary, fantasy, folktales, health, history, humor, multicultural, nature/environment, poetry, religion, science fiction, special needs, sports, suspense. Middle readers: animal, anthology, fantasy, folktales, health, hi-lo, history, humor, multicultural, nature/environment, poetry, religion, science fiction, special needs, sports, suspense. Young adults/teens: animal, anthology, contemporary, fantasy, folktales, health, hi-lo, history, humor, multicultural, nature/environment, poetry, religion, science fiction, special needs, sports, suspense. Submit outline/synopsis.

⊘ PLAN B PRESS

P.O. Box 4067, Alexandria VA 22303. (215)732-2663. **E-mail:** planbpress@gmail.com. **Website:** www.planbpress.com. **Contact:** Steven Allen May, president. Estab. 1999. **Pays author's copies.** Responds to queries in 1 month; mss in 3 months.

⊶ Plan B Press is a "small publishing company with an international feel. Our intention is to have Plan B Press be part of the conversation about the direction and depth of literary movements and genres. Plan B Press's new direction is to seek out authors rarely-to-never published, sharing new voices that might not otherwise be heard. Plan B Press is determined to merge text with image, writing with art." Publishes poetry and short fiction. Wants "experimental poetry, concrete/visual work." Has published poetry by Lamont B. Steptoe, Michele Belluomini, Jim Mancinelli, Lyn Lifshin, Robert Miltner, and Steven Allen May. Publishes 1 poetry book/year and 5-10 chapbooks/year. Manuscripts are selected through open submission and through competition (see below). Books/chapbooks are 24-48 pages, with covers with art/graphics.

POETRY Wants to see: experimental, concrete, visual poetry Does not want "sonnets, political or religious poems, work in the style of Ogden Nash." Query first, with a few sample poems and a cover letter with brief bio and publication credits. Book/chapbook mss may include previously published poems.

PLANNERS PRESS

Imprint of the American Planning Association, 122 S. Michigan Ave., Suite 1600, Chicago IL 60603. (312)431-9100. **Fax:** (312)431-9985. **E-mail:** plannerspress@planning.org. **Website:** www.planning.org/plannerspress/index.htm. **Contact:** Timothy Mennel, Ph.D. (planning practice, urban issues, land use, transportation). Estab. 1970. Publishes hardcover, electronic, and trade paperback originals; and trade paperback and electronic reprints. **Publishes 12 titles/year. 50 queries received/year. 35 mss received/year. 25% of books from first-time authors. 100% from unagented writers. Pays 10-15% royalty on wholesale price. Pays advance.** Publishes book 15 months after acceptance. Accepts simultaneous submissions. Responds in 1 month to queries; 2 months to proposals and mss. Catalog online www.planningbooks.com. Guidelines available by e-mail at plannerspress@planning.org.

⊶ "Our books often have a narrow audience of city planners and frequently focus on the tools of city planning."

NONFICTION Subjects include agriculture, business, economics, community, contemporary culture, economics, environment, finance, government, politics, history, horticulture, law, money, finance, nature, environment, politics, real estate, science, social sciences, sociology, transportation, world affairs. Submit proposal package, including: outline, 1 sample chapter and CV Submit completed ms. Reviews artwork/photos. Send photocopies.

TIPS "Our audience is professional planners but also anyone interested in community development, urban affairs, sustainability, and related fields."

⊕ ⊘ PLATYPUS MEDIA, LLC

725 Eighth St. SE, Washington DC 20003. (202)546-1674. **Fax:** (202)546-2356. **E-mail:** submissions@platypusmedia.com. **Website:** www.platypusmedia.com. **Contact:** Tracey Kilby, editorial assistant (children's—early childhood and science, birth, lactation). Estab. 2000. Publishes hardcover and trade paperback originals. **Publishes 3-4 titles/year. 100 queries received/year. 250 mss received/year. 5% of books from first-time authors. 100% from unagented writers. Pays royalty on wholesale price. Makes outright purchase.** Publishes book 9 months after acceptance. Accepts simultaneous submissions. Responds in 2-4 months to queries, proposals and mss. Catalog available free. Guidelines online.

NONFICTION Subjects include child guidance, education, health, medicine, womens issues, womens studies., breastfeeding, childbirth, children's science books. Query with SASE. *All unsolicited mss returned unopened.* Reviews artwork/photos. Send photocopies. No art will be returned. We are particularly interested in artists who can draw realistic images of mothers and babies, both in the human and mammal world.

FICTION Subjects include juvenile. Query with SASE. No electronic submissions.

TIPS Audience includes parents, children, teachers, and parenting professionals. We publish just a handful of books each year and most are generated in-house.

PLEXUS PUBLISHING, INC.

143 Old Marlton Pike, Medford NJ 08055. (609)654-6500. **Fax:** (609)654-4309. **E-mail:** jbryans@plexuspublishing.com. **Website:** www.plexuspublishing.com. **Contact:** John B. Bryans, editor-in-chief/publisher. Estab. 1977. Publishes hardcover and paperback originals. **Pays $500-1,000 advance.** Accepts simultaneous submissions. Responds in 3 months to proposals. Catalog and book proposal guidelines for 10×13 SASE.

⚟ Plexus publishes regional-interest (southern New Jersey and the greater Philadelphia area) fiction and nonfiction including mysteries, field guides, nature, travel and history. Also a limited number of titles in health/medicine, biology, ecology, botany, astronomy.

NONFICTION Query with SASE.

FICTION Mysteries and literary novels with a strong regional (southern New Jersey) angle. Query with SASE.

PLUM BLOSSOM BOOKS

Parallax Press, P.O. Box 7355, Berkeley CA 94707. (510)525-0101. **Fax:** (510)525-7129. **E-mail:** rachel@parallax.org. **Website:** www.parallax.org. **Contact:** Rachel Neuman, senior editor. Estab. 1985. **30% of books from first-time authors. Pays authors 20% based on wholesale price. Pays illustrators by the project.** Publishes book 9-12 months after acceptance. Responds to queries in 1-2 weeks; mss in 1 month. Catalog available for SASE. Writer's guidelines on website and for SASE.

⚟ "Plum Blossom Books publishes stories for children of all ages that focus on mindfulness in daily life, Buddhism, and social justice."

NONFICTION All levels: nature/environment, religion (Buddhist), Buddhist counting books.

FICTION Picture books: adventure, contemporary, folktales, multicultural, nature/environment, religion. Young readers: adventure, contemporary, folktales, multicultural, nature/environment, religion. Middle readers: multicultural, nature/environment, religion. Young adults/teens: nature/environment, religion.

TIPS "Read our books before approaching us. We are very specifically looking for mindfulness and Buddhist messages in high-quality stories where the Buddhist message is implied rather than stated outright."

🅐⊘ POCKET BOOKS

Simon & Schuster, 1230 Avenue of the Americas, New York NY 10020. (212)698-7000. **Website:** www.simonsays.com. **Contact:** Jennifer Bergstrom, editor-in-chief. Estab. 1939. Publishes paperback originals and reprints, mass market and trade paperbacks. Catalog available free. Guidelines online.

NONFICTION Subjects include cooking, foods, nutrition. *Agented submissions only.*

FICTION Subjects include mystery, romance, suspense, psychological suspense, thriller, western., *Star Trek. Agented submissions only.*

POCOL PRESS

Box 411, Clifton VA 20124. (703)830-5862. **Website:** www.pocolpress.com. **Contact:** J. Thomas Hetrick, editor. Estab. 1999. Publishes trade paperback originals. **Publishes 6 titles/year. 90 queries received/year. 20 mss received/year. 90% of books from first-time authors. 100% from unagented writers. Pays 10-12% royalty on wholesale price.** Publishes book less than 1 year after acceptance. Responds in 1 month to queries; 2 months too mss. Catalog and guidelines online.

FICTION Subjects include historical, horror, literary, mainstream, contemporary, military, war, mystery, short story collections, thematic, spiritual, sports, western., baseball fiction. "We specialize in thematic short fiction collections by a single author and baseball fiction. Expert storytellers welcome." Horror (psychological, supernatural), literary, mainstream/contemporary, short story collections, baseball. Does not accept or return unsolicited mss. Query with SASE or submit 1 sample chapter(s).

TIPS "Our audience is aged 18 and over. Pocol Press is unique; we publish good writing and great storytelling. Write the best stories you can. Read them to you friends/peers. Note their reaction. Publishes some of the finest fiction by a small press."

🌑⊘ POETRY SALZBURG

University of Salzburg, Department of English, Akademiestrasse 24, Salzburg A-5020, Austria. (43)(662)8044-4422. **Fax:** (43)(662)8044-167. **E-mail:** editor@poetrysalzburg.com. **Website:** www.poetrysalzburg.com. **Contact:** Dr. Wolfgang Goertschacher,

Andreas Schachermayr. Estab. 1971. **Payment varies.** Responds to queries in 1 month; mss in 3 months.

☞ Poetry Salzburg publishes "collections of at least 100 pages by mainly poets not taken up by big publishers." Publishes 6-8 paperbacks/year. Books are usually 100-350 pages, A5, professionally printed, perfect-bound, with card covers.

POETRY Query first, with a cover letter with brief bio and publication credits.

POISONED PEN PRESS

6962 E. 1st Ave., #103, Scottsdale AZ 85251. (480)945-3375. **Fax:** (480)949-1707. **E-mail:** editor@poisonedpenpress.com; info@poisonedpenpress.com. **E-mail:** submissions@poisonedpenpress.com. **Website:** www.poisonedpenpress.com. **Contact:** Jessica Tribble. Estab. 1996. Publishes hardcover originals, and hardcover and trade paperback reprints. **Publishes 36 titles/year. 1,000 queries received/year. 300 mss received/year. 35% of books from first-time authors. 65% from unagented writers. Pays 9-15% royalty on retail price.** Publishes book 10-12 months after acceptance. Responds in 2-3 months to queries and proposals; 6 months to mss. Catalog and guidelines online.

☞ "Our publishing goal is to offer well-written mystery novels of crime and/or detection where the puzzle and its resolution are the main forces that move the story forward."

FICTION Subjects include mystery. Mss should generally be longer than 65,000 words and shorter than 100,000 words. Member Publishers Marketing Associations, Arizona Book Publishers Associations, Publishers Association of West. Distributes through Ingram, Baker & Taylor, Brodart. Does not want novels centered on serial killers, spousal or child abuse, drugs, or extremist groups, although we do not entirely rule such works out. Accepts unsolicited mss. Electronic queries only. "Query with SASE. Submit clips, first 3 pages. We must receive both the synopsis and ms pages electronically as separate attachments to an e-mail message or as a disk or CD which we will not return."

TIPS "Audience is adult readers of mystery fiction."

POLYCHROME PUBLISHING CORP.

4509 N. Francisco, Chicago IL 60625. **E-mail:** info@polychromebooks.com. **Website:** www.polychromebooks.com. Estab. 1990. Publishes hardcover originals and reprints. **Publishes 4 titles/year. 3,000 que-**ries received/year. 7,500-8,000 mss received/year. 50% of books from first-time authors. 100% from unagented writers. Pays royalty Pays advance.** Publishes book 2 years after acceptance. Accepts simultaneous submissions. Responds in 8 months to mss. Catalog for #10 SASE. Guidelines for #10 SASE or on the website.

NONFICTION Subjects include ethnic. Subjects emphasize ethnic, particularly multicultural/Asian-American.

FICTION Subjects include ethnic, juvenile, multicultural, particularly Asian-American, picture books, young adult. "We do not publish fables, folktales, fairy tales, or anthropomorphic animal stories."

POPULAR WOODWORKING

F+W Media, Inc., 10151 Carver Road, Suite 200, Blue Ash OH 45242. (513)531-2690. **Website:** www.popularwoodworking.com. **Contact:** David Thiel, executive editor. **Publishes 6-8 titles/year. 30 queries received/year. 10 mss received/year. 20% of books from first-time authors. 95% from unagented writers.** Publishes book 1 year after acceptance. Accepts simultaneous submissions. Responds in 1 month.

NONFICTION Subjects include hobbies, woodworking, wood crafts. Query first. Proposal package should include an outline and digial photos.

TIPS "Our books are for beginning to advanced woodworking enthusiasts."

POSSIBILITY PRESS

1 Oakglade Circle, Hummelstown PA 17036. **E-mail:** info@possibilitypress.com. **Website:** www.possibilitypress.com. **Contact:** Mike Markowski, publisher. Estab. 1981. Publishes trade paperback originals. **Publishes 2-3 titles/year. 90% of books from first-time authors. 100% from unagented writers. Royalties vary.** Responds in 1 month to queries. Catalog available online. Guidelines online.

☞ "Our mission is to help the people of the world grow and become the best they can be, through the written and spoken word."

NONFICTION Subjects include psychology, pop psychology, self-help, leadership, relationships, attitude, business, success/motivation, inspiration, entrepreneurship, sales marketing, MLM and home-based business topics, and human interest success stories. Prefers submissions to be mailed. Include SASE. Submit ms in Microsoft Word. Your submission needs to be made both in hard copy and on a CD. Label it clearly with the book title and your name. Be sure to keep a backup CD for yourself. Save your ms as a .doc file name. Save your file a second time with an rtf (Rich Text Format) extension. See guidelines online. Reviews artwork/photos. Do not send originals.

FICTION Needs: parable that teach lessons about life and success.

TIPS "Our focus is on co-authoring and publishing short (15,000-30,000 words) bestsellers. We're looking for kind and compassionate authors who are passionate about making a difference in the world, and will champion their mission to do so, especially by public speaking. Our dream author writes well, knows how to promote, will champion their mission, speaks for a living, has a following and a platform, is cooperative and understanding, humbly handles critique and direction, is grateful, intelligent, and has a good sense of humor."

PPI (PROFESSIONAL PUBLICATIONS, INC.)

1250 Fifth Ave., Belmont CA 94002. (650)593-9119. **Fax:** (650)592-4519. **E-mail:** info@ppi2pass.com. **Website:** www.ppi2pass.com. Estab. 1975. Publishes hardcover, paperback, and electronic products, CD-ROMs and DVDs. **Publishes 10 titles/year. 5% of books from first-time authors. 100% from unagented writers.** Publishes book 4-18 months after acceptance. Accepts simultaneous submissions. Responds in 1 month to queries. Catalog and guidelines free.

⟐➻ "PPI publishes professional, reference, and licensing preparation materials. PPI wants submissions from both professionals practicing in the field and from experienced instructors. Currently emphasizing engineering, interior design, architecture, landscape architecture and LEED exam review."

NONFICTION Subjects include architecture, science., landscape architecture, engineering mathematics, engineering, surveying, interior design, greenbuilding, sustainable development, and other professional licensure subjects. Especially needs review and reference books for all professional licensing examinations. Please submit ms and proposal outlining market potential, etc. Proposal template available upon request. Reviews artwork/photos.

TIPS "We specialize in books for those people who want to become licensed and/or accredited professionals: engineers, architects, surveyors, interior

designers, LEED APs, etc. Exam Prep Lines generally include online and print products such as review manuals, practice problems, sample exams, E-Learning Modules, IPhone Apps, and more. Demonstrating your understanding of the market, competition, appropriate delivery methods, and marketing ideas will help sell us on your proposal."

◎ PRAIRIE JOURNAL PRESS

P.O. Box 68073, Calgary AB T3G 3N8, Canada. **E-mail:** prairiejournal@yahoo.com. **Website:** www.geocities.com/prairiejournal/. **Contact:** Anne Burke, literary editor. Estab. 1983. **Pays 1 author's copy; honorarium depends on grant/award provided by the government or private/corporate donations.**

FICTION Literary, short story collections. Submit with SAE with IRC for individuals. No U.S. stamps please. Accepts unsolicited mss. Sometimes comments on rejected mss.

TIPS "We wish we had the means to promote more new writers. We look for something different each time and try not to repeat types of stories if possible. We receive fiction of very high quality. Short fiction is preferable although excerpts from novels are considered if they stand alone on their own merit."

PRAKKEN PUBLICATIONS, INC.

P.O. Box 8623, Ann Arbor MI 48107. (734)975-2800. **Fax:** (734)975-2787. **E-mail:** pam@eddigest.com; susanne@eddigest.com. **Contact:** Susanne Peckham, book editor; Sharon K. Miller, art/design/production manager. Estab. 1934. Publishes educational hardcover and paperback originals, as well as educational magazines. **Publishes 3 titles/year.** Accepts simultaneous submissions. Responds in 2 months to queries. Catalog for #10 SASE.

⟐➻ "We publish books for educators in career/vocational and technology education, as well as books for the machine trades and machinists' education. Currently emphasizing machine trades."

NONFICTION Subjects include education. "We are currently interested in manuscripts with broad appeal in any of the specific subject areas of machine trades, technology education, career-technical education, and reference for the general education field." Submit outline, sample chapters.

TIPS "We have a continuing interest in magazine and book manuscripts which reflect emerging issues and trends in education, especially career-technical, industrial, and technology education."

PRB PRODUCTIONS

963 Peralta Ave., Albany CA 94706. (510)526-0722. **Fax:** (510)527-4763. **E-mail:** prbprdns@aol.com. **Website:** www.prbpro.com. **Contact:** Peter R. Ballinger and Leslie Gold. **Publishes 10-15 titles/year. Pays 10% royalty on retail price.** Accepts simultaneous submissions. Responds in 1 month to queries; 3 months to mss. Catalog online.

NONFICTION Subjects include music, dance. Query with SASE. Submit complete ms.

TIPS Audience is music schools, universities, libraries, professional music educators, and amateur/professional musicians.

PRESA :S: PRESS

P.O. Box 792, 8590 Belding Rd. NE, Rockford MI 49341. **E-mail:** presapress@aol.com. **Website:** www. presapress.com. **Contact:** Roseanne Ritzema, editor. Estab. 2003. **Pays 10-25 author\quotes copies.** Publishes book Time between acceptance and publication is 8-12 weeks. after acceptance of ms. Responds to queries in 2-4 weeks; to mss in 8-12 weeks. Guidelines available in magazine, for SASE, and by e-mail.

POETRY Needs poems, reviews, essays, photos, criticism, and prose. Dedicates 6-8 pages of each issue to a featured poet. Considers previously published poems. (Considers poetry posted on a public website/blog/forum and poetry posted on a private, password-protected forum as published.) Acquires first North American serial rights and the right to reprint in anthologies. Rights revert to poets upon publication. Accepts postal submissions only. Cover letter is preferred. Reads submissions year round. Poems are circulated to an editorial board. Never comments on rejected poems. Never publishes theme issues. Reviews books and chapbooks of poetry. Send materials for review consideration to Roseanne Ritzema Query first, with a few sample poems and a cover letter with brief bio and publication credits. Book/chapbook mss may include previously published poems.

PRESSES DE L'UNIVERSITÉ DE MONTREAL

Case postale 6128, Succursale Centre-ville, Montreal QC H3C 3J7, Canada. (514)343-6933. **Fax:** (514)343-2232. **E-mail:** pum@umontreal.ca. **Website:** www. pum.umontreal.ca. **Contact:** Sylvie Brousseau, rights and sales. Publishes hardcover and trade paperback

originals. **Publishes 40 titles/year.** Publishes book 6 months after acceptance. Responds in 1 month to queries and proposals; months to mss. Catalog and guidelines free.

NONFICTION Subjects include education, health, medicine, history, language, literature, philosophy, psychology, sociology, translation. Submit outline, 2 sample chapters.

MATHEW PRICE LTD.

Albany Court, Albury, Thame, Oxon OX9 2LP, United Kingdom. **E-mail:** info@mathewprice.com. **E-mail:** submissions@mathewprice.com. **Website:** www. mathewprice.com. **Contact:** Mathew Price, chairman. Estab. 1983.

Looking especially for stories for 2- to 4-yearolds and fiction for young adults, especially fantasy.

FICTION *Will accept e-mail submissions only.*

TIPS "Study the market; keep a copy of all your work."

PRICE STERN SLOAN, INC.

345 Hudson St., New York NY 10014. (212)366-2000. **Website:** us.penguingroup.com/youngreaders. **Contact:** Francesco Sedita, vice-president/publisher. Estab. 1963. Responds to queries in 6-8 weeks. Catalog available for 9x12 SASE and 5 first-class stamps. Ms guidelines available for SASE.

Price Stern Sloan does not accept e-mail submissions.

FICTION Publishes picture books and novelty/board books including Mad Libs Movie and Television Tie-ins, and unauthorized biographies. "We publish unique novelty formats and fun, colorful paperbacks and activity books.

TIPS "Price Stern Sloan publishes unique, fun titles."

PRICE WORLD PUBLISHING, LLC

1300 W. Belmont Ave., 20G, Chicago IL 60657. (866) S-WORKOUT; 888-234-6896. **Fax:** (216)803-0350. **E-mail:** publishing@priceworldpublishing.com. **Website:** www.priceworldpublishing.com. **Contact:** Robert Price, president/executive editor. Estab. 2002. Trade and mass market paperback and hardcover originals. **Publishes 10-20 titles/year titles/year. 35 queries received/year; 20 mss/year. 50% of books from first-time authors. 50% from unagented writers. Pays 8-15% royalty on wholesale price.**

NONFICTION Subjects include sports, fitness. Submit proposal package, including outline, completed ms; visit www.priceworldpublishing.com for proposal submission information. Reviews artwork/photos; send PDF or MS Word docs.

TIPS "The focus of our editorial scope is sports and fitness, with emphasis on instruction for training and performance. We now welcome all nonfiction proposals—visit our website for more information."

⊕ PRINCETON ARCHITECTURAL PRESS

37 E. 7th St., New York NY 10003. (212)995-9620. **Fax:** (212)995-9454. **E-mail:** submissions@papress.com. **Website:** www.papress.com. Publishes hardcover and trade paperback originals. **Publishes 50 titles/year. 300 queries received/year. 150 mss received/year. 65% of books from first-time authors. 95% from unagented writers. Pays royalty on wholesale price.** Publishes book 1 year after acceptance. Accepts simultaneous submissions. Responds in 2 months to queries, proposals and mss. Catalog and guidelines online.

NONFICTION Subjects include art, architecture. Submit proposal package, outline, 1 sample chapters, table of contents, sample of art, and survey of competitive titles. Reviews artwork/photos. Do not send originals.

TIPS "Princeton Architecture Press publishes fine books on architecture, design, photography, landscape, and visual culture. Our books are acclaimed for their strong and unique editorial vision, unrivaled design sensibility, and high production values at affordable prices."

PRINCETON UNIVERSITY PRESS

41 William St., Princeton NJ 08540. (609)258-4900. **Fax:** (609)258-6305. **Website:** www.pupress.princeton.edu. **Contact:** Hanne Winarsky, editor.

POETRY Submit hard copy of proposal with sample poems or full ms. Cover letter is required. Reads submissions year round. Mss will not be returned. Comments on finalists only. Responds in 3-4 months.

PRINTING INDUSTRIES OF AMERICA

200 Deer Run Rd., Sewickley PA 15143-2600, United States. (412)741-6860. **Fax:** (412)741-2311. **E-mail:** awoodall@printing.org. **Website:** www.printing.org. **Contact:** Amy Woodall, director (areas of interest: Printing, Graphic Arts, communication). Estab. 1921. Publishes trade paperback originals and hardcover reference texts. **Publishes 20 titles/year. Receives 20 ms/year; 30 queries/year. 50% of books from first-time authors. 100% from unagented writers. Pays 15-20% royalty on wholesale price.** Publishes book 18 months after acceptance. Accepts simultaneous submissions. Responds in 1 month to queries.

8—☛ "Printing Industries of America, along with its affiliates, delivers products and services that enhance the growth and profitability of its members and the industry through advocacy, education, research, and technical information."

NONFICTION Subjects include business, economics, education., communications, printing & graphic arts. Printing Industries of America's mission is to serve the graphic communications community as the major resource for technical information and services through research and education. Currently emphasizing technical textbooks as well as career guides for graphic communications and turnkey training curricula. Query with SASE, or submit outline, sample chapters, and SASE. Reviews artwork. Send photocopies.

PRUETT PUBLISHING

P.O. Box 2140, Boulder CO 80306. (303)449-4919. **Fax:** (303)443-9019. **Website:** www.pruettpublishing.com. **Contact:** Jim Pruett, publisher. Estab. 1959. Publishes hardcover and trade paperback originals, trade paperback reprints. **75-80 mss received/year. 90% of books from first-time authors. 90% from unagented writers.** Publishes book 18 months after acceptance. Accepts simultaneous submissions. Responds in 1 month to queries; 3 months to proposals and mss.

8—☛ "We are focused on the mountain West. Our trade books cover topics that range from fly fishing to hiking and biking, history, nature, and the environment. We also publish textbooks for grade-school students about the history of Colorado."

NONFICTION Subjects include alternative, Americana, education, history, nature, environment, sports, travel. Query with SASE. Submit outline, 2 sample chapters. Reviews artwork/photos. Send photocopies.

TIPS "We focus on outdoor recreationalists—hikers, fly-fishers, travelers. There has been a movement away from large publisher's mass market books toward small publisher's regional interest books, and in turn distributors and retail outlets are more interested in small publishers. Authors don't need to have a big name to have a good publisher. Look for similar books that you feel are well-produced—consider design, editing, overall quality, and contact those publishers. Get to know several publishers, and find the one that feels right—trust your instincts."

PRUFROCK PRESS, INC.

5926 Balcones Dr., Ste. 220, Austin TX 78731. (512)300-2220. **Fax:** (512)300-2221. **E-mail:** info@ prufrock.com. **Website:** www.prufrock.com. **Contact:** Sarah Morrison, Jennifer Robins, Lacy Compton. Publishes trade paperback originals and reprints. Catalog and guidelines free.

○→ "Prufrock Press publishes exciting, innovative and current resources supporting the education of special needs, gifted and advanced learners."

NONFICTION Subjects include child guidance, education. We publish for the education market. Our readers are typically teachers or parents of special needs, gifted and advanced learners. Our product line is built around professional development books for teachers and activity books for children. Our products support innovative ways of making learning more fun and exciting for children. Submit book prospectus (download form on website).

TIPS "We are looking for practical, classroom-ready materials that encourage children to creatively learn and think."

⊕⊘ PS BOOKS

Philadelphia Stories, Inc., 2021 S. 11th St., Philadelphia PA 19148. (215)551-5889. **Fax:** (215)635-0195. **E-mail:** info@psbookspublishing.org. **E-mail:** marc@psbookspublishing.org. **Website:** www.psbookspublishing.org. **Contact:** Marc Schuster, acquisitions editor. Estab. 2008. Publishes book 1 year after acceptance.

FICTION Humor, literary, mainstream, regional (Delaware valley, greater Philadelphia). Query with outline/synopsis and first 20 pages. Accepts queries by e-mail only. Include estimated word count, brief bio, list of publishing credits. Send disposable copy of ms and SASE for reply only. Responds to queries in 2 months. Considers simultaneous submissions, e-mail submissions. Rarely critiques/comments on rejected mss. Responds to mss in 3 months.

TIPS "We are looking for well written literary or up-market commercial fiction and non-fiction. We prefer novels to be under 300 pages (100,000 words) and expect authors to submit a marketing plan. Only send us polished work that fits our guidelines. We encourage authors to read our current titles and to read work published on the *Philadelphia Stories* website."

PUCKERBRUSH PRESS

413 Neville Hall, Orono ME 04469. (207)581-3832. **Website:** http://puckerbrushreview.com. **Contact:**

Sanford Phippen, editor. Estab. 1971. Publishes trade paperback originals and reprints of literary fiction and poetry. **Publishes 3-4 titles/year. Pays 10-15% royalty on wholesale price.** Responds in 1 month to queries; 2 months to proposals; 3 months to mss. Catalog for large SASE and 34¢. Guidelines for SASE.

NONFICTION Subjects include language, literature, translation. No religious subjects, crime per se, tired prose. Query with SASE.

FICTION Subjects include literary, short story collections, novels. Submit complete ms. Accepts queries by phone. Include brief bio, list of publishing credits.

POETRY Submit highest literary quality. Submit complete ms. Please submit your poetry, short stories, literary essays and reviews through the link on website. Hard-copy submissions will no longer be accepted.

TIPS "Be true to your vision, not to fashion. For sophisticated readers who retain love of literature. Maine writers continue to be featured."

THE PUDDIN'HEAD PRESS

P.O. Box 477889, Chicago IL 60647. (708)656-4900. **E-mail:** phbooks@att.net. **Website:** www.puddinheadpress.com. Estab. 1985. Responds to queries in 2 months.

○→ "In the last several years we have been increasingly active across the country. There are numerous readings and events that we sponsor. We do our own distribution, primarily in the Midwest, and also do distribution for other small presses. Please send a SASE for a list of our current publications and publication/distribution guidelines. We sell poetry books, not just print them. Submitted poetry is evaluated for its marketability and quality."

POETRY The Puddin'head Press is interested in "well-rounded poets who can support their work with readings and appearances." Wants "quality poetry by active poets who read and lead interesting lives. We occasionally publish chapbook-style anthologies and let poets on our mailing lists know what type of work we're interested in for a particular project." Does not want experimental, overly political poetry, or poetry with overt sexual content; no shock or novelty poems. Puddin'head Press publishes 2-3 books and 2-3 chapbooks per year. Books/chapbooks are 30-100 pages, perfect-bound or side-stapled ("we use various formats"). "Please visit our website for submission guidelines." Poets must include SASE with submission.

PUFFIN BOOKS

Imprint of Penguin Group (USA), Inc., 345 Hudson St., New York NY 10014. (212)366-2000. **Website:** www.penguinputnam.com. **Contact:** Kristin Gilson, editorial director. Sharyn November, senior editor Publishes trade paperback originals and reprints. **Publishes 175-200 titles/year. Receives 600 queries and mss/year. 1% of books from first-time authors. 5% from unagented writers. Royalty varies. Pays varies advance.** Publishes book 1 year after acceptance. Responds in 5 months. Catalog for 9×12 SAE with 7 first-class stamps.

⌐ "Puffin Books publishes high-end trade paperbacks and paperback reprints for preschool children, beginning and middle readers, and young adults."

NONFICTION Subjects include education, for teaching concepts and colors, not academic, history, women's issues/studies. Biography, illustrated books, young children's concept books (counting, shapes, colors). Subjects include education (for teaching concepts and colors, not academic), women in history. "Women in history books interest us." *No unsolicited mss.* Submit 5 pages of ms with SASE.

FICTION Subjects include picture books, young adult., middle grade, easy-to-read grades 1-3. Picture books, young adult novels, middle grade and easy-to-read grades 1-3: fantasy and science fiction, graphic novels, classics. *No unsolicited mss.* Submit 3 sample chapters with SASE.

TIPS "Our audience ranges from little children 'first books' to young adult (ages 14-16). An original idea has the best luck."

PURDUE UNIVERSITY PRESS

Stewart Center 370, 504 West State St., West Lafayette IN 47907-2058. (765)494-2038. **E-mail:** pupress@purdue.edu. **Website:** www.thepress.purdue.edu. **Contact:** Charles Watkinson, director; Katherine Purple, lead production editor. Estab. 1960. Publishes hardcover and trade paperback originals and trade paperback reprints. **Publishes 20-25 titles/year.** Catalog and guidelines for 9×12 SASE.

⌐ "We look for books that look at the world as a whole and offer new thoughts and insights into the standard debate. Currently emphasizing technology, human-animal issues, business. De-emphasizing literary studies."

NONFICTION Subjects include agriculture, Americana, business,government, politics, health, history, language, literary criticism, philosophy, regional, science, social sciences, sociology. Dedicated to the dissemination of scholarly and professional information, Purdue University Press provides quality resources in several key subject areas including business, technology, health, veterinary medicine, and other selected disciplines in the humanities and sciences. As the scholarly publishing arm of Purdue University and a unit of Purdue Libraries, the Press is also a partner for university faculty and staff, centers and departments, wishing to disseminate the results of their research. Query before submitting.

PUREPLAY PRESS

350 Judah St., Suite 302, San Francisco CA 94122. **E-mail:** info@pureplaypress.com; editor@pureplaypress.com. **Website:** www.pureplaypress.com. **Contact:** David Landau, editor/publisher. Estab. 2001.

⌐ "Founded in 2001 by writers and editors who felt the need to publish works about Cuba's history and culture. At present we have 12 books in print, all with Cuban themes, and we are beginning to publish on other subjects. Our byword is freedom from the status quo. The qualities we prize in the written word are sincerity, simplicity, elegance and clarity of expression. We are convinced that culture is infinite, and creativity general. We strive to be considerate to readers and encouraging to writers.Our books are closely edited, carefully designed, printed with high-quality materials and then marketed by all plausible means, including the World Wide Web. We are interested in fiction, history, poetry, politics and culture."

FICTION "While we cannot receive unsolicited manuscripts, we will consider proposals of up to 250 words in length. The most effective proposal is a statement about the work that might serve as copy for a book-jacket or a back cover."

○ PURICH PUBLISHING

Box 23032, Market Mall Post Office, Saskatoon SK S7J 5H3, Canada. (306)373-5311. **Fax:** (306)373-5315. **E-mail:** purich@sasktel.net. **Website:** www.purich-publishing.com. **Contact:** Donald Purich, publisher; Karen Bolstad, publisher. Estab. 1992. Publishes trade paperback originals. **Publishes 3-5 titles/year. 20% of books from first-time authors. 100% from unagented writers. Pays 8-12% royalty on retail price.** Publishes book 4 months after acceptance. Responds in 1 month to queries; months to mss. Catalog available free.

- 👁️➡ "Purich publishes books on law, Aboriginal/ Native American issues, and Western Canadian history for the academic and professional trade reference market."

NONFICTION, Aboriginal and social justice issues, Western Canadian history. "We are a specialized publisher and only consider work in our subject areas." Query with SASE.

Ⓐ PUSH

Scholastic, 557 Broadway, New York NY 10012. **E-mail:** DLevithan@Scholastic.com. **Website:** www.thisispush.com. Estab. 2002. **Publishes 6-9 titles/ year. 50% of books from first-time authors.**

- 👁️➡ PUSH publishes new voices in teen literature.

NONFICTION Young adults: memoir. *Does not accept unsolicited mss.*

FICTION Young adults: contemporary, multicultural, poetry. *Does not accept unsolicited mss.*

TIPS "We only publish first-time writers (and then their subsequent books), so authors who have published previously should not consider PUSH. Also, for young writers in grades 7-12, we run the PUSH Novel Contest with the Scholastic Art & Writing Awards. Every year it begins in October and ends in March. Rules can be found on our website."

Ⓐ G.P. PUTNAM'S SONS

Penguin Putnam, Inc., 345 Hudson St., New York NY 10014. (212)414-3610. **Fax:** (212)366-2664. **E-mail:** susan.kochan@us.penguingroup.com. **Website:** www.penguinputnam.com; www.us.penguingroup.com. **Contact:** Susan Kochan, associate editorial director. John Rudolph, executive editor; Timothy Travaglini, senior editor; Stacey Barney, editor. **Art Acquisitions:** Cecilia Yung, art director, Putnam and Philomel. **Pays author royalty based on retail price.** Responds in 4 months if interested.

NONFICTION Picture books: animal, biography, concept, history, nature/environment, science. Subjects must have broad appeal but inventive approach. Average word length: picture books—200-1,500.

FICTION Juvenile picture books: animal, concept, contemporary, humor, multicultural. Young readers: adventure, contemporary, history, humor, multicultural, special needs, suspense/mystery. Middle readers: adventure, contemporary, history, humor, fantasy, multicultural, problem novels, sports, suspense/mystery. Young adults: contemporary, history, fantasy, problem novels, special needs. Does not want to see series. Average word length: picture books—200-1,000; middle readers—10,000-30,000; young adults—40,000-50,000. Accepts unsolicited mss. No SASE required, as will only respond if interested. Picture books: send full mss. Fiction: Query with outline/synopsis and 10 ms pages. When submitting a portion of a longer work, please provide an accompanying cove letter that briefly describes your ms's plot, genre, the intended age group, and your publishing credits, if any. Do not send art unless requested.

TIPS "Study our catalogs and get a sense of the kind of books we publish, so that you know whether your project is likely to be right for us."

⊘ QED PRESS/CYPRESS HOUSE

Cypress House, 155 Cypress St., Fort Bragg CA 95437. (800)773-7782. **Fax:** (707)964-7531. **E-mail:** joeshaw@cypresshouse.com. **Website:** www.cypresshouse.com. **Contact:** Joe Shaw, editor. Estab. 1985. **Pays royalties of 7-12% and 25 author's copies.** Publishes book 1 year after acceptance. Responds to queries and mss in 1 month. Order sample books through website.

POETRY QED Press publishes "clear, clean, intelligent, and moving work." Wants "concrete, personal, and spare writing. No florid rhymed verse." Publishes no more than 1 poetry book/year. Books are usually about 96 pages (75-80 poems), digest-sized, offset-printed, perfect-bound, with full-color cover. Also offers book packaging, and promotion and marketing services to start-up publishers. We prefer to see 6 representative poems." Considers simultaneous submissions. Cover letter and SASE for return of materials are required.

◗ QED PUBLISHING

The Quarto Group, 226 City Rd., London EC1V 2TT, United Kingdom. +44 (0)20 7812 8633. **Fax:** +44 (0)20 7253 4370. **E-mail:** zetad@quarto.com. **Website:** www.quarto.com. **Contact:** Zeta Davies, associate publisher. Estab. 2003. **Publishes 70 titles/year.**

NONFICTION Picture books: animal, arts/crafts, biography, geography, reference, science. Young readers: activity books, animal, arts/crafts, biography, geography, reference, science. Middle readers: activity books, animal, arts/crafts, biography, geography, science. Average word length: picture books—500; young readers—3,000; middle readers—3,500. Query.

FICTION Average word length: picture books—500; young readers—3,000; middle readers—3,500. Query.

TIPS "Be persistent."

QUEST BOOKS

Imprint of Theosophical Publishing House, 306 W. Geneva Rd., P.O. Box 270, Wheaton IL 60187. **E-mail:** submissions@questbooks.net. **Website:** www.questbooks.net. **Contact:** Richard Smoley, editor. Idarmis Rodriguez, associate editor. Estab. 1965. Publishes hardcover and trade paperback originals and reprints. **Publishes 10 titles/year. 150 mss received/year; 350 queries received/year. 20% of books from first-time authors. 80% from unagented writers. Pays royalty on retail price. Pays varying advance.** Publishes book 1 year after acceptance. Accepts simultaneous submissions. Responds in 2 months to queries, proposals, and mss. Catalog available free. Guidelines available online at: www. questbooks.net/aboutquest. cfm#submission.

➣ "Quest Books is the imprint of the Theosophical Publishing House, the publishing arm of the Theosophical Society in America. Since 1965, Quest books has sold millions of books by leading cultural thinkers on such increasingly popular subjects as transpersonal psychology, comparative religion, deep ecology, spiritual growth, the development of creativity, and alternative health practices."

NONFICTION Subjects include philosophy, psychology, religion, spirituality., New Age, astrology/psychic. Our speciality is high-quality spiritual nonfiction with a self-help aspect. Great writing is a must. We seldom publish `personal spiritual awakening' stories. No submissions accepted that do not fit the needs outlined above. No fiction, poetry, children's books, or any literature based on channeling or personal psychic impressions. Submit proposal package, including outline, 1 sample chapter. Prefer online submissions; attachments must be sent as a single file in Microsoft Word, Rich Text, or PDF formats. Reviews artwork/photos. Hard copies of mss. and artwork will not be returned. Reviews artwork/photos. Writers should send photocopies or transparencies, but note that none will be returned.

⊘ QUITE SPECIFIC MEDIA GROUP, LTD.

7373 Pyramid Place, Hollywood CA 90046. (323)851-5797. **Fax:** (323)851-5798. **E-mail:** info@quitespecificmedia.com. **Website:** www.quitespecificmedia.com.

Contact: Ralph Pine, editor-in-chief. Estab. 1967. Publishes hardcover originals, trade paperback originals and reprints. **Publishes 12 titles/year. 300 queries received/year. 100 mss received/year. 75% of books from first-time authors. 85% from unagented writers. Pays royalty on wholesale price. Pays varies advance.** Publishes book 18 months after acceptance. Accepts simultaneous submissions. Responds to queries. Catalog online. Guidelines available free.

➣ "Quite Specific Media Group is an umbrella company of 5 imprints specializing in costume and fashion, theater and design."

NONFICTION Subjects include fashion, film, cinema, stage, history, literary criticism, translation. Accepts nonfiction and technical works in translations also. For and about performing arts theory and practice: acting, directing; voice, speech, movement; makeup, masks, wits; costumes, sets, lighting, sound; design and execution; technical theater, stagecraft, equipment; stage management; producing; arts management, all varieties; business and legal aspects; film, radio, television, cable, video; theory, criticism, reference; theater and performance history; costume and fashion. Query by e-mail please. Reviews artwork/photos.

QUIXOTE PRESS

3544 Blakslee St., Wever IA 52658. (800)571-2665. **Fax:** (319)372-7485. **Website:** www.heartsntummies.com. **Contact:** Bruce Carlson.

☺ Quixote Press specializes in humorous and/or regional folklore and special-interest cookbooks. Publishes trade paperback originals and reprints. Website: www.heartsntummies.com. Published many debut authors within the last year. Needs humor, short story collections. Query with SASE. Accepts simultaneous submissions. Pays 10% royalty on wholesale price. Publishes ms 1 year after acceptance.

TIPS "Carefully consider marketing considerations. Audience is women in gift shops, on farm sites, direct retail outlets, wineries, outdoor sport shops, etc. Contact us at *you idea* stage, not complete ms stage. Be receptive to design input by us."

☻ RADCLIFFE PUBLISHING LTD

70 Alston Dr., Bradwell Abbey, Milton Keynes MK13 9HG, United Kingdom. (44)(0)1908-326-941. **Fax:** (44)(0)-1908-326-960. **E-mail:** contact.us@radcliffe-publishing.com. **Website:** www.radcliffe-oxford.

com. **Contact:** Andrew Box, managing editor; Gillian Nineham, editorial director. Estab. 1987. **Publishes 90 or fewer titles/year. Pays royalty.** Guidelines available via e-mail.

RAGGED SKY PRESS

P.O. Box 312, Annandale NJ 08801. **E-mail:** info@raggedsky.com. **Website:** www.raggedsky.com. Publisher: Ellen Foos. Managing Editor: Vasiliki Katsarou. Editor: Arlene Weiner.

Produces books of poetry and inspired prose. Ragged Sky is a small, highly selective cooperative press. "We work with our authors closely." Learn more online.

RAINBOW PUBLISHERS

P.O. Box 261129, San Diego CA 92196. (858)277-1167. **E-mail:** editor@rainbowpublishers.com. **Website:** www.rainbowpublishers.com; www.legacypresskids.com. Estab. 1979. **For authors work purchased outright (range: $500 and up).** Accepts simultaneous submissions. Responds to queries in 6 weeks; mss in 3 months.

"Our mission is to publish Bible-based, teacher resource materials that contribute to and inspire spiritual growth and development in kids ages 2-12."

NONFICTION Young readers, middle readers, young adult/teens: activity books, arts/crafts, how-to, reference, religion.

TIPS "Our Rainbow imprint publishes reproducible books for teachers of children in Christian ministries, including crafts, activities, games and puzzles. Our Legacy imprint publishes titles for children such as devotionals, fiction and Christian living. Please write for guidelines and study the market before submitting material."

RAINCOAST BOOK DISTRIBUTION, LTD.

2440 Viking Way, Richmond BC V6V 1N2, Canada. (604)448-7100. **Fax:** (604)270-7161. **E-mail:** info@raincoast.com. **Website:** www.raincoast.com. Publishes hardcover and trade paperback originals and reprints. **Publishes 60 titles/year. 3,000 queries received/year. 10% of books from first-time authors. 40% from unagented writers. Pays 8-12% royalty on retail price. Pays $1,000-6,000 advance.** Publishes book within 2 years of acceptance. after acceptance of ms. Catalog for #10 SASE.

NONFICTION Subjects include animals, art, architecture, ethnic, history, nature, environment, photography, recreation, regional, sports, travel. *No unsolicited mss.* Query with SASE.

FICTION Subjects include literary, short story collections, young adult. *No unsolicited mss.*

RAIN TOWN PRESS

1111 E. Burnside St. #309, Portland OR 97214. (503)962-9612. **E-mail:** submissions@raintownpress.com. **Website:** www.raintownpress.com. **Contact:** Misty V'Marie, acquisitions editor; Ellery Harvey, art director. Estab. 2009. **Publishes 1-4 middle readers; 1-4 young adult titles/year. 100% of books from first-time authors. Pays 8-15% royalty on net sales. Does not pay advance.** Publishes book 1 year after acceptance. Accepts simultaneous submissions. Responds to queries and mss in 1-6 months. Catalog available on website. Imprints included in a single catalog. Guidelines available on website for writers, artists, and photographers.

NONFICTION Subjects include animals, contemporary culture, environment, health, history, multicultural, nature, sports. Middle Readers/YA/Teens: biography, concept, graphic novels, hi-lo, how-to. Query. Submit outline/synopsis and 2 sample chapters. See online submission guide for detailed instructions.

FICTION Subjects include fantasy, folktales, graphic novels, hi-lo, problem novels, science fiction, special needs., concept. Middle Readers/YA/Teens: Wants adventure, animal, contemporary, fantasy, folktales, graphic novels, health, hi-lo, history, humor, multicultural, nature/environment, problem novels, sci-fi, special needs, sports. Catalog available on website. Query. Submit complete ms. See online submission guide for detailed instructions.

TIPS "The middle grade and YA markets have sometimes very stringent conventions for subject matter, theme, etc. It's most helpful if an author knows his/her genre inside and out. Read, read, read books that have successfully been published for your genre. This will ultimately make your writing more marketable. Also, follow a publisher's submission guidelines to a tee. We try to set writers up for success. Send us what we're looking for."

RANDOM HOUSE AUDIO PUBLISHING GROUP

Subsidiary of Random House, Inc., 1745 Broadway, New York NY 10019. (212)782-9720. **Fax:** (212)782-9600. **Website:** www.randomhouse.com.

8—• "Audio publishing for adults and children, offering titles in both abridged and unabridged formats on cassettes, compact discs, and by digital delivery."

Ⓐ⊘ RANDOM HOUSE CHILDREN'S BOOKS

Random House, Inc., 1745 Broadway, New York NY 10019. (212)782-9000. **Website:** www.randomhouse. com. Estab. 1925.

◑ Submit mss through a literary agent.

FICTION "Random House publishes a select list of first chapter books and novels, with an emphasis on fantasy and historical fiction." Chapter books, middle-grade readers, young adult. *Does not accept unsolicited mss.*

TIPS "We look for original, unique stories. Do something that hasn't been done before."

Ⓐ RANDOM HOUSE-GOLDEN BOOKS FOR YOUNG READERS GROUP

1745 Broadway, New York NY 10019. **Contact:** Kate Klimo, publisher/vice president; Cathy Goldsmith, associate publisher/art director. Estab. 1935. **2% of books from first-time authors. Pays authors in royalties; sometimes buys mss outright.** Catalog free on request.

◑ Random House-Golden Books does not accept unsolicited manuscripts, only agented material. They reserve the right not to return unsolicited material.

Ⓐ⊘ RANDOM HOUSE INFORMATION GROUP

Division of Random House, Inc., 1745 Broadway, New York NY 10019. (212)782-9000. **Website:** www.randomhouse.com.

Ⓐ⊘ RANDOM HOUSE LARGE PRINT

Division of Random House, Inc., 1745 Broadway, New York NY 10019. (212)782-9720. **Fax:** (212)782-9600. **Website:** www.randomhouse.com. Estab. 1990. **Publishes 60 titles/year.**

⊜ RANSOM PUBLISHING

Radley House, 8 St. Cross Road, Winchester Hampshire SO23 9HXUK, United Kingdom. +44 (0) 01962 862307. **Fax:** +44 (0) 05601 148881. **E-mail:** ransom@ransom.co.uk. **Website:** www.ransom.co.uk. **Contact:** Jenny Ertle, editor. Estab. 1995. Publishes paperback originals. **Pays 10% royalty on net re-**

ceipts. Responds to mss in 3-4 weeks. Ms guidelines by e-mail.

8—• Independent UK publisher with distribution in English speaking markets throughout the world. Specializes in books for reluctant and struggling readers. Our high quality, visually stimulating, age appropriate material has achieved wide acclaim for its ability to engage and motivate those who either can't or won't read. One of the few English language publishers to publish books with very high interest age and very low reading age. Has a developing list of children's books for home and school use. Specializes in phonics and general reading programs.

FICTION Easy reading for young adults. Books for reluctant and struggling readers. Accepts unsolicited mss. Query with SASE or submit outline/proposal. Prefers queries by e-mail. Include estimated word count, brief bio, list of publishing credits.

RAVEN TREE PRESS

A Division of Delta Publishing Company, 1400 Miller Pkwy., McHenry IL 60050. (800)323-8270. **Fax:** (800)909-9901. **E-mail:** raven@deltapublishing.com; raven@raventreepress.com; acquisitions@deltapublishing.com. **Website:** www.raventreepress.com. Estab. 2000. Publishes hardcover and trade paperback originals. **Publishes 8-10 titles/year. 1,500 mss received/year. 50% of books from first-time authors. 90% from unagented writers. Pays royalty. Pays variable advance.** Publishes book 2 years after acceptance of ms. Accepts simultaneous submissions. Responds in 2 months to mss. Catalog and guidelines online.

8—• "We publish entertaining and educational picture books in a variety of formats. Bilingual (English/Spanish), English-only, Spanish-only, and wordless editions.

NONFICTION "Submission Guidelines online. Do not query or send mss without first checking submission guidelines on our website for most current information."

TIPS "Submit only based on guidelines. No e-mail or snail mail queries please. Word count is a definite issue, since we are bilingual."

RAZORBILL

Penguin Group, 345 Hudson St., New York NY 10014. (212)414-3448. **Fax:** (212)414-3343. **E-mail:** laura. schechter@us.penguingroup.com; Ben.Schrank@ us.penguingroup.com. **Website:** www.razorbillbooks.

com. **Contact:** Gillian Levinson, assistant edtor; Jessica Rothenberg, editor; Brianne Mulligan, editor. Estab. 2003. **Publishes 30 titles/year. Offers advance against royalties.** Publishes book 1-2 after acceptance. Responds to queries/mss in 1-3 months.

8→ "This division of Penguin Young Readers is looking for the best and the most original of commercial contemporary fiction titles for middle grade and YA readers. A select quantity of nonfiction titles will also be considered."

NONFICTION Middle readers and young adults/teens: concept. Submit outline/synopsis and 3 sample chapters along with query and SASE.

FICTION Middle Readers: adventure, contemporary, graphic novels, fantasy, humor, problem novels. Young adults/teens: adventure, contemporary, fantasy, graphic novels, humor, multicultural, suspense, paranormal, science fiction, dystopian, literary, romance. Average word length: middle readers—40,000; young adult—60,000. Submit outline/synopsis and 3 sample chapters along with query and SASE.

TIPS "New writers will have the best chance of acceptance and publication with original, contemporary material that boasts a distinctive voice and well-articulated world. Check out www.razorbillbooks.com to get a better idea of what we're looking for."

REALITY STREET

63 All Saints St., Hastings, E. Sussex TN34 3BN, United Kingdom. +44(0)1424 431271. **E-mail:** info@realitystreet.co.uk. **Website:** freespace.virgin.net/reality.street. **Contact:** Ken Edwards, editor/publisher. Estab. 1993. Publishes trade paperback originals. **Publishes 3-4 titles/year.** Catalog online.

8→ Reality Street is based in Hastings, UK, publishing new and innovative writing in English and in translation from other languages. Some established writers whose books they have published are Nicole Brossard, Allen Fisher, Barbara Guest, Fanny Howe, Denise Riley, Peter Riley, and Maurice Scully.

FICTION Subjects include poetry, poetry in translation, translation, experimental fiction, anthologies.

TIPS "Unsolicited submissions discouraged—please acquaint yourself with the output of the press, preferably by buying our books, before sending us any proposals."

○ RECLINER BOOKS

P.O. Box 64128, Calgary AB T2K 1A9, Canada. (403)668-9746. **E-mail:** info@reclinerbooks.com; submission@reclinerbooks.com. **Website:** www.reclinerbooks.com. **Contact:** Dustin Smith, editor (fiction, literary nonfiction). Estab. 2009. Publishes trade paperback originals. **Publishes 4-8 titles/year. 50% of books from first-time authors. 100% from unagented writers. Pays 10-15% royalty on retail price. Pays $250-500 advance.** Publishes book 1 year after acceptance. Accepts simultaneous submissions. Responds in 3 months on queries and proposals; 6 months on mss. Guidelines online.

NONFICTION Subjects include animals, anthropology, business, creative nonfiction, economics, environment, gay, health, history, language, law, lesbian, literature, medicine, memoirs, money, nature, politics, religion, science, sex, social sciences, sociology, womens issues, womens studies, world affairs, literary nonfiction. "We are currently seeking literary nonfiction titles only, the more literary the better." Submit proposal package, including: outline, 3 sample chapters; submit completed mss. Reviews artwork/photos as part of ms package; send photocopies.

FICTION Subjects include adventure, contemporary, experimental, feminist, gay, historical, humor, lesbian, literary, mainstream, military, multicultural, religious. "We are not currently accepting anything targeted at children, young adults, or science fiction readers." Submit proposal package, including: synopsis, 3 sample chapters, completed mss.

TIPS "Our audience is 24 years and older, 70% female, 30% male, 90% Canadian."

○ RED DEER PRESS

195 Allstate Pkwy., Markham ON L3R 4TB, Canada. (905)477-9700. **Fax:** (905)477-9179. **E-mail:** rdp@reddeerpress.com; dionne@reddeerpress.com; val@reddeerpress.com. **Website:** www.reddeerpress.com. **Contact:** Richard Dionne, publisher. Estab. 1975. **Pays 8-10% royalty.** Publishes book 18 months after acceptance. Accepts simultaneous submissions. Responds to queries in 6 months. Catalog for 9×12 SASE.

FICTION Publishes young adult, adult non-fiction, science fiction, fantasy, and paperback originals "focusing on books by, about, or of interest to Canadians." Books: offset paper; offset printing; hardcover/perfect-bound. Average print order: 5,000. First novel print order: 2,500. Distributes titles in Canada and the US, the UK, Australia and New Zealand. Young adult (juvenile and early reader), contemporary. No romance or horror. Accepts unsolicited mss. Query with SASE. No submissions on disk.

TIPS "We're very interested in young adult and children's fiction from Canadian writers with a proven track record (either published books or widely published in established magazines or journals) and for manuscripts with regional themes and/or a distinctive voice. We publish Canadian authors exclusively."

⊘ RED HEN PRESS

P.O. Box 3537, Granada Hills CA 91394. (818)831-0649. **Fax:** (818)831-6659. **E-mail:** redhenpressbooks.com. **Website:** www.redhen.org. **Contact:** Mark E. Cull, publisher/editor (fiction). Estab. 1993. Publishes trade paperback originals. **Publishes 22 titles/year. 2,000 queries received/year. 500 mss received/year. 10% of books from first-time authors. 90% from unagented writers.** Publishes book 1 year after acceptance. Accepts simultaneous submissions. Responds in 1 month to queries; 2 months to proposals. Catalog available free. Guidelines online.

8—✐ "*Red Hen Press is not currently accepting unsolicited material.* At this time, the best opportunity to be published by Red Hen is by entering one of our contests. Please find more information in our award submission guidelines."

NONFICTION Subjects include ethnic, gay, lesbian, language, literature, memoirs, women's issues/studies., political/social interest. Query with SASE. Reviews artwork/photos. Send photocopies.

FICTION Subjects include ethnic, experimental, feminist, gay, lesbian, historical, literary, mainstream, contemporary, poetry, poetry in translation, short story collections. Ethnic, experimental, feminist, gay/lesbian, historical, literary, mainstream/contemporary, short story collections. "We prefer high-quality literary fiction." Query with SASE.

POETRY Query and submit 5 sample poems. *Red Hen Press is not currently accepting unsolicited material.* At this time, the best opportunity to be published by Red Hen is by entering one of our contests. Please find more information in our award submission guidelines.

TIPS "Audience reads poetry, literary fiction, intelligent nonfiction. If you have an agent, we may be too small since we don't pay advances. Write well. Send queries first. Be willing to help promote your own book."

⊘ RED MOON PRESS

P.O. Box 2461, Winchester VA 22604. (540)722-2156. **E-mail:** jim.kacian@redmoonpress.com. **Website:** www.redmoonpress.com. **Contact:** Jim Kacian, editor/publisher. Estab. 1993.

8—✐ Red Moon Press "is the largest and most prestigious publisher of English-language haiku and related work in the world." Publishes 6-8 volumes/year, usually 3-5 anthologies and individual collections of English-language haiku, as well as 1-3 books of essays, translations, or criticism of haiku. Under other imprints, the press also publishes chapbooks of various sizes and formats.

POETRY Query with book theme and information, and 30-40 poems or draft of first chapter. Responds to queries in 2 weeks, to mss (if invited) in 3 months. "Each contract separately negotiated."

RED ROCK PRESS

331 W. 57th St., Suite 175, New York NY 10019. **Fax:** (212)362-6216. **E-mail:** info@redrockpress.com. **Website:** www.redrockpress.com. **Contact:** Ilene Barth. Estab. 1998. Publishes hardcover and trade paperback originals. **Publishes 6-8 titles/year. Pays royalty on wholesale price. The amount of the advance offered depends on the project.** Responds in 3-4 months to queries. Catalog for #10 SASE.

NONFICTION Subjects include creative nonfiction. All of our books are pegged to gift-giving holidays.

RED SAGE PUBLISHING, INC.

P.O. Box 4844, Seminole FL 33775. (727)391-3847. **E-mail:** submissions@eredsage.com. **Website:** www.eredsage.com. **Contact:** Alexandria Kendall, publisher; Theresa Stevens, managing editor. Estab. 1995. **Publishes 4 titles/year. 50% of books from first-time authors. Pays advance.** Guidelines online.

8—✐ Publishes books of romance fiction, written for the adventurous woman.

FICTION Submission guidelines online at http://www.eredsage.com/store/RedSageSubmissionGuidelines_HowToSendSubmission.html

○ RED TUQUE BOOKS, INC.

477 Martin St., Unit #6, Penticton BC V2A 5L2, Canada. (778)476-5750. **Fax:** (778)476-5651. **Website:** www.redtuquebooks.ca. **Contact:** David Korinetz, executive editor. **Pays 5-7% royalties on net sales. Pays**

$250 advance. Publishes book 1 year after acceptance. Responds in 3 weeks.

FICTION Adventure, short story collections, young adult and teen (specifically adventure and science fiction), graphic novels, and fantasy (space fantasy, sword and sorcery). Submit a query letter and first five pages. Include total word count. A one-page synopsis is optional. Accepts queries by e-mail and mail. SASE for reply only.

TIPS "Well-plotted, character-driven stories, preferably with happy endings, will have the best chance of being accepted. Keep in mind that authors who like to begin sentences with "and, or, and but" are less likely to be considered. Don't send anything gruesome or overly explicit; tell us a good story, but think PG."

ROBERT D. REED PUBLISHERS

P.O. Box 1992, Bandon OR 97411. (541)347-9882. **Fax:** (541)347-9883. **Website:** www.rdrpublishers. com. **Contact:** Cleone L. Reed; Kate Rakini, editor. Estab. 1991. Publishes hardcover and trade paperback originals. **Publishes 25-35 titles/year. 500 ms received/year; 2,000 queries received/year. 75% of books from first-time authors. 90% from unagented writers. Pays 12-17% royalty on wholesale price.** Publishes book 5 months after acceptance. Accepts simultaneous submissions. Responds in 1 month to queries, proposals, and mss. Catalog available online. Guidelines available online and by e-mail.

NONFICTION Subjects include alternative lifestyles, business, economics, child guidance, communications, contemporary contemporary culture, counseling, career guidance,education, ethnic, gay, lesbian, nonfiction, health, medicine, history, language, literature, memoirs, military, war, money, finance, multicultural, New Age, philosophy, psychology, sex, social sciences, spirituality, travel, womens issues, womens studies, world affairs. "We want titles that have a large audience with at least 10-year sales potential, and author's workshop, speaking and seminar participation. We like titles that are part of author's career." Submit proposal package with outline. Submit complete ms only upon request. Reviews artwork.

FICTION Subjects include adventure, fantasy, feminist, historical, humor, literary, military, war, multicultural, mystery, romance, sciencefiction, spiritual, western. "We look for high quality work—from authors who will work hard to display their work and travel, selling books." Query with SASE or e-mail.

Submit proposal package. Submit complete ms by request only.

TIPS "Target trade sales and sales to corporations, organizations and groups. Read over our website and see what we have done."

REFERENCE SERVICE PRESS

5000 Windplay Dr., Suite 4, El Dorado Hills CA 95762. (916)939-9620. **Fax:** (916)939-9626. **E-mail:** info@rsp-funding.com. **Website:** www.rspfunding.com. **Contact:** Stuart Hauser, acquisitions editor. Estab. 1977. Publishes hardcover originals. **Publishes 10-20 titles/year. 100% from unagented writers. Pays 10% royalty. Pays advance.** Publishes book 6 months after acceptance. Accepts simultaneous submissions. Responds in 2 months to queries. Catalog for #10 SASE.

"Reference Service Press focuses on the development and publication of financial aid resources in any format (print, electronic, e-book, etc.). We are interested in financial aid publications aimed at specific groups (e.g., minorities, women, veterans, the disabled, undergraduates majoring in specific subject areas, specific types of financial aid, etc.)."

NONFICTION Subjects include agriculture, art, architecture, business, economics, education, ethnic, health, medicine, history, religion, science, sociology, women's issues/studies., disabled. Submit outline, sample chapters.

TIPS "Our audience consists of librarians, counselors, researchers, students, re-entry women, scholars, and other fundseekers."

RENAISSANCE HOUSE

465 Westview Ave., Englewood NJ 07631. (800)547-5113. **E-mail:** raquel@renaissancehouse.net. **Website:** www.renaissancehouse.net. Publishes book 1 year after acceptance. Accepts simultaneous submissions. Responds to queries/mss in 2 months.

FICTION Subjects include fantasy, juvenile, picture books, legends, fables. Picture books: animal, folktales, multicultural. Young readers: animal, anthology, folktales, multicultural. Middle readers, young adult/teens: anthology, folktales, multicultural, nature/environment.

REPUBLIC OF TEXAS PRESS

Imprint of Taylor Trade Publishing, and part of Rowman and Littlefield Publishing Group, 5360 Manhattan Circle, #101, Boulder CO 80303. (303)543-7835, ext. 318. **E-mail:** tradeeditorial@rowman.com. **Web-**

site: www.rlpgtrade.com. **Contact:** Rick Rinehart, editorial director. Publishes trade and paperback originals. **Publishes 10-15 titles/year. 95% from unagented writers. Pays industry-standard royalty on net receipts. Pays small advance.** Publishes book 1 year after acceptance. Accepts simultaneous submissions. Responds in 2 months to queries.

NONFICTION "Republic of Texas Press specializes in Texas history and general Texana nonfiction, including ethnic, history, nature/environment, regional, sports, travel, women's issues/studies, Old West, Texas military, and ghost accounts." Proposals should be limited to a query letter; an e-mail will generate the quickest response. If querying by e-mail, please note in the memo box "book proposal." Send no attachments unless requested. What we look for at this stage is suitability of the proposed book to our publishing program (see categories) as well as the author's unique qualifications for writing his or her book.

TIPS "Do not submit any original materials, as they will not be returned. Our market is adult."

RIO NUEVO PUBLISHERS

Imprint of Treasure Chest Books, P.O. Box 5250, Tucson AZ 85703. **Fax:** (520)624-5888. **E-mail:** info@rionuevo.com. **Website:** www.rionuevo.com. Estab. 1975. Publishes hardcover and trade paperback originals and reprints. **Publishes 12-20 titles/year. 20 queries received/year. 10 mss received/year. 30% of books from first-time authors. 100% from unagented writers. Pays $1,000-4,000 advance.** Publishes book 1 year after acceptance. Accepts simultaneous submissions. Responds in 6 months to queries/proposals/mss. Catalog online. Guidelines available via e-mail.

NONFICTION Subjects include animals, cooking, foods, nutrition, gardening, history, nature, environment, regional, religion, spirituality, travel. "We cover the Southwest but prefer titles that are not too narrow in their focus. We want our books to be of broad enough interest that people from other places will also want to read them." Query with SASE. Submit proposal package, outline, 2 sample chapters. Reviews artwork/photos. Send photocopies.

TIPS "We have a general audience of intelligent people interested in the Southwest-nature, history, culture. Many of our books are sold in gift shops throughout the region; we are also distributed nationally by W.W. Norton."

RIVER CITY PUBLISHING

1719 Mulberry St., Montgomery AL 36106. **E-mail:** jgilbert@rivercitypublishing.com. **Website:** www.rivercitypublishing.com. **Contact:** Jim Gilbert, editor. Estab. 1989. Publishes hardcover and trade paperback originals. **Publishes 6 titles/year. Pays 10-15% royalty on retail price. Pays $500-5,000 advance.** Publishes book 1 year after acceptance. Accepts simultaneous submissions. Responds to mss in 9 months.

NONFICTION We do not publish self-help, how-to, business, medicine, religion, education, or psychology. Accepts unsolicited submissions and submissions from unagented authors, as well as those from established and agented writers. Submit 5 consecutive sample chapters or entire ms for review. "Please include a short biography that highlights any previous writing and publishing experience, sales opportunities the author could provide, ideas for marketing the book, and why you think the work would be appropriate for River City." Send appropriate-sized SASE or IRC, "otherwise, the material will be recycled." Also accepts queries by e-mail at: jgilbert@rivercitypublishing.com. "Please include your electronic query letter as inline text and not an as attachment; we do not open unsolicited attachments of any kind. Please do not include sample chapters or your entire manuscript as inline text. We do not field or accept queries by telephone. Please wait at least 3 months before contacting us about your submission." No multiple submissions. Rarely comments on rejected mss.

FICTION Literary fiction, narrative nonfiction, regional (southern), short story collections. No poetry, memoir, or children's books. See nonfiction submission guidelines.

TIPS "Only send your best work after you have received outside opinions. From approximately 1,000 submissions each year, we publish no more than 8 books and few of those come from unsolicited material. Competition is fierce, so follow the guidelines exactly. All first-time novelists should submit their work to the Fred Bonnie Award contest."

◐ ⊘ RIVERHEAD BOOKS

Penguin Putnam, 375 Hudson Street, Office #4079, New York NY 10014. **E-mail:** ecommerce@us.penguingroup.com; riverhead.web@us.penguingroup.com. **Website:** www.riverheadbooks.com. **Contact:** Megan Lynch, senior editor.

FICTION Literary, mainstream, contemporary. *Submit through agent only. No unsolicited mss.*

🅐 ROARING BROOK PRESS

175 Fifth Ave., New York NY 10010. (646)307-5151. **E-mail:** david.langva@roaringbrookpress.com. **E-mail:** press.inquiries@macmillanusa.com. **Website:** http://us.macmillan.com/RoaringBrook.aspx. **Contact:** David Langva. Estab. 2000. **Pays authors royalty based on retail price.**

NONFICTION Picture books, young readers, middle readers, young adults: adventure, animal, contemporary, fantasy, history, humor, multicultural, nature/environment, poetry, religion, science fiction, sports, suspense/mystery. *Not accepting unsolicited mss or queries.*

FICTION Picture books, young readers, middle readers, young adults: adventure, animal, contemporary, fantasy, history, humor, multicultural, nature/environment, poetry, religion, science fiction, sports, suspense/mystery. *Not accepting unsolicited mss or queries.*

TIPS "You should find a reputable agent and have him/her submit your work."

🅒 ROCKY MOUNTAIN BOOKS

406-13th Ave. NE, Calgary AB T2E 1C2, Canada. (403)249-9490. **Fax:** (403)249-2968. **E-mail:** rmb@heritagehouse.ca. **Website:** www.rmbooks.com. **Contact:** Fraser Seely, publisher. Publishes trade paperback and hardcover books. **Rarely offers advance.** Accepts simultaneous submissions. Responds in 2-6 months to queries. Catalog and guidelines online.

🔑 "RMB is a dynamic book publisher located in western Canada. We specialize in quality nonfiction on the outdoors, travel, environment, social & cultural issues."

NONFICTION Subjects include nonfiction outdoors, environment, travel & tourism and international mountain culture/history. Our main area of publishing is outdoor recreation guides to Western and Northern Canada.

🅒 RONSDALE PRESS

3350 W. 21st Ave., Vancouver BC V6S 1G7, Canada. (604)738-4688. **Fax:** (604)731-4548. **E-mail:** ronsdale@shaw.ca. **Website:** http://ronsdalepress.com. **Contact:** Ronald B. Hatch, director (fiction, poetry, social commentary); Veronica Hatch, managing director (children's literature). Estab. 1988. Publishes trade paperback originals. **Publishes 12 titles/year. 300 queries received/year. 800 mss received/year. 40% of books from first-time authors. 95% from unagented writers. Pays 10% royalty on retail price.** Publishes book 1 year after acceptance. Accepts simultaneous submissions. Responds to queries in 2 weeks; mss in 2 months. Catalog for #10 SASE. Guidelines online.

🔑 "Ronsdale Press is a Canadian literary publishing house that publishes 12 books each year, three of which are children's titles. Of particular interest are books involving children exploring and discovering new aspects of Canadian history."

NONFICTION Subjects include history, Canadian, language, literature, nature, environment, regional. Middle readers, young adults: animal, biography, history, multicultural, social issues. Average word length: young readers—90; middle readers-90. "We publish a number of books for children and young adults in the age 8 to 15 range. We are especially interested in YA historical novels. **We regret that we can no longer publish picture books.**" Submit complete ms.

FICTION Subjects include literary, short story collections., novels. Young adults: Canadian novels. Average word length: middle readers and young adults—50,000. Submit complete ms.

POETRY Poets should have published some poems in magazines/journals and should be well-read in contemporary masters. Submit complete ms.

TIPS "Ronsdale Press is a literary publishing house, based in Vancouver, and dedicated to publishing books from across Canada, books that give Canadians new insights into themselves and their country. We aim to publish the best Canadian writers."

ROSE ALLEY PRESS

4203 Brooklyn Ave. NE, #103A, Seattle WA 98105. (206)633-2725. **E-mail:** rosealleypress@juno.com. **Website:** www.rosealleypress.com. **Contact:** David Horowitz. Estab. 1995.

🔑 Rose Alley Press was founded by David D. Horowitz in November 1995. It was named for the London street where, on December 18th, 1679, poet and playwright John Dryden was brutally beaten by three thugs. Evidence suggests that an aristocrat who mistakenly attributed a satire's authorship to Dryden hired the assailants. Undaunted, Dryden continued writing, even more boldly than before the assault. Inspired by such perseverance, David established Rose Alley Press, which publishes rhymed and metered poetry, cultural commentary, and an annually updated booklet about writing and publication.

● ROTOVISION

Sheridan House, 114 Western Rd., Hove East Sussex BN3 IDD, England. (44)(127)371-6010. **Fax:** (44)(127)372-7269. **E-mail:** isheetam@rotovision.com. **Website:** www.rotovision.com. **Contact:** Isheeta Mustafi. Publishes hardcover and trade paperback originals, and trade paperback reprints. Accepts simultaneous submissions. Catalog available free. Guidelines available free.

NONFICTION Subjects include art, creative nonfiction, design, fashion, graphic design, photography. "Our books are aimed at keen amateurs and professionals who want to improve their skills." Submit an e-mail with "Book Proposal" in the subject line. Reviews artwork/photos. Send transparencies and PDFs.

TIPS "Our audience includes professionals, keen amateurs, and students of visual arts including graphic design, general design, advertising, and photography. Make your approach international in scope. Content not to be less than 35% US."

ROWMAN & LITTLEFIELD PUBLISHING GROUP

4501 Forbes Blvd., Suite 200, Lanham MD 20706. (301)459-3366. **Fax:** (301)429-5748. **E-mail:** jsisk@rowmanlittlefield.com. **Website:** www.rowmanlittlefield.com. **Contact:** Jonathan Sisk, vice president/executive editor (American government, public policy, political theory); Susan McEachern, vice president/editorial director (international studies); Sarah Stanton and Patti Davis, acquisitions editors. Estab. 1949. Publishes hardcover and trade paperback originals and reprints. **Pays advance.** Catalog online. Guidelines online.

⚷ "We are an independent press devoted to publishing scholarly books in the best tradition of university presses; innovative, thought-provoking texts for college courses; and crossover trade books intended to convey scholarly trends to an educated readership. Our approach emphasizes substance and quality of thought over ephemeral trends. We offer a forum for responsible voices representing the diversity of opinion on college campuses, and take special pride in several series designed to provide students with the pros and cons of hotly contested issues."

NONFICTION "Rowman & Littlefield is seeking proposals in the serious non-fiction areas of history, politics, current events, religion, sociology, philosophy, communication and education. All proposal inquiries can be e-mailed or mailed to the respective acquisitions editor listed on the contacts page on our website."

RUKA PRESS

P.O. Box 1409, Washington DC 20013. **E-mail:** contact@rukapress.com; submissions@rukapress.com. **Website:** www.rukapress.com. **Contact:** Daniel Kohan, owner. Estab. 2010. Publishes in trade paperback originals, electronic. **Publishes 2-4/year titles/year. Pays advance. Royalties are 10-25% on wholesale price.** Publishes book 9-12 months (between acceptance and publication). after acceptance of ms. Accepts simultaneous submissions. Responds in 1 month to queries, 1 month to proposals. Catalogue available online. Guidelines online.

⚷ "We publish nonfiction books with a strong environmental component for a general audience. We are looking for books that explain things, that make an argument, that demystify. We are interested in economics, science, nature, climate change, and sustainability. We like building charts and graphs, tables and timelines. Our politics are progressive, but our books need not be political."

NONFICTION Subjects include environment, nature, science. Submit proposal package, including outline, résumé, bio, or CV, and 1 sample chapter.

TIPS "We appeal to an audience of intelligent, educated readers with broad interests. Be sure to tell us why your proposal is unique, and why you are especially qualified to write this book. We are looking for originality and expertise."

SAFARI PRESS, INC.

15621 Chemical Lane, Building B, Huntington Beach CA 92649. (714)894-9080. **Fax:** (714)894-4949. **E-mail:** info@safaripress.com. **Website:** www.safaripress.com. **Contact:** Jacqueline Neufeld, editor. Estab. 1985. Publishes hardcover originals and reprints, and trade paperback reprints. **Publishes 25-30 titles/year. 70% of books from first-time authors. 80% from unagented writers. Pays 8-15% royalty on wholesale price.** Catalog for $1. Guidelines online.

💬 The editor notes that she receives many mss outside the areas of big-game hunting, wing-shooting, and sporting firearms, and these are always rejected.

NONFICTION "We discourage autobiographies, unless the life of the hunter or firearms maker has been exceptional. We routinely reject manuscripts along the lines of 'Me and my buddies went hunting for.. and a good time was had by all!" No outdoors topics (hiking, camping, canoeing, fishing, etc.) Query with SASE. Submit outline.

SAINT MARY'S PRESS

702 Terrace Heights, Winona MN 55987. (800)533-8095. **Fax:** (800)344-9225. **E-mail:** submissions@smp.org. **Website:** www.smp.org. Ms guidelines online or by e-mail.

NONFICTION Subjects include religion, prayers, spirituality. Titles for Catholic youth and their parents, teachers, and youth ministers. Query with SASE. Submit proposal package, outline, 1 sample chapter, SASE. Brief author biography.

TIPS "Request product catalog and/or do research online of Saint Mary Press book lists before submitting proposal."

⊕ SAKURA PUBLISHING & TECHNOLOGIES

P.O. Box 1681, Hermitage PA 16148. (330)360-5131. **E-mail:** skpublishing124@gmail.com. **Website:** www.sakura-publishing.com. **Contact:** Derek Vasconi, talent finder and CEO. Estab. 2010. Publishes hardcover, trade paperback, mass market paperback and electronic originals and reprints. **Publishes 10-12 titles/year. 90% of books from first-time authors. 99% from unagented writers. Pays royalty of 20-60% on wholesale price or retail price.** Publishes book 6 months after acceptance. Accepts simultaneous submissions. Responds in 1 month to queries, mss, proposals. Catalog available for #10 SASE. Guidelines available online or by e-mail.

NONFICTION Subjects include alternative lifestyles, Americana, animals, architecture, art, contemporary culture, creative nonfiction, entertainment, games, gay, history, hobbies, humanities, memoirs, military.

🌑 SALMON POETRY

Knockeven, Cliffs of Moher, County Clare, Ireland. 353(0)65 708 1941. **Fax:** 353(0)65 708 1941. **E-mail:** info@salmonpoetry.com. **E-mail:** jessie@salmonpoetry.com. **Website:** www.salmonpoetry.com. **Contact:** Jessie Lendennie, editor. Estab. 1981. Publishes mass market paperback originals.

POETRY "Salmon Press has become one of the most important publications in the Irish literary world, specialising in the promotion of new poets, particularly women poets. Established as an alternative voice. Walks tightrope between innovation and convention. Was a flagship for writers in the west of Ireland. Salmon has developed a cross-cultural, internatonal literary dialog, broadening Irish Literature and urging new perspectives on established traditions."

TIPS "If we are broad minded and willing to nurture the individual voice inherent in the work, the artist will emerge."

SALVO PRESS

E-mail: schmidt@salvopress.com; query@salvopress.com. **Website:** www.salvopress.com. **Contact:** Scott Schmidt, publisher. Estab. 1998. **75% from unagented writers. Pays 10% royalty.** Publishes book 9-12 months after acceptance. Responds in 5 minutes to 1 month to queries; 2 months to mss. Catalog and guidelines online.

FICTION, Adventure, literary, mystery (amateur sleuth, police procedural, private/hard-boiled), science fiction (hard science/technological), suspense, thriller/espionage. "We are a small press specializing in mystery, suspense, espionage and thriller fiction. Our press publishes in trade paperback and most e-book formats." Publishes hardcover, trade paperback originals and e-books in most formats. Books: 512×812; or 6×9 printing; perfect binding. **Published 6 debut authors within the last year.** Averages 6-12 fiction total titles/year, mostly fiction. "Our needs change, check our website." Query by e-mail only. Please place the word "Query" as the subject. Include estimated word count, brief bio, list of publishing credits, "and something to intrigue me so I ask for more."

SAMHAIN PUBLISHING, LTD

577 Mulberry St., Suite 1520, Macon GA 31201. (478)314-5144. **Fax:** (478)314-5148. **E-mail:** editor@samhainpublishing.com. **Website:** samhainpublishing.com. **Contact:** Laurie M. Rauch, executive editor. Estab. 2005. Publishes e-books and paperback originals. POD/offset printing; line illustrations. **Pays royalties 30-40% for e-books, average of 8% for trade paper, and author's copies (quantity varies).** Pub-

lishes book 18 months after acceptance. Responds in 4 months to queries and mss. Guidelines online.

FICTION Needs erotica and all genres and all heat levels of romance (contemporary, futuristic/time travel, gothic, historical, paranormal, regency period, romantic suspense, fantasy, action/adventure, etc.), as well as fantasy, urban fantasy or science fiction with strong romantic elements, with word counts between 12,000 and 120,000 words. "Samhain is now accepting submissions for our line of horror novels. We are actively seeking talented writers who can tell an exciting, dramatic and frightening story, and who are eager to promote their work and build their community of readers. We are looking for novels 'either supernatural or non-supernatural, contemporary or historical' that are original and compelling. Authors can be previously unpublished or established, agented or un-agented. Content can range from subtle and unsettling to gory and shocking. The writing is what counts." Accepts unsolicited mss. Query with outline/synopsis and either 3 sample chapters or the full ms. Accepts queries by e-mail only. Include estimated word count, brief bio, list of publishing credits, and "how the author is working to improve craft: association, critique groups, etc."

TIPS "Because we are an e-publisher first, we do not have to be as concerned with industry trends and can publish less popular genres of fiction if we believe the story and voice are good and will appeal to our customers. Please follow submission guidelines located on our website, include all requested information and proof your query/manuscript for errors prior to submission."

⊘ SAM'S DOT PUBLISHING

P.O. Box 782, Cedar Rapids IA 52406. **E-mail:** samsdot@samsdotpublishing.com. **Website:** www.samsdotpublishing.com. **Contact:** Tyree Campbell, managing editor. Estab. 2003. **Pays royalties of 12.5% minimum and 1-2 author's copies (out of a press run of 50-100).** Responds to queries in 2 weeks; mss in 4-6 weeks.

POETRY Sam's Dot Publishing prints collections of scifaiku, horror-ku, and minimalist poetry. Publishes 2-3 chapbooks/year and one anthology/year. Mss are selected through open submission. Chapbooks are 32 pages, offset-printed, saddle-stapled, with cardstock covers. Query first, with a few sample poems and a cover letter with brief bio and publication credits, up to 500 words. Chapbook mss may include previously published poems.

SANTA MONICA PRESS LLC

P.O. Box 850, Solana Beach CA 92075. (858)793-1890; (800)784-9553. **E-mail:** books@santamonicapress.com. **Website:** www.santamonicapress.com. Estab. 1994. Publishes hardcover and trade paperback originals. **Publishes 15 titles/year. 25% of books from first-time authors. 75% from unagented writers. Pays 4-10% royalty on wholesale price. Pays $500-2,500+ advance.** Publishes book 18 months after acceptance. Accepts simultaneous submissions. Responds in 1-2 months to proposals. Catalog for 9x12 SASE with $1.31 postage. Guidelines online.

⊶ "At Santa Monica Press, we're not afraid to cast a wide editorial net. Our eclectic list of lively and modern nonfiction titles includes books in such categories as popular culture, film history, photography, humor, biography, travel, and reference."

NONFICTION Subjects include Americana, architecture, art, contemporary culture, creative nonfiction, education, entertainment, film, games, humanities, language, literature, memoirs, regional, social sciences, sports, travel., Biography, coffee table book, general nonfiction, gift book, humor, illustrated book, reference. *All unsolicited mss returned unopened.* Submit proposal package, including outline, 2-3 sample chapters, biography, marketing and publicity plans, analysis of competitive titles, SASE with appropriate postage. Reviews artwork/photos. Send photocopies.

TIPS "Visit our website before submitting to view our author guidelines and to get a clear idea of the types of books we publish. Carefully analyze your book's competition and tell us what makes your book different— and what makes it better. Also let us know what promotional and marketing opportunities you, as the author, bring to the project."

SARABANDE BOOKS, INC.

2234 Dundee Rd., Suite 200, Louisville KY 40205. (502)458-4028. **Fax:** (502)458-4065. **E-mail:** info@sarabandebooks.org. **Website:** www.sarabandebooks.org. **Contact:** Sarah Gorham, editor-in-chief. Estab. 1994. Publishes trade paperback originals. **Publishes 10 titles/year. 1,500 queries received/year. 3,000 mss received/year. 35% of books from first-time authors. 75% from unagented writers. Pays royalty. 10% on actual income received. Also pays in author's copies.**

Pays $500-1,000 advance. Publishes book 18 months after acceptance. Accepts simultaneous submissions.

☞ "Sarabande Books was founded to publish poetry, short fiction, and creative nonfiction. We look for works of lasting literary value. Please see our titles to get an idea of our taste. Accepts submissions through contests and open submissions."

FICTION Subjects include literary, short story collections., novellas, short novels (300 pages maximum, 150 pages minimum). Literary, novellas, short novels, 250 pages maximum, 150 pages minimum. We consider novels and non-fiction in a wide variety of genres and subject matters with a special emphasis on mysteries and crime fiction. We do not consider science fiction, fantasy, or horror. Our target length is 70,000-90,000 words. Queries can be sent via e-mail, fax or regular post. Submissions to Mary McCarthy Prize in Short Fiction accepted January through February. Pays royalty of 10% on actual income received. Publishes ms 18 months after acceptance. Ms guidelines for #10 SASE.

POETRY Poetry of superior artistic quality; otherwise no restraints or specifications. Member: CLMP. Sarabande Books publishes books of poetry of 48 pages minimum. Wants "poetry that offers originality of voice and subject matter, uniqueness of vision, and a language that startles because of the careful attention paid to it—language that goes beyond the merely competent or functional. Manuscripts are selected through our literary contests, invitation, and recommendation by a well-established writer. At least half of our list is drawn from contest submissions to the Kathryn A. Morton Prize in Poetry."

TIPS "Sarabande publishes for a general literary audience. Know your market. Read-and buy-books of literature. Sponsors contests for poetry and fiction."

SASQUATCH BOOKS

119 S. Main, Suite 400, Seattle WA 98104. (206)467-4307. **Fax:** (206)467-4301. **E-mail:** ttabor@sasquatchbooks.com. **Website:** www.sasquatchbooks.com. **Contact:** Gary Luke, editorial director; Terence Maikels, acquisitions editor; Heidi Lenze, acquisitions editor. Estab. 1986. Publishes regional hardcover and trade paperback originals. **Publishes 30 titles/year. 20% of books from first-time authors. 75% from unagented writers. Pays royalty on cover price. Pays wide range advance.** Publishes book 6-9 months af-

ter acceptance. Accepts simultaneous submissions. Responds to queries in 3 months. Catalog for 9×12 envelope and 2 first-class stamps. Guidelines online.

NONFICTION Subjects include animals, art, architecture, business, economics, cooking, foods, nutrition, gardening, history, nature, environment, recreation, regional, sports, travel, women's issues/studies., outdoors. "We are seeking quality nonfiction works about the Pacific Northwest and West Coast regions (including Alaska to California). The literature of place includes how-to and where-to as well as history and narrative nonfiction." Picture books: activity books, animal, concept, nature/environment. Query first, then submit outline and sample chapters with SASE. Send submissions to The Editors. E-mailed submissions and queries are not recommended. Please include return postage if you want your materials back.

FICTION Young readers: adventure, animal, concept, contemporary, humor, nature/environment. Recently published *Amazing Alaska*, by Deb Vanasse, illustrated by Karen Lewis; *Sourdough Man*, by Cherie Stihler, illustrated by Barbara Lavallee.

TIPS "We sell books through a range of channels in addition to the book trade. Our primary audience consists of active, literate residents of the West Coast."

⊕ SATURNALIA BOOKS

105 Woodside Rd., Ardmore PA 19003. (267) 278-9541. **E-mail:** info@saturnaliabooks.com. **Website:** www.saturnaliabooks.org. **Contact:** Henry Israeli, publisher. Estab. 2002. Publishes trade paperback originals. **Publishes 4 titles/year. Receives 500 mss a year. 33% of books from first-time authors. 100% from unagented writers. Pays authors 4-6% royalty on retail price. Pays $400-2,000 advance.** Accepts simultaneous submissions. Responds in 4 months on mss. Catalog on website. Guidelines available on website.

☞ "We do not accept unsolicited submissions. We hold a contest, the Saturnalia Books Poetry Prize, annually in which 1 anonymously submitted title is chosen by a poet with a national reputation for publication. Submissions are accepted during the month of March. The submission fee is $30, and the prize is $2,000 and 20 copies of the book. See website for details."

POETRY "Saturnalia Books has no bias against any school of poetry, but we do tend to publish writers who take chances and push against convention in some way, whether it's in form, language, content, or musicality." Submit complete ms to contest only.

TIPS "Our audience tend to be young avid readers of contemporary poetry. Read a few sample books first."

✚ SCHIFFER PUBLISHING, LTD.

4880 Lower Valley Rd., Atglen PA 19310. (610)593-1777. **Fax:** (610)593-2002. **E-mail:** info@schifferbooks.com; Schifferbk@aol.com. **Website:** www.schifferbooks.com. **Contact:** Tina Skinner. Estab. 1975. **Publishes 10-20 titles/year. Pays royalty on wholesale price.** Responds in 2 weeks to queries. Catalog available free. Guidelines online.

NONFICTION Art-quality illustrated regional histories. Looking for informed, entertaining writing and lots of subject areas to provide points of entry into the text for non-history buffs who buy a beautiful book because they are from, or love, an area. Full color possible in the case of historic postcards. Fax or e-mail outline, photos, and book proposal.

TIPS "We want to publish books for towns or cities with relevant population or active tourism to support book sales. A list of potential town vendors is a helpful start toward selling us on your book idea."

⚫⊘ SCHOCKEN BOOKS

Imprint of Knopf Publishing Group, Division of Random House, Inc., 1745 Broadway 21-1, New York NY 10019. (212)572-9000. **Fax:** (212)572-6030. **Website:** www.schocken.com. Estab. 1945. Publishes hardcover and trade paperback originals and reprints. **Publishes 9-12 titles/year. Pays varied advance.** Accepts simultaneous submissions.

◯ Does not accept unsolicited mss.

SCHOLASTIC INC.

557 Broadway, New York NY 10012. (212)343-6100. **Website:** www.scholastic.com.

◯ Scholastic Trade Books is an award-winning publisher of original children's books. Scholastic publishes more than 600 new hardcover, paperback and novelty books each year. The list includes the phenomenally successful publishing properties Harry Potter®, Goosebumps®, The 39 Clues™, I Spy™, and The Hunger Games; best-selling and award-winning authors and illustrators, including Blue Balliett, Jim Benton, Meg Cabot, Suzanne Collins, Christopher Paul Curtis, Ann M. Martin, Dav Pilkey, J.K. Rowling, Pam Muñoz Ryan, Brian Selznick, David Shannon, Mark Teague, and Walter Wick,

among others; as well as licensed properties such as Star Wars® and Rainbow Magic®.

ⓐ SCHOLASTIC LIBRARY PUBLISHING

90 Old Sherman Turnpike, Danbury CT 06816. (203)797-3500. **Fax:** (203)797-3197. **Website:** www.scholastic.com/librarypublishing. **Contact:** Phil Friedman, vice president/publisher; Kate Nunn, editor-in-chief; Marie O'Neil, art director. Estab. 1895. Publishes hardcover and trade paperback originals. **Pays authors royalty based on net or work purchased outright. Pays illustrators at competitive rates.**

◯ *Accepts agented submissions only.*

NONFICTION Photo-illustrated books for all levels: animal, arts/crafts, biography, careers, concept, geography, health, history, hobbies, how-to, multicultural, nature/environment, science, social issues, special needs, sports. Average word length: young readers—2,000; middle readers—8,000; young adult—15,000. Query; submit outline/synopsis, résumé, and/or list of publications, and writing sample. SASE required for response.

FICTION Publishes 1 picture book series, Rookie Readers, for grades 1-2. Does not accept unsolicited mss. *Does not accept fiction proposals.*

⊘ SCIENCE & HUMANITIES PRESS

P.O. Box 7151, Chesterfield MO 63006. (636)394-4950. **E-mail:** banis@sciencehumanitiespress.com. **Website:** www.sciencehumanitiespress.com. **Contact:** Dr. Bud Banis, publisher. Publishes trade paperback originals and reprints, and electronic originals and reprints. **Publishes 20-30 titles/year. 1,000 queries received/year. 50 mss received/year. 25% of books from first-time authors. 100% from unagented writers. Pays 8% royalty on retail price.** Publishes book 1 year after acceptance. Accepts simultaneous submissions. Responds in 2 months to queries and proposals; 3 months to mss. Catalog and guidelines online.

NONFICTION Subjects include Americana, business, economics, child guidance, computers, electronics, creative nonfiction, education, government, politics, health, medicine, history, hobbies, language, literature, memoirs, military, war, money, finance, philosophy, psychology, recreation, regional, science, sex, sociology, software, spirituality, sports, travel, women's issues/studies, math/statistics, management science. "Submissions are best as brief descriptions by e-mail, including some description of the author's background/credentials, and thoughts on approach to nontraditional or specialized markets. Why is the book important and who would buy it? Prefer description by e-mail. Need not be a large format proposal. We prefer that you send proposals by e-mail with a brief description, marketing concept, and possibly a sample of the writing."

FICTION Subjects include adventure, historical, humor, literary, mainstream, contemporary, military, war, mystery, plays, poetry, regional, romance, short story collections, spiritual, sports, suspense, western, young adult. Adventure, historical, humor, literary, mainstream/contemporary, military/war, mystery, regional, romance, science fiction, short story collections, spiritual, sports, suspense, western, young adult. "We prefer books with a theme that gives a market focus." *Does not accept unsolicited mss* without a SASE. We prefer books with a theme that gives a market focus. Brief description by e-mail.

TIPS "Our expertise is electronic publishing for continuous short-run-in-house production."

SCRIBE PUBLICATIONS

18-20 Edward St., Brunswick VIC 3056, Australia. (61)(3)9388-8780. **Fax:** (61)(3)9388-8787. **E-mail:** info@scribepub.com.au. **Website:** www.scribepublications.com.au. Estab. 1976. **Publishes 70 titles/year. 10-25% of books from first-time authors. 10-20% from unagented writers.** Submission guidelines available on website under About Us.

NONFICTION Subjects include environment, government, politics, history, memoirs, nature, environment, psychology., current affairs, social history. "Please refer first to our website before contacting us or submitting anything, because we explain there who we will accept proposals from."

SEAL PRESS

1700 4th St., Berkeley CA 94710. (510)595-3664. **E-mail:** Seal.Press@perseusbooks.com. **E-mail:** sealacquisitions@avalonpub.com. **Website:** www.sealpress.com. Estab. 1976. Publishes trade paperback originals. **Publishes 30 titles/year. 1,000 queries received/year. 750 mss received/year. 25% of books from first-time authors. 50% from unagented writers. Pays 7-10% royalty on retail price. Pays variable royalty on retail price. Pays $3,000-10,000 advance. Pays variable advance.** Publishes book 1 year after acceptance. Accepts simultaneous submissions. Responds in 2 months to queries. Catalog and guidelines for SASE or online.

8→ "Seal Press is an imprint of Avalon Publishing Group, feminist book publisher interested in original, lively, radical, empowering and culturally diverse nonfiction by women addressing contemporary issues from a feminist perspective or speaking positively to the experience of being female. Currently emphasizing women outdoor adventurists, young feminists, political issues for women, health issues, and surviving abuse. *Not accepting fiction at this time.*"

NONFICTION Subjects include Americana, child guidance, contemporary culture, creative nonfiction, ethnic, gay, lesbian, memoirs, multicultural, nature, environment, sex, travel, women's issues/studies, popular culture, politics, domestic violence, sexual abuse. Query with SASE. Reviews artwork/photos. Send photocopies. No original art or photos accepted.

FICTION Ethnic, feminist, gay/lesbian, literary, multicultural. "We are interested in alternative voices." Query with SASE or submit outline, 2 sample chapters, synopsis.

TIPS "Our audience is generally composed of women interested in reading about women's issues addressed from a feminist perspective."

SEARCH INSTITUTE PRESS

Search Institute, 615 First Ave. NE, Suite 125, Minneapolis MN 55413. (612)399-0200. **Fax:** (612)692-5553. **E-mail:** acquisitions@search-institute.org. **Website:** www.search-institute.org. Estab. 1958. Publishes trade paperback originals. **Publishes 12-15 titles/year. Pays royalty.** Publishes book 1 year after acceptance. Accepts simultaneous submissions. Responds in 6 months to queries, proposals, mss. Catalog free on request, online. Guidelines online.

NONFICTION Subjects include career guidance, child guidance, community, counseling, education, entertainment, games, parenting, public affairs, social sciences., youth leadership, prevention, activities. Does not want children's picture books, poetry, New Age and religious-themes, memoirs, biographies, and autobiographies. Query with SASE.

TIPS "Our audience is educators, youth program leaders, mentors, parents."

SEAWEED SIDESHOW CIRCUS

P.O. Box 234, Jackson WI 53037. **E-mail:** sscircus@aol.com. **Website:** www.facebook.com/sscircus. **Contact:** Andrew Wright Milam, editor. Estab. 1994. **Pays 10 author's copies (out of a press run of 100).** Responds to queries in 6-9 weeks; to mss in 6-9 months. Query first, with 5-10 sample poems and cover letter with brief bio and publications credits.

SEAWORTHY PUBLICATIONS, INC.

3601 S. Banana River Blvd., A301, Cocoa Beach FL 32931. (262)268-9250. **Fax:** (262)268-9208. **E-mail:** orders@seaworthy.com. **Website:** www.seaworthy.com. **Contact:** Joseph F. Janson, publisher. Publishes trade paperback originals, hardcover originals, and reprints. **Publishes 8 titles/year. 150 queries received/year. 40 mss received/year. 60% of books from first-time authors. 100% from unagented writers. Pays 15% royalty on wholesale price. Pays $1,000 advance.** Publishes book 6 months after acceptance. Responds in 1 month to queries. Catalog and guidelines online.

⛐ "Seaworthy Publications is a nautical book publisher that primarily publishes books of interest to recreational boaters and bluewater cruisers, including cruising guides, how-to books about boating. Currently emphasizing cruising guides."

NONFICTION Subjects include regional., sailing, boating, regional, boating guide books. Regional guide books, first-person adventure, reference, technical—all dealing with boating. Query with SASE. Submit 3 sample chapters, TOC. Prefers electronic query via e-mail. Reviews artwork/photos. Send photocopies or color prints.

TIPS "Our audience consists of sailors, boaters, and those interested in the sea, sailing, or long-distance cruising."

⊜⊘ SECOND AEON PUBLICATIONS

19 Southminster Rd., Roath, Cardiff CF23 5AT, Wales. +44(29)2049-3093. **Fax:** +44(29)2049-3093. **E-mail:** peter@peterfinch.co.uk. **Website:** www.peterfinch.co.uk. **Contact:** Peter Finch, poetry editor. Estab. 1966.

⊘ Does not accept unsolicited mss.

POETRY *Does not accept unsolicited mss.*

⊙ SECOND STORY PRESS

20 Maud St., Suite 401, Toronto ON M5V 2M5, Canada. (416)537-7850. **Fax:** (416)537-0588. **E-mail:** info@secondstorypress.ca; marketing@secondstorypress.com. **Website:** www.secondstorypress.ca.

NONFICTION Picture books: biography. *Accepts appropriate material from residents of Canada only.* Submit complete ms or submit outline and sample chapters by postal mail only. No electronic submissions or queries.

FICTION Considers non-sexist, non-racist, and non-violent stories, as well as historical fiction, chapter books, picture books. *Accepts appropriate material from residents of Canada only.* Submit complete ms or submit outline and sample chapters by postal mail only. No electronic submissions or queries.

SEEDLING CONTINENTAL PRESS

520 E. Bainbridge St., Elizabethtown PA 17022. **E-mail:** bspencer@continentalpress.com. **Website:** www.continentalpress.com. **Contact:** Megan Bergonzi. **Work purchased outright from authors.** Publishes book 1-2 years after acceptance. Accepts simultaneous submissions. Responds to mss in 6 months.

⛐ Publishes books for classroom use only for the beginning reader in English. "Natural language and predictable text are requisite. Patterned text is acceptable, but must have a unique story line. Poetry, books in rhyme and full-length picture books are not being accepted. Illustrations are not necessary."

NONFICTION Young readers: animal, arts/crafts, biography, careers, concept, multicultural, nature/environment, science. Does not accept texts longer than 12 pages or over 300 words. Average word length: young readers—100. Submit complete ms.

FICTION Young readers: adventure, animal, folktales, humor, multicultural, nature/environment. Does not accept texts longer than 12 pages or over 300 words. Average word length: young readers—100. Submit complete ms.

TIPS "See our website. Follow writers' guidelines carefully and test your story with children and educators."

SENTIENT PUBLICATIONS

1113 Spruce St., Boulder CO 80302. **E-mail:** contact@sentientpublications.com. **Website:** www.sentientpublications.com. **Contact:** Connie Shaw, acquisitions editor. Estab. 2001. Publishes hardcover and trade paperback originals; trade paperback reprints. **Publishes 12 titles/year. 200 queries received/year. 100 mss received/year. 70% of books from first-time authors. 50% from unagented writers. Pays royalty on wholesale price. Pays advance.** Publishes book 6 months after acceptance. Accepts simultaneous submissions. Responds in 1 month to queries; 2 months to proposals and mss. Catalog online.

NONFICTION Subjects include audio, alternative, art, architecture, child guidance, contemporary culture, cooking, foods, nutrition, creative nonfiction, education, gardening, health, medicine, history, language, literature, memoirs, nature, environment, New Age, philosophy, photography, psychology, science, sex, social sciences, sociology, spirituality, travel, women's issues/studies. "We're especially looking for holistic health books that have something new to say." Submit proposal package, See our website. Submit complete ms.

⊕ SERIOUSLY GOOD BOOKS

999 Vanderbilt Beach Rd., Naples FL 34119. **E-mail:** seriouslygoodbks@aol.com. **Website:** www.seriously-goodbks.net. Estab. 2010. Publishes trade paperback and electronic originals. **Publishes 2-5 titles/year. Pays 15% minimum royalties.** Respons in 1 month to queries. Catalog and writers guidelines online.

⌐⊶ Publishes historial fiction only.

NONFICTION No nonfiction.

FICTION Subjects include historical. Query by e-mail.

TIPS "Looking for historial fiction with substance. We seek well-researched historical fiction in the vein of Rutherfurd, Mary Renault, Maggie Anton, Robert Harris, etc. Please don't query with historical fiction mixed with other genres (romance, time travel, vampires, etc.)."

SEVEN FOOTER PRESS / SEVEN FOOTER KIDS

247 W. 30th St., 11th Floor, New York NY 10001. **E-mail:** info@sevenfooterpress.com. **Website:** www.sevenfooterpress.com. **Contact:** Justin Heimberg, chief creative officer (humor, gift, nonfiction); David Gomberg, president and publisher (children's, illustrated, young adult, sports). Estab. 2004. Publishes hardcover, trade and mass market paperback originals. **Publishes 10-20 titles/year. 200 queries received/year. 50 mss received/year. 50% of books from first-time authors. 50% from unagented writers.** Publishes book 1 year after acceptance. Accepts simultaneous submissions. Catalog online.

NONFICTION Subjects include creative nonfiction, education, hobbies, regional, sex, sports, travel., college market, games/puzzles, high-concept. We specialize in hip, young audiences. We like books that are socially interactive or offer an experience beyond just reading. Submit proposal package, outline, 2 sample chapters, any visuals or illustrations. Reviews artwork/photos. Send photocopies and scanned artwork or design.

TIPS "The audience for Seven Footer Press titles is Gen X, Gen Y, college, young adults, young professionals, and pop culture fans. The audience for Seven Footer Kids titles is for all children."

⊘ SEVEN STORIES PRESS

140 Watts St., New York NY 10013. (212)226-8760. **Fax:** (212)226-1411. **E-mail:** anna@sevenstories.com. **Website:** www.sevenstories.com. **Contact:** Daniel Simon; Anna Lui. Estab. 1995. Publishes hardcover and trade paperback originals. **Publishes 40-50 titles/ year. 15% of books from first-time authors. 50% from unagented writers. Pays 7-15% royalty on retail price. Pays advance.** Publishes book 1-3 years after acceptance. Accepts simultaneous submissions. Responds in 1 month to queries and mss. Catalog and guidelines free.

⌐⊶ Founded in 1995 in New York City, and named for the seven authors who committed to a home with a fiercely independent spirit, Seven Stories Press publishes works of the imagination and political titles by voices of conscience. While most widely known for its books on politics, human rights, and social and economic justice, Seven Stories continues to champion literature, with a list encompassing both innovative debut novels and National Book Award–winning poetry collections, as well as prose and poetry translations from the French, Spanish, German, Swedish, Italian, Greek, Polish, Korean, Vietnamese, Russian, and Arabic.

NONFICTION Responds only if interested.

FICTION Subjects include literary. "We are currently unable to accept any unsolicited full manuscripts. We do accept query letters and sample chapters. Please send no more than a cover letter and two sample chapters, along with a 44-cent SASE or postcard for reply. (If you would like your submission materials returned to you, please include sufficient postage.)"

TIPS "Each year we also publish an annual compilation of censored news stories by Project Censored. Features of this series include the Top 25 Censored News Stories of the year—which has a history of identifying important neglected news stories and which is widely disseminated in the alternative press—as well as the "Junk Food News" chapter and chapters on hot-button topics for the year. Seven Stories also maintains a publishing partnership with Human Rights Watch through the yearly publication of the World

Report, a preeminent account of human rights abuse around the world—a report card on the progress of the world's nations towards the protection of human rights for people everywhere."

⚑☺ SEVERN HOUSE PUBLISHERS

9-15 High St., Sutton, Surrey SM1 1DF, United Kingdom. (44)(208)770-3930. **Fax:** (44)(208)770-3850. **Website:** www.severnhouse.com. **Contact:** Amanda Stewart, editorial director. Publishes hardcover and trade paperback originals and reprints. **Publishes 150 titles/year. 400-500 queries received/year. 50 mss received/year. Pays 7 ½-15% royalty on retail price. Pays $750-5,000 advance.** Accepts simultaneous submissions. Responds in 3 months to proposals. Catalog available free.

⚒➤ Severn House is currently emphasizing suspense, romance, mystery. Large print imprint from existing authors.

FICTION Subjects include adventure, fantasy, historical, horror, mainstream, contemporary, mystery, romance, short story collections, suspense. Adventure, fantasy, historical, horror, mainstream/contemporary, mystery, romance, short story collections, suspense. *Agented submissions only.*

SHAMBHALA PUBLICATIONS, INC.

300 Massachusetts Ave., P.O. Box 170358, Boston MA 02117. (617)424-0030. **Fax:** (617)236-1563. **E-mail:** editors@shambhala.com. **Website:** www.shambhala. com. Estab. 1969. Publishes hardcover and trade paperback originals and reprints. **Publishes 90-100 titles/year. 2,000 queries received/year. 500-700 mss received/year. 30% of books from first-time authors. 80% from unagented writers. Pays 8% royalty on retail price.** Publishes book 1 year after acceptance. Accepts simultaneous submissions. Responds in 1 month to queries; 2 months to proposals and mss. Catalog and guidelines free.

NONFICTION Subjects include alternative, art, architecture, creative nonfiction, health, medicine, humanities, language, literature, memoirs, philosophy, religion, spirituality, women's issues/studies. To send a book proposal, include a synopsis of the book, a table of contents or outline, a copy of the author's résumé or some other brief biographical statement, along with two or three sample chapters (they do not need to be in consecutive order). The chapters should be double-spaced. Include SASE. Publishes very little fiction or poetry. Reviews artwork/photos.

FICTION Query with SASE. Submit proposal package, outline, résumé, clips, 2 sample chapters, TOC. Submit complete ms.

SHEARSMAN BOOKS, LTD

50 Westons Hills Dr., Emersons Green Bristol BS16 7DF, United Kingdom. **E-mail:** editor@shearsman. com. **Website:** www.shearsman.com. **Contact:** Tony Frazer, editor. Estab. 1981. Publishes trade paperback originals. **Publishes 45-60 titles/year. Pays 10% royalty on retail price after 150 copies have sold; authors also receive 10 free copies of their books.** Responds in 2-3 months to mss. Catalog and guidelines online.

NONFICTION Subjects include memoirs, translation, essays.

POETRY "Shearsman only publishes poetry, poetry collections, and poetry in translation (from any language but with an emphasis on work in Spanish & in German). Some critical work on poetry and also memoirs and essays by poets. Mainly poetry by British, Irish, North American, & Australian poets." No children's books.

TIPS "Book ms submission: most of the ms must have already appeared in the UK or USA magazines of some repute, & it has to fill 70-72 pages of half letter or A5 pages. You must have sufficient return postage. Submissions can also be made by e-mail. It is unlikely that a poet with no track record will be accepted for publication as there is no obvious audience for the work. Try to develop some exposure to UK & US magazines & try to assemble a ms only later."

SHEED & WARD BOOK PUBLISHING

Imprint of Rowman & Littlefield Publishing Group, 4501 Forbes Blvd., Suite 200, Lanham MD 20706. (301)459-3366 ext. 5634. **Fax:** (301)429-5747. **E-mail:** sstanton@rowman.com;mboggs@rowman.com. **Website:** www.sheedandward.com. **Contact:** Sarah Stanton, acquisitions. Publishes hardcover and paperback originals. Catalog free or on website. Guidelines online.

⚒➤ "We are looking for books that help our readers, most of whom are college educated, gain access to the riches of the Catholic/Christian tradition. We publish in the areas of history, biography, spirituality, prayer, ethics, ministry, justice, liturgy."

NONFICTION Subjects include religion, spirituality., family life, theology, ethics. Submit proposal package to the appropriate acquistions editor, including outline, 2 sample chapters, strong cover letter indicating why the project is unique and compelling. Please do not send your entire ms. If an acquisitions editor would like to see the complete ms, he or she will let you know. Reviews artwork/photos. Send photocopies.

TIPS "We prefer that writers get our author guidelines either from our website or via mail before submitting proposals."

SHEN'S BOOKS

1547 Palos Verdes Mall #291, Walnut Creek CA 94597. (925)262-8108. **Fax:** (888)269-9092. **E-mail:** info@shens.com. **Website:** www.shens.com. **Contact:** Renee Ting, president. Estab. 1986. **Authors pay negotiated by project.** Publishes book 1-2 years after acceptance. Accepts simultaneous submissions. Responds to queries in 1-2 weeks; mss in 6-12 months. Catalog available on website.

NONFICTION Picture books, young readers: multicultural.

FICTION Picture books, young readers: folktales, multicultural with Asian Focus. Middle readers: multicultural.

TIPS "Be familiar with our catalog before submitting."

J. GORDON SHILLINGFORD PUBLISHING INC.

P.O. Box 86, RPO Corydon Ave., Winnipeg MB R3M 3S3, Canada. (204)779-6967. **Fax:** (204)779-6970. **E-mail:** jgshill@allstream.net. **Website:** www.jgshillingford.com. **Contact:** Clarise Foster, poetry editor; Glenda MacFarlane, drama editor, Gordon Shillingford, nonfiction editor. Estab. 1993. Publishes trade paperback originals. **Publishes 14 titles/year. 100 queries received/year. 50 mss received/year. 15% of books from first-time authors. 60% from unagented writers. Pays 10% royalty on retail price.** Accepts simultaneous submissions. Responds in 3-6 months to queries. Catalog and guidelines online.

Publishes nonfiction, drama, and poetry. Does not publish fiction, self-help or children's material. Only publishes Canadian citizens.

NONFICTION Subjects include government, politics, social history. Query with CV, 2-page sample, SASE.

SILVERFISH REVIEW PRESS

P.O. Box 3541, Eugene OR 97403. (541)344-5060. **E-mail:** sfrpress@earthlink.net. **Website:** www.silverfishreviewpress.com. **Contact:** Rodger Moody, series editor. Estab. 1978. Trade paperback originals. **Publishes 2-3 titles/year. 50% of books from first-time authors. 100% from unagented writers.** Guidelines online.

"Sponsors the Gerald Cable Book Award. This prize is awarded annually to a book length manuscript of original poetry by an author who has not yet published a full-length collection. There are no restrictions on the kind of poetry or subject matter; translations are not acceptable. Winners will receive one thousand dollars, publication, and twenty-five copies of the book. The winner will be announced in late March, 2012. Entries must be postmarked by October 15. Entries may be submitted by e-mail. See website for instructions."

TIPS "Read recent Silverfish titles."

SILVERLAND PRESS

E-mail: editor@silverlandpress.com. **Website:** www.silverlandpress.com. **Contact:** Karen Friesen, editor.

FICTION Subjects include fantasy, mystery, romance, science fiction, young adult. "We accept manuscripts between 40,000 words and 75,000 words targeting a young adult audience. At the current time we are especially interested in acquiring children's and young adult stories of all lengths where the work is part of a series." Submit via e-mail. In the subject line of the e-mail include the word "submission" and the title of the ms. Include a brief description of your story, word count, publishing history (if any), mailing address, and if ms is agented or not.

SILVER LEAF BOOKS, LLC

P.O. Box 6460, Holliston MA 01746. **E-mail:** editor@silverleafbooks.com. **Website:** www.silverleafbooks.com. **Contact:** Brett Fried, editor. **75% from unagented writers. Pays royalties, and provides author's copies.** Publishes book 1-2 years after acceptance. Responds to queries in 6 months; mss in 4 months. Guidelines online.

FICTION Fantasy (space fantasy, sword and sorcery), horror (dark fantasy, futuristic, psychological, supernatural), mystery/suspense (amateur sleuth, cozy, police procedural, private eye/hard-boiled), science fiction (hard science/technological, soft/sociological), young adult (adventure, fantasy/science fiction, horror, mystery/suspense). Query with outline/synopsis and 3 sample chapters. Accepts queries by snail mail. Include estimated word count, brief bio and marketing plan. Send SASE or IRC for return of ms or disposable copy of ms and SASE/IRC for reply only.

TIPS "Follow the online guidelines, be thorough and professional."

SILVER MOON PRESS

400 E. 85th St., New York NY 10028. (800)874-3320. **Fax:** (212)988-8112. **E-mail:** mail@silvermoonpress. com. **Website:** silvermoonpress.com. Publishes hardcover originals. **Publishes 1-2 prep workbooks and 1-2 historical fiction. titles/year. 600 queries received/year. 400 mss received/year. 60% of books from first-time authors. 70% from unagented writers. Pays 7-10% royalty. Pays 500-1,000 advance.** Publishes book 18 months after acceptance. Accepts simultaneous submissions. Responds in 6-12 months to queries, proposals and mss. Catalog with 9×12 SASE. Guidelines with #10 SASE.

○ *Does not accept unsolicited mss.*

NONFICTION Subjects include education, history, language, literature, multicultural.

FICTION Subjects include historical, multicultural., biographical. Middle readers: historical, multicultural and mystery. Average word length: 14,000.

TIPS "We do not accept biographies, poetry, or romance. We do not accept fantasy, science fiction, or historical fiction with elements of either. No picture books. Submissions that fit into New York State curriculum topics such as the Revolutionary War, Colonial times, and New York state history in general stand a greater chance of acceptance than those that do not."

Ⓐ SIMON & SCHUSTER ADULT PUBLISHING GROUP

1230 Avenue of the Americas, New York NY 10020. **E-mail:** ssonline@simonsays.com; Lydia.Frost@simonandschuster.com. **Website:** www.simonsays.com. Estab. 1924.

⚬━ The Simon & Schuster Adult Publishing Group includes a number of publishing units that offer books in several formats. Each unit has its own publisher, editorial group and publicity department. Common sales and business departments support all the units. The managing editorial, art, production, marketing, and subsidiary rights departments have staff members dedicated to the individual imprints.

FICTION *Agented submissions only.*

⊘ SIMON & SCHUSTER BOOKS FOR YOUNG READERS

Imprint of Simon & Schuster Children's Publishing, 1230 Avenue of the Americas, New York NY 10020.

(212)698-7000. **Fax:** (212)698-2796. **Website:** www. simonsayskids.com. Publishes hardcover originals. **Publishes 75 titles/year. Pays variable royalty on retail price.** Publishes book 2-4 years after acceptance. Accepts simultaneous submissions. Responds in 2 months to queries and mss. Guidelines for #10 SASE.

○ *No unsolicited mss.* All unsolicited mss returned unopened. Queries are accepted via mail.

NONFICTION Subjects include history, nature, environment., biography. Picture books: concept. All levels: narrative, current events, biography, history. "We're looking for picture books or middle grade nonfiction that have a retail potential. No photo essays." Recently published Insiders Series (picture book nonfiction, all ages). Query with SASE only.

FICTION Subjects include fantasy, historical, humor, juvenile, mystery, picture books, science fiction, young adult, adventure, historical, mystery, contemporary fiction. Query with SASE only.

TIPS "We're looking for picture books centered on a strong, fully-developed protagonist who grows or changes during the course of the story; YA novels that are challenging and psychologically complex; also imaginative and humorous middle-grade fiction. And we want nonfiction that is as engaging as fiction. Our imprint's slogan is 'Reading You'll Remember.' We aim to publish books that are fresh, accessible and family-oriented; we want them to have an impact on the reader."

Ⓐ⊘ SIMON & SCHUSTER CHILDREN'S PUBLISHING

Simon & Schuster, Inc., 1230 Avenue of the Americas, New York NY 10020. (212)698-7000. **Website:** www. simonsayskids.com. Publishes hardcover and paperback fiction, nonfiction, trade, library, mass market titles, and novelty books for preschool through young adult readers. **Publishes 650 titles/year.**

SKINNER HOUSE BOOKS

The Unitarian Universalist Association, 25 Beacon St., Boston MA 02108. (617)742-2100 ext. 603. **Fax:** (617)742-7025. **E-mail:** info@uua.org. **Website:** www. uua.org/skinner. **Contact:** Mary Benard, senior editor. Estab. 1975. Publishes trade paperback originals and reprints. **Publishes 10-20 titles/year. 50% of books from first-time authors. 100% from unagented writers.** Publishes book 1 year after acceptance. Accepts simultaneous submissions. Responds to queries in 3 weeks. Catalog for 6×9 SAE with 3 first-class stamps. Guidelines online.

- ☛ "We publish titles in Unitarian Universalist faith, liberal religion, history, biography, worship, and issues of social justice. Most of our children's titles are intended for religious education or worship use. They reflect Unitarian Universalist values. We also publish inspirational titles of poetic prose and meditations. Writers should know that Unitarian Universalism is a liberal religious denomination committed to progressive ideals. Currently emphasizing social justice concerns."

NONFICTION Subjects include gay, lesbian, memoirs, religion, women's issues/studies., inspirational, church leadership. All levels: activity books, multicultural, music/dance, nature/environment, religion. Query or submit outline/synopsis and 2 sample chapters. Reviews artwork/photos. Send photocopies.

FICTION All levels: anthology, multicultural, nature/environment, religion. Query or submit outline/synopsis and 2 sample chapters.

TIPS "From outside our denomination, we are interested in manuscripts that will be of help or interest to liberal churches, Sunday School classes, parents, ministers, and volunteers. Inspirational/spiritual and children's titles must reflect liberal Unitarian Universalist values."

SLACK, INC.

6900 Grove Rd., Thorofare NJ 08086. (856)848-1000. **Fax:** (856)853-5991. **E-mail:** bookspublishing@slack-inc.com. **Website:** www.slackbooks.com. **Contact:** John Bond, publisher. Estab. 1960. Publishes hardcover and paperback originals. **Publishes 35 titles/year. 80 queries received/year. 23 mss received/year. 75% of books from first-time authors. 100% from unagented writers. Pays 10% royalty. Pays advance.** Publishes book 8 months after acceptance. Accepts simultaneous submissions. Responds in 1 month to queries/proposals; 3 months to mss. Catalog and guidelines free. Guidelines online.

- ☛ SLACK INC. publishes academic textbooks and professional reference books on various medical topics in an expedient manner.

NONFICTION Subjects include health, medicine., ophthalmology. Submit proposal package, outline, 2 sample chapters, market profile and cv. Reviews artwork/photos. Send photocopies.

SMALL BEER PRESS

150 Pleasant St., #306, Easthampton MA 01027. (413) 203-1636. **Fax:** (413) 203-1636. **E-mail:** info@small-beerpress.com. **Website:** www.smallbeerpress.com. **Contact:** Gavin J. Grant, acquisitions. Estab. 2000. **Publishes 10 titles/year.**

FICTION Literary, experimental, speculative, story collections. "We do not accept unsolicited novel or short story collection manuscripts. Queries are welcome. Please send queries with an SASE by mail."

TIPS "Please be familiar with our books first to avoid wasting your time and ours, thank you."

⊕ SMALL DOGMA PUBLISHING, INC.

P.O. Box 91023, Lakeland FL 33804. (863)838-7251. **E-mail:** matt@smalldogma.com; submissions@smalldogma.com. **Website:** www.smalldogma.com. **Contact:** Matt Porricelli, president (fiction, self help, fantasy, sci-fi, religion, lit, poetry). Estab. 2006. Publishes hardcover and electronic originals, trade and mass market paperback originals; trade paperback reprints. **Publishes 20 titles/year. Receives 350 queries/year; 150 mss/year. 65% of books from first-time authors. 85% from unagented writers. Pays 23-50% royalty on wholesale price.** Publishes book 4-6 months after acceptance. Accepts simultaneous submissions. Responds in 2 months to queries and proposals; 3 months to mss. Catalog and guidelines available on website.

NONFICTION Subjects include business, career guidance, contemporary culture, counseling, creative nonfiction, economics, environment, finance, history, hobbies, humanities, literary criticism, military, money, nature, psychology, religion, sociology, travel, war, womens issues, womens studies, world affairs, young adult. "We are dedicated to making a difference and are always looking for new manuscripts that entertain, teach, challenge, inform or inspire. Please note: we do not accept material with gratuitous violence or sexual content." Submit complete ms along with query letter by e-mail.

FICTION Subjects include adventure, confession, fantasy, historical, humor, juvenile, literary, mainstream, multimedia, mystery, poetry, regional, religious, science fiction, short story collections, suspense, western, young adult. Submit complete ms along with query letter by e-mail.

POETRY Submit complete ms along with query letter by e-mail.

TIPS "Be different. Be passionate about your book. Be willing to do book signings/promotions. How do you plan to reach your target audience? What is your sales/ promotion strategy?"

SMALLFELLOW PRESS

9454 Wilshire Blvd. Suite 550, Beverly CA 90212. **E-mail:** asls@pacbell.net; tallfellow@pacbell.net. **Website:** www.smallfellow.com. **Contact:** Caudia Sloan.

Smallfellow no longer accepts ms/art submissions.

SOFT SKULL PRESS INC.

Counterpoint, 1919 Fifth St., Berkeley CA 94710. (510)704-0230. **Fax:** (510)704-0268. **E-mail:** info@softskull.com. **Website:** www.softskull.com. Publishes hardcover and trade paperback originals. **Publishes 40 titles/year. Pays 7-10% royalty. Average advance: $100-15,000.** Publishes book 6 months after acceptance. Responds in 2 months to proposals; 3 months to mss. Catalog and guidelines on website.

FICTION Confession, experimental, pop culture, gay/lesbian, erotica, graphic novels and comics, literary, mainstream/contemporary, multicultural, short story collections. Agented submissions encouraged. Soft Skull Press accepts unsolicited submissions. E-mail with a subject heading of "SUBMISSION OF Fiction/ Nonfiction/Graphic Novel" (whichever is appropriate). Include contact information on your attachment/s, be that a sample chapter or the whole manuscript. Attachments should be no bigger than 2 megabytes. For graphic novels, send a minimum of five fully inked pages of art, along with a synopsis of your storyline.

TIPS "See our website for updated submission guidelines. Submit electronically."

SOHO PRESS, INC.

853 Broadway, New York NY 10003. **E-mail:** soho@sohopress.com. **Website:** www.sohopress.com. **Contact:** Bronwen Hruska, publisher; Katie Herman, editor. Mark Doten, editor Estab. 1986. Publishes hardcover and trade paperback originals; trade paperback reprints. **Publishes 60-70 titles/year. 15-25% of books from first-time authors. 10% from unagented writers. Pays 10-15% royalty on retail price (varies under certain circumstances).** Publishes book 18 months after acceptance. Accepts simultaneous submissions. Responds in 3 months to queries and mss. Guidelines online.

Soho Press publishes primarily fiction, as well as some narrative literary nonfiction and mysteries set abroad. No electronic submissions, only queries by e-mail.

NONFICTION Subjects include creative nonfiction, ethnic, memoirs. "Independent publisher known for sophisticated fiction, mysteries set abroad, women's interest (no genre) novels and multicultural novels." Publishes hardcover and trade paperback originals and reprint editions. Books: perfect binding; halftone illustrations. First novel print order varies. We do not buy books on proposal. We always need to see a complete ms before we buy a book, though we prefer an initial submission of 3 sample chapters. We do not publish books with color art or photographs or a lot of graphical material." No self-help, how-to, or cookbooks. Submit 3 sample chapters and a cover letter with a synopsis and author bio; SASE. Send photocopies.

FICTION Subjects include ethnic, historical, humor, literary, mystery. In mysteries, we only publish series with foreign or exotic settings, usually procedurals. Adventure, ethnic, feminist, historical, literary, mainstream/contemporary, mystery (police procedural), suspense, multicultural. Submit 3 sample chapters and cover letter with synopsis, author bio, SASE. *No e-mailed submissions.*

TIPS "Soho Press publishes discerning authors for discriminating readers, finding the strongest possible writers and publishing them. Before submitting, look at our website for an idea of the types of books we publish, and read our submission guidelines."

SOLAS HOUSE/TRAVELERS' TALES

853 Alma St., Palo Alto CA 94301. (650)462-2110. **Fax:** (650)462-2114. **E-mail:** submit@travelerstales.com. **Website:** www.travelerstales.com. **Contact:** James O'Reilly and Larry Habegger, series editors; Sean O'Reilly, editor-at-large (sales/publicity). **Publishes 8-10 titles/year. Pays $100 honorarium for anthology pieces.** Accepts simultaneous submissions. Guidelines online.

Publishes inspirational travel books, mostly anthologies and travel advice books.

NONFICTION Subjects include all aspects of travel.

TIPS "We publish personal nonfiction stories and anecdotes—funny, illuminating, adventurous, frightening, or grim. Stories should reflect that unique alchemy that occurs when you enter unfamiliar territory and begin to see the world differently as a result. Stories that have already been published, including book excerpts, are welcome as long as the authors retain the copyright or can obtain permission from the copyright holder to reprint the material. We do not publish fiction."

SOUNDPRINTS/STUDIO MOUSE

Palm Publishing. LLC, 353 Main St., Norwalk CT 06851. (800)228-7839. **Fax:** (203)864-1776. **E-mail:** info@soundprints.com. **Website:** www.soundprints. com. Estab. 1947. Publishes book 1-2 years after acceptance. Responds to queries and mss in 6 months. Catalog available on website. Guidelines for SASE.

FICTION Picture books, young readers: adventure, animal, fantasy, history, multicultural, nature/environment, sports. Ages 18 months-5 years board book plus e-book and activities download Query or submit complete ms.

Ⓐ SOURCEBOOKS LANDMARK

Sourcebooks, Inc., P.O. Box 4410, Naperville IL 60567. **E-mail:** info@sourcebooks.com; romance@sourcebooks.com. **Website:** www.sourcebooks.com. **Contact:** Todd Stocke.

⭘━┓ "Our fiction imprint, Sourcebooks Landmark, publishes a variety of commercial fiction, including specialties in historical fiction and Austenalia. We are interested first and foremost in books that have a story to tell."

FICTION "We are actively acquiring single-title and single-title series Romance fiction (90,000 to 120,000 actual digital words) for our Casablanca imprint. We are looking for strong writers who are excited about marketing their books and building their community of readers, and whose books have something fresh to offer in the genre of Romance." Receipt of e-mail submissions will be acknowledged within 21 days via e-mail. Responds to queries in 6-8 weeks.

⊕ SOURCED MEDIA BOOKS, LLC

20 Via Cristobal, San Clemente CA 92673. (949)813-0182. **E-mail:** info@sourcedmediabooks.com. **E-mail:** submissions@sourcedmediabooks.com. **Website:** www.sourcedmediabooks.com. **Contact:** Amy Osmond Cook, Ph.D, acquisitions editor. Estab. 2009. Publishes hardcover originals, trade paperback originals, electronic originals. **Publishes 15-20 titles/year. 90% of books from first-time authors. 90% from unagented writers. Pays royalty of 50% on wholesale price.** Publishes book 3-6 months after acceptance. Accepts simultaneous submissions. Responds to que-

ries/proposals/mss in less than 1 month. Guidelines available free on request or by e-mail.

⭘━┓ "Sourced Media Books is a progressive publishing house specializing in books that reach across multiple media platforms. Sourced Media Books is committed to providing authors and readers with high-quality products. Each book is edited by a competent and thorough editorial team. In addition to high-quality books and ebooks, Sourced Media Books provides author mentorship, website development/hosting, and marketing/publicity materials upon request."

NONFICTION Subjects include business, cooking, economics, education, finance, foods, history, memoirs, money, nutrition, philosophy, religion, spirituality. "We especially enjoy working on the mss of experts who may or may not have an additional expertise in writing. If the content is professional and accurate, our editors are willing to do more extensive editing." Submit complete ms.

TIPS "We are especially interested in writers who are willing to use social media to market their books."

SOUTHERN METHODIST UNIVERSITY PRESS

P.O. Box 750415, Dallas TX 75275. (214)768-1436. **Fax:** (214)768-1428. **E-mail:** d-vance@tamu.edu. **Website:** www.tamupress.com. **Contact:** Diana Vance. Estab. 1937. Publishes hardcover and trade paperback originals and reprints. **Publishes 10-12 titles/year. 500 queries received/year. 500 mss received/year. 50% of books from first-time authors. 75% from unagented writers. Pays 10% royalty on wholesale price, 10 author's copies. Pays $500 advance.** Publishes book 1 year after acceptance. Accepts simultaneous submissions. Responds in 2 weeks to queries; 1 month to proposals; up to 1 year to mss. Catalog available free. Guidelines online.

⭘━┓ Known nationally as a publisher of the highest quality scholarly works and books for the "educated general reader," SMU Press publishes in the areas of ethics and human values, literary fiction, medical humanities, performing arts, Southwestern studies, and sport.

NONFICTION Subjects include creative nonfiction., medical ethics/human values. Proposals may be submitted in hard copy or as attachments to e-mails addressed to the appropriate acquisitions editor. To determine who that is, send a brief description of your ms to the acquisitionsassistant, Diana Vance. Query with SASE. Submit outline, bio, 3 sample chapters, TOC. Reviews artwork/photos. Send photocopies.

FICTION Subjects include literary, short story collections., novels. "We are willing to look at 'serious' or 'literary' fiction. No mass market, science fiction, formula, thriller, romance." Accepts unsolicited mss. Query with SASE. No simultaneous submissions. Sometimes comments on rejected mss. Proposals may be submitted in hard copy or as attachments to e-mails addressed to the appropriate acquisitions editor. To determine who that is, send a brief description of your manuscript to the acquisitions assistant, Diana Vance, at d-vance@tamu.edu. If one of our editors has invited your manuscript, please use this download-able proposal form. Because of the volume of proposals received, the Press cannot normally return material to authors. Please do not send original art or other irreplaceable materials.

SPEAK UP PRESS

P.O. Box 100506, Denver CO 80250. (303)715-0837. **Fax:** (303)715-0793. **E-mail:** info@speakuppress.org. **E-mail:** submit@speakuppress.org. **Website:** www. speakuppress.org. Estab. 1999.

○ *Only accepts submissions via e-mail.*

NONFICTION Nonfiction: Young adult nonfiction, with an emphasis on stories about overcoming adversity and finding a voice. No more than 2,500 words. Submit via e-mail only. Include work in body of e-mail. No attachments.

TIPS "Follow submission guidelines."

THE SPEECH BIN INC.

PO Box 1579, Appleton WI 54912-1579. (888)388-3224. **Fax:** (888)388-6344. **E-mail:** customercare@schoolspecialty.com. **Website:** www.speechbin.com. Estab. 1984.

8—π "The Speech Bin® products provide you with tools for children with speech, language, and communication needs. We equip you to help with articulation, phonology, oral-motor, apraxia, fluency, voice, early education, language and communication, auditory processing/listening, reading/literacy, autism/pervasive developmental delay, pragmatics and social skills, cognition, word finding, augmentative alternative communication, and more! Our products are hand-selected by experienced special needs professionals. Not only do they meet our high quality standards, they are also kid-tested and therapist, teacher and parent approved."

SPINNER BOOKS

University Games, 2030 Harrison St., San Francisco CA 94107. (415)503-1600. **Fax:** (415)503-0085. **E-mail:** info@ugames.com. **Website:** www.ugames.com. Estab. 1985. Publishes book 6 months after acceptance. Responds to queries in 3 months; mss in 2 months only if interested.

8—π "Spinners Books publishes books of puzzles, games and trivia."

NONFICTION Picture books: games & puzzles. *Only interested in agented material.* Query.

SPOUT PRESS

P.O. Box 581067, Minneapolis MN 55458. (612) 782-9629. **E-mail:** spoutpress@hotmail.com; editors@spoutpress.org. **Website:** www.spoutpress.org. **Contact:** Carrie Eidem, fiction editor. Estab. 1989. Publishes book 12-15 months after acceptance. Accepts simultaneous submissions. Responds in 1 month to queries; 3-5 months to mss. Ms guidelines for SASE or on website.

FICTION Subjects include ethnic, experimental, literary, short story collections. Ethnic, experimental, literary, short story collections. Runs annual. Accepts submissions all year around fall through spring. See website for specific dates and details. Does not accept unsolicited mss. Query with SASE. Accepts queries by mail. Include estimated word count, brief bio, list of publishing credits. Send SASE for return of ms or send a disposable ms and SASE for reply only.

POETRY Submit via mail with cover letter and SASE.

SPS STUDIOS, INC.

P.O. Box 1007, Dept. PM, Boulder CO 80306-1007. **E-mail:** editorial@spsstudios.com. **Website:** www.sps.com. **Contact:** Editorial Staff. Estab. 1971. **Pays $300/poem, all rights for each of the first 2 submissions chosen for publication (after which payment scale escalates), for the worldwide, exclusive right, $50/poem for one-time use in an anthology.** Responds in up to 6 months. Guidelines available for SASE or by e-mail.

POETRY SPS Studios publishes greeting cards, books, calendars, prints, and other gift items. Looking for poems, prose, and lyrics ("usually non-rhyming") appropriate for publication on greeting cards and in poetry anthologies. Also actively seeking "book-length manuscripts that would be appropriate for book and gift stores. We are also very interested in receiving book and card ideas that would be appropriate for college stores, as well as younger buyers. Poems should reflect a message, feeling, or sentiment that one person would want to share with another. We'd like to receive creative, original submissions about love relationships, family members, friendships, philosophies, and any other aspect of life. Poems and writings for specific holidays (Christmas, Valentine's Day, etc.) and special occasions, such as graduation, anniversary, and get well are also considered. Only a small portion of the material we receive is selected each year and the review process can be lengthy, but be assured every manuscript is given serious consideration." Submissions must be typewritten, one poem/page or sent by e-mail (no attachments). Include SASE. Simultaneous submissions "discouraged but okay with notification." Accepts fax and e-mail (pasted into body of message) submissions. Submit seasonal material at least 4 months in advance. Guidelines available for SASE or by e-mail. Responds in up to 6 months. Pays $300/poem, all rights for each of the first 2 submissions chosen for publication (after which payment scale escalates), for the worldwide, exclusive right, $50/poem for one-time use in an anthology.

STACKPOLE BOOKS

5067 Ritter Rd., Mechanicsburg PA 17055. **Fax:** (717)796-0412. **E-mail:** jschnell@stackpolebooks. com; cevans@stackpolebooks.com; kweaver@stackpolebooks.com; mallison@stackpolebooks.com; jnichols@stackpolebooks.com. **Website:** www.stackpolebooks.com. **Contact:** Judith Schnell, editorial director (outdoor sports); Chris Evans, editor (history); Mark Allison, editor (nature); Kyle Weaver, editor (regional/Pennsylvania). Estab. 1935. Publishes hardcover and trade paperback originals, reprints, and ebooks 100/yr. **Pays industry standard advance.** Publishes book 1 year after acceptance. Responds in 1 month to queries. Catalog and guidelines online.

> "Stackpole maintains a growing and vital publishing program by featuring authors who are experts in their fields."

NONFICTION Subjects include history, military., outdoor sports. "First of all, send your query to an individual editor. The more information you can supply, the better." Reviews artwork/photos.

TIPS "Stackpole seeks well-written, authoritative mss for specialized and general trade markets. Proposals

should include chapter outline, sample chapter, illustrations, and author's credentials."

STANDARD PUBLISHING

Standex International Corp., 8805 Governor's Hill Dr., Suite 400, Cincinnati OH 45249. (800)543-1353. **E-mail:** customerservice@standardpub.com; adult-ministry@standardpub.com; ministrytochildren@standardpub.com; ministrytoyouth@standardpub. com. **Website:** www.standardpub.com. Mark Taylor, adult ministry resources; Ruth Frederick, children and youth ministry resources; Diane Stortz, family resources. Estab. 1866. Guidelines and current publishing objectives available online.

> Publishes resources that meet church and family needs in the area of children's ministry.

STANFORD UNIVERSITY PRESS

1450 Page Mill Rd., Palo Alto CA 94304. (650)723-9434. **Fax:** (650)725-3457. **E-mail:** info@www.sup. org. **Website:** www.sup.org. **Contact:** Stacy Wagner (Asian studies, US foreign policy, Asian-American studies); Kate Wahl (law, political science, public policy); Margo Beth Crouppen (economics, finance, business). Estab. 1925. **Pays variable royalty (sometimes none). Pays occasional advance.** Guidelines online.

> "Stanford University Press publishes scholarly books in the humanities and social sciences, along with professional books in business, economics and management science; also high-level textbooks and some books for a more general audience."

NONFICTION Subjects include anthropology, archeology, business, economics, ethnic, studies, gay, lesbian, government, politics, history, humanities, language, literature, literary criticism, and literary theory, nature, environment, philosophy, psychology, religion, science, social sciences, sociology, political science, law, education, history and culture of China, Japan and Latin America, European history, linguistics, geology, medieval and classical studies. Query with prospectus and an outline. Reviews artwork/photos.

TIPS "The writer's best chance is a work of original scholarship with an argument of some importance."

ARIEL STARR PRODUCTIONS, LTD.

P.O. Box 17, Demarest NJ 07627. **E-mail:** arielstarrprod@aol.com. **Contact:** Attn: Acquisitions Editor. Estab. 1993. Trade and mass market paperback originals; electronic originals. **Publishes 5 titles/year.**

Receives 40 queries/year, 4 mss/year. 80% of books from first-time authors. 80% from unagented writers. Pays 5-15% royalty on wholesale price. Publishes book 12 months after acceptance of ms. Accepts simultaneous submissions. Responds in 2 months on queries and proposals, 6 months on mss. Guidelines available by e-mail.

NONFICTION Subjects include environment, nature, New Age, religion, spirituality. "We are open to other areas but we ask the person to submit a query letter, one-page outline, and a SASE first; nothing more unless we ask for it." Query with SASE. Reviews artwork/photos; send photocopies.

FICTION Subjects include adventure, fantasy, poetry, religious, science fiction, spiritual. Query with SASE and one-page proposal.

POETRY Query; submit 2 sample poems.

TIPS "We want books that stimulate the brain and inspire the mind. Be honest and decent in your queries."

ST. AUGUSTINE'S PRESS

P.O. Box 2285, South Bend IN 46680. (574)-291-3500. **Fax:** (574)291-3700. **E-mail:** bruce@staugustine.net. **Website:** www.staugustine.net. **Contact:** Bruce Fingerhut, president (philosophy). Publishes hardcover originals and trade paperback originals and reprints. **Publishes 20 titles/year. 350 queries received/year. 300 mss received/year. 2% of books from first-time authors. 95% from unagented writers. Pays 6-15% royalty. Pays $500-5,000 advance.** Publishes book 8 months after acceptance. Accepts simultaneous submissions. Responds in 2-6 months to queries; 3-8 months to proposals; 4-8 months to mss. Catalog available free.

"Our market is scholarly in the humanities. We publish in philosophy, religion, cultural history, and history of ideas only."

NONFICTION Query with SASE. Reviews artwork/photos. Send photocopies.

TIPS "Scholarly and college student audience."

STEEL TOE BOOKS

Department of English, Western Kentucky University, 1906 College Heights Blvd. #11086, Bowling Green KY 42101. (270)745-5769. **E-mail:** tom.hunley@wku.edu. **Website:** www.steeltoebooks.com. **Contact:** Dr. Tom C. Hunley, director. Estab. 2003.

Steel Toe Books publishes "full-length, single-author poetry collections. Our books are professionally designed and printed. We look for workmanship (economical use of language, high-energy verbs, precise literal descriptions, original figurative language, poems carefully arranged as a book); a unique style and/or a distinctive voice; clarity; emotional impact; humor (word plays, hyperbole, comic timing); performability (a Steel Toe poet is at home on the stage as well as on the page)." Does not want "dry verse, purposely obscure language, poetry by people who are so wary of being called 'sentimental' they steer away from any recognizable human emotions, poetry that takes itself so seriously that it's unintentionally funny." Publishes 1-3 poetry books/year. Manuscripts are normally selected through open submission.

POETRY "Check the website for news about our next open reading period." Book mss may include previously published poems. Responds to mss in 3 months. Pays $500 advance on 10% royalties and 10 author's copies. Order sample books by sending $12 to Steel Toe Books. *Must purchase a manuscript in order to submit.* See website for submission guidelines.

STEEPLE HILL BOOKS

Imprint of Harlequin Enterprises, 233 Broadway, Suite 1001, New York NY 10279. (212)553-4200. **Fax:** (212)227-8969. **Website:** www.eharlequin.com. **Contact:** Joan Marlow Golan, executive editor; Melissa Endlich, senior editor (inspirational contemporary romance, historical romance, romantic suspense); Tina James, senior editor (inspirational romantic suspense and historical romance); Emily Rodmell, associate editor. Estab. 1997. Publishes mass market paperback originals and reprints. **Publishes 144 titles/year. Pays royalty on retail price. Pays advance.** 3 months on proposals and mss. Guidelines available online, free on request, for #10 SASE.

"This series of contemporary, inspirational love stories portrays Christian characters facing the many challenges of life, faith, and love in today's world."

FICTION "We are looking for authors writing from a Christian worldview and conveying their personal faith and ministry values in entertaining fiction that will touch the hearts of believers and seekers everywhere." Query with SASE, submit completed ms.

TIPS "Drama, humor, and even a touch of mystery all have a place in Steeple Hill. Subplots are welcome and should further the story's main focus or intertwine in a meaningful way. Secondary characters (children, family, friends, neighbors, fellow church members, etc.) may all contribute to a substantial and satisfying story. These wholesome tales include strong family values and high moral standards. While there is no premarital sex between characters, in the case of romance, a vivid, exciting tone presented with a mature perspective is essential. Although the element of faith must clearly be present, it should be well integrated into the characterizations and plot. The conflict between the main characters should be an emotional one, arising naturally from the well-developed personalities you've created. Suitable stories should also impart an important lesson about the powers of trust and faith."

❂ STELLER PRESS LTD.

13, 4335 W. 10th Ave., Vancouver BC V6R 2H6, Canada. (604)222-2955. **Fax:** (604)222-2965. **E-mail:** info@stellerpress.com. **Website:** www.stellerpress.com. **Contact:** Steve Paton (regional interest, outdoors, gardening, history, travel). **Pays royalty on retail price.**

⌐■ "Most titles are specific to the Pacific Northwest, local interest, or by Canadian authors. Currently emphasizing regional interest, gardening, history, outdoors and travel and some fiction. De-emphasizing poetry."

NONFICTION Subjects include gardening, history, nature, environment, regional, travel.

STEMMER HOUSE PUBLISHERS

4 White Brook Rd., P.O. Box 89, Gilsum NH 03448. (800)345-6665. **Fax:** (603)357-2073. **E-mail:** info@stemmer.com; editor@stemmer.com. **Website:** www.stemmer.com. Estab. 1975. **Pays advance.** Publishes book 1-2 years after acceptance. Accepts simultaneous submissions. Catalog for 5 ½×8 ½ envelope and 2 first-class stamps. Guidelines for #10 SASE.

NONFICTION Subjects include animals, arts, multicultural, nature, environment. Query with SASE.

STERLING PUBLISHING CO., INC.

387 Park Ave. S 10th Floor, New York NY 10016. (212)532-7160. **Fax:** (212)981-0508. **E-mail:** ragis@sterlingpublishing.com; info@sterlingpublishing.com. **Website:** www.sterlingpublishing.com/kids. Brett Duquette Publishes hardcover and paperback originals and reprints. **15% of books from first-time authors. Pays royalty or work purchased outright. Offers advances (average amount: $2,000).** Accepts simultaneous submissions. Catalog available on website. Guidelines online.

⌐■ "Sterling publishes highly illustrated, accessible, hands-on, practical books for adults and children."

NONFICTION Subjects include alternative, animals, art, architecture, ethnic, gardening, health, medicine, hobbies, New Age, recreation, science, sports, fiber arts, games and puzzles, children's humor, children's science, nature and activities, pets, wine, home decorating, dolls and puppets, ghosts, UFOs, woodworking, crafts, medieval, Celtic subjects, alternative health and healing, new consciousness. Proposals on subjects such as crafting, decorating, outdoor living, and photography should be sent directly to Lark Books at their Asheville, North Carolina offices. Complete guidelines can be found on the Lark site: www.larkbooks.com/submissions. Publishes nonfiction only. Submit outline, publishing history, 1 sample chapter (typed and double-spaced), SASE. Explain your idea. Send sample illustrations where applicable. For children's books, please submit full mss. We do not accept electronic (e-mail) submissions. Be sure to include information about yourself with particular regard to your skills and qualifications in the subject area of your submission. It is helpful for us to know your publishing history—whether or not you've written other books and, if so, the name of the publisher and whether those books are currently in print. Reviews artwork/photocopies.

FICTION "At present we do not accept fiction."

TIPS "We are primarily a nonfiction activities-based publisher. We have a picture book list, but we do not publish chapter books or novels. Our list is not trend-driven. We focus on titles that will backlist well. "

STIPES PUBLISHING LLC

P.O. Box 526, Champaign IL 61824. (217)356-8391. **Fax:** (217)356-5753. **E-mail:** stipes01@sbcglobal. net. **Website:** www.stipes.com. **Contact:** Benjamin H. Watts, (engineering, science, business); Robert Watts (agriculture, music, and physical education). Estab. 1925. Publishes hardcover and paperback originals. **Publishes 15-30 titles/year. 50% of books from first-time authors. 95% from unagented writers. Pays 15% maximum royalty on retail price.** Publishes book 4 months after acceptance. Responds in 2 months to queries. Guidelines online.

"Stipes Publishing is oriented towards the education market and educational books with some emphasis in the trade market."

NONFICTION Subjects include agriculture, business, economics, music, dance, nature, environment, recreation, science. "All of our books in the trade area are books that also have a college text market. No books unrelated to educational fields taught at the college level." Submit outline, 1 sample chapter.

ST. JOHANN PRESS

P.O. Box 241, Haworth NJ 07641. (201)387-1529. **E-mail:** d.biesel@verizon.net. **Website:** www.stjohannpress.com. Estab. 1991. Publishes hardcover originals, trade paperback originals and reprints. **Publishes 6-8 titles/year. Receives 15 submissions/year. 50% of books from first-time authors. 95% from unagented writers. Pays 10-15% royalty on wholesale price.** Publishes book 15 months after acceptance. Accepts simultaneous submissions. Responds in 1 month on queries. Catalog online. Guidelines free on request.

NONFICTION Subjects include cooking, crafts, foods, history, hobbies, memoirs, military, nutrition, religion, sports (history), war (USMC)., Black history in sports. "We are a niche publisher with interests in titles that will sell over a long period of time. For example, the World Football League Encyclopedia, Chicago Showcase of Basketball, will not need to be redone. We do baseball but prefer soccer, hockey, etc." Query with SASE. Reviews artwork/photos as part of the ms package. Send photocopies.

TIPS "Our readership is libraries, individuals with special interests, (e.g. sports historians); we also do specialized reference."

STONE ARCH BOOKS

7825 Telegraph Rd., Minneapolis MN 55438. (952)224-0514. **Fax:** (952)933-2410. **E-mail:** info@stonearchbooks.com; author.sub@stonearchbooks.com. **Website:** www.stonearchbooks.com. **Contact:** Michael Dahl, acquisitions editor; Heather Kindseth, art director. **Work purchased outright from authors.** Catalog available on website.

FICTION Young readers, middle readers, young adults: adventure, contemporary, fantasy, humor, light humor, mystery, science fiction, sports, suspense. Average word length: young readers—1,000-3,000; middle readers and early young adults—5,000-10,000. Submit outline/synopsis and 3 sample chapters. Electronic submissions are preferred and should be sent to author.sub@stonearchbooks.com.

TIPS "A high-interest topic or activity is one that a young person would spend their free time on without adult direction or suggestion."

STONE BRIDGE PRESS

P.O. Box 8208, Berkeley CA 94707. **Website:** www.stonebridge.com. **Contact:** Peter Goodman, publisher. Estab. 1989. **75% from unagented writers. Pays royalty on wholesale price.** Publishes book 2 years after acceptance. Responds to queries in 4 months, mss in 8 months. Catalog for 2 first-class stamps and SASE. Ms guidelines online.

Stone Bridge Press received a Japan-U.S. Friendship Prize for *Life in the Cul-de-Sac*, by Senji Kuroi.

FICTION Experimental, gay/lesbian, literary, Japan-themed. "Primarily looking at material relating to Japan. Translations only." Does not accept unsolicited mss. Query with SASE. Accepts queries by e-mail, fax.

TIPS "Fiction translations only for the time being. No poetry."

STOREY PUBLISHING

210 MASS MoCA Way, North Adams MA 01247. (800)793-9396. **Fax:** (413)346-2196. **E-mail:** webmaster@storey.com. **Website:** www.storey.com. **Contact:** Deborah Balmuth, editorial director (building, sewing, gift). Estab. 1983. Publishes hardcover and trade paperback originals and reprints. **Publishes 40 titles/year. 600 queries received/year. 150 mss received/year. 25% of books from first-time authors. 60% from unagented writers. We offer both work-for-hire and standard royalty contracts. Pays advance.** Publishes book 2 years after acceptance. Accepts simultaneous submissions. Responds in 1 month to queries; 3 months to proposals/mss. Catalog available free. Guidelines online.

"The mission of Storey Publishing is to serve our customers by publishing practical information that encourages personal independence in harmony with the environment. We seek to do this in a positive atmosphere that promotes editorial quality, team spirit, and profitability. The books we select to carry out this mission include titles on gardening, small-scale farming, building, cooking, homebrewing, crafts, part-time business, home improvement, woodworking, animals, nature, natural living, personal care, and country living.We are always pleased to review new proposals, which we try to process expeditiously. We offer both work-for-hire and standard royalty contracts."

NONFICTION Subjects include animals, gardening, nature, environment, home, mind/body/spirit, birds, beer and wine, crafts, building, cooking. Reviews artwork/photos.

ST PAULS/ALBA HOUSE

Society of St. Paul, 2187 Victory Blvd., Staten Island NY 10314. (718)761-0047. **Fax:** (718)761-0057. **E-mail:** edmund_lane@juno.com; albabooks@aol.com. **Website:** www.stpauls.us; www.albahouse.org. **Contact:** Edmund C. Lane, SSP, acquisitions editor. Estab. 1957. Publishes trade paperback and mass market paperback originals and reprints. **Publishes 22 titles/ year. 250 queries received/year. 150 mss received/ year. 10% of books from first-time authors. 100% from unagented writers. Pays 5-10% royalty.** Publishes book 10 months after acceptance. Responds in 1 month to queries and proposals; 2 months to mss. Catalog and guidelines free.

NONFICTION Subjects include philosophy, religion, spirituality. Alba House is the North American publishing division of the Society of St. Paul, an International Roman Catholic Missionary Religious Congregation dedicated to spreading the Gospel message via the media of communications. Does not want fiction, children's books, poetry, personal testimonies, or autobiographies. Submit complete ms. Reviews artwork/ photos. Send photocopies.

TIPS "Our audience is educated Roman Catholic readers interested in matters related to the Church, spirituality, Biblical and theological topics, moral concerns, lives of the saints, etc."

STRIDER NOLAN PUBLISHING, INC.

702 Cricket Ave., Glenside PA 19038. **E-mail:** infostridernolan@yahoo.com. **Website:** www.stridernolanmedia.com. Publishes hardcover, trade paperback. **Publishes 5-10 titles/year. 1,000-2,000 queries received/year. 500-1,000 mss received/year. 50% of books from first-time authors. 50% from unagented writers. Pays royalty on retail price.** Accepts simultaneous submissions. Catalog and guidelines online.

"At this time, Strider Nolan is only seeking stories or art for our Visions anthology. Feel free to contact us via e-mail. If you would like to

submit a novel to us, we have plenty of material in the pipeline but are always willing to listen. We cannot guarantee anything, so your project would really have to be something special to get us to look at it. We do accept unagented material, although a prior history of published work (even self-published) is preferable. Favored genres include science fiction, horror, and historical fiction (especially westerns or Civil War)."

SUN BOOKS / SUN PUBLISHING

P.O. Box 5588, Santa Fe NM 87502. (505)471-5177. **E-mail:** info@sunbooks.com. **Website:** www.sunbooks. com. **Contact:** Skip Whitson, director. Estab. 1973. Publishes trade paperback originals and reprints. **Publishes 10-15 titles/year. 5% of books from first-time authors. 90% from unagented writers. Pays 5% royalty on retail price. Occasionally makes outright purchase.** Publishes book 16-18 months after acceptance. Will respond within 2 mos, via e-mail, to queries if interested. Catalog available online at www. sunbooks.com or www.abooksource.com. Queries via e-mail only, please.

NONFICTION Self-help, leadership, motivational, recovery, inspirational.

SUNBURY PRESS, INC.

2200 Market St., Camp Hill PA 17011. **E-mail:** info@ sunburypress.com; proposals@sunburypress.com. **Website:** www.sunburypress.com. Estab. 2004. Format publishes in hardcover and trade paperback originals and reprints; electronic originals and reprints. **Publishes 75 titles/year. 250 queries/year; 150 mss/ year 40% of books from first-time authors. 90% from unagented writers. Pays 10% royalty on wholesale price** Publishes book 3 months after acceptance of ms. Accepts simultaneous submissions. Responds in 1 months on queries, proposals, and mss. Catalog available online. Guidelines available by e-mail at: proposals@sunburypress.com.

Submit proposal package, including synopsis and 4 sample chapters.

NONFICTION Subjects include Americana, animals, anthropology, archeology, architecture, art, astrology, business, career guidance, child guidance, communications, computers, contemporary culture, counseling, crafts, creative nonfiction, dance, economics, education, electronics, entertainment, ethnic, government, health, history, hobbies, house and home, humanities, language, literature, memoirs, military, money, multicultural, music, nature, New Age, photography, regional, religion, science, sex, spirituality, sports, transportation, travel, war, world affairs, young adult. "We are currently seeking Civil War era memoirs and unpublished or new material regarding the Civil War. We are also seeking biographies / histories of local/regional figures who were noteworthy but unpublished or sparsely published." Reviews artwork.

FICTION Subjects include adventure, confession, contemporary, ethnic, experimental, fantasy, gothic, historical, horror, humor, juvenile, mainstream, military, multicultural, mystery, occult, picture books, poetry, regional, religious, romance, science fiction, short story collections, spiritual, sports, suspense, western, young adult. "We are especially seeking historical fiction regarding the Civil War and books of regional interest."

POETRY Submit complete ms.

TIPS "Our books appeal to very diverse audiences. We are building our list in many categories, focusing on many demographics. We are not like traditional publishers—we are digitally adept and very creative. Don't be surprised if we move quicker than you are accustomed to!"

SUNRISE RIVER PRESS

39966 Grand Ave., North Branch MN 55056. (800)895-4585. **Fax:** (651)277-1203. **E-mail:** editorial@sunriseriverpress.com. **Website:** www.sunriseriverpress.com. Estab. 1992. **Publishes 30 titles/year. Pays advance.** Accepts simultaneous submissions. Guidelines online.

⚮ "E-mail is preferred method of contact."

NONFICTION Subjects include cooking, foods, nutrition, health, medicine, genetics, immune system maintenance, fitness; also some professional healthcare titles. No phone calls, please; no originals.

FICTION "Although we don't solicit article-length manuscripts, short humour contributions or jokes are welcome." Submit online.

SUPERCOLLEGE

3286 Oak Ct., Belmont CA 94002. Phone/**Fax:** (650)618-2221. **E-mail:** supercollege@supercollege.com. **Website:** www.supercollege.com. Estab. 1998. Publishes trade paperback originals. **Publishes 8-10 titles/year. 50% of books from first-time authors. 70% from unagented writers. Pays royalty on wholesale price or makes outright purchase.** Publishes

book 7-9 months after acceptance. Catalog and writers guidelines online.

⚮ "We only publish books on admission, financial aid, scholarships, test preparation, student life, and career preparation for college and graduate students."

NONFICTION Subjects include education, admissions, financial aid, scholarships, test prep, student life, career prep. Submit complete ms. Reviews artwork/photos. Send photocopies.

TIPS "We want titles that are student and parent friendly, and that are different from other titles in this category. We also seek authors who want to work with a small but dynamic and ambitious publishing company."

✪ SWAN ISLE PRESS

P.O. Box 408790, Chicago IL 60640. (773)728-3780. **E-mail:** info@swanislepress.com. **Website:** www.swanislepress.com. Estab. 1999. Publishes hardcover and trade paperback originals. **Publishes 3 titles/year. 1,500 queries received/year. 0% of books from first-time authors. Pays 7 ½-10% royalty on wholesale price.** Publishes book 18 months after acceptance. Responds in 6 months to queries. Responds in 12 months to mss. Catalog and guidelines online.

💬 *"We do not accept unsolicited mss."*

NONFICTION Subjects include art, architecture, creative nonfiction, ethnic, history, humanities, language, literature, literary criticism, memoirs, multicultural, translation. Query with SASE. Submit complete mss only if author receives affirmative response to query. Reviews artwork/photos. Send photocopies.

FICTION Subjects include ethnic, historical, literary, multicultural, poetry, poetry in translation, short story collections, translation. Query with SASE. Submit complete mss.

POETRY Query and submit complete ms.

SWAN SCYTHE PRESS

515 P Street, #804, Sacramento CA 95814. **E-mail:** jimzbookz@yahoo.com. **Website:** www.swanscythe.com. **Contact:** James DenBoer, editor. Estab. 1999.

💬 Swan Scythe Press has been awarded a California Arts Council Multicultural Entry Grant and a Fideicomiso para la Cultura Mexico-EUA/US-Mexico Fund for Culture Grant.

POETRY "After publishing 25 chapbooks, a few full-sized poetry collections, and 1 anthology, then taking a short break from publishing, Swan Scythe Press is now re-launching its efforts with some new books, under a new editorship, in 2010. We have also begun a new series of books, called Poetas/Puentes, from emerging poets writing in Spanish, translated into English. We will also consider manuscripts in indigenous languages from North, Central and South America, translated into English. Query first before submitting a ms via e-mail or through website.

SWEETGUM PRESS

P.O. Drawer J, 304 Grover, Warrensburg MO 64093. (660)429-5773. **Fax:** (660)429-3487. **E-mail:** editors@sweetgumpress.com. **Website:** www.sweetgumpress.com. **Contact:** R.M. Kinder; Baird Brock; Kristine Lowe-Martin, editors. Estab. 2001. Publishes trade paperback originals. **Publishes 1-2 titles/year. 200 queries received/year. 50 mss received/year. 100% of books from first-time authors. 100% from unagented writers. Pays 10-15% royalty on retail price.** Publishes book 1 year after acceptance. Accepts simultaneous submissions. Responds in 1 month to queries; 3-6 months to mss. Catalog for #10 SASE. Guidelines online.

○━┱ "We will accept only work from midwestern writers."

NONFICTION Subjects include creative nonfiction, history, memoirs, regional, religion. Check website for current calls for manuscript. Then query, following guidelines. Query with SASE and first 3 pages of manuscript. Please do not submit synopses and sample chapters by e-mail unless asked to do so.

FICTION Subjects include experimental, historical, literary, mainstream, contemporary, mystery, regional, short story collections, suspense. Query with SASE and first 3 pages.

TIPS "Right now we are only interested in regional writers. Be straightforward about your goals and experience. Good writing is the most persuasive part of a submission, but make reading easy by sending your work in a professional format."

SWITCHGRASS BOOKS

Northern Illinois University Press, Switchgrass Books, 2280 Bethany Rd., DeKalb IL 60115. **E-mail:** lmanning2@niu.edu. **Website:** www.switchgrass.niu.edu. Estab. 2008. **Publishes 4 titles/year.** Guidelines are free and available online.

○━┱ E-mail submissions are not accepted.

FICTION "We publish only full-length novels set in or about the Midwest. Switchgrass authors must be from the Midwest, current residents of the region, or have significant ties to it. Briefly tell us in your cover letter why yours is an authentic Midwestern voice. We will not consider memoirs, short stories, novellas, graphic novels, poetry, or juvenile/YA literature. Agented mss will not be considered." Send your complete ms via U.S. mail. E-mail submissions will not be considered. No queries, calls, or e-mails, please. Please include a résumé or CV.

SYLVAN DELL PUBLISHING

612 Johnnie Dodds, Suite A2, Mt. Pleasant SC 29464. (843)971-6722. **Fax:** (843)216-3804. **E-mail:** donnagerman@sylvandellpublishing.com. **Website:** www.sylvandellpublishing.com. **Contact:** Donna German, editor. Estab. 2004. Publishes hardcover, trade paperback, and electronic originals. **Publishes 10 titles/year. 2,000 mss received/year. 50% of books from first-time authors. 100% from unagented writers. Pays 6-8% royalty on wholesale price. Pays small advance.** Publishes book 18 months after acceptance. May hold onto mss of interest for 1 year until acceptance. after acceptance of ms. Accepts simultaneous submissions. Acknowledges receipt of ms submission within one week. Catalog and guidelines online.

NONFICTION Subjects include science, math. "We are not looking for mss. about: pets (dogs or cats in particular); new babies; local or state-specific; magic; biographies; history-related; ABC books; poetry; series; young adult books or novels; holiday-related books. We do not consider mss. that have been previously published in any way, including e-books or self-published." Accepts electronic submissions only. Snail mail submissions are discarded without being opened. Reviews artwork/photos. Send 1-2 JPEGS.

FICTION Subjects include picture books. Picture books: animal, folktales, nature/environment, math-related. Word length—picture books: no more than 1500. Accepts electronic submissions only. Snail mail submissions are discarded without being opened.

TIPS "Please make sure that you have looked at our website to read our complete submission guidelines and to see if we are looking for a particular subject. Manuscripts must meet all four of our stated criteria. We look for fairly realistic, bright and colorful art-no cartoons. We want the children excited about the books. We envision the books being used at home and in the classroom."

SYNERGEBOOKS

205 S. Dixie Dr., Haines City FL 33844. (863)956-3015. **Fax:** (863)588-2198. **E-mail:** synergebooks@aol.com. **Website:** www.synergebooks.com. **Contact:** Debra Staples, publisher/acquisitions editor. Estab. 1999. Publishes trade paperback and electronic originals. **Publishes 40-60 titles/year. 250 queries received/year. 250 mss received/year. 95% of books from first-time authors. 99.9% from unagented writers. Pays 15-40% royalty; makes outright purchase.** Accepts simultaneous submissions. Catalog and guidelines online.

☞ "SynergEbooks is first and foremost a digital publisher, so most of our marketing budget goes to those formats. Authors are required to direct-sell a minimum of 100 digital copies of a title before it's accepted for print."

NONFICTION Subjects include New Age, philosophy, spirituality, travel, young adult. Submit proposal package, 1-3 sample chapters. Reviews artwork/photos. Send JPEG via attached mail.

FICTION Subjects include fantasy, historical, horror, humor, mainstream, contemporary, military, magic, mystery, philosophy, poetry, religious, romance, science fiction, short story collections, spiritual, suspense, western, young adult, and audio books. SynergEbooks publishes at least 40 new titles a year, and only 1-5 of those are put into print in any given year. "SynergEbooks is first and foremost a digital publisher, so most of our marketing budget goes to those formats. Authors are required to direct-sell a minimum of 100 digital copies of a title before it's accepted for print." Submit proposal package, including synopsis, 1-3 sample chapters, and marketing plans.

POETRY Anthologies must be a unique topic or theme. Query and submit 1-5 sample poems.

TIPS "At SynergEbooks, we work with the author to promote their work."

SYRACUSE UNIVERSITY PRESS

621 Skytop Rd., Suite 110, Syracuse NY 13244. (315)443-5534. **Fax:** (315)443-5545. **E-mail:** klbalens@syr.edu; jsbaines@syr.edu. **Website:** http://syracuseuniversitypress.syr.edu. **Contact:** Kelly Balenske, editorial assistant; Jennika Baines, acquisitions editor; Alice Randel Pfeiffer, director. Estab. 1943. **Publishes 50 titles/year. 25% of books from first-time authors. 95% from unagented writers.** Publishes

book 15 months after acceptance. Catalog available online. Guidelines online.

☞ "Currently emphasizing Middle East studies, Jewish studies, Irish studies, peace studies, dissability studies, television and popular culture, Native American studies, gender and ethnic studies, New York State."

NONFICTION Subjects include regional. "Special opportunity in our nonfiction program for freelance writers of books on New York state, sports history, Jewish studies, the Middle East, religious studies, television, and popular culture. Provide precise descriptions of subjects, along with background description of project. The author must make a case for the importance of his or her subject." Submit query with SASE or online, or submit outline and 2 sample chapters. Reviews artwork/photos.

TIPS "We're seeking well-written and well-researched books that will make a significant contribution to the subject areas listed above and will be well-received in the marketplace."

⬤ TAFELBERG PUBLISHERS

Imprint of NB Publishers, P.O. Box 879, Cape Town 8000, South Africa. (27)(21)406-3033. **Fax:** (27)(21)406-3812. **E-mail:** nb@nb.co.za. **Website:** www.tafelberg.com. **Contact:** Danita van Romburgh, editorial secretary; Louise Steyn, publisher. **Publishes 10 titles/year. Pays authors royalty of 15-18% based on wholesale price.** Publishes book 1 year after acceptance. Responds to queries in 2 weeks; mss in 6 months.

☞ General publisher best known for Afrikaans fiction, authoritative political works, children's/youth literature, and a variety of illustrated and nonillustrated nonfiction.

NONFICTION Subjects include health, medicine, memoirs, politics. Submit complete ms.

FICTION Subjects include juvenile, romance. Picture books, young readers: animal, anthology, contemporary, fantasy, folktales, hi-lo, humor, multicultural, nature/environment, scient fiction, special needs. Middle readers, young adults: animal (middle reader only), contemporary, fantasy, hi-lo, humor, multicultural, nature/environment, problem novels, science fiction, special needs, sports, suspense/mystery. Average word length: picture books—1,500-7,500; young readers—25,000; middle readers—15,000; young adults—40,000. Recently published *Because Pula*

Means Rain, by Jenny Robson (ages 12-15, realism); *BreinBliksem*, by Fanie Viljoen (ages 13-18, realism); *SuperZero*, by Darrel Bristow-Bovey (ages 9-12, realism/humor). Query or submit complete ms.

TIPS "Writers: Story needs to have a South African or African style. Illustrators: I'd like to look, but the chances of getting commissioned are slim. The market is small and difficult. Do not expect huge advances. Editorial staff attended or plans to attend the following conferences: IBBY, Frankfurt, SCBWI Bologna."

Ⓐ NAN A. TALESE

Imprint of Doubleday, Random House, Inco, 1745 Broadway, New York NY 10019. (212)782-8918. **Fax:** (212)782-8448. **Website:** www.nanatalese.com. **Contact:** Nan A. Talese, publisher and editorial director; Ronit Feldman, assistant editor. Publishes hardcover originals. **Publishes 15 titles/year. 400 queries received/year. 400 mss received/year. Pays variable royalty on retail price. Pays varying advance.** *Agented submissions only.*

➤ Nan A. Talese publishes nonfiction with a powerful guiding narrative and relevance to larger cultural interests, and literary fiction of the highest quality.

NONFICTION Subjects include contemporary culture, history, philosophy, sociology.

FICTION Subjects include literary. Well-written narratives with a compelling story line, good characterization and use of language. We like stories with an edge.

TIPS "Audience is highly literate people interested in story, information and insight. We want well-written material submitted by agents only. See our website."

TANGLEWOOD BOOKS

P.O. Box 3009, Terre Haute IN 47803. **E-mail:** ptierney@tanglewoodbooks.com. **Website:** www.tanglewoodbooks.com. **Contact:** Kairi Hamlin, acquisitions editor; Peggy Tierney, publisher. Estab. 2003. **Publishes 10 titles/year. 20% of books from first-time authors.** Publishes book 2 years after acceptance. Accepts simultaneous submissions. Responds to mss in up to 18 months.

➤ "Tanglewood Press strives to publish entertaining, kid-centric books."

NONFICTION Does not generally publish nonfiction.

FICTION Picture books: adventure, animal, concept, contemporary, fantasy, humor. Average word length: picture books—800. Query with 3-5 sample chapters.

TIPS "Please see lengthy 'Submissions' page on our website."

TAYLOR TRADE PUBLISHING

The Rowman & Littlefield Publishing Group, 5360 Manhattan Circle, #101, Boulder CO 80303. (303)543-7835. **Fax:** (303)543-0043. **E-mail:** rrinehart@rowman.com; tradeeditorial@rowman.com. **Website:** www.rlpgtrade.com. **Contact:** Acquisitions Editor. Rick Rinehart, editorial director Publishes hardcover originals, trade paperback originals and reprints. **Publishes 70 titles/year. 15% of books from first-time authors. 65% from unagented writers.** Publishes book 1 year after acceptance of ms. Responds in 2 months to queries. See catalog online. Submission guidelines available on website under "Author Resources.".

NONFICTION Subjects include child guidance, cooking, foods, nutrition, gardening, health, medicine, history, Texas/Western, nature, environment, sports, contemporary affairs, music, film, theater, art, nature writing, exploration, women's studies, African-American studies, literary studies. All proposals may be sent via e-mail. "Proposals should be limited to a query letter; an e-mail will generate the quickest response. If querying by e-mail, please note in the memo box 'book proposal.' Send no attachments unless requested. If using postal mail, query with SASE. What we look for at this stage is suitability of the proposed book to our publishing program (see categories) as well as the author's unique qualifications for writing his or her book."

⊕ TEACHER IDEAS PRESS

Libraries Unlimited, ABC-CLIO, P.O. Box 1911, Santa Barbara CA 93116. **E-mail:** scoatney@abc-clio.com. **Website:** www.teacherideaspress.com. **Contact:** Sharon Coatney, editor. Contact customer service by phone or e-mail for free updated catalog. Guidelines and catalog available online.

➤ "Teacher Ideas Press offers books written by teachers for teachers. Our books offer a clear and strong focus on literary and 21st century learning skills. We publish the best in innovative, practical, hands-on lessons and classroom-tested activities, all designed to help you teach 21st century literacy skills and improve student achievement. We are proud to be your partner in promoting excellence in the K-12 classroom. Whether you're a classroom, subject, or special area teacher or a library media specialist, you'll find instructional value in these resources. They include research-based strategies and materials for helping you differentiate for students who are gifted, are at risk, have special needs, or are English language learners. Send us proposals for books to teach reading comprehension, fluency, vocabulary, writing, and information literacy skills in collaboration with the school librarian."

⊘ TEBOT BACH

P.O. Box 7887, Huntington Beach CA 92615. (714)968-0905. **E-mail:** info@tebotbach.org. **Website:** www.tebotbach.org. **Contact:** Mifanwy Kaiser, editor/publisher. Publishes book 2 years after acceptance of ms. Responds to queries and mss, if invited, in 3 months.
POETRY Query first via e-mail, with a few sample poems and cover letter with brief bio.

TEMPLE UNIVERSITY PRESS

1852 N. 10th St., Philadelphia PA 19122. (215)926-2140. **Fax:** (215)926-2141. **E-mail:** tempress@temple.edu. **Website:** www.temple.edu/tempress/. **Contact:** Alex Holzman, director; Janet Francendese, editor-in-chief; Micah Kleit, executive editor; Mick Gusinde-Duffy, senior acquisitions editor. Estab. 1969. **Publishes 60 titles/year. Pays advance.** Publishes book 10 months after acceptance. Responds in 2 months to queries. Catalog available free. Guidelines online.
➤ "Temple University Press has been publishing path-breaking books on Asian-Americans, law, gender issues, film, women's studies and other interesting areas for nearly 40 years."
NONFICTION Subjects include ethnic, government, politics, health, medicine, history, photography, regional, Philadelphia, sociology, labor studies, urban studies, Latin American/Latino, Asian American, African American studies, public policy, women's studies. No memoirs, fiction or poetry. Query with SASE. Reviews artwork/photos.

TEN SPEED PRESS

The Crown Publishing Group, Attn: Acquisitions, 2625 Alcatraz Ave. #505, Berkeley CA 94705. (510)559-1600. **Fax:** (510)524-1052. **E-mail:** CrownBiz@randomhouse.com. **Website:** www.randomhouse.com/crown/tenspeed/. Estab. 1971. Publishes trade paperback originals and reprints. **Publishes 120 titles/year. 40% of books from first-time authors. 40% from unagented writers. Pays $2,500 average advance.** Pub-

lishes book 1 year after acceptance of ms. Accepts simultaneous submissions. Responds in 3 months to queries; 6-8 weeks to proposals. Catalog for 9×12 envelope and 6 first-class stamps. Guidelines online.
➤ "Ten Speed Press publishes authoritative books for an audience interested in innovative ideas. Currently emphasizing cookbooks, career, business, alternative education, and offbeat general nonfiction gift books."
NONFICTION Subjects include business, career guidance, cooking, crafts, relationships, how-to, humor, and pop culture. No fiction. "Please read our submission guidelines online. Before submitting your manuscript, you should first familiarize yourself with our publishing areas and imprints. Note that we do not consider certain genres, including fiction, poetry, memoir, and most photography." Query with SASE. Submit proposal package, sample chapters.
TIPS "We like books from people who really know their subject, rather than people who think they've spotted a trend to capitalize on. We like books that will sell for a long time, rather than 9-day wonders. Our audience consists of a well-educated, slightly weird group of people who like food, the outdoors, and take a light, but serious, approach to business and careers. Study the backlist of each publisher you're submitting to and tailor your proposal to what you perceive as their needs. Nothing gets a publisher's attention like someone who knows what he or she is talking about, and nothing falls flat like someone who obviously has no idea who he or she is submitting to."

TEXAS A&M UNIVERSITY PRESS

John H. Lindsey Building, Lewis St., 4354 TAMU, College Station TX 77843. (979)845-1436. **Fax:** (979)847-8752. **E-mail:** d-vance@tamu.edu. **Website:** www.tamupress.com. **Contact:** Mary Lenn Dixon, editor-in-chief; Thom Lemmons, managing editor; Shannon M. Davies, Louise Lindsey Merrick editor for the natural environment; Patricia Clabaugh, associate editor; Diana L. Vance, editorial assistant. Estab. 1974. **Publishes 60 titles/year. Pays royalty.** Publishes book 1 year after acceptance. Responds in 1 month to queries. Catalog available free. Guidelines online.
➤ "Texas A&M University Press publishes a wide range of nonfiction, scholarly, trade, and cross-over books of regional and national interest, reflecting the interests of the university, the

broader scholarly community, and the people of our state and region."

NONFICTION Subjects include agriculture, anthropology, archeology, art, architecture, language, literature, military, war, nature, environment, regional, Texas and the Southwest, Mexican-US borderlands studies, nautical archaeology, ethnic studies, presidential studies, history (American, Texas, western, military). Nonreturnable queries; e-mail preferred.

TIPS "Proposal requirements are posted on the website."

⊘ TEXAS TECH UNIVERSITY PRESS

P.O. Box 41037, Lubbock TX 79409. (806)742-2982. **Fax:** (806)742-2979. **E-mail:** judith.keeling@ttu.edu. **Website:** www.ttupress.org. **Contact:** Judith Keeling, editor-in-chief; Robert Mandel, director. Estab. 1971.

◯ Does not read unsolicited mss.

TEXAS WESTERN PRESS

The University of Texas at El Paso, 500 W. University Ave., El Paso TX 79968. (915)747-5688. **Fax:** (915)747-5345. **E-mail:** twpress@utep.edu; ctavarez@utep.edu. **Website:** twp.utep.edu. **Contact:** Robert L. Stakes, director. Estab. 1952. Publishes hardcover and paperback originals. **Publishes 1 title/year. Pays standard 10% royalty. Pays advance.** Responds in 2 months to queries. Catalog available free. Guidelines online.

⚷ "Texas Western Press publishes books on the history and cultures of the American Southwest, particularly historical and biographical works about West Texas, New Mexico, northern Mexico, and the U.S. borderlands. The Press also publishes selected books in the areas of regional art, photography, Native American studies, geography, demographics, border issues, politics, and natural history."

NONFICTION Subjects include education, health, medicine, history, language, literature, nature, environment, regional, science, social sciences. "Historic and cultural accounts of the Southwest (West Texas, New Mexico, northern Mexico). Also art, photographic books, Native American and limited regional fiction reprints. Occasional technical titles. Our *Southwestern Studies* use manuscripts of up to 30,000 words. Our hardback books range from 30,000 words and up. The writer should use good exposition in his work. Most of our work requires documentation. We favor a scholarly, but not overly pedantic, style. We specialize in superior book design." Query with SASE, or submit résumé, 2-3 sample chapters, cover letter,

description of ms and special features, TOC, list of competing titles.

TIPS "Texas Western Press is interested in books relating to the history of Hispanics in the US. Will experiment with photo-documentary books, and is interested in seeing more contemporary books on border issues. We try to treat our authors professionally, produce handsome, long-lived books and aim for quality, rather than quantity of titles carrying our imprint."

THIRD WORLD PRESS

P.O. Box 19730, Chicago IL 60619. (773)651-0700. **Fax:** (773)651-7286. **E-mail:** twpress3@aol.com; GWENMTWP@aol.com. **Website:** www.thirdworldpressinc.com. **Contact:** Bennett J. Johnson. Estab. 1967. Publishes hardcover and trade paperback originals and reprints. **Publishes 20 titles/year. 200-300 queries received/year. 200 mss received/year. 20% of books from first-time authors. 80% from unagented writers. Compensation based upon royalties. Individual arrangement with author depending on the book, etc.** Publishes book 18 months after acceptance. Accepts simultaneous submissions. Responds in 6 months to queries. Responds in 5 months to mss. Guidelines for #10 SASE.

◯ Third World Press is open to submissions in July only.

NONFICTION Subjects include anthropology, archeology, education, ethnic, government, politics, health, medicine, history, language, literature, literary criticism, philosophy, psychology, regional, religion, sociology, women's issues/studies, black studies. Query with SASE. Submit outline, 5 sample chapters. Reviews artwork/photos. Send photocopies.

FICTION Subjects include ethnic, feminist, historical, juvenile, animal, easy-to-read, fantasy, historical, contemporary, literary, mainstream, contemporary, picture books, plays, short story collections, young adult, easy-to-read/teen, folktales, historical, African-centered, African-American materials, preschool/picture book. "We primarily publish nonfiction, but will consider fiction by and about Blacks." Query with SASE. Submit outline, clips, 5 sample chapters.

POETRY Ethnic/African-centered and African-American materials. Submit complete ms.

☺ THISTLEDOWN PRESS LTD.

118 20th Street West, Saskatoon SK S7M 0W6, Canada. (306)244-1722. **Fax:** (306)244-1762. **Website:** www.

thistledownpress.com. **Contact:** Allan Forrie, publisher. **Pays authors royalty of 10-12% based on net dollar sales. Pays illustrators and photographers by the project (range: $250-750).** Publishes book 1 year after acceptance. Responds to queries in 4 months. Catalog free on request. Guidelines available for #10 envelope and IRC.

FICTION Middle readers, young adults: adventure, anthology, contemporary, fantasy, humor, poetry, romance, science fiction, suspense/mystery, short stories. Average word length: young adults—40,000. Submit outline/synopsis and sample chapters. *Does not accept mss.* Do not query by e-mail.

TIPS "Send cover letter including publishing history and SASE."

TIA CHUCHA PRESS

c/o Tia Chucha's Centro Cultural, 13197-A Gladstone Blvd., Sylmar CA 91342. **E-mail:** info@tiachucha.com. **Website:** www.tiachucha.com. **Contact:** Luis Rodriguez, director. Estab. 1989. Publishes hardcover and trade paperback originals. **Publishes 2-4 titles/year. 25-30 queries received/year. 150 mss received/year. Pays 10% royalty on wholesale price.** Publishes book 1 year after acceptance. Responds in 9 months to mss. Guidelines available free.

Tia Chucha's Centro Cultural is a nonprofit learning and cultural arts center. We support andpromote the continued growth, development and holistic learning of our community through the many powerful means of the arts. Tia Centra provides a positive space for people to activate what we all share as humans: the capacity to create, to imagine and to express ourselves in an effort to improve the quality of life for our community.

NONFICTION Subjects include agriculture, Americana, art, architecture, community, computers, electronics, contemporary culture, creative nonfiction, ethnic, government, politics, history, humanities, language, literature, memoirs, multicultural, music, dance, New Age, philosophy, photography, regional, sociology, software, translation, travel, womens issues, womens studies, world affairs. Celebrating Words, literature and art; festivals, book readings, signings.

FICTION Subjects include ethnic, feminist, historical, humor, juvenile, literary, mainstream, contemporary, multicultural, multimedia, plays, poetry, regional, short story collections, translation, young adult.

POETRY No restrictions as to style or content. We do cross-cultural and performance-oriented poetry. It has to work on the page, however. Query and submit complete ms.

TIPS We will cultivate the practice. Audience is those interested.

TIGHTROPE BOOKS

602 Markham St., Toronto ON M6G 2L8, Canada. (647)348-4460. **E-mail:** shirarose@tightropebooks. com. **Website:** www.tightropebooks.com. **Contact:** Shirarose Wilensky, editor. Estab. 2005. Publishes hardcover and trade paperback originals. **Publishes 12 titles/year. 70% of books from first-time authors. 100% from unagented writers. Pays 5-15% royalty on retail price. Pays advance of $200-300.** Publishes book 1 year after acceptance. Accepts simultaneous submissions. Responds if interested. Catalog and guidelines free on request and online.

NONFICTION Subjects include alternative lifestyles, architecture, art, contemporary culture, creative nonfiction, ethnic, gay, language, lesbian, literary criticism, literature, multicultural, womens issues. Query with SASE. Submit proposal package, including outline, 1 sample chapter and complete ms. Reviews artwork. Send photocopies.

FICTION Subjects include contemporary, ethnic, experimental, fantasy, feminist, gay, horror, juvenile, lesbian, literary, mainstream, multicultural, poetry, poetry in translation, short story collections, translation, young adult. Query with SASE. Submit proposal package, including: synopsis, 1 sample chapter and completed ms.

POETRY Query. Submit 10 sample poems. Submit complete ms.

TIPS "Audience is young, urban, literary, educated, unconventional."

TILBURY HOUSE

Harpswell Press, Inc., 103 Brunswick Ave., Gardiner ME 04345. (800)582-1899. **Fax:** (207)582-8227. **E-mail:** tilbury@tilburyhouse.com. **Website:** www.tilburyhouse.com. **Contact:** Karen Fisk, associate children's book editor; Jennifer Bunting, publisher. Estab. 1990. **Publishes 10 titles/year. Pays royalty based on wholesale price.** Publishes book 1 year after acceptance. Responds to mss in 2 months. Catalog available free. Guidelines online.

NONFICTION Regional adult biography/history/maritime/nature, and children's picture books that deal with issues, such as bullying, multiculturalism, etc. Submit complete ms or outline/synopsis. Reviews artwork/photos. Send photocopies.

FICTION Picture books: multicultural, nature/environment. Special needs include books that teach children about tolerance and honoring diversity. Submit complete ms or outline/synopsis.

TIPS "We are always interested in stories that will encourage children to understand the natural world and the environment, as well as stories with social justice themes. We really like stories that engage children to become problem solvers as well as those that promote respect, tolerance and compassion." We do not publish books with personified animal characters; historical fiction; chapter books; fantasy."

TIN HOUSE BOOKS

2617 NW Thurman St., Portland OR 97210. (503)473-8663. **Fax:** (503)473-8957. **E-mail:** meg@tinhouse.com. **Website:** www.tinhouse.com. **Contact:** Lee Montgomery, editorial director; Meg Storey, editor; Tony Perez, associate editor. Publishes hardcover originals, paperback originals, paperback reprints. **Publishes 8-10 titles/year. 20% from unagented writers.** Publishes book 1 year after acceptance. Accepts simultaneous submissions. Responds to queries in 2-3 weeks; mss in 2-3 months. Guidelines available on website.

"We are a small independent publisher dedicated to nurturing new, promising talent as well as showcasing the work of established writers. Our Tin House New Voice series features work by authors who have not previously published a book." Distributes/promotes titles through Publishers Group West.

NONFICTION *Agented mss only.* We no longer read unsolicited submissions by authors with no representation. We will continue to accept submissions from agents.

FICTION *Agented mss only.* We no longer read unsolicited submissions by authors with no representation. We will continue to accept submissions from agents.

TITAN PRESS

PMB 17897, Encino CA 91416. **E-mail:** titan91416@yahoo.com. **Website:** www.calwriterssfv.com. **Contact:** Stefanya Wilson, editor. Estab. 1981. Publishes hardcover and paperback originals. **Publishes 12 titles/year. 50% from unagented writers. Pays 20-40% royalty.** Publishes book 1 year after acceptance.

Responds to queries in 3 months. Ms guidelines for #10 SASE.

FICTION Literary, mainstream/contemporary, short story collections. Does not accept unsolicited mss. Query with SASE. Include brief bio, social security number, list of publishing credits.

TIPS "Look, act, sound, and *be* professional."

TO BE READ ALOUD PUBLISHING, INC.

P.O. Box 632426, Nacogdoches TX 75963. **E-mail:** michael@tobereadaloud.org; submissions@tobereadaloud.org. **Website:** www.tobereadaloud.org. **Contact:** Michael Powell, president (short stories); Stephen Powell, editor (poetry). Estab. 2006. Publishes trade paperback originals and reprints. **Publishes 4 titles/year. 250 queries received/year. 200 mss received/year. 90% of books from first-time authors. 90% from unagented writers. Makes outright purchase of $100-200.** Publishes book 4 months after acceptance. Accepts simultaneous submissions. Responds in 3 months to queries, proposals, and mss. Guidelines available via e-mail.

NONFICTION Subjects include community, contemporary culture, creative nonfiction, education, ethnic, military, war, multicultural, philosophy, sociology. "Submissions are for the purpose of supporting high school drama coaches and their oral interpretation competitors. Selections should be written to be read aloud. Selections should be less than 3,000 words." Submit complete ms.

FICTION Subjects include adventure, confession, ethnic, gothic, historical, horror, humor, juvenile, literary, multicultural, mystery, poetry, poetry in translation, science fiction, short story collections, sports, suspense, western. All submissions should be written by authors born in one of the following states: Alabama, Arkansas, Florida, Georgia, Louisiana, Kentucky, Mississippi, North Carolina, South Carolina, Tennessee, Virginia, or West Virginia. Submit complete ms. Attach as a Word .doc.

POETRY Submit complete ms.

TIPS "Our audience is high school drama students. Read your selection aloud before submitting. We service the UIL of Texas mostly; check their annual categories and write accordingly to match them."

TODD PUBLICATIONS

P.O. Box 1752, Boca Raton FL 33429. (561)910-0440. **E-mail:** toddpub@aol.com. **Website:** www.toddpub.info. **Contact:** Barry Klein, president. Estab. 1973.

Publishes reference books and trade paperback originals. **Publishes 10 titles/year. 10% of books from first-time authors. 100% from unagented writers.** Publishes book 3 months after acceptance. Accepts simultaneous submissions. Responds in 1 month to proposals. Book listing available via e-mail.

8—π "Todd Publications publishes/distributes reference books and directories of all types."

NONFICTION Subjects include ethnic, health, medicine & fitness. Submit outline and 2 sample chapters.

TOKYO ROSE RECORDS/ CHAPULTEPEC PRESS

4222 Chambers, Cincinnati OH 45223. **E-mail:** ChapultepecPress@hotmail.com. **Website:** www.tokyoroserecords.com. **Contact:** David Garza. Estab. 2001. Publishes trade paperback originals. **Publishes 1-2 titles/year. 50 queries received/year. 10 mss received/year. 50% of books from first-time authors. 100% from unagented writers. Pays 50% of profits and author's copies.** Publishes book 6 months after acceptance. Accepts simultaneous submissions. Catalog online.

NONFICTION Subjects include alternative, art, architecture, contemporary culture, creative nonfiction, ethnic, government, politics, history, humanities, language, literature, literary criticism, memoirs, multicultural, music, dance, nature, environment, philosophy, photography, recreation, regional, translation, world affairs. Submit proposal package, outline, 2-3 sample chapters, artwork samples. Reviews artwork/photos. Send photocopies.

FICTION Subjects include comic books, erotica, ethnic, experimental, humor, literary, multicultural, multimedia, occult, picture books, plays, poetry, poetry in translation, regional, short story collections stories, translation. Submit proposal package, clips, 2-3 sample chapters, artwork samples.

POETRY Chapultepec Press publishes books of poetry/literature, essays, social/political issues, art, music, film, history, popular science; library/archive issues, and bilingual works. Wants "poetry that works as a unit, that is caustic, fun, open-ended, worldly, mature, relevant, stirring, evocative. Bilingual. Looking for authors who have a publishing history. No poetry collections without a purpose, that are mere collections. Also looking for broadsides/posters/illuminations." Publishes 1-2 books/year. Books are usually 1-100 pages. Query first. Submit 5-15 sample poems.

TIPS Tokyo Rose Records/Chapultepec Press specializes in shorter-length publications (100 pages or less). Order sample books by sending $5 payable to David Garza.

⊘ TOP COW PRODUCTIONS

10390 Santa Monica Blvd., Suite 340, Los Angeles CA **Website:** http://www.topcow.com/Site/.

FICTION *No unsolicited submissions.* Prefers submissions from artists. See website for details and advice on how to break into the market.

TOP PUBLICATIONS, LTD.

3100 Independence Pkwy., Suite 311-349, Plano TX 75075. (972)490-9686. **Fax:** (972)233-0713. **E-mail:** info@toppub.com; submissions@toppub.com. **Website:** www.toppub.com. **Contact:** Sara Mendoza, editor. Estab. 1999. Publishes hardcover and paperback originals. **Publishes 2-3 titles/year. 200 queries received/year. 20 mss received/year. 90% of books from first-time authors. 95% from unagented writers. Pays 15-20% royalty on wholesale price. Pays $250-2,500 advance.** Publishes book 8 months after acceptance. Accepts simultaneous submissions. Acknowledges receipt of queries but only responds if interested in seeing ms. Responds in 6 months to mss. Tear sheets available on new titles. Guidelines online.

8—π Primarily a mainstream fiction publisher.

NONFICTION "We are primarily a fiction publisher and do not solicit submissions of non-fiction works."

FICTION Subjects include adventure, historical, horror, juvenile, mainstream, contemporary, military, war, mystery, regional, romance, science fiction, short story collections, suspense, young adult.

TIPS "We recommend that our authors write books that appeal to a large mainstream audience to make marketing easier and increase the chances of success. We only publish a few titles a year so the odds at getting published at TOP are slim. If we reject your work, it probably doesn't have any reflection on your work. We have to pass on a lot of good material each year simply by the limitations of our time and budget."

TOR BOOKS

175 Fifth Ave., New York NY 10010. **Website:** www.tor-forge.com. **Contact:** Juliet Pederson, publishing coordinator. Susan Change, senior editor **Publishes Publishes 5-10 middle readers/year; 5-10 young adult titles/year. titles/year. Pays author royalty. Pays illustrators by the project.** Catalog available

for 9x12 SAE and 3 first-class stamps. See website for latest submission guidelines.

NONFICTION Middle readers and young adult: geography, history, how-to, multicultural, nature/environment, science, social issues. Does not want to see religion, cooking. Average word length: middle readers—25,000-35,000; young adults—70,000.

FICTION Subjects include Middle readers, young adult titles: adventure, animal, anthology, concept, contemporary, fantasy, history, humor, multicultural, nature/environment, problem novel, science fiction, suspense/mystery. Average word length: middle readers—30,000; young adults—60,000-100,000. We do not accept queries.

TIPS "Know the house you are submitting to, familiarize yourself with the types of books they are publishing. Get an agent. Allow him/her to direct you to publishers who are most appropriate. It saves time and effort."

TORQUERE PRESS

P.O. Box 2545, Round Rock TX 78680. (512)586-3553. **Fax:** (866)287-2968. **E-mail:** editor@torquerepress.com; submissions@torquerepress.com. **Website:** www.torquerepress.com. **Contact:** Shawn Clements, submissions editor (homoerotica, suspense, gay/lesbian); Lorna Hinson, senior editor (gay/lesbian romance, historicals). Estab. 2003. Publishes trade paperback originals and electronic originals and reprints. **Publishes 140 titles/year. 500 queries received/year. 200 mss received/year. 25% of books from first-time authors. 100% from unagented writers. Pays 8-40% royalty. Pays $35-75 for anthology stories.** Publishes book 6 months after acceptance. Responds in 1 month to queries and proposals; 2-4 months to mss. Catalog and guidelines online.

"We are a gay and lesbian press focusing on romance and genres of romance. We particularly like paranormal and western romance."

FICTION Subjects include adventure, erotica, gay, lesbian, historical, horror, mainstream, contemporary, multicultural, mystery, occult, romance, science fiction, short story collections, suspense, western. All categories gay and lesbian themed. Adventure, erotica, historical, horror, mainstream, multicultural, mystery, occult, romance, science fiction, short story collections, suspense, western. Imprints accepting submissions. Submit proposal package, 3 sample chapters, clips.

TIPS "Our audience is primarily people looking for a familiar romance setting featuring gay or lesbian protagonists. Please read guidelines carefully and familiarize yourself with our lines."

TORREY HOUSE PRESS, LLC

P.O. Box 750196, Torrey UT 84775. (801)810-9THP. **E-mail:** mark@torreyhouse.com. **Website:** http://torreyhouse.com. **Contact:** Kirsten Allen, editor (literary fiction, creative nonfiction). Estab. 2010. Publishes hardcover, trade paperback, and electronic originals. **Publishes 10 titles/year. 500 queries/year; 200 mss/year. 80% of books from first-time authors. 80% from unagented writers. Pays 5-15% royalty on retail price.** Publishes book 6 months after acceptance. Accepts simultaneous submissions. Responds in 2 months to queries, proposals, and mss. Catalog online. Guidelines online or by e-mail.

Envisions reading audience of the American West literary fiction and creative nonfiction.

NONFICTION Subjects include anthropology, creative nonfiction, environment, nature. Query; submit proposal package, including: outline, sample chapter, bio.

FICTION Subjects include historical, literary. "THP publishes literary fiction and creative nonfiction about the people, cultures and resource management issues of the Colorado plateau and the American West." Submit proposal package including: synopsis, 3 sample chapters, bio.

POETRY Submit query, 3 sample poems.

TOTAL-E-BOUND PUBLISHING

Total-e-Ntwined Limited, 1 Faldingworth Road, Spridlington, Market Rasen, Lincolnshire LN8 2DE, United Kingdom. **Website:** http://www.total-e-bound.com; http://www.forum.totalebound.com. **Contact:** Claire Siemaszkiewicz, editor; Michele Paulin, editor; Janice Bennett, editor. Publishes paperback and e-book originals. **90% from unagented writers. Pays royalties 40% e-book, 10% print.** Publishes book 6 months after acceptance. Responds to queries in 2 weeks, mss in 2 months. Catalog online.

"The team at Total-e-bound came together to provide a unique service to our authors and readers. We are a royalty paying, full-service e-publisher. This means that there are no fees to the author tobecome published with us. Brought together by a mutual love of outstanding erotic fiction, we offer a mass of business experience in the form of editors, artists, marketeers, IT technicians and support staff to meet all of your needs. We love what we do and are totally dedicated, committed and loyal to providing the best service that we can to our authors and our readers. TEB publishes, markets and promotes top quality erotic romance e-books and paperback books."

FICTION "We are currently accepting manuscripts between 10,000 and 100,000+ words in the following genres: Action/Adventure, Bondage/BDSM, Comedy/Humour, Contemporary, Cowboy/Western, Fantasy/Fairytale, Futuristic/Sci-fi, Gay/Lesbian, Historical/Rubenesque, Ménage-á-trois/Multiple Partners, Multicultural, Older Woman/Younger Man, Paranormal/Timetravel, Thriller/Crime, Shapeshifters/Morphers, Vampire/Werewolf." Throughout the year we do special themed short stories. General guidelines: 10K - 15K word count Any genre (see below for specific themes) Anthologies are released every quarter—each with a distinctive theme. "We produce a series of four anthologies per year, six short stories in each. Query with outline/synopsis and first 3 and last chapters. Accepts queries by online submission e-mail. Include estimated word count, brief bio, list of publishing credits.

TIPS "First impressions are important. Send in a good intro letter with your synopsis and manuscript, giving details of what you will do yourself to promote your work. Always read and follow the submission guidelines."

☼ TOUCHWOOD EDITIONS

The Heritage Group, 340-1105 Pandora Ave., Victoria BC V8V 3P9, Canada. (250)360-0829. **Fax:** (250)386-0829. **E-mail:** info@touchwoodeditions.com. **Website:** www.touchwoodeditions.com. Ruth Linka Publishes trade paperback originals and reprints. **Publishes 20-25 titles/year. 40% of books from first-time authors. 70% from unagented writers. Pays 15% royalty on net price.** Publishes book 12-24 months after acceptance of ms. Accepts simultaneous submissions. Responds in 3 months to queries. Catalog and submission guidelines available online for free.

NONFICTION Subjects include anthropology, archeology, art, architecture, creative nonfiction, government, politics, history, nature, environment, recreation, regional., nautical. Submit TOC, outline, word count, 2-3 sample chapters, synopsis. Reviews artwork/photos. Send photocopies.

FICTION Subjects include historical, mystery. Submit TOC, outline, word count.

TIPS "Our area of interest is Western Canada. We would like more creative nonfiction and books about people of note in Canada's history."

TOWER PUBLISHING

588 Saco Rd., Standish ME 04084. (207)642-5400. **Fax:** (207)642-5463. **E-mail:** info@towerpub.com. **Website:** www.towerpub.com. **Contact:** Michael Lyons, president. Estab. 1772. Publishes hardcover originals and reprints, trade paperback originals. **Publishes 22 titles/year. 60 queries received/year. 30 mss received/year. 10% of books from first-time authors. 90% from unagented writers.** Publishes book 6 months after acceptance. Accepts simultaneous submissions. Responds in 1 month to queries; 2 months to proposals and mss. Catalog and guidelines online.

☛ Tower Publishing specializes in business and professional directories and legal books.

NONFICTION Subjects include business, economics. Looking for legal books of a national stature. Query with SASE. Submit outline.

⊘ TOY BOX PRODUCTIONS

7532 Hickory Hills Ct., Whites Creek TN 37189. (615)299-0822. **Fax:** (615)876-3931. **E-mail:** toybox@crttoybox.com. **Website:** www.crttoybox.com. Estab. 1995. Publishes mass market paperback originals. **Publishes 4 titles/year. 100% of books from first-time authors. 100% from unagented writers. Pays 10-15% royalty on wholesale price.** Catalog online.

◖ We are not accepting new submissions at this time.

NONFICTION Subjects include audio, Americana, education, religion. *All unsolicited mss returned unopened.*

☼ TRADEWIND BOOKS

202-1807 Maritime Mews, Granville Island, Vancouver BC V6H 3W7, Canada. (604)662-4405. **E-mail:** tradewindbooks@mail.lycos.com. **Website:** www.tradewindbooks.com. **Contact:** Michael Katz, publisher; Carol Frank, art director; R. David Stephens, senior editor. Publishes hardcover and trade paperback originals. **Publishes 5 titles/year. 15% of books from first-time authors. 50% from unagented writers. Pays 7% royalty on retail price. Pays variable advance.** Publishes book 3 years after acceptance. Accepts simultaneous submissions.

Responds to mss in 2 months. Catalog and guidelines online.

☛ "Tradewind Books publishes juvenile picture books and young adult novels. Requires that submissions include evidence that author has read at least 3 titles published by Tradewind Books."

FICTION Subjects include juvenile, picture books. Picture books: adventure, multicultural, folktales. Average word length: 900 words. *YA novels by Canadian authors only. Chapter books by US authors considered.*

TRAFALGAR SQUARE BOOKS

P.O. Box 257, 388 Howe Hill Road, North Pomfret VT 05053. (802)457-1911. **Website:** www.horseandrider-books.com. **Contact:** Martha Cook, managing director; Rebecca Didier, senior editor. Estab. 1985. Publishes hardcover and trade paperback originals. **Publishes 12 titles/year. 50% of books from first-time authors. 80% from unagented writers. Pays royalty. Pays advance.** Publishes book 18 months after acceptance. Responds in 1 month to queries, 2 months to proposals, 2-3 months to mss. Catalog free on request and by e-mail.

☛ "We publish high quality instructional books for horsemen and horsewomen, always with the horse's welfare in mind."

NONFICTION Subjects include animals, horses/dogs. We rarely consider books for complete novices. Query with SASE. Submit proposal package including outline, 1-3 sample chapters, letter of introduction including qualifications for writing on the subject and why the proposed book is an essential addition to existing publications. Reviews artwork/photos as part of the ms package. We prefer color laser thumbnail sheets or duplicate prints (do not send original photos or art!).

TIPS "Our audience is horse lovers and riders interested in doing what is best in the interest of horses."

TRAVIS LAKE PUBLISHING LLC

P.O. Box 410, City College Station TX 77841. **E-mail:** contact@travislakepublishing.com; submissions@travislakepublishing.com. **Website:** www.travislakepublishing.com. **Contact:** Sandra J. Smith, partner/editor-in-chief (mystery, thriller, science fiction, fantasy); Stephen D. Dealer, partner/publisher (history, civil rights, law, business). Estab. 2011. Publishes electronic originals, electronic reprints, trade paperback originals. **Publishes 10 titles/year. Advance range**

up to $200. **Royalties run from 8% (trades) to 50% (electronic).** Responds in 1 month on queries and proposals. Catalog available for #10 SASE or online. Guidelines available for #10 SASE or online.

NONFICTION Subjects include alternative lifestyles, Americana, animals, anthropology, archeology, business, community, computers, contemporary culture, crafts, creative nonfiction, electronics, ethnic, gardening, gay, history, hobbies, house and home, labor, law, memoirs, military, multicultural, real estate, recreation, science, social sciences. "We are looking for works that fall into two categories. The first is publications between 25,000 and 125,000 words. The second is short reference or how to works geared toward use on a mobile device." Submit a proposal packing including an outline, 2 sample chapters, and a "professional query letter which includes the title of your book, word count, genre, short bio, whether or not the proposed work has been previously published in any format, and your contact information."

FICTION Subjects include adventure, fantasy, historical, humor, mainstream, mystery, occult, regional, science fiction, suspense, young adult. "We are looking primarily for novel length manuscripts of between 35,000 and 125,000 words. Optimal length is around 82,000 words, approximately the length of a 328 page novel. At this time we do NOT publish romance or erotica. Depictions of sex should be no more explicit than what can be found in an R rated movie." Submit proposal package including synopsis, 3 sample chapters, a "professional query letter which includes the title of your novel, word count, genre, short bio, whether or not proposed work has been previously published in any format, and your contact information."

TRISTAN PUBLISHING

2355 Louisiana Ave. N, Golden Valley MO 55427. (763)545-1383. **Fax:** (763)545-1387. **E-mail:** info@tristanpublishing.com or manuscripts@tristanpublishing.com. **Website:** www.tristanpublishing.com. **Contact:** Brett Waldman, publisher. Estab. 2002. Publishes hardcover originals. **Publishes 6-10 titles/year. 1,000 queries and manuscripts/year. 15% of books from first-time authors. 100% from unagented writers. Pays royalty on wholesale or retail price; outright purchase.** Publishes book 2 years after acceptance. Accepts simultaneous submissions. Responds in 3 months on queries/proposals/mss. Catalog and guidelines free on request. Guidelines online.

NONFICTION Inspirational. "Our mission is to create books with a message that inspire and uplift in typically 1,000 words or less." Query with SASE; submit completed mss. Reviews artwork/photos; send photocopies.

FICTION Inspirational, gift books. Query with SASE; submit completed mss.

TIPS "Our audience is adults and children."

TRIUMPH BOOKS

542 Dearborn St., Suite 750, Chicago IL 60605. (312)939-3330; (800)335-5323. **Fax:** (312)663-3557. **Website:** www.triumphbooks.com. **Contact:** Tom Bast, editorial director. Estab. 1990. Publishes hardcover originals and trade paperback originals and reprints. Accepts simultaneous submissions. Catalog available free.

NONFICTION Subjects include recreation, sports., health, sports business/motivation. Query with SASE. Reviews artwork/photos. Send photocopies.

TRUMAN STATE UNIVERSITY PRESS

100 E. Normal St., Kirksville MO 63501-4221. (660)785-7336. **Fax:** (660)785-4480. **E-mail:** tsup@truman.edu. **Website:** tsup.truman.edu. **Contact:** Barbara Smith-Mandell, copy editor/acquisitions editor; Judith Sharp, production editor; Mark Hanley, chair. Estab. 1986. **Publishes 13 titles/year.** Guidelines online.

⚷ Truman State University Press (TSUP) publishes peer-reviewed research in the humanities for the scholarly community and the broader public, and publishes creative literary works. TSUP is a resource to the Truman campus community, where students explore their publishing interests and scholars seek publishing advice. Truman State University Press is a small, traditional publisher with a reputation for working closely with our authors. TSUP publishes high-quality and well-designed books authors are proud of and readers cherish.

NONFICTION Early modern, American studies, poetry.

○ TURNSTONE PRESS

206-100 Arthur St., Winnipeg MB R3B 1H3, Canada. (204)947-1555. **Fax:** (204)942-1555. **E-mail:** info@turnstonepress.com; editor@turnstonepress.com. **Website:** www.turnstonepress.com. Estab. 1976. Publishes book 2 years after acceptance. Responds in 4-7 months. Guidelines online.

⚷ "Turnstone Press is a literary publisher, not a general publisher, and therefore we are only interested in literary fiction, literary non-fiction—including literary criticism—and poetry. We do publish literary mysteries, thrillers, and noir under our Ravenstone imprint. We publish only Canadian authors or landed immigrants, we strive to publish a significant number of new writers, to publish in a variety of genres, and to have 50% of each year's list be Manitoba writers and/or books with Manitoba content."

NONFICTION "Samples must be 40 to 60 pages, typed/printed in a minimum 12 point serif typeface such as Times, Book Antiqua, or Garamond."

FICTION "Samples must be 40 to 60 pages, typed/printed in a minimum 12 point serif typeface such as Times, Book Antiqua, or Garamond."

POETRY Poetry manuscripts should be a minimum 70 pages. Submit complete ms. Include cover letter.

TIPS "As a Canadian literary press, we have a mandate to publish Canadian writers only. Do some homework before submitting works to make sure your subject matter/genre/writing style falls within the publishers area of interest."

TUTTLE PUBLISHING

364 Innovation Dr., North Clarendon VT 05759. (802)773-8930. **Fax:** (802)773-6993. **E-mail:** info@tuttlepublishing.com. **Website:** www.tuttlepublishing.com. Estab. 1832. Publishes hardcover and trade paperback originals and reprints. **Publishes 125 titles/year. 1,000 queries received/year. 20% of books from first-time authors. 40% from unagented writers. Pays 5-10% royalty on net or retail price, depending on format and kind of book. Pays advance.** Publishes book 18 months after acceptance. Accepts simultaneous submissions. Responds in 2-3 months to proposals.

⚷ Tuttle is America's leading publisher of books on Japan and Asia.

NONFICTION Query with SASE.

TWILIGHT TIMES BOOKS

P.O. Box 3340, Kingsport TN 37664. **Website:** www.twilighttimesbooks.com. **Contact:** Andy M. Scott, managing editor. Estab. 1999. **Publishes 50 titles/year. 10% from unagented writers. Pays 8-15% royalty.** Responds in 4 weeks to queries; 2 months to mss. Guidelines online.

⚷ "We publish compelling literary fiction by authors with a distinctive voice."

FICTION Accepts unsolicited mss. Do not send complete mss. Queries via e-mail only. Include estimated word count, brief bio, list of publishing credits, marketing plan.

TIPS "The only requirement for consideration at Twilight Times Books is that your novel must be entertaining and professionally written."

ⒶⓄ TYNDALE HOUSE PUBLISHERS, INC.

351 Executive Dr., Carol Stream IL 60188. (800)323-9400. **Fax:** (800)684-0247. **Website:** www.tyndale.com. **Contact:** Katara Washington Patton, acquisitions; Talinda Iverson, art acquisitions. Estab. 1962. Publishes hardcover and trade paperback originals and mass paperback reprints. **Publishes 15 titles/year. Pays negotiable royalty. Pays negotiable advance.** Accepts simultaneous submissions. Guidelines for 9×12 SAE and $2.40 for postage or visit website.

8—• "Tyndale House publishes practical, user-friendly Christian books for the home and family."

NONFICTION Subjects include child guidance, religion, devotional/inspirational. Prefers agented submissions.

FICTION Subjects include juvenile, romance., Christian (children's, general, inspirational, mystery/suspense, thriller, romance). "Christian truths must be woven into the story organically. No short story collections. Youth books: character building stories with Christian perspective. Especially interested in ages 10-14. We primarily publish Christian historical romances, with occasional contemporary, suspense, or standalones." Agented submissions only. *No unsolicited mss.*

TIPS "All accepted manuscripts will appeal to Evangelical Christian children and parents."

UNBRIDLED BOOKS

200 N. Ninth Street, Suite A, Columbia MO 65201. **Website:** http://unbridledbooks.com. Estab. 2004.

8—• "Unbridled Books is a premier publisher of works of rich literary quality that appeal to a broad audience."

FICTION Please query first by e-mail. Due to the heavy volume of submissions, we regret that at this time we are not able to consider uninvited mss. Please query either Fred Ramey or Greg Michalson, but not both.

TIPS "We try to read each ms that arrives, so please be patient."

UNITY HOUSE

Unity, 1901 N.W. Blue Pkwy., Unity Village MO 64065-0001. (816)524-3550. **Fax:** (816)347-5518. E-mail: unity@unityonline.org. **E-mail:** sartinson@unityonline.org. **Website:** www.unityonline.org. **Contact:** Sharon Sartin, executive assistant. Estab. 1889. Publishes hardcover, trade paperback, and electronic originals. **Publishes 5-7 titles/year. 50 queries received/year. 5% of books from first-time authors. 95% from unagented writers. Pays 10-15% royalty on retail price. Pays advance.** Publishes book 13 months after acceptance. Responds in 6-8 months. Catalog free on request & online: http://unityonline.org/publications/pdf/productcatalog.pdf. Guidelines free & available online & by e-mail.

8—• Unity House publishes metaphysical Christian books based on Unity principles, as well as inspirational books on metaphysics and practical spirituality. All manuscripts must reflect a spiritual foundation and express the Unity philosophy, practical Christianity, universal principles, and/or metaphysics.

NONFICTION Subjects include religion, spirituality, metaphysics, new thought. "Writers should be familiar with principles of metaphysical Christianity but not feel bound by them. We are interested in works in the related fields of holistic health, spiritual psychology, and the philosophy of other world religions." Submit proposal package, including: outline, 50 sample chapters. Reviews artwork/photos. Writers should send photocopies.

FICTION Subjects include spiritual, inspirational, metaphysical, visionary fiction. "We are a bridge between traditional Christianity and New Age spirituality. Unity is based on metaphysical Christian principles, spiritual values and the healing power of prayer as a resource for daily living." Submit complete mss (3 copies).

TIPS "We target an audience of spiritual seekers."

THE UNIVERSITY OF AKRON PRESS

120 E. Mill St., Suite 415, Akron OH 44325. (330)972-5342. **Fax:** (330)972-8364. **E-mail:** uapress@uakron.edu. **Website:** www.uakron.edu/uapress. **Contact:** Thomas Bacher, director and acquisitions. Estab. 1988. Publishes hardcover and paperback originals and re-issues. **Publishes 10-12 titles/year. 200-300 queries received/year. 50-75 mss received/year. 40% of books from first-time authors. 80% from unagented writers. Pays 7-15% royalty.** Publishes book 9-12 months after acceptance. Accepts simultaneous submissions. Responds in 2 weeks to queries/proposals;

3-4 months to solicited mss. Query prior to submitting. Catalog available free. Guidelines online.

⚭ "The University of Akron Press is the publishing arm of The University of Akron and is dedicated to the dissemination of scholarly, professional, and regional books and other content."

NONFICTION Subjects include Applied politics, early American literature, emerging technologies, history of psychology, history of technology, interdisciplinary studies, Northeast Ohio history and culture, Ohio politics, poetics. Query by e-mail. Mss cannot be returned unless SASE is included.

POETRY Follow the guidelines and submit mss only for the contest: www.uakron.edu/uapress/poetry. html. "We publish two books of poetry annually, one of which is the winner of The Akron Poetry prize. We also are interested in literary collections based around one theme, especially collections of translated works." If you are interested in publishing with The University of Akron Press, please fill out form online.

THE UNIVERSITY OF ALABAMA PRESS

P.O. Box 870380, Tuscaloosa AL 35487. (205)348-5180 or (205)348-1571. **Fax:** (205)348-9201. **E-mail:** rcook@uapress.ua.edu. **Website:** www.uapress.ua.edu. **Contact:** Rick Cook, production manager; Michele Myatt Quinn, designer; Kaci Lane Hindman, production editor. Publishes nonfiction hardcover and paperbound originals, and fiction paperback reprints. **Publishes 70-75 titles/year. 70% of books from first-time authors. 95% from unagented writers. Pays advance.** Responds in 2 weeks to queries. Catalog available free.

NONFICTION Subjects include anthropology, archeology, community, government, politics, history, language, literature, literary criticism, religion, translation. Considers upon merit almost any subject of scholarly interest, but specializes in communications, military history, public administration, literary criticism and biography, history, Jewish studies, and American archaeology. Accepts nonfiction translations. Query with SASE. Reviews artwork/photos.

FICTION Reprints of works by contemporary, Southern writers. Distributor of Fiction Collective 2 (FC@), avant garde fiction. Query with SASE.

TIPS "Please direct inquiry to appropriate acquisitions editor. University of Alabama Press responds to an author within 2 weeks upon receiving the ms. If they think it is unsuitable for Alabama's program,

they tell the author at once. If the ms warrants it, they begin the peer-review process, which may take 2-4 months to complete. During that process, they keep the author fully informed."

THE UNIVERSITY OF ARKANSAS PRESS

McIlroy House, 105 N. McIlroy Ave., Fayetteville AR 72701. (479)575-3246. **Fax:** (479)575-6044. **E-mail:** lmalley@uark.edu; jewatki@uark.edu. **Website:** uapress.com. **Contact:** Lawrence J. Malley, director and editor-in-chief and Julie Watkins, editor. Estab. 1980. Publishes hardcover and trade paperback originals and reprints. **Publishes 30 titles/year. 30% of books from first-time authors. 95% from unagented writers.** Publishes book 1 year after acceptance. Responds in 3 months to proposals. Catalog and guidelines on website or on request.

⚭ "The University of Arkansas Press publishes series on Ozark studies, the Civil War in the West, poetry and poetics, and sport and society."

NONFICTION Subjects include government, politics, history, Southern, humanities, literary criticism, nature, environment, regional, Arkansas. Accepted mss must be submitted on disk. Query with SASE. Submit outline, sample chapters, résumé.

POETRY University of Arkansas Press publishes four poetry books per year through the Miller Williams Poetry Prize. See Contests section of this book for more information.

◒ UNIVERSITY OF CALGARY PRESS

2500 University Dr. NW, Calgary AB T2N 1N4, Canada. (403)220-7578. **Fax:** (403)282-0085. **Website:** www.uofcpress.com. **Contact:** John King, senior editor. Publishes scholarly and trade paperback originals and reprints. **Publishes 20 titles/year.** Publishes book 20 months after acceptance of ms. Catalog available for free. Guidelines available online through ms submission website.

NONFICTION Subjects include art, architecture, philosophy women's studies, world affairs, Canadian studies, post-modern studies, native studies, history, international relations, arctic studies, Africa, Latin American and Caribbean studies, and heritage of the Canadian and American heartland.

⊘ THE UNIVERSITY OF CHICAGO PRESS

1427 E. 60th St., Chicago IL 60637. Voice-mail: (773)702-7700. **Fax:** (773)702-2705 or (773)702-9756. **Website:** www.press.uchicago.edu. **Contact:** Randolph Petilos, poetry editor. Estab. 1891.

○ *Poetry and fiction submissions by invitation only.*

UNIVERSITY OF GEORGIA PRESS

330 Research Dr., Athens GA 30602. (706)369-6130. **Fax:** (706)369-6131. **E-mail:** books@ugapress.uga. edu. **Website:** www.ugapress.org. Estab. 1938. Publishes hardcover originals, trade paperback originals, and reprints. **Publishes 85 titles/year. Pays 7-10% royalty on net receipts. Pays rare, varying advance.** Publishes book 1 year after acceptance. Responds in 2 months to queries. Catalog and guidelines for #10 SASE or online.

○➙ University of Georgia Press is a midsized press that publishes fiction only through the Flannery O'Connor Award for Short Fiction competition.

NONFICTION Subjects include government, politics, history, American, nature, environment, regional., environmental studies, literary nonfiction. Query with SASE. Submit bio, 1 sample chapter. Reviews artwork/photos. Send if essential to book.

FICTION Short story collections published in Flannery O'Connor Award Competition. Mss for Flannery O'Connor Award for Short Fiction accepted in April and May.

TIPS "Please visit our website to view our Catalogs and for all manuscript submission guidelines."

UNIVERSITY OF ILLINOIS PRESS

1325 S. Oak St., Champaign IL 61820-6903. (217)333-0950. **Fax:** (217)244-8082. **E-mail:** uipress@uillinois. edu. **Website:** www.press.uillinois.edu. **Contact:** Willis Regier, director (literature, classics, ancient religion, sports history); Larin McLaughlin, senior acquisitions editor (women's studies, American studies, religion); Laurie Matheson, senior acquisitions editor (history, appalachian studies, labor studies, music, folklore); Daniel Nasset, acquisitions editor (film studies, anthropology, communication studies. Estab. 1918. Publishes hardcover and trade paperback originals and reprints. **Publishes 150 titles/year. 35% of books from first-time authors. 95% from unagented writers. Pays $1,000-1,500 (rarely) advance.** Publishes book 1 year after acceptance of ms. Responds in 1 month to queries. Catalog for 9x12 envelope and 2 first-class stamps. Guidelines online.

○➙ University of Illinois Press publishes scholarly books and serious nonfiction with a wide range of study interests. Currently emphasiz-

ing American history, especially immigration, labor, African-American, and military; American religion, music, women's studies, and film.

NONFICTION Subjects include Americana, animals, cooking, foods, nutrition, government, politics, history, especially American history, language, literature, military, war, music, especially American music, dance, philosophy, regional, sociology, sports, translation., film/cinema/stage. "Always looking for solid, scholarly books in American history, especially social history; books on American popular music, and books in the broad area of American studies." Query with SASE. Submit outline.

TIPS "As a university press, we are required to submit all mss to rigorous scholarly review. Mss need to be clearly original, well written, and based on solid and thorough research. We cannot encourage memoirs or autobiographies."

UNIVERSITY OF IOWA PRESS

100 Kuhl House, 119 W. Park Rd., Iowa City IA 52242. (319)335-2000. **Fax:** (319)335-2055. **E-mail:** uipress@ uiowa.edu. **Website:** www.uiowapress.org. **Contact:** Holly Carver, director; Joseph Parsons, acquisitions editor. Estab. 1969. Publishes hardcover and paperback originals. **Publishes 35 titles/year. 30% of books from first-time authors. 95% from unagented writers. Pays 7-10% royalty on net receipts.** Publishes book 1 year after acceptance. Catalog available free. Guidelines online.

○➙ "We publish authoritative, original nonfiction that we market mostly by direct mail to groups with special interests in our titles, and by advertising in trade and scholarly publications."

NONFICTION Subjects include anthropology, archeology, creative nonfiction, history, regional, language, literature, nature, environment, American literary studies, medicine and literature. "Looks for evidence of original research, reliable sources, clarity of organization, complete development of theme with documentation, supportive footnotes and/ or bibliography, and a substantive contribution to knowledge in the field treated. Use *Chicago Manual of Style*." Query with SASE. Submit outline. Reviews artwork/photos.

FICTION Currently publishes the Iowa Short Fiction Award selections.

POETRY Currently publishes winners of the Iowa Poetry Prize Competition, Kuhl House Poets, poetry anthologies. Competition guidelines available on website.

UNIVERSITY OF NEBRASKA PRESS

1111 Lincoln Mall, Lincoln NE 68588. (800)755-1105. **Fax:** (402)472-6214. **E-mail:** pressmail@unl.edu; arold1@unl.edu. **Website:** nebraskapress.unl.edu. **Contact:** Heather Lundine, editor-in-chief; Alison Rold, production manager. Publishes hardcover and trade paperback originals and trade paperback reprints. Catalog available free. Guidelines online.

⚷ "We primarily publish nonfiction books and scholarly journals, along with a few titles per season in contemporary and regional prose and poetry. On occasion, we reprint previously published fiction of established reputation, and we have several programs to publish literary works in translation."

NONFICTION Subjects include agriculture, animals, anthropology, archeology, creative nonfiction, history, memoirs, military, war, multicultural, nature, environment, religion, sports, translation, women's issues/studies, Native American studies, American Lives series, experimental fiction by American-Indian writers. Submit book proposal with overview, audience, format, detailed chapter outline, sample chapters, sample bibliography, timetable, CV.

FICTION Series and translation only. Occasionally reprints fiction of established reputation.

POETRY Contemporary, regional.

UNIVERSITY OF NEVADA PRESS

Morrill Hall, Mail Stop 0166, Reno NV 89557. (775)784-6573. **Fax:** (775)784-6200. **Website:** www.unpress.nevada.edu. **Contact:** Joanne O'Hare, director. Estab. 1961. Publishes hardcover and paperback originals and reprints. **Publishes 25 titles/year.** Publishes book 18 months after acceptance. Responds in 2 months. Guidelines online.

⚷ "Small university press. Publishes fiction that primarily focuses on the American West." Member: AAUP

NONFICTION Subjects include anthropology, archeology, ethnic, studies, history, regional and natural, nature, environment, regional, history and geography., western literature, current affairs, gambling and gaming, Basque studies. No juvenile books. Submit proposal. No online submissions. Reviews artwork/photos. Send photocopies.

FICTION "We publish in Basque Studies, Gambling Studies, Western literature, Western history, Natural science, Environmental Studies, Travel and Outdoor books, Archeology, Anthropology, and Political Studies, all focusing on the West". The Press also publishes creative nonfiction and books on regional topics for a general audience. Submit proposal package, outline, clips, 2-4 sample chapters. Include estimated word count, brief bio, list of publishing credits. Send SASE or IRC. No e-mail submissions.

UNIVERSITY OF NEW MEXICO PRESS

1 University of New Mexico, MSC05 3185, Albuquerque NM 87131. (505)277-3324 or (800)249-7737. **Fax:** (505)277-3343. **E-mail:** clark@unm.edu; wcwhiteh@unm.edu. **Website:** www.unmpress.com. **Contact:** W. Clark Whitehorn, editor-in-chief. Estab. 1929. Publishes hardcover originals and trade paperback originals and reprints. **Pays variable royalty. Pays advance.** Catalog available for free. Please read and follow the submission query guidelines on the Author Information page online. Do not send your entire ms or additional materials until requested. If your book is accepted for publication, you will be notified.

⚷ "The Press is well known as a publisher in the fields of anthropology, archeology, Latin American studies, art and photography, architecture and the history and culture of the American West, fiction, some poetry, Chicano/a studies and works by and about American Indians. We focus on American West, Southwest and Latin American regions."

NONFICTION Subjects include Americana, anthropology, archeology, art, architecture, biography, creative nonfiction, ethnic, gardening, gay, lesbian, government, politics, history, language, literature, memoirs, military, war, multicultural, music, dance, nature, environment, photography, regional, religion, science, translation, travel, women's issues/studies, contemporary culture, cinema/stage, true crime, general nonfiction. No how-to, humor, juvenile, self-help, software, technical or textbooks. Query with SASE. Reviews artwork/photos. Send photocopies.

POETRY "The Press is well known as a publisher in the fields of anthropology, archeology, Latin American studies, art and photography, architecture and the history and culture of the American West, fiction, some poetry, Chicano/a studies and works by and about American Indians. We focus on American

West, Southwest and Latin American regions." Publishes hardcover originals and trade paperback originals and reprints. Pays variable royalty.

UNIVERSITY OF NORTH TEXAS PRESS

1155 Union Circle, #311336, Denton TX 76203. (940)565-2142. **Fax:** (940)565-4590. **E-mail:** ronald.chrisman@unt.edu; Karen.DeVinney@unt.edu. **Website:** http://untpress.unt.edu. **Contact:** Ronald Chrisman, director; Paula Oates, assistant editor; Lori Belew, administrative assistant. Estab. 1987. Publishes hardcover and trade paperback originals and reprints. **Publishes 14-16 titles/year. 500 queries received/year. 50% of books from first-time authors. 95% from unagented writers.** Publishes book 1-2 years after acceptance. Responds in 1 month to queries. Catalog for 8 ½×11 SASE. Guidelines online.

⌐ "We are dedicated to producing the highest quality scholarly, academic, and general interest books. We are committed to serving all peoples by publishing stories of their cultures and experiences that have been overlooked. Currently emphasizing military history, Texas history and literature, music, Mexican-American studies."

NONFICTION Subjects include Americana, ethnic, government, politics, history, music, dance, biography, military, war, nature, regional, women's issues/studies. Query with SASE. Reviews artwork/photos. Send photocopies.

FICTION "The only fiction we publish is the winner of the Katherine Anne Porter Prize in Short Fiction, an annual, national competition with a $1,000 prize, and publication of the winning ms each Fall."

POETRY "The only poetry we publish is the winner of the Vassar Miller Prize in Poetry, an annual, national competition with a $1,000 prize and publication of the winning ms each Spring." Query.

UNIVERSITY OF OKLAHOMA PRESS

2800 Venture Dr., Norman OK 73069. **E-mail:** cerankin@ou.edu. **Website:** www.oupress.com. **Contact:** Charles E. Rankin, editor-in-chief. Estab. 1928. Publishes hardcover and paperback originals and reprints. **Publishes 90 titles/year. Pays standard royalty.** Responds promptly to queries. Catalog for 9×12 SAE with 6 first-class stamps.

⌐ University of Oklahoma Press publishes books for both scholarly and nonspecialist readers.

NONFICTION Subjects include political science (Congressional, area and security studies), history (regional, military, natural), language/literature (American Indian, US West), American Indian studies, classical studies. Query with SASE or by e-mail. Submit outline, résumé, 1-2 sample chapters. Use *Chicago Manual of Style* for ms guidelines. Reviews artwork/photos.

⊘ UNIVERSITY OF PENNSYLVANIA PRESS

3905 Spruce St., Philadelphia PA 19104. (215)898-6261. **Fax:** (215)898-0404. **Website:** www.pennpress.org. **Contact:** Jerome Singerman, humanities editor; Peter Agree, editor-in-chief and social sciences editor; Jo Joslyn, art and architecture editor; Robert Lockhart, history editor; Bill Finan, politics, international relations; John Hubbard, art director. Estab. 1890. Publishes hardcover and paperback originals, and reprints. **Publishes 100+ titles/year. 20-30% of books from first-time authors. 95% from unagented writers. Royalty determined on book-by-book basis. Pays advance.** Publishes book 10 months after acceptance. Responds in 3 months to queries. Catalog and guidelines online.

⌐ "Manuscript submissions are welcome in fields appropriate for Penn Press's editorial program. The Press's acquiring editors, and their fields of responsibility, are listed in the Contact Us section of our website. Although we have no formal policies regarding manuscript proposals and submissions, what we need minimally, in order to gauge our degree of interest, is a brief statement describing the manuscript, a copy of the contents page, and a reasonably current vita. Initial inquiries are best sent by letter, in paper form, to the appropriate editor."

NONFICTION Subjects include Americana, art, architecture, history, American, art, architecture, literary criticism, sociology, anthropology, literary criticism, cultural studies, ancient studies, medieval studies, urban studies, human rights. Follow the *Chicago Manual of Style*. "Serious books that serve the scholar and the professional, student and general reader." *No unsolicited mss.* Query with SASE. Submit outline, résumé. Reviews artwork/photos. Send photocopies.

UNIVERSITY OF WISCONSIN PRESS

1930 Monroe St., 3rd Floor, Madison WI 53711. (608)263-1110. **Fax:** (608)263-1132. **E-mail:** uwiscpress@uwpress.wisc.edu. **E-mail:** kadushin@wisc.edu. **Website:** www.wisc.edu/wisconsinpress. **Con-**

tact: Raphael Kadushin, senior acquisitions editor. Gwen Walker, acquisitions editor Estab. 1937. Publishes hardcoveroriginals, paperback originals, and paperback reprints. **Publishes 98 total titles (average); 15 fiction titles/year. titles/year. Pays royalty.** Publishes book 9-18 months after acceptance. Responds in 2 weeks toqueries; 8 weeks to mss. Rarely comments on rejected mss.

NONFICTION Subjects include anthropology, dance, environment, film, foods, gay, history, lesbian, memoirs, travel., African Studies,autobiography, biography, classical studies, human rights, Irish studies,Jewish studies, Latin American studies, Latino/a memoirs, modern Western European history, performance studies, Slavic studies, Southeast Asian studies. Does not accept unsolicited mss. Query with SASE or submit outline, 1-2 sample chapter(s), synopsis. Accepts queries by e-mail, mail, fax. Include estimated word count, brief bio. Send copy of ms and SASE. Direct your inquiries in the areas of autobiography/memoir, biography, classical studies, dance and performance studies, film, food, gender studies, GLBT studies, Jewish studies, Latino/amemoirs, and travel to Raphael Kadushin, kadushin@wisc.edu. Agented fiction: 40%. Direct non-fiction inquiries in the areas of African studies, anthropology, environmental studies, human rights, Irish studies, Latin American studies, Slavic studies, Southeast Asian studies, and U.S. History to Gwen Walker, gcwalker@uwpress.wisc.edu. See website for more contact info.

FICTION Gay/lesbian, historical,lesbian, mystery, regional (Wisconsin), short story collections.

TIPS "Make sure the query letter and sample text are well-written, and read guidelines carefully to make sure we accept the genre you are submitting."

UNIVERSITY PRESS OF KANSAS

2502 Westbrooke Circle, Lawrence KS 66045. (785)864-4154. **Fax:** (785)864-4586. **E-mail:** upress@ku.edu. **Website:** www.kansaspress.ku.edu; facebook: www.facebook.com/kansaspress. **Contact:** Michael J. Briggs, editor-in-chief (military history, political science, law); Ranjit Arab, acquisitions editor (western history, American studies, environmental studies, women's studies); Fred M. Woodward, director, (political science, presidency, regional). Estab. 1946. Publishes hardcover originals, trade paperback originals and reprints. **Publishes 55 titles/year. 600 queries received/year. 20% of books from first-time authors.**

98% from unagented writers. Pays selective advance. Publishes book 10 months after acceptance. Responds in 1 month to proposals. Catalog and guidelines free.

✂➴ "The University Press of Kansas publishes scholarly books that advance knowledge and regional books that contribute to the understanding of Kansas, the Great Plains, and the Midwest."

NONFICTION Subjects include Americana, archeology, environment, government, military, nature, politics, regional, sociology, war, womens studies., American History, Native Studies, American Cultural Studies. "We are looking for books on topics of wide interest based on solid scholarship and written for both specialists and informed general readers. Do not send unsolicited, complete mss." Submit outline, sample chapters, cover letter, CV, prospectus. Reviews artwork/photos. Send photocopies.

UNIVERSITY PRESS OF MISSISSIPPI

3825 Ridgewood Rd., Jackson MS 39211. (601)432-6205. **Fax:** (601)432-6217. **E-mail:** press@mississippi.edu. **Website:** www.upress.state.ms.us. **Contact:** Craig Gill, editor-in-chief (regional studies, art, folklore, music). Estab. 1970. Publishes hardcover and paperback originals and reprints. **Publishes 60 titles/year. 20% of books from first-time authors. 90% from unagented writers. Competitive royalties and terms. Pays advance.** Publishes book 1 year after acceptance. Responds in 3 months to queries.

✂➴ "University Press of Mississippi publishes scholarly and trade titles, as well as special series, including: American Made Music; Conversations with Comic Artists; Conversations with Filmmakers; Faulkner and Yoknapatawpha; Literary Conversations; Studies in Popular Culture; Hollywood Legends; Caribbean Studies."

NONFICTION Subjects include Americana, art, architecture, ethnic, minority studies, government, politics, history, literature, literary criticism, music, photography, regional, Southern., folklife, literary criticism, popular culture with scholarly emphasis, literary studies. "We prefer a proposal that describes the significance of the work and a chapter outline." Submit outline, sample chapters, cv.

UNLIMITED PUBLISHING LLC

P.O. Box 99, Nashville IN 47448. **E-mail:** acquisitions@unlimitedpublishing.com. **Website:** www.unlimitedpublishing.com. Publisher (out-of-print books formerly from major publishers) Estab. 2000. **Publishes 25-50 titles/year. Receives 1,000 queries/year; 500 manuscripts/year. 20% of books from first-time authors. 40% from unagented writers. Pays 10-20% Royalty on retail price.** Publishes book 3 months after acceptance. 1 month on queries, proposal, and mss. Catalog online.

⊶ "We prefer short nonfiction and fiction with a clear audience, and expect authors to be actively involved in publicity. A detailed marketing plan is required with all submissions. Moderate to good computer skills are necessary."

NONFICTION Subjects include agriculture, alternative lifestyles, Americana, animals, anthropology, archaeology, architecture, art, business, career guidance, child guidance, communications, community, computers, contemporary culture, counseling, crafts, creative nonfiction, economics, education, electronics, environment, ethnic, finance, gardening, gay, government, health, history, hobbies, horticulture, humanities, labor, language, law, lesbian, literary criticism, literature, marine subjects, medicine, memoirs, military, money, multicultural, music, nature, parenting, philosophy, politics, psychology, real estate, recreation, regional, religion, science, sex, social sciences, sociology, software, sports, translation, transportation, travel, women's issues/studies, world affairs, young adult. "Unlimited Publishing LLC specializes in bringing back out-of-print books originally released by traditional publishers, and in publishing new books by professional writers. Our catalog currently includes books formerly published by many well-known book imprints, including Berkley Books, Houghton Mifflin, Kensington, Macmillan, Penguin, Wiley & Sons, Yale University Press and others. We prefer short nonfiction with a bare minimum of artwork and graphics, but are always interested in quality material, regardless of genre. UP functions like a traditional royalty book publisher, but uses revolutionary new print-on-demand book publishing technologies to slash the cost of getting books in print. UP does not publish books for a fee, nor charge inflated prices for books — from readers OR writers. Our policies are not suitable for vanity publishing or self-publishing. To learn more, please follow the guidelines online at our website." Submit proposal package, including: outline and 10-page excerpt in rich text format, a stan-

dard 'save-as option with Microsoft Word', author bio and detailed marketing plan.

FICTION Subjects include adventure, ethnic, experimental, fantasy, feminist, historical, horror, humor, juvenile, literary, mainstream, contemporary, military, war, multicultural, mystery, occult, regional, religious, science fiction fiction, short story collections, spiritual, sports, suspense, translation, war, western, young adult. Submit proposal package by e-mail, including: outline and 10-page excerpt in rich text format, author bio and detailed marketing plan.

TIPS "The growth of online bookselling allows authors and publishers to jointly cultivate a tightly targeted grassroots audience in specialty or niche markets before expanding to mainstream book industry channels based on proven public demand."

UNTAPPED TALENT LLC

P.O. Box 396, Hershey PA 17033. (717)707-0720. **E-mail:** rena@unt2.com. **Website:** www.unt2.com. **Contact:** Rena Wilson Fox, (Areas of interest: nonfiction, children's lit, fiction, middle grade). Estab. 2008. hardcover, trade and mass market paperbacks, and electronic originals. **Publishes 2-10 titles/year. Receives 2,000 queries/year; 400 mss/year. 80% of books from first-time authors. 80% from unagented writers. Pays 6-12% royalty on net price.** Publishes book 6-12 months after acceptance. Accepts simultaneous submissions. Responds in 2 months to queries, proposals, and mss. Catalog and guidelines online.

⊶ As a new publishing company, we only have published four titles, not enough for a catalog. Please feel free to view the books at our website.

NONFICTION Subjects include Americana, art, architecture, child guidance, parenting, computers, contemporary culture, cooking, foods, health, medicine, history, memoirs, music, dance, photography, psychology, religion, travel, women's issues/studies, world affairs, young adult. Submit by e-mail: proposal package, outline (if appropriate), 4 sample chapters, & synopsis. Reviews artwork/photos. Send photocopies, computer file.

FICTION Subjects include historical, humor, juvenile, literary, mainstream, contemporary, military, war, multicultural, mystery, regional, religious, romance, suspense, young adult. "We have a strong interest in historical fiction. We are looking for books that are current and fully formulated, modern interpretations—even if the story takes place in the past."

Submit proposal package with synopsis, 4 sample chapters, and any background information pertinent to the story.

TIPS Follow website instruction, make query brief; if 4 chapters are not many pages, add more; submit to acquisitions editor only.

⊕ UNTREED READS PUBLISHING

506 Kansas St., San Francisco CA 94107. (415)621-0465. **Fax:** (415)621-0465. **E-mail:** general@untreedreads.com; submissions@untreedreads.com. **Website:** www.untreedreads.com. **Contact:** Jay A. Hartman, editor-in-chief (fiction-all genres). K.D. Sullivan, CEO/publisher (nonfiction-all genres, especially business) Estab. 2009. Publishes electronic originals and reprints. **Publishes 35 titles/year. Receives 50 submissions/year. 80% of books from first-time authors. 75% from unagented writers. Pays 50-60% royalty on retail price.** Accepts simultaneous submissions. Responds in ½ month on queries, 1 month on proposals, and 1 ½ months on mss. Catalog and guidelines online.

NONFICTION Subjects include agriculture, alternative lifestyles, Americana, animals, anthropology, archeology, architecture, art, astrology, automotive, beauty, business, career guidance, child guidance, cinema, communications, community, computers, contemporary culture, cooking, counseling, crafts, creative nonfiction, dance, economics, education, electronics, entertainment, environment, ethnic, fashion, film, finance, foods, games, gardening, gay, government, health, history, hobbies, horticulture, house and home, humanities, labor, language, law, lesbian, literary criticism, literature, marine subjects, memoirs, military/war, money/finance, multicultural, music/dance, nature/environment/new age, philosophy, photography, psychology, real estate, recreation, regional, religion, science, sex, social sciences, sociology, software, spirituality, sports, translation, transportation, travel, women's issues/studies, world affairs, young adult. "We are very interested in developing our textbook market. Ereaders don't currently support graphs, tables, images, etc. as well as print books; however, we plan to be trendsetters in this as the technology in the ereaders improves. Also we are eager to increase our number of business books. We always look for series or works that could develop into a series." Submit proposal package, including 3 sample chapters. Submit completed mss. Reviews artwork/photos. Send photocopies. Author must provide signed release of permission to use the photographs.

FICTION Subjects include literary. "We look forward to long-terms relationships with our authors. We encourage works that are either already a series or could develop into a series. We are one of the few publishers publishing short stories and are happy to be a resource for these good works. We welcome short story collections. Also, we look forward to publishing children's books, cookbooks, and other works that have been known for illustrations in print as the technology in the multiple ereaders improves. We hope to be a large platform for diverse content and authors. We seek mainstream content, but if you're an author or have content that doesn't seem to always 'fit' into traditional market we'd like to hear from you." No erotica, picture books, poetry, poetry in translation, or romance Submit porposal package with 3 sample chapters. Submit completed ms.

POETRY "We are not accepting individual poems currently, but will accept proposals for poetry collections."

TIPS "For our fiction titles we lean toward a literary audience. For nonfiction titles, we want to be a platform for business people, entrepreneurs, and speakers to become well known in their fields of expertise. However, for both fiction and nonfiction we want to appeal to many audiences."

UPPER ACCESS, INC.

87 Upper Access Rd., Hinesburg VT 05461. (802)482-2988. **Fax:** (802)304-1005. **E-mail:** info@upperaccess.com. **Website:** www.upperaccess.com. **Contact:** Steve Carlson, publisher. Estab. 1986. Publishes hardcover and trade paperback originals; hardcover and trade paperback reprints. **Publishes 2-3 titles/year. 200 queries received/year. 40 mss received/year. 50% of books from first-time authors. 80% from unagented writers. Pays 10-20% royalty on wholesale price. $200-500 (Advances are tokens of our good faith; author earnings are from royalties a book sells.)** Publishes book 8 months after acceptance of ms. Accepts simultaneous submissions. Responds in 1 month to queries/manuscripts. Catalog online. Guidelines online.

🔑 Publishes nonfiction to improve the quality of life.

NONFICTION Subjects include alternative lifestyles, child guidance, community/public affairs, contemporary culture, cooking, foods, nutrition, creative non-fiction, education, ethnic, gardening, government, politics/politics, health, medicine, history, humor, humanities, language, literature, multicultural, nature, environment, philosophy, psychology, science, sex, social sciences, sociology, womens issues, womens studies, world affairs affairs, (gay, lesbian possible). "We are open to considering almost any nonfiction topic that has some potential for national general trade sales." Query with SASE. "We strongly prefer an initial e-mail describing your proposed title. No attachments please. We will look at paper mail if there is no other way, but e-mail will be reviewed much more quickly and thoroughly." Will request artwork, etc. if and when appropriate. "Discuss this with us in your initial e-mail query."

FICTION "Note: Please do not submit fiction, even if it relates to nonfiction subjects. We cannot take novels or poetry of any kind at this time."

TIPS "We target intelligent adults willing to challenge the status quo, who are interested in more self-sufficiency with respect for the environment. Most of our books are either unique subjects or unique or different ways of looking at major issues or basic education on subjects that are not well understood by most of the general public. We make a long-term commitment to each book that we publish, trying to find its market as long as possible."

⊕ URJ PRESS

633 Third Ave., 7th Floor, New York NY 10017. (212)650-4120. **Fax:** (212)650-4119. **E-mail:** press@urj.org. **Website:** www.urjpress.com. **Contact:** Rabbi Hara Person, editor. Publishes hardcover and trade paperback originals. **Publishes 22 titles/year. 500 queries received/year. 400 mss received/year. 70% of books from first-time authors. 90% from unagented writers. Pays 3-5% royalty on retail price. Makes outright purchase of 500-2,000. Pays $500-2,000 advance.** Publishes book 18-24 months after acceptance. Responds to queries/mss in 4 months. Catalog and guidelines free or on website.

◑ *URJ Press publishes books related to Judaism.*

NONFICTION Subjects include art, architecture, synagogue, child guidance, cooking, foods, nutrition, Jewish, education, ethnic, Judaism, government, politics, Israeli/Jewish, history, language, literature, Hebrew, military, war, as relates to Judaism, music, dance, nature, environment, philosophy, Jew-ish, religion, Judaism only, sex, as it relates to Judaism, spirituality, Jewish. Picture books, young readers, middle readers: religion. Average word length: picture books—1,500. Submit proposal package, outline, bio, 1-2 sample chapters.

FICTION Subjects include juvenile., children's picture books. Picture books: religion. Average word length: picture books—1,500. Submit complete ms with author bio.

TIPS "Look at some of our books. Have an understanding of the Reform Judaism community. In addition to bookstores, we sell to Jewish congregations and Hebrew day schools."

⟲ USBORNE PUBLISHING

83-85 Saffron Hill, London En EC1N 8RT, United Kingdom. (44)(020)7430-2800. **Fax:** (44)(020)7430-1562. **E-mail:** mail@usborne.co.uk; pippas@usborne.co.uk; alicep@usborne.co.uk; Graeme@usborne.co.uk. **Website:** www.usborne.com. **Pays authors royalty.**

⟐ "Usborne Publishing is a multiple-award winning, world-wide children's publishing company specializing in superbly researched and produced information books with a unique appeal to young readers."

FICTION Young readers, middle readers: adventure, contemporary, fantasy, history, humor, multicultural, nature/environment, science fiction, suspense/mystery, strong concept-based or character-led series. Average word length: young readers—5,000-10,000; middle readers—25,000-50,000.

TIPS "Do not send any original work and, sorry, but we cannot guarantee a reply."

VANDAMERE PRESS

P.O. Box 149, St. Petersburg FL 33731. **Fax:** (727) 556-2560. **E-mail:** webmaster@vandamere.com. **Website:** www.vandamere.com. **Contact:** Jerry Frank, senior acquisitions editor. Estab. 1984. Publishes hardcover and trade paperback originals and reprints. **Publishes 8-15 titles/year. 1,500 queries received/year and 500 mss received/year. 25% of books from first-time authors. 90% from unagented writers. Pays royalty. on revenues generated. Pays advance.** Publishes book 1 year after acceptance. Accepts simultaneous submissions. Responds in 6 months to queries.

⟐ "Vandamere publishes high-quality work with solid, well-documented research and minimum author/political bias."

NONFICTION Subjects include Americana, education, health, medicine, history, military, war, photography, regional, Washington D.C./Mid-Atlantic., disability/healthcare issues. No New Age. Submit outline, 2-3 sample chapters.

FICTION Subjects include adventure, mystery, suspense. Submit clips, 5-10 sample chapters.

TIPS "Authors who can provide endorsements from significant published writers, celebrities, etc., will always be given serious consideration. Clean, easy-to-read, dark copy is essential. Patience in waiting for replies is essential. All unsolicited work is looked at, but at certain times of the year our review schedule will stop. No response without SASE. No electronic submissions or queries!"

VANDERBILT UNIVERSITY PRESS

VU Station B 351813, Nashville TN 37235. (615)322-3585. **Fax:** (615)343-8823. **E-mail:** vupress@vanderbilt.edu. **Website:** www.vanderbiltuniversitypress.com. **Contact:** Michael Ames, director. Publishes hardcover originals and trade paperback originals and reprints. **Publishes 20-25 titles/year. 500 queries received/year. 25% of books from first-time authors. 90% from unagented writers. Pays rare advance.** Publishes book 10 months after acceptance. Accepts simultaneous submissions. Responds in 2 weeks to proposals. Catalog available free online. Guidelines online.

○ Also distributes for and co-publishes with Country Music Foundation.

NONFICTION Subjects include Americana, anthropology, archeology, education, ethnic, government, politics, health, medicine, history, language, literature, multicultural, music, dance, nature, environment, philosophy, women's issues/studies. Submit prospectus, sample chapter, cv. Does not accept electronic submissions. Reviews artwork/photos. Send photocopies.

TIPS "Our audience consists of scholars and educated, general readers."

⊕ VANHOOK HOUSE

925 Orchard St., Charleston WV 25302. **E-mail:** editor@vanhookhouse.com. **E-mail:** acquisitions@vanhookhouse.com. **Website:** www.vanhookhouse.com. **Contact:** Jim Whyte, acquisitions, all fiction/true crime/military/war. Estab. 2009. hardcover and trade paperback originals; trade paperback reprints. **Publishes 6 titles/year. Receives 20 mss/year. 100% of books from first-time authors. 100% from unagented writers. Pays authors 8-10% royalty on wholesale**

price. Advance negotiable. Publishes book 6 months after acceptance. Responds in 1 month on queries; 2 months on proposals; 3 months on mss. Catalog and guidelines free on request and available online.

⚷ "VanHook House is a small press focused on the talents of new, unpublished authors. We are looking for works of fiction and non-fiction to add to our catalog. No erotica or sci-fi, please. Query via e-mail. Queries accepted ONLY during submissions periods."

NONFICTION Subjects include agriculture, Americana, animals, anthropology, architecture, art, automotive, business, career guidance, child guidance, communications, community, computers, contemporary culture, cooking, counseling, crafts, creative nonfiction, dance, education, electronics, entertainment, environment, ethnic, foods, games, gardening, government, health, history, house and home, humanities, labor, language, law, literature, marine subjects, medicine, memoirs, military, muticultural, music, nature, New Age, nutrition, philosophy, photography, politics, psychology, public affairs, real estate, recreation, regional, religion, science, sex, social sciences, sociology, software, spirituality, sports, transportation, travel, women's issues/studies, war, world affairs. Reviews artwork.

POETRY "A collection MUST contain 200 individual poems to be considered." Query; submit 3 sample poems. "VanHook House is a small press focused on the talents of new, unpublished authors. We are looking for works of fiction and non-fiction to add to our catalog. No erotica or sci-fi, please. Query via e-mail. Queries accepted ONLY during submissions periods."

○ VÉHICULE PRESS

Box 125, Place du Parc Station, Montreal QC H2X 4A3, Canada. (514)844-6073. **Fax:** (514)844-7543. **E-mail:** vp@vehiculepress.com. **Website:** www.vehiculepress.com. **Contact:** Simon Dardick, president/publisher. Estab. 1973. Publishes trade paperback originals by Canadian authors mostly. **Publishes 15 titles/year. 20% of books from first-time authors. 95% from unagented writers. Pays 10-15% royalty on retail price. Pays $200-500 advance.** Publishes book 1 year after acceptance. Responds in 4 months to queries. Catalog for 9×12 SAE with IRCs.

⚷ "Montreal's Véhicule Press has published the best of Canadian and Quebec literature-fiction, poetry, essays, translations, and social history."

NONFICTION Subjects include government, politics, history, language, literature, memoirs, regional, sociology. Especially looking for Canadian social history. Query with SASE. Reviews artwork/photos.

FICTION Subjects include feminist, literary, translation., literary novels. Contact Andrew Steinmetz. Literary, regional, short story collections. No romance or formula writing. Query with SASE.

POETRY Contact Carmine Starnino with SASE. Vehicle Press is a "literary press with a poetry series, Signal Editions, publishing the work of Canadian poets only." Publishes flat-spined paperbacks. Publishes Canadian poetry that is "first-rate, original, content-conscious."

TIPS "Quality in almost any style is acceptable. We believe in the editing process."

⊘ VERTIGO

DC Universe, Vertigo-DC Comics, 1700 Broadway, New York NY 10019. **Website:** www.dccomics.com.

FICTION "The DC TALENT SEARCH program is designed to offer aspiring artists the chance to present artwork samples directly to the DC Editors and Art Directors. The process is simple: during your convention visit, drop off photocopied samples of your work and enjoy the show! No lines, no waiting. If the DC folks like what they see, a time is scheduled for you the following day to meet a DC representative personally and discuss your artistic interests and portfolio. At this time, DC Comics does not accept unsolicited writing submissions by mail. See submission guidelines online. "We're seeking artists for all our imprints, including the DC Universe, Vertigo, WildStorm, Mad magazine, Minx, kids comics and more!"

VIEWPOINT PRESS

PMB 400 785 Tucker Rd. #G, Tehachapi CA 93561. (661)821-5110. **Fax:** (661)821-7515. **E-mail:** joie99@aol.com. **Website:** http://www.viewpointpress.com/products.html.

○ *Not currently accepting mss.*

Ⓐ VIKING

Imprint of Penguin Group (USA), Inc., 375 Hudson St., New York NY 10014. (212)366-2000. **Website:** us.penguingroup.com/static/pages/publishers/adult/viking.html. Estab. 1925. Publishes hardcover and originals. **Publishes 100 titles/year. Pays 10-15% royalty on retail price.** Publishes book 18 months after acceptance. Accepts simultaneous submissions.

✖➛ Viking publishes a mix of academic and popular fiction and nonfiction.

NONFICTION Subjects include business, economics, child guidance, cooking, foods, nutrition, health, medicine, history, language, literature, music, dance, philosophy, womens issues, womens studies. Agented submissions only.

FICTION Subjects include literary, mainstream, contemporary, mystery, suspense. Literary, mainstream/contemporary, mystery, suspense. Agented submissions only.

Ⓐ VIKING CHILDREN'S BOOKS

345 Hudson St., New York NY 10014. **E-mail:** avery-studiopublicity@us.penguingroup.com. **Website:** www.penguingroup.com. **Contact:** Catherine Frank, executive editor. Joy Peskin, Anne Gunton, Tracy Gates, associate editorial editors; Joy Peskin, executive editor; Janet Pascal, editor; Kendra Levin, associate editor; Leila Sales, editorial assistant. Publishes hardcover originals. **Publishes 70 titles/year. Pays 2-10% royalty on retail price or flat fee. Pays negotiable advance.** Publishes book 1-2 years after acceptance. Responds to queries/mss in 6 months.

○ *Does not accept unsolicited submissions.*

✖➛ "Viking Children's Books is known for humorous, quirky picture books, in addition to more traditional fiction. We publish the highest quality fiction, nonfiction, and picture books for pre-schoolers through young adults."

NONFICTION All levels: biography, concept, history, multicultural, music/dance, nature/environment, science, and sports. Query with SASE, or submit outline, 3 sample chapters, SASE.

FICTION All levels: adventure, animal, contemporary, fantasy, history, humor, multicultural, nature/environment, poetry, problem novels, romance, science fiction, sports, suspense/mystery. *Accepts agented mss only.*

TIPS No "cartoony" or mass-market submissions for picture books.

Ⓐ VILLARD BOOKS

Imprint of Random House Publishing Group, 1745 Broadway, New York NY 10019. (212)572-2600. **Website:** www.atrandom.com. Estab. 1983. Publishes hardcover and trade paperback originals. **Pays negotiable royalty Pays negotiable advance.** Accepts simultaneous submissions.

✖➛ "Villard Books is the publisher of savvy and sometimes quirky, best-selling hardcovers and trade paperbacks."

NONFICTION, Commercial nonfiction. Agented submissions only.

FICTION Commercial fiction. Agented submissions only.

Ⓐ VINTAGE ANCHOR PUBLISHING

1745 Broadway, New York NY 10019. **E-mail:** vintageanchorpublicity@randomhouse.com. **Website:** www.randomhouse.com. **Contact:** Furaha Norton, editor. **Pays 4-8% royalty on retail price. Average advance: $2,500 and up.** Publishes book 1 year after acceptance.

FICTION Literary, mainstream/contemporary, short story collections. *Agented submissions only.* Accepts simultaneous submissions. No electronic submissions.

VIVISPHERE PUBLISHING

675 Dutchess Turnpike, Poughkeepsie NY 12603. (845)463-1100, ext. 314. **Fax:** (845)463-0018. **E-mail:** cs@vivisphere.com. **Website:** www.vivisphere.com. **Contact:** Lisa Mays. Estab. 1995. Publishes trade paperback originals and reprints and e-books. **Pays royalty.** Publishes book 6 months-2 years after acceptance. Accepts simultaneous submissions. Responds in 6-12 months to queries, proposals, mss. Catalog and guidelines online.

⚯➤ Vivisphere Publishing is now considering new submissions from any genre as follows: game of bridge (cards), nonfiction, history, military, new age, fiction, feminist/gay/lesbian, horror, contemporary, self-help, science fiction and cookbooks.

NONFICTION Subjects include history, military, New Age, Game of Bridge. "Query with SASE. Please submit a proposal package (printed paper copy) including: outline and 1st chapter along with your contact information to: Attn: New Submissions, at our address. Or, opt to submit via e-mail at cs@vivisphere.com."

FICTION Subjects include feminist, gay, lesbian, historical, horror, literary, contemporary, military, self help, science fiction. Query with SASE.

VIZ MEDIA LLC

P.O. Box 77010, 295 Bay St., San Francisco CA 94133. (415)546-7073. **E-mail:** evelyn.dubocq@viz.com. **Website:** www.viz.com.

⚯➤ "VIZ Media, LLC is one of the most comprehensive and innovative companies in the field of manga (graphic novel) publishing, animation and entertainment licensing of Japanese content. Owned by three of Japan's largest creators and licensors of manga and animation, Shueisha Inc., Shogakukan Inc., and Shogakukan-Shueisha Productions, Co., Ltd., VIZ Media is a leader in the publishing and distribution of Japanese manga for English speaking audiences in North America, the United Kingdom, Ireland, and South Africa and is a global ex-Asia licensor of Japanese manga and animation. The company offers an integrated product line including magazines such as SHONEN JUMP and SHOJO BEAT, graphic novels, and DVDs, and develops, markets, licenses, and distributes animated entertainment for audiences and consumers of all ages."

FICTION VIZ Media is currently accepting submissions and pitches for original comics. Keep in mind that all submissions must be accompanied by a signed release form.

VOYAGEUR PRESS

Quayside Publishing Group, 400 First Ave. N., Suite 300, Minneapolis MN 55401. (800)458-0454. **Fax:** (612)344-8691. **E-mail:** mdregni@voyageurpress.com. **Website:** voyageurpress.com. **Contact:** Michael Dregni, publisher. Estab. 1972. Publishes hardcover and trade paperback originals. **Publishes 80 titles/year. 1,200 queries received/year. 500 mss received/year. 10% of books from first-time authors. 90% from unagented writers. Pays royalty. Pays advance.** Publishes book 1 year after acceptance. Accepts simultaneous submissions. Responds in 3 months to queries.

⚯➤ "Voyageur Press (and its sports imprint MVP Books) is internationally known as a leading publisher of quality music, sports, country living, crafts, natural history, and regional books. No children's or poetry books."

NONFICTION Subjects include Americana, cooking, environment, history, hobbies, music, nature, regional, sports., collectibles, country living, knitting and quilting, outdoor recreation. Query with SASE. Submit outline. Send sample digital images or transparencies (duplicates and tearsheets only).

TIPS "We publish books for an audience interested in regional, natural, and cultural history on a wide variety of subjects. We seek authors strongly committed to helping us promote and sell their books. Please present as focused an idea as possible in a brief submission (1-page cover letter; 2-page outline or proposal). Note your credentials for writing the book. Tell all you know about the market niche and marketing possibilities for proposed book. We use more book designers than artists or illustrators, since most of our books are illustrated with photographs."

W&A PUBLISHING

One Peregrine Way, P.O. Box 849, Cedar Falls IA 50613. (319)266-0441; (800)927-8222. **Fax:** (319)266-1695. **E-mail:** kgolden@w-apublishing.com; editorial@w-apublishing.com. **Website:** www.w-apublishing.com. **Contact:** Karris Golden, executive editor. Estab. 2006. Publishes hardcover and electronic originals and hardcover reprints. **Publishes 10-12/year titles/year. 90% of books from first-time authors. 100% from unagented writers. Pays 15% royalty.** Publishes book 3-6 months after acceptance. Accepts simultaneous submissions. Responds in 1-2 months on queries and proposals. Catalog available online. Guidelines available online and by e-mail at editorial@w-apublishing.com.

NONFICTION Subjects include business, economics, finance, money, investing/trading; investment/trading strategies, systems, and techniques; hot trends; trading/investment psychology; trading guidelines and how-to; new, tested trading/investment methods; anthologies of articles related to the above. "We are always interested in great ideas, fresh voices, and new methods, strategies, and approaches that will educate readers interested in improving their skills as traders and investors." No proposals based on get-rich-quick schemes or 'foolproof, can't lose' strategies. Submit proposal packages, including: outline/synopsis, 1-3 sample chapters(s), table of contents and author's biographical information; prefer e-mailed submissions. Writers should send photocopies; scans; computer-generated graphics.

TIPS "Our readers have increased knowledge and awareness of discrete investment products and tools. They are interested in an education and want to learn from practicing financial professionals. Our goal is to offer readers materials highlighting new techniques, in-depth analysis, and solid information that helps them hone their skills and make informed decisions. We are interested in providing accompanying workbook materials in print and electronic form to augment the published book. (We prefer workbook/training materials that are supplemental rather than incorporated into the book.)"

⊘ WAKE FOREST UNIVERSITY PRESS

P.O. Box 7333, Winston-Salem NC 27109. (336)758-5448. **Fax:** (336)758-5636. **E-mail:** wfupress@wfu.edu.

Website: www.wfu.edu/wfupress. **Contact:** Jefferson Holdridge, director/poetry editor; Dillon Johnston, advisory editor. Estab. 1976. **Pays on 10% royalty contract, plus 6-8 author's copies. Negotiable advance.** Responds to queries in 1-2 weeks; to submissions (*if invited*) in 2-3 months.

⌘ "We publish only poetry from Ireland. I am able to consider only poetry written by native Irish poets. I must return, unread, poetry from American poets." Query with 4-5 samples and cover letter. Sometimes sends prepublication galleys. Buys North American or U.S. rights.

POETRY "We publish only poetry from Ireland. I am able to consider only poetry written by native Irish poets. I must return, unread, poetry from American poets."

WAKESTONE PRESS

200 Brook Hollow Rd., Nashville TN 37205. (615)739-6428. **E-mail:** submissions@wakestonepress.com. **Website:** www.wakestonepress.com. **Contact:** Frank Daniels III, editor. Estab. 2010. Publishes hardcover, trade paperback and electronic originals. **Publishes 6+ titles/year. 90% of books from first-time authors. 100% from unagented writers. Pays 7.5%-20% on wholesale price. Outright purchases $10,000-$20,000 maximum. Pays $2,000-$5,000 advance.** Publishes book 18 months after acceptance. Accepts simultaneous submissions. Responds 1 month to queries and proposals; 2 months to mss. Catalog free by request. Guidelines free by request.

NONFICTION Subjects include cooking, creative nonfiction, foods, history, house and home, law, memoirs, New Age, regional, sports, young adult. Submit in Microsoft Word file(s) a proposal package, including: book outline several (2-3) sample chapter(s) and author bio(s). Reviews art work and writers should send digital copies as part of submission file.

FICTION Subjects include erotica, gay, lesbian, occult, young adult. Submit in Microsoft Word file(s) a proposal package, including: book outline several (2-3) sample chapter(s) and author bio(s).

WALKER & COMPANY

175 Fifth Ave., New York NY 10010. **E-mail:** Emily.Easton@bloomsburyusa.com. **Website:** www.bloomsburykids.com and www.bloomsburyteens.com. **Contact:** Emily Easton, publisher; Stacy Cantor Abrams, editor; Mary-Kate Castellani, associate editor. Estab. 1959. **Publishes 45 titles/year. 5% of books**

from first-time authors. 15% from unagented writers. Pays authors royalty of 5-10%; pays illustrators royalty or flat fee. Offers advance payment against royalties. Writer's guidelines available for SASE.

NONFICTION Submit outline/synopsis and sample chapters; complete ms for picture books.

FICTION Picture books: adventure, history, humor. Middle readers: coming-of-age, adventure, contemporary, history, humor, multicultural. Young adults: adventure, contemporary, romance, humor, historical fiction, suspense/mystery, paranormal. Submit outline/synopsis and sample chapters; complete ms for picture books.

TIPS Writers: "Make sure you study our catalog before submitting. We are a small house with a tightly focused list. Illustrators: Have a well-rounded portfolio with different styles." Does not want to see folktales, ABC books, early readers, paperback series. "Walker and Company is committed to introducing talented new authors and illustrators to the children's book field."

⊕ WALTSAN PUBLISHING

5000 Barnett St., Ft. Worth TX 76103. **E-mail:** Sandra@Waltsan.com; acqs@WaltsanPublishing.com. **Website:** www.WaltsanPublishing.com. **Contact:** William Kercher, acquisitions editor. Estab. 2010. Trade paperback originals, mass market paperback originals, electronic originals. **Publishes 12 titles/year. Accepts electronic submissions only. "See website for details." Pays royalty minimum of 20%, maximum of 50% Does not pay advance.** Accepts simultaneous submissions. Responds in 1 month on queries, proposals, and mss. Cataog available for SAE with 1 first class stamp. Guidelines online.

ℝ Waltsan publishing publishes biographies, general nonfiction, how-tos, and illustrated, reference, scholary, self-help, technical books, and textbooks.

NONFICTION Interested in all topics. Reviews artwork as part of the ms package.

FICTION Interested in all topics. "Make sure your writing is polished, believable, and the ms is not too short. Pay attention to details and don't try to fool the readers. Check for continuity of details by making sure what is written in one chapter coincides with what is written in other chapters. Don't guess. Check your facts." Accepts electronic submissions ONLY. "See website for details."

POETRY Accepts electronic submissions ONLY. "See website for details."

TIPS "Waltsan Publishing's audience is the 'on-the-go' person, electronic reader or android in hand, that wants to read whenever and wherever they get a chance. Generally younger, technologically savvy, and intelligent. Truly a 21st century individual."

WASHINGTON STATE UNIVERSITY PRESS

P.O. Box 645910, Pullman WA 99164-5910. (800)354-7360. **Fax:** (509)335-8568. **E-mail:** wsupress@wsu.edu. **Website:** http://wsupress.wsu.edu. **Contact:** Acquisitions editor. Estab. 1928. Publishes hardcover originals, trade paperback originals, and reprints. **Publishes 4-6 titles/year. 40% of books from first-time authors. 95% from unagented writers. Pays 5% royalty graduated according to sales.** Publishes book 18 months after acceptance of ms. Responds in 2 months to queries. Submission Guidelines online.

ℝ WSU Press publishes scholarly nonfiction books on the history, pre-history, culture, and politics of the West, particularly the Pacific Northwest.

NONFICTION Subjects include, but are not limited to, archaeology, biography, cultural studies, cooking and food history, environment, government, history, politics, nature, railroads, science, essays. "We welcome engaging and thought-provoking mss that focus on the greater Pacific Northwest (primarily Washington, Oregon, Idaho, British Columbia, western Montana, and southeastern Alaska). Currently we are not accepting how-to books, literary criticism, memoirs, novels, or poetry." Submit outline, sample chapters. Reviews artwork/photos.

TIPS "We have developed our marketing in the direction of regional and local history, and use this as the base upon which to expand our publishing program. For history, the secret is to write strong narratives on significant topics or events. Stories should be told in imaginative, clever ways and be substantiated factually. Have visuals (photos, maps, etc.) available to help the reader envision what has happened. Explain stories in ways that tie them to wider-ranging regional, national—or even international—events. Weave them into the large pattern of history."

WASHINGTON WRITERS' PUBLISHING HOUSE

C/O Bravo Household, 3541 S. St., NW, Washington DC 20007. **E-mail:** wwphpress@gmail.com. **Website:**

www.washingtonwriters.org. **Contact:** Patrick Pepper, president. Estab. 1975.

FICTION Poetry Washington Writers' Publishing House publishes books by Washington, DC and Baltimore-area poets through its annual book competition. "No specific criteria, except literary excellence." Publishes 1-2 books/year." Washington Writers' Publishing House considers book-length mss for publication by fiction writers living within 60 driving miles of the U.S. Capitol, Baltimore area included, through competition only (see below). Offers $500 and 50 copies of published book plus additional copies for publicity use. Mss may include previously published stories and excerpts. Submit 2 copies of a short story collection or novel (no more than 350 pages, double or 1-½ spaced; author's name should not appear on any ms pages). Include separate page of publication acknowledgments plus 2 cover sheets: one with ms title, poet's name, address, telephone number, and e-mail address, the other with ms title only. Include SASE for results only; mss will not be returned (will be recycled). Guidelines available for SASE or on web site. "Author should indicate where they heard about WWPH." Entry fee: $25. Deadline: July 1-November 1 (postmark). Order sample fiction books on website or by sending $16 plus $3 s&h to Washington Writers' Publishing House, P.O. Box 15271, Washington DC 20003.

Ⓐ WATERBROOK MULTNOMAH PUBLISHING GROUP

Random House, 12265 Oracle Blvd., Suite 200, Colorado Springs CO 80921. (719)590-4999. **Fax:** (719)590-8977. **Website:** www.waterbrookmultnomah.com. Estab. 1996. Publishes hardcover and trade paperback originals. **Publishes 70 titles/year. 2,000 queries received/year. 15% of books from first-time authors. Pays royalty.** Publishes book 1 year after acceptance. Accepts simultaneous submissions. Responds in 2-3 months to queries/proposals/mss. Catalog online.

NONFICTION Subjects include child guidance, money, finance, religion, spirituality, marriage, Christian living. We publish books on unique topics with a Christian perspective. Agented submissions only.

FICTION Subjects include adventure, historical, literary, mainstream, contemporary, mystery, religious, inspirational, religious mystery/suspense, religious thriller, religious romance, romance, contemporary, historical, science fiction, spiritual, suspense. Agented submissions only.

WAVE BOOKS

1938 Fairview Ave. E., Suite 201, Seattle WA 98102. (206)676-5337. **E-mail:** info@wavepoetry.com. **Website:** www.wavepoetry.com. **Contact:** Charlie Wright, publisher; Joshua Beckman and Matthew Zapruder, editors; Heidi Broadhead, managing editor. Estab. 2005. Hardcover and trade paperback originals. Catalog online.

⚷ "Wave Books is an independent poetry press based in Seattle, Washington. Dedicated to publishing the best in contemporary American poetry and poetry in translation, Wave Books was founded in 2005, joining forces with already-established publisher Verse Press. Wave Books seeks to build on and expand the mission of Verse Press by publishing strong innovative work and encouraging our authors to expand and interact with their readership through nationwide readings and events, affirming our belief that the audience for poetry is larger and more diverse than commonly thought."

POETRY "We are dedicated to publishing the best in American poetry by new & established authors. We seek to build on & expand by publishing strong innovative work & encouraging our authors to expand & interact with their readership through nationwide readings & events, affirming our belief that the audience for poetry is larger & more diverse than commonly thought." No children's, fiction, or nonfiction for Wave library. No magazine contributions right now. Submit with cover letter. Galleys & advance reader's copies are acceptable.

WAVELAND PRESS, INC.

4180 Illinois Route 83, Suite 101, Long Grove IL 60047-9580. (847)634-0081. **Fax:** (847)634-9501. **E-mail:** info@waveland.com. **Website:** www.waveland.com. Estab. 1975.

⚷ Waveland Press, Inc. is a publisher of college textbooks and supplements. We are committed to providing reasonably priced teaching materials for the classroom and actively seek to add new titles to our growing lists in a variety of academic disciplines. If you are currently working on a project you feel serves a need and would have promise as an adopted text in the college market, we would like to hear from you.

TIPS "Mail stock list and price list."

WEIGL EDUCATIONAL PUBLISHERS LTD.

6325 10th St., SE, Calgary AB T2H 2Z9, Canada. (403)233-7747. **Fax:** (403)233-7769. **E-mail:** linda@weigl.com. **Website:** www.weigl.ca. Estab. 1979. Publishes hardcover originals and reprints, school library softcover. **Publishes 104 titles/year. 100% from unagented writers.** Catalog available for free.

 "Textbook publisher catering to juvenile and young adult audience (K-12)." Makes outright purchase. Responds ASAP to queries. Query with SASE.

NONFICTION Animals, education, government, politics, history, nature, environment, science.

WEIGL PUBLISHERS INC.

350 Fifth Ave. 59th Floor, New York NY 10118. (866)649-3445. **Fax:** (866)449-3445. **E-mail:** linda@weigl.com. **Website:** www.weigl.com. **Contact:** Heather Kissock, acquisitions. Estab. 2000. **Publishes 85 titles/year. 15% of books from first-time authors.** Publishes book 6-9 months after acceptance. Accepts simultaneous submissions. Catalog available for 912×11 SASE. Catalog available on website.

 Publishes 25 young readers/year; 40 middle readers/year; 20 young adult titles/year. "Our mission is to provide innovative high-quality learning resources for schools and libraries worldwide at a competitive price."

NONFICTION Young readers: animal, biography, geography, history, multicultural, nature/environment, science. Middle readers: animal, biography, geography, history, multicultural, nature/environment, science, social issues, sports. Young adults: biography, careers, geography, history, multicultural, nature/environment, social issues. Average word length: young readers—100 words/page; middle readers—200 words/page; young adults—300 words/page. Query by e-mail only.

WESLEYAN PUBLISHING HOUSE

P.O. Box 50434, Indianapolis IN 46250. **E-mail:** submissions@wesleyan.org. **Website:** www.wesleyan.org/wg. **Contact:** Rachael Stevenson, associate production editor. Estab. 1843. Publishes hardcover and trade paperback originals. **Publishes 25 titles/year. 150-175 submissions received/year. 50% of books from first-time authors. 90% from unagented writers. Pays royalty on wholesale price.** Publishes book 11 months after acceptance. Accepts simultaneous submissions. Responds in 2 months on proposals. Catalog available online. Guidelines online.

NONFICTION Subjects include Christianity/religion. No hard copy submissions. Submit proposal package, including outline, 3-5 sample chapters, bio. See writer's guidelines.

TIPS "Our books help evangelical Christians learn about the faith or grow in their relationship with God."

WESLEYAN UNIVERSITY PRESS

215 Long Lane, Middletown CT 06459. (860)685-7711. **Fax:** (860)685-7712. **E-mail:** stamminen@wesleyan.edu. **Website:** www.wesleyan.edu/wespress. **Contact:** Suzanna Tamminen, director and editor-in-chief. Estab. 1959. Publishes hardcover originals and paperbacks. Accepts simultaneous submissions. Catalog available free. Ms guidelines online or with #10 SASE.

 "Wesleyan University Press is a scholarly press with a focus on poetry, music, dance and cultural studies." Wesleyan University Press is one of the major publishers of poetry in the nation. Publishes 4-6 titles/year. Has published poetry by James Dickey, Joy Harjo, James Tate, and Yusef Komunyakaa. Guidelines available for SASE or on website. Responds to queries in 2 months; to mss in 4 months. Pays royalties plus 10 author's copies. Poetry publications from Wesleyan tend to get widely (and respectfully) reviewed. **"We are accepting manuscripts by invitation only until further notice."**

NONFICTION Subjects include music, dance., film/TV & media studies, science fiction studies, dance and poetry. Submit proposal package, outline, sample chapters, cover letter, CV, TOC, anticipated length of ms and date of completion. Reviews artwork/photos. Send photocopies.

POETRY We do not accept unsolicited manuscripts. Query first with SASE. Considers simultaneous submissions.

WESTERN PSYCHOLOGICAL SERVICES

625 Alaska Ave., Torrance CA 90503. (424)201-8800 or (800)648-8857. **Fax:** (424)201-6950. **E-mail:** review@wpspublish.com. **Website:** www.wpspublish.com; www.creativetherapystore.com. Estab. 1948. Publishes psychological and educational assessments and some trade paperback originals. **Publishes 2 titles/year. 60 queries received/year. 30 mss received/year. 90% of books from first-time authors. 95% from unagented writers. Pays 5-10% royalty on**

wholesale price. Publishes book 1 year after acceptance. Accepts simultaneous submissions. Responds in 2 months to queries. Catalog available free. Guidelines online.

☛ "Western Psychological Services publishes psychological and educational assessments that practitioners trust. Our products allow helping professionals to accurately screen, diagnose, and treat people in need. WPS publishes practical books and games used by therapists, counselors, social workers, and others in the helping professionals who work with children and adults."

NONFICTION Subjects include child guidance, psychology, autism, sensory processing disorders. "We publish children's books dealing with feelings, anger, social skills, autism, family problems." Submit complete ms. Reviews artwork/photos. Send photocopies.

FICTION Children's books dealing with feelings, anger, social skills, autism, family problems, etc. Submit complete ms.

WESTMINSTER JOHN KNOX PRESS

Division of Presbyterian Publishing Corp., 100 Witherspoon St., Louisville KY 40202. **Fax:** (502)569-5113. **E-mail:** submissions@wjkbooks.com. **Website:** www.wjkbooks.com. **Contact:** Jana Riess, acquisitions editor. Publishes hardcover and paperback originals and reprints. **Publishes 70 titles/year. 2,500 queries received/year. 750 mss received/year. 10% of books from first-time authors. Pays royalty on net price.** Responds in 3 months. Proposal guidelines online.

☛ "All WJK books have a religious/spiritual angle, but are written for various markets-scholarly, professional, and the general reader. Westminster John Knox is affiliated with the Presbyterian Church USA. No phone queries. We do not publish fiction, poetry, memoir, children's books, or dissertations. We will not return or respond to submissions without an accompanying SASE with sufficient postage."

NONFICTION Subjects include religion, spirituality. Submit proposal package according to the WJK book proposal guidelines found online.

⊘ WHITAKER HOUSE

1030 Hunt Valley Circle, New Kensington PA 15068. **E-mail:** publisher@whitakerhouse.com. **Website:** www.whitakerhouse.com. **Contact:** Tom Cox, managing editor. Estab. 1970. Publishes hardcover, trade

paperback, and mass market originals. **Publishes 50 titles/year. 600 queries received/year. 200 mss received/year. 15% of books from first-time authors. 60% from unagented writers. Pays 5-15% royalty on wholesale price.** Publishes book 7 months after acceptance. Accepts simultaneous submissions. Responds in 3 months to queries, proposals and mss. Catalog online. Guidelines available online and by e-mail.

NONFICTION Subjects include religion, Christian. Accepts submissions on topics with a Christian perspective. Subjects include Christian living, prayer, spiritual warfare, healing, gifts of the spirit, etc. Accepts submissions on any topic as long as they have a Christian perspective. Query with SASE.

FICTION Subjects include religious, Christian, historical romance, African American romance and Amish fiction. All fiction must have a Christian perspective. Query with SASE.

TIPS "Audience includes those seeking uplifting and inspirational fiction and nonfiction."

◎ WHITECAP BOOKS, LTD.

351 Lynn Ave., North Vancouver BC V7J 2C4, Canada. (640)980-9852. **Fax:** (604)980-8197. **E-mail:** whitecap@whitecap.ca. **Website:** www.whitecap.ca. Publishes hardcover and trade paperback originals. **Publishes 40 titles/year. 500 queries received/year; 1,000 mss received/year. 20% of books from first-time authors. 90% from unagented writers. Pays royalty. Pays negotiated advance.** Publishes book 1 year after acceptance. Accepts simultaneous submissions. Responds in 2-3 months to proposals. Catalog and guidelines online.

☛ "Whitecap Books is a general trade publisher with a focus on food and wine titles. Although we are interested in reviewing unsolicited ms submissions, please note that we only accept submissions that meet the needs of our current publishing program. Please see some of most recent releases to get an idea of the kinds of titles we are interested in."

NONFICTION Subjects include animals, cooking, foods, nutrition, gardening, history, nature, environment, recreation, regional, travel. Young children's and middle reader's nonfiction focusing mainly on nature, wildlife and animals. "Writers should take the time to research our list and read the submission guidelines on our website. This is especially important for children's writers and cookbook authors. We will only consider submissions that fall into these categories: cookbooks, wine and spirits, regional travel, home and garden, Canadian history, North American natural history, juvenile series-based fiction. At this time, we are not accepting the following categories: self-help or inspirational books, political, social commentary, or issue books, general how-to books, biographies or memoirs, business and finance, art and architecture, religion and spirituality." Submit cover letter, synopsis, SASE via ground mail. See guidelines online. Reviews artwork/photos. Send photocopies.

TIPS "We want well-written, well-researched material that presents a fresh approach to a particular topic."

WHITE MANE KIDS

73 W. Burd St., P.O. Box 708, Shippensburg PA 17257. (717)532-2237. **Fax:** (717)532-6110. **E-mail:** marketing@whitemane.com. **Website:** www.whitemane.com. **Contact:** Harold Collier, acquisitions editor. Estab. 1987. **Pays authors royalty of 7-10%. Pays illustrators and photographers by the project.** Publishes book 18 months after acceptance. Accepts simultaneous submissions. Responds to queries in 1 month, mss in 3 months. Catalog and writer's guidelines available for SASE.

NONFICTION Middle readers, young adults: history. Average word length: middle readers—30,000. Does not publish picture books. Submit outline/synopsis and 2-3 sample chapters.

FICTION Middle readers, young adults: history (primarily American Civil War). Average word length: middle readers—30,000. Does not publish picture books. Query.

TIPS "Make your work historically accurate. We are interested in historically accurate fiction for middle and young adult readers. We do *not* publish picture books. Our primary focus is the American Civil War and some America Revolution topics."

WHITE MANE PUBLISHING COMPANY INC.

73 W. Burd St., P.O. Box 708, Shippensburg PA 17257. (717)532-2237; (888)948-6263. **Fax:** (717)532-6110. **E-mail:** marketing@whitemane.com. **Website:** www.whitemane.com. Estab. 1987.

FICTION "Download and print out the Proposal Guidelines form. Fill out the form and mail it along with the title of the manuscript, statement of purpose, marketing ideas, a sample dust jacket paragraph, general manuscript information, and how you were referred to White Mane."

WHITE PINE PRESS

P.O. Box 236, Buffalo NY 14201. (716)627-4665. **Fax:** (716)627-4665. **E-mail:** wpine@whitepine.org. **Website:** www.whitepine.org. **Contact:** Dennis Maloney, editor. Estab. 1973. Publishes trade paperback originals. **Publishes 10-12 titles/year. 500 queries/yearly 1% of books from first-time authors. 100% from unagented writers. Pays contributor's copies.** Publishes book 18 months after acceptance. Accepts simultaneous submissions. Responds in 1 month to queries and proposals; 4 months to mss. Catalog available online; for #10 SASE. Guidelines online.

NONFICTION Subjects include language, literature, multicultural, translation., poetry. *"We are currently not considering nonfiction mss.* We do not review artwork/photos."

FICTION Subjects include poetry, poetry in translation, translation. "We are currently not reading U.S. fiction. We are currently reading unsolicited poetry only as part of our Annual Poetry Contest. The reading period is July 1 - November 30 for fiction and poetry in translation only." For fiction and poetry in translation only-query with SASE; submit proposal package, including synopsis and 2 sample chapters."

ALBERT WHITMAN & COMPANY

250 S. Northwest Hwy., Suite 320, Park Ridge IL 60068. (800)255-7675. **Fax:** (847)581-0039. **E-mail:** mail@awhitmanco.com. **Website:** www.albertwhitman.com. Estab. 1919. Publishes in original hardcover, paperback, boardbooks. **Publishes 40 titles/year. 10% of books from first-time authors. 50% from unagented writers. On retail price: Pays 10% royalty for novels; 5% for picture books. Pays advance.** Publishes book Publishes a book 18 months after acceptance. Accepts simultaneous submissions. Responds within 3 months to queries; 4 months to proposals and mss. "Send a self-addressed, stamped 9x12 envelope with your request, and address your letter to "Catalog Request" at our main address. Please include three first-class stamps (U.S. postage) with your SASE. Unless you specify otherwise, we will send our most recent catalog.". Guidelines available on website.

NONFICTION Subjects include Americana, animals, character education, disabilities, family issues, holidays, multicultural, sports. Picture books, young readers, middle readers: animal, arts/crafts, health, history, hobbies, multicultural, music/dance, nature/environment, science, sports, special needs. Does not want to see, "religion, any books that have to be written in, or fictionalized biographies. Submit query, outline, and sample chapter. For picture books send entire ms. Include cover letter. Reviews artwork/photos. Send photocopies.

FICTION Subjects include juvenile, picture books, sports. Picture books, young readers, middle readers: adventure, concept (to help children deal with problems), fantasy, history, humor, multicultural, suspense. Middle readers: problem novels, suspense/mystery. "We are interested in contemporary multicultural stories—stories with holiday themes, and exciting distinctive novels. We publish a wide variety of topics and are interested in stories that help children deal with their problems and concerns. Does not want to see, "religion-oriented, ABCs, pop-up, romance, counting." Submit query, outline, and sample chapter. For picture books send entire ms. Include cover letter.

TIPS "In both picture books and nonfiction, we are seeking stories showing life in other cultures and the variety of multicultural life in the U.S. We also want fiction and nonfiction about mentally or physically challenged children; some recent topics have been autism, stuttering, and diabetes. Look up some of our books first to be sure your submission is appropriate for Albert Whitman & Co. We publish trade books that are especially interesting to schools and libraries. We recommend you study our website before submitting your work."

WHITTLER'S BENCH PRESS

Dram Tree Books, P.O. Box 7183, Wilmington NC 28406. **E-mail:** dramtreebooks@ec.rr.com. **Website:** www.dramtreebooks.com. Estab. 2005. Publishes trade paperback originals and reprints. **Publishes 2-6 titles/year. 90% of books from first-time authors. 100% from unagented writers. Pays 10-15% royalty on retail price. Pays $250-500 advance.** Publishes book 1 year after acceptance. Responds in 2 months to queries and proposals; 4 months to mss. Guidelines available via e-mail.

FICTION Subjects include adventure, historical, humor, military, war, mystery, regional, suspense. Our main focus is on historical fiction, mysteries and humorous novels—and all of it must have some link to North Carolina. When submitting humorous novels you must make us laugh. Think in terms of books by authors like Michael Malone, T.R. Pearson, Clyde Edgerton, Terry Pratchett, etc.

Query with SASE. Submit proposal package, 3 sample chapters, clips.

TIPS Our readers are looking for compelling stories that will transport them away from the pressures of the 'real' world for however long they spend with our stories. The North Carolina tie-in is an important part of what will be a Whittler's Bench Press title. Remember they'll be paying good money to be entertained, so give them a story that satisfies. If historical fiction, make sure you get the history right. Finally, always remember: It must have a North Carolina angle of some kind.

WILD CHILD PUBLISHING

PO Box 4897, Culver City CA 90231. (310) 721-4461. **E-mail:** admin@wildchildpublishing.com. **Website:** www.wildchildpublishing.com. **Contact:** Marci Baun, editor-in-chief (genres not covered by other editors); Faith Bicknell-Brown, managing editor (horror and romance); S.R. Howen, editor (science fiction and nonfiction). Estab. 1999. **Publishes 12 titles/year. Pays royalties 10-40%.** Publishes book 2-4 months after acceptance. Responds in 1 month to queries and mss. Catalogs on website.

FICTION Adventure, children's/juvenile, erotica for Freya's Bower only, ethnic/multicultural, experimental, fantasy, feminist, gay, historical, horror, humor/satire, lesbian, literary, mainstream, military/war, mystery/suspense, New Age/mystic, psychic/supernatural, romance, science fiction, short story collections, thriller/espionage, western, young adult/teen (fantasy/science fiction). Multiple anthologies planned. Query with outline/synopsis and 1 sample chapter. Accepts queries by e-mail only. Include estimated word count, brief bio. Often critiques/comments on rejected mss.

TIPS "Read our submission guidelines thoroughly. Send in entertaining, well-written stories. Be easy to work with and upbeat."

WILDE PUBLISHING

P.O. Box 4581, Alburquerque NM 87196. **Fax:** (419)715-1430. **E-mail:** wilde@unm.edu. **Contact:** Josiah Simon, Dusty, McGowan, and David Wilde. Estab. 1989. Publishes hardcover and paperback originals. **Pay depends on grants and awards.** Publishes book 1 year after acceptance. Ms guidelines for #10 SASE.

FICTION Children's/juvenile, fantasy (sword and sorcery), historical, literary, military/war, mystery, psychic/supernatural, romance, short story collections, thriller/espionage, western, young adult. Does not accept unsolicited mss. Query with SASE. Accepts queries by e-mail, fax, mail. Include cover letter, brief bio, list of publishing credits. Send SASE for return of ms or send a disposable ms and SASE for reply only. Accepts submissions on disk. No simultaneous submissions.

TIPS "Check spelling, write frequently, avoid excuses!"

THE WILD ROSE PRESS

P.O. Box 708, Adams Basin NY 14410. (585) 752-8770. **E-mail:** queryus@thewildrosepress.com; rpenders@thewildrosepress.com. **Website:** www.thewildrosepress.com. **Contact:** Nicole D'Arienzo, editor. Estab. 2006. Publishes paperback originals, reprints, and e-books in a POD format. **Publishes approx. 10 fiction titles/year. Pays royalty of 7% minimum; 35% maximum.** Publishes book 1 year after acceptance. Responds in 1 month to queries; 3 months to mss. Guidelines available on website.

FICTION Subjects include contemporary, erotica, gothic, historical, regional, romance, suspense, war., *Subjects:* futuristic/time travel, regency, romantic suspense, and paranormal. Plans several anthologies "in several lines of the company in the next year, including Cactus Rose, Yellow Rose, American Rose, Black Rose, and Scarlet Rose.". "The American Rose line publishes stories about the French and Indian wars; Colonial America; the Revolutionary War; the war of 1812; the War Between the States; the Reconstruction era; the dawn of the new century. These are the struggles at the heart of the American Rose story. The central romantic relationship is the key driving force, set against historically accurate backdrop. These stories are for those who long for the courageous heroes and heroines who fought for their freedom and settled the new world; for gentle southern belles with spines of steel and the gallant gentlemen who sweep them away. This line is wide open for writers with a love of American history." Publishes paperback originals, reprints, and e-books in a POD format. Published 5 debut authors last year. Publishes approximately 10 fiction titles/year. Member: EPIC, Romance Writers of America. Distributes/promotes titles through major distribution chains, including Ingrams, Baker & Taylor, Sony, Kindle, Amazon.com, as well as smaller and online distributors. Please do not submit women's fiction, poetry, science fiction, fanfiction, or any type of nonfiction. *Does not accept unsolicited mss.*

Send query letter with outline and synopsis of up to 5 pages. Accepts all queries by e-mail. Include estimated word count, brief bio, and list of publishing credits. *Does not accept unsolicited mss.* Send query letter with outline and synopsis of up to 5 pages. Accepts all queries by e-mail. Include estimated word count, brief bio, and list of publishing credits. Agented fiction less than 1%. Always comments on rejected mss. Sends prepublication galleys to author. Only our full length (over 65K words) will go to print. For information on distribution visit our FAQ section.

TIPS "Polish your manuscript, make it as error free as possible, and follow our submission guidelines."

⊘ WILDSTORM

DC Universe, 1700 Broadway, New York NY 10019. **Website:** http://www.dccomics.com/wildstorm/.

▢ *Does not accept unsolicited mss.*

Ⓐ ⊘ WILLIAM MORROW

HarperCollins, 10 E. 53rd St., New York NY 10022. (212)207-7000. **Fax:** (212)207-7145. **Website:** www.harpercollins.com. Estab. 1926. **Pays standard royalty on retail price. Pays varying advance.** Catalog available free.

&—⚲ "William Morrow publishes a wide range of titles that receive much recognition and prestige—a most selective house."

NONFICTION Subjects include art, architecture, cooking, foods, nutrition, history. Length 50,000-100,000 words. *No unsolicited mss or proposals.* Agented submissions only.

FICTION Publishes adult fiction. Morrow accepts only the highest quality submissions in adult fiction. *No unsolicited mss or proposals.* Agented submissions only.

WILLIAMSON BOOKS

2630 Elm Hill Pike, Suite 100, Nashville TN 37214. **E-mail:** pjay@guideposts.org. **Website:** www.idealspublications.com. Estab. 1983. **Pays authors advance against future royalties based on wholesale price or purchases outright. Pays illustrators by the project. Pays photographers per photo.** Publishes book 1 year after acceptance. Responds to queries and mss in 4 months. Guidelines available for SASE.

&—⚲ Publishes "very successful nonfiction series (Kids Can! Series) on subjects such as history, science, arts/crafts, geography, diversity, multiculturalism. Little Hands series for ages 2-6, Kaleidoscope Kids series (age 7 and up) and

Quick Starts for Kids! series (ages 8 and up). Our goal is to help every child fulfill his/her potential and experience personal growth."

NONFICTION Hands-on active learning books, animals, African-American, arts/crafts, Asian, biography, diversity, careers, geography, health, history, hobbies, how-to, math, multicultural, music/dance, nature/ environment, Native American, science, writing and journaling. Does not want to see textbooks, picture books, fiction. "Looking for all things African American, Asian American, Hispanic, Latino, and Native American including crafts and traditions, as well as their history, biographies, and personal retrospectives of growing up in U.S. for grades pre K-8th. We are looking for books in which learning and doing are inseparable." Query with annotated TOC/synopsis and 1 sample chapter.

TIPS "Please do not send any fiction or picture books of any kind—those should go to Ideals Children's Books. Look at our books to see what we do. We're interested in interactive learning books with a creative approach packed with interesting information, written for young readers ages 3-7 and 8-14. In nonfiction children's publishing, we are looking for authors with a depth of knowledge shared with children through a warm, embracing style. Our publishing philosophy is based on the idea that all children can succeed and have positive learning experiences. Children's lasting learning experiences involve their participation."

WILLOW CREEK PRESS

P.O. Box 147, 9931 Highway 70 W., Minocqua WI 54548. (715)358-7010. **Fax:** (715)358-2807. **E-mail:** jpetrie@willowcreekpress.com. **Website:** www.willowcreekpress.com. **Contact:** Jeremy Petrie, vice president of sales. Estab. 1986. Publishes hardcover and trade paperback originals and reprints. **Publishes 25 titles/year. 400 queries received/year. 150 mss received/year. 15% of books from first-time authors. 50% from unagented writers. Pays 6-15% royalty on wholesale price. Pays $2,000-5,000 advance.** Publishes book 18 months after acceptance. Accepts simultaneous submissions. Responds in 2 months to queries. Guidelines online.

⚷ "We specialize in nature, outdoor, and sporting topics, including gardening, wildlife, and animal books. Pets, cookbooks, and a few humor books and essays round out our titles. Currently emphasizing pets (mainly dogs and cats), wildlife, outdoor sports (hunting, fishing). De-emphasizing essays, fiction."

NONFICTION Subjects include animals, cooking, foods, nutrition, gardening, nature, environment, recreation, sports, travel., wildlife, pets. Submit outline, 1 sample chapter, SASE. Reviews artwork/photos.

WILSHIRE BOOK COMPANY

9731 Variel Ave., Chatsworth CA 91311. (818)700-1522. **Fax:** (818)700-1527. **E-mail:** mpowers@mpowers.com. **Website:** www.mpowers.com. **Contact:** Rights Department. Estab. 1947. Publishes trade paperback originals and reprints. **Publishes 25 titles/ year. 1,200 queries received/year. 70% of books from first-time authors. 90% from unagented writers. Pays standard royalty. Pays advance.** Publishes book 6-9 months after acceptance. Accepts simultaneous submissions. Responds in 2 months. Ms guidelines online.

NONFICTION Subjects include psychology, personal success. Minimum 30,000 words Submit 3 sample chapters. Submit complete ms. Include outline, author bio, analysis of book's competition and SASE. No e-mail or fax submissions. Reviews artwork/photos. Send photocopies.

FICTION "You are not only what you are today, but also what you choose to become tomorrow." Looking for adult fables that teach principles of psychological growth. Distributes titles through wholesalers, bookstores and mail order. Promotes titles through author interviews on radio and television.Wants adult allegories that teach principles of psychological growth or offer guidance in living. Minimum 30,000 words. No standard fiction. Submit 3 sample chapters. Submit complete ms. Include outline, author bio, analysis of book's, competition and SASE.

TIPS "We are vitally interested in all new material we receive. Just as you are hopeful when submitting your manuscript for publication, we are hopeful as we read each one submitted, searching for those we believe could be successful in the marketplace. Writing and publishing must be a team effort. We need you to write what we can sell. We suggest you read the successful books similar to the one you want to write. Analyze them to discover what elements make them winners. Duplicate those elements in your own style, using a creative new approach and fresh material, and you will have written a book we can catapult onto the bestseller list. You are welcome to telephone or e-mail us for immediate feedback on any book concept you may have. To learn more about us and what we publish, and for complete ms guidelines, visit our website."

WINDRIVER PUBLISHING, INC.

72 N. WindRiver Rd., Silverton ID 83867. (208)752-1836. **Fax:** (208)752-1876. **E-mail:** info@windriver-publishing.com. **Website:** www.windriverpublishing.com. **Contact:** E. Keith Howick, Jr., president; Gail Howick, vice president/editor-in-chief. Estab. 2003. Publishes hardcover originals and reprints, trade paperback originals, and mass market originals. **Publishes 8 titles/year. 1,000 queries received/year. 300 mss received/year. 95% of books from first-time authors. 90% from unagented writers.** Publishes book 1 year after acceptance. Accepts simultaneous submissions. Responds in 1-2 months to queries; 4-6 months to proposals/mss. Catalog and guidelines online.

⚏ "Authors who wish to submit book proposals for review must do so according to our Submissions Guidelines, which can be found on our website, along with an on-line submission form, which is our preferred submission method. *We do not accept submissions of any kind by e-mail.*"

NONFICTION Subjects include business, computers, education, environment, gardening, government, health, history, hobbies, language, literature, medicine, nature, philosophy, religion, science, spirituality, sports, true crime., antiques/collectibles. *Does not accept unsolicited mss.* Reviews artwork/photos.

FICTION Subjects include adventure, fantasy, historical, horror, humor, juvenile, literary, military, war, mystery, occult, religious, romance, science fiction, short story collections, spiritual, sports, suspense, western, young adult, drama; espionage; political; psychological; fairy tales/folklore; graphic novels. *Does not accept unsolicited mss.*

TIPS "We do not accept manuscripts containing graphic or gratuitous profanity, sex, or violence. See online instructions for details."

WINDWARD PUBLISHING

Finney Company, 8075 215th St. W., Lakeville MN 55044. (952)469-6699. **Fax:** (952)469-1968. **E-mail:** feedback@finney-hobar.com. **Website:** www.finney-hobar.com. **Contact:** Alan E. Krysan, president. Estab. 1973. Publishes trade paperback originals. **Publishes 6-10 titles/year. 120 queries received/year. 50 mss received/year. 50% of books from first-time authors.**

100% from unagented writers. Pays 10% royalty on wholesale price. Pays advance. Publishes book 1 year after acceptance. Accepts simultaneous submissions. Responds in 8-10 weeks to queries.

⚏ Windward publishes illustrated natural history, recreation books, and children's books. "Covers topics of natural history and science, outdoor recreation, and children's literature. Its principal markets are book, retail, and specialty stores. While primarily a nonfiction publisher, we will occasionally accept fiction books with educational value."

NONFICTION Subjects include agriculture, animals, gardening, nature, environment, recreation, science, sports, natural history. Young readers, middle readers, young adults: activity books, animal, careers, nature/environment, science. Young adults: textbooks. Query with SASE. Does not accept e-mail or fax submissions. Reviews artwork/photos.

WISCONSIN HISTORICAL SOCIETY PRESS

816 State St., Madison WI 53706. (608)264-6465. **Fax:** (608)264-6486. **E-mail:** whspress@wisconsinhistory.org. **Website:** www.wisconsinhistory.org/whspress/. **Contact:** Kate Thompson, editor. Estab. 1855. Publishes hardcover and trade paperback originals; trade paperback reprints. **Publishes 12-14 titles/year. 60-75 queries received/year. 20% of books from first-time authors. 90% from unagented writers. Pays royalty on wholesale price.** Publishes book 2 years after acceptance. Catalog available free. Guidelines online.

NONFICTION Subjects include Wisconsin history and culture: archaeology, architecture, cooking, foods, ethnic, history (Wisconsin), memoirs, regional, sports. Submit proposal package, form from website. Reviews artwork/photos. Send photocopies.

TIPS "Our audience reads about Wisconsin. Carefully review the book."

WISDOM PUBLICATIONS

199 Elm St., Somerville MA 02144. (617)776-7416, ext. 28. **Fax:** (617)776-7841. **E-mail:** editors@wisdompubs.org. **Website:** www.wisdompubs.org. **Contact:** David Kittlestrom, senior editor. Estab. 1976. Publishes hardcover originals and trade paperback originals and reprints. **Publishes 20-25 titles/year. 300 queries received/year. 50% of books from first-time authors. 95% from unagented writers. Pays 4-8% royalty on wholesale price. Pays advance.** Publishes

book within 2 years of acceptance. after acceptance of ms. Catalog and guidelines online.

8━▪ "Wisdom Publications is dedicated to making available authentic Buddhist works for the benefit of all. We publish translations, commentaries, and teachings of past and contemporary Buddhist masters and original works by leading Buddhist scholars. Currently emphasizing popular applied Buddhism, scholarly titles."

NONFICTION Subjects include philosophy, Buddhist or comparative Buddhist/Western, psychology, religion, Buddhism, Tibet. Submissions should be made electronically.

POETRY Buddhist.

TIPS "We are basically a publisher of Buddhist books-all schools and traditions of Buddhism. Please see our catalog or our website before you send anything to us to get a sense of what we publish."

PAULA WISEMAN BOOKS

1230 Sixth Ave., New York NY 10020. (212)698-7272. **Fax:** (212)698-2796. **E-mail:** paula.wiseman@simonandschuster.com; Alexandra.Penfold@simonandschuster.com. **Website:** http://kids.simonandschuster.com. **Publishes 20 titles/year. 10% of books from first-time authors.**

NONFICTION Picture books: animal, biography, concept, history, nature/environment. Young readers: animal, biography, history, multicultural, nature/environment, sports. Average word length: picture books—500; others standard length. *Does not accept unsolicited or unagented mss.*

FICTION Considers all categories. Average word length: picture books—500; others standard length. *Does not accept unsolicited or unagented mss.*

WIZARDS OF THE COAST BOOKS FOR YOUNG READERS

P.O. Box 707, Renton WA 98057. (425)254-2287. **E-mail:** nina.hess@wizards.com. **Website:** www.wizards.com. **Contact:** Nina Hess. Estab. 2003. Publishes hardcover and trade paperback originals and trade paperback reprints. **Publishes 10 titles/year. 5% of books from first-time authors. Pays authors 4-6% based on retail price. Pays illustrators by project. Offers advances (average amount: $4,000).** Publishes book 9-24 months after acceptance. Catalog available on website. Ms guidelines available on website.

8━▪ Wizards of the Coast publishes only science fiction and fantasy shared-world titles. Currently emphasizing solid fantasy writers. De-emphasizing gothic fiction. Dragonlance; Forgotten Realms; Magic: The Gathering; Eberron. Wizard of the Coast publishes games as well, including Dungeons & Dragons® role-playing game.

FICTION Young readers, middle readers, young adults: fantasy only. Average word length: middle readers—30,000-40,000; young adults—60,000-75,000. Query with samples.

TIPS Editorial staff attended or plans to attend ALA conference.

WOLF DEN BOOKS

5794 SW. 40th St., #221, Miami FL 33155. (877)667-9737. **E-mail:** info@wolfdenbooks.com. **Website:** www.wolfdenbooks.com. **Contact:** Gail Shivel. Estab. 2000. Publishes hardcover, trade paperback and electronic originals and reprints. **Publishes 2 titles/year. 40 queries received/year. 10 mss received/year. 100% from unagented writers. Pays 7 ½% royalty on retail price.** Publishes book 1 year after acceptance. Accepts simultaneous submissions. Responds in 3 months to queries; 6 months to proposals; 8 months to mss. Catalog online. Guidelines available via e-mail.

NONFICTION Subjects include history, humanities, language, literature, literary criticism, philosophy. Query with SASE; submit proposal package, including outline; submit complete ms.

WOODBINE HOUSE

6510 Bells Mill Rd., Bethesda MD 20817. (301)897-3570. **Fax:** (301)897-5838. **E-mail:** ngpaul@woodbinehouse.com. **Website:** www.woodbinehouse.com. **Contact:** Nancy Gray Paul, acquisitions editor. Estab. 1985. Publishes trade paperback originals. **Publishes 10 titles/year. 15% of books from first-time authors. 90% from unagented writers. Pays 10-12% royalty.** Publishes book 18 months after acceptance. Accepts simultaneous submissions. Responds in 3 months to queries. Catalog for 6x9 SAE with 3 first-class stamps. No metered mail or international reply coupons (IRC's) please. Guidelines online.

8━▪ Woodbine House publishes books for or about individuals with disabilities to help those individuals and their families live fulfilling and satisfying lives in their homes, schools, and communities.

NONFICTION Subjects include specific issues related to a given disability (e.g., communication skills, social sciences skills, feeding issues) and practical guides to issues of concern to parents of children with disabilities (e.g., special education, sibling issues). Publishes books for and about children with disabilities. No personal accounts or general parenting guides. Submit outline, and at least 3 sample chapters. Reviews artwork/photos.

FICTION Subjects include picture books, children's. Receptive to stories re: developmental and intellectual disabilities, e.g., autism and cerebral palsy. Submit complete ms with SASE.

TIPS "Do not send us a proposal on the basis of this description. Examine our catalog or website and a couple of our books to make sure you are on the right track. Put some thought into how your book could be marketed (aside from in bookstores). Keep cover letters concise and to the point; if it's a subject that interests us, we'll ask to see more."

WOODLEY MEMORIAL PRESS

English Dept., Washburn University, Topeka KS 66621. **E-mail:** karen.barron@washburn.edu. **Website:** www.washburn.edu/reference/woodley-press. **Contact:** Kevin Rabas, acquisitions editor. Estab. 1980. Publishes paperback originals. Publishes book 1 year after acceptance. Responds in 2 weeks to queries; 6 months to mss. Guidelines available on website.

8— "Woodley Memorial Press is a small, nonprofit press which publishes novels and fiction collections by Kansas writers only; by 'Kansas writers' we mean writers who reside in Kansas or have a Kansas connection."

FICTION Literary, mainstream/contemporary, short story collections. Published KS Notable Book winner *Great Blues*, by Steve Semken; *The Trouble With Campus Security*, by G.W. Clift; and *Loading The Stone*, by Harley Elliot. "We prefer to work with authors of first books, for whom the book is an important step in a writing career. We rely heavily on the author's enthusiasm for the book, because almost all sales are generated by the author's promotion of the book through mailings (we'll pay), readings and book signings." Accepts unsolicited mss. Accepts queries by e-mail.

TIPS "We only publish one to three works of fiction a year, on average, and those will definitely have a Kansas connection. We seek authors who are dedicated to promoting their works."

WORDSONG

815 Church St., Honesdale PA 18431. **Fax:** (570)253-0179. **E-mail:** submissions@boydsmillspress.com;

eagarrow@boydsmillspress.com. **Website:** www.wordsongpoetry.com. Estab. 1990. **Pays authors royalty or work purchased outright.** Responds to mss in 3 months.

8— "We publish fresh voices in contemporary poetry."

NONFICTION Submit complete ms or submit through agent. Label package "Manuscript Submission" and include SASE. "Please send a book-length collection of your own poems. Do not send an initial query."

FICTION Submit complete ms or submit through agent. Label package "Manuscript Submission" and include SASE. "Please send a book-length collection of your own poems. Do not send an initial query."

POETRY Submit complete ms or submit through agent. Label package "Manuscript Submission" and include SASE. "Please send a book-length collection of your own poems. Do not send an initial query."

TIPS "Collections of original poetry, not anthologies, are our biggest need at this time. Keep in mind that the strongest collections demonstrate a facility with multiple poetic forms and offer fresh images and insights. Check to see what's already on the market and on our website before submitting."

WORD WARRIORS PRESS

930 Blackoaks Ln., Anoka MN 55303. **E-mail:** gail@wordwarriorspress.com. **Website:** www.wordwarriorspress.com. **Contact:** Gail Cerridwen, managing editor (creative nonfiction). Estab. 2003. Publishes trade paperback originals. **Publishes 1-2 titles/year. 100 queries received/year. 170 mss received/year. 100% of books from first-time authors. 100% from unagented writers. Pays 6-8% royalty on retail price.** Publishes book 9 months after acceptance. Accepts simultaneous submissions. Responds in 2 months to queries and proposals; 4 months to mss. Guidelines online.

NONFICTION Subjects include alternative, contemporary culture, creative nonfiction, ethnic, gay, lesbian, memoirs, multicultural, sex, womens issues, womens studies. We publish only authors in their 20s or late teens, especially those people and stories not well represented in mainstream publishing. We welcome raw, honest, edgy, and uncensored writing styles. Submit proposal package, outline, 2 sample chapters. Submit complete ms. Reviews artwork/photos. Send photocopies.

FICTION Subjects include ethnic, experimental, feminist, gay, lesbian, gothic, literary, mainstream, contemporary, multicultural, short story collections, young adult. Right now, we're publishing creative nonfiction (mostly written in the style of fiction). But we're also interested in edgy, experimental fiction for future publications. Submit proposal package, 2 sample chapters, clips. Submit complete ms.

TIPS Our target audience is younger and alternative people. We're especially interested right now in seeing personal experiences for any upcoming prison anthology. We'd also like to see more submissions from POC and LGBT authors.

WORLD BOOK, INC.

233 N. Michigan Ave. Suite 2000, Chicago IL 60601. (312)729-5800. **Fax:** (312)729-5600. **Website:** www. worldbook.com. **Contact:** Paul A. Kobasa, editor-in-chief. **Payment negotiated on project-by-project basis.** Publishes book 18 months after acceptance. Responds to queries in 2 months.

> World Book, Inc. (publisher of The World Book Encyclopedia), publishes reference sources and nonfiction series for children and young adults in the areas of science, mathematics, English-language skills, basic academic and social skills, social studies, history, and health and fitness. We publish print and non-print material appropriate for children ages 3-14. WB does not publish fiction, poetry, or wordless picture books."

NONFICTION Young readers: animal, arts/crafts, careers, concept, geography, health, reference. Middle readers: animal, arts/crafts, careers, geography, health, history, hobbies, how-to, nature/environment, reference, science. Young adult: arts/crafts, careers, geography, health, history, hobbies, how-to, nature/environment, reference, science. Submit outline/synopsis only; no mss.

WRITER'S DIGEST BOOKS

Imprint of F+W Media, Inc., 10151 Carver Rd., Suite #200, Blue Ash OH 45242. **E-mail:** writersdigest@fw-media.com. **Website:** www.writersdigest.com. **Contact:** Roseann Biederman. Estab. 1920. Publishes hardcover originals and trade paperbacks. **Publishes 18-20 titles/year. 300 queries received/year. 50 mss received/year. 30% from unagented writers. Pays average $3,000 advance.** Publishes book 1 year after acceptance. Accepts simultaneous submissions. Responds in

3 months to queries. "Our catalog of titles is available to view online at www.WritersDigestShop.com."

> "Writer's Digest Books is the premiere source for instructional books on writing and publishing for an audience of aspirational writers. Typical mss are 80,000 words. E-mail queries strongly preferred; no phone calls please."

NONFICTION "Our instruction books stress results and how specifically to achieve them. Should be well-researched, yet lively and readable. We do not want to see books telling readers how to crack specific nonfiction markets: *Writing for the Computer Market* or *Writing for Trade Publications*, for instance. We are most in need of fiction-technique books written by published authors. Be prepared to explain how the proposed book differs from existing books on the subject." No fiction or poetry Query with SASE. Submit outline, sample chapters, SASE.

TIPS "Most queries we receive are either too broad (how to write fiction) or too niche (how to write erotic horror), and don't reflect a knowledge of our large backlist of 150 titles. We rarely publish new books on journalism, freelancing, magazine article writing or marketing/promotion. We are actively seeking fiction and nonfiction writing technique books with fresh perspectives, interactive and visual writing instruction books, similar to *Pocket Muse*, by Monica Wood; and general reference works that appeal to an audience beyond writers."

✪ YBK PUBLISHERS, INC.

39 Crosby St., New York NY 10013. **E-mail:** info@ybkpublishers.com. **Website:** www.ybkpublishers.com. **Contact:** George Ernsberger, editor-in-chief. Estab. 2000. Publishes hardcover and trade paperback originals. **Publishes 12 titles/year. 90% of books from first-time authors. 100% from unagented writers. Pays -15% royalty on retail price.** Publishes book 3 months after acceptance. Accepts simultaneous submissions. Responds in 1 month only to nonfiction queries/proposals/mss. Catalog and guidelines online.

NONFICTION We seek highly directed niche subjects directed at a market that is narrow, identifiable, and economically reachable. Reviews artwork/photos.

TIPS "Our audience wants academic and special interest topics."

Ⓐⵔ YEARLING BOOKS

Imprint of Random House Children's Books/Random House, Inc., 1745 Broadway, New York NY

10019. (212)782-9000. **Website:** www.randomhouse. com/kids.

○ "Quality reprint paperback imprint for middle grade paperback books."

YELLOW SHOE FICTION SERIES

P.O. Box 25053, Baton Rouge LA 70894. **Website:** www.lsu.edu/lsupress. **Contact:** Michael Griffith, editor. Estab. 2004. **Publishes 2 titles/year. Pays royalty. Offers advance.**

FICTION Does not accept unsolicited mss. Accepts queries by mail, Attn: Rand Dotson. No electronic submissions.

YOGI IMPRESSIONS BOOKS PVT. LTD.

1711, Centre 1, World Trade Centre, Cuffe Parade Mumbai 400 005, India. **E-mail:** yogi@yogiimpressions.com. **Website:** www.yogiimpressions.com. Estab. 2000. Guidelines online.

⊶ "Yogi Impressions are Self-help, Personal Growth and Spiritual book publishers based in Mumbai, India. Established at the turn of the millennium, at Mumbai, Yogi Impressions publishes books which seek to revive interest in spirituality, enhance the quality of life and, thereby, create the legacy of a better world for future generations."

NONFICTION Subjects include audio, child guidance, multicultural, religion, spirituality., alternative health, enlightened business, self-improvement/ personal growth. Submit outline/proposal, bio, 2-3 sample chapters, market assessment, SASE.

⊕ YOUR CULTURE GIFTS

P.O. Box 1245, Ellicott City MD 21041. (410)461-5799. **E-mail:** info@yourculturegifts.com. **Website:** www. yourculturegifts.com. **Contact:** Frank Sauri, manager. Estab. 2007. Publishes trade paperback originals. **Publishes 5 titles/year. Pays 5-10% royalty on wholesale price.** Publishes book 18 months after acceptance. Accepts simultaneous submissions. Responds in 3 months to queries/proposals/mss. Catalog and guidelines online.

⊶ Limited to cultural, realistic, historical, creative nonfiction, with language and food components.

NONFICTION Subjects include children's/juvenile, cooking, foods, nutrition, creative nonfiction, history, multicultural, social sciences sciences, young adult. Query with SASE. Reviews artwork/photos. E-mail samples after request for ms.

FICTION Subjects include ethnic, historical, juvenile, multicultural, young adult. Query with SASE.

TIPS "Our audience is middle grade students, ESL students, unmotivated young adult readers, families. Be committed to a long-term project to share cultural information."

Ⓐ ZEBRA BOOKS

Kensington, 850 Third Ave., 16th Floor, New York NY 10022. (212)407-1500. **E-mail:** mrecords@kensingtonbooks.com. **Website:** www.kensingtonbooks.com. **Contact:** Megan Records, associate editor. Publishes hardcover originals, trade paperback and mass market paperback originals and reprints. Publishes book 12-18 months after acceptance. Accepts simultaneous submissions. Catalog online.

⊶ Zebra Books is dedicated to women's fiction, which includes, but is not limited to romance.

NONFICTION For non-fiction, send cover letter/ query, including the author's qualifications and connections relevant to the book's content and marketing, and summary or outline of book's content. All submissions should be double-spaced, paginated, cleanly printed and readable. Do not bind pages together.

FICTION Mostly historical romance. Some contemporary romance, westerns, horror, and humor. Agented submissions only.

ZENITH PRESS

Quayside Publishing Group, 400 First Avenue N., Suite 300, Minneapolis MN 55401. (612)344-8100; (800)328-0590. **Fax:** (612)344-8691. **E-mail:** spearson@quaysidepub.com; rkane@quaysidepub.com; spearson@quaysidepub.com. **Website:** www.qbookshop.com; zenithpress.com. **Contact:** Scott Pearson, acquisitions editor. Richard Kane, senior acquisitions editor (American military history, politics/current events) Estab. 2004. Publishes hardcover and trade paperback originals, electronic originals and reprints, hardcover and trade paperback reprints. **Publishes 210 titles/year. Receives 250 queries/year; 100 mss/ year. 25% of books from first-time authors. 50% from unagented writers. Pays authors 8-15% royalty on wholesale price.** Publishes book 1 year after acceptance. Accepts simultaneous submissions. Responds in 1 month on queries, proposals, and mss. Catalog available online. Guidelines available online at http:// www.quaysidepub.com/submissions.php.

⊶ "Zenith Press publishes an eclectic collection of historical nonfiction and current affairs in both narrative and illustrated formats. Building on a core of military history, particularly from World War II forward, Zenith reaches out to other historical, political, and science topics with compelling narrative hooks or eye-catching photography. From a history of nuclear weapons to contemporary coverage of the wars in Iraq and Afghanistan to an illustrated celebration of the space shuttle program, Zenith Books are engaging true stories with historical, military, or science foundations—sometimes all three at once."

NONFICTION Subjects include history, military, politics, science, world affairs. Submit proposal package, including outline, 1-3 sample chapters, and author biography. Reviews artwork. Send digital files.

ZOLAND BOOKS

Steerforth Press, 45 Lyme Rd., Suite 208, Hanover NH 03755. (603)643-4787. **Fax:** (603)643-4788. **Website:** www.steerforth.com/zoland/. **Contact:** Roland Pease, editor (Zoland Poetry annuals). Estab. 1987. Publishes trade paperback originals.

NONFICTION Subjects include translation, travel, book reviews.

FICTION Subjects include ethnic, experimental, fantasy, historical, horror, humor, literary, military, war, mystery, picture books, plays, poetry, regional, religious, romance, science fiction, short story collections, spiritual, suspense, translation, folklore.

POETRY Zoland annuals are meant to be read as a continuation of the Zoland Books line. Rather than 3-4 volumes of poetry by individual authors each year, there is instead one Zoland annual that includes a wide swath of individuals previously published by Zoland who were on the radar, and an individual that fits into the larger whole of each annual.

ZONDERVAN, A HARPERCOLLINS COMPANY

Division of HarperCollins Publishers, 5300 Patterson Ave. SE, Grand Rapids MI 49530. (616)698-6900. **Fax:** (616)698-3454. **E-mail:** submissions@zondervan. com; christianmanuscriptsubmissions.com. **Website:** www.zondervan.com. Estab. 1931. Publishes hardcover and trade paperback originals and reprints. **Publishes 200 titles/year. 10% of books from first-time authors. 60% from unagented writers. Pays 14% royalty on net amount received on sales of cloth and softcover trade editions; 12% royalty on net amount received on sales** of mass market paperbacks. Pays variable advance. Responds in 2 months to queries; 3 months to proposals; 4 months to mss. Guidelines online.

☛ "Our mission is to be the leading Christian communications company meeting the needs of people with resources that glorify Jesus Christ and promote biblical principles."

NONFICTION Subjects include history, humanities, memoirs, religion, Christian living, devotional, bible study resources, preaching, counseling, college and seminary textbooks, discipleship, worship, church renewal for pastors, professionals and lay leaders in ministry, theological, and biblical reference books. All religious perspective (evangelical). "We're currently accepting unsolicited book proposals only for the following categories: Academic (only college and seminary textbooks in the areas of theology, biblical studies, church history, etc.) Reference (commentaries, handbooks, encyclopedias, etc.) Ministry Resources (books and resources for pastors and ministry professionals). Proposals should be saved as a Microsoft Word document (unless it contains Hebrew, Greek, or language other than English, in which case it should be saved as an Adobe PDF document) and sent electronically as an attachment to submissions@ zondervan.com, putting the appropriate category in the subject line. Your proposal should include the book title a table of contents, including a 2 or 3-sentence description of each chapter, a brief description of the proposed book, including the unique contribution of the book and why you feel it must be published, your intended reader and your vita, including your qualifications to write the book. The proposal should be no more than 5 pages. If we're interested in reviewing more material from you, we'll respond within 6 weeks." *No longer accepts unsolicited mailed submissions.* Instead, submissions may be submitted electronically to (ChristianManuscriptSubmissions.com).

FICTION Refer to nonfiction. Inklings-style fiction of high literary quality. Christian relevance in all cases. Will not consider collections of short stories or poetry. Submit TOC, curriculum vitae, chapter outline, intended audience.

ZUMAYA PUBLICATIONS, LLC

3209 S. Interstate 35, #1086, Austin TX 78741. **E-mail:** submissions@zumayapublications.com. **E-mail:** submissions@zumayapublications.com. **Website:** www. zumayapublications.com. **Contact:** Elizabeth Burton, executive editor. Estab. 1999. Publishes trade paper-back and electronic originals and reprints. **Publishes 20-25 titles/year. 1,000 queries received/year. 100 mss received/year. 75% of books from first-time authors. 98% from unagented writers.** Publishes book 2 years after acceptance. Accepts simultaneous submissions. Responds in 6 months to queries and proposals; 9 months to mss. Guidelines online.

NONFICTION Subjects include creative nonfiction, memoirs, New Age, spirituality, true ghost stories. "The easiest way to figure out what I'm looking for is to look at what we've already done. Our main nonfiction interests are in collections of true ghost stories, ones that have been investigated or thoroughly documented, memoirs that address specific regions and eras and books on the craft of writing. That doesn't mean we won't consider something else." Electronic query only. Reviews artwork/photos. Send digital format.

FICTION Subjects include adventure, fantasy, bisexual, gay, lesbian, historical, horror, humor, juvenile, literary, mainstream, contemporary, multicultural, mystery, occult, romance, science fiction, short story collections, spiritual, suspense, transgender, western, young adult. "We are currently oversupplied with speculative fiction and are reviewing submissions in SF, fantasy and paranormal suspense by invitation only. We are much in need of GLBT and YA/middle grade, historical and western, New Age/inspirational (no overtly Christian materials, please), non-category romance, thrillers. As with nonfiction, we encourage people to review what we've already published so as to avoid sending us more of the same, at least, insofar as the plot is concerned. While we're always looking for good specific mysteries, we want original concepts rather than slightly altered versions of what we've already published." Electronic query only.

TIPS "We're catering to readers who may have loved last year's best seller but not enough to want to read 10 more just like it. Have something different. If it does not fit standard pigeonholes, that's a plus. On the other hand, it has to have an audience. And if you're not prepared to work with us on promotion and marketing, it would be better to look elsewhere."

CONSUMER MAGAZINES

Selling your writing to consumer magazines is as much an exercise of your marketing skills as it is of your writing abilities. Editors of consumer magazines are looking not only for good writing, but for good writing which communicates pertinent information to a specific audience—their readers.

APPROACHING THE CONSUMER MAGAZINE MARKET

Marketing skills will help you successfully discern a magazine's editorial slant, and write queries and articles that prove your knowledge of the magazine's readership. You can gather clues about a magazine's readership—and establish your credibility with the magazine's editor—in a number of ways:

- **READ** the magazine's listing in *Writer's Market*.
- **STUDY** a magazine's writer's guidelines.
- **CHECK** a magazine's website.
- **READ** several current issues of the target magazine.
- **TALK** to an editor by phone.

Writers who can correctly and consistently discern a publication's audience and deliver stories that speak to that target readership will win out every time over writers who submit haphazardly.

WHAT EDITORS WANT

In nonfiction, editors continue to look for short feature articles covering specialized topics. Editors want crisp writing and expertise. If you are not an expert in the area about which you are writing, make yourself one through research. Always query before sending your manuscript. Don't call or fax a query to an editor unless the listing mentions it is acceptable to do so.

Fiction editors prefer to receive complete manuscripts. Writers must keep in mind that marketing fiction is competitive, and editors receive far more material than they can publish. For this reason, they often do not respond to submissions unless they are interested in using the story. More comprehensive information on fiction markets can be found in *Novel & Short Story Writer's Market* (Writer's Digest Books).

PAYMENT

Most magazines listed here have indicated pay rates; some give very specific payment-per-word rates, while others state a range. Any agreement you come to with a magazine, whether verbal or written, should specify the payment you are to receive and when you are to receive it. Some magazines pay writers only after the piece in question has been published (on publication). Others pay as soon as they have accepted a piece and are sure they are going to use it (on acceptance).

So what is a good pay rate? There are no standards; the principle of supply and demand operates at full throttle in the business of writing and publishing. As long as there are more writers than opportunities for publication, wages for freelancers will never skyrocket. Rates vary widely from one market to the next. Smaller circulation magazines and some departments of the larger magazines will pay a lower rate.

Editors know the listings in *Writer's Market* are read and used by writers with a wide range of experience, from those unpublished writers just starting out, to those with a successful, profitable freelance career. As a result, many magazines publicly report pay rates in the lower end of their actual pay ranges. Experienced writers will be able to successfully negotiate higher pay rates for their material. Newer writers should be encouraged that as their reputation grows (along with their clip file), they will be able to command higher rates. The article "How Much Should I Charge?" gives you an idea of pay ranges for different freelance jobs, including those directly associated with magazines.

SPECIAL NOTE ABOUT LISTINGS

The *Writer's Market* staff works hard to update and verify information in the listings, but that information can sometimes change between the original update and when the book is published and/or read. So writers are always advised to check websites before submitting.

Also, due to space restrictions of the print product, the photography and tips information was removed from Consumer Magazine listings. This information is still present on WritersMarket.com, but it was either keep essential writing information of listings or cut listings. For more information on photography needs, check WritersMarket.com or the most recent *Photographer's Market*.

ANIMAL

$$ AKC GAZETTE

American Kennel Club, (212)696-8295. **Fax:** (212)696-8239. **Website:** www.akc.org/pubs/gazette. **Contact:** Tilly Grassa, creative director. **85% freelance written.** Monthly magazine. "Geared to interests of fanciers of purebred dogs as opposed to commercial interests or pet owners. We require solid expertise from our contributors—we are *not* a pet magazine." Estab. 1889. Circ. 60,000. Byline given. Offers 10% kill fee. Publishes ms an average of 6 months after acceptance. Submit seasonal material 6 months in advance. Accepts queries by mail. Responds in 2 months to queries. Guidelines for #10 SASE.

NONFICTION Needs general interest, how-to, humor, interview, photo feature, travel, dog art, training and canine performance sports. No poetry, tributes to individual dogs, or fiction. **Buys 30-40 mss/year.** Length: 1,000-3,000 words. **Pays $300-500.** Pays expenses of writers on assignment.

FICTION Annual short fiction contest only. Guidelines for #10 SASE. Send entries to AKC Publications Fiction Contest, The American Kennel Club, 260 Madison Avenue, New York, NY 10016.

$$ APPALOOSA JOURNAL

2720 West Pullman Rd., Moscow ID 83843. (208)882-5578. **Fax:** (208)882-8150. **E-mail:** editor@appaloosajournal.com; artdirector@appaloosajournal.com. **Website:** www.appaloosajournal.com. **Contact:** Dana Russell, editor; Laura Vander Hoek, art director. **40% freelance written.** Monthly magazine covering Appaloosa horses. We seek feature-length (1,500 to 1,800 words) and article-length (600 to 800 words) submissions about breeders, trainers, specific training methods, influential horses, youth and non-pro competitors, breed history, trail riding and artists using Appaloosa subjects. Article-length reports of timely and newsworthy events, such as shows, races and overseas competition, are welcome but must be pre-approved by the editor. Manuscripts exceeding the preferred word length will be evaluated according to relevance and content matter. Lengthy stories, opinion pieces or poorly written pieces will be rejected. Manuscripts may be sent on a CD or via e-mail in Microsoft Word or text-only format. If sent via CD, an accompanying hard copy should be printed, double spaced, following the guidelines. "*Appaloosa Journal* is the authoritative, association-based source for information about the Appaloosa Horse Club, the Appaloosa breed and the Appaloosa industry. Our mission is to cultivate a broader membership base and instill enthusiasm for the breed by recognizing the needs and achievements of the Appaloosa, ApHC members, enthusiasts and our readers. The Appaloosa Horse Club is a not-for-profit organization. Serious inquiries within specified budget only." In photographer's samples, wants to see "high-quality color photos of world-class, characteristic (coat patterned) Appaloosa horses in appealing, picturesque outdoor environments. Send a letter introducing yourself and briefly explaining your work. If you have inflexible preset fees, be upfront and include that information. Be patient. We are located at the headquarters; although an image might not work for the magazine, it might work for other printed materials. Work has a better chance of being used if allowed to keep on file. If work must be returned promptly, please specify. Otherwise, we will keep it for other departments' consideration." Estab. 1946. Circ. 25,000. Byline given. Publishes ms an average of 3 months after acceptance. Responds in 1 month to queries. Responds in 2 months to mss. Sample copy free. Guidelines available online.

NONFICTION Needs historical, interview, photo feature. **Buys 15-20 mss/year.** Send complete ms. *Appaloosa Journal* is not responsible for unsolicited materials. All freelance correspondence should be directed to Editor Dana Russell, editor@appaloosajournal.com, subject line "Freelance." Length: 800-1,800 words. **Pays $200-400.**

$$ AQUARIUM FISH INTERNATIONAL

Bowtie, Inc., P.O. Box 6050, Mission Viejo CA 92690-6050. (949)855-8822. **Fax:** (949)855-3045. **E-mail:** aquariumfish@bowtieinc.com. **Website:** www.fishchannel.com. **Contact:** Patricia Knight, managing editor; Clay Jackson, editor. **90% freelance written.** Monthly magazine covering fish and other aquatic pets. Estab. 1988. Byline given. Accepts queries by mail, e-mail, fax. Response times vary Guidelines with #10 SASE.

NONFICTION Needs general interest, species profiles, natural history with home care info, new product, press releases only for Product Showcase section, photo feature, caring for fish in aquariums. Special issues: "We do have 1 annual; freelancers should query." "No fiction, anthropomorphism, articles on sport fishing, or animals that cannot be kept as pets (i.e., whales, dolphins, manatees, etc.)." **Buys 60 mss/year.** Send complete ms. Length: 1,500-2,000 words. **Pays 15¢/word.**

FILLERS Length: 50-200 words.

⊘🐾 ARABIAN STUDS & STALLIONS ANNUAL

Vink Publishing, P.O. Box 8369, Woolloongabba QLD 4102 Australia. (61)(7)3334-8000. **Fax:** (61)(7)3391-5118. **E-mail:** montbrae@bigpond.net.au. **Website:** www.vinkpub.com.au. "Annual magazine covering International Arabian horses and people connected with the Arabian horse from Australia and around the world."

○ Query before submitting.

⊘🐾 THE AUSTRALIAN ARABIAN HORSE NEWS

Vink Publishing, P.O. Box 8369, Woolloongabba QLD 4102 Australia. (61)(7)3334-8000. **Fax:** (61)(7)3391-5118. **E-mail:** montbrae@bigpond.net.au. **Website:** www.vinkpub.com. **Contact:** Sharon Meyers, editor. Quarterly magazine covering Australian Arabian horses.

○ Query before submitting.

🐾💲 BIRDING WORLD

Sea Lawn, Coast Rd., Cley next the Sea, Holt Norfolk NR25 7RZ United Kingdom. (44)(126)374-0913. **E-mail:** steve@birdingworld.co.uk. **Website:** www.birdingworld.co.uk. **Contact:** Steve Gantlett. "Monthly magazine publishing notes about birds and birdwatching. The emphasis is on rarer British and Western Palearctic birds with topical interest." Estab. 1987. Accepts queries by mail, e-mail. Sample copy for free. Guidelines by email.

💲💲 CAT FANCY

Fancy Publications, BowTie Inc., P.O. Box 6050, Mission Viejo CA 92690. (949)855-8822. **Fax:** (949)855-3045. **E-mail:** query@catfancy.com; catsupport@catchannel.com; slogan@bowtieinc.com. **Website:** www.catfancy.com; www.catchannel.com. **Contact:** Susan Logan, editor. **90% freelance written.** Monthly magazine covering all aspects of responsible cat ownership. "*Cat Fancy* is the undisputed premier feline magazine that is dedicated to better lives for pet cats. Always a presence within the cat world, *Cat Fancy* and its sister website CatChannel.com are where cat owners, lovers and rescue organizations go for educa-

tion and entertainment." Estab. 1965. Circ. 290,000. Editorial lead time 6 months. Responds in 3 months to queries. Guidelines available online.

☛ "With a readership that is highly receptive to its credible advice, news, lifestyle information, *Cat Fancy* and CatChannel.com are the ultimate places to read about cat news, breeds, care and products and services."

NONFICTION Needs how-to, humor, photo feature, travel, behavior, health, lifestyle, cat culture, entertainment. "We no longer publish any fiction or poetry." **Buys 70 mss/year.** Feature Articles: We are open to working with new contributors and fresh voices in addition to drawing from a talented crop of established contributors. Each month, we provide our readers with a mix of informative articles on various topics, including breed profiles, feline health, nutrition, grooming, behavior, training, as well as lifestyle and special interest articles on cat culture, the human-animal bond and personalities. Query first. Length: 100-1,000 words. **Pays $50-450.**

💲💲 THE CHRONICLE OF THE HORSE

P.O. Box 46, Middleburg VA 20118-0046. (540)687-6341. **Fax:** (540)687-3937. **E-mail:** slieser@chronofhorse.com. **Website:** www.chronofhorse.com. **Contact:** Sara Lieser, managing editor. **80% freelance written.** Weekly magazine covering horses. "We cover English riding sports, including horse showing, grand prix jumping competitions, steeplechase racing, foxhunting, dressage, endurance riding, handicapped riding, and combined training. We are the official publication for the national governing bodies of many of the above sports. We feature news, how-to articles on equitation and horse care and interviews with leaders in the various fields." Estab. 1937. Circ. 18,000. Byline given. Pays for features on acceptance; news and other items on publication. Publishes ms an average of 4 months after acceptance. Submit seasonal material 3 months in advance. Accepts queries by mail, e-mail. Responds in 5-6 weeks to queries. Sample copy for $2 and 9×12 SASE. Guidelines available online.

NONFICTION Needs general interest, historical, history of breeds, use of horses in other countries and times, art, etc., how-to, trailer, train, design a course, save money, etc., humor, centered on living with horses or horse people, interview, of nationally known horsemen or the very unusual, technical, horse care, articles on feeding, injuries, care of foals, shoeing, etc. Special issues: Steeplechase Racing (January); American Horse in Sport and Grand Prix Jumping (February); Horse Show (March); Intercollegiate (April); Kentucky 4-Star Preview (April); Junior and Pony (April); Dressage (June); Horse Care (July); Combined Training (August); Hunt Roster (September); Amateur (November); Stallion (December). No poetry, Q&A interviews, clinic reports, Western riding articles, personal experience or wild horses. **Buys 300 mss/year.** Send complete ms. Length: 6-7 pages. **Pays $150-250.**

COLUMNS Dressage, Combined Training, Horse Show, Horse Care, Racing over Fences, Young Entry (about young riders, geared for youth), Horses and Humanities, Hunting, Vaulting, Handicapped Riding, Trail Riding, 1,000-1,225 words; News of major competitions (clear assignment with us first), 1,500 words. Query with or without published clips or send complete ms. **Pays $25-200.**

$ COONHOUND BLOODLINES

United Kennel Club, Inc., 100 E. Kilgore Rd., Kalamazoo MI 49002-5584. (269)343-9020. **Fax:** (269)343-7037. **E-mail:** vrand@ukcdogs.com. **Website:** www.ukcdogs.com. **Contact:** Vicki Rand, editor. **40% freelance written.** Monthly magazine covering all aspects of the 6 Coonhound dog breeds. Writers must retain the 'slang' particular to dog people and to our readers—many of whom are from the South. Estab. 1925. Circ. 16,000. Byline given. Publishes ms an average of 6 months after acceptance. Editorial lead time 6 months. Submit seasonal material 6 months in advance. Accepts queries by mail, e-mail, fax, phone. Accepts simultaneous submissions. Responds in 6 weeks to queries. Sample copy for $4.50.

NONFICTION Needs general interest, historical, humor, interview, new product, personal experience, photo feature, breed-specific. Special issues: Six of our 12 issues are each devoted to a specific breed of Coonhound. Treeing Walker (February); English (July); Black & Tan (April); Bluetick (May); Redbone (June); Plott Hound (August), 1,000-3,000 words and photos. **Buys 12-36 mss/year.** Query. Length: 1,000-5,000 words. **Pays variable amount.** Sometimes pays expenses of writers on assignment.

FICTION Must be about the Coonhound breeds or hunting with hounds. Needs adventure, historical, humorous, mystery. **Buys 3-6 mss/year.** Query. Length: 1,000-3,000 words. **Pay varies.**

$$ DOG FANCY

P.O. Box 6050, Mission Viejo CA 92690. (949)855-8822. **Fax:** (949)855-3045. **E-mail:** barkback@dogfancy.com. **Website:** www.dogfancy.com; www.dogchannel.com. **95% freelance written.** Monthly magazine for men and women of all ages interested in all phases of dog ownership. Estab. 1970. Circ. 268,000. Byline given. Offers kill fee. Publishes ms an average of 6 months after acceptance. Accepts queries by e-mail. Responds in 2 months to queries. Guidelines available online.

💬 Reading period from January through April.

NONFICTION Needs general interest, how-to, humor, inspirational, interview, photo feature, travel. "No stories written from a dog's point of view." **Buys 10 or fewer from new writers; 80 mss/year.** Query. Length: 800-1,200 words. **Pays 40¢/word.**

COLUMNS News hound, fun dog. **Buys 6 mss/year.** Query by e-mail. **Pays 40¢/word.**

$ DOG SPORTS MAGAZINE

Cher Car Kennels, 4215 S. Lowell Rd., St. Johns MI 48879. (989)224-7225. **Fax:** (989)224-6033. **E-mail:** suggestions@dogsports.com. **Website:** www.dogsports.com. **Contact:** Cheryl Carlson, editor. **5% freelance written.** Monthly tabloid covering working dogs. "Dog Sports online magazine is for ALL dog trainers. We focus on the "HOW" of dog training. You will find articles on Police K-9 training, Narcotics detection, Herding, Weight Pull, Tracking, Search and Rescue, and how to increase your dog training Business. We bring you the latest in techniques from the field, actual dog trainers that are out there, working, titling and training. French Ring, Mondio, Schutzhund, N.A.P.D. PPDA, K-9 Pro Sports all are featured, as well as spotlight articles on breeds, trainers, judges, or events." Estab. 1979. Circ. 2,000. Byline given. Publishes ms an average of 1 month after acceptance. Editorial lead time 1 month. Submit seasonal material 1 month in advance. Accepts queries by mail, e-mail. Accepts simultaneous submissions. Sample copy free or online.

NONFICTION Needs essays, general interest, how-to, working dogs, humor, interview, technical. **Buys 5 mss/year.** Send complete ms. **Pays $50.**

$$ EQUESTRIAN MAGAZINE

United States Equestrian Federation (USEF), 4047 Iron Works Pkwy., Lexington KY 40511. (859)225-6934. **Fax:** (859)231-6662. **E-mail:** bsosby@usef.org.

Website: www.usef.org. **Contact:** Brian Sosby, editor. **10-30% freelance written.** Magazine published 6 times/year covering the equestrian sport. Estab. 1937. Circ. 77,000. Byline given. Offers 50% kill fee. Editorial lead time 1-5 months. Accepts queries by mail, e-mail, fax, phone. Sample copy and writer's guidelines free.

NONFICTION Needs interview, technical, all equestrian-related. **Buys 20-30 mss/year.** Query with published clips. Length: 500-3,500 words. **Pays $200-400.**

$ EQUINE JOURNAL

103 Roxbury St., Keene NH 03431. (603)357-4271. **Fax:** (603)357-7851. **E-mail:** editorial@equinejournal.com. **Website:** www.equinejournal.com. **Contact:** Kelly Ballou, editor. **90% freelance written.** Monthly tabloid covering horses—all breeds, all disciplines. "The Equine Journal is a monthly, all-breed/discipline regional publication for horse enthusiasts. The purpose of our editorial is to educate, entertain and enable amateurs and professionals alike to stay on top of new developments in the field. Every month, the Equine Journal presents feature articles and columns spanning the length and breadth of horse-related activities and interests from all corners of the country." Estab. 1988. Circ. 26,000. Byline given. Editorial lead time 4 months. Accepts queries by mail, e-mail, fax, phone. Responds in 2 months to queries. Guidelines available online.

NONFICTION Needs general interest, how-to, interview. **Buys 100 mss/year.** Send complete ms. Length: 1,500-2,200 words.

COLUMNS Horse Health (health-related topics), 1,200-1,500 words. **Buys 12 mss/year.** Query.

$$ FIDO FRIENDLY MAGAZINE

Fido Friendly, Inc., P.O. Box 160, Marsing ID 83639. **E-mail:** fieldeditor@fidofriendly.com. **Website:** www.fidofriendly.com. **95% freelance written.** Bimonthly magazine covering travel with your dog. "We want articles about all things travel related with your dog." Estab. 2,000. Circ. 44,000. Byline given. Publishes ms an average of 2 months after acceptance. Editorial lead time 1-3 months. Submit seasonal material 3 months in advance. Accepts queries by e-mail. Accepts simultaneous submissions. Responds in 2 weeks to queries. Responds in 1 month to mss Sample copy for $7. Guidelines free.

NONFICTION **Contact:** Susan Sims, publisher. Needs essays, general interest, how-to, travel with your dog, humor, inspirational, interview, personal experience, travel. No articles about dog's point of view - dog's voice. **Buys 24 mss/yr. mss/year.** Query with published clips. Length: 600-1,200 words. **Pays 10-20¢ for assigned articles. Pays 10-20¢ for unsolicited articles.**

COLUMNS Fido Friendly City (City where dogs have lots of options to enjoy restaurants, dog retail stores, dog parks, sports activity.) **Buys 6 mss/yr. mss/year.** Query with published clips. **Pays 10-20¢/word**

$ THE GREYHOUND REVIEW

P.O. Box 543, Abilene KS 67410. (785)263-4660. **E-mail:** nga@ngagreyhounds.com. **Website:** www.ngagreyhounds.com. **20% freelance written.** Monthly magazine covering greyhound breeding, training, and racing. Estab. 1911. Circ. 3,500. Byline given. Submit seasonal material 2 months in advance. Responds in 2 weeks to queries. Responds in 1 month to mss. Sample copy for $3. Guidelines free.

NONFICTION Needs how-to, interview, personal experience. Do not submit gambling systems. **Buys 24 mss/year.** Query. Length: 1,000-10,000 words. **Pays $85-150.**

REPRINTS Send photocopy. Pays 100% of amount paid for original article.

$$$ HORSE&RIDER

2520 55th St., #210, Boulder CO 80301. **E-mail:** horseandrider@aimmedia.com. **Website:** www.horseandrider.com. **Contact:** Julie Preble, assistant editor. **10% freelance written.** Monthly magazine covering Western horse industry, competition, recreation. "*Horse&Rider* is THE leading Western training, how-to, and advice magazine for horse owners and enthusiasts. H&R is for goal-oriented horse owners who strive for excellence in riding, training, and horse management. Whether you're a competitive or recreational rider, H&R provides you with useful training articles, practical stable-management techniques, hands-on health care advice, safe trail riding practices, informative reports on the equine industry, and behind-the-scenes looks at equine events. H&R gives you access to valuable information from top trainers, clinicians, veterinarians, equine behaviorists, and industry experts." Estab. 1961. Circ. 164,000. Byline given. "Very little unsolicited freelance accepted." Publishes ms an average of 1 year after acceptance. Editorial lead time 2 months. Submit seasonal material 6 months in advance. Accepts queries by mail (must be on a cd in a digital format), e-mail (preferred). Responds in 3 months to queries and to mss. Sample copy and writer's guidelines online.

NONFICTION Needs book excerpts, general interest, how-to, horse training, horsemanship, humor, interview, new product, personal experience, photo feature, travel. **Buys 5-10 mss/year.** Send complete ms. Length: 1,000-3,000 words. **Pay depends on length, use, and quality.**

$ HORSE CONNECTION

Horse Connection, LLC, 333 Perry St., Suite 309, Castle Rock CO 80104. (303)663-1300. **Fax:** (303)663-1331. **E-mail:** gyoung@horseconnection.com. **Website:** www.horseconnection.com. **Contact:** Geoff Young, publisher/editor; Valerie Young, publisher/vice president of sales & marketing. **90% freelance written.** Magazine published 12 times/year covering horse owners and riders. Our readers are horse owners and riders. They specialize in English riding. We primarily focus on show jumping and hunters, dressage, and three-day events, with additional coverage of driving, polo, and endurance. Estab. 1995. Circ. 25,000. Byline given. Publishes ms an average of 1 month after acceptance. Editorial lead time 3 months. Submit seasonal material 3 months in advance. Accepts queries by e-mail. Responds in 1 month to queries. Sample copy for $3.50 or online. Guidelines for #10 SASE or online.

NONFICTION Needs humor, interview, personal experience, event reports. No general interest stories about horses. Nothing negative. No western, racing, or breed specific articles. No my first pony stories. **Buys 30-50 mss/year.** Query with published clips. Length: 500-1,000 words. **Pays $25 for assigned articles. Pays $75 for unsolicited articles.** Sometimes pays expenses of writers on assignment.

$$ HORSE ILLUSTRATED

BowTie, Inc., P.O. Box 8237, Lexington KY 40533. (859)260-9800. **Fax:** (859)260-1154. **E-mail:** horseillustrated@bowtieinc.com. **Website:** www.horseillustrated.com. **Contact:** Elizabeth Moyer, editor. **90% freelance written. Prefers to work with published/established writers but will work with new/unpublished writers.** Monthly magazine covering all aspects of horse ownership. "Our readers are adults, mostly women, between the ages of 18 and 40; stories should be geared to that age group and reflect responsible horse care." Estab. 1976. Circ. 160,660. Byline given. Publishes ms an average of 8 months after acceptance. Submit seasonal material 6 months in advance. Accepts queries by mail. Responds in 3 months to queries. Guidelines with #10 SASE and are available online at www.horsechannel.com/horse-magazines/horse-illustrated/submission-guidelines.aspx.

NONFICTION Needs general interest, how-to, horse care, training, veterinary care, inspirational, photo feature. "No little girl horse stories, cowboy and Indian stories or anything not *directly* relating to horses." **Buys 20 mss/year.** Query or send complete ms. Length: 1,000-2,000 words. **Pays $200-400.**

$$$ THE HORSE

P.O. Box 919003, Lexington KY 40591-9003. (859)278-2361. **Fax:** (859)276-4450. **E-mail:** editorial@thehorse.com. **Website:** www.thehorse.com. **85% freelance written.** Monthly magazine covering equine health, care, management and welfare. *The Horse* is an educational/news magazine geared toward the hands-on horse owner. Estab. 1983. Circ. 55,000. Byline given. Publishes ms an average of 6 months after acceptance. Accepts queries by mail, e-mail. Responds in 3 months to queries. Sample copy for $3.95 or online. Guidelines available online.

NONFICTION Needs how-to, technical, topical interviews. No first-person experiences not from professionals; this is a technical magazine to inform horse owners. **Buys 90 mss/year.** Query with published clips. Length: 250-4,000 words. **Pays $60-850.**

COLUMNS News Front (news on horse health), 100-500 words; Equinomics (economics of horse ownership); Step by Step (feet and leg care); Nutrition; Reproduction; Back to Basics, all 1,500-2,200 words. **Buys 50 column mss/year.** Query with published clips. **Pays $50-450.**

$$ JUST LABS

Village Press, 2779 Aero Park Dr., Traverse City MI 49686. (231)946-3712; (800)447-7367. **E-mail:** jake@villagepress.com. **Website:** www.justlabsmagazine.com. **Contact:** Jason Smith, editor. **50% freelance written.** Bimonthly magazine. "*Just Labs* is targeted toward the family Labrador Retriever, and all of our articles help people learn about, live with, train, take care of, and enjoy their dogs. We do not look for articles that pull at the heart strings (those are usually staff-written), but rather we look for articles that teach, inform, and entertain." Estab. 2001. Circ. 20,000. Byline given. Offers 40% kill fee. Publishes ms an average of 6 months after acceptance. Editorial lead time 6 months. Submit seasonal material 6-8 months in advance. Accepts queries by mail. Responds in 4-6 weeks to queries. Responds in 2 months to mss. Guidelines for #10 SASE.

NONFICTION Needs essays, how-to, (train, health, lifestyle), humor, inspirational, interview, photo feature, technical, travel. "We don't want tributes to dogs that have passed on. This is a privilege we reserve for our subscribers." **Buys 30 mss/year.** Query. Length: 1,000-1,800 words. **Pays $250-400 for assigned articles. Pays $250-400 for unsolicited articles.**

$ MINIATURE DONKEY TALK

Miniature Donkey Talk, Inc., P.O. Box 982, Cripple Creek CO 80813. (719)789-2904. **E-mail:** mike@donkeytalk.info. **Website:** www.miniaturedonkey.net; www.web-donkeys.com. **Contact:** Mike Gross. **65% freelance written.** Quarterly magazine covering donkeys, with articles on healthcare, promotion, and management of donkeys for owners, breeders, or donkey lovers. Estab. 1987. Circ. 4,925. Byline given. Publishes ms an average of 4 months after acceptance. Editorial lead time 2 months. Submit seasonal material 3 months in advance. Accepts queries by mail, e-mail, fax. Responds in 2 weeks to queries. Responds in 1 month to mss. Sample copy for $5. Guidelines free.

NONFICTION Needs book excerpts, humor, interview, personal experience. **Buys 6 mss/year.** Query with published clips. Length: 700-5,000 words. **Pays $25-150.**

COLUMNS Humor, 2,000 words; Healthcare, 2,000-5,000 words; Management, 2,000 words. **Buys 50 mss/year.** Query. **Pays $25-100.**

$$ PAINT HORSE JOURNAL

American Paint Horse Association, P.O. Box 961023, Fort Worth TX 76161-0023. (817)834-2742. **E-mail:** tonyag@apha.com; avasquez@apha.com. **Website:** www.painthorsejournal.com. **Contact:** Abigail Wilder, assistant editor. **10% freelance written. Works with a small number of new/unpublished writers each year.** Monthly magazine for people who raise, breed and show Paint Horses. Estab. 1966. Circ. 12,000. Byline given. Offers negotiable kill fee. Submit seasonal material 3 months in advance. Accepts queries by mail, e-mail, fax. Sample copy for $4.50. Guidelines available online.

NONFICTION Needs general interest, personality pieces on well-known owners of Paints, historical, Paint Horses in the past—particular horses and the breed in general, how-to, train and show horses, photo feature, Paint Horses. **Buys 4-5 mss/year.** Query. Length: 1,000-2,000 words. **Pays $100-500.**

$$ REPTILES

BowTie, Inc., P.O. Box 6050, Mission Viejo CA 92690. (949)855-8822. **E-mail:** reptiles@bowtieinc.com. **Website:** www.reptilesmagazine.com. **20% freelance written.** Monthly magazine covering reptiles and amphibians. *Reptiles* covers "a wide range of topics relating to reptiles and amphibians, including breeding, captive care, field herping, etc." Estab. 1992. Byline given. Offers 20% kill fee. Publishes ms an average of 6-8 months after acceptance. Accepts queries by mail, e-mail. Responds in 1 month to queries. Responds in 1-2 months to mss. Sample copy available online. Guidelines available online.

NONFICTION Needs general interest, historical, how-to, interview, personal experience, photo feature, travel. **Buys 10 mss/year.** Query. Length: 1,000-2,000 words. **Pays $250-500.**

$$ TROPICAL FISH HOBBYIST MAGAZINE

TFH Publications, Inc., One TFH Plaza, Neptune City NJ 07753. **E-mail:** associateeditor@tfh.com. **Website:** www.tfhmagazine.com. **90% freelance written.** Monthly magazine covering tropical fish. Manuscripts should be submitted as email attachments. Estab. 1952. Circ. 35,000. Byline given. Editorial lead time 3 months. Submit seasonal material 6 months in advance. Accepts queries by e-mail. Responds immediately on electronic queries. Guidelines available online.

NONFICTION **Buys 100-150 mss/year.** Manuscripts should be submitted as email attachments to associateeditor@tfh.com. Most articles are between 10,000 and 20,000 characters-with-spaces long. Please break up the text using subheads to categorize topics. We prefer articles that are submitted with photos. Do not insert photos into the text. Photos must be submitted separately. For more information regarding photos, please visit our Photographer's Guidelines page." Length: 10,000 - 20,000 characters-with-spaces **Pays $100-250.**

$$ USDF CONNECTION

United States Dressage Federation, 4051 Iron Works Pkwy., Lexington KY 40511. **E-mail:** connection@usdf.org. **E-mail:** editorial@usdf.org. **Website:** www.usdf.org. **40% freelance written.** Monthly magazine covering dressage (an equestrian sport). All material must relate to the sport of dressage in the US. Estab. 2000. Circ. 35,000. Byline given. Offers 50% kill fee. Publishes ms an average of 3 months after acceptance. Editorial lead time 3 months. Submit seasonal material 6 months in advance. Accepts queries by mail, e-mail. Responds in 1 month to queries. Responds in 1-2 months to mss. Sample copy for $5. Guidelines available online.

NONFICTION Needs book excerpts, essays, how-to, interview, opinion, personal experience. Does not want general interest equine material or stories that lack a US dressage angle. **Buys 40 mss/year.** Query. Length: 650-3,000 words. **Pays $100-500 for assigned articles. Pays $100-300 for unsolicited articles.** Sometimes pays expenses of writers on assignment.

COLUMNS Amateur Hour (profiles of adult amateur USDF members), 1,200-1,500 words; Under 21 (profiles of young USDF members), 1,200-1,500 words; Veterinary Connection (dressage-related horse health), 1,500-2,500 words; Mind-Body-Spirit Connection (rider health/fitness, sport psychology), 1,500-2,500 words. **Buys 24 mss/year.** Query with published clips. **Pays $150-400.**

ART AND ARCHITECTURE

$$ AMERICAN INDIAN ART MAGAZINE

American Indian Art, Inc., 7314 E. Osborn Dr., Scottsdale AZ 85251. (480)994-5445. **Fax:** (480)945-9533. **E-mail:** info@aiamagazine.com. **E-mail:** editorial@aiamagazine.com. **Website:** www.aiamagazine.com. **97% freelance written. Works with many new/unpublished writers/year.** Quarterly magazine covering Native American art, historic and contemporary, including new research on any aspect of Native American art north of the US-Mexico border. American Indian Art Magazine is a quarterly art journal that presents art by all North American Indians through articles and illustrations designed to be of interest to both casual readers and professionals. All articles, whether solicited or volunteered, are subject to review by members of the Magazine's Editorial Advisory Board and/or other authorities in the field. Articles reflecting original research are preferred over summaries and reviews of previously discussed material. The Magazine pays an author's fee of $400, upon publication, for research articles, $200 for museum collection articles and $400 for exhibition features. Estab. 1975. Circ. 22,000. Byline given. Publishes ms an average of 6 months after acceptance. Accepts queries by e-mail, online submission form. Responds in 6 weeks to queries. Responds in 3 months to mss. Guidelines for #10 SASE or online.

NONFICTION No previously published work or personal interviews with artists. **Buys 12-18 mss/year.** Query. Prefers email submissions as an attachment or on CD (prefers Microsoft Word) Length: 6,000-7,000 words. **Pays $150-300.**

$$$ AMERICANSTYLE MAGAZINE

The Rosen Group, 3000 Chestnut Ave., Suite 300, Baltimore MD 21211. (410)889-3093. **Fax:** (410)243-7089. **E-mail:** hoped@rosengrp.com. **Website:** www.americanstyle.com. **70% freelance written.** "*AmericanStyle* is a full-color lifestyle publication for people who love art. Our mandate is to nurture collectors with information that will increase their passion for contemporary art and craft and the artists who create it. *AmericanStyle*'s primary audience is contemporary craft collectors and enthusiasts. Readers are college-educated, age 35+, high-income earners with the financial means to collect art and craft, and to travel to national art and craft events in pursuit of their passions." Estab. 1994. Circ. 60,000. Publishes ms an average of 9-12 months after acceptance. Editorial lead time 9-12 months. Submit seasonal material at least 1 year in advance. Accepts queries by mail, e-mail. Sample copy for $3. Guidelines available online.

NONFICTION E-mailed submissions are to be followed by hard copy submissions. Length: 600-800 words. **Pays $400-800.** Sometimes pays expenses of writers on assignment.

COLUMNS Portfolio (profiles of emerging and established artists); Arts Tour; Arts Walk; Origins; One on One, all approximately 600 words. Query with published clips. **Pays $400-600.**

$$ THE ARTIST'S MAGAZINE

F+W Media, Inc., 10151 Carver Rd., Cincinnati OH 45242. (513)531-2690, ext. 11731. **Fax:** (513)891-7153. **Website:** www.artistsmagazine.com. **Contact:** Maureen Bloomfield, editor-in-chief; Brian Roeth, art director. **80% freelance written.** Magazine published 10 times/year covering primarily two-dimensional art for working artists. "Ours is a highly visual approach to teaching serious amateur and professional artists techniques that will help them improve their skills and market their work. The style should be crisp and immediately engaging, written in a voice that speaks directly to artists." Circ. 135,000. Bio note given for feature material. Offers 8% kill fee. Publishes ms an average of 6 months-1 year after acceptance. Responds in 6 months to queries. Sample copy for $5.99. Guidelines available online.

NONFICTION No unillustrated articles. **Buys 60 mss/year.** Length: 500-1,200 words. **Pays $300-500 and up.**

⬤⬤ ART PAPERS

Atlanta Art Papers, Inc., P.O. Box 5748, Atlanta GA 31107. (404)588-1837. **Fax:** (404)588-1836. **E-mail:** editor@artpapers.org. **Website:** www.artpapers.org. **Contact:** Sylvie Fortin, editor-in-chief. **95% freelance written.** Bimonthly magazine covering contemporary art and artists. *Art Papers*, about regional and national contemporary art and artists, features a variety of perspectives on current art concerns. Each issue presents topical articles, interviews, reviews from across the US, and an extensive and informative artists' classified listings section. Our writers and the artists they cover represent the scope and diversity of the country's art scene. Estab. 1977. Circ. 12,000. Byline given. Publishes ms an average of 3 months after acceptance. Editorial lead time 2 months. Submit seasonal material 2 months in advance.

NONFICTION Buys 240 mss/year. **Pays $60-325. unsolicited articles are on spec for unsolicited articles.**

COLUMNS Current art concerns and news. **Buys 8-10 mss/year.** Query. **Pays $100-175.**

○ ⬤⬤⬤⬤ AZURE DESIGN, ARCHITECTURE AND ART

460 Richmond St. W, Suite 601, Toronto ON M5V 1Y1 Canada. (416)203-9674. **Fax:** (416)203-9842. **E-mail:** editorial@azuremag.com; azure@azureonline.com. **Website:** www.azuremagazine.com. **Contact:** Nina Boccia, assistant editor. **75% freelance written.** Magazine covering design and architecture. Estab. 1985. Circ. 20,000. Offers variable kill fee. Publishes ms an average of 1 month after acceptance. Editorial lead time up to 45 days. Responds in 6 weeks to queries.

NONFICTION Buys 25-30 mss/year. Length: 350-2,000 words. **Pays $1/word (Canadian).**

COLUMNS Trailer (essay/photo on something from the built environment); and Forms & Functions (coming exhibitions, happenings in world of design), both 300-350 words. **Buys 30 mss/year.** Query. **Pays $1/word (Canadian).**

○ ⬤⬤

C The Visual Arts Foundation, P.O. Box 5, Station B, Toronto ON M5T 2T2 Canada. (416)539-9495. **Fax:** (416)539-9903. **E-mail:** amishmorrell@cmagazine.com. **Website:** www.cmagazine.com. **Contact:** Amish Morrell, editor. **80% freelance written.** Quarterly magazine covering international contemporary art. *C* provides a vital and vibrant forum for the presentation of contemporary art and the discussion of issues surrounding art in our culture, including feature articles, reviews and reports, as well as original artists' projects. Estab. 1983. Circ. 7,000. Byline given. Offers kill fee. Publishes ms an average of 4 months after acceptance. Editorial lead time 3 months. Accepts queries by mail, e-mail, fax. Accepts simultaneous submissions. Responds in 6 weeks to queries. Responds in 4 months to mss. Sample copy for $10 (US). Guidelines online.

NONFICTION Needs essays, general interest, opinion, personal experience. **Buys 50 mss/year.** Length: 1,000-3,000 words. **Pays $150-500 (Canadian), $105-350 (US).**

COLUMNS Reviews (review of art exhibitions), 500 words. **Buys 30 mss/year.** Query. **Pays $125 (Canadian)**

⬤⬤ DIRECT ART MAGAZINE

Slow Art Productions, 123 Warren St., Hudson NY 12534. **E-mail:** slowart@aol.com; directartmag@aol.com. **Website:** www.slowart.com. **75% freelance written.** Semiannual fine art magazine covering alternative, anti-establishment, left-leaning fine art. Estab. 1996. Circ. 10,000. Byline sometimes given. Editorial lead time 2 months. Submit seasonal material 3 months in advance. Accepts queries by mail, e-mail. Accepts simultaneous submissions. Responds in 2 weeks to queries. Responds in 1 month to mss. Sample copy for sae with 9×12 envelope and 10 first-class stamps. Guidelines for #10 SASE.

NONFICTION Needs essays, exposé, historical, how-to, humor, inspirational, interview, opinion, personal experience, photo feature, technical. **Buys 4-6 mss/year.** Query with published clips. Length: 1,000-3,000 words. **Pays $100-500.**

COLUMNS Query with published clips. **Pays $100-500.**

○⬤⬤ ESPACE

Le Centre de Diffusion 3D, 4888 rue Saint-Denis, Montreal QC H2J 2L6 Canada. (514)844-9858. **Fax:** (514)844-3661. **E-mail:** espace@espace-sculpture.com. **Website:** www.espace-sculpture.com. **Contact:**

Serge Fisette, editor. **95% freelance written.** Quarterly magazine covering sculpture events. Estab. 1987. Circ. 1,400. Byline given. Publishes ms an average of 3 months after acceptance. Editorial lead time 5 months. Submit seasonal material 3 months in advance. Accepts queries by mail. Accepts simultaneous submissions. Sample copy free.

🔑 Canada's only sculpture publication, *ESPACE*, represents a critical tool for the understanding of contemporary sculpture through analysis and reflection. Published 4 times a year, in English and French, *ESPACE* features interviews, in-depth articles, and special issues related to various aspects of three dimensionality. Foreign contributors guarantee an international perspective and diffusion. Deadlines to submit an article of 1,000 words/max are March 5, June 5, September 5, and December 5.

NONFICTION Needs essays, exposé. **Buys 60 mss/year.** Query. Length: 1,000 words. **Pays $65/page and a copy of the magazine.**

$$ THE MAGAZINE ANTIQUES

Brant Publications, 575 Broadway #5, New York NY 10012. (212)941-2800. **Fax:** (212)941-2819. **E-mail:** tmaedit@brantpub.com (JavaScript required to view). **Website:** www.themagazineantiques.com. **Contact:** Editorial. **75% freelance written.** Bimonthly magazine. "Articles should present new information in a scholarly format (with footnotes) on the fine and decorative arts, architecture, historic preservation, and landscape architecture." Estab. 1922. Circ. 61,754. Byline given. Publishes ms an average of 6 months after acceptance. Editorial lead time 6 months. Submit seasonal material 6 months in advance. Responds in 3 weeks to queries. Responds in 6 months to mss. Sample copy for $10.50 for back issue; $5 for current issue. Contact jbrentan@brantpub.com.

NONFICTION Needs historical, scholarly. **Buys 50 mss/year.** "For submission guidelines and questions about our articles, please contact the editorial department at tmaedit@brantpub.com; you need JavaScript enabled to view it." Length: 2,850-3,500 words. **Pays $250-500.** Sometimes pays expenses of writers on assignment.

$$$$ METROPOLIS

Bellerophon Publications, 61 W. 23rd St., 4th Floor, New York NY 10010. (212)627-9977. **Fax:** (212)627-9988. **E-mail:** edit@metropolismag.com. **Website:** www.metropolismag.com. **Contact:** Belinda Lanks, managing editor. **80% freelance written.** Monthly magazine (combined issue July/August) for consumers interested in architecture and design. "*Metropolis* examines contemporary life through design—architecture, interior design, product design, graphic design, crafts, planning, and preservation. Subjects range from the sprawling urban environment to intimate living spaces to small objects of everyday use. In looking for why design happens in a certain way, Metropolis explores the economic, environmental, social, cultural, political, and technological context. With its innovative graphic presentation and its provocative voice, *Metropolis* shows how richly designed our world can be." Estab. 1981. Circ. 45,000. Byline given. Pays 60-90 days after acceptance. Publishes ms an average of 3 months after acceptance. Submit seasonal material 3 months in advance. Accepts queries by mail, e-mail, fax. Responds in 8 months to queries. Sample copy for $7. Guidelines available online.

NONFICTION Contact: Martin Pedersen, executive editor. Needs essays, design, architecture, urban planning issues and ideas, interview, of multi-disciplinary designers/architects. No profiles on individual architectural practices, information from public relations firms, or fine arts. **Buys 30 mss/year.** Send query letters, not complete manuscripts, describing your idea and why it would be good for our magazine. Be concise, specific, and clear. Also, please include clips and a résumé. The ideal Metropolis story is based on strong reporting skills and includes an examination of current critical issues. A design firm's newest work isn't a story, but the issues that their work brings to light might be. We do not cover conferences or seminars. Please send these announcements to the general magazine address or email. Send query letters for potential articles for MetropolisMag.com, the online home of *Metropolis* Magazine, to edit@metropolismag.com. The same guidelines. Length: 1,500-4,000 words. **Pays $1,500-4,000.**

COLUMNS The Metropolis Observed (architecture, design, and city planning news features), 100-1,200 words, **pays $100-1,200**; Perspective (opinion or personal observation of architecture and design), 1,200 words, **pays $1,200**; Enterprise (the business/development of architecture and design), 1,500 words, **pays $1,500**; In Review (architecture and book review essays), 1,500 words, **pays $1,500**. Direct queries to

Belinda Lanks, managing editor. **Buys 40 mss/year.** Query with published clips.

⊗⊗ MODERNISM MAGAZINE

199 George St., Lambertville NJ 08530. (609)397-4104. **Fax:** (609)397-4409. **E-mail:** andrea@modernismmagazine.com. **Website:** www.modernismmagazine.com. **Contact:** Andrea Truppin, editor-in-chief. **70% freelance written.** "We are interested in design, architecture and decorative arts and the people who created them. Our coverage begins in the 1920s with Art Deco and related movements, and ends with 1980s Post-Modernism, leaving contemporary design to other magazines." Estab. 1998. Circ. 35,000. Byline given. Offers 25% kill fee. Publishes ms an average of 4 months after acceptance. Editorial lead time 6 months. Submit seasonal material 6 months in advance. Accepts queries by mail, e-mail. Accepts simultaneous submissions. Responds in 1 month to queries.

NONFICTION Needs book excerpts, essays, historical, interview, new product, photo feature. No first-person. **Buys 20 mss/year.** "To propose an article, send an email or letter to Andrea Truppin describing your subject matter, angle and illustration material. Please include a résumé and two samples of previously published writing, as well as a sample of unpublished writing. It helps to include images, but for the initial query, these can be low resolution digital files or photocopies. Proposals are submitted on a speculative basis." Length: 1,000-2,500 words. **Pays $300-600.**

ASSOCIATIONS

⊗⊗⊗⊗ AAA LIVING

Pace Communications, 1301 Carolina St., Greensboro NC 27401. **Fax:** (336)383-8272. **E-mail:** martha.leonard@paceco.com. **Website:** aaa.com/aaaliving. **Contact:** Martha Leonard. **70% freelance written.** Published 4 times a year/print; 6 times a year/digital. "AAA Living magazine, published for the Auto Club Group of Dearborn, Michigan, is for members of AAA clubs in 8 Midwest states (IL, N. IN, IA, MI, MN, NE, ND, & WI). Our magazine features lifestyle & travel articles about each state and the region, written by knowledgeable resident writers, as well as coverage of affordable, accessible travel getaways nationally & internationally & information about exclusive AAA products & services." Estab. 1917. Circ. 2.5 million. Byline givenmfor feature articles. Offers 10% kill fee. Publishes ms an average of 3 months after acceptance.

Editorial lead time 6 months. Submit seasonal material 6 months in advance. Accepts queries by mail, e-mail. Responds in 6 months to mss. Samples available online at aaa.com/aaaliving. Guidelines are not available online.

NONFICTION Needs travel. Query with published clips. Length: 150-1,600 words. **Pays $1/word for assigned articles.** Sometimes pays expenses of writers on assignment.

⊗⊗ ACTION

United Spinal Association, 75-20 Astoria Blvd., Jackson Heights NY 11370-1177. (718)803-3782, ext. 279. **E-mail:** action@unitedspinal.org. **Website:** www.unitedspinal.org/publications/action. **Contact:** Chris Pierson, managing editor. **75% freelance written.** Bimonthly magazine covering living with spinal cord injury. Estab. 1946. Circ. 12,000. Byline given. Publishes ms an average of 2-3 months after acceptance. Accepts queries by e-mail. Sample copy for SAE. Guidelines available on website.

NONFICTION Needs essays, general interest, how-to, humor, interview, new product, personal experience, photo feature, travel, medical research. Does not want "articles that treat disabilities as an affliction or cause for pity, or that show the writer does not get that people with disabilities are people like anyone else." **Buys 36 mss/year.** Query. "The editor prefers all submissions for *Action* to be in electronic form. We edit with MS Word and would appreciate writers to submit their articles or columns in Word or similar format, preferably as an attachment to an e-mail (sent to action@unitedspinal.org). Cutting and pasting your document into the e-mail message area is also acceptable. Electronic submissions do not have to be accompanied by hard copy. If you are sending your submission as hard copy, you must let the editor know ahead of time. Hard copy submissions will be accepted only in the event that a writer whose query has been approved has no other means of writing or submitting an article." Length: 1,000-1,800 words. **Pays $400.**

COLUMNS The Observatory (personal essays on subjects related to disability), 750 words. **Buys 60 mss/year.** Query with published clips. **Pays $200.**

⊗⊗⊗⊗ AMERICAN EDUCATOR

American Federation of Teachers, 555 New Jersey Ave. N.W., Washington DC 20001-2079. **E-mail:** amered@aft.org. **Website:** www.aft.org/newspubs/periodicals/

ae/index.cfm. **Contact:** Lisa Hansel, editor. **50% freelance written.** Quarterly magazine covering education, condition of children, and labor issues. *American Educator*, the quaterly magazine of the American Federation of Teachers, reaches over 800,000 public school teachers, higher education faculty, and education researchers and policymakers. The magazine concentrates on significant ideas and practices in education, civics, and the condition of children in America and around the world. Estab. 1977. Circ. 850,000. Byline given. Offers 50% kill fee. Publishes ms an average of 2-6 months after acceptance. Editorial lead time 1 year. Submit seasonal material 6 months in advance. Accepts queries by mail, e-mail. Accepts simultaneous submissions. Responds in 2 months to queries. Responds in 6 months to mss. Sample copy and guidelines available online.

NONFICTION Needs book excerpts, essays, historical, interview, discussions of educational research. No pieces that are not supportive of the public schools. **Buys 8 mss/year.** Query with published clips. Length: 1,000-7,000 words. **Pays $750-3,000 for assigned articles. Pays $300-1,000 for unsolicited articles.** Pays expenses of writers on assignment.

⊙⊙ DAC NEWS

Detroit Athletic Club, 241 Madison Ave., Detroit MI 48226. (313)442-1034. **Fax:** (313)442-1047. **E-mail:** kenv@thedac.com. **Website:** www.thedac.com. **20% freelance written**. Magazine published 10 times/year. *DAC News* is the magazine for Detroit Athletic Club members. It covers club news and events, plus general interest features. Estab. 1916. Circ. 5,000. Byline given. Publishes ms an average of 3 months after acceptance. Editorial lead time 3 months. Submit seasonal material 3 months in advance. Accepts queries by mail, phone. Responds in 1 month to queries. Sample copy free.

NONFICTION Needs general interest, historical, photo feature. No politics or social issues—this is an entertainment magazine. We do not acccept unsolicited manuscripts or queries for travel articles. **Buys 2-3 mss/year.** Length: 1,000-2,000 words. **Pays $100-500.** Sometimes pays expenses of writers on assignment.

⊙⊙⊙ DCM

AFCOM, 742 E. Chapman Ave., Orange CA 92866. **Fax:** (714)997-9743. **E-mail:** afcom@afcom.com; jmoore@afcom.com. **Website:** www.afcom.com. **Contact:** Karen Riccio, managing editor. **50% freelance written**. Bimonthly magazine covering data center management. *DCM* is the slick, 4-color, bimonthly publication for members of AFCOM, the leading association for data center management. Estab. 1988. Circ. 4,000 worldwide. Byline given. Pays on acceptance for assigned articles and on publication for unsolicited articles. Offers 0-10% kill fee. Publishes ms an average of 3 months after acceptance. Editorial lead time 6-12 months. Submit seasonal material 6 months in advance. Responds in 1-3 weeks to queries. Responds in 1-3 months to mss. Guidelines available online.

🖸 Prefers queries by e-mail.

NONFICTION Needs how-to, technical, management as it relates to and includes examples of data centers and data center managers. Special issues: The January/February issue is the annual 'Emerging Technologies' issue. Articles for this issue are visionary and product neutral. No product reviews or general tech articles. **Buys 15+ mss/year.** Query with published clips. Length: 2,000 word maximum **Pays 50¢/word and up, based on writer's expertise.**

⊙⊙ THE ELKS MAGAZINE

425 W. Diversey Pkwy., Chicago IL 60614-6196. (773)755-4740. **E-mail:** elksmag@elks.org. **Website:** www.elks.org/elksmag. **Contact:** Cheryl T. Stachura, editor/publisher. **25% freelance written**. Magazine covers nonfiction only; published 10 times/year with basic mission of being the voice of the elks. All material is written in-house. Estab. 1922. Circ. 1,037,000. Accepts queries by mail, e-mail. Responds in 1 month with a yes/no on ms purchase. Guidelines available online.

NONFICTION No fiction, religion, controversial issues, first-person, fillers, or verse. **Buys 20-30 mss/year.** Send complete ms. Length: 1,200-2,000 words. **Pays 25¢/word.**

COLUMNS "The invited columnists are already selected."

⊙⊙ HUMANITIES

National Endowment for the Humanities, 1100 Pennsylvania Ave. NW, Washington DC 20506. (202)606-8435. **Fax:** (202)606-8451. **E-mail:** dskinner@neh.gov. **Website:** www.neh.gov. **50% freelance written**. Bimonthly magazine covering news in the humanities focused on projects that receive financial support from the agency. Estab. 1980. Circ. 6,000. Byline given. Publishes ms an average of 2 months after acceptance.

Editorial lead time 3 months. Submit seasonal material 4 months in advance. Accepts queries by mail, e-mail, fax, phone. Sample copy available online.

NONFICTION Needs book excerpts, historical, interview, photo feature. **Buys 25 mss/year.** Query with published clips. Length: 400-2,500 words. **Pays $300-600.** Sometimes pays expenses of writers on assignment.

COLUMNS In Focus (directors of state humanities councils), 700 words; Breakout (special activities of state humanities councils), 750 words. **Buys 12 mss/year.** Query with published clips. **Pays $300.**

⊖⊖ ☺⊘ KIWANIS

Kiwanis International, 3636 Woodview Trace, Indianapolis IN 46268-3196. (317)875-8755; (800)549-2647 [dial 411] (US and Canada only). **Fax:** (317)879-0204. **E-mail:** magazine@kiwanis.org; shareyourstory@kiwanis.org. **Website:** www.kiwanis.org. **Contact:** Jack Brockley, editor. **10% freelance written.** Magazine published 6 times/year for business and professional persons and their families. Estab. 1917. Circ. 240,000. Byline given. Offers 40% kill fee. Publishes ms an average of 6 months after acceptance. Accepts queries by mail, e-mail, fax. Responds in 1 month to queries. Sample copy and writer's guidelines for 9×12 SAE with 5 first class stamps. Guidelines available online.

⛔ No unsolicited mss.

NONFICTION Needs "Most *Kiwanis* content is related to the activities of our Kiwanis clubs." No fiction, personal essays, profiles, travel pieces, fillers, or verse of any kind. A light or humorous approach is welcomed where the subject is appropriate and all other requirements are observed. **Buys 20 mss/year.** "See guidelines under Share Your Story in the Media Center section on the website. You must be 13 or older to submit your story and/or photographs. If you are age 18 or younger, you must have the permission of your parent or guardian to complete your submission." Length: 500-1,200 words. **Pays $300-600.** Sometimes pays expenses of writers on assignment.

⊖⊖ LION

Lions Clubs International, 300 W. 22nd St., Oak Brook IL 60523-8842. **Fax:** (630)571-1685. **E-mail:** magazine@lionsclubs.org. **Website:** www.lionsclubs.org. **Contact:** Jay Copp, senior editor. **35% freelance written. Works with a small number of new/unpublished writers each year.** Monthly magazine covering service club organization for Lions Club members and their families. Estab. 1918. Circ. 490,000. Byline given. Publishes ms an average of 5 months after acceptance. Accepts queries by mail, e-mail, fax, phone. Responds in 1 month to queries. Sample copy and writer's guidelines free.

NONFICTION Needs photo feature, must be of a Lions Club service project, informational (issues of interest to civic-minded individuals). No travel, biography, or personal experiences. **Buys 40 mss/year.** "Article length should not exceed 2,000 words, and is subject to editing. No gags, fillers, quizzes or poems are accepted. Photos must be color prints or sent digitally. *LION* magazine pays upon acceptance of material. Advance queries save your time and ours. Address all submissions to Jay Copp, senior editor, by mail or e-mail text and .tif or .jpg (300 dpi) photos." Length: 500-2,000 words. **Pays $100-750.** Sometimes pays expenses of writers on assignment.

⊖⊖ PENN LINES

Pennsylvania Rural Electric Association, 212 Locust St., Harrisburg PA 17108-1266. **E-mail:** reaenergy@reaenergy.com. **Website:** http://www.reaenergy.com/penn_lines.htm. Monthly magazine covering rural life in Pennsylvania. News magazine of Pennsylvania electric cooperatives. Features should be balanced, and they should have a rural focus. Electric cooperative sources (such as consumers) should be used. Estab. 1966. Circ. 140,000. Byline given. Publishes ms an average of 3 months after acceptance. Editorial lead time 4 months. Submit seasonal material 4 months in advance. Accepts queries by mail, e-mail. Sample copy available online. Guidelines available online.

NONFICTION Needs general interest, historical, how-to, interview, travel, rural PA only. **Buys 6 mss/year.** Query or send complete ms. Length: 500-2,000 words. **Pays $300-650.**

PHOTOS Captions required. Reviews transparencies, prints, GIF/JPEG files. Negotiates payment individually.

TIPS Find topics of statewide interest to rural residents. Detailed information on *Penn Lines'* readers, gleaned from a reader survey, is available online.

THE ROTARIAN

Rotary International, One Rotary Center, 1560 Sherman Ave., Evanston IL 60201. (847)866-3000. **Fax:** (847)328-8554. **E-mail:** rotarian@rotary.org. **Website:** www.rotary.org. **40% freelance written.** Monthly magazine for Rotarian business and professional men and women and their families, schools, libraries, hospitals, etc. "Articles should appeal to an international audience and in some way help Rotarians help other people. The organization's rationale is one of hope, encouragement, and belief in the power of individuals talking and working together." Estab. 1911. Circ. 510,000. Byline sometimes given. Offers kill fee. Kill fee negotiable Editorial lead time 4-8 months. Accepts queries by mail, e-mail. YesSample copy for $1 (edbrookc@rotaryintl.org). Guidelines available online.

NONFICTION Needs general interest, humor, inspirational, photo feature, technical, science, travel, lifestyle, sports, business/finance, environmental, health/medicine, social issues. No fiction, religious, or political articles. Query with published clips. Length: 1,500-2,500 words. **Pays negotiable rate.** Answer.

REPRINTS "Send tearsheet, photocopy or typed ms with rights for sale noted and information about when and where the material previously appeared." Negotiates payment.

COLUMNS Health; Management; Finance; Travel, all 550-900 words. Query.

⊛⊛⊛ SCOUTING

Boy Scouts of America, 1325 W. Walnut Hill Ln., P.O. Box 152079, Irving TX 75015-2079. **Website:** http://scoutingmagazine.org. **Contact:** John R. Clark, managing editor; Bryan Wendell, senior editor; Gretchen Sparling, associate editor; Linda Lawrence, assistant to the managing editor. **80% freelance written**. Magazine published 6 times/year covering Scouting activities for adult leaders of the Boy Scouts, Cub Scouts, and Venturing. Estab. 1913. Circ. 1 million. Byline given. Pays on acceptance for major features and some shorter features. Publishes ms an average of 18 months after acceptance. Editorial lead time 1 year. Submit seasonal material 1 year in advance. Accepts queries by mail. Accepts simultaneous submissions. Responds in 3 weeks to queries. Responds in 2 months to mss. Sample copy for $2.50 and 9×12 SAE with 4 first-class stamps or online. Guidelines available online.

NONFICTION Needs inspirational, interview. **Buys 20-30 mss/year.** Query with published clips and SASE. A query with a synopsis or outline of a proposed story is essential. Include a SASE. We do not buy fiction or poetry. We pay on acceptance. We purchase first rights unless otherwise specified (purchase does not necessarily guarantee publication). Photos, if of acceptable quality, are usually included in payment for certain assignments. (We normall assign a professional photographers to take photographs for major story assignments.) Payment rates depend on the professional quality the of an article. Payment is from $300 to $500 for a short feature, $650 to $800 for a major article, and more for quality articles by frequent contributors. Writers or photographers should be familiar with the Scouting program and *Scouting* magazine. A sample copy will be sent if you provide a SASE and $2.50. Length: short features of 500 to 700 words; some longer features, up to 1,200 words, usually the result of a definite assignment to a professional writer. **Pays $650-800 for major articles, $300-500 for shorter features.** Pays expenses of writers on assignment.

REPRINTS Send photocopy of article and information about when and where the article previously appeared. First-person accounts of meaningful Scouting experiences (previously published in local newspapers, etc.) are a popular subject.

COLUMNS Way It Was (Scouting history), 600-750 words; Family Talk (family—raising kids, etc.), 600-750 words. **Buys 8-12 mss/year.** Query. **Pays $300-500.**

FILLERS Limited to personal accounts of humorous or inspirational Scouting experiences. Needs anecdotes, short humor. **Buys 15-25 mss/year.** Length: 50-150 words. **Pays $25 on publication.**

⊛ ⊛⊛ THE TOASTMASTER

Toastmasters International, P.O. Box 9052, Mission Viejo CA 92690. (949)858-8255. **E-mail:** submissions@toastmasters.org. **Website:** www.toastmasters.org. **Contact:** Suzanne Frey, editor; Susan Campbell, graphic design manager. **50% freelance written.** Monthly magazine on public speaking, leadership, and club concerns. "This magazine is sent to members of Toastmasters International, a nonprofit educational association of men and women throughout the world who are interested in developing their communication and leadership skills. Members range from novice to professional speakers and from a wide variety of ethnic and cultural backgrounds, as Toastmasters is an international organization." Estab. 1933. Circ. 235,000 in 11,700 clubs worldwide. Byline given. Publishes ms an average of 1 year after acceptance. Submit seasonal material 3-4 months in advance. Accepts queries by mail, e-mail. Accepts simultaneous submissions. Responds in 6-8 weeks to queries. Sample copy for 9×12 SAE with 4 first-class stamps. Guidelines available online.

🔑 "Our readers are knowledgeable and experienced public speakers; therefore we accept only authentic, well-researched and well-crafted stories. Show, don't tell! Use sources, quotes from experts and other research to back up your views. The best articles have style, depth, emotional impact and take-away value to the reader. A potential feature article needs an unusual hook, compelling story or unique angle. Profiles of colorful, controversial, historically significant, amusing, unusual or unique people are welcome, but keep in mind that our readers live in 92 different countries, so stay away from profiles of American presidents or sports figures. All submissions must be in English, however. Please query first, or send a draft of your proposed article. We recommend you carefully study several issues of the magazine before submitting a query. We are not responsible for unsolicited articles, artwork, or photographs, so please don't send anything you can't afford to lose."

NONFICTION Needs how-to, humor, interview, well-known speakers and leaders, communications, leadership, language use. **Buys 50 mss/year.** "Please read our guidelines first, then when you are ready, submit through e-mail. Query with published clips." Length: 700-1,800 words. **"Compensation for accepted articles depends on whether our submission guidelines are followed, the amount of research involved, and the article's general value to us."** Sometimes pays expenses of writers on assignment.

REPRINTS Send typed ms with rights for sale noted and information about when and where the material previously appeared. Pays 50-70% of amount paid for an original article.

💲 TRAIL & TIMBERLINE

The Colorado Mountain Club, 710 10th St., Suite 200, Golden CO 80401. (303)996-2745. **Fax:** (303)279-3080. **E-mail:** editor@cmc.org. **Website:** www.cmc.org. **Contact:** Editor. **80% freelance written.** Official quarterly publication for the Colorado Mountain Club. "Articles in *Trail & Timberline* conform to the mission statement of the Colorado Mountain Club to unite the energy, interest, and knowledge of lovers of the Colorado mountains, to collect and disseminate information "regarding the Colorado mountains in the areas of art, science, literature and recreaetion", to stimulate public interest, and to encourage preservation of the mountains of Colorado and the Rocky Mountain region." Estab. 1918. Circ. 10,500. Byline given. Publishes ms an average of 2 months after acceptance. Editorial lead time 6 months. Submit seasonal material 6 months in advance. Accepts queries by mail, e-mail. Responds in 1 week to queries. Responds in 1 month to mss. Sample copy for $5. Guidelines available online.

NONFICTION Needs essays, humor, opinion, Switchbacks, personal experience, photo feature, travel, trip reports. **Buys 10-15 mss/year.** Send complete ms. Length: 500-2,000 words. **Pays $50.**

POETRY Contact: Jared Smith, poetry editor. Needs avant-garde, free verse, traditional. Buys 6-12 poems/year. **Pays $50.**

💲💲💲 UPDATE

New York Academy of Sciences, 2 E. 63rd St., New York NY 10021. **E-mail:** aburke@nyas.org; editorial@nyas.org. **Website:** www.nyas.org. **Contact:** Adrienne Burke, executive editor. **40% freelance written.** Magazine published 7 times/year covering science, health issues. Scientific newsletter for members of the New York Academy of Sciences. Estab. 2001. Circ. 25,000. Byline sometimes given. Publishes ms an average of 1 month after acceptance. Editorial lead time 2 months. Submit seasonal material 2 months in advance. Accepts queries by mail..

NONFICTION Needs book excerpts, essays, general interest, historical, interview, technical. No science fiction, any pieces exceeding 1,000 words, or subjects that aren't current. **Buys 6-7 mss/year.** Query. Length: 300-1,000 words. **Pays $200-1,200.** Sometimes pays expenses of writers on assignment.

ASTROLOGY, METAPHYSICAL AND NEW AGE

💲💲 FATE MAGAZINE

Fate Magazine, Inc., P.O. Box 460, Lakeville MN 55044 US. (952)431-2050. **Fax:** (952)891-6091. **E-mail:** submissions@fatemag.com. **Website:** www.fatemag.com. **Contact:** Phyllis Galde, editor-in-chief; David Godwin, managing editor. **75% freelance written.** Covering the paranormal, ghosts, ufos, strange science. "Reports a wide variety of strange and unknown phenomena. We are open to receiving any well-written, well-documented article. Our readers especially like reports of current investigations, experiments, theories, and experiences. See topics on website at http://www.fatemag.com/fatemagold/WritersGuidelines.pdf." Estab. 1948. Circ. 15,000. Byline given. Pays after publication. Publishes ms 3-6 months after acceptance. Editorial lead time 3-6 months. Accepts queries by mail, e-mail, fax. Accepts simultaneous submissions. Responds in 1-3 months to queries. Sample copy available for free online, by e-mail. Guidelines available online at www.fatemag.com/fatemagold/WritersGuidelines.pdf.

NONFICTION Contact: Editor. Needs general interest, historical, how-to, personal experience, photo feature, technical. "We do not publish poetry, fiction, editorial/opinion pieces, or book-length mss." **Buys 100 mss/year.** Query. 500-4,000 words **Pays 5¢/word.** Pays with merchandise or ad space if requested.

COLUMNS Contact: Editor. True Mystic Experiences: Short reader-submitted stories of strange experiences; My Proof of Survival: Short, reader-submitted stories of proof of life after death, 300-1,000 words. Writer should query. **$25**

FILLERS Fillers are especially welcomed and must be be fully authenticated also, and on similar topics. Length: 100-1,000 words. **Pays 5¢/word.**

🌓 WHOLE LIFE TIMES

Whole Life Media, LLC, 23705 Vanowen St., #306, West Hills CA 91307. (877)807-2599. **Fax:** (310)933-1693. **E-mail:** editor@wholelifemagazine.com. **Website:** www.wholelifemagazine.com. Bimonthly regional glossy on holistic living. *"Whole Life Times* relies almost entirely on freelance material. We depend on freelancers like you." Open to stories on natural health, alternative healing, green living, sustainable and local food, social responsibility, conscious business, the environment, spirituality and personal growth—anything that deals with a progressive, healthy lifestyle. Estab. 1979. Circ. 58,000. Byline given. Pays within 45 days. 50% kill fee on assigned stories. No kill fee to first-time WLT writers. 2-4 months Accepts queries by mail, e-mail. Sample copy for $3. Guidelines available online and via e-mail.

○ We are a regional publication and favor material that somehow links to our area via topics, sources, similar.

NONFICTION Special issues: Healing Arts, Food and Nutrition, Spirituality, New Beginnings, Re-

lationships, Longevity, Arts/Cultures Travel, Vitamins and Supplements, Women's Issues, Sexuality, Science and Metaphysics, eco lifestyle. **Buys 60 mss/year. Payment varies.** *WLT* **accepts up to 3 longer stories (800-1,100 words) per issue, and pay ranges from $150-200 depending on topic, research required and writer experience. In addition, we have a number of regular departments that pay $75-150 depending on topic, research required and writer experience.**

COLUMNS Local News, Taste of Health, Yoga & Spirit, Healthy Living, Art & Soul. Length: 750-900 words. City of Angels is our FOB section featuring short, newsy blurbs on our coverage topics, generally in the context of Los Angeles. These are generally 200-400 words and pay $25-35 depending on length and topic. This is a great section for writers who are new to us. BackWords is a 750-word personal essay that often highlights a seminal moment or event in the life of the writer and pays $100. One per issue.

🌓 WITCHES AND PAGANS

BBI Media, Inc., P.O. Box 687, Forest Grove OR 97116. (888)724-3966. **E-mail:** editor2@bbimedia.com. **Website:** www.witchesandpagans.com. Quarterly magazine covering paganism, wicca and earth religions. *Witches and Pagans* is dedicated to witches, wiccans, neo-pagans, and various other earth-based, pre-Christian, shamanic, and magical practitioners. We hope to reach not only those already involved in what we cover, but the curious and completely new as well. Estab. 2002. Circ. 15,000. Byline given. Offers 100% kill fee. Editorial lead time 3-4 months. Submit seasonal material 6 months in advance. Accepts queries by mail, e-mail, fax, phone. Responds in 1-2 weeks to queries. Responds in 1 month to mss. Sample copy for $6. Guidelines available online.

NONFICTION Needs book excerpts, essays, historical, how-to, humor, inspirational, interview, new product, opinion, personal experience, photo feature, religious, travel. Special issues: Features (articles, essays, fiction, interviews, and rituals) should range between 1,000 - 5,000 words. We most often publish items between 1500 - 3000 words; we prefer in-depth coverage to tidbits in most cases, and the upper ranges are usually reserved for lead pieces assigned to specific writers. Send complete ms. Submit all written material in electronic format. Our first choice is Open Office writer file attachments emailed directly to editor2@bbimedia.com. This e-mail address is being protected from spambots. You need JavaScript enabled to view it; other acceptable file attachment formats include text files and commonly used word processing programs; you may also paste the text of your ms directly into an email message. Use a plain, legible font or typeface large enough to read easily. Sidebars can be 500-1300 words or so. Reviews have specific lengths and formats, email editor2@bbimedia.com. This e-mail address is being protected from spambots. You need JavaScript enabled to view it . Length: 1,000-4,000 words. **"We offer a standard range of about $.025 per word for all written works except letters to the editor, as well as a contributor's copy of the issue in which your work appears. Occasionally we accept reprints (almost always solicited by us) at a rate of $.01 per word. These rates are** *inclusive* **of non-exclusive reprint and electronic rights. Short works such as reviews typically get a flat fee of $10. Payment for artwork, photography, and other visual works is negotiated individually; other exchanges, such as subscriptions or advertising space, may be possible and may be much more generous than cash payments."** Sometimes pays expenses of writers on assignment.

FICTION Needs adventure, erotica, ethnic, fantasy, historical, horror, humorous, mainstream, mystery, novel concepts, religious, romance, suspense. Does not want faction (fictionalized retellings of real events). Avoid gratuitous sex, violence, sentimentality and pagan moralizing. Don't beat our readers with the Rede or the Threefold Law. **Buys 3-4 mss/year.** Send complete ms. Length: 1,000-5,000 words. **Pays 2¢/word minimum**.

POETRY Needs avant-garde, free verse, haiku, light verse, traditional. Submit maximum 3-5 poems. **Pays $10.**

AUTOMOTIVE AND MOTORCYCLE

$ AMERICAN MOTORCYCLIST

American Motorcyclist Association, 13515 Yarmouth Dr., Pickerington OH 43147. (614)856-1900. **E-mail:** grassroots@ama-cycle.org. **Website:** www.americanmotorcyclist.com. **Contact:** Bill Wood, director of communications; Grant Parsons, managing editor. **10% freelance written**. Monthly magazine for enthusiastic motorcyclists investing considerable time

and money in the sport, emphasizing the motorcyclist, not the vehicle. Emphasizes people involved in, and events dealing with, all aspects of motorcycling. Readers are "enthusiastic motorcyclists, investing considerable time in road riding or all aspects of the sport." Estab. 1947. Circ. 260,000. Byline given. Editorial lead time 3 months. Submit seasonal material 4 months in advance. Accepts queries by mail, e-mail. Responds in 5 weeks to queries. Responds in 6 weeks to mss. Sample copy for $1.50. Guidelines free.

NONFICTION Needs interview, with interesting personalities in the world of motorcycling, personal experience, travel. **Buys 8 mss/year.** Send complete ms. Length: 1,000-2,500 words. **Pays minimum $8/ published column inch.**

TIPS "Our major category of freelance stories concerns motorcycling trips to interesting North American destinations. Prefers stories of a timeless nature."

$ $ AUTOMOBILE QUARTERLY

Automobile Heritage Publishing & Communications LLC, 800 E. 8th St., New Albany IN 47150. **Fax:** (812)948-2816. **E-mail:** info@autoquarterly.com; tpowell@autoquarterly.com. **Website:** www.autoquarterly.com. **Contact:** Tracy Powell, managing editor. **85% freelance written**. Quarterly magazine covering "automotive history, with excellent photography." Estab. 1962. Circ. 8,000. Byline given. Publishes ms an average of 1 year after acceptance. Editorial lead time 9 months. Responds in 1 month to queries. Responds in 2 months to mss. Sample copy for $19.95.

NONFICTION Needs historical, photo feature, technical, biographies. **Buys 25 mss/year.** Query. Length: 2,500-5,000 words. **Pays approximately 35¢/word or more.** Sometimes pays expenses of writers on assignment.

$ $ $ $ AUTOWEEK

Crain Communications, Inc., 1155 Gratiot Ave., Detroit MI 48207. (313)446-6000. **Fax:** (313)446-1027. **Website:** www.autoweek.com. **Contact:** Roger Hart, Executive Editor. **5% freelance written, most by regular contributors**. Biweekly magazine. *AutoWeek* is a biweekly magazine for auto enthusiasts. Estab. 1958. Circ. 300,000. Byline given. Publishes ms an average of 1 month after acceptance. Accepts queries by e-mail.

NONFICTION Needs historical, interview. **Buys 5 mss/year.** Query. Length: 100-400 words. **Pays $1/ word.**

✪ $$$ CANADIAN BIKER MAGAZINE

735 Market St., Victoria BC V8T 2E2 Canada. (250)384-0333. **Fax:** (250)384-1832. **E-mail:** edit@canadianbiker.com. **Website:** www.canadianbiker.com. **65% freelance written.** Magazine covering motorcycling. Estab. 1980. Circ. 20,000. Byline given. Publishes ms an average of 1 year after acceptance. Editorial lead time 3 months. Accepts queries by mail, e-mail, fax, phone. Responds in 6 weeks to queries. Responds in 6 months to mss. Sample copy for $5 or online. Guidelines free.

NONFICTION Needs general interest, historical, how-to, interview, Canadian personalities preferred, new product, technical, travel. **Buys 12 mss/year.** Send complete ms. Length: 500-1,500 words. **Pays $100-200 for assigned articles. Pays $80-150 for unsolicited articles.**

⊘ $$$$ CAR AND DRIVER

Hearst Communications, Inc., 1585 Eisenhower Place, Ann Arbor MI 48108. (734)971-3600. **Fax:** (734)971-9188. **E-mail:** editors@caranddriver.com. **Website:** www.caranddriver.com. **Contact:** Eddie Alterman, editor-in-chief. Monthly magazine for auto enthusiasts; college-educated, professional, median 24-35 years of age. Estab. 1956. Byline given. Offers 25% kill fee. Accepts queries by mail, e-mail, fax. Responds in 2 months to queries.

NONFICTION **Buys 1 mss/year. Pays maximum $3,000/feature; $750-1,500/short piece.** Pays expenses of writers on assignment.

$$ CLASSIC TRUCKS

Primedia/McMullen Argus Publishing, 1733 Alton Parkway, Irvine CA 92606. **E-mail:** inquiries@automotive.com. **Website:** www.classictrucks.com. Monthly magazine covering classic trucks from the 1930s to 1973. Estab. 1994. Circ. 60,000. Byline given. Editorial lead time 4 months. Submit seasonal material 4 months in advance. Guidelines free.

NONFICTION Needs how-to, interview, new product, technical, travel. Query. Length: 1,500-5,000 words. **Pays $75-200/page. Pays $100/page maximum for unsolicited articles.**

COLUMNS **Buys 24 mss/year.** Query.

$$$ FOUR WHEELER MAGAZINE

831 S. Douglas Street, El Segundo CA 90245. **Website:** www.fourwheeler.com. **20% freelance written. Works with a small number of new/unpublished writers each year.** Monthly magazine covering four-wheel-drive vehicles, back-country driving, competition, and travel adventure. Estab. 1963. Circ. 355,466. Publishes ms an average of 4 months after acceptance. Submit seasonal material 4 months in advance. Accepts queries by mail.

NONFICTION Query with photos. 1,200-2,000 words; average 4-5 pages when published. **Pays $200-300/feature vehicles; $350-600/travel and adventure; $100-800/technical articles.**

⊘ $$ FRICTION ZONE

44489 Town Center Way, Suite D497, Palm Desert CA 92260. (951)751-0442. **E-mail:** amy@friction-zone.com. **Website:** www.friction-zone.com. **60% freelance written.** Monthly magazine covering motorcycles. Estab. 1999. Circ. 26,000. Byline given. Publishes ms an average of 1 month after acceptance. Editorial lead time 6 weeks. Submit seasonal material 2 months in advance. NoResponds in to queries. Sample copy for $4.50 or on website.

NONFICTION Needs general interest, historical, how-to, humor, inspirational, interview, new product, opinion, photo feature, technical, travel, medical (relating to motorcyclists), book reviews (relating to motorcyclists). Does not accept first-person writing. **Buys 1 mss/year.** Query. Length: 1,000-3,000 words. **Pays 20¢/word.** Sometimes pays expenses of writers on assignment.

COLUMNS Health Zone (health issues relating to motorcyclists); Motorcycle Engines 101 (basic motorcycle mechanics); Road Trip (California destination review including hotel, road, restaurant), all 2,000 words. **Buys 60 mss/year.** Query. **Pays 20¢/word**

FICTION We want stories concerning motorcycling or motorcyclists. No 'first-person' fiction. Query. Length: 1,000-2,000 words. **Pays 20¢/word.**

FILLERS Needs anecdotes, facts, gags, newsbreaks, short humor. Length: 2,000-3,000 words. **Pays 20¢/word.**

$$ RIDER MAGAZINE

2575 Vista Del Mar Dr., Ventura CA 93001. (805)667-4314. **Fax:** (805)667-4378. **Website:** www.ridermagazine.com. **60% freelance written.** Monthly magazine covering motorcycling. *Rider* serves the all-brand motorcycle lifestyle/enthusiast with a slant toward travel and touring. Estab. 1974. Circ. 127,000. Byline given. Offers 25% kill fee. Publishes ms an average of 6-12

months after acceptance. Editorial lead time 3 months. Submit seasonal material 6 months in advance. Accepts queries by mail only. Responds in 2 months to queries. Sample copy for $2.95. Guidelines on website.
NONFICTION Needs general interest, historical, how-to, humor, interview, personal experience, travel. Does not want to see fiction or articles on 'How I Began Motorcycling.' **Buys 40-50 mss/year.** Query. Length: 750-1,800 words. **Pays $150-750.**
COLUMNS Favorite Rides (short trip), 850-1,100 words. **Buys 12 mss/year.** Query. **Pays $150-750.**

🟢🟢 ROADBIKE
TAM Communications, 1010 Summer St., Stamford CT 06905. (203)425-8777. **Fax:** (203)425-8775. **E-mail:** info@roadbikemag.com. **Website:** www.roadbikemag.com. **40% freelance written.** Monthly magazine covering motorcycling tours, project and custom bikes, products, news, and tech. Estab. 1993. Circ. 50,000. Byline given. Publishes ms an average of 6 months after acceptance. Editorial lead time 4 months. Submit seasonal material 6 months in advance. Accepts queries by mail, e-mail, fax, online submission form. Guidelines free.
NONFICTION Needs how-to, motorcycle tech, travel, camping, interview, motorcycle related, new product, photo feature, motorcycle events or gathering places with maximum of 1,000 words text, travel. No fiction. **Buys 100 mss/year.** Send complete ms. Length: 1,000-2,500 words. **Pays $15-400.**
FILLERS Needs facts.

🟢🟢 ROAD KING
Parthenon Publishing, 28 White Bridge Rd., Suite 209, Nashville TN 37205. **Website:** www.roadking.com. **25% freelance written.** Bimonthly magazine covering the trucking industry. Byline given. Pays 3 weeks from acceptance. Offers 30% kill fee. Publishes ms an average of 3 months after acceptance. Editorial lead time 3-4 months. Submit seasonal material 4 months in advance. Accepts queries by mail. Accepts simultaneous submissions. Responds in 3-4 weeks to queries. Sample copy for #10 SASE. Guidelines free.
NONFICTION No essays, no humor, no cartoons. **Buys 12 mss/year.** Query with published clips. Length: 100-1,000 words. **Pays $50-500.**

🟢 TRUCKIN' MAGAZINE
Source Interlink Media, Inc., 1733 Alton Parkway, Irvine CA 92606. **E-mail:** inquiries@automotive.com.

Website: www.truckinweb.com. Monthly magazine. Written for pickup drivers and enthusiasts. Circ. 186,606. Editorial lead time 3 months.

AVIATION

🟢 AFRICAN PILOT
Wavelengths 10 (Pty) Ltd., P.O. Box 30620, Kyalami 1684 South Africa. +27 11 466-8524. **Fax:** +27 11 466 8496. **E-mail:** Editor@Africanpilot.co.za. **Website:** www.africanpilot.co.za. **Contact:** Athol Franz, editor. **50% freelance written.** "*African Pilot* is southern Africa's premier monthly aviation magazine. It publishes a high-quality magazine that is well-known and respected within the aviation community of southern Africa. The magazine offers a number of benefits to readers and advertisers, including a weekly e-mail newsletter, annual service guide, pilot training supplement, executive wall calendar and an extensive website that mirrors the paper edition. The magazine offers clean layouts with outstanding photography and reflects editorial professionalism as well as a responsible approach to journalism. The magazine offers a complete and tailored promotional solution for all aviation businesses operating in the African region." Estab. 2001. Circ. 7,000+ online; 6,600+ print. Byline given. Editorial lead time 2-3 months. Accepts queries by e-mail. Accepts simultaneous submissions. Responds only if interested, send nonreturnable samples. Sample copies available upon request. Writer's guidelines online or via e-mail.
NONFICTION Needs general interest, historical, interview, new product, personal experience, photo feature, technical. No articles on aircraft accidents. **Buys up to 60 mss/year.** Send complete ms. Length: 1,200-2,800 words. Sometimes pays expenses of writers on assignment.

🟢🟢🟢 AIR & SPACE MAGAZINE
Smithsonian Institution, P.O. Box 37012, MRC 951, Washington DC 20013-7012. (202)633-6070. **Fax:** (202)633-6085. **E-mail:** editors@si.edu. **Website:** www.airspacemag.com. **80% freelance written.** Bimonthly magazine covering aviation and aerospace for a nontechnical audience. 'Emphasizes the human rather than the technological, on the ideas behind the events. Features are slanted to a technically curious, but not necessarily technically knowledgeable, audience. We are looking for unique angles to aviation/aerospace stories, history, events, personalities,

current and future technologies, that emphasize the human-interest aspect." Estab. 1985. Circ. 225,000. Byline given. Offers kill fee. Accepts queries by mail, e-mail, fax. Responds in 3 months to queries. Sample copy for $7. Guidelines available online.

NONFICTION Needs book excerpts, essays, general interest, on aviation/aerospace, historical, humor, photo feature, technical. **Buys 50 mss/year.** Query with published clips. Length: 1,500-3,000 words. **Pays $1,500-3,000.** Pays expenses of writers on assignment.

COLUMNS Above and Beyond (first person), 1,500-2,000 words; Flights and Fancy (whimsy), approximately 800 words. Soundings (brief items, timely but not breaking news), 500-700 words. **Buys 25 mss/year.** Query with published clips. **Pays $150-300.**

$ AUTOPILOT MAGAZINE

The AutoPilot Franchise Systems, 2310 Pendley Rd., Cumming GA 30041. (770)422-1505. **Fax:** (770)255-1016. **E-mail:** production@autopilotmagazine.com. **Website:** www.autopilotmagazine.com. **70% freelance written**. Bimonthly magazine covering aviation. *AutoPilot Magazine* is a lifestyle magazine for the aviation enthusiast. We currently have four editions circulating, including Alabama, Georgia, Florida and the Mid-Atlantic region. This magazine differs from other aviation publications, because its focus is specifically on the pilot. Estab. 2000. Circ. 90,000 for all four editions. Byline given. Editorial lead time 2-3 weeks. Accepts queries by mail, e-mail, fax, phone. Sample copy free. Guidelines free.

NONFICTION Needs book excerpts, essays, historical, personal experience, photo feature, travel. Query. Length: 500-900 words. **Pays $100.**

COLUMNS Airport Spotlight (general aviation airports), 500-800 words; Pilot Profiles, 500-800 words; Notable Aviation Organizations, 900 words; Aviation Museums, 900 words; Aviation Memorials, 600 words. **Pays $100.**

FILLERS Needs anecdotes.

$$ AVIATION HISTORY

Weider History Group, 19300 Promenade Dr., Leesburg VA 20176. **E-mail:** aviationhistory@weiderhistorygroup.com. **Website:** www.thehistorynet.com. **95% freelance written**. Bimonthly magazine covering military and civilian aviation from first flight to the jet age. "It aims to make aeronautical history not only factually accurate and complete, but also enjoyable to a varied subscriber and newsstand audience." Estab. 1990. Circ. 45,000. Byline given. Publishes ms an average of 2 years after acceptance. Editorial lead time 6 months. Submit seasonal material 1 year in advance. Accepts queries by mail, e-mail, fax. Accepts simultaneous submissions. Responds in 2 months to queries. Responds in 3 months to mss. Sample copy for $5. Guidelines with #10 SASE or online.

NONFICTION Needs historical, interview, personal experience. **Buys 24 mss/year.** Query. Feature articles should be 3,000-3,500 words, each with a 500-word sidebar where appropriate, author's biography, and book suggestions for further reading **Pays $300.**

COLUMNS Aviators, Restored, Extremes all 1,500 words or less. Pays $150 and up. Book reviews, 250-500 words, pays minimum $50.

$ BALLOON LIFE

9 Madeline Ave., Westport CT 06880. (203)629-1241. **E-mail:** bill_armstrong@balloonlife.com. **Website:** www.balloonlife.com. **75% freelance written.** Monthly magazine covering sport of hot air ballooning. Readers participate as pilots, crew, and official observers at events and spectators. Estab. 1986. Circ. 7,000. Byline given. Offers 50-100% kill fee. Publishes ms an average of 3-4 months after acceptance. Submit seasonal material 4 months in advance. Accepts queries by mail, e-mail. Accepts simultaneous submissions. Responds in 2 weeks to queries. Sample copy for 9×12 SAE with $2 postage. Guidelines available online.

NONFICTION Needs book excerpts, general interest, how-to, flying hot air balloons, equipment techniques, interview, new product, technical, events/rallies, safety seminars, balloon clubs/organizations, letters to the editor. **Buys 150 mss/year.** Send complete ms. Length: 1,000-1,500 words. **Pays $50-200.**

COLUMNS Crew Quarters (devoted to some aspect of crewing), 900 words; Preflight (a news and information column), 300-500 words; **pays $50**. Logbook (balloon events that have taken place in last 3-4 months), 300-500 words; **pays $20**. **Buys 60 mss/year.** Send complete ms.

$$ CESSNA OWNER MAGAZINE

Jones Publishing, Inc., N7528 Aanstad Rd., P.O. Box 5000, Iola WI 54945. (715)445-5000. **Fax:** (715)445-4053. **E-mail:** editor@cessnaowner.org. **Website:** www.cessnaowner.org. Keith Mathiowetz, editor. **50% freelance written.** Monthly magazine covering Cessna single and twin-engine aircraft. "*Cessna Own-*

er Magazine is the official publication of the Cessna Owner Organization (C.O.O.). Therefore, our readers are Cessna aircraft owners, renters, pilots, and enthusiasts. Articles should deal with buying/selling, flying, maintaining, or modifying Cessnas. The purpose of our magazine is to promote safe, fun, and affordable flying." Estab. 1975. Circ. 6,000. Byline given. Publishes ms an average of 3 months after acceptance. Editorial lead time 1 month. Submit seasonal material 3 months in advance. Accepts queries by mail, e-mail, fax, phone. Responds in 2 weeks to queries. Responds in 1 month to mss. Sample copy on website.

NONFICTION Needs historical, of specific Cessna models, how-to, aircraft repairs and maintenance, new product, personal experience, photo feature, technical, aircraft engines and airframes. Special issues: Engines (maintenance, upgrades); Avionics (purchasing, new products). **Buys 48 mss/year.** Query. Length: 1,500-2,000 words. **Pays 12¢/word.**

$$ FLIGHT JOURNAL

Air Age Publishing, 88 Danbury Road, Route 7, Wilton CT 06897. (203)431-9000. **Fax:** (203)529-3010. **E-mail:** flightjournal@airage.com. **Website:** www.flightjournal.com. Bimonthly magazine covering aviation-oriented material, for the most part with a historical overtone, but also with some modern history in the making reporting. "Flight Journal is like no other aviation magazine in the world, covering the world of flight from its simple beginnings to its high-tech, no-holds-barred future. We put readers in the cockpit and let them live the thrill and adventure of the aviation experience, narrated by those who know the technology and made the history. Each issue brings the stories of flight— past, present and future— to life." Accepts queries by mail, e-mail, fax. Guidelines available.

NONFICTION Needs exposé, historical, humor, interview, new product, personal experience, photo feature, technical. We do not want any general aviation articles like 'My Flight to Baja in my 172,' nor detailed recitations of the technical capabilities of an aircraft. Avoid historically accurate, but bland, chronologies of events. Lengthier pieces should be discussed in advance with the editors. Length: 2,500-3,000 words. **Pays $600.**

$$ FLYING ADVENTURES MAGAZINE

Aviation Publishing Corporation, El Monte Airport (EMT), P.O. Box 93613, Pasadena CA 91109-3613. (626)618-4000. **E-mail:** editor@flyingadventures.com; info@flyingadventures.com. **Website:** www.flyingadventures.com. **20% freelance written.** Bimonthly magazine covering lifestyle travel for owners and passengers of private aircraft. "Our articles cover upscale travelers." Estab. 1994. Circ. 135,858. Byline given for features. Editorial lead time 2 weeks to 2 months. Accepts queries by e-mail. Accepts simultaneous submissions. Responds immediately. Sample copy and guidelines free.

NONFICTION Needs travel, Lifestyle. Nothing nonrelevant, not our style. See magazine. Query with published clips. Length: 500-1,500 words. **Pays $150-300 for assigned and unsolicited articles.** Sometimes pays expenses of writers on assignment.

COLUMNS Contact: Editor. Numerous Departments, see magazine. **Buys 100+ mss/yr. mss/year.** Query with published clips. **Pays $-$150.**

$$ PIPERS MAGAZINE

Jones Publishing, Inc., N7450 Aanstad Rd., P.O. Box 5000, Iola WI 54945. (866)697-4737. **Website:** www.piperowner.org. **50% freelance written.** Monthly magazine covering Piper single and twin engine aircraft. *Pipers Magazine* is the official publication of the Piper Owner Society (P.O.S). Therefore, our readers are Piper aircraft owners, renters, pilots, mechanics, and enthusiasts. Articles should deal with buying/selling, flying, maintaining, or modifying Pipers. The purpose of our magazine is to promote safe, fun and affordable flying. Estab. 1988. Circ. 5,000. Publishes ms an average of 3 months after acceptance. Editorial lead time 1 month. Submit seasonal material 3 months in advance. Accepts queries by mail, e-mail, fax, phone. Responds in 2 weeks to queries. Responds in 1 month to mss. Sample copy free. Guidelines free.

NONFICTION Needs historical, of specific models of Pipers, how-to, aircraft repairs and maintenance, new product, personal experience, photo feature, technical, aircraft engines and airframes. **Buys 48 mss/year.** Query. Length: 1,500-2,000 words. **Pays 12¢/word.**

$$ PLANE AND PILOT

Werner Publishing Corp., 12121 Wilshire Blvd., 12th Floor, Los Angeles CA 90025-1176. (310)820-1500. **Fax:** (310)826-5008. **E-mail:** editor@planeandpilotmag.com. **Website:** www.planeandpilotmag.com. **80% freelance written.** Monthly magazine covering general aviation. Estab. 1964. Circ. 150,000. Byline given. Offers kill fee. Publishes ms an average of 4 months after acceptance. Submit seasonal material 4 months in advance. Responds in 4 months to queries. Sample copy for $5.50. Guidelines available online.

NONFICTION Needs how-to, new product, personal experience, technical, travel, pilot efficiency, pilot reports on aircraft. **Buys 75 mss/year.** Query. Length: 1,200 words. **Pays $200-500.** Pays expenses of writers on assignment.

COLUMNS Readback (any newsworthy items on aircraft and/or people in aviation), 1,200 words; Jobs & Schools (a feature or an interesting school or program in aviation), 900-1,000 words. **Buys 30 mss/year.** Send complete ms. **Pays $200-500.**

BUSINESS AND FINANCE

BUSINESS NATIONAL

$ $ $ $ CORPORATE BOARD MEMBER

Board Member Inc., 5110 Maryland Way, Suite 250, Brentwood TN 37027. **Fax:** (615)371-0899. **E-mail:** boardmember@boardmember.com. **Website:** www.boardmember.com. **100% freelance written.** Bimonthly magazine covering corporate governance. "Our readers are the directors and top executives of publicly-held US corporations. We look for detailed and preferably narrative stories about how individual boards have dealt with the challenges that face them on a daily basis: reforms, shareholder suits, CEO pay, firing and hiring CEOs, setting up new boards, firing useless directors. We're happy to light fires under the feet of boards that are asleep at the switch. We also do service-type pieces, written in the second person, advising directors about new wrinkles in disclosure laws, for example." Estab. 1999. Circ. 60,000. Byline given. Offers 25% kill fee. Publishes ms an average of 3 months after acceptance. Editorial lead time 4-5 months. Submit seasonal material 4-5 months in advance. Accepts queries by e-mail. Responds in 1 week. Sample copy available online. Guidelines by e-mail.

NONFICTION Special issues: Best Law Firms in America (July/August); What Directors Think (November/December). Does not want views from 35,000 feet, pontification, opinion, humor, anything devoid of reporting. **Buys 100 mss/year.** Query. Length: 650-2,500 words. **Pays $1,200-5,000.** Pays expenses of writers on assignment.

$ $ DOLLARS AND SENSE: THE MAGAZINE OF ECONOMIC JUSTICE

Economic Affairs Bureau, 29 Winter St., Boston MA 02108. (617)447-2177. **Fax:** (617)477-2179. **E-mail:** dollars@dollarsandsense.org. **Website:** www.dollarsandsense.org. **10% freelance written.** Bimonthly magazine covering economic, environmental, and social justice. "We explain the workings of the US and international economics, and provide left perspectives on current economic affairs. Our audience is a mix of activists, organizers, academics, unionists, and other socially concerned people." Estab. 1974. Circ. 8,000. Byline given. Publishes ms an average of 4 months after acceptance. Editorial lead time 3 months. Submit seasonal material 2 months in advance. Accepts queries by mail, e-mail, fax, phone. Guidelines available online.

NONFICTION Needs exposé, political economics. **Buys 6 mss/year.** Query with published clips. Length: 700-2,500 words. **Pays $0-200.** Sometimes pays expenses of writers on assignment.

$ $ ENTREPRENEUR MAGAZINE

Entrepreneur Media, 2445 McCabe Way, Suite 400, Irvine CA 92614. (949)261-2325. **Website:** www.entrepreneur.com. **60% freelance written.** *Entrepreneur* readers already run their own businesses. They have been in business for several years and are seeking innovative methods and strategies to improve their business operations. They are also interested in new business ideas and opportunities, as well as current issues that affect their companies. Circ. 600,000. Byline given. Publishes ms an average of 5 months after acceptance. Submit seasonal material 6 months in advance. Accepts queries by mail, e-mail. Responds in 3 months to queries. Sample copy for $7.20. Guidelines available online.

NONFICTION Needs how-to, information on running a business, dealing with the psychological aspects of running a business, profiles of unique entrepreneurs, current news/trends (and their effect on small business). **Buys 10-20 mss/year.** Query with published clips. Length: 1,800 words. **Payment varies**

COLUMNS Snapshots (profiles of interesting entrepreneurs who exemplify innovation in their marketing/sales technique, financing method or management style, or who have developed an innovative product/service or technology); Money Smarts (financial management); Marketing Smarts; Web Smarts (Internet news); Tech Smarts; Management Smarts; Viewpoint (first-person essay on entrepreneurship), all 300 words. **Pays $1/word.**

⊘ FORTUNE

Time, Inc., 1271 Avenue of the Americas, New York NY 10020. (212)522-1212. **Fax:** (212)522-0810. **E-mail:** letters@fortune.com. **Website:** www.fortune.com. Andrew Serwer, managing editor. **Contact:** Michele Hadlow, senior photo editor. Biweekly magazine. Edited primarily for high-demographic business people. Specializes in big stories about companies, business personalities, technology, managing, Wall Street, media, marketing, personal finance, politics, and policy. Circ. 1,066,000. Editorial lead time 6 weeks.

○ Does not accept freelance submissions.

$$$$ HISPANIC BUSINESS

Hispanic Business, Inc., 425 Pine Ave., Santa Barbara CA 93117-3709. (805)964-4554. **Fax:** (805)964-5539. **Website:** www.hispanicbusiness.com. **40-50% freelance written.** Monthly magazine covering Hispanic business. For more than 2 decades, *Hispanic Business* magazine has documented the growing affluence and power of the Hispanic community. Our magazine reaches the most educated, affluent Hispanic business and community leaders. Stories should have relevance for the Hispanic business community. Estab. 1979. Circ. 220,000 (rate base); 990,000 (readership base). Byline given. Offers 50% kill fee. Publishes ms an average of 1 month after acceptance. Editorial lead time 1-3 months. Submit seasonal material 2 months in advance. Accepts queries by mail. Accepts simultaneous submissions. Responds in 3 weeks to queries. Responds in 1 month to mss. Sample copy free.

NONFICTION Needs interview, travel. **Buys 120 mss/year.** Query résumé and published clips. Length: 650-2,000 words. **Pays $50-1,500.** Sometimes pays expenses of writers on assignment.

COLUMNS Tech Pulse (technology); Money Matters (financial), both 800 words. **Buys 40 mss/year.** Query with résumé and published clips. **Pays $50-450.**

🍁 $$ HOME BUSINESS REPORT

Impact Communications Ltd, 2625A Alliance St., Abbottsford BC V2S 3J9 Canada. (604)936-5815. **Fax:** (604)936-5805. **E-mail:** info@impactcommunicationsltd.com. **Website:** www.homebusinessreport.com. **95% freelance written.** Quarterly magazine covering home-based business/small business. "Our focus is on practical strategies that small and home-based business owners can use to increase their business success. We prefer articles about real people having real experiences, as opposed to lists of how-tos. We run 2 types of articles: features and Regional Reports, which profile successful Canadian home-based businesses." Estab. 1989. Circ. 125,000. Byline given. Publishes ms an average of 2 months after acceptance. Editorial lead time 1-3 months. Submit seasonal material 3-6 months in advance. Accepts queries by mail, e-mail. Responds in 1-6 weeks to queries. Responds in 1-6 months to mss. Sample copy and writer's guidelines online.

NONFICTION Needs interview, business articles. Special issues: Creating Cash Flow (October). Does not want articles solely on theory or 'puff' pieces that do little more than promote your own business or product. **Buys 35-40 mss/year.** Query. Length: 1,000-3,000 words. **Pays $200-350.**

$$$ MYBUSINESS MAGAZINE

Imagination Publishing, 600 W. Fulton St., Suite 600, Chicago IL 60661. (615)872-5800; (800)634-2669). **E-mail:** nfib@imaginepub.com. **Website:** www.mybusinessmag.com. **75% freelance written.** Bimonthly magazine for small businesses. "We are a guide to small business success, however that is defined in the new small business economy. We explore the methods and minds behind the trends and celebrate the men and women leading the creation of the new small business economy." Estab. 1999. Circ. 400,000. Byline given. Offers 30% kill fee. Publishes ms an average of 4 months after acceptance. Editorial lead time 4-6 months. Submit seasonal material 5 months in advance. Accepts queries by e-mail. Accepts simultaneous submissions. Responds in 3 weeks to queries. Sample copy free. Guidelines available online.

NONFICTION Needs how-to, new product. **Buys 8 mss/year.** "Query with résumé and 2 published clips. We accept pitches for feature stories, which fall under 1 of 3 categories: Own, Operate, and Grow. Story ideas should be small-business focused, with an emphasis on timely problems that small business owners face and real, workable solutions. Trend pieces are also of interest. Copy should be submitted as a Microsoft Word enclosure. Deadlines are 90 days before publication." Length: 200-1,800 words. **Pays $75-1,000.**

😊😊 THE NETWORK JOURNAL

The Network Journal Communication, 39 Broadway, Suite 2120, New York NY 10006. (212)962-3791. **Fax:** (212)962-3537. **E-mail:** tnjeditors@tnj.com. **Website:** www.tnj.com. **25% freelance written.** Monthly magazine covering business and career articles. *The Network Journal* caters to black professionals and small-business owners, providing quality coverage on business, financial, technology and career news germane to the black community. Estab. 1993. Circ. 25,000. Byline given. Editorial lead time 2 months. Submit seasonal material 3 months in advance. Accepts queries by mail, e-mail, fax, phone. Accepts simultaneous submissions. Sample copy for $1 or online. Writer's guidelines for SASE or online.

NONFICTION Needs how-to, interview. Send complete ms. Length: 1,200-1,500 words. **Pays $150-200.** Sometimes pays expenses of writers on assignment.

COLUMNS Book reviews, 700-800 words; career management and small business development, 800 words. **Pays $100.**

😊😊 😊😊😊😊 PROFIT

Rogers Media, 1 Mt. Pleasant Rd., 11th Floor, Toronto ON M4Y 2Y5 Canada. (416)764-1402. **Fax:** (416)764-1404. **Website:** www.profitguide.com. **80% freelance written.** Magazine published 6 times/year covering small and medium businesses. We specialize in specific, useful information that helps our readers manage their businesses better. We want Canadian stories only. Estab. 1982. Circ. 110,000. Byline given. Offers variable kill fee. Publishes ms an average of 2 months after acceptance. Submit seasonal material 6 months in advance. Accepts queries by mail, fax, phone. Responds in 1 month to queries. Responds in 6 weeks to mss. Sample copy for 9×12 SAE with 84¢ postage. Guidelines free.

NONFICTION Needs how-to, business management tips, strategies and Canadian business profiles. **Buys 50 mss/year.** Query with published clips. Length: 800-2,000 words. **Pays $500-2,000.** Pays expenses of writers on assignment.

COLUMNS Finance (info on raising capital in Canada), 700 words; Marketing (marketing strategies for independent business), 700 words. **Buys 80 mss/year.** Query with published clips. **Pays $150-600.**

😊😊 SFO MAGAZINE

Wasendorf & Associates, Inc., One Peregrine Way, Cedar Falls IA 50613. **E-mail:** editorial@sfomag.com. **Website:** www.sfomag.com. **Contact:** Michelle Van Dorn. **90% freelance written.** Monthly magazine covering trading of stocks, futures, options, exchange traded funds, and currency pairs. "We focus on issues and strategies for the retail individual trader." "Our articles are educational and nonpromotional in angle and tone. We try to offer our readers information they can apply immediately to their trading (expository types of articles)." Estab. 2000. Circ. 120,000. Byline given. Publishes ms an average of 2 months after acceptance. Editorial lead time 2.5 months. Accepts queries by e-mail. Accepts simultaneous submissions. Responds in 8 weeks to queries. Sample copy available online. Guidelines by e-mail.

NONFICTION Needs how-to, trading strategies, interview, in-depth on financial regulations, laws, etc. Special issues: "See editorial calendar. Each month, we have a 'spotlight' section that takes a look at an issue that may affect the way that an individual retail trader can access or take advantage of the financial markets. These are determined as the year progresses, but general areas of interest would be financial regulation, financial policy, taxes, etc. We do not run book excerpts or material that has been published elsewhere." **Buys 12 mss/year.** Query with published clips. Length: 600-800 words.

😊😊 TECHNICAL ANALYSIS OF STOCKS & COMMODITIES

4757 California Ave., SW, Seattle WA 98116. (206)938-0570. **E-mail:** editor@traders.com; jhutson@traders.com. **Website:** www.traders.com. **Contact:** Jack K. Huston, editor-in-chief; Elizabeth M.S. Flynn , managing editor. **95% freelance written.** "Magazine covers methods of investing and trading stocks, bonds and commodities (futures), options, mutual funds, and precious metals using technical analysis." Estab. 1982. Circ. 65,000. Byline given. Publishes ms an average of 6 months after acceptance. Responds in 3 months to queries. Sample copy for $8. Guidelines available online.

NONFICTION Needs how-to, trade, technical, cartoons, trading and software aids to trading, reviews, utilities, real world trading (actual case studies of trades and their results). No newsletter-type, buy-sell recommendations. The article subject must relate to technical analysis, charting or a numerical technique used to trade securities or futures. Almost universally requires graphics with every article. **Buys 150 mss/year.** Send complete ms. Length: 1,000-4,000 words. **Pays $100-500.**

COLUMNS Length: 800-1,600 words. **Buys 100 columns. mss/year.** Query. **Pays $50-300**

FILLERS Contact: Karen Wasserman, fillers editor. "Must relate to trading stocks, bonds, options, mutual funds, commodities, or precious metals." **Buys 20 fillers. mss/year.** Length: 500 words. **Pays $20-50.**

BUSINESS REGIONAL

🌑🌑 ALASKA BUSINESS MONTHLY

Alaska Business Publishing, 501 W. Northern Lights Blvd., Suite 100, Anchorage AK 99503-2577. (907)276-4373. **Fax:** (907)279-2900. **E-mail:** editor@akbizmag.com. **Website:** www.akbizmag.com. **Contact:** Susan Harrington, managing editor. **75% freelance written.** "Our audience is Alaska businessmen and women who rely on us for timely features and up-to-date information about doing business in Alaska." Estab. 1985. Circ. 12,000-15,000. Byline given. Offers $50 kill fee. Publishes ms an average of 2 months after acceptance. Editorial lead time 5 months. Submit seasonal material 6 months in advance. Accepts queries by e-mail, online submission form. Responds in 1 month to queries, 4 months to mss. Order sample copy through website store or download off website under "archives". Guidelines online.

NONFICTION Needs Alaska-centric, general interest, how-to, interview, new product, opinion, exposé, inspire, photo, technical, travel, business. No fiction, poetry, or anything not pertinent to Alaska business. **Buys approximately 130 mss/year.** Send query and clips of previously published articles. Length: 500-2,000 words. **Pays $100-350 for assigned articles. Pays $100-300 for unsolicited articles.**

☉ 🌑🌑🌑🌑 ALBERTA VENTURE

Venture Publishing Inc., 10259 - 105 St., Edmonton AB T5J 1E3 Canada. (780)990-0839. **E-mail:** admin@albertaventure.com. **Website:** www.albertaventure.com. **70% freelance written.** Monthly magazine covering business in Alberta. "Our readers are mostly business owners and managers in Alberta who read the magazine to keep up with trends and run their businesses better." Estab. 1997. Circ. 35,000. Byline given. Offers 30% kill fee. Publishes ms an average of 2 months after acceptance. Editorial lead time 3 months. Submit seasonal material 3 months in advance. Accepts queries by e-mail. Responds in 2 weeks to queries. Sample copy available online. Guidelines by email.

NONFICTION Needs how-to, business narrative related to Alberta. Does not want company or product profiles. **Buys 75 mss/year.** Query. Length: 1,000-3,000 words. **Pays $300-2,000 (Canadian).** Pays expenses of writers on assignment.

☉ 🌑🌑 ATLANTIC BUSINESS MAGAZINE

Communications Ten, Ltd., P.O. Box 2356, Station C, St. John's NL A1C 6E7 Canada. (709)726-9300. **Fax:** (709)726-3013. **Website:** www.atlanticbusinessmagazine.com. **80% freelance written.** Bimonthly magazine covering business in Atlantic Canada. We discuss positive business developments, emphasizing that the 4 Atlantic provinces are a great place to do business. Estab. 1989. Circ. 30,000. Byline given. Pays within 30 days of publication. Publishes ms an average of 2 months after acceptance. Editorial lead time 6 months. Accepts queries by mail, e-mail, fax. Sample copy and writer's guidelines free.

NONFICTION Needs exposé, general interest, interview, new product. We don't want religious, technical, or scholarly material. We are not an academic magazine. We are interested only in stories concerning business topics specific to the 4 Canadian provinces of Nova Scotia, New Brunswick, Prince Edward Island, and Newfoundland and Labrador. **Buys 36 mss/year.** Query with published clips. Length: 1,200-2,500 words. **Pays $300-750.** Sometimes pays expenses of writers on assignment.

COLUMNS Query with published clips.

🌑🌑 THE BUSINESS JOURNAL

American City Business Journals, Inc., 96 N. Third St., Suite 100, San Jose CA 95112. (408)295-3800. **Fax:** (408)295-5028. **Website:** sanjose.bizjournals.com. **Contact:** Moryt Milo, editor. **2-5% freelance written.** Weekly tabloid covering a wide cross-section of industries. Estab. 1983. Circ. 13,200. Byline given. Offers $75 kill fee. Editorial lead time 1 month. Responds in 2 weeks to queries. Sample copy free. Guidelines free.

○ Our stories are written for business people. Our audience is primarily upper-level management."

NONFICTION Buys 300 mss/year. Query. Length: 700-2,500 words. **Pays $175-400.**

🌑🌑 BUSINESS NH MAGAZINE

55 S. Commercial St., Manchester NH 03101. (603)626-6354. **Fax:** (603)626-6359. **E-mail:** hcopeland@BusinessNHmagazine.com. **Website:** www.

millyardcommunications.com. **Contact:** Heidi Copeland, publisher. **25% freelance written.** Monthly magazine covering business, politics, and people of New Hampshire. "Our audience consists of the owners and top managers of New Hampshire businesses." Estab. 1983. Circ. 15,000. Byline given. Publishes ms an average of 2 months after acceptance. Accepts queries by e-mail, fax.

NONFICTION Needs how-to, interview. No unsolicited mss; interested in New Hampshire writers only. **Buys 24 mss/year.** Query with published clips and résumé. Length: 750-2,500 words. **Payment varies.**

$$ CINCY MAGAZINE

Great Lakes Publishing Co., Cincinnati Club Building, 30 Garfield Place, Suite 440, Cincinnati OH 45202. (513)421-2533. **Fax:** (513)421-2542. **E-mail:** dgebhardt-french@cincymagazine.com. **Website:** www.cincymagazine.com. **Contact:** Dianne Gebhardt-French, editor; Tim Curtis, managing editor. **80% freelance written.** Glossy bimonthly color magazine written for business professionals in Greater Cincinnati, published 10 times annually. *Cincy* is written and designed for the interests of business professionals and executives both at work and away from work, with features, trend stories, news and opinions related to business, along with lifestyle articles on home, dining, shopping, travel, health and more. Estab. 2003. Circ. 15,300. Byline given. Offers 100% kill fee. Publishes ms an average of 3 months after acceptance. Editorial lead time 1-3 months. Submit seasonal material 4 months in advance. Accepts queries by mail, e-mail. No

NONFICTION Needs general interest, interview. Does not want stock advice. Length: 200-2,000 words. **Pays $75-600.**

$$ CORPORATE CONNECTICUT MAGAZINE

Corporate World LLC, P.O. Box 290726, Wethersfield CT 06129. **Fax:** (860)257-1924. **E-mail:** editor@corpct.com. **Website:** www.corpct.com. **50% freelance written.** Quarterly magazine covering regional reporting, global coverage of corporate/business leaders, entrepreneurs. *Corporate Connecticut* is devoted to people who make business happen in the private sector and who create innovative change across public arenas. Centered in the Northeast between New York and Boston, Connecticut is positioned in a coastal corridor with a dense affluent population who are highly mobile, accomplished and educated. Estab. 2001. Byline given. Offers 25% kill fee. Publishes ms an average of 2-3 months after acceptance. Editorial lead time 3-6 months. Submit seasonal material 10-12 months in advance. Accepts queries by mail, e-mail. Responds in 2 weeks to queries. Sample copy for #10 SASE.

NONFICTION Query with published clips. **Pays 35¢/word minimum with varying fees for excellence.**

$ CRAIN'S DETROIT BUSINESS

Crain Communications, Inc., 1155 Gratiot, Detroit MI 48207. (313)446-0419. **Fax:** (313)446-1687. **E-mail:** kcrain@crain.com. **Website:** www.crainsdetroit.com. **10% freelance written.** Weekly tabloid covering business in the Detroit metropolitan area—specifically Wayne, Oakland, Macomb, Washtenaw, and Livingston counties. Estab. 1985. Circ. 150,000. Byline given. Publishes ms an average of 1 month after acceptance. Accepts queries by mail, e-mail. Sample copy for $1.50. Guidelines available online.

💬 *Crain's Detroit Business* uses only area writers and local topics.

NONFICTION Needs new product, technical, business. **Buys 20 mss/year.** Query with published clips. 30-40 words/column inch **Pays $10-15/column inch.** Pays expenses of writers on assignment.

$$ INGRAM'S

Show-Me Publishing, Inc., P.O. Box 411356, Kansas City MO 64141. (816)842-9994. **Fax:** (816)474-1111. **E-mail:** editorial@ingramsonline.com. **Website:** www.ingramsonline.com. **Contact:** Joe Sweeney, editor in chief. **10% freelance written.** Monthly magazine covering Kansas City business and economic development. "*Ingram's* readers are top-level corporate executives and community leaders, officials and decision makers. Our editorial content must provide such readers with timely, relevant information and insights." Estab. 1975. Circ. 105,000. Byline given. Publishes ms an average of 1 month after acceptance. Editorial lead time 1 month. Submit seasonal material 5 months in advance. Accepts queries by e-mail. Sample copy free.

💬 Only accepts local writers; guest columnist are not paid articles.

NONFICTION Needs interview, technical. Does not want humor, inspirational, or anything not related to Kansas City business. **Buys 4-6 mss/year.** Query. Length: 500-1,500 words. **Pays $75-200 depending on research/feature length.** Sometimes pays expenses of writers on assignment.

COLUMNS Say So (opinion), 1,500 words. **Buys 12 mss/year. Pays $75-100 max.**

⊖⊖ THE LANE REPORT

Lane Communications Group, 201 E. Main St., 14th Floor, Lexington KY 40507. (859)244-3500. **Fax:** (859)244-3555. **E-mail:** markgreen@lanereport.com; editorial@lanereport.com. **Website:** www.lanereport.com. **70% freelance written.** Monthly magazine covering statewide business. Estab. 1986. Circ. 15,000. Byline given. Editorial lead time 6 weeks. Submit seasonal material 3 months in advance. Accepts queries by mail, e-mail, fax. Accepts simultaneous submissions. Responds in 1 month to queries. Sample copy and writer's guidelines free.

NONFICTION Needs essays, interview, new product, photo feature. No fiction. **Buys 30-40 mss/year.** Query with published clips. Length: 500-2,000 words. **Pays $150-375.** Sometimes pays expenses of writers on assignment.

COLUMNS Technology and Business in Kentucky; Advertising; Exploring Kentucky; Perspective; Spotlight on the Arts, all less than 1,000 words.

⊖ MERCER BUSINESS MAGAZINE

White Eagle Publishing Company, 1A Quakerbridge Plaza Drive, Suite 2, Mercerville NJ 08619. (609)689-9960. **Fax:** (609)586-9899. **E-mail:** info@mercer-chamber.org. **Website:** www.mercerchamber.org. **100% freelance written.** Monthly magazine covering national and local business-related, theme-based topics. *Mercer Business* is a Chamber of Commerce publication, so the slant is pro-business primarily. Also covers nonprofits, education and other related issues. Estab. 1924. Circ. 8,500. Byline given. Publishes ms an average of 1 month after acceptance. Editorial lead time 6 weeks. Submit seasonal material 6 weeks in advance. Accepts queries by e-mail. Accepts simultaneous submissions. Responds in 1 week to queries. Sample copy for #10 SASE. Guidelines by email.

NONFICTION Needs humor. Query with published clips. Length: 1,000-1,800 words. **Pays $150 for assigned articles.** Sometimes pays expenses of writers on assignment.

FILLERS Needs gags. **Buys 24 mss/year.** Length: 300-500 words.

⊘ ⊖⊖⊖⊖ OREGON BUSINESS

MEDIAmerica, Inc., 715 SW Morrison St, Suite 800, Portalnd OR 97205. (503)223-0304. **Fax:** (503)221-6544. **E-mail:** robind@oregonbusiness.com. **Website:** www.oregonbusiness.com. **15-25% freelance written.** Monthly magazine covering business in Oregon. Our subscribers inlcude owners of small and medium-sized businesses, government agencies, professional staffs of banks, insurance companies, ad agencies, attorneys and other service providers. We accept *only* stories about Oregon businesses, issues and trends. Estab. 1981. Circ. 50,000. Byline given. Editorial lead time 2 months. Accepts queries by mail, e-mail. Sample copy for $4. Guidelines available online.

NONFICTION Query with résumé and 2-3 published clips. Length: 1,200-3,000 words.

COLUMNS First Person (opinion piece on an issue related to business), 750 words; Around the State (recent news and trends, and how they might shape the future), 100-600 words; Business Tools (practical, how-to suggestions for business managers and owners), 400-600 words; In Character (profile of interesting or quirky member of the business community), 850 words. Query with résumé and 2-3 published clips.

⊖⊖ PACIFIC COAST BUSINESS TIMES

14 E. Carrillo St., Suite A, Santa Barbara CA 93101. (805)560-6950. **E-mail:** hdubroff@pacbiztimes.com. **Website:** www.pacbiztimes.com. **Contact:** Henry Dubroff, founder and editor. **10% freelance written.** Weekly tabloid covering financial news specific to Santa Barbara, Ventura, San Luis Obispo counties in California. Estab. 2000. Circ. 5,000. Byline given. Editorial lead time 1 month. Accepts queries by e-mail, phone. Sample copy free. Guidelines free.

NONFICTION Needs interview, opinion, personal finance. Does not want first person, promo or fluff pieces. **Buys 20 mss/year.** Query. Length: 500-800 words. **Pays $75-175.** Pays expenses of writers on assignment.

COLUMNS Harvey Mackay (management), 600 words. Query. **Pays $10-50.**

⊖⊖ PRAIRIE BUSINESS

Grand Forks (ND), Forum Communications Company, 808 Third Ave., #400, Fargo ND 58103. **Fax:** (701)280-9092. **E-mail:** avanormer@prairiebizmag.com. **Website:** www.prairiebizmag.com. **Contact:** Ryan Schuster, submissions editor. **30% freelance written.** Monthly magazine covering business on the Northern Plains (North Dakota, South Dakota, Minnesota). "We attempt to be a resource for business owners/managers, policymakers, educators, and nonprofit administrators, acting as a catalyst for growth

CONSUMER MAGAZINES

in the region by reaching out to an audience of decision makers within the region and also venture capitalists, site selectors, and angel visitors from outside the region." Estab. 2000. Circ. 20,000. Byline given. Pays within 2 weeks of mailing date. Publishes ms an average of 1-2 months after acceptance. Editorial lead time 2 months. Submit seasonal material 2 months in advance. Accepts queries by e-mail. Accepts simultaneous submissions. Responds in 2 weeks to queries. Sample copy free. Guidelines free.

NONFICTION Needs interview, technical, basic online research. "Does not want articles that are blatant self-promotion for any interest without providing value for readers." **Buys 36 mss/year.** Query. Length: 800-1,500 words. **Pays 15¢/word.**

$ ROCHESTER BUSINESS JOURNAL

Rochester Business Journal, Inc., 45 E. Ave., Suite 500, Rochester NY 14604. (585)546-8303. **Fax:** (585)546-3398. **E-mail:** rbj@rbj.net. **Website:** www.rbjdaily.com. **10% freelance written**. Weekly tabloid covering local business. The *Rochester Business Journal* is geared toward corporate executives and owners of small businesses, bringing them leading-edge business coverage and analysis first in the market. Estab. 1984. Circ. 10,000. Byline given. Publishes ms an average of 1 month after acceptance. Editorial lead time 6 weeks. Accepts queries by mail, fax. Responds in 1 week to queries. Sample copy for free or by e-mail. Guidelines available online.

NONFICTION Needs how-to, business topics, news features, trend stories with local examples. Do not query about any topics that do not include several local examples—local companies, organizations, universities, etc. **Buys 110 mss/year.** Query with published clips. Length: 1,000-2,000 words. **Pays $150.**

$$ SMARTCEO MAGAZINE

SmartCEO, 2700 Lighthouse Point E., Suite 220A, Baltimore MD 21224. (410)342-9510. **Fax:** (410)675-5280. **E-mail:** jeanine@smartceo.com. **Website:** www.smartceo.com. **Contact:** Jeanine Clingenpeel, editor. **25% freelance written**. Monthly magazine covering regional business in the Baltimore, MD and Washington, DC areas. "*SmartCEO* is a regional 'growing company' publication. We are not news; we are a resource full of smart ideas to help educate and inspire decision-makers in the Baltimore and DC areas. Each issue contains features, interviews, case studies, columns and other departments designed to help this region's CEOs face the daily challenges of running a business." Estab. 2001. Circ. 34,000. Byline given. Publishes ms an average of 2 months after acceptance. Editorial lead time 5 months. Submit seasonal material 5 months in advance. Accepts queries by e-mail, phone. Responds in 4 weeks to queries. Responds in 2 months to mss. Sample copy available online. Guidelines by email.

NONFICTION Needs essays, interview, business features or tips. "We do not want pitches on CEOs or companies outside the Baltimore, MD or Washington, DC areas; no product reviews, lifestyle content or book reviews, please." **Buys 20 mss/year.** Query. Length: 2,000-5,000 words. **Pays $300-600.** Sometimes pays expenses of writers on assignment.

COLUMNS Project to Watch (overview of a local development project in progress and why it is of interest to the business community), 600 words; Q&A and tip-focused coverage of business issues and challenges (each article includes the opinions of 10-20 CEOs), 500-1,000 words. **Buys 0-5 mss/year.** Query.

$ SOMERSET BUSINESS MAGAZINE

White Eagle Printing Company, P.O. Box 833, 360 Grove Street at Route 22 East, Somerville NJ 08876. (908)218-4300. **Fax:** (908)722-7823. **E-mail:** info@somersetbusinesspartnership.com. **Website:** www.scbp.org. **100% freelance written**. Monthly magazine covering national and local business-related, theme-based topics. *Somerset Business Magazine* is a Chamber of Commerce publication, so the slant is pro-business primarily. Also covers nonprofits, education and other related issues. Estab. 1924. Circ. 6,500. Publishes ms an average of 1 month after acceptance. Editorial lead time 6 weeks. Submit seasonal material 6 weeks in advance. Accepts queries by e-mail. Accepts simultaneous submissions. Responds in 1 week to queries. Sample copy for #10 SASE. Guidelines by email.

NONFICTION Needs humor. Query with published clips. Length: 1,000-1,800 words. **Pays $150 for assigned articles.** Sometimes pays expenses of writers on assignment.

$$ VERMONT BUSINESS MAGAZINE

365 Dorset Street, Burlington VT 05403. (802)863-8038. **Fax:** (802)863-8069. **Website:** www.vermontbiz.com. **Contact:** Tim McQuiston, editor. **80% freelance written**. Monthly tabloid covering business in Vermont. Circ. 8,000. Byline given. Publishes ms an average of 1 month after acceptance. Responds in 2

months to queries. Sample copy for sae with 11×14 envelope and 7 First-Class stamps.

NONFICTION Buys 200 mss/year. Query with published clips. Length: 800-1,800 words. **Pays $100-200.**

CAREER, COLLEGE AND ALUMNI

$$ AFRICAN-AMERICAN CAREER WORLD

Equal Opportunity Publications, Inc., 445 Broad Hollow Rd., Suite 425, Melville NY 11747. (631)421-9421. **Fax:** (631)421-1352. **E-mail:** info@eop.com. **Website:** www.eop.com. **60% freelance written.** Semiannual magazine focused on African-American students and professionals in all disciplines. Estab. 1969. Byline given. Publishes ms an average of 3 months after acceptance. Editorial lead time 3 months. Accepts queries by mail, e-mail, fax, phone. Accepts simultaneous submissions. Sample copy free. Guidelines free.

NONFICTION Needs how-to, get jobs, interview, personal experience. We do not want articles that are too general. Query. Length: 1,500-2,500 words. **Pays $350 for assigned articles.**

$$ AMERICAN CAREERS

Career Communications, Inc., 6701 W. 64th St., Overland Park KS 66202. (800)669-7795. **E-mail:** ccinfor@carcom.com. **Website:** www.carcom.com; www.americancareersonline.com. Jerry Kanabel, art director. **Contact:** Mary Pitchford. **10% freelance written.** "*American Careers* provides career, salary, and education information to middle school and high school students. Self-tests help them relate their interests and abilities to future careers." Estab. 1989. Circ. 500,000. Byline given. Pays 1 month after acceptance. Accepts queries by mail. Accepts simultaneous submissions. Sample copy for $4. Guidelines for #10 SASE.

NONFICTION No "preachy" advice to teens or articles that talk down to students. **Buys 5 mss/year.** Query by mail only with published clips. Length: 300-1,000 words. **Pays $100-450.**

$$ THE BLACK COLLEGIAN

IMDiversity, Inc., 140 Carondelet St., New Orleans LA 70130. (504)523-0154. **Website:** www.blackcollegian.com. **25% freelance written.** Semiannual magazine for African-American college students and recent graduates with an interest in career and job information, African-American cultural awareness, personalities, history, trends, and current events. Estab. 1970. Circ. 122,000. Byline given. Pays 1 month after publication. Submit seasonal material 2 months in advance. Accepts queries by mail. Responds in 6 months to queries. Guidelines for #10 SASE.

NONFICTION Needs book excerpts, exposé, general interest, historical, how-to, develop employability, inspirational, interview, opinion, personal experience. Query. Length: 900-1,900 words. **Pays $100-500 for assigned articles.**

$$ EQUAL OPPORTUNITY

Equal Opportunity Publications, Inc., 445 Broad Hollow Rd., Suite 425, Melville NY 11747. (631)421-9421. **Fax:** (631)421-0359. **E-mail:** jschneider@eop.com. **Website:** www.eop.com. **Contact:** James Schneider, director, editorial and production. **70% freelance written. Prefers to work with published/established writers.** Triannual magazine dedicated to advancing the professional interests of African Americans, Hispanics, Asian Americans, and Native Americans. "Our audience is 90% college juniors and seniors; 10% working graduates. An understanding of educational and career problems of minorities is essential." Estab. 1967. Circ. 11,000. Byline given. Publishes ms an average of 6 months after acceptance. Editorial lead time 6 months. Submit seasonal material 6 months in advance. Accepts queries by mail, e-mail, fax, phone. Responds in 2 weeks to queries. Responds in 1 month to mss. Sample copy and writer's guidelines for 9×12 SAE with 5 first-class stamps.

○ Distributed through college guidance and placement offices.

NONFICTION Needs general interest, specific minority concerns, how-to, job hunting skills, personal finance, better living, coping with discrimination, interview, minority role models, opinion, problems of minorities, personal experience, professional and student study experiences, technical, on career fields offering opportunities for minorites, coverage of minority interests. **Buys 10 mss/year.** Send complete ms. Length: 1,000-2,000 words. **Pays 10¢/word.** Sometimes pays expenses of writers on assignment.

$$$$ HARVARD MAGAZINE

7 Ware St., Cambridge MA 02138-4037. (617)495-5746. **Fax:** (617)495-0324. **E-mail:** harvard_magazine@harvard.edu. **Website:** www.harvardmagazine.com. **Contact:** Jonathan S. Shaw, managing editor. **35-50% freelance written.** Bimonthly magazine for Har-

vard University faculty, alumni, and students. Estab. 1898. Circ. 245,000. Byline given. Publishes ms an average of 4 months after acceptance. Editorial lead time 1 year. Accepts queries by mail, fax. Responds in 1 month. Sample copy available online.

NONFICTION Needs book excerpts, essays, interview, journalism on Harvard-related intellectual subjects. **Buys 20-30 mss/year.** Query with published clips. Length: 800-10,000 words. **Pays $400-3,000.** Pays expenses of writers on assignment.

$$ HISPANIC CAREER WORLD

Equal Opportunity Publications, Inc., 445 Broad Hollow Rd., Suite 425, Melville NY 11747. (631)421-9421. **Fax:** (631)421-1352. **E-mail:** info@eop.com. **Website:** www.eop.com. **Contact:** James Schneider, editorial and production director. **60% freelance written.** Semiannual magazine aimed at Hispanic students and professionals in all disciplines. Estab. 1969. Byline given. Publishes ms an average of 3 months after acceptance. Editorial lead time 3 months. Accepts queries by mail, e-mail, fax, phone. Accepts simultaneous submissions. Responds in 2 weeks to queries. Responds in 2 months to mss. Sample copy free. Guidelines free.

NONFICTION Needs how-to, find jobs, interview, personal experience. Query. Length: 1,500-2,500 words. **Pays $350 for assigned articles.**

$ NEXTSTEPU MAGAZINE

Next Step Publishing, Inc., 2 W. Main St., Suite 200, Victor NY 14564. **E-mail:** info@NextStepU.com. **Website:** www.nextstepmag.com. **75% freelance written.** Bimonthly magazine covering LINK Newsletter, Transfer Guide. "Our magazine is a 5-times-a-school-year objective publication that prepares students for life after high school." Articles cover college, careers, life, and financial aid. Estab. 1995. Circ. distributed in 20,500+ high schools. Editorial lead time 6 months. Submit seasonal material 6 months in advance. Accepts queries by e-mail. NoSample copy available online. Guidelines online a www.nextstepu. com/pdf-handouts/WriterGuidelines.pdf.

NONFICTION Needs book excerpts, general interest, how-to, interview, personal experience, travel. Special issues: *Link* is a newsletter published 5 times a year for high school counselors. Articles run 800-1,500 words and "should be focused on helping counselors do their jobs better." Past articles have included counseling

students with AD/HD, sports scholarships, and motivation tactics.

COLUMNS Contact: Laura Jeanne Hammond. College Planning (college types, making a decision, admissions); Financial Air (scholarships, financial aid options);SAT/ACT (preparing for the SAT/ACT, study tips), 400-1,000 words; Career Profiles (profile at least 3 professionals in different aspects of a specific industry), 800-1,000 words; Military (careers in the military, different branches, how to join), 400-600 words.

$$$$ NOTRE DAME MAGAZINE

University of Notre Dame, 538 Grace Hall, Notre Dame IN 46556-5612. (574)631-5335. **E-mail:** nd-mag@nd.edu. **Website:** magazine.nd.edu. Kerry Prugh, art director. **50% freelance written.** "We are a university magazine with a scope as broad as that found at a university, but we place our discussion in a moral, ethical, and spiritual context reflecting our Catholic heritage." Estab. 1972. Circ. 150,000. Byline given. Publishes ms an average of 1 year after acceptance. Accepts queries by mail, e-mail, fax. Responds in 2 months to queries. Sample copy available online and by request. Guidelines available online.

NONFICTION Needs opinion, personal experience, religious. **Buys 35 mss/year.** Query with published clips. Length: 600-3,000 words. **Pays $250-3,000.** Sometimes pays expenses of writers on assignment.

COLUMNS CrossCurrents (essays, deal with a wide array of issues—some topical, some personal, some serious, some light). Query with or without published clips or send complete ms.

$$ OREGON QUARTERLY

5228 University of Oregon, Eugene OR 97403. (541)346-5048. **Fax:** (541)346-5571. **E-mail:** quarterly@uoregon.edu. **Website:** www.oregonquarterly. com. **85% freelance written**. Quarterly magazine covering people and ideas at the University of Oregon and the Northwest. Estab. 1919. Circ. 100,000. Byline given. Offers 20% kill fee. Publishes ms an average of 3 months after acceptance. Accepts queries by mail (preferred), e-mail ("grumpily"). True; Only for excerpts sectionResponds in 2 months to queries Sample copy for 9×12 SAE with 4 first-class stamps. Guidelines available online.

NONFICTION Buys 30 mss/year. Query with published clips. Length: 300-3,000 words. **Payment varies—30¢-50C/per word for departments; fea-**

tures more. Sometimes pays expenses of writers on assignment.

FICTION Rarely publishes novel excerpts by UO professors or grads.

[C] $$ QUEEN'S ALUMNI REVIEW

Queen's University, 99 University Ave., Kingston ON K7L 3N6 Canada. **Fax:** (613)533-2060. **E-mail:** ken.cuthbertson@queensu.ca. **Website:** http://alumnireview.queensu.ca. **25% freelance written.** Quarterly magazine. Estab. 1927. Circ. 118,000. Byline given. Publishes ms an average of 3 months after acceptance. Editorial lead time 3 months. Submit seasonal material 9 months in advance. Accepts queries by mail, e-mail. Responds in 2 weeks to queries. Responds in 2 weeks to mss. Sample copy and writer's guidelines online.

NONFICTION "Does not want religious or political rants, travel articles, how-to, or general interest pieces that do not refer to or make some reference to our core audience." **Buys 10 mss/year.** Send complete ms. Length: 200-2,500 words. **Pays 50¢/word (Canadian), plus 10% e-rights fee for assigned articles.** Sometimes pays expenses of writers on assignment.

COLUMNS "Potential freelancers should study our magazine before submitting a query for a column." **Buys 10 mss/year.** Query with published clips or send complete ms. **Pays 50¢/word (Canadian), plus a 10% e-right fee.**

$$$ UAB MAGAZINE

UAB Publications and Periodicals (University of Alabama at Birmingham), AB 340, 1530 3rd Ave. S., Birmingham AL 35294-0103. (205)934-9420. **Fax:** (205)975-4416. **E-mail:** mwindsor@uab.edu;charlesb@uab.edu; periodicals@uab.edu. **Website:** www.uab.edu/uabmagazine. **Contact:** Matt Windsor, editor. **70% freelance written.** University magazine published 3 times/year covering University of Alabama at Birmingham. *UAB Magazine* informs readers about the innovation and creative energy that drives UAB's renowned research, educational, and health care programs. The magazine reaches active alumni, faculty, friends and donors, patients, corporate and community leaders, media and the public. Estab. 1980. Circ. 33,000. Byline given. Offers 50% kill fee. Publishes ms an average of 3-4 months after acceptance. Editorial lead time 3 months. Accepts queries by mail, e-mail. Sample copy available online. Guidelines free.

NONFICTION Needs general interest, interview. **Buys 40-50 mss/year.** Query with published clips. Length: 500-5,000 words. **Pays $100-1,200.** Sometimes pays expenses of writers on assignment.

$$ WORKFORCE DIVERSITY FOR ENGINEERING & IT PROFESSIONALS

Equal Opportunity Publications, Inc., 445 Broad Hollow Rd., Suite 425, Melville NY 11747. (631)421-9421. **Fax:** (631)421-1352. **E-mail:** info@eop.com. **Website:** www.eop.com. **60% freelance written.** Quarterly magazine addressing workplace issues affecting technical professional women, members of minority groups, and people with disabilities. Estab. 1969. Byline given. Publishes ms an average of 3 months after acceptance. Editorial lead time 3 months. Accepts queries by mail, e-mail, fax, phone. Accepts simultaneous submissions. Responds in 2 weeks to queries. Responds in 2 months to mss. Sample copy free. Guidelines free.

NONFICTION Needs how-to, find jobs, interview, personal experience. We do not want articles that are too general. Query. Length: 1,500-2,500 words. **Pays $350 for assigned articles.**

CHILD CARE AND PARENTAL GUIDANCE

$$$ AMERICAN BABY MAGAZINE

Meredith Corp., 375 Lexington Ave., 9th Floor, New York NY 10017. **E-mail:** abletters@americanbaby.com. **Website:** www.americanbaby.com. **70% freelance written.** Monthly magazine covering health, medical and childcare concerns for expectant and new parents, particularly those having their first child or those whose child is between the ages of birth and 2 years old. Mothers are the primary readers, but fathers' issues are equally important. Estab. 1938. Circ. 2,000,000. Byline given. Offers 25% kill fee. Publishes ms an average of 6 months after acceptance. Editorial lead time 5 months. Submit seasonal material 6 months in advance. Accepts queries by mail. Responds in 3 months to queries. Responds in 3 months to mss. Sample copy for 9×12 SAE with 6 first-class stamps. Guidelines for #10 sase.

- Prefers to work with published/established writers; works with a small number of new/unpublished writers each year.

NONFICTION Needs book excerpts, essays, general interest, how-to, some aspect of pregnancy or child

CONSUMER MAGAZINES

care, humor, new product, personal experience, fitness, beauty, health. No 'hearts and flowers' or fantasy pieces. **Buys 60 mss/year.** Send complete ms. Length: 1,000-2,000 words. **Pays $750-1,200 for assigned articles. Pays $600-800 for unsolicited articles.** Pays expenses of writers on assignment.

COLUMNS Personal essays (700-1,000 words) and shorter items for Crib Notes (news and features) and Health Briefs (50-150 words) are also accepted. **Pays $200-1,000.**

ATLANTA PARENT/ATLANTA BABY

2346 Perimeter Park Dr., Suite 100, Atlanta GA 30341. (770)454-7599. **E-mail:** atlantaparent@atlantaparent.com. **Website:** www.atlantaparent.com. **50% freelance written.** Byline given. Publishes ms an average of 3 months after acceptance. Submit seasonal material 6 months in advance. Accepts queries by mail, e-mail. Responds in 4 months to queries. Sample copy for $3.

NONFICTION Needs general interest, how-to, humor, interview, travel. Special issues: Private School (January); Camp (February); Birthday Parties (March and September); Maternity and Mothering (May and October); Childcare (July); Back-to-School (August); Teens (September); Holidays (November/December). No religious or philosophical discussions. **Buys 60 mss/year.** Send complete ms. Length: 800-1,500 words. **Pays $5-50.** Sometimes pays expenses of writers on assignment.

BABY TALK

Bonnier Corp., 460 No. Orlando Ave., Suite 200, Winter Park FL 32789. (212)522-4327. **Fax:** (212)522-8699. **E-mail:** letters@babytalk.com. **Website:** www.babytalk.com. Estab. 1935. Circ. 2,000,000. Byline given. Accepts queries by mail, online submission form. Responds in 2 months to queries.

Magazine published 10 times/year. *Baby Talk* is written primarily for women who are considering pregnancy or who are expecting a child, and parents of children from birth through 18 months, with the emphasis on pregnancy through first 6 months of life.

NONFICTION No phone calls. Query with SASE Length: 1,000-2,000 words. **Pays $500-2,000 depending on length, degree of difficulty, and the writer's experience.**

COLUMNS Several departments are written by regular contributors. 100-1,250 words. Query with SASE **Pays $100-1,000.**

BIRMINGHAM PARENT

Evans Publishing LLC, 700-C Southgate Dr., Pelham AL 35124. (205)739-0090. **Fax:** (205)739-0073. **E-mail:** editor@birminghamparent.com; carol@biringhamparent.com. **Website:** www.birminghamparent.com. **Contact:** Carol Muse Evans, publisher/editor; Lori Chandler Pruitt, associate editor. **75% freelance written.** Monthly magazine covering family issues, parenting, education, babies to teens, health care, anything involving parents raising children. "We are a free, local parenting publication in central Alabama. All of our stories carry some type of local slant. Parenting magazines abound: we are the source for the local market." Estab. 2004. Circ. 40,000. Byline given. Pays within 30 days of publication. Offers 20% kill fee. Publishes ms an average of 3-4 months after acceptance. Editorial lead time 3-4 months. Submit seasonal material 4 months in advance. Accepts queries by e-mail. Accepts simultaneous submissions. Responds in 2-3 weeks to queries. Responds in 2-3 months to mss. Sample copy for $3. Guidelines available online.

NONFICTION Needs book excerpts, general interest, how-to, interview, parenting. Does not want first person pieces. Our pieces educate and inform: we don't take stories without sources. **Buys 24 mss/year.** Send complete ms. Length: 350-2,500 words. **Pays $50-350 for assigned articles. Pays $35-200 for unsolicited articles.**

COLUMNS Parenting Solo (single parenting), 650 words; Baby & Me (dealing with newborns or pregnancy), 650 words; Teens (raising teenagers), 650-1,500 words. **Buys 36 mss/year.** Query with published clips or send complete ms. **Pays $35-200.**

CHESAPEAKE FAMILY

Jefferson Communications, 929 West St., Suite 307, Annapolis MD 21401. (410)263-1641. **Fax:** (410)280-0255. **E-mail:** editor@chesapeakefamily.com; calendar@chesapeakefamily.com. **Website:** www.chesapeakefamily.com. **Contact:** Betsy Stein, editor; Karen Gaspers, calendar editor. **80% freelance written.** Monthly magazine covering parenting. *Chesapeake Family* is a free, regional parenting publication serving readers in the Anne Arundel, Calvert, Prince George's, and Queen Anne's counties of Maryland. Our goal is to identify tips, resources, and products that will make our readers' lives easier. We answer the questions they don't have time to ask, doing the research for them so they have the information they need to make better decisions for their families' health, education, and well-being. Articles must have local angle and resources. Estab. 1990. Circ. 40,000. Byline given. Publishes ms an average of 2 months after acceptance. Editorial lead time 3-6 months. Submit seasonal material 4 months in advance. Accepts queries by mail, e-mail, fax. Accepts simultaneous submissions. Guidelines available online.

NONFICTION Needs how-to, parenting topics: sign your kids up for sports, find out if your child needs braces, etc., interview, local personalities, travel, family-fun destinations. No general, personal essays (however, personal anecdotes leading into a story with general applicability is fine). **Buys 25 mss/year.** Send complete ms. Length: 800-1,200 words. **Pays $75-125. Pays $35-50 for unsolicited articles.**

⊛⊛ CHICAGO PARENT

141 S. Oak Park Ave., Oak Park IL 60302. (708)386-5555. **Website:** www.chicagoparent.com. **Contact:** Tamara O'Shaughnessy, editor. **60% freelance written.** Monthly tabloid. "*Chicago Parent* has a distinctly local approach. We offer information, inspiration, perspective and empathy to Chicago-area parents. Our lively editorial mix has a 'we're all in this together' spirit, and articles are thoroughly researched and well written." Estab. 1988. Circ. 125,000 in 3 zones covering the 6-county Chicago metropolitan area. Byline given. Offers 10-50% kill fee. Publishes ms an average of 2 months after acceptance. Editorial lead time 4 months. Submit seasonal material 4 months in advance. Accepts queries by mail. Responds in 6 weeks to queries. Sample copy for $3.95 and 11×17 SAE with $1.65 postage. Guidelines for #10 SASE.

NONFICTION Needs essays, exposé, how-to, parent-related, humor, interview, travel, local interest. Special issues: include Chicago Baby and Healthy Child. No pot-boiler parenting pieces, simultaneous submissions, previously published pieces or non-local writers (from outside the 6-county Chicago metropolitan area). **Buys 40-50 mss/year.** Query with published clips. Length: 200-2,500 words. **Pays $25-300 for assigned articles. Pays $25-100 for unsolicited articles.** Pays expenses of writers on assignment.

COLUMNS Healthy Child (kids' health issues), 850 words; Getaway (travel pieces), up to 1,200 words; other columns not open to freelancers. **Buys 30 mss/year.** Query with published clips or send complete ms. **Pays $100.**

⊛⊛ COLUMBUS PARENT MAGAZINE

Consumer News Service, 34 S. Third St., Columbus OH 43215. (614)461-8878. **E-mail:** jhawes@columbusparent.com. **Website:** www.columbusparent.com. **Contact:** Jane Hawes, editor. **50% freelance written.** Monthly magazine covering parenting. A hip, reliable resource for Central Ohio parents who are raising children from birth to 18. Estab. 1988. Circ. 60,000. Byline given. Offers 10% kill fee. Publishes ms an average of 2 months after acceptance. Editorial lead time 3 months. Submit seasonal material 5 months in advance. Accepts queries by mail, e-mail, fax. Sample copy available online. Guidelines available online.

NONFICTION Needs general interest, how-to, interview, new product. Does not want personal essays. **Buys 80 mss/year.** Send complete ms. Length: 500-900 words. **Pays 10¢/word.**

⊛⊛⊛⊛ DISNEY FAMILYFUN

Disney Publishing, Inc., 47 Pleasant St., Northampton MA 01060. (413)585-0444. **Fax:** (413)586-5724. **E-mail:** queries.familyfun@disney.com. **Website:** www.familyfun.com. Magazine covering activities for families with kids ages 3-12. "*Diseny FamilyFun* is about all the great things families can do together. Our writers are either parents or authorities in a covered field." Estab. 1991. Circ. 2,100,000. Byline sometimes given. Offers 25% kill fee. Editorial lead time 6 months. Submit seasonal material 6 months in advance. Accepts simultaneous submissions. Responds in 3 months to queries. Sample copy for $5. Guidelines available online.

NONFICTION Needs book excerpts, essays, general interest, how-to, crafts, cooking, educational activities, humor, interview, personal experience, photo feature, travel. **Buys dozens of mss/year.** "Query with published clips. Articles are scheduled and assigned at least 5 months in advance of publication. Please send mss and queries by e-mail or standard mail only—not by telephone or fax. We do not accept unsolicited mss for feature stories; we do accept unsolicited mss for the following departments: Let's Go and Success Story. Queries should describe the content, structure, and tone of the proposed article. We receive many queries on the same topics, so please be as specific as possible about what makes your idea unique and why you are qualified to write about it. If appropriate, include photographs or sketches of the finished project, food, or craft. Due to the large volume of submissions, allow

6-8 weeks for a response. Supporting materials, such as photographs and clips, will be returned if accompanied by SASE with correct postage. Please note: Editorial responses to submissions will be sent via e-mail, so please provide an address for our reply." Length: 850-3,000 words. **Pays $1.25/word.** Pays expenses of writers on assignment.

COLUMNS "Everyday Fun: Debbie Way, senior editor (simple, quick, practical, inexpensive ideas and projects—outings, crafts, games, nature activities, learning projects, and cooking with children), 200-400 words; query or send ms; **pays per word or $200 for ideas.** Family Getaways: Becky Karush, associate editor (brief, newsy items about family travel, what's new, what's great, and especially, what's a good deal), 100-125 words; send ms; **pays per word or $50 for ideas.** Creative Solutions: Debra Immergut, senior editor (explains fun and inventive ideas that have worked for writer's own family), 1,000 words; query or send ms; **pays $1,250 on acceptance.** Also publishes best letters from writers and readers following column, send to My Great Idea: From Our Readers Editor, 100-150 words, **pays $100 on publication**." **Buys 60-80 letters/year; 10-12 mss/year.**

$ GRAND RAPIDS FAMILY MAGAZINE

Gemini Publications, 549 Ottawa Ave. NW, Suite 201, Grand Rapids MI 49503-1444. (616)459-4545. **Fax:** (616)459-4800. **E-mail:** cvalade@geminipub.com. **Website:** www.grfamily.com. **Contact:** Carole Valade. Monthly magazine covering local parenting issues. *Grand Rapids Family* seeks to inform, instruct, amuse, and entertain its readers and their families. Circ. 30,000. Byline given. Offers $25 kill fee. Editorial lead time 3 months. Submit seasonal material 4 months in advance. Accepts simultaneous submissions. Responds in 2 months to queries. Responds in 6 months to mss. Guidelines with #10 SASE.

NONFICTION Query. **Pays $25-50.**

COLUMNS All local: law, finance, humor, opinion, mental health. **Pays $25**

$ HOME EDUCATION MAGAZINE

P.O. Box 1083, Tonasket WA 98855. (800)236-3278; (509)486-1351. **Fax:** (509)486-2753. **E-mail:** articles@homeedmag.com. **Website:** www.homeedmag.com. **Contact:** Jeanne Faulconer, articles editor. **80% freelance written**. Bimonthly magazine covering home-based education. "We feature articles which address the concerns of parents who want to take a direct involvement in the education of their children—concerns such as socialization, how to find curriculums and materials, testing and evaluation, how to tell when your child is ready to begin reading, what to do when homeschooling is difficult, teaching advanced subjects, etc." Estab. 1983. Circ. 120,000. Byline given. Publishes ms an average of 6 months after acceptance. Submit seasonal material 6 months in advance. Accepts queries by mail. Responds in 2 months to queries. Sample copy for $6.50. Writer's guidelines with #10 SASE, via e-mail, or on website.

NONFICTION Needs essays, how-to, related to homeschooling, humor, interview, personal experience, photo feature, technical. **Buys 40-50 mss/year.** Send complete ms. Length: 750-2,500 words. **Pays $50-150.**

$ HOMESCHOOLING TODAY

P.O. Box 244, Abingdon VA 24212. (866)804-4478; 276-466-4478. **Fax:** (888)333-4478. **E-mail:** management@homeschooltoday.com. **Website:** www.homeschooltoday.com. **Contact:** Steve Murphy, publisher; Charles Humphrey, executive director; Marilyn Rockett, editor-in-chief; Erika Schanzenbach, art and design director. **75% freelance written**. Bimonthly magazine covering homeschooling. "We are a practical magazine for homeschoolers with a broadly Christian perspective." Estab. 1992. Circ. 13,000. Byline given. Offers 25% kill fee. Publishes ms an average of 1 year after acceptance. Editorial lead time 6 months. Submit seasonal material 1 year in advance. Accepts simultaneous submissions. Responds in 4 months to mss. Sample copy free. Guidelines available online at website.

NONFICTION Needs book excerpts, how-to, interview, new product. No fiction. **Buys 30 mss/year.** Send complete ms. Length: 500-2,000 words. **Pays 10¢/word.**

$ HUDSON VALLEY PARENT

The Professional Image, 174 South St., Newburgh NY 12550. **E-mail:** editor@excitingread.com. **Website:** www.hvparent.com. **95% freelance written**. Monthly magazine covering parents and families. Estab. 1994. Circ. 80,000. Byline given. Publishes ms an average of 3 months after acceptance. Editorial lead time 4 months. Submit seasonal material 4 months in advance. Accepts queries by e-mail. Responds in 2-4 weeks to mss. Sample copy free. Guidelines available online.

NONFICTION Needs exposé, general interest, humor, interview, personal experience. **Buys 20 mss/yr. mss/year.** Query. Length: 700-1,200 words. **Pays $70-120 for assigned articles. Pays $25-35 for unsolicited articles.**

☺☻ INDY'S CHILD MAGAZINE

Midwest Parenting Publications, 921 E. 86th St., Suite 130, Indianapolis IN 46240. **Website:** www.indyschild.com. **100% freelance written.** Monthly magazine covering a myriad of parenting topics and pieces of information relative to families and children in greater Cincinnati and Indianapolis. Sister publication is *Cincinnati Parent.* Estab. 1985. Byline given. Publishes ms an average of 6 months after acceptance. Editorial lead time 3 months. Submit seasonal material 6 months in advance. Accepts queries by mail, e-mail. Guidelines available online. "We ask that you read this entire page then complete the writer's agreement by clicking on the link at the bottom (or top) of the page. Please note that you must follow these guidelines for every piece of editorial that is submitted to our office. Failure to do so may prevent us from using your editorial."

Articles submitted should address current parenting issues with an Indianapolis and/or Cincinnati tie-in whenever possible. Strong emphasis is placed on how and where to find family-oriented events, as well as goods and services for children, in Central Indiana and the Cincinnati area.

NONFICTION Needs exposé, general interest, historical, how-to, family projects, crafts, humor, inspirational, interview, opinion, photo feature, travel. **Buys 50 mss/year.** Send complete ms. **Pays .10 cents per word for first publication rights to an article and no more. Feature articles must be no less than 1500-2000 words. Fees include the rights to use your article once published.**

COLUMNS Most Indy's Child Parenting Magazine articles are purchased from freelance writers. In a typical issue, readers will find a variety of regular columns. We also run two to three feature articles at 1500 words per article and six - 10 shorter articles at about 500-800 words per article which are reprints only. The topics must pertain to Indiana parents and families in general. Features consistently require indepth research and interviews with sources in Indiana (or Cincinnati, Ohio for our sister publication). Rave Reviews, Publisher's Note, Women's Health, Museum Note, Local Profiles, News You Can Use, Mayor's column, and more.

☯☻ ISLAND PARENT MAGAZINE

Island Parent Group, 830 Pembroke St., Suite A-10, Victoria BC V8T 1H9 Canada. (250)388-6905. **Fax:** (250)388-6920. **E-mail:** mail@islandparent.ca. **Website:** www.islandparent.ca. **Contact:** Sue Fast, editor. **98% freelance written.** Monthly magazine covering parenting. Estab. 1988. Circ. 20,000. Byline given. honorium. Publishes ms an average of 3 months after acceptance. Editorial lead time 3 months. Submit seasonal material 3 months in advance. Accepts queries by e-mail. Responds in 4-6 weeks to queries. Sample copy available online. Guidelines available online.

NONFICTION Contact: Sue Fast. Needs book excerpts, essays, general interest, how-to, humor, inspirational, interview, opinion, (does not mean letters to the editor), personal experience, travel. **Buys 80 mss/year.** Query. Length: 400-1,800 words. **Pays $35 for assigned articles. Pays $35 for unsolicited articles.**

FILLERS Needs anecdotes, facts, gags, newsbreaks, short humor. **Buys 10/year mss/year.** Length: 400-650 words. **Pays $35.**

☻ LIVING

Shalom Foundation, 1251 Virginia Ave., Harrisonburg VA 22802. **E-mail:** mediaforliving@gmail.com. **Website:** www.churchoutreach.com. **90% freelance written**. Quarterly tabloid covering family living. Articles focus on giving general encouragement for families of all ages and stages. Estab. 1985. Circ. 250,000. Byline given. Publishes ms an average of 6-12 months after acceptance. Editorial lead time 4-6 months. Submit seasonal material 6 months in advance. Accepts queries by mail, e-mail. Accepts simultaneous submissions. Responds in 2 months to queries. Responds in 2-4 months to mss. Sample copy for sae with 9×12 envelope and 4 First-Class stamps. Guidelines free.

"We want our stories and articles to be very practical and upbeat. Since we go to every home, we do not assume a Christian audience. Writers need to take this into account. Personal experience stories are welcome, but are not the only approach.Our audience? Children, teenagers, singles, married couples, right on through to retired persons. We cover the wide variety of subjects that people face in the home and workplace. (See theme list in our guidelines online.)"

NONFICTION Needs general interest, how-to, humor, inspirational, personal experience. We do not use devotional materials intended for Christian audiences. We seldom use pet stories and receive way too many grief/death/dealing with serious illness stories to use. We encourage stories from non-white writers (excuse the phrase). We publish in March, June, September, and December so holidays that occur in other months are not usually the subject of articles. **Buys 48-52 mss/year.** Query. Length: 500-1,200 words. **Pays $35-60.**

💲 **METROFAMILY MAGAZINE**

Inprint Publishing, 725 NW 11th St., Suite 204, Oklahoma City OK 73103. (405)3601-2081. **E-mail:** editor@metrofamilymagazine.com. **Website:** www.metrofamilymagazine.com. **Contact:** Mari Farthing, editor. **20% freelance written.** Monthly tabloid covering parenting. Circ. 35,000. Byline given. No kill fee; assignments given to local writers only. Publishes ms an average of 2-3 months after acceptance. Editorial lead time 3-6 months. Accepts queries by e-mail. Accepts simultaneous submissions. Responds in 3 weeks to queries (only if interested). Responds in 1 month to mss. Sample copy for sae with 10×13 envelope and 3 first-class stamps. Guidelines via e-mail or return with #10 SASE.

NONFICTION Family or mom-specific articles; see website for themes. No poetry, fiction (except for humor column), or anything that doesn't support good, solid family values. Send complete ms. Submit via e-mail only. Length: 800-1200 words. **Pays $40-60, plus 1 contributor's copy.**

💲💲 **METRO PARENT MAGAZINE**

Metro Parent Publishing Group, 22041 Woodward Ave., Ferndale MI 48220-2520. (248)398-3400. **Fax:** (248)3399-3970. **E-mail:** jelliott@metroparent.com; kkovelle@metroparent.com. **Website:** www.metroparent.com. **Contact:** Julia Elliott, executive editor; Kim Kovelle, associate editor. **75% freelance written.** Monthly magazine covering parenting, women's health, education. "MetroParent.com is an online parenting community offering expert advice, stories on parenting trends and issues, and numerous ways for parents to enrich their experience raising the next generation. It is part of Metro Parent Publishing Group, which began in suburban Detroit in 1986. Publications include Metro Parent magazine, Metro Baby, Going Places, Special Edition, Party Book and Big Book of Schools. Metro Parent Publishing Group

also brings family-friendly events to southeast Michigan as part of its events department." Circ. 80,000. Byline given. Publishes ms an average of 3 months after acceptance. Editorial lead time 3 months. Submit seasonal material 3 months in advance. Accepts queries by mail, e-mail. Accepts simultaneous submissions. Responds in 2 weeks to queries. Responds in 3 months to mss. Sample copy for $2.50.

NONFICTION Needs essays, humor, inspirational, personal experience. **Buys 100 mss/year.** Send complete ms. Length: 1,500-2,500 words. **Pays $50-300 for assigned articles.**

COLUMNS Women's Health (latest issues of 20-40 year olds), 750-900 words; Solo Parenting (advice for single parents); Family Finance (making sense of money and legal issues); Tweens 'N Teens (handling teen issues), 750-800 words. **Buys 50 mss/year.** Send complete ms. **Pays $75-150.**

💲💲 **PARENT:WISE AUSTIN**

Pleticha Publishing Inc., 7301 Ranch Rd. 620 N, Suite 155, 388, Austin TX 78726. (877)MAMA-304. **Fax:** (866)MAMA-591. **E-mail:** editor@parentwiseaustin.com. **Website:** www.parentwiseaustin.com. **25% freelance written.** Monthly magazine covering parenting news, features and issues; mothering issues; maternal feminism; feminism as it pertains to motherhood and work/life balance; serious/thoughtful essays about the parenting experience; humor articles pertaining to the parenting experience. "*Parent:Wise Austin* targets educated, thoughtful readers who want solid information about the parenting experience. We seek to create a warm, nurturing community by providing excellent, well researched articles, thoughtful essays, humor articles, and other articles appealing to parents. Our readers demand in-depth, well written articles; we do not accept, nor will we print, 're-worked' articles on boiler plate topics." Estab. 2004. Circ. 32,000. Byline given. Publishes ms an average of 2 months after acceptance. Editorial lead time 6 months. Submit seasonal material 6 months in advance. Accepts queries by e-mail. NoResponds in 1 week to queries. Responds in 1 month to mss. Sample copy for $1.50 postage. "However, sample copies can be viewed online." Guidelines available online.

NONFICTION Needs essays, humor, opinion, personal experience, travel, hard news, features on parenting issues. Special issues: Mother's Day issue (May); Father's Day issue (June). "Does not want boiler plate articles or generic articles that have been customized for our market." **Buys 12-20 mss/year.** All articles should be submitted in their entirety—no queries—via email. You should receive a response within 60-days (if not, please email us again to ensure that we received your submission). Please do NOT send us your article via snail mail (snail-mailed submissions will not be read or returned). Length: 500-2,500 words. **Pays $50-200.** Sometimes pays expenses of writers on assignment.

COLUMNS My Life as a Parent (humor), 500-700 words; Essay (first-person narrative), 500-1,000 words. **Buys 24-50 mss/year.** Send complete ms. **Pays $50.**

POETRY Needs avant-garde, free verse, haiku, light verse, traditional. "Does not want poetry that does not pertain to parenting or the parenting experience." Buys 3-5 poems/year. Submit maximum 3 poems. Length: 25 lines.

❸❸❸❸ PARENTING MAGAZINE (EARLY YEARS AND SCHOOL YEARS EDITIONS)

Bonnier Corporation, 2 Park Ave., 10th Floor, New York NY 10016. (212)779-5000. **Website:** www.parenting.com. Magazine published 10 times/year for mothers of children from birth to 12, and covering both the emotional and practical aspects of parenting. Estab. 1987. Circ. 2,100,000. Byline given. Offers 25% kill fee. Accepts queries by mail. Responds in 2 months. Samples not available. Guidelines for #10 SASE.

NONFICTION Contact: Articles Editor. Needs book excerpts, personal experience, child development/behavior/health. **Buys 20-30 mss/year.** Query. Length: 1,000-2,500 words. **Pays $1,000-3,000.** Pays expenses of writers on assignment.

COLUMNS Contact: Query to the specific departmental editor. **Buys 50-60 mss/year.** Query. **Pays $50-400.**

❸ PEDIATRICS FOR PARENTS

Pediatrics for Parents, Inc., 35 Starknaught Heights, Gloucester MA 01930. (215)253-4543. **Fax:** (973)302-4543. **E-mail:** richsagall@pedsforparents.com. **Website:** www.pedsforparents.com. **50% freelance written.** Monthly newsletter covering children's health. "*Pediatrics For Parents* emphasizes an informed, common-sense approach to childhood health care. We stress preventative action, accident prevention, when to call the doctor and when and how to handle a situation at home. We are also looking for articles that describe general, medical and pediatric problems, advances, new treatments, etc. All articles must be medically accurate and useful to parents with children—prenatal to adolescence." Estab. 1981. Circ. 120,000. Byline given. Publishes ms an average of 4 months after acceptance. Accepts queries by mail, e-mail, fax. Accepts simultaneous submissions. Responds in 1 month to queries. Sample copy available online. Guidelines available online.

NONFICTION No first person or experience. **Buys 25 mss/year.** Send complete ms. Length: 1,000-1,500 words. **Pays $10-25.**

❸ PIKES PEAK PARENT

The Gazette/Freedom Communications, 30 S. Prospect St., Colorado Springs CO 80903. **Fax:** (719)476-1625. **E-mail:** trudy@pikespeakparent.com. **Website:** www.pikespeakparent.com. **10% freelance written.** Monthly tabloid covering parenting, family and grandparenting. We prefer stories with local angle and local stories. We do not accept unsolicited manuscripts. Estab. 1994. Circ. 35,000. Byline given. Editorial lead time 3 months. Submit seasonal material 4 months in advance. Accepts queries by e-mail. Accepts simultaneous submissions. Responds in 1 month to queries. Sample copy available online.

NONFICTION Needs essays, general interest, how-to, medical related to parenting. **Buys 10 mss/year.** Query with published clips. Length: 800-1,000 words. **Pays $20-120.**

❸❸❸ PLUM MAGAZINE

Groundbreak Publishing, 276 Fifth Ave., Suite 302, New York NY 10001. (212)725-9201. **Fax:** (212)725-9203. **E-mail:** editor@plummagazine.com. **Website:** www.plummagazine.com. **90% freelance written.** Semi-annual magazine covering health and lifestyle for pregnant women over age 35. *Plum* is a patient education tool meant to be an adjunct to obstetrics care. It presents information on preconception, prenatal medical care, nutrition, fitness, beauty, fashion, decorating, and travel. It also covers newborn health with articles on baby wellness, nursery necessities, postpartum care, and more. Estab. 2004. Circ. 450,000. Byline sometimes given. Offers 20% kill fee. Publishes ms an average of 3-6 months after acceptance. Editorial lead time 6 months. Submit seasonal material 8 months in advance. Accepts queries by e-mail. Responds in 6 weeks to queries. Sample copy for $7.95. Guidelines by email.

NONFICTION Needs essays, how-to, interview. Query with published clips. Length: 300-3,500 words. **Pays 75¢-$1/word**

💲 SACRAMENTO PARENT

Family Publishing Inc., 457 Grass Valley Hwy., Suite 5, Auburn CA 95603. (530)888-0573. **Fax:** (530)888-1536. **E-mail:** lisa@sacramentoparent.com. **Website:** www.sacramentoparent.com. **Contact:** Lisa Thibodeau, editor. **50% freelance written.** Monthly magazine covering parenting in the Sacramento region. We look for articles that promote a developmentally appropriate, healthy and peaceful environment for children. Estab. 1992. Circ. 50,000. Byline given. Offers 10% kill fee. Publishes ms an average of 2 months after acceptance. Editorial lead time 3 months. Submit seasonal material 4 months in advance. Accepts queries by e-mail. Sample copy free. Guidelines by e-mail.

NONFICTION Needs book excerpts, general interest, how-to, humor, interview, opinion, personal experience. **Buys 36 mss/year.** Query. Length: 300-1,000 words. **Pays $50-200 for original articles.**

COLUMNS Let's Go! (Sacramento regional family-friendly day trips/excursions/activities), 600 words. **Pays $25-45.**

💲 SAN DIEGO FAMILY MAGAZINE

1475 Sixth Ave., 5th Floor, San Diego CA 92101-3200. (619)685-6970. **Fax:** (619)685-6978. **E-mail:** family@sandiegofamily.com. **Website:** www.sandiegofamily.com. **100% freelance written.** Monthly magazine for parenting and family issues. "*SDFM* is a regional family publication. We focus on providing current, informative and interesting editorial about parenting and family life that educates and entertains." Estab. 1982. Circ. 300,000. Byline given. Publishes ms an average of 1-6 months after acceptance. Editorial lead time 4 months. Submit seasonal material 6 months in advance. Accepts queries by mail, e-mail. Accepts simultaneous submissions. Responds in 1 month to queries. Responds in 2 months to mss. Sample copy for $4.50 to P.O. Box 23960, San Diego CA 92193. Guidelines available online.

NONFICTION Needs essays, general interest, how-to, interview, technical, travel, informational articles. Does not want humorous personal essays, opinion pieces, religious or spiritual. **Buys 350-500 mss/year.** Query. Length: 600-1,250 words. **Pays $22-90.**

FICTION "No adult fiction. We only want to see short fiction written for children: 'read aloud' stories, sto-

ries for beginning readers (400-500 words)." **Buys 0-12 fillers. mss/year.** Send complete ms.

💲 SCHOLASTIC PARENT & CHILD

Scholastic, Inc., 557 Broadway, New York NY 10012. (212)343-6100. **Fax:** (212)343-4801. **E-mail:** parentandchild@scholastic.com. **Website:** parentandchildonline.com. **Contact:** Nick Friedman, editor-in-chief. Bimonthly magazine published to keep active parents up-to-date on children's learning and development while in pre-school or child-care environment. Circ. 1,224,098. Editorial lead time 10 weeks.

💲💲 SOUTH FLORIDA PARENTING

1701 Green Rd., Suite B, Deerfield Beach FL 33441. (954)596-5607. **Fax:** (954)429-1207. **E-mail:** krlomer@tribune.com. **Website:** www.sfparenting.com. **Contact:** Kyara Lomer, editor. **90% freelance written.** Monthly magazine covering parenting, family. "*South Florida Parenting* provides news, information, and a calendar of events for readers in Southeast Florida (Palm Beach, Broward and Miami-Dade counties). The focus is on parenting issues, things to do, information about raising children in South Florida." Estab. 1990. Circ. 110,000. Byline given. Editorial lead time 4 months. Submit seasonal material 4 months in advance. Accepts queries by e-mail, fax. Responds in 3 months to queries.

○ Preference given to writers based in South Florida.

NONFICTION Needs how-to (parenting issues), interview/profile, family, parenting and children's issues. Special issues: family fitness, education, spring party guide, fall party guide, kids and the environment, toddler/preschool, preteen. Length: 500-1,000 words. **Pays $40-165.**

REPRINTS Pays $25-50.

COLUMNS Dad's Perspective, Family Deals, Products for Families, Health/Safety, Nutrition, Baby Basics, Travel, Toddler/Preschool, Preteen, South Florida News.

💲💲 SOUTHWEST FLORIDA PARENT & CHILD

The News-Press, A Gannett Company, 2442 Dr. Martin Luther King, Jr. Blvd., Fort Myers FL 33901. (239)335-0200. **Fax:** (239)344-0708. **E-mail:** editor@swflparentchild.com; phayford@Fortmyer.gannett.com. **Website:** http://news-press.com/moms. **Contact:** Pamela Smith Hayford, editor. **75% freelance written.** Monthly magazine covering parenting.

"*Southwest Florida Parent & Child* is a regional parenting magazine with an audience of mostly moms but some dads, too. With every article, we strive to give readers information they can use. We aim to be an indispensable resource for our local parents." Estab. 2000. Circ. 25,000. Byline given. Publishes ms an average of 2-3 months after acceptance. Editorial lead time 2-3 months. Submit seasonal material 3+ months in advance. Accepts queries by mail, e-mail, fax. Accepts simultaneous submissions.

NONFICTION Needs book excerpts, general interest, how-to, humor, interview, new product, personal experience, photo feature, religious, travel. Does not want personal experience or opinion pieces. **Buys 96-120 mss/year.** Send complete ms. Length: 500-700 words. **Pays $25-200.** Sometimes pays expenses of writers on assignment.

[Canada] $$$$ TODAY'S PARENT

Rogers Media, Inc., One Mt. Pleasant Rd., 8th Floor, Toronto ON M4Y 2Y5 Canada. (416)764-2883. **Fax:** (416)764-2894. **E-mail:** editors@todaysparent.com. **Website:** www.todaysparent.com. **Contact:** Jackie Shipley, art director. Monthly magazine for parents with children up to the age of 12. Circ. 175,000. Editorial lead time 5 months.

NONFICTION Length: 1,800-2,500 words. **Pays $1,500-2,200.**

COLUMNS Profile (Canadian who has accomplished something remarkable for the benefit of children), 250 words; **pays $250.** Your Turn (parents share their experiences), 800 words; **pays $200.** Beyond Motherhood (deals with topics not directly related to parenting), 700 words; **pays $800.** Education (tackles straightforward topics and controversial or complex topics), 1,200 words; **pays $1,200-1,500.** Health Behavior (child development and discipline), 1,200 words; **pays $1,200-1,500.** Slice of Life (explores lighter side of parenting), 750 words; **pays $650.**

[Canada] $$$$ TODAY'S PARENT PREGNANCY & BIRTH

Rogers Media, Inc., One Mt. Pleasant Rd., 8th Floor, Toronto ON M4Y 2Y5 Canada. (416)764-2883. **Fax:** (416) 764-2894. **E-mail:** editors@todaysparent.com. **Website:** www.todaysparent.com. **100% freelance written**. Magazine published 3 times/year. "*P&B* helps, supports and encourages expectant and new parents with news and features related to pregnancy, birth, human sexuality and parenting." Estab. 1973. Circ. 190,000. Publishes ms an average of 8 months after acceptance. Editorial lead time 6 months. Accepts queries by mail. Responds in 6 weeks to queries. Guidelines for SASE.

NONFICTION Buys 12 mss/year. Query with published clips; send detailed proposal. Length: 1,000-2,500 words. **Pays up to $1/word.** Sometimes pays expenses of writers on assignment.

$$ TOLEDO AREA PARENT NEWS

Adams Street Publishing, Co., 1120 Adams St., Toledo OH 43604. (419)244-9859. **E-mail:** cjacobs@toledocitypaper.com; editor@toledocitypaper.com. **Website:** www.toledoparent.com. **Contact:** Collette Jacobs, editor-in-chief and publisher; Christy Penka, assignment editor. Monthly tabloid for Northwest Ohio/Southeast Michigan parents. Estab. 1992. Circ. 40,000. Byline given. Publishes ms an average of 1 month after acceptance. Editorial lead time 3 months. Accepts queries by mail, e-mail, fax. Responds in 1 month to queries. Sample copy for $1.50.

NONFICTION Needs general interest, interview, opinion. **Buys 10 mss/year.** Length: 1,000-2,500 words. **Pays $75-125.**

$$ TWINS™ MAGAZINE

30799 Pinetree Road, #256, Cleveland OH 44124. (866) 586-7683. **Fax:** (866) 586-7683. **E-mail:** twinseditor@twinsmagazine.com. **Website:** www.twinsmagazine.com. **50% freelance written.** "We now publish eight (8) issues per year—4 print/4 digital covering all aspects of parenting twins/multiples. *Twins* is a national/international publication that provides informational and educational articles regarding the parenting of twins, triplets, and more. All articles must be multiple specific and have an upbeat, hopeful, and/or positive ending." Estab. 1984. Circ. 35,000. Byline given. Editorial lead time 4 months. Submit seasonal material 6 months in advance. Accepts queries by U.S. mail, e-mail only. Response time varies. Sample copy for $5 or on website. Guidelines available online.

NONFICTION Needs personal experience, first-person parenting experience, professional experience as it relates to multiples. Nothing on cloning, pregnancy reduction, or fertility issues. **Buys 12 mss/year.** Send complete ms. Length: 650-1,200 words. **Pays $25-250 for assigned articles. Pays $25-125 for unsolicited articles.**

COLUMNS A Word From Dad; Mom-2-Mom; LOL: Laugh Out Loud; Family Health; Resource Round Up;

Tales From Twins; & Research. Pays $25-75. **Buys 8-10 mss/year.** Query with or without published clips or send complete ms. **Pays $40-75.**

COMIC BOOKS

💲 THE COMICS JOURNAL

Fantagraphics Books, 7563 Lake City Way NE, Seattle WA 98115. (206)524-1967. **Fax:** (206)524-2104. **E-mail:** editorial@tcj.com. **Website:** www.tcj.com. Magazine covering the comics medium from an arts-first perspective on a six-week schedule. "*The Comics Journal* is one of the nation's most respected single-arts magazines, providing its readers with an eclectic mix of industry news, professional interviews, and reviews of current work. Due to its reputation as the American magazine with an interest in comics as an art form, the *Journal* has subscribers worldwide, and in this country serves as an important window into the world of comics for several general arts and news magazines." Byline given. Accepts queries by mail, e-mail. Guidelines available online.

NONFICTION Needs essays, interview, opinion, reviews. Send complete ms. Length: 2,000-3,000 words. **Pays 4¢/word, and 1 contributor's copy.**

COLUMNS On Theory, Art and Craft (2,000-3,000 words); Firing Line (reviews 1,000-5,000 words); Bullets (reviews 400 words or less). Send inquiries, samples **Pays 4¢/word, and 1 contributor's copy.**

NTH DEGREE

3502 Fernmoss Ct., Charlotte NC 28269. **E-mail:** submissions@nthzine.com. **Website:** www.nthzine.com. **Contact:** Michael Pederson. Estab. 2002.

CONSUMER SERVICE AND BUSINESS OPPORTUNITY

💲💲 HOME BUSINESS MAGAZINE

United Marketing & Research Co., Inc., P.O. Box 807, 20711 Holt Ave, Lakeville MN 55044. **E-mail:** editor@homebusinessmag.com; publisher@homebusinessmag.com. **Website:** www.homebusinessmag.com. **75% freelance written.** Covers every angle of the home-based business market including: cutting edge editorial by well-known authorities on sales and marketing, business operations, the home office, franchising, business opportunities, network marketing, mail order and other subjects to help readers choose, manage and prosper in a home-based busi-

ness; display advertising, classified ads and a directory of home-based businesses; technology, the Internet, computers and the future of home-based business; home-office editorial including management advice, office set-up, and product descriptions; business opportunities, franchising and work-from-home success stories. Estab. 1993. Circ. 105,000. Publishes ms an average of 6 months after acceptance. Editorial lead time 6 months. Submit seasonal material 6 months in advance. Accepts queries by e-mail. Accepts simultaneous submissions. Sample copy for sae with 9×12 envelope and 8 First-Class stamps. Guidelines for #10 sase.

NONFICTION Needs book excerpts, general interest, how-to, home business, inspirational, interview, new product, personal experience, photo feature, technical, mail order, franchise, business management, internet, finance network marketing. No non-home business related topics. **Buys 40 mss/year.** Send complete ms. Length: 200-1,000 words. **Pays 20¢/published word for work-for-hire assignments; 50-word byline for unsolicited articles.**

COLUMNS Marketing & Sales; Money Corner; Home Office; Management; Technology; Working Smarter; Franchising; Network Marketing, all 650 words. Send complete ms.

KIPLINGER'S PERSONAL FINANCE

1729 H St., NW, Washington DC 20006. (202)887-6400. **Fax:** (202)331-1206. **E-mail:** jbodnar@kiplinger.com. **Website:** www.kiplinger.com. **Contact:** Janet Bodnar, editor; Cynthia L. Currie, art director. **10% freelance written. Prefers to work with published/established writers.** Monthly magazine for general, adult audience interested in personal finance and consumer information. "*Kiplinger's* is a highly trustworthy source of information on saving and investing, taxes, credit, home ownership, paying for college, retirement planning, automobile buying, and many other personal finance topics." Estab. 1947. Circ. 800,000. Publishes ms an average of 2 months after acceptance. Responds in 1 month to queries.

NONFICTION Query with published clips. Pays expenses of writers on assignment.

CONTEMPORARY CULTURE

💲💲 A&U

Art & Understanding, Inc., 25 Monroe St., Suite 205, Albany NY 12210-2729. (518)426-9010. **Fax:** (518)436-5354. **E-mail:** mailbox@aumag.org; chaelneedle@mac.com. **Website:** www.aumag.org. **Contact:** Chael Needle, managing editor. **50% freelance written.** Monthly magazine covering cultural, political, and medical responses to HIV/AIDS. Estab. 1991. Circ. 205,000. Byline given. Pays 3 months after publication. Publishes ms an average of 3 months after acceptance. Editorial lead time 6 months. Accepts queries by mail, e-mail. Accepts simultaneous submissions. Responds in 1 month to queries. Responds in 2 months to mss. Sample copy for $5. Guidelines available online.

NONFICTION Needs AIDS-related book excerpts, essays, general interest, how-to, humor, interview, new product, opinion, personal experience, photo feature, travel, reviews (film, theater, art exhibits, video, music, other media), medical news, artist profiles. **Buys 6 mss/year.** Query with published clips. Length: 800-1,200 words. **Pays $150-300 for assigned articles.**

COLUMNS The Culture of AIDS (reviews of books, music, film), 300 words; Viewpoint (personal opinion), 750 words. **Buys 6 mss/year.** Send complete ms. **Pays $50-150.**

FICTION "Literary electronic submissions, as Word attachments, may be mailed to Brent Calderwood, literary editor, at aumaglit@gmail.com. Pay rate schedule available upon request." Send complete ms. Length: less than 1,500 words. **Pays $100.**

POETRY Any length/style (shorter works preferred). **Pays $25.**

🍁 $$$ ADBUSTERS

Adbusters Media Foundation, 1243 W. 7th Ave., Vancouver BC V6H 1B7 Canada. (604)736-9401. **Fax:** (604)737-6021. **E-mail:** editor@adbusters.org. **Website:** www.adbusters.org. **50% freelance written.** Bimonthly magazine. "We are an activist journal of the mental environment." Estab. 1989. Circ. 90,000. Byline given. Pays 1 month after publication. Accepts queries by mail, e-mail, fax. Accepts simultaneous submissions. Guidelines available online.

NONFICTION Needs essays, exposé, interview, opinion. **Buys variable mss/year.** Query. Length: 250-3,000 words. **Pays $100/page for unsolicited articles; 50¢/word for solicited articles.**

$$ ALBEMARLE

Carden Jennings Publishing Co., Ltd., 375 Greenbrier Dr., Suite 100, Charlottesville VA 22901. (434)817-2000. **Fax:** (434)817-2020. **E-mail:** albemarle@cjp.com. **Website:** www.cjp.com. **80% freelance written.** Bimonthly magazine covering lifestyle for central Virginia. Lifestyle magazine for central Virginia. Estab. 1987. Circ. 10,000. Byline given. Offers 30% kill fee. Publishes ms an average of 4 months after acceptance. Editorial lead time 6-8 months. Submit seasonal material 6 months in advance. Accepts queries by mail, e-mail, fax. Accepts simultaneous submissions. Responds in 1 month to queries. Responds in 2 months to mss. Sample copy for sae with 10×12 envelope and 5 first-class stamps. Guidelines for #10 SASE.

NONFICTION Needs essays, historical, interview, photo feature, travel. No fiction, poetry or anything without a direct tie to central Virginia. **Buys 30-35 mss/year.** Query with published clips. Length: 900-3,500 words. **Pays $75-225 for assigned articles and unsolicited articles.** Sometimes pays expenses of writers on assignment.

COLUMNS Etcetera (personal essay), 900-1,200 words; no food; Leisure (travel, sports), 3,000 words. **Buys 20 mss/year.** Query with published clips. **Pays $75-150.**

$ BOSTON REVIEW

P.O. Box 425786, Cambridge MA 02142. (617)324-1360. **Fax:** (617)452-3356. **E-mail:** review@bostonreview.net. **Website:** www.bostonreview.net. Timothy Donnelly. **Contact:** Dept. Editor. **90% freelance written.** Bimonthly magazine of cultural and political analysis, reviews, fiction, and poetry. "The editors are committed to a society and culture that foster human diversity and a democracy in which we seek common grounds of principle amidst our many differences. In the hope of advancing these ideals, the *Review* acts as a forum that seeks to enrich the language of public debate." Estab. 1975. Circ. 20,000. Byline given. Publishes ms an average of 4 months after acceptance. Accepts simultaneous submissions. Responds in 4 months to queries. Sample copy for $5 or online. Guidelines available online.

🔑 Reads submissions September 15-May 15.

NONFICTION Needs essays (book reviews). "*We do not accept unsolicited book reviews.* If you would like to be considered for review assignments, please send your résumé along with several published clips." **Buys 50 mss/year.** Query with published clips. You may submit query letters and unsolicited nonfiction up to 5,000 words via the online submissions system.

FICTION Contact: Junot Díaz , fiction editor. "I'm looking for stories that are emotionally and intellectually substantive and also interesting on the level of language. Things that are shocking, dark, lewd, comic, or even insane are fine so long as the fiction is *controlled* and purposeful in a masterly way. Subtlety, delicacy, and lyricism are attractive too." Needs ethnic, experimental, contemporary, prose poem. No romance, erotica, genre fiction. **Buys 5 mss/year.** Send complete ms. Length: 1,200-5,000 words. Average length: 2,000 words. **Pays $25-300, and 5 contributor's copies.**

POETRY Contact: Benjamin Paloff and Timothy Donnelly, poetry editors. *Boston Review*, published bimonthly, is a tabloid-format magazine of arts, culture, and politics. "We are open to both traditional and experimental forms. What we value most is originality and a strong sense of voice." Has published poetry by Frank Bidart, Lucie Brock-Broido, Peter Gizzi, Jorie Graham, Allen Grossman, John Koethe, and Karen Volkman. Receives about 5,000 submissions/year, accepts about 30 poems/year. Circulation is 20,000 nationally. Single copy: $5; subscription: $25. Sample: $5. Responds in 2-4 months. Acquires first serial rights. Reviews books of poetry, solicited reviews only. Send materials for review consideration. Reads poetry between September 15 and May 15 each year. Submit maximum 5-6 poems. **Payment varies.**

○ 💲💲 BROKEN PENCIL

P.O. Box 203, Station P, Toronto ON M5S 2S7 Canada. **E-mail:** editor@brokenpencil.com. **E-mail:** fiction@brokenpencil.com. **Website:** www.brokenpencil.com. **80% freelance written.** Quarterly magazine covering arts and culture. *Broken Pencil* is one of the few magazines in the world devoted exclusively to underground culture and the independent arts. We are a great resource and a lively read! *Broken Pencil* reviews the best zines, books, Web sites, videos and artworks from the underground and reprints the best articles from the alternative press. From the hilarious to the perverse, *Broken Pencil* challenges conformity and demands attention. Estab. 1995. Circ. 5,000. Byline given. Publishes ms an average of 2-3 months after acceptance. Accepts queries by mail, e-mail. Guidelines available online.

NONFICTION Needs essays, general interest, historical, humor, interview, opinion, personal experience, photo feature, travel, reviews. Does not want anything about mainstream art and culture. **Buys 8 mss/year.** Query with published clips. Length: 400-2,500 words.

Pays $100-400. Sometimes pays expenses of writers on assignment.

COLUMNS Contact: Contact Erin Kobayashi, books editor; James King, ezines editor; Terence Dick, music editor; Lindsay Gibb, film editor. Books (book reviews and feature articles); Ezines (ezine reviews and feature articles); Music (music reviews and feature articles); Film (film reviews and feature articles), all 200-300 words for reviews and 1,000 words for features. **Buys 8 mss/year.** Query with published clips. **Pays $100-400.**

FICTION Contact: Contact Hal Niedzviecki, fiction editor. We're particularly interested in work from emerging writers. Needs adventure, cond novels, confession, erotica, ethnic, experimental, fantasy, historical, horror, humorous, mystery, novel concepts, romance, science fiction, slice-of-life vignettes. **Buys 8 mss/year.** Send complete ms. Length: 500-3,000 words.

➕ 💲💲 BUST MAGAZINE

Bust, Inc., P.O. Box 1016, Cooper Station, New York NY 10276. **E-mail:** submissions@bust.com. **Website:** www.bust.com. **60% freelance written.** Bimonthly magazine covering pop culture for young women. "*Bust* is the groundbreaking, original women's lifestyle magazine & website that is unique in its ability to connect with bright, cutting-edge, influential young women." Estab. 1993. Circ. 100,000. Byline given. Publishes ms an average of 4 months after acceptance. Editorial lead time 3-4 months. Submit seasonal material 6 months in advance. Accepts queries by mail, e-mail. Accepts simultaneous submissions. Response time varies. Guidelines online at www.bust.com/info/submit.html.

NONFICTION Needs book excerpts, exposé, general interest, historical, how-to, humor, inspirational, interview, new product, personal experience, photo feature, travel. Special issues: No dates are currently set, but we usually have a fashion issue, a music issue and a *Men We Love* issue periodically. We do not want poetry; no stories not relating to women. **Buys 60+ mss/yr. mss/year.** Query with published clips. Length: 350-3,000 words. **Pays 0-$250/max for assigned articles. Pays 0-$250/max for unsolicited articles.** Sometimes pays expenses of writers on assignment.

COLUMNS Contact: Emily Rems, Managing Editor. Books (Reviews of books by women) assigned by us, Music (Reviews of music by/about women), Movies (Reviews of movies by/about women), 300 words; One-Handed-Read (Erotic Fiction for Women), 1,200 words. **Buys 6 mss/yr. mss/year.** Query with published clips. **Pays $-$100.**

FICTION Contact: Lisa Butterworth, Assoc. Editor. Needs erotica. "We only publish erotic fiction. All other content is nonfiction." **Buys 6 mss/yr. mss/year.** Query with published clips. Length: 1,000-1,500 words. **Pays $0-$100.**

🍁 $ CANADIAN DIMENSION

Dimension Publications, Inc., 91 Albert St., Room 2-E, Winnipeg MB R3B 1G5 Canada. (204)957-1519. **Fax:** (204)943-4617. **E-mail:** editor@canadiandimension.com; letters@canadiandimension.com. **Website:** www.canadiandimension.com. **Contact:** Cy Gonick, publisher and coordinating editor. **80% freelance written.** Bimonthly magazine covering socialist perspective. We bring a socialist perspective to bear on events across Canada and around the world. Our contributors provide in-depth coverage on popular movements, peace, labour, women, aboriginal justice, environment, third world and eastern Europe. Estab. 1963. Circ. 3,000. Publishes ms an average of 6 months after acceptance. Accepts simultaneous submissions. Responds in 6 weeks to queries. Sample copy for $2. Guidelines available online.

NONFICTION Needs interview, opinion, reviews. **Buys 8 mss/year.** Length: 500-2,000 words. **Pays $25-100.**

CLOUDBANK: JOURNAL OF CONTEMPORARY WRITING

P.O. Box 610, Corvallis OR 97339. **Website:** www.cloudbankbooks.com. **Contact:** Michael Malan, editor. Biannual journal of contemporary writing open to range of styles; never publishes theme issues. Estab. 2009. Publishes ms up to 6 months after acceptance. Accepts queries by mail. Accepts simultaneous submissions. Responds in 4 months. Guidelines available in magazine, for SASE, by email or on website.

🔑 Prefers submissions from skilled, experienced poets; will consider work from beginning poets. Considers poetry by teens. Previously published includes poetry posted on a public website/blog/forum. Reviews single-books of poetry in 500 words.

FICTION Digest-sized, 84 pages of print, perfect bound; color artwork on cover, includes ads. Receives 1,600 poems/year, accepts about 8%. Press run is 400. Subscribers: 300; shelf sales: 100 distributed free. Single copy $8; subscription: $15. Make checks payable to Cloudbank. Submit 5 poems or less at a time with SASE. Cover letter is preferred. Does not accept fax, email, or disk submissions. Reads year round. Never sends prepublication galleys. 150 lines/max. **Pays $200 prize for one poem or flash fiction piece per issue.**

POETRY Submit 5 poems or less at a time by mail with SASE. Cover letter is preferred. Does not accept fax, email, or disk submissions. Reads year round. Never sends prepublication galleys.

$$$ COMMENTARY

561 Seventh Ave., 16th Floor, New York NY 10018. (212)891-1400. **E-mail:** submissions@commentarymagazine.com. **Website:** www.commentarymagazine.com. Monthly magazine. Estab. 1945. Byline given. Publishes ms an average of 2 months after acceptance. Accepts queries by mail.

NONFICTION Needs essays, opinion. **Buys 4 mss/year.** Query. Length: 2,000-8,000 words. **Pays $400-1,200.**

🍁 $$ COMMON GROUND

Common Ground Publishing, 204-4381 Fraser St., Vancouver BC V5V 4G4 Canada. (604)733-2215. **Fax:** (604)733-4415. **E-mail:** admin@commonground.ca. **E-mail:** editor@commonground.ca. **Website:** www.commonground.ca. **90% freelance written.** Monthly tabloid covering health, environment, spirit, creativity, and wellness. "We serve the cultural creative community." Estab. 1982. Circ. 70,000. Byline given. Publishes ms an average of 1 month after acceptance. Editorial lead time 2 months. Submit seasonal material 3 months in advance. Accepts queries by e-mail. Accepts simultaneous submissions. Responds in 6 weeks to queries. Responds in 3 months to mss. Sample copy for $5. Guidelines available online.

NONFICTION Needs book excerpts, how-to, inspirational, interview, opinion, personal experience, travel, call to action. Send complete ms. Length: 500-2,500 words. **Pays 10¢/word (Canadian).**

$$$ FIRST THINGS

Institute on Religion & Public Life, 35 East 21st St., 6th floor, New York NY 10010. (212)627-1985. **E-mail:** ft@firstthings.com. **Website:** www.firstthings.com. **70% freelance written.** Covers social and intellectual commentary. "Intellectual journal published 10 times/year containing social and ethical commentary in a broad sense, religious and ethical perspectives on society, culture, law, medicine, church and state, morality, and more." Estab. 1990. Circ. 32,000. Byline given. Publishes ms an average of 4 months after acceptance. Editorial lead time 2 months. Submit seasonal material 5 months in advance. Responds in 3 weeks to mss. Sample copy and writer's guidelines for #10 SASE.

NONFICTION Needs essays, opinion. **Buys 60 mss/year.** Send complete ms. Length: 1,500-6,000 words. **Pays $400-1,000.** Sometimes pays expenses of writers on assignment.

POETRY Contact: Joseph Bettum, poetry editor. Needs traditional. Buys 25-30 poems/year. Length: 4-40 lines. **Pays $50.**

THE LIST

The List, Ltd., 14 High St., Edinburgh EH1 1TE Scotland. (44)(131)550-3050. **Fax:** (44)(131)557-8500. **Website:** www.list.co.uk. **25% freelance written.** Biweekly general interest magazine covering Glasgow and Edinburgh arts, events, listings, and lifestyle. "*The List* is pitched at educated 18-35 year olds in Scotland. All events listings are published free of charge and are accompanied by informative, independent critical comment offering a guide to readers as to what is worth seeing and why. Articles and features are also included previewing forthcoming events in greater detail." Estab. 1985. Circ. 500,000. Byline given. Offers 100% kill fee. Publishes ms an average of 2 weeks after acceptance. Editorial lead time 1 month. Submit seasonal material 1 month in advance. Accepts queries by mail, e-mail. Accepts simultaneous submissions.

NONFICTION Needs interview, opinion, travel. Query with published clips. Length: 300 words. **Pays £60-80.** Sometimes pays expenses of writers on assignment.

COLUMNS Reviews, 50-650 words, **pays £16-35**; Book Reviews, 150 words; **pays £14.** Comic Reviews, 100 words; **pays £10.** TV/Video Reviews, 100 words; **pays £10.** Record Reviews, 100 words; **pays £10.** Query with published clips.

MOTHER JONES

Foundation for National Progress, 222 Sutter St., Suite 600, San Francisco CA 94108. (415)321-1700. **E-mail:** query@motherjones.com. **Website:** www.motherjones.com. **Contact:** Monika Bauerlein and Clara Jeffery, editors. **80% freelance written.** Bimonthly magazine covering politics, investigative reporting, social issues, and pop culture. "*Mother Jones* is a 'progressive' magazine—but the core of its editorial well is reporting (i.e., fact-based). No slant required. MotherJones.com is an online sister publication." Estab. 1976. Circ. 240,000. Byline given. Offers 33% kill fee. Publishes ms an average of 4 months after acceptance. Editorial lead time 4 months. Submit seasonal material 6 months in advance. Responds in 2 months to queries. Sample copy for $6 and 9×12 SASE. Guidelines available online.

NONFICTION Needs exposé, interview, photo feature, current issues, policy, investigative reporting. **Buys 70-100 mss/year.** Query with published clips. "Please also include your rèsumè and two or three of your most relevant clips. If the clips are online, please provide the complete URLs. Web pieces are generally less than 1,500 words. Because we have staff reporters it is extremely rare that we will pay for a piece whose timeliness or other qualities work for the Web only. Magazine pieces can range up to 5,000 words. There is at least a two-month lead time. No phone calls please." Length: 2,000-5,000 words. **Pays $1/word.** Sometimes pays expenses of writers on assignment.

COLUMNS Outfront (short, newsy and/or outrageous and/or humorous items), 200-800 words; Profiles of Hellraisers, 500 words. **Pays $1/word.**

NATURALLY

Internaturally, Inc., P.O. Box 317, Newfoundland NJ 07435. (973)697-3552. **Fax:** (973)697-8313. **E-mail:** naturally@internaturally.com. **Website:** www.internaturally.com. **80% freelance written.** Quarterly magazine covering nudism and naturism. Write about nudists and naturists. More people stories than travel. Estab. 1980. Circ. 30,000. Byline given. Publishes ms an average of 3 months after acceptance. Editorial lead time 3-6 months. Submit seasonal material 6 months in advance. Accepts queries by mail, phone. Accepts simultaneous submissions. Responds in 2 weeks to queries. Responds in 3 months to mss. Sample copy available online. Guidelines available online.

NONFICTION Needs book excerpts, essays, exposé, general interest, historical, how-to, for first-time visitors to nudist park., humor, inspirational, interview, new product, personal experience, photo feature, travel. Special issues: Free-beach activities, public nude events. "We don't want opinion pieces and religious slants." **Buys 50 mss/year.** Send complete ms. Length: 500-2,000 words. **Pays $80 per page, text or photos minimum; $300 maximum for assigned articles.**

COLUMNS Health (nudism/naturism), Travel (nudism/naturism), Celebrities (nudism/naturism). **Buys 8 mss/year.** Send complete ms.

FICTION Needs humorous. Science fiction. **Buys 6-8 mss/year.** Send complete ms. Length: 800-2,000 words. **Pays $-$80 per page.**

POETRY Needs avant-garde, free verse, haiku, light verse, traditional. Buys 3-6/year poems/year. Submit maximum 3 poems.

FILLERS Needs anecdotes, facts, gags, newsbreaks, short humor. **Buys 4 mss/year.**

$ NEW HAVEN ADVOCATE

New Mass Media, Inc., 900 Chapel St., Suite 1100, New Haven CT 06510. (203)789-0010. **Fax:** (203)787-1418. **E-mail:** abromage@newhavenadvocate.com. **Website:** www.newhavenadvocate.com. **10% freelance written.** Weekly tabloid covering alternative, investigative, cultural reporting. Alternative, investigative, cultural reporting with a strong voice. We like to shake things up. Estab. 1975. Circ. 55,000. Byline given. Editorial lead time 1 month. Submit seasonal material 2 months in advance. Accepts simultaneous submissions. Responds in 1 month to queries.

NONFICTION Needs book excerpts, essays, exposé, general interest, humor, interview. **Buys 15-20 mss/year.** Query with published clips. Length: 750-2,000 words. **Pays $50-150.** Sometimes pays expenses of writers on assignment.

$ $ SHEPHERD EXPRESS

The Brooklyn Company, Inc., 207 E. Buffalo St., Suite 410, Milwaukee WI 53202. (414)276-2222. **Fax:** (414)276-3312. **E-mail:** info@expressmilwaukee. com. **Website:** http://expressmilwaukee.com. **Contact:** Louis Fortis, editor-in-chief and publisher. **50% freelance written.** Weekly tabloid covering news and arts with a progressive news edge and a hip entertainment perspective. Home of Sheprd Flickr interactive photo feature—Milwaukee-related photography. Estab. 1982. Circ. 58,000. Pays 1 month after publication. Publishes ms an average of 1 month after acceptance. Submit seasonal material 2 months in advance. Accepts simultaneous submissions. Sample copy for $3.

NONFICTION Needs book excerpts, essays, exposé, opinion. **Buys 200 mss/year.** Send complete ms. Length: 900-2,500 words. **Pays $35-300 for assigned**

articles. **Pays $10-200 for unsolicited articles.** Sometimes pays expenses of writers on assignment.

COLUMNS Opinions (social trends, politics, from progressive slant), 800-1,200 words; Books Reviewed (new books only: Social trends, environment, politics), 600-1,200 words. **Buys 10 mss/year.** Send complete ms.

$ $ $ THE SUN

107 N. Roberson St., Chapel Hill NC 27516. (919)942-5282. **Fax:** (919)932-3101. **Website:** www.thesunmagazine.org. Sy Safransky, editor. **Contact:** Luc Sanders, assistant editor. **90% freelance written.** Monthly magazine. "We are open to all kinds of writing, though we favor work of a personal nature." Estab. 1974. Circ. 69,500. Byline given. Publishes ms an average of 6-12 months after acceptance. Accepts queries by mail. Responds in 3-6 months to queries. Responds in 3-6 months to mss. Sample copy for $5. Guidelines available online.

NONFICTION Contact: Sy Safransky, editor. Needs essays, personal experience, spiritual, interview. **Buys 50 mss/year.** Send complete ms. 7,000 words maximum. **Pays $300-2,000.** .

FICTION Contact: Sy Safransky, editor. "We avoid stereotypical genre pieces like science fiction, romance, western, and horror. Read an issue before submitting." **Buys 20/year mss/year.** Send complete ms. 7,000 words maximum **Pays $300-1,500.**

POETRY Contact: Sy Safransky, editor. Needs free verse. Submit up to 6 poems at a time. Considers previously published poems but strongly prefers unpublished work; no simultaneous submissions. "Poems should be typed and accompanied by a cover letter and SASE." Guidelines available with SASE or on website. Responds within 3-6 months. Acquires first serial or one-time rights. Rarely publishes poems that rhyme. **Pays $100-500 on publication plus contributor's copies and subscription.** .

DISABILITIES

○ $ $ ABILITIES

Canadian Abilities Foundation, 340 College St., Suite 270, Toronto ON M5T 3A9 Canada. (416)923-1885. **Fax:** (416)923-9829. **Website:** www.abilities.ca. **50% freelance written.** Quarterly magazine covering disability issues. *Abilities* provides information, inspiration, and opportunity to its readers with articles and resources covering health, travel, sports, products, technology, profiles, employment, recreation, and more. Estab. 1987. Circ. 20,000. Byline given. Offers 50% kill fee. Publishes ms an average of 3 months after acceptance. Editorial lead time 3 months. Submit seasonal material 4 months in advance. Accepts queries by mail, e-mail, fax. Responds in 3 months to queries. Sample copy free. Writer's guidelines for #10 SASE, online, or by e-mail.

NONFICTION Needs general interest, how-to, humor, inspirational, interview, new product, personal experience, photo feature, travel. Does not want articles that 'preach to the converted'—this means info that people with disabilities likely already know, such as what it's like to have a disability. **Buys 30-40 mss/year.** Query or send complete ms. Length: 500-2,500 words. **Pays $50-400 (Canadian) for assigned articles. Pays $50-350 (Canadian) for unsolicited articles.**

COLUMNS The Lighter Side (humor), 700 words; Profile, 1,200 words.

$$$$ ARTHRITIS TODAY

Arthritis Foundation, 1330 W. Peachtree St., Suite 100, Atlanta GA 30309. (404)872-7100. **Fax:** (404)872-9559. **Website:** www.arthritistoday.org. **50% freelance written**. Bimonthly magazine covering living with arthritis and the latest in research/treatment. *Arthritis Today* is a consumer health magazine and is written for the more than 70 million Americans who have arthritis and for the millions of others whose lives are touched by an arthritis-related disease. The editorial content is designed to help the person with arthritis live a more productive, independent, and pain-free life. The articles are upbeat and provide practical advice, information, and inspiration. Estab. 1987. Circ. 650,000. Byline given. Offers kill fee. Offers kill fee Editorial lead time 6 months. Submit seasonal material 6 months in advance. Accepts queries by mail, online submission form. Accepts simultaneous submissions. Responds in 2 months to queries. Sample copy for 9×11 SAE with 4 first-class stamps. Guidelines available online.

NONFICTION Needs general interest, how-to, tips on any aspect of living with arthritis, inspirational, new product, arthritis related, opinion, personal experience, photo feature, technical, travel, tips, news, service, nutrition, general health, lifestyle. **Buys 12 unsolicited mss/year.** Query with published clips. Length: 150-2,500 words. **Pays $100-2,500.** Pays expenses of writers on assignment.

COLUMNS Nutrition, 100-600 words; Fitness, 100-600 words; Balance (emotional coping), 100-600 words; MedWatch, 100-800 words; Solutions, 100-600 words; Life Makeover, 400-600 words.

FILLERS Needs facts, gags, short humor. **Buys 2 mss/year.** Length: 40-100 words. **Pays $80-150.**

$$ CAREERS & THE DISABLED

Equal Opportunity Publications, 445 Broad Hollow Rd., Suite 425, Melville NY 11747. (631)421-9421. **Fax:** (631)421-0359. **E-mail:** info@eop.com. **Website:** www.eop.com. **60% freelance written**. Magazine published 6 times/year with Fall, Winter, Spring, Summer, and Expo editions; offering role-model profiles and career guidance articles geared toward disabled college students and professionals, and promotes personal and professional growth. Estab. 1967. Circ. 10,000. Byline given. Publishes ms an average of 6 months after acceptance. Editorial lead time 6 months. Submit seasonal material 6 months in advance. Accepts queries by mail, e-mail, fax, phone. Accepts simultaneous submissions. Responds in 3 weeks to queries. Sample copy for 9×12 SAE with 5 first-class stamps. Guidelines free.

NONFICTION Needs essays, general interest, how-to, interview, new product, opinion, personal experience. **Buys 30 mss/year.** Query. Length: 1,000-2,500 words. **Pays 10¢/word.** Sometimes pays expenses of writers on assignment.

$$ DIABETES HEALTH

365 Bel Marin Keys Blvd., Suite 100, Novato CA 94949. (415)883-1990. **Fax:** (415)883-1932. **E-mail:** editor@diabeteshealth.com. **Website:** www.diabeteshealth.com. **Contact:** Nadia Al-Samarrie, publisher and editor-in-chief. **40% freelance written**. Monthly tabloid covering diabetes care. *Diabetes Interview* covers the latest in diabetes care, medications, and patient advocacy. Personal accounts are welcome as well as medical-oriented articles by MDs, RNs, and CDEs (certified diabetes educators). Estab. 1991. Circ. 40,000. Byline given. Publishes ms an average of 2 months after acceptance. Editorial lead time 2 months. Submit seasonal material 2 months in advance. Accepts queries by e-mail, online submission form. Sample copy available online. Guidelines free.

NONFICTION Needs essays, how-to, humor, inspirational, interview, new product, opinion, personal experience. **Buys 25 mss/year.** Send complete ms. Length: 500-1,500 words. **Pays 20¢/word.**

PHOTOS State availability of or send photos. Negotiates payment individually.

TIPS "Be actively involved in the diabetes community or have diabetes. However, writers need not have diabetes to write an article, but it must be diabetes-related."

💲💲 DIABETES SELF-MANAGEMENT

R.A. Rapaport Publishing, Inc., 150 W. 22nd St., Suite 800, New York NY 10011. (212)989-0200. **Fax:** (212)989-4786. **E-mail:** editor@rapaportpublishing. com. **Website:** www.diabetesselfmanagement.com. **20% freelance written.** Bimonthly magazine. "We publish how-to health care articles for motivated, intelligent readers who have diabetes and who are actively involved in their own health care management. All articles must have immediate application to their daily living." Estab. 1983. Circ. 410,000. Byline given. Offers 20% kill fee. Submit seasonal material 6 months in advance. Accepts queries by mail, e-mail, fax. Responds in 6 weeks to queries. Sample copy for $4 and 9×12 SAE with 6 first-class stamps or online. Guidelines for #10 SASE.

NONFICTION Needs how-to, exercise, nutrition, diabetes self-care, product surveys, technical, reviews of products available, foods sold by brand name, pharmacology, travel, considerations and prep for people with diabetes. No personal experiences, personality profiles, exposés, or research breakthroughs. **Buys 10-12 mss/year.** Query with published clips. Length: 2,000-2,500 words. **Pays $400-700 for assigned articles. Pays $200-700 for unsolicited articles.**

💲 DIALOGUE

Blindskills, Inc., P.O. Box 5181, Salem OR 97304. **E-mail:** magazine@blindskills.com. **Website:** www. blindskills.com. **60% freelance written**. Quarterly journal covering visually impaired people. Estab. 1962. Circ. 1,100. Byline given. Publishes ms an average of 6 months after acceptance. Editorial lead time 3 months. Accepts queries by e-mail. One free sample on request. Available in large print, Braille, digital audio cassette, and e-mail. Guidelines available online.

NONFICTION Needs essays, general interest, historical, how-to, life skills methods used by visually impaired people, humor, interview, personal experience, sports, recreation, hobbies. No controversial, explicit sex, religious, or political topics. **Buys 50-60 mss/year.** Send complete ms. Length: 200-1,200/words. **Pays $15-35 for assigned articles. Pays $15-25 for unsolicited articles.**

COLUMNS All material should be relative to blind and visually impaired readers. Living with Low Vision, 1,000 words; Hear's How (dealing with sight loss), 1,000 words. Technology Answer Book, 1,000 words. **Buys 80 mss/year.** Send complete ms. **Pays $10-25.**

HEARING HEALTH

Hearing Health, 363 Seventh Avenue, 10th Floor, New York NY 10001. **E-mail:** info@drf.org. **Website:** www. drf.org/magazine. Magazine covering issues and concerns pertaining to hearing health and hearing loss. Byline given. Pays with contributor copies. Accepts queries by mail, e-mail. Accepts simultaneous submissions. Guidelines available online.

NONFICTION Send complete ms.

COLUMNS Features (800-1,500 words); First-person stories (500-1,500 words); Humor (500-750 words); Viewpoints/Op-Ed (350-500 words). Send complete ms.

💲 KALEIDOSCOPE

Kaleidoscope Press, 701 S. Main St., Akron OH 44311-1019. (330)762-9755. **Fax:** (330)762-0912. **E-mail:** mshiplett@udsakron.org. **Website:** www.udsakron. org/kaleidoscope.htm. **Contact:** Mildred Shiplett. **75% freelance written. Eager to work with new/unpublished writers**. Semiannual magazine. "Subscribers include individuals, agencies, and organizations that assist people with disabilities and many university and public libraries. Appreciates work by established writers as well. Especially interested in work by writers with a disability, but features writers both with and without disabilities. Writers without a disability must limit themselves to our focus, while those with a disability may explore any topic (although we prefer original perspectives about experiences with disability)." Estab. 1979. Circ. 1,000. Byline given. Accepts queries by mail, fax. Accepts simultaneous submissions. Responds in 3 weeks to queries. Responds in 6 months to mss. Sample copy for $6 prepaid. Double-space your work, number the pages, & include name. Guidelines available online.

NONFICTION Needs book excerpts, essays, humor, interview, personal experience, book reviews, articles related to disability. **Buys 8-15 mss/year.** 5,000 words maximum. **Pays $25, plus 2 copies**

FICTION Contact: Fiction Editor. Short stories, novel excerpts. Traditional and experimental styles. Works should explore experiences with disability. Use people-first language. Needs Well-developed plots, engaging characters, and realistic dialogue. We lean toward fiction that emphasizes character and emotions rather than action-oriented narratives. No fiction that is stereotypical, patronizing, sentimental, erotic, or maudlin. No romance, religious or dogmatic fiction; no children's literature. 5,000 words maximum **Pays $25, and 2 contributor's copies.**

POETRY "Do not get caught up in rhyme scheme. High quality with strong imagery and evocative language. Reviews any style." Buys 12-20 poems/year. Submit maximum 5 poems.

💲💲 PN

PVA Publications, 2111 E. Highland Ave., Suite 180, Phoenix AZ 85016-4702. (602)224-0500. **E-mail:** richard@pvamag.com. **Website:** www.pn-magazine.com. **Contact:** Richard Hoover, editor. Monthly magazine covering news and information for wheelchair users. Writing must pertain to people with disabilities—specifically mobility impairments. Estab. 1946. Circ. 40,000. Byline given. Publishes ms an average of 2-4 months after acceptance. Editorial lead time 3 months. Submit seasonal material 3 months in advance. Accepts queries by mail, e-mail, fax. Sample copy and guidelines free.

NONFICTION Needs how-to, interview, new product, opinion. **Buys 10-12 mss/year.** Send complete ms. Length: 1,200-2,500 words. **Pays $25-250.**

💲💲 SPECIALIVING

P.O. Box 1000, Bloomington IL 61702. (309)962-2003. **E-mail:** gareeb@aol.com. **Website:** www.specialiving. com. **90% freelance written**. Quarterly online magazine covering the physically disabled/mobility impaired. "We are now an online-only magazine. There is no subscription fee. Subject matter is the same. Payment is still the same, (max 800 words). Need photos with ms." Estab. 2001. Circ. 12,000. Byline given. Editorial lead time 3 months. Submit seasonal material 6 months in advance. Accepts queries by mail, e-mail, fax, phone. Accepts simultaneous submissions. Responds in 3 weeks to queries.

NONFICTION Needs how-to, humor, inspirational, interview, new product, personal experience, technical, travel. **Buys 40 mss/year.** Query. Length: 800 words. **Pays 10¢/word.**

COLUMNS Shopping Guide; Items. **Buys 30 mss/year.** Query.

💲💲 SPORTS 'N SPOKES

The Magazine for Wheelchair Sports and Recreation, PVA Magazines, 2111 E. Highland Ave., Suite 180, Phoenix AZ 85016-4702. (602)224-0500. **Fax:** (602)224-0507. **E-mail:** brenda@pvamag.com; richard@pvamag.com. **Website:** www.sportsnspokes. com. Richard Hoover, editor. **Contact:** Brenda Martin, editorial coordinator. Bimonthly magazine covering wheelchair sports and recreation. Writing must pertain to wheelchair sports and recreation. Estab. 1974. Circ. 25,000. Byline given. Publishes ms an average of 2-3 months after acceptance. Editorial lead time 2-3 months. Submit seasonal material 2-3 months in advance. Accepts queries by mail, e-mail, fax. Sample copy and guidelines free.

NONFICTION Needs general interest, interview, new product. **Buys 5-6 mss/year.** Send complete ms. Length: 1,200-2,500 words. **Pays $20-250.**

ENTERTAINMENT

💲 CINEASTE

Cineaste Publishers, Inc., 243 Fifth Ave., #706, New York NY 10016. (212)366-5720. **E-mail:** cineaste@ cineaste.com. **Website:** www.cineaste.com. **30% freelance written.** Quarterly magazine covering motion pictures with an emphasis on social and political perspective on cinema. Estab. 1967. Circ. 11,000. Byline given. Offers 50% kill fee. Publishes ms an average of 4 months after acceptance. Editorial lead time 3 months. Submit seasonal material 4 months in advance. Accepts queries by mail, e-mail, fax. Responds in 1 month to queries. Sample copy for $5. Writer's guidelines on website.

NONFICTION Needs book excerpts, essays, exposé, historical, humor, interview, opinion. **Buys 20-30 mss/year.** Query with published clips. Length: 2,000-5,000 words. **Pays $30-100.**

COLUMNS Homevideo (topics of general interest or a related group of films); A Second Look (new interpretation of a film classic or a reevaluation of an unjustly neglected release of more recent vintage); Lost and Found (film that may or may not be released or otherwise seen in the US but which is important enough to be brought to the attention of our readers), all 1,000-1,500 words. Query with published clips. **Pays $50 minimum.**

⚬ 💲 DANCE INTERNATIONAL

Scotiabant Dance Centre, Level 6 677 Davie St., Vancouver BC V6B 2G6 Canada. (604)681-1525. **Fax:** (604)681-7732. **E-mail:** Editor@DanceInternational. org. **Website:** www.danceinternational.org. **100% free-**

lance written. Quarterly magazine covering dance arts. Articles and reviews on current activities in world dance, with occasional historical essays; reviews of dance films, video, and books. Estab. 1973. Circ. 4,500. Byline given. Offers 50% kill fee. Publishes ms an average of 3 months after acceptance. Editorial lead time 3 months. Submit seasonal material 6 weeks in advance. Accepts queries by mail, e-mail, fax, phone. NoResponds in 2 weeks to queries. Responds in 1 month to mss. Sample copy for $7. Guidelines for #10 SASE.

NONFICTION Needs book excerpts, essays, historical, interview, personal experience, photo feature. **Buys 100 mss/year.** Query. Length: 1,200-2,200 words. **Pays $40-150.**

COLUMNS Dance Bookshelf (recent books reviewed), 700-800 words; Regional Reports (events in each region), 1,200 words. **Buys 100 mss/year.** Query. **Pays $80.**

$$ DIRECTED BY

Visionary Media, P.O. Box 1722, Glendora CA 91740-1722. **Fax:** (626)608-0309. **E-mail:** visionarycinema@yahoo.com. **Website:** www.directed-by.com. **10% freelance written.** Quarterly magazine covering the craft of directing a motion picture. "Our articles are for readers particularly knowledgeable about the art and history of movies from the director's point of view. Our purpose is to communicate our enthusiasm and interest in the craft of cinema." Estab. 1998. Circ. 42,000. Byline given. Offers 25% kill fee. Publishes ms an average of 3 months after acceptance. Editorial lead time 3 months. Submit seasonal material 3 months in advance. Accepts queries by mail, e-mail. Accepts simultaneous submissions. Responds in 6 weeks to queries. Sample copy for $5. Writer's guidelines free or by e-mail.

NONFICTION Needs interview, photo feature, onset reports. No gossip, celebrity-oriented material, or movie reviews. **Buys 5 mss/year.** Query. Length: 500-7,500 words. **Pays $50-750.** Sometimes pays expenses of writers on assignment.

COLUMNS Trends (overview/analysis of specific moviemaking movements/genres/subjects), 1,500-2,000 words; Focus (innovative take on the vision of a contemporary director), 1,500-2,000 words; Appreciation (overview of deceased/foreign director), 1,000-1,500 words; Final Cut (spotlight interview with contemporary director), 3,000 words; Perspectives (interviews/articles about film craftspeople who work with a featured director), 1,500-2,000 words. **Buys 5 mss/year.** Query. **Pays $50-750.**

$$ FANGORIA

The Brooklyn Company, 250 West 49th St., Suite 304, New York NY 10019-7454. **Website:** www.fangoria.com. **95% freelance written. Works with a small number of new/unpublished writers each year.** Magazine published 10 times/year covering horror films, TV projects, comics, videos, and literature, and those who create them. "We provide an assignment sheet (deadlines, info) to writers, thus authorizing queried stories that we're buying." Estab. 1979. Byline given. Pays 1-3 months after publication. Publishes ms an average of 3 months after acceptance. Submit seasonal material 4 months in advance. Accepts queries by mail. Responds in 6 weeks to queries. Sample copy for $9 and 10×13 SAE with 4 first-class stamps.. Guidelines for #10 SASE.

NONFICTION Needs interviews with technicians and filmmakers in the field. Avoids most articles on science-fiction films. **Buys 120 mss/year.** Query with published clips. Length: 1,000-3,500 words. **Pays $100-250.** Sometimes pays expenses of writers on assignment.

COLUMNS Monster Invasion (exclusive, early information about new film productions; also mini-interviews with filmmakers and novelists). Query with published clips. **Pays $45-75.**

$$ FLICK MAGAZINE

Decipher, Inc., 259 Granby St., 3rd Floor, Norfolk VA 23510. (757)623-3600. **Fax:** (757)623-8368. **E-mail:** julie.matthews@decipher.com. **Website:** www.flickmagazine.com. **30-40% freelance written.** Minimagazine distributed in movie theaters that comes out in conjunction with selected movies covering one specific movie per issue. *Flick*'s mission is to match the passion and personality of fans, taking readers inside Hollywood and increasing their connection to the film they are about to view. Estab. 2005. Circ. 2.5 million. Publishes ms an average of 4 months after acceptance. Editorial lead time 4-5 months. Accepts queries by mail, e-mail.

NONFICTION Needs essays, humor, interview, opinion, personal experience. Query. Length: 500-1,000 words. **Pays $200-500.** Sometimes pays expenses of writers on assignment.

FILLERS Needs gags, short humor. **Buys 5-10 mss/year. Pays $200-500.**

$ IN TOUCH WEEKLY

270 Sylvan Ave., Englewood Cliffs NJ 07632. (201)569-6699. **E-mail:** breakingnews@intouchweekly.com; contactintouch@intouchweekly.com. **Website:** www.intouchweekly.com. **10% freelance written.** Weekly magazine covering celebrity news and entertainment. Estab. 2002. Circ. 1,300,000. No byline given. Editorial lead time 1 week. Accepts queries by e-mail.

NONFICTION Needs interview, gossip. **Buys 1,300 mss/year.** Query. Send a tip about a celebrity by email. Length: 100-1,000 words. **Pays $50.**

$$ MOVIEMAKER MAGAZINE

MovieMaker Media LLC, 27 West 24th Street, Suite 9D, New York NY 10010. (646)405-5170. **Fax:** (646)405-5172. **E-mail:** jwood@moviemaker.com; rebecca@moviemaker.com. **Website:** www.moviemaker.com. **Contact:** Jennifer M. Wood, editor-in-chief; Rebecca Pahle, associate editor. **75% freelance written.** Bimonthly magazine covering film, independent cinema, and Hollywood. "*MovieMaker*'s editorial is a progressive mix of in-depth interviews and criticism, combined with practical techniques and advice on financing, distribution, and production strategies. Behind-the-scenes discussions with Hollywood's top moviemakers, as well as independents from around the globe, are routinely found in *MovieMaker*'s pages. Email is preferred submission method, but will accept via mail as well. Please, no telephone pitches. We want to read the idea with clips." Estab. 1993. Circ. 55,000. Byline given. Pays 30 days after newsstand publication. Offers kill fee. Offers variable kill fee. Publishes ms an average of 2 months after acceptance. Editorial lead time 3 months. Submit seasonal material 4 months in advance. Accepts queries by mail, e-mail. Accepts simultaneous submissions. Responds in 2-4 weeks to queries. Responds in 4-6 weeks to mss. Sample copy available online. Guidelines by email.

NONFICTION Needs exposé, general interest, historical, how-to, interview, new product, technical. **Buys 20 mss/year.** Query with published clips. Length: 800-3,000 words. **Pays $75-500 for assigned articles.**

COLUMNS Documentary; Home Cinema (home video/DVD reviews); How They Did It (first-person filmmaking experiences); Festival Beat (film festival reviews); World Cinema (current state of cinema from a particular country). Query with published clips **Pays $75-300.**

$$$ OK! MAGAZINE

American Media, Inc., 1155 Avenue of the Americas, New York NY 10036. **Website:** www.okmagazine.com. **10% freelance written.** Weekly magazine covering entertainment news. "We are a celebrity friendly magazine. We strive not to show celebrities in a negative light. We consider ourselves a cross between *People* and *In Style*." Estab. 2005. Circ. 1,000,000. Byline sometimes given. Pays after publication. Publishes ms an average of 1 month after acceptance. Editorial lead time 2 weeks. Accepts queries by mail, e-mail, fax.

NONFICTION Needs interview, photo feature. **Buys 50 mss/year.** Query with published clips. Length: 500-2,000 words. **Pays $100-1,000.**

🍁 $$ RUE MORGUE

Marrs Media, Inc., 2926 Dundas St. West, Toronto ON M6P 1Y8 Canada. **E-mail:** dave@rue-morgue.com. **Website:** www.rue-morgue.com. **Contact:** Dave Alexander, editor-in-chief. **50% freelance written.** Monthly magazine covering horror entertainment. "A knowledge of horror entertainment (films, books, games, toys, etc.)." Estab. 1997. Byline given. Publishes ms an average of 2-4 months after acceptance. Editorial lead time 2 months. Submit seasonal material 4 months in advance. Accepts queries by e-mail. NoResponds in 6 weeks to queries. Responds in 2 months to mss. Guidelines available by e-mail.

NONFICTION Needs essays, exposé, historical, interview, travel, new product. No reviews. Query with published clips or send complete ms. Length: 500-3,500 words.

COLUMNS Classic Cut (historical essays on classic horror films, books, games, comic books, music), 500-700 words. Query with published clips.

⊘ SOAP OPERA DIGEST

Source Interlink Media, 261 Madison Ave., 10th Floor, New York NY 10016. **Website:** www.soapdigest.com. Weekly magazine for the daytime and primetime soap opera viewer. Estab. 1976. Circ. 2 million.

💬 Does not buy freelance material or use freelance writers.

$$$$ SOUND & VISION

Bonnier Corp., 2 Park Ave., 10th Floor, New York NY 10016. (212)767-6000. **Fax:** (212)767-5615. **E-mail:** soundandvision@bonniercorp.com. **Website:** www.soundandvisionmag.com. **Contact:** Mike Mettler, editor-in-chief. **40% freelance written.** Magazine published 8 times/year. "Provides readers with authoritative information on the home entertainment technologies and products that will impact their lives." Estab. 1958. Circ. 400,000. Byline given. Publishes ms an average of 4 months after acceptance. Accepts queries by mail, e-mail, fax. Sample copy for SAE with 9×12 envelope and 11 first-class stamps.

NONFICTION **Buys 25 mss/year.** Query with published clips. Length: 1,500-3,000 words. **Pays $1,000-1,500.**

$ TELE REVISTA

304 Indian Trace #238, Weston FL (954)689-2428. **Fax:** (954)689-2428. **E-mail:** info@telerevista.com. **Website:** www.telerevista.com. **Contact:** Salvatore Trimarchi. **100% freelance written.** Monthly magazine written in Spanish covering Hispanic entertainment (US and Puerto Rico). We feature interviews, gossip, breaking stories, behind-the-scenes happenings, etc. Estab. 1986. Byline sometimes given. Publishes ms an average of 3 months after acceptance. Editorial lead time 2 months. Submit seasonal material 3 months in advance. Accepts queries by mail, e-mail, fax. Sample copy free.

NONFICTION Needs exposé, interview, opinion, photo feature. **Buys 200 mss/year.** Query. **Pays $25-75.**

COLUMNS **Buys 60 mss/year.** Query. **Pays $25-75.**

FILLERS Needs anecdotes, facts, gags, newsbreaks, short humor.

ETHNIC AND MINORITY

$$$$ AARP SEGUNDA JUVENTUD

AARP, 601 E St. NW, Washington DC 20049. **E-mail:** segundajuventud@aarp.org. **Website:** www.aarpsegundajuventud.org. **75% freelance written.** Bimonthly Spanish language magazine geared toward 50+ Hispanics. With fresh and relevant editorial content and a mission of inclusiveness and empowerment, *AARP Segunda Juventud* serves more than 800,000 Hispanic AARP members and their families in all 50 states, the District of Columbia, Puerto Rico, and the US Virgin Islands. Estab. 2002. Circ. 800,000. Byline given. Offers 33.33% kill fee. Publishes ms an average of 4 months after acceptance. Editorial lead time 2-12 months. Submit seasonal material 4-12 months in advance. Accepts queries by mail, e-mail. Accepts simultaneous submissions. Responds in 4 months to queries. Responds in 4 months to mss. Sample copy available online.

NONFICTION Needs general interest, interview, new product, travel, reviews (book, film, music). **Buys 36 mss/year.** Query with published clips. Length: 200-1,500 words. **Pays $1-2/word.** Sometimes pays expenses of writers on assignment.

COLUMNS Health; Finance; Travel; Celebrity profile; Encore (Hispanic 50+ individuals re-inventing themselves). **Buys 24 mss/year.** Query with published clips. **Pays $1-2/word.**

FILLERS Needs facts. **Buys 6 mss/year.** Length: 200-250 words. **Pays $1-2/word.**

AFRICAN VOICES

African Voices Communications, Inc., 270 W. 96th St., New York NY 10025. (212)865-2982. **Fax:** (212)316-3335. **E-mail:** africanvoices@aol.com. **Website:** www.africanvoices.com. **85% freelance written.** Quarterly magazine covering art, film, culture. *African Voices*, published quarterly, is an "art and literary magazine that highlights the work of people of color. We publish ethnic literature and poetry on any subject. We also consider all themes and styles: avant-garde, free verse, haiku, light verse, and traditional. We do not wish to limit the reader or author." Estab. 1992. Circ. 20,000. Byline given. Publishes ms an average of 3-6 months after acceptance. Editorial lead time 3 months. Submit seasonal material 3 months in advance. Accepts queries by mail. Accepts simultaneous submissions. Responds in 3 months to queries. Sample copy for $5.

NONFICTION Needs book excerpts, essays, historical, humor, inspirational, interview, photo feature, travel. Query with published clips. Length: 500-2,500 words. **Pays in contributor's copies.**

FICTION **Contact:** Contact Kim Horne, fiction editor. Needs adventure, cond novels, erotica, ethnic, experimental, fantasy, historical, general, horror, humorous, mainstream, mystery, novel concepts, religious, romance, science fiction, serialized, slice-of-life vignettes, suspense, African-American. **Buys 4 mss/year.** Send complete ms. Include short bio. Send SASE for return of ms. Responds in 3 months to queries. Accepts simultaneous and reprints submissions. Reviews fiction. Length: 500-2,500 words. **Pays $25-50. Pays on publication for first North American serial rights.**

POETRY **Contact:** Contact: Layding Kaliba, managing editor/poetry editor. Needs avant-garde, free verse, haiku, traditional. Submit no more than 2 poems at any 1 time. Accepts previously published poems and simultaneous submissions. Accepts submissions by e-mail (in text box), by fax, and by postal mail. Cover letter and SASE required. Seldom comments on rejected poems. Responds in 3 months. Pays 2 copies. Acquires first or one-time rights. Reviews books of poetry in 500-1,000 words. Send materials for review consideration to Layding Kaliba. Sponsors periodic poetry contests and readings. Send SASE for details. Buys 10 poems/year. Submit maximum 5 poems. Length: 5-100 lines. **Pays in contributor copies.**

$ AIM MAGAZINE

Aim Publication Association, P.O. Box 856, Forest Grove OR 97116. (253)815-9030. **E-mail:** apiladoone@aol.com; editor@aimmagazine.com;submissions@aimmagazine.org. **Website:** aimmagazine.org. **75% freelance written. Works with a small number of new/unpublished writers each year.** Quarterly magazine on social betterment that promotes racial harmony and peace for high school, college, and general audience. Publishes material to purge racism from the human bloodstream through the written word. Estab. 1975. Circ. 10,000. Byline given. Offers 60% kill fee. Publishes ms an average of 3 months after acceptance. Submit seasonal material 6 months in advance. Accepts queries by mail, e-mail. Does not accept previously published submissions.Responds in 2 months to queries. Responds in 1 month to mss. Sample copy and writer's guidelines for $5 and 9×12 SAE with correct postage or online. Guidelines available online: http://www.aimmagazine.org/submit.htm.

NONFICTION Needs exposé, education, general interest, social significance, historical, Black or Indian, how-to, create a more equitable society, interview, one who is making social contributions to community, book reviews, reviews of plays. No religious material. **Buys 16 mss/year.** Send complete ms. Length: 500-800 words. **Pays $25-35.**

FICTION Contact: Ruth Apilado, associate editor. Fiction that teaches the brotherhood of man. Needs ethnic, historical, mainstream, suspense. Open. No religious mss. **Buys 20 mss/year.** Send complete ms. Length: 1,000-1,500 words. **Pays $25-35.**

POETRY Needs avant-garde, free verse, light verse. No preachy poetry. Buys 20 poems/year. Submit maximum 5 poems. Length: 15-30 lines. **Pays $3-5.**

FILLERS Needs anecdotes, newsbreaks, short humor. **Buys 30 mss/year.** Length: 50-100 words. **Pays $5.**

$$ AMBASSADOR MAGAZINE

National Italian American Foundation, 1860 19th St. NW, Washington DC 20009. (202)939-3108. **Fax:** (202)387-0800. **E-mail:** don@niaf.org. **Website:** www.niaf.org. **Contact:** Don Oldenburg, editor. **50% freelance written.** Quarterly magazine for Italian-Americans covering Italian-American history and culture. We publish nonfiction articles on little-known events in Italian-American history and articles on Italian-American culture, traditions, and personalities living and dead. Estab. 1989. Circ. 25,000. Byline given. Pays on approval of final draft. Offers $50 kill fee. Editorial lead time 3 months. Accepts queries by mail, e-mail, fax. Accepts simultaneous submissions. Responds in 2 months to queries. Sample copy and writer's guidelines free.

NONFICTION Needs historical, interview, photo feature. **Buys 12 mss/year.** Send complete ms. Length: 800-1,500 words. **Pays $250 for photos and article.**

$$$ B'NAI B'RITH MAGAZINE

2020 K St. NW, 7th Floor, Washington DC 20006. (202)857-6527. **E-mail:** bbmag@bnaibrith.org. **Website:** http://bnaibrith.org. **90% freelance written.** Quarterly magazine specializing in social, political, historical, religious, cultural, `lifestyle,' and service articles relating chiefly to the Jewish communities of North America and Israel. Write for the American Jewish audience, i.e., write about topics from a Jewish perspective, highlighting creativity and innovation in Jewish life. Estab. 1886. Circ. 110,000. Byline given. Publishes ms an average of 6 months after acceptance. Editorial lead time 3 months. Submit seasonal material 5 months in advance. Accepts queries by mail, e-mail, fax. Accepts simultaneous submissions. Responds in 1 month to queries. Responds in 6 weeks to mss. Sample copy for $2. Writer's guidelines for #10 SASE or by e-mail.

NONFICTION Needs interview, photo feature, religious, travel. No Holocaust memoirs, first-person essays/memoirs, fiction, or poetry. **Buys 14-20 mss/year.** Query with published clips. Length: 1,000-2,500 words. **Pays $300-800 for assigned articles. Pays $300-700 for unsolicited articles.** Sometimes pays expenses of writers on assignment.

🍁 $ CELTICLIFE MAGAZINE

Clansman Publishing, Ltd., P.O. Box 8805, Station A, Halifax NS B3K 5M4 Canada. (902)835-2358. **Fax:** (902)835-0080. **E-mail:** editor@celticlife.ca. **Web-**

site: www.celticlife.ca. **Contact:** Alexa Thompson, editor-in-chief. **95% freelance written.** Quarterly magazine covering culture of North Americans of Celtic descent. "The magazine chronicles the stories of Celtic people who have settled in North America, with a focus on the stories of those who are not mentioned in history books. We also feature Gaelic language articles, history of Celtic people, traditions, music, and folklore. We profile Celtic musicians and include reviews of Celtic books, music, and videos." Estab. 1987. Circ. 5,000 (per issue). Byline given. Pays 2 months after publication. Publishes ms an average of 2 months after acceptance. Editorial lead time 2 months. Submit seasonal material 3 months in advance. Accepts queries by mail, e-mail, fax, phone. Responds in 1 week to queries. Responds in 1 month to mss Sample copy available online. Digital sample and guidelines available online.

80% of content must originate from Canadian citizens or Canadian landed immigrants.

NONFICTION Needs essays, general interest, historical, interview, opinion, personal experience, travel, Gaelic language, Celtic music reviews, profiles of Celtic musicians, Celtic history, traditions, and folklore. No fiction, poetry, historical stories already well publicized. **Buys 100 mss/year.** Query or send complete ms Length: 800-2,500 words. **Pays $50-75 (Canadian). All writers receive a complimentary subscription.**

$ FILIPINAS

Filipinas Publishing, Inc., GBM Bldg., 1580 Bryant St., Daly City CA 94015. (650)993-8943. **Website:** www.filipinasmag.com. Monthly magazine focused on Filipino-American affairs. *Filipinas* answers the lack of mainstream media coverage of Filipinos in America. It targets both Filipino immigrants and American-born Filipinos, gives in-depth coverage of political, social, and cultural events in the Philippines and in the Filipino-American community. Features role models, history, travel, food and leisure, issues, and controversies. Estab. 1992. Circ. 40,000. Byline given. Offers $10 kill fee. Publishes ms an average of 5 months after acceptance. Editorial lead time 2 months. Submit seasonal material 4 months in advance. Accepts queries by mail, e-mail, fax. Responds in 3 weeks to queries. Responds in 5 months to mss. Writer's guidelines for 9 ½x4 SASE or on website.

NONFICTION Needs exposé, general interest, historical, inspirational, interview, opinion, personal experience, travel. No academic papers. **Buys 80-100 mss/year.** Query with published clips. Length: 800-1,500 words. **Pays $50-75.**

COLUMNS Cultural Currents (Filipino traditions and beliefs), 1,000 words; New Voices (first-person essays by Filipino Americans ages 10-25), 800 words; First Person (open to all Filipinos), 800 words. Query with published clips. **Pays $50-75.**

$$ GERMAN LIFE

Zeitgeist Publishing, Inc., 1068 National Hwy., LaVale MD 21502. (301)729-6190. **Fax:** (301)729-1720. **E-mail:** mslider@germanlife.com. **Website:** www.germanlife.com. **Contact:** Mark Slider. **50% freelance written.** Bimonthly magazine covering German-speaking Europe. "*German Life* is for all interested in the diversity of German-speaking culture—past and present—and in the various ways that the US (and North America in general) has been shaped by its German immigrants. The magazine is dedicated to solid reporting on cultural, historical, social, and political events." Estab. 1994. Circ. 40,000. Byline given. Editorial lead time 4 months. Submit seasonal material 6 months in advance. Accepts queries by mail, e-mail. Responds in 2 months to queries. Responds in 3 months to mss. Sample copy for $4.95 and SASE with 4 first-class stamps. Guidelines available online.

NONFICTION Needs general interest, historical, interview, photo feature, travel. Special issues: Oktoberfest-related (October); Seasonal Relative to Germany, Switzerland, or Austria (December); Travel to German-speaking Europe (April). **Buys 50 mss/year.** Query with published clips. Length: 800-1,500 words. **Pays $200-500 for assigned articles. Pays $200-350 for unsolicited articles.**

COLUMNS German-Americana (regards specific German-American communities, organizations, and/or events past or present), 1,200 words; Profile (portrays prominent Germans, Americans, or German-Americans), 1,000 words; At Home (cuisine, etc. relating to German-speaking Europe), 800 words; Library (reviews of books, videos, CDs, etc.), 300 words. **Buys 30 mss/year.** Query with published clips. **Pays $50-150.**

FILLERS Needs facts, newsbreaks. Length: 100-300 words. **Pays $50-150.**

$$ HADASSAH MAGAZINE

50 W. 58th St., New York NY 10019. (212)688-0227. **Fax:** (212)446-9521. **E-mail:** magazine@hadassah.

org. **Website:** www.hadassah.org/magazine. **Contact:** Rachel Fyman Schwartzberg. **90% freelance written.** Monthly magazine. "*Hadassah* is a general interest Jewish feature and literary magazine. We speak to our readers on a vast array of subjects ranging from politics to parenting, to midlife crisis to Mideast crisis. Our readers want coverage on social and economic issues, Jewish women's (feminist) issues, the arts, travel and health." Circ. 300,000. NoResponds in 4 months to mss. Sample copy and writer's guidelines with 9×12 SASE.

NONFICTION Buys 10 unsolicited mss/year. Query. Length: 1,500-2,000 words. Sometimes pays expenses of writers on assignment.

COLUMNS "We have a family column and a travel column, but a query for topic or destination should be submitted first to make sure the area is of interest and the story follows our format."

FICTION Contact: Zelda Shluker, maaging editor. Short stories with strong plots and positive Jewish values. Needs ethnic, Jewish. No personal memoirs, schmaltzy or shelter magazine fiction. Length: 1,500-2,000 words. **Pays $500 minimum.**

$ INTERNATIONAL EXAMINER

622 S. Washington St., Seattle WA 98104. (206)624-3925. **Fax:** (206)624-3046. **E-mail:** editor@iexaminer.org. **Website:** www.iexaminer.org. **Contact:** Diem Ly, editor-in-chief. **75% freelance written.** Biweekly journal of Asian-American news, politics, and arts. "We write about Asian-American issues and things of interest to Asian-Americans. We do not want stuff about Asian things (stories on your trip to China, Japanese Tea Ceremony, etc. will be rejected). Yes, we are in English." Estab. 1974. Circ. 12,000. Publishes ms an average of 1 month after acceptance. Editorial lead time 1 month. Submit seasonal material 2 months in advance. Accepts simultaneous submissions. Guidelines for #10 SASE.

NONFICTION Needs essays, exposé, general interest, historical, humor, interview, opinion, personal experience, photo feature. **Buys 100 mss/year.** Query by mail, fax, or e-mail with published clips. 750-5,000 words, depending on subject. **Pays $25-100.** Sometimes pays expenses of writers on assignment.

FICTION Asian-American authored fiction by or about Asian-Americans. Needs novel concepts. **Buys 1-2 mss/year.** Query.

$$ ITALIAN AMERICA

219 E St. NE, Washington DC 20002. (202)547-2900. **Fax:** (202)546-8168. **E-mail:** ddesanctis@osia.org. **Website:** www.osia.org. **Contact:** Dona De Sanctis, editor. **20% freelance written.** Quarterly magazine. *Italian America* provides timely information about OSIA, while reporting on individuals, institutions, issues, and events of current or historical significance in the Italian-American community. Estab. 1996. Circ. 65,000. Byline given. Offers 50% kill fee. Publishes ms an average of 3 months after acceptance. Editorial lead time 3 months. Accepts queries by mail, e-mail, fax. Accepts simultaneous submissions. Sample copy free. Guidelines available online.

NONFICTION Needs historical, little known historical facts that must relate to Italian Americans, interview, opinion, current events. **Buys 8 mss/year.** Query with published clips. Length: 750-1,000 words. **Pays $50-250.**

TIPS "We pay particular attention to the quality of graphics that accompany the stories. We are interested in little known facts about historical/cultural Italian America."

$$ JEWISH ACTION

Orthodox Union, 11 Broadway, New York NY 10004. (212)613-8146. **Fax:** (212)613-0646. **E-mail:** ja@ou.org; carmeln@ou.org. **Website:** www.ou.org/jewish_action. **Contact:** Nechama Carmel, editor; Rashel Zywica, assistant editor; Yocheved Lefkovitz, art director. **80% freelance written.** Quarterly magazine covering a vibrant approach to Jewish issues, Orthodox lifestyle, and values. Estab. 1986. Circ. 40,000. Byline given. Pays 2 months after publication. Submit seasonal material 4 months in advance. Accepts queries by mail, e-mail, fax. Responds in 3 months to queries. Sample copy available online. Guidelines with #10 SASE or by e-mail.

💬 Prefers queries by e-mail. Mail and fax OK.

NONFICTION "We are not looking for Holocaust accounts. We welcome essays about responses to personal or societal challenges." **Buys 30-40 mss/year.** Query with published clips. Length: 1,000-3,000 words. **Pays $100-400 for assigned articles. Pays $75-150 for unsolicited articles.**

COLUMNS Just Between Us (personal opinion on current Jewish life and issues), 1,000 words. **Buys 4 mss/year.**

FICTION Must have relevance to Orthodox reader. Length: 1,000-2,000 words.

POETRY Buys limited number of poems/year. **Pays $25-75.**

JEWISH CURRENTS

P.O. Box 111, Accord NY 12404. (845)626-2427. **E-mail:** info@jewishcurrents.org. **Website:** www.jewishcurrents.org. **Contact:** Lawrence Bush, editor. *Jewish Currents*, published 4 times/year, is a progressive Jewish bimonthly magazine that carries on the insurgent tradition of the Jewish left through independent journalism, political commentary, and a 'countercultural' approach to Jewish arts and literature. *Jewish Currents* is 48 pages, magazine-sized, offset-printed, saddle-stapled with a full-color arts section, "Jcultcha & Funny Pages." Press run is 700. Subscription: $25/year. Estab. 1946. Circ. 16,000. Publishes ms 2 years after acceptance. Responds in 3 months.

POETRY Submit 4 poems at a time with a cover letter. No previously published poems or simultaneous submissions. Cover letter is required. "Include brief bio with author's publishing history." Poems should be typed, double-spaced; include SASE. **Pays 3 contributor's copies.**

⊗ KHABAR

Khabar, Inc., 3790 Holcomb Bridge Rd., Suite 101, Norcross GA 30092. (770)451-7666, ext. 115. **Fax:** (770)234-6115. **E-mail:** parthiv@khabar.com;info@khabar.com. **Website:** www.khabar.com. **50% freelance written.** "Monthly magazine covering the Asian Indian community in and around Georgia." Content relating to Indian-American and/or immigrant experience. Estab. 1992. Circ. 27,000. Offers 25% kill fee. Publishes ms an average of 2 months after acceptance. Editorial lead time 2 months. Submit seasonal material 2 months in advance. Accepts queries by e-mail. Accepts simultaneous submissions. Sample copy free. Guidelines by e-mail.

NONFICTION Needs essays, interview, opinion, personal experience, travel. **Buys 5 mss/year.** Send complete ms. Length: 750-4,000 words. **Pays $100-300 for assigned articles. Pays $75 for unsolicited articles.**

COLUMNS Book Review, 1,200 words; Music Review, 800 words; Spotlight (profiles), 1,200-3,000 words. **Buys 5 mss/year.** Query with or without published clips or send complete ms. **Pays $75+.**

FICTION Needs ethnic, Indian American/Asian immigrant. **Buys 5 mss/year.** Query or send complete ms. **Pays $50-100.**

⊗⊗⊗⊗ LATINA MAGAZINE

Latina Media Ventures, LLC, 625 Madison Ave., 3rd Floor, New York NY 10022. (212)642-0200. **E-mail:** editor@latina.com. **Website:** www.latina.com. **40-50% freelance written.** Monthly magazine covering Latina lifestyle. *Latina Magazine* is the leading bilingual lifestyle publication for Hispanic women in the US today. Covering the best of Latino fashion, beauty, culture, and food, the magazine also features celebrity profiles and interviews. Estab. 1996. Circ. 250,000. Byline given. Offers 25% kill fee. Publishes ms an average of 2-3 months after acceptance. Editorial lead time 3 months. Submit seasonal material 4-5 months in advance. Accepts queries by e-mail. Responds in 1 month to queries. Responds in 1-2 months to mss. Sample copy available online.

NONFICTION Needs essays, how-to, humor, inspirational, interview, new product, personal experience. Special issues: The 10 Latinas Who Changed the World (December). We do not feature an extensive amount of celebrity content or entertainment content, and freelancers should be sensitive to this. The magazine does not contain book or album reviews, and we do not write stories covering an artist's new project. We do not attend press junkets and do not cover press conferences. Please note that we are a lifestyle magazine, not an entertainment magazine. **Buys 15-20 mss/year.** Query with published clips. Length: 300-2,200 words. **Pays $1/word.** Pays expenses of writers on assignment.

⊗⊗⊗ MOMENT

4115 Wisconsin Ave. NW, Suite 102, Washington DC 20016. (202)363-6422. **Fax:** (202)362-2514. **E-mail:** editor@momentmag.com. **Website:** www.momentmag.com. **90% freelance written.** Bimonthly magazine. *Moment* is committed to portraying intellectual, political, cultural, and religious debates within the community, and to educating readers about Judaism's rich history and contemporary movements, ranging from left to right, fundamentalist to secular. Estab. 1975. Circ. 65,000. Byline given. Publishes ms an average of 6 months after acceptance. Editorial lead time 3 months. Submit seasonal material 6 months in advance. Accepts queries by mail, e-mail, fax. Accepts simultaneous submissions. Responds in 1 month to queries. Responds in 3 months to mss. Sample copy for $4.50 and SAE. Guidelines available online.

NONFICTION **Buys 25-30 mss/year.** Query with published clips. Length: 2,500-7,000 words. **Pays $200-1,200 for assigned articles. Pays $40-500 for unsolicited articles.**

COLUMNS 5765 (snappy pieces about quirky events in Jewish communities, news and ideas to improve Jewish living), 250 words maximum; Olam (first-person pieces, humor, and colorful reportage), 600-1,500 words; Book reviews (fiction and nonfiction) are accepted but generally assigned, 400-800 words. **Buys 30 mss/year.** Query with published clips. **Pays $50-250.**

$$ NATIVE PEOPLES MAGAZINE

5333 N. 7th St., Suite C-224, Phoenix AZ 85014. (602)265-4855. **Fax:** (602)265-3113. **E-mail:** dgibson@nativepeoples.com; kcoochwytewa@nativepeoples.com. **Website:** www.nativepeoples.com. **Contact:** Daniel Gibson, editor; Kevin Coochwytewa, art director. Bimonthly magazine covering Native Americans. High-quality reproduction with full color throughout. The primary purpose of this magazine is to offer a sensitive portrayal of the arts and lifeways of native peoples of the Americas. Estab. 1987. Circ. 40,000. Byline given. Accepts queries by mail, e-mail, fax. Responds in 2 months to queries. Guidelines available online.

NONFICTION Needs interviews of interesting and leading Natives from all walks of life, with an emphasis on arts, personal experience. **Buys 35 mss/year.** Length: 1,000-2,500 words. **Pays 25¢/word.**

$$ RUSSIAN LIFE

RIS Publications, P.O. Box 567, Montpelier VT 05601. **Website:** www.russianlife.net. **75% freelance written.** Bimonthly magazine covering Russian culture, history, travel, and business. "Our readers are informed Russophiles with an avid interest in all things Russian. But we do not publish personal travel journals or the like." Estab. 1956. Circ. 15,000. Byline given. Publishes ms an average of 3-6 months after acceptance. Editorial lead time 2 months. Submit seasonal material 3 months in advance. Accepts queries by mail. TrueResponds in 1 month to queries. Sample copy with 9×12 SASE and 6 first-class stamps. Guidelines available online.

NONFICTION Needs general interest, photo feature, travel. No personal stories, i.e., How I came to love Russia. **Buys 15-20 mss/year.** Query. Length: 1,000-6,000 words. **Pays $100-300.**

$$ SCANDINAVIAN REVIEW

The American-Scandinavian Foundation, 58 Park Ave., New York NY 10016. (212)779-3587. **E-mail:** info@amscan.org. **Website:** www.amscan.org. **75% freelance written.** Triannual magazine for contemporary Scandinavia. Audience: Members, embassies, consulates, libraries. Slant: Popular coverage of contemporary affairs in Scandinavia. Estab. 1913. Circ. 4,000. Byline given. Publishes ms an average of 2 months after acceptance. Editorial lead time 3 months. Submit seasonal material 3 months in advance. Responds in 6 weeks to queries. Sample copy available online. Guidelines free.

NONFICTION Needs general interest, interview, photo feature, travel, must have Scandinavia as topic focus. Special issues: Scandinavian travel. No pornography. **Buys 30 mss/year.** Query with published clips. Length: 1,500-2,000 words. **Pays $300 maximum.**

SKIPPING STONES: A MULTICULTURAL LITERARY MAGAZINE

P.O. Box 3939, Eugene OR 97403-0939. (541)342-4956. **E-mail:** editor@skippingstones.org. **Website:** www.skippingstones.org. **Contact:** Arun Toke, editor. **80% freelance written.** "*Skipping Stones* is an award-winning multicultural, nonprofit magazine designed to promote cooperation, creativity and celebration of cultural and ecological richness. We encourage submissions by children of color, minorities and under-represented populations. We want material meant for children and young adults/teenagers with multicultural or ecological awareness themes. Think, live and write as if you were a child, tween or teen. Wants material that gives insight to cultural celebrations, lifestyle, customs and traditions, glimpse of daily life in other countries and cultures. Photos, songs, artwork are most welcome if they illustrate/highlight the points. Translations are invited if your submission is in a language other than English. Upcoming themes will include cultural celebrations, living abroad, challenging, hospitality customs of various cultures, cross-cultural understanding, African, Asian and Latin American cultures, humor, international understanding, turning points and magical moments in life, caring for the earth, spirituality, and multicutural awareness." Estab. 1988. Circ. 2,200 print, plus web. Byline given. Publishes ms an average of 4-8 months after acceptance. Editorial lead time 3-4 months. Submit seasonal material 4 months in advance. Accepts queries by mail, e-mail. Accepts simultaneous submissions. Responds only if interested, send nonreturnable samples. Sample copy for $6. Writer's guidelines online or for business-sized envelope.

NONFICTION Needs essays, general interest, humor, inspirational, interview, opinion, personal experience, photo feature, travel, All levels: animal, biography, cooking, games/puzzles, history, humorous, interview/profile, multicultural, nature/environment, creative problem-solving, religion and cultural celebrations, sports, travel, social and international awareness. Does not want to see preaching, violence or abusive language; no poems by authors over 18 years old; no suspense or romance stories. No 'preachy' or 'screetchy' articles. **Buys 20-30 mss/year.** Send complete ms. Length: 400-800 words.

FICTION Middle readers, young adult/teens: contemporary, meaningful, humorous. All levels: folktales, multicultural, nature/environment. Multicultural needs include: bilingual or multilingual pieces; use of words from other languages; settings in other countries, cultures or multi-ethnic communities. Needs adventure, ethnic, historical, humorous, multicultural, international, social issues. **Buys 20 mss/year.** Send complete ms. Length: 300-800 words. **Pays with contributor copies.**

POETRY Only accepts poetry from youth under age 18. Buys 100-150 poems/year. Submit maximum 4 poems. Length: 30 lines maximum.

🍁 $ WINDSPEAKER

Aboriginal Multi-Media Society of Alberta, 13245-146 St., Edmonton AB T5L 4S8 Canada. (780)455-2700. **Fax:** (780)455-7639. **E-mail:** dsteel@ammsa.com. **Website:** www.ammsa.com/windspeaker. **Contact:** Debora Steel, editor. **25% freelance written.** Monthly tabloid covering native issues. Focus on events and issues that affect and interest native peoples, national or local. Estab. 1983. Circ. 27,000. Byline given. Offers kill fee. Publishes ms an average of 1 month after acceptance. Editorial lead time 1 month. Submit seasonal material 2 months in advance. Accepts queries by mail, e-mail, phone. Accepts simultaneous submissions. Sample copy free. Guidelines available online.

NONFICTION Needs opinion, photo feature, travel, news interview/profile, reviews: books, music, movies. Special issues: Powwow (June); Travel supplement (May). **Buys 200 mss/year.** Query with published clips and SASE or by phone. Length: 500-800 words. **Pays $3-3.60/published inch.** Sometimes pays expenses of writers on assignment.

FOOD AND DRINK

⊕ AMERICAN WINE SOCIETY JOURNAL

American Wine Society, 2881 S. Lake Leelanau Dr., Lake Leelanau MI 49653. (586)946-0049. **E-mail:** rink@americanwinesociety.org. **Website:** www.americanwinesociety.org. **Contact:** Jim Rink, editor. **100% freelance written.** "The non-profit American Wine Society is the largest consumer based wine education organization in the US The *Journal* reflects the varied interests of AWS members, which may include wine novices, experts, grape growers, amateur and professional winemakers, chefs, wine appreciators, wine educators, restauranteurs, and anyone wanting to learn more about wine and gastronomy." Estab. 1967. Circ. 5,000. Byline given. Publishes 3 months after acceptance. Editorial lead time is 3 months. Accepts queries by mail, e-mail. Accepts simultaneous submissions. Responds in 2 weeks on queries, 3 months on mss. Sample copy online.

NONFICTION Needs general interest, historical, how-to, nostalgic, technical, travel. Submit query with published clips.

COLUMNS Columns include wine reviews, book reviews, food and wine articles. Writer should send query with published clips.

$$$ DRAFT

Draft Publishing, 4742 N. 24th St., Suite 210, Phoenix AZ 85016. (888)806-4677. **E-mail:** jessica.daynor@draftmag.com. **Website:** www.draftmag.com. **60% freelance written.** Bimonthly magazine covering beer and men's lifestyle (including food, travel, sports and leisure). "*DRAFT* is a national men's magazine devoted to beer, breweries and the lifestyle and culture that surrounds it. Read by nearly 300,000 men aged 21-45, *DRAFT* offers formal beer reviews, plus coverage of food, travel, sports and leisure. Writers need not have formal beer knowledge (though that's a plus!), but they should be experienced journalists who can appreciate beer and beer culture." Estab. 2006. Circ. 275,000. Byline given. Offers 20% kill fee. Publishes ms an average of 2 months after acceptance. Editorial lead time 4 months. Submit seasonal material 6 months in advance. Accepts queries by e-mail. Accepts simultaneous submissions. Responds in 3 weeks to queries. Sample copy for $3 (magazine can also be found on most newsstands for $4.99). Guidelines available at www.draftmag.com/submissions.

NONFICTION Needs features, short front-of-book pieces, how-to's, interviews, travel, food, restaurant and bar pieces, sports and adventure; anything guy-related. Special issues: The editorial calendar is as follows: November/December: Holiday issue; Jan/Feb:

Best of issue; May/June: Food issue; Mar/Apr: Travel issue; July/Aug: All-American issue; Sept/Oct Anniversary issue. Do not want unsolicited mss., beer reviews, brewery profiles. **Buys 80/year. mss/year.** Query with published clips. Length: 250-2,500 words. **50-90¢ for assigned articles.** sometimes (limit agreed upon in advance).

COLUMNS Contact: Chris Staten, associate editor, (chris.staten@draftmag.com) for OnTap and OnTap llife, Jessica Daynor, managing editor, for all other departments. 'On Tap' (short FOB pieces on beer-related subjects, 350 words; 'On Tap Life' (short FOB pieces on NON -beer-related subjects (travel, food, sports, home, leisure), 350 words; 'Trek' (travel pieces [need not relate to beer, but it's a plus]), 950 words; 'Taste' (beer-and-food-related incident or unique perspective on beer), 750 words. **Buys 50 mss/year.** Query with published clips. **Pays 50¢-80¢.**

GOURMET TRAVELLER WINE

ACP Magazines, Ltd., 54-58 Park St., GP.O. Box 4088, Sydney NSW 2000 Australia. (61)(2)9282-8000. **Fax:** (61)(2)9267-4361. **Website:** www.gourmettraveller-wine.com.au. **Contact:** Judy Sarris, editor. Bimonthly magazine for the world of wine, celebrating both local and overseas industries. *"Gourmet Traveller WINE* is for wine lovers: It's for those who love to travel, to eat out and to entertain at home, and for those who want to know more about the wine in their glass." Circ. 22,088.

Target men 25-54, professionals & managers.
NONFICTION Needs general interest, how-to, interview, new product, travel. Query.

KASHRUS MAGAZINE

The Kashrus Institute, P.O. Box 204, Brooklyn NY 11204. (718)336-8544. **E-mail:** editorial@kashrusmagazine.com. **Website:** www.kashrusmagazine.com. **Contact:** Rabbi Wikler, editor. Estab. 1981. Circ. 10,000. Byline given. Offers 50% kill fee. Publishes ms an average of 2 months after acceptance. Submit seasonal material 2 months in advance. Accepts queries by mail, phone. Accepts simultaneous submissions. Responds in 2 weeks. Sample copy for $2.

NONFICTION Needs general interest, interview, new product, personal experience, photo feature, religious, technical, travel. Special issues: International Kosher Travel (October); Passover Shopping Guide (March); Domestic Kosher Travel Guide (June). **Buys 8-12 mss/year.** Query with published clips. Length: 1,000-1,500 words. **Pays $100-250 for assigned articles. Pays up to $100 for unsolicited articles.** Sometimes pays expenses of writers on assignment.

COLUMNS Book Review (cookbooks, food technology, kosher food), 250-500 words; People In the News (interviews with kosher personalities), 1,000-1,500 words; Regional Kosher Supervision (report on kosher supervision in a city or community), 1,000-1,500 words; Food Technology (new technology or current technology with accompanying pictures), 1,000-1,500 words; Travel (international, national—must include Kosher information and Jewish communities), 1,000-1,500 words; Regional Kosher Cooking, 1,000-1,500 words. **Buys 8-12 mss/year.** Query with published clips. **Pays $50-250.**

TEA A MAGAZINE

1000 Germantown Pike., F-2, Plymouth Meeting PA 19462. (484)688-0300. **Fax:** (484)688-0303. **E-mail:** teamag@teamag.com; Dan@teamag.com. **Website:** www.teamag.com. **Contact:** Dan Bolton, editor and publisher. **75% freelance written**. Quarterly magazine covering anything tea related. "TEA is a lifestyle publication celebrating tea and tea culture. It exists to encourage people to drink fine tea. Online and in print it articulates a forward-looking vision of nourishing, healthy, modern tea. TEA's content educates and excites enthusiasts. It offers new energy, new direction – with opportunities for tea enthusiasts young and old to share their discoveries via mobile, web and at retail locations where the publication is sold." Estab. 1994. Circ. 9,500. Byline given. Publishes ms an average of 1 year after acceptance. Editorial lead time 9 months. Submit seasonal material 6 months in advance. Responds in 6 months to mss. Guidelines by email.

NONFICTION Needs book excerpts, essays, general interest, historical, how-to, humor, interview, personal experience, photo feature, travel. Send complete ms. **Pays negotiable amount.** Sometimes pays expenses of writers on assignment.

COLUMNS Readers' Stories (personal experience involving tea); Book Reviews (review on tea books). Send complete ms. **Pays negotiable amount**

FICTION Does not want anything that is not tea related. Send complete ms. **Pays negotiable amount.**

POETRY Needs avant-garde, free verse, haiku, light verse, traditional. Does not want anything that is not tea related.

❸❸❸❸ WINE ENTHUSIAST MAGAZINE

Wine Enthusiast Media, 333 North Bedford Rd., Mt. Kisco NY 10549. **E-mail:** editor@wineenthusiast.net. **Website:** www.winemag.com. **40% freelance written.** Monthly magazine covering the lifestyle of wine. "Our readers are upscale and educated, but not necessarily super-sophisticated about wine itself. Our informal, irreverent approach appeals to savvy enophiles and newbies alike." Estab. 1988. Circ. 80,000. Byline given. Offers 25% kill fee. Editorial lead time 4 months. Submit seasonal material 5 months in advance. Accepts queries by e-mail. Responds in 2 weeks to queries; 2 months to mss.

NONFICTION Needs essays, humor, interview, new product, personal experience. **Buys 5 mss/year. Pays $750-2,500 for assigned articles. Pays $750-2,000 for unsolicited articles. Pays 50¢/word for website.**

❸❸ WINE PRESS NORTHWEST

333 W. Canal Dr., Kennewick WA 99336. (509)582-1564. **Fax:** (509)585-7221. **E-mail:** editor@winepressnw.com; edegerman@winepressnw.com. **Website:** www.winepressnw.com. **Contact:** Andy Perdue, editor-in-chief; Eric Degerman, managing editor. **50% freelance written.** Quarterly magazine covering Pacific Northwest wine (Washington, Oregon, British Columbia, Idaho). "Wine Press Northwest is a quarterly magazine for those with an interest in wine, from the novice to the veteran. We publish in March, June, September and December.We focus on Washington, Oregon, Idaho and British Columbia's talented winemakers and the wineries, vintners and restaurants that showcase Northwest wines. We are dedicated to all who savor the fruits of their labor." Estab. 1998. Circ. 12,000. Byline given. Offers 20% kill fee. Publishes ms an average of 3 months after acceptance. Editorial lead time 3 months. Submit seasonal material 3 months in advance. Accepts queries by mail, e-mail, fax. Accepts simultaneous submissions. Responds in 1 month to queries. Sample copy free or online. Guidelines free.

NONFICTION Needs general interest, historical, interview, new product, photo feature, travel. No beer, spirits, non-NW (California wine, etc.) **Buys 30 mss/year.** Query with published clips. Length: 1,500-2,500 words. **Pays $300.** Sometimes pays expenses of writers on assignment.

❸❸❸ WINE SPECTATOR

M. Shanken Communications, Inc., 387 Park Ave. S., New York NY 10016. **E-mail:** wsonline@mshanken. com. **Website:** www.winespectator.com. **20% freelance written. Prefers to work with published/established writers.** Monthly news magazine. Estab. 1976. Circ. 350,000. Byline given. Pays within 30 days of publication. Publishes ms an average of 2 months after acceptance. Submit seasonal material 4 months in advance. Accepts queries by mail, fax. Responds in 3 months to queries. Guidelines for #10 SASE.

NONFICTION Needs general interest, news about wine or wine events, interview, of wine, vintners, wineries, opinion, photo feature, travel, dining and other lifestyle pieces. No winery promotional pieces or articles by writers who lack sufficient knowledge to write below just surface data. Query. Length: 100-2,000 words. **Pays $100-1,000.**

GAMES AND PUZZLES

❸ THE BRIDGE BULLETIN

American Contract Bridge League, 6575 Windchase Dr., Horn Lake MS 38637-1523. (662)253-3156. **Fax:** (662)253-3187. **E-mail:** editor@acbl.org. **E-mail:** brent. manley@acbl.org. **Website:** www.acbl.org. Paul Linxwiler, managing editor. **Contact:** Brent Manley, editor. **20% freelance written.** Monthly magazine covering duplicate (tournament) bridge. Estab. 1938. Circ. 155,000. Byline given. Publishes ms an average of 3 months after acceptance. Editorial lead time 2 months. Accepts queries by mail, e-mail. Accepts simultaneous submissions.

NONFICTION Needs book excerpts, essays, how-to, play better bridge, humor, interview, new product, personal experience, photo feature, technical, travel. **Buys 6 mss/year.** Query. Length: 500-2,000 words. **Pays $100/page.**

❸❸ CHESS LIFE

P.O. Box 3967, Crossville TN 38557-3967. (931)787-1234. **Fax:** (931)787-1200. **E-mail:** dlucas@uschess. org; fbutler@uschess.org. **Website:** www.uschess.org. **Contact:** Daniel Lucas, editor; Francesca "Frankie" Butler, art director. **15% freelance written. Works with a small number of new/unpublished writers/ year.** Monthly magazine. "*Chess Life* is the official publication of the United States Chess Federation, covering news of most major chess events, both here and abroad, with special emphasis on the triumphs and exploits of American players." Estab. 1939. Circ. 85,000. Byline given. Publishes ms an average of 6 months after acceptance. Submit seasonal material 6 months in advance. Accepts queries by mail, e-mail, fax, phone. TrueAccepts simultaneous submissions. Responds in 3 months to mss. Sample copy and writer's guidelines with 9×11 SASE with 5 first-class stamps.

NONFICTION Needs general interest, historical, humor, interview, of a famous chess player or organizer, photo feature, chess centered, technical. No stories about personal experiences with chess. **Buys 30-40 mss/year.** Query with samples if new to publication. 3,000 words maximum. **Pays $100/page (800-1,000 words).** Sometimes pays expenses of writers on assignment.

FILLERS Submit with samples and clips. Buys first or negotiable rights to cartoons and puzzles. **Pays $25 upon acceptance.**

⊖⊖⊖ GAMES MAGAZINE

Kappa Publishing Group, Inc., 6198 Butler Pike, Suite 200, Blue Bell PA 19422. (215)643-6385. **Fax:** (215)628-3571. **E-mail:** games@kappapublishing.com. **Website:** www.gamesmagazine-online.com. **Contact:** R. Wayne Schmittberger, editor-in-chief. **50% freelance written.** Online magazine covering puzzles and games. *Games* is a magazine of puzzles, contests, and features pertaining to games and ingenuity. It is aimed primarily at adults and has an emphasis on pop culture. Estab. 1977. Circ. 75,000. Byline given. Offers 25% kill fee. Publishes ms an average of 4 months after acceptance. Editorial lead time 3 months. Submit seasonal material 6 months in advance. Accepts queries by mail, e-mail. Accepts simultaneous submissions. Responds in 6 weeks to queries. Responds in 3 months to mss. Sample copy for $5. Guidelines for #10 sase.

NONFICTION Needs photo feature, puzzles. **Buys 100 puzzles/year and 3 mss/year.** Query. Length: 1,500-2,500 words. **Pays $300-1,000.** Sometimes pays expenses of writers on assignment.

COLUMNS Gamebits (game/puzzle news), 250 words; Games & Books (product reviews), 350 words; Wild Cards (short text puzzles), 100 words. **Buys 50 mss/year.** Query. **Pays $25-250.**

FICTION Needs adventure, interactive, mystery. **Buys 1-2 mss/year.** Query. Length: 1,500-2,500 words. **Pays $500-1,200.**

HIGHLIGHTS HIGH FIVE

807 Church St., Honesdale PA 18431. **Fax:** (570)251-7847. **Website:** www.highlights.com/high-five. **Contact:** Kathleen Hayes, editor. "*Highlights High Five* was created to help you encourage your young child's development—and have fun together at the same time. Based on sound educational principles and widely accepted child-development theories, each monthly issue brings a 40-page, high-quality mix of read-aloud stories and age appropriate activities that will help you set your child firmly on the path to becoming a lifelong learner. Stories for younger readers should have 170 words or less and should appeal to children ages 2-6." Estab. 2009. See guidelines on the website. Accepts queries by mail.

GAY AND LESBIAN INTEREST

⊖⊖ THE ADVOCATE

Here Media, Inc., 10990 Wilshire Blvd., Penthouse, Los Angeles CA 90024. (310)943-5858. **Fax:** (310)806-6350. **E-mail:** newsroom@advocate.com. **Website:** www.advocate.com. **Contact:** Winston Gieseke, managing editor. Biweekly magazine covering national news events with a gay and lesbian perspective on the issues. Estab. 1967. Circ. 120,000. Byline given. Responds in 1 month to queries. Sample copy for $3.95. Guidelines on website.

NONFICTION Needs exposé, interview, news reporting and investigating. Query. Length: 1,200 words. **Pays $550.**

COLUMNS Arts & Media (news and profiles of well-known gay or lesbians in entertainment) is most open to freelancers, 750 words. Query. **Pays $100-500.**

⊖⊖ CURVE MAGAZINE

P.O Box 467, New York NY 10034. **E-mail:** editor@curvemag.com. **Website:** www.curvemag.com. **60% freelance written.** Magazine published 10 times/year covering lesbian entertainment, culture, and general interest categories. "We want dynamic and provocative articles that deal with issues, ideas, or cultural moments that are of interest or relevance to gay women." Estab. 1990. Circ. 80,000. Byline given. Offers 25% kill fee. Editorial lead time 6 months. Submit seasonal material 6 months in advance. Accepts queries by mail, e-mail, fax. Sample copy for $4.95 with $2 postage. Guidelines available online.

NONFICTION Needs general interest, photo feature, travel, celebrity interview/profile. Special issues: Sex (February); Travel (March); Fashion + Design (April); Weddings (May); Pride (June); Green/Music (July/August); [Travel/Tech] (September); Sexy & Powerful Women (October); Food/Wine/Holiday (November); Gift Guide (December). No fiction or poetry. **Buys 100 mss/year.** Query. Length: 200-2,000 words. **Pays 15¢/word.**

⊕ ECHO MAGAZINE

ACE Publishing, Inc., P.O. Box 16630, Phoenix AZ 85011-6630. (602)266-0550. **Fax:** (602)266-0773. **E-mail:** editor@echomag.com. **Website:** www.echomag.com. **Contact:** Glenn Gullickson, managing editor. **30-40% freelance written**. Biweekly magazine covering gay and lesbian issues. *Echo Magazine* is a newsmagazine for gay, lesbian, bisexual, and transgendered persons in the Phoenix metro area and throughout the state of Arizona. Editorial content needs to be pro-gay, that is, supportive of GLBT equality in all areas of American life. Estab. 1989. Circ. 15,000-18,000. Byline given. Publishes ms an average of less than 1 month after acceptance. Editorial lead time 1-2 months. Submit seasonal material 1-2 months in advance. Accepts queries by e-mail. Responds in 2 weeks to queries. Responds in 1 month to mss. Sample copy available online. Guidelines by e-mail.

NONFICTION Needs book excerpts, essays, historical, humor, interview, opinion, personal experience, photo feature, travel. Special issues: Pride Festival (April); Arts issue (August); Holiday Gift/Decor (December). No articles on topics unrelated to our GLBT readers, or anything that is not pro-gay. **Buys 10-20 mss/year.** Query. Length: 500-2,000 words. **Pays $30-40.**

COLUMNS Guest Commentary (opinion on GLBT issues), 500-1,000 words; Arts/Entertainment (profiles of GLBT or relevant celebrities, or arts issues), 800-1,500 words. **Buys 5-10 mss/year.** Query. **Pays $30-40.**

⊕ THE GAY & LESBIAN REVIEW

Gay & Lesbian Review, Inc., P.O. Box 180300, Boston MA 02118. (617)421-0082. **E-mail:** editor@glreview.com. **Website:** www.glreview.com. **100% freelance written**. Bimonthly magazine covers gay and lesbian history, culture, and politics. In-depth essays on GLBT history, biography, the arts, political issues, written in clear, lively prose targeted to the 'literate nonspecialist.' Estab. 1994. Circ. 12,000. Byline given. Editorial lead time 2 months. Accepts queries by mail, e-mail, phone. Accepts simultaneous submissions. Sample copy free. Guidelines free.

NONFICTION Needs essays, historical, humor, interview, opinion, book reviews. Does not want fiction, memoirs, personal reflections. Query. Length: 1,500-5,000 words. **Pays $100.**

POETRY Needs avant-garde, free verse, traditional. **No payment for poems.**

⊕⊕⊕⊕ THE GUIDE

491 Church Street, Suite 200, Toronto ON M4Y 2C6. (416)925-6665. **Fax:** (416)925-6674. **E-mail:** matt.mills@xtra.ca; info@guidemag.com. **Website:** www.guidemag.com. **Contact:** Mark Sullivan, managing editor. **75% freelance written**. Monthly magazine on the gay and lesbian news, features, and travel. Estab. 1981. Circ. 45,000. Offers negotiable kill fee. Publishes ms an average of 2 months after acceptance. Submit seasonal material 4 months in advance. Accepts queries by mail, e-mail. Accepts simultaneous submissions. Responds in 3 months to queries.

NONFICTION Needs book excerpts, if yet unpublished, essays, exposé, general interest, historical, humor, interview, opinion, personal experience, photo feature, religious. **Buys 48 mss/year.** Send complete ms. Length: 500-2,500 words. **Pays $100-1,750**

⊕⊕ INSTINCT MAGAZINE

303 N. Glenoaks Blvd., Suite L-120, Burbank CA 91502. (818)286-0071; (818)843-1536 x102. **E-mail:** editor@instinctmag.com. **Website:** http://instinctmag.com. **Contact:** Mike Wood, editor-in-chief. **40% freelance written**. Gay men's monthly lifestyle and entertainment magazine. "*Instinct* is a blend of *Cosmo* and *Maxim* for gay men. We're smart, sexy, irreverent, and we always have a sense of humor—a unique style that has made us the #1 gay men's magazine in the US." Estab. 1997. Circ. 115,000. Byline given. Offers 20% kill fee. Editorial lead time 2-3 months. Accepts queries by mail, e-mail. Accepts simultaneous submissions. Sample copy available online. Guidelines available online. Register online first.

NONFICTION Needs exposé, general interest, humor, interview, celebrity and non-celebrity, travel, basically anything of interest to gay men will be considered. Does not want first-person accounts or articles. Send complete ms. via online submissions manager

Length: 850-2,000 words. **Pays $50-300.** Sometimes pays expenses of writers on assignment.

COLUMNS Health (gay, off-kilter), 800 words; Fitness (irreverent), 500 words; Movies, Books (edgy, sardonic), 800 words; Music, Video Games (indie, underground), 800 words. **Pays $150-250.**

MENSBOOK JOURNAL

CQS Media, Inc., P.O. Box 418, Sturbridge MA 01566. **Fax:** (508)347-8150. **E-mail:** features@mensbook.com. **Website:** www.mensbook.com. **Contact:** P.C. Carr, editor/publisher. **75% freelance written.** Quarterly online download. "We target bright, inquisitive, discerning gay men who want more non-commercial substance from gay media. We seek primarily first-person autobiographical pieces—then: biographies, political and social analysis, cartoons, short fiction, commentary, travel, humor." Estab. 2008. Circ. 5,000. Byline given. Editorial lead time 4 months. Submit seasonal material 6 months in advance. Accepts queries by e-mail. Responds in 8 weeks to queries. Sample copy sent free by PDF. Guidelines online at www.mensbook.com/writersguidelines.htm.

NONFICTION Needs first-person pieces; essays; think-pieces; exposé; humor; inspirational profiles of courage and triumph over adversity; interview/profile; religion/philosophy vis-a-vis the gay experience; opinion; travel. "We do not want celebrity profiles/commentary, chatty, campy gossip; sexual conjecture about famous people; or film reviews." **Buys 25 mss/year.** Query by e-mail. Length: 1,000-2,500 words. **Pays stipend for assigned articles and for unsolicited articles.**

FICTION Contact: Contact Payson Fitch, managing editor. Needs adventure, erotica, fantasy, mystery/suspense, slice-of-life vignettes. **Buys 10-12 fiction mss/year.** Send complete ms. Length: 750-3,000 words.

POETRY Contact: Contact J.K. Small, poetry editor. Needs avant-garde, free verse, haiku, light verse, traditional. Buys 8 poems/year. poems/year.

METROSOURCE MAGAZINE

137 W. 19th St., 2nd Floor, New York NY 10011. (212)691-5127. **E-mail:** letters@metrosource.com. **Website:** www.metrosource.com. **75% freelance written.** Magazine published 6 times/year. "*MetroSource* is an upscale, glossy, 4-color lifestyle magazine targeted to an urban, professional gay and lesbian readership." Estab. 1990. Circ. 145,000. Byline given. Publishes ms an average of 2 months after acceptance.

Editorial lead time 4 months. Submit seasonal material 4 months in advance. Accepts queries by mail, e-mail, fax, phone. Accepts simultaneous submissions. Sample copy for $5.

NONFICTION Contact: Paul Hagen, editor-in-chief. Needs exposé, interview, opinion, photo feature, travel. **Buys 20 mss/year.** Query with published clips. Length: 1,000-1,800 words. **Pays $100-400.**

COLUMNS Book, film, television, and stage reviews; health columns; and personal diary and opinion pieces. Word lengths vary. Query with published clips. **Pays $200.**

THE WASHINGTON BLADE

529 14th St., NW, Washington D.C. 20045. (202)747-2077. **Fax:** (202)747-2070. **E-mail:** info@washblade.com; knaff@washblade.com. **Website:** www.washblade.com. **Contact:** Kevin Naff, editor. **20% freelance written.** Nation's oldest and largest weekly newspaper covering the lesbian, gay, bisexual and transgender issues. Articles (subjects) should be written from or directed to a gay perspective. Estab. 1969. Circ. 30,000. Byline given. Submit seasonal material one month in advance. Accepts queries by mail, e-mail, fax. Responds in within one month to queries.

COLUMNS Send feature submissions to Joey DiGuglielmo, arts editor. Sent opinion submission to Kevin Naff, editor. Pay varies. No sexually explicit material.

XTRA

Pink Triangle Press, 2 Carlton St., Suite 1600, Toronto ON M5B 1J3 Canada. (416)925-6665; (800)268-9872. **Fax:** (416)925-6674. **E-mail:** info.toronto@xtra.ca. **E-mail:** matt.mills@xtra.ca. **Website:** www.xtra.ca. **Contact:** Matt Mills, associate publisher and editor-in-chief. **80% freelance written.** Biweekly tabloid covering gay, lesbian, bisexual, and transgender issues, news, arts, and events of interest in Toronto. "*Xtra* is dedicated to lesbian and gay sexual liberation. We publish material that advocates this end, according to the mission statement of the not-for-profit organization Pink Triangle Press, which operates the paper." Estab. 1984. Circ. 45,000. Byline given. Editorial lead time 1 month. Accepts queries by e-mail. Accepts simultaneous submissions. Responds in 2 weeks to queries. Sample copy available online. Guidelines by e-mail.

NONFICTION Needs book excerpts, essays, interview, opinion, personal experience, travel. Does not want US-based stories or profiles of straight people who do not have a direct connection to the LGBT community. Query with published clips. Length: 200-1,600 words. Sometimes pays expenses of writers on assignment. Payment: Limit agreed upon in advance.

COLUMNS *Xtra* rarely publishes unsolicited columns. **Buys 6 columns/year. mss/year.** Query with published clips.

GENERAL INTEREST

$$ THE AMERICAN LEGION MAGAZINE

P.O. Box 1055, Indianapolis IN 46206-1055. (317)630-1200. **Fax:** (317)630-1280. **E-mail:** magazine@legion.org. **E-mail:** mgrills@legion.org;hsoria@legion.org. **Website:** www.legion.org. **Contact:** Matt Grills, cartoon editor; Holly Soria, art director. **70% freelance written. Prefers to work with published/established writers, but works with a small number of new/unpublished writers each year.** Monthly magazine. "Working through 15,000 community-level posts, the honorably discharged wartime veterans of The American Legion dedicate themselves to God, country, and traditional American values. They believe in a strong defense; adequate and compassionate care for veterans and their families; community service; and the wholesome development of our nation's youth. We publish articles that reflect these values. We inform our readers and their families of significant trends and issues affecting our nation, the world and the way we live. Our major features focus on the American flag, national security, foreign affairs, business trends, social issues, health, education, ethics and the arts. We also publish selected general feature articles, articles of special interest to veterans, and question-and-answer interviews with prominent national and world figures." Estab. 1919. Circ. 2,550,000. Byline given. Publishes ms an average of 6 months after acceptance. Accepts queries by mail, e-mail, fax. Responds in 2 months to queries. Sample copy for $3.50 and 9×12 SAE with 6 first-class stamps. Guidelines for #10 SASE.

NONFICTION Needs general interest, interview. No regional topics or promotion of partisan political agendas. No personal experiences or war stories. **Buys 50-60 mss/year.** Query with SASE should explain the subject or issue, article's angle and organization, writer's qualifications, and experts to be interviewed. Length: 300-2,000 words. **Pays 40¢/word and up.**

THE ATLANTIC MONTHLY

The Watergate, 600 New Hampshire Ave., NW, Washington DC 20037. (202)266-6000. **Website:** www.theatlantic.com. **Contact:** James Bennet, editor; C. Michael Curtis, fiction editor; David Barber, poetry editor. Covering poetry, fiction, and articles of the highest quality. General magazine for an educated readership with broad cultural and public-affairs interests. "The Atlantic considers unsolicited manuscripts, either fiction or nonfiction. A general familiarity with what we have published in the past is the best guide to our needs and preferences. Manuscripts must be typewritten and double-spaced. Receipt of manuscripts will be acknowledged if accompanied by a self-addressed stamped envelope. Manuscripts will not be returned. **At this time, the print magazine does not read submissions sent via fax or e-mail.** TheAtlantic.com no longer accepts unsolicited submissions." Estab. 1857. Circ. 500,000. Byline given. Accepts queries by mail. Guidelines available onine.

NONFICTION Needs book excerpts, essays, general interest, humor, travel. Query with or without published clips or send complete ms to 'Editorial Department' at address above. All unsolicited mss must be accompanied by SASE. A general familiarity with what we have published in the past is the best guide to our needs and preferences. Simply send your manuscript—typewritten, double-spaced—to the Editorial Director, The Atlantic. Receipt of manuscripts will be acknowledged if accompanied by a self-addressed stamped envelope. Manuscripts will not be returned. Length: 1,000-6,000 words **Payment varies** Sometimes pays expenses.

FICTION Seeks fiction that is clear, tightly written with strong sense of 'story' and well-defined characters. No longer publishes fiction in the regular magazine. Instead, it will appear in a special newsstand-only fiction issue. Send complete ms. Preferred length: 2,00-6,000 words **True**.

POETRY *The Atlantic Monthly* publishes some of the most distinguished poetry in American literature. "We read with interest and attention every poem submitted to the magazine and, quite simply, we publish those that seem to us to be the best." Receives about 60,000 poems/year. Subscription: $24.50 for 10 issues. Sample: $7.50 (back issue). Buys 30-35 poems/year poems/year. Submit maximum 6 poems/max poems.

⑨ CAPPER'S

Ogden Publications, Inc., 1503 SW 42nd St., Topeka KS 66609-1265. (800)678-4883. **E-mail:** editor@cappers.com; tsmith@cappers.com. **Website:** www.cappers.com. **Contact:** Hank Will, editor-in-chief. **90% freelance written.** Monthly tabloid emphasizing home and family for readers who live mainly in the rural Midwest. "*CAPPER's* is upbeat, focusing on the homey feelings people like to share, as well as hopes and dreams. *CAPPER's* is a bimonthly rural lifestyle magazine that focuses on small town life, country and rural lifestyles and 'hobby' farms. Buys shared rights. *CAPPER's* no longer publishes poetry and fiction. No unsolicited mss accepted; authors must query first. Send queries via e-mail (editor@cappers.com). Articles (except Heart of the Home) are assigned; no editorial calendar is published. A great way to have a first article published is to become a *CAPPER's* blogger. For blogger information, send e-mail." Estab. 1879. Circ. 100,000. Byline given. Pays for articles on publication. Publishes ms an average of 2-12 months after acceptance. Submit seasonal queries 6-8 months in advance. Accepts queries by e-mail. Responds in 2-3 weeks to queries. Sample copy available online. Guidelines available online or by e-mail.

NONFICTION feature-length articles (800-1,500 words with photos) on topics of interest to those living in rural areas, on farms or ranches, or those simply interested in the rural lifestyle; department articles (500-1,500 words with photos) on nostalgia, farm equipment and animals, DIY projects, gardening and cooking. Paid upon publication.

COLUMNS Heart of the Home: Send complete ms. **Pays approximately $2/printed inch.**

THE CHRISTIAN SCIENCE MONITOR

The Home Forum Page, 210 Massachussetts Ave., P02-30, Boston MA 02115. **E-mail:** homeforum@csmonitor.com. **Website:** www.csmonitor.com. **Contact:** Susan Leach, Marjorie Kehe, editors. *The Christian Science Monitor*, an international daily newspaper, regularly features poetry in The Home Forum section. Wants "finely crafted poems that explore and celebrate daily life; that provide a respite from daily news and from the bleakness that appears in so much contemporary verse." Considers free verse and fixed forms. Estab. 1908.

POETRY Submit up to 5 poems at a time. Lines/poem: Prefers short poems under 20 lines. No previously published poems or simultaneous submissions. Accepts e-mail submissions only (by attachment in MS Word, 1 poem/e-mail). Pays $20/haiku; $40/poem. Does not want "work that presents people in helpless or hopeless states; poetry about death, aging, or illness; or dark, violent, sensual poems. No poems that are overtly religious or falsely sweet."

⑨⑨ FASHION FORUM

Business Journals, Inc., 1384 Broadway, 11th Floor, New York NY 10018. (212)710-7442. **E-mail:** jillians@busjour.com. **Website:** www.busjour.com. **Contact:** Jillian Sprague, managing editor. **80% freelance written.** Semiannual magazine covering luxury fashion (men's 70%, women's 30%), luxury lifestyle. "*Forum* directly targets a very upscale reader interested in profiles and service pieces on upscale designers, new fashion trends, and traditional suiting. Lifestyle articles—including wine and spirits, travel, cars, boating, sports, collecting, etc.—are upscale top of the line (i.e., don't write how expensive taxis are)." Circ. 150,000. Byline given. Offers 50% kill fee. Publishes ms an average of 3-4 months after acceptance. Editorial lead time 6 months. Submit seasonal material 6 months in advance. Accepts queries by mail, e-mail. NoResponds in 2-3 weeks to queries. Guidelines by e-mail.

NONFICTION Needs general interest, interview, travel, luxury lifestyle trends, fashion service pieces. Does not want personal essays ("we run a few but commission them"). No fiction or single product articles; "in other words, an article should be on whats new in Italian wines, not about 1 superspecial brand." **Buys 20-25 mss/year.** Query. Length: 600-1,500 words. **Pays $300-500.**

COLUMNS Travel, 1,000-1,500 words; Wine + Spirits, 600-1,200 words; Gourmet, 600-1,200 words; Wheels, 600 words. **Buys 10-15 mss/year.** Query. **Pays $300-500.**

⑨⑨ GRIT

Ogden Publications, 1503 SW 42nd St., Topeka KS 66609. (785)274-4300. **Fax:** (785)274-4305. **E-mail:** Grit@Grit.com; cregan@grit.com. **Website:** www.grit.com. **Contact:** Caleb Regan, managing editor. **90% freelance written. Open to new writers.** Bimonthly magazine. "*Grit* focuses on rural lifestyles, country living and smallfarming. We are looking for useful, practical information on livestock,gardening, farm equipment, home and yard improvement and related topics." Estab. 1882. Circ. 230,000. Byline given. Submit seasonal material 6 months in advance. Accepts queries by mail, e-mail. Responds within 3 months. Sample copyavailable for $6 with 9×12 SASE. Guidelines available online.

FICTION "We do not accept fiction or poetry submissions."

$$$$ HARPER'S MAGAZINE

666 Broadway, 11th Floor, New York NY 10012. (212)420-5720. **Fax:** (212)228-5889. **E-mail:** readings@harpers.org. **Website:** www.harpers.org. **90% freelance written.** Monthly magazine for well-educated, socially concerned, widely read men and women who value ideas and good writing. *Harper's Magazine* encourages national discussion on current and significant issues in a format that offers arresting facts and intelligent opinions. By means of its several shorter journalistic forms—Harper's Index, Readings, Forum, and Annotation—as well as with its acclaimed essays, fiction, and reporting, *Harper's* continues the tradition begun with its first issue in 1850: to inform readers across the whole spectrum of political, literary, cultural, and scientific affairs. Estab. 1850. Circ. 230,000. Offers negotiable kill fee. Publishes ms an average of 3 months after acceptance. Responds in 6 weeks to queries. Sample copy for $5.95.

NONFICTION Needs humor. **Buys 2 mss/year.** Query. Length: 4,000-6,000 words.

FICTION Will consider unsolicited fiction. Needs humorous. **Buys 12 mss/year.** Query. Length: 3,000-5,000 words. **Generally pays 50¢-$1/word.**

$$$$ NATIONAL GEOGRAPHIC MAGAZINE

1145 17th St. NW, Washington DC 20036. (202)857-7000. **Fax:** (202)492-5767. **Website:** www.nationalgeographic.com. Chris Johns, editor-in-chief. **60% freelance written. Prefers to work with published/established writers.** Monthly magazine for members of the National Geographic Society. Estab. 1888. Circ. 6,800,000.

NONFICTION Query (500 words with clips of published articles) by mail to senior assitant editor Oliver Payne. Do not send mss. Length: 2,000-8,000 words. Pays expenses of writers on assignment.

$$$ NEWSWEEK

The Daily Beast, 251 W. 57th St., New York NY 10019. (212)445-4000. **E-mail:** editors@newsweek.com. **Website:** www.newsweek.com. *Newsweek* is edited to report the week's developments on the newsfront of the world and the nation through news, commentary, and analysis. Circ. 3,180,000.

COLUMNS Contact: myturn@newsweek.com. "We are no longer accepting submissions for the print edition. To submit an essay to our website, please e-mail it to: myturn@newsweek.com. The My Turn essay should be: A) an original piece, B) 850-900 words, C) generally personal in tone, and D) about any topic, but not framed as a response to a Newsweek story or another My Turn essay. Submissions must not have been published elsewhere. Please include your full name, phone number, and address with your entry. The competition is very stiff-we get 600 entries per month-and we can only print 1 a week. *Due to the number of submissions we receive, we cannot respond unless we plan to publish your essay;* if your story is tied to current events, it may not be appropriate. We are fully aware of the time and effort involved in preparing an essay, and each ms is given careful consideration. For an automated message with further details about My Turn, you may call: (212) 445-4547." **Pays $1,000 on publication.**

THE NEW YORKER

4 Times Square, New York NY 10036. (212) 286-5900. **E-mail:** beth_lusko@newyorker.com; toon@cartoonbank.com. **Website:** www.newyorker.com; www.cartoonbank.com. **Contact:** Bob Mankoff, cartoon; David Remnick, editor-in-chief. A quality weekly magazine of distinct news stories, articles, essays, and poems for a literate audience. Estab. 1925. Circ. 938,600. Accepts queries by mail, e-mail. NoResponds in 3 months to mss.

💬 *The New Yorker* receives approximately 4,000 submissions per month.

NONFICTION Submissions: Fiction, poetry, Shouts & Murmurs, and newsbreaks should be sent as pdf attachments. Do not paste them into the message field. Due to volume, we cannot consider unsolicited "Talk of the Town" stories or other nonfiction. Read more www.newyorker.com/contact/contactus#ixzz1IZ1dgwWo.

FICTION Publishes 1 ms/issue. Send complete ms. Fiction, poetry, Shouts & Murmurs, and newsbreaks should be sent as pdf attachments. Do not paste them into the message field. **Payment varies.**

POETRY Send poetry to Poetry Department. Submit maximum 6 poems.

⊛⊛⊛ THE NEW YORK TIMES MAGAZINE

620 8th Ave., New York NY 10018. (212)556-1234. **Fax:** (212)556-3830. **E-mail:** magazine@nytimes.com; thearts@nytimes.com. **Website:** www.nytimes.com/pages/magazine. *The New York Times Magazine* appears in *The New York Times* on Sunday. The *Arts and Leisure* section appears during the week. The *Op Ed* page appears daily. Circ. 1.8 million.

⊛⊛⊛ THE OLD FARMER'S ALMANAC

Yankee Publishing, Inc., P.O. Box 520, Dublin NH 03444. (603)563-8111. **Website:** www.Almanac.com. **Contact:** Janice Stillman, editor. **95% freelance written.** Annual magazine covering weather, gardening, history, oddities, lore. "*The Old Farmer's Almanac* is the oldest continuously published periodical in North America. Since 1792, it has provided useful information for people in all walks of life: tide tables for those who live near the ocean; sunrise tables and planting charts for those who live on the farm or simply enjoy gardening; recipes for those who like to cook; and forecasts for those who don't like the question of weather left up in the air. The words of the *Almanac*'s founder, Robert B. Thomas, guide us still: 'Our main endeavor is to be useful, but with a pleasant degree of humour.'" Estab. 1792. Circ. 3,750,000. Byline given. Offers 25% kill fee. Publishes ms an average of 9 months after acceptance. Editorial lead time 6 months. Submit seasonal material 1 year in advance. Accepts queries by mail. Responds in 3 weeks to queries. Responds in 2 months to mss. Guidelines available online.

NONFICTION Needs general interest, historical, how-to, garden, cook, save money, humor, weather, natural remedies, obscure facts, history, popular culture. No personal recollections/accounts, personal/family histories. Query with published clips. Length: 800-2,500 words. **Pays 65¢/word.** Sometimes pays expenses of writers on assignment.

FILLERS Needs anecdotes, short humor. **Buys 1-2 mss/year.** Length: 100-200 words. **Pays $25.**

⊛⊛⊛ OPEN SPACES

Open Spaces Publications, Inc., PMB 134, 6327-C SW Capitol Hwy., Portland OR 97239-1937. (503)313-4361. **Fax:** (503)227-3401. **E-mail:** info@open-spaces.com. **Website:** www.open-spaces.com. **95% freelance written.** Quarterly general interest magazine. "*Open Spaces* is an online quarterly which gives voice to the Northwest on issues that are regional, national and international in scope. Our readership is thoughtful, intelligent, widely read and appreciative of ideas and writing of the highest quality. With that in mind, we seek thoughtful, well-researched articles and insightful fiction, essays and poetry on a variety of subjects from a number of different viewpoints." Estab. 1997. Byline given. Offers 20% kill fee. Publishes ms an average of 6 months after acceptance. Editorial lead time 9 months. Accepts queries by mail, fax. Accepts simultaneous submissions. Sample copy for $10. Guidelines available online.

NONFICTION Needs essays, general interest, historical, how-to, if clever, humor, interview, personal experience, travel. **Buys 35 mss/year.** Query first. 1,500-4,00 words. **Pays variable amount.**

COLUMNS Contact: David Williams, departments editor. Books (substantial topics such as the Booker Prize, The Newbery, etc.); Travel (must reveal insight); Sports (past subjects include rowing, and swing dancing); Unintended Consequences, 1,500-2,500 words. **Buys 20-25 mss/year.** Send complete ms. **Payment varies**

FICTION Contact: Ellen Teicher, fiction editor. Quality is far more important than type. Read the magazine. Excellence is the issue—not subject matter. **Buys 8 mss/year.** Send complete ms with SASE. Length: 2,000-5,000 words. **Payment varies.**

POETRY Contact: Susan Juve-Hu Bucharest, poetry editor. Again, quality is far more important than type. Submit 3 poems with SASE. "No epics, please."

FILLERS Needs anecdotes, short humor, cartoons.

⊛⊛⊛⊛ OUTSIDE

Mariah Media, Inc., 400 Market St., Santa Fe NM 87501. (505)989-7100. **Fax:** (505)989-4700. **Website:** www.outsidemag.com. **60% freelance written.** Monthly magazine covering active lifestyle. Estab. 1977. Circ. 665,000. Byline given. Offers 25% kill fee. Publishes ms an average of 3-6 months after acceptance. Accepts queries by mail. Responds is 6-8 weeks. Guidelines on website.

NONFICTION Needs book excerpts, new product, travel. **Buys 300 mss/year.** Query with 2 or 3 relevant clips along with a SASE to: Editorial Department, *Outside* magazine, 400 Market St., Santa Fe, New Mexico, 87501. Length: 100-5,000 words. **Pays $1.50-2/word for assigned articles. Pays $1-1.50/word for unsolicited articles.** Pays expenses of writers on assignment.

COLUMNS Pays $1.50-$2.

💲💲💲💲 PARADE

ParadeNet, Inc., 711 Third Ave., New York NY 10017-4014. (212)450-7000. **Website:** www.parade.com. **Contact:** Megan Brown, articles editor. **95% freelance written.** Weekly magazine for a general interest audience. Estab. 1941. Circ. 32,000,000. Offers kill fee. Kill fee varies in amount. Publishes ms an average of 5 months after acceptance. Editorial lead time 1 month. Accepts queries by mail, online submission form. Accepts simultaneous submissions. Sample copy available online. Guidelines available online.

NONFICTION Spot news events are not accepted, as *Parade* has a 2-month lead time. No fiction, fashion, travel, poetry, cartoons, nostalgia, regular columns, personal essays, quizzes, or fillers. Unsolicited queries concerning celebrities, politicians or sports figures are rarely assigned. **Buys 150 mss/year.** Query with published clips. Length: 1,200-1,500 words. **Pays very competitive amount.** Pays expenses of writers on assignment.

⊘ PEOPLE

Time, Inc., 1271 Avenue of the Americas, New York NY 10020. (212)522-1212. **Fax:** (212)522-1359. **E-mail:** editor@people.com. **Website:** www.people.com. Weekly magazine. Designed as a forum for personality journalism through the use of short articles on contemporary news events and people. Circ. about 3.7 million. Editorial lead time 3 months.

> ○ Does not buy freelance materials or use freelance writers.

💲💲 READER'S DIGEST

The Reader's Digest Association, Inc., Box 100, Pleasantville NY 10572-0100. **E-mail:** articleproposals@rd.com. **Website:** www.rd.com. Monthly magazine. **COLUMNS** Life; @Work; Off Base, **pays $300.** Laugh; Quotes, **pays $100.** Address your submission to the appropriate humor category.

💲💲💲💲 ROBB REPORT

CurtCo Media Labs, 29160 Heathercliff Rd., Suite #200, Malibu CA 90265. (310)589-7700. **Fax:** (310)589-7701. **E-mail:** editorial@robbreport.com. **Website:** www.robbreport.com. **Contact:** Russ Rocknak, design director. **60% freelance written.** Monthly lifestyle magazine geared toward active, affluent readers. Addresses upscale autos, luxury travel, boating, technology, lifestyles, watches, fashion, sports, investments, collectibles. "For over 30 years, Robb Report magazine has served as the definitive authority on connoisseurship for ultra-affluent consumers. Robb Report not only showcases the products and services available from the most prestigious luxury brands around the globe, but it also provides its sophisticated readership with detailed insight into a range of these subjects, which include sports and luxury automobiles, yachts, real estate, travel, private aircraft, fashion, fine jewelry and watches, art, wine, state-of-the-art home electronics and much more. For connoisseurs seeking the very best that life has to offer, Robb Report remains the essential luxury resource." Estab. 1976. Circ. 111,000. Byline given. Offers 25% kill fee. Submit seasonal material 5 months in advance. Accepts queries by mail, fax. Responds in 2 months to queries. Responds in 1 month to mss. Sample copy for $10.95, plus shipping and handling. Guidelines for #10 SASE.

NONFICTION Needs new product, autos, boats, aircraft, watches, consumer electronics, travel, international and domestic, dining. Special issues: Home (October); Recreation (March). **Buys 60 mss/year.** Query with published clips. Length: 500-2,000 words. **Pays $1/word.** Sometimes pays expenses of writers on assignment.

💲💲 THE SATURDAY EVENING POST

The Saturday Evening Post Society, 1100 Waterway Blvd., Indianapolis IN 46202. (317)634-1100. **Website:** www.saturdayeveningpost.com. Steve Slon, editorial director. **30% freelance written.** Bimonthly general interest, family-oriented magazine focusing on lifestyle, physical fitness, and preventive medicine. "Ask almost any American if he or she has heard of *The Saturday Evening Post*, and you will find that many have fond recollections of the magazine from their childhood days. Many readers recall sitting with their families on Saturdays awaiting delivery of their *Post* subscription in the mail. *The Saturday Evening Post* has forged a tradition of 'forefront journalism.' *The Saturday Evening Post* continues to stand at the journalistic forefront with its coverage of health, nutrition, and preventive medicine." Estab. 1728. Circ. 350,000. Byline given. Publishes ms an average of 3 months after acceptance. Submit seasonal material 4 months in advance. Accepts queries by mail, fax. Accepts simultaneous submissions. Responds in 3 weeks to queries. Responds in 6 weeks to mss.

NONFICTION Needs how-to, gardening, home improvement, humor, interview, medical, health, fitness. No political articles or articles containing sexual innuendo or hypersophistication. **Buys 25 mss/year.** Send complete ms. Length: 1,000-2,500 words. **Pays $25-400.**

COLUMNS Travel (destinations); Post Scripts (well-known humorists); Post People (activities of celebrities). Length 750-1,500. **Buys 16 mss/year.** Query with published clips or send complete ms. **Pays $150 minimum, negotiable maximum.**

POETRY Needs light verse.

FILLERS Contact: Post Scripts Editor. Needs anecdotes, short humor. **Buys 200 mss/year.** Length: 300 words. **Pays $15.**

⊛ SENIOR LIVING

Stratis Publishing Ltd, 153, 1581-H Hillside Ave., Victoria BC V8T 2CI Canada. (250)479-4705. **Fax:** (250)479-4808. **E-mail:** editor@seniorlivingmag.com. **Website:** www.seniorlivingmag.com. **Contact:** Bobbie Jo Reid, managing editor. **100% freelance written.** 12 times per yr. magazine covering active 50+ living. "Inspiring editorial profiling 'seniors' (50+) who are active & lead interesting lives. Include articles on health, housing, accessibility, sports, travel, recipes, etc." Estab. 2004. Circ. 41,000. Byline given. Pays quarterly. Publishes an average of 2-3 months after acceptance. Editorial lead time 3 months. Submit seasonal material 6 months in advance. Accepts queries by e-mail. Accepts simultaneous submissions. Sample copy available online. Guidelines available.

NONFICTION Needs historical, how-to, humor, inspirational, interview, personal experience, travel, active living for 50+. Do not want politics, religion, promotion of business, service or products, humor that demeans 50+ demographic or aging process. **Buys 150 mss/year.** Query. Does not accept previously published material. Length: 500-1,200 words. **Pays $35-150 for assigned articles. Pays $35-150 for unsolicited articles.** Sometimes pays expenses (limit agreed upon in advance).

⊛⊛⊛⊛ SMITHSONIAN MAGAZINE

Capital Gallery, Suite 6001, MRC 513, P.O. Box 37012, Washington DC 20013-7012. (202)275-2000. **E-mail:** smithsonianmagazine@si.edu. **Website:** www.smithsonianmag.com. **Contact:** Molly Roberts, photo editor; Jeff Campagna, art services coordinator. **90% freelance written.** Monthly magazine for associate members of the Smithsonian Institution; 85% with college education. "*Smithsonian Magazine's* mission is to inspire fascination with all the world has to offer by featuring unexpected and entertaining editorial that explores different lifestyles, cultures and peoples, the arts, the wonders of nature and technology, and much more. The highly educated, innovative readers of *Smithsonian* share a unique desire to celebrate life, seeking out the timely as well as timeless, the artistic as well as the academic, and the thought-provoking as well as the humorous." Circ. 2,300,000. Offers 33% kill fee. Publishes ms an average of 6 months after acceptance. Editorial lead time 2 months. Submit seasonal material 3 months in advance. Accepts queries by online submission form only. Responds in 3 weeks to queries from the web form. Sample copy for $5. Guidelines available online.

NONFICTION Buys 120-130 feature (up to 5,000 words) and 12 short (500-650 words) mss/year. Use online submission form. **Pays various rates per feature, $1,500 per short piece.** Pays expenses of writers on assignment.

COLUMNS Buys 12-15 department articles/year. Length: 1,000-2,000 words. Last Page humor, 550-700 words. Use online submission form. **Pays $1,000-1,500.**

⊛ SOFA INK QUARTERLY

Sofa Ink, P.O. Box 625, American Fork UT 84003. **E-mail:** publisher@sofaink.com. **E-mail:** acquisitions@sofaink.com. **Website:** www.sofaink.com; www.sofainkquarterly.com. **Contact:** David Cowsert. **95% freelance written.** Quarterly magazine. "Sofa Ink Quarterly offers wonderful original stories, poetry, and nonfiction that is entertaining yet wholesome. Sofa Ink Quarterly showcases original writing and art that avoids sensationalism. There is no swearing, profaning deity, excessive gore, gratuitous violence or gratuitous sex. You will find exceptional storytelling, delightful poetry, and beautiful art." Estab. 2005. Circ. 650. Byline given. Publishes ms an average of 3 months after acceptance. Submit seasonal material 4 months in advance. Accepts queries by mail, e-mail. Accepts simultaneous submissions. Responds in 1-3 months to queries. Responds in 1-3 months to mss. Sample copy for $6. Guidelines available online.

NONFICTION Needs essays, general interest, historical, humor, inspirational, interview, personal experience. Send complete ms. Length: 7,500 words. **Pays $5, plus 3 contributor copies.**

PHOTOS Identification of subjects, model releases required. Offers no additional payment for photos accepted with ms.

FICTION Needs adventure, ethnic, experimental, fantasy, historical, humorous, mainstream, mystery, romance, science fiction, slice-of-life vignettes, suspense, western. Does not want erotic, religious. **Buys 24-30 mss/year.** Send complete ms. Length: 7,500 words. **Pays $5.**

POETRY Needs avant-garde, free verse, haiku, light verse, traditional. Submit 5 poems maximum at a time. Considers simultaneous submissions. Accepts e-mail submissions (as attachment in Word). Submit seasonal poems 4 months in advance. Time between acceptance and publication is about 3 months. Guidelines available for SASE or on website. Responds in 1-3 months. Pays $5 and 3 contributor's copies. Acquires first North American serial rights. Buys 9-15 poems/year. Submit maximum 5 poems.

⊘ TIME

Time/Life Building, 1271 Avenue of the Americas, New York NY 10020. **E-mail:** letters@time.com. **Website:** www.time.com. **Contact:** Art director. Weekly magazine. *TIME* covers the full range of information that is important to people today—breaking news, national and world affairs, business news, societal and lifestyle issues, culture and entertainment news and reviews. Estab. 1923. Circ. 4,034,000.

○ *TIME* does not accept unsolicited material for publication. The magazine is entirely staff written and produced.

⊗⊗⊗ YES! MAGAZINE

284 Madrona Way NE, Suite 116, Bainbridge Island WA 98110. **E-mail:** editors@yesmagazine.org. **E-mail:** submissions@yesmagazine.org. **Website:** www.yesmagazine.org. **70% freelance written.** Quarterly magazine covering sustainability, social justice, grassroots activism, contemporary culture; nature, conservation, ecology, politics, and world affairs. "*YES! Magazine* documents how people are creating a more just, sustainable and compassionate world. Each issue includes articles focused on a theme—about solutions to a significant challenge facing our world—and a number of timely, non-theme articles. Our non-theme section provides ongoing coverage of issues like health, climate change, globalization, media reform, faith, democracy, economy and labor, social and racial justice and peace building. To inquire about upcoming themes, send an email to submissions@yesmagazine.org; please be sure to type 'themes' as the subject line." Estab. 1997. Circ. 55,000. Byline given. Rarely offers kill fee. Publishes ms an average of 1-6 months after acceptance. Editorial lead time 3-6 months. Submit seasonal material 2-6 months in advance. Accepts queries by e-mail. Sample copy and writer's guidelines online.

NONFICTION Needs book excerpts, opinion. "We don't want stories that are negative or too politically partisan." **Buys 30 mss/year.** Query with published clips. Length: 100-2,500 words. **Pays $50-1,250 for assigned articles. Pays $50-600 for unsolicited articles.**

COLUMNS Signs of Life (positive news briefs), 100-250 words; Commentary (opinion from thinkers and experts), 500 words; Book and film reviews, 500-800 words. **Pays $20-$300.**

HEALTH AND FITNESS

⊗⊗ AMERICAN FITNESS

15250 Ventura Blvd., Suite 200, Sherman Oaks CA 91403. (800)446-2322, ext. 200. **E-mail:** americanfitness@afaa.com. **Website:** www.afaa.com. **Contact:** Meg Jordan, editor. **75% freelance written.** Bimonthly magazine covering exercise and fitness, health, and nutrition. "We need timely, in-depth, informative articles on health, fitness, aerobic exercise, sports nutrition, age-specific fitness, and outdoor activity. Absolutely no first-person accounts. Need well-researched articles for professional readers." Estab. 1983. Circ. 42,900. Byline given. Pays 30 days after publication. Publishes ms an average of 6 months after acceptance. Submit seasonal material 4 months in advance. Accepts queries by mail, fax. Accepts simultaneous submissions. Responds in 2 months to queries. Sample copy for $4.50 and SASE with 6 first-class stamps.

NONFICTION Needs historical, history of various athletic events, inspirational, sport's leaders motivational pieces, interview, fitness figures, new product, plus equipment review, personal experience, successful fitness story, photo feature, on exercise, fitness, new sport, travel, activity adventures. No articles on unsound nutritional practices, popular trends, or unsafe exercise gimmicks. **Buys 18-25 mss/year.** Send complete ms. Length: 800-1,200 words. **Pays $200 for features, $80 for news.** Sometimes pays expenses of writers on assignment.

COLUMNS Research (latest exercise and fitness findings); Alternative paths (nonmainstream approaches to health, wellness, and fitness); Strength (latest breakthroughs in weight training); Clubscene (profiles and highlights of fitness club industry); Adventure (treks, trails, and global challenges); Food (low-fat/nonfat, high-flavor dishes); Homescene (home-workout alternatives); Clip 'n' Post (concise exercise research to post in health clubs, offices or on refrigerators). Length: 800-1,000 words. Query with published clips or send complete ms. **Pays $100-200.**

◉◉ CLIMBING

Primedia Enthusiast Group, Box 420034, Palm Coast FL 32142. (970)963-9449. **Fax:** (970)963-9442. **E-mail:** msamet@climbing.com. **Website:** www.climbing.com. Magazine published 9 times/year covering climbing and mountaineering. Provides features on rock climbing and mountaneering worldwide. Estab. 1970. Circ. 51,000. Editorial lead time 6 weeks. Accepts queries by e-mail. Sample copy for $4.99. Guidelines available online.

> ◐ We pride ourselves on running the best, most exciting, and most experimental climbing photography and writing in the world. We're glad that you are interested in helping us convey passion and creativity for the sport. For more information contact Matt Samet: msamet@climbing.com."

NONFICTION Needs interview, interesting climbers, personal experience, climbing adventures, surveys of different areas. Query. Length: 1,500-3,500 words. **Pays 35¢/word.**

◉◉◉◉ FITNESS MAGAZINE

Meredith Corp., 805 Third Ave., 25th Floor, New York NY 10022. **E-mail:** fitnessmail@fitnessmagazine.com. **Website:** www.fitnessmagazine.com. Monthly magazine for women in their 20s and 30s who are interested in fitness and living a healthy life. Circ. 1.5 million. Byline given. Offers 20% kill fee. Responds in 2 months to queries.

NONFICTION Buys 60-80 mss/year. Query. Length: 1,500-2,500 words. **Pays $1,500-2,500.** Pays expenses of writers on assignment.

COLUMNS Length: 600-1,200 words **Buys 30 mss/year.** Query. **Pays $800-1,500.**

◉◉ HEALING LIFESTYLES & SPAS

P.O. Box 271207, Louisville CO 80027. (202)441-9557. **Fax:** (303)926-4099. **E-mail:** melissa@healinglife-styles.com; editorial@healinglifestyles.com. **Website:** www.healinglifestyles.com. **Contact:** Melissa B. Williams, editor-in-chief. **90% freelance written.** Estab. 1996. Circ. 45,000. Publishes ms an average of 2-10 months after acceptance. Editorial lead time 6 months. Submit seasonal material 6-9 months in advance. Accepts queries by mail, e-mail. Responds in 6 weeks to queries.

NONFICTION Needs travel, domestic and international. No fiction or poetry. Query. Length: 1,000-2,000 words. **Pays $150-500, depending on length, research, experience, and availability and quality of images.**

COLUMNS All Things New & Natural (short pieces outlining new health trends, alternative medicine updates, and other interesting tidbits of information), 50-200 words; Urban Retreats (focuses on a single city and explores its spas and organic living features), 1,200-1,600 words; Health (features on relevant topics ranging from nutrition to health news and updates), 900-1,200 words; Food (nutrition or spa-focused food articles and recipes), 1,000-1,200 words; Ritual (highlights a specific at-home ritual), 500 words; Seasonal Spa (focuses on a seasonal ingredient on the spa menu), 500-700 words; Spa Origins (focuses on particular modalities and healing beliefs from around the world, 1,000-1,200 words; Yoga, 400-800 words; Retreat (highlights a spa or yoga retreat), 500 words; Spa a la carte (explores a new treatment or modality on the spa menu), 600-1,000 words; Insight (focuses on profiles, theme-related articles, and new therapies, healing practices, and newsworthy items), 1,000-2,000 words. Query.

◑ ◉◉ IMPACT MAGAZINE

IMPACT Productions, 2007 2nd St. SW, Calgary AB T2S 1S4 Canada. (403)228-0605. **E-mail:** editor@impactmagazine.ca. **Website:** www.impactmagazine.ca. **Contact:** Chris Welner, editor. **10% freelance written.** Bimonthly magazine covering fitness and sport performance. "A leader in the industry, *IMPACT Magazine* is committed to publishing content provided by the best experts in their fields for those who aspire to higher levels of health, fitness, and sport performance." Estab. 1992. Circ. 90,000. Byline given. Pays 30 days after publication. Offers 25% kill fee. Publishes ms an average of 4-6 months after acceptance. Editorial lead time 6 months. Submit seasonal material 6 months in advance. Accepts queries by e-mail.

Accepts simultaneous submissions. Responds in 4 weeks to queries. Sample copy and guidelines available online.

NONFICTION Needs general interest, how-to, interview, new product, opinion, technical. **Buys 4 mss/year.** Query. Length: 600-1,800 words. **Pays $0.25/max. for assigned articles. Pays $0.25/max. for unsolicited articles.**

$$$$ MEN'S HEALTH

Rodale, 33 E. Minor St., Emmaus PA 18098. (610)967-5171. **Fax:** (610)967-7725. **E-mail:** mhletters@rodale.com. **Website:** www.menshealth.com. **50% freelance written.** Magazine published 10 times/year covering men's health and fitness. *Men's Health* is a lifestyle magazine showing men the practical and positive actions that make their lives better, with articles covering fitness, nutrition, relationships, travel, careers, grooming, and health issues. Estab. 1986. Circ. 1,600,000. Offers 25% kill fee. Accepts queries by mail, fax. Responds in 3 weeks to queries. Guidelines for #10 SASE.

NONFICTION Buys 30 features/year; 360 short mss/year. Query with published clips. 1,200-4,000 words for features, 100-300 words for short pieces **Pays $1,000-5,000 for features; $100-500 for short pieces.**

COLUMNS Length: 750-1,500 words. **Buys 80 mss/year. Pays $750- 2,000.**

$$$ MUSCLE & FITNESS

Weider Publications, part of American Media, Inc., 21100 Erwin St., Woodland Hills CA 91367. (818)884-6800. **Fax:** (818)595-0463. **Website:** www.muscleandfitness.com. **50% freelance written.** Monthly magazine covering bodybuilding and fitness for healthy, active men and women. *Muscle & Fitness* contains a wide range of features and monthly departments devoted to all areas of bodybuilding, health, fitness, sport, injury prevention and treatment, and nutrition. Editorial fulfills 2 functions: information and entertainment. Special attention is devoted to how-to advice and accuracy. Estab. 1950. Circ. 500,000. Publishes ms an average of 2 months after acceptance. Editorial lead time 5 months. Submit seasonal material 6 months in advance. Accepts queries by mail. Responds in 1 month to queries.

NONFICTION Needs book excerpts, how-to, training, humor, interview, photo feature. **Buys 120 mss/year.** Query with published clips. Length: 800-1,800 words. **Pays $400-1,000.** Pays expenses of writers on assignment.

🍁 ➜ MUSCLEMAG

RK Publishing, Inc., 400 Matheson Blvd. W., Mississauga ON L5R 3M1 Canada. (905)507-3545. **Fax:** (905)507-2372. **E-mail:** editorial@emusclemag.com. **Website:** www.emusclemag.com. **80% freelance written.** Covers hardcore bodybuilding. "Monthly magazine building health, fitness, and physique." Circ. . Byline given. Publishes ms an average of 6 months after acceptance. Accepts queries by mail, e-mail. Responds in 4 months to queries. Responds in 4 months to mss. Guidelines available.

NONFICTION Needs how-to, interview, new product, personal experience, photo feature, bodybuilding, strenth training, health, nutrition & fitness. **Pays $80-400 for assigned accepted articles submitted on spec.**

FILLERS Needs anecdotes, facts, gags, newsbreaks, fitness, nutrition, health, short humor. **Buys 50-100 mss/year.** Length: 100-200 words.

🍁 $$$ OXYGEN

Robert Kennedy Publishing, 400 Matheson Blvd. W., Mississauga ON L5R 3M1 Canada. (905)507-3545; (888)254-0767. **Fax:** (905)507-2372. **Website:** www.oxygenmag.com. **70% freelance written.** Monthly magazine covering women's health and fitness. *Oxygen* encourages various exercise, good nutrition to shape, and condition the body. Estab. 1997. Circ. 340,000. Byline given. Offers 25% kill fee. Publishes ms an average of 4 months after acceptance. Editorial lead time 3 months. Submit seasonal material 6 months in advance. Accepts queries by mail, fax. Responds in 5 weeks to queries. Responds in 2 months to mss. Sample copy for $5.

NONFICTION Needs exposé, how-to, training and nutrition, humor, inspirational, interview, new product, personal experience, photo feature. No poorly researched articles that do not genuinely help the readers toward physical fitness, health, and physique. **Buys 100 mss/year.** Send complete ms with SASE and $5 for return postage. Length: 1,400-1,800 words. **Pays $250-1,000.** Sometimes pays expenses of writers on assignment.

COLUMNS Nutrition (low-fat recipes), 1,700 words; Weight Training (routines and techniques), 1,800 words; Aerobics (how-tos), 1,700 words. **Buys 50 mss/year.** Send complete ms. **Pays $150-500.**

⊕⊕⊕⊕ POZ

CDM Publishing, LLC, 462 Seventh Ave., 19th Floor, New York NY 10118-7424. (212)242-2163. **Fax:** (212)675-8505. **E-mail:** editor-in-chief@poz.com. **Website:** www.poz.com. **Contact:** Regan Hofmann, editor-in-chief; Michael Halliday, art production manager. **25% freelance written.** Monthly national magazine for people impacted by HIV and AIDS. "*POZ* is a trusted source of conventional and alternative treatment information, investigative features, survivor profiles, essays and cutting-edge news for people living with AIDS and their caregivers. *POZ* is a lifestyle magazine with both health and cultural content." Estab. 1994. Circ. 125,000. Byline given. Pays 30 days after publication. Offers 25% kill fee. Publishes ms an average of 3 months after acceptance. Editorial lead time 4 months. Submit seasonal material 4 months in advance. Accepts simultaneous submissions. Sample copy and writer's guidelines free.

NONFICTION Needs book excerpts, essays, exposé, historical, how-to, humor, inspirational, interview, opinion, personal experience, photo feature. Query with published clips. "We take unsolicited mss on speculation only." Length: 200-3,000 words. **Pays $1/word.** Sometimes pays expenses of writers on assignment.

⊕⊕⊕⊕ SHAPE MAGAZINE

Weider Publications, Inc., 21100 Erwin St., Woodland Hills CA 91367. (818)595-0593. **Fax:** (818)704-7620. **Website:** www.shapemag.com. **70% freelance written. Prefers to work with published/established writers.** Monthly magazine covering health, fitness, nutrition, and beauty for women ages 18-34. *Shape* reaches women who are committed to healthful, active lifestyles. Our readers are participating in a variety of fitness-related activities, in the gym, at home and outdoors, and they are also proactive about their health and are nutrition conscious. Estab. 1981. Circ. 1,600,000. Offers 33% kill fee. Submit seasonal material 8 months in advance. Accepts queries by mail. Responds in 2 months to queries. Sample copy for sae with 9×12 envelope and 4 First-Class stamps. Guidelines available online.

NONFICTION Needs book excerpts, exposé, health, fitness, nutrition related, how-to, get fit, health/fitness, recipes. "We rarely publish celebrity question and answer stories, celebrity profiles, or menopausal/hormone replacement therapy stories." **Buys 27 features/**year; **36-54 short mss/year.** Query with published clips. 2,500 words/features; 1,000 words/shorter pieces **Pays $1.50/word (on average).**

⊕⊕⊕ SPIRITUALITY & HEALTH MAGAZINE

Spirituality & Health Media, LLC, 425 Boardman Ave., Suite C, Traverse City MI 49684. (231)933-5660. **E-mail:** editors@spiritualityhealth.com. **Website:** www.spiritualityhealth.com. **Contact:** Stephen Kiesling, editor-in-chief; Matt Sutherland, managing editor. Bimonthly magazine covering research-based spirituality and health. "We look for formally credentialed writers in their fields. We are non-denominational and non-proselytizing. We are not New Age. We appreciate well-written work that offers spiritual seekers from all different traditions help in their unique journeys." Estab. 1998. Circ. 95,000. Byline given. Offers 50% kill fee. Editorial lead time 4 months. Submit seasonal material 6 months in advance. Accepts queries by e-mail. Accepts simultaneous submissions. Responds in 3-4 months to queries. Responds in 2-4 months to mss. Sample copy and writer's guidelines online.

NONFICTION Needs book excerpts, how-to, news shorts. Does not want proselytizing, New Age cures with no scientific basis, "how I recovered from a disease personal essays," psychics, advice columns, profiles of individual healers or practitioners, pieces promoting one way or guru, reviews, poetry or columns. Send complete ms. 300 words for news shorts, otherwise 700 -1,500 words. Sometimes pays expenses of writers on assignment. Limit agreed upon in advance

⊘ ⊕⊕ VIBRANT LIFE

Review and Herald Publishing Association, 55 W. Oak Ridge Dr., Hagerstown MD 21740-7390. (301)393-4019. **Website:** www.vibrantlife.com. **80% freelance written. Enjoys working with published/ established writers; works with a small number of new/unpublished writers each year.** Bimonthly magazine covering health articles (especially from a prevention angle and with a Christian slant). Estab. 1885. Circ. 30,000. Byline given. Offers 50% kill fee. Submit seasonal material 9 months in advance. Accepts queries by mail, e-mail, fax. Responds in 1 month to queries. Sample copy for $1. Guidelines available online.

NONFICTION Needs interview, with personalities on health. **Buys 50-60 feature articles/year and 6-12 short mss/year.** Send complete ms. 500-1,500 words for features, 25-250 words for short pieces. **Pays $75-300 for features, $50-75 for short pieces.**

COLUMNS Buys 12-18 department articles/year. Length: 500-650 words. **Pays $75-175.**

💲💲💲💲 VIM & VIGOR

1010 E. Missouri Ave., Phoenix AZ 85014-2601. (602)395-5850. **Fax:** (602)395-5853. **Website:** www.comhs.org/vim_vigor/. **90% freelance written.** Quarterly magazine covering health and healthcare. Estab. 1985. Circ. 800,000. Byline given. Publishes ms an average of 6 months after acceptance. Sample copy for 9×12 SAE with 8 first-class stamps. Guidelines for #10 SASE.

NONFICTION Send published clips and résumé by mail or e-mail. Length: 500-1,200 words. **Pays 90¢-$1/word.** Pays expenses of writers on assignment.

💲💲 WHJ/HRHJ

Rian Enterprises, LLC, 4808 Courthouse St., Suite 204, Williamsburg VA 23188. **Fax:** (757)645-4473. **E-mail:** editorial@thehealthjournals.com. **Website:** www.thehealthjournals.com. **70% freelance written.** Monthly tabloid covering consumer/family health and wellness in Virginia. "Articles accepted of local and national interest. Health-savvy, college educated audience of all gender, ages, and backgrounds." Estab. 2005. Circ. 81,000. Byline given on most pieces. Publishes ms an average of 1-2 months after acceptance. Editorial lead time 4-6 months. Submit seasonal material 4-6 months in advance. Accepts queries by e-mail. Accepts simultaneous submissions. Only responds to mss of interest. Sample copy available online. Guidelines available by request only.

NONFICTION Needs book excerpts, essays, exposé, general interest, historical, how-to, humor, inspirational, interview, new product, opinion, personal experience, photo feature, technical, travel. Does not want promotion of products, religious material, anything over 1,000 words. **Buys 100 mss/year.** Query with published clips. Length: 400-1,000 words. **Pays 15¢/word (starting rate), $50/reprint.** Sometimes pays expenses of writers on assignment.

💲💲💲💲 YOGA JOURNAL

Active Interest Media, Healthy Living Group, 475 Sansome St., Suite 850, San Francisco CA 94111. (415)591-0555. **Fax:** (415)591-0733. **E-mail:** queries@yjmag.com. **Website:** www.yogajournal.com. **Contact:** Kaitlin Quistgaard, editor-in-chief. **75% freelance writ-ten.** Magazine published 9 times a year covering the practice and philosophy of yoga. "With comprehensive features on the practice, fitness, well-being, and everyday balance, we deliver the yoga tradition suited to today's lifestyle. We welcome professional queries for these departments: **Om:** Covers myriad aspects of the yoga lifestyle (150-400 words). This department includes Yoga Diary, a 250-word story about a pivotal moment in your yoga practice. **Eating Wisely:** A popular, 1,400-word department about relationship to food. Most stories focus on vegetarian and whole-foods cooking, nutritional healing, and contemplative pieces about the relationship between yoga and food. **Well Being:** This 1,500-word department presents reported pieces about holistic health practices." Estab. 1975. Circ. 300,000. Byline given. Pays within 90 days of acceptance. Offers kill fee. Offers kill fee on assigned articles. Publishes ms an average of 10 months after acceptance. Submit seasonal material 7 months in advance. Accepts queries by e-mail. Responds in 6 weeks to queries if interested. Sample copy for $4.99. Guidelines on website.

NONFICTION Needs book excerpts, how-to, yoga, exercise, etc., inspirational, yoga or related, interview, opinion, photo feature, travel, yoga-related. Does not want unsolicited poetry or cartoons. "Please avoid New Age jargon and in-house buzz words as much as possible." **Buys 50-60 mss/year.** Query with SASE. Length: 3,000-5,000 words. **Pays $800-2,000.**

COLUMNS Health (self-care; well-being); Body-Mind (hatha Yoga, other body-mind modalities, meditation, yoga philosophy, Western mysticism); Community (service, profiles, organizations, events), all 1,500-2,000 words. **Pays $400-800.** Living (books, video, arts, music), 800 words. **Pays $200-250.** World of Yoga, Spectrum (brief yoga and healthy living news/events/fillers), 150-600 words. **Pays $50-150.**

HISTORY

AMERICAN HISTORY

Weider History Group, 19300 Promenade Dr., Leesburg VA 20176-6500. (703)771-9400. **Fax:** (703)779-8345. **Website:** www.historynet.com. **60% freelance written**. Bimonthly magazine of cultural, social, military, and political history published for a general audience. "Presents the history of America to a broad spectrum of general-interest readers in an authoritative, informative, thought-provoking and entertaining style. Lively narratives take readers on an adventure with history, complemented by rare photographs, paintings, illustrations and maps." Estab. 1966. Circ. 95,000. Byline given. Responds in 10 weeks to queries. Sample copy and guidelines for $5 (includes 3rd class postage) or $4 and 9×12 SAE with 4 first-class stamps. Guidelines for #10 SASE.

NONFICTION Key prerequisites for publication are thorough research and accurate presentation, precise English usage, and sound organization, a lively style, and a high level of human interest. *Unsolicited manuscripts not considered.* Inappropriate materials include: book reviews, travelogues, personal/family narratives not of national significance, articles about collectibles/antiques, living artists, local/individual historic buildings/landmarks, and articles of a current editorial nature. **Buys 20 mss/year.** Query by mail only with published clips and SASE. 2,000-4,000 words depending on type of article.

🜚🜚 AMERICA'S CIVIL WAR

Weider History Group, 19300 Promenade Dr., Leesburg VA 20176-6500. (703)771-9400. **Fax:** (703)779-8345. **E-mail:** acw@weiderhistorygroup.com. **Website:** www.historynet.com. **95% freelance written.** Bimonthly magazine covering popular history and straight historical narrative for both the general reader and the Civil War buff covering strategy, tactics, personalities, arms, and equipment. Estab. 1988. Circ. 78,000. Byline given. Accepts queries by mail, e-mail. Sample copy for $5. Writer's guidelines for #10 SASE.

NONFICTION Needs historical, book notices, preservation news. **Buys 24 mss/year.** "Query. Submit a page outlining the subject and your approach to it, and why you believe this would be an important article for the magazine. Briefly summarize your prior writing experience in a cover note." Length: 3,500-4,000 words and a 500-word sidebar. **Pays $300 and up.**

COLUMNS Personality (profiles of Civil War personalities); Men & Material (about weapons used); Commands (about units); Eyewitness to War (historical letters and diary excerpts). Length: 2,000 words. **Buys 24 mss/year.** Query. **Pays $150 and up.**

🜚 THE ARTILLERYMAN

Historical Publications, Inc., 234 Monarch Hill Rd., Tunbridge VT 05077. (802)889-3500. **Fax:** (802)889-5627. **E-mail:** mail@artillerymanmagazine.com. **Website:** www.artillerymanmagazine.com. **Contact:** Kathryn Jorgensen, editor. **60% freelance writ-**

ten. Quarterly magazine covering antique artillery, fortifications, and crew-served weapons 1750-1900 for competition shooters, collectors, and living history reenactors using artillery. "Emphasis on Revolutionary War and Civil War but includes everyone interested in pre-1900 artillery and fortifications, preservation, construction of replicas, etc." Estab. 1979. Circ. 1,500. Byline given. Publishes ms an average of 6 months after acceptance. Accepts queries by mail, e-mail, fax. Accepts simultaneous submissions. Responds in 3 weeks to queries. Sample copy and writer's guidelines for 9×12 SAE with 4 first-class stamps.

NONFICTION Needs historical, how-to, interview, photo feature, technical, travel. **Buys 12 mss/year.** Send complete ms. 300 words minimum. **Pays $40-60.**

🜚 BRITISH HERITAGE

Weider History Group, 19300 Promenade Dr., Leesburg VA 20176. (703)771-9400. **Fax:** (703)779-8345. **E-mail:** dana.huntley@weiderhistorygroup.com. **Website:** www.thehistorynet.com. Bimonthly magazine covering British travel and culture. "The magazine of travel, culture and adventure, especially written for those who love England, Scotland, Ireland and Wales. A must-read for Anglophiles, British Heritage shows them what they can see and do, how to get there and where to stay, with information that even veteran travelers may overlook." Circ. 77,485. Pays kill fee though never had to. Editorial lead time 6 months. Accepts queries by e-mail. No

NONFICTION **Buys 50 mss/year.** Query by e-mail. Length: 1,000-2,500 words.

🜚🜚🜚 CIVIL WAR TIMES

Weider History Group, 19300 Promenade Dr., Leesburg VA 20176-6500. (703)779-8371. **Fax:** (703)779-8345. **E-mail:** cwt@weiderhistorygroup.com. **Website:** www.historynet.com. **90% freelance written. Works with a small number of new/unpublished writers each year.** Magazine published 6 times/year. "*Civil War Times* is the full-spectrum magazine of the Civil War. Specifically, we look for nonpartisan coverage of battles, prominent military and civilian figures, the home front, politics, military technology, common soldier life, prisoners and escapes, period art and photography, the naval war, blockade-running, specific regiments, and much more." Estab. 1962. Circ. 108,000. Pays on acceptance and on publication. Publishes ms an average of 18 months after acceptance. Submit seasonal material 1 year in advance. Responds in 3-6 months to queries. Sample copy for $6. Guidelines for #10 SASE.

NONFICTION Needs interview, photo feature, Civil War historical material. "Don't send us a comprehensive article on a well-known major battle. Instead, focus on some part or aspect of such a battle, or some group of soldiers in the battle. Similar advice applies to major historical figures like Lincoln and Lee. Positively no fiction or poetry." **Buys 20 freelance mss/year.** Query with clips and SASE **Pays $75-800.**

🟢🟢 COBBLESTONE

A Division of Carus Publishing, 30 Grove St., Suite C, Peterborough NH 03458. (800)821-0115. **Fax:** (603)924-7380. **E-mail:** customerservice@caruspub.com. **Website:** www.cobblestonepub.com. **50% freelance written.** Covers material for ages 9-14. "We are interested in articles of historical accuracy and lively, original approaches to the subject at hand. Our magazine is aimed at youths from ages 9 to 14. Writers are encouraged to study recent COBBLESTONE back issues for content and style. (Sample issues are available for $6.95 plus $2.00 shipping and handling. Sample issues will not be sent without prepayment.) All material must relate to the theme of a specific upcoming issue in order to be considered. To be considered, a query must accompany each individual idea (however, you can mail them all together) and must include the following: a brief cover letter stating the subject and word length of the proposed article, a detailed one-page outline explaining the information to be presented in the article, an extensive bibliography of materials the author intends to use in preparing the article, a SASE. Authors are urged to use primary resources and up-to-date scholarly resources in their bibliography. Writers new to COBBLESTONE® should send a writing sample with the query. If you would like to know if your query has been received, please also include a stamped postcard that requests acknowledgment of receipt. In all correspondence, please include your complete address as well as a telephone number where you can be reached. A writer may send as many queries for one issue as he or she wishes, but each query must have a separate cover letter, outline, bibliography, and SASE. All queries must be typed. **Please do not send unsolicited manuscripts - queries only!** Prefers to work with published/established writers. Each issue presents a particular theme, making it exciting as well as informative. Half of all subscriptions are for schools. All material must relate to monthly theme." Circ. 15,000. Byline given. Offers 50% kill fee. Accepts queries by mail, fax. Accepts simultaneous submissions. Guidelines available on website or with SASE; sample copy for $6.95, $2 shipping/handling, 10×13 SASE.

NONFICTION Needs historical, humor, interview, personal experience, photo feature, travel, crafts, recipes, activities. No material that editorializes rather than reports. **Buys 45-50 mss/year.** Query with writing sample, 1-page outline, bibliography, SASE. 800 words/feature articles; 300-600 words/supplemental nonfiction; up to 700 words maximum/activities. **Pays 20-25¢/word.**

FICTION Needs adventure, historical, biographical, retold legends, folktales, multicultural. **Buys 5 mss/year.** Query. Length: 800 words maximum. **Pays 20-25¢/word.**

POETRY Contact: Meg Chorlian. Needs free verse, light verse, traditional. Serious and light verse considered. Must have clear, objective imagery. Buys 3 poems/year. 100 lines maximum. **Pays on an individual basis. Acquires all rights.**

FILLERS "Crossword and other word puzzles (no word finds), mazes, and picture puzzles that use the vocabulary of the issue's theme or otherwise relate to the theme." **Pays on an individual basis.**

🟢🟢 GATEWAY

Missouri History Museum, P.O. Box 11940, St. Louis MO 63112-0040. (314)746-4558. **Fax:** (314)746-4548. **E-mail:** vwmonks@mohistory.org. **Website:** www.mohistory.org. **75% freelance written.** Annual magazine covering Missouri history and culture. *Gateway* is a popular cultural history magazine that is primarily a member benefit of the Missouri History Museum. Thus, we have a general audience with an interest in the history and culture of Missouri, and St. Louis in particular. Estab. 1980. Circ. 11,000. Byline given. Offers $100 kill fee. Publishes ms an average of 6 months to 1 year after acceptance. Editorial lead time 6 months. Accepts queries by mail, e-mail, fax. Responds in 1 month to queries. Responds in 2 months to mss. Sample copy for $10. online or send #10 SASE.

NONFICTION Needs book excerpts, interview, photo feature, Interviews; historical, scholarly essays; Missouri biographies; photo essays; viewpoints on events; first-hand historical accounts; book excerpts; regional architectural history; literary history. No genealogies. No genealogies. **Buys 4-6 mss/year.** Query with writing samples. Length: 4,000-5,000 words. **Pays $300-400 (average).**

$ GOOD OLD DAYS

Dynamic Resource Group, 306 E. Parr Rd., Berne IN 46711. **Fax:** (260)589-8093. **E-mail:** editor@goodolddaysonline.com. **Website:** www.goodolddaysonline.com. **Contact:** Ken Tate, editor. **75% freelance written**. Bi-Monthly magazine of first person nostalgia, 1935-1965. "We look for strong narratives showing life as it was in the middle decades of the 20th century. Our readership is comprised of nostalgia buffs, history enthusiasts, and the people who actually lived and grew up in this era." Byline given. Pays on contract. Publishes ms an average of 8 months after acceptance. Submit seasonal material 10 months in advance. Accepts queries by fax, online submission form. Responds in 2 months to queries. Sample copy for $2. Guidelines available online.

NONFICTION Needs historical, humor, personal experience, photo feature, favorite food/recipes, year-round seasonal material, biography, memorable events, fads, fashion, sports, music, literature, entertainment. No fiction accepted. **Buys 350 mss/year.** Query or send complete ms. Length: 500-1,500 words. **Pays $20-100, depending on quality and photos.**

✪ $$ HISTORY MAGAZINE

Moorshead Magazines, 505 Consumers Rd., Suite 312, Toronto ON M2J 4V8 Canada. **E-mail:** edward@moorshead.com. **Website:** www.history-magazine.com. **Contact:** Edward Zapletal, publisher and. **90% freelance written.** Bimonthly magazine covering social history. A general interest history magazine, focusing on social history up to the outbreak of World War II. Estab. 1999. Byline given. Publishes ms an average of 6 months after acceptance. Editorial lead time 6 months. Submit seasonal material 6 months in advance. Accepts queries by mail, e-mail. Responds in 1 month. Sample copy available online. Guidelines available online.

NONFICTION Needs book excerpts, historical. Does not want first-person narratives or revisionist history. **Buys 50 mss/year.** Query. Length: 400-2,500 words. **Pays $50-250.**

$ LEBEN

City Seminary Press, 2150 River Plaza Dr., #150, Sacramento CA 95833. **E-mail:** editor@leben.us. **Website:** www.leben.us. **40% freelance written**. Estab. 2004. Circ. 5,000. Byline given. Offers 25% kill fee. Publishes ms an average of 6 months after acceptance. Editorial lead time 6 months. Submit seasonal material 6 months in advance. Accepts queries by online submission form. Accepts simultaneous submissions. Responds in 3 weeks to queries. Responds in 2 months to mss. Sample copy for $1.50 (order online or request via e-mail). Guidelines by email.

NONFICTION Needs historical, reformed biography. Does not want articles that argue theological issues. There is a place for that, but not in a popular history/biography magazine aimed at general readership. Query. Length: 500-2,500 words. **Pays up to $100.**

LIGHTHOUSE DIGEST

Lighthouse Digest, P.O. Box 250, East Machias ME 04630. (207)259-2121. **E-mail:** Editor@Lighthouse-Digest.com. **Website:** www.lighthousedigest.com. **Contact:** Tim Harrison, editor. **15% freelance written**. Monthly magazine covering historical, fiction and news events about lighthouses and similar maritime stories. Estab. 1989. Circ. 24,000. Byline given. Publishes ms an average of 4 months after acceptance. Editorial lead time 3 months. Submit seasonal material 3 months in advance. Accepts queries by e-mail. Accepts simultaneous submissions. Responds in 6 weeks to queries. Sample copy free.

NONFICTION Needs exposé, general interest, historical, humor, inspirational, personal experience, photo feature, religious, technical, travel. No historical data taken from books. **Buys 30 mss/year.** Send complete ms. 2,500 words maximum

FICTION Needs adventure, historical, humorous, mystery, religious, romance, suspense. **Buys 2 mss/year.** Send complete ms. 2,500 words maximum.

$$ PERSIMMON HILL

1700 NE 63rd St., Oklahoma City OK 73111. (405)478-6404. **Fax:** (405)478-4714. **E-mail:** editor@nationalcowboymuseum.org. **Website:** www.nationalcowboymuseum.org. **Contact:** Judy Hilovsky. **70% freelance written. Prefers to work with published/established writers; works with a small number of new/unpublished writers each year.** Quarterly magazine for an audience interested in Western art, Western history, ranching, and rodeo, including historians, artists, ranchers, art galleries, schools, and libraries. Estab. 1970. Circ. 7,500. Byline given. Publishes ms an average of 18 months after acceptance. Responds in 3 months to queries. Sample copy for $10.50, including postage. Writer's guidelines available on website. **NONFICTION** Buys 50-75 mss/year. Query by mail with clips. Word length: 1,500 words. **Pays $150-300**

💲💲💲 TIMELINE

Ohio Historical Society, 1982 Velma Ave., Columbus OH 43211-2497. (614)297-2360. **Fax:** (614)297-2367. **E-mail:** timeline@ohiohistory.org. **Website:** www.ohiohistory.org/resource/publicat/timeline. **90% freelance written. Works with a small number of new/unpublished writers each year.** Quarterly magazine covering history, prehistory, and the natural sciences, directed toward readers in the Midwest. Estab. 1984. Circ. 7,000. Byline given. Pays on final edit. Offers $75 minimum kill fee. Publishes ms an average of 1 year after acceptance. Submit seasonal material 6 months in advance. Accepts queries by mail, e-mail, fax. Responds in 3 weeks to queries. Responds in 6 weeks to mss. Sample copy for $12 and 9×12 SAE. Guidelines for #10 SASE.

NONFICTION Needs book excerpts, essays, historical, photo feature. **Buys 22 mss/year.** Query. 1,500-6,000 words. Also vignettes of 500-1,000 words. **Pays $100-800.**

💲 TOMBIGBEE COUNTRY MAGAZINE

Tombigbee Country Magazine, P.O. Box 621, Gu-Win AL 35563. (205)412-9750; (205)412-8557. **E-mail:** tombigbeecountrymagazine@yahoo.com. **Website:** www.tombigbeecountry.com. **Contact:** Bo Webster, editor. **50% freelance written**. Monthly magazine covering nostalgia - history. "Tombigbee Country is a Magazine dedicated to theOld Time Tales, History, & Humor of Northeast Mississippi &Northwest Alabama.TomBigbee Country is a regional, nostalgia, monthly magazine which featureshuman interest articles concerning the area surrounding the Upper TombigbeeRiver (Tenn-Tom Waterway).We take pride in being a country magazine that uses a mixture of irony, witand humor with good folk history." Estab. 2,000. Circ. 10,000. Byline given. Publishes ms an average of 1 month after acceptance. Editorial lead time 2 months. Submit seasonal material 2 months in advance. Accepts queries by mail, e-mail. Accepts simultaneous submissions. Responds in 1 week to queries. Responds in 1 month to mss. Sample copy $2. Guidelines free.

NONFICTION Needs book excerpts, essays, general interest, historical, humor, inspirational, personal experience, religious. Special issues: We are eager for stories on personal experience with celebrities—country musicians, famous southerners. We do not want tributes to family members. **Buys 24+ mss/year.** Query. Length: 800-2,000 words. **Pays $24 for assigned articles. Pays $24 for unsolicited articles.**

💲 THE TOMBSTONE EPITAPH

Tombstone Epitaph, Inc., P.O. BOX 1880, Tombstone AZ 85638. (520)457-2211. **E-mail:** info@tombstoneepitaph.com. **Website:** www.tombstoneepitaph.com. **Contact:** Frederick Schoemehl, editor. **60% freelance written**. Monthly tabloid covering American west to 1900 (-1935, if there's an Old West connection). "We seek lively, well-written, sourced articles that examine the history and culture of the Old West." Estab. 1880. Byline given. End of calendar year. Publishes ms an average of 3 months after acceptance. Editorial lead time 3 months. Submit seasonal material 6 months in advance. Accepts queries by e-mail. Responds in 2 weeks to queries. Responds in 1 month to mss. Sample copy for $3. Guidelines by email.

NONFICTION Needs essays, historical, humor, personal experience, (if historically grounded), travel, Past events as interpreted in film, books, magazines, etc. "We do not want poorly sourced stories, contemporary West pieces, fiction, poetry, big 'tell-all' stories." **Buys 25-40 mss/year.** Query. Length: 1,000-5,000 words. **Pays $30-50 for assigned articles. Pays $30 max. for unsolicited articles.**

💲💲 TRACES OF INDIANA AND MIDWESTERN HISTORY

Indiana Historical Society, 450 W. Ohio St., Indianapolis IN 46202-3269. (317)232-1877. **Fax:** (317)233-0857. **E-mail:** rboomhower@indianahistory.org. **Website:** www.indianahistory.org. **Contact:** Ray E. Boomhower, senior editor. **80% freelance written.** Quarterly magazine on Indiana history. "Conceived as a vehicle to bring to the public good narrative and analytical history about Indiana in its broader contexts of region and nation, *Traces* explores the lives of artists, writers, performers, soldiers, politicians, entrepreneurs, homemakers, reformers, and naturalists. It has traced the impact of Hoosiers on the nation and the world. In this vein, the editors seek nonfiction articles that are solidly researched, attractively written, and amenable to illustration, and they encourage scholars, journalists, and freelance writers to contribute to the magazine." Estab. 1989. Circ. 6,000. Byline given. Publishes ms an average of 6 months after acceptance. Submit seasonal material 1 year in advance. Responds in 3 months to mss. Guidelines available online.

NONFICTION **Buys 20 mss/year.** Send complete ms. Length: 2,000-4,000 words. **Pays $100-500.**

⊘ $$$ TRUE WEST

True West Publishing, Inc., P.O. Box 8008, Cave Creek AZ 85327. (888)687-1881. **Fax:** (480)575-1903. **E-mail:** editor@twmag.com. **Website:** twmag.com. Bob Boze Bell, executive editor. **Contact:** Meghan Saar, Editor-in-Chief. **45% freelance written. Works with a small number of new/unpublished writers each year.** Magazine published 10 times/year covering Western American history from prehistory 1800 to 1930. "We want reliable research on significant historical topics written in lively prose for an informed general audience. More recent topics may be used if they have a historical angle or retain the Old West flavor of trail dust and saddle leather. True West magazine's features and departments tie the history of the American West (between 1800-1930) to the modern western lifestyle through enticing narrative and intelligent analyses." Estab. 1953. Byline given. Kill fee applicable only to material assigned by the editor, not for stories submitted on spec based on query written to the editor. 50% of original fee should the story have run in the publication. Editorial lead time 6 months. Accepts queries by mail, e-mail. Sample copy for $3. Guidelines available online.

NONFICTION No fiction, poetry, or unsupported, undocumented tales. **Buys 30 mss/year.** Send query to Meghan Saar at editor@twmag.com Length: no more than 1,500 words. **Pays $50-800. "Features pay $150-500 with a $20 payment for each photo the author provides that is published with the article and not already part of True West archives."**

FILLERS Needs anecdotes, facts, gags, newsbreaks, short humor. **Buys 30 mss/year.** Length: 50-300 words.

$$ WILD WEST

Weider History Group, 19300 Promenade Dr., Leesburg VA 20176-6500. (703)771-9400. **Fax:** (703)779-8345. **E-mail:** wildwest@weiderhistorygroup.com. **Website:** www.historynet.com. **Contact:** Eric Weider, publisher. **95% freelance written.** Bimonthly magazine covering the history of the American frontier, from its eastern beginnings to its western terminus. "*Wild West* covers the popular (narrative) history of the American West—events, trends, personalities, anything of general interest." Estab. 1988. Circ. 83,500. Byline given. Publishes ms an average of 2 years after acceptance. Editorial lead time 10 months. Submit seasonal material 1 year in advance. Accepts queries by mail, e-mail. Accepts simultaneous submissions. Responds in 3 months to queries. Responds in 6 months to mss. Sample copy for $6. Writer's guidelines for #10 SASE or online.

NONFICTION Needs historical, Old West. No excerpts, travel, etc. Articles can be adapted from book. No fiction or poetry—nothing current. **Buys 36 mss/year.** Query. 3,500 words with a 500-word sidebar. **Pays $300.**

COLUMNS Gunfighters & Lawmen, 2,000 words; Westerners, 2,000 words; Warriors & Chiefs, 2,000 words; Western Lore, 2,000 words; Guns of the West, 1,500 words; Artists West, 1,500 words; Books Reviews, 250 words. **Buys 36 mss/year.** Query. **Pays $150 for departments; book reviews paid by the word, minimum $40.**

$$ WORLD WAR II

Weider History Group, 19300 Promenade Dr., Leesburg VA 20176. **E-mail:** worldwar2@weiderhistorygroup.com. **Website:** www.historynet.com. **Contact:** Editor, *World War II*. **25% freelance written. "Most of our stories are assigned by our staff to professional writers. However, we do accept written proposals for features and for our Time Travel department."** Bimonthly magazine covering military operations in World War II—events, personalities, strategy, the home front, etc. Estab. 1986. Circ. 146,000. Byline given. Kill fee. Accepts queries by mail, e-mail. Writer's guidelines available on website or for SASE.

NONFICTION **Buys 24 mss/year.** Query. "Your proposal should convince the editors to cover the subject, describe how you would treat the subject, and give the editors an opportunity to judge your writing ability. Please include your writing credentials and background with your proposal. A familiarity with recent issues of the magazine is the best guide to our editorial needs. The magazine does not consider simultaneous submissions or material that has been previously published." Features: 2,500-4,000 words.

HOBBY AND CRAFT

$$$$ AMERICAN CRAFT

American Craft Council, 1224 Marshall St. NE, Suite 200, Minneapolis MN 55413. (612)206-3100. **E-mail:**

letters@craftcouncil.org; mmoses@craftcouncil.org. **Website:** www.americancraftmag.org. **Contact:** Monica Moses, editor. **75% freelance written**. Bimonthly magazine covering art/craft/design. Estab. 1943. Circ. 40,000. Byline given. Pays 30 days after acceptance. Offers 25% kill fee. Publishes ms an average of 2 months after acceptance. Editorial lead time 3 months. Submit seasonal material 3 months in advance. Accepts queries by mail, e-mail. Accepts simultaneous submissions. Responds in 1 month to queries. Responds in 2 months to mss. Sample copy free. Guidelines by email.

NONFICTION Needs essays, general interest, interview, new product, opinion, photo feature, travel. Query with published clips. Length: 1,200-3,000 words. Pays expenses of writers on assignment.

COLUMNS Critics's Corner (critical essays), 200-2,500 words; Wide World of Craft (travel), 800-1,000 words; Material Culture (material studies), 600-800 words; outskirts (a look at peripheral disciplines), 600-800 words. **Buys 10-12 mss/year.** Query with published clips. **Pays $1-1.50/word.**

⊖ AUTOGRAPH COLLECTOR

Odyssey Publications, 510-A South Corona Mall, Corona CA 92879. (951)734-9636. **Fax:** (951)371-7139. **E-mail:** editorev@telus.net. **Website:** http://autograph-magazine.com. **80% freelance written.** Monthly magazine covering the autograph collecting hobby. The focus of *Autograph Collector* is on documents, photographs, or any collectible item that has been signed by a famous person, whether a current celebrity or historical figure. Articles stress how and where to locate celebrities and autograph material, authenticity of signatures and what they are worth. Byline given. Offers negotiable kill fee. Editorial lead time 2 months. Submit seasonal material 3 months in advance. Accepts queries by mail, e-mail, fax, phone. Responds in 2 weeks to queries. Sample copy and writer's guidelines free.

NONFICTION Needs historical, how-to, interview, personal experience. **Buys 25-35 mss/year.** Query. Length: 1,600-2,000 words. **Pays 5¢/word.** Sometimes pays expenses of writers on assignment.

COLUMNS *Autograph Collector* buys 8-10 columns per month written by regular contributors. **Buys 90-100 mss/year.** Query. **Pays $50 or as determined on a per case basis.**

FILLERS Needs anecdotes, facts. **Buys 20-25 mss/year.** Length: 200-300 words. **$15.**

⊖⊖ BEAD & BUTTON

Kalmbach Publishing, P.O. Box 1612, 21027 Crossroads Circle, Waukesha WI 53187. **E-mail:** editor@beadandbutton.com. **Website:** www.beadandbutton.com. **Contact:** Julia Gerlach, editor; Anna Elizabeth Draeger, associate editor; Anna Elizabeth Draeger, associate editor; Stacy Werkheiser, associate editor; Lora Groszkiewicz, editorial assistant. **50% freelance written.** "*Bead & Button* is a bimonthly magazine devoted to techniques, projects, designs and materials relating to making beaded jewelry. Our readership includes both professional and amateur bead and button makers, hobbyists, and enthusiasts who find satisfaction in making beautiful things." Estab. 1994. Circ. 100,000. Byline given. Offers $75 kill fee. Publishes ms an average of 4-12 months after acceptance. Accepts queries by mail, e-mail, fax. Guidelines available online.

NONFICTION Needs historical, on beaded jewelry history, how-to, make beaded jewelry and accessories, humor, inspirational, interview. **Buys 20-25 mss/year.** Send complete ms. Length: 750-1,500 words. **Pays $100-400.**

⊖⊖ BLADE MAGAZINE

F+W Media, Inc., 700 E. State St., Iola WI 54990-0001. (715)445-2214. **Fax:** (715)445-4087. **E-mail:** joe.kertzman@fwmedia.com. **Website:** www.blademag.com. **Contact:** Joe Kertzman, managing editor. **5% freelance written.** Monthly magazine covering working and using collectible, popular knives. *Blade* prefers in-depth articles focusing on groups of knives, whether military, collectible, high-tech, pocket knives or hunting knives, and how they perform. Estab. 1973. Circ. 39,000. Byline given. Publishes ms an average of 9 months after acceptance. Editorial lead time 9 months. Submit seasonal material 9 months in advance. Accepts queries by mail, e-mail, fax. Responds in 3 months to queries. Responds in 6 months to mss. Sample copy for $4.99. Guidelines for sae with 8x11 envelope and 3 first-class stamps.

NONFICTION Needs general interest, historical, how-to, interview, new product, photo feature, technical. "We assign profiles, show stories, hammer-in stories, etc. We don't need those. If you've seen the story on the Internet or in another knife or knife/gun magazine, we don't need it. We don't do stories on knives used for self-defense." Send complete ms. Length: 700-1,400 words. **Pays $150-300.**

FILLERS Needs anecdotes, facts, newsbreaks. **Buys 1-2 fillers. mss/year.** Length: 50-200 words. **Pays $25-50.**

⑨ BREW YOUR OWN

Battenkill Communications, 5515 Main St., Manchester Center VT 05255. (802)362-3981. **Fax:** (802)362-2377. **E-mail:** edit@byo.com. **Website:** www.byo.com; www.byo.com/about/guidelines. **85% freelance written.** Monthly magazine covering home brewing. "Our mission is to provide practical information in an entertaining format. We try to capture the spirit and challenge of brewing while helping our readers brew the best beer they can." Estab. 1995. Circ. 50,000. Byline given. Offers 25% kill fee. Publishes ms an average of 4 months after acceptance. Editorial lead time 3 months. Submit seasonal material 3 months in advance. Accepts queries by mail, e-mail, fax. Responds in 2 months to queries. Guidelines available online.

NONFICTION Needs historical, how-to, home brewing, humor, related to home brewing, interview, of professional brewers who can offer useful tips to home hobbyists, personal experience, trends. **Buys 75 mss/year.** Query with published clips or description of brewing expertise Length: 800-3,000 words. **Pays $50-350, depending on length, complexity of article, and experience of writer.** Sometimes pays expenses of writers on assignment.

COLUMNS News (humorous, unusual news about homebrewing), 50-250 words; Last Call (humorous stories about homebrewing), 700 words. **Buys 12 mss/year.** Query with or without published clips. **Pays $75**

♻ ⑨⑨ CANADIAN WOODWORKING AND HOME IMPROVEMENT

Sawdust Media, Inc., 51 Maple Ave. N., RR #3, Burford ON N0E 1A0 Canada. (519)449-2444. **Fax:** (519)449-2445. **E-mail:** pfulcher@canadianwoodworking.com. **Website:** www.canadianwoodworking.com. Paul Fulcher, publisher. **20% freelance written.** Bimonthly magazine covering woodworking; only accepts work from Canadian writers. Estab. 1999. Byline given. Offers 50% kill fee. Accepts queries by e-mail. Sample copy available online. Guidelines by e-mail.

NONFICTION Needs how-to, humor, inspirational, new product, personal experience, photo feature, technical. Does not want profile on a woodworker. Query. Length: 500-4,000 words. **Pays $100-600 for assigned articles. Pays $50-400 for unsolicited articles.**

⑨ CARVING MAGAZINE

All American Crafts, P.O. Box 611, Faribault MN 55021. **E-mail:** editors@carvingmagazine.com. **Website:** www.carvingmagazine.com. **Contact:** Chris Whillock, editor. **95% freelance written.** Quarterly magazine covering woodcarving. *Carving Magazine* specialzing in woodcarving articles including step-by-steps, techniques, profiles and photo galleries. Estab. 2002. Circ. 20,000. Byline given. Publishes ms an average of 6 months after acceptance. Editorial lead time 6 months. Submit seasonal material 6 months in advance. Accepts queries by mail, e-mail.

NONFICTION Needs general interest, historical, how-to, interview, photo feature. Does not want anything other than woodcarving. **Buys 40 mss/year.** Length: 2,000 words. **Pays $50-100.**

⑨⑨ CERAMICS MONTHLY

600 N. Cleveland Ave., Suite 210, Westerville OH 43082. (614)792-5867. **Fax:** (614)891-8960. **E-mail:** editorial@ceramicsmonthly.org. **Website:** www.ceramicsmonthly.org. **70% freelance written.** Monthly magazine (except July and August) covering the ceramic art and craft field. "Each issue includes articles on potters and ceramics artists from throughout the world, exhibitions, and production processes, as well as critical commentary, book and video reviews, clay and glaze recipes, kiln designs and firing techniques, advice from experts in the field, and ads for available materials and equipment. While principally covering contemporary work, the magazine also looks back at influential artists and events from the past." Estab. 1953. Circ. 39,000. Byline given. Editorial lead time 3 months. Submit seasonal material 6 months in advance. Accepts queries by mail, e-mail, fax, phone. Responds in 2 months to mss. Guidelines available online.

NONFICTION Needs essays, how-to, interview, opinion, personal experience, technical. **Buys 100 mss/year.** Send complete ms. Length: 500-3,000 words. **Pays 10¢/word.**

COLUMNS Upfront (workshop/exhibition review), 500-1,000 words. **Buys 20 mss/year.** Send complete ms.

⑨⑨ CLASSIC TOY TRAINS

Kalmbach Publishing Co., P.O. Box 1612, 21027 Crossroads Cir., Waukesha WI 53187-1612. (262)796-8776, ext. 524. **Fax:** (262)796-1142. **E-mail:** manuscripts@classictoytrains.com. **Website:** www.classictoytrains.com. **Contact:** Carl Swanson, editor. **80% freelance written.** Magazine published 9 times/

year covering collectible toy trains (O, S, Standard) like Lionel and American Flyer, etc. "For the collector and operator of toy trains, *CTT* offers full-color photos of layouts and collections of toy trains, restoration tips, operating information, new product reviews and information, and insights into the history of toy trains." Estab. 1987. Circ. 50,000. Byline given. Publishes ms an average of 1 year after acceptance. Editorial lead time 3 months. Submit seasonal material 6 months in advance. Accepts queries by mail, e-mail. Responds in 3 weeks to queries. Responds in 1 month to mss. Sample copy for $5.95, plus postage. Guidelines available online.

NONFICTION Needs general interest, historical, how-to, restore toy trains; design a layout; build accessories; fix broken toy trains, interview, personal experience, photo feature, technical. **Buys 90 mss/year.** Query. Length: 500-5,000 words. **Pays $75-500.** Sometimes pays expenses of writers on assignment.

CQ AMATEUR RADIO

CQ Communications, Inc., 25 Newbridge Rd., Hicksville NY 11801. (516)681-2922. **Fax:** (516)681-2926. **E-mail:** cq@cq-amateur-radio.com. **E-mail:** w2vu@cq-amateur-radio.com. **Website:** www.cq-amateur-radio.com. **Contact:** Richard Moseson, editor. **40% freelance written.** Monthly magazine covering amateur (ham) radio. "*CQ* is published for active ham radio operators and is read by radio amateurs in over 100 countries. All articles must deal with amateur radio. Our focus is on operating and on practical projects. A thorough knowledge of amateur radio is required." Estab. 1945. Circ. 60,000. Byline given. Publishes ms an average of 6 months after acceptance. Editorial lead time 4 months. Submit seasonal material 4 months in advance. Accepts queries by mail, e-mail, fax. Responds in 3 weeks to queries. Responds in 3 months to mss. Sample copy free. Guidelines available online.

NONFICTION Needs historical, how-to, interview, personal experience, technical, all related to amateur radio. **Buys 50-60 mss/year.** Query. Length: 2,000-4,000 words. **Pays $40/published page.**

CREATING KEEPSAKES

Creative Crafts Group, LLC, 14850 Pony Express Rd., Bluffdale UT 84065. (801)984-2070. **E-mail:** editorial@CreatingKeepsakes.com. **Website:** www.creatingkeepsakes.com. Monthly magazine covering scrapbooks. Written for scrapbook lovers and those

with a box of photos high in the closet. Circ. 100,000. Editorial lead time 6 weeks. Accepts queries by mail, e-mail. Guidelines available online.

NONFICTION Query with 2 visuals to illustrate your suggested topic. Length: 800-1,200 words.

DESIGNS IN MACHINE EMBROIDERY

Great Notions News Corp., 2517 Manana Dr., Dallas TX 75220. (888)739-0555. **Fax:** (413)723-2027. **E-mail:** eroche@dzgns.com. **Website:** www.dzgns.com. **75% freelance written.** Bimonthly magazine covering machine embroidery. Projects in *Designs in Machine Embroidery* must feature machine embroidery and teach readers new techniques. Estab. 1998. Circ. 50,000. Byline given. Publishes ms an average of 2 months after acceptance. Editorial lead time 4 months. Submit seasonal material 4 months in advance. Accepts queries by mail, e-mail. NoResponds in 2-3 weeks to queries. Guidelines available online.

NONFICTION Needs how-to, interview, new product, technical. Does not want previously published items. **Buys 60 mss/year.** Query. Length: 250-1,000 words. **Pays $250-500.**

DOLLHOUSE MINIATURES

68132 250th Ave., Kasson MN 55944. (507)634-3143. **E-mail:** usoffice@ashdown.co.uk. **Website:** www.dhminiatures.com. **80% freelance written.** Monthly magazine covering dollhouse scale miniatures. *Dollhouse Miniatures* is America's best-selling miniatures magazine and the definitive resource for artisans, collectors, and hobbyists. It promotes and supports the large national and international community of miniaturists through club columns, short reports, and by featuring reader projects and ideas. Estab. 1971. Circ. 25,000. Byline given. Editorial lead time 6 months. Submit seasonal material 6 months in advance. Accepts queries by mail. Responds in 1 month to queries. Responds in 2 months to mss. Sample copy for $4.95. Guidelines available online.

NONFICTION Needs how-to, miniature projects of various scales in variety of media, interview, artisans, collectors, photo feature, dollhouses, collections, museums. No articles on miniature shops or essays. **Buys 50-60 mss/year.** Send complete ms. Length: 500-1,500 words. **Pays $50-350 for assigned articles. Pays $0-200 for unsolicited articles.**

PHOTOS Send photos. Captions, identification of subjects required. Reviews 35mm slides and larger,

3x5 prints. Photos are paid for with ms. Seldom buys individual photos.

TIPS Familiarity with the miniatures hobby is very helpful. Accuracy to scale is extremely important to our readers. A complete package (manuscripts/photos) has a better chance of publication.

🟡🟢 DOLLS

Jones Publishing, Inc., P.O. Box 5000, N7528 Aanstad Rd., Iola WI 54945. (715)445-5000. **Fax:** (715)445-4053. **E-mail:** carief@jonespublishing.com;jonespub@jonespublishing.com. **Website:** www.dollsmagazine.com. **75% freelance written.** "Magazine published 10 times/year covering dolls, doll artists, and related topics of interest to doll collectors and enthusiasts." "*Dolls* enhances the joy of collecting by introducing readers to the best new dolls from around the world, along with the artists and designers who create them. It keeps readers up-to-date on shows, sales and special events in the doll world. With beautiful color photography, *Dolls* offers an array of easy-to-read, informative articles that help our collectors select the best buys." Estab. 1982. Circ. 100,000. Byline given. Accepts queries by mail, e-mail. Responds in 1 month to queries.

NONFICTION Needs historical, how-to, interview, new product, photo feature. **Buys 55 mss/year.** Send complete ms. Length: 750-1,200 words. **Pays $75-300.**

F+W MEDIA, INC. (MAGAZINE DIVISION)

10151 Carver Rd., Suite 200, Cincinnati OH 45242. (513)531-2690. **E-mail:** dave.pulvermacher@fwmedia.com. **Website:** www.fwmedia.com. "Each month, millions of enthusiasts turn to the magazines from F+W for inspiration, instruction, and encouragement. Readers are as varied as our categories, but all are assured of getting the best possible coverage of their favorite hobby." Publishes magazines in the following categories: **antiques and collectibles** (*Antique Trader*); **automotive** (*Military Vehicles, Old Cars Report Price Guide, Old Cars Weekly*); **coins and paper money** (*Bank Note Reporter, Coins Magazine, Coin Prices, Numismatic News, World Coin News*); **comics** (*Comics Buyer's Guide*); **construction** (*Frame Building News, Metal Roofing, Rural Builder*); **fine art** (*Collector's Guide, Pastel Journal, Southwest Art, The Artist's Magazine, Watercolor Artist*); **firearms and knives** (*Blade, Gun Digest—The Magazine, Gun-Knife Show Calendar*); **genealogy** (*Family Tree Magazine*); **graphic design** (*HOW Magazine, PRINT*); **horticul-**

ture (*Horticulture*); **militaria** (*Military Trader*); **outdoors and hunting** (*Deer & Deer Hunting, Trapper & Predator Caller, Turkey & Turkey Hunting*); **records and CDs** (*Goldmine*); **sports** (*Sports Collectors Digest*); **woodworking** (*Popular Woodworking Magazine);* **writing** (*Writer's Digest*).

🔘 Please see individual listings in the Consumer Magazines and Trade Journals sections for specific submission information about each magazine.

🟡🟢🟢 FAMILY TREE MAGAZINE

F+W Media, Inc., 10151 Carver Rd., Suite #200, Cincinnati OH 45242. (513)531-2690. **Fax:** (513)891-7153. **Website:** www.familytreemagazine.com. **75% freelance written**. Magazine covering family history, heritage, and genealogy research. "*Family Tree Magazine* is a general-interest consumer magazine that helps readers discover, preserve, and celebrate their family's history. We cover genealogy, ethnic heritage, genealogy websites and software, photography and photo preservation, and other ways that families connect with their past." Estab. 1999. Circ. 75,000. Byline given. Offers 25% kill fee. Publishes ms an average of 6 months after acceptance. Editorial lead time 8 months. Submit seasonal material 8 months in advance. Accepts queries by mail, e-mail. Responds in 1 month to queries. Sample copy for $8 from website. Guidelines available online.

NONFICTION Needs book excerpts, historical, how-to, genealogy, new product, photography, computer, technical, genealogy software, photography equipment. **Buys 60 mss/year.** Query with published clips. Length: 250-4,500 words. **Pays $25-800.** Does not pay expenses.

♻ 🟢 FIBRE FOCUS

Magazine of the Ontario Handweavers & Spinners, 17 Robinson Rd., RR4, Waterford ON N0E 1Y0 Canada. (519)443-7104. **E-mail:** ffpublisher@bell.net. **Website:** www.ohs.on.ca. **Contact:** Graham McCracken. **90% freelance written.** Quarterly magazine covering handweaving, spinning, basketry, beading, and other fibre arts. "Our readers are weavers and spinners who also do dyeing, knitting, basketry, feltmaking, papermaking, sheep raising, and craft supply. All articles deal with some aspect of these crafts." Estab. 1957. Circ. 1,000. Byline given. Pays within 30 days after publication. Editorial lead time 6 months. Submit seasonal material 6 months in advance. Responds in

1 month to queries. Sample copy for $8 (Canadian). Guidelines available online.

NONFICTION Needs how-to, interview, new product, opinion, personal experience, technical, travel, book reviews. **Buys 40-60 mss/year.** "Please contact the *Fibre Focus* editor before undertaking a project or an article. Mss may be submitted c/o Graham McCracken by phone or e-mail for anything you have to contribute for upcoming issues. **Feature article deadlines: December 31, March 31, June 30, and September 15.** Please read the guidelines for contributing an article to *Fibre Focus*." Word length varies. **Pays $30 (Canadian) per published page.**

💲💲 FINE BOOKS & COLLECTIONS

OP Media, LLC, 4905 Pine Cone Drive #2, Durham NC 27707. (800)662-4834. **Fax:** (919)489-4767. **E-mail:** rebecca@finebooksmagazine.com. **Website:** www.finebooksmagazine.com. **90% freelance written.** Bimonthly magazine covering used and antiquarian bookselling and book collecting. We cover all aspects of selling and collecting out-of-print books. We emphasize good writing, interesting people, and unexpected view points. Estab. 2002. Circ. 5,000. Byline given. Offers negotiable kill fee. Publishes ms an average of 4 months after acceptance. Editorial lead time 6+ months. Submit seasonal material 4 months in advance. Accepts queries by mail, e-mail. Accepts simultaneous submissions. Responds in 2 months to queries and mss. Sample copy for $6.50 + shipping. Guidelines available online.

NONFICTION Needs book excerpts, essays, exposé, general interest, historical, how-to, humor, opinion, personal experience, photo feature, travel. Does not want tales of the 'gold in my attic' vein; how to collect; bibliographies/lists; stories emphasizing books/art as an investment **Buys 25 mss/year.** Query with published clips. Length: 500-2,000 words. **Pays $125-400.** Sometimes pays expenses of writers on assignment.

COLUMNS Digest (news about collectors, booksellers, and bookselling), 500 words.

💲 FINESCALE MODELER

Kalmbach Publishing Co., 21027 Crossroads Circle, P.O. Box 1612, Waukesha WI 53187. (414)796-8776. **Website:** www.finescale.com. **80% freelance written. Eager to work with new/unpublished writers.** "Magazine published 10 times/year devoted to how-to-do-it modeling information for scale model builders who build non-operating aircraft, tanks, boats, automo-biles, figures, dioramas, and science fiction and fantasy models." Circ. 60,000. Byline given. Publishes ms an average of 14 months after acceptance. Responds in 6 weeks to queries. Responds in 3 months to mss. Sample copy with 9×12 SASE and 3 first-class stamps.

NONFICTION Needs how-to, build scale models, technical, research information for building models. Query or send complete ms. Length: 750-3,000 words. **Pays $60/published page minimum.**

COLUMNS *FSM* Showcase (photos plus description of model); *FSM* Tips and Techniques (model building hints and tips). **Buys 25-50 mss/year.** Send complete ms. **Pays $25-50.**

💲💲 FINE TOOL JOURNAL

Antique & Collectible Tools, Inc., 27 Fickett Rd., Pownal ME 04069. (207)688-4962. **Fax:** (207)688-4831. **E-mail:** ceb@finetoolj.com. **Website:** www.finetoolj.com. **90% freelance written.** "Quarterly magazine specializing in older or antique hand tools from all traditional trades. Readers are primarily interested in woodworking tools, but some subscribers have interests in such areas as leatherworking, wrenches, kitchen, and machinist tools. Readers range from beginners just getting into the hobby to advanced collectors and organizations." Estab. 1970. Circ. 2,500. Byline given. Offers $50 kill fee. Publishes ms an average of 6 months after acceptance. Editorial lead time 9 months. Submit seasonal material 6 months in advance. Accepts queries by mail, online submission form. Responds in 2 months to queries. Responds in 3 months to mss. Sample copy for $5. Guidelines for #10 SASE.

NONFICTION Needs general interest, historical, how-to, make, use, fix and tune tools, interview, personal experience, photo feature, technical. **Buys 24 mss/year.** Send complete ms. Length: 400-2,000 words. **Pays $50-200.** Pays expenses of writers on assignment.

COLUMNS Stanley Tools (new finds and odd types), 300-400 words; Tips of the Trade (how to use tools), 100-200 words. **Buys 12 mss/year.** Send complete ms. **Pays $30-60.**

💲💲 FINE WOODWORKING

The Taunton Press, Inc., 63 South Main St., P.O. Box 5506, Newtown CT 06470-5506. (203)426-8171. **Fax:** (203)426-3434. **E-mail:** fw@taunton.com. **Website:** www.finewoodworking.com. **Contact:** Tom McKenna, senior editor. Bimonthly magazine on woodworking in the small shop. "All writers are also skilled woodworkers. It's more important that a contributor be a woodworker than a writer. Our editors (also woodworkers) will provide assistance and travel to shops to shoot all photography needed." Estab. 1975. Circ. 270,000. Byline given. Offers variable kill fee. Submit seasonal material 6 months in advance. Accepts simultaneous submissions. Responds in 1 month to queries. Guidelines online at www.finewoodworking.com/pages/fw_authorguideline.asp.

NONFICTION Needs how-to, woodworking. **Buys 120 mss/year.** Send article outline, helpful drawings or photos, and proposal letter. **Pays $150/magazine page.** Sometimes pays expenses of writers on assignment.

COLUMNS Fundamentals (basic how-to and concepts for beginning woodworkers); Master Class (advanced techniques); Finish Line (finishing techniques); Question & Answer (woodworking Q&A); Methods of Work (shop tips); Tools & Materials (short reviews of new tools). **Buys 400 mss/year. Pays $50-150/published page.**

$$ THE HOME SHOP MACHINIST

P.O. Box 629, Traverse City MI 49685. (231)946-3712. **Fax:** (231)946-6180. **E-mail:** gbulliss@villagepress.com; daronklooster@villagepress.com. **Website:** www.homeshopmachinist.net. **Contact:** George Bulliss, editor; Daron Klooster, managing editor. **95% freelance written.** Bimonthly magazine covering machining and metalworking for the hobbyist. Circ. 34,000. Byline given. Publishes ms an average of 2 years after acceptance. Responds in 2 months to queries. Sample copy free. Guidelines for 9×12 SASE.

NONFICTION Needs how-to, projects designed to upgrade present shop equipment or hobby model projects that require machining, technical, should pertain to metalworking, machining, drafting, layout, welding or foundry work for the hobbyist. No fiction or people features. **Buys 40 mss/year.** Send complete ms. Length: open—"whatever it takes to do a thorough job." **Pays $40/published page, plus $9/published photo.**

COLUMNS "Become familiar with our magazine before submitting." Book Reviews; New Product Reviews; Micro-Machining; Foundry. Length: 600-1,500 words. **Buys 25-30 mss/year.** Query. **Pays $40-70.**

FILLERS Buys 12-15 mss/year. Length: 100-300 words. **Pays $30-48.**

$$ KITPLANES

Belvoir Media Group LLC, 203 Argonne Ave., Suite B105, Long Beach CA 90803. **E-mail:** editorial@kitplanes.com. **Website:** www.kitplanes.com. **Contact:** Mary Bernard, editor-in-chief. **50% freelance written. Eager to work with new/unpublished writers.** Monthly magazine covering self-construction of private aircraft for pilots and builders. Estab. 1984. Circ. 72,000. Byline given. Publishes ms an average of 3 months after acceptance. Submit seasonal material 6 months in advance. Accepts queries by mail, e-mail. Responds in 4 weeks to queries. Responds in 6 weeks to mss. Sample copy for $6. Guidelines available online.

NONFICTION Needs general interest, how-to, interview, new product, personal experience, photo feature, technical. No general-interest aviation articles, or "My First Solo" type of articles. **Buys 80 mss/year.** Query. Length: 500-3,000 words. **Pays $150-500, including story photos.**

$$ KNIVES ILLUSTRATED

4635 McEwen RD., Dallas TX 75244. (714)939-9991. **Fax:** (714)456-0146. **E-mail:** BVoyles@Beckett.com. **Website:** www.knivesillustrated.com. **40-50% freelance written.** Bimonthly magazine covering high-quality factory and custom knives. We publish articles on different types of factory and custom knives, how-to make knives, technical articles, shop tours, articles on knife makers and artists. Must have knowledge about knives and the people who use and make them. We feature the full range of custom and high tech production knives, from miniatures to swords, leaving nothing untouched. We're also known for our outstanding how-to articles and technical features on equipment, materials and knife making supplies. We do not feature knife maker profiles as such, although we do spotlight some makers by featuring a variety of their knives and insight into their background and philosophy. Estab. 1987. Circ. 35,000. Byline given. Editorial lead time 3 months. Accepts queries by mail, e-mail, fax. Responds in 2 weeks to queries. Sample copy available. Guidelines for #10 SASE.

NONFICTION Needs general interest, historical, how-to, interview, new product, photo feature, technical. **Buys 35-40 mss/year.** Query. Length: 400-2,000 words. **Pays $100-500.**

$ LINN'S STAMP NEWS

Amos Press, P.O. Box 29, Sidney OH 45365. (937)498-0801. **Fax:** (937)498-0886. **E-mail:** linns@linns.com. **Website:** www.linns.com. **Contact:** Michael Baadke, editor. **50% freelance written.** Weekly tabloid on the stamp collecting hobby. "All articles must be about philatelic collectibles. Our goal at *Linn's* is to create a weekly publication that is indispensable to stamp collectors." Estab. 1928. Circ. 32,000. Byline given. Pays within 1 month of publication. Publishes ms an average of 4 months after acceptance. Submit seasonal material 2 months in advance. Responds in 6 weeks to queries. Sample copy online. Guidelines available online.

NONFICTION Needs general interest, historical, how-to, interview, technical, club and show news, current issues, auction realization, and recent discoveries. "No articles merely giving information on background of stamp subject. Must have philatelic information included." **Buys 40 mss/year.** Send complete ms. 750 words maximum. **Pays $40-100.** Sometimes pays expenses of writers on assignment.

$ LOST TREASURE, INC.

P.O. Box 451589, Grove OK 74345. (866)469-6224. **Fax:** (918)786-2192. **E-mail:** managingeditor@losttreasure.com. **Website:** www.losttreasure.com. **75% freelance written.** Monthly and annual magazines covering lost treasure. Estab. 1966. Circ. 55,000. Byline given. Accepts queries by mail, e-mail, fax. Responds in 1 month to queries. Responds in 2 months to mss. Sample copy for #10 SASE. Guidelines for 10×13 SAE with $1.70 postage or online.

NONFICTION **Buys 225 mss/year.** Query on *Treasure Cache* only. Length: 1,000-2,000 words. **Pays 4¢/word.**

$$ MILITARY VEHICLES

F+W Media, Inc., 700 E. State St., Iola WI 54990-0001. (715)445-4612. **Fax:** (715)445-4087. **Website:** www.militaryvehiclesmagazine.com. **50% freelance written.** Bimonthly magazine covering historic military vehicles. Dedicated to serving people who collect, restore, and drive historic military vehicles. Circ. 18,500. Byline given. Publishes ms an average of 1 month after acceptance. Accepts queries by mail, e-mail. Accepts simultaneous submissions. Responds in 1 week to queries. Responds in 1 month to mss. Sample copy for $5.

NONFICTION Needs historical, how-to, technical. **Buys 20 mss/year.** Send complete ms. Length: 1,300-2,600 words. **Pays $0-200.**

$ MODEL CARS MAGAZINE

Golden Bell Press, 2403 Champa St., Denver CO 80205. (808)754-1378. **E-mail:** gregg@modelcarsmag.com. **Website:** www.modelcarsmag.com. **25% freelance written.** Magazine published 9 times year covering model cars, trucks, and other automotive models. "*Model Cars Magazine* is the hobby's how-to authority for the automotive modeling hobbiest. We are on the forefront of the hobby, our editorial staff are model car builders, and every single one of our writers have a passion for the hobby that is evident in the articles and stories that we publish. We are the model car magazine written by and for model car builders." Estab. 1999. Circ. 7,00. Byline given. Publishes ms an average of 2-3 months after acceptance. Editorial lead time 2-3 months. Accepts queries by mail, e-mail. Sample copy online.

NONFICTION Needs how-to. Length: 600-3,000 words. **Pays $50/page. Pays $25/page for unsolicited articles.**

$ MONITORING TIMES

Grove Enterprises, Inc., 7546 Hwy. 64 W., Brasstown NC 28902-0098. (828)837-9200. **E-mail:** editor@monitoringtimes.com. **Website:** www.monitoringtimes.com. **15% freelance written.** Monthly magazine for radio hobbyists. Estab. 1982. Circ. 15,000. Byline given. Publishes ms an average of 4 months after acceptance. Submit seasonal material 4 months in advance. Accepts queries by mail, e-mail. Responds in 1 month to queries. Sample copy for 9×12 SAE and 9 first-class stamps. Guidelines available online.

NONFICTION Needs general interest, how-to, humor, interview, personal experience, photo feature, technical. **Buys 50 mss/year.** Query. Length: 1,500-3,000 words. **Pays average of $50/published page.**

$ NATIONAL COMMUNICATIONS MAGAZINE

Norm Schrein, Inc., P.O. Box 291918, Kettering OH 45429. (937)299-7226. **Fax:** (937)299-1323. **E-mail:** norm@bearcat1.com. **Website:** www.nat-com.org. **Contact:** Norm Schrein. **100% freelance written.** Bimonthly magazine covering radio as a hobby. Estab. 1990. Circ. 5,000. Byline given. Publishes ms an average of 2 months after acceptance. Editorial lead time 2 months. Submit seasonal material 2 months in advance. Accepts queries by phone. Accepts simultaneous submissions. Sample copy for $4.

NONFICTION Needs how-to, interview, new product, personal experience, photo feature, technical. Does not want articles off topic of the publication's audience (radio hobbyists). **Buys 2-3 mss/year.** Query. Length: 300 words. **Pays $75+.**

$ $ PAPER CRAFTS MAGAZINE

Primedia Magazines, 14850 Pony Express Rd., Suite 200, Bluffdale UT 84065. (801)816-8300. **Fax:** (801)816-8302. **E-mail:** editor@papercraftsmag.com. **Website:** www.papercraftsmag.com. **Contact:** Jennifer Schaerer, editor-in-chief; Kerri Miller, managing editor. Magazine published 10 times/year designed to help readers make creative and rewarding handmade crafts. The main focus is fresh, craft-related projects our reader can make and display in her home or give as gifts. Estab. 1978. Circ. 300,000. Byline given. Editorial lead time 6 months. Accepts queries by mail, e-mail. Responds in 1 month to queries. Guidelines for #10 SASE.

NONFICTION Needs how-to. **Buys 300 mss/year.** Query with photo or sketch of how-to project. Do not send the actual project until request. **Pays $100-500.**

$ PIECEWORK MAGAZINE

Interweave Press, Inc., 201 E. 4th St., Loveland CO 80537-5655. (800) 272-2193. **Fax:** (970)669-6117. **E-mail:** piecework@interweave.com. **Website:** www. interweave.com. **90% freelance written.** Bimonthly magazine covering needlework history. *PieceWork* celebrates the rich tradition of needlework and the history of the people behind it. Stories and projects on embroidery, cross-stitch, knitting, crocheting, and quilting, along with other textile arts, are featured in each issue. Estab. 1993. Circ. 30,000. Byline given. Offers 25% kill fee. Editorial lead time 6 months. Submit seasonal material 6 months in advance. Accepts queries by mail, e-mail, fax, phone. Responds in 6 months to queries. Sample copy and writer's guidelines free.

NONFICTION Needs book excerpts, historical, how-to, interview, new product. No contemporary needlework articles. **Buys 25-30 mss/year.** Send complete ms. Length: 1,000-5,000 words. **Pays $100/printed page.**

$ POPULAR COMMUNICATIONS

CQ Communications, Inc., 25 Newbridge Rd., Hicksville NY 11801. (516)681-2922. **Fax:** (516)681-2926. **E-mail:** cq@cq-amateur-radio.com. **Website:** www.popular-communications.com. **25% freelance written.** Monthly magazine covering the radio communications hobby. Estab. 1982. Circ. 40,000. Byline given. Publishes ms an average of 6 months after acceptance. Editorial lead time 3 months. Submit seasonal material 6 months in advance. Accepts queries by mail, e-mail. Responds in 1 month to queries. Responds in

2 months to mss. Sample copy free. Guidelines for #10 SASE.

NONFICTION Needs general interest, how-to, antenna construction, humor, new product, photo feature, technical. **Buys 6-10 mss/year.** Query. Length: 1,800-3,000 words. **Pays $135/printed page.**

$ $ $ $ POPULAR MECHANICS

Hearst Corp., 300 W. 57th St., New York NY 10019. (212)649-2000. **E-mail:** popularmechanics@hearst.com. **Website:** www.popularmechanics.com. **Up to 50% freelance written.** Monthly magazine on technology, science, automotive, home, outdoors. We are a men's service magazine that addresses the diverse interests of today's male, providing him with information to improve the way he lives. We cover stories from do-it-yourself projects to technological advances in aerospace, military, automotive and so on. Estab. 1902. Circ. 1,200,000. Offers 25% kill fee. Publishes ms an average of 6 months after acceptance. Submit seasonal material 6 months in advance.

NONFICTION Pays $1/word and up.

$ $ POPULAR WOODWORKING MAGAZINE

F+W Media, Inc., 8469 Blue Ash Rd., Suite 100, Cincinnati OH 45236. (513)531-2690, ext. 11348. **E-mail:** megan.fitzpatrick@fwmedia.com. **Website:** www.popularwoodworking.com. **45% freelance written.** Magazine published 7 times/year. "*Popular Woodworking Magazine* invites woodworkers of all skill levels into a community of professionals who share their hard-won shop experience through in-depth projects and technique articles, which help the readers hone their existing skills and develop new ones for both hand and power tools. Related stories increase the readers' understanding and enjoyment of their craft. Any project submitted must be aesthetically pleasing, of sound construction, and offer a challenge to readers. On the average, we use 2 freelance features per issue. Our primary needs are 'how-to' articles on woodworking. Our secondary need is for articles that will inspire discussion concerning woodworking. Tone of articles should be conversational and informal but knowledgeable, as if the writer is speaking directly to the reader. Our readers are the woodworking hobbyist and small woodshop owner. Writers should have an extensive knowledge of woodworking and excellent woodworking techniques and skills." Estab. 1981. Circ. 150,000. Byline given. Publishes ms an average of 10 months after acceptance. Submit seasonal material

6 months in advance. Accepts queries by mail, e-mail, phone. Responds in 2 months to queries. Sample copy for $5.99 and 9×12 SAE with 6 first-class stamps or online. Guidelines available online.

NONFICTION Needs how-to (on woodworking projects, with plans), humor (woodworking anecdotes), technical (woodworking techniques). No tool reviews. **Buys 12 mss/year.** Send complete ms. **Pay starts at $250/published page.**

COLUMNS Tricks of the Trade (helpful techniques), End Grain (thoughts on woodworking as a profession or hobby, can be humorous or serious), 500-550 words. **Buys 20 columns/yr mss/year.** Query.

THE QUILTER

All American Crafts, Inc., 7 Waterloo Rd., Stanhope NJ 07874. (973)347-6900, ext. 135. **E-mail:** editors@ thequiltermag.com. **Website:** www.thequiltermag. com. **Contact:** Laurette Koserowski, editor. **45% freelance written.** Bimonthly magazine on quilting. Estab. 1988. Byline given. Publishes ms an average of 6 months after acceptance. Submit seasonal material 6 months in advance. Accepts queries by mail, phone. Responds in 6 weeks to queries. Sample copy for SAE with 9×12 envelope and 4 first-class stamps. Guidelines available online.

NONFICTION Query with published clips. Length: 350-1,000 words. **Pays $150-250/article for original, unpublished mss. Project payments are a flat rate of $175-$375/project.**

COLUMNS Feature Teacher (qualified quilt teachers with teaching involved—with slides); Profile (award-winning and interesting quilters). Length: 1,000 words maximum. **Pays 10¢/word, $15/photo.**

QUILTER'S WORLD

185 Sweet Rd., Lincoln ME 04457. **Website:** www.quilters-world.com. **100% freelance written. Works with a small number of new/unpublished writers each year.** Bimonthly magazine covering quilting. "*Quilter's World* is a general quilting publication. We accept articles about special quilters, techniques, coverage of unusual quilts at quilt shows, special interest quilts, human interest articles and patterns. We include 2 articles and 12-15 patterns in every issue. Reader is 30-70 years old, midwestern." Circ. 130,000. Byline given. Pays 45 days after acceptance. Submit seasonal material 10 months in advance. Accepts queries by mail, e-mail. Responds in 3 months to queries. Guidelines available online.

NONFICTION Needs how-to, interview, new product, photo feature feature, technical, quilters, quilt products. Query or send complete ms **Pays $100-$200 for articles; $50-550 for quilt designs**

RENAISSANCE MAGAZINE

80 Hathaway Dr., Stratford CT 06615. (800)232-2224. **Fax:** (800)775-2729. **E-mail:** editortom@renaissancemagazine.com. **Website:** www.renaissancemagazine.com. **Contact:** Tom Hauck, editor. **90% freelance written.** Bimonthly magazine covering the history of the Middle Ages and the Renaissance. "Our readers include historians, reenactors, roleplayers, medievalists, and Renaissance Faire enthusiasts." Estab. 1996. Circ. 33,000. Byline given. Publishes ms an average of 1 year after acceptance. Editorial lead time 6 months. Submit seasonal material 4 months in advance. Accepts queries by mail, e-mail, fax, phone. Responds in 3 weeks to queries. Responds in 2 months to mss. Sample copy for $9. Guidelines available online.

NONFICTION Needs essays, exposé, historical, how-to, interview, new product, opinion, photo feature, religious, travel. **Buys 25 mss/year.** Query or send ms Length: 1,000-5,000 words. **Pays 8¢/word.**

ROCK & GEM

Miller Magazines, Inc., 3585 Maple St., Suite 232, Ventura CA 93003. (805)644-3824. **Fax:** (805)644-3875. **E-mail:** editor@rockngem.com. **Website:** www. rockngem.com. **99% freelance written.** Monthly magazine covering rockhounding field trips, how-to lapidary projects, minerals, fossils, gold prospecting, mining, etc. See guidelines. This is not a scientific journal. Its articles appeal to amateurs, beginners, and experts, but its tone is conversational and casual, not stuffy. It's for hobbyists. Estab. 1971. Circ. 55,000. Byline given. Editorial lead time 4 months. Submit seasonal material 6 months in advance. Accepts queries by mail. Guidelines available online.

Contributor agreement required.

NONFICTION Needs general interest, how-to, personal experience, photo feature, travel. Does not want to see The 25th Anniversary of the Pet Rock, or anything so scientific that it could be a thesis. **Buys 156-200 mss/year.** Send complete ms. Length: 2,000-4,000 words. **Pays $100-250.**

SEW NEWS

Creative Crafts Group, 741 Corporate Circle, Suite A, Golden CO 80401. (303)215-5600. **Fax:** (303)215-5601.

E-mail: sewnews@sewnews.com. **Website:** www.sewnews.com. **70% freelance written. Works with a small number of new/unpublished writers each year.** Monthly magazine covering fashion, gift, and home-dec sewing. "Our magazine is for the beginning home sewer to the professional dressmaker. It expresses the fun, creativity, and excitement of sewing." Estab. 1980. Circ. 185,000. Byline given. Publishes ms an average of 6 months after acceptance. Submit seasonal material 6 months in advance. Accepts queries by mail, e-mail, fax. Responds in 2 months to mss. Sample copy for $5.99. Guidelines for #10 SAE with 2 first-class stamps or online.

NONFICTION Needs how-to, sewing techniques, interview, interesting personalities in home-sewing field. **Buys 200-240 mss/year.** Query with published clips if available Length: 500-2,000 words. **Pays $25-500.**

$ SHUTTLE SPINDLE & DYEPOT

Handweavers Guild of America, Inc., 1255 Buford Hwy., Suite 211, Suwanee GA 30024. (678)730-0010. **Fax:** (678)730-0836. **E-mail:** hga@weavespindye.org. **Website:** www.weavespindye.org. **60% freelance written.** Quarterly magazine. "Quarterly membership publication of the Handweavers Guild of America, Inc., *Shuttle Spindle & Dyepot* magazine seeks to encourage excellence in contemporary fiber arts and to support the preservation of techniques and traditions in fiber arts. It also provides inspiration for fiber artists of all levels and develops public awareness and appreciation of the fiber arts. *Shuttle Spindle & Dyepot* appeals to a highly educated, creative, and very knowledgeable audience of fiber artists and craftsmen, weavers, spinners, dyers, and basket makers." Estab. 1969. Circ. 30,000. Byline given. Publishes ms an average of 6 months after acceptance. Editorial lead time 8 months. Submit seasonal material 8 months in advance. Accepts queries by mail, e-mail, fax, phone. Sample copy for $8.00 plus shipping. Guidelines available online.

NONFICTION Needs inspirational, interview, new product, personal experience, photo feature, technical, travel. No self-promotional and no articles from those without knowledge of area/art/artists. **Buys 40 mss/year.** Query with published clips. Length: 1,000-2,000 words. **Pays $75-150.**

COLUMNS Books and Videos, News and Information, Calendar and Conference, Travel and Workshop (all fiber/art related).

$ SUNSHINE ARTIST

Palm House Publishing Inc., 4075 L.B. McLeod Rd., Suite E, Orlando FL 32811. (800)597-2573. **Fax:** (407)228-9862. **E-mail:** business@sunshineartist.com. **Website:** www.sunshineartist.com. Monthly magazine covering art shows in the US. We are the premiere marketing/reference magazine for artists and crafts professionals who earn their living through art shows nationwide. We list more than 2,000 shows monthly, critique many of them, and publish articles on marketing, selling and other issues of concern to professional show circuit artists. Estab. 1972. Circ. 12,000. Byline given. Publishes ms an average of 3 months after acceptance. Responds in 2 months to queries. Sample copy for $5.

NONFICTION No how-to. **Buys 5-10 freelance mss/year.** Send complete ms. Length: 1,000-2,000 words. **Pays $50-150.**

$$ TATTOO REVUE

Art & Ink Enterprises, Inc., c/o Outlaw Biker/Art & Ink Publications, 1000 Seaboard Street Suite B4, Charlotte NC 28206-2991. (704)333-3331. **Fax:** (704)333-3433. **E-mail:** inked@skinartmag.com. **Website:** www.skinart.com. **25% freelance written.** Interview and profile magazine published 4 times/year covering tattoo artists, their art and lifestyle. All writers must have knowledge of tattoos. Features include interviews with tattoo artists and collectors. Estab. 1990. Circ. 100,000. Byline given. Publishes ms an average of 3 months after acceptance. Editorial lead time 3 months. Submit seasonal material 5 months in advance. Accepts queries by mail, e-mail, fax. Responds in 2 weeks to queries. Sample copy for $5.98. Guidelines for #10 SASE.

NONFICTION Needs book excerpts, historical, humor, interview, photo feature. Special issues: Publishes special convention issues—dates and locations provided upon request. No first-time experiences—our readers already know. **Buys 10-30 mss/year.** Send complete ms. Length: 500-2,500 words. **Pays $25-200.**

COLUMNS Buys 10-30 mss/year. Query with or without published clips or send complete ms. **Pays $25-50.**

FILLERS Needs anecdotes, facts, gags, newsbreaks, short humor. **Buys 10-20 mss/year.** Length: 50-2,000 words.

$$ TEDDY BEAR REVIEW

Jones Publishing, Inc., P.O. Box 5000, Iola WI 54945-5000. (800)331-0038. **Fax:** (715)445-4053. **Website:**

www.teddybearreview.com. **65% freelance written. Works with a small number of new/unpublished writers each year.** Bimonthly magazine on teddy bears for collectors, enthusiasts and bearmakers. Estab. 1985. Byline given. Payment upon publication on the last day of the month the issue is mailed. Submit seasonal material 6 months in advance. Sample copy and writer's guidelines for $2 and 9×12 SAE.

NONFICTION Needs historical, how-to, interview. No articles from the bear's point of view. **Buys 30-40 mss/year.** Query with published clips. Length: 900-1,500 words. **Pays $100-350.**

⊖⊖ THREADS

Taunton Press, 63 S. Main St., P.O. Box 5506, Newtown CT 06470. (203)426-8171. **Fax:** (203)426-3434. **E-mail:** th@taunton.com. **Website:** www.threadsmagazine.com. Bimonthly magazine covering garment sewing, garment design, and embellishments (including quilting and embroidery). "We're seeking proposals from hands-on authors who first and foremost have a skill. Being an experienced writer is of secondary consideration." Estab. 1985. Circ. 129,000. Byline given. Offers $150 kill fee. Editorial lead time 4 months. Responds in 1-2 months to queries. Guidelines available online.

COLUMNS Product reviews; Book reviews; Tips; Closures (stories of a humorous nature). Query. **Closures pays $150/page. Each sewing tip printed pays $25.**

⊖⊖ TOY FARMER

Toy Farmer Publications, 7496 106 Ave. SE, LaMoure ND 58458-9404. (701)883-5206. **Fax:** (701)883-5209. **E-mail:** info@toyfarmer.com. **Website:** www.toyfarmer.com. **70% freelance written**. Monthly magazine covering farm toys. Estab. 1978. Circ. 27,000. Byline given. Editorial lead time 2 months. Submit seasonal material 3 months in advance. Accepts queries by mail, e-mail, fax, phone. Responds in 1 month to queries. Responds in 2 months to mss. Writer's guidelines available upon request.

NONFICTION Needs general interest, historical, interview, new product, personal experience, technical, book introductions. **Buys 100 mss/year.** Query with published clips. Length: 800-1,500 words. **Pays 10¢/word.** Sometimes pays expenses of writers on assignment.

⊖⊖ TOY TRUCKER & CONTRACTOR

Toy Farmer Publications, 7496 106th Ave. SE, LaMoure ND 58458-9404. (701)883-5206. **Fax:** (701)883-5209. E-

mail: info@toyfarmer.com. **Website:** www.toytrucker. com. **40% freelance written**. Monthly magazine covering collectible toys. "We are a magazine on hobby and collectible toy trucks and construction pieces." Estab. 1990. Circ. 6,500. Byline given. Editorial lead time 2 months. Submit seasonal material 3 months in advance. Accepts queries by mail, e-mail, fax, phone. Responds in 1 month to queries. Responds in 2 months to mss. Writer's guidelines available on request.

NONFICTION Needs historical, interview, new product, personal experience, technical. **Buys 35 mss/year.** Query. Length: 800-1,400 words. **Pays 10¢/word.** Sometimes pays expenses of writers on assignment.

⊖ TREASURES: ANTIQUE TO MODERN COLLECTIBLES

P.O. Box 306, Grundy Center IA 50638. (319)824-6981. **Fax:** (319)824-3414. **E-mail:** lkruger@pioneermagazines.com. **Website:** www.treasuresmagazine.com; www.collectors-news.com. **Contact:** Linda Kruger, executive director. **20% freelance written. Works with a small number of new/unpublished writers each year.** Ten issues/year; magazine-size publication on glossy stock, full cover, covering antiques, collectibles, and nostalgic memorabilia and modern collectibles. Estab. 1959. Circ. 11,000. Byline given. Publishes ms an average of 1 year after acceptance. Submit seasonal material 3 months in advance. Accepts queries by e-mail. Responds in 2 weeks to queries. Responds in 6 weeks to mss. Sample copy for $4 and 9×12 SAE. Guidelines free.

NONFICTION Needs general interest, collectibles, antique to modern, historical, relating to collections or collectors, how-to, display your collection, care for, restore, appraise, locate, add to, etc., interview, covering individual collectors and their hobbies, unique or extensive; celebrity collectors, and limited edition artists, technical, in-depth analysis of a particular antique, collectible, or collecting field, travel, hot antiquing places in the US. Special issues: Twelve-month listing of antique and collectible shows, flea markets, and conventions (January includes events January-December; June includes events June-May); Care & Display of Collectibles (September); holidays (October-December). **Buys 36 mss/year.** Query with sample of writing. Length: 800-1,000 words. **Pays $1.10/column inch.**

⊖ WESTERN & EASTERN TREASURES

People's Publishing Co., Inc., P.O. Box 219, San Anselmo CA 94979. **Website:** www.treasurenet.com.

100% freelance written. Monthly magazine covering hobby/sport of metal detecting/treasure hunting. *"Western & Eastern Treasures provides concise, yet comprehensive coverage of every aspect of the sport/hobby of metal detecting and treasure hunting with a strong emphasis on current, accurate information; innovative, field-proven advice and instruction; and entertaining, effective presentation."* Estab. 1966. Circ. 50,000. Byline given. Publishes ms an average of 4+ months after acceptance. Editorial lead time 4 months. Submit seasonal material 3-4 months in advance. No-Responds in 3 months to mss. Sample copy for sae with 9×12 envelope and 5 First-Class stamps. Guidelines for #10 SASE.

NONFICTION Needs how-to, tips and finds for metal detectorists, interview, only people in metal detecting, personal experience, positive metal detector experiences, technical, only metal detecting hobby-related, helping in local community with metal detecting skills (i.e., helping local police locate evidence at crime scenes—all volunteer basis). Special issues: *Silver & Gold Annual* (editorial deadline February each year)—looking for articles 1,500+ words, plus photos on the subject of locating silver and/or gold using a metal detector. No fiction, poetry, or puzzles. **Buys 150+ mss/year.** Send complete ms. Length: 1,000-1,500 words. **Pays 3¢/word for articles.**

💲💲 WOODSHOP NEWS

Cruz Bay Publishing Inc., an Active Interest Media company, 10 Bokum Rd., Essex CT 06426. (860)767-8227. **Fax:** (860)767-1048. **E-mail:** editorial@woodshopnews.com. **Website:** www.woodshopnews.com. **Contact:** Tod Riggio, editor. **20% freelance written.** Monthly tabloid covering woodworking for professionals. Solid business news and features about woodworking companies. Feature stories about interesting professional woodworkers. Some how-to articles. Estab. 1986. Circ. 60,000. Byline given. Publishes ms an average of 3 months after acceptance. Submit seasonal material 4 months in advance. Accepts queries by mail, e-mail, fax. Responds in 1 month to queries. Sample copy available online. Guidelines free.

NONFICTION Needs how-to, query first, interview, new product, opinion, personal experience, photo feature. Key word is newsworthy. No general interest profiles of folksy woodworkers. **Buys 15-25 mss/year.** Send complete ms. Length: 100-1,200 words. **Pays $50-500 for assigned articles. Pays $40-250**

for unsolicited articles. Pays expenses of writers on assignment.

COLUMNS Pro Shop (business advice, marketing, employee relations, taxes, etc., for the professional written by an established professional in the field); Finishing (how-to and techniques, materials, spraybooths, staining; written by experienced finishers), both 1,200-1,500 words. **Buys 18 mss/year.** Query. **Pays $200-300.**

HOME AND GARDEN

💲💲 THE AMERICAN GARDENER

7931 E. Boulevard Dr., Alexandria VA 22308-1300. (703)768-5700. **Fax:** (703)768-7533. **E-mail:** editor@ahs.org; myee@ahs.org. **Website:** www.ahs.org. **Contact:** Mary Yee, art director. **60% freelance written.** Bimonthly, 64-page, four-color magazine covering gardening and horticulture. "This is the official publication of the American Horticultural Society (AHS), a national, nonprofit, membership organization for gardeners, founded in 1922. The AHS mission is 'to open the eyes of all Americans to the vital connection between people and plants, and to inspire all Americans to become responsible caretakers of the earth, to celebrate America's diversity through the art and science of horticulture, and to lead this effort by sharing the society's unique national resources with all Americans.' All articles are also published on members-only website." Estab. 1922. Circ. 20,000. Byline given. Offers 25% kill fee. Publishes ms an average of 6 months after acceptance. Editorial lead time 6 months. Submit seasonal material at least 1 year in advance. Accepts queries by mail with SASE. NoResponds in 3 months to queries. Sample copy for $5. Writer's guidelines by e-mail and online.

NONFICTION Buys 20 mss/year. Query with published clips. No fax, phone, or e-mail submissions. Length: 1,500-2,500 words. **Pays $300-500, depending on complexity and author's experience.**

COLUMNS Natural Connections (explains a natural phenomenon—plant and pollinator relationships, plant and fungus relationships, parasites—that may be observed in nature or in the garden), 750-1,200 words. Homegrown Harvest (articles on edible plants delivered in a personal, reassuring voice. Each issue focuses on a single crop, such as carrots, blueberries, or parsley), 800-900 words; Plant in the Spotlight (profiles of a single plant species or cultivar, including a personal perspective on why it's a favored plant), 600 words. **Buys 5 mss/year.** Query with published clips. **Pays $100-250.**

💲💲 ATLANTA HOMES AND LIFESTYLES

Network Communications, Inc., 1100 Johnson Ferry Rd., Suite 595, Atlanta GA 30342. (404)252-6670. **Fax:** (404)252-6673. **Website:** www.atlantahomesmag.com. **65% freelance written.** Magazine published 12 times/year. *Atlanta Homes and Lifestyles* is designed for the action-oriented, well-educated reader who enjoys his/her shelter, its design and construction, its environment, and living and entertaining in it. Estab. 1983. Circ. 33,091. Byline given. Publishes ms an average of 6 months after acceptance. Accepts queries by mail, fax. Responds in 3 months to queries. Sample copy for $3.95. Guidelines available online.

NONFICTION Needs interview, new product, photo feature, well-designed homes, gardens, local art, remodeling, food, preservation, entertaining. We do not want articles outside respective market area, not written for magazine format, or that are excessively controversial, investigative or that cannot be appropriately illustrated with attractive photography. **Buys 35 mss/year.** Query with published clips. Length: 500-1,200 words. **Pays $100-500.** Sometimes pays expenses of writer on assignment

🌢 AUSTRALIAN COUNTRY COLLECTIONS

Universal Magazines, Ltd., Unit 5, 6-8 Byfield St., North Ryde NSW 2113 Australia. (61)(2)9887-0399. **Fax:** (61)(2)9805-0714. **E-mail:** countrycollections@universalmagazines.com.au. **Website:** http://www.completecraft.com.au/. Bimonthly magazine featuring a variety of stunning Australian country homes in every issue, creating a sense of country style for our readers' world. "Your country lifestyle magazine, Country Collections caters to those wanting to live the country life wherever they live; be them passionate homemakers, collectors or those aspiring to own a country dream home. Be inspired by the variety of stunning homes and successful tree change stories in every issue." Circ. 30,000.

NONFICTION Needs general interest, inspirational, photo feature. Query.

💲 BACKHOME

Wordsworth Communications, Inc., P.O. Box 70, Hendersonville NC 28793. (828)696-3838. **Fax:** (828)696-0700. **E-mail:** backhome@ioa.com. **Website:** www.backhomemagazine.com. **80% freelance written.** Bimonthly magazine. "*BackHome* encourages readers to take more control over their lives by doing more for themselves: productive organic gardening; building and repairing their homes; utilizing renewable energy systems; raising crops and livestock; building furniture; toys and games and other projects; creative cooking. *BackHome* promotes respect for family activities, community programs, and the environment." Estab. 1990. Circ. 42,000. Byline given. Offers $25 kill fee at publisher's discretion. Publishes ms an average of 1 year after acceptance. Editorial lead time 3 months. Submit seasonal material 6 months in advance. Accepts queries by mail, e-mail, fax, phone. Responds in 6 weeks to queries. Responds in 2 months to mss. Sample copy $5 or online. Guidelines available online.

○ The editor reports an interest in seeing more renewable energy experiences, *good* small houses, workshop projects (for handy persons, not experts), and community action others can copy.

NONFICTION Needs how-to, gardening, construction, energy, homebusiness, interview, personal experience, technical, self-sufficiency. No essays or old-timey reminiscences. **Buys 80 mss/year.** Query. Length: 750-5,000 words. **Pays $35 (approximately)/printed page.**

💲💲💲💲 BETTER HOMES AND GARDENS

1716 Locust St., Des Moines IA 50309-3023. (515)284-3044. **Fax:** (515)284-3763. **Website:** www.bhg.com. Brenda Lesch, creative director. **Contact:** Doug Crichton, editor-in-chief. **10-15% freelance written.** Magazine "providing home service information for people who have a serious interest in their homes." "We read all freelance articles, but much prefer to see a letter of query rather than a finished manuscript." Estab. 1922. Circ. 7,605,000.

NONFICTION Needs travel, education, gardening, health, cars, home, entertainment. "We do not deal with political subjects or with areas not connected with the home, community, and family. No poetry or fiction." **Pay rates vary.**

💲💲 BIRDS & BLOOMS

Reiman Media Group, 5925 Country Ln., Greendale WI 53129-1404. (414)423-0100. **E-mail:** editors@birdsandblooms.com. **Website:** www.birdsandblooms.

com. **15% freelance written.** "Bimonthly magazine focusing on the beauty in your own backyard. *Birds & Blooms* is a sharing magazine that lets backyard enthusiasts chat with each other by exchanging personal experiences. This makes *Birds & Blooms* more like a conversation than a magazine, as readers share tips and tricks on producing beautiful blooms and attracting feathered friends to their backyards." "See contributor's guidelines at: http://www.birdsandblooms.com/contributor-s-guidelines." Estab. 1995. Circ. 1,900,000. Byline given. Publishes ms an average of 7 months after acceptance. Editorial lead time 2 months. Submit seasonal material 4 months in advance. Accepts queries by mail, online submission form. Accepts simultaneous submissions. Responds in 2 months to queries & mss. Sample copy for $2, 9×12 SAE and $1.95 postage. Guidelines online or for #10 SASE.

NONFICTION Needs essays, how-to, humor, inspirational, personal experience, photo feature, natural crafting and plan items for building backyard accents. No bird rescue or captive bird pieces. **Buys 12-20 mss/year.** Send complete ms to us, along with your full name, daytime phone number, e-mail address and mailing address. If you're submitting for a particular column, note that as well. Each reader contributor whose story, photo or short item is published receives a *Birds & Blooms* tote bag. See guidelines online. Length: 250-1,000 words. **Pays $100-400.**

COLUMNS Backyard Banter (odds, ends & unique things); Bird Tales (backyard bird stories); Local Lookouts (community backyard happenings), all 200 words. **Buys 12-20 mss/year.** Send complete ms. **Pays $50-75.**

FILLERS Needs anecdotes, facts, gags. **Buys 25 mss/year.** Length: 10-250 words. **Pays $10-75.**

🟢🟢 CALIFORNIA HOMES

McFadden-Bray Publishing Corp., 417 31st St., Suite B, Newport Beach CA 92663. (949)640-1484. **Fax:** (949)640-1665. **E-mail:** edit@calhomesmagazine. com; susan@calhomesmagazine.com; larissa@papercakesdesign.com. **Website:** www.calhomesmagazine.com. Larissa Linn, art director. **Contact:** Kathy Bryant, managing editor; Vanessa Brunner, assistant editor. **80% freelance written.** Bimonthly magazine covering California interiors, architecture, some food, travel, history, and current events in the field. Estab. 1997. Circ. 80,000. Byline given. Offers 50% kill fee.

Publishes ms an average of 3 months after acceptance. Editorial lead time 3 months. Submit seasonal material 6 months in advance. Accepts queries by mail, e-mail, fax. Responds in 1 month to queries. Responds in 2 months to mss. Sample copy for $7.50. Guidelines for #10 SASE.

NONFICTION Query. Length: 500-1,000 words. **Pays $250-750.** Sometimes pays expenses of writers on assignment.

🟢⊘ CANADIAN HOMES & COTTAGES

The In-Home Show, Ltd., 2650 Meadowvale Blvd., Unit 4, Mississauga ON L5N 6M5 Canada. (905)567-1440. **Fax:** (905)567-1442. **E-mail:** jnaisby@homesandcottages.com. **E-mail:** oliver@homesandcottages. com. **Website:** www.homesandcottages.com. **Contact:** Oliver Johnson, managing editor. **75% freelance written.** Magazine published 6 times/year covering building and renovating. "Publishes articles that have a technical slant, as well as those with a more general lifestyle feel." Estab. 1987. Circ. 92,340. Byline given. Offers 10% kill fee. Publishes ms an average of 6 months after acceptance. Editorial lead time 3 months. Submit seasonal material 6 months in advance. Accepts queries by mail. Sample copy for SAE. Guidelines for #10 SASE.

NONFICTION Needs humor, building and renovation related, new product, technical. **Buys 32 mss/year.** Query. Length: 800-1,500 words. **Pays $3500-650.** Sometimes pays expenses of writers on assignment.

🟢 🟢🟢 THE CANADIAN ORGANIC GROWER

1205 Route 915, New Horton NB E4H 1W1 Canada. **E-mail:** janet@cog.ca; office@cog.ca; publications@cog. ca. **Website:** www.cog.ca/magazine.htm. **Contact:** Janet Wallace, managing editor. **100% freelance written.** Quarterly magazine covering organic gardening and farming. "We publish articles that are of interest to organic gardeners, farmers and consumers in Canada. We're always looking for practical how-to articles, as well as farmer profiles. At times, we include news about the organic community, recipes and stories about successful marketing strategies." Estab. 1975. Circ. 4,000. Byline given. Publishes ms an average of 2-3 months after acceptance. Editorial lead time 6 months. Submit seasonal material 6 months in advance. Accepts queries by mail, e-mail. Responds in 3 weeks to queries. Responds in 1 month to mss. Sample copy available online. Guidelines available online.

NONFICTION Needs essays, general interest, how-to, garden, farm, market, process organic food, interview, new product, opinion, technical, "If you would like to write an article for *The Canadian Organic Grower*, please email the editor to discuss your idea before you start to write. If you would like to submit a book review, please contact the COG Librarian for detailed guidelines and, if necessary, suggestions about books to review: library@cog.ca." Does not want "rants." **Buys 25 mss/year.** Query. Length: 500-2,500 words. **Pays $150-350 for assigned articles. Pays $150-350 for unsolicited articles.**

💲💲💲💲 COASTAL LIVING

Southern Progress Corp., 2100 Lakeshore Dr., Birmingham AL 35209. (205)445-6007. **Fax:** (205)445-8655. **E-mail:** mamie_walling@timeinc.com. **Website:** www.coastalliving.com. **Contact:** Mamie Walling. "Bimonthly magazine for those who live or vacation along our nation's coasts. The magazine emphasizes home design and travel, but also covers a wide variety of other lifestyle topics and coastal concerns." Estab. 1997. Circ. 660,000. Offers 25% kill fee. Responds in 2 months to queries. Sample copy available online. Guidelines available online.

NONFICTION Query with clips and SASE. **Pays $1/word.**

💲💲 COLORADO HOMES & LIFESTYLES

Network Communications, Inc., 1777 S. Harrison St., Suite 903, Denver CO 80210. (303)248-2060. **Fax:** (303)248-2066. **E-mail:** mabel@coloradohomesmag.com. **Website:** www.coloradohomesmag.com. **Contact:** Mary Barthelme Abel, editor-in-chief. **75% freelance written.** Upscale shelter magazine published 9 times/year containing beautiful homes, landscapes, architecture, calendar, antiques, etc. All of Colorado is included. Geared toward home-related and lifestyle areas, personality profiles, etc. Estab. 1981. Circ. 36,000. Byline given. Offers 15% kill fee. Publishes ms an average of 3 months after acceptance. Editorial lead time 3 months. Submit seasonal material 1 year in advance. Accepts queries by mail, e-mail. Accepts simultaneous submissions. Responds in 2 months to queries. Sample copy for #10 SASE.

NONFICTION No personal essays, religious, humor, or technical submissions. **Buys 50-75 mss/year.** Query with published clips. Length: 900-1,500 words. **Pays $200-400.** Sometimes pays expenses of writers on assignment. Provide sources with phone numbers

COUNTRY LIVING

The Hearst Corp., 300 W. 57th St., New York NY 10019. (212)649-3501. **E-mail:** clmail@hearst.com. **Website:** www.countryliving.com. Monthly magazine covering home design and interior decorating with an emphasis on country style. Estab. 1978. Circ. 1,600,000.

💬 "A lifestyle magazine for readers who appreciate the warmth and traditions associated with American home and family life. Each monthly issue embraces American country decorating and includes features on furniture, antiques, gardening, home building, real estate, cooking, entertaining and travel." Verify the market is active and accepting submissions before sending your manuscript via regular mail.

NONFICTION **Buys 20-30 mss/year.** Send complete ms and SASE. **Payment varies.**

COLUMNS Query first.

💲💲 EARLY AMERICAN LIFE

Firelands Media Group LLC, P.O. Box 221228, Shaker Heights OH 44122-0996. **E-mail:** queries@firelands-media.com. **Website:** www.ealonline.com. **Contact:** Tess Rosch, publisher. **60% freelance written.** Bimonthly magazine for people who are interested in capturing the warmth and beauty of the 1600-1840 period and using it in their homes and lives today. They are interested in antiques, traditional crafts, architecture, restoration, and collecting. Estab. 1970. Circ. 90,000. Byline given. 25% kill fee. Publishes ms an average of 1 year after acceptance. Accepts queries by mail, e-mail. Responds in 3 months to queries. Sample copy and writer's guidelines for 9×12 SAE with $2.50 postage. Guidelines available online at: www.ealonline.com/editorial/guidelines.php.

NONFICTION **Buys 40 mss/year.** Query us first before sending ms. Length: 750-3,000 words. **Pays $250-700, additionally for photos.**

💲💲💲💲 ECOHOME DESIGNS

Hanley Wood, 1 Thomas Cir., #600, Washington DC 20005-5811. **E-mail:** hgottemoeller@hanleywood.com. **Website:** www.hanleywood.com. **Contact:** Hillary Gottemoeller. **75% freelance written.** Semiannual magazine covering sustainable building, green design, predrawn blueprints. "Whether your definition of green building is about the use of sustainable materials or about high performance and energy savings, *Eco-Home Designs* is the perfect place to find the latest editorial about the green building phenomenon as well as predrawn house plans that feature comfortable green designs. Readers will find a wealth of insights about the newest building materials and construction methods, as well as tried-and-true tips on building an energy-efficient custom home." Estab. 2009. Byline given. Offers 50% kill fee. Publishes ms an average of 2 months after acceptance. Editorial lead time 6 months. Submit seasonal material 3 months in advance. Accepts queries by e-mail. Accepts simultaneous submissions. Responds in 1 week to queries. Responds in 1 month to mss. Guidelines available.

NONFICTION **Contact:** Simon Hyoun, editor. Needs how-to, choose green building materials; practice green building concepts, new product, photo feature, technical. No personal stories of home building experiences. **Buys 12 mss/year.** Query with published clips. Length: 500-1,000 words. **Pays $.80-$1/word for assigned or unsolicted articles.**

$$$ FINE GARDENING

Taunton Press, 63 S. Main St., P.O. Box 5506, Newtown CT 06470-5506. (203)426-8171. **Fax:** (203)426-3434. **E-mail:** fg@taunton.com. **Website:** www.finegardening.com. Bimonthly magazine. High-value magazine on landscape and ornamental gardening. Articles written by avid gardeners—first person, handson gardening experiences. Estab. 1988. Circ. 200,000. Byline given. Publishes an average of 6 months after acceptance. Editorial lead time 1 year. Submit seasonal material 1 year in advance. Accepts queries by mail, e-mail. Guidelines free.

NONFICTION Needs how-to, personal experience, photo feature.

$$ FINE HOMEBUILDING

The Taunton Press, Inc., 63 S. Main St., P.O. Box 5506, Newtown CT 06470-5506. (203)426-8171. **Fax:** (203)426-3434. **E-mail:** fh@taunton.com. **Website:** www.finehomebuilding.com. Bimonthly magazine for builders, architects, contractors, owner/builders and others who are seriously involved in building new houses or reviving old ones. Estab. 1981. Circ. 300,000. Byline given. Pays half on acceptance, half on publication. Offers kill fee. Offers on acceptance payment as kill fee. Publishes ms an average of 1 year after acceptance. Responds in 1 month to queries. Writer's guidelines for SASE and on website.

NONFICTION Query with outline, description, photographs, sketches and SASE. **Pays $150/published page.**

COLUMNS Tools & Materials, Reviews, Questions & Answers, Tips & Techniques, Cross Section, What's the Difference?, Finishing Touches, Great Moments, Breaktime, Drawing Board (design column). Query with outline, description, photographs, sketches and SASE. **Payment varies**

$ GARDEN COMPASS

Streamopolis, 1450 Front St., San Diego CA 92101. **Website:** www.gardencompass.com. Bert Wahlen, Jr. **70% freelance written**. Magazine covering gardening. *Garden Compass* is entertaining and offers sound practical advice for West Coast gardeners. Estab. 1992. Circ. 112,000. Byline given. Offers $50 kill fee. Publishes ms an average of 10 weeks after acceptance. Editorial lead time 6 months. Submit seasonal material 6 months in advance. Accepts queries by mail, e-mail. Accepts simultaneous submissions. Responds in 1 month to queries. Sample copy free.

COLUMNS Pest Patrol (plant posts/diseases), 400-800 words; e-Gardening (garden info on the Web), 400-800 words; Book Review (gardening books), 400-600 words; Fruit Trees, 800-1,200 words. Query with published clips. **Payment varies.**

FILLERS Needs anecdotes, facts, newsbreaks. Length: 30-150 words. **Pays $25.**

$$$ HIGH COUNTRY HOUSE AND HOME

Colorado Resort Publishing, P.O. Box 8, Vail CO 81658. (970)748-2970. **E-mail:** knicoletti@cmnm.org. **E-mail:** Kim Nicoletti, managing editor. **Website:** www.highcountryhouseandhome.com. **80% freelance written**. Quarterly magazine covering building, remodeling Colorado homes. "We cater to an affluent population of homeowners (including primary, second and third homeowners) who are planning to build or remodel their Colorado home in the mountains or on the western slope. While we feature luxury homes, we also have a slant toward green building." Estab. 2005. Circ. 35,000. Byline given. Publishes ms an average of 2-3 months after acceptance. Editorial lead time 12 months. Submit seasonal material 6 months in advance. Accepts queries by e-mail. Responds in 2-4 weeks to queries. Responds in month to mss. Sample copy available online.

NONFICTION Needs interview, new product, Profiles of Colorado homes and features related to them. We do not want do-it-yourself projects. Query with published clips. **Pays $200-650 for assigned articles. We do not buy articles; we only assign articles.**

COLUMNS Your Green Home (tips for environmentally-conscious building, remodeling and living), 300 words. **Buys 4 mss/year.** Query.

$$$$ HORTICULTURE

F+W Media, Inc., 10151 Carver Rd., Suite #200, Cincinnati OH 45242. (513)531-2690. **Fax:** (513)891-7153. **E-mail:** edit@hortmag.com. **Website:** www.hortmag.com. Bimonthly magazine. *Horticulture*, the country's oldest gardening magazine, is designed for active home gardeners. Our goal is to offer a blend of text, photographs and illustrations that will both instruct and inspire readers. Circ. 160,000. Byline given. Offers kill fee. Submit seasonal material 10 months in advance. Accepts queries by mail, e-mail, fax. Responds in 3 months to queries. Guidelines for SASE or by e-mail.

NONFICTION Buys 70 mss/year. Query with published clips, subject background material and SASE. Length: 800-1,000 words. **Pays $500.**

COLUMNS Length: 200-600 words. Query with published clips, subject background material and SASE. Include disk where possible. **Pays $250.**

$$$$ HOUSE BEAUTIFUL

The Hearst Corp., 300 W. 57th St., 24th Floor, New York NY 10019. (212)903-5000. **E-mail:** readerservices@housebeautiful.com. **Website:** www.housebeautiful.com. Monthly magazine. Targeted toward affluent, educated readers ages 30-40. Covers home design and decoration, gardening and entertaining, interior design, architecture and travel. Circ. 865,352. Editorial lead time 3 months.

💬 Query first.

LOG HOME LIVING

Home Buyer Publications, Inc., 4125 Lafayette Center Dr., Suite 100, Chantilly VA 20151. (703)222-9411; (800)826-3893. **Fax:** (703)222-3209. **E-mail:** editor@loghomeliving.com; ksmith@homebuyerpubs.com. **Website:** www.loghomeliving.com. **90% freelance written.** Monthly magazine for enthusiasts who are dreaming of, planning for, or actively building a log home. Estab. 1989. Circ. 132,000. Byline given. Offers $100 kill fee. Publishes ms an average of 6 months after acceptance. Editorial lead time 6 months. Submit seasonal material 6 months in advance. Accepts queries by mail, e-mail. Responds in 6 weeks to queries. Sample copy for $4. Guidelines available online.

NONFICTION Needs how-to, build or maintain log home, interview, log home owners, personal experience, photo feature, log homes, technical, design/decor topics, travel. **Buys 60 mss/year.** Query with SASE. Length: 1,000-2,000 words. **Payment depends on length, nature of the work and writer's expertise.** Pays expenses of writers on assignment.

$$ MOUNTAIN LIVING

Network Communications, Inc., 1777 S. Harrison St., Suite 903, Denver CO 80210. (303)248-2062; (303)248-2063. **Fax:** (303)248-2064. **E-mail:** hscott@mountainliving.com; cdeorio@mountainliving.com. **Website:** www.mountainliving.com. **Contact:** Holly Scott, publisher; Christine DeOrio, editor-in-chief. **50% freelance written.** Magazine published 10 times/year covering architecture, interior design ,and lifestyle issues for people who live in, visit, or hope to live in the mountains. Estab. 1994. Circ. 48,000. Byline given. Offers 15% kill fee. Publishes ms an average of 4 months after acceptance. Editorial lead time 6 months. Submit seasonal material 8-12 months in advance. Accepts queries by mail, e-mail. NoResponds in 6 weeks to queries. Responds in 2 months to mss. Sample copy for $7. Guidelines by e-mail.

NONFICTION Needs photo feature, travel, home features. **Buys 30 mss/year.** Query with published clips. Length: 500-1,000 words. **Pays $250-600.** Sometimes pays expenses of writers on assignment.

COLUMNS ML Recommends; Short Travel Tips; New Product Information; Art; Insider's Guide; Entertaining. Length: 300-800 words. **Buys 35 mss/year.** Query with published clips. **Pays $50-500.**

$$$$ ORGANIC GARDENING

Rodale, 33 E. Minor St., Emmaus PA 18098. **E-mail:** ogdcustserv@rodale.com. **Website:** www.organicgardening.com. **75% freelance written**. Bimonthly magazine. "*Organic Gardening* is for gardeners who enjoy gardening as an integral part of a healthy lifestyle. Editorial shows readers how to grow flowers, edibles, and herbs, as well as information on ecological landscaping. Also covers organic topics including soil building and pest control." Estab. 1942. Circ. 300,000. Byline given. Pays between acceptance and publication. Accepts queries by mail, fax. Responds in 3 months to queries.

NONFICTION Query with published clips and outline **Pays up to $1/word for experienced writers.**

⊖⊛ ROMANTIC HOMES

Y-Visionary Publishing, 2400 East Katella Avenue, Suite 300, Orange CA 92868. **E-mail:** jdemontravel@beckett.com. **Website:** www.romantichomesmag.com. **Contact:** Jacqueline Demontravel, editor. **70% freelance written**. Monthly magazine covering home decor. *Romantic Homes* is the magazine for women who want to create a warm, intimate, and casually elegant home—a haven that is both a gathering place for family and friends and a private refuge from the pressures of the outside world. The *Romantic Homes* reader is personally involved in the decor of her home. Features offer unique ideas and how-to advice on decorating, home furnishings, and gardening. Departments focus on floor and wall coverings, paint, textiles, refinishing, architectural elements, artwork, travel, and entertaining. Every article responds to the reader's need to create a beautiful, attainable environment, providing her with the style ideas and resources to achieve her own romantic home. Estab. 1994. Circ. 200,000. Byline given. Pays 30-60 days upon receipt of invoice. Publishes ms an average of 4 months after acceptance. Editorial lead time 5 months. Submit seasonal material 6 months in advance. Accepts queries by mail, fax. Accepts simultaneous submissions. Responds in 2 weeks to queries. Responds in 2 months to mss. Guidelines for #10 SASE.

NONFICTION Needs essays, how-to, new product, personal experience, travel. **Buys 150 mss/year.** Query with published clips. Length: 1,000-1,200 words. **Pays $500.**

COLUMNS Departments cover antiques, collectibles, artwork, shopping, travel, refinishing, architectural elements, flower arranging, entertaining, and decorating. Length: 400-600 words. **Pays $250.**

⊖⊛ SAN DIEGO HOME/GARDEN LIFESTYLES

McKinnon Enterprises, Box 719001, San Diego CA 92171-9001. (858)571-1818. **Fax:** (858)571-1889. **E-mail:** donoho@sdhg.net. **Website:** www.sdhg.net. **30% freelance written**. Monthly magazine covering homes, gardens, food, intriguing people, real estate, art and culture for residents of San Diego city and county. Estab. 1979. Circ. 50,000. Byline given. Publishes ms an average of 3 months after acceptance. Submit seasonal material 3 months in advance. Accepts queries by mail. Responds in 3 months to queries. Sample copy for $5.

NONFICTION Query with published clips. Length: 500-1,000 words. **Pays $50-375.**

⊖⊛⊛ SU CASA

Hacienda Press, 4100 Wolcott Ave. NE, Suite B, Albuquerque NM 87109. (505)344-1783. **Fax:** (505)345-3795. **E-mail:** ddelling@santafean.com; akellogg@sucasamagazine.com. **Website:** www.sucasamagazine.com. **Contact:** Diana Delling, editor; Alicia Kellog, senior editor. **80% freelance written**. Magazine published 5 times/year covering southwestern homes, building, design, architecture for the reader comtemplating building, remodeling, or decorating a Santa Fe style home. Su Casa is tightly focused on Southwestern home building, architecture and design. In particular, we feature New Mexico homes. We also cover alternative construction, far-out homes and contemporary design. Estab. 1995. Circ. 40,000. Byline given. Offers 50% kill fee. Publishes ms an average of 6 months after acceptance. Editorial lead time 6-9 months. Submit seasonal material 9 months in advance. Accepts queries by mail, e-mail, fax, phone. NoResponds in 1 week to queries. Responds in 1 month to mss. Sample copy free. Guidelines free.

NONFICTION Needs book excerpts, essays, interview, personal experience, photo feature. Special issues: The summer issue covers kitchen and bath topics. Does not want how-to articles, product reviews or features, no trends in southwest homes. **Buys 30 mss/year.** Query with published clips. Length: 1,000-2,500 words. **Pays $250-1,000.** Sometimes pays expenses of writers on assignment. Limit agreed upon in advance

⊖⊛ TEXAS GARDENER

Suntex Communications, Inc., P.O. Box 9005, Waco TX 76714-9005. (254)848-9393. **Fax:** (254)848-9779. **E-mail:** info@texasgardener.com. **Website:** www.texasgardener.com. **80% freelance written. Works with a small number of new/unpublished writers each year.** Bimonthly magazine covering vegetable and fruit production, ornamentals, and home landscape information for home gardeners in Texas. Estab. 1981. Circ. 20,000. Byline given. Publishes ms an average of 4 months after acceptance. Submit seasonal material 6 months in advance. Accepts queries by mail, e-mail, fax. Responds in 2 months to queries. Sample copy for $4.25 and SAE with 5 first-class stamps. Writers' guidelines available online at website.

NONFICTION Needs how-to, humor, interview, photo feature. **Buys 50-60 mss/year.** Query with published clips. Length: 800-2,400 words. **Pays $50-200.**

COLUMNS Between Neighbors. **Pays $25.**

🟢🟢 TEXAS HOME & LIVING

Publications & Communications, Inc., 13581 Pond Springs Rd., Suite 450, Austin TX 78729. (512)381-0576. **Fax:** (512)331-3950. **E-mail:** bronas@pcinews.com. **Website:** www.texasHomeandLiving.com. **75% freelance written.** Bimonthly magazine. "*Texas Home & Living*..the magazine of design, architecture and Texas lifestyle." Estab. 1994. Circ. 50,000. Byline given. Offers 100% kill fee. Publishes ms an average of 4 months after acceptance. Editorial lead time 4 months. Submit seasonal material 6 months in advance. Accepts queries by mail, e-mail, fax. Responds in 1 month to queries; 2 months to mss. Sample copy free. Guidelines available online.

NONFICTION Needs how-to, interview, new product, travel. **Buys 18 mss/year.** Query with published clips. Length: 500-2,000 words. **Pays $200 for assigned articles.** Pays expenses of writers on assignment.

🟢🟢 VICTORIAN HOMES

Y-Visionary Publishing, LP, 2400 East Katella Ave., Suite 300, Anaheim CA 92806. (714)939-9991. **Fax:** (714)939-9909. **E-mail:** hblack@beckett.com. **Website:** www.victorianhomesmag.com. **Contact:** Hillary Black, editor; Jacqueline deMontravel, editorial director. **90% freelance written.** Bimonthly magazine covering Victorian home restoration and decoration. *Victorian Homes* is read by Victorian home owners, restorers, house museum management, and others interested in the Victorian revival. Feature articles cover home architecture, interior design, furnishings, and the home's history. Photography is very important to the feature. Estab. 1981. Circ. 100,000. Byline given. Offers $50 kill fee. Publishes ms an average of 1 year after acceptance. Editorial lead time 4 months. Submit seasonal material 1 year in advance. Accepts queries by mail, e-mail, fax. Accepts simultaneous submissions. Responds in 6 weeks to queries. Responds in 2 months to mss. Sample copy and writer's guidelines for SAE.

NONFICTION Needs how-to, create period style curtains, wall treatments, bathrooms, kitchens, etc., photo feature. **Buys 30-35 mss/year.** Query. Length: 800-1,800 words. **Pays $300-500.** Sometimes pays expenses of writers on assignment.

HUMOR

🟢 FUNNY TIMES

Funny Times, Inc., P.O. Box 18530, Cleveland Heights OH 44118. (216)371-8600. **Fax:** (216)371-8696. **E-mail:** info@funnytimes.com. **Website:** www.funnytimes.com. **50% freelance written.** Monthly tabloid for humor. *Funny Times* is a monthly review of America's funniest cartoonists and writers. We are the *Reader's Digest* of modern American humor with a progressive/peace-oriented/environmental/politically activist slant. Estab. 1985. Circ. 70,000. Byline given. Publishes ms an average of 3 months after acceptance. Editorial lead time 2 months. Accepts simultaneous submissions. Responds in 3 months to mss. Sample copy for $3 or 9×12 SAE with 3 first-class stamps ($1.14 postage). Guidelines available online.

NONFICTION Needs essays, funny, humor, interview, opinion, humorous, personal experience, absolutely funny. **Buys 60 mss/year.** Send complete ms. Length: 500-700 words. **Pays $60 minimum.**

COLUMNS Query with published clips.

FICTION Contact: Ray Lesser and Susan Wolpert, editors. Anything funny. **Buys 6 mss/year.** Query with published clips. Length: 500-700 words. **Pays $50-150.**

FILLERS Needs short humor. **Buys 6 mss/year. Pays $20.**

INFLIGHT

🟢🟢🟢 GO

INK Publishing, 68 Jay St., Suite 315, Brooklyn NY 11201. (347)294-1220. **Fax:** (917)591-6247. **E-mail:** editorial@airtranmagazine.com. **Website:** www.airtranmagazine.com. **Contact:** Orion Ray-Jones, editor-in-chief; Peter Koch, executive editor; Sophie Hoeller, assistant editor. **80% freelance written.** Monthly magazine covering travel. "*Go Magazine* is an inflight magazine covering travel, general interest and light business." Estab. 2003. Circ. 100,000. Byline given. net 45 days upon receipt of invoice. Offers 50% kill fee. Publishes ms an average of 3 months after acceptance. Editorial lead time 4 months. Submit seasonal material 5 months in advance. Accepts queries by e-mail. Sample copy available online. Guidelines online at website.

NONFICTION Needs general interest, interview, photo feature, travel, light business. Does not want first-person travelogues. **Buys 200 mss/year.** Query with published clips. Length: 400-2,000 words. **Pay is negotiable.**

$$$ HEMISPHERES

Ink Publishing, 68 Jay St., Brooklyn NY 11201. (347)294-1220. **Fax:** (917)591-6247. **E-mail:** editorial@hemispheresmagazine.com. **Website:** www.hemispheresmagazine.com. **Contact:** Joe Keohane, editor-in-chief. **95% freelance written.** Monthly magazine for the educated, business, and recreational frequent traveler on an airline that spans the globe. "Inflight magazine that interprets 'inflight' to be a mode of delivery rather than an editorial genre. *Hemispheres'* task is to engage, intrigue and entertain its primary readers—an international, culturally diverse group of affluent, educated professionals and executives who frequently travel for business and pleasure on United Airlines. The magazine offers a global perspective and a focus on topics that cross borders as often as the people reading the magazine. Emphasizes ideas, concepts, and culture rather than products, presented in a fresh, artful and sophisticated graphic environment." Estab. 1992. Circ. 12.3 million. Byline given. Offers 20% kill fee. Publishes ms an average of 4-6 months after acceptance. Editorial lead time 8 months. Submit seasonal material 8 months in advance. Accepts queries by mail. Responds in 2 months to queries. Responds in 4 months to mss. Sample copy for $7.50. Guidelines on website.

NONFICTION Needs general interest, humor, personal experience. No 'in this country' phraseology. 'Too American' is a frequent complaint for queries. Query with published clips. Length: 500-3,000 words. **Pays 50¢/word and up.**

COLUMNS Making a Difference (Q&A format interview with world leaders, movers, and shakers; a 500-600 word introduction anchors the interview. "We want to profile an international mix of men and women representing a variety of topics or issues, but all must truly be making a difference. No puffy celebrity profiles.); 15 Fascinating Facts (a snappy selection of 1- or 2-sentence obscure, intriguing, or travel-service-oriented items that the reader never knew about a city, state, country, or destination.); Executive Secrets (things that top executives know); Case Study (business strategies of international companies or organizations. No lionizations of CEOs. Strategies should be the emphasis. "We want international candidates.); Weekend Breakaway ("takes us just outside a major city after a week of business for several activities for an action-packed weekend"); Roving Gourmet (insider's guide to interesting eating in major city, resort area, or region. The slant can be anything from ethnic to expensive; not just best. The 4 featured eateries span a spectrum from hole in the wall, to expense account lunch, and on to big deal dining.); Collecting (occasional 800-word story on collections and collecting that can emphasize travel); Eye on Sports (global look at anything of interest in sports); Vintage Traveler (options for mature, experienced travelers); Savvy Shopper (insider's tour of best places in the world to shop. Savvy Shopper (steps beyond all those stories that just mention the great shopping at a particular destination. A shop-by-shop, gallery-by-gallery tour of the best places in the world.); Science and Technology (substantive, insightful stories on how technology is changing our lives and the business world. "Not just another column on audio components or software. No gift guides!"); Aviation Journal (for those fascinated with aviation; topics range widely.); Terminal Bliss ("a great airports guide series"); Grape And Grain (wine and spirits with emphasis on education, "not one-upmanship"); Show Business (films, music, and entertainment); Musings (humor or just curious musings); Quick Quiz (tests to amuse and educate); Travel Trends (brief, practical, invaluable, global, trend-oriented); Book Beat (tackles topics like the Wodehouse Society, the birth of a book, the competition between local bookshops, and national chains. "Please, no review proposals."); What the World's Reading (residents explore how current bestsellers tell us what their country is thinking). Length: 1,400 words. Query with published clips. **Pays 50¢/word and up.**

FICTION Needs adventure, ethnic, historical, humorous, mainstream, mystery, explorations of those issues common to all people but within the context of a particular culture. **Buys 14 mss/year.** Send complete ms. Length: 1,000-4,000 words. **Pays 50¢/word and up.**

$$$$ SPIRIT MAGAZINE

Pace Communications, Inc., Suite 360, 2811 McKinney Ave., Dallas TX 75204. (214)580-8070. **Fax:** (214)580-2491. **Website:** www.spiritmag.com. **Contact:** Jay Heinrichs, editorial director. Monthly magazine for passengers on Southwest Airlines. Estab. 1992. Circ. 380,000. Byline given. Responds in 1 month to queries. Guidelines available online.

NONFICTION Buys about 40 mss/year. Query by mail only with published clips. 3,000-6,000 words (features). **Pays $1/word.** Pays expenses of writers on assignment.

COLUMNS Length: 800-900 words. **Buys about 21 mss/year.** Query by mail only with published clips.

FILLERS Buys 12 mss/year. 250 words. **variable amount.**

JUVENILE

$ $ $ $ BOYS' LIFE

Boy Scouts of America, P.O. Box 152079, 1325 West Walnut Hills Ln., Irving TX 75015. (972)580-2366. **Fax:** (972)580-2079. **Website:** www.boyslife.org. **Contact:** J.D. Owen, editor-in-chief; Michael Goldman, managing editor; Aaron Derr, senior writer. **75% freelance written. Prefers to work with published/ established writers; works with small number of new/unpublished writers each year.** *Boys' Life* is a monthly 4-color general interest magazine for boys 7-18, most of whom are Cub Scouts, Boy Scouts or Venturers. Estab. 1911. Circ. 1.1 million. Byline given. Publishes approximately one year after acceptance. Accepts queries by mail. Responds to queries/mss in 2 months. Sample copies for $3.95 plus 9×12 SASE. Guidelines available with SASE and online.

NONFICTION Contact: Send article queries to the attention of the senior editor; column queries to the attention of the associate editor. Scouting activities and general interests (nature, Earth, health, cars, sports, science, computers, space and aviation, entertainment, history, music, animals, how-to's, etc.). **Buys 60 mss/year.** Query with SASE. No phone queries Averge word length for articles: 500-1,500 words, including sidebars and boxes. Average word length for columns: 300-750. **Pay ranges from $300 and up.** Pays expenses of writers on assignment.

COLUMNS Contact: Columns query associate editor with SASE for response.

FICTION All fiction is assigned.

BRILLIANT STAR

1233 Central St., Evanston IL 60201. (847)853-2354. **Fax:** (847)256-1372. **E-mail:** brilliant@usbnc.org; sengle@usbnc.org. **Website:** www.brilliantstarmagazine.org. **Contact:** Susan Engle, associate editor; Amethel Parel-Sewell, art director. "*Brilliant Star* presents Bahá'í history and principles through fiction, nonfiction, activities, interviews, puzzles, car-

toons, games, music, and art. Universal values of good character, such as kindness, courage, creativity, and helpfulness are incorporated into the magazine." Estab. 1969. Byline given. Pays 2 contributor's copies. Guidelines available for SASE or via e-mail.

NONFICTION Middle readers: arts/crafts, games/ puzzles, geography, how-to, humorous, multicultural, nature/environment, religion, social issues. Buys 6 mss/year. Query. Length: 300-700 words.

FICTION Needs Middle readers: contemporary, fantasy, folktale, multicultural, nature/environment, problem-solving, religious. Submit complete ms. Length: 700-1,400 words.

POETRY "We only publish poetry written by children at the moment."

$ CADET QUEST MAGAZINE

P.O. Box 7259, Grand Rapids MI 49510-7259. (616)241-5616. **Fax:** (616)241-5558. **E-mail:** submissions@calvinistcadets.org. **Website:** www.calvinistcadets.org. **Contact:** G. Richard Broene, editor. **40% freelance written. Works with a small number of new/unpublished writers each year.** Magazine published 7 times/ year. "*Cadet Quest Magazine* shows boys 9-14 how God is at work in their lives and in the world around them." Estab. 1958. Circ. 7,500. Byline given. Publishes ms an average of 4-11 months after acceptance. Accepts simultaneous submissions. Responds in 2 months to mss. Sample copy for 9×12 SASE. Guidelines for #10 SASE.

NONFICTION Needs how-to, humor, inspirational, interview, personal experience, informational. Special issues: Write for new themes list in February. Send complete ms. Length: 500-1,500 words. **Pays 4-6¢/word.**

COLUMNS Project Page (uses simple projects boys 9-14 can do on their own made with easily accessible materials; must provide clear, accurate instructions).

FICTION Considerable fiction is used. Fast-moving stories that appeal to a boy's sense of adventure or sense of humor are welcome. Needs adventure, religious, spiritual, sports, comics. Avoid preachiness. Avoid simplistic answers to complicated problems. Avoid long dialogue and little action. No fantasy, science fiction, fashion, horror or erotica. Send complete ms. Length: 900-1,500 words. **Pays 4-6¢/word, and 1 contributor's copy.**

$ $ CALLIOPE

Cobblestone Publishing Co., 30 Grove St., Suite C, Peterborough NH 03458-1454. (603)924-7209. **Fax:**

(603)924-7380. **E-mail:** cfbakeriii@meganet.net. **Website:** www.cobblestonepub.com. **Contact:** Rosalie Baker and Charles Baker, co-editors; Lou Waryncia, editorial director; Ann Dillon, art director. **50% freelance written.** Magazine published 9 times/year covering world history (East and West) through 1800 AD for 8 to 14-year-old kids. Articles must relate to the issue's theme. Lively, original approaches to the subject are the primary concerns of the editors in choosing material. Estab. 1990. Circ. 13,000. Byline given. Kill fee. Accepts queries by mail. If interested, responds 5 months before publication date. Sample copy for $5.95, $2 shipping and handling, and 10×13 SASE. Guidelines available online.

NONFICTION Needs essays, general interest, historical, how-to, crafts/woodworking, humor, interview, personal experience, photo feature, technical, travel, recipes. No religious, pornographic, biased, or sophisticated submissions. **Buys 30-40 mss/year.** Query with writing sample, 1-page outline, bibliography, SASE. 400-1000/feature articles; 300-600 words/supplemental nonfiction. **Pays 20-25¢/word.**

FICTION Middle readers and young adults: adventure, folktales, plays, history, biographical fiction. Material must relate to forthcoming themes. Needs adventure, historical, biographical, retold legends. **Buys 10 mss/year.** Length: 1000 words maximum **Pays 20-25¢/word.**

FILLERS Crossword and other word puzzles (no word finds), mazes, and picture puzzles that use the vocabulary of the issue's theme or otherwise relate to the theme. **Pays on an individual basis.**

💲💲 CLUBHOUSE MAGAZINE

Focus on the Family, 8605 Explorer Dr., Colorado Springs CO 80920. **Website:** www.clubhousemagazine.com. **25% freelance written.** Monthly magazine. *Clubhouse* readers are 8-12 year old boys and girls who desire to know more about God and the Bible. Their parents (who typically pay for the membership) want wholesome, educational material with Scriptural or moral insight. The kids want excitement, adventure, action, humor, or mystery. Your job as a writer is to please both the parent and child with each article. Estab. 1987. Circ. 85,000. Byline given. Publishes ms an average of 12-18 months after acceptance. Editorial lead time 5 months. Submit seasonal material 9 months in advance. Responds in 2 months to mss. Sample copy for $1.50 with 9×12 SASE. Guidelines for #10 SASE.

NONFICTION Contact: Jesse Florea, editor. Needs essays, how-to, humor, inspirational, interview, personal experience, photo feature, religious. Avoid Bible stories. Avoid informational-only, science, or educational articles. Avoid biographies told encyclopedia or textbook style. **Buys 6 mss/year.** Send complete ms. Length: 800-1,200 words. **Pays $25-450 for assigned articles. Pays 15-25¢/word for unsolicited articles.**

FICTION Contact: Jesse Florea, editor. Needs adventure, humorous, mystery, religious, suspense, holiday. Avoid contemporary, middle-class family settings (existing authors meet this need), poems (rarely printed), stories dealing with boy-girl relationships. **Buys 10 mss/year.** Send complete ms. Length: 400-1,500 words. **Pays $200 and up for first time contributor and 5 contributor's copies; additional copies available.**

FILLERS Needs facts, newsbreaks. **Buys 2 mss/year.** Length: 40-100 words.

💲💲 CRICKET

Carus Publishing Co., 700 E. Lake St., Suite 300, Chicago IL 60601. (312)701-1720, ext. 10. **Website:** www.cricketmag.com. **Contact:** Marianne Carus, editor-in-chief; Lonnie Plecha, executive editor; Karen Kohn, senior art director. Monthly magazine for children ages 9-14. "*Cricket* is looking for more fiction and nonfiction for the older end of its 9-14 age range, as well as contemporary stories set in other countries. It also seeks humorous stories and mysteries (not detective spoofs), fantasy and original fairy tales, stand-alone excerpts from unpublished novels, and well-written/researched science articles." Estab. 1973. Circ. 73,000. Byline given. Accepts queries by mail. Responds in 4-6 months to mss. Guidelines available online.

NONFICTION Middle readers, young adults/teens: adventure, architecture, archaeology, biography, foreign culture, games/puzzles, geography, natural history, science and technology, social science, sports, travel. Multicultural needs include articles on customs and cultures. Requests bibliography with submissions. Buys 30 mss/year. Submit complete ms, SASE. Length: 200-1,500 words. **Pays 25¢/word maximum.**

FICTION Middle readers, young adults/teens: contemporary, fantasy, folk and fairy tales, history, humorous, science fiction, suspense/mystery. Buys 70 mss/year. Recently published work by Aaron Shepard, Arnold Adoff, and Nancy Springer. Needs fantasy, historical, humorous, mystery, science fiction, realistic, contemporary, folk tales, fairy tales, legends, myths.

No didactic, sex, religious, or horror stories. **Buys 75-100 mss/year.** Submit complete ms. Length: 200-2,000 words. **Pays 25¢/word maximum, and 6 contributor's copies; $2.50 charge for extras.**

POETRY Reviews poems. Limit submission to 5 poems or less. Serious, humorous, nonsense rhymes. Buys 20-30 poems/year. 50 lines maximum **Pays $3/line maximum.**

FILLERS Crossword puzzles, logic puzzles, math puzzles, crafts, recipes, science experiments, games and activities from other countries, plays, music, art.

$$ DIG MAGAZINE

Carus Publishing Co., 30 Grove St., Suite C, Peterborough NH 03458. (603)924-7209. **Fax:** (603)924-7380. **Website:** www.digonsite.com. **Contact:** Rosalie Baker, editor. **75% freelance written.** Magazine published 9 times/year covering archaeology for kids ages 9-14. Estab. 1999. Circ. 20,000. Byline given. Publishes ms an average of 1 year after acceptance. Editorial lead time 1 year. Accepts queries by mail. Responds in several months. Sample copy for $5.95 with 8x11 SASE or $10 without SASE. Guidelines available online.

NONFICTION Needs personal experience, photo feature, travel, archaeological excavation reports. No fiction. Occasional paleontology stories accepted. **Buys 30-40 mss/year.** Query with published clips. Length: 100-1,000 words. **Pays 20-25¢/word.**

$$ FACES

Cobblestone Publishing, 30 Grove St., Suite C, Peterborough NH 03458. (603)924-7209; (800)821-0115. **Fax:** (603)924-7380. **E-mail:** customerservice@caruspub.com. **Website:** www.cobblestonepub.com. **90-100% freelance written.** "Publishes monthly throughout the year, *Faces* covers world culture for ages 9-14. It stands apart from other children's magazines by offering a solid look at one subject and stressing strong editorial content, color photographs throughout, and original illustrations. *Faces* offers an equal balance of feature articles and activities, as well as folktales and legends." Estab. 1984. Circ. 15,000. Byline given. Offers 50% kill fee. Accepts queries by mail, e-mail. Accepts simultaneous submissions. Sample copy for $6.95, $2 shipping and handling, 10×13 SASE. Guidelines with SASE or online.

NONFICTION Needs historical, humor, interview, personal experience, photo feature, travel, recipes, activities, crafts. **Buys 45-50 mss/year.** Query with writing sample, 1-page outline, bibliography, SASE. Length: 800 words/feature articles; 300-600/supplemental nonfiction; up to 700 words/activities. **Pays 20-25¢/word.**

FICTION Needs ethnic, historical, retold legends/folktales, original plays. Length: 800 words maximum. **Pays 20-25¢/word.**

POETRY Serious and light verse considered. Must have clear, objective imagery. Length: 100 lines maximum. **Pays on an individual basis.**

FILLERS "Crossword and other word puzzles (no word finds), mazes, and picture puzzles that use the vocabulary of the issue's theme or otherwise relate to the theme." **Pays on an individual basis.**

$$ GIRLS' LIFE

Monarch Publishing, 4529 Harford Rd., Baltimore MD 21214. (410)426-9600. **Fax:** (410)254-0991. **E-mail:** jessica@girlslife.com. **Website:** www.girlslife.com. **Contact:** Jessica D'Argenio Waller, senior editor. Bimonthly magazine covering girls ages 9-15. Estab. 1994. Circ. 400,000. Byline given. Publishes ms an average of 3 months after acceptance. Editorial lead time 4 months. Submit seasonal material 5 months in advance. Accepts queries by mail, e-mail. Responds in 1 month to queries. Sample copy for $5 or online. Guidelines available online.

NONFICTION Needs book excerpts, essays, general interest, how-to, humor, inspirational, interview, new product, travel, "Features and articles should speak to young women ages 10-15 looking for new ideas about relationships, family, friends, school, etc. with fresh, savvy advice. Front-of-the-book columns and quizzes are a good place to start." Special issues: Back to School (August/September); Fall, Halloween (October/November); Holidays, Winter (December/January); Valentine's Day, Crushes (February/March); Spring, Mother's Day (April/May); and Summer, Father's Day (June/July). **Buys 40 mss/year.** Query by mail with published clips. Submit complete mss on spec only. Length: 700-2,000 words. **Pays $350/regular column; $500/feature.**

COLUMNS Buys 20 mss/year. Query with published clips. **Pays $150-450.**

FICTION "We accept short fiction. They should be stand-alone stories and are generally 2,500-3,500 words."

$ HIGHLIGHTS FOR CHILDREN

803 Church St., Honesdale PA 18431. (570)253-1080. **Fax:** (570)251-7847. **Website:** www.highlights.com.

Contact: Christine French Clark, editor-in-chief; Cindy Faber Smith, art director. **80% freelance written.** Monthly magazine for children up to age 12. "This book of wholesome fun is dedicated to helping children grow in basic skills and knowledge, in creativeness, in ability to think and reason, in sensitivity to others, in high ideals, and worthy ways of living—for children are the world's most important people. We publish stories for beginning and advanced readers. Up to 500 words for beginners (ages 3-7), up to 800 words for advanced (ages 8-12)." Estab. 1946. Circ. Approximately 2.5 million. Accepts queries by mail. Responds in 2 months to queries. Sample copy free. Guidelines on website in "About Us" area.

NONFICTION "Generally we prefer to see a manuscript rather than a query. However, we will review queries regarding nonfiction." Length: 800 words maximum. **Pays $25 for craft ideas and puzzles; $25 for fingerplays; $150 and up for articles.**

FICTION Meaningful stories appealing to both girls and boys, up to age 12. Vivid, full of action. Engaging plot, strong characterization, lively language. Prefers stories in which a child protagonist solves a dilemma through his or her own resources. Seeks stories that the child ages 8-12 will eagerly read, and the child ages 2-7 will like to hear when read aloud (500-800 words). Stories require interesting plots and a number of illustration possiblities. Also need rebuses (picture stories 120 words or under), stories with urban settings, stories for beginning readers (100-500 words), sports and humorous stories, adventures, holiday stories, and mysteries. We also would like to see more material of 1-page length (300 words), both fiction and factual. Needs adventure, fantasy, historical, humorous, animal, contemporary, folktales, multi-cultural, problem-solving, sports. No war, crime or violence. Send complete ms. **Pays $150 minimum plus 2 contributor's copies.**

POETRY Lines/poem: 16 or less ("most poems are shorter"). Considers simultaneous submissions ("please indicate"); no previously published poetry. No e-mail submissions. "Submit typed manuscript with very brief cover letter." Occasionally comments on submissions "if manuscript has merit or author seems to have potential for our market." Guidelines available for SASE. Responds "generally within one month." Always sends prepublication galleys. Pays 2 contributor's copies; "money varies." Acquires all rights.

😊😊 JACK AND JILL

Children's Better Health Institute, P.O. Box 567, Indianapolis IN 46206-0567. (317)636-8881. **E-mail:** j.goodman@cbhi.org. **Website:** www.jackandjill-mag.org. **50% freelance written.** Bimonthly magazine published 6 times/year for children ages 8-12. "Write entertaining and imaginative stories for kids, not just about them. Writers should understand what is funny to kids, what's important to them, what excites them. Don't write from an adult 'kids are so cute' perspective. We're also looking for health and healthful lifestyle stories and articles, but don't be preachy." Estab. 1938. Circ. 200,000. Byline given. Publishes ms an average of 8 months after acceptance. Submit seasonal material 8 months in advance. Responds to mss in 3 months. Guidelines available online.

NONFICTION Young readers, middle readers: animal, arts, crafts, cooking, games, puzzles, history, hobbies, how-to, humorous, interviews, profile, nature, science, sports. Buys 8-10 mss/year. Submit complete ms. Queries not accepted. Length: 500 words.

FICTION Young readers and middle readers: adventure, contemporary, folktales, health, history, humorous, nature, sports. Buys 30-35 mss/year. Submit complete ms. Queries not accepted. Length: 500 words. **Pays up to 25¢/word.**

POETRY Wants light-hearted poetry appropriate for the age group. Reviews submissions for possible use in all Children's Better Health Institute publications. Mss must be typewritten with poet's contact information in upper right-hand corner of each poem's page. SASE required. **Pays $35 minimum for poetry.**

😊😊😊 JUNIOR SCHOLASTIC

Scholastic, Inc., 557 Broadway, New York NY 10012-3902. (212)343-6100. **Fax:** (212)343-6945. **E-mail:** junior@scholastic.com. **Website:** www.juniorscholastic.com. Magazine published 18 times/year. Edited for students ages 11-14. Circ. 535,000. Editorial lead time 6 weeks.

😊😊 LADYBUG

Carus Publishing Co., 700 E. Lake St., Suite 300, Chicago IL 60601. (312)701-1720. **Website:** www.cricket-mag.com. **Contact:** Marianne Carus, editor-in-chief; Suzanne Beck, managing art director. Monthly magazine for children ages 2-6. "We look for quality literature and nonfiction." Subscription: $35.97/year (12 issues). sample: $5; sample pages available on website.

Estab. 1990. Circ. 125,000. Byline given. Responds in 6 months to mss. Guidelines available online.

NONFICTION Picture-oriented material: activities, animal, arts/crafts, concept, cooking, humorous, math, nature/environment, problem-solving, science. **Buys 35 mss/year.** Send complete ms, SASE. Length: 400-700 words. **Pays 25¢/word ($25 minimum).**

FICTION Picture-oriented material: adventure, animal, fantasy, folktales, humorous, multicultural, nature/environment, problem-solving, science fiction, sports, suspense/mystery. "Open to any easy fiction stories." Buys 50 mss/year. **Buys 30 mss/year.** Submit complete ms, include SASE. Length: 800 words maximum. **Pays 25¢/word ($25 minimum).**

POETRY Needs light verse, traditional. *LADYBUG Magazine*, published monthly, is a reading and listening magazine for young children (ages 2-6). Wants poetry that is "rhythmic, rhyming; serious, humorous, active." Buys 40 poems/year. Submit maximum 5 poems. 20 lines maximum. **Pays $3/line ($25 minimum).**

FILLERS Learning activities, games, crafts, songs, finger games. See back issues for types, formats, and length.

MAGIC DRAGON

Association for Encouragement of Children's Creativity, P.O. Box 687, Webster NY 14580. **E-mail:** magicdragon@rochester.rr.com. **Website:** www.magicdragonmagazine.com. Quarterly magazine covering children's writing and art (no photography). "All work is created by children up to age 12 (elementary school grades). We consider stories, poems, and artwork. Queries, writing, and art accepted by USPS mail and by e-mail." Estab. 2005. Circ. 3,500. Byline given. Pays 1 contributor copy on publication. Editorial lead time 3-6 months. Submit seasonal material 6 months in advance. Accepts queries by mail, e-mail. Responds in 2 weeks to queries. Sample copy for $4. Guidelines available online.

NONFICTION Needs essays, humor, inspirational, personal experience. Send complete ms. Length: 250 words maximum.

FICTION Needs adventure, fantasy, historical, humorous.

POETRY Needs free verse, haiku, light verse, traditional. Length: 30 lines maximum.

NATIONAL GEOGRAPHIC KIDS

National Geographic Society, 1145 17th St. NW, Washington DC 20036. **Website:** www.kidsnational-geographic.com. **70% freelance written.** Magazine published 10 times/year. It's our mission to excite kids about their world. We are the children's magazine that makes learning fun. Estab. 1975. Circ. 1.3 million. Byline given. Offers 10% kill fee. Publishes ms an average of 6 months after acceptance. Editorial lead time 6+ months. Submit seasonal material 6+ months in advance. Accepts queries by mail. Accepts simultaneous submissions. Sample copy for #10 SAE. Guidelines free.

NONFICTION Needs general interest, humor, interview, technical, travel, animals, human interest, science, technology, entertainment, archaeology, pets. "We do not want poetry, sports, fiction, or story ideas that are too young—our audience is between ages 8-14." Query with published clips and résumé. Length: 100-1,000 words. **Pays $1/word for assigned articles.** Pays expenses of writers on assignment.

COLUMNS Amazing Animals (animal heroes, stories about animal rescues, interesting/funny animal tales), 100 words; Inside Scoop (fun, kid-friendly news items), 50-70 words. Query with published clips. **Pays $1/word.**

NATURE FRIEND MAGAZINE

4253 Woodcock Lane, Dayton VA 22821. (540)867-0764. **E-mail:** photos@naturefriendmagazine.com. **Website:** www.dogwoodridgeoutdoors.com; www.naturefriendmagazine.com. **Contact:** Kevin Shank, editor. **80% freelance written.** Monthly magazine covering nature. Picture-oriented material, conversational, no talking animal stories. No evolutionary material. "*Nature Friend* includes stories, puzzles, science experiments, nature experiments—all submissions need to honor God as creator." Estab. 1982. Circ. 13,000. Byline given. Editorial lead time 4 months. Submit seasonal material 6 months in advance. Accepts simultaneous submissions. Responds in 6 months to mss. Sample copy and writer's guidelines for $10 postage paid.

NONFICTION Needs how-to, nature, science experiments, photo feature, articles about interesting/unusual animals. No poetry, evolution, animals depicted in captivity. **Buys 50 mss/year.** Send complete ms. Length: 250-900 words. **Pays 5¢/word.**

COLUMNS Learning By Doing, 500-900 words. **Buys 12 mss/year.** Send complete ms.

FILLERS Needs facts, puzzles, short essays on something current in nature. **Buys 35 mss/year.** Length: 150-250 words. **5¢/word.**

☺☺ NEW MOON

New Moon Publishing, Inc., P.O. Box 161287, Duluth MN 55816. (218)728-5507. **Fax:** (218)728-0314. **E-mail:** girl@newmoon.org. **Website:** www.newmoon.org. **25% freelance written.** Bimonthly magazine covering girls ages 8-14, edited by girls aged 8-14. "In general, all material should be pro-girl and feature girls and women as the primary focus. *New Moon* is for every girl who wants her voice heard and her dreams taken seriously. *New Moon* celebrates girls, explores the passage from girl to woman, and builds healthy resistance to gender inequities. The *New Moon* girl is true to herself and *New Moon* helps her as she pursues her unique path in life, moving confidently into the world." Estab. 1992. Circ. 30,000. Byline given. Publishes ms an average of 6 months after acceptance. Editorial lead time 6 months. Submit seasonal material 8 months in advance. Accepts queries by mail, e-mail, fax. Accepts simultaneous submissions. Responds in 2 months to mss. Sample copy for $7 or online. Guidelines for SASE or online.

NONFICTION Needs essays, general interest, humor, inspirational, interview, opinion, personal experience, written by girls, photo feature, religious, travel, multicultural/girls from other countries. No fashion, beauty, or dating. **Buys 20 mss/year.** Send complete ms. Length: 600 words. **Pays 6-12¢/word.**

COLUMNS Women's Work (profile of a woman and her job relating the the theme), 600 words; Herstory (historical woman relating to theme), 600 words. **Buys 10 mss/year.** Query. **Pays 6-12¢/word**

FICTION Prefers girl-written material. All girl-centered. Needs adventure, fantasy, historical, humorous, slice-of-life vignettes. **Buys 6 mss/year.** Send complete ms. Length: 1,200-1,400 words. **Pays 6-12¢/word.**

POETRY No poetry by adults.

☺☺ POCKETS

Upper Room, P.O. Box 340004, 1908 Grand Ave., Nashville TN 37203-0004. (800)972-0433. **Fax:** (615)340-7275. **E-mail:** pockets@upperroom.org. **Website:** pockets.upperroom.org/. **Contact:** Lynn W. Gilliam, editor. **60% freelance written.** Monthly (except February) magazine covering children's and families' spiritual formation. Magazine published 11 times/year. "*Pockets* is a Christian devotional magazine for children ages 8-12. Stories should help children experience a Christian lifestyle that is not always a neatly wrapped moral package but is open to the continuing revelation of God's will." Estab. 1981. Byline given. Publishes ms an average of 1 year after acceptance. Submit seasonal material 1 year in advance. Responds in 8 weeks to mss. Each issue reflects a specific theme. Sample copy available with a 9×12 SASE with 4 First-Class stamps attached to envelope. Guidelines on website.

○ Does not accept e-mail or fax submissions.

NONFICTION Picture-oriented, young readers, middle readers: cooking, games/puzzles. "*Pockets* seeks biographical sketches of persons, famous or unknown, whose lives reflect their Christian commitment, written in a way that appeals to children." Does not accept how-to articles. "Nonfiction reads like a story." Multicultural needs include: stories that feature children of various racial/ethnic groups and do so in a way that is true to those depicted. Buys 10 mss/year. **Buys 10 mss/year.** Length: 400-1,000 words. **Pays 14¢/word.**

COLUMNS Poetry and Prayer (related to themes), maximum 20 lines; Family Time, 200-300 words; Peacemakers at Work (profiles of children working for peace, justice, and ecological concerns), 400-600 words. **Pays 14¢/word.** Activities/Games (related to themes). **Pays $25 and up.** Kids Cook (simple recipes children can make alone or with minimal help from an adult). **Pays $25.**

FICTION adventure, ethnic/multicultural, historical (general), religious/inspirational, slice-of-life vignettes. No fantasy, science fiction, talking animals. "All submissions should address the broad theme of the magazine. Each issue is built around one theme with material which can be used by children in a variety of ways. Scripture stories, fiction, poetry, prayers, art, graphics, puzzles and activities are included. Submissions do not need to be overtly religious. They should help children experience a Christian lifestyle that is not always a neatly-wrapped moral package, but is open to the continuing revelation of God's will. Seasonal material, both secular and liturgical, is desired." Needs adventure, ethnic, historical, general, religious. No violence, science fiction, romance, fantasy, or talking animal stories. **Buys 25-30 mss/year.** Send complete ms with SASE. Length: 600-1,400 words. **Pays 14¢/word.**

POETRY *Pockets*, published monthly (except February), is an interdenominational magazine for children ages 8-12. "Each issue is built around a specific theme, with material (including poetry) that can be used by children in a variety of ways. Submissions do not need to be overly religious; they should help children experience a Christian lifestyle that is not always a neatly wrapped moral package but is open to the continuing revelation of God's will." Considers poetry by children. Buys 14 poems/year. Length: 4-20 lines. **$25 minimum.**

$ SHINE BRIGHTLY

GEMS Girls' Clubs, P.O. Box 7259, Grand Rapids MI 49510. (616)241-5616. **Fax:** (616)241-5558. **E-mail:** shinebrightly@gemsgc.org. **Website:** www.gemsgc.org. **Contact:** Jan Boone, editor; Kelli Ponstein, managing editor. **80% freelance written. Works with new and published/established writers.** Monthly magazine (with combined June/July, August summer issue). "Our purpose is to lead girls into a living relationship with Jesus Christ and to help them see how God is at work in their lives and the world around them. Puzzles, crafts, stories, and articles for girls ages 9-14." Estab. 1970. Circ. 17,000. Byline given. Publishes ms an average of 1 year after acceptance. Submit seasonal material 1 year in advance. Accepts simultaneous submissions. Responds in 2 months to queries; 3 months to mss. Sample copy with 9×12 SASE with 3 first class stamps and $1. Guidelines available online.

NONFICTION Needs humor, inspirational, seasonal and holiday, interview, personal experience, avoid the testimony approach, photo feature, query first, religious, travel, adventure, mystery. **Buys 35 unsolicited mss/year.** Submit complete ms in body of e-mail. No attachments. Length: 100-900 words. **Pays 3-5¢/word, plus 2 copies.**

COLUMNS How-to (crafts); puzzles and jokes; quizzes. Length: 200-400 words. Send complete ms. **Pay varies.**

FICTION Does not want "unrealistic stories and those with trite, easy endings. We are interested in manuscripts that show how girls can change the world." Needs adventure, that girls could experience in their hometowns or places they might realistically visit, ethnic, historical, humorous, mystery, believable only, religious, nothing too preachy, romance, slice-of-life vignettes, suspense,. **Buys 30 mss/year.** Submit complete ms in body of e-mail. No attachments. Length: 400-900 words. **Pays up to $35.**

POETRY Needs free verse, haiku, light verse, traditional. **Pays $5-15.**

$ SPARKLE

GEMS Girls' Clubs, P.O. Box 7259, Grand Rapids MI 49510. (616)241-5616. **Fax:** (616)241-5558. **E-mail:** kelli@gemsgc.org. **Website:** www.gemsgc.org. **Contact:** Sara Lynn Hilton, senior editor; Sara DeRidder, art director/photo editor. **80% freelance written.** "Our mission is to prepare young girls to live out their faith and become world-changers-. We strive to help girls make a difference in the world. We look at the application of scripture to everyday life. We strive to delight the reader and cause the reader to evalute her own life in light of the truth presented. Finally, we strive to teach practical life skills." Estab. 2002. Circ. 5,000. Byline given. Offers $20 kill fee. Editorial lead time 3 months. Submit seasonal material 1 year in advance. Accepts queries by mail, e-mail. Accepts simultaneous submissions. Responds in 3 weeks to queries. Responds in 3 months to mss. Sample copy for 9x13 SAE, 3 first-class stamps, and $1 for coverage/publication cost. Writer's guidelines for #10 SASE or online.

NONFICTION Needs how-to, crafts/recipes, humor, inspirational, personal experience, photo feature, religious, travel, Young readers: animal, arts/crafts, biography, careers, cooking, concept, games/puzzles, geography, health, history, hobbies, how-to, interview/profile, math, multicultural, nature/environment, problem-solving, quizzes, science, social issues, sports, travel, personal experience, inspirational, music/drama/art. Constant mention of God is not necessary if the moral tone of the story is positive. **Buys 15 mss/year.** Send complete ms. Length: 100-400 words. **Pays $20/article**

COLUMNS Crafts; puzzles and jokes; quizzes, all 200-400 words. Send complete ms. **Payment varies.**

FICTION Young readers: adventure, animal, contemporary, fantasy, folktale, health, history, humorous, multicultural, music and musicians, nature/environment, problem-solving, religious, recipes, service projects, sports, suspense/mystery, interacting with family and friends. We currently Looking for inspirational biographies, stories form Zambia, Africa, and ideas on how to live a green lifestyle. Needs adventure, ethnic, fantasy, humorous, mystery, religious, slice-of-life vignettes. **Buys 10 mss/year.** Send complete ms. Length: 100-400 words. **Pays $20/story.**

POETRY Needs free verse, haiku, light verse, traditional. We do not wish to see anything that is too difficult for a first grader to read. We wish it to remain light. The style can be fun, but also teach a truth. No violence or secular material. Buys 4 poems/year. Submit maximum 4 poems.

FILLERS Needs facts, short humor. **Buys 6 mss/year.** Length: 50-150 words. **Pays $10-15.**

⊖⊖ SPIDER

Cricket Magazine Group, 70 East Lake St., Suite 300, Chicago IL 60601. (312)701-1720. **Fax:** (312)701-1728. **Website:** www.cricketmag.com. **85% freelance written.** Monthly reading and activity magazine for children ages 6 to 9. *Spider* introduces children to the highest quality stories, poems, illustrations, articles, and activities. It was created to foster in beginning readers a love of reading and discovery that will last a lifetime. We're looking for writers who respect children's intelligence. Estab. 1994. Circ. 70,000. Byline given. Accepts simultaneous submissions. Responds in 6 months to mss. Guidelines available online.

NONFICTION Submit complete ms, bibliography, SASE. Length: 300-800 words. **Pays up to 25¢/word.**

FICTION Stories should be easy to read. Recently published work by Polly Horvath, Andrea Cheng, and Beth Wagner Brust. Needs fantasy, humorous, science fiction, folk tales, fairy tales, fables, myths. No romance, horror, religious. Submit complete ms and SASE. Length: 300-1,000 words. **Pays up to 25¢/word.**

POETRY Needs free verse, traditional. Submit maximum 5 poems. Length: 20 lines maximum. **Pays $3/ line maximum.**

FILLERS Recipes, crafts, puzzles, games, brainteasers, math and word activities. 1-4 pages. **Pays for fillers.**

⊖ STONE SOUP

Children's Art Foundation, P.O. Box 83, Santa Cruz CA 95063-0083. (831)426-5557. **Fax:** (831)426-1161. **E-mail:** editor@stonesoup.com. **Website:** www.stonesoup.com. **Contact:** Ms. Gerry Mandel, editor. **100% freelance written.** Bimonthly magazine of writing and art by children, including fiction, poetry, book reviews, and art by children through age 13. *Stone Soup* is 48 pages, 7x10, professionally printed in color on heavy stock, saddle-stapled, with coated cover with full-color illustration. Receives 5,000 poetry submissions/year, accepts about 12. Press run is 15,000 (14,000 subscribers, 3,000 shelf sales, 500 other). Subscription: membership in the Children's Art Foundation includes a subscription, $37/year. *Stone Soup*, published 6 times/year, showcases writing and art by children ages 13 and under. "We have a preference for writing and art based on real-life experiences; no formula stories or poems. We only publish writing by children ages 8 to 13. We do not publish writing by adults." Estab. 1973. Circ. 15,000. Publishes ms an average of 4 months after acceptance. Submit seasonal material 6 months in advance. Sample copy by phone only. Guidelines available online.

NONFICTION Needs historical, personal experience, book reviews. **Buys 12 mss/year.** Submit complete ms; no SASE. **Pays $40.**

FICTION Contact: Ms. Gerry Mandel, editor. Needs adventure, ethnic, experimental, fantasy, historical, humorous, mystery, science fiction, slice-of-life vignettes, suspense. We do not like assignments or formula stories of any kind. **Buys 60 mss/year.** Send complete ms; no SASE. Length: 150-2,500 words. **Pays $40 for stories. Authors also receive 2 copies, a certificate, and discounts on additional copies and on subscriptions.**

POETRY Needs avant-garde, free verse. *Stone Soup*, published 6 times/year, showcases writing and art by children ages 13 and under. Wants free verse poetry. Does not want rhyming poetry, haiku, or cinquain. Buys 12 poems/year. **Pays $40/poem, a certificate, and 2 contributor's copies plus discounts.**

⊘ ⊖⊖ TURTLE MAGAZINE FOR PRESCHOOL KIDS

Children's Better Health Institute, 1100 Waterway Blvd., Indianapolis IN 46202. **Website:** www.turtlemag.org. Bimonthly magazine. *Turtle Magazine for Preschool Kids*, published by Childen's Better Health Institute, is a magazine for children ages 3-5. "Colorful and entertaining..perfect for reading aloud." Wants light-hearted poetry appropriate for the age group. Reviews submissions for possible use in all Children's Better Health Institute publications. Estab. 1978. Circ. 300,000. Byline given. Submit seasonal material 8 months in advance. Responds in 3 months to queries. Sample copy for $3.99. Guidelines for #10 sase.

NONFICTION Length: 250 words or less. **Pays up to $70.**

FICTION Writers should present their material in a way that is appropriate for kids, but which does not talk down to them. Reading our editorial guidelines is not enough. Careful study of current issues will acquaint writers with each title's personality, various departments, and regular features. Short stories 350 words or less. No queries. Send complete ms. Length: 150-350 words. **Pays up to $70.**

POETRY We use short verse on our inside front cover and back cover. Length: 4-12 lines. **Pays up to $35.**

YES MAG

3968 Long Gun Place, Victoria BC V8N 3A9 Canada. **Fax:** (250)477-5390. **E-mail:** editor@yesmag.ca; jude@yesmag.com. **Website:** www.yesmag.ca. **Contact:** Jude Isabella, managing editor; David Garrison, publisher; Shannon Hunt, editor. Bimonthly magazine. "*YES Mag* is designed to make science accessible, interesting, exciting, and fun. Written for children ages 10 to 15, *YES Mag* covers a range of topics including science and technology news, environmental updates, do-at-home projects and articles about Canadian science and scientists." Emphasis on Canadian writers. Estab. 1996. Circ. 22,000. Byline given. Publishes mss 3 months after acceptance. Accepts queries by e-mail. Responds to queries/mss in 6 weeks. Sample copies available for $5. Writer's guidelines available on the website under "Contact" information. **NONFICTION** science, biology, math, engineering, physics, chemistry, etc. Query with published clips. Prefers e-mailed queries. Average Length: 250-800 words. **Pays $70-200 for stories and articles.**

TIPS "We do not publish fiction or science fiction or poetry. Visit our website for more information and sample articles. Articles relating to the physical sciences and mathematics are encouraged."

LITERARY AND LITTLE

ACORN

OutOfPocket Press, 122 Calistoga Rd., #135, Santa Rose CA 95409. **E-mail:** acornhaiku@mac.com. **Website:** www.acornhaiku.com. **Contact:** Carolyn Hall, editor. Biannual magazine dedicated to publishing the best of contemporary English language haiku, and in particular to showcasing individual poems that reveal the extraordinary moments found in everyday life. Estab. 1998. Publishes ms an average of 1-3 months after acceptance. Reads submissions in January-February and July-August only. NoResponds in 3 weeks to mss. Guidelines and sample poems available online at www.acornhaiku.com.

POETRY Needs HAIKU. "Decisions made by editor on a rolling basis. Poems judged purely on merit." Sometimes acceptance conditional on minor edits. Often comments on rejected poems. Accepts submissions via mail or e-mail, however e-mail is preferred. "Does NOT want epigrams, musings, and overt emotion poured into 17 syllables; surreal, science fiction, or political commentary 'ku;' strong puns or raunchy humor. A 5-7-5 syllable count is not necessary or encouraged." Length: 1-5 lines; 17 or fewer syllables.

THE ADIRONDACK REVIEW

Black Lawrence Press, 8405 Bay Parkway, Apt C8, Brooklyn NY 11214. **E-mail:** editors@theadirondackreview.com; angela@blacklawrencepress.com. **Website:** www.adirondackreview.homestead.com. **Contact:** Angela Leroux-Lindsey, Kara Christenson, Diane Goettel, editor. *The Adirondack Review*, published quarterly online, is a literary journal dedicated to quality free verse poetry and short fiction as well as book and film reviews, art, photography, and interviews. "We are open to both new and established writers. Our only requirement is excellence. We would like to publish more French and German poetry translations as well as original poems in these languages. We publish an eclectic mix of voices and styles, but all poems should show attention to craft. We are open to beginners who demonstrate talent, as well as established voices. The work should speak for itself." Estab. 2000. Responds to queries in 1-2 months. Responds to mss in 2-4 months.

FICTION Needs adventure, experimental, historical. Send complete ms with cover letter. Accepts submissions by e-mail. Include estimated word count, brief bio, list of publications, and "how they learned about the magazine." Send either SASE (or IRC) for return of ms or disposable copy of ms and #10 SASE for reply only. Considers simultaneous submissions, multiple submissions.

POETRY Needs "Well-crafted, thoughtful writing full of imagery." Does not want "religious, overly sentimental, horror/gothic, rhyming, greeting card, pet-related, humor, or science fiction poetry." Has published poetry by Bob Hicok, Timothy Liu, Lola Haskins, D.C. Berry, David Rigsbee, and Paul Guest. Accepts about 3-5% of poems submitted.

AFRICAN AMERICAN REVIEW

St. Louis University, 317 Adorjan Hall, 3800 Lindell Blvd., St. Louis MO 63108. (314)977-3688. **Fax:** (314)977-1514. **E-mail:** keenanam@slu.edu. **Website:** aar.slu.edu. Nathan Grant, editor. **65% freelance written.** Quarterly journal covering African-American literature and culture. Essays on African-American literature, theater, film, art and culture generally; interviews; poetry and fiction by African-American authors; book reviews. Estab. 1967. Circ. 2,000. Byline given. Publishes ms an average of 1 year after acceptance. Editorial lead time 1 year. Responds in 1 week to queries. Responds in 3-6 months to mss. Sample copy for $12. Guidelines available online.

NONFICTION Needs essays, interview. **Buys 30 mss/year.** Query. Length: 6,000-8,500 words.

FICTION Contact: Nathan Grant, editor. Needs ethnic, experimental, mainstream. No children's/juvenile/young adult/teen. **Buys 30 mss/year.** Length: No more than 1,500 words. **1 contributor's copy and 5 offprints.**

$ AGNI

Creative Writing Program, Boston University, 236 Bay State Rd., Boston MA 02215. (617)353-7135. **Fax:** (617)353-7134. **E-mail:** agni@bu.edu. **Website:** www.agnimagazine.org. **Contact:** Sven Birkerts, editor. Biannual magazine. "Eclectic literary magazine publishing first-rate poems, essays, translations, and stories." Estab. 1972. Circ. 3,000 in print, plus more than 60,000 distinct readers online per year. Byline given. Publishes ms an average of 6 months after acceptance. Editorial lead time 1 year. Accepts queries by mail. Accepts simultaneous submissions. Responds in 2 weeks to queries. Responds in 4 months to mss. Sample copy for $10 or online. Guidelines available online.

FICTION Buys stories, prose poems. "No science fiction or romance." **Buys 20+ mss/year. Pays $10/page up to $150, a one-year subscription, and for print publication: 2 contributor's copies and 4 gift copies.**

POETRY Buys 120+ poems/year poems/year. Submit maximum 5 poems. **Pays $20/page up to $150.**

$ $ ALASKA QUARTERLY REVIEW

ESB 208, University of Alaska-Anchorage, 3211 Providence Dr., Anchorage AK 99508. (907)786-6916. **E-mail:** aqr@uaa.alaska.edu. **Website:** www.uaa.alaska.edu/aqr. **Contact:** Ronald Spatz. **95% freelance written.** Semiannual magazine publishing fiction, poetry, literary nonfiction, and short plays in traditional and experimental styles. "*AQR* publishes fiction, poetry, literary nonfiction and short plays in traditional and experimental styles." Estab. 1982. Circ. 2,200. Byline given. Honorariums on publication when funding permits. Publishes ms an average of 6 months after acceptance. Accepts queries by mail. Responds in 1 month to queries. Responds in 6 months to mss. Sample copy for $6. Guidelines available online.

NONFICTION Buys 0-5 mss/year. Query. Length: 1,000-20,000 words. **Pays $50-200 subject to funding.**

FICTION Contact: Ronald Spatz, fiction editor. "Works in AQR have certain characteristics: freshness, honesty, and a compelling subject. The voice of the piece must be strong—idiosyncratic enough to create a unique persona. We look for craft, putting it in a form where it becomes emotionally and intellectually complex. Many pieces in AQR concern everyday life. We're not asking our writers to go outside themselves and their experiences to the absolute exotic to catch our interest. We look for the experiential and revelatory qualities of the work. We will champion a piece that may be less polished or stylistically sophisticated, if it engages me, surprises me, and resonates for me. The joy in reading such a work is in discovering something true. Moreover, in keeping with our mission to publish new writers, we are looking for voices our readers do not know, voices that may not always be reflected in the dominant culture and that, in all instances, have something important to convey." Needs experimental and traditional literary forms., contemporary, prose poem, novel excerpts, drama: experimental & traditional one-acts. No romance, children's, or inspirational/religious. **Buys 20-26 mss/year; 0-2 mss/year drama. mss/year.** not exceeding 100 pages **Pays $50-200 subject to funding; pays in contributor's copies and subscriptions when funding is limited.**

POETRY Needs avant-garde, free verse, traditional. No light verse. Buys 10-30 poems/year. Submit maximum 10 poems. **Pays $10-50 subject to availability of funds; pays in contributor's copies and subscriptions when funding is limited. Acquires first North American serial rights.**

🍁 $ THE ANTIGONISH REVIEW

St. Francis Xavier University, P.O. Box 5000, Antigonish NS B2G 2W5 Canada. (902)867-3962. **Fax:** (902)867-5563. **E-mail:** tar@stfx.ca. **Website:** www.antigonishreview.com. **Contact:** Bonnie McIsaac, office manager. **100% freelance written.** Quarterly magazine. Literary magazine for educated and creative readers. Estab. 1970. Circ. 850. Byline given. Offers variable kill fee. Publishes ms an average of 8 months after acceptance. Editorial lead time 4 months. Submit seasonal material 4 months in advance. Accepts queries by mail, fax. Responds in 1 month to queries. Responds in 6 months to mss. Sample copy for $7 or online. Writer's guidelines for #10 SASE or online.

NONFICTION Needs essays, interview, book reviews/articles. No academic pieces. **Buys 15-20 mss/year.** Query. Length: 1,500-5,000 words **Pays $50-150.**

FICTION Literary. No erotica. **Buys 35-40 mss/year.** Send complete ms. Length: 500-5,000 words. **Pays $100 for stories.**

POETRY *The Antigonish Review*, published quarterly, tries "to produce the kind of literary and visual mosaic that the modern sensibility requires or would respond to. Has published poetry by Andy Wainwright, W.J. Keith, Michael Hulse, Jean McNeil, M. Travis Lane, and Douglas Lochhead. No previously published poems or simultaneous submissions. Buys 100-125 poems/year. Submit maximum 5 poems. Submit 6-8 poems at a time. Lines/poem: not over 80, i.e., 2 pages. **Pays $30/full page and 2 contributor's copies. Acquires first North American serial rights.**

ANTIOCH REVIEW

P.O. Box 148, Yellow Springs OH 45387-0148. **E-mail:** mkeyes@antiochreview.org. **Website:** http://antioch-college.org/antioch_review/. Judith Hall, poetry editor. **Contact:** Muriel Keyes. Quarterly magazine for general, literary, and academic audience. Literary and cultural review of contemporary issues, and literature for general readership. Estab. 1941. Circ. 5,000. Byline given. Publishes ms an average of 10 months after acceptance. Responds in 3-6 months to mss. Sample copy for $7. Guidelines available online.

NONFICTION Length: 2,000-8,000 words. **Pays $15/printed page.**

FICTION Contact: Fiction editor. Quality fiction only, distinctive in style with fresh insights into the human condition. Needs experimental, contemporary. No science fiction, fantasy, or confessions. generally under 8,000 **Pays $15/printed page.**

POETRY *The Antioch Review* "is an independent quarterly of critical and creative thought. For well over 50 years, creative authors, poets, and thinkers have found a friendly reception—regardless of formal reputation. We get far more poetry than we can possibly accept, and the competition is keen. Here, where form and content are so inseparable and reaction is so personal, it is difficult to state requirements or limitations. Studying recent issues of *The Antioch Review* should be helpful." Has published poetry by Peter Marcus, Jacqueline Osherow, Joanna Rawson, David Yezzi, and others. Receives about 3,000 submissions/year. Circulation is 3,000; 70% distributed

through bookstores and newsstands. Subscription: $40. Sample: $7. Work published in *The Antioch Review* has been included frequently in *The Best American Poetry, The Best New Poets* and *The Pushcart Prize*. No light or inspirational verse. **Pays $15/printed page.**

ARC

Arc Poetry Society, P.O. Box 81060, Ottawa ON K1P 1B1 Canada. **E-mail:** editor@arcpoetry.ca; managingeditor@arcpoetry.ca. **Website:** www.arcpoetry.ca. **Contact:** Katia Grubisic, editor; Monty Reid, managing editor. Semiannual magazine featuring poetry, poetry-related articles, and criticism. Our focus is poetry, and Canadian poetry in general, although we do publish writers from elsewhere. We are looking for the best poetry from new and established writers. We often have special issues. Send a SASE for upcoming special issues and contests. Estab. 1978. Circ. 1,500. Byline given. Publishes ms an average of 6 months after acceptance. Responds in 4 months. Guidelines for #10 SASE.

NONFICTION Needs essays, interview, book reviews. Query first. Length: 500-4,000 words. **Pays $40/printed page (Canadian), and 2 copies.**

POETRY Needs avant-garde, free verse. E-mail submissions not accepted. Buys 60 poems/year. Submit maximum 5 poems. **Pays $40/printed page (Canadian).**

ARTFUL DODGE

Dept. of English, College of Wooster, Wooster OH 44691. (330)263-2577. **E-mail:** artfuldodge@wooster.edu. **Website:** www.wooster.edu/artfuldodge. **Contact:** Daniel Bourne, editor-in-chief; Karin Lin-Greenberg, fiction editor; Marcy Campbell, associate fiction editor; Carolyne Wright, translation editor. Annual magazine that takes a strong interest in poets who are continually testing what they can get away with successfully in regard to subject, perspective, language, etc., but who also show mastery of the current American poetic techniques—its varied textures and its achievement in the illumination of the particular. There is no theme in this magazine, except literary power. We also have an ongoing interest in translations from Central/Eastern Europe and elsewhere. Estab. 1979. Circ. 1,000. Accepts queries by mail. Accepts simultaneous submissions. Responds in 1-6 months to mss. Sample copy for $7. Guidelines for #10 SASE.

FICTION Contact: Marcy Campbell, fiction editor. Needs experimental, prose poem. We judge by literary quality, not by genre. We are especially interested in fine English translations of significant prose writers. Translations should be submitted with original texts. **Pays 2 contributor's copies and honorarium of $5/page, thanks to funding from the Ohio Arts Council.**

POETRY Contact: Philip Brady, poetry editor. We are interested in poems that utilize stylistic persuasions both old and new to good effect. We are not afraid of poems which try to deal with large social, political, historical, and even philosophical questions—especially if the poem emerges from one's own life experience and is not the result of armchair pontificating. We don't want cute, rococo surrealism, someone's warmed-up, left-over notion of an avant-garde that existed 10-100 years ago, or any last bastions of rhymed verse in the civilized world. Buys 20 poems/year. Submit maximum 6 poems. **Pays $5/page honorarium and 2 contributor's copies.**

ATLANTA REVIEW

P.O. Box 8248, Atlanta GA 31106. **E-mail:** atlrev@yahoo.com. **Website:** www.atlantareview.com. **Contact:** Dan Veach, Editor/Publisher. *Atlanta Review,* published semiannually, is devoted primarily to poetry, but occasionally features interviews and b&w artwork. Wants "quality poetry of genuine human appeal." Has published poetry by Seamus Heaney, Billy Collins, Derek Walcott, Maxine Kumin, Alicia Stallings, Gunter Grass, Eugenio Montale, and Thomas Lux. Atlanta Review is 128 pages, digest-sized, professionally printed on acid-free paper, flat-spined, with glossy color cover. Receives about 10,000 poems/year, accepts about 1%. Press run is 2,500. Single copy: $6; subscription: $10. Sample: $5. Estab. 1994.

POETRY Submit no more than 5 poems at a time. No previously published poems. No e-mail submissions from within the U.S.; postal submissions only. Include SASE for reply. "Authors living outside the United States and Canada may submit work via e-mail." Cover letter is preferred. Include brief bio. Put name and address on each poem. Reads submissions according to the following deadlines: June 1 for Fall; December 1 for Spring. "While we do read year round, response time may be slower during summer and the winter holidays." Time between acceptance and publication is 6 months. Seldom comments on rejected poems. Guidelines available for SASE, by e-mail, or on website. Responds in 1 month. Pays 2 contribu-

tor's copies, author's discounts on additional copies. Acquires first North American serial rights.

BARN OWL REVIEW

Olin Hall 342, The University of Akron, Akron OH 44325. **E-mail:** info@barnowlreview.com. **Website:** www.barnowlreview.com. **Contact:** Mary Biddinger and Jay Robinson, editors-in-chief. "We are a handsomely designed print journal looking for work that takes risks while still connecting with readers. We aim to publish the highest quality poetry from both emerging and established writers." Accepts simultaneous submissions.

POETRY Contact: Poetry editors: Susan Grimm, Michael Krutel, Eric Morris, Amy Bracken Sparks. Barn Owl Review favors no particular poetic school or style; "however, we look for innovation and risk-taking in the poems that we publish." Submit 3-5 poems (in single attachment) via Submishmash between June 1-November 1. **Contributors receive 2 copies of the issue.**

BELLINGHAM REVIEW

Mail Stop 9053, Western Washington University, Bellingham WA 98225. (360)650-4863. **E-mail:** bhreview@wwu.edu. **Website:** wwww.bhreview.org. Brenda Miller, editor-in-chief. **Contact:** Marilyn Bruce, managing editor. **100% freelance written.** Annual small press literary magazine covering poems, stories, and essays. No limitations on form or subject matter. Annual nonprofit magazine published once a year in the Spring. Seeks "Literature of palpable quality: poems stories and essays so beguiling they invite us to touch their essence. The *Bellingham Review* hungers for a kind of writing that nudges the limits of form, or executes traditional forms exquisitely." Estab. 1977. Circ. 1,500. Byline given. Pays on publication when funding allows. Publishes ms an average of 6 months after acceptance. Editorial lead time 6 months. Accepts simultaneous submissions. Responds in 1-6 months. Sample copy for $12. Guidelines available online.

NONFICTION Contact: Danielle Smith, nonfiction editor; Erica Nold, nonfiction editor. Needs essays, personal experience. Does not want anything non-literary. **Buys 4-6 mss/year.** Send complete ms. 6,000 words maximum. **Pays as funds allow, plus contributor copies.**

FICTION Contact: Jason Styles, fiction editor; Chantelle Diaz, fiction editor; Tom Graham, fiction editor. Experimental, humor/satire, literary, regional (Northwest). Does not want anything nonliterary. Needs experimental, humorous. **Buys 4-6 mss/year.** Send complete ms. 6,000 words maximum. **Pays as funds allow.**

POETRY Contact: Britt Ashley, poetry editor; George Such, poetry editor. Needs avant-garde, free verse, traditional. *Bellingham Review*, published twice/year, has no specific preferences as to form. Wants "well-crafted poetry, but are open to all styles." Has published poetry by David Shields, Tess Gallagher, Gary Soto, Jane Hirshfield, Albert Goldbarth, and Rebecca McClanahan. Accepts submissions by postal mail and e-mail. Include SASE. Reads submissions September 15-December 1 only (submissions must be postmarked within this reading period). Responds in 2 months. Will not use light verse. Buys 10-30 poems/year. Submit maximum 3-5/poems at a time. poems. Indicate approximate word count on prose pieces. **Pays contributor's copies, a year's subscription, plus monetary payment (if funding allows).**

BELOIT POETRY JOURNAL

Beloit Poetry Journal, P.O. Box 151, Farmington ME 04938. (207)778-0020. **E-mail:** bpj@bpj.org. **Website:** www.bpj.org. Quarterly magazine covering contemporary poetry. *Poetry Beloit Poetry Journal*, published quarterly, prints "the most outstanding poems we receive, without bias as to length, school, subject, or form. For more than 60 years of continuous publication, we have been distinguished for the extraordinary range of our poetry and our discovery of strong new poets." Wants "visions broader than the merely personal; language that makes us laugh and weep, recoil, resist—and pay attention. We're drawn to poetry that grabs hold of the whole body, not just the head." Estab. 1950. Circ. 1,350. Responds in 1-16 weeks to queries. Sample copy for $5. Guidelines available on website.

POETRY Limit submissions to 5 pages or a single long poem. **Pays 3 contributor's copies.**

💲💲 BOULEVARD

Opojaz, Inc., 6614 Clayton Rd., Box 325, Richmond Heights MO 63117. (314)862-2643. **Fax:** (314)862-2982. **E-mail:** kellyleavitt@boulevardmagazine.org; richardburgin@att.net; richardburgin@netzero.net. **E-mail:** http://boulevard.submishmash.com/submit. **Website:** www.boulevardmagazine.org. Kelly Leavitt, managing editor. **Contact:** Richard Burgin, editor. **100% freelance written**. Triannual magazine covering fiction, poetry, and essays. "*Boulevard* is a diverse literary magazine presenting original creative work by well-known authors, as well as by writers of exciting promise." Estab. 1985. Circ. 11,000. Byline given. Offers Publishes ms an average of 9 months after acceptance. Accepts queries by mail. Accepts simultaneous submissions. Responds in 2 weeks to queries. Responds in 3 months to mss. Sample copy for $10. Guidelines available online.

NONFICTION Needs book excerpts, essays, interview, opinion, photo feature. No pornography, science fiction, children's stories, or westerns. **Buys 10 mss/year.** Send complete ms. Now has online submissions link. 10,000 words maximum. **Pays $20/page, minimum $150.**

FICTION Contact: Richard Burgin, editor. Also sponsors the Short Fiction Contest for Emerging Writers. $1,500 and publication in Boulevard awarded to the winning story by a writer who has not yet published a book of fiction, poetry, or creative non-fiction with a nationally distributed press. All entries must be postmarked by December 31, 2010. Entry fee is $15 for each individual story, with no limit per author. Entry fee includes a one-year subscription to Boulevard (one per author). Make check payable to Boulevard. Needs confession, experimental, mainstream, novel excerpts. "We do not want erotica, science fiction, romance, western, horror, or children's stories." **Buys 20 mss/year.** Send complete ms. Now takes online submissions: pdf, doc, docx, txt, rtf, jpg, gif, mp3, mp4, m4a, zip, tiff, png 8,000 words maximum. **$50-$500 (sometimes higher) for accepted work**.

POETRY Needs avant-garde, free verse, haiku, traditional. *Boulevard*, published 3 times/year, strives "to publish only the finest in fiction, poetry, and nonfiction (essays and interviews). While we frequently publish writers with previous credits, we are very interested in publishing less experienced or unpublished writers with exceptional promise. We've published everything from John Ashbery to Donald Hall to a wide variety of styles from new or lesser known poets. We're eclectic. We are interested in original, moving poetry written from the head as well as the heart. It can be about any topic." Has published poetry by Albert Goldbarth, Molly Peacock, Bob Hicok, Alice Friman, Dick Allen, and Tom Disch. *Boulevard* is 175-250 pages, digest-sized, professionally printed, flat-spined, with glossy card cover. Subscription: $15 for 3 issues, $22 for 6 issues, $25 for 9 issues. "Foreign subscribers, please add $6." Sample: $8 plus 5 first-class stamps and SASE. Make checks payable to Opojaz, Inc. Considers simultaneous submissions with notification; no previously published poems. Guidelines available for SASE, by e-mail, or on website. Responds in less than 2 months. Acquires first-time publication and anthology rights. Does not consider book reviews. "Do not send us light verse. Does not want "poetry that is uninspired, formulaic, self-conscious, unoriginal, insipid." Buys 80 poems/year. Submit maximum 5 poems. Length: 200/max lines. **$25-300 (sometimes higher) depending on length, plus one contributor's copy.**

🍁 $$ BRICK

Brick, P.O. Box 609, Station P, Toronto ON M5S 2Y4 Canada. **E-mail:** info@brickmag.com. **Website:** www.brickmag.com. **Contact:** Nadia Szilvassy, publisher and managing editor. **90% freelance written**. Semiannual magazine covering literature and the arts. "We publish literary nonfiction of a very high quality on a range of arts and culture subjects." Estab. 1977. Circ. 4,000. Byline given. Publishes ms 3-5 months after acceptance. Editorial lead time 5 months. Responds in 6 months to mss. Sample copy for $15, plus shipping. Guidelines available online.

NONFICTION Needs essays, historical, interview, opinion, travel. No fiction, poetry, personal memoir, or art. **Buys 30-40 mss/year.** Send complete ms. Length: 250-3,000 words. **Pays $75-500 (Canadian).**

$ BUTTON

P.O. Box 77, Westminster MA 01473. **E-mail:** sally@moonsigns.net. **Website:** www.moonsigns.net. **10% freelance written**. Annual literary magazine. *"Button* is New England's tiniest magazine of poetry, fiction, and gracious living, published once a year. As 'gracious living' is on the cover, we like wit, brevity, cleverly-conceived essay/recipe, poetry that isn't sentimental or song lyrics. I started *Button* so that a century from now, when people read it in landfills or, preferably, libraries, they'll say, 'Gee, what a great time to have lived. I wish I lived back then.' Submit only between April 1 and September 30 please." Estab. 1993. Circ. 1,500. Byline given. Publishes ms an average of 3-9 months after acceptance. Editorial lead time 6 months. Responds in 1 month to queries. Responds in 2 months to mss. Sample copy for $2.50. Guidelines available online.

NONFICTION Needs personal experience, cooking stories. Does not want "the tired, the trite, the sexist, the multiply-folded, the single-spaced, the sentimental, the self-pitying, the swaggering, the infantile (i.e., coruscated whimsy and self-conscious quaint), poems about Why You Can't Be Together and stories about How Complicated Am I. Before you send us anything, sit down and read a poem by Stanley Kunitz or a story by Evelyn Waugh, Louisa May Alcott, or anyone who's visited the poles, and if you still think you've written a damn fine thing, have at it. A word-count on the top of the page is fine—a copyright or 'all rights reserved' reminder makes you look like a beginner." **Buys 1-2 mss/year.** Length: 300-2,000 words. **Pays small honorarium and copies.**

FICTION Contact: W.M. Davies, fiction editor. Seeking quality fiction. No genre fiction, science fiction, techno-thriller. "Wants more of anything Herman Melville, Henry James, or Betty MacDonald would like to read." **Buys 1-2 mss/year.** Send complete ms. Length: 300-2,000 words. **Pays honorarium and subscriptions.**

POETRY Contact: Maude Piper, poetry editor. Needs free verse, traditional. *Button*, published annually, is "New England's tiniest magazine of fiction, poetry, and gracious living." Buys 2-4 poems/year. Submit maximum 3 poems. **Pays $10-25 (honorarium) and at least 2 contributor's copies.**

🍁 $$ THE CAPILANO REVIEW

2055 Purcell Way, North Vancouver BC V7J 3H5 Canada. (604)984-1712. **E-mail:** contact@thecapilanoreview.ca; tcr@capilanou.ca. **E-mail:** tcr@capilanou.ca. **Website:** www.thecapilanoreview.ca. **Contact:** Tamara Lee, managing editor. **100% freelance written**. *The Capilano Review* has a long history of publishing new and established Canadian writers and artists who are experimenting with or expanding the boundaries of conventional forms and contexts. International writers and artists appear in our pages too. Now in its 38th year, the magazine continues to favour the risky, the provocative, the innovative, and the dissident. Tri-annual visual and literary arts magazine that "publishes only what the editors consider to be the very best fiction, poetry, drama, or visual art being produced. *TCR* editors are interested in fresh, original work that stimulates and challenges readers. Over the years, the magazine has developed a reputation for pushing beyond the boundaries of traditional art and writing. We are interested in work that is new in concept and in execution." Estab. 1972. Circ. 800. Byline given. Publishes ms an average of within 1 year after acceptance. Accepts queries by mail. Only by mail. Does not accept e-mail submissions. Please refer to website for submission guidelines.Responds in 4 months to mss. Sample copy for $10 (outside of Canada, USD). Guidelines with #10 SASE with IRC or Canadian stamps.

FICTION Send complete ms with SASE and Canadian postage or IRCs. Needs experimental, novel concepts, previously unpublished only, literary. No traditional, conventional fiction. Want to see more innovative, genre-blurring work. **Buys 10-15 mss/year.** Does not accept submissions through email or on disks. 6,000 words **Pays $50-200.**

POETRY Needs avant-garde, free verse, previously unpublished poetry. Buys 40 poems/year. Submit maximum 6-8 poems (with SASE and Canadian postage or IRCs) CAD, subscription, and 2 contributor's copies. Acquires first North American serial rights. poems. Length: No more than 4 pages. **Pays $50-200.**

$$ CHICKEN SOUP FOR THE SOUL PUBLISHING, LLC

Chicken Soup for the Soul Publishing, LLC, **Fax:** (203)861-7194. **E-mail:** for all inquires: webmaster@chickensoupforthesoul.com. **Website:** www.chickensoup.com for submissions/information. **95% freelance written.** Paperback with 12 publications/year featuring inspirational, heartwarming, uplifting short stories. Estab. 1993. Circ. Over 200 titles; 100 million books in print. Byline given. Accepts simultaneous submissions. Responds upon consideration. Guidelines available online.

NONFICTION No sermon, essay, eulogy, term paper, journal entry, political, or controversial issues. **Buys 1,000 mss/year.** Send complete ms. Length: 300-1,200 words. **Pays $200.**

POETRY Needs traditional. No controversial poetry.

$$ CHRYSALIS READER

1745 Gravel Hill Rd., Dillwyn VA 23936. (434)983-3021. **E-mail:** editor@swedenborg.com; rlawson@sover.net. **E-mail:** chrysalis@hovac.com. **Website:** www.swedenborg.com/chrysalis. **Contact:** Robert F. Lawson, editor. **90% freelance written**. Annual magazine published in the fall. Each issue focuses on a theme: Bridges: Paths Between Worlds (2010), The Marketplace: Exchange (2011) Deadline was Nov. 15, 2010. "*The Chrysalis Reader* is a contemporary journal of spiritual discovery published in honor of Emanuel Swedenborg. Each issue focuses on a meaningful theme that inspires current writings and artwork that address today's questions on spirituality. Essays, fiction, poetry, and artwork give fresh and diverse perspectives from many traditions, personal experiences, and fields of study. As Swedenborg says, 'the essence of a thing cannot come into being unless it unites with a means that can express it." *The Chrysalis Reader* is published annually in the fall. Content of fiction, articles, poetry, etc. should be focused on that issue's theme and directed to the intellectual reader. Estab. 1985. Circ. 2,000. Byline given. Publishes ms an average of 15 months after acceptance. Accepts queries by mail or e-mail. Accepts simultaneous submissions. Responds in 4 weeks to queries. Responds in 6 months to mss. Sample copy for $10. Guidelines and themes by email and online at website.

NONFICTION Needs essays, interviews, personal experiences. Special issues: Upcoming special issues will explore contemporary questions on spiruality. Every anthology has its own theme. 2011 theme: The Marketplace. "We do not want inspirational or religious articles." Manuscripts should be typed, double-spaced, and no longer than 3,000 words. Manuscripts will not be returned to authors without an SASE. Please keep a copy of your submission for your records. It is very important to send for writer's guidelines and sample copies before submitting. Length: 1,500-3,000 words. **Pays $75 for assigned articles.**

FICTION Contact: Robert Tucker, fiction editor. Needs adventure, fantasy, historical, science fiction: none of an overtly religious nature. Length: 1,500-3,000 words.

POETRY Contact: Rob Lawson, series editor. "We are interested in all forms of poetry, but none of an overtly religious nature." (Specialized: spirituality; themes) Does not want anything "overly religious or sophomoric." Buys 20 poems/year. Submit maximum of 6 poems. **Pays $75 for prose and $25 for poetry**.

CIMARRON REVIEW

English Dept., Oklahoma State Univ., 205 Morrill Hall, Stillwater OK 74078. **E-mail:** cimarronreview@okstate.edu. **Website:** http://cimarronreview.okstate.edu. **Contact:** Toni Graham, fiction editor. Quarterly magazine covering fiction, poetry, essays, and art. "We want strong literary writing. We are partial to fic-

CONSUMER MAGAZINES

tion in the modern realist tradition and distinctive poetry—lyrical, narrative, etc." Estab. 1967. Accepts simultaneous submissions. Responds in 3-6 months to mss. Guidelines available.

POETRY Contact: Lisa Lewis, Alfred Corn, and Ai, poetry editors. *Cimarron Review*, published quarterly, is a literary journal "that takes pride in our eclecticism. We like evocative poetry (lyric or narrative) controlled by a strong voice. No restrictions as to subject matter." Wants "poems whose surfaces and structures risk uncertainty and which display energy, texture, intelligence, and intense investment." Has published poetry by William Stafford, John Ashbery, Grace Schulman, Barbara Hamby, Patricia Fargnoli, Phillip Dacey, Holly Prado, and Kim Addonizio. Submit 3-5 poems at a time. **Pays 2 contributor's copies. Acquires first North American serial rights only.**

$ COLORADO REVIEW

Center for Literary Publishing, Colorado State University, 9105 Campus Delivery, Fort Collins CO 80523. (970)491-5449. **E-mail:** creview@colostate.edu. **Website:** http://coloradoreview.colostate.edu. **Contact:** Stephanie G'Schwind, editor-in-chief and nonfiction editor. Literary magazine published 3 times/year. Circ. 1,000. Byline given. Publishes ms an average of 6 months after acceptance. Editorial lead time 1 year. Accepts simultaneous submissions. Responds in 2 months to mss. Sample copy for $10. Guidelines available online.

NONFICTION Buys 6-9 mss/year. Mss are read from August 1 to April 30. Mss received between May 1 and July 31 will be returned unread.S end no more than 1 story at a time.

FICTION Contact: Steven Schwartz. Needs contemporary, ethnic, experimental, mainstream, short fiction. No genre fiction. Send complete ms. Mss are read from August 1 to April 30. Mss received between May 1 and July 31 will be returned unread. Send no more than 1 story at a time. Length: under 30 ms pages. **Pays $5/page.**

POETRY Contact: Don Revell, Sasha Steensen, and Matthew Cooperman, poetry editors; Dan Beachy-Quick, book review editor. Considers poetry of any style. Send no more than 5 poems atone time. Mss are read from August 1 to April 30. Mss received between May 1 and July 31 will be returned unread. Has published poetry by Sherman Alexie, Laynie Browne, John Gallaher, Kevin Prufer, Craig Morgan Teicher, Susan Tichy, Elizabeth Robinson, Elizabeth Willis, and Keith Waldrop. Buys 60-100 poems/year. Submit maximum 5 poems. **Pays minimum of $25 or $5/page.**

$ $ CONFRONTATION

English Department, C.W. Post Campus Long Island University, Brookville NY 11548. (516)299-2720. **Fax:** (516)299-2735. **E-mail:** confrontationmag@gmail.com. **Website:** confrontationmagazine.org. **Contact:** Jonna Semeiks, editor-in-chief. **75% freelance written.** Semiannual magazine covering all forms and genres of stories, poems, essays, memoirs, and plays. A special section contains book reviews and cultural commentary. "We are eclectic in our taste. Excellence of style is our dominant concern. We bring new talent to light. We are open to all submissions, each issue contains original work by famous and lesser-known writers and also contains a thematic supplement that 'confront' a topic; the ensuing confrontation is an attempt to see the many sides of an issue rather than a formed conclusion." - Martin Tucker, director Confrontation Publications Estab. 1968. Circ. 2,000. Byline given. Offers kill fee. Publishes ms an average of 1 year after acceptance. Accepts queries by mail, e-mail, phone. Accepts simultaneous submissions. Responds in 3 weeks to queries. Responds in 2 months to mss. Sample copy for $3.

NONFICTION Needs essays, personal experience. **Buys 15 mss/year.** Send complete ms. Length: 1,500-5,000 words. **Pays $100-300 for assigned articles. Pays $15-300 for unsolicited articles.**

FICTION We judge on quality, so genre is open. Needs experimental, mainstream, novel excerpts, slice-of-life vignettes, contemporary, prose poem. No 'proselytizing' literature or genre fiction. **Buys 60-75 mss/year.** Send complete ms. 6,000 words **Pays $25-250.**

POETRY Contact: Belinda Kremer, poetry editor. Needs avant-garde, free verse, haiku, light verse, traditional. *Confrontation Magazine*, published semiannually, is interested "in all forms. Our only criterion is high literary merit. We think of our audience as an educated, lay group of intelligent readers. Has published poetry by David Ray, T. Alan Broughton, David Ignatow, Philip Appleman, Jane Mayhall, and Joseph Brodsky. Submit no more than 10 pages at a time (up to 6 poems). No sentimental verse. No previously published poems. Buys 60-75 poems/year. Lines/poem: Length should generally be kept to 2 pages **Pays $10-100. Pays $5-50 and 1 contributor's copy with discount available on additional copies.**

CONNECTICUT REVIEW

Connecticut State University, 39 Woodland St., Hartford CT 06105-2337. **E-mail:** ctreview@southernct.edu. **Website:** www.ctstateu.edu/ctreview/index.html. JP Briggs, Jian-Zhong Lin, Mary Collins. **Contact:** Vivian Shipley, editor. **98% freelance written.** Semiannual magazine. "*Connecticut Review* is a high-quality literary magazine. We take both traditional literary pieces and those on the cutting edge of their genres. We are looking for poetry, fiction, short-shorts, creative essays, and scholarly articles accessible to a general audience. Each issue features an 8-page color fine art section with statements from the painters or photographers featured." Estab. 1967. Circ. 3,000. Byline given. Publishes ms an average of 18 months after acceptance. Accepts queries by mail. Accepts simultaneous submissions. Responds in 6 weeks to queries. Responds in 4 months to mss Sample copy for $12 and 3 first-class stamps. Guidelines for #10 SASE.

NONFICTION Special issues: Virtuality (2007); Parable and Culture (2008). Send complete ms. Length: 500-4,000 words.

FICTION Needs experimental, literary. "No 'entertainment' fiction, though we don't mind if you entertain us while you plumb for the truth." **Buys 14 mss/year.** Send complete ms. Length: 50-4,000 words.

POETRY Needs avant-garde, free verse, haiku, traditional. No doggerel poetry. Buys 80 poems/year. Submit maximum 5 poems.

CRAB CREEK REVIEW

7315 34th Ave. NW, Seattle WA 98117. **E-mail:** crabcreekreview@gmail.com. **Website:** www.crabcreekreview.org. Byline given. Accepts queries by e-mail. Accepts simultaneous submissions. Responds in 3-5 months to mss. Guidelines available online.

NONFICTION Contact: Star Rockers, nonfiction editor. short personal essays that don't sidestep the truth. "No academic or critical essays. "

FICTION Contact: Jen Betterley, fiction editor. Accepts only the strongest fiction. Prefers shorter work. Needs confession, experimental, humorous, mainstream. Send complete ms. Length: 3,500 words. **Pays in 2 copies.**

POETRY Contact: Ronda Broatch, poetry editor. Needs avant-garde, free verse, traditional. Has published poetry by Oliver de la Paz, Dorianne Laux, Greg Nicholl, and translations by Ilya Kaminsky and

Matthew Zapruder. Fiction by karen Heuler and Daniel Homan. *Crab Creek Review* is an 80- to 120-page, perfect-bound paperback. Subscription: $15/year, $28/2 year. Sample: $6. Submit maximum 3 poems. **Pays 1 copy.**

CRAB ORCHARD REVIEW

Department of English, Mail Code 4503, Faner Hall 2380, Southern Illinois University at Carbondale, Carbondale IL 62901. (618)453-6833. **Fax:** (618)453-8224. **Website:** www.craborchardreview.siuc.edu/. "We are a general interest literary journal published twice/year. We strive to be a journal that writers admire and readers enjoy. We publish fiction, poetry, creative nonfiction, fiction translations, interviews and reviews." Estab. 1995. Circ. 2,500. Publishes ms an average of 9-12 months after acceptance. Accepts simultaneous submissions. Responds in 3 weeks to queries. Responds in 9 months to mss. Sample copy for $8. Guidelines for #10 SASE.

FICTION Contact: Jon Tribble, managing editor. Needs ethnic, excerpted novel. No science fiction, romance, western, horror, gothic or children's. Wants more novel excerpts that also stand alone as pieces. Length: 1,000-6,500 words. **Pays $100 minimum; $20/page maximum, 2 contributor's copies and a year subscription.**

CRAZYHORSE

College of Charleston, Dept. of English, 66 George St., Charleston SC 29424. (843)953-7740. **E-mail:** crazyhorse@cofc.edu. **Website:** www.crazyhorsejournal.org. Semiannual magazine. We like to print a mix of writing regardless of its form, genre, school, or politics. We're especially on the lookout for original writing that doesn't fit the categories and that engages in the work of honest communication. Estab. 2,000. Circ. 1,500. Publishes ms an average of 6-12 months after acceptance. Accepts simultaneous submissions. Responds in 1 week to queries. Responds in 3-5 months to mss. Sample copy for $5. Writer's guidelines for SASE or by e-mail.

FICTION Accepts all fiction of fine quality, including short shorts and literary essays. **Buys 12-15 mss/year. Pays 2 contributor's copies and $20 per page.**

POETRY No previously published poems. No fax, e-mail or disk submissions. Cover letter is preferred. Reads submissions year round, but slows down during the summer. Buys 80 poems/year. Submit maximum 5

poems. **Pays 2 contributor's copies, plus 1-year subscription (2 issues).**

🍁 $ DESCANT

P.O. Box 314, Station P, Toronto ON M5S 2S8 Canada. (416)593-2557. **Fax:** (416)593-9362. **E-mail:** info@descant.ca. **Website:** descant.ca. Quarterly journal. Estab. 1970. Circ. 1,200. Publishes ms an average of 16 months after acceptance. Editorial lead time 1 year. Accepts queries by mail, e-mail, phone. Sample copy for $8.50 plus postage. Guidelines available online.

NONFICTION Needs book excerpts, essays, interview, personal experience, historical.

FICTION Contact: Karen Mulhallen, editor. Short stories or book excerpts. Maximum length 6,000 words; 3,000 words or less preferred. Needs ethnic, experimental, historical, humorous. No gothic, religious, beat. Send complete ms. **Pays $100 (Canadian); additional copies $8.**

POETRY Needs free verse, light verse, traditional. "*Descant* seeks high quality poems and stories in both traditional and innovative form." Annual. Circ. 500-750. Member CLMP. Literary. Submit maximum 6 poems. **Pays $100. Pays on pubication.**

DIAGRAM

Dept. of English, Univ. of Arizona, P.O. Box 210067, Tucson AZ 85721-0067. **E-mail:** editor@thediagram.com. **Website:** www.thediagram.com. Online journal covers poetry, fiction and nonfiction. We sponsor a yearly chapbook competition. "*Diagram* is an electronic journal of text and art, found and created. We're interested in representations, naming, indicating, schematics, labelling and taxonomy of things; in poems that masquerade as stories; in stories that disguise themselves as indices or obituaries." Accepts queries by e-mail. Responds in 1 month to mss.

NONFICTION Contact: Nicole Walker, nonfiction editor.

DMQ REVIEW

E-mail: editors@dmqreview.com. **Website:** www.dmqreview.com. **Contact:** Sally Ashton, editor-in-chief; Marjorie Manwaring, editor. Quarterly website covering poetry and artwork. We seek work that represents the diversity of contemporary poetry and demonstrates literary excellence, whether it be lyric, free verse, prose, or experimental form. Estab. 1999. Publishes ms 1-3 months after acceptance. Accepts queries by e-mail. Accepts simultaneous submissions. Responds in 3 months. Guidelines available online.

POETRY Needs avant-garde, free verse, traditional. Has published poetry by David Lehman, Ellen Bass, Amy Gerstler, Bob Hicok, Ilya Kaminsky, and Jane Hirshfield. Receives about 3,000-5,000 poems/year, accepts about 1%. E-mail submissions only; NO attachments. Include a brief bio, 50 words/max. Type Poetry Submission followed by your name in the subject line. Submit maximum 3 poems.

$ DOWNSTATE STORY

1825 Maple Ridge, Peoria IL 61614. (309)688-1409. **E-mail:** ehopkins@prairienet.org. **Website:** www.wiu.edu/users/mfgeh/dss. Annual magazine covering short fiction with some connection with Illinois or the Midwest. Estab. 1992. Circ. 500. Publishes ms an average of 1 year after acceptance. Accepts simultaneous submissions. Responds ASAP. Sample copy for $8. Guidelines available online.

FICTION Contact: Elaine Hopkins, editor. Needs adventure, ethnic, experimental, historical, horror, humorous, mainstream, mystery, romance, science fiction, suspense, western. No porn. **Buys 10 mss/year.** Length: 300-2,000 words. **Pays $50.**

TIPS Wants more political fiction. Publishes short shorts and literary essays.

$ EPOCH

Cornell University, 251 Goldwin Smith Hall, Cornell University, Ithaca NY 14853. (607)255-3385. **Fax:** (607)255-6661. **100% freelance written.** Magazine published 3 times/year. "Well-written literary fiction, poetry, personal essays. Newcomers always welcome. Open to mainstream and avant-garde writing." Estab. 1947. Circ. 1,000. Byline given. Offers 100% kill fee. Publishes ms an average of 6 months after acceptance. Editorial lead time 6 months. Submit seasonal material 8 months in advance. Accepts queries by mail. Responds in 2 weeks to queries. Responds in 6 weeks to mss. Sample copy for $5. Guidelines for #10 SASE.

NONFICTION Needs essays, interview. No inspirational. **Buys 6-8 mss/year.** Send complete ms. **Pays $5-10/printed page.**

FICTION Contact: Joseph Martin, senior editor. Needs ethnic, experimental, mainstream, novel concepts, literary short stories. No genre fiction. Would like to see more Southern fiction (Southern US). **Buys 25-30 mss/year.** Send complete ms. **Pays $5 and up/printed page.**

POETRY Contact: Nancy Vieira Couto. Needs avant-garde, free verse, haiku, light verse, traditional. Buys

30-75 poems/year. Submit maximum 7 poems. **Pays $5 up/printed page.**

○ ⊖⊖ EVENT

Douglas College, P.O. Box 2503, New Westminster BC V3L 5B2 Canada. (604)527-5293. **Fax:** (604)527-5095. **E-mail:** event@douglascollege.ca. **Website:** www. event.douglas.bc.ca. **100% freelance written.** Magazine published 3 times/year containing fiction, poetry, creative nonfiction, notes on writing, and reviews. "We are eclectic and always open to content that invites involvement. Generally, we like strong narrative." Estab. 1971. Circ. 1,250. Byline given. Publishes ms an average of 8 months after acceptance. Accepts queries by mail. Accepts simultaneous submissions. Responds in 1 month to queries. Responds in 6 months to mss. Guidelines available online.

FICTION "We look for readability, style, and writing that invites involvement." Submit maximum 2 stories. Needs humorous, contemporary. No technically poor or unoriginal pieces. **Buys 12-15 mss/year.** Send complete ms. 5,000 words maximum **Pays $25/ page up to $500.**

POETRY Needs free verse. "We tend to appreciate the narrative and sometimes the confessional modes." No light verse. Buys 30-40 poems/year. Submit maximum 10 poems. **Pays $25-500.**

FAULTLINE

Dept. of English and Comparative Literature, University of California at Irvine, Irvine CA 92697-2650. **E-mail:** faultline@uci.edu. **Website:** www.humanities. uci.edu/faultline. **100% freelance written.** Annual magazine covering poetry, fiction, essays, interviews, translations, and art. Estab. 1992. Circ. 1,000. Byline given. Publishes ms an average of 5 months after acceptance. Editorial lead time 4 months. Accepts queries by mail. Accepts simultaneous submissions. Responds in 4 weeks to queries. Responds in 4 months to mss. Sample copy for $5 or online. Writer's guidelines for #10 SASE or online.

NONFICTION Needs book excerpts, essays, humor, interview, personal experience, photo feature, travel. **Buys up to 2 mss/year.** Send complete ms. Maximum 5,000 words.

FICTION Needs ethnic, experimental, humorous, slice-of-life vignettes. **Buys 6-9 mss/year.** Send complete ms. "While simultaneous submissions are accepted, multiple submissions are not accepted. Please restrict your submissions to one story at a time, re-gardless of length." Maximum 5,000 words. **Pays in contributor copies.**

POETRY Needs avant-garde, free verse, haiku, light verse, traditional. Buys 8-15 poems/year. Submit maximum 5 poems. **Pays in contributor copies.**

⊖ FICTION

c/o Dept. of English, City College, 138th St. & Covenant Ave., New York NY 10031. **Website:** www.fictioninc.com. Semiannual magazine. "As the name implies, we publish only fiction; we are looking for the best new writing available, leaning toward the unconventional. *Fiction* has traditionally attempted to make accessible the inaccessible, to bring the experimental to a broader audience." Estab. 1972. Circ. 4,000. Publishes ms an average of 1 year after acceptance. Accepts simultaneous submissions. Responds in 3 months to mss. Sample copy for $7. Guidelines available online.

○ Reading period for unsolicited mss is September 15-May 15.

FICTION Needs experimental, humorous, satire, contemporary, literary. translations. No romance, science fiction, etc. **Buys 24-40 mss/year.** Length: 5,000 words. **Pays $114.**

⊖ FIELD: CONTEMPORARY POETRY & POETICS

Oberlin College Press, 50 N. Professor St., Oberlin OH 44074-1091. (440)775-8408. **Fax:** (440)775-8124. **E-mail:** oc.press@oberlin.edu. **Website:** www.oberlin.edu/ocpress. **Contact:** managing editor. **60% freelance written.** Biannual magazine of poetry, poetry in translation, and essays on contemporary poetry by poets. *FIELD: Contemporary Poetry and Poetics*, published semiannually in April and October, is a literary journal with "emphasis on poetry, translations, and essays by poets." Has published poetry by Michelle Glazer, Tom Lux, Carl Phillips, Betsy Sholl, Charles Simic, Jean Valentine and translations by Marilyn Hacker and Stuart Friebert. *FIELD* is 100 pages, digest-sized, printed on rag stock, flat-spined, with glossy color card cover. Subscription: $16/year, $28 for 2 years. Sample: $8 postpaid. Estab. 1969. Circ. 1,500. Byline given. Editorial lead time 4 months. Accepts queries by mail, e-mail, fax, phone, online submission form. Responds in 6-8 weeks to mss. Sample copy for $8. Guidelines available online and for #10 SASE.

POETRY Needs Contemporary, prose poems, free verse, traditional. Submissions are read August 1 through May 31. Submit 3-5 of your best poems. No previously published poems or simultaneous submissions. No e-mail submissions. Include cover letter and SASE. Reads submissions year round. Submit using our submission manager at http://www.oberlin.edu/ocpress/submissions.html. Buys 120 poems/year. Submit maximum 5 poems. **Pays $15/page and 2 contributor's copies.**

FIVE POINTS

Georgia State University, P.O. Box 3999, Atlanta GA 30302-3999. **E-mail:** info@langate.gsu.edu. **Website:** www.webdelsol.com/Five_Points. Triannual. *Five Points* is committed to publishing work that compels the imagination through the use of fresh and convincing language. Estab. 1996. Circ. 2,000. Publishes ms an average of 6 months after acceptance. Sample copy for $7.

FICTION Contact: Megan Sexton, executive editor. **Pays $15/page minimum; $250 maximum, free subscription to magazine and 2 contributor's copies; additional copies $4.**

THE FOURTH RIVER

Chatham College, Woodland Rd., Pittsburgh PA 15232. **E-mail:** 4thriver@gmail.com. **Website:** http://fourthriver.chatham.edu. **Contact:** Sheryl St. Germain, executive editor; Peter Oresick, editor-in-chief. **100% freelance written.** "*The Fourth River*, an annual publication of Chatham University's MFA in Creative Writing Programs, features "literature that engages and explores the relationship between humans and their environments." Wants "writings that are richly situated at the confluence of place, space, and identity, or that reflect upon or make use of landscape and place in new ways." *The Fourth River* is digest-sized, perfect-bound, with full-color cover by various artists. Accepts about 30-40 poems/year. Press run is 500. Single copy: $10; subscription: $16 for 2 years. Back issues: $5. Make checks payable to Chatham University." Estab. 2005. Byline given. Pays with contributor copies only. Accepts queries by mail. Accepts simultaneous submissions. Responds in 3 months to mss. Sample copy for $10. Guidelines available online.

NONFICTION Contact: Marc Nieson, nonfiction editor. Needs Accepts previously unpublished book excerpts, essays, exposé, general interest, historical, humor, opinion, personal experience, travel. Send complete ms. Maximum 25 pages (double-spaced).

FICTION Contact: Robert Yune, fiction editor. Needs adventure, cond novels, confession, ethnic, experimental, fantasy, historical, horror, humorous, mainstream, mystery, novel concepts, romance, science fiction, slice-of-life vignettes, suspense, western, literary. Send complete ms. Maximum 25 pages (double-spaced).

POETRY Contact: Heather McNaugher, poetry editor. Needs avant-garde, free verse, haiku, light verse, traditional. Submit 7 poems at a time. Lines/poem: submit 25 pages maximum. No previously published poems. Submit by post or through Submittable. Cover letter is preferred. "SASE is required for response." Reads submissions September 1-March 15. Time between acceptance and publication is 5-8 months. Poems are circulated to an editorial board. Sometimes comments on rejected poems. Sometimes publishes theme issues. Guidelines available on website. Responds in 3-5 months. Acquires first North American serial rights. Maximum 7 poems.

GARGOYLE

Paycock Press, 3819 N. 13th St., Arlington VA 22201. (703)525-9296. **E-mail:** hedgehog2@erols.com. **Website:** www.gargoylemagazine.com. **Contact:** Richard Peabody, co-editor, Lucinda Ebersole, co-editor. **75%**. Literary magazine: 512×812; 200 pages; illustrations; photos. "*Gargoyle Magazine* has always been a scallywag magazine, a maverick magazine, a bit too academic for the underground and way too underground for the academics. We are a writer's magazine in that we are read by other writers and have never worried about reaching the masses." Annual. Wants "edgy realism or experimental works. We run both." Wants to see more Canadian, British, Australian, and Third World fiction. Receives 50-200 unsolicited mss/month. Accepts 10-15 mss/issue. Accepts submissions during June, July, and Aug. Agented fiction 5%. **Publishes 2-3 new writers/year.** Recently published work by Stephanie Allen, Tom Carson, Michael Casey, Kim Chinquee, Susan Cokal, Ramola D., Janice Eidus, Thaisa Frank, James Grady, Colette Inez, Susan Smith Nash, Zena Polin, Wena Poon, Pilar Quintana, Kris Saknussem, Tomaz Salamun, Lynda Sexson, Elisabeth Sheffield, Barry Silesky, Curtis Smith, Patricia Smith, Marilyn Stablein, Ronald Wallace. Length: 30 pages maximum; average length: 5-10 pages. Publishes short shorts. Also publishes literary essays, literary criticism, poetry. Sometimes comments on rejected mss. "We prefer electronic submissions. Please use submission engine online." For snail mail, send SASE for reply, return of ms; or send a disposable copy of ms. Sends galleys to author. Estab. 1976. Circ. 2,000. 12 months Accepts queries by online submission form. Accepts simultaneous submissions. Responds in 1month to queries, proposals, and to mss. Sample copy for $12.95. Catalog available online at FAQ link. "We don't have guidelines; we have never believed in them."

NONFICTION Needs memoir, photo feature, creative nonfiction, literary criticism. **Pays 10% of print run and so-so split (after/if) we break even. Sends galleys to author.**

FICTION Needs experimental, poetry, literary, short story collections. No romance, horror, science fiction **Buys 10-15 mss/year.** Query in an email. Reviews artwork. Length: 1,000-4,500 words.

THE GEORGIA REVIEW

The University of Georgia, Athens GA 30602. (706)542-3481. **Fax:** (706)542-0047. **E-mail:** garev@uga.edu. **Website:** www.uga.edu/garev. **Contact:** Stephen Corey, editor. **99% freelance written.** Quarterly journal. Our readers are educated, inquisitive people who read a lot of work in the areas we feature, so they expect only the best in our pages. All work submitted should show evidence that the writer is at least as well-educated and well-read as our readers. Essays should be authoritative but accessible to a range of readers. Estab. 1947. Circ. 3,500. Byline given. Publishes ms an average of 6 months after acceptance. Accepts queries by mail. Responds in 2 weeks to queries. Responds in 2-3 months to mss. Sample copy for $10. Guidelines available online.

NONFICTION Needs essays. For the most part we are not interested in scholarly articles that are narrow in focus and/or overly burdened with footnotes. The ideal essay for *The Georgia Review* is a provocative, thesis-oriented work that can engage both the intelligent general reader and the specialist. **Buys 12-20 mss/year.** Send complete ms. **Pays $40/published page.**

FICTION We seek original, excellent writing not bound by type. Ordinarily we do not publish novel excerpts or works translated into English, and we strongly discourage authors from submitting these. **Buys 12-20 mss/year.** Send complete ms. Open **Pays $50/published page.**

POETRY We seek original, excellent poetry. Submit 3-5 poems at a time. We do not accept submissions via fax or e-mail. If a submission is known to be included in a book already accepted by a publisher, please notify us of this fact (and of the anticipated date of book publication) in a cover letter. Reads year-round, but submissions postmarked May 15-August 15 will be returned unread. Always sends prepublication galleys. Pays $4/line, one-year subscription, and 1 contributor's copy. Acquires first North American serial rights. Reviews books of poetry. "Our poetry reviews range from 500-word 'Book Briefs' on single volumes to 5,000-word essay reviews on multiple volumes." Buys 60-75 poems/year. Submit maximum 5 poems. **Pays $4/line.**

$ THE GETTYSBURG REVIEW

Gettysburg College, Gettysburg PA 17325. (717)337-6770. **Fax:** (717)337-6775. **Website:** www.gettysburgreview.com. Quarterly magazine. "Our concern is quality. Manuscripts submitted here should be extremely well written. Reading period September-May." Estab. 1988. Circ. 3,000. Byline given. Publishes ms an average of 6 months after acceptance. Editorial lead time 1 year. Submit seasonal material 9 months in advance. Accepts queries by mail, fax. Accepts simultaneous submissions. Responds in 1 month to queries. Responds in 3-6 months to mss. Sample copy for $11. Guidelines available online.

NONFICTION Needs essays. **Buys 20 mss/year.** Send complete ms. Length: 3,000-7,000 words. **Pays $30/page.**

FICTION Contact: Mark Drew, assisant editor. High quality, literary. Needs experimental, historical, humorous, mainstream, novel concepts, serialized, contemporary. "We require that fiction be intelligent and esthetically written." **Buys 20 mss/year.** Send complete ms. Length: 2,000-7,000 words. **Pays $30/page.**

POETRY Buys 50 poems/year. Submit maximum 5 poems. **Pays $2.50/line.**

$$ GLIMMER TRAIN STORIES

Glimmer Train Press, Inc., 1211 NW Glisan St., Suite 207, Portland OR 97209. **Fax:** (503)221-0837. **E-mail:** eds@glimmertrain.org. **Website:** www.glimmertrain.org. **90% freelance written**. Quarterly magazine of literary short fiction. "We are interested in literary short stories, particularly by new and lightly published writers." Estab. 1991. Circ. 12,000. Byline given. Publishes ms an average of 18 months after acceptance. Accepts simultaneous submissions. Responds

CONSUMER MAGAZINES

in 2 months to mss. Sample copy for $12 on website. Guidelines available online.

FICTION Buys 40 mss/year. Submit via the website. In a pinch, send paper. up to 12,000 **Pays $700.**

GREEN MOUNTAINS REVIEW

Johnson State College, 337 College Hill, Johnson VT 05656. (802)635.1350. **E-mail:** gmr@jsc.vsc.edu. **Website:** http://greenmountainsreview.com/. **Contact:** Elizabeth Powell, poetry editor. Semiannual magazine covering poems, stories and creative nonfiction by both well-known authors and promising newcomers. The editors are open to a wide rane of styles and subject matter. Publishes ms 6-12 months after acceptance. Accepts queries by mail. Responds in 1 month to queries; 6 months to mss. Sample copy for $7. Guidelines available free.

NONFICTION Needs essays, book reviews, interview, literary criticism. Special issues: There may be special issues, as in the past.

FICTION Contact: Jacob White, fiction editor. Adventure, experimental, humor/satire, literary, mainstream, serialized novels, translations. Recently published work by Tracy Daugherty, Terese Svoboda, Walter Wetherell, T.M. McNally, J. Robert Lennon, Louis B. Jones, and Tom Whalen. Publishes short shorts. Also publishes literary criticism, poetry. Sometimes comments on rejected mss. Length: 1,000-7,500 words. **Pays contributor's copies, 1-year subscription and small honorarium, depending on grants.**

POETRY Contact: Elizabeth Powell, poetry editor. Has published poetry by Carol Frost, Sharon Olds, Carl Phillips, David St. John, and David Wojahn. Submit no more than 5 poems at a time.

$ $ GUD MAGAZINE

Greatest Uncommon Denominator Publishing, P.O. Box 1537, Laconia NH 03247. **E-mail:** editor@gudmagazine.com. **Website:** www.gudmagazine.com. **99% freelance written.** Semiannual magazine covering literary content and art. "*GUD Magazine* transcends and encompasses the audiences of both genre and literary fiction by featuring fiction, art, poetry, essays and reports, comics, and short drama." Estab. 2006. Byline given. Publishes ms an average of 6-12 months after acceptance. Editorial lead time 6 months. Submit seasonal material 6 months in advance. Accepts queries by online submission form. Accepts simultaneous submissions. Responds in 6 months to mss. Guidelines available online.

NONFICTION Needs book excerpts, essays, historical, humor, interview, personal experience, photo feature, travel, interesting event. **Buys 2-4 mss/year.** submit complete ms using online form Length: 1-15,000 words. **Pays $.03/word for first rights.**

FICTION Needs adventure, erotica, ethnic, experimental, fantasy, horror, humorous, science fiction, suspense. **Buys 40 mss/year.** Length: 1-15,000 words. **Pays $450.**

POETRY Needs avant-garde, free verse, haiku, light verse, traditional. Does not want anything that rhymes 'love' with 'above.' Buys 12-20 poems/year. **Pays $.03/word for first rights.**

FILLERS Buys comics. Reviews GIF/JPEG files. **Pays $12.**

$ GULF COAST: A JOURNAL OF LITERATURE AND FINE ARTS

University of Houston, Dept. of English, University of Houston, Houston TX 77204-3013. (713)743-3223. **E-mail:** editors@gulfcoastmag.org. **Website:** www.gulfcoastmag.org. Christine Ha, Eric Howerton, Edward Porter, fiction editors. **Contact:** The Editors. Biannual magazine covering innovative fiction, nonfiction, and poetry for the literary-minded. Buys 5-10 ms/year. Receives 300 unsolicited mss/month. Accepts 4-8 mss/issue; 12-16 mss/year. Agented fiction 5%. **Publishes 2-8 new writers/year.** Recently published work by Matt Bell, Megan Mayhew Bergman, Sarah Shun-Lien Bynum, Jenine Capot Crucet, Benjamin Percy, John Weir. Publishes short shorts. Sometimes comments on rejected mss. Estab. 1986. 6 months-1 year Accepts queries by mail, phone. Accepts simultaneous submissions. Responds in 4-6 months to mss. Writer's guidelines for #10 SASE or on website.

NONFICTION Contact: Nonfiction editor. Needs interview, reviews. **Gulf Coast reads general submissions, submitted by post or through the online submissions manager, from September 1 through March 1.** Submissions e-mailed directly to the editors, or postmarked between March 1 and Sept. 1, will not be read or responded to. Please visit our contest page for contest submission guidelines. **Pays $50 per review, and $100 per interview.**

FICTION Contact: Fiction editor. Buys 5-10 ms/year. Receives 300 unsolicited mss/month. Accepts 4-8 mss/issue; 12-16 mss/year. Publishes ms 6 months-1 year after acceptance. Agented fiction 5%. **Publishes 2-8 new writers/year.** Recently published work by

Matt Bell, Megan Mayhew Bergman, Sarah Shun-Lien Bynum, Jenine Capot Crucet, Benjamin Percy, John Weir. Publishes short shorts. Sometimes comments on rejected mss. Back issue for $7, 7×10 SASE with 4 first-class stamps. Please do not send multiple submissions; we will read only one submission per author at a given time, except in the case of our annual contests. Needs ethnic, experimental, multicultural, literary, regional, translations, contemporary. No children's, genre, religious/inspirational. **Gulf Coast reads general submissions, submitted by post or through the online submissions manager, from September 1 through March 1.** Submissions e-mailed directly to the editors, or postmarked between March 1 and Sept. 1, will not be read or responded to. Please visit our contest page for contest submission guidelines. Responds in 4-6 months to mss. Accepts simultaneous submissions. **Pays $-$100.**

POETRY Contact: Poetry editor. Submit maximum 1-5 poems.

THE G.W. REVIEW

The George Washington University, 800 21st St. NW, Marvin Center Box 20, Washington DC 20052. (202)994-7779. **E-mail:** gwreview@gwu.edu. **Website:** http://thegwreview.weebly.com. **100% freelance written.** Biannual magazine. "*The G.W. Review* seeks to exposé readers to new and emerging writers from both the United States and abroad. New, innovative writing—both in style and subject—is valued above the author's previous publishing history." Estab. 1980. Circ. 1,000. Byline given. Publishes ms an average of 3-6 months after acceptance. Editorial lead time 3 months. Submit seasonal material 4 months in advance. Accepts queries by mail, e-mail. Accepts simultaneous submissions. Responds in 2 months to queries. Responds in 3-6 months to mss. Sample copy for $7. Writer's guidelines on website or by e-mail.

NONFICTION "We are not accepting nonfiction pieces at this time."

FICTION Needs experimental, mainstream and novel concepts. "We do not publish genre fiction (i.e., romance, mystery, crime, etc.)." Send complete ms. Publishes 6 mss a year. Length: 1,000-6,000 words.

POETRY Needs avant-garde, traditional and free verse. Publishes 20 poems a year.

HARPUR PALATE

English Department, P.O. Box 6000, Binghamton University, Binghamton NY 13902-6000. **E-mail:** har-pur.palate@gmail.com. **Website:** http://harpurpalate.blogspot.com. **Contact:** Barrett Bowlin, managing editor. **100% freelance written.** Semiannual literary magazine. "We have no restrictions on subject matter or form. Quite simply, send us your highest-quality fiction and poetry." Estab. 2000. Circ. 700. Byline given. Publishes ms an average of 1-2 months after acceptance. Accepts simultaneous submissions. Responds in 8 months to mss. Sample copy for $8. Guidelines available online.

FICTION No more than 1 submission per envelope. Length: 250-8,000 words. **Pays 2 contributor copies.**

POETRY No more than 10 pages total. No response without SASE. Submit maximum 3-5 poems. **Pays 2 contributor copies.**

HAWAII REVIEW

University of Hawaii Board of Publications, 2445 Campus Rd., Hemenway Hall 107, Honolulu HI 96822. (808)956-3030. **Fax:** (808)956-3083. **E-mail:** hawaiireview@gmail.com. **Website:** www.kaleo.org/hawaii_review. **100% freelance written.** Semiannual magazine covering fiction, poetry, reviews, and art. Estab. 1973. Circ. 2,000. Byline given. Publishes ms an average of 3 months after acceptance. Accepts queries by e-mail, fax, phone. Accepts simultaneous submissions. Responds in 3 months to mss. Sample copy for $10. Guidelines available online.

NONFICTION Needs essays, interview. Send complete ms. Length: 0-10,000 words.

FICTION Needs confession, experimental, humorous, novel concepts, short fiction, short stories. Send complete ms.

POETRY Needs avant-garde, free verse, haiku, traditional. Submit maximum 6 poems.

🌐 HAYDEN'S FERRY REVIEW

c/o Virginia G. Piper Center for Creative Writing, Arizona State University, P.O. Box 875002, Tempe AZ 85287-5002. (480)965-1337. **E-mail:** HFR@asu.edu. **Website:** www.haydensferryreview.org. **Contact:** Beth Staples, managing editor. **85% freelance written.** Semiannual magazine. "*Hayden's Ferry Review* publishes the best quality fiction, poetry, and creative nonfiction from new, emerging, and established writers." Estab. 1986. Circ. 1,300. Byline given. Publishes ms an average of 6 months after acceptance. Editorial lead time 5 months. Accepts queries by online submission form. Accepts simultaneous submissions. Responds in 1 week or less to e-mail queries. Responds in

3-4 months to mss. Sample copy for $7.50. Guidelines available online.

NONFICTION Needs essays, interview, personal experience. **Buys 2 mss/year.** Send complete ms. Word length open **Pays $50.**

FICTION Contact: Editors change every 1-2 years. Needs ethnic, experimental, humorous, slice-of-life vignettes, contemporary, prose poem. **Buys 10 mss/year.** Send complete ms. Word length open.

POETRY Needs avant-garde, free verse, haiku, light verse, traditional. Buys 60 poems/year. Submit maximum 6 poems. Word length open. **Pays $50.**

$ HOBART

P.O. Box 1658, Ann Arbor MI 48103. **E-mail:** aaron@hobartpulp.com. **Website:** www.hobartpulp.com. Website covering short stories, personal essays, short interviews, comics, roundtable discussions. "We tend to like quirky stories like truck driving, mathematics and vagabonding. We like stories with humor (humorous but engaging, literary but not stuffy). We want to get excited about your story and hope you'll send your best work." Accepts queries by e-mail. "If our response time is longer than 3 mos., feel free to inquire." Responds in 1-3 months to mss.

NONFICTION Needs essays, personal., humor, interview, short., Roundtable Discussions. **Pays $50-150.**

$ THE HOLLINS CRITIC

P.O. Box 9538, Hollins University, Roanoke VA 24020-1538. **E-mail:** acockrell@hollins.edu. **Website:** www.hollins.edu/academics/critic. **Contact:** Cathryn Hankla. **100% freelance written.** Magazine published 5 times/year. Estab. 1964. Circ. 400. Byline given. Publishes ms an average of 1 year after acceptance. Accepts queries by online submission form. Submit at www.hollinscriticssubmissions.com. Accepts simultaneous submissions. Responds in 2 months to mss. Sample copy for $3. Guidelines for #10 SASE.

POETRY Needs avant-garde, free verse, traditional. Submit up to 5 poems at a time using the online submission form at www.hollinscriticsubmissions.com, available from September 15-December 1. Submissions received at other times will be returned unread. Responds in 6 weeks. Pays $25/poem plus 5 contributor's copies. "We read poetry only from September 1-December 15." Buys Publishes 16-20 poems/year. poems/year.

$ THE HUDSON REVIEW

The Hudson Review, Inc., 684 Park Ave., New York NY 10065. **Website:** www.hudsonreview.com. **Contact:** Paula Deitz. **100% freelance written.** Quarterly magazine publishing fiction, poetry, essays, book reviews; criticism of literature, art, theatre, dance, film and music; and articles on contemporary cultural developments. Estab. 1948. Circ. 2,000. Byline given. Publishes ms an average of 6 months after acceptance. Editorial lead time 3 months. Accepts queries by mail. Responds in 6 months. Sample copy for $10. Guidelines for #10 SASE or online.

NONFICTION Contact: Paula Deitz. Needs essays, general interest, historical, opinion, personal experience, travel. **Buys 4-6 mss/year.** Send complete ms between January 1 and March 31 only 3,500 words maximum **Pays 2½¢/word.**

FICTION Reads between September 1 and November 30 only. **Buys 4 mss/year.** 10,000 words maximum. **Pays 2½¢/word.**

POETRY Reads poems only between April 1 and June 30. Buys 12-20 poems/year. Submit maximum 7 poems. **Pays 50¢/line.**

$ HUNGER MOUNTAIN

Vermont College of Fine Arts, 36 College St., Montpelier VT 05602. (802)828-8517. **E-mail:** hungermtn@vermontcollege.edu. **Website:** www.hungermtn.org. Monthly online publication and annual perfect-bound journal covering high quality fiction, poetry, creative nonfiction, craft essaus, writing for children, and artwork. Accepts high quality work from unknown, emerging, or successful writers. No genre fiction, drama, or academic articles, please. Estab. 2002. Byline given. Publishes ms an average of 1 year after acceptance. "Submit online or by mail. Please see www.hungermtn.org for complete guidelines before submitting." Submit seasonal material 1 year in advance. Accepts simultaneous submissions. Responds in 4 months to mss. Sample copy for $10. Writer's guidelines online.

NONFICTION No informative or instructive articles, please. Prose for young adults is acceptable. Payment varies. Prose for children and young adults is acceptable. Payment varies. Query with published clips.

FICTION Needs adventure, high quality short stories and short shorts. No genre fiction, meaning science fiction, fantasy, horror, erotic, etc. Query with published clips. **Pays $25-100.**

POETRY Needs avant-garde, free verse, traditional. No light verse, humor/quirky/catchy verse, greeting card verse. Buys 10 poems/year.

$ IDEAGEMS

IdeaGems Publications, P.O. Box 4748, Portland ME 04112. (202)746-5160. **E-mail:** ideagems@aol.com. **Website:** www.ideagems.com. **Contact:** Laurie Notch, managing editor. **40-50% freelance written.** Hard-copy periodical AND e-zine containing serial stories (fact and fiction), serial graphic novels, poetry, flash fiction, articles, and artwork on women-centered experiences and adventures. "Monthly feuilleton that includes women-centered adventure, suspense, and mystery stories laced with romance and intrigue. We present a variety of serial stories, flash fiction, articles, and illustrations similar to the days of yore when Dickensian frame stories, dime novels, and penny dreadfuls were all the rage. Most of our tales are made up, but some are based on truth. We also include poetry, photography, and original artwork to add eye-pleasing color to our non-glossy journal. We do not deal with women's issues or offer lifestyle tips. Our stories portray average women in fantastic, nail-biting situations." Estab. 2006. Circ. 2,000. Byline given. Publishes ms an average of 1-3 months after acceptance. Editorial lead time 1-3 months. Submit seasonal material 3 months in advance. Accepts queries by mail, e-mail. Accepts simultaneous submissions. Free sample PDF copy opon request. Guidelines by email and on website.

NONFICTION Needs book excerpts, essays, exposé, historical, humor, inspirational, interview, opinion, personal experience, photo feature, photo feature essays of women on the job, technical, travel, exotic journeys—not touristy travelogues, women running their own businesses, encounters with the paranormal. Special issues: New special issue, "TOUGH LIT" is out regularly now. Dedicated to crime, grit, mystery, and suspense writers. Send submissions to e-mail. Does not want religious, pornographic, or conservative political material. **Buys 1-4 mss/year.** Query. Length: 500-7,500 words. **"Sorry, we can no longer pay for accepted submissions. We offer free publicity and promotion online and in print plus a complimentary PDF copy."**

FICTION "We are open to any work of imagination and whimsy where women play central roles. We love stories that tackle issues; however, we do not invite stories with strong religions overtones, racial/gender prejudice, or political bents for the purposes of zealous expostulating. We are not able to review any full-length novels or graphic novels at this time, but you can always send a query and a sample chapter for us to consider running as serialized material." Needs adventure, ethnic, experimental, fantasy, historical, horror, humorous, mystery, novel concepts, romance, science fiction, serialized, slice-of-life vignettes, suspense, "Get us your ghoulish, gory, ghastly, ghostly stories, poems, photos, and artwork for our fearsome fall issue!. Query. Length: 150-7,500 words. Flash Fiction: 100-500 words. Article: 500 to 2,500 words. Novel excerpt: up to 3 chapters. Short story: 1,500 to 5,000 words.

POETRY Needs avant-garde, free verse, haiku, light verse, traditional. Buys 1-10 poems/year. Submit maximum 2 poems. Length: 3-50 lines.

$ ILLUMEN

Sam's Dot Publishing, P.O. Box 782, Cedar Rapids IA 52406-0782. **E-mail:** illumensdp@yahoo.com. **Website:** www.samsdotpublishing.com/aoife/cover.htm. **Contact:** Karen L. Newman, editor. **100% freelance written.** Semiannual magazine. "*Illumen* publishes speculative poetry and articles about speculative poetry, and reviews of poetry and collections." Estab. 2004. Circ. 40. Byline given. Offers 100% kill fee. Editorial lead time 2 months. Submit seasonal material 6 months in advance. Accepts queries by e-mail. Responds in 2 weeks to queries. Responds in 3-4 months to mss. Sample copy for $8. Guidelines available online.

NONFICTION **Buys 5-8 mss/year.** Send complete ms. Length: 2,000 words. **Pays $10 for unsolicited articles.**

POETRY Needs avant-garde, free verse, haiku, light verse, traditional. "Scifaiku is a difficult sell with us because we also publish a specialty magazine—*Scifaikuest*—for scifaiku and related forms." Buys 40-50 poems/year. Submit maximum 5 poems. Length: 200 lines. **Pays 1-2¢/word.**

$ INDIANA REVIEW

Ballantine Hall 465, 1020 E. Kirkwood, Indiana University, Bloomington IN 47405-7103. (812)855-3439. **E-mail:** inreview@indiana.edu. **Website:** www.indiana.edu/~inreview. **100% freelance written.** Biannual magazine. "*Indiana Review*, a nonprofit organization run by IU graduate students, is a journal of previously

CONSUMER MAGAZINES

unpublished poetry and fiction. Literary interviews and essays are also considered. We publish innovative fiction, nonfiction, and poetry. We're interested in energy, originality, and careful attention to craft. While we publish many well-known writers, we also welcome new and emerging poets and fiction writers." Estab. 1976. Circ. 5,000. Byline given. Publishes ms an average of 3-6 months after acceptance. Accepts queries by mail, e-mail. Accepts simultaneous submissions. Responds in 2 or more weeks to queries. Responds in 4 or more months to mss. Sample copy for $9. Guidelines available online.

NONFICTION Needs essays, interview, creative nonfiction, reviews. No coming of age/slice of life pieces. **Buys 5-7 mss/year.** Send complete ms. 9,000 words maximum. **Pays $5/page ($10 minimum), plus 2 contributor's copies.**

FICTION Contact: Danny Nguyen, fiction editor. "We look for daring stories which integrate theme, language, character, and form. We like polished writing, humor, and fiction which has consequence beyond the world of its narrator." Needs ethnic, experimental, mainstream, novel concepts, literary, short fictions, translations. No genre fiction. **Buys 14-18 mss/year.** Send complete ms. Length: 250-10,000 words. **Pays $5/page ($10 minimum), plus 2 contributor's copies.**

POETRY Contact: Hannah Faith Notess, poetry editor. "We look for poems that are skillful and bold, exhibiting an inventiveness of language with attention to voice and sonics. Experimental, free verse, prose poem, traditional form, lyrical, narrative." Buys 80 poems/year. Submit maximum 6 poems. 5 lines minimum **Pays $5/page ($10 minimum), plus 2 contributor's copies.**

$ $ INKWELL

Manhattanville College, 2900 Purchase St., Purchase NY 10577. (914)323-7239. **Fax:** (914)323-3122. **E-mail:** inkwell@mville.edu. **Website:** www.inkwelljournal.org. **100% freelance written**. Semiannual magazine covering poetry, fiction, essays, artwork, and photography. Estab. 1995. Byline given. Publishes ms an average of 4 months after acceptance. Editorial lead time 4 months. Accepts simultaneous submissions. Responds in 1 month to queries. Responds in 4-6 months to mss. Sample copy for $6. Guidelines free.

NONFICTION Needs book excerpts, essays, literary essays, memoirs. Does not want children's literature, erotica, pulp adventure, or science fiction. **Buys 3-4 mss/year.** Send complete ms. 5,000 words maximum **Pays $100-350.**

FICTION Needs mainstream, novel concepts, literary. Does not want children's literature, erotica, pulp adventure, or science fiction. **Buys 20 mss/year.** Send complete ms. 5,000 words maximum **Pays $75-150.**

POETRY Needs avant-garde, free verse, traditional. Does not want doggerel, funny poetry, etc. Buys 40 poems/year. Submit maximum 5 poems. **Pays $5-10/page.**

$ IRREANTUM

The Association for Mormon Letters, P.O. Box 1315, Salt Lake City UT 84110-1315. **E-mail:** editor@amlpubs.org. **Website:** www.irreantum.org. Literary journal published 2 times/year. "While focused on Mormonism, *Irreantum* is a cultural, humanities-oriented magazine, not a religious magazine. Our guiding principle is that Mormonism is grounded in a sufficiently unusual, cohesive, and extended historical and cultural experience that it has become like a nation, an ethnic culture. We can speak of Mormon literature at least as surely as we can of a Jewish or Southern literature. *Irreantum* publishes stories, one-act dramas, stand-alone novel and drama excerpts, and poetry by, for, or about Mormons (as well as author interviews, essays, and reviews). The journal's audience includes readers of any or no religious faith who are interested in literary exploration of the Mormon culture, mindset, and worldview through Mormon themes and characters either directly or by implication. *Irreantum* is currently the only magazine devoted to Mormon literature." Estab. 1999. Circ. 500. Publishes ms an average of 3-12 months after acceptance. Accepts queries by e-mail. Accepts simultaneous submissions. Responds in 2 weeks to queries. Responds in 2 months to mss. Sample copy for $6. Guidelines by email.

FICTION Needs adventure, ethnic, Mormon, experimental, fantasy, historical, horror, humorous, mainstream, mystery, religious, romance, science fiction, suspense. **Buys 12 mss/year.** Length: 1,000-5,000 words. **Pays $0-100.**

$ ISLAND

P.O. Box 210, Sandy Bay Tasmania 7006 Australia. (61)(3)6226-2325. **E-mail:** island.magazine@utas.edu.au. **Website:** www.islandmag.com. Quarterly magazine. "*Island* seeks quality fiction, poetry, essays, and articles. A literary magazine with an environmental heart." Circ. 1,500. Accepts queries by e-mail and submissions only online via website. Subscriptions and sample copies available for purchase online. Guidelines available online.

NONFICTION Pays $150 (Australian)/1,000 words.

FICTION Length: up to 2,500 words. **Pays $150 (Australian).**

POETRY Pays $100.

$ THE JOURNAL

The Ohio State University, 164 W. 17th Ave., Columbus OH 43210. (614)292-4076. **Fax:** (614)292-7816. **E-mail:** thejournal@osu.edu; thejournalmag@gmail.com. **Website:** english.osu.edu/research/journals/thejournal/. **100% freelance written**. Semiannual magazine. "We're open to all forms; we tend to favor work that gives evidence of a mature and sophisticated sense of the language." Estab. 1972. Circ. 1,500. Byline given. Publishes ms an average of 1 year after acceptance. Accepts queries by mail, online submission form. Accepts simultaneous submissions. Responds in 2 weeks to queries. Responds in 2 months to mss. Sample copy for $7 or online. Guidelines available online.

NONFICTION Needs essays, interview. **Buys 2 mss/year.** Query. Length: 2,000-4,000 words. **Pays $20 maximum.**

COLUMNS Reviews of contemporary poetry, 1,500 words maximum **Buys 2 mss/year.** Query. **Pays $20.**

FICTION Needs novel concepts, literary short stories. No romance, science fiction or religious/devotional. Open **Pays $20.**

POETRY Needs avant-garde, free verse, traditional. Buys 100 poems/year. Submit maximum 5 poems. **Pays $20.**

$ THE KENYON REVIEW

Finn House, 102 W. Wiggin, Gambier OH 43022. (740)427-5208. **Fax:** (740)427-5417. **E-mail:** kenyonreview@kenyon.edu. **Website:** KenyonReview.org. **Contact:** Marlene Landefeld. **100% freelance written**. Quarterly magazine covering contemporary literature and criticism. "An international journal of literature, culture, and the arts, dedicated to an inclusive representation of the best in new writing (fiction, poetry, essays, interviews, criticism) from established and emerging writers." Estab. 1939. Circ. 6,000. Byline given. Publishes ms an average of 1 year after acceptance. Editorial lead time 1 year. Submit seasonal material 1 year in advance. Responds in 4 months to mss. Sample copy $10, includes postage and handling. Please call or e-mail to order. Guidelines available online.

FICTION Needs condensed novels, ethnic, experimental, historical, humorous, mainstream, contemporary. 3-15 typeset pages preferred **Pays $30-40/page.**

$ THE KIT-CAT REVIEW

244 Halstead Ave., Harrison NY 10528. (914)835-4833. **E-mail:** kitcatreview@gmail.com. **Contact:** Claudia Fletcher, editor. **100% freelance written**. Quarterly magazine. "*The Kit-Cat Review* is named after the 18th Century Kit-Cat Club, whose members included Addison, Steele, Congreve, Vanbrugh, and Garth. It is part of the collections of the Univ. of Wisconsin, Madison, and the State Univ. of New York, Buffalo. Its purpose is to promote/discover excellence and originality." Estab. 1998. Circ. 500. Byline given. Publishes ms an average of 6-12 months after acceptance. Accepts queries by mail, phone. Accepts simultaneous submissions. Responds in 1 week to queries. Responds in 2 months to mss. Sample copy for $7 (payable to Claudia Fletcher). Guidelines for SASE.

NONFICTION Needs book excerpts, essays, general interest, historical, humor, interview, personal experience, travel. **Buys 6 mss/year.** Send complete ms with brief bio and SASE 5,000 words maximum **Pays $25-100.**

FICTION Needs ethnic, experimental, novel concepts, slice-of-life vignettes. No stories with O. Henry-type formula endings. Shorter pieces stand a better chance of publication. No science fiction, fantasy, romance, horror, or new age. **Buys 20 mss/year.** Send complete ms. 5,000 words maximum **Pays $25-100 and 2 contributor's copies; additional copies $5.**

POETRY Needs free verse, traditional. No excessively obscure poetry. Buys 100 poems/year. **Pays $20-100.**

✪ $ THE MALAHAT REVIEW

The University of Victoria, P.O. Box 1700, STN CSC, Victoria BC V8W 2Y2 Canada. (250)721-8524. **E-mail:** malahat@uvic.ca (for queries only). **Website:** www.malahatreview.ca. **Contact:** John Barton, editor. **100% freelance written. Eager to work with new/unpublished writers**. Quarterly magazine covering poetry, fiction, creative nonfiction, and reviews. "We try to achieve a balance of views and styles in each issue. We strive for a mix of the best writing by both established and new writers." Estab. 1967. Circ. 1,500. Byline given. Publishes ms an average of 6 months after acceptance. Accepts queries by mail. NoResponds in 2 weeks to queries. Responds in 3-10 months to mss. Sample copy for $16.95 (US). Guidelines available online.

NONFICTION Include SASE with Canadian postage or IRCs. **Pays $30/magazine page.**

FICTION Needs general fiction and creative nonfiction. **Buys 12-14 mss/year.** Send complete ms. 8,000 words max. **Pays $30/magazine page.**

POETRY Needs avant-garde, free verse, traditional. Buys 100 poems/year. 5-10 pages **Pays $20/magazine page.**

$ $ MANOA

English Dept., University of Hawaii, Honolulu HI 96822. (808)956-3070. **Fax:** (808)956-3083. **E-mail:** mjournal-l@listserv.hawaii.edu. **Website:** manoajournal.hawaii.edu. **Contact:** Frank Stewart, Poetry Editor. Semiannual magazine. "High quality literary fiction, poetry, essays, personal narrative. In general, each issue is devoted to new work from Pacific and Asian nations. Our audience is international. US writing need not be confined to Pacific settings or subjects. Please note that we seldom publish unsolicited work." Estab. 1989. Circ. 2,000 print, 10,000 digital. Byline given. Editorial lead time 9 months. Accepts simultaneous submissions. Responds in 3 weeks to queries; 1 month to poetry mss; 6 months to fiction. Sample copy for $15 (US). Guidelines available online.

NONFICTION No Pacific exotica. Query first. Length: 1,000-5,000 words. **Pays $25/printed page.**

FICTION Query first and/or see website. Needs mainstream, contemporary, excerpted novel. No Pacific exotica. **Buys 1-2 in the US (excluding translation) mss/year.** Send complete ms. Length: 1,000-7,500 words. **Pays $100-500 normally ($25/printed page).**

POETRY No light verse. Buys 10-20 poems/year. Submit maximum 5-6 poems. **Pays $25/poem.**

$ THE MASSACHUSETTS REVIEW

South College, University of Massachusetts, Amherst MA 01003-9934. (413)545-2689. **Fax:** (413)577-0740. **E-mail:** massrev@external.umass.edu. **Website:** www.massreview.org. Quarterly magazine. Estab. 1959. Circ. 1,200. Publishes ms an average of 18 months after acceptance. Accepts queries by mail. Accepts simultaneous submissions. Responds in 3 months to mss. Sample copy for $8. Guidelines available online.

💬 Does not respond to mss without SASE.

NONFICTION No reviews of single books. Send complete ms or query with SASE 6,500 words maximum. **Pays $50.**

FICTION short stories. Wants more prose less than 30 pages. **Buys 10 mss/year.** Send complete ms. 25-30 pages maximum.

POETRY Submit maximum 6 poems. **Pays 50¢/line to $25 maximum.**

$ MICHIGAN QUARTERLY REVIEW

0576 Rackham Bldg., 915 E. Washington, University of Michigan, Ann Arbor MI 48109-1070. (734)764-9265. **E-mail:** mqr@umich.edu. **Website:** www.umich.edu/~mqr. **Contact:** Jonathan Freedman, editor; Vicki Lawrence, managing editor. **75% freelance written.** Quarterly magazine. "MQR is an eclectic interdisciplinary journal of arts and culture that seeks to combine the best of poetry, fiction, and creative nonfiction with outstanding critical essays on literary, cultural, social, and political matters. The flagship journal of the University of Michigan, MQR draws on lively minds here and elsewhere, seeking to present accessible work of all varieties for sophisticated readers from within and without the academy." Estab. 1962. Circ. 1,000. Byline given. Publishes ms an average of 1 year after acceptance. Accepts queries by mail. Responds in 2 months to queries. Responds in 2 months to mss. Sample copy for $4. Guidelines available online.

NONFICTION Buys 35 mss/year. Query. Length: 2,000-5,000 words. **Pays $10/published page.**

FICTION Contact: Fiction Editor. "No restrictions on subject matter or language. We are very selective. We like stories which are unusual in tone and structure, and innovative in language. No genre fiction written for a market. Would like to see more fiction about social, political, cultural matters, not just centered on a love relationship or dysfunctional family." **Buys 10 mss/year.** Send complete ms. Length: 1,500-7,000 words. **Pays $10/published page.**

POETRY Pays $10/published page.

$ MID-AMERICAN REVIEW

Bowling Green State University, Department of English, Box W, Bowling Green OH 43403. (419)372-2725. **E-mail:** mikeczy@bgsu.edu. **Website:** www.bgsu.edu/midamericanreview. **Contact:** Michael Czyzniejewski. **Willing to work with new/unpublished writers.** Biannual magazine of the highest quality fiction, poetry, and translations of contemporary poetry and fiction. Also publishes critical articles and book reviews of contemporary literature. "We try to put the best possible work in front of the biggest possible audience. We publish serious fiction and poetry, as well as critical studies in contemporary literature, translations and book reviews." Estab. 1981. Circ. 700. Byline given. Pays on publication when funding is available. Publishes ms an average of 6 months after acceptance. Accepts queries by online submission form. Responds in 5 months to mss. Sample copy for $7 (current issue); $5 (back issue); $10 (rare back issues). Guidelines available online.

NONFICTION Needs essays, articles focusing on contemporary authors and topics of current literary interest, short book reviews (500-1,000 words). **Pays $10/page up to $50, pending funding.**

FICTION Contact: Michael Czyzniejewski, fiction editor. Character-oriented, literary, experimental, short short. Needs experimental, Memoir, prose poem, traditional. No genre fiction. Would like to see more short shorts. **Buys 12 mss/year.** 6,000 words **Pays $10/page up to $50, pending funding.**

POETRY Contact: Contacts: Brad Modlin, poetry editor; Angela Gentry and David D. Williams, assistant poetry editors. Buys 60 poems/year. **Pays $10/page up to $50, pending funding.**

THE MIDWEST QUARTERLY

406b Russ Hall, Pittsburg State University, Pittsburg KS 66762. (620)235-4369; (620)235-4317. **E-mail:** midwestq@pittstate.edu; smeats@pittstate.edu. **Website:** www.pittstate.edu/department/english/midwest-quarterly. **Contact:** James B. M. Schick. Quarterly magazine covering scholarly articles for the academic audience dealing with a broad range of subjects of current interest, and poetry. *The Midwest Quarterly* publishes "articles on any subject of contemporary interest, particularly literary criticism, political science, philosophy, education, biography, and sociology. Each issue contains a section of poetry usually 12 poems in length. We seek discussions of an analytical and speculative nature and well-crafted poems. Poems of interest to us use intense, vivid, concrete and/or surrealistic images to explore the mysterious and surprising interactions of the nature and inner human worlds." Estab. 1959. Contest winnings. Accepts queries by mail, e-mail, fax, phone. Accepts simultaneous submissions. Guidelines available online.

NONFICTION Needs essays. No heavily documented research studies.

COLUMNS "*TMQ* no longer publishes book reviews."

POETRY Contact: Dr. Stephen Meats, poetry editor. Needs avant-garde, traditional.

MISSISSIPPI REVIEW

Univ. of Southern Mississippi, 118 College Dr., #5144, Hattiesburg MS 39406-0001. (601)266-4321. **Fax:** (601)266-5757. **E-mail:** elizabeth@mississippireview.com. **Website:** www.mississippireview.com. Semiannual. "Literary publication for those interested in contemporary literature—writers, editors who read to be in touch with current modes." Estab. 1972. Circ. 1,500. Sample copy for $10.

FICTION Contact: Rie Fortenberry, managing editor. Needs experimental, fantasy, humorous, contemporary, avant-garde and art fiction. No juvenile or genre fiction. 30 pages maximum.

THE MISSOURI REVIEW

357 McReynolds Hall, University of Missouri, Columbia MO 65211. (573)882-4474. **Fax:** (573)884-4671. **E-mail:** tmr@missourireview.com. **Website:** www.missourireview.com. **90% freelance written.** Quarterly magazine. Estab. 1978. Circ. 6,500. Byline given. Offers signed contract. Editorial lead time 6 months. Accepts queries by mail. Responds in 2 weeks to queries. Responds in 10 weeks to mss. Sample copy for $8.95 or online. Guidelines available online.

NONFICTION Contact: Evelyn Somers, associate editor. Needs book excerpts, essays. No literary criticism. **Buys 10 mss/year.** Send complete ms. **Pays $1,000.**

FICTION Contact: Speer Morgan, editor. Needs ethnic, humorous, mainstream, novel concepts, literary. No genre or flash fiction. **Buys 25 mss/year.** Send complete ms. no preference. **Pays $30/printed page.**

POETRY Contact: Jason Koo, poetry editor. Publishes 3-5 poetry features of 6-12 pages per issue. Please familiarize yourself with the magazine before submitting poetry. Buys 50 poems/year. **Pays $30/printed page.**

MODERN HAIKU

P.O. Box 33077, Santa Fe NM 87594-3077. **E-mail:** modernhaiku@gmail.com. **Website:** http://modernhaiku.org. **85% freelance written.** Magazine published 3 times/year. "*Modern Haiku* publishes high quality material only. Haiku and related genres, articles on haiku, haiku book reviews, and translations comprise its contents. It has an international circulation; subscribers include many university, school, and public libraries." Estab. 1969. Circ. 650. Byline given. Publishes ms an average of 6 months after acceptance. Editorial lead time 4 months. Accepts queries by mail, e-mail. "Now accepts submissions by e-mail; please review submission guidelines on website." Responds in 1 week to queries. Responds in 6-8 weeks to mss. Sample copy for $13 in North America, $14 in Canada, $17 in Mexico, $30 overseas. Payment possible by PayPal on the *Modern Haiku* website. Guidelines available online.

NONFICTION Needs essays, anything related to haiku. Send complete ms. **Pays $5/page.**

COLUMNS Haiku & Senryu; Haibun; Essays (on haiku and related genres); Reviews (books of haiku or related genres). **Buys 40 essay and review mss/year (most are commissioned). mss/year.** Send complete ms. **Pays $5/page.**

POETRY Needs haiku, senryu, haibun, haiga. Submissions: Guidelines available for SASE or on website. No previously published haiku or simultaneous submissions. Responds in 4-6weeks. No contributor's copies. Acquires first international serial rights. Postal submissions: "Send 5-15 haiku on 1 or 2 letter-sized sheets. Put name and address at the top of each sheet. Include SASE." Pays $1 per haiku. E-mail submissions: "May be attachments (recommended) or pasted in body of message. Subject line must read: MH submission. Adhere to guidelines on the website. No payment for accepted haiku." Reviews of books of haiku by staff and freelancers by invitation in 350-1,000 words, usually single-book format. Send materials for review consideration with complete ordering information. Reviews of books of haiku by staff and freelancers by invitation in 350-1,000 words, usually single-book format. Send materials for review consideration with complete ordering information Does not want "general poetry, tanka, linked verse forms." Buys 750 poems/year. Submit maximum 24 poems. **Pays $1 per haiku by postal mail only (not for e-mail).**

$ NEW ENGLAND REVIEW

Middlebury College, Middlebury VT 05753. (802)443-5075. **E-mail:** nereview@middlebury.edu. **Website:** go.middlebury.edu/nereview; www.nereview.com. Quarterly magazine. Literary only. Reads September 1-May 31 (postmarked dates). Estab. 1978. Circ. 2,000. Byline given. Publishes ms an average of 6 months after acceptance. Accepts simultaneous submissions. Responds in 2 weeks to queries. Responds in 3 months to mss. Sample copy for $10 (add $5 for overseas). Guidelines available online.

💬 No e-mail submissions.

NONFICTION Buys 20-25 mss/year. Send complete ms. 7,500 words maximum, though exceptions may be made. **Pays $10/page ($20 minimum), and 2 copies.**

FICTION Send 1 story at a time, unless it is very short. Serious literary only, novel excerpts. **Buys 25 mss/year.** Send complete ms. Prose length: not strict on word count **Pays $10/page ($20 minimum), and 2 copies.**

POETRY Buys 75-90 poems/year. Submit maximum 6 poems. **Pays $10/page ($20 minimum), and 2 copies.**

TIPS "We consider short fiction, including short-shorts, novellas, and self-contained extracts from novels in both traditional and experimental forms. In nonfiction, we consider a variety of general and literary, but not narrowly scholarly essays; we also publish long and short poems; screenplays; graphics; translations; critical reassessments; statements by artists working in various media; testimonies; and letters from abroad. We are committed to exploration of all forms of contemporary cultural expression in the US and abroad. With few exceptions, we print only work not published previously elsewhere."

$ NEW LETTERS

University of Missouri-Kansas City, 5101 Rockhill Rd., Kansas City MO 64110. (816)235-1168. **Fax:** (816)235-2611. **E-mail:** newletters@umkc.edu. **Website:** www.newletters.org. **100% freelance written.** Quarterly magazine. Estab. 1934. Circ. 5,000. Byline given. Publishes ms an average of 6 months after acceptance. Editorial lead time 6 months. Submit seasonal material 6 months in advance. Accepts queries by mail. Responds in 1 month to queries; 5 months to mss. Sample copy for $10 or sample articles on website. Guidelines available online.

NONFICTION Needs essays. No self-help, how-to, or nonliterary work. **Buys 8-10 mss/year.** Send complete ms. 5,000 words maximum. **Pays $40-100.**

FICTION Contact: Robert Stewart, editor. Needs ethnic, experimental, humorous, mainstream, contemporary. No genre fiction. **Buys 15-20 mss/year.** Send complete ms. 5,000 words maximum. **Pays $30-75.**

POETRY Needs avant-garde, free verse, haiku, traditional. No light verse. Buys 40-50 poems/year. Submit maximum 6 poems. Open. **Pays $10-25.**

⊛ NEW ORLEANS REVIEW

Box 195, Loyola University, New Orleans LA 70118. (504)865-2295. **E-mail:** noreview@loyno.edu. **Website:** http://neworleansreview.org. **Contact:** Christopher Chambers, editor; Amberly Fox, managing editor. Biannual magazine publishing poetry, fiction, translations, photographs, and nonfiction on literature, art and film. Readership: those interested in contemporary literature and culture. New Orleans Review is a journal of contemporary literature and culture, publishing new poetry, fiction, nonfiction, art, photography, film and book reviews. The journal was founded in 1968 and has since published an eclectic variety of work by established and emerging writers including Walker Percy, Pablo Neruda, Ellen Gilchrist, Nelson Algren, Hunter S. Thompson, John Kennedy Toole, Richard Brautigan, Barry Spacks, James Sallis, Jack Gilbert, Paul Hoover, Rodney Jones, Annie Dillard, Everette Maddox, Julio Cortazar, Gordon Lish, Robert Walser, Mark Halliday, Jack Butler, Robert Olen Butler, Michael Harper, Angela Ball, Joyce Carol Oates, Diane Wakoski, Dermot Bolger, Roddy Doyle, William Kotzwinkle, Alain Robbe-Grillet, Arnost Lustig, Raymond Queneau, Yusef Komunyakaa, Michael Martone, Tess Gallagher, Matthea Harvey, D. A. Powell, Rikki Ducornet, and Ed Skoog. Estab. 1968. Circ. 1,500. Accepts queries by online submission form. Accepts simultaneous submissions. Responds in 4 months to mss. Sample copy for $5.

FICTION Contact: Christopher Chambers, editor. Good writing, from conventional to experimental. We are now using an online submission system and require a $3 fee. See website for details. Length: up to 6,500 words. **Pays $25-50 and 2 copies.**

POETRY Submit maximum 3-6 poems.

◯ ⊛⊛ THE NEW QUARTERLY

St. Jerome's University, 290 Westmount Rd. N., Waterloo ON N2L 3G3 Canada. (519)884-8111, ext. 28290. **E-mail:** editor@tnq.ca; pmulloy@tnq.ca. **Website:** www.tnq.ca. **95% freelance written**. Quarterly book covering Canadian fiction and poetry. "Emphasis on emerging writers and genres, but we publish more traditional work as well if the language and narrative structure are fresh." Estab. 1981. Circ. 1,000. Byline given. Publishes ms an average of 4 months after acceptance. Editorial lead time 6 months. Accepts queries by mail. Accepts simultaneous submissions. Responds in 2 weeks to queries. Responds in 4 months

to mss. Sample copy for $16.50 (cover price, plus mailing). Guidelines for #10 SASE or online.

◯ Open to Canadian writers only.

FICTION "*Canadian work only.* We are not interested in genre fiction. We are looking for innovative, beautifully crafted, deeply felt literary fiction." **Buys 20-25 mss/year.** Send complete ms. Does not accept submissions by e-mail. Accepts simultaneoues submissions if indicated in cover letter. 20 pages maximum **Pays $200/story**.

POETRY Needs avant-garde, free verse, traditional. *Canadian work only.* Buys 40 poems/year. Submit maximum 3 poems. **Pays $40/poem.**

⊜ ⊛ THE NEW WRITER

P.O. Box 60, Cranbrook Kent TN17 2ZR United Kingdom. (44)(158)021-2626. **E-mail:** editor@thenewwriter.com. **Website:** www.thenewwriter.com. **Contact:** Sarah Jackson, poetry editor. Publishes 6 issues per annum. "Contemporary writing magazine which publishes the best in fact, fiction and poetry." Estab. 1996. Circ. 1,500. Publishes ms an average of 1 year after acceptance. Accepts queries by e-mail, fax. Accepts simultaneous submissions. Responds in 2 months to queries. Responds in 4 months to mss. Sample copy for SASE and A4 SAE with IRCs only. Guidelines for SASE.

NONFICTION Query. Length: 1,000-2,000 words. **Pays £20-40.**

FICTION *No unsolicited mss.* Accepts fiction from subscribers only. "We will consider most categories apart from stories written for children. No horror, erotic, or cosy fiction." Query with published clips. Length: 2,000-5,000 words. **Pays £10 per story by credit voucher; additional copies for £1.50.**

POETRY Buys 50 poems/year. Submit maximum 3 poems. 40 lines maximum **Pays £3/poem.**

⊛ NORTH AMERICAN REVIEW

University of Northern Iowa, 1222 W. 27th St., Cedar Falls IA 50614. (319)273-6455. **Fax:** (319)273-4326. **E-mail:** nar@uni.edu. **Website:** northamericanreview.org. **Contact:** Kim Groninga, nonfiction editor. **90% freelance written.** Published 4 times/year. "The *NAR* is the oldest literary magazine in America and one of the most respected; though we have no prejudices about the subject matter of material sent to us, our first concern is quality." Estab. 1815. Circ. under 5,000. Byline given. Publishes ms an average of 1 year after acceptance. Accepts queries by mail. Responds in 4 months to mss. Sample copy for $7. Guidelines available online.

NONFICTION Contact: Ron Sandvik, nonfiction editor. Length: Open. **Pays $5/350 words; $20 minimum, $100 maximum.**

FICTION Open (literary). "No flat narrative stories where the inferiority of the character is the paramount concern." Wants to see more "well-crafted literary stories that emphasize family concerns. We'd also like to see more stories engaged with environmental concerns." Reads fiction mss all year. Publishes ms an average of 1 year after acceptance. **Publishes 2 new writers/year.** Recently published work by Lee Ann Roripaugh, Dick Allen, Rita Welty Bourke. Wants more well-crafted literary stories that emphasize family concerns. No flat narrative stories where the inferiority of the character is the paramount concern. Accepts submissions by USPS mail only. Send complete ms with SASE. Responds in 3 months to queries; 4 months to mss. No simultaneous submissions. Sample copy for $7. Writer's guidelines online. **Pays $5/350 words; $20 minimum, $100 maximum.**

POETRY No restrictions; highest quality only. **Pays $1/line; $20 minimum, $100 maximum.**

NOTRE DAME REVIEW

University of Notre Dame, 840 Flanner Hall, Notre Dame IN 46556. (574)631-6952. **Fax:** (574)631-4795. **E-mail:** english.ndreview.1@nd.edu. **Website:** www.nd.edu/~ndr/review.htm. Semiannual magazine. The *Notre Dame Review* is an indepenent, noncommercial magazine of contemporary American and international fiction, poetry, criticism, and art. We are especially interested in work that takes on big issues by making the invisible seen, that gives voice to the voiceless. In addition to showcasing celebrated authors like Seamus Heaney and Czelaw Milosz, the *Notre Dame Review* introduces readers to authors they may have never encountered before, but who are doing innovative and important work. In conjunction with the *Notre Dame Review*, the online companion to the printed magazine, the *Notre Dame Re-view* engages readers as a community centered in literary rather than commercial concerns, a community we reach out to through critique and commentary as well as aesthetic experience. Estab. 1995. Circ. 2,000. Publishes ms an average of 6 months after acceptance. Accepts simultaneous submissions. Responds in 4 or more months to mss. Sample copy for $6. Guidelines available online.

FICTION Contact: William O'Rourke, fiction editor. "We're eclectic. Upcoming theme issues planned. List of upcoming themes or editorial calendar available for SASE. Does not read mss May-August." No genre fiction. **Buys 100 (90 poems, 10 stories) mss/year.** Length: 3,000 words. **Pays $5-25.**

NTHPOSITION

E-mail: val@nthposition.com. **Website:** www.nthposition.com. **Contact:** Rufo Quintavalle, poetry editor; Val Stevenson, managing editor. **5% freelance written.** *nthposition*, published monthly online, is "an eclectic, London-based journal with politics and opinion, travel writing, fiction and poetry, art reviews and interviews, and some high weirdness." Guidelines available online.

NONFICTION Needs essays, reviews, opinion, travel.

POETRY Contact: Todd Swift. Accepts e-mail submissions only (pasted into body of message; no attachments). Cover letter is required. "Please include a brief (2 sentences) biographical note." Reads submissions throughout the year. Time between acceptance and publication is 4 months. "Poems are read and selected by the poetry editor, who uses his own sense of what makes a poem work online to select." Never comments on rejected poems. Occasionally publishes theme issues. Guidelines available by e-mail or on website. Responds in 6 weeks. No payment. Does not request rights but expects proper acknowledgement if poems reprinted later. Publishes special theme e-books from time to time, such as 100 Poets Against the War. "No racism, nastiness, silkworm farming or diabetes articles." Submit maximum Submit 2-4 poems at a time poems.

ONE-STORY

One-Story, LLC, 232 3rd St., #A111, Brooklyn NY 11215. **Website:** www.one-story.com. **Contact:** Maribeth Batcha, publisher. **100% freelance written.** literary magazine covering 1 short story. "*One-Story* is a literary magazine that contains, simply, 1 story. It is a subscription-only magazine. Every 3 weeks subscribers are sent *One-Story* in the mail. *One-Story* is artfully designed, lightweight, easy to carry, and ready to entertain on buses, in bed, in subways, in cars, in the park, in the bath, in the waiting rooms of doctor's offices, on the couch, or in line at the supermarket. Subscribers also have access to a website, where they can learn more about *One-Story* authors, and hear about *One-Story* readings and events. There is always time to read *One-Story*." Estab. 2002. Circ. 3,500. Byline given. Publishes ms an average of 3-6 months after acceptance. Editorial lead time 3-4 months. Accepts simultaneous submissions. Responds in 2-6 months to mss. Sample copy for $5. Guidelines available online.

FICTION *One-Story* only accepts short stories. Do not send excerpts. Do not send more than 1 story at a time. **Buys 18 mss/year.** Send complete ms. Length: 3,000-8,000 words. **Pays $100.**

$ PALABRA

P.O. Box 86146, Los Angeles CA 90086-0146. **E-mail:** info@palabralitmag.com. **Website:** www.palabralitmag.com. Annual magazine featuring poetry, fiction, short plays, and more. "*PALABRA* is about exploration, risk, and ganas—the myriad intersections of thought, language, story and art—*el mas alla of letters*, symbols and spaces into meaning." Byline given. Responds in 3-4 months to mss.

NONFICTION **Pays $25-35.**

FICTION Needs experimental/hybrid, mainstream, novel excerpts, flash fiction, short plays. Does not want genre work (mystery, romance, science fiction, etc.). Send complete ms; unpublished work only. Length: 4,000 words. **Pays $25-$35.**

POETRY Needs avant garde, free verse, traditional. Submit maximum 5 poems.

$$$ THE PARIS REVIEW

62 White St., New York NY 10013. (212)343-1333. **E-mail:** queries@theparisreview.org. **Website:** www.theparisreview.org. Nathaniel Rich, fiction editor. **Contact:** Lorin Stein, editor. Quarterly magazine. "Fiction and poetry of superlative quality, whatever the genre, style or mode. Our contributors include prominent, as well as less well-known and previously unpublished writers. Writers at Work interview series includes important contemporary writers discussing their own work and the craft of writing." Accepts queries by mail. Accepts simultaneous submissions. Responds in 4 months to mss. Sample copy for $12 (includes postage). Guidelines available online.

💬 Address submissions to proper department. Do not make submissions via e-mail.

FICTION Study the publication. Annual Aga Khan Fiction Contest award of $1,000. Recently published work by Karl Taro Greenfeld, J. Robert Lennon, and Belle Boggs. Send complete ms. **Pays $500-1,000.**

POETRY **Contact:** Richard Howard, poetry editor. Submit no more than six poems at a time. Poetry can be sent to the poetry editor (please include a self-addressed, stamped envelope), or submitted online at http://www.theparisreview.org/poetry/. **Pays $35 minimum varies according to length. Awards $1,000 in Bernard F. Conners Poetry Prize contest.**

$$ PARNASSUS: POETRY IN REVIEW

Poetry in Review Foundation, 205 W. 89th St., #8F, New York NY 10024. (212)362-3492. **E-mail:** parnew@aol.com. **Website:** www.parnassusreview.com. **Contact:** Herbert Leibowitz, editor and publisher. Annual magazine covering poetry and criticism. "We now publish 1 double issue a year." Estab. 1972. Circ. 1,800. Byline given. Publishes ms an average of 12-14 months after acceptance. Accepts queries by mail. Responds in 2 months to mss. Sample copy for $15.

NONFICTION Needs essays. **Buys 30 mss/year.** Query with published clips. Length: 1,500-7,500 words. **Pays $200-750.**

POETRY Needs avant garde, free verse, traditional. Accepts most types of poetry. Buys 3-4 unsolicited poems/year.

PEARL

3030 E. Second St., Long Beach CA 90803. (562)434-4523. **E-mail:** pearlmag@aol.com. **Website:** www.pearlmag.com. **Contact:** Joan Jobe Smith, Marilyn Johnson, and Barbara Hauk, poetry editors. Biannual magazine featuring poetry, short fiction, and black and white artwork. We also sponsor the Pearl Poetry Prize, an annual contest for a full length book, as well as the Pearl Short Story Prize. "*Pearl* is an eclectic publication, a place for lively, readable poetry and prose that speaks to real people about real life in direct, living language, profane or sublime." Estab. 1974. Pays with contributor's copy. Publishes ms an average of 6-12 months after acceptance. Accepts queries by mail. Accepts simultaneous submissions. Sample copy for $8. Guidelines available online.

FICTION "Our annual fiction issue features the winner of our Pearl Short Story Prize contest as well as 'short-shorts,' and some of the longer stories in our contest. Length: 1,200 words. No obscure, experimental fiction. The winner of the Pearl Short Story Prize receives 4250 and 10 copies of the issue the story appears in . A $10 entry fee includes a copy of the magazine; all entries are considered for publication." Nothing sentimental, obscure, predictable, abstract or cliché-ridden poetry or fiction. Length: 1,200 words.

Short Story Prize of $250, 100 copies of the issue the story appears in.

POETRY "Our poetry issue contains a 12-15 page section featuring the work of a single poet. Entry fee for the Pearl Poetry Prize is $20, which includes a copy of the winning book." No sentimental, obscure, predictable, abstract or cliché-ridden poetry. Submit maximum 3-5 poems. 40 lines max. Send with cover letter and SASE.

THE PEDESTAL MAGAZINE

6815 Honors Court, Charlotte NC 28210. (704)643-0244. **E-mail:** pedmagazine@carolina.rr.com. **Website:** www.thepedestalmagazine.com. **Contact:** Nathan Leslie, fiction editor; John Amen, editor-in-chief. Bimonthly website currently accepting submissions of poetry, fiction, and nonfiction. "We are committed to promoting diversity and celebrating the voice of the individual." Estab. 2000. Accepts queries by e-mail. Accepts simultaneous submissions. Responds in 4-6 weeks to mss. Guidelines available online.

NONFICTION Needs essays, Reviews, interview. **Pays 2¢/word. Pays for unsolicited articles.**

FICTION "We are receptive to all sorts of high-quality literary fiction. Genre fiction is encouraged as long as it crosses or comments upon its genre and is both character-driven and psychologically acute. We encourage submissions of short fiction, no more than 3 flash fiction pieces at a time. There is no need to query prior to submitting; please submit via the submission form—no email to the editor." Needs traditional literary, experimental, horror, mainstream, mystery, romance, science fiction, Works that don't fit into a specific category. **Buys 10-25 mss/year.** For the December issue (reading cycle October 28-December 14), Bruce Boston and Marge Simon will be jointly guest-editing a special speculative fiction issue. Speculative includes science fiction, fantasy, horror, slipstream, surreal, and experimental. All fiction submitted between October 28 and December 14 should be speculative and not exceed 1,500 words. NOTE: Do not submit speculative work intended to be considered for the December issue until afer October 28, 2011. Length: 4,000 words. **Pays $40/poem ; 8¢/word.**

POETRY "We are open to a wide variety of poetry, ranging from the highly experimental to the traditionally formal. Submit all poems in 1 form. No need to query before submitting." Submit maximum 6 poems. No length restriction. Pays $40/poem.

[icon] $ PLANET-THE WELSH INTERNATIONALIST

P.O. Box 44, Aberystwyth Ceredigion SY23 3ZZ United Kingdom. **E-mail:** planet.enquiries@planetmagazine.org.uk. **Website:** www.planetmagazine.org.uk. **Contact:** Emily Trahair, acting editor. Bimonthly journal. A literary/cultural/political journal centered on Welsh affairs but with a strong interest in minority cultures in Europe and elsewhere. *Planet: The Welsh Internationalist*, published quarterly, is a cultural magazine "centered on Wales, but with broader interests in arts, sociology, politics, history, and science." Wants "good poetry in a wide variety of styles. No limitations as to subject matter; length can be a problem." Has published poetry by Nigel Jenkins, Anne Stevenson, and Les Murray. *Planet* is 128 pages, A5, professionally printed, perfect-bound, with glossy color card cover. Receives about 500 submissions/year, accepts about 5%. Press run is 1,550 (1,500 subscribers, about 10% libraries, 200 shelf sales). Single copy: £6.75; subscription: £22 (£38 overseas). Sample available. Estab. 1970. Circ. 1,400. Publishes ms 4-6 months after acceptance. Responds in 3 months. Sample copy for £4. Guidelines available online.

FICTION Would like to see more inventive, imaginative fiction that pays attention to language and experiments with form. No magical realism, horror, science fiction. No submissions returned unless accompanied by an SASE. Writers submitting from abroad should send at least 3 IRCs for return of typescript; 1 IRC for reply only. E-mail queries accepted. Writer's guidelines online. Length: 1,500-4,000 words. **Pays £50/1,000 words.**

POETRY Please submit 4-6 poems at a time. No previously published poems or simultaneous submissions. Accepts e-mail (as attachment) and disk submissions. SASE or SAE with IRCs essential for reply. **Pays £30 minimum.**

$ PLEIADES

Pleiades Press, Department of English, University of Central Missouri, Martin 336, Warrensburg MO 64093. (660)543-4425. **Fax:** (660)543-8544. **E-mail:** pleiades@ucmo.edu. **Website:** www.ucmo.edu/englphil/pleiades. **Contact:** G.B. Crump, Matthew Eck and Phong Nguyen, prose editors. **100% freelance written.** Semiannual journal (5½x8½ perfect bound). "We publish contemporary fiction, poetry, interviews, literary essays, special-interest personal essays, reviews for a general and literary audience from authors from around the world." Estab. 1991. Circ. 3,000. Byline given. Publishes ms an average of 9 months after acceptance. Editorial lead time 9 months. Accepts queries by mail. Accepts simultaneous submissions. Responds in 2 months to queries. Responds in 1-4 months to mss. Sample copy for $5 (back issue); $6 (current issue). Guidelines available online.

NONFICTION Contact: Phong Nguyen and Matthew Eck, nonfiction editor. Needs book excerpts, essays, interview, reviews. "Nothing pedantic, slick, or shallow. Do not send submissions after May 31. We résumé reading nonfiction Sept. 1." **Buys 4-6 mss/year.** Send complete ms. Length: 2,000-4,000 words. **Pays $10.**

FICTION Contact: Matthew Eck and Phong Nguyen. We read fiction year-round. Needs ethnic, experimental, humorous, mainstream, novel concepts, magic realism. No science fiction, fantasy, confession, erotica. **Buys 16-20 mss/year.** Send complete ms. Length: 2,000-6,000 words. **Pays $10.**

POETRY Contact: Kevin Prufer and Wayne Miller. Needs avant-garde, free verse, haiku, light verse, traditional. "Nothing didactic, pretentious, or overly sentimental. Do not send poetry after May 31. We résumé reading poetry on Sept. 1." Buys 40-50 poems/year. Submit maximum 6 poems. **Pays $3/poem, and contributor copies**.

🏦🏦 PLOUGHSHARES

Emerson College, Ploughshares, 120 Boylston St., Boston MA 02116. **Website:** www.pshares.org. **Contact:** Ladette Randolph, editor. *Ploughshares*, published 3 times/year, is "a journal of new writing guest-edited by prominent poets and writers to reflect different and contrasting points of view. Translations are welcome if permission has been granted. Our mission is to present dynamic, contrasting views on what is valid and important in contemporary literature and to discover and advance significant literary talent. Each issue is guest-edited by a different writer. We no longer structure issues around preconceived themes." Editors have included Carolyn Forché, Gerald Stern, Rita Dove, Chase Twichell, and Marilyn Hacker. Has published poetry by Donald Hall, Li-Young Lee, Robert Pinsky, Brenda Hillman, and Thylias Moss. Ploughshares is 200 pages, digest-sized. Receives about 11,000 poetry, fiction, and essay submissions/year. Press run is 6,000. Subscription: $30 domestic,

$30 plus shipping (see website) foreign. Sample: $14 current issue, $7 back issue, please inquire for shipping rates. Estab. 1971. Circ. 6,000. Publishes ms an average of 6 months after acceptance. Accepts queries by mail, online submission form. Accepts simultaneous submissions. Responds in 5 months to mss. Guidelines available online.

NONFICTION Needs essays. Length: 3,00-10,000 words. **Pays $25/printed page; $50 minimum, $250 maximum.**

FICTION Recently published work by ZZ Packer, Antonya Nelson, Stuart Dybek. Needs mainstream, literary. "No genre (science fiction, detective, gothic, adventure, etc.), popular formula or commerical fiction whose purpose is to entertain rather than to illuminate."

POETRY Needs avant-garde, free verse, traditional. Submit 1-3 poems at a time.

🏦 POETRY

The Poetry Foundation, 61 W. Superior St., Chicago IL 60654. (312)787-7070. **Fax:** (312)787-6650. **E-mail:** editors@poetrymagazine.org. **Website:** www.poetrymagazine.org. Christian Wiman, Editor. **Contact:** Helen Klaviter. **100% freelance written.** Monthly magazine. *Poetry*'s website offers featured poems, letters, reviews, interviews, essays, and web-exclusive features. *Poetry*, published monthly by The Poetry Foundation (see separate listing in Organizations), "has no special manuscript needs and no special requirements as to form or genre: We examine in turn all work received and accept that which seems best." Has published poetry by the major voices of our time as well as new talent. *Poetry* is 512x9, elegantly printed, flat-spined. Receives 90,000 submissions/year, accepts about 300-350. Press run is 16,000. Single copy: $3.75; subscription: $35 ($38 for institutions). Sample: $5.50. Estab. 1912. Circ. 31,000. Byline given. Publishes ms an average of 9 months after acceptance. Accepts queries by mail. Responds in 1 month to queries and to mss. Sample copy for $3.75 or online at website. Guidelines available online.

NONFICTION Buys 14 mss/year. Query. Length: 1,000-2,000 words. **Pays $150/page.**

POETRY Accepts all styles and subject matter. Submit no more than 4 poems at a time. No previously published poems or simultaneous submissions. Electronic submission preferred. When submitting by post put return address on outside of envelope; include SASE.

Submissions must be typed, single-spaced, with poet's name and address on every page. Guidelines available for SASE. Responds in 1-2 months. Pays $10/line (with a minimum payment of $300). Reviews books of poetry in multi-book formats of varying lengths. Does not accept unsolicited reviews. Buys 180-250 poems/year. Submit maximum 4 poems. Open **Pays $10/line ($150 minimum payment).**

POETRY INTERNATIONAL

San Diego State University, 5500 Campanile Dr., San Diego CA 92182-6020. (619)594-1522. **Fax:** (619)594-4998. **E-mail:** poetryinternational@yahoo.com. **Website:** http://poetryinternational.sdsu.edu. **Contact:** Fred Moramarco, Founding Editor. Annual journal covering new poems from emerging and well-established poets, offering commentary on poetry anthologies, books by individual poets, and poetic criticism, art from around the world. "We intend to continue to publish poetry that makes a difference in people's lives, and startles us anew with the endless capacity of language to awaken our senses and expand our awareness." Estab. 1997. No kill fee Accepts queries by mail. Accepts simultaneous submissions. Responds in 6-8 months to mss. Guidelines available on web site.

NONFICTION Translations, query first for book reviews. Special issues: Reprints photos.

FICTION Query.

POETRY Features the poetry of a different nation of the world as a special section in each issue. Submit maximum 5 poems.

POETRY NEW ZEALAND

34B Methuen Rd., Avondale Auckland New Zealand. **E-mail:** alstair@ihug.co.nz. **Website:** www.poetrynz. net. "Each issue has 15-20 pages of poetry from a developing or established poet. The rest of the issue is devoted to a selection of poetry from New Zealand and abroad, plus essays, reviews, and general criticism to a total of 112 pages." Estab. 1951. Accepts queries by mail. Responds in 3 months to mss. Guidelines available online.

NONFICTION Submit a copy of the magazine. **Featured poets and essayists receive 1 copy of the magazine and a fee.**

POETRY Accepts any theme/style of poetry. Send complete ms, bio, and SASE.

THE PORTLAND REVIEW

Portland State University, P.O. Box 347, Portland OR 97207-0347. (503)725-4533. **E-mail:** theportlandre-view@gmail.com. **Website:** portlandreview.tumblr. com. **Contact:** Jacqueline Treiber, editor. **98% freelance written.** Triannual magazine covering short prose, poetry, photography, and art. Estab. 1956. Circ. 1,500. Byline given. Publishes ms an average of 3-6 months after acceptance. Accepts simultaneous submissions. Responds in 2-4 months to mss. Sample copy for $9. Guidelines available online. "Automatic rejection of mss not following guidelines."

FICTION Flash, vignette, and reviews of small-press publications or emergent authors. No fantasy, detective, or western. **Buys 40 mss/year.** Send complete ms. 5,000 words maximum. **Pays contributor's copies.**

POETRY Needs Avant garde, free verse, haiku, light verse, traditional. Buys 50 poems/year. Submit maximum 5 poems.

THE PRAIRIE JOURNAL

P.O. Box 68073, 28 Crowfoot Terrace NW, Calgary AB Y3G 3N8 Canada. **E-mail:** editor@prairiejournal.org (queries only); prairiejournal@yahoo.com. **Website:** prairiejournal.org. **Contact:** A.E. Burke, literary editor. **100% freelance written.** Semiannual magazine publishing quality poetry, short fiction, drama, literary criticism, reviews, bibliography, interviews, profiles, and artwork. "The audience is literary, university, library, scholarly, and creative readers/writers." Estab. 1983. Circ. 600. Byline given. Publishes ms an average of 4-6 months after acceptance. Editorial lead time 4-6 months. Accepts queries by mail, e-mail. NoResponds in 2 weeks to queries. Responds in 6 months to mss. Sample copy for $5. Guidelines available online.

NONFICTION Needs essays, humor, interview, literary. No inspirational, news, religious, or travel. **Buys 25-40 mss/year.** Query with published clips. Length: 100-3,000 words. **Pays $50-100, plus contributor's copy.**

COLUMNS Reviews (books from small presses publishing poetry, short fiction, essays, and criticism), 200-1,000 words. **Buys 5 mss/year.** Query with published clips. **Pays $10-50.**

FICTION No genre (romance, horror, western—sagebrush or cowboys), erotic, science fiction, or mystery. **Buys 6 mss/year.** Send complete ms. Length: 100-3,000 words. **Pays $10-75.**

POETRY Needs avant-garde, free verse, haiku. No heroic couplets or greeting card verse. Buys 25-35 poems/year. Submit maximum 6-8 poems. Length: 3-50 lines. **Pays $5-50.**

PRAIRIE SCHOONER

The University of Nebraska Press, Prairie Schooner, 123 Andrews Hall, University of Nebraska, Lincoln NE 68588-0334. (402)472-7211, 1-800-715-2387. **E-mail:** jengelhardt2@unlnotes.unl.edu. **Website:** http://prairieschooner.unl.edu. **100% freelance written.** Quarterly magazine. "We look for the best fiction, poetry, and nonfiction available to publish, and our readers expect to read stories, poems, and essays of extremely high quality. We try to publish a variety of styles, topics, themes, points of view, and writers with a variety of backgrounds in all stages of their careers. We like work that is compelling—intellectually or emotionally—either in form, language, or content." Estab. 1926. Circ. 2,500. Byline given. Publishes ms an average of 1 year after acceptance. Editorial lead time 6 months. Accepts queries by mail, e-mail. Responds in 1 week to queries. Responds in 3-4 months to mss. Sample copy for $6. Guidelines for #10 SASE.

NONFICTION Needs essays, literary/personal, literary or creative nonfiction, memoir, or essays on literature. No scholarly papers that require footnotes. No pieces written only to express a moral lesson or to inspire. There must be depth and literary quality as well. **Buys 6-8 mss/year.** Send complete ms. Length: 250-20,000 words. **Pays 3 copies of the issue in which the writer's work is published.**

FICTION "We try to remain open to a variety of styles, themes, and subject matter. We look for high-quality writing, 3-D characters, well-wrought plots, setting, etc. We are open to realistic and/or experimental fiction." Needs ethnic, experimental, mainstream, novel concepts, literary. **Buys 15-25 mss/year.** Send complete ms. **Pays 3 copies of the issue in which the writer's work is published.**

POETRY Needs avant garde, free verse, haiku, light verse, traditional. Buys 100-120 poems/year. Submit maximum 7 poems. **Pays 3 copies of the issue in which the writer's work is published.**

○ ⑤ PRISM INTERNATIONAL

Department of Creative Writing, Buch E462, 1866 Main Mall, University of British Columbia, Vancouver BC V6T 1Z1 Canada. (604)822-2514. **Fax:** (604)822-3616. **Website:** www.prismmagazine.ca. **100% freelance written. Works with new/unpublished writers.** A quarterly international journal of contemporary writing—fiction, poetry, drama, creative nonfiction and translation. Readership: public and university li-

braries, individual subscriptions, bookstores—a worldwide audience concerned with the contemporary in literature. Estab. 1959. Circ. 1,200. Publishes ms an average of 4 months after acceptance. Accepts queries by mail. Responds in 4 months to queries. Responds in 3-6 months to mss. Sample copy for $11, more info online. Guidelines available online.

NONFICTION No reviews, tracts, or scholarly essays. **Pays $20/printed page, and 1-year subscription.**

FICTION For Drama: one-acts/excerpts of no more than 1500 words preferred. Also interested in seeing dramatic monologues. Needs experimental, novel concepts, traditional. "New writing that is contemporary and literary. Short stories and self-contained novel excerpts. Works of translation are eagerly sought and should be accompanied by a copy of the original. Would like to see more translations. No gothic, confession, religious, romance, pornography, or science fiction." **Buys 12-16 mss/year.** Send complete ms. 25 pages maximum **Pays $20/printed page, and 1-year subscription.**

POETRY Needs avant-garde, traditional. **Buys 10 poems/issue.** Submit maximum 6 poems. **Pays $40/printed page, and 1-year subscription.**

QUARTERLY WEST

University of Utah, 255 S. Central Campus Dr., Room 3500, Salt Lake City UT 84112. **E-mail:** quarterlywest@gmail.com. **Website:** www.utah.edu/quarterlywest. **Contact:** Matt Kirkpatrick & Cami Nelson, editors. Semiannual magazine. "We publish fiction, poetry, and nonfiction in long and short formats, and will consider experimental as well as traditional works." Estab. 1976. Circ. 1,900. Publishes ms an average of 6 months after acceptance. Accepts queries by mail. Accepts simultaneous submissions. Responds in 6 months to mss. Sample copy for $7.50 or online. Guidelines available online.

NONFICTION Needs essays, interview, personal experience, travel, book reviews. **Buys 6-8 mss/year.** Send complete ms. 10,000 words maximum **Pays $20-100.**

FICTION No preferred lengths; interested in longer, fuller short stories and short shorts. Needs ethnic, experimental, humorous, mainstream, novel concepts, slice-of-life vignettes, short shorts, translations. No detective, science fiction or romance. **Buys 6-10 mss/year.** Send complete ms. **Pays $15-100, and 2 contributor's copies.**

CONSUMER MAGAZINES

POETRY Needs avant-garde, free verse, traditional. Buys 40-50 poems/year. Submit maximum 5 poems. **Pays $15-100.**

☺ ☺☺ QUEEN'S QUARTERLY

144 Barrie St., Queen's University, Kingston ON K7L 3N6 Canada. (613)533-2667. **Fax:** (613)533-6822. **E-mail:** queens.quarterly@queensu.ca. **Website:** www.queensu.ca/quarterly. **Contact:** Joan Harcourt, editor. **95% freelance written.** Quarterly magazine covering a wide variety of subjects, including science, humanities, arts and letters, politics, and history for the educated reader. "A general interest intellectual review, featuring articles, book reviews, poetry, and fiction." Estab. 1893. Circ. 3,000. Byline given. Publishes ms on average 6-12 months after acceptance. Accepts queries by e-mail. Responds in 2-3 months to queries. Free sample copy online. Writer's guidelines online.

NONFICTION Contact: Boris Castel, Editor (articles, essays and reviews).

FICTION Contact: Joan Harcourt, Literary Editor (fiction and poetry). short stories. Submissions over 3,000 words shall not be accepted. Length: 2,500-3,000 words.

POETRY Buys 25 poems/year. Submit maximum 6 poems.

☺ RATTAPALLAX

Rattapallax Press, 217 Thompson St., Suite 353, New York NY 10012. (212)560-7459. **E-mail:** info@rattapallax.com. **Website:** www.rattapallax.com. **Contact:** Alan Cheuse, fiction editor. **10% freelance written.** Annual magazine covering international fiction and poetry. *Rattapallax* is a literary magazine that focuses on issues dealing with globalization. Estab. 1999. Circ. 3,000. Byline given. Publishes ms an average of 6 months after acceptance. Editorial lead time 6 months. Submit seasonal material 6 months in advance. Accepts queries by e-mail. Responds in 2 weeks to queries. Responds in 6 months to mss. Sample copy available online. Guidelines available online.

POETRY Needs avant-garde, free verse, traditional. Submit maximum 5 poems. Length: 5-200 lines.

REDACTIONS: POETRY, POETICS, & PROSE

58 S. Main St., 3rd Floor, Brockport NY 14420. **E-mail:** redactionspoetry@yahoo.com (poetry); redactionsprose@yahoo.com (prose). **Website:** www.redactions.com. Every 9 months covering poems, reviews of new books of poems, translations, manifestos, interviews, essays concerning poetry, poetics, poetry movements, or concerning a specific poet or a group of poets; and anything dealing with poetry. "We now also publish fiction and creative nonfiction." Accepts queries by e-mail. Accepts simultaneous submissions.

NONFICTION Needs essays on poetics, reviews of new books of poems, interviews with poets., art, translation. We are also now accepting creative nonfiction.

POETRY "Anything dealing with poetry."

RED ROCK REVIEW

College of Southern Nevada, CSN Department of English, J2A, 3200 E. Cheyenne Ave., North Las Vegas NV 89030. (702)651-4094. **Fax:** (702)651-4639. **E-mail:** redrockreview@csn.edu. **Website:** sites.csn.edu/english/redrockreview/. **Contact:** Rich Logsdon, Senior Editor. Semiannual magazine covering poetry, fiction and creative nonfiction as well as book reviews. "We are dedicated to the publication of fine contemporary literature." Estab. 1994. Accepts queries by e-mail. No longer accepting snail mail submissions. Send all submissions as MS. Word, RTF, or PDF file attachment to redrockreview@csn.edu. Guidelines available online. Occasionally comments on rejections.

NONFICTION Needs essays. No literary criticism. Length: 5,000 words.

FICTION Contact: John Ziebell (john.zeibell@csn.edu). Length: 7,500 words.

POETRY Contact: Jean French (jean.french@csn.edu). Length: 80 lines.

RHINO

The Poetry Forum, Inc., P.O. Box 591, Evanston IL 60204. **E-mail:** editors@rhinopoetry.org. **Website:** www.rhinopoetry.org. **Contact:** Ralph Hamilton Sr., Editor; Helen Degen Cohen, Sr. Editor and Founder. Annual magazine covering high-quality, diverse poetry, short/shorts and translations by new and established writers. "This eclectic annual journal of more than 30 years accepts poetry, flash fiction (1,000 words or less), and poetry-in-translation from around the world that experiments, provokes, compels. More than 80 poets are showcased. The regular call for poetry is from April 1 to October 1st, and the Founder's Contest submission period has been changed to July 1 to October 1st." Accepts simultaneous submissions. Response time may exceed 6 weeks. Guidelines available online.

NONFICTION. Needs essays, on poetry, humor, translation.

FICTION Needs humorous, flash fiction, (1,000 words or less), poetry, poetry-in-translation. Submit by mail or online. Include SASE for USPS mail only. Short shorts: 1,000 words or less.

POETRY Needs avant-garde, free verse, light verse, traditional. "Please label each poem with your name, address, telephone number, and email address for ease in contacting you." Submit maximum 5 poems.

⊛ RIVER STYX MAGAZINE

Big River Association, 3547 Olive St., Suite 107, St. Louis MO 63103. (314)533-4541. **E-mail:** bigriver@ riverstyx.org. **Website:** www.riverstyx.org. **Contact:** Richard Newman, Editor. Triannual magazine. *"River Styx* publishes the highest quality fiction, poetry, interviews, essays, and visual art. We are an internationally distributed multicultural literary magazine. Mss read May-November." Estab. 1975. Byline given. Publishes ms an average of 1 year after acceptance. Accepts queries by mail. Accepts simultaneous submissions. Responds in 4 months to mss. Sample copy for $8. Guidelines available online.

NONFICTION Needs essays, interview. **Buys 2-5 mss/year.** Send complete ms. **Pays 2 contributor copies, plus 1 year subscription; plus cash payment as funds permit.**

FICTION Contact: Richard Newman, editor. Needs ethnic, experimental, mainstream, novel concepts, short stories, literary. No genre fiction, less thinly veiled autobiography. **Buys 6-9 mss/year.** Send complete ms. no more than 23-30 manuscript pages. **Pays 2 contributor copies, plus 1-year subscription; plus cash payment as funds permit.**

POETRY Needs avant-garde, free verse. *River Styx Magazine*, published 3 times/year in April, August, and December, is "an international, multicultural journal publishing both award-winning and previously undiscovered writers. We feature poetry, short fiction, essays, interviews, fine art, and photography." Wants "excellent poetry—original, energetic, musical, and accessible." Does not want "chopped prose or opaque poetry that isn't about anything." Has published poetry by Jennifer Perrine, Louis Simpson, Molly Peacock, Marilyn Hacker, Yusef Komunyakaa, Andrew Hudgins, and Catie Rosemurgy. *River Styx Magazine* is 100-120 pages, digest-sized, professionally printed on coated stock, perfect-bound, with color cover, includes ads. Receives about 8,000 poems/year, accepts 60-75. Press run is 2,500 (1,000 subscribers, 80 libraries). Subscription: $20/year, $35/2 years. Sample: $9. Sometimes comments on rejected poems. Publishes 1 theme issue/year. Upcoming themes available in magazine or on website. Guidelines available for SASE or on website. Responds in up to 5 months. Pays 2 contributor's copies and one-year subscription, plus a small cash payments as funds permit. Acquires one-time rights. No religious. Buys 40-50 poems/year. Submit maximum 3-5 poems. **Pays 2 contributor copies, plus a 1-year subscription; plus small cash payments as funds permit.**

⟳ ⊛ THE SAVAGE KICK LITERARY MAGAZINE

Murder Slim Press, 29 Alpha Rd., Gorleston Norfolk NR31 0EQ United Kingdom. **E-mail:** moonshine@ murderslim.com. **Website:** www.murderslim.com. **100% freelance written.** Semiannual magazine. "*Savage Kick* primarily deals with viewpoints outside the mainstream..honest emotions told in a raw, simplistic way. It is recommended that you are very familiar with the *SK* style before submitting. We have only accepted 8 new writers in 4 years of the magazine. Ensure you have a distinctive voice and story to tell." Estab. 2005. Circ. 500+. Byline given. Publishes ms an average of up to 2 months after acceptance. Accepts queries by mail, e-mail. Accepts simultaneous submissions. Responds in 7-10 days to queries. Guidelines free.

NONFICTION Needs interview, personal experience. **Buys 10-20 mss/year.** Send complete ms. Length: 500-3,000 words. **Pays $25-35.**

COLUMNS Buys up to 4 mss/year. Query. **Pays $25-35.**

FICTION Needs mystery, slice-of-life vignettes, crime. "Real-life stories are preferred, unless the work is distinctively extreme within the crime genre. No Poetry of any kind, no mainstream fiction, Oprah-style fiction, Internet/chat language, teen issues, excessive Shakespearean language, surrealism, overworked irony, or genre fiction (horror, fantasy, science fiction, western, erotica, etc.)." **Buys 10-25 mss/ year.** Send complete ms. Length: 500-6,000 words. **Pays $35.**

⊛ THE SEATTLE REVIEW

Box 354330, University of Washington, Seattle WA 98195. (206)543-2302. **E-mail:** seaview@u.washington.edu. **Website:** www.seattlereview.org. Semiannual magazine. Includes general fiction, poetry, craft essays on writing, and one interview per issue with a Northwest writer. Estab. 1978. Circ. 1,000. Responds in 8 months to mss. Sample copy for $6. Guidelines available online.

FICTION Wants more creative nonfiction. "We also publish a series called Writers and their Craft, which deals with aspects of writing fiction (also poetry)—point of view, characterization, etc, rather than literary criticism, each issue." Needs ethnic, experimental, fantasy, historical, horror, humorous, mainstream, mystery, novel concepts, suspense, western, contemporary, feminist, gay, lesbian, literary, psychic/supernatural/occult, regional, translations. "Nothing in bad taste (porn, racist, etc.). No genre fiction or science fiction." **Buys 4-10 mss/year.** Send complete ms. Length: 500-10,000 words. **Pays $0-100.**

SENECA REVIEW

Hobart and William Smith Colleges, Geneva NY 14456. (315)781-3392. **E-mail:** senecareview@hws.edu. **Website:** www.hws.edu/academics/senecareview/index.aspx. Semiannual magazine *Seneca Review* publishes mss of poetry, translations, essays on contemporary poetry, and lyric essays (creative nonfiction that borders on poetry). "The editors have special interest in translations of contemporary poetry from around the world. Publisher of numerous laureates and award-winning poets, we also publish emerging writers and are always open to new, innovative work. Poems from *SR* are regularly honored by inclusion in *The Best American Poetry* and *Pushcart Prize* anthologies. Distributed internationally." Accepts queries by mail or online at http://senecareview.submishmash.com/submit. Responds in 3 months to mss. Guidelines available online. E-mail quetions to senecareview@hws.edu.

NONFICTION Accepts essays, (up to 20 pages), translation. Special issues: Past special features include Irish women's poetry; Israeli women's poetry; Polish, Catalan, and Albanian poetry; excerpts from the notebooks of 32 contemporary American poets, an issue of essays devoted to Hayden Carruth; issuede dicated to editor Deborah Tall; The Lyric Body, Anthology of Poets, Essayists and Artists Intimately Address Difference and Disability.

POETRY Submit maximum 3-5 poems.

THE SEWANEE REVIEW

University of the South, 735 University Ave., Sewanee TN 37383-1000. (931)598-1000. **Website:** www.sewanee.edu/sewanee_review. "A literary quarterly, publishing original fiction, poetry, essays on literary and related subjects, and book reviews for well-educated readers who appreciate good American and English literature." Estab. 1892. Circ. 2,200. Responds in 6-8 weeks to mss. Sample copy for $8.50 ($9.50 outside US). Guidelines available online.

💬 Does not read mss June 1-August 31.

FICTION Send query letter for reviews. Send complete ms for fiction. No erotica, science fiction, fantasy or excessively violent or profane material. **Buys 10-15 mss/year.** Length: 3,500-7,500 words.

POETRY Send complete ms. Submit maximum 6 poems. Length: 40 lines.

$ SHENANDOAH

Washington and Lee University, Mattingly House, 2 Lee Ave., Lexington VA 24450-2116. (540)458-8765. **Fax:** (540)458-8461. **E-mail:** shenandoah@wlu.edu. **Website:** shenandoah.wlu.edu/faq.html. **Contact:** R. T. Smith, editor. Triannual magazine. "Unsolicited manuscripts will not be read between January 1 and October 1, 2010. All manuscripts received during this period will be recycled unread." Estab. 1950. Circ. 2,000. Byline given. Publishes ms an average of 10 months after acceptance. Responds in 3 months to mss. Sample copy for $12. Guidelines available online.

NONFICTION Needs essays, Book reviews. **Buys 6 mss/year.** Send complete ms. **Pays $25/page ($250 max).**

FICTION Needs mainstream, short stories. No sloppy, hasty, slight fiction. **Buys 15 mss/year.** Send complete ms. **Pays $25/page ($250 max).**

POETRY Considers simultaneous submissions "only if we are immediately informed of acceptance elsewhere." No e-mail submissions. All submissions should be typed on 1 side of the paper only, with name and address clearly written on the upper right corner of the ms. Include SASE. Reads submissions September 1-May 15 only. Responds in 3 months. Pays $2.50/line, one-year subscription, and 1 contributor's copy. Acquires first publication rights. Staff reviews books of poetry in 7-10 pages, multi-book format. Send materials for review consideration. (Most reviews are solicited.) "No inspirational, confessional poetry." Buys 70 poems/year. Submit maximum 5 poems. **Pays $2.50/line ($200 max).**

⊘ SHORT STUFF

Bowman Publications, Short Stuff Magazine, Bowman Publications, 2001 I St., #500, Fairbury NE 68352. (402)587-5003. **E-mail:** shortstf89@aol.com.

98% freelance written. Bimonthly magazine. "We are perhaps an enigma in that we publish only clean stories in any genre. We'll tackle any subject, but don't allow obscene language or pornographic description. Our magazine is for grown-ups, not X-rated 'adult' fare." Estab. 1989. Circ. 5,000. Byline given. Payment and contract upon publication. Editorial lead time 3 months. Submit seasonal material 3 months in advance. Responds in 6 months to mss. Sample copy - send 9×12 SAE with 5 first-class (44¢) stamps. Guidelines for #10 SASE.

NONFICTION Needs humor. Special issues: "We are holiday oriented and each issue reflects the appropriate holidays." **Buys 30 mss/year.** Send complete ms. Include cover letter about the author and synopsis of the story. Length: 500-1,500 words. **Payment varies.**

FICTION Needs adventure, historical, humorous, mainstream, mystery, romance, science fiction, (seldom), suspense, western. "We want to see more humor—not essay format—real stories with humor; 1,000-word mysteries, modern lifestyles. The 1,000-word pieces have the best chance of publication. No erotica; nothing morbid or pornographic. **Buys 144 mss/year.** Send complete ms. Length: 500-1,500 words. **Payment varies.**

FILLERS Needs anecdotes, short humor. **Buys 200 mss/year.** Length: 20-500 words. **Filler pays variable amount.**

SOUTHERN HUMANITIES REVIEW

Auburn University, 9088 Haley Center, Auburn University AL 36849. (334)844-9088. **E-mail:** shrengl@auburn.edu. **E-mail:** shrsubmissions@auburn.edu. **Website:** www.auburn.edu/english/shr/home.htm. **Contact:** Karen Beckwith. **99% freelance written.** Quarterly perfect-bound journal covering general humanities. *Southern Humanities Review* publishes fiction, poetry, and critical essays on the arts, literature, philosophy, religion, and history for a well-read, scholarly audience. Estab. 1967. Circ. approximately 700. Byline given. Accepts queries by mail, e-mail. NoResponds in 1-2 weeks to queries. Sample copy for $5 in U.S.; $7 everywhere else. Guidelines for #10 SASE or at www.auburn.edu/shr.

FICTION **Buys 4-8 mss/year.** Send complete ms. Length: 15,000 words. **Pays 2 contributor copies.**

POETRY Any kind; short poems preferred. Buys 10-25 poems/year. Submit maximum 5 poems. **Pays 2 contributor copies.**

⊕ THE SOUTHERN REVIEW

Louisiana State University, Old President's House, Baton Rouge LA 70803-5001. (225)578-5108. **Fax:** (225)578-5098. **E-mail:** southernreview@lsu.edu. **Website:** www.lsu.edu/tsr. **Contact:** Jeanne Leiby, Editor. **100% freelance written. Works with a moderate number of new/unpublished writers each year; reads unsolicited mss.** Quarterly magazine with emphasis on contemporary literature in the US and abroad. Reading period: September1-June 1. All mss. submitted during summer months will be recycled. Estab. 1935. Circ. 2,900. Byline given. Publishes ms an average of 6 months after acceptance. Accepts queries by mail. Does not accept previously published work.Responds in 2 months. Sample copy for $8. Guidelines available online.

NONFICTION Buys 25 mss/year. Length: 4,000-10,000 words. **Pays $30/page.**

FICTION **Contact:** Jessica Faust-Spitzfaden, assistant editor. Short stories of lasting literary merit, with emphasis on style and technique; novel excerpts. "We emphasize style and substantial content. No mystery, fantasy or religious mss." Submit one ms. in any genre at a time. "We rarely publish work that is longer than 8,000 words. We consider novel excerpts if they stand alone." Length: 4,000-8,000 words. **Pays $30/page.**

POETRY Submit maximum 5/time poems. 1-4 pages **Pays $30/page.**

THE SOW'S EAR POETRY REVIEW

217 Brookneill Dr., Winchester VA 22602. **E-mail:** sowsearpoetry@yahoo.com. **Website:** www.sows-ear.kitenet.net. **Contact:** Kristin Camitta Zimet. **100% freelance written.** Quarterly magazine. "*The Sow's Ear* prints fine poetry of all styles and lengths, complemented by b&w art. We also welcome reviews, interviews, and essays related to poetry. We are open to group submissions. Our 'Crossover' section features poetry married to any other art form, including prose, music, and visual media." Estab. 1988. Circ. 700. Publishes ms an average of 1-6 months after acceptance. Editorial lead time 1-6 months. Submit seasonal material 3 months in advance. Accepts queries by mail, e-mail. Accepts simultaneous submissions. Responds in 2 weeks to queries. Responds in 3 months to mss. Sample copy for $8. Guidelines available for SASE, by e-mail, or on website.

NONFICTION Needs essays related to poetry, interviews of poets, reviews of poetry books. Query. Length: 1,000-3,000 words.

COLUMNS Review of poetry book published within a year (1,000-3,000 words); interview with a poet; essay related to poetry. Query.

POETRY Needs avant-garde, free verse, haiku, light verse, traditional. Features groups of poets and "Crossovers" combining poetry with another art form. Submit up to 5 poems at a time. Considers simultaneous submissions "if you tell us promptly when work is accepted elsewhere"; no previously published poems, although will consider poems from chapbooks if they were never published in a magazine. Previously published poems may be included in 'Crossover' if rights are cleared. No e-mail submissions, except for poets outside the US; postal submissions only. Include brief bio and SASE. Pays 2 contributor's copies. Inquire about reviews, interviews, and essays. Contest/Award offerings: *The Sow's Ear* Poetry Competition and *The Sow's Ear* Chapbook Contest (separate listings in Contests & Awards). Open to any style or length. Buys 100 poems/year. No limits on line length.

STAND MAGAZINE

School of English, University of Leeds, Leeds LS2 9JT United Kingdom. (44)(113)343-4794. **E-mail:** stand@leeds.ac.uk. **Website:** www.standmagazine.org. "Quarterly literary magazine." Estab. 1952. Accepts queries by mail. Guidelines available online at website.

THE STORYTELLER

2441 Washington Rd., Maynard AR 72444. (870)647-2137. **E-mail:** storytellermag1@@yahoo.com. **Website:** www.thestorytellermagazine.com. **95% freelance written.** Quarterly magazine featuring short stories, essays, nonfiction and poetry. Estab. 1996. Circ. 700. Byline given. Publishes ms an average of 1-12 months after acceptance. Editorial lead time 6 months. Submit seasonal material 4 months in advance. Accepts queries by mail, e-mail. Accepts simultaneous submissions. Responds in 1 week to queries. Responds in 2 weeks to mss. Sample copy for 4 first-class stamps. Guidelines for #10 SASE.

NONFICTION Needs essays, general interest, historical, how-to, humor, inspirational, opinion, personal experience. Does not want anything graphic, pornographic, or based on Star Trek or Star Wars. Be original with all your work. We don't want 'poor me' articles or stories about how life is hard. We all understand that, but give us something at the end where we can see that things are looking up. **Buys 80 mss/year.** Send complete ms with SASE. Length: 1,500 words.

FICTION Needs adventure, fantasy, historical, horror, humorous, mainstream, mystery, romance, science fiction, slice-of-life vignettes, suspense, western. Does not want anything graphic, religious or bashing—even in fiction. **Buys 180 mss/year.** Send complete ms with SASE. Length: 1,500 words.

POETRY Needs avant-garde, free verse, haiku, light verse, traditional. Submit with SASE. Does not want long rambling. Buys 220 poems/year. Submit maximum 3 poems. Length: 40 lines.

FILLERS Needs anecdotes, facts, short humor. **Buys 5-6 mss/year.** Length: 15-50 words.

SUBTROPICS

University of Florida, P.O. Box 112075, 4008 Turlington Hall, Gainesville FL 32611-2075. **E-mail:** dleavitt@ufl.edu; subtropics@english.ufl.edu. **Website:** www.english.ufl.edu/subtropics. **Contact:** David Leavitt. **100% freelance written.** "Magazine published 3 times/year through the University of Florida's English department. *Subtropics* seeks to publish the best literary fiction, essays, and poetry being written today, both by established and emerging authors. We will consider works of fiction of any length, from short shorts to novellas and self-contained novel excerpts. We give the same latitude to essays. We appreciate work in translation and, from time to time, republish important and compelling stories, essays, and poems that have lapsed out of print by writers no longer living." Estab. 2005. Byline given. Publishes ms an average of 6 months after acceptance. Responds in 1 month to queries and mss. Guidelines available online.

NONFICTION Needs essays, literary nonfiction. No book reviews. **Buys 15 mss/year.** Send complete ms. **Pays $1,000.**

FICTION Literary fiction only, including short-shorts. No genre fiction. **Buys 20 mss/year.** Send complete ms. **Pays $500 for short-shorts; $1,000 for full stories.**

POETRY Buys 50 poems/year. Submit maximum 5 poems. **Pays $100.**

SYCAMORE REVIEW

Purdue University Dept. of English, 500 Oval Dr., West Lafayette IN 47907. (765) 494-3783. **Fax:** (765) 494-3780. **E-mail:** sycamore@purdue.edu. **Website:** www.sycamorereview.com. Semiannual magazine publishing poetry, fiction and nonfiction, books reviews and art. "Strives to publish the best writing by new and established writers. Looks for well crafted and engaging work, works that illuminate our lives in the collective human search for meaning. We would like to publish more work that takes a reflective look at our national identity and how we are perceived by the world. We look for diversity of voice, pluralistic worldviews, and political and social context." Accepts queries by mail.

NONFICTION **Contact:** Jess Mehr. Needs essays, Personal, humor, Literary Memoir, Translation. No outside interviews, previously published work (except translations) or genre pieces (conventional sci fi, romance, horror, etc.) No scholarly articles or journalistic pieces. Please query for book reviews, brief critical essays as well as all art.

POETRY Submissions should be typed, double-spaced,with numbered pages and the author's name and the title easily visible on each page. Does not publish creative work by any student currently attending Purdue University. Former students should wait one year before submitting. Submit maximum Submit 4-5 poems in one envelope. "Wait until you have received a response to submit again." poems.

⊘ $ THEMA

Thema Literary Society, P.O. Box 8747, Metairie LA 70011-8747. **E-mail:** thema@cox.net. **Website:** http://themaliterarysociety.com. **100% freelance written.** Triannual magazine covering a different theme for each issue. Upcoming themes for SASE. "*Thema* is designed to stimulate creative thinking by challenging writers with unusual themes, such as 'The Box Under the Bed' and 'Put It In Your Pocket, Lillian'. Appeals to writers, teachers of creative writing, and general reading audience." Estab. 1988. Circ. 350. Byline given. Publishes ms an average of within 6 months after acceptance. Accepts queries by mail. Accepts simultaneous submissions. Responds in 1 week to queries. Responds in 5 months to mss. Sample copy for $10. Guidelines for #10 SASE.

FICTION **Contact:** Virginia Howard, editor. Needs adventure, ethnic, experimental, fantasy, historical, humorous, mainstream, mystery, novel concepts, religious, science fiction, slice-of-life vignettes, suspense, western, contemporary, sports, prose poem. No erotica. **Buys 30 mss/year.** fewer than 6,000 words preferred **Pays $10-25.**

POETRY Needs avant-garde, free verse, haiku, light verse, traditional. No erotica. Buys 27 poems/year. Submit maximum 3 poems. Length: 4-50 lines. **Pays $10.**

$$$ TIN HOUSE

McCormack Communications, P.O. Box 10500, Portland OR 97210. (503)274-4393. **Fax:** (503)222-1154. **E-mail:** info@tinhouse.com. **Website:** www.tinhouse.com. **Contact:** Cheston Knapp, managing editor; Holly Macarthur, founding editor. **90% freelance written.** "We are a general interest literary quarterly. Our watchword is quality. Our audience includes people interested in literature in all its aspects, from the mundane to the exalted." Estab. 1998. Circ. 11,000. Byline given. Publishes ms an average of 6 months after acceptance. Editorial lead time 6 months. Submit seasonal material 6 months in advance. Accepts queries by mail, online submission form. Accepts simultaneous submissions. Responds in 6 weeks to queries. Responds in 3 months to mss. Sample copy for $15. Guidelines available online.

NONFICTION Needs book excerpts, essays, interview, personal experience. Send complete ms September 1-May 31 via regular mail or online submission form. No fax or e-mail submissions. 5,000 words maximum **Pays $50-800 for assigned articles. Pays $50-500 for unsolicited articles.** Sometimes pays expenses of writers on assignment.

COLUMNS Lost and Found (mini-reviews of forgotten or underappreciated books), up to 500 words; Readable Feasts (fiction or nonfiction literature with recipes), 2,000-3,000 words; Pilgrimage (journey to a personally significant place, especially literary), 2,000-3,000 words. **Buys 15-20 mss/year.** Send complete ms. **Pays $50-500.**

FICTION **Contact:** Rob Spillman, fiction editor. Needs experimental, mainstream, novel concepts, literary. **Buys 15-20 mss/year.** Send complete ms September 1-May 31 via regular mail or online submission form. No fax or e-mail submissions. 5,000 words maximum **Pays $200-800.**

POETRY **Contact:** Brenda Shaunessy, poetry editor. Needs avant-garde, free verse, traditional. "No prose masquerading as poetry." Send complete ms September 1-May 31 via regular mail or online submission form. No fax or e-mail submissions. Buys 40 poems/year. Submit maximum 5 poems. **Pays $50-150.**

TIPS "Remember to send an SASE with your submission."

$$ VERBATIM

Word, Inc., P.O. BOX 1774, Burlingame ILCA 94011. (800)897-3006. **E-mail:** editor@verbatimmag.com.

Website: www.verbatimmag.com. **75-80% freelance written**. Quarterly magazine covering language and linguistics. "*Verbatim* is the only magazine of language and linguistics for the lay person." Estab. 1974. Circ. 1,600. Byline given. Publishes ms an average of 6-9 months after acceptance. Editorial lead time 3 months. Submit seasonal material 6 months in advance. Accepts queries by e-mail (only). Responds in 3 weeks to queries. Responds in 2 months to mss. E-mail for sample copy. Guidelines available online.

NONFICTION Needs essays, humor, personal experience. Does not want puns or overly cranky prescriptivism. **Buys 24-28 mss/year.** Query. Submissions only accepted online. **Pays $25-400 for assigned articles. Pays $25-300 for unsolicited articles.**

POETRY "We only publish poems explicitly about language. Poems written in language not enough." Buys 4-6 poems/year. Submit maximum 3 poems. Length: 3-75 lines. **Pays $25-50.**

VERSAL

Postbus 3865, Amsterdam 1054 EJ The Netherlands. **Website:** www.wordsinhere.com. **Contact:** Shayna Schapp, assistant art editor (artists); Megan Garr, editor (writers and designers). Annual print magazine. "*Versal*, published each May by *wordsinhere*, is the only literary magazine of its kind in the Netherlands and publishes new poetry, prose, and art from around the world. *Versal* and the writers behind it are also at the forefront of a growing translocal European literary scene, which includes exciting communities in Amsterdam, Paris and Berlin. *Versal* seeks work that is urgent, involved and unexpected." Estab. 2002. Circ. 650. Publishes ms an average of 3-4 months after acceptance. Accepts queries by e-mail. Accepts simultaneous submissions. Responds in 2 months. Sample copies available for $10. Guidelines available online.

NONFICTION Query.

FICTION Contact: Robert Glick, editor. Needs experimental, mainstream, novel concepts, Flash fiction, prose poetry. **Buys 10 mss/year. pays in copies.**

POETRY Contact: Megan M. Garr, editor. Needs avant-garde, free verse. Submit 3-5 poems at a time. Considers simultaneous submissions; no previously published poems. Accepts submissions online only (online submission system can be found on website. Reads submissions September 15–January 15. Time between acceptance and publication is 4-7 months. Poems are circulated to an editorial board. Sometimes

comments on rejected poems. Guidelines available on website. Responds in 2 months. Sends prepublication PDF galleys. Pays 1 contributor's copy. Acquires one-time rights. Rights revert to poet upon publication. Buys 35 poems/year. Submit maximum 5 poems. **Pays in copies**.

VESTAL REVIEW

2609 Dartmouth Dr., Vestal NY 13850. **E-mail:** submissions@vestalreview.net. **Website:** www.vestalreview.net. Semi-annual print magazine specializing in flash fiction. "We accept submissions only through our submission manager." Circ. 1,500. Publishes ms an average of 3-4 months after acceptance. Accepts queries by e-mail. Accepts simultaneous submissions. Responds in 1 week to queries. Responds in 4 months to mss. Guidelines available online.

FICTION Needs ethnic, horror, mainstream, speculative fiction. Does not read new submissions in January, June, July, and December. All submissions received during these months will be returned unopened. Length: 50-500 words. **Pays 3-10¢/word and 1 contributor's copy; additional copies $10 (plus postage).**

WEST BRANCH

Stadler Center for Poetry, Bucknell University, Lewisburg PA 17837-2029. (570)577-1853. **Fax:** (570)577-1885. **E-mail:** westbranch@bucknell.edu. **Website:** www.bucknell.edu/westbranch. Semiannual literary magazine. *West Branch* publishes poetry, fiction, and nonfiction in both traditional and innovative styles. Byline given. Accepts queries by online submission form. Sample copy for $3. Guidelines available online.

NONFICTION Needs essays, general interest, literary. **Buys 4-5 mss/year.** Send complete ms. **Pays $20-100 ($10/page).**

FICTION Needs novel excerpts, short stories. No genre fiction. **Buys 10-12 mss/year.** Send complete ms. **Pays $20-100 ($10/page).**

POETRY Needs free and formal verse. Buys 30-40 poems/year. Submit maximum 6 poems. **Pays $20-100 ($10/page).**

WESTERN HUMANITIES REVIEW

University of Utah, English Department, 255 S. Central Campus Dr., Room 3500, Salt Lake City UT 84112-0494. (801)581-6070. **Fax:** (801)585-5167. **E-mail:** whr@mail.hum.utah.edu. **Website:** www.hum.utah.edu/whr. **Contact:** Dawn Lonsinger, Managing Editor. A tri-annual magazine for educated readers.

Estab. 1947. Circ. 1,000. Pays in contributor copies. Publishes ms an average of 1 year after acceptance. Accepts simultaneous submissions. Sample copy for $10. Guidelines available online.

NONFICTION Contact: Barry Weller, editor-in-chief. **Buys 6-8unsolicited/year mss/year.** Send complete ms. **Pays $5/published page.**

FICTION Contact: Lance Olsen, Fiction Editor. Needs experimental, and innovative voices. Does not want genre (romance, sci-fi, etc.). **Buys 5-8 mss/year.** Send complete ms. Length: 5,000 words. **Pays $5/published page (when funds available).**

POETRY Contact: Richard Howard, poetry editor.

🍁 $ WINDSOR REVIEW

Dept. of English, University of Windsor, Windsor ON N9B 3P4 Canada. (519)253-3000; (519) 253-4232 ext. 2290. **Fax:** (519)971-3676. **E-mail:** uwrevu@uwindsor.ca. **Website:** www.uwindsor.ca. **Contact:** Marty Gervais, art editor. Semiannual magazine. "We try to offer a balance of fiction and poetry distinguished by excellence." Estab. 1965. Circ. 250. Publishes ms an average of 6 months after acceptance. Accepts queries by e-mail. Responds in 1 month to queries; 6 weeks to mss. Sample copy for $7 (US). Guidelines available online.

FICTION Contact: Alistair MacLeod, fiction editor. Needs experimental. No genre fiction (science fiction, romance), but would consider if writing is good enough. Send complete ms. Length: 1,000-5,000 words. **Pays $25, 1 contributor's copy and a free subscription.**

POETRY Submit maximum 6 poems.

$ THE YALOBUSHA REVIEW

University of Mississippi, P.O. Box 1848, Dept. of English, University MS 38677. (662)915-3175. **E-mail:** yreditor@yahoo.com. **Website:** www.olemiss.edu/yalobusha. Annual literary journal seeking quality submissions from around the globe. Reading period is July 15-November 15. Estab. 1995. Circ. 500. Accepts queries by mail. Does not accept previously published workAccepts simultaneous submissions. Responds in 2-4 months to mss. Sample copy for $5. Guidelines for #10 SASE.

NONFICTION Contact: Nonfiction Editor. Needs essays, memoir, travel, experimental pieces. Does not want sappy confessional or insights into parenthood. Send complete ms with cover letter and SASE. Length: 10,000 words. **Pays honorarium when funding available.**

FICTION Contact: Fiction Editor. Needs experimental, historical, humorous, mainstream, novel excerpts, short shorts. **Buys 3-6 mss/year.** Send complete ms with cover letter and SASE. Length: 10,000 words. **Pays honorarium when funding available.**

POETRY Contact: Poetry Editor. Needs avant-garde, free verse, traditional. Interested in publishing a variety of voices, both new and established. Submit maximum up to 5 poems. **Send cover letter and SASE. Pays 2 contributor's copies.**

$ ZAHIR

Zahir Publishing, 315 South Coast Hwy. 101, Suite U8, Encinitas CA 92024. **E-mail:** zahirtales@gmail.com. **Website:** www.zahirtales.com. **Contact:** Sheryl Tempchin, editor. **100% freelance written.** Quarterly online magazine. "We publish literary speculative fiction." Estab. 2003. Byline given. Publishes ms an average of 2-12 months after acceptance. Accepts queries by mail, e-mail. Responds in 1-2 weeks to queries. Responds in 1-3 months to mss. Writer's guidelines for #10 SASE, by e-mail, or online.

FICTION Needs fantasy, surrealism, magical realism, science fiction, surrealism, magical realism. No children's stories or stories that deal with excessive violence or anything pornographic. **Buys 18-25 mss/year.** Send complete ms. or submit through online submission form. 6,000 words maximum. **Pays $10 and one copy of the annual print anthology.**

$$$ ZOETROPE: ALL-STORY

Zoetrope: All-Story, The Sentinel Bldg., 916 Kearny St., San Francisco CA 94133. (415)788-7500. **Website:** www.all-story.com. Quarterly magazine specializing in the best of contemporary short fiction. *Zoetrope: All Story* presents a new generation of classic stories. Estab. 1997. Circ. 20,000. Byline given. Publishes ms an average of 5 months after acceptance. Accepts queries by mail. Accepts simultaneous submissions. Responds in 8 months (if SASE included). Sample copy for $8.00. Guidelines available online.

FICTION Buys 25-35 mss/year. "Writers should submit only one story at a time and no more than two stories a year. We consider unsolicited submissions of short stories and one-act plays no longer than 7,000 words. Excerpts from larger works, screenplays, treatments, and poetry will be returned unread. We do not accept artwork or design submissions. We do not accept unsolicited revisions nor respond to writers who don't include an SASE." Send complete ms.

by mail to: *Zoetrope:All-Story* Attn: Fiction Editor. **Pays $1,000.**

$ ZYZZYVA

466 Geary Street, Suite 401, San Francisco CA 94102. (415)440-1510. **E-mail:** editor@zyzzyva.org. **Website:** www.zyzzyva.org. **Contact:** Howard Junker. **100% freelance written. Works with a small number of new/unpublished writers each year.** Magazine published in March, August, and November. "We feature work by writers currently living on the West Coast or in Alaska and Hawaii only. We are essentially a literary magazine, but of wide-ranging interests and a strong commitment to nonfiction." Estab. 1985. Circ. 2,500. Byline given. Publishes ms an average of 3 months after acceptance. Accepts queries by mail, e-mail. Responds in 1 week to queries. Responds in 1 month to mss. Sample copy for $7 or online. Guidelines available online.

NONFICTION Needs book excerpts, general interest, historical, humor, personal experience. **Buys 50 mss/year.** Query by mail or e-mail. Open **Pays $50.**

FICTION Needs ethnic, experimental, humorous, mainstream. **Buys 60 mss/year.** Send complete ms. Length: 100-7,500 words. **Pays $50.**

POETRY Buys 20 poems/year. Submit maximum 5 poems. Length: 3 200 lines. **Pays $50.**

MEN'S

$$$$ ESQUIRE

300 W. 57th St., 21st Floor, New York NY 10019. (212)649-4020. **Website:** www.esquire.com. Monthly magazine covering the ever-changing trends in American culture. *Esquire* is geared toward smart, well-off men. General readership is college educated and sophisticated, between ages 30 and 45. Written mostly by contributing editors on contract. Rarely accepts unsolicited mss. Estab. 1933. Circ. 720,000. Publishes ms an average of 2-6 months after acceptance. Editorial lead time at least 2 months. Accepts simultaneous submissions. Guidelines for SASE.

NONFICTION Buys 4 features and 12 shorter mss/year. Magazine no longer accepts paper submissions. To submit, use online submission manager at http://esquiresubmissions.com. Columns average 1,500 words; features average 5,000 words; short front of book pieces average 200-400 words. **Payment varies.**

FICTION "Literary excellence is our only criterion." Needs novel concepts, short stories, memoirs, plays. No pornography, science fiction or 'true romance' stories. Send complete ms. To submit a story, use online submission manager at http://esquiresubmissions.com.

$$$$ KING

Harris Publications, Inc., 1115 Broadway, 8th Floor, New York NY 10010. **Fax:** (212)807-0216. **E-mail:** king@harris-pub.com. **Website:** www.king-mag.com. **75% freelance written.** Men's lifestyle magazine published 80 times/year. *King* is a general interest men's magazine with a strong editorial voice. Topics include lifestyle, entertainment, news, women, cars, music, fashion, investigative reporting. Estab. 2001. Circ. 270,000. Byline given. Offers 25% kill fee. Editorial lead time 2-3 months. Submit seasonal material 4 months in advance. Accepts queries by e-mail. Responds in 1 month to queries. Guidelines free.

NONFICTION Needs essays, exposé, general interest. Does not want completed articles. Pitches only. Query with published clips. Length: 2,000-5,000 words. **Pays $1-1.50/word.** Sometimes pays expenses of writers on assignment.

MILITARY

🍁 $$ AIRFORCE

Air Force Association of Canada, P.O Box 2460, Stn D, Ottawa ON K1P 5W6 Canada. (613)232-2303. **Fax:** (613)232-2156. **E-mail:** director@airforce.ca. **Website:** www.airforce.ca. **5% freelance written.** Quarterly magazine covering Canada's air force heritage. Stories center on Canadian military aviation—past, present and future. Estab. 1977. Circ. 16,000. Byline given. Publishes ms an average of 6 months after acceptance. Editorial lead time 3 months. Submit seasonal material 3 months in advance. Accepts queries by mail, e-mail, fax, phone. Accepts simultaneous submissions. Responds in 2 weeks to queries. Responds in 1 month to mss. Sample copy free. Guidelines by email.

NONFICTION Needs historical, interview, personal experience, photo feature. **Buys 2 mss/year.** Query with published clips. Length: 1,500-3,500 words. Sometimes pays expenses of writers on assignment. Limit agreed upon in advance

FILLERS Needs anecdotes, facts. About 800 words. **Negotiable.**

$$ AIR FORCE TIMES

Army Times Publishing Co., 6883 Commercial Dr., Springfield VA 22159. (703)750-8646. **Fax:** (703)750-

8601. **E-mail:** airlet@airforcetimes.com. **Website:** www.airforcetimes.com. **Contact:** Becky Iannotta, managing editor. "Weeklies edited separately for Army, Navy, Marine Corps, and Air Force military personnel and their families. They contain career information such as pay raises, promotions, news of legislation affecting the military, housing, base activities and features of interest to military people." Estab. 1940. Byline given. Offers kill fee. Accepts queries by mail, e-mail, phone. Accepts simultaneous submissions. Responds in 1 month to queries. Sample copy for #10 SASE. Guidelines for #10 SASE.

NONFICTION No advice pieces. **Buys 150-175 mss/year.** Query. Length: 750-2,000 words. **Pays $100-500.**

COLUMNS Length: 500-900. **Buys 75 mss/year. Pays $75-125.**

💲💲 ARMY MAGAZINE

2425 Wilson Blvd., Arlington VA 22201. (703)841-4300. **Fax:** (703)841-3505. **E-mail:** armymag@ausa.org. **Website:** www.ausa.org. **70% freelance written. Prefers to work with published/established writers.** Monthly magazine emphasizing military interests. Estab. 1904. Circ. 90,000. Byline given. Publishes ms an average of 5 months after acceptance. Submit seasonal material 3 months in advance. Accepts queries by mail. Sample copy and writer's guidelines for 9×12 SAE with $1 postage or online.

NONFICTION Needs historical, military and original, humor, military feature-length articles and anecdotes, interview, photo feature. Special issues: "We would like to see more pieces about little-known episodes involving interesting military personalities. We especially want material lending itself to heavy, contributor-supplied photographic treatment. The first thing a contributor should recognize is that our readership is very savvy militarily. 'Gee-whiz' personal reminiscences get short shrift, unless they hold their own in a company in which long military service, heroism and unusual experiences are commonplace. At the same time, *ARMY* readers like a well-written story with a fresh slant, whether it is about an experience in a foxhole or the fortunes of a corps in battle." No rehashed history. No unsolicited book reviews. **Buys 40 mss/year.** Submit complete ms (hard copy and disk). Length: 1,000-1,500 words. **Pays 12-18¢/word.**

💲💲💲 MILITARY OFFICER

201 N. Washington St., Alexandria VA 22314-2539. (800)234-6622. **Fax:** (703)838-8179. **E-mail:** editor@moaa.org. **Website:** www.moaa.org. **Contact:** Managing editor. **60% freelance written. Prefers to work with published/established writers.** Monthly magazine for officers of the 7 uniformed services and their families. Estab. 1945. Circ. 325,000. Byline given. Publishes ms an average of 1 year after acceptance. Accepts queries by e-mail. Responds in 3 months to queries. Sample copy and guidelines available online.

NONFICTION "We rarely accept unsolicited mss." **Buys 50 mss/year.** Query with résumé, sample clips. Length: 1,000-2,000 words (features). **Pays 80¢/word (features).**

💲💲 PROCEEDINGS

U.S. Naval Institute, 291 Wood Rd., Annapolis MD 21402. (410)268-6110. **Fax:** (410)295-7940. **E-mail:** articlesubmissions@usni.org. **Website:** www.usni.org. **Contact:** Paul Merzlak, editor-in-chief; Amy Voight, photo editor. **80% freelance written.** Monthly magazine covering Navy, Marine Corps, Coast Guard issues. Estab. 1873. Circ. 60,000. Byline given. Publishes ms an average of 9 months after acceptance. Editorial lead time 3 months. Responds in 2 months to queries. Sample copy for $3.95. Guidelines available on website.

NONFICTION Needs essays, historical, interview, photo feature, technical. **Buys 100-125 mss/year.** Send complete ms. 3,000 words. **Pays $60-150/printed page for unsolicited articles.**

COLUMNS Comment & Discussion (letters to editor), 500 words; Commentary (opinion), 700 words; Nobody Asked Me, But.. (opinion), less than 700 words. **Buys 150-200 mss/year.** Query or send complete ms. **Pays $34-150.**

FILLERS Needs anecdotes. **Buys 20 fillers/year mss/year.** Length: 100 words. **Pays $25.**

💲💲💲💲 SOLDIER OF FORTUNE

2135 11th St., Boulder CO 80302-4045. (303)449-3750. **E-mail:** editorsof@aol.com. **Website:** www.sofmag.com. **Contact:** Lt. Col. Robert A. Brown, editor/publisher. **50% freelance written.** Monthly magazine covering military, paramilitary, police, combat subjects, and action/adventure. "We are an action-oriented magazine; we cover combat hot spots around the world. We also provide timely features on state-of-the-art weapons and equipment; elite military and police units; and historical military operations. Readership is primarily active-duty military, veterans, and law enforcement." Estab. 1975. Circ. 60,000. Byline given. Offers 25% kill fee. Responds in 3 weeks to queries. Responds in 1 month to mss. Sample copy for $5. Guidelines with #10 SASE.

NONFICTION Needs exposé, general interest, historical, how-to, on weapons and their skilled use, humor, interview, new product, personal experience, photo feature, No. 1 on our list, technical, travel, combat reports, military unit reports, and solid Vietnam and Operation Iraqi Freedom articles. No `How I won the war' pieces; no op-ed pieces unless they are fully and factually backgrounded; no knife articles (staff assignments only). All submitted articles should have good art; art will sell us on an article. **Buys 75 mss/year.** Query with or without published clips or send complete ms. Send mss to articles editor; queries to managing editor Length: 2,000-3,000 words. **Pays $150-250/page.**

FILLERS Contact: Bulletin board editor. Needs newsbreaks, military/paramilitary related has to be documented. Length: 100-250 words. **Pays $50.**

MUSIC CONSUMER

ALARM

Alarm Press, 205 N. Michigan Ave. Suite 3200, Chicago IL 60601. (312)341-1290. **E-mail:** info@alarmpress.com. **Website:** www.alarmpress.com. *ALARM*, published 6 times/year, "does one thing, and it does it very well: it publishes the best new music and art in *ALARM* magazine and alarmpress.com. From our headquarters in a small Chicago office, along with a cast of contributing writers spread across the country, we listen to thousands of CDs, view hundreds of gallery openings, and attend lectures and live concerts in order to present inspirational artists who are fueled by an honest and contagious obsession with their art." Accepts queries by mail, e-mail. Only responds if interested. Submit by e-mail with the subject line "ALARM Magazine Submissions. Please send your work as part of the body of an e-mail; we cannot accept attachments." Alternatively, submissions may be sent by regular mail to Submissions Dept. "*ALARM* is not responsible for the return, loss of, or damage to unsolicited manuscripts, unsolicited art work, or any other unsolicited materials. Those submitting manuscripts, art work, or any other materials should not send originals."

🌀🌀 BLUEGRASS UNLIMITED

Bluegrass Unlimited, Inc., P.O. Box 771, Warrenton VA 20188-0771. (540)349-8181 or (800)BLU-GRAS. **Fax:** (540)341-0011. **E-mail:** editor@bluegrassmusic.

com. **Website:** www.bluegrassmusic.com. **10% freelance written. Prefers to work with published/established writers.** Monthly magazine covering bluegrass, acoustic, and old-time country music. Estab. 1966. Circ. 27,000. Byline given. Offers negotiated kill fee. Publishes ms an average of 4 months after acceptance. Submit seasonal material 4 months in advance. Accepts queries by mail, e-mail, fax. Responds in 2 weeks to queries. Responds in 2 months to mss. Sample copy free. Guidelines for #10 SASE.

NONFICTION Needs general interest, historical, how-to, interview, personal experience, photo feature, travel. No fan-style articles. **Buys 30-40 mss/year.** Query. Open **Pays 10-13¢/word.**

FICTION Needs ethnic, humorous. **Buys 3-5 mss/year.** Query. Negotiable **Pays 10-13¢/word.**

🌀🌀 CHAMBER MUSIC

Chamber Music America, 305 Seventh Ave., 5th Floor, New York NY 10001-6008. (212)242-2022. **Fax:** (212)242-7955. **E-mail:** egoldensohn@chamber-music.org. **Website:** www.chamber-music.org. Bimonthly magazine covering chamber music. Estab. 1977. Circ. 13,000. Byline given. Offers kill fee. Publishes ms an average of 5 months after acceptance. Editorial lead time 4 months. Accepts queries by mail, phone.

NONFICTION Needs book excerpts, essays, humor, opinion, personal experience, issue-oriented stories of relevance to the chamber music fields written by top music journalists and critics, or music practitioners. No artist profiles, no stories about opera or symphonic work. **Buys 35 mss/year.** Query with published clips. Length: 2,500-3,500 words. **Pays $500 minimum.** Sometimes pays expenses of writers on assignment.

🌀 CHURCH MUSIC QUARTERLY

The Royal School of Church Music, 19 The Close, Salisbury SP1 2EB United Kingdom. (44)(1722)424848. **Fax:** (44)(172)242-4849. **E-mail:** cmq@rscm.com. **Website:** www.rscm.com. Quarterly publication that offers advice, information, and inspiration to church music enthusiasts around the world. Each issue offers a variety of articles and interviews by distinguished musicians, theologians, and scholars. Circ. 13,500. Accepts queries by e-mail. Guidelines by email.

NONFICTION Submit ms, bio. Length: 1,200-1,400 words

GUITAR WORLD

149 5th Ave., 9th Floor, New York NY 10010. (650)872-1642. **E-mail:** gwedit@aol.com; soundingboard@

guitarworld.com. **Website:** www.guitarworld.com. Monthly magazine. Written for guitar players categorized as either professionals, semi-professionals or amateur players. Every issue offers broad-ranging interviews that cover technique, instruments, and lifestyles. "To submit a GuitarWorldBlips story, you must be logged in. If you already have an account on GuitarWorldBlips, please log in. Or join GuitarWorldBlips—it's free and fast. Just fill out the form and enter the URL, title, and description. Your story will appear once we've validated your e-mail address." Circ. 150,000. Editorial lead time 2 months.

⊘ ROLLING STONE

Wenner Media, 1290 Avenue of the Americas, New York NY 10104. (212)484-1616. **Fax:** (212)484-1664. **E-mail:** letters@rollingstone.com; photo@rollingstone.com. **Website:** www.rollingstone.com. **Contact:** Jann S. Wenner; John Gara, photo editor. Biweekly magazine geared towards young adults interested in news of popular music, entertainment and the arts, current news events, politics and American culture. Circ. 1,254,200. Editorial lead time 1 month.

💬 Query before submitting.

$$$ SYMPHONY

American Symphony Orchestra League, 33 W. 60th St., Fifth Floor, New York NY 10023. (212)262-5161. **Fax:** (212)262-5198. **E-mail:** rsandla@americanorchestras.org; clane@americanorchestras.org; jmelick@americanorchestras.org; editor@americanorchestras.org. **Website:** www.symphony.org. **Contact:** Robert Sandla, editor; Chester Lane, senior editor; Jennifer Melick, managing editor. **50% freelance written**. Bimonthly magazine for the orchestra industry and classical music enthusiasts covering classical music, orchestra industry, musicians. "Symphony, the quarterly magazine of the League of American Orchestras, reports on the critical issues, trends, personalities, and developments of the orchestra world. Every issue includes news, provocative essays, in-depth articles, and cutting-edge research relevant to the entire orchestra field. Symphony profiles take readers behind the scenes to meet the people who are making a difference in the orchestra world, while wide-ranging survey articles reveal the strategies and tactics that are helping orchestras meet the challenges of the 21st century. Symphony is a matchless source of meaningful information about orchestras, and serves as an advocate and connector for the orchestra field." Circ. 18,000. Byline given. Publishes ms an average of 10 weeks after acceptance. Editorial lead time 6 months. Submit seasonal material 8 months in advance. Accepts queries by mail, e-mail. Accepts simultaneous submissions. Guidelines available online.

NONFICTION Needs book excerpts, essays, inspirational, interview, opinion, personal experience, rare, photo feature, rare, issue features, trend pieces (by assignment only; pitches welcome). Does not want to see reviews, interviews. **Buys 30 mss/year.** Query with published clips. Length: 1,500-3,500 words. **Pays $500-900.** Sometimes pays expenses of writers on assignment.

COLUMNS Repertoire (orchestral music—essays); Comment (personal views and opinions); Currents (electronic media developments); In Print (books); On Record (CD, DVD, video), all 1,000-2,500 words. **Buys 12 mss/year.** Query with published clips.

MYSTERY

$ ELLERY QUEEN'S MYSTERY MAGAZINE

Dell Magazines Fiction Group, 267 Broadway, 4th Floor, New York NY 10017. (212)686-7188. **Fax:** (212)686-7414. **E-mail:** elleryqueenmm@dellmagazines.com. **Website:** www.themysteryplace.com/eqmm. **100% freelance written**. Featuring mystery fiction. "*Ellery Queen's Mystery Magazine* welcomes submissions from both new and established writers. We publish every kind of mystery short story: the psychological suspense tale, the deductive puzzle, the private eye case—the gamut of crime and detection from the realistic (including the policeman's lot and stories of police procedure) to the more imaginative (including 'locked rooms' and 'impossible crimes'). We look for strong writing, an original and exciting plot, and professional craftsmanship. We encourage writers whose work meets these general criteria to read an issue of *EQMM* before making a submission." Estab. 1941. Circ. 100,000. Byline given. Publishes ms an average of 6-12 months after acceptance. Accepts queries by online submission form. Accepts simultaneous submissions. Responds in 3 months to mss. Sample copy for $5.50. Guidelines for SASE or online.

FICTION Contact: Janet Hutchings, editor. "We always need detective stories. Special consideration given to anything timely and original." Needs mystery. No explicit sex or violence, no gore or horror. Seldom publishes parodies or pastiches. "We do not want true detective or crime stories." **Buys up to 120 mss/year.** *EQMM* uses an online submission system (http://eqmm.magazinesubmissions.com) that has been designed to streamline our process and improve communication with authors. We ask that all submissions be made electronically, using this system, rather than on paper. All stories should be in standard manuscript format and submitted in .DOC format. We cannot accept .DOCX, .RTF, or .TXT files at this time. For detailed submission instructions, see http://eqmm.magazinesubmissions.com or our writers guidelines page (http://www.themysteryplace.com/eqmm/guidelines). Most stories 2,500-8,000 words. Accepts longer and shorter submissions—including minute mysteries of 250 words, and novellas of up to 20,000 words from established authors **Pays 5-8¢/word; occasionally higher for established authors**.

POETRY Short mystery verses, limericks. Length: 1 page, double spaced maximum.

NATURE, CONSERVATION AND ECOLOGY

[🍁] $ ALTERNATIVES JOURNAL

University of Waterloo, Faculty of Environmental Studies, Waterloo ON N2L 3G1 Canada. (519)888-4442. **Fax:** (519)746-0292. **E-mail:** editor@alternativesjournal.ca. **Website:** www.alternativesjournal.ca. **Contact:** Nicola Ross, editor-in-chief; Marcia Ruby, production coordinator. **90% freelance written**. Estab. 1971. Circ. 5,000. Byline given. Offers 50% kill fee. Publishes ms an average of 5 months after acceptance. Editorial lead time 7 months. Submit seasonal material 5 months in advance. Accepts queries by mail, e-mail, fax. Accepts simultaneous submissions. Sample copy free for Canadian writers only. Guidelines available online.

NONFICTION Needs book excerpts, essays, exposé, humor, interview, opinion. **Buys 50 mss/year.** Query with published clips. Length: 800-3,000 words. **Pays $50-150 (Canadian).** Sometimes pays expenses of writers on assignment.

ARIZONA WILDLIFE VIEWS

2221 W. Greenway Rd., Phoenix AZ 85053. (800)777-0015. **E-mail:** awv@azgfd.gov. **Website:** www.azgfd.gov/magazine. **50% freelance written**. Bimonthly magazine covering Arizona wildlife, wildlife management and outdoor recreation (specifically hunting, fishing, wildlife watching, boating and off-highway vehicle recreation). *Arizona Wildlife Views* is a general interest magazine about Arizona wildlife, wildlife management and outdoor recreation. We publish material that conforms to the mission and policies of the Arizona Game and Fish Department. In addition to Arizona wildlife and wildlife management, topics include habitat issues, outdoor recreation involving wildlife, boating, fishing, hunting, bird-watching, animal observation, off-highway vehicle use, etc., and historical articles about wildlife and wildlife management. Circ. 22,000. Byline given. Publishes ms an average of 10 months after acceptance. Editorial lead time 1 year. Submit seasonal material 2 months in advance. Accepts queries by mail, e-mail. Accepts simultaneous submissions. Responds in 1 month to queries. Responds in 2 months to mss. Sample copy free. Guidelines free and available online.

NONFICTION Needs general interest, historical, how-to, interview, photo feature, technical, travel, scientific for a popular audience. Does not want me and Joe articles, anthropomorphism of wildlife or opinionated pieces not based on confirmable facts. **Buys 20 mss/year.** Query. Length: 1,000-2,500 words. **Pays $450-800.**

[🍁] $$$ THE ATLANTIC SALMON JOURNAL

The Atlantic Salmon Federation, P.O. Box 5200, St. Andrews NB E5B 3S8 Canada. (506)529-1033. **Fax:** (506)529-4438. **E-mail:** savesalmon@asf.ca. **Website:** www.asf.ca. **Contact:** Martin Silverstone. **50-68% freelance written**. Quarterly magazine covering conservation efforts for the Atlantic salmon, catering to the dedicated angler and conservationist. Circ. 11,000. Byline given. Publishes ms an average of 6 months after acceptance. Submit seasonal material 3 months in advance. Accepts simultaneous submissions. Responds in 2 months to queries. Sample copy for 9×12 SAE with $1 (Canadian), or IRC. Guidelines free.

NONFICTION Needs exposé, historical, how-to, humor, interview, new product, opinion, personal experience, photo feature, technical, travel, conservation. **Buys 15-20 mss/year.** Query with published clips. Length: 2,000 words. **Pays $400-800 for articles with photos.** Sometimes pays expenses of writers on assignment.

COLUMNS Fit To Be Tied (Conservation issues and salmon research; the design, construction and success of specific flies); interesting characters in the sport and opinion pieces by knowledgeable writers, 900 words; Casting Around (short, informative, entertaining reports, book reviews and quotes from the world of Atlantic salmon angling and conservation). Query. **Pays $50-300.**

🐻🐻 THE BEAR DELUXE MAGAZINE

Orlo, 810 SE Belmont, Studio 5, Portland OR 97214. (503)242-1047. **E-mail:** bear@orlo.org. **Website:** www.orlo.org. **Contact:** Tom Webb, editor-in-chief; Kristin Rogers Brown, art director. **80% freelance written.** Covers fiction/essay/poetry/other. 750-4,500 words. Do not combine submissions, rather submit poetry, fiction and essay in separate packages. News essays, on occasion, are assigned out if they have a strong element of reporting. Artists contribute to *The Bear Deluxe* in various ways, including: editorial illustration, editorial photography, spot illustration, independent art, cover art, graphic design, and cartoons. "*The Bear Deluxe Magazine* is a national independent environmental arts magazine publishing significant works of reporting, creative nonfiction, literature, visual art and design. Based in the Pacific Northwest, it reaches across cultural and political divides to engage readers on vital issues effecting the environment. Published twice per year, *The Bear Deluxe* includes a wider array and a higher-percentage of visual art work and design than many other publications. Artwork is included both as editorial support and as stand alone or independent art. It has included nationally recognized artists as well as emerging artists. As with any publication, artists are encouraged to review a sample copy for a clearer understanding of the magazine's approach. Unsolicited submissions and samples are accepted and encouraged. *The Bear Deluxe* has been recognized for both its editorial and design excellence. Over the years, awards and positive reviews have been handed down from *Print* magazine, *Utne Reader, Literary Arts, Adbusters*, the Bumbershoot Arts Festival, *Orion, Fact Sheet 5*, the Regional Arts and Culture Council, *The Oregonian*, and the *Library Journal*, among others." Estab. 1993. Circ. 19,000. Byline given. Offers 25% kill fee. Publishes ms an average of 6 months after acceptance. Editorial lead time 6 months. Submit seasonal material 9 months in advance. Accepts queries by mail, e-mail. Accepts simultaneous submissions. Responds in 3-6 months to mail queries. Only re-

sponds to e-mail queries if interested. Sample copy for $3. Guidelines for #10 SASE or on website.

NONFICTION Needs book excerpts, essays, exposé, general interest, interview, new product, opinion, personal experience, photo feature, travel, artist profiles. Special issues: Publishes 1 theme/2 years. **Buys 40 mss/year.** Query with published clips. Length: 250-4,500 words. Essays: 750-3,000 words. **Pays $25-400, depending on piece.** Sometimes pays expenses.

COLUMNS Reviews (almost anything), 300 words; Front of the Book (mix of short news bits, found writing, quirky tidbits), 300-500 words; Portrait of an Artist (artist profiles), 1,200 words; Back of the Book (creative opinion pieces), 650 words. **Buys 16 mss/year.** Query with published clips. **Pays $25-400, depending on piece.**

FICTION Stories must have some environmental context, but we view that in a broad sense. Needs adventure, condensed novels, historical, horror, humorous, mystery, novel concepts, western. No detective, children's or horror. **Buys 8 mss/year.** Query or send complete ms. Length: 750-4,500 words. **Pays free subscription to the magazine, contributor's copies and $25-400, depending on piece; additional copies for postage.**

POETRY Needs avant-garde, free verse, haiku, light verse, traditional. Buys 16-20 poems/year. Submit maximum 3-5 poems. 50 lines maximum **Pays $20, subscription, and copies.**

FILLERS Needs facts, newsbreaks, short humor. **Buys 10 mss/year.** Length: 100-750 words. **$25, subscription, and copies.**

BIRD WATCHER'S DIGEST

P.O. Box 110, Marietta OH 45750. (740)373-5285; (800)879-2473. **Fax:** (740)373-8443. **E-mail:** editor@birdwatchersdigest.com. **E-mail:** submissions@birdwatchersdigest.com. **Website:** www.birdwatchersdigest.com. **Contact:** Bill Thompson III, editor. **60.** Bimonthly magazine covering natural history—birds and bird watching. "*BWD* is a nontechnical magazine interpreting ornithological material for amateur observers, including the knowledgeable birder, the serious novice and the backyard bird watcher; we strive to provide good reading and good ornithology. Works with a small number of new/unpublished writers each year." Estab. 1978. Circ. 125,000. Byline given. Publishes ms an average of 2 years after acceptance. Submit seasonal material 6 months in advance. TrueResponds in 10-12 weeks to queries. Sample copy for $3.99 or access online. Guidelines available online.

NONFICTION Needs book excerpts, how-to, relating to birds, feeding and attracting, etc., humor, personal experience, travel, limited. No articles on pet or caged birds; none on raising a baby bird. **Buys 45-60 mss/year.** We gladly accept e-mail queries and manuscript submissions but are not able to respond immediately to most inquiries via e-mail. When submitting by e-mail, please make the subject line read "Submission—your topic." Attach your submission to your e-mail in either MS Word (.doc) or RichText Format (.rtf). Please do not copy and paste your submission into the body of the e-mail. Whether submitting by regular mail or e-mail, please include your full contact information on every page. We ask that you allow 10 to 12 weeks for a response. Length: 600-3,500 words. **Pays from $100.**

EARTH ISLAND JOURNAL

Earth Island Institute, 300 Broadway, Suite 28, San Francisco CA 94133. **E-mail:** editor@earthisland.org. **Website:** www.earthislandjournal.org. **80% freelance written.** Quarterly magazine covering the environment/ecology. We are looking for in-depth, vigorously reported stories that reveal the connections between the environment and other contemporary issues. Our audience, though modest, includes many of the leaders of the environmental movement. Article pitches should be geared toward this sophisticated audience. Estab. 1985. Circ. 10,000. Byline given. Publishes ms an average of 4 months after acceptance. Editorial lead time 4 months. Submit seasonal material 4 months in advance. Accepts queries by e-mail. Responds in 4 weeks to queries. Responds in 1 month to mss. Sample copy for $5. Guidelines available online.

NONFICTION Needs book excerpts, essays, exposé, general interest, interview, opinion, personal experience, photo feature. We do not want product pitches, services, or company news. **Buys 20/year mss/year.** Query with published clips. Length: 750-4,000 words. **Pays 20¢ a word for unsolicited articles.** Sometimes pays expenses of writers on assignment.

COLUMNS Voices (first person reflection about the environment in a person's life.), 750 words. **Buys 4 mss/year.** Query. **Pays $50.00.**

E THE ENVIRONMENTAL MAGAZINE

Earth Action Network, 28 Knight St., Westport CT 06851. (203)854-5559. **Fax:** (203)866-0602. **E-mail:** info@emagazine.com; brita@emagazine.com. **Website:** www.emagazine.com. **60% freelance written.** Bimonthly magazine. *E Magazine* was formed for the purpose of acting as a clearinghouse of information, news, and commentary on environmental issues. Estab. 1990. Circ. 50,000. Byline given. Editorial lead time 3 months. Submit seasonal material 6 months in advance. Accepts queries by mail, e-mail, fax. Accepts simultaneous submissions. Sample copy for $5 or online. Guidelines available online.

NONFICTION Needs exposé, environmental, how-to, new product, book review, feature (in-depth articles on key natural environmental issues). **Buys 100 mss/year.** Query with published clips. Length: 100-4,000 words. **Pays 30¢/word.**

COLUMNS On spec or free contributions welcome. In Brief/Currents (environmental news stories/trends), 400-1,000 words; Conversations (Q&As with environmental movers and shakers), 2,000 words; Tools for Green Living; Your Health; Eco-Travel; Eco-Home; Eating Right; Green Business; Consumer News (each 700-1,200 words). Query with published clips.

HIGH COUNTRY NEWS

119 Grand Ave., P.O. Box 1090, Paonia CO 81428. (970)527-4898. **E-mail:** editor@hcn.org. **Website:** www.hcn.org. **Contact:** Cindy Wehling, art director. **70% freelance written.** Biweekly nonprofit magazine covering environment, rural communities, and natural resource issues in 11 western states for environmentalists, politicians, companies, college classes, government agencies, grass roots activists, public land managers, etc. Estab. 1970. Circ. 25,000. Byline given. Kill fee of 1/3 of agreed rate. Publishes ms an average of 2 months after acceptance. Accepts queries by e-mail. Responds in 2 weeks to queries. Sample copy available online. Guidelines available online at: hcn.org/about/submissions.

NONFICTION **Buys 100 mss/year.** Query. up to 3,000 words **Pay negotiable.** Sometimes pays expenses of writers on assignment.

NATIONAL PARKS MAGAZINE

National Parks Conservation Association, 777 6th St., NW, Suite 700, Washington D.C. 20001-3723. (202)223-6722; (800)628-7275. **Fax:** (202)454-3333. **E-mail:** npmag@npca.org. **Website:** www.npca.org/magazine/. **Contact:** Scott Kirkwood, editor-in-chief.

60% freelance written. Prefers to work with published/established writers. Quarterly magazine for a largely unscientific but highly educated audience interested in preservation of National Park System units, natural areas, and protection of wildlife habitat. "*National Parks* magazine publishes articles about areas in the National Park System, proposed new areas, threats to parks or park wildlife, scientific discoveries, legislative issues, and endangered species of plants or animals relevant to national parks. We do not publish articles on general environmental topics, nor do we print articles about land managed by the Fish and Wildlife Service, Bureau of Land Management, or other federal agencies." Estab. 1919. Circ. 340,000. Offers 33% kill fee. Publishes ms an average of 2 months after acceptance. Responds in 3-4 months to queries. Sample copy for $3 and 9×12 SASE or online. Guidelines available online.

NONFICTION Needs exposé, on threats, wildlife problems in national parks, descriptive articles about new or proposed national parks and wilderness parks. No poetry, philosophical essays, or first-person narratives. No unsolicited mss. Length: 1,500 words. **Pays $1,300 for 1,500-word features and travel articles.**

✪ 🌑🌑🌑 NATURE CANADA

75 Albert St., Suite 300, Ottawa ON K1P 5E7 Canada. (613)562-3447. **Fax:** (613)562-3371. **E-mail:** info@ naturecanada.ca. **Website:** www.naturecanada.ca. Quarterly magazine covering conservation, natural history and environmental/naturalist community. "Editorial content reflects the goals and priorities of Nature Canada as a conservation organization with a focus on our program areas: federally protected areas (national parks, national wildlife areas, etc.), endangered species, and bird conservation through Canada's important bird areas. Nature Canada is written for an audience interested in nature conservation. Nature Canada celebrates, preserves, and protects Canadian nature. We promote the awareness and understanding of the connection between humans and nature and how natural systems support life on Earth. We strive to instill a sense of ownership and belief that these natural systems should be protected." Estab. 1971. Circ. 27,000. Byline given. Offers $100 kill fee. Publishes ms an average of 3 months after acceptance. Editorial lead time 4 months. Submit seasonal material 6 months in advance. Responds in 4 months to mss. Sample copy for $5. Guidelines available online.

NONFICTION Buys 12 mss/year. Query with published clips. Length: 650-2,000 words. **Pays up to 50¢/ word (Canadian).**

🌑🌑 NORTHERN WOODLANDS MAGAZINE

Center for Woodlands Education, Inc., 1776 Center Rd., P.O. Box 471, Corinth VT 05039-0471. (802)439-6292. **Fax:** (802)439-6296. **E-mail:** dave@northern-woodlands.org. **Website:** www.northernwoodlands. org. **40-60% freelance written.** Quarterly magazine covering natural history, conservation, and forest management in the Northeast. "*Northern Woodlands* strives to inspire landowners' sense of stewardship by increasing their awareness of the natural history and the principles of conservation and forestry that are directly related to their land. We also hope to increase the public's awareness of the social, economic, and environmental benefits of a working forest." Estab. 1994. Circ. 15,000. Byline given. Pays 1 month prior to publication Publishes ms an average of 6 months after acceptance. Editorial lead time 6 months. Submit seasonal material 6 months in advance. Accepts queries by mail, e-mail. Accepts simultaneous submissions. Responds in 1 month to queries. Responds in 1-2 months to mss Sample copy available online. Guidelines available online.

NONFICTION No product reviews, first-person travelogues, cute animal stories, opinion, or advocacy pieces. **Buys 15-20 mss/year.** Query with published clips. Length: 500-3,000 words. **Pay varies per piece.** Sometimes pays expenses of writers on assignment.

🌑🌑 OCEAN MAGAZINE

P.O. Box 84, Rodanthe NC 27968-0084. (252)256-2296. **Website:** www.oceanmagazine.org. **100% freelance written.** "*OCEAN Magazine* serves to celebrate and protect the greatest, most comprehensive resource for life on earth, our world's ocean. *OCEAN* publishes articles, stories, poems, essays, and photography about the ocean—observations, experiences, scientific and environmental discussions—written with fact and feeling, illustrated with images from nature." Estab. 2004. Circ. 40,000. Byline given. Publishes ms an average of 2-4 months after acceptance. Editorial lead time 3-6 months. Submit seasonal material 3-6 months in advance. Accepts queries by e-mail. Accepts simultaneous submissions. Responds in 1 day to 2 months. Sample copy available for $3 digital, $8.45 print. Guidelines available online.

NONFICTION Needs book excerpts, essays, general interest, historical, inspirational, interview, opinion, personal experience, photo feature, technical, travel, spiritual. Does not want poor writing. **Buys 24-36 mss/year.** Query. Length: 75-5,000 words. **Pays $75-250.**

FICTION Needs adventure, fantasy, historical, novel concepts, romance, slice-of-life vignettes. **Buys 1-2 mss/year.** Query. Length: 100-2,000 words. **Pays $75-150.**

POETRY Needs avant-garde, free verse, haiku, light verse, traditional. Buys 12 poems/year. Submit maximum 6 poems. **Pays $25-75.**

FILLERS Needs anecdotes, facts. **Buys Reflections facts 4-12 mss/year.** Length: 20-100 words. **Pays $25-75.**

💲💲💲 OUTDOOR AMERICA

Izaak Walton League of America, 707 Conservation Ln., Gaithersburg MD 20878. (301)548-0150. **Fax:** (301)548-9409. **E-mail:** oa@iwla.org. **Website:** www.iwla.org. **Contact:** Dawn Merritt, communications director. Quarterly magazine covering national conservation efforts/issues related to and involving members of the Izaak Walton League. A 4-color publication, *Outdoor America* is received by League members, as well as representatives of Congress and the media. Our audience, located predominantly in the midwestern and mid-Atlantic states, enjoys traditional recreational pursuits, such as fishing, hiking, hunting, as well as conservation activities and educating youth. All have a keen interest in protecting the future of our natural resources and outdoor recreation heritage. Estab. 1922. Circ. 36,500. Offers 1/3 original rate kill fee. Publishes ms an average of 2 months after acceptance. Accepts queries by mail, e-mail. Responds in 2 months to queries. Sample copy for $2.50. Guidelines available online.

NONFICTION No fiction, poetry, or unsubstantiated opinion pieces. Query or send ms for short columns/news pieces (500 words or less). Features are planned 6-12 months in advance. **Pays $1,000-1,500 for features.**

💲💲💲💲 SIERRA

85 Second St., 2nd Floor, San Francisco CA 94105. (415)977-5656. **Fax:** (415)977-5799. **E-mail:** sierra.magazine@sierraclub.org. **Website:** www.sierraclub.org. **Contact:** Martha Geering, art director. **Works with a small number of new/unpublished writers each year.** Bimonthly magazine emphasizing conservation and environmental politics for people who are well educated, activist, outdoor-oriented, and politically well informed with a dedication to conservation. Estab. 1893. Circ. 695,000. Byline given. Offers negotiable kill fee. Publishes ms an average of 4 months after acceptance. Accepts queries by mail, fax. Responds in 2 months to queries. Sample copy for $3 and SASE, or online. Guidelines available online.

NONFICTION Needs exposé, well-documented articles on environmental issues of national importance such as energy, wilderness, forests, etc., general interest, well-researched nontechnical pieces on areas of particular environmental concern, interview, photo feature, photo feature essays on threatened or scenic areas, journalistic treatments of semitechnical topic (energy sources, wildlife management, land use, waste management, etc.). "No 'My trip to ..' or 'Why we must save wildlife/nature' articles; no poetry or general superficial essays on environmentalism; no reporting on purely local environmental issues. **Buys 30-36 mss/year.** Query with published clips. Length: 1,000-3,000 words. **Pays $800-3,000.**

COLUMNS Food for Thought (food's connection to environment); Good Going (adventure journey); Hearth & Home (advice for environmentally sound living); Body Politics (health and the environment); Profiles (biographical look at environmentalists); Hidden Life (exposure of hidden environmental problems in everyday objects); Lay of the Land (national/international concerns), 500-700 words; Mixed Media (essays on environment in the media; book reviews), 200-300 words. **Pays $50-500.**

💲💲💲💲 WILDLIFE CONSERVATION

2300 Southern Blvd., Bronx NY 10460. (718)220-5100. **E-mail:** nsimmons@wcs.org; membership@wcs.org. **Website:** www.wcs.org. Bimonthly magazine for environmentally aware readers. Offers 25% kill fee. Accepts simultaneous submissions. Responds in 1 month to queries. Sample copy for $4.95 (plus $1 postage). Writer's guidelines available for SASE or via e-mail.

NONFICTION Buys 30 mss/year. Query with published clips. Length: 300-2,000 words. **Pays $1/word for features and department articles, and $150 for short pieces**

PERSONAL COMPUTERS

💲💲💲 SMART COMPUTING

Sandhills Publishing, 131 W. Grand Dr., Lincoln NE 68521. (800)544-1264. **Fax:** (402)479-2104. **E-mail:** editor@smartcomputing.com. **Website:** www.smartcomputing.com. **Contact:** Bob Chester, editor; Ron Kobler, editor-in-chief. **45% freelance written.** Monthly magazine. "We focus on plain-English computing articles with an emphasis on tutorials that improve productivity without the purchase of new hardware." Estab. 1990. Circ. 200,000. Byline given. Offers 25% kill fee. Publishes ms an average of 2 months after acceptance. Editorial lead time 4 months. Submit seasonal material 4 months in advance. Accepts queries by mail, e-mail. Accepts simultaneous submissions. Responds in 1 month to queries. Sample copy for $7.99. Guidelines for #10 SASE.

NONFICTION Needs how-to, new product, technical. No humor, opinion, personal experience. **Buys 250 mss/year.** Query with published clips. Length: 800-3,200 words. **Pays $240-960.** Pays expenses of writers on assignment up to $75

PHOTOGRAPHY

APOGEE PHOTO

11121 Wolf Way, Westminster CO 80031. (904)619-2010 (Florida contact). **E-mail:** meier@qadas.com. **Website:** apogeephoto.com. **Contact:** Marla Meier, editorial director. A free online monthly magazine designed to inform, educate and entertain photographers of all ages and levels. Take online photography courses, read photo articles covering a wide range of photo topics and see listings of photo workshops and tours, camera clubs, and books. Submit your articles for publication.

🔑 Please do a search by subject before submitting your article to see if your article covers a new subject or brings a new perspective on a particular subject or theme.

PHOTOGRAPHER'S FORUM MAGAZINE

813 Reddick St., Santa Barbara CA 93103. (805)963-6425. **Fax:** (805)965-0496. **E-mail:** julie@serbin.com. **Website:** www.pfmagazine.com. **Contact:** Julie Simpson, managing editor. Quarterly magazine for the serious student and emerging professional photographer. Includes feature articles on historic and con-

temporary photographers, interviews, book reviews, workshop listings, new products.

NONFICTION Needs historical, interview, new product, photo feature, profile, reviews.

POLITICS AND WORLD AFFAIRS

💲💲 CHURCH & STATE

518 C St. NE, Washington DC 20002. (202)466-3234. **Fax:** (202)466-2587. **E-mail:** americansunited@au.org. **Website:** www.au.org. **10% freelance written.** Monthly magazine emphasizing religious liberty and church/state relations matters. "Strongly advocates separation of church and state. Readership is well-educated." Estab. 1947. Circ. 40,000. Publishes ms an average of 2 months after acceptance. Accepts queries by mail. Accepts simultaneous submissions. Responds in 2 months to queries. Sample copy and writer's guidelines for 9×12 SAE with 3 first-class stamps.

NONFICTION Needs exposé, general interest, historical, interview. **Buys 11 mss/year.** Query. Length: 800-1,600 words. **Pays $150-300.** Sometimes pays expenses of writers on assignment.

💲 COMMONWEAL

Commonweal Foundation, 475 Riverside Dr., Room 405, New York NY 10115. (212)662-4200. **Fax:** (212)662-4183. **E-mail:** editors@commonwealmagazine.org. **Website:** www.commonwealmagazine.org. **Contact:** Paul Baumann, editor; Tiina Aleman, production editor. Biweekly journal of opinion edited by Catholic lay people, dealing with topical issues of the day on public affairs, religion, literature, and the arts. Estab. 1924. Circ. 20,000. Byline given. Submit seasonal material 4 months in advance. Responds in 2 months to queries. Sample copy free. Guidelines available online.

NONFICTION Needs essays, general interest, interview, personal experience, religious. **Buys 30 mss/year.** Query with published clips. Length: 2,000-2,500 words. **Pays $200-300 for longer mss; $100-200 for shorter pieces.**

COLUMNS Upfronts (brief, newsy reportorials, giving facts, information and some interpretation behind the headlines of the day), 750-1,000 words; Last Word (usually of a personal nature, on some aspect of the human condition: spiritual, individual, political, or social), 800 words.

POETRY Contact: Rosemary Deen, editor. Needs free verse, traditional. *Commonweal*, published every 2 weeks, is a Catholic general interest magazine for college-educated readers. Does not publish inspirational poems. Buys 20 poems/year. Length: 75 lines/poem max **Pays 75¢/line plus 2 contributor's copies. Acquires all rights. Returns rights when requested by the author.**

🟡🟢 THE FREEMAN: IDEAS ON LIBERTY

30 S. Broadway, Irvington-on-Hudson NY 10533. (914)591-7230. **Fax:** (914)591-8910. **E-mail:** srichman@fee.org. **Website:** www.thefreemanonline.org. **Contact:** Sheldon Richman, editor. **85% freelance written.** Monthly publication for the layman and fairly advanced students of liberty. Estab. 1946. Byline given. Publishes ms an average of 5 months after acceptance. Sample copy for 7 ½×10 ½ SASE with 4 first-class stamps. Guidelines available on website.

NONFICTION Buys 100 mss/year. Query with SASE. Length: 3,500 words. **Pays 10¢/word.** Sometimes pays expenses of writers on assignment.

🟡🟢 THE PROGRESSIVE

409 E. Main St., Madison WI 53703. (608)257-4626. **Fax:** (608)257-3373. **E-mail:** editorial@progressive.org; mattr@progressive.org. **Website:** www.progressive.org. **Contact:** Matthew Rothschild, editor. **75% freelance written.** Monthly magazine of investigative reporting, political commentary, cultural coverage, activism, interviews, poetry, and humor. Estab. 1909. Byline given. Publishes ms an average of 6 weeks after acceptance. Accepts queries by mail. Responds in 1 month to queries. Sample copy for 9×12 SASE with 4 first-class stamps or sample articles online. Guidelines available online.

NONFICTION Query. Length: 500-4,000 words. **Pays $500-1,300.**

POETRY Publishes 1 original poem a month. "We prefer poems that connect up—in 1 fashion or another, however obliquely—with political concerns." **Pays $150.**

🔵 THEORIA

Berghahn Books, University of KwaZulu-Natal, Private Bag X17, Belville Western Cape 7535 South Africa. (27)(21)959-2404. **E-mail:** sherranclarence@gmail.com. **Website:** http://journals.berghahnbooks.com/th. **Contact:** Ms. Sherran Clarence, managing editor. **100% freelance written.** "Academic journal published 4 times/year. *Theoria* is an engaged, multidisciplinary peer-reviewed journal of social and political theory. Its purpose is to address—through scholarly debate—the many challenges posed to intellectual life by the major social, political, and economic forces that shape the contemporary world. Thus, it is principally concerned with questions such as how modern systems of power, processes of globalization, and capitalist economic organization bear on matters such as justice, democracy, and truth." Estab. 1947. Circ. 300. Byline sometimes given. Publishes ms an average of 6 months after acceptance. Editorial lead time 3 months. Submit seasonal material 3 months in advance. Accepts queries by mail, e-mail, fax, phone. Responds in 1 week to queries. Responds in 3-4 months to mss. Sample copy free online. Writer's guidelines online or via e-mail. "Ms must comply with guidelines."

NONFICTION Needs book excerpts, essays, exposé, general interest, historical, interview, review articles, book reviews, theoretical, philosophical, political, articles. **Buys 1 mss/year.** Send complete ms. Length: 6,000-9,000 words. "Ms must be ready for blind peer review." **No pay.**

COLUMNS Book Reviews, 1,000-1,500 words; Review Articles, 3,000-5,000 words. **Buys 1 mss/year.** Send complete ms.

PSYCHOLOGY AND SELF-IMPROVEMENT

🟡 SPOTLIGHT ON RECOVERY MAGAZINE

R. Graham Publishing Company, 9602 Glenwood Rd., #140, Brooklyn NY 11236. (347)831-9373. **E-mail:** rgraham_100@msn.com. **Website:** www.spotlightonrecovery.com. **Contact:** Robin Graham, publisher and editor-in-chief. **85% freelance written.** Quarterly magazine covering self-help, recovery, and empowerment. "This is the premiere outreach and resource magazine in New York. Its goal is to be the catalyst for which the human spirit could heal. Everybody knows somebody who has mental illness, substance abuse issues, parenting problems, educational issues, or someone who is homeless, unemployed, physically ill, or the victim of a crime. Many people suffer in silence. *Spotlight on Recovery* will provide a voice to those who suffer in silence and begin the dialogue of recovery." Estab. 2001. Circ. 1,500-2,500. Byline sometimes given. Publishes ms an average of 2 months after acceptance. Editorial lead time 1 month. Submit seasonal material 1 month in advance. Accepts queries by mail, e-mail. Accepts simultaneous submissions. Responds in 2 weeks to queries. Responds in 1 month to mss. Sample copy and writer's guidelines free.

NONFICTION Needs book excerpts, interview, opinion, personal experience. **Buys 30-50 mss/year.** Query with published clips. Length: 150-1,500 words. **Pays 5¢/word or $75-80/article.**

COLUMNS Buys 4 mss/year. Query with published clips. **Pays 5¢/word or $75-80/column.**

FICTION Needs ethnic, mainstream, slice-of-life vignettes.

FILLERS Needs facts, newsbreaks, short humor. **Buys 2 mss/year. Pays 5¢/word.**

REGIONAL

ALABAMA

💲 ALABAMA LIVING

Alabama Rural Electric Assn., P.O. Box 244014, Montgomery AL 36124. (334)215-2732. **Fax:** (334)215-2733. **E-mail:** dgates@areapower.com. **Website:** www.alabamaliving.com. Michael Cornelison, art director. **Contact:** Darryl Gates, editor. **80% freelance written.** Monthly magazine covering topics of interest to rural and suburban Alabamians. "Our magazine is an editorially balanced, informational and educational service to members of rural electric cooperatives. Our mix regularly includes Alabama history, Alabama features, gardening, outdoor, and consumer pieces." Estab. 1948. Circ. 400,000. Byline given. Editorial lead time 4 months. Submit seasonal material 4 months in advance. Accepts queries by mail, e-mail. Accepts simultaneous submissions. Responds in 1 month to queries. Sample copy free.

NONFICTION Needs historical, rural-oriented, Alabama slant, Alabama. Special issues: Gardening (March); Travel (April); Home Improvement (May); Holiday Recipes (December). **Buys 20 mss/year.** Send complete ms. Length: 500-750 words. **Pays $250 minimum for assigned articles. Pays $150 minimum for unsolicited articles.**

ARIZONA

💲💲 ARIZONA FOOTHILLS MAGAZINE

8132 N. 87th Place, Scottsdale AZ 85258. (480)460-5203. **Fax:** (480)443-1517. **E-mail:** editorial@azfoothillsmag.com; editorial@mediathatdeelivers.com. **Website:** www.azfoothillsmag.com. **10% freelance written.** Monthly magazine covering Arizona lifesyle. Estab. 1996. Circ. 60,000. Byline given. Publishes ms an average of 6 months after acceptance. Editorial lead time 6 months. Submit seasonal material at least 4 months in advance. Accepts queries by mail, e-mail. Responds in 1 month to queries. Sample copy for #10 SASE.

NONFICTION Needs general interest, photo feature, travel, fashion, decor, arts, interview. **Buys 10 mss/ year.** Query with published clips. Length: 900-2,000 words. **Pays 35-40¢/word for assigned articles.**

COLUMNS Travel, dining, fashion, home decor, design, architecture, wine, shopping, golf, performance & visual arts.

💲 PHOENIX MAGAZINE

Cities West Publishing, Inc., 15169 N. Scottsdale Road, Ste. C-310, Scottsdale AZ 85254. (866)481-6970. **Fax:** (602)604-0169. **E-mail:** aklawonn@citieswestpub. com. **Website:** www.phoenixmag.com. **Contact:** Adam Klawonn, managing editor. **70% freelance written.** Monthly magazine covering regional issues, personalities, events, neighborhoods, customs, and history of metro Phoenix. Estab. 1966. Circ. 60,000. Byline given. Publishes ms an average of 3 months after acceptance. Submit seasonal material 1 year in advance. Accepts queries by mail, e-mail. Responds in 2 months to queries. Responds in 2 months to mss. Sample copy for $3.95 and 9×12 SASE with 5 first-class stamps.. Guidelines for #10 sase.

NONFICTION Needs general interest, interview, investigative, historical, service pieces (where to go and what to do around town). "We do not publish fiction, poetry, personal essays, book reviews, music reviews, or product reviews, and our travel stories are staff written. With the exception of our travel stories, all of the content in *Phoenix* magazine is geographically specific to the Phoenix-metro region. We do not publish any non-travel news or feature stories that are outside the Phoenix area, and we prefer that our freelancers are located in the Phoenix metro area." **Buys 50 mss/year.** Query with published clips via e-mail. "Include a short summary, a list of sources, and an explanation of why you think your idea is right for the magazine and why you're qualified to write it." Length: 150-2,000 words.

CALIFORNIA

$ CALIFORNIA NORTHERN MAGAZINE

P.O. Box 2268, Sacramento CA 95822. **E-mail:** editorial@calnorthern.net. **E-mail:** submissions@calnorthern.net. **Website:** www.calnorthern.net. **Contact:** Casey Mills, editor. **60% freelance written.** Biannual publication exploring the region's cultures, environments, histories, and identities. It provides a rare California-based forum for exceptional essays, long-form journalism, literature, and photography, and distinguishes itself from traditional regional media by balancing its local emphasis with a level of sophistication and depth typically found in larger national publications. Estab. 2010. Circ. 500. Byline given. Accepts queries by mail, e-mail, fax. Responds in 3 weeks to queries; 2 months to ms. Guidelines by e-mail.

NONFICTION Contact: Richard Mills, executive editor. Needs book excerpts, essays, historical, interview, nostalgic, opinion, personal experience, photo feature, profile. **Buys 6 mss/year.** Query. Length: 2,500-12,00 words. **Pays $.05-.07/word.**

COLUMNS Contact: Richard Mills, executive editor. Notes From The Field: vignettes that provide readers a window into a part of Northern California that is often overlooked, or a well-known place that the writer has a unique connection to. 500-700 words. **Buys 8 mss/year.** Query.

FICTION Contact: Paul Barrett, executive editor. Fiction should be submitted by writers who reside in the region or have some strong connection to it. No genre fiction. **Buys 2 mss/year.** Send complete ms. Accepts 2,000-8,500 words.

POETRY Needs Avant-garde, free verse, haiku, light verse, traditional. Buys 5 poems/year poems/year. Submit maximum 3 poems.

$$ CARLSBAD MAGAZINE

Wheelhouse Media, P.O. Box 2089, Carlsbad CA 92008. (760)729-9099. **Fax:** (760)729-9011. **E-mail:** tim@wheelhousemedia.com. **Website:** www.clickoncarlsbad.com. **Contact:** Tim Wrisley. **80% freelance written.** Bimonthly magazine covering people, places, events, arts in Carlsbad, California. "We are a regional magazine highlighting all things pertaining specifically to Carlsbad. We focus on history, events, people and places that make Carlsbad interesting and unique. Our audience is both Carlsbad residents and visitors or anyone interested in learning more about Carlsbad. We favor a conversational tone that still adheres to standard rules of writing." Estab. 2004. Circ. 35,000. Byline given. Publishes ms an average of 6 months after acceptance. Editorial lead time 4 months. Submit seasonal material 6-12 months in advance. Accepts queries by mail, e-mail. Accepts simultaneous submissions. Responds in 2 months to queries and to mss. Sample copy for $2.31. Guidelines by email.

NONFICTION Needs historical, interview, photo feature, home, garden, arts, events. Does not want self-promoting articles for individuals or businesses, real estate how-to's, advertorials. **Buys 3 mss/year.** Query with published clips. Length: 300-2,700 words. **Pays 20-30¢/word for assigned articles. Pays 20¢/word for unsolicited articles.** Sometimes pays expenses of writers on assignment.

COLUMNS Carlsbad Arts (people, places or things related to cultural arts in Carlsbad); Happenings (events that take place in Carlsbad); Carlsbad Character (unique Carlsbad residents who have contributed to Carlsbad's character); Commerce (Carlsbad business profiles); Surf Scene (subjects pertaining to the beach/surf in Carlsbad), all 500-700 words. Garden (Carlsbad garden feature); Home (Carlsbad home feature), both 700-1,200 words. **Buys 60 columns. mss/year.** Query with published clips. **Pays $50 flat fee or 20¢/word.**

$$ THE EAST BAY MONTHLY

The Berkeley Monthly, Inc., 1301 59th St., Emeryville CA 94608. (510)658-9811. **Fax:** (510)658-9902. **E-mail:** editorial@themonthly.com; letters@themonthly.com. **Website:** www.eastbaymonthly.com. **95% freelance written.** Monthly general interest tabloid covering the San Francisco Bay Area. "We feature distinctive, intelligent articles of interest to *East Bay* readers." Estab. 1970. Circ. 81,000. Byline given. Editorial lead time 2+ months. Submit seasonal material 3 months in advance. Accepts queries by mail, e-mail. Accepts simultaneous submissions. Responds in 1 month. Sample copy for $1. Writer's guidelines for #10 SASE or by e-mail.

NONFICTION No fiction or poetry. Query with published clips. Length: 1,500-3,000 words. **Pays $200-700.**

COLUMNS Shopping Around (local retail news), 2,000 words; First Person, 2,000 words. Query with published clips.

$ JOURNAL PLUS MAGAZINE

654 Osos St., San Luis Obispo CA 93401. (805)546-0609; (805)544-8711. **Fax:** (805)546-8827. **E-mail:** slo-journal@fix.net. **Website:** www.slojournal.com. **Contact:** Steve Owens, publisher. "*The Journal* is strictly local to the Central Coast of California, and the writers are local as well." Sample copy for SASE with $2 postage. Guidelines available online.

NONFICTION Needs general interest. Query. Length: 600-1,400 words. **Pays $50 for articles under 850 words, with artwork or photos; $75 for articles under 850 words, with artwork or photos.**

$ NOB HILL GAZETTE

Nob Hill Gazette, Inc., 5 Third St., Suite 222, San Francisco CA 94103. (415)227-0190. **Fax:** (415)974-5103. **E-mail:** claudia@nobhillgazette.com; email@nobhillgazette.com. **Website:** www.nobhillgazette.com. **Contact:** Claudia Zaik, editor; Lois Lehrman, publisher. **95% freelance written**. Monthly magazine covering upscale lifestyles in the Bay Area. *Nob Hill Gazette* is for an upscale readership. Estab. 1978. Circ. 82,000. Byline given. Pays on 15th of month following publication. Offers $50 kill fee. Publishes ms an average of 2-3 months after acceptance. Editorial lead time 1-2 months. Submit seasonal material 1-2 months in advance. Accepts queries by e-mail. Responds in 2 weeks to queries. Responds in 2 months to mss. Sample copy available online. Guidelines free.

NONFICTION Needs general interest, historical, interview, opinion, photo feature, trends, lifestyles, fashion, health, fitness, entertaining, decor, real estate, charity and philanthropy, culture and the arts. Does not want first person articles, anything commercial (from a business or with a product to sell), profiles of people not active in the community, anything technical, anything on people or events not in the Bay Area. **Buys 75 mss/year.** Query with published clips. Length: 1,200-2,000 words. **Pays $100.** Sometimes pays expenses of writers on assignment.

COLUMNS Contact: Contact Lois Lehrman, publisher. All our columnists are freelancers, but they write for us regularly, so we don't take other submissions.

$ $ SACRAMENTO NEWS & REVIEW

Chico Community Publishing, 1124 Del Paso Blvd., Sacramento CA 95815. (916)498-1234. **Fax:** (916)498-7920. **E-mail:** melindaw@newsreview.com; kelm@newsreview.com. **Website:** www.newsreview.com. **Contact:** Melinda Welsh, editor. **25% freelance written.** Alternative news and entertainment weekly magazine. We maintain a high literary standard for submissions; unique or alternative slant. Publication aimed at a young, intellectual audience; submissions should have an edge and strong voice. We have a decided preference for stories with a strong local slant. "Our mission: To publish great newspapers that are successful and enduring. To create a quality work environment that encourages employees to grow professionally while respecting personal welfare. To have a positive impact on our communities and make them better places to live. " Estab. 1989. Circ. 87,000. Byline given. Offers 10% kill fee. Publishes ms an average of 2 months after acceptance. Editorial lead time 2 months. Submit seasonal material 2 months in advance. Accepts queries by mail, e-mail. Accepts simultaneous submissions. Responds in 1 month to queries. Responds in 2 months to mss. Sample copy for 50¢. Guidelines available online.

💬 Prefers to work with Sacramento-area writers.

NONFICTION Needs essays, exposé, general interest, humor, interview, personal experience. Does not want to see travel, product stories, business profile. **Buys 20-30 mss/year.** Query with published clips. Length: 750-5,000 words. **Pays $40-500.** Sometimes pays expenses of writers on assignment.

CANADA/INTERNATIONAL

$ $ ABACO LIFE

Caribe Communications, P.O. Box 37487, Raleigh NC 27627. (919)859-6782. **Fax:** (919)859-6769. **E-mail:** jimkerr@mindspring.com. **Website:** www.abacolife.com. **Contact:** Jim Kerr, publisher and editor. **50% freelance written**. Quarterly magazine covering Abaco, an island group in the Northeast Bahamas. "*Abaco Life* editorial focuses entirely on activities, history, wildlife, resorts, people and other subjects pertaining to the Abacos. Readers include locals, vacationers, second-home owners, and other visitors whose interests range from real estate and resorts to scuba, sailing, fishing, and beaches. The tone is upbeat, adventurous, humorous. No fluff writing for an audience already familiar with the area." Estab. 1979. Circ. 10,000. Byline given. Offers 40% kill fee. Publishes ms an average of 2 months after acceptance. Editorial lead time 2 months. Submit seasonal material 4 months in advance. Accepts queries by mail, e-mail. Accepts simultaneous submissions. Responds in 2 weeks to queries.

Responds in 2 months to mss. Sample copy for $2. Guidelines free.

NONFICTION Needs general interest, historical, how-to, interview, personal experience, photo feature, travel. No general first-time impressions. Articles must be specific, show knowledge and research of the subject and area—'Abaco's Sponge Industry'; 'Diving Abaco's Wrecks'; 'The Hurricane of '36.' **Buys 8-10 mss/year.** Query or send complete ms Length: 700-2,000 words. **Pays $400-1,000.**

🍁 $$$$ ALBERTAVIEWS

AlbertaViews, Ltd., Suite 208-320 23rd Ave. SW, Calgary AB T2S 0J2 Canada. (403)243-5334 or 1-877-212-5334. **Fax:** (403)243-8599. **E-mail:** editor@albertaviews.ab.ca. **Website:** www.albertaviews.ab.ca. **Contact:** Evan Osenton, editor. **50% freelance written.** Bimonthly magazine covering Alberta culture: politics, economy, social issues, and art. We are a regional magazine providing thoughtful commentary and background information on issues of concern to Albertans. Most of our writers are Albertans. Estab. 1997. Circ. 30,000. Byline given. Offers 50% kill fee. Publishes ms an average of 3 months after acceptance. Editorial lead time 4 months. Submit seasonal material 3 months in advance. Accepts queries by e-mail. Responds in 6 weeks to queries. Responds in 2 months to mss. Sample copy free. Guidelines available online.

NONFICTION Needs essays. **Buys 18 mss/year.** "Query with written proposal of 300–500 words outlining your intended contribution to Alberta Views, why you are qualified to write about your subject and what sources you intend to use; a résumé outlining your experience and education; recent examples of your published work (tear sheets)." Length: 3,000-5,000 words. **Pays $1,000-1,500 for assigned articles. Pays $350-750 for unsolicited articles.** Sometimes pays expenses of writers on assignment.

FICTION Only fiction by Alberta writers. **Buys 6 mss/year.** Send complete ms. Length: 2,500-4,000 words. **Pays $1,000 maximum.**

🍁 $$ COTTAGE

OP Publishing, Ltd., Suite 500-200, West Esplanade, North Vancouver BC V7M 1A4 Canada. (604)998-3327. **Fax:** (604)998-3320. **E-mail:** editor@cottagemagazine.com. **Website:** www.cottagemagazine.com. **80% freelance written.** "Bimonthly magazine covering do-it-yourself projects, profiles of people and their innovative solutions to building and maintaining their country homes, issues that affect rural individuals and communities, and the R&R aspect of country living." "Our readers want solid, practical information about living in the country—including alternative energy and sustainable living. They also like to have fun in a wide range of recreational pursuits, from canoeing, fishing, and sailing to water skiing, snowmobiling, and entertaining." Estab. 1992. Circ. 20,000. Byline given. Pays within 1 month of publication. Offers 25% kill fee. Publishes ms an average of 6 months after acceptance. Accepts queries by e-mail. Accepts simultaneous submissions. Responds in 1 month to queries.

NONFICTION Buys 18-24 mss/year. Query. Up to 1,500 words. **Pays $100-450 (including visuals).**

COLUMNS Utilities (solar and/or wind power), 800 words; Weekend Project (a how-to most homeowners can do themselves), 800 words; Government (new regulations, processes, problems), 800 words; Diversions (advisories, ideas, and how-to's about the fun things that people do), 800 words; InRoads (product reviews), 50-600 words; This Land (personal essays or news-based story with a broader context), 800 words; Last Word or Cabin Life (personal essays and experiences), 800 words; Elements (short articles focusing on a single feature of a cottage), 600 words; Alternatives (applied alternative energy), 600 words. Query. **Pays $75-250.**

FILLERS Needs anecdotes, facts, newsbreaks, seasonal tips. **Buys 12 mss/year.** Length: 50-200 words. **20¢/word.**

🍁 $$$$ HAMILTON MAGAZINE

Town Media, 1074 Cooke Blvd., Burlington ON L7T 4A8 Canada. (905)522-6117 or (905)634-8003. **Fax:** (905)634-7661 or (905)634-8804. **E-mail:** mskulnick@townmedia.ca; info@townmedia.ca. **Website:** www.hamiltonmagazine.com. **Contact:** Marc Skulnick, editor; Kate Sharrow, art director. **50% freelance written.** Quarterly magazine devoted to the Greater Hamilton and Golden Horseshoe area. "Mandate: to entertain and inform by spotlighting the best of what our city and region has to offer. We invite readers to take part in a vibrant community by supplying them with authoritative and dynamic coverage of local culture, food, fashion and design. Each story strives to expand your view of the area, every issue an essential resource for exploring, understanding and unlocking the region. Packed with insight, intrigue and suspense, *Hamilton Magazine* delivers the city to your doorstep." Estab. 1978. Byline given. Offers 50% kill fee. Editorial lead time 2-3 months. Submit seasonal material 2-3 months in advance. Accepts queries by e-mail. NoResponds in 1 week to queries and to mss. Sample copy with #10 SASE. Guidelines by e-mail.

NONFICTION Needs book excerpts, essays, exposé, historical, how-to, humor, inspirational, interview, personal experience, photo feature, religious, travel. Does not want generic articles that could appear in any mass-market publication. Send complete ms. Length: 800-2,000 words. **Pays $200-1,600 for assigned articles. Pays $100-800 for unsolicited articles.** Sometimes pays expenses of writers on assignment.

COLUMNS A&E Art, 1,200-2,000 words; A&E Music, 1,200-2,000 words; A&E Books, 1,200-1,400 words. **Buys 12 columns. mss/year.** Send complete ms. **Pays $200-400.**

○ ●● MONDAY MAGAZINE

Black Press Ltd., 818 Broughton St., Victoria BC V8W 1E4 Canada. **E-mail:** editor@mondaymag.com. **Website:** www.mondaymag.com. **Contact:** Grant McKenzie, editor-in-chief. **10% freelance written.** Weekly tabloid covering local news. "*Monday Magazine* is Victoria's only alternative newsweekly. For more than 35 years, we have published fresh, informative, and alternative perspectives on local events. We prefer lively, concise writing with a sense of humor and insight." Estab. 1975. Circ. 25,000. Byline given. Pays 1 month after publication. Publishes ms an average of 1 month after acceptance. Editorial lead time 1-2 months. Submit seasonal material 2 months in advance. Accepts queries by e-mail (preferred). Responds in 6-8 weeks to queries. Responds in up to 3 months to mss "See Writer's Guidelines on our website."

NONFICTION Needs local exposé, general interest, humor, interview, personal experience. Special issues: Body, Mind, Spirit (October); Student Survival Guide (August). Does not want fiction, poetry, or conspiracy theories. Send complete ms. Length: 300-1,000 words. **Pays $25to $50.**

○ ●● ⊘ OUTDOOR CANADA MAGAZINE

25 Sheppard Ave. W, Suite 100, Toronto ON M2N 6S7 Canada. (416)733-7600. **Fax:** (416)227-8296. **E-mail:** editorial@outdoorcanada.ca. **Website:** www.outdoorcanada.ca. **90% freelance written. Works with a small number of new/unpublished writers each year.**

Estab. 1972. Circ. 90,000. Byline given. Publishes ms an average of 8 months after acceptance. Submit seasonal material 1 year in advance. Accepts queries by mail, e-mail. Responds in 1 month to queries. Guidelines available online.

NONFICTION Needs how-to, fishing, hunting, outdoor issues, outdoor destinations in Canada. **Buys 35-40 mss/year.** Does not accept unsolicited mss. 2,500 words **Pays $500 and up.**

FILLERS Buys 30-40 mss/year. Length: 100-500 words. **Pays $50 and up.**

○ UP HERE

P.O. Box 1350, Yellowknife NT X1A 3T1 Canada. (867)766-6710. **Fax:** (867)873-9876. **E-mail:** aaron@uphere.ca; katharine@uphere.ca. **Website:** www.uphere.ca. **Contact:** Aaron Spitzer, editor; Katharine Sandiford, managing editor. **50% freelance written.** Magazine published 8 times/year covering general interest about Canada's Far North. We publish features, columns, and shorts about people, wildlife, native cultures, travel, and adventure in Yukon, Northwest Territories, and Nunavut. Be informative, but entertaining. Estab. 1984. Circ. 22,000. Byline given. Offers 50% kill fee. Editorial lead time 6 months. Accepts queries by e-mail. Sample copy for $4.95 (Canadian) and 9×12 SASE.

NONFICTION Needs essays, general interest, how-to, humor, interview, personal experience, photo feature, technical, travel, lifestyle/culture, historical. **Buys 25-30 mss/year.** Query. Length: 1,500-3,000 words. **Fees are negotiable.**

COLUMNS Write for updated guidelines, visit website, or e-mail. **Buys 25-30 mss/year.** Query with published clips.

COLORADO

● SOUTHWEST COLORADO ARTS PERSPECTIVE MAGAZINE

Shared Vision Publishing, P.O. Box 3042, Durango CO 81302. (970)739-3200. **E-mail:** director@artsperspective.com; denise@sharedvisiononline.com. **Website:** www.artsperspective.com. **100% freelance written.** Quarterly tabloid covering art. "*Arts Perspective Magazine* offers a venue for all of the arts. Artists, writers, musicians, dancers, performers and galleries are encourage to showcase their work. A resource for supporters of the arts to share a common thread in the continuum of creative expression." Estab. 2004.

Circ. 30,000+. Byline given. Publishes ms an average of 2 months after acceptance. Editorial lead time 2-5 months. Submit seasonal material 2-5 months in advance. Accepts queries by mail, e-mail, phone. Responds in 2 weeks to queries. Responds in 1 month to mss. Sample copy free. www.artsperspective.com/submissions.php.

POETRY Needs avant-garde, free verse, haiku, light verse, traditional. Buys 4 poems/year. Submit maximum 3 poems. Length: 4-45 lines.

💲💲 STEAMBOAT MAGAZINE

Ski Town Publications, Inc., 1120 S. Lincoln Ave., Suite F, Steamboat Springs CO 80487. (970)871-9413. **Fax:** (970)871-1922. **E-mail:** info@steamboatmagazine.com. **Website:** www.steamboatmagazine.com. **Contact:** Deborah Olsen, president; Jennie Lay, editor. **80% freelance written**. Quarterly magazine showcasing the history, people, lifestyles, and interests of Northwest Colorado. Our readers are generally well-educated, well-traveled, upscale, active people visiting our region to ski in winter and recreate in summer. They come from all 50 states and many foreign countries. Writing should be fresh, entertaining, and informative. Estab. 1978. Circ. 20,000. Byline given. Pays 50% on acceptance, 50% on publication. Submit seasonal material 1 year in advance. Accepts queries by mail, e-mail, fax, phone. Responds in 3 months to queries. Sample copy for $5.95 and SAE with 10 first-class stamps. Guidelines free.

NONFICTION Needs book excerpts, essays, general interest, historical, humor, interview, photo feature, travel. **Buys 10-15 mss/year.** Query with published clips. Length: 150-1,500 words. **Pays $50-300 for assigned articles.** Sometimes pays expenses of writers on assignment.

CONNECTICUT

💲💲💲 CONNECTICUT MAGAZINE

Journal Register Co., 35 Nutmeg Dr., Trumbull CT 06611. (203)380-6600. **Fax:** (203)380-6610. **E-mail:** cmonagan@connecticutmag.com. **Website:** www.connecticutmag.com. **Contact:** Charles A. Monagam, editor; Dale B. Salm, managing editor. **75% freelance written**. "Prefers to work with published/established writers who know the state and live/have lived here. Monthly magazine for an affluent, sophisticated, suburban audience. We want only articles that pertain to living in Connecticut." Estab. 1971. Circ.

93,000. Byline given. Offers 20% kill fee. Publishes ms an average of 4 months after acceptance. Submit seasonal material 4 months in advance. Accepts queries by mail, e-mail, fax. Responds in 6 weeks to queries. Guidelines for #10 SASE.

NONFICTION Needs book excerpts, exposé, general interest, interview, topics of service to Connecticut readers. Special issues: Dining/entertainment, northeast/travel, home/garden and Connecticut bride twice/year. Also, business (January) and healthcare 4-6x/year. No personal essays. **Buys 50 mss/year.** Query with published clips. 3,000 words maximum. **Pays $600-1,200.** Sometimes pays expenses of writers on assignment.

COLUMNS Business, Health, Politics, Connecticut Calendar, Arts, Dining Out, Gardening, Environment, Education, People, Sports, Media, From the Field (quirky, interesting regional stories with broad appeal). Length: 1,500-2,500 words. **Buys 50 mss/year.** Query with published clips. **Pays $400-700.**

FILLERS Short pieces about Connecticut trends, curiosities, interesting short subjects, etc. Length: 150-400 words. **Pays $75-150.**

DELAWARE

💲💲 DELAWARE TODAY

3301 Lancaster Pike, Suite 5C, Wilmington DE 19805. (302)656-1809. **Fax:** (302)656-5843. **E-mail:** editors@delawaretoday.com. **Website:** www.delawaretoday.com. **50% freelance written**. Monthly magazine geared toward Delaware people, places and issues. All stories must have Delaware slant. No pitches such as Delawareans will be interested in a national topic. Estab. 1962. Circ. 25,000. Byline given. Offers 50% kill fee. Publishes ms an average of 4 months after acceptance. Editorial lead time 3 months. Submit seasonal material 6 months in advance. Responds in 2 months to queries. Sample copy for $2.95.

NONFICTION Needs historical, interview, photo feature, lifestyles, issues. Special issues: Newcomer's Guide to Delaware. **Buys 40 mss/year.** Query with published clips. Length: 100-3,000 words. **Pays $50-750.** Sometimes pays expenses of writers on assignment.

COLUMNS Business, Health, History, People, all 1,500 words. **Buys 24 mss/year.** Query with published clips. **Pays $150-250.**

FILLERS Needs anecdotes, newsbreaks, short humor. **Buys 10 mss/year.** Length: 100-200 words. **Pays $50-75.**

DISTRICT OF COLUMBIA

💲💲 WASHINGTON CITY PAPER

2390 Champlain St., NW, Washington DC 20009. (202)332-2100. **Fax:** (202)332-8500. **E-mail:** abaca@ washingtoncitypaper.com. **Website:** www.washingtoncitypaper.com. **Contact:** Alex Baca, assistant editor. **50% freelance written**. Relentlessly local alternative weekly in nation's capital covering city and regional politics, media and arts. No national stories. Estab. 1981. Circ. 95,000. Byline given. Offers kill fee. Offers 10% kill fee for assigned stories. Publishes ms an average of 6 weeks after acceptance. Editorial lead time 7-10 days. Responds in 1 month to queries. Guidelines available online.

NONFICTION Buys 100 mss/year. District Line: 800-1,500 words; Covers: 2,500-10,000 words **Pays 10-40¢/word.** Sometimes pays expenses of writers on assignment.

COLUMNS Music Writing (eclectic). **Buys 100 mss/year.** Query with published clips or send complete ms. **Pays 10-40¢/word.**

FLORIDA

💲💲💲💲 BOCA RATON MAGAZINE

JES Publishing, 5455 N. Federal Highway, Suite M, Boca Raton FL 33487. (561)997-8683. **Fax:** (561)997-8909. **Website:** www.bocamag.com. **Contact:** Marie Speed, editor-in-chief; Kevin Kaminski, editor. **70% freelance written**. Bimonthly lifestyle magazine devoted to the residents of South Florida, featuring fashion, interior design, food, people, places, and issues that shape the affluent South Florida market. Estab. 1981. Circ. 20,000. Byline given. Publishes ms an average of 3 months after acceptance. Submit seasonal material 7 months in advance. Accepts simultaneous submissions. Responds in 1 month to queries. Sample copy for $4.95 and 10×13 SAE with 10 first-class stamps. Guidelines for #10 SASE.

NONFICTION Needs general interest, historical, humor, interview, photo feature, travel. Special issues: Interior Design (September-October); Real Estate (March-April); Best of Boca (July-August). Send complete ms. Length: 800-2,500 words. **Pays $350-1,500.**

COLUMNS Body & Soul (health, fitness and beauty column, general interest); Hitting Home (family and social interactions); History or Arts (relevant to South Florida), all 1,000 words. Query with published clips or send complete ms. **Pays $350-400.**

💲💲 EMERALD COAST MAGAZINE

Rowland Publishing, Inc., 1932 Miccosukee Rd., Tallahassee FL 32308. (850)878-0554. **Fax:** (850)656-1871. **E-mail:** editorial@rowlandinc.com. **Website:** www.emeraldcoastmagazine.com. **25% freelance written**. Bimonthly magazine. Lifestyle publication celebrating life on Florida's Emerald Coast. All content has an Emerald Coast (Northwest Florida) connection. This includes Sandestin, Destin, Fort Walton Beach. Estab. 2000. Circ. 18,000. Byline given. Publishes ms an average of 3 months after acceptance. Editorial lead time 4 months. Submit seasonal material 6 months in advance. Accepts queries by mail, e-mail. Accepts simultaneous submissions. Responds in 3 months to queries. Responds in 3 months to mss. Sample copy for $4. Guidelines by e-mail.

NONFICTION Needs essays, historical, inspirational, interview, new product, personal experience, photo feature. No fiction, poetry, or travel. No general interest—be Northwest Florida specific. **Buys 5 mss/year.** Query with published clips. Length: 1,800-2,000 words. **Pays $100-250.**

💲 FT. MYERS MAGAZINE

And Pat, LLC, 15880 Summerlin Rd., Suite 189, Fort Myers FL 33908. (941)433-3884. **E-mail:** ftmyers@ optonline.net. **Website:** www.ftmyersmagazine.com. **90% freelance written**. Bimonthly magazine covering regional arts and living for educated, active, successful and creative residents of Lee & Collier counties (FL) and guests at resorts and hotels in Lee County. "Content: Arts, entertainment, media, travel, sports, health, home, garden, environmental issues." Estab. 2001. Circ. 20,000. Byline given. 30 days after publication. Publishes ms an average of 2-6 months after acceptance. Editorial lead time 2-4 months. Submit seasonal material 2-4 months in advance. Accepts queries by e-mail. Accepts simultaneous submissions. Responds in 3 months to queries and to mss. Guidelines available online.

NONFICTION Needs essays, general interest, historical, how-to, humor, interview, personal experience, reviews, previews, news, informational. **Buys 10-25 mss/year.** Send complete ms. Length: 750-1,500 words. **Pays $50-150 or approximately 10¢/word.** Sometimes pays expenses of writers on assignment.

COLUMNS Media: books, music, video, film, theater, Internet, software (news, previews, reviews, interviews, profiles), 750-1,500 words. Lifestyles: art & design, science & technology, house & garden, health & wellness, sports & recreation, travel & leisure, food & drink (news, interviews, previews, reviews, profiles, advice), 750-1,500 words. **Buys 60 mss/year.** Query with or without published clips or send complete ms. **Pays $50-150.**

💲💲 TALLAHASSEE MAGAZINE

Rowland Publishing, Inc., 1932 Miccosukee Rd., Tallahassee FL 32308. **E-mail:** editorial@rowlandpublishing.com. **Website:** www.rowlandpublishing.com. **20% freelance written.** Bimonthly magazine covering life in Florida's Capital Region. All content has a Tallahassee, Florida connection. Estab. 1978. Circ. 18,000. Byline given. Publishes ms an average of 2 months after acceptance. Editorial lead time 4 months. Submit seasonal material 6 months in advance. Accepts queries by mail, e-mail. Accepts simultaneous submissions. Responds in 3 months to queries & mss. Sample copy for $4. Guidelines by e-mail.

NONFICTION Needs book excerpts, essays, historical, inspirational, interview, new product, personal experience, photo feature, travel, sports, business, Calendar items. No fiction, poetry, or travel. No general interest. **Buys 15 mss/year.** Query with published clips. Length: 500-2,500 words. **Pays $100-350.**

THE THIRTY-A REVIEW

227 Sandy Springs Place, Suite D-297, Sandy Springs GA 30328. **E-mail:** miles@thirtyareview.com. **Website:** thirtyareview.com. Monthly magazine focusing on 30-A and the surrounding areas. "We tell the human interest stories that make 30-A's entrepreneurs, developers and artists tick, making the magazine appealing to both tourists and locals alike." Accepts queries by e-mail.

NONFICTION Needs general interest, interview. Query with published clips.

💲💲 WHERE MAGAZINE (WHERE GUESTBOOK, WHERE MAP, WHERE NEWSLETTER)

Morris Visitor Publications, 7300 Corporate Center Dr., Suite 303, Miami FL 33126. **Fax:** (305)892-2991. **E-mail:** aurora.rodriguez@wheremagaziine.com. **Website:** www.wheretraveler.com. **Contact:** Aurora Rodriguez, editor. **40% freelance written.** Monthly magazine covering Miami tourism. "We cover Miami only. We are a tourism guide, so features are only about where to go and what to do in Miami. Writers must be very familiar with Miami." Estab. 1936. Circ. 30,000. Byline for features only, but all writers listed on masthead. Editorial lead time 3 months. Submit seasonal material 3 months in advance. Accepts queries by mail, e-mail. Responds in 1 week to queries Sample copy available online. Guidelines by e-mail.

NONFICTION Needs new product, photo feature, travel, (in Miami). Query. Length: 500 words.

COLUMNS Dining; Entertainment; Museums & Attractions; Art Galleries; Shops & Services; Navigating around Miami, 50 words. Queries for writer clips only per page of 1 blurbs per page.

GENERAL REGIONAL

💲💲 BLUE RIDGE COUNTRY

Leisure Publishing, 3424 Brambleton Ave., Roanoke VA 24018. (540)989-6138. **Fax:** (540)989-7603. **E-mail:** krheinheimer@leisurepublishing.com. **Website:** www.blueridgecountry.com. **Contact:** Kurt Rheinheimer, editor. **90% freelance written.** Bimonthly, full-color magazine embracing the feel and spirit of the Blue Ridge region, the traditions and recipes, the husbandry and farming, the country stores and bed-and-breakfast inns, the things to visit and learn about—everything that will allow and encourage the reader to take a trip home for the weekend even if he or she has never lived in the region. "The magazine is designed to celebrate the history, heritage and beauty of the Blue Ridge region. It is aimed at adult, upscale readers who enjoy living or traveling in the mountain regions of Virginia, North Carolina, West Virginia, Maryland, Kentucky, Tennessee, South Carolina, Alabama, and Georgia." Estab. 1988. Circ. 425,000. Byline given. Offers kill fee. Offers $50 kill fee for commissioned pieces only. Publishes ms an average of 8 months after acceptance. Submit seasonal material 6 months in advance. Accepts queries by mail, e-mail, fax; prefer e-mail. Responds in 3-4 months to queries. Responds in 2 months to mss. Sample copy with 9×12 SASE with 6 first-class stamps. Guidelines available online.

NONFICTION Needs essays, general interest, historical, personal experience, photo feature, travel, The photo essay will continue to be part of each issue, but for the foreseeable future will be a combination of book and gallery/museum exhibit previews, and also

essays of work by talented individual photographers—though we cannot pay, this is a good option for those who are interested in editorial coverage of their work. Those essays will include short profile, web link and contact information, with the idea of getting them, their work and their business directly in front of 425,000 readers' eyes. **Buys 25-30 mss/year.** Send complete ms. Length: 200-1,500 words. **Pays $50-250.**
COLUMNS Inns and Getaways (reviews of inns); Mountain Delicacies (cookbooks and recipes); Country Roads (shorts on regional news, people, destinations, events, history, antiques, books); Inns and Getaways (reviews of inns); On the Mountainside (first-person outdoor recreation pieces excluding hikes). **Buys 30-42 mss/year.** Query. **Pays $25-125.**

⊘ MIDWEST LIVING

Meredith Corp., 1716 Locust St., Des Moines IA 50309. (515)284-3000. **Fax:** (515)284-3836. **E-mail:** midwestliving@meredith.com. **Website:** www.midwestliving.com. Bimonthly magazine covering Midwestern families. Regional service magazine that celebrates the interest, values, and lifestyles of Midwestern families. Estab. 1987. Circ. 915,000. Editorial lead time 6 months. Accepts queries by mail, e-mail. Sample copy for $3.95. Guidelines by email.
NONFICTION Needs general interest, good eating, festivals and fairs, historical, interesting slices of Midwestern history, customs, traditions and the people who preserve them, interview, towns, neighborhoods, families, people whose stories exemplify the Midwest spirit an values, travel, Midwestern destinations with emphasis on the fun and affordable. Query.

THE OXFORD AMERICAN

201 Donaghey Ave., Main 107, Conway AR 72035. (501)450-5376. **Fax:** (501)450-3490. **E-mail:** info@oxfordamerican.org. **Website:** www.oxfordamerican.org. **Contact:** Carol Ann Fitzgerald, managing editor; Wes Enzinna, associate editor; Warwick Sabin, publisher. Quarterly literary magazine from the South with a national audience. Circ. 20,000. Accepts queries by mail. NoResponds in 2-3 months or sooner to mss. Guidelines available online at http://www.oxfordamerican.org/pages/submission-guidelines.
NONFICTION Needs short and long essays (500 to 3,000 words), general interest, how-to, humor, personal experience, travel, reporting, business. Query with SASE or send complete ms.

COLUMNS Odes, Travel, Politics, Business, Writing on Writing, Southerner Abroad, Reports, Literature.
FICTION Stories should be from or about the South. Send complete ms.
POETRY Poems should be from or about the South. Submit maximum 3-5 poems.

⊘ SOUTHCOMM PUBLISHING COMPANY, INC.

541 Buttermilk Pike, Suite 100, Crescent Springs KY 41017. (678)624-1075. **Fax:** (678)623-9979. **E-mail:** cwwalker@southcomm.com. **Website:** http://southcommpublishing.com. **Contact:** Carolyn Williams-Walker. "Our magazines primarily are used as marketing and economic development pieces, but they are also used as tourism guides and a source of information for newcomers. As such, our editorial supplies entertaining and informative reading for those visiting the communities for the first time, as well as those who have lived in the area for any period of time. We are looking for writers who are interested in writing dynamic copy about Georgia, Tennessee, South Carolina, North Carolina, Alabama, Virginia, Florida, Pennsylvania, Texas, and many other states." Estab. 1985. Byline given. Pays 30 days after acceptance. Publishes ms an average of 1-2 months after acceptance. Accepts queries by mail, e-mail, fax. Sample copy and writer's guidelines free.
NONFICTION "We are not looking for article submissions. We will assign stories to writers in which we're interested. Queries should include samples of published works and biographical information." **Buys 50+ mss/year.** Query or send complete ms. Length: 100-1,000 words. **Pays $25-200.**

GEORGIA

⊘⊘ GEORGIA MAGAZINE

Georgia Electric Membership Corp., P.O. Box 1707, Tucker GA 30085. (770)270-6951. **Fax:** (770)270-6995. **E-mail:** aorowski@georgiaemc.com. **Website:** www.georgiamagazine.org. **Contact:** Ann Orowski, editor. **50% freelance written.** We are a monthly magazine for and about Georgians, with a friendly, conversational tone and human interest topics. Estab. 1945. Circ. 509,000. Byline given. Publishes ms an average of 6 months after acceptance. Editorial lead time 2 months. Submit seasonal material 6 months in advance. Accepts simultaneous submissions. Responds in 1 month to subjects of interest. Sample copy for $2. Guidelines for #10 SASE, or by e-mail.

NONFICTION Needs general interest, Georgia-focused, historical, how-to, in the home and garden, humor, inspirational, interview, photo feature, travel. Query with published clips. 1,000-1,200 words; 800 words for smaller features and departments. **Pays $350-500.**

THE PIEDMONT REVIEW

P.O. Box 12047, Atlanta GA 30355. **E-mail:** mneiman@piedmontreview.com. **Website:** www.piedmontreview.com. Monthly magazine covering local business, dining, cultural and charity events, fashion, home and garden features, art reviews, travel, and various personal success stories. *The Piedmont Review* is one of Atlanta's most popular lifestyle magazines. Accepts queries by e-mail.

NONFICTION Needs general interest, interview, new product, opinion, personal experience. Query with published clips.

$$ POINTS NORTH MAGAZINE

All Points Interactive Media Corp., 568 Peachtree Pkwy., Cumming GA 30041-6820. (770)844-0969. **Fax:** (770)844-0968. **E-mail:** bre@ptsnorth.com; heather@ptsnorth.com; editorial@ptsnorth.com. **Website:** www.ptsnorth.com. **Contact:** Bre Humphries, editor; Heather Brown, senior editor. **15% freelance written**. Monthly magazine covering lifestyle (regional). "*Points North* specializes in providing pertinent information for our prestigious audience. In each issue we feature intriguing personalities that have a connection to the Atlanta area, fabulous travel destinations, upcoming local and regional events, topics relating to home improvement, recreation, cultural arts and entertainment, fashion, health, retail shopping and the latest news and information from those north Atlanta communities in our primary coverage area." Estab. 2000. Circ. 81,000. Byline given. Offers negotiable (for assigned articles only) kill fee. Publishes ms an average of 3 months after acceptance. Editorial lead time 3 months. Submit seasonal material 6 months in advance. Accepts queries by e-mail only. Responds in 6-8 weeks to queries. Responds in 6-8 months to mss. Sample copy for $3.

NONFICTION Contact: Managing Editor. Needs general interest, only topics pertaining to Atlanta area, historical, interview, travel. **Buys 50-60 mss/year.** Query with published clips. Length: 1,200-2,500 words. **Pays $250-500.**

$$ SAVANNAH MAGAZINE

Morris Publishing Group, P.O. Box 1088, Savannah GA 31402-1088. **Fax:** (912)525-0611. **E-mail:** editor@savannahmagazine.com. **Website:** www.savannahmagazine.com. **95% freelance written**. Bimonthly magazine focusing on homes and entertaining covering coastal lifestyle of Savannah and South Carolina area. "*Savannah Magazine* publishes articles about people, places and events of interest to the residents of the greater Savannah areas, as well as coastal Georgia and the South Carolina low country. We strive to provide our readers with information that is both useful and entertaining—written in a lively, readable style." Estab. 1990. Circ. 16,000. Byline given. Offers 20% kill fee. Publishes ms an average of 2 months after acceptance. Editorial lead time 2 months. Submit seasonal material 4 months in advance. Accepts queries by mail, e-mail, fax. Accepts simultaneous submissions. Responds in 4 weeks to queries. Responds in 6 weeks to mss. Sample copy free. Guidelines by e-mail.

NONFICTION Needs general interest, historical, humor, interview, travel. Does not want fiction or poetry. Query with published clips. Length: 500-750 words. **Pays $250-450.**

HAWAII

$$$ HONOLULU MAGAZINE

PacificBasin Communications, 1000 Bishop St., Suite 405, Honolulu HI 96813. (808)537-9500. **Fax:** (808)537-6455. **E-mail:** akamn@honolulumagazine.com; kathrynw@honolulumagazine.com. **Website:** www.honolulumagazine.com. **Contact:** A. Kam Napier, editor; Kathryn Drury Wagner, executive editor. **Prefers to work with published/established writers.** Monthly magazine covering general interest topics relating to Hawaii residents. Estab. 1888. Circ. 30,000. Byline given. Pays about 30 days after publication. Where appropriate, kill fee of half of assignment fee. Accepts queries by mail, e-mail. Guidelines available online.

NONFICTION Needs historical, interview, sports, politics, lifestyle trends, all Hawaii-related. "We write for Hawaii residents, so travel articles about Hawaii are not appropriate." Send complete ms. determined when assignments discussed. **Pays $250-1,200.** Sometimes pays expenses of writers on assignment.

COLUMNS Length determined when assignments discussed. Query with published clips or send complete ms. **Pays $100-300.**

IDAHO

⊛⊛ SUN VALLEY MAGAZINE

Valley Publishing, LLC, 111 First Ave. N #1M, Meriwether Building, Hailey ID 83333. (208)788-0770. **Fax:** (208)788-3881. **E-mail:** michael@sunvalleymag.com; robinleahy@sunvalleymag.com. **Website:** www.sunvalleymag.com. **Contact:** Mike McKenna, editor; Robin Leahy, art director. **95% freelance written.** Quarterly magazine covering the lifestyle of the Sun Valley area. *Sun Valley Magazine* presents the lifestyle of the Sun Valley area and the Wood River Valley, including recreation, culture, profiles, history and the arts. Estab. 1973. Circ. 17,000. Byline given. Publishes ms an average of 5 months after acceptance. Editorial lead time 1 year. Submit seasonal material 14 months in advance. Accepts queries by mail. Accepts simultaneous submissions. Responds in 5 weeks to queries. Responds in 2 months to mss. Sample copy for $4.95 and $3 postage. Guidelines for #10 SASE.

NONFICTION Needs historical, interview, photo feature, travel. Special issues: Sun Valley home design and architecture, Spring; Sun Valley weddings/wedding planner, summer. Query with published clips. **Pays $40-500.** Sometimes pays expenses of writers on assignment.

COLUMNS Conservation issues, winter/summer sports, health & wellness, mountain-related activities and subjects, home (interior design), garden. All columns must have a local slant. Query with published clips. **Pays $40-300.**

ILLINOIS

⊛⊛⊛⊛ CHICAGO MAGAZINE

435 N. Michigan Ave., Suite 1100, Chicago IL 60611. (312)222-8999. **E-mail:** bfenner@chicagomag.com; cwalker@chicagomag.com. **Website:** www.chicagomag.com. **Contact:** Elizabeth Fenner, editor-in-chief; Cassie Walker Burke, executive editor. **50% freelance written. Prefers to work with published/established writers.** Monthly magazine for an audience which is 95% from Chicago area; 90% college educated; upper income, overriding interests in the arts, politics, dining, good life in the city and suburbs. Most are

in 25-50 age bracket, well-read and articulate. "Produced by the city's best magazine editors and writers, Chicago Magazine is the definitive voice on top dining, entertainment, shopping and real estate in the region. It also offers provocative narrative stories and topical features that have won numerous awards. Chicago Magazine reaches 1.5 million readers and is published by Tribune Company." Estab. 1968. Circ. 182,000. Publishes ms an average of 3 months after acceptance. Submit seasonal material 4 months in advance. Accepts queries by mail, e-mail. Responds in 1 month to queries. For sample copy, send $3 to Circulation Department. Guidelines for #10 SASE.

NONFICTION Needs exposé, humor, personal experience, think pieces, profiles, spot news, historical articles. Does not want anything about events outside the city or profiles on people who no longer live in the city. **Buys 100 mss/year.** Query; indicate specifics, knowledge of city and market, and demonstrable access to sources. Length: 200-6,000 words. **Pays $100-3,000 and up.** Pays expenses of writers on assignment.

⊛⊛⊛⊛ CHICAGO READER

Chicago Reader, Inc., 11 E. Illinois St., Chicago IL 60611. (312)828-0350. **Fax:** (312)828-9926. **E-mail:** mshalhoup@chicagoreader.com; jludwig@chicagoreader.com; letters@chicagoreader.com. **Website:** www.chicagoreader.com. **Contact:** Mara Shalhoup, editor; Jerome Ludwig, managing editor. **50% freelance written.** Weekly Alternative tabloid for Chicago. Estab. 1971. Circ. 120,000. Byline given. Occasional kill fee. Publishes ms an average of 2 weeks after acceptance. Editorial lead time up to 6 months. Accepts queries by mail, e-mail, fax. Accepts simultaneous submissions. Responds if interested. Sample copy free. Writer's guidelines free or online.

NONFICTION **Buys 500 mss/year.** Send complete ms. Length: 250-2,500 words. **Pays $100-3,000.** Sometimes pays expenses of writers on assignment.

COLUMNS Local color, 500-2,500 words; arts and entertainment reviews, up to 1,200 words.

⊛⊛ CHICAGO SCENE MAGAZINE

233 E. Erie, Suite 603, Chicago IL 60611. **Fax:** (312)587-7397. **E-mail:** email@chicago-scene.com. **Website:** www.chicago-scene.com. **Contact:** Ted Widen, publisher; Robert Luce, editor. **95% freelance written.** Monthly magazine covering dining, nightlife, travel, beauty, entertainment, fitness, style, drinks. *Chicago Scene Magazine* is the premier news and entertain-

ment publication for Chicago's young professional. Estab. 2001. Byline given. Publishes ms an average of 2 months after acceptance. Submit seasonal material 3 months in advance. Accepts queries by e-mail. Sample copy available online. Guidelines free.

NONFICTION Needs how-to, interview, new product, travel. Does not want personal experiences, essays, technical. Query with published clips. Length: 600-2,400 words. **Pays $25-250.**

COLUMNS Beauty, 840 words; Dining, 1,260-1,680 words; Drinks, 1,260-1,680 words; Fitness, 420-630 words; Travel, 1,260-1,680 words; Nightlife, 1,050-1,680 words; Personal Style, 420 words. Query with published clips. **Pays $25-250.**

$ ILLINOIS ENTERTAINER

4223 W. Lake Street, Suite 420, Chicago IL 60624. (773)533-9333. **Fax:** (312)922-9341. **E-mail:** ieeditors@aol.com. **Website:** www.illinoisentertainer.com. **80% freelance written.** Monthly free magazine covering popular and alternative music, as well as other entertainment: film, media. Estab. 1974. Circ. 55,000. Byline given. Offers 50% kill fee. Publishes ms an average of 2 months after acceptance. Editorial lead time 2 months. Submit seasonal material 2 months in advance. Accepts queries by mail. Accepts simultaneous submissions. Responds in 2 months to queries. Sample copy for $5.

NONFICTION Needs exposé, how-to, humor, interview, new product, reviews. No personal, confessional, inspirational articles. **Buys 75 mss/year.** Query with published clips. Length: 600-2,600 words. **Pays $15-160.** Sometimes pays expenses of writers on assignment.

COLUMNS Spins (LP reviews), 100-400 words. **Buys 200-300 mss/year.** Query with published clips. **Pays $8-25.**

$ MIDWESTERN FAMILY MAGAZINE

P.O. Box 9302, Peoria IL 61612. (309)303-7309. **Fax:** (866)412-3835. **E-mail:** jrudd@midwesternfamily.com. **Website:** www.midwesternfamily.com. **90% freelance written.** Bimonthly magazine covering family living in Central Illinois. *Midwestern Family* is a comprehensive guide to fun, health and happiness for Central Illinois families. Estab. 2003. Circ. 23,000. Byline given. Publishes ms an average of 2 months after acceptance. Editorial lead time 4-6 weeks. Submit seasonal material 4-6 weeks in advance. Accepts queries by e-mail, online submission form. Responds in 2 weeks to queries. Responds in 4 months to mss. Sample copy for $1.50. Guidelines by e-mail.

NONFICTION Query. Length: 1,000-1,500 words. **Pays $100.** Sometimes pays expenses of writers on assignment.

COLUMNS Home; Fun; Life; Food; Health; Discovery, all 1,000-1,250 words. **Buys 40 mss/year.** Query. **Pays $100.**

$$ NEWCITY

New City Communications, Inc., 770 N. Halsted, Chicago IL 60622. (312)243-8786. **Fax:** (312)243-8802. **E-mail:** brian@newcity.com. **Website:** www.newcitychicago.com. **Contact:** Brian Hieggelke, editor and publisher;. **50% freelance written.** Weekly magazine. Estab. 1986. Circ. 50,000. Byline given. Pays 2-12 months after publication. Offers kill fee. Offers 20% kill fee in certain cases. Publishes ms an average of 1 month after acceptance. Editorial lead time 2 months. Submit seasonal material 2 months in advance. Responds in 1 month to mss. Sample copy for $3. Guidelines available on website: http://newcitynetwork.com/editorialart/publicitypr-proposing-stories-submitting-listings/.

NONFICTION Needs essays, exposé, general interest, interview, personal experience, travel, related to traveling from Chicago and other issues particularly affecting travelers from this area, service. **Buys 100 mss/year.** Query by e-mail only Length: 100-4,000 words. **Pays $10-200.** Rarely pays expenses of writers on assignment.

COLUMNS Lit (literary supplement), 300-2,000 words; Music, Film, Arts (arts criticism), 150-800 words; Chow (food writing), 300-2,000 words. **Buys 50 mss/year.** Query by e-mail **Pays $15-300.**

$$ NORTHWEST QUARTERLY MAGAZINE

Hughes Media Inc., 728 N. Prospect St., Rockford IL 61101. **Fax:** (815)316-2301. **E-mail:** janine@northwestquarterly.com. **Website:** www.northwestquarterly.com. **20% freelance written.** Quarterly magazine covering regional lifestyle of Northern Illinois and Southern Wisconsin, and also Kane and McHenry counties (Chicago collar counties), highlighting strengths of living and doing business in the area. Estab. 2004. Circ. 42,000. Byline given. Publishes ms an average of 4-6 months after acceptance. Editorial lead time 6 months. Submit seasonal material 6 months in advance. Accepts queries by mail, e-mail. Responds in 2 weeks to queries. Responds in 2 months to mss. Sample copy and guidelines by e-mail.

NONFICTION Needs historical, interview, photo feature, regional features. Does not want opinion, fiction, anything unrelated to our geographic region. **Buys 150 mss/year.** Query. Length: 700-2,500 words. **Pays $25-500.** Sometimes pays expenses of writers on assignment.

COLUMNS Health & Fitness, 1,000-2,000 words; Home & Garden, 1,500 words; Destinations & Recreation, 1,000-2,000 words; Environment & Nature, 2,000-3,000 words. **Buys 120 mss/year.** Query. **Pays $100-500.**

FILLERS Needs short humor. **Buys 24 mss/year.** Length: 100-200 words. **Pays $30-50.**

💲💲 OUTDOOR ILLINOIS

Illinois Department of Natural Resources, P.O. Box 19225, Dept. NL, Springfield IL 62794-9225. (217)785-4193. **E-mail:** dnr.editor@illinois.gov. **Website:** www.dnr.state.il.us/oi. **25% freelance written.** Monthly magazine covering Illinois cultural and natural resources. *Outdoor Illinois* promotes outdoor activities, Illinois State parks, Illinois natural and cultural resources. Estab. 1973. Circ. 30,000. Byline given. Editorial lead time 4 months. Submit seasonal material 1 year in advance. Accepts queries by mail, e-mail. Responds in 2 weeks to queries. Sample copy free. Guidelines by email.

NONFICTION Needs historical, how-to, humor, interview, photo feature, travel. Does not want first person unless truly has something to say. Query with published clips. Length: 350-1,500 words. **Pays $100-250.**

💲💲 WEST SUBURBAN LIVING

C2 Publishing, Inc., P.O. Box 111, Elmhurst IL 60126. (630)834-4995. **Fax:** (630)834-4996. **Website:** www.westsuburbanliving.net. **Contact:** Chuck Cozette, editor. **80% freelance written.** Bimonthly magazine focusing on the western suburbs of Chicago. Estab. 1996. Circ. 25,000. Byline given. Publishes ms an average of 2-4 months after acceptance. Accepts queries by mail, e-mail, fax. NoSample copy available online.

NONFICTION Needs general interest, how-to, travel. "Does not want anything that does not have an angle or tie-in to the area we cover—Chicago's western suburbs." **Buys 15 mss/year. Pays $100-500.** Sometimes pays expenses of writers on assignment.

INDIANA

💲💲 EVANSVILLE LIVING

Tucker Publishing Group, 223 NW Second St., Suite 200, Evansville IN 47708. (812)426-2115. **Fax:** (812)426-2134. **Website:** www.evansvilleliving.com. **80-100% freelance written.** Bimonthly magazine covering Evansville, Indiana, and the greater area. *Evansville Living* is the only full-color, glossy, 100+ page city magazine for the Evansville, Indiana, area. Regular departments include: Home Style, Garden Style, Day Tripping, Sporting Life, and Local Flavor (menus). Estab. 2000. Circ. 50,000. Byline given. Publishes ms an average of 3 months after acceptance. Editorial lead time 6 months. Submit seasonal material 6 months in advance. Accepts queries by mail, e-mail, fax. YesSample copy for $5 or online. Guidelines for free or by e-mail.

NONFICTION Needs essays, general interest, historical, photo feature, travel. **Buys 60-80 mss/year.** Query with published clips. Length: 200-2,000 words. **Pays $100-300.** Sometimes pays expenses of writers on assignment.

COLUMNS Home Style (home); Garden Style (garden); Sporting Life (sports); Local Flavor (menus), all 1,500 words. Query with published clips. **Pays $100-300.**

💲💲💲 INDIANAPOLIS MONTHLY

Emmis Communications, 1 Emmis Plaza, 40 Monument Circle, Suite 100, Indianapolis IN 46204. (317)237-9288. **E-mail:** deborah@emmis.com. **Website:** www.indianapolismonthly.com. **Contact:** Deborah Paul, editorial director. **30% freelance written. Prefers to work with published/established writers.** "*Indianapolis Monthly* attracts and enlightens its upscale, well-educated readership with bright, lively editorial on subjects ranging from personalities to social issues, fashion to food. Its diverse content and attention to service make it the ultimate source by which the Indianapolis area lives." Estab. 1977. Circ. 50,000. Byline given. Offers kill fee. Offers negotiable kill fee. Publishes ms an average of 2 months after acceptance. Editorial lead time 3 months. Submit seasonal material 3 months in advance. Accepts queries by mail, e-mail. Responds in 6 weeks to queries. Sample copy for $6.10.

NONFICTION Needs book excerpts, by Indiana authors or with strong Indiana ties, essays, exposé, general interest, interview, photo feature. "No poetry, fiction, or domestic humor; no 'How Indy Has Changed Since I Left Town', 'An Outsider's View of the 500', or generic material with no or little tie to Indianapolis/Indiana." **Buys 35 mss/year.** Query by mail with published clips. Length: 200-3,000 words. **Pays $50-1,000.**

🌑🌑 NORTHERN INDIANA LAKES MAGAZINE

1415 W. Coliseum Blvd., Fort Wayne IN 46808. (260)484-0546. **Fax:** (260)469-0454. **E-mail:** editor@nilakes.com. **Website:** www.nilakes.com. **Contact:** Sue Rawlinson, editor-in-chief. Magazine published 8 times/year that defines lake living at its best. "*Northern Indiana LAKES Magazine* is the official publication for the good life in northern Indiana. The LAKES country market area is essentially defined as 20 northern Indiana counties: Adams, Allen, DeKalb, Elkhart, Huntington, Jasper, Kosciusko, LaGrange, Lake, LaPorte, Marshall, Newton, Noble, Porter, Pulaski, St. Joseph, Starke, Steuben, Wells and Whitley. Now reaches into Southern Michigan and Lake Michigan's shoreline. Byline given. Pays within 30 days of publication. Accepts queries by mail. Guidelines by e-mail and online at website.

NONFICTION Needs general interest, humor, interview, travel. Does not want "personal essays, stories about your vacation, celebrity profiles (with rare exceptions), routine pieces on familiar destinations, completed manuscripts, previously published works." Query with published clips. **Pays 10-35¢/word.**

IOWA

🌑🌑 THE IOWAN

Pioneer Communications, Inc., 300 Walnut, Suite 6, Des Moines IA 50309. **Fax:** (515)282-0125. **E-mail:** editor@iowan.com. **Website:** www.iowan.com. **Contact:** Beth Wilson, editor. **75% freelance written.** Bimonthly magazine covering the state of Iowa. "Our mission statement is: To celebrate the people and communities, the history and traditions, and the culture and events of Iowa that make our readers proud of our state." Estab. 1952. Circ. 25,000. Byline given. Offers $100 kill fee. Publishes ms an average of 3 months after acceptance. Editorial lead time 9-10 months. Submit seasonal material 6 months in advance. Accepts queries by mail, e-mail. Responds to queries received twice/year. Sample copy for $4.50 + s&h.

NONFICTION Needs book excerpts, essays, general interest, historical, interview, photo feature, travel. **Buys 30 mss/year.** Query with published clips. Length: 500-1,500 words. **Pays $250-450.** Sometimes pays expenses of writers on assignment.

COLUMNS Last Word (essay), 800 words. **Buys 6 mss/year.** Query with published clips. **Pays $100.**

KANSAS

🌑🌑 KANSAS!

Kansas Department of Commerce, 1000 SW Jackson St., Suite 100, Topeka KS 66612-1354. (785)296-3479. **Fax:** (785)296-6988. **E-mail:** ksmagazine@kansascommerce.com. **Website:** www.kansmag.com. **90% freelance written.** Quarterly magazine emphasizing Kansas travel attractions and events. Estab. 1945. Circ. 45,000. Byline and courtesy bylines are given to all content. Purchased content will publish an average of 1 year after acceptance. Submit seasonal material 8 months in advance. Accepts queries by mail. Responds in 2 months to queries. Guidelines available online.

NONFICTION Needs general interest, photo feature, travel. Query by mail. Length: 750-1,250 words. **Pays $200-350.** Mileage reimbursement is available for writers on assignment in the state of Kansas; TBD by assignment editor.

KENTUCKY

FORT MITCHELL LIVING

Community Publications, Inc., 179 Fairfield Ave., Bellevue KY 41073. (859)291-1412. **Fax:** (859)291-1417. **E-mail:** fortmitchell@livingmagazines.com. **Website:** www.livingmagazines.com. Estab. 1983. Circ. 4,700. Byline given. Editorial lead time 2 months. Submit seasonal material 3 months in advance. Guidelines by email.

NONFICTION Query.

FORT THOMAS LIVING

Community Publications, Inc., 179 Fairfield Ave., Bellevue KY 41073. (859)291-1412. **Fax:** (859)291-1417. **E-mail:** fortthomas@livingmagazines.com. **Website:** www.livingmagazines.com. **Contact:** Linda Johnson, editor. Monthly magazine covering Fort Thomas community. "Magazine focuses upon people living and working in Fort Thomas and promoting acitvities of interest to this community." Estab. 1977. Circ. 4,400.

Byline given. Editorial lead time 2 months. Submit seasonal material 3 months in advance. Accepts queries by mail, e-mail. Guidelines by email.

NONFICTION Does not want any material unrelated to Fort Thomas, Kentucky. Query. Prefers email submissions.

💲💲 KENTUCKY LIVING

Kentucky Association of Electric Co-Ops, P.O. Box 32170, Louisville KY 40232. (502)451-2430. **Fax:** (502)459-1611. **E-mail:** e-mail@kentuckyliving.com. **Website:** www.kentuckyliving.com. **Mostly freelance written. Prefers to work with published/established writers.** Monthly feature magazine primarily for Kentucky residents. Estab. 1948. Circ. 500,000. Byline given. Publishes ms an average of 12 months after acceptance. Submit seasonal material at least 6 months in advance. Accepts simultaneous submissions. Responds in 1 month to queries. Sample copy with SASE (9×12 envelope and 4 first-class stamps).

NONFICTION Emphasis on electric industry and ties to Kentucky's electric co-op areas of readership. **Buys 18-24 mss/year.** Send complete ms. **Pays $75-935** Sometimes pays expenses of writers on assignment.

💲💲 KENTUCKY MONTHLY

P.O. Box 559, Frankfort KY 40602-0559. (502)227-0053; (888)329-0053. **Fax:** (502)227-5009. **E-mail:** kymonthly@kentuckymonthly.com; steve@kentuckymonthly.com. **Website:** www.kentuckymonthly.com. **Contact:** Stephen Vest, editor. **50% freelance written.** Monthly magazine. "We publish stories about Kentucky and by Kentuckians, including those who live elsewhere." Estab. 1998. Circ. 42,000. Byline given. Pays within 3 months of publication. Publishes ms an average of 3 months after acceptance. Editorial lead time 3 months. Submit seasonal material 4 months in advance. Accepts queries by mail, e-mail, fax. Accepts simultaneous submissions. Responds in 1 month. Sample copy and writer's guidelines online.

NONFICTION Needs book excerpts, general interest, historical, how-to, humor, interview, photo feature, religious, travel, all with a Kentucky angle. **Buys 50 mss/year.** Query. Length: 300-2,000 words. **Pays $75-350 for assigned articles. Pays $50-200 for unsolicited articles.**

FICTION Needs adventure, historical, mainstream, novel concepts, all Kentucky-related stories. **Buys 10 mss/year.** Query with published clips. Length: 1,000-5,000 words. **Pays $50-100.**

LOUISIANA

💲💲 PRESERVATION IN PRINT

Preservation Resource Center of New Orleans, 923 Tchoupitoulos St., New Orleans LA 70130. (504)581-7032. **Fax:** (504)636-3073. **E-mail:** mfitzpatrick@prcno.org; prc@prcno.org. **Website:** www.prcno.org. **Contact:** Mary Fitzpatrick, editor. **30% freelance written.** Monthly magazine covering preservation. "We want articles about interest in the historic architecture of New Orleans." Estab. 1974. Circ. 10,000. Byline given. Publishes ms an average of 1 month after acceptance. Editorial lead time 1 month. Submit seasonal material 1-2 months in advance. Accepts queries by mail, e-mail, fax, phone. Accepts simultaneous submissions. Sample copy available online. Guidelines free.

NONFICTION Needs essays, historical, interview, photo feature, technical. **Buys 30 mss/year.** Query. Length: 700-1,000 words. **Pays $100-200 for assigned articles.** Sometimes pays expenses of writers on assignment.

MAINE

💲 DISCOVER MAINE MAGAZINE

10 Exchange St., Suite 208, Portland ME 04101. (207)874-7720. **Fax:** (207)874-7721. **E-mail:** info@discovermainemagazine.com. **Website:** www.discovermainemagazine.com. **100% freelance written.** Monthly magazine covering Maine history and nostalgia. Sports and hunting/fishing topics are also included. "Discover Maine Magazine is dedicated to bringing the amazing history of the great state of Maine to readers in every corner of the state and to those from away who love the rich heritage and traditions of Maine. From the history of Maine's mill towns, to the traditions of family farming and coastal fishing, nine times a year Discover Maine's stories tell of life in the cities and towns across Maine as it was years ago." Estab. 1992. Circ. 12,000. Byline given. Publishes ms an average of 2-3 months after acceptance. Editorial lead time 3 months. Submit seasonal material 3 months in advance. Accepts queries by mail, fax, phone. Accepts simultaneous submissions. Responds in 2 weeks to queries. Responds in 1 month to mss.

NONFICTION Needs historical. Does not want to receive poetry. **Buys 200 mss/year.** Send complete ms. Length: 500-2,000 words. **Pays $20-30**

MARYLAND

❸❸ BALTIMORE MAGAZINE

Inner Harbor, E. 1000 Lancaster St., Suite 400, Baltimore MD 21202. (410)752-4200. **Fax:** (410)625-0280. **E-mail:** Send correspondence to the appropriate editor. **Website:** www.baltimoremagazine.net. **Contact:** Department editors (Max Weiss—lifestyle, film, sports, general inquiries; Suzanne Loudermilk—Food; Ken Eglehart—business, special editions; John Lewis—arts and culture; Amy Mulvihill—calendar, coming events, party pages); Amanda White-Iseli, art director; Kathryn Mychailysyzn, associate art director. **50-60% freelance written**. Monthly city magazine featuring news, profiles and service articles. "Pieces must address an educated, active, affluent reader and must have a very strong Baltimore angle." Estab. 1907. Circ. 70,000. Byline given. Pays within 1 month of publication. Offers kill fee in some cases Submit seasonal material 4 months in advance. Accepts queries by mail, e-mail (preferred). Sample copy for $4.99. Guidelines available online.

NONFICTION Needs book excerpts, Baltimore subject or author, essays, exposé, general interest, historical, humor, interview, with a Baltimorean, new product, personal experience, photo feature, travel, local and regional to Maryland. "Nothing that lacks a strong Baltimore focus or angle. Unsolicited personal essays are almost never accepted. We've printed only two over the past few years; the last was by a 19-year veteran city judge reminiscing on his time on the bench and the odd stories and situations he encountered there. Unsolicited food and restaurant reviews, whether positive or negative, are likewise never accepted." Query by e-mail or mail with published clips or send complete ms. Length: 1,600-2,500 words. **Pays 30-40¢/word.** Sometimes pays expenses.

COLUMNS "The shorter pieces are the best places to break into the magazine." Hot Shot, Health, Education, Sports, Parenting, Politics. Length: 1,000-2,500 words. Query with published clips.

MASSACHUSETTS

❸❸ CAPE COD LIFE

Cape Cod Life, Inc., 13 Steeple Street, Ste. 204, P.O. Box 1439, Mashpee MA 02649. (508)419-7381. **Fax:** (508)477-1225. **Website:** www.capecodlife.com. **Contact:** Susan Dewey, managing editor. **80% freelance written**. Magazine published 6 times/year focusing on area lifestyle, history and culture, people and places, business and industry, and issues and answers for year-round and summer residents of Cape Cod, Nantucket, and Martha's Vineyard as well as nonresidents who spend their leisure time here. Cape Cod Life Magazine has become the premier lifestyle magazine for the Cape & Islands, featuring topics ranging from arts and events, history and heritage, beaches and boating as well as a comprehensive resource for planning the perfect vacation. Circ. 45,000. Byline given. Pays 90 days after acceptance. Offers 20% kill fee. Submit seasonal material 6 months in advance. Accepts queries by mail. Responds in 3 months to queries. Responds in 3 months to mss. Sample copy for $5. Guidelines for #10 SASE.

NONFICTION Needs book excerpts, general interest, historical, interview, photo feature, travel, outdoors, gardening, nautical, nature, arts, antiques. **Buys 20 mss/year.** Query. Length: 800-1,500 words. **Pays $200-400.**

❸❸ CAPE COD MAGAZINE

Rabideau Media Group, P.O. Box 208, Yarmouth Port MA 02765. (508)771-6549. **Fax:** (508)771-3769. **E-mail:** editor@capecodmagazine.com. **Website:** www.capecodmagazine.com. **80% freelance written**. Magazine published 9 times/year covering Cape Cod lifestyle. Estab. 1996. Circ. 16,000. Byline given. Pays 30 days after publication. Offers 25% kill fee. Publishes ms an average of 3 months after acceptance. Editorial lead time 6 months. Submit seasonal material 1 year in advance. Accepts queries by mail, e-mail. Responds in 3 weeks to queries. Responds in 2 months to mss. Sample copy for $5. Guidelines by e-mail.

NONFICTION Needs book excerpts, essays, general interest, historical, humor, interview, personal experience. Does not want clichéd pieces, interviews, and puff features. **Buys 3 mss/year.** Send complete ms. Length: 800-2,500 words. **Pays $300-500 for assigned articles. Pays $100-300 for unsolicited articles.** Sometimes pays expenses of writers on assignment.

COLUMNS Last Word (personal observations in typical back page format), 700 words. **Buys 4 mss/year.** Query with or without published clips or send complete ms. **Pays $150-300.**

❸❸ CHATHAM MAGAZINE

Rabideau Publishing, P.O. Box 208, Yarmouth Port MA 02675. (508)771-6549. **Fax:** (508)771-3769. **E-**

mail: editor@capecodmagazine.com. **Website:** www. chathammag.com. **Contact:** Michael Rabideau, publisher; Liz Rabideau, associate publisher. **80% freelance written.** Annual magazine covering Chatham lifestyle. Estab. 2006. Byline given. Pays 30 days after publication. Offers 25% kill fee. Publishes ms an average of 3 months after acceptance. Editorial lead time 6 months. Submit seasonal material 1 year in advance. Accepts queries by mail, e-mail. Responds in 3 weeks to queries. Responds in 2 months to mss. Sample copy for $5. Guidelines by e-mail.

NONFICTION Needs book excerpts, essays, general interest, historical, humor, interview, personal experience. Send complete ms. Length: 800-2,500 words. **Pays $300-500 for assigned articles. Pays $100-300 for unsolicited articles.** Sometimes pays expenses of writers on assignment.

COLUMNS Hooked (fishing issues), 700 words. **Buys 4 mss/year.** Query with or without published clips or send complete ms. **Pays $150-300.**

💲💲 PROVINCETOWN ARTS

Provincetown Arts, Inc., 650 Commercial St., P.O. Box 35, Provincetown MA 02657. (508)487-3167. **E-mail:** cbusa@comcast.net. **Website:** www.provincetownarts. org. **90% freelance written**. Annual magazine covering contemporary art and writing. "*Provincetown Arts* focuses broadly on the artists and writers who inhabit or visit the Lower Cape, and seeks to stimulate creative activity and enhance public awareness of the cultural life of the nation's oldest continuous art colony. Drawing upon a 75-year tradition rich in visual art, literature, and theater, *Provincetown Arts* offers a unique blend of interviews, fiction, visual features, reviews, reporting, and poetry. Has published poetry by Bruce Smith, Franz Wright, Sandra McPherson, and Cyrus Cassells. 170 pages, magazine-sized, perfect-bound, with full-color glossy cover. Press run is 10,000. Estab. 1985. Circ. 8,000. Offers 50% kill fee. Publishes ms an average of 4 months after acceptance. Editorial lead time 6 months. Submit seasonal material 6 months in advance. Accepts simultaneous submissions. Responds in 3 weeks to queries; 2 months to mss. Sample copy for $10. Guidelines for #10 sase.

NONFICTION Needs book excerpts, essays, humor, interview. **Buys 40 mss/year.** Send complete ms. Length: 1,500-4,000 words. **Pays $150 minimum for assigned articles. Pays $125 minimum for unsolicited articles.**

FICTION Contact: Christopher Busa, editor. Needs mainstream, novel concepts. **Buys 7 mss/year.** Send complete ms. Length: 500-5,000 words. **Pays $75-300.**

POETRY Submit up to 3 poems at a time. No e-mail submissions; "all queries and submissions should be sent via postal mail." Submissions must be typed. Buys 25 poems/year poems/year. Submit maximum 3 poems. **Pays $25-100/poem plus 2 contributor's copies. Acquires first rights.**

💲💲 WORCESTER MAGAZINE

101 Water St., Worcester MA 01604. (508)749-3166. **Fax:** (508)749-3165. **E-mail:** editor@worcestermag. com. **Website:** www.worcestermag.com. **Contact:** Doreen Manning, editor; Gareth Charter, publisher. **10% freelance written.** Weekly tabloid emphasizing the central Massachusetts region, especially the city of Worcester. Estab. 1976. Circ. 40,000. Byline given. Publishes ms an average of 3 weeks after acceptance. Submit seasonal material 2 months in advance. Accepts queries by mail, e-mail, fax.

NONFICTION Needs essays, exposé, area government, corporate, general interest, historical, humor, opinion, local, personal experience, photo feature, religious, interview (local). **Buys less than 75 mss/year.** Length: 500-1,500 words. **Pays 10¢/word.**

MICHIGAN

💲💲💲 ANN ARBOR OBSERVER

Ann Arbor Observer Co., 201 E. Catherine, Ann Arbor MI 48104. **Fax:** (734)769-3375. **E-mail:** hilton@ aaobserver.com. **Website:** www.arborweb.com. **50% freelance written**. Monthly magazine. "We depend heavily on freelancers and we're always glad to talk to new ones. We look for the intelligence and judgment to fully explore complex people and situations, and the ability to convey what makes them interesting." Estab. 1976. Circ. 60,000. Byline given in some sections. Publishes ms an average of 2 months after acceptance. Accepts queries by mail, e-mail, fax, phone. Responds in 3 weeks to queries. Responds in several months to mss. Sample copy for 12½x15 SAE with $3 postage. Guidelines for #10 SASE.

NONFICTION Buys 75 mss/year. Length: 100-2,500 words. **Pays up to $1,000.** Sometimes pays expenses of writers on assignment.

COLUMNS Up Front (short, interesting tidbits), 150 words. **Pays $100.** Inside Ann Arbor (concise stories), 300-500 words. **Pays $200.** Around Town (unusual, compelling ancedotes), 750-1,500 words. **Pays $150-200.**

💲💲 GRAND RAPIDS MAGAZINE

Gemini Publications, 549 Ottawa Ave., NW, Suite 201, Grand Rapids MI 49503-1444. (616)459-4545. **Fax:** (616)459-4800. **E-mail:** cvalade@geminipub.com. **Website:** www.grmag.com. *Grand Rapids* is a general interest life and style magazine designed for those who live in the Grand Rapids metropolitan area or desire to maintain contact with the community. Estab. 1964. Circ. 20,000. Byline given. Editorial lead time 2 months. Submit seasonal material 2 months in advance. Sample copy for $2 and SASE with $1.50 postage. Guidelines with #10 SASE.

NONFICTION Query. **Pays $25-500.**

💲💲 MICHIGAN HISTORY

The Historical Society of Michigan, 5815 Executive Dr., Lansing MI 48911. (517)332-1828. **Fax:** (517)324-4370. **E-mail:** mhmeditor@hsmichigan.org. **E-mail:** majher@hsmichigan.org. **Website:** www.hsmichigan. org. **Contact:** Patricia Majher, editor. Covers exciting stories of Michigan people and their impact on their communities, the nation and the world. *Michigan History* overflows with intriguing feature articles, bold illustrations and departments highlighting history-related books, travel and events 6 time each year. Bimonthly magazine, 64 colorful pages. "A thoroughly entertaining read, Michigan History specializes in stories from Michigan's colorful past. Within its pages, you'll learn about logging, mining, manufacturing, and military history as well as art and architecture, music, sports, shipwrecks, and more. Requires idea queries first." In addition to payment, authors receive 5 free copies of issues in which their work appears. Estab. 1917. Circ. 22,000. Byline given. Publishes ms 6 months after acceptance. Editorial lead time 1 year. Accepts queries by mail, e-mail. Guidelines for authors at www.hsmichigan.org/mhm/pub_guidelines.html.

NONFICTION Needs feature articles, bold illustrations and departments highlighting history-related books, travel and events., Remember the Time features (first-person, factual, personal experiences that happened in Michigan—750 words) pay $100. Other features pay $200-$400, depending on word length and cooperation in gathering photos. "We are not a scholarly journal and do not accept academic papers." **Buys 50-55/mss/year.** "When you are ready to submit a manuscript, please provide a digital copy of the text, and also list your research sources for fact-checking purposes. Include with your ms a summary of your writing experience and "in the interest of full disclosure" any relationship you have to your subject. You are expected to gather your own graphics (provided digitally and with captions, if possible) or at least suggest possible graphics." Length: 750-2,500 words. **Pays $100-400.**

MINNESOTA

💲💲 LAKE COUNTRY JOURNAL MAGAZINE

P.O. Box 978, Brainerd MN 56401. (218)828-6424, ext. 14. **Fax:** (218)825-7816. **E-mail:** jodi@lakecountryjournal.com. **Website:** www.lakecountryjournal.com. **Contact:** Jodi Schwen, editor. **90% freelance written.** Bimonthly magazine covering central Minnesota's lake country. "Lake Country is one of the fastest-growing areas in the midwest. Each bimonthly issue of Lake Country Journal Magazine captures the essence of why we work, play, and live in this area. Through a diverse blend of articles from features and fiction, to recreation, recipes, gardening, and nature, this quality lifestyle magazine promotes positive family and business endeavors, showcases our natural and cultural resources, and highlights the best of our people, places, and events." Estab. 1996. Circ. 14,500. Byline given. Offers 25% kill fee. Publishes ms an average of 6 months after acceptance. Submit seasonal material 1 year in advance. Accepts queries by mail, e-mail. Responds in 2 months to queries. Responds in 3 months to mss. Sample copy for $6. Guidelines available online.

NONFICTION Needs essays, general interest, how-to, humor, interview, personal experience, photo feature. "No articles that come from writers who are not familiar with our target geographical location." **Buys 30 mss/year.** Query with or without published clips Length: 1,000-1,500 words. **Pays $100-200.** Sometimes pays expenses of writers on assignment.

COLUMNS Profile-People from Lake Country, 800 words; Essay, 800 words; Health (topics pertinent to central Minnesota living), 500 words. **Buys 40 mss/year.** Query with published clips **Pays $50-75.**

FICTION Needs adventure, humorous, mainstream, slice-of-life vignettes, literary, also family fiction appropriate to Lake Country and seasonal fiction. **Buys 6 mss/year.** Length: 1,500 words. **Pays $100-200.**

POETRY Needs free verse. "Never use rhyming verse, avant-garde, experimental, etc." Buys 6 poems/year. Submit maximum 4 poems. Length: 8-32 lines. **Pays $25.**

FILLERS Needs anecdotes, short humor. **Buys 20 fillers/year mss/year.** Length: 100-300 words. **$25/filler.**

🟢🟢 LAKE SUPERIOR MAGAZINE

Lake Superior Port Cities, Inc., P.O. Box 16417, Duluth MN 55816-0417. (218)722-5002. **Fax:** (218)722-4096. **E-mail:** edit@lakesuperior.com. **Website:** www.lakesuperior.com. **40% freelance written. Works with a small number of new/unpublished writers each year. Please include phone number and address with e-mail queries.** Bimonthly magazine covering contemporary and historic people, places and current events around Lake Superior. Estab. 1979. Circ. 20,000. Byline given. Publishes ms an average of 10 months after acceptance. Submit seasonal material 1 year in advance. Accepts queries by mail, e-mail. Responds in 3 months to queries. Sample copy for $4.95 and 6 first-class stamps. Guidelines available online.

NONFICTION Needs book excerpts, general interest, historical, humor, interview, local, personal experience, photo feature, local, travel, local, city profiles, regional business, some investigative. **Buys 15 mss/year.** Query with published clips. Length: 300-1,800 words. **Pays $60-400.** Sometimes pays expenses of writers on assignment. , with assignments.

COLUMNS Current events and things to do (for Events Calendar section), less than 300 words; Around The Circle (media reviews; short pieces on Lake Superior; Great Lakes environmental issues; themes, letters and short pieces on events and highlights of the Lake Superior Region); Essay (nostalgic lake-specific pieces), up to 1,100 words; Profile (single personality profile with photography), up to 900 words. Other headings include Destinations, Wild Superior, Lake Superior Living, Heritage, Recipe Box. **Buys 20 mss/year.** Query with published clips. **Pays $60-90.**

FICTION Ethnic, historic, humorous, mainstream, novel excerpts, slice-of-life vignettes, ghost stories. Must be targeted regionally. Wants stories that are Lake Superior related. **Buys 2-3 mss/year.** Query with published clips. Length: 300-2,500 words. **Pays $50-125.**

🟢🟢🟢 MPLS. ST. PAUL MAGAZINE

MSP Communications, 220 S. 6th St., Suite 500, Minneapolis MN 55402. (612)339-7571. **Fax:** (612)339-5806.

E-mail: edit@mspmag.com. **E-mail:** APlatt@mspmag.com. **Website:** www.mspmag.com. Stephanie March (food and dining), StephM@mspmag.com; Stephanie Davila (front-of-the-book Scene + Heard), SDavila@mspcommunications.com; Tad Simons (arts and entertainment subjects), tsimons@mspmag.com; Melissa Colgan (fashion/lifestyle/shopping), MColgan@mspmag.com. **Contact:** Adam Platt, executive editor. Monthly magazine. *Mpls. St. Paul Magazine* is a city magazine serving upscale readers in the Minneapolis-St. Paul metro area. Circ. 80,000. Editorial lead time 3 months. Accepts queries by mail, e-mail, fax. Sample copy for $10. Guidelines available online.

NONFICTION Needs book excerpts, essays, general interest, historical, interview, personal experience, photo feature, travel. **Buys 150 mss/year.** Query with published clips. Length: 500-4,000 words. **Pays 50-75¢/word for assigned articles.**

MISSISSIPPI

🟢🟢 MISSISSIPPI MAGAZINE

Downhome Publications, 5 Lakeland Circle, Jackson MS 39216. (601)982-8418. **Fax:** (601)982-8447. **E-mail:** editor@mismag.com. **Website:** www.mississippimagazine.com. **Contact:** Editor. **90% freelance written.** Bimonthly magazine covering Mississippi—the state and its lifestyles. "We are interested in positive stories reflecting Mississippi's rich traditions and heritage and focusing on the contributions the state and its natives have made to the arts, literature, and culture. In each issue we showcase homes and gardens, in-state travel, food, design, art, and more." Estab. 1982. Circ. 40,000. Byline given. Offers 25% kill fee. Publishes ms an average of 6 months after acceptance. Editorial lead time 6 months. Submit seasonal material 1 year in advance. Accepts queries by mail, fax. Responds in 2 months to queries. Guidelines for #10 SASE or online.

NONFICTION Needs general interest, historical, how-to, home decor, interview, personal experience, travel, in-state. No opinion, political, sports, exposé. **Buys 15 mss/year.** Query. Length: 100-1,200 words. **Pays $25-350.**

COLUMNS Southern Scrapbook (see recent issues for example), 100-600 words; Gardening (short informative article on a specific plant or gardening technique), 800-1,200 words; Culture Center (story about an event or person relating to Mississippi's art, music, theatre, or literature), 800-1,200 words; On

Being Southern (personal essay about life in Mississippi; only ms submissions accepted), 750 words. **Buys 6 mss/year.** Query. **Pays $150-225.**

MISSOURI

💲💲 417 MAGAZINE

Whitaker Publishing, 2111 S. Eastgate Ave., Springfield MO 65809. (417)883-7417. **Fax:** (417)889-7417. **E-mail:** editor@417mag.com. **Website:** www.417mag.com. **Contact:** Katie Pollock, editor. **50% freelance written.** Monthly magazine. *"417 Magazine* is a regional title serving southwest Missouri. Our editorial mix includes service journalism and lifestyle content on home, fashion and the arts; as well as narrative and issues pieces. The audience is affluent, educated, mostly female." Estab. 1998. Circ. 20,000. Byline given. Publishes ms an average of 2-3 months after acceptance. Editorial lead time 6 months. Accepts queries by e-mail. Responds in 1-2 months to queries. Sample copy by e-mail. Guidelines available online.

NONFICTION Needs essays, exposé, general interest, how-to, humor, inspirational, interview, new product, personal experience, photo feature, travel, local book reviews. "We are a local magazine, so anything not reflecting our local focus is something we have to pass on." **Buys 175 mss/year.** Query with published clips. Length: 300-3,500 words. **Pays $30-500, sometimes more.** Sometimes pays expenses of writers on assignment.

💲💲 KANSAS CITY HOMES & GARDENS

Network Communications, Inc., 9647 Lackman Rd., Lenexa KS 66219. (913)648-5757. **Fax:** (913)648-5783. **E-mail:** bpearl@nci.com. **Website:** www.kchandg.com. **Contact:** Brooke Pearl, editor. Magazine published 8 times annually. *"KCH&G* creates inspirational, credible, and compelling content about trends and events in local home and design for affluent homeowners, with beautiful photography, engaging features, and expert insight. We help our readers get smarter about where to find and how to buy the best solutions for enhancing their homes." Estab. 1986. Circ. 18,000. Byline given. Editorial lead time 4 months. Submit seasonal material 4 months in advance. Accepts queries by mail, e-mail, fax. Accepts simultaneous submissions. Responds in 1 month. Sample copy for $5.

NONFICTION Buys 8 mss/year. Query with published clips. Length: 600-1,000 words. **Pays $100-350.** Sometimes pays expenses of writers on assignment.

KANSAS CITY MAGAZINE

7101 College Blvd., Suite 400, Overland Park KS 66210. (913)894-6923. **E-mail:** eswanson@anthempublishing.com. **Website:** www.kcmag.com. **Contact:** Leigh Elmore, editor. **75% freelance written.** Monthly magazine. "Our mission is to celebrate living in Kansas City. We are a consumer lifestyle/general interest magazine focused on Kansas City, its people and places." Estab. 1994. Circ. 31,000. Byline given. Offers 10% kill fee. Publishes ms an average of 3 months after acceptance. Editorial lead time 4 months. Submit seasonal material 6 months in advance. Accepts queries by mail, e-mail, fax. Accepts simultaneous submissions. Sample copy for 8 ½x11 SAE or online.

NONFICTION Needs exposé, general interest, interview, photo feature. **Buys 15-20 mss/year.** Query with published clips. Length: 250-3,000 words.

COLUMNS Entertainment (Kansas City only), 1,000 words; Food (Kansas City food and restaurants only), 1,000 words. **Buys 12 mss/year.** Query with published clips.

💲💲 MISSOURI LIFE

Missouri Life, Inc., 501 High St., Suite A, Boonville MO 65233. (660)882-9898. **Fax:** (660)882-9899. **E-mail:** sarah@missourilife.com. **Website:** www.missourilife.com. **Contact:** Sarah Herrera, associate art director. **85% freelance written.** Bimonthly magazine covering the state of Missouri. *"Missouri Life*'s readers are mostly college-educated people with a wide range of travel and lifestyle interests. Our magazine discovers the people, places, and events—both past and present—that make Missouri a great place to live and/or visit." Estab. 1973. Circ. 74,000. Byline given. Editorial lead time 6 months. Submit seasonal material 6 months in advance. Accepts queries by mail, e-mail, fax. Responds in approximately 2 months to queries. Sample copy available for $4.95 and SASE with $2.44 first-class postage (or a digital version can be purchased online). Guidelines available online.

NONFICTION Needs general interest, historical, travel, all Missouri related. Length: 300-2,000 words. **No set amount per word.**

COLUMNS "All Around Missouri (people and places, past and present, written in an almanac style); Missouri Artist (features a Missouri artist), 500 words; Made in Missouri (products and businesses native to Missouri), 500 words. Contact assistant manager for restaurant review queries.

⊖⊖ RELOCATING TO THE LAKE OF THE OZARKS

Cliffside Corporate Center, 2140 Bagnell Dam Blvd., Suite 303E, Lake Ozark MO 65049. (573)365-2323. **Fax:** (573)365-2351. **E-mail:** spublishingco@msn.com. **Website:** www.relocatingtothelakeoftheozarks.com. **Contact:** Dave Leathers. Annual relocation guides; free for people moving to the area. Byline given. Publishes ms an average of 6 months after acceptance. Accepts queries by e-mail. Sample copy for $8.95.

NONFICTION Needs historical, travel, local issues. Length: 600-1,000 words.

⊖ RIVER HILLS TRAVELER

Traveler Publishing Co., P.O. Box 220, Valley Park MO 63088. (800)874-8423. **Fax:** (800)874-8423. **E-mail:** stories@rhtrav.com. **Website:** www.riverhillstraveler.com. **80% freelance written.** Monthly tabloid covering outdoor sports and nature in the southeast quarter of Missouri, the east and central Ozarks. Topics like those in *Field & Stream* and *National Geographic*. Estab. 1973. Circ. 5,000. Byline given. Publishes ms an average of 2 months after acceptance. Editorial lead time 2 months. Submit seasonal material 1 year in advance. Accepts queries by e-mail. Accepts simultaneous submissions. Responds in 2 months to queries. Sample copy for SAE or online. Guidelines available online.

NONFICTION Needs historical, how-to, humor, opinion, personal experience, photo feature, technical, travel. No stories about other geographic areas. **Buys 80 mss/year.** Query with writing samples. 1,500 word maximum. **Pays $15-50.**

⊖ RURAL MISSOURI MAGAZINE

Association of Missouri Electric Cooperatives, P.O. Box 1645, Jefferson City MO 65102. **E-mail:** hberry@ruralmissouri.coop. **Website:** www.ruralmissouri.coop. **5% freelance written.** Monthly magazine covering rural interests in Missouri; people, places and sights in Missouri. "Our audience is comprised of rural electric cooperative members in Missouri. We describe our magazine as 'being devoted to the rural way of life.'" Estab. 1948. Circ. 535,000. Byline given. Publishes ms an average of 6 months after acceptance. Editorial lead time 6 months. Submit seasonal material 6 months in advance. Accepts queries by mail, e-mail. Responds in 6-8 weeks to queries and to mss. Sample copy available online. Guidelines available online.

NONFICTION Needs general interest, historical. Does not want personal experiences or nostalgia pieces. Send complete ms. Length: 1,000-1,100 words. **Pays variable amount for each piece.**

MONTANA

⊖⊖ MONTANA MAGAZINE

Lee Enterprises, P.O. Box 5630, Helena MT 59604-5630. **E-mail:** editor@montanamagazine.com. **E-mail:** butch.larcombe@lee.net. **Website:** www.montanamagazine.com. **Contact:** Butch Larcombe, editor. **90% freelance written.** Bimonthly magazine. Strictly Montana-oriented magazine that features community profiles, contemporary issues, wildlife and natural history, travel pieces. Estab. 1970. Circ. 40,000. Byline given. Publishes ms an average of 1 year after acceptance. Submit seasonal material 1 year in advance. Accepts simultaneous submissions. Responds in 6 months to queries. Sample copy for $5 or online. Guidelines available online.

⚪ Accepts queries by e-mail. No phone calls.

NONFICTION Needs essays, general interest, interview, photo feature, travel. Special issues: Special features on summer and winter destination points. No 'me and Joe' hiking and hunting tales; no blood-and-guts hunting stories; no poetry; no fiction; no sentimental essays. **Buys 30 mss/year.** Query with samples and SASE. Length: 800-1,000 words. **Pays 20¢/word.** Sometimes pays expenses of writers on assignment.

COLUMNS Memories (reminisces of early-day Montana life), 800-1,000 words; Outdoor Recreation, 1,500-2,000 words; Community Festivals, 500 words, plus b&w or color photo; Montana-Specific Humor, 800-1,000 words. Query with samples and SASE.

NEVADA

⊖⊖ NEVADA MAGAZINE

401 N. Carson St., Carson City NV 89701. (775)687-5416. **Fax:** (775)687-6159. **E-mail:** editor@nevadamagazine.com. **Website:** www.nevadamagazine.com. **25% freelance written. Works with a small number of new/unpublished writers each year.** Bimonthly magazine published by the state of Nevada to promote tourism. Estab. 1936. Circ. 20,000. Byline given. Publishes ms an average of 6 months after acceptance. Submit seasonal material 6 months

in advance. Accepts queries by e-mail (preferred). Responds in 1 month to queries.

NONFICTION Length: 700-1,000 words. **Pays $50-250.**

NEW HAMPSHIRE

💲❋ NEW HAMPSHIRE MAGAZINE

McLean Communications, Inc., 150 Dow St., Manchester NH 03101. (603)624-1442. **E-mail:** editor@nhmagazine.com; bcoles@nhmagazine.com. **Website:** www.nhmagazine.com. **Contact:** Rick Broussard, executive editor; Barbara Coles, editor. **50% freelance written.** Monthly magazine devoted to New Hampshire. "We want stories written for, by, and about the people of New Hampshire with emphasis on qualities that set us apart from other states. We feature lifestyle, adventure, and home-related stories with a unique local angle.' Estab. 1986. Circ. 32,000. Byline given. Offers 25% kill fee. Editorial lead time 3 months. Submit seasonal material 3 months in advance. Accepts queries by mail, e-mail, fax. Accepts simultaneous submissions. Responds in 2 months to queries. Responds in 3 months to mss. Guidelines available online.

NONFICTION Needs essays, general interest, historical, photo feature, business. **Buys 30 mss/year.** Query with published clips. Length: 800-2,000 words. **Pays $50-500.** Sometimes pays expenses of writers on assignment.

FILLERS Length: 200-400 words.

NEW JERSEY

💲💲💲💲 NEW JERSEY MONTHLY

New Jersey Monthly, LLC, 55 Park Place, P.O. Box 920, Morristown NJ 07963-0920. (973)539-8230. **Fax:** (973)538-2953. **E-mail:** dingram@njmonthly.com; dcarter@njmonthly.com. **E-mail:** research@njmonthly.com. **Website:** www.njmonthly.com. **75-80% freelance written.** Monthly magazine covering just about anything to do with New Jersey, from news, politics, and sports to decorating trends and lifestyle issues. Our readership is well-educated, affluent, and on average our readers have lived in New Jersey 20 years or more. Estab. 1976. Circ. 92,000. Byline given. Pays on completion of fact-checking. Offers 20% kill fee. Publishes ms an average of 3 months after acceptance. Editorial lead time 3 months. Submit seasonal material 6 months in advance. Accepts queries by mail, e-mail, fax, phone. Accepts simultaneous submissions. Responds in 2-3 months to queries.

NONFICTION Needs book excerpts, essays, exposé, general interest, historical, humor, interview, personal experience, photo feature, travel, within New Jersey, arts, sports, politics. No experience pieces from people who used to live in New Jersey or general pieces that have no New Jersey angle. **Buys 90-100 mss/year.** Query with published magazine clips and SASE. Length: 250-3,000 words. **Pays $750-2,500.** Pays reasonable expenses of writers on assignment with prior approval.

COLUMNS Exit Ramp (back page essay usually originating from personal experience but written in a way that tells a broader story of statewide interest), 1,200 words. **Buys 12 mss/year.** Query with published clips. **Pays $400.**

FILLERS Needs anecdotes, for front-of-book. **Buys 12-15 mss/year.** Length: 200-250 words. **$100.**

💲❋ NEW JERSEY SAVVY LIVING

CTB, LLC, P.O. Box 607, Short Hills NJ 07078-0607. (973)966-0997. **Fax:** (973)966-0210. **E-mail:** njsavvyliving@ctbintl.com. **Website:** www.njsavvyliving.com. **90% freelance written.** Bimonthly magazine covering New Jersey residents with affluent lifestyles. "*Savvy Living* is a regional magazine for an upscale audience, ages 35-65. We focus on lifestyle topics such as home design, fashion, the arts, travel, personal finance, and health and well being." Estab. 1997. Circ. 50,000. Byline given. Offers $50 kill fee. Publishes ms an average of 3 months after acceptance. Editorial lead time 3 months. Accepts queries by mail. Accepts simultaneous submissions. Response time varies. Sample copy for sae with 9×12 envelope.

NONFICTION Needs interview, people of national and regional importance, photo feature, travel, home/decorating, finance, health, fashion, beauty. No investigative, fiction, personal experience, and non-New Jersey topics (excluding travel). **Buys 50 mss/year.** Query with published clips. Length: 900-2,000 words. **Pays $250-500.**

COLUMNS Savvy Shoppers (inside scoop on buying); Dining Out (restaurant review); Home Gourmet (gourmet cooking and entertaining). **Buys 25 mss/year.** Query with published clips. **Pays $300.**

💲💲 THE SANDPAPER

The SandPaper, Inc., 1816 Long Beach Blvd., Surf City NJ 08008-5461. (609)494-5900. **Fax:** (609)494-1437. **E-mail:** jaymann@thesandpaper.net; letters@thesandpaper.net; photo@thesandpaper.net. **Website:** www.thesandpaper.net. **Contact:** Jay Mann, managing editor; Gail Travers, executive editor; Ryan Morrill, photography editor. Weekly tabloid covering subjects of interest to Long Island Beach area residents and visitors. Each issue includes a mix of news, human interest features, opinion columns, and entertainment/calendar listings. Estab. 1976. Circ. 30,000. Byline given. Offers 100% kill fee. Publishes ms an average of 1 month after acceptance. Submit seasonal material 3 months in advance. Accepts queries by mail, e-mail, fax, phone. Accepts simultaneous submissions. Responds in 1 month to queries.

COLUMNS Speakeasy (opinion and slice-of-life, often humorous); Commentary (forum for social science perspectives); both 1,000-1,500 words, preferably with local or Jersey Shore angle. **Buys 50 mss/year.** Send complete ms. **Pays $40.**

NEW MEXICO

🌑🌑 NEW MEXICO MAGAZINE

Lew Wallace Bldg., 495 Old Santa Fe Trail, Santa Fe NM 87501. (505)827-7447. **E-mail:** letters@nmmagazine.com. **E-mail:** queries@nmmagazine.com. **Website:** www.nmmagazine.com. **70.** Covers areas throughout the state. "We want to publish a lively editorial mix, covering both the down-home (like a diner in Tucumcari) and the upscale (a new bistro in world-class Santa Fe)." Explore the gamut of the Old West and the New Age. "Our magazine is about the power of place—in particular more than 120,000 sq. miles of mountains, desert, grasslands, and forest inhabited by a culturally rich mix of individuals. It is an enterprise of the New Mexico Tourism Dept., which strives to make potential visitors aware of our state's multicultural heritage, climate, environment, and uniqueness." Estab. 1923. Circ. 100,000. 20% kill fee. Publishes ms an average of 3 months after acceptance. Submit seasonal material 1 year in advance. Accepts queries by mail, e-mail (preferred). Does not accept previously published submissions.Responds to queries if interested. Sample copy for $5. Guidelines with SASE.

○ No unsolicited mss. Does not return unsolicited material.

NONFICTION "Submit your story idea along with a working head and subhead and a paragraph synopsis. Include published clips and a short sum-up about your strengths as a writer. We will consider your proposal as well as your potential to write stories we've conceptualized."

NEW YORK

🌑🌑 ADIRONDACK LIFE

P.O. Box 410, Jay NY 12941-0410. (518)946-2191. **Fax:** (518)946-7461. **E-mail:** astoltie@adirondacklife.com. **Website:** www.adirondacklife.com. Kelly Hofschneider, photo editor. **Contact:** Annie Stoltie, editor. **70% freelance written. Prefers to work with published/established writers.** Magazine published 8 issues/year, including special Annual Outdoor Guide, emphasizes the Adirondack region and the North Country of New York State in articles covering outdoor activities, history, and natural history directly related to the Adirondacks. Estab. 1970. Circ. 50,000. Byline given. Pays 30 days after publication. Publishes ms an average of 10 months after acceptance. Submit seasonal material 1 year in advance. Accepts queries by mail, e-mail. Does not accept previously published work.Sample copy for $3 and 9×12 SAE. Guidelines available online.

NONFICTION Special issues: Outdoors (May); Single-topic Collector's issue (September). **Buys 20-25 unsolicited mss/year.** Query with published clips. Accepts queries, but not unsolicited mss, via e-mail. Length: 1,000-4,000 words. **Pays 30¢/word.** Sometimes pays expenses of writers on assignment.

COLUMNS Special Places (unique spots in the Adirondack Park); Watercraft; Barkeater (personal essays); Wilderness (environmental issues); Working (careers in the Adirondacks); Home; Yesteryears; Kitchen; Profile; Historical Preservation; Sporting Scene. Length: 1,200-2,100 words. Query with published clips. **Pays 30¢/word.**

FICTION Considers first-serial novel excerpts in its subject matter and region.

🌑 ARTSNEWS

ArtsWestchester, 31 Mamaroneck Ave., White Plains NY 10601. **Fax:** (914)428-4306. **E-mail:** jormond@artswestchester.org. **Website:** www.artswestchester.org. **Contact:** Jim Ormond, editor. **20% freelance written.** Monthly tabloid covering arts and entertainment in Westchester County, New York. "We profile artists, arts organizations and write teasers about upcoming exhibitions, concerts, events, theatrical performances, etc." Estab. 1975. Circ. 20,000. Byline given. Editorial lead time 1 month. Submit seasonal material 2 months in advance. Accepts queries by mail, e-mail. Sample copy free.

NONFICTION Query with published clips. Length: 400-500 words. **Pays $75-100.** Pays expenses of writers on assignment.

$$ BUFFALO SPREE MAGAZINE

Buffalo Spree Publishing, Inc., 100 Corporate Pkwy., Suite 200, Buffalo NY 14226. (716)783-9119. **Fax:** (716)783-9983. **E-mail:** elicata@buffalospree.com. **Website:** www.buffalospree.com. **Contact:** Elizabeth Licata, editor. **90% freelance written.** City regional magazine published 12 times/year. Estab. 1967. Circ. 25,000. Byline given. Publishes ms an average of 2 months after acceptance. Accepts queries by e-mail. Responds in 6 months to queries. Sample copy for $4.95 and 9×12 SAE with 12 first-class stamps.

NONFICTION Needs interview, travel, issue-oriented features, arts, living, food, regional. Query with résumé and published clips. Length: 1,000-2,000 words. **Pays $125-250.**

CITY LIMITS

Community Service Society of New York, 105 E. 22nd St., Suite 901, New York NY 10010. (212)614-5397. **E-mail:** citylimits@citylimits.org; magazine@citylimits.org; editor@citylimits.org. **Website:** www.citylimits.org. **Contact:** Mark Anthony Thomas, director; Jarrett Murphy, editor-in-chief. **50% freelance written.** Monthly magazine covering urban politics and policy. "*City Limits* is a nonprofit print and online magazine focusing on issues facing New York City and its neighborhoods, particularly low-income communities. The magazine is strongly committed to investigative journalism, in-depth policy analysis, and hard-hitting profiles." Estab. 1976. Circ. 5,000. Byline given. Offers 50% kill fee. Publishes ms an average of 3 months after acceptance. Editorial lead time 2 months. Accepts queries by mail, e-mail, fax. Accepts simultaneous submissions. Responds in 1 month. Sample copy for $2.95. Guidelines free.

NONFICTION Needs book excerpts, exposé, humor, interview, opinion, photo feature. No essays, polemics. **Buys 25 mss/year.** Query with published clips. Length: 400-3,500 words. **Pays $150-2,000 for assigned articles. Pays $100-800 for unsolicited articles.** Pays expenses of writers on assignment.

COLUMNS Making Change (nonprofit business), Big Idea (policy news), Book Review—all 800 words; Urban Legend (profile), First Hand (Q&A)—both 350 words. **Buys 15 mss/year.** Query with published clips.

$ HUDSON VALLEY LIFE

The Professional Image, 174 South St., Newburgh NY 12550. (845)562-3606. **E-mail:** editor@excitingread.com. **Website:** www.hvlife.com. **Contact:** M.J. Goff, editor. **95% freelance written.** Monthly magazine serving parents and active adults by providing reliable local information of interest. Estab. 1999. Circ. 15,000. Publishes ms an average of 3 months after acceptance. Guidelines available online.

NONFICTION Needs exposé, general interest, humor, interview, personal experience. **Buys 15 mss/yr. mss/year.** Query. Length: 700-1,200 words. **Pays $60-120 for assigned articles. Pays $25-35 for unsolicited articles.**

$$$$ NEW YORK MAGAZINE

New York Media Holdings, LLC, 75 Varick Street, New York NY 10013. **Website:** www.newyorkmag.com. **25% freelance written.** Weekly magazine focusing on current events in the New York metropolitan area. Circ. 433,813. Offers 25% kill fee. Submit seasonal material 2 months in advance. Responds in 1 month to queries. Sample copy for $3.50 or on website.

NONFICTION Query by mail. No unsolicited mss. **Pays $1/word.** Pays expenses of writers on assignment.

NORTH CAROLINA

$$ AAA CAROLINAS GO MAGAZINE

6600 AAA Dr., Charlotte NC 28212. **Fax:** (704)569-7815. **Website:** www.aaacarolinas.com. **Contact:** Tom Crosby, VP of communications. **20% freelance written.** Member publication for the Carolina affiliate of American Automobile Association covering travel, auto-related issues. "We prefer stories that focus on travel and auto safety in North and South Carolina and surrounding states." Estab. 1922. Circ. 1.1 million. Byline given. Editorial lead time 2 months. Accepts queries by mail. Sample copy and writer's guidelines for #10 SASE.

NONFICTION Needs travel, auto safety. Length: 750 words. **Pays $150.**

$$ CARY MAGAZINE

S&A Cherokee, Westview at Weston, 301 Cascade Pointe Lane, #101, Cary NC 27513. (919)674-6020. **Fax:** (919)674-6027. **E-mail:** editor@carymagazine.com. **Website:** www.carymagazine.com. **Contact:** Tara Croft, co-editor. **40% freelance written.** Publishes 8 times/year. "Lifestyle publication for the affluent communities of Cary, Apex, Morrisville, Holly Springs and Fuquay-Varina. Our editorial objective is to entertain, enlighten and inform our readers with unique and engaging editorial and vivid photography." Estab. 2004. Circ. 18,000. Byline given. Kill fee negotiated. Editorial lead time 3 months. Submit seasonal material 3 months in advance. Accepts queries by mail, e-mail. Responds in 2-4 weeks to queries. Responds in 1 month to mss. Sample copy for $4.95. Guidelines free.

NONFICTION Needs historical, specific to Western Wake County, North Carolina, inspirational, interview, human interest, personal experience. Don't submit articles with no local connection. **Buys 2 mss/ year.** Query with published clips. Sometimes pays expenses of writers on assignment.

😊😊 CHARLOTTE MAGAZINE

Morris Visitor Publications, 309 E. Morehead St., Suite 50, Charlotte NC 28202. (704)335-7181. **Fax:** (704)335-3757. **E-mail:** richard.thurmond@charlottemagazine.com. **Website:** www.charlottemagazine.com. Carrie Campbell, art director (carrie.campbell@charlottemagazine.com). **75% freelance written.** Monthly magazine covering Charlotte life. This magazine tells its readers things they didn't know about Charlotte, in an interesting, entertaining, and sometimes provocative style. Circ. 40,000. Byline given. Pays within 30 days of acceptance. Offers 25% kill fee. Publishes ms an average of 3 months after acceptance. Editorial lead time 3 months. Submit seasonal material 6 months in advance. Accepts queries by mail, e-mail. Accepts simultaneous submissions. Responds in 6 months to mss. Sample copy for 8 ½ ×11 SAE and $5.

NONFICTION Needs book excerpts, exposé, general interest, interview, photo feature, travel. **Buys 35-50 mss/year.** Query with published clips. Length: 200-3,000 words. **Pays 20-40¢/word.** Sometimes pays expenses of writers on assignment.

COLUMNS Buys 35-50 mss/year. Pays 20-40¢/word

😊😊 FIFTEEN 501

Weiss and Hughes Publishing, 189 Wind Chime Ct., Raleigh NC 27615. (919)870-1722. **Fax:** (919)719-5260. **E-mail:** djackson@whmags.com. **Website:** www.fifteen501.com. **Contact:** Danielle Jackson, editor. **50% freelance written.** Quarterly magazine covering lifestyle issues relevant to residents in the US 15/501 corridor of Durham, Orange and Chatham counties. "We cover issues important to residents of Durham, Orange and Chatham counties. We're committed to improving our readers' overall quality of life and keeping them informed of the lifestyle amenities there." Estab. 2006. Circ. 30,000. Byline given. within 30 days of publication. Offers 25% kill fee. Publishes ms an average of 2 months after acceptance. Editorial lead time 2-3 months. Submit seasonal material 6 months in advance. Accepts queries by mail, e-mail. Accepts simultaneous submissions. Responds in 2-4 weeks to queries. Sample copy available online. Guidelines by e-mail.

NONFICTION Needs general interest, historical, how-to, home interiors, landscaping, gardening, technology, inspirational, interview, personal experience, photo feature, technical, travel. Does not want opinion pieces, political or religious topics. Query. Length: 600-1,200 words. **Pays 35¢/word.** Sometimes pays expenses of writers on assignment.

COLUMNS Around Town (local lifestyle topics), 1,000 words; Hometown Stories, 600 words; Travel (around North Carolina), 1,000 words; Home Interiors/Landscaping (varies), 1,000 words; Restaurants (local, fine dining), 600-1,000 words. **Buys 20-25 mss/ year.** Query. **Pays 35¢/word.**

😊😊 OUR STATE

Mann Media, P.O. Box 4552, Greensboro NC 27404. (336)286-0600. **Fax:** (336)286-0100. **E-mail:** editorial@ourstate.com. **Website:** www.ourstate.com. **95% freelance written.** Monthly magazine covering North Carolina. *Our State* is dedicated to providing editorial about the history, destinations, out-of-the-way places, and culture of North Carolina. Estab. 1933. Circ. 130,000. Byline given. Publishes ms an average of 6-24 months after acceptance. Editorial lead time 4-6 months. Submit seasonal material 4 months in advance. Accepts queries by mail, e-mail, fax. Responds in 6 weeks to queries. Responds in 2 months to mss. Sample copy for $6. Guidelines for #10 SASE.

NONFICTION Needs historical, travel, North Carolina culture, folklore. **Buys 250 mss/year.** Send complete ms. Length: 1,400-1,600 words. **Pays $300-500.**

COLUMNS Tar Heel Memories (remembering something specific about North Carolina), 1,000 words; Tar Heel Profile (profile of interesting North Carolinian), 1,500 words; Tar Heel Literature (review of books by North Carolina writers and about North Carolina), 300 words.

⊛⊛ WAKE LIVING

Weiss and Hughes Publishing, 189 Wind Chime Ct., Suite 104, Raleigh NC 27615. (919)870-1722. **Fax:** (919)719-5260. **E-mail:** dhughes@wakeliving.com; djackson@whmags.com. **Website:** www.wakeliving. com. **Contact:** David Hughes, president and publisher; Danielle Jackson, editor. **50% freelance written.** Quarterly magazine covering lifestyle issues in Wake County, North Carolina. "We cover issues important to residents of Wake County. We are committed to improving our readers' overall quality of life and keeping them informed of the lifestyle amenities here." Estab. 2003. Circ. 40,000. Byline given. Pays within 30 days of publication. Offers 25% kill fee. Publishes ms an average of 2 months after acceptance. Editorial lead time 2-3 months. Submit seasonal material 6 months in advance. Accepts queries by mail, e-mail. Accepts simultaneous submissions. Responds in 2-4 weeks to queries. Sample copy available online. Guidelines available online.

NONFICTION Needs general interest, historical, how-to, home interiors, technology, landscaping, gardening, inspirational, interview, personal experience, photo feature, technical, travel. Does not want opinion pieces, political topics, religious articles. Query. Length: 600-1,200 words. **Pays 35¢/word.** Sometimes pays expenses of writers on assignment.

COLUMNS Around Town (local lifestyle topics); Hometown Stories, 600 words; Travel (around North Carolina); Home Interiors/Landscaping, all 1,000 words. Restaurants (local restaurants, fine dining), 600-1,000 words. **Buys 20-25 mss/year.** Query. **Pays 35¢/word.**

NORTH DAKOTA

⊛⊛ NORTH DAKOTA LIVING MAGAZINE

North Dakota Association of Rural Electric Cooperatives, 3201 Nygren Dr. NW, P.O. Box 727, Mandan ND 58554-0727. (701)663-6501. **Fax:** (701)663-3745. **E-mail:** kbrick@ndarec.com; cdevney@ndarec. com. **Website:** www.ndarec.com/dakotaLiving. **20% freelance written.** Monthly magazine covering information of interest to memberships of electric cooperatives and telephone cooperatives. "We publish a general interest magazine for North Dakotans. We treat subjects pertaining to living and working in the northern Great Plains. We provide progress reporting on electric cooperatives and telephone cooperatives." Estab. 1954. Circ. 70,000. Byline given. Publishes ms an average of 6 months after acceptance. Editorial lead time 6 months. Submit seasonal material 6 months in advance. Accepts queries by mail, e-mail. Accepts simultaneous submissions. Sample copy and writer's guidelines not available.

NONFICTION Needs general interest, historical, how-to, humor, interview, new product, travel. **Buys 20 mss/year.** Query with published clips. Length: 1,500-2,000 words. **Pays $100-500 minimum for assigned articles. Pays $300-600 for unsolicited articles.** Sometimes pays expenses of writers on assignment.

COLUMNS Energy Use and Financial Planning, both 750 words. **Buys 6 mss/year.** Query with published clips. **Pays $100-300.**

FICTION Needs historical, humorous, slice-of-life vignettes, western. **Buys 1 mss/year.** Query with published clips. Length: 1,000-2,500 words. **Pays $100-400.**

OHIO

⊛⊛ AKRON LIFE

Baker Media Group, 90 S. Maple St., Akron OH 44302. (330)253-0056. **Fax:** (330)253-5868. **E-mail:** kmoorhouse@bakermediagroup.com; editor@bakermediagroup.com. **Website:** www.akronlife.com. **Contact:** Georgina Carson, editor; Kathy Moorhouse, art director. **10% freelance written.** Monthly regional magazine covering Summit, Stark, Portage and Medina counties. "*Akron Life & Leisure* is a monthly lifestyles publication committed to providing information that enhances and enriches the experience of living in or visiting Akron and the surrounding region of Summit, Portage, Medina and Stark Counties. Each colorful, thoughtfully designed issue profiles interesting places, personalities and events in the arts, sports, entertainment, business, politics and social scene. We cover issues important to the Greater Akron area and significant trends affecting the lives of those who live here." Estab. 2002. Circ. 15,000. Byline given. Offers 50% kill fee. Publishes ms an average of 4-6 months after acceptance. Editorial lead time 2+ months. Submit seasonal material 6 months in advance. Accepts queries by mail, e-mail, fax. Sample copy free. Guidelines free.

NONFICTION Needs essays, general interest, historical, how-to, humor, interview, photo feature, travel. Query with published clips. Length: 300-

2,000 words. **Pays $0.10 max/word for assigned and unsolicited articles.**

$ BEND OF THE RIVER MAGAZINE

P.O. Box 859, Maumee OH 43537. (419)893-0022. **Website:** http://bendoftherivermagazine.com. **98% freelance written. This magazine reports that it is eager to work with all writers. "We buy material that we like whether it is by an experienced writer or not."** Monthly magazine for readers interested in northwestern Ohio history and nostalgia. Estab. 1972. Circ. 6,500. Byline given. Publishes ms an average of 1 month after acceptance. Submit seasonal material 2 months in advance. Responds in 1 week to queries. Sample copy for $1.25.

NONFICTION Needs historical. **Buys 75 unsolicited mss/year.** Send complete ms. 1,500 words. **Pays $50 on average.**

$$$ CINCINNATI MAGAZINE

Emmis Publishing Corp., 441 Vine St., Suite 200, Cincinnati OH 45202-2039. (513)421-4300. **Fax:** (513)562-2746. **Website:** www.cincinnatimagazine.com. **Contact:** Jay Stowe, editor; Amanda Boyd Walters, deputy editor. Monthly magazine emphasizing Cincinnati living. Circ. 38,000. Byline given. Accepts queries by mail, e-mail. Send SASE for writer's guidelines; view content on magazine website.

NONFICTION Buys 12 mss/year. Query. Length: 2,500-3,500 words. **Pays $500-1,000.**

COLUMNS Topics are Cincinnati media, arts and entertainment, people, politics, sports, business, regional. Length: 1,000-1,500 words. **Buys 10-15 mss/year.** Query. **Pays $200-400.**

$$$ CLEVELAND MAGAZINE

City Magazines, Inc., 1422 Euclid Ave., Suite 730, Cleveland OH 44115. (216)771-2833. **Fax:** (216)781-6318. **E-mail:** gleydura@clevelandmagazine.com; miller@clevelandmagazine.com; kessen@clevelandmagazine.com. **Website:** www.clevelandmagazine.com. **Contact:** Kristen Miller, art director; Steve Gleydura, editor. **60% freelance written. Mostly by assignment.** Monthly magazine with a strong Cleveland/Northeast Ohio angle. Estab. 1972. Circ. 50,000. Byline given. Publishes ms an average of 3 months after acceptance. Editorial lead time 6 months. Submit seasonal material 8 months in advance. Accepts queries by mail, e-mail, fax. Accepts simultaneous submissions. Responds in 2 months to queries.

NONFICTION Needs general interest, historical, humor, interview, travel, home and garden. Query with published clips. Length: 800-4,000 words. **Pays $250-1,200.**

COLUMNS Talking Points (opinion or observation-driven essay), approx. 1,000 words Query with published clips. **Pays $300**

$$$ COLUMBUS MONTHLY

5255 Sinclair Rd., P.O. Box 29913, Columbus OH 43229-7513. (614)888-4567. **Fax:** (614)848-3838. **Website:** www.columbusmonthly.com. **Contact:** Ray Paprocki, editor; Jill Hawes, senior editor. **40-60% freelance written. Prefers to work with published/established writers.** Monthly magazine emphasizing subjects specifically related to Columbus and Central Ohio. Circ. 35,000. Byline given. Publishes ms an average of 2 months after acceptance. Responds in 1 month to queries. Sample copy for $6.50.

NONFICTION Buys 2-3 unsolicited mss/year. Query. Length: 250-4,000 words. **Pays $85-900.** Sometimes pays expenses of writers on assignment.

$$$ OHIO MAGAZINE

Great Lakes Publishing Co., 1422 Euclid Ave., Suite 730, Cleveland OH 44115. (216)771-2833. **E-mail:** editorial@ohiomagazine.com. **Website:** www.ohiomagazine.com. **Contact:** Lesley Blake, art director. **50% freelance written.** Monthly magazine emphasizing Ohio-based travel, news and feature material that highlights what's special and unique about the state. Estab. 1978. Circ. 80,000. Byline given. 20% kill fee. Publishes ms an average of 6 months after acceptance. Submit seasonal material 6 months in advance. Accepts queries by mail, e-mail, fax. Responds in 3 months to queries. Responds in 3 months to mss. Sample copy for $3.95 and 9×12 SAE or online. Guidelines available online.

NONFICTION Length: 1,000-3,000 words. **Pays $300-1,200.** Sometimes pays expenses of writers on assignment.

COLUMNS Buys minimum 5 unsolicited mss/year. Pays $100-600.

OKLAHOMA

⊕ $$ INTERMISSION

Langdon Publishing, 110 E. 2nd St., Tulsa OK 74103-3212. (918)596-2368. **Fax:** (918)596-7144. **E-mail:** nbizjack@cityoftulsa.org. **Website:** www.tulsapac.com.

CONSUMER MAGAZINES

30% freelance written. Monthly magazine covering entertainment. "We feature profiles of entertainers appearing at our center, Q&As, stories on the events and entertainers slated for the Tulsa PAC." Byline given. Offers 50% kill fee. Publishes ms an average of 1 month after acceptance. Editorial lead time 2 months. Submit seasonal material 2 months in advance. Accepts queries by mail, e-mail. Accepts simultaneous submissions. Responds in 2 weeks to queries. Sample copy available online. Guidelines by email.

NONFICTION Needs general interest, interview. Does not want personal experience. **Buys 35 mss/ year.** Query with published clips. Length: 600-1,400 words. **Pays $100-200.**

COLUMNS Q&A (personalities and artists tied into the events at the Tulsa PAC), 1,100 words. **Buys 12 mss/year.** Query with published clips. **Pays $100-150.**

💲💲 OKLAHOMA TODAY

P.O. Box 1468, Oklahoma City OK 73101-1468. (405)230-8450. **Fax:** (405)230-8650. **E-mail:** steffie@ oklahomatoday.com. **Website:** www.oklahomatoday. com. **Contact:** Steffie Corcoran, editor. **80% freelance written. Works with approximately 25 new/unpublished writers each year.** Bimonthly magazine covering people, places, and things Oklahoma. "We are interested in showing off the best Oklahoma has to offer; we're pretty serious about our travel slant but regularly run history, nature, and personality profiles." Estab. 1956. Circ. 45,000. Byline given. Publishes ms an average of 6 months after acceptance. Submit seasonal material 1 year in advance. Accepts queries by mail, e-mail. Responds in 4 months to queries. Sample copy for $4.95 and 9×12 SASE or online. Guidelines available online.

NONFICTION Needs book excerpts, on Oklahoma topics, historical, Oklahoma only, interview, Oklahomans only, photo feature, in Oklahoma, travel, in Oklahoma. No phone queries. **Buys 20-40 mss/year.** Query with published clips. Length: 250-3,000 words. **Pays $25-750.**

FICTION Needs novel concepts, occasionally short fiction.

OREGON

💲💲 OREGON COAST

4969 Highway 101 N. #2, Florence OR 97439. **E-mail:** Rosemary@nwmags.com. **Website:** www.northwest-magazines.com. **Contact:** Rosemary Camozzi. **65%**

freelance written. Bimonthly magazine covering the Oregon Coast. Estab. 1982. Circ. 50,000. Byline given. Pays after publication. Offers 33% (on assigned stories only, not on stories accepted on spec) kill fee. Publishes ms an average of up to 1 year after acceptance. Submit seasonal material 6 months in advance. Accepts queries by mail, e-mail. Responds in 3 months to queries. Sample copy for $4.50. Guidelines available on website.

NONFICTION Buys 55 mss/year. Query with published clips. Length: 500-1,500 words. **Pays $75-350, plus 2 contributor copies.**

PENNSYLVANIA

💲💲 BERKS COUNTY LIVING

201 Washington St., Suite 525, GoggleWorks Center for the Arts, Reading PA 19601. (610)898-1928. **Fax:** (610)898-1933. **E-mail:** fscoboria@berkscountyliving.com. **Website:** www.berkscountyliving.com. **Contact:** Francine Scoboria. **90% freelance written.** Bimonthly magazine covering topics of interest to people living in Berks County, Pennsylvania. Estab. 2000. Circ. 36,000. Byline given. Offers 25% kill fee. Publishes ms an average of 4 months after acceptance. Editorial lead time 3 months. Submit seasonal material 4 months in advance. Accepts queries by mail, e-mail. Accepts simultaneous submissions. Responds in 1 week to queries. Responds in 1 month to mss. Sample copy for sae with 9×12 envelope and 2 first-class stamps. Guidelines available online.

NONFICTION Needs exposé, general interest, historical, how-to, humor, inspirational, interview, new product, photo feature, travel, food, health. **Buys 25 mss/year.** Query. Length: 750-2,000 words. **Pays $150-400.** Sometimes pays expenses of writers on assignment.

💲💲 MAIN LINE TODAY

Today Media, Inc., 4699 West Chester Pike, Newtown Square PA 19073. (610)848-6037. **Fax:** (610)325-5215. **E-mail:** hrowland@mainlinetoday.com; tbehan@ mainlinetoday.com. **Website:** www.mainlinetoday. com. **Contact:** Hobart Rowland, editor; Tara Behan, senior editor. **60% freelance written.** Monthly magazine serving Philadelphia's main line and western suburbs. *Main Line Today*'s high-quality print and electronic media provide authoritative, current and entertaining information on local lifestyle trends, while examining the people, issues and institutions that shape life in Philadelphia's western suburbs. Estab. 1996. Circ. 20,000. Byline given. Offers 25% kill fee. Publishes ms an average of 3 months after acceptance. Editorial lead time 5 months. Submit seasonal material 5 months in advance. Accepts queries by fax. Accepts simultaneous submissions. Responds in 2 weeks to queries. Responds in 1 month to mss. Sample copy free. Guidelines free.

NONFICTION Needs book excerpts, historical, how-to, humor, interview, opinion, photo feature, travel. Special issues: Health & Wellness Guide (September and March). Query with published clips. Length: 400-3,000 words. **Pays $125-650.** Sometimes pays expenses of writers on assignment.

COLUMNS Profile (local personality); Neighborhood (local people/issues); End of the Line (essay/humor); Living Well (health/wellness), all 1,600 words. **Buys 50 mss/year.** Query with published clips. **Pays $125-350.**

🟡🟡 PENNSYLVANIA

Pennsylvania Magazine Co., P.O. Box 755, Camp Hill PA 17001-0755. (717)697-4660. **E-mail:** editor@pa-mag.com. **Website:** www.pa-mag.com. **90% freelance written.** Bimonthly magazine covering people, places, events, and history in Pennsylvania. Estab. 1981. Circ. 33,000. Byline given. Pays on acceptance except for articles (by authors unknown to us) sent on speculation. Offers kill fee. 25% kill fee for assigned articles. Publishes ms an average of 9 months after acceptance. Submit seasonal material 9 months in advance. Accepts queries by mail, e-mail. Responds in 4-6 weeks to queries. Sample copy free. Guidelines for #10 SASE or by e-mail.

NONFICTION Nothing on Amish topics, hunting, or skiing. **Buys 75-120 mss/year.** Query. Length: 750-2,500 words. **Pays 15¢/word.**

COLUMNS Round Up (short items about people, unusual events, museums, historical topics/events, family and individually owned consumer-related businesses), 250-1,300 words; Town and Country (items about people or events illustrated with commissioned art), 500 words. Include SASE. Query. **Pays 15¢/word.**

🟡🟡 PENNSYLVANIA HERITAGE

Pennsylvania Historical and Museum Commission and the Pennsylvania Heritage Society, Commonwealth Keystone Bldg., Plaza Level, 400 North St., Harrisburg PA 17120-0053. (717)787-2407. **Fax:** (717)346-9099. **E-mail:** miomalley@state.pa.us.

Website: www.paheritage.org. **Contact:** Michael J. O'Malley III, editor; Kim Krammes-Stone, art director. **75% freelance written. Prefers to work with published/established writers.** Quarterly magazine. *Pennsylvania Heritage* introduces readers to Pennsylvania's rich culture and historic legacy; educates and sensitizes them to the value of preserving that heritage; and entertains and involves them in such a way as to ensure that Pennsylvania's past has a future. The magazine is intended for intelligent lay readers. Estab. 1974. Circ. 10,000. Byline given. Publishes ms an average of 1 year after acceptance. Accepts queries by mail, e-mail. Responds in 10 weeks to queries. Responds in 8 months to mss. Sample copy for $5 and 9×12 SAE or online. Guidelines for #10 SASE.

NONFICTION No articles which do not relate to Pennsylvania history or culture. **Buys 20-24 mss/year.** Prefers to see mss with suggested illustrations. Length: 2,000-3,500 words. **Pays $100-500.**

🟡🟡 PHILADELPHIA STYLE

Philadelphia Style Magazine, LLC, 141 League St., Philadelphia PA 19147. (215)468-6670. **Fax:** (215)223-3095. **E-mail:** info@phillystylemag.com. **Website:** www.phillystylemag.com. **Contact:** Sarah Schaffer, editor in chief. **50% freelance written.** "Bimonthly magazine covering upscale living in the Philadelphia region. Topics include: celebrity interviews, fashion (men's and women's), food, home and design, real estate, dining, beauty, travel, arts and entertainment, and more. Our magazine is a positive look at the best ways to live in the Philadelphia region. Submitted articles should speak to an upscale, educated audience of professionals that live in the Delaware Valley." Estab. 1999. Circ. 60,000. Byline given. Offers 25% kill fee. Publishes ms an average of 3 months after acceptance. Editorial lead time 2-4 months. Submit seasonal material 6 months in advance. Accepts queries by mail, e-mail, fax.

NONFICTION Needs general interest, interview, travel, region-specific articles. "We are not looking for articles that do not have a regional spin." **Buys 100+ mss/year.** Send complete ms. Length: 300-2,500 words. **Pays $50-500.**

COLUMNS Declarations (celebrity interviews and celebrity contributors); Currents (fashion news); Manor (home and design news); Liberties (beauty and travel news); Dish (dining news); Life in the City (fresh, quirky, regional reporting on books, real estate, art, retail, dining, events, and little-known stories/facts about the region), 100-500 words; Vanguard (people on the forefront of Philadelphia's arts, media, fashion, business, and social scene), 500-700 words; In the Neighborhood (reader-friendly reporting on up-and-coming areas of the region including dining, shopping, attractions, and recreation), 2,000-2,500 words. Query with published clips or send complete ms. **Pays $50-500.**

$$$$ PITTSBURGH MAGAZINE

WiesnerMedia, 600 Waterfront Drive, Suite 100, Pittsburgh PA 15222-4795. (412)304-0900. **Fax:** (412)304-0938. **E-mail:** editors@pittsburghmagazine.com. **Website:** www.pittsburghmag.com. **Contact:** Julie Talerico, editor-in-chief; Betsy Benson, publisher and vice president. **70% freelance written.** Monthly magazine. "*Pittsburgh* presents issues, analyzes problems, and strives to encourage a better understanding of the community. Our region is Western Pennsylvania, Eastern Ohio, Northern West Virginia, and Western Maryland." Estab. 1970. Circ. 75,000. Byline given. Offers kill fee. Offers kill fee. Publishes ms an average of 2 months after acceptance. Submit seasonal material 6 months in advance. Accepts queries by mail. Responds in 2 months to queries. Sample copy for $2 (old back issues). Writer's guidelines online or via SASE.

NONFICTION Needs exposé, lifestyle, sports, informational, service, business, medical, profile. "We have minimal interest in historical articles and we do not publish fiction, poetry, advocacy, or personal reminiscence pieces." Query in writing with outline and clips. Length: 1,200-4,000 words. **Pays $300-1,500+.**

$ SUSQUEHANNA LIFE

637 Market St., Lewisburg PA 17837. (800)232-1670. **Fax:** (570)524-7796. **E-mail:** susquehannalife@gmail.com. **Website:** www.susquehannalife.com. **80% freelance written.** Quarterly magazine covering Central Pennsylvania lifestyle. Estab. 1993. Circ. 45,000. Byline given. Offers 50% kill fee. Publishes ms an average of 6-9 months after acceptance. Editorial lead time 3-6 months. Submit seasonal material 4-6 months in advance. Accepts queries by e-mail. Responds in 4-6 weeks to queries. Responds in 1-3 months to mss. Sample copy for $4.95, plus 5 first-class stamps. Guidelines for #10 SASE.

NONFICTION Needs book excerpts, general interest, historical, how-to, inspirational, related to the region, interview, photo feature, travel. Does not want fiction. **Buys 30-40 mss/year.** Query or send complete ms. Length: 800-1,200 words. **Pays $75-125.** Sometimes pays expenses of writers on assignment.

RHODE ISLAND

$$$ RHODE ISLAND MONTHLY

The Providence Journal Co., 717 Allens Ave., Suite 105, Providence RI 02905. (401)649-4800. **E-mail:** dwelshman@rimonthly.com. **Website:** www.rimonthly.com. **Contact:** Dean Welshman, art director. **50% freelance written.** Monthly magazine. *Rhode Island Monthly* is a general interest consumer magazine with a strict Rhode Island focus. Estab. 1988. Circ. 41,000. Byline given. Offers 25% kill fee. Publishes ms an average of 3 months after acceptance. Editorial lead time 3 months. Submit seasonal material 6 months in advance. Accepts queries by mail, e-mail, fax. Responds in 6 weeks to queries. Guidelines free.

NONFICTION Needs exposé, general interest, interview, photo feature. **Buys 40 mss/year.** Query with published clips. Length: 1,800-3,000 words. **Pays $600-1,200.** Sometimes pays expenses of writers on assignment.

SOUTH CAROLINA

CHARLESTON MAGAZINE

P.O. Box 1794, Mt. Pleasant SC 29465-1794. (843)971-9811 or (888)242-7624. **E-mail:** dshankland@charlestonmag.com; anna@charlestonmag.com; jed@charlestonmag.com. **Website:** www.charlestonmag.com. **Contact:** Darcy Shankland, editor-in-chief; Anna Evans, managing editor; Jed Drew, publisher. **80% freelance written.** Bimonthly magazine covering current issues, events, arts and culture, leisure pursuits, travel, and personalities, as they pertain to the city of Charleston and surrounding areas. A Lowcountry institution for more than 30 years, *Charleston Magazine* captures the essence of Charleston and her surrounding areas—her people, arts and architecture, culture and events, and natural beauty. Estab. 1972. Circ. 25,000. Byline given. Pays 1 month after publication. Submit seasonal material 4 months in advance. Accepts queries by mail, e-mail, fax. Sample copies may be ordered at cover price from office. Guidelines for #10 sase.

NONFICTION Needs general interest, humor, interview, opinion, photo feature, travel, food, architecture, sports, current events/issues, art. Not interested in 'Southern nostalgia' articles or gratuitous history pieces. **Buys 40 mss/year.** Query with published clips and SASE. Length: 150-1,500 words. **Payment negotiated** Sometimes pays expenses of writers on assignment.

COLUMNS Channel Markers (general local interest), 50-400 words; Local Seen (profile of local interest), 500 words; In Good Taste (restaurants and culinary trends in the city), 1,000-1,200 words, plus recipes; Chef at Home (profile of local chefs), 1,200 words, plus recipes; On the Road (travel opportunities near Charleston), 1,000-1,200 words; Southern View (personal experience about Charleston life), 750 words; Doing Business (profiles of exceptional local businesses and entrepreneurs), 1,000-1,200 words; Native Talent (local profiles), 1,000-1,200 words; Top of the Shelf (reviews of books with Southern content or by a Southern author), 750 words.

⊕⊛ HILTON HEAD MONTHLY

P.O. Box 5926, Hilton Head Island SC 29938. **Fax:** (843)842-5743. **E-mail:** editor@hiltonheadmonthly.com. **Website:** www.hiltonheadmonthly.com. **Contact:** Jeff Vrabel, Editor. **75% freelance written.** Monthly magazine covering the people, business, community, environment, and lifestyle of Hilton Head, South Carolina and the surrounding Lowcountry. Our mission is to offer lively, fresh writing about Hilton Head Island, an upscale, environmentally conscious and intensely pro-active resort community on the coast of South Carolina." Circ. 35,000. Byline given. Offers 50% kill fee. Publishes ms an average of 6 months after acceptance. Editorial lead time 3 months. Submit seasonal material 4 months in advance. Accepts queries by mail, e-mail, . Accepts simultaneous submissions. Responds in 1 week to queries. Responds in 4 months to mss. Sample copy for $3.

NONFICTION Needs general interest, historical, history only, how-to, home related, humor, interview, Hilton Head residents only, opinion, general humor or Hilton Head Island community affairs, personal experience, travel. Everything is local, local, local, so we're especially interested in profiles of notable residents (or those with Lowcountry ties) and original takes on home design/maintenance, environmental issues, entrepreneurship, health, sports, arts and entertainment, humor, travel and volunteerism. We like to see how national trends/issues play out on a local level." **Buys 225-250 mss/year.** Query with published clips.

COLUMNS News; Business; Lifestyles (hobbies, health, sports, etc.); Home; Around Town (local events, charities and personalities); People (profiles, weddings, etc.). Query with synopsis. **Pays 20¢/word.**

TENNESSEE

⊕⊛ AT HOME TENNESSEE

671 N. Ericson Rd., Suite 200, Cordova TN 38018. (901)684-4155. **Fax:** (901)684-4156. **Website:** www. athometn.com. **Contact:** Margaret Monger, publisher and editorial director; Janna Herbison, editor. **50% freelance written.** Monthly magazine. Estab. 2002. Circ. 37,000. Byline given. Offers 50% kill fee. Editorial lead time 2 months. Submit seasonal material 2-3 months in advance. Accepts queries by e-mail. No-Responds in 1-2 months to queries. Sample copy for $4.99. Guidelines free.

NONFICTION Needs general interest, how-to, interview, travel, landscaping, arts, design. Does not want opinion. Query with published clips. Length: 400-900 words. **Pays $50-200.**

⊕⊛ MEMPHIS

Contemporary Media, P.O. Box 1738, Memphis TN 38101. (901)521-9000. **Fax:** (901)521-0129. **E-mail:** murtaugh@memphismagazine.com. **Website:** www. memphismagazine.com. **Contact:** Frank Murtaugh, managing editor. **30% freelance written. Works with a small number of new/unpublished writers.** Monthly magazine covering Memphis and the local region. Our mission is to provide Memphis with a colorful and informative look at the people, places, lifestyles and businesses that make the Bluff City unique. Estab. 1976. Circ. 24,000. No byline given. Submit seasonal material 3 months in advance. Accepts queries by mail, e-mail, fax.

NONFICTION Needs essays, general interest, historical, interview, photo feature, travel, Interiors/exteriors, local issues and events. Special issues: Restaurant Guide and City Guide. **Buys 20 mss/year.** Query with published clips. Length: 500-3,000 words. **Pays 10-30¢/word.** Sometimes pays expenses of writers on assignment.

FICTION One story published annually as part of contest. Open only to those within 150 miles of Memphis. See website for details.

⊕⊛ MEMPHIS DOWNTOWNER MAGAZINE

Downtown Productions, Inc., 408 S. Front St., Suite 109, Memphis TN 38103. (901)525-7118. **Fax:**

(901)525-7128. **E-mail:** editor@memphisdowntown-er.com. **Website:** www.memphisdowntowner.com. **Contact:** Terre Gorham, editor. **50% freelance written.** Monthly magazine covering features on positive aspects with a Memphis tie-in, especially to downtown. "We feature people, companies, nonprofits, and other issues that the general Memphis public would find interesting, entertaining, and informative. All editorial focuses on the positives Memphis has. No negative commentary or personal judgements. Controversial subjects should be treated fairly and balanced without bias." Estab. 1991. Circ. 30,000. Byline given. Pays on 15th of month in which assignment is published. Offers 25% kill fee. Publishes ms an average of 2-6 months after acceptance. Editorial lead time 3-6 months. Submit seasonal material 3-6 months in advance. Accepts queries by mail, e-mail. Responds in 2 weeks to queries. Sample copy free. Guidelines by e-mail.

NONFICTION Needs general interest, historical, how-to, humor, interview, personal experience, photo feature. **Buys 40-50 mss/year.** Query with published clips. Length: 600-2,000 words. **Pays scales vary depending on scope of assignment, but typically runs 15¢/word.** Sometimes pays expenses of writers on assignment.

COLUMNS So It Goes (G-rated humor), 600-800 words; Discovery 901 (Memphis one-of-a-kinds), 1,000-1,200 words. **Buys 6 mss/year.** Query with published clips. **Pays $100-150.**

FILLERS "Unusual, interesting, or how-to or what to look for appealing to a large, general audience." Needs facts.

TEXAS

💲💲💲 HOUSTON PRESS

1621 Milam, Suite 100, Houston TX 77002. (713)280-2400. **Fax:** (713)280-2444. **Website:** www.houstonpress.com. **Contact:** Margaret Downing, editor. **40% freelance written.** "Weekly tabloid covering news and arts stories of interest to a Houston audience. If the same story could run in Seattle, then it's not for us." Estab. 1989. Byline given. Publishes ms an average of 2 weeks after acceptance. Editorial lead time 2 months. Submit seasonal material 3 months in advance. Sample copy for $3.

NONFICTION Needs exposé, general interest, interview, arts reviews. Query with published clips.

Length: 300-4,500 words. **Pays $10-1,000.** Sometimes pays expenses of writers on assignment.

💲💲💲 TEXAS HIGHWAYS

P.O. Box 141009, Austin TX 78714-1009. (800)839-4997. **Website:** www.texashighways.com. **70% freelance written.** Monthly magazine encourages travel within the state and tells the Texas story to readers around the world. Estab. 1974. Circ. 250,000. Publishes ms an average of 1 year after acceptance. Accepts queries by mail. Responds in 2 months to queries. Guidelines available online.

NONFICTION Query with description, published clips, additional background materials (charts, maps, etc.) and SASE. Length: 1,200-1,500 words. **Pays 40-50¢/word.**

💲💲💲💲 TEXAS MONTHLY

Emmis Publishing LP, P.O. Box 1569, Austin TX 78767-1569. (512)320-6900. **Fax:** (512)476-9007. **E-mail:** lbaldwin@texasmonthly.com. **Website:** www.texasmonthly.com. **Contact:** Jake Silverstein, editor; Leslie Baldwin, photo editor; Scott Dadich, art director. **10% freelance written.** Monthly magazine covering Texas. Estab. 1973. Circ. 300,000. Byline given. Pays on acceptance, $1/word and writer's expenses. Publishes ms an average of 1-3 months after acceptance. Editorial lead time 2 months. Submit seasonal material 3 months in advance. Accepts queries by mail, e-mail, fax. NoResponds in 6-8 weeks to queries. Responds in 6-8 weeks to mss. Sample copy for $7. Guidelines available online.

NONFICTION Contact: Contact John Broders, associate editor (jbroders@texasmonthly.com). Needs book excerpts, essays, exposé, general interest, interview, personal experience, photo feature, travel. Does not want articles without a Texas connection. **Buys 15 mss/year.** Query. Length: 2,000-5,000 words. Pays expenses of writers on assignment.

💲💲 TEXAS PARKS & WILDLIFE

4200 Smith School Rd., Bldg. D, Austin TX 78744. (512)389-8793. **Fax:** (512)707-1913. **E-mail:** louie.bond@tpwd.state.tx.us; brandon.jakobeit@tpwd.state.tx.us. **Website:** www.tpwmagazine.com. **Contact:** Louie Bond, editor; Brandon Jakobeit, assistant art director. **80% freelance written.** Monthly magazine featuring articles about "Texas hunting, fishing, birding, outdoor recreation, game and nongame wildlife, state parks, environmental issues." All articles

must be about Texas. Estab. 1942. Circ. 150,000. Byline given. Offers kill fee. Kill fee determined by contract, usually $200-250. Publishes ms an average of 4 months after acceptance. Accepts queries by mail. Responds in 1 month to queries. Responds in 3 months to mss. Sample copy and guidelines available online.
NONFICTION Needs general interest (Texas only), how-to, outdoor activities, photo feature, travel, state parks, and small towns. **Buys 60 mss/year.** Query with published clips; follow up by e-mail 1 month after submitting query. Length: 500-2,500 words. **Pays 50¢/word.**

VIRGINIA

😊😊 THE ROANOKER

Leisure Publishing Co., Leisure Publishing Co., 3424 Brambleton Ave., Roanoke VA 24018. (540)989-6138. **Fax:** (540)989-7603. **E-mail:** krheinheimer@leisure-publishing.com. **Website:** www.theroanoker.com. **Contact:** Kurt Rheinheimer, editor; Austin Clark, creative director; Patty Jackson, production director. **75% freelance written. Works with a small number of new/unpublished writers each year.** Magazine published 6 times/year. "*The Roanoker* is a general interest city magazine for the people of Roanoke, Virginia and the surrounding area. Our readers are primarily upper-income, well-educated professionals between the ages of 35 and 60. Coverage ranges from hard news and consumer information to restaurant reviews and local history." Estab. 1974. Circ. 10,000. Byline given. Publishes ms an average of 4 months after acceptance. Submit seasonal material 4 months in advance. Accepts queries by mail, e-mail, fax. Responds in 2 months to queries. Sample copy for $2 with 9×12 SASE and 5 first-class stamps or online.
NONFICTION Needs exposé, historical, how-to, live better in western Virginia, interview, of well-known area personalities, photo feature, travel, Virginia and surrounding states, periodic special sections on fashion, real estate, media, banking, investing. **Buys 30 mss/year.** Send complete ms. 1,400 words maximum. **Pays $35-200.**
COLUMNS Skinny (shorts on people, Roanoke-related books, local issues, events, arts and culture).

😊😊 VIRGINIA LIVING

Cape Fear Publishing, 109 E. Cary St., Richmond VA 23219. (804)343-7539. **Fax:** (804)649-0306. **E-mail:** RichardErnsberger@capefear.com. **Website:** www.

virginialiving.com. **Contact:** Richard Ernsberger, Jr. **80% freelance written.** Bimonthly magazine covering life and lifestyle in Virginia. "We are a large-format (10×13) glossy magazine covering life in Virginia, from food, architecture, and gardening, to issues, profiles, and travel." Estab. 2002. Circ. 70,000. Byline given. Publishes ms an average of 4-6 months after acceptance. Editorial lead time 2-6 months. Submit seasonal material 1 year in advance. Accepts queries by mail. Accepts simultaneous submissions. Responds in 1 month. Sample copy for $5.
NONFICTION Needs book excerpts, essays, exposé, general interest, historical, interview, new product, personal experience, photo feature, travel, architecture, design. No fiction, poetry, previously published articles, or stories with a firm grasp of the obvious. **Buys 180 mss/year.** Query with published clips or send complete ms. Length: 300-3,000 words. **Pays 50¢/word.**
COLUMNS Beauty; Travel; Books; Events; Sports (all with a unique Virginia slant), all 1,000-1,500 words. **Buys 50 mss/year.** Send complete ms. **Pays $120-200.**

WASHINGTON

😊😊 PUGET SOUND MAGAZINE

2115 Renee Place, Port Townsend WA 98368. (206)414-1589. **Fax:** (206)932-2574. **E-mail:** editorial@pugetsoundmagazine.com. **Website:** www.pugetsoundmagazine.com. **Contact:** David Petrich. **50% freelance written.** Online magazine covering regional focus on adventure, travel, recreation, art, food, wine, culture, wildlife, plants, and healthy living on the shoreline communities of Puget Sound and the Salish Sea. Olympia WA to Campbell River, BC. Writing from a personal experience, human interest perspective. We do profiles, historic pieces, how to—mostly features on water-centric lifestyles. Estab. 2008. Circ. 30,000 when go to print in 2011 as a quarterly. Byline given. Publishes ms an average of 2 months after acceptance. Editorial lead time 2 months. Accepts queries by mail, e-mail. Accepts simultaneous submissions. Responds in 4 weeks to queries. Sample copy free. Guidelines available online.
NONFICTION **Contact:** Kathleen McKelvey. Needs book excerpts, essays, general interest, historical, how-to, humor, inspirational, interview, personal experience, photo feature, travel. Special issues: No special issues at this time. Nothing negative, political,

pornographic, religious. Send complete ms. Length: 800-2,000 words. **Pays 10¢ for assigned articles and for unsolicited articles.**

FICTION Contact: Katherine McKelvey. Needs adventure, historical, humorous, mainstream, mystery, western. **Buys 6 mss/year.** Query with published clips. Word length: 800-1,000 words. **Pays 10¢.word.**

POETRY Contact: Terry Persun, editor. Needs free verse, traditional. Buys 6/yr. poems/year. Submit maximum 3 poems. Length: 25 lines.

💲💲 SEATTLE MAGAZINE

Tiger Oak Publications Inc., 1518 First Ave. S, Suite 500, Seattle WA 98134. (206)284-1750. **Fax:** (206)284-2550. **E-mail:** rachel.hart@tigeroak.com. **Website:** www.seattlemagazine.com. **Contact:** Rachel Hart, editorial director; Kristen Russell, managing editor. **75% freelance written.** "Monthly magazine serving the Seattle metropolitan area. Articles should be written with our readers in mind. They are interested in social issues, the arts, politics, homes and gardens, travel and maintaining the region's high quality of life." Estab. 1992. Circ. 45,000. Byline given. Pays on or about 30 days after publication. Offers 25% kill fee. Publishes ms an average of 3 months after acceptance. Editorial lead time 6 months. Submit seasonal material 6 months in advance. Accepts queries by mail, e-mail, fax. Responds in 2 months to queries. Sample copy for #10 SASE. Guidelines available online.

NONFICTION Needs book excerpts, local, essays, exposé, general interest, humor, interview, photo feature, travel, local/regional interest. No longer accepting queries by mail. Query with published clips. Length: 200-4,000 words. **Pays $50 minimum.**

COLUMNS Scoop, Urban Safari, Voice, Trips, People, Environment, Hot Button, Fitness, Fashion, Eat and Drink Query with published clips. **Pays $225-400.**

💲💲💲 SEATTLE WEEKLY

Village Voice, 1008 Western Ave., Suite 300, Seattle WA 98104. (206)623-0500. **Fax:** (206)467-4338. **Website:** www.seattleweekly.com. **20% freelance written.** Weekly tabloid covering arts, politics, food, business and books with local and regional emphasis. Estab. 1976. Circ. 105,000. Byline given. Offers variable kill fee. Publishes ms an average of 1 month after acceptance. Submit seasonal material 2 months in advance. Responds in 1 month to queries. Sample copy for $3. Guidelines available online.

NONFICTION Needs book excerpts, exposé, general interest, historical, Northwest, humor, interview, opinion. **Buys 6-8 mss/year.** Query with cover letter, résumé, published clips and SASE. Length: 300-4,000 words. **Pays $50-800.** Sometimes pays expenses of writers on assignment.

WISCONSIN

💲💲 MADISON MAGAZINE

Morgan Murphy Media, 7025 Raymond Rd., Madison WI 53719. (608)270-3600. **Fax:** (608)270-3636. **E-mail:** bnardi@madisonmagazine.com. **Website:** www.madisonmagazine.com. **Contact:** Brennan Nardi, editor. **75% freelance written.** Monthly magazine. Estab. 1978. Byline given. Offers 33% kill fee. Publishes ms an average of 2 months after acceptance. Editorial lead time 3 months. Submit seasonal material 3-4 months in advance. Accepts queries by mail, e-mail. Accepts simultaneous submissions. Responds in 3 weeks to queries. Responds in 3 weeks to mss. Sample copy free. Guidelines available online.

NONFICTION Needs book excerpts, essays, exposé, general interest, historical, how-to, humor, inspirational, interview, new product, opinion, personal experience, photo feature, religious, technical, travel.

COLUMNS Your Town (local events) and OverTones (local arts/entertainment), both 300 words; Habitat (local house/garden) and Business (local business), both 800 words. **Buys 120 mss/year.** Query with published clips. **Pays variable amount.**

FILLERS Needs anecdotes, facts, gags, newsbreaks, short humor. Length: 100 words. **Pays 20-30¢/word.**

💲💲💲💲 MILWAUKEE MAGAZINE

126 N. Jefferson St., Milwaukee WI 53202. (414)273-1101. **Fax:** (414)273-0016. **E-mail:** milmag@milwaukeemagazine.com; cristina.daglas@milwaukeemag.com. **Website:** www.milwaukeemagazine.com. **Contact:** Cristina Daglas, editor; Kurt Chandler, senior editor; Ann Christianson, senior editor/dining critic; Howie Magner, senior editor. **40% freelance written.** Monthly magazine. "We publish stories about Milwaukee, of service to Milwaukee-area residents and exploring the area's changing lifestyle, business, arts, politics, and dining. Our goal has always been to create an informative, literate and entertaining magazine that will challenge Milwaukeeans with in-depth reporting and analysis of issues of the day, provide useful service features, and enlighten readers with thoughtful sto-

ries, essays and columns. Underlying this mission is the desire to discover what is unique about Wisconsin and its people, to challenge conventional wisdom when necessary, criticize when warranted, heap praise when deserved, and season all with affection and concern for the place we call home." Circ. 40,000. Byline given. Offers 20% kill fee. Publishes ms an average of 2 months after acceptance. Submit seasonal material 6 months in advance. Accepts queries by mail, e-mail. Responds in 6 weeks to queries. Sample copy for $6. Guidelines available online.

NONFICTION Needs essays, exposé, general interest, historical, interview, photo feature, travel, food and dining, and other services. "No articles without a strong Milwaukee or Wisconsin angle. Length: 2,500-5,000 words for full-length features; 800 words for 2-page breaker features (short on copy, long on visuals)." **Buys 30-50 mss/year.** Query with published clips. **Pays $700-2,000 for full-length articles.** Sometimes pays expenses of writers on assignment.

COLUMNS Insider (inside information on Milwaukee, exposé, slice-of-life, unconventional angles on current scene), up to 500 words; Mini Reviews for Insider, 125 words. Query with published clips.

WISCONSIN NATURAL RESOURCES

Wisconsin Department of Natural Resources, P.O. Box 7921, Madison WI 53707-7921. (608)266-1510. **Fax:** (608)264-6293. **E-mail:** natasha.kassulke@wisconsin.gov. **E-mail:** Natasha Kassulke. **Website:** www.wnrmag.com. **30% freelance written.** Bimonthly magazine covering environment, natural resource management, and outdoor skills. "We cover current issues in Wisconsin aimed to educate and advocate for resource conservation, outdoor recreation, and wise land use." Estab. 1931. Circ. 77,000. Byline given. Publishes ms an average of 8 months after acceptance. Editorial lead time 6 months. Submit seasonal material 1 year in advance. Accepts queries by mail, e-mail. Accepts simultaneous submissions. Responds in 3 weeks to queries. Responds in 6 months to mss. Sample copy free. Guidelines available online.

NONFICTION Needs essays, how-to, photo feature, features on current outdoor issues and environmental issues. Does not want animal rights pieces, poetry or fiction. Query. Length: 1,500-2,700 words.

💲💲 WISCONSIN TRAILS

333 W. State St., Milwaukee WI 53201. **Fax:** (414)647-4723. **E-mail:** clewis@wistrails.com. **Website:** http://

wisconsintrails.com. **Contact:** Chelsey Lewis. **40% freelance written**. Bimonthly magazine for readers interested in Wisconsin and its contemporary issues, personalities, recreation, history, natural beauty, and arts. Estab. 1960. Circ. 55,000. Byline given. Pays 1 month from publication. Kill fee 20%, up to $75. Publishes ms an average of 6 months after acceptance. Submit seasonal material 1 year in advance. Accepts queries by mail, e-mail, fax. Responds in 2-3 months to queries. Sample copy for $4.95. Guidelines for #10 SASE or online.

NONFICTION Does not accept unsolicited mss. Query or send outline Length: 250-1,500 words. **Pays 25¢/word.** Sometimes pays expenses of writers on assignment.

RELIGIOUS

💲💲 AMERICA

106 W. 56th St., New York NY 10019. (212)581-4640. **Fax:** (212)399-3596. **E-mail:** america@americamagazine.org. **E-mail:** articles@americamagazine.org; reviews@americamagazine.org. **Website:** www.americamagazine.org. "Published weekly for adult, educated, largely Roman Catholic audience. Founded by the Jesuit order and directed today by Jesuits and lay colleagues, *America* is a resource for spiritual renewal and social analysis guided by the spirit of charity. The print and web editions of *America* feature timely and thought-provoking articles written by prestigious writers and theologians, and incisive book, film and art reviews." Estab. 1909. Byline given. Responds in 3 weeks to queries. Guidelines available online.

NONFICTION "We are not interested in purely informational pieces or personal narratives which are self-contained and have no larger moral interest." Length: 1,500-2,000 words. **Pays $50-300.**

POETRY Contact: Rev. James S. Torrens, poetry editor. "Only 10-12 poems published a year, thousands turned down." Buys 10-12 poems/year. Length: 15-30 lines.

💲 BIBLE ADVOCATE

Bible Advocate, Church of God (Seventh Day), P.O. Box 33677, Denver CO 80233. (303)452-7973. **E-mail:** bibleadvocate@cog7.org. **Website:** http://baonline.org/. **Contact:** Sherri Langton, associate editor. **25% freelance written.** Religious magazine published 6 times/year. "Our purpose is to advocate the Bible and represent the Church of God (Seventh Day) to a

Christian audience." Estab. 1863. Circ. 13,500. Byline given. Offers 50% kill fee. Publishes ms an average of 9 months after acceptance. Editorial lead time 3 months. Submit seasonal material 6 months in advance. Accepts queries by mail, e-mail; prefers e-mail; attachments ok. Accepts simultaneous submissions. Responds in 2 months to queries. Sample copy for sae with 9×12 envelope and 3 first-class stamps. Guidelines available online.

NONFICTION Needs inspirational, personal experience, religious, Biblical studies. No articles on Christmas or Easter. **Buys 15-20 mss/year.** Send complete ms and SASE. Length: 1,000-1,200 words. **Pays $25-55.**

POETRY Needs free verse, traditional, Christian/Bible themes. Prefers e-mail submissions. Cover letter is preferred. "No handwritten submissions, please." Time between acceptance and publication is up to 1 year. "I read them first and reject those that won't work for us. I send good ones to editor for approval." Seldom comments on rejected poems. No avant-garde. Buys 10-12 poems/year. Submit maximum 5/poems. poems. Length: 5-20 lines. **Pays $20 and 2 contributor's copies.**

FILLERS Needs anecdotes, facts. **Buys 5 mss. mss/year.** Length: 50-400 words. **Pays $10-20.**

💲💲 CATHOLIC DIGEST

P.O. Box 6015, New London CT 06320. (800)321-0411. **Fax:** (860)457-3013. **E-mail:** queries@catholicdigest.com; cartoons@catholicdigest.com. **Website:** www.catholicdigest.com. **12% freelance written.** Monthly magazine. Publishes features and advice on topics ranging from health, psychology, humor, adventure, and family, to ethics, spirituality, and Catholics, from modern-day heroes to saints through the ages. Helpful and relevant reading culled from secular and religious periodicals. Estab. 1936. Circ. 275,000. Byline given. Editorial lead time 3 months. Submit seasonal material 4-5 months in advance. Accepts queries by mail, e-mail. Responds in 2 months to mss. Sample copy free. Guidelines available online.

NONFICTION Needs book excerpts, essays, general interest, historical, how-to, humor, inspirational, interview, personal experience, religious, travel. Does not accept unsolicited submissions. Send complete ms. Length: 350-1,500 words. **Pays $200-300.**

FILLERS Contact: Filler Editor. Open Door (statements of true incidents through which people are brought into the Catholic faith, or recover the Cath-

olic faith they had lost), 350-600 words. Send to opendoor@catholicdigest.com. Good Egg (stories about a Catholic who has demonstrated their faith through commitment to their family, community, and church), 350-600 words. Send to goodegg@catholicdigest.com. **Buys 200 mss/year.** 350-600 words.

💲💲 CATHOLIC FORESTER

Catholic Order of Foresters, 355 Shuman Blvd., P.O. Box 3012, Naperville IL 60566-7012. **Fax:** (630)983-3384. **E-mail:** magazine@catholicforester.org. **Website:** www.catholicforester.org. **Contact:** Patricia Baron, associate editor; Danielle Marsh, art director. **20% freelance written.** Quarterly magazine for members of the Catholic Order of Foresters, a fraternal insurance benefit society. "*Catholic Forester,*is a quarterly magazine filled with product features, member stories, and articles affirming fraternalism, unity, friendship, and true Christian charity among members. Although a portion of each issue is devoted to the organization and its members, a few freelance pieces are published in most issues. These articles cover varied topics to create a balanced issue for the purpose of informing, educating, and entertaining our readers." Estab. 1883. Circ. 137,000. Editorial lead time 6 months. Submit seasonal material 6 months in advance. TrueResponds in 3 months to mss. Sample copy for 9×12 SAE and 4 first-class stamps. Guidelines available online.

NONFICTION Needs health and wellness, money management and budgeting, parenting and family life, interesting travels, insurance, nostalgia, humor, inspirational, religious, Will consider previously published work. **Buys 12-16 mss/year.** Send complete ms by mail, fax, or e-mail. Rejected material will not be returned without accompanying SASE. Length: 500-1,500 words. **Pays 50¢/word.**

FICTION Needs humorous, religious, inspirational. **Buys 12-16 mss/year.** Length: 500-1,500 words. **Pays 50¢/word.**

POETRY Needs light verse, traditional. Buys 3 poems/year. 15 lines maximum **Pays 30¢/word.**

💲💲 CELEBRATE LIFE

American Life League, P.O. Box 1350, Stafford VA 22555. (540)659-4171. **Fax:** (540)659-2586. **E-mail:** clmag@all.org. **Website:** www.clmagazine.org. **Contact:** Editor. **50% freelance written.** Bimonthly magazine "publishing educational articles and human-interest stories on the right to life and dignity of all human beings." Estab. 1979. Circ. 30,000. Byline given. Submit seasonal material 4 months in advance. Accepts queries by mail, e-mail. No.Accepts simultaneous submissions. Responds in 6 months to mss. For sample copy, send 9×12 SAE envelope and 4 first-class stamps. Guidelines available on website.

NONFICTION "Nonfiction only; no fiction, poetry, songs, music, allegory, or devotionals." Does not publish reprints. Query with published clips or send complete ms. Length: 400-1,600 words.

$$$ CHARISMA & CHRISTIAN LIFE

Charisma Media, 600 Rinehart Rd., Lake Mary FL 32746. (407)333-0600. **Fax:** (407)333-7133. **E-mail:** charisma@charismamedia.com. **Website:** www.charismamag.com. **Contact:** Marcus Yoars. **80% freelance written.** Monthly magazine covering items of interest to the Pentecostal or independent charismatic reader. Now also online. "More than half of our readers are Christians who belong to Pentecostal or independent charismatic churches, and numerous others participate in the charismatic renewal in mainline denominations." Estab. 1975. Circ. 250,000. Byline given. Offers $50 kill fee. Publishes ms an average of 3 months after acceptance. Editorial lead time 4 months. Submit seasonal material 5 months in advance. Accepts queries by mail, e-mail. Sample copy for $4. Guidelines by e-mail and online.

NONFICTION Needs book excerpts, exposé, general interest, interview, religious. No fiction, poetry, COLUMNS, or sermons. **Buys 40 mss/year.** Query. Length: 1,800-2,500 words. Pays expenses of writers on assignment.

$$ THE CHRISTIAN CENTURY

104 S. Michigan Ave., Suite 700, Chicago IL 60603-5901. (312)263-7510. **Fax:** (312)263-7540. **E-mail:** main@christiancentury.org. **E-mail:** submissions@christiancentury.org; poetry@christiancentury.org. **Website:** www.christiancentury.org. **Contact:** Jill Peláez Baumgaertner, poetry editor. **90% freelance written. Works with new/unpublished writers.** Biweekly magazine for ecumenically-minded, progressive Protestants, both clergy and lay. "We seek manuscripts that articulate the public meaning of faith, bringing the resources of religious tradition to bear on such topics as poverty, human rights, economic justice, international relations, national priorities and popular culture. We are also interested in pieces that examine or critique the theology and ethos of individual religious communities. We welcome articles that find fresh meaning in old traditions and that adapt or apply religious traditions to new circumstances. Authors should assume that readers are familiar with main themes in Christian history and theology, are accustomed to the historical-critical study of the Bible and are already engaged in relating faith to social and political issues. Many of our readers are ministers or teachers of religion at the college level. Book reviews are solicited by our books editor. Please note that submissions via e-mail will not be considered. If you are interested in becoming a reviewer for the *Christian Century*, please send your rèsumè and a list of subjects of interest to Attn: Book reviews. Authors must have a critical and analytical perspective on the church and be familiar with contemporary theological discussion." Estab. 1884. Circ. 37,000. Byline given. Editorial lead time 1 month. Submit seasonal material 4 months in advance. Accepts queries by mail, e-mail. Responds in 4-6 week to queries. Responds in 2 months to mss. Sample copy for $3.50. Guidelines available online.

NONFICTION Needs essays, humor, interview, opinion, religious. No inspirational. **Buys 150 mss/year.** Send complete ms; query appreciated, but not essential. Length: 1,000-3,000 words. **Pays variable amount for assigned articles. Pays $100-300 for unsolicited articles.**

COLUMNS "We do not accept unsolicited submissions for our regular columns."

POETRY Contact: Jill Pelàez Baumgaertner, poetry editor. Needs avant-garde, free verse, haiku, traditional. (Specialized: Christian; social issues) *The Christian Century*, an "ecumenical biweekly," is a liberal, sophisticated journal of news, articles of opinion, and reviews. Uses approximately 1 poem/issue, not necessarily on religious themes but in keeping with the literate tone of the magazine. Has published poetry by Jeanne Murray Walker, Ida Fasel, Kathleen Norris, Luci Shaw, J. Barrie Shepherd, and Wendell Berry. "Prefer shorter poems." Inquire about reprint permission. No sentimental or didactic poetry. Buys 50 poems/year. Length: 20 lines/max. **Pays usually $20/poem plus 1 contributor's copy and discount on additional copies. Acquires all rights.**

$$ CHRISTIAN HOME & SCHOOL

Christian Schools International, 3350 E. Paris Ave. SE, Grand Rapids MI 49512. (616)957-1070, ext. 239.

Fax: (616)957-5022. **E-mail:** rheyboer@csionline.org. **Website:** www.csionline.org/chs. **30% freelance written. Works with a small number of new/unpublished writers each year.** Magazine published 2 times/year during the school year covering family life and Christian education. In addition, a special high school issue is published each Spring. *Christian Home & School* is designed for parents in the United States and Canada who send their children to Christian schools and are concerned about the challenges facing Christian families today. These readers expect a mature, Biblical perspective in the articles, not just a Bible verse tacked onto the end. Estab. 1922. Circ. 66,000. Byline given. Publishes ms an average of 4 months after acceptance. Submit seasonal material 4 months in advance. Accepts queries by mail, e-mail. Responds in 1 month to queries. Sample copy and writer's guidelines for 9×12 SAE with 4 first-class stamps. Writer's guidelines only for #10 SASE or online. For article topics please refer to the editorial calendar posted at website: www.csionline.org/chs.

NONFICTION Needs book excerpts, interview, opinion, personal experience, articles on parenting and school life. **Buys 30 mss/year.** Send complete ms. Length: 1,000-2,000 words. **Pays $175-250.**

COLUMBIA

1 Columbus Plaza, New Haven CT 06510. (203)752-4398. **Fax:** (203)752-4109. **E-mail:** columbia@kofc.org. **Website:** www.kofc.org/columbia. **Contact:** Alton Pelowski, managing editor. Monthly magazine for Catholic families. Caters primarily to members of the Knights of Columbus. Estab. 1921. Circ. 1,500,000. Accepts queries by mail, e-mail. Sample copy and writer's guidelines free.

NONFICTION No reprints, poetry, cartoons, puzzles, short stories/fiction. Query with SASE or by e-mail. Length: 750-1,500 words.

CONSCIENCE

Catholics for Choice, 1436 U St. NW, Suite 301, Washington D.C. 20009-3997. (202)986-6093. **E-mail:** conscience@catholicsforchoice.org. **Website:** www.catholicsforchoice.org. **Contact:** Kim Puchir; David Nolan. **80% written by nonstaff writers. Publishes 40 freelance submissions yearly; 10% by unpublished writers, 50% by authors who are new to the magazine, 70% by experts.** "Conscience offers in-depth coverage of a range of topics, including contemporary politics, Catholicism, women's rights in society and in religions, U.S. politics, reproductive rights, sexuality and gender, ethics and bioethics, feminist theology, social justice, church and state issues, and the role of religion in formulating public policy." Estab. 1980. Circ. 12,000. Byline given. Publishes ms an average of 2 months after acceptance. Accepts queries by mail, e-mail. Responds in 4 months to queries. Sample copy free with 9×12 envelope and $1.85 postage. Guidelines with #10 SASE.

NONFICTION Needs book excerpts, interview, opinion, personal experience, a small amount, issue analysis. **Buys 4-8 mss/year.** Send complete ms. Length: 1,500-3,500 words. **Pays $200 negotiable.**

COLUMNS Book Reviews, 600-1,200 words. **Buys 4-8 mss/year. Pays $75.**

💲💲 DECISION

Billy Graham Evangelistic Association, 1 Billy Graham Pkwy., Charlotte NC 28201-0001. (704)401-2432. **Fax:** (704)401-3009. **E-mail:** submissions@bgea.org. **Website:** www.decisionmag.org. **Contact:** Bob Paulson, editor. **5% freelance written. Works each year with small number of new/unpublished writers.** "Magazine published 11 times/year with a mission to extend the ministry of Billy Graham Evangelistic Association; to communicate the Good News of Jesus Christ in such a way that readers will be drawn to make a commitment to Christ; and to encourage, strengthen and equip Christians in evangelism and discipleship." Estab. 1960. Circ. 400,000. Byline given. Publishes ms an average of up to 18 months after acceptance. Editorial lead time 6 months. Submit seasonal material 6 months in advance. Sample copy for sae with 9×12 envelope and 4 first-class stamps. Guidelines available online.

NONFICTION Needs personal experience, testimony. **Buys approximately 8 mss/year.** Send complete ms. Length: 400-1,500 words. **Pays $200-400.** Pays expenses of writers on assignment.

COLUMNS Finding Jesus (people who have become Christians through Billy Graham Ministries), 500-900 words. **Buys 11 mss/year.** Send complete ms. **Pays $200.**

💲💲 EFCA TODAY

Evangelical Free Church of America, 418 Fourth St., NE, Charlottesville VA 22902. **E-mail:** dianemc@journeygroup.com. **Website:** www.efca.org. **30% freelance written.** Quarterly digital magazine. "*EFCA Today*'s purpose is to unify church leaders around the overall mission of the EFCA by bringing its stories and vision to life, and to sharpen those leaders by generating conversations over topics pertinent to faith and life in this 21st century." Estab. 1931. Byline given. Offers 50% kill fee. Publishes ms an average of 3 months after acceptance. Editorial lead time 5 months. Submit seasonal material 6 months in advance. Accepts queries by mail, e-mail. Rarely accepts previously published material.Responds in 6 weeks. Sample copy for $1 with SAE and 5 first-class stamps. Guidelines by email.

NONFICTION Needs interview, of EFCA-related subjects, feature articles of EFCA interest, highlighting EFCA subjects. No general-interest inspirational articles. Send complete ms. Length: 200-1,100 words and related/approved expenses for assigned articles. **Pays 23¢/word for first rights, including limited subsidiary rights (free use within an EFCA context).**

COLUMNS Engage (out of the church and into the world); Leader to Leader (what leaders are saying, doing, learning); Catalyst (the passion of EFCA's young leaders; Face to Face (our global family), all between 200 and 600/words. Send complete ms. **Pays 23¢/word and related/approved expenses for assigned articles.**

$$ ENRICHMENT

The General Council of the Assemblies of God, 1445 N. Boonville Ave., Springfield MO 65802. (417)862-2781. **Fax:** (417)862-0416. **E-mail:** enrichmentjournal@ag.org. **Website:** www.enrichmentjournal.ag.org. **Contact:** Rick Knoth, managing editor. **15% freelance written.** Quarterly journal covering church leadership and ministry. "*Enrichment* offers enriching and encouraging information to equip and empower spirit-filled leaders." Circ. 33,000. Byline given. 50% kill fee. Publishes ms an average of 1 year after acceptance. Editorial lead time 18 months. Submit seasonal material 18 months in advance. Accepts queries by mail, e-mail. Sample copy for $7. Guidelines free.

NONFICTION Needs religious. Send complete ms. Length: 1,000-3,000 words. **Pays up to 15¢/word.**

$ EVANGELICAL MISSIONS QUARTERLY

Billy Graham Center/Wheaton College, P.O. Box 794, Wheaton IL 60187. (630)752-7158. **Fax:** (630)752-7155. **E-mail:** emq@wheaton.edu. **Website:** www.emqonline.com. **Contact:** Managing editor. **67% freelance written.** Quarterly magazine covering evangelical missions. This is a professional journal for evangelical missionaries, agency executives, and church members who support global missions ministries. Estab. 1964. Circ. 7,000. Byline given. Offers negotiable kill fee. Publishes ms an average of 18 months after acceptance. Editorial lead time 1 year. Accepts queries by e-mail. Responds in 2 weeks to queries. Sample copy free. Guidelines available online.

NONFICTION Needs essays, interview, opinion, personal experience, religious, book reviews. No sermons, poetry, or straight news. **Buys 24 mss/year.** Query. Length: 800-3,000 words. **Pays $25-100.**

COLUMNS In the Workshop (practical how to's), 800-2,000 words; Perspectives (opinion), 800 words. **Buys 8 mss/year.** Query. **Pays $50-100.**

✪ $$ FAITH & FRIENDS

The Salvation Army, 2 Overlea Blvd., Toronto ON M4H 1P4 Canada. (416)422-6226. **Fax:** (416)422-6120. **E-mail:** faithandfriends@can.salvationarmy.org. **Website:** www.faithandfriends.ca. **25% freelance written.** Monthly magazine covering Christian living and religion. "Our mission statement: to show Jesus Christ at work in the lives of real people, and to provide spiritual resources for those who are new to the Christian faith." Estab. 1996. Circ. 50,000. Byline given. Offers $50 kill fee. Publishes ms an average of 3 months after acceptance. Editorial lead time 3 months. Submit seasonal material 6 months in advance. Accepts queries by mail, e-mail. TrueResponds in 1 week to queries and to mss. Sample copy available online. Guidelines by e-mail.

NONFICTION Needs book excerpts, humor, inspirational, interview, personal experience, photo feature, religious, travel. Does not want sermons, devotionals, or Christian-ese. **Buys 12-24 mss/year.** Query. Length: 500-1,250 words. **Pays $50-200.**

COLUMNS God in My Life (how life changed by accepting Jesus); Someone Cares (how life changed through someone's intervention), 750 words. **Buys 12-18 mss/year.** Query. **Pays $50.**

✪ $$ FAITH TODAY

Evangelical Fellowship of Canada, MIP Box 3745, Markham ON L3R 0Y4 Canada. (905)479-5885. **Fax:** (905)479-4742. **Website:** www.faithtoday.ca. Bimonthly magazine. "*FT* is the magazine of an association of more than 40 evangelical denominations, but serves evangelicals in all denominations. It focuses on church issues, social issues and personal faith as they are tied to the Canadian context. Writing should explicitly acknowledge that Canadian evangelical context." Estab. 1983. Circ. 18,000. Byline given. Offers 30-50% kill fee. Publishes ms an average of 4 months after acceptance. Editorial lead time 4 months. Accepts queries by mail, e-mail, fax. Responds in 6 weeks to queries. Sample copy for SASE in Canadian postage. Guidelines available online at www.faithtoday.ca/writers. "View a sample copy at www.faithtoday.ca/digitalsample. Or download one of our apps from www.faithtoday.ca."

NONFICTION Needs book excerpts, Canadian authors only, essays, Canadian authors only, interview, Canadian subjects only, opinion, religious, news feature. **Buys 75 mss/year.** Query. Length: 400-2,000 words. **Pays $100-500 Canadian.** Sometimes pays expenses of writers on assignment.

🜄 FORWARD IN CHRIST

WELS Communication Services, 2929 N. Mayfair Rd., Milwaukee WI 53222. (414)256-3210. **Fax:** (414)256-3899. **E-mail:** fic@wels.net. **Website:** www.wels.net. **Contact:** Julie K. Wietzke, managing editor; John A. Braun, executive editor. **5% freelance written.** Official monthly magazine covering Wisconsin Evangelical Lutheran Synod (WELS) news, topics, issues. The material usually must be written by or about WELS members. Estab. 1913. Circ. 42,000. Byline given. Publishes ms an average of 6 months after acceptance. Editorial lead time 3 months. Submit seasonal material 4 months in advance. Accepts queries by mail, e-mail, fax. Responds in 2 months to queries. Sample copy and writer's guidelines free. Guidelines available on website.

NONFICTION Needs personal experience, religious. Query. Length: 550-1,200 words. **Pays $75/page, $125/2 pages.** Sometimes pays expenses of writers on assignment.

🜨 THE FRIEND

The Friend Publications Ltd, 173 Euston Rd., London England NW1 2BJ United Kingdom. (44)(207)663-1010. **Fax:** (44)(207)663-1182. **E-mail:** editorial@the-friend.org. **Website:** www.thefriend.org. Weekly magazine. Completely independent, *The Friend* brings readers news and views from a Quaker perspective, as well as from a wide range of authors whose writings are of interest to Quakers and non-Quakers alike. There are articles on issues such as peace, spirituality, Quaker belief, and ecumenism, as well as news of Friends from Britain and abroad. Circ. 3,250. Byline

given. Accepts queries by mail, e-mail, phone. Guidelines available online.

NONFICTION Query. 550 words/full page; 1,100 words/double page spread.

COLUMNS Art reviews (new books, plays, videos, exhibitions), 550 words.

POETRY There are no rules regarding poetry, but doesn't want particularly long poems.

🜨🜨 GUIDEPOSTS MAGAZINE

Box 5814, Harlan IA 51593. (800)431-2344. **E-mail:** submissions@guidepostsmag.com. **Website:** www.guideposts.com. **40% freelance written. Works with a small number of new/unpublished writers each year.** Monthly magazine. "*Guideposts* is an inspirational monthly magazine for people of all faiths, in which men and women from all walks of life tell in true, first-person narrative how they overcame obstacles, rose above failures, handled sorrow, gained new spiritual insight, and became more effective people through faith in God." Estab. 1945. Offers kill fee. Offers 20% kill fee on assigned stories, but not to first-time freelancers. Publishes ms an average of several months after acceptance. Guidelines available online.

NONFICTION Buys 40-60 unsolicited mss/year. Length: 250-1,500 words. **Pays $100-500.** Pays expenses of writers on assignment.

HIGHWAY NEWS

Transport For Christ, P.O. Box 117, 1525 River Rd., Marietta PA 17547. (717)426-9977. **Fax:** (717)426-9980. **E-mail:** editor@transportforchrist.org. **Website:** www.transportforchrist.org. **Contact:** Inge Koenig. **50% freelance written.** Monthly magazine covering trucking and Christianity. "We publish human interest stories, testimonials, and teachings that have a foundation in Biblical/Christian values. Since truck drivers and their families are our primary readers, we publish works that they will find edifying and helpful." Estab. 1957. Circ. 29,000. Byline given. Publishes ms an average of 1 year after acceptance. Submit seasonal material 1 year in advance. Accepts queries by mail, e-mail, fax. Accepts simultaneous submissions. Responds in 1 month to queries. Responds in 2 months to mss. Sample copy free. Writer's guidelines by e-mail.

NONFICTION Needs essays, general interest, humor, inspirational, interview, personal experience, photo feature, religious, trucking. No sermons full of personal opinions. **Buys 20-25 mss/year.** Send complete ms. Length: 600-800 words.

COLUMNS From the Road (stories by truckers on the road); Devotionals with Trucking theme, both 600 words. Send complete ms.

FICTION Needs humorous, religious, slice-of-life vignettes. No romance or fantasy. We use very little fiction. **Buys 1 or fewer mss/year.** Send complete ms. Length: 600-800 words.

POETRY Needs traditional. Accepts very little poetry. Don't send anything unrelated to the trucking industry. Buys 2 poems/year. Submit maximum 10 poems. Length: 4-20 lines.

FILLERS Needs anecdotes, facts, short humor. Length: 20-200 words.

💲 HORIZONS

100 Witherspoon St., Louisville KY 40202-1396. (502)569-5897. **Fax:** (502)569-8085. **E-mail:** susan.jackson-dowd@pcusa.org. **Website:** www.pcusa.org/horizons/. **Contact:** Susan Jackson Dowd, communications coordinator. Bimonthly. "Magazine owned and operated by Presbyterian women offering information and inspiration for Presbyterian women by addressing current issues facing the church and the world." Estab. 1988. Circ. 25,000. Publishes ms an average of 4 months after acceptance. Sample copy for $4 and 9×12 SAE. Guidelines for #10 SASE.

FICTION Send complete ms. Length: 800-1,200 words. **Pays $50/600 words and 2 contributor's copies.**

💲💲 LEADERS IN ACTION

CSB Ministries, P.O. Box 150, Wheaton IL 60189. (630)582-0630. **Fax:** (630)582-0623. **Website:** csbministries.org. Magazine published 3 times/year covering leadership issues for CSB Ministries leaders. "*Leaders in Action* is distributed to leaders with CSB Ministries across North America. CSB is a nonprofit, non-denominational agency dedicated to winning and training boys and girls to serve Jesus Christ. Hundreds of churches throughout the U.S. and Canada make use of our wide range of services." Estab. 1960. Circ. 6,000. Byline given. Offers $35 kill fee. Publishes ms an average of 3 months after acceptance. Editorial lead time 3 months. Responds in 1 week to queries. Sample copy for $1.50 and 10×13 SAE with 4 first-class stamps. Guidelines for #10 sase.

NONFICTION Buys 8 mss/year. Query. Length: 500-1,500 words. **Pays 5-10¢/word.** Sometimes pays expenses of writers on assignment.

💲💲 LIGHT & LIFE MAGAZINE [LLM]

Free Methodist Church-USA, 770 N. High School Rd., Indianapolis IN 46214. (317)616-4776. **Fax:** (317)244-1247. **E-mail:** jeff.finley@fmcusa.org. **Website:** http://llcomm.org; http://fmcusa.org. **Contact:** Jeff Finley, managing editor. **20%.** "Light & Life Magazine [LLM] is a monthly magazine by Light & Life Communications, the publishing arm of the Free Methodist Church–USA. Each issue focuses on a specific theme with a cohesive approach in which the articles complement each other." Estab. 1868. Circ. 53,000 (English); 6,000 (Spanish). Byline given. Accepts queries by e-mail. Responds in 2 months. Sample copy for $4. Guidelines available online at http://llcom.org/writersguidelines.

NONFICTION Query. Length: 325 words (feature: 1,100 words). **Pays $75/article ($200/feature).**

💲💲 LIGUORIAN

One Liguori Dr., Liguori MO 63057-9999. (636)464-2500. **Fax:** (636)464-8449; (636)464-2503. **E-mail:** liguorianeditor@liguori.org. **Website:** www.liguorian.org. **Contact:** Cheryl Plass, managing editor. **25% freelance written. Prefers to work with published/established writers.** Magazine published 10 times/year for Catholics. "Our purpose is to lead our readers to a fuller Christian life by helping them better understand the teachings of the gospel and the church and by illustrating how these teachings apply to life and the problems confronting them as members of families, the church, and society." Estab. 1913. Circ. 100,000. Submit seasonal material 8 months in advance. Accepts queries by mail, e-mail, fax, phone. Responds in 3 months to mss. Sample copy for 9×12 SAE with 3 first-class stamps or online. Guidelines for #10 SASE and on website.

NONFICTION "No travelogue approach or un-researched ventures into controversial areas. Also, no material found in secular publications—fad subjects that already get enough press, pop psychology, negative or put-down articles. *Liguorian* does not consider retold Bible stories." **Buys 30-40 unsolicited mss/year.** Length: 400-2,400 words. **Pays 12-15¢/word and 5 contributor's copies.**

FICTION Needs religious, senior citizen/retirement. Send complete ms. 1,500-2,000 words preferred **Pays 12-15¢/word and 5 contributor's copies.**

💲💲 LIVE

Gospel Publishing House, 1445 N. Boonville Ave., Springfield MO 65802-1894. (417)862-1447. **Fax:**

(417)862-6059. **E-mail:** rl-live@gph.org. **Website:** www.gospelpublishing.com. **100% freelance written.** Weekly magazine for weekly distribution covering practical Christian living. "*LIVE* is a take-home paper distributed weekly in young adult and adult Sunday school classes. We seek to encourage Christians in living for God through fiction and true stories which apply Biblical principles to everyday problems." We seek to encourage Christians in living for God through fiction and true stories which apply Biblical principles to everyday problems." Estab. 1928. Circ. 35,000. Byline given. Publishes ms an average of 18 months after acceptance. Editorial lead time 12 months. Submit seasonal material 18 months in advance. Accepts queries by mail, e-mail. Accepts simultaneous submissions. Responds in 2 weeks to queries. Responds in 6 weeks to mss. Sample copy for #10 SASE. Guidelines for #10 SASE or on website: www.gospelpublishing.com/store/startcat.cfm?cat=tWRITGUID.

NONFICTION Needs inspirational, religious. No preachy articles or stories that refer to religious myths (e.g., Santa Claus, Easter Bunny, etc.) **Buys 50-100 mss/year.** Send complete ms. Length: 400-1,100 words. **Pays 7-10¢/word.**

FICTION Contact: Richard Bennett, editor. Needs religious, inspirational, prose poem. No preachy fiction, fiction about Bible characters, or stories that refer to religious myths (e.g., Santa Claus, Easter Bunny, etc.). No science or Bible fiction. No controversial stories about such subjects as feminism, war or capital punishment. **Buys 20-50 mss/year.** Send complete ms. Length: 800-1,200 words. **Pays 7-10¢/word.**

POETRY Needs free verse, haiku, light verse, traditional. Buys 15-24 poems/year. Submit maximum 3 poems. Length: 12-25 lines. **Pays $35-60.**

⊕ $ THE LIVING CHURCH

Living Church Foundation, P.O. Box 514036, Milwaukee WI 53203-3436. (414)276-5420. **Fax:** (414)276-7483. **E-mail:** tlc@livingchurch.org. **Website:** www.livingchurch.org. **Contact:** Douglas LeBlanc, editor at large; John Schuessler, managing editor. **50% freelance written.** Magazine covering news or articles of interest to members of the Episcopal Church. "Weekly magazine that presents news and views of the Episcopal Church and the wider Anglican Communion, along with articles on spirituality, Anglican heritage, and the application of Christianity in daily life. There are commentaries on scripture, book reviews, editorials, letters to the editor, and special thematic issues." Estab. 1878. Circ. 9,500. Byline given. Does not pay unless article is requested. Publishes ms an average of 3 months after acceptance. Editorial lead time 3 weeks. Submit seasonal material 2 months in advance. Accepts queries by mail, e-mail, fax. Responds in 2 weeks to queries. Responds in 1 month to mss. Sample copy free.

NONFICTION Needs opinion, personal experience, photo feature, religious. **Buys 10 mss/year.** Send complete ms. Length: 1,000 words. **Pays $25-100.** Sometimes pays expenses of writers on assignment.

COLUMNS Benediction (devotional), 250 words; Viewpoint (opinion), under 1,000 words. Send complete ms. **Pays $50 maximum.**

POETRY Needs light verse, traditional.

$ $ THE LOOKOUT

Standard Publishing, 8805 Governor's Hill Dr., Suite 400, Cincinnati OH 45249. (513)931-4050. **Fax:** (513)931-0950. **E-mail:** lookout@standardpub.com. **Website:** www.lookoutmag.com. Sheryl Overstreet, assistant editor. **Contact:** Shawn McMullen, editor. **50% freelance written.** Weekly magazine for Christian adults, with emphasis on spiritual growth, family life, and topical issues. "Our purpose is to provide Christian adults with practical, Biblical teaching and current information that will help them mature as believers." Estab. 1894. Circ. 45,000. Byline given. Offers 33% kill fee. Publishes ms an average of 1 year after acceptance. Editorial lead time 9 months. Submit seasonal material 1 year in advance. Accepts queries by mail, e-mail. No previously published material-Accepts simultaneous submissions. Responds in 10 weeks to queries. Responds in 10 weeks to mss. Sample copy for $1. Guidelines by e-mail or online.

NONFICTION Needs inspirational, interview, opinion, personal experience, religious. No fiction or poetry. **Buys 100 mss/year.** Send complete ms. Check guidelines. **Pays 11-17¢/word.**

$ $ THE LUTHERAN

8765 W. Higgins Rd., 5th Floor, Chicago IL 60631-4183. (770)380-2540. **Fax:** (773)380-2409. **E-mail:** lutheran@lutheran.org. **Website:** www.thelutheran.org. Michael D. Watson, art director. **Contact:** Daniel J. Lehmann, editor. **15% freelance written.** Monthly magazine for lay people in church. News and activities of the Evangelical Lutheran Church in America, news of the world of religion, ethical reflections on issues in society, personal Christian experience. Estab. 1988. Circ. 300,000. Byline given. Offers 50% kill fee. Publishes ms an average of 6 months after acceptance. Submit seasonal material 4 months in advance. Accepts queries by mail, e-mail. Responds in 6 weeks to queries. Sample copy free. Guidelines available online.

NONFICTION Needs inspirational, interview, personal experience, photo feature, religious. No articles unrelated to the world of religion. **Buys 40 mss/ year.** Query with published clips. Length: 250-1,200 words. **Pays $75-600.** Pays expenses of writers on assignment.

THE LUTHERAN DIGEST

The Lutheran Digest, Inc., 6160 Carmen Ave. E, Inver Grove Heights MN 55076. (952)933-2820. **Fax:** (952)933-5708. **E-mail:** editor@lutherandigest.com. **Website:** www.lutherandigest.com. David Tank, editor. **Contact:** Nicholas A. Skapyak, editor. **95% freelance written.** Quarterly magazine covering Christianity from a Lutheran perspective. Publishes articles and poetry. "Articles frequently reflect a Lutheran Christian perspective, but are not intended to be sermonettes. Popular stories show how God has intervened in a person's life to help solve a problem." Estab. 1953. Circ. 70,000. Byline given. Publishes ms an average of 6 months after acceptance. Editorial lead time 9 months. Submit seasonal material 9 months in advance. Accepts queries by e-mail mss only as Microsoft Word or PDF attachments. Accepts simultaneous submissions. Responds in 1 month to queries. Responds in 4 months to mss. No response to e-mailed mss unless selected for publication. Sample copy for $3.50. Guidelines available online.

NONFICTION Needs general interest, historical, how-to, personal or spiritual growth, humor, inspirational, personal experience, religious, nature, God's unique creatures. Does not want "to see personal tributes to deceased relatives or friends. They are seldom used unless the subject of the article is well known. We also avoid articles about the moment a person finds Christ as his or her personal savior." Buys 50-60 mss/year. Send complete ms. Length: 1,500 words. **Pays $35-50.**

POETRY Submit 3 poems at a time. Lines/poem: 25 maximum. Considers previously published poems and simultaneous submissions. Accepts fax and e-mail (as attachment) submissions. Cover letter is preferred. "Include SASE if return is desired." Time

between acceptance and publication is up to 9 months. "Poems are selected by editor and reviewed by publication panel." Guidelines available for SASE or on website. Responds in 3 months. Pays credit and 1 contributor's copy. Acquires one-time rights.

MESSAGE MAGAZINE

Review and Herald Publishing Association, 55 West Oak Ridge Dr., Hagerstown MD 21740. (301)393-4099. **Fax:** (301)393-4103. **E-mail:** wjohnson@rhpa. org. **E-mail:** Message@rhpa.org. **Website:** www.messagemagazine.org. **Contact:** Washington Johnson. **10-20% freelance written.** Bimonthly magazine. "*Message* is the oldest religious journal addressing ethnic issues in the country. Our audience is predominantly Black and Seventh-day Adventist; however, *Message* is an outreach magazine for the churched and un-churched across cultural lines." Estab. 1898. Circ. 110,000. Byline given. Publishes ms an average of 12 months after acceptance. Editorial lead time 6 months. Submit seasonal material 6 months in advance. Responds in 9 months to queries. Sample copy by e-mail. Guidelines by e-mail and online.

NONFICTION Needs general interest; how-to (overcome depression, overcome defeat, get closer to God, learn from failure, deal with the economic crises, etc.). **Buys variable number of mss/year.** Send complete ms. Length: 800-1,200 words. **Payment varies. Payment upon acceptance.**

THE MESSENGER OF THE SACRED HEART

Apostleship of Prayer, 661 Greenwood Ave., Toronto ON M4J 4B3 Canada. (416)466-1195. **Website:** http://sacredheartcanada.com. **20% freelance written.** "Monthly magazine for Canadian and U.S. Catholics interested in developing a life of prayer and spirituality; stresses the great value of our ordinary actions and lives." Estab. 1891. Circ. 11,000. Byline given. Submit seasonal material 5 months in advance. NoResponds in 1 month to queries. Sample copy for $1 and 7½x10½ SAE. Guidelines for #10 SASE.

FICTION Contact: Rev. F.J. Power, S.J. and Alfred DeManche, editors. Needs religious, stories about people, adventure, heroism, humor, drama. No poetry. **Buys 12 mss/year.** Send complete ms. Length: 750-1,500 words. **Pays 8¢/word, and 3 contributor's copies.**

MY DAILY VISITOR

Our Sunday Visitor, Inc., Publishing Division, 200 Noll Plaza, Huntington IN 46750. (260)356-8400. **Fax:**

(260)356-8472. **E-mail:** mdvisitor@osv.com; mhogan@osv.com. **Website:** www.osv.com. **Contact:** Michelle Hogan, executive assistant. **99% freelance written.** Bimonthly magazine of Scripture meditations based on the day's Catholic Mass readings. Circ. 33,000. Byline given. Publishes ms an average of 6 months after acceptance. Accepts queries by mail, e-mail. Responds in 2 months to queries. Sample copy and writer's guidelines for #10 SAE with 3 first-class stamps.

NONFICTION Needs inspirational, personal experience, religious. **Buys 12 mss/year.** Query with published clips. 130-140 words times the number of days in month. **Pays $500 for 1 month (28-31) of meditations and 5 free copies.**

A NEW HEART

Hospital Christian Fellowship, Inc., P.O. Box 4004, San Clemente CA 92674. (949)496-7655. **Fax:** (949)496-8465. **E-mail:** hcfusa@gmail.com. **Website:** www.hcfusa.com. **50% freelance written.** Quarterly magazine covering articles and true stories that are health-related, with a Christian message, to encourage healthcare workers, patients, and volunteers to meet specific needs. Estab. 1978. Circ. 5,000. Byline given. Publishes ms an average of 4-6 months after acceptance. Editorial lead time 6 months. Submit seasonal material 6 months in advance. Accepts queries by mail, e-mail, fax, phone. Accepts simultaneous submissions. Responds in 2 weeks to queries. Sample copy free. Guidelines free.

NONFICTION Needs humor, inspirational, personal experience, religious. No fiction. **Buys 10-20 mss/year.** Query. Length: 500-1,500 words.

COLUMNS Book Review (medical/Christian), 200 words; Events (medical/Christian), 100-200 words; Chaplains (medical/Christian/inspirational), 200-250 words; On the Lighter Side (medical/clean fun), 100-200 words. **Buys 4-6 mss/year.** Send complete ms. **Pays in copies.**

FILLERS Needs anecdotes, gags, short humor. **Buys 4-10 mss/year.** Length: 50-100 words. **Pays in copies.**

$$ ONE

Catholic Near East Welfare Association, 1011 First Ave., New York NY 10022. (212)826-1480. **Fax:** (212)838-1344. **E-mail:** cnewa@cnewa.org. **Website:** www.cnewa.org. **75% freelance written.** Bimonthly magazine for a Catholic audience with interest in the Near East, particularly its current religious, cultural and political aspects. Estab. 1974. Circ. 100,000. Byline given. Publishes ms an average of 6 months after acceptance. Accepts queries by mail, fax. Responds in 1 month to queries. Sample copy and writer's guidelines for 7 ½×10 ½ SAE with 2 first-class stamps.

NONFICTION Length: 1,200-1,800 words. **Pays 20¢/edited word.**

$$ ON MISSION

North American Mission Board, SBC, 4200 North Point Pkwy., Alpharetta GA 30022-4176. **E-mail:** onmission@namb.net. **Website:** www.onmission.com. **25% freelance written.** Quarterly lifestyle magazine that popularizes evangelism, church planting and missions. "*On Mission*'s primary purpose is to tell the story of southern baptist missionaries in North America and to help readers and churches become more intentional about personal evangelism, church planting, and missions in North America. *On Mission* equips Christians for leading people to Christ and encourages churches to reach people through new congregations." Estab. 1998. Circ. 200,000. Byline given. Publishes ms an average of 6 months after acceptance. Editorial lead time 9 months. Submit seasonal material 9 months in advance. Accepts queries by mail, e-mail (prefers e-mail). Responds in 6 weeks to queries. Responds in 4 months to mss. Sample copy free or online. Guidelines available online.

NONFICTION Needs how-to, humor, personal experience, stories of sharing your faith in Christ with a non-Christian. **Buys 30 mss/year.** Query with published clips. Length: 350-1,200 words. **Pays 25¢/word, more for cover stories.** Pays expenses of writers on assignment.

COLUMNS **Buys 8 mss/year.** Blog posts Buys 48 per year. Query. **Pays 25¢/word.**

$$ OUR SUNDAY VISITOR

Our Sunday Visitor, Inc., 200 Noll Plaza, Huntington IN 46750. (260)356-8400. **Fax:** (260)356-8472. **E-mail:** oursunvis@osv.com; jnorton@osv.com. **Website:** www.osv.com. **Contact:** John Norton, editor. **70% freelance written. (Mostly assigned.).** Weekly publication covering world events and culture from a Catholic perspective. "We are a Catholic publishing company seeking to educate and deepen our readers in their faith. Currently emphasizing devotional, inspirational, catholic identity, apologetics, and catechetics." Estab. 1912. Circ. 60,000. Byline given. Publishes ms an average of 2-3 weeks after acceptance. Accepts queries by mail, e-mail. Sample copy for $2. Send a 10×13 SASE with 93 cents in postage affixed.

✿✿ OUTREACH MAGAZINE

Outreach, Inc., 2230 Oak Ridge Way, Vista CA 92081-2314. (760)940-0600. **Fax:** (760)597-2314. **E-mail:** tellus@outreachmagazine.com. **Website:** www.outreachmagazine.com. **80% freelance written.** Bimonthly magazine covering outreach. "*Outreach* is designed to inspire, challenge, and equip churches and church leaders to reach out to their communities with the love of Jesus Christ." Circ. 30,000, plus newsstand. Byline given. Offers 10% kill fee. Publishes ms an average of 2-4 months after acceptance. Editorial lead time 6 months. Submit seasonal material 6 months in advance. Accepts queries by mail, e-mail, fax. Mail submissions to Editor. Mark Query or Unsolicited manuscript on your envelope. E-mail submissions to editor@outreach.com. No phone calls, please. Accepts simultaneous submissions. Responds in 2 months to queries. Responds in 8 months to mss. Sample copy free. Guidelines free and online.

NONFICTION Needs book excerpts, how-to, humor, inspirational, interview, personal experience, photo feature, religious. Special issues: Vacation Bible School (January); Church Growth—America's Fastest-Growing Churches (Special Issue). Does not want fiction, poetry, non-outreach-related articles. **Buys 30 mss/year.** Query with published clips. Length: 1,500-2,500 words. **Pays $375-600 for assigned articles. Pays $375-500 for unsolicited articles.** Sometimes pays expenses of writers on assignment.

COLUMNS Contact: Lindy Lowry, editor. Pulse (short stories about outreach-oriented churches and ministries), 250-350 words; Soulfires (an as-told-to interview with a person about the stories and people that have fueled their passion for outreach), 900 words; Ideas (a profile of a church that is using a transferable idea or concept for outreach), 300 words, plus sidebar; Soulfires (short interviews with known voices about the stories and people that have informed their worldview and faith perspective), 600 words. **Buys 6 mss/year.** Query with published clips. **Pays $100-375.**

FILLERS Needs facts, gags. **Buys 6/year. mss/year.** Length: 25-100 words.

✿ THE PENTECOSTAL MESSENGER

Messenger Publishing House/Pentecostal Church of God, P.O. Box 850, Joplin MO 64802-0850. (417)624-7050. **Fax:** (417)624-7102. **E-mail:** charlotteb@pcg.

org. **Website:** www.pcg.org. **Contact:** Charlotte Beal. Monthly magazine covering Christian, inspirational, religious, leadership news. "Our organization is Pentecostal in nature. Our publication goes out to our ministers and laypeople to educate, inspire and inform them of topics around the world and in our organization that will help them in their daily walk." Estab. 1919. Circ. 5,000. Byline given. Editorial lead time 6 months. Submit themed material 6 months in advance. Accepts queries by mail. Accepts simultaneous submissions. May contact the *Pentecostal Messenger* for a list of monthly themes.

NONFICTION Needs book excerpts, essays, exposé, general interest, inspirational, interview, new product, personal experience, religious. **Buys 12-24 mss/year.** Send complete ms. Length: 750-2,000 words. **Pays $15-40.**

⊘ ✿✿ THE PLAIN TRUTH

Plain Truth Ministries, 300 W. Green St., Pasadena CA 91129. (800)309-4466. **Fax:** (626)358-4846. **E-mail:** managing.editor@ptm.org. **Website:** www.ptm.org. **90% freelance written.** Bimonthly magazine. "We seek to reignite the flame of shattered lives by illustrating the joy of a new life in Christ." Estab. 1935. Circ. 70,000. Byline given. Offers $50 kill fee. Publishes ms an average of 8 months after acceptance. Editorial lead time 6 months. Submit seasonal material 6 months in advance. Accepts queries by mail, e-mail. Accepts simultaneous submissions. Sample copy for sae with 9×12 envelope and 5 First-Class stamps. Guidelines available online.

NONFICTION Needs inspirational, interview, personal experience, religious. **Buys 48-50 mss/year.** Query with published clips and SASE. *No unsolicited mss.* Length: 750-2,500 words. **Pays 25¢/word.**

✿✿ POINT

Converge Worldwide (Baptist General Conference), 2002 S. Arlington Heights Rd., Arlington Heights IL 60005. **Fax:** (847)228-5376. **E-mail:** bob.putman@convergeww.org. **Website:** www.convergeworldwide.org. **5% freelance written.** Nonprofit, religious, evangelical Christian magazine published 4 times/year covering Converge Worldwide. "*Point* is the official magazine of Converge Worldwide (BCG). Almost exclusively uses articles related to Converge, our churches, or by/about Converge people." Circ. 43,000. Byline given. Offers 50% kill fee. Editorial lead time 6 months. Submit seasonal material 6 months in advance. Accepts queries by e-mail. Responds in 1 month to queries. Responds in 3 months to mss. Sample copy for #10 SASE. Writer's guidelines, theme list free.

NONFICTION Articles about our people, churches, missions. View online at: www.convergeworldwide.org. before sending anything. **Buys 20-30 mss/year.** Query with published clips. Length: 300-1,500 words. **Pays $60-280.** Sometimes pays expenses of writers on assignment.

COLUMNS Converge Connection (blurbs of news happening in Converge Worldwide), 50-150 words. Send complete ms. **Pays $30.**

🍁 $ PRAIRIE MESSENGER

Benedictine Monks of St. Peter's Abbey, P.O. Box 190, Muenster SK S0K 2Y0 Canada. 1+(306)682-1772. **Fax:** 1+(306)682-5285. **E-mail:** pm.canadian@stpeterspress.ca. **Website:** www.prairiemessenger.ca. **Contact:** Maureen Weber, associate editor. **10% Freelance written.** Weekly Catholic publication published by the Benedictine Monks of St. Peter's Abbey. Has a strong focus on ecumenism, social justice, interfaith relations, aboriginal issues, arts and culture. Estab. 1904. Circ. 5,000. Byline given. Publishes ms an average of 4 months after acceptance. Submit seasonal material 3 months in advance. Accepts queries by mail, e-mail, fax, phone. TrueAccepts simultaneous submissions. Responds only if interested, send nonreturnable samples. Sample copy for 9×12 SASE with $1 Canadian postage or IRCs. Guidelines available online. "Because of government subsidy regulations, we are no longer able to accept non-Canadian freelance material."

NONFICTION Needs interview, opinion, religious. "No articles on abortion." **Buys 15 mss/year.** Send complete ms. Length: 500-800 words. **Pays $60** Sometimes pays expenses of writers on assignment.

$ $ PRESBYTERIANS TODAY

Presbyterian Church (U.S.A.), 100 Witherspoon St., Louisville KY 40202-1396. (502)569-5520. **Fax:** (502)569-8887. **E-mail:** today@pcusa.org. **Website:** www.pcusa.org/today. **Contact:** Eva Stimson, editor; Shellee Marie Layman, art director. **25% freelance written. Prefers to work with published/established writers.** Denominational magazine published 10 times/year covering religion, denominational activities, and public issues for members of the Presbyterian Church (U.S.A.). "The magazine's purpose is to increase understanding and appreciation of what the church and its members are doing to live out their Christian faith." Estab. 1867. Circ. 40,000. Byline given. Offers 50% kill fee. Publishes ms an average of 6 months after acceptance. Editorial lead time 3 months. Submit seasonal material 3 months in advance. Accepts queries by mail, e-mail, fax, phone. Responds in 2 weeks to queries. Sample copy free. Guidelines available online.

NONFICTION Needs how-to, inspirational, Presbyterian programs, issues, people, everyday Christian issues. **Buys 20 mss/year.** Send complete ms. Length: 1,000-1,800 words. **Pays $300 maximum for assigned articles. Pays $75-300 for unsolicited articles.**

$ $ PRISM MAGAZINE

Evangelicals for Social Action, 6 E. Lancaster Ave., Wynnewood PA 19096. (484)384-2990. **E-mail:** kkomarni@eastern.edu. **Website:** www.prismmagazine.org. **50% freelance written.** Bimonthly magazine covering Christianity and social justice. "For holistic, Biblical, socially-concerned, progressive Christians." Estab. 1993. Circ. 2,500. Byline given. Publishes ms an average of 4-6 months after acceptance. Editorial lead time 4 months. Submit seasonal material 4 months in advance. Accepts queries by mail, e-mail. Responds in 1 month to queries; 3 months to mss. Hardcover sample copy for $3. PDF sample copy free. Request via website. Guidelines on website.

NONFICTION Needs essays on culture/faith, interviews, ministry profiles, reviews, etc. **Buys 10-12/year mss/year.** Send complete ms. Length: 500-3,000 words. **Pays $50-75 per printed page.**

$ PURPOSE

616 Walnut Ave., Scottdale PA 15683. (724)887-8500. **Fax:** (724)887-3111. **E-mail:** CarolD@MennoMedia.org; purposeeditor@mpn.net. **Website:** www.mpn.net. **Contact:** Carol Duerksen, editor. **75% freelance written.** Monthly magazine for adults, young and old, general audience with varied interests. Magazine focuses on Christian discipleship—how to be a faithful Christian in the midst of everyday life situations. Uses personal story form to present models and examples to encourage Christians in living a life of faithful discipleship. Estab. 1968. Circ. 8,500. Publishes ms an average of 18 months after acceptance. Submit seasonal material 1 year in advance. Accepts queries by e-mail. Accepts simultaneous submissions. Responds in 3 months to queries. Sample copy and writer's guidelines for 6×9 SAE and $2.

NONFICTION Buys 140 mss/year. E-mail submissions preferred.

FICTION Contact: Carol Duerksen, editor. Produce the story with specificity so that it appears to take place somewhere and with real people. Needs historical, related to discipleship theme, humorous, religious. No militaristic/narrow patriotism or racism. Send complete ms. Length: 600 words. **Pays up to 7¢ for stories, and 2 contributor's copies.**

POETRY Needs free verse, light verse, traditional. Buys 140 poems/year. Length: 12 lines. **Pays $7.50-20/poem depending on length and quality. Buys one-time rights only.**

FILLERS 6¢/word maximum.

QUAKER LIFE

Friends United Meeting, 101 Quaker Hill Dr., Richmond IN 47374. (765)962-7573. **Fax:** (765)966-1293. **E-mail:** quakerlife@fum.org. **Website:** www.fum. org. **Contact:** Katie Wonsik. **50% freelance written.** A Christian Quaker magazine published 6 times/year that covers news, inspirational, devotional, peace, equality, and justice issues. Estab. 1960. Circ. 3,000. Byline given. Publishes ms an average of 3-6 months after acceptance. Editorial lead time 2-3 months. Submit seasonal material 4-6 months in advance. Accepts queries by mail, e-mail. Accepts simultaneous submissions. Responds in 1 week to queries. Responds in 1-3 months to mss. Sample copy and writer's guidelines free.

NONFICTION Needs book excerpts, general interest, humor, inspirational, interview, personal experience, photo feature, religious, travel, bible study. No poetry or fiction. Query. Length: 400-1,500 words. **Pays 3 contributor's copies.**

COLUMNS News Brief (newsworthy events among Quakers), 75-200 words; Devotional/Inspirational (personal insights or spiritual turning points), 750 words; Ideas That Work (ideas from meetings that could be used by others), 750 words; Book/Media Reviews, 75-300 words.

RADIX MAGAZINE

Radix Magazine, Inc., P.O. Box 4307, Berkeley CA 94704. (510)548-5329. **E-mail:** radixmag@aol.com. **Website:** www.radixmagazine.com. **Contact:** Sharon Gallagher, editor. **10% freelance written.** Quarterly magazine. "*Radix Magazine*, published quarterly, is named for the Latin word for "root" and "has its roots both in the 'real world' and in the truth

of Christ's teachings." Wants poems "that reflect a Christian world-view, but aren't preachy." Has published poetry by John Leax, Czeslaw Milosz, Madeleine L'Engle, and Luci Shaw. *Radix* is 32 pages, magazine-sized, offset-printed, saddle-stapled, with 60-lb. self cover. Receives about 120 poems/year, accepts about 10%. Press run varies. Subscription: $15. Sample: $5. Make checks payable to *Radix Magazine*." Estab. 1979. Circ. 3,000. Byline given. Publishes ms 3 months to 3 years after acceptance. Editorial lead time 6 months. Submit seasonal material 6 months in advance. Accepts queries by e-mail. Responds in 2 months to queries and to mss. Sample copy for $5. Guidelines by e-mail.

NONFICTION Contact: Sharon Gallagher, editor. Needs essays, religious. Query. Length: 500-2,000 words.

POETRY Needs avant-garde, free verse, haiku. "Needs poetry." Submit 1-4 poems at a time. Buys 8 poems/year. Submit maximum 4 poems. Length: 4-20 lines. **Pays 2 contributor copies.**

RAILROAD EVANGELIST

Railroad Evangelist Association, Inc., P.O. Box 5026, Vancouver WA 98668. (360)699-7208. **E-mail:** rrjoe@ comcast.net. **Website:** www.railroadevangelist.com. **80% freelance written.** Magazine published 3 times/ year covering the railroad industry. "The *Railroad Evangelist*'s purpose and intent is to reach people everywhere with the life-changing gospel of Jesus Christ. The railroad industry is our primary target, along with model railroad and rail fans." Estab. 1938. Circ. 3,000/issue. Byline sometimes given. Editorial lead time 6 weeks. Submit seasonal material 6 weeks in advance. Accepts queries by mail, e-mail. Sample copy for SAE with 10×12 envelope and 3 first-class stamps. Guidelines for #10 SASE.

○ All content must be railroad related.

NONFICTION Needs inspirational, interview, personal experience, religious. Query. Length: 300-800 words.

COLUMNS Right Track (personal testimony), 300-800 words; Ladies Line (personal testimony), 300-500 words; Kids Corner (geared toward children), 50-100 words. Query. **Pays in contributor copies.**

FICTION Needs historical, religious. Query. Length: 300-800 words. **Pays in contributor copies.**

POETRY Needs traditional. Length: 10-100 lines. **Pays in contributor copies.**

⊕ ⊕ REFORM JUDAISM

633 Third Ave., 7th Floor, New York NY 10017-6778. (212)650-4240. **Fax:** (212)650-4249. **E-mail:** rjmagazine@urj.org. **Website:** www.reformjudaismmag.org. **30% freelance written.** Quarterly magazine of Jewish issues for contemporary Jews. "*Reform Judaism* is the official voice of the Union for Reform Judaism, linking the institutions and affiliates of Reform Judaism with every Reform Jew. *RJ* covers developments within the Movement while interpreting events and Jewish tradition from a Reform perspective." Estab. 1972. Circ. 310,000. Byline given. Offers kill fee for commissioned articles. Publishes ms an average of 3 months after acceptance. Submit seasonal material 6 months in advance. Accepts simultaneous submissions. Responds in 2 months to queries and to mss. Sample copy for $3.50. Guidelines available online.

NONFICTION **Buys 30 mss/year.** Submit complete ms. SASE is preferrable and will elicit a faster response. Cover stories: 2,500-3,500 words; major feature: 1,800-2,500 words; secondary feature: 1,200-1,500 words; department (e.g., travel): 1,200 words. **Pays 30¢/published word.** Sometimes pays expenses of writers on assignment.

FICTION Needs humorous, religious, sophisticated, cutting-edge, superb writing. **Buys 4 mss/year.** Send complete ms. Length: 600-2,500 words. **Pays 30¢/published word.**

⊕ ⊕ RELEVANT

Relevant Media Group, 900 N. Orange Ave., Winter Park FL 32789. (407)660-1411. **Fax:** (407)660-8555. **E-mail:** ryan@relevantmediagroup.com; alyce@relevantmediagroup.com. **Website:** www.relevantmagazine.com. **Contact:** Ryan Hamm, managing editor; Alyca Giligan, associate editor. **80% freelance written.** Bimonthly magazine covering God, life, and progressive culture. *Relevant* is a lifestyle magazine for Christians in their 20s and 30s. Estab. 2002. Circ. 83,000. Byline given. Pays 45 days after publication. Offers 50% kill fee. Publishes ms an average of 6 months after acceptance. Editorial lead time 4 months. Submit seasonal material 5 months in advance. Accepts queries by e-mail. Accepts simultaneous submissions. Responds in 6 weeks to queries. Responds in 3 months to mss. Sample copy available online. Guidelines available online.

NONFICTION Needs general interest, how-to, inspirational, interview, new product, personal experience, religious. Don't submit anything that doesn't target ages 18-34. Query with published clips. Length: 600-1,000 words. **Pays 10-15¢/word for assigned articles. Pays 10¢/word for unsolicited articles.** Sometimes pays expenses of writers on assignment.

⊕ RIVER REGION'S JOURNEY

P.O. Box 230367, Montgomery AL 36123. (334)213-7940. **Fax:** (334)213-7990. **E-mail:** info@readjourneymagazine.com. **Website:** www.readjourneymagazine.com. **Contact:** DeAnne Watson, editor. **50% freelance written.** Monthly magazine covering Christian living. Includes Protestant Christian writing, topical articles on Christian living, and Christian living articles with helpful information for walking with Christ daily. Estab. 1999. Circ. 8,000. Byline given. Offers 25% kill fee. Publishes ms an average of 6-12 months after acceptance. Editorial lead time 1 year. Submit seasonal material 1 year in advance. Accepts queries by e-mail. Accepts simultaneous submissions. Sample copy for $1.75 and self-addressed magazine-size envelope. Guidelines by e-mail.

NONFICTION Needs inspirational, religious. No fiction, poetry, or autobiography. Submit query or complete ms. Length: 1,300-2,200 words. **Pays $25-50 for assigned articles. Pays $25 for unsolicited articles.**

SACRED JOURNEY

Fellowship in Prayer, Inc., 291 Witherspoon St., Princeton NJ 08542. (609)924-6863. **Fax:** (609)924-6910. **E-mail:** submissions@sacredjourney.org. **Website:** www.fellowshipinprayer.org. **70% freelance written.** *Sacred Journey: The Journal of Fellowship in Prayer* is a quarterly multi-faith journal published winter, spring, summer, and autumn. Estab. 1950. Circ. 5,000. Editorial lead time 3 months. Submit seasonal material 4 months in advance. Accepts queries by e-mail (preferably). Accepts simultaneous submissions. Responds within 4 months of receipt. Submission is considered permission for publication. "We reserve the right to edit. We will make every effort to contact the author with content revisions. Please include or be prepared to provide a bio of 50-words or less and/or a headshot phot to accompany your work, should it be selected for the print journal." Free sample copy available online. Writer Guidelines are available online or by request.

NONFICTION **Buys 30 mss/year.** Send complete ms. Length: Approx. 750-1,500 words, double-spaced. **"If your work is selected for publication in the journal or on our website, you will receive a complimenta-**

ry 1-year subscription to *Sacred Journey* **if you work is selected for publication in the journal or on our website. For publication in the print journal you will also receive 5 copies of the issue in which your work appears.**"

POETRY "No poetry highly specific to a certain faith tradition. Nothing laden with specific faith terminology, nor a lot of Bibe quotes or other quotes." Submit maximum 5 per submission poems. Limited to 35 lines (occasionally longer).

🌐 THE SECRET PLACE

American Baptist Home Mission Societies, ABC/USA, P.O. Box 851, Valley Forge PA 19482-0851. (610)768-2434. **E-mail:** thesecretplace@abc-usa.org. **100% freelance written.** Quarterly devotional covering Christian daily devotions. Estab. 1937. Circ. 250,000. Byline given. Editorial lead time 1 year. Submit seasonal material 9 months in advance. For free sample and guidelines, send 6×9 SASE.

NONFICTION Needs inspirational. **Buys about 400 mss/year.** Send complete ms. Length: 100-200 words. **Pays $20.**

POETRY Needs avant-garde, free verse, light verse, traditional. Buys Publishes 12-15 poems/year. poems/year. Submit maximum Maximum number of poems: 6. poems. Length: 4-30 lines. **Pays $20.**

🌐🌐 SHARING THE VICTORY

Fellowship of Christian Athletes, 8701 Leeds Rd., Kansas City MO 64129. (816)921-0909. **Fax:** (816)921-8755. **E-mail:** stv@fca.org. **Website:** www.fca.org. **Contact:** Jill Ewert, managing editor; Matt Casner, art director. **50% freelance written. Prefers to work with published/established writers, but works with a growing number of new/unpublished writers each year.** Published 9 times/year. "We seek to serve as a ministry tool of the Fellowship of Christian Athletes by informing, inspiring and involving coaches, athletes and all whom they influence, that they may make an impact for Jesus Christ." Estab. 1959. Circ. 80,000. Byline given. Publishes ms an average of 4 months after acceptance. Submit seasonal material 6 months in advance. Responds to queries/mss in 3 months. Sample copy for $1 and 9×12 SASE with 3 first-class stamps. Guidelines available online.

NONFICTION Needs inspirational, interview, with name athletes and coaches solid in their faith, personal experience, photo feature. **Buys 5-20 mss/year.** Query. Considers electronic sumbissions via e-mail.

Length: 700-1,200 words. **Pays $150-400 for assigned and unsolicited articles.**

🌐 SOCIAL JUSTICE REVIEW

3835 Westminster Place, St. Louis MO 63108. (314)371-1653. **Fax:** (314)371-0889. **Website:** www.socialjusticereview.org. **25% freelance written. Works with a small number of new/unpublished writers each year.** Bimonthly magazine "to promote a true Christian Humanism with respect for the dignity and rights of all human beings." Estab. 1908. Publishes ms an average of 1 year after acceptance. Accepts queries by mail. Sample copy for SAE with 9×12 envelope and 3 first-class stamps.

NONFICTION Query by mail only with SASE. Length: 2,500-3,000 words. **Pays about 2¢/word.**

🌐 SPIRITUAL LIFE

2131 Lincoln Rd. NE, Washington DC 20002-1199. (888)616-1713; (202)832-5505. **Fax:** (202)832-5711. **E-mail:** edodonnell@aol.com. **Website:** www.spiritual-life.org. **Contact:** Edward O'Donnell, editor. **80% freelance written. Prefers to work with published/established writers.** Quarterly magazine for largely Christian, well-educated, serious readers. Circ. 12,000. Publishes ms an average of 1 year after acceptance. Responds in 2 months to queries. Sample copy and writer's guidelines for 7x10 or larger SAE with 5 first-class stamps.

NONFICTION Sentimental articles or those dealing with specific devotional practices not accepted. No fiction or poetry. **Buys 20 mss/year.** Length: 3,000-5,000 words. **Pays $50 minimum, and 2 contributor's copies.**

🌐🌐 ST. ANTHONY MESSENGER

28 W. Liberty St., Cincinnati OH 45202-6498. (513)241-5615. **Fax:** (513)241-0399. **E-mail:** mageditors@americancatholic.org. **Website:** www.americancatholic.org. **Contact:** John Feister. **55% freelance written.** Monthly general interest magazine for a national readership of Catholic families, most of which have children or grandchildren in grade school, high school, or college. *St. Anthony Messenger* is a Catholic family magazine which aims to help its readers lead more fully human and Christian lives. We publish articles which report on a changing church and world, opinion pieces written from the perspective of Christian faith and values, personality profiles, and fiction which entertains and informs. Estab. 1893.

CONSUMER MAGAZINES

Circ. 305,000. Byline given. Publishes ms an average of 1 year after acceptance. Submit seasonal material 6 months in advance. Accepts queries by mail, e-mail, fax. Responds in 3 weeks to queries. Responds in 2 months to mss. Sample copy for 9×12 SAE with 4 first-class stamps. Guidelines available online.

NONFICTION Needs how-to, on psychological and spiritual growth, problems of parenting/better parenting, marriage problems/marriage enrichment, humor, inspirational, interview, opinion, limited use; writer must have special qualifications for topic, personal experience, if pertinent to our purpose, photo feature, informational, social issues. **Buys 35-50 mss/year.** Query with published clips. Length: 2,000-2,500 words. **Pays 20¢/word.** Sometimes pays expenses of writers on assignment.

FICTION Contact: Father Pat McCloskey, O.F.M., editor. Needs mainstream, religious, senior citizen/retirement. "We do not want mawkishly sentimental or preachy fiction. Stories are most often rejected for poor plotting and characterization; bad dialogue—listen to how people talk; inadequate motivation. Many stories say nothing, are 'happenings' rather than stories. No fetal journals, no rewritten Bible stories." **Buys 12 mss/year.** Send complete ms. Length: 2,000-2,500 words. **Pays 16¢/word maximum and 2 contributor's copies; $1 charge for extras.**

POETRY Our poetry needs are very limited. Submit maximum 4-5 poems. Up to 20-25 lines; the shorter, the better. **Pays $2/line; $20 minimum.**

SUCCESS STORIES

Franklin Publishing Company, 2723 Steamboat Circle, Arlington TX 76006. (817)548-1124. **E-mail:** ludwigotto@sbcglobal.net. **Website:** www.franklinpublishing.net; www.londonpress.us. **Contact:** Dr. Ludwig Otto. **59% freelance written.** Monthly journal covering positive responses to the problems in life. Estab. 1983. Circ. 1,000. Byline given. Does not pay, but offers 15% discount on issues purchased and 1-year free membership in the International Association of Professionals. Publishes ms an average of 1 month after acceptance. Editorial lead time 1 month. Submit seasonal material 3 months in advance. Accepts queries by mail, e-mail. Accepts simultaneous submissions. Responds in 1 week to queries and to mss. Guidelines available online.

NONFICTION Needs book excerpts, essays, general interest, historical, how-to, humor, inspirational, interview, new product, opinion, personal experience, religious, technical, travel. Send complete ms. Length: 750-6,000 words.

FICTION Needs adventure, condensed novels, ethnic, horror, humorous, mainstream, mystery, novel concepts, religious, science fiction, slice-of-life vignettes of life, suspense, western. Send complete ms.

POETRY Needs avant-garde, free verse, haiku, light verse, traditional.

FILLERS Needs anecdotes, facts, gags.

⊙ ⊙ THIS ROCK

Catholic Answers, P.O. Box 199000, San Diego CA 92159. (619)387-7200. **Fax:** (619)387-0042. **Website:** www.catholic.com. **60% freelance written.** Monthly magazine covering Catholic apologetics and evangelization. Our content explains, defends and promotes Catholic teaching. Estab. 1990. Circ. 24,000. Byline given. Offers variable kill fee. Publishes ms an average of 4 months after acceptance. Accepts queries by e-mail. Responds in 2-4 weeks to queries. Responds in 1-2 months to mss. Sample copy available online. Guidelines by e-mail.

NONFICTION Needs book excerpts, essays, religious, conversion stories. **Buys 50 mss/year.** Send complete ms. Length: 1,500-3,000 words. **Pays $200-350.**

COLUMNS Damascus Road (stories of conversion to the Catholic Church), 2,000 words. **Buys 10 mss/year.** Send complete ms. **Pays $200.**

⊙ ⊙ THRIVE - THE EB ONLINE

Fellowship of Evangelical Baptist Churches in Canada, P.O. Box 457, Guelph ON N1H 6K9 Canada. 519-821-4830, ext. 229. **Fax:** 519-821-9829. **E-mail:** eb@fellowship.ca. **Website:** www.thrive-magazine.ca; www.fellowship.ca. **10% freelance written.** Online magazine covering religious, spiritual, Christian living, denominational, and missionary news. "We exist to enhance the life and ministry of the church leaders and members in Fellowship Congregations." Estab. 1953. Byline given. Publishes ms an average of 6 months after acceptance. Editorial lead time 4 months. Accepts queries by e-mail. Accepts simultaneous submissions. Sample copy available online. Guidelines available online.

NONFICTION Needs religious. No poetry, fiction, puzzles. **Buys 4-6 mss/year.** Send complete ms. Length: 600-2,400 words. **Pays $50.**

TRICYCLE

1115 Broadway Suite 1113, New York NY 10010. (6460461-9847. **E-mail:** editorial@tricycle.com. **Web-**

site: www.tricycle.com. **80% freelance written**. Quarterly magazine covering the impact of Buddhism on Western culture. *Tricycle* readers tend to be well educated and open minded. Estab. 1991. Circ. 60,000. Byline given. Offers 25% kill fee. Editorial lead time 3 months. Accepts queries by mail, e-mail, fax. Accepts simultaneous submissions. Responds in 3 months to queries & mss Sample copy for $7.95 or online at website. Guidelines available online.

NONFICTION Needs book excerpts, essays, general interest, historical, humor, inspirational, interview, personal experience, photo feature, religious, travel. **Buys 4-6 mss/year.** Length: 1,000-5,000 words.

COLUMNS Reviews (film, books, tapes), 600 words; Science and Gen Next, both 700 words. **Buys 6-8 mss/year.** Query.

🌙 $ THE UPPER ROOM

1908 Grand Ave., P.O. Box 340004, Nashville TN 37203. (615)340-7252. **Fax:** (615)340-7267. **E-mail:** theupperroommagazine@upperroom.org. **Website:** www.upperroom.org. **95% freelance written. Eager to work with new/unpublished writers.** Bimonthly magazine offering a daily inspirational message which includes a Bible reading, text, prayer, 'Thought for the Day,' and suggestion for further prayer. Each day's meditation is written by a different person and is usually a personal witness about discovering meaning and power for Christian living through scripture study which illuminates daily life. Circ. 2.2 million (U.S.); 385,000 outside U.S. Byline given. Publishes ms an average of 1 year after acceptance. Submit seasonal material 14 months in advance. Sample copy and writer's guidelines with a 4×6 SAE and 2 first-class stamps. Guidelines only for #10 SASE or online.

NONFICTION Needs inspirational, personal experience, Bible-study insights. Special issues: Lent and Easter; Advent. No poetry, lengthy spiritual journey stories. **Buys 365 unsolicited mss/year.** Send complete ms by mail or e-mail. Length: 300 words. **Pays $25/meditation.**

$ $ U.S. CATHOLIC

Claretian Publications, 205 W. Monroe St., Chicago IL 60606. (312)236-7782. **Fax:** (312)236-8207. **E-mail:** editors@uscatholic.org. **E-mail:** submissions@uscatholic.org. **Website:** www.uscatholic.org. **100% freelance written.** Monthly magazine covering Roman Catholic spirituality. "*U.S. Catholic* is dedicated to the belief that it makes a difference whether you're Catholic. We invite and help our readers explore the wisdom of their faith tradition and apply their faith to the challenges of the 21st century." Estab. 1935. Circ. 40,000. Byline given. Publishes ms an average of 2-3 months after acceptance. Editorial lead time 8 months. Submit seasonal material 6 months in advance. Accepts queries by mail, e-mail, fax, phone. Responds in 1 month to queries. Responds in 2 months to mss. Sample copy for large SASE. Guidelines by e-mail or on website.

⭕ Please include SASE with written ms.

NONFICTION Needs essays, inspirational, opinion, personal experience, religious. **Buys 100 mss/year.** Send complete ms. Length: 2,500-3,500 words. **Pays $250-600.** Sometimes pays expenses of writers on assignment.

COLUMNS Pays $250-600.

FICTION Contact: Maureen Abood, literary editor. Accepts short stories. "Topics vary, but unpublished fiction should be no longer than 2,500 words and should include strong characters and cause readers to stop for a moment and consider their relationships with others, the world, and/or God. Specifically religious themes are not required; subject matter is not restricted. E-mail literaryeditor@uscatholic.org. Usually responds in 8-10 weeks. Minimum payment is $300." Needs ethnic, mainstream, religious, slice-of-life vignettes. **Buys 4-6 mss/year.** Send complete ms. Length: 2,500-3,000 words. **Pays $300.**

POETRY Contact: Maureen Abood, literary editor. Needs free verse. Submit 3-5 poems at a time. Lines/poem: 50 maximum. Considers simultaneous submissions; no previously published poems. Accepts e-mail submissions (pasted into body of message; no attachments). Cover letter is preferred. "Always include SASE." Time between acceptance and publication is 3 months. Poems are circulated to an editorial board. Seldom comments on rejected poems. Guidelines available for SASE or on website. Responds in 3 months. Pays $75/poem and 5 contributor's copies. Acquires first North American serial rights. No light verse. Buys 12 poems/year. Submit maximum 5 poems. Length: 50 lines. **Pays $75.**

$ $ THE WAR CRY

The Salvation Army, 615 Slaters Lane, Alexandria VA 22314. (703)684-5500. **Fax:** (703)684-5539. **E-mail:** war_cry@usn.salvationarmy.org. **5% freelance written.** Biweekly magazine covering evangelism and

Christian growth stories. Estab. 1881. Circ. 250,000. Byline given. Publishes ms an average of 2 months to 1 year after acceptance. Editorial lead time 6 weeks. Submit seasonal material 1 year in advance. Responds in 3-4 weeks to mss. Sample copy, theme list, and writer's guidelines free for #10 SASE or online.

NONFICTION Needs inspirational, interview, personal experience, religious. No missionary stories, confessions. **Buys 25 mss/year.** Send complete ms. **Pays 15¢/word for articles.**

FILLERS Needs anecdotes, inspirational. **Buys 10-20 mss/year.** Length: 200-500 words. **Pays 15¢/word.**

⑤ WESLEYAN LIFE

The Wesleyan Publishing House, P.O. Box 50434, Indianapolis IN 46250. (317)774-7909. **Fax:** (317)774-3924. **E-mail:** communications@wesleyan.org. **Website:** www.wesleyanlifeonline.com. Quarterly magazine of The Wesleyan Church. Estab. 1842. Circ. 50,000. Byline given. Submit seasonal material 6 months in advance. Accepts simultaneous submissions.

NONFICTION Needs inspirational, religious. No poetry accepted. Send complete ms. Length: 250-400 words. **Pays $25-150.**

⦿ ⑤ WOMAN ALIVE

Christian Publishing and Outreach, Garcia Estate, Canterbury Rd., Worthing West Sussex BN13 1BW United Kingdom. 44)(190)360-4379. **E-mail:** womanalive@cpo.org.uk. **Website:** www.womanalive.co.uk. **Contact:** Jackie Harris, editor; Sharon Barnard, assistant editor. "Christian magazine geared specifically toward women. It covers all denominations and seeks to inspire, encourage, and provide resources to women in their faith, helping them to grow in their relationship with God and providing practical help and biblical perspective on the issues impacting their lives." Accepts queries by mail, e-mail. Sample copy for £1.50, plus postage. Guidelines by email.

NONFICTION Needs how-to, personal experience, travel, also, building life skills and discipleship, interviews with Christian women in prominent positions or who are making a difference in their communities/jobs, women facing difficult challenges or taking on new challenges, affordable holiday destinations written from a Christian perspective. Submit clips, bio, article summary, ms, SASE. 750-900/1-page article; 1,200-1,300/2-page article; 1,500-1,600/3-page article. **Pays £75/1-page article; £95/2-page article; £125/3-page article.**

PHOTOS Send photos. Reviews 300 dpi digital images.

RETIREMENT

⑤⑤⑤⑤ AARP THE MAGAZINE

AARP, c/o Editorial Submissions, 601 E. St. NW, Washington DC 20049. **E-mail:** aarpmagazine@aarp.org. **Website:** www.aarp.org/magazine. **Contact:** Editorial Submissions. **50% freelance written. Prefers to work with published/established writers.** Bimonthly magazine. "*AARP The Magazine* is devoted to the varied needs and active life interests of AARP members, age 50 and over, covering such topics as financial planning, travel, health, careers, retirement, relationships, and social and cultural change. Its editorial content serves the mission of AARP seeking through education, advocacy and service to enhance the quality of life for all by promoting independence, dignity, and purpose." Circ. 21,500,000. Byline given. Offers 25% kill fee. Publishes ms an average of 6 months after acceptance. Submit seasonal material 6 months in advance. Accepts queries by mail, e-mail only. No-Responds in 3 months to queries. Sample copy free. Guidelines available online.

NONFICTION No previously published articles. Query with published clips. *No unsolicited mss.* Length: Up to 2,000 words. **Pays $1/word.** Sometimes pays expenses of writers on assignment.

⑤ MATURE LIVING

Lifeway Christian Resources, 1 Lifeway Plaza, Nashville TN 37234. (615)251-2000. **E-mail:** matureliving@lifeway.com. **Website:** www.lifeway.com. **Contact:** Rene Holt. **90% freelance written.** "Monthly leisure reading magazine for senior adults 55 and older. *Mature Living* is Christian in content and the material required is what would appeal to 55 and over age group: inspirational, informational, nostalgic, humorous. Our magazine is distributed mainly through churches (especially Southern Baptist churches) that buy the magazine in bulk and distribute it to members in this age group." Estab. 1977. Circ. 320,000. Byline given. Publishes ms an average of 7-8 weeks after acceptance. Submit seasonal material 1 year in advance. Responds in 3 months to mss. Sample copy for 9×12 SAE with 4 first-class stamps. Guidelines for #10 sase.

NONFICTION Needs general interest, historical, how-to, humor, inspirational, interview, personal experience, travel, crafts. No pornography, profanity, occult, liquor, dancing, drugs, gambling. **Buys 100 mss/year.** Length: 600-1,200 words. **Pays $85-115**

COLUMNS Cracker Barrel (brief, humorous, original quips and verses), **pays $15**; Grandparents' Brag Board (something humorous or insightful said or done by your grandchild or great-grandchild), **pays $15**; Inspirational (devotional items), **pays $25**; Food (introduction and 4-6 recipes), **pays $50**; Over the Garden Fence (vegetable or flower gardening), **pays $40**; Crafts (step-by-step procedures), **pays $40**; Game Page (crossword or word-search puzzles and quizzes), **pays $40.**

FICTION Contact: David Seay, editor-in-chief. Needs humorous, religious, senior citizen/retirement. No reference to liquor, dancing, drugs, gambling; no pornography, profanity or occult. **Buys 12 mss/year.** Send complete ms. 900-1,200 words preferred **Pays $85-115; 3 contributor's copies.**

POETRY Buys 24 poems/year. Submit maximum 5 poems. Length: 12-16 lines. **Pays $-25.**

$ MATURE YEARS

The United Methodist Publishing House, 201 Eighth Ave. S., P.O. Box 801, Nashville TN 37202-0801. (615)749-6292. **Fax:** (615)749-6512. **E-mail:** matureyears@umpublishing.org. **80% freelance written. Prefers to work with published/established writers.** Quarterly magazine designed to help persons in and nearing the retirement years understand and appropriate the resources of the Christian faith in dealing with specific problems and opportunities related to aging. Estab. 1954. Circ. 55,000. Publishes ms an average of 1 year after acceptance. Submit seasonal material 14 months in advance. Responds in 2 weeks to queries. Responds in 2 months to mss. Sample copy for $6 and 9×12 SAE. Writer's guidelines for #10 SASE or by e-mail.

NONFICTION Needs how-to, hobbies, inspirational, religious, travel, special guidelines, older adult health, finance issues. **Buys 75-80 mss/year.** Send complete ms; e-mail submissions preferred. Length: 900-2,000 words. **Pays $45-125.** Sometimes pays expenses of writers on assignment.

COLUMNS Health Hints (retirement, health), 900-1,500 words; Going Places (travel, pilgrimage), 1,000-1,500 words; Fragments of Life (personal inspiration), 250-600 words; Modern Revelations (religious/inspirational), 900-1,500 words; Money Matters (personal finance), 1,200-1,800 words; Merry-Go-Round (cartoons, jokes, 4-6 line humorous verse); Puzzle Time (religious puzzles, crosswords). **Buys 4 mss/year.** Send complete ms. **Pays $25-45.**

FICTION Contact: Marvin Cropsey, editor. Needs humorous, religious, slice-of-life vignettes, retirement years nostalgia, intergenerational relationships. "We don't want anything poking fun at old age, saccharine stories, or anything not for older adults. Must show older adults (age 55 plus) in a positive manner." **Buys 4 mss/year.** Send complete ms. Length: 1,000-2,000 words. **Pays $60-125.**

POETRY Needs free verse, haiku, light verse, traditional. Buys 24 poems/year. Submit maximum 6 poems. Length: 3-16 lines. **Pays $5-20.**

RURAL

$$ BACKWOODS HOME MAGAZINE

P.O. Box 712, Gold Beach OR 97444. (541)247-8900. **Fax:** (541)247-8600. **E-mail:** editor@backwoodshome.com; letters@backwoodshome.com. **E-mail:** article-submission@backwoodshome.com. **Website:** www.backwoodshome.com. **Contact:** Dave Duffy, editor and publisher. **90% freelance written.** Bimonthly magazine covering self-reliance. "*Backwoods Home Magazine* is written for people who have a desire to pursue personal independence, self-sufficiency, and their dreams. We offer 'how-to' articles on self-reliance." Estab. 1989. Circ. 38,000. Byline given. Editorial lead time 4-6 months. Submit seasonal material 4-6 months in advance. Accepts queries by mail, e-mail. Sample copy for 9x10 SAE and 6 first-class stamps. Guidelines free online.

NONFICTION Needs general interest, how-to, humor, personal experience, technical. **Buys 120 mss/year.** Send complete ms, no attachments. Length: 500 words. **Pays $30-200.**

🍁 $$ THE COUNTRY CONNECTION

Pinecone Publishing, 691 Pinecrest Rd., Boulter ON K0L 1G0 Canada. (866)332-3651; (613)332-3651. **Website:** www.pinecone.on.ca. **Contact:** Gus Zylstra, publisher. **100% freelance written.** Magazine published 4 times/year covering nature, environment, history, heritage, nostalgia, travel and the arts. *The Country Connection* is a magazine for true nature lovers and the rural adventurer. Building on our commitment to heritage, cultural, artistic, and environmental themes, we continually add new topics to illuminate the country experience of people living within na-

CONSUMER MAGAZINES

ture. Our goal is to chronicle rural life in its many aspects, giving 'voice' to the countryside. Estab. 1989. Circ. 4,000. Byline given. Publishes ms an average of 4 months after acceptance. Editorial lead time 4 months. Accepts queries by mail, e-mail, phone. Sample copy for $5.64. Guidelines available online.

NONFICTION Needs general interest, historical, humor, opinion, personal experience, travel, lifestyle, leisure, art and culture, vegan recipes. No hunting, fishing, animal husbandry, or pet articles. **Buys 60 mss/year.** Send complete ms. Length: 500-2,000 words. **Pays 10¢/word.**

FICTION Needs adventure, fantasy, historical, humorous, slice-of-life vignettes, country living. **Buys 10 mss/year.** Send complete ms. Length: 500-1,500 words. **Pays 10¢/word.**

🌐💲 FARM & RANCH LIVING

Reiman Media Group, 5400 S. 60th St., Greendale WI 53129. (414)423-0100. **Fax:** (414)423-8463. **E-mail:** editors@farmandranchliving.com. **Website:** www.farmandranchliving.com. **30% freelance written. Eager to work with new/unpublished writers.** Bimonthly magazine aimed at families that farm or ranch full time. *F&RL* is *not* a 'how-to' magazine—it focuses on people rather than products and profits. Estab. 1978. Circ. 400,000. Byline given. Publishes ms an average of 6 months after acceptance. Submit seasonal material 6 months in advance. Accepts queries by mail, e-mail, fax. Responds in 6 weeks to queries. Sample copy for $2. Guidelines for #10 SASE.

NONFICTION Needs humor, rural only, inspirational, interview, personal experience, farm/ranch related, photo feature, nostalgia, prettiest place in the country (photo/text tour of ranch or farm). No issue-oriented stories (pollution, animal rights, etc.). **Buys 30 mss/year.** Send complete ms. Length: 600-1,200 words. **Pays up to $300 for text/photo package. Payment for Prettiest Place negotiable.**

MONADNOCK TABLE: THE GUIDE TO OUR REGION'S FOOD, FARMS, & COMMUNITY

P.O. Box 1504, Keene NH 03431. **E-mail:** editor@monadnocktable.com. **Website:** www.monadnocktable.com. **Contact:** Marcia Passos Duffy, managing editor and editorial director. Quarterly Magazine for local food/farms in the Monadnock Region of New Hampshire. Estab. 2010. Circ. 10,000. Byline given. Publishes ms an average of 3 months after acceptance. 25% Kill fee. Editorial lead time 3 months. Submit seasonal material

3 months in advance. Accepts queries by e-mail. Reports in 4 weeks on queries; 1 month mss. Sample copy available online. Guidelines are available on website.

NONFICTION Contact: Marcia Passos Duffy, editorial director. Needs book excerpts, essays, how-to, interview, opinion, personal experience. 500-1,000. **Pays 10¢ per word.** Sometimes pays expenses of writers on assignment. (limit agreed upon in advance)

COLUMNS Our Local Farmer (profile of local farmer in Monadnock Region), up to 800 words; Local Eats (profile of local chef and/or restaurant using local food), up to 800 words; Feature (how-to or "think" piece about local foods), up 1,000; Books/Opinion/Commentary (review of books, book excerpt, commentary, opinion pieces about local food), up to 500 words. **Buys 10 mss/year.** Query.

💲 MOTHER EARTH NEWS

Ogden Publications, 1503 SW 42nd St., Topeka KS 66609-1265. (785)274-4300. **E-mail:** letters@motherearthnews.com. **Website:** www.motherearthnews.com. **Contact:** Cheryl Long, editor-in-chief. **Mostly written by staff and team of established freelancers.** Bimonthly magazine emphasizing country living, country skills, natural health and sustainable technologies for both long-time and would-be ruralists. *"Mother Earth News* promotes self-sufficient, financially independent and environmentally aware lifestyles. Many of our feature articles are written by our Contributing Editors, but we also assign articles to freelance writers, particularly those who have experience with our subject matter (both firsthand adn writing experience." Circ. 350,000. Byline given. Submit seasonal material 5 months in advance. Responds in 6 months to mss. Sample copy for $5. Guidelines for #10 SASE.

NONFICTION Needs how-to, green building, do-it-yourself, organic gardening, whole foods & cooking, natural health, livestock & sustainable farming, renewable energy, 21st century homesteading, nature-environment-community, green transportation. No fiction, please. **Buys 35-50 mss/year.** "Query. Please send a short synopsis of the idea, a one-page outline and any relevant digital photos, and samples. If available, please send us copies of one or two published articles, or tell us where to find them online." "Country Lore" length: 100-300/words. "Firsthand Reports" length: 1,500-2,000/words **Pays $25-150.**

COLUMNS Country Lore (helpful how-to tips); 100-300/words; Firsthand Reports (first-person stories about sustainable lifestyles of all sorts), 1,500-2,000/words.

💲💲 RANGE MAGAZINE

Purple Coyote Corp., 106 E. Adams St., Suite 201, Carson City NV 89706. (775)884-2200. **Fax:** (775)884-2213. **E-mail:** edit@rangemagazine.com. **Website:** www.rangemagazine.com. **70% freelance written.** Quarterly magazine. *RANGE* magazine covers ranching and farming and the issues that affect agriculture. Estab. 1991. Publishes ms an average of 6 months after acceptance. Accepts queries by e-mail. Responds in 6-8 weeks to queries. Responds in 3-6 months to mss. Sample copy for $2. Guidelines available online.

NONFICTION Needs personal experience, photo feature, Major ranch features in American west, issues that affect ranchers, profiles, short book excerpts that suit range, humor, photo essays. No sports or events. Writer must be familiar with range. No rodeos or events. No rodeos or anything by a writer not familiar with *RANGE*. Query. Length: 500-2,000 words. **Pays $50-400.**

💲 RURAL HERITAGE

P.O. Box 2067, Cedar Rapids IA 52406. (319)362-3027. **E-mail:** editor@ruralheritage.com. **Website:** www.ruralheritage.com. **Contact:** Gail Damerow, editor. **98% freelance written. Willing to work with a small number of new/unpublished writers.** Bimonthly magazine devoted to the training and care of draft animals. Estab. 1976. Circ. 9,500. Byline given. Publishes ms an average of 6 months after acceptance. Submit seasonal material 6 months in advance. Accepts queries by mail, e-mail. Responds in 3 months to queries. Sample copy for $8. Guidelines available online.

NONFICTION Needs how-to, farming with draft animals, interview, people using draft animals, photo feature. No articles on *mechanized* farming. **Buys 200 mss/year.** Query or send complete ms. Length: 1,200-1,500 words. **Pays 5¢/word.**

POETRY Needs traditional. **Pays $5-25.**

💲💲 RURALITE

P.O. Box 558, Forest Grove OR 97116-0558. (503)357-2105. **Fax:** (503)357-8615. **E-mail:** editor@ruralite.org. **E-mail:** curtisc@ruralite.org. **Website:** www.ruralite.org. **80% freelance written. Works with new, unpublished writers.** Monthly magazine aimed at members of consumer-owned electric utilities throughout 10 western states, including Alaska. Publishes 48 region-al editions. Estab. 1954. Circ. 325,000. Byline given. Accepts queries by mail. Responds in 1 month to queries. Sample copy for 9×12 SAE with $1.28 of postage affixed. Guidelines available online.

NONFICTION Buys 50-60 mss/year. Query. Length: 100-2,000 words. **Pays $50-500.**

SCIENCE

💲💲💲💲 AMERICAN ARCHAEOLOGY

The Archaeological Conservancy, 5301 Central Ave. NE, #902, Albuquerque NM 87108. (505)266-9668. **Fax:** (505)266-0311. **E-mail:** tacmag@nm.net. **Website:** www.americanarchaeology.org. **Contact:** Michael Bawaya, editor; Vicki Singer, art director. **60% freelance written.** Quarterly magazine. "We're a popular archaeology magazine. Our readers are very interested in this science. Our features cover important digs, prominent archaeologists, and most any aspect of the science. We only cover North America." Estab. 1997. Circ. 35,000. Byline given. Offers 20% kill fee. Publishes ms an average of 3 months after acceptance. Editorial lead time 3 months. Accepts queries by mail, e-mail, fax. Responds in 3 weeks to queries. Responds in 1 month to mss

NONFICTION No fiction, poetry, humor. **Buys 15 mss/year.** Query with published clips. Length: 1,500-3,000 words. **Pays $1,000-2,000.** Pays expenses of writers on assignment.

PHOTOS State availability. Identification of subjects required. Reviews transparencies, prints. Pays $50 and up for occasional stock images; assigns work by project (pay varies); negotiable. Credit line given. Buys one-time rights. Offers $400-600/photo shoot. Negotiates payment individually.

💲💲💲💲 ARCHAEOLOGY

Archaeological Institute of America, 36-36 33rd St., Long Island NY 11106. (718)472-3050. **Fax:** (718)472-3051. **E-mail:** cvalentino@archaeology.org. **E-mail:** editorial@archaeology.org. **Website:** www.archaeology.org. **Contact:** Editor-in-chief. **50% freelance written.** *ARCHAEOLOGY* combines worldwide archaeological findings with photography, specially rendered maps, drawings, and charts. Covers current excavations and recent discoveries, and includes personality profiles, technology updates, adventure, travel and studies of ancient cultures. "*ARCHAEOLOGY* magazine is a publication of the Archaeological Institute of America, a 130-year-old nonprofit organization.

The magazine has been published continuously for more than 60 years. We have a total audience of nearly 750,000, mostly in the United States and Canada. Our readership is a combination of the general public, enthusiastic amateurs, and scholars in the field. Publishing bimonthly, we bring our readers all the exciting aspects of archaeology: adventure, discovery, culture, history, technology, and travel. Authors include both professional journalists and professional archaeologists. If you are a scientist interested in writing about your research for *ARCHAEOLOGY*, see tips and suggestions on writing for a general audience online." Estab. 1948. Circ. 750,000. Byline given. Offers 25% kill fee. Submit seasonal material 6 months in advance. Accepts queries by mail, e-mail, fax. Accepts simultaneous submissions. Sample copy and writer's guidelines free. Guidelines online. Request photographer's sample copy for $6 through paypal to scribblesbyshannon@yahoo.com.

NONFICTION Needs essays, general interest. "Our reviews department looks for short (250- to 500-word) articles on museums, books, television shows, movies, websites, and games of interest to our readers. While the material reviewed may not be purely archaeological in nature, it should have a strong archaeological element to it. Reviews should not simply summarize the material, but provide a critical evaluation." **Buys 6 mss/year.** Query preferred. "Preliminary queries should be no more than 1 or 2 pages (500 words max.) in length and may be sent to the Editor-in-Chief by mail or via e-mail to editorial@archaeology.org. We do not accept telephone queries. Check our online index and search to make sure that we have not already published a similar article. Your query should tell us the following: who you are, why you are qualified to cover the subject, how you will cover the subject (with an emphasis on narrative structure, new knowledge, etc.), and why our readers would be interested in the subject." Length: 1,000-3,000 words. **Pays $2,000 maximum.** Sometimes pays expenses of writers on assignment.

COLUMNS Insider is a piece of about 2,500 words dealing with subject matter with which the author has an intimate, personal interest. **Conversation** is a one-page interview in a Q&A format with someone who has made a considerable impact on the field of archaeology or has done something unusual or intriguing. **Letter From..** is an account of a personal experience involving a particular topic or site. "Letters" have included a visit to an alien-archaeology theme park, the account of an archaeologist caught in a civil war, and an overnight stay with the guards at Angkor Wat. "Letters" are usually about 2,500 to 3,000 words in length. **Artifact** is the last editorial page of the magazine. Its purpose is to introduce the reader to a single artifact that reveals something surprising about a site or an historical event. Unusual artifacts recently excavated are preferred and visuals must be of the highest quality. The writer must explain the archaeological context, date, site found, etc., as well as summarize the artifact's importance in about 200 words or less. First person accounts by the actual excavators or specialists are preferred, although exceptions are be made.

$ $ ASTRONOMY

Kalmbach Publishing, 21027 Crossroads Circle, P.O. Box 1612, Waukesha WI 53187-1612. (800)533-6644. **Fax:** (262)796-1615. **Website:** www.astronomy.com. David J. Eicher, editor. **Contact:** LuAnn Williams Belter, art director (for art and photography). **50% of articles submitted and written by science writers; includes commissioned and unsolicited.** Monthly magazine covering the science and hobby of astronomy. "Half of our magazine is for hobbyists (who are active observers of the sky); the other half is directed toward armchair astronomers who are intrigued by the science." Estab. 1973. Circ. 122,000. Byline given. Responds in 1 month to queries. Responds in 3 months to mss. Guidelines for #10 SASE or on website.

NONFICTION Needs book excerpts, new product, announcements, photo feature, technical, space, astronomy. **Buys 75 mss/year.** Query. Length: 500-3,000 words. **Pays $100-1,000.**

$ $ $ $ BIOSCIENCE

American Institute of Biological Sciences, 1900 Campus Commons Dr., Suite 200, Reston VA 20191. (202)628-1500. **Fax:** (202)628-1509. **E-mail:** tbeardsley@aibs.org. **Website:** www.aibs.org. James Verdier, managing editor, jverdier@aibs.org. **Contact:** Dr. Timothy M. Beardsley, editor-in-chief. **5% freelance written.** Monthly peer-reviewed scientific journal covering organisms from molecules to the environment. "We contract professional science writers to write features on assigned topics, including organismal biology and ecology, but excluding biomedical topics." Estab. 1951. Byline given. Publishes ms an average of 3 months after acceptance. Editorial lead time 2 months. Accepts queries by e-mail. Responds in 2-3 weeks to queries. Sample copy on website. Guidelines free.

NONFICTION Does not want biomedical topics. **Buys 10 mss/year.** Query. Length: 1,500-3,000 words. **Pays $1,500-3,000.** Sometimes pays expenses of writers on assignment.

$$$ CHEMICAL HERITAGE

Chemical Heritage Foundation (CHF), 315 Chestnut St., Philadelphia PA 19106. (215)925-2222. **E-mail:** editor@chemheritage.org. **Website:** www.chemheritage.org. **40% freelance written.** The magazine is published three times per year. *Chemical Heritage* reports on the history of the chemical and molecular sciences and industries, on CHF activities, and on other activities of interest to our readers. Estab. 1982. Circ. 20,000. Byline given. Publishes ms an average of 6-12 months after acceptance. Editorial lead time 4 months. Accepts queries by mail, e-mail, phone. Responds in 1 month to queries and to mss. Sample copy free.

NONFICTION Needs book excerpts, essays, historical, interview. No exposés or excessively technical material. Many of our readers are highly educated professionals, but they may not be familiar with, for example, specific chemical processes. **Buys 3-5 mss/year.** Query. Length: 1,000-3,500 words. **Pays 50¢ to $1/word.**

COLUMNS Contact: Associate Editor: Jennifer Dionisio, jdionisio@chemheritage.org). Book reviews: 200 or 750 words; CHF collections: 300-500 words; policy: 1,000 words; personal remembrances: 750 words; profiles of CHF awardees and oral history subjects: 600-900 words: buys 3-5 mms/year. **Buys 10 mss/year.** Query.

🌐 $$ COSMOS MAGAZINE

Luna Media Pty Ltd., Level 1, 49 Shepherd St., Chippendale, Sydney NSW 2008 Australia. (61)(2)9310-8500. **Fax:** (61)(2)9698-4899. **E-mail:** submissions@cosmosmagazine.com. **Website:** www.cosmosmagazine.com. **90% freelance written.** Bimonthly magazine covering science. "An Australian brand with a global outlook, *COSMOS* internationally respected for its literary writing, excellence in design and engaging breadth of content. Won the 2009 Magazine of the Year and twice Editor of the Year at the annual Bell Awards for Publishing Excellence; the American Institute of Physics Science Writing Award; the Reuters/IUCN Award for Excellence in Environmental Journalism; the City of Sydney Lord Mayor's Sustainability Award and an Earth Journalism Award. *COSMOS* is the brainchild of Wilson da Silva, a former ABC TV science reporter and past president of the World Federation of Science Journalists. It is backed by an editorial advisory Board that includes Apollo 11 astronaut Buzz Aldrin, ABC Radio's Robyn Williams, and is chaired by Dr. Alan Finkel, the neuroscientist and philanthropist who is the Chancellor of Monash University in Melbourne." Estab. 2005. Circ. 25,000. Byline given. Offers up to 50% kill fee. Publishes ms an average of 1 month after acceptance. Editorial lead time 2 months. Submit seasonal material 3 months in advance. Accepts queries by e-mail, fax. Accepts simultaneous submissions. Responds in 1 month to queries. Responds in 3 months to mss. Guidelines available online.

NONFICTION Needs book excerpts, essays, exposé, historical, humor, interview, opinion, photo feature, travel. **Buys 250 mss/year.** Query with published clips. Length: 700-5,000 words. **Pays 60¢/word for assigned articles. Pays 30¢/word for unsolicited articles.** Sometimes pays expenses of writers on assignment.

COLUMNS Travelogue (travel to an intriguing/unusual place that involves science), 1,500-2,000 words. Query. **Pays $1,200-1,700**

FICTION Needs science fiction. No fantasy—science fiction only. **Buys 8 mss/year.** Length: 2,000-4,000 words. **Pays flat $300 per story.**

$$$$ INVENTORS DIGEST

Inventors Digest, LLC, 520 Elliot St., Suite 200, Charlotte NC 28202. (704)369-7312. **Fax:** (704)333-5115. **E-mail:** info@inventorsdigest.com. **Website:** www.inventorsdigest.com/about-us. **50% freelance written.** Monthly magazine covering inventions, technology, engineering, intellectual property issues. Inventors Digest is committed to educating and inspiring entry- and enterprise-level inventors and professional innovators. As the leading print and online publication for the innovation culture, *Inventors Digest* delivers useful, entertaining and cutting-edge information to help its readers succeed. Estab. 1983. Circ. 40,000. Byline given. Offers 40% kill fee. Publishes ms an average of 2 months after acceptance. Editorial lead time 2 months. Submit seasonal material 4 months in advance. Accepts queries by mail, e-mail. Responds in 3 weeks to queries. Responds in 1 month to mss. Sample copy available online. Guidelines free.

NONFICTION Needs book excerpts, historical, how-to, secure a patent, find a licensing manufacturer, avoid scams, inspirational, interview, new product, opinion, (does not mean letters to the editor), personal experience, technical. Special issues: Our editorial calendar is available at our website, http://inventorsdigest.com/images/Inventors%20Digest%20Media%20Kit_R08.pdf. "We don't want poetry. No stories that talk about readers—stay away from 'one should do X' construction. Nothing that duplicates what you can read elsewhere." **Buys 4 mss/year.** Query. Length: 2,500 words. **Pays $50-TBD for assigned articles. Pays $50-TBD for unsolicited articles.**

COLUMNS Contact: Brandon Phillips. Cover (the most important package-puts a key topic in compelling context), 2,000-3,000 words; Radar (news/product snippets), 1,200; Bookshelf (book reviews), 700; Pro Bono (legal issues), 850; Profile (human interest stories on inventors and innovators), BrainChild (celebration of young inventors and innovators), FirstPerson (inventors show how they've overcome hurdles), 1,000; MeetingRoom (learn secrets to success of best inventor groups in the country), 900; TalkBack (Q&A with manufacturers, retailers, etc. in the innovation industry), Five Questions With..(a conversation with some of the brightest and most controversial minds in Technology, manufacturing, academia and other fields), 800. **Buys 4 mss/year.** Query. **Pays $20.**

💲💲💲💲 SCIENTIFIC AMERICAN

415 Madison Ave., New York NY 10017. (212)754-0550. **Fax:** (212)755-1976. **E-mail:** editors@sciam.com. **Website:** www.sciam.com. **Contact:** Emily Harrison, photography editor; Edward Bell, art director. Monthly magazine covering developments and topics of interest in the world of science. Query before submitting. *Scientific American* brings its readers directly to the wellspring of exploration and technological innovation. The magazine specializes in first-hand accounts by the people who actually do the work. Their personal experience provides an authoritative perspective on future growth. Over 100 of our authors have won Nobel Prizes. Complementing those articles are regular departments written by *Scientific American*'s staff of professional journalists, all specialists in their fields. *Scientific American* is the authoritative source of advance information. Authors are the first to report on important breakthroughs, because they're the people who make them. It all goes back to *Scientific American*'s corporate mission: to link those who use knowledge with those who create it. Estab. 1845. Circ. 710,000.

NONFICTION Pays $1/word average. Pays expenses of writers on assignment.

💲💲 SKY & TELESCOPE

New Track Media, 90 Sherman St., Cambridge MA 02140. (617)864-7360. **Fax:** (617)864-6117. **E-mail:** editors@SkyandTelescope.com. **Website:** skyandtelescope.com. **Contact:** Dennis di Cicco, senior editor. **15% freelance written.** Monthly magazine covering astronomy. "*Sky & Telescope* is the magazine of record for astronomy. We cover amateur activities, research news, equipment, book, and software reviews. Our audience is the amateur astronomer who wants to learn more about the night sky." Estab. 1941. Circ. 110,000. Byline given. Publishes ms an average of 6 months after acceptance. Editorial lead time 4 months. Submit seasonal material 1 year in advance. Accepts queries by mail, e-mail, fax. Responds in 3 weeks to queries. Responds in 1 month to mss. Sample copy for $6.99. Guidelines available online.

NONFICTION Needs essays, historical, how-to, opinion, personal experience, photo feature, technical. No poetry, crosswords, New Age, or alternative cosmologies. **Buys 10 mss/year.** Query. Length: 1,500-2,500 words. **Pays at least 25¢/word.** Sometimes pays expenses of writers on assignment.

COLUMNS Focal Point (opinion), 700 words; Books & Beyond (reviews), 800 words; The Astronomy Scene (profiles), 1,500 words. **Buys 20 mss/year.** Query. **Pays 25¢/word.**

⊘ 💲💲💲💲 STARDATE

University of Texas, 1 University Station, A2100, Austin TX 78712. (512)471-5285. **Fax:** (512)471-5060. **Website:** http://stardate.org. **80% freelance written.** Bimonthly magazine covering astronomy. "*StarDate* is written for people with an interest in astronomy and what they see in the night sky, but no special astronomy training or background." Estab. 1975. Circ. 10,000. Byline given. Offers 25% kill fee. Publishes ms an average of 4 months after acceptance. Editorial lead time 6 months. Submit seasonal material 6 months in advance. Accepts queries by mail, e-mail, fax. Responds in 6 weeks to queries. Sample copy and writer's guidelines free.

NONFICTION Needs general interest, historical, interview, photo feature, technical, travel, research in astronomy. No first-person; first stargazing experiences; paranormal. **Buys 8 mss/year.** Query with published clips. Length: 1,500-3,000 words. **Pays $500-1,500.** Sometimes pays expenses of writers on assignment.

COLUMNS Astro News (short astronomy news item), 250 words. **Buys 6 mss/year.** Query with published clips. **Pays $100-200.**

WEATHERWISE

Taylor & Francis Group, 325 Chestnut St., Suite 800, Philadelphia PA 19106. (215)625-8900. **E-mail:** margaret.benner@taylorandfrancis.com. **Website:** www.weatherwise.org. **Contact:** Margaret Benner, editor-in-chief. **75% freelance written.** Bimonthly magazine covering weather and meteorology. "*Weatherwise* is America's only magazine about the weather. Our readers range from professional weathercasters and scientists to basement-bound hobbyists, but all share a common interest in craving information about weather as it relates to the atmospheric sciences, technology, history, culture, society, art, etc." Estab. 1948. Circ. 11,000. Byline given. Publishes ms an average of 6 months after acceptance. Editorial lead time 6-9 months. Submit seasonal material 9 months in advance. Accepts queries by mail, e-mail, fax, phone. Responds in 2 months to queries. Guidelines available online.

NONFICTION Needs book excerpts, essays, general interest, historical, how-to, interview, new product, opinion, personal experience, photo feature, technical, travel. Special issues: Photo Contest (September/October deadline June 2). No blow-by-blow accounts of the biggest storm to ever hit your backyard. **Buys 15-18 mss/year.** Query with published clips. Length: 2,000-3,000 words. **Pays $200-500 for assigned articles. Pays $0-300 for unsolicited articles.**

COLUMNS Weather Front (news, trends), 300-400 words; Weather Talk (folklore and humor), 650-1,000 words. **Buys 12-15 mss/year.** Query with published clips. **Pays $0-200.**

SCIENCE FICTION, FANTASY AND HORROR

A COMPANION IN ZEOR

1622 Swallow Crest Dr., Apt. B, Edgewood MD 21040-1751. **Website:** www.simegen.com/sgfandom/rimonslibrary/cz/. **Contact:** Karen MacLeod, editor. *A Companion in Zeor*, published irregularly online, is a science fiction/fantasy fanzine. Estab. 1978. Accepts queries by mail, e-mail, fax. Guidelines available for SASE, by fax, email, or on website.

FICTION Accepts fax, e-mail (pasted into body of message), and disk submissions. For regular mail submissions, "note whether to return or dispose of rejected mss." Cover letter is preferred. Sometimes sends prepublication galleys. Always willing to work with authors or poets to help in improving their work." Reviews books of poetry. Poets may send material for review consideration.

POETRY Accepts fax, e-mail (pasted into body of message), and disk submissions. For regular mail submissions, "note whether to return or dispose of rejected mss." Cover letter is preferred. Sometimes sends prepublication galleys. "Always willing to work with authors or poets to help in improving their work." Reviews books of poetry. Poets may send material for review consideration.

AOIFE'S KISS

The Speculative Fiction Foundation, P.O. Box 782, Cedar Rapids IA 52406-0782. **E-mail:** aoifeskiss@yahoo.com. **Website:** www.samsdotpublishing.com. **Contact:** Tyree Campbell, Managing Editor. **100%.** "Aoife's Kiss is a print and online magazine of fantasy, science fiction, horror, sword & sorcery, and slipstream, published quarterly in March, June, September, and December. Aoife's Kiss publishes short stories, poems, illustrations, articles, and movie/book/chapbook reviews, and interviews with noted individuals in those genres." Estab. 2002. Offers 100% kill fee. Editorial lead time is 2 months. Submit seasonal material 2 months in advance. Accepts queries by e-mail. Responds in 2 weeks to queries.

NONFICTION Buys 10-16 mss/year. Send complete ms Length: 4,000 words

FICTION *Aoife's Kiss*, published quarterly, prints "fantasy, science fiction, sword and sorcery, alternate history, dark fantasy short stories, poems, illustrations, and movie and book reviews." Wants "fantasy, science fiction, spooky horror, and speculative poetry with minimal angst." **Buys 16-20 mss/year.** Accepts e-mail submissions (pasted into body of message); no disk submissions. "Submission should include snail mail address and a short (1-2 lines) bio." Reads submissions year-round.

THE MAGAZINE OF FANTASY & SCIENCE FICTION

P.O. Box 3447, Hoboken NJ 07030. (201) 876-2551. **E-mail:** fandsf@aol.com. **Website:** www.fandsf.com. **Contact:** Gordon Van Gelder, editor. **100%.** *"The Magazine of Fantasy and Science Fiction publishes various types of science fiction and fantasy short stories and novellas, making up about 80% of each issue. The balance of each issue is devoted to articles about science fiction, a science column, book and film reviews, cartoons, and competitions."* Bimonthly." Estab. 1949. Circ. 40,000. Byline given. Publishes ms an average of 9-12 months after acceptance. Submit seasonal material 8 months in advance. Responds in 2 months to queries. Sample copy for $6. Guidelines for SASE, by e-mail or website.

COLUMNS Curiosities (Reviews of odd & obscure books), 270 words max. Accepts 6 mss/year. Query. **Pays $-$50.**

FICTION Contact: Gordon Van Gelder, Editor. "Prefers character-oriented stories. We receive a lot of fantasy fiction, but never enough science fiction." Needs adventure, fantasy, horror, space fantasy, sword & sorcery, dark fantasy, futuristic, psychological, supernatural, science fiction, hard science/technological, soft/sociological. **Buys 60-90/mss. mss/year.** No electronic submissions. Send complete Ms. Length: up to 25,000 words **Pays 5-9¢/word.**

POETRY *The Magazine of Fantasy & Science Fiction,* published bimonthy, is "one of the longest-running magazines devoted to the literature of the fantastic." Wants only poetry that deals with the fantastic or the science-fictional. Has published poetry by Rebecca Kavaler, Elizabeth Bear, Sophie M. White, and Robert Frazier. "I buy poems very infrequently—just when one hits me right." Seldom comments on rejected poems. Guidelines available for SASE or on website. Responds in up to 1 month. Always sends prepublication galleys. **Pays $50/poem and 2 contributor's copies. Acquires first North American serial rights.**

🌑 MORPHEUS TALES

116 Muriel St., London N1 9QU UK. **E-mail:** morpheustales@blueyonder.co.uk. **Website:** www.morpheustales.com. **Contact:** Adam Bradley, publisher. **100% freelance written.** Quarterly magazine covering horror, science fiction, fantasy. "We publish the best in horror, science fiction and fantasy, both fiction and nonfiction." Estab. 2008. Circ. 1,000. Publishes

ms an average of 18 months after acceptance. Editorial lead time 3 months. Submit seasonal material 6 months in advance. Accepts queries by e-mail. Responds in 1 week to queries. Responds in 1 month to mss. Sample copy for $7. Guidelines available online.

NONFICTION Needs book excerpts, essays, general interest, how-to, inspirational, interview, new product, opinion, photo feature, Letters to the Editor. All material must be based on horror, science fiction or fantasy genre. **Buys 6 mss/year.** Query. Length: 1,000-3,000 words. Sometimes pays expenses of writers on assignment.

FICTION Needs experimental, fantasy, horror, mystery, novel concepts, science fiction, serialized, suspense. **Buys 20 mss/year.** Send complete ms. Length: 800-3,000 words.

💲 APEX MAGAZINE

Apex Publications, LLC, P.O. Box 24323, Lexington KY 40524. (859)312-3974. **E-mail:** jason@apexbookcompany.com. **Website:** www.apexbookcompany.com. **Contact:** Catherynne M. Valente, subm. editor. **100% freelance written.** Monthly e-zine publishing dark speculative fiction. "An elite repository for new and seasoned authors with an other-worldly interest in the unquestioned and slightly bizarre parts of the universe." Estab. 2004. Circ. 10,000 unique visits per month. Byline given. Offers 30% kill fee. Publishes ms an average of 2 months after acceptance. Editorial lead time 2 months. Submit seasonal material 2 months in advance. Accepts queries by e-mail. Responds in 20-30 days to queries and to mss. Sample copy available online. Guidelines available online.

FICTION dark speculative fiction. Does not want monster fiction. **Buys 24 mss/year.** Send complete ms. Length: 100-7,500 words. **Pays $20-200.**

💲 ASIMOV'S SCIENCE FICTION

Dell Magazine Fiction Group, 267 Broadway, 4th Floor, New York NY 10007. (212)686-7188. **Fax:** (212)686-7414. **E-mail:** asimovssf@dellmagazines.com. **Website:** www.asimovs.com. **Contact:** Brian Bieniowski, managing editor; Sheila Williams, editor; Victoria Green, senior art director; June Levine, associate art director. **98% freelance written. Works with a small number of new/unpublished writers each year.** Magazine published 10 times/year, including 2 double issues. "Magazine consists of science fiction and fantasy stories for adults and young adults. Publishes the best short science fiction available." Estab. 1977. Circ. 50,000. Publishes ms an average of 6-12 months after acceptance. Accepts queries by mail. NoResponds in 2 months to queries. Responds in 3 months to mss. Sample copy for $5. Guidelines for #10 SASE or online.

FICTION "Science fiction primarily. Some fantasy and humor but no sword and sorcery. No explicit sex or violence that isn't integral to the story. It is best to read a great deal of material in the genre to avoid the use of some very old ideas. Send complete ms and SASE with *all* submissions." Needs fantasy, science fiction, hard science, soft sociological. No horror or psychic/supernatural. Would like to see more hard science fiction. **Buys 10 mss/issue mss/year.** Length: 750-15,000 words. **Pays 5-8¢/word.**

POETRY 40 lines maximum. **Pays $1/line.**

⊗ LEADING EDGE

4087 JKB, Provo UT 84602. **E-mail:** editor@leadingedgemagazine.com. **Website:** www.leadingedgemagazine.com. **90% freelance written.** Semiannual magazine covering science fiction and fantasy. Twice yearly magazine. "We strive to encourage developing and established talent and provide high quality speculative fiction to our readers." Does not accept mss with sex, excessive violence, or profanity. "*Leading Edge* is a magazine dedicated to new and upcoming talent in the field of science fiction and fantasy." Has published work by Orson Scott Card, Brandon Sanderson, and Dave Wolverton. Has published poetry by Michael Collings, Tracy Ray, Susan Spilecki, and Bob Cook. Estab. 1980. Circ. 200. Byline given. Publishes ms an average of 2-4 months after acceptance. Responds in 2-4 months to mss. Sample copy for $5.95. Guidelines available online at website.

○ Accepts unsolicited submissions.

FICTION Needs fantasy, science fiction. **Buys 14-16 mss/year.** Send complete ms with cover letter and SASE. Include estimated word count. Length: 15,000 words maximum **Pays 1¢/word; $10 minimum.**

POETRY Needs avant-garde, haiku, light verse, traditional. "Publishes 2-4 poems per issue. Poetry should reflect both literary value and popular appeal and should deal with science fiction- or fantasy-related themes." Submit 1 or more poems at a time. No e-mail submissions. Cover letter is preferred. Include name, address, phone number, length of poem, title, and type of poem at the top of each page. Please include SASE with every submission." Submit maxi-

mum 10 poems. Pays $10 for first 4 pages; $1.50/each subsequent page.

⊗ MINDFLIGHTS

Double-Edged Publishing Inc., 9618 Misty Brook Cove, Cordova TN 38016. (901)213-3768. **E-mail:** editor@mindflights.com; MindFlightsEditors@gmail.com. **Website:** www.mindflights.com. **Contact:** Selena Thomason, managing editor. **100% freelance written.** Monthly online magazine and annual print magazine covering science fiction, fantasy, all genres of speculative fiction and poetry, grounded in a Christian or Christian-friendly worldview. "Paving new roads for Christ-reflected short fiction. Not preachy, but still a reflection of the truth and light. Examples of this are in the writings of C.S. Lewis and Tolkien. We strive to provide quality fiction and poetry, all in means that respect traditional values and Christian principles. Be uplifting, encouraging with something interesting to our audience—fans of sci-fi and fantasy who are comfortable with an environment committed to a Christian world view." Estab. 2007. Byline given. Publishes ms an average of 2 months after acceptance. Editorial lead time 3-4 months. Submit seasonal material 4 months in advance. Accepts queries by online submission form. NoResponds in 3-4 weeks to mss. Sample copy available online. Guidelines available online at mindflights.com/guidelines.php.

NONFICTION **Buys 1 mss/year.** Send complete ms. Length: 300-5,000 words. **Pays $5-25.**

FICTION "Illustrations are compensated with $10 gratuity payment." Needs fantasy, science fiction, work with strong speculative element. Does not want to see any work that would be offensive to a Christian audience. **Buys 25 mss/year.** "We only accept submissions via our online form. Send complete ms. after August 1, when we plan to résumé taking submissions." Length: 50-5,000 words. **Pays $5-25.**

POETRY Needs avant-garde, free verse, haiku, light verse, traditional. "We accept all forms of poetry, but the work must be speculative in nature." Does not want to see any work that would be offensive to a Christian audience. Buys 25 poems/year. Submit maximum 3 poems. **Pays ½¢ per word, $5/min.-$25/max.**

⊗⊗⊗ ON SPEC

P.O. Box 4727, Station South, Edmonton AB T6E 5G6 Canada. (780)413-0215. **Fax:** (780)413-1538. **E-mail:** onspec@onspec.ca. **E-mail:** onspecmag@gmail.com.

Website: www.onspec.ca. **95% freelance written.** Quarterly magazine covering Canadian science fiction, fantasy and horror. "We publish speculative fiction and poetry by new and established writers, with a strong preference for Canadian authored works." Estab. 1989. Circ. 2,000. Byline given. Publishes ms an average of 6-18 months after acceptance. Editorial lead time 6 months. Accepts queries by mail. Accepts simultaneous submissions. Responds in 2 weeks to queries. 3 months after deadline to mss. Sample copy for $8. Guidelines for #10 SASE or on website.

FICTION Needs fantasy, horror, science fiction, magic realism, ghost stories, fairy stories. No media tie-in or shaggy-alien stories. No condensed or excerpted novels, religious/inspirational stories, fairy tales. **Buys 50 mss/year.** Send complete ms. Length: 1,000-6,000 words. **Pays $50-180 for fiction. Short stories (under 1,000 words): $50 plus 1 contributor's copy.**

POETRY Needs avant-garde, free verse. No rhyming or religious material. Buys 6 poems/year. Submit maximum 10 poems. Length: 4-100 lines. **Pays $50 and 1 contributor's copy.**

ⓢ TALES OF THE TALISMAN

Hadrosaur Productions, P.O. Box 2194, Mesilla Park NM 88047-2194. **E-mail:** hadrosaur@zianet.com. **Website:** www.talesofthetalisman.com. **Contact:** David Lee Summers, editor. **95% freelance written.** Quarterly magazine covering science fiction and fantasy. "*Tales of the Talisman* is a literary science fiction and fantasy magazine. We publish short stories, poetry, and articles with themes related to science fiction and fantasy. Above all, we are looking for thought-provoking ideas and good writing. Speculative fiction set in the past, present, and future is welcome. Likewise, contemporary or historical fiction is welcome as long as it has a mythic or science fictional element. Our target audience includes adult fans of the science fiction and fantasy genres along with anyone else who enjoys thought-provoking and entertaining writing." Estab. 1995. Circ. 200. Byline given. Offers 100% kill fee. Publishes ms an average of 9 months after acceptance. Editorial lead time 9-12 months. Submit seasonal material 1 year in advance. Accepts queries by mail, e-mail. Responds in 1 week to queries. Responds in 1 month to mss. Sample copy for $8. Guidelines available online.

NONFICTION Needs interview, technical, articles on the craft of writing. "We do not want to see unsolicited articles—please query first if you have an idea that you think would be suitable for *Tales of the Talisman*'s audience. We do not want to see negative or derogatory articles." **Buys 1-3 mss/year.** Query. Length: 1,000-3,000 words. **Pays $10 for assigned articles.**

FICTION Contact: David L. Summers, editor. Needs fantasy, space fantasy, sword and sorcery, horror, science fiction, hard science/technological, soft/sociological. "We do not want to see stories with graphic violence. Do not send 'mainstream' fiction with no science fictional or fantastic elements. Do not send stories with copyrighted characters, unless you're the copyright holder." **Buys 25-30 mss/year.** Send complete ms. Length: 1,000-6,000 words. **Pays $6-10.**

POETRY Needs avant-garde, free verse, haiku, light verse, traditional. "Do not send 'mainstream' poetry with no science fictional or fantastic elements. Do not send poems featuring copyrighted characters, unless you're the copyright holder." Buys 24-30 poems/year. Submit maximum 5 poems. Length: 3-50 lines.

ⓢ VAMPIRES 2 MAGAZINE

Man's Story 2 Publishing Co., 1321 Snapfinger Rd., Decatur GA 30032. **E-mail:** mansstory2@aol.com. **Website:** www.vampires2.us. **80% freelance written.** "Online E-Zine that strives to re-create Vampire Romance in the pulp fiction style of the 1920s through the 1970s with strong emphasis on 3D graphic art." Also features Illustrated Stories, Online Magazine, Online Photo Galleries and more. Estab. 1999. Circ. 2,500. Publishes ms an average of 1-6 months after acceptance. Accepts queries by e-mail only. Accepts simultaneous submissions. Guidelines available online.

FICTION Needs adventure, erotica, fantasy, horror, suspense, pulp fiction involving vampires. **Buys 30-50 mss/year.** Send complete ms. Length: 3,500 words more or less. **Pays $25.**

SEX

ⓢⓢ EXOTIC MAGAZINE

X Publishing Inc., 818 SW 3rd Ave., Suite 1324, Portland OR 97204. (503)816-4174. **Fax:** (503)241-7239. **E-mail:** editor@xmag.com; info@xmag.com. **Website:** www.xmag.com. Monthly magazine covering adult entertainment, sexuality. "*Exotic* is pro-sex, informative, amusing, mature, and intelligent. Our readers rent and/or buy adult videos, visit strip clubs, and are interested in topics related to the adult entertainment industry and sexuality/culture. Don't talk down to them or fire too far over their heads. Many readers are computer literate and well-traveled. We're also interested in insightful fetish material. We are not a 'hard core' publication." Estab. 1993. Circ. 75,000+. Byline given. Pays 30 days after publication. Accepts queries by fax. Accepts simultaneous submissions. Responds in 2 weeks to queries. Responds in 2 months to mss. Sample copy for SAE with 9×12 envelope and 5 first-class stamps. Guidelines for #10 SASE.

NONFICTION Needs exposé, general interest, historical, how-to, humor, interview, travel, News. No men writing as women, articles about being a "horny guy", opinion pieces pretending to be fact pieces. **Buys 36 mss/year.** Send complete ms. Length: 1,000-1,800 words. **Pays 10¢/word up to $150.**

FICTION "We are currently overwhelmed with fiction submissions. Please only send fiction if it's really amazing." Needs erotica, slice-of-life vignettes, must present either erotic element or some vice of modern culture, such as gambling, music, dancing. Send complete ms. Length: 1,000-1,800 words. **Pays 10¢/word up to $150.**

🚫🚫🚫🚫 HUSTLER

HG Inc., 8484 Wilshire Blvd., Suite 900, Beverly Hills CA 90211. **Fax:** (323)651-2741. **Website:** www.hustler.com. **60% freelance written.** Magazine published 13 times/year. *Hustler* is the no-nonsense men's magazine, one that is willing to speak frankly about society's sacred cows and exposé its hypocrites. The *Hustler* reader expects honest, unflinching looks at hard topicsÂ³sexual, social, political, personality profile, true crime. Estab. 1974. Circ. 750,000. Byline given. Pays as boards ship to printer. Offers 20% kill fee. Publishes ms an average of 3 months after acceptance. Editorial lead time 4 months. Submit seasonal material 6 months in advance. Accepts queries by mail, e-mail, fax. Responds in 2 weeks to queries. Responds in 1 month to mss. Guidelines for #10 SASE.

NONFICTION Needs book excerpts, exposé, general interest, how-to, interview, personal experience, trends. **Buys 30 mss/year.** Query. Length: 3,500-4,000 words. **Pays $1,500.** Sometimes pays expenses of writers on assignment.

COLUMNS Sex play (some aspect of sex that can be encapsulated in a limited space), 2,500 words. **Buys 13 mss/year.** Send complete ms. **Pays $750.**

FILLERS Jokes and Graffilthy, bathroom wall humor. **Pays $50-100.**

🚫🚫🚫 ⊘ PENTHOUSE

General Media Communications, 2 Penn Plaza, 11th Floor, New York NY 10121. (212)702-6000. **Fax:** (212)702-6279. **E-mail:** pbloch@pmgi.com. **Website:** www.penthouse.com. Monthly magazine. *Penthouse* is for the sophisticated male. Its editorial scope ranges from outspoken contemporary comment to photography essays of beautiful women. *Penthouse* features interviews with personalities, sociological studies, humor, travel, food and wine, and fashion and grooming for men. Estab. 1969. Circ. 640,000. Byline given. Pays 2 months after acceptance. Offers 25% kill fee. Editorial lead time 3 months. Accepts simultaneous submissions. Guidelines for #10 SASE.

NONFICTION Needs exposé, general interest, to men, interview. **Buys 50 mss/year.** Send complete ms. Length: 4,000-6,000 words. **Pays $3,000.**

COLUMNS Length: 1,000 words. **Buys 25 mss/year.** Query with published clips or send complete ms. **Pays $500.**

SPORTS

ARCHERY AND BOWHUNTING

🚫🚫 BOW & ARROW HUNTING

Beckett Media LLC, 22840 Savi Rancy Pkwy., Suite 200, Yorba Linda CA 92887. (714)200-1900. **Fax:** (800)249-7761. **E-mail:** JBell@Beckett.com; editorial@bowandarrowhunting.com. **Website:** www.bowandarrowhunting.com. **70% freelance written.** Magazine published 9 times/year covering bowhunting. "Dedicated to serve the serious bowhunting enthusiast. Writers must be willing to share their secrets so our readers can become better bowhunters." Estab. 1962. Circ. 90,000. Byline given. Publishes ms an average of 2 months after acceptance. Submit seasonal material 6 months in advance. Accepts queries by mail, e-mail. Accepts simultaneous submissions. Responds in 1 month to queries. Responds in 6 weeks to mss. Sample copy and writer's guidelines free.

NONFICTION Needs how-to, humor, interview, opinion, personal experience, technical. **Buys 60 mss/year.** Send complete ms. Length: 1,700-3,000 words. **Pays $200-450.**

FILLERS Needs facts, newsbreaks. **Buys 12 mss/year.** Length: 500 words. **Pays $20-100.**

$$ BOWHUNTER

InterMedia Outdoors, 6385 Flank Dr., Suite 800, Harrisburg PA 17112. (717)695-8085. **Fax:** (717)545-2527. **E-mail:** curt.wells@imoutdoors.com. **Website:** www.bowhunter.com. Mark Olszewski, art director; Jeff Waring, publisher. **Contact:** Curt Wells, editor. **50% freelance written.** Bimonthly magazine covering hunting big and small game with bow and arrow. "We are a special-interest publication, produced by bowhunters for bowhunters, covering all aspects of the sport. Material included in each issue is designed to entertain and inform readers, making them better bowhunters." Estab. 1971. Circ. 126,480. Byline given. Submit seasonal material 8 months in advance. Accepts queries by mail, e-mail, fax. Responds in 1 month to queries. Responds in 2 months to mss. Sample copy for $2 and 8 ½ x 11 SASE with appropriate postage. Guidelines for #10 SASE or on website.

NONFICTION Needs general interest, how-to, interview, opinion, personal experience, photo feature. **Buys 60 plus mss/year.** Query. Length: 250-2,000 words. **Pays $500 maximum for assigned articles. Pays $100-400 for unsolicited articles.** Sometimes pays expenses of writers on assignment.

$$ BOWHUNTING WORLD

Grand View Media Group, 5959 Baker Rd., Suite 300, Minnetonka MN 55345. (888)431-2877. **E-mail:** mark@grandviewmedia.com; mikes@grandviewmedia.com. **Website:** www.bowhuntingworld.com. **Contact:** Mark Melotick; Mike Strandlund. **50% freelance written.** Bimonthly magazine with 3 additional issues for bowhunting and archery enthusiasts who participate in the sport year-round. Estab. 1952. Circ. 95,000. Byline given. Publishes ms an average of 5 months after acceptance. Responds in 1 week (e-mail queries). Responds in 6 weeks to mss. Sample copy for $3 and 9×12 SASE with 10 first-class stamps. Guidelines with #10 SASE.

Accepts queries by mail, but prefers e-mail.

NONFICTION Buys 60 mss/year. Send complete ms. Length: 1,500-2,500 words. **Pays $350-600.**

BASEBALL

$ JUNIOR BASEBALL

JSAN Publishing LLC, Wilton CT 06897. (203)210-5726. **E-mail:** jim@juniorbaseball.com. **Website:** www.juniorbaseball.com. **Contact:** Jim Beecher, publisher. **25% freelance written.** Bimonthly magazine covering youth baseball. Focused on youth baseball players ages 7-17 (including high school) and their parents/coaches. Edited to various reading levels, depending upon age/skill level of feature. Estab. 1996. Circ. 20,000. Byline given. Publishes ms an average of 4 months after acceptance. Editorial lead time 3 months. Submit seasonal material 4 months in advance. Accepts simultaneous submissions. Responds in 2 weeks to queries; 1 month to mss. Sample copy for $5 and online.

NONFICTION Needs how-to, skills, tips, features, how-to play better baseball, etc., interview, with major league players; only on assignment, personal experience, from coaches' or parents' perspective. No trite first-person articles about your kid. No fiction or poetry. **Buys 8-12 mss/year.** Query. Length: 500-1,000 words. **Pays $50-100.**

COLUMNS When I Was a Kid (a current Major League Baseball player profile); Parents Feature (topics of interest to parents of youth ball players); all 1,000-1,500 words. In the Spotlight (news, events, new products), 50-100 words; Hot Prospect (written for the 14 and older competitive player. High school baseball is included, and the focus is on improving the finer points of the game to make the high school team, earn a college scholarship, or attract scouts, written to an adult level), 500-1,000 words. **Buys 8-12 columns mss/year. Pays $50-100.**

BICYCLING

$$$ ADVENTURE CYCLIST

Adventure Cycling Assn., Box 8308, Missoula MT 59807. (406)721-1776, ext. 222. **Fax:** (406)721-8754. **E-mail:** magazine@adventurecycling.org. **Website:** www.adventurecycling.org. **Contact:** Greg Siple, art director; Michael Deme, editor. **75% freelance written.** Published 9 times/year for Adventure Cycling Association members, emphasizing bicycle tourism and travel. Estab. 1975. Circ. 45,500. Byline given. Kill fee 25%. Submit seasonal material 12 months in advance. Sample copy and guidelines for 9×12 SAE with 4 first-class stamps. Info available at www.adventurecycling.org/mag.

NONFICTION Needs first-person bike-travel accounts (U.S. and worldwide), essays, how-to, profiles, photo feature, technical, U.S. or foreign tour accounts. **Buys 20-25 mss/year.** Send complete ms. Length:

1,400-3,500 words. **Inquiries requested prior to complete manuscripts. Pays sliding scale per word.**

💲💲 BIKE MAGAZINE

Source Interlink Media, P.O. Box 1028, Dana Point CA 926229. (949)325-6200. **Fax:** (949)325-6196. **E-mail:** bikemag@sorc.com. **Website:** www.bikemag.com. **Contact:** Joe Parkin, editor; Brice Minnigh, managing editor. **35% freelance written.** Magazine publishes 8 times/year covering mountain biking. Estab. 1993. Circ. 170,000. Byline given. Offers 25% kill fee. Publishes ms an average of 2 months after acceptance. Editorial lead time 4 months. Submit seasonal material 6 months in advance. Responds in 2 months to queries. Sample copy for $8. Guidelines for #10 SASE.

NONFICTION Needs humor, interview, personal experience, photo feature, travel. **Buys 20 mss/year.** Length: 1,000-2,500 words. **Pays 50¢/word.** Sometimes pays expenses of writers on assignment. $500 maximum.

COLUMNS Splatter (news), 300 words; Urb (details a great ride within 1 hour of a major metropolitan area), 600-700 words. **Buys 20 mss/year. Pays 50¢/word.**

💲💲 CYCLE CALIFORNIA! MAGAZINE

1702-L Meridian Ave., #289, San Jose CA 95125. (408)924-0270. **Fax:** (408)292-3005. **E-mail:** tcorral@cyclecalifornia.com; BMack@cyclecalifornia.com. **Website:** www.cyclecalifornia.com. **Contact:** Tracy L. Corral; Bob Mack, publisher. **75% freelance written.** Magazine published 11 times/year covering Northern California bicycling events, races, people. Issues (topics) covered include bicycle commuting, bicycle politics, touring, racing, nostalgia, history, anything at all to do with riding a bike. Estab. 1995. Circ. 26,000 print; 4,700 digital. Byline given. Publishes ms an average of 3 months after acceptance. Editorial lead time 6 weeks. Submit seasonal material 6 weeks in advance. Accepts queries by e-mail. Accepts simultaneous submissions. Responds in 1 month to queries. Sample copy with 10×13 SASE and 3 first-class stamps. Guidelines with #10 SASE.

NONFICTION Needs historical, how-to, interview, opinion, personal experience, technical, travel. Special issues: Bicycle Tour & Travel (January/February). No articles about any sport that doesn't relate to bicycling, no product reviews. **Buys 36 mss/year.** Query. Length: 500-1,500 words. **Pays 10-15¢/word.**

PHOTOS Send photos. Identification of subjects required. Reviews 3 x 5 prints. Negotiates payment individually.

COLUMNS **Buys 2-3 mss/year.** Query with published clips. **Pays 10-15¢/word.**

TIPS "E-mail us with good ideas. While we don't exclude writers from other parts of the country, articles really should reflect a Northern California slant, or be of general interest to bicyclists. We prefer stories written by people who like and use their bikes."

💲💲 VELONEWS

Inside Communications, Inc., 3002 Sterling Circle, Suite 100, Boulder CO 80301. (303)440-0601. **Fax:** (303)444-6788. **E-mail:** velonews@pcspublink.com. **Website:** www.velonews.com. **40% freelance written.** Monthly tabloid covering bicycle racing. Estab. 1972. Circ. 48,000. Byline given. Publishes ms an average of 1 month after acceptance. Responds in 3 weeks to queries.

NONFICTION **Buys 80 mss/year.** Query. Length: 300-1,200 words. **Pays $100-400.**

REPRINTS Send typed manuscript with rights for sale noted and information about when and where the material previously appeared.

PHOTOS State availability. Captions, identification of subjects required.

BOATING

💲💲 BOATING WORLD MAGAZINE

Duncan McIntosh Co., 17782 Cowan, Suite C, Irvine CA 92614. (949)660-6150. **Fax:** (949)660-6172. **Website:** www.boatingworld.com. Mike Werling, managing editor, mikew@boatingworld.com. **Contact:** Alan Jones, executive editor. **60% freelance written.** Magazine published 8 times/year covering recreational trailer boats. "Typical reader owns a power boat between 14 and 32 feet long and has 3-9 years experience. Boat reports are mostly written by staff while features and most departments are provided by freelancers. We are looking for freelancers who can write well and who have at least a working knowledge of recreational power boating and the industry behind it." Estab. 1997. Circ. 100,000. Publishes ms an average of 4 months after acceptance. Accepts simultaneous submissions. Responds in 3 months to queries. Sample copy free. Guidelines for #10 SASE.

NONFICTION Needs general interest, how-to, humor, new product, personal experience, travel. **Buys**

20-25 mss/year. Query. Length: 1,400-1,600 words. **Pays $150-450.** Sometimes pays expenses of writers on assignment.

FILLERS Needs anecdotes, facts, newsbreaks. Length: 250-500 words. **Pays $50-100.**

😊😊😊 CANOE & KAYAK

Source Interlink Media, 236 Avenida Fabricante, Suite 201, San Clemente CA 92672. (425)827-6363. **E-mail:** jeff@canoekayak.com; joe@canoekayak.com; dave@canoekayak.com. **Website:** www.canoekayak.com. **Contact:** Jeff Moag, editor-in-chief; Joe Carberry, senior editor; Dave Shively, managing editor. **75% freelance written.** Bimonthly magazine. *Canoe & Kayak Magazine* is North America's No. 1 paddlesports resource. Our readers include flatwater and whitewater canoeists and kayakers of all skill levels. We provide comprehensive information on destinations, technique and equipment. Beyond that, we cover canoe and kayak camping, safety, the environment, and the history of boats and sport. Estab. 1972. Circ. 70,000. Byline given. Publishes ms an average of 6 months after acceptance. Editorial lead time 6 months. Submit seasonal material 8 months in advance. Accepts queries by mail, e-mail. Responds in 2 months to queries. Sample copy and writer's guidelines for 9×12 SAE with 7 first-class stamps.

NONFICTION Needs historical, how-to, canoe, kayak camp, load boats, paddle whitewater, etc., personal experience, photo feature, technical, travel. Special issues: Whitewater Paddling; Beginner's Guide; Kayak Touring; Canoe Journal. No cartoons, poems, stories in which bad judgement is portrayed or 'Me and Molly' articles. **Buys 25 mss/year.** Send complete ms. Length: 400-2,500 words. **Pays $100-800 for assigned articles. Pays $100-500 for unsolicited articles.**

COLUMNS Put In (environment, conservation, events), 500 words; Destinations (canoe and kayak destinations in US, Canada), 1,500 words; Essays, 750 words. **Buys 40 mss/year.** Send complete ms. **Pays $100-350.**

FILLERS Needs anecdotes, facts, newsbreaks. **Buys 20 mss/year.** Length: 200-500 words. **Pays $25-50.**

😊😊😊 CHESAPEAKE BAY MAGAZINE

1819 Bay Ridge Ave., Annapolis MD 21403. (410)263-2662, ext. 32. **Fax:** (410)267-6924. **E-mail:** chesapeakeboating@gmail.com. **Website:** www.chesapeakeboating.net. **Contact:** Ann Levelle, managing editor; Karen Ashley, art director; T.F. Sayles, editor.

60% freelance written. Monthly magazine covering boating and the Chesapeake Bay. "Our readers are boaters. Our writers should know boats and boating. Read the magazine before submitting." Estab. 1972. Circ. 46,000. Byline given. Pays within 2 months after acceptance. Publishes ms an average of 1 year after acceptance. Editorial lead time 1 year. Submit seasonal material 1 year in advance. Accepts queries by mail, e-mail, fax, phone. Accepts simultaneous submissions. Responds in 2 months to queries. Responds in 3 months to mss. Sample copy for $5.19 prepaid.

NONFICTION Buys 30 mss/year. Query with published clips. Length: 300-3,000 words. **Pays $100-1,000.** Pays expenses of writers on assignment.

😊😊😊😊 CRUISING WORLD

The Sailing Co., 55 Hammarlund Way, Middletown RI 02842. (401)845-5100. **Fax:** (401)845-5180. **E-mail:** elaine.lembo@cruisingworld.com; bill.roche@bonniercorp.com. **Website:** www.cruisingworld.com. **Contact:** Elaine Lembo; Bill Roche, art director. **60% freelance written**. Monthly magazine covering sailing, cruising/adventuring, do-it-yourself boat improvements. "*Cruising World* is a publication by and for sailboat owners who spend time in home waters as well as voyaging the world. Its readership is extremely loyal, savvy, and driven by independent thinking." Estab. 1974. Circ. 155,000. Byline given. **Pays on acceptance for articles;** on publication for photography. Publishes ms an average of 18 months after acceptance. Editorial lead time 3 months. Submit seasonal material 1 year in advance. Accepts queries by mail. Responds in 2 months to queries. Responds in 4 months to mss. Sample copy free. Guidelines available online.

NONFICTION Needs book excerpts, essays, exposé, general interest, historical, how-to, humor, interview, new product, opinion, personal experience, photo feature, technical, travel. No travel articles that have nothing to do with cruising aboard sailboats from 20-50 feet in length. **Buys dozens mss/year.** Send complete ms. **Pays $50-1,500 for assigned articles. Pays $50-1,000 for unsolicited articles.** Sometimes pays expenses of writers on assignment.

COLUMNS Shoreline (sailing news, people, and short features; contact Elaine Lembo), 300 words maximum; Hands-on Sailor (refit, voyaging, seamanship, how-to; contact Mark Pillsbury), 1,000-1,500 words. **Buys dozens mss/year.** Query with or without published clips or send complete ms.

GOOD OLD BOAT

Partnership for Excellence, Inc., 7340 Niagara Lane N., Maple Grove MN 55311. (763)494-0314. **E-mail:** karen@goodoldboat.com. **Website:** www.goodold-boat.com. **Contact:** Karen Larson, editor. **90% free-lance written.** Bimonthly magazine covering sailing. "*Good Old Boat* magazine focuses on maintaining, upgrading, and loving cruising sailboats that are 10 years old and older. Readers see themselves as part of a community of sailors who share similar maintenance and replacement concerns which are not generally addressed in the other sailing publications. Our readers do much of the writing about projects they have done on their boats and the joy they receive from sailing them." Estab. 1998. Circ. 30,000. Pays 2 months in advance of publication. Publishes ms an average of 12-18 months after acceptance. Editorial lead time 4 months. Submit seasonal material 12-15 months in advance. Accepts queries by mail, e-mail. Accepts simultaneous submissions. Responds in 1-2 weeks to queries. Responds in 2-6 months to mss. Sample copy free. Guidelines available online.

NONFICTION Needs general interest, historical, how-to, interview, personal experience, photo feature, technical. Articles which are written by non-sailors serve no purpose for us. **Buys 150 mss/year.** Query or send complete ms. **Payment varies, refer to published rates on website.**

HEARTLAND BOATING

The Waterways Journal, Inc., 319 N. Fourth St., Suite 650, St. Louis MO 63102. (314)241-4310. **Fax:** (314)241-4207. **E-mail:** lbraff@heartlandboating.com. **Website:** www.heartlandboating.com. **Contact:** John R. Cassady, art director. **90% freelance written.** Magazine published 8 times/year covering recreational boating on the inland waterways of mid-America, from the Great Lakes south to the Gulf of Mexico and over to the east. "Our writers must have experience with, and a great interest in, boating, particularly in the area described above. *Heartland Boating*'s content is both informative and humorous—describing boating life as the heartland boater knows it. The content reflects the challenge, joy, and excitement of our way of life afloat. We are devoted to both power and sailboating enthusiasts throughout middle America; houseboats are included. The focus is on the freshwater inland rivers and lakes of the heartland, primarily the waters of the Arkansas, Tennessee, Cumberland, Ohio,

Missouri, Illinois, and Mississippi rivers, the Tennessee-Tombigbee Waterway, The Gulf Intracoastal Waterway, and the lakes along these waterways." Estab. 1989. Circ. 12,000. Byline given. Editorial lead time 3 months. Accepts queries by mail. Responds only if interested. Sample copy online at website. Choose the Try It For Free! button. Fill out the form, and you will receive 3 free copies. Guidelines for #10 SASE.

Submission window is May 1–July 15.

NONFICTION Needs how-to, articles about navigation maintenance, upkeep, or making time spent aboard easier and more comfortable, humor, personal experience, technical, Great Loop leg trips, along waterways and on-land stops. Special issues: Annual houseboat issue in March looks at what is coming out on the houseboat market for the coming year. **Buys 100 mss/year.** Send complete ms. Length: 850-1,500 words. **Pays $40-285.**

COLUMNS Books Aboard (assigned book reviews), 400 words. Buys 8-10 mss/year. Pays $40. Handy Hints (boat improvement or safety projects), 1,000 words. Buys 8 mss/year. Pays $180. Heartland Haunts (waterside restaurants, bars or B&Bs), 1,000 words. Buys 16 mss/year. Pays $160. Query with published clips or send complete ms.

HOUSEBOAT MAGAZINE

Harris Publishing, Inc., 360 B St., Idaho Falls ID 83402. **Fax:** (208)522-5241. **E-mail:** blk@houseboat-magazine.com. **Website:** www.houseboatmagazine.com. **35% freelance written.** "Quarterly magazine for houseboaters, who enjoy reading everything that reflects the unique houseboating lifestyle. If it is not a houseboat-specific article, please do not query." Estab. 1990. Circ. 25,000. Byline given. Offers 25% kill fee. Publishes ms an average of 3 months after acceptance. Editorial lead time 6 months. Submit seasonal material 6 months in advance. Accepts simultaneous submissions. Responds in 1 month to queries. Sample copy for $5. Guidelines by e-mail.

No unsolicited mss. Accepts queries by mail and fax, but e-mail strongly preferred.

NONFICTION Needs how-to, interview, new product, personal experience, travel. **Buys 36 mss/year.** Query. Length: 1,500-2,200 words. **Pays $200-500.**

COLUMNS Pays $150-300.

LAKELAND BOATING

O'Meara-Brown Publications, Inc., 727 S. Dearborn St., Suite 812, Chicago IL 60605. (312)276-0610. **Fax:**

(312)276-0619. **E-mail:** ljohnson@lakelandboating.com. **Website:** www.lakelandboating.com. **Contact:** Lindsey Johnson, editor. **50% freelance written.** Magazine covering Great Lakes boating. Estab. 1946. Circ. 60,000. Byline given. Accepts queries by e-mail. Responds in 4 months to queries. Sample copy for $5.50 and 9×12 SAE with 6 first-class stamps. Guidelines free.

NONFICTION Needs book excerpts, historical, how-to, interview, personal experience, photo feature, technical, travel, must relate to boating in Great Lakes. No inspirational, religious, expose or poetry. **Buys 20-30 mss/year.** Length: 300-1,500 words. **Pays $100-600.**

COLUMNS Bosun's Locker (technical or how-to pieces on boating), 100-1,000 words. **Buys 40 mss/year.** Query. **Pays $25-200.**

$ LIVING ABOARD

FTW Publishing, P.O. Box 668, Redondo Beach CA 90277. (888)893-7245. **Fax:** (310)789-3448. **E-mail:** editor@livingaboard.com. **Website:** www.livingaboard.com. **95% freelance written.** Bimonthly magazine covering living on boats/cruising. Estab. 1973. Circ. 10,000. Byline given. Publishes ms an average of 3-6 months after acceptance. Accepts queries by mail, e-mail, fax. Responds in 1-2 weeks to queries. Responds in 1-2 months to mss. Sample copy available online. Guidelines free.

NONFICTION Needs how-to, buy, furnish, maintain, provision a boat, interview, personal experience, technical, as relates to boats, travel, on the water, Cooking Aboard with Recipes. Send complete ms. **Pays 5¢/word.**

COLUMNS Cooking Aboard (how to prepare healthy and nutritious meals in the confines of a galley; how to entertain aboard a boat), 1,000-1,500 words; Environmental Notebook (articles pertaining to clean water, fish, waterfowl, water environment), 750-1,000 words. **Buys 40 mss/year.** Send complete ms. **Pays 5¢/word**

$ NORTHERN BREEZES, SAILING MAGAZINE

Northern Breezes, Inc., 3949 Winnetka Ave. N, Minneapolis MN 55427. (763)542-9707. **Fax:** (763)542-8998. **E-mail:** info@sailingbreezes.com. **Website:** www.sailingbreezes.com. **70% freelance written.** Magazine published 8 times/year for the Great Lakes and Midwest sailing community. Focusing on regional cruising, racing, and day sailing. Estab. 1989. Circ. 22,300. Byline given. Editorial lead time 1 months. Submit seasonal material 3 months in advance. Accepts queries by mail, e-mail, fax, phone. Responds in 1 month to queries. Responds in 2 months to mss. Sample copy free. Guidelines available online.

NONFICTION Needs book excerpts, how-to, sailing topics, humor, inspirational, interview, new product, personal experience, photo feature, technical, travel. No boating reviews. **Buys 24 mss/year.** Query with published clips. Length: 300-3,500 words.

COLUMNS This Old Boat (sailboat), 500-1,000 words; Surveyor's Notebook, 500-800 words. **Buys 8 mss/year.** Query with published clips. **Pays $50-150.**

🍁 $$ PACIFIC YACHTING

OP Publishing, Ltd., 200 West Esplanade, Suite 500, North Vancouver BC V7M 1A4 Canada. (604)998-3310. **Fax:** (604)998-3320. **E-mail:** editor@pacificyachting.com. **Website:** www.pacificyachting.com. **Contact:** Dale Miller, editor. **90% freelance written.** Monthly magazine covering all aspects of recreational boating in the Pacific Northwest. "The bulk of our writers and photographers not only come from the local boating community, many of them were longtime *PY* readers before coming aboard as a contributor. The *PY* reader buys the magazine to read about new destinations or changes to old haunts on the British Columbia coast and the Pacific Northwest and to learn the latest about boats and gear." Estab. 1968. Circ. 19,000. Byline given. Publishes ms an average of 6 months after acceptance. Editorial lead time 4 months. Submit seasonal material 6 months in advance. Accepts queries by mail, e-mail, fax. Sample copy for $6.95, plus postage charged to credit card. Guidelines available online.

NONFICTION Needs historical, British Columbia coast only, how-to, humor, interview, personal experience, technical, boating related, travel, cruising, and destination on the British Columbia coast. "No articles from writers who are obviously not boaters!" Query. Length: 800-2,000 words. **Pays $150-500. Pays some expenses of writers on assignment for unsolicited articles.** Pays expenses of writers on assignment.

COLUMNS Currents (current events, trade and people news, boat gatherings, and festivities), 50-250 words. Reflections; Cruising, both 800-1,000 words. Query. **Pay varies.**

$$ PONTOON & DECK BOAT

Harris Publishing, Inc., 360 B. St., Idaho Falls ID 83402. (208)524-7000. **Fax:** (208)522-5241. **E-mail:**

blk@pdbmagazine.com. **Website:** www.pdbmagazine.com. **15% freelance written.** Magazine published 11 times/year. "We are a boating niche publication geared toward the pontoon and deck boating lifestyle and consumer market. Our audience is comprised of people who utilize these boats for varied family activities and fishing. Our magazine is promotional of the PDB industry and its major players. We seek to give the reader a twofold reason to read our publication: to celebrate the lifestyle, and to do it aboard a first-class craft." Estab. 1995. Circ. 84,000. Byline given. Editorial lead time 2 months. Submit seasonal material 3 months in advance. Accepts simultaneous submissions. Responds in 6 weeks to queries. Responds in 3 months to mss. Sample copy and writer's guidelines free.

NONFICTION Needs how-to, personal experience, technical, remodeling, rebuilding. We are saturated with travel pieces; no general boating, humor, fiction, or poetry. **Buys 15 mss/year.** Send complete ms. Length: 600-2,000 words. **Pays $50-300.** Sometimes pays expenses of writers on assignment.

COLUMNS No Wake Zone (short, fun quips); Better Boater (how-to). **Buys 6-12 mss/year.** Query with published clips. **Pays $50-150.**

$$$ POWER & MOTORYACHT

Source Interlink Media, 261 Madison Ave., 6th Floor, New York NY 10016. (212)915-4313; (212)915-4000. **Fax:** (212)915-4328. **E-mail:** richard.thiel@powerandmotoryacht.com. **Website:** www.powerandmotoryacht.com. Aimee Colon, art director. **Contact:** Richard Thiel, editor-in-chief. **25% freelance written.** Monthly magazine covering powerboats 24 feet and larger with special emphasis on the 35-foot-plus market. "Readers have an average of 33 years experience boating, and we give them accurate advice on how to choose, operate, and maintain their boats as well as what electronics and gear will help them pursue their favorite pastime. In addition, since powerboating is truly a lifestyle and not just a hobby for them, *Power & Motoryacht* reports on a host of other topics that affect their enjoyment of the water: chartering, sportfishing, and the environment, among others. Articles must therefore be clear, concise, and authoritative; knowledge of the marine industry is mandatory. Include personal experience and information for marine industry experts where appropriate." Estab. 1985. Circ. 157,000. Byline given. Offers 33% kill fee. Publishes ms an average of 4-6 months after acceptance. Editorial lead time 4-6 months. Submit seasonal material 4-6 months in advance. Accepts queries by mail, e-mail. Responds in 1 month to queries. Sample copy with 10×12 SASE. Guidelines with #10 SASE or via e-mail.

NONFICTION Needs how-to, interview, personal experience, photo feature, travel. No unsolicited mss or articles about sailboats and/or sailing yachts (including motorsailers or cruise ships). **Buys 20-25 mss/year.** Query with published clips. Length: 800-1,500 words. **Pays $500-1,000 for assigned articles.** Sometimes pays expenses of writers on assignment.

⊘ $$$ POWERBOAT

Affinity Group Inc., 2575 Vista Del Mar, Ventura CA 93001. (805)667-4100. **Fax:** (805)667-4336. **E-mail:** edit-dept@powerboatmag.com; jason@powerboatmag.com. **Website:** www.powerboatmag.com. Jim Hendricks, editorial director, jhendricks@affinitygroup.com. **Contact:** Jason Johnson, senior editor. **25% freelance written.** Magazine published 11 times/year covering performance boating. Estab. 1973. Circ. 50,000. Byline given. Offers negotiable kill fee. Publishes ms an average of 3 months after acceptance. Editorial lead time 3 months. Submit seasonal material 4 months in advance. Accepts queries by mail, e-mail, fax. Sample copy available online.

○ No unsolicited mss.

NONFICTION Needs how-to, interview, new product, photo feature. No general interest boating stories. **Buys numerous mss/year.** Query. Length: 300-2,000 words. **Pays $125-1,200.** Sometimes pays expenses of writers on assignment.

✪ $$ POWER BOATING CANADA

1121 Invicta Drive Unit 2, Oakville ON L6H 2R2 Canada. (800)354-9145. **Fax:** (905)844-5032. **E-mail:** editor@powerboating.com. **Website:** www.powerboating.com. **70% freelance written.** Bimonthly magazine covering recreational power boating. *Power Boating Canada* offers boating destinations, how-to features, boat tests (usually staff written), lifestyle pieces—with a Canadian slant—and appeal to recreational power boaters across the country. Estab. 1984. Circ. 42,000. Byline given. Publishes ms an average of 3 months after acceptance. Editorial lead time 2 months. Submit seasonal material 3 months in advance. Responds in 1 month to queries. Responds in 2 months to mss. Sample copy free.

NONFICTION Needs historical, how-to, interview, personal experience, travel, boating destinations. No general boating articles or personal anecdotes. **Buys 40-50 mss/year.** Query. Length: 1,200-2,500 words. **Pays $150-300 (Canadian).** Sometimes pays expenses of writers on assignment.

💲💲💲 SAIL

98 N. Washington St., Suite 107, Boston MA 02114. (617)720-8600. **Fax:** (617)723-0912. **E-mail:** sailmag@sailmagazine.com. **Website:** www.sailmagazine.com. **Contact:** Peter Nielsen, editor-in-chief. **30% freelance written.** Monthly magazine written and edited for everyone who sails—aboard a coastal or bluewater cruiser, trailerable, one-design or offshore racer, or daysailer. How-to and technical articles concentrate on techniques of sailing and aspects of design and construction, boat systems, and gear; the feature section emphasizes the fun and rewards of sailing in a practical and instructive way. Estab. 1970. Circ. 180,000. Byline given. Publishes ms an average of 1 year after acceptance. Accepts queries by mail, e-mail, fax. Responds in 3 months to queries. Guidelines with SASE or online (download).

NONFICTION Needs how-to, personal experience, technical, distance cruising, destinations. Special issues: Cruising, chartering, commissioning, fitting-out, special race (e.g., America's Cup), Top 10 Boats. **Buys 50 mss/year.** Query. Length: 1,500-3,000 words. **Pays $200-800.** Sometimes pays expenses of writers on assignment.

COLUMNS Sailing Memories (short essay); Sailing News (cruising, racing, legal, political, environmental); Under Sail (human interest). Query. **Pays $50-400.**

💲💲💲 SAILING MAGAZINE

125 E. Main St., Port Washington WI 53074. (262)284-3494. **Fax:** (262)284-7764. **E-mail:** editorial@sailing-magazine.net. **Website:** www.sailingmagazine.net. Monthly magazine for the experienced sailor. Estab. 1966. Circ. 45,000. Pays after publication. Accepts queries by mail, e-mail. Responds in 2 months to queries.

NONFICTION Needs book excerpts, how-to, tech pieces on boats and gear, interview, personal experience, travel, by sail. **Buys 15-20 mss/year.** Length: 750-2,500 words. **Pays $100-800.**

💲💲 SAILING WORLD

World Publications, 55 Hammarlund Way, Middletown RI 02842. (401)845-5100. **Fax:** (401)848-5180. E-mail: editor@sailingworld.com. **Website:** www.sailingworld.com. **Contact:** Dave Reed, editor; Shannon Cain, associate art director. **40% freelance written.** Magazine published 10 times/year covering performance sailing. Estab. 1962. Circ. 65,000. Byline given. Publishes ms an average of 4 months after acceptance. Responds in 1 month to queries. Sample copy for $5. Guidelines available online at website.

NONFICTION Needs how-to, for racing and performance-oriented sailors, interview, photo feature, Regatta sports and charter. No travelogs. **Buys 5-10 unsolicited mss/year.** Prospective contributors to Sailing World should study recent issues of the magazine to determine appropriate subject matter. The emphasis here is on performance sailing: keep in mind that the Sailing World readership is relatively educated about the sport. Unless you are dealing with a totally new aspect of sailing, you can and should discuss ideas on an advanced technical level; however, extensive formulae and graphs don't play well to our audience. When in doubt as to the suitability of an article or idea, submit a written query before time and energy are misdirected. (Because of the volume of queries received, editors cannot accept phone calls.) Length: 400-1,500 words. **Pays $400 for up to 2,000 words.** Does not pay expenses of writers on assignment unless pre-approved.

💲💲 SEA KAYAKER

Sea Kayaker, Inc., P.O. Box 17029, Seattle WA 98127. (206)789-1326. **Fax:** (206)781-1141. **E-mail:** editorial@seakayakermag.com. **Website:** www.seakayakermag.com. **95% freelance written.** *Sea Kayaker* is a bimonthly publication with a worldwide readership that covers all aspects of kayak touring. It is well known as an important source of continuing education by the most experienced paddlers. Estab. 1984. Circ. 30,000. Byline given. Offers 10% kill fee. Publishes ms an average of 6 months after acceptance. Editorial lead time 4 months. Submit seasonal material 4 months in advance. Accepts queries by mail, e-mail, fax, phone. Responds in 2 months to queries. Sample copy for $7.30 (US), samples to other countries extra. Guidelines available online.

NONFICTION Needs essays, historical, how-to, on making equipment, humor, new product, personal experience, technical, travel. Unsolicited gear reviews are not accepted. **Buys 50 mss/year.** Send complete ms. Length: 1,500-5,000 words. **Pays 18-20¢/word**

for assigned articles. Pays 15-17¢/word for unsolicited articles.

COLUMNS Technique; Equipment; Do-It-Yourself; Food; Safety; Health; Environment; Book Reviews; all 1,000-2,500 words. **Buys 40-45 mss/year.** Query. **Pays 15-20¢/word.**

SEA MAGAZINE

Duncan McIntosh Co., 17782 Cowan, Suite A, Irvine CA 92614. (949)660-6150, ext. 253. **Fax:** (949)660-6172. **E-mail:** mike@seamag.com. **Website:** www.goboatingamerica.com. **Contact:** Mike Werling, managing editor. Monthly magazine covering West Coast power boating. Estab. 1908. Circ. 55,000. Byline given. Publishes ms an average of 6 months after acceptance. Editorial lead time 3 months. Submit seasonal material 6 months in advance. Accepts simultaneous submissions. Responds in 3 months to queries.

NONFICTION Needs how-to, new product, personal experience, technical, travel. **Buys 36 mss/year.** Send complete ms. Length: 1,000-1,500 words. **Payment varies** Pays expenses of writers on assignment.

🌐 $$$$ SHOWBOATS INTERNATIONAL

Published by Boat International Media, 41-47 Hartfield Rd., London SW19 3RQ United Kingdom. (954)522-2628 (U.S. number). **Fax:** (954)522-2240. **E-mail:** marilyn.mower@boatinternationalmedia.com. **Website:** www.boatinternational.com. **Contact:** Marilyn Mower, editorial director - U.S.; Richard Taranto, art director. **70% freelance written.** Magazine published 10 times/year covering luxury superyacht industry. Estab. 1995. Circ. 55,000. Byline given. Offers 30% kill fee. Editorial lead time 2 months. Submit seasonal material 4 months in advance. Accepts queries by e-mail. Responds in 2 months to mss. Sample copy for $6.00. Guidelines free.

NONFICTION Travel/destination pieces that are superyacht related. **Buys 3/year mss/year.** Query. Length: 700-2,500 words. **Pays $300 minimum, $2,000 maximum for assigned articles.** Sometimes pays expenses of writers on assignment.

$$ SOUTHERN BOATING MAGAZINE

Southern Boating & Yachting, Inc., 330 N. Andrews Ave., Ft. Lauderdale FL 33301. (954)522-5515. **Fax:** (954)522-2260. **E-mail:** info@southernboating.com. **Website:** www.southernboating.com. **Contact:** Louisa Beckett. **50% freelance written.** Monthly boating magazine. Upscale monthly yachting magazine focusing on the Southeast U.S., Bahamas, Caribbean, and Gulf of Mexico. Estab. 1972. Circ. 40,000. Byline given. Pays within 30 days of publication. Publishes ms an average of 2 months after acceptance. Editorial lead time 3 months. Submit seasonal material 3 months in advance. Accepts queries by e-mail. Sample copy for $8.

NONFICTION Needs how-to, boat maintenance, travel, boating related, destination pieces. **Buys 50 mss/year.** Query. Length: 900-1,200 words. **Pays $500-750 with art.**

COLUMNS Weekend Workshop (how-to/maintenance), 900 words; What's New in Electronics (electronics), 900 words; Engine Room (new developments), 1,000 words. **Buys 24 mss/year.** Query first, see media kit for special issue focus. **Pays $600.**

$ WATERFRONT TIMES

Storyboard Media Inc., 2787 E. Oakland Park Blvd., Suite 205, Ft. Lauderdale FL 33306. (954)524-9450. **Fax:** (954)524-9464. **E-mail:** editor@waterfronttimes.com. **Website:** www.waterfronttimes.com. **Contact:** Jennifer Heit, editor. **20% freelance written.** Monthly tabloid covering marine and boating topics for the Greater Ft. Lauderdale waterfront community. Estab. 1984. Circ. 20,000. Byline given. Publishes ms an average of 2 months after acceptance. Submit seasonal material 3 months in advance. Responds in 1 month to queries. Sample copy for SAE with 9×12 envelope and 4 first-class stamps.

NONFICTION Needs interview, of people important in boating, i.e., racers, boat builders, designers, etc. from south Florida, Regional articles on south Florida's waterfront issues; marine communities; travel pieces of interest to boaters, including docking information. Length: 500-1,000 words. **Pays $100-125 for assigned articles.**

$$ WATERWAY GUIDE

P.O. Box 1125, 16273 General Puller Hwy., Deltaville VA 23043. (804)776-8999. **Fax:** (804)776-6111. **E-mail:** slandry@waterwayguide.com. **Website:** www.waterwayguide.com. **Contact:** Susan Landry, editor. **90% freelance written.** Triannual magazine covering intracoastal waterway travel for recreational boats. "Writer must be knowledgeable about navigation and the areas covered by the guide." Estab. 1947. Circ. 30,000. Byline given. Publishes ms an average of 3 months after acceptance. Editorial lead time 4 months. Submit seasonal material 3 months in advance. Ac-

CONSUMER MAGAZINES

cepts queries by mail, phone. Responds in 6 weeks to queries. Responds in 2 months to mss. Sample copy for $39.95 with $3 postage.

NONFICTION Needs essays, historical, how-to, photo feature, technical, travel. **Buys 6 mss/year.** Send complete ms. Length: 250-5,000 words. **Pays $50-500.**

WATERWAYS WORLD

Waterways World Ltd, 151 Station St., Burton-on-Trent Staffordshire DE14 1BG United Kingdom. 01283 742950. **E-mail:** editorial@waterwaysworld.com. **Website:** www.waterwaysworld.com. **Contact:** Richard Fairhurst, editor. Monthly magazine publishing news, photographs, and illustrated articles on all aspects of inland waterways in Britain, and on limited aspects of waterways abroad. Estab. 1972. Editorial lead time 2 months. Accepts queries by mail, e-mail. NoGuidelines by email.

NONFICTION Does not want poetry or fiction. Submit query letter or complete ms, SAE.

WAVELENGTH MAGAZINE

Wild Coast Publishing, P.O. Box 24 Stn A, Nanaimo BC V9R 5K4 Canada. (250)244-6437; (866)984-6437. **Fax:** (250)244-1937; (866)654-1937. **E-mail:** editor@wavelengthmagazine.com. **Website:** www.wavelengthmagazine.com. **Contact:** John Kimantas, editor. **75% freelance written.** Quarterly magazine with a major focus on paddling the Pacific coast. We promote safe paddling, guide paddlers to useful products and services and explore coastal environmental issues. Estab. 1991. Circ. 65,000 print and electronic readers. Byline given. Publishes ms an average of 4 months after acceptance. Editorial lead time 4 months. Submit seasonal material 4 months in advance. Accepts queries by mail, e-mail. Sample copy available online. Guidelines available online.

NONFICTION Needs how-to, paddle, travel, humor, new product, personal experience, technical, travel, trips. **Buys 25 mss/year.** Query. Length: 1,000-1,500 words. **Pays $50-75.**

WOODENBOAT MAGAZINE

WoodenBoat Publications, Inc., P.O. Box 78, 41 WoodenBoat Ln., Brooklin ME 04616. (207)359-4651. **Fax:** (207)359-8920. **E-mail:** woodenboat@woodenboat.com. **E-mail:** matt@woodenboat.com. **Website:** www.woodenboat.com. **Contact:** Matt Murphy. **50% freelance written.** Bimonthly magazine for wooden boat owners, builders, and designers. "We are devoted exclusively to the design, building, care, preservation, and use of wooden boats, both commercial and pleasure, old and new, sail and power. We work to convey quality, integrity, and involvement in the creation and care of these craft, to entertain, inform, inspire, and to provide our varied readers with access to individuals who are deeply experienced in the world of wooden boats." Estab. 1974. Circ. 90,000. Byline given. Offers variable kill fee. Publishes ms an average of 1 year after acceptance. Accepts simultaneous submissions. Responds in 2 months to queries. Responds in 2 months to mss. Sample copy for $5.99. Guidelines available online.

NONFICTION Needs technical, repair, restoration, maintenance, use, design, and building wooden boats. No poetry, fiction. **Buys 50 mss/year.** Query with published clips. Length: 1,500-5,000 words. **Pays $300/1,000 words.** Sometimes pays expenses of writers on assignment.

COLUMNS Currents pays for information on wooden boat-related events, projects, boatshop activities, etc. Uses same columnists for each issue. Length: 250-1,000 words. Send complete information. **Pays $5-50.**

YACHTING

Bonnier Corporation, 55 Hammarlund Way, Middletown RI 02842. **Fax:** (401)845-5180. **E-mail:** letters@yachtingmagazine.com. **Website:** www.yachtingmagazine.com. **30% freelance written.** Monthly magazine. Monthly magazine written and edited for experienced, knowledgeable yachtsmen. Estab. 1907. Circ. 132,000. Byline given. Editorial lead time 2 months. Submit seasonal material 6 months in advance. Accepts queries by mail, e-mail, fax. Responds in 1 month to queries. Responds in 3 months to mss. Sample copy free. Guidelines available online.

NONFICTION Needs personal experience, technical. **Buys 50 mss/year.** Query with published clips. Length: 750-800 words. **Pays $150-1,500.** Pays expenses of writers on assignment.

GENERAL INTEREST

OUTDOORS NW

PMB Box 331, 10002 Aurora Ave. N. #36, Seattle WA 98133. (206)418-0747; (800) 935-1083. **Fax:** (206)418-0746. **E-mail:** info@outdoorsnw.com. **Website:** www.outdoorsnw.com. **80% freelance written.** Monthly magazine covering outdoor recreation in the Pacific Northwest. "Writers must have a solid knowledge of the sport they are writing about. They must be doers." Estab. 1988. Circ. 40,000. Byline given. Publishes ms an average of 3 months after acceptance. Editorial lead time 2 months. Submit seasonal material 4 months in advance. Accepts queries by mail, e-mail, fax. Accepts simultaneous submissions. Sample copy and writer's guidelines for $3.

NONFICTION Needs interview, new product, travel. Query with published clips. Length: 750-1,500 words. **Pays $25-125.** Sometimes pays expenses of writers on assignment.

COLUMNS Faces, Places, Puruits (750 words). **Buys 4-6 mss/year.** Query with published clips. **Pays $40-75.**

$ SILENT SPORTS

Journal Community Publishing Group, 600 Industrial Dr., P.O. Box 609, Waupaca WI 54981. (715)258-5546; (800)236-3313. **Fax:** (715)258-8162. **E-mail:** info@silentsports.net. **Website:** www.silentsports.net. **75% freelance written.** Monthly magazine covering running, cycling, cross-country skiing, canoeing, kayaking, snowshoeing, in-line skating, camping, backpacking, and hiking aimed at people in Wisconsin, Minnesota, northern Illinois, and portions of Michigan and Iowa. "Not a coffee table magazine. Our readers are participants from rank amateur weekend athletes to highly competitive racers." Estab. 1984. Circ. 10,000. Byline given. Offers 20% kill fee. Publishes ms an average of 3 months after acceptance. Submit seasonal material 4 months in advance. Accepts queries by mail, e-mail, fax. Responds in 3 months to queries. Sample copy and writer's guidelines for 10×13 SAE with 7 first-class stamps.

NONFICTION Needs general interest, how-to, interview, opinion, technical, travel. **Buys 25 mss/year.** Query. 2,500 words maximum. **Pays $15-100.** Sometimes pays expenses of writers on assignment.

SPORTS ILLUSTRATED

Time, Inc., 1271 Avenue of the Americas, New York NY 10020. (212)522-1212. **E-mail:** story_queries@simail.com. **Website:** www.si.com. Terry McDonell, editor. Weekly magazine. *Sports Illustrated* reports and interprets the world of sport, recreation, and active leisure. It previews, analyzes, and comments upon major games and events, as well as those noteworthy for character and spirit alone. It features individuals connected to sport and evaluates trends concerning the part sport plays in contemporary life. In addition, the magazine has articles on such subjects as sports gear and swim suits. Special departments deal with sports equipment, books, and statistics. Estab. 1954. Circ. 3,339,000. Accepts queries by mail. Responds in 4-6 weeks to queries.

💬 Do not send photos or graphics. Include a SASE for return of materials.

NONFICTION Query.

GOLF

$$ AFRICAN AMERICAN GOLFER'S DIGEST

80 Wall St., Suite 720, New York NY 10005. (212)571-6559. **E-mail:** debertcook@aol.com. **Website:** www.africanamericangolfersdigest.com. **Contact:** Debert Cook, managing editor. **100% freelance written.** Quarterly. Covering golf lifestyle, health, travel destinations and reviews, golf equipment, golfer profiles. "Editorial should focus on interests of our market demographic of African Americans with historical, artistic, musical, educational (higher learning), automotive, sports, fashion, entertainment, and other categories of high interest to them." Estab. 2003. Circ. 20,000. Byline given. Publishes ms an average of 3 months after acceptance. Editorial lead time 3-6 months. Submit seasonal material 3-6 months in advance. Accepts queries by e-mail. Accepts simultaneous submissions. Responds in 3 weeks to queries. Responds in 3 months to mss. Sample copy for $6. Guidelines by e-mail.

NONFICTION Needs how-to, interview, new product, personal experience, photo feature, technical, travel., golf-related. **Buys 3 mss/year.** Query. Length: 250-1,500 words. **Pays 10-50¢/word.**

COLUMNS Profiles (celebrities, national leaders, entertainers, corporate leaders, etc., who golf); Travel (destination/golf course reviews); Golf Fashion (jewelry, clothing, accessories). **Buys 3 mss/year.** Query. **Pays 10-50¢/word.**

FILLERS Needs anecdotes, facts, gags, newsbreaks, short humor. **Buys 3 mss/year.** Length: 20-125 words. **Pays 10-50¢/word.**

$$ ARIZONA, THE STATE OF GOLF

Arizona Golf Association, 7226 N. 16th St., Suite 200, Phoenix AZ 85020. (602)944-3035. **Fax:** (602)944-3228. **Website:** www.azgolf.org. **Contact:** Brian Foster, director of marketing and communications. **50% freelance written.** Quarterly magazine covering golf in Arizona, the official publication of the Arizona Golf Association. Estab. 1999. Circ. 45,000. By-

CONSUMER MAGAZINES

line given. Editorial lead time 6 months. Submit seasonal material 3 months in advance. Accepts queries by mail. Accepts simultaneous submissions. Sample copy and writer's guidelines free.

NONFICTION Needs book excerpts, essays, historical, how-to, golf, humor, inspirational, interview, new product, opinion, personal experience, photo feature, travel, destinations. **Buys 5-10 mss/year.** Query. Length: 500-2,000 words. **Pays $50-500.** Sometimes pays expenses of writers on assignment.

COLUMNS Short Strokes (golf news and notes), Improving Your Game (golf tips), Out of Bounds (guest editorial, 800 words). Query.

GOLF CANADA

Chill Media Inc., 77 John St., Suite 4, Oakville ON L6K 3W3 Canada. (905)337-1886. **Fax:** (905)337-1887. **E-mail:** scotty@chillmag.ca; stacy@ichill.ca. **Website:** www.golfcanada.ca. Stacy Bradshaw, editor. **Contact:** Scott Stevenson, publisher. **80% freelance written.** Magazine published 4 times/year covering Canadian golf. *Golf Canada* is the official magazine of the Royal Canadian Golf Association, published to entertain and enlighten members about RCGA-related activities and to generally support and promote amateur golf in Canada. Estab. 1994. Circ. 159,000. Byline given. Offers 100% kill fee. Editorial lead time 3 months. Submit seasonal material 6 months in advance. Accepts queries by mail, e-mail, fax, phone. YesSample copy free.

NONFICTION Needs historical, interview, new product, opinion, photo feature, travel. No professional golf-related articles. **Buys 42 mss/year.** Query with published clips. Length: 750-3,000 words. **Pays 60¢/word, including electronic rights.** Sometimes pays expenses of writers on assignment.

COLUMNS Guest Column (focus on issues surrounding the Canadian golf community), 700 words. Query. **Pays 60¢/word, including electronic rights.**

THE GOLFER

59 E. 72nd St., New York NY 10021. (212)867-7070. **Fax:** (212)867-8550. **E-mail:** info@thegolferinc.com. **Website:** www.thegolfermag.com; www.thegolferinc. com. **40% freelance written.** Bimonthly magazine covering golf. A sophisticated tone for a lifestyle-oriented magazine. "The Golfer Inc. is an international luxury brand, a new media company that is a driving force in the game. Its website is the source for those who want the best the game has to offer—the clas-

sic courses, great destinations, finest accoutrements, most intriguing personalities and latest trends on and off the course.The magazine has distinguished itself as the highest quality, most innovative in its field. It is written for the top of the market—those who live a lifestyle shaped by their passion for the game. With its stunning photography, elegant design and evocative writing, The Golfer speaks to its affluent readers with a sense of style and sophistication—it is a world class publication with an international flair, celebrating the lifestyle of the game." Estab. 1994. Circ. 253,000. Byline given. Offers negotiable kill fee. Publishes ms an average of 2 months after acceptance. Editorial lead time 2 months. Submit seasonal material 4 months in advance. Accepts queries by mail, e-mail, fax. Accepts simultaneous submissions. Sample copy free.

NONFICTION Needs book excerpts, essays, general interest, historical, how-to, humor, inspirational, interview, new product, opinion, personal experience, photo feature, technical, travel. Send complete ms. Length: 300-2,000 words. **Pays $150-600.**

GOLFING MAGAZINE

Golfer Magazine, Inc., 274 Silas Dean Hwy., Wethersfield CT 06109. (860)563-1633. **Fax:** (646)607-3001. **E-mail:** tlanders@golfingmagazine.net; JTorsiello@golfingMagazine.net. **Website:** www.golfingmagazineonline.com. **Contact:** Tom Landers, president and publisher; John Torsiello, editor. **30% freelance written.** Bimonthly magazine covering golf, including travel, products, player profiles and company profiles. Estab. 1999. Circ. 175,000. Byline given. Offers negotiable kill fee. Editorial lead time 2 months. Submit seasonal material 2 months in advance. Accepts queries by mail, e-mail. YesSample copy free.

NONFICTION Needs book excerpts, new product, photo feature, travel. **Buys 4-5 mss/year.** Query. Length: 700-2,500 words. **Pays $250-1,000 for assigned articles. Pays $100-500 for unsolicited articles.**

FILLERS Needs facts, gags. **Buys 2-3 mss/year.** Payment individually determined.

GOLF NEWS MAGAZINE

Golf News Magazine, P.O. Box 1040, Rancho Mirage CA 92270. (760)321-8800. **Fax:** (760)328-3013. **E-mail:** golfnews@aol.com. **Website:** www.golfnewsmag.com. **Contact:** Dan Poppers, editor-in-chief. **40% freelance written.** Monthly magazine covering golf. "Our publication specializes in the creative treatment of the sport of golf, offering a variety of themes and slants as related to golf. If it's good writing and relates to golf, we're interested." Estab. 1984. Circ. 15,000. Byline given. Publishes ms an average of 3 months after acceptance. Editorial lead time 2 months. Submit seasonal material 2 months in advance. Accepts queries by mail, e-mail, fax. Accepts simultaneous submissions. Responds in 3 weeks to queries. Responds in 3 weeks to mss. Sample copy for $2 and 9×12 SAE with 4 first class stamps.

NONFICTION Needs book excerpts, essays, exposé, general interest, historical, humor, inspirational, interview, opinion, personal experience, real estate. **Buys 20 mss/year.** Query with published clips. **Pays $75-350.**

COLUMNS Submit ideas. **Buys 10 mss/year.** Query with published clips.

GOLF TIPS

Werner Publishing Corp., 12121 Wilshire Blvd., 12th Floor, Los Angeles CA 90025-1176. (310)820-1500. **Fax:** (310)826-5008. **E-mail:** editors@golftipsmag. com. **Website:** www.golftipsmag.com. **95% freelance written.** Magazine published 9 times/year covering golf instruction and equipment. "We provide mostly concise, very clear golf instruction pieces for the serious golfer." Estab. 1986. Circ. 300,000. Byline given. Offers 33% kill fee. Publishes ms an average of 2 months after acceptance. Editorial lead time 3 months. Submit seasonal material 4 months in advance. Responds in 1 month to queries. Sample copy free. Guidelines on website.

NONFICTION Needs book excerpts, how-to, interview, new product, photo feature, technical, travel, all golf related. "Generally, golf essays rarely make it." **Buys 125 mss/year.** Send complete ms. Length: 250-2,000 words. **Pays $300-1,000 for assigned articles. Pays $300-800 for unsolicited articles.** Sometimes pays expenses of writers on assignment.

COLUMNS Stroke Saver (very clear, concise instruction), 350 words; Lesson Library (book excerpts—usually in a series), 1,000 words; Travel Tips (formatted golf travel), 2,500 words. **Buys 40 mss/year.** Query with or without published clips or send complete ms. **Pays $300-850.**

MINNESOTA GOLFER

6550 York Ave. S., Suite 211, Edina MN 55435. (952)927-4643. **Fax:** (952)927-9642. **E-mail:** wp@mngolf.org; editor@mngolf.org. **Website:** www.mngolfer.

com. **Contact:** W.P. Ryan, editor. **75% freelance written.** Bimonthly magazine covering golf in Minnesota, the official publication of the Minnesota Golf Association. Estab. 1975. Circ. 66,000. Byline given. Pays on acceptance or publication. Editorial lead time 3 months. Accepts queries by mail, e-mail, fax.

NONFICTION Needs historical, interview, new product, travel, book reviews, instruction, golf course previews. Query with published clips. Length: 400-2,000 words. **Pays $50-750.** Sometimes pays expenses of writers on assignment.

COLUMNS Punch shots (golf news and notes); Q School (news and information targeted to beginners, junior golfers and women); Great Drives (featuring noteworthy golf holes in Minnesota); Instruction.

TEXAS GOLFER MAGAZINE

Texas Golder Media, 15721 Park Row, Suite 100, Houston TX 77084. (888)863-9899. **E-mail:** george@texasgolfermagazine.com. **Website:** www.texasgolfermagazine.com. **Contact:** George Fuller, editor-in-chief and associate publisher. **10% freelance written.** Bi-monthly magazine covering golf in Texas. Estab. 1984. Circ. 50,000. Byline given. Pays 10 days after publication. Publishes ms an average of 2 months after acceptance. Editorial lead time 2 months. Submit seasonal material 3 months in advance. Responds in 2 weeks to queries. Responds in 1 month to mss. Sample copy free. Prefers direct phone discussion for writer's guidelines.

NONFICTION Needs book excerpts, humor, personal experience, all golf-related. Travel pieces accepted about golf outside of Texas. **Buys 20 mss/year.** Query. **Pays 25-40¢/word.**

VIRGINIA GOLFER

Touchpoint Publishing, Inc., 600 Founders Bridge Blvd., Midlothian VA 23113. (804)378-2300, ext. 12. **Fax:** (804)378-2369. **E-mail:** ablair@vsga.org. **Website:** www.vsga.org. **Contact:** Andrew Blair, editor. **65% freelance written.** Bimonthly magazine covering golf in Virginia, the official publication of the Virginia State Golf Association. Estab. 1983. Circ. 45,000. Byline given. Editorial lead time 6 months. Submit seasonal material 3 months in advance. Accepts queries by mail, e-mail. Accepts simultaneous submissions. Sample copy and writer's guidelines free.

NONFICTION Needs book excerpts, essays, historical, how-to, golf, humor, inspirational, interview, personal experience, photo feature, technical, golf equipment, where to play, golf business. **Buys 30-40 mss/year.** Send complete ms. Length: 500-2,500 words. **Pays $50-200.** Sometimes pays expenses of writers on assignment.

COLUMNS Chip ins & Three Putts (news notes), Rules Corner (golf rules explanations and discussion), Your Game, Golf Travel (where to play), Great Holes, Q&A, Golf Business (what's happening?), Fashion. Query.

GUNS

💲💲 MUZZLE BLASTS

P.O. Box 67, Friendship IN 47021. (812)667-5131. **Fax:** (812)667-5136. **E-mail:** mblastdop@seidata.com. **Website:** www.nmlra.org. **65% freelance written.** Monthly magazine. "Articles must relate to muzzleloading or the muzzleloading era of American history." Estab. 1939. Circ. 18,500. Byline given. Offers $50 kill fee. Publishes ms an average of 6 months after acceptance. Editorial lead time 4 months. Submit seasonal material 6 months in advance. Responds in 1 month to mss. Sample copy and writer's guidelines free.

NONFICTION Needs book excerpts, general interest, historical, how-to, humor, interview, new product, personal experience, photo feature, technical, travel. No subjects that do not pertain to muzzleloading. **Buys 80 mss/year.** Query. Length: 2,500 words. **Pays $150 minimum for assigned articles. Pays $50 minimum for unsolicited articles.**

COLUMNS Buys 96 mss/year. Query. **Pays $50-200.**

FICTION Must pertain to muzzleloading. Needs adventure, historical, humorous. **Buys 6 mss/year.** Query. Length: 2,500 words. **Pays $50-300.**

FILLERS Needs facts. **Pays $50.**

HIKING AND BACKPACKING

💲💲💲💲 BACKPACKER MAGAZINE

Cruz Bay Publishing, Inc., an Active Interest Media Co., 2520 55th St., Suite 210, Boulder CO 80301. **E-mail:** gfullerton@backpacker.com. **Website:** www.backpacker.com. Dennis Lewon, deputy editor (Features & People), dlewon@backpacker.com; Shannon Davis, senior editor (Destinations), sdavis@backpacker.com; Kristin Bjornsen, associate editor (Skills(, kbjornsen@aimmedia.com; Kristin Hostetter, gear editor (Gear), khostetter1@gmail.com. **Contact:** Jonathan Dorn, editor-in-chief. **50% freelance written.** Magazine published 9 times/year covering wilderness travel for backpackers. Estab. 1973. Circ. 340,000. Byline given. 6 months. Accepts queries by mail (include SASE for returns), e-mail (preferred, with attachments and web links), fax. Responds in 2-4 weeks to queries. Free sample copy. Guidelines available online.

NONFICTION Needs essays, exposé, historical, how-to, humor, inspirational, interview, new product, personal experience, technical, travel, BACKPACKER primarily covers hiking. When warranted, we cover canoeing, kayaking, snowshoeing, cross-country skiing, and other human-powered modes of travel. Wilderness or backcountry: The true backpacking experience means getting away from the trailhead and into the wilds. Whether a dayhike or a weeklong trip, out-of-the-way, unusual destinations are what we're looking for. No step-by-step accounts of what you did on your summer vacation—stories that chronicle every rest stop and gulp of water. Query with published clips before sending complete ms. Length: 750-4,000 words. **Pays 60¢-$1/word.**

COLUMNS Signpost, News From All Over (adventure, environment, wildlife, trails, techniques, organizations, special interests—well-written, entertaining, short, newsy item), 50-500 words; Getaways (great hiking destinations, primarily North America), includes weekend, 250-500 words, weeklong, 250-1000, multi-destination guides, 500-1500 words, and dayhikes, 50-200 words, plus travel news and other items; Fitness (in-the-field health column), 750-1,200 words; Food (food-related aspects of wilderness: nutrition, cooking techniques, recipes, products and gear), 500-750 words; Know How (ranging from beginner to expert focus, written by people with solid expertise, details ways to improve performance, how-to-do-it instructions, information on equipment manufacturers, and places readers can go), 300-1,000 words; Senses (capturing a moment in backcountry through sight, sound, smell, and other senses, paired with an outstanding photo), 150-200 words. **Buys 50-75 mss/year.**

HOCKEY

💲💲 MINNESOTA HOCKEY JOURNAL

Touchpoint Sports, 505 N. Hwy 169, Ste. 465, Minneapolis MN 55441. (763)595-0808. **Fax:** (763)595-0016. **E-mail:** mhj@touchpointsports.com; greg@touchpointsports.com. **Website:** www.minnesotahockeyjournal.com. **50% freelance written**. Journal published 4 times/year. Estab. 2000. Circ. 40,000. Byline given. Editorial lead time 6 months. Submit seasonal material 4 months in advance. Accepts simultaneous submissions. Sample copy and writer's guidelines free.

NONFICTION Needs essays, general interest, historical, how-to, play hockey, humor, inspirational, interview, new product, opinion, personal experience, photo feature, travel, hockey camps, pro hockey, juniors, college, Olympics, youth, etc. **Buys 3-5 mss/year.** Query. Length: 500-1,500 words. **Pays $100-300.**

USA HOCKEY MAGAZINE

Touchpoint Sports, 1775 Bob Johnson Dr., Colorado Springs CO 80906. (719)576-8724. **Fax:** (763)538-1160. **E-mail:** usah@usahockey.org; info@touchpointsports.com. **Website:** www.usahockeymagazine.com; www.usahockey.com. **Contact:** Harry Thompson, editor-in-chief. **60% freelance written.** Magazine published 10 times/year covering amateur hockey in the US. The world's largest hockey magazine, *USA Hockey Magazine* is the official magazine of USA Hockey, Inc., the national governing body of hockey. Estab. 1980. Circ. 444,000. Byline given. Pays on acceptance or publication. Editorial lead time 6 months. Submit seasonal material 4 months in advance. Accepts simultaneous submissions. Sample copy and writer's guidelines free.

NONFICTION Needs essays, general interest, historical, how-to, play hockey, humor, inspirational, interview, new product, opinion, personal experience, photo feature, travel, hockey camps, pro hockey, juniors, college, NCAA hockey championships, Olympics, youth, etc. **Buys 20-30 mss/year.** Query. Length: 500-5,000 words. **Pays $50-750.** Pays expenses of writers on assignment.

COLUMNS Short Cuts (news and notes); Coaches' Corner (teaching tips); USA Hockey; Inline Notebook (news and notes). **Pays $150-250.**

FICTION Needs adventure, humorous, slice-of-life vignettes. **Buys 10-20 mss/year. Pays $150-1,000.**

FILLERS Needs anecdotes, facts, gags, newsbreaks, short humor. **Buys 20-30 mss/year.** Length: 10-100 words. **Pays $25-250.**

HORSE RACING

HOOF BEATS

750 Michigan Ave., Columbus OH 43215. **E-mail:** hoofbeats@ustrotting.com. **Website:** www.hoof-

beatsmagazine.com. **60% freelance written.** Monthly magazine covering harness racing and standardbred horses. "Articles and photos must relate to harness racing or standardbreds. We do not accept any topics that do not touch on these subjects." Estab. 1933. Circ. 13,500. Byline given. Offers 25% kill fee. Publishes ms an average of 2-4 months after acceptance. Editorial lead time 6 months. Submit seasonal material 6 months in advance. Accepts queries by mail, e-mail, fax. Accepts simultaneous submissions. Responds in 2 weeks to queries. Responds in 1 month to mss. Sample copy available online. Guidelines free.

NONFICTION Needs general interest, how-to, interview, personal experience, photo feature, technical. "We do not want any fiction or poetry." **Buys 48-72 mss/year.** Query. Length: 750-3,000 words. **Pays $100-500. Pays $100-500 for unsolicited articles.**

COLUMNS Equine Clinic (standardbreds who overcame major health issues), 900-1,200 words; Profiles (short profiles on people or horses in harness racing), 600-1,000 words; Industry Trends (issues impacting standardbreds & harness racing), 1,000-2,000 words. **Buys 60 mss/year.** Query. **Pays $100-500.**

HUNTING AND FISHING

ALABAMA GAME & FISH

Game & Fish, 2250 Newmarket Pkwy., Suite 110, Marietta GA 30067. (770)953-9222. **Fax:** (678)279-7512. **E-mail:** ken.dunwoody@imoutdoors.com. **Website:** www.alabamagameandfish.com. Jimmy Jacobs, editor. **Contact:** Ken Dunwoody, editorial director. See *Game & Fish*. Pays a kill fee.

AMERICAN ANGLER

P.O. Box 810, Arlington VA 05250. (706)823-3538. **E-mail:** steve.walburn@morris.com; wayne.knight@morris.com. **Website:** www.americanangler.com. **Contact:** Steve Walburn, editor; Wayne Knight, art director. **95% freelance written.** Bimonthly magazine covering fly fishing. "*American Angler* is devoted exclusively to fly fishing. We focus mainly on coldwater fly fishing for trout, steelhead, and salmon, but we also run articles about warmwater and saltwater fly fishing. (Our sister magazine, Saltwater Fly Fishing, is devoted exclusively to the latter.) Our mission is to supply our readers with well-written, accurate articles on every aspect of the sport—angling techniques and methods, reading water, finding fish, selecting flies, tying flies, fish behavior, places to fish, casting, managing line, rigging, tackle, accessories, entomology, and any other relevant topics. Each submission should present specific, useful information that will increase our readers' enjoyment of the sport and help them catch more fish." Estab. 1976. Circ. 60,000. Byline given. Publishes ms an average of 6 months after acceptance. Editorial lead time 3 months. Submit seasonal material 5 months in advance. Accepts queries by mail, fax. Accepts simultaneous submissions. Responds in 6 weeks to queries. Responds in 2 months to mss. Sample copy for $6. Guidelines with #10 SASE.

NONFICTION Needs how-to, most important, personal experience, photo feature, seldom, technical. No superficial, broad-brush coverage of subjects. **Buys 45-60 mss/year.** Query with published clips. Length: 800-2,200 words. **Pays $200-400.**

COLUMNS One-page shorts (problem solvers), 350-750 words. Query with published clips. **Pays $100-300.**

AMERICAN HUNTER

11250 Waples Mill Rd., Fairfax VA 22030-9400. (703)267-1336. **Fax:** (703)267-3971. **E-mail:** publications@nrahq.org; americanhunter@nrahq.org, lcromwell@nrahq.org. **Website:** www.americanhunter.org. **Contact:** J. Scott Olmsted, editor-in-chief. Monthly magazine for hunters who are members of the National Rifle Association (NRA). "*American Hunter* contains articles dealing with various sport hunting and related activities both at home and abroad. With the encouragement of the sport as a prime game management tool, emphasis is on technique, sportsmanship and safety. In each issue hunting equipment and firearms are evaluated, legislative happenings affecting the sport are reported, lore and legend are retold and the business of the Association is recorded in the Official Journal section." Circ. 1,000,000. Byline given. Accepts queries by mail, e-mail. Responds in 6 months to queries. Guidelines with #10 SASE.

NONFICTION Special issues: Pheasants, whitetail tactics, black bear feed areas, mule deer, duck hunters' transport by land and sea, tech topics to be decided; rut strategies, muzzleloader moose and elk, fall turkeys, staying warm, goose talk, long-range muzzleloading. Not interested in material on fishing, camping, or firearms knowledge. Query. Length: 1,800-2,000 words. **Pays up to $1,000.**

COLUMNS Hunting Guns, Hunting Loads, destination and adventure, and Public Hunting Grounds.

Study back issues for appropriate subject matter and style. Length: 800-1,500 words. **Pays $300-800.**

TIPS "Although unsolicited manuscripts are accepte

ARKANSAS SPORTSMAN

Game & Fish, 2250 Newmarket Pkwy., Suite 110, Marietta GA 30067. (770)953-9222. **Fax:** (678)279-7512. **E-mail:** ken.dunwoody@imoutdoors.com. **Website:** www.arkansassportsmanmag.com. Nick Gilmore, editor. **Contact:** Ken Dunwoody, editorial director. See *Game & Fish*. Pays a kill fee.

BACON BUSTERS

Yaffa Publishing, 17-21 Bellevue St., Surry Hills NSW 2010 Australia. (61)(2)9281-2333. **Fax:** (61)(2)9281-2750. **E-mail:** editor@baconbusters.com.au. **Website:** www.yaffa.com.au. **Contact:** Clint Magro, editor. Bimonthly magazine covering the hog hunting scene in Australia. "*Bacon Busters* content includes readers' short stories, how-to articles, pig hunting features, technical advice, pig dog profiles, and Australia's biggest collection of pig hunting photos. Not to mention the famous Babes & Boars section!" Estab. 1995.

NONFICTION Needs exposé, general interest, how-to, interview. Query.

BC OUTDOORS HUNTING AND SHOOTING

Keywest Marketing LTD., 202 9644 54 Ave., Edmonton AB T6E 5V1 Canada. (604)464-1876. **Fax:** (604)464-3186. **E-mail:** info@outdoorgroupmedia.com; mmitchell@outdoorgroupmedia.com; production@outdoorgroupmedia.com; sswanson@oppublishing.com; imc@outdoorgroupmedia.com. **Website:** www.bcoutdoorsmagazine.com. **Contact:** Mike Mitchell, editor. **80% freelance written.** Biannual magazine covering hunting, shooting, camping, and backroads. "*BC Outdoors Magazine* publishes 7 sport fishing issues a year with 2 hunting and shooting supplement issues each summer and fall. Our magazine is about the best outdoor experiences in BC. Whether you're camping on an ocean shore, hiking into your favorite lake, or learning how to fly-fish on your favourite river, we want to showcase what our province has to offer to sport fishing and outdoor enthusiasts. *BC Outdoors Hunting and Shooting* provides trusted editorial for trapping, deer hunting, big buck, bowhunting, bag limits, baitling, decoys, calling, camouflage, tracking, trophy hunting, pheasant hunting, goose hunting, hunting regulations, duck hunting, whitetail hunting, hunting regulations, hunting trips and mule deer hunting." Estab. 1945. Circ. 30,000. Byline given. Offers kill fee. Publishes ms an average of 3 months after acceptance. Accepts queries by e-mail. Writer's guidelines for 8×10 SASE with 7 Canadian first-class stamps. Guidelines available online.

NONFICTION Needs how-to, new or innovative articles on hunting subjects, personal experience, outdoor adventure, outdoor topics specific to British Columbia. **Buys 50 mss/year.** "Please query the publication before submitting. Please do not send unsolicited manuscripts or photos. Your pitch should be no more than 100-words outlining exactly what your story will be. You should be able to encapsulate the essence of your story and show us why our readers would be interested in reading or knowing what you are writing about. Queries need to be clear, succinct and straight to the point. Show us why we should publish your article in 150 words or less." Length: 1,700-2,000 words. **Pays $300-500.**

COLUMNS Column needs basically supplied in-house.

💲💲 THE BIG GAME FISHING JOURNAL

Informational Publications, Inc., 1800 Bay Ave., Point Pleasant NJ 08742. **Fax:** (732)223-2449. **Website:** www.biggamefishingjournal.com. **90% freelance written,**. Bimonthly magazine covering big game fishing. Estab. 1994. Circ. 45,000. Byline given. Offers 50% kill fee. Editorial lead time 3 months. Submit seasonal material 3 months in advance. Accepts queries by mail, online submission form. Accepts simultaneous submissions. Responds in 2 weeks to queries. Responds in 1 month to mss. Guidelines free.

NONFICTION Needs how-to, interview, technical. **Buys 50-70 mss/year.** Send complete ms. Length: 2,000-3,000 words. **Pays $200-400.** Sometimes pays expenses of writers on assignment.

💲💲 CALIFORNIA GAME & FISH

Game & Fish, 2250 Newmarket Pkwy., Suite 110, Marietta GA 30067. (770)953-9222. **Fax:** (678)279-7512. **E-mail:** ken.dunwoody@imoutdoors.com. **Website:** www.californiagameandfish.com. Daniel McElrath, editor. See *Game & Fish*. Pays a kill fee.

💲💲 DEER & DEER HUNTING

F+W Media, Inc., 700 E. State St., Iola WI 54990-0001. (715)445-2214. **E-mail:** dan.schmidt@fwmedia.com. **Website:** www.deeranddeerhunting.com. **Contact:** Dan Schmidt, editor-in-chief. **95% free-lance written.** Magazine published 10 times/year covering white-tailed deer. "Readers include a cross section of the deer hunting population—individuals who hunt with bow, gun, or camera. The editorial content of the magazine focuses on white-tailed deer biology and behavior, management principle and practices, habitat requirements, natural history of deer, hunting techniques, and hunting ethics. We also publish a wide range of how-to articles designed to help hunters locate and get close to deer at all times of the year. The majority of our readership consists of 2-season hunters (bow & gun) and approximately one-third camera hunt." Estab. 1977. Circ. 200,000. Byline given. Publishes ms an average of 18 months after acceptance. Editorial lead time 6 months. Submit seasonal material 12 months in advance. Accepts queries by mail, e-mail. Responds in 1 month to queries. Responds in 2 months to mss. Sample copy for 9×12 SASE. Guidelines available online.

NONFICTION Needs general interest, historical, how-to, photo feature, technical. No "Joe and me" articles. **Buys 100 mss/year.** Send complete ms. Length: 1,000-2,000 words. **Pays $150-600 for assigned articles. Pays $150-400 for unsolicited articles.** Sometimes pays expenses of writers on assignment.

COLUMNS Deer Browse (odd occurrences), 500 words. **Buys 10 mss/year.** Query. **Pays $50-300.**

FICTION Mood deer hunting pieces. **Buys 9 mss/year.** Send complete ms.

FILLERS Needs facts, newsbreaks. **Buys 40-50 mss/year.** Length: 100-500 words. **Pays $15-150.**

💲💲 THE DRAKE MAGAZINE

1600 Maple St., Fort Collins CO 80521. (949)218-8642. **E-mail:** info@drakemag.com. **Website:** www.drake-mag.com. **70% freelance written.** Quarterly magazine for people who love flyfishing. Estab. 1998. Byline given. Pays 1 month after publication. Publishes ms an average of 1 year after acceptance. Editorial lead time 1 year. Submit seasonal material 1 year in advance. Accepts queries by e-mail. Responds in 6 months to mss. Guidelines available online.

NONFICTION Needs flyfishing news items from your local area, historical, humor, opinion, personal experience, photo feature, short essays, travel, flyfishing related. **Buys 20-30 mss/year.** Query. Length: 650-2,000 words. **Pays 25¢/word depending on the amount of work we have to put into the piece.**

$$$ FIELD & STREAM

2 Park Ave., New York NY 10016. (212)779-5296. **Fax:** (212)779-5114. **E-mail:** fsletters@bonniercorp.com. **Website:** www.fieldandstream.com. **50% freelance written.** Broad-based monthly service magazine for the hunter and fisherman. Editorial content consists of articles of penetrating depth about national hunting, fishing, and related activities. Also humor, personal essays, profiles on outdoor people, conservation, sportsmen's insider secrets, tactics and techniques, and adventures. Estab. 1895. Circ. 1,500,000. Byline given. Pays on acceptance for most articles. Accepts queries by mail. Responds in 1 month to queries. Guidelines available online.

$$ FLORIDA GAME & FISH

Game & Fish, 2250 Newmarket Pkwy., Suite 110, Marietta GA 30067. (770)953-9222. **Fax:** (678)279-7512. **E-mail:** ken.dunwoody@imoutdoors.com. **Website:** www.floridagameandfish.com. Jimmy Jacobs, editor. **Contact:** Ken Dunwoody, editorial director. See *Game & Fish*. Pays a kill fee.

$$ FLORIDA SPORTSMAN

Wickstrom Communications, Intermedia Outdoors, 2700 S. Kanner Hwy., Stuart FL 34994. (772)219-7400. **Fax:** (772)219-6900. **E-mail:** editor@floridasportsman.com. **Website:** www.floridasportsman.com. **30% freelance written.** Monthly magazine covering fishing, boating, hunting, and related sports—Florida and Caribbean only. Edited for the boatowner and offshore, coastal, and fresh water fisherman. It provides a how, when, and where approach in its articles, which also includes occasional camping, diving, and hunting stories—plus ecology; in-depth articles and editorials attempting to protect Florida's wilderness, wetlands, and natural beauty. Circ. 115,000. Byline given. Publishes ms an average of 6 months after acceptance. Submit seasonal material 6 months in advance. Accepts queries by mail, e-mail. Responds in 2 months to queries. Responds in 1 month to mss. Sample copy free. Guidelines available at www.floridasportsman.com/submission_guidelines.

NONFICTION Needs essays, environment or nature, how-to, fishing, hunting, boating, humor, outdoors angle, personal experience, in fishing, etc., technical, boats, tackle, etc., as particularly suitable for Florida specialties. **Buys 40-60 mss/year.** Query. Length: 1,500-2,500 words. **Pays $475.**

$$ FLW BASS FISHING MAGAZINE, FLW WALLEYE FISHING MAGAZINE

FLW Outdoors, 30 Gamble Lane, Benton KY 42025. **E-mail:** cmoore@flwoutdoors.com. **Website:** www.flwoutdoors.com. **Contact:** Colin Moore, editor. **40% freelance written.** Magazines published 8 times/year in 2 editions (16 magazines/year) covering bass and walleye. "*FLW Bass Fishing Magazine* and *FLW Walleye Fishing Magazine* caters to all anglers from beginning weekend anglers to hardcore professional anglers. Our magazine seeks to educate as well as entertain anglers with cutting-edge techniques and new product innovations being used by America's top fishermen." Estab. 1979. Circ. 100,000+. Byline given. Publishes ms an average of 4 months after acceptance. Editorial lead time 5 months. Submit seasonal material 1 year in advance. Accepts queries by mail, e-mail. NoSample copy free. Guidelines free.

NONFICTION Needs how-to, new product, photo feature, technical, travel. Does not want "me-and-Bubba-went-fishing type stories"; stories about author's first trip to catch a certain type of fish; orstories in the first person about catching a fish. **Buys 50-75 mss/year.** Query. Length: 2,000-2,500 words. **Pays $400-500.** Sometimes pays expenses of writers on assignment.

COLUMNS Destinations; Environment; Boat Tech; Tackle Maintenance. **Buys 20-30 mss/year.** Query. **Pays $100-300.**

$ FLY FISHERMAN MAGAZINE

P.O. Box 420235, Palm Coast FL 32142. **E-mail:** flyfish@emailcustomerservice.com. **Website:** www.flyfisherman.com. **Contact:** Jeff Simpson. Published 6 times/year covering fly fishing. Written for anglers who fish primarily with a fly rod and for other anglers who would like to learn more about fly fishing. Circ. 120,358.

$$ FUR-FISH-GAME

2878 E. Main St., Columbus OH 43209-9947. **E-mail:** ffgcox@ameritech.net. **Website:** www.furfishgame.com. **Contact:** Mitch Cox, editor. **65% freelance written**. Monthly magazine for outdoorsmen of all ages who are interested in hunting, fishing, trapping, dogs, camping, conservation, and related topics. Estab. 1900. Circ. 111,000. Byline given. Publishes ms an average of 7 months after acceptance. Responds in 2 months to queries. Sample copy for $1 and 9×12 SASE. Guidelines with #10 SASE.

NONFICTION Query. Length: 500-3,000 words. **Pays $50-250 or more for features depending upon quality, photo support, and importance to magazine.**

⊘⊘ GAME & FISH

2250 Newmarket Pkwy., Suite 110, Marietta GA 30067. (770)953-9222. **Fax:** (678)279-7512. **E-mail:** ken.dunwoody@imoutdoors.com. **Website:** www.gameandfishmag.com. **Contact:** Ken Dunwoody, editorial director; Ron Sinfelt, photo editor; Allen Hansen, graphic artist. **90% freelance written.** Publishes 28 different monthly outdoor magazines, each 1covering the fishing and hunting opportunities in a particular state or region (see individual titles to contact editors). Estab. 1975. Circ. 570,000 for 28 state-specific magazines. Byline given. Pays 3 months prior to cover date of issue. Offers negotiable kill fee. Publishes ms an average of 7 months after acceptance. Submit seasonal material 8 months in advance. Accepts queries by mail, e-mail, fax. Responds in 3 months to queries. Sample copy for $3.50 and 9×12 SASE. Guidelines for #10 SASE.

NONFICTION Length: 1,500-2,400 words. **Pays $150-300; additional payment made for electronic rights.**

⊘⊘ GEORGIA SPORTSMAN

Game & Fish, 2250 Newmarket Pkwy., Suite 110, Marietta GA 30067. (770)953-9222. **Fax:** (678)279-7512. **E-mail:** ken.dunwoody@imoutdoors.com. **Website:** www.georgiasportsmanmag.com. Jimmy Jacobs, editor. **Contact:** Ken Dunwoody, editorial director. See *Game & Fish*. Pays a kill fee.

⊘⊘⊘ GRAY'S SPORTING JOURNAL

Morris Communications Corp., 735 Broad St., Augusta GA 30901. (706)724-0851. **E-mail:** russ@lumpkin@morris.com. **Website:** www.gra012ssportingjournal.com. **75% freelance written.** 7 issues per year magazine High-end hunting and fishing—think *Field & Stream* meets *The New Yorker*. "We expect competent, vividly written prose—fact or fiction—that has high entertainment value for a very sophisticated audience of experienced hunters and anglers. We do not consider previously published material. We do, however, occasionally run prepublication book excerpts. To get a feel for what Gray's publishes, review several back issues. Note that we do not, as a rule, publish 'how-to' articles; this is the province of our regular columnists." Estab. 1975. Circ. 32,000. Byline given. Publishes ms an average of 1 year after acceptance. Editorial lead time 14 months. Submit seasonal material 16 months in advance. Accepts simultaneous submissions. Responds in 3 months to mss. Guidelines available online.

NONFICTION Needs essays, historical, humor, personal experience, photo feature, travel. Special issues: Gray's publishes three themed issues each year: August is always entirely devoted to upland birdhunting; April to fly fishing; December to sporting travel. All other issues—February, May, September, November—focus on seasonally appropriate themes. Each issue always features a travel piece, from exotic destinations to right around the corner. We publish no how-to of any kind. **Buys 20-30 mss/year.** Send complete ms. Length: 1,500-12,000 words. **Pays $600-1,000 for unsolicited articles.**

FICTION Accepts quality fiction with some aspect of hunting or fishing at the core. Needs adventure, experimental, historical, humorous, slice-of-life vignettes. If some aspect of hunting or fishing isn't at the core of the story, it has zero chance of interesting *Gray's*. **Buys 20 mss/year.** Send complete ms. Length: 1,500-12,000 words. **Pays $600-1,000.**

POETRY Needs avant-garde, haiku, light verse, traditional. Buys 7/year poems/year. Submit maximum 3 poems. Length: 10-40 lines.

⊘⊘ GREAT PLAINS GAME & FISH

Game & Fish, 2250 Newmarket Pkwy., Suite 110, Marietta GA 30067. (770)953-9222. **Fax:** (678)279-7512. **E-mail:** ken.dunwoody@imoutdoors.com. **Website:** www.greatplainsgameandfish.com. Daniel McElrath, editor. **Contact:** Ken Dunwoody, editorial director. See *Game & Fish*. Pays a kill fee.

⊘⊘ ILLINOIS GAME & FISH

Game & Fish, 2250 Newmarket Pkwy., Suite 110, Marietta GA 30067. (770)953-9222. **Fax:** (678)279-7512. **E-mail:** ken.dunwoody@imoutdoors.com. **Website:** www.illinoisgameandfish.com. Daniel McElrath, editor. **Contact:** Ken Dunwoody, editorial director. See *Game & Fish*. Pays a kill fee.

⊘⊘ IOWA GAME & FISH

Game & Fish, 2250 Newmarket Pkwy., Suite 110, Marietta GA 30067. (770)953-9222. **Fax:** (678)279-7512. **E-mail:** ken.dunwoody@imoutdoors.com. **Website:** www.iowagameandfish.com. Daniel McElrath, editor. **Contact:** Ken Dunwoody, editorial director. See *Game & Fish*. Pays a kill fee.

$$ KENTUCKY GAME & FISH

Game & Fish, 2250 Newmarket Pkwy., Suite 110, Marietta GA 30067. (770)953-9222. **Fax:** (678)279-7512. **E-mail:** ken.dunwoody@imoutdoors.com. **Website:** www.kentuckygameandfish.com. Jimmy Jacobs, editor. **Contact:** Ken Dunwoody, editorial director. See *Game & Fish*. Pays a kill fee.

$$ THE MAINE SPORTSMAN

183 State St., Augusta ME 04330. (207)622-4242. **Fax:** (207)622-4255. **E-mail:** harry@mainesportsman.com. **Website:** www.mainesportsman.com. **80% freelance written.** Monthly tabloid. "Eager to work with new/unpublished writers, but because we run over 30 regular columns, it's hard to get into *The Maine Sportsman* as a beginner." Estab. 1972. Circ. 30,000. Byline given. Pays during month of publication. Publishes ms an average of 3 months after acceptance. Accepts queries by mail, e-mail. Responds in 2 weeks to queries.

NONFICTION **Buys 25-40 mss/year.** Send complete ms via e-mail Length: 200-2,000 words. **Pays $20-300.** Sometimes pays expenses of writers on assignment.

$$ MARLIN

P.O. Box 8500, Winter Park FL 32790. (407)628-4802. **Fax:** (407)628-7061. **E-mail:** editor@marlinmag.com. **Website:** www.marlinmag.com. **90% freelance written.** Magazine published 8 times/year covering the sport of big game fishing (billfish, tuna, dorado, and wahoo). Our readers are sophisticated, affluent, and serious about their sport—they expect a high-class, well-written magazine that provides information and practical advice. Estab. 1982. Circ. 50,000. Byline given. Publishes ms an average of 3 months after acceptance. Submit seasonal material 3 months in advance. YesSample copy free with SASE. Guidelines available online.

NONFICTION Needs general interest, how-to, bait-rigging, tackle maintenance, etc., new product, personal experience, photo feature, technical, travel. No freshwater fishing stories. No 'Me & Joe went fishing' stories. **Buys 30-50 mss/year.** Query with published clips. Length: 800-3,000 words. **Pays $250-500.**

COLUMNS Tournament Reports (reports on winners of major big game fishing tournaments), 200-400 words; Blue Water Currents (news features), 100-400 words. **Buys 25 mss/year.** Query. **Pays $75-250.**

$ MICHIGAN OUT-OF-DOORS

P.O. Box 30235, Lansing MI 48909. (517)371-1041. **Fax:** (517)371-1505. **E-mail:** thansen@mucc.org; magazine@mucc.org. **Website:** www.michiganoutofdoors.com. **Contact:** Tony Hansen, editor. **75% freelance written.** Monthly magazine emphasizing Michigan hunting and fishing with associated conservation issues. Estab. 1947. Circ. 40,000. Byline given. Publishes ms an average of 6 months after acceptance. Submit seasonal material 6 months in advance. Accepts queries by e-mail only. Responds in 1 month to queries. Sample copy for $3.50. Guidelines for free.

NONFICTION Needs exposé, historical, how-to, interview, opinion, personal experience, photo feature. All topics must pertain to hunting and fishing topics in Michigan. Special issues: Archery Deer and Small Game Hunting (October); Firearm Deer Hunting (November); Cross-country Skiing and Early-ice Lake Fishing (December or January); Camping/Hiking (May); Family Fishing (June). No humor or poetry. **Buys 96 mss/year.** Send complete ms. Length: 1,000-2,000 words. **Pays $150 minimum for feature stories. Photos must be included with story.**

$$ MICHIGAN SPORTSMAN

Game & Fish, 2250 Newmarket Pkwy., Suite 110, Marietta GA 30067. (770)953-9222. **Fax:** (678)279-7512. **E-mail:** ken.dunwoody@imoutdoors.com. **Website:** www.michigansportsmanmag.com. Nick Gilmore, editor. **Contact:** Ken Dunwoody, editorial director. See *Game & Fish*. Pays a kill fee.

$$ MINNESOTA SPORTSMAN

Game & Fish, 2250 Newmarket Pkwy., Suite 110, Marietta GA 30067. (770)953-9222. **Fax:** (678)279-7512. **E-mail:** ken.dunwoody@imoutdoors.com. **Website:** www.minnesotasportsmanmag.com. Nick Gilmore, editor. **Contact:** Ken Dunwoody, editorial director. See *Game & Fish*. Pays a kill fee.

$$ MISSISSIPPI/LOUISIANA GAME & FISH

Game & Fish, 2250 Newmarket Pkwy., Suite 110, Marietta GA 30067. (770)953-9222. **Fax:** (678)279-7512. **E-mail:** ken.dunwoody@imoutdoors.com. **Website:** www.mississippigameandfish.com. Jimmy Jacobs, editor. **Contact:** Ken Dunwoody, editorial director. See *Game & Fish*. Pays a kill fee.

⬤⬤ MISSOURI GAME & FISH

Game & Fish, 2250 Newmarket Pkwy., Suite 110, Marietta GA 30067. (770)953-9222. **Fax:** (678)279-7512. **E-mail:** ken.dunwoody@imoutdoors.com. **Website:** www.missourigameandfishmag.com. Nick Gilmore, editor. **Contact:** Ken Dunwoody, editorial director. See *Game & Fish*. Pays a kill fee.

⬤⬤ MUSKY HUNTER MAGAZINE

P.O. Box 340, 7978 Hwy. 70 E., St. Germain WI 54558. (715)477-2178. **Fax:** (715)477-8858. **E-mail:** editor@muskyhunter.com. **Website:** www.muskyhunter.com. **Contact:** Jim Saric, editor. **90% freelance written.** Bimonthly magazine on musky fishing. Serves the vertical market of musky fishing enthusiasts. "We're interested in how-to, where-to articles." Estab. 1988. Circ. 37,000. Byline given. Publishes ms an average of 4 months after acceptance. Submit seasonal material 4 months in advance. Responds in 2 months to queries. Sample copy with 9×12 SASE and $2.79 postage. Guidelines with #10 SASE.

NONFICTION Needs historical, related only to musky fishing, how-to, catch muskies, modify lures, boats, and tackle for musky fishing, personal experience, must be musky fishing experience, technical, fishing equipment, travel, to lakes and areas for musky fishing. **Buys 50 mss/year.** Send complete ms. Length: 1,000-2,500 words. **Pays $100-300 for assigned articles. Pays $50-300 for unsolicited articles.**

⬤⬤ NEW ENGLAND GAME & FISH

Game & Fish, 2250 Newmarket Pkwy., Suite 110, Marietta GA 30067. (770)953-9222. **Fax:** (678)279-7512. **E-mail:** ken.dunwoody@imoutdoors.com. **Website:** www.newenglandgameandfish.com. David Johnson, editor. **Contact:** Ken Dunwoody, editorial director. See *Game & Fish*. Pays a kill fee.

⬤⬤ NEW YORK GAME & FISH

Game & Fish, 2250 Newmarket Pkwy., Suite 110, Marietta GA 30067. (770)953-9222. **Fax:** (678)279-7512. **E-mail:** ken.dunwoody@imoutdoors.com. **Website:** www.newyorkgameandfish.com. David Johnson, editor. **Contact:** Ken Dunwoody, editorial director. See *Game & Fish*. Pays a kill fee.

⬤⬤ NORTH AMERICAN WHITETAIL

Game & Fish, 2250 Newmarket Pkwy., Suite 110, Marietta GA 30067. (770)953-9222. **Fax:** (678)279-7512. **E-mail:** ken.dunwoody@imoutdoors.com. **Website:** www.northamericanwhitetail.com. **Contact:** Ken Dunwoody, editorial director. **70% freelance written.** Magazine published 8 times/year about hunting trophy-class white-tailed deer in North America, primarily the US. "We provide the serious hunter with highly sophisticated information about trophy-class whitetails and how, when, and where to hunt them. We are not a general hunting magazine or a magazine for the very occasional deer hunter." Estab. 1982. Circ. 150,000. Byline given. Pays 65 days prior to cover date of issue. Offers negotiable kill fee. Publishes ms an average of 6 months after acceptance. Submit seasonal material 10 months in advance. Accepts queries by mail, e-mail, phone. Responds in 3 months to mss. Sample copy for $3.50 and 9×12 SAE with 7 first-class stamps. Guidelines for #10 SASE.

NONFICTION Needs how-to, interview. **Buys 50 mss/year.** Query. Length: 1,000-3,000 words. **Pays $150-400.**

COLUMNS Trails and Tails (nostalgic, humorous, or other entertaining styles of deer-hunting material, fictional or nonfictional), 1,200 words. **Buys 8 mss/year.** Send complete ms. **Pays $150.**

⬤⬤ NORTH CAROLINA GAME & FISH

Game & Fish, 2250 Newmarket Pkwy., Suite 110, Marietta GA 30067. (770)953-9222. **Fax:** (678)279-7512. **E-mail:** ken.dunwoody@imoutdoors.com. **Website:** www.ncgameandfish.com. David Johnson, editor. **Contact:** Ken Dunwoody, editorial director. See *Game & Fish*. Pays a kill fee.

⬤⬤ OHIO GAME & FISH

Game & Fish, 2250 Newmarket Pkwy., Suite 110, Marietta GA 30067. (770)953-9222. **Fax:** (678)279-7512. **E-mail:** ken.dunwoody@imoutdoors.com. **Website:** www.ohiogameandfish.com. David Johnson, editor. **Contact:** Ken Dunwoody, editorial director. See *Game & Fish*. Pays a kill fee.

⬤⬤ OKLAHOMA GAME & FISH

Game & Fish, 2250 Newmarket Pkwy., Suite 110, Marietta GA 30067. (770)953-9222. **Fax:** (678)279-7512. **E-mail:** ken.dunwoody@imoutdoors.com. **Website:** www.oklahomagameandfish.com. Nick Gilmore, editor. **Contact:** Ken Dunwoody, editorial director. See *Game & Fish*. Pays a kill fee.

✪ ⬤⬤ ONTARIO OUT OF DOORS

Ontario Federation of Anglers and Hunters, P.O. Box 8500, Peterborough ON K9J 0B4 Canada. (705)748-0076. **Fax:** (705)748-9577. **Website:** www.ontariooutofdoors.com. **Contact:** John Kerr, editor-in-chief. **80% freelance written.** Magazine published 10 times/year covering the outdoors (hunting, fishing). Estab. 1968. Circ. 93,865. Byline given. Publishes ms an average of 6 months after acceptance. Editorial lead time 1 year. Submit seasonal material 2 months in advance. Accepts queries by mail, e-mail, fax. Responds in 3 months to queries. Writer's guidelines free.

NONFICTION Needs interview, opinion, technical, travel, wildlife management. No 'Me and Joe' features. **Buys 100 mss/year.** Length: 500-2,500 words. **Pays $950 maximum for assigned articles.**

FICTION **Pays $500 maximum.**

[⊘] $$ PENNSYLVANIA ANGLER & BOATER

Pennsylvania Fish & Boat Commission, P.O. Box 67000, Harrisburg PA 17106-7000. (717)705-7835. **E-mail:** ra-pfbcmagazine@state.pa.us. **Website:** www.fish.state.pa.us. **40% freelance written.** Bimonthly magazine covering fishing, boating, and related conservation topics in Pennsylvania. Circ. 28,000. Byline given. Pays 2 months after acceptance. Publishes ms an average of 8 months after acceptance. Submit seasonal material 8 months in advance. Responds in 1 month to queries. Responds in 2 months to mss. Sample copy for 9×12 SAE with 9 first-class stamps. Guidelines for #10 SASE.

[○] No unsolicited mss.

NONFICTION Needs how-to, and where-to, technical. No saltwater or hunting material. **Buys 75 mss/year.** Query. Length: 500-2,500 words. **Pays $25-300.**

PHOTOS Send photos. Captions, identification of subjects, model releases required. Reviews 35mm and larger transparencies, hi-res digital submissions on CD (preferred). Offers no additional payment for photos accompanying mss.

$$ PENNSYLVANIA GAME & FISH

Game & Fish, 2250 Newmarket Pkwy., Suite 110, Marietta GA 30067. (770)953-9222. **Fax:** (678)279-7512. **E-mail:** ken.dunwoody@imoutdoors.com. **Website:** www.pagameandfish.com. David Johnson, editor. **Contact:** Ken Dunwoody, editorial director. See *Game & Fish*. Pays a kill fee.

$$ RACK MAGAZINE

Buckmasters, Ltd., 10350 U.S. Hwy. 80 E., Montgomery AL 36117. (800)240-3337. **Fax:** (334)215-3535. **E-mail:** mhandley@buckmasters.com. **Website:** www.buckmasters.com. **50% freelance written.** Monthly, July-December magazine covering big game hunting. "All features are either first- or third-person narratives detailing the successful hunts for world-class, big game animals—mostly white-tailed deer and other North American species." Estab. 1998. Circ. 75,000. Byline given. Publishes ms an average of 9 months after acceptance. Editorial lead time 9-12 months. Submit seasonal material 9 months in advance. Accepts queries by e-mail. Accepts simultaneous submissions. Responds in 1 month to queries. Responds in 2 months to mss. Sample copy free. Guidelines free.

NONFICTION Needs personal experience. "We're interested only in articles chronicling successful hunts." **Buys 40-50 mss/year.** Query. Length: 1,000 words. **Pays $100-325 for assigned and unsolicited articles.**

$$ ROCKY MOUNTAIN GAME & FISH

Game & Fish, 2250 Newmarket Pkwy., Suite 110, Marietta GA 30067. (770)935-9222. **Fax:** (678)279-7512. **E-mail:** ken.dunwoody@imoutdoors.com. **Website:** www.rmgameandfish.com. Daniel McElrath, editor. **Contact:** Ken Dunwoody, editorial director. See *Game & Fish*. Pays a kill fee.

$$ SALT WATER SPORTSMAN

Bonnier Corporation, 460 N. Orlando Ave., Suite 200, Winter Park FL 32789. (407)628-4802. **E-mail:** editor@saltwatersportsman.com. **Website:** www.saltwatersportsman.com. **85% freelance written.** Monthly magazine. *Salt Water Sportsman* is edited for serious marine sport fishermen whose lifestyle includes the pursuit of game fish in US waters and around the world. It provides information on fishing trends, techniques, and destinations, both local and international. Each issue reviews offshore and inshore fishing boats, high-tech electronics, innovative tackle, engines, and other new products. Coverage also focuses on sound fisheries management and conservation. Circ. 170,000. Byline given. Offers kill fee. Publishes ms an average of 5 months after acceptance. Submit seasonal material 8 months in advance. Accepts queries by mail, e-mail, fax. Responds in 1 month to queries. Sample copy for #10 SASE. Guidelines available online.

NONFICTION Needs how-to, personal experience, technical, travel, to fishing areas. **Buys 100 mss/year.** Query. Length: 1,200-2,000 words. **Pays $300-750.**

COLUMNS Sportsman's Tips (short, how-to tips and techniques on salt water fishing, emphasis is on building, repairing, or reconditioning specific items or gear). Send complete ms.

💲💲 SOUTH CAROLINA GAME & FISH

Game & Fish, 2250 Newmarket Pkwy., Suite 110, Marietta GA 30067. (770)953-9222. **Fax:** (678)279-7512. **E-mail:** ken.dunwoody@imoutdoors.com. **Website:** www.scgameandfish.com. David Johnson, editor. **Contact:** Ken Dunwoody, editorial director. See *Game & Fish*. Pays a kill fee.

💲💲💲💲 SPORT FISHING

Bonnier Corporation, 460 N. Orlando Ave., Suite 200, Winter Park FL 32789. (407)628-4802. **Fax:** (407)628-7061. **E-mail:** missie.prichard@bonniercorp.com. **Website:** www.sportfishingmag.com. **50% freelance written.** Magazine published 10 times/year covering saltwater angling, saltwater fish and fisheries. "*Sport Fishing*'s readers are middle-aged, affluent, mostly male, who are generally proficient in and very educated to their sport. We are about fishing from boats, not from surf or jetties." Estab. 1985. Circ. 250,000. Byline given. Offers 25% kill fee. Publishes ms an average of 6-12 months after acceptance. Editorial lead time 2-12 months. Submit seasonal material 1 year in advance. Accepts queries by e-mail. Responds in 1 week to queries. Responds in 1 month to mss. Sample copy with #10 SASE. Guidelines available online.

NONFICTION Needs general interest, how-to. Query. Length: 2,500-3,000 words. **Pays $500-750 for text only; $1,500+ possible for complete package with photos.** Answer.

💲💲💲 SPORTS AFIELD

Field Sports Publishing, 15621 Chemical Ln., Suite B, Huntington Beach CA 92649. (714)373-4910. **E-mail:** letters@sportsafield.com. **Website:** www.sportsafield.com. **Contact:** Jerry Gutierrez, art director. **60% freelance written.** Magazine published 6 times/year covering big game hunting. "We cater to the upscale hunting market, especially hunters who travel to exotic destinations like Alaska and Africa. We are not a deer hunting magazine, and we do not cover fishing." Estab. 1887. Circ. 50,000. Byline given. Pays 1 month prior to publication. Publishes ms an average of 6 months after acceptance. Editorial lead time 4 months. Submit seasonal material 5 months in advance. Accepts queries by mail, e-mail. Responds in 2 months to queries and to mss Sample copy for $7.99. Guidelines available online.

NONFICTION Needs personal experience, travel. **Buys 6-8 mss/year.** Query. Length: 1,500-2,500 words. **Pays $500-800.**

FILLERS Needs newsbreaks. **Buys 30 mss/year.** Length: 200-500 words. **Pays $75-150.**

💲💲 TENNESSEE SPORTSMAN

Game & Fish, 2250 Newmarket Pkwy., Suite 110, Marietta GA 30067. (770)953-9222. **Fax:** (678)279-7512. **E-mail:** ken.dunwoody@imoutdoors.com. **Website:** www.tennesseesportsmanmag.com. Jimmy Jacobs, editor. **Contact:** Ken Dunwoody, editorial director. See *Game & Fish*. Pays a kill fee.

💲💲 TEXAS SPORTSMAN

Game & Fish, 2250 Newmarket Pkwy., Suite 110, Marietta GA 30067. (770)953-9222. **Fax:** (678)279-7512. **E-mail:** ken.dunwoody@imoutdoors.com. **Website:** www.texassportsmanmag.com. Nick Gilmore, editor. **Contact:** Ken Dunwoody, editorial director. See *Game & Fish*. Pays a kill fee.

💲💲 TRAPPER & PREDATOR CALLER

F+W Media, Inc., 700 E. State St., Iola WI 54990. (715)445-2214. **E-mail:** jared.blohm@fwmedia.com. **Website:** www.trapperpredatorcaller.com. **75% freelance written.** Tabloid published 10 times/year covering trapping and predator calling, fur trade. "Must have mid-level to advanced knowledge, because *T&PC* is heavily how-to focused." Estab. 1975. Circ. 42,000. Byline given. Publishes ms an average of 6 months after acceptance. Editorial lead time 1 year. Submit seasonal material 1 year in advance. Accepts queries by e-mail.

NONFICTION Needs how-to, interview, personal experience, travel. **Buys 100 mss/year.** Send complete ms. Length: 1,500-2,500 words. **Pays $250 for assigned articles.**

💲💲 TURKEY & TURKEY HUNTING

F+W Media, Inc., 700 E. State St., Iola WI 54990-0001. (715)445-4612. **E-mail:** brian.lovett@fwmedia.com. **Website:** www.turkeyandturkeyhunting.com. Brian Lovett, editor. **Contact:** Brian Lovett, editor. **50% freelance written.** Bimonthly magazine filled with practical and comprehensive information for wild turkey hunters. Estab. 1982. Circ. 40,000. Byline given. Offers 50% kill fee. Publishes ms an average of 8 months after acceptance. Editorial lead time 1 year. Submit seasonal material 1 year in advance. Accepts queries by mail, e-mail. Responds in 1 month to queries. Responds in 6 months to mss. Sample copy for $4. Ms and photo guidelines online.

NONFICTION Does not want "Me and Joe went hunting and here's what happened" articles. **Buys 20 mss/year.** Send complete ms. Length: 1,500-2,500 words. **Pays $275-400.**

🌑💲 TURKEY COUNTRY

National Wild Turkey Federation, P.O. Box 530, Edgefield SC 29824-0530. (803)637-3106. **Fax:** (803)637-0034. **E-mail:** info@nwtf.net; turkeycountry@nwtf.net. **E-mail:** klee@nwtf.net. **Website:** www.turkeycountrymagazine.com. Gregg Powers, managing editor; P.J. Perea, senior editor; Matt Lindler, photo editor. **Contact:** Karen Lee, editor. **50-60% freelance written.** "Bimonthly educational magazine for members of the National Wild Turkey Federation. Topics covered include hunting, history, restoration, management, biology, and distribution of wild turkey." Estab. 1973. Circ. 180,000. Byline given. Publishes ms an average of 6 months after acceptance. Editorial lead time 1 year. Accepts queries by mail, e-mail. Responds in 2 months to queries Sample copy for $3 and 9×12 SAE. Guidelines available online.

NONFICTION Query (preferred) or send complete ms. Length: 700-2,500 words. **Pays $100 for short fillers; $200-500 for features.**

FICTION Must contribute to the education, enlightenment, or entertainment of readers in some special way.

🌑💲 VIRGINIA GAME & FISH

Game & Fish, 2250 Newmarket Pkwy., Suite 110, Marietta GA 30067. (770)953-9222. **Fax:** (678)279-7512. **E-mail:** ken.dunwoody@imoutdoors.com. **Website:** www.virginiagameandfish.com. David Johnson, editor. **Contact:** Ken Dunwoody, editorial director. See *Game & Fish*. Pays a kill fee.

🌑💲 WASHINGTON-OREGON GAME & FISH

Game & Fish, 2250 Newmarket Pkwy., Suite 110, Marietta GA 30067. (770)953-9222. **Fax:** (678)279-7512. **E-mail:** ken.dunwoody@imoutdoors.com. **Website:** www.wogameandfish.com. Daniel McElrath, editor. **Contact:** Ken Dunwoody, editorial director. See *Game & Fish*. Pays a kill fee.

🌑💲 WEST VIRGINIA GAME & FISH

Game & Fish, 2250 Newmarket Pkwy., Suite 110, Marietta GA 30067. (770)953-9222. **Fax:** (678)279-7512.

E-mail: ken.dunwoody@imoutdoors.com. **Website:** www.wvgameandfish.com. Jimmy Jacobs, editor. **Contact:** Ken Dunwoody, editorial director. "This is the ultimate resource for West Virginia outdoor enthusiasts that are passionate about hunting, shooting and fishing." Pays a kill fee.

◯ See *Game & Fish*.

🌑💲 WISCONSIN SPORTSMAN

Game & Fish, 2250 Newmarket Pkwy., Suite 110, Marietta GA 30067. (770)953-9222. **Fax:** (678)279-7512. **E-mail:** ken.dunwoody@imoutdoors.com. **Website:** www.wisconsinsportsmanmag.com. Nick Gilmore, editor. **Contact:** Ken Dunwoody, editorial director. See *Game & Fish*. Pays a kill fee.

MARTIAL ARTS

🌑💲 BLACK BELT

Black Belt Communications, LLC, 24900 Anza Dr., Unit E, Valencia CA 91355. **Fax:** (661)257-3028. **E-mail:** byoung@aimmedia.com. **Website:** www.blackbeltmag.com. **Contact:** Robert W. Young, executive editor. **80% freelance written. Works with a small number of new/unpublished writers each year.** Monthly magazine emphasizing martial arts for both experienced practitioner and layman. Estab. 1961. Circ. 100,000. Publishes ms an average of 1 year after acceptance. Accepts queries by mail, e-mail, fax. Accepts simultaneous submissions. Responds in 3 weeks to queries. Guidelines available online.

NONFICTION Needs exposé, how-to, interview, new product, personal experience, technical, travel, Informational. We never use personality profiles. **Buys 40-50 mss/year.** Query with outline 1,200 words minimum. **Pays $100-300.**

🌑💲 JOURNAL OF ASIAN MARTIAL ARTS

Via Media Publishing Co., 941 Calle Mejia, #822, Santa Fe NM 87501. (505)983-1919. **E-mail:** info@goviamedia.com. **Website:** www.goviamedia.com. **90% freelance written.** "Quarterly magazine covering all historical and cultural aspects related to Asian martial arts, offering a mature, well-rounded view of this uniquely fascinating subject. Although the journal treats the subject with academic accuracy (references at end), writing need not lose the reader!". Estab. 1991. Circ. 10,000. Byline given. Publishes ms an average of 1 year after acceptance. Submit seasonal material 6 months in advance. Responds in 1 month to queries.

Responds in 2 months to mss. Sample copy for $10. Guidelines with #10 SASE or online.

NONFICTION Needs essays, exposé, historical, how-to, martial art techniques and materials, e.g., weapons, interview, personal experience, photo feature, place or person, religious, technical, travel. No articles overburdened with technical/foreign/scholarly vocabulary, or material slanted as indirect advertising or for personal aggrandizement. **Buys 30 mss/year.** Query with short background and martial arts experience. Length: 1,000-10,000 words. **Pays $150-500.**

COLUMNS Location (city, area, specific site, Asian or non-Asian, showing value for martial arts, researchers, history); Media Review (film, book, video, museum for aspects of academic and artistic interest). Length: 1,000-2,500 words. **Buys 16 mss/year.** Query. **Pays $50-200.**

FICTION Needs adventure, historical, humorous, slice-of-life vignettes, translation. No material that does not focus on martial arts culture. **Buys 1 mss/year.** Query. Length: 1,000-10,000 words. **Pays $50-500, or copies.**

POETRY Needs avant-garde, free verse, haiku, light verse, traditional. No poetry that does not focus on martial arts culture. Buys 2 poems/year. Submit maximum 10 poems. **Pays $10-100, or copies.**

FILLERS Needs anecdotes, facts, gags, newsbreaks, short humor. **Buys 2 mss/year.** Length: 25-500 words. **Pays $1-50, or copies.**

💲💲 T'AI CHI

Wayfarer Publications, P.O. Box 39938, Los Angeles CA 90039. (323)665-7773. **Fax:** (323)665-1627. **E-mail:** taichi@tai-chi.com. **Website:** www.tai-chi. com. **Contact:** Marvin Smalheiser, editor. **90% freelance written.** Quarterly magazine covering T'ai Chi Ch'uan as a martial art and for health and fitness. "Covers T'ai Chi Ch'uan and other internal martial arts, plus qigong and Chinese health, nutrition, and philosophical disciplines. Readers are practitioners or laymen interested in developing skills and insight for self-defense, health, and self-improvement." Estab. 1977. Circ. 50,000. Byline given. Publishes ms an average of 3 months after acceptance. Editorial lead time 3 months. Submit seasonal material 6 months in advance. Accepts queries by mail, e-mail, fax. Responds in 3 weeks to queries. Responds in 3 months to mss. Sample copy for $5.99. Guidelines available online.

NONFICTION Needs essays, how-to, on T'ai Chi Ch'uan, qigong, and related Chinese disciplines, interview, personal experience. "Do not want articles promoting an individual, system, or school." Send complete ms. Length: 1,200-4,500 words. **Pays $75-500.**

💲💲 ULTIMATE MMA

Apprise Media, 2400 E. Katella Ave., Suite 300, Anaheim CA 92806. (714)939-9991. **Fax:** (714)939-9909. **E-mail:** djeffrey@beckett.com. **Website:** wwww.ultimatemmamag.com. Monthly magazine covering mixed martial arts, grappling. "We are interested in anything and everything about mixed martial arts.. lifestyle to events to training to strategy." Estab. 2000. Byline given. Offers 20% kill fee. Publishes ms an average of 1-3 months after acceptance. Editorial lead time 3 months. Submit seasonal material 3 months in advance. Accepts queries by mail, e-mail. Responds in 2 months to mss. Sample copy free. Guidelines free.

NONFICTION Needs book excerpts, exposé, general interest, historical, how-to, inspirational, interview, new product, personal experience, photo feature, technical. **Buys 30 mss/year.** Query. Length: 500-1,500 words. **Pays $150-500 for assigned articles. Pays $150-500 for unsolicited articles.** Sometimes pays expenses of writers on assignment.

COLUMNS Beyond Fighting (lifestyle of fighters); Exercises to bolster MMA game and general fitness. **Buys 30 mss/year.** Query with or without published clips. **Pays $-$125.**

MISCELLANEOUS SPORTS

💲 ACTION PURSUIT GAMES

Beckett Media, 2400 E. Katella Ave., Suite 300, Anaheim CA 92806. (714)939-9991. **E-mail:** editor@actionpursuitgames.com. **E-mail:** bryansullivanapg@gmail.com; liisa.sullivan@verizon.net. **Website:** www.actionpursuitgames.com. Editors Bryan Sullivan and Liisa Sullivan. **Contact:** Daniel Reeves, editor. **60% freelance written.** Monthly magazine covering paintball. Estab. 1987. Circ. 85,000. Byline given. Publishes ms an average of 2 months after acceptance. Editorial lead time 3 months. Submit seasonal material 6 months in advance. Accepts queries by e-mail. Sample copy for sae with 9×12 envelope and 5 First-Class stamps. Guidelines available online.

NONFICTION Needs essays, exposé, general interest, historical, how-to, humor, interview, new product, opinion, personal experience, technical, travel, all paintball-related. No sexually oriented material. **Buys 100+ mss/year.** Length: 500-1,000 words. **Pays $100.** Sometimes pays expenses of writers on assignment.

COLUMNS Guest Commentary, 400 words; TNT (tournament news), 500-800 words; Young Guns, 300 words; Scenario Game Reporting, 300-500 words. **Buys 24 mss/year. Pays $100.**

FICTION Needs adventure, historical, must be paintball related. **Buys 1-2 mss/year.** Send complete ms. Length: 500 words. **Pays $100.**

POETRY Needs avant-garde, free verse, haiku, light verse, traditional. Buys 1-2 poems/year. Submit maximum 1 poems. Length: 20 lines.

FILLERS Needs anecdotes, gags. **Buys 2-4 mss/year.** Length: 20-50 words. **Pays $25.**

$$ AMERICAN CHEERLEADER

Macfadden Performing Arts Media LLC, 110 William St., 23rd Floor, New York NY 10038. (646)459-4800. **Fax:** (646)459-4900. **E-mail:** mwalker@americancheerleader.com; acmail@americancheerleader.com. **Website:** www.americancheerleader.com. **Contact:** Joanna Schwartz, publisher; Marisa Walker, editor. **30% freelance written.** Bimonthly magazine covering high school, college, and competitive cheerleading. We try to keep a young, informative voice for all articles—'for cheerleaders, by cheerleaders.' Estab. 1995. Circ. 200,000. Byline given. Offers 25% kill fee. Publishes ms an average of 4 months after acceptance. Editorial lead time 3 months. Submit seasonal material 4 months in advance. Accepts queries by mail, e-mail, online submission form. Responds in 4 weeks to queries. Responds in 2 months to mss. Sample copy for $2.95. Guidelines free.

NONFICTION Young adults: biography, interview/profile (sports personalities), careers, fashion, beauty, health, how-to (cheering techniques, routines, pep songs, etc.), problem-solving, sports, cheerleading-specific material. "We're looking for authors who know cheerleading." Buys 20 mss/year. Special issues: Tryouts (April); Camp Basics (June); College (October); Competition (December). No professional cheerleading stories, i.e., no Dallas Cowboy cheerleaders. **Buys 12-16 mss/year.** Query with published clips; provide résumé, business card, tearsheets to be kept on file. Length: 750-2,000 words. **Pays $100-250 for assigned articles. Pays $100 maximum for unsolicited articles.** Sometimes pays expenses of writers on assignment.

COLUMNS Gameday Beauty (skin care, celeb how-tos), 600 words; Health & Fitness (teen athletes), 1,000 words; Profiles (winning squads), 1,000 words. **Buys 12 mss/year.** Query with published clips. **Pays $100-250.**

$$$ ATV MAGAZINE/ATV SPORT

Ehlert Publishing, 6420 Sycamore Lane, Maple Grove MN 55369. **Fax:** (763)383-4499. **E-mail:** jprusak@affinitygroup.com. **Website:** www.atvmagonline.com; www.atvsport.com. **Contact:** John Prusak, editor. **20% freelance written.** Bimonthly magazine covering all-terrain vehicles. Devoted to covering all the things ATV owners enjoy, from hunting to racing, farming to trail riding. Byline given. Pays on magazine shipment to printer. Editorial lead time 6 months. Accepts queries by mail, e-mail, fax. Responds in 3 weeks to queries. Sample copy and writer's guidelines for #10 SASE.

NONFICTION Needs how-to, interview, new product, personal experience, photo feature, technical, travel. **Buys 15-20 mss/year.** Query with published clips. Length: 200-2,000 words. **Pays $100-1,000.** Sometimes pays expenses of writers on assignment.

🍁 $ CANADIAN RODEO NEWS

Canadian Rodeo News, Ltd., 272245 RR 2, Airdrie AB T4A 2L5 Canada. (403)945-7393. **Fax:** (403)945-0936. **E-mail:** editor@rodeocanada.com. **Website:** www.rodeocanada.com. **80% freelance written.** Monthly tabloid covering Canada's professional rodeo (CPRA) personalities and livestock. Read by rodeo participants and fans. Estab. 1964. Circ. 4,000. Byline given. Publishes ms an average of 1 month after acceptance. Editorial lead time 1 month. Submit seasonal material 1 month in advance. Accepts queries by mail, e-mail, fax. Accepts simultaneous submissions. Responds in 1 month to queries. Responds in 2 months to mss.

NONFICTION Needs general interest, historical, interview. **Buys 70-80 mss/year.** Query. Length: 400-1,200 words. **Pays $30-60.**

$ LACROSSE MAGAZINE

113 W. University Pkwy., Baltimore MD 21210. (410)235-6882. **Fax:** (410)366-6735. **E-mail:** gferraro@uslacrosse.org; blogue@uslacrosse.org. **Website:** www.uslacrosse.org. **Contact:** Gabriella O'Brien, art director; Brian Logue, director of communications. **60% freelance written.** *Lacrosse* is the only national feature publication devoted to the sport of lacrosse. It is a benefit of membership in U.S. Lacrosse, a nonprofit organization devoted to promoting the growth of la-

crosse and preserving its history. U.S. Lacrosse maintains *Lacrosse Magazine Online* (LMO) at www.lax-magazine.com. *LMO* features daily lacrosse news and scores directly from lacrosse-playing colleges. *LMO* also includes originally-produced features and news briefs covering all levels of play. Occasional feature articles printed in *Lacrosse* are re-published at *LMO*, and vice versa. The online component of *Lacrosse* will do things that a printed publication can't—provide news, scores and information in a timely manner. Estab. 1978. Circ. 235,000. Byline given. Publishes ms an average of 2 months after acceptance. Editorial lead time 2 months. Submit seasonal material 2 months in advance. Sample copy free. Guidelines free.

NONFICTION Needs book excerpts, general interest, historical, how-to, drills, conditioning, x's and o's, etc., interview, new product, opinion, personal experience, photo feature, technical. **Buys 30-40 mss/year.** Length: 500-1,750 words. **Payment negotiable.** Sometimes pays expenses of writers on assignment.

COLUMNS First Person (personal experience), 1,000 words; Fitness (conditioning/strength/exercise), 500-1,000 words; How-to, 500-1,000 words. **Buys 10-15 mss/year. Payment negotiable.**

POINTE MAGAZINE

MacFadden Performing Arts Media, LLC, 110 William St., 23rd Floor, New York NY 10038. (646)459-4800. **Fax:** (646)459-4900. **E-mail:** pointe@dancemedia.com. **Website:** www.pointemagazine.com. **Contact:** Amy Cogan, publisher. Bimonthly magazine covering ballet. *Pointe Magazine* is the only magazine dedicated to ballet. It offers practicalities on ballet careers as well as news and features. Estab. 2000. Circ. 38,000. Byline given. NoResponds in 1 month. Sample copy for SAE with 9×12 envelope and 6 First-Class stamps.

NONFICTION Needs historical, how-to, interview, biography, careers, health, news. **Buys 60 mss/year.** Query with published clips. Length: 400-1,500 words. **Pays $125-400.**

POLO PLAYERS' EDITION

9011 Lake Worth Rd., Suite B, Lake Worth FL 33467. (561)968-5208. **Fax:** (561)968-5208. **E-mail:** gwen@poloplayersedition.com. **Website:** www.poloplayersedition.com. **Contact:** Gwen Rizzo. Monthly magazine on the sport and lifestyle polo. "Our readers are affluent, well educated, well read, and highly sophisticated." Circ. 6,150. Offers kill fee. Kill fee varies.

Publishes ms an average of 2 months after acceptance. Submit seasonal material 3 months in advance. Accepts queries by mail, e-mail, fax. Accepts simultaneous submissions. Responds in 3 months to queries. Guidelines for #10 SAE with 2 stamps.

NONFICTION Needs historical, interview, personal experience, photo feature, technical, travel. Special issues: Annual Art Issue/Gift Buying Guide; Winter Preview/Florida Supplement. **Buys 20 mss/year.** Send complete ms. Length: 800-3,000 words. **Pays $150-400 for assigned articles. Pays $100-300 for unsolicited articles.** Sometimes pays expenses of writers on assignment.

COLUMNS Yesteryears (historical pieces), 500 words; Profiles (clubs and players), 800-1,000 words. **Buys 15 mss/year.** Query with published clips. **Pays $100-300.**

PRORODEO SPORTS NEWS

Professional Rodeo Cowboys Association, 101 ProRodeo Dr., Colorado Springs CO 80919. (719)593-8840. **Fax:** (719)548-4889. **Website:** www.prorodeo.com. **Contact:** Neal Reid, managing editor. **10% freelance written.** Biweekly magazine covering professional rodeo. "Our readers are extremely knowledgeable about the sport of rodeo, and anyone who writes for us should have that same in-depth knowledge. Estab. 1952. Circ. 27,000. Byline given. Publishes ms an average of 1 month after acceptance. Editorial lead time 2 months. Submit seasonal material 2 months in advance. Responds in 2 weeks to queries Sample copy for #10 SASE. Guidelines free.

NONFICTION Needs historical, how-to, interview, photo feature, technical. **Pays $50-100.**

RUGBY MAGAZINE

Rugby Press, Ltd., 459 Columbus Ave., #1200, New York NY 10024. (212)787-1160. **Fax:** (212)787-1161. **E-mail:** alex@rugbymag.com. **Website:** www.rugbymag.com. **Contact:** Alex Goff, editor-in-chief. **75% freelance written.** Monthly magazine. Estab. 1975. Circ. 10,000. Byline given. Publishes ms an average of 2 months after acceptance. Editorial lead time 1 month. Submit seasonal material 2 months in advance. Accepts queries by mail, e-mail, fax, phone. Accepts simultaneous submissions. Responds in 2 weeks to queries. Responds in 1 month to mss. Sample copy for $4. Guidelines free.

NONFICTION Needs book excerpts, essays, general interest, historical, how-to, humor, interview, new product, opinion, personal experience, photo feature, technical, travel. **Buys 15 mss/year.** Send complete ms. Length: 600-2,000 words. **Pays $50 minimum.** Pays expenses of writers on assignment.

COLUMNS Nutrition (athletic nutrition), 900 words; Referees' Corner, 1,200 words. **Buys 2-3 mss/year.** Query with published clips. **Pays $50 maximum.**

FICTION Needs cond novels, humorous, novel concepts, slice-of-life vignettes. **Buys 1-3 mss/year.** Query with published clips. Length: 1,000-2,500 words. **Pays $100.**

$ SKYDIVING

1725 N. Lexington Ave., DeLand FL 32724. (386)736-9779. **Fax:** (386)736-9786. **E-mail:** sue@skydivingmagazine.com. **Website:** www.skydivingmagazine.com. **Contact:** Sue Clifton, editor; Mike Truffer, publisher. **25% freelance written.** Monthly tabloid featuring skydiving for sport parachutists, worldwide dealers and equipment manufacturers. *Skydiving* is a news magazine. Its purpose is to deliver timely, useful and interesting information about the equipment, techniques, events, people and places of parachuting. Our scope is national. *Skydiving*'s audience spans the entire spectrum of jumpers, from first-jump students to veterans with thousands of skydives. Some readers are riggers with a keen interest in the technical aspects of parachutes, while others are weekend "fun" jumpers who want information to help them make travel plans and equipment purchases. Estab. 1979. Circ. 14,200. Byline given. Publishes ms an average of 3 months after acceptance. Accepts simultaneous submissions. Responds in 1 month to queries. Sample copy for $2. Guidelines available online.

NONFICTION No personal experience or human interest articles. Query. Length: 500-1,000 words. **Pays $25-100.** Sometimes pays expenses of writers on assignment.

FILLERS Needs newsbreaks. Length: 100-200 words. **$25 minimum.**

MOTOR SPORTS

$ DIRT RIDER

Source Interlink Media, Inc., 1733 Alton Pkwy., Irvine CA 92606. **E-mail:** drmail@sorc.com. **Website:** www.dirtrider.com. Monthly magazine devoted to the sport of off-road motorcycle riding that showcases the many ways enthusiast can enjoy dirt bikes. Circ. 201,342. Guidelines on website.

$ THE HOOK MAGAZINE

P.O. Box 51324, Bowling Green KY 42104. (270)202-6742. **E-mail:** editor@hookmagazine.com; rblively@hotmail.com. **Website:** www.hookmagazine.com. **Contact:** Bryan Lively, editor-in-chief. **80% freelance written.** Bimonthly magazine covering tractor pulling. Estab. 1992. Circ. 6,000. Byline given. Editorial lead time 6 months. Submit seasonal material 6 months in advance. Accepts queries by mail, e-mail, fax. Accepts simultaneous submissions. Responds in 3 weeks to queries. Responds in 2 months to mss. Sample copy for 8 ½x11 SAE with 4 first-class stamps or online. Guidelines for #10 SASE.

NONFICTION Needs how-to, interview, new product, personal experience, photo feature, technical, event coverage. **Buys 25 mss/year.** Send complete ms. Length: 500-1,500 words. **Pays $70 for technical articles; $35 for others.**

FILLERS Needs anecdotes, short humor. **Buys 6 mss/year.** Length: 100 words.

$$ ROAD RACER X

Filter Publications, 122 Vista del Rio Dr., Morgantown WV 26508. (304)284-0080. **Fax:** (304)284-0081. **E-mail:** letters@roadracerx.com. **Website:** www.roadracerx.com. **25% freelance written.** 8 issues per year magazine covering motorcycle road racing. "We cover the sport from a lifestyle/personality perspective. We don't do many technical stories or road tests." Estab. 2003. Circ. 35,000. Byline given. Publishes ms an average of 2 months after acceptance. Editorial lead time 2 months. Submit seasonal material 1 month in advance. Accepts queries by e-mail. Responds in 1 month to queries. Sample copy for #10 SASE. Guidelines available.

NONFICTION Needs historical, (road racing), interview, (racers). Special issues: "We publish official event programs for several important events, including the Red Bull U.S. Grand Prix & the Miller Motorsports Park World Superbike race. We do not want road tests." **Buys 8 mss/yr. mss/year.** Query. Length: 2,000-3,000 words. **Pays $400-600 for assigned articles. Pays $400-600 for unsolicited articles.** Sometimes pays expenses of writers on assignment. (limit agreed upon in advance)

COLUMNS **Contact:** Chris Jonnum. **Buys 8 mss/yr. mss/year.** Query. **Pays $25-$100.**

$$ SAND SPORTS MAGAZINE

Wright Publishing Co., Inc., P.O. Box 2260, Costa Mesa CA 92628. (714)979-2560, ext. 107. **Fax:**

(714)979-3998. **E-mail:** msommer@hotvws.com. **Website:** www.sandsports.net. **Contact:** Michael Sommer, editor. **20% freelance written**. Bimonthly magazine covering vehicles for off-road and sand dunes. Estab. 1995. Circ. 35,000. Byline given. Editorial lead time 3 months. Submit seasonal material 6 months in advance. Accepts queries by mail. Sample copy and writer's guidelines free.

NONFICTION Needs how-to, technical-mechanical, photo feature, technical. **Buys 20 mss/year.** Query. 1,500 words minimum **Pays $175/page.** Sometimes pays expenses of writers on assignment.

RUNNING

💲 INSIDE TEXAS RUNNING

2470 Gray Falls, Suite 110, Houston TX 77077. (281)759-0555. **Fax:** (281)759-7766. **E-mail:** lance@runningmags.com. **Website:** www.insidetexasrunning.com. **70% freelance written**. Monthly (except June and August) tabloid covering running and running-related events. Our audience is made up of Texas runners who may also be interested in cross training. Estab. 1977. Circ. 10,000. Byline given. Publishes ms an average of 2 months after acceptance. Submit seasonal material 2 months in advance. Responds in 1 month to mss. Sample copy for $4.95. Guidelines for #10 SASE.

NONFICTION Special issues: Shoe Review (March); Fall Race Review (September); Marathon Focus (October); Resource Guide (December). **Buys 20 mss/year.** Send complete ms. Length: 500-1,500 words. **Pays $100 maximum for assigned articles. Pays $50 maximum for unsolicited articles.**

💲💲 NEW YORK RUNNER

New York Road Runners, 9 E. 89th St., New York NY 10128. (212)860-4455. **Fax:** (212)423-0879. **E-mail:** webmaster@nyrr.org. **Website:** www.nyrr.org. Quarterly magazine covering running, walking, nutrition, and fitness. Estab. 1958. Circ. 45,000. Byline given. Submit seasonal material 4 months in advance. Accepts queries by mail, e-mail, fax. Responds in 2 months to queries. Sample copy for $3.

NONFICTION Needs interview, of runners. **Buys 15 mss/year.** Query. Length: 750-1,000 words. **Pays $50-350.**

COLUMNS Running Briefs (anything noteworthy in the running world), 250-500 words. Query.

💲💲💲💲 RUNNER'S WORLD

Rodale, 135 N. 6th St., Emmaus PA 18098. (610)967-8441. **Fax:** (610)967-8883. **E-mail:** rwwebedit@rodale.com. **Website:** www.runnersworld.com. **Contact:** David Willey, editor-in-chief; Kory Kennedy, design director. **5% freelance written.** Monthly magazine on running, mainly long-distance running. Estab. 1966. Circ. 500,000. Byline given. Publishes ms an average of 6 months after acceptance. Submit seasonal material 6 months in advance. Accepts queries by mail. Responds in 2 months to queries. Guidelines available online.

NONFICTION Needs how-to, train, prevent injuries, interview, personal experience. No "my first marathon" stories. No poetry. **Buys 5-7 mss/year.** Query. **Pays $1,500-2,000.** Pays expenses of writers on assignment.

COLUMNS Finish Line (back-of-the-magazine essay, personal experience, humor). **Buys 24 mss/year.** Send complete ms. **Pays $300.**

💲💲 RUNNING TIMES

Rodale, Inc., P.O. Box 20627, Boulder CO 80308. (203)761-1113. **Fax:** (203)761-9933. **E-mail:** editor@runningtimes.com. **Website:** www.runningtimes.com. **Contact:** Jonathan Beverly, editor-in-chief. **40% freelance written**. Magazine published 10 times/year covering distance running and racing. "*Running Times* is the national magazine for the experienced running participant and fan. Our audience is knowledgeable about the sport and active in running and racing. All editorial relates specifically to running: improving performance, enhancing enjoyment, or exploring events, places, and people in the sport." Estab. 1977. Circ. 102,000. Byline given. Publishes ms an average of 3 months after acceptance. Editorial lead time 4-6 months. Submit seasonal material 6 months in advance. Accepts queries by mail, e-mail. Responds in 1 month to queries. Responds in 2 months to mss. Sample copy for $8. Guidelines available online.

NONFICTION Needs book excerpts, essays, historical, how-to, training, humor, inspirational, interview, new product, opinion, personal experience, with theme, purpose, evidence of additional research and/or special expertise, photo feature, news, reports. No basic, beginner how-to, generic fitness/nutrition, or generic first-person accounts. **Buys 35 mss/year.** Query. Length: 1,500-3,000 words. **Pays $200-1,000 for assigned articles. Pays $150-300 for unsolicited**

articles. Sometimes pays expenses of writers on assignment.

COLUMNS Training (short topics related to enhancing performance), 1,000 words; Sports-Med (application of medical knowledge to running), 1,000 words; Nutrition (application of nutritional principles to running performance), 1,000 words. **Buys 10 mss/year.** Query. **Pays $50-200.**

FICTION Any genre, with running-related theme or characters. Buys 1 ms/year. Send complete ms. Length: 1,500-3,000 words. **Pays $100-500.**

TIPS "Thoroughly get to know runners and the running culture, both at the participant level and the professional, elite level."

$$ TRAIL RUNNER

Big Stone Publishing, 2567 Dolores Way, Carbondale CO 81623. (970)704-1442. **Fax:** (970)963-4965. **E-mail:** aarnold@bigstonepub.com. **Website:** www.trailrunnermag.com. **Contact:** Michael Benge, editor; Ashley Arnold, associate editor. **50% freelance written.** Bimonthly magazine covering trail running, adventure racing, snowshoeing. Covers all aspects of off-road running. "North America's only magazine dedicated to trail running. In-depth editorial and compelling photography informs, entertains and inspires readers of all ages and abilities to enjoy the outdoors and to improve their health and fitness through the sport of trail running." Estab. 1999. Circ. 29,000. Byline given. Offers $50 kill fee. Publishes ms an average of 2 months after acceptance. Editorial lead time is 3 months. Submit seasonal material 5 months in advance. Accepts queries by e-mail. Accepts simultaneous submissions. Responds in 4 weeks to queries. Sample copy for $5. Guidelines available online at http://trailrunnermag.com/contri_guidelines.php.

NONFICTION Needs exposé, historical, how-to, humor, inspirational, interview, personal experience, technical, travel, racing. Does not want "My first trail race." **Buys 30-40 mss/year.** Query with one or two writing samples (preferably previously published articles), including your name, phone number and email address. Identify which department your story would be best suited for. **Pays 30¢/word for assigned and unsolicited articles.**

COLUMNS Contact: Michael Benge, editor, or Ashley Arnold, associate editor. Making Tracks (news, race reports, athlete Q&A, nutrition tips), 300-800 words; Adventure (adventure stories, athlete profiles); Nutrition (sports nutrition, health news), 800-1,000 words; Great Escapes (running destinations/trails), 1,200 words **Buys 30 mss/year.** Query with published clips. **Pays 30 cents/word.**

FICTION Pays 25-35 cents/word.

FILLERS Needs anecdotes, facts, newsbreaks, short humor. **Buys 10 mss/year.** Length: 75-400 words. **Pays 30 cents/word.**

SKIING AND SNOW SPORTS

$ AMERICAN SNOWMOBILER

Kalmbach Publishing Co., 21027 Crossroads Circle, P.O. Box 1612, Waukesha WI 53187-1612. **E-mail:** editor@amsnow.com. **Website:** www.amsnow.com. **Contact:** Mark Savage, editor. **30% freelance written.** Magazine published 6 times seasonally covering snowmobiling. Estab. 1985. Circ. 54,000. Byline given. Publishes an average of 4 months after acceptance. Editorial lead time 4 months. Submit seasonal material 6 months in advance. Accepts queries by mail, e-mail, fax. Responds in 1 month to queries. Responds in 2 months to mss. Guidelines available online.

NONFICTION Needs general interest, historical, how-to, interview, personal experience, photo feature, travel. **Buys 10 mss/year.** Query with published clips. Length: 500-1,200 words. **Pay varies for assigned articles. Pays $100 minimum for unsolicited articles.**

$ SKATING

United States Figure Skating Association, 20 First St., Colorado Springs CO 80906. (719)635-5200. **Fax:** (719)635-9548. **E-mail:** info@usfigureskating.org. **Website:** www.usfsa.org. "Magazine published 10 times/year. *Skating* magazine is the official publication of U.S. Figure Skating, and thus we cover skating at both the championship and grass roots level." Estab. 1923. Circ. 45,000. Byline given. Publishes ms an average of 3 months after acceptance. Accepts queries by mail, e-mail, fax.

NONFICTION Needs general interest, historical, how-to, interview, background and interests of skaters, volunteers, or other U.S. Figure Skating members, photo feature, technical and competition reports, figure skating issues and trends, sports medicine. **Buys 10 mss/year.** Query. Length: 500-2,500 words. **Payment varies**

COLUMNS Ice Breaker (news briefs); Foreign Competition Reports; Health and Fitness; In Synch (synchronized skating news); Takeoff (up-and-coming athletes), all 500-2,000 words.

$$$$ SKIING

Bonnier Corporation, 5720 Flatiron Pkwy., Boulder CO 80301. (303)253-6300. **E-mail:** editor@skiingmag.com. **Website:** www.skiingmag.com. **Contact:** Sam Bass, editor. Magazine published 7 times/year for skiers who "deeply love winter, and who live for travel, adventure, instruction, gear, and news." "*Skiing* is the user's guide to winter adventure. It is equal parts jaw-dropping inspiration and practical information, action and utility, attitude and advice. It relates the lifestyles of dedicated skiers and captures their spirit of daring and exploration. Dramatic photography transports readers to spine-tingling mountains with breathtaking immediacy. Reading *Skiing* is almost as much fun as being there." Estab. 1948. Circ. 400,000. Byline given. Offers 40% kill fee. No

NONFICTION **Buys 10-15 feature (1,500-2,000 words) and 12-24 short (100-500 words) mss/year.** Query. **Pays $1,000-2,500/feature; $100-500/short piece.**

COLUMNS Length: 200-1,000 words. **Buys 2-3 mss/year.** Query. **Pays $150-1,000.**

⊘ $$$ SKIING MAGAZINE

Bonnier Corp., 5720 Flatiron Pkwy., Boulder CO 80301. (303)448-7600. **Fax:** (303)448-7638. **E-mail:** editor@skiingmag.com. **Website:** www.skinet.com/skiing. **60% freelance written.** Magazine published 8 times/year. *Skiing Magazine* is an online ski-lifestyle publication written and edited for recreational skiers. Its content is intended to help them ski better (technique), buy better (equipment and skiwear), and introduce them to new experiences, people, and adventures. Estab. 1936. Circ. 430,000. Byline given. Offers 15% kill fee. Publishes ms an average of 3 months after acceptance. Submit seasonal material 8 months in advance. Accepts queries by mail, e-mail. Sample copy with 9×12 SASE and 5 first-class stamps.

- Does not accept unsolicited mss, and assumes no responsibility for their return.

NONFICTION Needs essays, historical, how-to, humor, interview, personal experience. **Buys 5-10 mss/year.** Send complete ms. Length: 1,000-3,500 words. **Pays $500-1,000 for assigned articles. Pays $300-700 for unsolicited articles.** Pays expenses of writers on assignment.

FILLERS Needs facts, short humor. **Buys 10 mss/year.** Length: 60-75 words. **Pays $50-75.**

$$ SNOWEST MAGAZINE

Harris Publishing, 360 B St., Idaho Falls ID 83402. (208)524-7000. **Fax:** (208)522-5241. **E-mail:** lindstrm@snowest.com. **Website:** snowest.com. **10-25% freelance written.** Monthly magazine. "*SnoWest* covers the sport of snowmobiling, products, and personalities in the western states. This includes mountain riding, deep powder, and trail riding, as well as destination pieces, tech tips, and new model reviews." Estab. 1972. Circ. 140,000. Byline given. Publishes ms an average of 2 months after acceptance. Editorial lead time 6 months. Submit seasonal material 3 months in advance. Sample copy and writer's guidelines free.

NONFICTION Needs how-to, fix a snowmobile, make it high performance, new product, technical, travel. **Buys 3-5 mss/year.** Query with published clips. Length: 500-1,500 words. **Pays $150-300.**

$$ SNOW GOER

Affinity Media, 300 Fernbrook Lane N, Suite #2000, Plymouth MN 55447. **Fax:** (763)-383-4499. **Website:** www.snowgoer.com. **5% freelance written.** Magazine published 7 times/year covering snowmobiling. "*Snow Goer* is a hard-hitting, tell-it-like-it-is magazine designed for the ultra-active snowmobile enthusiast. It is fun, exciting, innovative, and on the cutting edge of technology and trends." Estab. 1967. Circ. 66,000. Byline given. Publishes ms an average of 5 months after acceptance. Editorial lead time 5 months. Submit seasonal material 6 months in advance. Accepts queries by mail. Accepts simultaneous submissions. Responds in 3 months to queries. Sample copy for sae with 8×10 envelope and 4 First-Class stamps.

NONFICTION Needs general interest, how-to, interview, new product, personal experience, photo feature, technical, travel. **Buys 6 mss/year.** Query. Length: 500-4,000 words. **Pays $50-500.** Sometimes pays expenses of writers on assignment.

WATER SPORTS

$$ ROWING NEWS

The Independent Rowing News, Inc., Rivermill Suite 440, 85 Mechanic St., Suite 440, Lebanon NH 03766. (603)448-5090. **E-mail:** editor@rowingnews.com. **Website:** www.rowingnews.com. **Contact:** Ed Winchester. **75% freelance written.** Monthly magazine covering rowing (the Olympic sport). We write for a North American readership, serving the rowing community with features, how-to, and dispatches from the rowing world at large. Estab. 1994. Circ. 20,000. Byline given. Publishes ms an average of 1-2 months after acceptance. Editorial lead time 1-12 months. Submit seasonal material 1-2 months in advance. Responds in 6 weeks to queries. Sample copy available online. Guidelines free.

NONFICTION Needs essays, how-to, rowing only, interview, new product, personal experience, rowing, travel. Everything must be directedly related to rowing. **Buys 12 mss/year.** Query with published clips. Length: 1,500-5,000 words. Sometimes pays expenses of writers on assignment.

⊘ $ SURFER MAGAZINE

Source Interlink, P.O. Box 1028, Dana Point CA 92629-5028. (949)325-6212. **E-mail:** brendon@surfermag.com. **Website:** www.surfermag.com. **Contact:** Brendon Thomas, editor. Monthly magazine edited for the avid surfers and those who follow the beach, wave riding scene. Circ. 118,570. Editorial lead time 10 weeks.

💬 Query before submitting.

$$ SWIMMING WORLD MAGAZINE

Sports Publications International, P.O. Box 20337, Sedona AZ 86341. (928)284-4005. **Fax:** (928)284-2477. **Website:** www.swimmingworldmagazine.com. **Contact:** Jason Marsteller, managing editor. **30% freelance written.** Bimonthly magazine about competitive swimming. Readers are fitness-oriented adults from varied social and professional backgrounds who share swimming as part of their lifestyle. Submit 250-word synopsis of your article. Estab. 1960. Circ. 50,000. Byline given. Editorial lead time 2 months. Submit seasonal material 3 months in advance. Accepts queries by mail, e-mail, fax. Accepts simultaneous submissions. Responds in 1 month to queries. Guidelines available online.

NONFICTION Needs book excerpts, essays, exposé, general interest, historical, how-to, training plans and techniques, humor, inspirational, interview, people associated with fitness and competitive swimming, new product, articles describing new products for fitness and competitive training, personal experience, photo feature, technical, travel, general health. **Buys 30 mss/year.** Query. Length: 250-2,500 words. **Pays $75-400.**

$ THE WATER SKIER

1251 Holy Cow Rd., Polk City FL 33868. (863)324-4341. **Fax:** (863)325-8259. **E-mail:** satkinson@usawaterski.org. **Website:** www.usawaterski.org. **Contact:** Scott Atkinson, editor. **10-20% freelance written.** Magazine published 7 times/year. *The Water Skier* is the membership magazine of USA Water Ski, the national governing body for organized water skiing in the United States. The magazine has a controlled circulation and is available only to USA Water Ski's membership, which is made up of 20,000 active competitive water skiers and 10,000 members who are supporting the sport. These supporting members may participate in the sport but they don't compete. The editorial content of the magazine features distinctive and informative writing about the sport of water skiing only. Estab. 1951. Circ. 30,000. Byline given. Offers 30% kill fee. Editorial lead time 4 months. Submit seasonal material 6 months in advance. Responds in 2 weeks to queries. Sample copy for $3.50. Guidelines with #10 SASE.

NONFICTION Needs historical, has to pertain to water skiing, interview, call for assignment, new product, boating and water ski equipment, travel, water ski vacation destinations. **Buys 10-15 mss/year.** Query. Length: 1,500-3,000 words. **Pays $100-150.**

COLUMNS The Water Skier News (small news items about people and events in the sport), 400-500 words. Other topics include safety, training (3-event, barefoot, disabled, show ski, ski race, kneeboard, and wakeboard); champions on their way; new products. Query. **Pays $50-100.**

SHOOTING SHOTGUNS

$$ SHOTGUN SPORTS MAGAZINE

P.O. Box 6810, Auburn CA 95604. (530)889-2220. **Fax:** (530)889-9106. **E-mail:** shotgun@shotgunsportsmagazine.com. **Website:** www.shotgunsportsmagazine.com. **Contact:** Linda Martin, production coordinator. **50% freelance written. Welcomes new writers.** Monthly magazine covering all the shotgun sports and shotgun hunting—sporting clays, trap, skeet, hunting, gunsmithing, shotshell patterning, shotsell reloading, mental training for the shotgun sports, shotgun tests, anything shotgun. Publishes ms an average of 1-6 months after acceptance. Sample copy and writer's guidelines available by contacting Linda Martin, or via the website.

🗩 Responds within 3 weeks. Subscription: $32.95 (U.S.); $49.95 (Canada); $79.95 (foreign).

NONFICTION Needs Currently needs anything with a 'shotgun' subject. Think pieces, roundups, historical, interviews, etc. No articles promoting a specific club or sponsored hunting trip, etc. Submit complete ms with photos by mail with SASE. Can submit by e-mail. Make Length: 1,500-3,000 words. **Pays $50-150.**

TEEN AND YOUNG ADULT

🟡🟢 CICADA MAGAZINE

Cricket Magazine Group, 70 E. Lake St., Suite 300, Chicago IL 60601. (312)701-1720. **Fax:** (312)701-1728. **E-mail:** dvetter@caruspub.com. **Website:** www.cicadamag.com. **Contact:** Marianne Carus, editor-in-chief; Deborah Vetter, executive editor; John Sandford, art director. **80% freelance written.** Bimonthly literary magazine for ages 14 and up. Publishes original short stories, poems, and first-person essays written for teens and young adults. *Cicada* publishes fiction and poetry with a genuine teen sensibility, aimed at the high school and college-age market. The editors are looking for stories and poems that are thought-provoking but entertaining. Estab. 1998. Circ. 10,000. Byline given. Accepts simultaneous submissions. Responds in 2 months to mss. Guidelines available online.

NONFICTION Needs essays, personal experience, book reviews. Young adults: first-person, coming-of-age experiences that are relevant to teens and young adults (example: life in the Peace Corps). Buys up to 6 mss/year. Submit complete ms, SASE. Length: 5,000 words maximum; 300-500 words/book reviews. **Pays up to 25¢/word.**

FICTION Young adults: adventure, contemporary, fantasy, historical, humor/satire, multicultural, nature/environment, romance, science fiction, sports, suspense/mystery. Buys up to 42 mss/year. The main protagonist should be at least 14 and preferably older. Stories should have a genuine teen sensibility and be aimed at readers in high school or college. Needs adventure, fantasy, historical, humorous, mainstream, novel concepts, romance, science fiction, contemporary, realistic, novellas (1/issue). 5,000 words maximum (up to 15,000 words/novellas). **Pays up to 25¢/word.**

POETRY Needs free verse, light verse, traditional. Reviews serious, humorous, free verse, rhyming (if done well) poetry. Limit submissions to 5 poems. Length: 25 lines maximum. **Pays up to $3/line on publication.**

🟡 INSIGHT

The Review and Herald Publishing Association, 55 W. Oak Ridge Dr., Hagerstown MD 21740. (301)393-4038. **E-mail:** insight@rhpa.org. **Website:** www.insightmagazine.org. **80% freelance written.** Weekly magazine covering spiritual life of teenagers. *Insight* publishes true dramatic stories, interviews, and community and mission service features that relate directly to the lives of Christian teenagers, particularly those with a Seventh-day Adventist background. Estab. 1970. Circ. 16,000. Byline given. Publishes ms an average of 4 months after acceptance. Editorial lead time 6 months. Submit seasonal material 6 months in advance. Accepts queries by mail, e-mail, fax. Responds in 1 month to mss. Sample copy for $2 and #10 SASE. Guidelines available online.

NONFICTION Needs how-to, teen relationships and experiences, humor, interview, personal experience, photo feature, religious. **Buys 120 mss/year.** Send complete ms. Length: 500-1,500 words. **Pays $25-150 for assigned articles. Pays $25-125 for unsolicited articles.**

COLUMNS Big Deal (topic of importance to teens) 1,000-1,500 words; Interviews (Christian culture figures, especially musicians), 1,500 words; It Happened to Me (first-person teen experiences containing spiritual insights), 1,000 words; On the Edge (dramatic true stories about Christians), 1,000-1,500 words; So I Said..(true short stories in the first person of common, everyday events and experiences that taught the writer something), 300-500 words. Send complete ms. **Pays $25-125.**

🟡🟡 LISTEN MAGAZINE

The Health Connection, 55 W. Oak Ridge Dr., Hagerstown MD 21740. (301)393-4010; (301)393-4082. **E-mail:** editor@listenmagazine.org. **Website:** www.listenmagazine.org. **Contact:** Celeste Perrino-Walker, editor. **80% freelance written.** Monthly magazine specializing in tobacco, drug, and alcohol prevention, presenting positive alternatives to various tobacco, drug, and alcohol dependencies. *Listen* is used in many high school classes and by professionals: medical personnel, counselors, law enforcement officers, educators, youth workers, etc. Circ. 12,000. Byline given. Publishes ms an average of 6 months after acceptance. Accepts queries by mail, e-mail. Accepts simultaneous submissions. Responds in 2 months to queries. Sample copy for $2 and 9×12 SASE. Guidelines available online.

NONFICTION Buys 30-50 unsolicited mss/year. Query.

💲💲 THE NEW ERA

50 E. North Temple St., Room 2414, Salt Lake City UT 84150-0024. (801)240-2951. **Fax:** (801)240-2270. **E-mail:** newera@ldschurch.org. **Website:** www.newera. lds.org. **Contact:** Richard M. Romney, managing editor. **20% freelance written.** Monthly magazine for young people (ages 12-18) of the Church of Jesus Christ of Latter-day Saints (Mormon), their church leaders and teachers. Estab. 1971. Circ. 230,000. Byline given. Publishes ms an average of 1 year after acceptance. Submit seasonal material 1 year in advance. Accepts queries by mail, e-mail, fax. Responds in 2 months to queries. Sample copy for $1.50. Guidelines available online.

NONFICTION Needs how-to, humor, inspirational, interview, personal experience, informational. Query. Length: 150-1,200 words. **Pays $25-350/article.**

COLUMNS What's Up? (news of young Mormons around the world); How I Know; Scripture Lifeline. **Pays $25-125/article.**

POETRY Needs free verse, light verse, traditional, all other forms. Must relate to editorial viewpoint. **Pays $25 and up.**

💲💲💲💲 SEVENTEEN

300 W. 57th St., 17th Floor, New York NY 10019. (917)934-6500. **Fax:** (917)934-6574. **Website:** www.seventeen.com. **20% freelance written.** Monthly magazine. *Seventeen* is a young woman's first fashion and beauty magazine. Tailored for young women in their teens and early twenties, *Seventeen* covers fashion, beauty, health, fitness, food, college, entertainment, fiction, plus crucial personal and global issues. Estab. 1944. Circ. 2,400,000. Byline given. Offers 25% kill fee. Publishes ms an average of 6 months after acceptance. Accepts queries by mail. Responds in 3 months to queries.

NONFICTION Length: 1,200-2,500 words. **Pays $1/word, occasionally more.** Pays expenses of writers on assignment.

TRAVEL, CAMPING AND TRAILER

💲💲 AAA MIDWEST TRAVELER

AAA Auto Club of Missouri, 12901 N. 40 Dr., St. Louis MO 63141. (314)523-7350 ext. 6301. **Fax:** (314)523-6982. **E-mail:** dreinhardt@aaamissouri.com. **Website:** www.aaa.com/traveler. **Contact:** Deborah Reinhardt, managing editor. **80% freelance written.** Bimonthly magazine covering travel and automotive safety. "We provide members with useful information on travel, auto safety and related topics." Estab. 1901. Circ. 500,000. Byline given. Offers $50 kill fee. Editorial lead time 1 year. Submit seasonal material 6 months in advance. Accepts queries by mail, e-mail, fax. Accepts simultaneous submissions. Responds in 1 month. Sample copy with 10×13 SASE and 4 First-Class stamps. Guidelines with #10 SASE.

NONFICTION Needs travel. No humor, fiction, poetry or cartoons. **Buys 20-30 mss/year.** Query; query with published clips the first time. Length: 800-1,200 words. **Pays $400.**

💲 CAMPERWAYS, MIDWEST RV TRAVELER, FLORIDA RV TRAVELER, NORTHEAST OUTDOORS, SOUTHERN RV

Woodall Publications Corp., 2575 Vista Del Mar Dr., Ventura CA 93001. (888)656-6669. **E-mail:** info@ woodallpub.com. **Website:** www.woodalls.com. **75% freelance written.** Monthly tabloids covering RV lifestyle. "We're looking for articles of interest to RVers. Lifestyle articles, destinations, technical tips, interesting events, and the like make up the bulk of our publications. We also look for region-specific travel and special interest articles." Circ. 30,000. Byline given. Offers 50% kill fee. Accepts queries by mail, e-mail. Sample copy free. Guidelines for #10 SASE.

Accepts queries in June, July, and August for upcoming year.

NONFICTION Needs how-to, personal experience, technical, travel. No "Camping From Hell" articles. **Buys approximately 500 mss/year.** Length: 500-2,000 words. **Payment varies.**

💲 CAMPING TODAY

126 Hermitage Rd., Butler PA 16001-8509. (724)283-7401. **E-mail:** d_johnston01@msn.com. **Website:** www.fcrv.org. **Contact:** DeWayne Johnston, editor. **30% freelance written.** Bimonthly official membership publication of the FCRV. "*Camping Today* is the largest nonprofit family camping and RV organization in the U.S. and Canada. Members are heavily oriented toward RV travel. Concentration is on member activities in chapters. Group is also interested in conservation and wildlife. The majority of members are retired." Estab. 1983. Circ. 10,000. By-

line given. Publishes ms an average of 6 months after acceptance. Submit seasonal material 3 months in advance. Accepts simultaneous submissions. Responds in 2 months to queries and to mss. Sample copy and guidelines for 4 first-class stamps. Guidelines for #10 SASE.

NONFICTION Needs humor, camping or travel related, interview, interesting campers, new product, technical, RVs related, travel, interesting places to visit by RV, camping. **Buys 10-15 mss/year.** Query by mail or email or send complete ms with photos. Length: 750-2,000 words. **Pays $50-150.**

$$$ COAST TO COAST MAGAZINE

Affinity Group, Inc., 2575 Vista Del Mar Dr., Ventura CA 93001. (805)667-4100. **E-mail:** editor@coastresorts.com. **Website:** www.coastresorts.com. **80% freelance written.** Quarterly magazine for members of Coast to Coast Resorts. "*Coast to Coast* focuses on North American travel, outdoor recreation, camping and RV parks; circulation is 60,000." Estab. 1983. Byline given. Offers 33% kill fee. Publishes ms an average of 4 months after acceptance. Editorial lead time 5 months. Submit seasonal material 5 months in advance. Accepts queries by mail, e-mail, fax. Accepts simultaneous submissions. Responds in 6-8 weeks to queries. Responds in 1-2 months to mss. Sample copy for $4 and 9×12 SASE. Guidelines for #10 SASE.

NONFICTION Needs book excerpts, essays, general interest, how-to, interview, new product, personal experience, photo feature, technical, travel. No poetry, cartoons. **Buys 70 mss/year.** Send complete ms. Length: 800-2,500 words. **Pays $75-1,200.**

COLUMNS Pays $ 150-400.

$$ FAMILY MOTOR COACHING

8291 Clough Pike, Cincinnati OH 45244. (513)474-3622. **Fax:** (513)388-5286. **E-mail:** rgould@fmca.com; magazine@fmca.com. **Website:** www.fmca.com. **Contact:** Robbin Gould, editor. **80% freelance written. We prefer that writers be experienced RVers.** Monthly magazine emphasizing travel by motorhome, motorhome mechanics, maintenance, and other technical information. "*Family Motor Coaching* magazine is edited for the members and prospective members of the Family Motor Coach Association who own or are about to purchase self-contained, motorized recreational vehicles known as motorhomes. Featured are articles on travel and recreation, association news and activities, plus articles on new products and motorhome maintenance and repair. Approximately 1/3 of editorial content is devoted to travel and entertainment, 1/3 to association news, and 1/3 to new products, industry news, and motorhome maintenance." Estab. 1963. Circ. 140,000. Byline given. Publishes ms an average of 8 months after acceptance. Submit seasonal material 4 months in advance. Accepts queries by mail, e-mail, fax. Responds in 3 months to queries. Sample copy for $3.99; $5 if paying by credit card. Guidelines with #10 SASE or request PDF by e-mail.

NONFICTION Needs how-to, do-it-yourself motorhome projects and modifications, humor, interview, new product, technical, motorhome travel (various areas of North America accessible by motorhome), bus conversions, nostalgia. **Buys 50-75 mss/year.** Query with published clips. Length: 1,000-2,000 words. **Pays $100-500, depending on article category.**

$$ HIGHROADS

AAA Arizona, 3144 N. 7th Ave., Phoenix AZ 85013. (602)650-2732. **Fax:** (602)241-2917. **E-mail:** highroads@arizona.aaa.com. **Website:** www.aaa.com. **50% freelance written.** Bimonthly magazine covering Travel/Automotive. Our magazine goes out to our 470,000+ AAA Arizona members on a bimonthly basis. The mean age of ur audience is around 60 years old. We look for intelligent, engaging writing covering auto and travel-related topics. Byline given. Offers 30% kill fee. Editorial lead time 6 months. Submit seasonal material 6 months in advance. Accepts queries by mail, e-mail, fax. Accepts simultaneous submissions. Sample copy for #10 SASE. Guidelines by e-mail.

NONFICTION Needs travel, Auto-related. Articles unrelated to travel, automotive or Arizona living. **Buys 21 mss/year.** Query with published clips. Length: 500-2,000 words. **Pays $0.35/word for assigned articles. Pays $0.35/word for unsolicited articles.**

COLUMNS Contact: Jill Schildhouse. Weekender (Weekend destinations near Arizona), Road Trip (Day activities in Arizona), Charming Stays (A charming inn or B&B in Arizona); 500 to 700 words. **Buys 10 mss/year. Pays $0-35.**

$$ HIGHWAYS

Affinity Group, Inc., 2575 Vista Del Mar Dr., Ventura CA 93001. (805)667-4100. **E-mail:** highways@goodsamclub.com. **Website:** www.goodsamclub.com/highways. **30% freelance written.** Monthly magazine covering recreational vehicle lifestyle. "All of our readers own some type of RV—a motorhome, trailer, pop-up, tent—so our stories need to include places that you can go with large vehicles, and campgrounds in and around the area where they can spend the night." Estab. 1966. Circ. 975,000. Byline given. Offers 50% kill fee. Publishes ms an average of 6 months after acceptance. Accepts queries by e-mail. Responds in 2 weeks to queries. Sample copy and writer's guidelines free or online.

NONFICTION Needs how-to, repair/replace something on an RV, humor, technical, travel, all RV related. **Buys 15-20 mss/year.** Query. Length: 800-1,100 words.

COLUMNS On the Road (issue related); RV Insight (for people new to the RV lifestyle); Action Line (consumer help); Tech Topics (tech Q&A); Camp Cuisine (cooking in an RV); Product Previews (new products). No plans on adding new COLUMNS.

INTERNATIONAL LIVING

International Living Publishing, Ltd., Elysium House, Ballytruckle, Waterford Ireland (800)643-2479. **Fax:** 353-51-304-561. **E-mail:** editor@internationalliving.com. **Website:** www.internationalliving.com. **Contact:** Eoin Bassett, managing editor. **50% freelance written**. Monthly magazine covering retirement, travel, investment, and real estate overseas. "We do not want descriptions of how beautiful places are. We want specifics, recommendations, contacts, prices, names, addresses, phone numbers, etc. We want offbeat locations and off-the-beaten-track spots." Estab. 1981. Circ. 500,000. Byline given. Offers 25-50% kill fee. Publishes ms an average of 3 months after acceptance. Editorial lead time 2 months. Submit seasonal material 3 months in advance. Accepts queries by mail, e-mail, fax. Accepts simultaneous submissions. Responds in 2 months to mss. Sample copy for #10 SASE. Guidelines available online.

NONFICTION Needs how-to, get a job, buy real estate, get cheap airfares overseas, start a business, etc., interview, entrepreneur or retiree abroad, new product, travel, personal experience, travel, shopping, cruises. No descriptive, run-of-the-mill travel articles. **Buys 100 mss/year.** Send complete ms. Length: 500-2,000 words. **Pays $200-500 for assigned articles. Pays $100-400 for unsolicited articles.**

FILLERS Needs facts. **Buys 20 mss/year.** Length: 50-250 words. **Pays $25-50.**

THE INTERNATIONAL RAILWAY TRAVELER

Hardy Publishing Co., Inc., P.O. Box 3747, San Diego CA 92163. (619)260-1332. **Fax:** (619)296-4220. **E-mail:** irteditor@aol.com. **Website:** www.irtsociety.com. **100% freelance written**. Monthly newsletter covering rail travel. Estab. 1983. Circ. 3,500. Byline given. Pays within 1 month of the publication date. Offers 25% kill fee. Editorial lead time 4 months. Submit seasonal material 6 months in advance. Responds in 1 month to queries. Responds in 2 months to mss. Sample copy for $6. Guidelines for #10 SASE or via e-mail..

NONFICTION Needs general interest, how-to, interview, new product, opinion, personal experience, travel, book reviews. **Buys 48-60 mss/year.** Send complete ms. Length: 800-1,200 words. **Pays 3¢/word.**

ISLANDS

Bonnier Corp., 460 N. Orlando Ave., Suite 200, Winter Park FL 32789. (407)628-4802. **E-mail:** story-ideas@islands.com. **Website:** www.islands.com. **80% freelance written**. Magazine published 8 times/year. "We cover accessible and once-in-a-lifetime islands from many different perspectives: travel, culture, lifestyle. We ask our authors to give us the essence of the island and do it with literary flair." Estab. 1981. Circ. 250,000. Byline given. Offers 25% kill fee. Publishes ms an average of 8 months after acceptance. Accepts queries by e-mail. Responds in 2 months to queries. Responds in 6 weeks to mss. Sample copy for $6. "E-mail us for writer's guidelines."

NONFICTION Needs book excerpts, essays, general interest, interview, photo feature, travel, service shorts, island-related material. **Buys 25 feature mss/year.** Send complete ms. Length: 2,000-4,000 words. **Pays $750-2,500.** Sometimes pays expenses of writers on assignment.

COLUMNS Discovers section (island related news), 100-250 words; Taste (island cuisine), 900-1,000 words; Travel Tales (personal essay), 900-1,100 words; Live the Life (island expat Q&A). Query with published clips. **Pays $25-1,000.**

MOTORHOME

Affinity Group Inc., 2575 Vista Del Mar Dr., Ventura CA 93001. (805)667-4100. **Fax:** (805)667-4484. **E-mail:** info@motorhomemagazine.com. **Website:** www.motorhomemagazine.com. **Contact:** Eileen Hubbard, editor. **60% freelance written**. Monthly magazine. "*MotorHome* is a magazine for owners and prospective buyers of motorized recreational vehicles who are active outdoorsmen and wide-ranging travelers. We cover all aspects of the RV lifestyle; editorial material is both technical and nontechnical in nature. Regular features include tests and descriptions of various models of motorhomes, travel adventures, and hobbies pursued in such vehicles, objective analysis of equipment and supplies for such vehicles, and do-it-yourself articles. Guides within the magazine provide listings of manufacturers, rentals, and other sources of equipment and accessories of interest to enthusiasts. Articles must have an RV slant and excellent photography accompanying text." Estab. 1968. Circ. 150,000. Byline given. Offers 30% kill fee. Publishes ms an average of within 1 year after acceptance. Editorial lead time 4 months. Submit seasonal material 6 months in advance. Accepts queries by mail, fax. Responds in 1 month to queries. Responds in 2 months to mss. Sample copy free. Guidelines available online or for #10 SASE.

NONFICTION Needs general interest, historical, how-to, humor, interview, new product, personal experience, photo feature, technical, travel, celebrity profiles, recreation, lifestyle, legislation, all RV related. No diaries of RV trips or negative RV experiences. **Buys 120 mss/year.** Query with published clips. Length: 250-2,500 words. **Pays $300-600.**

COLUMNS Crossroads (offbeat briefs of people, places, and events of interest to travelers), 100-200 words; Keepers (tips, resources). Query with published clips or send complete ms. **Pays $100**

○ ❸❸ NORTH AMERICAN INNS MAGAZINE

Harworth Publishing Inc., Box 998, Guelph ON N1H 6N1 Canada. (519)767-6059. **Fax:** (519)821-0479. **E-mail:** editor@harworthpublishing.com. **Website:** www.innsmagazine.com. **Contact:** Mary Hughes, editor. *North American Inns* is a national publication for travel, dining and pastimes. It focuses on inns, beds & breakfasts, resorts and travel in North America. The magazine is targeted to travelers looking for exquisite getaways. Accepts queries by e-mail. Guidelines by e-mail.

NONFICTION Needs general interest, interview, new product, opinion, personal experience, travel. Query. Length: 300-600 words. **Pays $175-250 (Canadian).**

FILLERS Short quips or nominations at 75 words are **$25 each.** All stories submitted have to accompany

photos. Please e-mail photos to designer@harworthpublishing.com.

❸ PATHFINDERS

6325 Germantown Ave., Philadelphia PA 19144. (215)438-2140. **Fax:** (215)438-2144. **E-mail:** editors@pathfinderstravel.com. **Website:** www.pathfinderstravel.com. **75% freelance written.** Bimonthly magazine covering travel for people of color, primarily African-Americans. We look for lively, original, well-written stories that provide a good sense of place, with useful information and fresh ideas about travel and the travel industry. Our main audience is African-Americans, though we do look for articles relating to other persons of color: Native Americans, Hispanics and Asians. Pathfinders Travel Magazine for People of Color is is published quarterly. The magazine, which enjoys circulation of 100,000 copies, reaches an affluent audience of African American travelers interested in enjoying the good life. Pathfinders tells readers where to go, what to do, where to dine and how to 'get there from a cultural perspective. Pathfinders covers domestic and international destinations. The slick, glossy, color magazine is available nationally in Barnes & Nobel, Crown, Borders, Hastings and other independent book stores. Estab. 1997. Circ. 100,000. Byline given. Accepts queries by mail, e-mail. Responds in 1 month to queries. Responds in 2 months to mss. Sample copy at bookstores (Barnes & Noble, Borders). Guidelines available online.

NONFICTION Needs essays, historical, how-to, personal experience, photo feature, travel, all vacation travel oriented. No more pitches on Jamaica. We get these all the time. **Buys 16-20 mss/year.** Send complete ms. 1,200-1,400 words for cover stories; 1,000-1,200 words for features. **Pays $200.**

COLUMNS Chef's Table, Post Cards from Home; Looking Back; City of the Month, 500-600 words. Send complete ms. **Pays $150.**

❸❸ PILOT GETAWAYS MAGAZINE

Airventure Publishing LLC, P.O. Box 550, Glendale CA 91209-0550. (818)241-1890. **Fax:** (818)241-1895. **E-mail:** info@pilotgetaways.com; editor@pilotgetaways.com. **Website:** www.pilotgetaways.com. **Contact:** John T. Kounis, editor. **90% freelance written.** Bimonthly magazine covering aviation travel for private pilots. *Pilot Getaways* is a travel magazine for private pilots. Our articles cover destinations that are easily accessible by private aircraft, including details such as airport transportation, convenient hotels, and attractions. Other regular features include fly-in dining, flying tips, and bush flying. Estab. 1999. Circ. 25,000. Byline given. Editorial lead time 4 months. Submit seasonal material 9 months in advance. Accepts queries by mail, e-mail, fax, phone. Accepts simultaneous submissions. Responds in 2 weeks to queries. Responds in 2 months to mss. Sample copy and writer's guidelines free.

NONFICTION Needs travel, specifically travel guide articles. "We rarely publish articles about events that have already occurred, such as travel logs about trips the authors have taken or air show reports." **Buys 30 mss/year.** Query. Length: 1,000-3,500 words. **Pays $100-500.**

COLUMNS Weekend Getaways (short fly-in getaways), 2,000 words; Fly-in Dining (reviews of airport restaurants), 1,200 words; Flying Tips (tips and pointers on flying technique), 1,000 words; Bush Flying (getaways to unpaved destinations), 1,500 words. **Buys 20 mss/year.** Query. **Pays $100-500.**

⚙⚙⚙ PORTHOLE CRUISE MAGAZINE

Panoff Publishing, 4517 NW 31st Ave., Ft. Lauderdale FL 33309-3403. (954)377-7777. **Fax:** (954)377-7000. **E-mail:** editorial@ppigroup.com. **Website:** www.porthole.com. **70% freelance written.** Bimonthly magazine covering the cruise industry. *Porthole Cruise Magazine* entices its readers to take a cruise vacation by delivering information that is timely, accurate, colorful, and entertaining. Estab. 1992. Circ. 80,000. Byline given. Offers 20% kill fee. Publishes ms an average of 6 months after acceptance. Editorial lead time 8 months. Submit seasonal material 5 months in advance. Accepts queries by e-mail. Accepts simultaneous submissions. Guidelines available online.

NONFICTION Needs general interest, cruise related, historical, how-to, pick a cruise, not get seasick, travel tips, humor, interview, crew on board or industry executives, new product, personal experience, photo feature, travel, off-the-beaten-path, adventure, ports, destinations, cruises, onboard fashion, spa articles, duty-free shopping, port shopping, ship reviews. No articles on destinations that can't be reached by ship. **Buys 60 mss/year.** Length: 1,000-1,200 words. **Pays $500-600 for assigned feature articles.**

⚙⚙⚙⚙ SPA

Bonnier Corp., 415 Jackson St., San Francisco CA 94111. (415)632-1633. **Fax:** (415)632-1640. **Website:** www.spamagazine.com. Bimonthly magazine covering health spas: treatments, travel, cuisine, fitness, beauty. Approachable and accessible, authoritative and full of advice, *Spa* is the place to turn for information and tips on nutrition, spa cuisine/recipes, beauty, health, skin care, spa travel, fitness, well-being and renewal. Byline given. Offers 25% kill fee. Editorial lead time 3 months. Accepts queries by mail. Sample copy for $6.

COLUMNS In Touch (spa news, treatments, destinations); Body (nutrition, health & fitness, spa therapies); Rituals (spa at home, beauty, home, books and music, mind/body).

☉ ⚙⚙ SPA LIFE

Harworth Publishing, Inc., P.O. Box 998, Guelph ON N1H 6N1 Canada. (519)767-6059. **Fax:** (519)821-0479. **E-mail:** editor@harworthpublishing.com. **Website:** www.spalifemagazine.com. "*Spa Life* is about more than just spas. With favorite recipes from featured spa destinations, mouth-watering treats are at your fingertips. *Spa Life* is also dedicated to personal and health issues." Estab. 2000. Accepts queries by e-mail. Guidelines by e-mail.

NONFICTION Needs general interest, interview, new product, personal experience, travel. Length: 300-600 words. **Pays $25-50 (Canadian).**

⚙ ⚙⚙ TIMES OF THE ISLANDS

Times Publications, Ltd., P.O. Box 234, Lucille Lightbourne Bldg., #7, Providenciales Turks & Caicos Islands British West Indies. (649)946-4788. **Fax:** (649)946-4788. **E-mail:** timespub@tciway.tc. **Website:** www.timespub.tc. **60% freelance written.** Quarterly magazine covering the Turks & Caicos Islands. "*Times of the Islands* is used by the public and private sector to inform visitors and potential investors/developers about the Islands. It goes beyond a superficial overview of tourist attractions with in-depth articles about natural history, island heritage, local personalities, new development, offshore finance, sporting activities, visitors' experiences, and Caribbean fiction." Estab. 1988. Circ. 10,000. Byline given. Publishes ms an average of 6 months after acceptance. Editorial lead time 4 months. Submit seasonal material at least 4 months in advance. Accepts queries by e-mail. Accepts simultaneous submissions. Responds in 6 weeks to queries. Responds in 2 months to mss. Sample copy for $6. Guidelines available online.

NONFICTION Needs book excerpts, essays, general interest, Caribbean art, culture, cooking, crafts, historical, humor, interview, locals, personal experience, trips to the Islands, photo feature, technical, island businesses, travel, book reviews, nature, ecology, business (offshore finance), watersports. **Buys 20 mss/year.** Query. Length: 500-3,000 words. **Pays $150-500.**

COLUMNS On Holiday (unique experiences of visitors to Turks & Caicos), 500-1,500 words. **Buys 4 mss/year.** Query. **Pays $150.**

FICTION Needs adventure, sailing, diving, ethnic, Caribbean, historical, Caribbean, humorous, travel-related, mystery, novel concepts. **Buys 2-3 mss/year.** Query. Length: 1,000-3,000 words. **Pays $250-400.**

💲💲 TRAILER LIFE

Affinity Group, Inc., 2575 Vista Del Mar Dr., Ventura CA 93001. **Fax:** (805)667-4484. **E-mail:** info@trailerlife.com. **Website:** www.trailerlife.com. **40% freelance written.** Monthly magazine. *"Trailer Life* magazine is written specifically for active people whose overall lifestyle is based on travel and recreation in their RV. Every issue includes product tests, travel articles, and other features—ranging from lifestyle to vehicle maintenance."* Estab. 1941. Circ. 270,000. Byline given. Offers kill fee. Offers 30% kill fee for assigned articles that are not acceptable. Publishes ms an average of 6 months after acceptance. Editorial lead time 4 months. Submit seasonal material 6 months in advance. Accepts queries by mail. Responds in 2 months to queries. Responds in 2 months to mss. Sample copy free. Guidelines for #10 SASE.

NONFICTION Needs historical, how-to, technical, humor, new product, opinion, personal experience, travel. "No vehicle tests, product evaluations or road tests; tech material is strictly assigned. No diaries or trip logs, no non-RV trips; nothing without an RV-hook." **Buys 75 mss/year.** Query. Length: 250-2,500 words. **Pays $125-700.** Sometimes pays expenses of writers on assignment.

COLUMNS Around the Bend (news, trends of interest to RVers), 100 words. **Buys 70 mss/year.** Query or send complete ms **Pays $75-250.**

💲💲💲💲 TRAVEL + LEISURE

American Express Publishing Corp., 1120 Avenue of the Americas, New York NY 10036. (212)382-5600. **Website:** www.travelandleisure.com. **80% freelance written.** *Travel + Leisure* is a monthly magazine edited for affluent travelers. It explores the latest resorts, hotels, fashions, foods, and drinks, as well as political, cultural, and economic issues affecting travelers. Circ. 925,000. Byline given. Offers 25% kill fee. Accepts queries by mail, e-mail. Responds in 6 weeks to queries. Responds in 6 weeks to mss. Sample copy for $5.50 from (800)888-8728. Guidelines available online.

NONFICTION Needs travel. **Buys 40-50 feature (3,000-5,000 words) and 200 short (125-500 words) mss/year.** Query (e-mail preferred) **Pays $4,000-6,000/feature; $100-500/short piece.** Pays expenses of writers on assignment.

COLUMNS Length: 2,500-3,500 words. **Buys 125-150 mss/year. Pays $2,000-3,500.**

💲 TRAVEL NATURALLY

Internaturally, Inc., P.O. Box 317, Newfoundland NJ 07435-0317. (973)697-3552. **Fax:** (973)697-8313. **E-mail:** naturally@internaturally.com. **Website:** www.internaturally.com. **90% freelance written.** Quarterly magazine covering wholesome family nude recreation and travel locations. *Travel Naturally* looks at why millions of people believe that removing clothes in public is a good idea, and at places specifically created for that purpose—with good humor, but also in earnest. *Travel Naturally* takes you to places where your personal freedom is the only agenda, and to places where textile-free living is a serious commitment. Estab. 1981. Circ. 35,000. Byline given. Editorial lead time 4 months. Submit seasonal material 4 months in advance. Accepts queries by mail, e-mail, fax. Accepts simultaneous submissions. Sample copy for $9. Guidelines available online.

NONFICTION Needs general interest, interview, personal experience, photo feature, travel. **Buys 12 mss/year.** Send complete ms. Length: 2 pages. **Pays $80/published page, including photos.**

POETRY Wants poetry about the naturalness of the human body and nature, any length. Consideers previously published poems and simultaneous submissions. Accepts e-mail and fax submissions. "Name and address must be submitted with e-mail."

FILLERS Needs anecdotes, facts, gags, newsbreaks, short humor, poems, artwork. **Payment is pro-rated based on length.**

💲 TRAVEL SMART

Communications House, Inc., P.O. Box 397, Dobbs Ferry NY 10522. **E-mail:** travelsmartnow@aol.com. **Website:** www.travelsmartnewsletter.com. Monthly newsletter covering information on good-value travel. Estab. 1976. Circ. 20,000. Accepts queries by mail, e-mail. Responds in 6 weeks to queries. Responds in 6 weeks to mss. Sample copy for sae with 9×12 envelope and 3 First-Class stamps. Guidelines for sae with 9×12 envelope and 3 First-Class stamps.

NONFICTION Query. Length: 100-1,500 words. **Pays $150 maximum.**

🍁 $$ VERGE MAGAZINE

Verge Magazine Inc., P.O. Box 147, Peterborough ON K9J 6Y5 Canada. **E-mail:** contributing@vergemagazine.com. **Website:** www.vergemagazine.com. **Contact:** Jessica Lockhart, contributing editor. **60% freelance written.** Quarterly magazine. "Each issue takes you around the world, with people who are doing something different and making a difference doing it. This is the magazine resource for those wanting to volunteer, work, study or adventure overseas." "*Verge* is the magazine for people who travel with purpose. It explores ways to get out and see the world by volunteering, working, and studying overseas. Our readers are typically young (17-40 years), or young at heart, active, independent travelers. Editorial content is intended to inform and motivate the reader by profiling unique individuals and experiences that are timely and socially relevant. We look for articles that are issue driven and combine an engaging and well-told story with nuts and bolts how-to information. Wherever possible and applicable, efforts should be made to provide sources where readers can find out more about the subject, or ways in which readers can become involved in the issue covered." Estab. 2002. Circ. 10,000. Byline given. Publishes ms an average of 6 months after acceptance. Submit seasonal material 8-12 months in advance. Accepts queries by mail, e-mail. Responds in 8 weeks to queries. Responds in 2 months to mss. Sample copy for $6, plus shipping. Guidelines available online.

NONFICTION Contact: Jessica Lockhart. Needs how-to, humor, interview, news, travel. "We do not want pure travelogues, predictable tourist experiences, luxury travel, stories highighting a specific company, or organisation." **Buys 30-40 mss/year.** Send complete ms. Length: 800-2,500 words. **Pays $0.10 (CAD) per word to first-time contributors.**

COLUMNS Contact: Jessica Lockhart. **Buys 20-30 mss/year.** Query with published clips. **Pays $0.10 (CAD) per word to first-time contributors.**

$$ WOODALL'S REGIONALS

2575 Vista Del Mar Dr., Ventura CA 93001. **Website:** www.woodalls.com. Monthly magazine for RV and camping enthusiasts. Woodall's Regionals include *CamperWays, Midwest RV Traveler, Northeast Outdoors, Florida RV Traveler.* Byline given. Accepts queries by mail, e-mail. Responds in 1-2 months to queries. Sample copy free. Guidelines free.

NONFICTION Buys 300 mss/year. Query with published clips. Length: 1,000-1,400 words. **Pays $180-220/feature; $75-100/department article and short piece.**

WOMEN'S

$$$ BRIDAL GUIDE

RFP, LLC, 330 Seventh Ave., 10th Floor, New York NY 10001. (212)838-7733; (800)472-7744. **Fax:** (212)308-7165. **E-mail:** editorial@bridalguide.com. **Website:** www.bridalguide.com. **20% freelance written.** Bimonthly magazine covering relationships, sexuality, fitness, wedding planning, psychology, finance, and travel. Only works with experienced/published writers. Accepts queries by mail. Responds in 3 months to queries and mss. Sample copy for $5 and SAE with 4 first-class stamps. Guidelines available.

NONFICTION "Please do not send queries concerning beauty, fashion, or home design stories since we produce them in-house. We do not accept personal wedding essays, fiction, or poetry. Address travel queries to travel editor. All correspondence accompanied by an SASE will be answered." **Buys 100 mss/year.** Query with published clips from national consumer magazines. Length: 1,000-2,000 words. **Pays 50¢/word.**

🌐 $$ THE BROADSHEET

Broad Universe, 1812 E. Madison St. #8, Seattle WA 98122. **E-mail:** broadsheet@broaduniverse.org. **Website:** http://broaduniverse.org. **Contact:** Lee-Anne Phillips, editor-in-chief. Covers articles about women writers of science fiction, fantasy, and horror genre fiction. "*The Broadsheet* is a small web-based zine published three times a year. *The Broadsheet* accepts art, articles, interviews, book reviews and commentaries about any topic involving women writers and artists in science fiction, fantasy and horror. It also accepts general articles on the writing or marketing of science fiction/fiction/horror. We only print nonfiction. Anyone may submit, whether female or male, new writer or experienced pro. Interviews should be between 3,000 and 5,000 words. Brief articles (2,000 words or less) are preferred for Create, Sell, Read, and Think. However, excellent interviews and articles of shorter or longer lengths will also receive consideration." Pays for articles specifically targeting their marketplace and membership. Estab. 2000. Accepts queries by e-mail. Query first via e-mail, according to topic: For Art: Constance Burris at art@broaduniverse.org. For Read: JJ Pionke at editor1@broaduniverse.org. For Create: Carol Ullmann at editor3@broaduniverse.org. All other topics: Broadsheet Editor Lee-Anne Phillips at broadsheet@broaduniverse.org. Accepts simultaneous submissions.

NONFICTION **Contact:** JJ Pionke. **Art and Interviews: $50; Create, Sell, Think: $40; Read: $25 for the usual brief review; up to $40 for pieces that deliver something more. A brief biography of the contributor, including any link to the artist or author's website, will also run with the piece if so desired. Art and articles appearing in past issues of** ***The Broadsheet*** **are made available in our public archives unless the artist or author states otherwise in writing.**

🍁 $$$$ CHATELAINE

One Mount Pleasant Rd., 8th Floor, Toronto ON M4Y 2Y5 Canada. (416)764-1888. **Fax:** (416)764-2891. **E-mail:** storyideas@chatelaine.rogers.com. **Website:** www.chatelaine.com. **Contact:** Samantha Grice, managing editor. Monthly magazine. "*Chatelaine* is edited for Canadian women ages 25-49, their changing attitudes and lifestyles. Key editorial ingredients include health, finance, social issues and trends, as well as fashion, beauty, food and home decor. Regular departments include Health pages, Entertainment, Money, Home, Humour, How-to." Byline given. Offers 25-50% kill fee. Accepts queries by mail, e-mail (preferred). Responds in 4-6 weeks to 1 month to queries; up to 2 months to proposals. See writers' guidelines online at website.

💬 *Does not accept unsolicited manuscripts.* Submit story ideas online.

$$ COMPLETE WOMAN

Associated Publications, Inc., 875 N. Michigan Ave., Suite 3434, Chicago IL 60611. (312)266-8680. **Fax:** (312)573-3020. **Website:** www.thecompletewomanmagazine.com. Kourtney McKay, art director. **90% freelance written.** Estab. 1980. Circ. 300,000. Byline given. Pays 45 days after acceptance. Publishes ms an average of 6 months after acceptance. Editorial lead time 6 months. Submit seasonal material 5 months in advance. Accepts queries by mail. Accepts simultaneous submissions. Responds in 2 months to queries. Responds in 2 months to mss. Guidelines with #10 SASE.

NONFICTION Needs book excerpts, exposé, of interest to women, general interest, how-to, beauty/diet-related, humor, inspirational, interview, celebrities, new product, personal experience, photo feature, sex, love, relationship advice. **Buys 60-100 mss/year.** Send complete ms. Length: 800-2,000 words. **Pays $160-500.** Sometimes pays expenses of writers on assignment.

COUNTRY WOMAN

Reiman Publications, 5400 South 60th St., Greendale WI 53129. (414)423-0100. **E-mail:** editors@countrywomanmagazine.com. **Website:** www.countrywomanmagazine.com. **Contact:** Lori Lau Grzybowski, editor. **75-85% freelance written.** Bimonthly magazine. *Country Woman* is for contemporary rural women of all ages and backgrounds and from all over the U.S. and Canada. It includes a sampling of the diversity that makes up rural women's lives—love of home, family, farm, ranch, community, hobbies, enduring values, humor, attaining new skills and appreciating present, past and future all within the context of the lifestyle that surrounds country living. Estab. 1970. Byline given. Submit seasonal material 5 months in advance. Accepts queries by mail. Accepts simultaneous submissions. Responds in 2 months to queries. Responds in 3 months to mss. Sample copy for $2 and SASE. Guidelines with #10 SASE.

NONFICTION Needs general interest, historical, how-to, crafts, community projects, decorative, antiquing, etc., humor, inspirational, interview, personal experience, photo feature, packages profiling interesting country women-all pertaining to rural women's interests. Query. 1,000 words maximum.

COLUMNS Why Farm Wives Age Fast (humor), I Remember When (nostalgia) and Country Decorating. Length: 500-1,000 words. **Buys 10-12 mss/year.** Query or send ms.

FICTION **Contact:** Kathleen Anderson, managing editor. Main character *must* be a country woman. All fiction must have a country setting. Fiction must have a positive, upbeat message. Includes fiction in every issue. Would buy more fiction if stories suitable for our audience were sent our way. No contemporary, urban pieces that deal with divorce, drugs, etc. Send complete ms. Length: 750-1,000 words.

POETRY Needs light verse, traditional. Poetry must have rhythm and rhyme! It must be country-related, positive and upbeat. Always looking for seasonal poetry. Buys 6-12 poems/year. Submit maximum 6 poems. Length: 4-24 lines.

$$$$ ELLE

Hachette Filipacchi Media U.S., Inc., 1271 Avenue of the Americas, 41st Floor, New York NY 10020. (212)767-5800. **Fax:** (212)489-4210. **Website:** www.elle.com. Monthly magazine. Edited for the modern, sophisticated, affluent, well-traveled woman in her twenties to early thirties. Circ. 1,100,000. Editorial lead time 3 months.

💬 Query first.

$$$$ FAMILY CIRCLE

Meredith Corporation, 375 Lexington Ave., 9th Floor, New York NY 10017. **Website:** www.familycircle.com. Lisa Kelsey, art director. **80% freelance written**. Magazine published every 3 weeks. We are a national women's service magazine which covers many stages of a woman's life, along with her everyday concerns about social, family, and health issues. Submissions should focus on families with children ages 8-16. Estab. 1932. Circ. 4,200,000. Byline given. Offers 20% kill fee. Editorial lead time 4 months. Submit seasonal material 4 months in advance. Responds in 2 months to queries. Responds in 2 months to mss. For back issues, send $6.95 to P.O. Box 3156, Harlan IA 51537. Guidelines available online.

NONFICTION Needs essays, opinion, personal experience, women's interest subjects such as family and personal relationships, children, physical and mental health, nutrition and self-improvement. No fiction or poetry. **Buys 200 mss/year.** Submit detailed outline, 2 clips, cover letter describing your publishing history, SASE or IRCs. Length: 1,000-2,500 words. **Pays $1/word.**

🍁 $$$$ FLARE MAGAZINE

Rogers Communications, One Mt. Pleasant Rd., 8th Floor, Toronto ON M4Y 2Y5 Canada. (416)764-1829. **Fax:** (416)764-2866. **E-mail:** editors@flare.com. **Website:** www.flare.com. Monthly magazine for women ages 17-35. Byline given. Offers 50% kill fee. Accepts queries by e-mail. Response time varies. Sample copy for #10 SASE. Guidelines available online.

NONFICTION Buys 24 mss/year. Query. Length: 200-1,200 words. **Pays $1/word.** Pays expenses of writers on assignment.

GIRLFRIENDZ

The Word Source, LLC, 6 Brookville Dr., Cherry Hill NJ 08003. **E-mail:** tobi@girlfriendzmag.com. **Website:** www.girlfriendzmag.com; www.facebook.com/girlfriendz. **80% freelance written**. Bimonthly magazine covering Baby Boomer women. "As a publication by and for Baby Boomer women, we are most interested in entertaining, educating, and empowering our readers. Our target is smart women born between 1946 and 1964. We like a little humor in our articles, but only if it's appropriate and subtle. And most importantly, all facts must be checked for accuracy. We insist on well-researched and well-documented information." Estab. 2007. Circ. 30,000. Byline given. Headshot and bio included. "As a startup, we are unable to pay our writers." Editorial lead time 3 months. Submit seasonal material 6 months in advance. Accepts queries by e-mail. Accepts simultaneous submissions. Responds in 2 weeks to queries. Sample copy for $5. Guidelines available online.

NONFICTION Needs book excerpts, exposé, historical, how-to, humor, interview, (celebrities only), new product, articles of interest to women born 1946-1964; "especially interested in local and national celebrities. Examples of those we've already profiled: Dr. Ruth, Joan Lunden, Fran Drescher." "We do not want fiction, essays, or poetry." **Buys 20 mss/year.** Query. Length: 735-1,200 words. Sometimes pays expenses of writers on assignment.

$$$$ GLAMOUR

Conde Nast Publications, Inc., 4 Times Square, 16th Floor, New York NY 10036. (212)286-2860. **Fax:** (212)286-8336. **Website:** www.glamour.com. Cynthia Leive, editor-in-chief. Monthly magazine covering subjects ranging from fashion, beauty and health, personal relationships, career, travel, food and entertainment. "*Glamour* is edited for the contemporary woman, and informs her of the trends and recommends how she can adapt them to her needs, and motivates her to take action." Estab. 1939. Circ. 2,320,325. Accepts queries by mail. Not available online.

NONFICTION Needs personal experience, relationships, travel. **Pays 75¢-$1/word**

$$$$ GOOD HOUSEKEEPING

Hearst Corp., 300 W. 57th St., 28th Floor, New York NY 10019. (212)649-2200. **Website:** www.goodhousekeeping.com. Monthly magazine. "*Good Housekeeping* is edited for the 'new traditionalist.' Articles which focus on food, fitness, beauty, and child care draw upon the resources of the Good Housekeeping Institute. Editorial includes human interest stories, articles that focus on social issues, money management, health news, travel." Circ. 5,000,000. Byline given. Offers 25% kill fee. Submit seasonal material 6 months in advance. Responds in 2-3 months to queries. Responds in 2-3 months to mss. For sample copy, call (212)649-2359. Guidelines with #10 SASE.

NONFICTION **Buys 4-6 mss/issue mss/year.** Query. Length: 1,500-2,500 words. Pays expenses of writers on assignment.

COLUMNS Profiles (inspirational, activist or heroic women), 400-600 words. Query with published clips. **Pays $1/word for items 300-600 words.**

FICTION **Contact:** Laura Mathews, fiction editor. No longer accepts unagented fiction submissions. Because of heavy volume of fiction submissions, *Good Housekeeping* is not accepting unsolicited submissions at this time. Agented submissions only. 1,500 words (short-shorts); novel according to merit of material; average 5,000 word short stories. **Pays $1,000 minimum.**

$$ GRACE ORMONDE WEDDING STYLE

Elegant Publishing, Inc., P.O. Box 89, Barrington RI 02806. (401)245-9726. **Fax:** (401)245-5371. **E-mail:** jessica@weddingstylemagazine.com. **Website:** www.weddingstylemagazine.com. **Contact:** Jessica Latimer. **90% freelance written.** Semiannual magazine covering weddings catering to the affluent bride. Estab. 1997. Circ. 500,000. Publishes ms an average of 4 months after acceptance. Editorial lead time 1 month. Sample copy available online. Guidelines by e-mail.

💬 Does not accept queries.

⊘ $$$$ LADIES' HOME JOURNAL

Meredith Corp., 375 Lexington Ave., 9th Floor, New York NY 10017. (212)557-6600. **E-mail:** lhj@mdp.com. **Website:** www.lhj.com. **50% freelance written.** Monthly magazine focusing on issues of concern to women 30-45. "*Ladies' Home Journal* is for active, empowered women who are evolving in new directions. It addresses informational needs with highly focused features and articles on a variety of topics: self, style, family, home, world, health, and food." Estab. 1882. Circ. 4.1 million. Offers 25% kill fee. Publishes ms an average of 4-12 months after acceptance. Editorial lead time 4 months. Accepts queries by mail, e-mail. Accepts simultaneous submissions. Responds in 3 months to queries. Guidelines available online at www.lhj.com/lhj/file.jsp?item=/help/writersGuidelines.

NONFICTION Send 1-2 page query, SASE, résumé, and clips via mail or e-mail (preferred). Length: 2,000-3,000 words. **Pays $2,000-4,000.** Pays expenses of writers on assignment.

FICTION Only short stories and novels submitted by an agent or publisher will be considered. No poetry of any kind. **Buys 12 mss/year.** Send complete ms. 2,000-2,500.

🍁 $$ THE LINK & VISITOR

Canadian Baptist Women of Ontario and Quebec, 100-304 The East Mall, Etobicoke ON M9B 6E2 Canada. (416)651-8967. **E-mail:** rsejames@gmail.com. **Website:** www.baptistwomen.com. **Contact:** Renee James, editor/director of communications. **50% freelance written.** Magazine published 6 times/year designed to help Baptist women grow their world, faith, relationships, creativity, and mission vision—evangelical, egalitarian, Canadian. Estab. 1878. Circ. 3,500. Byline given. Publishes ms an average of 6 months after acceptance. Editorial lead time 2 months. Submit seasonal material 4 months in advance. Accepts simultaneous submissions. Sample copy for 9×12 SAE with 2 first-class Canadian stamps. Guidelines available online.

NONFICTION Needs inspirational, interview, religious. **Buys 30-35 mss/year.** Send complete ms. Length: 750-2,000 words. **Pays 5-12¢/word (Canadian).** Sometimes pays expenses of writers on assignment.

$ LONG ISLAND WOMAN

Maraj, Inc., P.O. Box 176, Malverne NY 11565. (516)505-0555. **Fax:** (516)505-1753. **E-mail:** editor@liwomanonline.com. **Website:** www.liwomanonline.com. **40% freelance written.** Monthly magazine covering issues of importance to women—health, family, finance, arts, entertainment, fitness, travel, home. Estab. 2001. Circ. 40,000. Byline given. Pays within 1 month of publication. Offers 33% kill fee. Publishes ms an average of 3 months after acceptance. Editorial lead time 3 months. Submit seasonal material 3 months in advance. Accepts queries by mail, e-mail. Accepts simultaneous submissions. Responds in 8 weeks to queries. Responds in 3 months to mss. Sample copy for $5. Guidelines available online.

NONFICTION Needs book excerpts, general interest, how-to, humor, interview, new product, travel, reviews. **Buys 25-30 mss/year.** Send complete ms. Length: 500-1,800 words. **Pays $35-150.**

COLUMNS Humor; Health Issues; Family Issues; Financial and Business Issues; Book Reviews and Books; Arts and Entertainment; Travel and Leisure; Home and Garden; Fitness.

MADISON

ACP Magazines, Ltd., 54-58 Park St., Sydney NSW 2000 Australia. (61)(2)9282-8000. **Fax:** (61)(2)9267-4361. **E-mail:** madison@acpmagazines.com.au. **Website:** www.madisonmag.com.au. **Contact:** Elizabeth Renkert, editor. Monthly magazine offering intelligent news and features, real women and their stories, beautiful fashion, sexy beauty, inspiring homes and impress-your-friends food. "She is 25-39. Ambitious, sexy and socially aware. The MADISON woman actively enjoys her life. She loves fashion but will dress to suit a style she's developed. She's seriously interested in beauty but her health is just as important as finding the perfect lip-gloss."

MARIE CLAIRE

The Hearst Publishing Corp., Feature Submissions, Marie Claire Magazine, 300 W. 57th St., 34th Floor, New York NY 10019-1497. (212)649-5000. **Fax:** (212)649-5050. **E-mail:** JoannaColes@hearst.com. **Website:** www.marieclaire.com. **Contact:** Joanna Coles, editor-in-chief. Monthly magazine written for today's younger working woman with a smart service-oriented view. Estab. 1937. Circ. 952,223. Editorial lead time 6 months.

MS. MAGAZINE

433 S. Beverly Dr., Beverly Hills CA 90212. (310)556-2515. **Fax:** (310)556-2514. **E-mail:** mkort@msmagazine.com. **Website:** www.msmagazine.com. **Contact:** Michele Kort, senior editor. **70% freelance written.** Quarterly magazine on women's issues and news. Estab. 1972. Circ. 150,000. Byline given. Offers 25% kill fee. Responds in 3 months to queries. Responds in 3 months to mss. Sample copy for $9. Guidelines available online.

NONFICTION Buys 4-5 feature (2,000-3,000 words) and 4-5 short (500 words) mss/year. Query with published clips. Length: 300-3,500 words. **Pays $1/word, 50¢/word for news stories and book review.**
COLUMNS Buys 6-10 mss/year. Pays $1/word.
FICTION "*Ms.* welcomes the highest-quality original fiction and poetry, but is publishing these infrequently as of late."

PREGNANCY

Pregnancy Magazine Group, 4000 Shoreline Ct., Suite 400, S. San Francisco CA 94080-1960. **E-mail:** editors@pregnancymagazine.com. **Website:** www.pregnancymagazine.com. **40% freelance written.** Magazine covering products, wellness, technology fashion, and beauty for pregnant women; and products, health, and child care for babies up to 12 months old. "A large part of our audience is first-time moms who seek advice and information about health, relationships, diet, celebrities, fashion, and green living for pregnant women and babies up to 12 months old. Our readers are first-time and experienced moms (and dads) who want articles that are relevant to their modern lives. Our goal is to help our readers feel confident and prepared for pregnancy and parenthood by providing the best information for today's parents." Estab. 2000. Circ. 250,000. Offers kill fee. Editorial lead time 5 months. Submit seasonal material 5-6 months in advance. Guidelines available at www.pregnancymagazine.com/writers.

NONFICTION Buys 60 mss/year. Length: 350-2,000 words.

P31 WOMAN

Proverbs 31 Ministries, 616-G Matthews-Mint Hill Rd., Charlotte NC 28105. (704)849-2270. **E-mail:** janet@proverbs31.org. **Website:** www.proverbs31.org. Janet Burke. **Contact:** Glynnis Whitwer, editor. **50% freelance written.** Monthly magazine covering Christian issues for women. "The *P31 Woman* provides Christian wives and mothers with articles that encourage them in their faith and support them in the many roles they have as women. We look for articles that have a Biblical foundation and offer inspiration, yet have a practical application to everyday life." Estab. 1992. Circ. 10,000. Byline given. Publishes ms an average of 6 months after acceptance. Editorial lead time 5 months. Submit seasonal material 5-6 months in advance. Accepts queries by mail, e-mail. Accepts simultaneous submissions. Responds in 2-4 weeks to queries; 1-2 months to mss. Sample copy online or $2 for hard copy. Guidelines available online.

NONFICTION Needs humor, inspirational, personal experience, religious. No biographical stories or articles about men's issues. Send complete ms. Length: 200-1,000 words. **Pays in contributor copies.**

$$$ ⊘ REDBOOK MAGAZINE

Hearst Corp., Articles Dept., Redbook, 300 W. 57th St., 22nd Floor, New York NY 10019. **Website:** www. redbookmag.com/writersguidelines. Monthly magazine. "*Redbook* is targeted to women between the ages of 25 and 45 who define themselves as smart, capable, and happy with their lives. Many, but not all, of our readers are going through one of two key life transitions: single to married and married to mom. Each issue is a provocative mix of features geared to entertain and inform them, including: News stories on contemporary issues that are relevant to the reader's life and experience, and explore the emotional ramifications of cultural and social changes; First-person essays about dramatic pivotal moments in a woman's life; Marriage articles with an emphasis on strengthening the relationship; Short parenting features on how to deal with universal health and behavioral issues; Reporting on exciting trends in women's lives." Estab. 1903. Circ. 2,300,000. Publishes ms an average of 6 months after acceptance. Responds in 3 months to queries. Responds in 3 months to mss. Guidelines available online.

NONFICTION Query with published clips and SASE 2,500-3,000 words/articles; 1,000-1,500 words/short articles

⟳ RESOURCES FOR FEMINIST RESEARCH

RFR/DRF (Resources for Feminist Research), OISE, University of Toronto, 252 Bloor St. W., Toronto ON M5S 1V6 Canada. **E-mail:** rfr@utoronto.ca. **Website:** www.oise.utoronto.ca/rfr. Semiannual academic journal covering feminist research in an interdisciplinary, international perspective. Estab. 1972. Circ. 2,500. Byline given. Publishes ms an average of 1 year after acceptance. Editorial lead time 1 year. Accepts queries by e-mail. Responds in 2 weeks to queries. Responds in 6-8 months to mss. Guidelines free.

NONFICTION Needs essays, academic articles and book reviews. Does not want nonacademic articles. Send complete ms. Length: 3,000-5,000 words.

$$$$ SELF

Conde Nast, 4 Times Square, New York NY 10036. (212)286-2860. **Fax:** (212)286-8110. **E-mail:** comments@self.com. **Website:** www.self.com. Monthly magazine for women ages 20-45. Self-confidence, self-assurance, and a healthy, happy lifestyle are pivotal to *Self* readers. This healthy lifestyle magazine delivers by addressing real-life issues from the inside out, with unparalleled energy and authority. From beauty, fitness, health and nutrition to personal style, finance, and happiness, the path to total well-being begins with *Self*. Circ. 1,300,000. Byline given on features and most short items. Accepts queries by online submission form. Accepts simultaneous submissions. Responds in 1 month to queries. Guidelines for #10 sase.

NONFICTION **Buys 40 mss/year.** Query with published clips. Length: 1,500-5,000 words. **Pays $1-2/ word.**

COLUMNS Uses short, news-driven items on health, fitness, nutrition, money, jobs, love/sex, psychology and happiness, travel. Length: 300-1,000 words. **Buys 50 mss/year.** Query with published clips. **Pays $1-2/word.**

$$ SKIRT! MAGAZINE

Morris Communications, 7 Radcliffe St., Suite 302, Charleston SC 29403. (843)958-0027. **Fax:** (843)958-0029. **E-mail:** submissions@skirt.com; digitalmedia@skirt.com. **Website:** www.skirt.com. **Contact:** Nikki Hardin, publisher. **50% freelance written.** Monthly magazine covering women's interest. "*Skirt!* is all about women—their work, play, families, creativity, style, health, wealth, bodies, and souls. The magazine's attitude is spirited, independent, outspoken, serious, playful, irreverent, sometimes controversial, and always passionate." Estab. 1994. Circ. 285,000. Byline given. Publishes ms an average of 2 months after acceptance. Editorial lead time 2-3 months. Submit seasonal material 2-3 months in advance. Accepts queries by e-mail (preferred). Accepts simultaneous submissions. Responds in 6-8 weeks to queries. Responds in 1-2 months to mss. Guidelines on website.

NONFICTION Needs essays, humor, personal experience. "Do not send feature articles. We only accept submissions of completed personal essays that will work with our monthly themes available online." **Buys 100+ mss/year.** Send complete ms. "We prefer e-mail submissions." Length: 900-1,200 words. **Pays $150-200.**

⦿ ⊖⊖ ⊖ THAT'S LIFE!

H Bauer Publishing, Academic House, 24-28 Oval Rd., London England NW1 7DT United Kingdom. (44) (207)241-8000. **E-mail:** stories@thatslife.co.uk. **Website:** www.thatslife.co.uk. **Contact:** Sophie Hearsey, editor. "*that's life!* is packed with the most amazing true-life stories and fab puzzles offering big money prizes including family sunshine holidays and even a car! We also have bright, up-to-date fashion, health, and beauty pages with top tips and readers' letters. And just to make sure we get you smiling too, there's our rib-tickling rude jokes and 'aren't men' daft tales." Estab. 1995. Circ. 550,000. Submit seasonal material 3 months in advance. Accepts queries by mail. NoResponds in 6 weeks to mss. Guidelines by e-mail.

FICTION "Stories should have a strong plot and a good twist. A sexy relationships/scene can feature strongly, but isn't essential—the plot twist is much more important. The writing should be chronological and fast moving. A maximum of 4 characters is advisable. Avoid straightforward romance, historical backgrounds, science fiction, and stories told by animals or small children. Graphic murders and sex crimes—especially those involving children—are not acceptable." Send complete ms. Length: 700 words. **Pays £400.**

⦿ ⊖⊖ TODAY'S BRIDE

Family Communications, 65 The East Mall, Toronto ON M8Z SW3 Canada. (416)537-2604. **Fax:** (416)538-1794. **E-mail:** info@canadianbride.com. **Website:** www.todaysbride.ca; www.canadianbride.com. **20% freelance written**. Semiannual magazine. Magazine provides information to engaged couples on all aspects of wedding planning, including tips, fashion advice, etc. There are also beauty, home, groom, and honeymoon travel sections. Estab. 1979. Circ. 102,000. Byline given. Editorial lead time 6 months. Accepts queries by mail, e-mail, fax. Accepts simultaneous submissions. Responds in 2 weeks-1 month.

NONFICTION Needs humor, opinion, personal experience. No travel pieces. Send complete ms. Length: 800-1,400 words. **Pays $250-300.**

⊖⊖ WOMAN'S LIFE

A Publication of Woman's Life Insurance Society, 1338 Military St., P.O. Box 5020, Port Huron MI 48061-5020. (800)521-9292, ext. 281. **Fax:** (810)985-6970. **E-mail:** wkrabach@womanslife.org. **Website:** www.womanslife.org. **Contact:** Wendy Krabach, managing editor. **30% freelance written**. Quarterly magazine published for a primarily female membership to help them care for themselves and their families. Estab. 1892. Circ. 32,000. Byline given. Publishes ms an average of 1 year after acceptance. Submit seasonal material 6 months in advance. Accepts queries by mail, e-mail, fax. Accepts simultaneous submissions. Responds in 1 year to queries and to mss. Sample copy for sae with 9×12 envelope and 4 first-class stamps. Guidelines for #10 SASE.

NONFICTION Buys 4-10 mss/year. Send complete ms. Length: 1,000-2,000 words. **Pays $150-500.**

⊖⊖⊖ WOMAN'S WORLD

Bauer Publishing Co., 270 Sylvan Ave., Englewood Cliffs NJ 07632. (201)569-6699. **Fax:** (201)569-3584. **E-mail:** dearww@aol.com. **Website:** http://winit. womansworldmag.com. **Contact:** Stephanie Saible, editor-in-chief. Weekly magazine covering human interest and service pieces of interest to family-oriented women across the nation. *Woman's World* is a women's service magazine. It offers a blend of fashion, food, parenting, beauty, and relationship features coupled with the true-life human interest stories. "We publish short romances and mini-mysteries for all women, ages 18-68." Estab. 1980. Circ. 1,625,779. Publishes ms an average of 4 months after acceptance. Submit seasonal material 4 months in advance. Accepts queries by mail. Responds in 2 months to mss. Guidelines for #10 SASE.

NONFICTION Pays $500/1,000 words.

FICTION Contact: Johnene Granger, fiction editor. "Short story, romance, and mainstream of 800 words and mini-mysteries of 1,000 words. Each of our stories has a light romantic theme and can be written from either a masculine or feminine point of view. Women characters may be single, married, or divorced. Plots must be fast moving with vivid dialogue and action. The problems and dilemmas inherent in them should be contemporary and realistic, handled with warmth and feeling. The stories must have a positive resolution. Specify Fiction on envelope. Always enclose SASE. Responds in 4 months. No phone or fax queries. Pays $1,000 for romances on acceptance for North American serial rights for 6 months. The 1,000 word mini-mysteries may feature either a 'whodunnit' or 'howdunnit' theme. The mystery may revolve around anything from a theft to murder. However, we are not interested in sordid or grotesque crimes.

Emphasis should be on intricacies of plot rather than gratuitous violence. The story must include a resolution that clearly states the villain is getting his or her come-uppance. Submit complete mss. Specify Mini-Mystery on envelope. Enclose SASE. No phone queries." Needs mystery, romance, contemporary. Not interested in science fiction, fantasy, historical romance, or foreign locales. No explicit sex, graphic language, or seamy settings. Send complete ms. Romances—800 words; mysteries—1,000 words. **Pays $1,000/romances; $500/mysteries.**

$ WOMEN IN BUSINESS

American Business Women's Association (The ABWA Co., Inc.), 9100 Ward Pkwy., P.O. Box 8728, Kansas City MO 64114-0728. (816)361-6621. **Fax:** (816)361-4991. **E-mail:** abwa@abwa.org. **Website:** www.abwa.org. **Contact:** Rene Street, executive director. **30% freelance written.** Bimonthly magazine covering issues affecting working women. "How-to features for career women on business trends, small-business ownership, self-improvement, and retirement issues. Profiles business women." Estab. 1949. Circ. 45,000. Byline given. Publishes ms an average of 3 months after acceptance. Editorial lead time 3 months. Accepts queries by mail, e-mail, fax. Accepts simultaneous submissions. Responds in 3 weeks to queries. Responds in 2 months to mss. Sample copy for sae with 9×12 envelope and 4 First-Class stamps. Guidelines for #10 SASE.

NONFICTION Needs how-to, interview, computer/Internet. No fiction or poetry. **Buys 3% of submitted mss/year.** Query. Length: 500-1,000 words. **Pays $100/500 words.**

COLUMNS Life After Business (concerns of retired business women); It's Your Business (entrepreneurial advice for business owners); Health Spot (health issues that affect women in the work place). Length: 500-750 words. Query. **Pays $100/500 words**

TRADE JOURNALS

Many writers who pick up *Writer's Market* for the first time do so with the hope of selling an article to one of the popular, high-profile consumer magazines found on newsstands and in bookstores. Many of those writers are surprised to find an entire world of magazine publishing exists outside the realm of commercial magazines—trade journals. Writers who *have* discovered trade journals have found a market that offers the chance to publish regularly in subject areas they find interesting, editors who are typically more accessible than their commercial counterparts, and pay rates that rival those of the big-name magazines.

Trade journal is the general term for any publication focusing on a particular occupation or industry. Other terms used to describe the different types of trade publications are business, technical, and professional journals. They are read by truck drivers, bricklayers, farmers, fishermen, heart surgeons, and just about everyone else working in a trade or profession. Trade periodicals are sharply angled to the specifics of the professions on which they report. They offer business-related news, features, and service articles that will foster their readers' professional development.

An ideal way to begin your foray into trade journals is to write for those that report on your present profession. Whether you've been teaching dance, farming, or working as a paralegal, begin by familiarizing yourself with the magazines that serve your occupation. After you've read enough issues to have a feel for the kinds of pieces the magazines run, approach the editors with your own article ideas. If you don't have experience in a profession but can demonstrate an ability to understand (and write about) the intricacies and issues of a particular trade that interests you, editors will still be willing to hear from you.

ADVERTISING, MARKETING AND PR

$$$ BRAND PACKAGING

BNP Media, 155 Pfingsten Rd., Suite 205, Deerfield IL 60015. (847)405-4000. **Fax:** (847)405-4100. **E-mail:** acevedoj@bnpmedia.com. **Website:** www.brandpackaging.com. **Contact:** Jennifer Acevedo, executive editor. **15% freelance written.** Magazine published 10 times/year covering how packaging can be a marketing tool. "We publish strategies and tactics to make products stand out on the shelf. Our market is brand managers who are marketers but need to know something about packaging." Estab. 1997. Circ. 33,000. Byline given. Publishes ms an average of 2 months after acceptance. Editorial lead time 3 months. Submit seasonal material 3 months in advance. Accepts queries by mail, fax. Guidelines available on website.

NONFICTION Needs how-to, interview, new product. **Buys 10 mss/year.** Send complete ms. Length: 600-2,400 words. **Pays 40-50¢/word.**

COLUMNS Emerging Technology (new packaging technology), 600 words. **Buys 10 mss/year.** Query. **Pays $150-300.**

$ DECA DIMENSIONS

1908 Association Dr., Reston VA 20191. (703)860-5000. **Fax:** (703)860-4013. **E-mail:** publications@deca.org. **Website:** www.deca.org. **30% freelance written.** Quarterly magazine covering marketing, professional development, business, career training during school year (no issues published May-August). *DECA Dimensions* is the membership magazine for DECA—The Association of Marketing Students, primarily ages 15-19 in all 50 states, the U.S. territories, Germany, and Canada. The magazine is delivered through the classroom. Students are interested in developing professional, leadership, and career skills. Estab. 1947. Circ. 160,000. Byline given. Editorial lead time 3 months. Submit seasonal material 4 months in advance. Accepts queries by mail, e-mail, fax, phone. Accepts simultaneous submissions.

NONFICTION Needs essays, general interest, how-to, get jobs, start business, plan for college, etc., interview, business leads, personal experience, working, leadership development. **Buys 10 mss/year.** Send complete ms. Length: 800-1,000 words. **Pays $125 for assigned articles. Pays $100 for unsolicited articles.**

COLUMNS Professional Development; Leadership, 350-500 words. **Buys 6 mss/year.** Send complete ms. **Pays $ 75-100.**

$$ O'DWYER'S PR REPORT

271 Madison Ave., #600, New York NY 10016. (212)679-2471; (866)395-7710. **Fax:** (212)683-2750. **E-mail:** john@odwyerpr.com. **Website:** www.odwyerpr.com. **Contact:** John O'Dwyer. Monthly magazine providing PR articles. *O'Dwyer's* has been covering public relations, marketing communications, and related fields for over 40 years. The company provides the latest news and information about PR firms and professionals, the media, corporations, legal issues, jobs, technology, and much more through its website, weekly newsletter, monthly magazine, directories, and guides. Many of the contributors are PR people publicizing themselves while analyzing something. Byline given. Accepts queries by mail.

NONFICTION Needs opinion. Query. **Pays $250.**

SHOPPER MARKETING

Path to Purchase Institute, 7400 Skokie Blvd., Skokie IL 60077. (847)675-7400. **Fax:** (847)675-7494. **E-mail:** shoppermarketing@p2pi.org. **Website:** www.shoppermarketingmag.com. **80% freelance written.** Monthly tabloid covering advertising and primarily the in-store marketing industry. "We cover how brands market to the shopper at retail, what insights/research did they gather to reach that shopper and how did they activate the program at retail. We write case studies on shopper marketing campaigns, displays, packaging, retail media, and events. We write major category reports, company profiles, trends features, and more. Our readers are marketers and retailers, and a small selection of P-O-P producers (the guys that build the displays)." Estab. 1988. Circ. 20,000. Byline given. Offers Editorial lead time 2 months. Submit seasonal material 3 months in advance. Accepts queries by e-mail. Accepts simultaneous submissions. Responds in 1 month to queries. Guidelines free.

$$ SIGN BUILDER ILLUSTRATED

Simmons-Boardman Publishing Corp., 345 Hudson St., 12th Floor, New York NY 10014. (252)355-5806. **E-mail:** jwooten@sbpub.com; abray@sbpub.com. **Website:** www.signshop.com. **Contact:** Jeff Wooten, editor; Ashley Bray, associate editor. **40% freelance written,.** Monthly magazine covering sign and graphic industry. Estab. 1987. Circ. 14,500. Byline given. Offers 10% kill fee. Publishes ms an average of 3 months after acceptance. Editorial lead time 3 months. Submit seasonal material 4 months in advance. Accepts queries by mail, e-mail, fax, phone. Accepts simultaneous submissions. Responds in 1 month to queries. Sample copy and writer's guidelines free.

NONFICTION Needs historical, how-to, humor, interview, photo feature, technical. **Buys 50-60 mss/year.** Query. Length: 1,000-1,500 words. **Pays $250-550 for assigned articles.**

$$ SIGNCRAFT

SignCraft Publishing Co., Inc., P.O. Box 60031, Fort Myers FL 33906. (239)939-4644. **Fax:** (239)939-0607. **E-mail:** signcraft@signcraft.com. **Website:** www.signcraft.com. **10% freelance written.** Bimonthly magazine covering the sign industry. Estab. 1980. Circ. 14,000. Byline given. Offers negotiable kill fee. Publishes ms an average of 6 months after acceptance. Accepts queries by mail, e-mail, fax. Responds in 1 month to queries. Sample copy and writer's guidelines for $3.

NONFICTION Needs interview. **Buys 10 mss/year.** Query. Length: 500-2,000 words.

$$$ SOCAL MEETINGS + EVENTS MAGAZINE

Tiger Oak Publications, One Tiger Oak Plaza, 900 S. Third St., Minneapolis MN 55415. **Fax:** (612)338-0532. **E-mail:** meghan.mcandrews@tigeroak.com. **Website:** http://meetingsmags.com. **Contact:** Meghan McAndrews, managing editor. **80% freelance written.** "*SoCal Meetings & Events* magazine is the premier trade publication for meetings planners and hospitality service providers in Southern California. This magazine aims to report on and promote businesses involved in the meetings and events industry. The magazine covers current and emerging trends, people and venues in the meetings and events industry in Southern California." Quarterly magazine. Estab. 1993. Circ. 20,000. Byline given. Offers 20% kill fee. Publishes ms an average of 4 months after acceptance. Editorial lead time 4-6 months. Submit seasonal material 6 months in advance. Accepts queries by mail. Accepts simultaneous submissions. Responds in 1-2 weeks to queries.

NONFICTION Needs general interest, historical, interview, new product, opinion, personal experience, photo feature, technical, travel. **Buys 30 mss/year.** "Each query should tell us: What the story will be about; how you will tell the story (what sources you will use, how you will conduct research, etc.); why is the story pertinent to the market audience. Please also attach PDFs of 3 published magazine articles." Length: 600-1,500 words. **The average department length story (4-700 words) pays about $2-300 and the average feature length story (1,000-1,200 words) pays from $5-600, depending on the story. These rates are not guaranteed and vary.**

COLUMNS Meet + Eat (restaurant reviews); Facility Focus (venue reviews); Regional Spotlight (city review), 1,000 words. **Buys 30 mss/year.** Query with published clips. **Pays $400-600.**

$$$ TEXAS MEETINGS + EVENTS

Tiger Oak Publications, One Tiger Oak Plaza, 900 S. 3rd St., Minneapolis MN 55401. (612)548-3180. **Fax:** (612)548-3181. **E-mail:** meghan.mcandrews@tigeroak.com. **Website:** http://meetingsmags.com. **80% freelance written.** Quarterly magazine covering meetings and events industry. Estab. 1993. Circ. 20,000. Byline given. Offers 20% kill fee. Publishes ms an average of 4 months after acceptance. Editorial lead time 4-6 months. Submit seasonal material 6 months in advance. Accepts queries by mail. Accepts simultaneous submissions. Responds in 1-2 weeks to queries.

NONFICTION Needs general interest, historical, interview, new product, opinion, personal experience, photo feature, technical, travel. **Buys 30 mss/year.** Query with published clips. Length: 600-1,500 words. **Pays $400-800.**

COLUMNS Meet + Eat (restaurant reviews); Facility Focus (venue reviews); Regional Spotlight (city review), 1,000 words. **Buys 30 mss/year.** Query with published clips. **Pays $400-600.**

ART, DESIGN AND COLLECTIBLES

$$ AIRBRUSH ACTION MAGAZINE

Action, Inc., 3209 Atlantic Ave., P.O. Box 438, Allenwood NJ 08720. (732)223-7878; (800)876-2472. **Fax:** (732)223-2855. **E-mail:** ceo@airbrushaction.com. **Website:** www.airbrushaction.com. **80% freelance written.** Bimonthly magazine covering the spectrum of airbrush applications: automotive and custom paint applications, illustration, T-shirt airbrushing, fine art, automotive and sign painting, hobby/craft applications, wall murals, fingernails, temporary tattoos, artist profiles, reviews, and more. Estab. 1985. Circ. 35,000. Byline given. Pays 1 month after publication. Publishes ms an average of 6 months after acceptance. Editorial lead time 6 months. Submit seasonal material 6 months in advance. Accepts queries by mail, e-mail, fax, phone. Accepts simultaneous submissions.

NONFICTION Needs how-to, humor, inspirational, interview, new product, personal experience, technical. Nothing unrelated to airbrush. Query with published clips. **Pays 15¢/word.** Sometimes pays expenses of writers on assignment.

COLUMNS Query with published clips.

🌓 ANTIQUEWEEK

MidCountry Media, 27 N. Jefferson St., P.O. Box 90, Knightstown IN 46148. (800)876-5133, ext. 189. **Fax:** (800)345-3398. **E-mail:** connie@antiqueweek.com; tony@antiqueweek.com. **Website:** www.antiqueweek.com. **Contact:** Connie Swaim, managing editor; Tony Gregory, publisher. **80% freelance written.** Weekly tabloid covering antiques and collectibles with 3 editions: Eastern, Central, and National, plus the monthly *AntiqueWest*. "*AntiqueWeek* has a wide range of readership from dealers and auctioneers to collectors, both advanced and novice. Our readers demand accurate information presented in an entertaining style." Estab. 1968. Circ. 50,000. Byline given. Offers 10% kill fee or $25. Submit seasonal material 1 month in advance. Accepts queries by mail, e-mail. Guidelines by e-mail.

NONFICTION Needs historical, how-to, interview, opinion, personal experience, antique show and auction reports, feature articles on particular types of antiques and collectibles. **Buys 400-500 mss/year.** Query. Length: 1,000-2,000 words. **Pays $50-250.**

🌑 THE APPRAISERS STANDARD

New England Appraisers Association, 6973 Crestridge Dr., Memphis TN 38119. (901)758-2659. **E-mail:** ETuten551@aol.com. **Website:** www.newenglandappraisers.net. **Contact:** Edward Tuten, editor. **50% freelance written. Works with a small number of new/unpublished writers each year**. Quarterly publication covering the appraisals of antiques, art, collectibles, jewelry, coins, stamps, and real estate. "The writer should be knowledgeable on the subject, and the article should be written with appraisers in mind, with prices quoted for objects, good pictures, and descriptions of articles being written about." Estab. 1980. Circ. 1,000. Short bio and byline given. Publishes ms an average of 1 year after acceptance. Submit seasonal material 2 months in advance. Accepts queries by mail, e-mail. Accepts simultaneous submissions. Responds in 1 month to queries. Responds in 2 months to mss. Sample copy for 9x12 SAE with $1 postage. Guidelines for #10 SASE.

NONFICTION Needs interview, personal experience, technical, travel. Send complete ms. Length: 700 words. **Pays $60.**

🌓 FAITH+FORM

47 Grandview Terrace, Essex CT 06426. (860)575-4702. **E-mail:** mcrosbie@faithandform.com. **Website:** www.faithandform.com. **Contact:** Michael J. Crosbie, editor-in-chief. **50% freelance written.** Quarterly magazine covering relgious buildings and art. *Faith + Form*, devoted to religious art and architecture, is read by artists, designers, architects, clergy, congregations, and all who care about environments for worship. Writers must be knowledgeable about environments for worship, or able to explain them. Estab. 1967. Circ. 4,500. Byline given. Publishes ms an average of 6 months after acceptance. Editorial lead time 6 months. Submit seasonal material 6 months in advance. Accepts queries by online submission form. Accepts simultaneous submissions. Responds in 2 weeks to queries. Responds in 1 month to mss. Guidelines available.

NONFICTION Needs book excerpts, essays, how-to, inspirational, interview, opinion, personal experience, photo feature, religious, technical. **Buys 6 mss/year.** Query. Length: 500-2,500 words.

COLUMNS News, 250-750 words; Book Reviews, 250-500 words. **Buys 3 mss/year.** Query.

🌕 HOW

F+W Media, Inc., 10151 Carver Rd., Suite 200, Blue Ash OH 45242. (513)531-2690. **Fax:** (513)531-2902. **E-mail:** editorial@howdesign.com. **Website:** www.howdesign.com. **75% freelance written.** Bi-monthly magazine covering graphic design profession. Estab. 1985. Circ. 40,000. Byline given. Responds in 6 weeks to queries.

⚷ "The HOW brand now extends beyond the print magazine to annual events for design professionals, yearly design competitions, digital products and books."

NONFICTION Special issues: Self-Promotion Annual (September/October); Business Annual (November/December); International Annual of Design

(March/April); Creativity/Paper/Stock Photography (May/June); Digital Design Annual (July/August). No how-to articles for beginning artists or fine-art-oriented articles. **Buys 40 mss/year.** Query with published clips and samples of subject's work, artwork, or design. Length: 1,500-2,000 words. **Pays $700-900.** Sometimes pays expenses of writers on assignment.

COLUMNS Creativity (focuses on creative exercises and inspiration) 1,200-1,500 words. In-House Issues (focuses on business and creativity issues for corporate design groups), 1,200-1,500 words. Business (focuses on business issue for design firm owners), 1,200-1,500 words. **Buys Number of columns: 35. mss/year.** Query with published clips. **Pays $250-400.**

💲💲 THE PASTEL JOURNAL

F+W Media, Inc., 10151 Carver Rd., Suite #200, Cincinnati OH 45242. (513)531-2690. **Fax:** (513)891-7153. **Website:** www.pasteljournal.com. **Contact:** Anne Hevener. Bimonthly magazine covering pastel art. "*The Pastel Journal* is the only national magazine devoted to the medium of pastel. Addressing the working professional as well as passionate amateurs, *The Pastel Journal* offers inspiration, information, and instruction to our readers." Estab. 1999. Circ. 22,000. Byline given. Offers 25% kill fee. Publishes ms an average of 3-6 months after acceptance. Editorial lead time 6 months. Submit seasonal material 6 months in advance. Accepts queries by mail. Accepts simultaneous submissions. Responds in 4-6 weeks to queries. Writer's guidelines free.

NONFICTION Needs how-to, interview, new product, profile. Does not want articles that aren't art-related. Review magazine before submitting. Query with or without published clips. Length: 500-2,500 words. **Pays $150-750.**

💲💲💲 PRINT

F+W Media, Inc., 38 E. 29th St., 4th Floor, New York NY 10016. (212)447-1400. **Fax:** (212)447-5231. **E-mail:** Aaron.Kenedi@fwmedia.com. **E-mail:** info@print-mag.com. **Website:** www.printmag.com. **Contact:** Aaron Kenedi. **75% freelance written.** Bimonthly magazine covering graphic design and visual culture. "*PRINT*'s articles, written by design specialists and cultural critics, focus on the social, political, and historical context of graphic design, and on the places where consumer culture and popular culture meet. We aim to produce a general interest magazine for professionals with engagingly written text and lavish

illustrations. By covering a broad spectrum of topics, both international and local, we try to demonstrate the significance of design in the world at large." Estab. 1940. Circ. 45,000. Byline given. Offers 25% kill fee. Publishes ms an average of 3 months after acceptance. Editorial lead time 3 months. Submit seasonal material 3 months in advance. Accepts queries by e-mail. Responds in 2 weeks to queries. Responds in 1 month to mss.

NONFICTION Needs essays, interview, opinion. **Buys 35-40 mss/year.** Query with published clips. Length: 1,000-2,500 words. **Pays $1,250.** Sometimes pays expenses of writers on assignment.

💲💲 PROFESSIONAL ARTIST

Turnstile Publishing, 1500 Park Center Dr., Orlando FL 32835. (407)563-7000. **Fax:** (407)563-7099. **E-mail:** khall@artcalendar.com. **Website:** www.profession-alartistmag.com. Louise Buyo at lbuyo@profession-alartistmag.com. **Contact:** Kim Hall. **75% freelance written.** Monthly magazine. Estab. 1986. Circ. 20,000. Sample print copy for $5. Guidelines available online.

NONFICTION Needs essays, the psychology of creativity, how-to, interview, successful artists with a focus on what made them successful, networking articles, marketing topics, technical articles (new equipment, new media, computer software, Internet marketing.), cartoons, art law, including pending legislation that affects artists (copyright law, Internet regulations, etc.). "We like nuts-and-bolts information about making a living as an artist. We do not run reviews or art historical pieces, nor do we like writing characterized by 'critic-speak,' philosophical hyperbole, psychological arrogance, politics, or New Age religion. Also, we do not condone a get-rich-quick attitude." Send complete ms. **Pays $250.**

COLUMNS "If an artist or freelancer sends us good articles regularly, and based on results we feel that he is able to produce a column at least 3 times per year, we will invite him to be a contributing writer. If a gifted artist-writer can commit to producing an article on a monthly basis, we will offer him a regular column and the title contributing editor." Send complete ms.

💲 TEXAS ARCHITECT

Texas Society of Architects, 500 Chicon St., Austin TX 78702. (512)478-7386. **Fax:** (512)478-0528. **Website:** www.texasarchitect.org. **Contact:** Stephen Sharpe, editor. **30% freelance written. Mostly written by unpaid members of the professional society.** Bimonthly journal covering architecture and architects of Texas. "*Texas Architect* is a highly visually-oriented look at Texas architecture, design, and urban planning. Articles cover varied subtopics within architecture. Readers are mostly architects and related building professionals." Estab. 1951. Circ. 12,500. Byline given. Publishes ms an average of 3 months after acceptance. Submit seasonal material 4 months in advance. Accepts queries by mail, e-mail. Responds in 6 weeks to queries. Guidelines available online.

NONFICTION Needs interview, photo feature, technical, book reviews. Query with published clips. Length: 100-2,000 words. **Pays $50-100 for assigned articles.**

COLUMNS News (timely reports on architectural issues, projects, and people), 100-500 words. **Buys 10 articles/year mss/year.** Query with published clips. **Pays $50-100.**

🌕🌓 WATERCOLOR ARTIST

F+W Media, Inc., 10151 Carver Rd., Suite #200, Cincinnati OH 45242. (513)531-2690. **Fax:** (513)891-7153. **Website:** www.watercolorartistmagazine.com. **Contact:** Jennifer Hoffman, art director; Kelly Kane, editor. Bimonthly magazine covering water media arts. Estab. 1984. Circ. 45,000. Byline given. Offers 10% kill fee. Publishes ms an average of 3-6 months after acceptance. Editorial lead time 6 months. Submit seasonal material 6 months in advance. Accepts queries by mail. Accepts simultaneous submissions. Responds in 4-6 weeks to queries. Writer's guidelines available at http://www.artistsnetwork.com/contactus.

NONFICTION Needs book excerpts, essays, how-to, inspirational, interview, new product, personal experience. Does not want articles that aren't art-related. Review magazine before submitting. **Buys 36 mss/year.** Send query letter with images. Length: 350-2,500 words. **Pays $150-600.**

AUTO AND TRUCK

AFTERMARKET BUSINESS WORLD

Advanstar Communications, 24950 Country Club Blvd., Suite 200, North Olmsted OH 44070. (440)891-2746. **Fax:** (440)891-2675. **E-mail:** kmcnamara@advanstar.com. **Website:** www.aftermarketbusiness.com. **Contact:** Krista McNamara, content manager. "The mission of *Aftermarket Business World* (formerly Aftermarket Business) involves satisfying the needs of US readers who want to do business here and elsewhere and helping readers in other countries who want to do business with U. companies. Being an electronic publication assures us that we can reach just about anybody, anywhere. New editorial material for *Aftermarket Business World* will focus on news, trends, and analysis about the international automotive aftermarket. Written for corporate executives and key decision makers responsible for buying automotive products (parts, accessories, chemicals) and other services sold at retail to consumers and professional installers. It's the oldest continuously published business magazine covering the retail automotive aftermarket and is the only publication dedicated to the specialized needs of this industry." Estab. 1936. Circ. 120,000. Byline given. "Corporate policy requires all freelancers to sign a print and online usage contract for stories." Pay negotiable. Sample copies available; call (888)527-7008 for rates.

🌓 AUTO RESTORER

Bowtie, Inc., P.O. Box 6050, Mission Viejo CA 92690. (949)855-8822. **Fax:** (949)855-3045. **E-mail:** tkade@fancypubs.com; editors@mmminc.org. **Website:** www.autorestorermagazine.com. **Contact:** Ted Kade, editor. **85% freelance written.** Monthly magazine covering auto restoration. "Our readers own old cars and they work on them. We help our readers by providing as much practical, how-to information as we can about restoration and old cars." Estab. 1989. Circ. 60,000. Publishes mss 3 months after acceptance. Submit seasonal material 4 months in advance. Accepts queries by mail, e-mail, fax. Responds in 2 months to queries. Sample copy for $7. Guidelines free.

☛ "Interview the owner of a restored car. Present advice to others on how to do a similar restoration. Seek advice from experts. Go light on history and nonspecific details. Make it something that the magazine regularly uses. Do automotive how-tos."

NONFICTION Needs how-to, auto restoration, new product, photo feature, technical product evaluation. **Buys 60 mss/year.** Query first. Length: 250-2,000/words. **Pays $150/published page, including photos and illustrations.**

🌕🌓 BUSINESS FLEET

Bobit Publishing, 3520 Challenger St., Torrance CA 90501. (310)533-2400. **E-mail:** chris.brown@bobit.com. **Website:** www.businessfleet.com. **Contact:**

Chris Brown, executive editor. **10% freelance written.** Bimonthly magazine covering businesses which operate 10-50 company vehicles. Estab. 2000. Circ. 100,000. Byline given. Offers 25% kill fee. Publishes ms an average of 3 months after acceptance. Editorial lead time 2 months. Submit seasonal material 2 months in advance. Accepts queries by mail, e-mail, fax. Responds in 3 weeks to queries. Responds in 2 months to mss. Sample copy and writer's guidelines free.

NONFICTION Needs how-to, interview, new product, personal experience, photo feature, technical. **Buys 16 mss/year.** Query with published clips. Length: 500-2,000 words. **Pays $100-400.** Sometimes pays expenses of writers on assignment.

💲💲 FENDERBENDER

DeWitt Publishing, 1043 Grand Ave. #372, St. Paul MN 55105. (651)224-6207. **Fax:** (651)224-6212. **E-mail:** news@fenderbender.com; jweyer@fenderbender.com. **Website:** www.fenderbender.com. **Contact:** Jake Weyer, editor. **50% freelance written.** Monthly magazine covering automotive collision repair. Estab. 1999. Circ. 58,000. Byline given. Offers 20% kill fee. Publishes ms an average of 2 months after acceptance. Editorial lead time 3 months. Submit seasonal material 6 months in advance. Accepts queries by e-mail. Accepts simultaneous submissions. Responds in 1-2 months to queries. Responds in 2-3 months to mss. Sample copy for SAE with 10x13 envelope and 6 first-class stamps. Guidelines available online.

NONFICTION Needs exposé, how-to, inspirational, interview, technical. Does not want personal narratives or any other first-person stories. No poems or creative writing mss. Query with published clips. Length: 1,800-2,500 words. **Pays 25-60¢/word.** Sometimes pays expenses of writers on assignment.

COLUMNS Q&A, 600 words; Shakes, Rattles & Roll-overs; Rearview Mirror. Query with published clips. **Pays 25-35¢/word.**

💲💲 FLEET EXECUTIVE

NAFA Fleet Management Association, 125 Village Blvd., Suite 200, Princeton NJ 08540. (609)986-1053; (609)720-0882. **Fax:** (609)720-0881; (609)452-8004. **E-mail:** publications@nafa.org; info@nafa.org. **Website:** www.nafa.org. **10% freelance written.** Magazine published 6 times/year covering automotive fleet management. Estab. 1957. Circ. 4,000. Publishes ms an average of 4 months after acceptance. Editorial

lead time 2 months. Accepts queries by mail. Accepts simultaneous submissions. Responds in 1 month to queries. Guidelines free.

NONFICTION Needs interview, technical. **Buys 24 mss/year.** Query with published clips. Length: 500-3,000 words. **Pays $500 maximum.**

OLD CARS WEEKLY

a Division of F+W Media, Inc., 700 E. State St., Iola WI 54990-0001. (715)445-4612. **Fax:** (715)445-2214. **E-mail:** angelo.vanbogart@fwmedia.com. **Website:** www.oldcarsweekly.com. **Contact:** Angelo Van Bogart. **30% freelance written.** Weekly tabloid for anyone restoring, selling or driving an old car. Estab. 1971. Circ. 55,000. Byline given. Pays within 3 months after publication date. Publishes ms an average of 6 months after acceptance. Call circulation department for sample copy. Guidelines for #10 SASE.

NONFICTION Needs how-to, technical, auction prices realized lists. No "Grandpa's Car," "My First Car," or "My Car" themes from freelance contributors. **Buys 1,000 mss/year.** Send complete ms. Length: 400-1,600 words. **Payment varies.**

💲💲💲 OVERDRIVE

Randall-Reilly Publishing, 3200 Rice Mine Rd. NE, Tuscaloosa AL 35406. (205)349-2990. **Fax:** (205)750-8070. **E-mail:** mheine@rrpub.com. **Website:** www.etrucker.com. **Contact:** Max Heine, editorial director. **5% freelance written.** Monthly magazine for independent truckers. Estab. 1961. Circ. 100,000. Byline given. Offers 10% kill fee. Publishes ms an average of 2 months after acceptance. Responds in 2 months to queries. Sample copy for 9x12 SASE.

NONFICTION Needs essays, exposé, how-to, truck maintenance and operation, interview, successful independent truckers, personal experience, photo feature, technical. Send complete ms. Length: 500-2,500 words. **Pays $300-1,500 for assigned articles.**

💲 PML

PML Consulting, P.O. 365, Ridgecrest CA 98555. (888)928-9111. **E-mail:** thom@pmletter.com. **Website:** www.pmletter.com/blog. **100% freelance written.** Monthly magazine covering technical tips, personality profiles, and race coverage of Porsche automobiles. Estab. 1981. Circ. 1,500. Byline given. Publishes ms an average of 2 months after acceptance. Editorial lead time 2 months. Submit seasonal material 2 months in advance. Accepts queries by mail, e-mail, fax, phone. Accepts simultaneous submissions.

Responds in 2 weeks to queries. Responds in 1 month to mss. Sample copy for $5. Guidelines for #10 SASE. **NONFICTION** Needs general interest, historical, how-to, humor, interview, new product, personal experience, photo feature, technical, travel, race results. **Buys 30-40 mss/year.** Query with published clips. Length: 500-2,000 words. **Pays $30-50 and up, depending on length and topic.** Sometimes pays expenses of writers on assignment.
FILLERS Needs anecdotes, facts, gags, newsbreaks, short humor. **Negotiable amount.**

☺ 💲💲 TIRE NEWS

Rousseau Automotive Communication, 455, Notre-Dame Est, Suite 311, Montreal QC H2Y 1C9 Canada. (514)289-0888; 1-877-989-0888. **Fax:** (514)289-5151. **E-mail:** info@autosphere.ca; 104420.662@compuserve.com; daniel.lafrance@autosphere.ca. **Website:** www.publicationsrousseau.com; http://autosphere.ca/en/tires.html. Daniel Lafrance, web editor. Bimonthly magazine covering Canadian tire industry. *Tire News* focuses on education/training, industry image, management, new tires, new techniques, marketing, HR, etc. Estab. 2004. Circ. 16,000. Byline given. Publishes ms an average of 2 months after acceptance. Editorial lead time 2 months. Submit seasonal material 2 months in advance. Accepts simultaneous submissions. Responds in 2 weeks to queries. Responds in 2 months to mss. Guidelines by e-mail.
NONFICTION Needs general interest, how-to, inspirational, interview, new product, technical. Does not want opinion pieces. **Buys 5 mss/year.** Query with published clips. Length: 550-610 words. **Pays up to $200 (Canadian).**
FILLERS Needs facts. **Buys 2 mss/year.** Length: 550-610 words. **Pays $0-200.**

☺ 💲💲 WESTERN CANADA HIGHWAY NEWS

Craig Kelman & Associates, 2020 Portage Ave., 3rd Floor, Winnipeg MB R3J 0K4 Canada. (204)985-9785. **Fax:** (204)985-9795. **E-mail:** terry@kelman.ca. **Website:** http://highwaynews.ca. **Contact:** Terry Ross, editor. **30% freelance written.** Quarterly magazine covering trucking. "The official magazine of the Alberta, Saskatchewan, and Manitoba trucking associations." Estab. 1995. Circ. 4,500. Byline given. Publishes ms an average of 2 months after acceptance. Editorial lead time 3 months. Submit seasonal material 3 months in advance. Accepts simultaneous submissions. Re-

sponds in 1 month to queries and mss. Sample copy for 10x13 SAE with 1 IRC. Guidelines for #10 SASE.
NONFICTION Needs essays, general interest, how-to, run a trucking business, interview, new product, opinion, personal experience, photo feature, technical, profiles in excellence (bios of trucking or associate firms enjoying success). **Buys 8-10 mss/year.** Query. Length: 500-3,000 words. **Pays 18-25¢/word.** Sometimes pays expenses of writers on assignment.
COLUMNS Safety (new safety innovation/products), 500 words; Trade Talk (new products), 300 words. Query. **Pays 18-25¢/word.**

AVIATION AND SPACE

💲💲 AEROSAFETY WORLD MAGAZINE

Flight Safety Foundation, 801 N. Fairfax St., Suite 400, Alexandria VA 22314-1774. (703)739-6700. **Fax:** (703)739-6708. **E-mail:** donoghue@flightsafety.org. **Website:** www.flightsafety.org. **Contact:** J.A. Donoghue, editor-in-chief. Monthly newsletter covering safety aspects of airport operations. Estab. 1974. Accepts queries by mail, e-mail, fax.
NONFICTION Needs technical. Query.

💲💲 AVIATION INTERNATIONAL NEWS

The Convention News Co., 214 Franklin Ave., Midland Park NJ 07432. (201)444-5075. **Fax:** (201)444-4647. **E-mail:** nmoll@ainonline.com; editor@ainonline.com. **Website:** www.ainonline.com. Annmarie Yannaco, managing editor, ayannaco@ainonline.com. **Contact:** Nigel Moll, editor. **30-40% freelance written.** Monthly magazine, with daily onsite issues published at 3 conventions and 2 international air shows each year, and twice-weekly AINalerts via e-mail covering business and commercial aviation with news features, special reports, aircraft evaluations, and surveys on business aviation worldwide, written for business pilots and industry professionals. "While the heartbeat of *AIN* is driven by the news it carries, the human touch is not neglected. We pride ourselves on our people stories about the industry's 'movers and shakers' and others in aviation who make a difference." Estab. 1972. Circ. 40,000. Byline given. Pays on acceptance and upon receipt of writer's invoice. Offers variable kill fee. Publishes ms an average of 2 months after acceptance. Editorial lead time 2 months. Submit seasonal material 3 months in advance. Accepts queries by mail, e-mail, fax. Responds in 6 weeks to queries. Responds in 2 months to mss. Sample copy for $10. Writer's guidelines for 9x12 SAE with 3 first-class stamps.

NONFICTION Needs how-to, aviation, interview, new product, opinion, personal experience, photo feature, technical. No puff pieces. "Our readers expect serious, real news. We don't pull any punches. *AIN* is not a 'good news' publication; it tells the story, both good and bad." **Buys 150-200 mss/year.** Query with published clips. Do not send mss by e-mail unless requested. Length: 200-3,000 words. **Pays 40¢/word to first timers, higher rates to proven *AIN* freelancers.** Pays expenses of writers on assignment.

⊖⊖ GROUND SUPPORT WORLDWIDE MAGAZINE

Cygnus Business Media, 1233 Janesville Ave., Fort Atkinson WI 53538. (800)547-7377, ext. 1370. **Fax:** (920)563-1699. **E-mail:** brad.mcallister@Aviation-Pros.com. **Website:** www.groundsupportworldwide.com. **Contact:** Brad McAllister. **20% freelance written.** Magazine published 10 times/year. "Our readers are those aviation professionals who are involved in ground support—the equipment manufacturers, the suppliers, the ramp operators, ground handlers, and airport and airline managers. We cover issues of interest to this community—deicing, ramp safety, equipment technology, pollution, etc." Estab. 1993. Circ. 15,000+. Publishes ms an average of 2 months after acceptance. Editorial lead time 2 months. Accepts queries by mail, e-mail, fax. Responds in 3 weeks to queries. Responds in 3 months to mss. Sample copy for SAE with 9x11 envelope and 5 first-class stamps.

NONFICTION Needs how-to, use or maintain certain equipment, interview, new product, opinion, photo feature, technical aspects of ground support and issues, industry events, meetings, new rules and regulations. **Buys 12-20 mss/year.** Send complete ms. Length: 500-2,000 words. **Pays $100-300.**

⊖⊖⊖ PROFESSIONAL PILOT

Queensmith Communications, 30 S. Quaker Lane, Suite 300, Alexandria VA 22314. (703)370-0606. **Fax:** (703)370-7082. **E-mail:** editor@propilotmag.com; prose@propilotmag.com; editorial@propilotmag.com. **Website:** www.propilotmag.com. Murray Smith, publisher. **Contact:** Phil Rose, editor. **75% freelance written.** Monthly magazine covering corporate, non-combat government, law enforcement, and various other types of professional aviation. "The typical reader of *Professional Pilot* has a sophisticated grasp

of piloting/aviation knowledge and is interested in articles that help him/her do the job better or more efficiently." Estab. 1967. Circ. 40,000. Byline given. Offers kill fee. Kill fee negotiable. Publishes ms an average of 2-3 months after acceptance. Accepts queries by mail, e-mail, fax.

NONFICTION Buys 40 mss/year. Query. Length: 750-2,500 words. **Pays $200-1,000, depending on length. A fee for the article will be established at the time of assignment.** Sometimes pays expenses of writers on assignment.

BEAUTY AND SALON

⊖⊖ BEAUTY STORE BUSINESS

Creative Age Communications, 7628 Densmore Ave., Van Nuys CA 91406. (818)782-7328, ext. 353; (800)442-5667. **Fax:** (818)782-7450. **E-mail:** mbatist@creativeage.com; mbirenbaum@creativeage.com; skelly@creativeage.com. **Website:** www.beautystorebusiness.com. Shelley Moench-Kelly, managing editor. **Contact:** Manyesha Batist, editor/online editor. **50% freelance written.** Monthly magazine covering beauty store business management, news, and beauty products. Estab. 1994. Circ. 15,000. Byline given. Offers kill fee. Offers negotiable kill fee. Publishes ms an average of 3 months after acceptance. Editorial lead time 3 months. Submit seasonal material 4 months in advance. Accepts queries by mail, e-mail, fax. Responds in 1 week to queries. Responds in 2 weeks, if interested.

NONFICTION Needs how-to, business management, merchandising, e-commerce, retailing, interview, industry leaders/beauty store owners. **Buys 20-30 mss/year.** Query. Length: 1,800-2,200 words. **Pays $250-525 for assigned articles.** Sometimes pays expenses of writers on assignment.

☺ ⊖⊖ COSMETICS

Rogers, One Mount Pleasant Rd., 7th Floor, Toronto ON M4Y 2Y5 Canada. (416)764-1680. **Fax:** (416)764-1704. **E-mail:** kristen.vinakmens@cosmetics.rogers.com. **Website:** www.cosmeticsmag.com. **Contact:** Kristen Vinakmens, editor. **10% freelance written.** Bimonthly magazine. Estab. 1972. Circ. 13,000. Byline given. Offers 50% kill fee. Publishes ms an average of 3 months after acceptance. Editorial lead time 4 months. Submit seasonal material 4 months in advance. Accepts queries by mail. Responds in 1 month to queries. Sample copy for $6 (Canadian) and 8% GST.

NONFICTION Needs general interest, interview, photo feature. **Buys 1 mss/year.** Query. Length: 250-1,200 words. **Pays 25¢/word.** Sometimes pays expenses of writers on assignment.

COLUMNS "All articles assigned on a regular basis from correspondents and columnists that we know personally from the industry."

$$ DAYSPA

Creative Age Publications, 7628 Densmore Ave., Van Nuys CA 91406. (818)782-7328, ext. 301. **Fax:** (818)782-7450. **Website:** www.dayspamagazine.com. **Contact:** Linda Kossoff, consulting editor. **50% freelance written.** Monthly magazine covering the business of day spas, multi-service/skincare salons, and resort/hotel spas. "*Dayspa* includes only well-targeted business and trend articles directed at the owners and managers. It serves to enrich, enlighten, and empower spa/salon professionals." Estab. 1996. Circ. 31,000. Byline given. Publishes ms an average of 4 months after acceptance. Editorial lead time 4 months. Submit seasonal material 4 months in advance. Accepts queries by mail, e-mail, fax, phone, online submission form. Responds in 2 months to queries. Sample copy for $5.

NONFICTION **Buys 40 mss/year.** Query. Length: 1,500-1,800 words. **Pays $150-500.**

COLUMNS Legal Pad (legal issues affecting salons/spas); Money Matters (financial issues); Management Workshop (spa management issues); Health Wise (wellness trends), all 1,200-1,500 words. **Buys 20 mss/year.** Query. **Pays $150-400.**

DERMASCOPE MAGAZINE

Aesthetics International Association, 310 E. I-30, Suite B107, Garland TX 75043. (469)429-9300. **Fax:** (469)429-9301. **E-mail:** amckay@dermascope.com; press@dermascope.com. **Website:** www.dermascope.com. **Contact:** Amy McKay. Monthly magazine covering aesthetics (skin care) and body and spa therapy. "Our magazine is a source of practical advice and continuing education for skin care, body, and spa therapy professionals. Our main readers are salon, day spa, and destination spa owners, managers, or technicians and aesthetics students. How-tos, skin therapy, body therapy, diet, nutrition, spa, equipment, medical procedures, makeup, and business articles should be approximately 1,500-2,000 words. Feature stories are should be between 1,800-2,500 words. Sidebars are a plus. Stories exceeding 2,500 may be printed in part and run in concurrent issues." Estab. 1978. Circ. 16,000. Publishes ms an average of 6 months after acceptance. Editorial lead time 3 months. Submit seasonal material 6 months in advance. Accepts queries by mail, e-mail, fax. Responds in 4-6 months. Sample copy available by phone. Guidelines available online at website.

NONFICTION Needs book excerpts, general interest, historical, how-to, inspirational, personal experience, photo feature, technical. Query with published clips. Length: 1,500-2,500 words. Does not accept reprints.

$$ IMPRESSIONS

Nielsen Business Media, 1145 Sanctuary Pkwy., Suite 355, Alpharetta GA 30009-4772. (770)291-5574. **Fax:** (770)777-8733. **E-mail:** mderryberry@impressionsmag.com; jlaster@impressionsmag.com. **Website:** www.impressionsmag.com. **Contact:** Marcia Derryberry, editor-in-chief; Jamar Laster, managing editor. **30% freelance written.** Monthly magazine covering computerized embroidery and digitizing design. "Authoritative, up-to-date information on screen printing, embroidery, heat-applied graphics and inkjet-to-garment printing. Readable, practical business and/or technical articles that show our readers how to succeed in their profession." Published 13 times a year. Estab. 1994. Circ. 20,000. Byline given. Publishes ms an average of 3 months after acceptance. Editorial lead time 3 months. Submit seasonal material 6 months in advance. Accepts queries by mail, e-mail. Accepts simultaneous submissions. Sample copy for $10.

NONFICTION Needs how-to, embroidery, sales, marketing, design, general business info, interview, new product, photo feature, technical, computerized embroidery. **Buys 40 mss/year.** Query. Length: 800-2,000 words. **Pays $200 and up for assigned articles.**

$$ MASSAGE MAGAZINE

5150 Palm Valley Rd., Suite 103, Ponte Vedra Beach FL 32082. (904)285-6020. **Fax:** (904)285-9944. **E-mail:** kmenahan@massagemag.com. **Website:** www.massagemag.com. **Contact:** Karen Menehan. **60% freelance written.** Bimonthly magazine covering massage and other touch therapies. Estab. 1985. Circ. 50,000. Byline given. Publishes ms an average of 2 months-24 months after acceptance. Accepts queries by e-mail. Responds in 2 months to queries. Responds in 3 months to mss. Sample copy for $6.95. Guidelines available online.

NONFICTION Needs book excerpts, essays, general interest, how-to, interview, personal experience,

photo feature, technical, experiential. No multiple submissions. Length: 600-2,000 words. **Pays $50-400.**
COLUMNS Profiles; News and Current Events; Practice Building (business); Technique; Body/Mind. Length: 800-1,200 words. **Pays $75-300 for assigned articles.**
FILLERS Needs facts, newsbreaks. Length: 100-800 words. **Pays $125 maximum.**

⊖⊖ NAILPRO

Creative Age Publications, 7628 Densmore Ave., Van Nuys CA 91406. (818)782-7328. **Fax:** (818)782-7450. **E-mail:** nailpro@creativeage.com. **Website:** www.nailpro.com. **75% freelance written.** Monthly magazine written for manicurists and nail technicians working in a full-service salon or nails-only salons. Estab. 1989. Circ. 65,000. Byline given. Publishes ms an average of 6 months after acceptance. Editorial lead time 3 months. Submit seasonal material 3 months in advance. Accepts queries by mail, e-mail, fax. Accepts simultaneous submissions. Responds in 6 weeks to queries. Sample copy for $2 and 9x12 SASE.
NONFICTION Needs book excerpts, how-to, humor, inspirational, interview, personal experience, photo feature, technical. No general interest articles or business articles not geared to the nail-care industry. **Buys 50 mss/year.** Query. Length: 1,000-3,000 words. **Pays $150-450.**
COLUMNS All Business (articles on building salon business, marketing and advertising, dealing with employees), 1,500-2,000 words; Attitudes (aspects of operating a nail salon and trends in the nail industry), 1,200-2,000 words. **Buys 50 mss/year.** Query. **Pays $250-350.**

⊘ ⊖⊖ NAILS

Bobit Business Media, 3520 Challenger St., Torrance CA 90503. (310)533-2457. **Fax:** (310)533-2507. **E-mail:** judy.lessin@bobit.com. **Website:** www.nailsmag.com. **Contact:** Judy Lessin, features editor. **10% freelance written.** Monthly magazine. *NAILS* seeks to educate its readers on new techniques and products, nail anatomy and health, customer relations, working safely with chemicals, salon sanitation, and the business aspects of running a salon. Estab. 1983. Circ. 55,000. Byline given. Submit seasonal material 4 months in advance. Accepts queries by mail, e-mail, fax. Responds in 1 month to queries. Sample copy and writer's guidelines for #10 SASE.
NONFICTION Needs historical, how-to, inspirational, interview, personal experience, photo feature, technical. "No articles on 1 particular product, company profiles, or articles slanted toward a particular company or manufacturer." **Buys 20 mss/year.** Query with published clips. Length: 1,200-3,000 words. **Pays $200-500.** Sometimes pays expenses of writers on assignment.

⊖⊖ PULSE MAGAZINE

HOST Communications Inc., 2365 Harrodsburg Rd., Suite A325, Lexington KY 40504. (859)425-5062. **Fax:** (859)226-4445. **E-mail:** mae.manacap-johnson@ispastaff.com. **Website:** www.experienceispa.com/media/pulse-magazine. **Contact:** Mae Manacap-Johnson, editor. **20% freelance written.** Magazine published 10 times/year covering spa industry. Estab. 1991. Circ. 5,300. Byline given. Publishes ms an average of 1 month after acceptance. Editorial lead time 3 months. Submit seasonal material 4 months in advance. Accepts queries by e-mail. Sample copy for #10 SASE. Guidelines by e-mail.
NONFICTION Needs general interest, how-to, interview, new product. Does not want articles focused on spas that are not members of ISPA, consumer-focused articles (market is the spa industry professional), or features on hot tubs ("not *that* spa industry"). **Buys 8-10 mss/year.** Query with published clips. Length: 800-2,000 words. **Pays $250-500.** Sometimes pays expenses of writers on assignment.

⊖⊖ SKIN DEEP

Associated Skin Care Professionals, 25188 Genesee Trail Rd., Suite 200, Golden CO 80401. (800)789-0411. **E-mail:** cpatrick@ascpskincare.com. **Website:** www.ascpskincare.com. **Contact:** Carrie Patrick, editor. **80% freelance written.** Bimonthly magazine covering technical, educational, and business information for estheticians with an emphasis on solo practitioners and spa/salon employees or independent contractors. "Our audience is the US individual skin care practitioner who may work on her own and/or in a spa or salon setting. We keep her up to date on skin care trends and techniques and ways to earn more income doing waxing, facials, peels, microdermabrasion, body wraps and other skin treatments. Our product-neutral stories may include novel spa treatments within the esthetician scope of practice. We do not cover mass-market retail products, hair care, nail care, makeup, physician only treatments/products, cosmetic surgery, or invasive treatments like colonics or ear candling. Successful stories have included how-tos on paraffin facials, aromatherapy body wraps, waxing tips, how to read ingredient labels, how to improve word-of-mouth advertising, and how to choose an online scheduling software package." Estab. 2003. Circ. 11,000+. Byline given. Publishes ms an average of 4-6 months after acceptance. Editorial lead time 4-5 months. Submit seasonal material 7 months in advance. Accepts queries by e-mail. Responds in 2 weeks to queries. Guidelines available.

NONFICTION "We don't run general consumer beauty material or products that are very rarely run a new product that is available through retail outlets. 'New' products means introduced in the last 12 months. We do not run industry personnel announcements or stories on individual spas/salons or getaways. We don't cover hair or nails." **Buys 12 mss/year.** Query. Length: 800-1,800 words. **Pays $75-$300 for assigned articles.**

⊖⊖ SKIN INC. MAGAZINE

Allured Business Media, 336 Gundersen Dr., Suite A, Carol Stream IL 60188. (630)653-2155. **Fax:** (630)653-2192. **E-mail:** taschetta-millane@allured.com. **Website:** www.skininc.com. **Contact:** Melinda Taschetta-Millane, editor. **30% freelance written.** Magazine published 12 times/year. "Mss considered for publication that contain original and new information in the general fields of skin care and makeup, dermatological and esthetician-assisted surgical techniques. The subject may cover the science of skin, the business of skin care and makeup, and plastic surgeons on healthy (i.e., nondiseased) skin." Estab. 1988. Circ. 30,000. Byline given. Publishes ms an average of 6 months after acceptance. Editorial lead time 6 months. Submit seasonal material 1 year in advance. Accepts queries by mail, e-mail, fax, phone. Responds in 3 weeks to queries. Responds in 1 month to mss. Sample copy and writer's guidelines free.

NONFICTION Needs general interest, how-to, interview, personal experience, technical. **Buys 6 mss/year.** Query with published clips. Length: 2,000 words. **Pays $100-300 for assigned articles. Pays $50-200 for unsolicited articles.**

COLUMNS Finance (tips and solutions for managing money), 2,000-2,500 words; Personnel (managing personnel), 2,000-2,500 words; Marketing (marketing tips for salon owners), 2,000-2,500 words; Retail (retailing products and services in the salon environment), 2,000-2,500 words. Query with published clips. **Pays $50-200.**

FILLERS Needs facts, newsbreaks. **Buys 6 mss/year.** Length: 250-500 words. **Pays $50-100.**

BEVERAGES AND BOTTLING

AMERICAN BAR ASSOCIATION JOURNAL

321 N. Clark St., 20th Floor, Chicago IL 60654. (312)988-6018; (800)285-2221. **E-mail:** debora.clark@americanbar.org. **Website:** www.abajournal.com. **Contact:** Debora Clark, deputy design director. Monthly magazine of the American Bar Association. Emphasizes law and the legal profession. Readers are lawyers. Estab. 1915. Circ. 500,000.

✪ ⊖⊖ BAR & BEVERAGE BUSINESS MAGAZINE

Mercury Publications, 1740 Wellington Ave., Winnipeg MB R3H 0E8 Canada. (204)954-2085. **Fax:** (204)954-2057. **E-mail:** elaine@mercury.mb.ca; editorial@mercury.mb.ca. **Website:** www.barandbeverage.com. **Contact:** Elaine Dufault, associate publisher and national account manager. **33% freelance written.** Bimonthly magazine providing information on the latest trends, happenings, buying-selling of beverages and product merchandising. Estab. 1998. Circ. 16,077. Byline given. Pays 30-45 days from receipt of invoice. Offers 33% kill fee. Submit seasonal material 3 months in advance. Accepts simultaneous submissions. Sample copy and writer's guidelines free or by e-mail.

NONFICTION Needs how-to, making a good drink, training staff, etc., interview. Industry reports, profiles on companies. Query with published clips. Length: 500-9,000 words. **Pays 25-35¢/word.** Sometimes pays expenses of writers on assignment.

COLUMNS Out There (bar and beverage news in various parts of the country), 100-500 words. Query. **Pays $0-100.**

⊖⊖ THE BEVERAGE JOURNAL

MI Licensed Beverage Association, 920 N. Fairview, Lansing MI 48912. (517)374-9611; (800)292-2896. **Fax:** (517)374-1165. **E-mail:** editor@mlba.org. **Website:** www.mlba.org. **Contact:** Peter Broderick, editor. **40-50% freelance written.** Monthly magazine. Estab. 1983. Circ. 4,200. Editorial lead time 3 months. Submit seasonal material 3 months in advance. Accepts queries by mail, e-mail. Responds in 2 weeks to queries. Responds in 1 month to mss. Sample copy for $5 or online.

NONFICTION Needs essays, general interest, historical, how-to, make a drink, human resources, tips, etc. , humor, interview, new product, opinion, personal experience, photo feature, technical. **Buys 24 mss/year.** Send complete ms. Length: 1,000 words. **Pays $20-200.**

COLUMNS Open to essay content ideas. Interviews (legislators, others), 750-1,000 words; personal experience (waitstaff, customer, bartenders), 500 words. **Buys 12 mss/year.** Send complete ms. **Pays $25-100.**

⊛⊛ PRACTICAL WINERY & VINEYARD

PWV, Inc., 58-D Paul Dr., San Rafael CA 94903-2054. (415)479-5819. **Fax:** (415)492-9325. **E-mail:** office@practicalwinery.com; tina@practicalwinery.com. **Website:** www.practicalwinery.com. **Contact:** Don Neel, publisher/editor; Tina Vierra, associate publisher. **50% freelance written.** Bimonthly magazine covering winemaking, grapegrowing, and wine marketing. *"Practical Winery & Vineyard* is a technical trade journal for winemakers and grapegrowers. All articles are fact-checked and peer-reviewed prior to publication to ensure 100% accuracy, readability, and practical useful application for readers. No consumer-focused wine articles, please." Estab. 1979. Circ. 4,000. Byline given. Publishes ms an average of 6-9 months after acceptance. Editorial lead time 6-9 months. Submit seasonal material 9 months in advance. Accepts queries by mail, e-mail, fax. Responds in 1-2 weeks to queries. Responds in 1 month to mss. Guidelines by e-mail.

NONFICTION **Contact:** Tina L. Vierra, associate publisher. Needs how-to, technical. Special issues: "Each issue has a specific topic/focus. Please see Editorial Calendar. We do not want any wine consumer trends, retail info, or wine tasting notes; no food, travel, wine lifestyles." **Buys 25 mss/year.** Query with published clips. Length: 1,000-3,000 words. **Pays 25-50¢ a word for assigned articles. Pays 25-35¢ a word for unsolicited articles.**

⊛⊛⊛ VINEYARD & WINERY MANAGEMENT

P.O. Box 14459, Santa Rosa CA 95402. (707)577-7700. **Fax:** (707)577-7705. **E-mail:** tcaputo@vwm-online.com. **Website:** www.vwm-online.com. **Contact:** Tina Caputo, editor-in-chief. **80% freelance written.** Bimonthly magazine of professional importance to grape growers, winemakers, and winery sales and business people. "Headquartered in Sonoma County,

California, we proudly remain as a leading independent wine trade magazine serving all of North America." Estab. 1975. Circ. 6,500. Byline given. 20% kill fee. Accepts queries by e-mail. Responds in 3 weeks to queries. Responds in 1 month to mss. Guidelines for by e-mail.

NONFICTION Needs how-to, interview, new product, technical. **Buys 30 mss/year.** Query. Length: 1,500-2,000 words. **Pays approximately $500/feature.** Sometimes pays expenses of writers on assignment.

⊛⊛ WINES & VINES

Wine Communications Group, 65 Mitchell Blvd., Suite A, San Rafael CA 94903. (415)453-9700. **Fax:** (415)453-2517. **E-mail:** edit@winesandvines.com. **Website:** www.winesandvines.com. **Contact:** Kerry Kirkham, technical editor. **50% freelance written.** Monthly magazine covering the North American winegrape and winemaking industry. "Since 1919, *Wines & Vines Magazine* has been the authoritative voice of the wine and grape industry—from prohibition to phylloxera, we have covered it all. Our paid circulation reaches all 50 states and many foreign countries. Because we are intended for the trade—including growers, winemakers, winery owners, wholesalers, restauranteurs, and serious amateurs—we accept more technical, informative articles. We do not accept wine reviews, wine country tours, or anything of a wine consumer nature." Estab. 1919. Circ. 5,000. Byline given. Pays 30 days after acceptance. Publishes ms an average of 3 months after acceptance. Editorial lead time 2 months. Submit seasonal material 4 months in advance. Accepts queries by e-mail. Responds in 2-3 weeks to queries. Sample copy for $5. Guidelines free.

NONFICTION Needs interview, new product, technical. "No wine reviews, wine country travelogues, 'lifestyle' pieces, or anything aimed at wine consumers. Our readers are professionals in the field." **Buys 60 mss/year.** Query with published clips. Length: 1,000-2,000 words. **Pays flat fee of $500 for assigned articles.**

BOOK AND BOOKSTORE

⊛ THE BLOOMSBURY REVIEW

Dept. WM, Owaissa Communications Co., Inc., P.O. Box 8928, Denver CO 80201. (303)455-3123. **Fax:** (303)455-7039. **E-mail:** bloomsb@aol.com. **75% freelance written.** Quarterly tabloid covering books and book-related matters. "We publish book reviews, interviews with writers and poets, literary essays, and original poetry. Our audience consists of educated, literate, nonspecialized readers." Estab. 1980. Circ. 35,000. Byline given. Publishes ms an average of 4-6 months after acceptance. Accepts queries by mail. Responds in 4 months to queries. Sample copy for $5 and 9x12 SASE. Guidelines for #10 SASE.

NONFICTION Needs essays, interview, book reviews. **Buys 60 mss/year.** Send complete ms. Length: 800-1,500 words. **Pays $10-20. Sometimes pays writers with contributor copies or other premiums if writer agrees.**

COLUMNS Book reviews and essays, 500-1,500 words. **Buys 6 mss/year.** Query with published clips or send complete ms. **Pays $10-20.**

POETRY Contact: Ray Gonzalez, poetry editor. Needs Needs avant-garde, free verse, haiku, traditional. Buys 20 poems/year. Submit maximum 5 poems. **Pays $5-10.**

⊖⊖ FOREWORD REVIEWS

425 Boardman Ave., Suite B, Traverse City MI 49684. (231)933-3699. **Fax:** (231)933-3899. **E-mail:** victoria@ forewordreviews.com. **Website:** www.forewordreviews.com. **Contact:** Victoria Sutherland, publisher. **95% freelance written.** Bimonthly magazine covering reviews of good books independently published. "In each issue of the magazine, there are 3 to 4 feature *ForeSight* articles focusing on trends in popular categories. These are in addition to the 75 or more critical reviews of forthcoming titles from independent presses in our *Review* section. While we try very hard to communicate with publicity departments concerning calls for submissions to the *ForeSight* features, we also hope that publishers will keep these forms handy to track what's happening at *ForeWord.* Look online for our review submission guidelines or view the 2012 editorial calendar. Be sure to read the *ForeWord* Ten-Point Tip Sheet, which outlines how to make sure you know how to present your book for best results." Estab. 1998. Circ. 20,000 (about 85% librarians, 12% bookstores, 3% publishing professionals). Byline given. Pays 2 months after publication. Publishes ms an average of 2-3 months after acceptance. Editorial lead time 3-4 months. Submit seasonal material 5 months in advance. Accepts queries by mail, e-mail. Responds in 1 month to queries. Responds in 1 month to mss. Sample copy for $10 and 8 ½ x11 SASE with $1.50 postage.

NONFICTION Query with published clips. All review submissions should be sent to the Book Review

Editor. Submissions should include a fact sheet or press release. Length: 400-1,500 words. **Pays $25-200 for assigned articles.**

THE HORN BOOK MAGAZINE

The Horn Book, Inc., 56 Roland St., Suite 200, Boston MA 02129. (617)628-0225. **Fax:** (617)628-0882. **Website:** www.hbook.com. Cynthia Ritter, editorial assistant. **75% freelance written. Prefers to work with published/established writers.** Bimonthly magazine covering children's literature for librarians, booksellers, professors, teachers and students of children's literature. Estab. 1924. Circ. 8,000. Byline given. Publishes ms an average of 4 months after acceptance. Submit seasonal material 6 months in advance. Accepts queries by mail, e-mail, fax. Accepts simultaneous submissions. Responds in 3 months to queries. Sample copy and writer's guidelines online.

NONFICTION Needs , interviews with children's book authors and illustrators, topics of interest to the children's bookworld. **Buys 20 mss/year.** Query or send complete ms. Preferred length: 1,000-2,500 words. **Pays honorarium upon publication.**

⊖ VIDEO LIBRARIAN

3435 NE Nine Boulder Dr., Poulsbo WA 98370. (360)626-1259. **Fax:** (360)626-1260. **E-mail:** vidlib@ videolibrarian.com. **Website:** www.videolibrarian.com. **75% freelance written.** Bimonthly magazine covering DVD reviews for librarians. "*Video Librarian* reviews approximately 225 titles in each issue: children's, documentaries, how-to's, movies, TV, music and anime." Estab. 1986. Circ. 2,000. Byline given. Publishes ms an average of 2 months after acceptance. Editorial lead time 2 months. Accepts queries by e-mail. Accepts simultaneous submissions. Responds in 1 week to queries. Sample copy for $11.

NONFICTION **Buys 500+ mss/year.** Query with published clips. Length: 200-300 words. **Pays $10-20/review.**

BRICK, GLASS AND CERAMICS

⊖⊖ GLASS MAGAZINE

National Glass Association, 8200 Greensboro Dr., Suite 302, McLean VA 22102. (866)342-5642, ext. 150. **Fax:** (703)442-0630. **E-mail:** editorialinfo@glass.org. **Website:** www.glassmagazine.com. **Contact:** Jenni Chase, editor. **10% freelance written. Prefers to work**

with published/established writers. Monthly magazine covering the architectural glass industry. Estab. 1948. Circ. 23,000. Byline given. Offers kill fee. Kill fee varies. Publishes ms an average of 6 months after acceptance. Accepts queries by mail, e-mail, fax. Responds in 2 months to mss. Sample copy for $5 and 9x12 SASE with 10 first-class stamps.

NONFICTION Needs interview, of various glass businesses; profiles of industry people or glass business owners, new product, technical, about glazing processes. **Buys 5 mss/year.** Query with published clips. 1,000 words minimum. **Pays $150-300.**

$ STAINED GLASS

Stained Glass Association of America, 9313 East 63rd St., Raytown MO 64133. (800)438-9581. **Fax:** (816)737-2801. **E-mail:** quarterly@sgaaonline.com; webmaster@sgaaonline.com. **Website:** www.stainedglass.org. **Contact:** Richard Gross, editor and media director. **70% freelance written.** Quarterly magazine. "Since 1906, *Stained Glass* has been the official voice of the Stained Glass Association of America. As the oldest, most respected stained glass publication in North America, *Stained Glass* preserves the techniques of the past as well as illustrates the trends of the future. This vital information, of significant value to the professional stained glass studio, is also of interest to those for whom stained glass is an avocation or hobby." Estab. 1906. Circ. 8,000. Byline given. Publishes ms an average of 1 year after acceptance. Editorial lead time 6 months. Submit seasonal material 8 months in advance. Accepts queries by mail, e-mail, fax. Responds in 3 months to queries. Guidelines on website.

NONFICTION Needs how-to, humor, interview, new product, opinion, photo feature, technical. **Buys 9 mss/year.** Query or send complete ms, but must include photos or slides—very heavy on photos. Length: 2,500-3,500 words. **Pays $125/illustrated article; $75/nonillustrated.**

COLUMNS Columns must be illustrated. Teknixs (technical, how-to, stained and glass art), word length varies by subject. **Buys 4 mss/year.** Query or send complete ms, but must be illustrated.

BUILDING INTERIORS

$ $ FABRICS + FURNISHINGS INTERNATIONAL

SIPCO Publications + Events, 3 Island Ave., Suite 6i, Miami Beach FL 33139. **E-mail:** eric@sipco.net.

Website: www.fandfi.com. **Contact:** Eric Schneider, editor/publisher. **10% freelance written.** Bimonthly magazine covering commercial, hospitality interior design, and manufacturing. *F+FI* covers news from vendors who supply the hospitality interiors industry. Estab. 1990. Circ. 11,000+. Byline given. Offers $100 kill fee. Editorial lead time 3 months. Submit seasonal material 3 months in advance. Accepts queries by e-mail. Accepts simultaneous submissions.

NONFICTION Needs interview, technical. "Does no opinion, consumer pieces. Our readers must learn something from our stories." Query with published clips. Length: 500-1,000 words. **Pays $250-350.**

$ $ QUALIFIED REMODELER

Cygnus Business Media, 1233 Janesville Ave., Fort Atkinson WI 53538. **E-mail:** Rob.Heselbarth@cygnusb2b.com. **Website:** www.qualifiedremodeler.com. **Contact:** Rob Heselbarth, editorial director. **5% freelance written.** Monthly magazine covering residential remodeling. Estab. 1975. Circ. 83,500. Byline given. Publishes ms an average of 1 month after acceptance. Editorial lead time 3 months. Submit seasonal material 2 months in advance. Accepts queries by mail, e-mail, fax, phone.

NONFICTION Needs how-to, business management, new product, photo feature, best practices articles, innovative design. **Buys 12 mss/year.** Query with published clips. Length: 1,200-2,500 words. **Pays $300-600 for assigned articles. Pays $200-400 for unsolicited articles.** Sometimes pays expenses of writers on assignment.

COLUMNS Query with published clips. **Pays $400**

$ $ $ $ REMODELING

HanleyWood, LLC, One Thomas Circle NW, Suite 600, Washington D.C. 20005. (202)452-0800. **Fax:** (202)785-1974. **E-mail:** salfano@hanleywood.com; ibush@hanleywood.com. **Website:** www.remodelingmagazine.com. **Contact:** Sal Alfano, editorial director; Ingrid Bush, managing editor. **10% freelance written.** Monthly magazine covering residential and light commercial remodeling. "We cover the best new ideas in remodeling design, business, construction and products." Estab. 1985. Circ. 80,000. Byline given. Offers 5¢/word kill fee. Publishes ms an average of 3 months after acceptance. Accepts queries by mail, e-mail, fax.

NONFICTION Needs interview, new product, technical, small business trends. **Buys 6 mss/year.** Query with published clips. Length: 250-1,000 words. **Pays $1/word.** Sometimes pays expenses of writers on assignment.

BUSINESS MANAGEMENT

➍ $$$$$ BEDTIMES

International Sleep Products Association, 501 Wythe St., Alexandria VA 22314. (571)482-5442. **E-mail:** jpalm@sleepproducts.org. **Website:** www.bedtimes-magazine.com; www.sleepproducts.org. **Contact:** Julie Palm, editor. **20-40% freelance written.** Monthly magazine covering the mattress manufacturing industry. "Our news and features are straightforward—we are not a lobbying vehicle for our association. No special slant." Estab. 1917. Circ. 3,800. Byline given. Publishes ms an average of 3 months after acceptance. Editorial lead time 2 months. Accepts queries by e-mail. Accepts simultaneous submissions. Responds in 1 month to queries. Sample copy for $4. Guidelines by e-mail.

NONFICTION No pieces that do not relate to business in general or mattress industry in particular. **Buys 15-25/year mss/year.** Query with published clips. Length: 500-2,500 words. **Pays 50-$1/word for short features; $2,000 for cover story.**

$$$ BUSINESS TRAVEL EXECUTIVE

11 Ryerson Ave., Suite 201, Pompton Plains NJ 07444. **E-mail:** jallison@askbte.com; DBooth@askbte.com. **Website:** www.askbte.com. Editorial Office: 5768 Remington Dr., Winston-Salem, NC 27104, (336)766-1961. **Contact:** Gerald Allison, publisher. **90% freelance written.** Monthly magazine covering corporate procurement of travel services. "We are not a travel magazine. We publish articles designed to help corporate purchasers of travel negotiate contracts, enforce policy, select automated services, track business travelers, and account for their safety and expenditures, understand changes in the various industries associated with travel. Do not submit mss without an assignment. Look at the website for an idea of what we publish." Byline given. Publishes ms an average of 2 months after acceptance. Editorial lead time 0-3 months. Accepts queries by e-mail.

NONFICTION Needs how-to, technical. **Buys 48 mss/year.** Query. Length: 800-2,000 words. **Pays $200-800.**

COLUMNS Meeting Place (meeting planning and management); Hotel Pulse (hotel negotiations, con-

tracting and compliance); Security Watch (travel safety); all 1,000 words. **Buys 24 mss/year.** Query. **Pays $200-400.**

$$ CBA RETAILERS + RESOURCES

CBA, the Association for Christian Retail, 9240 Explorer Dr., Suite 200, Colorado Springs CO 80920. **Fax:** (719)272-3510. **E-mail:** ksamuelson@cbaonline.org. **Website:** www.cbaonline.org. **30% freelance written.** Monthly magazine covering the Christian retail industry. "Writers must have knowledge of and direct experience in the Christian retail industry. Subject matter must specifically pertain to the Christian retail audience." Estab. 1968. Byline given. Publishes ms an average of 3 months after acceptance. Editorial lead time 3 months. Submit seasonal material 6 months in advance. Accepts queries by e-mail. Responds in 2 months to queries. Sample copy for $9.50 or online.

NONFICTION **Buys 24 mss/year.** Query. Length: 750-1,500 words. **Pays 30¢/word upon publication.**

$$ CONTRACTING PROFITS

Trade Press Publishing, 2100 W. Florist Ave., Milwaukee WI 53209. (414)228-7701; (800)727-7995. **Fax:** (414)228-1134. **E-mail:** dan.weltin@tradepress.com. **Website:** www.cleanlink.com/cp. **Contact:** Dan Weltin, editor-in-chief. **40% freelance written.** Magazine published 10 times/year covering building service contracting and business management advice. "We are the pocket MBA for this industry—focusing not only on cleaning-specific topics, but also discussing how to run businesses better and increase profits through a variety of management articles." Estab. 1995. Circ. 32,000. Byline given. Pays within 30 days of acceptance. Editorial lead time 2 months. Submit seasonal material 3 months in advance. Accepts queries by mail, e-mail. Responds in weeks to queries. Guidelines free.

NONFICTION Needs exposé, how-to, interview, technical. No product-related reviews or testimonials. **Buys 30 mss/year.** Query with published clips. Length: 1,000-1,500 words. **Pays $100-500.** Sometimes pays expenses of writers on assignment.

COLUMNS Query with published clips.

$$$ EXPO

Red 7 Media, 10 Norden Place, Norwalk CT 06855. (203)899-8438. **E-mail:** traphael@red7media.com; lbarney@red7media.com. **E-mail:** tsilber@red7media.com. **Website:** www.expoweb.com. **Contact:** Tony Silber, general manager; T.J. Raphael, associate editor; Lee Barney, executive editor. **80% freelance written.** Magazine covering expositions. Byline given. Offers 50% kill fee. Editorial lead time 3 months. Accepts queries by mail, e-mail, fax. Responds in 3 weeks to queries. Sample copy and guidelines free.

NONFICTION Needs how-to, interview. Query with published clips. Length: 600-2,400 words. **Pays 50¢/word.** Pays expenses of writers on assignment.

COLUMNS Profile (personality profile), 650 words; Exhibitor Matters (exhibitor issues) and EXPOTech (technology), both 600-1,300 words. **Buys 10 mss/year.** Query with published clips.

💲💲💲 FAMILY BUSINESS MAGAZINE

Family Business Publishing Co., Family Business Magazine, 1845 Walnut St., Philadelphia PA 19103. **Fax:** (215)405-6078. **E-mail:** bspector@familybusinessmagazine.com. **Website:** www.familybusinessmagazine.com. **Contact:** Barbara Spector, editor-in-chief. **50% freelance written.** Quarterly magazine covering family-owned companies. "Written expressly for family company owners and advisors. Focuses on business and human dynamic issues unique to family enterprises. Offers practical guidance and tried-and-true solutions for business stakeholders." Estab. 1989. Circ. 6,000. Byline given. Offers 30% kill fee. Publishes ms an average of 9-12 months after acceptance. Editorial lead time 6 months. Submit seasonal material 6 months in advance. Accepts queries by e-mail only. Guidelines available online.

NONFICTION Needs how-to, family business related only, interview, personal experience. "No small business articles, articles that aren't specifically related to multi-generational family companies (no general business advice). No success stories—there must be an underlying family or business lesson. No payment for articles written by family business advisors and other service providers." **Buys 24 mss/year.** Query with published clips. E-mail queries required. Length: 1,500-2,000 words. **Pays $50-1,400 for articles written by freelance reporters.**

💲💲 INTENTS

Industrial Fabrics Association International, 1801 County Rd. B W, Roseville MN 55113-4061. (651)225-2508; (800)-225-4324. **Fax:** (651)631-9334. **E-mail:** srniemi@ifai.com; jclafferty@ifai.com; generalinfo@ifai.com. **Website:** www.ifai.com. **Contact:** Susan R. Niemi, pub-

lisher; Jill C. Lafferty, editor. **50% freelance written.** Bimonthly magazine covering tent-rental and special-event industries. Estab. 1994. Circ. 12,000. Byline given. Publishes ms an average of 2 months after acceptance. Editorial lead time 3 months. Accepts queries by mail, e-mail, fax. Sample copy and writer's guidelines free.

NONFICTION Needs how-to, interview, new product, photo feature, technical. **Buys 12-18 mss/year.** Query. Length: 800-2,000 words. **Pays $300-500.** Sometimes pays expenses of writers on assignment.

💲💲 MAINEBIZ

Mainebiz Publications, Inc., 2 Cotton St., 3rd Floor, Portland ME 04101. (207)761-8379. **Fax:** (207)761-0732. **E-mail:** ccoultas@mainebiz.biz. **Website:** www.mainebiz.biz. **Contact:** Carol Coultas, editor. **25% freelance written.** Biweekly tabloid covering business in Maine. *Mainebiz* is read by business decision makers across the state. They look to the publication for business news and analysis. Estab. 1994. Circ. 13,000. Byline given. Offers 10% kill fee. Publishes ms an average of 1 month after acceptance. Editorial lead time 1 month. Submit seasonal material 2 months in advance. Accepts queries by mail, e-mail. Responds in 3 weeks to queries.

NONFICTION Needs essays, exposé, interview, business trends. Special issues: See website for editorial calendar. **Buys 50+ mss/year.** Query with published clips. Length: 500-2,500 words. **Pays $50-250.** Pays expenses of writers on assignment.

💲💲 RETAIL INFO SYSTEMS NEWS

Edgell Communications, 4 Middlebury Blvd., Randolph NJ 07869. (973)607-1300. **Fax:** (973)607-1395. **E-mail:** ablair@edgellmail.com; jskorupa@edgellmail.com. **Website:** www.risnews.com. **Contact:** Adam Blair, editor; Joe Skorupa, group editor-in-chief. **65% freelance written.** Monthly magazine covering retail technology. Estab. 1988. Circ. 22,000. Byline sometimes given. Publishes ms an average of 2 months after acceptance. Editorial lead time 3 months. Submit seasonal material 3 months in advance. Accepts queries by mail.

NONFICTION Needs essays, exposé, how-to, humor, interview, technical. **Buys 80 mss/year.** Query with published clips. Length: 700-1,900 words. **Pays $600-1,200 for assigned articles.** Sometimes pays expenses of writers on assignment.

COLUMNS News/trends (analysis of current events), 150-300 words. **Buys 4 articles/year mss/year.** Query with published clips. **Pays $100-300.**

⊖⊖ RTOHQ: THE MAGAZINE

1504 Robin Hood Trail, Austin TX 78703. (800)204-2776. **Fax:** (512)794-0097. **E-mail:** bkeese@rtohq.org. **Website:** www.rtohq.org. **Contact:** Bill Keese, executive editor. **50% freelance written.** Bimonthly magazine covering the rent-to-own industry. *RTOHQ: The Magazine* is the only publication representing the rent-to-own industry and members of APRO. The magazine covers timely news and features affecting the industry, association activities, and member profiles. Awarded best 4-color magazine by the American Society of Association Executives in 1999. Estab. 1980. Circ. 5,500. Byline given. Offers 25% kill fee. Publishes ms an average of 2 months after acceptance. Editorial lead time 2 months. Submit seasonal material 4 months in advance. Accepts queries by mail, e-mail, fax, phone, online submission form. Accepts simultaneous submissions. Responds in 1 month to queries. Responds in 2 months to mss.

NONFICTION Needs exposé, general interest, how-to, inspirational, interview, technical, industry features. **Buys 12 mss/year.** Query with published clips. Length: 1,200-2,500 words. **Pays $150-700.** Sometimes pays expenses of writers on assignment.

⊖⊖ STAMATS MEETINGS MEDIA

655 Montgomery St., Suite 900, San Francisco CA 94111. **Fax:** (415)788-1358. **E-mail:** tyler.davidson@meetingsfocus.com. **Website:** www.meetingsmedia.com. **Contact:** Tyler Davidson, chief content director. **75% freelance written.** Monthly tabloid covering meeting, event, and conference planning. Estab. 1986. Circ. *Meetings East* and *Meetings South* 22,000; *Meetings West* 26,000. Byline given. Pays 1 month after publication. Publishes ms an average of 1 month after acceptance. Editorial lead time 3 months. Submit seasonal material 3 months in advance. Accepts queries by mail, e-mail, fax. Responds in 3 weeks to queries. Sample copy for DSR with 9x13 envelope and 5 first-class stamps.

NONFICTION Needs how-to, travel, as it pertains to meetings and conventions. "No first-person fluff—this is a business magazine." **Buys 150 mss/year.** Query with published clips. Length: 1,200-2,000 words. **Pays $500 flat rate/package.**

⊖ THE STATE JOURNAL

WorldNow, P.O. Box 11848, Charleston WV 25339-1848. (304)344-1630; (304)395-3649. **E-mail:** bgryan@statejournal.com. **Website:** www.statejournal.com.

Contact: Beth Gorczyca Ryan, managing editor. **30% freelance written.** "We are a weekly journal dedicated to providing stories of interest to the business community in West Virginia." Estab. 1984. Circ. 10,000. Byline given. Publishes ms an average of 3 weeks after acceptance. Submit seasonal material 4 months in advance. Accepts queries by mail, e-mail, fax. Sample copy and writer's guidelines for #10 SASE.

NONFICTION Needs general interest, interview, new product, (all business related). **Buys 400 mss/year.** Query. Length: 250-1,500 words. **Pays $50.** Sometimes pays expenses of writers on assignment.

⊖⊖ SUSTAINABLE INDUSTRIES

Sustainable Industries Media, LLC, P.O. Box 460324, San Francisco CA 94146. (415)762-3945. **E-mail:** sarah@sustainableindustries.com. **Website:** www.sustainableindustries.com. **Contact:** Sara Stroud, associate editor. **20% freelance written.** Bimonthly magazine covering environmental innovation in business. "We seek high quality, balanced reporting aimed at business readers. More compelling writing than is typical in standard trade journals." Estab. 2003. Circ. 2,500. Byline sometimes given. Publishes ms an average of 1-3 months after acceptance. Editorial lead time 1-2 months. Accepts queries by mail, e-mail. Accepts simultaneous submissions.

NONFICTION Needs general interest, how-to, interview, new product, opinion, news briefs. Special issues: Themes rotate on the following topics: Agriculture & Natural Resources; Green Building; Energy; Government; Manufacturing & Technology; Retail & Service; Transportation & Tourism—though all topics are covered in each issue. No prosaic essays or extra-long pieces. Query with published clips. Length: 500-1,500 words. **Pays $0-500.**

COLUMNS Guest columns accepted, but not compensated. Business trade columns on specific industries: 500-1,000 words. Query.

⊖ ⊖⊖ VENECONOMY/VENECONOMA

VenEconomia, Edificio Gran Sabana, Piso 1, Ave. Abraham Lincoln, No. 174, Blvd. de Sabana Grande, Caracas Venezuela. (58)(212)761-8121. **Fax:** (58)(212)762-8160. **E-mail:** mercadeo@veneconomia.com. **Website:** www.veneconoma.com; www.veneconomy.com. **70% freelance written.** Monthly business magazine covering business, political, and social issues in Venezuela. "*VenEconomy*'s subscribers are mostly business people, both Venezuelans and foreigners doing business in Venezuela. Some academics and diplomats also read our magazine. The magazine is published monthly both in English and Spanish—freelancers may query us in either language. Our slant is decidedly pro-business, but not dogmatically conservative. Development, human rights, political, and environmental issues are covered from a business-friendly angle." Estab. 1983. Byline given. Offers 50% kill fee. Publishes ms an average of 1 month after acceptance. Editorial lead time 1-2 months. Submit seasonal material 1 month in advance. Accepts queries by e-mail. Accepts simultaneous submissions. Responds in 2 weeks to queries. Responds in 4 months to mss. Sample copy by e-mail.

NONFICTION Contact: Francisco Toro, political editor. Needs essays, exposé, interview, new product, opinion. No first-person stories or travel articles. **Buys 50 mss/year.** Query. Length: 1,100-3,200 words. **Pays 10-15¢/word for assigned articles.** Sometimes pays expenses of writers on assignment.

$$$ WORLD TRADE

20900 Farnsleigh Rd., Shaker Heights OH 44122. (424)634-2499; (216)991-4861. **E-mail:** hardings@worldtradewt100.com; walzm@bnpmedia.com. **Website:** www.worldtrademag.com. **Contact:** Sarah Harding, publisher; Martha L. Walz, editor-in-chief; Mike Powell, art director. **50% freelance written.** Monthly magazine covering international business. Estab. 1988. Circ. 75,000. Byline given. Publishes ms an average of 1 month after acceptance. Editorial lead time 3 months. Accepts queries by mail, fax.

NONFICTION Needs interview, technical, market reports, finance, logistics. **Buys 40-50 mss/year.** Query with published clips. Length: 450-1,500 words. **Pays 50¢/word.**

COLUMNS International Business Services, 800 words; Shipping, Supply Chain Management, Logistics, 800 words; Software & Technology, 800 words; Economic Development (US, International), 800 words. **Buys 40-50 mss/year. Pays 50¢/word.**

CHURCH ADMINISTRATION AND MINISTRY

$ CHRISTIAN COMMUNICATOR

9118 W. Elmwood Dr., Suite 1G, Niles IL 60714-5820. (847)296-3964. **Fax:** (847)296-0754. **E-mail:** ljohnson@wordprocommunications.com. **Website:** acwriters.com. **Contact:** Lin Johnson, managing editor. **70% freelance written.** Monthly magazine covering Christian writing and speaking. Circ. 4,000. Byline given. Publishes ms an average of 6-12 months after acceptance. Editorial lead time 3 months. Submit seasonal material 9 months in advance. Accepts queries by e-mail. Responds in 6-8 weeks to queries. Responds in 8-12 weeks to mss. Sample copy for SAE and 5 first-class stamps. Writer's guidelines for SASE, by e-mail, or online.

NONFICTION Needs how-to, interview, book reviews. **Buys 90 mss/year.** Query or send complete ms only by e-mail. Length: 650-1,000 words. **Pays $10. $5 for reviews. ACW CD for anecdotes.**

COLUMNS Speaking, 650-1,000 words. **Buys 11 mss/year.** Query. **Pays $10.**

POETRY Needs free verse, light verse, traditional. Buys Publishes 22 poems/year. poems/year. Submit maximum Maximum number of poems: 3. poems. Length: 4-20 lines. **Pays $5.**

FILLERS Needs anecdotes, short humor. **Buys 10-30 mss/year.** Length: 75-300 words. **Pays CD.**

$ CREATOR MAGAZINE

P.O. Box 3538, Pismo Beach CA 93448. (800)777-6713. **E-mail:** customerservice@creatormagazine.com. **Website:** www.creatormagazine.com. **Contact:** Bob Burroughs, editor. **35% freelance written.** Bimonthly magazine. Most readers are church music directors and worship leaders. Content focuses on the spectrum of worship styles from praise and worship to traditional to liturgical. All denominations subscribe. Articles on worship, choir rehearsal, handbells, children's/youth choirs, technique, relationships, etc. Estab. 1978. Circ. 6,000. Byline given. Publishes ms an average of 3 months after acceptance. Editorial lead time 3 months. Submit seasonal material 4 months in advance. Accepts queries by mail. Accepts simultaneous submissions. Sample copy for SAE with 9x12 envelope and 5 first-class stamps. Guidelines free.

NONFICTION Needs essays, how-to, be a better church musician, choir director, rehearsal technician, etc., humor, short personal perspectives, inspirational, interview, call first, new product, call first, opinion, personal experience, photo feature, religious, technical, choral technique. Special issues: July/August is directed toward adult choir members, rather than directors. **Buys 20 mss/year.** Query or send complete ms. Length: 1,000-10,000 words. **Pays $30-75 for as-**

signed articles. **Pays $30-60 for unsolicited articles.** Pays expenses of writers on assignment.

COLUMNS Hints & Humor (music ministry short ideas, cute anecdotes, ministry experience), 75-250 words; Inspiration (motivational ministry stories), 200-500 words; Children/Youth (articles about specific choirs), 1,000-5,000 words. **Buys 15 mss/year.** Query or send complete ms. **Pays $20-60.**

💲💲 GROUP MAGAZINE

Simply Youth Ministry, 1515 Cascade Ave., Loveland CO 80538. (970)669-3836. **E-mail:** sfirestone@group.com. **Website:** http://groupmagazine.com. **Contact:** Scott Firestone. **50% freelance written.** Bimonthly magazine for Christian youth workers. "*Group* is the interdenominational magazine for leaders of Christian youth groups. *Group*'s purpose is to supply ideas, practical help, inspiration, and training for youth leaders." Estab. 1974. Circ. 55,000. Byline sometimes given. Editorial lead time 4 months. Submit seasonal material 5 months in advance. Accepts queries by mail, e-mail, fax. Responds in 8-10 weeks to queries. Responds in 2 months to mss. Sample copy for $2, plus 10x12 SAE and 3 first-class stamps. Guidelines available online.

NONFICTION Needs inspirational, personal experience, religious. No fiction, prose, or poetry. **Buys 30 mss/year.** Query. Length: 200-2,000 words. **Pays $50-250.** Sometimes pays expenses of writers on assignment.

COLUMNS "Try This One" section needs short ideas (100-250 words) for youth group use. These include games, fund-raisers, crowdbreakers, Bible studies, helpful hints, outreach ideas, and discussion starters. "Hands-on Help" section needs mini-articles (100-350 words) that feature practical tips for youth leaders on working with students, adult leaders, and parents. **Pays $50.**

💲💲 THE JOURNAL OF ADVENTIST EDUCATION

General Conference of SDA, 12501 Old Columbia Pike, Silver Spring MD 20904-6600. (301)680-5069. **Fax:** (301)622-9627. **E-mail:** rumbleb@gc.adventist.org; goffc@gc.adventist.org. **Website:** http://jae.adventist.org. Chandra Goff. **Contact:** Beverly J. Robinson-Rumble, editor. Bimonthly (except skips issue in summer) professional journal covering teachers and administrators in Seventh Day Adventist school systems. Published 5 times/year in English, 2 times/year in French, Spanish, and Portuguese. Emphasizes procedures, philosophy and subject matter of Christian education. Estab. 1939. Circ. 14,000 in English; 13,000 in other languages. Byline given. Publishes ms an average of 1 year after acceptance. Editorial lead time 1 year. Accepts queries by mail, e-mail, fax, phone. Responds in 6 weeks to queries. Responds in 4 months to mss. Sample copy for sae with 10x12 envelope and 5 First-Class stamps. Guidelines available online.

NONFICTION Needs book excerpts, essays, how-to, education-related, personal experience, photo feature, religious, education. "No brief first-person stories about Sunday Schools." "Query. Articles submitted on disk or by e-mail as attached files are welcome. Store in MS Word or WordPerfect format. If you submit a CD, be sure to include a printed copy of the article with the CD. Articles should be 6-8 pages long, with a max of 10 pages, including references. Two-part articles will be considered." Length: 1,000-1,500 words. **Pays $25-300.**

💲 KIDS' MINISTRY IDEAS

Review and Herald Publishing Association, 55 W. Oak Ridge Dr., Hagerstown MD 21740. (301)393-3178. **Fax:** (301)393-3209. **E-mail:** kidsmin@rhpa.org. **Website:** www.kidsministryideas.com. **Contact:** Editor. **95% freelance written.** "A quarterly resource for children's leaders, those involved in Vacation Bible School and Story Hours, home school teachers, etc., *Kids' Ministry Ideas* provides affirmation, pertinent and informative articles, program ideas, resource suggestions, and answers to questions from a Seventh-day Adventist Christian perspective." Estab. 1991. Circ. 3,000. Byline given. Publishes ms an average of 3 months after acceptance. Editorial lead time 3 months. Submit seasonal material 6 months to one year in advance. Accepts queries by mail, e-mail, fax. Responds in 3 weeks to queries. Responds in 3 months to mss. Writer's guidelines online.

NONFICTION Needs inspirational, new product, related to children's ministry, articles fitting the mission of *Kids' Ministry Ideas*. **Buys 40-60 mss/year.** Send complete ms. **Features:** Articles generally cover a 2-page spread and should be no more than 800 words. One-page articles should be 300 words. Queries are welcome. Length: 300-800 words. **Pays $20-100 for assigned articles. Pays $20-70 for unsolicited articles. Writers can expect payment within 5-6 weeks of acceptance. Upon publication, authors are sent**

1 complimentary copy of the issue in which their material appears.

COLUMNS **Buys 20-30 mss/year.** Query. **Pays $20-100.**

$ MOMENTUM

National Catholic Educational Association, 1005 N. Glebe Rd., Suite 525, Arlington VA 22201. (571)257-0010. **Fax:** (703)243-0025. **E-mail:** momentum@ncea.org. **Website:** www.ncea.org. **Contact:** Brian E. Gray, editor. **65% freelance written.** Quarterly educational journal covering educational issues in Catholic schools and parishes. *Momentum* is a membership journal of the National Catholic Educational Association. The audience is educators and administrators in Catholic schools K-12, and parish programs. Estab. 1970. Circ. 20,000. Byline given. Publishes ms an average of 3 months after acceptance. Accepts queries by e-mail. Sample copy for $5 SASE and 8 first-class stamps. Guidelines available online.

NONFICTION No articles unrelated to educational and catechesis issues. **Buys 40-60 mss/year.** Query and send complete ms. Length: 1,500 words for feature articles; 3,500-5,000 for research articles; 500-750 words for book reviews. **Pays $75 maximum.**

COLUMNS From the Field (practical application in classroom); DRE Directions (parish catechesis), both 700 words. **Buys 10 columns. mss/year.** Query and send complete ms. **Pays $50.**

$ $ THE PRIEST

Our Sunday Visitor, Inc., 200 Noll Plaza, Huntington IN 46750. (800)348-2440. **Fax:** (260)359-9117. **E-mail:** tpriest@osv.com. **Website:** www.osv.com. **Contact:** Editorial Department. **40% freelance written.** Monthly magazine. Byline given. Editorial lead time 3 months. Submit seasonal material 4 months in advance. Accepts queries by mail, e-mail, fax, phone. Responds in 5 weeks to queries. Responds in 3 months to mss. Writer's guidelines on website.

NONFICTION Needs essays, historical/nostalgic, humor, inspirational, interview/profile, opinion, personal experience, photo feature, religious. **Buys 96 mss/year.** Send complete ms. Length: 1,500 words maximum. **Pays $200 minimum for assigned articles. Pays $50 minimum for unsolicited articles.**

COLUMNS Viewpoints (whatever applies to priests and the Church); 1,000 words or less; send complete ms.

$ RTJ'S CREATIVE CATECHIST

Twenty-Third Publications, P.O. Box 6015, New London CT 06320. (800)321-0411, ext. 188. **Fax:** (860)437-6246. **E-mail:** rosanne.coffey@bayard-inc.com. **Website:** www.rtjscreativecatechist.com. **Contact:** Rosanne Coffey, editor. Monthly magazine for Catholic catechists and religion teachers. Estab. 1966. Circ. 30,000. Byline given. Publishes ms an average of 3-20 months after acceptance. Editorial lead time 4 months. Submit seasonal material 6 months in advance. Accepts queries by mail, e-mail. Accepts simultaneous submissions. Responds in 1-2 weeks to queries. Responds in 1-2 months to mss. Sample copy for SAE with 9x12 envelope and 3 first-class stamps. Guidelines free.

NONFICTION Needs how-to, inspirational, personal experience, religious, articles on celebrating church seasons, sacraments, on morality, on prayer, on saints. Special issues: Sacraments; Prayer; Advent/Christmas; Lent/Easter. All should be written by people who have experience in religious education, or a good background in Catholic faith. Does not want fiction, poems, plays, articles written for Catholic school teachers (i.e., math, English, etc.), or articles that are academic rather than catechetical in nature. **Buys 35-40 mss/year.** Send complete ms. Length: 600-1,300 words. **Pays $100-125 for assigned articles. Pays $75-125 for unsolicited articles.**

COLUMNS Catechist to Catechist (brief articles on crafts, games, etc., for religion lessons); Faith and Fun (full-page religious word games, puzzles, mazes, etc., for children). **Buys 30 mss/year.** Send complete ms. **Pays $20-125.**

$ $ TODAY'S CATHOLIC TEACHER

Peter Li Education Group, 2621 Dryden Rd., Suite 300, Dayton OH 45439. (937)293-1415; (800)523-4625, x1139. **Fax:** (937)293-1310. **E-mail:** mthomas@peterli.com. **E-mail:** bshepard@peterli.com. **Website:** www.catholicteacher.com. **Contact:** Betsy Shepard, editor; Michael D. Thomas, editor-in-chief. **60% freelance written.** Magazine published 6 times/year during school year covering Catholic education for grades K-12. "We look for topics of interest and practical help to teachers in Catholic elementary schools in all curriculum areas including religion technology, discipline, and motivation." Estab. 1972. Circ. 50,000. Byline given. Publishes ms an average of 2 months after acceptance. Editorial lead time 3 months. Submit seasonal material 6 months in advance. Accepts queries by mail, e-mail, fax. Accepts simultaneous submissions. Responds in 1 month to queries. Responds in 3 months to mss. Sample copy for $3 or on website. Guidelines available online.

NONFICTION Needs essays, how-to, humor, interview, personal experience. No articles pertaining to public education. **Buys 15 mss/year.** Query or send complete ms. Query letters are encouraged. E-mail, write, call, or fax the editor for editorial calendar. Articles may be submitted as hard copy; submission by e-mail with accompanying hard copy is appreciated. Length: 1,500-3,000 words. **Pays $150-300.** Sometimes pays expenses of writers on assignment.

💲💲💲 WORSHIP LEADER MAGAZINE

32234 Paseo Adelanto, Suite A, San Juan Capistrano CA 92675. (888)881-5861. **Fax:** (949)240-0038. **E-mail:** jeremy@wlmag.com. **Website:** www.worshipleader.com. **Contact:** Jeremy Armstrong, managing editor. **80% freelance written.** Bimonthly magazine covering all aspects of Christian worship. "*Worship Leader Magazine* exists to challenge, serve, equip, and train those involved in leading the 21st century church in worship. The intended readership is the worship team (all those who plan and lead) of the local church." Estab. 1990. Circ. 40,000. Byline given. Offers 50% kill fee. Editorial lead time 3 months. Submit seasonal material 6 months in advance. Responds in 6 weeks to queries. Responds in 3 months to mss. Sample copy for $5.

NONFICTION Needs general interest, how-to, related to purpose/audience, inspirational, interview, opinion. **Buys 15-30 mss/year.** Query with published clips. "*Worship Leader* magazine does not accept unsolicited articles for the print version of the magazine. However, we do accept submissions for our Web properties. This is often the first step in creating a relationship with us and our readers, which could lead to more involvement as a writer. Web articles should be between 700 and 900 words and have beneficial qualities to a person who is involved in creating devotional arts or planning a service of worship. Web articles are published on a gratis basis. Please send finished articles to Jeremy Armstrong, jeremy@wlmag.com and potential articles to feedback@wlmag.com." Length: 1,200-2,000 words for print version articles. **Pays $200-800 for assigned articles. Pays $200-500 for unsolicited articles.** Sometimes pays expenses of writers on assignment.

FICTION "You can also submit a song; see www.songdiscovery.com/submit-a-song."

💲 YOUTH AND CHRISTIAN EDUCATION LEADERSHIP

Pathway Press, 1080 Montgomery Ave., Cleveland TN 37311. (800)553-8506. **Fax:** (800)546-7590. **E-mail:** tammy_hatfield@pathwaypress.org. **Website:** www.leadershipmag@pathwaypress.org. **Contact:** Sheila Stewart, editor. **25% freelance written.** Quarterly magazine covering Christian education. *Youth and Christian Education Leadership* is written for teachers, youth pastors, children's pastors, and other local Christian education workers. Estab. 1976. Circ. 12,000. Publishes ms an average of 6 months after acceptance. Editorial lead time 3 months. Submit seasonal material 6 months in advance. Accepts queries by mail, e-mail. Accepts simultaneous submissions. Responds in 3 months to mss. Sample copy for $1.25 and 9x12 SASE. Writer's guidelines online or by e-mail.

NONFICTION Needs how-to, humor, in-class experience, inspire, interview, motivational, seasonal short skits. **Buys 16 mss/year.** Send complete ms; include SSN. Send SASE for return of ms. Internet submissions are accepted. They should be sent as attachments to email and not as part of the email message itself. Length: 500-1,000 words. **Pays $25-50.**

COLUMNS Sunday School Leadership; Reaching Out (creative evangelism); The Pastor and Christian Education; Preschool; Elementary; Teen; Adult; Drawing Closer; Kids Church, all 500-1,000 words. Send complete ms with SASE. **Pays $25-50.**

💲💲 YOUTHWORKER JOURNAL

Salem Publishing/CCM Communications, 402 BNA Dr., Suite 400, Nashville TN 37217-2509. **E-mail:** articles@youthworker.com. **E-mail:** ALee@SalemPublishing.com. **Website:** www.youthworker.com. **Contact:** Steve Rabey, editor; Amy L. Lee, managing editor. **100% freelance written.** Website and bimonthly magazine covering professional youth ministry in the church and parachurch. "We exist to help meet the personal and professional needs of career, Christian youth workers in the church and parachurch. Proposals accepted on the posted theme, according to the writer's guidelines on our website. It's not enough to write well—you must know youth ministry." Estab.

1984. Circ. 20,000. Byline given. Publishes ms an average of 3 months after acceptance for print; immediately online. Editorial lead time 6 months for print; immediately online. Submit seasonal material 6 months in advance for print. Accepts queries by e-mail, online submission form. Responds within 6 weeks to queries. Sample copy for $5. Guidelines available online.

NONFICTION Needs essays, new product, youth ministry books only, personal experience, photo feature, religious. Query. Length: 250-3,000 words. **Pays $15-200.**

CLOTHING

❂❂❂ FOOTWEAR PLUS

9 Threads, 36 Cooper Square, 4th Floor, New York NY 10003. (646)278-1550. **Fax:** (646)278-1553. **Website:** www.footwearplusmagazine.com. **20% freelance written.** Monthly magazine covering footwear fashion and business. "A business-to-business publication targeted at footwear retailers. Covering all categories of footwear and age ranges with a focus on new trends, brands and consumer buying habits, as well as retailer advice on operating the store more effectively." Estab. 1990. Circ. 18,000. Byline given. Publishes ms an average of 1-2 months after acceptance. Editorial lead time 1-2 months. Sample copy for $5.

NONFICTION Needs interview, new product, technical. Does not want pieces unrelated to footwear/fashion industry. **Buys 10-20 mss/year.** Query. Length: 500-2,500 words. **Pays $1,000 maximum.** Sometimes pays expenses of writers on assignment.

CONSTRUCTION AND CONTRACTING

❂❂ AUTOMATED BUILDER

CMN Associates, Inc., 2401 Grapevine Dr., Oxnard CA 93036. (805)351-5931. **Fax:** (805)351-5755. **E-mail:** cms03@pacbell.net. **Website:** www.automatedbuilder.com. **Contact:** Don O. Carlson, editor/publisher. **10% freelance written.** "*Automated Builder* provides management, production and marketing information on all 7 segments of home, apartment and commercial construction, including: (1) production builders, (2) panelized home manufacturers, (3) hud-code (mobile) home manufacturers, (4) modular home manufacturers, (5) component manufacturers, (6) special unit (commercial) manufacturers, and (7) MH

builders and builders/dealers. The material is technical in content and concerned with new technologies or improved methods for in-plant building and components related to building. Online content is uploaded from the monthly print material." Estab. 1964. Circ. 25,000. Byline given. Publishes ms an average of 3 months after acceptance. Editorial lead time 2 months. Submit seasonal material 2 months in advance. Accepts queries by mail, e-mail, fax. Responds in 2 weeks to queries.

NONFICTION "No architect or plan 'dreams.' Housing projects must be built or under construction." **Buys 6-8 mss/year.** Query. Phone queries OK. Length: 250-500 words. **Pays $350 for stories including photos.**

❂❂ BUILDERNEWS MAGAZINE

PNW Publishing, BUILDERnews Magazine, 2105 C St., Vancouver WA 98663. (360)906-0793; (800)401-0696. **Fax:** (360)906-0794. **E-mail:** editing@bnmag.com. **Website:** www.bnmag.com. Estab. 1996. Circ. 35,000. Byline given. Pays on acceptance of revised ms. Publishes ms an average of 1 month after acceptance. Editorial lead time 2 months. Submit seasonal material 3 months in advance. Accepts queries by mail, e-mail, fax. Responds in 1 week to queries. Responds in 1 month to mss. Sample copy for free or online. Guidelines free.

NONFICTION Needs how-to, interview, new product, technical. "No personal bios, unless they teach a valuable lesson to those in the building industry." **Buys 400 mss/year.** Query. Length: 500-2,500 words. **Pays $200-500.** Sometimes pays expenses of writers on assignment.

COLUMNS Engineering; Construction; Architecture & Design; Tools & Materials; Heavy Equipment; Business & Economics; Legal Matters; E-build; Building Green; all 750-2,500 words. Query.

❂❂❂ THE CONCRETE PRODUCER

Hanley-Wood, LLC, 8725 W. Higgins Rd., Suite 600, Chicago IL 60631. (773)824-2400; (773)824-2496. **E-mail:** smitchell@hanleywood.com; ryelton@hanleywood.com. **Website:** www.theconcreteproducer.com. **Contact:** Shelby O. Mitchell, managing editor; Rick Yelton, commercial editorial program and events manager. **25% freelance written.** Monthly magazine covering concrete production. "Our audience consists of producers who have succeeded in making concrete the preferred building material through management, operating, quality control, use of the latest technology, or use of superior materials." Estab. 1982. Circ. 18,000. Byline given. Publishes ms an average of 2 months after acceptance. Editorial lead time 4 months. Accepts queries by mail, e-mail, fax, phone. Responds in 1 week to queries. Responds in 2 months to mss. Sample copy for $4. Guidelines free.

NONFICTION Needs how-to, promote concrete, new product, technical. **Buys 10 mss/year.** Send complete ms. Length: 500-2,000 words. **Pays $200-1,000.** Sometimes pays expenses of writers on assignment.

⊖⊖ FRAME BUILDING NEWS

F+W Media, Inc., 700 E. State St., Iola WI 54990-0001. (715)445-4612, ext. 428. **Fax:** (715)445-4087. **E-mail:** jim.austin@fw.media.com. **Website:** www.framebuildingnews.com. **10% freelance written.** Magazine published 5 times/year covering post-frame building. "*Frame Building News* is the official publication of the National Frame Builders Association, which represents contractors who specialize in post-frame building construction." Estab. 1990. Circ. 20,000. Byline given. Publishes ms an average of 3 months after acceptance. Editorial lead time 3 months. Submit seasonal material 3 months in advance. Accepts queries by mail. Accepts simultaneous submissions.

NONFICTION Needs book excerpts, historical, how-to, interview, new product, opinion, photo feature, technical. No advertorials. **Buys 15 mss/year.** Query with published clips. 750 words minimum. **Pays $100-500 for assigned articles.**

COLUMNS Money Talk (taxes for business); Tech Talk (computers for builders); Tool Talk (tools); Management Insights (business management); all 1,000 words. **Buys 15 mss/year.** Send complete ms. **Pays $0-500.**

⊖ HARD HAT NEWS

Lee Publications, Inc., 6113 State Hwy. 5, P.O. Box 121, Palatine Bridge NY 13428. (518)673-3237. **Fax:** (518)673-2381. **E-mail:** jcasey@leepub.com. **Website:** www.hardhat.com. **Contact:** Jon Casey, editor. **50% freelance written.** Biweekly tabloid covering heavy construction, equipment, road, and bridge work. "Our readers are contractors and heavy construction workers involved in excavation, highways, bridges, utility construction, and underground construction." Estab. 1980. Circ. 15,000. Byline given. Editorial lead time 2 weeks. Submit seasonal material 2 weeks in

advance. Accepts queries by mail, e-mail, fax, phone. Sample copy and writer's guidelines free.

NONFICTION Needs interview, new product, opinion, photo feature, technical. Send complete ms. Length: 800-2,000 words. **Pays $2.50/inch.** Sometimes pays expenses of writers on assignment.

COLUMNS Association News; Parts and Repairs; Attachments; Trucks and Trailers; People on the Move.

⊖⊖ HOME ENERGY MAGAZINE

Home Energy Magazine, 1250 Addison St., Suite 211B, Berkeley CA 94702. (510)524-5405. **Fax:** (510)981-1406. **E-mail:** contact@homeenergy.org. **Website:** www.homeenergy.org. Alan Meier, publisher. **Contact:** Jim Gunshinan, managing editor. **10% freelance written.** Bimonthly magazine covering green home building and renovation. Estab. 1984. Circ. 5,000. Byline given. Offers 10% kill fee. Publishes ms an average of 4 months after acceptance. Editorial lead time 4 months. Accepts queries by e-mail. Responds in 2 weeks to queries. Responds in 2 months to mss. Guidelines by email.

NONFICTION Needs interview, technical. "We do not want articles for consumers/general public." **Buys 6 mss/year.** Query with published clips. Length: 900-3,500 words. **Pays 20¢/word; $400 maximum for assigned articles. Pays 20¢/word; $400 maximum for unsolicited articles.**

⊖⊖⊖ INTERIOR CONSTRUCTION

Ceilings & Interior Systems Construction Association, 405 Illinois Ave., Unit 2B, St. Charles IL 60174. (630)584-1919. **Fax:** (630)584-2003. **E-mail:** rmgi@comcast.net; cisca@cisca.org. **Website:** www.cisca.org. **Contact:** Rick Reuland, publisher. Quarterly magazine on acoustics and commercial specialty ceiling construction. Estab. 1950. Circ. 3,000. Byline given. Publishes ms an average of 1 1/2 months after acceptance. Editorial lead time 2-3 months. Accepts queries by e-mail. Sample copy by e-mail. Guidelines available.

NONFICTION Needs new product, technical. Query with published clips. Publishes 1-2 features per issue. Length: 700-1,700 words. **Pays $400 minimum, $800 maximum for assigned articles.**

⊖⊖ METAL ROOFING MAGAZINE

a Division of F+W Media, Inc., 700 E. Iola St., Iola WI 54990-0001. (715)445-4612, ext. 13281. **Fax:** (715)445-4087. **E-mail:** jim.austin@fwmedia.com.

Website: www.metalroofingmag.com. **Contact:** Jim Austin. **10% freelance written.** Bimonthly magazine covering roofing. *Metal Roofing Magazine* offers contractors, designers, suppliers, architects, and others in the construction industry a wealth of information on metal roofing—a growing segment of the roofing trade. Estab. 2000. Circ. 26,000. Byline given. Publishes ms an average of 3 months after acceptance. Editorial lead time 3 months. Submit seasonal material 3 months in advance. Accepts queries by mail. Accepts simultaneous submissions.

NONFICTION Needs book excerpts, historical, how-to, interview, new product, opinion, photo feature, technical. No advertorials. **Buys 15 mss/year.** Query with published clips. 750 words minimum. **Pays $100-500 for assigned articles.**

COLUMNS Gutter Opportunities; Stay Cool; Metal Roofing Details; Spec It. **Buys 15 mss/year.** Send complete ms. **Pays $0-500.**

🌑 💲💲 NETCOMPOSITES

4a Broom Business Park, Bridge Way Chesterfield S41 9QG UK. **E-mail:** info@netcomposites.com. **Website:** www.netcomposites.com. **1% freelance written.** Bimonthly newsletter covering advanced materials and fiber-reinforced polymer composites, plus a weekly electronic version called *Composite eNews*, reaching over 15,000 subscribers and many more pass-along readers. *Advanced Materials & Composites News* covers markets, applications, materials, processes, and organizations for all sectors of the global hi-tech materials world. Audience is management, academics, researchers, government, suppliers, and fabricators. Focus on news about growth opportunities. Estab. 1978. Circ. 15,000+. Byline sometimes given. Publishes ms an average of 1 month after acceptance. Editorial lead time 2 weeks. Submit seasonal material 1 month in advance. Accepts queries by e-mail. Responds in 1 week to queries. Responds in 1 month to mss. Sample copy for #10 SASE.

NONFICTION Needs new product, technical, industry information. **Buys 4-6 mss/year.** Query. 300 words. **Pays $200/final printed page.**

💲💲 POB MAGAZINE

BNP Media, 2401 W. Big Beaver Rd., Suite 700, Troy MI 48084. (248)362-3700. **E-mail:** pobeditor@bnpmedia.com. **Website:** www.pobonline.com. **Contact:** Christine Grahl. **5% freelance written,.** Monthly magazine covering surveying, mapping, and geomatics. Estab. 1975. Circ. 39,000. Byline given. Publishes ms an average of 3 months after acceptance. Editorial lead time 3 months. Accepts queries by e-mail, phone. Sample copy and guidelines available online.

NONFICTION "Query. Please ensure the document is saved in MS-Word or text-only format. Please also include an author byline and biography." Length: 1,700-2,200 words, with 2 graphics included. **Pays $400.**

💲💲 RURAL BUILDER

a Division of F+W Media, Inc., 700 E. State St., Iola WI 54990-0001. (715)445-4612, ext. 13644. **Fax:** (715)445-4087. **E-mail:** sharon.thatcher@fwmedia.com. **Website:** www.ruralbuilder.com. **10% freelance written.** Magazine published 8 times/year covering rural building. "*Builder* serves diversified town and country builders, offering them help managing their businesses through editorial and advertising material about metal, wood, post-frame, and masonry construction." Estab. 1967. Circ. 30,000. Byline given. Publishes ms an average of 3 months after acceptance. Editorial lead time 3 months. Submit seasonal material 3 months in advance. Accepts queries by mail, e-mail. Accepts simultaneous submissions.

NONFICTION Needs how-to, new product, opinion, photo feature, technical. No advertorials. **Buys 15 mss/year.** Query with published clips. 750 words minimum. **Pays $100-300.**

COLUMNS Money Talk (taxes for business); Tech Talk (computers for builders); Tool Talk (tools); Management Insights (business management); all 1,000 words. **Buys 15 mss/year.** Send complete ms. **Pays $0-500.**

💲💲 UNDERGROUND CONSTRUCTION

Oildom Publishing Company of Texas, Inc., P.O. Box 941669, Houston TX 77094-8669. (281)558-6930, ext. 220. **Fax:** (281)558-7029. **E-mail:** rcarpenter@oildom.com; oklinger@oildom.com. **Website:** www.undergroundconstructionmagazine.com. **Contact:** Robert Carpenter, editor; Oliver Klinger, publisher. **35% freelance written.** Monthly magazine covering underground oil and gas pipeline, water and sewer pipeline, cable construction for contractors, and owning companies. Circ. 38,000. Publishes ms an average of 6 months after acceptance. Accepts queries by mail, e-mail, fax, phone. Responds in 1 month to mss. Sample copy for SAE.

NONFICTION Needs how-to, , job stories and industry issues. Query with published clips. Length: 1,000-2,000 words. **Pays $3-500.** Sometimes pays expenses of writers on assignment.

DRUGS, HEALTH CARE AND MEDICAL PRODUCTS

$$$$ ⊘ ACP INTERNIST/ACP HOSPITALIST

American College of Physicians, 191 N. Independence Mall W., Philadelphia PA 19106-1572. (215)351-2400. **E-mail:** acpinternist@acponline.org; acphospitalist@acponline.org. **Website:** www.acpinternist.org; www.acphospitalist.org. **Contact:** Jennifer Kearney-Strouse, editor of *ACP Internist*; Jessica Berthold, editor of *ACP Hospitalist*. **40% freelance written.** Monthly magazine covering internal medicine/hospital medicine. "We write for specialists in internal medicine, not a consumer audience. Topics include clinical medicine, practice management, health information technology, and Medicare issues." Estab. 1981. Circ. 85,000 (Internist), 24,000 (Hospitalist). Byline given. Offers kill fee. Negotiable. Publishes ms an average of 2 months after acceptance. Editorial lead time 4 months. Submit seasonal material 6 months in advance. Accepts queries by e-mail. Guidelines free.
NONFICTION Needs interview. Query with published clips. Length: 700-2,000 words. **Pays $500-2,000 for assigned articles.** Pays expenses of writers on assignment.

● AUSTRALIAN HEALTH REVIEW

CSIRO Publishing, 150 Oxford St., Collingwood VIC 3066 Australia. (61)(2)9562-6640. **Fax:** (61)(2)9562-6699. **E-mail:** publishing.ahr@csiro.au. **Website:** www.publish.csiro.au/journals/ahr. Quarterly magazine for the Australian Healthcare and Hospitals Association. "*AHR* provides information for decision makers in the health care industry and is read by health care professionals, managers, planners, and policy makers throughout Australia and the region." Byline given. Guidelines available online.
NONFICTION Needs opinion, feature articles, research notes, case studies, book reviews, editorials. Send complete ms. Length: 500-5,000 words.

$$ LABTALK

LabTalk, P.O. Box 1945, Big Bear Lake CA 92315. (909)866-5590. **Fax:** (909)866-5577. **E-mail:** cwalker@framesdata.com. **Website:** www.LabTalkOnline.com. **20% freelance written.** Magazine published 6 times/year for the eye wear industry. Estab. 1970. Accepts simultaneous submissions.

$$$ VALIDATION TIMES

Washington Information Source Co., 19-B Wirt St. SW, Leesburg VA 20175. (703)779-8777. **Fax:** (703)779-2508. **E-mail:** kreid@fdainfo.com. **Website:** www.fdainfo.com. **Contact:** Ken Reid. Monthly newsletters covering regulation of pharmaceutical and medical devices. "We write to executives who have to keep up on changing FDA policies and regulations, and on what their competitors are doing at the agency." Estab. 1999. Byline given. Publishes ms an average of 1 month after acceptance. Editorial lead time 1 month. Submit seasonal material 1 month in advance. Accepts queries by mail. Responds in 1 month to queries. Sample copy and writer's guidelines free.
NONFICTION Needs how-to, technical, regulatory. No lay interest pieces. **Buys 50-100 mss/year.** Query. Length: 600-1,500 words. **Pays $100/half day; $200 full day to cover meetings and same rate for writing.** Sometimes pays expenses of writers on assignment.

EDUCATION AND COUNSELING

○ $ THE ATA MAGAZINE

11010 142nd St. NW, Edmonton AB T5N 2R1 Canada. (780)447-9400. **Fax:** (780)455-6481. **E-mail:** government@teachers.ab.ca. **Website:** www.teachers.ab.ca. **Contact:** Editor. Quarterly magazine covering education. Estab. 1920. Circ. 42,100. Byline given. Publishes ms an average of 4 months after acceptance. Editorial lead time 2 months. Submit seasonal material 2 months in advance. Accepts queries by mail, e-mail, fax, phone. Accepts simultaneous submissions. Responds in 2 months to queries. Guidelines available online.
NONFICTION Query with published clips. Length: 500-1,500 words. **Pays $75 (Canadian).**

● AUSTRALASIAN JOURNAL OF EARLY CHILDHOOD

Early Childhood Australia, P.O. Box 86, Deakin West ACT 2600 Australia. (61)(2)6242-1800. **Fax:** (61)(2)6242-1818. **E-mail:** publishing@earlychildhood.org.au. **Website:** www.earlychildhoodaustralia.org.au. **Contact:** Chris Jones, publishing manager. Nonprofit early childhood advocacy organisation, acting in the interests of young children aged from bith to eight years of age, their families and those in the early childhood field. Specialist publisher of early childhood magazines, journals, and booklets. Guidelines available online.

NONFICTION Needs essays. Send complete ms. Length: Magazine articles, 600-1,000 words; research-based papers, 3,000-6,500 words; submissions for booklets, approximately 5,000 words.

THE FORENSIC TEACHER

Wide Open Minds Educational Services, P.O. Box 5263, Wilmington DE 19808. **E-mail:** admin@theforensicteacher.com. **Website:** www.theforensicteacher.com. **Contact:** Mark R. Feil, editor. **70% freelance written.** Quarterly magazine covering forensic education. "Our readers are middle, high and post-secondary teachers who are looking for better, easier and more engaging ways to teach forensics as well as law enforcement and scientific forensic experts. Our writers understand this and are writing from a forensic or educational background, or both. Prefer a first person writing style." Estab. 2006. Circ. 30,000. Byline given. Pays 60 days after publication. Publishes ms an average of 6 months after acceptance. Editorial lead time 6 months. Submit seasonal material 6 months in advance. Accepts queries by mail, e-mail. Accepts simultaneous submissions. Responds in 2 weeks to queries. Responds in 2 months to mss. Sample copy for $5. Guidelines available online.

NONFICTION Needs how-to, personal experience, photo feature, technical, lesson plans. Does not want poetry, fiction or anything unrelated to medicine, law, forensics or teaching. **Buys 18 mss/year.** Send complete ms. Length: 400-2,000 words. **Pays 2¢/word.**

COLUMNS Needs lesson experiences or ideas, personal or professional experiences with a branch of forensics. "If you've done it in your classroom please share it with us. Also, if you're a professional, please tell our readers how they can duplicate the lesson/demo/experiment in their classrooms. Please share what you know."

FILLERS Needs : facts, newsbreaks. **Buys 15 fillers/year. mss/year.** Length: 50-200 words. **Pays 2¢/word.**

PTO TODAY

PTO Today, Inc., 100 Stonewall Blvd., Suite 3, Wrentham MA 02093. (800)644-3561. **Fax:** (508)384-6108. **E-mail:** editor@ptotoday.com. **Website:** www.ptoto-

day.com. **Contact:** Craig Bystrynski, editor-in-chief. **50% freelance written.** Magazine published 6 times during the school year covering the work of school parent-teacher groups. "We celebrate the work of school parent volunteers and provide resources to help them do that work more effectively." Estab. 1999. Circ. 80,000. Byline given. Offers 30% kill fee. Publishes ms an average of 4-6 months after acceptance. Editorial lead time 4 months. Submit seasonal material 4 months in advance. Accepts queries by e-mail. Guidelines by e-mail.

NONFICTION Needs general interest, how-to, interview, personal experience. **Buys 20 mss/year.** Query. We review but do not encourage unsolicited submissions. Features run roughly 1,200 to 2,200 words. Average assignment is 1,200 words. Department pieces run 600 to 1,200 words. **Payment depends on the difficulty of the topic and the experience of the writer. "We pay by the assignment, not by the word; our pay scale ranges from $200 to $700 for features and $150 to $400 for departments. We occasionally pay more for high-impact stories and highly experienced writers. We buy all rights, and we pay on acceptance (within 30 days of invoice)."** Sometimes pays expenses of writers on assignment.

SCHOOLARTS MAGAZINE

Davis Art, Production Department, Attn: Article Submissions, 50 Portland St., Worcester MA 01608. **E-mail:** nwalkup@davisart.com. **Website:** www.davisart.com. **Contact:** Nancy Walkup, editor. **85% freelance written.** Monthly magazine (August/September-May/June), serving arts and craft education profession, K-12, higher education, and museum education programs written by and for art teachers. Estab. 1901. Pays on publication (honorarium and 4 copies). Publishes ms an average of 24 months after acceptance. Accepts queries by mail. Responds in 1-2 months to queries. Guidelines available online.

NONFICTION Query or send complete ms and SASE. Mail a CD containing article's text and photographs, along with signed permission forms (online under Guidelines). No e-mail submissions. Length: 600-1,400 words. **Pays $30-150.**

TEACHERS & WRITERS MAGAZINE

Teachers & Writers Collaborative, 520 Eighth Ave., Suite 2020, New York NY 10018. (212)691-6590. **Fax:** (212)675-0171. **E-mail:** editors@twc.org. **Website:** www.twc.org/magazine. **75% freelance written.**

Quarterly magazine covering how to teach creative writing (kindergarten through university). *"Teachers & Writers Magazine* covers a cross-section of contemporary issues and innovations in education and writing, and engages writers, educators, critics, and students in a conversation on the nature of creativity and the imagination." Estab. 1967. Circ. 5,000. Byline given. Publishes ms an average of 4-6 months after acceptance. Editorial lead time 4 months. Submit seasonal material 4-6 months in advance. Accepts queries by e-mail, as an attachment (preferred). Accepts simultaneous submissions. Responds in 4-8 weeks to queries. Responds in 3-6 months to mss. Sample copy for $5. Guidelines by e-mail.

NONFICTION Needs book excerpts, on creative writing education, essays, interview, opinion, personal experience, creative writing exercises. 500-2,500/words

✪ TEACHERS OF VISION

A Publication of Christian Educators Association, 227 N. Magnolia Ave., Suite 2, Anaheim CA 92801. (714)761-1476. **E-mail:** TOV@ceai.org. **Website:** www.ceai.org. **70% freelance written**. Magazine published 4 times/year for Christians in public education. *"Teachers of Vision*'s articles inspire, inform, and equip teachers and administrators in the educational arena. Readers look for teacher tips, integrating faith and work, and general interest education articles. Topics include subject matter, religious expression and activity in public schools, and legal rights of Christian educators. Our audience is primarily public school educators. Other readers include teachers in private schools, university professors, school administrators, parents, and school board members." Estab. 1953. Circ. 10,000. Byline given. Publishes ms an average of 6 months after acceptance. Editorial lead time 4 months. Submit seasonal material 4 months in advance. Accepts queries by mail, e-mail. Accepts simultaneous submissions. Responds in 1 month to queries. Responds in 3-4 months to mss. Sample copy for sae with 9x12 envelope and 4 first-class stamps. Guidelines available online.

NONFICTION Needs how-to, humor, inspirational, interview, opinion, personal experience, religious. No preaching. **Buys 50-60 mss/year.** Query or send complete ms if 2,000 words or less. Length: 1,500 words. **Pays $40-50.**

COLUMNS Query. **Pays $10-40.**

POETRY Will accept poetry if pertains to public schools.

FILLERS Send with SASE—must relate to public education.

TEACHING MUSIC

MENC: The National Association for Music Education, 1806 Robert Fulton Dr., Reston VA 20191. **E-mail:** lindab@nafme.org. **Website:** www.menc.org. **Contact:** Linda C. Brown, editor. Journal covering music education issued 6 times a year. *"Teaching Music* offers music educators a forum for the exchange of practical ideas that will help them become more effective teachers. Written in an easy-to-read, conversational style, the magazine includes timely information to interest, inform, and inspire music teachers and those who support their work." Byline given. *Does not pay writers at this time.* Publishes ms an average of 24 months after acceptance. Editorial lead time 12-18 months. Accepts queries by e-mail (preferably in Word). Responds in 2 weeks to queries. Responds in 3 months to mss. Guidelines available online.

NONFICTION Needs how-to, inspirational, personal experience, mss for the Lectern section that describe effective and innovative instructional strategies or thoughtful solutions to problems faced by music educators at all levels, from PreK through college. Major article categories are General Music, Band, Orchestra, Chorus, Early Childhood, Advocacy, and Teacher Education/Professional Development. Send complete ms. Length: 1,000-1,400 words.

✪✪✪✪ TEACHING TOLERANCE

The Southern Poverty Law Center, 400 Washington Ave., Montgomery AL 36104. (334)956-8200. **Fax:** (334)956-8488. **Website:** www.teachingtolerance. org. **30% freelance written.** Semiannual magazine. Estab. 1991. Circ. 400,000. Byline given. Editorial lead time 6 months. Submit seasonal material 6 months in advance. Accepts queries by mail, fax, online submission form. Sample copy and writer's guidelines free or online.

NONFICTION Needs essays, how-to, classroom techniques, personal experience, classroom, photo feature. No jargon, rhetoric or academic analysis. No theoretical discussions on the pros/cons of multicultural education. **Buys 2-4 mss/year.** Submit outlines or complete mss. Length: 1,000-3,000 words. **Pays $500-3,000.** Pays expenses of writers on assignment.

COLUMNS Essays (personal reflection, how-to, school program), 400-800 words; Idea Exchange (special projects, successful anti-bias activities), 250-500 words; Student Writings (short essays dealing with diversity, tolerance, justice), 300-500 words. **Buys 8-12 mss/year.** Query with published clips. **Pays $50-1,000.**

$ TECH DIRECTIONS

Prakken Publications, Inc., P.O. Box 8623, P, Ann Arbor MI 48107-8623. (734)975-2800. **Fax:** (734)975-2787. **E-mail:** susanne@techdirections.com. **Website:** www.techdirections.com. **Contact:** Susanne Peckham, managing editor. **100% freelance written. Eager to work with new/unpublished writers.** Monthly (except June and July) magazine covering issues, trends, and activities of interest to science, technical, and technology educators at the elementary through post-secondary school levels. Estab. 1934. Circ. 40,000. Byline given. Publishes ms an average of 1 year after acceptance. Responds in 1 month to queries. Sample copy for $5. Guidelines available online.

NONFICTION Needs general interest, how-to, personal experience, technical, think pieces. **Buys 50 unsolicited mss/year.** Length: 2,000-3,000 words. **Pays $50-150.**

COLUMNS Direct from Washington (education news from Washington DC); Technology Today (new products under development); Technologies Past (profiles the inventors of last century); Mastering Computers, Technology Concepts (project orientation).

ELECTRONICS AND COMMUNICATION

$$ THE ACUTA JOURNAL

Information Communications Technology in Higher Education, ACUTA, 152 W. Zandale Dr., Suite 200, Lexington KY 40503. (859)278-3338. **Fax:** (859)278-3268. **E-mail:** aburton@acuta.org; pscott@acuta.org. **Website:** www.acuta.org. **Contact:** Amy Burton; Patricia Scott, director of communications. **20% freelance written.** Quarterly professional association journal covering information communications technology (ICT) in higher education. "Our audience includes, primarily, middle to upper management in the IT/telecommunications department on college/university campuses. They are highly skilled, technology-oriented professionals who provide data, voice, and video communications services for residential and academic purposes." Estab. 1997. Circ. 2,200. Byline given. Publishes ms an average of 6 months after acceptance. Editorial lead time 6 months. Accepts queries by mail, e-mail, fax, phone. Responds in 1 month to queries. Responds in 2 months to mss. Sample copy for SAE with 9x12 envelope and 6 first-class stamps. Guidelines free.

NONFICTION Needs how-to, ICT, technical, technology, case study, college/university application of technology. **Buys 6-8 mss/year.** Query. Length: 1,200-4,000 words. **Pays 8-10¢/word.** Sometimes pays expenses of writers on assignment.

$$ CABLING BUSINESS MAGAZINE

Cabling Publications, Inc., 12035 Shiloh Rd., Suite 350, Dallas TX 75228. (214)328-1717. **Fax:** (214)319-6077. **E-mail:** russell@cablingbusiness.com. **Website:** www.cablingbusiness.com. **Contact:** Russell Paulov, editor-in-chief; Margaret Patterson, managing editor. **30% freelance written.** Monthly magazine covering telecommunications, cable manufacturing, volP, wireless, broadband, and structured cabling. Estab. 1991. Circ. 15,000. Byline given. Publishes ms an average of 1-2 months after acceptance. Editorial lead time 2 months. Submit seasonal material 2 months in advance. Accepts queries by e-mail. Accepts simultaneous submissions. Responds in 1 week to queries and to mss. Guidelines by e-mail.

NONFICTION Needs how-to, interview, new product, opinion, personal experience, technical. No vendor/product specific infomercials. **Buys 6 mss/year.** Query. Length: 1,500-2,500 words. **Pays $400 maximum for assigned and unsolicited articles.**

COLUMNS New Products (latest technology from industry), 350 words; Testing Equipment Q&A (work with specific companies on testing information), Cable Q&A (work with specific companies on cable questions from around the industry), 800 words; Terminology/Calendar, 200 words. Query. **Pays $-$400.**

$$$ SOUND & VIDEO CONTRACTOR

NewBay Media, LLC, 28 E. 28th St., 12th Floor, New York NY 10016. (818)236-3667. **Fax:** (913)514-3683. **E-mail:** cwisehart@nbmedia.com; jgutierrez@nbmedia.com. **Website:** www.svconline.com. Cynthia Wisehart, editor. **Contact:** Jessaca Gutierrez, managing and online editor. **60% freelance written.** Monthly magazine covering professional audio, video, security, acoustical design, sales, and marketing.

Estab. 1983. Circ. 24,000. Byline given. Publishes ms an average of 3 months after acceptance. Editorial lead time 3 months. Accepts queries by mail, e-mail, fax, phone. Accepts simultaneous submissions. Responds ASAP to queries. Sample copy and writer's guidelines free.

NONFICTION Needs historical, how-to, photo feature, technical, professional audio/video applications, installations, product reviews. No opinion pieces, advertorial, interview/profile, exposé/gossip. **Buys 60 mss/year.** Query. Length: 1,000-2,500 words. **Pays $200-1,200 for assigned articles. Pays $200-650 for unsolicited articles.**

COLUMNS Security Technology Review (technical install information); Sales & Marketing (techniques for installation industry); Video Happenings (Pro video/projection/storage technical info), all 1,500 words. **Buys 30 mss/year.** Query. **Pays $200-350.**

⬤ TECH TRADER MAGAZINE

The Intermedia Group, Ltd., Tech Trader Magazine, 41 Bridge Rd.,, Glebe NSW 2037 Australia. (61)(2)9660-2113. **Fax:** (61)(2)9660-0885. **E-mail:** kymberly@intermedia.com.au. **Website:** www.intermedia.com.au. "Tech Trader Magazine delivers the latest news, opinion, features, product reviews, overseas reports, and new products together in one lively publication."

NONFICTION Needs general interest, new product. Query.

ENERGY AND UTILITIES

⬤⬤ ELECTRICAL APPARATUS

Barks Publications, Inc., Suite 901, 500 N. Michigan Ave., Chicago IL 60611. (312)321-9440. **Fax:** (312)321-1288. **E-mail:** eamagazine@barks.com. **Website:** www.barks.com/eacurr.html. **Contact:** Elsie Dickson, associate publisher; Kevin Jones, senior editor. Monthly magazine for persons working in electrical and electronic maintenance, in industrial plants and service and sales centers, who install and service electric motors, transformers, generators, controls, and related equipment. Contact staff members by telephone for their preferred e-mail addresses. Estab. 1967. Circ. 16,000. Byline given. Publishes ms an average of 1 month after acceptance. Accepts queries by mail, fax. Responds in 1 week to queries. Responds in 2 weeks to mss.

NONFICTION Needs technical. Length: 1,500-2,500 words. **Pays $250-500 for assigned articles.**

⬤ ELECTRICAL BUSINESS

CLB Media, Inc., 222 Edward St., Aurora ON L4G 1W6 Canada. (905)727-0077; (905)713-4391. **Fax:** (905)727-0017. **E-mail:** acapkun@annexweb.com. **Website:** www.ebmag.com. **Contact:** Anthony Capkun, editor. **35% freelance written.** Tabloid published 10 times/year covering the Canadian electrical industry. *Electrical Business* targets electrical contractors and electricians. It provides practical information readers can use right away in their work and for running their business and assets. Estab. 1964. Circ. 18,097. Byline given. Offers 50% kill fee. Publishes ms an average of 1-2 months after acceptance. Editorial lead time 3 months. Submit seasonal material 6 months in advance. Accepts queries by e-mail, phone. Accepts simultaneous submissions. Responds in 1 month to queries. Responds in 1 month to mss. Guidelines free.

NONFICTION Needs how-to, technical. Special issues: Summer Blockbuster issue (June/July); Special Homebuilders' issue (November/December). **Buys 15 mss/year.** Query. Length: 800-1,200 words. **Pays 40¢/word.** Sometimes pays expenses of writers on assignment.

COLUMNS Atlantic Focus (stories from Atlantic Canada); Western Focus (stories from Western Canada, including Manitoba); Trucks for the Trade (articles pertaining to the vehicles used by electrical contractors); Tools for the Trade (articles pertaining to tools used by contractors); all 800 words. **Buys 6 mss/year.** Query. **Pays 40¢/word.**

⬤⬤ PUBLIC POWER

1875 Connecticut Ave., NW, Suite 1200, Washington D.C. 20009-5715. (202)467-2900. **Fax:** (202)467-2910. **E-mail:** magazine@publicpower.org; dblaylock@publicpower.org. **Website:** www.publicpowermedia.org. **Contact:** David L. Blaylock, editor. **60% freelance written. Prefers to work with published/established writers.** Publication of the American Public Power Association, published 8 times a year. Emphasizes electric power provided by cities, towns, and utility districts. Estab. 1942. Byline given. Publishes ms an average of 3 months after acceptance. Accepts queries by mail, e-mail, fax. Responds in 6 months to queries. Sample copy and writer's guidelines free.

NONFICTION Pays $500 and up.

⬤⬤ SOLAR INDUSTRY

Zackin Publications, Inc., P.O. Box 2180, Waterbury CT 06722. (800)325-6745. **Fax:** (203)262-4680. E-mail: jlillian@solarindustrymag.com. **Website:** www.solarindustrymag.com. **Contact:** Jessica Lillian, editor. **5% freelance written. Prefers to work with published/established writers.** *Solar Industry* magazine is a monthly trade publication serving professionals in the solar energy industry. Estab. 1980. Circ. 10,000. Publishes ms an average of 2 months after acceptance. Submit seasonal material 4 months in advance. Accepts queries by mail, e-mail, fax, phone. Responds in 2 weeks to queries. "To read sample copies, view digital archive at www.solarindustrymag.com.". Guidelines available online.

🔑 "Publishes 2 types of timely articles: features that examine and analyze solar energy industry trends; and features that give readers nuts and bolts information about how to improve their operations. These features are written by professional industry staff and contract journalists, and also by industry experts."

NONFICTION Needs how-to, improve retail profits and business know-how, interview, of successful retailers in this field. No general business articles not adapted to this industry. **Buys 10 mss/year.** Query. Length: 1,500-2,000 words. **Pay varies.**

ENGINEERING AND TECHNOLOGY

🍁 $$$ CANADIAN CONSULTING ENGINEER

Business Information Group, 80 Valleybrook Dr., Toronto ON M3B 2S9 Canada. (416)510-5119. **Fax:** (416)510-5134. **E-mail:** bparsons@ccemag.com. **Website:** www.canadianconsultingengineer.com. **Contact:** Bronwen Parsons, editor. **20%% freelance written.** Bimonthly magazine covering consulting engineering in private practice. Estab. 1958. Circ. 8,900. Byline given depending on length of story. Offers 50% kill fee. Publishes ms an average of 4 months after acceptance. Editorial lead time 6 months. Responds in 3 months to mss.

💬 Canadian content only. Impartial editorial required.

NONFICTION Needs historical, new product, technical, engineering/construction projects, environmental/construction issues. **Buys 8-10 mss/year.** Length: 300-1,500 words. **Pays $200-1,000 (Canadian).** Sometimes pays expenses of writers on assignment.

COLUMNS Export (selling consulting engineering services abroad); Management (managing consulting engineering businesses); On-Line (trends in CAD systems); Employment; Business; Construction and Environmental Law (Canada), all 800 words. **Buys 4 mss/year.** Query with published clips. **Pays $250-400.**

$$ COMPOSITES MANUFACTURING MAGAZINE

(formerly *Composites Fabrication Magazine*), American Composites Manufacturers Association, 1010 N. Glebe Rd., Suite 450, Arlington VA 22201. (703)525-0511. **Fax:** (703)525-0743. **E-mail:** mskea@acmanet.org. **Website:** www.acmanet.org. **Contact:** Melinda Skea, editor. Monthly magazine covering any industry that uses reinforced composites: marine, aerospace, infrastructure, automotive, transportation, corrosion, architecture, tub and shower, sports, and recreation. "Primarily, we publish educational pieces, the how-to of the shop environment. We also publish marketing, business trends, and economic forecasts relevant to the composites industry." Estab. 1979. Circ. 12,000. Byline given. Publishes ms an average of 2-3 months after acceptance. Editorial lead time 2 months. Accepts queries by e-mail. Accepts simultaneous submissions. Responds in 1 week to queries. Responds in 1 month to mss. Guidelines by e-mail and online.

NONFICTION Needs how-to, composites manufacturing, new product, technical, marketing, related business trends and forecasts. Special issues: "Each January we publish a World Market Report where we cover all niche markets and all geographic areas relevant to the composites industry. Freelance material will be considered strongly for this issue.". No need to query company or personal profiles unless there is an extremely unique or novel angle. **Buys 5-10 mss/year.** Query. Length: 1,500-4,000 words. **Pays 20-40¢/word (negotiable).** Sometimes pays expenses of writers on assignment.

COLUMNS "We publish columns on HR, relevant government legislation, industry lessons learned, regulatory affairs, and technology. Average word length for columns is 500 words. We would entertain any new column idea that hits hard on industry matters." Query. **Pays $300-350.**

$$$ ENTERPRISE MINNESOTA MAGAZINE

Enterprise Minnesota, Inc., 310 4th Ave. S., Suite 7050, Minneapolis MN 55415. (612)373-2900; (800)325-

3073. **Fax:** (612)373-2901. **E-mail:** editor@enterpriseminnesota.org. **Website:** www.enterpriseminnesota.org. **Contact:** Tom Mason, editor. **90% freelance written.** Magazine published 5 times/year. Estab. 1991. Circ. 16,000. Byline given. Offers 10% kill fee. Publishes ms an average of 3 months after acceptance. Editorial lead time 1 month. Submit seasonal material 1 year in advance. Accepts queries by mail, e-mail. Guidelines free.

NONFICTION Needs general interest, how-to, interview. **Buys 60 mss/year.** Query with published clips. **Pays $150-1,000.**

COLUMNS Feature Well (Q&A format, provocative ideas from Minnesota business and industry leaders), 2,000 words; Up Front (mini profiles, anecdotal news items), 250-500 words. Query with published clips.

⊝⊛ LD+A

Illuminating Engineering Society of North America, 120 Wall St., 17th Floor, New York NY 10005-4001. (212)248-5000, ext. 108. **Fax:** (212)248-5017. **E-mail:** ptarricone@ies.org. **Website:** www.ies.org. **Contact:** Paul Tarricone, editor/associate publisher. **10% freelance written.** Estab. 1971. Circ. 10,000. Byline given. Publishes ms an average of 4 months after acceptance. Editorial lead time 2 months. Submit seasonal material 4 months in advance. Accepts queries by mail, e-mail, fax, phone. Accepts simultaneous submissions. Responds in 2 weeks to queries. Guidelines available on website.

NONFICTION Needs historical, how-to, opinion, personal experience, photo feature, technical. No articles blatantly promoting a product, company, or individual. **Buys 6-10 mss/year.** Query. Length: 1,500-2,000 words.

COLUMNS Essay by Invitation (industry trends), 1,200 words. Query. **Does not pay for columns.**

⊝⊛ MANUFACTURING & TECHNOLOGY EJOURNAL

Manufacturers Group Inc., P.O. Box 4310, Lexington KY 40544. **E-mail:** editor@mfrtech.com. **Website:** www.mfrtech.com. **40% freelance written.** Weekly website covering manufacturing and technology. Editorial targets middle and upper management—presidents, plant managers, engineering, purchasing. Editorial includes features on operations and management, new plants, acquisitions, expansions, new products. Estab. 1976 (print). Circ. 10,000 plus weekly (e-mail); 5,000 weekly online. Byline given. 30 days

followiong publication. Offers 25% kill fee. Publishes ms an average of 2 weeks after acceptance. Editorial lead time 2 weeks. Submit seasonal material 2 weeks in advance. Guidelines by e-mail.

NONFICTION Needs new product, opinion, technical, New plants, expansions, acquisitions. Most articles are assignments. Special issues: "We have assigned features on timely issues relating to economics, environmental, manufacturing trends, employment. Open to feature suggestions by outline only." General interest, inspirational, personal, travel, book excerpts. "You can include up to 2 photo or graphic images and must come as an attachment to your e-mail as JPEGs and no larger than 300x300 pixels each." Length: 750-1,200 words. **Pays $0.20/word published.**

COLUMNS New Plants, Acquisitions, New Technology, Expansions. Query. **Pays $-$0.20/word.**

⊝⊛ MINORITY ENGINEER

Equal Opportunity Publications, Inc., 445 Broad Hollow Rd., Suite 425, Melville NY 11747. (631)421-9421. **Fax:** (516)421-0359. **E-mail:** jschneider@eop.com; info@eop.com. **Website:** www.eop.com. **Contact:** James Schneider, director, editorial and production. **60% freelance written. Prefers to work with published/established writers.** Triannual magazine covering career guidance for minority engineering students and minority professional engineers. Estab. 1969. Circ. 15,000. Byline given. Publishes ms an average of 3 months after acceptance. Editorial lead time 3 months. Accepts queries by mail, e-mail, fax, phone. Accepts simultaneous submissions. Responds in 2 weeks to queries. Responds in 2 months to mss. Sample copy and writer's guidelines for 9x12 SAE with 5 first-class stamps. Guidelines free.

NONFICTION Needs book excerpts, general interest, on specific minority engineering concerns, how-to, land a job, keep a job, etc., interview, minority engineer role models, opinion, problems of ethnic minorities, personal experience, student and career experiences, technical, on career fields offering opportunities for minority engineers, articles on job search techniques, role models. No general information. Query. Length: 1,500-2,500 words. **Pays $350 for assigned articles.** Sometimes pays expenses of writers on assignment.

⊝⊛⊝⊛ RAILWAY TRACK AND STRUCTURES

Simmons-Boardman Publishing, 20 S. Clark St., Suite 2450, Chicago IL 60603. (312)683-0130. **Fax:**

(312)683-0131. **E-mail:** mischa@sbpub-chicago.com. **Website:** www.rtands.com. **Contact:** Mischa Wanek-Libman, editor. **1% freelance written.** Monthly magazine covering railroad civil engineering. "*RT&S* is a nuts-and-bolts journal to help railroad civil engineers do their jobs better." Estab. 1904. Circ. 9,500. Byline given. Offers 90% kill fee. Publishes ms an average of 1 month after acceptance. Editorial lead time 2 months. Submit seasonal material 3 months in advance. Accepts queries by mail, fax, phone. Accepts simultaneous submissions. Responds in 1 month to queries and to mss.

NONFICTION Needs how-to, new product, technical. Does not want nostalgia or "railroadiana." **Buys 1 mss/year.** Query. Length: 900-2,000 words. **Pays $500-1,000.** Sometimes pays expenses of writers on assignment.

🟢🟢 WOMAN ENGINEER

Equal Opportunity Publications, Inc., 445 Broad Hollow Rd., Suite 425, Melville NY 11747. (631)421-9421. **Fax:** (631)421-1352. **E-mail:** info@eop.com; jschneider@eop.com. **Website:** www.eop.com. **Contact:** James Schneider, editor. **60% freelance written. Works with a small number of new/unpublished writers each year.** Triannual magazine aimed at advancing the careers of women engineering students and professional women engineers. Estab. 1968. Circ. 16,000. Byline given. Publishes ms an average of 3 months after acceptance. Editorial lead time 3 months. Accepts queries by mail, e-mail, fax, phone. Responds in 2 weeks to queries. Responds in 2 months to mss. Sample copy and writer's guidelines free.

NONFICTION Needs how-to, find jobs, interview, personal experience. Query. Length: 1,500-2,500 words. **Pays $350 for assigned articles.**

ENTERTAINMENT AND THE ARTS

🟢🟢🟢 AMERICAN CINEMATOGRAPHER

American Society of Cinematographers, 1782 N. Orange Dr., Hollywood CA 90028. (800)448-0145; outside US: (323)969-4333. **Fax:** (323)876-4973. **E-mail:** stephen@ascmag.com. **Website:** www.theasc.com. **Contact:** Stephen Pizzello, executive editor. **90% freelance written.** Monthly magazine covering cinematography (motion picture, TV, music video, commercial). "*American Cinematographer* is a trade publication devoted to the art and craft of cinematography. Our readers are predominantly film-industry professionals." Estab. 1919. Circ. 45,000. Byline given. Offers 50% kill fee. Publishes ms an average of 2-3 months after acceptance. Editorial lead time 2 months. Submit seasonal material 3 months in advance. Accepts queries by mail, e-mail, phone. Responds in 2 weeks to queries. Responds in 2 months to mss. Sample copy and writer's guidelines free.

NONFICTION Contact: Stephen Pizzello, editor. Needs interview, new product, technical. No reviews or opinion pieces. **Buys 20-25 mss/year.** Query with published clips. Length: 1,500-4,000 words. **Pays $600-1,200.** Sometimes pays expenses of writers on assignment.

🟢🟢 BOXOFFICE MAGAZINE

Boxoffice Media, LLC, 230 Park Ave., Suite 1000, New York NY 10169. (212)922-9800. **E-mail:** help@boxoffice.com; amy@boxoffice.com; peter@boxoffice.com; ken@boxoffice.com. **Website:** www.BoxOffice.com; www.BoxOfficeMagazine.com. **Contact:** Amy Nicholson, editor; Peter Cane, publisher; Kenneth James Bacon, creative director; Phil Contrino, boxoffice.com editor: phil@boxoffice.com. **15% freelance written.** Providing news and numbers to the film industry since 1920. Magazine about the motion picture industry for executives and managers working in the film business, including movie theater owners and operators, Hollywood studio personnel and leaders in allied industries. Estab. 1920. Circ. 6,000. Byline given. Publishes ms an average of 3 months after acceptance. Submit seasonal material 5 months in advance. Accepts queries by mail, e-mail, fax. Sample copy for $5 in US; $10 outside U.S.

NONFICTION Needs book excerpts, essays, interview, new product, personal experience, photo feature, technical, investigative all regarding movie theatre business. Query with published clips. Length: 800-2,500 words. **Pays 10¢/word.**

🟢🟢 CAMPUS ACTIVITIES

Cameo Publishing Group, 1520 Newberry Rd., Blair SC 29015. (800)728-2950. **Fax:** (803)712-6703. **E-mail:** info@cameopublishing.com; ian@cameopublishing.com. **Website:** www.campusactivitiesmagazine.com; www.cameopublishing.com. **Contact:** Ian Kirby, editor/general manager; W.C. Kirby, publisher. **75% freelance written.** Magazine published 8 times/year covering entertainment on college campuses. *Campus*

Activities goes to entertainment buyers on every campus in the US. Features stories on artists (national and regional), speakers, and the programs at individual schools. Estab. 1991. Circ. 9,872. Byline given. Offers kill fee. Offers 15% kill fee if accepted and not run. Publishes ms an average of 2 months after acceptance. Editorial lead time 2 months. Submit seasonal material 2 months in advance. Accepts queries by mail, e-mail, fax. Accepts simultaneous submissions. Responds in 1 month to queries. Responds in 2 months to mss. Sample copy for $3.50. Guidelines free.

NONFICTION Needs interview, photo feature. Accepts no unsolicited articles. **Buys 40 mss/year.** Query. Length: 1,400-3,000 words. **Pays 13¢/word.** Sometimes pays expenses of writers on assignment.

⊗⊗ DANCE TEACHER

McFadden Performing Arts Media, 333 Seventh Ave., 11th Floor, New York NY 10001. **Fax:** (646)459-4000. **E-mail:** khildebrand@dancemedia.com. **Website:** www.dance-teacher.com. **Contact:** Karen Hildebrand, editor-in-chief. **60% freelance written.** Monthly magazine. Estab. 1979. Circ. 25,000. Byline given. Publishes ms an average of 3 months after acceptance. Submit seasonal material 6 months in advance. Accepts queries by mail, e-mail, fax, phone, online submission form. Responds in 3 months to mss. Sample copy for SAE with 9x12 envelope and 6 first-class stamps. Guidelines available for free.

    "Our readers are professional dance educators, business persons, and related professionals in all forms of dance."

NONFICTION Needs how-to, teach, health, business, legal. Special issues: Summer Programs (January); Music & More (May); Costumes and Production Preview (November); College/Training Schools (December). No PR or puff pieces. All articles must be well researched. **Buys 50 mss/year.** Query. Length: 700-2,000 words. **Pays $100-300.**

DRAMATICS MAGAZINE

Educational Theatre Association, 2343 Auburn Ave., Cincinnati OH 45219. (513)421-3900. **E-mail:** dcorathers@edta.org. **Website:** www.edta.org. **Contact:** Don Corathers, editors. "*Dramatics* is for students (mainly high school age) and teachers of theater. Mix includes how-to (tech theater, acting, directing, etc.), informational, interview, photo feature, humorous, profile, technical. We want our student readers to grow as theater artists and become a more discerning and appreciative audience. Material is directed to both theater students and their teachers, with strong student slant." Pays $100-500 for plays; $50-500 for articles; up to $100 for illustrations. Estab. 1929. Circ. 35,000. Byline given. Publishes ms 3 months after acceptance. Accepts simultaneous submissions. Sample copy available for 9x12 SAE with 4-ounce first-class postage. Guidelines available for SASE.

NONFICTION Needs Young adults: arts/crafts, careers, how-to, interview/profile, multicultural (all theater-related). "We try to portray the theater community in all its diversity.". Does not want to see academic treatises. **Buys 50 mss/year.** Submit complete ms. Length: 750-3,000 words.

FICTION Needs: Young adults—drama (one-act and full-length plays). "We prefer unpublished scripts that have been produced at least once." Does not want to see plays that show no understanding of the conventions of the theater. No plays for children, no Christmas or didactic "message" plays. Submit complete ms. Buys 5-9 plays/year. Emerging playwrights have better chances with résumé of credits. Length: 750-3,000 words.

⊗⊗⊗ EMMY MAGAZINE

Academy of Television Arts & Sciences, 5220 Lankershim Blvd., North Hollywood CA 91601-3109. **E-mail:** emmymag@emmys.org. **Website:** www.emmys.tv. **Contact:** Gail Polevoi, editor. **90% freelance written. Prefers to work with published/established writers.** Bimonthly magazine on television for TV professionals. Circ. 14,000. Byline given. Pays on publication or within 6 months. Offers 25% kill fee. Publishes ms an average of 4 months after acceptance. Accepts queries by mail. Responds in 1 month to queries. Sample copy for sae with 9x12 envelope and 6 first-class stamps. Guidelines available online.

NONFICTION Query with published clips. Length: 1,500-2,000 words. **Pays $1,000-1,200.**

COLUMNS Mostly written by regular contributors, but newcomers can break in with filler items with In the Mix or short profiles in Labors of Love. Length: 250-500 words, depending on department. Query with published clips. **Pays $250-500.**

⊗⊗ MAKE-UP ARTIST MAGAZINE

12808 NE 95th St., Vancouver WA 98682. (360)882-3488. **E-mail:** news@makeupmag.com. **Website:** www.makeupmag.com, www.makeup411.com, www.imats.net. **Contact:** Heather Wisner, managing editor; Michael Key, editor-in-chief. **90% freelance written.** Bimonthly magazine covering all types of professional make-up artistry. "Our audience is a mixture of high-level make-up artists, make-up students, and movie buffs. Writers should be comfortable with technical writing, and should have substantial knowledge of at least 1 area of makeup, such as effects or fashion. This is an entertainment-industry magazine, so writing should have an element of fun and storytelling. Good interview skills required." Estab. 1996. Circ. 16,000. Byline given. Pays within 30 days of publication. Editorial lead time 6 weeks. Submit seasonal material 2 months in advance. Accepts queries by e-mail. Accepts simultaneous submissions. Sample copy for $7. Guidelines available via e-mail.

NONFICTION Needs features, how-to, new products, photo features, profile. "Does not want fluff pieces about consumer beauty products." **Buys 20+ mss/year.** Query with published clips. Length: 500-3,000 words. **Pays 20-50¢/word.** Sometimes pays expenses of writers on assignment.

COLUMNS : Cameo (short yet thorough look at a make-up artist not covered in a feature story), 800 words (15 photos); Lab Tech (how-to advice for effects artists, usually written by a current make-up artist working in a lab), 800 words (3 photos); Backstage (analysis, interview, tips, and behind the scenes info on a theatrical production's make-up), 800 words (3 photos). **Buys 30 columns/year. mss/year.** Query with published clips. **Pays $100.**

$ SCREEN MAGAZINE

Screen Enterprises, Inc., 676 N. LaSalle Blvd., #501, Chicago IL 60654. (312)640-0800. **Fax:** (312)640-1928. **E-mail:** editor@screenmag.com. **Website:** www.screenmag.com. **Contact:** Andrew Schneider, editor. **5% freelance written.** Biweekly Chicago-based trade magazine covering advertising and film production in the Midwest and national markets. *Screen* is written for Midwest producers (and other creatives involved) of commercials, AV, features, independent corporate, and multimedia. Estab. 1979. Circ. 15,000. Byline given. Accepts queries by e-mail. Responds in 3 weeks to queries.

NONFICTION Needs interview, new product, technical. No general AV; nothing specific to other markets; no no-brainers or opinion. **Buys 26 mss/year.** Query with published clips. Length: 750-1,500 words. **Pays $50.**

FARM

AGRICULTURAL EQUIPMENT

$ AG WEEKLY

Lee Agri-Media, P.O. Box 918, Bismarck ND 58501. (701)255-4905. **Fax:** (701)255-2312. **E-mail:** mark.conlon@lee.net. **Website:** www.agweekly.com. **Contact:** Mark Conlon, editor. **40% freelance written.** Monthly tabloid covering regional farming and ranching, with emphasis on Idaho. *Ag Weekly* is an agricultural publication covering production, markets, regulation, politics. Writers need to be familiar with Idaho agricultural commodities. Circ. 12,402. Byline given. Publishes ms an average of 1 month after acceptance. Editorial lead time 1 month. Submit seasonal material 1 month in advance. Accepts queries by e-mail. Accepts simultaneous submissions. Responds in 2 weeks to queries. Responds in 1 month to mss. Guidelines with #10 SASE.

NONFICTION Needs interview, new product, opinion, travel, ag-related. Does not want anything other than local/regional ag-related articles. No cowboy poetry. **Buys 100 mss/year.** Query. Length: 250-700 words. **Pays $40-70.**

CROPS AND SOIL MANAGEMENT

$$ AMERICAN/WESTERN GROWER

Meister Media Worldwide, 37733 Euclid Ave., Willoughby OH 44094. (440)942-2000. **E-mail:** avazzano@meistermedia.com; deddy@meistermedia.com. **Website:** www.fruitgrower.com. **Contact:** Ann-Marie Vazzano, managing editor; David Eddy, editor. **3% freelance written.** Annual magazine covering commercial fruit growing. "How-to articles are best." Estab. 1880. Circ. 44,000. Byline given. Publishes ms an average of 4 months after acceptance. Editorial lead time 2 months. Submit seasonal material 4 months in advance. Accepts queries by mail, e-mail, fax, phone. Responds in 2 weeks to queries. Responds in 2 months to mss. Sample copy and writer's guidelines free.

NONFICTION Needs how-to, better grow fruit crops. **Buys 6-10 mss/year.** Send complete ms. Length: 800-1,200 words. **Pays $200-250.** Sometimes pays expenses of writers on assignment.

$ FRUIT GROWERS NEWS

Great American Publishing, P.O. Box 128, Sparta MI 49345. (616)887-9008. **Fax:** (616)887-2666. **E-mail:** fgnedit@fruitgrowersnews.com. **Website:** www.fruitgrowersnews.com. **Contact:** Matt Milkovich, managing editor; Kathy Gibbons, editorial director. **10% freelance written.** Monthly tabloid covering agriculture. "Our objective is to provide commercial fruit growers of all sizes with information to help them succeed." Estab. 1961. Circ. 16,429. Publishes ms an average of 2 months after acceptance. Editorial lead time 1-2 months. Submit seasonal material 3 months in advance. Accepts queries by mail, e-mail, fax. Accepts simultaneous submissions. Responds in 2 weeks to queries. Responds in 1 month to mss.

NONFICTION Needs general interest, interview, new product. No advertorials or other puff pieces. **Buys 25 mss/year.** Query with published clips and résumé. Length: 600-1,000 words. **Pays $150-250.** Sometimes pays expenses of writers on assignment.

$$ GOOD FRUIT GROWER

Washington State Fruit Commission, 105 S. 18th St., #217, Yakima WA 98901-2177. (509)575-2315. **E-mail:** jim.black@goodfruit.com. **Website:** www.goodfruit.com. **Contact:** Jim Black, managing editor. **10% freelance written.** Semi-monthly magazine covering tree fruit/grape growing. Estab. 1946. Circ. 11,000. Byline given. Publishes ms an average of 2 months after acceptance. Accepts queries by mail, e-mail. Accepts simultaneous submissions. Responds in 1 week to queries. Responds in 1 month to mss. Guidelines free.

NONFICTION **Buys 20 mss/year.** Query. Length: 500-1,500 words. **Pays 40-50¢/word.** Sometimes pays expenses of writers on assignment.

$ GRAIN JOURNAL

Country Journal Publishing Co., 3065 Pershing Ct., Decatur IL 62526. (800)728-7511. **E-mail:** ed@grainnet.com. **Website:** www.grainnet.com. **Contact:** Ed Zdrojewski, editor. **5% freelance written.** Bimonthly magazine covering grain handling and merchandising. *Grain Journal* serves the North American grain industry, from the smallest country grain elevators and feed mills to major export terminals. Estab. 1972. Circ. 12,000. Byline sometimes given. Publishes ms an average of 2 months after acceptance. Editorial lead time 2 months. Submit seasonal material 2 months in advance. Accepts simultaneous submissions.

NONFICTION Needs how-to, interview, new product, technical. Query. 750 words maximum. **Pays $100.**

$ ONION WORLD

Columbia Publishing, 8405 Ahtanum Rd., Yakima WA 98903. (509)248-2452, ext. 105. **Fax:** (509)248-4056. **E-mail:** dbrent@columbiapublications.com. **Website:** www.onionworld.net. **Contact:** Brent Clement, editor. **25% freelance written.** Monthly magazine covering the world of onion production and marketing for onion growers and shippers. Estab. 1985. Circ. 5,500. Byline given. Publishes ms an average of 1 month after acceptance. Submit seasonal material 1 month in advance. Accepts queries by e-mail or phone. Accepts simultaneous submissions. Responds in 1 month to queries. Sample copy for SAE with 9x12 envelope and 5 first-class stamps.

NONFICTION Needs general interest, historical, interview. **Buys 30 mss/year.** Query. Length: 1,200-1,250 words. **Pays $100-250 per article, depending upon length. Mileage paid, but query first.**

$ SPUDMAN

Great American Publishing, P.O. Box 128, Sparta MI 49345. (616)887-9008. **Fax:** (616)887-2666. **E-mail:** bills@spudman.com. **Website:** www.spudman.com. **Contact:** Bill Schaefer, managing editor. **10% freelance written.** Monthly magazine covering potato industry's growing, packing, processing, and chipping. Estab. 1964. Circ. 10,000. Byline given. Offers $75 kill fee. Publishes ms an average of 2 months after acceptance. Editorial lead time 2 months. Submit seasonal material 4 months in advance. Accepts queries by mail, e-mail. Responds in 2-3 weeks to queries. Sample copy for SAE with 8 ½x11 envelope and 3 first-class stamps. Guidelines for #10 SASE.

$ THE VEGETABLE GROWERS NEWS

Great American Publishing, P.O. Box 128, Sparta MI 49345. (616)887-9008, ext. 102. **Fax:** (616)887-2666. **E-mail:** vgnedit@vegetablegrowersnews.com. **Website:** www.vegetablegrowersnews.com. **Contact:** Matt Milkovich, managing editor. **10% freelance written.** Monthly tabloid covering agriculture. Estab. 1970. Circ. 16,000. Publishes ms an average of 2 months after acceptance. Editorial lead time 1-2 months. Submit seasonal material 3 months in advance. Accepts queries by mail, e-mail, fax. Accepts simultaneous submissions. Responds in 2 weeks to queries. Responds in 1 month to mss.

NONFICTION Needs general interest, interview, new product. No advertorials, other puff pieces. **Buys 25 mss/year.** Query with published clips and résumé. Length: 800-1,200 words. **Pays $100-125.** Sometimes pays expenses of writers on assignment.

DAIRY FARMING

$ $ HOARD'S DAIRYMAN

W.D. Hoard and Sons, Co., 28 Milwaukee Ave., W., P.O. Box 801, Fort Atkinson WI 53538. (920)563-5551. **Fax:** (920)563-7298. **E-mail:** editors@hoards.com. **Website:** www.hoards.com. Tabloid published 20 times/year covering dairy industry. "We publish semi-technical information published for dairy-farm families and their advisors. If you have a handy way to handle something on your farm, submit it as 1 of our famed Handy Hints." Estab. 1885. Circ. 100,000. Byline given. Publishes ms an average of 4 months after acceptance. Editorial lead time 2 months. Submit seasonal material 3 months in advance. Accepts queries by mail, e-mail, fax. Responds in 2 weeks to queries. Responds in 1 month to mss. Sample copy for 12x15 SAE and $3. Guidelines for #10 SASE.

NONFICTION Needs how-to, technical. **Buys 60 mss/year.** Query. Length: 800-1,500 words. **Pays $150-350.**

$ $ WESTERN DAIRYBUSINESS

Dairy Business Communications, 1200 W. Laurel Ave., Visalia CA 93277. (800)934-7872; (559)802-3743. **Fax:** (559)802-3746. **E-mail:** rgoble@dairybusiness.com. **Website:** www.dairybusiness.com. **10% freelance written. Prefers to work with published/established writers.** Monthly magazine dealing with large-herd commercial dairy industry. Rarely publishes information about non-Western producers or dairy groups and events. Estab. 1922. Circ. 10,051. Byline given. Publishes ms an average of 3 months after acceptance. Submit seasonal material 3 months in advance. Accepts queries by e-mail. Responds in 1 month to queries.

NONFICTION Needs interview, new product, opinion, industry analysis, industry analysis. No religion, nostalgia, politics, or 'mom and pop' dairies. Query, or e-mail complete ms. Length: 300-1,500 words. **Pays $50-400.**

🍁 $ WESTERN DAIRY FARMER

Sun Media, 4504 61 Ave., Leduc, AB T9E 3Z1, Canada. (780)986-2271. **Fax:** (780)986-6397. **E-mail:** john.greig@sunmedia.ca; paul.mahon@sunmedia.ca. Paul Mahon, publisher, editor-in-chief. **Contact:** John Greig, editor. **70% freelance written.** Eight-times yearly magazine covering the dairy industry. *Western Dairy Farmer* is a trade publication dealing with issues surrounding the dairy industry. The magazine features innovative articles on animal health, industry changes, new methods of dairying, and personal experiences. Sometimes highlights successful farmers. Estab. 1991. Circ. 4,700. Byline given. Publishes ms an average of 1 month after acceptance. Editorial lead time 1 month. Submit seasonal material 1 month in advance. Accepts queries by mail, e-mail. Responds in 2 days to queries. Responds in 1 week to mss. Sample copy for 9×12 SAE.

NONFICTION Needs general interest, how-to, interview, new product, personal experience, only exceptional stories, technical. Not interested in anything not dairy related. **Buys 50 mss/year.** Query or send complete ms. Length: 900-1,200 words. **Pays $120-400.** Pays expenses of writers on assignment..

LIVESTOCK

$ $ ANGUS BEEF BULLETIN

Angus Productions, Inc., 3201 Frederick Ave., St. Joseph MO 64506-2997. (816)383-5270. **Fax:** (816)233-6575. **E-mail:** shermel@angusjournal.com. **Website:** www.angusbeefbulletin.com. **Contact:** Shauna Rose Hermel, editor. **45% freelance written.** Tabloid published 5 times/year covering commercial cattle industry. The *Bulletin* is mailed free to commercial cattlemen who have purchased an Angus bull and had the registration transferred to them and to others who sign a request card. Estab. 1985. Circ. 65,000-70,000. Byline given. Publishes ms an average of 3 months after acceptance. Editorial lead time 3 months. Submit seasonal material 3 months in advance. Accepts queries by mail, e-mail. Accepts simultaneous submissions. Responds in 3 weeks to queries. Responds in 3 months to mss. Sample copy for $5. Guidelines for #10 SASE.

NONFICTION Needs how-to, cattle production, interview, technical, cattle production. **Buys 10 mss/year.** Query with published clips. Length: 800-2,500 words. **Pays $50-600.** Pays expenses of writers on assignment.

BACKYARD POULTRY

Countryside Publications, Ltd., 145 Industrial Dr., Medford WI 54451. (715)785-7979. **Fax:** (715)785-

7414. **E-mail:** byp@tds.net. **Website:** www.backyard-poultrymag.com. **Contact:** Elaine Belanger, editor. Bimonthly magazine covering breed selection, housing, management, health and nutrition, and other topics of interest to promote more and better raising of small-scale poultry. Query first.

$$ THE CATTLEMAN

Texas and Southwestern Cattle Raisers Association, 1301 W. 7th St., Suite 201, Fort Worth TX 76102. **E-mail:** ehbrisendine@tscra.org. **Website:** www.thecattlemanmagazine.com. **Contact:** Ellen H. Brisendine, editor. **25% freelance written.** Monthly magazine covering the Texas/Oklahoma beef cattle industry. "We specialize in in-depth, management-type articles related to range and pasture, beef cattle production, animal health, nutrition, and marketing. We want 'how-to' articles." Estab. 1914. Circ. 15,400. Byline given. Publishes ms an average of 2 months after acceptance. Editorial lead time 2 months. Submit seasonal material 6 months in advance. Accepts queries by mail, e-mail. Guidelines available online.

NONFICTION Needs how-to, interview, new product, personal experience, technical, ag research. Special issues: Editorial calendar themes include: Horses (January); Range and Pasture (February); Livestock Marketing (July); Hereford and Wildlife (August); Feedlots (September); Bull Buyers (October); Ranch Safety (December). Does not want to see anything not specifically related to beef production in the Southwest. **Buys 20 mss/year.** Query with published clips. Length: 1,500-2,000 words. **Pays $200-350 for assigned articles. Pays $100-350 for unsolicited articles.** Sometimes pays expenses of writers on assignment.

$$ FEED LOT MAGAZINE

Feed Lot Magazine, Inc., P.O. Box 850, Dighton KS 67839. (620)397-2838. **Fax:** (620)397-2839. **E-mail:** feedlot@st-tel.net. **Website:** www.feedlotmagazine.com. **40% freelance written.** Bimonthly magazine that provides readers with the most up-to-date information on the beef industry in concise, easy-to-read articles designed to increase overall awareness among the feedlot community. "The editorial information content fits a dual role: large feedlots and their related cow/calf operations, and large 500pl cow/calf, 100pl stocker operations. The information covers all phases of production from breeding, genetics, animal health, nutrition, equipment design, research through finishing fat cattle. *Feed Lot* publishes a mix of new information and timely articles which directly affect the cattle industry." Estab. 1993. Circ. 12,000. Byline given. Offers 50% kill fee. Publishes ms an average of 2 months after acceptance. Editorial lead time 2 months. Submit seasonal material 6 months in advance. Accepts queries by mail, e-mail, fax. Responds in 1 month to queries. Sample copy and writer's guidelines for $1.50.

NONFICTION Needs interview, new product, cattle-related, photo feature. Send complete ms. Length: 100-400 words. **Pays 20¢/word.**

$ SHEEP! MAGAZINE

Countryside Publications, Ltd., 145 Industrial Dr., Medford WI 54451. (715)785-7979; (800)551-5691. **Fax:** (715)785-7414. **E-mail:** sheepmag@tds.net. **Website:** www.sheepmagazine.com. **35% freelance written. Prefers to work with published/established writers.** Bimonthly magazine published in north-central Wisconsin. Estab. 1980. Circ. 11,000. Byline given. Offers $30 kill fee. Submit seasonal material 3 months in advance.

NONFICTION Needs book excerpts, how-to, on innovative lamb and wool marketing and promotion techniques, efficient record-keeping systems, or specific aspects of health and husbandry, interview, on experienced sheep producers who detail the economics and management of their operation, new product, of value to sheep producers; should be written by someone who has used them, technical, on genetics health and nutrition. **Buys 80 mss/year.** Send complete ms. Length: 750-2,500 words. **Pays $45-150.**

MANAGEMENT

$ AG JOURNAL

Arkansas Valley Publishing, 422 Colorado Ave., (P.O. Box 500), La Junta CO 81050. (719)384-1453. **E-mail:** publisher@ljtdmail.com. **Website:** www.agjournalonline.com. **Contact:** Candi Hill, publisher/editor. **20% freelance written.** Weekly journal covering agriculture. Estab. 1949. Circ. 11,000. Byline given. Publishes ms an average of 2 weeks after acceptance. Editorial lead time 1 month. Submit seasonal material 1 month in advance. Accepts queries by e-mail. Responds in 2 weeks to queries. Sample copy and writer's guidelines free.

NONFICTION Needs how-to, interview, new product, opinion, photo feature, technical. Query by e-mail only. **Pays 4¢/word.** Sometimes pays expenses of writers on assignment.

⊜ $ SMALLHOLDER MAGAZINE

Newsquest Media Group, Hook House, Hook Rd., Wimblington, March Cambs PE15 0QL United Kingdom. Phone/**Fax:** (44)(135)474-1538. **E-mail:** liz.wright1@btconnect.com. **Website:** www.smallholder.co.uk. **Contact:** Liz Wright. Accepts queries by e-mail. Guidelines by email.

NONFICTION Length: 700-1,400 words. **Pays 4£/word.**

MISCELLANEOUS FARM

$ $ ACRES U.S.A.

P.O. Box 91299, Austin TX 78709-1299. (512)892-4400. **Fax:** (512)892-4448. **E-mail:** editor@acresusa.com. **Website:** www.acresusa.com. "Monthly trade journal written by people who have a sincere interest in the principles of organic and sustainable agriculture." Estab. 1970. Circ. 18,000. Byline given. Editorial lead time 4 months. Submit seasonal material 6 months in advance. Accepts queries by mail, e-mail, fax. Accepts simultaneous submissions. Sample copy and writer's guidelines free.

NONFICTION Needs exposé, how-to, personal experience. Special issues: Seeds (January), Poultry (February), Compost/Compost Tea (April), Cattle & Grazing (May), Dairy (June), Grains (August), Soil Fertility & Testing (October). Does not want poetry, fillers, product profiles, or anything with a promotional tone. **Buys about 50 mss/year.** Send complete ms. Length: 1,000-2,500 words. **Pays 10¢/word**

$ $ BEE CULTURE

P.O. Box 706, Medina OH 44256-0706. **Fax:** (330)725-5624. **E-mail:** kim@beeculture.com. **Website:** www.beeculture.com. **Contact:** Mr. Kim Flottum, editor. **50% freelance written.** Covers the natural science of honey bees. "Monthly magazine for beekeepers and those interested in the natural science of honey bees, with environmentally-oriented articles relating to honey bees or pollination." Estab. 1873. Publishes ms an average of 4 months after acceptance. Accepts queries by mail, e-mail, fax, phone. Responds in 1 month to mss. Sample copy with 9x12 SASE and 5 first-class stamps. Guidelines and

NONFICTION Needs interview, personal experience, photo feature. No "How I Began Beekeeping" articles. Highly advanced, technical, and scientific abstracts accepted for review for quarterly Refered section. 2,000 words average. **Pays $200-250.**

REGIONAL FARM

$ $ AMERICAN AGRICULTURIST

5227 Baltimore Pike, Littlestown PA 17340. (717)359-0150. **Fax:** (717)359-0250. **E-mail:** jvogel@farmprogress.com. **Website:** www.farmprogress.com. **20% freelance written.** Monthly magazine covering "cutting-edge technology and news to help farmers improve their operations.". "We publish cutting-edge technology with ready on-farm application." Estab. 1842. Circ. 32,000. Publishes ms an average of 3 months after acceptance. Editorial lead time 3 months. Submit seasonal material 3 months in advance. Accepts queries by e-mail, fax. Accepts simultaneous submissions. Responds in 2 weeks to queries. Responds in 1 month to mss. Guidelines for #10 SASE.

NONFICTION Needs how-to, humor, inspirational, interview, new product, personal experience, photo feature feature, technical, "No stories without a strong tie to Mid-Atlantic farming.". **Buys 20 mss/year.** Query. Length: 500-1,000 words. **Pays $300-500.** Sometimes pays expenses of writers on assignment.

COLUMNS Country Air (humor, nostalgia, inspirational), 300-400 words. **Buys 12 mss/year mss/year.** Send complete ms. **Pays $100.**

$ THE LAND

Free Press Co., P.O. Box 3169, Mankato MN 56002-3169. (507)345-4523. **E-mail:** editor@thelandonline.com. **Website:** www.thelandonline.com. **40% freelance written.** Weekly tabloid covering farming in Minnesota and Northern Iowa. Although we're not tightly focused on any one type of farming, our articles must be of interest to farmers. In other words, will your article topic have an impact on people who live and work in rural areas? Prefers to work with Minnesota or Iowa writers. Estab. 1976. Circ. 33,000. Byline given. Publishes ms an average of 2 months after acceptance. Editorial lead time 2 months. Submit seasonal material 2 months in advance. Accepts queries by mail, e-mail. Responds in 3 weeks to queries. Responds in 2 months to mss. Guidelines with #10 SASE.

NONFICTION Needs general interest, ag, how-to, crop, livestock production, marketing. **Buys 80 mss/year.** Query. Length: 500-750 words. **Pays $50-70 for assigned articles.**

COLUMNS Query. **Pays $10-50.**

FINANCE

⟳ $$$ ADVISOR'S EDGE

Rogers Media, Inc., 333 Bloor St. E., 6th Floor, Toronto ON M4W 1G6 Canada. **E-mail:** philip.porado@advisor.rogers.com. **Website:** www.advisor.ca. **Contact:** Philip Porado, executive editor. Monthly magazine covering the financial industry (financial advisors and investment advisors). "*Advisor's Edge* focuses on sales and marketing opportunities for the financial advisor (how they can build their business and improve relationships with clients)." Estab. 1998. Circ. 36,000. Byline given. Offers 25% kill fee. Publishes ms an average of 3 months after acceptance. Editorial lead time 3 months. Accepts queries by e-mail.

NONFICTION Needs how-to, interview. No articles that aren't relevant to how a financial advisor does his/her job. **Buys 12 mss/year.** Query with published clips. Length: 1,500-2,000 words. **Pays $900 (Canadian).**

$$$ COLLECTIONS & CREDIT RISK

SourceMedia, One State St. Plaza, 27th Floor, New York NY 10004. **E-mail:** darren.waggoner@sourcemedia.com. **Website:** www.creditcollectionsworld.com. **Contact:** Darren Waggoner, chief editor. **33% freelance written.** Monthly journal covering debt collections and credit risk management. "*Collections & Credit Risk* is the only magazine that brings news and trends of strategic and competitive importance to collections and credit-policy executives who are driving the collections industry's growth and diversification in both commercial and consumer credit. These executives work for financial institutions, insurance companies, collections agencies, law firms and attorney networks, health-care providers, retailers, telecoms and utility companies, manufacturers, wholesalers, and government agencies." Estab. 1996. Circ. 30,000. Byline given. Offers kill fee. Kill fee determined case by case. Publishes ms an average of 3 months after acceptance. Editorial lead time 3 months. Accepts queries by mail. Sample copy free or online.

NONFICTION Needs interview, technical, business news and analysis. No unsolicited submissions accepted—freelancers work on assignment only. **Buys 30-40 mss/year.** Query with published clips. Length: 1,000-2,500 words. **Pays $800-1,000.** Sometimes pays expenses of writers on assignment.

$$$ CREDIT TODAY

P.O. Box 720, Roanoke VA 24004. (540)343-7500. **E-mail:** robl@credittoday.net; editor@credittoday.net. **Website:** www.credittoday.net. **Contact:** Rob Lawson, publisher. **50% freelance written.** Monthly newsletter covering business or trade credit. Estab. 1997. Publishes ms an average of 2 months after acceptance. Editorial lead time 1-2 months. Accepts queries by e-mail. NoGuidelines free.

NONFICTION Needs how-to, interview, technical. Does not want "puff" pieces promoting a particular product or vendor. **Buys 20 mss/year.** Send complete ms. Length: 700-1,800 words. **Pays $200-1,400.**

$$ CREDIT UNION MANAGEMENT

Credit Union Executives Society, 5510 Research Park Dr., Madison WI 53711-5377. (608)271-2664. **E-mail:** lisa@cues.org; cues@cues.org. **Website:** www.cumanagement.org. **Contact:** Lisa Hochgraf, editor. **44% freelance written.** Monthly magazine covering credit union, banking trends, management, HR, and marketing issues. "Our philosophy mirrors the credit union industry of cooperative financial services." Estab. 1978. Circ. 7,413. Publishes ms an average of 2 months after acceptance. Editorial lead time 3 months. Submit seasonal material 4 months in advance. Accepts queries by mail. Accepts simultaneous submissions. Responds in 2 weeks to queries. Responds in 1 month to mss. Sample copy and writer's guidelines free.

NONFICTION Needs book excerpts, how-to, be a good mentor/leader, recruit, etc., interview, technical. **Buys 74 mss/year.** Query with published clips. Length: 700-2,400 words. **$250-350 for assigned features.** Phone expenses only

COLUMNS Management Network (book/Web reviews, briefs), 300 words; e-marketing, 700 words; Point of Law, 700 words; Best Practices (new technology/operations trends), 700 words. Query with published clips.

$$$ THE FEDERAL CREDIT UNION

National Association of Federal Credit Unions, 3138 10th St. N., Arlington VA 22201. (703)522-4770; (800)336-4644. **Fax:** (703)524-1082. **E-mail:** sbroaddus@nafcu.org. **Website:** www.nafcu.org. **Contact:** Susan Broaddus, managing editor. **30% freelance written.** Estab. 1967. Circ. 8,000. Byline given. Publishes ms an average of 3 months after acceptance. Submit seasonal material 5 months in advance. Accepts queries by mail, e-mail, fax. Accepts simultaneous submissions. Responds in 2 months to queries. Sample copy for SAE with 10x13 envelope and 5 first-class stamps. Guidelines for #10 SASE.

NONFICTION Needs humor, inspirational, interview. Query with published clips and SASE. Length: 1,200-2,000 words. **Pays $400-1,000.**

💲💲 SERVICING MANAGEMENT

Zackin Publications, P.O. Box 2180, Waterbury CT 06722. (800)325-6745. **Fax:** (203)262-4680. **E-mail:** hall@sm-online.com. **Website:** www.sm-online.com. **Contact:** Phil Hall, editor. **15% freelance written.** Monthly magazine covering residential mortgage servicing. Estab. 1989. Circ. 20,000. Byline given. Publishes ms an average of 2 months after acceptance. Accepts queries by mail, e-mail, fax, phone. Responds in 2 weeks to queries. Guidelines available online.

NONFICTION Needs how-to, interview, new product, technical. **Buys 10 mss/year.** Query. Length: 1,500-2,500 words.

COLUMNS Buys 5 mss/year. Query. **Pays $200.**

💲💲💲💲 USAA MAGAZINE

USAA, 9800 Fredericksburg Rd., San Antonio TX 78288. **E-mail:** usaamagazine@usaa.com. **Website:** www.usaa.com/maglinks. **80% freelance written.** Quarterly magazine covering financial security for USAA members. "Conservative, common-sense approach to personal finance issues. Especially interested in how-to articles and pieces with actionable tips." Estab. 1970. Circ. 4.2 million. Byline given. Offers 25% kill fee. Publishes ms an average of 4 months after acceptance. Editorial lead time 6 months. Submit seasonal material 6 months in advance. Accepts queries by e-mail. Responds in 6-8 weeks to queries. No mss accepted. Guidelines by email.

NONFICTION Needs general interest, (finance), historical, (military), how-to, (personal finance), interview, (military/financial), personal experience, (finance). No poetry, photos, lifestyle unrelated to military or personal finance. **Buys 20 mss/year.** Query with published clips. Length: 750-1,500 words. **Pays $750-1,500 for assigned articles.** Sometimes pays expenses of writers on assignment.

💲💲💲💲 WEALTH MANAGER

Summit Business Media, 5081 Olympic Blvd., Erlanger KY 41018. (201)526-2344. **Fax:** (201)526-1260. **E-mail:** jgreen@sbmedia.com. **Website:** www.wealth-managermag.com. **Contact:** James Green, group

editor-in-chief. **90% freelance written.** Magazine published 11 times/year for financial advisors. Estab. 1999. Circ. 50,000. Byline given. Publishes ms an average of 3 months after acceptance. Editorial lead time 4 months. Submit seasonal material 4 months in advance. Accepts queries by e-mail. Responds in 1 month to queries.

NONFICTION Needs book excerpts, interview, technical. Do not submit anything that does not deal with financial planning issues or the financial markets. **Buys 30-40 mss/year.** Query with published clips. Length: 1,500-3,000 words. **Pays $1.50/word for assigned articles.**

FLORIST, NURSERIES AND LANDSCAPERS

💲💲 DIGGER

Oregon Association of Nurseries, 29751 S.W. Town Center Loop W., Wilsonville OR 97070. (503)682-5089; (800) 342-6401. **Fax:** (503)682-5099. **E-mail:** ckipp@oan.org; info@oan.org. **Website:** www.oan.org. **Contact:** Curt Kipp, publications manager. **50% freelance written.** Monthly magazine covering nursery and greenhouse industry. "*Digger* is a monthly magazine that focuses on industry trends, regulations, research, marketing, and membership activities. In August the magazine becomes *Digger Farwest Edition*, with all the features of *Digger* plus a complete guide to the annual Farwest Show, 1 of North America's top-attended nursery industry trade shows." Circ. 8,000. Byline given. Pays on receipt of copy. Offers 100% kill fee. Publishes ms an average of 2 months after acceptance. Editorial lead time 6 weeks. Submit seasonal material 2 months in advance. Accepts queries by mail, e-mail, fax, phone. Sample copy and writer's guidelines free.

NONFICTION Needs general interest, how-to, propagation techniques, other crop-growing tips, interview, personal experience, technical. Special issues: "Farwest Edition (August)—this is a triple-size issue that runs in tandem with our annual trade show (14,500 circulation for this issue)." No articles not related or pertinent to nursery and greenhouse industry. **Buys 20-30 mss/year.** Query. Length: 800-2,000 words. **Pays $125-400 for assigned articles. Pays $100-300 for unsolicited articles.** Sometimes pays expenses of writers on assignment.

$ GROWERTALKS

Ball Publishing, 622 Town Rd,, P.O. Box 1660, West Chicago IL 60186. (630)588-3385; (630)588-3401. **Fax:** (630)208-9350. **E-mail:** jzurko@ballpublishing.com; cbeytes@growertalks.com. **Website:** www.growertalks.com. **Contact:** Jen Zurko. **50% freelance written.** Monthly magazine. Estab. 1937. Circ. 9,500. Byline given. Publishes ms an average of 3 months after acceptance. Editorial lead time 4 months. Submit seasonal material 3 months in advance. Accepts queries by mail, e-mail, fax. Responds in 1 month to queries. Sample copy and writer's guidelines free.

NONFICTION Needs how-to, time- or money-saving projects for professional flower/plant growers, interview, ornamental horticulture growers, personal experience, of a grower, technical, about growing process in greenhouse setting. No articles that promote only 1 product. **Buys 36 mss/year.** Query. Length: 1,200-1,600 words. **Pays $125 minimum for assigned articles. Pays $75 minimum for unsolicited articles.**

GOVERNMENT AND PUBLIC SERVICE

$ $ AMERICAN CITY & COUNTY

Penton Media, 6151 Powers Ferry Rd. NW, Suite 200, Atlanta GA 30339. (770)618-0199. **Fax:** (770)618-0349. **E-mail:** bill.wolpin@penton.com; lindsay.isaacs@penton.com. **Website:** www.americancityandcounty.com. **Contact:** Lindsay Isaacs, managing editor; Bill Wolpin, editorial director. **40% freelance written.** Monthly magazine covering local and state government in the U.S. Estab. 1909. Circ. 75,000. Byline given. Offers 25% kill fee. Publishes ms an average of 2 months after acceptance. Editorial lead time 3 months. Accepts queries by e-mail. Accepts simultaneous submissions. Guidelines by e-mail.

NONFICTION Needs new product, local and state government news analysis. **Buys 36 mss/year.** Query. Length: 600-2,000 words. **Pays 30¢/published word.** Sometimes pays expenses of writers on assignment.

COLUMNS Issues & Trends (local and state government news analysis), 500-700 words. **Buys 24 ms/year. mss/year.** Query. **Pays $150-250.**

EVIDENCE TECHNOLOGY MAGAZINE

P.O. Box 555, Kearney MO 64060. **E-mail:** kmayo@evidencemagazine.com. **Website:** www.evidencemagazine.com. **Contact:** Kristi Mayo, editor. Bimonthly magazine providing news and information relating to the collection, processing and preservation of evidence. "This is a business-to-business publication, not a peer reviewed journal. We look for mainstream pieces. Our readers want general crime scenes and forensic science articles." Accepts queries by e-mail. Guidelines available online.

NONFICTION Needs general interest, how-to, interview, new product, technical. Query. **Pays 2 contributor copies.**

FIRE APPARATUS & EMERGENCY EQUIPMENT

21-00 Rt. 208 South, Fair Lawn NJ 07410. (973)251-5050. **Fax:** (973)251-5065. **E-mail:** news@firemagazine.com. **Website:** www.fireapparatus.com. **Contact:** Robert Halton, editor-in-chief. Monthly magazine focused on fire trucks, tools, and new technology.

NONFICTION Needs general interest, how-to, new product, technical. Query.

FIRE ENGINEERING

PennWell Corporation, 21-00 Route 208 S., Fair Lawn NJ 07410. (800)962-6484, ext. 5047. **E-mail:** dianef@pennwell.com. **Website:** www.fireengineering.com. **Contact:** Diane Feldman, executive editor. Monthly magazine covering issues of importance to firefighters. Estab. 1877. Accepts queries by mail, e-mail. Responds in 2-3 months to mss. Guidelines available online.

NONFICTION Needs how-to, new product,, incident reports, training. Send complete ms.

COLUMNS Volunteers Corner; Training Notebook; Rescue Company; The Engine Company; The Truck Company; Fire Prevention Bureau; Apparatus; The Shops; Fire Service EMS; Fire Service Court; Speaking of Safety; Fire Commentary; Technology Today; and Innovations: Homegrown. Send complete ms.

$ $ FIREHOUSE MAGAZINE

Cygnus Business Media, 3 Huntington Quadrangle, Suite 301N, Melville NY 11747. (631)845-2700. **Fax:** (631)845-7109. **E-mail:** Elizabeth.Friszell@cygnuspub.com. **Website:** www.firehouse.com. **Contact:** Elizabeth Friszell-Nerouslas, managing editor. **85% freelance written. Works with a small number of new/unpublished writers each year.** Monthly magazine. *Firehouse* covers major fires nationwide, controversial issues and trends in the fire service, the latest firefighting equipment and methods of firefighting, historical fires, firefighting history and memorabilia.

TRADE JOURNALS

Fire-related books, fire safety education, hazardous-materials incidents, and the emergency medical services are also covered. Estab. 1976. Circ. 83,538 (print). Byline given. Accepts queries by mail, e-mail, fax, online submission form. Sample copy for SAE with 9x12 envelope and 8 first-class stamps.

NONFICTION Needs book excerpts, of recent books on fire, EMS, and hazardous materials, historical, great fires in history, fire collectibles, the fire service of yesteryear, how-to, fight certain kinds of fires, buy and maintain equipment, run a fire department, technical on almost any phase of firefighting, techniques, equipment, training, administration, trends in the fire service. "No profiles of people or departments that are not unusual or innovative, reports of nonmajor fires, articles not slanted toward firefighters' interests. No poetry." **Buys 100 mss/year.** Query. "If you have any story ideas, questions, hints, tips, etc., please do not hesitate to call." Length: 500-3,000 words. The average length of each article is between 2-3 pages, including visuals. **Pays $50-400 for assigned articles.**

COLUMNS Training (effective methods); Book Reviews; Fire Safety (how departments teach fire safety to the public); Communicating (PR, dispatching); Arson (efforts to combat it). Length: 750-1,000 words. **Buys 50 mss/year.** Query or send complete ms. **Pays $100-300.**

FIRE PROTECTION CONTRACTOR

550 High St., Suite 220, Auburn CA 95603. (530)823-0706. **Fax:** (530)823-6937. **E-mail:** info@fpcmag.com. **Website:** www.fpcmag.com. **Contact:** Brant Brumbeloe, editor. Monthly magazine for the benefit of fire protection contractors, engineers, designers, sprinkler fitters, apprentices, fabricators, manufacturers, and distributors of fire protection products used in automatic fire sprinkler systems. Estab. 1978. Guidelines available online at website.

NONFICTION Needs general interest, how-to, interview, new product, technical. Query.

$ $ LAW ENFORCEMENT TECHNOLOGY MAGAZINE

Cygnus Business Media, 1233 Janesville Ave., Fort Atkinson WI 53538. (800)547-7377. **E-mail:** officer@corp.officer.com; tabatha.wethal@cygnusb2b.com. **Website:** www.officer.com. **Contact:** Tabatha Wethal. **40% freelance written.** Monthly magazine covering police management and technology. Estab. 1974. Circ. 30,000. Byline given. Publishes ms an average of 4 months after acceptance. Editorial lead time 6 months. Responds in 1 month to queries. Responds in 2 months to mss. Guidelines free.

NONFICTION Needs how-to, interview, photo feature, police management and training. **Buys 30 mss/year.** Query. Length: 1,200-2,000 words. **Pays $75-400 for assigned articles.**

$ $ 9-1-1MAGAZINE.COM

Official Publications, Inc., 18201 Weston Place, Tustin CA 92780. (714)544-7776. **Fax:** (714)838-9233. **E-mail:** editor@9-1-1magazine.com. **Contact:** Randall Larson, editor. **85% freelance written.** Trade magazine published 9 times/year for knowledgeable emergency communications professionals and those associated with this respectful profession. "Serving law enforcement, fire, and emergency medical services, with an emphasis on communications, *9-1-1 Magazine* provides valuable information to readers in all aspects of the public safety communications and response community. Each issue contains a blending of product-related, technical, operational, and people-oriented stories, covering the skills, training, and equipment which these professionals have in common." Estab. 1988. Circ. 18,000. Byline given. Offers 20% kill fee. Publishes ms an average of 4-6 months after acceptance. Accepts queries by mail, e-mail, fax. Responds in 1 month to queries and to mss. Sample copy for sae with 9x12 envelope and 5 first-class stamps. Guidelines available online.

NONFICTION Needs new product, photo feature, technical, incident report. **Buys 15-25 mss/year.** Query by e-mail. "We prefer queries, but will look at mss on speculation. Most positive responses to queries are considered on spec, but occasionally we will make assignments. Each ms should include a 25-word bio of the author. All submissions must include social security number, address, and phone number." Length: 1,000-2,500 words. **Pays 10-20¢/word.**

$ $ PLANNING

American Planning Association, 205 N. Michigan Ave., Suite 1200, Chicago IL 60601. (312)431-9100. **Fax:** (312)786-6700. **E-mail:** slewis@planning.org. **Website:** www.planning.org. **Contact:** Sylvia Lewis, editor; Richard Sessions, art director. **30% freelance written.** Monthly magazine emphasizing urban planning for adult, college-educated readers who are regional and urban planners in city, state, or federal agencies or in private business, or university faculty or students. Estab. 1972. Circ. 44,000. Byline given.

Publishes ms an average of 2 months after acceptance. Accepts queries by mail, e-mail, fax. Responds in 5 weeks to queries. Guidelines available online.

NONFICTION Special issues: Transportation Issue. Also needs news stories up to 500 words. **Buys 44 features and 33 news story mss/year.** Length: 500-3,000 words. **Pays $150-1,500.**

$$ POLICE AND SECURITY NEWS

DAYS Communications, Inc., 1208 Juniper St., Quakertown PA 18951-1520. (215)538-1240. **Fax:** (215)538-1208. **E-mail:** jdevery@policeandsecuritynews.com; dyaw@policeandsecuritynews.com. **Website:** www.policeandsecuritynews.com. **Contact:** James Devery, editor; David Yaw, publisher. **40% freelance written.** Bimonthly periodical on public law enforcement and Homeland Security. "Our publication is designed to provide educational and entertaining information directed toward management level. Technical information written for the expert in a manner the nonexpert can understand." Estab. 1984. Circ. 24,000. Byline given. Publishes ms an average of 2 months after acceptance. Accepts queries by mail, e-mail, fax, phone, online submission form. Accepts simultaneous submissions. Sample copy and writer's guidelines with 10x13 SASE with $2.53 postage.

NONFICTION Contact: Al Menear, articles editor. Needs exposé, historical, how-to, humor, interview, opinion, personal experience, photo feature, technical. **Buys 12 mss/year.** Query. Length: 200-2,500 words. **Pays 10¢/word. Sometimes pays in trade-out of services.**

FILLERS Needs facts, newsbreaks, short humor. **Buys 6 mss/year.** Length: 200-2,000 words. **10¢/word.**

THE POLICE CHIEF

International Association of Chiefs of Police, 515 N. Washington St., Alexandria VA 22301. (703)836-6767. **Fax:** (703)836-4543. **E-mail:** higginboth@theiacp.org. **Website:** www.policechiefmagazine.org. **Contact:** Charles Higginbotham, editor. Monthly magazine covering law enforcement issues. "Articles are contributed by practitioners in law enforcement or related fields. Manuscripts must be original work, previously unpublished and not simultaneously submitted to another publisher. No word rate is paid or other remuneration given. Contributors' opinions and statements are not purported to define official IACP policy or imply IACP endorsement." Byline given. Responds in 3-6 months Guidelines available online at website.

NONFICTION Needs general interest, administration, innovative techniques, new technological developments/applications, success stories, operational procedures, research, and other topics of interest to law enforcement administrators and practitioners. Authors are encouraged to submit PC disks in MS Word or WordPerfect (up to 6.1), or by e-mail to higginboth@theiacp.org. Brief biographical sketch of each author containing author's name, position title, agency, and complete mailing address must accompany manuscripts. 2,000-4,000/words. **Byline credit and 5 complimentary copies of issue with your article.**

$$$$ YOUTH TODAY

American Youth Work Center, 1200 17th St. NW, 4th Floor, Washington DC 20036. (202)785-0764. **E-mail:** pboyle@youthtoday.org. **Website:** www.youthtoday.org. **Contact:** Patrick Boyle, editor. **50% freelance written.** Newspaper published 10 times a year covering businesses that provide services to youth. Audience is people who run youth programs—mostly nonprofits and government agencies—who want help in providing services and getting funding. Estab. 1994. Circ. 9,000. Byline given. Offers $200 kill fee for features. Editorial lead time 2 months. Accepts queries by mail, e-mail, or disk. Accepts simultaneous submissions. Responds in 2 weeks to queries. Responds in 1 month to mss. Sample copy for $5. Guidelines available online.

NONFICTION Needs exposé, general interest, technical. "No feel-good stories about do-gooders. We examine the business of youth work." **Buys 5 mss/year.** Query. Send rèsumè, short cover letter, clips. Length: 600-2,500 words. **Pays $150-2,000 for assigned articles.** Pays expenses of writers on assignment.

COLUMNS "Youth Today also publishes 750-word guest columns, called Viewpoints. These pieces can be based on the writer's own experiences or based on research, but they must deal with an issue of interest to our readership and must soundly argue an opinion, or advocate for a change in thinking or action within the youth field."

GROCERIES AND FOOD PRODUCTS

$$$ CONVENIENCE DISTRIBUTION

American Wholesale Marketers Association, 2750 Prosperity Ave., Suite 530, Fairfax VA 22031. (703)208-

3358. **Fax:** (703)573-5738. **E-mail:** info@awmanet.org. **Website:** www.awmanet.org. **70% freelance written.** Magazine published 10 times/year. "We cover trends in candy, tobacco, groceries, beverages, snacks, and other product categories found in convenience stores, grocery stores, and drugstores, plus distribution topics. Contributors should have prior experience writing about the food, retail, and/or distribution industries. Editorial includes a mix of columns, departments, and features (2-6 pages). We also cover AWMA programs." Estab. 1948. Circ. 11,000. Byline given. Publishes ms an average of 2 months after acceptance. Editorial lead time 3-4 months. Accepts queries by e-mail only. Guidelines available online.

NONFICTION Needs how-to, technical, industry trends, also profiles of distribution firms. No comics, jokes, poems, or other fillers. **Buys 40 mss/year.** Query with published clips. Length: 1,200-3,600 words. **Pays 50¢/word.** Pays expenses of writers on assignment.

$$$$ FOOD PRODUCT DESIGN MAGAZINE

P.O. Box 3439, Northbrook IL 60065-3439. (480)990-1101 ext. 1241; (800)581-1811. **E-mail:** lkuntz@vpico.com. **Website:** www.foodproductdesign.com. **Contact:** Lynn A. Kuntz, editor-in-chief. **50% freelance written.** Monthly magazine covering food processing industry. Magazine written for food technologists by food technologists. No foodservice/restaurant, consumer, or recipe development. Estab. 1991. Circ. 30,000. Byline given. Publishes ms an average of 2 months after acceptance. Editorial lead time 4 months. Sample copy for SAE with 9×12 envelope and 5 first-class stamps.

NONFICTION Needs technical. **Buys 30 mss/year.** Length: 1,500-7,000 words. **Pays $100-1,500.** Sometimes pays expenses of writers on assignment.

COLUMNS Pays $100-500.

$ FRESH CUT MAGAZINE

Great American Publishing, P.O. Box 128, 75 Applewood Dr., Suite A, Sparta MI 49345. (616)887-9008. **Fax:** (616)887-2666. **E-mail:** fcedit@freshcut.com. **Website:** www.freshcut.com. **20% freelance written.** Monthly magazine covering the value-added and precut fruit and vegetable industry. The editor is interested in articles that focus on what different fresh-cut processors are doing. Estab. 1993. Circ. 16,000. Byline given. Publishes ms an average of 2 months after acceptance. Editorial lead time 2 months. Accepts queries by mail, e-mail, fax, phone, online submission form. Responds in 1 month to queries. Responds in 2 months to mss. Sample copy for SAE with 9x12 envelope. Guidelines for #10 SASE.

NONFICTION Needs historical, new product, opinion, technical. **Buys 2-4 mss/year.** Query with published clips.

COLUMNS Packaging; Food Safety; Processing/Engineering. **Buys 20 mss/year.** Query. **Pays $125-200.**

$$$ NATURAL FOOD NETWORK MAGAZINE

1030 W. Higgins Rd., Suite 230, Park Ridge IL 60068. (847)720-5600. **E-mail:** news@naturalfoodnet.com; pan@m2media360.com. **Website:** www.naturalfoodnet.com. **Contact:** Pan Demetrakakes, editor. **70% freelance written.** Bimonthly magazine covering natural and certified organic food industry (domestic and international). Estab. 2003. Circ. 15,000. Byline given. Offers 10% (up to $50 maximum) kill fee. Publishes ms an average of 2 months after acceptance. Editorial lead time 2 months. Submit seasonal material 2 months in advance. Accepts queries by e-mail. Accepts simultaneous submissions. Responds in 1 week to queries. Responds in 1 month to mss. Sample copy and guidelines free.

NONFICTION Does not want work with a consumer angle. **Buys 50 mss/year.** Query. Length: 250-1,500 words. **Pays $250-750.** Sometimes pays expenses of writers on assignment.

COLUMNS Q&A with industry leaders (natural and organic specialists in academia, trade associations and business); Worldview (interviews with internationally recognized leaders in organic food supply), both 750 words. **Buys 6 mss/year mss/year.** Query. **Pays $500.**

$$ THE PRODUCE NEWS

800 Kinderkamack Rd., Suite 100, Oradell NJ 07649. (201)986-7990. **Fax:** (201)986-7996. **E-mail:** groh@theproducenews.com. **Website:** www.theproducenews.com. **Contact:** John Groh, editor and publisher. **10% freelance written. Works with a small number of new/unpublished writers each year.** Weekly magazine for commercial growers and shippers, receivers, and distributors of fresh fruits and vegetables, including chain store produce buyers and merchandisers. Estab. 1897. Publishes ms an average of 2 weeks after acceptance. Accepts queries by mail, e-mail, fax. Responds in 1 month to queries. Sample copy and writer's guidelines for 10×13 SAE and 4 first-class stamps.

NONFICTION Query. **Pays $1/column inch minimum.** Sometimes pays expenses of writers on assignment.

💲💲 PRODUCE RETAILER

Vance Publishing Corp., 400 Knightsbridge Pkwy., Lincolnshire IL 60069. (512)906-0733. **E-mail:** pamelar@produceretailer.com. **Website:** http://produceretailer.com. **Contact:** Pamela Riemenschneider, editor; Tony Reyes, art director. **10% freelance written.** Monthly magazine. "*Produce Merchandising* is the only monthly journal on the market that is dedicated solely to produce merchandising information for retailers. Our purpose is to provide information about promotions, merchandising, and operations in the form of ideas and examples." Estab. 1988. Circ. 12,000. Byline given. Publishes ms an average of 3 months after acceptance. Editorial lead time 3 months. Accepts queries by mail. Responds in 2 weeks to queries.

NONFICTION Needs how-to, interview, new product, photo feature, technical, contact the editor for a specific assignment. **Buys 48 mss/year.** Query with published clips. Length: 1,000-1,500 words. **Pays $200-600.** Pays expenses.

COLUMNS Contact: Contact editor for a specific assignment. **Buys 30 mss/year.** Query with published clips. **Pays $200-450.**

🔄 💲💲 WESTERN GROCER MAGAZINE

Mercury Publications Ltd., 1740 Wellington Ave., Winnipeg MB R3H 0E8 Canada. (204)954-2085, ext. 291; (800)337-6372. **Fax:** (204)954-2057. **E-mail:** editorial@mercury.mb.ca. **Website:** www.westerngrocer.com. **Contact:** Nicole Sherwood, editorial coordinator. **75% freelance written.** Bimonthly magazine covering the grocery industry. Reports for the Western Canadian grocery, allied non-food and institutional industries. Each issue features a selection of relevant trade news and event coverage from the West and around the world. Feature reports offer market analysis, trend views, and insightful interviews from a wide variety of industry leaders. *The Western Grocer* target audience is independent retail food stores, supermarkets, manufacturers and food brokers, distributors and wholesalers of food, and allied non-food products, as well as bakers, specialty and health food stores, and convenience outlets. Estab. 1916. Circ. 15,500. Byline given. Pays 30-45 days from receipt of invoice. Offers 33% kill fee. Submit seasonal material 3 months in advance. Sample copy and writer's guidelines free.

NONFICTION Needs how-to, interview. Does not want industry reports and profiles on companies. Query with published clips. Length: 500-9,000 words. **Pays 25-35¢/word.** Sometimes pays expenses of writers on assignment.

HOME FURNISHINGS AND HOUSEHOLD GOODS

HOME LIGHTING & ACCESSORIES

Doctorow Communications, Inc., 180 Phillips Hill Rd., New City NY 10956. (973)779-1600. **Fax:** (845)708-5166. **Website:** www.homelighting.com. **25% freelance written. Prefers to work with published/established writers.** Monthly magazine for lighting showrooms/department stores. Estab. 1923. Circ. 10,000. Publishes ms an average of 6 months after acceptance. Submit seasonal material 6 months in advance. Accepts queries by mail. Responds in 2 months to queries. Sample copy for sae with 9x12 envelope and 4 first-class stamps.

NONFICTION Needs interview, with lighting retailers, personal experience, as a businessperson involved with lighting, technical, concerning lighting or lighting design, profile (of a successful lighting retailer/lamp buyer). Special issues: Outdoor (March); Tribute To Tiffanies (August). **Buys less than 10 mss/year.** Query.

HOSPITALS, NURSING AND NURSING HOMES

💲💲 CURRENT NURSING IN GERIATRIC CARE

Freiberg Press Inc., P.O. Box 612, Cedar Falls IA 50613. (319)553-0642; (800)354-3371. **Fax:** (319)553-0644. **E-mail:** bfreiberg@cfu.net. **Website:** www.care4elders.com. **Contact:** Bill Freiberg. **25% freelance written.** Bimonthly trade journal covering medical information and new developments in research for geriatric nurses and other practitioners. Estab. 2006. Byline sometimes given. Accepts queries by e-mail. Sample copy free; send e-mail to Kathy Freiderg at kfreiberg@cfu.net.

NONFICTION Query. Length: 500-1,500 words. **Pays 15¢/word for assigned articles.**

🔄 💲💲 LONG TERM CARE

Ontario Long Term Care Association, 345 Renfrew Dr., Third Floor, Markham ON L3R 9S9 Canada. (905)470-8995. **Fax:** (905)470-9595. **E-mail:** info@

oltca.com. **Website:** www.oltca.com. Quarterly magazine covering professional issues and practical articles of interest to staff working in a long-term care setting (nursing home, retirement home). Information must be applicable to a Canadian setting; focus should be on staff and on resident well-being. Estab. 1990. Circ. 6,000. Byline given. Publishes ms an average of 4 months after acceptance. Editorial lead time 3 months. Submit seasonal material 5 months in advance. Responds in 3 months to queries. Sample copy and guidelines free.

NONFICTION Needs general interest, how-to, practical, of use to long term care practitioners, inspirational, interview. No product-oriented articles. Query with published clips. Individuals should submit their ideas and/or completed articles to: justwrite@powergate.ca. Electronic versions in either Wordperfect or MS Word are preferred. Length:400-2,500 words. **Pays up to $500 (Canadian).**

COLUMNS Query with published clips. **Pays up to $500 (Canadian).**

🌐🌐🌐 NURSEWEEK

Gannett Healthcare Group, 1721 Moon Lake Blvd., Suite 540, Hoffman Estates IL 60169. **E-mail:** editor@nurse.com. **Website:** www.nurse.com. **Contact:** Jennifer Thew, RN. **98% freelance written.** Biweekly magazine covering nursing news. "Registered nurses read our magazine, which they receive for free by mail. We cover nursing news about people, practice, and the profession. Before you begin to write, we recommend that you review several of our magazines for content and style. We also suggest e-mailing your idea to the editorial director in your region (See list online). The editorial director can help you with the story's focus or angle, along with the organization and development of ideas." Estab. 1999. Circ. 155,000. Byline given. Offers $200 kill fee. Publishes ms an average of 2 months after acceptance. Editorial lead time 2-3 months. Submit seasonal material 4 months in advance. Accepts queries by e-mail. Accepts simultaneous submissions. Guidelines on website.

NONFICTION Needs interview, personal experience, , articles on innovative approaches to clinical care and evidence-based nursing practice, health-related legislation and regulation, community health programs, healthcare delivery systems, and professional development and management, advances in nursing specialties such as critical care, geriatrics,

perioperative care, women's health, home care, long-term care, emergency care, med/surg, pediatrics, advanced practice, education, and staff development. "We don't want poetry, fiction, or technical pieces." **Buys 20 mss/year.** Query. Length: 900 words. **Pays $200-800 for assigned or unsolicited articles.**

HOTELS, MOTELS, CLUBS, RESORTS AND RESTAURANTS

💲💲 BARTENDER MAGAZINE

Foley Publishing, P.O. Box 158, Liberty Corner NJ 07938. (908)766-6006. **Fax:** (908)766-6607. **E-mail:** barmag@aol.com. **Website:** www.bartender.com. Doug Swenson, art director. **Contact:** Jackie Foley, editor. **100% freelance written. Prefers to work with published/established writers; eager to work with new/unpublished writers.** Quarterly magazine emphasizing liquor and bartending for bartenders, tavern owners, and owners of restaurants with full-service liquor licenses. Estab. 1979. Circ. 150,000. Byline given. Publishes ms an average of 3 months after acceptance. Submit seasonal material 3 months in advance. Accepts simultaneous submissions. Responds in 2 months to mss. Sample copy with 9 x 12 SAE and 4 first-class stamps.

NONFICTION Needs general interest, historical, how-to, humor, interview with famous bartenders or ex-bartenders, new product, opinion, personal experience, photo feature, travel, nostalgia, unique bars, new techniques, new drinking trends, bar sports, bar magic tricks. Special issues: Annual Calendar and Daily Cocktail Recipe Guide. Send complete ms and SASE. Length: 100-1,000 words.

COLUMNS Bar of the Month; Bartender of the Month; Creative Cocktails; Bar Sports; Quiz; Bar Art; Wine Cellar; Tips from the Top (from prominent figures in the liquor industry); One For the Road (travel); Collectors (bar or liquor-related items); Photo Essays. Length: 200-1,000 words. Query by mail only with SASE. **Pays $50-200.**

FILLERS Needs anecdotes, newsbreaks, short humor, clippings, jokes, gags. Length: 25-100 words. **Pays $5-25.**

♻ 💲💲 HOTELIER

Kostuch Publications, Ltd., 23 Lesmill Rd., Suite 101, Toronto ON M3B 3P6 Canada. (416)447-0888. **Fax:** (416)447-5333. **E-mail:** rcaira@foodservice.ca. **Web-**

site: www.hoteliermagazine.com. **Contact:** Rosanna Caira, editor and publisher. **40% freelance written.** Magazine published 8 times/year covering the Canadian hotel industry. Estab. 1989. Circ. 9,000. Byline given. Editorial lead time 3 months. Submit seasonal material 2 months in advance. Accepts queries by mail, fax. Sample copy and writer's guidelines free.

NONFICTION Needs how-to, new product. No case studies. **Buys 30-50 mss/year.** Query. Length: 700-1,500 words. **Pays 35¢/word (Canadian) for assigned articles.** Sometimes pays expenses of writers on assignment.

⑨⑨⑨ PIZZA TODAY

Macfadden Protech, LLC, 908 S. 8th St., Suite 200, Louisville KY 40203. (502)736-9500. **Fax:** (502)736-9502. **E-mail:** jwhite@pizzatoday.com. **Website:** www.pizzatoday.com. Mandy Detwiler, managing editor. **Contact:** Jeremy White, editor-in-chief. **30% freelance written. Works with published/established writers; occasionally works with new writers.** Monthly magazine for the pizza industry, covering trends, features of successful pizza operators, business and management advice, etc. Estab. 1984. Circ. 44,000. Byline given. Publishes ms an average of 2 months after acceptance. Submit seasonal material 3 months in advance. Accepts queries by mail, e-mail, fax. Responds in 2 months to queries. Responds in 3 weeks to mss. Sample copy for sae with 10x13 envelope and 6 first-class stamps. Guidelines for #10 SASE and online.

NONFICTION Needs interview, entrepreneurial slants, pizza production and delivery, employee training, hiring, marketing, and business management. No fillers, humor, or poetry. **Buys 85 mss/year.** Length: 1,000 words. **Pays 50¢/word, occasionally more.** Sometimes pays expenses of writers on assignment.

⑨⑨⑨ SANTÉ MAGAZINE

On-Premise Communications, 100 South St., Bennington VT 05201. (802)442-6771. **Fax:** (802)442-6859. **E-mail:** mvaughan@santemagazine.com. **Website:** www.isantemagazine.com. **Contact:** Mark Vaughan, editor. **75% freelance written.** Four-issues-per-year magazine covering food, wine, spirits, and management topics for restaurant professionals. "Information and specific advice for restaurant professionals on operating a profitable food and beverage program. Writers should 'speak' to readers on a professional-to-professional basis." Estab. 1996. Circ. 45,000. Byline given. Offers 50% kill fee. Publishes

ms an average of 2 months after acceptance. Editorial lead time 3 months. Submit seasonal material 6 months in advance. Accepts queries by e-mail. Responds in 2 weeks to queries. "We do not accept mss." Sample copy available. Guidelines by email.

NONFICTION Needs interview, Restaurant business news. "We do not want consumer-focused pieces." **Buys 20 mss/year.** Query with published clips. Length: 650-1,800 words. Sometimes pays expenses of writers on assignment.

COLUMNS "Due to a Redesign, 650 words; Bar Tab (focuses on 1 bar's unique strategy for success), 1,000 words; Restaurant Profile (a business-related look at what qualities make 1 restaurant successful), 1,000 words; Maximizing Profits (covers 1 great profit-maximizing strategy per issue from several sources), Signature Dish (highlights 1 chef's background and favorite dish with recipe), Sommeliers Choice (6 top wine managers recommend favorite wines; with brief profiles of each manager), Distillations (6 bar professionals offer their favorite drink for a particular type of spirit; with brief profiles of each manager), 1,500 words; Provisions (like The Goods only longer; an in-depth look at a special ingredient), 1,500 words. **Buys 20 mss/year.** Query with published clips. **Pays $300-$800.**

◐ ⑨⑨ WESTERN HOTELIER MAGAZINE

Mercury Publications, Ltd., 1740 Wellington Ave., Winnipeg MB R3H 0E8 Canada. (204)954-2085. **Fax:** (204)954-2057. **E-mail:** editorial@mercury.mb.ca. **Website:** www.mercury.mb.ca. **Contact:** Nicole Sherwood, editorial coordinator. **33% freelance written.** Quarterly magazine covering the hotel industry. "*Western Hotelier* is dedicated to the accommodation industry in Western Canada and US western border states. *WH* offers the West's best mix of news and feature reports geared to hotel management. Feature reports are written on a sector basis and are created to help generate enhanced profitability and better understanding." Circ. 4,342. Byline given. Pays 30-45 days from receipt of invoice. Offers 33% kill fee. Submit seasonal material 3 months in advance. Accepts queries by mail, fax. Accepts simultaneous submissions. Responds in 2 weeks to queries. Sample copy and writer's guidelines free.

NONFICTION Needs how-to, train staff, interview. Industry reports and profiles on companies. Query with published clips. Length: 500-9,000 words. **Pays 25-35¢/word.** Sometimes pays expenses of writers on assignment.

☺ 💲💲 WESTERN RESTAURANT NEWS

Mercury Publications, Ltd., 1740 Wellington Ave., Winnipeg MB R3H 0E8 Canada. (204)954-2085. **Fax:** (204)954-2057. **E-mail:** editorial@mercury.mb.ca. **Website:** www.westernrestaurantnews.com; www.mercury.mb.ca. **Contact:** Nicole Sherwood, editorial director. **20% freelance written.** Bimonthly magazine covering the restaurant trade. Reports profiles and industry reports on associations, regional business developments, etc. *"Western Restaurant News Magazine* is the authoritative voice of the foodservice industry in Western Canada. Offering a total package to readers, *WRN* delivers concise news articles, new product news, and coverage of the leading trade events in the West, across the country, and around the world." Estab. 1994. Circ. 14,532. Byline given. Pays 30-45 days from receipt of invoice. Offers 33% kill fee. Submit seasonal material 3 months in advance. Accepts queries by mail, fax. Accepts simultaneous submissions. Sample copy and writer's guidelines free.

NONFICTION Needs how-to, interview. Industry reports and profiles on companies. Query with published clips. Length: 500-9,000 words. **Pays 25-35¢/word.** Sometimes pays expenses of writers on assignment.

INDUSTRIAL OPERATIONS

☺ 💲💲 COMMERCE & INDUSTRY

Mercury Publications, Ltd., 1740 Wellington Ave., Winnipeg MB R3H 0E8 Canada. (204)954-2085. **Fax:** (204)954-2057. **E-mail:** editorial@mercury.mb.ca. **Website:** www.mercury.mb.ca. **Contact:** Nicole Sherwood, editorial coordinator. **75% freelance written.** Bimonthly magazine covering the business and industrial sectors. Industry reports and company profiles provide readers with an in-depth insight into key areas of interest in their profession. Estab. 1947. Circ. 18,876. Byline given. Pays 30-45 days from receipt of invoice. Offers 33% kill fee. Submit seasonal material 3 months in advance. Accepts queries by mail, e-mail, fax. Accepts simultaneous submissions. Responds in 2 weeks to queries. Sample copy and writer's guidelines free or by e-mail.

NONFICTION Needs how-to, interview. Industry reports and profiles on companies. Query with published clips. Length: 500-9,000 words. **Pays 25-35¢/word.** Sometimes pays expenses of writers on assignment.

💲💲 MODERN MATERIALS HANDLING

Peerless Media, 111 Speen St., Suite 200, Framingham MA 01701. (508)663-1500. **E-mail:** mlevans@ehpub.com; robert.trebilcock@myfairpoint.net. **Website:** www.mmh.com. **Contact:** Michael Levans, editorial director. **40% freelance written.** Magazine published 13 times/year covering warehousing, distribution centers, inventory. *"Modern Materials Handling* is a national magazine read by managers of warehouses and distribution centers. We focus on lively, well-written articles telling our readers how they can achieve maximum facility productivity and efficiency. We cover technology, too." Estab. 1945. Circ. 81,000. Byline given. Pays on acceptance (allow 4-6 weeks for invoice processing). Publishes ms an average of 1 month after acceptance. Editorial lead time 3 months. Accepts queries by mail, e-mail, fax. Sample copy and guidelines free.

NONFICTION Needs how-to, new product, technical. Special issues: State-of-the-Industry Report, Peak Performer, Salary and Wage survey, Warehouse of the Year. Doesn't want "anything that doesn't deal with our topic—warehousing. No general-interest profiles or interviews." Buys 25 mss/year. Query with published clips. **Pays $300-650.**

INFORMATION SYSTEMS

💲💲💲 DESKTOP ENGINEERING

Level 5 Communications, Inc., 1283 Main St., P.O. Box 1039, Dublin NH 03444. (603)563-1631. **Fax:** (603)563-8192. **E-mail:** jgooch@deskeng.com. **E-mail:** de-editors@deskeng.com. **Website:** www.deskeng.com. **Contact:** Jamie Gooch, managing editor. **90% freelance written.** Monthly magazine covering computer hardware/software for hands-on design and mechanical engineers, analysis engineers, and engineering management. Ten special supplements/year. Estab. 1995. Circ. 63,000. Byline given. Pays in month of publication. Kill fee for assigned story. Publishes ms an average of 2 months after acceptance. Editorial lead time 3 months. Accepts queries by mail, e-mail, phone. Responds in 2 weeks to queries. Responds in 1 month to mss. Sample copy for free with 8x10 SASE. Guidelines available on website.

NONFICTION Needs how-to, new product, reviews, technical, design. No fluff. **Buys 50-70 mss/year.** Query. Submit outline before you write an article. Length: 1,000-1,200 words. **Pays per project. Pay negotiable for unsolicited articles.** Sometimes pays expenses of writers on assignment.

COLUMNS Product Briefs (new products), 50-100 words; Reviews (software, hardware), 500-1,500 words.

$$$ GAME DEVELOPER

United Business Media LLC, 303 Second St., South Tower, 9th Floor, San Francisco CA 94107. (415)947-6000. **Fax:** (415)947-6090. **E-mail:** bsheffield@gdmag.com; jen.steele@ubm.com. **E-mail:** editors@gdmag.com. **Website:** www.gdmag.com. **Contact:** Brandon Sheffield, editor-in-chief; Jen Steele. **90% freelance written.** Monthly magazine covering computer game development. Estab. 1994. Circ. 35,000. Byline given. Publishes ms an average of 3-6 months after acceptance. Editorial lead time 3 months. Submit seasonal material 4 months in advance. Accepts queries by e-mail. Guidelines available online.

NONFICTION Needs how-to, personal experience, technical. **Buys 50 mss/year.** Query. Length: 3,500 words for Feature articles and the Postmortem column; 600-1,200 words for product reviews (game development tools). **Pays $150/page.**

$ JOURNAL OF INFORMATION ETHICS

McFarland & Co., Inc., Publishers, P.O. Box 611, Jefferson NC 28640. (336)246-4460. **E-mail:** hauptman@stcloudstate.edu. **90% freelance written.** Semiannual scholarly journal covering all of the information sciences. "Addresses ethical issues in all of the information sciences with a deliberately interdisciplinary approach. Topics range from electronic mail monitoring to library acquisition of controversial material to archival ethics. The *Journal*'s aim is to present thoughtful considerations of ethical dilemmas that arise in a rapidly evolving system of information exchange and dissemination." Estab. 1992. Byline given. Publishes ms an average of 2 years after acceptance. Submit seasonal material 8 months in advance. Accepts queries by mail, e-mail, phone. Sample copy for $30. Guidelines free.

NONFICTION Needs essays, opinion, Also book reviews. **Buys 10-12 mss/year.** Send complete ms. Length: 500-3,500 words. **Pays $25-50, depending on length.**

$$$ SYSTEM INEWS

Penton Technology Media, 748 Whalers Way, Fort Collins CO 80525. (970)663-4700; (800)621-1544. **E-mail:** editors@systeminetwork.com. **Website:** www.iseriesnetwork.com. **40% freelance written.** Magazine, published 12 times/year, focused on programming, networking, IS management, and technology for users of IBM AS/400, iSERIES, SYSTEM i, AND IBM i platform. Estab. 1982. Circ. 30,000 (international). Byline given. Offers 50% kill fee. Publishes ms an average of 3 months after acceptance. Editorial lead time 4 months. Submit seasonal material 4 months in advance. Accepts queries by e-mail. Responds in 3 weeks to queries. Responds in 5 weeks to mss. Guidelines available online.

NONFICTION Needs technical. Query. Length: 1,500-2,500 words. **Pays $300/$500 flat fee for assigned articles, depending on article quality and technical depth.**

COLUMNS Load'n'go (complete utility).

$$$$ TECHNOLOGY REVIEW

MIT, One Main St., 13th Floor, Cambridge MA 02142. (617)475-8000. **Fax:** (617)475-8042. **E-mail:** jason.pontin@technologyreview.com; david.rotman@technologyreview.com. **Website:** www.technologyreview.com. **Contact:** Jason Pontin, editor-in-chief; David Rotman, editor. Magazine published 10 times/year covering information technology, biotech, material science, and nanotechnology. *Technology Review* promotes the understanding of emerging technologies and their impact. Estab. 1899. Circ. 310,000. Byline given. Accepts queries by mail, e-mail.

NONFICTION Length: 2,000-4,000 words. **Pays $1-3/word.**

FILLERS Short tidbits that relate laboratory prototypes on their way to market in 1-5 years. Length: 150-250 words. **Pays $1-3/word.**

INSURANCE

$$$$ ADVISOR TODAY

NAIFA, 2901 Telestar Court, Falls Church VA 22042. (703)770-8204. **E-mail:** amseka@naifa.org. **Website:** www.advisortoday.com. **Contact:** Ayo Mseka. **25% freelance written.** Monthly magazine covering life insurance and financial planning. "Writers must demonstrate an understanding at what insurance agents and financial advisors do to earn business and serve their clients." Estab. 1906. Circ. 110,000. Pays on acceptance or publication (by mutual agreement with editor). Publishes ms an average of 3 months after acceptance. Editorial lead time 3 months. Submit seasonal material 6 months in advance. Accepts queries by mail, e-mail, fax, phone. Accepts simultaneous submissions. Guidelines available online at www.advisortoday.com/about/contribute.cfm.

NONFICTION **Buys 8 mss/year.** "We prefer e-mail submissions in Microsoft Word format. For other formats and submission methods, please query first. For all articles and queries, contact Ayo Mseka. Web articles should cover the same subject matter covered in the magazine. The articles can be between 300-800 words and should be submitted to Ayo Mseka. Please indicate where a story has been previously published articles have been accepted." Length: 1,500-6,000 words. **Pays $800-2,000.**

JEWELRY

+ $ ADORNMENT

Association for the Study of Jewelry & Related Arts, 246 N. Regent St., Port Chester NY 10573. **E-mail:** ekarlin@usa.net. **Website:** www.jewelryandrelatedarts.com; www.asjra.net. **50% freelance written.** Quarterly magazine covering jewelry—antique to modern. Estab. 2002. Circ. 1,000+. Byline given. Publishes ms an average of 3 months after acceptance. Editorial lead time 3 months. Accepts queries by mail, e-mail. Responds in 1-2 weeks to queries. Responds in 1 month to mss. Sample copy free as a PDF e-mailed or $10 for hard copy mailed . Guidelines free.

NONFICTION Needs book excerpts, (reviews), (articles on jewelry), interview, (of jewelry artists), Exhibition reviews—in-depth articles on jewelry subjects. We do not want articles about retail jewelry. We write about ancient, antique, period, and unique and studio jewelers. **Buys 12-15 mss/year mss/year.** Query with published clips. Length: 1,000-3,000 words. **Pays $125 max. for assigned articles. Pays $0 for unsolicited articles.**

$ THE DIAMOND REGISTRY

580 Fifth Ave., New York NY 10036. (212)575-0444; (888)669-4747. **E-mail:** info@diamondregistry.com. **Website:** www.diamondregistry.com. **50% freelance written.** "Our publication is the first independent insider newsletter of diamond information. Regularly quoted in *The New York Times* and other financial publications—*Fortune, Forbes* and *Newsweek*— The *Diamond Registry* contains analyses and forecasts on diamond supplies prices and trends, worldwide mining updates, exclusive interviews with some of the most important players in the industry, and the latest breaking news." Estab. 1969. Submit seasonal material 1 month in advance. Accepts queries by mail, e-mail. Accepts simultaneous submissions. Responds in about 3 weeks to mss. Sample copy for $5.

NONFICTION Needs how-to, ways to increase sales in diamonds, improve security, etc., interview, of interest to diamond dealers or jewelers, prevention advice (on crimes against jewelers). Send complete ms. Length: 50-500 words. **Pays $75-150.**

$$ THE ENGRAVERS JOURNAL

P.O. Box 318, Brighton MI 48116. (810)229-5725. **Fax:** (810)229-8320. **E-mail:** editor@engraversjournal.com. **Website:** www.engraversjournal.com. **Contact:** Managing Editor. **70% freelance written.** Monthly magazine covering the recognition and identification industry (engraving, marking devices, awards, jewelry, and signage). "We provide practical information for the education and advancement of our readers, mainly retail business owners." Estab. 1975. Byline given. Publishes ms an average of 3-9 months after acceptance. Accepts queries by mail, e-mail, fax. Responds in 2 weeks to mss. Guidelines free.

NONFICTION Needs general interest, industry related, how-to, small business subjects, increase sales, develop new markets, use new sales techniques, etc., technical. No general overviews of the industry. Length: 1,000-5,000 words. **Pays $200 and up.**

JOURNALISM AND WRITING

$ AUTHORSHIP

National Writers Association, 10940 S. Parker Rd., #508, Parker CO 80134. (303)841-0246. **E-mail:** natlwritersassn@hotmail.com. **Website:** www.webmasternationalwriters.com. Quarterly magazine covering writing articles only. "Association magazine targeted to beginning and professional writers. Covers how-to, humor, marketing issues. Disk and e-mail submissions preferred." Estab. 1950s. Circ. 4,000. Byline given. Editorial lead time 3 months. Submit seasonal material 6 months in advance. Accepts simultaneous submissions. Responds in 2 months to queries. Sample copy for stamped, self-addressed, 8½x11 envelope.

NONFICTION Buys 25 mss/year. Query or send complete ms. Length: 1,200 words. **Pays $10, or discount on memberships and copies.**

🌀 BOOK DEALERS WORLD

North American Bookdealers Exchange, P.O. Box 606, Cottage Grove OR 97424. (541)942-7455. **Fax:** (541)942-7455. **E-mail:** nabe@bookmarketingprofits.com. **Website:** www.bookmarketingprofits.com. **50% freelance written.** Quarterly magazine covering writing, self-publishing, and marketing books by mail. Circ. 20,000. Byline given. Publishes ms an average of 3 months after acceptance. Accepts simultaneous submissions. Responds in 1 month to queries. Sample copy for $3.

NONFICTION Needs book excerpts, writing, mail order, direct mail, publishing, how-to, home business by mail, advertising, interview, of successful self-publishers, positive articles on self-publishing, new writing angles, marketing. **Buys 10 mss/year.** Send complete ms. Length: 1,000-1,500 words. **Pays $25-50.**

COLUMNS Publisher Profile (on successful self-publishers and their marketing strategy). Length: 250-1,000 words. **Buys 20 mss/year.** Send complete ms. **Pays $5-20.**

FILLERS Fillers concerning writing, publishing, or books. **Buys 6 mss/year.** Length: 100-250 words. **Pays $3-10.**

🌀 🌀 🌀 CANADIAN SCREENWRITER

Writers Guild of Canada, 366 Adelaide St. W., Suite 401, Toronto ON M5V 1R9 Canada. (416)979-7907. **Fax:** (416)979-9273. **E-mail:** info@wgc.ca; m.parker@wgc.ca. **Website:** www.wgc.ca/magazine. **Contact:** Maureen Parker, executive director. **80% freelance written.** Magazine published 3 times/year covering screenwriting for television, film, radio, and digital media. *Canadian Screenwriter* profiles Canadian screenwriters, provides industry news, and offers practical writing tips for screenwriters. Estab. 1998. Circ. 4,000. Byline given. Offers 50% kill fee. Publishes ms an average of 1 month after acceptance. Editorial lead time 2 months. Submit seasonal material 2 months in advance. Accepts queries by e-mail. Responds in 1 week to queries. Responds in 1 month to mss. Guidelines by e-mail.

NONFICTION Needs how-to, humor, interview. Does not want writing on foreign screenwriters. The focus is on Canadian-resident screenwriters. **Buys 12 mss/year.** Query with published clips. Length: 750-

2,200 words. **Pays 50¢/word.** Sometimes pays expenses of writers on assignment.

🌀 🌀 CANADIAN WRITER'S JOURNAL

Box 1178, New Liskeard ON P0J 1P0 Canada. (705)647-5424. **Fax:** (705)647-8366. **E-mail:** editor@cwj.ca. **Website:** www.cwj.ca. **Contact:** Deborah Ranchuk, editor. **75% freelance written.** Bimonthly magazine for writers. "Digest-size magazine for writers emphasizing short 'how-to' articles, which convey easily understood information useful to both apprentice and professional writers. General policy and postal subsidies require that the magazine must carry a substantial Canadian content. We try for about 90% Canadian content, but prefer good material over country of origin, or how well you're known. Writers may query, but unsolicited mss are welcome." Estab. 1984. Circ. 350. Byline given. Publishes ms an average of 2-9 months after acceptance. Accepts queries by mail, e-mail, fax, phone; preference will be given to the article that can be submitted electronically. Responds in 2 months to queries. Sample copy for $8, including postage. Guidelines available online.

NONFICTION Needs how-to, articles for writers, , humorous and seasonal items. **Buys 200 mss/year.** Query optional. 400-2,500/words for articles; 250-500/words for book reviews **Pays $7.50/published magazine page (approx. 450 words), plus 1 complimentary copy. A $2 premium is paid for electronic submissions.**

FICTION Fiction is published only through semi-annual short fiction contest with April 30 deadline. Send SASE for rules, or see guidelines on website. Does not want gratuitous violence or sex subject matters. Accepts submissions by e-mail. Responds in 2 months to queries. Pays on publication for one-time rights.

POETRY Poetry must be unpublished elsewhere; short poems or extracts used as part of articles on the writing of poetry. Submit up to 5 poems at a time. No previously published poems. Accepts e-mail submissions (pasted into body of message, with 'Submission' in the subject line). Include SASE with postal submissions. "U.S. postage accepted; do not affix to envelope. Poems should be titled." Responds in 3-6 months. **Pays $2-5 per poem published (depending on length) and 1 contributor's copy. SASE required for response and payment.**

🌀 🌀 🌀 ECONTENT MAGAZINE

Online, Inc., 143 Old Marlton Pike, Medford NJ 08055. (203)761-1466; (800)248-8466. **Fax:** (203)761-1444;

(203)304-9300. **E-mail:** theresa.cramer@infotoday.com. **Website:** www.econtentmag.com. **Contact:** Theresa Cramer, editor. **90% freelance written.** Monthly magazine covering digital content trends, strategies, etc. "*EContent* is a business publication. Readers need to stay on top of industry trends and developments." Estab. 1979. Circ. 12,000. Byline given. Pays within 1 month of publication. Editorial lead time 3-4 months. Accepts queries by email. Responds in 3 weeks to queries. Responds in 1 month to mss. Sample copy and writer's guidelines online.

NONFICTION Needs exposé, how-to, interview, new product, opinion, technical, news features, strategic and solution-oriented features. No academic or straight Q&A. **Buys 48 mss/year.** Query with published clips. Submit electronically as e-mail attachment. Length: 500-700 words. **Pays 40-50¢/word.** Sometimes pays expenses of writers on assignment.

COLUMNS Profiles (short profile of unique company, person or product), 1,200 words; New Features (breaking news of content-related topics), 500 words maximum. **Buys 40 mss/year.** Query with published clips. **Pays 30-40¢/word.**

🍁 $ FELLOWSCRIPT

InScribe Christian Writers' Fellowship, *FellowScript*, c/o P.O. Box 6201, Wetaskiwin AB T9A 2E9 Canada. **E-mail:** fellowscript@gmail.com. **Website:** www.inscribe.org. **Contact:** Bonnie Way, editor. **100% freelance written.** Quarterly writers' newsletter featuring Christian writing. "Our readers are Christians with a commitment to writing. Among our readership are best-selling authors and unpublished beginning writers. Submissions to us should include practical information, something the reader can immediately put into practice." Estab. 1983. Circ. 200. Byline given. Publishes ms an average of 6-12 months after acceptance. Editorial lead time 3 months. Submit seasonal material 4 months in advance. Accepts queries by e-mail, prefers full ms by email; postal submissions only accepted from InScribe members. Accepts simultaneous submissions. Responds in 1 month to queries and mss. Sample copy for $5, 9 x 12 SAE, and 3 first-class stamps (Canadian) or IRCs. Guidelines available online.

NONFICTION Needs essays, exposé, how-to, for writers, interview, new product. Does not want poetry, fiction, personal experience, testimony or think piece, commentary articles. **Buys 30-45 mss/year.** Send complete ms attached in rtf or doc format. Length: 400-1,200 words. **Pays 2 1/2¢/word (first rights); 1 1/2¢/word reprints (Canadian funds).**

COLUMNS Book reviews, 150-300 words; Market Updates, 50-300 words. **Buys 1-3. mss/year.** Send complete ms. **Pays 1 copy.**

FILLERS Needs facts, newsbreaks. **Buys 5-10 mss/year.** Length: 25-300 words. **Pays 1 copy.**

🌐 $ FREELANCE MARKET NEWS

The Writers Bureau Ltd., 8-10 Dutton St., Manchester M3 1LE England. (44)(161)819-9922. **Fax:** (44)(161)819-2842. **E-mail:** fmn@writersbureau.com. **Website:** www.freelancemarketnews.com. **15% freelance written.** Monthly newsletter covering freelance writing. Estab. 1968. Byline given. Publishes ms an average of 3 months after acceptance. Editorial lead time 3 months. Submit seasonal material 3 months in advance. Accepts queries by mail, e-mail, fax. Sample copy and guidelines available online.

NONFICTION Needs how-to sell your writing/improve your writing. **Buys 12 mss/year.** Length: 700 words. **Pays £50/1,000 words.**

COLUMNS New Markets (magazines which have recently been published); Fillers & Letters; Overseas Markets (obviously only English-language publications); Market Notes (established publications accepting articles, fiction, reviews, or poetry). All should be between 40 and 200 words. **Pays £40/1,000 words.**

$$ FREELANCE WRITER'S REPORT

CNW Publishing, Inc., 45 Main St., P.O. Box A, North Stratford NH 03590-0167. (603)922-8338. **E-mail:** fwrwm@writers-editors.com. **Website:** www.writers-editors.com. **25% freelance written.** Monthly newsletter. "*FWR* covers the marketing and business/office management aspects of running a freelance writing business. Articles must be of value to the established freelancer; nothing basic." Estab. 1982. Byline given. Publishes ms an average of 6 months after acceptance. Editorial lead time 2 months. Submit seasonal material 2 months in advance. Accepts simultaneous submissions. Responds in 1 week to queries. Responds in 2 weeks to mss. Sample copy for 6x9 SAE with 2 first-class stamps (for back copy); $4 for current copy. Guidelines and

NONFICTION Needs book excerpts, how-to (market, increase income or profits). "No articles about the basics of freelancing." **Buys 50 mss/year.** Send complete ms by e-mail. Length: Up to 900 words. **Pays 10¢/word.**

$$ MSLEXIA

Mslexia Publications Ltd., P.O. Box 656, Newcastle upon Tyne NE99 1PZ United Kingdom. [(44)(191)233-3860. **E-mail:** submissions@mslexia.co.uk; postbag@mslexia.co.uk. **Website:** www.mslexia.co.uk. **Contact:** Debbie Taylor, editorial director. **60% freelance written.** Quarterly magazine offering advice and publishing opportunities for women writers, plus poetry and prose submissions on a different theme each issue. "*Mslexia* tells you all you need to know about exploring your creativity and getting into print. No other magazine provides *Mslexia*'s unique mix of advice and inspiration; news, reviews, interviews; competitions, events, grants; all served up with a challenging selection of new poetry and prose. *Mslexia* is read by authors and absolute beginners. A quarterly master class in the business and psychology of writing, it's the essential magazine for women who write." Estab. 1998. Circ. 9,000. Byline given. Offers 50% kill fee. Publishes ms an average of 1 month after acceptance. Editorial lead time 3 months. Submit seasonal material 3 months in advance. Accepts queries by mail, e-mail, phone. Accepts simultaneous submissions. Responds in 3 months to mss. Writer's guidelines online or by e-mail.

NONFICTION Needs how-to, interview, opinion, personal experience. No general items about women or academic features. We are only interested in features (for tertiary-educated readership) about women's writing and literature. **Buys 40 mss/year.** Query with published clips. Length: 500-2,200 words. **Pays $70-400 for assigned articles. Pays $70-300 for unsolicited articles.** Sometimes pays expenses of writers on assignment.

COLUMNS We are open to suggestions, but would only commission 1 new column/year, probably from a UK-based writer. **Buys 12 mss/year.** Query with published clips.

FICTION See guidelines on website. "Submissions not on one of our current themes will be returned (if submitted with a SASE) or destroyed." **Buys 30 mss/year.** Send complete ms. Length: 50-2,200 words.

POETRY Needs avant-garde, free verse, haiku, traditional. Buys 40 poems/year. Submit maximum 4 poems. **Pays £25 per poem; £15 per 1,000 words prose; features by negotiation. Plus contributors' copies.**

$$ NOVEL & SHORT STORY WRITER'S MARKET

F+W Media, Inc., 10151 Carver Rd., Suite 200, Blue Ash OH 45242. (513)531-2690. **Fax:** (513)531-2686. **E-mail:** marketbookupdates@fwmedia.com. **Website:** www.writersmarket.com. **Contact:** Editor. **85% freelance written.** Annual resource book covering the fiction market. "In addition to thousands of listings for places to get fiction published, we feature articles on the craft and business of fiction writing, as well as interviews with successful fiction writers, editors, and agents. Our articles are unique in that they always offer an actionable take-away. In other words, readers must learn something immediately useful about the creation or marketing of fiction." Estab. 1981. Byline given. Pays on acceptance plus 45 days. Offers 25% kill fee. Accepts queries by e-mail only. Include "NSSWM Query" in the subject line. Responds in 4 weeks to queries.

Accepts proposals during the summer.

NONFICTION Needs how-to, write, sell and promote fiction; find an agent; etc., interview, personal experience. **Buys 12-15 mss/year.** Length: 1,500-2,500 words. **Pays $400-650.**

$$ POETS & WRITERS MAGAZINE

90 Broad St., Suite 2100, New York NY 10004. (212)226-3586. **E-mail:** editor@pw.org. **Website:** www.pw.org. **Contact:** Suzanne Pettypiece, managing editor. **95% freelance written.** Bimonthly professional trade journal for poets and fiction writers and creative nonfiction writers. Estab. 1987. Circ. 60,000. Byline given. Pays on acceptance of finished draft. Offers 25% kill fee. Publishes ms an average of 4 months after acceptance. Submit seasonal material 4 months in advance. Accepts queries by mail, e-mail. Responds in 2 months to mss. Sample copy for $5.95 to Sample Copy Dept. Guidelines available online.

NONFICTION Needs how-to, craft of poetry, fiction or creative nonfiction writing, interviews, with poets or writers of fiction and creative nonfiction, personal essays about literature, regional reports of literary activity, reports on small presses, service pieces about publishing trends. "We do not accept submissions by fax." **Buys 35 mss/year.** Send complete ms. Length: 500-2,500 (depending on topic) words.

COLUMNS Literary and Publishing News, 500-1,000 words; Profiles of Emerging and Established Poets, Fiction Writers and Creative Nonfiction Writers,

2,000-3,000 words; Regional Reports (literary activity in US and abroad), 1,000-2,000 words. Query with published clips or send complete ms. **Pays $150-500.**

$$ QUILL & SCROLL MAGAZINE

Quill and Scroll International Honorary Society for High School Journalists, University of Iowa, School of Journalism and Mass Communication, 100 Adler Journalism Bldg., Iowa City IA 52242. (319)335-3457. **Fax:** (319)335-3989. **E-mail:** quill-scroll@uiowa.edu. **Website:** www.uiowa.edu/~quill-sc. **Contact:** Vanessa Shelton, publisher/editor. **20% freelance written.** Bimonthly magazine covering scholastic journalism-related topics during school year. "Our primary audience is high school journalism students working on and studying topics related to newspapers, yearbooks, radio, television, and online media; secondary audience is their teachers and others interested in this topic. We invite journalism students and advisers to submit mss about important lessons learned or obstacles overcome." Estab. 1926. Circ. 10,000. Byline given. Pays on acceptance and publication. Publishes ms an average of 4 months after acceptance. Editorial lead time 2 months. Accepts queries by mail, e-mail. Accepts simultaneous submissions. Responds in 2 weeks to queries. Guidelines available.

NONFICTION Needs essays, how-to, humor, interview, new product, opinion, personal experience, photo feature, technical, travel, types on topic. Does not want articles not pertinent to high school student journalists. Query. Length: 600-1,000 words. **Pays $100-500 for assigned articles. Pays complementary copy and $200 maximum for unsolicited articles.** Sometimes pays expenses of writers on assignment.

$$$ QUILL MAGAZINE

Society of Professional Journalists, 3909 N. Meridian St., Indianapolis IN 46208. **Fax:** (317)920-4789. **E-mail:** sleadingham@spj.org. **Website:** www.spj.org/quill.asp. **Contact:** Scott Leadingham, editor. **75% freelance written.** Monthly magazine covering journalism and the media industry. "*Quill* is a how-to magazine written by journalists. We focus on the industry's biggest issues while providing tips on how to become better journalists." Estab. 1912. Circ. 10,000. Byline given. Offers 25% kill fee. Publishes ms an average of 2 months after acceptance. Editorial lead time 2-3 months. Submit seasonal material 2-3 months in advance. Accepts queries by e-mail. Accepts simultaneous submissions.

NONFICTION Needs general interest, how-to, technical. Does not want personality profiles and straight research pieces. **Buys 12 mss/year.** Query. Length: 800-2,500 words. **Pays $150-800.**

$$$ WRITER'S DIGEST

F+W Media, Inc., 10151 Carver Rd., Suite #200, Cincinnati OH 45242. (513)531-2690, ext. 11483. **E-mail:** wdsubmissions@fwmedia.com. **Website:** www.writersdigest.com. **75% freelance written.** Magazine for those who want to write better, get published and participate in the vibrant culture of writers. "Our readers look to us for specific ideas and tips that will help them succeed, whether success means getting into print, finding personal fulfillment through writing or building and maintaining a thriving writing career and network." Estab. 1920. Byline given. Offers 25% kill fee. Publishes ms an average of 6-9 months after acceptance. Accepts queries by e-mail only. Responds in 2-4 months to queries. Responds in 2-4 months to mss. Guidelines and editorial calendar available online (writersdigest.com/submissionguidelines).

💬 The magazine does not accept or read e-queries with attachments.

NONFICTION Needs essays, how-to, humor, inspirational, interviews, profiles. Does not accept phone, snail mail, or fax queries. "We don't buy newspaper clippings or reprints of articles previously published in other writing magazines. Book and software reviews are handled in-house, as are most *WD* interviews." **Buys 40 mss/year.** Send complete ms. Length: 800-1,500 words. **Pays 30-50¢/word.**

$ WRITING THAT WORKS

Communications Concepts, Inc., 7481 Huntsman Blvd., #720, Springfield VA 22153-1648. (703)643-2200. **E-mail:** concepts@writingthatworks.com. **Website:** www.apexawards.com. Monthly newsletter on business writing and communications. "Our readers are company writers, editors, communicators, and executives. They need specific, practical advice on how to write well as part of their job." Estab. 1983. Byline sometimes given. Pays within 45 days of acceptance. Publishes ms an average of 3 months after acceptance. Editorial lead time 3 months. Accepts queries by mail, e-mail, online submission form. Responds in 1 month to queries. Sample copy and writer's guidelines online.

NONFICTION Needs how-to. **Buys 90 mss/year.** Accepts electronic final mss. E-mail attached word processing files. Length: 100-600 words. **Pays $35-150.**
COLUMNS Writing Techniques (how-to business writing advice); Style Matters (grammar, usage, and editing); Online Publishing (writing, editing, and publishing for the Web); Managing Publications; PR & Marketing (writing).
FILLERS Short tips on writing or editing. Mini-reviews of communications websites for business writers, editors, and communicators. Length: 100-250 words. **Pays $35.**

$$$$ WRITTEN BY

7000 W. Third St., Los Angeles CA 90048. (323)782-4522. **Fax:** (323)782-4800. **Website:** www.wga.org. **40% freelance written.** Magazine published 9 times/year. "*Written By* is the premier magazine written by and for America's screen and TV writers. We focus on the craft of screenwriting and cover all aspects of the entertainment industry from the perspective of the writer. We are read by all screenwriters and most entertainment executives." Estab. 1987. Circ. 12,000. Byline given. Offers 10% kill fee. Publishes ms an average of 2 months after acceptance. Editorial lead time 4 months. Submit seasonal material 4 months in advance. Accepts queries by mail, e-mail, fax, phone, online submission form. Guidelines for #10 SASE.
NONFICTION Needs book excerpts, essays, historical, humor, interview, opinion, personal experience, photo feature, technical, software. No beginner pieces on how to break into Hollywood, or how to write scripts. **Buys 20 mss/year.** Query with published clips. Length: 500-3,500 words. **Pays $500-3,500 for assigned articles.** Sometimes pays expenses of writers on assignment.
COLUMNS Pays $1,000 maximum.

LAW

$$$$ ABA JOURNAL

American Bar Association, 321 N. Clark St., 20th Floor, Chicago IL 60654. (312)988-6018. **Fax:** (312)988-6014. **E-mail:** releases@americanbar.org. **Website:** www.abajournal.com. **Contact:** Allen Pusey, editor and publisher. **10% freelance written.** Monthly magazine covering the trends, people and finances of the legal profession from Wall Street to Main Street to Pennsylvania Avenue. The *ABA Journal* is an independent, thoughtful, and inquiring observer of the law and the legal profession. The magazine is edited for members of the American Bar Association. Circ. 380,000. Byline given. Accepts queries by e-mail, fax. Guidelines available online.
NONFICTION "We don't want anything that does not have a legal theme. No poetry or fiction." **Buys 5 mss/year.** "We use freelancers with experience reporting for legal or consumer publications; most have law degrees. If you are interested in freelancing for the *Journal*, we urge you to include your résumé and published clips when you contact us with story ideas." Length: 500-3,500 words. **Pays $300-2,000 for assigned articles.**
COLUMNS The National Pulse/Ideas from the Front (reports on legal news and trends), 650 words; eReport (reports on legal news and trends), 500-1,500 words. "The *ABA Journal eReport* is our weekly online newsletter sent out to members." **Buys 25 mss/year.** Query with published clips. **Pays $300, regardless of story length.**

$$$ BENCH & BAR OF MINNESOTA

Minnesota State Bar Association, 600 Nicollet Mall #380, Minneapolis MN 55402. (612)333-1183; 800-882-6722. **Fax:** (612)333-4927. **E-mail:** jhaverkamp@mnbar.org. **Website:** www.mnbar.org. **Contact:** Judson Haverkamp, editor. **5% freelance written.** Magazine published 11 times/year. *Bench & Bar* seeks reportage, analysis, and commentary on trends and issues in the law and the legal profession, especially in Minnesota. Preference to items of practical/professional human interest to lawyers and judges. Audience is mostly Minnesota lawyers. Estab. 1931. Circ. 17,000. Byline given. Publishes ms an average of 3 months after acceptance. Responds in 1 month to queries. Guidelines for free online or by mail.
NONFICTION Needs analysis and exposition of current trends, developments and issues in law, legal profession, especially in Minnesota. Balanced commentary and "how-to" considered. "We do not want one-sided opinion pieces or advertorial." **Buys 2-3 mss/year.** Send query or complete ms. Length: 1,000-3,500 words. **Pays $500-1,500.** Some expenses of writers on assignment.

$$$ JCR

National Court Reporters Association, 8224 Old Courthouse Rd., Vienna VA 22180. **E-mail:** jschmidt@ncrahq.org. **Website:** www.ncraonline.org. **Contact:** Jacqueline Schmidt, editor. **10% freelance**

written. Monthly, except bimonthly July/August and November/December magazine covering court reporting, captioning, and CART provision. "The *JCR* has 2 complementary purposes: to communicate the activities, goals and mission of its publisher, the National Court Reporters Association; and, simultaneously, to seek out and publish diverse information and views on matters significantly related to the court reporting and captioning professions." Estab. 1899. Circ. 20,000. Byline sometimes given. Publishes ms an average of 4-5 months after acceptance. Editorial lead time 4 months. Submit seasonal material 4 months in advance. Accepts queries by mail, e-mail. Ms guidelines are available on the NCRAonline.org website under *JCR*.

NONFICTION Needs book excerpts, how-to, interview, technical, legal issues. **Buys 6-10 mss/year mss/year.** Query. Length: 1,000-2,500 words. **Pays $1,000 maximum for assigned articles. Pays $100 maximum for unsolicited articles.** Sometimes pays expenses of writers on assignment.

COLUMNS Language (proper punctuation, grammar, dealing with verbatim materials); Technical (new technologies, using mobile technology, using technology for work); Book excerpts (language, crime, legal issues)—all 1,000 words. **Pays $100.**

$$$ JOURNAL OF COURT REPORTING

National Court Reporters Association, 8224 Old Courthouse Rd., Vienna VA 22180. (800)272-6272, ext. 164. **E-mail:** jschmidt@ncrahq.org. **Website:** www.ncraonline.org. **Contact:** Jacqueline Schmidt, editor. **10% freelance written.** Monthly (bimonthly July/August and November/December) magazine. "The *Journal of Court Reporting* has 2 complementary purposes: to communicate the activities, goals and mission of its publisher, the National Court Reporters Association; and, simultaneously, to seek out and publish diverse information and views on matters significantly related to the court reporting and captioning professions." Estab. 1899. Circ. 20,000. Byline sometimes given. Publishes ms an average of 4-5 months after acceptance. Editorial lead time 4 months. Submit seasonal material 4 months in advance. Accepts queries by mail, e-mail. Accepts simultaneous submissions. Guidelines free.

NONFICTION Needs book excerpts, how-to, interview, technical, legal issues. **Buys 10 mss/year.** Query. Length: 1,000-2,500 words. **Pays 1,000 max. for assigned articles. Pays $100 maximum for unsolicited articles.** Sometimes pays expenses of writers on assignment.

COLUMNS Language (proper punctuation, grammar, dealing with verbatim materials); Technical (new technologies, using mobile technology, using technology for work); Book excerpts (language, crime, legal issues), all 1,000 words; Puzzles (any, but especially word-related games). **Pays $100.**

✪ $$$$ NATIONAL

The Canadian Bar Association, 500-865 Carling Ave., Ottawa ON K1S 5S8 Canada. (613)237-2925. **Fax:** (613)237-0185. **E-mail:** beverleys@cba.org; national@cba.org. **Website:** www.cba.org/national. **Contact:** Beverley Spencer editor-in-chief. **90% freelance written.** Magazine published 8 times/year covering practice trends and business developments in the law, with a focus on technology, innovation, practice management, and client relations. Estab. 1993. Circ. 37,000. Byline given. Offers 50% kill fee. Publishes ms an average of 2 months after acceptance. Editorial lead time 2 months. Accepts queries by e-mail.

NONFICTION Buys 25 mss/year. Query with published clips. Length: 1,000-2,500 words. **Pays $1/word.** Sometimes pays expenses of writers on assignment.

$ PARALEGAL TODAY

Conexion International Media, Inc., Editorial Department, 118 Steiner Dr., Pittsburgh PA 15236. (412)653-2262. **E-mail:** skane@conexionmedia.com. **Website:** www.paralegaltoday.com; www.conexioninternationalltd.com. **Contact:** Sally A. Kane, Esq., editor-in-chief. "Quarterly magazine geared toward all legal assistants/paralegals throughout the US and Canada, regardless of specialty (litigation, corporate, bankruptcy, environmental law, etc.). How-to articles to help paralegals perform their jobs more effectively are most in demand, as are career and salary information, technolgoy tips, and trends pieces.". Estab. 1983. Circ. 8,000. Byline given. Editorial lead time is 10 weeks. Submit seasonal material 3 months in advance. Accepts queries by mail, e-mail, fax, online submission form. Accepts simultaneous submissions. Responds in 2 months to mss. Sample copy and writer's guidelines available online.

NONFICTION Needs interview, unique and interesting paralegals in unique and particular work-related situations, news (brief, hard news topics regarding paralegals), features (present information to help paralegals advance their careers). Send query letter first; if electronic, send as attachment. **Pays $75-300.**

😊😊 THE PENNSYLVANIA LAWYER

Pennsylvania Bar Association, P.O. Box 186, Harrisburg PA 17108. **E-mail:** editor@pabar.org; donsarvey@earthlink.net. **Website:** www.pabar.org. **Contact:** Donald C. Sarvey, editorial director. **25% freelance written. Prefers to work with published/ established writers.** Bimonthly magazine published as a service to the legal profession and the members of the Pennsylvania Bar Association. Estab. 1979. Circ. 30,000. Byline given. Publishes ms an average of 6 months after acceptance. Submit seasonal material 6 months in advance. Accepts queries by mail, e-mail, online submission form. Responds in 2 months to queries and to mss. Sample copy for $2. Writer's guidelines for #10 SASE or by e-mail.

NONFICTION Needs how-to, interview, law-practice management, technology. **Buys 8-10 mss/year.** Query. Length: 1,200-1,500 words. **Pays $50 for book reviews; $75-400 for assigned articles. Pays $150 for unsolicited articles.** Sometimes pays expenses of writers on assignment.

THE PUBLIC LAWYER

American Bar Association Government and Public Sector Lawyers Division, ABA GPS LD, 321 N. Clark St., MS 19.1, Chicago IL 60610. (312)988-5809. **Fax:** (312)988-5709. **E-mail:** katherine.mikkelson@americanbar.org. **Website:** www.governmentlawyer.org. **60% freelance written.** Semiannual magazine covering government attorneys and the legal issues that pertain to them. "The mission of *The Public Lawyer* is to provide timely, practical information useful to all public lawyers regardless of practice setting. We publish articles covering topics that are of universal interest to a diverse audience of public lawyers, such as public law office management, dealing with the media, politically motivated personnel decisions, etc. Articles must be national in scope." Estab. 1993. Circ. 6,500. Byline given. Publishes ms an average of 4 months after acceptance. Editorial lead time 6 months. Accepts queries by e-mail. Accepts simultaneous submissions. Responds in 1 month to queries. Responds in 2 months to mss. Guidelines available online.

NONFICTION Needs interview, opinion, technical, book reviews. Does not want pieces that do not relate to the status of government lawyers or that are not

legal issues exclusive to government lawyers. We accept very few articles written by private practice attorneys. **Buys 6-8 mss/year.** Query. Length: 2,000-5,000 words. **Pays contributor copies.**

😊😊😊😊 SUPER LAWYERS

Thomson Reuters, 610 Opperman Dr., Eagan MN 55123. (877)787-5290. **Website:** www.superlawyers. com. **Contact:** Adam Wahlberg. **100% freelance written.** Monthly magazine covering law and politics. "We publish glossy magazines in every region of the country; all serve a legal audience and have a storytelling sensibility. We write profiles of interesting attorneys exclusively." Estab. 1990. Byline given. Offers 25% kill fee. Publishes ms an average of 1 month after acceptance. Editorial lead time 6 months. Submit seasonal material 6 months in advance. Accepts queries by phone, online submission form. Accepts simultaneous submissions. Guidelines free.

NONFICTION Needs general interest, historical. Query. Length: 500-2,000 words. **Pays 50¢-$1.50/ word.**

LUMBER

😊😊 PALLET ENTERPRISE

Industrial Reporting, Inc., 10244 Timber Ridge Dr., Ashland VA 23005. (804)550-0323. **Fax:** (804)550-2181. **E-mail:** edb@ireporting.com; chaille@ireporting.com. **Website:** www.palletenterprise.com. **Contact:** Edward C. Brindley, Jr., Ph.D., publisher. **40% freelance written.** Monthly magazine covering lumber and pallet operations. "The *Pallet Enterprise* is a monthly trade magazine for the sawmill, pallet, remanufacturing, and wood processing industries. Articles should offer technical, solution-oriented information. Anti-forest articles are not accepted. Articles should focus on machinery and unique ways to improve profitability/make money." Estab. 1981. Circ. 14,500. Editorial lead time 2 months. Submit seasonal material 2 months in advance. Accepts queries by mail, e-mail, fax, phone. Accepts simultaneous submissions. Guidelines free.

NONFICTION Needs interview, new product, opinion, technical, industry news, environmental, forests operation/plant features. No lifestyle, humor, general news, etc. **Buys 20 mss/year.** Query with published clips. Length: 1,000-3,000 words. **Pays $200-400 for assigned articles. Pays $100-400 for unsolicited articles.** Sometimes pays expenses of writers on assignment.

COLUMNS Green Watch (environmental news/opinion affecting US forests), 1,500 words. **Buys 12 mss/year.** Query with published clips. **Pays $200-400.**

$$ TIMBERLINE

Industrial Reporting, Inc., 10244 Timber Ridge Dr., Ashland VA 23005. (804)550-0323. **Fax:** (804)550-2181. **E-mail:** chaille@ireporting.com. **Website:** www.timberlinemag.com. **Contact:** Chaille Brindley, assistant publisher. **50% freelance written.** Monthly tabloid covering the forest products industry. Estab. 1994. Circ. 30,000. Byline given. Editorial lead time 2 months. Submit seasonal material 2 months in advance. Accepts queries by mail, e-mail, fax, phone. Accepts simultaneous submissions. Guidelines free.

NONFICTION Contact: Tim Cox, editor. Needs historical, interview, new product, opinion, technical, industry news, environmental operation/plant features. No lifestyles, humor, general news, etc. **Buys 25 mss/year.** Query with published clips. Length: 1,000-3,000 words. **Pays $200-400 for assigned articles. Pays $100-400 for unsolicited articles.** Sometimes pays expenses of writers on assignment.

COLUMNS Contact: Tim Cox, editor. From the Hill (legislative news impacting the forest products industry), 1,800 words; Green Watch (environmental news/opinion affecting US forests), 1,500 words. **Buys 12 mss/year.** Query with published clips. **Pays $200-400.**

$$ TIMBERWEST

TimberWest Publications, LLC, P.O. Box 610, Edmonds WA 98020-0160. **Fax:** (425)771-3623. **E-mail:** diane@forestnet.com. **Website:** www.forestnet.com. **Contact:** Diane Mettler, managing editor. **75% freelance written.** Monthly magazine covering logging and lumber segment of the forestry industry in the Northwest. "We publish primarily profiles on loggers and their operations—with an emphasis on the machinery—in Washington, Oregon, Idaho, Montana, Northern California, and Alaska. Some timber issues are highly controversial, and although we will report on the issues, this is a pro-logging publication. We don't publish articles with a negative slant on the timber industry." Estab. 1975. Circ. 10,000. Byline given. Editorial lead time 3 months. Accepts queries by mail, fax. Responds in 3 weeks to queries. Sample copy for $2. Guidelines for #10 sase.

NONFICTION Needs historical, interview, new product. "No articles that put the timber industry in a bad light—such as environmental articles against logging." **Buys 50 mss/year.** Query with published clips. Length: 1,100-1,500 words. **Pays $350.** Pays expenses of writers on assignment.

FILLERS Needs facts, newsbreaks. **Buys 10 mss/year.** Length: 400-800 words. **Pays $100-250.**

MACHINERY AND METAL

$$$ AMERICANMACHINIST.COM

Penton Media, 1300 E. 9th St., Cleveland OH 44114. (216)931-9240. **Fax:** (913)514-6386. **E-mail:** robert.brooks@penton.com. **Website:** www.americanmachinist.com. **Contact:** Robert Brooks, editor-in-chief. **10% freelance written.** Monthly online website covering all forms of metalworking covering all forms of metalworking. Accepts contributed features and articles. "*AmericanMachinist.com* is the oldest magazine dedicated to metalworking in the United States. Our readers are the owners and managers of metalworking shops. We publish articles that provide the managers and owners of job shops, contract shops, and captive shops the information they need to make their operations more efficient, more productive, and more profitable. Our articles are technical in nature and must be focused on technology that will help these shops to become more competitive on a global basis. Our readers are skilled machinists. This is not the place for lightweight items about manufacturing, and we are not interested in articles on management theories." Estab. 1877. Circ. 80,000. Byline sometimes given. Offers 20% kill fee. Publishes ms an average of 1-2 months after acceptance. Editorial lead time 3-6 months. Submit seasonal material 4-6 months in advance. Accepts queries by mail, e-mail, phone. Responds in 1-2 weeks to queries. Responds in 1 month to mss.

NONFICTION Needs general interest, how-to, new product, opinion, personal experience, photo feature, technical. Query with published clips. Length: 600-2,400 words. **Pays $300-1,200.** Sometimes pays expenses of writers on assignment.

FILLERS Needs anecdotes, facts, gags, newsbreaks, short humor. **Buys 12-18 mss/year.** Length: 50-200 words. **Pays $25-100.**

$$$ CUTTING TOOL ENGINEERING

CTE Publications, Inc., 40 Skokie Blvd., Suite 450, Northbrook IL 60062-1698. (847)714-0175. **Fax:** (847)559-4444. **E-mail:** alanr@jwr.com. **Website:** www.ctemag.com. **Contact:** Alan Richter, editor. **40% freelance written.** Monthly magazine covering industrial metal cutting tools and metal cutting operations. "*Cut-*

ting Tool Engineering serves owners, managers, and engineers who work in manufacturing, specifically manufacturing that involves cutting or grinding metal or other materials. Writing should be geared toward improving manufacturing processes." Circ. 48,000. Byline given. Offers 50% kill fee. Publishes ms an average of 2 months after acceptance. Editorial lead time 2 months. Accepts queries by mail, fax. Responds in 2 months to mss. Sample copy and writer's guidelines free.

NONFICTION Needs how-to, opinion, personal experience, technical. "No fiction or articles that don't relate to manufacturing." **Buys 10 mss/year.** Length: 1,500-3,000 words. **Pays $750-1,500.** Pays expenses of writers on assignment.

⚙ 💲💲 EQUIPMENT JOURNAL

Pace Publishing, 5160 Explorer Dr., Unit 6, Mississauga ON L4W 4T7 Canada. (416)459-5163. **E-mail:** Editor@Equipmentjournal.com. **Website:** www.Equipmentjournal.com. **10% freelance written.** "We are Canada's national heavy equipment newspaper. We focus on the construction, material handling, mining, forestry and on-highway transportation industries." Estab. 1964. Circ. 23,000 subscribers. Byline given. Publishes ms an average of 1-2 months after acceptance. Editorial lead time 2-3 months. Submit seasonal material 2 months in advance. Accepts queries by mail. Accepts simultaneous submissions. Responds within 1 week. Sample copy and guidelines free.

NONFICTION Needs how-to, interview, new product, photo feature, technical. No material that falls outside of *EJ*'s mandate—the Canadian equipment industry. **Buys 15/year mss/year.** Send complete ms. We prefer electronic submissions. We do not accept unsolicited freelance submissions. Length: 500-1,500 words. **$250-$400 for assigned and unsolicited articles.** Sometimes pays expenses of writers on assignment.

💲💲💲 THE FABRICATOR

833 Featherstone Rd., Rockford IL 61107. (815)399-8700. **Fax:** (815)381-1370. **E-mail:** kateb@thefabricator.com; timh@thefabricator.com. **Website:** www.thefabricator.com. **Contact:** Kate Bachman, editor; Tim Heston, senior editor. **15% freelance written.** Monthly magazine covering metal forming and fabricating. "Our purpose is to disseminate information about modern metal forming and fabricating techniques, machinery, tooling, and management concepts for the metal fabricator." Estab. 1971. Circ. 58,000. Byline given. Editorial lead time 6 months. Accepts queries by mail, e-mail. Responds in 2 weeks to queries. Responds in 1 month to mss. Guidelines available online.

NONFICTION Needs how-to, technical, company profile. Query with published clips. Length: 1,200-2,000 words. **Pays 40-80¢/word.**

MACHINE DESIGN

Penton Media, Penton Media Bldg., 1300 E. 9th St., Cleveland OH 44114. (216)931-9412. **Fax:** (216)621-8469. **E-mail:** mdeditor@penton.com. **Website:** www.machinedesign.com. Semimonthly magazine covering machine design. Covers the design engineering of manufactured products across the entire spectrum of the idustry for people who perform design engineering functions. Circ. 185,163. Editorial lead time 10 weeks. Accepts queries by mail, e-mail. No

NONFICTION Needs how-to, new product, technical. Send complete ms.

COLUMNS Query with or without published clips or send complete ms.

💲💲 SPRINGS

Spring Manufacturers Institute, 2001 Midwest Rd., Suite 106, Oak Brook IL 60523-1335. (630)495-8588. **Fax:** (630)495-8595. **E-mail:** lynne@smihq.org. **Website:** www.smihq.org. **Contact:** Lynne Carr, general manager. **10% freelance written.** Quarterly magazine covering precision mechanical spring manufacture. Articles should be aimed at spring manufacturers. Estab. 1962. Circ. 10,800. Byline given. Publishes ms an average of 3-6 months after acceptance. Editorial lead time 4 months. Accepts simultaneous submissions. Guidelines available online.

NONFICTION Needs general interest, how-to, interview, opinion, personal experience, technical. **Buys 4-6 mss/year.** Length: 2,000-10,000 words. **Pays $100-600 for assigned articles.**

💲💲💲 STAMPING JOURNAL

Fabricators & Manufacturers Association (FMA), 833 Featherstone Rd., Rockford IL 61107-6302. (815)381-0382. **Fax:** (815)381-1370. **E-mail:** kateb@thefabricator.com. **Website:** www.thefabricator.com. **15% freelance written.** Bimonthly magazine covering metal stamping. "We look for how-to and educational articles—nonpromotional." Estab. 1989. Circ. 35,000. Byline given. Editorial lead time 6 months. Accepts queries by mail, e-mail, fax, phone. Responds in 2 weeks to queries. Responds in 2 months to mss. Sample copy and writer's guidelines free.

NONFICTION Needs how-to, technical, company profile. Special issues: Forecast issue (January). No unsolicited case studies. **Buys 5 mss/year.** Query with published clips. 1,000 words **Pays 40-80¢/word.** Sometimes pays expenses of writers on assignment.

PHOTOS State availability. Captions, identification of subjects required. Reviews contact sheets. Negotiates payment individually.

TIPS Articles should be impartial and should not describe the benefits of certain products available from certain companies. They should not be biased toward the author's or against a competitor's products or technologies. The publisher may refuse any article that does not conform to this guideline.

$$$$ TODAY'S MACHINING WORLD

Screw Machine World, Inc., 4235 W. 166th St., Oak Forest IL 60452. (708)535-2237. **Fax:** (708)535-0103. E-mail: emily@todaysmachiningworld.com; lloydgraff-tmw@yahoo.com. **Website:** www.todaysmachining-world.com. **Contact:** Emily Aniakou; Lloyd Graff. **40% freelance written.** Monthly magazine covering metal turned parts manufacturing in the US and global. "We hire writers to tell a success story or challenge regarding our industry. There are **no** advertorials coming from advertisers." Estab. 2001. Circ. 18,500. Byline given. Offers $500 kill fee. Publishes ms an average of 2 months after acceptance. Editorial lead time 2-4 months. Submit seasonal material 2 months in advance. Responds in 1 month to mss. Guidelines free.

NONFICTION Needs general interest, how-to. "We do not want unsolicited articles." **Buys 12-15 mss/year.** Query. Length: 1,500-2,500 words. **Pays $1,500-2,000 for assigned articles.**

COLUMNS Shop Doc (manufacturing problem/solution), 500 words. Query. **Pays $-$250.**

MAINTENANCE AND SAFETY

$$ AMERICAN WINDOW CLEANER MAGAZINE

12 Publishing Corp., 750-B NW Broad St., Southern Pines NC 28387. (910)693-2644. **Fax:** (910)246-1681. **Website:** www.awcmag.com. Bob Lawrence; Karen Grinter, creative director. **Contact:** Gary Mauer. **20% freelance written.** Bimonthly magazine on window cleaning. Articles to help window cleaners become more profitable, safe, professional, and feel good about what they do. Estab. 1986. Circ. 8,000. Byline given. Offers 33% kill fee. Publishes ms an average

of 4-8 months after acceptance. Editorial lead time 2 months. Submit seasonal material 3 months in advance. Responds in 2 weeks to queries. Responds in 1 month to mss. Guidelines available online.

NONFICTION Needs how-to, humor, inspirational, interview, personal experience, photo feature, technical, add on business. "We do not want PR-driven pieces. We want to educate—not push a particular product." **Buys 20 mss/year.** Query. Length: 500-5,000 words. **Pays $50-250.**

COLUMNS Window Cleaning Tips (tricks of the trade); 1,000-2,000 words; Humor-anecdotes-feel good-abouts (window cleaning industry); Computer High-Tech (tips on new technology), all 1,000 words **Buys 12 mss/year.** Query. **Pays $50-100.**

$$ EXECUTIVE HOUSEKEEPING TODAY

The International Executive Housekeepers Association, 1001 Eastwind Dr., Suite 301, Westerville OH 43081-3361. (614)895-7166. **Fax:** (614)895-1248. E-mail: ldigiulio@ieha.org. **Website:** www.ieha.org. **Contact:** Laura DiGiulio, editor. **50% freelance written.** "Monthly magazine for nearly 5,000 decision makers responsible for housekeeping management (cleaning, grounds maintenance, laundry, linen, pest control, waste management, regulatory compliance, training) for a variety of institutions: hospitality, healthcare, education, retail, government.". Estab. 1930. Circ. 5,500. Byline given. Publishes ms an average of 6 months after acceptance. Editorial lead time 2 months. Submit seasonal material 3 months in advance. Accepts queries by mail, e-mail, fax, phone.

NONFICTION Needs general interest, interview, new product, related to magazine's scope, personal experience, in housekeeping profession, technical. **Buys 30 mss/year.** Query with published clips. Length: 500-1,500 words.

COLUMNS Federal Report (OSHA/EPA requirements), 1,000 words; Industry News; Management Perspectives (industry specific), 500-1,500 words. Query with published clips.

MANAGEMENT AND SUPERVISION

$$ INCENTIVE

Northstar Travel Media LLC, 100 Lighting Way, Secaucus NJ 07094-3626. (201)902-2000; (201)902-1975. E-mail: lcioffi@ntmllc.com. **Website:** www.incentivemag.com. **Contact:** Lori Cioffi, editorial director. Monthly magazine covering sales promotion and employee motivation: managing and marketing through motivation. Estab. 1905. Circ. 41,000. Byline given. Publishes ms an average of 3 months after acceptance. Accepts queries by mail, e-mail, fax. Responds in 1 month to queries. Responds in 2 months to mss. Sample copy for SAE with 9x12 envelope.

NONFICTION Needs general interest, motivation, demographics, how-to, types of sales promotion, buying product categories, using destinations, interview, sales promotion executives, travel, incentive-oriented, corporate case studies. **Buys 48 mss/year.** Query with published clips. Length: 1,000-2,000 words. **Pays $250-700 for assigned articles. Does not pay for unsolicited articles.** Pays expenses of writers on assignment.

💲💲 PLAYGROUND MAGAZINE

Harris Publishing, 360 B St., Idaho Falls ID 83402. (208)542-2271. **Fax:** (208)522-5241. **E-mail:** lindstrm@playgroundmag.com. **Website:** www.playgroundmag.com. **Contact:** Lane Lindstrom, editor. **25% freelance written.** Magazine published quarterly covering playgrounds, play-related issues, equipment and industry trends. *"Playground Magazine* targets park and recreation management, elementary school teachers and administrators, child care facilities and parent-group leader readership. Articles should focus on play and the playground market as a whole, including aquatic play and surfacing."* Estab. 2000. Circ. 35,000. Byline given. Publishes ms an average of 6 months after acceptance. Editorial lead time 2 months. Submit seasonal material 1 year in advance. Accepts queries by mail, e-mail. Accepts simultaneous submissions. Responds in 1 month to queries. Responds in 2 months to mss. Sample copy for $5. Guidelines for #10 SASE.

NONFICTION Needs how-to, interview, new product, opinion, personal experience, photo feature, technical, travel. *Playground Magazine* does not publish any articles that do not directly relate to play and the playground industry. **Buys 4-6 mss/year.** Query. Length: 800-1,500 words. **Pays $50-300 for assigned articles.** Sometimes pays expenses of writers on assignment.

COLUMNS Dream Spaces (an article that profiles a unique play area and focuses on community involvement, unique design, or human interest), 800-1,200 words. **Buys 2 mss/year.** Query. **Pays $100-300.**

MARINE AND MARITIME INDUSTRIES

💲💲 PROFESSIONAL MARINER

Navigator Publishing, P.O. Box 461510, Escondido CA 92046. (207)772-2466, ext. 204. **Fax:** (207)772-2879. **E-mail:** jgormley@professionalmariner.com. **Website:** www.professionalmariner.com. **Contact:** John Gormley, editor. **75% freelance written.** Bimonthly magazine covering professional seamanship and maritime industry news. Estab. 1993. Circ. 29,000. Byline given. Editorial lead time 3 months. Accepts queries by mail, e-mail, fax, phone. Accepts simultaneous submissions.

NONFICTION Buys 15 mss/year. Query. Length: varies; short clips to long profiles/features. **Pays 25¢/word.** Sometimes pays expenses of writers on assignment.

💲 WORK BOAT WORLD

Baird Publications, Suite 3, 20 Cato St., Hawthorn East 3123 Australia. (61)(3)9824-6055. **Fax:** (61)(3)9824-6588. **E-mail:** marinfo@baird.com.au. **Website:** www.bairdmaritime.com. Monthly magazine covering all types of commercial, military and government vessels to around 130 meters in length. Maintaining close contact with ship builders, designers, owners and operators, suppliers of vessel equipment and suppliers of services on a worldwide basis, the editors and journalists of *Work Boat World* seek always to be informative. They constantly put themselves in the shoes of readers so as to produce editorial matter that interests, educates, informs and entertains. Estab. 1982.

NONFICTION Needs general interest, how-to, interview, new product. Query.

MEDICAL

💲 ADVANCE FOR RESPIRATORY CARE & SLEEP MEDICINE

Merion Publications, Inc., 2900 Horizon Dr., Box 61556, King of Prussia PA 19406-0956. (800)355-5627, ext. 1324. **Fax:** (610)278-1425. **E-mail:** sgeorge@advanceweb.com; advance@merion.com. **Website:** http://respiratory-care-sleep-medicine.advanceweb.com; www.advanceweb.com. **Contact:** Sharlene George, editor. **50% freelance written.** Biweekly magazine covering clinical, technical and business management trends for professionals in pulmonary, respiratory care, and sleep. "*ADVANCE for Respiratory Care & Sleep Medicine* welcomes original articles, on speculation, from members of the respiratory care and sleep professions. Once accepted, mss become the property of *ADVANCE for Respiratory Care & Sleep Medicine* and cannot be reproduced elsewhere without permission from the editor. An honorarium is paid for published articles. **For information on preparing your manuscript, please** download our Writer's Guidelines (PDF format)." Estab. 1988. Circ. 45,500. Byline given. Offers 75% kill fee. Publishes ms an average of 6 months after acceptance. Editorial lead time 1 month. Submit seasonal material 3 months in advance. Accepts queries by mail, e-mail. Accepts simultaneous submissions. Responds in 2 weeks to queries. Responds in up to 6 months to mss. Guidelines available at http://respiratory-care-sleep-medicine.advanceweb.com/Editorial/Content/editorial.aspx?CTIID=3587.

NONFICTION Needs technical. "We do not want to get general information articles about specific respiratory care related diseases. For example, our audience is all too familiar with cystic fibrosis, asthma, COPD, bronchitis, Alpha 1 Antitrypsin Defiency, pulmonary hypertension and the like." **Buys 2-3 mss/year.** Query. E-mail article and send printout by mail. Length: 1,500-2,000/words; double-spaced, 4-7 pages. **Pays honorarium.** Sometimes pays expenses of writers on assignment.

$ ADVANCE NEWSMAGAZINES

Merion Publications Inc., 2900 Horizon Dr., King of Prussia PA 19406. (610)278-1400. **Fax:** (610)278-1425. **E-mail:** advance@merion.com. **Website:** www.advanceweb.com. More than 30 magazines covering allied health fields, nursing, age management, long-term care, and more. Byline given. Editorial lead time 3 months. Accepts queries by e-mail only.

NONFICTION Needs interview, new product, personal experience, technical. Query with published clips. Include name, and phone and fax number for verification. Length: 2,000 words.

COLUMNS Phlebotomy Focus, Safety Solutions, Technology Trends, POL Perspectives, Performance in POCT, Eye on Education.

$ AT THE CENTER

Right Ideas, Inc., P.O. Box 309, Fleetwood PA 19522. (800)588-7744. **Fax:** (800)588-7744. **E-mail:** publications@rightideas.us. **Website:** www.atcmag.com. **20% freelance written.** Webzine published 4 times/year that provides encouragement and education to the staff, volunteers, and board members working in crisis pregnancy centers. Estab. 2000. Circ. 30,000. Byline given. Publishes ms an average of 1 year after acceptance. Editorial lead time 6 months. Submit seasonal material 1 year in advance. Accepts queries by mail, e-mail, fax. Accepts simultaneous submissions. Responds in 1 month to queries. Responds in 3-4 months to mss. Online at www.atcmag.com. Writer's guidelines for #10 SASE or by e-mail.

NONFICTION Buys about 12 mss/year. Query. Length: 800-1,200 words. **Pays $150 for assigned articles. Pays $50-150 for unsolicited articles.**

$$$ BIOTECHNOLOGY HEALTHCARE

BioCommunications LLC, 780 Township Line Rd., Yardley PA 19067. (267)685-2783. **Fax:** (267)685-2966. **E-mail:** editors@biotechnologyhealthcare.com. **Website:** www.biotechnologyhealthcare.com. **75% freelance written.** Bimonthly magazine. "We are a business magazine (not an academic journal) that covers the economic, regulatory, and health policy aspects of biotech therapies and diagnostics. Our audience includes third-party payers, employer purchasers of healthcare, public healthcare agencies, and healthcare professionals who prescribe biotech therapies. Articles should be written in business magazine-style prose and should be focused on the concerns of these audiences." Estab. 2004. Circ. 36,000 (digital); 12,431 (print). Byline given. Offers $300 kill fee. Publishes ms an average of 3 months after acceptance. Editorial lead time 4 months. Accepts queries by mail, e-mail, fax. Responds in 2 weeks to queries. Responds in 1 month to mss. Guidelines by e-mail.

NONFICTION Needs book excerpts, essays, how-to, manage the cost of biologics, case studies, interview, opinion, technical, about biotech therapies, diagnostics, or devices, regulatory developments, cost analyses studies, coverage of hot-button issues in the field. **Buys 24 mss/year.** Query with published clips. Length: 1,650-3,300 words. **Pays 75-85¢/word. Pays $300-1,870 for unsolicited articles.** Pays expenses of writers on assignment.

COLUMNS "Our columns are 'spoken for,' but I am always interested in pitches for new columns from qualified writers." **Buys 18 mss/year.** Query with pub-

lished clips. **Pays $300 minimum for a full piece; 75¢/ word maximum for ms 600-1,200 words.**
FILLERS Needs gags. Buys 3 cartoons mss/year. Pays $300 for cartoons upon publication.

💲💲 JEMS

Elsevier Public Safety, 525 B St., Suite 1900, San Diego CA 92101. **Fax:** (619)699-6396. **E-mail:** jems.editor@ elsevier.com; a.j.heightman@elsevier.com; je.berry@ elsevier.com. **Website:** www.jems.com. **Contact:** A.J. Heightman, MPA, EMT-P, editor-in-chief. **95% freelance written.** Monthly magazine directed to personnel who serve the pre-hospital emergency medicine industry: paramedics, EMTs, emergency physicians and nurses, administrators, EMS consultants, etc. Estab. 1980. Circ. 45,000. Byline given. Publishes ms an average of 6 months after acceptance. Submit seasonal material 6 months in advance. Accepts queries by mail, e-mail, fax, online submission form. Responds in 2-3 months to queries. Guidelines available online.
NONFICTION Needs essays, exposé, general interest, how-to, humor, interview, new product, opinion, personal experience, photo feature, technical, continuing education. **Buys 50 mss/year.** Query. "All story ideas must be submitted via our online system at http://ees. elsevier.com/jems." **Pays $200-400.**
COLUMNS Length: 850 words maximum. Query with or without published clips. **Pays $50-250.**

💲💲💲 MANAGED CARE

780 Township Line Rd., Yardley PA 19067. (267)685-2788. **Fax:** (267)685-2966. **E-mail:** jmarcille@medi-media.com. **Website:** www.managedcaremag.com. **Contact:** John Marcille, editor. **75% freelance written.** Monthly magazine. "We emphasize practical, usable information that helps HMO medical directors and pharmacy directors cope with the options, challenges, and hazards in the rapidly changing health care industry." Estab. 1992. Circ. 44,000. Byline given. Offers 20% kill fee. Publishes ms an average of 6 weeks after acceptance. Editorial lead time 3 months. Submit seasonal material 4 months in advance. Accepts queries by mail, e-mail, fax. Responds in 3 weeks to queries. Responds in 2 months to mss. Writer's guidelines on request.
NONFICTION Needs book excerpts, general interest, trends in health-care delivery and financing, quality of care, and employee concerns, how-to, deal with requisites of managed care, such as contracts with health plans, affiliation arrangements, accreditation, com-

puter needs, etc., original research and review articles that examine the relationship between health care delivery and financing. Also considered occasionally are personal experience, opinion, interview/profile, and humor pieces, but these must have a strong managed care angle and draw upon the insights of (if they are not written by) a knowledgeable managed care professional. **Buys 40 mss/year.** Query with published clips. Length: 1,000-3,000 words. **Pays 75¢/word.** Pays expenses of writers on assignment.

MEDESTHETICS

Creative Age Publications, 7628 Densmore Ave., Van Nuys CA 91406. **E-mail:** ihansen@creativeage.com. **Website:** www.medestheticsmagazine.com. **50% freelance written.** Bimonthly magazine covering noninvasive medical aesthetic services such as laser hair removal, skin rejuvenation, injectable fillers, and neurotoxins. *"Medesthetics* is a business to business magazine written for and distributed to dermatologists, plastic surgeons and other physicians offering noninvasive medical aesthetic services. We cover the latest equipment and products as well as legal and management issues specific to medspas, laser centers and other medical aesthetic practices." Estab. 2005. Circ. 20,000. Byline given. Publishes ms an average of 3 months after acceptance. Editorial lead time 3 months. Submit seasonal material 3 months in advance. Accepts queries by e-mail. Responds in 1 month to queries.
NONFICTION Needs new product, technical. "Does not want articles directed at consumers." **Buys 25 mss/year.** Query.

MIDWIFERY TODAY

P.O Box 2672, Eugene OR 97402-0223. (541)344-7438. **Fax:** (541)344-1422. **E-mail:** editorial@midwifery-today.com and jan@midwiferytoday.com (editorial only); layout@midwiferytoday.com (photography). **Website:** www.midwiferytoday.com. **Contact:** Jan Tritten, editor-in-chief and publisher. **95% freelance written.** Quarterly magazine. Estab. 1986. Circ. 3,000. Byline given. Publishes ms an average of 5 months after acceptance. Editorial lead time 3-9 months. Submit seasonal material 6 months in advance. Accepts queries by e-mail. Accepts simultaneous submissions. Responds in 2 weeks to queries. Responds in 1 month to mss. Sample copy and guidelines available online.
NONFICTION Needs book excerpts, essays, how-to, humor, inspirational, interview, opinion, personal ex-

perience, photo feature, clinical research, herbal articles, birth stories, business advice. **Buys 60 mss/year.** Send complete ms. Length: 300-3,000 words.

COLUMNS News: "In My Opinion" (150-750 words). **Buys 8 columns/year. mss/year.** Send complete ms.

POETRY Needs avant-garde, haiku, light verse, traditional. Accepts e-mail submissions (pasted into body of message or as attachment). Cover letter is required. Does not want poetry unrelated to pregnancy or birth. Does not want poetry that is "off subject or puts down the subject." Buys 4/year poems/year. Maximum line length: 25. **Pays 2 contributor's copies. Acquires first rights.**

FILLERS Needs Needs anecdotes, facts, newsbreaks. Length: 100-600 words.

◎◎◎◎ MODERN PHYSICIAN

Crain Communications, 360 N. Michigan Ave., Chicago IL 60601-3806. (312)649-5439. **Fax:** (312)280-3183. **E-mail:** dburda@modernhealthcare.com. **Website:** www.modernphysician.com. **Contact:** David Burda, editor. **10% freelance written.** Monthly magazine covering business and management news for doctors. "*Modern Physician* offers timely topical news features with lots of business information—revenues, earnings, financial data." Estab. 1997. Circ. 24,000. Byline given. Publishes ms an average of 2 months after acceptance. Editorial lead time 2 months. Accepts queries by mail, e-mail. Responds in 6 weeks to queries. Writer's guidelines sent after query.

NONFICTION Length: 750-1,000 words. **Pays 75¢-$1/word. (Does not pay for Guest Commentaries.)**

◎ ◎◎ OPTICAL PRISM

250 The East Mall, Suite 1113, Toronto ON M9B 6L3 Canada. (416)233-2487. **Fax:** (416)233-1746. **E-mail:** info@opticalprism.ca. **Website:** www.opticalprism.ca. **30% freelance written.** Magazine published 10 times/year. "We cover the health, fashion, and business aspects of the optical industry in Canada. Estab. 1982. Circ. 10,000. Byline given. Publishes ms an average of 2 months after acceptance. Editorial lead time 3 months. Submit seasonal material 3 months in advance. Accepts queries by mail, e-mail. Accepts simultaneous submissions.

NONFICTION Needs interview, related to optical industry. Query. Length: 1,000-1,600 words. **Pays 40¢/word (Canadian).** Sometimes pays expenses of writers on assignment.

COLUMNS Insight (profiles on people in the eyewear industry—also sometimes schools and businesses), 700-1,000 words. **Buys 5 mss/year.** Query. **Pays 40¢/word.**

◎◎ PLASTIC SURGERY NEWS

American Society of Plastic Surgeons, 444 E. Algonquin Rd., Arlington Heights IL 60005. **Fax:** (847)981-5458. **E-mail:** mss@plasticsurgery.org. **Website:** www.plasticsurgery.org. **Contact:** Mike Stokes, managing editor. **15% freelance written.** Monthly tabloid covering plastic surgery. *Plastic Surgery News* readership is comprised primarily of plastic surgeons and those involved with the specialty (nurses, techs, industry). The magazine is distributed via subscription and to all members of the American Society of Plastic Surgeons. The magazine covers a variety of specialty-specific news and features, including trends, legislation, and clinical information. Estab. 1960. Circ. 6,000. Byline given. Offers 25% kill fee. Publishes ms an average of 1-2 months after acceptance. Editorial lead time 1-3 months. Accepts queries by e-mail. Accepts simultaneous submissions. Responds in 2 weeks to queries. Responds in 3 months to mss. Sample copy for 10 first-class stamps. Guidelines by e-mail.

NONFICTION Needs exposé, how-to, new product, technical. Does not want celebrity or entertainment based pieces. **Buys 20 mss/year.** Query with published clips. Length: 1,000-3,500 words. **Pays 20-40¢/word.** Sometimes pays expenses of writers on assignment.

COLUMNS Digital Plastic Surgeon (technology), 1,500-1,700 words.

◎◎ PODIATRY MANAGEMENT

Kane Communications, Inc., P.O. Box 750129, Forest Hills NY 11375. (718)897-9700. **Fax:** (718)896-5747. **E-mail:** bblock@podiatrym.com. **Website:** www.podiatrym.com. Magazine published 9 times/year for practicing podiatrists. "Aims to help the doctor of podiatric medicine to build a bigger, more successful practice, to conserve and invest his money, to keep him posted on the economic, legal, and sociological changes that affect him." Estab. 1982. Circ. 16,500. Byline given. $75 kill fee. Submit seasonal material 4 months in advance. Accepts queries by e-mail. Accepts simultaneous submissions. Responds in 2 weeks to queries. Sample copy for $5 and 9x12 SAE. Guidelines for #10 SASE.

NONFICTION Buys 35 mss/year. Length: 1,500-3,000 words. **Pays $350-600.**

⊖⊖ PRIMARY CARE OPTOMETRY NEWS

SLACK Inc., 6900 Grove Rd., Thorofare NJ 08086-9447. (856)848-1000. **Fax:** (856)848-5991. **E-mail:** editor@pconsupersite.com. **Website:** www.pconsupersite.com. **Contact:** Nancy Hemphill, editor-in-chief. **5% freelance written.** Monthly tabloid covering optometry. "*Primary Care Optometry News* strives to be the optometric professional's definitive information source by delivering timely, accurate, authoritative and balanced reports on clinical issues, socioeconomic and legislative affairs, ophthalmic industry, and research developments, as well as updates on diagnostic and thereapeutic regimens and techniques to enhance the quality of patient care." Estab. 1996. Circ. 39,000. Byline given. Offers 50% kill fee. Publishes ms an average of 2 months after acceptance. Editorial lead time 2 months. Accepts queries by mail, e-mail, fax, phone. Responds in 2 weeks to queries. Guidelines by e-mail.

NONFICTION Needs how-to, interview, new product, opinion, technical. **Buys 20 mss/year.** Query. Length: 800-1,000 words. **Pays $350-500.** Sometimes pays expenses of writers on assignment.

COLUMNS What's Your Diagnosis (case presentation), 800 words. **Buys 40 mss/year.** Query. **Pays $100-500.**

⊖⊖ SOUTHERN CALIFORNIA PHYSICIAN

LACMA Services, Inc., 707 Wilshire Blvd., Suite 3800, Los Angeles CA 90017. (213)226-0335. **Fax:** (213)226-0350. **E-mail:** cheryle@lacmanet.org. **Website:** www.socalphysician.net. **Contact:** Cheryl England, publisher/editor. **25% freelance written.** Monthly magazine covering non-technical articles of relevance to physicians. "We want professional, well-researched articles covering policy, issues, and other concerns of physicians. No personal anecdotes or patient viewpoints." Estab. 1908. Circ. 18,000. Byline given. Offers 10% kill fee. Publishes ms an average of 2-3 months after acceptance. Editorial lead time 2-3 months. Accepts queries by e-mail. Accepts simultaneous submissions. Responds in 4 weeks to queries. Responds in 2 months to mss.

NONFICTION Needs general interest. **Buys 12-24 mss/year.** Query with published clips. Length: 600-3,000 words. **Pays $200-600 for assigned articles.**

COLUMNS Medical World (tips/how-to's), 800-900 words. Query with published clips. **Pays $$200-$600.**

⊘ ⊖⊖ STRATEGIC HEALTH CARE MARKETING

Health Care Communications, 11 Heritage Lane, P.O. Box 594, Rye NY 10580. (914)967-6741. **Fax:** (914)967-3054. **E-mail:** healthcomm@aol.com. **Website:** www.strategichealthcare.com. **Contact:** Michele von Dambrowski, publisher. **90% freelance written.** Monthly newsletter covering health care marketing and management in a wide range of settings, including hospitals, medical group practices, home health services, and managed care organizations. Emphasis is on strategies and techniques employed within the health care field and relevant applications from other service industries. Works with published/established writers only. *Strategic Health Care Marketing* is specifically seeking writers with expertise/contacts in managed care, patient satisfaction, and e-health. Estab. 1984. Byline given. Offers 25% kill fee. Publishes ms an average of 2 months after acceptance. Accepts queries by mail, e-mail. Responds in 1 month to queries. Sample copy for SAE with 9x12 envelope and 3 first-class stamps. Guidelines sent with sample copy only.

NONFICTION Needs how-to, interview, new product, technical. **Buys 50 mss/year.** Query. Length: 1,000-1,800 words. **Pays $100-500.** Sometimes pays expenses of writers on assignment with prior authorization.

MUSIC TRADE

⊖ CLASSICAL SINGER MAGAZINE

Classical Publications, Inc., P.O. Box 1710, Draper UT 84020. (801)254-1025, ext. 14. **Fax:** (801)254-3139. **E-mail:** editorial@classicalsinger.com. **Website:** www.classicalsinger.com. **Contact:** Sara Thomas. Monthly magazine covering classical singers. Estab. 1988. Circ. 7,000. Byline given, plus bio and contact info. Publishes ms an average of 3 months after acceptance. Editorial lead time 3 months. Submit seasonal material 3 months in advance. Accepts queries by e-mail. Responds in 1 month to queries. Potential writers will be given password to website version of magazine and writer's guidelines online.

NONFICTION Needs book excerpts, exposé, carefully done, how-to, humor, interview, new product, personal experience, photo feature, religious, technical, travel, , crossword puzzles on opera theme. Does not want reviews unless they are assigned. Query with published clips. Length: 500-3,000 words. **Pays 5¢/**

word ($50 minimum). Writers also receive 10 copies of the magazine. Pays telephone expenses of writers with assignments when Xerox copy of bill submitted.

Ø $ INTERNATIONAL BLUEGRASS

International Bluegrass Music Association, 2 Music Circle S., Suite 100, Nashville TN 37203. (615)256-3222. **Fax:** (615)256-0450. **E-mail:** info@ibma.org. **Website:** www.ibma.org. **10% freelance written.** Bimonthly newsletter. "We are the business publication for the bluegrass music industry. IBMA believes that our music has growth potential. We are interested in hard news and features concerning how to reach that potential and how to conduct business more effectively." Estab. 1985. Circ. 4,500. Byline given. Publishes ms an average of 2 months after acceptance. Submit seasonal material 4 months in advance. Accepts queries by mail, e-mail, phone. Accepts simultaneous submissions. Responds in 1 month to queries. Sample copy for sae with 6x9 envelope and 2 first-class stamps.

NONFICTION Needs book excerpts, essays, how-to, conduct business effectively within bluegrass music, new product, opinion. No interview/profiles/feature stories of performers (rare exceptions) or fans. **Buys 6 mss/year.** Query. Length: 1,000-1,200 words. **Pays up to $150/article for assigned articles.**

COLUMNS Staff written.

MUSIC CONNECTION

Music Connection, Inc., 14654 Victory Blvd., 1st Floor, Encino CA 91436. (818)995-0101. **Fax:** (818)995-9235. **E-mail:** markn@musicconnection.com. **Website:** www.musicconnection.com. **Contact:** Mark Nardone, associate publisher. **40% freelance written.** Monthly magazine geared toward working musicians and/or other industry professionals, including producers/engineers/studio staff, managers, agents, publicists, music publishers, record company staff, concert promoters/bookers, etc. Found in select major booksellers and all Guitar Centers in America. "Check out our Digital Edition (including video and audio content) at www.musicconnection.com/digital.". Estab. 1977. Circ. 75,000. Byline given. Pays after publication. Offers kill fee. Kill fee varies. Publishes ms an average of 2 months after acceptance. Editorial lead time 2 months. Submit seasonal material 2 months in advance. Sample copy for $5.

NONFICTION Needs how-to, music industry related, interview, new product, technical. Query with published clips. Length: 1,000-5,000 words. **Payment varies.** Sometimes pays expenses of writers on assignment.

MUSIC EDUCATORS JOURNAL

MENC: The National Association for Music Education, Sage Publications, Inc., 2455 Teller Rd., Thousand Oaks CA 91320. (805)499-0721. **Fax:** (805)499-8096. **E-mail:** ellaw@menc.org. **Website:** http://mej.sagepub.com. **Contact:** Ella Wilcox, editor. Quarterly music education journal published in March, June, September, and December. "Offers scholarly and practical articles on music teaching approaches and philosophies, instructional techniques, current trends, and issues in music education in schools and communities and the latest in products and services. Especially welcome are topics of value, assistance, or inspiration to practicing music teachers." Accepts queries by e-mail. Sample copy available. Guidelines available on website.

NONFICTION "Music Educators Journal (MEJ) encourages music education professionals to submit mss about all phases of music education in schools and communities, practical instructional techniques, teaching philosophy, and current issues in music teaching and learning. The main goal of MEJ is to advance music education.". Authors should avoid personal asides that are not relevant to the primary topic, as well as content that promotes a person, performing group, institution, or product. Submissions should be grounded in the professional literature. Articles with no citations or reference to previous work in the area will not be considered for publication. Manuscripts should be submitted electronically to http://mc.manuscriptcentral.com/mej. Length: 1,800-3,500/words. **Each author receives 2 copies of the issue in which his or her article appears; authors may also order additional copies.**

$$$ OPERA NEWS

Metropolitan Opera Guild, Inc., 70 Lincoln Center Plaza, 6th Floor, New York NY 10023-6593. (212)769-7080. **Fax:** (212)769-8500. **E-mail:** info@operanews.com. **Website:** www.operanews.com. **Contact:** Kitty March. **75% freelance written.** Monthly magazine for people interested in opera—the opera professional as well as the opera audience. Estab. 1936. Circ. 105,000. Byline given. Publishes ms an average of 4 months after acceptance. Editorial lead time 4 months. Accepts queries by e-mail. Sample copy for $5.

NONFICTION Needs historical, interview, informational, think pieces, opera, and CD, DVD and book reviews. "We do not accept works of fiction or personal remembrances. No phone calls, please." Query. Length: 1,500-2,800 words. **Pays $450-1,200.** Sometimes pays expenses of writers on assignment.

COLUMNS Buys 24 mss/year.

$$ VENUES TODAY

18350 Mt. Langley, Suite 201, Fountain Valley CA 92708. **Fax:** (714)378-0040. **E-mail:** linda@venuestoday.com. **Website:** www.venuestoday.com. **Contact:** Linda Deckard, publisher/editor-in-chief. **70% freelance written.** Weekly magazine covering the live entertainment industry and the buildings that host shows and sports. "We need writers who can cover an exciting industry from the business side, not the consumer side. The readers are venue managers, concert promoters, those in the concert and sports business, not the audience for concerts and sports. So we need business journalists who can cover the latest news and trends in the market." Estab. 2002. Byline given. Publishes ms an average of 1 month after acceptance. Editorial lead time 1-2 months. Submit seasonal material 1-2 months in advance. Accepts queries by mail, e-mail, fax. Accepts simultaneous submissions. Responds in 1 week to queries. Guidelines free.

NONFICTION Needs interview, photo feature, technical, travel. Does not want customer slant, marketing pieces. Query with published clips. Length: 500-1,500 words. **Pays $100-250.** Pays expenses of writers on assignment.

COLUMNS Venue News (new buildings, trend features, etc.); Bookings (show tours, business side); Marketing (of shows, sports, convention centers); Concessions (food, drink, merchandise). Length: 500-1,200 words. **Buys 250 mss/year.** Query with published clips. **Pays $100-250.**

FILLERS Needs gags. **Buys 6 mss/year. Pays $100-300.**

PAPER

$$ THE PAPER STOCK REPORT

McEntee Media Corp., 9815 Hazelwood Ave., Cleveland OH 44149-2305. (440)238-6603. **Fax:** (440)238-6712. **E-mail:** ken@recycle.cc. **Website:** www.recycle.cc. **Contact:** Ken McEntee, editor/publisher. Biweekly newsletter covering market trends and news in the paper recycling industry. "Audience is interested in new innovative markets, applications for recovered scrap paper, as well as new laws and regulations impacting recycling." Estab. 1990. Circ. 2,000. Byline given. Publishes ms an average of 1 month after acceptance. Editorial lead time 2 months. Submit seasonal material 2 months in advance. Accepts queries by mail, e-mail, fax, phone. Accepts simultaneous submissions. Responds in 1 month to queries. Sample copy for #10 SAE with 55¢ postage.

NONFICTION Needs book excerpts, essays, exposé, general interest, historical, interview, new product, opinion, photo feature, technical, all related to paper recycling. **Buys 0-13 mss/year.** Send complete ms. Length: 250-1,000 words. **Pays $50-250 for assigned articles. Pays $25-250 for unsolicited articles.** Pays expenses of writers on assignment.

$$ RECYCLED PAPER NEWS

McEntee Media Corp., 9815 Hazelwood Ave., Strongsville OH 44149. (440)238-6603. **Fax:** (440)238-6712. **E-mail:** ken@recycle.cc. **Website:** www.recycle.cc. **Contact:** Ken McEntee. **10% freelance written.** Monthly newsletter. "We are interested in any news impacting the paper recycling industry, as well as other environmental issues in the paper industry, i.e., water/air pollution, chlorine-free paper, forest conservation, etc., with special emphasis on new laws and regulations." Estab. 1990. Publishes ms an average of 2 months after acceptance. Editorial lead time 1 month. Submit seasonal material 1 month in advance. Accepts queries by mail, e-mail, fax, phone. Accepts simultaneous submissions. Responds in 2 months to queries. Sample copy for 9x12 SAE and 55¢ postage. Guidelines for #10 sase.

NONFICTION Needs book excerpts, essays, how-to, interview, new product, opinion, personal experience, photo feature, technical, new business, legislation, regulation, business expansion. **Buys 0-5 mss/year.** Query with published clips. **Pays $10-500.**

COLUMNS Query with published clips. **Pays $10-500.**

PETS

$$ PET PRODUCT NEWS INTERNATIONAL

BowTie News, P.O. Box 6050, Mission Viejo CA 92690. (949)855-8822. **Fax:** (949)855-3045. **E-mail:** scollins@bowtieinc.com. **E-mail:** bhutchins@bowtieinc.com. **Website:** www.petproductnews.com. Lisa MacDonald, marketing director. **Contact:** Sherri Collins, ed-

TRADE JOURNALS

itor; Brian Hutchins, news director. **70% freelance written.** Monthly magazine. "*Pet Product News* covers business/legal and economic issues of importance to pet product retailers, suppliers, and distributors, as well as product information and animal care issues. We're looking for straightforward articles on the proper care of dogs, cats, birds, fish, and exotics (reptiles, hamsters, etc.) as information the retailers can pass on to new pet owners." Estab. 1947. Circ. 26,000. Byline given. Offers $50 kill fee. Editorial lead time 3 months. Submit seasonal material 4 months in advance. Accepts queries by mail, fax. Responds in 2 weeks to queries. Sample copy for $5.50. Guidelines for #10 SASE.

NONFICTION Needs general interest, interview, new product, photo feature, technical. "No 'cute' animal stories or those directed at the pet owner." **Buys 150 mss/year.** Query. Length: 500-1,500 words. **Pays $175-350.**

COLUMNS The Pet Dealer News™ (timely news stories about business issues affecting pet retailers), 800-1,000 words; Industry News (news articles representing coverage of pet product suppliers, manufacturers, distributors, and associations), 800-1,000 words; Pet Health News™ (pet health and articles relevant to pet retailers); Dog & Cat (products and care of), 1,000-1,500 words; Fish & Bird (products and care of), 1,000-1,500 words; Small Mammals (products and care of), 1,000-1,500 words; Pond/Water Garden (products and care of), 1,000-1,500 words. **Buys 120 mss/year.** Query. **Pays $150-300.**

PLUMBING, HEATING, AIR CONDITIONING AND

○ $$ HPAC: HEATING PLUMBING AIR CONDITIONING

80 Valleybrook Dr., Toronto ON M3B 2S9 Canada. (416)764-1549. **E-mail:** kerry.turner@hpacmag.rogers.com. **Website:** www.hpacmag.com. **Contact:** Kerry Turner, editor. **20% freelance written.** Monthly magazine. For a prompt reply, enclose a sheet on which is typed a statement either approving or rejecting the suggested article which can either be checked off, or a quick answer written in and signed and returned. Estab. 1923. Circ. 16,500. Publishes ms an average of 3 months after acceptance. Accepts queries by mail, e-mail, phone. Responds in 2 months to queries.

NONFICTION Needs how-to, technical. Length: 1,000-1,500 words. **Pays 25¢/word.** Sometimes pays expenses of writers on assignment.

$$ SNIPS MAGAZINE

BNP Media, 2401 W. Big Beaver Rd., Suite 700, Troy MI 48084. (248)244-6416. **Fax:** (248)362-0317. **E-mail:** mcconnellm@bnpmedia.com. **Website:** www.snipsmag.com. **Contact:** Michael McConnell. **2% freelance written.** Monthly magazine for sheet metal, heating, ventilation, air conditioning, and metal roofing contractors. Estab. 1932. Publishes ms an average of 3 months after acceptance. Accepts queries by mail, e-mail, fax, phone. Call for writer's guidelines.

NONFICTION Length: under 1,000 words unless on special assignment. **Pays $200-300.**

PRINTING

$$ THE BIG PICTURE

ST Media Group International, 11262 Cornell Park Dr., Cincinnati OH 45242. (513)421-2050. **E-mail:** gregory.sharpless@stmediagroup.com. **Website:** http://bigpicture.net. **Contact:** Gregory Sharpless. **20% freelance written.** Monthly magazine covering wide-format digital printing. "*The Big Picture* covers wide-format printing as well as digital workflow, finishing, display, capture, and other related topics. Our 21,500 readers include digital print providers, sign shops, commercial printers, in-house print operations, and other print providers across the country. We are primarily interested in the technology and work processes behind wide-format printing, but also run trend features on segments of the industry (innovations in point-of-purchase displays, floor graphics, fine-art printing, vehicle wrapping, textile printing, etc.)." Estab. 1996. Circ. 21,500 controlled. Byline given. Offers 20% kill fee. Publishes ms an average of 2 months after acceptance. Editorial lead time 2 months. Accepts queries by e-mail. Accepts simultaneous submissions. Responds in 2 weeks to queries. Responds in 1 month to mss. Guidelines available.

NONFICTION Needs how-to, interview, new product, technical. Does not want broad consumer-oriented pieces that do not speak to the business and technical aspects of producing print for pay. **Buys 15-30 mss/year.** Query with published clips. Length: 1500-2500 words. **Pays $500-700 for assigned articles.** Sometimes (limit agreed upon in advance).

$ $ IN-PLANT GRAPHICS

North American Publishing Co., 1500 Spring Garden St., 12th Floor, Philadelphia PA 19130. (215)238-5321. **Fax:** (215)238-5457. **E-mail:** bobneubauer@napco.com. **Website:** www.ipgonline.com. **Contact:** Bob Neubauer, editor. **40% freelance written.** Estab. 1951. Circ. 23,100. Byline given. Publishes ms an average of 3 months after acceptance. Editorial lead time 2 months. Submit seasonal material 3 months in advance. Accepts queries by mail, e-mail, fax. Guidelines available online.

NONFICTION Needs new product, graphic arts, technical, graphic arts/printing/prepress. No articles on desktop publishing software or design software. No Internet publishing articles. **Buys 5 mss/year.** Query with published clips. Length: 800-1,500 words. **Pays $350-500.**

$ $ SCREEN PRINTING

ST Media Group International, 11262 Cornell Park Dr., Cincinnati OH 45242. (513)421-2050, ext. 331. **Fax:** (513)421-5144. **E-mail:** gail.flower@stmediagroup.com. **Website:** www.screenweb.com. **Contact:** Gail Flower. **30% freelance written.** Monthly magazine for the screen printing industry, including screen printers (commercial, industrial, and captive shops), suppliers and manufacturers, ad agencies, and allied profession. Estab. 1953. Circ. 17,500. Byline given. Publishes ms an average of 3 months after acceptance. Accepts queries by mail, e-mail, fax. Sample copy available. Guidelines for #10 SASE.

NONFICTION Unsolicited mss not returned. **Buys 10-15 mss/year.** Query. **Pays $400 minimum for major features.**

PROFESSIONAL PHOTOGRAPHY

$ $ NEWS PHOTOGRAPHER

National Press Photographers Association, Inc., 6677 Whitemarsh Valley Walk, Austin TX 78746-6367. **E-mail:** magazine@nppa.org. **Website:** www.nppa.org. Published 12 times/year. "*News Photographer* magazine is dedicated to the advancement of still and television news photography. The magazine presents articles, interviews, profiles, history, new products, electronic imaging, and news related to the practice of photojournalism." Estab. 1946. Circ. 11,000. Byline given. Offers 100% kill fee. Publishes ms an average

of 4 months after acceptance. Editorial lead time 2 months. Submit seasonal material 2 months in advance. Accepts queries by mail, e-mail, fax, phone. Accepts simultaneous submissions. Responds in 1 month to queries. Sample copy for SAE with 9x12 envelope and 3 first-class stamps. Guidelines free.

NONFICTION Needs historical, how-to, interview, new product, opinion, personal experience, photo feature, technical. **Buys 10 mss/year.** Query. 1,500 words **Pays $300.** Pays expenses of writers on assignment.

COLUMNS Query.

$ $ THE PHOTO REVIEW

140 E. Richardson Ave., Suite 301, Langhorne PA 19047. (215)891-0214. **Fax:** (215)891-9358. **E-mail:** info@photoreview.org. **Website:** www.photoreview.org. **50% freelance written.** Quarterly magazine covering art photography and criticism. "*The Photo Review* publishes critical reviews of photography exhibitions and books, critical essays, and interviews. We do not publish how-to or technical articles." Estab. 1976. Circ. 2,000. Byline given. Publishes ms an average of 9-12 months after acceptance. Editorial lead time 3 months. Submit seasonal material 6 months in advance. Accepts queries by mail. Accepts simultaneous submissions. Responds in 2 months to queries. Responds in 3 months to mss. Sample copy for $7. Guidelines for #10 SASE.

NONFICTION Needs interview, photography essay, critical review. No how-to articles. **Buys 20 mss/year.** Send complete ms. 2-20 typed pages **Pays $10-250.**

REAL ESTATE

☼ ☽ $ $ CANADIAN PROPERTY MANAGEMENT

Mediaedge Communications Inc., 5255 Yonge St., Toronto ON M2N 6P4 Canada. (416)512-8186. **Fax:** (416)512-8344. **E-mail:** paulm@mediaedge.ca; robertt@mediaedge.ca. **Website:** www.mediaedge.ca. **10% freelance written.** Magazine published 8 times/year covering Canadian commercial, industrial, institutional (medical and educational), and residential properties. *Canadian Property Management* magazine is a trade journal supplying building owners and property managers with Canadian industry news, case law reviews, technical updates for building operations and events listings. Building and professional profile articles are regular features. Estab. 1985. Circ. 12,500. Byline given. Publishes ms an average of 3 months after acceptance. Editorial lead time 2 months. Submit seasonal material 2 months in advance. Accepts queries by mail, e-mail, fax, phone. Accepts simultaneous submissions. Responds in 3 weeks to queries. Responds in 2 months to mss. Sample copy for $5, subject to availability. Guidelines free.

NONFICTION Needs interview, technical. No promotional articles (i.e., marketing a product or service geared to this industry) Query with published clips. Length: 700-1,200 words. **Pays 35¢/word.**

💲💲 THE COOPERATOR

Yale Robbins, Inc., 102 Madison Ave., 5th Floor, New York NY 10016. (212)683-5700. **Fax:** (212)545-0764. **E-mail:** editorial@cooperator.com. **Website:** www.cooperator.com. **70% freelance written.** Monthly tabloid covering real estate in the New York City metro area. *The Cooperator* covers condominium and cooperative issues in New York and beyond. It is read by condo unit owners and co-op shareholders, real estate professionals, board members and managing agents, and other service professionals. Estab. 1980. Circ. 40,000. Byline given. Publishes ms an average of 3 months after acceptance. Submit seasonal material 3 months in advance. Accepts queries by mail, e-mail, fax. Responds in 1 month to queries. Sample copy and writer's guidelines free.

NONFICTION Needs interview, new product, personal experience. No submissions without queries. Query with published clips. Length: 1,500-2,000 words. **Pays $325-425.** Sometimes pays expenses of writers on assignment.

COLUMNS Profiles of co-op/condo-related businesses with something unique; Building Finance (investment and financing issues); Buying and Selling (market issues, etc.); Design (architectural and interior/exterior design, lobby renovation, etc.); Building Maintenance (issues related to maintaining interior/exterior, facades, lobbies, elevators, etc.); Legal Issues Related to Co-Ops/Condos; Real Estate Trends, all 1,500 words. **Buys 100 mss/year.** Query with published clips.

💲💲 FLORIDA REALTOR MAGAZINE

Florida Association of Realtors, 7025 Augusta National Dr., Orlando FL 32822-5017. (407)438-1400. **Fax:** (407)438-1411. **E-mail:** flrealtor@floridarealtors.org. **Website:** www.floridarealtormagazine.com. **Contact:** Doug Damerst, editor-in-chief. **70% freelance written.** Journal published 10 times/year covering the Florida real estate profession. "As the official publication of the Florida Association of Realtors, we provide helpful articles for our 115,000 members. We report new practices that lead to successful real estate careers and stay up on the trends and issues that affect business in Florida's real estate market." Estab. 1925. Circ. 112,205. Byline given. Publishes ms an average of 2 months after acceptance. Editorial lead time 3 months. Accepts queries by mail, e-mail, fax.

NONFICTION No fiction or poetry. **Buys varying number of mss/year.** Query with published clips. Length: 800-1,500 words. **Pays $500-700.** Sometimes pays expenses of writers on assignment.

COLUMNS Some written in-house: Law & Ethics, 900 words; Market It, 600 words; Technology & You, 800 words; ManageIt, 600 words. **Buys varying number of mss/year. Payment varies.**

💲💲 PROPERTIES MAGAZINE

Properties Magazine, Inc., 3826 W. 158th St., Cleveland OH 44111. (216)251-0035. **Fax:** (216)251-0064. **E-mail:** kkrych@propertiesmag.com. **Website:** www.propertiesmag.com. **Contact:** Kenneth C. Krych, editor/publisher. **25% freelance written.** Monthly magazine covering real estate, residential, commercial construction. "*Properties Magazine* is published for executives in the real estate, building, banking, design, architectural, property management, tax, and law community—busy people who need the facts presented in an interesting and informative format." Estab. 1946. Circ. over 10,000. Byline given. Publishes ms an average of 2 months after acceptance. Editorial lead time 2 months. Submit seasonal material 2 months in advance. Accepts queries by mail, fax. Responds in 3 weeks to queries. Sample copy for $3.95.

NONFICTION Needs general interest, how-to, humor, new product. Special issues: Environmental issues (September); Security/Fire Protection (October); Tax Issues (November); Computers In Real Estate (December). **Buys 30 mss/year.** Send complete ms. Length: 500-2,000 words. **Pays 50¢/column line.** Sometimes pays expenses of writers on assignment.

COLUMNS Buys 25 mss/year. Query or send complete ms. **Pays 50¢/column line.**

⟳ 💲💲 REM

2255 B #1178 Queen St. East, Toronto ON M4E 1G3 Canada. (416)425-3504. **E-mail:** jim@remonline.com. **Website:** www.remonline.com. **Contact:** Jim Adair, managing editor. **35% freelance written**. Monthly Canadian trade journal covering real estate. "*REM* provides Canadian real estate agents and brokers with news and opinions they can't get anywhere else. It is an independent publication and not affiliated with any real estate board, association, or company." Estab. 1989. Circ. 38,000. Offers 25% kill fee. Publishes ms an average of 2 months after acceptance. Editorial lead time 3 months. Submit seasonal material 3 months in advance. Accepts queries by mail, e-mail, fax. Accepts simultaneous submissions.

NONFICTION Needs book excerpts, exposé, inspirational, interview, new product, personal experience. "No articles geared to consumers about market conditions or how to choose a realtor. Must have Canadian content." **Buys 60 mss/year.** Query. Length: 500-1,500 words. **Pays $200-400.**

💲💲 ZONING PRACTICE

American Planning Association, 205 N. Michigan Ave., Suite 1200, Chicago IL 60601. (312)431-9100. **Fax:** (312)786-6700. **E-mail:** zoningpractice@planning.org. **Website:** www.planning.org/zoningpractice/index.htm. **90% freelance written.** Monthly newsletter covering land-use regulations including zoning. "Our publication is aimed at practicing urban planners and those involved in land-use decisions, such as zoning administrators and officials, planning commissioners, zoning boards of adjustment, land-use attorneys, developers, and others interested in this field. The material we publish must come from writers knowledgeable about zoning and subdivision regulations, preferably with practical experience in the field. Anything we publish needs to be of practical value to our audience in their everyday work." Estab. 1984. Circ. 2,900. Byline given. Offers 50% kill fee. Publishes ms an average of 3 months after acceptance. Editorial lead time 6 months. Accepts queries by mail, e-mail, fax, phone. Responds in 2 weeks to queries. Responds in 1 month to mss. Guidelines available atwww.planning.org/zoningpractice/contribguidelines.htm.

NONFICTION Needs technical. "See our description. We do not need general or consumer-interest articles about zoning because this publication is aimed at practitioners." **Buys 12 mss/year.** Query. Length: 3,000-5,000 words. **Pays $300 minimum for assigned articles.** Sometimes pays expenses of writers on assignment.

RESOURCES AND WASTE REDUCTION

💲💲💲 EROSION CONTROL

Forester Media Inc., 2946 De La Vina St., Santa Barbara CA 93105. (805)682-1300. **Fax:** (805)682-0200. **E-mail:** eceditor@forester.net. **Website:** www.erosion-control.com. **Contact:** Janice Kaspersen, editor. **60% freelance written.** Magazine published 7 times/year covering all aspects of erosion prevention and sediment control. "*Erosion Control* is a practical, hands-on, 'how-to' professional journal. Our readers are civil engineers, landscape architects, builders, developers, public works officials, road and highway construction officials and engineers, soils specialists, farmers, landscape contractors, and others involved with any activity that disturbs significant areas of surface vegetation." Estab. 1994. Circ. 23,000. Byline given. Pays 1 month after acceptance. Publishes ms an average of 3 months after acceptance. Editorial lead time 4 months. Submit seasonal material 4 months in advance. Accepts queries by mail, e-mail, fax, phone. Responds in 3 weeks to queries. Sample copy and writer's guidelines free.

NONFICTION Needs photo feature, technical. **Buys 15 mss/year.** Query with published clips. Length: 3,000-4,000 words. **Pays $700-850.** Sometimes pays expenses of writers on assignment.

💲💲 MSW MANAGEMENT

Forester Media Inc., P.O. Box 3100, Santa Barbara CA 93130. (805)682-1300. **Fax:** (805)682-0200. **E-mail:** jtrotti@forester.net. **Website:** www.mswmanagement.com. **Contact:** John Trotti, group editor. **70% freelance written.** Bimonthly magazine. "*MSW Management* is written for public sector solid waste professionals—the people working for the local counties, cities, towns, boroughs, and provinces. They run the landfills, recycling programs, composting, and incineration. They are responsible for all aspects of garbage collection and disposal; buying and maintaining the associated equipment; and designing, engineering, and building the waste processing facilities, transfer stations, and landfills." Estab. 1991. Circ. 25,000. Byline given. Pays 30 days after acceptance. Editorial lead time 4 months. Submit seasonal material 4 months in advance. Accepts queries by mail, e-mail, fax, phone. Accepts simultaneous submissions. Responds in 6 weeks to queries. Responds in 2 months to mss. Sample copy and writer's guidelines free.

NONFICTION Needs photo feature, technical. "No rudimentary, basic articles written for the average person on the street. Our readers are experienced professionals with years of practical, in-the-field experience. Any material submitted that we judge as too fundamental will be rejected." **Buys 15 mss/year.** Query. Length: 3,000-4,000 words. **Pays $350-750.** Sometimes pays expenses of writers on assignment.

💲💲 WATER WELL JOURNAL

National Ground Water Association, 601 Dempsey Rd., Westerville OH 43081. **Fax:** (614)898-7786. **E-mail:** tplumley@ngwa.org. **Website:** www.ngwa.org. **Contact:** Thad Plumley, director of publications; Mike Price, associate editor. Each month the *Water Well Journal* covers the topics of drilling, rigs and heavy equipment, pumping systems, water quality, business management, water supply, on-site waste water treatment, and diversification opportunities, including geothermal installations, environmental remediation, irrigation, dewatering, and foundation installation. It also offers updates on regulatory issues that impact the ground water industry. Circ. 24,000. Byline given. Publishes ms an average of 3 months after acceptance. Editorial lead time 6 weeks. Submit seasonal material 3 months in advance. Accepts queries by mail. Responds in 2 weeks to queries. Responds in 1 month to mss. Guidelines free.

NONFICTION Needs essays, sometimes, historical, sometimes, how-to, recent examples include how-to chlorinate a well; how-to buy a used rig; how-to do bill collections, interview, new product, personal experience, photo feature, technical, business management. No company profiles or extended product releases. **Buys up to 30 mss/year.** Query with published clips. Length: 1,000-3,000 words. **Pays $150-400.**

SELLING AND MERCHANDISING

💲💲 BALLOONS & PARTIES MAGAZINE

PartiLife Publications, 65 Sussex St., Hackensack NJ 07601. (201)441-4224. **Fax:** (201)342-8118. **E-mail:** mark@balloonsandparties.com. **Website:** www.balloonsandparties.com. **Contact:** Mark Zettler, publisher. **10% freelance written.** International trade journal published bi-monthly for professional party

decorators and gift delivery businesses. "*BALLOONS & Parties Magazine* is published 6 times a year by PartiLife Publications, L.L.C., for the balloon, party and event fields. New product data, letters, mss, and photographs should be sent as 'Attention: Editor' and should include sender's full name, address, and telephone number. SASE required on all editorial submissions. All submissions considered for publication unless otherwise noted. Unsolicited materials are submitted at sender's risk and *BALLOONS & Parties*/PartiLife Publications, L.L.C., assumes no responsibility for unsolicited materials." Estab. 1986. Circ. 7,000. Byline given. Publishes ms an average of 3 months after acceptance. Submit seasonal material 6 months in advance. Accepts queries by mail, e-mail, fax, phone. Responds in 6 weeks to queries. Sample copy for SAE with 9x12 envelope.

NONFICTION Needs essays, how-to, interview, new product, personal experience, photo feature, technical, craft. **Buys 12 mss/year.** Send complete ms. Length: 500-1,500 words. **Pays $100-300 for assigned articles. Pays $50-200 for unsolicited articles.** Sometimes pays expenses of writers on assignment.

COLUMNS Problem Solver (small business issues); Recipes That Cook (centerpiece ideas with detailed how-to); 400-1,000 words. Send complete ms with photos.

🔁 C&I RETAILING

Convenience & Impulse Retailing; Berg Bennett, Pty Ltd., Suite 6, The Atrium, 340 Darling St., Balmain NSW 2041 Australia. (61)(2)9555-1355. **Fax:** (61)(2)9555-1434. **E-mail:** magazine@c-store.com.au. **Website:** www.c-store.com.au. Bimonthly magazine covering retail store layout, consumer packaged goods, forecourt, impulse retailing as well as convenience food. Circ. 22,750.

NONFICTION Needs general interest, how-to, new product, Also industry news. Query.

💲💲 CASUAL LIVING MAGAZINE

Sandow Media Furniture/Today Group, 7025 Albert Pick Rd., Suite 200, Greensboro NC 27409. (336)605-1115. **Fax:** (336)605-1158. **E-mail:** ncrews@casualliving.com. **Website:** www.casualliving.com. **Contact:** Nicole Crews, executive editor. **10% freelance written.** Monthly magazine covering outdoor furniture and accessories, barbecue grills, spas, and more. "Casual Living is a trade only publication for the casual furnishings and related industries, published monthly. We write about new products, trends, and casual fur-

niture retailers, plus industry news." Estab. 1958. Circ. 10,000. Publishes ms an average of 1-2 months after acceptance. Editorial lead time 1-2 months. Submit seasonal material 2 months in advance. Accepts queries by mail, e-mail. Responds in 2 weeks to queries.
NONFICTION Needs how-to, interview. **Buys 20 mss/year.** Query with published clips. Length: 300-1,000 words. **Pays $300-700.** Sometimes pays expenses of writers on assignment.

❸❸❸❸ CONSUMER GOODS TECHNOLOGY

Edgell Communications, 4 Middlebury Blvd., Randolph NJ 07869. (973)607-1300. **Fax:** (973)607-1395. **E-mail:** aackerman@edgellmail.com. **Website:** www.consumergoods.com. **Contact:** Alliston Ackerman, editor. **40% freelance written.** Monthly tabloid benchmarking business technology performance. Estab. 1987. Circ. 25,000. Byline given. Publishes ms an average of 2 months after acceptance. Editorial lead time 3 months. Accepts queries by e-mail. Guidelines by e-mail.
NONFICTION Needs essays, exposé, interview. **Buys 60 mss/year.** Query with published clips. Length: 700-1,900 words. **Pays $600-1,200.** Sometimes pays expenses of writers on assignment.
COLUMNS Columns 400-750 words—featured columnists. **Buys 4 mss/year.** Query with published clips. **Pays 75¢-$1/word**

❸❸ NICHE

The Rosen Group, 3000 Chestnut Ave., Suite 304, Baltimore MD 21211. (410)889-3093, ext. 231. **Fax:** (410)243-7089. **E-mail:** info@rosengrp.com; hoped@rosengrp.com. **Website:** www.nichemagazine.com. **Contact:** Hope Daniels, editor-in-chief. **80% freelance written.** Quarterly trade magazine for the progressive craft gallery retailer. Each issue includes retail gallery profiles, store design trends, management techniques, financial information, and merchandising strategies for small business owners, as well as articles about craft artists and craft mediums. Estab. 1988. Circ. 25,000. Byline given. Publishes ms an average of 6-9 months after acceptance. Editorial lead time 9 months. Submit queries for seasonal material 1 year in advance. Accepts queries by e-mail. Responds in 4-6 weeks to queries. Responds in 3 months to mss. Sample copy for $3.
NONFICTION Needs interview, photo feature, articles targeted to independent retailers and small busi-

ness owners. **Buys 15-20 mss/year.** Query with published clips. **Pays $300-700.** Sometimes pays expenses of writers on assignment.
COLUMNS Retail Details (short items at the front of the book, general retail information); Artist Profiles (short biographies of American Craft Artists); Retail Resources (including book/video/seminar reviews and educational opportunities pertaining to retailers). Query with published clips. **Pays $25-100 per item.**

❸ O&A MARKETING NEWS

KAL Publications, Inc., 559 S. Harbor Blvd., Suite A, Anaheim CA 92805-4525. (714)563-9300. **Fax:** (714)563-9310. **E-mail:** kathy@kalpub.com. **Website:** www.kalpub.com. **3% freelance written.** Bimonthly tabloid. *O&A Marketing News* is editorially directed to people engaged in the distribution, merchandising, installation, and servicing of gasoline, oil, TBA, quick lube, carwash, convenience store, alternative fuel, and automotive aftermarket products in the 13 Western states. Estab. 1966. Circ. 7,500. Byline sometimes given. Publishes ms an average of 2 months after acceptance. Editorial lead time 1 month. Submit seasonal material 1 month in advance. Accepts queries by mail, e-mail, fax. Accepts simultaneous submissions. Responds in 2 months to queries. Responds in 2 months to mss. Sample copy for SASE with 9x13 envelope and 10 first-class stamps.
NONFICTION Needs interview, photo feature, industry news. Does not want anything that doesn't pertain to the petroleum marketing industry in the 13 Western states. **Buys 35 mss/year.** Send complete ms. Length: 100-500 words. **Pays $1.25/column inch.**
COLUMNS Oregon News (petroleum marketing news in state of Oregon). **Buys 7 mss/year.** Send complete ms. **Pays $1.25/column inch.**
FILLERS Needs gags, short humor. **Buys 7 fillers/year mss/year.** Length: 1-200 words. **Pays per column inch.**

➕ ❸❸ SMART RETAILER

Emmis Communications, 707 Kautz Rd., St. Charles IL 60174. (630)377-8000; (888)228-7624. **Fax:** (630)377-8194. **E-mail:** edit@smart-retailer.com; cbiz@sampler.emmis.com. **E-mail:** swagner@smart-retailer.com. **Website:** www.smart-retailer.com. **Contact:** Susan Wagner, editor. **50% freelance written.** Magazine published 7 times/year covering independent retail, gift, and home decor. *Smart Retailer* is a trade publication for independent retailers of gifts and home accents. Estab. 1993. Circ. 32,000. Byline given. Pays 1 month after acceptance of final ms. Offers $50 kill fee. Publishes ms an average of 4-6 months after acceptance. Editorial lead time 4-6 months. Submit seasonal material 8-10 months in advance. Accepts queries by mail, e-mail, fax. Accepts simultaneous submissions. Usually responds in 4-6 weeks (only if accepted). Sample articles are available on website. Guidelines by e-mail.

NONFICTION Needs how-to, pertaining to retail, interview, new product, finance, legal, marketing, small business. No fiction, poetry, fillers, photos, artwork, or profiles of businesses, unless queried and first assigned. **Buys 20 mss/year.** Send résumé and published clips to: Writers Query, *Smart Retailer*. Send complete ms. Length: 1,000-2,500 words. **Pays $275-500 for assigned articles. Pays $200-350 for unsolicited articles.** Sometimes pays expenses of writers on assignment. Limit agreed upon in advance.

COLUMNS Display & Design (store design and product display), 1,500 words; Retailer Profile (profile of retailer—assigned only), 1,800 words; Vendor Profile (profile of manufacturer—assigned only), 1,200 words; Technology (Internet, computer-related articles as applies to small retailers), 1,500 words; Marketing (marketing ideas and advice as applies to small retailers), 1,500 words; Finance (financial tips and advice as applies to small retailers), 1,500 words; Legal (legal tips and advice as applies to small retailers), 1,500 words; Employees (tips and advice on hiring, firing, and working with employees as applies to small retailers), 1,500 words. **Buys 15 mss/year.** Query with published clips or send complete ms. **Pays $250-350.**

§§ TRAVEL GOODS SHOWCASE

Travel Goods Association, 301 North Harrison St., #412, Princeton NJ 08540-3512. (877)842-1938. **Fax:** (877)842-1938. **E-mail:** info@travel-goods.org; cathy@travel-goods.org. **Website:** www.travel-goods.org. **Contact:** Cathy Hays. **5-10% freelance written.** Magazine published quarterly. *"Travel Goods Showcase* contains articles for retailers, dealers, manufacturers, and suppliers about luggage, business cases, personal leather goods, handbags, and accessories. Special articles report on trends in fashion, promotions, selling and marketing techniques, industry statistics, and other educational and promotional improvements and advancements." Estab. 1975. Circ. 21,000. Byline given. Offers $50 kill fee. Publishes

ms an average of 2 months after acceptance. Editorial lead time 3 months. Submit seasonal material 2 months in advance. Accepts queries by mail, e-mail. Responds in 2 weeks to queries. Responds in 1 month to mss. Sample copy and writer's guidelines free.

NONFICTION Needs interview, new product, technical, travel, retailer profiles with photos. No manufacturer profiles. **Buys 3 mss/year.** Query with published clips. Length: 1,200-1,600 words. **Pays $200-400.**

§§§ VERTICAL SYSTEMS RESELLER

Edgell Communications, Inc., 4 Middlebury Blvd., Suite 1, Randolph NJ 07869. (973)607-1300. **Fax:** (973)607-1395. **E-mail:** alorden@edgellmail.com. **Website:** www.verticalsystemsreseller.com. **Contact:** Abigail Lorden, editor-in-chief. **60% freelance written.** Monthly journal covering channel strategies that build business. Estab. 1992. Circ. 30,000. Byline given. Publishes ms an average of 2 months after acceptance. Editorial lead time 3 months. Accepts queries by mail, e-mail, fax. Accepts simultaneous submissions. Responds in 2 weeks to queries. Responds in 2 months to mss.

NONFICTION Needs interview, opinion, technical, technology/channel issues. **Buys 36 mss/year.** Query with published clips. Length: 1,000-1,700 words. **Pays $200-800 for assigned articles.** Sometimes pays expenses of writers on assignment.

§§§ VM+SD

ST Media Group International, 11262 Cornell Park Dr., Cincinnati OH 45242. (513)421-2050. **Fax:** (513)421-5144. **E-mail:** anne.dinardo@stmediagroup.com. **Website:** www.vmsd.com. **Contact:** Anne DiNardo, editor. **10% freelance written.** Monthly magazine covering retailing store design, store planning, visual merchandising, brand marketing. "Our articles need to get behind the story, tell not only what retailers did when building a new store, renovating an existing store, mounting a new in-store merchandise campaign, but also why they did what they did: specific goals, objectives, strategic initiatives, problems to solve, target markets to reach, etc." Estab. 1872. Circ. 20,000. Byline given. Offers $100 kill fee. Publishes ms an average of 1-2 months after acceptance. Editorial lead time 2-3 months. Submit seasonal material 3-4 months in advance. Accepts queries by e-mail. Guidelines free.

NONFICTION **Buys 2-3 mss/year.** Query. Length: 500-1,000 words. **Pays $400-1,000.**

COLUMNS Contact: Contact Anne Dinardo, editor. Please ask for an editorial calendar. **Buys 5-6 mss/year.** Query. **Pays $500-750.**

SPORT TRADE

$ $ AQUATICS INTERNATIONAL

Hanley Wood, LLC, 6222 Wilshire Blvd., Suite 600, Los Angeles CA 90048. **Fax:** (503)288-4402. **E-mail:** gthill@hanleywood.com. **Website:** www.aquaticsintl. com. **Contact:** Gary Thill, editor. Magazine published 10 times/year covering public swimming pools and waterparks. Devoted to the commercial and public swimming pool industries. The magazine provides detailed information on designing, building, maintaining, promoting, managing, programming, and outfitting aquatics facilities. Estab. 1989. Circ. 30,000. Byline given. Publishes ms an average of 3 months after acceptance. Editorial lead time 3 months. Responds in 1 month to queries. Sample copy for $10.50. **NONFICTION** Needs how-to, interview, technical. **Buys 6 mss/year.** Send query letter with published clips/samples. Length: 1,500-2,500 words. **Pays $525 for assigned articles.**
COLUMNS Pays $250.

$ $ ARROWTRADE MAGAZINE

Arrow Trade Publishing Corp., 3479 409th Ave. NW, Braham MN 55006. (320)396-3473. **Fax:** (320)396-3206. **E-mail:** timdehn@arrowtrademag.com. **Website:** www.arrowtrademag.com. **Contact:** Tim Dehn. **60% freelance written.** Bimonthly magazine covering the archery industry. "Our readers are interested in articles that help them operate their businesses better. They are primarily owners or managers of sporting goods stores and archery pro shops." Estab. 1996. Circ. 10,500. Byline given. Publishes ms an average of 2 months after acceptance. Editorial lead time 2 months. Accepts queries by mail, e-mail, fax. Responds in 2 weeks to queries. Responds in 2 weeks to mss. Sample copy for SAE with 9x12 envelope and 10 First-Class stamps.
NONFICTION Needs interview, new product. "Generic business articles won't work for our highly specialized audience." **Buys 24 mss/year.** Query with published clips. Length: 2,400-4,800 words. **Pays $350-550.** Sometimes pays expenses of writers on assignment.

$ $ BOWLING CENTER MANAGEMENT

Luby Publishing, 122 S. Michigan Ave., Suite 1806, Chicago IL 60603. (312)341-1110. **Fax:** (312)341-1180.

E-mail: mikem@lubypublishing.com. **Website:** www. bcmmag.com. **50% freelance written,.** Monthly magazine covering bowling centers, family entertainment. "Our readers are looking for novel ways to draw more customers. Accordingly, we look for articles that effectively present such ideas." Estab. 1995. Circ. 12,000. Byline given. Publishes ms an average of 3 months after acceptance. Editorial lead time 3 months. Submit seasonal material 6 months in advance. Accepts queries by e-mail. Accepts simultaneous submissions. Responds in 2-3 weeks to queries. Sample copy for $10.
NONFICTION Needs how-to, interview. **Buys 10-20 mss/year.** Query. Length: 750-1,500 words. **Pays $150-350.**

$ $ GOLF COURSE MANAGEMENT

Golf Course Superintendents Association of America, 1421 Research Park Dr., Lawrence KS 66049. (800)472-7878. **Fax:** (785)832-3643. **E-mail:** shollister@gcsaa.org; bsmith@gcsaa.org; tcarson@gcsaa. org. **Website:** www.gcsaa.org. **Contact:** Scott Hollister, editor-in-chief; Bunny Smith, managing editor; Teresa Carson, science editor. **50% freelance written.** Monthly magazine covering the golf course superintendent. *GCM* helps the golf course superintendent become more efficient in all aspects of their job. Estab. 1924. Circ. 40,000. Byline given. Publishes ms an average of 6 months after acceptance. Editorial lead time 6 months. Submit seasonal material 6 months in advance. Accepts simultaneous submissions. Responds in 3 weeks to queries. Responds in 1 month to mss. Guidelines available at www2.gcsaa.org/gcm/ed_features.asp and www2.gcsaa.org/gcm/ed_research.asp.
NONFICTION Needs how-to, interview. No articles about playing golf. **Buys 40 mss/year.** Query for either feature, research, or superintendent article. Submit electronically, preferably as e-mail attachment. Send 1-page synopsis or query for feature article to Scott Hollister (shollister@gcsaa.org). For research articles, submit to Teresa Carson (tcarson@gcsaa.org). If you are a superintendent, contact Bunny Smith (bsmith@gcsaa.org). Length: 1,500-2,000 words. **Pays $400-600.** Sometimes pays expenses of writers on assignment.

$ $ INTERNATIONAL BOWLING INDUSTRY

B2B Media, Inc., 13245 Riverside Dr., Suite 501, Sherman Oaks CA 91423. (818)789-2695. **Fax:** (818)789-2812. **E-mail:** info@bowlingindustry.com. **Website:** www.bowlingindustry.com. **40% freelance written.**

Monthly magazine covering ownership and management of bowling centers (alleys) and pro shops. "*IBI* publishes articles in all phases of bowling center and bowling pro shop ownership and management, among them finance, promotion, customer service, relevant technology, architecture, and capital improvement. The magazine also covers the operational areas of bowling centers and pro shops such as human resources, food and beverage, corporate and birthday parties, ancillary attractions (go-karts, gaming and the like), and retailing. Articles must have strong how-to emphasis. They must be written specifically in terms of the bowling industry, although content may be applicable more widely." Estab. 1993. Circ. 10,200. Byline given. Offers $50 kill fee. Publishes ms an average of 3 months after acceptance. Submit seasonal material 3 months in advance. Accepts queries by mail, e-mail, fax. Accepts simultaneous submissions. Responds in 2 weeks to queries. Responds in 1 month to mss. Sample copy for #10 SASE. Guidelines free.

NONFICTION Needs how-to, interview, new product, technical. **Buys 40 mss/year.** Send complete ms. Length: 1,100-1,400 words. **Pays $250.** Sometimes pays expenses of writers on assignment.

⊛⊛ POOL & SPA NEWS

Hanley Wood, LLC, 6222 Wilshire Blvd., Suite 600, Los Angeles CA 90048. (323)801-4972. **Fax:** (323)801-4986. **E-mail:** etaylor@hanleywood.com. **Website:** http://poolspanews.com. **Contact:** Erika Taylor, editor. **15% freelance written.** Semimonthly magazine covering the swimming pool and spa industry for builders, retail stores, and service firms. Estab. 1960. Circ. 16,300. Publishes ms an average of 2 months after acceptance. Accepts queries by mail, e-mail. Responds in 1 month to queries. Sample copy for $5 and 9x12 SAE and 11 first-class stamps.

NONFICTION Needs interview, technical. Send résumé with published clips. Length: 500-2,000 words. **Pays $150-550.** Pays expenses of writers on assignment.

⊛⊛ REFEREE

Referee Enterprises, Inc., 2017 Lathrop Ave., Racine WI 53405. **Fax:** (262)632-5460. **E-mail:** submissions@referee.com. **Website:** www.referee.com. **Contact:** Julie Sternberg, managing editor. **75% freelance written.** Monthly magazine covering sports officiating. *Referee* is a magazine for and read by sports officials of all kinds with a focus on baseball, basketball, foot-

ball, softball, and soccer officiating. Estab. 1976. Circ. 40,000. Byline given. Offers kill fee. Kill fee negotiable. Publishes ms an average of 6 months after acceptance. Editorial lead time 6 months. Accepts queries by mail, e-mail. Responds in 2 weeks to queries. Responds in 1 month to mss. Sample copy with #10 SASE. Guidelines available online.

NONFICTION Needs book excerpts, essays, historical, how-to, sports officiating related, humor, interview, opinion, photo feature, technical, as it relates to sports officiating. "We don't want to see articles with themes not relating to sport officiating. General sports articles, although of interest to us, will not be published." **Buys 40 mss/year.** Query with published clips. Length: 500-3,500 words. **Pays $50-400.** Sometimes pays expenses of writers on assignment.

⊛⊛ THE RINKSIDER

Target Publishing Co., Inc., 2470 E. Main St., Columbus OH 43209. (614)235-1022. **Fax:** (614)235-3584. **E-mail:** story@rinksider.com; editor@rinksider.com. **Website:** www.rinksider.com. **Contact:** Suzy Weinland, editor. **90% freelance written.** Bimonthly magazine of interest to owners/operators of roller skating facilities, promotions, games, snack bars, roller hockey competitive programs, music, decor, features on new or successful skating centers, competitive amusements, etc. Estab. 1953. Circ. 1,600. Byline given. Offers 100% (unless poorly done) kill fee. Publishes ms an average of 2 months after acceptance. Editorial lead time 1 month. Accepts queries by e-mail. Accepts simultaneous submissions. Responds in 2 weeks to queries. Responds in 1 month to mss. Sample copy for $5. Guidelines free.

NONFICTION Needs essays, historical, how-to, humor, inspirational, interview, new product, personal experience, photo feature, travel. Does not want opinion pieces. Query with published clips. Length: 250-1,000 words. **Pays $75-200.**

COLUMNS Finance; Roller Skating News; Marketing; Technology. **Buys 20 mss/year.** Query with published clips. **Pays $75-200.**

⊛⊛ SKI AREA MANAGEMENT

Beardsley Publications, 45 Main St. N, P.O. Box 644, Woodbury CT 06798. (303)652-0285. **Fax:** (303)652-0461. **E-mail:** samedit@saminfo.com. **E-mail:** rick@saminfo.com. **Website:** www.saminfo.com. **Contact:** Rick Kahl, editor. **85% freelance written.** Bimonthly magazine covering everything involving the management and development of ski resorts. "We are the publication of record for the North American ski industry. We report on new ideas, developments, marketing, and regulations with regard to ski and snowboard resorts. Everyone from the CEO to the lift operator of winter resorts reads our magazine to stay informed about the people and procedures that make ski areas successful." Estab. 1962. Circ. 4,500. Byline given. Offers kill fee. Offers kill fee. Editorial lead time 2 months. Submit seasonal material 3 months in advance. Accepts queries by mail, e-mail. Responds in 2 weeks to queries. Sample copy for 9x12 SAE with $3 postage or online. Guidelines for #10 SASE.

NONFICTION Needs historical, how-to, interview, new product, opinion, personal experience, technical. "We don't want anything that does not specifically pertain to resort operations, management, or financing." **Buys 25-40 mss/year.** Query. Length: 500-2,500 words. **Pays $50-400.**

💲💲 SKI PATROL MAGAZINE

National Ski Patrol, 133 S. Van Gordon St., Suite 100, Lakewood CO 80228. (303)988-1111, ext. 2625. **Fax:** (303)988-3005. **E-mail:** chorgan@nsp.org. **Website:** www.nsp.org. **Contact:** Candace Horgan, editor. **80% freelance written.** Covers the National Ski Patrol, skiing, snowboarding, and snowsports safety. *Ski Patrol Magazine* is a triannual publication for the members and affiliates of the National Ski Patrol. Topics are related to patrolling, mountain rescue, and the ski industry. Estab. 1962. Circ. 26,000. Byline given. Editorial lead time is 3 months. Submit seasonal material 3 months in advance. Accepts queries by mail, e-mail, fax. "If you choose to fax, be sure to include a cover page that indicates your intent to submit to *Ski Patrol Magazine*.". Accepts simultaneous submissions. Responds in 1-2 weeks on queries; 2 months on decisions Sample copy available for SASE with $1.90 postage. Guidelines available for SASE with 1 first-class stamp.

NONFICTION Needs essays, exposé, general interest, historical, how-to, humor, interview, nostalgic, opinion, personal experience, photo feature, profile, technical. **Buys 10-15 mss/year.** Query with published clips. Length: 700-3,000 words. Does not pay expenses of writers on assignment.

COLUMNS OEC, Medical; MTR, Transport/Rescue; Sweep, Personal Experience; 1,000 words each. **Buys 8-12 mss/year.** Query with published clips. **Pays $100-200.**

💲💲 THOROUGHBRED TIMES

2008 Mercer Rd., P.O. Box 8237, Lexington KY 40533. (859)260-9800. **E-mail:** tlaw@thoroughbredtimes.com. **Website:** www.thoroughbredtimes.com. **10% freelance written.** Weekly tabloid written for professionals who breed and/or race thoroughbreds at tracks in the US and around the world. Articles must help owners and breeders understand racing to help them realize a profit. Estab. 1985. Circ. 20,000. Byline given. Offers 50% kill fee. Publishes ms an average of 1 month after acceptance. Submit seasonal material 2 months in advance. Responds in 2 weeks to mss.

NONFICTION Needs historical, interview, technical. **Buys 52 mss/year.** Query. Length: 500-2,500 words. **Pays 10-20¢/word.** Sometimes pays expenses of writers on assignment.

COLUMNS Vet Topics; Business of Horses; Pedigree Profiles; Bloodstock Topics; Tax Matters; Viewpoints; Guest Commentary.

STONE, QUARRY AND MINING

☺ 💲💲 CANADIAN MINING JOURNAL

Business Information Group, 80 Valleybrook Dr., Toronto ON M3B 2S9 Canada. (416)510-6742. **Fax:** (416)510-5138. **E-mail:** rnoble@canadianminingjournal.com. **Website:** www.canadianminingjournal.com. **Contact:** Russell Noble, editor. **5% freelance written.** Magazine covering mining and mineral exploration by Canadian companies. *Canadian Mining Journal* provides articles and information of practical use to those who work in the technical, administrative, and supervisory aspects of exploration, mining, and processing in the Canadian mineral exploration and mining industry. Estab. 1882. Circ. 11,000. Byline given. Publishes ms an average of 3 months after acceptance. Submit seasonal material 3 months in advance. Accepts queries by mail, e-mail, fax, phone. Responds in 1 week to queries. Responds in 1 month to mss.

NONFICTION Needs opinion, technical, operation descriptions. **Buys 6 mss/year.** Query with published clips. Length: 500-1,400 words. **Pays $100-600.** Pays expenses of writers on assignment.

COLUMNS Guest editorial (opinion on controversial subject related to mining industry), 600 words. **Buys 3 mss/year.** Query with published clips. **Pays $150.**

🅢🅢 PIT & QUARRY

Questex Media Group, 600 Superior Ave. E., Suite 1100, Cleveland OH 44114. (216)706-3700; (216)706-3747. **Fax:** (216)706-3710. **E-mail:** info@pitandquarry.com; dconstantino@questex.com. **Website:** www.pitandquarry.com. **Contact:** Darren Constantino, editor-in-chief. **10-20% freelance written.** Monthly magazine covering nonmetallic minerals, mining, and crushed stone. Audience has knowledge of construction-related markets, mining, minerals processing, etc. Estab. 1916. Circ. 23,000. Byline given. Publishes ms an average of 2 months after acceptance. Editorial lead time 2 months. Accepts queries by e-mail. Accepts simultaneous submissions. Responds in 1 month to queries. Responds in 4 months to mss. **NONFICTION** Needs how-to, interview, new product, technical. No humor or inspirational articles. **Buys 3-4 mss/year.** Query. Length: 2,000-2,500 words. **Pays $250-500 for assigned articles. Does not pay for unsolicited articles.** Sometimes pays expenses of writers on assignment.
COLUMNS Brand New; Techwatch; E-business; Software Corner; Equipment Showcase. Length: 250-750 words. **Buys 5-6 mss/year.** Query. **Pays $250-300.**

🅢 STONE WORLD

BNP Media, 210 Rt. 4 E., Suite 203, Paramus NJ 07652. (201)291-9001. **Fax:** (201)291-9002. **E-mail:** michael@stoneworld.com. **Website:** www.stoneworld.com. **Contact:** Michael Reis, editor/publisher. Monthly magazine on natural building stone for producers and users of granite, marble, limestone, slate, sandstone, onyx, and other natural stone products. Estab. 1984. Circ. 21,000. Byline given. Publishes ms an average of 4 months after acceptance. Submit seasonal material 6 months in advance. Responds in 2 months to queries. Sample copy for $10.
NONFICTION Needs how-to, fabricate and/or install natural building stone, interview, photo feature, technical, architectural design, artistic stone uses, statistics, factory profile, equipment profile, trade show review. **Buys 10 mss/year.** Send complete ms. Length: 600-3,000 words. **Pays $6/column inch.** Pays expenses of writers on assignment.
COLUMNS News (pertaining to stone or design community); New Literature (brochures, catalogs, books, videos, etc., about stone); New Products (stone products); New Equipment (equipment and machinery for working with stone); Calendar (dates and locations of events in stone and design communities). Query or send complete ms. Length 300-600 words. **Pays $6/inch.**

TOY, NOVELTY AND HOBBY

PEN WORLD

Masterpiece Litho, Inc., P.O. Box 550246, Houston TX 77255-0246. (713)869-9997. **Fax:** (713)869-9993. **E-mail:** editor@penworld.com. **Website:** www.penworld.com. **Contact:** Laura Chandler, editor. Magazine published 6 times/year. Published for writing instrument enthusiasts. Circ. 30,000.

TRANSPORTATION

LIMOUSINE DIGEST

(*Limousine Digest*), Digest Publications, 3 Reeves Station Rd., Medford NJ 08055. (609)953-4900. **Fax:** (609)953-4905. **E-mail:** info@limodigest.com. **Website:** www.limodigest.com. **Contact:** Susan Rose, editor/assistant publisher. **10% freelance written.** Monthly magazine covering ground transportation. "*Limousine Digest* is 'the voice of the luxury ground transportation industry.' We cover all aspects of ground transportation, from vehicles to operators, safety issues, and political involvement." Estab. 1990. Circ. 10,000. Byline given. Publishes ms an average of 3 months after acceptance. Editorial lead time 1 year. Submit seasonal material 3 months in advance. Accepts queries by mail, e-mail, fax. Accepts simultaneous submissions.
NONFICTION Needs historical, how-to, start a company, market your product, humor, inspirational, interview, new product, personal experience, photo feature, technical, travel, industry news, business. **Buys 7-9 mss/year.** Send complete ms. Length: 700-1,900 words. **Negotiates flat-fee and per-word rates individually. Will pay authors in advertising trade-outs.**
COLUMNS New Model Showcase (new limousines, sedans, buses), 1,000 words; Player Profile (industry members profiled), 700 words; Hall of Fame (unique vehicles featured), 500-700 words. **Buys 5 mss/year.** Query. **Negotiates flat-fee and per-word rates individually. Will pay authors in advertising trade-outs.**

🅢🅢 METRO MAGAZINE

Bobit Publishing Co., 3520 Challenger St., Torrance CA 90503. (310)533-2400. **Fax:** (310)533-2502. **E-mail:** info@metro-magazine.com. **E-mail:** alex.roman@bobit.com. **Website:** www.metro-magazine.com. **Con-**

tact: Alex Roman, managing editor. **10% freelance written.** Magazine published 10 times/year covering transit bus, passenger rail, and motorcoach operations. METRO's coverage includes both public transit systems and private bus operators, addressing topics such as funding mechanisms, procurement, rolling stock maintenance, privatization, risk management and sustainability. *Metro Magazine* delivers business, government policy, and technology developments that are *industry specific* to public transportation. Estab. 1904. Circ. 20,500. Byline given. Offers 10% kill fee. Publishes ms an average of 2 months after acceptance. Editorial lead time 3 months. Submit seasonal material 3 months in advance. Accepts queries by e-mail. Responds in 2 weeks to queries. Responds in 1 month to mss. Sample copy for $8. Guidelines by e-mail.

NONFICTION Needs how-to, interview, of industry figures, new product, related to transit—bus and rail—private bus, technical. **Buys 6-10 mss/year.** Query. Length: 400-1,500 words. **Pays $80-400.**

COLUMNS Query. **Pays 20¢/word**

💲💲 SCHOOL BUS FLEET

Bobit Business Media, 3520 Challenger St., Torrance CA 90503. (310)533-2400. **Fax:** (310)533-2512. **E-mail:** sbf@bobit.com. **Website:** www.schoolbusfleet.com. Magazine covering school transportation of K-12 population. "Most of our readers are school bus operators, public and private." Estab. 1956. Circ. 24,000. Byline given. Offers 25% kill fee or $50. Publishes ms an average of 3 months after acceptance. Editorial lead time 3 months. Submit seasonal material 3 months in advance. Accepts queries by mail, e-mail, fax. Responds in 1 month to queries. *Not currently accepting submissions.* .

TRAVEL TRADE

💲💲 CRUISE INDUSTRY NEWS

441 Lexington Ave., Suite 809, New York NY 10017. (212)986-1025. **Fax:** (212)986-1033. **E-mail:** oivind@cruiseindustrynews.com. **Website:** www.cruiseindustrynews.com. **Contact:** Oivind Mathisen, editor. **20% freelance written.** Quarterly magazine covering cruise shipping. "We write about the business of cruise shipping for the industry. That is, cruise lines, shipyards, financial analysts, etc." Estab. 1991. Circ. 10,000. Byline given. Pays on acceptance or on publication. Offers 25% kill fee. Publishes ms an average of 4 months after acceptance. Editorial lead time 3

months. Accepts queries by mail. Reponse time varies. Sample copy for $15. Guidelines for #10 SASE.

NONFICTION Needs interview, new product, photo feature, business. No travel stories. **Buys more than 20 mss/year.** Query with published clips. Length: 500-1,500 words. **Pays $.50/word published.** Sometimes pays expenses of writers on assignment.

💲💲 LEISURE GROUP TRAVEL

Premier Tourism Marketing, 621 Plainfield Rd., Suite 406, Willowbrook IL 60527. (630)794-0696. **Fax:** (630)794-0652. **E-mail:** randy@ptmgroups.com. **E-mail:** editor@ptmgroups.com. **Website:** www.premiertourismmarketing.com. **Contact:** Randy Mink, managing editor. **35% freelance written.** Bimonthly magazine covering group travel. "We cover destinations and editorial relevant to the group travel market." Estab. 1994. Circ. 15,012. Byline given. Editorial lead time 6 months. Submit seasonal material 6 months in advance. Accepts queries by mail, e-mail.

NONFICTION Needs travel. **Buys 75 mss/year.** Query with published clips. Length: 1,200-3,000 words. **Pays $0-1,000.**

💲💲 MIDWEST MEETINGS®

Hennen Publishing, 302 6th St. W, Brookings SD 57006. (605)692-9559. **Fax:** (605)692-9031. **E-mail:** info@midwestmeetings.com; editor@midwestmeetings.com. **Website:** www.midwestmeetings.com. **Contact:** Serenity J. Banks, editor. **20% freelance written.** Quarterly magazine covering meetings/conventions industry. We provide information and resources to meeting/convention planners with a Midwest focus. Estab. 1996. Circ. 28,500. Byline given. Publishes ms an average of 5 months after acceptance. Editorial lead time 3 months. Submit seasonal material 3 months in advance. Accepts queries by e-mail. Guidelines by e-mail.

NONFICTION Needs essays, general interest, historical, how-to, humor, interview, personal experience, travel. Does not want marketing pieces related to specific hotels/meeting facilities. **Buys 15-20 mss/year.** Send complete ms. Length: 500-1,000 words. **Pays 5-50¢/word.**

💲💲💲 RV BUSINESS

G&G Media Group, 2901 E. Bristol St., Suite B, Elkhart IN 46514. (574)266-7980, ext. 13. **Fax:** (574)266-7984. **E-mail:** bhampson@rvbusiness.com; bhampson@g-gmediagroup.com. **Website:** www.rvbusiness.com. **Contact:** Bruce Hampson, editor. **50% freelance written.** Bimonthly magazine covers a specific audience of people who manufacture, sell, market, insure, finance, service and supply, components for recreational vehicles. *RV Business* caters to a specific audience of people who manufacture, sell, market, insure, finance, service and supply, components for recreational vehicles. Estab. 1972. Circ. 21,000. Byline given. Offers kill fee. Publishes ms an average of 2 months after acceptance. Editorial lead time 2 months. Accepts queries by e-mail only.

NONFICTION Needs new product, photo feature, industry news and features. "No general articles without specific application to our market." **Buys 50 mss/year.** Query with published clips. Length: 125-2,200 words. **Pays $50-1,000.** Sometimes pays expenses of writers on assignment.

COLUMNS Top of the News (RV industry news), 75-400 words; Business Profiles, 400-500 words; Features (indepth industry features), 800-2,000 words. **Buys 300 mss/year.** Query. **Pays $50-1,000.**

⊗⊗ SPECIALTY TRAVEL INDEX

Alpine Hansen, P.O. Box 458, San Anselmo CA 94979. (415)455-1643. **E-mail:** info@specialtytravel.com. **Website:** www.specialtytravel.com. **90% freelance written.** Semiannual magazine covering adventure and special interest travel. Estab. 1980. Circ. 35,000. Byline given. Pays on receipt and acceptance of all materials. Editorial lead time 3 month. Submit seasonal material 3 months in advance. Accepts queries by mail, e-mail. Writer's guidelines on request.

NONFICTION Needs how-to, personal experience, photo feature, travel. **Buys 15 mss/year.** Query. Length: 1,250 words. **Pays $300 minimum.**

⊗ STAR SERVICE TRAVEL 42

NORTHSTAR Travel Media, 200 Brookstown Ave., Suite 301, Winston-Salem NC 27101. (336)714-3328. **Fax:** (336)714-3168. **E-mail:** csheaffer@ntmllc.com. **Website:** www.starserviceonline.com; www.travel-42.com/. **Contact:** Cindy Sheaffer, editorial director. Estab. 2011. Pays 1 month after acceptance. Accepts queries by e-mail preferred.

VETERINARY

ANIMAL SHELTERING

2100 L St. NW, Washington D.C. 20037. (202)452-1100. **Fax:** (301)721-6468. **E-mail:** asm@humane-society.org. **Website:** www.animalsheltering.org. **Contact:** Shevaun Brannigan, production/marketing manager; Carrie Allan, editor. **20% freelance written.** Magazine for animal care professionals and volunteers, dealing with animal welfare issues faced by animal shelters, animal control agencies, and rescue groups. Emphasis on news for the field and professional, hands-on work. Readers are shelter and animal control directors, kennel staff, field officers, humane investigators, animal control officers, animal rescuers, foster care volunteers, general volunteers, shelter veterinarians, and anyone concerned with local animal welfare issues. Estab. 1978. Circ. 6,000. Sample copies are free; contact Shevaun Brannigan at sbrannigan@hsus.org. Guidelines available by e-mail.

NONFICTION Approximately 6-10 submissions published each year from non-staff writers; of those submissions, 50% are from writers new to the publication. **"Payment varies depending on length and complexity of piece. Longer features generally $400–600; short news pieces generally $200. We rarely take unsolicited work, so it's best to contact the editor with story ideas."**

⊗ DOG SPORTS MAGAZINE

Cher Car Kennels, 4215 S. Lowell Rd., St. Johns MI 48879. (989)224-7225. **Fax:** (989)224-6033. **E-mail:** suggestions@dogsports.com. **Website:** www.dogsports.com. **Contact:** Cheryl Carlson, editor. **5% freelance written.** Monthly tabloid covering working dogs. "Dog Sports online magazine is for ALL dog trainers. We focus on the "HOW" of dog training. You will find articles on Police K-9 training, Narcotics detection, Herding, Weight Pull, Tracking, Search and Rescue, and how to increase your dog training Business. We bring you the latest in techniques from the field, actual dog trainers that are out there, working, titling and training. French Ring, Mondio, Schutzhund, N.A.P.D. PPDA, K-9 Pro Sports all are featured, as well as spotlight articles on breeds, trainers, judges, or events." Estab. 1979. Circ. 2,000. Byline given. Publishes ms an average of 1 month after acceptance. Editorial lead time 1 month. Submit seasonal material 1 month in advance. Accepts queries by mail, e-mail. Accepts simultaneous submissions. Sample copy free or online.

NONFICTION Needs essays, general interest, how-to, working dogs, humor, interview, technical. **Buys 5 mss/year.** Send complete ms. **Pays $50.**

CONTESTS & AWARDS

The contests and awards listed in this section are arranged by subject. Nonfiction writers can turn immediately to nonfiction awards listed alphabetically by the name of the contest or award. The same is true for fiction writers, poets, playwrights and screenwriters, journalists, children's writers, and translators. You'll also find general book awards, fellowships offered by arts councils and foundations, and multiple category contests.

New contests and awards are announced in various writer's publications nearly every day. However, many lose their funding or fold—and sponsoring magazines go out of business just as often. We have contacted the organizations whose contests and awards are listed here with the understanding that they are valid through 2012-2013.

To make sure you have all the information you need about a particular contest, always send a SASE to the contact person in the listing before entering a contest. The listings in this section are brief, and many contests have lengthy, specific rules and requirements that we could not include in our limited space. Often a specific entry form must accompany your submission.

When you receive a set of guidelines, you will see that some contests are not applicable to all writers. The writer's age, previous publication, geographic location, and length of the work are common matters of eligibility. Read the requirements carefully to ensure you don't enter a contest for which you are not qualified.

Winning a contest or award can launch a successful writing career. Take a professional approach by doing a little extra research. Find out who the previous winner of the award was by investing in a sample copy of the magazine in which the prize-winning article, poem, or short story appeared. Attend the staged reading of an award-winning play. Your extra effort will be to your advantage in competing with writers who simply submit blindly.

PLAYWRITING & SCRIPTWRITING

APPALACHIAN FESTIVAL OF PLAYS & PLAYWRIGHTS

Barter Theatre, Box 867, Abingdon VA 24212-0867. (276)619-3316. **Fax:** (276)619-3335. **E-mail:** apfestival@ bartertheatre.com. **Website:** www.bartertheatre.com/ festival. **Contact:** Nick Piper, associate director/director, New Play Development. "With the annual Appalachian Festival of New Plays & Playwrights, Barter Theatre wishes to celebrate new, previously unpublished/unproduced plays by playwrights from the Appalachian region. If the playwrights are not from Appalachia, the plays themselves must be about the region." Deadline: March 1. Prize: $250, a staged reading performed at Barter's Stage II theater, and some transportation compensation and housing during the time of the festival. There may be an additional award for the best staged readings.

APPALACHIAN FILM FESTIVAL SCREENPLAY CONTEST

Appalachian Film Festival, c/o Huntington Regional Film Commission, P.O. Box 347, Huntington WV 25708. **E-mail:** appyfilmfest@gmail.com. **Website:** www.appyfilmfest.com. Filmmakers must have resided during either of the last 2 years (or been a full-time student attending a college) in any of the 13 states that make up the Appalachian region - WV, OH, KY, NY, PA, MD, VA, TN, SC, GA, AL and MS. Categories: Micro, Short, Documentary, Feature Film, Young Filmmaker, Screenplay. Complete guidelines available on website. Prize: Up to $1,000

BAKER'S PLAYS HIGH SCHOOL PLAYWRITING CONTEST

45 W. 25th St., New York NY 10010. **E-mail:** publications@bakersplays.com. **Website:** www.bakersplays. com. **Contact:** Roxanne Heinze-Bradshaw. **Open to any high school students.** Annual contest. Purpose of the contest: to encourage playwrights at the high school level and to ensure the future of American theater. Unpublished submissions only. Postmark deadline: January 30. Notification: May. SASE for contest rules and entry forms. No entry fee. Awards $500 to the first place playwright with publication by Baker's Plays; $250 to the second place playwright with an honorable mention; and $100 to the third place playwright with an honorable mention in the series. Judged anonymously.

BIG BREAK INTERNATIONAL SCREENWRITING COMPETITION

Final Draft, Inc., 26707 W. Agoura Rd., Suite 205, Calabasas CA 91302. (818)995-8995. **Website:** www. finaldraft.com/bigbreak. **Contact:** Shelly Mellott, VP events and services. "Big Break, a Final Draft, Inc. contest, is an annual, global screenwriting competition designed to promote emerging creative talent. Big Break rewards screenwriters with cash, prizes and A-list executive meetings. Contest is open to any writer. Guidelines and rules available online." No paper submissions. Submissions must be unpublished. Enter online. The contest objective is to bring recognition to promising screenwriters. June 1/ June 15 (extended). Prize: "Over $30,000 in cash and prizes, plus Hollywood industry meetings!" 1st Place prizes: $15,000 total cash, plus finalist prizes, airfare to L.A., 3-night hotel stay (unless winner resides in or around L.A.), lunch with executives. 2nd Place prizes: $4,000 total cash, plus finalist prizes, airfare to L.A., 3-night hotel stay (unless winner resides in or around L.A.), lunch with executives. 3rd Place prizes: $2,000 total cash, plus finalist prizes, airfare to L.A., 3-night hotel stay (unless winner resides in or around L.A.), lunch with executives. 4th and 5th Place prizes: $250 total cash, plus finalist prizes. See 6th through 20th Place Finalist Prizes on website.

SHUBERT FENDRICH MEMORIAL PLAYWRITING CONTEST

Pioneer Drama Service, Inc., P.O. Box 4267, Englewood CO 80155. (303)779-4035. **Fax:** (303)779-4315. **E-mail:** editors@pioneerdrama.com. **E-mail:** submissions@pioneerdrama.com. **Website:** www.pioneerdrama.com. **Contact:** Lori Conary, submissions editor. Purpose of the contest: "To encourage the development of quality theatrical material for educational and family theater." Previously unpublished submissions only. Open to all writers not currently published by Pioneer Drama Service. Deadline for entries: December 31. SASE for contest rules and guidelines or view online. No entry fee. Cover letter, SASE for return of ms, and proof of production or staged reading must accompany all submissions. Awards $1,000 royalty advance and publication. Upon receipt of signed contracts, plays will be published and made available in our next catalog. Judging by editors. All rights acquired with acceptance of contract for publication. Restrictions for entrants: Any writers currently published by Pioneer Drama Service are not eligible.

GOTHAM SCREEN FILM FESTIVAL AND SCREENPLAY CONTEST

291 Broadway, Suite 701, New York NY 10007. E-mail: info@gothamscreen.com. **Website:** www.gothamscreen.com. "Submit via Withoutabox account or download form at website. The contest is open to anyone. Feature length screenplays should be properly formatted and have an approximate length of 80-120 pages. On the cover page, please put the title, the writer's name(s) and the contact details." Deadline: September. Prize: $2,500. In addition, excerpts from selected contest entries will be performed live by professional actors at a staged reading during the festival.

☉ GOVERNOR GENERAL'S LITERARY AWARD FOR DRAMA

Canada Council for the Arts, 350 Albert St., P.O. Box 1047, Ottawa ON K1P 5V8 Canada. (613)566-4414, ext. 5573. **Fax:** (613)566-4410. **Website:** www.canadacouncil.ca/prizes/ggla. Offered for the best English-language and the best French-language work of drama by a Canadian. Publishers submit titles for consideration. Deadline depends on the book's publication date. Books in English: March 15, June 1 or August 7. Books in French: March 15 or July 15. Prize: Each laureate receives $25,000; non-winning finalists receive $1,000.

⊕ THE MARILYN HALL AWARDS FOR YOUTH THEATRE

P.O. Box 148, Beverly Hills CA 90213. **Website:** www.beverlyhillstheatreguild.com. **Contact:** Candace Coster, competition coordinator. Purpose of contest: "To encourage the creation and development of new plays for youth theatre." Unpublished submissions only. Authors must be U.S. citizens or legal residents and must sign entry form personally. Deadline for entries: between January 15 and last day of February each year (postmark accepted). Playwrights may submit up to two scripts. One nonprofessional production acceptable for eligibility. SASE for contest rules and entry forms. No entry fee. Awards: $700, 1st prize; $300, 2nd prize. Judging by theatre professionals cognizant of youth theatre and writing/producing.

HENRICO THEATRE COMPANY ONE-ACT PLAYWRITING COMPETITION

P.O. Box 90775, Henrico VA 23273. (804)501-5138. **Fax:** (804)501-5284. **E-mail:** per22@co.henrico.va.us. **Contact:** Amy A. Perdue, cultural arts senior coordinator. "Offered annually for previously unpublished or unproduced plays or musicals to produce new dramatic works in one-act form. Scripts with small casts and simpler sets given preference. Controversial themes and excessive language should be avoided. Only one-act plays or musicals will be considered. The manuscript should be a one-act original (not an adaptation), unpublished, and unproduced, free of royalty and copyright restrictions. Scripts with smaller casts and simpler sets may be given preference. Controversial themes and excessive language should be avoided. Standard play script form should be used. All plays will be judged anonymously; therefore, there should be two title pages; the first must contain the play's title and the author's complete address and telephone number. The second title page must contain only the play's title. The playwright must submit two excellent quality copies. Receipt of all scripts will be acknowledged by mail. Scripts will be returned if SASE is included. No scripts will be returned until after the winner is announced. The HTC does not assume responsibility for loss, damage or return of scripts. All reasonable care will be taken." Deadline: July 1. Prize: Prizes: $300 prize. $200 to runner-up. Winning entries may be produced; videotape sent to author.

HOLIDAY SCREENPLAY CONTEST

P.O. Box 450, Boulder CO 80306. (303)629-3072. **E-mail:** Cherubfilm@aol.com. **Website:** www.HolidayScreenplayContest.com. "Scripts must be centered around 1 holiday (New Year's Day, President's Day, Valentine's Day, St. Patrick's Day, April Fool's Day, Easter, 4th of July, Halloween, Thanksgiving, Hanukkah, Christmas, Kwanzaa, or any other world holiday you would like to feature). This contest is limited to the first 400 entries." Screenplays must be in English. Screenplays must not have been previously optioned, produced, or purchased prior to submission. Multiple submissions are accepted, but each submission requires a separate online entry and separate fee. Screenplays must be between 90-125 pages. Deadline: November 30. Prize: Up to $500.

HORROR SCREENPLAY CONTEST

Cherub Productions, P.O. Box 540, Boulder Co 80306. (303)629-3072. **E-mail:** Cherubfilm@aol.com. **Website:** www.horrorscreenplaycontest.com. "This contest is looking for horror scripts." Contest is limited to the first 600 entries. Screenplays must be between 90-125 pages. Deadline: July 20. Prize: More than $5,000 in cash and prizes.

NATIONAL CHILDREN'S THEATRE FESTIVAL

Actors' Playhouse at the Miracle Theatre, 280 Miracle Mile, Coral Gables FL 33134. (305)444-9293, ext. 615. **Fax:** (305)444-4181. **E-mail:** maulding@actorsplayhouse.org. **Website:** www.actorsplayhouse.org. **Contact:** Earl Maulding. Purpose of contest: to bring together the excitement of the theater arts and the magic of young audiences through the creation of new musical works and to create a venue for playwrights/composers to showcase their artistic products. Submissions must be unpublished. Submissions are made by author or author's agent. Deadline for entries: April 1 annually. Visit website or send SASE for contest rules and entry forms. Entry fee is $10. Awards: first prize of $500, full production, and transportation to Festival weekend based on availability. Past judges include Joseph Robinette, Moses Goldberg and Luis Santeiro.

NATIONAL LATINO PLAYWRITING AWARD

Arizona Theatre Co., 343 S. Scott Ave., Tucson AZ 85701. (520)884-8210. **Fax:** (520)628-9129. **E-mail:** jbazzell@arizonatheatre.org. **Website:** www.arizonatheatre.org. **Contact:** Jennifer Bazzell, literary manager. Offered annually for unproduced, unpublished plays over 50 pages in length. Plays may be in English, bilingual, or in Spanish (with English translation). The award recognizes exceptional full-length plays by Latino playwrights on any subject. Open to Latino playwrights currently residing in the US, its territories, and/or Mexico. Guidelines online or via e-mail. Deadline: December 31. Prize: $1,000

DON AND GEE NICHOLL FELLOWSHIPS IN SCREENWRITING

Academy of Motion Picture Arts & Sciences, 1313 N. Vine St., Hollywood CA 90028-8107. (310)247-3010. **E-mail:** nicholl@oscars.org. **Website:** www.oscars.org/nicholl. "Offered annually for unproduced feature film screenplays to identify talented new screenwriters. Open to writers who have not earned more than $5,000 writing for films or TV." Deadline: May 1. Prize: Up to 5 $35,000 fellowships awarded each year.

ONE-ACT PLAY CONTEST

Tennessee Williams/New Orleans Literary Festival, 938 Lafayette St., Suite 328, New Orleans LA 70113. (504)581-1144. **E-mail:** info@tennesseewilliams.net. **Website:** www.tennesseewilliams.net/contests. **Contact:** Paul J. Willis. "Annual contest for an unpublished play." "The One-Act Play Competition is an opportunity for playwrights to see their work fully produced before a large audience during one of the largest literary festivals in the nation, and for the festival to showcase undiscovered talent." Deadline: November 1 yearly. Prize: $1,500, a VIP All Access Pass ($500 value), publication, and a staged reading at the festival. The play will also be fully produced at the following year's festival. The Tennessee Williams/New Orleans Literary Festival reserves the right to publish. Judged by an anonymous expert panel.

THE PAGE INTERNATIONAL SCREENWRITING AWARDS

The PAGE Awards Committee, 7510 Sunset Blvd., #610, Hollywood CA 90046-3408. **E-mail:** info@PAGEawards.com. **Website:** www.PAGEawards.com. **Contact:** Zoe Simmons, contest coordinator. Annual competition to discover the most talented new screenwriters from across the country and around the world. "Each year, awards are presented to 31 screenwriters in 10 different genre categories: action/adventure, comedy, drama, family film, historical film, science fiction, thriller/horror, short film script, TV drama pilot, and TV sitcom pilot. Guidelines and entry forms are online. The contest is open to all writers 18 years of age and older who have not previously earned more than $25,000 writing for film and/or television. Please visit contest website for a complete list of rules and regulations." Deadline: January 15 (early); March 1 (regular); April 1 (late). Prize: Over $50,000 in cash and prizes, including a $25,000 grand prize, plus gold, silver, and bronze prizes in all 10 categories. Most importantly, the award-winning writers receive extensive publicity and industry exposure. Judging is done entirely by Hollywood professionals, including industry script readers, consultants, agents, managers, producers, and development executives. Entrants retain all rights to their work.

SCRIPTAPALOOZA SCREENPLAY COMPETITION

Supported by Write Brothers, 7775 Sunset Blvd., #200, Hollywood CA 90046. (323)654-5809. **E-mail:** info@scriptapalooza.com. **Website:** www.scriptapalooza.com. **Contact:** Mark Andrushko, president. "Annual competition for unpublished scripts from any genre. Open to any writer, 18 or older. Submit 1 copy of a 90- to 130-page screenplay. Body pages must be numbered, and scripts must be in industry-standard format. All entered scripts will be read and judged by more than 90 production companies." Early Deadline: January 7; Deadline: March 5; Late Deadline: April 16. Prize: 1st Place: $10,000 and software package from Write Brothers, Inc.; 2nd Place, 3rd Place, and 10 Runners-Up: Software package from Write Brothers, Inc. The top 100 scripts will be considered by over 90 production companies.

SCRIPTAPALOOZA TELEVISION WRITING COMPETITION

7775 Sunset Blvd., Suite #200, Hollywood CA 90046. (323)654-5809. **E-mail:** info@scriptapalooza.com. **Website:** www.scriptapaloozatv.com. "Seeking talented writers who have an interest in American television writing." Prize: $500, $200, and $100 in each category (total $3,200); production company consideration. Categories: Sitcoms, pilots, 1-hour dramas, and reality shows. Entry fee: $40; accepts PayPal credit card, or make checks payable to Scriptapalooza. Deadline: April 15 and October 1 of each year. Length: Standard television format whether 1 hour, 1-half hour, or pilot. Open to any writer 18 or older. Guidelines available now for SASE or on website. Accepts inquiries by e-mail, phone. Deadline: October 1 and April 15. Prize: 1st Place: $500; 2nd Place: $200; 3rd Place: $100 (in each category); production company consideration.

SOUTHEASTERN THEATRE CONFERENCE HIGH SCHOOL NEW PLAY CONTEST

SETC, 1175 Revolution Mill Dr., Suite 14, Greensboro NC 27405. **E-mail:** chadrunyon@hotmail.com. **Website:** www.setc.org. **Contact:** Chad Runyon. Annual contest for one-act plays (no musicals, adaptations, or collaborations) on any subject. The script should be a one-act play that has not been published or professionally produced. Each applicant may submit one play only. E-mail play as a PDF and application form to chadrunyon@hotmail.com.Visit website for additional details and required application form. High school student playwrights who currently reside in 1 of the 10 states in the SETC region are eligible. These states include Alabama, Florida, Georgia, Kentucky, Mississippi, North Carolina, South Carolina, Tennessee, Virginia, and West Virginia. Deadline: Submit October 1-December 1. Prize: $250, subsidy to attend the annual SETC convention in March with an adult chaperone, and a staged reading followed by a talkback.

SOUTHERN PLAYWRIGHTS COMPETITION

Jacksonville State University, 700 Pelham Rd. N., Jacksonville AL 36265-1602. (256)782-5469. **Fax:** (256)782-5441. **E-mail:** jmaloney@jsu.edu; swhitton@jsu.edu. **Website:** www.jsu.edu/depart/english/southpla.htm. **Contact:** Joy Maloney, Steven J. Whitton. "Offered annually to identify and encourage the best of Southern playwriting. Playwrights must be a native or resident of Alabama, Arkansas, District of Columbia, Florida, Georgia, Kentucky, Louisiana, Missouri, North Carolina, South Carolina, Tennessee, Texas, Virginia, or West Virginia." Deadline: January 15. Prize: $1,000 and production of the play.

SOUTHWEST WRITERS

3721 Morris NE, Suite A, Albuquerque NM 87111. (505)265-9485. **Fax:** (505)265-9483. **E-mail:** swwriters@juno.com. **Website:** www.southwestwriters.com. The SouthWest Writers Writing Contest encourages and honors excellence in writing. In addition to competing for cash prizes and the coveted Storyteller Award, contest entrants may receive an optional written critique of their entry from a qualified contest critiquer. Deadline: May 1-May 16. Prize: Up to $1,000 grand prize.

THEATRE CONSPIRACY ANNUAL NEW PLAY CONTEST

Theatre Conspiracy, 10091 McGregor Blvd., Ft. Myers FL 33919. (239)936-3239. **Fax:** (239)936-0510. **E-mail:** info@theatreconspiracy.org. **Contact:** Bill Taylor, producing artistic director. Offered annually for full-length plays that are unproduced or have received up to 3 productions with 8 or less actors and simple to moderate production demands. No musicals. One entry per year. Send SASE for contest results. Deadline: March 30. Prize: $700 and full production.

TRUSTUS PLAYWRIGHTS' FESTIVAL

Trustus Theatre, 520 Lady St., Columbia SC 29201. (803)254-9732. **Fax:** (803)771-9153. **E-mail:** shammond@trustus.org. **Website:** www.trustus.org. **Contact:** Sarah Hammond, literary manager. Offered annually for professionally unproduced full-length plays; cast limit of 8. Prefers challenging, innovative dramas and comedies. No musicals, plays for young audiences, or "hillbilly" southern shows. Send SASE or consult the Trustus website for guidelines and application. Deadline: See website. Prize: $500 and a

1-year development period with full production and travel/accommodations to attend the public opening.

☼ ㊉㊉ THE HERMAN VOADEN NATIONAL PLAYWRITING COMPETITION

Drama Department, Queen's University, Kingston ON K7L 3N6 Canada. (613)533-2104. **E-mail:** carolanne. hanna@queensu.ca; drama@queensu.ca. **Website:** www.queensu.ca/drama. **Contact:** Carol Anne Hanna. Offered every 2 years for unpublished plays to discover and develop new Canadian plays. See website for deadlines and guidelines. Open to Canadian citizens or landed immigrants. Prize: $3,000, $2,000, and 8 honorable mentions. 1st- and 2nd-prize winners are offered a 1-week workshop and public reading by professional director and cast. The 2 authors will be playwrights-in-residence for the rehearsal and reading period.

ANNA ZORNIO MEMORIAL CHILDREN'S THEATRE PLAYWRITING COMPETITION

University of New Hampshire, Department of Theatre and Dance, PCAC, 30 Academic Way, Durham NH 03824. (603)862-3044. **Fax:** (603)862-0298. **E-mail:** mike.wood@unh.edu. **Website:** www.unh.edu/theatre-dance/zornio. **Contact:** Michael Wood. "Offered every 4 years for unpublished well-written plays or musicals appropriate for young audiences with a maximum length of 60 minutes. May submit more than 1 play, but not more than 3. All plays will be performed by adult actors. Guidelines and entry forms available as downloads on the website. Open to all playwrights in US and Canada. All ages are invited to participate." Purpose of the award: "to honor the late Anna Zornio, an alumna of The University of New Hampshire, for dedication to and inspiration of playwriting for young people, K-12th grade. Open to playwrights who are residents of the U.S. and Canada. Plays or musicals should run about 45 minutes." Unpublished submissions only. Submissions made by the author. Deadline for entries: March 2, 2012. No entry fee. Awards $500 plus guaranteed production. Judging by faculty committee. Acquires rights to campus production. For entry form and more information visit www.unh.edu/theatre-dance/zornio.

ARTS COUNCILS & FELLOWSHIPS

$50,000 GIFT OF FREEDOM

A Room of Her Own Foundation, P.O. Box 778, Placitas NM 87043. **E-mail:** info@aroomofherownfounda-

tion.org. **Website:** www.aroomofherownfoundation. org. **Contact:** Tracey Cravens-Gras, associate director. "The publicly funded award provides very practical help—both materially and in professional guidance and moral support with mentors and advisory council—to assist women in making their creative contribution to the world. The Gift of Freedom competition will determine superior finalists from each of 4 genres: Creative nonfiction, fiction, playwrighting, and poetry. One genre finalist will be awarded the $50,000 Gift of Freedom grant, distributed over 2 years in support of the production of a particular creative project. The 3 remaining genre finalists will each receive a $5,000 prize." Open to female residents of the US. Guidelines, deadlines, and application available at www.aroomofherownfoundation.org. Prize: Award is $50,000 over 2 years in support of the production of a particular creative project.

ALABAMA STATE COUNCIL ON THE ARTS INDIVIDUAL ARTIST FELLOWSHIP

201 Monroe St., Montgomery AL 36130-1800. (334)242-4076, ext. 236. **Fax:** (334)240-3269. **E-mail:** anne.kimzey@arts.alabama.gov. **Website:** www.arts. state.al.us. **Contact:** Anne Kimzey, literature program manager. Purpose: To recognize the achievements and potential of Alabama writers. Must be a legal resident of Alabama who has lived in the state for 2 years prior to application. Competition receives 25 submissions annually. Accepts inquiries by e-mail and phone. Guidelines available in January on website. Deadline: March 1. Applications must be submitted online by eGRANT. Judged by independent peer panel. Winners notified by mail and announced on website in June.

ARROWHEAD REGIONAL ARTS COUNCIL INDIVIDUAL ARTIST SUPPORT GRANT

Arrowhead Regional Arts Council, 1301 Rice Lake Rd., Suite 120, Duluth MN 55811. (218)722-0952 or (800)569-8134. **E-mail:** info@aracouncil.org. **Website:** www.aracouncil.org. Award is to provide financial support to regional artists wishing to take advantage of impending, concrete opportunities that will advance their work or careers. Applicants must live in the 7-county region of Northeastern Minnesota. Deadline: August, November, March. Prize: up to $2,500. Judged by the ARAC Board.

GEORGE BENNETT FELLOWSHIP

Phillips Exeter Academy, 20 Main St., Exeter NH 03833-2460. **E-mail:** teaching_opportunities@exeter.

edu. **Website:** www.exeter.edu. Annual award for fellow and family "to provide time and freedom from material considerations to a person seriously contemplating or pursuing a career as a writer. Applicants should have a ms in progress which they intend to complete during the fellowship period." Duties: To be in residency for the academic year; and to make oneself available informally to students interested in writing. The committee favors writers who have not yet published a book with a major publisher. Residence at the Academy during the fellowship period required. Deadline for application: December 1. Prize: Cash stipend, room and board. Judged by committee of the English department.

CHLA RESEARCH GRANTS

Children's Literature Association, P.O. Box 138, Battle Creek MI 49016. (269)965-8180. **Fax:** (269)965-3568. **E-mail:** info@childlitassn.org. **Website:** www.childlitassn.org. **Contact:** ChLA Grants Chair. Offered annually. Two types of grants area available: Faculty Research Grants and Beiter Graduate Student Research Grants. The grants are awarded for proposals dealing with criticism or original scholarship with the expectation that the undertaking will lead to publication (or a conference presentation for student awards) and make a significant contribution to the field of children's literature in the area of scholarship or criticism. Funds are not intended for work leading to the completion of a professional degree. Guidelines available online. Deadline: February 1 annually. Prize: $500-1,500.

CREATIVE & PERFORMING ARTISTS & WRITERS FELLOWSHIP

American Antiquarian Society, 185 Salisbury St., Worcester MA 01609. (508)471-2131. **Fax:** (508)753-3311. **Website:** www.americanantiquarian.org. **Contact:** James David Moran. Annual contest for published writers and performers to conduct research in pre-20th century history. To find creative and performing artists, writers, filmmakers, journalists, and other persons whose goals are to produce imaginative, non-formulaic works dealing with pre-20th century American history. Deadline: October 5. Prize: The stipend will be $1,350 for fellows residing on campus (rent-free) in the society's scholars' housing, located next to the main library building. The stipend will be $1,850 for fellows residing off campus. Fellows will not be paid a travel allowance." AAS staff and outside reviewers.

DELAWARE DIVISION OF THE ARTS

820 N. French St., Wilmington DE 19801. (302)577-8278. **Fax:** (302)577-6561. **E-mail:** kristin.pleasanton@state.de.us. **Website:** www.artsdel.org. Award "to help further careers of emerging and established professional artists." For Delaware residents only. Prize: $10,000 for masters; $6,000 for established professionals; $3,000 for emerging professionals. Judged by out-of-state, nationally recognized professionals in each artistic discipline. No entry fee. Guidelines available after May 1 on website. Accepts inquiries by e-mail, phone. Expects to receive 25 fiction entries. Deadline: August 1. Open to any Delaware writer. Results announced in December. Winners notified by mail. Results available on website. **Contact:** Kristin Pleasanton, coordinator.

DOBIE PAISANO FELLOWSHIPS

University Station (G0400), Austin TX 78712-0531. (512)471-7620. **E-mail:** adameve@mail.utexas.edu. **Website:** www.utexas.edu/ogs/Paisano. The annual Dobie Paisano fellowships provide an opportunity for creative or nonfiction writers to live and write for an extended period in an environment that offers isolation and tranquility. At the time of application, the applicant must: be a native Texan, have lived in Texas at some time for at least three years, or have published significant work with a Texas subject. The Ralph A. Johnston Memorial Fellowship, aimed at writers who have demonstrated some publishing and critical success, offers a $20,000 stipend over four months. The Jesse H. Jones Writing Fellowship offers an $18,000 stipend over five and a half months. Criteria for making the awards include quality of work, character of the proposed project, and suitability of the applicant for life at Paisano, the late J. Frank Dobie's ranch near Austin, TX. Annual deadline in January; awards announced in May. Application fee: $20/one fellowship, $30 both fellowships. Applications and detailed information are available on the website.

JOSEPH R. DUNLAP FELLOWSHIP

William Morris Society in the US, Department of English, University of Iowa, Iowa City IA 52242. **E-mail:** us@morrissociety.org. **Website:** www.morrissociety.org. **Contact:** Prof. Florence Boos. Offered annually "to promote study of the life and work of William Morris (1834-96), British poet, designer, and socialist. Award may be for research or a creative project." Curriculum vitae, 1-page proposal, and 2 letters of recommendation

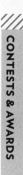

CONTESTS & AWARDS

required for application. Applicants must be US citizens or permanent residents. Deadline: December 15 of the year before the award is to be applied. Prize: Up to $1,000; multiple and partial awards possible

GAP (GRANTS FOR ARTIST PROJECTS) PROGRAM

Artist Trust, 1835 12th Ave., Seattle WA 98122. (206)467-8734 ext. 11. **Fax:** (206)467-9633. **E-mail:** miguel@artisttrust.org. **Website:** www.artisttrust.org. **Contact:** Miguel Guillén, program manager. The GAP grant is awarded annually to 60 Washington state artists of all disciplines. Artist projects may include (but are not limited to): The development, completion or presentation of new work; publication; travel for artistic research or to present or complete work; documentation of work; and advanced workshops for professional development. Full-time students are not eligible. Guidelines will be posted on website in March. Deadline: May. Prize: Award: Up to $1,500 for artist-generated projects.

MINNESOTA EMERGING WRITERS' GRANT

The Loft Literary Center, 1011 Washington Ave. S., Suite 200, Open Book, Minneapolis MN 55415. (612)215-2575. **Fax:** (612)215-2576. **E-mail:** loft@loft.org. **Website:** www.loft.org. **Contact:** Jerod Santek. "The Minnesota Emerging Writers' Grant provides writers financial support and professional assistance to develop and implement multifaceted plans to help them with their artistic endeavors. Two to 4 winners will be selected to receive grants of up to $10,000 to underwrite projects of their own design." Deadline: June 2013. Watch for application guidelines in March 2013.

JENNY MCKEAN MOORE VISITING WRITER

English Deptartment, George Washington University, Rome Hall, 801 22nd St. NW, Suite 760, Washington DC 20052. (202)994-6180. **Fax:** (202)994-7915. **E-mail:** tvmallon@gwu.edu. **Website:** http://columbian.gwu.edu/departmentsprograms/english/creativewriting/activitiesevents. **Contact:** Thomas Mallon, director of Creative Writing. Application Deadline: November 1. Prize: Annual stipend varies, depending on endowment performance; most recently, stipend was $58,000, plus reduced-rent townhouse (not guaranteed).

NEBRASKA ARTS COUNCIL INDIVIDUAL ARTISTS FELLOWSHIPS

Nebraska Arts Council, 1004 Farnam St., Plaza Level, Omaha NE 68102. (402)595-2122. **Fax:** (402)595-2334.

E-mail: jayne.hutton@nebraska.gov. **Website:** www.nebraskaartscouncil.org. **Contact:** J.D. Hutton. Offered every 3 years (literature alternates with other disciplines) to recognize exemplary achievements by originating artists in their fields of endeavor and support the contributions made by Nebraska artists to the quality of life in this state. Generally, distinguished achievement awards are $5,000 and merit awards are $1,000-2,000. Must be a resident of Nebraska for at least 2 years prior to submission date; 18 years of age; and not enrolled in an undergraduate, graduate, or certificate-granting program in English, creative writing, literature, or related field. Deadline: November 15, 2014.

NORTH CAROLINA ARTS COUNCIL REGIONAL ARTIST PROJECT GRANTS

North Carolina Arts Council, Dept. of Cultural Resources, MSC #4632, Raleigh NC 27699-4634. (919)807-6500. **Fax:** (919)807-6532. **E-mail:** david.potorti@ncdcr.gov. **Website:** www.ncarts.org. Open to any writer living in North Carolina. See website for contact information for the local arts councils that distribute these grants. $500-3,000 awarded to writers to pursue projects that further their artistic development. **Contact:** David Potorti, literature director. Deadline: Generally late summer/early fall. Prize: $500-3,000 awarded to writers to pursue projects that further their artistic development.

RHODE ISLAND ARTIST FELLOWSHIPS AND INDIVIDUAL PROJECT GRANTS

Rhode Island State Council on the Arts, One Capitol Hill, 3rd Floor, Providence RI 02908. (401)222-3880. **Fax:** (401)222-3018. **E-mail:** Cristina.DiChiera@arts.ri.gov. **Website:** www.arts.ri.gov. **Contact:** Cristina DiChiera, director of individual artist programs. Annual fellowship competition is based upon panel review of mss for poetry, fiction, and playwriting/screenwriting. Project grants provide funds for community-based arts projects. Rhode Island artists may apply without a nonprofit sponsor. Applicants for all RSCA grant and award programs must be at least 18 years old and not currently enrolled in an arts-related degree program. Online application and guidelines can be found at www.arts.ri.gov/grants/guidelines/. Deadline: April 1 and October 1. Prize: Fellowship awards: $5,000 and $1,000. Grants range from $500-10,000, with an average of around $3,000.

FICTION

AMERICAN SHORT STORY CONTEST

American Short Fiction, P.O. Box 301209, Austin TX 78703. (512)538-1305. **Fax:** (512)538-1306. **Website:** www.americanshortfiction.org. **Contact:** Jill Meyers, editor. "Contest offered annually to reward and recognize short stories under 1,000 words." 1st Place: $500 and publication; 2nd Place: $250 and publication. Submissions accepted only via the online submission manager on website. Please see website for full guidelines. Submissions accepted between February 15 and May 1. Prize: 1st Place: $500 & publication; 2nd Place: $250 & publication.

THE SHERWOOD ANDERSON FOUNDATION FICTION AWARD

264 Tobacco Rd., Madison NC 27025. (336)427-4450. **E-mail:** dspear003@gmail.com. **Website:** sherwood-andersonfoundation.org. **Contact:** David M. Spear, foundation co-president. Contest is to honor, preserve and celebrate the memory and literary work of Sherwood Anderson, American realist for the first half of the 20th century. Annual award supports developing writers of short stories and novels. Entrants must have published at least one book of fiction or have had several short stories published in major literary and/or commercial publication. Self-published stories do not qualify. Send a detailed resumé that includes a bibliography of your publications. Include a cover letter that provides a history of your writing experience and your plans for writing projects. Also, submit 2 or 3 examples of what you consider to be your best work. Do not send manuscripts by e-mail. Only mss in English will be accepted. Open to any writer who meets the qualifications listed above. Accepts inquiries by e-mail. Mail your application to the above address. No mss or publications will be returned. Deadline: April 1. Prize: $15,000 grant award.

BARD FICTION PRIZE

Bard College, P.O. Box 5000, Annandale-on-Hudson NY 12504-5000. (845)758-7087. **E-mail:** bfp@bard.edu. **Website:** www.bard.edu/bfp. The Bard Fiction Prize is intended to encourage and support young writers of fiction to pursue their creative goals and to provide an opportunity to work in a fertile and intellectual environment. Prize: $30,000 cash award and appointment as writer-in-residence at Bard College for 1 semester. Judged by committee of 5 judges (authors associated with Bard College). No entry fee. Cover letter should include name, address, phone, e-mail and name of publisher where book was previously published. Guidelines available by SASE, fax, phone, e-mail, or on website. Deadline: July 15. Entries must be previously published. Open to U.S. citizens aged 39 and below. Results announced by October 15. Winners notified by phone. For contest results, e-mail, or visit website. **Contact:** Irene Zedlacher.

✪ BELLEVUE LITERARY REVIEW GOLDENBERG PRIZE FOR FICTION

Bellevue Literary Review, NYU Dept of Medicine, 550 First Ave., OBV-A612, New York NY 10016. (212)263-3973. **Fax:** (212)263-3206. **E-mail:** info@blreview.org; stacy@blreview.org. **Website:** www.blreview.org. The BLR prizes award outstanding writing related to themes of health, healing, illness, the mind and the body. Annual. Competition/award for short stories. Prize: $1,000 and publication in *The Bellevue Literary Review*. Receives about 200-300 entries per category. BLR editors select semi-finalists to be read by an independent judge who chooses the winner. Previous judges include Amy Hempel, Rick Moody, Rosellen Brown, and Andre Dubus III. **Entry fee:** $15, or $20 to include 1-year subscription to *The Bellevue Literary Review*. Send credit card information or make checks payable to Bellevue Literary Review. Guidelines available in February. Accepts inquiries by e-mail, phone, mail. Submissions open in February. **Entry deadline:** July 1. Entries should be unpublished. Anyone may enter contest. Length: No minimum; maximum of 5,000 words. Cover letter should include name, address, phone, e-mail, story title. Title and word count should appear on ms. Writers may submit own work. Results announced in December and made available to entrants with SASE, by e-mail, on website. Winners notified by mail, by e-mail. **Contact:** Stacy Bodziak, managing editor.

BINGHAMTON UNIVERSITY JOHN GARDNER FICTION BOOK AWARD

Creative Writing Program, Binghamton University, Department of English, General LIterature, and Rhetoric, P.O. Box 6000, Binghamton NY 13902-6000. (607)777-2713. **E-mail:** cwpro@binghamton.edu. **Website:** http://english.binghamton.edu/cwpro. **Contact:** Maria Mazziotti Gillan, director. Offered annually for a novel or collection of short stories published that year in a press run of 500 copies or more. Each book submitted must be accompanied by an application form. Publisher may submit more than 1 book for prize consideration. Send 3 copies of each book. Guidelines available on website. Award's purpose is "to serve the literary community by calling attention to outstanding books of fiction." Deadline: March 1. Prize: $1,000. Judged by a professional writer not on Binghamton University faculty.

✪ CANADIAN SHORT STORY COMPETITION

Red Tuque Books, Unit #6, 477 Martin St., Penticton BC V2A 5L2 Canada. (778)476-5750. **Fax:** (778)476-5750. **E-mail:** dave@redtuquebooks.ca. **Website:** www.redtuquebooks.ca. **Contact:** David Korinetz, contest director. Offered annually for unpublished works. Purpose of award is "to promote Canada and Canadian publishing. Stories require a Canadian element. There are three ways to qualify. They can be written by a Canadian, or written about Canadians, or take place somewhere in Canada." Deadline: December 31. Prize: 1st Place: $500; 2nd Place: $150; 3rd Place: $100; and 10 prizes of $25 will be given to honourable mentions. All 13 winners will be published in an anthology. They will each receive a complimentary copy. Judged by Canadian authors in the fantasy/sci-fi/horror field. Acquires first print rights. Contest open to anyone.

KAY CATTARULLA AWARD FOR BEST SHORT STORY

Texas Institute of Letters, P.O. Box 609, Round Rock TX 78680. **E-mail:** tilsecretary@yahoo.com. **Website:** http://texasinstituteofletters.org. Offered annually for work published January 1-December 31 of previous year to recognize the best short story. The story submitted must have appeared in print for the first time to be eligible. Writers must have been born in Texas, must have lived in Texas for at least 2 consecutive years, or the subject matter of the work must be associated with Texas. See website for guidelines and deadline date. Prize: $1,000.

JACK DYER FICTION PRIZE

Crab Orchard Review, Department of English, Mail Code 4503, Faner Hall 2380, Southern Illinois University at Carbondale, Carbondale IL 62901. **E-mail:** jtribble@siu.edu. **Website:** www.craborchardreview.siu.edu. **Contact:** Jon C. Tribble, man. editor. Offered annually for unpublished short fiction. *Crab Orchard Review* acquires first North American serial rights

to all submitted work. Open to any writer; US citizens only. Entries must be unpublished. Length: 6,000 words maximum. "Please note that no stories will be returned." Results announced by end of August. Winners notified by mail. Contest results on website or send SASE. Guidelines available after January for SASE or on website. Deadline: March 1-May 4. Prize: $2,000 and publication and 1-year subscription to *Crab Orchard Review*. Judged by editorial staff (prescreening); winner chosen by genre editor.

MARY KENNEDY EASTHAM FLASH FICTION PRIZE

Category in the Soul Making Keats Literary Competition, The Webhallow House, 1544 Sweetwood Dr., Broadmoor Village CA 94015-2029. **E-mail:** pennobhill@aol.com. **Website:** www.soulmakingcontest.us. **Contact:** Eileen Malone. "Three flash fiction (short-short) stories per entry, under 500 words. Previously published material is accepted. Indicate category on each story. Identify only with 3x5 card. Open annually to any writer." Deadline: November 30 (annually). Prize: 1st Place: $100; 2nd Place: $50; 3rd Place: $25.

➕ ✪ THE FAR HORIZONS AWARD FOR SHORT FICTION

The Malahat Review, University of Victoria, P.O. Box 1700, Stn CSC, Victoria BC V8W 2Y2 Canada. (250)721-8524. **Fax:** (250)472-5051. **E-mail:** malahat@uvic.ca. **Website:** www.malahatreview.ca. **Contact:** John Barton, editor. Open to "emerging short fiction writers from Canada, the US, and elsewhere" who have not yet published their fiction in a full-length book (48 pages or more). Guidelines available on website. Deadline: May 1 of odd-numbered years. Prize: Offers $1,000 CAD, publication in fall issue of *The Malahat Review*. Announced in fall on website, Facebook page, and in quarterly e-newsletter, *Malahat Lite*.

FIRSTWRITER.COM INTERNATIONAL SHORT STORY CONTEST

firstwriter.com, United Kingdom. **Website:** www.firstwriter.com. **Contact:** J. Paul Dyson, managing editor. "Accepts short stories up to 3,000 words on any subject and in any style." Deadline: April 1. Prize: Prize total about $300. Ten special commendations will also be awarded and all the winners will be published in *firstwriter* magazine and receive a $36 subscription voucher, allowing an annual subscription to be taken out for free. All submissions are automatically considered for publication in *firstwriter* magazine and may be published there online. Judged by *firstwriter* magazine editors.

GIVAL PRESS NOVEL AWARD

Gival Press, LLC, P.O. Box 3812, Arlington VA 22203. (703)351-0079. **E-mail:** givalpress@yahoo.com. **Website:** www.givalpress.com. **Contact:** Robert L. Giron. Offered annually for a previously unpublished original novel (not a translation). Guidelines by phone, on website, via e-mail, or by mail with SASE. Length: 30,000-100,000 words. Cover letter should include name, address, phone, e-mail, word count, novel title; include a short bio and short synopsis. Only the title and word count should appear on the actual ms. Writers may submit own work. "Review the types of mss Gival Press has published. We stress literary works." "To award the best literary novel." Deadline: May 30. Prize: $3,000, plus publication of book with a standard contract and author's copies. Final judge is announced after winner is chosen. Entries read anonymously.

GIVAL PRESS SHORT STORY AWARD

Gival Press, P.O. Box 3812, Arlington VA 22203. (703)351-0079. **E-mail:** givalpress@yahoo.com. **Website:** www.givalpress.com. "To award the best literary short story." Annual. Prize: $1,000 and publication on website. Category: Literary short story. Receives about 100-150 entries per category. Entries are judged anonymously. **Entry fee:** $25. Make checks payable to Gival Press, LLC. Guidelines available online, via e-mail, or by mail. **Deadline:** August 8. Entries must be unpublished. Open to anyone who writes original short stories in English. Length: 5,000-15,000 words. Include name, address, phone, e-mail, word count, title on cover letter; include short bio. Only the title and word count should be found on ms. Writers may submit their own ficiton. "We publish literary works." Results announced in the fall of the same year. Winners notified by phone. Results available with SASE, by e-mail, on website. **Contact:** Robert L. Giron, publisher..

GLIMMER TRAIN'S FAMILY MATTERS

Glimmer Train, 4763 SW Maplewood Rd., P.O. Box 80430, Portland OR 97280. (503)221-0836. **Fax:** (503)221-0837. **E-mail:** eds@glimmertrain.org. **Website:** www.glimmertrain.org. **Contact:** Linda Swanson-Davies. "Offered for stories about family. Submissions to this category generally range from 1,500-6,000 words, but up to 12,000 is fine. Open in the months of April and October. Submit online at www.glimmertrain.org. Winners will be called 2 months after the close of the contest." Prize: 1st Place: $1,500, publicationin *Glimmer Train Stories*, and 20 copies of that issue; 2nd Place: $500; 3rd Place: $300.

GLIMMER TRAIN'S FICTION OPEN

Glimmer Train, Inc., Glimmer Train Press, Inc., 4763 SW Maplewood Rd., P.O. Box 80430, Portland OR 97280. (503)221-0836. **Fax:** (503)221-0837. **E-mail:** eds@glimmertrain.org. **Website:** www.glimmertrain. org. **Contact:** Linda Swanson-Davies. "Submissions to this category generally range from 2,000-8,000 words, but up to 20,000 is fine. Open in the months of March, June, September, and December. Submit online at www.glimmertrain.org. Winners will be called 2 months after the close of the contest." Prize: 1st Place $2,500, publication in *Glimmer Train Stories*, and 20 copies of that issue; 2nd Place $1,000; 3rd Place: $600.

GLIMMER TRAIN'S SHORT-STORY AWARD FOR NEW WRITERS

Glimmer Train Press, Inc., 1211 NW Glisan St., Suite 207, Portland OR 97209. (503)221-0836. **Fax:** (503)221-0837. **E-mail:** eds@glimmertrain.org. **Website:** www.glimmertrain.org. **Contact:** Linda Swanson-Davies. "Offered for any writer whose fiction hasn't appeared in a nationally distributed print publication with a circulation over 5,000. Submissions to this category generally range from 1,500-6,000 words, but up to 12,000 is fine. Open in the months of February, May, August, and November. Submit online at www.glimmertrain.org. Winners will be called 2 months after the close of the contest." Prize: 1st Place: $1,500, publication in *Glimmer Train Stories*, and 20 copies of that issue; 2nd Place: $500; 3rd Place: $300.

GLIMMER TRAIN'S VERY SHORT FICTION AWARD (JANUARY)

Glimmer Train Press, Inc., 4763 SW Maplewood Rd., P.O. Box 80430, Portland OR 97280. (503)221-0836. **Fax:** (503)221-0837. **E-mail:** eds@glimmertrain.org. **Website:** www.glimmertrain.org. eds@glimmertrain. org; www.glimmertrain.org; **Contact:** Linda Swanson-Davies. Award to encourage the art of the very short story. "We want to read your original, unpublished, very short story—word count not to exceed 3,000 words." Prize: $1,200 and publication in Glimmer Train Stories and 20 author's copies (1st place); First/Second runners-up: $500/$300 respectively and possible publication. Entry fee: $15/story. **Con-**

test open in the months of January and July. Open to all writers. Make your submissions online at www. glimmertrain.org. Winners will be called and results announced two months after the close of each contestt

GLIMMER TRAIN'S VERY SHORT FICTION CONTEST (JULY)

Glimmer Train Press, Inc., 4763 SW Maplewood Rd., P.O. Box 80430, Portland OR 97280. (503)221-0836. **Fax:** (503)221-0837. **E-mail:** eds@glimmertrain.org. **Website:** www.glimmertrain.org. **Contact:** Linda Swanson-Davies. "Offered to encourage the artof the very short story. Word count: 3,000 maximum. Open July 1-31. Submit online at www.glimmertrain.org. Winners will be called on October 1." Prize: 1st Place: $1,500, publication in *Glimmer Train Stories*, and 20 copies of that issue; 2nd Place: $500; 3rd Place: $300.

⊙ GOVERNOR GENERAL'S LITERARY AWARD FOR FICTION

Canada Council for the Arts, 350 Albert St., P.O. Box 1047, Ottawa ON K1P 5V8 Canada. (613)566-4414, ext. 5573. **Fax:** (613)566-4410. **Website:** www.canadacouncil.ca/prizes/ggla. Offered annually for the best English-language and the best French-language work of fiction by a Canadian. Publishers submit titles for consideration. Deadline depends on the book's publication date. Books in English: March 15, June 1 or August 7. Books in French: March 15 or July 15. Prize: Each laureate receives $25,000; non-winning finalists receive $1,000.

G. S. SHARAT CHANDRA PRIZE FOR SHORT FICTION

BkMk Press, University of Missouri-Kansas City, 5100 Rockhill Rd., Kansas City MO 64110-2499. (816)235-2558. **Fax:** (816)235-2611. **E-mail:** bkmk@ umkc.edu. **Website:** www.umkc.edu/bkmk. Offered annually for the best book-length ms collection (unpublished) of short fiction in English by a living author. Translations are not eligible. Initial judging is done by a network of published writers. Final judging is done by a writer of national reputation. Guidelines for SASE, by e-mail, or on website. Deadline: January 15 (postmarked). Prize: $1,000, plus book publication by BkMk Press.

◔ LYNDALL HADOW/DONALD STUART SHORT STORY COMPETITION

Fellowship of Australian Writers (WA), P.O. Box 6180, Swanbourne WA 6910 Australia. (61)(8)9384-4771. **Fax:** (61)(8)9384-4854. **E-mail:** admin@fawwa.org.

au. **Website:** www.fawwa.org.au. Annual contest for unpublished short stories (maximum 3,000 words). "We reserve the right to publish entries in a FAWWA publication or on its website." Guidelines online or for SASE. Deadline: June 1. Prize: 1st Place: $400; 2nd Place; $100; Highly Commended: $50.

LORIAN HEMINGWAY SHORT STORY COMPETITION

Hemingway Days Festival, P.O. Box 993, Key West FL 33041-0993. **E-mail:** shortstorykw@gmail.com. **Website:** www.shortstorycompetition.com. **Contact:** Eva Eliot, editorial assistant; Joanne Denning, contest development director. Award to "encourage literary excellence and the efforts of writers whose voices have yet to be heard." Offered annually for unpublished short stories up to 3,500 words. Guidelines available via mail, e-mail, or online. Deadline: May 15. Prize: 1st Place: $1,500, plus publication of his or her winning story in *Cutthroat: A Journal of the Arts*; 2nd-3rd Place: $500; honorable mentions will also be awarded.

THE HILLERMAN MYSTERY NOVEL COMPETITION

Wordharvest & St. Martins Press, 304 Calle Oso, Santa Fe NM 87501. (505)471-1565. **E-mail:** wordharvest@wordharvest.com. **Website:** www.hillermanconference.com. No entry fee. Accepts inquiries by e-mail, phone. **Deadline:** June 1. Entries should be unpublished; self-published work is generally accepted. Length: no less than 220 typewritten pages, or approximately 60,000 words. Cover letter should include name, address, phone, e-mail, list of publishing credits. Please include SASE for response. Writers may submit their own work. "Make sure murder or another serious crime or crimes is at the heart of the story, and emphasis is on the solution rather than the details of the crime. The story's primary setting should be the southwest US, which includes CA, AZ, CO, NV, NM, OK, TX, and UT." **Contact:** Anne Hillerman and Jean Schaumberg, co-organizers.

TOM HOWARD/JOHN H. REID SHORT STORY CONTEST

c/o Winning Writers, 351 Pleasant St., PMB 222, Northampton MA 01060-3961. (866)946-9748. **E-mail:** johnreid@mail.qango.com. **Website:** www.winningwriters.com. Now in its 20th year. Open to all writers. Prizes of $3,000, $1,000, $400 and $250 will be awarded, plus 6 Most Highly Commended Awards of $150 each. Submit any type of short story, essay or other work of prose. Submit online or by mail. Early submission encouraged. Contest is sponsored by Tom Howard Books and assisted by Winning Writers. Judges: John H. Reid and Dee C. Konrad. See the complete guidelines and past winners. Guidelines available in July on website. Prefers inquiries by e-mail. **Deadline:** March 31. "Both published and unpublished works are accepted. In the case of published work, the contestant must own the online publication rights." Length: 5,000 words max per entry.

L. RON HUBBARD'S WRITERS OF THE FUTURE CONTEST

P.O. Box 1630, Los Angeles CA 90078. (323)466-3310. **Fax:** (323)466-6474. **E-mail:** contests@authorservicesinc.com. **Website:** www.writersofthefuture.com. Foremost competition for new and amateur writers of unpublished science fiction or fantasy short stories or novelettes. Offered "to find, reward and publicize new speculative fiction writers so they may more easily attain professional writing careers." Open to writers who have not professionally published a novel or short novel, more than 1 novelette, or more than 3 short stories. Prize (awards quarterly): 1st Place: $1,000; 2nd Place: $750; and 3rd Place: $500. Annual grand prize: $5,000. "Contest has 4 quarters. There shall be 3 cash prizes in each quarter. In addition, at the end of the year, the 4 first-place, quarterly winners will have their entries rejudged, and a grand prize winner shall be determined." **Deadline:** December 31, March 31, June 30, September 30.

THE IOWA SHORT FICTION AWARD

Iowa Writers' Workshop, 507 N. Clinton St., 102 Dey House, Iowa City IA 52242-1000. **Website:** www.uiowapress.org. **Contact:** Jim McCoy, director. Annual award "to give exposure to promising writers who have not yet published a book of prose." Open to any writer. Current University of Iowa students are not eligible. No application forms are necessary. Announcement of winners made early in year following competition. Winners notified by phone. No application forms are necessary. Do not send original ms. Include SASE for return of ms. Entries must be unpublished, but stories previously published in periodicals are eligible for inclusion. "The ms must be a collection of short stories of at least 150 word-processed, double-spaced pages." Submission period: August 1-September 30. Prize: publication by University of Iowa Press Judged by senior Iowa Writers' Workshop members who screen mss; published fiction author of note makes final selections.

JESSE JONES AWARD FOR FICTION

P.O. Box 609, Round Rock TX 78680. **E-mail:** tilsecretary@yahoo.com. **Website:** http://texasinstituteofletters.org. Offered annually by Texas Institute of Letters for work published January 1-December 31 of year before award is given to recognize the writer of the best book of fiction entered in the competition. Writers must have been born in Texas, have lived in the state for at least 2 consecutive years at some time, or the subject matter of the work should be associated with the state. President changes every 2 years. See website for guidelines. Deadline: See website for exact date. Prize: $6,000.

JAMES JONES FIRST NOVEL FELLOWSHIP

Wilkes University, Creative Writing Department, 245 S. River St., Wilkes-Barre PA 18766. (570)408-4547. **Fax:** (570)408-3333. **E-mail:** Jamesjonesfirstnovel@wilkes.edu. **Website:** www.wilkes.edu/pages/1159.asp. Offered annually for unpublished novels, novellas, and closely-linked short stories (all works in progress). "The award is intended to honor the spirit of unblinking honesty, determination, and insight into modern culture exemplified by the late James Jones." The competition is open to all American writers who have not previously published novels. Deadline: March 1. Prize: $10,000; 2 runners-up get $750 honorarium.

LITERAL LATTÉ FICTION AWARD

Literal Latté, 200 E. 10th St., Suite 240, New York NY 10003. (212)260-5532. **E-mail:** litlatte@aol.com. **Website:** www.literal-latte.com. **Contact:** Edward Estlin, contributing editor. "Award to provide talented writers with 3 essential tools for continued success: money, publication, and recognition. Offered annually for unpublished fiction (maximum 10,000 words). Guidelines online. Open to any writer." Deadline: January 15. Prize: 1st Place: $1,000 and publication in *Literal Latté*; 2nd Place: $300; 3rd Place: $200; also up to 7 honorable mentions.

LITERAL LATTE SHORT SHORTS CONTEST

Literal Latte, 200 E. 10th St., Suite 240, New York NY 10003. (212)260-5532. **E-mail:** litlatte@aol.com. **Website:** www.literal-latte.com. **Contact:** Jenine Gordon Bockman, editor. Postmarked by June 30th. Prize: $500. The Editors.

THE LONG STORY CONTEST, INTERNATIONAL

A. E. Coppard Prize for Fiction, White Eagle Coffee Store Press, P.O. Box 383, Fox River Grove IL 60021. (847)639-9200. **E-mail:** wecspress@aol.com. **Website:** whiteeaglecoffeestorepress.com. Offered annually since 1993 for unpublished work to recognize and promote long short stories of 8,000-14,000 words (about 30-50 pages, double-spaced, 12-point font). Sample of previous winner: $6.95, including postage. Open to any writer, no restrictions on materials. Prize: A.E. Coppard Prize of $1,000 and publication, plus 25 copies of chapbook and 10 press kits. Categories: "No limits on style or subject matter." Entry fee: $15 fee; $10 for second story in same envelope. Guidelines available in April by SASE, e-mail, or on website. Accepts inquiries by e-mail. Length: 8,000-14,000 words (30-50 pages double-spaced, 12-point font) single story; may have multi-parts or be a self-contained novel segment. Deadline: December 15. Accepts previously unpublished submissions, but previous publication of small parts with acknowledgment is okay. Simultaneous submissions OK. Send cover with name, address, phone; second title page with title only. Submissions are not returned; they are recycled. "SASE for most current information." Results announced in late spring. Winners notified by phone. For contest results, send SASE or visit website in late spring. "Write with richness and depth. This has become the premiere competition in the world for long stories, giving many winners and finalists the opportunity to move to the next level of publishing success." **Contact:** Frank E. Smith, publisher.

THE MARY MACKEY SHORT STORY PRIZE

Category in the Soul Making Keats Literary Competition, The Webhallow House, 1544 Sweetwood Dr., Broadmoor Village CA 94015-2029. **E-mail:** pennobhill@aol.com. **Website:** www.soulmakingcontest.us. Open annually to any writer. "One story/entry, up to 5,000 words. All prose works must be typed, page numbered, and double-spaced. Identify only with 3x5 card. ." $5/entry (make checks payable to NLAPW). Needs fiction, short stories. **Deadline:** November 30 (annually). **Prizes:** 1st Place: $100; 2nd Place: $50; 3rd Place: $25. **Contact:** Eileen Malone.

○ THE MALAHAT REVIEW NOVELLA PRIZE

The Malahat Review, University of Victoria, P.O. Box 1700 STN CSC, Victoria BC V8W 2Y2 Canada. (250)721-8524. **E-mail:** malahat@uvic.ca. **Website:** malahatreview.ca. **Contact:** John Barton, editor. "Held in alternate years with the Long Poem Prize. Offered to promote unpublished novellas. Obtains first world rights. After publication rights revert to the author. Open to any writer." Submit novellas between 10,000 and 20,000 words in length. Include separate page with author's name, address, e-mail, and novella title; no identifying information on mss. pages. No e-mail submissions. Do not include SASE for results; mss will not be returned. Guidelines available on website. Deadline: February 1 (even years). Prize: $1,500 CAD and one year's subscription. 2010 winner was Tony Tulathimutte. Winner and finalists contacted by e-mail. Winner published in summer issue of *The Malahat Review* and announced on website, Facebook page, and in quarterly e-newsletter, *Malahat Lite*.

MARY MCCARTHY PRIZE IN SHORT FICTION

Sarabande Books, P.O. Box 4456, Louisville KY 40204. (502)458-4028. **Fax:** (502)458-4065. **E-mail:** info@sarabandebooks.org. **Website:** www.sarabandebooks.org. **Contact:** Kirby Gann, managing editor. Offered annually to publish an outstanding collection of stories, novellas, or a short novel (less than 250 pages). All finalists considered for publication. Deadline: January 1-February 15. Prize: $2,000 and publication (standard royalty contract).

DAVID NATHAN MEYERSON PRIZE FOR FICTION

Southwest Review, P.O. Box 750374, Dallas TX 75275-0374. (214) 768-1037. **Fax:** (214) 768-1408. **E-mail:** swr@smu.edu. **Website:** www.smu.edu/southwestreview. **Contact:** Jennifer Cranfill, senior editor. Annual award given to awriter who has not published a first book of fiction, either a novel or collection of stories. Submissions must be no longer than 8,000 words. Work should be printed without the author's name. Name and address should appear only on the cover letter. Submissions will not be returned. For notification of the winning submission, include a SASE. Winner announced in August. Postmarked deadline for entry is May 1. Prize: $1,000 and publication in the *Southwest Review*.

MILKWEED NATIONAL FICTION PRIZE

Milkweed Editions, 1011 Washington Ave. S., Suite 300, Minneapolis MN 55415. (612)332-3192. **Fax:** (612)215-2550. **E-mail:** editor@milkweed.org. **Web-**

site: www.milkweed.org. **Contact:** Daniel Slager, award director. Purpose of the award: to recognize an outstanding literary novel for readers ages 8-13 and encourage writers to turn their attention to readers in this age group. Unpublished submissions only "in book form." Please send SASE or visit website for award guidelines. The prize is awarded to the best work for children ages 8-13 that Milkweed agrees to publish in a calendar year. The prize consists of a $5,000 advance against royalties agreed to at the time of acceptance. Submissions must follow our usual children's guidelines.

⊕ THE HOWARD FRANK MOSHER SHORT FICTION PRIZE

Vermont College, 36 College St., Montpelier VT 05602. (802)828-8517. **E-mail:** hungermtn@vcfa.edu. **Website:** www.hungermtn.org. **Contact:** Miciah Bay Gault, editor. The annual Howard Frank Mosher Short Fiction Prize offers $1,000 and publication in *Hunger Mountain*; 2 runners-up receive $100 and are considered for publication. Submit story under 10,000 words. Guidelines available on website. Deadline: June 30.

NATIONAL WRITERS ASSOCIATION NOVEL WRITING CONTEST

The National Writers Association, 10940 S. Parker Rd. #508, Parker CO 80134. (303)841-0246. **E-mail:** natlwritersassn@hotmail.com. **Website:** www.nationalwriters.com. **Contact:** Sandy Whelchel, director. Categories: Open to any genre or category. Entry fee: $35. Opens December 1. Open to any writer. Entries must be unpublished. Length: 20,000-100,000 words. Annual contest to help develop creative skills, to recognize and reward outstanding ability, and to increase the opportunity for the marketing and subsequent publication of novel mss. Deadline: April 1. Prize: 1st Place: $500; 2nd Place: $250; 3rd Place: $150. Judged by editors and agents.

NATIONAL WRITERS ASSOCIATION SHORT STORY CONTEST

The National Writers Association, 10940 S. Parker Rd. #508, Parker CO 80134. (303)841-0246. **Fax:** (303)841-2607. **E-mail:** natlwritersassn@hotmail.com. **Website:** www.nationalwriters.com. **Contact:** Sandy Whelchel, director. Annual contest to encourage writers in this creative form, and to recognize those who excel in fiction writing. Deadline: July 1. Prize: 1st Place: $200; 2nd Place: $100; 3rd Place: $50.

FRANK O'CONNOR AWARD FOR SHORT FICTION

descant, Texas Christian University's literary journal, TCU Box 297270, Fort Worth TX 76129. (817)257-6537. **Fax:** (817)257-6239. **E-mail:** descant@tcu.edu. **Website:** www.descant.tcu.edu. Offered annually for unpublished short stories. Publication retains copyright but will transfer it to the author upon request. fiction, short stories. **Deadline:** September-March. **Prize:** $500. **Contact:** Dan Williams and Alex Lemon, editors. Offered annually for unpublished short stories. Publication retains copyright but will transfer it to the author upon request. Deadline: September-March. Prize: $500.

ON THE PREMISES CONTEST

On The Premises, LLC, 4323 Gingham Court, Alexandria VA 22310. (202) 262-2168. **E-mail:** questions@onthepremises.com. **Website:** www.onthepremises.com. "*On the Premises* aims to promote newer and/or relatively unknown writers who can write what we feel are creative, compelling stories told in effective, uncluttered and evocative prose. Each contest challenges writers to produce a great story based on a broad premise that our editors supply as part of the contest." Competition/award for short stories. 1st Prize: $180; 2nd Prize: $140; 3rd Prize: $100; Honorable Mentions recieve $40. Length: minimum 1,000 words; maximum 5,000. **Contact:** Tarl Roger Kudrick or Bethany Granger, co-publishers.

PEARL SHORT STORY PRIZE

3030 E. Second St., Long Beach CA 90803-5163. (562)434-4523. **E-mail:** Pearlmag@aol.com. **Website:** www.pearlmag.com. Award to "provide a larger forum and help widen publishing opportunities for fiction writers in the small press and to help support the continuing publication of Pearl." Prize: $250, publication in Pearl and 10 copies of the journal. Judged by the editors of Pearl: Marilyn Johnson, Joan Jobe Smith, Barbara Hauk. Entry fee: $10/story. Include a brief bio and SASE for reply or return of mss. Accepts simultaneous submissions, but asks to be notified if story is accepted elsewhere. **Submission period: April 1-May 31(postmark).** Entries must be unpublished. "Although we are open to all types of fiction, we look most favorably on coherent, well-crafted narratives containing interesting, believable characters in meaningful situations." Length: 4,000 words maximum. Open to any writer. Guidelines for SASE or on website. Accepts queries by e-mail or fax. Results announced in September. Winners notified by mail. For contest results, send SASE, e-mail, or visit website. **Contact:** Marilyn Johnson, fiction editor.

EDGAR ALLAN POE AWARD

1140 Broadway, Suite 1507, New York NY 10001. (212)888-8171. **Fax:** (212)888-8107. **E-mail:** mwa@ mysterywriters.org. **Website:** www.mysterywriters. org. Mystery Writers of America is the leading association for professional crime writers in the United States. Members of MWA include most major writers of crime fiction and non-fiction, as well as screenwriters, dramatists, editors, publishers, and other professionals in the field. We welcome everyone who is interested in mysteries and crime writing to join MWA. Purpose of the award: to honor authors of distinguished works in the mystery field. Previously published submissions only. Submissions made by the author, author's agent; "normally by the publisher." Work must be published/produced the year of the contest. Deadline for entries: Must be received by November 30. Submission information can be found at: www.mysterywriters.org. No entry fee. Awards ceramic bust of "Edgar" for winner; scrolls for all nominees. Judging by professional members of Mystery Writers of America (writers). Nominee press release sent in mid January. Winner announced at the Edgar® Awards Banquet, held in late April/early May.

THE KATHERINE ANNE PORTER PRIZE FOR FICTION

Nimrod International Journal, The University of Tulsa, 800 S. Tucker Dr., Tulsa OK 74104. (918)631-3080. **Fax:** (918)631-3033. **E-mail:** nimrod@utulsa.edu. **Website:** www.utulsa.edu/nimrod. **Contact:** Francine Ringold. "This annual award was established to discover new, unpublished writers of vigor and talent. Open to US residents only." 7,500-word maximum for short stories Deadline: April 30. Prize: Prizes: 1st Place: $2,000 and publication; 2nd Place: $1,000 and publication. *Nimrod* retains the right to publish any submission. The *Nimrod* editors select the finalists and a recognized author selects the winners.

☺ THE ROGERS WRITERS' TRUST FICTION PRIZE

The Writers' Trust of Canada, 90 Richmond St. E., Suite 200, Toronto ON M5C 1P1 Canada. (416)504-8222. **Fax:** (416)504-9090. **E-mail:** info@writerstrust. com. **Website:** www.writerstrust.com. **Contact:** Amanda Hopkins. "Awarded annually for a distinguished work of fiction—either a novel or short story collection—published within the previous year. Presented at the Writers' Trust Awards event held in Toronto each fall. Open to Canadian citizens and permanent residents only." Deadline: August 1. Prize: $25,000 and $2,500 to 4 finalists.

RROFIHE TROPHY

Anderbo.com, 270 Lafayette St., #705, New York NY 10012. **E-mail:** rrofihe@yahoo.com. **Website:** www. anderbo.com/anderbo1/anderrrofihetrophy2011. html. **Contact:** Rick Rofihe, editor. "Ninth annual contest for an unpublished short story (up to 5,000 words). Stories should be typed, double-spaced, on 8 1/2 x 11 paper with the author's name and contact information on the first page, and name and story title on the upper right corner of remaining pages. Limit 1 submission/author. Author must not have been previously published in *Open City*. Enclose SASE to receive names of winner and honorable mentions. All mss are nonreturnable and will be recycled. Acquires first North American serial rights (from winner only)." Deadline: October 15 (postmarked). Prize: $500, a trophy, and publication on Anderbo.com. Judge: Rick Rofihe.

☺ SASKATCHEWAN FICTION AWARD

Saskatchewan Book Awards, Inc., 100-2400 College Ave., Regina SK S4P 0K1 Canada. (306)569-1585. **Fax:** (306)569-4187. **E-mail:** director@bookawards.sk.ca. **Website:** www.bookawards.sk.ca. **Contact:** Executive director, book submissions. Offered annually. "This award is presented to a Saskatchewan author for the best book of fiction (novel or short fiction), judged on the quality of writing." Deadline: November 1. Prize: $2,000 (CAD).

⊕ THE SATURDAY EVENING POST GREAT AMERICAN FICTION CONTEST

The Saturday Evening Post Society, 1100 Waterway Blvd., Indianapolis IN 46202. **E-mail:** fictioncontest@saturdayeveningpost.com. **Website:** www.saturdayeveningpost.com/fiction-contest. "We are looking for stories with universal appeal touching on shared experiences and themes that will resonate with readers from diverse backgrounds and experience." Stories must be submitted by the author and previously unpublished (excluding personal websites and blogs), and 1,500-5,000 words in length. No extreme profanity or graphic sex scenes. Deadline: July 1. Prize: The winning story will receive $500 and publication in the magazine and online. Five runners-up will be published online and receive $100 each.

THE SCENT OF AN ENDING™

White Eagle Coffee Store Press, P.O. Box 383, Fox River Grove IL 60021-0383. (847)639-9200. **E-mail:** scentofanending@aol.com. **Website:** www.thescentofanending.com, or www.whiteeaglecoffeestorepress.com. **Contact:** Frank Edmund Smith, publisher. "Contest is offered annually for unpublished submissions. We're searching for the best bad ending to an imaginary novel—an ending that's a real stinker. We're looking for a memorably bad ending to a novel that has not been written. Submit the invented title of the novel and the final 25-125 words. The entry must be completely your own invention and cannot be taken from or closely based on anything actually published." Initial publication on website, then in chapbook format. "All winners will be required to sign a contract verifying originality." Deadline: September 30 annually. Prize: 1st place: $89.25; 2nd place: $67.32; 3rd place: $31.18, "plus dubious fame and publication for winner and all finalists. Initial publication on website, then publication in chapbook format. Winners and finalists receive copies of the published chapbook." Rights to any winning and published materials revert to author upon publication. WECSPress holds the rights to first publication in print and on the Internet and to permanent reprint rights. Please see website for complete contest information and sample endings and current finalists. Judged by editors of White Eagle Coffee Store Press.

JOANNA CATHERINE SCOTT NOVEL EXCERPT PRIZE

Category in the Soul Making Keats Literary Competition, The Webhallow House, 1544 Sweetwood Dr., Broadmoor Village CA 94015-2029. **E-mail:** pennobhill@aol.com. **Website:** www.soulmakingcontest.us. **Contact:** Eileen Malone. Open annually to any writer. "Send first chapter or the first 20 pages, whichever comes first. Include a 1-page synopsis indicating category at top of page. Identify with 3x5 card only." Deadline: November 30 (annually). Prize: 1st Place: $100; 2nd Place: $50; 3rd Place: $25.

MICHAEL SHAARA AWARD FOR EXCELLENCE IN CIVIL WAR FICTION

Civil War Institute at Gettysburg College, 300 N. Washington St., Campus Box 435, Gettysburg PA 17325. (717)337-6590. **Fax:** (717)337-6596. **E-mail:** civilwar@gettysburg.edu. **Website:** www.gettysburg.edu/cwi. Offered annually for fiction published January 1-December 31. Contest "to encourage examination of the Civil War from unique perspectives or by taking an unusual approach." All Civil War novels are eligible. Publishers should make nominations, but authors and critics can nominate as well. Prize: $5,000, which includes travel stipend. No entry fee. **Deadline: December 31.** Entries must be previously published. Judged for presentation of unique perspective, use of unusual approach, effective writing, contribution to existing body of Civil War literature. Competition open to authors of Civil War novels published for the first time in the year designated by the award (i.e. for 2008 award, only novels published in 2008 are eligible). Guidelines available on website. Accepts inquiries by fax, e-mail, and phone. Cover letter should include name, address, phone, e-mail, and title. Need 4 copies of novel. "Enter well before deadline. Results announced in July. Winners notified by phone. For contest results, visit website." **Contact:** Diane Brennan.

STEVEN TURNER AWARD FOR BEST FIRST WORK OF FICTION

6335 W. Northwest Hwy., #618, Dallas TX 75225. **Website:** www.texasinstituteofletters.org. Writers must have been born in Texas, have lived in the state for at least 2 consecutive years at some time, or the subject matter of the work should be associated with the state. Guidelines online. Deadline: normally first week in January; see website for specific date. Prize: $1,000.

THREE CHEERS AND A TIGER

E-mail: editors@toasted-cheese.com. **Website:** www.toasted-cheese.com. Purpose of contest is to write a short story (following a specific theme) within 48 hours. Contests are held first weekend in spring (mystery) and first weekend in fall (sf/f). Prize: Amazon gift certificates and publication. Categories: Short stories. Blind-judged by 2 *Toasted Cheese* editors. Each judge uses his or her own criteria to choose entries. No entry fee. Entries must be unpublished. Word limit announced at the start of the contest. Contest-specific information is announced 48 hours before the contest submission deadline. Open to any writer. Accepts inquiries by e-mail. "Follow the theme, word count and other contest rules. We have more suggestions at our website." Results announced in April and October. Winners notified by e-mail. List of winners on website. **Contact:** Stephanie Lenz, editor.

WAASMODE SHORT FICTION PRIZE

Passages North, Department of English, Northern Michigan University, 1401 Presque Isle Ave., Marquette MI 49855. (906)227-1203. **Fax:** (906)227-1096. **E-mail:** passages@nmu.edu. **Website:** www.passagesnorth.com. **Contact:** Kate Myers Hanson. Offered every 2 years to publish new voices in literary fiction (maximum 5,000 words). Guidelines for SASE or online. "In association with the Just Desserts Contest, we have our Waasmode Short Fiction Prize, which is also $1,000 1st Place prize and publication. It is a 7,500 word maximum word count. It is also given every other year. When we are not having our fiction contest, we are having our poetry and nonfiction contests. Elinor Benedict Poetry Prize: $1,000 1st Place prize and publication; $15 for up to 3 poems entry fee ($3 for each additional poem after that). Thomas J. Hruska Memorial Prize in Nonfiction: $1,000 1st Place prize and publication; $15 per essay entry fee. Submissions accepted at www.passagesnorth.com. Deadline: Submit October 15-February 15. Prize: $1,000 and publication for winner; 2 honorable mentions are also published; all entrants receive a copy of *Passages North*.

GARY WILSON SHORT FICTION AWARD

descant, Texas Christian University's literary journal, TCU, Box 297270, Fort Worth TX 76129. (817)257-6537. **Fax:** (817)257-6239. **E-mail:** descant@tcu.edu. **Website:** www.descant.tcu.edu. "Offered annually for an outstanding story in an issue." **Prize:** $250. **Contact:** David Kuhne, editor. "Offered annually for an outstanding story in an issue."

TOBIAS WOLFF AWARD IN FICTION

Bellingham Review, Mail Stop 9053, Western Washington University, Bellingham WA 98225. (360)650-4863. **E-mail:** bhreview@wwu.edu. **Website:** www. bhreview.org. Offered annually for unpublished work. Prize: $1,000, plus publication and subscription. Categories: Novel excerpts and short stories. Entry fee: $18 for 1st entry; $10 each additional entry. Guidelines available in September for SASE or on website. **Deadline:** Contest runs December 1-March 15. Entries must be unpublished. Length: 6,000 words or less per story or chapter. Open to any writer. *"Bellingham Review* accepts electronic and mailed submissions. Enter electronic submissions through Submittable, a

link to which is available on the website." Winner announced in August and notified by mail or e-mail. For contest results, send SASE with mailed submissions. **Contact:** Brenda Miller.

NONFICTION

THE SHAUGHNESSY COHEN PRIZE FOR POLITICAL WRITING

The Writers' Trust of Canada, 90 Richmond St. E., Suite 200, Toronto ON M5C 1P1 Canada. (416)504-8222. **Fax:** (416)504-9090. **E-mail:** info@writerstrust. com. **Website:** www.writerstrust.com. **Contact:** Amanda Hopkins, program coordinator. "Awarded annually for a nonfiction book of outstanding literary merit that enlarges our understanding of contemporary Canadian political and social issues. Presented at the Politics & the Pen event each spring in Ottawa. Open to Canadian citizens and permanent residents only." Prize: $25,000 and $2,500 to 4 finalists.

CARR P. COLLINS AWARD FOR NONFICTION

The Texas Institute of Letters, P.O. Box 609, Round Rock TX 78680. **E-mail:** tilsecretary@yahoo.com. **Website:** http://texasinstituteofletters.org/. Offered annually for work published January 1-December 31 of the previous year to recognize the best nonfiction book by a writer who was born in Texas, who has lived in the state for at least 2 consecutive years at one point, or a writer whose work has some notable connection with Texas. See website for guidelines. Deadline: See website for exact date. Prize: $5,000.

DIAGRAM ESSAY CONTEST

Department of English, University of Arizona, P.O. Box 210067, Tucson AZ 85721-0067. **E-mail:** nmp@ thediagram.com; editor@thediagram.com. **Website:** www.thediagram.com/contest.html. **Contact:** Ander Monson, editor. Contest for essays up to 10,000 words. Deadline: End of October each year. Check website for more details. Prize: $1,000 and publication. Finalist essay also published. Judges: Ander Monson and Nicole Walker

EVANS BIOGRAPHY & HANDCART AWARDS

Mountain West Center for Regional Studies, Utah State University, 0735 Old Main Hill, Logan UT 84322-0735. (435)797-0299. **Fax:** (435)797-1092. **E-mail:** mwc@usu.edu. **Website:** http://mountainwest.

usu.edu/evans.aspx. **Contact:** Patricia Lambert, director. "Offered to encourage the writing of biography about people who have played a role in the interior West. Publishers or authors may nominate books. Criteria for consideration: Work must be a biography or autobiography on someone who lived in or significantly contributed to the history of the Interior West; annual must be submitted for consideration for publication year's award; new editions or reprints are not eligible; mss are not accepted. Submit 6 copies." Deadline: January 1 for books published in the previous calendar years. Prize: $10,000 and $2,500.

⊙ EVENT NONFICTION CONTEST

Event, Poetry and Prose., P.O. Box 2503, New Westminster BC V3L 5B2 Canada. (604)527-5293. **Fax:** (604)527-5095. **E-mail:** event@douglascollege.ca. **Website:** http://event.douglas.bc.ca. Offered annually for unpublished creative nonfiction. Maximum length: 5,000 words. Acquires first North American serial print rights and limited non-exclusive digital rights for the winning entries. Open to any writer, except Douglas College employees. Previously published material, including that which has appeared online or has been accepted for publication elsewhere, cannot be considered. No simultaneous submissions. The writer should not be identified on the entry. Include separate cover sheet with name, address, phone number/email, and title(s). Send to address above. Include a SASE (Canadian postage/IRCs/US $1). Multiple entries are allowed; however, each entry must be accompanied by its own entry fee. Make check or international money order payable to EVENT. Deadline: April 15. Prize: Judges reserve the right to award 2 or 3 prizes: 3 at $500 or 2 at $750.

JOHN GUYON LITERARY NONFICTION PRIZE

Crab Orchard Review, English Department, Southern Illinois University at Carbondale, Carbondale IL 62901. **E-mail:** jtribble@siu.edu. **Website:** www.craborchardreview.siu.edu. **Contact:** Jon C. Tribble, managing editor. "Offered annually for unpublished work. This competition seeks to reward excellence in the writing of creative nonfiction. This is not a prize for academic essays. *Crab Orchard Review* acquires first North American serial rights to submitted works. Open to US citizens only." Deadline: March 1-May 4. Prize: $2,000 and publication.

⊕ THOMAS J. HRUSKA MEMORIAL PRIZE IN NONFICTION

Passages North, Department of English, Northern Michigan University, 1401 Presque Isle Ave., Marquette MI 49855. (906) 227-1203. **Fax:** (906) 227-1096. **Website:** www.passagesnorth.com. **Contact:** Kate Myers Hanson, acquisitions. "When we are not having our fiction contest, we are having our poetry and nonfiction contests." Send SASE for announcement of winners. Author's name may appear anywhere on ms or cover letter. Manuscripts will not be returned. All entrants receive a contest issue. Honorable mentions will also be chosen for each contest and may or may not be published according to the needs of the editors. Deadline: February 15. Prize: $1,000 1st Place prize and publication.

⊕ THE HUNGER MOUNTAIN CREATIVE NONFICTION PRIZE

Vermont College, 36 College St., Montpelier VT 05602. (802)828-8517. **E-mail:** hungermtn@vcfa.edu. **Website:** www.hungermtn.org. **Contact:** Miciah Bay Gault, editor. The annual Hunger Mountain Creative Nonfiction Prize offers $1,000 and publication in *Hunger Mountain* online; 2 runners-up receive $100 and are considered for publication. Submit essay under 10,000 words. Guidelines available on website. Deadline: September 10.

TILIA KLEBENOV JACOBS RELIGIOUS ESSAY PRIZE

Category in the Soul Making Keats Literary Competition, The Webhallow House, 1544 Sweetwood Dr., Broadmoor Village CA 94015-2029. **E-mail:** pennobhill@aol.com. **Website:** www.soulmakingcontest.us. **Contact:** Eileen Malone. "Call for thoughtful writings of up to 3,000 words. No preaching, no proselytizing." Open annually to any writer. Previously published material is accepted. Indicate category on cover page and on identifying 3x5 card. Deadline: November 30 (annually). Prize: 1st Place: $100; 2nd Place $50; 3rd Place $25.

KATHERINE SINGER KOVACS PRIZE

Modern Language Association of America, 26 Broadway, 3rd Floor, New York NY 10004-1789. (646)576-5141. **Fax:** (646)458-0030. **E-mail:** awards@mla.org. **Website:** www.mla.org. **Contact:** Coordinator of Book Prizes. Offered annually for a book published during the previous year in English or Spanish in the field of Latin American and Spanish literatures and cultures. Books should be broadly interpretive works that enhance understanding of the interrelations among literature, the other arts, and society. Author must be a current member of the MLA. Deadline: May 1. Prize: A cash award and a certificate to be presented at the Modern Language Association's annual convention in January.

KATHERYN KROTZER LABORDE LITERARY NONFICTION PRIZE

Category in the Soul Making Keats Literary Competition, The Webhallow House, 1544 Sweetwood Dr., Broadmoor Village CA 94015-2029. **E-mail:** pennobhill@aol.com. **Website:** www.soulmakingcontest. us. **Contact:** Eileen Malone. All prose works must be typed, page numbered, and double-spaced. Each entry up to 3,000 words. Identify only with 35 card. Open annually to any writer. Deadline: November 30 (annually). Prize: 1st Place: $100; 2nd Place: $50; 3rd Place: $25.

⊕ LITERAL LATTE ESSAY AWARD

Literal Latte, 200 E. 10th St., Suite 240, New York NY 10003. (212)260-5532. **E-mail:** litlatte@aol.com. **Website:** www.literal-latte.com. **Contact:** Jenine Gordon Bockman. "Open to any writer. Send previously unpublished personal essays, 10,000 words max. All topics accepted. Include email address for reply." Acquires first rights. To give support and exposure to great writing. Postmark by Sept. 15. Prize: 1st Prize: $1,000; 2nd: $300; 3rd: $200. The Editors

☯ LITERARY NONFICTION CONTEST

PRISM International, Creative Writing Program, UBC, Buch E462—1866 Main Mall, Vancouver BC V6T 1Z1 Canada. **E-mail:** prismwritingcontest@gmail.com. **Website:** www.prismmagazine.ca. **Contact:** Contest manager. Offered annually for published and unpublished writers to promote and reward excellence in literary nonfiction writing. "*PRISM* buys first North American serial rights upon publication. We also buy limited Web rights for pieces selected for the website. Open to anyone except students and faculty of the Creative Writing Program at UBC or people who have taken a creative writing course at UBC in the 2 years prior to contest deadline. All entrants receive a 1-year subscription to *PRISM*. Guidelines for SASE (Canadian postage only), via e-mail, or visit our website." Deadline: November 30. Prize: $1,500 for the winning entry, plus $20/page for the publication of the winner in *PRISM*'s spring issue.

RICHARD J. MARGOLIS AWARD

c/o Margolis & Bloom, LLP, 535 Boylston St., 8th Floor, Boston MA 02116. (617)267-9700, ext. 517. **E-mail:** harry@margolis.com. **Website:** www.margolis.com/award. **Contact:** Harry S. Margolis. "Sponsored by the Blue Mountain Center, this annual award is given to a promising new journalist or essayist whose work combines warmth, humor, wisdom, and concern with social justice. Submit 3 copies of at least 2 examples of your published or unpublished work (maximum 30 pages) and a short biographical note. Submissions may be by mail or e-mail." Deadline: July 1. Prize: $5,000 and a 1-month residency at the Blue Mountain Center—a writers and artists colony in the Adirondacks in Blue Mountain Lake, New York.

HOWARD R. MARRARO PRIZE

Modern Language Association of America, 26 Broadway, 3rd Floor, New York NY 10004-1789. (646)576-5141. **Fax:** (646)458-0030. **E-mail:** awards@mla.org. **Website:** www.mla.org. **Contact:** Coordinator of Book Prizes. Offered in even-numbered years for a scholarly book or essay on any phase of Italian literature or comparative literature involving Italian, published in previous year. Authors must be members of the MLA. Deadline: May 1. Prize: A cash award and a certificate to be presented at the Modern Language Association's annual convention in January.

KENNETH W. MILDENBERGER PRIZE

Modern Language Association of America, 26 Broadway, 3rd Floor, New York NY 10004-1789. (646)576-5141. **Fax:** (646)458-0030. **E-mail:** awards@mla.org. **Website:** www.mla.org. **Contact:** Coordinator of Book Prizes. Offered in odd-numbered years for a publication from the previous year in the field of language culture, literacy, or literature with a strong application to the teaching of languages other than English. Author need not be a member. Deadline: May 1. Prize: A cash award, and a certificate, to be presented at the Modern Language Association's annual convention in January, and a year's membership in the MLA.

C. WRIGHT MILLS AWARD

The Society for the Study of Social Problems, 901 McClung Tower, University of Tennessee, Knoxville TN 37996-0490. (865)689-1531. **Fax:** (865)689-1534. **E-mail:** mkoontz3@utk.edu. **Website:** www.sssp1.org. **Contact:** Michele Smith Koontz, administrative officer and meeting manager. "Offered annually for a book published the previous year that most effectively critically addresses an issue of contemporary public importance; brings to the topic a fresh, imaginative perspective; advances social scientific understanding of the topic; displays a theoretically informed view and empirical orientation; evinces quality in style of writing; and explicitly or implicitly contains implications for courses of action." Deadline: December 15. Prize: $500 stipend.

MLA PRIZE FOR A DISTINGUISHED SCHOLARLY EDITION

Modern Language Association of America, 26 Broadway, 3rd Floor, New York NY 10004-1789. (646)576-5141. **Fax:** (646)458-0030. **E-mail:** awards@mla.org. **Website:** www.mla.org. **Contact:** Coordinator of Book Prizes. Offered in odd-numbered years. "To qualify for the award, an edition should be based on an examination of all available relevant textual sources; the source texts and the edited text's deviations from them should be fully described; the edition should employ editorial principles appropriate to the materials edited, and those principles should be clearly articulated in the volume; the text should be accompanied by appropriate textual and other historical contextual information; the edition should exhibit the highest standards of accuracy in the presentation of its text and apparatus; and the text and apparatus should be presented as accessibly and elegantly as possible." Editor need not be a member of the MLA. Deadline: May 1. Prize: A cash award and a certificate to be presented at the Modern Language Association's annual convention in January.

MLA PRIZE FOR A FIRST BOOK

Modern Language Association of America, 26 Broadway, 3rd Floor, New York NY 10004-1789. (646)576-5141. **Fax:** (646)458-0030. **E-mail:** awards@mla.org. **Website:** www.mla.org. **Contact:** Coordinator of Book Prizes. Offered annually for the first book-length scholarly publication by a current member of the association. To qualify, a book must be a literary or linguistic study, a critical edition of an important work, or a critical biography. Studies dealing with literary theory, media, cultural history, and interdisciplinary topics are eligible; books that are primarily translations will not be considered. Deadline: April 1. Prize: A cash award and a certificate to be presented at the Modern Language Association's annual convention in January.

MLA PRIZE FOR INDEPENDENT SCHOLARS

Modern Language Association of America, 26 Broadway, 3rd Floor, New York NY 10004-1789. (646)576-5141. **Fax:** (646)458-0030. **E-mail:** awards@mla.org. **Website:** www.mla.org. **Contact:** Coordinator of Book Prizes. Offered in even-numbered years for a book in the field of English, or another modern language, or literature published in the previous year. Authors who are enrolled in a program leading to an academic degree or who hold tenured or tenure-track positions in higher education are not eligible. Authors need not be members of MLA. Guidelines and application form for SASE. Deadline: May 1. Prize: A cash award, a certificate, and a year's membership in the MLA.

LINDA JOY MYERS VIGNETTE MEMOIR PRIZE

Category in the Soul Making Keats Literary Competition, Webhallow House, 1544 Sweetwood Dr., Broadmoor Village CA 94015-2029. **E-mail:** pennobhill@aol.com. **Website:** www.soulmakingcontest.us. **Contact:** Eileen Malone. Open annually to any writer. "One memoir/entry, up to 1,500 words, double spaced. Previously published material is acceptable. Indicate category on first page. Identify only with 3x5 card." Deadline: November 30 (annually). Prize: 1st Place: $100; 2nd Place $50; 3rd Place $25.

NATIONAL PEACE ESSAY CONTEST

1200 17th St. NW, Washington DC 20036. (202)457-1700. **Fax:** (202)429.6063. **E-mail:** essaycontest@usip.org. **Website:** www.usip.org/NPEC. "The contest gives students the opportunity to do valuable research, writing and thinking on a topic of importance to international peace and conflict resolution. Teaching guides are available for teachers who allow the contest to be used as a classroom assignment." Deadline for entries is February 1, 2012. "Interested students, teachers and others may visit the website to download or request contest materials. Please do not include SASE." Guidelines and rules on website. No entry fee. State-level awards are $1,000 college scholarships. National winners are selected from among the 1st place state winners. National winners receive scholarships in the following amounts: first place $10,000; second $5,000; third $2,500. National amount includes state award. First-place state winners invited to an expenses-paid awards program in Washington, DC in June.

Judging is conducted by education professionals from across the country and by the board of directors of the United States Institute of Peace. "All submissions become property of the U.S. Institute of Peace to use at its discretion and without royalty or any limitation. Students grades 9-12 in the U.S., its territories and overseas schools may submit essays for review by completing the application process. U.S. citizenship required for students attending overseas schools. National winning essays will be published by the U.S. Institute of Peace."

PRESERVATION FOUNDATION CONTESTS

The Preservation Foundation, Inc., 2213 Pennington Bend, Nashville TN 37214. **E-mail:** preserve@storyhouse.org. **Website:** www.storyhouse.org. **Contact:** Richard Loller, publisher. "Two contests offered annually for unpublished nonfiction. General nonfiction category (1,500-5,000 words)—any appropriate nonfiction topic. Travel nonfiction category (1,500-5,000 words)—must be true story of trip by author or someone known personally by author. E-mail entries only (no mss). Open to any previously unpublished writer. Defined as having earned no more than $750 by creative writing in any previous year." Deadline: August 31. Prize: 1st Place: $100 in each category; certificates for finalists.

☼ SASKATCHEWAN NONFICTION AWARD

Saskatchewan Book Awards, Inc., 100-2400 College Ave., Regina SK S4P 0K1 Canada. (306)569-1585. **Fax:** (306)569-4187. **E-mail:** director@bookawards.sk.ca. **Website:** www.bookawards.sk.ca. **Contact:** Executive director. Offered annually for work published. "This award is presented to a Saskatchewan author for the best book of nonfiction, judged on the quality of writing." Deadline: November 1. Prize: $2,000 (CAD).

☼ SASKATCHEWAN SCHOLARLY WRITING AWARD

Saskatchewan Book Awards, Inc., 100-2400 College Ave., Regina SK S4P 0K1 Canada. (306)569-1585. **Fax:** (306)569-4187. **E-mail:** director@bookawards.sk.ca. **Website:** www.bookawards.sk.ca. **Contact:** Executive director, book submissions. Offered annually. "This award is presented to a Saskatchewan author for the best contribution to scholarship. The work must recognize or draw on specific theoretical work within a community of scholars, and participate in the creation and transmission of scholarly knowledge." Deadline: November 1. Prize: $2,000 (CAD).

ALDO AND JEANNE SCAGLIONE PRIZE FOR COMPARATIVE LITERARY STUDIES

Modern Language Association of America, 26 Broadway, 3rd Floor, New York NY 10004-1789. (646)576-5141. **Fax:** (646)458-0030. **E-mail:** awards@mla.org. **Website:** www.mla.org. **Contact:** Coordinator of Book Prizes. Offered annually for outstanding scholarly work published in the preceding year in the field of comparative literary studies involving at least 2 literatures. *Author must be a member of the MLA.* Works of scholarship, literary history, literary criticism, and literary theory are eligible; books that are primarily translations are not eligible. Deadline: May 1. Prize: A cash award and a certificate to be presented at the Modern Language Association's annual convention in January.

ALDO AND JEANNE SCAGLIONE PRIZE FOR FRENCH AND FRANCOPHONE STUDIES

Modern Language Association of America, 26 Broadway, 3rd Floor, New York NY 10004-1789. (646)576-5141. **Fax:** (646)458-0030. **E-mail:** awards@mla.org. **Website:** www.mla.org. **Contact:** Coordinator of Book Prizes. Offered annually for work published in the preceding year that is an outstanding scholarly work in the field of French or francophone linguistic or literary studies. *Author must be a member of the MLA.* Works of scholarship, literary history, literary criticism, and literary theory are eligible; books that are primarily translations are not eligible. Deadline: May 1. Prize: a cash award and a certificate to be presented at the Modern Language Association's annual convention in January.

ALDO AND JEANNE SCAGLIONE PRIZE FOR ITALIAN STUDIES

Modern Language Association of America, 26 Broadway, 3rd Floor, New York NY 10004-1789. (646)576-5141. **Fax:** (646)458-0030. **E-mail:** awards@mla.org. **Website:** www.mla.org. **Contact:** Coordinator of Book Prizes. Offered in odd-numbered years for a scholarly book on any phase of Italian literature or culture, or comparative literature involving Italian, including works on literary or cultural theory, science, history, art, music, society, politics, cinema, and linguistics, preferably but not necessarily relating other disciplines to literature. Books must have been published in year prior to competition. *Authors must be members of the MLA.* Deadline: May 1. Prize: A cash award and a certificate to be presented at the Modern Language Association's annual convention in January.

ALDO AND JEANNE SCAGLIONE PRIZE FOR STUDIES IN GERMANIC LANGUAGES & LITERATURE

Modern Language Association of America, 26 Broadway, 3rd Floor, New York NY 10004-1789. (646)576-5141. **Fax:** (646)458-0030. **E-mail:** awards@mla.org. **Website:** www.mla.org. **Contact:** Coordinator of Book Prizes. Offered in even-numbered years for outstanding scholarly work appearing in print in the previous 2 years and written by a member of the MLA on the linguistics or literatures of the Germanic languages. Works of literary history, literary criticism, and literary theory are eligible; books that are primarily translations are not eligible. Deadline: May 1. Prize: A cash award, and a certificate to be presented at the Modern Language Association's annual convention in January.

ALDO AND JEANNE SCAGLIONE PRIZE FOR STUDIES IN SLAVIC LANGUAGES AND LITERATURES

Modern Language Association of America, 26 Broadway, 3rd Floor, New York NY 10004-1789. (646)576-5141. **Fax:** (646)458-0030. **E-mail:** awards@mla.org. **Website:** www.mla.org. **Contact:** Coordinator of Book Prizes. Offered in odd-numbered years for books published in the previous 2 years. Membership in the MLA is not required. Works of literary history, literary criticism, philology, and literary theory are eligible; books that are primarily translations are not eligible. Deadline: May 1. Prize: A cash award and a certificate to be presented at the Modern Language Association's annual convention in January.

ALDO AND JEANNE SCAGLIONE PUBLICATION AWARD FOR A MANUSCRIPT IN ITALIAN LITERARY STUDIES

Modern Language Association, 26 Broadway, 3rd Floor, New York NY 10004-1789. (646)576-5141. **Fax:** (646)458-0030. **E-mail:** awards@mla.org. **Website:** www.mla.org. **Contact:** Coordinator of Book Prizes. Awarded annually to an author of a ms dealing with any aspect of the languages and literatures of Italy, including medieval Latin and comparative studies, or intellectual history if main thrust is clearly relat-

ed to the humanities. Materials from ancient Rome are eligible if related to post-classical developments. Also translations of classical works of prose and poetry produced in Italy prior to 1900 in any language (i.e., neo-Latin, Greek) or in a dialect of Italian (i.e., Neapolitan, Roman, Sicilian). Work can be in English or Italian. *Authors must be members of the MLA* and currently reside in the US or Canada. Deadline: August 1. Prize: A cash award and a certificate to be presented at the Modern Language Association's annual convention in January.

SCIENCE WRITING AWARDS IN PHYSICS AND ASTRONOMY

American Institute of Physics, 1 Physics Ellipse, College Park MD 20740-3843. (301)209-3096. **Fax:** (301)209-0846. **Website:** www.aip.org/aip/writing. Offered for published articles, booklets, or books that improve the general public's appreciation and understanding of physics and astronomy. Four categories: articles or books intended for children, preschool-15 years old; broadcast media for radio or television programming; journalism, written by a professional journalist; books or articles by a scientist. Guidelines by phone, e-mail, or online. Deadline: February 17. Prize: $3,000, an engraved Windsor chair, and a certificate awarded in each category.

MINA P. SHAUGHNESSY PRIZE

Modern Language Association of America, 26 Broadway, 3rd Floor, New York NY 10004-1789. (646)576-5141. **Fax:** (646)458-0030. **E-mail:** awards@mla.org. **Website:** www.mla.org. **Contact:** Coordinator of Book Prizes. Offered in even-numbered years for a scholarly book in the fields of language, culture, literacy, or literature with strong application to the teaching of English published during preceding year. Authors need not be members of the MLA. Deadline: May 1. Prize: A cash prize, a certificate, to be presented at the Modern Language Association's annual convention in January, and a 1-year membership in the MLA.

VFW VOICE OF DEMOCRACY

Veterans of Foreign Wars of the U.S., 406 W. 34th St., Kansas City MO 64111. (816)968-1117. **E-mail:** kharmer@vfw.org. **Website:** www.vfw.org. **Open to high school students.** Annual contest. Purpose of contest: to give high school students the opportunity to voice their opinions about their responsibility to our country and to convey those opinions via the broadcast media to all of America. Deadline for entries: November 1. No entry fee. Winners receive awards ranging from $1,000-30,000. Requirements for entrants: "Ninth-twelfth grade students in public, parochial, private and home schools are eligible to compete. Former first place state winners are not eligible to compete again. Contact your participating high school teacher, counselor, our website www.vfw.org or your local VFW Post to enter."

☮ THE HILARY WESTON WRITERS' TRUST PRIZE FOR NONFICTION

The Writers' Trust of Canada, 90 Richmond St. E., Suite 200, Toronto ON M5C 1P1 Canada. (416)504-8222. **Fax:** (416)504-9090. **E-mail:** info@writerstrust.com. **Website:** www.writerstrust.com. **Contact:** Amanda Hopkins. "Offered annually for a work of nonfiction published in the previous year. Award presented at a a gala event held in Toronto each fall. Open to Canadian citizens and permanent residents only." Deadline: August 1. Prize: $25,000 (Canadian), and $2,500 to 4 finalists.

WILLIAM SANDERS SCARBOROUGH PRIZE

Modern Language Association of America, 26 Broadway, 3rd Floor, New York NY 10004-1789. (646)576-5141. **Fax:** (646)458-0030. **E-mail:** awards@mla.org. **Website:** www.mla.org. **Contact:** Coordinator of book prizes. Offered annually for work published in the previous year. "Given in honor of a distinguished man of letters and the first African-American member of the Modern Language Association, this prize will be awarded to an outstanding scholarly study of black American literature or culture." Open to MLA members and nonmembers. Authors or publishers may enter titles. Guidelines for SASE or by e-mail. Deadline: May 1. Prize: A cash award, and a certificate to be presented at the Modern Language Association's annual convention in January.

WRITING FOR CHILDREN & YOUNG ADULTS

☮ MARILYN BAILLIE PICTURE BOOK AWARD

The Canadian Children's Book Centre, 40 Orchard View Blvd., Suite 101, Toronto ON M4R 1B9 Canada. (416)975-0010. **Fax:** (416)975-8970. **E-mail:** meghan@bookcentre.ca. **Website:** www.bookcentre.ca. "To be

eligible, the book must be an original work in English, aimed at children ages 3-8, written and illustrated by Canadians and first published in Canada. Eligible genres include fiction, non-fiction and poetry. Books must be published between Jan. 1 and Dec. 31 of the previous calendar year." "Honors excellence in the illustrated picture book format." Prize: $20,000.

JOHN AND PATRICIA BEATTY AWARD

950 Glenn Drive, Suite 150, Folsom CA 95630. (916)233-3298. **Fax:** (916)932-2209. **E-mail:** hollym@cla-net.org. **Website:** www.cla-net.org. **Contact:** Holly Macriss, executive director. Purpose of award: "The purpose of the John and Patricia Beatty Award is to encourage the writing of quality children's books highlighting California, its culture, heritage and/or future." Previously published submissions only. Submissions made by the author, author's agent or review copies sent by publisher. The award is given to the author of a children's book published the preceding year. Deadline for entries: Submissions may be made January-December. Contact CLA Executive Director who will liaison with Beatty Award Committee. Awards cash prize of $500 and an engraved plaque. Judging by a 5-member selection committee appointed by the president of the California Library Association. Requirements for entrants: "Any children's or young adult book set in California and published in the U.S. during the calendar year preceding the presentation of the award is eligible for consideration. This includes works of fiction as well as nonfiction for children and young people of all ages. Reprints and compilations are not eligible. The California setting must be depicted authentically and must serve as an integral focus for the book." Winning selection is announced through press release during National Library Week in April. Author is presented with award at annual California Library Association Conference in November.

☮ THE GEOFFREY BILSON AWARD FOR HISTORICAL FICTION FOR YOUNG PEOPLE

The Canadian Children's Book Centre, 40 Orchard View Blvd., Suite 217, Toronto ON M4R 1B9 Canada. (416)975-0010. **Fax:** (416)975-8970. **Website:** www.bookcentre.ca. **Contact:** Meghan Howe. Created in Geoffrey Bilson's memory in 1988. Awarded annually to reward excellence in the writing of an outstanding work of historical fiction for young readers, by a Canadian author, published in the previous calendar year. Open to Canadian citizens and residents of Canada for at least 2 years. **Deadline:** Mid- December. **Prize:** $5,000. Please visit website for submissions guidelines and eligibility criteria, as well as specific submission deadline.

BOSTON GLOBE-HORN BOOK AWARDS

The Boston Globe, Horn Book, Inc., 56 Roland St., Suite 200, Boston MA 02129. (617)628-0225. **Fax:** (617)628-0882. **E-mail:** info@hbook.com; khedeen@hbook.com. **Website:** hbook.com/bghb/. **Contact:** Katrina Hedeen. Offered annually for excellence in literature for children and young adults (published June 1-May 31). Categories: picture book, fiction and poetry, nonfiction. Judges may also name several honor books in each category. Books must be published in the US, but may be written or illustrated by citizens of any country. The Horn Book Magazine publishes speeches given at awards ceremonies. Guidelines for SASE or online. **Deadline for entries:** May 31. **Prize:** Winners receive $500 and an engraved silver bowl; honor book recipients receive an engraved silver plate. Judged by a panel of 3 judges selected each year.

✪ ANN CONNOR BRIMER AWARD

P.O. Box 36036, Halifax NS B3J 3S9 Canada. **Website:** www.nsla.ns.ca/index.php/about/awards/ann-connor-brimer-award/ann-connor-brimer/. **Contact:** Heather MacKenzie, award director. Purpose of the contest: to recognize excellence in writing. Given to an author of a children's book who resides in Atlantic Canada. Previously published submissions only. Submissions made by the author's agent or nominated by a person or group of people. Must be published in previous year. **Deadline for entries:** October 15. SASE for contest rules and entry forms. Please go to website for contest rules and entry forms: http://www.nsla.ns.ca/index.php/about/awards/ann-connor-brimer-award/ann-connor-brimer/. No entry fee but four copies of the title must accompany the submission. Awards $2,000 and framed certificate. Judging by a selection committee. Requirements for entrants: Book must be intended for use up to age 15; in print and readily available; fiction or nonfiction except textbooks

✪ THE NORMA FLECK AWARD FOR CANADIAN CHILDREN'S NONFICTION

The Canadian Children's Book Centre, 40 Orchard View Blvd., Suite 217, Toronto ON M4R 1B9 Canada. (416)975-0010. **Fax:** (416)975-8970. **E-mail:** info@bookcentre.ca. **Website:** www.bookcentre.ca. **Contact:** Meghan Howe, library coordinator. The Norma Fleck Award was established by the Fleck Family Foundation in May 1999 to honour the life of Norma Marie Fleck, and to recognize exceptional Canadian nonfiction books for young people. Publishers are welcome to nominate books using the online form. Offered annually for books published between January 1 and December 31 of the previous calendar year. Open to Canadian citizens or landed immigrants. The jury will always include at least 3 of the following: a teacher, a librarian, a bookseller, and a reviewer. A juror will have a deep understanding of, and some involvement with, Canadian children's books. The Canadian Children's Book Centre will select the jury members. **Deadline: Mid-December (annually).** Prize: $10,000 goes to the author (unless 40% or more of the text area is composed of original illustrations, in which case the award will be divided equally between the author and the artist).

GOLDEN KITE AWARDS

Society of Children's Book Writers and Illustrators (SCBWI), 8271 Beverly Blvd., Los Angeles CA 90048-4515. (323)782-1010. **E-mail:** awards@scbwi.org. **Website:** www.scbwi.org. Society of Children's Book Writers and Illustrators, 8271 Beverly Blvd. Los Angeles CA 90048. (323)782-1010. **E-mail:** scbwi@scbwi.org. **Website:** www.scbwi.org. **Contact:** SCBWI Golden Kite Coordinator. Annual award. Estab. 1973. "The works chosen will be those that the judges feel exhibit excellence in writing, and in the case of the picture-illustrated books—in illustration, and genuinely appeal to the interests and concerns of children. For the fiction and nonfiction awards, original works and single-author collections of stories or poems of which at least half are new and never before published in book form are eligible—anthologies and translations are not. For the picture-illustration awards, the art or photographs must be original works (the texts—which may be fiction or nonfiction—may be original, public domain or previously published). **Deadline for entries:** December 15. SASE for award rules. No entry fee. Awards, in addition to statuettes and plaques, the four winners receive $2,500 cash award plus trip to LA SCBWI Conference. The panel of judges will consist of professional authors, illustrators, editors or agents." Requirements for entrants: "must be a member of SCBWI and books must be published in that year." Winning books will be displayed at national conference in August. Books to be entered, as well as further inquiries, should be submitted to: The Society of Children's Book Writers and Illustrators, above address.

GOVERNOR GENERAL'S LITERARY AWARD FOR CHILDREN'S LITERATURE

Canada Council for the Arts, 350 Albert St., P.O. Box 1047, Ottawa ON K1P 5V8 Canada. (613)566-4414, ext. 5573. **Fax:** (613)566-4410. **Website:** www.canadacouncil.ca/prizes/ggla. Offered for the best English-language and the best French-language works of children's literature by a Canadian in 2 categories: text and illustration. Publishers submit titles for consideration. Deadline depends on the book's publication date. Books in English: March 15, June 1, or August 7. Books in French: March 15 or July 15. Prize: Each laureate receives $25,000; non-winning finalists receive $1,000.

CAROL OTIS HURST CHILDREN'S BOOK PRIZE

Westfield Athenaeum, 6 Elm St., Westfield MA 01085. (413)568-7833. **Website:** www.westath.org. **Contact:** Ralph Melnick, assistant director, Westfield Athenaeum. The Carol Otis Hurst Children's Book Prize honors outstanding works of fiction and nonfiction written for children and young adults through the age of 18. For a work to be considered, the writer must either be a native or a current resident of New England. While the prize (together with a monetary award of $500) is presented annually to an author whose work best exemplifies the highest standards of writing for this age group regardless of genre or topic or geographical setting, the prize committee is especially interested in those books that treat life in the region.

IRA CHILDREN'S AND YOUNG ADULT'S BOOK AWARD

800 Barksdale Rd., P.O. Box 8139, Newark DE 19714-8139. (302)731-1600. **Fax:** (302)731-1057. **E-mail:** kbaughman@reading.org; exec@reading.org. **Website:** www.reading.org. **Contact:** Kathy Baughman. Awards are given for an author's first or second published book for fiction and nonfiction in 3 categories: primary (ages preschool-8), intermediate (ages 9-13), and young adult (ages 14-17). This award is intended for newly published authors who show unusual promise in the children's book field. Deadline for entries: See website. Awards $1,000. For guidelines, write or e-mail.

EZRA JACK KEATS/KERLAN MEMORIAL FELLOWSHIP

113 Elmer L. Andersen Library, 222 21st Ave. S., University of Minnesota, Minneapolis MN 55455. **Website:** http://special.lib.umn.edu/clrc/. This fellowship from the Ezra Jack Keats Foundation will provide $1,500 to a "talented writer and/or illustrator of children's books who wishes to use the Kerlan Collection for the furtherance of his or her artistic development." Special consideration will be given to someone who would find it difficult to finance a visit to the Kerlan Collection. The Ezra Jack Keats Fellowship recipient will receive transportation costs and a per diem allotment.

THE VICKY METCALF AWARD FOR CHILDREN'S LITERATURE

The Writers' Trust of Canada, 90 Richmond St. E., Suite 200, Toronto ON M5C 1P1 Canada. (416)504-8222. **Fax:** (416)504-9090. **E-mail:** info@writerstrust.com. **Website:** www.writerstrust.com. **Contact:** Amanda Hopkins, program coordinator. "The Metcalf Award is presented to a Canadian writer for a body of work in children's literature at The Writers' Trust Awards event held in Toronto each Fall. Open to Canadian citizens and permanent residents only."

MUNICIPAL CHAPTER OF TORONTO IODE JEAN THROOP BOOK AWARD

40 St. Clair Ave. E.Suite 205, Toronto ON M4T 1M9 Canada. (416)925-5078. **Fax:** (416)925-5127. **E-mail:** ioedtoronto@bellnet.ca. **Website:** www.bookcentre.ca/awards/iode_book_award_municipal_chapter_toronto. **Contact:** Jennifer Werry, contest director. Submit entries to: Theo Heras, Lillian Smith Library, 239 College St., Toronto. Annual contest. Estab. 1974. Previously published submissions only. Submissions made by author. Deadline for entries: November 1. No entry fee. Awards: $1,000. If the illustrator is different from the author, the prize money is divided. Judging by Book Award Committee comprised of members of Toronto Municipal Chapter IODE. Requirements for entrants: Authors and illustrators must be Canadian and live within the GTA.

JOHN NEWBERY MEDAL

Association for Library Service to Children, Division of the American Library Association, 50 E. Huron, Chicago IL 60611. (800)545-2433, ext. 2153. **Fax:** (312)280-5271. **E-mail:** library@ala.org. **Website:** www.ala.org. Purpose of award: to recognize the most distinguished contribution to American children's literature published in the U.S. Previously published submissions only; must be published prior to year award is given. Deadline for entries: December 31. SASE for award rules. Entries not returned. No entry fee. Medal awarded at Caldecott/Newbery banquet during ALA annual conference. Judging by Newbery Award Selection Committee.

PATERSON PRIZE FOR BOOKS FOR YOUNG PEOPLE

The Poetry Center at Passaic County Community College, One College Blvd., Paterson NJ 07505-1179. (973)523-6085. **Fax:** (973)523-6085. **E-mail:** mgillan@pccc.edu. **Website:** www.pccc.edu/poetry. **Contact:** Maria Mazziotti Gillan, executive director. Part of the Poetry Center's mission is "to recognize excellence in books for young people." Published submissions only. Submissions made by author, author's agent or publisher. Must be published between January 1-December 31 of year previous to award year. Deadline for entries: March 15. SASE for contest rules and entry forms or visit website. Awards $500 for the author in either of 3 categories: PreK-Grade 3; Grades 4-6, Grades 7-12. Judging by a professional writer selected by the Poetry Center. Contest is open to any writer/illustrator.

⊕ THE KATHERINE PATERSON PRIZE FOR YOUNG ADULT AND CHILDREN'S WRITING

Vermont College, 36 College St., Montpelier VT 05602. (802)828-8517. **E-mail:** hungermtn@vcfa.edu. **Website:** www.hungermtn.org. **Contact:** Miciah Bay Gault, editor. The annual Katherine Paterson Prize for Young Adult and Children's Writing offers $1,000 and publication in *Hunger Mountain*; 3 runners-up receive $100 and are also published. Submit young adult or middle grade mss, and writing for younger children, short stories, picture books, or novel excerpts, under 10,000 words. Guidelines available on website. Deadline: June 30.

PEN/PHYLLIS NAYLOR WORKING WRITER FELLOWSHIP

588 Broadway, New York NY 10012. **E-mail:** awards@pen.org. **Website:** www.pen.org. **Contact:** Nick Burd, awards program director. Offered annually to a writer of children's or young-adult fiction in financial need, who has published 2 books for children and young adults which may have been well reviewed and warmly received by literary critics, but which have not generated sufficient income to support the author. Previous works must be released through a US publisher. Writers must be nominated by an editor or fellow writer. The nominator should write a letter of support, describing in some detail how the candidate meets the criteria for the Fellowship. The nominator should also provide: 1) A list of the candidate's published work, accompanied by copies of reviews, where possible. 2) Three copies of the outline of the current novel in progress, together with 50-75 pages of the text. Picture books are not eligible. 3) On a separate piece of paper, a brief description of the candidate's recent earnings and a statement about why monetary support will make a particular difference in the applicant's writing life at this time. If the candidate is married or living with a domestic partner, please include a brief description of total family income and expenses. Awards $5,000.

POCKETS FICTION-WRITING CONTEST

P.O. Box 340004, Nashville TN 37203-0004. (615)340-7333. **Fax:** (615)340-7267. **E-mail:** pockets@upperroom.org; theupperroommagazine@upperroom.org. **Website:** www.pockets.upperroom.org. **Contact:** Lynn W. Gilliam, senior editor. *Pockets* is a devotional magazine for children between the ages of 6 and 11. Contest offered annually for unpublished work to discover new children's writers. Prize: $1,000 and publication in *Pockets*. Categories: short stories. Judged by *Pockets* staff and staff of other Upper Room Publications. No entry fee. Guidelines available on website or send #10 SASE. **Deadline: Must be postmarked between March 1-August 15.** Entries must be unpublished. Because the purpose of the contest is to discover new writers, previous winners are not eligible. No violence, science fiction, romance, fantasy or talking animal stories. Word length 1,000-1,600 words. Open to any writer. Winner announced November 1 and notified by U.S. mail. Contest submissions accompanied by SASE will be returned Nov. 1. "Send SASE with 4 first-class stamps to request guidelines and a past issue, or go to: http://pockets.upperroom.org."

MICHAEL L. PRINTZ AWARD

Young Adult Library Services Association, Division of the American Library Association, 50 E. Huron, Chicago IL 60611. **Fax:** (312)280-5276. **E-mail:** yalsa@ala.org. **Website:** www.ala.org/yalsa/printz. Annual award. The Michael L. Printz Award is an award for a book that exemplifies literary excellence in young adult literature. It is named for a Topeka, Kansas school librarian who was a long-time active member of the Young Adult Library Services Association. It will be selected annually by an award committee that can also name as many as 4 honor books. The award-winning book can be fiction, nonfiction, poetry or an anthology, and can be a work of joint authorship or editorship. The books must be published between January 1 and December 31 of the preceding year and be designated by its publisher as being either a young adult book or one published for the age range that YALSA defines as young adult, e.g. ages 12 through 18. The deadline for both committee and field nominations will be December 1.

QUILL AND SCROLL INTERNATIONAL WRITING/PHOTO CONTEST

School of Journalism, Univ. of Iowa, 100 Adler Journalism Bldg., Iowa City IA 52242-2004. (319)335-3457. **Fax:** (319)335-3989. **E-mail:** quill-scroll@uiowa.edu; vanessa-shelton@uiowa.edu. **Website:** www.uiowa. edu/~quill-sc. **Contact:** Vanessa Shelton, contest director. **Open to students.** Annual contest. Previously published submissions only. Submissions made by the author or school newspaper adviser. Must be published within the last year. Deadline for entries: February 5. Visit website for more information and entry forms. Entry fee is $2/entry. Engraved plaque awarded to sweepstakes winners. Judging by various judges. *Quill and Scroll* acquires the right to publish submitted material in its magazine or website if it is chosen as a winning entry. Requirements for entrants: must be students in grades 9-12 for high school division. Entry form available on website. Winners will receive *Quill and Scroll*'s National Award Gold Key and, if seniors, are eligible to apply for one of the scholarships offered by *Quill and Scroll*. All winning entries are automatically eligible for the International Writing and Photo Sweepstakes Awards. Engraved plaque awarded to sweepstakes winners.

TOMÁS RIVERA MEXICAN AMERICAN CHILDREN'S BOOK AWARD

601 University Dr., San Marcos TX 78666-4613. (512)245-2357. **Website:** http://www.education.tx-state.edu/about/Map-Directions.html. **Contact:** Dr. Jesse Gainer, award director. Competition open to adults. Annual contest. Competition open to adults. Annual contest. Estab. 1995. Purpose of award: "To encourage authors, illustrators and publishers to produce books that authentically reflect the lives of Mexican Americans appropriate for children and young adults in the United States." Unpublished mss not accepted. Submissions made by "any interested individual or publishing company." Must be published during the two years prior to the year of consideration for the appropriate category "Works for Younger Children" or " Works for Older Children." Deadline for entries: November 1 of publication year. Contact Dr. Jesse Gainer for information and send copy of book. No entry fee. Awards $2,000 per book.

☺ SASKATCHEWAN CHILDREN'S LITERATURE AWARD

Saskatchewan Book Awards, Inc., 100-2400 College Ave., Regina SK S4P 0K1 Canada. (306)569-1585. **Fax:** (306)569-4187. **E-mail:** director@bookawards.sk.ca. **Website:** www.bookawards.sk.ca. **Contact:** Executive director, book submissions. Offered annually award. "This award is presented to a Saskatchewan author or pair of authors, or to Saskatchewan author and a Saskatchewan illustrator, for the best book of children's literature, for ages 0-11, judged on the quality of the writing and illustration." Deadline: November 1. Prize: $2,000 (CAD).

✚ SYDNEY TAYLOR BOOK AWARD

Association of Jewish Libraries, P.O. Box 1118, Teaneck NJ 07666. (212)725-5359. **E-mail:** chair@sydneytaylorbookaward.org; heidi@cbiboca.org. **Website:** www.sydneytaylorbookaward.org. **Contact:** Barbara Bietz, chair. Offered annually for work published during the current year. "Given to distinguished contributions to Jewish literature for children. One award for younder readers, one for older readers, and one for teens." Publishers submit books. Deadline: December 31, but we cannot guarantee that books received after December 1 will be considered. Guidelines on website. Awards certificate, cash award, and gold or silver seals for cover of winning book.

SYDNEY TAYLOR MANUSCRIPT COMPETITION

Association of Jewish Libraries, Sydney Taylor Manuscript Award Competition, 204 Park St., Montclair NJ 07042. **E-mail:** stmacajl@aol.com. **Contact:** Aileen Grossberg. **Open to students** and to any unpublished writer of fiction. Annual contest. Estab. 1985. Purpose of the contest: "This competition is for unpublished writers of fiction. Material should be for readers ages 8-11, with universal appeal that will serve to deepen the understanding of Judaism for all children, revealing positive aspects of Jewish life." Unpublished submissions only. Deadline for entries: December 15. Download rules and forms from website. No entry fee. Awards $1,000. Award winner will be notified in April, and the award will be presented at the convention in June. Judging by qualified judges from within the Association of Jewish Libraries. Requirements for entrants: must be an unpublished fiction writer; also, books must range from 64-200 pages in length. "AJL assumes no responsibility for publication, but hopes this cash incentive will serve to encourage new writers of children's stories with Jewish themes for all children."

○ TD CANADIAN CHILDREN'S LITERATURE AWARD

The Canadian Children's Book Centre, 40 Orchard View Blvd., Suite 217, Toronto ON M4R 1B9 Canada. (416)975-0010. **Fax:** (416)975-8970. **Website:** www.bookcentre.ca. "All books, in any genre, written and illustrated by Canadians and for children ages 1-12 are eligible. Only books first published in Canada are eligible for submission. Books must be published between January 1 and December 31 of the previous calendar year. Open to Canadian citizens and/or permanent residents of Canada. To honour the most distinguished book of the year for young people in both English and French." Submission deadline: Mid-December. Prize: Two prizes of $25,000, 1 for English, 1 for French. $10,000 will be divided among the Honour Book English titles and Honour Book French titles, to a maximum of 4; $2,500 shall go to each of the publishers of the English and French grand-prize winning books for promotion and publicity.

RITA WILLIAMS YOUNG ADULT PROSE PRIZE

National League of American Pen Women, Nob Hill, San Francisco Branch, The Webhallow House, 1544 Sweetwood Dr., Broadmoor Vlg. CA 94015. **E-mail:** pennobhill@aol.com. **Website:** www.soulmakingcontest.us. **Contact:** Eileen Malone. **Open to students.** Up to 3,000 words in story, essay, journal entry, creative nonfiction, or memoir by writers in grades 9-12. See judges online at website. Annual prize. Deadline: November 30. Guidelines for SASE or at www.soulmakingcontest.us. Charges $5/entry (make checks payable to NLAPW, Nob Hill Branch) International

entrants please send Travelers Check drawn on a USA bank. Prize: 1st Place: $100; 2nd Place: $50; 3rd Place: $25. Open to any writer in grade 9-12 or equivalent. No e-mail entries or those mailed special delivery, certified or registered will be accepted. Do enclose SASE in your entry package if you wish to receive contest results.

ALICE WOOD MEMORIAL OHIOANA AWARD FOR CHILDREN'S LITERATURE

Ohioana Library Association, 274 E. First Ave., Suite 300, Columbus OH 43201. (614)466-3831. **Fax:** (614)728-6974. **E-mail:** ohioana@ohioana.org. **Website:** www.ohioana.org. **Contact:** Linda R. Hengst. Offered to an author whose body of work has made, and continues to make, a significant contribution to literature for children or young adults, and through their work as a writer, teacher, administrator, and community member, interest in children's literature has been encouraged and children have become involved with reading. Nomination forms for SASE. Recipient must have been born in Ohio or lived in Ohio at least 5 years. Guidelines for SASE. Accepts inquiries by phone and e-mail. Results announced in August or September. Winners notified by letter in May. For contest results, call or e-mail Ohioana Library: Linda Hengst, executive director. Deadline: December 31. Prize is $1,000.

WORK-IN-PROGRESS GRANT

Society of Children's Book Writers and Illustrators (SCBWI), 8271 Beverly Blvd., Los Angeles CA 90048. (323)782-1010. **E-mail:** scbwi@scbwi.org. **Website:** www.scbwi.org. Four grants—one designated specifically for a contemporary novel for young people, one for nonfiction, one for an unpublished writer, one general fiction—to assist SCBWI members in the completion of a specific project. Open to SCBWI members only. Applications received only between February 15 and March 15.

WRITE IT NOW!

SmartWriters.com, 10823 Worthing Ave., San Diego CA 92126-2220. (858)689-2665. **E-mail:** editor@SmartWriters.com. **Website:** www.SmartWriters.com. **Contact:** Roxyanne Young, editorial director. Annual contest. "Our purpose is to encourage new writers and help get their manuscripts into the hands of people who can help further their careers." Unpublished submissions only. Submissions made by author. Deadline for entries: May 1. SASE for contest rules and entry forms; also see website. Entry fee is $15 for initial entry, $10 for additional entries. Awards a cash prize, books about writing, and an editorial review of the winning mss. Judging by published writers and editors. Requirement for entrants: "This contest is open to all writers age 18 and older. There are 5 categories: Young Adult, Mid-grade, Picture Book, Nonfiction, and Illustration."

♻ YOUNG ADULT CANADIAN BOOK AWARD

1150 Morrison Dr., Suite 400, Ottawa ON K2H 8S9 Canada. (613)232-9625. **Fax:** (613)563-9895. **Website:** www.cla.ca. This award recognizes an author of an outstanding English language Canadian book which appeals to young adults between the ages of 13 and 18. To be eligible for consideration, the following must apply; it must be a work of fiction (novel, collection of short stories, or graphic novel), the title must be a Canadian publication in either hardcover or paperback, and the author must be a Canadian citizen or landed immigrant. The award is given annually, when merited, at the Canadian Library Association's annual conference. Established in 1980 by the Young Adult Caucus of the Saskatchewan Library Association. Nominations should be sent by December 31, annually.

GENERAL

⊘ ☯ AUSTRALIAN CHRISTIAN BOOK OF THE YEAR AWARD

Australian Christian Literature Society, c/o SPCK-Australia, P.O. Box 198, Forest Hill Victoria 3131 Australia. **E-mail:** acls@spcka.org.au. **Website:** www.spcka.org.au. **Contact:** Book of the Year coordinator. "Annual contest for an Australian Christian book published between April 1 and March 31." Deadline: March 31. Prize: $2,500 (AUD) and a framed certificate.

JAMIE CAT CALLAN HUMOR PRIZE

Category in the Soul Making Keats Literary Competition, The Webhallow House, 1544 Sweetwood Dr., Broadmoor Village CA 94015-2029. **E-mail:** pennobhill@aol.com. **Website:** www.soulmakingcontest.us. **Contact:** Eileen Malone. "Any form, 2,500 words or less, 1 piece per entry. Previously published material is accepted. Indicate category on cover page. Identify only with 3x5 card. Open annually to any writer." Deadline: November 30. Prize: 1st Place: $100; 2nd Place: $50; 3rd Place: $25.

MLA PRIZE IN UNITED STATES LATINA & LATINO AND CHICANA & CHICANO LITERARY AND CULTURAL STUDIES

Modern Language Association of America, 26 Broadway, 3rd Floor, New York NY 10004-1789. (646)576-5141. **Fax:** (646)458-0030. **E-mail:** awards@mla.org. **Website:** www.mla.org. **Contact:** Coordinator of Book Prizes. Offered in odd-numbered years. Award for an outstanding scholarly study in any language of United States Latina and Latino and Chicana and Chicano literature or culture. *Open to current MLA members only.* Authors or publishers may submit titles. Deadline: May 1. Prize: A cash award, and a certificate to be presented at the Modern Language Association's annual convention in January.

NACUSA YOUNG COMPOSERS' COMPETITION

Box 49256 Barrington Station, Los Angeles CA 90049 United States. (541)765-2406. **E-mail:** nacusa@music-usa.org. **Website:** www.music-usa.org/nacusa. **Contact:** Greg Steinke. Encourages the composition of new American concert hall music. Deadline: October 30. Prize: 1st Prize: $400; 2nd Prize: $100; and possible Los Angeles performances. Applications are judged by a committee of experienced NACUSA composer members.

OHIOANA WALTER RUMSEY MARVIN GRANT

Ohioana Library Association, 274 E. First Ave., Suite 300, Columbus OH 43201. (614)466-3831. **Fax:** (614)728-6974. **E-mail:** ohioana@ohioana.org. **Website:** www.ohioana.org. Award "to encourage young, unpublished writers 30 years of age or younger." Competition for short stories or novels in progress. Prize: $1,000. **No entry fee.** Up to 6 pieces of prose may be submitted; maximum 60 pages, minimum 10 pages double-spaced, 12-point type. **Deadline:** January 31. Entries must be unpublished. Open to unpublished authors born in Ohio or who have lived in Ohio for a minimum of 5 years. Must be 30 years of age or younger. Guidelines for SASE or on website. Winner notified in May or June. Award given in October. **Contact:** Linda Hengst.

PULITZER PRIZES

The Pulitzer Prize Board, Columbia University, 709 Journalism Building, 2950 Broadway, New York NY 10027. (212)854-3841. **E-mail:** pulitzer@www.pulitzer.org. **Website:** www.pulitzer.org. **Contact:** Sig

Gissler, administrator. Journalism in US newspapers and news websites (published daily or weekly), and in letters, drama, and music by Americans. Deadline: December 31 (music); January 25 (journalism); June 15 and October 15 (letters); December 31 (drama). Prize: $10,000.

DAVID RAFFELOCK AWARD FOR PUBLISHING EXCELLENCE

National Writers Association, 10940 S. Parker Rd., #508, Parker CO 80134. (303)841-0246. **Fax:** (303)841-2607. **E-mail:** natlwritersassn@hotmail.com. **Website:** www.nationalwriters.com. **Contact:** Sandy Whelchel. "Contest is offered annually for books published the previous year." Published works only. Open to any writer. Guidelines for SASE, by e-mail or on website. Winners announced in June at the NWAF conference and notified by mail or phone. List of winners available for SASE or visit website. Its purpose is to assist published authors in marketing their works and to reward outstanding published works. Deadline: May 15. Prize: Publicity tour, including airfare, valued at $5,000.

BYRON CALDWELL SMITH AWARD

The University of Kansas, Hall Center for the Humanities, 900 Sunnyside Ave., Lawrence KS 66045. (785)864-4798. **E-mail:** vbailey@ku.edu. **Website:** www.hallcenter.ku.edu. **Contact:** Victor Bailey, director. Offered in odd years. To qualify, applicants must live or be employed in Kansas and have written an outstanding book published within the previous 2 calendar years. Translations are eligible. Guidelines for SASE or online. Deadline: March 1, 2013. Prize: $1,500

TEXAS INSTITUTE OF LETTERS AWARD FOR MOST SIGNIFICANT SCHOLARLY BOOK

The Texas Institute of Letters, P.O. Box 609, Round Rock TX 78680. **E-mail:** tilsecretary@yahoo.com. **Website:** http://texasinstituteofletters.org. Offered annually for submissions published January 1-December 31 of previous year to recognize the writer of the book making the most important contribution to knowledge. Writer must have been born in Texas, have lived in the state at least 2 consecutive years at some time, or the subject matter of the book should be associated with the state. See website for guidelines. Deadline: Visit website for exact date. Prize: $2.500.

FRED WHITEHEAD AWARD FOR DESIGN OF A TRADE BOOK

Texas Institute of Letters, P.O. Box 609, Round Rock TX 78680. **E-mail:** tilsecretary@yahoo.com. **Website:** http://texasinstituteofletters.org. Offered annually for the best design for a trade book. Open to Texas residents or those who have lived in Texas for 2 consecutive years. See website for guidelines. Deadline: Early January; see website for exact date. Prize: $750.

☺ THE WRITERS' TRUST ENGEL/ FINDLEY AWARD

The Writers' Trust of Canada, 90 Richmond St. E., Suite 200, Toronto ON M5C 1P1 Canada. (416)504-8222. **Fax:** (416)504-9090. **E-mail:** info@writerstrust.com. **Website:** www.writerstrust.com. **Contact:** Amanda Hopkins. "The Writers' Trust Engel/Findley Award is presented annually at The Writers' Trust Awards Event, held in Toronto each fall, to a Canadian writer for a body of work in hope of continued contribution to the richness of Canadian literature. Open to Canadian citizens and permanent residents only." Prize: $25,000.

JOURNALISM

THE AMERICAN LEGION FOURTH ESTATE AWARD

The American Legion, 700 N. Pennsylvania, Indianapolis IN 46204. (317)630-1253. **E-mail:** pr@legion.org. **Website:** www.legion.org/presscenter/fourthestate. Offered annually for journalistic works published the previous calendar year. Subject matter must deal with a topic or issue of national interest or concern. Entry must include cover letter explaining entry, and any documenation or evidence of the entry's impact on the community, state, or nation. No printed entry form. Guidelines for SASE or on website. Deadline: February 28. Prize: $2,000 stipend to defray expenses of recipient accepting the award at The American Legion National Convention in August. Members of The National Public Relations Commission of The American Legion.

☺☺ AMY WRITING AWARDS

The Amy Foundation, P.O. Box 16091, Lansing MI 48901. (517)323-6233. **Fax:** (517)321-2572. **E-mail:** amyfoundtn@aol.com. **Website:** www.amyfound.org. "Offered annually to recognize creative, skillful writing that applies biblical principles. Submitted articles must be published in a secular, non-religious publication (either printed or online) and must be reinforced with at least one passage of scripture. The article must have been published between January 1 and December 31 of the current calendar year." Deadline: January 31. Prize: 1st Prize: $10,000; 2nd Prize: $5,000; 3rd Prize: $4,000; 4th Prize: $3,000; 5th Prize: $2,000; and 10 prizes of $1,000.

⊕ STANLEY WALKER AWARD FOR NEWSPAPER JOURNALISM

The Texas Institute of Letters, P.O. Box 609, Round Rock TX 78680. **E-mail:** tilsecretary@yahoo.com. **Website:** http://texasinstituteofletters.org. Offered annually for work published January 1-December 31 of previous year to recognize the best writing appearing in a daily newspaper. Writer must have been born in Texas, have lived in the state for 2 consecutive years at some time, or the subject matter of the article must be associated with the state. See website for guidelines. Deadline: See website for exact date. Prize: $1,000.

TRANSLATION

DER-HOVANESSIAN PRIZE

New England Poetry Club, 654 Green St., No. 2, Cambridge MA 02139. **E-mail:** contests@nepoetryclub.org. **Website:** www.nepoetryclub.org. **Contact:** NEPC contest coordinator. For a translation from any language into English. Send a copy of the original. Funded by John Mahtesian. "Contest open to members and nonmembers. Poems should be typed and submitted in duplicate with author's name, address, phone, and e-mail address of writer on only 1 copy. (Judges receive copies without names.) Copy only. Label poems with contest name. Entries should be sent by regular mail only. Special delivery or signature required mail will be returned by the post office. Entries should be original, unpublished poems in English. No poem should be entered in more than 1 contest, nor have won a previous contest. No entries will be returned. NEPC will not engage in correspondence regarding poems or contest decisions." Deadline: May 31. Prize: $250. Judges are well-known poets and sometimes winners of previous NEPC contests.

FENIA AND YAAKOV LEVIANT MEMORIAL PRIZE IN YIDDISH STUDIES

Modern Language Association of America, 26 Broadway, 3rd Floor, New York NY 10004-1789. (646)576-5141. **Fax:** (646)458-0030. **E-mail:** awards@mla.org. **Website:** www.mla.org. **Contact:** Coordinator of book prizes. This prize is to honor, in alternating years, an outstanding English translation of a Yiddish literary work or an outstanding scholarly work in any language in the field of Yiddish. Offered in even-numbered years. Open to MLA members and nonmembers. Authors or publishers may submit titles. Guidelines for SASE or by e-mail. Deadline: May 1. Prize: A cash prize, and a certificate, to be presented at the Modern Language Association's annual convention in January.

SOEURETTE DIEHL FRASER AWARD FOR BEST TRANSLATION OF A BOOK

P.O. Box 609, Round Rock TX 78680. **E-mail:** tilsecretary@yahoo.com. **Website:** http://texasinstituteofletters.org. Offered every 2 years to recognize the best translation of a literary book into English. Translator must have been born in Texas or have lived in the state for at least 2 consecutive years at some time. Deadline: Early January; see website for exact date. Prize: $1,000.

✪ GOVERNOR GENERAL'S LITERARY AWARD FOR TRANSLATION

Canada Council for the Arts, 350 Albert St., P.O. Box 1047, Ottawa ON K1P 5V8 Canada. (613)566-4414, ext. 5573. **Fax:** (613)566-4410. **Website:** www.canadacouncil.ca/prizes/ggla. Offered for the best English-language and the best French-language work of translation by a Canadian. Publishers submit titles for consideration Deadline depends on the book's publication date. Books in English: March 15, June 1, or August 7. Books in French: March 15 or July 15. Prize: Each laureate receives $25,000; non-winning finalists receive $1,000.

PEN AWARD FOR POETRY IN TRANSLATION

PEN American Center, 588 Broadway, Suite 303, New York NY 10012. (212)334-1660, ext. 108. **E-mail:** awards@pen.org. **Website:** www.pen.org. **Contact:** Literary awards manager. This award recognizes book-length translations of poetry from any language into English, published during the current calendar year. All books must have been published in the US. Translators may be of any nationality. US residency/citizenship not required. Nominations must be received between October 1, 2012 and February 1, 2013. Early submissions are strongly recommended. Three copies of book-length translations published between

January 1, 2012 and December 31, 2012, may be submitted by publishers, agents, or the translators themselves. Self-published books are not eligible. Books with more than 2translators are not eligible. How to submit: 1) Pay the $50 entry fee online and proceed to checkout. If paying by check, skip to step 2. 2) Fill out the online submission form and click "Submit Form." 3) Mail 1 copy of the candidate's book, your printed submission form, and proof of online payment or a check to above address. Deadline: February 1. Prize: $3,000. Judged by a single translator of poetry appointed by the PEN Translation Committee.

PEN TRANSLATION PRIZE

PEN American Center, 588 Broadway, Suite 303, New York NY 10012. (212)334-1660, ext. 108. **Fax:** (212)334-2181. **E-mail:** awards@pen.org. **Contact:** Literary Awards coordinator. Offered for a literary book-length translation into English published in the calendar year. No technical, scientific, or reference books. Publishers, agents, or translators may submit 3 copies of each eligible title. All eligible titles must have been published in the US. Self-published books are not eligible. 1) Pay the $50 entry fee online and proceed to checkout. If paying by check, skip to step 2. 2) Fill out the online submission form and click "Submit Form." 3) Mail 3 copies of the candidate's book, your printed submission form, and proof of online payment or a check. Nominations must be received between October 1, 2012 and February 1, 2013. Early submissions are strongly recommended. Prize: $3,000 .

LOIS ROTH AWARD FOR A TRANSLATION OF A LITERARY WORK

Modern Language Association, 26 Broadway, 3rd Floor, New York NY 10004-1789. (646)576-5141. **Fax:** (646)458-0030. **E-mail:** awards@mla.org. **Website:** www.mla.org. **Contact:** Coordinator of Book Prizes. Offered every 2 years (odd years) for an outstanding translation into English of a book-length literary work published the previous year. Translators need not be members of the MLA. Deadline: April 1. Prize: A cash award and a certificate to be presented at the Modern Language Association's annual convention in January.

ALDO AND JEANNE SCAGLIONE PRIZE FOR A TRANSLATION OF A LITERARY WORK

Modern Language Association, 26 Broadway, 3rd Floor, New York NY 10004-1789. (646)576-5141. **Fax:** (646)458-0030. **E-mail:** awards@mla.org. **Website:**

www.mla.org. **Contact:** Coordinator of Book Prizes. Offered in even-numbered years for the translation of a book-length literary work appearing in print during the previous year. Translators need not be members of the MLA. Deadline: April 1. Prize: A cash award and a certificate to be presented at the Modern Language Association's annual convention in January.

ALDO AND JEANNE SCAGLIONE PRIZE FOR A TRANSLATION OF A SCHOLARLY STUDY OF LITERATURE

Modern Language Association of America, 26 Broadway, 3rd Floor, New York NY 10004-1789. (646)576-5141. **Fax:** (646)458-0030. **E-mail:** awards@mla.org. **Website:** www.mla.org. **Contact:** Coordinator of Book Prizes. Offered in odd-numbered years for an outstanding translation into English of a book-length work of literary history, literary criticism, philology, or literary theory published during the previous biennium. Translators need not be members of the MLA. Deadline: May 1. Prize: A cash award and a certificate to be presented at the Modern Language Association's annual convention in January.

POETRY

☉ ACORN-PLANTOS AWARD FOR PEOPLES POETRY

Acorn-Plantos Award Committee, 36 Sunset Ave., Hamilton ON L8R 1V6 Canada. **E-mail:** jeffseff@allstream.net. **Contact:** Jeff Seffinga. "Annual contest for work that appeared in print in the previous calender year. This award is given to the Canadian poet who best (through the publication of a book of poems) exemplifies populist or peoples poetry in the tradition of Milton Acorn, Ted Plantos, et al. Work may be entered by the poet or the publisher; the award goes to the poet. Entrants must submit 5 copies of each title. Poet must be a citizen of Canada or a landed immigrant. Publisher need not be Canadian." Deadline: June 30. Prize: $500 (CDN) and a medal. Judged by a panel of poets in the tradition who are not entered in the current year.

AKRON POETRY PRIZE

The University of Akron Press, 120 E. Mill St., Suite 415, Akron OH 44308. (330)972-5342. **Fax:** (330)972-8364. **E-mail:** uapress@uakron.edu; marybid@uakron.edu. **Website:** www3.uakron.edu/uapress/poetryprize.html. Offers annual award of $1,500 plus publication of a book-length ms. Submissions must be unpublished. Considers simultaneous submissions (with notification of acceptance elsewhere). Submit 48 or more pages, typed, single-spaced; optional self-addressed postcard for confirmation. Mss will not be returned. Do not send mss bound or enclosed in covers. See website for complete guidelines. **Entry fee:** $25. **Deadline:** Entries accepted May 1-June 15 only. Competition receives 500+ entries. 2011 winner was Emily Rosko for *Prop Rockery*. 2012 judge: Dara Wier. Winner posted on website by September 30. "Intimate friends, relatives, current and former students of the final judge (students in an academic, degree-conferring program or its equivalent) are not eligible to enter the 2013 Akron Poetry Prize competition." **Contact:** Mary Biddinger, editor/award director.

ANNUAL GIVAL PRESS OSCAR WILDE AWARD

Gival Press, LLC, P.O. Box 3812, Arlington VA 22203. (703)351-0079. **E-mail:** givalpress@yahoo.com. **Website:** www.givalpress.com. **Contact:** Robert L. Giron. "Award given to the best previously unpublished original poem—written in English of any length, in any style, typed, double-spaced on 1 side only—which best relates gay/lesbian/bisexual/transgendered life, by a poet who is 18 years or older. Entrants are asked to submit their poems without any kind of identification (with the exception of titles) and with a separate cover page with the following information: name, address (street, city, and state with zip code), telephone number, e-mail address (if available), and a list of poems by title. Checks drawn on American banks should be made out to Gival Press, LLC." Deadline: June 27 (postmarked). Prize: $100 and the poem, along with information about the poet, will be published on the Gival Press website.

⊘ ANNUAL WORLD HAIKU COMPETITION & ANNUAL WORLD TANKA CONTEST

P.O. Box 17331, Arlington VA 22216. **E-mail:** lpezinesubmissions@gmail.com. **Website:** http://lyricalpassionpoetry.yolasite.com. **Contact:** Raquel D. Bailey. Contest is open to all writers. Requires first rights for all previously unpublished works. "Promotes Japanese short form poetry." Deadline: November 30, 2012. (Dates are subject to change each year. See website for details.). Prize: Monetary compensation and publication. Judged by experienced editors and award-winning writers from the contemporary writing community.

THE PATRICIA BIBBY FIRST BOOK AWARD

Tebot Bach, P.O. Box 7887, Huntington Beach CA 92615-7887. **E-mail:** mifanwy@tebotbach.org. **Website:** www.tebotbach.org. **Contact:** Mifanwy Kaiser. The Patricia Bibby First Book Award offers $1,000 and publication of a book-length poetry ms by Tebot Bach (see separate listing in Book/Chapbook Publishers). Open to "all poets writing in English who have not committed to publishing collections of poetry of 36 poems or more in editions of over 400 copies." Complete guidelines available by e-mail or on website. Deadline: October 31 (postmark), annually. Judges are selected annually. Winner announced each year in April.

BLUE MOUNTAIN ARTS/SPS STUDIOS POETRY CARD CONTEST

P.O. Box 1007, Boulder CO 80306. (303)449-0536. **Fax:** (303)447-0939. **E-mail:** poetrycontest@sps.com. **Website:** www.sps.com. "We're looking for original poetry that is rhyming or non-rhyming, although we find that non-rhyming poetry reads better. Poems may also be considered for possible publication on greeting cards or in book anthologies. Contest is offered biannually. Guidelines available online." Deadline: December 31 and June 30. Prize: 1st Place: $300; 2nd Place: $150; 3rd Place: $50. Blue Mountain Arts editorial staff.

THE FREDERICK BOCK PRIZE

Poetry, 61 W. Superior St., Chicago IL 60654. (312)787-7070. **E-mail:** poetry@poetrymagazine.org. **Website:** www.poetrymagazine.org. Offered annually for poems published in *Poetry* during the preceding year (October through September). Upon acceptance, *Poetry* licenses exclusive worldwide first serial rights, including electronic rights, for publication, as well as non-exclusive rights to reprint, reuse, and archive the work, in any format, in perpetuity. Copyright reverts to author upon first publication. Any writer may submit poems to *Poetry*. Prize: $500

BARBARA BRADLEY PRIZE

New England Poetry Club, 654 Green St., No. 2, Cambridge MA 02139 . **E-mail:** contests@nepoetryclub.org. **Website:** www.nepoetryclub.org. **Contact:** NEPC contest coordinator. For a lyric poem under 21 lines, written by a woman. "Contest open to members and nonmembers. Poems should be typed and submitted in duplicate with author's name, address, phone, and e-mail address of writer on only 1 copy. (Judges receive copies without names.) Copy only. Label poems with contest name. Entries should be sent by regular mail only. Special delivery or signature required mail will be returned by the post office. Entries should be original, unpublished poems in English. No poem should be entered in more than 1 contest, nor have won a previous contest. No entries will be returned. NEPC will not engage in correspondence regarding poems or contest decisions." Deadline: May 31. Prize: $200. Judges are well-known poets and sometimes winners of previous NEPC contests.

⊕ BRICK ROAD POETRY BOOK CONTEST

Brick Road Poetry Press, Inc., P.O. Box 751, Columbus GA 31902. (706)649-3080. **Fax:** (706)649-3094. **E-mail:** editor@brickroadpoetrypress.com. **Website:** www.brickroadpoetrypress.com. Offers annual award. The 1st Prize winner will receive a publication contract with Brick Road Poetry Press, $1,000, and 25 copies of the printed book. The winning book will be published in both print and e-book formats. "We may also offer publication contracts to the top finalists." Submissions must be unpublished as a collection, but individual poems may have been previously published elsewhere. Submit 70-100 pages of poetry. Guidelines available by e-mail or online. **Entry fee:** $25. **Deadline:** November 1. Competition receives 150 entries/year. Judged by Ron Self and Keith Badowski. Winners notified February 15. Copies of winning books available for $15.95. "The mission of Brick Road Poetry Press is to publish and promote poetry that entertains, amuses, edifies and surprises a wide audience of appreciative readers. We are not qualified to judge who deserves to be published, so we concentrate on publishing what we enjoy. Our preference is for poetry geared toward dramatizing the human experience in a language rich with sensory image and metaphor, recognizing that poetry can be, at one and the same time, both familiar as the perspiration of daily labor and outrageous as a carnival sideshow." **Contact:** Ron Self and Keith Badowski, co-editors/founders.

BRIGHT HILL PRESS POETRY CHAPBOOK AWARD

Bright Press Hill & Literary Center, P.O. Box 193, 94 Church St., Treadwell NY 13846. (607)829-5055. **E-mail:** brighthillpress@stny.rr.com. **Website:** www. brighthillpress.org. The annual Bright Hill Press Chapbook Award offers $300, publication of a chap-book-length ms, and 25 author's copies. Guidelines available for SASE, by e-mail, or on website. Submissions must be unpublished as a collection, but individual poems may have been previously published elsewhere. Considers simultaneous submissions if Bright Hill Press is notified of acceptance elsewhere. Submit 16-24 pages of poetry, paginated and secured with bulldog or spring clip. Include bio, table of contents, and acknowledgments page. Include 2 title pages: 1 with ms title, poet's name, address, and phone number; 1 with ms title only. Include SASE for results only; mss will not be returned. Multiple entries accepted with separate fee for each. Competition receives over 300 entries/year. Copies of winning chapbooks available from Bright Hill Press (see website); include with entry only a 5x7 SASE with $1.31 postage affixed and receive a free copy of a recent winning Bright Hill Press poetry chapbook. Deadline: July 31 (postmark).

BRITTINGHAM PRIZE IN POETRY; FELIX POLLAK PRIZE IN POETRY

University of Wisconsin Press, Department of English, 600 N. Park St., University of Wisconsin, Madison WI 53706. **E-mail:** rwallace@wisc.edu. **Website:** www.wisc.edu/wisconsinpress/poetryguide.html. **Contact:** Ronald Wallace, contest director. Offered for unpublished book-length mss of original poetry. Submissions must be received by the press during the month of September, accompanied by a required SASE for contest results. Does not return mss. One entry fee covers both prizes. Guidelines for SASE or online. 2012 Brittingham Prize winner was Jazzy Danziger, *Darkroom*. Prize: $2,500 ($1,000 cash prize and $1,500 honorarium for campus reading) and publication of the 2 winning mss.

CAKETRAIN CHAPBOOK COMPETITION

P.O. Box 82588, Pittsburgh PA 15218. **E-mail:** caketrainjournal@hotmail.com. **Website:** www.caketrain.org/competitions. Annual chapbook contest sponsored by *Caketrain* literary journal. Can submit by mail with SASE or by e-mail. See website for guidelines. Winner receives a $250 cash prize and 25 copies of their chapbook. **Entry fee:** $15 for reading fee only or $20 for entry fee and copy of winning chapbook. **Deadline:** October 1. Recent winners include Claire Hero's *afterpastures* (2008); Tina May Hall's *All the Day's Sad Stories* (2009); Ben Mirov's *Ghost Machine* (2010); Sarah Rose Etter's *Tongue Party* (2011); and Meredith Stricker's *Mistake* (2012). .

THE CENTER FOR BOOK ARTS POETRY CHAPBOOK COMPETITION

The Center for Book Arts, 28 W. 27th St., 3rd Floor, New York NY 10001. (212)481-0295. **Fax:** (866)708-8994. **E-mail:** info@centerforbookarts.org. **Website:** www.centerforbookarts.org. Contest needs poetry chapbooks. Offered annually for unpublished collections of poetry. Individual poems may have been previously published. Collection must not exceed 500 lines or 24 pages (does not include cover page, title pages, table of contents, or acknowledgements pages). Copies of winning chapbooks available through website. "The cover page should contain, on a single detachable page, the ms title and author's name, along with address, phone number, and e-mail. The author's name should not appear anywhere else. A second title page should be provided without the author's name or other identification. Please provide a table of contents and a separate acknowledgements page containing prior magazine or anthology publication of individual poems. Mss should be bound with a simple spring clip. Poems may have appeared in journals or anthologies but not as part of a book-length collection. Competition is open to all poets writing in English who have published no more than 2 full-length books. Poets may not have studied with either judge in a degree-granting program for the last 5 years. "Center for Book Arts is a nonprofit organization dedicated to the traditional crafts of bookmaking and contemporary interpretations of the book as an art object. Through the Center's Education, Exhibition, and Workspace Programs, we ensure that the ancient craft of the book remains a viable and vital part of our civilization." Deadline: December 1 (postmarked). Prize: $500 award, $500 honorarium for a reading, publication, and 10 copies of chapbook. 2012 judges were Phillis Levin and Sharon Dolin.

CIDER PRESS REVIEW BOOK AWARD

P.O. Box 33384, San Diego CA 92163. **E-mail:** editor@ciderpressreview.com. **Website:** http://ciderpressreview.com/bookaward. **Contact:** Contest director. Annual award from *Cider Press Review*. Submissions must be unpublished as a collection, but individual poems may have been previously published elsewhere. Submit book-length ms of 48-80 pages. "Submissions can be made online using the submission form on the website or by mail. If sending by mail, include 2 cover sheets—1 with title, author's name, and complete contact information; and 1 with title only, all bound with a spring clip. Check website for change of address coming in the future. Include SASE for results only if no email address included; notification via email and on the website; manuscripts cannot be returned. Online submissions must be in Word for PC or PDF format, and should not include title page with author's name. The editors strongly urge contestants to use online delivery if possible." Review the complete submission guidelines and learn more online at website. Deadline: submit September 1 - November 30 (postmark). Prize: $1,500, publication, and 25 author's copies of a book length collection of poetry. Author receives a standard publishing contract. Initial print run is not less than 1,000 copies. CPR acquires first publication rights. 2012 judge was Gray Jacobik. The 2011 winner was Joseph Fasano.

CLOCKWISE CHAPBOOK AWARD

Tebot Bach, 20592 Minerva Lane, Huntington Beach CA 92646. (714)968-0905. **Fax:** (714)968-4677. **E-mail:** mifanwy@tebotbach.org. **Website:** www.tebotbach.org. **Contact:** Gail Wrongsky. Must be previously unpublished poetry for the full collection; individual poems may have been published. Purpose of award is to honor the winning entry. Deadline: April 30. Prize: $500 award, chapbook publication. Judged by Gail Wronsky.

THE COLORADO PRIZE FOR POETRY

Colorado Review/Center for Literary Publishing, Department of English, Colorado State University, 9105 Campus Delivery, Ft. Collins CO 80523-9105. (970)491-5449. **E-mail:** creview@colostate.edu. **Website:** http://coloradoprize.colostate.edu. The annual Colorado Prize for Poetry awards an honorarium of $2,000 and publication of a book-length ms. Submission must be unpublished as a collection, but individual poems may have been published elsewhere. Submit mss of 48-100 pages of poetry (no set minimum or maximum) on any subject, in any form, double- or single-spaced. Include 2 titles pages: 1 with ms title only, the other with ms title and poet's name, address, and phone number. Enclosed SASP for notification of receipt and SASE for results; mss will not be returned. Guidelines available for SASE or by e-mail. **Entry fee:** $25; includes 1-year subscription to *Colorado Review*. **Deadline:** January 14. Winner was Eric Baus. 2011 judge was Cole Swensen. **Contact:** Stephanie G'Schwind, editor.

⊕ CPR EDITOR'S PRIZE BOOK AWARD

P.O. Box 33384, San Diego CA 92163. **E-mail:** editor@ciderpressreview.com. **Website:** http://ciderpressreview.com/bookaward. **Contact:** Contest director. Annual award from *Cider Press Review*. Submissions must be unpublished as a collection, but individual poems may have been previously published elsewhere. Submit book-length ms of 48-80 pages. "Submissions can be made online using the submission form on the website or by mail. If sending by mail, include 2 cover sheets—1 with title, author's name, and complete contact information; and 1 with title only, all bound with a spring clip. Check website for change of address coming in the future. Include SASE for results only if no email address included; notification via email and on the website; manuscripts cannot be returned. Online submissions must be in Word for PC or PDF format, and should not include title page with author's name. The editors strongly urge contestants to use online delivery if possible." Review the complete submission guidelines and learn more online at website. Deadline: submit April 1 - June 30 (postmark). Prize: $1,000, publication, and 25 author's copies of a book length collection of poetry. Author receives a standard publishing contract. Initial print run is not less than 1,000 copies. CPR acquires first publication rights. Judged by *Cider Press Review* editors.

CRAB ORCHARD SERIES IN POETRY FIRST BOOK AWARD

Department of English, Mail Code 4503, Faner Hall 2380, Southern Illinois University of Carbondale, Carbondale IL 62901. **E-mail:** jtribble@siu.edu. **Website:** www.craborchardreview.siu.edu. **Contact:** Jon Tribble, series editor. Annual award. 2011 winner was Tyler Mills (*Tongue Lyre*). "Mss should be 50-75 pages of original poetry, in English, by a US citizen or permanent resident who has neither published, nor committed to publish, a volume of poetry 40 pages or more in length (individual poems may have been previously published). Current students and employees of Southern Illinois University and authors published by Southern Illinois University Press are not eligible." See guidelines for complete formatting instructions. Guidelines available for SASE or on website. Deadline: See guidelines or check website. Prize: Offers $2,500 ($1,000 prize plus $1,500 honorarium for a reading at Southern Illinois University Carbondale) and publication.

CRAB ORCHARD SERIES IN POETRY OPEN COMPETITION AWARDS

Department of English, Mail Code 4503, Faner Hall 2380, Southern Illinois University at Carbondale, Carbondale IL 62901. **E-mail:** jtribble@siu.edu. **Website:** www.craborchardreview.siu.edu. **Contact:** Jon Tribble, series editor. Annual competition. 2011 winners were Jacob Shores-Arguello ("In the Absence of Clocks") and Wally Swist ("Huang Po and the Dimensions of Love"). Submissions must be unpublished as a collection, but individual poems may have been previously published elsewhere. Considers simultaneous submissions, but series editor must be informed immediately upon acceptance. Mss should be typewritten or computer-generated (letter quality only; no dot matrix), single-spaced; clean photocopy is recommended as mss are not returned. See guidelines for complete formatting instructions. Guidelines available for SASE or on website. Deadline: See guidelines or check website. Prize: Offers 2 winners $3,500 and publication of a book-length ms. Cash prize totals reflect a $1,500 honorarium for each winner for a reading at Southern Illinois University Carbondale. Publication contract is with Southern Illinois University Press.

THE ROBERT DANA ANHINGA PRIZE FOR POETRY

Anhinga Press, P.O. Box 3665, Tallahassee FL 32315. (850)442-1408. **Fax:** (850)442-6323. **E-mail:** info@anhinga.org. **Website:** www.anhinga.org. **Contact:** Rick Campbell, poetry editor. Offered annually for a book-length collection of poetry by an author who has not published more than 1 book of poetry. Guidelines for SASE or on website. Open to any writer writing in English. Deadline: February 15-May 1. Prize: $2,000, and publication Past judges include Donald Hall, Joy Harjo, Robert Dana, Mark Jarman, and Tony Hoagland. Past winners include Frank X. Gaspar, Earl S. Braggs, Julia Levine, Keith Ratzlaff, and Lynn Aarti Chandhok, and Rhett Iseman Trull.

T.S. ELIOT PRIZE FOR POETRY

Truman State University Press, 100 E. Normal Ave., Kirksville MO 63501-4221. (660)785-7336. **Fax:** (660)785-4480. **E-mail:** tsup@truman.edu. **Website:** tsup.truman.edu. **Contact:** Nancy Rediger. Offers annual award of $2,000 and publication. "The manuscript may include individual poems previously published in journals or anthologies, but may not include a significant number of poems from a published chapbook or self-published book." Submit 60-100 pages. Include 2 title pages: 1 with poet's name, address, phone number, and ms title; the other with ms title only. Include SASE for acknowledgment of ms receipt only; mss will not be returned. Guidelines available for SASE or on website. Competition receives about 500 entries/year. 2012 winner was David Livewell (*Shackamaxon*). Deadline: October 31. 2012 judge: Sandra McPherson.

⊕ FALL POETRY CHAPBOOK CONTEST

White Eagle Coffee Store Press, P.O. Box 383, Fox River Grove IL 60021-0383. (847)639-9200. **E-mail:** wecspress@aol.com. **Website:** whiteeaglecoffeestorepress.com. **Contact:** Frank Edmund Smith, publisher. Collection as a whole must be unpublished, though individual poems can be previously published. Credit to original publication must be given. "This contest is designed to promote and reward the writing of a small collection of poetry—20-22 pages. Typically, poets wish to publish chapbooks early in their careers, as a way of marking an achievement and having inexpensive books to sell at poetry readings. Many poets continue to publish chapbooks throughout their careers. This press especially welcomes writers of any age who have just begun to publish, but it is open to more successful writers, too." Deadline: October 31. Prize: Publication, $500, and 25 copies of the published chapbook; 10 copies for press kits. All contest entrants receive a copy of the book. "The final judge is always announced and is someone who has already published with the press, usually a previous contest winner. Thus, the press is always open to new styles and new writers. Author maintains copyright. White Eagle Coffee Store Press acquires first publishing rights and the exclusive right to print and reprint the chapbook."

JANICE FARRELL POETRY PRIZE

Category in the Soul Making Keats Literary Competition, The Webhallow House, 1544 Sweetwood Dr., Broadmoor Village CA 94015-2029. **E-mail:** pennobhill@aol.com. **Website:** www.soulmakingcontest.us. "Poetry may be double- or single-spaced. One-page poems only, and only 1 poem/page. All poems must be titled. Three poems/entry. Indicate category on each poem. Identify with 3x5 card only. Open to all writers." $5/entry (make checks payable to NLAPW). **Deadline:** November 30 (annually). **Prizes:** 1st Place:

$100; 2nd Place: $50; 3rd Place: $25. Judged by a local San Francisco successfully published poet. **Contact:** Eileen Malone.

FIELD POETRY PRIZE

Oberlin College Press/FIELD, 50 N. Professor St., Oberlin OH 44074. (440)775-8408. **Fax:** (440)775-8124. **E-mail:** oc.press@oberlin.edu. **Website:** www.oberlin.edu/ocpress/prize.htm. The annual FIELD Poetry Prize for a book-length collection of poems offers $1,000 and publication in the FIELD Poetry Series. Mss of 50-80 pages must be submitted during May through our online submissions manager. See our website for details. Entry Fee: $28; includes one-year subscription to FIELD: Contemporary Poetry and Poetics. **Deadline:** submit during May only. 2011 winner was Mark Neely (Beasts of the Hill). **Contact:** Drew Krewer, managing editor.

THE FINCH PRIZE FOR POETRY

The National Poetry Review, P.O. Box 2080, Aptos CA 95001-2080. **E-mail:** editor@nationalpoetry review.com. **Website:** www.nationalpoetryreview.com. **Contact:** C.J. Sage, editor. The Finch Prize for Poetry offers $500 plus publication in *The National Poetry Review*. All entries will be considered by the editor for publication. 2011 winner was Susan Rothbard. Submissions must be unpublished and uncommitted. Considers simultaneous submissions, "but if the work is selected by *The National Poetry Review* for the prize or for publication, it must be withdrawn from elsewhere unless you have withdrawn it from us 2 weeks before our acceptance." Submit up to 3 poems/entry (10 pages maximum per group of 3). Include cover letter with bio and contact information, including e-mail address for results. Complete guidelines available on website. Deadline: June 30 (postmark).

FIRMAN HOUGHTON PRIZE

New England Poetry Club, 654 Green St., No. 2, Cambridge MA 02139 . **E-mail:** contests@nepoetryclug.org. **Website:** www.nepoetryclub.org. **Contact:** NEPC contest coordinator. For a lyric poem in honor of the former president of NEPC. "Contest open to members and nonmembers. Poems should be typed and submitted in duplicate with author's name, address, phone, and e-mail address of writer on only 1 copy. (Judges receive copies without names.) Copy only. Label poems with contest name. Entries should be sent by regular mail only. Special delivery or signature required mail will be returned by the post office. Entries should be original, unpublished poems in English. No poem should be entered in more than 1 contest, nor have won a previous contest. No entries will be returned. NEPC will not engage in correspondence regarding poems or contest decisions." Deadline: May 31. Prize: $250. Judges are well-known poets and sometimes winners of previous NEPC contests.

GERTRUDE PRESS POETRY CHAPBOOK CONTEST

P.O. Box 83948, Portland OR 97283. **E-mail:** editor@gertrudepress.org. **Website:** www.gertrudepress.org. Gertrude Press (see separate listing in Books/Chapbooks) sponsors an annual chapbook competition. Individual poems may have been previously published; unpublished poems are welcome. Submit 16-20 pages of poetry (electronic submissions preferred, but postal submissions accepted). "Poetry may be of any subject matter, and writers from all backgrounds are encouraged to submit." Include list of acknowledgments and cover letter indicating how poet learned of the contest. Include 1 title page with identifying information and 1 without. Guidelines available in *Gertrude*, for SASE, by e-mail, or on website. Deadline: April 15. Prize: Offers $100, publication, and 50 author copies (out of a press run of 200) to the winning poet.

ALLEN GINSBERG POETRY AWARDS

The Poetry Center at Passaic County Community College, One College Blvd., Paterson NJ 07505-1179. (973)684-6555. **Fax:** (973)523-6085. **E-mail:** mgillan@pccc.edu. **Website:** www.pccc.edu/poetry. The Allen Ginsberg Poetry Awards offer annual prizes of 1st Prize: $1,000; 2nd Prize: $200; and 3rd Prize: $100. All winning poems, honorable mentions, and editor's choice poems will be published in *Paterson Literary Review*. Winners will be asked to participate in a reading that will be held in the Paterson Historic District. Submissions must be unpublished. Submit up to 5 poems (no poem more than 2 pages long). Send 4 copies of each poem entered. Include cover sheet with poet's name, address, phone number, e-mail address and poem titles. Poet's name should not appear on poems. Include SASE for results only; poems will not be returned. Guidelines available for SASE or on website. **Entry fee:** $18 (includes subscription to *Paterson Literary Review*). Write "poetry contest" in memo section of check and make payable to PCCC. **Deadline:** April 1 (postmark). Winners will be announced the following summer by mail and in newspaper an-

nouncements. 2011 winners: Christopher Bursk and Charlotte Muse (1st); Mark Hillringhouse and Sander Zulauf (2nd); and Antoinette Libro (3rd). **Contact:** Maria Mazziotti Gillan, executive director.

GIVAL PRESS POETRY AWARD

Gival Press, LLC, P.O. Box 3812, Arlington VA 22203. (703)351-0079. **E-mail:** givalpress@yahoo.com. **Website:** www.givalpress.com. **Contact:** Robert L. Giron, editor. "Offered annually for a previously unpublished poetry collection as a complete ms, which may include previously published poems; previously published poems must be acknowledged, and poet must hold rights. The competition seeks to award well-written, original poetry in English on any topic, in any style. Guidelines for SASE, by e-mail, or online. Entrants are asked to submit their poems without any kind of identification (with the exception of the titles) and with a separate cover page with the following information: Name, address (street, city, state, and zip code), telephone number, e-mail address (if available), short bio, and a list of the poems by title. Checks drawn on American banks should be made out to Gival Press, LLC." Deadline: December 15 (postmarked). Prize: $1,000, publication, and 20 author's copies. The editor narrows entries to the top 10; previous winner selects top 5 and chooses the winner—all done anonymously.

GOLDEN ROSE AWARD

New England Poetry Club, 654 Green St., No. 2, Cambridge MA 02139. **Website:** www.nepoetryclub.org. **Contact:** NEPC contest coordinator. "Given annually to the poet who has done the most for the art in the previous year or in a lifetime. Chosen by board." "Contest open to members and nonmembers. Poems should be typed and submitted in duplicate with author's name, address, phone, and e-mail address of writer on only 1 copy. (Judges receive copies without names.) Copy only. Label poems with contest name. Entries should be sent by regular mail only. Special delivery or signature required mail will be returned by the post office. Entries should be original, unpublished poems in English. No poem should be entered in more than 1 contest, nor have won a previous contest. No entries will be returned. NEPC will not engage in correspondence regarding poems or contest decisions." May 31. Judges are well-known poets and sometimes winners of previous NEPC contests.

◯ GOVERNOR GENERAL'S LITERARY AWARD FOR POETRY

Canada Council for the Arts, 350 Albert St., P.O. Box 1047, Ottawa ON K1P 5V8 Canada. (613)566-4414, ext. 5573. **Fax:** (613)566-4410. **Website:** www.canadacouncil.ca/prizes/ggla. Offered for the best English-language and the best French-language work of poetry by a Canadian. Publishers submit titles for consideration. Deadline depends on the book's publication date. Books in English: March 15, June 1, or August 7. Books in French: March 15 or July 15. Prize: Each laureate receives $25,000; non-winning finalists receive $1,000.

THE GREEN ROSE PRIZE IN POETRY

New Issues Poetry & Prose, Deptartment of English, Western Michigan University, 1903 W. Michigan Ave., Kalamazoo MI 49008-5331. (269)387-8185. **Fax:** (269)387-2562. **Website:** www.wmich.edu/newissues. The Green Rose Prize in Poetry offers $2,000 and publication of a book of poems by an established poet who has published 1 or more full-length collections of poetry. *New Issues* may publish as many as 3 additional mss from this competition. Considers simultaneous submissions, but *New Issues* must be notified of acceptance elsewhere. Submit a ms of at least 48 pages, typed; single-spaced preferred. Clean photocopies acceptable. Do not bind; use manila folder or metal clasp. Include cover page with poet's name, address, phone number, and title of the ms. Also include brief bio, table of contents, and acknowledgments page. Submissions are also welcome through the online submission manager www.submishmash.com. "For hardcopy manuscripts only, you may include SASP for notification of receipt of ms and SASE for results only; mss will be recycled." Guidelines available for SASE, by fax, e-mail, or on website. **Entry fee:** $25. Make checks payable to New Issues Poetry & Prose. **Deadline:** Submit May 1-September 30 (postmark).

KATHRYN HANDLEY PROSE POEM PRIZE

Category in the Soul Making Keats Literary Competition, The Webhallow House, 1544 Sweetwood Dr., Colma CA 94015-2029. **E-mail:** pennobhill@aol.com. **Website:** www.soulmakingcontest.us. Open annually to all writers. Poetry may be double- or single-spaced. 1-page poems only, and only 1 prose poem/page. Three poems/entry. Indicate category on each poem. Identify only with 3x5 card. **Entry fee:** $5/entry (make checks payable to NLAPW). **Deadline:** November 30. Prizes: 1st Place: $100; 2nd Place: $50; 3rd Place: $25. **Contact:** Eileen Malone.

THE BESS HOKIN PRIZE

Poetry, 61 W. Superior St., Chicago IL 60654. (312)787-7070. **E-mail:** poetry@poetrymagazine.org. **Website:** www.poetrymagazine.org. Offered annually for poems published in *Poetry* during the preceding year (October-September). Upon acceptance, *Poetry* licenses exclusive worldwide first serial rights, including electronic rights, for publication, as well as non-exclusive rights to reprint, reuse, and archive the work, in any format, in perpetuity. Copyright reverts to author upon first publication. Prize: $1,000.

TOM HOWARD/JOHN H. REID POETRY CONTEST

Tom Howard Books, c/o Winning Writers, 351 Pleasant St., PMB 222, Northampton MA 01060-3961. (866)946-9748. **Fax:** (413)280-0539. **E-mail:** johnreid@mail.qango.com. **Website:** www.winningwriters.com. Offers annual award of 1st Prize: $3,000; 2nd Prize: $1,000; 3rd Prize: $400; 4th Prize: $250; 6 Most Highly Commended Awards of $150 each; plus a new $250 bonus prize for humorous verse. The top 10 entries will be published on the Winning Writers website. Submissions may be published or unpublished and may have won prizes elsewhere. Considers simultaneous submissions. Submit poems in any form, style, or genre. "There is no limit on the number of lines or poems you may submit." No name on ms pages; type or computer-print on letter-size white paper, single-sided. Submit online or by regular mail. Guidelines available for SASE or on website. **Entry fee:** $7 USD for every 25 lines (exclude poem titles and any blank lines from line count). **Deadline:** December 15-September 30. **Contact:** John Reid, award director.

JUNIPER PRIZE FOR POETRY

University of Massachusetts Press, Amherst MA 01003. (413)545-2217. **Fax:** (413)545-1226. **E-mail:** info@umpress.umass.edu. **Website:** www.umass.edu/umpress. **Contact:** Carla J. Potts. The University of Massachusetts Press offers the annual Juniper Prize for Poetry, awarded in alternate years for the first and subsequent books. Considers simultaneous submissions, "but if accepted for publication elsewhere, please notify us immediately. Mss by more than 1 author, entries of more than 1 mss simultaneously or within the same year, and translations are not eligible." Submit paginated ms of 50-70 pages of poetry, with paginated contents page, credits page, and information on previously published books. Include 2 cover sheets: 1 with contract information, 1 without. Mss will not be returned. Guidelilnes available for SASE or on website. Deadline: August 1 - September 29 (postmark). Winners announced online in April on the press website. Prize: includes publication and $1,500 in addition to royalties. In even-numbered years (2012, etc.), only "subsequent" books will be considered—mss whose authors have had at least 1 full-length book or chapbook (of at least 30 pages) of poetry published or accepted for publication. Self-published work is not considered to lie within this "books and chapbooks" category. In odd-numbered years (2013, etc.), only "first books' will be considered—mss by writers whose poems may have appeared in literary journals and/or anthologies but have not been published or accepted for publication in book form.

THE LAUREATE PRIZE FOR POETRY

The National Poetry Review, P.O. Box 2080, Aptos CA 95001-2080. **E-mail:** editor@nationalpoetryreview.com. **Website:** www.nationalpoetryreview.com. **Contact:** C.J. Sage, editor. Honors "1 new poem that *The National Poetry Review* believes has the greatest chance, of those entered, of standing the test of time and becoming part of the literary canon." Submit via e-mail and PayPal (preferred; see website for instructions) or via mail. Poems must be uncommitted (not accepted for first publication elsewhere). Deadline: September 30. Prize: $500, plus publication in *The National Poetry Review*.

THE LEVINSON PRIZE

Poetry, 61 W. Superior St., Chicago IL 60654. (312)787-7070. **Fax:** (312)787-6650. **E-mail:** poetry@poetrymagazine.org. **Website:** www.poetrymagazine.org. Offered annually for poems published in *Poetry* during the preceding year (October-September). Upon acceptance, *Poetry* licenses exclusive worldwide first serial rights, including electronic rights, for publication, as well as non-exclusive rights to reprint, reuse, and archive the work, in any format, in perpetuity. Copyright reverts to author upon first publication. Prize: $500.

LEVIS READING PRIZE

Virginia Commonwealth University, Department of English, P.O. Box 842005, Richmond VA 23284-2005. (804)828-1329. **Fax:** (804)828-8684. **E-mail:** tndida-

to@vcu.edu. **Website:** www.has.vcu.edu/eng/resources/levis_prize/levis_prize.htm. **Contact:** Thom Didato. "Offered annually for books of poetry published in the previous year to encourage poets early in their careers. The entry must be the writer's first or second published book of poetry. Previously published books in other genres, or previously published chapbooks or self-published material, do not count as books for this purpose." Deadline: January 15. Prize: $1,500 honorarium and an expense-paid trip to Richmond to present a public reading.

THE RUTH LILLY POETRY PRIZE

Poetry, 61 W. Superior St., Chicago IL 60654. **E-mail:** poetry@poetrymagazine.org. **Website:** www.poetrymagazine.org. Offered annually to a poet whose accomplishments in the field of poetry warrant extraordinary recognition. No applicants or nominations are accepted. Deadline: Varies. Prize: $100,000.

LITERAL LATTÉ POETRY AWARD

Literal Latté, 200 E. 10th St., Suite 240, New York NY 10003. (212)260-5532. **E-mail:** LitLatte@aol.com. **Website:** www.literal-latte.com. **Contact:** Jenine Gordon Bockman, editor. "Offered annually to any writer for unpublished poetry (maximum 2,000 words per poem). All styles welcome. Winners published in *Literal Latté*." Acquires first rights. Deadline: Postmark by July 15. Prize: 1st Place: $1,000; 2nd Place: $300; 3rd Place: $200. The Editors.

THE MACGUFFIN NATIONAL POET HUNT CONTEST

The MacGuffin, 18600 Haggerty Rd., Livonia MI 48152. (734)462-4400, ext. 5327. **Fax:** (734)462-4679. **E-mail:** macguffin@schoolcraft.edu. **Website:** www.macguffin.org. Work is judged blindly by a renowned, published poet. Offered annually for unpublished work. Guidelines available by mail, e-mail, or on the website. Acquires first rights (if published). Once published, all rights revert to the author. Open to any writer. All non-winning poems will also be considered by staff for publication in an upcoming issue of *The MacGuffin*. Also accepting unpublished stories up to 5,000 words and poetry up to 400 lines for normal publication. Please direct all correspondence to Gordon Krupsky. **Costs:** $15 for a 5-poem entry. Check or MO payable to Schoolcraft College. **Deadline:** April 2-June 4 (postmarked). Prize: 1st Place: $500; 2 Honorable Mentions will be published. 2012 Judge: Dorianne Laux. Past judges include Terry Blackhawk, Jim

Daniels, Thomas Lynch, and Vivian Shipley. **Contact:** Gordon Krupsky, managing editor.

NAOMI LONG MADGETT POETRY AWARD

Lotus Press, Inc., P.O. Box 21607, Detroit MI 48221. **E-mail:** lotuspress@comcast.net. **Website:** www.lotuspress.org. Offered annually to recognize an unpublished poetry ms by an African American. Guidelines for SASE, by e-mail, or online. **Deadline:** January 2-March 1. Prize: $500 and publication by Lotus Press. **Contact:** Constance Withers.

☾ THE MALAHAT REVIEW LONG POEM PRIZE

The Malahat Review, Box 1700 STN CSC, Victoria BC V8W 2Y2 Canada. **E-mail:** malahat@uvic.ca (queries only). **Website:** www.malahatreview.ca. The biennial Long Poem Prize offers 2 awards of $1,000 CAD each for a long poem or cycle (10-20 printed pages). Includes publication in The Malahat Review. Open to "entries from Canadian, American, and overseas authors." Submissions must be unpublished. No simultaneous submissions. Submit a single poem or cycle of poems, 10-20 published pages (a published page equals 32 lines or less, including breaks between stanzas); no restrictions on subject matter or aesthetic approach. Include separate page with poet's name, address, e-mail, and title; no identifying information on mss pages. No e-mail submissions. Do not include SASE for results; mss will not be returned. Guidelines available on website. **Entry fee:** $35 CAD for Canadian entries, $40 USD for US entries ($45 USD for entries from Mexico and outside North America); includes 1-year subscription to *The Malahat Review*. **Deadline:** February 1 (postmark) of alternate years (2011, 2013, etc.). 2011 winners: Julie Joosten, Maggie Schwed. 2011 judges: Jeffrey Donaldson, Barbara Colebrook Peace, Elizabeth Philips. Winners published in the summer issue of *The Malahat Review*, announced in summer on website, Facebook page, and in quarterly e-newsletter *Malahat lite*. **Contact:** John Barton, editor.

THE MORTON MARR POETRY PRIZE

Southern Methodist University, P.O. Box 750374, Dallas TX 75275-0374. (214)768-1037. **Fax:** (214)768-1408. **E-mail:** swr@mail.smu.edu. **Website:** www.smu.edu/southwestreview. The annual Morton Marr Poetry Prize awards 1st Prize: $1,000 and 2nd Prize: $500 to a poet who has not yet published a first book of poetry. Winners will be published in Southwest Review.

Submit 6 poems in a "traditional" form (e.g., sonnet, sestina, villanelle, rhymed stanzas, blank verse, et al). Include cover letter with poet's name, address, and other relevant information; no identifying information on entry pages. Manuscripts will not be returned. Guidelines available on website. **Entry fee:** $5/poem. **Deadline:** September 30 (postmark). **Contact:** Prize coordinator.

KATHLEEN MCCLUNG SONNET PRIZE CATEGORY

Category in the Soul Making Keats Literary Competition, National League of American Pen Women, The Webhallow House, 1544 Sweetwood Dr., Broadmoor Village CA 94015-2029. **E-mail:** pennobhill@aol.com. **Website:** www.soulmakingcontest.us. **Contact:** Eileen Malone. "Call for Shakespearean and Petrarchan sonnets on the theme of the 'beloved.'" Previously published material is accepted. Indicate category on cover page and on identifying 3x5 card. Open annually to any writer. Deadline: November 30 (annually). Prize: 1st Place: $100; 2nd Place: $50; 3rd Place: $25.

THE KATHRYN A. MORTON PRIZE IN POETRY

Sarabande Books, Inc., P.O. Box 4456, Louisville KY 40204. (502)458-4028. **E-mail:** info@sarabandebooks.org. **Website:** www.SarabandeBooks.org. **Contact:** Sarah Gorham, editor-in-chief. Member: CLMP. The Kathryn A. Morton Prize in Poetry is awarded annually to a book-length ms (at least 48 pages). All finalists are considered for publication. Competition receives approximately 1,400 entries. 2011 winner was Lauren Shapiro for her collection, *Easy Math*. 2012 judge was Cole Swensen. "To avoid conflict of interest, students in a degree-granting program or close friends of a judge are ineligible to enter the contest in the genre for which their friend or teacher is serving as judge. Sarabande, as a member of CLMP, complies with its Contest Code of Ethics." Entry form and SASE are required. Accepts simultaneous submissions, but must be notified immediately if manuscript is accepted elsewhere. Guidelines available for SASE, by e-mail, or on website. Deadline: Submit January 1-February 15 (postmark) only. Prize: $2,000, publication, and a standard royalty contract.

SHEILA MARGARET MOTTON PRIZE

New England Poetry Club, 2 Farrar St., Cambridge MA 02138. **E-mail:** contests@nepoetryclub.org. **Website:** www.nepoetryclub.org. **Contact:** NEPC contest coordinator. Checks for all contests should be made to New England Poetry Club. All entries should be sent in duplicate with name, address, phone, and email of writer on only one copy. (Judges receive copies without names). Send 2 copies of book of poetry published in the last 2 years and $5 handling fee. "Contest open to members and nonmembers. Poems should be typed and submitted in duplicate with author's name, address, phone, and e-mail address of writer on only 1 copy. (Judges receive copies without names.) Copy only. Label poems with contest name. Entries should be sent by regular mail only. Special delivery or signature required mail will be returned by the post office. Entries should be original, unpublished poems in English. No poem should be entered in more than 1 contest, nor have won a previous contest. No entries will be returned. NEPC will not engage in correspondence regarding poems or contest decisions." Deadline: May 31. Prize: $500. Judges are well-known poets and sometimes winners of previous NEPC contests.

ERIKA MUMFORD PRIZE

New England Poetry Club, 654 Green St., No. 2, Cambridge MA 02139. **E-mail:** contests@nepoetryclub.org. **Website:** www.nepoetryclub.org/contests.htm. **Contact:** NEPC contest coordinator. Offered annually for a poem in any form about foreign culture or travel. Funded by Erika Mumford's family and friends. "Contest open to members and nonmembers. Poems should be typed and submitted in duplicate with author's name, address, phone, and e-mail address of writer on only 1 copy. (Judges receive copies without names.) Copy only. Label poems with contest name. Entries should be sent by regular mail only. Special delivery or signature required mail will be returned by the post office. Entries should be original, unpublished poems in English. No poem should be entered in more than 1 contest, nor have won a previous contest. No entries will be returned. NEPC will not engage in correspondence regarding poems or contest decisions." Deadline: May 31. Prize: $250. Judges are well-known poets and sometimes winners of previous NEPC contests.

THE NATIONAL POETRY REVIEW BOOK PRIZE

The National Poetry Review, P.O. Box 2080, Aptos CA 95001-2080. **E-mail:** editor@nationalpoetryreview.com. **Website:** www.nationalpoetryreview.com. **Contact:** C.J. Sage, editor. *The National Poetry Review*

Book Prize offers $1,000, publication of a book-length ms, and 15 author copies. All entries will be considered for publication. 2011 winner was John Mann. Submit 45-80 pages of poetry via e-mail and PayPal (strongly preferred) or via mail. Include cover letter with bio and acknowledgments page. Include e-mail address (no SASEs; mss will be recycled). Guidelines available on website. Deadline: June 30 (postmark).

NATIONAL WRITERS ASSOCIATION POETRY CONTEST

The National Writers Association, 10940 S. Parker Rd. #508, Parker CO 80134. (303)841-0246. **E-mail:** natlwritersassn@hotmail.com. **Website:** www.nationalwriters.com. **Contact:** Sandy Whelchel, director. "Annual contest to encourage the writing of poetry, an important form of individual expression but with a limited commercial market." Deadline: October 1. Prize: 1st Place: $100; 2nd Place: $50; 3rd Place: $25.

HOWARD NEMEROV SONNET AWARD

320 Hunter Dr., Evansville IN 47711. **E-mail:** mona.3773@yahoo.com. **Website:** http://theformalist.evansville.edu/Home.htm. **Contact:** Mona Baer, contest coordinator. *The Formalist* sponsors the annual Howard Nemerov Sonnet Award. 2011 winner was Robert W. Crawford. 2011 judge was A. M. Juster. Submit original, unpublished sonnets; no translations; sonnet sequences are acceptable, but each sonnet will be considered individually. Poets may enter as many sonnets as they wish. Poet's name, address, phone number, and e-mail address should be typed on the **back** of each entry. Enclose SASE for contest results; mss will not be returned. Guidelines available for SASE or on website. Deadline: November 15, 2012 (postmark). Prize: Offers $1,000 prize for a single sonnet. Winner and 11 finalists will be published in *Measure: A Review of Formal Poetry*.

THE PABLO NERUDA PRIZE FOR POETRY

Nimrod International Journal, 800 S. Tucker Dr., Tulsa OK 74104. (918)631-3080. **Fax:** (918)631-3033. **E-mail:** nimrod@utulsa.edu. **Website:** www.utulsa.edu/nimrod. The annual Nimrod Literary Awards include The Pablo Neruda Prize for Poetry, which offers: 1st Prize—$2,000 and publication in *Nimrod: International Journal of Prose and Poetry*; and 2nd Prize—$1,000 and publication. *Nimrod* retains the right to publish any submission. Submissions must be unpublished. Work must be in English or translated by original author. Submit 3-10 pages of poetry (1 long poem or several short poems). Poet's name must not appear on ms. Include cover sheet with poem title(s), poet's name, address, phone and fax numbers, and e-mail address (poet must have a US address by October of contest year to enter). Mark "Contest Entry" on submission envelope and cover sheet. Include SASE for results only; mss will not be returned. Guidelines available for #10 SASE or on website. **Entry fee:** $20; includes 1-year subscription (2 issues) to *Nimrod*. Make checks payable to *Nimrod*. 2011 winners were Hayden Saunider ("Sideways Glances in the Rear-View Mirror") and Suzanne Cleary ("Amazing" and other poems). Winners will be announced on *Nimrod*'s website. **Contact:** Francine Ringold.

THE NEW ISSUES POETRY PRIZE

New Issues Poetry & Prose, New Issues Poetry & Prose, Department of English, Western Michigan University, 1903 W. Michigan Ave., Kalamazoo MI 49008-5331. (269)387-8185. **Fax:** (269)387-2562. **E-mail:** new-issues@wmich.edu. **Website:** www.wmich.edu/newissues. The New Issues Poetry Prize offers $2,000, plus publication of a book-length ms. Open to "poets writing in English who have not previously published a full-length collection of poems. Additional mss will be considered from those submitted to the competition for publication. Considers simultaneous submissions, but *New Issues* must be notified of acceptance elsewhere. Submit ms of at least 48 pages, typed, single-spaced preferred. Clean photocopies acceptable. Do not bind; use manila folder or metal clasp. Include cover page with poet's name, address, phone number, and title of the ms. Also include brief bio and acknowledgments page. Submissions are also welcome through the online submission manager www.submishmash.com. For hardcopy submissions only, you may include SASP for notification of receipt of ms and SASE for results only; no mss will be returned. **Entry fee:** $20. Make checks payable to New Issues Poetry & Prose. **Deadline:** November 30 (postmark).

THE JOHN FREDERICK NIMS MEMORIAL PRIZE

Poetry, 61 W. Superior St., Chicago IL 60654. (312)787-7070. **E-mail:** poetry@poetrymagazine.org. **Website:** www.poetrymagazine.org. Offered annually for poems published in *Poetry* during the preceding year (October-September). Upon acceptance, *Poetry* licenses exclusive worldwide first serial rights, including electronic rights, for publication, as well as non-exclusive rights to reprint, reuse, and archive the work, in any format, in perpetuity. Copyright reverts to author upon first publication. Copyrights are returned to the authors on request. Prize: $500.

GUY OWEN PRIZE

Department of Languages, Literature and Philosophy, Armstrong Atlantic State Univ., 11935 Abercorn St., Savannah GA 31419-1997. (912)344-3123. **E-mail:** tonyraymorris@gmail.com (inquiries only). **Website:** www.southernpoetryreview.org. **Contact:** Tony Morris, managing editor. The annual Guy Owen Prize offers $1,000 and publication in Southern Poetry Review to the winning poem selected by a distinguished poet. All entries will be considered for publication. 2011 winner was Catherine Staples. Submissions must be unpublished. "We consider work published online or posted there as previously published." Considers simultaneous submissions if indicated as such. Submit 3-5 poems (10 pages maximum). Include cover sheet with poet's name and contact information; no identifying information on ms pages. No e-mail or disk submissions. Include SASE for results only; mss will not be returned. Guidelines available in magazine, for SASE, by e-mail, or on website. **Deadline:** March 1-June 15 (postmark).

THE PATERSON POETRY PRIZE

The Poetry Center at Passaic County Community College, One College Blvd., Paterson NJ 07505-1179. (973)684-6555. **Fax:** (973)523-6085. **E-mail:** mgillan@pccc.edu. **Website:** www.pccc.edu/poetry. The Paterson Poetry Prize offers an annual award of $1,000 for the strongest book of poems (48 or more pages) published in the previous year. The winner will be asked to participate in an awards ceremony and to give a reading at The Poetry Center. Minimum press run: 500 copies. Publishers may submit more than 1 title for prize consideration; 3 copies of each book must be submitted. Include SASE for results; books will not be returned (all entries will be donated to The Poetry Center Library). Guidelines and application form (required) available for SASE or on website. **Entry fee:** None. **Deadline:** February 1 (postmark).

PAVEMENT SAW PRESS CHAPBOOK AWARD

321 Empire St., Montpelier OH 43543-1301. **E-mail:** info@pavementsaw.org. **Website:** www.pavementsaw.org. **Contact:** David Baratier, editor. "Pavement Saw Press has been publishing steadily since the fall of

1993. Each year since 1999, we have published at least 4 full-length paperback poetry collections, with some printed in library edition hard covers, 1 chapbook and a yearly literary journal anthology. We specialize in finding authors who have been widely published in literary journals but have not published a chapbook or full-length book." 2012 winner was Amy Wright. Submit up to 32 pages of poetry. Include signed cover letter with poet's name, address, phone number, e-mail, publication credits, a brief biography, and ms title. Also include 2 cover sheets: 1 with poet's contact information and ms title, 1 with the ms title only. Do not put poet's name on mss pages except for first title page. No mss will be returned. Deadline: December 31 (postmark). Prize: Chapbook Award offers $500, publication, and 50 author copies.

PEARL POETRY PRIZE

Pearl Editions, 3030 E. Second St., Long Beach CA 90803. (562)434-4523. **Fax:** (562)434-4523. **E-mail:** pearlmag@aol.com. **Website:** www.pearlmag.com. The annual Pearl Poetry Prize awards $1,000, publication, and 25 author's copies for a book-length ms. Guidelines available for SASE or on website. **Entry fee:** $20. **Deadline:** Submit May 1-June 30 only. 2010 winner was Jerry Neren (*Once Upon a Time in Vietnam*). 2012 judge: Andrea Carter Brown. **Contact:** Marilyn Johnson, editor/publisher. "Offered annually to provide poets with further opportunity to publish their poetry in book-form and find a larger audience for their work. Mss must be original works written in English. Guidelines for SASE or online. Open to all writers." Deadline: Submit May 1-June 30 only. Prize: $1,000 and publication by Pearl Editions

JEAN PEDRICK PRIZE

New England Poetry Club, 2 Farrar St., Cambridge MA 02138. **E-mail:** contests@nepoetryclub.org. **Website:** www.nepoetryclub.org. **Contact:** NEPC contest coordinator. "Contest open to members and non-members. Poems should be typed and submitted in duplicate with author's name, address, phone, and e-mail address of writer on only 1 copy. (Judges receive copies without names.) Copy only. Label poems with contest name. Entries should be sent by regular mail only. Special delivery or signature required mail will be returned by the post office. Entries should be original, unpublished poems in English. No poem should be entered in more than 1 contest, nor have won a previous contest. No entries will be returned. NEPC

will not engage in correspondence regarding poems or contest decisions." Deadline: May 31. Prize: $100. Judges are well-known poets and sometimes winners of previous NEPC contests.

PEN/JOYCE OSTERWEIL AWARD FOR POETRY

PEN American Center, 588 Broadway, Suite 303, New York NY 10012. (212)334-1660, ext. 126. **E-mail:** awards@pen.org. **Website:** www.pen.org. **Contact:** Jasmine Davey, literary awards coordinator. *Candidates may only be nominated by members of PEN.* This award recognizes the high literary character of the published work to date of a new and emerging American poet of any age, and the promise of further literary achievement. Nominated writer may not have published more than 1 book of poetry. Offered in odd-numbered years and alternates with the PEN/Voelcker Award for Poetry. Deadline: February 1, 2013. Prize: $5,000. Judged by a panel of 3 judges selected by the PEN Awards Committee.

PEN/VOELCKER AWARD FOR POETRY

PEN American Center, 588 Broadway, Suite 303, New York NY 10012. (212)334-1600, ext. 108. **E-mail:** awards@pen.org. **Website:** www.pen.org. **Contact:** Jasmine Davey, literary awards coordinator. Deadline: See website. Prize: $5,000 stipend. Judged by a panel of 3 poets or other writers.

PERUGIA PRESS PRIZE

Perugia Press, P.O. Box 60364, Florence MA 01062. **E-mail:** info@perugiapress.com. **Website:** www.perugiapress.com. The Perugia Press Prize for a first or second poetry book by a woman offers $1,000 and publication. Poet must have no more than 1 previously published book of poems (chapbooks don't count). Submissions must be unpublished as a collection, but individual poems may have been previously published in journals, chapbooks, and anthologies. Considers simultaneous submissions if notified of acceptance elsewhere. "Follow online guidelines carefully. Electronic submissions available through our website." No translations or self-published books. Multiple submissions accepted if accompanied by separate entry fee for each. **Entry fee:** $25. Make checks payable to Perugia Press. **Deadline:** Submit August 1-November 15 (postmark). "Use USPS or electronic submission, not FedEx or UPS." Winner announced by April 1 by e-mail or SASE (if included with entry).

Judges: Panel of Perugia authors, booksellers, scholars, etc. **Contact:** Susan Kan.

A. POULIN, JR. POETRY PRIZE

BOA Editions, Ltd., 250 N. Goodman St., Suite 306, Rochester NY 14607. **E-mail:** conners@boaeditions. org. **Website:** www.boaeditions.org. BOA Editions, Ltd. sponsors the annual A. Poulin, Jr. Poetry Prize for a poet's first book. Published books in other genres do not disqualify contestants from entering this contest. Send by first class or priority mail (recommended). Entrants must be a citizen or legal resident of the US. Poets, who are at least 18 years of age, who have yet to publish a full-length book collection of poetry. Translations are not eligible. Individual poems may have been previously published in magazines, journals, anthologies, chapbooks of 32 pages or less, or self-published books of 46 pages or less, but must be submitted in ms form. Considers simultaneous submissions. Submit 48-100 pages of poetry, paginated consecutively, typed or computer-generated in 11 point font. Bind with spring clip (no paperclips). Include cover/title page with poet's name, address, and telephone number. Also include table of contents; list of acknowledgments; and entry form (available for download on website). Multiple entries accepted with separate entry fee for each. No e-mail submissions. Include SASP for notification of receipt and SASE for results. Mss will not be returned. Guidelines available on website in May. Deadline: Submit between August 1-Nov. 30 (annually). Prize: Awards $1,500 honorarium and book publication in the A. Poulin, Jr. New Poets of America Series.

MARGARET REID POETRY CONTEST FOR TRADITIONAL VERSE

c/o Winning Writers, 351 Pleasant St., PMB 222, Northampton MA 01060-3961. **E-mail:** johnreid@ mail.qango.com. **Website:** www.winningwriters.com. Offers annual award of 1st Prize: $3,000; 2nd Prize: $1,000; 3rd Prize: $400; 4th Prize: $250; and 6 Most Highly Commended Awards of $150 each. The top 10 entries will be published on the Winning Writers website. Submissions may be published or unpublished, may have won prizes elsewhere, and may be entered in other contests. Submit poems in traditional verse forms; see website for guidelines. No limit on number of lines or number of poems submitted. No name on ms pages; type or computer-print on letter-size white paper, single-sided. Guidelines available for SASE or on website. Submit online or by mail. **Entry fee:** $8 USD for every 25 lines (exclude poem title and any blank lines from count). **Deadline:** November 15-June 30. 2011 winner was Jacie Ragan ("In the Shadow of the Condor"). 2011 judges: John H. Reid and Dee C. Konrad. Winners announced in December at WinningWriters.com; entrants who provide valid e-mail addresses also receive notification. **Contact:** John Reid. "Seeks poems in traditional verse forms, such as sonnets." Both unpublished and published work accepted. 2011 winner was Jacie Ragan ("In the Shadow of the Condor").

ERNEST SANDEEN PRIZE IN POETRY

Dept. of English, University of Notre Dame, Notre Dame IN 46556-5639. (574)631-7526. **Fax:** (574)631-4795. **E-mail:** creativewriting@nd.edu. **Website:** http://english.nd.edu/creative-writing/publications/ sandeen-sullivan-prizes. The Sandeen Prize in Poetry offers $1,000 (a $500 award and a $500 advance against royalties from the Notre Dame Press) and publication of a book-length ms. Open to poets who have published at least 1 volume of poetry. "Please include a photocopy of the copyright and the title page of your previous volume. Vanity press publications do not fulfill this requirement. We will pay special attention to second volumes. Please include a vita and/or a biographical statement that includes your publishing history. We will be glad to see a selection of reviews of the earlier collection." Submit 2 copies of ms (inform if ms is available on computer disk). Include SASE for acknowledgment of receipt of ms and SASE for return of ms. **Entry fee:** $15; includes one-year subscription to Notre Dame Review. Make checks payable to University of Notre Dame. **Deadline:** Submit May 1- September 1. 2011 winner was Janet Kaplan (*Dreamlife of a Philanthropist*).

MAY SARTON AWARD

New England Poetry Club, 654 Green St., No. 2, Cambridge MA 02139. **Website:** www.nepoetryclub. org. **Contact:** NEPC contest coordinator. "Given intermittently to a poet whose work is an inspiration to other poets. Recipients are chosen by the board." "Contest open to members and nonmembers. Poems should be typed and submitted in duplicate with author's name, address, phone, and e-mail address of writer on only 1 copy. (Judges receive copies without names.) Copy only. Label poems with contest name. Entries should be sent by regular mail only.

Special delivery or signature required mail will be returned by the post office. Entries should be original, unpublished poems in English. No poem should be entered in more than 1 contest, nor have won a previous contest. No entries will be returned. NEPC will not engage in correspondence regarding poems or contest decisions." Deadline: May 31. Prize: $250. Judges are well-known poets and sometimes winners of previous NEPC contests.

☼ SASKATCHEWAN POETRY AWARD

Saskatchewan Book Awards, Inc., 100-2400 College Ave., Regina SK S4P 0K1 Canada. (306)569-1585. **Fax:** (306)569-4187. **E-mail:** director@bookawards.sk.ca. **Website:** www.bookawards.sk.ca. **Contact:** Executive director, book submissions. Offered annually. "This award is presented to a Saskatchewan author for the best book of poetry, judged on the quality of writing." Deadline: November 1. Prize: $2,000 (CAD).

☼ SHORT GRAIN CONTEST

Box 67, Saskatoon SK S7K 3K1 Canada. (306)244-2828. **Fax:** (306)244-0255. **E-mail:** grainmag@sasktel.net. **Website:** www.grainmagazine.ca. The annual Short Grain Contest includes a category for poetry of any style up to 100 lines, offering 3 prizes with a 1st Prize of $1,000, plus publication in *Grain Magazine*. "Each entry must be original, unpublished, not submitted elsewhere for publication or broadcast, nor accepted elsewhere for publication or broadcast, nor entered simultaneously in any other contest or competition for which it is also eligible to win a prize. Entries must be typed on 8- ½x 11 paper. It must be legible. Faxed and/or electronic entries not accepted. No simultaneous submissions. A separate covering page must be attached to the text of your entry, and must provide the following information: Poet's name, complete mailing address, telephone number, e-mail address, entry title, category name, and line count. An absolutely accurate word or line count is required. No identifying information on the text pages. Entries will not be returned. Names of the winners and titles of the winning entries will be posted on the *Grain Magazine* website in August; only the winners will be notified. Entry fee: $35 CAD; $40 for US and international entrants, in US funds; includes 1 year subscription to *Grain Magazine*. Deadline: April 1." **Contact:** Mike Thompson, business administrator (inquiries only).

SLIPSTREAM ANNUAL POETRY CHAPBOOK COMPETITION

Slipstream, Box 2071, Niagara Falls NY 14301. **E-mail:** editors@slipstreampress.org. **Website:** www.slipstreampress.org. The annual Slipstream Poetry Chapbook Contest awards $1,000, publication of a chapbook ms, and 50 author's copies. All entrants receive copy of winning chapbook and an issue of *Slipstream*. Considers simultaneous submissions if informed of status. Accepts previously published work with acknowledgments. Submit up to 40 pages of poetry, any style, format, or theme. Manuscripts will not be returned. Guidelines available for SASE or on website. **Entry fee:** $20. **Deadline:** December 1. Latest winner is Moriah Erickson for *Three Crows Laughing*. **Contact:** Dan Sicoli, co-editor.

HELEN C. SMITH MEMORIAL AWARD FOR POETRY

The Texas Institute of Letters, P.O. Box 609, Round Rock TX 78680. **E-mail:** tilsecretary@yahoo.com. **Website:** http://texasinstituteofletters.org/. Offered annually for the best book of poems published January 1-December 31 of previous year. Poet must have been born in Texas, have lived in the state at some time for at least 2 consecutive years, or the subject matter must be associated with the state. See website for guidelines. Deadline: Early January. Prize: $1,200. Offered annually for the best book of poems published January 1-December 31 of previous year. Poet must have been born in Texas, have lived in the state at some time for at least 2 consecutive years, or the subject matter must be associated with the state. See website for guidelines. Deadline: Early January; see website for details. Prize: $1,200.

THE SOW'S EAR CHAPBOOK COMPETITION

The Sow's Ear Review, P.O. Box 127, Millwood VA 22646. (540)955-3955. **E-mail:** rglesman@gmail.com. **Website:** www.sows-ear.kitenet.net. **Contact:** Robert G. Lesman, managing editor. *The Sow's Ear Poetry Review* sponsors an annual chapbook competition. Open to adults. Submissions may be previously published individually if poet holds publication rights. Considers simultaneous submissions, "but if your chapbook is accepted elsewhere, you must withdraw promptly from our competition." Submit 22-26 pages of poetry; no length limit on poems, but no more than 1 poem on a page. Include title page and table of contents. Poet's name should not appear on poems, title page, or table of contents. Include separate sheet with chapbook title, poet's name, address, phone number, e-mail address (if available), and publication credits for submitted poems, if any. Include SASE or e-mail address for results only; entries will not be returned. Guidelines available for SASE, by e-mail, or on website. Submit in March and April. Deadline: May 1 (postmark). Prize: Offers $1,000, publication as the spring issue of the magazine, and 25 author's copies.

THE SOW'S EAR POETRY COMPETITION

The Sow's Ear Review, P.O. Box 127, Millwood VA 22646. **E-mail:** rglesman@gmail.com. **Website:** www. sows-ear.kitenet.net. *The Sow's Ear Poetry Review* sponsors an annual contest for unpublished poems. Offers $1,000 and publication in *The Sow's Ear Poetry Review.* Submit up to 5 unpublished poems. Include separate sheet with poem titles, poet's name, address, phone number, and e-mail address (if available). "We will check with finalists regarding publication status of poems before sending to final judge." Poet's name should not appear on poems. Include SASE for results only; entries will not be returned. Guidelines available for SASE, by e-mail, or on website. **Entry fee:** $27 for up to 5 poems. Contestants receive a year's subscription. Make checks payable to The Sow's Ear Poetry Review. Submit in September or October. **Deadline:** November 1 (postmark). Past judges include Gregory Orr and Marge Piercy. "Four criteria help us judge the quality of submissions: 1) Does the poem make the strange familiar or the familiar strange, or both? 2) Is the form of the poem vital to its meaning? 3) Do the sounds of the poem make sense in relation to the theme? 4) Does the little story of the poem open a window on the Big Story of the human situation?" **Contact:** Robert G. Lesman, managing editor.

SRPR EDITORS' PRIZE CONTEST

Spoon River Poetry Review, 4241 Department of English, Publications Unit, Illinois State University, Normal IL 61790-4241. (309)438-3025. **Website:** www. litline.org/spoon. Offered annually for unpublished poetry to identify and reward excellence. Guidelines available online. Open to all writers. Submit 2 copies of 3 unpublished poems; maximum of 10 pages total. Name, address, and phone number of poet should appear on each page of 1 copy only. Entries must be unpublished and will not be returned. Entries cannot be received by fax or e-mail. Deadline: April 15. Prize: 1st

Place: $1,000 and publication; Runners-Up (2): $100 each and publication.

WALLACE E. STEGNER FELLOWSHIPS

Creative Writing Program, Stanford University, Stanford CA 94305-2087. (650)723-0011. **Fax:** (650)723-3679. **E-mail:** krystalg@stanford.edu. **Website:** www. stanford.edu/group/creativewriting/stegner. Offers 5 fellowships in poetry and 5 in fiction of $26,000 plus tuition of over $7,000/year for promising writers who can benefit from 2 years of instruction and participation in the program. "We do not require a degree for admission. No school of writing is favored over any other. Chronological age is not a consideration." Accepts applications between September 1 and December 1 (postmark). Applicants may apply online. Competition receives about 1,700 entries/year. **Contact:** Admissions coordinator: Krystal Griffiths, program assistant.

THE RUTH STONE PRIZE IN POETRY

Vermont College, 36 College St., Montpelier VT 05602. (802)828-8517. **E-mail:** hungermtn@vcfa. edu. **Website:** www.hungermtn.org. The annual Ruth Stone Prize in Poetry offers $1,000 and publication in *Hunger Mountain: The VCFA Journal of the Arts*; 2 runners-up receive $100 and are also published. Submit up to 3 poems, not to exceed 6 pages. **Entry fee:** $20. **Deadline:** December 10. Guidelines available on website. "Include SASE and index card with poem titles and address; do not put name on poems." **Contact:** Miciah Bay Gault, editor.

THE ELIZABETH MATCHETT STOVER MEMORIAL AWARD

Southwest Review, Southern Methodist University, P.O. Box 750374, Dallas TX 75275-0374. (214)768-1037. **Fax:** (214)768-1408. **E-mail:** swr@mail.smu.edu. **Website:** www.smu.edu/southwestreview. **Contact:** Jennifer Cranfill, senior editor, and Willard Spiegelman, editor-in-chief. "Offered annually to the best works of poetry that have appeared in the magazine in the previous year. Please note that mss are submitted for publication, not for the prizes themselves. Guidelines for SASE and online." Prize: $300 Judged by Jennifer Cranfill and Willard Spiegelman.

● STROKESTOWN INTERNATIONAL POETRY COMPETITION

Strokestown International Poetry Festival, Strokestown Poetry Festival Office, Strokestown,

County Roscommon Ireland. (+353) 71 9633759. **E-mail:** office@strokestownpoetry.org. **Website:** www.strokestownpoetry.org. **Contact:** Director. This annual competition was established to promote excellence in poetry and participation in the reading and writing of it. Acquires first publication rights. Deadline: January. Prize: 1st Prize: 4,000 euros (approximately $3,900) for a poem in English of up to 70 lines, plus others totalling about $3,000. Up to 10 shortlisted poets will be invited to read at the Strokestown International Poetry Festival and paid a reading fee.

⊕ TEXAS INSTITUTE OF LETTERS BOB BUSH MEMORIAL AWARD FOR FIRST BOOK OF POETRY

Texas Institute of Letters, P.O. Box 609, Round Rock TX 78680. **Website:** http://texasinstituteofletters.org. Offered annually for best first book of poetry published in previous year. Writer must have been born in Texas, have lived in the state at least 2 consecutive years at some time, or the subject matter should be associated with the state. Deadline: See website for exact date. Prize: $1,000. Offered annually for best first book of poetry published in previous year. Writer must have been born in Texas, have lived in the state at least 2 consecutive years at some time, or the subject matter should be associated with the state. Deadline: See website for exact date. Prize: $1,000.

TRANSCONTINENTAL POETRY AWARD

Pavement Saw Press, 321 Empire St., Montpelier OH 43543. (419)485-0524. **E-mail:** info@pavementsaw.org. **Website:** pavementsaw.org. The Transcontinental Poetry Award offers $1,000, publication, and a percentage of the print run for a first or second book. "Each year, Pavement Saw Press will seek to publish at least 1 book of poetry and/or prose poems from manuscripts received during this competition, which is open to anyone who has not previously published a volume of poetry or prose. Poets who have not published a book, who have published 1 collection, or who have published a second collection of fewer than 40 pages, or who have published a second full-length collection with a print run of no more than 500 copies are eligible. More than 1 prize may be awarded." Submit 48-70 pages of poetry (1 poem/page), paginated and bound with a single clip. Include 2 cover sheets: 1 with ms title, poet's name, address, phone number, and e-mail; if available, the second with ms title only (this sheet should be clipped to ms). Also include 1-page cover letter (a brief biography, ms title, poet's name, address, and telephone number, e-mail, and poet's signature) and acknowledgments page (journal, anthology, chapbook, etc., and poem published). Include SASP for acknowledgment of receipt; SASE unnecessary as result will be sent with free book and no mss will be returned. Guidelines available for SASE or on website. **Entry fee:** $20; electronic submissions $27. "All US entrants will receive books, chapbooks, and journals equal to, or more than, the entry fee. Add $3 (USD) for other countries to cover the extra postal charge if sending by mail." Make checks payable to Pavement Saw Press. **Deadline:** Reads submissions in June, July, and until August 15 (must have August 15 or earlier postmark). **Contact:** David Baratier, editor.

TUFTS POETRY AWARDS

Claremont Graduate University, 160 E. 10th St., Harper East B7, Claremont CA 91711-6165. (909)621-8612. **Website:** www.cgu.edu/tufts. **Contact:** Wendy Martin, program director. The annual Kingsley Tufts Poetry Award offers $100,000 for a work by an emerging poet, "one who is past the very beginning but has not yet reached the acknowledged pinnacle of his/her career." 2012 winner is Timothy Donnelly (*The Cloud Corporation*). The Kate Tufts Discovery Award ($10,000) is for a first book. 2012 winner is Katherine Larson (*Radial Symmetry*). To be considered for the 2013 awards, books must have been published between September 1, 2011 and August 31, 2012. Entry form and guidelines available for SASE or on website. Check website for updated deadlines and award information.

☺ UTMOST CHRISTIAN POETRY CONTEST

Utmost Christian Writers Foundation, 121 Morin Maze, Edmonton AB T6K 1V1 Canada. **E-mail:** nnharms@telusplanet.net. **Website:** www.utmost-christianwriters.com. **Contact:** Nathan Harms, executive director. The Utmost Christian Poetry Contest opens annually for entries on September 1 "for Christian poets only!" $3,000 in cash prizes. The purpose of this contest is "to promote excellence in poetry by poets of Christian faith. All entries are eligible for most of the cash awards, but there is a special category for rhyming poetry with prizes of $300 and $100. All entries must be unpublished." See rules and entry form online at website. Deadline: February 28 annually. Prize: 1st Place: $1,000; 2nd Place: $600; 10 prizes of $100 are offered for honorable mention. Rights are acquired to post winning entries on the organization's website. Judged by a committee of the Directors of Utmost Christian Writers Foundation (who work under the direction of Barbara Mitchell, chief judge).

DANIEL VAROUJAN AWARD

New England Poetry Club, 654 Green St., No. 2, Cambridge MA 02139. **E-mail:** contests@nepoetryclub.org. **Website:** www.nepoetryclub.org. **Contact:** NEPC contest coordinator. "For an unpublished poem (not a translation)worthy of Daniel Varoujan, a poet killed by the Turks in the genocide that destroyed three-fourths of the Armenian population. Previous winners may not enter again." "Contest open to members and nonmembers. Poems should be typed and submitted in duplicate with author's name, address, phone, and e-mail address of writer on only 1 copy. (Judges receive copies without names.) Copy only. Label poems with contest name. Entries should be sent by regular mail only. Special delivery or signature required mail will be returned by the post office. Entries should be original, unpublished poems in English. No poem should be entered in more than 1 contest, nor have won a previous contest. No entries will be returned. NEPC will not engage in correspondence regarding poems or contest decisions." Deadline: May 31. Prize: $1,000. Judges are well-known poets and sometimes winners of previous NEPC contests.

THE WASHINGTON PRIZE

Dearlove Hall, Adirondack Community College, 640 Bay Rd., Queensbury NY 12804. **E-mail:** editor@ wordworksdc.com. **Website:** www.wordworksdc.com. **Contact:** Nancy White, Washington Prize administrator. Additional information available on website. Winners announced in August. Book publication planned for January 2013. "Submit a ms of 48-64 pages. Include 2 title pages, 1 with and 1 without author information, an acknowledgments page, a table of contents and a cover letter containing a brief bio. Use a binder clip to secure the ms. Mss will be recycled. Indicate the information source where you learned about The Washington Prize (for example, AWP newsletter, *Poets & Writers Magazine*, the Word Works website). Send entries to Nancy White at address above." Deadline: Submit January 15-March 15 (postmark). Prize: Offers $1,500 and publication of a book-length ms of original poetry in English by a living American poet (US or Canadian citizen or resident).

WERGLE FLOMP HUMOR POETRY CONTEST

Winning Writers, 351 Pleasant St., PMB 222, Northampton MA 01060-3961. (866)946-9748. **Fax:** (413)280-0539. **E-mail:** adam@winningwriters.com. **Website:** www.winningwriters.com. Offers annual award of 1st Prize: $1,500; 2nd Prize: $800; 3rd Prize: $400; plus 12 Honorable Mentions of $75 each. Both published and unpublished poems are welcome. Final judge: Jendi Reiter. See the complete guidelines and past winners. All prizewinners receive online publication at WinningWriters.com. Submissions may be previously published. Considers simultaneous submissions. Submit 1 humorous poem of any length, in any form. See website for examples." Entries accepted only through website; no entries by regular mail. Guidelines available on website. **Entry fee:** None. **Deadline:** April 1. Competition receives about 2,000 entries/year. **Contact:** Adam Cohen.

WHITE PINE PRESS POETRY PRIZE

White Pine Press, P.O. Box 236, Buffalo NY 14201. **E-mail:** wpine@whitepine.org. **Website:** www.whitepine.org. **Contact:** Dennis Maloney, editor. Offered annually for previously published or unpublished poets. Manuscript: Up to 80 pages of original work; translations are not eligible. Poems may have appeared in magazines or limited-edition chapbooks. Open to any US citizen. Deadline: November 30 (postmarked). Prize: $1,000 and publication. Final Judge is a poet of national reputation. All entries are screened by the editorial staff of White Pine Press.

STAN AND TOM WICK POETRY PRIZE

301 Satterfield Hall, Kent State University, P.O. Box 5190, Kent OH 44242-0001. (330)672-2067. **E-mail:** wickpoet@kent.edu. **Website:** www.dept.kent.edu/ wick. Offers annual award of $2,500 and publication by Kent State University Press. Open to poets writing in English who have not yet published a full-length collection. Submissions must be unpublished as a collection, but individual poems may have been previously published elsewhere. Considers simultaneous submissions as long as the Wick Poetry Center receives notice upon acceptance elsewhere. Submit 50-70 pages of poetry. Include cover sheet with poet's name, address, telephone number, e-mail address, and title of ms. Guidelines available for SASE or on website. **Reading fee:** $25. **Deadline:** Submit Febru-

ary 1-May 1. Competition receives700-800 entries. **Contact:** David Hassler, director.

THE J. HOWARD AND BARBARA M.J. WOOD PRIZE

Poetry, 61 W. Superior St., Chicago IL 60654. (312)787-7070. **E-mail:** poetry@poetrymagazine.org. **Website:** www.poetrymagazine.org. Offered annually for poems published in *Poetry* during the preceding year (October-September). Upon acceptance, *Poetry* licenses exclusive worldwide first serial rights, including electronic rights, for publication, as well as nonexclusive rights to reprint, reuse, and archive the work, in any format, in perpetuity. Copyright reverts to author upon first publication. Prize: $5,000.

WORKING PEOPLE'S POETRY COMPETITION

Blue Collar Review, P.O. Box 11417, Norfolk VA 23517. **E-mail:** red-ink@earthlink.net. **Website:** www.partisanpress.org. The Working People's Poetry Competition offers $100 and a 1-year subscription to *Blue Collar Review* and "1 year posting of winning poem on our website. Poetry should be typed as you would like to see it published, with your name and address on each page. Include cover letter with entry." Guidelines available on website. Deadline: May 15. Previous winner was Gregg Shotwell.

MULTIPLE WRITING AREAS

⟲ AESTHETICA CREATIVE WORKS COMPETITION

P.O. Box 371, York YO23 1WL United Kingdom. **E-mail:** pauline@aestheticamagazine.com. **E-mail:** submissions@aestheticamagazine.com. **Website:** www.aestheticamagazine.com. The Aesthetica Creative Works Competition represents the scope of creative activity today, and provides an opportunity for both new and established artists to nurture their reputations on an international scale. There are three categories: Short Film Festival, Art Prize, and Creative Writing. Art Prize has four sub-categories, Creative writing has two. See website for guidelines and more details. The Aesthetica Creative Works Competition represents the scope of creative activity today, and provides an opportunity for both new and established artists to nurture their reputations on an international scale. There are three categories: Artwork & Photography, Fiction and Poetry. See guidelines online. The Aesthetica Creative Works Competition is looking to discover talented artists and writers. The editor of Aesthetica is a Fellow of the Royal Society of Arts. See guidelines online. Works should be done in English August 31, 2011. Prize: £500-1,000, Each winner will receive an additional prize from our competition partners. Winners will be published in the Aesthetica Creative Works Annual. Winners will receive a complimentary copy of the Aesthetica Creative Works Annual and publication of the work in their creative section (3 winners).

AMERICAS AWARD

University of Wisconsin-Milwaukee, P.O. Box 413, Milwaukee WI 53201. **Website:** http://www4.uwm.edu/clacs/aa/index.cfm. **Contact:** Julie Kline. Annual award. Purpose of contest: Up to 2 awards are given each spring in recognition of U.S. published works (from the previous year) of fiction, poetry, folklore or selected nonfiction (from picture books to works for young adults) in English or Spanish which authentically and engagingly relate to Latin America, the Caribbean, or to Latinos in the United States. By combining both and linking the "Americas," the intent is to reach beyond geographic borders, as well as multicultural-international boundaries, focusing instead upon cultural heritages within the hemisphere. Previously published submissions only. Submissions open to anyone with an interest in the theme of the award. Deadline for entries: January 15. Visit website or send SASE for contest rules and any committee changes. Awards $500 cash prize, plaque and a formal presentation at the Library of Congress, Washington DC. Judging by a review committee consisting of individuals in teaching, library work, outreach and children's literature specialists.

ARTIST TRUST FELLOWSHIP AWARD

1835 12th Ave., Seattle WA 98122. (209)467-8734 ext. 9. **Fax:** (206)467-9633. **E-mail:** miguel@artisttrust.org. **Website:** artisttrust.org. **Contact:** Miguel Guillen, Program Manager. "The fellowship is a merit-based award of $7,500 to practicing professional Washington State artists of exceptional talent and demonstrated ability. Literature fellowships are offered every other year. The award is made on the basis of work of the past 5 years. Applicants must be individual artists; Washington State residents; not matriculated students; and generative artists. Offered every 2 years in even years. Guidelines and application online." Deadline: February 26. Prize: $7,500.

AUTUMN HOUSE POETRY, FICTION, AND NONFICTION PRIZES

P.O. Box 60100, Pittsburgh PA 15211. (412)381-4261. **E-mail:** msimms@autumnhouse.org. **Website:** http://autumnhouse.org. Offers annual prize of $2,500 and publication of book-length ms with national promotion. Submission must be unpublished as a collection, but individual poems, stories, and essays may have been previously published elsewhere. Considers simultaneous submissions. Submit 50-80 pages of poetry or 200-300 pages of prose ("blind judging—2 cover sheets requested"). Guidelines available for SASE, by e-mail, or on website. **Entry fee:** $30/ms. **Deadline:** June 30 annually. Competition receives 1,500 entries/year. 2012 judges were Stephen Dunn, Stewart O'Nan, and Phillip Lopate. Winners announced through mailings, website, and ads in *Poets & Writers*, *American Poetry Review*, and *Writer's Chronicle* (extensive publicity for winner). Copies of winning books available from Amazon.com, Barnes & Noble, and other retailers. "Autumn House is a nonprofit corporation with the mission of publishing and promoting poetry and other fine literature. We have published books by Gerald Stern, Ruth L. Schwartz, Ed Ochester, Andrea Hollander Budy, George Bilgere, Jo McDougall, and others." **Contact:** Michael Simms, editor.

THE BASKERVILLE PUBLISHERS POETRY AWARD & THE BETSY COLQUITT POETRY AWARD

descant, Texas Christian University's literary journal, TCU, Box 297270, Fort Worth TX 76129. (817)257-6537. **Fax:** (817)257-6239. **E-mail:** descant@tcu.edu. **Website:** www.descant.tcu.edu. "Annual award for an outstanding poem published in an issue of *descant*." Deadline: September - April. $250 for Baskerville Award; $500 for Betsy Colquitt Award. Publication retains copyright, but will transfer it to the author upon request. **Contact:** Dan Williams and Alex Lemon.

CANADA COUNCIL GOVERNOR GENERAL'S LITERARY AWARDS

350 Albert St., P.O. Box 1047, Ottawa ON K1P 5V8 Canada. (613)566-4410, ext. 5573. **Fax:** (613)566-4410. **Website:** www.canadacouncil.ca/prizes/ggla. Annual award. Purpose of award: given to the best English-language and the best French-language work in each of the 7 categories of Fiction, Literary Nonfiction, Poetry, Drama, Children's Literature (text), Children's Literature (illustration) and Translation. Books must be first-edition trade books that have been written, translated or illustrated by Canadian citizens or permanent residents of Canada. In the case of translation, the original work written in English or French, must also be a Canadian-authored title. Books must be submitted by publishers. Deadline depends on the book's publication date. For books published in English: March 15, June 1 and August 7. For books published in French: March 15 and July 15. The awards ceremony is scheduled mid-November. Amount of award: $25,000 to winning authors; $1,000 to non-winning finalists.

THE CITY OF VANCOUVER BOOK AWARD

Cultural Services Dept., 111 W. Hasting St., Suite 501, Vancouver BC V6B 1H4 Canada. (604) 829-2007. **Fax:** (604)871-6005. **E-mail:** marnie.rice@vancouver.ca. **Website:** vancouver.ca/bookaward. "Offered annually for books published in the previous year which exhibit excellence in the categories of content, illustration, design, and format. The book must contribute significantly to the appreciation and understanding of the city of Vancouver and heighten awareness of 1 or more of the following: Vancouver's history, the city's unique character, or achievements of the city's residents. The book may be fiction, nonfiction, poetry, or drama written for adults or children, and may deal with any aspects of the city—history, geography, current affairs, or the arts. Guidelines online." Prize: $2,000.

CWW ANNUAL WISCONSIN WRITERS AWARDS COMPETITION

Council for Wisconsin Writers, **Website:** www.wisconsinwriters.org. **Contact:** Geoff Gilpin; Karla Huston, awards co-chairs; and Carolyn Washburne, Christopher Latham Sholes Award and Major Achievement Award co-chair. Offered annually for work published by Wisconsin writers the previous calendar year. Nine awards: Major/life achievement alternate years; short fiction; short nonfiction; nonfiction book; poetry book; fiction book; children's literature; Lorine Niedecker Poetry Award; Sholes Award for Outstanding Service to Wisconsin Writers Alternate Years; Essay Award for Young Writers. Open to Wisconsin residents. Guidelines, rules, and entry form on website. Deadline: January 31 (postmark). Prizes: $500 and a week-long residency at Shake Rag Alley in Mineral Point. Essay Contest: $150. "This year only the Essay Award for Young Writers prize will be $250."

DANA AWARDS IN THE NOVEL, SHORT FICTION, ESSAY AND POETRY

www.danaawards.com, 200 Fosseway Dr., Greensboro NC 27445. (336)644-8028. **E-mail:** danaawards@pipeline.com; danaawards@gmail.com. **Website:** www.danaawards.com. **Contact:** Mary Elizabeth Parker, chair. Four awards offered annually for unpublished work written in English. Purpose is monetary award for work that has not been previously published or received monetary award, but will accept work published simply for friends and family. Works previously published online are not eligible. No work accepted by or for persons under 16 for any of the 4 awards: **Novel**—For the first 40 pages of a novel completed or in progress; **Fiction**—short fiction (no memoirs) up to 10,000 words; **Essay**—personal essay, memoir, or creative nonfiction up to 10,000 words; **Poetry**—for best group of 5 poems based on excellence of all 5 (no light verse, no single poem over 100 lines). Deadline: October 31 (postmarked). Prize: Awards: $1,000 for each of the 4 awards.

EATON LITERARY AGENCY'S ANNUAL AWARDS PROGRAM

Eaton Literary Agency, P.O. Box 49795, Sarasota FL 34230. (941)366-6589. **Fax:** (941)365-4679. **E-mail:** eatonlit@aol.com. **Website:** www.eatonliterary.com. Offered biannually for unpublished mss. Prize: $2,500 (over 10,000 words); $500 (under 10,000 words). Judged by an independent agency in conjunction with some members of Eaton's staff. No entry fee. Guidelines available for SASE, by fax, e-mail, or on website. Accepts inquiries by fax, phone and e-mail. Deadline: **March 31** (mss under 10,000 words); **August 31** (mss over 10,000 words). Entries must be unpublished. Open to any writer. Results announced in April and September. Winners notified by mail. For contest results, send SASE, fax, e-mail, or visit website. **Contact:** Richard Lawrence, V.P. Offered biannually for unpublished mss. Entries must be unpublished. Open to any writer. Guidelines available for SASE, by fax, e-mail, or on website. Accepts inquiries by fax, phone and e-mail. Results announced in April and September. Winners notified by mail. For contest results, send SASE, fax, e-mail, or visit website. Deadline: March 31 (mss under 10,000 words); August 31 (mss over 10,000 words). Prize: $2,500 (over 10,000 words); $500 (un-

der 10,000 words). Judged by an independent agency in conjunction with some members of Eaton's staff.

THE VIRGINIA FAULKNER AWARD FOR EXCELLENCE IN WRITING

Prairie Schooner, 123 Andrews Hall, University of Nebraska-Lincoln, Lincoln NE 68588-0334. (402)472-0911. **Fax:** (402)472-9771. **E-mail:** PrairieSchooner@unl.edu. **Website:** www.prairieschooner.unl.edu. **Contact:** Kwame Dawes. Offered annually for work published in *Prairie Schooner* in the previous year. Categories: short stories, essays, novel excerpts and translations. Guidelines for SASE or on website. Accepts inquiries by fax and e-mail. "We only read mss from September 1 through May 1." Winning entry must have been published in *Prairie Schooner* in the year preceeding the award. Results announced in the Spring issue. Winners notified by mail in February or March. Prize: $1,000. Judged by Editorial Board.

☼ FIRST BOOK AWARD

Saskatchewan Book Awards, Inc., 100-2400 College Ave., Regina SK S4P 0K1 Canada. (306)569-1585. **Fax:** (306)569-4187. **E-mail:** director@bookawards.sk.ca. **Website:** www.bookawards.sk.ca. **Contact:** Executive director, book submissions. Offered annually. "This award is presented to a Saskatchewan author for the best first book, judged on the quality of writing." Books from the following categories will be considered: Children's; drama; fiction (short fiction by a single author, novellas, novels); nonfiction (all categories of nonfiction writing except cookbooks, directories, how-to books, or bibliographies of minimal critical content); and poetry. Deadline: November 1. Prize: $2,000 (CAD).

☼ FREEFALL SHORT PROSE AND POETRY CONTEST

Freefall Literary Society of Calgary, 922 9th Ave. SE, Calgary AB T2G 0S4 Canada. **E-mail:** freefallmagazine@yahoo.ca. **Website:** www.freefallmagazine.ca. **Contact:** Lynn C. Fraser, managing editor. Offered annually for unpublished work in the categories of poetry (5 poems/entry) and prose (3,000 words or less). The purpose of the award in both categories is to recognize writers and offer publication credits in a literary magazine format. Contest rules and entry form online. Acquires first Canadian serial rights; ownership reverts to author after one-time publication. Deadline: December 31. Prize: 1st Place: $300 (CAD); 2nd Place: $150 (CAD); 3rd Place: $75; Honourable Mention: $25. All prizes include publication in the spring edition of *FreeFall Magazine*. Winners will also be invited to read at the launch of that issue if such a launch takes place. Honorable mentions in each category will be published and may be asked to read. Travel expenses not included. Judged by current guest editor for issue (who are also published authors in Canada).

GEORGETOWN REVIEW

Georgetown Review, 400 East College St., Box 227, Georgetown KY 40324. (502) 863-8308. **Fax:** (502) 863-8888. **E-mail:** gtownreview@georgetowncollege. edu. **Website:** http://georgetownreview.georgetown-college.edu. **Contact:** Steve Carter, editor. "Annual. Publishes short stories, poetry, and creative non-fiction. Reading period September 1-December 31. Also sponsors yearly writing contest for short stories, poetry, and creative nonfiction." Receives about 300 entries for each category. Entries are judged by the editors. Guidelines available in July. Accepts inquiries by e-mail. Contest open to anyone except family and friends of the editors. "Sometimes our contests are themed, so check the website for details." Results announced Februry or March. Winners notified by e-mail. Results made available to entrants with SASE. Cover letter and ms should include name, address, phone, e-mail, novel/story title. Writers may submit own work. Entries should be unpublished. Purpose is to publish quality work. Deadline: October 15. Prize: $1,000 and publication; runners-up receive publication.

✚ ◯ GOVERNOR GENERAL'S LITERARY AWARDS

Canada Council for the Arts, 350 Albert St., P.O. Box 1047, Ottawa ON K1P 5V8 Canada. (613)566-4414, ext. 4075. **Website:** www.canadacouncil.ca/prizes/ggla. (Specialized: Canadian citizens/permanent residents; English- and French-language works) Established by Parliament, the Canada Council for the Arts "provides a wide range of grants and services to professional Canadian artists and art organizations in dance, media arts, music, theater, writing, publishing, and the visual arts." The Governor General's Literary Awards, valued at $25,000 CAD each, are given annually for the best English-language and best French-language work in each of 7 categories, including poetry. Non-winning finalists each receive $1,000 CAD. Books must be first edition trade books written,

translated, or illustrated by Canadian citizens or permanent residents of Canada and published in Canada or abroad during the previous year (September 1 through the following September 30). Collections of poetry must be at least 48 pages long, and at least half the book must contain work not published previously in book form. In the case of translation, the original work must also be a Canadian-authored title. Books must be submitted by publishers with a Publisher's Submission Form, which is available on request from the Writing and Publishing Section of the Canada Council for the Arts. Guidelines and current deadlines on the website and available by mail, telephone, fax, or e-mail.

GREAT LAKES COLLEGES ASSOCIATION NEW WRITERS AWARD

535 W. William, Suite 301, Ann Arbor MI 48103. (734)661-2350. **Fax:** (734)661-2349. **E-mail:** wegner@glca.org. **Website:** www.glca.org. The New Writers Award is given for an author's first published volume, 1 in each category of fiction, creative nonfiction, and poetry. Writer must be nominated by publisher, and a publisher can submit only 1 entry for a given genre. The writer can submit a work directly if it is self-published. Prize: Winners are invited to tour the GLCA colleges. An honorarium of $500 will be guaranteed the author by each GLCA member college they visit. Judges are professors of literature and creative writing at GLCA's member colleges. No entry fee. Submitted volumes must be written in English and published in the US or Canada. Submit 4 copies of the book to Gregory R. Wegner, director of program development, at the GLCA mailing address listed above. Guidelines are published in February for a given year's award. Accepts inquiries by e-mail. Results announced in January of each year. Offers annual award to the best first book of poetry, fiction, and creative nonfiction among those submitted by publishers. The winning authors tour several of the 13 GLCA-member colleges (as invited) reading, lecturing, visiting classes, doing workshops, and publicizing their books. **Contact:** Gregory R. Wegner.

HACKNEY LITERARY AWARDS

1305 2nd Ave. North, #103, Birmingham AL 35203. (205)226-4921. **E-mail:** info@hackneyliteraryawards. org. **Website:** www.hackneyliteraryawards.org. **Contact:** Myra Crawford, PhD, executive director. Offered annually for unpublished novels, short stories (maximum 5,000 words) and poetry (50 line limit). Guidelines on website. Deadline: September 30 (novels), November 30 (short stories and poetry). Prize: $5,000 in annual prizes for poetry and short fiction ($2,500 national and $2,500 state level). 1st Place: $600; 2nd Place: $400; 3rd Place: $250; plus $5,000 for an unpublished novel. Competition winners will be announced on the website each March.

➕ ERIC HOFFER AWARD

Hopewell Publications, LLC, P.O. Box 11, Titusville NJ 08560-0011. **Fax:** (609)964-1718. **E-mail:** info@hopepubs.com. **Website:** www.hofferaward.com. **Contact:** Christopher Klim, chair. "Annual contest for previously published books. Recognizes excellence in independent publishing in many unique categories: Art (titles capture the experience, execution, or demonstration of the arts); Poetry (all styles); General Fiction (nongenre-specific fiction); Commercial Fiction (genre-specific fiction); Children (titles for young children); Young Adult (titles aimed at the juvenile and teen markets); Culture (titles demonstrating the human or world experience); Memoir (titles relating to personal experience); Business (titles with application to today's business environment and emerging trends); Reference (titles from traditional and emerging reference areas); Home (titles with practical applications to home or home-related issues, including family); Health (titles promoting physical, mental, and emotional well-being); Self-help (titles involving new and emerging topics in self-help); Spiritual (titles involving the mind and spirit, including religion); Legacy (titles over 2 years of age that hold particular relevance to any subject matter or form). Open to any writer of published work within the last 2 years, including categores for older books." "This contest recognizes excellence in independent publishing in many unique categories: Art, Poetry, General Fiction, Commercial Fiction, Children, Young Adult, Culture, Memoir, Business, Reference, Home, Health, Self-help, Spiritual, and Legacy (fiction and nonfiction)." January 21. Prize: $2,000 Grand Prize, the Montaigne Medal for the most thought-provoking book, the Da Vinci Eye for the best cover, and the New Horizons Award for best new authors, international press/media, and coverage in *The US Review of Books*. Judges include authors, editors, agents, publishers, book producers, artists, experienced category readers, and health and business professionals.

INDIANA REVIEW (SHORT-SHORT/ PROSE-POEM) CONTEST

Indiana Review, Ballantine Hall 465, 1020 E. Kirkwood Ave., Indiana University, Bloomington IN 47405-7103. (812)855-3439. **Fax:** (812)855-9535. **E-mail:** inreview@indiana.edu. **Website:** http://indianareview.org. **Contact:** Alessandra Simmons, editor. Offered annually for unpublished work. Maximum story/poem length is 500 words. Guidelines available in March for SASE, by phone, e-mail, on website, or in publication. Open to any writer. Cover letter should include name, address, phone, e-mail, word count and title. No identifying information on ms. "We look for command of language and form." Results announced in August. Winners notified by mail. For contest results, send SASE or visit website. Deadline: June. Prize: $1,000, plus publication, contributor's copies, and a year's subscription to *Indiana Review*. Guest judge for 2011 was Ander Monson.

INSIGHT WRITING CONTEST

Insight Magazine, 55 W. Oak Ridge Dr., Hagerstown MD 21740. **Fax:** (301)393-4055. **E-mail:** insight@rhpa.org. **Website:** www.insightmagazine.org. **Contact:** Dwain Esmond, editor. Annual contest for writers in the categories of student short story, general short story, and student poetry. Unpublished submissions only. General category is open to all writers; student categories must be age 22 and younger. Deadline: May 31. Prize: **Student Short Story** and **General Short Story:** 1st Prize: $250; 2nd Prize: $200; 3rd Prize: $150. **Student Poetry:** 1st Prize: $100; 2nd Prize: $75; 3rd Prize: $50. Entries must include cover sheet. Form available with SASE or on website. See website for rules and more information.

THE IOWA REVIEW AWARD IN POETRY, FICTION, AND NONFICTION

308 EPB, University of Iowa, Iowa City IA 52242. **E-mail:** iowa-review@uiowa.edu. **Website:** www.iowareview.org. **Contact:** Contest Coordinator. *The Iowa Review* Award in Poetry, Fiction, and Nonfiction presents $1,500 to each winner in each genre, $750 to runners-up. Winners and runners-up published in *The Iowa Review*. 2011 winners were Emily Van Kley, John Van Kirk, and Helen Phillips. Submissions must be unpublished. Considers simultaneous submissions (with notification of acceptance elsewhere). Submit up to 25 pages of prose, (double-spaced) or 10 pages of poetry (1 poem or several, but no more than

1 poem per page). Submit online or by mail. Include cover page with writer's name, address, e-mail and/ or phone number, and title of each work submitted. Personal identification must not appear on ms pages. Label mailing envelope as a contest entry, E.G., "Contest: Fiction." One entry per envelope. Include SASP for confirmation of receipt of entry, SASE for results. Guidelines available on website. Deadline: Submit January 1-31 (postmark). 2012 Judges: Timothy Donnelly, Ron Currie, Jr., and Meghan Daum.

THE MCGINNIS-RITCHIE MEMORIAL AWARD

Southwest Review, P.O. Box 750374, Dallas TX 75275-0374. (214)768-1037. **Fax:** (214)768-1408. **E-mail:** swr@mail.smu.edu. **Website:** www.smu.edu/southwestreview. **Contact:** Jennifer Cranfill, senior editor, and Willard Spiegelman, editor-in-chief. "The McGinnis-Ritchie Memorial Award is given annually to the best works of fiction and nonfiction that appeared in the magazine in the previous year. Mss are submitted for publication, not for the prizes themselves. Guidelines for SASE or online." Prize: 2 cash prizes of $500 each. Judged by Jennifer Cranfill and Willard Spiegelman.

NEW LETTERS LITERARY AWARDS

New Letters, UMKC, University House, Room 105, 5101 Rockhill Rd., Kansas City MO 64110-2499. (816)235-1168. **Fax:** (816)235-2611. **Website:** www. newletters.org. Award has 3 categories (fiction, poetry, and creative nonfiction) with 1 winner in each. Offered annually for previously unpublished work. "For guidelines, send an SASE to *New Letters*, or visit www. newletters.org." Deadline: May 18. Prize: "1st place: $1,500, plus publication; first runners-up: a copy of a recent book of poetry or fiction courtesy of our affiliate BkMk Press. Preliminary judges are regional writers of prominence and experience. All judging is done anonymously. Winners picked by a final judge of national repute. Previous judges include Maxine Kumin, Albert Goldbarth, Charles Simic, Janet Burroway."

NEW MILLENNIUM AWARDS FOR FICTION, POETRY, AND NONFICTION

P.O. Box 2463, Room M2, Knoxville TN 37901. (423)428-0389. **Website:** www.newmillenniumwritings.com/awards; www.writingawards.com. "No restrictions as to style, content or number of submissions. Previously published pieces OK if online or under 5,000 print circulation. Send any time between now and midnight, June 17, for the Summer Awards program, January 31 for the Winter Awards. Simultaneous and multiple submissions welcome. Each fiction or nonfiction piece is a separate entry and should total no more than 6,000 words, except for the Short-Short Fiction Award, which should total no more than 1,000 words. (Nonfiction includes essays, profiles, memoirs, interviews, creative nonfiction, travel, humor, etc.) Each poetry entry may include up to 3 poems, not to exceed 5 pages total. All 20 poetry finalists will be published. Include name, phone, address, e-mail, and category on cover page only." Apply online via submissions manager. "Send SASE or IRC for list of winners or await your book." Entries should be postmarked on or before June 17 or January 31. Prize: $1,000 for Best Poem; $1,000 for Best Fiction; $1,000 for Best Nonfiction; $1,000 for Best Short-Short Fiction.

NEW SOUTH WRITING CONTEST

Georgia State University, Campus Box 1894, MSC 8R0322, Unit 8, Atlanta GA 30303-3083. **E-mail:** newsouth@gsu.edu. **Website:** www.review.gsu.edu. **Contact:** Editor. Offered annually to publish the most promising work of up-and-coming writers of poetry (up to 3 poems) and fiction (9,000 word limit). Rights revert to writer upon publication. Guidelines online. Deadline: March 5. Prize: 1st Place: $1,000 in each category; 2nd Place: $250; and publication to winners.

OHIOANA BOOK AWARDS

Ohioana Library Association, 274 E. First Ave., Suite 300, Columbus OH 43201-3673. (614)466-3831. **Fax:** (614)728-6974. **E-mail:** ohioana@ohioana.org. **Website:** www.ohioana.org. **Contact:** Linda Hengst, executive director. Offered annually to bring national attention to Ohio authors and their books, published in the last 2 years. (Books can only be considered once.) Categories: Fiction, nonfiction, juvenile, poetry, and books about Ohio or an Ohioan. Writers must have been born in Ohio or lived in Ohio for at least 5 years, but books about Ohio or an Ohioan need not be written by an Ohioan. Prize: certificate and glass sculpture. Judged by a jury selected by librarians, book reviewers, writers and other knowledgeable people. Each winter the jury considers all books received since the previous jury. No entry fee. **Deadline: December 31.** A copy of the book must be received by the Ohioana Library by December 31 prior to the year the award is given; literary quality of the book must be outstanding. No entry forms are needed, but they are available July 1 of each year. Specific questions should be sent to Ohioana. Results announced in August or September. Winners notified by mail in May.

JUDITH SIEGEL PEARSON AWARD

Wayne State University/Family of Judith Siegel Pearson, Attn: Writing Awards Committee, 5057 Woodward Ave., Suite 9408, Detroit MI 48202. (313)577-2450. **Fax:** (313)577-8618. **E-mail:** ad2073@wayne.edu. Offers an annual award of up to $500 for the best creative or scholarly work on a subject concerning women. The type of work accepted rotates each year: Drama in 2012; poetry in 2013 (poetry, 20 pages maximum); essays in 2014; fiction in 2015. Open to all interested writers and scholars. Submissions must be unpublished. Guidelines available by e-mail. No late or electronic submissions accepted. Deadline: Mid-late February. Offers an annual award of up to $500 for the best creative or scholarly work on a subject concerning women. The type of work accepted rotates each year: Drama in 2012; poetry in 2013 (poetry, 20 pages maximum); essays in 2014; fiction in 2015. Open to all interested writers and scholars. Submissions must be unpublished. Guidelines available by e-mail. No late or electronic submissions accepted. Deadline: Mid-late February. **Contact:** Royanne Smith, contest coordinator.

THE PINCH LITERARY AWARD IN FICTION AND POETRY

The University of Memphis/Hohenberg Foundation, Department of English, 435 Patterson Hall, Memphis TN 38152. (901)678-4591. **E-mail:** editor@thepinchjournal.com. **Website:** www.thepinchjournal.com. Offered annually for unpublished short stories of 5,000 words maximum or up to three poems. Guidelines on website. Cost: $20, which is put toward one issue of *The Pinch*. Deadline: March 15. Prize: 1st place Fiction: $1,500 and publication; 1st place Poetry: $1,000 and publication. Offered annually for unpublished short stories of 5,000 words maximum or up to three poems. Guidelines on website. Cost: $20, which is put toward one issue of *The Pinch*. Deadline: March 15. Prize: 1st place Fiction: $1,500 and publication; 1st place Poetry: $1,000 and publication. Offered annually for unpublished short stories of 5,000 words maximum or up to three poems. Guidelines on website. Deadline: March 15. Prize: 1st place Fic-

tion: $1,500 and publication; 1st place Poetry: $1,000 and publication.

PNWA LITERARY CONTEST

Pacific Northwest Writers Association, PMB 2717-1420 NW Gilman Blvd, Suite 2, Issaquah WA 98027. (425)673-2665. **Fax:** (206)824-4559. **E-mail:** staff@pnwa.org. **Website:** www.pnwa.org. **Contact:** Kelli Liddane. **Open to students.** Annual contest. Purpose of contest: "Valuable tool for writers as contest submissions are critiqued (2 critiques)." Unpublished submissions only. Submissions made by author. Deadline for entries: February 18, 2011. Entry fee is $35/entry for members, $50/entry for nonmembers. Awards $700-1st; $300-2nd. Awards in all 12 categories.

THE PRESIDIO LA BAHIA AWARD

Sons of the Republic of Texas, 1717 Eighth St., Bay City TX 77414-5033. (979)245-6644. **Fax:** (979)244-3819. **E-mail:** srttexas@srttexas.org. **Website:** www.srttexas.org. **Contact:** Scott Dunbar, chairman. Offered annually to promote suitable preservation of relics, appropriate dissemination of data, and research into Texas heritage, with particular attention to the Spanish Colonial period. Deadline: September 30. Prize: $2,000 total; 1st Place: Minimum of $1,200; 2nd and 3rd prizes at the discretion of the judges Judged by members of the Sons of the Republic of Texas on the Presidio La Bahia Award Committee.

✪ THE RBC BRONWEN WALLACE AWARD FOR EMERGING WRITERS

The Writers' Trust of Canada, 90 Richmond St. East, Suite 200, Toronto, Ontario M5C 1P1 Canada. (416)504-8222. **Fax:** (416)504-9090. **E-mail:** info@writerstrust.com. **Website:** www.writerstrust.com. **Contact:** Amanda Hopkins. Presented annually to "a Canadian writer under the age of 35 who is not yet published in book form. The award, which alternates each year between poetry and short fiction, was established in memory of poet Bronwen Wallace." Prize: $5,000 and $1,000 to 2 finalists.

✪ REGINA BOOK AWARD

Saskatchewan Book Awards, Inc., 100-2400 College Ave., Regina SK S4P 0K1 Canada. (306)569-1585. **Fax:** (306)569-4187. **E-mail:** director@bookawards.sk.ca. **Website:** www.bookawards.sk.ca. **Contact:** Executive director, book submissions. Offered annually. "In recognition of the vitality of the literary community in Regina, this award is presented to a

Regina author for the best book, judged on the quality of writing." Books from the following categories will be considered: Children's; drama; fiction (short fiction by a single author, novellas, novels); nonfiction (all categories of nonfiction writing except cookbooks, directories, how-to books, or bibliographies of minimal critical content); poetry. Deadline: November 1. Prize: $2,000 (CAD).

SUMMERFIELD G. ROBERTS AWARD

Sons of the Republic of Texas, 1717 Eighth St., Bay City TX 77414-5033. (979)245-6644. **Fax:** (979)244-3819. **E-mail:** srttexas@srttexas.org. **Website:** www. srttexas.org. **Contact:** David Hanover, chairman. Offered annually for submissions published during the previous calendar year to encourage literary effort and research about historical events and personalities during the days of the Republic of Texas, 1836-1846, and to stimulate interest in the period. Deadline: January 15. Prize: $2,500 the last 3 winners of the contest.

☉ SASKATCHEWAN BOOK OF THE YEAR AWARD

Saskatchewan Book Awards, Inc., 100-2400 College Ave., Regina SK S4P OK1 Canada. (306)569-1585. **Fax:** (306)569-4187. **E-mail:** director@bookawards. sk.ca. **Website:** www.bookawards.sk.ca. **Contact:** Executive director, book submissions. Offered annually. "This award is presented to a Saskatchewan author for the best book, judged on the quality of writing. Books from the following categories will be considered: children's; drama; fiction (short fiction by a single author, novellas, novels); nonfiction (all categories of nonfiction writing except cookbooks, directories, how-to books, or bibliographies of minimal critical content); poetry. Visit website for more details." Deadline: November 1. Prize: $3,000 (CAD).

☉ SASKATOON BOOK AWARD

Saskatchewan Book Awards, Inc., 100-2400 College Ave., Regina SK S4P OK1 Canada. (306)569-1585. **Fax:** (306)569-4187. **E-mail:** director@bookawards.sk.ca. **Website:** www.bookawards.sk.ca. **Contact:** Executive director, book submissions. Offered annually. "This award is presented to a Saskatoon author (or pair of authors) for the best book, judged on the quality of writing." Books from the following categories will be considered: Children's; drama; fiction (short fiction by a single author, novellas, novels); nonfiction (all categories of nonfiction writing except cookbooks, directories, how-to books, or bibliographies of mini-mal critical content); poetry. Deadline: November 1. Prize: $2,000 (CAD).

THE MONA SCHREIBER PRIZE FOR HUMOROUS FICTION & NONFICTION

3940 Laurel Canyon Blvd., #566, Studio City CA 91604. **E-mail:** brad.schreiber@att.net. **Website:** www.brashcyber.com. **Contact:** Brad Schreiber. "The purpose of the contest is to award the most creative humor writing, in any form less than 750 words, in either fiction or nonfiction, including but not limited to stories, articles, essays, speeches, shopping lists, diary entries, and anything else writers dream up." Deadline: December 1. Prize: 1st Place: $500; 2nd Place: $250; 3rd Place: $100. Brad Schreiber, author, journalist, consultant, and instructor at MediaBistro.com. Complete rules and previous winning entries on website.

KAY SNOW WRITERS' CONTEST

9045 SW Barbur Blvd. #5A, Portland OR 97219-4027. (503)452-1592. **Fax:** (503)452-0372. **E-mail:** wilwrite@teleport.com. **Website:** www.willamettewriters.com. **Contact:** Lizzy Shannon, contest director. Annual contest. **Open to students.** Purpose of contest: "to encourage beginning and established writers to continue the craft." Unpublished, original submissions only. Submissions made by the author. Deadline for entries: April 23rd. SASE for contest rules and entry forms. Entry fee is $10, Williamette Writers' members; $15, nonmembers; free for student writers grades 1-12. Awards cash prize of $300 per category (fiction, nonfiction, juvenile, poetry, script writing), $50 for students in three divisions: 1-5, 6-8, 9-12. Judges are anonymous.

☉ SUBTERRAIN ANNUAL LITERARY AWARDS COMPETITION: THE LUSH TRIUMPHANT

P.O. Box 3008 MPO, Vancouver BC V6B 3X5 Canada. (604)876-8710. **Fax:** (604)879-2667. **E-mail:** subter@ portal.ca. **Website:** www.subterrain.ca. Entrants may submit as many entries in as many categories as they like. Fiction: Max of 3,000 words. Poetry: A suite of 5 related poems (max of 15 pages). Creative Nonfiction based on fact, adorned with fiction): Max of 4,000 words. "All entries MUST be previously unpublished material and not currently under consideration in any other contest or competition." Deadline: May 15. Prize: Winners in each category will receive $750 cash (plus payment for publication) and publication in the Winter issue. First runner-up in each category will received a $250 cash prize and be published in the Spring issue of *subTerrain*. All entrants receive a complimentary 1-year subscription to *subTerrain*.

☯ TORONTO BOOK AWARDS

City of Toronto c/o Toronto Protocol, 100 Queen St. W., City Clerk's Office, 2nd floor, West Tower, Toronto ON M5H 2N2 Canada. (416)392-7805. **Fax:** (416)392-1247. **E-mail:** bkurmey@toronto.ca. **Website:** www. toronto.ca/book_awards. **Contact:** Bev Kurmey, protocol officer. The Toronto Book Awards honor authors of books of literary or artistic merit that are evocative of Toronto. Annual award for short stories, novels, poetry or short story collections. Prize: $15,000. Each short-listed author (usually 4-6) receives $1,000 and the winner receives the remainder. Categories: No separate categories—novels, short story collections, books of poetry, biographies, history, books about sports, children's books—all are judged together. Judged by jury of five who have demonstrated interest and/or experience in literature, literacy, books and book publishing. No entry fee. Cover letter should include name, address, phone, e-mail and title of entry. Six copies of the entry book are also required. **Deadline: last week of March.** Entries must be previously published. Guidelines available in September on website. Accepts inquires by fax, e-mail, phone. Finalists announced in June; winners notified in September at a gala reception. Guidelines and results available on website.

WORLD'S BEST SHORT-SHORT STORY FICTION CONTEST, NARRATIVE NONFICTION CONTEST & SOUTHEAST REVIEW POETRY CONTEST

English Department, Florida State University, Tallahassee FL 32306. **E-mail:** southeastreview@gmail. com. **Website:** www.southeastreview.org. **Contact:** Katie Cortese, acquisitions editor. Annual award for unpublished short-short stories (500 words or less), poetry, and narrative nonfiction (6,000 words or less). Deadline: March 15. Prize: $500 per category. Winners and finalists will be published in *The Southeast Review*.

WRITER'S DIGEST WRITING COMPETITION

F+W Media, Inc., 700 E. State St., Iola WI 54990. (513)531-2690, ext. 1328. **E-mail:** writing-competition@fwmedia.com; nicole.florence@fwmedia.com. **Website:** www.writersdigest.com. **Contact:** Nicki Florence. Annual awards in multiple categories, including, inspirational writing, memoir/personal essay, magazine feature article, short story, rhyming poetry, nonrhyming poetry, stage play, TV/movie script. Guidelines available online. Open to any writer. Deadline: May 2. Grand Prize: $3,000 and trip to New York City to meet with editors and agents. Each category has 1st Place ($1,000), 2nd Place ($500), 3rd Place ($250), and more.

☯ WRITERS GUILD OF ALBERTA AWARDS

Writers Guild of Alberta, Percy Page Centre, 11759 Groat Rd., Edmonton AB T5M 3K6 Canada. (780)422-8174. **Fax:** (780)422-2663. **E-mail:** mail@ writersguild.ab.ca. **Website:** www.writersguild. ab.ca. **Contact:** Executive Director. Offers the following awards: Wilfrid Eggleston Award for Nonfiction; Georges Bugnet Award for Fiction; Howard O'Hagan Award for Short Story; Stephan G. Stephansson Award for Poetry; R. Ross Annett Award for Children's Literature; Gwen Pharis Ringwood Award for Drama; Jon Whyte Memorial Essay Prize; James H. Gray Award for Short Nonfiction; Amber Bowerman Memorial Travel Writing Award. Eligible entries will have been published anywhere in the world between January 1 and December 31 of the current year; the authors must have been residents of Alberta for at least 12 of the 18 months prior to December 31. Unpublished mss, except in the drama, essay, and short nonfiction categories, are not eligible. Anthologies are not eligible. Works may be submitted by authors, publishers, or any interested parties. Deadline: December 31. Prize: Winning authors receive $1,500; essay prize winners receive $700. Other awards: Isabel Miller Young Writers Award; authors must be 12-18 years of age and a resident of Alberta.

PROFESSIONAL ORGANIZATIONS

//

AGENTS' ORGANIZATIONS

ASSOCIATION OF AUTHORS' AGENTS (AAA), David Higham Associates Ltd, 5-8 Lower John Street, Golden Square, London W1F 9HA . (020) 7434 5900. E-mail: anthonygoff@david-higham.co.uk. Website: www.agentsassoc.co.uk.

ASSOCIATION OF AUTHORS' REPRESENTATIVES (AAR). E-mail: info@aar-online.org. Website: www.aar-online.org.

ASSOCIATION OF TALENT AGENTS (ATA), 9255 Sunset Blvd., Suite 930, Los Angeles CA 90069. (310)274-0628. Fax: (310)274-5063. E-mail: shellie@agentassociation.com. Website: www.agentassociation.com.

WRITERS' ORGANIZATIONS

ACADEMY OF AMERICAN POETS 584 Broadway, Suite 604, New York NY 10012-5243. (212)274-0343. Fax: (212)274-9427. E-mail: academy@poets.org. Website: www.poets.org.

AMERICAN CRIME WRITERS LEAGUE (ACWL), 17367 Hilltop Ridge Dr., Eureka MO 63205. Website: www.acwl.org.

AMERICAN INDEPENDENT WRITERS (AIW), 1001 Connecticut Ave. NW, Suite 701, Washington DC 20036. (202)775-5150. Fax: (202)775-5810. E-mail: info@aiwriters.org. Website: www.americanindependentwriters.org.

AMERICAN MEDICAL WRITERS ASSOCIATION (AMWA), 30 West Gude Drive, Suite 525, Rockville MD 20850-4347. (301)294-5303. Fax: (301)294-9006. E-mail: amwa@amwa.org. Website: www.amwa.org.

AMERICAN SCREENWRITERS ASSOCIATION (ASA), 269 S. Beverly Dr., Suite 2600, Beverly Hills CA 90212-3807. (866)265-9091. E-mail: asa@goasa.com. Website: www.asascreenwriters.com.

AMERICAN TRANSLATORS ASSOCIATION (ATA), 225 Reinekers Lane, Suite 590, Alexandria VA 22314. (703)683-6100. Fax: (703)683-6122. E-mail: ata@atanet.org. Website: www.atanet.org.

EDUCATION WRITERS ASSOCIATION (EWA), 2122 P St., NW Suite 201, Washington DC 20037. (202)452-9830. Fax: (202)452-9837. E-mail: ewa@ewa.org. Website: www.ewa.org.

GARDEN WRITERS ASSOCIATION (GWA), 10210 Leatherleaf Ct., Manassas VA 20111. (703)257-1032. Fax: (703)257-0213. E-mail: info@gardenwriters.org. Website: www.gardenwriters.org.

HORROR WRITERS ASSOCIATION (HWA), 244 5th Ave., Suite 2767, New York NY 10001. E-mail: hwa@horror.org. Website: www.horror.org.

THE INTERNATIONAL WOMEN'S WRITING GUILD (IWWG),P.O. Box 810, Gracie Station, New York NY 10028-0082. (212)737-7536. Fax: (212)737-9469. E-mail: dirhahn@aol.org. Website: www.iwwg.com.

MYSTERY WRITERS OF AMERICA (MWA), 1140 Broadway, Suite 1507, New York NY 10001. (212)888-8171. Fax: (212)888-8107. E-mail: mwa@mysterywriters.org. Website: www.mysterywriters.org.

NATIONAL ASSOCIATION OF SCIENCE WRITERS (NASW), P.O. Box 7905, Berkeley, CA 94707. (510)647-9500. E-mail: LFriedmann@nasw.org. website: www.nasw.org.

NATIONAL ASSOCIATION OF WOMEN WRITERS (NAWW), 24165 IH-10 W., Suite 217-637, San Antonio TX 78257. Phone/Fax: (866)821-5829. Website: www.naww.org.

ORGANIZATION OF BLACK SCREENWRITERS (OBS). Golden State Mutual Life Insurance Bldg., 1999 West Adams Blvd., Rm. Mezzanine Los Angeles, CA 90018. Website: www.obswriter.com.

OUTDOOR WRITERS ASSOCIATION OF AMERICA (OWAA), 121 Hickory St., Suite 1, Missoula MT 59801. (406)728-7434. Fax: (406)728-7445. E-mail: krhoades@owaa.org. Website: www.owaa.org.

POETRY SOCIETY OF AMERICA (PSA), 15 Gramercy Park, New York NY 10003. (212)254-9628. website: www.poetrysociety.org. Poets & Writers, 90 Broad St., Suite 2100, New York NY 10004. (212)226-3586. Fax: (212)226-3963. Website: www.pw.org.

ROMANCE WRITERS OF AMERICA (RWA), 114615 Benfer Road, Houston TX 77069. (832)717-5200. Fax: (832)717-5201. E-mail: info@rwanational.org. Website: www.rwanational.org.

SCIENCE FICTION AND FANTASY WRITERS OF AMERICA (SFWA), P.O. Box 877, Chestertown MD 21620. E-mail: execdir@sfwa.org. Website: www.sfwa.org.

SOCIETY OF AMERICAN BUSINESS EDITORS & WRITERS (SABEW), University of Missouri, School of Journalism, 30 Neff Annex, Columbia MO 65211. (602) 496-7862. E-mail: sabew@sabew.org. Website: www.sabew.org.

SOCIETY OF AMERICAN TRAVEL WRITERS (SATW), 7044 S. 13 St., Oak Creek WI 53154. (414)908-4949. Fax: (414)768-8001. E-mail: satw@satw.org. Website: www.satw.org.

SOCIETY OF CHILDREN'S BOOK WRITERS & ILLUSTRATORS (SCBWI), 8271 Beverly Blvd., Los Angeles CA 90048. (323)782-1010. Fax: (323)782-1892. E-mail: scbwi@scbwi.org. Website: www.scbwi.org.

WESTERN WRITERS OF AMERICA (WWA). E-mail: spiritfire@kc.rr.com. Website: www.westernwriters.org.

INDUSTRY ORGANIZATIONS

AMERICAN BOOKSELLERS ASSOCIATION (ABA), 200 White Plains Rd., Suite 600, Tarrytown NY 10591. (914)591-2665. Fax: (914)591-2720. E-mail: info@bookweb.org. Website: www.bookweb.org.

AMERICAN SOCIETY OF JOURNALISTS & AUTHORS (ASJA), 1501 Broadway, Suite 302, New York NY 10036. (212)997-0947. Fax: (212)937-2315. E-mail: director@asja.org. Website: www.asja.org.

ASSOCIATION FOR WOMEN IN COMMUNICATIONS (AWC), 3337 Duke St., Alexandria VA 22314. (703)370-7436. Fax: (703)342-4311. E-mail: info@womcom.org. Website: www.womcom.org.

ASSOCIATION OF AMERICAN PUBLISHERS (AAP), 71 5th Ave., 2nd Floor, New York NY 10003. (212)255-0200. Fax: (212)255-7007. Or, 50 F St. NW, Suite 400, Washington DC 20001. (202)347-3375. Fax: (202)347-3690. Website: www.publishers.org.

THE ASSOCIATION OF WRITERS & WRITING PROGRAMS (AWP), Mail Stop 1E3, George Mason University, Fairfax VA 22030. (703)993-4301. Fax: (703)993-4302. E-mail: services@awp-writer.org. website: www.awpwriter.org.

THE AUTHORS GUILD, INC., 31 E. 32nd St., 7th Floor, New York NY 10016. (212)563-5904. Fax: (212)564-5363. E-mail: staff@authorsguild.org. website: www.authorsguild.org.

CANADIAN AUTHORS ASSOCIATION (CAA), P.O. Box 581, Stn. Main Orilla ON L3V 6K5 Canada. (705)653-0323. Fax: (705)653-0593. E-mail: admin@canauthors.org. Website: www.canauthors.org.

CHRISTIAN BOOKSELLERS ASSOCIATION (CBA), P.O. Box 62000, Colorado Springs CO 80962-2000. (800)252-1950. Fax: (719)272-3510. E-mail: info@cbaonline.org. website: www.cba-online.org.

THE DRAMATISTS GUILD OF AMERICA, 1501 Broadway, Suite 701, New York NY 10036. (212)398-9366. Fax: (212)944-0420. Website: www.dramatistsguild.com.

NATIONAL LEAGUE OF AMERICAN PEN WOMEN (NLAPW), 1300 17th St. NW, Washington DC 20036-1973. (202)785-1997. Fax: (202)452-8868. E-mail: nlapw1@verizon.net. Website: www.americanpenwomen.org.

NATIONAL WRITERS ASSOCIATION (NWA), 10940 S. Parker Rd., #508, Parker CO 80134. (303)841-0246. Fax: (303)841-2607. E-mail: natlwritersassn@hotmail.com. Website: www.nationalwriters.com

NATIONAL WRITERS UNION (NWU), 256 West 38th Street, Suite 703, New York, NY 10018. (212)254-0279. Fax: (212)254-0673. E-mail: nwu@nwu.org. Website: www.nwu.org.

PEN AMERICAN CENTER, 588 Broadway, Suite 303, New York NY 10012-3225. (212)334-1660. Fax: (212)334-2181. E-mail: pen@pen.org. Website: www.pen.org.

THE PLAYWRIGHTS GUILD OF CANADA (PGC), 215 Spadina Ave., Suite #210, Toronto ON M5T 2C7 Canada. (416)703-0201. Fax: (416)703-0059. E-mail: info@playwrightsguild.ca. Website: www.playwrightsguild.com.

VOLUNTEER LAWYERS FOR THE ARTS (VLA), One E. 53rd St., 6th Floor, New York NY 10022. (212)319-2787. Fax: (212)752-6575. Website: www.vlany.org.

WOMEN IN FILM (WIF), 6100 Wilshire Blvd., Suite 710, Los Angeles CA 90048. (323)935-2211. Fax: (323)935-2212. E-mail: info@wif.org. Website: www.wif.org.

WOMEN'S NATIONAL BOOK ASSOCIATION (WNBA), P.O. Box 237, FDR Station, New York NY 10150. (212)208-4629. Fax: (212)208-4629. E-mail: publicity@bookbuzz.com. Website: www.wnba-books.org.

WRITERS GUILD OF ALBERTA (WGA), 11759 Groat Rd., Edmonton AB T5M 3K6 Canada. (780)422-8174. Fax: (780)422-2663. E-mail: mail@writersguild.ab.ca. Website: writersguild. ab.ca.

WRITERS GUILD OF AMERICA-EAST (WGA), 555 W. 57th St., Suite 1230, New York NY 10019. (212)767-7800. Fax: (212)582-1909. e-mail: info@wgaeast.org. Website: www.wgaeast.org.

WRITERS GUILD OF AMERICA-WEST (WGA), 7000 W. Third St., Los Angeles CA 90048. (323)951-4000. Fax: (323)782-4800. Website: www.wga.org.

WRITERS UNION OF CANADA (TWUC), 90 Richmond St. E., Suite 200, Toronto ON M5C 1P1 Canada. (416)703-8982. Fax: (416)504-9090. E-mail: info@writersunion.ca. Website: www.writersunion.ca.

GLOSSARY

#10 ENVELOPE. A standard, business-size envelope.

ADVANCE. A sum of money a publisher pays a writer prior to the publication of a book. It is usually paid in installments, such as one-half on signing the contract; one-half on delivery of a complete and satisfactory manuscript.

AGENT. A liaison between a writer and editor or publisher. An agent shops a manuscript around, receiving a commission when the manuscript is accepted. Agents usually take a 10-15% fee from the advance and royalties.

ARC. Advance reader copy.

ASSIGNMENT. Editor asks a writer to produce a specific article for an agreed-upon fee.

AUCTION. Publishers sometimes bid for the acquisition of a book manuscript that has excellent sales prospects. The bids are for the amount of the author's advance, advertising and promotional expenses, royalty percentage, etc. Auctions are conducted by agents.

AVANT-GARDE. Writing that is innovative in form, style, or subject.

BACKLIST. A publisher's list of its books that were not published during the current season, but that are still in print.

BIMONTHLY. Every two months.

BIO. A sentence or brief paragraph about the writer; can include education and work experience.

BIWEEKLY. Every two weeks.

BLOG. Short for weblog. Used by writers to build platform by posting regular commentary, observations, poems, tips, etc.

BLURB. The copy on paperback book covers or hard cover book dust jackets, either promoting the book and the author or featuring testimonials from book reviewers or well-known people in the book's field. Also called flap copy or jacket copy.

BOILERPLATE. A standardized contract.

BOUND GALLEYS. A prepublication edition of a book, usually prepared from photocopies of the final galley proofs; also known as ``bound proofs.'' Designed for promotional purposes, bound galleys serve as the first set of review copies to be mailed out.

BYLINE. Name of the author appearing with the published piece.

CATEGORY FICTION. A term used to include all types of fiction.

CHAPBOOK. A small booklet usually paperback of poetry, ballads or tales.

CIRCULATION. The number of subscribers to a magazine.

CLIPS. Samples, usually from newspapers or magazines, of a writer's published work.

COFFEE-TABLE BOOK. An heavily illustrated oversize book.

COMMERCIAL NOVELS. Novels designed to appeal to a broad audience. These are often broken down into categories such as western, mystery and romance. See also genre.

CONTRIBUTOR'S COPIES. Copies of the issues of magazines sent to the author in which the author's work appears.

CO-PUBLISHING. Arrangement where author and publisher share publications costs and profits of a book. Also known as cooperative publishing.

COPYEDITING. Editing a manuscript for grammar, punctuation, printing style and factual accuracy.

COPYRIGHT. A means to protect an author's work. See ``Minding the Details'' for more information.

COVER LETTER. A brief letter that accompanies the manuscript being sent to and agent or editor.

CREATIVE NONFICTION. Nonfictional writing that uses an innovative approach to the subject and creative language.

CRITIQUING SERVICE. Am editing service in which writers pay a fee for comments on the salability or other qualities of their manuscript. Fees vary, as do the quality of the critiques.

CV. Curriculum vita. A brief listing of qualifications and career accomplishments.

ELECTRONIC RIGHTS. Secondary or subsidiary rights dealing with electronic/multimedia formats (i.e., the Internet, CD-ROMs, electronic magazines).

ELECTRONIC SUBMISSION. A submission made by modem or on computer disk.

EROTICA. Fiction or art that is sexually oriented.

EVALUATION FEES. Fees an agent may charge to evaluate material. The extent and quality of this evaluation varies, but comments usually concern the salability of the manuscript.

FAIR USE. A provision of the copyright law that says short passages from copyrighted material may be used without infringing on the owner's rights.

FEATURE. An article giving the reader information of human interest rather than news.

FILLER. A short item used by an editor to "fill" out a newspaper column or magazine page. It could be a joke, an anecdote, etc.

FILM RIGHTS. Rights sold or optioned by the agent/author to a person in the film industry, enabling the book to be made into a movie.

FOREIGN RIGHTS. Translation or reprint rights to be sold abroad.

FRONTLIST. A publisher's list of books that are new to the current season.

GALLEYS. The first typeset version of a manuscript that has not yet been divided into pages.

GENRE. Refers either to a general classification of writing, such as the novel or the poem, or to the categories within those classifications, such as the problem novel or the sonnet.

GHOSTWRITER. A writer who puts into literary form an article, speech, story or book based on another person's ideas or knowledge.

GRAPHIC NOVEL. A story in graphic form, long comic strip, or heavily illustrated story; of 40 pages or more.

HI-LO. A type of fiction that offers a high level of interest for readers at a low reading level.

HIGH CONCEPT. A story idea easily expressed in a quick, one-line description.

HONORARIUM. Token payment--small amount of money, or a byline and copies of the publication.

HOOK. Aspect of the work that sets it apart from others and draws in the reader/viewer.

HOW-TO. Books and magazine articles offering a combination of information and advice in describing how something can be accomplished.

IMPRINT. Name applied to a publisher's specific line of books.

JOINT CONTRACT. A legal agreement between a publisher and two or more authors, establishing provisions for the division of royalties the book generates.

KILL FEE. Fee for a complete article that was assigned and then cancelled.

LEAD TIME. The time between the acquisition of a manuscript by an editor and its actual publication.

LITERARY FICTION. The general category of serious, non-formulaic, intelligent fiction.

MAINSTREAM FICTION. Fiction that transcends popular novel categories such as mystery, romance and science fiction.

MARKETING FEE. Fee charged by some agents to cover marketing expenses. It may be used to cover postage, telephone calls, faxes, photocopying or any other expense incurred in marketing a manuscript.

MASS MARKET. Non-specialized books of wide appeal directed toward a large audience.

MEMOIR. A narrative recounting a writer's (or fictional narrator's) personal or family history; specifics may be altered, though essentially considered nonfiction.

MIDDLE GRADE OR MID-GRADE. The general classification of books written for readers approximately ages 9-11. Also called middle readers.

MIDLIST. Those titles on a publisher's list that are not expected to be big sellers, but are expected to have limited/modest sales.

MODEL RELEASE. A paper signed by the subject of a photograph giving the photographer permission to use the photograph.

MULTIPLE CONTRACT. Book contract with an agreement for a future book(s).

MULTIPLE SUBMISSIONS. Sending more than one book or article idea to a publisher at the same time.

NARRATIVE NONFICTION. A narrative presentation of actual events.

NET ROYALTY. A royalty payment based on the amount of money a book publisher receives on the sale of a book after booksellers' discounts, special sales discounts and returns.

NOVELLA. A short novel, or a long short story; approximately 7,000 to 15,000 words.

ON SPEC. An editor expresses an interest in a proposed article idea and agrees to consider the finished piece for publication "on speculation." The editor is under no obligation to buy the finished manuscript.

ONE-TIME RIGHTS. Rights allowing a manuscript to be published one time. The work can be sold again by the writer without violating the contract.

OPTION CLAUSE. A contract clause giving a publisher the right to publish an author's next book.

PAYMENT ON ACCEPTANCE. The editor sends you a check for your article, story or poem as soon as he decides to publish it.

PAYMENT ON PUBLICATION. The editor doesn't send you a check for your material until it is published.

PEN NAME. The use of a name other than your legal name on articles, stories or books. Also called a pseudonym.

PHOTO FEATURE. Feature in which the emphasis is on the photographs rather than on accompanying written material.

PICTURE BOOK. A type of book aimed at preschoolers to 8-year-olds that tells a story using a combination of text and artwork, or artwork only.

PLATFORM. A writer's speaking experience, interview skills, website and other abilities which help form a following of potential buyers for that author's book.

POD. Print on demand.

PROOFREADING. Close reading and correction of a manuscript's typographical errors.

PROPOSAL. A summary of a proposed book submitted to a publisher, particularly used for nonfiction manuscripts. A proposal often contains an individualized cover letter, one-page overview of the book, marketing information, competitive books, author information, chapter-by-chapter outline, and two to three sample chapters.

QUERY. A letter that sells an idea to an editor or agent. Usually a query is brief (no more than one page) and uses attention-getting prose.

REMAINDERS. Copies of a book that are slow to sell and can be purchased from the publisher at a reduced price.

REPORTING TIME. The time it takes for an editor to report to the author on his/her query or manuscript.

REPRINT RIGHTS. The rights to republish a book after its initial printing.

ROYALTIES, STANDARD HARDCOVER BOOK. 10 percent of the retail price on the first 5,000 copies sold; 121/2 percent on the next 5,000; 15 percent thereafter.

ROYALTIES, STANDARD MASS PAPERBACK BOOK. 4-8 percent of the retail price on the first 150,000 copies sold.

ROYALTIES, STANDARD TRADE PAPERBACK BOOK. No less than 6 percent of list price on the first 20,000 copies; 7½ percent thereafter.

SASE. Self-addressed, stamped envelope; should be included with all correspondence.

SELF-PUBLISHING. In this arrangement the author pays for manufacturing, production and marketing of his book and keeps all income derived from the book sales.

SEMIMONTHLY. Twice per month.

SEMIWEEKLY. Twice per week.

SERIAL. Published periodically, such as a newspaper or magazine.

SERIAL FICTION. Fiction published in a magazine in installments, often broken off at a suspenseful spot.

SERIAL RIGHTS. The right for a newspaper or magazine to publish sections of a manuscript.

SHORT-SHORT. A complete short story of 1,500 words.

SIDEBAR. A feature presented as a companion to a straight news report (or main magazine article) giving sidelights on human-interest aspects or sometimes elucidating just one aspect of the story.

SIMULTANEOUS SUBMISSIONS. Sending the same article, story or poem to several publishers at the same time. Some publishers refuse to consider such submissions.

SLANT. The approach or style of a story or article that will appeal to readers of a specific magazine.

SLICE-OF-LIFE VIGNETTE. A short fiction piece intended to realistically depict an interesting moment of everyday living.

SLUSH PILE. The stack of unsolicited or misdirected manuscripts received by an editor or book publisher.

SOCIAL NETWORKS. Websites that connect users: sometimes generally, other times around specific interests. Four popular ones at the moment are MySpace, Facebook, Twitter and LinkedIn.

SUBAGENT. An agent handling certain subsidiary rights, usually working in conjuction with the agent who handled the book rights. The percentage paid the book agent is increased to pay the subagent.

SUBSIDIARY RIGHTS. All right other than book publishing rights included in a book publishing contract, such as paperback rights, book club rights and movie rights. Part of an agent's job is to negotiate those rights and advise you on which to sell and which to keep. For more information, read "Minding the Details."

SUBSIDY PUBLISHER. A book publisher who charges the author for the cost to typeset and print his book, the jacket, etc., as opposed to a royalty publisher who pays the author.

SYNOPSIS. A brief summary of a story, novel or play. As part of a book proposal, it is a comprehensive summary condensed in a page or page and a half, single-spaced.

TABLOID. Newspaper format publication on about half the size of the regular newspaper page.

TEARSHEET. Page from a magazine or newspaper containing your printed story, article, poem or ad.

TOC. Table of Contents.

TRADE BOOK. Either a hardcover or softcover book; subject matter frequently concerns a special interest for a general audience; sold mainly in bookstores.

TRADE PAPERBACK. A soft-bound volume, usually around 5X8, published and designed for the general public; available mainly in bookstores.

TRANSLATION RIGHTS. Sold to a foreign agent or foreign publisher.

UNSOLICITED MANUSCRIPT. A story, article, poem or book that an editor did not specifically ask to see.

YA. Young adult books.

INDEX

2M Communications, Ltd. 184

$50,000 Gift of Freedom 818

A

AAA Carolinas Go Magazine 646

AAA Living 479

AAA Midwest Traveler 718

AandU, America's AIDS Magazine 508

AARP Segunda Juventud 519

AARP The Magazine 674

Abaco Life 625

ABA Journal 787

Abbeville Family 223

ABC-CLIO 223

Abel Literary Agency, Inc., Dominick 184

Abilities 513

Abrams Books for Young Readers 223

Abrams Inc., Harry N. 223

Absey & Co. 223

Ace Science Fiction and Fantasy 224

Acme Press 224

Acorn 575

Acorn-Plantos Award for Peoples Poetry 845

ACP Internist/ACP Hospitalist 757

Acres U.S.A. 770

Acropolis Books Inc. 224

Action 479

Action Publishing 224

Action Pursuit Games 709

Acuta Journal, The 760

Adams-Blake Publishing 224

Adams-Hall Publishing 225

Adams Literary 184

Adams Media 225

Adbusters 509

Addicus Books, Inc. 225

Adirondack Life 645

Adirondack Review, The 575

Adornment 782

ADVANCE for Respiratory Care & Sleep Medicine 793

ADVANCE Newsmagazines 794

Adventure Cyclist 686

Advisor's Edge 771

Advisor Today 781

Advocate, The 528

Aeronautical Publishers 225

AeroSafety World Magazine 739

Aesthetica Creative Works Competition 863

Affluent Publishing Corporation 226

African-American Career World 497

African American Golfer's Digest 695

African American Review 575

African Pilot 487

African Voices 519

Aftermarket Business World 737

Ag Journal 769

Agni 576

Ag Weekly 766

Ahsahta Press 226

Aim Magazine 520

Air and Space Magazine 487

Airbrush Action Magazine 734

Airforce 612

Air Force Times 612

AKC Gazette 470

Akron Life 648

Akron Poetry Prize 845

Alabama Game & Fish 699

Alabama Living 623

Alabama State Council on the Arts
    Individual Artist Fellowship 818

Aladdin/Pulse 226

Alarm 614

Alaska Business Monthly 493

Alaska Quarterly Review 576

Albemarle 509

Alberta Venture 493

AlbertaViews 626

Alive Communications, Inc. 184

Allworth Press 227

Alondra Press, LLC 227

Alpine Publications 227

Alternatives Journal 616

Althouse Press, The 227

Amacom Books 228

Amadeus Press 228

Ambassador Books, Inc. 228

Ambassador Magazine 520

Amber Communications Group, Inc. 229

America 657

American Agriculturist 770

American Angler 699

American Archaeology 677

American Baby Magazine 499

American Bar Association Journal 743

American Bar Association Publishing 229

American Careers 497

American Carriage House Publishing 229

American Catholic Press 229

American Cheerleader 710

American Chemical Society 230

American Cinematographer 764

American City & County 773

American Correctional Association 230

American Counseling Association 230

American Craft 546

American Educator 479

American Federation of Astrologers 230

American Fitness 537

American Gardener, The 558

American History 541

American Hunter 700

American Indian Art Magazine 476

American Legion Fourth Estate Award,
    The 843

American Legion Magazine, The 531

AmericanMachinist.com 790

American Motorcyclist 485

American Press 231

American Quilter's Society 231

American Short Story Contest 821

American Snowmobiler 714

AmericanStyle Magazine 476

American Water Works Association 231

American/Western Fruit Grower 766

American Window Cleaner Magazine 792

American Wine Society Journal 525

Americas Award 863

America's Civil War 542

America West Publishers 231

Amherst Media Inc. 232

Amigadget Publishing Co. 232

Amster Literary Enterprises, Betsy 185

Amsterdam Press 232

Amulet Books 232

Amy Writing Awards 843

Anacus Press and Ecopress 232

Anaphora Literary Press 232

Anderson Foundation Fiction Award, The
    Sherwood 821

Andrews McMeel Universal 233

Angoor Press LLC 233

Angus Beef Bulletin 768

Anhinga Press 233

Animal Sheltering 812

Ann Arbor Observer 639

Annick Press, Ltd. 233

Annual Gival Press Oscar Wilde Award 846

Annual World Haiku Competition & Annual
    World Tanka Contest 846

Antigonish Review, The 576

Antioch Review 577

Antiqueweek 735

Anvil Press 234

Aoife's Kiss 681

APA Books 234

Apex Magazine 682

Apogee Photo 621

Appalachian Festival of Plays &

Playwrights 814

Appalachian Film Festival Screenplay
    Contest 814

Appalachian Mountain Club Books 234

Appaloosa Journal 470

Appraisers Standard, The 735

Aquarium Fish International 470

Aquatics International 807

Arabian Studs & Stallions Annual 471

Arc 577

Arcade Publishing 235

Arcadia 185

Arcadia Publishing 235

Archaeology 677

Archaia 235

Arc Publications 235

Arctos Press 235

A-R Editions, Inc. 235

Arizona Foothills Magazine 623

Arizona, the State of Golf 695

Arizona Wildlife Views 616

Arkansas Sportsman 700

Arkham Bridge Publishing 236

ARMY Magazine 613

Arrowhead Regional Arts Council Individual
    Artist Support Grant 818

ArrowTrade Magazine 807

Arsenal Pulp Press 236

Arte Publico Press 237

Artful Dodge 577

Arthritis Today 514

Artilleryman, The 542

Artist's Magazine, The 476

Artist Trust Fellowship Award 863

Art Papers 477

ArtsNews 645

ASA, Aviation Supplies & Academics 237

Asabi PUblishing 237

ASCE Press 238

Ashland Poetry Press 238

Asimov's Science Fiction 682

ASM Press 238

Astragal Press 238

Astronomy 678

ATA Magazine, The 757

Atheneum Books For Young Readers 238

At Home Tennessee 653

Atlanta Homes and Lifestyles 559

Atlanta Parent/Atlanta Baby 500

Atlanta Review 578

Atlantic Business Magazine 493

Atlantic Monthly, The 531

Atlantic Salmon Journal, The 616

A.T. Publishing 239

Atriad Press, LLC 239

At the Center 794

ATV Magazine/ATV Sport 710

AustralasianJournal of Early Childhood 757

Australian Arabian Horse News, The 471

Australian Christian Book of the Year
    Award 842

Australian Country Collections 559

Australian Health Review 757

Authorship 782

Autograph Collector 547

Automated Builder 754

Automobile Quarterly 485

AutoPilot Magazine 488

Auto Restorer 737

AutoWeek 485

Autumn House Press 240

Autumn House Poetry, Fiction, and
    Nonfiction Prizes 864

Avalon Books 240

Aviation History 488

Aviation International News 739

Avon Books 240

Azro Press 241

Azure Design, Architecture and Art 477

B

Baby Talk 500

Backbeat Books 241

BackHome 559

Backpacker Magazine 698

Backwoods Home Magazine 675

Backyard Poultry 768

Bacon Busters 700

Baen Books 241

Bailiwick Press 241

Baillie Picture Book Award, Marilyn 836

Baker Academic 242

Baker Books 242

Baker's Plays High School Playwriting
    Contest 814

Balloon Life 488

BALLOONS & Parties Magazine 804

Baltimore Magazine 638

Balzer & Bray 242

Bancroft Press 242

Bantam Books 243

Bar & Beverage Business Magazine 743

Bard Fiction Prize 821

Barn Owl Review 578

Barrett Books, Inc., Loretta 186

Barricade Books, Inc. 243

Bartender Magazine 778

Basic Health Publications, Inc. 243

Baskerville Publishers Poetry Award & the
    Betsy Colquitt Poetry Award, The 864

Baylor University Press 244

BC Outdoors Hunting and Shooting 700

Bead & Button 547

Bear Deluxe Magazine, The 617

BearManor Media 244

Beatty Award, John and Patricia 836
Beauty Store Business 740
Beck Publishing, Goodman 310
Bedford/St. Martin's 244
Bedtimes 747
Bee Culture 770
Behrman House Inc. 244
Beil, Publisher, Inc., Frederic C. 244
Bellevue Literary Press 245
Bellevue Literary Review Goldenberg Prize
   for Fiction 821
Bellingham Review 578
Beloit Poetry Journal 579
BenBella Books 245
Bench & Bar of Minnesota 787
Bendall Books 245
Bend of the River Magazine 649
Bender Literary Agency, Faye 186
Bennett Fellowship, George 818
Bentley Publishers 245
Berkley Publishing Group, The 245
Berks County Living 650
Berrett-Koehler Publishers, Inc. 246
Bethany House Publishers 246
Better Homes and Gardens 559
Betterway Home Books 246
Beverage Journal, The 743
Bibby First Book Award, The Patricia 846
Bible Advocate 657
Bick Publishing House 246
Big Break International Screenwriting
   Competition 814
Big Game Fishing Journal, The 701
Big Picture, The 800
Bijur Literary Agency, Vicky 186
Bike Magazine 687
Bilson Award for Historical Fiction for
   Young People, The Geoffrey 836

Binghamton University John Gardner
   Fiction Book Award 821
BioScience 678
Biotechnology Healthcare 794
Birding World 471
Birds & Blooms 559
Birdsong Books 247
Bird Watcher's Digest 617
Birmingham Parent 500
BkMk Press 247
Black Belt 708
Black Collegian, The 497
Black Dome Press Corp. 247
Black Heron Press 247
Black Lawrence Press 248
Black Literary Agency, David 187
Black Mountain Press 248
Black Ocean 248
Black Rose Writing 248
Black Velvet Seductions Publishing 249
Blade Magazine 547
Blair, Publisher, John F. 249
Bloomberg Press 249
Blooming Tree Press 250
Bloomsbury Children's Books 250
Bloomsbury Review, The 744
BlueBridge 250
Bluegrass Unlimited 614
Blue Light Press 251
Blue Moon Books, Inc. 251
Blue Mountain Arts/SPS Studios Poetry
   Card Contest 846
Blue Mountain Press 251
Blue Poppy Press 251
Blue Ridge Country 630
Blue River Press 251
BNA Books 252
B'nai B'rith Magazine 520

BOA Editions, Ltd. 252

Boating World Magazine 687

Bobo Strategy 252

Boca Raton Magazine 629

Bock Prize, The Frederick 846

Bold Strokes Books, Inc. 253

Bold Strummer, Ltd., The 253

Book Dealers World 783

BookEnds, LLC 187

Books & Such Literary Agency 187

Borealis Press, Ltd. 253

Boston Globe-Horn Book Awards 837

Boston Review 509

Bottom Dog Press, Inc. 253

Boulevard 579

Bow & Arrow Hunting 685

Bowhunter 686

Bowhunting World 686

Bowling Center Management 807

Boxoffice Magazine 764

Boys' Life 567

Bradley Prize, Barbara 846

Branden Publishing Co., Inc 253

Brand Packaging 733

Braun Associates, Inc., Barbara 188

Brealey Publishing, Nicholas 254

Brenner Information Group 254

Brewers Publications 254

Brew Your Own 548

Brick 580

Brick Books 254

Brick House Literary Agents 188

Brick Road Poetry Book Contest 847

Brick Road Poetry Press, Inc. 255

Bridal Guide 724

Bridge Bulletin, The 527

Bright Hill Press Poetry Chapbook Award 847

Brighter Books Publishing House 255

Bright Mountain Books, Inc. 256

Bright Ring Publishing, Inc. 256

Brilliant Star 567

Brimer Award, Ann Connor 837

Brittingham Prize in Poetry; Felix Pollak Prize in Poetry 847

British Heritage 542

Broadsheet, The 724

Broadway Books 256

Broken Jaw Press 256

Broken Pencil 510

Bronze Man Books 257

Brooks Books 256

Browne & Miller Literary Associates 189

Brown, Ltd., Curtis 188

Brucedale Press, The 257

Buffalo Spree Magazine 646

Buildernews Magazine 754

Business Fleet 737

Business Journal, The 493

Business NH Magazine 493

Business Travel Executive 747

Buster Books 257

Bust Magazine 510

Button 580

By Light Unseen Media 257

Bykofsky Associates, Inc., Sheree 189

C

Cabling Business Magazine 760

Cadet Quest Magazine 567

Caketrain Chapbook Competition 847

Calamari Press 258

California Game & Fish 701

California Homes 560

California Northern Magazine 624

Calkins Creek 258

Calliope 567

Camino Books, Inc. 259

Camperway, Midwest RV Traveler, Florida
RV Traveler, Northeast Outdoors,
Southern RV 718
Camping Today 718
Campus Activities 764
Canada Council Governor General's Literary
Awards 864
Canadian Biker Magazine 486
Canadian Consulting Engineer 762
Canadian Dimension 511
Canadian Homes & Cottages 560
Canadian Mining Journal 809
Canadian Organic Grower, The 560
Canadian Property Management 801
Canadian Rodeo News 710
Canadian Screenwriter 783
Canadian Short Story Competition 822
Canadian Woodworking 548
Canadian Writer's Journal 783
Candlewick Press 259
Canoe & Kayak 688
Cape Cod Life 638
Cape Cod Magazine 638
Capilano Review, The 580
CAPPER's 532
Car And Driver 486
Careers & the disABLED 514
Carlsbad Magazine 624
Carolrhoda Books, Inc. 259
Carstens Publications, Inc. 259
Cartwheel Books 260
Carvainis Agency, Inc., Maria 190
Carving Magazine 548
Cary Magazine 646
Castiglia Literary Agency 190
Casual Living Magazine 804
Cat Callan Humor Prize, Jamie 842
Cat Fancy 471

Catholic Digest 658
Catholic Forester 658
Catholic University of America Press 260
Cattarulla Award for Best Short Story, Kay 822
Cattleman, The 769
Cave Hollow Press 260
Cavendish Children's Books, Marshall 261
Caxton Press 261
CBA Retailers + Resources 747
Cedar Fort, Inc. 261
Celebrate Life 658
Cellar Door Publishing, LLC 262
CelticLife Magazine 520
Center for Book Arts Poetry Chapbook
Competition, The 848
Center for Thanatology Research &
Education, Inc. 262
Center One Publishing 262
Centerstream Publishing 263
Ceramics Monthly 548
Cessna Owner Magazine 488
Chalice Press 263
Chamber Music 614
Chandra Prize for Short Fiction,
G. S. Sharat 824
Channel Lake, Inc. 263
Charisma & Christian Life 659
Charlesbridge Publishing 263
Charles River Media 264
Charleston Magazine 652
Charlotte Magazine 647
Chatelaine 725
Chatham Magazine 638
Chelsea Green Publishing Co. 264
Chemical Heritage 679
Chemical Publishing Co., Inc. 265
Chesapeake Bay Magazine 688
Chesapeake Family 500

Chess Life 527

Chicago Magazine 633

Chicago Parent 501

Chicago Reader 633

Chicago Review Press 265

Chicago Scene Magazine 633

Chicken Soup for the Soul Publishing, LLC 581

Children's Brains are Yummy (CBAY)
Books 265

Children's Press/Franklin Watts 266

Child's Play (International) Ltd. 266

Child Welfare League Of America 267

Chivalry Bookshelf 267

ChLa Research Grants 819

Choate Agency, LLC, The 191

Chosen Books 267

Christian Books Today Ltd 267

Christian Century, The 659

Christian Communicator 750

Christian Ed. Publishers 268

Christian Focus Publications 268

Christian Home & School 659

Christian Science Monitor, The 532

Chronicle Books 268

Chronicle Books for Children 269

Chronicle of the Horse, The 471

Chrysalis Reader 581

Church Growth Institute 269

Church Music Quarterly 614

Church Publishing Inc. 270

Church & State 621

Cicada Magazine 717

Cider Press Review 848

Cimarron Review 581

Cincinnati Magazine 649

Cincy Magazine 494

Cineaste 516

C&I Retailing 804

City Limits 646

City of Vancouver Book Award, The 864

Civil War Times 542

Clarion Books 270

Clarity Press, Inc. 270

Clark Associates, WM 220

Classical Singer Magazine 797

Classic Toy Trains 548

Classic Trucks 486

Clear Light Publishers 270

Cleis Press 271

Cleveland Magazine 649

Cleveland State University Poetry Center 271

Climbing 538

Clockwise Chapbook Award 848

Cloudbank 511

Clover Park Press 271

Clubhouse Magazine 568

Coach House Books 272

Coastal Living 561

Coast to Coast Magazine 719

Cobblestone 543

Coffe House Press 272

Cohen Prize for Political Writing, The
Shaughnessy 830

Collections & Credit Risk 771

College Press Publishing Co. 272

Collin, Literary Agent, Frances 191

Collins Award For Nonfiction, Carr P. 830

Colorado Homes & Lifestyles 561

Colorado Prize for Poetry, The 848

Colorado Review 582

Columbia 660

Columbus Monthly 649

Columbus Parent Magazine 501

Comics Journal, The 508

Commentary 511

Commerce & Industry 780

Common Courage Press 273

Common Ground 511

Commonweal 621

Companion in Zeor, A 681

Complete Woman 725

Composites Manufacturing Magazine 762

Conari Press 273

Concordia Publishing House 273

Concrete Producer, The 754

Confrontation 582

Connecticut Magazine 628

Connecticut Review 583

Conscience 660

Consortium Publishing 273

Constable & Robinson, Ltd. 274

Consumer Goods Technology 805

Consumer Press 274

Contracting Profits 747

Convenience Distribution 775

Coonhound Bloodlines 472

Cooperator, The 802

Copper Canyon Press 274

Corporate Board Member 490

Corporate Connecticut Magazine 494

Corwin Press, Inc. 274

Cosmetics 740

Cosmos Magazine 679

Coteau Books 275

Cottage 626

Council on Social Work Education 275

Country Connection, The 675

Country Living 561

Countryman Press, The 275

Country Woman 725

Covenant Communications, Inc. 276

Cowley Publications 276

CPR Editor's Prize Book Award 849

CQ Amateur Radio 549

CQ Press 276

Crab Creek Review 583

Crab Orchard Review 583

Crab Orchard Series in Poetry First Book
    Award 849

Crab Orchard Series in Poetry Open
    Competition Awards 849

Crabtree Publishing Company 276

Craftsman Book Co. 277

Crain's Detroit Business 494

Crazyhorse 583

Creating Keepsakes 549

Creative & Performing Artists & Writers
    Fellowship 819

Creative Company 277

Creative Culture, Inc., The 191

Creative Editions 277

Creative Homeowner 277

Creator Magazine 750

Credit Today 771

Credit Union Management 771

Crescent Moon Publishing 278

Cricket 568

Cricket Books 278

Crimson Romance 278

Cross-Cultural Communications 278

Crossquarter Publishing Group 279

Crown Books for Young Readers 279

Crown Business 279

Crown Publishing Group 279

C&R Press 258

Cruise Industry News 811

Cruising World 688

Current Nursing in Geriatric Care 777

Curve Magazine 528

Cutting Tool Engineering 790

CWW Annual Wisconsin Writers Awards
    Competition 864

Cycle California! Magazine 687

Cycle Publications Inc. 279

Cyclotour Guide Books 279

D

Da Capo Press 280

DAC News 480

Dana Anhinga Prize For Poetry, The Robert 849

Dana Awards in the Novel, Short Fiction, Essay and Poetry 865

Dance International 516

DanceTeacher 765

Daniel & Daniel Publishers, Inc. 280

Dante University Of America Press, Inc. 280

Darhansoff & Verrill Literary Agents 191

Davenport, Publishers, May 280

David Publishers Inc., Jonathan 281

Dawbert Press, Inc. 281

DAW Books, Inc. 281

Dawn Publications 281

Dawson Associates, Liza 192

Dayspa 741

DBS Productions 281

DCM 480

Deca Dimensions 733

Decision 660

Deer & Deer Hunting 701

DeFiore & Co. 192

Delacorte Pess Books for Young Readers 282

Delaware Division of the Arts 819

Delaware Today 628

Del Rey Books 282

Demontreville Press, Inc. 282

Denali Press, The 282

Der-Hovanessian Prize 844

Dermascope Magazine 741

descant 584

Describe Adonis Press 283

Designs in Machine Embroidery 549

Desktop Engineering 780

Diabetes Health 514

Diabetes Self-Management 515

Diagram 584

DIAGRAM Essay Contest 830

Dial Books for Young Readers 283

Dialogue 515

Diamond Registry, The 782

Digger 772

Dig Magazine 569

Dijkstra Literary Agency, Sandra 193

Direct Art Magazine 477

DIRECTED BY 517

Dirt Rider 712

Discover Maine Magazine 637

Diskus Publishing 283

Disney FamilyFun 501

Disney Hyperion Books for Children 284

Diversion Press 284

Divertir 284

DK Publishing 285

DMQ Review 584

DNA Press and Nartea Publishing 285

Dobie Paisano Fellowships 819

Dog-Eared Publications 285

Dog Fancy 472

Dog Sports Magazine 472, 812

Dollars and Sense 490

Dollhouse Miniatures 549

Dolls 550

Doral Publishing, Inc. 285

Dorchester Publishing Co., Inc. 285

Doubleday Books for Young Readers 286

Doubleday Religious Publishing 286

Dover Publications, Inc. 286

Down East Books 286

Downstate Story 584

Down the Shore Publishing 286
Draft 525
Dragonfly 286
Drake Magazine, The 701
Dramatics Magazine 765
Dreamland Books Inc. 287
Dreisbach Literary Management 193
Dufour Editions 287
Dundurn Press, Ltd. 287
Dunedin Academic Press, Ltd. 287
Dunham Literary, Inc. 193
Dunlap Memorial Fellowship, Joseph R. 819
Dunne Books, Thomas 287
Duquesne University Press 288
Dutton 288
Dutton Children's Books 288
Dyer Fiction Prize, Jack 822
Dystel & Goderich Literary Management 194

E

Eagle's View Publishing 288
Eakin Press 289
Early American Life 561
Earth Island Journal 618
East Bay Monthly, The 624
Eastham Flash Fiction Prize.
    Mary Kennedy 822
Eastland Press 289
Eaton Literary Agency's Annual Awards
    Program 865
Ecco Press, The 289
Echo Magazine 529
EcoHome Designs 561
EContent Magazine 783
Écrits des Forges 289
EDCON Publishing Group 289
Edge Science Fiction and Fantasy
    Publishing/Tesseract Books 290
Educator's International Press, Inc. 290

Edupress, Inc. 290
Eerdmans Books for Young Readers 290
Eerdmans Publishing Co., William 291
EFCA Today 660
Egmont USA 291
Electrical Apparatus 761
Electrical Business 761
Elgar Publishing Inc., Edward 291
Eliot Prize for Poetry, T.S. 849
Elixirist 291
Elks Magazine, The 480
Elle 726
Ellora's Cave Publishing, Inc. 292
Elohi Gadugi / The Habit of Rainy Nights
    Press 292
Emerald Coast Magazine 629
Emis, Inc. 292
Emmy Magazine 765
Encounter Books 293
Enete Enterprises 293
English Literary Agency, The Elaine P. 194
English Tea Rose Press 293
Engravers Journal, The 782
Enrichment 661
Enslow Publishers Inc. 293
Enterprise Minnesota Magazine 762
Entrepreneur Magazine 490
Eos 294
Epicenter Press, Inc. 294
Epoch 584
Equal Opportunity 497
Equestrian Magazine 472
Equine Journal 473
Equipment Journal 791
Erie Canal Productions 294
Erosion Control 803
Escape Collective Publishing 294
ESPACE 477

Esquire 612

ETC Publications 294

E The Environmental Magazine 618

Eth Literary Representation, Felicia 195

Evangelical Missions Quarterly 661

Evans Biography & Handcart Award 830

Evansville Living 635

Event 585

Event Nonfiction Contest 831

Evidence Technology Magazine 773

Executive Housekeeping Today 792

Exotic Magazine 684

EXPO 747

F

F+W Crime 295

F+W Media, Inc. (Book Division) 295

F+W Media, Inc. (Magazine Division) 550

Fabricator, The 791

Fabrics + Furnishings International 746

Faces 569

Facts On File, Inc. 295

Fairleigh Dickinson University Press 296

Faith and Friends 661

Faith + Form 735

Faith Today 661

Fall Poetry Chapbook Contest 850

Family Business Magazine 748

Family Circle 726

Family Motor Coaching 719

Family Tree Magazine 550

Fangoria 517

Farcountry Press 296

Far Horizons Award for Short Fiction, The 822

Farm & Ranch Living 676

Farrar, Straus & Giroux 296

Farrar, Straus & Giroux/Books for Young
    Readers 297

Farrell Poetry Prize, Janice 850

Fashion Forum 532

Fate Magazine 483

Father's Press 297

Faulkner Award for Excellence in Writing,
    The Virginia 865

Faultline 585

FC2 297

Federal Credit Union, The 771

Feed Lot Magazine 769

FellowScript 784

Fell Publishers, Inc., Frederick 297

Fence Books 298

FenderBender 738

Fendrich Memorial Playwriting Contest,
    Shubert 814

Ferguson Publishing Co. 298

Fibre Focus 550

Fickling Books, David 298

Fiction 585

Fido Friendly Magazine 473

FIELD 585

Field & Stream 702

FIELD Poetry Prize 850

Fifteen 501 647

Fifth House Publishers 298

Filipinas 521

Filter Press, LLC 299

Finch Literary Agency, Diana 195

Finch Prize for Poetry, The 850

Findhorn Press 299

Fine Books & Collections 551

Fine Gardening 562

Fine Homebuilding 562

FinePrint Literary Management 195

Finescale Modeler 551

Fine Tool Journal 551

Fine Woodworking 551

Finney Company, Inc. 299

Fire Apparatus & Emergency Equipment 773

Fire Engineering 773

Firehouse Magazine 773

Fire Protection Contractor 774

First Book Award 865

First Edition Design Publishing 299

First Things 511

firstwriter.com International Short Story
   Contest 822

Fitness Magazine 538

Fitzhenry & Whiteside Ltd. 299

Five Points 586

Five Star Publications, Inc. 299

Flare Magazine 726

Flarestack Poets 300

Flashlight Press 300

Fleck Award for Canadian Children's Nonfiction, The Norma 837

Fleet Executive 738

Flick Magazine 517

Flight Journal 489

Floating Bridge Press 300

Floricanto Press 300

Florida Academic Press 300

Florida Game & Fish 702

Florida Realtor Magazine 802

Florida Sportsman 702

Flux 301

FLW Bass Fishing Magazine, FLW Walleye
   Fishing Magazine 702

Fly Fisherman Magazine 702

Flying Adventures Magazine 489

Flying Pen Press LLC 301

Focal Press 301

Fodor's Travel Publications, Inc. 302

Food Product Design Magazine 776

Footwear Plus 754

Foreign Policy Association 302

Forensic Teacher, The 758

ForeWord Reviews 745

Fort Mitchell Living 636

Fortress Press 302

Fort Ross Inc. International Rights 303

Fort Thomas Living 636

Fortune 491

Forward in Christ 662

Forward Movement 303

Foster Publishing, Inc., Walter 303

four-seventeen 417 Magazine 642

Fourth River, The 586

Four Wheeler Magazine 486

Fox Chapel Publishing 303

Frame Building News 755

Frances Lincoln Children's Books 303

Fraser Award For Best Translation of a Book,
   Soeurette Diehl 844

Fredericks Literary Agency, Inc., Jeanne 196

FreeFall Short Prose and Poetry Contest 865

Freelance Market News 784

Freelance Writer's Report 784

Freeman
   Ideas on Liberty, The 622

Free Spirit Publishing, Inc. 304

Freestone/Peachtree, Jr. 304

Fresh Cut Magazine 776

Friction Zone 486

Friedrich Agency, The 196

Friend, The 662

Front Street 304

Fruit Growers News 767

Ft. Myers Magazine 629

Fulcrum Publishing 305

FunnelBrain LLC 305

Funny Times 565

Fur-Fish-Game 702

FutureCycle Press 305

G

Gambit Publishing 305
Game Developer 781
Game & Fish 703
Games Magazine 528
GAP (Grants for Artist Projects) Program 820
Garden Compass 562
Gargoyle 586
Gaslight Publications 306
Gateway 543
Gauthier Publications, Inc. 306
Gay & Lesbian Review, The 529
Gay Sunshine Press and Leyland
   Publications 306
Gelfman Schneider Literary Agents, Inc. 196
Gem Guides Book Co. 306
Genesis Press, Inc. 307
Georgetown Review 866
Georgia Magazine 631
Georgia Review, The 6, 587
Georgia Sportsman 703
German Life 521
Gertrude Press Poetry Chapbook Contest
   851
Gettysburg Review, The 587
Ghost Pony Press 307
Gibbs Smith 307
Gifted Education Press 307
Ginsberg Poetry Awards, Allen 851
Girlfriendz 726
Girls' Life 569
Gival Press 308
Gival Press Novel Award 823
Gival Press Poetry Award 851
Gival Press Short Story Award 823
Glamour 726
Glass Magazine 745
Glass Page Books 308

GLB Publishers 308
Glenbridge Publishing, Ltd. 308
Glencannon Press, The 309
Glimmer Train Stories 587
Glimmer Train's Family Matters 823
Glimmer Train's Fiction Open 823
Glimmer Train's Short-Story Award for New
   Writers 823
Glimmer Train's Very Short Fiction Award
   (January) 823
Glimmer Train's Very Short Fiction Contest
   (July) 824
Go 565
Godine, Publisher, David R. 309
Goldblatt Literary, LLC, Barry 197
Golden Kite Awards 837
Golden Rose Award 851
Golden West Books 309
Golf Canada 696
Golf Course Management 807
Golfer, The 696
Golfing Magazine 696
Golf News Magazine 696
Golf Tips 697
Gollehon Press, Inc. 309
Good Fruit Grower 767
Good Housekeeping 727
Good Old Boat 689
Good Old Days 544
Goose Lane Editions 310
Gotham Screen Film Festival and Screenplay
   Contest 815
Gourmet Traveller Wine 526
Governor General's Literary Award for
   Children's Literature 838
Governor General's Literary Award for
   Drama 815
Governor General's Literary Award for

Fiction 824

Governor General's Literary Award for
   Poetry 852

Governor General's Literary Award for
   Translation 844

Governor General's Literary Awards 866

Grace Ormonde Wedding Style 727

Grain Journal 767

Grand Canyon Association 311

Grand Rapids Family Magazine 502

Grand Rapids Magazine 640

Granite Publishing, LLC 311

Graphia 311

Gray's Sporting Journal 703

Grayson Literary Agency, Ashley 197

Graywolf Press 311

Great Lakes Colleges Association New
   Writers Award 866

Great Northwest Publishing & Dist. Co.,
   Inc. 312

Great Plains Game & Fish 703

Great Potential Press 312

Great Quotations Publishing 312

Great Source Education Group 313

Greenburger Associates, Inc., Sanford J. 197

Green Rose Prize in Poetry, The 852

Greene Bark Press 313

Greenhaven Press 313

Green Mountains Review 588

Greenwillow Books 313

Greenwood Press 313

Greenwood Publishing Group 314

Grey Gecko Press 314

Greyhaus Literary 198

Greyhound Review, The 473

Grit 532

Grit City Publications 314

Grosset & Dunlap Publishers 315

Ground Support Worldwide Magazine 740

Groundwood Books 315

Group Magazine 751

Group Publishing, Inc. 315

Grove/Atlantic, Inc. 315

GrowerTalks 773

Gryphon House, Inc. 316

Gryphon Publications 316

GUD Magazine 588

Guernica Editions 316

Guideposts Magazine 662

Guide, The 529

Guitar World 614

Gulf Coast 588

Gulf Publishing Company 317

Gun Digest Books 317

Guyon Literary Nonfiction Prize, John 831

G.W. Review, The 589

H

Hachai Publishing 318

Hackney Literary Awards 866

Hadassah Magazine 521

Hadley Rille Books 318

Hadow/Donald Stuart Short Story
   Competition, Lyndall 824

Half Halt Press, Inc. 318

Hall Awards for Youth Theatre,
   The Marilyn 815

Hamilton Institute, Alexander 319

Hamilton Magazine 626

Hampton Roads Publishing Co., Inc. 319

Hancock House Publishers 319

Handley Prose Poem Prize, Kathryn 852

Hanser Publications 320

Hard Hat News 755

Harlan Davidson Inc. 320

HarperBusiness 320

HarperCollins Children's Books/

HarperCollins Publishers 320
Harper's Magazine 533
Harpur Palate 589
Harris Literary Agency, Inc., The Joy 198
Harvard Business Review Press 321
Harvard Common Press, The 321
Harvard Magazine 497
Harvest House Publishers 321
Hastings House/Daytrips Publishers 321
Hatala Geroproducts 322
Hawaii Review 589
HAWK Publishing Group 322
Hayden's Ferry Review 589
Hayes School Publishing Co. Inc. 322
Hay House Inc. 322
Healing Lifestyles & Spas 538
Health Communications, Inc. 323
Hearing Health 515
Heartland Boating 689
Hein & Co., Inc., William S. 323
Heinemann Educational Publishers 323
Hellgate Press 323
Hellicious Horrors Epublishing 323
Hemingway Short Story Competition,
    Lorian 824
Hemispheres 566
Hendrick-Long Publishing Co., Inc. 323
Hendrickson Publishers, Inc. 324
Henrico Theatre Company One-Act
    Playwriting Competition 815
Henshaw Group, Richard 198
Heritage Books, Inc. 324
Heritage House Publishing Co., Ltd. 324
Heyday Books 324
Hibbard Publishers 325
HiddenSpring 325
High Country House and Home 562
High Country News 618

Highland Press Publishing 325
Highlights for Children 569
Highlights High Five 528
Highroads 719
High Tide Press 325
Highway News 662
Highways 719
Hillerman Mystery Novel Competition, The
    824
Hilton Head Monthly 653
Hinkler 326
Hippocrene Books Inc. 326
Hippopotamus Press 326
Hispanic Business 491
Hispanic Career World 498
History Magazine 544
History Publishing Company, Inc. 326
His Work Christian Publishing 327
Hoard's Dairyman 768
Hobart 590
Hoffer Award, Eric 867
Hokin Prize, The Bess 852
Holiday House, Inc. 327
Holiday Screenplay Contest 815
Hollins Critic, The 590
Homa & Sekey Books 327
Home Business Magazine 508
Home Business Report 491
Home Education Magazine 502
Home Energy Magazine 755
Home Lighting & Accessories 777
Homeschooling Today 502
Home Shop Machinist, The 552
Honolulu Magazine 632
Hoof Beats 699
Hook Magazine, The 712
Hopewell Publications 328
Horizons 663

Horn Book Magazine, The 745

Horror Screenplay Contest 815

Horse Connection 474

Horse Illustrated 474

Horse&Rider 473

Horse, The 474

Horticulture 563

Hotelier 778

Houghton Mifflin Harcourt Books for
    Children 328

Houghton Mifflin Harcourt Co. 328

Houghton Prize, Firman 850

House Beautiful 563

Houseboat Magazine 689

House of Anansi Press 328

Houston Press 654

HOW 735

HOW Books 329

Howard/John H. Reid Poetry Contest,
    Tom 852

Howard/John H. Reid Short Story Contest,
    Tom 824

HPAC
    Heating Plumbing Air Conditioning 800

HQN Books 329

Hruska Memorial Prize in Nonfiction,
    Thomas J. 831

H&S Publishing, LLC 317

Hubbard's Writers of the Future Contest, L.
    Ron 825

Hudson Hills Press, Inc. 329

Hudson Review, The 590

Hudson Valley Life 646

Hudson Valley Parent 502

Humanities 480

Hunger Mountain 590

Hunger Mountain Creative Nonfiction Prize,
    The 831

Hunter House Publishers 329

Hurst Children's Book Prize, Carol Otis 838

Hustler 685

H & W Publishing Inc 317

I

Ibex Publishers 330

Ibis Editions 330

Iconografix, Inc. 330

IdeaGems 591

Ideals Publications Inc. 330

IDW Publishing 331

Idyll Arbor, Inc. 331

Ilium Press 331

Illinois Entertainer 634

Illinois Game & Fish 703

Illumen 591

Illumination Arts 332

Image Comics 332

Immedium 332

IMPACT Books 332

Impact Magazine 538

Impact Publishers, Inc. 333

Impressions 741

Incentive 792

Indianapolis Monthly 635

Indiana Review 591

Indiana Review ½ K (Short-Short/Prose-
    Poem) Contest 867

Indy's Child Magazine 503

Information Today, Inc. 333

Ingalls Publishing Group, Inc. 333

Ingram's 494

Inkwell 592

In-Plant Graphics 801

Inside Texas Running 713

Insight 717

Insight Writing Contest 867

Insomniac Press 333

Instinct Magazine 529

InTents 748

Interior Construction 755

Interlink Publishing Group, Inc. 334

Intermission 649

International Bluegrass 798

International Bowling Industry 807

International Examiner 522

International Living 720

International Press 334

International Publishers Co., Inc. 334

International Railway Traveler, The 720

International Wealth Success 335

InterVarsity Press 335

In Touch Weekly 518

Inventors Digest 679

Iowa Game & Fish 703

Iowa Review Award in Poetry, Fiction, and
    Nonfiction, The 867

Iowa Short Fiction Award, The 825

Iowan, The 636

IRA Children's and Young Adult's Book
    Award 838

Irish Academic Press 336

Iron Gate Publishing 336

Irreantum 592

Island 592

Island Parent Magazine 503

Islands 720

Italian America 522

Italica Press 336

J

Jack and Jill 570

Jacobs Religious Essay Prize,
    Tilia Klebenov 831

Jain Publishing Co. 336

James Books, Alice 337

JCR 787

Jems 795

Jewish Action 522

Jewish Currents 523

Jewish Lights Publishing 337

Jist Publishing 337

Johns Hopkins University Press, The 338

Jones Award for Fiction, Jesse 825

Jones First Novel Fellowship, James 825

Journal Of Adventist Education, The 751

Journal of Asian Martial Arts 708

Journal of Court Reporting 788

Journal of Information Ethics 781

Journal Plus Magazine 625

Journal, The 593

JourneyForth 338

Junior Baseball 686

Junior Scholastic 570

Juniper Prize For Poetry 852

Jupiter Gardens Press 339

Just Labs 474

K

Kaeden Books 339

Kaleidoscope 515

Kalmbach Publishing Co. 339

Kamehameha Publishing 340

Kane/Miller Book Publishers 340

Kansas! 636

Kansas City Homes & Gardens 642

Kansas City Magazine 642

Kar-Ben Publishing 340

Kashrus Magazine 526

Keats/Kerlan Memorial Fellowship, Ezra
    Jack 838

Kentucky Game & Fish 704

Kentucky Living 637

Kentucky Monthly 637

Kenyon Review, The 593

Key Curriculum Press 341

Khabar 523

Kids Can Press 341

Kids' Ministry Ideas 751

Kindred Productions 341

King 612

Kiplinger's Personal Finance 508

Kirchoff/Wohlberg, Inc. 199

Kit-Cat Review, The 593

Kitplanes 552

Kitsune Books 342

Kiwanis 481

Klinger, Inc., Harvey 199

Knives Illustrated 552

Knoll, Publishers, Allen A. 342

Knopf, Alfred A. 342

Knox Robinson Publishing 342

Koala Books 343

Koenisha Publications 343

Konner Literary Agency, Linda 199

Kouts, Literary Agent, Barbara S. 200

Kovacs Prize, Katherine Singer 831

Krause Publications 343

KRBY Creations, LLC 343

Kregel Publications 344

Krichevsky Literary Agency, Inc., Stuart 200

L

Laborde Literary Nonfiction Prize,
    Katheryn Krotzer 832

LabTalk 757

Lacrosse Magazine 710

Ladies' Home Journal 727

Ladybug 570

LadybugPress 344

Lake Claremont Press 344

Lake Country Journal Magazine 640

Lakeland Boating 689

Lake Superior Magazine 641

Lamb Books, Wendy 345

Land, The 770

Lane Report, The 495

Lapwing Publications 345

Larsen/Elizabeth Pomada, Literary Agents,
    Michael 200

Latina Magazine 523

Laureate Prize for Poetry, The 853

Laurel-Leaf 345

Law Enforcement Technology Magazine 774

Lawyers & Judges Publishing Co. 345

Lazin Books, Sarah 201

LD+A 763

Leaders in Action 663

Leading Edge 683

Leben 544

Lectio Publishers 345

Lee & Low Books 346

Legacy Press 346

Leisure Group Travel 811

Leonard Books, Hal 346

Lescher & Lescher, Ltd. 201

Lethe Press 346

Leviant Memorial Prize in Yiddish Studies,
    Fenia and Yaakov 844

Levine Books, Arthur A. 346

Levine Greenberg Literary Agency, Inc. 201

Levinson Prize, The 853

Levis Reading Prize 853

Life Cycle Books 347

Light and Life Magazine [LLM] 663

Lighthouse Digest 544

Lighthouse Point Press 347

Liguorian 663

Lillenas Publishing Co. 347

Lilly Poetry Prize, The Ruth 853

Limousine Digest 810

Linden Publishing, Inc. 347

Link & Visitor, The 727

Linn's Stamp News 552
LION 481
Liquid Silver Books 347
Listen & Live Audio 348
Listen Magazine 717
List, The 512
Literal Latte Essay Award 832
Literal Latté Fiction Award 825
Literal Latté Poetry Award 853
Literal Latte Short Shorts Contest 825
Literary Nonfiction Contest 832
Little, Brown and Co. 348
Little, Brown and Co. Adult Trade Books 348
Little, Brown and Co. Books for Young
    Readers 348
Little Tiger Press 349
LIVE 663
Living 503
Living Aboard 690
Living Church, The 664
Living Word Literary Agency 201
Livingston Press 349
Llewellyn Publications 349
Loft Press, Inc. 349
Log Home Living 563
Lollipop Power Books 349
Long Island Woman 727
Long Story Contest, International, The 826
Long Term Care 777
Lookout, The 664
Lord Literistic, Inc., Sterling 216
Lost Horse Press 349
Lost Treasure, Inc. 553
Louisiana State University Press 350
Love Spell 350
Loving Healing Press Inc. 350
Lowenstein Associates Inc. 201
LRP Publications, Inc. 351

Lucent Books 351
Luna Bisonte Prods 351
Lutheran Digest, The 665
Lutheran, The 664
Lyons Literary, LLC 202
Lyons Press, The 351

M
Maass Literary Agency, Donald 203
MacGuffin National Poet Hunt Contest,
    The 853
Machine Design 791
Mackey Short Story Prize, The Mary 826
Madgett Poetry Award, Naomi Long 854
Madison 728
Madison Magazine 656
Magazine Antiques, The 478
Magazine of Fantasy & Science Fiction,
    The 682
Magenta Publishing for the Arts 351
Magical Child 351
Magic Dragon 571
Magination Press 352
Magnus Press 352
Mainebiz 748
Maine Sportsman, The 704
Main Line Today 650
Make-up Artist Magazine 765
Malahat Review, The 593
Malahat Review Long Poem Prize, The 854
Malahat Review Novella Prize, The 826
Managed Care 795
Management Advisory Publications 352
Mandala Publishing 352
Mann Agency, Carol 203
Manoa 594
Manor House Publishing, Inc. 353
Mantra Lingua 353
Manufacturing & Technology eJournal 763

Manus & Associates Literary Agency, Inc. 203

Margolis Award, Richard J. 832

Marie Claire 728

Marine Techniques Publishing 353

Marlin 704

Marlor Press, Inc. 354

Marraro Prize, Howard R. 832

Marr Poetry Prize, The Morton 854

Marshall Agency, The Evan 204

Martin Literary Management 204

Martin Sisters Publishing, LLC 354

Maskew Miller Longman 354

Massachusetts Review, The 594

Massage Magazine 741

Master Books 355

Mature Living 674

Mature Years 675

Maupin House Publishing, Inc. 355

Maverick Duck Press 355

Maverick Musicals and Plays 355

McBooks Press 355

McBride Literary Agency, Margret 205

McCarthy Prize in Short Fiction, Mary 826

McClung Sonnet Prize Category, Kathleen 854

McDonald & Woodward Publishing Co., The 356

McElderry Books, Margaret K. 356

McFarland & Co., Inc., Publishers 357

McGinnis-Ritchie Memorial Award, The 868

MC Press 357

Meadowbrook Press 357

Medesthetics 795

Medical Group Management Association 358

Mellen Poetry Press 358

Me & Mi Publishing 357

Memphis 653

Memphis Downtowner Magazine 653

Mendel Media Group, LLC 205

Mensbook Journal 530

Men's Health 539

Mercer Business Magazine 495

Meriwether Publishing Ltd. 358

Merriam Press 359

MESSAGE Magazine 665

Messenger of the Sacred Heart, The 665

Messianic Jewish Publishers 359

Metal Roofing Magazine 755

Metcalf Award for Children's Literature, The Vicky 838

MetroFamily Magazine 504

Metro Magazine 810

Metro Parent Magazine 504

Metropolis 478

MetroSource Magazine 530

Meyerson Prize for Fiction, David Nathan 826

Miami University Press 359

Michigan History 640

Michigan Out-of-Doors 704

Michigan Quarterly Review 594

Michigan Sportsman 704

Michigan State University Press 359

Microsoft Press 359

Mid-American Review 594

Mid-List Press 360

Midmarch Arts Press 360

Midwestern Family Magazine 634

Midwest Living 631

Midwest Meetings® 811

Midwest Quarterly, The 595

Midwifery Today 795

Mildenberger Prize, Kenneth W. 832

Military Officer 613

Military Vehicles 553

Milkweed Editions 360

Milkweed National Fiction Prize 826

Milkweeds for Young Readers 360

Millbrook Press, The 361

Mills Award, C. Wright 832

Milwaukee Magazine 656

MindFlights 683

Miniature Donkey Talk 475

Minnesota Emerging Writers' Grant 820

Minnesota Golfer 697

Minnesota Hockey Journal 698

Minnesota Sportsman 704

Minority Engineer 763

Mississippi/Louisiana Game & Fish 704

Mississippi Magazine 641

Mississippi Review 595

Missouri Game & Fish 705

Missouri Life 642

Missouri Review, The 595

MLA Prize for a Distinguished Scholarly
    Edition 833

MLA Prize for a First Book 833

MLA Prize for Independent Scholars 833

MLA Prize in United States Latina & Latino
    and Chicana & Chicano Literary and
    Cultural Studies 842

Model Cars Magazine 553

Modern Haiku 595

Modernism Magazine 479

Modern Materials Handling 780

Modern Physician 796

Modern Publishing 361

Moment 523

Momentum 752

Momentum Books, LLC 361

Monadnock Table 676

Monday Magazine 627

Mondial 361

Monitoring Times 553

Montana Magazine 643

Moody Publishers 361

Moon Shadow Press 362

Moon Tide Press 362

Moore Visiting Writer, Jenny McKean 820

Moose Enterprise Book & Theatre Play
    Publishing 362

Morehouse Publishing Co. 362

Morgan James Publishing 363

Morhaim Literary Agency, Howard 206

Morpheus Tales 682

Morris Agency, Inc., William 206

Morton Prize in Poetry, The Kathryn A. 854

Mosher Short Fiction Prize, The Howard
    Frank 827

Mother Earth News 676

Mother Jones 512

Motorbooks 363

Motorcycling 363

Motorhome 720

Motton Prize, Sheila Margaret 854

Mountain Living 563

Mountain Press Publishing Co. 364

MovieMaker Magazine 518

Moving Parts Press 364

Mpls. St. Paul Magazine 641

MSI Press 364

Mslexia 785

Ms. Magazine 728

MSW Management 803

Multicultural Books 364

Mumford Prize, Erika 855

Municipal Chapter of Toronto IODE Book
    Award 838

Muscle & Fitness 539

MuscleMag 539

Music Connection 798

Music Educators Journal 798

Musky Hunter Magazine 705

Muzzle Blasts 698

MVP Books 365

MyBusiness Magazine 491

My Daily Visitor 665

Myers Memoir Vignette Prize, Linda Joy 833

Mystic Ridge Books 365

N

NACUSA Young Composers' Competition 842

Naggar Literary Agency, Inc., Jean V. 206

Nailpro 742

Nails 742

Napoleon & Company 365

NAR Associates 366

National 788

National Association for Music Education 366

National Children's Theatre Festival 816

National Communications Magazine 553

National Geographic Kids 571

National Geographic Magazine 533

National Latino Playwriting Award 816

National Parks Magazine 618

National Peace Essay Contest 833

National Poetry Review 855

National Writers Association Novel Writing Contest 827

National Writers Association Poetry Contest 855

National Writers Association Short Story Contest 827

Native Peoples Magazine 524

Natural Food Network Magazine 776

Naturally 512

Nature Canada 619

Nature Friend Magazine 571

Naturegraph Publishers, Inc. 366

Nautical & Aviation Publishing Company of America, The 366

Naval Institute Press 366

NavPress, (The Publishing Ministry of the Navigators) 367

NBM Publishing 367

Neal-Schuman Publishers, Inc. 367

Nebraska Arts Council Individual Artists Fellowships 820

Nelson Literary Agency 207

Nemerov Sonnet Award, Howard 855

Neruda Prize for Poetry, The Pablo 855

NetComposites 756

Network Journal, The 492

Nevada Magazine 643

Newbery Medal, John 838

New Canaan Publishing Company LLC. 367

NewCity 634

New England Game & Fish 705

New England Review 596

New Era, The 718

New Forums Press 367

New Hampshire Magazine 644

New Haven Advocate 513

New Heart, A 666

New Issues Poetry & Prose 368

New Issues Poetry Prize, The 856

New Jersey Monthly 644

New Jersey Savvy Living 644

New Letters 596

New Letters Literary Awards 868

New Libri Press 368

New Mexico Magazine 645

New Millennium Awards for Fiction, Poetry, and Nonfiction 868

New Moon 572

New Native Press 369

New Orleans Review 597

New Quarterly, The 597

New Rivers Press 369

Newsage Press 369

New South Writing Contest 868

News Photographer 801

Newsweek 533

New Victoria Publishers 369

New Writer, The 597

New Yorker, The 533

New York Game & Fish 705

New York Magazine 646

New York Runner 713

New York Times Magazine, The 534

Next Decade, Inc. 370

NextStepU Magazine 498

NICHE 805

Nicholl Fellowships in Screenwriting, Don
   and Gee 816

Nims Memorial Prize, The John Frederick 856

9-1-1Magazine.com 774

Ninety-Six Press 370

Nob Hill Gazette 625

Nomad Press 370

North American Inns Magazine 721

North American Review 597

North American Whitetail 705

North Carolina Arts Council Regional Artist
   Project Grants 820

North Carolina Game & Fish 705

North Carolina Office of Archives and
   History 370

North Dakota Living Magazine 648

Northern Breezes, Sailing Magazine 690

Northern Indiana LAKES Magazine 636

Northern Woodlands Magazine 619

North Light Books 370

Northwest Quarterly Magazine 634

Nortia Press 371

Norton Co., Inc., W.W. 371

Notre Dame Magazine 498

Notre Dame Review 598

Nova Press 371

Novel & Short Story Writer's Market 785

Nth Degree 508

nthposition 598

Nursebooks.org 371

NurseWeek 778

O

Oak Knoll Press 372

Oak Tree Press 372

O&A Marketing News 805

Ober Associates, Harold 207

Oberlin College Press 372

Obrake Books 373

OCEAN Magazine 619

Oceanview Publishing 373

O'Connor Award for Short Fiction, Frank 827

Octameron Press 373

O'Dwyer's PR Report 733

Ohioana Book Awards 868

Ohioana Walter Rumsey Marvin Grant 842

Ohio Game & Fish 705

Ohio Magazine 649

Oklahoma Game & Fish 705

Oklahoma Today 650

OK! Magazine 518

Old Cars Weekly 738

Old Farmer's Almanac, The 534

One 666

One-Act Play Contest 816

One-Story 598

Oneworld Publications 373

Onion World 767

On Mission 666

On Spec 683

OnStage Publishing 374

Ontario Out Of Doors 705

On The Premises Contest 827

Ooligan Press 374

Open Court Publishing Co. 375

Open Road Travel Guides 375

Open Spaces 534

Opera News 798

Optical Prism 796

Orange Frazer Press, Inc. 375

Orca Book Publishers 375

Orchard Books 376

Orchises Press 376

Oregon Business 495

Oregon Coast 650

Oregon Quarterly 498

Organic Gardening 563

OTTN Publishing 376

Our Child Press 376

Our State 647

Our Sunday Visitor 666

Our Sunday Visitor, Inc. 376

Outdoor America 620

Outdoor Canada Magazine 627

Outdoor Illinois 635

Outdoors NW 694

Outreach Magazine 667

Outrider Press, Inc. 377

Outside 534

Overdrive 738

Overlook Press, The 377

Owen Prize, Guy 856

Owen Publishers, Inc., Richard C. 377

Oxford American, The 631

Oxford University Press 378

Oxygen 539

Ozark Mountain Publishing, Inc. 378

P

Pacific Coast Business Times 495

Pacific Press 378

Pacific View Press 379

Pacific Yachting 690

PAGE International Screenwriting Awards,
   The 816

Paint Horse Journal 475

Palabra 599

Palari Publishing 379

Palettes & Quills 379

Pallet Enterprise 789

Pantheon Books 380

Paper Crafts Magazine 554

Paper Stock Report, The 799

Parade 535

Paradise Cay Publications 380

Paradise Research Publications, Inc. 380

Paragon House Publishers 380

Paralegal Today 788

Parent Wise Austin 504

Parenting Magazine 505

Paris Review, The 599

Parkway Publishers, Inc. 381

Parnassus 599

Passkey Publications 381

Pastel Journal, The 736

Paterson Poetry Prize, The 856

Paterson Prize for Books for Young People 839

Paterson Prize for Young Adult and
   Children's Writing, The Katherine 839

Pathfinders 721

Path Press, Inc. 381

Paul Dry Books 381

Pauline Books & Media 382

Paulist Press 382

Pavement Saw Press Chapbook Award 856

Paycock Press 382

Peace Hill Press 383

Peachtree Children's Books 383

Pearl 599

Pearl Poetry Prize 857

Pearl Short Story Prize 827

Pearson Award, Judith Siegel 869

Pecan Grove Press 383

Pedestal Magazine, The 600

Pediatrics for Parents 505

Pedlar Press 383

Pedrick Prize, Jean 857

Pelican Publishing Company 384

Pemmican Publications 384

Pemmican Publications, Inc. 385

PEN Award for Poetry in Translation 844

Penguin Group USA 385

PEN/Joyce Osterweil Award for Poetry 857

Penn Lines 481

Pennsylvania 651

Pennsylvania Angler & Boater 706

Pennsylvania Game & Fish 706

Pennsylvania Heritage 651

Pennsylvania Lawyer, The 789

Penny-Farthing Press Inc. 385

PEN/Phyllis Naylor Working Writer
    Fellowship 839

Pentecostal Messenger, The 667

Penthouse 685

PEN Translation Prize 845

PEN/Voelcker Award for Poetry 857

Pen World 810

People 535

Perennial 386

Permanent Press, The 386

Persimmon Hill 544

Perugia Press 386

Perugia Press Prize 857

Peter Pauper Press, Inc. 386

Pet Product News International 799

Pflaum Publishing Group 387

Philadelphia Style 651

Philomel Books 387

Phoenix Magazine 623

Photographer's Forum Magazine 621

Photo Review, The 801

Piano Press 387

Piatkus Books 388

Picador USA 388

Piccadilly Books, Ltd. 388

Piccadilly Press 388

PieceWork Magazine 554

Piedmont Review, The 632

Pikes Peak Parent 505

Pilot Getaways Magazine 721

Piñata Books 389

Pinch Literary Award in Fiction and
    Poetry, The 869

Pineapple Press, Inc. 388

Pipers Magazine 489

Pit & Quarry 810

Pitspopany Press 389

Pittsburgh Magazine 652

Pizza Today 779

Plain Truth, The 667

Plan B Press 390

Plane and Pilot 489

PLANET-The Welsh Internationalist 600

Planners Press 390

Planning 774

Plastic Surgery News 796

Platypus Media, LLC 390

Playground Magazine 793

Pleiades 600

Plexus Publishing, Inc. 391

Ploughshares 601

Plum Blossom Books 391

Plum Magazine 505

PML 738

PN 516
PNWA Literary Contest 869
POB Magazine 756
Pocket Books 391
Pockets 572
POCKETS Fiction-Writing Contest 839
Pocol Press 391
Podiatry Management 796
Poe Award, Edgar Allan 828
Poetry 601
Poetry International 602
Poetry New Zealand 602
Poetry Salzburg 391
Poets & Writers Magazine 785
Point 667
Pointe Magazine 711
Points North Magazine 632
Poisoned Pen Press 392
Police and Security News 775
Police Chief, The 775
Polo Players' Edition 711
Polychrome Publishing Corp. 392
Pontoon & Deck Boat 690
Pool & Spa News 808
Popular Mechanics 554
Popular Woodworking 392
Popular Woodworking Magazine 554
Porter Prize for Fiction,
    The Katherine Anne 828
Porthole Cruise Magazine 722
Portland Review, The 602
Possibility Press 392
Poulin, Jr. Poetry Prize, A. 858
Powerboat 691
Power Boating Canada 691
Power & Motoryacht 691
POZ 540
PPI (Professional Publications, Inc.) 393

Practical Winery & Vineyard 744
Prairie Business 495
Prairie Journal Press 393
Prairie Journal, The 602
Prairie Messenger 668
Prairie Schooner 603
Prakken Publications, Inc. 393
Pratt, Inc., Helen F. 207
PRB Productions 394
Pregnancy 728
Presa S Press 394
Presbyterians Today 668
Preservation Foundation Contests 834
Preservation in Print 637
Presidio La Bahia Award, The 869
Presses de l'Universite de Montreal 394
Price Ltd. Mathew 394
Price Stern Sloan, Inc. 394
Price World Publishing, LLC 394
Priest, The 752
Priest Literary Agency, Aaron M. 207
Primary Care Optometry News 797
Princeton Architectural Press 395
Princeton University Press 395
Print 736
Printing Industries of America 395
Printz Award, Michael L. 839
Prism International 603
Prism Magazine 668
Proceedings 613
Produce News, The 776
Produce Retailer 777
Professional Artist 736
Professional Mariner 793
Professional Pilot 740
Profit 492
Progressive, The 622
Properties Magazine 802

Prorodeo Sports News 711
Provincetown Arts 639
P & R Publishing Co. 378
Pruett Publishing 395
Prufrock Press, Inc. 396
PS Books 396
Pthirty-one Woman 728
PTO Today 758
Public Lawyer, The 789
Public Power 761
Puckerbrush Press 396
Puddin'head Press, The 396
Puffin Books 397
Puget Sound Magazine 655
Pulitzer Prizes 842
Pulse Magazine 742
Purdue University Press 397
Pureplay Press 397
Purich Publishing 397
Purpose 668
PUSH 398
Putnam's Sons, G.P. 398

Q

QED Press/Cypress House 398
QED Publishing 398
Quaker Life 669
Qualified Remodeler 746
Quarterly West 603
Queen's Alumni Review 499
Queen's Mystery Magazine, Ellery 615
Queen's Quarterly 604
Quest Books 399
Quill Magazine 786
Quill & Scroll Magazine 786
Quill and Scroll International Writing/Photo
    Contest 840
Quilter's World 555
Quilter, The 555

Quite Specific Media Group, Ltd. 399
Quixote Press 399

R

Rack Magazine 706
Radcliffe Publishing Ltd. 399
Radix Magazine 669
Raffelock Award for Publishing Excellence,
    David 843
Ragged Sky Press 400
Railroad Evangelist 669
Railway Track and Structures 763
Rainbow Publishers 400
Raincoast Book Distribution, Ltd. 400
Rain Town Press 400
Random House Audio Publishing Group 400
Random House Children's Books 401
Random House/Golden Books for Young
    Readers Group 401
Random House Information Group 401
Random House Large Print 401
RANGE Magazine 677
Ransom Publishing 401
Rattapallax 604
Raven Tree Press 401
Razorbill 401
RBC Bronwen Wallace Memorial Award,
    The 869
Reader's Digest 535
Reality Street 402
Recliner Books 402
Recycled Paper News 799
Redactions
    Poetry, Poetics, & Prose 604
Redbook Magazine 729
Red Deer Press 402
Red Hen Press 403
Red Moon Press 403
Red Rock Press 403

Red Rock Review 604

Red Sage Publishing, Inc. 403

Red Tuque Books, Inc. 403

Reed Publishers, Robert D. 404

Rees Literary Agency, Helen 208

Referee 808

Reference Service Press 404

Reform Judaism 670

Regal Literary Agency 208

Regina Book Award 869

Reid Poetry Contest for Traditional Verse,
Margaret 858

Relevant 670

Relocating to the Lake of the Ozarks 643

REM 802

Remodeling 746

Renaissance House 404

Renaissance Magazine 555

Reptiles 475

Republic of Texas Press 404

Resources for Feminist Research 729

Retail Info Systems News 748

Rhino 604

Rhode Island Artist Fellowships and
Individual Project Grants 820

Rhode Island Monthly 652

Rhodes Literary Agency, Jodie 208

Rider Magazine 486

Rights Factory, The 209

Rinaldi Literary Agency, Angela 209

Rinksider, The 808

Rio Nuevo Publishers 405

Rittenberg Literary Agency, Inc., Ann 209

River City Publishing 405

Riverhead Books 405

River Hills Traveler 643

River Region's Journey 670

River Styx Magazine 605

Rivera Mexican American Children's Book
Award, Tomás 840

RLR Associates, Ltd. 210

RoadBike 487

Road King 487

Road Racer X 712

Roanoker, The 655

Roaring Brook Press 406

Robb Report 535

Roberts Award, Summerfield G. 870

Robbins Literary Agency, B.J. 210

Rochester Business Journal 496

Rock & Gem 555

Rocky Mountain Books 406

Rocky Mountain Game & Fish 706

Rogers Writers' Trust Fiction Prize, The 828

Rolling Stone 615

Romantic Homes 564

Ronsdale Press 406

Rose Alley Press 406

Rosenberg Group, The 210

Rosenkranz Literary Agency, Rita 211

Ross Yoon Agency 211

Rotarian, The 481

Roth Award for a Translation of a Literary
Work, Lois 845

Rotovision 407

Rotrosen Agency LLC, Jane 211

Rowing News 715

Rowland Agency, The Damaris 212

Rowman & Littlefield Publishing Group 407

Rrofihe Trophy 828

RTJ's Creative Catechist 752

RTOHQ
The Magazine 749

Rue Morgue 518

Rugby Magazine 711

Ruka Press 407

Runner's World 713

Running Times 713

Rural Builder 756

Rural Heritage 677

Ruralite 677

Rural Missouri Magazine 643

Russell & Volkening 212

Russian Life 524

RV Business 811

S

Sacramento News & Review 625

Sacramento Parent 506

Sacred Journey 670

Safari Press Inc. 407

Sagalyn Agency, The 212

Sail 692

Sailing Magazine 692

Sailing World 692

Saint Mary's Press 408

Sakura Publishing & Technologies 408

Salmon Poetry 408

Salt Water Sportsman 706

Salvo Press 408

Samhain Publishing, Ltd 408

Sam's Dot Publishing 409

Sandeen Prize in Poetry, Ernest 858

San Diego Family Magazine 506

San Diego Home/Garden Lifestyles 564

Sandpaper, The 644

Sand Sports Magazine 712

Sanders & Associates, Victoria 213

Santa Monica Press LLC 409

Santé Magazine 779

Sarabande Books, Inc. 409

Sarton Award, May 858

Saskatchewan Book of the Year Award 870

Saskatchewan Children's Literature
    Award 840

Saskatchewan Fiction Award 828

Saskatchewan Nonfiction Award 834

Saskatchewan Poetry Award 859

Saskatchewan Scholarly Writing Award 834

Saskatoon Book Award 870

Sasquatch Books 410

Saturday Evening Post, The 535

Saturday Evening Post Great American
    Fiction Contest, The 828

Saturnalia Books 410

Savage Kick Literary Magazine, The 605

Savannah Magazine 632

Scaglione Prize for a Translation of a
    Literary Work, Aldo and Jeanne 845

Scaglione Prize for a Translation of a
    Scholarly Study of Literature, Aldo and
    Jeanne 845

Scaglione Prize for Comparative Literary
    Studies, Aldo and Jeanne 834

Scaglione Prize for French and Francophone
    Studies, Aldo and Jeanne 834

Scaglione Prize for Italian Studies, Aldo and
    Jeanne 834

Scaglione Prize for Studies in Germanic
    Languages & Literature, Aldo and
    Jeanne 835

Scaglione Prize for Studies in Slavic
    Languages and Literatures, Aldo and
    Jeanne 835

Scaglione Publication Award for a
    Manuscript in Italian Literary Studies,
    Aldo and Jeanne 835

Scandinavian Review 524

Scarborough Prize, William Sanders 836

Scent of an Ending™, The 829

Schiffer Publishing, Ltd. 411

Schmidt, Harold Literary Agency 213

Schocken Books 411

Scholastic Inc. 411

Scholastic Library Publishing 411

Scholastic Parent & Child 506

SchoolArts Magazine 758

School Bus Fleet 811

Schreiber Prize for Humorous Fiction &
    Nonfiction, The Mona 870

Schulman Literary Agency, Susan 213

Science & Humanities Press 411

Science Writing Awards in Physics and
    Astronomy 835

Scientific American 680

Scott Novel Excerpt Prize,
    Joanna Catherine 829

Scouting 482

Scovil Galen Ghosh Literary
    Agency, Inc. 214

Screen Magazine 766

Screen Printing 801

Scribe Publications 412

Scriptapalooza Screenplay Competition 816

Scriptapalooza Television Writing
    Competition 817

Sea Kayaker 692

Seal Press 412

Sea Magazine 693

Search Institute Press 412

Seattle Magazine 656

Seattle Review, The 605

Seattle Weekly 656

Seaweed Sideshow Circus 412

Seaworthy Publications, Inc. 413

Second Aeon Publications 413

Second Story Press 413

Secret Place, The 671

Seedling Continental Press 413

Self 729

Seneca Review 606

Senior Living 536

Sentient Publications 413

Seriously Good Books 414

Servicing Management 772

Seven Footer Press / Seven Footer Kids 414

Seven Stories Press 414

Seventeen 718

Severn House Publishers 415

Sewanee Review, The 606

Sew News 555

Seymour Agency, The 214

SFO Magazine 492

Shaara Award for Excellence in Civil War
    Fiction, Michael 829

Shambhala Publications, Inc. 415

Shannon Literary Agency, Inc., Denise 214

Shape Magazine 540

Sharing the Victory 671

Shaughnessy Prize, Mina P. 835

Shearsman Books, LTD 415

Sheed & Ward Book Publishing 415

Sheep! Magazine 769

Shenandoah 606

Shen's Books 416

Shepherd Express 513

Sherman Associates, Inc., Wendy 214

Shillingford Publishing Inc., J. Gordon 416

SHINE brightly 573

Shopper Marketing 733

Short Grain Contest 859

Short Stuff 606

Shotgun Sports Magazine 716

ShowBoats International 693

Shuttle Spindle & Dyepot 556

Siegel, International Literary Agency, Inc.,
    Rosalie 215

Sierra 620

Sign Builder Illustrated 733

SignCraft 734

Silent Sports 695

Silverfish Review Press 416

Silverland Press 416

Silver Leaf Books, LLC 416

Silver Moon Press 417

Simon & Schuster Adult Publishing
   Group 417

Simon & Schuster Books for Young
   Readers 417

Simon & Schuster Children's Publishing 417

Skating 714

Ski Area Management 808

Skiing 715

Skiing Magazine 715

Skin Deep 742

Skin Inc. Magazine 743

Skinner House Books 417

Ski Patrol Magazine 809

Skipping Stones
   A Multicultural Literary Magazine 524

Skirt! Magazine 729

Skydiving 712

Sky & Telescope 680

Slack, Inc. 418

Slipstream Annual Poetry Chapbook
   Competition 859

Small Beer Press 418

Small Dogma Publishing, Inc. 418

Smallfellow Press 419

Smallholder Magazine 770

SmartCEO Magazine 496

Smart Computing 621

Smart Retailer 805

Smith Book Award, Byron Caldwell 843

Smith Memorial Award for Best Book of
   Poetry, Helen C. 859

Smithsonian Magazine 536

Snips Magazine 800

SnoWest Magazine 715

Snow Goer 715

Snow Writers' Contest, Kay 870

Soap Opera Digest 518

SoCal Meetings + Events Magazine 734

Social Justice Review 671

Sofa Ink Quarterly 536

Soft Skull Press Inc. 419

Soho Press, Inc. 419

Solar Industry 761

Solas House/Travelers' Tales 419

Soldier of Fortune 613

Somerset Business Magazine 496

Soundprints/Studio Mouse 420

Sound & Video Contractor 760

Sound & Vision 518

Souothern California Physician 797

Sourcebooks Landmark 420

Sourced Media Books, LLC 420

South Carolina Game & Fish 707

SouthComm Publishing Company, Inc. 631

Southeastern Theatre Conference High
   School New Play Contest 817

Southern Boating Magazine 693

Southern Humanities Review 607

Southern Methodist University Press 420

Southern Playwrights Competition 817

Southern Review, The 607

South Florida Parenting 506

Southwest Colorado Arts Perspective
   Magazine 627

Southwest Florida Parent & Child 506

Southwest Writers 817

Sow's Ear 859

Sow's Ear Poetry Competition, The 860

Sow's Ear Poetry Review, The 607

Spa 722

Spa Life 722

Sparkle 573

Speak Up Press 421

SpeciaLiving 516

Specialty Travel Index 812

Speech Bin Inc., The 421

Spencerhill Associates 215

Spider 574

Spinner Books 421

Spirit Magazine 566

Spirituality & Health Magazine 540

Spiritual Life 671

Spitzer Literary Agency, Inc., Philip G. 215

Sport Fishing 707

Sports Afield 707

Sports Illustrated 695

SPORTS 'N SPOKES 516

Spotlight on Recovery Magazine 622

Spout Press 421

Springs 791

SPS Studios, Inc. 421

Spudman 767

SRPR Editors' Prize Contest 860

Stackpole Books 422

Stained Glass 746

Stamats Meetings Media 749

Stamping Journal 791

Standard Publishing 422

Stand Magazine 608

Stanford University Press 422

St. Anthony Messenger 671

StarDate 680

Starr Productions, Ltd., Ariel 422

Star Service Travel42 812

State Journal, The 749

St. Augustine's Press 423

Steamboat Magazine 628

Steel Toe Books 423

Steele-Perkins Literary Agency 215

Steeple Hill Books 423

Stegner Fellowships, Wallace E. 860

Steller Press Ltd. 424

Stemmer House Publishers 424

Sterling Publishing Co., Inc. 424

Stipes Publishing LLC 424

St. Johann Press 425

Stone Arch Books 425

Stone Bridge Press 425

Stone Prize in Poetry, The Ruth 860

Stone Soup 574

Stone World 810

Storey Publishing 425

Storyteller, The 608

Stover Memorial Award, The Elizabeth
    Matchett 860

ST PAULS/Alba House 426

Strategic Health Care Marketing 797

Straus Agency, Inc., Robin 216

Strickler Author Management, Pam 216

Strider Nolan Publishing, Inc. 426

Stringer Literary Agency, LLC, The 216

Strokestown International Poetry
    Competition 860

Strothman Agency, LLC, The 217

subTERRAIN Annual Literary Awards
    Competition 870

Subtropics 608

Su Casa 564

Success Stories 672

Sun Books / Sun Publishing 426

Sunbury Press, Inc. 426

Sunrise River Press 427

Sunshine Artist USA 556

Sun, The 513

Sun Valley Magazine 633

SuperCollege 427

Super Lawyers 789

Surfer Magazine 716

Susquehanna Life 652

Sustainable Industries 749

Swan Isle Press 427

Swan Scythe Press 427

Sweetgum Press 428

Sweeney Agency, LLC, Emma 217

Swimming World Magazine 716

Switchgrass Books 428

Sycamore Review 608

Sylvan Dell Publishing 428

Symphony 615

SynergEbooks 429

Syracuse University Press 429

System iNEWS 781

T

Tafelberg Publishers 429

T'ai Chi 709

Talese, Nan A. 430

Tales of the Talisman 684

Tallahassee Magazine 630

Tanglewood Books 430

Tattoo Revue 556

Taylor Book Award, Sydney 840

Taylor Manuscript Competition, Sydney 840

Taylor Trade Publishing 430

TD Canadian Children's Literature
    Award 841

Tea A Magazine 526

Teacher Ideas Press 430

Teachers of Vision 759

Teachers & Writers Magazine 758

Teaching Music 759

Teaching Tolerance 759

Teal Literary Agency, Patricia 217

Tebot Bach 431

Tech Directions 760

Technical Analysis of Stocks &
    Commodities 492

Technology Review 781

Tech Trader Magazine 761

Teddy Bear Review 556

Tele Revista 519

Temple University Press 431

Tennessee Sportsman 707

Ten Speed Press 431

Tessler Literary Agency, LLC 218

Texas A&M University Press 431

Texas Architect 736

Texas Gardener 564

Texas Golfer Magazine 697

Texas Highways 654

Texas Home & Living 565

Texas Institute of Letters Award for Most
    Significant Scholarly Book 843

Texas Institute of Letters Bob Bush Memorial
    Award for First Book of Poetry 861

Texas Meetings + Events 734

Texas Monthly 654

Texas Parks & Wildlife 654

Texas Sportsman 707

Texas Tech University Press 432

Texas Western Press 432

that's life! 730

Theatre Conspiracy Annual New Play
    Contest 817

THEMA 609

Theoria 622

Third World Press 432

Thirty-A Review, The 630

This Rock 672

Thistledown Press Ltd. 432

Thoroughbred Times 809

Threads 557

Three Cheers and a Tiger 829

Thrive - The EB Online 672
Tia Chucha Press 433
Tightrope Books 433
Tilbury House 433
Timberline 790
TimberWest 790
TIME 537
Timeline 545
Times of the Islands 722
Tin House 609
Tin House Books 434
Tire News 739
Titan Press 434
Toastmaster, The 482
To Be Read Aloud Publishing, Inc. 434
Today's Bride 730
Today's Catholic Teacher 752
Today's Machining World 792
Today's Parent 507
Today's Parent Pregnancy & Birth 507
Todd Publications 434
Tokyo Rose Records/Chapultepec Press 435
Toledo Area Parent News 507
Tombigbee Country Magazine 545
Tombstone Epitaph, The 545
Top Cow Productions 435
Top Publications, Ltd. 435
Tor Books 435
Toronto Book Awards 871
Torquere Press 436
Torrey House Press, LLC 436
Total-e-bound Publishing 436
Touchwood Editions 437
Tower Publishing 437
Toy Box Productions 437
Toy Farmer 557
Toy Trucker & Contractor 557
Traces of Indiana and Midwestern

History 545
Tradewind Books 437
Trafalgar Square Books 438
Trailer Life 723
Trail Runner 714
Trail & Timberline 483
Transaction Publishers 226
Transcontinental Poetry Award 861
Trapper & Predator Caller 707
Travel Goods Showcase 806
Travel + Leisure 723
Travel Naturally 723
Travel Smart 723
Travis Lake Publishing LLC 438
Treasures 557
Treimel NY, S©ott 218
Tricycle 672
Trident Media Group 218
Tristan Publishing 438
Triumph Books 439
Tropical Fish Hobbyist Magazine 475
Truckin' Magazine 487
True West 546
Truman State University Press 439
Trustus Playwrights' Festival 817
Tufts Poetry Awards 861
Turkey Country 708
Turkey & Turkey Hunting 707
Turner Award for Best First Work of Fiction,
    Steven 829
Turnstone Press 439
Turtle Magazine for
    Preschool Kids 574
Tuttle Publishing 439
Twenty-Three House Publishing 223
Twilight Times Books 439
Twins™ Magazine 507
Tyndale House Publishers, Inc. 440

U

UAB Magazine 499

Ultimate MMA 709

Unbridled Books 440

Underground Construction 756

Unity House 440

University of Akron Press 440

University of Alabama Press, The 441

University of Arkansas Press, The 441

University of Calgary Press 441

University of Chicago Press, The 441

University of Georgia Press 442

University of Illinois Press 442

University of Iowa Press 442

University of Nebraska Press 443

University of Nevada Press 443

University of New Mexico Press 443

University of North Texas Press 444

University of Oklahoma Press 444

University of Pennsylvania Press 444

University of Wisconsin Press 444

University Press of Kansas 445

University Press of Mississippi 445

Unlimited Publishing LLC 445

UnTapped Talent LLC 446

Untreed Reads Publishing 447

Update 483

Up Here 627

Upper Access, Inc. 447

Upper Room, The 673

URJ Press 448

USAA Magazine 772

USA Hockey Magazine 699

Usborne Publishing 448

U.S. Catholic 673

USDF Connection 475

Utmost Christian Poetry Contest 861

V

Validation Times 757

Vampires 2 Magazine 684

Vandamere Press 448

Vanderbilt University Press 449

VanHook House 449

Varoujan Award, Daniel 862

Vegetable Growers News, The 767

Vehicule Press 449

VeloNews 687

VenEconomy/VenEconoma 749

Venues Today 799

Verbatim 609

Verge Magazine 724

Veritas Literary Agency 219

Vermont Business Magazine 496

Versal 610

Vertical Systems Reseller 806

Vertigo 450

Vestal Review 610

VFW Voice of Democracy 835

Vibrant Life 540

Victorian Homes 565

Video Librarian 745

Viewpoint Press 450

Viking 450

Viking Children's Books 450

Villard Books 450

Vim & Vigor 541

Vineyard & Winery Management 744

Vintage Anchor Publishing 451

Virginia Game & Fish 708

Virginia Golfer 697

Virginia Living 655

Vivisphere Publishing 451

Viz Media LLC 451

VM+SD 806

Voaden National Playwriting Competition,

The Herman 818
Voyageur Press 451

W
Waasmode Short Fiction Prize 830
Wake Forest University Press 452
Wake Living 648
Wakestone Press 452
Wales Literary Agency, Inc. 219
Walker & Company 452
Walker Award for Newspaper Journalism, Stanley 844
Waltsan Publishing 453
W&A Publishing 452
War Cry, The 673
Ward & Balkin Agency, Inc., The 185
Washington Blade, The 530
Washington City Paper 629
Washington-Oregon Game & Fish 708
Washington Prize, The 862
Washington State University Press 453
Washington Writers' Publishing House 453
WaterBrook Multnomah Publishing Group 454
Watercolor Artist 737
Waterfront Times 693
Water Skier, The 716
Waterway Guide 693
Waterways World 694
Water Well Journal 804
Wave Books 454
Waveland Press, Inc. 454
WaveLength Magazine 694
Wealth Manager 772
Weatherwise 681
Weed Literary 219
Weigl Educational Publishers Ltd. 455
Weigl Publishers Inc. 455
Weil Agency, Inc., The Wendy 219

Wergle Flomp Humor Poetry Contest 862
Wesleyan Life 674
Wesleyan Publishing House 455
Wesleyan University Press 455
West Branch 610
Western Canada Highway News 739
Western DairyBusiness 768
Western Dairy Farmer 768
Western & Eastern Treasures 557
Western Grocer Magazine 777
Western Hotelier Magazine 779
Western Humanities Review 610
Western Psychological Services 455
Western Restaurant News 780
Westminster John Knox Press 456
Weston Writers' Trust Prize for Nonfiction, The Hilary 836
West Suburban Living 635
West Virginia Game & Fish 708
Where Magazine (Where Guestbook, Where Map, Where Newsletter) 630
Whitaker House 456
Whitecap Books, Ltd. 456
Whitehead Award for Design of a Trade Book, Fred 843
White Mane Kids 457
White Mane Publishing Company Inc. 457
White Pine Press 457
White Pine Press Poetry Prize 862
Whitman & Company, Albert 457
Whittler's Bench Press 458
WHJ/HRHJ 541
Whole Life Times 484
Wick Poetry Prize, Stan and Tom 862
Wild Child Publishing 458
Wilde Publishing 458
Wildlife Conservation 620
Wild Rose Press 459

Wildstorm 459

Wild West 546

William Morrow 459

Williamson Books 459

Williams Young Adult Prose Prize, Rita 841

Willow Creek Press 460

Wilshire Book Company 460

Wilson Short Fiction Award, Gary 830

WindRiver Publishing, Inc. 461

Windsor Review 611

Windspeaker 525

Windward Publishing 461

Wine Enthusiast Magazine 527

Wine Press Northwest 527

Wine Spectator 527

Wines & Vines 744

Wisconsin Historical Society Press 461

Wisconsin Natural Resources 657

Wisconsin Sportsman 708

Wisconsin Trails 657

Wisdom Publications 461

Wiseman Books, Paula 462

Witches and Pagans 484

Wizards of The Coast Books for Young
    Readers 462

Wolf Den Books 462

Wolff Award in Fiction, Tobias 830

Woman Alive 674

Woman Engineer 764

Woman's Life 730

Woman's World 730

Women in Business 731

Woodall's Regionals 724

Woodbine House 462

Woodenboat Magazine 694

Woodley Memorial Press 463

Wood Memorial Ohioana Award for
    Children's Literature, Alice 841

Wood Prize, The J. Howard and Barbara M.J. 863

Woodshop News 558

Worcester Magazine 639

Wordsong 463

Word Warriors Press 463

Work Boat World 793

Workforce Diversity For Engineering & IT
    Professionals 499

Working People's Poetry Competition 863

Work-In-Progress Grant 841

World Book, Inc. 464

World's Best Short Short Story Fiction
    Contest, Narrative Nonfiction Contest, &
    Southeast Review Poetry Contest 871

World Trade 750

World War II 546

Worship Leader Magazine 753

Write It Now! 841

Writer's Digest 786

Writer's Digest Books 464

Writers-Editors Network Annual
    International Writing Competition 871

Writers Guild of Alberta Awards 871

Writers House 220

Writers' Trust Engel/Findley Award, The 843

Writing that Works 786

Written By 787

X

Xtra 530

Y

Yachting 694

Yalobusha Review, The 611

YBK Publishers, Inc. 464

Yearling Books 464

Yellow Shoe Fiction Series 465

YES Mag 575

Yes! Magazine 537